A BIBLIOGRAPHY OF
BRITISH HISTORY
1914–1989

A BIBLIOGRAPHY OF BRITISH HISTORY

1914–1989

COMPILED AND EDITED BY

KEITH ROBBINS

CLARENDON PRESS · OXFORD

1996

Oxford University Press, Walton Street, Oxford OX2 6DP

Oxford New York

Athens Auckland Bangkok Bombay
Calcutta Cape Town Dar es Salaam Delhi
Florence Hong Kong Istanbul Karachi
Kuala Lumpur Madras Madrid Melbourne
Mexico City Nairobi Paris Singapore
Taipei Tokyo Toronto
and associated companies in
Berlin Ibadan

Oxford is a trade mark of Oxford University Press

Published in the United States
by Oxford University Press Inc., New York

British Library Cataloguing in Publication Data
Data available

Library of Congress Cataloging in Publication Data
Data available
ISBN 0–19–822496–6

1 3 5 7 9 10 8 6 4 2

Typeset by Hope Services (Abingdon) Ltd.
Printed in Great Britain
on acid-free paper by
Bookcraft Ltd., Midsomer-Norton,
Nr. Bath, Avon.

To Paul, Daniel, Lucy, and Adam
who grew up with this unwelcome sibling

PREFACE

IT was in 1975, when I was a young Professor of History at the University of Wales, Bangor that I was approached on behalf of the Royal Historical Society with the suggestion that I should undertake the task of compiling a Bibliography of Writings on British History since 1914. It would constitute the final volume in a well-established series. Its predecessor, compiled by Professor H. J. Hanham, had just appeared. The initial hope was that the work would begin in 1976 and be completed within five years. It was difficult to resist the challenge which such a task represented, even if, in retrospect, it may appear that it would have been prudent to do so.

There is an argument for suggesting that such an enterprise should only have been undertaken by a specialist bibliographer whose full-time labour could have been devoted to the project. However, it was thought appropriate that the editor, like his predecessors, should be an active historian, committed to teaching and writing in the area and period to be covered by the bibliography. The end-product, after all, was to be a tool for practitioners and it was their concerns which an active historian might comprehend more fully. The corollary of this decision, however, has been that the compilation has had to take its place alongside that active writing life and the multifarious professional and other responsibilities that have subsequently ensued. The consequence has been that the time taken to complete the work has extended long beyond that which had originally been tentatively envisaged. Even so, to use the word 'complete' begs many questions.

The task might have been expedited if, from the outset, the editor had 'farmed out' sections to other contributors and had limited his own role to co-ordination. In retrospect, there might seem to have been much to commend such a policy. On the other hand, experience of other joint enterprises had led to the conclusion that completion was as likely to have been delayed because, for reasons good and bad, contributors would not have been able to adhere to a common timetable. More fundamentally, however, apart from certain subject areas where limits and boundaries were reasonably self-evident, a major problem has precisely been the delimitation of categories. While it was possible to devise initial outline frameworks, the detailed contents could only be decided 'on the job'. The possibilities of overlap, duplication, and disagreement were considerable and could have jeopardized progress. It was for this reason that it was agreed that the editor would undertake the work himself, receiving such assistance along the way as might become available. The folly of this willingness has become evident to the editor, and no doubt to many others, as the enthusiasm of youth has mellowed into middle age. It follows that the taxonomy of the bibliography as a whole is his doing and he takes responsibility for its structure and contents. Unfortunately, it also follows that the editor has necessarily had to develop or deepen an awareness of relevant literature beyond the initial specialist knowledge in particular areas which he possessed at the outset. Such a comprehensive acquaintance is not achieved overnight. It has been reinforced by the observations of specialists who are duly thanked, in what follows, for their assistance in commenting on initial drafts.

Such indebtedness is in no way lessened by the fact that it could also pose problems for the editor which come to the heart of the enterprise and should at least be aired here. The brief to cover 'British history since 1914' proved to be deceptively simple. All three elements—'British', 'history', and 'since 1914'—have proved problematic and incapable of producing universal agreement. It scarcely needs to be said that throughout the period in which this work has been executed what has been thought by historians to be worthy of study has been steadily expanding. Historians have tended to specialize in sub-disciplines within the broad field of historiography. Naturally, fashions come and go, but now there are few areas in which there is no interest amongst historians. Editors of previous volumes in this series were not unaware of this problem, but they did not have to deal with a virtually limitless historical imperialism. On the other hand, while historians have wished to probe issues way beyond what an earlier generation would have recognized as 'history', and at least an attempt has had to be made to cater for their actual and anticipated needs, non-historian specialists who have been consulted have, naturally, pressed for even more comprehensiveness and suggested that, within their disciplines, things would have been ordered differently and even more extensively. Such opinions have been respected but not invariably accepted. To have deployed all the material suggested or pointed to would, in some cases at least, have led to an undesirable imbalance as between categories and also, perhaps, have transformed an already bulky production into an unmanageable one.

In short, this is a bibliography compiled by a historian, a historian aware that the archetypical historian no longer exists and who has therefore ranged widely but who has none the less not attempted, in certain specialist areas which are still not conventionally regarded as 'history', to replicate what is in some cases already available or attempted to operate at such a depth that a non-historian specialist would feel that completeness had been achieved. It is, however, not simply a bibliography for historians. It is also designed to meet the needs of students and scholars from a range of disciplines, and by no means at an introductory level. The needs of such users have been kept in mind, though it must be apparent that their 'needs' are not in fact self-evident.

The scope of a twentieth-century bibliography which purports to be 'British' is also extraordinarily problematic and could have produced a variety of outcomes. How, over such a period of time, should Britain/The British Empire-Commonwealth be handled, on the one hand, and how should Britain/Ireland and the nations of Britain be handled on the other? What may appear to be appropriate in 1914 may no longer be appropriate at subsequent quarter-century intervals. Since there is manifestly no solution that is invariably satisfactory, the decision was taken to focus on Britain itself and to regard the internal development of overseas possessions and self-governing territories as largely extraneous. Such a conclusion may appear premature, at least as far as the initial decades are concerned, but at least in the later decades it would not have made sense to regard their internal history as 'British'.

Likewise, the United Kingdom of Great Britain and Ireland came to an end before the initial decade of the bibliography's span was out. To have continued to include the internal history of the Irish Free State and the Republic of Ireland in 'British' history would have caused offence, notwithstanding the continuing interaction between Irish and British developments. To have excluded a part of the United Kingdom, namely Northern Ireland, on the ground that it was not 'British' (and even such a definition is of course highly contentious), would have seemed arbitrary, given that authority in the province rested, and rests, ultimately or immediately, with the British Parliament. Yet, the history of Northern

Ireland cannot be properly understood without reference to developments south of the border. In short, no solution is fully satisfactory, and the editor trusts that his solution gives no offence in the island of Ireland.

Even within 'Britain' itself there are methodological problems of equal complexity. A solution which has been adopted in the past, within this series, is to have discrete sections for 'Scotland' and 'Wales' into which can be poured the entire relevant range of material. Such an arrangement is, of course, not without merit. Users with particular national interests can focus their attention readily and do not need, because of its subject arrangement, to hunt throughout the bibliography as a whole. However, such compartmentalization can perpetuate the view that the history of Scotland and Wales is somehow marginal to the history of 'Britain'. Such a view goes against the thrust of much recent historiography which has sought to loosen an Anglocentric perspective on Britain. Therefore, although Scottish and Welsh sub-sections have been identified within particular categories, there are no comprehensive Scottish and Welsh sections. Such a course enables the editor to avoid the assumption that every other section of the book is really about 'England'. On the other hand, ironically given the fact that the bibliography has very largely been compiled in Wales and Scotland, the editor may be vulnerable to a charge that in stressing their importance within a bibliography of 'Britain' he has not given sufficient emphasis to their individuality. In mitigation, it must be emphasized that there is no answer which satisfies all sensitivities. In any event, as is true throughout, individual authors conspire constantly to frustrate the neat categories adopted by the bibliographer. Books which purport to be about one or other aspect of British history turn out on inspection to be about English history. Likewise, books on English history turn out in fact to be about British history.

There is one final difficulty with the term 'British', particularly in certain areas and since 1945. It concerns the global reach of the English language. In literature, the arts generally, and in science, but not confined to these areas, there can be a certain arbitrariness in supposing an individual or a work to be 'British'. A career or a discovery may be 'Anglo-American'. On the whole, it has not seemed wise to be too rigid in this respect but it is only right to observe that there can be something highly artificial about the concept, for example, of 'British biology' or 'British jazz'. A comparable, though as yet less acute, problem exists in rather different areas, arising, for example out of membership of NATO and of the European Community. Arguably, what is 'British' can only be understood if it is considered in a multilateral context.

'Since 1914' has also brought considerable difficulty. In part, this is because, as has already been mentioned, different time reference points conjure up very different notions of 'Britain'. Its initial open-ended character, however, left the compiler with the difficult and perhaps impossible task of trying to decide on the nature of the material which it was appropriate to include. Certain monographs, articles, reports, and papers seemed, on investigation, to have carved out a status for themselves—at least judged from the 1980s—which meant that their inclusion was not problematic. That seemed not to be the case with other items whose importance seemed largely to be limited to the immediate period of publication. Their enduring merit was questionable. On the other hand, and this was particularly true of some material in the social sciences, potential users should certainly be directed to such works because they were indubitably 'typical' of their time in theme, structure, and substance. Once again, it proved impossible to adopt a hard and fast division and users will find a wide range of material which has been listed. Of course, it is entirely possible that what may seem to be ephemeral at this juncture may turn out to have an enduring importance.

'Since 1914' has been difficult in other respects. Previous editors in this series have known from the outset what their period was to be. Initially, in this case, it was thought that it should probably cover the period from 1914 until 1975/6 when the work of compilation began. It was in 1975 that the first of the annual bibliographies on British and Irish History, sponsored by the Royal Historical Society, made its appearance. Perhaps they would carry the burden henceforward and make the appearance of a successor to this enterprise redundant. In the event, however, it proved impossible to resist the temptation to embrace and incorporate material which appeared in an unending stream covering the years after 1975. Yet, once that temptation had been yielded to, it began to be ever more difficult to decide where a date-line should be drawn. The editor only found himself able to proceed by moving inexorably through one field after another with the sad consequence that there was a seemingly never ending discrepancy in the 'up-to-dateness' of particular sections. It was not apparent that there was any particular date post-1975 which obviously suggested itself as a 'logical' conclusion. It was therefore decided to end the scope in 1989, an arbitrary but not altogether unsatisfying three quarters of a century. All sections have been looked at with this concluding date in mind and, while there have been a few tentative ventures beyond it, the temptation to resume the labour of Sisyphus into the indefinite future has been resisted.

It should be added that in the two decades during which this work has been undertaken the editor's task has been both assisted and complicated by the rapid developments in technology. These developments have meant that within intervals of five years the means of storing information have shifted significantly. Latter-day sophistication has been a bonus, particularly when a mishap at a late stage threatened all that had been achieved. Nevertheless, the need to upgrade earlier records added to the labour along the way. In general, however, the rate of technological change has been such as to call into question, for the future, a published bibliography of this type. The Royal Historical Society has this matter very much in hand and Dr John Morrill presides over projects on its behalf which will take historical bibliography into the twenty-first century.

I am grateful for the initial support of the officers of the Royal Historical Society, particularly the then President, the late Professor Sir Geoffrey Elton. He and his distinguished successors have continued, from time to time, to express their interest in the project and, more or less, to contain their scepticism about its ultimate conclusion.

I am also grateful for the transatlantic support offered by Professor Henry R. Winkler and, through him, officers of the American Historical Association, who were able to assist me in my work and who received aid from the National Endowment for the Humanities for this purpose.

Professor H. J. Hanham, editor of the preceding volume, gave me initial advice from across the Atlantic, and, since his return to this country, has offered appreciated sympathy as the pain of his own experience has faded into the past.

In North Wales, I was helped initially by the then Librarian at Bangor, Glynne Heywood. I was assisted in initial searches by Miss Arfona Roberts (Mrs Jones).

In 1985, while teaching in the summer in Vancouver, I was graciously allowed to make use of the resources of the Library of the University of British Columbia.

In Scotland, I am above all grateful to the Librarian of the University of Glasgow, Mr Henry Heaney, and to the many members of his staff who tolerated my unexpected presence on floors of the library where historians were not normally expected to tread. The specialist librarians gave me a great deal of help in locating material. I also made use of the admirable resources of the Mitchell Library in Glasgow and the National Library of Scotland in Edinburgh.

I also owe a debt to my wife who was able, for a time, to use her scientific background on my behalf and identify suitable material and suggest ways in which it might be categorized.

A grant from the Leverhulme Trustees enabled me to employ Dr Jacqueline Jenkinson in Glasgow as my research assistant for a year. I am grateful to the Trustees and to Dr Jenkinson for her help and encouragement at a time when I was particularly pressed with other commitments. The same is true of Miss Patricia Ferguson, my secretary in the Department of Modern History.

In Lampeter I am grateful for the help of Ms Corinne Brown, Mrs Lynda Cadman, Mr Stuart Martin, Mr Carl Williams and a group of postgraduate students for help in the final stages; and for a grant from the Pantyfedwen Fund of the University of Wales, Lampeter, towards expenses.

At Oxford University Press I have received support and encouragement, at different stages, from Dr Ivon Asquith, Dr Anthony Morris, and Ms Anne Gelling in particular.

The colleagues and friends in universities in the United Kingdom and beyond whom I have buttonholed and requested information from at all times of the day, and often of the night, are too numerous to mention individually. However, I should like to single out the following who, at one stage or another, kindly looked at drafts and made suggestions: Professor Anthony Bottoms (in relation to legal matters and crime), Dr Catherine Delano Smith and Professor Robert Steel (geography), Dr J. A. Mangan and Professor J. Walvin (sport and leisure), Professor Judith Brown (Britain and India), Professor Owen Chadwick (the churches), Professor Michael Biddiss (historiography), Professor George Boyce and Professor Colin Seymour-Ure (the press and the media), Professor Jan MacDonald (theatre, film, and television), Professor David Harkness (Northern Ireland), Dr Michael Black (books and publishing), Professor Robin Downie (philosophy), Professor J. McEwen (public health), Professor Philip Beaumont (industrial and employment questions). If I have inadvertently omitted any other specific name I hope my apologies can be accepted and sufficient thanks offered in my initial general acknowledgement.

It is certain that without this assistance offered at different times and in different places the bibliography could not have been completed. The responsibility, however, remains with the editor. He would not claim that he has read every word of every item which has been included. He has, however, studied a very high proportion and scanned at least a significant amount of the remainder. The question of the extent to which it was possible or helpful to add a commentary, replete with value-judgments, was debated from the beginning. In the event, that has only occurred to a small extent. To have gone further would have added to the bulk in a way which would not have been desirable. In addition, a bibliographer quickly runs out of descriptive adjectives and few items are equally 'good' or 'informative' or 'insightful' from the perspective of potential users whose needs are rarely uniform. The great danger in a verbal commentary (or a lettered 'scale of utility' or equivalent shorthand device) is that the bibliographer supposes that his own needs are universal. However, to give the reader additional help beyond the messages implicit in the internal arrangement of particular sections, each section is prefaced by a short commentary which gives a general comment on the nature of the material following, indicating, where appropriate, some of the problems in the arrangement, some of the potential overlap with other sections (for example, should we look for 'drugs' or 'alcoholism' in a social or medical category), and some of the matters on which comparatively little appears to have been written. It should be added that, with the exception of a few entries written in French or in German, this is an English-language bibliography. The editor is aware that this outcome understates the extent to which German historians, in particular, have made a most helpful contribution to the study of recent British history.

It is scarcely conceivable that the result of such a complex and protracted process will be without error and, no doubt, if one were beginning again, some things, at least, would have been done differently. However, whatever its possible imperfections it is offered as a pathway into the extraordinary history of twentieth-century Britain. Beyond all the assistance and advice offered by professional colleagues, however, I am grateful to the members of my family who have kept me to the task when more public pursuits might have fatally distracted me. I mention again my wife, Janet, but also my four children. Adam has had the misfortune to become ensnared into helping and deserves a special mention. I have noticed, however, that the 'children' have grown up during the lifespan of this enterprise. The dedication may be a little compensation for delights they might have experienced without it.

K. R.

University of Wales, Lampeter
January 1994

CONTENTS

Abbreviations   xxx

1. GENERAL   1

   A. Bibliographies and other Reference Books   1
      1. Abstracts   1
      2. General Bibliographies   1
      3. Biography   1
      4. Databases and Banks   2
      5. Directories   2
      6. Factual Handbooks   2
      7. Guide to Sources   2
      8. Indexes   3
      9. Library Guides and Catalogues   3
      10. Maps and Atlases   3
      11. Newspaper and Periodical Guides   4
      12. Official Publications   5
      13. Photographic and Film Archives   5
      14. Polls and Surveys   6
      15. Reference Material   6
      16. Statutes   6
      17. Yearbooks   7

   B. General Histories and Studies   7
      1. Collections of Documents   7
      2. General Histories   7
      3. Historical Bibliographies   10

2. CONSTITUTIONAL AND POLITICAL HISTORY   11

   A. The Monarchy   11
      1. General   11
      2. The Royal Family   12

   B. Parliament   14
      1. Parliament as a Whole   15
      2. General Works   15
      3. The House of Commons   16
      4. The House of Lords   17
      5. Miscellaneous   18

   C. Central Institutions   18
      1. General   19
      2. The Cabinet   19

3. Whitehall and Westminster	20
4. Ministerial Responsibility	20
5. The Opposition	20
6. Cabinet Secretariat	20
7. Cabinet and Official Secrecy	20
8. Public Employment	20
9. Reform Proposals	21
10. The Treasury	21
11. Departments	21
12. Civil Service: General/Individuals/Administrative Procedures and Values	22
D. Politicians	25
1. Prime Ministers	26
2. Cabinet Ministers (Except Lord Chancellors)	30
3. Other Political Figures	36
4. General Works on Politicians and Parliament	41
E. Political Parties	41
1. General	42
2. The Conservative Party	43
3. The Labour Party	44
4. The Liberal Party	47
5. Social Democratic Party	48
6. Green Party (Formerly the Ecology Party)	48
7. Independent Labour Party	48
8. The Co-operative Party	49
9. The Common Wealth Party	49
10. Communist Politics in Britain	49
11. Socialist Party of Great Britain	51
12. Socialist Workers' Party	51
13. Trotskyism in Great Britain	51
14. General Works on Left-Wing Politics in Britain	51
15. The Radical Right	52
16. Pressure Groups and Quangos	53
F. Political Thought	53
1. General	54
2. Socialist Thought	54
3. Liberalism	55
4. Conservatism	56
G. The Electoral System	56
1. Election Results	56
2. Religious and Racial Factors	57
3. Women Voters	58
4. General Elections 1918–1987	58
5. General	60

H. Regionalism and General Studies on Devolution   61
    1. General   62
    2. Combined Studies of Celtic Nationalism   62
    3. Scotland   62
        (a) General and Political History   62
        (b) Scottish Nationalism and the Scottish National Party 64
        (c) Scottish Labour History and the Labour Party in Scotland 64
        (d) The Conservative Party in Scotland   65
    4. Wales   65
        (a) Government and Politics   65
        (b) Welsh Nationalism   66
    5. The Isle of Man: Government and Politics   67
    6. Ireland   67
        (a) General   67
        (b) Irish Nationalism and Rebellion   69
        (c) Northern Ireland, Ulster, and Ulster Unionism   70
            (i) Northern Ireland   70
            (ii) Ulster and Ulster Unionism   73
        (d) Anglo-Irish Relations   74
        (e) Irish Politicians   75

I. Local Government   77
    1. Reference   77
    2. General   78
    3. Local Government and National Government   80
    4. Local Government Service   81
    5. Local Government Finance   81
    6. Local Government in London   82
    7. Local Politics   83
    8. Local Government in English Cities and Boroughs   83
    9. English County Councils   84
    10. Scottish Cities and Burghs   85
    11. Welsh Authorities   85
    12. Northern Ireland   85

3. THE ECONOMY AND INDUSTRY   86

A. The History of the British Economy   86
    1. Bibliographies and General Surveys   86
    2. Economic History   90
        (a) 1918 to the Present (Excluding the Second World War) 90
        (b) Anglo-American Economic Relations   93
        (c) Wartime Economics   94
        (d) Tariffs   95

B. Property, Income, Pensions   95
    1. Property, Inheritance, and Wealth   95
    2. Income, Prices, and Incomes Policy   96

3. Wages and Salaries   97
4. Employment Pension Schemes   100
5. Inflation   100

C. National Insurance, Social Security, Health, and Safety at Work   101
   1. Unemployment and National Insurance   101
   2. Pensions and Benefits   102
   3. Health Insurance, Safety at Work, and Industrial Arbitration   103

D. Finance   105
   1. Accounting   105
   2. Insurance   106
   3. 'The City'   107
   4. Advertising   108
   5. Savings Banks   109
   6. Building Societies   109
   7. Banks and Banking   110
      (a) General Surveys   110
      (b) Clearing Banks and Merchant Banking   111
      (c) Banks—Individual Histories   112
   8. Miscellany   113
   9. Finance and Monetary Policy   113
  10. The Fate of Sterling   116
  11. Decimal Currency   117
  12. Investment   117
  13. Public Expenditure   118
  14. Overseas Trade   119
  15. Taxation   120
  16. Local Authority Finance   120
  17. National Income   121
  18. Budgets   121
  19. Balance of Payments   122

E. Industry   122
   1. Business History   123
   2. Regional Economies   126
      (a) General Studies   126
      (b) English Regional Studies   128
      (c) Scottish Regional Studies   130
      (d) Welsh Regional Studies   132
      (e) Northern Ireland Regional Studies   133
      (f) Economics of Urban Areas   134
   3. Industrial Management   134
      (a) Management and Managers   134
      (b) Mergers, Monopolies, and Multinationals   136
   4. Industrial Relations (Including Industrial Psychology and Psychology
      and Sociology)   137

5. The Labour Force   145
   (a) Occupations (General Works; Manpower; Employment Training   145
   (b) Profits and Productivity; Industrial Democracy   147
6. Nationalized Industries, Public Ownership, Planning   149
7. Particular Industries   151
8. Trade Unionism   163
9. Strikes   168
10. Employment/Unemployment   169
11. Miscellaneous   171
12. Oddments   175

4. BRITISH SOCIETY   177
   1. Population, Migration, and Immigration   177
   2. Mortality, Birth Rate, and Birth Control   178
      (a) Mortality   178
      (b) Birth Rate and Birth Control   183
   3. Social Change   184
   4. The Status of Women   186
   5. Sociology, Social Science, and Modern British Society   192
   6. Children and Childhood   196
   7. Youth   203
   8. Middle Age   206
   9. The Elderly   206
   10. Social Policy, Social Welfare, and Social Work   209
   11. Poverty and the Welfare State   215
   12. Charities and Voluntary Work   218
   13. Social Administration   221
   14. Local Communities and Community Concerns   221
   15. Class and Status   226
   16. The Working Classes   230
   17. The Middle Classes   232
   18. The Upper Classes   232
   19. Professional Occupations   233
   20. Students   235
   21. Social Behaviour and Customs   236
   22. Marriage, Divorce, and Family Life   237
   23. Unclassified   241
   24. Crime, Criminals, and Criminology   241
      (a) General   241
      (b) The Courts   244
      (c) Punishment and the Penal System   245
      (d) Prisons, Prisoners, and Prison Officers   246
      (e) Probation and After-Care   248
      (f) Young Offenders, Borstals, and Delinquency   249
      (g) Police   253

(*h*) Murder 255

(*i*) Suicide 256

(*j*) Drugs 256

(*k*) Sexual Offences 256

(*l*) Miscellany 257

25. Race Relations 257

(*a*) General 257

(*b*) Race Relations and Government Legislation 262

(*c*) Racism, Prejudice, and Racial Disadvantage 263

(*d*) Nationalities 265

    (i)   Asian Communities 265

    (ii)   Afro-Caribbeans 265

    (iii)   Jews 266

    (iv)   Anti-Semitism 268

    (v)   Gypsies 268

    (vi)   Irish 268

    (vii) Poles 268

    (viii) Chinese 269

    (ix)   Italians 269

    (x)   Cypriots 269

    (xi)   Maltese 269

    (xii) Vietnamese 269

    (xiii) General 269

(*e*) Immigration 269

(*f*) Regional Studies 270

    (i)   London 270

    (ii)   Birmingham 271

    (iii)   Manchester 271

    (iv)   Liverpool 271

    (v)   Cardiff and South Wales 271

    (vi)   Miscellaneous Areas 271

(*g*) Housing 272

(*h*) Students 272

(*i*) Autobiographies 272

(*j*) Bibliographies 272

5. RELIGION AND THE CHURCHES 274

1. General 274

2. Histories 275

3. The Church of England 276

4. Social Questions 281

5. Politics 281

6. Doctrine 282

7. Theological Education 283

8. The Bible, Preaching, Music 283

9. Roman Catholicism in England and Wales   283

10. The Free Churches   285
    (a) Baptists   285
    (b) Congregationalists and United Reformed Church   286
    (c) Methodism   286
    (d) Smaller Free Churches   287
    (e) Quakers   288

11. Ireland   288
    (a) General   288
    (b) Presbyterianism   289
    (c) Church of Ireland   289
    (d) Methodism   289
    (e) Roman Catholicism   289

12. Scotland   289
    (a) General   289
    (b) Presbyterianism   289
    (c) Non-Presbyterian Protestants   291
    (d) Episcopalianism   291
    (e) Roman Catholicism   291

13. Wales   291

14. Ecumenism   292

15. Missions   293

16. Sociology of Religion   294

17. Moral Re-armament   294

18. Judaism   294

19. Afro-Caribbean Movements   295

20. Miscellaneous   295

21. Non-Christian Religions   296

6. EXTERNAL RELATIONS   297

A. The British Empire/Commonwealth   297
    1. General   297
    2. The 'Old Dominions'   300
       (a) Australia   300
       (b) Canada   301
       (c) New Zealand   302
    3. Africa   302
       (a) General   302
       (b) High Commission Territories   303
       (c) South Africa   303
       (d) West Africa   303
            (i)   General   303
            (ii) Ghana   304
            (iii) Nigeria   304
            (iv) Sierra Leone   304

(v)   The Gambia   304
(vi) British Cameroons   304
(e) Central Africa   305
(i)   Northern Rhodesia/Zambia   305
(ii)   Central African Federation   305
(iii) Southern Rhodesia/Zimbabwe   305
(f) East Africa   306
(i)   General   306
(ii)   Kenya   306
(iii) Uganda   306
(iv)   Tanganyika/Zanzibar/Tanzania   306
(v)   British Somaliland/Somalia   306

4. Mediterranean   306
(a) Gibraltar   306
(b) Malta   306
(c) Cyprus   307

5. The Pacific   307
(a) General   307
(b) Fiji   307
(c) The Gilbert and Ellice Islands (Kiribati and Tuvalu) and Nauru 307
(d) New Hebrides/Vanuatu   307
(e) Pitcairn Island   307
(f) Western Samoa   307
(g) Solomon Islands   307
(h) Tonga   307

6. South-East Asia   308
(a) Malaya/Malaysia   308
(b) Sarawak   309
(c) Brunei   309
(d) North Borneo/Sabah   309
(e) Singapore   309
(f) Hong Kong   309
(g) Ceylon/Sri Lanka   310

7. West Indies   310
(a) General   310
(b) Bahamas   311
(c) Belize/British Honduras   311
(d) British Guiana/Guyana   311
(e) Cayman Islands   311
(f) Jamaica   311
(g) Leeward Islands   312
(i)   Antigua and Barbuda   312
(ii)   St. Kitts-Nevis and Anguilla   312
(iii) British Virgin Islands   312
(h) Trinidad and Tobago   312

(*i*) Windward Islands   312
   (i)   Barbados   312
   (ii)   Dominica   312
   (iii) Grenada   312
   (iv) St. Lucia   312
   (v)   St. Vincent and the Grenadines   312
(*j*) West Indian Federation   312
  8. Indian Sub-Continent   313
    (*a*) India   313
    (*b*) Pakistan   315
    (*c*) Indian Ocean   315
    (*d*) Burma   315

B. Foreign Relations (Outside the Empire/Commonwealth)   315
  1. Foreign Policy: General Surveys   316
  2. Diplomats and Diplomacy   317
  3. Diplomacy/Foreign Policy in the First World War   320
  4. Peacemaking 1919   321
  5. Peace Movements, the League of Nations, and the United Nations   321
  6. The Labour Party and Foreign Policy   324
  7. Policy towards East Asia   325
    (*a*) General   325
    (*b*) Japan   325
    (*c*) China   326
  8. Policy towards Germany in the 1920s   327
  9. Policy towards Germany in the 1930s   327
  10. Policy towards Italy 1920–1939   330
  11. Policy towards the Middle East   331
  12. Policy towards Northern Europe   333
  13. Policy towards Poland 1919–1945   333
  14. Policy towards the Soviet Union 1917–1945   333
  15. Policy towards Spain and Portugal 1919–1951   335
  16. Policy towards the United States   336
  17. Policy towards the Vatican   339
  18. Policy towards Western Europe since 1945   339
  19. Policy towards France 1919–1942   342
  20. Policy towards Palestine/Israel   343
    (*a*) General   343
    (*b*) The Suez Crisis 1956   345
    (*c*) Egypt   346
    (*d*) Sudan   346

7. WAR AND THE ARMED SERVICES   347
A. The First World War   347
  1. General (Domestic)   347

2. General (Fighting)   348
3. The Experience of Soldiers   348
4. Military Commanders   349
5. Africa   349
6. The Balkans   349
7. The Dardanelles   349
8. The Italian Front   350
9. Mesopotamia/Transcaspia   350
10. The Russian Front   350
11. The Western Front   350
12. Blockade   351
13. Medical Services   351
14. The Indian Army   351
15. Intelligence   351
16. Photography   351
17. Air Power   351
18. Transport   352
19. Naval Operations   352
20. Women and the First World War   353
21. Operations: Ireland   353

B. The Second World War   353
1. General   353
2. Re-armament in the 1930s   353
3. Official Histories   354
4. Military Theorists   354
5. Generals   354
6. The Battle of the Atlantic   355
7. The Battle of Britain 1940   355
8. Air Defence   356
9. The Dakar Expedition   356
10. The Dieppe Raid 1942   356
11. Dunkirk Evacuation 1940   356
12. War in Greece   356
13. The War in Italy   357
14. War in the Levant   357
15. War in the Mediterranean   357
16. War in North Africa   357
17. War in Scandinavia   358
18. The 'Second Front'   358
19. War in South-East Asia   358
20. War in South-East Europe   358
21. Victory in Europe   358
22. The R.A.F.   359
23. The Navy   360
24. British Prisoners of War   360

25. Detention in Britain 360
26. War in Asia 361
27. Special Operations 361
28. Evacuation 361
29. Deception 361
30. Electronic Warfare 362
31. Convoys and Merchant Shipping 362
32. Civil Defence 362
33. Home Guard 362
34. The Home Front 363
35. Intelligence 363
36. Science 364
37. Propaganda (and in the First World War) 364

C. The Royal Navy 364
  1. General 364
  2. Admirals 365
  3. Profiles 365
  4. Memoirs 366
  5. Other Service 366
  6. Naval Policy and Strategy 366
  7. Ships 367
  8. The Royal Marines 368
  9. Naval Aviation 368
  10. Naval Intelligence 368

D. The British Army 369
  1. General 369
  2. The British Soldier 369
  3. Organizational Structure 369
  4. Weaponry 370
  5. Regiments 371
    (a) General 371
    (b) Irish Regiments 371
    (c) Scottish Regiments 371
    (d) English Regiments 372
    (e) Welsh Regiments 375
    (f) Auxiliary Corps 376
  6. Education: The Armed Forces 376

E. The Royal Air Force 376
  1. General 376
  2. The Royal Air Force 377
  3. Aircraft 377
  4. Airmen 378
  5. Support Services 379
  6. Formations: First and Second World Wars 379

7. Air Operations 379
8. Commanders 380
9. Bombing 380
10. Air Policy 380

F. Intelligence 381
1. General 381
2. MI6 381
3. MI5 381
4. GCHQ 381
5. Universities 381
6. Individuals 382

G. Post-1945 383
1. National Service 383
2. Operations 383
   (a) The Falklands Campaign 383
   (b) Korea 384
   (c) Malaya 384
3. Subversion and Counter-Insurgency 385
4. British Army on the Rhine 385

8. TRANSPORT 386
1. General History and Economics, Traffic and Commuting, Local Transport Studies, the Channel Tunnel, Miscellany 387
2. Canals and Inland Waterways 390
3. Shipping 392
   (a) Reference and General Shipping Works 392
   (b) Shipping Lines, Shipowners, Types of Ships 394
   (c) Shipbuilding 395
   (d) Ports, Docks, and Harbours 396
4. Railways 398
   (a) Reference and General Works 398
   (b) Company and Station Histories; Underground Railways 400
   (c) Steam Railways, Railway Construction, Traction Engines 404
5. Roads and Road Vehicles 406
   (a) Roads 406
   (b) Bicycles 407
   (c) Motorcycles 407
   (d) Trams and Tramways 408
   (e) Trolley Buses 409
   (f) Buses and Coaches 409
   (g) Motor Cars, the Motor Car Industry, other Road Vehicles 411
      (i) Motor Cars 411
      (ii) The Motor Car Industry 412
      (iii) Other Motor Vehicles 413
6. Aviation 414

(*a*) Flight and Aviation—General and Early Histories   414

(*b*) Aircraft Development   415

(*c*) The British Aircraft Industry and British Airlines   416

(*d*) Air Transport, Civil Aviation, and Airports   417

(*e*) Rocket Technology and Air-Cushioned Vehicles   418

9. URBAN AND RURAL LIFE, STANDARD OF LIVING, HOUSING, AND THE ENVIRONMENT 420

A. Towns   421

   1. General   421

   2. Towns: Large   427

   3. Towns: Small   429

   4. Towns: Scotland   430

   5. Towns: Wales   431

   6. Towns: Ireland   431

   7. New Towns   431

   8. Urban Geography   433

   9. Urban Sociology   434

  10. Suburbia   434

  11. London   434

B. Housing   436

C. Town and Country Planning   445

   1. General Studies   445

   2. Town and Country Planning by Area (Excluding London) 446

   3. London Planning   448

   4. Conservation and Preservation of Villages, Towns, and Cities

     (General and Specific Works)   449

   5. New Towns and Villages   450

D. Rural Life   451

   1. General Studies   451

   2. Villages   453

   3. English Villages and Rural Communities 453

   4. Scottish Villages and Rural Communities 455

   5. Villages and Rural Communities in Wales and Northern Ireland 456

   6. Parishes in England   457

   7. Parishes in Scotland and Wales   458

E. Agriculture, Fishing, Forestry, and Gardening   459

   1. Farming and Agriculture: Bibliographical and Survey Works 459

   2. Farming and Agriculture: Chronological Studies 460

   3. Farming in Scotland, Wales, and Northern Ireland/Agricultural

     Trade with Overseas Countries   464

   4. Farm Workers, Machinery, Techniques   465

   5. Forestry   466

   6. The Fishing Industry   468

   7. Market Gardening   469

8. Gardens and Gardening 469
F. The Environment 470
  1. General 470
  2. Pollution 472
    (a) General Studies 472
    (b) Specific Studies 473
      (i) Air Pollution 473
      (ii) Water Pollution 474
      (iii) Pesticides and Chemicals 475
      (iv) Nuclear Radiation and Waste 475
      (v) Noises Pollution 476
      (vi) Lead Pollution 476
      (vii) Flood Pollution 477
      (viii) Floods 477
  3. Conservation of Natural Resources 477
  4. Environmentalism 478
  5. Land Use 479
  6. Landscape 480
  7. Planning and the Law 480
  8. Theorists 482
  9. Conservation 482
  10. Economics of Urban Areas 482
  11. Geography 483
G. Food and Living Standards 483
  1. General Consumerism 483
  2. Nutrition and Diet 485
  3. Food—General History 486
  4. Foodstuffs 488
    (a) Milk 488
    (b) Meat 488
    (c) Sugar and Confectionery 489
    (d) Other Foodstuffs 489
    (e) Alcoholic Beverages and Public Houses 489

10. MEDICINE AND HEALTH 491
  1. Medical Education, Professional Bodies, Great Medical Men, Institutes 491
  2. Medicine 495
  3. General on Man and Medicine 501
  4. Medicine—the World 503
  5. Miscellaneous 503
  6. Health Care 504
  7. Hospitals 506
  8. General Practice 509
  9. National Health Service 510
  10. Nursing 514

11. Mental and Physical Handicap   515
12. Social Medicine/Public Health   520
13. Medical Services: Armed Forces   524
14. Alcoholism   525
15. Drugs   526
16. Disease Distribution   527
17. Genetics   528
18. Pharmacy, etc.   528
19. Physiology   529
20. Virology, etc.   530
21. Dentistry   531
22. Psychology, Psychotherapy, Psychiatry   532

11. EDUCATION   533
   1. Education in General   533
   2. Educational Documents, etc.   537
   3. History of Education   538
   4. Teachers   539
   5. Teacher-Training Institutions   540
   6. Aspects of Instruction   541
   7. Planning and Administration   541
   8. Education and Society   542
   9. Reference   543
   10. Education and Religion   543
   11. Examinations   544
   12. Education: Politics   544
   13. Secondary Modern, Comprehensive, Grammar Schools   545
   14. Preparatory Schools   546
   15. Public Schools   546
   16. Schools for Girls   549
   17. Education: Handicaps   549
   18. Education: Young Children   549
   19. Education: Immigrants   550
   20. Costs of Education   551
   21. Headmasters   551
   22. Scottish Schools   551
   23. Miscellaneous   551
   24. Further Education   552
   25. Universities: General   553
   26. Particular Universities   556
   27. Education: Scotland   560
   28. Education: Wales   561
   29. Education: Northern Ireland   561
   30. Adult Education   561
   31. The Second World War   563

12. CULTURE, RECREATION, LEISURE, AND SPORT — 564
   1. Culture in General — 565
   2. British Languages — 566
   3. Architecture — 568
   4. Art — 569
   5. Design and Fashion — 573
   6. Sculpture — 574
   7. Ballet — 574
   8. Music — 575
   9. Film — 581
   10. Photography — 584
   11. Radio — 584
   12. Television — 586
   13. Books and Publishing — 588
   14. The Press — 590
   15. Writers and Literature — 597
   16. Theatre — 607
   17. Comedy — 613
   18. Anthropology — 615
   19. Archaeology — 615
   20. Astronomy and Astronomers — 615
   21. Biochemistry — 617
   22. Biology and Biologists — 618
   23. Botany — 619
   24. Classical Scholarship — 619
   25. Economics and Economists — 620
   26. Geography — 621
   27. Historians and the Discipline of History — 623
   28. Philosophy and Philosophers — 626
   29. Political Science — 627
   30. Censorship — 627
   31. Leisure — 627
   32. Tourism — 628
   33. Recreation and National Parks — 628
   34. Gardens — 629
   35. Holidays — 629
   36. Sport — 630
   37. Rugby — 630
   38. Football — 630
   39. Cricket — 631
   40. Boxing — 632
   41. Gambling — 632
   42. Horse Racing and Show-Jumping and Fox-Hunting — 632
   43. Cycling and Motorsport — 632
   44. Athletics — 632

45. Tennis   632
46. Golf   633
47. Miscellaneous   633
48. Exploration   633
49. Science and Theology   635

Index   637

ABBREVIATIONS

A. Geog.	Acta Geographica
Aberd. Univ. Rev.	Aberdeen University Review
Acta Hist. Acad. Sci. Hung.	Acta Historica Academia Scientiarum Hungarica
Acta Sociol.	Acta Sociologica
Adult Educ.	Adult Education
Advan. Science	Advancement of Science
Afr. Affs	African Affairs
Africa Q.	Africa Quarterly
Agric. Hist.	Agricultural History
Agric. Hist. Rev.	Agricultural History Review
Amenag. Territ. Develop. Region.	Aménagement du Territoire et Développement Régional
Amer. Behavioral Scientist	American Behavioral Scientist
Amer. Econ. Rev.	American Economic Review
Amer. Hist. Rev.	American Historical Review
Amer. Inst. Plan. J.	American Institute of Planning Journal
Amer. J. Econ. Sociol.	American Journal of Economics and Sociology
Amer. J. Inl. Law	American Journal of International Law
Amer. J. Pub. Health	American Journal of Public Health
Amer. J. Sociol.	American Journal of Sociology
Amer. Jewish Hist. Q.	American Jewish Historical Quarterly
Amer. Pol. Sci. Rev.	American Political Science Review
Amer. Scientist	American Scientist
Anal. et Prévis.	Analyse et Prévision
Ann. Med. Hist.	Annals of Medical History
Ann. Rev. Anthrop.	Annual Review of Anthropology
Ann. Rev. Physiol	Annual Review of Physiology
Ann. Roy. Coll. Surgeons	Royal College of Surgeons
Ann. Sci.	Annals of Science
Arch. Iberoamer. Hist. Med.	Archivo Iberoamericano de Historia de la Medicina y Antropologia Medica
Arch. Opthalmol.	Archives of Opthamology
Architects J.	Architects Journal
Architectural Rev.	Architectural Review
Archiv. Eur. Sociol.	Archives Europeennes de Sociologie
Army Q.	Army Quarterly
Asian J. Pub. Admin.	Asian Journal of Public Administration
ASLIB Procs	ASLIB Proceedings
Austral. J. Pol. Hist.	Australian Journal of Politics and History
Austral. Outlook	Australian Outlook
Bankers Mag.	Bankers Magazine
Baptist Q.	Baptist Quarterly
Boll. Soc. Geog. Ital.	Bolletino della Societá Geografica Italiana
Brit. J. Addiction	British Journal of Addiction
Brit. J. Aesthetics	British Journal of Aesthetics
Brit. J. Criminol.	British Journal of Criminology
Brit. J. Delinquency	British Journal of Delinquency
Brit. J. Educ. Studs	British Journal of Educational Studies

Brit. J. Hist. Sci.	British Journal for the History of Science
Brit. J. Indust. Relns	British Journal of Industrial Relations
Brit. J. Inl. Studs	British Journal of International Studies
Brit. J. Med. Educ.	British Journal of Medical Education
Brit. J. Pol. Sci.	British Journal of Political Science
Brit. J. Prev. Soc. Med.	British Journal of Preventative and Social Medicine
Brit. J. Psychiatry	British Journal of Psychiatry
Brit. J. Soc. Psych. Comm. Health	British Journal of Social Psychiatry and Community Health
Brit. J. Soc. Clin. Psychol.	British Journal of Social and Clinical Psychology
Brit. J. Social Work	British Journal of Social Work
Brit. J. Sociol.	British Journal of Sociology
Brit. J. Sports Hist.	British Journal of Sports History
Brit. J. Stat. Psychol.	British Journal of Statistical Psychology
Brit. Med. J.	British Medical Journal
Brit. Mus. Q.	British Museum Quarterly
Brooklyn Bot. Gard. Rec.	Brooklyn Botanical Gardens Record
Bull. Amer. Lib. Assoc.	Bulletin of the American Library Association
Bull. Bd. Celtic Studs	Bulletin of the Board of Celtic Studies
Bull. Eastern Caribb. Affs	Bulletin of Eastern Caribbean Affairs
Bull. Econ. Res.	Bulletin of Economic Research
Bull. Hist. Med.	Bulletin of the History of Medicine
Bull. Inst. Hist. Res.	Bulletin of the Institute of Historical Research
Bull. Narcotics	Bulletin on Narcotics
Bull. N. Y. Acad. Med.	Bulletin of the New York Academy of Medicine
Bull. Oxf. Univ. Inst. Econ. Stats	Bulletin of the Oxford University Institute of Economics and Statistics
Bull. Soc. Stud. Ind. Hist.	Bulletin of the Society for the Study of Industrial History
Bull. Soc. Stud. Lab. Hist.	Bulletin of the Society for the Study of Labour History
Bus.	Business
Busin. Econ.	Business Economics
Bus. Hist. Rev.	Business History Review
Bus. Hist.	Business History
C. Int. Sociol.	Cahiers Internationaux de Sociologie
C. Sociol. Demogr. medic.	Cahiers de Sociologie et de Démographie médicale
C. Sociol. Econ.	Cahiers de Sociologie Economique
Camb. J.	Cambridge Journal
Camb. Law J.	Cambridge Law Journal
Cambrian Law Rev.	Cambrian Law Review
Can. Dimension	Canadian Dimension
Can. J. Afr. Studs	Canadian Journal of African Studies
Can. J. Hist.	Canadian Journal of History
Can. J. Econ. Pol. Sci.	Canadian Journal of Economics and Political Science
Can. Geog. J.	Canadian Geographical Journal
Can. J. Pol. Sci.	Canadian Journal of Political Science
Can. J. Pub. Admin.	Canadian Journal of Public Administration
Can. Rev. Studs in Nationalism	Canadian Review of Studies in Nationalism
Carib. Hist. Rev.	Caribbean History Review
Carib. Studs	Caribbean Studies
Cath. Hist. Rev.	Catholic Historical Review
Cent. Environ. Studs Rev.	Centre for Environmental Studies Review
Chemy. Br.	Chemistry in Britain
China Q.	China Quarterly

Church Hist.	Church History
Church Q.	Church Quarterly
Church Q. Rev.	Church Quarterly Review
Ciba Rev.	Ciba Review
Clergy Rev.	Clergy Review
Columbia Law Rev.	Columbia Law Review
Comm. Dvlpt. J.	Community Development Journal
Comp. Pols/Comp. Pol.	Comparative Politics
Comp. Pol. Studs	Comparative Political Studies
Comp. Studs Soc. Hist.	Comparative Studies in Society and History
Contemp. Record	Contemporary Record
Contemp. Rev.	Contemporary Review
Co-op. Conflict	Co-operation and Conflict
Crim. Law Rev.	Criminal Law Review
Critical Q.	Critical Quarterly
Curr. Legal Probl.	Current Legal Problems
Current Sociol.	Current Sociology
Cwealth J.	Commonwealth Journal
Def. Occident	Défense de l'Occident
Dipl. Hist.	Diplomatic History
Disarmt. Arms Control	Disarmament and Arms Control
Dominican Studs	Dominican Studies
Dublin Rev.	Dublin Review
Durham Res. Rev.	Durham Research Review
Durham Univ. J	Durham University Journal
East European Q.	East European Quarterly
Eastern Churches Rev.	Eastern Churches Review
Econ. Dvlpt. Cult. Change	Economic Development and Cultural Change
Econ. Hist. Rev.	Economic History Review
Econ. J.	Economic Journal
Econ. Record	Economic Record
Econ. Soc. Rev.	Economic and Social Review
Econ. Soc.	Economics and Society
Educ. Forum	Educational Forum
Educ. Theatre J.	Educational Theatre Journal
Employee Relns J.	Employee Relations Journal
Eng. Hist. Rev.	English Historical Review
Environt. & Behavior	Environment & Behavior
Eugenics Rev.	Eugenics Review
Eur. Econ. Rev	European Economic Review
Eur. Hist. Q.	European History Quarterly
Eur. J. Soc. Psychol.	European Journal of Social Psychology
Eur. Studs Rev.	European Studies Review
Evergreen Rev.	Evergreen Review
Explor. Econ. Res.	Explorations in Economic Research
Far Eastern Econ. Rev.	Far Eastern Economic Review
Fiscal Studs	Fiscal Studies
For. Affs	Foreign Affairs
Forth Rev.	Forth Review
Fort. Rev.	Fortnightly Review
Friends Q.	Friends Quarterly
Garden Hist.	Garden History

Geog.	Geography
Geog. J.	Geographical Journal
Geog. Mag.	Geographical Magazine
Geog. Rev.	Geographical Review
Ger. Hist.	German History
GLC Intelligence Unit Q. Bull.	GLC Intelligence Unit Quarterly Bulletin
Gvt. Opp.	Government and Opposition
Gtr. London Intelligence J.	Greater London Intelligence Journal
Hibbert J.	Hibbert Journal
Higher Ed.	Higher Education
Higher Ed. J.	Higher Education Journal
Hist.	History
Hist. Educ.	History of Education
Hist. Educ. Q.	History of Education Quarterly
Hist. Europ. Ideas	History of European Ideas
Hist. J.	Historical Journal
Hist. J. Film Tele.	Historical Journal of Film and Television
Hist. Mag. Prot. Episc. Ch.	Historical Magazine of the Protestant Episcopal Church
Hist. Pol. Econ.	History of Political Economy
Hist. Sci.	History of Science
Hist. Studs [Dublin]	Historical Studies
Hist. Studs Australia and New Zealand	Historical Studies, Australia and New Zealand
Hist. Today	History Today
Hist. Workshop	History Workshop
Housing Rev.	Housing Review
Howard J.	Howard Journal
Housing & Planning Rev.	Housing & Planning Review
Housing Studs	Housing Studies
Human Relns	Human Relations
Huntington Lib. Q.	Huntington Library Quarterly
Ind. Relns J.	Industrial Relations Journal
Ind. J. Public Admin.	Indian Journal of Public Administration
India Q.	India Quarterly
Info. Soc. Sci.	Information sur les Sciences Sociales
Inl. Affs	International Affairs
Inl. Affs (Moscow)	International Affairs, Moscow
Inl. J. Comp. Sociol.	International Journal of Comparative Sociology
Inl. J. Ethics	International Journal of Ethics
Inl. J. Health Serv.	International Journal of Health Services
Inl. Hist. Rev.	International History Review
Inl. J. Hist. Sport	International Journal of the History of Sport
Inl. J. Offend. Therapy	International Journal of Offender Therapy and Comparative Criminology
Inl. J. Pols	International Journal of Politics
Inl. J. Soc. Work	International Journal of Social Work
Inl. J. Urban and Regional Res.	International Journal of Urban and Regional Research
Inl. Lab. Rev.	International Labour Review
Inl. Law J.	International Law Journal
Inl. Migration Rev.	International Migration Review
Inl. Organization	International Organization
Inl. Rev. Educ.	International Review of Education

Inl. Rev. Soc. Hist.	International Review of Social History
Inl. Soc Sci. J.	International Social Science Journal
Inl. J. Agrarian Affs	International Journal of Agrarian Affairs
Irish Econ. Soc. Hist.	Irish Economic and Social History
Irish Hist. Studs	Irish Historical Studies
J. Admin. Overseas	Journal of Administration Overseas
J. Afr. Hist.	Journal of African History
J. Amer. Dietetic Assoc.	Journal of the American Dietetic Association
J. Amer. Hist.	Journal of American History
J. Agric. Econ.	Journal of Agricultural Economics
J. Amer. Pharm. Ass.	Journal of the American Pharmaceutical Association
J. Amer. Studs	Journal of American Studies
J. Biosoc. Sci.	Journal of Biosocial Science
J. Brit. Astron. Ass.	Journal of the British Astronomical Association
J. Brit. Inst. Inl. Affs	Journal of the British Institute of International Affairs
J. Brit. Studs	Journal of British Studies
J. Can. Studs	Journal of Canadian Studies
J. Cent. Eur. Affs	Journal of Central European Affairs
J. Chem. Educ.	Journal of Chemical Education
J. Child Psychol. Psychiatry	Journal of Child Psychology and Psychiatry
J. Church State	Journal of Church and State
J. Com. Markt. Studs	Journal of Common Market Studies
J. Contemp. Afr. Studs	Journal of Contemporary African Studies
J. Contemp. Hist.	Journal of Contemporary History
J. Contemp. Legisl.	Journal of Contemporary Legislation
J. Corr. Work	Journal of Correctional Work
J. Cwealth. Comp. Pol.	Journal of Commonwealth and Comparative Politics
J. Cwealth. Pol. Studs	Journal of Commonwealth Political Studies
J. Crim. Law Criminol. Pol. Sci.	Journal of Criminal Law, Criminology and Police Science
J. Eccl. Hist.	Journal of Ecclesiastical History
J. Econ. Hist.	Journal of Economic History
J. Econ. Lit.	Journal of Economic Literature
J. Educ. Admin. Hist.	Journal of Educational Administration and History
J. Finance	Journal of Finance
J. Genetic Psychol.	Journal of Genetic Psychology
J. Health Politics, Policy and Law	Journal of Health Politics, Policy and Law
J. Health. Soc. Behav.	Journal of Health and Social Behavior
J. Hist. Behav. Sci.	Journal of the History of the Behavioral Sciences
J. Hist. Biol.	Journal of the History of Biology
J. Hist. Geog.	Journal of Historical Geography
J. Hist. Ideas	Journal of the History of Ideas
J. Hist. Med.	Journal of the History of Medicine
J. Hum. Resources	Journal of Human Resources
J. Indust. Econ.	Journal of Industrial Economics
J. Imp. Cwealth. Hist.	Journal of Imperial and Commonwealth History
J. Ind. Hygiene	Journal of Industrial Hygiene
J. Inst. Actuaries	Journal of the Institute of Actuaries
J. Inst. Transport	Journal of the Institute of Transport
J. Inter-Amer. Studs	Journal of Inter-American Studies
J. Lat. Amer. Studs	Journal of Latin American Studies
J. Law Econ.	Journal of Law and Economics
J. Lib. Hist.	Journal of Library History

J. Marr. Fam. Liv.	Journal of Marriage and Family Living
J. Mental. Sci	Journal of Mental Science
J. Min. Agric.	Journal of the Ministry of Agriculture
J. Mod. Afr. Studs	Journal of Modern African Studies
J. Mod. Hist.	Journal of Modern History
J. Navigation	Journal of Navigation
J. Negro Hist.	Journal of Negro History
J. N. E. Lab. Hist.	Journal of North East Labour History
J. Palestine Studs	Journal of Palestine Studies
J. Photography	Journal of Photography
J. Planning & Environment Law	Journal of Planning and Environment Law
J. Pol. Econ.	Journal of Political Economy
J. Pols	Journal of Politics
J. Procs Agric. Econ. Soc.	Journal of the Proceedings of the Agricultural Economics Society
J. Pub. Law	Journal of Public Law
J. Roy. Agric. Soc. Eng.	Journal of the Royal Agricultural Society of England
J. Roy. Army Med. Corps	Journal of the Royal Army Medical Corps
J. Roy. Central Asian Soc.	Journal of the Royal Central Asian Society
J. Roy. Coll. Gen. Practitioners	Journal of the Royal College of General Practitioners
J. Roy. Coll. Physicians	Journal of the Royal College of Physicians
J. Roy. Inst. Brit. Arch.	Journal of the Royal Institute of British Architects
J. Roy. Soc. Arts	Journal of the Royal Society of Arts
J. Roy. Stat. Soc.	Journal of the Royal Statistical Society
J. Roy. United Services Inst. Def. Studs	Journal of the Royal United Services Institute for Defence Studies
J. Sci. Stud. Rel.	Journal for the Scientific Study of Religion
J. Soc. Hist.	Journal of Social History
J. Soc. Issues	Journal of Social Issues
J. Social Pol.	Journal of Social Policy
J. Soc. Film Television Arts	Journal of the Society for Film and Television Arts
J. Soc. Welfare Law	Journal of Social Welfare Law
J. Soc. Bibliogr. Nat. Hist.	Journal of the Society for the Bibliography of Natural History
J. Southeast Asian Hist.	Journal of Southeast Asian History
J. South East Asian Studs	Journal of South East Asian Studies
J. State Medicine	Journal of State Medicine
J. Strat. Studs	Journal of Strategic Studies
J. Transport Econ. Policy	Journal of Transport Economics and Policy
J. Transport Hist.	Journal of Transport History
J. Tropic. Med.	Journal of Tropical Medicine
J. Unit. Reformed Ch. Hist. Soc.	Journal of the United Reformed Church History Society
J. Urban Hist.	Journal of Urban History
J. Welsh Eccl. Hist.	Journal of Welsh Ecclesiastical History
J. World Hist.	Journal of World History
Jew. J. Sociol.	Jewish Journal of Sociology
Jewish Soc. Studs	Jewish Social Studies
Journalism Q.	Journalism Quarterly
Kenyon Rev.	Kenyon Review
Lab. Monthly	Labour Monthly
Labor Hist.	Labor History
Land Econ.	Land Economics
Landscape Hist.	Landscape History

Law and Contemp. Probs	Law and Contemporary Problems
Law. Q. Rev.	Law Quarterly Review
Legislative Studs Q.	Legislative Studies Quarterly
Leisure Studs	Leisure Studies
Lloyds Bank Rev.	Lloyds Bank Review
Local Gvt. Policy Making	Local Government Policy Making
Local Gvt. Studs	Local Government Studies
London Rev. Pub. Admin.	London Review of Public Administration
London J.	London Journal
Management in Gvt.	Management in Government
Manch. Sch. Econ. Soc. Studs	Manchester School of Economic and Social Studies
Manch. Lit. Phil. Soc.	Manchester Literary and Philosophical
Memoirs and Procs	Society Memoirs and Proceedings
Med. Hist.	Medical History
Med. World	Medical World
Medico-Legal J.	Medico-Legal Journal
Mental Handicap Bull.	Mental Handicap Bulletin
Mid. East J.	Middle East Journal
Mid. Hist.	Midland History
Middle East Affs	Middle East Affairs
Midwest Q.	Midwest Quarterly
Mil. Mitt.	Militarische Mitteilungen
Millbank Mem. Fund. Q.	Millbank Memorial Fund Quarterly
Min. of Labour Gazette	Ministry of Labour Gazette
Mod. Asian Studs	Modern Asian Studies
Mod. Churchman	Modern Churchman
Mod. Law	Modern Law
Mod. Law Rev.	Modern Law Review
Monthly Lab. Rev.	Monthly Labour Review
Municipal Rev.	Municipal Review
Nat. Bureau Econ. Res.	National Bureau of Economic Research
Nat. Civic Rev.	National Civic Review
Nat. Inst. Econ. Soc. Res. Q. Rev.	National Institute of Economic and Social Research Quarterly Review
Nat. Lib. Wales J.	National Library of Wales Journal
Nat. Rev.	National Review
Nat. West. Bank Q. Rev.	National Westminster Bank Quarterly Review
New Left Rev.	New Left Review
New Lit. Hist.	New Literary History
N.Z. J. Public Admin.	New Zealand Journal of Public Administration
New Rev. East Eur. Hist.	New Review of East European History
New World Q.	New World Quarterly
North Amer. Rev.	North American Review
North Staffs. J. Field Studs	North Staffordshire Journal of Field Studies
Northern Hist.	Northern History
Notes Rec. Roy. Soc. Lond.	Notes and Records of the Royal Society of London
Oral Hist.	Oral History
Oxf. Agrarian Studs	Oxford Agrarian Studies
Oxf. Econ Papers	Oxford Economic Papers
Pacific Affs	Pacific Affairs
Pac. Community	Pacific Community
Pac. Hist. Rev	Pacific Historical Review

Pac. Sociol. Rev.	Pacific Sociology Review
Parl. Affs	Parliamentary Affairs
Partisan Rev.	Partisan Review
Pass. Pres.	Passato e Presente
Perspect. Biol. Med.	Perspectives in Biology and Medicine
Pharm. J.	Pharmaceutical Journal
Phil. Soc. Sci.	Philosophy of the Social Sciences
Phil. Trans. Roy. Soc. London	Philosophical Transactions of the Royal Society of London
Philosophical J.	Philosophical Journal
Pol. Affs	Political Affairs
Pol. Scientist	Political Scientist
Police Studs	Police Studies
Polish Rev.	Polish Review
Pol. Geog. Q.	Political Geography Quarterly
Pol. Q.	Political Quarterly
Pol. Sci.	Political Science
Pol. Sci. Q.	Political Science Quarterly
Pol. Studs	Political Studies
Pop.	Population
Pop. Index	Population Index
Pop. Studs	Population Studies
Postgrad. Med. J.	Postgraduate Medical Journal
Proc. Brit. Acad.	Proceedings of the British Academy
Proc. Brit. Assoc. Jap. Studs	Proceedings of the British Association of Japanese Studies
Proc. Inst. Elec. Eng.	Proceedings of the Institute of Electrical Engineers
Proc. Indust. Relns Res. Assoc.	Proceedings of the Industrial Relations Research Association
Proc. Roy. Microsc. Soc.	Proceedings of the Royal Microscopical Society
Proc. Roy. Phil. Soc. Glasgow	Proceedings of the Royal Philosophical Society of Glasgow
Proc. Roy. Soc. London	Proceedings of the Royal Society of London
Proc. Roy. Soc. Med.	Proceedings of the Royal Society of Medicine
Proc. Wes. Hist. Soc.	Proceedings of the Wesley Historical Society
Proc. Western Soc. Fr. Hist.	Proceedings of the Annual Meeting of the Western Society for French History
Pub. Law	Public Law
Public Admin.	Public Administration
Public Admin. (Sydney)	Public Administration (Sydney)
Public Admin. Bull.	Public Administration Bulletin
Public Admin. Rev.	Public Administration Review
Pub. Op. Q.	Public Opinion Quarterly
Publ. Management	Public Management
Publishing Hist.	Publishing History
Q. J. Econ.	Quarterly Journal of Economics
Q. J. Forestry	Quarterly Journal of Forestry
Q. J. Roy. Astronom. Soc.	Quarterly Journal of the Royal Astronomical Society
Q. J. Roy. Meteorological Soc.	Quarterly Journal of the Royal Meteorological Society
Q. J. Studs Alcohol	Quarterly Journal of Studies on Alcohol
Quart. Rev.	Quarterly Review
Q. Rev. Agric. Econ.	Quarterly Review of Agricultural Economics
Queen's Q.	Queen's Quarterly
R. Sci. Financ.	Revue de Science Financière
Records Scot. Church Hist. Soc.	Records of the Scottish Church History Society
Regional Studs	Regional Studies

Relig. in Life	Religion in Life
Ren. Mod. Studs	Renaissance and Modern Studies
Rev. d'Hist. Diplo.	Revue d'Histoire Diplomatique
Rev. Econ. Stats	Review of Economics and Statistics
Rev. Econ. Studs	Review of Economic Studies
Rev. Franc. Sci. Polit.	Revue Française de Science Politique
Rev. Franc. Sociol.	Revue Française de Sociologie
Rev. Inl. Studs	Review of International Studies
Rev. Pol.	Review of Politics
Rev. of Revs	Review of Reviews
Rev. Sociol.	Revue de Sociologie
Riv. Ital. Sci. Pol.	Rivista Italiana di Scienze Politiche
Riv. Sociol.	Rivista di Sociologia
Roy. Inst. Great Brit. Procs	Royal Institution of Great Britain: Proceedings
Rural Sociol.	Rural Sociology
Scand. J. Hist.	Scandinavian Journal of History
Sci. Mthly.	Scientific Monthly
Sci. Prog.	Science Progress
Scot. Agric. Econ.	Scottish Agricultural Economics
Scot. Art Rev.	Scottish Art Review
Scot. Ecclesiol. Soc. Trans.	Scottish Ecclesiological Society Transactions
Scot. Hist. Rev.	Scottish Historical Review
Scot. Geog. Mag.	Scottish Geographical Magazine
Scot. J. Pol. Econ.	Scottish Journal of Political Economy
Scot. J. Sociol.	Scottish Journal of Sociology
Scot. Lab. Hist. Soc. Rev.	Scottish Labour History Society Review
Slav. E. Eur. Rev.	Slavonic and East European Review
Soc. Casework	Social Casework
Soc. Econ. Admin.	Social and Economic Administration
Soc. Econ. Studs	Social and Economic Studies
Soc. Hist.	Social History
Soc. Pol.	Social Policy
Soc. Probs	Social Problems
Soc. Pol. Studs	Social and Political Studies
Soc. Serv. Q.	Social Service Quarterly
Soc. Serv. Rev.	Social Service Review
Soc. Reg.	Socialist Register
Soc. Res.	Social Research
Soc. Sci.	Social Science
Soc. Sci. Q.	Social Science Quarterly
Soc. Studs	Social Studies
Soc. Stud. Sci.	Social Studies of Science
Soc. Work	Social Work
Sociol. B.	Sociological Bulletin
Sociol. Rev.	Sociological Review
Sociol. Rur.	Sociologia Ruralis
Sociol. Soc. Res.	Sociology and Social Research
South Atl. Q.	South Atlantic Quarterly
Southeast Asian Affs	Southeast Asian Affairs
Southern Econ. J.	Southern Economic Journal
Southern Hist.	Southern History
Southwestern Soc. Sci. Q.	Southwestern Social Science Quarterly

Stud. Comp. Loc. Gvt.	Studies in Comparative Local Government
Studio Inl.	Studio International
Swansea Geog.	Swansea Geographer
Temps Mod.	Temps Modernes
Theatre Q.	Theatre Quarterly
Tijd. Econ. Soc. Geog.	Tijdschrift voor Economische en Sociale Geografie
Town & Country Plan.	Town & Country Planning
Town Plan. Rev.	Town Planning Rev.
Trans. Amer. Phil. Soc.	Transactions of the American Philosophical Society
Trans. Gaelic Soc. Inverness	Transactions of the Gaelic Society of Inverness
Trans. Hon. Soc. Cymmr.	Transactions of the Honourable Society of Cymmrodorion
Trans. Inc. San. Assn. Scot.	Transactions of the Incorporated Sanitary Association of Scotland
Trans. Inst. Brit. Geog.	Transactions of the Institute of British Geography
Trans. Jewish Hist. Soc. Eng.	Transactions of the Jewish Historical Society of England
Trans. Manch. Stat. Soc.	Transactions of the Manchester Statistical Society
Trans. Newcomen Soc.	Transactions of the Newcomen Society
Trans NE Coast Inst. Eng. Shipbuilders	Transactions of the NE Coast Institute of Engineers and Shipbuilders
Trans. Roy. Ent. Soc. Lond.	Transactions of the Royal Entomological Society of London
Trans. Roy. Hist. Soc.	Transactions of the Royal Historical Society
Trans. Roy. Soc. Trop. Med. Hyg.	Transactions of the Royal Society of Tropical Medicine and Hygiene
Transport Hist.	Transport History
Trends in Educ.	Trends in Education
Twentieth Cent.	Twentieth Century
United States Dept. of State Bull.	United States Department of State Bulletin
Univ. Q.	Universities Quarterly
Univ. Rev.	Universities Review
Univ. Birm. Hist. J.	University of Birmingham Historical Journal
Univ. Leeds Rev.	University of Leeds Review
Univ. Left. Rev.	Universities and Left Review
Univ. Toronto Law J.	University of Toronto Law Journal
Unpartizan Rev.	Unpartizan Review
Update Rev.	Update Review
Urban Affs Q.	Urban Affairs Quarterly
Urban Studs	Urban Studies
Vie Econ. Soc.	Vie Economique et Sociale
Virginia Q. Rev.	Virginia Quarterly Review
Vistas Astronom.	Vistas in Astronomy
Welsh Hist. Rev.	Welsh History Review
West Eur. Pols	West European Politics
Western Pol. Q.	Western Political Quarterly
Wiener Lib. Bull.	Wiener Library Bulletin
Wiseman Rev.	Wiseman Review
World Affs Q.	World Affairs Quarterly
World Pol.	World Politics
World Rev. Nutrition & Dietetics	World Review of Nutrition and Dietetics
Yale Rev.	Yale Review
Ybook. World Affs	Yearbook of World Affairs
Yorks. Bull. Econ. Soc. Res.	Yorkshire Bulletin of Economic and Social Research

1

GENERAL

A. BIBLIOGRAPHIES AND OTHER REFERENCE BOOKS

1. ABSTRACTS

1 Historical Abstracts. Oxf. 1955+.

2 INTERNATIONAL POLITICAL SCIENCE ASSOCIATION. International Political Science Abstracts. Oxf. 1951–1972. 1973+.

3 Human Resources Abstracts. 1965+.

4 SOCIOLOGICAL ABSTRACTS INC. Sociological Abstracts 1953+. Five times per annum.

2. GENERAL BIBLIOGRAPHIES

5 British National Bibliography.

6 Books in English. 1971–.

7 Whitaker's Cumulative Book List. 1924–.

8 Whitaker's Books of the Month and Books to Come. 1970–.

9 BESTERMAN (THEODORE). A World Bibliography of Bibliographies and of Bibliographical Catalogues, Calendars, Abstracts, Digests, Indexes and the Like. 5 vols 4th edn 1965–1966.

10 TOOMEY (ALICE F.) *comp.* A World Bibliography of Bibliographies 1964–1974. 2 vols. Totowa, New Jersey. 1977.

11 Bibliographical Index: A Cumulative Bibliography of Bibliographies. N.Y. 1937–.

12 ROBERTS (N.) *ed.* Use of Social Science Literature. 1977.

13 GRAY (RICHARD A.) *comp.* Serial Bibliographies in the Humanities and Social Sciences. 1969.

3. BIOGRAPHY

14 DAVIS (HENRY WILLIAM CARLESS) *and* WEAVER (JOHN REGINALD HOMER) *eds.* The Dictionary of National Biography 3rd Supplement [1912–21.]. Oxf. 1927.

15 WEAVER (JOHN REGINALD HOMER) *ed.* The Dictionary of National Biography 4th Supplement [1922–30.]. Oxf. 1937.

16 LEGG (LEOPOLD GEORGE WICKHAM) *ed.* The Dictionary of National Biography 5th Supplement [1931–40.]. Oxf. 1949.

17 LEGG (LEOPOLD GEORGE WICKHAM) *and* WILLIAMS (E. T.) *eds.* The Dictionary of National Biography 6th Supplement [1941–50.]. Oxf. 1959.

18 WILLIAMS (E. T.) *and* PALMER (HELEN M.) *eds.* The Dictionary of National Biography 7th Supplement [1951–60.]. Oxf. 1971.

19 WILLIAMS (E. T.) *and* NICHOLLS (CHRISTINE S.) *eds.* The Dictionary of National Biography 8th Supplement [1961–70.]. Oxf. 1981.

20 BLAKE (ROBERT N. W.) *Baron, and* NICHOLLS (CHRISTINE S.) *eds.* The Dictionary of National Biography 9th Supplement [1971–80.]. Oxf. 1986.

21 10th Supplement [1981–85.]. Oxf. 1990.

22 The Dictionary of National Biography: The Concise Dictionary. Part II: 1901–1970. Oxf. 1982.

23 Who's Who. 1897+.

24 Who was Who, 1897–1915. 1920.

25 1916–1928. 1929.

26 1929–1940. 1947.

27 1941–1950. 1952.

28 1951–1960. 1961.

29 1961–1970. 1972.

30 1971–1980. 1981.

31 Who was Who: A Cumulated Index, 1897–1980. 1981.

32 Vacher's Biographical Guide. 1987.

33 OXBURY (HAROLD). Great Britons: Twentieth Century Lives. Oxf. 1985.

34 Burke's Peerage and Baronetage 1826+. Latterly appearing irregularly.

35 Debrett's Peerage and Baronetage 1769+. Now quinquennial.

36 PINE (LESLIE GILBERT). The New Extinct Peerage 1884–1971, Containing Extinct, Abeyant, Dormant and Suspended Peerages with Genealogies and Arms. 1972.

37 LEESON (FRANCIS L.). A Directory of British Peerages. 1984.

38 Kelly's Handbook to the Titled, Landed and Official Classes. 1977.

39 Distinguished People of Today. 1988+. Annual. It replaces Debrett's Handbook. 1982–1986.

40 ROBERTS (FRANK C.) *comp.* Obituaries from The Times, 1951–1960. 1979.

41 Obituaries from *The Times*, 1961–1970.

42 Obituaries from *The Times*, 1971–1975.

43 Current Biography. 1940+. N.Y. Monthly.

44 KIFFER (MARY E.). Current Biography: Cumulated Index 1940–1985. N.Y. 1986. [Supersedes Current Biography Cumulative Index 1940–1970.].

45 BELLAMY (JOYCE M.) *and* SAVILLE (JOHN) *eds.* Dictionary of Labour Biography. 8 vols 1972–. The cumulated index is in vol. 8.

46 MAITRON (JEAN) *ed.* Dictionnaire Biographique du Mouvement Ouvrier International: Grande Bretagne. Vol. 1 Paris. 1979.

47 Proceedings of the British Academy, 1903+. Annual. [Contains obituaries of deceased Fellows.].

48 ROBBINS (KEITH GILBERT) *ed.* The Blackwell Biographical Dictionary of British Political Life in the Twentieth Century. Oxf. 1990.

49 LLOYD (*Sir* JOHN EDWARD) *and* JENKINS (R. T.) *eds.* The Dictionary of Welsh Biography down to 1940. 1959. Y Bywgraffiadur Cymreig hyd 1940. 1959.

50 JENKINS (R. T.) *and* JONES (E. D.). Y Bywgraffiadur Cymreig 1941–1950. 1970.

51 BOYLAN (HENRY). A Dictionary of Irish Biography. 2nd edn Dublin. 1980.

4. DATABASES AND BANKS

52 HALL (JAMES LOGAN) *and* BROWN (M. J.). Online Bibliographical Databases: A Directory and Sourcebook. 4th edn 1986.

53 BRITISH LIBRARY. Inventory of Bibliographic Databases Produced in the UK. Boston Spa. 1976.

54 ROYAL INSTITUTE OF PUBLIC ADMINISTRATION. RIPALIS. [Only available to members of the Institute.].

55 ESRC. Data Archive based at the University of Essex, Wivenhoe Park, Colchester, CO4 3SQ.

56 ACOMPLINE and URBALINE. [Originally initiatives of the now defunct Greater London Council, they cover a wide range of urban issues: Details of Research Library, London Research Centre, Parliament House, Black Prince Road, London SE1 7SJ.].

57 CENTRAL STATISTICAL OFFICE. [Details from Databank Manager, Central Statistical Office, Room 52/4, Government Buildings, Great George Street, London SW1P 3AQ.].

5. DIRECTORIES

58 SHAW (GARETH) *and* TIPPER (ALISON). British Directories: A Bibliography and Guide to Directories Published in England and Wales (1850–1950) and Scotland (1773–1950). 1988.

59 HENDERSON (C. A. P.) *ed.* Current British Directories. 10th edn 1985.

60 The Top 2000 Directories and Annuals. 1980+.

61 The Top 3000 Directories and Annuals. 1985+.

62 SELLER (LINDSAY). Councils, Committees and Boards: A Handbook of Advisory, Consultative, Executive and Similar Bodies in British Public Life. 6th edn 1984.

63 HENDERSON (G. P.) *and* HENDERSON (S. P. A.). Directory of British Associations and Associations in Ireland. 9th edn 1988.

6. FACTUAL HANDBOOKS

64 BUTLER (DAVID EDGEWORTH) *and* BUTLER (GARETH). British Political Facts 1900–1985. 1986.

65 COOK (CHRIS) *and* STEVENSON (JOHN). The Longman Handbook of Modern British History 1714–1987. 2nd edn 1988.

66 FOOTE (GEOFFREY). A Chronology of Post-War British Politics. 1988.

67 ROSE (RICHARD) *and* McALLISTER (IAN). United Kingdom Facts. 1982.

68 HUGGETT (FRANK EDWARD). A Dictionary of British History 1815–1973. 1974.

69 FRYDE (E. B.), GREENWAY (D. E.), *and* ROY (I.) *eds.* Handbook of British Chronology. 3rd edn 1986.

7. GUIDE TO SOURCES

70 SELDON (ANTHONY) *ed.* Contemporary History: Practice and Method. Oxf. 1988.

71 FOSTER (JANET) *and* SHEPPARD (JULIA). British Archives. 2nd edn 1988.

72 DOWNS (ROBERT B.). British and Irish Library Resources: A Bibliographical Guide. 1981.

73 HISTORICAL MANUSCRIPTS COMMISSION. Accessions to Repositories and Reports Added to the National Register of Archives. 1954–. 1923–1953: this was published by the Institute of Historical Research in their Bulletin. 1953–1956: it appeared as part of the Bulletin of the National Register of Archives. Since then it has been a separate publication.

74 Archives. 1948–.

75 Journal of the Society of Archivists. 1972–.

76 HISTORICAL MANUSCRIPTS COMMISSION. Record Repositories in Great Britain: A Geographical Directory. 8th edn 1987.

77 STOREY (RICHARD) *and* TOUGH (ALISTAIR) *comp.* Consolidated Guide to the Modern Records Centre. University of Warwick, Coventry. 1986.

78 COOK (CHRIS). Sources in British Political History 1900–1951. 6 vols 1975–85.

79 HAZLEHURST (CAMERON) *and* WOODLAND (CHRISTINE). A Guide to the Papers of British Cabinet Ministers 1900–1951. 1974.

8. INDEXES

80 British Humanities Index. 1962–.

81 Subject Index to Periodicals. 1918–.

82 Public Affairs Information Service Bulletin. 1915–. N.Y.

83 BLACKMORE (RUTH MATTESON) *ed.* Cumulative Subject Index to the Public Affairs Information Service Bulletin 1915–74. 1977.

84 MACDONALD (K. I.). The Essex Reference Index: British Journals of Politics and Sociology 1950–1973. 1975.

85 Recently Published Articles. 1976–.

86 Index to Theses Accepted for the Higher Degrees in the Universities of Great Britain and Ireland. 1953–.

87 Dissertation Abstracts International. 1938–. Ann Arbor, Michigan.

88 American Doctoral Dissertations. 1934–. N.Y.

89 JACOB (P. M.). History Theses 1901–1970: Historical Research for Higher Degrees in the Universities of the United Kingdom. 1976.

90 HORN (JOYCE M.). History Theses 1971–1980: Historical Research for Higher Degrees in the Universities of the United Kingdom. 1984.

91 Comprehensive Dissertations Index 1861–1972: Volume 28: History. 1973.

92 KUEHL (WARREN F.). Dissertations in History 1970–June 1980: An Index to Dissertations Completed in History Departments of United States and Canadian Universities. Oxf. 1985.

9. LIBRARY GUIDES AND CATALOGUES

93 CODLIN (ELLEN M.). Aslib Directory of Information Sources in the United Kingdom. 2 vols, 5th edn 1984.

94 BURKETT (JACK). Library and Information Networks in the United Kingdom. 5th edn 1979.

95 Library and Information Networks in Western Europe. 1983.

96 ROBERTS (STEPHEN A.), COOPER (ALAN), *and* GILDER (LESLEY). Research Libraries and Collections in the United Kingdom. A Selective Inventory and Guide. 1978.

97 DALE (PETER). Guide to Libraries and Information Units. 29th edn 1990 succeeds Guide to Government

Departments and Other Libraries *ed.* by R. T. Atkins. 28th edn 1988.

98 LEVINE (H. M.) *and* OWEN (D. B.). An American Guide to British Social Science Abstracts. 1976.

99 COLLISON (ROBERT). Published Library Catalogues: An Introduction to Their Contents and Use. 1973.

100 The British Library General Catalogue of Printed Books to 1975. 360 vols 1979–87.

101 Subject Index of Modern Books Acquired 1946–1950. 4 vols 1961.

102 1951–1955. 6 vols 1974.

103 1956–1960. 6 vols 1965.

104 1961–1970. 12 vols 1982.

105 1971–1975. 14 vols and 1 Supplement. 1986.

106 The British Library General Subject Catalogue 1975–1985. 75 vols 1986.

107 The National Union Catalog Pre-1956 Imprints: A Cumulative Author List Representing Library of Congress Printed Cards and Titles Reported and Other American Libraries: Compiled and Edited with the Co-operation of the Library of Congress and the National Union Catolog Sub-Committee of the Resources and Technical Services Division, American Library Association. 754 vols 1968–81.

108 The National Union Catalog. 1958–1962. 54 vols N.Y. 1963.

109 The National Union Catalog. Motion Pictures and Filmstrips 1963–1967. 2 vols Ann Arbor, Mich. 1969.

110 The National Union Catalog. Motion Pictures and Filmstrips 1968–1972. 4 vols Ann Arbor, Mich. 1973.

111 The National Union Catalog. Author List 1968–1972. 119 vols Ann Arbor, Mich. 1973.

112 The National Union Catalog. Films 1973–1977. 7 vols Totowa, New Jersey. 1978.

113 The National Union Catalog. Author List 1973–1977. 135 vols Totowa, N. J. 1978.

114 Library of Congress Catalog: A Cumulative List of Works Represented by Library of Congress Printed Cards: Books: Subjects 1950–1954. 20 vols Ann Arbor, Mich. 1955.

115 1955–1959. 22 vols Paterson, N. J. 1960.

116 1960–1964. 25 vols Ann Arbor, Mich. 1965.

117 1965–1969. 42 vols Ann Arbor, Mich. 1970.

118 1970–1974. 100 vols Totowa, N. J. 1976.

119 A London Bibliography of the Social Sciences. 4 vols 1931–.

10. MAPS AND ATLASES

120 The Ordnance Survey Atlas of Great Britain. 1983.

121 The Ordnance Survey Gazetteer of Great Britain. 1987. 2nd edn 1989.

122 MASON (OLIVER) *comp*. Bartholomew Gazetteer of Britain. 1986.

123 BICKMORE (D. P.) *and* SHAW (M. A.). The Atlas of Britain and Northern Ireland. Oxf. 1963.

124 The 'Reader's Digest' Complete Atlas of the British Isles. 1966.

125 FOTHERGILL (STEPHEN) *and* VINCENT (JILL). The State of the Nation. 1985.

126 OSMAN (TERRY). The Facts of Everyday Life. 1985.

127 The Ordnance Survey Map Catalogue. Annual.

128 HARLEY (J. B.). Ordnance Survey Maps: A Descriptive Manual. 1975.

129 LOCK (C. B. MURIEL). Modern Maps and Atlases: An Outline Guide to Twentieth Century Production. 1969. 3rd edn 1976.

130 Business Atlas of Great Britain. 1974.

131 DIAMOND (DEREK) *and* EDWARDS (ROGER) *comps*. Business in Britain: A Philip Management Planning Atlas. 1975.

132 BARTHOLOMEW. Road Atlas Britain. 1943+. Annual.

133 MINISTRY OF HOUSING AND LOCAL GOVERNMENT. Planning Maps of England and Wales. 1962 [1931–61.].

134 DEPARTMENT OF THE ENVIRONMENT. Planning Maps of England and Wales. 2 vols 1975.

135 Atlas of the Environment: England and Wales 1976+.

136 SCOTTISH DEVELOPMENT DEPARTMENT. Planning Maps Series. Scotland. 1966.

137 CARTER (HAROLD) *et al*. National Atlas of Wales. Cardiff. 1980.

138 IRISH NATIONAL COMMITTEE FOR GEOGRAPHY. Atlas of Ireland. Dublin. 1979.

139 FALKUS (MALCOLM) *and* GILLINGHAM (JOHN) *eds*. Historical Atlas of Britain. 1981.

140 HORNER (A. A.), WALSH (J. A.), *and* HARRINGTON (V. P.). Population in Ireland: A Census Atlas. Dept of Geography. University College, Dublin. 1987.

141 COMPTON (PAUL A.). Northern Ireland: A Census Atlas. Dublin. 1978.

142 CENSUS RESEARCH UNIT, UNIVERSITY OF DURHAM. People in Britain: A Census Atlas. H.M.S.O. 1980.

143 POPE (REX) *ed*. Atlas of British Social and Economic History. 1989.

144 FREEMAN-GRENVILLE (G. S. P.). Atlas of British History. 1979.

II. NEWSPAPER AND PERIODICAL GUIDES

145 BRITISH MUSEUM PUBLICATIONS. Catalogue of the Newspaper Library at Colindale. 8 vols 1975.

146 WEBBER (ROSEMARY) *comp*. World List of National Newspapers in Libraries in the British Isles. 1976.

147 Benn's Media Directory. 2 vols 1978+ Annual. [Until 1948 published by Mitchell, and until 1978 by Benn as the Newspaper Press Directory.].

148 BRITISH MEDIA PUBLICATIONS. Willing's Press Guide. Annual. 1890+.

149 BOWKER PUBLICATIONS. Ulrich's International Periodicals Directory. 2 vols 1932+. 27th edn 3 vols 1988–9.

150 Irregular Series and Annuals: An International Directory. 3 vols 1967–87.

151 Ulrich's Update: A Quarterly Update. 1988+.

152 EBSCO PUBLISHING. The Serials Directory: An International Reference Book. 3 vols Birmingham, Ala. 5th edn 1991.

153 STEWART (JAMES D.) *ed*. British Union Catalogue of Periodicals: A Record of the Periodicals of the World from the Seventeenth Century to the Present Day in British Libraries. 4 vols 1955.

154 Supplement (to 1960). 1962.

155 PORTER (KENNETH I.) *and* KOSTER (C. J.) *eds*. New Periodical Titles, 1960–1968. 1970.

156 GASCOIGNE (J.). New Periodical Titles, 1969–1973. 1976.

157 Annual Supplements 1974–1981. Retitled and issued quarterly as Serials in the British Library 1981+.

158 TITUS (EDNA BROWN) *ed*. Union List of Serials in Libraries in the United States and Canada. 5 vols 3rd edn N.Y. 1965. Continued as New Serial Titles: A Union List of Serials commencing Publication after December 31 1949: 1950–70 Cumulative. 4 vols 1973. 1971–5. 1975. 2 vols 1976. 1976–80. 2 vols 1981. 1981–5. 6 vols 1986. 1986–7. 4 vols 1988. Update quarterly.

159 WOODWORTH (DAVID P.) *and* GOODAIR (CHRISTINE M.). Current British Periodicals: A Bibliographical Guide. Wetherby. 4th edn 1986.

160 WALFORD (A. J.) *and* HARVEY (JOAN M.) *eds*. Walford's Guide to Current British Periodicals in the Humanities and Social Sciences. 1985.

161 CENTRAL OFFICE OF INFORMATION. Technical and Specialised Periodicals published in Britain: A Selected List. 1972.

162 BOEHM (ERIC H.), POPE (BARBARA H.) *and* ENSIGN (MARIE S.) *eds*. Historical Periodicals Directory. 5 vols Oxf. 1981–6.

163 KIRBY (JOHN LAVAN). A Guide to Historical Periodicals in the English Language. 1970.

164 LIBRARY ASSOCIATION. A Union List of Statistical Serials in British Libraries. 1973.

165 WAPSIEC (JAN). Sociology: An International Bibliography of Serial Literature, 1880–1980. 1983.

166 HARRIS (CHAUNCEY D.) *and* FELLMAN (JAMES D.). International List of Geographical Serials. 3rd edn 1980. Dept. of Geography, University of Chicago.

167 HARRIS (CHAUNCEY D.). Annotated World List of Selected Current Geographical Serials. 4th edn 1980. Dept. of Geography, University of Chicago.

168 THE TIMES. The Official Index to The Times 1906–1956.

169 The Times Index 1957+.

170 FINANCIAL TIMES BUSINESS INFORMATION. Monthly Index to the Financial Times. 1981+.

171 THE GUARDIAN. 1986+.

12. OFFICIAL PUBLICATIONS

172 HORROCKS (SIDNEY). The State as Publisher: A Librarian's Guide to the Publications of His Majesty's Stationery Office. 1952.

173 RICHARD (STEPHEN). Directory of British Official Publications: A Guide to Sources. 2nd edn 1984.

174 PEMBERTON (JOHN E.). British Official Publications. Oxf. 1973.

175 RODGERS (FRANK). Guide to British Government Publications. N.Y. 1980.

176 BUTCHER (DAVID). Official Publications in Britain. 1983.

177 HAKIM (CATHERINE). Secondary Analysis in Social Research: A Guide to Data Sources with Examples. 1982.

178 OLLE (JAMES G.). An Introduction to British Government Publications. 1965. 2nd edn 1973.

179 Government Publications: Monthly and Consolidated Lists. 1936–1954.

180 Government Publications 1954–1985.

181 Annual Catalogue 1985+.

182 MALLABER (K. A.). 'The Sale Catalogues of British Government Publications 1836 to 1965'. *J. Librarianship* 5/2 (1973), 116–31.

183 BLACKMORE (RUTH MATTESON) *comp.* Cumulative Index to the Annual Catalogues of Her Majesty's Stationery Office 1922–1972. 2 vols 1976.

184 NURCOMBE (VALERIE J.) *ed.* Whitehall and Westminster. 1984.

185 Catalogue of British Official Publications not published by H.M.S.O. 1980+. Camb. 1981+.

186 Directory of Specialists in Official Publications. 1985. 2nd edn 1988.

187 British Official Publications online: A Review of sources, services and developments: Proceedings of a one–day seminar held by ISG, SCOOP at the Department of Trade and Industry, Victoria Street, London on 20 Sept. 1989 and 4 Oct. 1989.

188 RICHARD (STEPHEN). British Government Publications: An Index to Chairmen and Authors. Vol. II 1900–1940. 1974. Vol. III: 1941–1978. 1982. Vol. IV: 1979–1982. 1984.

189 MORGAN (A. MARY) *ed.* British Government Publications: An Index to Chairmen and Authors, 1941–1966. 1969.

190 H.M.S.O. Index to Chairmen of Committees. 1982+ Annual.

191 FINNIE (HAZEL) *comp.* Checklist of British Official Serial Publications. 12th edn 1987.

192 FORD (PERCY) *and* FORD (GRACE). A Guide to Parliamentary Papers. 3rd edn Oxf. 1972.

193 A Breviate of Parliamentary Papers 1900–1916. Oxf. 1957.

194 A Breviate of Parliamentary Papers 1917–1939. Oxf. 1951.

195 A Breviate of Parliamentary Papers 1940–1954: War and Reconstruction. Oxf. 1961.

196 FORD (PERCY), FORD (GRACE), *and* MARSHALLSAY (DIANA). Select List of British Parliamentary Papers, 1955–1964. Dublin. 1970.

197 MARSHALLSAY (DIANA) *and* SMITH (J. H.) *eds.* Ford's List of British Parliamentary Papers 1965–1974, together with Specialist Commentaries. Camb. 1979.

198 MARSHALLSAY (DIANA) *and* RICHARDS (PETER GODFREY) *eds.* Ford's List of British Parliamentary Papers 1974–1983, together with Specialist Commentaries. Camb. 1989.

199 H.M.S.O. General Index to Parliamentary Papers, 1900–1949. 1960.

200 General Alphabetical Index for 1950 to 1958–9. 1963.

201 1959 to 1969. 1975.

202 RODGERS (FRANK). Serial Publications in the British Parliamentary Papers 1900–1968: A Bibliography. 1971.

203 DI ROMA (EDWARD) *and* ROSENTHAL (JOSEPH A.) *comps.* A Numerical Finding List of British Command Papers Published 1832–1961/2. N.Y. 1967.

204 McBRIDE (ELIZABETH A.). British Command Papers: A Numerical Finding List 1962/3–1976/7. Emory University, Atlanta, Georgia. 1982.

205 VOGEL (ROBERT). A Breviate of British Diplomatic Blue Books 1919–1939. Montreal. 1963.

206 MALTBY (ARTHUR). The Government of Northern Ireland: A Catalogue and Breviate of Parliamentary Papers. Shannon. 1974.

13. PHOTOGRAPHIC AND FILM ARCHIVES

207 CORNISH (GRAHAM PETER). Archival Collections of Non-Book Material. 2nd edn 1986.

208 WALL (JOHN) *comp.* Directory of British Photographic Collections. 1977.

209 NUNN (G. W. A.) *ed.* British Sources of Photographs and Pictures. 1952.

210 Classified Index to the Library of Aerial Photographs. 1954.

211 EVANS (HILARY) *and* EVANS (MARY). Picture Researchers Handbook: An International Guide to Picture Sources and How to Use Them. Newton Abbot. 1975. 3rd edn Wokingham. 1986.

212 BRADSHAW (DAVID N.) *and* HAHN (CATHERINE). World Photography Sources. N.Y. 1982.

213 ORMOND (RICHARD) *and* ROGERS (MALCOLM) *eds*. Dictionary of British Portraiture. Vol. iv: The Twentieth Century: Historical Figures born before 1900. 1981.

214 NATIONAL PORTRAIT GALLERY. 20th Century Portraits. 1978.

215 Complete Illustrated Catalogue. 1876–1979. 1981.

216 OLIVER (ELIZABETH) *ed*. Researcher's Guide to British Film and Television Collections. 2nd edn 1985.

217 THORPE (FRANCES) *ed*. A Directory of British Film and Television Libraries. 1975.

218 *Ed*. International Directory of Film and TV Documentation Centres. Chicago/London. 1988.

219 ELTON (*Sir* ARTHUR). 'The Film as Source Material For History'. *ASLIB Procs*. 7/4 (1955), 207–39.

220 BALLANTYNE (JAMES) *ed*. Researcher's Guide to British Newsreels. 1983 and 1988.

221 BRITISH UNIVERSITIES FILM AND VIDEO COUNCIL/INSTITUTE OF CONTEMPORARY BRITISH HISTORY. Post-War British History: A Select List of Videos and Films Available in the U.K. 1988.

222 McNULTY (ANNE) *and* TROOP (HILARY). Directory of British Oral History Collections. Vol. 1 1981. [Oral History Society.].

223 FOREMAN (NELL) *comp*. Archive Sound Collections: An Interim Directory of Institutional Collections of Sound Recordings in Great Britain Holding Material other than that Currently Commercially Available. Aberystwyth. 1974.

224 WEERASINGHE (LALI) *comp*. Directory of Recorded Sound Resources in the United Kingdom. British Library. 1989.

225 SELDON (ANTHONY) *and* PAPPWORTH (JOANNA). By Word of Mouth: Elite Oral History. 1983.

226 BRITISH INSTITUTE OF RECORDED SOUND becomes NATIONAL SOUND ARCHIVE in 1983 as part of the British Library.

227 BBC SOUND ARCHIVES LIBRARY. Broadcasting House. London. W1A 1AA.

228 Catalogue of Records Talks and Speeches. 3 vols 1966–7.

14. POLLS AND SURVEYS

229 CALDER (ANGUS) *and* SHERIDAN (DOROTHY) *eds*. Speak for Yourself: A Mass Observation Anthology 1937–1949. 1984.

230 GALLUP (GEORGE H.) *ed*. The Gallup International Public Opinion Polls: Great Britain 1937–1975. 2 vols. Vol. 1 1937–64. Vol. 2 1965–75. N.Y. 1976.

231 HEALD (GORDON) *and* WHYBROW (ROBERT J.). The Gallup Survey of Britain. 1986.

232 WHYBROW (ROBERT J.). Britain Speaks Out, 1937–1987: A Social History as seen through Gallup Data. 1989.

233 Gallup Political Index. 1960+. Monthly.

234 NATIONAL OPINION POLLS. NOP Political Bulletin. 1963–1975.

235 NOP MARKET RESEARCH. Political, Social, Economic Review. 1975+. Every two months.

236 MORI. British Public Opinion. Irregular. Ten times per annum since 1983.

237 British Social Attitudes. 1984+.

238 ABRAMS (MARK), GERARD (DAVID), *and* TIMMS (NOEL) *eds*. Values and Social Change in Britain. 1985.

239 HARDING (STEPHEN D.) *and* PHILLIPS (DAVID) *with* FOGARTY (MICHAEL P.). Contrasting Values in Western Europe: Unity, Diversity and Change. 1986.

15. REFERENCE MATERIAL

240 WALFORD (A. J.). Guide to Reference Material. 3 vols 4th edn 1980–1987.

241 HIGGENS (GAVIN L.). Printed Reference Material. 2nd edn 1984.

242 SHEEHY (EUGENE P.) *ed*. Guide to Reference Books. 10th edn Chicago. 1986.

243 HARZFELD (LOIS A.). Periodical Indexes in the Social Sciences and Humanities: A Subject Guide. Folkestone. 1978.

244 TAYLOR (PETER J.). Information Guides: A Survey of Subject Guides to Sources of Information Produced by Library and Information Services in the United Kingdom. 1978.

245 STEPHENS (J.). Inventory of Abstracting and Indexing Services Produced in the United Kingdom. 2nd edn 1983.

246 STAVELEY (RONALD) *and* PIGGOTT (MARY) *eds*. Government Information and the Research Worker. 1952. Rev. edn 1965.

247 COMFORT (A. F.) *and* LOVELESS (C.). Guide to Government Data: A Survey of Unpublished Social Science Material in Libraries of Government Departments in London. 1974.

248 Guide to Government and Other Libraries and Research Bureaux. 1975.

16. STATUTES

249 H.M.S.O. Public General Acts and Measures. 1945+.

250 Statutes in Force. 1972+.

251 Index to the Statutes Covering the Legislation in Force on 31 December 1985. 2 vols 1987.

252 Chronological Table of the Statutes. Part I. 1235–1950. Part II 1950–31 December 1985. 2 vols 1987.

253 The Statutory Rules and Orders and Statutory Instruments Revised to December 31 1948. 25 vols 3rd edn 1949–1952.

254 Statutory Rules and Orders 1945–. 1946–.

255 Table of Government Orders Covering the General Instruments to 31 December 1986. 1988.

256 List of Statutory Instruments. 1900+. Monthly.

257 Index to Government Orders in Force on 31 December 1985. 2 vols 1987.

258 Index to Local and Personal Acts and Special Orders and Special Procedure Orders, 1801–1947. 1949.

259 Supplementary Index to Local and Personal Acts, 1948–1966. 1967.

260 Local and Personal Acts 1800+.

261 THE LAW COMMISSION AND THE SCOTTISH LAW COMMISSION. Chronological Table of Local Legislation Part II: Local and Personal Acts 1909–1973, Private Acts 1539–1973. 1985.

262 Current Law Statutes Annotated. 1948+.

17. YEARBOOKS

263 Annual Register: A Record of World Events. 1974+.

264 Whitaker's Almanack. 1868+.

265 The Statesman's Year Book. 1864+.

266 PAXTON (JOHN) *ed.* The Statesman's Year Book Historical Companion. 1988.

267 The Year Book of World Affairs. 1947+.

268 The Times Yearbook of World Affairs. 1978+.

269 Keesings Contemporary Archives. 1931+. [Weekly until 1983 and monthly since then.].

270 Britain: An Official Handbook. 1954+. [An earlier version first appeared in 1946.].

271 Commonwealth Survey. 1953–1967. [Fortnightly.].

272 Survey of British and Commonwealth Affairs. 1967–1970. [Fortnightly.].

273 Survey of Current Affairs. 1971–1985. [Monthly.].

274 Vacher's Parliamentary Companion: A Reference Book for Parliament, National Organisations and Public Offices. 1831+. [Quarterly.].

275 British Political Yearbook, 1947. 1947.

276 OAKLEY (ROBIN) *and* ROSE (PETER). The Political Year, 1970. 1970.

277 —— The Political Year, 1971. 1971.

278 NORRIS (W.). One from Seven Hundred: A Year in the Life of Parliament. Oxf. 1966.

279 BAX (ANTHONY) *and* FAIRFIELD (S.) *eds.* The Macmillan Guide to the UK 1978–1979. 1979.

B. GENERAL HISTORIES AND STUDIES

1. COLLECTIONS OF DOCUMENTS

280 BARKER (WILLIAM ALAN) *ed.* Documents of English History 1832–1950. 1954.

281 BETTEY (JOSEPH HAROLD) *ed.* English Historical Documents 1906–1939. 1967.

282 BRIGGS (ASA) *Baron, comp.* 'They saw it Happen'. Vol. iv. 1897–1940. Oxf. 1960.

283 REYNOLDS (REGINALD ARTHUR) *ed.* British Pamphleteers. Vol. ii. From the French Revolution to the Nineteen-Thirties. 1951.

284 WROUGHTON (JOHN). Documents on British political history. Vol. iii. 1914–1970. 1973.

2. GENERAL HISTORIES

285 TAYLOR (ALAN JOHN PERCIVALE). English History, 1914–1945. Oxf. 1965. Vol. xv of the *Oxford History of England*. A brilliantly opinionated study which is beginning to show its age.

286 WEBB (ROBERT KIEFER). Modern England: From the Eighteenth Century to the Present. N.Y. 1968. Other American textbooks include Alfred Freeman Havighurst, Britain in Transition: The Twentieth Century. Evanston, Ill. 1979 (appeared as Twentieth Century Britain. Evanston, Ill. 1962. 4th edn 1985) and Walter Leonard Arnstein (appeared as Britain, Yesterday and Today: 1830

to the Present. Boston. 1966). Also Bentley Brinkerhoff Gilbert, Britain since 1918. 1967.

287 ROBBINS (KEITH GILBERT). The Eclipse of a Great Power: Modern Britain, 1870–1975. 1983. 2nd edn [to 1992] 1994.

288 MARWICK (ARTHUR JOHN BRERETON). Britain in the Century of Total War: War, Peace and Social Change, 1900–1967. 1968.

289 —— Britain in Our Century: Images and Controversies. 1984.

290 LLOYD (TREVOR O.). Empire to Welfare State: English History, 1906–1976. Oxf. 1979. 3rd edn 1986 [to 1985.].

291 MEDLICOTT (WILLIAM NORTON). Contemporary England, 1914–1964. 1967. New edn with epilogue 1964–1974. 1976.

292 BELOFF (MAX). Wars and Welfare: Britain 1914–1945. 1984.

293 PELLING (HENRY MATHISON). Modern Britain, 1885–1955. 1960.

294 THOMSON (DAVID). England in the Twentieth Century. Harmondsworth. 1965. 2nd rev. edn by Geoffrey Warner. Harmondsworth. 1981.

295 BLAKE (ROBERT N. W.) *Baron.* The Decline of Power, 1915–1964. 1985.

296 SOMERVELL (DAVID CHURCHILL). Modern Britain, 1870–1950. 1952.

297 JARMAN (THOMAS LECKIE). Democracy and World Conflict, 1868–1970. 1971: a history of modern Britain. The above are widely used texts not without their own influence on modern British history; older works which can be similarly categorized include: Sir James Ramsay Montague Butler. A history of England, 1815–1939. 1928. 2nd edn 1960 [1918–39 added.]. Sir John Arthur Ransome Marriott. Modern England, 1885–1945. 1934. 4th edn 1960. John Alfred Spender, Great Britain: Empire and Commonwealth, 1886–1935. 1936.

298 SEAMAN (LEWIS CHARLES BERNARD). Post-Victorian Britain, 1902–1951. 1966. A useful school text. See also Roger Raymond Sellman, Modern British History, 1815–1970: a practical guide, 1976. Leslie William Herne, A Guide to British History, 1868–1959, 1966.

299 MOWAT (CHARLES LOCH). Britain Between the Wars, 1918–1940. 1955. Although out of date in places, it remains superior to its later competitors, William Lloyd McElwee, Britain's Locust Years, 1918–1940, 1962; Marion Yass, Britain between the world wars, 1918–1939, 1975; Noreen Branson, Britain in the Nineteen Twenties, 1978; Noreen Branson and Margot Heinemann, Britain in the Nineteen Thirties, 1971; Ronald Blythe, The Age of Illusion: England in the Twenties and Thirties, 1919–1940. 1963. Our own Times, 1913–1934, by Sir Stephen King Hall, is instant history, as is John Cobb Fossey, Prelude to 1937: Being a Sketch of the Critical Years 1931–1936, 1937. Both only have value for that reason. Decennial sketches by contemporaries and others have limited value. Malcolm Muggeridge, The Thirties: 1930–1940 in Great Britain, 1940, new edn 1967, has inspired others: John Montgomery, The Twenties: An Informal Social History, 1957; Richard Bennett, A Picture of the Twenties, 1961; Alan Jenkins, The Thirties, 1976; Julian Symons, The Angry Thirties, 1976; Collin Brooks, Devil's Decade: Portraits of the Nineteen Thirties, 1948. John Raymond ed., The Baldwin Age, 1960, is slightly superior.

300 BARTLETT (CHRISTOPHER JOHN). A History of Post-war Britain, 1945–1974. 1977. Other 'post-war' assessments include Peter Calvocoressi, The British Experience, 1940–1975, 1978; Christopher Montague Woodhouse, Post-War Britain, 1966; Alan Sked and C. P. Cook, Post-War Britain: A Political History. Harmondsworth, 1979. Michael Sissons and Philip N. French, eds, The Age of Austerity, 1945–1951, 1963, and Vernon Bogdanor, ed., The Age of Affluence, 1951–1964, 1970, both contain useful essays. Sketches are attempted by John Montgomery, The Fifties, 1965, Alan Thompson, The Day Before Yesterday: An Illustrated History of Britain from Attlee to Macmillan, 1971, Bernard Levin, The Pendulum Years: Britain and the Sixties, 1970, Alan Jenkins, The Forties, 1977, Alan C. S. Ross, The Forties: A Period Piece, 1950, and T. E. B. Howarth, Prospect and Reality: Great Britain 1945–1955, 1985.

301 HAIGH (CHRISTOPHER) ed. The Cambridge Historical Encyclopaedia of Great Britain and Ireland. 1985.

302 ALDERMAN (GEOFFREY). Modern Britain 1700–1983: A Domestic History. 1986.

303 ROYLE (EDWARD). Modern Britain, A Social History 1750–1985. 1987.

304 TOMPSON (RICHARD S.). The Atlantic Archipelago. A Political History of the British Isles. Lewiston, N.Y. 1986.

305 THE ANNUAL REGISTER. 1758+.

306 GILBERT (MARTIN) ed. A Century of Conflict, 1850–1950: Essays for A. J. P. Taylor. 1966.

307 READ (DONALD). The English Provinces, c.1760–1960: A Study in Influence. 1964.

308 TIERNEY (MARK). Modern Ireland, 1850–1950. 1972.

309 O'BRIEN (CONOR CRUISE) ed. The Shaping of Modern Ireland. 1960.

310 MURPHY (JOHN AUGUSTINE). Ireland in the Twentieth Century. 1975.

311 LYONS (FRANCIS STEWART LELAND). Ireland since the Famine. 1973.

312 FARRELL (MICHAEL). Northern Ireland: The Orange State. 1976.

313 CURTIS (EDMUND). A History of Ireland. 1936. 6th edn 1961.

314 PRYDE (GEORGE SMITH). A New History of Scotland. Vol. II, Scotland from 1603 to the Present Day. 1962.

315 KELLAS (JAMES GRANT). Modern Scotland, the Nation since 1870. 1968.

316 FERGUSON (WILLIAM). Scotland: 1689 to the Present. Edin. Hist. of Scotland IV. Edin./Lond. 1968.

317 WILLIAMS (DAVID). History of Modern Wales. 1950. New edn 1977.

318 BARRACLOUGH (GEOFFREY). An Introduction to Contemporary History. 1964.

319 CHURCHILL (Sir WINSTON LEONARD SPENCER). Great Contemporaries. 1937. Rev. edn 1938.

320 BROGAN (Sir DENIS WILLIAM). The English People: Impressions and Observations. 1943.

321 BARKER (Sir ERNEST). The Character of England. 1947.

322 WILSON (FRANCESCA MARY) ed. Strange Island: Britain through Foreign Eyes, 1395–1940. 1955.

323 WILLIAMS (RAYMOND). Culture and Society, 1780–1950. 1958.

324 WEST (Sir ALGERNON). Contemporary Portraits. 1920.

325 RUSSELL (BERTRAND ARTHUR WILLIAM) Earl. Portraits from Memory and other Essays. 1956.

326 MALLABY (Sir GEORGE). Each in his Office: Studies of Men in Power. 1972.

327 LOCKHART (Sir ROBERT HAMILTON BRUCE). Friends, Foes and Foreigners. 1957.

328 KEYNES (JOHN MAYNARD) Baron. Essays in Biography. 1933. New edn 1951. Repr. 1961.

329 GREGG (PAULINE). A Social and Economic History of Britain, 1760–1972. 7th edn 1973.

330 BARNETT (CORRELLI). The Collapse of British Power. 1972.

331 BARKER (WILLIAM ALAN) *et al.* A General History of England, 1832–1960. 2 vols 2nd edn 1960.

332 BREACH (ROBERT WALTER). A History of our own Times: Britain 1900–1964. 1968.

333 BROWN (ALFRED VICTOR). A History of Britain, 1939–1968. Oxf. 1970.

334 REYNOLDS (ERNEST EDWIN) *and* BRASHER (NORMAN HENRY). Britain in the Twentieth Century, 1900–1964. Camb. 1966.

335 RICHARDS (DENIS GEORGE) *and* QUICK (ANTHONY). Twentieth Century Britain. 1968.

336 MACDONALD (DONALD FARQUHAR). The Age of Transition: Britain in the Nineteenth and Twentieth Centuries. 1967.

337 FEILING (*Sir* KEITH GRAHAME). Study of the Modern History of Great Britain, 1862–1946. 1947.

338 ALLEN (ARTHUR BRUCE). Twentieth Century Britain. 1958.

339 NAYLOR (JOHN F.) *ed.* Britain, 1919–1970. Chicago. 1971.

340 GRAHAM (JOHN GEOFFREY). British History, 1914 to the Present Day. 1971.

341 PICK (FREDERICK WALTER). Contemporary History. Oxf. 1949.

342 RAY (JOHN). A History of Britain, 1900–1939. 1968.

343 RAYNER (ROBERT MACEY). Recent Times: A History of Britain and its Continental Background, 1868–1939. 1949.

344 PEACOCK (HERBERT LEONARD). A History of Modern Britain, 1815–1968. 1968.

345 HOPEWELL (SYDNEY). One Hundred and Fifty Years of Modern Britain, 1815 to the Present Day. Oxf. 1965.

346 HOWAT (GERALD MALCOLM DAVID). From Chatham to Churchill: British History, 1760–1965. 1966.

347 UNSTEAD (ROBERT JOHN). Britain in the Twentieth Century. 1966.

348 WEYMOUTH (ANTHONY). This Century of Change, 1853–1952. 1953.

349 DERRY (KINGSTON). British History from 1782 to 1933. 1935.

350 CLEMENT (HENRY ANTHONY). British History, 1865–1965. 1966.

351 BRETT (SIDNEY REED). British History, 1901–1961. 1966.

352 GRETTON (RICHARD HENRY). A Modern History of the English People, 1910–1922. 1929.

353 COLLIER (JOHN) *and* LANG (IAIN). Just the other Day: an Informal History of Great Britain since the War. 1932.

354 FURTH (CHARLES). Life since 1900. 3rd edn 1966.

355 HEARD (GERALD). These Hurrying Years: an Historical Outline, 1900–1933. 1934.

356 HERD (HAROLD). Panorama, 1900–1942. 1942.

357 COLE (GEORGE DOUGLAS HOWARD). Great Britain in the Post-war World. 1942.

358 LIPSON (EPHRAIM). Europe, 1914–1939. 4th edn 1947.

359 TAYLOR (DON). Years of Challenge. 1959.

360 TAYLOR (ALAN JOHN PERCIVALE). The Struggle for Mastery in Europe, 1848–1918. Oxf. 1954. New edn Oxf. 1971.

361 SOUTHGATE (GEORGE WALTER). England, 1867–1939. 1951.

362 RICKER (JOHN C.). The Modern Era. 1960.

363 NIEMEYER (NANNIE) *and* SPALDING (ETHEL HOWARD). England: A Social and Economic History, 1830–1936. 6th edn 1957.

364 NEAL (TERENCE ARTHUR). Democracy and Responsibility: British History, 1880–1965. 1969.

365 NEW CAMBRIDGE MODERN HISTORY. 12 vols Camb. 1957+. XII. The Shifting Balance of World Forces, 1898–1945. Ed. by Charles Loch Mowat. Camb. 1968.

366 MEECH (THOMAS COX). This Generation: A History of Great Britain and Ireland from 1900 to 1926. 2 vols 1927–1928.

367 MONK (LEONARD ASHBY). Britain, 1945–1970. 1976.

368 TAYLOR (ALAN JOHN PERCIVALE). Essays in English History. 1976.

369 —— Europe: Grandeur and Decline. 1967.

370 —— From Napoleon to Stalin. 1950.

371 THOMPSON (LAURENCE). 1940: Year of Legend, Year of History. 1966.

372 WINKLER (H. R.). 'Some Recent Writings on Twentieth Century Britain', in Elizabeth Furber *ed.* Changing Views on British History: Essays on Historical Writing since 1939. Camb., Mass. 1966.

373 BIRMINGHAM UNIVERSITY. Centre for Contemporary Cultural Studies. Report. Birm. 1964.

374 ARMSTRONG (NOEL). Let's Make Britain Great Again. Norwich. 1964.

375 MAUDE (ANGUS EDMUND UPTON). The Consuming Society. 1967.

376 MAGEE (BRYAN EDGAR). Towards 2000: The World we Make. 1915.

377 WINGFIELD-STRATFORD (ESMÉ CECIL). Beyond Empire. 1964.

378 NOSSITER (BERNARD D.). Britain: A Future that Works. 1978.

379 MIDDLETON (D.). The British. 1957. [U.S. edn 'These are the British'.].

380 TUMELTY (JAMES). Britain Today. 2nd edn 1970.

381 KOESTLER (ARTHUR) *ed.* Suicide of a Nation? An Inquiry into the State of Britain Today. By Henry Fairlie and others. 1963.

382 ROUTH (HAROLD VICTOR). The Diffusion of English Culture Outside England: A Problem for Post-war Reconstruction. Camb. 1941.

383 MONTAGUE (JOEL BENJAMIN) *Jnr.* Class and Nationality: English and American Studies. 1963.

384 MARCHANT (*Sir* JAMES) *ed.* Post-War Britain. 1945.

385 WATKINS (ERNEST). The Cautious Revolution. 1951.

386 JOHNSON (WALFORD), WHYMAN (JOHN), *and* WYKES (GEORGE). A Short Economic and Social History of Twentieth Century Britain. 1967.

387 MADGWICK (P. J.), STEEDS (D.), *and* WILLIAMS (L. J.). Britain since 1945. 1982.

388 SCOTT (J. D.). Life in Britain. N.Y. 1956.

389 CANNING (JOHN) *ed.* Living History: 1914. 1968.

390 MOWAT (CHARLES LOCH). England in the Twentieth Century. *History* li (1966), 188–196.

391 ROBBINS (KEITH GILBERT). 'The Great 20th Century Serial'. *History* lvii (1972), 248–50.

3. HISTORICAL BIBLIOGRAPHIES

392 HAVIGHURST (ALFRED FREEMAN). Modern England 1901–1970. Camb. 1976. 2nd edn 1987.

393 MOWAT (CHARLES LOCH). British History since 1926: A Select Bibliography. 1960.

394 WESTERGAARD (JOHN), WEYMAN (ANNE), *and* WILES (PAUL) *eds.* Modern British Society: A Bibliography. 1974. 2nd edn 1977.

395 CHALONER (W. H.) *and* RICHARDSON (R. C.). Bibliography of British Economic and Social History. 1984. 2nd edn Manch. 1984.

396 INSTITUTE OF HISTORICAL RESEARCH. Bibliography of Historical Works Issued in the United Kingdom. *Ed.* by Joan Lancaster 1946–56. 1957.

397 KELLAWAY (WILLIAM) *ed.* 1957–1960. 1962.

398 —— *ed.* 1961–1965. 1967.

399 —— *ed.* 1966–1970. 1972.

400 TAYLOR (ROSEMARY) *ed.* 1971–1975. 1977.

401 INSTITUTE OF HISTORICAL RESEARCH. Writings on British History.

402 MILNE (ALEXANDER TAYLOR) *ed.* 1901–1933. 5 vols 1968–1970.

403 —— *ed.* 1934–1945. 8 vols 1937–60.

404 MUNRO (D. J.) *ed.* 1946–1948. 1973.

405 —— *ed.* 1949–1951. 1975.

406 SIMS (J. M.) *ed.* 1952–1954. 1975.

407 SIMS (J. M.) *and* JACOBS (P. M.) *eds.* 1955–1957. 1977.

408 CREATON (HEATHER J.) *ed.* 1958–1959. 1977.

409 PHILPIN (CHARLES H. E.) *and* CREATON (HEATHER J.) *eds.* 1960–1961. 1978.

410 CREATON (HEATHER) *ed.* 1962–1964. 1979.

411 —— *ed.* 1965–1966. 1981.

412 —— *ed.* 1967–1968. 1982.

413 —— *ed.* 1969–1970. 1984.

414 —— *ed.* 1971–1972. 1985.

415 —— *ed.* 1973–1974. 1986.

416 ROYAL HISTORICAL SOCIETY. Annual Bibliography of British and Irish History. 1976+.

417 HISTORICAL ASSOCIATION. Annual Bibliography of Historical Literature. 1911+.

418 ENGLISH HISTORICAL REVIEW. [Lists annually articles on British History.].

419 International Bibliography of Historical Sciences. 1935+.

420 UNESCO. International Bibliography of Political Science. 1954+.

421 International Bibliography of Sociology. 1950+.

422 STEVENSON (BRUCE). Reader's Guide to Great Britain: A Bibliography. 1977.

423 LEWIS (PETER R.). The Literature of the Social Sciences. 1960.

424 BRITISH LIBRARY LENDING DIVISION. British Reports, Translations and Theses. 1981+. [Replaces BLLD Announcements Bulletin.].

425 CATTERALL (PETER). 'The State of the Literature on Post-War British History'. In Post-War Britain 1945–64: Themes and Perspectives *ed.* by Tony Gorst, Lewis Johnman, and Scott Lucas. 1989.

426 —— British History 1945–1987: An Annotated Bibliography. Oxf. 1990.

2

CONSTITUTIONAL AND POLITICAL HISTORY

A. THE MONARCHY

The historiography of the monarchy, perhaps predictably, displays a wider ranger of material than many other categories. Studies by historians and political scientists focus on the powers and status of the monarchy within a political and constitutional context. Alongside them stand certain polemical works which marry historical scholarship with opinion on the desirability of monarchy. There are also many biographies of monarchs, consorts, and other leading and not so leading members of the royal family. They vary in tone between the severe and the sentimental. In the longer term, the value of interim studies may be limited, yet the exclusion of ephemeral portraits from a bibliography would deprive the scholar of valuable insights into contemporary attitudes to monarchy which biographers unwittingly disclose by their unspoken assumptions or omissions. The cleavage between 'academic' and 'popular' approaches does mean, however, that it is difficult to identify books which give a rounded account of the significance of the monarchy in twentieth-century British history.

I. GENERAL

427 CANNON (JOHN) *and* GRIFFITHS (RALPH). The Oxford Illustrated History of the British Monarchy. Oxf. 1988.

428 HARDIE (FRANK MARTIN). The Political Influence of the British Monarchy, 1868–1952. 1970.

429 PETRIE (*Sir* CHARLES ALEXANDER). The Modern British Monarchy. 1961.

430 DUNCAN (ANDREW). The Reality of Monarchy. 1970.

431 COUNIHAN (DAVID). Royal Progress: Britain's Changing Monarchy. 1977.

432 HOWARD (PHILIP). The British Monarchy in the Twentieth Century. 1977.

433 LOCKYER (ROGER WALTER). The Monarchy. 1966.

434 MacDONAGH (MICHAEL). The English King: A Study of the Monarchy and the Royal Family, Historical, Constitutional and Social. N.Y. 1971.

435 MICHIE (ALLAN ANDREW). The Crown and the People. 1952.

436 MARTIN (BASIL KINGSLEY). The Crown and the Establishment. 1962.

437 MURRAY-BROWN (JEREMY) *ed.* The Monarchy and its Future. 1969.

438 THOMPSON (JOSEPH ALLEN) *and* MEJIA (ARTHUR). Modern British Monarchy. 1971.

439 GOLBY (JOHN) *and* PURDUE (WILLIAM). The Monarchy and the British People 1760 to the Present. 1987.

440 KEITH (ARTHUR BERRIEDALE). The King and the Imperial Crown: The Powers and Duties of His Majesty. 1936.

441 —— The Privileges and Rights of the Crown. 1936.

442 —— The King, the Constitution, the Empire and Foreign Affairs, 1936–1937. 1938.

443 BENEMY (FRANK WILLIAM GEORGESON). The Queen Reigns, She does not rule. 1963.

444 HARRIS (LEONARD MORTIMER). Long to Reign over Us? The Status of the Royal Family in the Sixties. 1966.

445 SINCLAIR (DAVID). Two Georges: The Making of the Modern Monarchy. 1988.

446 NAIRN (TOM). The Enchanted Glass: Britain and Its Monarchy. 1988.

447 BRENDON (PIERS). Our Own Dear Queen. 1986.

448 BOLITHO (HENRY HECTOR). A Century of British Monarchy. 1951. Edn with epilogue, 1953.

449 HALE (THOMAS F.). 'The Labour Party and the Monarchy'. *Contemp. Rev.* 219 (1971), 73–9.

450 ROSE (RICHARD) *and* KAVANAGH (DENNIS). 'Monarchy in Contemporary Political Culture'. *Comp. Pols.* viii (1976), 548–76.

451 CANNADINE (DAVID). 'The Context, Performance and Meaning of Ritual: The British Monarchy and "The Invention of Tradition" c. 1820–1977'. In The Invention of Tradition, by Eric Hobsbawm and Terence Ranger, *eds* Camb. 1983.

452 CANNON (JOHN). 'The Survival of the British Monarchy'. *Trans. Roy. Hist. Soc.* 5th ser. 36 (1986), 143–64.

453 MARPLES (MORRIS). Princes in the Making: A Study of Royal Education. 1965.

454 HUGHES (EMRYS). The Prince, the Crown and the Cash. 1969.

455 WILLIAMS (NEVILLE). Royal Houses of Great Britain from Medieval to Modern Times. 1971.

456 —— The Royal Residences of Great Britain: A Social History. 1960.

457 HOWARD (PHILIP). The Royal Palaces. 1970.

458 MANSFIELD (ALAN). Ceremonial Costume: Court, Civil and Civic Costume from 1660 to the Present Day. 1980.

459 SQUIBB (G. D.). Precedence in England and Wales. Oxf. 1981.

460 SHINN (R. F.). 'The King's Title, 1926: A Note on a Critical Document'. *Eng. Hist. Rev.* 98 (1983), 349–53.

461 EVATT (HERBERT VERE). The King and His Dominion Governors: A Study of the Reserve Powers of the Crown in Great Britain and the Dominions. 1936. New edn 1967. An Australian perspective.

462 BARKER (Sir ERNEST). British Constitutional Monarchy. 1944. Rev. edn 1952.

Specific constitutional questions are considered in W. P. M. Kennedy, 'The Regency Acts, 1937–1953', *Univ. Toronto Law J.* x (1954), 248–54; C. L. Berry, 'The Coronation Oath and the Church of England', *J. Eccl. Hist.* xi (1960), 98–105; John D. Fair, 'Walter Bagehot, Royal Mediation, and the Modern British Constitution, 1869–1931', *The Historian* 43/1 (1980), 36–54; Graeme Cochrane Moodie, 'The Monarch and the Selection of a Prime Minister: A Re-examination of the Crisis of 1931', *Pol. Stud.* v (1957), 1–20; Andrew Alexander, 'British Politics and the Royal Prerogative of Appointment since 1945', *Parl. Affs* xxiii (1970), 248–57; D. J. Heasman, 'The Monarch, the Prime Minister and the Dissolution of Parliament', *Parl. Affs.* xiv (1960–1), 94–107.

463 FLEMING (TOM) *comp.* Voices out of the Air: The Royal Christmas Broadcasts, 1932–1981. 1981.

464 HARDIE (FRANK). 'The King and the Constitutional Crisis'. *History Today* xx (1970), 338–47.

465 HART-DAVIS (DUFF) *ed.* End of an Era: Letters and Journals of Sir Alan Lascelles 1887–1920. 1986.

2. THE ROYAL FAMILY

466 PAKENHAM (ELIZABETH) *Countess of Longford.* The Royal House of Windsor. 1974.

467 JUDD (DENIS). The House of Windsor. 1973.

468 ROSE (KENNETH). Kings, Queens and Courtiers: Intimate Portraits of the Royal House of Windsor. 1985.

469 BERTON (PIERRE). The Royal Family: The Story of the British Monarchy from Victoria to Elizabeth. N.Y. 1954.

470 ACLAND (ERIC) *and* BARTLETT (ERNEST HENRY). The House of Windsor, George V to George VI. Toronto. 1937.

471 BATTISCOMBE (GEORGINA). Queen Alexandra. 1969.

472 CARRINGTON (CHARLES EDMUND). The Life and Reign of King George V. 1936.

473 ROSE (KENNETH). King George V. 1983.

This witty but weighty work must be read with Sir Harold George Nicolson, *King George the Fifth: His Life and Reign*, 1952. Other modest studies include John Francis Gore, *King George V: A Personal Memoir*, 1941; and Denis Judd, *The Life and Times of George V*, 1973; Sir Arthur Wynne Morgan Bryant, *George V*, 1936; and John Buchan, Baron Tweedsmuir, *The King's Grace*, 1910–1935, 1935, are interesting as period pieces. David Churchill Somervell, *The Reign of King George V: An English Chronicle*, 1935, is another contemporary assessment. So is Richard Jebb, *His Britannic Majesty: A Political View of the Crown in the Jubilee Year 1935*, 1935.

474 WATSON (F.). 'The Death of George V'. *History Today* 36/12 (1986), 21–30.

475 POPE-HENNESSY (JAMES). Queen Mary, 1867–1953. 1959.

Pictures abound in Louis Wolff, *Her Majesty Queen Mary: An Authoritative Portrait of a Great Lady in Her Years as Queen Mother*, 1949; Marguerite Dorothea Peacocke, *Queen Mary: Her Life and Times*, 1953, is modest. David Duff, *Queen Mary*, 1985, adds a little.

476 EDWARD VIII. A King's Story: The Memoirs of H.R.H. The Duke of Windsor, K.G. 1951.

Henry Hector Bolitho, *King Edward VIII*, 1937, new edn 1954, is a competent life. Sir Edward Montague Compton Mackenzie, *The Windsor Tapestry*, 1938, offers one immediate assessment. Different perspectives are found in Lewis Broad, *The Abdication Twenty-Five Years After: A Re-appraisal*, 1961; Robert Sencourt, *The Reign of Edward VIII*, 1962; Alan John Percivale Taylor, ed. William Maxwell Aitken, *Baron Beaverbrook, The Abdication of King Edward VIII*, 1966; Brian Inglis, *Abdication*, 1966. The autobiography of the Duchess of Windsor is *The Heart has its Reasons*, 1956; Michael Pye,

The King over the Water: The Windsors in the Bahamas, 1940–45, 1981, is one view of the Windsors' war.

477 WELLS (WARRE BRADLEY). Why Edward Went: Crown, Clique and Church. N.Y. 1937.

478 MARTIN (RALPH GUY). The Woman he Loved. 1974.

479 MOSLEY (DIANA). The Duchess of Windsor. 1980.

480 BIRMINGHAM (STEPHEN). Duchess: The Story of Wallis Warfield Simpson. 1981.

481 MAINE (BASIL STEPHEN). Edward VIII: Duke of Windsor. 1937.

482 —— Our Ambassador King: King Edward VIII's Life of Devotion and Service as Prince of Wales. 1936.

483 HIBBERT (CHRISTOPHER). Edward, the Uncrowned King. 1972.

484 GRAY (ROBERT). Edward VIII: The Man we Lost: A Pictorial Study. Salisbury. 1972.

485 EDWARD VIII. The Crown and the People, 1902–1953. 1953.

486 DONALDSON (FRANCES). Edward VIII. 1974.

487 HOOD (DINA WELLS). Working for the Windsors. 1957.

488 BOCCA (GEOFFREY). She might have been Queen. 1955.

489 THORNTON (MICHAEL). Royal Feud: The Queen Mother and the Duchess of Windsor. 1985.

490 BLOOM (URSULA). The Duke of Windsor. 1972.

491 BALFOUR (JOHN PATRICK DOUGLAS) *Lord Kinross*. The Windsor Years: The Life of Edward, as Prince of Wales, King and Duke of Windsor. 1967.

492 WHITE (J. LINCOLN). The Abdication of Edward VIII. A Record with all the Published Documents. 1937.

493 BLOCH (MICHAEL) *ed.* Wallis and Edward: Letters 1931–1937: The Intimate Correspondence of the Duke and Duchess of Windsor. 1986.

494 —— The Duke of Windsor's War. 1982.

495 —— Operation Widi: The Plot to Kidnap the Duke of Windsor, July 1940. 1984.

496 —— The Secret File of the Duke of Windsor. 1988.

497 HIGHAM (CHARLES). Wallis: Secret Lives of the Duchess of Windsor. 1988.

498 WARWICK (CHRISTOPHER). Abdication. 1986.

499 JENNINGS (*Sir* WILLIAM IVOR). 'The Abdication of King Edward VIII'. *Politica* ii (1937), 287–311.

500 —— 'Notes on Constitutional Developments, 1 January–August 1937'. *Politica* ii (1937), 495–506.

501 KNAPPEN (M. M.). 'Review article: the Abdication of Edward VIII'. *J. Mod. Hist.* x (1938), 242–50.

502 ROSENZWEIG (L. W.). 'The Abdication of Edward VIII: A Psycho–Historical Explanation'. *J. Brit. Studs* xiv (1975), 102–19.

503 WHEELER-BENNETT (*Sir* JOHN WHEELER). King George VI: His Life and Reign. 1958.

Slighter studies include John Sleigh Pudney, *His Majesty King George VI: A Study;* Sir Roger Thomas Baldwin Fulford, *The Pictorial Life Story of King George VI*, 1952; Keith Middlemas, *The Life and Times of George VI*, 1974; Keith V. Gordon, *The King in Peace and War*, 1940, has its own flavour. *King George VI to his Peoples, 1936–1951: Selected Broadcasts and Speeches*, 1952, is a useful collection of addresses.

504 BOLITHO (HENRY HECTOR). George VI. 1937.

505 JUDD (DENIS). George VI: 1895–1952. 1982.

506 HOWARTH (PATRICK). George VI: A Biography. 1987.

507 DUFF (DAVID SKENE). Elizabeth of Glamis. 1973.

No scholarly study exists. Other information can be gleaned from Lady Cynthia Mary Evelyn Asquith, *The Duchess of York*, 1928; Betty Spencer Shew, *Queen Elizabeth, the Queen Mother*, 1955; Dorothy Laird, *Queen Elizabeth the Queen Mother and Her Support to the Throne During Four Reigns*, 1966; Godfrey Talbot, *Queen Elizabeth, The Queen Mother*, 1973; Lady Frances Donaldson, *King George VI and Queen Elizabeth*, 1977; Anthony Holden, *The Queen Mother: A Birthday Tribute*, 1985.

508 LACEY (ROBERT). Majesty. Elizabeth II and the House of Windsor. 1977.

509 LONGFORD (ELIZABETH) *Countess of Longford*. Elizabeth R: A Biography. 1983.

An informative but incomplete climax to the studies of the Queen which may be said to have begun with Michael Chance, *Our Princesses and their Dogs*, 1936, and to have continued with Louis Wolff, *Elizabeth and Philip*, 1947; Godfrey Herbert Winn, *The Young Queen: The Life Story of Her Majesty Queen Elizabeth II*, 1952; L. A. Nickolls, *The Crowning of Elizabeth II: A Diary of the Coronation Year*, 1953; Dermot MacGregor Morrah, *The Work of the Queen*, 1958; Dorothy Laird, *How the Queen Reigns: An Authentic Study of the Queen's Personality and Life Work*, 1959; Douglas Liversidge, *Queen Elizabeth II: The British Monarchy Today*, 1974; Graham Fisher, *The Queen's Life and Her Twenty-Five Years of Monarchy*, 1976; Reginald Davis, *Elizabeth our Queen*, 1976, without greatly adding to historical understanding.

510 BOCCA (GEOFFREY). Elizabeth and Philip. N.Y. 1953.

511 CAMPBELL (JUDITH). Elizabeth and Philip. 1972.

512 ALLISON (RONALD). The Queen: The Life and Work of Elizabeth II. 1973.

513 BARKER (BRIAN). When the Queen was Crowned. 1976.

514 BROWN (MICHELE) *comp.* Queen Elizabeth II: The Silver Jubilee Book, 1952–1977. Newton Abbot. 1976.

515 HILTON (JAMES). The Duke of Edinburgh. 1956.

516 HOLLIS (*Sir* LESLIE CHASEMORE). The Captain General: A Life of H.R.H. Prince Philip. 1961.

517 BOOTHROYD (JOHN BASIL). Philip: An Informal Biography. Harlow. 1971.

518 LIVERSIDGE (DOUGLAS). Prince Philip: First Gentleman of the Realm. 1976.

519 JUDD (DENIS). Prince Philip: A Biography. 1980.

520 HALL (UNITY). Philip: The Man Behind the Monarchy. 1987.

521 BLOOM (URSULA). The Great Queen Consort. 1976.

522 H.R.H. THE PRINCE PHILIP, DUKE OF EDINBURGH. Selected Speeches 1948–1955. 1957.

523 THOMAS (ALFRED NOYES). The Queen's Sister: An Intimate Portrait of Princess Margaret. 1955.

524 WINN (GODFREY HERBERT). The Younger Sister: An Intimate Portrait Study of H.R.H. Princess Margaret. 1951.

525 WARWICK (CHRISTOPHER). Princess Margaret. 1983.

526 CATHCART (HELEN). Princess Margaret. 1974.

527 LIVERSIDGE (DOUGLAS). Prince Charles: Monarch in the Making. 1975.

528 HOLDEN (ANTHONY). Charles, Prince of Wales. 1979.

529 LANE (PETER). Prince Charles: A Study in Development. 1988.

530 JUNOR (PENNY). Charles. 1987.

531 HAMILTON (ALAN). The Real Charles. 1988.

532 CATHCART (HELEN). Prince Charles: The Biography. 1976.

533 FISHER (GRAHAM). Prince Andrew: Boy, Man and Prince. 1982.

534 CATHCART (HELEN). Anne, The Princess Royal: A Princess for our Times. 1988.

535 COURTNEY (NICHOLAS). Princess Anne: A Biography. 1986.

536 JUNOR (PENNY). Diana: Princess of Wales: A Biography. 1982.

537 MORTON (ANDREW). Duchess. 1988.

538 FRANKLAND (NOBLE). Prince Henry, Duke of Gloucester. 1980.

539 PRINCESS ALICE, DUCHESS OF GLOUCESTER. The Memoirs of Princess Alice, Duchess of Gloucester. 1983.

540 HOLMAN (DENNIS). Lady Louis. Life of the Countess Mountbatten of Burma. 1952.

541 PRINCESS MARIE LOUISE. My Memories of Six Reigns. 1956.

542 PONSONBY (FREDERICK EDWARD GREY) *Lord Sysonby.* Recollections of Three Reigns. *Ed.* by Colin Welch. 1952.

543 HARDINGE (HELEN MARY) *Lady Hardinge of Penshurst.* Loyal to Three Kings. 1967.

544 BARRYMAINE (NORMAN). The Story of Peter Townsend. 1958.

545 HAMILTON (WILLIAM). My Queen and I. 1975.

B. PARLIAMENT

It is only to be expected that the long tradition of 'constitutional history' should continue to result in substantial general surveys of parliament. By the 1960s, however, the expansion of 'politics' as an independent academic discipline resulted in studies and articles which tended to reflect more critically on the functioning of parliament. Compared with the magisterial surveys which approached the British parliament as 'the mother of parliaments' and were generally laudatory, studies frequently suggested, as their titles indicate, that parliament stood in need of reform. Simultaneously, the nature of the constitution also came under scrutiny. The manifest inadequacies of 'British constitutions' as implemented in ex-colonial territories, together with the impact of membership of the European Community and the awareness of other constitutional conventions, led to intense, though often contradictory, scrutiny of British assumptions. The body of literature which has been produced in recent decades understandably straddles the boundary between prescription and description. The prevailing mood also led to a reluctance on the part of historians to write general constitutional histories. It was also the case that fashion suggested to many historians that constitutional history, once conceived as being close to the heart of their discipline, was no longer a proper study. Perfectly properly, scholars of politics and government have filled this gap with considerable success but their own training and orientation has not permitted them to marry the study of parliament with an awareness of history often displayed by an earlier generation which came to the study of parliament with a strong historical sense.

1. Parliament as a Whole

546 JENNINGS (*Sir* WILLIAM IVOR). Parliament. Camb. 1939. 2nd edn 1957.

547 CORMACK (PATRICK). Westminster Palace and Parliament. 1980.

548 RUSH (MICHAEL). Parliament and the Public. 1976.

549 HANSARD SOCIETY. Parliamentary Reform, 1933–1960: A Survey of Suggested Reforms. 1961.

550 CAMPION (GILBERT FRANCIS MONTRIOU) *Baron Campion et al.* Parliament: A Survey. 1952.

551 PALMER (HERBERT JOHN). Government and Parliament in Britain: A Bibliography. 1960.

552 CRICK (BERNARD ROWLAND). The Crisis of British Government in the Nineteen Sixties. 1964.

553 —— *Ed.* Essays on reform: A centenary tribute. 1967.

554 WORLOCK (DAVID). Parliament and the People, 1780–1970. 1970.

555 WILDING (NORMAN WILLIAM) *and* LAUNDY (PHILIP ALAN CHARLES). An Encyclopedia of Parliament. 1958. 4th rev. edn 1972.

556 BOND (MAURICE FRANCIS). Guide to the Records of Parliament. 1971.

557 NORRIS (HERBERT WILLIAM). One from Seven Hundred: A Year in the Life of Parliament. Oxf. 1966.

558 RICHARDS (PETER GODFREY). Parliament and Conscience. 1970.

559 NICOLSON (NIGEL). People and Parliament. 1958.

560 MOSLEY (RICHARD KENNETH). Westminster Workshop: A Student's Guide to the British Constitution.

561 MORRISON (HERBERT STANLEY) *Baron Morrison.* Government and Parliament. 1954.

562 British Parliamentary Democracy. 1962.

563 ILBERT (*Sir* COURTENAY PEREGRINE). Parliament: Its History, Constitution and Practice.

564 CRICK (BERNARD ROWLAND). The Reform of Parliament. 1964. 2nd edn 1968.

565 COOMBES (DAVID L.). Westminster to Brussels: The Significance for Parliament of Accession to the European Community. 1973.

566 GORDON (STRATHEARN). Our Parliament. 1945. 6th and enlgd. edn 1964.

2. General Works

567 SMELLIE (KINGSLEY BRYCE SPEAKMAN). A Hundred Years of British Government. 1937.

568 KEITH (*Sir* ARTHUR BERRIEDALE). The Constitution of England from Queen Victoria to George VI. 2 vols 1940.

569 BIRCH (ANTHONY HAROLD). Representative and Responsible Government: An Essay on the British Constitution. 1964.

570 LASKI (HAROLD JOSEPH). Parliamentary Government in England: A Commentary. 1938.

571 GREAVES (HAROLD RICHARD GORING). The British Constitution. 1938.

572 LASKI (HAROLD JOSEPH). The Crisis of the Constitution: 1931 and After. 1932.

573 KEITH (*Sir* ARTHUR BERRIEDALE). The Constitution Under Strain: Its Working from the Crisis of 1938 down to the Present Time. 1942.

574 EHRLICH (LUDWIK). The War and the English Constitution. 1917.

575 CHRIMES (STANLEY BERTRAM). English Constitutional History. 1948.

576 KEIR (*Sir* DAVID LINDSAY). The Constitutional History of Modern Britain. 1938. 9th edn 1969.

577 AMERY (LEOPOLD CHARLES MAURICE STENNETT). Thoughts on the Constitution. 1947.

578 AMOS (*Sir* MAURICE SHELDON). The English Constitution. 1930.

579 WHEARE (*Sir* KENNETH CLINTON). Government by Committee: An Essay on the British Constitution. Oxf. 1955.

580 MARSHALL (GEOFFREY). Constitutional Conventions: The Rules and Forms of Political Accountability. Oxf. 1984.

581 TURPIN (COLIN). British Government and the Constitution. A Selection of Legal and Non–Legal Materials with Commentary. 1985.

582 KELLAS (J.). 'The Politics of Constitution-making: The Experience of the United Kingdom'. In The Politics of Constitutional Change in Industrial Nations, by K. G. Banting and R. Simeon *eds.* 1985.

583 JOWELL (J.) *and* OLIVER (D.) *eds.* The Changing Constitution. Oxf. 1985.

584 NORTON (PHILIP). 'The House of Commons and the Constitution: The Challenge of the 1970s'. *Parl. Affs* 34 (1981), 253–71.

585 SHELL (F. R.). 'The British Constitution in 1980'. *Parl. Affs* 34 (1981), 149–64.

586 DÖRING (H.). 'Krisenbewusstsein im Establishment?—timmen zur Verfassungsverein seit 1974'. In Krise in Grossbritannien? Gustav Schmidt and K. Rohe, *eds* (1987), 162–82.

587 NORTON (PHILIP) *ed.* Parliament in the 1980s. 1985.

588 CRICK (BERNARD ROWLAND). 'The Prospects for Parliamentary Reform'. *Pol. Q.* xxxvi (1965), 333–46.

589 GREAVES (HAROLD RICHARD GORING). 'The Last Revolution and the Next, 1930–1970'. *Pol. Q.* xli (1970), 83–8.

590 HAMPTON (W. A.). 'Parliament and the Civil Service'. *Parl. Affs* xvii (1964), 430–8.

591 LEE (J. M.). 'Parliament and the Reorganisation of Central Government'. *Parl. Affs* xxiv (1971), 164–73.

592 BUTT (RONALD). The Power of Parliament. 1967.

593 VIOLETTE (EUGENE MORROW) *ed.* English Constitutional Documents Since 1832. N.Y. 1936.

594 MINOGUE (MARTIN) *ed.* Documents on Contemporary British Government. 2 vols. Camb. 1977.

595 STEPHENSON (CARL) *and* MARCHAM (FREDERICK GEORGE) *eds.* Sources of English Constitutional History. 2 vols. Rev. edn 1972.

596 LeMAY (GODFREY HUGH LANCELOT) *comp.* British Government, 1914–1953: Select Documents. 1955.

597 ANSON (*Sir* WILLIAM REYNELL). The Law and Custom of the Constitution. 2 vols. 1935.

598 MOSLEY (RICHARD KENNETH). The Story of the Cabinet Office. 1969.

599 SCHUYLER (ROBERT LIVINGSTON) *and* WESTON (CORINNE COMSTOCK). British Constitutional History Since 1832. Princeton. 1957.

600 JENNINGS (*Sir* WILLIAM IVOR). Law and the Constitution. 1933. 4th edn 1954.

601 HALL (DANIEL GEORGE EDWARD). A Brief Survey of English Constitutional History. 1939.

602 MARCHAM (FREDERICK GEORGE). A Constitutional History of Modern England, 1485 to the Present. 1960.

603 LOVELL (COLIN RHYS). English Constitutional and Legal History: A Survey. N.Y. 1962.

604 MARRIOTT (*Sir* JOHN ARTHUR RANSOME). The Constitution in Transition, 1910–1924. Oxf. 1924.

605 —— This Realm of England: Monarchy, Aristocracy, Democracy. 1938.

606 McILWAIN (CHARLES HOWARD). Constitutionalism and the Changing World. 1939.

607 KEIR (*Sir* DAVID LINDSAY) *and* LAWSON (FREDERICK HENRY) *eds.* Cases in Constitutional Law. Oxf. 5th edn 1967.

608 WADE (EMLYN CAPEL STUART) *and* PHILLIPS (GEORGE GODFREY). Constitutional Law. 6th edn 1960.

609 CRACKNELL (DOUGLAS GEORGE). Constitutional Law and the English Legal System. 1963.

610 JENNINGS (*Sir* WILLIAM IVOR). The British Constitution. Camb. 1941. 3rd edn 1950.

611 MARSHALL (GEOFFREY) *and* MOODIE (GRAEME COCHRANE). Some Problems of the Constitution. 1959. 2nd edn 1961.

612 SAINSBURY (K.). 'The Constitution: Some Disputed Points'. *Parl. Affs* xiv (1962), 213–63.

613 HARVEY (JACK) *and* BATHER (LESLIE). The British Constitution. 1963.

614 MARSHALL (GEOFFREY). 'Parliament and the Constitution'. *Pol. Q.* xxxvi (1965), 266–76.

615 BEATTIE (A. J.). 'Recent Developments in the British Constitution'. *Jahrbuch des Öffentlichen Rechts*, xiv (1965), 321–48.

616 HAYNES (CHARLES EDWARD). The Essentials of the British Constitution. Oxf. 1965.

617 HOGG (QUINTIN McGAREL) *Lord Hailsham.* New charter: Some Proposals for Constitutional Reform. 1969.

618 GILMOUR (*Sir* IAN HEDWORTH JOHN). The Body Politic. 1969.

619 JEWELL (RICHARD EDWARD COXHEAD). The British Constitution. 1970.

620 PHILLIPS (OWEN HOOD). Reform of the Constitution. 1970.

621 BROMHEAD (PETER ALEXANDER). Britain's Developing Constitution. 1974.

622 BROMHEAD (PETER ALEXANDER) *and* SHELL (D.). 'The British Constitution in 1974'. *Parl. Affs* xxviii (1975), 105–24.

623 —— 'The British Constitution in 1975'. *Parl. Affs* xxix (1976), 135–54.

624 WALES (PETER). The British Constitution: An Introduction. 1974.

625 HARTLEY (TREVOR CLAYTON). Government and Law: An Introduction to the Working of the Constitution in Britain. 1975.

626 JOHNSON (NEVIL). In Search of the Constitution: Reflections on State and Society in Britain. Oxf. 1977.

627 MARSHALL (GEOFFREY). Parliamentary Sovereignty and the Commonwealth. 1957.

628 HOLLIS (CHRISTOPHER). Parliament and its Sovereignty. 1973.

629 CHRIMES (STANLEY BERTRAM) *and* ROOTS (IVAN ALAN). English Constitutional History: A Select Bibliography. 1958.

3 · THE HOUSE OF COMMONS

630 MARSDEN (PHILIP). The Officers of the Commons, 1363–1965. 1966.

631 LAUNDY (PHILIP). The Office of Speaker. 1964.

632 TAYLOR (ERIC). The House of Commons at Work. 1951.

633 HANSON (ALBERT HENRY) *and* CRICK (BERNARD ROWLAND) *eds.* The Commons in Transition. 1970.

634 RYDZ (D. L.). The Parliamentary Agents: A History. 1979.

635 BAKER (ARTHUR). The House is Sitting. 1958.

636 WALKLAND (STUART ALAN) *and* RYLE (MICHAEL) *eds.* The Commons in the Seventies. 1970. 2nd edn 1977.

637 LIVERSIDGE (DOUGLAS). The House of Commons. 1974.

638 WALKLAND (STUART ALAN). The Legislative Process in Great Britain. 1968.

639 MIDDLETON (R.). 'The Problems and Consequences of Parliamentary Government: An Historical View'. *Parl. Affs* xxiii (1969–70), 55–60.

640 A BIBLIOGRAPHY OF PARLIAMENTARY DEBATES OF GREAT BRITAIN *comp.* by WOODS (JOHN A.). *House of Commons Library* Document No. 2. 1956.

641 ROSS (CHARLES). The Parliamentary Record, 1861–1939. [Issued weekly during the parliamentary session.].

642 LAW (WILLIAM). Our Hansard: Or, the True Mirror of Parliament: A Full Account of the Official Reporting of the Debates in the House of Commons. 1950.

643 RODGERS (FRANK). Serial Publications in the British Parliamentary Papers, 1900–1968: A bibliography. 1971.

644 PEMBERTON (JOHN EDWARD). British Official Publications. 1971.

645 MAY (THOMAS ERSKINE) *Baron Farnborough*. A Treatise on the Law, Privileges, Proceedings, and Usage of Parliament. 1944.

646 WITTKE (CARL FREDERICK). The History of English Parliamentary Privilege. Columbus, Ohio. 1921.

647 HANSON (ALBERT HENRY) *and* WISEMAN (HERBERT VICTOR). Parliament at Work: A Case-Book of Parliamentary Procedure. 1962.

See also Valentine Herman, 'Adjournment Debates in the House of Commons'. *Parl. Affs* xxvi (1973), 92–104; Richard Kimber *et al.* 'Parliamentary Questions and the Allocation of Departmental Responsibilities'. *Parl. Affs* xxvii (1974), 287–93; K. Swinhoe, 'Lines of Division Among Members of Parliament over Procedural Reform in the House of Commons'. *Polit. Studs* xviii (1970), 400–2.

648 GRIFFITH (J. A. G.). Parliamentary Scrutiny of Government Bills. 1974.

649 HAWTREY (S. C.) *and* BARCLAY (H. M.). Parliamentary Dictionary. 1956. 3rd edn 1970.

650 CAMPION (GILBERT FRANCIS MONTRIOU) *Baron Campion*. An Introduction to the Procedure of the House of Commons. 3rd edn 1958.

651 DREWRY (G.). 'The Outsider and House of Commons Reform: Some Evidence from the Crossman Diaries'. *Parl. Affs* xxxi (1978), 424–35.

652 ROBINSON (MADELINE R.). 'Parliamentary Privilege and Political Morality in Britain, 1939–57'. *Pol. Sci. Q.* lxxiii (1958), 179–205.

653 JOHNSON (NEVIL). Parliament and Administration: The Estimates Committee 1945–1965. 1966.

654 LEE (JOHN MICHAEL). 'Select Committees and the Constitution'. *Pol. Q.* xli (1970), 182–94.

655 WALKLAND (STUART ALAN). 'Science and Parliament: The Role of the Select Committees of the House of Commons'. *Parl. Affs* xviii (1965), 266–78.

656 COOMBES (DAVID L.). The Member of Parliament and the Administration: The Case of the Select Committee on Nationalised Industries. 1966.

657 NEAVE (AIREY). Control by Committee: The Reform of the Committee System of the House of Commons. 1968.

658 PARTINGTON (MARTIN). 'Parliamentary Committees: Recent Developments'. *Parl. Affs* xxiii (1970), 366–79.

659 WISEMAN (HERBERT VICTOR). 'Supply and Ways and Means: Procedural Changes in 1966'. *Parl. Affs* xxi (1968), 10–15.

660 RICHARDSON (JEREMY J.) *and* KIMBER (RICHARD). 'The Role of All-Party Committees in the House of Commons'. *Parl. Affs* xxv (1972), 339–49.

661 MORRIS (ALFRED J.) *ed.* The Growth of Parliamentary Scrutiny by Committee. Oxf. 1970.

662 HICKS (URSULA KATHLEEN). British Public Finances: Their Structure and Development, 1880–1952. 1954.

663 EINZIG (PAUL). The Control of the Purse: Progress and Decline of Parliament's Financial Control. 1959.

664 HANSON (ALBERT HENRY). Parliament and Public Ownership. 1961.

665 RYLE (MICHAEL). 'Parliamentary Control of Expenditure and Taxation'. *Pol. Q.* xxxviii (1967), 435–46.

666 KORAH (VALENTINE). 'Counter-Inflation Legislation: Whither Parliamentary Sovereignty?' *Law Q. Rev.* xcii (1976), 42–61.

667 REID (GORDON STANLEY). The Politics of Financial Control: The Role of the House of Commons. 1966.

4. THE HOUSE OF LORDS

668 SAINTY (JOHN CHRISTOPHER). Leaders and Whips in the House of Lords, 1783–1964. *House of Lords Record Office* memo. 31. 1964.

669 —— Officers of the House of Lords, 1485–1971. 1971.

670 BROMHEAD (PETER ALEXANDER). The House of Lords and Contemporary Politics, 1911–1957. 1958.

671 NORTON (PHILIP). 'The Forgotten Whips: Whips in the House of Lords'. *The Parliamentarian* lvii (1976), 86–92.

672 BROMHEAD (PETER ALEXANDER). 'Mr Wedgwood Benn, the Peerage and the Constitution'. *Parl. Affs* xiv (1961).

673 VINCENT (JOHN RUSSELL). 'The House of Lords'. *Parl. Affs* ixx (1966), 475–85.

674 SKENE (NORMAN HENRY). The British Peerage in Parliament. Ilfracombe. 1962.

675 BOSSOM (ALFRED CHARLES) *Baron Bossom*. Our House. 1965.

676 SKEFFINGTON (JOHN) *Baron Massereene and Ferrard*. The Lords. 1973.

677 BAILEY (SYDNEY DAWSON) *ed.* The Future of the House of Lords. 1954.

678 SEAMAN (ROBERT DONALD HAROLD). The Reform of the Lords. 1971.

679 ALLYN (EMILY). Lords versus Commons: A Century of Conflict and Compromise, 1830–1930. Philadelphia. 1931.

680 MORGAN (JANET P.). The House of Lords and the Labour Government, 1964–1970. Oxf. 1975.

681 ABSHAGEN (KARL HEINZ). King, Lords and Gentlemen: Influence and Power of the English Upper Classes. 1939.

682 WILKINSON (RUPERT HUGH). Gentlemanly Power: British Leadership and the Public School Tradition; a Comparative Study in the Making of Rulers. 1964.

5. MISCELLANEOUS

683 RHODES (GERALD). Committees of Inquiry. 1975.

684 GABINÉ (BERNARD LUTHARD). A Finding List of British Royal Commission Reports, 1860–1935. Camb., Mass. 1935.

685 CHAPMAN (RICHARD ARNOLD) ed. The Role of Commissions in Policy Making. 1973.

686 CARTWRIGHT (T. J.). Royal Commissions and Departmental Committees in Britain: A Case Study in Institutional Adaptiveness and Public Participation in Government. 1975.

687 JOHNSON (NEVIL). 'The Royal Commission on the Constitution'. *Public Admin* lii (1974), 1–12.

688 H.M.S.O. Royal Commission on the Constitution, 1969–1973. 2 vols. 1973.

689 SHAW (CHARLES JAMES DALRYMPLE) *Lord Kilbrandon*. A Background to Constitutional Reform. Brighton. 1975.

690 VERNON (ROLAND VENABLES) *and* MANSERGH (NICHOLAS). Advisory Bodies: A Study of their Uses in Relation to Central Government, 1919–1939. 1940.

691 RICHARDS (PETER GODFREY). Honourable Members: A Study of the British Backbencher. 1959. 2nd edn 1964.

692 ——The Backbenchers. 1972.

693 BROMHEAD (PETER ALEXANDER). Private Members' Bills in the British Parliament. 1956.

694 KERR (D.). 'The Changing Role of the Backbencher'. *The Parliamentarian* I (1969), 7–11.

695 MACKINTOSH (JOHN PITCAIRN). The Influence of the Backbencher, Now and a Hundred Years Ago. Manch. 1970.

696 LYNSKEY (JAMES J.). 'The Role of British Backbenchers in the Modification of Government Policy'. *Western Pol. Q.* xxiii (1970), 333–47.

697 ——'Backbench Tactics and Parliamentary Party Structure'. *Parl. Affs* xxvii (1974), 28–37.

698 LEONARD (RICHARD LAWRENCE) *and* HERMAN (VALENTINE) *eds.* The Backbencher and Parliament: A Reader. 1972.

699 BERRINGTON (HUGH BAYARD). Backbench Opinion in the House of Commons, 1945–1955. Oxf. 1973.

700 JUDGE (DAVID). 'Backbench Specialisation: A Study in Parliamentary Questions'. *Parl. Affs* xxvii (1974), 171–86.

701 NORTON (PHILIP) *ed.* Dissension in the House of Commons: Intra-party Dissent in the House of Commons Division Lobbies, 1945–1974. 1975.

702 ——'Private Legislation and the Influence of the Backbench M.P.'. *Parl. Affs* xxx (1977), 356–62.

C. CENTRAL INSTITUTIONS

Mutatis mutandis, the same remarks apply to the study of central government. The rich variety of material available ranges from institutional studies of particular ministries to assessments of the machinery of government overall. Major changes in that machinery both produced and reflected growing academic interest in these matters. The books and articles published in the post-1945 period indicate a pervasive concern with 'modernization' and the emergence of new organizational and management perspectives. The growth of government produced more books on government until, in turn, the mood changed. Writers spoke of the paralyisis caused by 'government overload'. In some eyes, it became necessary to roll back the frontiers of government. The results, too, of central government reorganization proved disappointing in particular instances and led to a certain scepticism about the managerial insights which were allegedly deployed. The titles of books and their dates of publication frequently give clear indications of concerns which were current at the time. Debate about the role and function of the Civil Service rarely ceased and at times produced a rash of publications in response to particular reports and enquiries. Alongside these exchanges, histories of government departments of a traditional kind continued to appear, supplemented by memoirs by retired officials and the occasional biography. That such 'inside' insight was not more widespread no doubt reflected the traditions and conventions of secrecy and confidentiality within the Civil Service itself. 'Official Secrecy' also continued to be a substantial constraint on politicians, or at least some of them and has only been seriously but not universally breached in the most recent decades. Taken in the round, therefore, while the material for the study of British central institutions is in total substantial, it is curiously segmented. There is no lack of technical studies but they are all too frequently self-contained. The issue of the relationship between institutions and processes, between 'officials', 'politicians', and 'the public', is too often ignored by scholars who have addressed themselves to one side or other of this relationship with exemplary thoroughness.

1. GENERAL

703 BODELSEN (CARL ADOLF GOTLIEB). The Government and Institutions of England. 8th edn Copenhagen. 1965.

704 MUIR (JOHN RAMSAY BRYCE). How Britain is Governed: A Critical Analysis of Modern Developments in the British System of Government. 1930. 4th edn 1940.

705 CAMPION (GILBERT FRANCIS MONTRIOU) *Lord Campion, et al.* British Government since 1918. 1950.

706 JENNINGS (*Sir* WILLIAM IVOR). The Queen's Government. 1954.

707 PARRIS (HENRY WALTER). Constitutional Bureaucracy: The Development of British Central Administration Since the Eighteenth Century. 1969.

708 HEARDER (HARRY) *and* LOYN (HENRY ROYSTON) *eds.* British Government and Administration: Studies presented to S.B. Chrimes. Cardiff. 1974.

709 FRY (GEOFFREY KINGDON). The Growth of Government: The Development of Ideas About the Role of the State and the Machinery and Functions of Government in Britain Since 1780. 1979.

710 CHAPMAN (BRIAN). The Profession of Government. 1959.

711 CHESTER (*Sir* DANIEL NORMAN) *and* WILSON (FRANCIS MICHAEL GLENN) *eds.* The Organisation of British Central Government, 1914–1956. 1957. 2nd edn (to 1964) 1968.

712 MACKENZIE (WILLIAM JAMES MILLAR) *and* GROVE (JACK WILLIAM). Central Administration in Britain. 1957.

713 HALDANE COMMITTEE REPORT. Report of the Machinery of Government Committee. Chairman: Viscount Haldane. Ministry of Reconstruction. Cd. 9230. H.C. (1918), xii, 1.

714 HANKEY (MAURICE PASCAL ALERS) *Baron Hankey.* The Development of the Higher Control of the Machinery of Government. 1942.

2. THE CABINET

715 KEITH (*Sir* ARTHUR BERRIEDALE). The British Cabinet System 1830–1938. 1939. 2nd rev. edn by Norman H. Gibbs. 1952.

716 JENNINGS (*Sir* WILLIAM IVOR). Cabinet Government. 1936. 3rd edn Camb. 1959.

717 DAALDER (HANS). Cabinet Reform in Britain, 1914–1963. Stanford, Calif. 1964.

718 HERMAN (VALENTINE) *and* ALT (JAMES E.). Cabinet Studies: A Reader. 1975.

719 MACKINTOSH (JOHN PITCAIRN). The British Cabinet. 1962. 3rd edn 1977.

720 GORDON-WALKER (PATRICK CHRESTIEN) *Baron Gordon-Walker.* The Cabinet: Political Authority in Britain. 1970. 2nd edn 1972.

721 HENNESSY (PETER). Cabinet. Oxf. 1986.

722 EAVES (JOHN). Emergency Powers and the Parliamentary Watchdog: Parliament and the Executive in Great Britain, 1939–1951. 1957.

723 HEADEY (BRUCE WYNDHAM). British Cabinet Ministers: The Role of Politicians in Executive Office. 1974.

724 EHRMAN (JOHN PATRICK WILLIAM). Cabinet Government and War, 1890–1940. 1958.

725 SEYMOUR-URE (COLIN). 'British "War Cabinets" in Limited Wars: Korea, Suez and the Falklands'. *Public Admin.* Summer (1984), 181–200.

726 FINER (HERMAN). 'The British Cabinet, the House of Commons and the War'. *Pol. Sci. Q.* lvi (1941), 321–60.

727 RUSH (MICHAEL). The Cabinet and Policy Formation. 1984.

728 BROOKSHIRE (J. H.). 'Clement Attlee and Cabinet Reform 1930–1945'. *Hist. J.* 24 (1981), 175–88.

729 HENNESSY (PETER) *and* ARENDS (ANDREW). Mr Attlee's Engine Room: Cabinet Committee Structure and the Labour Governments 1945–51. Glasgow. 1983.

730 JORDAN (HENRY D.). 'Foreign Government and Politics: The British Cabinet and the Ministry of Defence'. *Amer. Pol. Sci. Rev.* 43 (1949), 73–82.

731 MILNE (R. S.). 'The Experiment with "Co-ordinating Ministers" in the British Cabinet 1951–3'. *Can. J. Econ. Pol. Sci.* (1955), 365–9.

732 ALDERMAN (R. K.) *and* CROSS (J. A.). 'Problems of Ministerial Turnover in Two Labour Cabinets'. *Pol. Studs* 29 (1981), 425–30.

733 SILKIN (ARTHUR). 'The "Agreement to Differ" of 1975 and its Effects on Ministerial Responsibility'. *Pol. Q.* 48 (1977), 65–77.

734 BURCH (MARTIN). 'The British Cabinet: A Residual Executive'. *Parl. Affs* 41 (1988), 34–48.

735 WISEMAN (HERBERT VICTOR). Parliament and the Executive: an Analysis with Readings. 1966.

3. WHITEHALL AND WESTMINSTER

736 BRUCE-GARDYNE (JOCK) *Baron*. Ministers and Mandarins. 1986.

737 WASS (*Sir* DOUGLAS). Government and the Governed. 1984.

738 HOSKYNS. (*Sir* JOHN). 'Whitehall and Westminster: An Outsider's View'. *Parl. Affs* 36 (1983), 137–47.

739 ROSE (RICHARD). 'The Making of Cabinet Ministers'. *Brit. J. Pol. Sci.* 1/4 (1971), 393–414.

740 WILLSON (FRANCIS MICHAEL GLENN). 'The Routes of Entry of New Members of the British Cabinet, 1868–1958'. *Pol. Studs* vii (1959), 222–32.

741 —— 'Entry to the Cabinet, 1959–1968'. *Pol. Studs* xviii (1970), 236–38.

742 HEASMAN (D. J.). 'The Ministerial Hierarchy'. *Parl. Affs* xiv (1962), 307–30.

743 'Parliamentary Paths to High Office'. *Parl. Affs* xvi (1963), 315–30.

4. MINISTERIAL RESPONSIBILITY

744 ALDERMAN (R. K.) *and* CROSS (J. A.). The Tactics of Resignation: A Study in British Cabinet Government. 1967.

745 —— 'The Timing of Cabinet Reshuffles'. *Parl. Affs* 40 (1987), 1–19.

746 —— 'Rejuvenating the Cabinet: The Records of Post-War British Prime Ministers Compared'. *Pol. Studs* 34 (1986), 639–46.

747 FINER (SAMUEL E.). 'The Individual Responsibility of Ministers'. *Public Admin* 34 (1956), 377–96.

748 FRY (GEOFFREY KINGDON). 'Thoughts on the Present State of the Convention of Ministerial Responsibility'. *Parl. Affs* xxiii (1969–70), 10–20.

749 TURPIN (C.). 'Ministerial Responsibility: Myth or Reality?' in The Changing Constitution, Jeffrey Jowell and Dawn Oliver *eds*. Oxf. 1985.

750 MARSHALL (GEOFFREY) *ed*. Ministerial Responsibility. Oxf. 1989.

5. THE OPPOSITION

751 TURNER (DUNCAN ROBERT). The Shadow Cabinet in British Politics. 1969.

752 PUNNETT (ROBERT MALCOLM). Front Bench Opposition: The Role of the Leader of the Opposition, the Shadow Cabinet and Shadow Government in British Politics. 1973.

6. CABINET SECRETARIAT

753 LINGE (G. J. R.). The Functions of the Cabinet Secretariat. 1952.

754 MOSLEY (RICHARD KENNETH). The Story of the Cabinet Office. 1969.

755 NAYLOR (JOHN F.). A Man and an Institution: Sir Maurice Hankey, the Cabinet Secretariat and the Custody of Cabinet Secrecy. Camb. 1984.

756 —— 'The Establishment of the Cabinet Secretariat'. *Hist. J.* xiv (1971), 783–803.

757 JONES (THOMAS). A Diary with Letters, 1930–1950. 1954.

758 —— Whitehall Diary. *Ed.* Robert Keith Middlemas. 3 vols 1969–71.

7. CABINET AND OFFICIAL SECRECY

759 *Report of a Committee of Privy Councillors on Ministerial Memoirs*. Cmnd 6386 *Parliamentary Papers* xiii (1975–6).

760 MIDDLEMAS (ROBERT KEITH). 'Cabinet Secrecy and the Crossman Diaries'. *Pol. Q.* xlvii (1976), 39–51.

761 YOUNG (HUGO). The Crossman Affair. 1976.

762 FRASER (PETER). 'Cabinet Secrecy and War Memoirs'. *Hist.* 70 (1985), 397–409.

763 WILLIAMS (DAVID). Not in the Public Interest. 1965.

764 PONTING (CLIVE). The Right to Know. 1985.

765 NORTON-TAYLOR (RICHARD). The Ponting Affair. 1985.

766 HOOPER (DAVID). Official Secrets: The Use and Abuse of the Act. 1987.

767 AITKEN (JONATHAN). Officially Secret. 1971.

768 MICHAEL (JAMES). The Politics of Secrecy. Harmondsworth. 1982.

769 PYPER (ROBERT). 'Sarah Tisdall, Ian Willmore and the Civil Servant's "Right to Leak"'. *Pol. Q.* 56 (1985), 72–81.

770 ZELLICK (GRAHAM). 'National Security, Official Information and the Law'. *Contemp. Rev.* 249 (1986), 189–96.

771 CHAPMAN (RICHARD ARNOLD) *and* HUNT (M.) *eds*. Open Government. 1987.

772 ROYAL INSTITUTE OF PUBLIC ADMINISTRATION, Policy and Practice: The Experience of Government. 1980.

773 Parliament and the Executive. 1982.

774 LEE (JOHN MICHAEL). Reviewing the Machinery of Government 1942–1952. An Essay on the Anderson Committee and its Successors. Bristol. 1977.

8. PUBLIC EMPLOYMENT

775 ABRAMOVITZ (MOSES) *and* ELIASBERG (VERA F.). The Growth of Public Employment in Great Britain 1890–1950. *Nat. Bureau Econ. Res.* Princeton. 1957.

776 KNOX (FRANCIS). The Growth of Central Government Manpower. 1969.

9. REFORM PROPOSALS

777 STACEY (FRANK ARTHUR). British Government, 1966–1975: Years of Reform. 1975.

778 BRASHER (NORMAN HENRY). Studies in British Government. 1965.

779 BRAY (JEREMY). Decision in Government. 1970.

780 ROBERTSON (JAMES HUGH). Reform of British Central Government. 1971.

781 THORNHILL (WILLIAM) ed. The Modernization of British Government. 1975.

782 CHAPMAN (RICHARD ARNOLD) and GREENAWAY (J. R.). The Dynamics of Administrative Reform. 1980.

783 STRAPPERT (A.). Die Reorganisation der Britischen Zentralregierung seit dem Ende der 50er Jahre, in Besondere die Zentrale Lenkung. Berlin. 1975.

784 GREAVES (HAROLD RICHARD GORING). 'British Central Government, 1914–1956'. Pol. Q. xxviii (1957), 383–9.

785 BELOFF (MAX) Lord. 'The Whitehall Factor: The Role of the Higher Civil Service 1919–1939'. In The Politics of Reappraisal 1918–1939, Gillian Peele and Chris Cook. 1975.

786 CLARKE (Sir RICHARD WILLIAM BARNES). New Trends in Government. 1971.

787 GARRETT (JOHN). The Management of Government. 1972.

788 RADCLIFFE (JAMES). The Reorganisation of British Central Government. 1991.

789 HARRIS (JOHN SHARP). British Government Inspection: The Local Services and the Central Departments. 1955.

790 WILLIS (JOHN). The Parliamentary Powers of English Government Departments. Camb., Mass. 1933.

791 HAGUE (DOUGLAS CHALMERS) et al. Public Policy and Private Interests: The Institutions of Compromise. 1975.

792 PUGH (RALPH BERNARD). The Crown Estate. 1960.

793 BURK (KATHLEEN) ed. War and the State: The Transformation of British Government 1914–1919. 1982.

794 TURNER (JOHN A.). 'The Formation of Lloyd George's "Garden Suburb": "Fabian-like Milnerite Infiltration"?'. Hist. J. xx (1977), 165–84.

795 SCOTT (JOHN DICK) and HUGHES (RICHARD). The Administration of War Production. 1956.

796 McGUCKEN (W.). 'The Central Organisation of Scientific and Technical Advice in the United Kingdom During the Second World War'. Minerva 17 (1979), 33–69.

797 BOOTH (A.) and COATS (A. W.). 'Some Wartime Observations on the Role of the Economist in Government'. Oxf. Econ Papers 32 (1980), 177–99.

798 COATS (A. W.). 'Britain: The Rise of Specialists'. Hist. Pol. Econ. 13 (1981), 365–404.

799 MacLEOD (ROY) ed. Government and Expertise: Specialists, Administrators and Professionals 1860–1919. Camb. 1988.

800 PARKER (HENRY MICHAEL DENNE). Manpower: A Study of Wartime Policy and Administration. 1957.

801 FRANKS (OLIVER SHEWELL) Baron. Central Planning and Control in War and Peace. 1947.

802 ROBSON (WILLIAM ALEXANDER). 'The Machinery of Government, 1939–1947'. Pol. Q. xix (1948), 1–14.

10. THE TREASURY

803 KYNASTON (DAVID). The Chancellor of the Exchequer. Lavenham. 1980.

804 BRIDGES (EDWARD ETTINGDENE) Baron. The Treasury. 1964. 2nd edn 1967.

805 ROSEVEARE (HENRY). The Evolution of a British Institution: The Treasury. 1969.

806 BROWNING (PETER). The Treasury and Economic Policy 1964–1985. 1986.

807 PLIATZKY (Sir LEO). The Treasury under Mrs Thatcher. Oxf. 1989.

808 HECLO (HUGH) and WILDAVSKY (AARON). The Private Government of Public Money. 1974. 2nd edn 1981.

809 BEER (SAMUEL HUTCHISON). Treasury Control: The Co-ordination of Financial and Economic Policy. Oxf. 1956. 2nd edn 1957.

810 McLEOD (R. M.). Treasury Control and Social Administration. 1968.

811 PLIATZKY (Sir LEO). Getting and Spending: Public Expenditure, Employment and Inflation. Oxf. 2nd edn 1984.

812 WILLIAMS (ALAN). Output Budgeting and the Contribution of Microeconomics to Efficiency in Government. 1967. 2nd edn 1974.

813 NEWTON (TREVOR). Cost–Benefit Analysis in Administration. 1972.

814 BAILEY (S. D.). 'This Colossal Engine of Finance'. Parl. Affs vi (1953), 354–64.

815 MORAN (M.). 'Monetary Policy and the Machinery of Government'. Public Admin 59 (1981), 265–70.

816 BARNETT (JOEL). Inside the Treasury. 1982.

817 HILL (MICHAEL J.). The Sociology of Public Administration. 1972.

818 The State, Administration and the Individual. 1976.

11. DEPARTMENTS

819 HOOD (CHRISTOPHER), DUNSIRE (ANDREW) and THOMPSON (KENNETH A.). 'So you think you know what Government Departments are . . .?'. Public Admin Rev. 27 (1978), 20–32.

820 PITT (DOUGLAS C.) and SMITH (BRIAN CHARLES). Government Departments: An Organisational Perspective. 1981.

821 POLLITT (CHRISTOPHER). Manipulating the Machine: Changing the Pattern of Ministerial Departments 1960–83. 1984.

822 JOHNSON (FRANKLYN ARTHUR). Defence by Committee: The British Committee of Imperial Defence, 1885–1959. 1960.

823 —— Defence by Ministry: The British Ministry of Defence 1944–74. 1980.

824 TAYLOR (BRIAN). 'Coming of Age: A Study of the Evolution of the Ministry of Defence Headquarters 1974–1982'. *J. Roy. United Services Inst. Defe. Studs* 128 (1983), 44–51.

825 HOWARD (*Sir* MICHAEL ELIOT). The Central Organisation of Defence. 1970.

826 JORDAN (H. D.). 'The British Cabinet and the Ministry of Defence'. *Amer. Pol. Sci. Rev.* xliii, (1949), 73–82.

827 BROADBENT (*Sir* EWEN). The Military and Government: From Macmillan to Heseltine. 1988.

828 GORDON (HAMPDEN CHARLES). The War Office. 1935.

829 FAY (*Sir* SAMUEL). The War Office at War. 1973.

830 GREY (CHARLES GREY). A History of the Air Ministry. 1940.

831 RODGER (N. A. M.). The Admiralty. Lavenham. 1979.

832 WILLIAMS (*Sir* GRIFFITH). 'The First Ten Years of the Ministry of Education'. *Brit. J. Educ. Studs* 3 (1955), 101–14.

833 PILE (*Sir* WILLIAM D.). The Department of Education and Science. 1979.

834 McLAINE (I.). Ministry of Morale: Home Front Morale and the Ministry of Information in World War II. 1979.

835 WILLCOX (TEMPLE). 'Projection or Publicity? Rival Concepts in the Pre-war Planning of the British Ministry of Information'. *J. Contemp. Hist.* 18 (1983), 97–116.

836 LOWE (RODNEY). Adjusting to Democracy: The Role of the Ministry of Labour in British Politics, 1916–1939. Oxf. 1986.

837 KIRBY (MAURICE W.). 'The Politics of State Coercion in Inter-war Britain: The Mines Department of the Board of Trade, 1920–1942'. *Hist. J.* 22 (1979), 373–96.

838 BENN (*Sir* ERNEST). 'Recollections of the Ministry of Reconstruction'. *Quart. Rev.* ccxci (1953), 334–9.

839 JONES (*Sir* THOMAS GEORGE). The Unbroken Front: The Ministry of Food, 1916–1944: Personalities and Problems. 1944.

12. CIVIL SERVICE:
GENERAL/INDIVIDUALS/ADMINISTRATIVE PROCEDURES AND VALUES

840 ROYAL INSTITUTE OF PUBLIC ADMINISTRATION. British Public Administration: Select Bibliography. 1963.

841 FINER (HERMAN). The British Civil Service: An Introductory Essay. 1927.

842 STOUT (HIRAM MILLER). Public Service in Great Britain. Chapel Hill, 1938.

843 COHEN (EMMELINE WALEY). The Growth of the British Civil Service, 1780–1939. 1941. Repr. 1965.

844 DALE (HAROLD EDWARD). The Higher Civil Service of Great Britain. Oxf. 1941.

845 GREAVES (HAROLD RICHARD GORING). The Civil Service in the Changing State. 1947.

846 CRITCHLEY (THOMAS ALAN). The Civil Service Today. 1951.

847 GRIFFITH (LLEWELYN WYN). The British Civil Service, 1854–1954. 1954.

848 CAMPBELL (GEORGE ARCHIBALD). The Civil Service in Britain. 1955. 2nd edn 1965.

849 CRAIG (*Sir* JOHN HERBERT McCUTCHEON). A History of Red Tape. 1955.

850 KELSALL (ROGER KEITH). Higher Civil Servants in Britain, from 1870 to the Present Day. 1955.

851 ROBSON (WILLIAM ALEXANDER). The Governors and the Governed. 1964.

852 —— *Ed.* The Civil Service in Britain and France. 1956.

853 *Report of the Committee on the Civil Service 1966–1968* Cmnd 3638 *Parliamentary Papers* xviii (1967–8) ['The Fulton Report'.].

854 THOMAS (HUGH SWYNNERTON) *Baron ed.* Crisis in the Civil Service. 1968.

855 SELF (P.). 'The Reform of the Civil Service'. *Pol. Q.* xxxviii (1967), 32–9.

856 ROBERTSON (J. F.). 'Civil Service Reform in Britain'. *N. Z. J. Public Admin* xxxi (1968), 83–100.

857 CHAPMAN (RICHARD ARNOLD). 'The Fulton Report: A Summary'. *Public Admin* xlvi (1968), 443–51.

858 FRY (GEOFFREY KINGDON). 'Some Weaknesses in the Fulton Report on the British Home Civil Service'. *Pol. Studs* xvii (1969), 484–94.

859 —— 'Some Developments in the British Home Civil Service Since the Fulton Report'. *Public Admin* (Sydney) xxix (1970), 32–50.

860 PAINTER (C.). 'The Civil Service: Post-Fulton Malaise'. *Public Admin* liii (1975), 427–41.

861 DUNNETT (*Sir* JAMES). 'The Civil Service: Seven Years after Fulton'. *Public Admin* 54 (1976), 371–9.

862 CHAPMAN (RICHARD ARNOLD) *and* LOFTS (DUDLEY). 'The Civil Service after Fulton'. *Public Admin Bull.* 27 (1978), 41–53.

863 MacDONALD (JAMES) *and* FRY (GEOFFREY KINGDON). 'Policy Planning Units—Ten Years on'. *Public Admin* 58 (1980), 421–38.

864 HENNESSY (PETER). 'Fulton: 20 Years On'. *Contemp. Record* 2/2 (1988), 44–55.

865 RIDLEY (F. F.). Specialists and Generalists. 1968.

866 WILLIAMS (R.). 'Administrative Modernisation in British Government'. *Int. Soc. Sci. J.* i (1969), 100–15.

867 FRY (GEOFFREY KINGDON). Statesmen in Disguise: The Changing Role of the Administrative Class of the British Home Civil Service, 1853–1966. 1969.

868 CHAPMAN (RICHARD ARNOLD). The Higher Civil Service in Britain. 1970.

869 RUSSELL-SMITH (*Dame* ENID). Modern Bureaucracy: The Home Civil Service. 1974.

870 SHERIFF (PETA). Career Patterns in the Higher Civil Service. 1976.

871 KELLNER (PETER) *and* CROWTHER-HUNT (NORMAN) *Lord*. The Civil Servants: An Inquiry into Britain's Ruling Class. 1980.

872 PONTING (CLIVE). Whitehall: Tragedy and Farce. 1986.

873 HENNESSY (PETER). Whitehall. 1988.

874 DREWRY (GAVIN) *and* BUTCHER (TONY). The Civil Service Today. Oxf. 1988.

875 Civil Service Commission: Annual Report 1855+.

876 READER (K. M.). The Civil Service Commission: 1855–1975. 1981.

877 MALLABY (*Sir* GEORGE). 'The Civil Service Commission: Its Place in the Machinery of Government'. *Public Admin* xlii (1964), 1–10.

878 PARRIS (HENRY WALTER). Staff Relations in the Civil Service: Fifty Years of Whitleyism. 1973.

879 WHITE (L. D.). Whitley Councils in the British Civil Service. Chicago. 1933.

880 NATIONAL WHITLEY COUNCIL. Fulton—The Reshaping of the Civil Service, Developments since 1970. 1971.

881 STACK (FRIEDA). 'Civil Service Associations and the Whitley Report of 1917'. *Pol. Q.* xl (1969), 283–95.

882 BEAUMONT (PHILIP B.). Government as Employer—Setting an Example? 1981.

883 MOORE (N. E. A.). 'The Civil Service College: What it is and what it is not'. *Management in Gvt.* 39 (1984), 96–103.

884 WALKER (NIGEL). Morale in the Civil Service: A Study of the Desk Worker. Edin. 1961.

885 GLADDEN (EDGAR NORMAN). Civil Service or Bureaucracy? 1956.

886 —— British Public Service Administration. 1961.

887 —— A History of Public Administration. 2 vols 1972.

888 SISSON (C. H.). The Spirit of British Administration. 1968.

889 DELAFONS (J.). 'Working in Whitehall: Changes in Public Administration, 1952–1982'. *Public Admin* 60 (1982), 253–72.

890 *Report of the Committee on the Political Activities of Civil Servants* Cmnd 7718 *Parliamentary Papers* xii (1948–9).

891 *Political Activities of Civil Servants: Report of the Committee* Cmnd 7057 *Parliamentary Papers* (1977–8).

892 EMDEN (CECIL STUART). The Civil Servant in the Law and the Constitution. 1923.

893 MUSTOE (NELSON EDWIN). The Law and Organisation of the British Civil Service. 1932.

894 CH'EN (WEI-KIUNG). The Doctrine of Civil Service Neutrality in Party Conflicts in the United States and Great Britain. Chicago. 1937.

895 WHEARE (*Sir* KENNETH CLINTON). The Civil Service in the Constitution. 1954.

896 ROSE (RICHARD). Ministers and Ministries: A Functional Analysis. Oxf. 1987.

897 DUNSIRE (ANDREW), HOOD (CHRISTOPHER), *with* HUBY (MEG). Cutback Management in Public Bureaucracies: Popular Theories and Observed Outcomes in Whitehall. Camb. 1989.

898 TORSTENDAHL (ROLF). Bureaucratisation in Northwestern Europe 1880–1985: Domination and Governance. 1990. [The systems discussed are the British, the French, the German; and the Swedish.].

899 CHRISTOPH (J. B.). 'Political Rights and Administrative Impartiality in the British Civil Service'. *Amer. Pol. Sci. Rev.* 51 (1) (1957), 67–87.

900 EPSTEIN (LEON D.). 'Political Sterilization of Civil Servants: The United States and Great Britain'. *Public Admin Rev.* x (1950), 281–90.

901 BONTECOU (ELEANOR). 'The English Policy as to Communists and Fascists in the Civil Service'. *Columbia Law Rev.* 51 (1951), 564–86.

902 WRIGHT (MAURICE). 'Ministers and Civil Servants: Relations and Responsibilities'. *Parl. Affs* xxx (1977), 293–313.

903 RIDLEY (F. F.). 'The British Civil Service and Politics: Principles in Question and Traditions in Flux'. *Parl. Affs* 36 (1983), 28–48.

904 BLAIR (L.). 'The Civil Servant: Political Reality and Legal Myth'. *Pub. Law* i (1958), 32–49.

905 GORDON (MICHAEL R.). 'Civil Servants, Politicians and Parties: Shortcomings in the British Policy Process'. *Comp. Pol.* xli (1971), 29–58.

906 CROSS (JOHN A.). 'Ministerial Responsibility and the British Civil Service'. *The Parliamentarian* li (1970), 191–6.

907 GUNN (L. A.). 'Politicians and Officials: Who is Answerable?' *Pol. Q.* xliii (1972), 253–60.

908 PONTING (CLIVE). The Right to Know: The Inside Story of the Belgrano Affair. 1985.

909 HODGETTS (JOHN EDWIN). Organisation, Staffing and Control of the British Civil Service. Chicago. 1946.

910 HENNESSY (PETER), MORRISON (SUSAN), *and* TOWNSEND (RICHARD). Routine Punctuated by Orgies: The Central Policy Review Staff, 1970–83. Glasgow. 1985.

911 DUNSIRE (ANDREW). The Making of an Administrator. Manchester. 1956.

912 BROWN (R. G. S.) *and* STEEL (D. R.). The Administrative Process in Britain. 1970. 2nd edn 1979.

913 GARRETT (JOHN). Managing the Civil Service. 1980.

914 CHAPMAN (RICHARD ARNOLD). Leadership in the British Civil Service: A Study of Sir Percival Waterfield and the Creation of the Civil Service Selection Board. 1984.

915 WATERFIELD (PERCIVAL). 'Civil Service Recruitment'. *Public Admin* 26 (1) (1958), 3–8.

916 BLUME (S. S.) *and* CHENNELLS (E.). 'Professional Civil Servants: A Study in the Sociology of Public Administration'. *Public Admin* liii (1975), 111–31.

917 ROBINSON (K.). 'Selection and the Social Background of the Administrative Class'. *Public Admin* 33(4) (1955), 383–8 and 34 (2) (1956), 169–74.

918 PICKERING (J. F.). 'Recruitment to the Administrative Class, 1960–1964'. *Public Admin* xiv (1967), 169–99.

919 KEELING (DESMOND). 'The Development of Central Training in the Civil Service, 1963–1970'. *Public Admin* xlix (1971), 51–71.

920 CHAPMAN (RICHARD A.). 'Administrative Culture and Personnel Management: The British Civil Service in the 1980s'. *Teaching Public Administration* 4 (1984), 1–14.

921 MURRAY (MILDRED OCTAVIA) *Lady*. The Making of a Civil Servant: Sir Oswyn Murray, G.C.B., Secretary of the Admiralty, 1917–36. 1940.

922 SALTER (JAMES ARTHUR) *Lord*. Memoirs of a Public Servant. 1961.

923 —— Slave of the Lamp. 1967.

924 BRIDGES (EDWARD ETTINGDENE) *Baron*. Portrait of a Profession: the Civil Service. Camb. 1950.

925 CHAPMAN (RICHARD A.). Ethics in the British Civil Service. 1988. [A study centred on the career and values of Lord Bridges.].

926 JONES (JAMES HARRY). Josiah Stamp, Public Servant: The Life of the first Baron Stamp of Shortlands. 1964.

927 MUNRO (CHARLES KIRKPATRICK). The Fountains in Trafalgar Square: Some Reflections on the Civil Service. 1952.

928 KEMPE (*Sir* JOHN ARROW). Reminiscences of an old Civil Servant, 1846–1927. 1928.

929 DUNNILL (FRANK). The Civil Service: Some Human Aspects. 1956.

930 CARSWELL (JOHN PATRICK). The Civil Servant and his World. 1966.

931 COWLES (E.). Sand-hills and Mountains: Memoirs of a Civil Servant. 1932.

932 GLADDEN (EDGAR NORMAN). 'An Old Hand Remembers: A Personal Account, 1932–1947'. *Public Admin* l (1972), 305–12.

933 HARRIS (RICHARD WILLIAM). Not So Humdrum: The Autobiography of a Civil Servant. 1939.

934 HAMILTON (*Sir* H. P.). 'Sir Warren Fisher and the Public Service'. *Public Admin* xxix (1951), 3–38.

935 LOWE (RODNEY) *and* ROBERTS (RICHARD). 'Sir Horace Wilson, 1900–35: The Making of a Mandarin'. *Hist. J.* 30 (1987), 641–62.

936 WEIR (*Sir* CECIL). Civilian Assignment. 1953.

937 HASSELL (CHRISTOPHER). Edward Marsh: Patron of the Arts. 1959.

938 MALLABY (*Sir* GEORGE). From My Level. 1965.

939 PART (*Sir* ANTHONY). The Making of a Mandarin. 1990.

940 REDCLIFFE-MAUD (JOHN) *Baron*. Experience of an Optimist. 1981.

941 MacDOUGALL (*Sir* DONALD). Don and Mandarin: Memoirs of an Economist. 1987.

942 ROLL (ERIC) *Baron*. Crowded Hours. 1985.

943 PLIATSKY (*Sir* LEO). Getting and Spending. 1982.

944 PLOWDEN (EDWIN) *Baron*. An Industrialist in the Treasury. 1989.

945 WILLSON (FRANCIS MICHAEL GLENN). Administrators in Action: British Case Studies. 1961.

946 EVANS (DOROTHY ELIZABETH). Women and the Civil Service: A History of the Development of the Employment of Women in the Civil Service. 1934.

947 MARTINDALE (HILDA). Women Servants of the State, 1870–1938: A History of Women in the Civil Service. 1938.

948 ZIMMECK (M.). 'Strategies and Strategems for the Employment of Women in the British Civil Service, 1919–1939'. *Hist. J.* 27 (1984), 901–24.

949 MEYNELL (ALIX). Public Servant, Private Woman: An Autobiography. 1988.

950 ROWLANDS (EDWARD). 'The Politics of Regional Administration: The Establishment of the Welsh Office'. *Public Admin* l (1972), 333–51.

951 THOMAS (IAN C.). The Creation of the Welsh Office: Conflicting Purposes in Institutional Change. Glasgow. 1981.

952 RHODES (R. A. W.). Beyond Westminster and Whitehall: The Sub-Central Governments of Britain. 1988.

953 PUNNETT (ROBERT MALCOLM). 'The Structure of the Macmillan Government 1957–1963'. *Quart. Rev.* cccii (1964), 12–23.

D. POLITICIANS

It is not surprising that the rich tradition of British political biography has been sustained into the late twentieth century. Notwithstanding the increased attention given to the study of elections and all of the mechanisms of politics, the importance of individual politicians in the political process has continued to be affirmed. In part this is because politicians have themselves implicitly asserted their own significance by continuing to write their own memoirs or to encourage biographers on a scale unusual in Europe. The result is a profusion of material which varies substantially in the quality of the writing and the degree of 'revelation' but which, cumulatively, provides the reader with insights into the everyday realities of British political life. Even so, the reader must necessarily be aware of the complexities which surround the disclosure of political 'truth'. Political memoirs and even political biographies can be designed as much to exonerate as to illuminate. The purposes for which political diaries are kept and published are various. Even a cursory examination of diaries relating to the same meeting or event discloses differences of perception. It would be unwise, therefore, to suppose that the 'right to publish' which politicians increasingly asserted from the 1960s onwards has produced a wholly new and authoritative source of information. It has also sadly been the case that the training in, and awareness of, history has significantly diminished amongst post-1945 politicians, with certain exceptions. It follows that memoirs and autobiographies do not display that awareness of historical context which a historian would like to see.

Not unexpectedly, the density of material is greatest at the Prime Ministerial level. There, frequently but not invariably, a full cycle can be traced—contemporary biographies (laudatory, denigratory, or 'neutral') written as often as not by journalists rather than historians and compiled without access to private papers, speeches (still frequently important until eclipsed in the television age), memoir, or autobiography, posthumous and more or less 'official' biography, followed by substantial and frequently 'revisionist' lives on a similar scale. All of this material is often supplemented by 'short studies' and scholarly articles which scrutinize particular episodes in considerable detail. Naturally, this cycle is not complete in the case of recent and still living Prime Ministers. On the other hand, for whatever reason, Prime Ministers since 1945 have generally felt obliged to publish their accounts of their stewardship whereas their predecessors resisted this temptation or did not live long enough to embark on the task.

The same cycle can be observed, though it is less comprehensive, in the case of holders of other major offices of state. It even applies to some holders of minor offices or even backbenchers whose careers had brief moments of glory.

It should be noted, however, that there are lacunae even amongst such a plethora of material. While biographies of individual Prime Ministers abound, there are comparatively few studies of the office of Prime Minister. Indeed, there are comparatively few historical studies of any of the major offices, that is to say studies which give the reader insight into how the holders of these offices actually functioned over time. Likewise, to take an example at the opposite extreme, it is hard to gain a comprehensive picture of how 'ordinary' MPs functioned—where they lived, how often they visited their constituencies, etc.—despite the existence of many backbench memoirs and biographies.

I. PRIME MINISTERS

954 CARTER (BYRUM E.). The Office of Prime Minister. 1956.

955 BERKELEY (HUMPHREY JOHN). The Power of the Prime Minister. 1968.

956 BENEMY (FRANK WILLIAM GEORGESON). The Elected Monarch: The Development of the Power of the Prime Minister. 1965.

957 ALDERMAN (R. K.). 'The Prime Minister and the Appointment of Ministers: An Exercise in Political Bargaining'. *Parl. Affs* xxix (1976), 101–34.

958 PUNNETT (R. M.). 'The Prime Minister and the Dissolution of Parliament'. *Contemp. Rev.* ccviii (1966), 77–82.

959 JONES (G. W.). 'Prime Ministers' Advisers'. *Pol. Studs* xxi (1973), 363–75.

960 WILLIAMS (FRANCIS) *Baron Francis-Williams*. A Pattern of Rulers. 1965.

961 WILLIAMS (MARCIA) *Baroness Falkender*. Inside No. 10. 1972.

962 BROAD (CHARLIE LEWIS). The Path to Power: The Rise to the Premiership from Rosebery to Wilson. 1965.

963 HAZLEHURST (CAMERON) *and* WOODLAND (CHRISTINE) *comps.* A Guide to the Papers of British Cabinet Ministers, 1900–1951. 1974.

964 HOWARD (ANTHONY) *and* WEST (RICHARD). The Making of the Prime Minister. 1965.

965 FISHER (*Sir* NIGEL). The Tory Leaders: Their Struggle for Power. 1977.

966 ALEXANDER (ANDREW). The Making of the Prime Minister, 1970. 1970.

967 MACKINTOSH (JOHN PITCAIRN) *ed.* British Prime Ministers in the Twentieth Century. 2 vols 1977–8.

968 MACMILLAN (HAROLD) *Earl of Stockton.* The Past Masters: Politics and Politicians, 1906–1939. 1975.

969 VAN THAL (HERBERT) *ed.* The Prime Ministers. Vol. II. 1975.

970 FARR (DIANA). Five at 10: Prime Ministers' Consorts Since 1957. 1985.

Asquith

971 *Asquith*, by Roy Harris Jenkins, *Baron Jenkins of Hillhead.* 1964. 3rd edn 1986.

A good official life is John Alfred Spender and Cyril Asquith, Baron Asquith of Bishopstone, *Life of Herbert Henry Asquith, Lord Oxford and Asquith*, 2 vols, 1932; Ronald Buchanan McCallum, *Asquith*, 1936, is a sketch. Stephen Edward Koss, *Asquith*, 1976, is a substantial biography. Cameron Hazlehurst, 'Asquith as Prime Minister, 1908–1916', *Eng. Hist. Rev.* lxxxv (1970), 532–59, is a critical assessment. Michael and Eleanor Brock, *eds. H. H. Asquith: Letters to Venetia Stanley*, Oxf. 1982, is a remarkable compilation. Asquith's own sifted recollections appeared in *The Genesis of the War*, 1923; *Studies and Sketches*, 1924; *Fifty Years of Parliament*, 2 vols, 1926, and

Memories and Reflections, 1852–1927, 2 vols, 1928; Sir Desmond MacCarthy, *ed. H. H. A.: Letters . . . to a Friend, 1915–27*, 2 ser. 1933–4.

Margot (Emma Alice Margaret), Countess of Oxford and Asquith, *The Autobiography of Margot Asquith*, 2 vols, 1920–2, new edn 1962; *Places and Persons*, 1925; *More Memories*, 1933; *More or Less about Myself*, 1934; and *Off the Record*, 1943. D. Bennett, *Margot*, 1984 is lively but not altogether reliable. See also Herbert Asquith, *Moments of Memory: Recollections and Impressions*, 1937, and Frances Horner, *Lady Horner, Time Remembered*, 1933.

972 McGILL (BARRY). 'Asquith's Predicament, 1914–1918'. *J. Mod. Hist.* xxxix (1967), 283–303.

973 PRICE (DENIS). 'The Fall of Asquith: A Matter of Opinion'. *Contemp. Rev.* ccxxx (1977), 143–7.

Speeches

974 *Speeches by the Earl of Oxford and Asquith*, ed. by Jesse Basil Herbert, 1927, is standard. *Occasional Addresses, 1893–1916*, 1918, is non-political. See also *The Justice of our Case . . . Four Speeches*, 1914; *The War, its Causes and its Messages: Speeches . . . August–October 1914*, 1914; *The Paisley Policy, 1920*, 1920.

Attlee

975 *Attlee* by Kenneth Harris, 1982; *Attlee: A Political Biography* by Trevor Burridge, 1985; Roy Harris Jenkins, *Baron Jenkins of Hillhead, Mr Attlee: An Interim Biography* 1948, is more perceptive than John Thomas Murphy, *Labour's Big Three: A Biographical Study of Clement Attlee, Herbert Morrison and Ernest Bevin*, 1948, or Cyril Clemens, *The Man from Limehouse: Clement Richard Attlee*, Missouri, 1946. Clement Richard Attlee, Earl Attlee, *As it Happened*, 1954, is thin as is Francis Williams, *Baron Francis-Williams, A Prime Minister Remembers: The War and Post-war Memoirs of the Rt. Hon Earl Attlee, Based on his Private Papers and on a Series of Recorded Conversations*, 1961. There is useful assessment in J. Vernon Jenson, 'Clement R. Attlee and Twentieth Century Parliamentary Speaking', *Parl. Affs* xxiii (1970), 277–85; D. J. Heasman, ' "My Station and its Duties"—The Attlee Version', *Parl. Affs* xxi (1967), 75–84; W. Golant's articles are useful, 'The Early Political Thought of C. R. Attlee', *Pol. Q.* xl (1969), 246–55; 'C. R. Attlee in the First and Second Labour Governments', *Parl. Affs* xxvi (1973), 318–35; 'The Emergence of C. R. Attlee as Leader of the Parliamentary Labour Party in 1935', *Hist. J.* xiii (1970), 318–32; 'Mr Attlee', *History Today* 33/9 (1983), 12–17.

Speeches

976 *War comes to Britain. Speeches . . . Edited, with biographical introduction by John Dugdale*, 1940; *Purpose and Policy: Selected Speeches*, 1947; *The Social Worker*, 1920; *The Labour Party Perspective*, 1937, 2nd edn 1949; 'Eight Decades of Change', *Contemp. Rev.* ccviii (1966), 281–5.

Baldwin

977 *Baldwin, a Biography*, by Robert Keith Middlemas and Anthony John Lane Barnes, 1969. A substantial work, though rather careless. Arthur Windham Baldwin, *Earl Baldwin, My Father: The True Story*, 1955, is a filial response to the negative tone of George Malcolm Young, *Stanley Baldwin*, 1952. Harford Montgomery Hyde, *Baldwin: The Unexpected Prime Minister*, 1973, and Kenneth Young, *Stanley Baldwin*, 1976, are competent. Roy Harris Jenkins, *Baron Jenkins of Hillhead, Baldwin*, 1987 is an elegant interpretation.

Charles Loch Mowat, 'Baldwin Restored', *J. Mod. Hist.* xxvii (1955), 169–74 assesses the early biographies; Reginald Bassett, 'Telling the Truth to the People: The Myth of the Baldwin "Confession" ', *Camb. J.* ii (1948), 84–95, and Cameron Hazlehurst, 'The Baldwinite Conspiracy', *Hist. Studs* xvi (1974), 167–91.

Speeches, etc.

978 *On England, and Other Addresses*, 1926, 4th edn 1938; *Our Inheritance: Speeches and Addresses*, 1928; *Service of our Lives: Last Speeches as Prime Minister*, 1937; *This Torch of Freedom: Speeches and Addresses*, 1935.

979 Handlist of the Political Papers of Stanley Baldwin in the Library of the University of Cambridge. Compiled by Arthur Ernest Bion Owen. Camb. 1973.

Balfour

980 *Balfour: International Statesman*, by Ruddock F. Mackay. Oxf. 1985.

Blanche Elizabeth Campbell Dugdale, *Arthur James Balfour, First Earl of Balfour*, 2 vols, 1936, is still useful. Max Egremont, *A List of Arthur James Balfour*, 1980 is superior to Kenneth Young, *Arthur James Balfour: The Happy Life of the Politician, Prime Minister, Statesman and Philosopher, 1848–1930*, 1963. Sydney Henry Zebel, *Balfour: A Political Biography*, Camb. 1973, is useful.

Speeches

981 Some of his later speeches can be found in *Opinions and Argument from Speeches and Addresses of the Earl of Balfour . . . 1910–1927*, ed. by Blanche E. C. Dugdale, 1927.

Callaghan

982 *Callaghan: The Road to Number Ten*, by Peter Kellner. 1976. *Time and Chance* by James Callaghan, 1987.

Chamberlain

983 *The Life of Neville Chamberlain*, by *Sir* Keith Grahame Feiling, 1946, reissued, with a new preface and bibliography, 1970. *Neville Chamberlain: Vol. 1: Pioneering and Reform, 1869–1929*, by David N. Dilks. Camb. 1984.

Contemporary studies include *Sir* Charles Alexander Petrie, *The Chamberlain Tradition*, 1938; Duncan Keith-Shaw, *Prime Minister Neville Chamberlain*, 1939; *Sir* Derek Walker-Smith, *Neville Chamberlain*, 1940, and have only period interest. Iain Norman Macleod, *Neville Chamberlain*, 1961; Charles Bothwell Pyper, *Chamberlain and his Critics: A Statesman Vindicated*, Isleworth, 1962; Harford Montgomery Hyde, *Neville Chamberlain*, 1976, and William R. Rock, *Neville Chamberlain*, 1969, are competent.

David Dilks, 'New Perspectives on Chamberlain', *The Listener*, xcvi (1976), 598–600, offers a foretaste. *Sir*

Douglas Savory, 'Chamberlain, Macleod and the Facts', *Contemp. Rev.* cci (1962), 142–51 states one view. Roy Douglas, 'Chamberlain and Eden, 1937–38', *J. Contemp. Hist.* xiii (1978), 97–116, examines a relationship. L. W. Fuchser, *Neville Chamberlain and Appeasement: A Study in the Politics of History*, N.Y./Lond. 1983.

984 Jorgen Scott Rasmussen, 'Party Discipline in Wartime: The Downfall of the Chamberlain Government', *J. Pol.* xxxii (1970), 379–406.

985 David M. Roberts, 'Clement Davies and the Fall of Neville Chamberlain, 1939–1940', *Welsh Hist. Rev.* viii (1976), 188–215.

986 Lindsay Rogers, 'The Last Tory Prime Minister'. *Polit. Sci. Q.* lxii (1947), 287–94.

Speeches

987 *In Search of Peace*, ed. Arthur Bryant, 1938, reissued in 1939 as *The Struggle for Peace*.

Churchill

988 Randolph Spencer Churchill and Martin John Gilbert, *Churchill*, 6 vols, 1968–83. Martin John Gilbert, *Churchill*, 1979.

There are many one-volume lives which, while dwarfed factually by the major life, nevertheless are historiographically interesting. Philip Guedalla, *Mr Churchill: A Portrait*, 1941; Charles Lewis Broad, *Mr Churchill*, 1941; Guy Eden, *Portrait of Churchill*, 1945; Virginia Cowles, *Winston Churchill: The Era and the Man*, 1953; Charles Eade, ed. *Churchill by his Contemporaries*, 1953; Reginald William Thompson, *The Yankee Marlborough*, 1963; David N. Dilks, *Sir Winston Churchill*, 1965; Hugo Stafford Northcote, *Winston Churchill: Man of Destiny*, 1965; Alan John Percivale Taylor, ed. *Churchill: Four Faces and the Man*, 1969; Peter Stansky, ed. *Churchill: A Profile*, 1973; Robert Payne, *The Great Man: A Portrait of Winston Churchill*, N.Y. 1974; Henry Mathison Pelling, *Churchill*, 1974; Piers Brendon, *Winston Churchill*, 1984 and Ted Morgan, *Churchill 1874–1915*, 1983; William Manchester, *The Last Lion: Winston Spencer Churchill: Visions of Glory 1874–1932*, 2 vols, 1983 and 1987.

One relationship is examined in Kenneth Young, *Churchill and Beaverbrook: A Study in Friendship and Politics*, 1966, and George Malcolm Thomson, *Vote of Censure*, 1968.

Personal impressions, from various angles, appear in Violet Bonham-Carter, *Baroness Asquith, Winston Churchill as I Knew him*, 1965; Charles McMoran Wilson, *Baron Moran, Churchill: The Struggle for Survival, 1940–1965*, 1966; *Sir* John Wheeler Wheeler-Bennett, ed. *Action This Day: Working with Churchill*, 1968; Reginald William Thompson, *Churchill and Morton*, 1976; Phyllis Moir, *I was Winston Churchill's Private Secretary*, 1941; Shafto Gerald Pawle, *The War and Colonel Warden: Based on the Recollections of Commander C. R. Thompson, Personal Assistant to the Prime Minister, 1940–45*, 1963.

The best of the photographic books are: Randolph

Spencer Churchill and Helmut Gernsheim, *comps. Churchill: His Life in Photographs*, 1955; Martin John Gilbert, *Churchill: A Photographic Portrait*, 1974; H. Tatlock Miller and Loudon Sainthill, *Churchill: The Walk with Destiny*, 1979.

Particular facets of Churchill's career and character are covered by Robert H. Pilpel, *Churchill in America, 1895–1961: An Affectionate Portrait*, 1976; Robert Rhodes James, *Churchill: A Study in Failure, 1900–1939*, 1970; Martin John Gilbert, *Winston Churchill: The Wilderness Years*, 1981; Denis C. Bardens, *Churchill in Parliament*, 1967; J. D. Bruce Miller, *Sir Winston Churchill and the Commonwealth of Nations*, St Lucia, Queensland, 1967; Herbert Leslie Stewart, *Winged Words: Sir Winston Churchill as Writer and Speaker*, Toronto, 1953; Oskar K. Rabinowicz, *Winston Churchill on Jewish Problems: A Half Century Survey*, 1956; *Sir* Isaiah Berlin, *Mr Churchill in 1940*, the essay first appeared in 1949; Mary Cogan Brommage, *Churchill and Ireland*, Notre Dame, 1964; Bill Adler, *ed. The Churchill Wit*, N.Y. 1965; Kay Halle, *comp., Impossible Churchill: A Treasury of Winston Churchill's Wit*, N.Y., 1966; *Sir* Peter Gretton, *Former Naval Person: Winston Churchill and the Royal Navy*, 1968; James C. Humes, *Churchill: Speaker of the Century*, N.Y., 1980; Brian Gardner, *Churchill in his Times: A Study in a Reputation, 1939–1945*, 1978; *Sir* John Colville, *The Churchillians*, 1981, is a study of his associates by one of them. Martin John Gilbert, *Churchill's Political Philosophy*, 1981, and Paul Addison, 'The Political Beliefs of Winston Churchill', *Trans. Roy. Hist. Soc.* 5th ser. (1980), 23–47 speculate on ideas.

Churchill's estimates of his *Great Contemporaries*, 1937, rev. edn 1938 remain interesting. His *The World Crisis*, 6 vols 1923–31, 2 vols 1939 has been examined by Robin Prior, *Churchill's 'World Crisis' as History*, 1983. His *A History of the English-Speaking Peoples*, 1956–8, 4 vols, has prompted comments from two men who were associated with his historical enterprises, Maurice Percy Ashley, *Churchill as Historian*, 1968 and *Sir* Frederick William Dampier Deakin. His *The Second World War*, 5 vols, 1948–54, would benefit from the critical attentions of a Prior.

989 CHURCHILL (WINSTON LEONARD SPENCER). Arms and the Covenant. 1938.

990 —— Step by Step, 1936–1939. 1939.

991 —— Into Battle. 1941.

992 —— The Unrelenting Struggle. 1942.

993 —— Onwards to Victory. 1943.

994 —— The End of the Beginning. 1943.

995 —— The Dawn of Liberation. 1945.

996 —— Victory. 1945.

997 —— The Sinews of Peace. 1948.

998 —— Europe Unite. 1950.

999 —— In the Balance. 1951.

1000 —— Stemming the Tide. 1953.

1001 Bernard James Farmer, *Bibliography of the Works of Sir Winston S. Churchill*, 1958, and Frederick Woods, *A Bibliography of the Works of Sir Winston Churchill*, 1969, 2nd rev. edn, 1975 are useful guides to Churchill research.

Speeches

1002 Robert Rhodes James, *ed. The Complete Speeches of Sir Winston Churchill, 1897–1963*, 8 vols N.Y., 1974.

1003 CHURCHILL (WINSTON LEONARD SPENCER). War Speeches, 1940–1945. 1946; Secret Session Speeches. 1946; The Unwritten Alliance: Speeches, 1953–1959. 1961.

Douglas-Home

1004 *Sir Alec Douglas-Home*, by Kenneth Young, 1970.

See also Emrys Hughes, *Sir Alec Douglas-Home*, 1964, and John Dickie, *The Uncommon Commoner: A Study of Sir Alec Douglas-Home*, 1964; *Sir* Alec Douglas-Home, *Baron Home of the Hirsel, The Way the Wind Blows: An Autobiography*, 1976.

Speeches

1005 *Peaceful Change: A Selection of Speeches by Sir Alec Douglas-Home with a Portrait of the Author by Eldon Griffiths*, 1964.

Eden

1006 *Anthony Eden: A Biography*, by David Carlton, 1981.

1007 Sidney Aster, *Anthony Eden*, 1976, is also good. The new prime minister was assessed in three contemporary studies: Alan Campbell-Johnson, *Sir Anthony Eden: a Biography*, 1955; Charles Lewis Broad, *Sir Anthony Eden: The Chronicles of a Career*, 1955; *Sir* William Rees-Mogg, *Sir Anthony Eden*, 1956. Randolph Spencer Churchill, *The Rise and Fall of Sir Anthony Eden*, 1959, rushes to judgment.

1008 EDEN (ROBERT ANTHONY) Earl of Avon, Memoirs: *Full Circle*, 1960; *Facing the Dictators*, 1962; *The Reckoning*, 1965.

1009 McDERMOTT (*Sir* GEOFFREY LYSTER). The Eden Legacy and the Decline of British Diplomacy. 1969.

1010 CAMPBELL-JOHNSON (ALAN). Eden: The Making of a Statesman. Westport, Conn. 1976.

1011 BARKER (ELISABETH). Churchill and Eden at War. 1978.

1012 PETERS (ANTHONY R.). Anthony Eden at the Foreign Office, 1931–1938. Aldershot. 1986.

1013 JAMES (ROBERT RHODES). Anthony Eden. 1986.

1014 ROSE (NORMAN ANTHONY). 'The Resignation of Anthony Eden'. *Hist. J.* 25 (1982), 911–31, deals with 1938.

Speeches, etc.

1015 *Foreign Affairs*, 1939; *Freedom and Order: Selected Speeches, 1939–1946*, 1947; *Days for Decison*, 1949.

Heath

1016 *Edward Heath: A Personal and Political Biography*, by George Hutchinson, 1970, is instant biography but Margaret Laing, *Edward Heath: Prime Minister*, 1972, adds little. Andrew Roth, *Heath and the Heathmen*, 1972, discerned a new phenomenon.

Speeches

1017 HEATH (EDWARD RICHARD GEORGE). *Old World, New Horizons: Britain, the Common Market, and the Atlantic Alliance*, 1970, is a good statement of intent.

Lloyd George

1018 *Lloyd George*, by Kenneth Owen Morgan, 1974. The same author has written shorter studies, *David Lloyd George: Welsh Radical as World Statesman*, Cardiff 1963, and *David Lloyd George, 1863–1945*, Cardiff, 1981, which appeared in both Welsh and English. He has also edited *Lloyd George Family Letters, 1885–1936*, Cardiff/London, 1973 and a collection of documents, with introduction, *The Age of Lloyd George*, 1971.

A comprehensive multi-volumed life is being written by John Grigg.

Albert James Sylvester, *The Real Lloyd George*, 1947, needs to be read alongside *Life with Lloyd George: The Diary of A. J. Sylvester, 1931–45*, ed. by Colin Cross, 1975; Malcolm Thomson, *David Lloyd George: The Official Biography*, 1948, had the assistance of his widow; Thomas Jones, *Lloyd George*, 1951, is stately; Frank Owen, *Tempestuous Journey: Lloyd George, his Life and Times*, 1954, is massive; George Donald K. MacCormick, *The Mask of Merlin: A Critical Study of David Lloyd George*, 1963, adds little; Martin John Gilbert, comp., *Lloyd George*, Englewood Cliffs, N.J., 1968, and Charles Loch Mowat, *Lloyd George*, 1964, are introductions; Alan John Percivale Taylor, *The Rise and Fall of Lloyd George*, 1961, is a stimulating lecture and he has also edited a useful collection, *Lloyd George: Twelve Essays*, 1971. Peter Rowland, *Lloyd George*, 1975, is solid. The third volume of John Grigg's biography has now reached the war, *Lloyd George: From Peace to War, 1912–1916*, 1985. Martin Pugh, *Lloyd George*, 1988, is an excellent short study. William Maxwell Aitken, *Baron Beaverbrook, The Decline and Fall of Lloyd George: And Great was the Fall Thereof*, 1963, 2nd edn 1966, should be read with Michael Kinnear, *The Fall of Lloyd George: The Political Crisis of 1922*, 1973; John Campbell, *Lloyd George: The Goat in the Wilderness, 1922–1931*, 1977, is an excellent study; John Ray, *Lloyd George and Churchill*, 1970, adds little. Family perspectives appear in William George, *My Brother and I*, 1958; Richard Lloyd George, *Earl Lloyd George, Lloyd George*, 1960; *My Darling Pussy: The Letters of Lloyd George and Frances Stevenson, 1913–1941*, ed. by Alan John Percivale Taylor, 1975; Frances Louise, *Countess Lloyd-George, Lloyd George: A Diary*, 1971; Frances Louise, *Countess Lloyd-George, The Years that are Past*, 1967.

1019 LLOYD GEORGE (DAVID). War Memoirs. 6 vols 1933–6; 2 vols edn 1938.

1020 —— The Truth About Reparations and War Debts. 1932.

1021 —— The Truth About the Peace Treaties. 2 vols. 1938.

1022 ADAMS (R. J. Q.). Arms and the Wizard: Lloyd George and the Ministry of Munitions, 1915–1916. College Station. 1978.

1023 BROOKS (D.). 'Lloyd George—For and Against'. *Hist. J.* 24 (1981).

1024 SPENDER (STEPHEN). 'The Character of Lloyd George'. *Twentieth Century* cl (1951), 511–20.

1025 ADAMS (W. S.). 'Lloyd George and the Labour Movement'. *Past & Present* iii (1953), 55–64.

1026 EHRMAN (JOHN). 'Lloyd George and Churchill as War Ministers'. *Trans. Roy. Hist. Soc.* 5th ser. xi (1961), 101–15.

1027 MORGAN (KENNETH OWEN). 'Lloyd George's Premiership: A Study in "Prime-Ministerial" Government'. *Hist. J.* xiii (1970), 130–57.

1028 —— 'Lloyd George and the Historians'. *Trans. Hon. Soc. Cymmr.* (1971), 65–85.

1029 KOSS (STEPHEN EDWARD). 'Lloyd George and Nonconformity: The Last Rally'. *Eng. Hist. Rev.* lxxxix (1974), 77–108.

1030 DESMARAIS (RALPH H.). 'Lloyd George and the Development of the British Government's Strikebreaking Organisation'. *Inl Rev. Soc. Hist.* xx (1975), 1–15.

Speeches

1031 *Through Terror to Triumph: Speeches and Pronouncements . . . since the Beginning of the War*, ed. by Frances Louise Stevenson, afterwards Lloyd-George, 1915; *Is it Peace? Articles and Addresses on the European Situation*, 2nd edn 1923; *The Great Crusade: Extracts from Speeches Delivered During the War*, ed. by Frances Louise Stevenson, 1918; *Slings and Arrows: Sayings Chosen from the Speeches of the Rt. Hon. D. Lloyd George*, ed. Philip Guedalla, 1929; Herbert Rohmann, *Intonation und Lautgebung in der Sprache von Lloyd George*, 1939.

MacDonald

1032 *Ramsay MacDonald*, by David Ian Marquand, 1977. Godfrey Elton, *Baron Elton, The Life of James Ramsay MacDonald*, 1939, does not extend beyond 1919; Mary Agnes Hamilton, *J. Ramsay MacDonald*, 1929, Hubert Hessell, *James Ramsay MacDonald: Labour's Man of Destiny*, 1929, and Lauchlan Macneill Weir, *The Tragedy of Ramsay MacDonald: A Political Biography*, 1938, reflect their dates of publication; Benjamin Sacks, *J. Ramsay MacDonald in Thought and Action*, Albuquerque, N. Mex., 1952, is full but unperceptive; Austen Morgan, *J. Ramsay MacDonald*, Manchester, 1987, is a useful short study; M.S. Venkataramani, 'Ramsay MacDonald and Britain's Domestic Politics and Foreign Relations, 1919–1931', *Pol. Studs*, viii (1960), 231–49; Richard Wall Lyman, 'James Ramsay MacDonald and the Leadership of the Labour Party, 1918–1922', *J. Brit. Studs*, ii (1962), 132–60; Charles Loch Mowat, 'Ramsay MacDonald and the Labour Party', in *Essays in Labour History, 1886–1923*, ed. by Asa Briggs and John Saville, 1971; Rodney Barker, 'Political Myth: Ramsay MacDonald and the Labour Party', *Hist.* lxi (1976), 46–56; Trevor Lloyd, 'Ramsay MacDonald: Socialist or Gentleman?', *Can. J. Hist.* 15 (1980), 399–407.

Speeches, etc.

1033 *Wanderings and Excursions, 1925; At Home and Abroad: Essays, 1936; American Speeches, 1930; Ramsay MacDonald's Political Writings, ed. by Bernard Barker, 1972.*

Macmillan

1034 FISHER (NIGEL). Harold Macmillan: A Biography. 1982.

1035 SAMPSON (ANTHONY). Macmillan: A Study in Ambiguity. 1967.

1036 HUGHES (EMRYS). Macmillan: Portrait of a Politician. 1962.

1037 HORNE (ALISTAIR). Macmillan, 1894–1956. 1988.

1038 —— Macmillan, 1957–1986. 1989.

1039 MACMILLAN (HAROLD) *Earl of Stockton.* Memoirs:

1040 —— Winds of Change, 1914–1939. 1966.

1041 —— The Blast of War, 1939–1945. 1967.

1042 —— Tides of Fortune, 1945–1955. 1969.

1043 —— Riding the Storm, 1956–1959. 1971.

1044 —— Pointing the Way, 1959–1961. 1972.

1045 —— At the End of the Day, 1961–1963. 1973.

1046 Photographs from his collection appear in Ruth Dudley Edwards, *Harold Macmillan: A Life in Pictures*, 1983; His *War Diaries: The Mediterranean, 1943–45*, 1984, refer to his period as British Minister Resident in North Africa.

Works

1047 *Reconstruction: A Plea for National Policy, 1933; The Next Five Years, 1935; The Middle Way: A Study of the Problem of Economic and Social Progress in a Free and Democratic Society, 1938, rev. edn 1966; Economic Aspects of Defence, 1939.*

Thatcher

1048 *Margaret Thatcher: A Personal and Political Biography* by Russell Lewis, 1975, is only an early assessment, as are George Gardiner, *Margaret Thatcher: From Childhood to Leadership*, 1975, and Ernle Money, *Margaret Thatcher: First Lady of the House*, 1975. A clutch of later studies take the story further but add little in depth: Patrick Cosgrave, *Margaret Thatcher: A Tory and Her Party*, 1978; Nicholas Wapshott and George Brock, *Thatcher*, 1983; Penny Junor, *Margaret Thatcher: Woman, Mother, Prime Minister*, 1983; Bruce Arnold, *Margaret Thatcher: A Study in Power*, 1984. Two interim assessments of her first government are Patrick Cosgrave, *Thatcher: The First Term*, 1985, and Jock Bruce-Gardyne, *Mrs Thatcher's First Administration: Confounding the Prophets*, 1984.

1049 ROSS (JOHN). Thatcher and Friends: The Anatomy of the Tory Party. c.1983.

1050 RIDDELL (PETER). The Thatcher Government. Oxford. 1983.

1051 DALYELL (TAM). Thatcher's Torpedo. 1983.

1052 COLE (JOHN). The Thatcher Years: A Decade of Revolution in British Politics. 1987.

1053 SKIDELSKY (ROBERT). Thatcherism. 1988.

1054 JESSOP (BOB), BONNETT (KEVIN), BROMLEY (SIMON), *and* LING (TOM). Thatcherism: A Tale of Two Nations. Camb. 1988.

1055 KAVANAGH (DENNIS). Thatcherism and British Politics: The End of Consensus? Oxf. 1987.

1056 CREWE (IVOR). Thatcherism: Its Origins, Electoral Impact and Implications for Downs's Theory of Party Strategy. Colchester. 1986.

1057 YOUNG (HUGO). The Thatcher Phenomenon. 1986.

1058 —— Thatcherism: Personality and Politics. Basingstoke. 1987.

1059 —— One of Us: A Biography of Margaret Thatcher. 1989.

Wilson

1060 *Harold Wilson: A Critical Biography*, by Dudley Smith, 1964, is an early outline, as are Leslie Smith, *Harold Wilson: The Authentic Portrait*, 1964, Ernest Kay, *Pragmatic Premier: An Intimate Portrait of Harold Wilson*, 1967, Gerard Eyre Noel, *Harold Wilson and the 'New Britain'*, 1964, and Paul Foot, *The Politics of Harold Wilson*, Harmondsworth, 1968.

Speeches and Works

1061 *Purpose in Politics: Selected Speeches, 1964; The New Britain: Labour's Plans Outlined, Selected Speeches, Harmondsworth, 1964; Ernest Kay, comp. The Wit of Harold Wilson, 1967; The Labour Government, 1964–1970: A Personal Record, 1971; Final Term: The Labour Government, 1974–1976, 1979; Memoirs: The Making of a Prime Minister 1916–1964, 1975.*

2. CABINET MINISTERS (EXCEPT LORD CHANCELLORS)

Addison

1062 MORGAN (KENNETH OWEN) *and* MORGAN (JANE). Portrait of a Progressive: The Political Career of Christopher, Viscount Addison. Oxf. 1980.

1063 MINNEY (RUBEIGH JAMES). Viscount Addison: Leader of the Lords. 1958.

1064 ADDISON (CHRISTOPHER) *Viscount Addison.* Politics from Within, 1911–1918. 2 vols. 1924.

1065 —— Four and a Half Years: A Personal Diary from June 1914 to January 1919. 2 vols 1934.

Amery

1066 AMERY (LEOPOLD CHARLES MAURICE STENNETT). My Political Life. 3 vols 1953–5.

Amory

1067 ALLEN (WALTER GORE). The Reluctant Politician: Derick Heathcote Amory. 1958.

1068 BARNES (JOHN) *and* NICHOLSON (DAVID) *eds.* The Leo Amery Diaries: Vol. 1: 1886–1929. 1980. Vol. 2: The Empire at Bay 1929–1945. 1987.

Anderson

1069 WHEELER-BENNETT (*Sir* JOHN). John Anderson, Viscount Waverley. 1962.

Balfour

1070 BALFOUR (HAROLD) *Baron Balfour of Inchrye*. Wings over Westminster. 1973.

Barnes

1071 BARNES (GEORGE NICOLL). From Workshop to War Cabinet. 1924.

Beaverbrook

1072 TAYLOR (ALAN JOHN PERCIVALE). Beaverbrook. 1972.

1073 FARRER (DAVID). G—For God Almighty. A Personal Memoir of Lord Beaverbrook. 1969.

1074 VINES (C. M.). A Little Nut-Brown Man: My Three Years with Lord Beaverbrook. 1969.

1075 WOOD (ALAN). The True History of Lord Beaverbrook. 1965.

1076 YOUNG (KENNETH). Churchill and Beaverbrook: A Study in Friendship and Politics. 1966.

1077 BEAVERBROOK (WILLIAM MAXWELL AITKEN) *Lord*. My Early Life. Fredericton, New Brunswick. 1965.

1078 GOURLAY (LOGAN). The Beaverbrook Years. 1983.

1079 —— *Ed*. The Beaverbrook I Knew. 1985. Repr. 1987.

Benn

1080 BENN (TONY). The Regeneration of Britain. 1965.

1081 —— Out of the Wilderness: Diaries 1963–1967. 1987.

1082 —— Office without Power: Diaries 1968–1972. 1988.

1083 —— Against the Tide: Diaries 1973–1976. 1989.

1084 —— Conflicts of Interest: Diaries 1977–1980. 1990.

1085 —— Speeches by Tony Benn. 1974.

1086 —— Arguments for Socialism. 1979.

1087 —— Arguments for Democracy. 1981.

1088 —— Parliament, People and Power: Agenda for a Free Society. 1982.

1089 —— Fighting Back: Speaking out for Socialism in the Eighties. 1988.

1090 HIGGINS (SYDNEY). The Benn Inheritance: The Story of a Radical Family. 1984.

1091 FREEMAN (ALAN). The Benn Heresy. 1982.

1092 LEWIS (RUSSELL). Tony Benn: A Critical Biography. 1978.

1093 BUTLER (DAVID). 'The Benn Archive'. *Contemp. Record* 1 (1987), 13–14.

1094 COCKS (MICHAEL). Labour and the Benn Factor. 1989.

Bevan

1095 BEVAN (ANEURIN). In Place of Fear. 1952. 2nd edn 1961.

1096 BROME (HERBERT VINCENT). Aneurin Bevan: A Biography. 1953.

1097 KRUG (MARK M.). Aneurin Bevan: A Cautious Rebel. N.Y. 1961.

1098 FOOT (MICHAEL MacKINTOSH). Aneurin Bevan. 2 vols 1962 and 1973.

1099 FAIRLIE (HENRY). 'Aneurin Bevan and the Art of Politics'. *History Today* 10 (1960), 661–7.

1100 CAMPBELL (JOHN). Nye Bevan and the Mirage of British Socialism. 1987.

Bevin

1101 BULLOCK (ALAN LOUIS CHARLES) *Baron Bullock*. The Life and Times of Ernest Bevin. 3 vols 1960. 1967. 1983.

1102 EVANS (TREVOR MALDWYN). Bevin. 1946.

1103 FRANCIS WILLIAMS (EDWARD) *Lord*. Ernest Bevin: Portrait of a Great Englishman. 1952.

1104 —— Ernest Bevin: An Illustrated Life, 1881–1951. Aylesbury. 1974.

Bevins

1105 BEVINS (REGINALD). The Greasy Pole: A Personal Account of the Realities of British Politics. 1965.

Birkenhead

1106 SMITH (FREDERICK EDWIN) *Earl of Birkenhead*. The Last Phase. 1935. [Vol 2 of biography which covers post-1914 period.].

1107 —— The Speeches of Lord Birkenhead. 1929. [With a preface by Lord Hugh Cecil.].

1108 —— Contemporary Personalities. 1924.

1109 —— Law, Life and Letters. 2 vols 1927.

1110 —— Last Essays. 1930.

1111 SMITH (FREDERICK WINSTON FURNEAUX) *Lord Birkenhead*. F. E.: The Life of F. E. Smith, First Earl of Birkenhead. 1959.

1112 CAMP (WILLIAM NEWTON ALEXANDER) *Comp*. The Glittering Prizes: A Biographical Study of F. E. Smith, First Earl of Birkenhead. 1960.

1113 CAMPBELL (JOHN). F. E. Smith, First Earl of Birkenhead. 1984.

Bondfield

1114 BONDFIELD (MARGARET). A Life Work. 1949.

Boyd-Carpenter

1115 BOYD-CARPENTER (JOHN). Memoirs. 1980.

Brentford

1116 TAYLOR (HENRY ARCHIBALD). Jix, Viscount Brentford. 1933.

Brown

1117 CONNOR (['CASSANDRA'] *Sir* WILLIAM NEIL). George Brown: A Profile and Pictorial Biography. Oxf. 1964.

1118 BROWN (GEORGE) *Lord George-Brown*. In My Way: The Political Memoirs of Lord George-Brown. 1971.

Burns

1119 COLE (GEORGE DOUGLAS HOWARD). John Burns. 1943.

1120 KENT (WILLIAM R. G.). John Burns, Labour's Lost Leader: A Biography. 1950.

1121 BROWN (KENNETH DOUGLAS). John Burns. 1977.

Butler

1122 HARRIS (RALPH). Politics without Prejudice: A Political Appreciation of the Rt. Hon. Richard Austen Butler. 1956.

1123 BOYD (FRANCIS). Richard Austen Butler. 1956.

1124 SPARROW (GERALD). 'R. A. B.': Study of a Statesman. 1965.

1125 BUTLER (RICHARD AUSTEN) *Lord Butler*. The Art of the Possible: The Memoirs of Lord Butler, K.G. C.H. 1971.

1126 —— The Art of Memory: Friends in Perspective. 1982.

1127 BUTLER *and* SULLIVAN (F. B.). Lord Butler: The 1944 Act in Perspective. 1980.

1128 STAFFORD (PAUL). 'Political Autobiography and the Art of the Possible: R. A. Butler at the Foreign Office 1938–1939'. *Hist. J.* 28 (1985), 901–22.

1129 COSGRAVE (PATRICK). R. A. Butler: An English Life. 1981.

1130 BUTLER (MOLLIE). August and Rab: A Memoir. 1987.

1131 HOWARD (ANTHONY). Rab: The Life of R. A. Butler. 1987.

Carrington

1132 COSGRAVE (PATRICK). Carrington: A Life and a Policy. 1985.

1133 CARRINGTON (PETER ALEXANDER RUPERT) *Lord*. Reflect on Things Past: The Memoirs of Lord Carrington. 1988.

Carson

1134 HYDE (HARFORD MONTGOMERY). Carson: The Life of Sir Edward Carson, Lord Carson of Duncairn. 1953.

1135 MARJORIBANKS (EDWARD). The Life of Edward Carson. Vol.1. Toronto. 1932.

1136 COLVIN (IAN DUNCAN). The Life of Edward Carson. Vols 2 and 3. London. 1932. 1936.

1137 STEWART (ANTHONY TERENCE QUINCEY). Edward Carson. Dublin. 1981.

Castle

1138 THANE (PAT). 'Towards Equal Opportunities? Women in Britain since 1945' in *eds*. Terry Gourvish and Alan O'Day, Britain since 1945. 1991. 183–208.

1139 CASTLE (BARBARA). The Castle Diaries, 1974–1976. 1980.

1140 —— The Castle Diaries, 1964–1970. 1984.

1141 DE'ATH (WILFRID). Barbara Castle: A Portrait from Life. 1970.

Chamberlain, (Austen)

1142 PETRIE (*Sir* CHARLES ALEXANDER). The Chamberlain Tradition. 1938.

1143 —— The Life and Letters of Rt. Hon. Austen Chamberlain. 2 vols, 1939–40; vol 2 begins in 1914.

1144 CHAMBERLAIN (*Sir* JOSEPH AUSTEN). Peace in our Time: Addresses on Europe and the Empire. 1928.

1145 —— Down the Years: A Volume of Essays on Men and Affairs. 1934.

1146 —— Seen in Passing . . . (1937). [A travel book.].

1147 DUTTON (DAVID). Austen Chamberlain: Gentleman in Politics. Bolton. 1985.

Clynes

1148 CLYNES (JOHN ROBERT). Memoirs. 2 vols 1937.

Cooper

1149 COOPER (ALFRED DUFF) *Viscount Norwich*. Old Men Forget. 1953.

1150 COOPER (ARTEMIS) *ed*. A Durable Fire: The Letters of Duff and Diana Cooper, 1913–1950. 1983.

1151 CHARMLEY (JOHN). Duff Cooper: The Authorized Biography. 1986.

Crewe

1152 POPE-HENNESSY (JAMES). Lord Crewe, 1858–1945: The Likeness of a Liberal. 1955.

Cripps

1153 TYLER (FROOM). Cripps: A Portrait and a Prospect. 1942.

1154 STRAUSS (PATRICIA). Cripps: Advocate and Rebel. 1943.

1155 ESTORICK (ERIC). Stafford Cripps. 1949.

1156 COOKE (COLIN ARTHUR). The Life of Richard Stafford Cripps. 1957.

1157 GORODETSKY (GABRIEL). Stafford Cripps' Mission to Moscow 1940–1942. Camb. 1984.

Crosland

1158 CROSLAND (ANTHONY). The Future of Socialism. 1956.

1159 —— The Politics of Education. Harmondsworth. 1971.

1160 —— Socialism Now, and other Essays. 1974.

1161 LIPSEY (DAVID) *and* LEONARD (DICK). The Socialist Agenda: Crosland's Legacy. 1981.

1162 CROSLAND (SUSAN). Tony Crosland. 1982.

[See also book by VAIZEY (JOHN) below, under Gaitskell, but which also discusses Crosland.].

Crossman

1163 DALYELL (TAM). Dick Crossman. 1989.

1164 CROSSMAN (RICHARD HOWARD STAFFORD). The Diaries of a Cabinet Minister. 3 vols 1975–7.

1165 —— The Backbench Diaries of Richard Crossman. 1981. *Ed.* MORGAN (JANET).

1166 —— Inside View: Three Lectures on Prime Ministerial Government. 1950.

1167 HOWARD (ANTHONY) *ed.* The Crossman Diaries: Selections from the Diaries of a Cabinet Minister, 1964–1970. 1979.

1168 YOUNG (HUGO). The Crossman Affair. 1976.

Cunliffe-Lister

1169 CUNLIFFE-LISTER (PHILIP) *Earl Swinton*. Sixty Years of Power: Some Memories of the Men who Wielded it. 1966. [In collaboration with MARGACH (JAMES).].

1170 CROSS (JOHN ARTHUR). Lord Swinton. 1982.

Curzon

1171 CURZON (GEORGE NATHANIEL) *Baron Scarsdale*. Selections of the Day: Being a Selection of Speeches and Writings. 1915.

1172 —— Leaves from a Viceroy's Note-Book and other Papers. 1926.

1173 MOSLEY (LEONARD). The Glorious Fault: The Life of Lord Curzon. N.Y. 1960.

1174 ZETLAND (GEORGE DUNDAS) *Marquis*. The Life of Lord Curzon. . . 3 vols 1928.

1175 PARKER (JAMES G.). Lord Curzon: A Biography. 1989.

Dalton

1176 DALTON (HUGH NEALE) *Baron*. Call Back Yesterday: Memoirs, 1887–1931. 1953.

1177 —— The Fateful Years: Memoirs, 1931–1945. 1957.

1178 —— High Tide and After: Memoirs, 1945–1960. 1962.

1179 PIMLOTT (BEN). Hugh Dalton. 1985.

1180 —— *Ed.* The Second World War Diary of Hugh Dalton 1940–1945. 1986.

1181 —— *Ed.* The Political Diary of Hugh Dalton, 1918–1940, 1945–1960. 1987.

Davidson

1182 DAVIDSON (JOHN COLIN CAMPBELL). Memoirs of a Conservative: J. C. C. Davidson's Memoirs and Papers, 1910–1937. 1969.

Derby

1183 CHURCHILL (RANDOLPH S.). Lord Derby . . . : The Official Life of Edward, Lord Derby, 17th Earl of Derby 1865–1948. 1959.

1184 BAGLEY (J. J.). The Earls of Derby 1485–1985. 1985.

Eccles

1185 ECCLES (DAVID McADAM) *Viscount Eccles*. Life and Politics: A Moral Diagnosis. 1967.

1186 —— By Safe Hand: The Wartime Letters of Sybil and David Eccles, 1939–1942. 1983.

Elliot

1187 COOTE (*Sir* COLIN REITH). A Companion of Honour: The Story of Walter Elliot. 1965.

Elwyn-Jones

1188 ELWYN-JONES (FREDERICK) *Baron*. In My Time: An Autobiography. 1983.

Esher

1189 FRASER (PETER). Lord Esher: A Political Biography. 1973.

1190 BRETT (MAURICE V.) *and* BRETT (OLIVER SYLVAIN BALIOL). Journals and Letters of Reginald, Viscount Esher. 4 vols 1934–1938.

1191 LEES-MILNE (JAMES). The Enigmatic Edwardian: The Life of Reginald, 2nd Viscount Esher. 1986.

Foot

1192 HOGGART (SIMON DAVID) *and* LEIGH (DAVID). Michael Foot: A Portrait. 1981.

1193 FOOT (MICHAEL MacKINTOSH). Another Heart and other Pulses: The Alternative to the Thatcher Society. 1984.

Gaitskell

1194 WILLIAMS (PHILIP M.). Hugh Gaitskell. 1979.

1195 —— *Ed.* The Diary of Hugh Gaitskell, 1945–1956. 1983.

1196 JENKINS (ROY). 'Hugh Gaitskell: A Political Memoir'. *Encounter* 22 (1964), 3–10.

1197 RODGERS (WILLIAM THOMAS) *ed.* Hugh Gaitskell, 1906–1963. 1964.

1198 HASELER (STEPHEN). The Gaitskellites: Revisionism in the British Labour Party, 1951–1954. 1969.

1199 McDERMOTT (GEOFFREY). Leader Lost: A Biography of Hugh Gaitskell. 1972.

1200 VAIZEY (JOHN). In Breach of Promise: Gaitskell, MacLeod, Titmuss, Crosland, Boyle: Five Men Who Shaped a Generation. 1983.

Grey

1201 HALDANE (RICHARD BURDON) *Viscount Haldane*. Viscount Grey of Fallodon. 1928.

1202 TREVELYAN (GEORGE MACAULAY). Grey of Fallodon. 1937.

1203 ROBBINS (KEITH GILBERT). Sir Edward Grey: A Biography of Lord Grey of Fallodon. 1971.

1204 HINSLEY (FRANCIS HARRY) *ed.* British Foreign Policy under Sir Edward Grey. Camb. 1977.

1205 GREY (EDWARD) *Viscount Grey of Fallodon*. Thoughts on Public Life. 1923.

1206 —— Twenty Five Years 1892–1916. 2 vols 1925.

Griffiths

1207 GRIFFITHS (JAMES). Pages from Memory. 1969.

1208 SMITH (JENKYN BEVERLEY) *et al.* James Griffiths and his Times. Cardiff. 1977.

Hailsham

1209 HOGG (QUINTIN) *Baron Hailsham*. The Door Wherein I Went. 1975.

1210 —— A Sparrow's Flight: Memoirs. 1990.

1211 —— The Purpose of Parliament. 1946.

Haldane

1212 HALDANE (RICHARD BURDON) *Viscount Haldane*. An Autobiography. 1929.

1213 MAURICE (*Sir* FREDERICK BARTON). Haldane, 1856–1928: The Life of Viscount Haldane of Cloan. 2 vols 1937 and 1939.

1214 SOMMER (DUDLEY). Haldane of Cloan: His Life and Times, 1856–1928. 1960.

1215 KOSS (STEPHEN EDWARD). Lord Haldane: A Scapegoat for Liberalism. 1969.

1216 SPIERS (EDWARD M.). Haldane: An Army Reformer. Edin. 1980.

Halifax

1217 WOOD (EDWARD FREDERICK LINLEY) *Earl of Halifax*. Fulness of Days. 1957.

1218 CRASTER (*Sir* HERBERT HENRY EDMUND) *ed.* Speeches on Foreign Policy by Viscount Halifax. 1940.

1219 HODGSON (STUART). Lord Halifax: An Appreciation. 1941.

1220 JOHNSON (ALAN CAMPBELL). Viscount Halifax: A Biography. 1941.

1221 SMITH (FREDERICK WINSTON FURNEAUX). Lord Birkenhead. Halifax. 1965.

Hankey [Maurice Pascal Alers]

1222 ROSKILL (STEPHEN WENTWORTH). Hankey: Man of Secrets. 3 vols 1970–4.

1223 HANKEY (MAURICE PASCAL ALERS) *Baron.* Diplomacy by Conference: Studies in Public Affairs 1926–1946. 1946.

Hattersley

1224 HATTERSLEY (ROY). Goodbye to Yorkshire. 1976.

1225 —— A Yorkshire Boyhood. 1983.

1226 —— Choose Freedom: The Future for Democratic Socialism. 1987.

Healey

1227 REED (BRUCE) *and* WILLIAMS (GEOFFREY). Denis Healey and the Politics of Power. 1971.

1228 HEALEY (DENIS WINSTON). The Time of my Life. 1989.

Henderson

1229 JENKINS (EDWIN ALFRED). From Foundry to Foreign Office: The Romantic Life Story of the Rt. Hon. Arthur Henderson M.P. 1933.

1230 HAMILTON (MARY AGNES). Arthur Henderson: A Biography. 1938.

1231 CARLTON (DAVID). MacDonald versus Henderson: The Foreign Policy of the Second Labour Government. 1970.

1232 LEVENTHAL (FRED MARC). Arthur Henderson: A Biography. Manch. 1989.

Heseltine

1233 HESELTINE (MICHAEL). Where there's a Will. 1987.

1234 CRITCHLEY (JULIAN). Heseltine: The Unauthorised Biography. 1987.

Hoare

1235 HOARE (SAMUEL JOHN GURNEY) *Viscount Templewood.* Nine Troubled Years. 1954.

1236 CROSS (JOHN ARTHUR). Sir Samuel Hoare: A Political Biography. 1977.

Hollis

1237 HOLLIS (CHRISTOPHER). Along the Road to Frome. 1958.

Hore-Belisha

1238 MINNEY (RUBEIGH JAMES) *ed.* The Private Papers of Hore-Belisha. 1960.

1239 TRYTHALL (A. J.). 'The Downfall of Leslie Hore-Belisha'. *J. Contemp. Hist.* 16 (1981), 391–411.

Howe

1240 HILLMAN (JUDY) *and* CLARKE (PETER). Geoffrey Howe: A Quiet Revolutionary. 1988.

Hurd

1241 HURD (DOUGLAS). An End to Promises: Sketch of a Government, 1970–1974. 1979.

Isaacs

1242 EASTWOOD (G. G.). George Isaacs: Printer, Trade Union Leader, Cabinet Minister. 1952.

Jay

1243 JAY (DOUGLAS PATRICK THOMAS) *Baron.* Change and Fortune. 1980.

Jenkins

1244 CAMPBELL (JOHN F.). Roy Jenkins: A Biography. Lond./N.Y. 1983.

1245 JENKINS (ROY HARRIES) *Baron Jenkins of Hillhead.* European Diary, 1977–1981. 1989.

1246 LESTER (ANTHONY) *ed.* Essays and Speeches by Roy Jenkins. 1967.

1247 LINDLEY (CLIVE) *ed.* Partnership of Principle: Writings and Speeches on the Making of the Alliance by Roy Jenkins. 1985.

Johnston

1248 JOHNSTON (THOMAS). Memories. 1952.

1249 —— The History of the Working Classes in Scotland. Glasg. 1920. 4th edn 1946.

1250 WALKER (GRAHAM). Thomas Johnston 1881–1965. Manch. 1988.

Joseph

1251 HALCROW (MORRISON). Keith Joseph: A Single Mind. 1989.

Kilmuir

1252 KILMUIR (DAVID MAXWELL-FYFE) *Earl.* Political Adventure: The Memoirs of the Earl of Kilmuir. 1964.

Llewellin

1253 THOMAS (GILBERT). [John Jestin] Llewellin: A Biography. 1961.

Lloyd

1254 LLOYD (SELWYN) *Baron.* Mr. Speaker, Sir. 1976.

1255 —— Suez 1956: A Personal View. 1978.

1256 THORPE (DAVID R.). Selwyn Lloyd. 1989.

Long

1257 PETRIE (*Sir* CHARLES ALEXANDER). Walter Long and his Times. 1936.

1258 LONG (WALTER HUME) *Viscount.* Memories. . . 1923.

Longford

1259 PAKENHAM (FRANCIS AUNGIER) *Earl of Longford.* Born to Believe: An Autobiography. 1953.

1260 —— Five Lives. 1964.

1261 —— The Grain of Wheat. 1974.

1262 —— Eleven at No. 10: A Personal View of Prime Ministers, 1931–1984. 1984.

1263 CRAIG (MARY). Longford: A Biographical Portrait. 1978.

1264 LONGFORD (ELIZABETH) *Countess of Longford.* The Pebbled Shore: Memoirs of Elizabeth Longford. 1986.

Lyttelton

1265 LYTTELTON (OLIVER) *Lord Chandos.* The Memoirs of Lord Chandos. 1962.

MacDonald

1266 MacDONALD (MALCOLM). People and Places: Random Reminiscences. 1969.

McKenna

1267 McKENNA (STEPHEN). Reginald McKenna, 1863–1943: A Memoir. 1948.

MacLeod

1268 FISHER (*Sir* NIGEL). Iain Macleod. 1973. [See also book by VAIZEY (JOHN) above, under Gaitskell, but which also discusses Macleod.].

Marsh

1269 MARSH (RICHARD WILLIAM) *Baron Marsh*. Off the Rails. 1978.

Masterman

1270 MASTERMAN (LUCY). C. F. G. Masterman: A Biography. 1939.

Maudling

1271 MAUDLING (REGINALD). Memoirs. 1978.

Milner

1272 WRENCH (*Sir* JOHN EVELYN LESLIE). Alfred, Lord Milner: The Man of No Illusions, 1854–1925. 1958.

1273 GOLLIN (ALFRED MANUEL). Proconsul in Politics: A Study of Lord Milner in Opposition and in Power. 1964.

1274 MARLOWE (JOHN). Milner: Apostle of Empire: A Life of Alfred George, the Right Honourable Viscount Milner . . . 1854–1925. 1976.

1275 O'BRIEN (TERENCE H.). Milner: Viscount Milner of St. James's and Cape Town, 1854–1925. 1979.

Monckton

1276 SMITH (FREDERICK WINSTON FURNEAUX) *Lord Birkenhead*. Walter Monckton: The Life of Viscount Monckton of Brenchley. 1969.

Montagu

1277 WALEY (*Sir* SIGISMUND DAVID). Edwin Montagu. 1964.

Morley

1278 MORLEY (JOHN) *Viscount Morley of Blackburn*. Recollections. 2 vols 1917.

1279 —— Memorandum on Resignation, August 1914. 1928.

1280 KNICKERBOCKER (FRANCES WENTWORTH). Free Minds: John Morley and his Friends. Camb. Mass. 1943.

1281 HAMER (DAVID ALLAN). John Morley: Liberal Intellectual. Oxf. 1968.

Morrison

1282 MORRISON (HERBERT) *Baron*. An Autobiography. 1960.

1283 DONOUGHUE (BERNARD) *and* JONES (GEORGE WILLIAM). Herbert Morrison: Portrait of a Politician. 1972.

1284 MORRISON *Lady*. Memoirs of a Marriage. 1977.

Owen

1285 HARRIS (KENNETH). David Owen: Personally Speaking. 1987.

Percy of Newcastle

1286 PERCY (EUSTACE) *Lord Percy of Newcastle*. Some Memories. 1958.

Pethick-Lawrence

1287 PETHICK-LAWRENCE (FREDERICK WILIAM) *Lord*. Fate has been Kind. 1943.

1288 BRITTAIN (VERA MARY). Pethick-Lawrence: A Portrait. 1963.

Powell

1289 UTLEY (THOMAS EDWIN). Enoch Powell: The Man and His Thinking. 1968.

1290 ROTH (ANDREW). Enoch Powell: Tory Tribune. 1970.

1291 NAPAL (DOOJEN). Enoch Powell: A Study in Personality and Politics. Wolverhampton. 1975.

1292 FOOT (PAUL MacKINTOSH). The Rise of Enoch Powell. 1969.

1293 SCHOEN (DOUGLAS E.). Enoch Powell and the Powellites. 1977.

1294 LEWIS (ERNEST MICHAEL ROY). Enoch Powell: Principle in Politics. 1979.

1295 BERKELEY (HUMPHREY). The Odyssey of Enoch: A Political Memoir. 1977.

1296 WOOD (JOHN) *ed*. A Nation not Afraid: The Thinking of Enoch Powell. 1965.

1297 POWELL (JOHN ENOCH). Freedom and Reality. 1969.

1298 —— Still to Decide. 1972.

1299 —— A Nation—No Nation? 1978. *Ed.* by Richard Ritchie.

1300 COSGRAVE (PATRICK). The Lives of Enoch Powell. 1989.

Prior

1301 PRIOR (JIM). A Balance of Power. 1986.

Pym

1302 PYM (FRANCIS). The Politics of Consent. 1984.

Reading

1303 ISAACS (GERALD RUFUS) *2nd Marquess of Reading*. Rufus Isaacs, First Marquess of Reading, 1860–1935. 2 vols 1942. 1945.

1304 HYDE (HARFORD MONTGOMERY). Lord Reading: The Life of Rufus Isaacs, First Marquess of Reading. 1967.

1305 JUDD (DENIS). Lord Reading. 1982.

Samuel

1306 SAMUEL (HERBERT LOUIS) *Viscount Samuel*. Memoirs. 1945.

1307 —— The War and Liberty. 1917.

1308 BOWLE (JOHN EDWARD). Viscount Samuel: A Biography. 1957.

Shinwell

1309 SHINWELL (EMMANUEL) *Baron Shinwell*. Conflict Without Malice. 1955.

1310 —— I've Lived through it all. 1973.

1311 —— Lead with the Left: My First Ninety-Six Years. 1981.

1312 SHINWELL *and* DOXAT (JOHN). Shinwell Talking: A Conversational Biography to Celebrate his 100th Birthday. 1984.

Shore

1313 SHORE (PETER). Entitled to Know. 1966.

Simon

1314 SIMON (JOHN ALLESBROOK) *Viscount Simon*. Retrospect. 1952.

1315 BECHHOFER-ROBERTS (CARL ERIC). Sir John Simon: Being an Account of the Life and Career . . . 1938.

Smith (See under Birkenhead, First Earl).

Snowden

1316 SNOWDEN (PHILIP) *Viscount Snowden*. An Autobiography. 2 vols 1934.

1317 LAYBOURN (K.) *and* JAMES (D.) *eds*. Philip Snowden. Bradford. 1987.

1318 CROSS (COLIN). Philip Snowden. 1966.

1319 ANDREADES (ANDREAS MICHAEL). Philip Snowden: The Man and his Financial Policy. 1930.

1320 BECHHOFER-ROBERTS (CARL ERIC). Philip Snowden: An Impartial Portrait. 1929.

Stewart

1321 STEWART (MICHAEL) *Baron*. Life and Labour. 1980.

Strachey

1322 THOMAS (HUGH SWYNNERTON) *Baron*. John Strachey. 1973.

1323 NEWMAN (MICHAEL). John Strachey. Manch. 1989.

Stuart

1324 STUART (JAMES) *Viscount Stuart of Findhorn*. Within the Fringe. 1967.

Swinton (See under Cunliffe-Lister).

Tebbit

1325 TEBBIT (NORMAN). Upwardly Mobile. 1988.

Thomas

1326 THOMAS (GEORGE) *Viscount Tonypandy*. Mr. Speaker: Memoirs of Viscount Tonypandy. 1985.

Thomas

1327 BLAXLAND (WILLIAM GREGORY). J. H. Thomas: A Life for Unity. 1964.

Tomlinson

1328 BLACKBURN (FRED). George Tomlinson. 1954.

Watkinson

1329 WATKINSON (HAROLD ARTHUR) *Baron*. Turning Points. 1986.

Wheatley

1330 HOWELL (DAVID). A Lost Left: Three Studies in Socialism and Nationalism. Manch. 1986. [One of the Studies features John Wheatley.].

Whitelaw

1331 WHITELAW (WILLIAM STEPHEN IAN) *Lord*. The Whitelaw Memoirs. 1989.

Wigg

1332 WIGG (GEORGE) *Baron*. George Wigg. 1972.

Wilkinson

1333 VERNON (BETTY D.). Ellen Wilkinson, 1891–1947. 1982.

Williams, Shirley

1334 WILLIAMS (SHIRLEY). Politics is for People. 1981.

Williams, Thomas

1335 WILLIAMS (THOMAS) *Baron*. Digging for Britain. 1965.

Woolton

1336 WOOLTON (FREDERICK JAMES) *Earl*. The Memoirs of the Rt. Hon. the Earl of Woolton. 1959.

1337 LANGLEY (H. M.). 'The Woolton Papers'. *Bod. Lib. Record* 11 (1984), 320–37.

3. OTHER POLITICAL FIGURES

Abse

1338 ABSE (LEO). Private Member. 1973.

Allen

1339 MARWICK (ARTHUR JOHN BRERETON). Clifford Allen: The Open Conspirator. Edin. 1974.

1340 GILBERT (MARTIN JOHN) *ed*. Plough My Own Furrow: The Story of Lord Allen of Hurtwood as Told through his Writings and Correspondence. 1965.

Amery

1341 AMERY (JULIAN). Approach March: A Venture in Autobiography. 1973.

Archer

1342 MANTLE (JONATHAN). In for a Penny: The Unauthorised Biography of Jeffrey Archer. 1988.

Ashley

1343 ASHLEY (JACK). Journey into Silence. 1973.

Astor, Nancy

1344 COLLIS (M. S.). Nancy Astor. 1960.

1345 SYKES (CHRISTOPHER). Nancy: The Story of Lady Astor. 1972.

1346 LANGHORNE (ELIZABETH). Nancy Astor and her Friends. 1974.

1347 MASTERS (ANTHONY). Nancy Astor: A Life. 1981.

1348 MARLOWE (DEREK). Nancy Astor: The Lady from Virginia. 1984. [See also books below on the Astor family.].

Astor, William Waldorf

1349 ASTOR (WILLIAM WALDORF) *Viscount*. Temperance and Politics. 1925.

1350 GATES (JOHN D.). The Astor Family. N.Y. 1981.

1351 SINCLAIR (DAVID). Dynasty: The Astors and their Times. 1983.

1352 ASTOR (WILLIAM WALDORF). Our Imperial Future. 1943.

[See also books above on the Astor family.].

Atholl (Duchess of)

1353 HETHERINGTON (S. J.). Katharine Atholl. Aberdeen. 1989.

Bayford

1354 RAMSDEN (JOHN). Real Old Tory Politics: The Political Diaries of Sir Robert Sanders, First Lord Bayford, 1910–1935. 1984.

Berkeley

1355 BERKELEY (HUMPHREY). Crossing the Floor. 1972.

Beveridge

1356 BEVERIDGE (WILLIAM HENRY) *Baron*. Why I am a Liberal. 1945.

1357 MAIR (PHILIP BEVERIDGE). 'Shared Enthusiasm': William Beveridge. 1982.

1358 MOOS (SIEGFRIED). A Pioneer of Social Advance: William Henry Beveridge. Durham. 1963.

1359 HARRIS (JOSÉ). William Beveridge: A Biography. Oxf. 1977.

Blackburn

1360 BLACKBURN (RAYMOND). I am an Alcoholic. 1954.

Boothby

1361 BOOTHBY (ROBERT JOHN GRAHAM) *Baron*. I Fight to Live. 1947.

1362 —— My Yesterday, your Tomorrow. 1962.

1363 —— Boothby: Recollections of a Rebel. 1978.

Bottomley

1364 SYMONS (JULIAN). Horatio Bottomley. 1955.

1365 HYMAN (ALAN). The Rise and Fall of Horatio Bottomley: The Biography of a Swindler. 1972.

1366 FELSTEAD (SIDNEY T.). Horatio Bottomley. 1936.

1367 DEESON (ARTHUR F. L.). Great Swindlers. [On Horatio Bottomley and others.]. 1971.

Bracken

1368 BOYLE (ANDREW). 'Poor Dear Bracken': The Quest for Brendan Bracken. 1974.

1369 LYSAGHT (CHARLES EDWARD). Brendan Bracken. 1979.

Braddock

1370 TOOLE (MILLIE). Mrs Bessie Braddock, M.P. 1957.

1371 BRADDOCK (JOHN) *and* BRADDOCK (MARGARET ELIZABETH). The Braddocks. 1963.

Brockway

1372 BROCKWAY (ARCHIBALD FENNER) *Baron*. Inside the Left: Thirty Years of Platform, Press, Prison and Parliament. 1942.

1373 —— German Diary. 1946.

1374 —— Outside the Right. 1963.

1375 —— Towards Tomorrow: The Autobiography of Fenner Brockway. 1977.

1376 —— 98 Not Out. 1986.

Brodrick

1377 BRODRICK (WILLIAM S. JOHN FREMANTLE) *Earl of Midleton*. Records and Reactions, 1856–1939. 1939.

Bruce-Gardyne

1378 BRUCE-GARDYNE (JOCK). Ministers and Mandarins: Inside the Whitehall Village. 1986.

Bryce

1379 BRYCE (JAMES) *Viscount Bryce of Dechmont*. Essays and Addresses in Wartime. 1918.

1380 FISHER (HERBERT ALFRED LAURENS). James Bryce, Viscount Bryce of Dechmont, O.M. 2 vols 1927.

1381 IONS (EDMUND). James Bryce and American Democracy, 1870–1922. 1968.

1382 TULLOCH (HUGH). James Bryce's American Commonwealth: The Anglo-American Background. Woodbridge. 1988.

Buchan [Baron Tweedsmuir]

1383 SMITH (JANET BUCHANAN ADAM). John Buchan. 1965.

1384 BUCHAN (WILLIAM). John Buchan: A Memoir. 1982.

1385 BUCHAN (SUSAN C.) *Baroness Tweedsmuir*. John Buchan. 1947.

Buxton, Charles Roden

1386 DE BUNSEN (VICTORIA ALEXANDRINA). Charles Roden Buxton: A Memoir. 1948.

Buxton, Noel

1387 ANDERSON (MOSA). Noel Buxton: A Life. 1952.

Cartland

1388 CARTLAND (BARBARA). Ronald Cartland. 1945.

Cazalet

1389 JAMES (ROBERT RHODES). Victor Cazalet: A Portrait. 1976.

Cecil

1390 ROSE (KENNETH). The Later Cecils. 1975.

1391 [GASCOYNE-]CECIL ([EDGAR ALGERNON] ROBERT) *Viscount Cecil*. All the Way. 1949.

1392 —— A Great Experiment. 1941. [Autobiography. Mostly concerns the League of Nations.].

Channon

1393 JAMES (ROBERT RHODES) *ed.* 'Chips': The Diaries of Sir Henry Channon. 1967.

Churchill

1394 HALLE (KAY) *Comp.* Randolph Churchill: The Young Unpretender: Essays by His Friends. 1971.

1395 ROBERTS (BRIAN). Randolph: A Story of Churchill's Son. 1984.

Colquhoun

1396 COLQUHOUN (MAUREEN). A Woman in the House. 1980.

Courtney

1397 COURTNEY (ANTHONY). Sailor in a Russian Frame. 1968.

Crawley

1398 CRAWLEY (AIDAN). Leap Before You Look: A Memoir. 1988.

Critchley

1399 CRITCHLEY (JULIAN). Westminster Blues. 1986.

Currie

1400 CURRIE (EDWINA). Life Lines. 1989.

Davies

1401 GRIFFITHS (ROBERT). S. O. Davies: A Socialist Faith. 1983.

Dodds-Parker

1402 DODDS-PARKER (DOUGLAS). Political Eunuch. 1986.

Donnelly

1403 DONNELLY (DESMOND). Gaderene '68: The Crimes, Follies and Misfortunes of the Wilson Government. 1968.

Donner

1404 DONNER (*Sir* PATRICK). Crusade: A Life against the Calamitous Twentieth Century. 1984.

Driberg

1405 DRIBERG (TOM). The Best of Both Worlds: A Personal Diary. 1953.

1406 —— Ruling Passions. 1977.

Ewart-Biggs

1407 EWART-BIGGS (JANE) *Baroness.* Lady in the Lords. 1988.

Fairbairn

1408 FAIRBAIRN (NICHOLAS). A Life is too Short. [Autobiography Vol. 1.]. 1987.

Finch

1409 FINCH (HAROLD). Memoirs of a Bedwellty M.P. 1972.

Fisher

1410 OGG (DAVID). Herbert Fisher 1865–1940: A Short Biography. 1947.

1411 FISHER (HERBERT ALBERT LAURENS). An Unfinished Autobiography. 1940.

Fletcher

1412 FLETCHER (ERIC GEORGE MOLYNEAUX) *Baron.* Random Reminiscences. 1986.

Gallacher

1413 GALLACHER (WILLIAM). Revolt on the Clyde. 1936. New edn 1949.

1414 —— The Chosen Few: A Sketch of Men and Events in Parliament, 1936–1940. 1940.

1415 —— The Rolling of the Thunder. 1948.

1416 —— Rise Like Lions. 1951.

1417 —— The Tyrant's Might is Passing. 1954.

1418 —— The Last Memoirs of William Gallacher. 1966.

Gardiner

1419 BOX (MURIEL). Rebel Advocate: A Biography of Gerald Gardiner. 1983.

Grigg

1420 GRIGG (*Sir* PERCY JAMES). Prejudice and Judgement. 1948.

Grimond

1421 GRIMOND (JO) *Lord.* Memoirs. 1979.

1422 —— A Personal Manifesto. 1983.

Hardie

1423 MORGAN (KENNETH OWEN). Keir Hardie: Radical and Socialist. 1975.

1424 HUGHES (EMRYS). Keir Hardie. 1956.

1425 SMILLIE (ROBERT), MacDONALD (RAMSAY), *and* MacARTHUR (MARY). Memoir of James Keir Hardie M.P. and Tributes to his Work. Glasg. 1915.

1426 STEWART (WILLIAM). James Keir Hardie: A Biography. 1921.

1427 McLEAN (IAIN). Keir Hardie. 1975.

1428 REID (FRED). Keir Hardie: The Making of a Socialist. 1978.

Harvey

1429 HARVEY (IAN). To Fall Like Lucifer. 1971.

Harvie-Watt

1430 HARVIE-WATT (G. S.). Most of My Life. 1980.

Herbert

1431 HERBERT (ALAN PATRICK). Independent Member. 1950.

1432 POUND (REGINALD). A. P. Herbert: A Biography. 1976.

Hewins

1433 HEWINS (WILLIAM ALBERT SAMUEL). The Apologia of an Imperialist: Forty Years of Empire Policy. 2 vols 1929.

Jenkins

1434 JENKINS (HUGH). The Culture Gap: An Experience of Government and the Arts. 1979.

Johnson

1435 JOHNSON (DONALD McINTOSH). A Cassandra at Westminster. 1967.

1436 —— On Being an Independent M.P. 1964.

1437 —— A Doctor in Parliament. 1958.

1438 —— A Doctor Reflects: Miracles and Mirages. 1975.

Jowett

1439 BROCKWAY (ARCHIBALD FENNER) *Baron.* Socialism over Sixty Years: The Life of Jowett of Bradford, 1864–1944. 1946.

Kilroy-Silk

1440 KILROY-SILK (ROBERT). Hard Labour: The Political Diary of Robert Kilroy-Silk. 1986.

King

1441 KING (EVELYN MANSFIELD). Closest Correspondence: The Inside Story of an M.P. 1989.

Kinnock

1442 HARRIS (ROBERT). The Making of Neil Kinnock. 1984.

1443 DROWER (G. M. F.). Neil Kinnock: The Path to Leadership. 1984.

1444 LEAPMAN (MICHAEL). Kinnock. 1987.

Kirkwood

1445 KIRKWOOD (DAVID) *Baron.* My Life of Revolt. 1935.

Lansbury

1446 POSTGATE (RAYMOND). The Life of George Lansbury. 1951.

1447 LANSBURY (GEORGE). My Life. 1928.

1448 —— What I Saw in Russia. 1920.

Lee

1449 LEE ([JANET] JENNIE) *Baroness.* Tomorrow is a New Day. 1939.

1450 —— This Great Journey: A Volume of Autobiography, 1904–1945. 1963.

1451 —— My Life with Nye. 1980.

Livingstone

1452 LIVINGSTONE (KEN). If Voting Changed Anything They'd Abolish it. 1987. [Autobiography.].

1453 CARVELL (JOHN). Citizen Ken. 1984.

Lloyd

1454 ADAM (COLIN FORBES). Life of Lord [George Ambrose] Lloyd. 1948.

1455 CHARMLEY (JOHN). Lord Lloyd and the Decline of the British Empire. 1987.

Lloyd George

1456 PRICE (EMYR). Megan Lloyd George. Caernarfon. 1983.

Lothian

1457 BUTLER (*Sir* JAMES RAMSAY MONTAGU). Lord Lothian 1882–1940. 1960.

1458 KERR (PHILIP HENRY) *Marquess of Lothian*. The American Speeches of Lord Lothian, July 1939 to December 1940. 1941.

McGovern

1459 McGOVERN (JOHN). Neither Fear nor Favour. 1960.

Mackinder

1460 GILBERT (EDWARD W.). Sir Halford Mackinder. 1961.

1461 BLOUET (BRIAN W.). Sir Halford Mackinder 1861–1947: Some New Perspectives. Oxf. 1975.

McNeill

1462 McNEILL (JOHN GORDON SWIFT). What I have Seen and Heard. 1925.

Mann

1463 MANN (JEAN). Woman in Parliament. 1962.

Manning

1464 MANNING (*Dame* [ELIZABETH] LEAH). A Life for Education. 1970.

1465 —— What I Saw in Spain. 1935.

Markievicz

1466 O'FAOLAIN (SEAN). Constance Markievicz. 1934. Repr. 1987.

1467 MARRECO (CONSTANCE GEORGINA). The Rebel Countess: The Life and Times of Constance Markievicz. Philadelphia. 1967.

1468 VAN VORIS (JACQUELINE). Constance de Markievicz: In the Cause of Ireland. Amherst, Mass. 1967.

Maxton

1469 McALLISTER (GILBERT). James Maxton: The Portrait of a Rebel. 1935.

1470 McNAIR (JOHN). James Maxton: The Beloved Rebel. 1955.

1471 BROWN (GORDON). Maxton: A Biography. Edin. 1986.

1472 KNOX (WILLIAM). James Maxton. Manch. 1987.

Mayhew

1473 MAYHEW (CHRISTOPHER). Party Games. 1969.

1474 —— Time to Explain. 1987.

Mikardo

1475 MIKARDO (IAN). Backbencher. 1988.

Milne

1476 MILNE (EDWARD). No Shining Armour. 1976.

Mitchell

1477 MITCHELL (*Sir* HAROLD P.). In My Stride. Edin. 1951.

Mond

1478 MOND (ALFRED) *Lord Melchett*. Industry and Politics. 1927.

1479 BOLITHO (HENRY HECTOR). Alfred Mond, First Lord Melchett. 1933.

Morel

1480 COCKS (FREDERICK SEYMOUR). E. D. Morel: The Man and His Work. 1920.

1481 CLINE (CATHERINE ANNE). E. D. Morel, 1873–1924: The Strategies of Protest. Belfast. 1980.

Morris-Jones

1482 MORRIS-JONES (*Sir* HENRY). Doctor in the Whip's Room. 1955.

Mosley (Cynthia Blanche)
[See book by MOSLEY (NICHOLAS) below.].

Mosley

1483 MOSLEY (*Sir* OSWALD ERNALD). My Life. 1968.

1484 SKIDELSKY (ROBERT JACOB ALEXANDER). Oswald Mosley. 1975. 2nd edn 1981.

1485 MOSLEY (NICHOLAS). Rules of the Game: Sir Oswald and Lady Cynthia Mosley, 1896–1933. 1982.

1486 —— Beyond the Pale: Sir Oswald Mosley, 1933–1980. 1983.

1487 CHESTERTON (A. K.). Mosley: Portrait of a Leader. 1936.

Mott-Radclyffe

1488 MOTT-RADCLYFFE (*Sir* CHARLES). Foreign Body in the Eye. 1975.

Nabarro

1489 NABARRO (*Sir* GERALD). NAB 1: Portrait of a Politician. 1969.

1490 —— Exploits of a Politician. 1973.

Newton

1491 LEGH (THOMAS WODEHOUSE) *Baron Newton*. Retrospection. 1941.

Nicolson

1492 NICOLSON (NIGEL) *ed.* Harold Nicolson: Diaries and Letters. 3 vols 1966–8.

1493 —— Portrait of a Marriage. 1973. [Harold Nicolson and Vita Sackville-West.].

1494 WOLFF (L.). 'The Public Faces of Harold Nicolson: The Thirties'. *Biography* 5 (1982), 240–52.

Noel-Baker

1495 WHITAKER (DAVID J.). Fighter for Peace: Philip Noel-Baker, 1889–1982. York. 1989.

O'Connor

1496 FYFE (HENRY HAMILTON). T. P. O'Connor. 1934.

1497 O'CONNOR (THOMAS POWER). Memoirs of an Old Parliamentarian, 1885–1929. N.Y. 2 vols 1929.

1498 BRADY (L. W.). T. P. O'Connor and the Liverpool Irish. 1983.

O'Malley

1499 O'MALLEY (WILLIAM). Glancing Back. 1933.

O'Mara

1500 LAVELLE (PATRICIA). James O'Mara: A Staunch Sinn Feiner 1873–1948. Dublin. 1961.

Parker

1501 PARKER (JOHN). Father of the House: Fifty Years in Politics. 1982.

Parmoor

1502 PARMOOR (CHARLES ALFRED CRIPPS) *Baron*. A Retrospect: Looking Back over a Life of More than Eighty Years. 1936.

Penhaligon

1503 PENHALIGON (ANNETTE). Penhaligon. 1989.

Ponsonby

1504 PONSONBY (ARTHUR) *Baron*. Falsehood in Wartime. 1928.

1505 JONES (RAYMOND A.). Arthur Ponsonby. 1989.

Ponsonby

1506 PONSONBY (*Sir* CHARLES). Ponsonby Remembers. 1965.

Power

1507 EDWARDS (J. G.). 'Sir John Cecil Power, Bart. 1870–1950'. *Bull. Inst. Hist. Res.* 23 (1950), 139–46.

Price

1508 PRICE (MORGAN PHILIPS). My Three Revolutions. 1969.

Pritt

1509 PRITT (DENIS NOWELL). The Autobiography of D. N. Pritt. 3 vols 1965–6.

Rathbone

1510 STOCKS (MARY DANVERS) *Baroness*. Eleanor Rathbone. 1949.

Rawlinson

1511 RAWLINSON (PETER) *Baron*. A Price Too High. 1989.

Redmond

1512 GWYNN (DENIS ROLLESTON). The Life of John Redmond. 1932.

1513 GWYNN (STEPHEN L.). Redmond's Last Years. 1919.

1514 WELLS (W. B.). John Redmond: A Biography. 1919.

Riddell

1515 RIDDELL (GEORGE ALLARDICE) *Baron*. Lord Riddell's War Diary, 1914–1918. 1923.

Saklatvala

1516 GALLACHER (WILLIAM). 'Shapurji Saklatvala 1874–1936'. *Labour Monthly* Jan. 1937, 51–3.

Shakespeare

1517 SHAKESPEARE (*Sir* GEOFFREY). Let Candles be Brought In. 1949.

Short

1518 SHORT (EDWARD). Whip to Wilson. 1989.

1519 —— I Knew my Place. 1983.

Silverman

1520 HUGHES (EMRYS). Sydney Silverman: Rebel in Parliament. 1969.

Simmons

1521 SIMMONS (CHARLES JAMES). Soap Box Evangelist. 1972.

Simon

1522 STOCKS (MARY DANVERS) *Baroness*. Ernest Simon of Manchester. 1963.

Smillie

1523 SMILLIE (ROBERT). My Life for Labour. 1924.

Smith

1524 SMITH (*Sir* CYRIL). Big Cyril. 1977.

Smyth

1525 SMYTH (*Sir* JOHN). Only Enemy. 1959.

Steel

1526 BARTRAM (PETER). David Steel: His Life and Politics. 1981.

1527 STEEL (DAVID). Against Goliath: David Steel's Story. 1989.

Stevas

1528 STEVAS (NORMAN ST JOHN) *Baron*. The Two Cities. 1984.

Summerskill

1529 SUMMERSKILL (EDITH) *Baroness*. Letters to my Daughter. 1957.

1530 —— A Woman's World. 1967. [An Autobiography.].

Taylor of Mansfield

1531 TAYLOR OF MANSFIELD ([HARRY] BERNARD TAYLOR) *Baron*. Uphill all the Way. 1973.

Teeling

1532 TEELING ([LUKE] WILLIAM BURKE). Corridors of Frustration. 1970.

Thorpe

1533 CHESTER (LEWIS), LINKLATER (MAGNUS), *and* MAY (DAVID). Jeremy Thorpe: A Secret Life. 1979.

1534 BESSELL (PETER). Cover-Up: The Jeremy Thorpe Affair. 1980.

Tillett

1535 SCHNEER (JONATHON). Ben Tillett: Portrait of a Labour Leader. 1982.

1536 LIGHT (GEORGE) *ed*. Ben Tillett: Fighter and Pioneer. 1943.

1537 TILLETT (BEN). Memoirs and Reflections. 1931.

Tree

1538 TREE (RONALD). When the Moon was High: Memoirs of Peace and War. 1975.

Trevelyan

1539 MORRIS (A. J. ANTHONY). C. P. Trevelyan, 1870–1958. Belfast. 1977.

Walters

1540 WALTERS (DENNIS). Not Always with the Pack. 1989.

Wedgwood

1541 WEDGWOOD (JOSIAH CLEMENT) *Baron*. Memoirs of a Fighting Life. 1941.

1542 WEDGWOOD (CICELEY VERONICA). The Last of the Radicals: Josiah Wedgwood, M.P. 1951.

Wilson

1543 MARLOWE (JOHN). Late Victorian: The Life of Sir Arnold Talbot Wilson. 1967.

1544 WILSON (*Sir* ARNOLD TALBOT). Loyalties: Mesopotamia, 1914–1917: A Personal and Historical Record. 1930.

1545 ——Thoughts and Talks, 1935–1937. 1938.

1546 ——More Thoughts and Talks. 1939.

Windlesham

1547 HENNESSY (DAVID JAMES GEORGE) *Baron Windlesham*. Politics in Practice. 1975.

Winterton

1548 BRODRICK (ALAN HOUGHTON). Near to Greatness: A Life of the Sixth Earl Winterton. 1965.

1549 TURNOUR (EDWARD) *Earl Winterton*. Orders of the Day. 1953.

1550 ——Fifty Tumultuous Years. 1955.

Woodhouse

1551 WOODHOUSE (CHRISTOPHER MONTAGUE). Something Ventured. 1982.

Wyatt

1552 WYATT (WOODROW). Confessions of an Optimist. 1985.

4. GENERAL WORKS ON POLITICIANS AND PARLIAMENT

1553 VALLANCE (ELIZABETH). Women in the House. 1979.

1554 SILK (PAUL) *with* WALTERS (RHODA). How Parliament Works. 1987.

1555 BUCK (PHILIP WALLENSTEIN). Amateurs and Professionals in British Politics, 1918–1959. 1963.

1556 ——'First Time Winners in the British House of Commons since 1918'. *Amer. Pol. Sci. Rev.* 58 (1964), 662–7.

1557 ELLIS (JOHN) *and* JOHNSON (RICHARD WILLIAM). Members from the Unions. 1974.

1558 PENTNEY (JOHN). 'Worms that Turned: The Inter-Party Mobility of Parliamentary Candidates since 1945'. *Parl. Affs* 30 (1977), 363–72.

1559 WATT (DAVID). 'The Politics of 1951–1971'. *History Today* 22 (1972), 3–11.

1560 JONES (J. BARRY). A Research Register of Territorial Politics in the United Kingdom. Glasg. 1980.

1561 MULLER (WILLIAM D.). British Politics Group Research Register 1981. Glasg. 1981.

1562 POLITICAL PARTY YEARBOOKS, 1885–1948. 128 vols Hassocks, Sussex. 1974.

1563 FOOT (*Sir* DINGLE). British Political Crises. 1976.

1564 PLATT (D. C. M.). 'The Commercial and Industrial Interests of Ministers of the Crown'. *Pol. Studs* 9 (1961), 267–90.

1565 WILLSON (FRANCIS MICHAEL GLENN). 'Some Career Patterns in British Politics: Whips in the House of Commons, 1906–1966'. *Parl. Affs* 24 (1970–1), 33–42.

1566 HANNINGTON (WALTER). Never on Our Knees. 1967.

1567 BONHAM-CARTER (VIOLET) *Baroness Asquith*. The Impact of Personality in Politics. Oxf. 1963.

1568 WILLIAMS (EDWARD FRANCIS) *Baron Francis-Williams*. A Pattern of Rulers. 1965.

1569 ROSKILL (STEPHEN WENTWORTH). The Art of Leadership. 1964.

1570 VERNON (BETTY D.). Margaret Cole 1893–1980. 1986.

1571 SALVIDGE (STANLEY). Salvidge of Liverpool: Behind the Political Scenes, 1890–1928. 1934.

1572 BENN (*Sir* ERNEST). Happier Days: Recollections and Reflections. 1949.

1573 ABEL (DERYCK). Ernest Benn: Counsel for Liberty. 1960.

E. POLITICAL PARTIES

The study of political parties has expanded significantly over the period, reflecting in part the growth of 'politics' as a self-contained discipline. Questions concerning structure, organization, and finance have been treated with increasing sophistication and thoroughness. Such studies have tended to make certain conventional party histories seem unacceptably straightforward. It has also been the case that some historians whose focus of attention has been on 'high politics' have been indifferent towards party politics as perceived and carried out at the 'grass roots'. The result has been that the study of 'political parties' has been diminished rather than enhanced by being squeezed within the boundaries of one academic discipline or another. The extent of the gap should not be overstated but it rarely takes the reader long before becoming aware that the assumptions and methodologies of authors on 'political parties' place them in either a 'history' or a 'politics' camp.

It also becomes apparent that the focus of scholarly concern frequently reflects the political concerns of the moment—the 'inevitability' of the rise or fall of a particular political party being seen in relation to a specific point in time. It is appropriate to include material which is largely driven by this concern even though it cannot be regarded as 'definitive'. Writers whose own sympathies have sometimes been explicit have used their analysis of historical developments as a weapon in a contemporary political debate. It has indeed been the case, largely, that the study of particular parties has engaged the attention of writers sympathetic to those parties. Paradoxically perhaps, it also appears to be the case that writers have been more attracted by the study of a spasmodically successful party (Labour) rather than the more consistently successful party (Conservative). The rise and fall of smaller parties appears, in general, to be adequately treated.

1. GENERAL

1574 JENNINGS (*Sir* WILLIAM IVOR). Party Politics. 3 vols Camb. 1960–2.

1575 BULMER-THOMAS (IVOR). The Growth of the British Party System. 2 vols 1965. 2nd edn 1967.

1576 McKENZIE (ROBERT TRELFORD). British Political Parties: The Distribution of Power Within the Conservative and Labour Parties. 1955. 2nd edn 1963.

1577 BEATTIE (ALAN) *ed.* English Party Politics. 2 vols 1970. (vol. 2—Twentieth Century).

1578 JAMES (ROBERT RHODES). The British Revolution: British Politics, 1880–1939. Vol. 2. 1914–1939. 1977.

1579 —— Ambitions and Realities: British Politics 1964–70. 1972.

1580 THOMAS (NEVILLE PENRY). A History of British Politics from the Year 1900. 1956.

1581 SOMERVELL (DAVID CHURCHILL). British Politics Since 1900. 1950. 2nd edn 1953.

1582 BALL (ALAN R.). British Political Parties: The Emergence of a Modern Party System. 1981. 2nd edn 1987.

1583 PUGH (MARTIN DAVID). The Making of Modern British Politics 1867–1939. Oxf. 1982.

1584 MACFARLANE (LESLIE JOHN). British Politics 1918–1964. Oxf. 1965.

1585 BEER (SAMUEL HUTCHISON). Modern British Politics: A Study of Parties and Pressure Groups. 1965. 2nd edn 1969.

1586 LEES (JOHN DAVID) *and* KIMBER (RICHARD). Political Parties in Modern Britain: An Organisational and Functional Guide. 1972.

1587 INGLE (STEPHEN). The British Party System. Oxf. 1987. 2nd edn 1989.

1588 FINER (SAMUEL E.). The Changing British Party System 1945–79. Washington. 1980.

1589 HOBSBAWM (ERIC JOHN). 'Twentieth Century British Politics'. *Past and Present* xi (1957), 100–8.

1590 GREENLEAF (W. H.). 'The Character of Modern British Politics'. *Parl. Affs* (1975), 368–85.

1591 WALLER (P. J.) *ed.* Politics and Social Change in Modern Britain. 1987. [A volume in honour of A. F. Thompson, contains essays on industrial, political, and social aspects of inter-war Britain.].

1592 BUTLER (DAVID EDGEWORTH) *and* HALSEY (A. H.) *eds.* Policy and Politics: Essays in honour of Norman Chester. 1978.

1593 PEELE (GILLIAN). British Party Politics: Competing for Power in the 1980s. Deddington. 1988.

1594 HARRISON (MARTIN). 'Political Finance in Britain'. *J. Pol.* 25 (1963), 664–85.

1595 PINTO-DUSCHINSKY (MICHAEL). British Political Finance 1830–1980. Washington. 1981.

1596 —— 'Trends in British Political Funding 1979–1983'. *Parl. Affs* 38 (1985), 328–49.

1597 JOHNSTON (R. J.). 'A Further Look at British Political Finance'. *Pol. Studs* 25 (1986), 466–73.

1598 EWING (KEITH). The Funding of Political Parties in Britain. Camb. 1987.

1599 FAIR (JOHN D.). British Interparty Conferences: A Study of the Procedure of Conciliation in British Politics, 1867–1921. Oxf. 1980.

1600 ROSE (RICHARD). The Problems of Party Government. 1974.

1601 JACKSON (ROBERT J.). Rebels and Whips: An Analysis of Dissension, Discipline and Cohesion in British Political Parties. 1968.

1602 DOWSE (ROBERT E.) *and* SMITH (TREVOR). 'Party Discipline in the House of Commons'. *Parl. Affs* xvi (1963), 159–64.

1603 NORTON (PHILIP). 'Party Organisation in the House of Commons'. *Parl. Affs* xxxi (1978), 406–23.

1604 JONES (CHARLES). 'Inter-Party Competition in Britain, 1950–1959'. *Parl. Affs* xvii (1964), 50–6.

1605 PLANT (RAYMOND). Ideology in Modern British Politics. Deddington. 1988.

1606 ROSE (RICHARD). 'The Political Ideas of English Party Activists'. *Amer. Pol. Sci. Rev.* 56 (1962), 360–71.

1607 WILSON (DAVID JACK). Power and Party Bureaucracy in Britain: Regional Organisation in the Conservative and Labour Parties. Farnborough. 1975.

1608 COMFORT (GEORGE O.). Professional Politicians: A Study of British Party Agents. Washington. 1958.

1609 FRASURE (ROBERT) *and* KORNBERG (ALLAN). 'Constituency Agents and British Politics'. *Brit. J. Pol. Sci.* 5 (1975), 459–76.

2. THE CONSERVATIVE PARTY

1610 BLOCK (GEOFFREY DAVID MAURICE). A Source Book of Conservatism. 1964.

1611 CONSERVATIVE PARTY ANNUAL CONFERENCE REPORTS 1948+.

1612 BLAKE (ROBERT NORMAN WILLIAM) *Baron.* The Conservative Party from Peel to Thatcher. 1985.

1613 LANE (PETER). The Conservative Party. 1973.

1614 LINDSAY (THOMAS FANSHAWE) *and* HARRINGTON (MICHAEL). The Conservative Party, 1918–1970. 1974. (To 1979), 2nd edn 1979.

1615 SOUTHGATE (DONALD GEORGE) *ed.* The Conservative Leadership, 1832–1932. 1974.

1616 McKENZIE (ROBERT TRELFORD) *and* SILVER (ALLAN). Angels in Marble: Working Class Conservatives in Urban England. 1968.

1617 NORDLINGER (E.). The Working-Class Tories: Authority, Deference and Stable Democracy. 1967.

1618 PUGH (MARTIN DAVID). The Tories and the People 1880–1935. 1985.

1619 BUTLER (RICHARD AUSTEN) *Baron.* The Conservatives. 1977.

1620 RAMSDEN (JOHN A.). A History of the Conservative Party: The Age of Balfour and Baldwin. 1978.

1621 NUGENT (NEIL) *and* KING (ROGER) *eds.* The British Right: Conservative and Right-Wing Politics in Britain. Farnborough. 1977.

1622 GAMBLE (ANDREW). The Conservative Nation. 1974.

1623 JESSOP (BOB). Traditionalism, Conservatism and British Political Culture. 1974.

1624 BEHRENS (ROBERT). The Conservative Party from Heath to Thatcher: Policies and Politics 1974–1979. Farnborough. 1980.

1625 LAYTON-HENRY (ZIG) *ed.* Conservative Party Politics. 1980.

1626 NORTON (PHILIP) *and* AUGHEY (ARTHUR). Conservatives and Conservatism. 1981.

1627 BROWN (KENNETH DOUGLAS) *ed.* Essays in Anti-Labour History: Responses to the Rise of Labour in Britain. 1974.

1628 CLOSE (DAVID). 'Conservatives and Coalition After the First World War'. *J. Mod. Hist.* xlv (1973), 240–60.

1629 SELF (ROBERT C.). Tories and Tariffs: The Conservative Party and the Politics of Tariff Reform 1922–1932. 1986.

1630 COOPER (ANDREW F.). British Agricultural Policy, 1912–36: A Study in Conservative Politics. Manchester. 1989.

1631 GOODHART (PHILIP). The 1922: The Story of the Conservative Backbenchers Parliamentary Committee. 1973.

1632 PETRIE (*Sir* CHARLES ALEXANDER). The Carlton Club. 1955.

1633 RASMUSSEN (JORGEN SCOTT). 'Government and Intra-party Opposition: Dissent within the Conservative Parliamentary Party in the 1930s'. *Pol. Studs* xix (1971), 172–83.

1634 HOFFMAN (JOHN DAVID). The Conservative Party in Opposition, 1945–1951. 1964.

1635 RAMSDEN (JOHN A.). ' "A Party for Owners or a Party for Earners?" How Far did the British Conservative Party Really Change after 1945?'. *Trans. Roy. Hist. Soc.* 5th ser. 37 (1987), 49–63.

1636 BURTON (HYDE CLARKE). The Great Betrayal: An Indictment of the Conservative Governments' Departure from Conservative Principles, 1951–1963. 1963.

1637 BERRINGTON (HUGH B.). 'The Conservative Party: Revolts and Pressures, 1955–1961'. *Pol. Q.* xxxii (1961), 363–73.

1638 THOMSON (G.). 'Parties in Parliament, 1959–1963: The Conservatives'. *Pol. Q.* xxxiv (1963), 249–55.

1639 CHURCHILL (RANDOLPH SPENCER). The Fight for the Tory Leadership: A Contemporary Chronicle. 1964.

1640 LAYTON-HENRY (ZIG). 'The Young Conservatives 1945–1970'. *J. Contemp. Hist.* viii (1973), 143–76.

1641 HOLLIS (CHRISTOPHER). 'The Conservative Party in History'. *Pol. Q.* xxxii (1961), 214–28.

1642 SCHWARZ (J. E.) *and* LAMBERT (G.). 'Career Objectives, Group Feeling and Legislative Party Voting Cohesion: The British Conservatives, 1959–68'. *J. Pols.* xxxxiii (1971), 399–421.

1643 CROSS (JOHN ARTHUR). 'Withdrawal of the Conservative Party Whip'. *Parl. Affs* 212 (1967–8), 166–75.

1644 FRASURE (ROBERT C.). 'Backbench Opinion Revisited: The Case of the Conservatives'. *Pol. Studs* xx (1972), 325–8.

1645 NORTON (PHILIP). Conservative Dissidents: Dissent within the Conservative Parliamentary Party 1970–74. 1978.

1646 RAMSDEN (JOHN A.). The Making of Conservative Party Policy: The Conservative Research Department since 1929. 1980.

1647 BECHMANN (ARNOLD). 'The Conservative Research Department: The Care and Feeding of Future British Political Elites'. *J. Brit. Studs* 13 (1974), 92–113.

1648 PINTO-DUCHINSKY (MICHAEL). 'Central Office and "Power" in the Conservative Party'. *Pol. Studs* 20 (1972), 1–16.

1649 KELLY (RICHARD N.). Conservative Party Conferences: The Hidden System. Manchester. 1989.

1650 GREENWOOD (J. R.). 'Promoting Working Class Candidatures in the Conservative Party: The Limits of Central Office Power'. *Parl. Affs* 41 (1988), 456–68.

1651 ROSE (RICHARD). 'The Bow Group's Role in British Politics'. *Western Pol. Q.* 14 (1961), 265–78.

1652 SEYD (PATRICK). 'Factionalism within the Conservative Party: The Monday Club'. *Govt. and Opp.* 7 (1972), 464–87.

1653 BEHRENS (ROBERT). '"Blinkers for the Cart-Horse": The Conservative Party and the Trade Unions 1974–8'. *Pol. Q.* 49 (1978), 457–66.

1654 MORAN (MICHAEL). 'The Conservative Party and the Trade Unions since 1974'. *Pol. Studs* 27 (1979), 38–53.

1655 GRANT (WYN). 'Business Interests and the British Conservative Party'. *Govt. and Opp.* 15 (1980), 143–61.

3 . THE LABOUR PARTY

1656 THE LABOUR PARTY. Labour Party Bibliography. 1967.

1657 THE LABOUR PARTY. Report of the Annual Conference. 1901+.

1658 SOCIETY FOR THE STUDY OF LABOUR HISTORY. Bulletin 1+ Sheffield. 1964.

1659 SMITH (HAROLD). The British Labour Movement to 1970: A Bibliography. 1981.

1660 GILBERT (VICTOR F.) *comp.* Labour and Social History Theses: American, British and Irish University Theses and Dissertations in the Field of British and Irish Labour History, Presented Between 1900 and 1978. 1982.

1661 BELLAMY (JOYCE M.) *and* SAVILLE (JOHN) *eds.* Dictionary of Labour Biography. 8 vols 1972–1984. The cumulated index is in vol. 8.

1662 HARRISON (ROYDEN), WOOLVEN (GILLIAN), *and* DUNCAN (ROBERT). The Warwick Guide to British Labour Periodicals 1790–1970: A Check List. Brighton. 1977.

1663 WOLFE (WILLARD). 'A Century of Books on the History of Socialism in Britain, Part 1: Before 1950'. *British Studies Monitor* 10 (1980), 46–65.

1664 —— 'Writings on the History of Socialism in Britain, Part 2: Since 1950'. *British Studies Monitor* 10 (1981), 18–46.

1665 MAEHL (WILLIAM H.). ' "Jerusalem Deferred": Recent Writings in the History of the British Labour Movement'. *J. Mod. Hist.* xli (1969), 335–67.

1666 BRIGGS (ASA) *Baron, and* SAVILLE (JOHN) *eds.* Essays in Labour History in Memory of G. D. H. Cole. 1960.

1667 —— 2nd ser. 1971.

1668 —— 3rd ser. 1977.

1669 THE LABOUR PARTY. A Pictorial History of the Labour Party, 1900–1975 to Celebrate the Seventy-fifth Anniversary of its Birth. 1975.

1670 RODGERS (WILLIAM T.) *and* DONOUGHUE (BERNARD). The People in Parliament: An Illustrated History of the Labour Party 1966.

1671 LONGMATE (NORMAN RICHARD). Milestones in Working Class History. 1975.

1672 TRACEY (HERBERT) *ed.* The Book of the Labour Party: its History, Growth, Policy and Leaders. 3 vols 1925.

1673 COLE (GEORGE DOUGLAS HOWARD). A Short History of the British Working Class Movement, 1789–1947. 1948.

1674 WILLIAMS (FRANCIS) *Baron Francis-Williams.* Fifty Years March: The Rise of the Labour Party. 1949.

1675 BROGAN (COLM). Fifty Years On: British Socialism, 1900–1950. 1950.

1676 TRACEY (HERBERT) *ed.* The British Labour Party: Its History, Growth, Policy and Leaders. 3 vols 1948.

1677 BRAND (CARL FREMONT). The British Labour Party: A Short History. Stanford. 1965. 2nd edn 1974.

1678 PELLING (HENRY MATHISON). A Short History of the Labour Party. 1961. 8th edn 1985.

1679 WILMOT (EDWARD P.). The Labour Party: A Short History. 1968.

1680 COLE (GEORGE DOUGLAS HOWARD). A History of the Labour Party from 1914. 1969.

1681 JARMAN (THOMAS LECKIE). Socialism in Britain. 1972.

1682 KAVANAGH (DENNIS) *ed.* The Politics of the Labour Party. 1982.

1683 COOK (CHRIS) *and* TAYLOR (IAN) *eds.* The Labour Party: An Introduction to its History, Structure and Politics. 1980.

1684 HINTON (JAMES). Labour and Socialism: A History of the British Labour Movement 1867–1974. Brighton. 1983.

1685 LAYBOURN (KEITH). The Rise of Labour: The British Labour Party 1890–1979: Problems and Perspectives of Interpretation. 1988.

1686 JONES (BARRY) *and* KEATING (MICHAEL). Labour and the British State. Oxf. 1985.

1687 SAVILLE (JOHN). The Labour Movement in Britain: A Commentary. 1988.

1688 BLACKWELL (TREVOR) *and* SEABROOK (JEREMY). The Politics of Hope: Britain at the End of the Twentieth Century. 1988.

1689 MORGAN (KENNETH OWEN). Labour People: Leaders and Lieutenants Hardie to Kinnock. Oxf. 1987.

1690 —— 'The High and Low Politics of Labour: Keir Hardie to Michael Foot', in High and Low Politics in Modern Britain, *eds.* Michael J. Bentley and John Stevenson, 1983. 285–312.

1691 DRUCKER (HENRY M.). 'Leadership Selection in the Labour Party'. *Parl. Affs* 29 (1976), 378–95.

1692 —— 'Changes in the Labour Party Leadership'. *Parl. Affs* 34 (1981), 369–91.

1693 —— 'Intra-party Democracy in Action: The Election of the Leader and Deputy Leader by the Labour Party in 1983'. *Parl. Affs* 37 (1984), 283–300.

1694 WINTER (JAY MURRAY). Socialism and the Challenge of War: Ideas and Politics in Britain 1912–1918. 1974.

1695 CLINE (CATHERINE ANN). Recruits to Labour: The British Labour Party 1914–1931. N.Y. 1963.

1696 SHAPIRO (STANLEY). 'The Great War and Reform: Liberals and Labour, 1917–1919'. *Labor Hist.* xii (1971), 323–44.

1697 WINTER (JAY MURRAY). 'Arthur Henderson, the Russian Revolution and the Reconstruction of the Labour Party'. *Hist. J.* xv (1972), 753–73.

1698 THOMIS (MALCOLM I.). 'Conscription and Consent: British Labour and the Resignation Threat of January 1916'. *Austral. J. Pol. Hist.* xxxiii (1977), 10–18.

1699 BARKER (BERNARD). 'Anatomy of Reformism: The Social and Political Ideas of the Labour Leadership in Yorkshire'. *Inl. Rev. Soc. Hist.* xviii (1973), 1–27.

1700 McKIBBIN (ROSS). The Evolution of the Labour Party 1910–1924. 1974.

1701 COWLING (MAURICE). The Impact of Labour, 1920–1924: The Beginning of Modern British Politics. 1971.

1702 BRANSON (NOREEN). Poplarism 1919–25: George Lansbury and the Councillors' Revolt. 1979.

1703 WEBB (SIDNEY JAMES) *Baron Passfield*. 'The First Labour Government'. *Pol. Q.* xxxii (1961), 6–44.

1704 LYMAN (RICHARD WALL). The First Labour Government. 1957.

1705 —— 'The British Labour Party: The Conflict between Socialist Ideals and Practical Politics between the Wars'. *J. Brit. Studs* v (1965), 140–52.

1706 HOWELL (DAVID). A Lost Left: Three Studies in Socialism and Nationalism. Manch. 1986. [Case studies of James Connolly, John Maclean, and John Wheatley form the core of the book.].

1707 RENSHAW (PATRICK). 'Anti-Labour Politics in Britain, 1918–1927'. *J. Contemp. Hist.* xii (1977), 693–706.

1708 MACINTYRE (STUART). 'British Labour, Marxism and Working Class Apathy in the Nineteen Twenties'. *Hist. J.* xx (1977), 479–96.

1709 DOWSE (ROBERT EDWARD). 'The Left-wing Opposition During the First Two Labour Governments'. *Parl. Affs* xiv (1960–61), 80–93.

1710 TAYLOR (ALAN JOHN PERCIVALE). 'A Look Back at British Socialism, 1922–1937'. *Encounter* liv (1958), 27–33.

1711 MANSFIELD (NORMAN). Failure of the Left, 1919–1939. 1947.

1712 MOWAT (CHARLES LOCH). 'The Fall of the Labour Government in Great Britain, August 1931'. *Huntington Lib. Q.* vii (1944), 356–83.

1713 EATWELL (ROGER) *and* WRIGHT (ANTHONY W.). 'Labour and the Lessons of 1931'. *Hist.* lxiii (1978), 38–53.

1714 DARE (R.). 'Instinct and Organization: Intellectuals and British Labour After 1931'. *Hist. J.* 26 (1983), 677–97.

1715 WARREN (FRANK A.). An Alternative Vision: The Socialist Party in the 1930s. 1974.

1716 JUPP (JAMES). The Radical Left in Britain, 1931–1941. 1982.

1717 SAMUELS (STUART). 'The Left Book Club'. *J. Contemp. Hist.* i (1966), 65–86.

1718 PIMLOTT (BENJAMIN). Labour and the Left in the 1930s. Camb. 1977.

1719 —— 'The Socialist League: Intellectuals and the Labour Left in the 1930s'. *J. Contemp. Hist.* vi (1971), 12–38.

1720 McHENRY (DEAN EUGENE). The Labour Party in Transition. 1938.

1721 GOLLANCZ (*Sir* VICTOR) *ed.* Betrayal of the Left. 1941.

1722 BEALEY (FRANK W.) *and* DYER (MICHAEL). 'Size of Place and the Labour Vote in Britain, 1918–66'. *Western Pol. Q.* xxiv (1971), 84–113.

1723 McCULLOCH (G.). 'Labour, the Left and the British General Election of 1945'. *J. Brit. Studs* 24 (1985), 465–89.

1724 WARDE (ALAN). Consensus and Beyond: The Development of Labour Party Strategy since the Second World War. Manchester. 1982.

1725 ALDERMAN (R. KEITH). 'Discipline in the Parliamentary Labour Party, 1945–1951'. *Parl. Affs* xviii (1965), 293–305.

1726 PARKER (JOHN). Labour Marches on. Harmondsworth. 1947.

1727 SHAW (ERIC). Discipline and Discord in the Labour Party: The Politics of Managerial Control in the Labour Party, 1951–86. Manchester. 1988.

1728 ALDERMAN (R. KEITH). 'Parliamentary Party Discipline in Opposition: The Parliamentary Labour Party, 1951–1964'. *Parl. Affs* xxi (1968), 124–36.

1729 BONNOR (JEAN). 'The Four Labour Cabinets'. *Sociol. Rev.* vi (1958), 37–48.

1730 STECK (H. J.). 'Grassroots, Militants and Ideology: The Bevanite Revolt'. *Polity* (Amherst, Mass.) ii (1970), 426–42.

1731 JENKINS (MARK). Bevanism—Labour's High Tide: The Cold War and the Democratic Mass Movement. Nottingham. 1979.

1732 SCHNEER (JONATHAN). Labour's Conscience: The Labour Left 1945–51. 1988.

1733 RUBINSTEIN (DAVID). The Labour Left and Domestic Policy 1945–1950. 1979.

1734 LOEWENBERG (GERHARD). 'The Transformation of the British Labour Party Policy Since 1945'. *J. Pol.* xxi (1959), 234–57.

1735 ANDERSON (PERRY). 'The Left in the Fifties'. *New Left Rev.* xxix (1965), 3–18.

1736 HASELER (STEPHEN). The Gaitskellites: Revisionism in the British Labour Party 1951–1964. 1969.

1737 HINDELL (K.) *and* WILLIAMS (P.). 'Scarborough and Blackpool: An Analysis of some Votes at the Labour Party Conferences of 1960 and 1961'. *Pol. Q.* 33 (1962), 306–20.

1738 MULLER (WILLIAM DALE). 'Trade Union Sponsored Members of Parliament in the Defence Dispute of 1960–1'. *Parl. Affs* 23 (1970), 258–76.

1739 MILIBAND (RALPH). Parliamentary Socialism: A Study in the Politics of Labour. 1961. 2nd edn 1972.

1740 HUNTER (LESLIE DAVID STEVENSON). The Road to Brighton Pier. 1959.

1741 RATTRAY (ROBERT FLEMING). 'The Decline and Fall of the Labour Party'. *Q. Rev.* ccxcv (1957), 249–59.

1742 EVANS (E. W.). 'British Labour and the Common Market'. *Bankers Mag.* clxxxxiv (1962), 238–46.

1743 DOWSE (ROBERT EDWARD). 'The Parliamentary Labour Party in Opposition'. *Parl. Affs* xiii (1960), 520–9.

1744 HORNBY (R.). 'Parties in Parliament, 1959–1963: The Labour Party'. *Pol. Q.* xxxiv (1963), 240–8.

1745 KAUFMAN (GERALD) *ed.* The Left: A Symposium. 1966.

1746 EPSTEIN (LEON D.). 'New MPs and the Politics of the PLP'. *Pol. Studs* x (1962), 121–9.

1747 HOUGHTON (DOUGLAS). 'The Labour Backbencher'. *Pol. Q.* xl (1969), 454–63.

1748 THE LABOUR PARTY (Research Department). Twelve Wasted Years. 1963.

1749 BECKERMAN (WILFRED) *ed.* The Labour Government's Economic Record, 1964–1970. 1972.

1750 PIPER (JOHN RICHARD). 'Backbench Rebellion, Party Government and Consensus Politics: The Case of the Parliamentary Labour Party 1966–1970'. *Parl. Affs* xxvii (1974), 384–96.

1751 MINKIN (LEWIS). The Labour Party Conference: A Study in the Politics of Intra-party Democracy. 1977.

1752 COATES (KENNETH). The Crisis of British Socialism: Essays on the Rise of Harold Wilson and the Fall of the Labour Party. 1971.

1753 HARRISON (ROYDEN). 'Labour Government: Then and Now'. *Pol. Q.* xli (1970), 67–82.

1754 WAKEFORD (GEOFFREY). The Great Labour Mirage: An Indictment of Socialism in Britain. 1969.

1755 CHAMBERLAIN (CHRISTOPHER). 'The Growth of Support for the Labour Party in Britain'. *Brit. J. Soc.* xxiv (1973), 474–89.

1756 STEWART (MARGARET). Protest or Power? A Study of the Labour Party. 1974.

1757 COATES (DAVID). The Labour Party and the Struggle for Socialism. 1975.

1758 —— Labour in Power? A Study of the Labour Government, 1974–1979. 1980.

1759 LAYTON-HENRY (ZIG). 'Labour's Lost Youth'. *J. Contemp. Hist.* xi (1976), 275–308.

1760 HOWELL (DAVID). British Social Democracy: A Study in Development and Decay. 1976. 2nd edn 1980.

1761 HATFIELD (MICHAEL). The House the Left Built: Inside Labour Policy Making 1970–1975. 1978.

1762 MARTIN (COLIN) *and* MARTIN (DICK). 'The Decline of Labour Party Membership'. *Pol. Q.* 48 (1977), 459–71.

1763 COATES (KENNETH) *ed.* What Went Wrong? Nottingham. 1979.

1764 HASELER (STEPHEN). The Tragedy of Labour. Oxf. 1980.

1765 McALLISTER (IAN) *and* MUGHAN (A.). 'Attitudes, Issues and Labour Party Decline in England, 1974–1979'. *Comp. Pol. Studs* 18 (1985), 37–57.

1766 KOGAN (DAVID) *and* KOGAN (MAURICE). The Battle for the Labour Party. 1982.

1767 HOBSBAWM (ERIC) *ed.* The Forward March of Labour Halted? 1981.

1768 MITCHELL (AUSTIN). Four Years in the Death of the Labour Party. 1983.

1769 HOBSBAWM (ERIC). Politics for a Rational Left: Political Writing 1977–1988. 1989.

1770 SILKIN (JOHN). Changing Battlefields: The Challenge to the Labour Party. 1987.

1771 WAINWRIGHT (HILARY). Labour: A Tale of Two Parties. 1987.

1772 RUSTIN (MICHAEL). 'Different Conceptions of Party: Labour's Constitutional Debates'. *New Left Rev.* 126 (1981), 17–42.

1773 SEYD (PATRICK). The Rise and Fall of the Labour Left. 1987.

1774 COCKS (MICHAEL). Labour and the Benn Factor. 1989.

1775 JENKINS (HUGH). Rank and File. 1980.

1776 POTTS (A.) *and* JONES (E. R.) *comps.* Northern Labour History: A Bibliography. 1981.

1777 JANOSIK (EDWARD GABRIEL). Constituency Labour Parties in Britain. 1968.

1778 COX (DAVID). 'The Labour Party in Leicester: A Study in Branch Development'. *Inl. Rev. Soc. Hist.* vi (1961), 197–211.

1779 WYNCOLL (P.). The Nottingham Labour Movement, 1880–1939. 1985.

1780 BUSH (J.). Behind the Lines: East London Labour, 1914–1919. 1984.

1781 MOORE (B.). All Out: The Dramatic Story of the Sheffield Demonstration against Dole Cuts on February 6th 1935. Sheffield. 1985.

1782 WRIGHT (ANTHONY W.) *and* SHACKLETON (RICHARD) *eds.* Worlds of Labour: Essays in Birmingham Labour History. Birmingham. 1983.

1783 HASTINGS (R. F.). 'The Birmingham Labour Movement 1918–1945'. *Mid. Hist.* 5 (1979–80), 78–92.

1784 ROLF (D.). 'Labour and Politics in the West Midlands Between the Wars'. *North Staffs J. Field Studs* 18 (1978), 42–52.

1785 CALLCOTT (M.). 'The Nature and Extent of Political Change in the Inter-war Years: The Example of County Durham'. *Northern Hist.* 16 (1980), 215–37.

1786 HOWELL-THOMAS (DOROTHY). Socialism in West Sussex: A History of the Chichester Constituency Labour Party. Chichester. 1983.

1787 YOUNG (ALISON). The Reselection of MPs. 1983.

1788 BOCHEL (JOHN) *and* DENVER (DAVID). 'Candidate Selection in the Labour Party: What the Selectors Seek'. *Brit. J. Pol. Sci.* 23 (1983), 45–69.

1789 McCORMICK (PAUL). Enemies of Democracy. 1979.

1790 —— 'Prentice and the Newham North East Constituency: The Making of Historical Myths'. *Pol. Studs* 29 (1981), 73–90.

1791 —— 'The Labour Party: Three Unnoticed Changes'. *Brit. J. Pol. Sci.* 10 (1980), 381–8.

1792 TATCHELL (PETER). The Battle for Bermondsey. 1983.

1793 TURNER (JOHN E.). Labour's Doorstep Politics in London. 1978. [Includes Bermondsey.].

1794 CRICK (MICHAEL). The March of Militant. 2nd edn 1986.

1795 BERRY (DAVID). The Sociology of Grass Roots Politics: A Study of Party Membership. 1970. [Liverpool.].

1796 HINDESS (BARRY). The Decline of Working-Class Politics. 1971.

1797 BAXTER (R.). 'The Working Class and Labour Politics'. *Pol. Studs* xx (1972), 97–107.

1798 EPSTEIN (LEON D.). British Class Consciousness and the Labour Party'. *J. Brit. Studs* v (1962), 136–50.

1799 FORESTER (TOM). The Labour Party and the Working Class. 1976.

1800 HAYTER (DIANE). The Labour Party: Crisis and Prospects. 1977. [A Fabian Society Tract.].

1801 WHITELEY (PAUL). The Labour Party in Crisis. 1983.

1802 GORDON (I.) *and* WHITELEY (PAUL). 'Social Class and Political Attitudes: The Case of Labour Councillors'. *Pol. Studs* 27 (1979), 99–113.

1803 MIDDLETON (LUCY) *ed.* Women in the Labour Movement: The British Experience. 1977.

1804 TODD (NIGEL). 'Labour Women: A Study of Women in the Bexley Branch of the British Labour Party, 1945–1950'. *J. Contemp. Hist.* viii (1973), 159–73.

1805 PERRIGO (SARAH). Trouble and Strife: Women and the Labour Party. 1985.

1806 PANITCH (LEO VICTOR). Social Democracy and Industrial Militancy: The Labour Party and Incomes Policy, 1945–1974. Camb. 1976.

1807 TAYLOR (R.). 'The Uneasy Alliance—Labour and the Unions'. *Pol. Q.* xlvii (1976), 398–407.

4. THE LIBERAL PARTY

1808 SLESSER (*Sir* HENRY HERMAN). A History of the Liberal Party. 1944.

1809 DOUGLAS (ROY). The History of the Liberal Party, 1895–1970. 1971.

1810 WILSON (TREVOR GORDON). The Downfall of the Liberal Party, 1914–1935. 1966.

1811 KOSS (STEPHEN EDWARD). 'The Destruction of Britain's Last Liberal Government'. *J. Mod. Hist.* 40 (1968), 257–77.

1812 DAVID (EDWARD). 'The Liberal Party Divided, 1916–1918'. *Hist. J.* xiii (1970), 509–32.

1813 GOOCH (JOHN). 'The Maurice Debate, 1918'. *J. Contemp. Hist.* iii (1968), 211–28.

1814 MORGAN (KENNETH OWEN). Consensus and Disunity: The Lloyd George Coalition Government 1918–22. Oxf. 1979.

1815 KELLEY (ROBERT). 'Asquith at Paisley: The Content of British Liberalism at the End of its Era'. *J. Brit. Stud.* iv (1964), 133–59.

1816 WALKER (WILLIAM M.). 'Dundee's Disenchantment with Churchill: A Comment upon the Downfall of the Liberal Party'. *Scot. Hist. Rev.* xlix (1970), 85–108.

1817 DOWSE (ROBERT EDWARD). 'The Entry of Liberals into the Labour Party, 1910–1920'. *Yorks. Bull. Econ. Soc. Res.* (1961), 78–87.

1818 BENTLEY (MICHAEL J.). 'Liberal Politics and the Grey Conspiracy of 1921'. *Hist. J.* xx (1977), 461–78.

1819 COOK (CHRIS). A Short History of the Liberal Party 1900–1976. 1976. 3rd edn (1900–88). 1988.

1820 ADELMAN (PAUL). The Decline of the Liberal Party, 1910–1931. 1981.

1821 LANE (PETER). The Liberal Party. 1973.

1822 THOMPSON (JOSEPH ALLEN). The Collapse of the British Liberal Party: Fate or Self-Destruction? Lexington, Mass. 1969.

1823 RASMUSSEN (JORGEN SCOTT). The Liberal Party: A Study of Retrenchment and Revival. 1965.

1824 LORT-PHILLIPS (PATRICK). 'The British Liberal Revival'. *For. Affs* xxxviii (1959), 121–31.

1825 INGLE (S. J.). 'The Recent Revival of the British Liberal Party: Some Geographical, Social and Political Aspects'. *Pol. Sci.* 2 (1966), 39–48.

1826 CYR (ARTHUR). Liberal Party Politics in Britain. 1977.

1827 BOGDANOR (VERNON) *ed.* Liberal Party Politics. Oxf. 1983.

1828 WILSON (DES). Battle for Power. 1987.

5. SOCIAL DEMOCRATIC PARTY

1829 TAVERNE (DICK). The Future of the Left: Lincoln and After. 1974. [Campaign for Social Democracy.].

1830 BRADLEY (IAN). Breaking the Mould? The Birth and Prospects of the Social Democratic Party. 1981.

1831 TRACEY (N.). The Origins of the Social Democratic Party. 1983.

1832 JUPP (JAMES). 'The British Social Democrats and Crisis in the British Labour Party'. *Politics* (Australia) 16 (1981), 253–60.

1833 ZENTNER (PETER). Social Democracy in Britain: Must Labour Lose? 1982.

1834 OWEN (DAVID). Face the Future. 1981.

1835 —— A Future that Will Work: Competitiveness and Compassion. 1984.

1836 RODGERS (WILLIAM THOMAS). The Politics of Change. 1982.

1837 WILLIAMS (SHIRLEY). Politics is for People. Harmondsworth. 1981.

1838 STEPHENSON (HUGH). Claret and Chips: The Rise of the SDP. 1982.

1839 SEYMOUR-URE (COLIN KNOWLTON). 'The SDP and the Media'. *Pol. Q.* 53 (1982), 433–42.

1840 RICHARDS (P. G.). 'The SDP in Parliament'. *Parl. Affs* 35 (1982), 136–42.

1841 JOSEPHS (JEREMY). Inside the Alliance: An Inside Account of the Development and Prospects of the Liberal–SDP Alliance. 1983.

1842 STUDLAR (DONLEY T.) *and* McALLISTER (IAN). Protest and Survive: Alliance Support in the 1983 British General Election. Glasg. 1985.

1843 SOCIAL DEMOCRATIC PARTY. Decentralising Government. 1982. [SDP Policy Dept.].

1844 —— The Politics of Prosperity and the Politics of Poverty. 1983. [OWEN (DAVID).].

1845 —— (Policy Dept.) Attacking Poverty. 1983.

1846 —— Caring about People—Caring about Costs: Policy Guidelines for the Local Elections. 1984.

1847 —— Education Matters. 1984.

1848 —— Housing: A Choice for All. 1984.

1849 —— Policy for Women. 1984.

1850 JOINT LIBERAL PARTY/ SDP ALLIANCE COMMISSION ON ELECTORAL REFORM. Electoral Reform: Fairer Voting in Natural Communities: First Report . . . 1982.

1851 SDP/LIBERAL ALLIANCE. Let's Get Europe Working Together: Manifesto of the SDP/Liberal Alliance for the European Elections, 1984. 1984.

1852 —— Britain United: The Time has come: the SDP/Liberal Alliance Programme for Government. 1987.

1853 WILLIAMS (GEOFFREY LEE) *and* WILLIAMS (ALAN LEE). The Rise of the Social Democratic Party. 1988.

1854 —— Labour's Decline and the Social Democrats' Fall. 1989.

6. THE GREEN PARTY (FORMERLY THE ECOLOGY PARTY)

1855 RUDIG (WOLFGANG) *and* LOWE (PHILIP D.). 'The Withered "Greening" of British Politics: A Study of the Ecology Party'. *Pol. Studs* 34 (1986), 262–84.

1856 IRVINE (SANDY) *and* PANTON (ALEC). A Green Manifesto: Policies for a Green Future. 1988.

1857 PARKIN (SARA). Green Parties: An International Guide. 1989.

1858 PORRITT (JONATHON). Seeing Green: The Politics of Ecology Explained. Oxf. 1984.

1859 ECOLOGY PARTY. Working for the Future. 1980. [Green Economics.].

1860 —— How to Survive the Nuclear Age: What the Government Will not Tell you. 1980.

1861 —— Nuclear Disarmament and Beyond. 1981.

1862 —— Politics for Life. [1983 General Election Manifesto.] 1983.

1863 —— Towards a Green Europe. [Common Programme of Action of the European Green Parties.] 1984.

1864 GREEN PARTY. Green Politics. (1985).

1865 —— Will They Thank Us For This? 1986.

1866 —— General Election Manifesto. 1987.

7. INDEPENDENT LABOUR PARTY

1867 BEER (MAX). 'The Independent Labour Party'. Ch. in 'A History of British Socialism'. Vol. 2. 1919. Rev. edn 1929.

1868 COLE (GEORGE DOUGLAS HOWARD). 'The Independent Labour Party'. *New Statesman* 14 April 1928.

1869 JOHNSON (FRANCIS). The ILP in War and Peace: A Short Account of the Party from its Foundation to the Present Day. 1942.

1870 DOWSE (ROBERT EDWARD). Left in the Centre: The Independent Labour Party, 1893–1940. 1960.

1871 —— 'The ILP 1914–1932: A Bibliographical Study'. *Bull. Soc. Stud. Lab. Hist.* 2 (1962), 3–8.

1872 OLDFIELD (A.). 'The Independent Labour Party and Planning, 1920–1926'. *Inl. Rev. Soc. Hist.* 21 (1976), 1–29.

1873 MARWICK (ARTHUR JOHN BRERETON). 'The Independent Labour Party in the 1920s'. *Bull. Inst. Hist. Res.* 35 (1962), 62–74.

1874 PARRY (CYRIL). 'The Independent Labour Party and Gwynedd Politics, 1900–1920'. *Welsh Hist. Rev.* 4 (1968), 47–66.

1875 WOOLVEN (GILLIAN). Publications of the Independent Labour Party, 1893–1932. Coventry. 1977.

1876 STRACHEY (JOHN). Revolution by Reason: An Account of the Financial Proposals Submitted by Oswald Mosley at the 33rd Independent Labour Party Conference . . . 1925.

1877 INDEPENDENT LABOUR PARTY. Annual Conference Report . . . [58th–1950, Whitley Bay.] 1950.

1878 —— Accept Churchill's Challenge . . . [Conf. report 1951] 1951.

1879 —— Socialism through Peace . . . [Conf. report, 1952] 1952.

1880 —— Which Way to Worker's Control?: Towards a Socialist Policy for Industry. [GRAHAM (ALISTAIR).] 1971.

1881 McKIBBIN (ROSS). The Evolution of the Labour Party 1910–1924. 1974.

8. THE CO-OPERATIVE PARTY

1882 LUCAS (JAMES). Co-operation in Scotland. 1920. [Co-operative Union Pub.].

1883 WEBB (SIDNEY) *and* WEBB (BEATRICE). The Consumers Co-operative Movement. 1921.

1884 BARNES (ALFRED). The Political Aspect of Co-operation. 1926. [Co-operative Union Pub.].

1885 CARR-SAUNDERS (*Sir* ALEXANDER M.) *et al.* Consumers Co-operation in Britain. 1938.

1886 COLE (GEORGE DOUGLAS HOWARD). A Century of Co-operation. 1944.

1887 —— The British Co-operative Movement in a Socialist Society. 1951.

1888 TOPHAM (EDWARD) *and* HOUGH (JOHN ASPEY). The Co-operative Movement in Britain. 1944. Repr. 1946.

1889 RHODES (G. W.). Co-operative Labour Relations 1900–1962. 1962.

1890 BAILEY (*Sir* JACK). The British Co-operative Movement. 1955. 2nd edn 1960.

1891 UNION COOPERATIVE (MANCHESTER). 'Le Mouvement Cooperatif Britannique et la Problème de la Cogestion'. *Amer. Econ. Coll.* 43 (1955), 397–416.

1892 U.K. CENTRAL OFFICE OF INFORMATION. The Co-operative Movement in Britain. 1962. [HMSO].

1893 POLLARD (SIDNEY). 'The Foundation of the Co-operative Party'. Ch. in BRIGGS (ASA) *and* SAVILLE (JOHN), 'Essays in Labour History', 1886–1923. 1971.

1894 BONNER (ARNOLD). British Co-operation: The History, Principles and Organisation of the British Co-operative Movement. Manch. 1961.

1895 CARBERRY (THOMAS F.). Consumers in Politics: A History and General Review of the Co-operative Party. Manch. 1969.

1896 SMITH (BARBARA) *and* OSTERGAARD (GEOFFREY NIELSEN). Constitutional Relations Between the Labour and Co-operative Parties: An Historical Review. 1960.

1897 OSTERGAARD *and* HALSEY (ALBERT HENRY). Power in Co-operatives: A Study of the Internal Politics of British Retail Societies. Oxf. 1965.

1898 ADAMS (TONY). 'The Formation of the Co-operative Party Re-Considered'. *Inl. Rev. Soc. Hist.* 32 (1987), 48–68.

1899 CO-OPERATIVE PARTY. The People's Industry: A Statement on Social Ownership. 1952. [Discussion Guides Series, No. 1.].

1900 —— (Discussion Pamphlets) Co-operation and Modern Socialism. [BAILEY (JACK).] 1957.

1901 —— The Challenge of Monopoly. [WOOD (JAMES MAXWELL).] 1960.

9. THE COMMON WEALTH PARTY

1902 PRYNN (D. L.). 'Common Wealth—A British "Third Party" of the 1940s'. *J. Contemp. Hist.* 7 (1972), 169–79.

1903 WALKER (G. S.). 'The Common Wealth Labour Party in Northern Ireland 1942–1947'. *Irish Hist. Studs* 24 (1984), 69–91.

1904 CALDER (ANGUS). 'Never Again: December 1942 to August 1945'. Ch. in 'The People's War', *passim.* 1969.

1905 ACLAND (*Sir* RICHARD). The Forward March. 1941.

1906 —— What it Will be Like in the New Britain. 1942.

1907 —— How it can be Done. 1943.

1908 —— COMMON WEALTH INFORMATION BULLETIN. 1943–1946.

1909 —— COMMON WEALTH REVIEW. 1944–1949.

1910 —— COMMON WEALTH NEWS LETTER. 1950–1954.

1911 —— COMMON WEALTH PARTY. A New Kind of Politics: A Party in the Making. 1958.

1912 —— We Hold These Truths: A Manifesto for Libertarians. Devon. 1969.

10. COMMUNIST POLITICS IN BRITAIN

1913 MACKENZIE (ALAN J.). 'Communism in Britain: A Bibliography'. *Bull. Soc. Stud. Lab. Hist.* 44 (1982), 23–41.

1914 KENDALL (WALTER). The Revolutionary Movement in Britain: 1900–1921: The Origins of British Communism. 1969.

1915 —— The History of the Communist Party of Great Britain. 1986.

1916 MACFARLANE (LESLIE JOHN). The British Communist Party: Its Origin and Development until 1929. 1966.

1917 KLUGMANN (JAMES). History of the Communist Party of Great Britain: Vol. 1 Formation and Early Years, 1919–1924. 1968. Vol. 2 The General Strike, 1925–1927. 1969.

1918 BRANSON (NOREEN). A History of the Communist Party of Great Britain, 1927–1981. 1985.

1919 PELLING (HENRY MATHISON). The British Communist Party: A Historical Profile. 1958.

1920 —— 'The Early History of the Communist Party of Great Britain, 1920–1929'. *Trans. Roy. Hist. Soc.* 5th ser. 8 (1958), 41–57.

1921 TAYLOR (HENRY ARCHIBALD). Communism in Great Britain: A Short History of the British Communist Party. 1951.

1922 BELL (TOM). The Communist Party: A Short History. 1937.

1923 HERMANN (P. W.). Die Communist Party of Great Britain: Untersuchungen zur Geschichtlichen Entwicklung, Organisation, Ideologie und Politik der C.P.G.B. von 1920–1970. Königstein. 1976.

1924 WOODHOUSE (MICHAEL). Essays on the History of Communism in Britain. 1975.

1925 PEARCE (BRIAN). The Early History of the Communist Party in Great Britain. 1966.

1926 CHALLINOR (RAYMOND). The Origins of British Bolshevism. 1977.

1927 NEWTON (KENNETH). The Sociology of British Communism. 1969.

1928 WOOD (NEAL). Communism and British Intellectuals. 1959.

1929 DEWAR (HUGO). Communist Politics in Britain: The CPGB from its Origins to the Second World War. 1976.

1930 CAMPBELL (JOHN ROSS). Forty Fighting Years, the Communist Record, 1920–1960: Some Highlights in the Life of the Communist Party of Great Britain. 1960.

1931 ATTFIELD (JOHN W.) *and* WILLIAMS (STEPHEN) eds. 1939: The Communist Party of Great Britain and the War. 1984.

1932 HEINEMANN (MARGOT). '1956 and the Communist Party'. *Soc. Reg.* 13 (1976), 43–57.

1933 SAVILLE (JOHN). 'The XXth Congress and the British Communist Party'. *Soc. Reg.* 13 (1976), 1–23.

1934 HINTON (JAMES) *and* HYMAN (RICHARD). Trade Unions and Revolution: The Industrial Politics of the Early British Communist Party. 1975.

1935 WEINBERGER (B.). 'Communism and the General Strike'. *Bull. Soc. Stud. Lab. Hist.* 48 (1984), 31–57.

1936 MARTIN (RODERICK). Communism and the British Trade Unions, 1924–1933: A Study of the National Minority Movement. Oxf. 1969.

1937 HAYBURN (R.). 'The National Unemployed Workers' Movement 1921–1936: A Re-appraisal'. *Inl. Rev. Soc. Hist.* 28 (1983), 279–95.

1938 HOBSBAWM (ERIC JOHN ERNEST). 'The British Communist Party'. *Pol. Q.* 15 (1954), 30–43.

1939 JOHNSTONE (MONTY). 'The Communist Party in the 1920's'. *New Left Rev.* 16 (1967), 47–63.

1940 MITCHELL (DAVID). 'A Ghost of a Chance: British Revolutionaries in 1919'. *History Today* 20 (1970), 753–61.

1941 CAMERON (J. M.). 'The Thirties in Britain: The Marxist Mood'. *Listener* 74 (1965), 613–14.

1942 ROSENHAFT (EVE). 'Communism and Communists: Britain and Germany Between the Wars'. *Hist. J.* 26 (1983), 221–36.

1943 STANSKY (PETER) *and* ABRAHAMS (WILLIAM). Journey to the Frontier: Julian Bell and John Cornford: Their Lives and the 1930s. 1966.

1944 BLAKE (ROBERT NORMAN WILLIAM) *Baron Blake*. Stalinism in Britain. 1970.

1945 COPEMAN (FREDERICK). Reason in Revolt. 1948.

1946 POLLITT (HARRY). Serving My Time: An Apprenticeship in Politics. 1940.

1947 MAHON (JOHN). Harry Pollitt: A Biography. 1976.

1948 PIRATIN (PHIL). Our Flag Stays Red. 1978.

1949 PAYNTER (WIL). My Generation. 1972.

1950 McSHANE (HARRY). No Mean Fighter. 1978.

1951 MACINTYRE (STUART). Little Moscows: Communism and Working Class Militancy in Inter-war Britain. 1980.

1952 SAMUEL (RAPHAEL). 'The Lost World of British Communism'. *New Left Rev.* 154 (1985), 3–53.

1953 BORNSTEIN (SAM) *and* RICHARDSON (AL). Two Steps Back: Communists and the Wider Labour Movement, 1939–1945: A Study in Relations between 'Vanguard' and Class. 1982.

1954 DARKE (BOB). The Communist Technique in Britain. 1952.

1955 MILES (A.). 'Workers Education: The Communist Party and the Plebs League in the 1920's'. *Hist. Workshop* 18 (1984), 102–14.

1956 BAKER (BLAKE). 'The Communist Party'. Ch. in The Far Left: An Exposé of the Extreme Left in Britain. 1981.

1957 COMMUNIST PARTY OF GREAT BRITAIN. The British Road to Socialism. Rev. edn 1952. 3rd rev. edn 1968. New edn 1977.

1958 —— Forging the Weapon: A Handbook for Members of the Communist Party. 1955.

1959 —— A Policy for Britain: General Election Programme of the Communist Party. 1955.

1960 —— Communist Policy for Great Britain: The General Election. 1964.

1961 —— Speeches and Documents of the 6th (Manchester) Conference of the Communist Party of Great Britain . . . 1924. 1970.

1962 —— (Historians Group) Labour-Communist Relations, 1920–1939. 1957.

1963 COMMUNIST PARTY OF BRITAIN (MARXIST/LENINIST). Congress '76. [First Congress Report.] 1976.

1964 —— Counter Attack. 1985.

1965 —— The Protracted Struggle of the Working Class. 1986.

1966 PITCAIRN (LEE). 'Crisis in British Communism: An Insider's View'. *New Left Rev.* 153 (1985), 102–20.

11. SOCIALIST PARTY OF GREAT BRITAIN

1967 BEER (MAX). 'The Reorganisations of the Socialist Parties'. Ch. in A History of British Socialism. Vol. 2. 1919. Rev. edn 1929.

1968 BARLTROP (ROBERT). The Monument: The Story of the Socialist Party of Great Britain. 1975.

1969 SOCIALIST PARTY OF GREAT BRITAIN. The Socialist Party and War. 1950.

1970 —— Questions of the Day. 4th rev. edn 1953.

1971 —— From Capitalism to Socialism. 1986.

1972 —— Socialism as a Practical Alternative. 1987.

12. SOCIALIST WORKERS' PARTY

1973 FOOT (PAUL). Why you Should be a Socialist: The Case for a New Socialist Party. 1977.

1974 CANNON (JAMES P.). The Socialist Workers' Party in World War Two: Writings and Speeches, 1940–1943. [*Ed.* Les Evans.] 1975.

1975 BIRCHALL (IAN). The Smallest Mass Party in the World: Building the Socialist Worker's Party 1951–1979. 1981.

1976 SOCIALIST WORKER'S PARTY. Why Labour Fails. 1979.

1977 —— The Labour Party: Myth and Reality. [HALLAS (DUNCAN).] 1981.

1978 —— Permanent Revolution: A Re-examination. [CLIFF (TONY).] 1983.

1979 —— How Marxism Works. 1983.

1980 —— Socialism from Below. [McNALLY (DAVID).] 1984.

1981 —— The Future Socialist Society. 1987.

13. TROTSKYISM IN BRITAIN

1982 BORNSTEIN (SAM) *and* RICHARDSON (AL). Against the Stream: A History of the Trotskyist Movement in Britain 1924–1938. 1986.

1983 BORNSTEIN (SAM). The War and the International: A History of the Trotskyist Movement in Britain 1937–1949. 1986.

1984 GROVES (REG). The Balham Group: How British Trotskyism Began. 1974.

1985 ALI (TARIQ). The Coming British Revolution. 1972.

1986 CALLAGHAN (JOHN). British Trotskyism: Theory and Practice. Oxf. 1984.

1987 SOCIALIST LABOUR LEAGUE. In Defence of Trotskyism. 1973.

1988 WORKER'S REVOLUTIONARY PARTY (Pamphlet). Scargill, Solidarity and the Worker's Revolutionary Party. 1983.

1989 —— (Pamphlet). Studies in Dialectical Materialism. [HEALY (G.).] 1982.

1990 SHIPLEY (PETER). Militant Tendency: Trotskyism in the Labour Party. 1983.

1991 CRICK (MICHAEL). The March of Militant. Rev. and updated, 1986.

1992 MILITANT. A History of the Labour Party: Articles Reprinted from 'Militant'. 1979.

1993 —— (Pamphlet). Stop the Cuts. 1979.

1994 —— (Pamphlet). Nuclear Time Bomb. 1986.

1995 MILITANT LIVERPOOL BLACK CAUCUS. The Racial Politics of Militant in Liverpool . . . 1980–1986. L/pool. 1986.

14. GENERAL WORKS ON LEFT-WING POLITICS IN BRITAIN

1996 SPEIRS (JOHN), SEXSMITH (ANN). *and* EVERITT (ALASTAIR). The Left in Britain: A Checklist and Guide. Brighton. 1976.

1997 BINYON (GILBERT CLIVE). The Christian Socialist Movement in England. 1931.

1998 LE MIRE (E. D.). 'The Socialist League Leaflets and Manifestoes: An Annotated Checklist'. *Inl. Rev. Soc. Hist.* 22 (1977), 21–9.

1999 WIDGERY (DAVID). The Left in Britain, 1956–68. Harmondsworth. 1976.

2000 YOUNG (NIGEL). An Infantile Disorder? Crisis and Decline of the New Left. 1977.

2001 CALLAGHAN (JOHN). The Far Left in British Politics. Oxf. 1987.

2002 SHIPLEY (PETER). Revolutionaries in Modern Britain. 1976.

2003 MAIR (PETER). 'The Marxist Left'. Ch. in Multi-Party Britain, Henry Matthew Drucker, ed. 1979.

2004 TOMLINSON (JOHN). Left–Right: The March of Political Extremism in Britain. 1981.

2005 ALI (TARIQ). 'The Critical Condition of British Socialism'. Ch. in ALI (TARIQ) *ed.* 1968 and After: Inside the Revolution. 1978.

2006 —— Street Fighting Years: An Autobiography of the Sixties. 1987.

2007 HAIN (PETER) *with* BENN (TONY). The Crisis and the Future of the Left: The Debate of the Decade. 1980.

2008 CARR (GORDON). The Angry Brigade: The Cause and the Case. 1973.

2009 BAKER (BLAKE). The Far Left: An Exposé of the Extreme Left in Britain. 1981.

15. THE RADICAL RIGHT

2010 REES (PHILIP). Fascism in Britain. [A Bibliography.] Hassocks. 1974. Repr. 1978.

2011 BILLIG (MICHAEL) *and* BELL (ANDREW). 'Fascist Parties in Post-War Britain'. *Sage Race Relations Abstracts* 5/1 (1980), 1–30.

2012 STUBBS (J. O.). 'Lord Milner and Patriotic Labour, 1914–1918'. *Eng. Hist. Rev.* 87 (1972), 717–54.

2013 DOUGLAS (ROY). 'The National Democratic Party and the British Worker's League'. *Hist. J.* 15 (1972), 533–52.

2014 TURNER (JOHN A.). 'The British Commonwealth Union and the General Election of 1918'. *Eng. Hist. Rev.* 93 (1978), 528–59.

2015 DRENNAN (JAMES). British Union of Fascists: Oswald Mosley and British Fascism. 1934.

2016 RUDLIN (W. A.). The Growth of Fascism in Great Britain. 1935.

2017 STRACHEY (JOHN). The Menace of Fascism. 1933.

2018 MULLALLY (FREDERIC). Fascism Inside Britain. 1946.

2019 BONDY (LOUIS T.). Racketeers of Hatred. 1948.

2020 WEST (REBECCA). The Meaning of Treason. 1949.

2021 CROSS (COLIN). The Fascists in Britain. 1961.

2022 MANDLE (WILLIAM FREDERICK). Anti-Semitism and the British Union of Fascists. 1968.

2023 BREWER (JOHN D.). 'The British Union of Fascists and Anti-Semitism in Birmingham'. *Mid. Hist.* 9 (1984), 109–22.

2024 —— Mosley's Men: The British Union of Fascists in the West Midlands. Aldershot. 1984.

2025 SHERMER (DAVID). Blackshirts: Fascism in Britain. 1971.

2026 BENEWICK (ROBERT J.). The Fascist Movement in Britain. Rev. edn 1972. [First pub. under the title 'Political Violence and Public Order'. 1969.

2027 GRIFFITHS (RICHARD). Fellow Travellers of the Right: British Enthusiasts for Nazi Germany 1933–1939. 1980.

2028 LUNN (KENNETH) *and* THURLOW (RICHARD C.). British Fascism: Essays on the Radical Right in Inter-war Britain. 1980.

2029 THURLOW (RICHARD C.). Fascism in Britain: A History, 1918–1985. Oxf. 1987.

2030 LEWIS (D. S.). Illusions of Grandeur: Mosley, Fascism and British Society 1931–1981. Manch. 1987.

2031 EISENBERG (DENNIS). The Re-emergence of Fascism. 1967. [Great Britain is dealt with at 33–69.].

2032 WEBBER (G. C.). 'Patterns of Membership and Support for the British Union of Fascists'. *J. Contemp. Hist.* 19 (1984), 575–605.

2033 MANDLE (WILLIAM FREDERICK). 'The Leadership of the British Union of Fascists'. *Austral. J. Pol. Hist.* 12 (1966), 360–83.

2034 —— 'Sir Oswald Mosley's Resignation from the Labour Government'. *Hist. Studs Australia and New Zealand* 10 (1963), 493–510.

2035 MOSLEY (*Sir* OSWALD). The Greater Britain. 1932. Rev. 1934.

2036 —— One Hundred Questions Answered. 1936.

2037 —— Tomorrow We Live. 1938.

2038 —— My Answer. 1946.

2039 —— The Alternative. 1948.

2040 —— Mosley—Right or Wrong? 1961.

2041 —— My Life. 1962.

2042 WALKER (MARTIN). The National Front. 1977.

2043 —— 'The National Front'. Ch. in DRUCKER (HENRY MATTHEW) *ed.* Multi-Party Britain. 1979.

2044 BILLIG (MICHAEL). Fascists: A Psychological View of the National Front. 1978.

2045 EDGAR (DAVID). 'Racism, Fascism and the Politics of the National Front'. *Race and Class* 19 (1977), 111–31.

2046 WALKER (MARTIN). The National Front. Glasg. 1977.

2047 FIELDING (NIGEL). The National Front. 1981.

2048 ZHIGALOV (I. I.). '[Neo-Fascism in Great Britain: Sources, Aims, Peculiarities.]'. *Voprosi Istorii* 7 (1980), 61–78.

2049 TAYLOR (STAN). The National Front in English Politics. 1982.

2050 HUSBANDS (CHRISTOPHER T.). Racial Exclusionism and the City: The Urban Support of the National Front. 1983.

2051 HUSBANDS (CHRISTOPHER T.), HARROP (M.), *and* ENGLAND (J.). 'The Basis for National Front Support'. *Pol. Studs* 28 (1980), 271–83.

2052 LABOUR PARTY RESEARCH DEPARTMENT. The National Front Investigated. 1978.

2053 NATIONAL FRONT. (Policy Committee). The Case for Economic Nationalism. [TYNDALL (JOHN).] Croydon. 1975.

2054 —— (Policy Cttee). The Money Manufacturers: An Exposé of the Root Cause of the Financial and Economic Crisis. [MacDONALD (CLARE).] Croydon. 1975.

2055 —— Education for National Survival. Teddington. 1976.

2056 NUGENT (NEILL) *and* KING (ROGER) *eds.* The British Right. Farnborough 1977.

2057 SPRING (DAVID). The League of British Covenanters: A Study in English Extremism. 1987.

2058 KNIGHT (D.). Beyond the Pale: The Christian Fringe. 1982.

16. Pressure Groups and Quangos

2059 SHIPLEY (PETER). Directory of Pressure Groups and Representative Associations. Epping. 1979. 2nd edn 1980.

2060 JORDAN (A. G.) *and* RICHARDSON (JOHN JEREMY). Government and Pressure Groups in Britain. Oxf. 1987.

2061 ALDERMAN (GEOFFREY). Pressure Groups and Government in Great Britain. 1984.

2062 COXALL (W. N.). Political Realities: Parties and Pressure Groups. 2nd edn 1986.

2063 WOOTTON (GRAHAM). Pressure Politics in Contemporary Britain. Lexington, Mass. 1978.

2064 FINER (S. E.). Anonymous Empire: A Study of the Lobby in Great Britain. 1958.

2065 STEWART (J. D.). British Pressure Groups: Their Role in Relation to the House of Commons. Oxf. 1958.

2066 POTTER (ALLEN M.). Organised Groups in British National Politics. 1961.

2067 MACKENZIE (R. T.) *ed.* 'Parties, Pressure Groups and the British Political Process'. *Pol. Q.* 29/1 (1958).

2068 WILSON (HARPER HUBERT). Pressure Group: The Campaign for Commercial Television. 1961.

2069 RIVERS (PATRICK). Politics. 1974.

2070 WILSON (DES). Pressure: The A to Z of Campaigning Britain. 1984.

2071 MILLER (CHARLES). Lobbying Government: Understanding and Influencing the Corridors of Power. Oxf. 1987.

2072 DUBS (ALF). Lobbying: An Insider's Guide to the Parliamentary Process. 1988.

2073 KIMBER (RICHARD) *and* RICHARDSON (JOHN JEREMY) *eds.* Pressure Groups in Britain: A Reader. 1974.

2074 ALDERMAN (GEOFFREY) *et al.* 'Symposium: Pressure Groups'. *Contemp. Record* 2/1 (1988), 2–15.

2075 GRANT (WYN). Pressure Groups: Politics and Democracy in Britain. 1989.

2076 FROST (BRIAN) *ed.* The Tactics of Pressure: A Critical Review of Six British Pressure Groups. 1975.

2077 KING (ROGER) *and* NUGENT (NEILL) *eds.* Respectable Rebels: Middle Class Campaigns in Britain in the 1970's. 1979.

2078 GARRARD (JOHN) *et al. eds.* The Middle Class in Politics. Farnborough. 1978.

2079 ELLIOTT (BRIAN) *et al.* 'Bourgeois Social Movements in Britain: Repertoires and Responses'. *Sociol. Rev.* n.s. 30 (1982), 71–96.

2080 BARKER (A.) *ed.* Quangos in Britain. Basingstoke. 1982.

F. POLITICAL THOUGHT

The literature on this subject reflects its chequered history and uncertain location on the boundary between the general world of ideas and prevailing philosophical fashions on the one hand, and the exigencies of party rhetoric on the other. Books purporting to present or to analyse the political thought of a particular party have been ignored or ridiculed by other writers who find such doctrines as at best tangentially relevant to the manœuvres of everyday politics. In general political commentary, particularly amongst writers of a Conservative disposition, there are considerable traces of the belief that a supposed British genius for politics consists in an indifference towards grand doctrine. It is not altogether surprising, therefore, that such studies of writers who may be classified as 'British political theorists' focus on writers of the Left. Scepticism about 'political thought' received some incidental support from a post-1945 philosophical outlook which found a good deal of metaphysical nonsense in previous discourse on 'the State'. It is not surprising, therefore, that the literature on British political thought reveals these mixed intellectual origins and assumptions. It is only in the last decade or so that the study of political thought has regained a certain confidence and has begun to produce work which reflects systematically on how 'political thought' must be approached in twentieth-century Britain.

1. GENERAL

2081 GREENLEAF (W. H.). The British Political Tradition: Vol. 1. The Rise of Collectivism. Vol. 2. The Ideological Heritage. 1983. Vol. 3. Much Govern'd Nation (2 parts). 1988.

2082 MILLER (DAVID) ed. The Blackwell Encyclopaedia of Political Thought. Oxf. 1986.

2083 PHILIP (P. J.). English Political Ideas from 1918 to 1939. 1950.

2084 BARKER (RODNEY). Political Ideas in Modern Britain. 1978.

2085 SCRUTON (ROGER). A Dictionary of Political Thought. 1982.

2086 DE CRESPIGNY (ANTHONY) and MINOGUE (KENNETH) eds. Contemporary Political Philosophers. 1976.

2087 INGLIS (FRED). Radical Earnestness and English Social Theory 1880–1980. 1982.

2088 OAKESHOTT (MICHAEL). Rationalism in Politics and Other Essays. 1962.

2089 —— On Human Conduct. Oxf. 1975.

2090 GREENLEAF (W. H.). Oakeshott's Philosophical Politics. 1956.

2091 FRANCO (PAUL). The Political Philosophy of Michael Oakeshott. New Haven. 1990.

2092 WIENER (MARTIN J.). Between Two Worlds: The Political Thought of Graham Wallas. Oxf. 1971.

2093 COWLEY (BRIAN LEE). The Self, the Individual and the Community: Liberalism in the Political Thought of F. A. Hayek and Sidney and Beatrice Webb. Oxf. 1987.

2094 HAYEK (FRIEDRICH AUGUST) von. The Road to Serfdom. 1944.

2095 HAYEK (FRIEDRICH AUGUST) von. Law, Legislation and Liberty. 3 vols 1973.

2096 BARRY (NORMAN P.). Hayek's Road to Serfdom Revisited: Essays by Economists, Philosophers and Political Scientists on 'The Road to Serfdom' after Forty Years. 1984.

2097 —— Hayek's Social and Economic Philosophy. 1979.

2. SOCIALIST THOUGHT

2098 COLE (GEORGE DOUGLAS HOWARD). A History of Socialist Thought. 5 vols in 7. 1953–60.

2099 BEALEY (FRANK WILLIAM) ed. The Social and Political Thought of the British Labour Party. 1970.

2100 WRIGHT (ANTHONY W.). British Socialism: Socialist Thought from the 1880s to the 1960s. 1983.

2101 FOOTE (GEOFFREY). The Labour Party's Political Thought: A History. 1985.

2102 BARKER (RODNEY). Education and Politics, 1900–1951: A Study of the Labour Party. Oxf. 1972.

2103 —— 'The Labour Party and Education for Socialism'. *Inl Rev. Soc. Hist.* xiv (1969), 22–53.

2104 JONES (S. G.). The British Labour Movement and Film, 1918–1939. 1987.

2105 DENNIS (NORMAN) and HALSEY (A. H.). English Ethical Socialism: Thomas More to R. H. Tawney. Oxf. 1988.

2106 MACBRIAR (ALAN MARNE). Fabian Socialism and English Politics, 1884–1918. Camb. 1962.

2107 McCARRAN (MARGARET PATRICIA). Fabianism in the Political Life of Britain, 1919–1931. 1952. 2nd edn Chicago. 1954.

2108 COLE (MARGARET ISABEL) ed. The Story of Fabian Socialism. 1961.

2109 PUGH (PATRICIA). Educate, Agitate, Organise: 100 Years of Fabian Socialism. 1984.

2110 PIMLOTT (BEN) ed. Fabian Essays in Socialist Thought. 1984.

2111 TSUZUKI (CHUSHICHI). Edward Carpenter 1844–1929: Prophet of Human Fellowship. Camb. 1980.

2112 CATLIN (*Sir* GEORGE E. C.). For God's Sake, Go! An Autobiography. Gerrard's Cross. 1972.

2113 FREEDEN (MICHAEL) ed. Reappraising J. A. Hobson: Humanism and Welfare. 1990.

2114 DEANE (HERBERT ANDREW). The Political Ideas of Harold Laski. N.Y. 1955.

2115 MARTIN (BASIL KINGSLEY). Harold Laski 1893–1950: A Biographical Memoir. 1953.

2116 EASTWOOD (G. G.). Harold Laski. 1977.

2117 GREENLEAF (W. H.). 'Laski and British Socialism'. *Hist. Pol. Thought* I (1981), 573–9.

2118 LASKI (HAROLD JOSEPH) et al. Programme for Victory: A collection of Essays Prepared for the Fabian Society. 1941.

2119 CARPENTER (L. P.). G. D. H. Cole: An Intellectual Portrait. Camb. 1973.

2120 —— 'Corporatism in Britain 1930–1945'. *J. Contemp. Hist.* xi (1976), 3–25.

2121 BARKER (RODNEY). 'Guild Socialism Revisited?'. *Pol. Q.* 46 (1975), 246–54.

2122 COLE (*Dame* MARGARET ISABEL). The Life of G. D. H. Cole. 1971.

2123 —— Growing up into Revolution. 1949.

2124 VERNON (BETTY D.). Margaret Cole 1893–1980: A Political Biography. 1986.

2125 WRIGHT (ANTHONY W.). G. D. H. Cole and Socialist Democracy. Oxf. 1979.

2126 WOOLF (LEONARD SIDNEY). Sowing: An Autobiography of the Years 1880–1904. 1961.

2127 —— Growing: An Autobiography of the Years 1904–1911. 1961.

2128 —— Beginning Again: An Autobiography of the Years 1911–1918. 1964.

2129 —— Downhill all the Way: An Autobiography of the Years 1919–1939. 1967.

2130 EISENBERG (J.). Leonard Woolf: A Political Biography. 1978.

2131 WOOTTON (BARBARA FRANCES) *Baroness.* In a World I Never Made: Autobiographical Reflections. 1967.

2132 HARDING (D. W.). 'Political Scepticism in Britain'. *Pol. Q.* xxx (1959), 18–28.

2133 MARWICK (ARTHUR JOHN BRERETON). 'Middle Opinion in the Thirties: Planning, Progress and Political Agreement'. *Eng. Hist. Rev.* lxxix (1964), 285–98.

2134 ANDERSON (PERRY) *and* BLACKBURN (ROBIN) eds. Towards Socialism. 1965.

2135 GORER (GEOFFREY). The Danger of Equality and Other Essays. 1966.

2136 ABEL-SMITH (BRIAN) *et al.* Socialism and Affluence: Four Fabian Essays. 1967.

2137 CRICK (BERNARD ROWLAND) *and* ROBSON (WILLIAM ALEXANDER) eds. Protest and Discontent. Harmondsworth. 1970.

2138 STRACHEY (EVELYN JOHN ST LOE). The Coming Struggle for Power. 1932.

2139 —— Contemporary Capitalism. 1956.

2140 TAWNEY (RICHARD HENRY). The Acquisitive Society. 1921.

2141 —— Equality. 1931. 4th edn 1952.

2142 —— Beatrice Webb. 1945.

2143 WRIGHT (ANTHONY W.). R. H. Tawney. Manchester. 1987.

2144 TERRILL (ROSS). R. H. Tawney and His Times. Camb. Mass. 1973.

2145 WINTER (JAY M.). 'A Bibliography of the Published Writings of R. H. Tawney'. *Econ. H. R.* 2nd ser. xv (1972), 137–53.

2146 HINDEN (RITA) ed. R. H. Tawney: The Radical Tradition. Harmondsworth. 1966.

2147 COLE (MARGARET ISABEL) *Dame.* Beatrice Webb. 1946.

2148 RADICE (LISANNE). Beatrice and Sidney Webb: Fabian Socialists. 1984.

2149 MUGGERIDGE (KITTY) *and* ADAM (RUTH). Beatrice Webb: A Life, 1858–1943. 1968.

2150 MACKENZIE (NORMAN) ed. The Letters of Sidney and Beatrice Webb III Pilgrimage 1912–1947. Camb. 1978.

2151 MACKENZIE (JEANNE) *and* MACKENZIE (NORMAN) eds. The Diary of Beatrice Webb. Vol. 3 1905–1924. 1984. Vol. 4 1924–1943.

2152 HIMMELFARB (GERTRUDE). 'The Intellectual in Politics: The Case of the Webbs'. *J. Contemp. Hist.* vi (1971), 3–11.

2153 MARQUAND (DAVID I.). 'The Politics of Deprivation: Reconsidering the Failure of Utopianism'. *Encounter* xxxii (1969), 36–44.

2154 MILIBAND (RALPH). The State in Capitalist Society. 1970.

2155 ANDERSON (PERRY) *et al.* Towards Socialism. 1965.

2156 YOUNG (NIGEL). An Infantile Disorder? The Crisis and Decline of the New Left. 1977.

2157 HOLLAND (STUART). The Socialist Challenge. 1975.

2158 DRUCKER (HENRY). Doctrine and Ethos in the Labour Party. 1979.

2159 ANDERSON (PERRY). Arguments within English Marxism. 1980.

2160 WILLIAMS (RAYMOND HENRY). 'Notes on Marxism in Britain since 1945'. *New Left Rev.* (1976–7), 81–94.

2161 CRICK (BERNARD ROWLAND). 'Socialist Literature in the 1950s'. *Pol. Q.* 31 (3) (1960), 361–73.

2162 YEO (STEPHEN) ed. New Views of Co-operation. 1989.

3. LIBERALISM

2163 BULLOCK (ALAN LOUIS CHARLES) *Baron and* SHOCK (MAURICE) eds. The Liberal Tradition from Fox to Keynes. 1956.

2164 ECCLESHALL (ROBERT). British Liberalism: Liberal Thought from the 1640s to the 1980s. 1986.

2165 BENTLEY (MICHAEL J.). The Liberal Mind, 1914–1929. Camb. 1977.

2166 —— The Climax of Liberal Politics: British Liberalism in Theory and Practice 1868–1918. 1987.

2167 NATHAN (H. L.) *Baron and* WILLIAMS (H. H.) eds. Liberal Points of View. 1927.

2168 —— Liberalism and Some Problems of Today. 1929.

2169 BENN (*Sir* ERNEST J. P.). The Return to Laissez-Faire. 1928.

2170 —— Modern Government as a Busybody in other Men's Matters. 1936.

2171 —— State the Enemy. 1953.

2172 LASKI (HAROLD JOSEPH). The Decline of Liberalism. 1940.

2173 WATSON (GEORGE GRIMES) ed. The Unservile State: Essays in Liberty and Welfare. 1957.

2174 FULFORD (*Sir* ROGER THOMAS BALDWIN). The Liberal Case. Harmondsworth. 1959.

2175 WATSON (GEORGE GRIMES) ed. Radical Alternative: Studies in Liberalism. 1962.

2176 MORRIS (JAMES/JAN). The Outriders: A Liberal View of Britain. 1963.

2177 WATKINS (ALAN R.). The Liberal Dilemma. 1966.

2178 MINOGUE (KENNETH). The Liberal Mind. 1963.

2179 HAIN (PETER). Radical Liberalism and Youth Politics. 1973.

2180 BEITH (ALAN). The Case for the Liberal Party and the Alliance. 1983.

2181 FREEDEN (MICHAEL). Liberalism Divided: A Study in British Political Thought 1914–1939. Oxf. 1986.

4. CONSERVATISM

2182 WHITE (REGINALD JAMES) *ed.* The Conservative Tradition. 1950. 2nd edn 1964.

2183 O'GORMAN (FRANK). British Conservatism: Conservative Thought from Burke to Thatcher. 1986.

2184 BUCK (PHILIP W.) *ed.* How Conservatives Think. Harmondsworth. 1985.

2185 FAIR (JOHN D.) *and* HUTCHESON (JOHN A.). 'British Conservatism in the Twentieth Century: An Emerging Ideological Tradition'. *Albion* 19 (1987), 549–78.

2186 BOOTHBY (ROBERT JOHN GRAHAM) *Baron, et al.* Industry and the State: A Conservative View. 1927.

2187 BRYANT (*Sir* ARTHUR WYNNE MORGAN). The Spirit of Conservatism. 1929.

2188 JONES (AUBREY). The Pendulum of Politics. 1946.

2189 HOGG (QUINTIN McGAREL). The Case for Conservatism. 1947. Rev. edn 1959.

2190 LAW (RICHARD KIDSTON). Return from Utopia. 1950.

2191 POWELL (J. ENOCH) *and* MAUDE (ANGUS). The New Conservatism: An Anthology of Post-War Thought. 1955.

2192 RAISON (TIMOTHY). Why Conservative? Harmondsworth. 1964.

2193 GLICKMAN (HARVEY). 'The Toryism of English Conservatism'. *J. Brit. Studs* I (1961), 111–43.

2194 MAUDE (ANGUS) *Baron.* The Common Problem. 1969.

2195 JOSEPH (*Sir* KEITH). Reversing the Trend. 1975.

2196 GILMOUR (*Sir* IAN). Inside Right: A Study of Conservatism. 1977.

2197 GREENLEAF (W. H.). 'The Character of Modern British Conservatism' in *eds* R. Benewick, R. N. Berki, and B. Parekh, Knowledge and Belief in Politics: The Problem of Ideology. 1973.

2198 QUINTON (ANTHONY) *Baron.* The Politics of Imperfection: The Religious and Secular Traditions of Conservative Thought in England from Hooker to Oakeshott. 1978.

2199 COWLING (MAURICE) *ed.* Conservative Essays. 1980.

2200 WALDEGRAVE (WILLIAM). The Binding of Leviathan: Conservatism and the Future. 1978.

2201 SCRUTON (ROGER). The Meaning of Conservatism. Harmondsworth. 1980. 2nd edn 1984.

2202 WEBBER (G. C.). The Ideology of the British Right, 1918–39. 1986.

2203 CULLEN (S.). 'The Development of the Ideals and Policy of the British Union of Fascists, 1932–40'. *J. Contemp. Hist.* 22 (1987), 115–36.

G. THE ELECTORAL SYSTEM

The study of elections and the electoral system has been a major preoccupation of academic study after 1945 when the first thorough contemporaneous election study was undertaken. While still including regular General Election studies, the publication of electoral data together with analysis and interpretation has now extended to all elections whether for the European Parliament, the House of Commons, or local elections. Such general studies are accompanied by particular gender, ethnic, or regional electoral studies, though these are patchy. The analysis of electoral data has naturally been facilitated by the advent of the computer, and the ability to handle and compare large numbers has resulted in an electoral science which rests heavily upon statistical sophistication. By the same token, however, the transmission and discussion of this material has begun to transcend the traditional forms of publication represented in this bibliography.

1. ELECTION RESULTS

2204 CRAIG (FREDERICK WALTER SCOTT). British Parliamentary Election Results, 1885–1918. 1974. 2nd edn Aldershot. 1989.

2205 —— British Parliamentary Election Results, 1918–1949. 1969. 3rd edn, 1989.

2206 —— British Parliamentary Election Results, 1950–1970. Chichester. 1971. 2nd edn [to 1973], 1981.

2207 —— British Parliamentary Election Results, 1974–1983. Aldershot. 1984.

2208 —— British Parliamentary Election Statistics, 1918–1970. Chichester. 1971.

2209 —— Britain Votes Four: British Parliamentary Election Results 1983–1987. 1987.

2210 —— British Electoral Facts 1832–1987. Aldershot. 1988.

2211 —— Boundaries of Parliamentary Constituencies, 1885–1972. 1973.

2212 —— British General Election Manifestos, 1900–1974. Aldershot. 1975.

2213 —— Minor Parties at British Parliamentary Elections, 1885–1974. 1975.

2214 —— Chronology of British Parliamentary By-Election Results, 1833–1987. 1987.

2215 ROSS (JAMES FREDERICK STANLEY). Parliamentary Representation. 1943. 2nd edn 1948.

2216 —— Elections and Electors. 1955.

2217 MITCHELL (BRIAN REDMAN) *and* BOEHM (KLAUS). British Parliamentary Election Results, 1950–1964. Camb. 1966.

2218 KINNEAR (MICHAEL). The British Voter: An Atlas and Survey Since 1885. 1968. 2nd edn 1981.

2219 ALLEN (A. J.). The English Voter. 1964.

2220 WALLER (ROBERT). The Almanac of British Politics. 1983 and 1987.

2221 CREWE (IVOR) *and* FOX (ANTHONY). British Parliamentary Constituencies: A Statistical Compendium. 1984.

2222 BUTLER (DAVID EDGEWORTH). The Electoral System in Britain Since 1918. Oxf. 2nd edn 1963.

2223 —— 'The Redistribution of Seats'. *Public Admin* xxxiii (1955), 125–47.

2224 BUTLER (DAVID EDGEWORTH) *and* STOKES (DONALD ELKINTON). Political Change in Britain: Forces Shaping Electoral Choice. 1969. 2nd edn 1974.

2225 BENEWICK (ROBERT J.) *et al.* 'The Floating Voter and the Liberal View of Representation'. *Pol. Studs* xvii (1961), 177–95.

2226 HERMENS (F. A.). 'Electoral System and Political Systems: Recent Developments in Britain'. *Parl. Affs* xxix (1976), 47–59.

2227 ABRAMSON (PAUL R.). 'Generational Change and Continuity and British Partisan Choice'. *Brit. J. Pol. Sci.* 6 (1976), 364–8.

2228 JOHNSON (NEVIL). 'Servicemen and Parliamentary Elections'. *Parl. Affs* xvi (1963), 207–12; 440–4.

2229 MILLER (WILLIAM L.). Electoral Dynamics in Britain Since 1918. 1977.

2230 MILLER (WILLIAM L.) *and* RAAB (GILLIAN). 'The Religious Alignment of English Elections Between 1918 and 1970'. *Pol. Studs* xxv (1977), 227–51.

2231 ALFORD (R. R.). Party and Society. 1964.

2. RELIGIOUS AND RACIAL FACTORS

2232 ALDERMAN (GEOFFREY). The Jewish Vote in Great Britain Since 1945. Glasgow. 1980.

2233 DEAKIN (NICHOLAS) *ed.* Colour and the British Electorate: Six Case Studies. 1965.

2234 —— 'Colour and the 1966 General Election'. *Race* 8 (1966), 17–42.

2235 NANDY (D.). 'Immigrants and the Election'. *Lab. Monthly* 46 (1964), 449–53.

2236 WOOD (JOHN B.) *ed.* Powell and the 1970 Election. 1970.

2237 DEAKIN (NICHOLAS) *and* BOURNE (J.). 'Powell, the Minorities and the 1970 Election'. *Pol. Q.* 41 1970. 399–415.

2238 STUDLAR (DONLEY T.). 'Policy Voting in Britain: The Coloured Immigration Vote in the 1964, 1966 and 1970 General Elections'. *Amer. Pol. Sci. Rev.* 72 (1978), 46–64.

2239 ANWAR (MUHAMMAD). 'Asian Participation in the October 1974 General Election'. *New Community* 4 (1975), 376–83.

2240 —— Votes and Policies: Ethnic Minorities and the General Election 1979. 1980.

2241 —— Ethnic Minorities and the 1983 General Election: A Research Report. 1984.

2242 —— Race and Politics: Ethnic Minorities in the British Political System. 1986.

2243 FITZGERALD (M.). Ethnic Minorities and the 1983 General Election. 1984.

2244 LE LOHE (M. J.). 'Voter Discrimination Against Asian and Black Candidates in the 1983 General Election'. *New Community* 11 (1983), 101–8.

2245 —— 'Ethnic Minority Participation in Local Elections. Bradford. 1984.

2246 STUDLAR (DONLEY T.). 'The Ethnic Vote: Problems of Analysis and Interpretation'. *New Community* 11 (1983), 92–100.

2247 WELCH (SUSAN) *and* STUDLAR (DONLEY T.). 'The Impact of Race on Political Behaviour in Britain'. *Brit. J. Pol. Sci.* 15 (1985), 528–39.

2248 LAYTON-HENRY (ZIG) *and* STUDLAR (DONLEY T.). 'The Electoral Participation of Black and Asian Britons: Integration or Alienation?'. *Parl. Affs* 38 (1985), 307–18.

2249 SANDERSON (G. N.). 'The "Swing of the Pendulum" in British General Elections 1832–1966'. *Pol. Studs* xiv (1966), 349–59.

2250 JUST (MARION R.). 'Causal Models of Voter Rationality, Great Britain 1959 and 1963'. *Pol. Studs* xxi (1973).

2251 TAYLOR (A. H.). 'The Effect of Electoral Pacts on the Decline of the Liberal Party'. *Brit. J. Pol. Sci* III (1973), 243–8.

2252 TAYLOR (A. H.). 'The Proportional Decline Hypothesis in English Elections'. *Roy. State. Soc. J.* ser. A cxxxv (1972), 365–9.

2253 BLONDEL (JEAN). Voters, Parties and Leaders: The Social Fabric of British Politics. 1963. Rev. edn 1974.

2254 HIMMELWEIT (HILDE T.), HUMPHREYS (PATRICK), *and* JAEGER (MARIANNE). How Voters Decide: A Longitudinal Study of Political Attitudes and Voting Extending over Fifteen Years. 2nd edn Milton Keynes. 1985.

2255 BONHAM (JOHN). The Middle Class Vote. 1954.

3. WOMEN VOTERS

2256 FULFORD (*SIR* ROGER). Votes for Women: The Story of a Struggle. 1957.

2257 MONTEFIORE (DORA B.). From a Victorian to a Modern. 1927.

2258 FAWCETT (*DAME* MILLICENT GARRETT). The Women's Victory—and after: Personal Reminiscences, 1911–1918. 1920.

2259 CURRELL (MELVILLE). Political Women. 1974.

2260 MITCHELL (HANNAH MARIA). The Hard Way Up: The Autobiography of Hannah Mitchell, Suffragette and Rebel. Edited by Geoffrey Mitchell. 1968.

2261 ROSS (JAMES FREDERICK STANLEY). 'Women and Parliamentary Elections'. *Brit. J. Sociol.* iv (1953), 14–24.

2262 RASMUSSEN (JORGEN S.). 'The Electoral Costs of Being a Woman in the 1979 British General Election'. *Comp. Pol.* 15 (1983), 462–75.

2263 VALLANCE (ELIZABETH). 'Women Candidates in the 1983 General Election'. *Parl. Affs* 37 (1984), 301–9.

2264 HILLS (J.). 'Candidates: The Impact of Gender'. *Parl. Affs* 34 (1981), 221–8.

2265 NORRIS (PIPPA). 'Conservative Attitudes in Recent British Elections: An Emerging Gender Gap'. *Pol. Studs* 34 (1986), 120–8.

2266 CAMPBELL (BEATRIX). The Iron Ladies: Why do Women Vote Tory? 1987.

4. GENERAL ELECTIONS 1918–1987

2267 HODDER-WILLIAMS (RICHARD). Public Opinion Polls and British Politics. 1970.

2268 ABRAMS (MARK). 'Public Opinion Polls and the British General Election'. *Pub. Op. Q.* 14 (1950), 40–52.

2269 ELDERSVELD (S. J.). 'British Polls and the 1950 General Election'. *Pub. Op. Q.* 15 (1951), 115–32.

2270 ROSE (RICHARD). The Polls and the 1970 Election. Glasg. 1970.

2271 ABRAMS (MARK). 'Opinion Polls and the 1970 British General Election'. *Pub. Op. Q.* 34 (1970), 317–24.

2272 ROSE (RICHARD). Towards Normality—Public Opinion Polls in the 1979 Election. Glasgow. 1979.

2273 BOOTH (ARTHUR HAROLD). British Hustings, 1924–1950. 1957.

1918–1929

2274 HOBBS (ARTHUR O.) *and* OGDEN (F. J.). A Guide to the Representation of the People Act of 1918. 1918.

2275 TERRY (GEORGE PERCY WARNER). The Representation of the People Acts 1918 to 1928 and Amending Acts, and the Law Relating to the Registration of Jurors. 1939.

2276 CLOSE (DAVID H.). 'The Collapse of Resistance to Democracy: Conservatism, Adult Suffrage and Second Chamber Reform, 1911–1928'. *Pol. Studs* xxv (1977), 871–91.

2277 MILLER (WILLIAM L.). 'Cross Voting and the Dimensionality of Party Conflict in Britain During the Period of Realignment, 1918–31'. *Pol. Studs* ixx (1971), 455–64.

2278 MCEWEN (J. M.). 'The Coupon Election of 1918 and Unionist Members of Parliament'. *J. Mod. Hist.* xxxiv (1962), 294–306.

2279 DOUGLAS (ROY). 'The Background to the "Coupon" Election Arrangements'. *Eng. Hist. Rev.* lxxxvi (1971), 318–36.

2280 COOK (CHRIS). The Age of Alignment: Electoral Politics 1922–1929. 1975.

2281 MATTHEW (HENRY COLIN GRAY) *et al.* 'The Franchise Factor in the Rise of the Labour Party'. *Eng. Hist. Rev.* xci (1976), 723–52.

2282 CLARKE (PETER FREDERICK). 'Liberals, Labour and the Franchise'. *Eng. Hist. Rev.* xcii (1977), 725–39.

2283 BOOTH (WILLIAM). 'The Liberals and the 1923 General Election. 1. The Campaign'. *Contemp. Rev.* ccvi (1965), 247–53. 2. The Result. *Contemp. Rev.* ccvi (1965), 312–15.

2284 ROWE (E. A.). 'Broadcasting and the 1929 General Election'. *Ren. Mod. Studs* xii (1968), 108–19.

2285 HELLER (RICHARD). 'East Fulham Revisited'. *J. Contemp. Hist.* vi (1971), 172–96.

1935

2286 ROBERTSON (JAMES C.). 'The British General Election of 1935'. *J. Contemp. Hist.* ix (1974), 149–64. ˙

2287 HUMPHREYS (JOHN H.). The General Election 1935 and Constitutional Reform. 1936.

1945

2288 MCCALLUM (RONALD BUCHANAN) *and* READMAN (ALISON). The British General Election of 1945. Oxf. 1947.

2289 COLE (G. D. H.). 'Why Britain Went Socialist'. *Virginia Q. Rev.* 23 (1947), 509–20.

2290 GILBERT (BENTLEY BRINKERHOFF). 'Third Parties and Voters' Decisions: The Liberals and the General Election of 1945'. *J. Brit. Studs* 11 (1972), 131–41.

2291 ARNSTEIN (WALTER L.). 'The Liberals and the General Election of 1945: A Skeptical Note'. *J. Brit. Studs* xiv (1975), 120–6.

2292 GILBERT (BENTLEY BRINKERHOFF). 'The Liberals and the General Election of 1945: A Modest Rejoinder'. *J. Brit. Studs* xiv (1975), 127–8.

2293 PELLING (HENRY MATHISON). 'The 1945 General Election Reconsidered'. *Hist. J.* 23 (1980), 399–414.

2294 BURRIDGE (TREVOR). 'A Postscript to Potsdam: The Churchill–Laski Electoral Clash'. *J. Contemp. Hist.* 12 (1977), 725–39.

2295 HARRINGTON (WILLIAM) *and* YOUNG (PETER). The 1945 Revolution. 1978.

2296 McCULLOCH (GARY). 'Labour, the Left and the British General Election of 1945'. *J. Brit. Studs* 24 (1985), 465–89.

2297 SCHNEER (JONATHAN). 'The Labour Left and the General Election of 1945' in J. M. W. Bean, *ed*. The Political Culture of Modern Britain: Studies in Memory of Stephen Koss. 1987. 243–61.

2298 ROLF (DAVID). 'Birmingham Labour and the Background to the 1945 General Election', in Worlds of Labour: Essays in Birmingham Labour History. Anthony Wright and Richard Shackleton, *eds*. Birmingham. 1983. 127–55.

2299 BUSSEY (SARAH). 'The Labour Victory in Winchester in 1945'. *Southern Hist.* 8 (1986), 144–52.

1950

2300 NICHOLAS (HERBERT GEORGE). The British General Election of 1950. 1951.

2301 CHRIMES (STANLEY BERTRAM) *ed*. The General Election in Glasgow, February 1950. 1950.

2302 BENNEY (MARK) *et al*. How People Vote: A Study of Electoral Behaviour in Greenwich. 1956.

2303 RICHARDS (PETER GODFREY). 'General Election (1950)'. *Pol. Q.* 21 (1950), 114–21.

2304 BRAND (C. F.). 'The British General Election of 1950'. *S. Atl. Q.* 50 (1951), 478–98.

1951

2305 BUTLER (DAVID EDGEWORTH). The British General Election of 1951. 1952.

2306 WILLIAMS (J. R.). 'The British General Election of 1951: Candidates and Parties'. *Parl. Affs* 5 (1952), 480–94.

2307 BRAND (C. F.). 'The British General Election of 1951'. *S. Atl. Q.* 52 (1953), 29–53.

2308 JENKIN (T. P.). 'The British General Election of 1951'. *Western Pol. Q.* 5 (1952), 51–65.

2309 MILNE (R. S.) *and* MACKENZIE (H. C.). Straight Fight: A Study of Voting Behaviour in the Constituency of Bristol North-East at the General Election of 1951. 1954.

2310 CLEARY (E. J.) *and* POLLINS (H.). 'Liberal Voting at the General Election of 1951'. *Sociol. Rev.* n.s. 1 (1953), 27–41.

1955

2311 BUTLER (DAVID EDGEWORTH). The British General Election of 1955. 1955.

2312 MILNE (R. S.) *and* MACKENZIE (H. C.). Marginal Seat: A Study of Voting Behaviour in the Constituency of Bristol North-East at the General Election of 1955. 1958.

2313 BRAND (C. F.). 'The British General Election of 1955'. *S. Atl. Q.* 55 (1956), 289–312.

2314 BIRCH (ANTHONY H.), CAMPBELL (P. W.), *and* LUCAS (P. G.). 'The Popular Press in the British General Election of 1955'. *Pol. Studs* 4 (1956), 297–306.

1959

2315 BUTLER (DAVID EDGEWORTH) *and* ROSE (RICHARD). The British General Election of 1959. 1960.

2316 ABRAMS (MARK) *and* ROSE (RICHARD). Must Labour Lose? Harmondsworth. 1960.

2317 BRAND (C. F.). 'The British General Election of 1959'. *S. Atl. Q.* 59 (1960), 521–42

2318 McCALLUM (R. B.). 'Thoughts on the General Election'. *Contemp. Rev.* 196 (1959), 263–9.

1964

2319 BUTLER (DAVID EDGEWORTH) *and* KING (ANTHONY). The British General Election of 1964. 1965.

2320 BERRINGTON (HUGH B.). 'The General Election of 1964'. *Roy. Stats. Soc. J.* 128 (1965), 17–66.

2321 BRAND (C. F.). 'The British General Election of 1964'. *S. Atl. Q.* 64 (1965), 332–50.

2322 LEES (J. D.). 'Aspects of Third Party Campaigning in the 1964 General Election'. *Parl. Affs* 19 (1965–6), 83–90.

2323 EPSTEIN (LEON D.). 'The Nuclear Deterrent and the British General Election of 1964'. *J. Brit. Studs* 5 (1965), 139–63.

2324 HOLT (A. T.) *and* TURNER (J. E.). Political Parties in Action: The Battle of Barons Court. 1968.

1966

2325 BUTLER (DAVID EDGEWORTH) *and* KING (ANTHONY). The British General Election of 1966. 1966.

2326 BRAND (C. F.). 'The British General Election of 1966'. *S. Atl. Q.* 66 (1967), 131–47.

2327 BELOFF (MAX). 'Reflections on the British General Election 1966'. *Gvt and Opp.* 1 (1966), 529–45.

2328 BROMHEAD (PETER A.). 'The General Election of 1966'. *Parl. Affs* 19 (1965–6), 332–45.

1970

2329 BUTLER (DAVID EDGEWORTH) *and* PINTO-DUSCHINSKY (MICHAEL). The British General Election of 1970. 1971.

2330 BRAND (C. F.). 'The British General Election of 1970'. *S. Atl. Q.* 70 (1971), 350–64.

February 1974

2331 BUTLER (DAVID EDGEWORTH) *and* KAVANAGH (DENNIS). The British General Election of February 1974. 1974.

2332 ALT (JAMES E.), CREWE (IVOR), *and* SARLVIK (BO). 'Partisanship and Policy Choice: Issue Preference in the British Electorate, February 1974'. *Brit. J. Pol. Sci.* 6 (1976), 273–90.

2333 '"Angels in Plastic": The Liberal Surge in 1974'. *Pol. Studs* 25 (1977), 343–68.

2334 BERRINGTON (HUGH B.) *and* BEDEMAN (TREVOR). 'The February Election (1974)'. *Parl. Affs* 27 (1974), 317–32.

2335 JOHNSTON (R. J.). 'Campaign Expenditure and the Efficiency of Advertising at the 1974 Elections in England'. *Pol. Studs* 27 (1979), 114–19.

2336 MILLER (WILLIAM L.). 'The Religious Alignment in England at the General Elections of 1974'. *Parl. Affs* 30 (1977), 258–68.

2337 LEMIEUX (PETER H.). 'Political Issues and Liberal Support in the February 1974 British General Election'. *Pol. Studs* xxv (1977), 323–42.

October 1974
2338 BUTLER (DAVID EDGEWORTH) *and* KAVANAGH (DENNIS). The British General Election of October 1974. 1975.

1979
2339 BUTLER (DAVID EDGEWORTH) *and* KAVANAGH (DENNIS). The British General Election of 1979. 1980.

2340 MITCHELL (AUSTIN). Can Labour Win Again? 1979.

2341 McALLISTER (IAN) *and* MUGHAN (ANTHONY). 'Attitudes, Issues, and Labour Party Decline in England 1974–79'. *Comp. Pol. Studs* 18 (1985), 37–57.

2342 PULZER (PETER J. G.). 'British General Election of 1979: Back to the Fifties or on to the Eighties? *Parl. Affs* 32 (1979), 361–75.

1983
2343 BUTLER (DAVID EDGEWORTH) *and* KAVANAGH (DENNIS). The British General Election of 1983. 1984.

2344 RANNEY (AUSTIN) *ed.* Britain at the Polls 1983. Durham, N.C. 1985.

2345 —— 'Review Article: Thirty Years of Psephology'. *Brit. J. Pol. Sci.* 6 (1976), 217–30. [Concentrates on the Nuffield Election series.].

2346 McALLISTER (IAN) *and* ROSE (RICHARD). The Nationwide Competition for Votes: The 1983 British General Election. 1984.

2347 JOHNSON (ROBERT J.). The Geography of English Politics: The 1983 General Election.

2348 —— 'Places, Campaigns and Votes'. *Pol. Geog. Q.* 5 (1986), 105–17.

2349 MILLER (WILLIAM L.). 'There Was No Alternative: The British General Election in 1983'. *Parl. Affs* 4 (1983), 364–84.

2350 LIVINGSTONE (KEN) *and* ALI (TARIQ). 'Why Labour Lost'. *New Left Rev.* 140 (1983), 23–39.

2351 RASMUSSEN (JORGEN S.). 'How Remarkable was 1983?'. *Parl. Affs* 36 (1983), 371–88.

2352 SANDERS (DAVID), WARD (HUGH), *and* MARSH (DAVID). 'Government Popularity and the Falklands War: A Reassessment'. *Brit. J. Pol. Sci.* 17 (1987), 281–314.

2353 THATCHER (CAROL). Diary of an Election: With Margaret Thatcher on the Campaign Trail. 1983.

2354 LAVER (MICHAEL). 'Party Policy, Polarisation and the Breaking of Moulds: The 1983 British Party Manifestos in Context'. *Parl. Affs* 37 (1984), 33–9.

1987
2355 CREWE (IVOR) *and* HARROP (MARTIN) *eds.* Political Communications: The General Election Campaign of 1987. Camb. 1989.

By-elections
2356 COOK (CHRIS) *and* RAMSDEN (JOHN) *eds.* By-elections in British Politics. 1973.

2357 MUGHAM (ANTHONY). Party and Participation in British Elections. 1986. [Extensive evidence on by-elections.].

2358 NORRIS (PIPPA). British By-Elections: The Volatile Electorate. Oxf. 1990.

5. GENERAL

2359 PULZER (PETER JULIUS GEORGE). Political Representation and Elections in Britain. 1967. 3rd edn 1975.

2360 MOODIE (GRAEME COCHRANE) *and* STUDDERT-KENNEDY (GERALD). Opinions, Publics and Pressure Groups: An Essay on Vox Populi and Representative Government. 1970.

2361 ALDERMAN (GEOFFREY). British Elections: Myth and Reality. 1978.

2362 BUDGE (IAN). 'Strategic Issues and Votes: British General Elections 1950–1979'. *Comp. Pol. Studs* 15 (1982), 249–82.

2363 CURTICE (JOHN) *and* STEED (MICHAEL). 'Electoral Choice and the Production of Government: The Changing Operation of the Electoral System in the United Kingdom since 1955'. *Brit. J. Pol. Sci.* 12 (1982), 249–82.

2364 BUTLER (DAVID EDGEWORTH). British General Elections since 1945. 1989.

Regional
2365 JONES (BETI). Etholiadau Seneddol yng Nghymru 1900–1975. Talybont. 1977.

2366 HARVIE (CHRISTOPHER). 'Labour in Scotland During the Second World War'. *Hist. J.* 26 (1983), 921–44.

2367 SCOTT (ROGER). 'The 1970 General Election in Ulster'. *Parl. Affs* (1970–1), 16–32.

2368 JAENSCH (DEAN). 'The Scottish Vote 1974: A Realigning Party System'. *Pol. Studs* 24 (1976), 306–19.

2369 DENVER (D. T.). 'Political Communication: Scottish Local Newspapers and the General Election of February 1974'. *Scot. J. Sociol.* 2 (1977), 11–30.

2370 TAYLOR (A. H.). 'Some Recent Parliamentary Changes and the February 1974 General Election'. *Cambria* 1 (1974), 85–97.

2371 JOHNSTON (R. J.). 'The Electoral Geography of an Election Campaign: Scotland in October 1974'. *Scot. Geog. Mag.* 93 (1977), 98–109.

2372 BRAND (JACK) *and* MILLER (WILLIAM L.). The Labour Party in Scotland in 1979: Advance or Retreat? Glasgow. 1983.

2373 WALLER (ROBERT). The Atlas of British Politics. 1985.

2374 COX (W. HARVEY). 'The 1983 General Election in Northern Ireland: Anatomy and Consequences'. *Parl. Affs* 37 (1983), 40–58.

2375 COUSINS (P. E.). 'London Votes 1983: The General Election'. *Lond. Rev. Pub. Admin* 16 (1984), 2–13.

2376 Etholiad Cyffredinol 1987 yng Nghymru: The 1987 General Election in Wales. Aberystwyth. 1988.

European Parliament

2377 CRAIG (F. W. S.) and MACHIE (T. T.) *eds.* Europe Votes I. Chichester. 1980.

2378 CRAIG (F. W. S.) *ed.* Europe Votes II. Chichester. 1985.

2379 The Times Guide to the European Parliament. 1980.

2380 BUTLER (DAVID EDGEWORTH) and MARQUAND (DAVID). European Elections and British Politics. 1981.

2381 COOK (CHRIS) and FRANCIS (MARY). The First European Elections: A Handbook and Guide. 1979.

2382 BUTLER (DAVID EDGEWORTH) and JOWETT (PAUL). Party Strategies in Britain: A Study of the 1984 European Elections. 1985.

2383 HEARL (DEREK). 'The United Kingdom' in Juliet Lodge, *ed.* Direct Elections to the European Parliament 1984. 1986.

2384 LODGE (JULIET). 'Euro-Elections and the European Parliament: The Dilemma over Turnout and Powers'. *Parl. Affs* 38 (1984), 40–55.

Referenda

2385 GOODHART (PHILIP). The Referendum. 1971.

2386 ALDERSON (STANLEY). Yea or Nay? Referenda in the United Kingdom. 1975.

2387 'The Referendum Under the British Constitution'. *Contemp. Rev.* ccxxiii (1973), 247–50.

2388 GRIMOND (JO) and NEVE (BRIAN). The Referendum. 1975.

2389 BUTLER (DAVID EDGEWORTH) and KITZINGER (UWE). The 1975 Referendum. 1976.

2390 KING (ANTHONY). Britain Says Yes. Washington, DC. 1977.

2391 GOODHART (PHILIP). Full Hearted Consent: The Story of the Referendum Campaign and the Campaign for the Referendum. 1976.

2392 BOGDANOR (VERNON). The People and the Party System: The Referendum and Electoral Reform in British Politics. Camb. 1981.

2393 BRISTOW (STEPHEN L.). 'Partisanship, Participation and Legitimacy in Britain's E.E.C. Referendum'. *J. Com. Market Studs* ixvv (1976), 297–310.

2394 WRIGHT (E.). 'The British Referendum: The Constitutional Significance'. *Parliamentarian* lvi (1975), 159–66.

H. REGIONALISM AND GENERAL* STUDIES ON DEVOLUTION

The methodological problems posed by an 'all-British' bibliographical approach have been alluded to in the initial introduction. The importance of the 'sub-central' level has been increasing in British political life since 1945, though in contentious ways. The distinctive features of the political life of Wales and Scotland have become more apparent and it has therefore been found appropriate to accommodate this development by means of a separate section. Politics and government in these areas cannot be understood outside the United Kingdom context but nor can they be understood without a recognition of their distinctive features. It must also be evident that questions of political identity are in turn linked to economic performance and much additional material relating to this aspect of 'regionalism' will be found in the chapter on the Economy and Industry.

The issues which can loosely be linked under the heading 'devolution' have fluctuated in their importance but have remained of underlying significance. It is within this section, too, that it has been thought most appropriate to include as a separate category the politics of Northern Ireland where again, even more strongly, local and United Kingdom issues intermingle and have produced various 'solutions' whose permanence has been temporary. At a certain level, it is impossible to detach the politics of Northern Ireland from the politics of the Irish Free State/the Republic of Ireland. It has already been explained that coverage of that state's internal development has not been attempted, yet in this section some items have been included since they have a direct bearing on the triangular relationship between Belfast, Dublin, and London.

* For specific studies of Scottish and Welsh Devolution proposals see appropriate section below.

1. GENERAL

2395 HECHTER (MICHAEL). 'Regional Inequality and National Integration: The Case of the British Isles'. *J. Soc. Hist.* 5 (1971), 96–117.

2396 'The Persistence of Regionalism in the British Isles'. *Amer. J. Sociol.* 79 (1973), 319–42.

2397 PEATE (IORWERTH). Studies in Regional Consciousness and Environment. Oxf. 1930.

2398 KOLINSKY (MARTIN) *ed.* Divided Loyalties: British Regional Assertion and European Integration. Manch. 1978.

2399 NAIRN (TOM). The Break-Up of Britain: Crisis and Neo-Nationalism 1965–1975. 1977.

2400 WISEMAN (HERBERT VICTOR). 'Regional Government in the United Kingdom'. *Parl. Affs* 19 (1965–6), 58–62.

2401 CROSS (J. A.). 'The Regional Decentralisation of British Government Departments'. *Public Admin* 48 (1970), 423–41.

2402 LAW (CHRISTOPHER M.). British Regional Development Since World War One. Newton Abbot. 1980.

2403 FAWCETT (CHARLES BUNGAY). Provinces of England: A Study of Some Geographical Aspects of Devolution. 1919. Rev. edn 1960.

2404 HOGWOOD (BRIAN W.) *and* KEATING (MICHAEL) *eds.* Regional Government in England. Oxf. 1982.

2405 McDONALD (J. F.). The Lack of Political Identity in English Regions: Evidence from MPs. Glasg. 1979.

2406 MACKINTOSH (JOHN PITCAIRN). The Devolution of Power. 1968.

2407 DALYELL (TAM). Devolution: The End of Britain. 1977.

2408 BOGDANOR (VERNON). The Constitution and Political Consequence of Devolution. 1978.

2409 —— Devolution. 1979.

2410 CRAVEN (EDWARD). Regional Devolution and Social Policy. 1975.

2411 BALSOM (DENIS) *and* McALLISTER (IAN). 'The Scottish and Welsh Devolution Referenda of 1979'. *Parl. Affs* 32 (1979).

2412 U.K. POLICY STUDIES INSTITUTE. Westminster and Devolution. 1978.

2413 U.K. ROYAL COMMISSION ON THE CONSTITUTION 1969–1973. Devolution within the United Kingdom: Some Alternatives for Discussion. 1974. [HMSO].

2414 U.K. LORD PRESIDENT OF THE COUNCIL, The SCOTTISH OFFICE and The WELSH OFFICE. Our Changing Democracy: Devolution to Scotland and Wales. 1975. [HMSO].

2415 Devolution to Scotland and Wales: Supplementary Statement. 1976. [HMSO].

2416 DRUCKER (HENRY MATTHEW). The Politics of Nationalism and Devolution. 1980.

2417 HEALD (DAVID). Making Devolution Work. 1976.

2. COMBINED STUDIES OF CELTIC NATIONALISM

2418 COUPLAND (*SIR* REGINALD). Welsh and Scottish Nationalism: A Study. 1954.

2419 EDWARDS (OWEN DUDLEY) *et al.* Celtic Nationalism. 1968.

2420 HECHTER (MICHAEL). Internal Colonialism: The Celtic Fringe in British National Development 1536–1966. 1975.

2421 STURM (ROLAND). Nationalismus in Schottland und Wales 1966–1988: Eine Analyse Seiner Ursachen und Konsequenzen. Bochum. 1981.

2422 GRANT (W. P.) *and* PREECE (R. J. C.). 'Welsh and Scottish Nationalism'. *Parl. Affs* 21 (1968), 255–63.

2423 MISHLER (W.). 'Scotching Nationalism in the British Parliament: Crosscutting Cleavages among MP's'. *Legislative Studs Q.* 8 (1983), 5–28.

2424 ELLIS (PETER BERRESFORD). Celtic Inheritance. 1985.

2425 MACNEILL (EOIN). Celtic Ireland. Dublin/Lond. 1921.

2426 O'LEARY (CORNELIUS). Celtic Nationalism. Belfast. 1982.

2427 CELTIC LEAGUE ANNUAL. 1969–1972.

2428 THOMPSON (FRANCIS G.) *ed.* The Significance of Freedom. Dublin. 1969.

2429 —— *Ed.* The Celt in the Seventies. Dublin. 1970.

2430 —— *Ed.* Celtic Unity Ten Years On. Dublin. 1971.

2431 —— *Ed.* The Celtic Experience Past and Present. Dublin. 1972.

2432 DAVIES (ELWYN). Celtic Studies in Wales: A Survey Prepared for the Second International Congress of Celtic Studies. Cardiff. 1963.

3. SCOTLAND

(a) General and Political History

2433 FERGUSON (WILLIAM). Scotland 1689 to the Present. (Edinburgh History of Scotland Volume 4). Edin./Lond. 1968. 2nd edn 1975.

2434 PRYDE (GEORGE SMITH). Scotland from 1603 to the Present Day. 1962. [A New History of Scotland, Vol. 3.].

2435 CAMPBELL (ROY HUTCHESON). Scotland Since 1707. Oxf. 1965.

2436 MITCHISON (ROSALIND). A History of Scotland. 1970. 2nd edn 1982.

2437 FINLAYSON (IAIN). The Scots. 1987.

2438 GLOVER (JANET REAVELEY). The Story of Scotland. 1960. Rev. edn 1977.

2439 MACKIE (JOHN DUNCAN). A History of Scotland. Harmondsworth. 1964. 2nd edn 1968.

2440 KELLAS (JAMES GRANT). Modern Scotland: The Nation Since 1870. 1968. 2nd edn 1980.

2441 —— The Scottish Political System. Camb. 1973. 4th edn 1989.

2442 HARVIE (CHRISTOPHER). No Gods and Precious Few Heroes: Scotland 1914–1980. [New History of Scotland Vol. 8.] 1981.

2443 —— Scotland and Nationalism: Scottish Society and Politics 1701–1977. 1977.

2444 HANCOCK (PHILIP D.). A Bibliography of Works on Scotland 1916–1950. 2 vols Edin. 1960.

2445 MacNEILL (DUNCAN). The Scottish Realm: An Approach to the Political and Constitutional History of Scotland. Glasg. 1947.

2446 FRY (MICHAEL). Patronage and Principle: A Political History of Modern Scotland. Aberd. 1987.

2447 REID (JAMES MacARTHUR). Scotland's Progress: The Survival of a Nation. 1971.

2448 SMOUT (T. CHRISTOPHER). A Century of the Scottish People 1830–1950. 1986.

2449 WHITTINGTON (GRAEME) *and* WHITE (I. D.). A Historical Geography of Scotland. 1983.

2450 TURNOCK (DAVID). The Historical Geography of Scotland Since 1707: Geographical Aspects of Modernisation. Camb. 1982.

2451 —— The New Scotland. Newton Abbot. 1979.

2452 GORDON (GEORGE) *and* DICKS (BRIAN) *eds.* Scottish Urban History. Aberd. 1983.

2453 ADAMS (IAN H.). The Making of Urban Scotland. 1978.

2454 HUMES (WALTER M.) *and* PATTERSON (HAMISH M.) *eds.* Scottish Culture and Scottish Education 1800–1980. Edin. 1983.

2455 McARTHUR (COLIN). Scotch Reels: Scotland in Cinema and Television. 1982.

2456 STEEL (TOM). Scotland's Story. 1984. [Linked to STV/Channel 4 TV series.].

2457 SCOTT (PAUL HENDERSON). In Bed with an Elephant. [Anglo-Scottish Relations 1200–1984.] Edin. 1985.

2458 CLOUGH (MONICA). The Field of Thistles: Scotland's Past and Scotland's People. Edin. 1983.

2459 CARGILL (KENNETH). Scotland 2000: Eight Views on the State of a Nation. Glasg. 1987.

2460 MOODY (DAVID). Scottish Local History: An Introductory Guide. 1986.

2461 KAY (BILLY). Odyssey: Voices from Scotland's Recent Past. Edin. 1982.

2462 WITHERS (CHARLES W. J.). Gaelic in Scotland, 1698–1981: The Geographical History of a Language. Edin. 1984.

2463 —— Gaelic Scotland and the Transformation of a Culture Region. 1988.

2464 CAMPBELL (ROY HUTCHESON) *ed.* Scottish Industrial History: A Miscellany. 1978.

2465 SCOTTISH HISTORICAL REVIEW. 1903/4–.

2466 BRANDER (MICHAEL). The Emigrant Scots. 1982.

2467 DONALDSON (GORDON). The Scots Overseas. 1966.

2468 CAGE (R. A.). The Scots Abroad. 1985.

2469 HARPER (MARJORY). Emigration from North-East Scotland. Aberd. 1988.

2470 HEALD (DAVID) *and* KEATING (MICHAEL J.). 'The Impact of the Devolution Commitment on the Scottish Body Politic'. *Austral. J. Pol. Hist.* 26 (1980), 386–402.

2471 KEATING (MICHAEL J.). 'Administrative Devolution in Practice: The Secretary of State for Scotland and the Scottish Office'. *Public Admin* 54 (1976), 133–45.

2472 JUDGE (DAVID) *and* FINLAYSON (D. A.). 'Scottish Members of Parliament: Problems of Devolution'. *Parl. Affs* 28 (1975), 278–92.

2473 MERCER (JOHN). Scotland: The Devolution of Power. 1978.

2474 BOCHEL (JOHN). The Referendum Experience: Scotland 1979. Aberd. 1981.

2475 BUDGE (IAN) *and* URWIN (DEREK W.). Scottish Political Behaviour. 1966.

2476 MILLER (WILLIAM L.). The End of British Politics? Scots and English Political Behaviour in the Seventies. Oxf. 1981.

2477 FERGUSSON (*Sir* JAMES). The Sixteen Peers of Scotland: An Account of the Elections of the Representative Peers of Scotland, 1707–1959. Oxf. 1960.

2478 BURNS (JAMES H.). 'The Scottish Committees of the House of Commons, 1948–1959'. *Pol. Studs* 8 (1960), 272–96.

2479 EDWARDS (G. E.). 'The Scottish Grand Committee, 1958 to 1970'. *Parl. Affs* 25 (1972), 303–25.

2480 POTTINGER (GEORGE). The Secretaries of State for Scotland, 1926–1976: Fifty Years of the Scottish Office. Edin. 1979.

2481 GIBSON (JOHN SIBBALD). The Thistle and the Crown: A History of the Scottish Office. Edin. 1985.

2482 CAMPBELL (ROY HUTCHESON). 'The Scottish Office and the Special Areas in the 1930's'. *Hist. J.* (1979), 167–83.

2483 McKAY (DONALD IAIN). Scotland 1980: The Economics of Self-Government. Edin. 1977.

2484 —— Scotland: The Framework for Change. Edin. 1979.

2485 SILLARS (JIM). Scotland: The Case for Optimism. Edin. 1986.

2486 MILLER (WILLIAM L.) *et al.* Oil and the Scottish Voter 1974–1979. 1980. [SSRC].

2487 PARRY (RICHARD). Scottish Political Facts. Edin. 1988.

2488 SCOTTISH COUNCIL FOR SOCIAL SERVICE. Party Lines: A Guide to Contacts in the Political Parties of Scotland. Edin. 1981. Rev. 1982. 1984. [1984. edn pub. by SCOTTISH COUNCIL FOR COMMUNITY AND VOLUNTARY ORGANISATIONS.].

2489 DICKSON (TONY) *ed.* Scottish Capitalism: Class, State and Nation from before the Union to the Present. 1980.

2490 —— *Ed.* Capital and Class in Scotland. Edin. 1982.

2491 HOGWOOD (BRIAN). The Tartan Fringe: Quangos and other Associated Animals in Scotland. Glasg. 1979.

(b) *Scottish Nationalism and the Scottish National Party*

2492 PRYDE (GEORGE SMITH). 'The Development of Nationalism in Scotland'. *Sociol. Rev.* 1st ser. 27 (1935), 264–80.

2493 HANHAM (HAROLD JOHN). Scottish Nationalism. 1969.

2494 AGNEW (JOHN A.). 'Political Regionalism and Scottish Nationalism in Gaelic Scotland'. *Can. Rev. Studies in Nationalism* 8 (1981), 115–29.

2495 WOLFE (JAMES NATHANIEL) *ed.* Government and Nationalism in Scotland: An Enquiry by Members of the University of Edinburgh. Edin. 1969.

2496 BRAND (JACK). The National Movement in Scotland. 1978.

2497 TURNER (ARTHUR CAMPBELL). Scottish Home Rule. Oxf. 1952.

2498 FRASER (K. C.). A Bibliography of the Scottish National Movement 1844–1973. Dollar. 1976.

2499 McLEAN (IAIN). 'The Rise and Fall of the Scottish National Party'. *Pol. Studs* 18 (1970), 357–72.

2500 WEBB (KEITH). The Growth of Nationalism in Scotland. Glasg. 1977.

2501 YOUNG (JAMES D.). 'Marxism and the Scottish National Question'. *J. Contemp. Hist.* 18 (1983), 141–63.

2502 BOCHEL (JOHN M.) *and* DENVER (D. T.). 'The Decline of the Scottish National Party—An Alternative View'. *Pol. Studs* 20 (1972), 311–16.

2503 MULLIN (W. A. ROGER). 'The Scottish National Party'. Ch. in Henry Matthew Drucker, *ed.* Multi-party Britain. 1979.

2504 MacCORMACK (NEIL). The Scottish Debate: Essays on Scottish Nationalism. 1970.

2505 McCRONE (GAVIN). Scotland's Future: The Economics of Nationalism. N.Y. 1969.

2506 WOLFE (BILLY). Scotland Lives. Edin. 1973. [History of the SNP.].

2507 MacCORMACK (JOHN MACDONALD). The Flag in the Wind: The Story of the National Movement in Scotland. 1955.

2508 PAMPHLETS RELATING TO SCOTTISH NATIONALISM, 1844–1973. Wakefield, EP Microform. 1978.

2509 BRYAN (GORDON). Scottish Nationalism and Cultural Identity in the Twentieth Century: An Annotated Bibliography of Secondary Sources. Westport, Conn./Lond. 1984.

2510 SCOTTISH NATIONAL PARTY. Choose Scotland: The Challenge of Independence: SNP Manifesto, 1983. Edin. 1983.

2511 —— Play the Scottish Card: SNP General Election Manifesto, 1987. Edin. 1987.

2512 —— Scotland's Future: Independence in Europe: SNP Manifesto, European Elections 15 June 1989. Edin. 1989.

(c) *Scottish Labour History and the Labour Party in Scotland*

2513 DONNACHIE (IAN), HARVIE (CHRISTOPHER), *and* WOOD (IAN S.). *eds.* Forward! Labour Politics in Scotland 1888–1988. Edin. 1989.

2514 HARVIE (CHRISTOPHER). 'Labour in Scotland During the Second World War'. *Hist. J.* 26 (1983), 921–44.

2515 YOUNG (JAMES D.). The Rousing of the Scottish Working Class. 1979.

2516 MIDDLEMAS (KEITH). The Clydesiders: A Leftwing Struggle for Parliamentary Power. 1965.

2517 McLEAN (IAIN). The Legend of Red Clydeside. Edin. 1983.

2518 UNGER (DAVID CHARLES). The Roots of Red Clydeside: Economic and Social Relations and Working Class Politics in the West of Scotland 1900–1919. 1981.

2519 REID (A.). 'Glasgow Socialism'. *Soc. Hist.* 11 (1986), 89–97.

2520 JOHNSTON (THOMAS). The History of the Working Classes in Scotland. Glasg. 1920. 4th edn 1946.

2521 MARWICK (WILLIAM HUTTON). A Short History of Labour in Scotland. Edin. 1967.

2522 DRUCKER (HENRY MATTHEW). Breakaway: The Scottish Labour Party. Edin. 1978.

2523 BRAND (JACK) *and* MILLER (WILLIAM). The Labour Party in Scotland in 1979: Advance or Retreat? Glasg. 1983.

2524 HOLFORD (JOHN). Reshaping Labour: Organisation, Work and Politics: Edinburgh in the Great War and After. 1987.

2525 STUART (JAMES GIBB). The Mind Benders: The Gradual Revolution and Scottish Independence. Glasg. 1979.

2526 HOWELL (DAVID). A Lost Left: Three Studies in Socialism and Nationalism. Manch. 1986. [Two of the Case Studies in this book cover John Maclean and John Wheatley.].

2527 MILTON (NAN). John Maclean. 1973. [By his daughter.].

2528 BROOM (JOHN). John MacLean. Loanhead. 1973.

2529 MCGRATH (JOHN). The Game's a Bogey: 7:84's John MacLean Show. Edin. 1975.

2530 LAW (T. S.). Homage to John Maclean. Edin. 1973. Repr. 1979.

2531 MARWICK (ARTHUR JOHN BRERETON). 'James Maxton: His Place in Scottish Labour History'. *Scot. Hist. Rev.* 43 (1964), 25–43.

2532 MCALLISTER (GILBERT). James Maxton: The Portrait of a Rebel. 1935.

2533 MCNAIR (JOHN). James Maxton: The Beloved Rebel. 1955.

2534 BROWN (GORDON). Maxton: A Biography. Edin. 1986.

2535 KNOX (WILLIAM). James Maxton. Manch. 1987.

2536 LABOUR PARTY. Scottish Election Special. 1964.

2537 LABOUR PARTY IN SCOTLAND. The Better Way for Scotland: The Labour Party Manifesto for Scotland, 1979. Glasg. 1979.

2538 —— Scotland Will Win: Manifesto of the Labour Party in Scotland, 1987. Glasg. 1987.

2539 LABOUR PARTY SCOTTISH COUNCIL. Labour: The Real Voice of Scotland in Europe: Labour's Campaign Document for the European Elections, 1989. Glasg. 1989.

(d) The Conservative Party in Scotland

2540 WARD (JOHN TOWER). The First Century: A History of Scottish Tory Organisation, 1882–1982. Edin. 1982.

2541 WARNER (GERALD). The Scottish Tory Party: A History. 1988. [Foreword by Margaret Thatcher.].

2542 CONSERVATIVE AND UNIONIST PARTY. The Conservative Manifesto for Scotland, 1983. 1983.

2543 (Scottish Constitutional Committee) Scotland's Government: A Report . . . 1970.

(e) Scottish Liberals and the Social Democrats.

2544 SCOTTISH LIBERAL PARTY. The Scottish Liberal Manifesto. Edin. 1979.

2545 SOCIAL DEMOCRATIC PARTY and the SCOTTISH LIBERAL PARTY. Working Together for Scotland: A Joint Programme for Government. 1983.

4. WALES

(a) Government and Politics

2546 MORGAN (KENNETH OWEN). Wales 1880–1980: The Rebirth of a Nation. Oxf./Cardiff. 1981.

2547 —— Wales in British Politics, 1868–1922. Cardiff. 1963. 3rd edn 1980.

2548 —— 'Post-War Reconstruction in Wales, 1918 and 1945'. Ch. in The Working Class in Modern British History: Essays in honour of Henry Pelling. Jay M. Winter, *ed.* Camb. 1983.

2549 —— 'Peace Movements in Wales, 1899–1945'. *Welsh Hist. Rev.* 10 (1980/81), 398–430.

2550 JONES (GARETH ELWYN). People, Protest and Politics in the Twentieth Century: Case Studies in Twentieth Century Wales. Llandysul. 1987.

2551 —— Modern Wales: A Concise History 1585–1979. Camb. 1984.

2552 WILLIAMS (GWYN ALFRED). The Welsh in their History. 1982. [Collected Papers.].

2553 —— 'Women Workers in Wales 1968–1982'. *Welsh Hist. Rev.* 11 (1982/3), 530–48.

2554 JONES (IDRIS DEANE). Modern Welsh History . . . [1715 to the Present Day.] 1934.

2555 WILLIAMS (DAVID). A History of Modern Wales, 1485–1939. 1950.

2556 DAVIES (R. R.), GRIFFITHS (R. A.), JONES (IEUAN GWYNEDD), *and* MORGAN (KENNETH OWEN) *eds.* Welsh Society and Nationhood: Historical Essays Presented to Glanmor Williams. Cardiff. 1984.

2557 JENKINS (GERAINT H.) *and* SMITH (J. BEVERLEY). Politics and Society in Wales, 1840–1922: Essays in honour of Ieuan Gwynedd Jones. Cardiff. 1988.

2558 MORRIS (JAN). The Matter of Wales. 1984.

2559 LUCAS (ROWLAND). The Voice of a Nation?: A Concise Account of the BBC in Wales, 1923–1973. Llandysul. 1983.

2560 MOR-O'BRIEN (ANTHONY). 'The Merthyr Boroughs Election, November 1915'. *Welsh Hist. Rev.* 12 (1985), 538–66.

2561 PARRY (CYRIL). The Radical Tradition in Welsh Politics: A Study of Liberal and Labour Politics in Gwynedd, 1900–1920. Hull. 1970.

2562 JONES (J. GRAHAM). 'Wales and the New Liberalism, 1926–1929'. *Nat. Lib. Wales J.* 22 (1982), 321–46.

2563 —— 'Wales and "War Socialism", 1926–1929'. *Welsh Hist. Rev.* 11 (1982), 173–99.

2564 MORGAN (KENNETH OWEN). 'Cardiganshire Politics: The Liberal Ascendancy, 1885–1923'. *Ceredigion* 5 (1967), 311–46.

2565 —— 'The New Liberalism and the Challenge of Labour: The Welsh Experience, 1885–1929'. *Welsh Hist. Rev.* 6 (1973), 288–312.

2566 STEAD (PETER). 'Working Class Leadership in South Wales 1900–1920'. *Welsh. Hist. Rev.* 6 (1972), 329–53.

2567 COX (IDRIS). The Fight for Socialism in South Wales, 1848–1948. Cardiff. 1948.

2568 —— Forward to a New Life for South Wales. Cardiff. 1944. [Communist Party of Great Britain, South Wales Committee.].

2569 —— Drive the Spectre from Wales. 1947. [CPGB, Wales Cttee.].

2570 GOTTS (G. L.). Party Politics in Local Government in South Wales, with Special Reference to Cardiff, Glamorgan and Pontypridd. Cardiff. 1970.

2571 RANDALL (P. J.). 'Wales in the Structure of Central Government'. *Public Admin* I (1972), 353–71.

2572 MADGWICK (PETER JONES). Government by Consultation: The Case of Wales. Glasg. 1979.

2573 MADGWICK (PETER JONES), GRIFFITHS (NON), and WALKER (VALERIE). The Politics of Rural Wales: A Study of Cardiganshire. 1973.

2574 WILLIAMS (D. G. T.). 'Wales and Legislative Devolution'. *Cambrian Law Rev.* 6 (1975).

2575 OSMOND (JOHN). Creative Conflict: The Politics of Welsh Devolution. Llandysul/Lond. 1978.

2576 JONES (J. BARRY). The Welsh Veto: The Politics of the Devolution Campaign in Wales. Glasg. 1979.

2577 FOULKES (DAVID), JONES (J. BARRY), and WILFORD (R.). The Welsh Veto: The Wales Act 1978 and the Referendum. Cardiff. 1983.

2578 HUGHES (CLEDWYN) *Baron Cledwyn of Penrhos.* The Referendum: The End of an Era: A Lecture . . . Cardiff. 1980.

2579 THOMAS (IAN C.). The Creation of the Welsh Office: Conflicting Purposes in Institutional Change. Glasg. 1981.

2580 EVANS (THOMAS JOHN). Sir Rhys Hopkin Morris: . . . the Man and his Character. Llandysul. 1958.

2581 MOR-O'BRIEN (ANTHONY). ' "Conchie": Emrys Hughes and the First World War'. *Welsh Hist. Rev.* 13 (1986/7), 328–52.

2582 JAMES (ARNOLD J.) and THOMAS (JOHN E.). Wales at Westminster: A History of Parliamentary Representation of Wales 1801–1979. Llandysul. 1982.

2583 BALSOM (DENIS) *and* BURCH (MARTIN). A Political and Electoral Handbook for Wales. Farnborough. 1980.

2584 COX (KEVIN). Geography, Social Contexts and Welsh Voting Behaviour 1861–1951. Brussels. 1967.

2585 THOMAS (G. H.). 'The Changing Pattern of Parliamentary Representation in Wales, 1945–1966'. *Swansea Geog.* 6 1968.

2586 U.K. BOUNDARY COMMISSION FOR WALES. 1983 Review of European Assembly Constituencies. 1983.

2587 GEORGE (K. D.) and MAINWARING (LYNN) *eds.* The Welsh Economy. Cardiff. 1988.

2588 REES (GARETH). Poverty and Social Inequality in Wales. 1980.

2589 WILLIAMS (GLYN). Social and Cultural Change in Contemporary Wales. 1980.

2590 THOMAS (NED). The Welsh Extremist: A Culture in Crisis. 1971.

2591 WELSH HISTORICAL REVIEW. 1960–.

(b) Welsh Nationalism

2592 CHAPPELL (EDGAR LEYSHON). Wake Up Wales!: A Survey of Welsh Home Rule Activities. 1934.

2593 JENKINS (R. T.). 'The Development of Nationalism in Wales'. *Sociol. Rev.* 1st ser. 27 (1935), 162–82.

2594 DANIEL (JOHN EDWARD). Welsh Nationalism, What it Stands for. 1937.

2595 BELL (*SIR* HAROLD IDRIS). 'Welsh Nationalism Today'. Ch. in The Crisis of Our Time and other Essays. 1954.

2596 EDWARDS (H. W. J.). 'The Course of Welsh Nationalism Today'. *Dublin Rev.* 228 (1954), 268–80.

2597 POWELL (W. R.). 'Nationalism in Wales'. *Contemp. Rev.* 202, (1956), 97–106.

2598 DAVIES (EDNYFED HUDSON). 'Welsh Nationalism'. *Pol. Q.* 39 (1968), 322–32.

2599 CONNOLLY (L. W.). 'Politics and Royalty: Welsh Nationalism and the Investiture of the Prince of Wales, 1969'. *Queen's Q.* 76 (1969), 412–23.

2600 MORGAN (KENNETH OWEN). 'Welsh Nationalism, the Historical Background'. *J. Contemp. Hist.* 6 (1971), 153–72.

2601 BUTT PHILIP (ALAN). The Welsh Question: Nationalism in Welsh Politics, 1945–1970. Cardiff. 1975.

2602 MAYO (PATRICIA ELTON). The Roots of Identity: Three National Movements in Contemporary European Politics. 1974. [One of the Case Studies is on Welsh Nationalism.].

2603 MORGAN (WILLIAM JOHN) *ed.* The Welsh Dilemma: Some Essays on Nationalism in Wales. Llandybie. 1973.

2604 WILLIAMS (COLIN H.). 'Cultural Nationalism in Wales'. *Can. Rev. Studies in Nationalism* 4 (1976), 15–38.

2605 —— National Separatism. Cardiff. 1982.

2606 DAVIES (D. HYWEL). The Welsh Nationalist Party, 1925–1945: A Call to Nationhood. Cardiff. 1983.

2607 JONES (J. GRAHAM). 'Forming Plaid Cymru: Laying the Foundations, 1926–1936'. *Nat. Lib. Wales J.* 22 (1982), 427–61.

2608 'Forming Plaid Cymru: Searching for a Policy, 1926–1930'. *Nat. Lib. Wales J.* 23 (1983), 175–208.

2609 JONES (JOHN EDWARD). 1925–1955: Cylchwyn Plaid Cymru. Cardiff. 1955.

2610 BALSOM (DENIS). 'Plaid Cymru: The Welsh National Party'. Ch. in Henry Matthew Drucker, *ed.* Multi-party Britain. 1979.

2611 —— The Nature and Distribution of Support for Plaid Cymru. Glasg. 1979.

2612 OSMOND (JOHN). The Centralist Enemy. Ammanford. 1974.

2613 ELLIS (PETER BERRESFORD). Wales, A Nation Again: The Nationalist Struggle for Freedom. 1968.

5. THE ISLE OF MAN: GOVERNMENT AND POLITICS

2614 YOUNG (GEORGE VAUGHAN CHICHESTER). Subject Guide and Chronological Table Relating to the Acts of the Tynwald, 1776–1975. Douglas. 1977.

2615 CORRAN (HENRY STANLEY). The Isle of Man. Newton Abbot. 1977.

2616 KINVIG (ROBERT HENRY). The Isle of Man: A Social, Cultural and Political History. L/pool. 1944. 2nd edn 1950. 3rd edn 1975. Repr. 1978.

2617 KNEEN (J. J.). The Place-Names of the Isle of Man, with their Origin and History. 2 vols Douglas. Vol. 1 1925. Vol. 2 1927.

2618 KILLIP (CHRISTOPHER). The Isle of Man: A Book about the Manx. 1980.

2619 SHERRATT (TOM) comp. Isle of Man Parliamentary Election Results 1919–1979. Warrington. 1979.

2620 KERMODE (D. G.). 'The Legislative-Executive Relationship in the Isle of Man'. *Pol. Studs* 16 (1968), 18–42.

2621 —— Devolution at Work: A Case Study of the Isle of Man. Farnborough. 1978.

2622 The Changing Pattern of Manx Devolution. Glasg. 1980.

2623 HORNER (SIMON A.). The Isle of Man and the Channel Islands: A Study of their Status in Constitutional, International and European Law. Florence. 1984.

2624 KEETON (GEORGE W.). The United Kingdom: The Development of its Laws and Constitutions: England and Wales, Northern Ireland, the Isle of Man. 1955.

2625 BIRCH (JACK WILLIAM). The Isle of Man: A Study in Economic Geography. Bristol. 1964.

(See also in Newspapers Section—GIBSON (J. S. W.). Local Newspapers, 1750–1920: England and Wales, the Channel Islands, the Isle of Man. Birm. 1987.)

2626 ISLE OF MAN OFFICIAL YEARBOOK 1983–. Ramsay. 1983.

2627 TYNWALD REPORT OF THE PROCEEDINGS OF THE LEGISLATIVE COUNCIL 1954–. Douglas. 1954.

2628 —— REPORT OF THE PROCEEDINGS OF THE HOUSE OF KEYS 1954–. Douglas. 1954.

2629 —— Report of the Possible Effects on the Isle of Man of United Kingdom Entry into the Common Market. Douglas, 1969. [By THURSTON (HUGH)].

2630 Report of the Committee of Tynwald Appointed to Examine the Representation of the People Acts, 1951 to 1961. Douglas. 1963.

2631 U.K. GENERAL REGISTER OFFICE. Census 1921: Isle of Man. 1924.

2632 ISLE OF MAN REGISTRAR-GENERAL. Annual Report and Statistical Review of Births, Marriages and Deaths in the Isle of Man, 1951–. Douglas. 1951.

2633 Census 1951. Report on Isle of Man. Douglas. 1956.

2634 Census 1961. Report on Isle of Man. Douglas. 1965/6.

2635 ISLE OF MAN SUMMERLAND FIRE COMMISSION. Report . . . Douglas. 1974.

2636 BOYD (JAMES I. C.). The Isle of Man Railway . . . 1962. 3rd edn 1973.

2637 DEANE (CHARLES). The Isle of Man T.T. Camb. 1975.

6. IRELAND

(a) General

2638 EAGER (ALAN). Guide to Irish Bibliographical Material: A Bibliography of Irish Bibliographies and Sources of Information. 1980.

2639 SHANNON (MICHAEL OWEN) ed. Modern Ireland: A Bibliography on Politics, Planning, Research and Development. Westport. 1981.

2640 MOODY (THEODORE W.) ed. Irish Historiography 1936–1970. Dublin. 1971.

2641 LEE (JOSEPH) ed. Irish Historiography 1970–1979. Cork. 1981.

2642 BECKETT (JAMES CAMLIN). The Making of Modern Ireland, 1603–1923. 1966, with a rev. bibliog. 1981.

2643 LYONS (FRANCIS STEWART LELAND). Ireland since the Famine: 1850 to the Present. 1971.

2644 —— Culture and Anarchy in Ireland 1890–1939. Oxf. 1979.

2645 FOSTER (ROY F.). Modern Ireland 1600–1972. 1988.

2646 DALY (MARY E.). Social and Economic History of Ireland since 1800. Dublin. 1981.

2647 HOPPEN (KARL THEODORE). Ireland since 1800: Conflict and Conformity. 1989.

2648 LEE (JOSEPH J.). Ireland, 1912–1985: Politics and Society. Camb. 1990.

2649 GOLDSTROM (J. M.) and CLARKSON (LESLIE ALBERT) eds. Irish Population, Economy and Society: Essays in Honour of the late K. H. Connell. Oxf. 1981.

2650 de PAOR (LIAM). The Peoples of Ireland: From Pre-history to Modern Times. 1986.

2651 MURPHY (JOHN A.). Ireland in the Twentieth Century. Dublin. 1975.

2652 MEENAN (JAMES). The Irish Economy since 1922. L/pool. 1970.

2653 MACDONAGH (OLIVER). Ireland: The Union and its Aftermath. 1977.

2654 FITZGERALD (GARRET ERNEST). Towards a New Ireland. 1972. Dublin. 1973.

2655 de BREFFNY (BRIAN) *ed*. The Irish World. 1977.

2656 LAUGHREY (PATRICK). The People of Ireland. Belfast. 1988.

2657 O'BRIEN (CONOR CRUISE). States of Ireland. 1972.

2658 COOGAN (TIM PAT). Ireland, A Personal View. 1975.

2659 BOYLAN (HENRY). A Dictionary of Irish Biography. Dublin. 1978.

2660 GALLAGHER (TOM) *and* O₃CONNELL (JAMES) *eds*. Contemporary Irish Studies. Manch. 1983.

2661 IRISH HISTORICAL STUDIES. 1938–.

2662 IRISH ECONOMIC AND SOCIAL HISTORY. 1974–.

2663 FREEMAN (THOMAS WALTER). Ireland: Its Physical, Historical, Social and Economic Geography. 1950. 2nd rev. edn under new title, 'Ireland: A General and Regional Geography'. 1960. 4th edn 1969.

2664 EDWARDS (RUTH DUDLEY). An Atlas of Irish History. 1973. 2nd edn 1981.

2665 HESLINGA (MARCUS WILLEM). The Irish Border as a Cultural Divide: A Contribution to the Study of Regionalism in the British Isles. Assen. 1962.

2666 REPORT OF THE IRISH BOUNDARY COMMISSION, 1923. [Introduced by HAND (GEOFFREY J.).] Shannon. 1969.

2667 MAIR (PETER). The Break-Up of the United Kingdom: The Irish Experience of Regional Change 1918–1949. Glasg. 1978.

2668 ELLIS (PETER BERRESFORD). A History of the Irish Working Class. 1972. New edn 1985.

2669 BOYD (ANDREW). The Rise of the Irish Trade Unions 1729–1970. Tralee. 1972.

2670 McCARTHY (C.). Trade Unions in Ireland, 1894–1960. Dublin. 1977.

2671 SHEEHY (JEANNE). The Rediscovery of Ireland's Past: The Celtic Revival, 1830–1930. 1980.

2672 JOHNSON (DAVID S.). 'The Economic History of Ireland between the Wars'. *Irish Econ. Soc. Hist.* 1 (1974), 49–61.

2673 BARKER (*Sir* ERNEST). Ireland in the Last Fifty Years (1866–1916). Oxf. 1917. 2nd edn 1919.

2674 OWENS (ROSEMARY CULLEN). Smashing Times: A History of the Irish Women's Suffrage Movement 1889–1922. Dublin. 1984.

2675 FITZPATRICK (DAVID) *ed*. Ireland and the First World War. Dublin. 1986.

2676 WARD (ALAN J.). Ireland and Anglo-American Relations, 1899–1921. 1969.

2677 CARROLL (F. M.). American Opinion and the Irish Question, 1910–1923: A Study in Opinion and Policy. Dublin. 1978.

2678 MAGUIRE (MARIA). A Bibliography of Published Works on Irish Foreign Relations, 1921–1978. Dublin. 1981.

2679 LAWLOR (SHEILA M.). 'Ireland from Truce to Treaty: War or Peace? July to October 1921'. *Irish Hist. Studs* 22 (1980), 49–64.

2680 GWYNN (DENNIS ROLLESTON). The Irish Free State, 1922–1927. 1928.

2681 —— The History of Partition, 1912–1925. Dublin. 1950.

2682 LAFFAN (MICHAEL). The Partition of Ireland 1911–1925. Dublin. 1985.

2683 BOYLE (KEVIN). 'The Tallents Report on the Craig-Collins Pact of 30 March 1922'. *Irish Jurist.* 12 (1977), 148–75.

2684 AKENSON (DONALD HARMAN) *and* FALLIN (J. F.). 'The Irish Civil War and the Drafting of the Free-State Constitution'. *Eire/Ireland* 5 (1970), pt.1: 10–26, pt.2: 42–93, pt.4: 28–70.

2685 KOHN (LEO). The Constitution of the Irish Free State. 1932.

2686 CURRAN (JOSEPH M.). The Birth of the Irish Free State 1921–1923. Alabama. 1980.

2687 MacMANUS (FRANCIS) *ed*. The Years of the Great Test. Cork. 1967.

2688 CROZIER (FRANK PERCY). A Word to Gandhi: The Lesson of Ireland. 1931.

2689 MANSERGH (PHILIP NICHOLAS SETON). The Prelude to Partition: Concepts and Aims in Ireland and India. Camb. 1978.

2690 HACHEY (THOMAS E.). The Problem of Partition: Peril to World Peace. Chicago. 1972.

2691 —— Britain and Irish Separatism: From the Fenians to the Free State, 1867–1922. Chicago. 1977.

2692 PYNE (PETER). 'The Politics of Parliamentary Absenteeism: Ireland's Four Sinn Fein Parties, 1905–1926'. *J. Cwealth Comp. Pol.* 12 (1974), 206–27.

2693 —— 'The Third Sinn Fein Party, 1923–1926'. *Econ. Soc. Rev.* 1 (1969/70), 29–50, 229–57.

2694 —— 'The New Irish State and the Decline of the Republican Sinn Fein Party'. *Eire/Ireland* 11 (1976), 33–65.

2695 MAIR (PETER). 'Labour and the Irish Party System Revisited: Party Competition in the 1920s'. *Econ. Soc. Rev.* 9 (1977), 59–69.

2696 MITCHELL (ARTHUR). Labour in Irish Politics 1890–1930: The Irish Labour Movement in an Age of Revolution. Dublin. 1974.

2697 BOWDEN (TOM). The Breakdown of Public Security: The Case of Ireland 1916–21 and Palestine 1936–39. 1977.

2698 McCARDLE (DOROTHY). The Irish Republic: A Documented Chronicle of the Anglo-Irish Conflict and the Partitioning of Ireland, with a Detailed Account of the Period, 1916–1923. 1937.

2699 O'MALLEY (ERNIE). The Singing Flame. Dublin. 1978.

2700 —— On Another Man's Wound. 1936. 1961.

[Above two books on the Anglo-Irish War and the Civil War.].

2701 GALLAGHER (FRANK). The Indivisible Island: The History of the Partition of Ireland. 1957.

2702 FITZPATRICK (DAVID). Irish Emigration 1801–1921. Dublin. 1984.

2703 —— Politics and Irish Life 1913–1921. Dublin. 1977.

2704 CARROLL (JOSEPH THOMAS). Ireland in the War Years. Newton Abbot. 1975.

2705 NOWLAN (KEVIN BARRY) and WILLIAMS (T. DESMOND). Ireland and the War Years and After 1939–1951. 1969.

2706 RAYMOND (R. J.). 'American Public Opinion and Irish Neutrality, 1939–1945'. Eire/Ireland 18 (1983), 20–45.

2707 FISK (ROBERT). In Time of War: Ireland, Ulster and the Price of Neutrality 1939–1945. 1983.

2708 DWYER (T. RYLE). Strained Relations: Ireland at Peace and the USA at War, 1941–1945. Dublin. 1988.

2709 —— Irish Neutrality and the U.S.A. 1939–1947. Dublin. 1977.

2710 SHARE (BERNARD). The Emergency: Neutral Ireland. Dublin. 1978.

2711 DUGGAN (JOHN P.). Neutral Ireland and the Third Reich. Dublin/Totowa, N.J. 1985.

2712 CARTER (CAROLLE J.). The Shamrock and the Swastika: German Espionage in Ireland in World War Two. Palo Alto CA. 1977.

2713 ROSENBERG (JOSEPH L.). 'The Consecration of Expediency: The Wartime Neutrality of Ireland'. Austral. J. Pol. Hist. 25 (1980), 327–31.

2714 HARKNESS (DAVID W.). The Restless Dominion. 1969.

2715 —— 'The Constitution of Ireland and the Development of National Identity'. J. Cwealth Comp Pol. 36 (1988), 135–46.

2716 LEE (JOSEPH) ed. Ireland 1945–1970. Dublin. 1970.

2717 AKENSON (DONALD HARMAN). Small Differences: Irish Catholics and Irish Protestants, 1815–1922: An International Perspective. Kingston, Ontario. 1988.

2718 SPENCER (A. E. C. W.). 'Catholics in Britain and Ireland: Regional Contrasts'. In Demography of Immigrants and Minority Groups in the United Kingdom. D. A. Coleman, ed. 1982.

2719 CORISH (PATRICK J.). The Irish Catholic Experience: A Historical Survey. Dublin. 1985.

2720 KEOGH (DERMOT). The Vatican, the Bishops and Irish Politics 1919–1939. Camb. 1986.

2721 Ireland and Europe, 1919–1948. Totowa N.J. 1988.

(b) Irish Nationalism and Rebellion

2722 BOYCE (DAVID GEORGE). Nationalism in Ireland. 1982.

2723 —— Ed. The Revolution in Ireland 1879–1923. 1988.

2724 —— The Irish Question and British Politics, 1868–1986. 1988.

2725 GARVIN (TOM). Nationalist Revolutionaries in Ireland 1858–1928. Oxf. 1987.

2726 CRONIN (SEAN). Irish Nationalism: A History of its Roots and Ideology. Dublin. 1980.

2727 KEE (ROBERT). The Green Flag: A History of Irish Nationalism. 1972.

2728 RUMPF (ERHARD). Nationalism and Socialism in Twentieth Century Ireland. L/pool. 1977.

2729 BEW (PAUL). 'The Problem of Irish Unionism'. Economics and Society 6 (1977), 89–109.

2730 KING (JAMES CLIFFORD). The Orange and the Green. 1965.

2731 HEPBURN (A. C.) comp. The Conflict of Nationality in Modern Ireland. 1980.

2732 TOWNSHEND (CHARLES). Political Violence in Ireland: Government and Resistance since 1848. Oxf. 1983.

2733 WARD (MARGARET). Unmanageable Revolutionaries: Women and Irish Nationalism. 1983.

2734 FERGUSSON (Sir JAMES). The Curragh Incident. 1964.

2735 RYAN (ALFRED PATRICK). Mutiny at the Curragh. 1956.

2736 CAULFIELD (MAX). The Easter Rebellion. 1964.

2737 DUFF (CHARLES ST LAWRENCE). Six Days to Shake an Empire: Events and Factors behind the Irish Rebellion of 1916. 1966.

2738 COFFEY (THOMAS M.). Agony at Easter: The 1916 Uprising. 1970.

2739 EDWARDS (OWEN DUDLEY) and PYLE (FERGUS) eds. 1916: The Easter Rising. 1968.

2740 MARTIN (FRANCIS XAVIER). Leaders and Men of the Easter Rising: Dublin 1916. 1967.

2741 NOWLAN (KEVIN BARRY) ed. Making of 1916: Studies in the History of the Rising. Dublin. 1969.

2742 GRANT (NEIL). The Easter Rising, Dublin 1916: The Irish Rebel Against British Rule. 1973.

2743 O'BROIN (LEON). Dublin Castle and the 1916 Rising. 1966.

2744 RYAN (DESMOND). The Rising. 1949.

2745 GREAVES (CHARLES DESMOND). The Easter Rising in Song and Ballad. 1980.

2746 HOLT (EDGAR CRAWSHAW). Protest in Arms: The Irish Troubles, 1916–1923. 1960.

2747 WILLIAMS (T. DESMOND) ed. The Irish Struggle, 1916–1926. 1966.

2748 O'BROIN (LEON). Protestant Nationalists in Revolutionary Ireland: The Stopford Connection. Dublin. 1985.

2749 YOUNGER (CALTON). Ireland's Civil War. 1968.

2750 BARRY (THOMAS B.). Guerilla Days in Ireland: A First Hand Account of the Black and Tan War, 1919–1921. Dublin. 1949.

2751 BENNETT (RICHARD LAWRENCE). The Black and Tans. 1959. Rev. edn 1976.

2752 O'CONNOR (ULICK). A Terrible Beauty is Born: The Irish Troubles, 1912–1922. 1975.

2753 O'FARRELL (PADRAIC). Who's Who in the Irish War of Independence 1916–1921. Dublin. 1980.

2754 MARTIN (FRANCIS XAVIER) *ed.* The Irish Volunteers, 1913–1915: Recollections and Documents. Dublin. 1963.

2755 —— *Ed.* The Howth Gun-running and the Kilcoole Gun-running, 1914: Recollections and Documents. Dublin. 1964.

2756 HOBSON (BULMER). A Short History of the Irish Volunteers. Dublin. 1918.

2757 FOX (RICHARD MICHAEL). The History of the Irish Citizen Army. Dublin. 1943.

2758 O'CASEY (SEAN). The Story of the Irish Citizen Army, 1919. Dublin. 1971.

2759 ROBBINS (FRANK). Under the Starry Plough: Recollections of the Irish Citizen Army. Dublin. 1977.

2760 O'BROIN (LEON). Revolutionary Underground: The Story of the Irish Republican Brotherhood, 1858–1924. Dublin. 1976.

2761 O'BEIRNE-RANELAGH (JOHN). 'The Irish Republican Brotherhood, 1858–1924'. *Irish Hist. Studs* 20 (1976), 26–39.

2762 O'NEILL (THOMAS PATRICK). 'In Search of a Political Path: Irish Republicanism 1922–1927'. *Hist. Studs* (Dublin), 10 (1976), 141–71.

2763 BELL (J. BOWYER). The Secret Army: The IRA 1916–1979. Rev. edn 1979.

2764 —— 'The Escalation of Insurgency: The Provisional Irish Republican Army's Experience, 1969–1971'. *Rev. Pol.* 35 (1973), 398–411.

2765 O'DOHERTY (EAMON). An Illustrated History of the I.R.A. 1985.

2766 BISHOP (PATRICK). The Provisional IRA. 1987.

2767 COOGAN (TIM PAT). The IRA. 1970.

2768 McGUIRE (MARIA). To Take Arms: A Year in the Provisional IRA. 1973.

2769 FALIGOT (ROGER). La Résistance Irlandaise, 1916–1976. Paris. 1977.

2770 —— Nous avons tué Mountbatten: L'I.R.A. Parle. Paris. 1981.

2771 MacSTIOFAIN (SEAN). Memoirs of a Revolutionary. 1975.

2772 BOWDEN (TOM). 'The I.R.A. and the Changing Tactics of Terrorism'. *Pol. Q.* 47 (1976), 42, 5–37.

2773 MULLIN (CHRIS). Error of Judgement: The Birmingham Bombings. 1986.

(c) *Northern Ireland, Ulster, and Ulster Unionism*

(i) *Northern Ireland*

2774 Social and Economic Trends. 1975–80. HMSO

2775 Ulster Year Book. 1926–38, 1947+. Annual.

2776 DEUTSCH (RICHARD R.). Northern Ireland, 1921–1974: A Select Bibliography. N.Y./Lond. 1975.

2777 Northern Ireland Statutes. 1922+.

2778 Chronological Table of the Statutes: Northern Ireland. 19th edn 1987.

2779 MALTBY (ARTHUR). The Government of Northern Ireland, 1922–1972: A Catalogue and Breviate of Parliamentary Papers. Dublin. 1979.

2780 COLLETT (R. J.). Northern Ireland Statistics: A Guide to Principal Sources. Belfast. 1979.

2781 ROLSTON (BILL) *et al. comps.* A Social Science Bibliography of Northern Ireland, 1945–1983: Material Published since 1945 Relating to Northern Ireland since 1921. Belfast. 1987.

2782 BUCKLAND (PATRICK). A History of Northern Ireland. Dublin. 1981.

2783 —— The Factory of Grievances: Devolved Government in Northern Ireland 1921–1939. Dublin. 1979.

2784 ARTHUR (PAUL) *and* JEFFERY (KEITH). Northern Ireland since 1968. Oxf. 1988.

2785 TOWNSHEND (CHARLES) *ed.* Consensus in Ireland: Approaches and Recessions. Oxf. 1988.

2786 HARKNESS (DAVID W.). Northern Ireland since 1920. Dublin. 1983.

2787 BEW (PAUL), GIBBON (PETER), *and* PATTERSON (HENRY). The State in Northern Ireland, 1921–1971: Political Forces and Social Causes. Manch. 1979.

2788 FARRELL (MICHAEL). The Poor Law and the Workhouse in Belfast 1838–1948. 1978.

2789 —— The Struggle in the North. 1970.

2790 —— Northern Ireland: The Orange State. 1976. 2nd edn 1980.

2791 —— *Ed.* Twenty Years on. 1988.

2792 DEVLIN (P.). Yes, We Have No Bananas: Outdoor Relief in Belfast 1920–1939. Belfast. 1981.

2793 MOXON-BROWNE (EDWARD). Nation, Class and Creed in Northern Ireland. 1983.

2794 PATTERSON (HENRY). Class Conflict and Sectarianism: The Protestant Working Class and the Belfast Labour Movement, 1868–1920. Belfast. 1981.

2795 JOHNSON (DAVID S.). 'The Belfast Boycott 1920–1922'. In *eds.* J. M. Goldstrom and Leslie Albert Clarkson, Irish Population, Economy and Society: Essays in Honour of the Late K. H. Connell. 1981.

2796 KNIGHT (JAMES). Northern Ireland: The Elections of the Twenties. 1972.

2797 ELLIOTT (SYDNEY). Northern Ireland Parliamentary Election Results, 1921–1972. Chichester. 1973.

2798 DUTTER (L. E.). 'The Structure of Vote Preferences: The 1921, 1925, 1973 and 1975 Northern Irish Parliamentary Elections'. *Comp. Pol. Studs* 15 (1982), 171–96.

2799 JOHNSON (DAVID S.). 'Northern Ireland as a Problem in the Economic War, 1932–1938'. *Irish Hist. Studs* 22 (1980), 144–61.

2800 BOYCE (DAVID GEORGE). '"Normal Policing": Public Order in Ireland since Partition'. *Eire/Ireland* 14 (1979), 35–52.

2801 MANSERGH (PHILIP NICHOLAS SETON). The Government of Northern Ireland: A Study in Devolution. 1936.

2802 LAWRENCE (REGINALD JAMES). The Government of Northern Ireland: Public Finance and Public Services, 1921–1964. Oxf. 1965.

2803 —— 'Politics and Public Administration in Northern Ireland'. *Administration* [Dublin] 15 (1968), 112–20.

2804 ARTHUR (PAUL). 'Devolution as Administrative Convenience: A Case Study of Northern Ireland'. *Parl. Affs* 30 (1977), 97–106.

2805 —— The Government and Politics of Northern Ireland. Harlow. 1980.

2806 BIRRELL (DEREK) *and* MURIE (ALAN). Policy and Government in Northern Ireland: Lessons of Devolution. Dublin. 1980.

2807 BIRRELL (DEREK). 'The Stormont–Westminster Relationship'. *Parl. Affs* 26 (1972–3), 471–91.

2808 BRETT (C. E. B.). 'The Lessons of Devolution in Northern Ireland'. *Pol. Q.* 41 (1970), 261–80.

2809 LAWRENCE (REGINALD J.). 'Northern Ireland at Westminster'. *Parl. Affs* 20 (1966–7), 90–6.

2810 WALLACE (MARTIN). Northern Ireland: Fifty Years of Self-Government. Newton Abbot. 1971.

2811 HARKNESS (DAVID W.). 'Aspects of Government and Society in Northern Ireland 1920–1968'. Ch. in Revue Française de Civilisation Britannique: L'Irelande du Nord. Brest. 1988.

2812 —— 'Reforms in Northern Ireland'. *Ireland: Politics and Society* (Paris), 1 (1987), 29–40.

2813 GREEN (ARTHUR JOHN). Devolution and Public Finance: Stormont from 1921 to 1972. Glasg. 1979.

2814 SHEA (PATRICK). Voices and the Sound of Drums. [Memoirs of a Catholic Civil Servant.] Belfast. 1981.

2815 BIRRELL (DEREK). 'The Northern Ireland Civil Service from Devolution to Direct Rule'. *Public Admin* 56 (1978), 305–19.

2816 OLIVER (JOHN A.). Working at Stormont. Dublin. 1978.

2817 McALLISTER (IAN) *and* WILSON (BRIAN). Bi-Confessionalism in a Confessional Party System: The Northern Ireland Alliance Party. Glasg. 1979.

2818 WATT (DAVID) *ed.* The Constitution of Northern Ireland: Problems and Prospects. 1981.

2819 DEUTSCH (RICHARD R.) *and* MAGOWAN (VIVIENNE). Northern Ireland, 1968–1974: A Chronology of Events. 3 vols Belfast. 1973–5.

2820 BLAKE (JOHN W.). Northern Ireland in the Second World War. Belfast. 1956.

2821 FLACKES (W. D.). Northern Ireland: A Political Directory, 1968–1979. Dublin. 1980.

2822 —— Northern Ireland: A Political Directory 1968–1983. [Rev. edn of above, for the BBC.] London. 1983.

2823 TEAGUE (PAUL) *ed.* Beyond the Rhetoric: Politics, the Economy and Social Policy in Northern Ireland. 1987.

2824 DARBY (JOHN). Conflict in Northern Ireland: The Development of a Polarised Community. Dublin. 1976.

2825 DARBY (JOHN) *and* WILLIAMSON (ARTHUR) *eds.* Violence and the Social Services in Northern Ireland. 1978.

2826 BARRITT (DENIS PHILLIPS) *and* CARTER (SIR CHARLES FREDERICK). The Northern Ireland Problem: A Study in Group Relations. 1962. 2nd edn 1972.

2827 CALVERT (HENRY). The Northern Ireland Problem. 1972.

2828 LIJPHART (AREND). 'The Northern Ireland Problem: Cases, Theories and Solutions'. *Brit. J. Pol. Sci.* 5 (1975), 83–106.

2829 U.K. SECRETARY OF STATE FOR NORTHERN IRELAND. The Future of Northern Ireland: A Paper for Discussion. 1972. [HMSO].

2830 U.K. NORTHERN IRELAND OFFICE. The Government of Northern Ireland: Proposals for Further Discussion. 1980.

2831 HARKNESS (DAVID W.). 'The Difficulties of Devolution: The Post-War Debate at Stormont'. *Irish Jurist.* 12 (1977), 176–86.

2832 ROSE (RICHARD). Governing without Consensus: An Irish Perspective. 1971.

2833 —— Northern Ireland: A Time of Choice. 1976.

2834 O'LEARY (CORNELIUS). 'North Ireland: The Politics of Illusion'. *Pol. Q.* 11 (1961), 307–15.

2835 KELLY (HENRY). How Stormont Fell. 1972.

2836 CALLAGHAN (JAMES). A House Divided: The Dilemma of Northern Ireland. 1973.

2837 YOUNGER (CALTON). A State of Disunion. 1972.

2838 BECKETT (JAMES CAMLIN). 'Northern Ireland'. *J. Contemp. Hist.* 6 (1971), 121–34.

2839 BOWDEN (TOM). 'Bloody Sunday: A Reappraisal'. *Europ. Studs Rev.* 2 (1972), 25–42.

2840 BOYD (ANDREW). Holy War in Belfast. Tralee. 1969.

2841 EDWARDS (OWEN DUDLEY). The Sins of the Fathers. Dublin. 1970.

2842 O'MALLEY (PADRAIG). The Uncivil Wars: Ireland Today. Belfast. 1983.

2843 HEWITT (JAMES). The Irish Question. Hove. 1986.

2844 WARD (ALAN J.) ed. Northern Ireland: Living with the Crisis. N.Y. 1987.

2845 GREAVES (CHARLES DESMOND). The Irish Crisis. 1972.

2846 DILLON (MARTIN) and LEHANE (DENIS CHARLES). Political Murder in Northern Ireland. 1973.

2847 SCARMAN (LESLIE GEORGE) Baron. Violence and Civil Disturbances in Northern Ireland in 1969: Report of a Tribunal of Inquiry. Belfast. 1972. [HMSO].

2848 NORTHERN IRELAND COMMUNITY RELATIONS COMMISSION. Register of Completed and Ongoing Research into the Irish Conflict. Belfast. 1972.

2849 FIELDS (RONA M.). A Society on the Run: A Psychology of Northern Ireland. Harmondsworth. 1973.

2850 EVELEGH (R.). Peacekeeping in a Democratic Society: The Lessons of Northern Ireland. 1978.

2851 FEENEY (V. E.). 'The Civil Rights Movement in Northern Ireland'. Eire/Ireland 9 (1974), 3–13.

2852 HEWITT (CHRISTOPHER). 'Catholic Grievances, Catholic Nationalism and Violence in Northern Ireland during the Civil Rights Period: A Reconsideration'. Brit. J. Sociology 32 (1981), 362–80.

2853 CALVERT (HARRY GREENALL). Constitutional Law in Northern Ireland: A Study in Regional Government. 1968.

2854 BOYLE (KEVIN), HADDEN (TOM), and HILLYARD (PADDY). Justice in Northern Ireland: A Study in Social Confidence. 1973.

2855 —— Law and the State: The Case of Northern Ireland. 1975.

2856 —— Ten Years On: The Legal Control of Political Violence. 1980.

2857 McCANN (EAMONN). War and an Irish Town. Harmondsworth. 1974.

2858 TAYLOR (PETER). Beating the Terrorists. Harmondsworth. 1989.

2859 —— Families at War. 1989.

2860 FRASER (MORRIS). Children in Conflict. 1973.

2861 BLEAKLEY (DAVID). Crisis in Ireland. 1974.

2862 COMPTON (PAUL A.). 'Fertility, Nationality and Religion in Northern Ireland', in Demography of Immigrants and Minority Groups in the United Kingdom. D. A. Coleman. 1982.

2863 AKENSON (DONALD HARMAN). Education and Enmity: The Control of Schooling in Northern Ireland 1920–1950. Newton Abbot/N.Y. 1973.

2864 EVERSLEY (DAVID). Religion and Employment in Northern Ireland. London. 1989.

2865 McGUFFIN (JOHN). The Guinea Pigs. Harmondsworth. 1974.

2866 —— Internment. Tralee. 1973.

2867 BISHOP (J. W.). 'Law in the Control of Terrorism and Insurrection: The British Laboratory Experience'. Law and Contemp. Probs. 42 (1978), 140–201.

2868 FINN (J. E.). 'Public Support for Emergency/Anti-Terrorist Legislation in Northern Ireland: A Preliminary Analysis'. Terrorism 10 (1987), 113–24.

2869 WALSH (DERMOT). The Use and Abuse of Emergency Legislation in Northern Ireland. 1983.

2870 GIFFORD (TONY). Supergrasses: The Use of Accomplice Evidence in Northern Ireland: A Report. 1984.

2871 ROBERTSON (GEOFFREY). Reluctant Judas: The Life and Death of the Special Branch Informer, Kenneth Lennon. 1976.

2872 Report of the Commission to Consider Legal Procedures to deal with Terrorist Activities in Northern Ireland. Cmnd 5185. Parliamentary Papers, xxvi (1972–3).

2873 Report of a Committee to Consider, in the Context of Civil Liberties and Human Rights, Measures to Deal with Terrorism in Northern Ireland. Cmnd 5874. Parliamentary Papers, xxviii (1974–5).

2874 Review of the Operation of the Prevention of Terrorism (Temporary Provisions) Acts 1974 and 1976. Cmnd 7324. Parliamentary Papers, xxiii (1977–8).

2875 Review of the Operation of the Prevention of Terrorism (Temporary Provisions) Act 1976. Cmnd 8803. Parliamentary Papers (1982–3).

2876 SCORER (CATHERINE). 'The United Kingdom Prevention of Terrorism Acts 1974 and 1976'. Inl J. Pols. 10 (1980), 105–11.

2877 MAGEE (JOHN) ed. Northern Ireland: Crisis and Conflict. 1974.

2878 HULL (ROGER HAROLD). The Irish Triangle: Conflict in Northern Ireland. 1976.

2879 PROBERT (BELINDA). Beyond Orange and Green: The Political Economy of the Northern Ireland Crisis. 1978.

2880 BELL (J. BOWYER). 'The Chroniclers of Violence in Northern Ireland: The First Wave Interpreted'. Rev. of Politics 34 (1972), 147–57.

2881 —— 'The Chroniclers Revisited: The Analysis of Tragedy'. Rev. of Politics 36 (1974), 521–34.

2882 WINCHESTER (SIMON). In Holy Terror: Reporting the Ulster Troubles. 1974.

2883 BAILEY (ANTHONY). Acts of Union: Reports on Ireland, 1973–1979. N.Y. 1980.

2884 CURTIS (LIZ). Ireland and the Propaganda War: The Media and the Battle for 'Hearts and Minds'. 1984.

2885 FERGUSON (ROB). Television on History: Representations of Ireland. 1985.

2886 CATHCART (REX). The Most Contrary Region: The B.B.C. in Northern Ireland, 1924–1984. Belfast. 1984.

2887 HESKIN (KEN). Northern Ireland: A Psychological Analysis. Dublin. 1980.

2888 HOLLAND (JACK). Too Long a Sacrifice: Life and Death in Ireland since 1969. N.Y. 1981.

2889 COOGAN (TIM PAT). On the Blanket: The H-Block Story. Dublin. 1980.

2890 WILKINSON (PAUL). 'The Provisional I.R.A.: An Assessment in the wake of the 1981 Hunger Strike'. *Govt and Opp.* 7 (1982), 140–56.

2891 CLARKE (L.). Broadening the Battlefield: The H-Blocks and the Rise of Sinn Fein. Dublin. 1987.

2892 BERESFORD (DAVID). Ten Men Dead: The Story of the 1981 Irish Hunger Strikes. 1987.

2893 SANDS (BOBBY). One Day in my Life. Cork. 1983.

2894 FEEHAN (JOHN M.). Bobby Sands and the Tragedy of Ireland. Cork. 1983.

2895 BUFWACK (MARY S.). Village without Violence: An Examination of a Northern Irish Community. Camb., Mass. 1982.

2896 AUNGER (E. A.). 'Religion and Occupational Class in Northern Ireland'. *Econ. Soc. Hist.* 7 (1975), 1–18.

2897 HAMILL (DESMOND). Pig in the Middle: The Army in Northern Ireland, 1969–1984. 1985.

2898 BARZILAY (DAVID). The British Army in Ulster. 4 vols 1973–81.

2899 ARTHUR (MAX). Northern Ireland—Soldiers Talking. 1969 to today. 1988.

2900 KITSON (FRANK). Low-Intensity Operations: Subversion, Insurgency and Peace-Keeping. 1971.

2901 CHARTERS (DAVID A.). 'Intelligence and Psychological Warfare Operations in Northern Ireland'. *J. Roy. United Services Inst. Def. Studs* 122 (1977). 22–7.

(ii) Ulster and Ulster Unionism

2902 STEWART (ANTHONY TERENCE QUINCEY). The Narrow Ground: Aspects of Ulster 1609–1969. 1977.

2903 —— The Ulster Crisis. 1967.

2904 MOODY (THEODORE W.) *and* BECKETT (JAMES CAMLIN) *eds.* Ulster since 1800: A Political and Economic Survey. 1955.

2905 MOODY (THEODORE W.). The Ulster Question, 1603–1973. Dublin. 1974.

2906 KENNEDY (LIAM) *and* OLLERENSHAW (PHILIP). An Economic History of Ulster, 1820–1940. Manch. 1985.

2907 ROEBUCK (PETER) *ed.* Plantation to Partition: Essays in honour of J. L. McCracken. Belfast. 1981.

2908 BUDGE (IAN) *and* O'LEARY (CORNELIUS). Belfast: Approach to Crisis: A Study of Belfast Politics, 1613–1970. 1973.

2909 FITZGIBBON (CONSTANTINE). Red Hand: The Ulster Colony. 1973. 2nd edn 1981.

2910 MORRISON (H. S.). Modern Ulster: Its Character, Customs, Politics and Industries. 1920.

2911 MCNEILL (RONALD) *Baron Cushendun.* Ulster's Stand for Union. 1922.

2912 —— The Irish Boundary Question. 1924.

2913 WALLACE (MARTIN). Drums and Guns: Revolution in Ulster. 1970.

2914 HASTINGS (MAX). Ulster '69: The Fight for Civil Rights in Northern Ireland. 1970.

2915 RIDDELL (PATRICK). Fire Over Ulster. 1970.

2916 SMYTH (CLIFFORD). Ulster Assailed. Belfast. 1971.

2917 DE PAOR (LIAM). Divided Ulster. Harmondsworth. 1971.

2918 ELLIOT (R. S. P.) *and* HICKIE (JOHN). Ulster: A Case Study in Conflict Theory. 1971.

2919 STUDY GROUP OF THE INSTITUTE FOR THE STUDY OF CONFLICT. The Ulster Debate. 1972.

2920 JANKE (PETER) *and* PRICE (D. L.). Ulster: Consensus and Coercion. 1974.

2921 FISK (ROBERT). The Point of No Return: The Strike which Broke the British in Ulster. 1975.

2922 CARLTON (CHARLES). Bigotry and Blood: Documents on the Ulster Troubles. Chicago. 1977.

2923 ROSE (RICHARD). 'Ulster Politics: A Select Bibliography of Political Discord'. *Pol. Studs* 20 (1972), 206–12.

2924 PAKENHAM (FRANCIS AUNGIER) *Earl of Longford, and* MCHARDY (ANNE). Ulster. 1981.

2925 GALLAGHER (ERIC). Christians in Ulster, 1968–1980. Oxf. 1982.

2926 HARRIS (ROSEMARY). Prejudice and Tolerance in Ulster. Manch./Totowa, N.J. 1972.

2927 BLEAKLEY (DAVID). Peace in Ulster. Lond./Oxf. 1972.

2928 COCHRANE (D. G.). 'Britannic Irish and Hibernian Irish in Ulster's Racial Conflict'. *Sociologus* 22 (1972), 87–101.

2929 WILSON (THOMAS BRIGHT) *ed.* Ulster under Home Rule: A Study of the Political and Economic Problems of Northern Ireland. 1955.

2930 —— Ulster Divided. Oxf. 1989.

2931 FARRELL (MICHAEL). Arming the Protestants: The Formation of the Ulster Special Constabulary and the Royal Ulster Constabulary 1920–1927. 1983.

2932 HEZLET (SIR ARTHUR). The 'B' Specials: A History of the Ulster Special Constabulary. Belfast. 1975.

2933 WEITZER (RONALD). 'Policing a Divided Society: Obstacles to Normalisation in Northern Ireland'. *Soc. Probs* 33 (1985), 41–55.

2934 —— 'Accountability and Complaints against the Police in Northern Ireland'. *Police Studs* 9 (1986), 99–109.

2935 STALKER (JOHN). Stalker. 1988.

2936 TAYLOR (PETER). Stalker: The Search for Truth. 1987.

2937 DOHERTY (FRANK). The Stalker Affair. Cork. 1986.

2938 BREATHNACH (S.). The Irish Police: From Earliest Times to the Present Day. Dublin. 1974. [See ch. on the R.U.C.].

2939 RYDER (CHRIS). The R.U.C. 1989.

2940 GRAY (TONY). The Orange Order. 1972.

2941 ROBERTS (D. A.). 'The Orange Order in Ireland: A Religious Institution?'. *Brit. J. Sociol.* 22 (1971), 269–82.

2942 MILLER (DAVID W.). Queen's Rebels: Ulster Loyalism in Historical Perspective. Dublin. 1978.

2943 CARSON (WILLIAM ARTHUR). Ulster and the Irish Republic. Belfast. 1956.

2944 UTLEY (THOMAS EDWIN). Lessons of Ulster. 1975.

2945 CRAWFORD (ROBERT GEORGE). Loyal to King Billy: A Profile of the Ulster Protestants. 1987.

2946 BELL (GEOFFREY). The Protestants of Ulster. 1976.

2947 —— The British in Ireland. 1984.

2948 BUCKLAND (PATRICK). Irish Unionism. 2 vols Dublin. 1972. 1973.

2949 —— 'The Unity of Ulster Unionism, 1886–1939'. *Hist.* 9 (1975), 211–23.

2950 —— Irish Unionism, 1885–1923: A Documentary History. Belfast. 1973. [HMSO].

2951 BIGGS-DAVISON (JOHN). The Hand is Red. 1973.

2952 BIGGS-DAVISON and CHOWDHARAY-BEST (GEORGE). The Cross of Saint Patrick: The Catholic Unionist Tradition in Ireland. Kensal. 1984.

2953 HARBINSON (JOHN FITZSIMONS). The Ulster Unionist Party, 1882–1973: Its Development and Organisation. Belfast, 1973.

2954 KINGHAN (NANCY). United We Stood: The Official History of the Ulster Women's Unionist Council, 1911–1974. Belfast. 1975.

2955 DISKIN (MICHAEL). The Development of Party Competition among Unionists in Ulster 1966–1982. Glasg. 1984.

2956 DAVIS (R.). 'Ulster Protestants and the Sinn Fein Press'. *Eire/Ireland* 15 (1980), 60–85.

2957 WALKER (GRAHAM). '"Protestantism before Party!": The Ulster Protestant League in the 1930's'. *Hist. J.* 28 (1985), 961–7.

2958 BOULTON (DAVID). The U.V.F. 1966–1973: An Anatomy of Loyalist Rebellion. Dublin. 1973.

2959 NELSON (SARA). Ulster's Uncertain Defenders: Protestant Political Paramilitary and Community Groups and the Northern Ireland Conflict. Belfast. 1984.

2960 AUGHEY (ARTHUR) and MCILHENEY (COLIN). 'Law Before Violence? The Protestant Paramilitaries in Ulster Politics'. *Eire/Ireland* 19 (1984), 55–74.

(d) Anglo-Irish Relations

2961 O₃FARRELL (PATRICK). Ireland's English Question: Anglo-Irish Relations, 1534–1970. 1971.

2962 —— England and Ireland since 1800. Oxf. 1980.

2963 MacDONAGH (OLIVER). States of Mind: A Study of Anglo-Irish Conflict 1780–1980. 1983.

2964 HARTLEY (STEPHEN). The Irish Question as a Problem in British Foreign Policy 1914–1918. Basingstoke. 1987.

2965 LAWLOR (SHEILA). Britain and Ireland, 1914–1923. Dublin. 1983.

2966 TOWNSHEND (CHARLES). The British Campaign in Ireland 1919–1921: The Development of Political and Military Policies. 1975.

2967 CANNING (PAUL). British Policy Towards Ireland 1921–1941. 1985.

2968 SHEARMAN (HUGH FRANCIS). Anglo-Irish Relations. 1948.

2969 GALLAGHER (FRANK). The Anglo-Irish Treaty. 1965.

2970 McCOLGAN (JOHN). British Policy and Irish Administration 1920–1922. 1983.

2971 HACHEY (THOMAS E.). 'The Neutrality Issue in Anglo-Irish Relations during World War Two'. *S. Atlantic Q.* 78 (1979), 157–71.

2972 O'HALPIN (EUNAN). The Decline of the Union: British Government in Ireland 1892–1920. Dublin. 1987.

2973 DRUDY (P. J.) ed. Ireland and Britain since 1922. Camb. 1986.

2974 BECKETT (JAMES CAMLIN). The Anglo-Irish Tradition. 1976.

2975 PAKENHAM (FRANCIS AUNGIER) *Earl of Longford.* Peace by Ordeal: An Account from First Hand Sources of the Negotiation and Signature of the Anglo-Irish Treaty, 1921. 1935. New edn 1972.

2976 FANNING (J. RONAN). 'The Response of the London and Belfast Governments to the Declaration of the Republic of Ireland, 1948–1949'. *Inl Affs* 58 (1981–2), 95–114.

2977 O'BRIEN (JOHN). 'Ireland's Departure from the British Commonwealth'. *Round Table* 306 (1988), 179–94.

2978 KENDLE (JOHN EDWARD). 'The Round Table Movement and "Home Rule All Round"'. *Hist. J.* 11 (1968), 332–53.

2979 —— 'Federalism and the Irish Problem 1918'. *Hist* 56 (1971), 207–30.

2980 BOYCE (DAVID GEORGE). 'British Conservative Opinion, the Ulster Question and the Partition of Ireland 1912–1921'. *Irish Hist. Studs* 17 (1970), 89–112.

2981 —— Englishmen and Irish Troubles: British Public Opinion and the Making of Irish Policy, 1918–1922. 1972.

2982 —— 'From War to Neutrality: Anglo-Irish Relations, 1921–1950'. *Brit. J. Inl Studs* 5 (1979), 15–36.

2983 SAVAGE (DAVID W.) *et al.* 'Ireland and British Politics, 1914–1921'. *J. Brit. Studs* 12 (1971), 84–149.

2984 SCHNEIDER (FRED D.). 'British Labour and Ireland, 1918–1921: The Retreat to Houndsditch'. *Rev. of Pol.* 11 (1978), 368–91.

2985 MCMAHON (DEIRDRE). Republicans and Imperialists: Anglo-Irish Relations in the 1930's. 1984.

2986 —— 'A Transient Apparition: British Policy Towards the De Valera Government 1932–1935'. *Irish Hist. Studs* 22 (1981), 331–61.

2987 DOWNEY (JAMES E.). Us and them: Britain, Ireland and the Northern Ireland Question, 1962–1982. Dublin. 1983.

2988 ARNOLD (BRUCE). What Kind of Country? Modern Irish Politics, 1968–1983. 1984.

2989 HARKNESS (DAVID W.). 'Mr De Valera's Dominion: Irish Relations with Britain and the Commonwealth, 1932–1938'. *J. Cwealth Pol. Studs* 8 (1970), 206–28.

2990 MANSERGH (PHILIP NICHOLAS SETON). The Irish Question, 1840–1921: A Commentary on Anglo-Irish Relations . . . 1940. Rev. edn 1965.

2991 STRAUSS (ERICH). Irish Nationalism and British Democracy. 1951.

2992 PECK (JOHN). Dublin from Downing Street. Dublin. 1978. [View of Anglo-Irish Relations in the 1970s by former British Ambassador.].

2993 JONES (THOMAS). Whitehall Diary No. 3: Ireland, 1918–1925. 1971. *Ed.* Keith Middlemas.

2994 O'BRIEN (CONOR CRUISE). Neighbours. 1980. [Anglo-Irish Relations.].

2995 JOHNSTON (A.). 'Britain, Ireland and Ulster'. *Rev. Inl Studs* 7 (1981), 187–98.

2996 GIRVIN (BRIAN) *and* STURM (ROLAND) *eds.* Politics and Society in Contemporary Ireland. Aldershot. 1986. [Essays on the Anglo-Irish Agreement.].

2997 POWER (PAUL F.). 'The Sunningdale Strategy and the Northern Majority Consent Doctrine in Anglo-Irish Relations'. *Eire-Ireland* 12 (1977), 35–67.

2998 KENNY (ANTHONY). The Road to Hillsborough: The Shaping of the Anglo-Irish Agreement. Oxf. 1986.

2999 HADDEN (TOM) *and* BOYLE (KEVIN). The Anglo-Irish Agreement: Commentary, Text and Official Review. 1987.

3000 O'LEARY (BRENDAN). 'The Anglo-Irish Agreement: Statecraft or Folly?'. *West Eur. Pols.* 10 (1987), 5–32.

3001 —— 'The Limits to Coercive Consocialisation in Northern Ireland'. *Pol. Studs* 37 (1989), 562–88.

3002 McGARRY (JOHN). 'The Anglo-Irish Agreement and Unlikely Prospects for Power-Sharing in Northern Ireland'. *Eire-Ireland* 23 (1988), 111–28.

3003 McKITTERICK (DAVID). Despatches from Belfast. Belfast. 1989.

3004 AUGHEY (ARTHUR). Ulster Unionism and the Anglo-Irish Agreement. 1989.

3005 COUGHLAN (A.). Fooled Again? The Anglo-Irish Agreement and After. Cork. 1986.

3006 HASLETT (E.). The Anglo-Irish Agreement: Northern Ireland Perspectives. Belfast. 1986.

3007 O'HALLORAN (CLARE). Partition and the Limits of Irish Nationalism. Dublin. 1987.

3008 KENNEDY (DENIS). The Widening Gulf: Northern Attitudes to the Independent Irish State, 1919–1949. Belfast. 1988.

3009 O'CLEARY (CONOR). 'The Effects of the European Monetary System on Anglo-Irish Relations'. *Pol. Q.* 50 (1979), 182–91.

(e) Irish Politicians

Browne

3010 BROWNE (NOEL). Against the Tide. Dublin. 1986.

Dillon

3011 LYONS (FRANCIS STEWART LELAND). John Dillon: A Biography. 1968.

Healy

3012 HEALY (TIMOTHY MICHAEL). Letters and Leaders of My Day. 2 vols 1928.

3013 O'FLAHERTY (LIAM). The Life of Tim Healy. 1927.

Redmond

3014 GWYNN (DENIS ROLLESTON). The Life of John Redmond. 1932.

3015 GWYNN (STEPHEN L.). Redmond's Last Years. 1932.

3016 WELLS (W. B.). John Redmond: A Biography. 1919.

Casement

3017 SAVORY (ROGER). Casement: The Flawed Hero. 1984.

3018 GWYNN (DENIS ROLLESTON). The Life and Death of Roger Casement. 1930.

3019 HYDE (HARFORD MONTGOMERY) *ed.* The Trial of Sir Roger Casement. 1960.

3020 INGLIS (BRIAN). Roger Casement. 1973.

3021 MacCOLL (RENÉ). Roger Casement: A New Judgement. 1956.

3022 REID (B. L.). The Lives of Roger Casement. 1976.

3023 KNOTT (GEORGE H.). Trial of Sir Roger Casement. Edin. 1917.

3024 SINGLETON-GATES (PETER). The Black Diaries: An Account of Roger Casement's Life and Times, With a Collection of his Diaries and Public Writings. 1959.

Collins

3025 FORESTER (MARGERY). Michael Collins: The Lost Leader. 1971.

3026 TAYLOR (REX). Michael Collins. 1958.

3027 RYAN (DESMOND). The Invisible Army: A Story of Michael Collins. 1932.

3028 O'BROIN (LEON). Michael Collins. Dublin. 1980.

3029 DWYER (T. RYLE). Michael Collins and the Treaty: His Differences with De Valera. Dublin. 1981.

Connolly

3030 GREAVES (CHARLES DESMOND). The Life and Times of James Connolly. 1961.

3031 EDWARDS (RUTH DUDLEY). James Connolly. Dublin. 1981.

3032 LEVENSON (SAMUEL). James Connolly: A Biography. 1973.

3033 REEVE (CARL). James Connolly and the United States: The Road to the 1916 Irish Rebellion. Atlantic Highlands, N.J. 1978.

3034 Mac an BEATHA (PROINSIAS). James Connolly and the Workers Republic. Baile atha Cliath. 1978.

3035 FALIGOT (ROGER). James Connolly et le Mouvement Révolutionnaire Irlandais. Paris. 1978.

3036 RYAN (DESMOND). James Connolly, His Life, Work and Writings. Dublin. 1924.

3037 RANSOM (B.). Connolly's Marxism. 1980.

3038 O'BRIEN (NORA CONNOLLY). James Connolly: Portrait of a Rebel Father. Dublin. 1975.

3039 —— Comp. James Connolly Wrote for Today. Dublin. 1978.

3040 ELLIS (PETER BERRESFORD) ed. James Connolly: Selected Writings. Harmondsworth. 1973. N.Y. 1974.

3041 FOX (RICHARD MICHAEL). James Connolly: The Forerunner. Tralee. 1943.

3042 MORGAN (AUSTEN). James Connolly: A Political Biography. 1988.

De Valera

3043 PAKENHAM (FRANCIS AUNGIER) Earl of Longford, and O'NEILL (THOMAS PATRICK). Eamon De Valera. 1970.

3044 MARX (ROLAND). Eamon De Valera. Paris. 1990.

3045 DWYER (T. RYLE). De Valera's Darkest Hour: In Search of National Independence 1919–1932. Dublin. 1982.

3046 —— De Valera's Finest Hour: In Search of National Independence 1932–1959. Dublin. 1982.

3047 BOWMAN (JOHN). De Valera and the Ulster Question, 1917–1973. Oxf. 1982.

3048 MOYNIHAN (MAURICE) ed. Speeches and Statements by Eamon De Valera, 1917–1973. Dublin. 1980.

3049 O'CARROLL (J. P.) and MURPHY (JOHN A.) eds. De Valera and His Times. Cork. 1983.

3050 BROMAGE (MARY COGAN). De Valera and the March of a Nation. N.Y. 1956.

3051 O'FAOLAIN (SEAN). De Valera. Harmondsworth. 1934.

3052 FITZGIBBON (C.) and MORRISON (G.). The Life and Times of Eamon de Valera. Dublin. 1973.

3053 EDWARDS (OWEN DUDLEY). Eamon De Valera. Cardiff. 1987.

Fitzgerald

3054 FITZGERALD (FERGUS) ed. Memoirs of Desmond Fitzgerald, 1913–1916. 1968.

Griffith

3055 YOUNGER (CALTON). Arthur Griffith. Dublin. 1981.

3056 DAVIS (RICHARD P.). Arthur Griffith. Dundalk. 1976.

3057 —— Arthur Griffith and Non-Violent Sinn Fein. Dublin. 1974.

3058 GRIFFITH (ARTHUR). The Resurrection of Hungary: A Parallel for Ireland, with Appendices on Pitt's Policy and Sinn Fein. 1918. 1st edn 1907. 3rd edn Dublin.

Hobson

3059 HOBSON (BULMER). Ireland Yesterday and Tomorrow. Tralee. 1968.

Larkin

3060 LARKIN (EMMET). James Larkin, Irish Labour Leader, 1876–1947. Lond./Camb. Mass. 1965.

MacNeill

3061 TIERNEY (MICHAEL). Eoin MacNeill: Scholar and Man of Action 1867–1945. [Ed. by Francis Xavier Martin.] Oxf. 1980.

3062 MARTIN (FRANCIS XAVIER) and BYRNE (F. J.) eds. The Scholar Revolutionary: Eoin MacNeill 1867–1945. Shannon. 1973.

McGilligan

3063 HARKNESS (DAVID W.). 'Patrick McGilligan, Man of Commonwealth'. J. Imp. Cwealth Hist. 8 (1979), 117–35.

O'Higgins

3064 WHITE (TERENCE DE VERE). Kevin O'Higgins. 1948.

O'Malley

3065 O'MALLEY (WILLIAM). Glancing Back. 1933.

O'Mara

3066 LAVELLE (PATRICIA). James O'Mara: A Staunch Sinn Feiner 1873–1948. Dublin. 1961.

Pearse

3067 PEARSE (PADRAIC H.). The Letters of Padraic H. Pearse. Gerrards Cross. 1980.

3068 CANNING (BERNARD J.). Padraig H. Pearse and Scotland: Cuimhneachan an Phiarsaigh, 1879–1979. Glasg. 1979. [Glasgow Padraig Pearse Centenary Committee.].

3069 EDWARDS (RUTH DUDLEY). Patrick Pearse: The Triumph of Failure. 1977.

3070 O'BUACHALLA (SEAMUS) ed. A Significant Educationalist: The Educational Writings of P. H. Pearse. Dublin. 1980.

Plunkett

3071 WEST (TREVOR). Horace Plunkett: Co-operation and Politics. Gerrards Cross. 1986.

Brookeborough

3072 BARTON (BRIAN). Brookeborough: The Making of a Prime Minister. Belfast. 1988.

Craig

3073 BUCKLAND (PATRICK). James Craig. Dublin. 1980.

3074 ERVINE (ST JOHN GREER). Craigavon: Ulsterman. 1949.

Paisley

3075 MARRINAN (PATRICK). Paisley: Man of Wrath. Tralee. 1973.

3076 BRUCE (STEVE). God Save Ulster: The Religion and Politics of Paisleyism. Oxf. 1986.

3077 MOLONEY (ED) *and* POLLAK (ANDY). Paisley. Dublin. 1986.

3078 SMYTH (CLIFFORD). Ian Paisley: Voice of Protestant Ulster. Edin. 1987.

3079 PAISLEY (RHONDA). Ian Paisley, My Father. Basingstoke. 1988.

3080 PAISLEY (IAN). Why I am a Protestant. 1968.

O'Neill

3081 O'NEILL (TERENCE) *Lord O'Neill of the Maine*. The Autobiography of Terence O'Neill. London. 1972.

3082 ——Ulster at the Crossroads. 1969. [With an introduction by John Cole.].

Midgley

3083 WALKER (GRAHAM). The Politics of Frustration: Harry Midgley and the Failure of Labour in Northern Ireland. Manch. 1985.

Faulkner

3084 FAULKNER (BRIAN) *Baron Faulkner*. Memoirs of a Statesman. 1978. [*Ed.* by John Houston.].

3085 BLEAKLEY (DAVID). Faulkner: Conflict and Consent in Irish Politics. 1974.

3086 BOYD (ANDREW). Brian Faulkner and the Crisis of Ulster Unionism. Tralee. 1972.

Devlin

3087 DEVLIN (BERNADETTE). The Price of My Soul. 1969.

3088 TARGET (GEORGE WILLIAM). Bernadette: The Story of Bernadette Devlin. 1975.

Hume

3089 WHITE (BARRY). John Hume: Statesman of the Troubles. Belfast. 1984.

I. LOCAL GOVERNMENT

The previous section on 'regionalism' and on 'devolution' leaves the question of 'local government' problematic. Indeed, 'local government' in the United Kingdom as a whole can be thought to be in protracted and unresolved crisis throughout this period. The growth in central government has left great uncertainty about the role of local authorities, an uncertainty which has in some places at some times issued in open hostility and conflict on such matters as finance and education. The literature reflects both the scholarly concern with these issues and also includes some polemical contribution to the debate. In addition, 'reform' of local government both as advocated and as sometimes implemented has raised contentious issues of identity. What is a 'locality'? Questions such as this also find a place elsewhere in the bibliography as discussed by geographers, sociologists, and town planners. In very recent decades, the form and nature of local government has become particularly important in England given the regional/national assertiveness elsewhere in the United Kingdom and which has resulted—entering at different times and for somewhat different reasons—in the presence of 'territorial' Secretaries of State in the United Kingdom cabinet—except for England. Are there English 'regions' and how can they be defined? How does local government as traditionally conceived relate to the 'regional identities' of the European Community? In other words, 'local government' is not a static category. What might have been thought its boundaries and responsibilities in 1914 sometimes had scant connection with the world of 1989. The literature naturally reflects this shifting picture.

1. REFERENCE

3090 YOUNGS (FREDERICK A.). Guide to the Local Administration Units of England. Vol. 1: Southern England. 2nd edn 1981.

3091 Godwin's Concise Guide to Local Authorities in England and Wales. 1974.

3092 GOLDING (LEWIS). Dictionary of Local Government in England and Wales. 1962.

3093 MINOGUE (MARTIN) ed. Documents on Contemporary British Government. Vol. 2: Local Government in Britain. Camb. 1977.

3094 Municipal Year Book and Public Services Directory. 1898–.

3095 Local Government Trends. 1973–83, 1987.

3096 JEFFERIES (ROGER). Tackling the Town Hall: A Local Authority Handbook. 1982.

3097 ROBINSON (MARY) comp. Local Authority Information Sources: A Guide to Publications, Databases and Services. 1986.

3098 HALASZ (D.). Metropolis. Den Haag. 1967.

3099 Local Government Annotations Service. Romford. 1965.

3100 ROWAT (DONALD C.) ed. International Handbook on Local Government Reorganization: Contemporary Developments. 1980.

3101 BARKER (W.). Local Government Statistics: A Guide to Statistics on Local Government Finance and Service in the United Kingdom at August 1964. 1965.

3102 —— Local Government Financial Statistics. 1953.

3103 —— Local Government Comparative Statistics. 1981.

3104 —— Who's Who in Local Government 1984/5. 1984.

3105 CROSS (CHARLES) and BAILEY (STEPHEN). Cross on Local Government Law. 7th edn 1986.

3106 DAVIES (KEITH). Local Government Law. 1983.

3107 SCHOFIELD (A. NORMAN). Local Government Elections. 1949. After many editions, now published as A. J. Little, ed. Schofield's Local Government Elections. 8th edn 1979.

2. GENERAL

3108 BASSETT (P.). A List of the Historical Records of the County Councils Association. (Now the Association of County Councils). 1980. SSRC.

3109 LIPMAN (VIVIAN DAVID). Local Government Areas, 1834–1945. Oxf. 1949.

3110 MORRIS (J. HERWALD). Local Government Areas. 1960.

3111 RICHARDS (MELVILLE). Welsh Administrative and Territorial Units: Medieval and Modern. Cardiff. 1969.

3112 REDLICH (JOSEF) and HIRST (FRANCIS WRIGLEY). The History of Local Government in England. 1903. Reissue of Book I with introduction and epilogue by Bryan Keith-Lucas. 1958. 2nd edn 1970.

3113 GRIFFITHS (ERNEST S.). The Modern Development of City Government in the United Kingdom and the United States. 2 vols. 1926–7.

3114 HILL (H. A.) and OLIVER (A. M.). The Local Government Act 1929 (Annotated). 1929.

3115 SMELLIE (KINGSLEY BRYCE SPEAKMAN). A History of Local Government. 1946. 4th edn 1968.

3116 HASLUCK (EUGENE LEWIS). Local Government in England. Camb. 1936. 2nd edn 1948.

3117 HARRIS (GEORGE MONTAGU). Local Government in Many Lands: A Comparative Study. 1933.

3118 —— Municipal Self-Government in Britain: A Study of the Practice of Local Government in Ten of the Larger British Cities. 1939.

3119 —— Comparative Local Government. 1948.

3120 CHESTER (DANIEL NORMAN). Central and Local Government: Financial and Administrative Relations. 1951.

3121 MIDWINTER (ARTHUR F.). The Politics of Local Spending. Edin. 1984. [Scotland.].

3122 MARSHALL (ARTHUR HEDLEY). Financial Administration in Local Government. 1960.

3123 KEITH-LUCAS (BRYAN) and RICHARDS (PETER GODFREY). A History of Local Government in the Twentieth Century. 1978.

3124 KEITH-LUCAS (BRYAN). English Local Government in the Nineteenth and Twentieth Centuries. 1977.

3125 HARRISON (MARY M. M.) and NORTON (ALAN). Local Government Administration in England and Wales. 1967.

3126 SEELEY (IVOR H.). Local Government Explained. 1978.

3127 ALEXANDER (ALAN). The Politics of Local Government in the United Kingdom. 1982.

3128 ALEXANDER (ALAN) and WRIGLEY (CHRIS). 'Symposium: Local Government'. Contemp. Record 2/6 (1989), 2–8.

3129 MABILEAU (ALBERT), MOYSER (GEORGE), PARRY (GERAINT), and QUANTIN (PATRICK). Local Politics and Participation in France and Britain. Camb. 1989.

3130 LOUGHLIN (MARTIN), GELFAND (M. DAVID), and YOUNG (KEN) eds. Half a Century of Municipal Decline 1935–1985. 1985.

3131 BRAND (JACK). Local Government Reform in England 1888–1974. 1974.

3132 PEARCE (CLIFFORD). The Machinery of Change in Local Government 1888–1974: A Study of Central Involvement. 1980.

3133 FREEMAN (T. W.). Geography and Regional Administration: England and Wales 1830–1968. 1968.

3134 THORNHILL (W.) ed. The Growth and Reform of English Local Government. 1971.

3135 ELCOCK (HOWARD). Local Government: Politicians, Professionals and the Public in Local Authorities. 2nd edn 1986.

3136 ROBSON (WILLIAM A.). The Development of Local Government. 1931. 3rd edn 1954.

3137 —— Local Government in Crisis. 1966. 2nd edn 1968.

3138 BYRNE (TONY). Local Government in Britain: Everyone's Guide to how it all works. 5th edn Harmondsworth. 1987.

3139 STOKER (GERRY). The Politics of Local Government. 1988.

3140 HAMPTON (WILLIAM). Local Government and Local Politics. 1987.

3141 MILLER (WILLIAM L.). Irrelevant Elections? The Quality of Local Democracy in Britain. Oxf. 1988.

3142 BULPITT (JAMES GRAHAM). Party Politics in English Local Government. 1967.

3143 MELLORS (COLIN) and COPPERTHWAITE (NIGEL). Local Government in the Community. Camb. 1987.

3144 GYFORD (JOHN) and WILSON (MARI). National Parties and Local Politics. 1983.

3145 GYFORD (JOHN), LEACH (STEVE), and GAME (CHRIS). The Changing Politics of Local Government. 1989.

3146 CROSS (C.) and MALLEN (D.). Local Government and Politics. 3rd edn 1987.

3147 WARREN (J. H.). 'The Party System in Local Government'. Parl. Affs 5 (1951–2), 179–94.

3148 SHARPE (L. J.) and NEWTON (KENNETH). Does Politics Matter? The Determinants of Public Policy. Oxf. 1984.

3149 LEACH (STEVE) and STEWART (J. D.). 'The Politics and Management of Hung Authorities'. Public Admin 66 (1988), 35–55.

3150 RICHARDS (PETER GODFREY). The Local Government System. 1983.

3151 —— The Reformed Local Government System. 1980.

3152 GYFORD (JOHN). Local Politics in Britain. 1976.

3153 JACKSON (RICHARD MEREDITH). The Machinery of Local Government. 1958. 2nd edn 1965.

3154 JACKSON (WILLIAM ERIC). The Structure of Local Government in England and Wales. 1949. 4th edn 1960.

3155 JACKSON (P. W.). Local Government. 1967. 3rd edn 1976.

3156 BENEMY (FRANK WILLIAM GEORGESON). Whitehall—Town Hall: A Brief Account of Central and Local Government. 1962. 6th edn 1967.

3157 CLARKE (JOHN JOSEPH). A History of Local Government of the United Kingdom. 1955.

3158 —— The Local Government of the United Kingdom. 1919. 20th edn 1969.

3159 FINER (HERMAN). English Local Government. 3rd edn 1950.

3160 MAUD (JOHN PRIMATT REDCLIFFE). Local Government in Modern England. 1932.

3161 MAUD (JOHN PRIMATT REDCLIFFE) and FINER (HERMAN). Local Government in England and Wales. 2nd edn Oxf. 1953.

3162 RHODES (R. A. W.). 'The Lost World of British Local Politics'. Local Gvt Studs 1 (1975), 39–59.

3163 CROUCH (W. W.). 'Local Government under the British Labour Government'. J. Pol. 12 (1950), 232–59.

3164 HAWKSWORTH (J. M.). 'Some Developments in Local Government 1944–1948'. Public Admin 29 (1948), 262–8.

3165 WISEMAN (HERBERT VICTOR) ed. Local Government in England 1958–69. 1970.

3166 Royal Commission on Local Government in England 1966–1969. Cmnd 4040, Parliamentary papers xxxviii (1968–9). [Chairman: Lord Redcliffe-Maud.].

3167 SHAW (JAMES E.). Local Government in Scotland: Past, Present and Future. Edin. 1942.

3168 Royal Commission on Local Government in Scotland 1966–1969. Cmnd 4150, Parliamentary Papers xxxix (1968–9) [Chairman Lord Wheatley.].

3169 The New Scottish Local Authorities: Organisation and Management Structures. 1973.

3170 Committee of Inquiry into Local Government in Scotland: Report. Cmnd 8115, Parliamentary Papers (1980–1). [Chairman Anthony Stodart.].

3171 Committee of Inquiry into the Functions and Powers of the Islands Councils in Scotland. Cmnd 9216, Parliamentary Papers (1983–4). [Chairman Sir David Montgomery.].

3172 WELSH (L.) ed. Royal Commission on Local Government: Evidence in Brief: Summaries of Evidence to the Commission and other Material on the Subject Published in the Local Government Chronicle. 1967.

3173 JONES (GEORGE W.). 'Mr Crossman and the Reform of Local Government, 1964–1966'. Parl. Affs 20 (1966), 77–89.

3174 BENJAMIN (ROGER W.). 'Local Government in Post-Industrial Britain; Studies of the Royal Commission on Local Government' in Comparing Urban Delivery Systems: Structure and Performance, Vincent Ostrom and Francis Bish, eds. 1977.

3175 WOOD (BRUCE). The Process of Local Government Reform 1966–74. 1976.

3176 SHARPE (L. J.). 'Elected Representatives in Local Government'. Brit. J. Sociol. xiii, 3 (1967).

3177 —— 'Leadership and Representation in Local Government'. Pol. Q. xxxvii, 2 (1966).

3178 MACKINTOSH (JOHN PITCAIRN). 'The Royal Commission on Local Government in Scotland 1966–1969'. Public Admin 48 (1970), 49–56.

3179 YOUNG (RONALD G.). The Search for Democracy: A Guide to and Polemic about Local Government in Scotland. Milngavie. 1977.

3180 PAGE (EDWARD C.) and MIDWINTER (ARTHUR F.). Remote Bureaucracy or Administrative Efficiency? Scotland's New Local Government System. Glasgow. 1979.

3181 DAWSON (ANDREW H.). 'The Idea of the Region: The Reorganisation of Scottish Local Government'. Public Admin 59 (1981), 279–94.

3182 SHARPE (L. J.). 'The Failure of Local Government Modernisation in Britain: A Critique of Functionalism'. *Can. J. Pub. Admin* 24 (1981).

3183 RICHARDS (PETER GODFREY). The Local Government Act 1972: Problems of Implementation. 1975.

3184 RICHARDSON (ANN). 'Decision-Making by Non-elected members: An Analysis of New Provisions in the 1972 Local Government Act'. *J. Social Pol.* 6 (1977), 171–84.

3185 Conduct in Local Government: Prime Minister's Committee on Local Government Rules of Conduct. Cmnd 4636, Parliamentary Papers viii (1974) [Chairman Lord Redcliffe-Maud—to consider the implications of the Poulson Affair.].

3186 GILLARD (MICHAEL) and TOMKINSON (MARTIN). Nothing to Declare: The Political Corruptions of John Poulson. 1980.

3187 ALEXANDER (ALAN). Local Government since Reorganisation. 1982.

3188 DEARLOVE (JOHN). The Reorganisation of British Local Government: Old Orthodoxies and Political Perspectives. Camb. 1979.

3189 Streamlining the Cities: Government Proposals for Reorganising Local Government in Greater London and the Metropolitan Counties Cmnd 9063, Parliamentary Papers (1983–4).

3190 —— The Conduct of Local Authority Business. Cmnd 9797–9801, Parliamentary Papers (1985–6).

3191 KEITH-LUCAS (BRYAN). The English Local Government Franchise. Oxf. 1952.

3192 JENNINGS (R. E.). 'The Changing Representational Role of the Local Councillor in England'. *Local Gvt Studs* 8 (1985), 67–86.

3193 ISAAC-HENRY (KESTER). 'Taking Stock of the Local Authority Associations'. *Public Admin* 62 (1984).

3194 GYFORD (JOHN) and JAMES (MARI). 'The Development of Party Politics in the Local Authority Associations'. *Local Gvt Studs* 8 (1982), 23–46.

3195 BINDER (B. J. A.). 'Relations between Central and Local Government since 1975: Are the Associations Failing?'. *Local Gvt Studs* 8 (1982), 35–44.

3196 SAMUELS (HARRY). The County Council: What it is and What it does. 1925. [Fabian Tract.].

3197 COHEN (EMMELINE W.). Autonomy and Delegation in County Government. 1952.

3198 KEITH-LUCAS (BRYAN). 'The Government of the County in England'. *Western Pol. Q.* 9 (1956), 44–55.

3199 STANYER (JEFFERY). County Government in England and Wales. 1967.

3200 YOUNG (KENNETH) *ed.* New Directions for County Government. 1989.

3201 CLARK (DAVID). Battle for the Counties: A Guide to the County Council Elections. 1977.

3202 SHARPE (L. J.) *ed.* Voting in Cities: The 1964 Borough Elections. 1967.

3203 BOCHEL (JOHN) *and* DENVER (DAVID T.). The Scottish Local Elections 1974: Results and Statistics. Edin. 1975.

3204 CRAIG (F. W. S.) *ed.* City and Royal Burgh of Glasgow: Municipal Election Results 1948–73. 1984.

3. LOCAL GOVERNMENT AND NATIONAL GOVERNMENT

3205 SADEK (S. E. M.). The Balance Point between Local Autonomy and National Control. The Hague. 1972. [England is discussed 11–70.].

3206 RHODES (R. A. W.). The National World of Local Government. 1986.

3207 —— Control and Power in Central-Local Relations. 1981.

3208 —— 'Continuity and Change in British Central-Local Relations: The "Conservative Threat"'. *Brit. J. Pol. Sci.* 14 (1984), 261–83.

3209 —— 'Intergovernmental Relations in the Post-War Period'. *Local Government Studs* 8 (1985), 35–56.

3210 ASHFORD (DOUGLAS E.). British Dogmatism and French Pragmatism: Central-Local Policymaking in the Welfare State. 1982.

3211 KEATING (MICHAEL). The City—Power and Policy: A Comparative Study of the United States, Britain and France. Aldershot. 1991.

3212 ELLIOTT (BRIAN) *and* MCCRONE (DAVID). 'Austerity and the Politics of Resistance'. In Cities in Recession: Critical Responses to the Urban Policies of the New Right, Ivan Szelenyi, 1984.

3213 JONES (GEORGE W.). Central-Local Relations in Britain. 1980.

3214 PAGE (EDWARD C.). Why Should Central/Local Relations in Scotland be any different from that in England? Glasgow. 1978.

3215 OULIHAN (BRIAN). The Politics of Local Government: Central-Local Relations. 1986.

3216 LOUGHLIN (MARTIN). Local Government in the Modern State. 1986.

3217 RANSON (STEWART), JONES (GEORGE W.), *and* WALSH (KIERON) *eds.* Between Centre and Locality: The Politics of Public Policy. 1985.

3218 GOLDSMITH (M.) *ed.* New Research in Central-Local Relations. 1986.

3219 YOUNG (KEN) *ed.* National Interests and Local Government. 1983.

3220 JONES (GEORGE W.) *ed.* New Approaches to the Study of Central-Local Government Relations. 1980.

3221 CHESTER (DANIEL NORMAN). Central and Local Government: Financial and Administrative Relations. 1951.

3222 CENTRAL POLICY REVIEW STAFF. Relations Between Central Government and Local Authorities. 1977.

3223 ELLIOTT (MICHAEL J.). The Role of Law in Central-Local Relations. 1981.

3224 LAFFIN (M.). Professionalism and Policy: The Role of the Professions in the Central/Local Relationship. 1986.

3225 GRIFFITH (JOHN ANEURIN GREY). Central Departments and Local Authorities. 1966.

3226 RHODES (GERALD) ed. Central-Local Relations: The Experience of the Environmental Health and Trading Services. 1986.

3227 JACOBS (BRIAN). 'Labour Against the Centre: The Clay Cross Syndrome'. *Local Government Studs* 10 (1984), 75–87.

3228 RICHARDS (PETER GODFREY). Delegation in Local Government: County to District Councils. 1956.

3229 LEACH (S. N.) and MOGRE (N.). 'County/District Relations in Shire and Metropolitan Counties in the Field of Town and Country Planning: A Comparison'. *Policy and Politics* 7 (1979), 165–79.

3230 LANSLEY (STEWART), GOSS (SUE), and WOLMAR (CHRISTIAN). Councils in Conflict: The Rise and Fall of the Municipal Left. 1989.

4. LOCAL GOVERNMENT SERVICE

3231 WARREN (J. H.). The Local Government Service. 1952.

3232 RIPLEY (B. J.). Administration in Local Authorities. 1970.

3233 POOLE (K. P.). The Local Government Service in England and Wales. 1978.

3234 WILSON (N.). 'The Local Government Service since the War'. *Public Admin* 30 (1952), 131–8.

3235 MINISTRY OF HOUSING AND LOCAL GOVERNMENT. Committee on the Staffing of Local Government. Report of the Committee. 1967.

3236 SMITH (TREVOR A.). Town and County Hall: Problems of Recruitment and Training. 1966.

3237 BOADEN (NOEL T.). 'Innovation and Change in English Local Government'. *Pol. Studs* 19 (1971), 416–29.

3238 GREENWOOD (ROYSTON) et al. Patterns of Management in Local Government. 1981.

3239 —— In Pursuit of Corporate Rationality: Organisational Developments in the Post—Reorganisation Period. Birmingham. 1977.

3240 RHODES (R. A. W.) and MIDWINTER (ARTHUR F.). Corporate Management: The New Conventional Wisdom in British Local Government. Glasg. 1980.

3241 GREENWOOD (ROYSTON) and STEWART (J. D.). Corporate Planning in English Local Government: An Analysis with Readings 1967–72. 1974.

3242 STEWART (J. D.). 'Developments in Corporate Planning in British Local Government: The Bains Report and Corporate Planning'. *Local Govt Studs* 5 (1973), 13–30.

3243 PINKUS (CHARLES E.) and DIXSON (ANNE). Solving Local Government Problems: Practical Applications of Operations Research in Cities and Regions. 1981.

3244 BOYNTON (Sir JOHN). Job at the Top: The Chief Executive in Local Government. 1986.

3245 HEADRICK (T. E.). The Town Clerk in English Local Government. 1962.

3246 BARRATT (Sir C.). 'The Town Clerk in British Local Government'. *Public Admin.* 41 (1963), 157–71.

3247 LAFFIN (M.) and YOUNG (KEN). 'The Changing Role and Responsibilities of Local Authority Chief Officers'. *Public Admin.* 63 (1985), 41–59.

3248 POYNTON (THOMAS LLEWELYN) et al. The Institute of Municipal Treasurers and Accountants: A Short History 1885–1960. 1960.

3249 DAVIES (R. V.) ed. Watchdog's Tales: The District Audit Service: The First 138 Years. 1986.

3250 HELMORE (LEONARD MERVYN). The District Auditor. 1961.

3251 WILSON (A.). 'The District Audit Service'. *Public Admin.* 28 (1950), 189–98.

3252 MOORE (V.) and SALES (H.). The Local Ombudsman: A Review of the First Five Years. 1980.

3253 LEWIS (NORMAN) and GATESHILL (BERNARD). The Commission for Local Administration: A Preliminary Appraisal. 1978.

3254 YARDLEY (D. C. M.). 'Local Ombudsmen in England: Recent Trends and Developments'. *Public Law* (1983), 522–31.

3255 CHINKIN (C. M.) and BAILEY (R. J.). 'The Local Ombudsman' *Public Admin.* 54 (1976), 267–82.

3256 COOK (P.). Ombudsman: An Autobiography. 1981.

3257 DEAKIN (NICHOLAS). 'Research and the Policy-Making Process in Local Government'. *Policy and Politics* 10 (1982), 303–16.

5. LOCAL GOVERNMENT FINANCE

3258 TRAVERS (TONY). The Politics of Local Government Finance. 1986.

3259 NEWTON (KEN) and KARRAN (T. J.). The Politics of Local Expenditure. 1985.

3260 HEPWORTH (N. P.). The Finance of Local Government. 7th edn 1984.

3261 DRUMMOND (JOSEPH MARGACH). The Finance of Local Government: England and Wales. 2nd edn 1962.

3262 FOSTER (C. D.), JACKSON (R. A.), and PERLMAN (M.). Local Government Finance in a Unitary State. 1980.

3263 CRAWFORD (C.) *and* MOORE (V.). The Free Two Pence: Section 137 of Local Government Act 1972 and Section 83 of the Local Government (Scotland) Act 1973. 1983.

3264 Local Government Finance: Report of the Committee of Inquiry Cmnd 6453, Parliamentary Papers xxi (1975–6).

3265 WARD (IAN) *and* WILLIAMS (PETER). 'The Government and Local Accountability since Layfield'. *Local Government Studs* 18 (1986), 21–32.

3266 BIRDSEYE (P.) *and* WEBB (T.). 'Why the Rate Burden is Cause for Concern'. *Nat. West Bank Q. Rev.* (Feb 1984), 2–15.

3267 BURGESS (TYRRELL) *and* TRAVERS (TONY). Ten Billion Pounds: Whitehall's Takeover of the Town Halls. 1980.

3268 BAILEY (S.) *and* MEADOWS (J.). 'High Spending Cities: An Historical Perspective'. *Public Money* 4 (1984), 21–6.

3269 HOGGART (KEITH). 'Property Tax Resources and Political Party Control in England 1974–1984'. *Urban Studs* 23 (1986), 33–46.

3270 ROSE (RICHARD) *and* PAGE (EDWARD) *eds.* Fiscal Stress in Cities. Camb. 1983.

3271 JACKSON (P. M.), MEADOWS (J.), *and* TAYLOR (A. B.). 'Urban Fiscal Decay in U.K. Cities'. *Local Government Studs* 8 (1985), 23–43.

3272 HOGGART (KEITH). 'Responses to Local Fiscal Stress: Local Government Expenditures in England 1976–85'. *Progress in Planning* 27 (1987), 137–220.

3273 ASHFORD (DOUGLAS E.). 'The Effects of Central Finance on the British Local Government System'. *Brit. J. Pol. Sci.* 6 (1976), 305–22.

3274 CRISPIN (A.). 'Local Government Finance: Assessing the Central Government's Contribution'. *Public Admin.* 54 (1976), 45–61.

3275 ATKINSON (R.). The Development of the Rate Support Grant (R.S.G.) System. Portsmouth. 1984.

3276 OLIVER (F. R.) *and* STANYER (JEFFREY). 'Some Aspects of the Financial Behaviour of County Boroughs'. *Public Admin.* 47 (1969), 169–84.

3277 GREENWOOD (ROYSTON). 'Changing Patterns of Budgeting in English Local Government'. *Public Admin.* 61 (1983), 149–68.

6. LOCAL GOVERNMENT IN LONDON

3278 ROBSON (WILLIAM A.). The Government and Misgovernment of London. 1939.

3279 RUCK (SYDNEY K.) *and* RHODES (GERALD). The Government of Greater London. 1970.

3280 YOUNG (KEN) *and* GARSIDE (PATRICIA L.). Metropolitan London: Politics and Urban Change 1837–1981. 1982.

3281 SAINT (ANDREW) *ed.* Politics and the People of London: The London County Council 1889–1965. 1989.

3282 FELDMAN (DAVID) *and* JONES (GARETH STEDMAN). Metropolis: London Histories and Representations since 1800. 1989.

3283 JACKSON (WILLIAM ERIC). Achievement: A Short History of the London County Council. 1965.

3284 MORRISON (HERBERT). How London is Governed. 1949.

3285 Royal Commission on Local Government in Greater London 1957–1960 Cmnd 1164, Parliamentary Papers xviii (1959–60).

3286 SHARPE (H.). 'The Politics of Local Government in Greater London'. *Public Admin.* xxxviii (1960).

3287 RHODES (GERALD). The Government of London: The Struggle for Reform. 1970.

3288 SMALLWOOD (F.). Greater London: The Politics of Metropolitan Reform. Indianapolis, Indiana. 1965.

3289 FOLEY (DONALD L.). Governing the London Region: Reorganisation and Planning in the Sixties. Berkeley, Ca. 1972.

3290 RHODES (GERALD) *ed.* The New Government of London: The First Five Years. 1972.

3291 CUTLER (HORACE). The Cutler Files. 1981.

3292 SEACOMBE (WALLY). 'Sheila Rowbotham on Labour and the Greater London Council'. *Can. Dimension* 21 (1987), 32–7.

3293 SOFER (ANNE). The London Left Takeover. 1987.

3294 MACKINTOSH (MAUREEN) *and* WAINWRIGHT (HILARY). A Taste of Power: The Politics of Local Economics. 1987.

3295 O'LEARY (BRENDAN). 'Why Was the GLC Abolished?'. *Inl J. Urban and Regional Res.* 11 (1987), 193–217.

3296 FORRESTER (A.), LANSLEY (S.), *and* PAULEY (R.). Beyond Our Ken: A Guide to the Battle for London. 1985.

3297 CRAIG (F. W. S.). Greater London Votes 1: The Greater London Council 1964–1970. 1971.

3298 ROWLEY (GWYN). 'The Greater London Council Elections of 1964 and 1967: A Study in Electoral Geography'. *Trans. Inst. Brit. Geog.* 53 (1971), 117–32.

3299 COUSINS (PAUL). 'The GLC Election 1981'. *London J.* 8 (1982), 39–62.

3300 BARTLEY (JEFF) *and* GORDON (IAN). 'London at the Polls: A Review of the 1981 GLC Election and Analysis'. *London J.* 8 (1982), 39–62.

3301 YOUNG (KEN). Local Politics and the Rise of the Party: The London Municipal Society and the Conservative Intervention in Local Elections 1894–1963. Leicester. 1975.

3302 'The Conservative Strategy for London 1855–1975'. *London J.* 1 (1975), 56–81.

3303 FULTON (H. W.). 'The GLC's Parliamentary Business'. *Gtr London Intelligence J.* 42 (1979), 18–23.

3304 MACE (R.) *ed.* Taking Stock: A Documentary History of the Greater London Council Supplies Department: Celebrating Seventy Five Years of Working for London. 1984.

7. LOCAL POLITICS

3305 GLASSBERG (ANDREW D.). Representation and the Urban Community. 1981.

3306 HUSBANDS (CHRISTOPHER TEMPLE). 'The London Borough Council Elections of 6 May 1982: Results and Analysis'. *London J.* 8 (1982), 177–90.

3307 COUSINS (P. F.). '1982: The Battle for the Boroughs'. *London Rev. Public Admin.* 15 (1983), 12–24.

3308 HUSBANDS (CHRISTOPHER TEMPLE). 'The London Borough Council Elections of 8 May 1986: Results and Analysis'. *London J.* 12 (1986), 146–66.

3309 REES (A. M.) *and* SMITH (T. A.). Town Councillors: A Study of Barking. 1964.

3310 WISTRICH (ENID). Local Government Reorganisation: The First Years of Camden. 1972.

3311 MESSINA (A. M.). 'Ethnic Minority Representation and Party Competition in Britain: The Case of Ealing Borough'. *Pol. Studs* 35 (1987), 224–38.

3312 BUTTERWORTH (R.). 'Islington Borough Council: Some Characteristics of Single-Party Rule'. *Politics* 1 (1966), 21–31.

3313 DEARLOVE (JOHN). The Politics of Policy in Local Government: The Making and Maintenance of Public Policy in the Royal Borough of Kensington and Chelsea. Camb. 1973.

3314 RODRIGUES (J.). 'Ted Knight Interviewed'. *Marxism Today* 25 (1981), 11–16.

3315 GOSS (SUE). Local Labour and Local Government: A Study of Interests, Politics and Policy in Southwark 1919 to 1982. Edin. 1989.

3316 MORPHET (JANICE). 'Local Authority Decentralisation— Tower Hamlets goes all the way'. *Policy and Politics* 15 (1987), 119–26.

3317 HUGHES (P.). 'Decentralisation in Tower Hamlets'. *Local Govt Policy Making* 14 (1987), 29–36.

3318 BERESFORD (PAUL). Good Council Guide: Wandsworth 1978–1987. 1987.

3319 'Struggles in the Welfare State: Wandsworth—The Cuts and the Fightback'. *Critical Social Policy* 1 (1981), 67–94.

8. LOCAL GOVERNMENT IN ENGLISH CITIES AND BOROUGHS

Birmingham.

3320 BLACK (H. J.). History of the Corporation of Birmingham Vol.6. 1936–50. Bham. 1957.

3321 NEWTON (KENNETH). Second City Politics: Democratic Processes and Decision Making in Birmingham. Oxf. 1976.

3322 MORRIS (D. S.) *and* NEWTON (KENNETH). 'The Social Composition of a City Council: Birmingham 1925–1966'. *Soc. Econ. Admin.* (1971), 29–33.

3323 MADDICK (H.) *and* PRITCHARD (E. P.). 'Conventions of Local Authorities in the West Midlands'. *Public Admin.* 36 (1958), 145–55 and 37 (1959), 135–43.

3324 SUTCLIFFE (ANTHONY). 'Political Leadership in Labour-controlled Birmingham: The Contrasting Style of Henry Watton (1959–66) and Stanley Yapp (1972–74)'. *Local. Gvt Studs* ii (1976), 15–32.

Bristol.

3325 CLEMENTS (ROGER VICTOR). Local Notables and the City Council (1969).

Derby.

3326 STUART (DENIS). County Borough: The History of Burton upon Trent 1901–74: Part 2: 1914–74. Burton on Trent. 1977.

Eastbourne.

3327 ASPDEN (J. C.). A Municipal History of Eastbourne 1938–1974. Eastbourne. 1979.

3328 GLOSSOP. BIRCH (ANTHONY HAROLD). Small Town Politics: A Study of Political Life in Glossop. 1959.

Leeds.

3329 WISEMAN (HERBERT VICTOR). Local Government at Work: A Case Study of a County Borough. 1967.

Liverpool.

3330 BERRY (DAVID). The Sociology of Grass Roots Politics: A Study of Party Membership. 1970.

3331 PARKINSON (MICHAEL). Liverpool on the Brink: One City's Struggle against Government Cuts. 1985.

3332 TAAFE (PETER) *and* MULHEARN (TONY). Liverpool: A City that Dared to Fight. 1988. [A 'Militant' perspective.].

3333 MIDWINTER (ARTHUR F.). 'Setting the Rate: Liverpool Style'. *Local. Gvt Studs* 11 (1985), 25–33.

Newcastle-Under-Lyme.

3334 BEALEY (FRANK WILLIAM), BLONDEL (JEAN), *and* MCCANN (WILLIAM). Constituency Politics: A Study of Newcastle-under-Lyme. 1965.

Newcastle-Upon-Tyne.

3335 GREEN (D. G.). Power and Party in an English City: An Account of Single-Party Rule. 1981.

3336 SMITH (T. DAN). 'Local Government in Newcastle: the Background to some Recent Developments'. *Public Admin.* 43 (1965), 413–18.

3337 An Autobiography. Newcastle. 1970.

Portsmouth.

3338 Borough Government in Portsmouth 1835–1974. Portsmouth. 1975.

Reading.

3339 ALEXANDER (ALAN). Borough Government and Politics: Reading 1835–1985. 1985.

Sheffield.

3340 HAMPTON (WILLIAM). Democracy and Community: A Study of Politics in Sheffield. Oxf. 1970.

3341 Forty Years of Labour Rule in Sheffield. Sheffield. 1967. [Sheffield Trades and Labour Council.].

3342 BLUNKETT (DAVID) *and* JACKSON (KEITH). Democracy in Crisis: The Town Halls Respond. [A book which draws on, but is not confined to, Sheffield experience.].

Wolverhampton.

3343 JONES (GEORGE W.). Borough Politics: A Study of the Wolverhampton Town Council 1888–1964. 1969.

York.

3344 MORRELL (J. B.) *and* WATSON (A. G.) *eds.* How York governs itself. 1928.

3345 —— *Eds.* Whitehall at York: How York is Governed by the Ministers of the Crown. 1933.

3346 MINISTRY OF HOUSING AND LOCAL GOVERNMENT. Report of the Inspector appointed by the Minister of Housing and Local government to hear Objections to the Proposals of the Local Government Commission for England for the City of York and surrounding areas. 1966.

9. ENGLISH COUNTY COUNCILS

Bedfordshire.

3347 Bedfordshire County Council: A Hundred Years at Your Service 1889–1989. Bedfordshire C.C. 1988.

Berkshire.

3348 DAVIES (E. R.). A History of the First Berkshire County Council. Berkshire C.C. 1981.

Cheshire.

3349 LEE (JOHN MICHAEL). Social Leaders and Public Persons: A Study of County Government in Cheshire Since 1888. Oxf. 1963.

3350 WOOD (BRUCE), SOLOMON (BARBARA W.), *and* WALTERS (PETER). The Scope of Local Initiative: A Study of Cheshire County Council 1961–1974. 1974.

Cornwall.

3351 DAVIES (A. L.) *ed.* Cornwall County Council 1889–1989: A History of 100 Years of County Government. Cornwall C.C. 1989.

Cumbria.

3352 A Century of Service 1889–1989. Cumbria C.C. 1989. [Cumbria consists of Cumberland, Westmorland and part of Lancashire.].

Devon.

3353 STANYER (JEFFERY). A History of Devon County Council 1889–1989. Exeter. 1989.

East Sussex.

3354 BELL (CHRISTOPHER RICHARD VINCENT). A History of East Sussex Council 1889–1974. Chichester. 1976.

Essex.

3355 100 Not Out: A Centenary of Service: Essex County Council 1889–1989. Essex C.C. 1989.

Hampshire.

3356 RUSHTON (G. A.). 100 Years of Progress; Hampshire County Council 1889–1989. Hampshire C.C. 1989.

Hertfordshire.

3357 SHELDRICK (G.). The Hart Reguardant: Hertfordshire County Council 1889–1989. 1989.

Humberside.

3358 ELCOCK (HOWARD). 'English Local Government Reformed: The Politics of Humberside'. *Public Admin* 53 (1975), 159–66.

Kent.

3359 MOYLAN (P. A.). The Form and Reform of County Government: Kent 1889–1974. Leicester. 1978.

3360 1889–1974. Kent C.C. 1975.

Lancashire.

3361 MARSHALL (JOHN D.) *and* MCCLINTOCK (MARION E.) *eds.* The History of Lancashire County Council 1889–1974. 1977.

Lincolnshire (Lindsey).

3362 WICKSTEAD (A.). Lincolnshire, Lindsey: The Story of the County Council 1889–1974. 1978.

Manchester (Greater).

3363 FRANGOPULO (N. J.). Tradition in Action: The Historical Evolution of the Greater Manchester County. Wakefield. 1977.

Norfolk.

3364 WILKINS-JONES (C.) *ed.* Centenary: A Hundred Years of County Government in Norfolk 1889–1989. Norwich. 1989.

3365 Norfolk County Council 1889–1974. Norwich. 1974.

3366 JOHNSON (R. W.). 'The Nationalisation of English Rural Politics: Norfolk South-West 1945–1970'. *Parl. Affs* 26 (1972), 8–55.

Shropshire.

3367 BAUGH (G. C.). Shropshire and its Rulers: A Thousand Years. Shrewsbury. 1979.

Staffordshire.

3368 FOWLES (D.) *et al.* 100 Not Out: A Look Back at 100 Years of Staffordshire County Council. Staffordshire C.C. Stafford. 1989.

Warwickshire.

3369 MITCHELL (D. J.). A History of Warwickshire County Council 1889–1989. Warwickshire C.C. 1988.

West Sussex.

3370 GODFREY (J.) *et al.* West Sussex County Council: The First Hundred Years. West Sussex C.C. 1988.

Wiltshire.

3371 ROGERS (K.). Wiltshire County Council: The First Hundred Years 1889–1989. Wiltshire C.C. 1989.

Yorkshire (North Riding).

3372 ASHCROFT (M. Y.) *ed.* A History of the North Riding of Yorkshire County Council 1889–1974. North Riding of Yorkshire C.C. Northallerton. 1974.

Yorkshire (West Riding)

3373 BARBER (B. J.) *and* BERESFORD (M. W.). The West Riding County Council 1889–1974: Historical Studies. West Yorkshire Metropolitan C.C. 1979.

10. SCOTTISH CITIES AND BURGHS

Edinburgh.

3374 ELLIOTT (BRIAN), McCRONE (DAVID), *and* SKELTON (VALERIE). 'Property and Political Power: Edinburgh 1875–1975'. In The Middle Class in Politics, John Garrard *et al.*, eds. Farnborough. 1978.

Glasgow.

3375 BUDGE (IAN), BRAND (JACK), MARGOLIS (MICHAEL) *and* SMITH (A. L. M.), Political Stratification and Democracy. 1972.

3376 BUDGE (IAN). 'Electors' Attitudes towards Local Government. A Survey of a Glasgow Constituency'. *Pol. Studs* 13, (1965), 386–92.

3377 KEATING (MICHAEL). The City that Refused to Die: Glasgow: The Politics of Urban Regeneration. Aberd. 1988.

Peterhead.

3378 BEALEY (FRANK WILLIAM) *and* SEWEL (JOHN). The Politics of Independence: A Study of a Scottish Town. Aberd. 1981.

11. WELSH AUTHORITIES

3379 REES (IOAN BOWEN). Government by Community. 1971.

Haverfordwest.

3380 DICKMAN (H. J.). Haverfordwest Rural District Council: A History of the Council 1894–1974. Haverfordwest. 1976.

3381 FOULKES (DAVID). 'The Work of the Local Commissioner for Wales'. *Public Law* (1978), 264–89.

3382 BRENNAN (T.), COONEY (E. W.), *and* POLLINS (H.). 'Party Politics and Local Government in Western South Wales'. *Pol. Q.* 25, (1954), 76–83.

3383 MORGAN (PRYS TOMOS JON) *ed.* Glamorgan Society 1780–1980. Cardiff. 1988.

3384 JOHN (ARTHUR H.) *and* WILLIAMS (GLANMOR) *eds.* Glamorgan County History 5: Industrial Glamorgan from 1700 to 1970. Cardiff. 1980.

3385 AMBROSE (G. P.). Monmouthshire County Council 1888–1974. Gwent C.C. 1974.

12. NORTHERN IRELAND

3386 CONNOLLY (MICHAEL) *ed.* 'Local Government in Northern Ireland'. *Local Gvt Studs* 12 (1986), 13–60.

3

THE ECONOMY AND INDUSTRY

A. THE HISTORY OF THE BRITISH ECONOMY

General surveys and histories of the British economy have become steadily more plentiful. They are listed in this section alongside general studies of particular aspects of the economy. As in other areas of British public life, a perception of decline has led economic historians and economists in some cases to combine analysis with prescription. It has been the alleged peculiarities of the British economy which have particularly attracted attention in recent general assessments. The more detailed chronologically located studies reflect the consolidation of economic history as a sub-discipline, even though one author writes of its 'rise and decline'. These studies of sub-periods blend both contemporary or near-contemporary assessments and later interpretations since, as always, what contemporaries believed to be happening was not infrequently a factor in what subsequently happened. Such has been the close relationship between economic history and economic planning that it makes little sense to suppose that economic history is 'academic' and economic policy is 'practical'. It is also clear, however, particularly in the decades since 1945, that there is a certain artificiality in supposing that the British economy can be understood without reference to the economies of the United States and of Western Europe with which, to greater or lesser degree, it has become linked. There is indeed a considerable body of literature which specifically addresses Anglo-American economic relations but its existence brings into relief how limited are the studies of the relationship, over time, between the British economy and other European, Asian, or Commonwealth economies.

1. BIBLIOGRAPHIES AND GENERAL SURVEYS

3387 CHALONER (WILLIAM HENRY) *and* RICHARDSON (ROGER CHARLES). British Economic and Social History: A Bibliographical Guide. Manch. 1976. 2nd edn 1984.

3388 HAMILTON (FREDERICK EDWIN IAN). Regional Economic Analysis in Britain and the Commonwealth: A Bibliographical Guide. 1968.

3389 HALL (LAURA MARGARET) *Lady et al.* A Bibliography in Economics. 1957. 2nd edn 1959.

3390 PRATT (ALAN FREDERICK WESTON). Economic and Social History: A Booklist for Schools. 1938.

3391 ECONOMIC HISTORY REVIEW. 'List of Publications on the Economic History of Great Britain and Ireland'. *Econ. Hist. Rev.* 1– (1927–). [Pub. annually.].

3392 HARTE (NEGLEY BOYD). 'Trends in Publications on the Economic and Social History of Great Britain and Ireland, 1925–1974'. *Econ. Hist. Rev.* 2nd ser. 30 (1977), 20–41.

3393 —— *Ed.* The Study of Economic History. 1971.

3394 GILBERT (VICTOR F.) *and* HOLMES (COLIN). Theses and Dissertations in Economic and Social History in Yorkshire Universities, 1920–1974. Sheffield. 1975.

3395 STURGES (RODNEY PAUL). Economists' Papers, 1750–1950: A Guide to Archive and other Manuscript Sources for the History of British and Irish Economic Thought. 1975.

3396 LANE (PETER). Documents on British Economic and Social Policy, vol. 2 [1870–1939], 1968, and vol. 3 [1945–1967], 1969.

3397 WILLIAMS (THOMAS GEORGE). The Main Currents of Social and Industrial Change 1870–1924. 1925.

3398 REES (*Sir* JAMES FREDERICK). A Survey of Economic Development, with Special Reference to Great Britain. 1933.

3399 DERRY (THOMAS KINGSTON). Outlines of English Economic History. 1932.

3400 HOLLIS (MAURICE CHRISTOPHER). The Two Nations: A Financial Study of English History. 1935.

3401 WHITE (LESLIE WILLIAM). Industrial and Social Revolution, 1750–1937. 1938.

3402 LEWIS (*Sir* WILLIAM ARTHUR). An Economic Survey, 1919–1939. 1949.

3403 SLATER (GILBERT). The Growth of Modern England. 1939.

3404 DIETZ (FREDERICK CHARLES). An Economic History of England. 1942.

3405 ALDCROFT (DEREK HOWARD) *and* FEARON (PETER) *eds.* British Economic Fluctuations, 1790–1939. 1972.

3406 —— *Eds.* Economic Growth in 20th Century Britain. 1969.

3407 ALDCROFT (DEREK HOWARD) *and* RICHARDSON (HENRY WARD). The British Economy, 1870–1939. 1969.

3408 ALDCROFT (DEREK HOWARD). British Railways in Transition: The Economic Problems of Britain's Railways since 1914. 1968.

3409 —— British Transport since 1914: An Economic History. 1975.

3410 ASHWORTH (WILLIAM). An Economic History of England, 1870–1939. 1960.

3411 LENMAN (BRUCE). An Economic History of Modern Scotland, 1660–1976. 1977.

3412 TOMLINSON (JIM). Problems of British Economic Policy, 1870–1945. 1981.

3413 CHALONER (WILLIAM HENRY) *and* RATCLIFFE (BARRIE M.) *eds.* Trade and Transport: Essays in Economic History in Honour of T. S. Willan. Manch. 1977.

3414 McDOUGALL (*Sir* DONALD). Studies in Economic Policy. 2 vols 1975.

3415 GAMBLE (ANDREW). Britain in Decline: Economic Policy, Political Strategy and the British State. 1981. 2nd edn 1985.

3416 MORRIS (JOSEPH ACTON). The Growth of Industrial Britain: A Work Book and Study Guide in Social and Economic History. 1971.

3417 SMITH (HENRY). A Select Bibliography on the Monetary System. Leicester. 1937.

3418 RICHARDS (RICHARD DAVID). Money and Banking: A Select Bibliography. Camb. 1929.

3419 OTTLEY (GEORGE) *ed.* A Bibliography of British Railway History. 1965.

3420 U.K. MINES DEPARTMENT. Catalogue of Publications Relating to the Mining, Quarrying and Petroleum Industries. 1937.

3421 BUXTON (NEIL K.). The Economic Development of the British Coal Industry: From the Industrial Revolution to the Present Day. 1979.

3422 HORROCKS (SIDNEY) *comp.* Lancashire Business Histories. Manch. 1971.

3423 SAVAGE (CHRISTOPHER I.). An Economic History of Transport. 1959.

3424 SHEPERD (WILLIAM G.). 'Changes in British Industrial Concentration, 1951–1958'. *Oxf. Econ. Papers* 18 (1966), 126–32.

3425 FOGARTY (MICHAEL P.). Prospects of the Industrial Areas of Great Britain. 1945.

3426 —— Further Studies in Industrial Organisation. 1948.

3427 ALLEN (GEORGE). The Structure of Industry in Britain: A Study in Economic Change. 1961. [Covers period 1900–60.].

3428 KAHN (ALFRED EDWARD). Great Britain in the World Economy. 1946.

3429 KINDLEBERGER (CHARLES POOR). Economic Growth in France and Britain, 1851–1950. Camb., Mass. 1964.

3430 LEONARD (A.). Britain's Economy. Ilfracombe. 1970.

3431 HANNAH (LESLIE). The Rise of the Corporate Economy. 1976.

3432 DEVONS (ELY). An Introduction to British Economic Statistics. Camb. 1950.

3433 LEWES (FREDERICK MARTIN MEREDITH). Statistics of the British Economy. 1967.

3434 PHELPS (EDMUND STRUTHER) *ed.* Economic Justice, Selected Readings. Harmondsworth. 1973.

3435 HICKS (*Sir* JOHN RICHARD). The Social Framework: An Introduction to Economics. Oxf. 1942. 3rd edn 1960.

3436 WALKER (GILBERT). Economic Planning by Programme and Control in Great Britain. 1957.

3437 DENTON (GEOFFREY) *et al.* Economic Planning in Britain, France, and Germany. 1968.

3438 BURRAGE (MICHAEL). 'Culture and Britain's Economic Growth'. *Brit. J. Sociol.* 20 (1969), 117–33.

3439 ASHLEY (*Sir* WILLIAM JAMES). The Economic Organisation of England: An Outline History. [With a new chapter on economic instability and state intervention.] 1935.

3440 BRANTON (NOEL). The Economic Organisation of Modern Britain. 1966.

3441 RUNDLE (RAYMOND NORMAN). Britain's Economic and Social Development from 1700 to the Present Day. 1973.

3442 ASHWORTH (WILLIAM). Contracts and Finance. 1953.

3443 JONES (GWILYM PEREDUR) *and* POOL (CHARLES GEORGE). A Hundred Years of Economic Development in Great Britain. 1940.

3444 BREACH (ROBERT WALTER) *and* HARTWELL (RONALD MAX) *eds*. British Economy and Society, 1870–1970: Documents, Descriptions, Statistics. 1972.

3445 PREST (ALAN RICHMOND) *ed*. The U.K. Economy: A Manual of Applied Economics. 1966. 8th edn 1980.

3446 LIVINGSTONE (JAMES MCCARDLE). The British Economy in Theory and Practice. 1974.

3447 SMITH (WILFRED). An Economic Geography of Great Britain. 2nd edn 1953.

3448 MUSGRAVE (PETER WILLIAM). The Economic Structure. 1969.

3449 MORRIS (DEREK) *ed*. The Economic System in the United Kingdom. Oxf. 3rd edn 1985.

3450 SELLMAN (GEORGE RAYMOND STANLEY). A Practical Guide to Modern British Economic History, from 1700 to the Present Day. 1947.

3451 LE RUEZ (JACQUES). Economic Planning and Politics in Britain. N.Y. 1975. [Covers 1945–74.].

3452 ROLL (ERIC). The Uses and Abuses of Economics. 1978.

3453 HAWKE (GARY RICHARD). Economics for Historians. Camb. 1980.

3454 WRIGHT (J. F.). Britain in the Age of Economic Management: An Economic History since 1939. N.Y./Oxf. 1979.

3455 ROBERTS (DAVID WILLIAM). An Outline of the Economic History of England to 1952. 6th edn 1954. 1st edn 1931, which covered period to 1930.

3456 THOMAS (MAURICE WALTON) *ed*. A Survey of English Economic History. 1957.

3457 CLAPHAM (*Sir* JOHN HAROLD). An Economic History of Modern Britain. Vol. 3, epilogue 1914–1929. Camb. 1938. Repr. 1950–52.

3458 PHILLIPS (GORDON ASHTON) *and* MADDOCK (ROWLAND THOMAS). The Growth of the British Economy 1918–1968. 1973.

3459 SOUTHGATE (GEORGE WALTER). English Economic History. [With full summaries.] 1948.

3460 MCDONNELL (KEVIN GEORGE THOMAS) *et al*. A Survey of English Economic History. 1960.

3461 LIPSON (EPHRAIM). The Growth of English Society: A Short Economic History. 1954. 4th edn 1959.

3462 NIEMEYER (NANNIE) *and* SPALDING (ETHEL HOWARD). England: A Social and Economic History, 1830 to 1936. 1937. 5th edn 1953.

3463 CROOME (HONORIA RENÉE MINTURN) *and* HAMMOND (RICHARD JAMES). The Economy of Britain: A History. 1938. 2nd edn 1947.

3464 JOHNSON (EDGAR AUGUSTUS JEROME). An Economic History of Modern England. N.Y. 1939.

3465 JACKSON (JOHN HAMPDEN). England since the Industrial Revolution, 1815–1948. 1949.

3466 MEREDITH (HUGH OWEN). Economic History of England: A Study in Social Development. 5th edn 1949.

3467 COLE (GEORGE DOUGLAS HOWARD). Introduction to Economic History, 1750–1950. 1952.

3468 FAY (CHARLES RULE). Great Britain from Adam Smith to the Present Day. 1928.

3469 LYTHE (SAMUEL GEORGE EDGAR). British Economic History since 1760. 1951.

3470 —— An Economic History of Scotland, 1100–1939. Glasg. 1975.

3471 CAIRNCROSS (*Sir* ALEXANDER KIRKLAND) *ed*. The Scottish Economy: A Statistical Account of Scottish Life. 1954.

3472 CAMPBELL (ROY HUTCHESON). 'Scottish Economic History'. [Review article] *Scot. J. Pol. Econ.* 23 (1976), 183–92.

3473 SMOUT (T. CHRISTOPHER). 'US Consular Reports: A Source for Scottish Economic Historians'. *Scot. Hist. Rev.* 58 (1979), 179–85.

3474 PROUDFOOT (B.). 'A Perspective on the Scottish Economy'. *Scot. Geog. Mag.* 100 (1984), 96–103.

3475 GEORGE (K. D.) *and* MAINWARING (LYNN). The Welsh Economy. Cardiff. 1981.

3476 COURT (WILLIAM HENRY BASSANO). A Concise Economic History of Britain from 1750 to Recent Times. 1954.

3477 HOBLEY (LEONARD FRANK). Living and Working: A Social and Economic History of England, 1760–1960. 1974.

3478 FEINSTEIN (CHARLES) *ed*. The Managed Economy: Essays in British Economic Policy since 1929. 1983.

3479 FLINN (MICHAEL WALTER). An Economic and Social History of Britain since 1700. 1963.

3480 PERRY (DONALD GORDON). A Social and Economic History Notebook, 1750–1960. 1955. 3rd edn 1963.

3481 SAYERS (RICHARD SIDNEY). The Vicissitudes of an Export Economy: Britain since 1880. Sydney. 1965.

3482 —— A History of Economic Change in England, 1880–1939. 1967.

3483 HOLLAND (A. J.). The Age of Industrial Expansion: British Economic and Social History since 1700. 1968. 2nd edn 1976.

3484 READER (KEITH STANLEY). The Modern British Economy in Historical Perspective. Harlow. 1969.

3485 BRANDON (LEONARD GEORGE). A Short Economic and Social History of England. [Book 2: Modern Times.] 1942. 3rd rev. edn 1951.

3486 BRIGGS (MILTON) *and* JORDAN (PERCY). An Economic History of England. 1914. 11th edn 1964.

3487 CARUS-WILSON (ELEANORA MARY) *ed*. Essays in Economic History . . . 3 vols 1954. 1962.

3488 CLIFFORD (JAMES). Aspects of Economic Development, 1760–1960. 1967.

3489 WALKER (JAMES). British Economic and Social History, 1700–1977. 2nd edn Plymouth 1979. [1st pub. 1968, covering period 1700–1967.].

3490 MURPHY (BRIAN). A History of the British Economy, 1086–1970. 1973.

3491 PARKER (MICHAEL ST. JOHN) and REID (DAVID JAMES). The British Revolution, 1750–1970: A Social and Economic History. 1972.

3492 JOHNSON (WALFORD) et al. A Short Economic and Social History of 20th Century Britain. 1967.

3493 HOBSBAWM (ERIC JOHN ERNEST). Industry and Empire: An Economic History of Britain since 1750. 1968.

3494 JONES (RICHARD BENJAMIN). The Economic and Social History of England, 1770–1977. 1979. [1st pub. 1971, covering the period 1700–1970.].

3495 POLLARD (SIDNEY). The Development of the British Economy, 1914–1980. 1962. 3rd edn 1983.

3496 COURT (WILLIAM HENRY BASSANO). Scarcity and Choice in History. 1970.

3497 COWIE (LEONARD WALLACE). The Industrial Revolution 1750 to the Present Day. 1970.

3498 ADAMS (DAVID PHILIP). The Evolution of Modern Britain. 1970.

3499 CAIRNCROSS (Sir ALEXANDER KIRKLAND) and SINCLAIR (PETER). An Introduction to Economics. 6th edn 1982. 1st edn 1944.

3500 CAIRNCROSS (Sir ALEXANDER KIRKLAND). Changing Perceptions of Economic Policy: Essays in Honour of the Seventieth Birthday of Sir Alec Cairncross. 1981. Ed. Frances Cairncross.

3501 SINCLAIR (PETER). 'Economic Debates'. Ch. in Trends in British Politics since 1945. Chris Cook and John Ramsden, eds. 1978.

3502 PEACOCK (ALAN). 'The British Economy and its Problems'. Ch. in British Progress and Decline. William B. Gwyn and Richard Rose, eds. 1980.

3503 McCLOSKEY (DONALD NANSEN) ed. Essays on a Mature Economy: Britain after 1840. 1971.

3504 GREGG (PAULINE). A Social and Economic History of Britain 1760–1972. 1950. 7th edn 1973.

3505 TITLEY (DAVID PAUL). Machines, Money and Men: An Economic and Social History of Great Britain from 1700 to the 1970s. 1973.

3506 HILL (CHARLES PETER). British Economic and Social History, 1700–1975. 4th edn 1977.

3507 ROBERTS (JIM) and ROWE (ALBERT W.). Making the Present: A Social and Economic History of Britain, 1918–1972. 1975.

3508 YOUNGSON (ALEXANDER JOHN). The British Economy, 1920–1957. 1960. [Repr. as 'Britain's Economic Growth, 1920–1966'. 1968.].

3509 ASHLEY (MAURICE). The People of England: A Short Social and Economic History. 1982. Repr. 1984.

3510 PAISH (FRANK WALTER). How the Economy Works and other Essays. 1970.

3511 POPE (REX) and HOYLE (BERNARD) eds. British Economic Performance, 1880–1980. 1984.

3512 KIRBY (MAURICE W.). The Decline of British Economic Power since 1870. 1981.

3513 FLOUD (RODERICK) and MCCLOSKEY (DONALD NANSEN) eds. The Economic History of Britain since 1700: vol. 2. 1860 to the 1970s. Camb. 1981.

3514 MATTHEWS (ROBERT CHARLES OLIVER), FEINSTEIN (CHARLES), and ODLING-SMEE (J. C.). British Economic Growth, 1856–1973. 1982.

3515 ROBBINS (LIONEL CHARLES) Baron. Political Economy Past and Present: A Review of Leading Theories in Economic Policy. 1976.

3516 KALDOR (NICHOLAS) Baron. Essays on Economic Policy. 2 vols 1964. Repr. 1980.

3517 HOSKINS (WILLIAM GEORGE). Provincial England: Essays in Social and Economic History. 1963.

3518 WRIGHT (J. F.). 'British Economic Growth, 1688–1959'. Econ. Hist. Rev. 18 (1965), 397–412.

3519 GAYLER (JOSHUA LEONARD) et al. A Sketch Map Economic History of Britain. 1957.

3520 HARROD (ROY F.). The British Economy. N.Y. 1963.

3521 ASH (JOHN COLIN KEITH). Forecasting the United Kingdom Economy. Farnborough. 1973.

3522 TOMLINSON (JIM). British Macroeconomic Policy since 1940. 1986.

3523 ALDCROFT (DEREK HOWARD). The British Economy. Brighton. 1988.

3524 DONALDSON (PETER). A Guide to the British Economy. 1965. 4th edn Harmondsworth. 1976.

3525 DUNNETT (ANDREW). Understanding the British Economy. 1982.

3526 FINE (BEN) and HARRIS (LAURENCE). The Peculiarities of the British Economy. 1985.

3527 MAY (TREVOR). An Economic and Social History of Britain, 1760–1970. Harlow. 1987.

3528 WINCH (DONALD). Economics and Policy: A Historical Study. 1969.

3529 HARE (P. G.). An Introduction to British Economic Policy. Brighton. 1984.

3530 —— Planning the British Economy. Basingstoke. 1985.

3531 WILSON (THOMAS BRIGHT). Planning and Growth. 1984.

3532 BONNER (ARNOLD). Economic Planning and the Co-operative Movement. 1950.

3533 WOOTTON (BARBARA) Baroness. Plan or No Plan? 1934.

3534 ROBINSON (EDWARD AUSTIN GOSSAGE). Economic Planning in the United Kingdom: Some Lessons. 1967.

3535 COLE (GEORGE DOUGLAS HOWARD). Economic Planning. 1971.

3536 MORE (CHARLES). The Industrial Age: Economy and Society in Britain 1750–1985. 1989.

3537 HARBURY (COLIN DESMOND) *and* LIPSEY (RICHARD G.). An Introduction to the United Kingdom Economy. 1st edn 1983, 3rd edn 1989.

3538 POLLINS (HAROLD). An Economic History of the Jews in England. 1982.

3539 BENYON (V. H.). Agriculture and Economics [in Britain, 1920–1977]. Exeter. 1979.

3540 SMITHIES (EDWARD). The Black Economy in England since 1914. Dublin. 1984.

3541 WORSWICK (GEORGE DAVID NORMAN). 'Two Great Recessions: The 1980s and the 1930s in Britain'. *Scot. J. Pol. Econ.* 31 (1984), 209–28.

3542 KOOT (GERALD M.). English Historical Economy, 1870–1926: The Rise of Economic History. Camb. 1987.

3543 McCLOSKEY (DONALD NANSEN). Economic History. Basingstoke. 1987.

3544 WILSON (CHARLES) *ed.* Economic History and the Historian: A Collection of Essays. 1969.

3545 COLEMAN (DONALD CUTHBERT). History and the Economic Past: An Account of the Rise and Decline of Economic History in Britain. Oxf. 1987.

2. ECONOMIC HISTORY

(a) 1918 to the Present (excluding the Second World War)

3546 DOWIE (J. A.). '1919–1920 is in Need of Attention'. *Econ. Hist. Rev.* 28 (1975), 429–50.

3547 —— 'Growth in the Inter-War Period: Some More Arithmetic'. *Econ. Hist. Rev.* 21 (1968), 93–112.

3548 PAISH (FRANK WALTER). 'British Floating Debt Policy from 1919 to 1939'. *Economica* 7 (1940), 225–47.

3549 TAWNEY (RICHARD H.). 'The Abolition of Economic Controls, 1918–1921'. *Econ. Hist. Rev.* 1st ser. 13 (1943), 1–30.

3550 SAYERS (RICHARD S.). 'The Springs of Technical Progress in Britain, 1919–1939'. *Econ. J.* 60 (1950), 275–91.

3551 ATKIN (JOHN). 'Official Regulation of British Overseas Investment 1914–1931'. *Econ. Hist. Rev.* 23 (1970), 324–35.

3552 PAYNE (W. F.). Business Behaviour, 1919–1922: An Account of Post-War Inflation and Depression. 1943.

3553 BODINGTON (CLIVE EATON). The Baldwin–Bruce Economic Policy: Its Scientific Basis. 1923.

3554 BAXENDALE (ARTHUR SALISBURY). Britain's Coming Great Crash. 1924.

3555 CRAMMOND (EDGAR). The Economic Position of Great Britain. 1924.

3556 BATTEN (EDGAR). National Economics for Britain's Day of Need. 1926.

3557 PIGOU (ARTHUR CECIL). Aspects of British Economic History, 1918–1925. 1947.

3558 CLARK (COLIN GRANT). England's Fight against Communism and its Relation to the Industrial Crisis. 1926.

3559 RICHARDSON (HENRY WARD). 'Over-Commitment in Britain before 1930'. *Oxf. Econ. Papers.* 17 (1965), 237–62.

3560 PLACHY (FRANK). Britain's Economic Plight. 1926.

3561 ALDCROFT (DEREK HOWARD). 'Economic Progress in Britain in the 1920's'. *Scot. J. Pol. Econ.* 13 (1966), 297–316.

3562 BUXTON (NEIL K.). 'Economic Progress in Britain in the 1920's: A Reappraisal'. *Scot. J. Pol. Econ.* 14 (1967), 175–86. [Criticism of above article.].

3563 ALDCROFT (DEREK HOWARD). 'Economic Progress in Britain in the 1920's: A Rejoinder'. *Scot. J. Pol. Econ.* 14 (1967), 187–91. [Reply to Buxton's criticism.].

3564 BOOTH (ALAN) *and* PACK (MELVYN). Employment, Capital and Economic Policy: Great Britain 1918–1939. Oxf. 1985.

3565 ALFORD (BERNARD WILLIAM ERNEST). Depression and Recovery? British Economic Growth, 1918–1939. 1972.

3566 GLYNN (SEAN) *and* OXBORROW (JOHN). Inter-War Britain: A Social and Economic History. 1976.

3567 FERGUSON (N. A.). 'Women's Work: Employment Opportunities and Economic Roles, 1918–1939'. *Albion* 7 (1975), 55–68.

3568 MILNER (FREDERIC). Economic Evolution in England. 1930.

3569 McKIBBIN (ROSS). 'The Economic Policy of the Second Labour Government, 1929–1931'. *Past and Present* 68 (1975), 95–123.

3570 WILLIAMS (DAVID). 'London and the 1931 Financial Crisis'. *Econ. Hist. Rev.* 2nd ser. 15 (1963), 513–28.

3571 ALLEN (G. C.). 'Advice from Economists Forty Five Years Ago'. *Three Banks Rev.* 106 (1975), 35–50.

3572 MOGGRIDGE (DONALD EDWARD). 'The 1931 Financial Crisis: A New View'. *Banker* 120 (1970), 832–9.

3573 BENN (*Sir* ERNEST JOHN PICKSTONE). Honest Doubt: Being a Collection of Papers on the Price of Modern Politics. 1932.

3574 VARGA (E.). The Great Crisis and its Political Consequences: Economics and Politics, 1928–1934. 1934.

3575 JAMES (FRANK CYRIL). England Today: A Survey of the Economic Situation. 1932.

3576 SALTER (JAMES ARTHUR) *Baron*. Recovery: The Second Effort. 1932.

3577 ROBBINS (LIONEL CHARLES) *Baron*. The Great Depression. 1934.

3578 HENDERSON (HUBERT DOUGLAS). The Inter-war Years and other Papers. Oxf. 1955. *Ed*. Henry Clay.

3579 RICHARDSON (HENRY WARD). 'The Basis of Economic Recovery in the 1930's: A Review and a New Interpretation'. *Econ. Hist. Rev.* 15 (1962), 344–63.

3580 —— Economic Recovery in Britain, 1932–1939. 1967.

3581 —— 'The Economic Significance of the Depression in Britain'. *J. Contemp. Hist.* 4 (1969), 3–19.

3582 HODSON (HENRY VINCENT). Slump and Recovery, 1929–1937: A Survey of World Economic Affairs. 1938.

3583 THOMAS (MARK). 'Rearmament and Economic Recovery in the Late 1930's'. *Econ. Hist. Rev.* 26 (1983), 552–73.

3584 CAPIE (FORREST). Depression and Protectionism: Britain between the Wars. 1983.

3585 FLINN (MICHAEL WALTER). 'Exports and the Scottish Economy in the Depresssion of the 1930's'. Ch. in Trade and Transport: Essays in Honour of T. S. Willan. William Henry Chaloner and Barrie M. Ratcliffe, *eds*. Manch. 1977.

3586 BUXTON (NEIL K.). 'Economic Growth in Scotland Between the Wars: The Role of Production Structure and Rationalization'. *Econ. Hist. Rev.* 33 (1980), 538–55.

3587 ARNDT (HEINZ WOLFGANG). The Economic Lessons of the 1930's. 1944.

3588 STEVENSON (JOHN) *and* COOK (CHRIS). The Slump. 1977.

3589 ALDCROFT (DEREK HOWARD). 'Economic Growth in Britain in the Inter-war Years: A Reassessment'. *Econ. Hist. Rev.* 20 (1967), 311–26.

3590 —— The Inter-war Economy: Britain 1918–1939. 1970.

3591 —— The British Economy between the Wars. 1983.

3592 CAPIE (FORREST) *and* COLLINS (MICHAEL). The Inter-War British Economy: A Statistical Abstract. Manch. 1983.

3593 BROADBERRY (S. N.). The British Economy Between the Wars: A Macroeconomic Survey. Oxf. 1986.

3594 DRUMMOND (IAN M.). British Economic Policy and the Empire, 1919–1939. 1972.

3595 BANK OF ENGLAND. The UK Recovery in the 1930s. 1988.

3596 YASS (MARION). The Great Depression. 1970.

3597 HUTT (GEORGE ALLEN). The Final Crisis. 1935.

3598 DAVIES (ERNEST ALBERT JOHN). 'National' Capitalism: The Government's Record as Protector of Private Monopoly. 1939.

3599 U.S. LIBRARY OF CONGRESS. A List of Reference on the Economic Policy of Great Britain, 1930–1940. 1940.

3600 REES (GORONWY). The Great Slump: Capitalism in Crisis 1929–1933. 1970.

3601 MACMILLAN (HAROLD) *Earl of Stockton*. The Middle Way: A Study of the Problem of Economic and Social Progress in a Free and Democratic Society. 1938.

3602 CLARK (COLIN GRANT) *and* PIGOU (ARTHUR CECIL). The Economic Position of Great Britain. 1935.

3603 CLARK (COLIN GRANT). The Conditions of Economic Progress. 1940. 3rd edn 1957.

3604 —— The Economics of 1960. 1942.

3605 MEDLICOTT (WILLIAM NORTON). Economic Blockade. 2 vols 1952 and 1959.

3606 BIRNIE (ARTHUR). An Economic History of the British Isles. 1950.

3607 RATTRAY (R. F.). 'Basic Realities of the Economic Crisis'. *Quart. Rev.* (1947), 423–36.

3608 HUTCHISON (TERENCE WILMOT). Economics and Economic Policy in Britain 1946–1966: Some Aspects of their Interrelations. 1968.

3609 DE JOUVENEL (BERTRAND). Problems of Socialist England. 1949.

3610 HUTCHISON (KEITH). The Decline and Fall of British Capitalism. 1951. 2nd edn 1966.

3611 MATTHEWS (ROBERT CHARLES OLIVER). 'Why has Britain had Full Employment since the War?'. *Econ. J.* 78 (1968), 555–69.

3612 MITCHELL (JOAN EILEEN). Crisis in Britain, 1951. 1963.

3613 CROSLAND (CHARLES ANTHONY RAVEN). Britain's Economic Problem. 1953.

3614 AMERY (LEOPOLD STENNETT). A Balanced Economy. 1954.

3615 COLE (GEORGE DOUGLAS HOWARD). The Post-War Condition of Britain. 1956.

3616 WORSWICK (GEORGE DAVID NORMAN) *and* ADY (PETER HONORINE). The British Economy 1945–1950. Oxf. 1952.

3617 —— The British Economy in the 1950s. 1962.

3618 WILSON (JAMES HAROLD) *Baron*. Post-War Economic Policies in Britain. 1957.

3619 HARROD (*Sir* HENRY ROY FORBES). Policy against Inflation. 1958.

3620 SHONFIELD (ANDREW AKIBA). British Economic Policy since the War. 1958.

3621 YOUNG (MICHAEL DUNLOP). Labour's Plan for Plenty. 1947.

3622 REDDAWAY (WILLIAM BRIAN) *and* SMITH (A. D.). 'Progress in British Manufacturing Industries in the Period 1948–1954'. *Econ. J.* 70 (1960), 17–37.

3623 SCHWARTZ (GEORGE LEOPOLD). Bread and Circuses, 1945–1958. 1959.

3624 CAIRNCROSS (*Sir* ALEXANDER KIRKLAND). Years of Recovery: British Economic Policy, 1945–1951. 1985.

3625 DOW (JOHN CHRISTOPHER RODER). The Management of the British Economy 1945–1960. Camb. 1964. 2nd edn 1970.

3626 ALFORD (BERNARD WILLIAM ERNEST). British Economic Performance, 1945–1975. Basingstoke. 1988.

3627 MISHAN (EZRA J.). 'A Survey of Welfare Economics, 1939–1951'. *Econ. J.* 70 (1960), 197–265.

3628 PREST (ALAN RICHMOND). 'The British Economy, 1945–1960'. *Manch. Sch. Econ. Soc. Studs* 33 (1965), 141–8.

3629 O'DEA (DESMOND JAMES). Cyclical Indicators for the Post-War British Economy. Camb. 1975.

3630 NERLOVE (MARC). 'A Quarterly Econometric Model for the United Kingdom'. *Amer. Econ. Rev.* 52 (1962), 154–76.

3631 MACRAE (NORMAN ALISTAIR DUNCAN). Sunshades in October: An Analysis of the Main Mistakes in British Economic Policy since the Mid-1950's. 1963.

3632 MOORE (BARRY) *and* RHODES (JOHN). 'Evaluating the Effects of British Regional Economic Policy [1950–1971]'. *Econ. J.* 83 (1973), 87–110.

3633 KNAPP (JOHN) *and* LOMAX (KENNETH). 'Britain's Growth Performance: The Enigma of the 1950's'. *Lloyds Bank Rev.* 74 (1967), 1–24.

3634 HARRIS (RALPH) *ed.* Radical Reaction: Essays in Competition and Affluence. 1961.

3635 SHANKS (MICHAEL JAMES). The Stagnant Society: A Warning. Harmondsworth. 1961.

3636 U.K. ECONOMIC INTELLIGENCE UNIT. The Economic Effects of Disarmament. 1963.

3637 U.K. CABINET OFFICE. The Economic Situation: A Statement by H.M. Government, 26 October 1964.

3638 U.K. POLITICAL *and* ECONOMIC PLANNING. Growth in the British Economy: A Study of Economic Problems and Policies in Contemporary Britain. 1960.

3639 HARROD (*Sir* HENRY ROY FORBES). The British Economy. 1963.

3640 CARTER (CHARLES FREDERICK) *and* WILLIAMS (BRUCE E.). 'Government Scientific Policy and the Growth of the British Economy'. *Manch. Sch. Econ. Soc. Studs* 32 (1964), 197–214.

3641 MALIK (REX). What's Wrong with British Industry? Harmondsworth. 1964.

3642 MATTHEWS (ROBERT CHARLES OLIVER). 'Some Aspects of Post-War Growth in the British Economy in Relation to Historical Experience'. *Trans. Manch. Stat. Soc.* (1964), 3–25.

3643 DAVENPORT (NICHOLAS ERNEST HAROLD). The Split Society. 1964.

3644 BENEMY (FRANK WILLIAM GEORGESON). Industry, Income and Investment: The Common Sense of Economics. 1962.

3645 ESHAG (EPRIME). The Present System of Trade and Payments versus Full Employment and Welfare State. 1966.

3646 COHEN (CHARLES DESMOND). British Economic Policy, 1960–1969. 1971.

3647 BLACKABY (F. T.) *et al.* British Economic Policy, 1960–1974. Camb. 1978.

3648 HUGHES (J. R. T.). 'Measuring British Economic Growth'. *J. Econ. Hist.* 24 (1964), 60–83.

3649 SHONFIELD (ANDREW AKIBA). Modern Capitalism: The Changing Balance of Public and Private Power. 1965.

3650 BECKERMAN (WILFRED) *et al.* 'The National Plan: A Discussion before the Royal Statistical Society, November 24 1965'. *J. Roy. Stat. Soc.* [Series A], 129 (1966), 1–24.

3651 RHYS-WILLIAMS (JULIET EVANGELINE) *Lady.* A New Look at Britain's Economic Policy. Harmondsworth. 1965.

3652 HENDERSON (PATRICK DAVID) *ed.* Economic Growth in Britain. 1966.

3653 HARRIS (JOHN). The Big Slump. 1967.

3654 HICKS (*Sir* JOHN RICHARD). After the Boom: Thoughts on the 1966 Economic Crisis. 1966.

3655 SPRINGHAM (BETTY). Problems of the British Economy. 1967.

3656 JONES (GLYN) *and* BARNES (MICHAEL). Britain on Borrowed Time. 1967.

3657 CAVES (RICHARD EARL) *et al.* Britain's Economic Prospects. Washington. 1968.

3658 WINCOTT (HAROLD). The Business of Capitalism: A Selection of Unconventional Essays on Economic Problems of the 1960's. 1968.

3659 SARGENT (JOHN RICHARD). 'Recent Growth Experience in the Economy of the United Kingdom'. *Econ. J.* 78 (1968), 19–42.

3660 MARLOW (BARBARA). Charting the British Economy. 1968.

3661 BROWN (*Sir* ERNEST HENRY PHELPS). 'The Brookings Study of the Poor Performance of the British Economy'. *Economica* 36 (1969), 235–52.

3662 SURREY (M. J. C.). 'The National Plan in Retrospect'. *Bull. Oxf. Univ. Inst. Econ. Stats.* 34 (1972), 249–68.

3663 PISSARIDES (C. A.). 'A Model of British Macro-Economic Policy, 1955–1969'. *Manch. Sch. Econ. Soc. Studs* 11 (1972), 245–59.

3664 MANSER (WILLIAM ARTHUR PEETE). Britain in Balance. 1971.

3665 BECKERMAN (WILFRED) *ed.* Labour's Economic Record, 1964–1970. 1972.

3666 SANDFORD (CEDRIC THOMAS). Economic Policy. 1970.

3667 CAIRNCROSS (*Sir* ALEXANDER KIRKLAND) *ed.* Britain's Economic Prospects Reconsidered. 1971.

3668 NOBBS (JACK). Economic Problems of the 1970s. 1971.

3669 PEAKER (ANTHONY). Economic Growth in Modern Britain. 1974.

3670 HARRIS (RALPH) *and* SEWILL (BRENDAN). British Economic Policy 1970–1974. 1975.

3671 POLLARD (SIDNEY). The British Economic Miracle. 1976.

3672 STEWART (MICHAEL). The Jekyll and Hyde Years: Politics and Economic Policy since 1964. 1977.

3673 HOLMES (MARTIN). Political Pressure and Economic Policy: The British Government 1970–1974. 1982.

3674 BECKERMAN (WILFRID). The British Economy in 1975. 1965.

3675 HICKS (*Sir* JOHN RICHARD). Crisis '75. 1975.

3676 HOLMES (MARTIN). The Labour Government 1974–1979. 1985.

3677 HOOD (CHRISTOPHER). Big Government in Hard Times. Oxf. 1981.

3678 KEEGAN (WILLIAM). Who Runs the Economy?: Control and Influence in British Economic Policy. 1979.

3679 MAUNDER (PETER). The British Economy in the 1970's. 1980.

3680 BACON (ROBERT WILLIAM). Britain's Economic Problem: Too Few Producers. 1976. 2nd edn 1978.

3681 BLACK (JOHN). The Economics of Modern Britain: An Introduction to Macroeconomics. Oxf. 1979. 4th edn 1985.

3682 GLYN (ANDREW). The British Economic Disaster. 1980.

3683 HAWKINS (CHRIS). The British Economy: What Will our Children Think? 1982.

3684 CROSS (ROD). Economic Theory and Policy in the U.K.: An Outline and Assessment of the Controversies. 1982.

3685 EATWELL (JOHN). Whatever Happened to Britain? The Economics of Decline. 1982.

3686 POLLARD (SIDNEY). The Wasting of the British Economy: British Economic Policy, 1945 to the Present. 1982. 2nd edn 1984.

3687 MORRELL (JAMES). Britain Through the 80's: An Evaluation of Market and Business Prospects. Farnborough. 1980.

3688 SMITH (GERRY M.). Britain in Decline?: A Select Bibliography. Hartlepool. 1979.

3689 HOLMES (MARTIN). The First Thatcher Government, 1979–1983: Contemporary Conservatism and Economic Change. Boulder, Colorado. 1985.

3690 WALTERS (*Sir* ALAN A.). Britain's Economic Renaissance: Margaret Thatcher's Reforms 1979–1984. Oxf./N.Y. 1986.

3691 KEEGAN (WILLIAM). Mrs Thatcher's Economic Experiment. 1984.

3692 BARCLAYS BANK. UK Economic Survey. 1984.

3693 SMITH (KEITH). The British Economic Crisis: Its Past and Future. Harmondsworth. 1984.

3694 BODINGTON (STEPHEN), GEORGE (MIKE), *and* MICHAELSON (JOHN). Developing the Socially Useful Economy. 1986.

3695 DURBIN (ELIZABETH). New Jerusalem: The Labour Party and the Economics of Democratic Socialism. 1985.

3696 THOMPSON (GRAHAME). The Conservatives' Economic Policy. 1986.

3697 ELBAUM (BERNARD) *and* LAZONICK (WILLIAM). The Decline of the British Economy. Oxf. 1986.

3698 LABOUR RESEARCH DEPARTMENT. A State of Collapse: The UK Economy under the Tories. 1987.

3699 COATES (DAVID). The Economic Decline of Modern Britain: The Debate Between Left and Right. Brighton. 1986.

3700 —— The Economic Revival of Modern Britain: The Debate Between Left and Right. Aldershot. 1987.

3701 JONES (AUBREY). Britain's Economy: The Roots of Stagnation. Camb. 1986.

3702 SKED (ALAN). Britain's Decline: Problems and Perspectives. Oxf. 1987.

3703 VANE (HOWARD R.) *and* LASLIN (TERRY). Current Controversies in Economics. Oxf. 1987.

3704 MAYNARD (GEOFFREY). The Economy under Mrs. Thatcher. Oxf. 1988.

3705 SMITH (DAVID). Mrs Thatcher's Economics. 1988.

3706 GREEN (FRANCIS). The Restructuring of the United Kingdom Economy. 1989.

3707 BALL (MICHAEL) *et al.* The Transformation of Britain. 1989.

(b) Anglo-American Economic Relations

3708 BAGWELL (PHILIP SIDNEY) *and* MINGAY (GORDON EDMUND). Britain and America 1850–1939: A Study of Economic Change. 1970.

3709 COSTIGLIOLA (FRANK C.). 'Anglo-American Financial Rivalry in the 1920's'. *J. Econ. Hist.* 37 (1977), 911–34.

3710 THOMAS (BRINLEY). Migration and Economic Growth: A Study of Great Britain and the Atlantic Economy. 1954. 2nd edn Camb. 1973.

3711 HOLMES (GRAEME). Britain and America: A Comparative Economic History, 1850–1939. Newton Abbot. 1976.

3712 KREIDER (CARL JONAS). The Anglo-American Trade Agreement: A Study of British and American Commercial Policies, 1934–1939. Princeton, N.J. 1943.

3713 DENNY (LOWELL). America Conquers Britain: A Record of Economic War. 1930.

3714 MALLALIEU (WILLIAM C.). British Reconstruction and American Policy 1945–1955. 1956.

3715 ROSENSON (ALEX). 'The Terms of the Anglo-American Financial Agreement'. *Amer. Econ. Rev.* 37 (1947), 178–87.

3716 DOBSON (ALAN P.). The Politics of the Anglo-American Economic Special Relationship, 1940–1987. 1988.

3717 GINSBURG (ALAN L.) *and* STERN (ROBERT M.). 'The Determination of the Factors Affecting American and British Exports in the Inter-War and Post-War Periods'. *Oxf. Econ. Papers* 17 (1965), 263–78.

3718 KIMBALL (WARREN F.). 'Beggar My Neighbour: America and the British Interim Finance Crisis, 1940–1941'. *J. Econ. Hist.* 29 (1969), 758–72.

3719 McCURRAGH (D. F.). 'Britain's U.S. Dollar Problems, 1939–1945'. *Econ. J.* 58 (1948), 356–72.

3720 ZUPNICK (ELLIOT). 'Consumer Credit and Monetary Policy in the United States and the United Kingdom'. *J. Finance* 17 (1962), 342–54.

3721 STERN (R.). 'British and American Productivity and Comparative Costs in International Trade'. *Oxf. Econ. Papers* 14 (1962), 275–96.

3722 MERRETT (A. J.) *and* WHITAKER (JOHN). 'The Profitability of British and American Industry'. *Lloyds Bank Rev.* 83 (1967), 1–11.

3723 DE NOVO (JOHN A.). 'The Culberston Economic Mission and Anglo-American Tensions in the Middle East, 1944–1945'. *J. Amer. Hist.* 63 (1977), 913–36.

3724 COWIE (H. T.). 'American Investment in British Industry'. *Pol. Q.* 30, (1959), 254–61.

3725 AMERY (LEO S.). The Washington Loans Agreement. 1946.

3726 WINDLE (ROBERT). British and American Economic History, 1850–1950. 1971.

3727 CLARKE (*Sir* RICHARD). Anglo-American Collaboration in War and Peace 1942–1949. Oxf. 1982. *Ed.* Sir Alexander Kirkland Cairncross.

3728 DOBSON (ALAN P.). U.S. Wartime Aid to Britain, 1940–1946. 1986.

3729 PELLING (HENRY MATHISON). Britain and the Marshall Plan. Basingstoke. 1988.

(c) Wartime Economics

3730 LAUX (JAMES MICHAEL). War, Crises and Transformation: The British Economy in the 20th Century. Cincinnati, Ohio. 1961.

3731 MILWARD (ALAN STEELE). The Economic Effects of the Two World Wars in Britain. 1970. New edn 1984.

3732 MURPHY (MARY ELIZABETH). The British War Economy, 1939–1943. N.Y. 1943.

3733 UNWIN (JOSEPH DANIEL). Our Economic Problems and their Solution. 1944.

3734 CHESTER (*Sir* DANIEL NORMAN). Lessons of the British War Economy. Camb. 1951.

3735 BOOTHBY (ROBERT JOHN GRAHAM) *Baron.* The New Economy. 1943.

3736 BELLERBY (JOHN ROTHERFORD) *et al.* Economic Reconstruction. 1943.

3737 SMITH (HENRY NORMAN). The Politics of Plenty. 1944.

3738 OLSON (MANCUR) *Jnr.* The Economics of Wartime Shortage: A History of British Food Supplies in the Napoleonic Wars and in World Wars One and Two. Durham, N.C. 1963.

3739 WINTER (JAY MURRAY) *ed.* War and Economic Development: Essays in Memory of David Joslin. 1975.

3740 EATON (JOHN). Economics of Peace and War: An Analysis of Britain's Economic Problems. 1952.

3741 BULKLEY (MILDRED EMILY). A Bibliographical Survey of Contemporary Sources for the Economic and Social History of the War. Oxf. 1922.

3742 GRAY (HOWARD LEVY). War-Time Control of Industry: The Experience of England. N.Y. 1918.

3743 BRAND (ROBERT HENRY). War and National Finance. 1921.

3744 DEARLE (NORMAN BURRELL). The Labour Costs of the World War to Great Britain 1914–1922. 1940.

3745 ANDREWS (IRENE OSGOOD). Economic Effects of the War upon Women and Children in Great Britain. N.Y. 1918.

3746 STAMP (JOSIAH CHARLES) *Baron.* The Financial Aftermath of War. 1932.

3747 BOWLEY (ARTHUR L.). Some Economic Consequences of the Great War. 1930.

3748 HIRST (FRANCIS WRIGLEY). The Consequences of the War to Great Britain. 1934.

3749 LAUTERBACH (ALBERT T.). 'Economic Demobilization in Great Britain after the First World War'. *Pol. Sci. Q.* 57 (1942), 376–93.

3750 LITMAN (SIMON). Prices and Price Control in Great Britain and the United States during the World War. N.Y. 1920.

3751 GRADY (HENRY F.). British War Finance, 1914–1919. N.Y. 1927.

3752 FRASURE (CARL MAYNARD). British Policy on War Debts and Reparations. Phil., PA. 1940.

3753 HALPERN (LOUIS). British War Finance, 1939–1944. N.Y. 1949.

3754 HANCOCK (*Sir* WILLIAM KEITH) *and* GOWING (MARGARET MARY). The British War Economy. 1949.

3755 POSTAN (*Sir* MOSEI MIKHAIL EFIMOVICH). British War Production. 1952.

3756 MOGGRIDGE (DONALD EDWARD). 'Economic Policy in the Second World War'. Ch. in Essays on John Maynard Keynes. W. Milo Keynes, *ed.* Camb. 1975.

(d) Tariffs

3757 SNYDER (RIXFORD KINNEY). The Tariff Problem in Great Britain, 1918–1923. Stanford, Calif. 1944.

3758 CAPIE (FORREST). 'The British Tariff and Industrial Protection in the 1930's'. *Econ. Hist. Rev.* 31 (1978), 399–409.

3759 McGUIRE (EDWARD). The British Tariff System. 1939. 2nd edn 1951.

3760 HUTCHINSON (*Sir* HERBERT JOHN). Tariff-Making and Industrial Reconstruction: An Account of the Work of the Import Duties Advisory Committee, 1932–1939. 1965.

3761 ABEL (DERYCK ROBERT ENDSLEIGH). A History of British Tariffs, 1923–1942. 1945.

3762 MEREDITH (DAVID). 'The British Government and Colonial Economic Policy, 1919–1939'. *Econ. Hist. Rev.* 28 (1975), 484–99.

3763 GLICKMAN (DAVID L.). 'The British Imperial Preference System'. *Q. J. Econ.* 61 (1947), 439–70.

3764 BENHAM (FREDERICK CHARLES). Great Britain under Protection. 1941.

B. PROPERTY, INCOME, PENSIONS

This section brings together literature which treats, from varying perspectives, the issue of 'wealth'—what it is conceived to be, how it is expressed, how it is earned, invested, and transmitted. While authors sometimes discuss and debate relative wealth on the bases of agreed statistical series, the relevant data can be particularly difficult to identify. The literature therefore reflects the fact that attitudes to wealth on the part of authors explicitly or implicitly determine the nature of the evidence which is held to be relevant. Comparison is made particularly difficult at a time of rapid inflation when different kinds of asset do not uniformly fluctuate in value. Attempts by successive governments to establish 'incomes policies' naturally produced further studies which attempted to analyse their differential impact on various social categories. These built upon official or unofficial investigation of the consequences of various taxation policies. The material which has been identified in this section is largely 'economic' but shades into a 'social' category. Approaches to 'the rich' and 'the poor' which are avowedly sociological feature more prominently in subsequent chapters.

1. PROPERTY, INHERITANCE, AND WEALTH

3765 HARGREAVES (A. D.). 'Modern Real Property'. *Mod. Law. Rev.* 19 (1956), 14–25.

3766 KLEIN (L. R.) *et al.* 'Savings and Finances of the Upper Income Classes'. *Bull. Oxf. Univ. Inst. Econ. Stats* 18 (1956), 293–319.

3767 MORGAN (EDWARD VICTOR). The Structure of Property Ownership in Great Britain. 1960.

3768 HARBURY (COLIN DESMOND). 'Inheritance and the Economic Distribution of Personal Wealth in Great Britain'. *Econ. J.* 72 (1962), 845–68.

3769 HARBURY (COLIN DESMOND) *and* HITCHINS (D. M. W. N.). 'Wealth, Women and Inheritance'. *Econ. J.* 87 (1977), 124–31.

3770 SHORRUCKS (A. F.). 'Age-Wealth Relationships: A Cross-Section and Cohort Analysis'. *Rev. Econ. Stats* 57 (1975), 155–63.

3771 WEDGEWOOD (JOSIAH). The Economics of Inheritance. 1929.

3772 ROKELING (G. D.). A British Index of National Prosperity, 1920–1927. 1928.

3773 CLAYTON (DAVID) *et al.* Capital Taxation and Land Ownership in England and Wales: A Preliminary Assessment. Reading. 1967.

3774 CAMPION (HARRY). Public and Private Property in Great Britain. 1939.

3775 HILTON (JOHN). Rich Man, Poor Man. 1944.

3776 MEADE (JAMES EDWARD). Efficiency, Equality and the Ownership of Property. 1964.

3777 POLLARD (SIDNEY) *and* CROSSLEY (DAVID W.). The Wealth of England 1085–1966. 1968.

3778 REVELL (JACK ROBERT STEPHEN). The Wealth of the Nation: The National Balance Sheet of the United Kingdom, 1957–1961. Camb. 1967.

3779 REVELL (JACK ROBERT STEPHEN) *and* MOYLE (JOHN). The Owners of Quoted Ordinary Shares: A Survey for 1963. 1966.

3780 MOYLE (JOHN). The Pattern of Ordinary Share Ownership 1957–1970. Camb. 1971.

3781 SANDFORD (CEDRIC THOMAS). Taxing Personal Wealth: An Analysis of Capital Taxation in the United Kingdom: History, Present Structure and Future Possibilities. 1971.

3782 TOWNSEND (PETER) and BOSANQUET (NICHOLAS) eds. Labour and Inequality. 1972.

3783 RUBINSTEIN (W. D.) ed. Wealth and the Wealthy in the Modern World. 1980.

3784 —— Men of Property: The Very Wealthy in Britain since the Industrial Revolution. 1981.

3785 —— Wealth and Inequality in Britain. 1986.

3786 TURVEY (RALPH). 'The Effect of Price Level Changes on Real Private Incomes in the United Kingdom, 1954–1960'. *Economica* 29 (1962), 171–5.

3787 MILLER (JOHN GARETH). Family Property and Financial Provision. 1974.

3788 COUNTER INFORMATION SERVICES. The Wealthy. 1979.

3789 RYAN (ALAN). Property and Political Theory. Oxf. 1984.

3790 FIELD (FRANK) ed. The Wealth Report. Vol. 1, 1979: vol. 2, 1983.

3791 ATKINSON (ANTHONY BARNES). Unequal Shares: Wealth in Britain. 1972.

3792 —— Ed. Wealth, Income and Inequality: Selected Readings. Harmondsworth. 1973. 2nd edn Oxf. 1980.

3793 —— The Economics of Inequality. Oxf. 1975.

3794 ATKINSON (ANTHONY BARNES) and HARRISON (A. J.). The Distribution of Personal Wealth in Britain. 1978.

3795 LAWRENCE (REGINALD FREDERICK). Inheritance Tax. 1987.

2. INCOME, PRICES, AND INCOMES POLICY

3796 DALTON (HUGH). 'The Measurement of the Inequality of Incomes'. *Econ. J.* 30 (1920), 348–61.

3797 BALCHIN (NIGEL MARLIN). Income and Outcome: A Study of Personal Finance. 1936.

3798 FORD (PERCY). Incomes, Means Tests and Personal Responsibility. 1939.

3799 CAMPBELL (A. D.). 'Changes in Scottish Incomes, 1924–1949'. *Econ. J.* 65 (1955), 225–40.

3800 ASHTON (ELWYN THOMAS). 'Problem Families and their Household Budgets'. *Eugenics Rev.* 48 (1956), 95–101.

3801 LYDALL (HAROLD FRENCH). British Incomes and Savings. Oxf. 1955.

3802 —— 'The Long-Term Trend in the Size and Distribution of Incomes'. *J. Roy. Stat. Soc.* [Series A], 122 (1959), 1–37.

3803 —— 'The Life Cycle in Income, Saving and Asset Ownership'. *Econometrica* 23 (1955), 31–50.

3804 LYDALL (HAROLD FRENCH) and LANSING (JOHN B.). 'A Comparison of the Distribution of Personal Income and Wealth in the United States and Great Britain'. *Amer. Econ. Rev.* 49 (1959), 43–67.

3805 SEERS (DUDLEY GEORGE). The Levelling of Incomes since 1938. Oxf. 1951.

3806 —— Changes in the Cost-of-Living and the Distribution of Income since 1938. Oxf. 1949.

3807 CARTTER (ALAN MURRAY). The Redistribution of Income in Post-War Britain: A Study of the Effects of the Central Government Fiscal Program in 1948–1949. New Haven, Conn. 1955.

3808 BECKERMAN (WILFRED). An Introduction to National Income Analysis. 1968.

3809 SERGEANT (WINSLEY) and ROYDHOUSE (ERIC). Prices and Wages Freeze: A Narrative Guide to the Prices and Incomes Act 1966, together with the Text of the Act. 1966.

3810 PREST (ALAN RICHMOND) and STARK (THOMAS). 'Some Aspects of Income Distribution in the U.K. since World War Two'. *Manch. Sch. Econ. Soc. Studs* 35 (1967), 217–43.

3811 NEILD (ROBERT RALPH). Pricing and Employment in the Trade Cycle: A Study of British Manufacturing Industry, 1950–1961. Camb. 1963.

3812 ALLEN (R. G. D.). 'Movements in Retail Prices since 1953'. *Economica* 28 (1958), 14–25.

3813 CAMPBELL (J. R.). 'The Development of Incomes Policy in Britain'. *Marxism Today* 9 (1965), 69–75.

3814 MILLWARD (ROBERT). 'Price Restraint, Anti-Inflation Policy and Public and Private Industry in the United Kingdom, 1948–1973'. *Econ. J.* 86 (1976), 226–42.

3815 BELL (G.). 'Incomes Policy: The British Experience'. *Busin. Econ.* 6 (1971), 18–22.

3816 FELS (ALLAN). The British Prices and Incomes Board. Camb. 1972.

3817 MITCHELL (JOAN). The National Board for Prices and Incomes. 1972.

3818 THATCHER (ARTHUR ROGER). Prices and Earnings 1951–1969. 1971.

3819 WOOTTON (BARBARA) Baroness. Incomes Policy: An Inquest and a Proposal. 1974.

3820 NICHOLSON (ROBERT JOHN). 'Distribution of Personal Incomes'. *Lloyds Bank Rev.* 74 (1967).

3821 YOUNG (MICHAEL). 'The Distribution of Income within the Family'. *Brit. J. Sociol.* 3 (1952), 305–21.

3822 STARK (THOMAS). The Distribution of Personal Income in the U.K, 1949–1963. Camb. 1972.

3823 TITMUSS (RICHARD MORRIS). Income Distribution and Social Change: A Study in Criticism. 1962.

3824 TODD (JUDITH). The Conjurers: Wealth and Welfare in the Upper Income Brackets. 1966.

3825 DORRINGTON (J. G.). 'A Structural Approach to Estimating the Built-In Flexibility of United Kingdom Taxes on Personal Income'. *Econ. J.* 84 (1974), 576–94.

3826 HAWTREY (*Sir* RALPH GEORGE). Incomes and Money. 1967.

3827 —— An Incomes Policy. 1965.

3828 NICHOLSON (JOHN LEONARD). Distribution of Income in the United Kingdom in 1959, 1957 and 1953. Camb. 1965.

3829 BARNA (TIBOR). The Redistribution of Incomes through Public Finance in 1937. Oxf. 1945.

3830 BEHREND (HILDE), LYNCH (HARRIET), *and* DAVIES (JEAN). A National Survey of Attitudes to Inflation and Incomes Policy. 1966.

3831 BOWEN (IAN). Acceptable Inequalities: An Essay on the Distribution of Income. 1970.

3832 PEN (JAN). Income Distribution. Harmondsworth. 1971.

3833 PETERS (B. G.). 'Income Inequality in Sweden and the United Kingdom: A Longitudinal Analysis'. *Acta Sociol.* 16 (1973), 108–20.

3834 PRESTON (BARBARA). 'Statistics of Inequality'. *Sociol. Rev.* 22 (1974), 103–18.

3835 ATKINSON (ANTHONY BARNES). The Tax Credit Scheme and the Redistribution of Income. 1973.

3836 —— *Ed.* The Personal Distribution of Incomes. 1976.

3837 U.K. BOARD OF INLAND REVENUE. The Survey of Personal Incomes 1969/1970. 1972. [Pub. annually.].

3838 U.K. CENTRAL STATISTICAL OFFICE. National Income and Expenditure. 1970. [Pub. annually.].

3839 EVERSLEY (DAVID). 'Employment Planning and Income Maintenance'. *Town and Country Planning* 43 (1975), 206–9.

3840 KNOX (PAUL L.). 'Social Indicators and the Concept of Level of Living'. *Sociol. Rev.* 22 (1974), 249–57.

3841 MUELLBAUER (J.). 'Prices and Inequality: The United Kingdom Experience'. *Econ. J.* 84 (1974), 32–55.

3842 —— 'Inequality Measures, Prices and Household Composition'. *Rev. Econ. Studs* 41 (1974), 498–504.

3843 —— 'Household Composition, Engel Curves and Welfare Comparisons between Households'. *Eur. Econ. Rev.* 5 (1974), 103–22.

3844 CHAMPERNOWNE (DAVID GAWEN). 'Comparisons of Measures of Inequality of Income Distribution'. *Econ. J.* 84 (1974), 787–816.

3845 —— The Distribution of Incomes between Persons. 1973.

3846 —— 'A Model of Income Distribution'. *Econ. J.* 68 (1957), 318–51.

3847 PAISH (FRANK WALTER). The Rise and Fall of Incomes Policy. 1969. 2nd edn 1971.

3848 CLEGG (HUGH ARMSTRONG). How to Run an Incomes Policy: And Why we Made such a Mess of the Last One. 1971.

3849 BLACKABY (FRANK). An Incomes Policy for Britain: Policy Proposals and Research Needs. 1972.

3850 BALFOUR (CAMPBELL). Incomes Policy and the Public Sector. 1972.

3851 TURNER (HERBERT ARTHUR). The Progress and Poverty of Incomes Policy. 1967.

3852 WEBB (ADRIAN) *and* SIEVE (JACK). Income Distribution and the Welfare State. 1971.

3853 DANIEL (WILLIAM WENTWORTH). The Next Stage of Incomes Policy. 1976.

3854 HENRY (S. G. B.) *and* ORMEROD (P.). 'Incomes Policy and Wage Inflation: Empirical Evidence for the U.K., 1976–1977'. *Nat. Inst. Econ. Soc. Res. Q.* 85 (1978), 31–9.

3855 KING (JOHN) *and* REGAN (PHILIP). Relative Income Shares. 1976.

3856 DINWIDDY (ROBERT). The Effects of Certain Social and Demographic Changes on Income Distribution. 1977.

3857 COWELL (FRANK A.). Measuring Inequality. 1977.

3858 ABRAMS (PHILIP) *ed.* Work, Urbanism and Inequality: U.K. Society Today. 1978.

3859 HARRIS (DONALD J.). Capital Accumulation and Income Distribution. 1978.

3860 TANFIELD (JENNIFER). The Impact of the 1982 Budget on Individual Incomes and Real Income Movements since 1979. 1982.

3861 MALLANDER (JACQUELINE). Incomes In and Out of Work 1978–1982. 1984.

3. WAGES AND SALARIES

3862 COLE (GEORGE DOUGLAS HOWARD). The Payment of Wages. 1918. [Fabian Society Research Dept.].

3863 BELL (*Sir* HUGH). High Wages: Their Cause and Effect. 1921.

3864 ROWE (J. W. F.). Wages in Price and Theory. 1928. Reissued 1969.

3865 DOBB (MAURICE HERBERT). Wages. 1928. 4th edn 1956.

3866 HICKS (*Sir* JOHN RICHARD). The Theory of Wages. 1935.

3867 DUNLOP (J. T.). 'Cyclical Variations in the Wage Structure'. *Rev. Econ. Stats.* 21 (1939), 30–9.

3868 MORRIS (WILLIAM A.). Earnings and Spending. 1939.

3869 MARLEY (JOAN G.) *and* CAMPION (HARRY). 'Changes in Salaries in Great Britain, 1924–1939'. *J. Roy. Stat. Soc.* 103 (1940).

3870 DOUTY (H. M.). 'Union Impact on Wage Structures'. *Proc. Indust. Relns Res. Assoc.* 6 (1953), 61–76, 125–8.

3871 U.K. MINISTRY OF LABOUR. 'Average Earnings and Hours of Men in Manufacturing: Analysis by Establishment'. *Min. of Labour Gazette* 67 (1959), 524–33.

3872 WILKINSON (R.). 'Differences in Earnings and the Distribution of Manpower in the U.K., 1948–1957'. *Yorks. Bull. Econ. and Soc. Res.* 14 (1962), 46–54.

3873 HART (PETER EDWARD). 'The Dynamics of Earnings, 1963–1973'. *Econ. J.* 86 (1976), 551–65.

3874 KAHN (HILDA R.). Salaries in the Public Sector in England and Wales. 1962.

3875 SEARLE-BARNES (ROBERT GRIFFITHS). Pay and Productivity Bargaining: A Study of the Effects of National Wage Agreements in the Nottinghamshire Coal Fields. Manch. 1969.

3876 SAUNDERS (CHRISTOPHER) *and* MARSDEN (DAVID). Pay Inequalities in the European Community. 1981.

3877 HEINEMANN (MARGOT). Wages Front. 1947.

3878 METCALF (DAVID). Low Pay, Occupational Mobility and Minimum Wage Policy in Great Britain. Washington, D.C. 1981.

3879 SLOANE (PETER J.) *ed.* Women and Low Pay. 1980.

3880 BEHREND (HILDE). 'A Fair Day's Work'. *Scot. J. Pol. Econ.* 8 (1961), 102–18.

3881 BOWLEY (*Sir* ARTHUR LYON). Wages, Earnings and Hours of Work in the United Kingdom, 1914–1947. 1947.

3882 —— Wages and Income in the United Kingdom since 1860. Camb. 1937.

3883 —— Prices and Wages in the United Kingdom, 1914–1920. Oxf. 1921.

3884 BIENEFELD (M. A.). Working Hours in British Industry: An Economic History. 1972.

3885 —— Wages, Relative Prices and the Export of Capital. Brighton. 1977.

3886 BURNS (EVELINE MABEL). Wages and the State: A Comparative Study of the Problems of State Wage Regulation. 1926.

3887 CHAPMAN (AGATHA LOUISA) *and* KNIGHT (ROSE). Wages and Salaries in the United Kingdom, 1920–1938. Camb. 1953.

3888 PEACOCK (*Sir* ALAN TURNER) *and* RYAN (W. J. L.). 'Wage Claims and the Pace of Inflation [1948–1951]'. *Econ. J.* 63 (1953), 385–92.

3889 AMPHLETT (EDGAR MONTAGUE). 'Employers' Wage Policy'. *Pol. Q.* 27 (1956), 293–302.

3890 ROBERTS (BENJAMIN CHARLES). National Wages Policy in War and Peace. 1958.

3891 ROUTH (GERALD GUY CUMMING). Occupation and Pay in Great Britain, 1906–1960. 1965. 2nd edn covering 1906–1979, 1980.

3892 RUBNER (ALEXANDER). Fringe Benefits: The Golden Chains. 1962.

3893 REID (GRAHAM LIVINGSTONE) *and* ROBERTSON (DONALD JAMES) *eds.* Fringe Benefits, Labour Costs and Social Security. 1965.

3894 WOOTTON (BARBARA) *Baroness, et al.* The Social Foundations of Wage Policy: A Study of Contemporary British Wage and Salary Structure. 1955. 2nd edn 1962.

3895 SPRAOS (JOHN). 'Linking Wages to Productivity'. *Bankers' Mag.* 185 (1958), 300–3.

3896 THOMAS (R. L.). 'Cross-Sectional Phillips Curve'. *Manch. Sch. Econ. Soc. Studs* 42 (1974), 205–39.

3897 MACKAY (D. I.) *and* HART (R. A.). 'Wage Inflation and the Phillips Relationship'. *Manch. Sch. Econ. Soc. Studs* 42 (1974), 131–61.

3898 MCCALLUM (B. T.). 'Wage Rate Changes and the Excess Demand for Labour: An Attractive Formulation'. *Economica* 41 (1974), 269–77.

3899 GROSSMAN (HERSCHEL I.). 'The Cyclical Pattern of Unemployment Wage Inflation'. *Economica* 41 (1974), 403–13.

3900 TYLECOTE (ANDREW B.). 'The Effect of Monetary Policy on Wage Inflation'. *Oxf. Econ. Papers* 27 (1975), 240–4.

3901 LYDALL (HAROLD FRENCH). The Structure of Earnings. Oxf. 1968.

3902 JAQUES (ELLIOT). Measurement of Responsibility: A Study of Work, Payment and Individual Progress. 1961.

3903 —— Equitable Payment: A General Theory of Work, Differential Payment and Individual Progress. 1961.

3904 —— Time-Span Handbook: The Use of Time-Span Discretion to Measure the Level of Work in Employment Roles and to Arrange an Equitable Payment Structure. 1964.

3905 HAWTREY (*Sir* RALPH GEORGE). Cross Purposes in Wage Policy. 1955.

3906 U.K. DEPT. OF EMPLOYMENT AND PRODUCTIVITY. A National Minimum Wage: Report of an Inter-departmental Working Party. 1969.

3907 BROWN (*Sir* ERNEST HENRY PHELPS) *and* BROWNE (MARGARET H.). A Century of Pay: The Course of Pay and Production in France, Germany, Sweden, the United Kingdom and the United States of America, 1860–1960. 1968.

3908 —— 'Earnings in Industries of the United Kingdom, 1948–1959'. *Econ. J.* 72 (1962), 517–49.

3909 BROWN (*Sir* ERNEST HENRY PHELPS). 'Equal Pay for Equal Work'. *Econ. J.* 59 (1949), 384–98.

3910 —— The Inequality of Pay. 1977.

3911 —— Pay and Profits. 1968.

3912 BROWN (*Sir* ERNEST HENRY PHELPS) *and* HOPKINS (SHEILA). A Perspective of Wages and Prices. 1981.

3913 PENCAVEL (JOHN H.). 'Relative Wages and Trade Unions in the United Kingdom'. *Economica* 41 (1974), 194–210.

3914 EDWARDS (*Sir* RONALD STANLEY) *and* ROBERTS (ROBERT DAVID). Status, Productivity and Pay: A Major Experiment: A Study of the Electricity Supply Industry's Agreements and their Outcome 1961–1971. 1971.

3915 U.K. NATIONAL BOARD FOR PRICES AND INCOMES. Top Salaries in the Private Sector and Nationalised Industries. 1969. [Report no. 107.].

3916 HOOD (W.) *and* REES (R. D.). 'Inter-industry Wage Levels in United Kingdom Manufacturing'. *Manch. Sch. Econ. Soc. Studs* 42 (1974), 171–85.

3917 PATTERSON (WILLIAM DAVID). The Lansdowne Earnings Survey. 1974.

3918 LUPTON (THOMAS). Wages and Salaries. Harmondsworth. 1975.

3919 SHAPIRO (JUDITH CLAIRE). Inter-industry Wage Determination: The Post-War U.K. Experience. 1966.

3920 MARQUAND (JUDITH). Wage Drift: Origins, Measurement and Behaviour. 1967.

3921 FISHBEIN (WARREN H.). Wage Restraint by Consensus, Britain's Search for an Incomes Policy Agreement, 1965–1979. 1984.

3922 MOSES (LEON N.). 'Income, Leisure and Wage Pressure'. *Econ. J.* 72 (1962), 320–34.

3923 ALLSOP (KATHLEEN). A New Deal for Young Workers. 1966.

3924 PHILLIPS (A. W.). 'The Relation between Unemployment and the Rate of Change in Money Wage Rates in the United Kingdom, 1861–1957'. *Economica* 25 (1958), 283–99.

3925 DEVONS (ELY) *and* CROSSLEY (JOHN RODNEY). The "*Guardian*" Wages Index: A Series of Indexes of Wages Rates in British Industry since 1948. Manch. 1962.

3926 DEVONS (ELY). 'Wage Rates by Industry, 1948–1965'. *Economica* 35 (1968), 392–423.

3927 BROWN (ALAN). Profits, Wages and Wealth. 1961.

3928 MASTERS (STANLEY H.). 'An Inter-Industry Analysis of Wages and Plant Size'. *Rev. Econ. Stat.* 51 (1969), 341–59.

3929 SAWYER (MICHAEL C.). 'The Earnings of Manual Workers: A Cross-Section Analysis'. *Scot. J. Pol. Econ.* 20 (1973), 141–57.

3930 KNOWLES (K. G. J. C.) *and* ROBERTSON (DONALD JAMES). 'Earnings and Engineering, 1926–1948'. *Bull. Oxf. Univ. Inst. Stats* 13 (1951), 179–200.

3931 —— 'Some Notes on Engineering Earnings'. *Bull. Oxf. Univ. Inst. Stats* 13 (1951), 223–8.

3932 —— 'Differences between the Wages of Skilled and Unskilled Workers, 1880–1950'. *Bull. Oxf. Univ. Inst. Econ. Stats.* 13 (1951), 109–27.

3933 FOGARTY (MICHAEL). The Just Wage. 1961.

3934 DERRICK (P.). 'Wages and Dividends'. *Contemp. Rev.* 201 (1962), 1–6.

3935 JOHNSTON (THOMAS LOTHIAN). 'Pay Policy after the Pause'. *Scot. J. Pol. Econ.* 9 (1962), 1–16.

3936 ROBINSON (DEREK). 'Wage Rates, Wage Income and Wage Policy'. *Bull. Oxf. Univ. Inst. Econ. Stats.* 25 (1963), 47–76.

3937 HILL (T. P.). 'Wages and Labour Turnover'. *Bull. Oxf. Univ. Inst. Econs. Stats.* 24 (1962), 184–234.

3938 MITCHELL (D. J. B.). 'British Incomes Policy, the Competitive Effect and the 1967 Devaluation'. *Southern Econ. J.* 37 (1970), 88–92.

3939 U.K. OFFICE OF MANPOWER ECONOMICS. Equal Pay: First Report on the Implementation of the 1970 Act. 1972.

3940 McKERSIE (R. B.) *and* HUNTER (L. C.). Pay, Productivity and Collective Bargaining. 1973.

3941 ROBINSON (OLIVE) *and* WALLACE (JOHN). 'Part-Time Employment and Low Pay in Retail Distribution in Britain'. *Ind. Relns J.* 5 (1974), 38–53.

3942 BURKITT (BRIAN). Trade Unions and Wages. Bradford. 1975.

3943 HEBDEN (J.). 'Men and Women's Pay in Britain, 1968–1975'. *Ind. Relns J.* 9 (1978), 56–70.

3944 WOOD (ADRIAN). A Theory of Pay. Camb. 1978.

3945 SLOANE (PETER J.). *ed.* Women and Low Pay. 1980.

3946 FALLICK (LESLIE J.) *and* ELLIOTT (ROBERT F.) *eds.* Incomes Policies, Inflation and Relative Pay. 1981.

3947 ELLIOTT (ROBERT F.) *and* FALLICK (LESLIE J.). Pay in the Public Sector. 1981.

3948 —— Pay Differentials in Perspective: A Study of Manual and Non-Manual Worker's Pay over the Period 1951–1975. Aberd. 1977.

3949 —— Salary Changes and Salary Structure: A Study of Clerical Workers Pay. Aberd. 1977.

3950 POND (CHRIS). Low Pay-1980s Style. 1981. [Low Pay Unit.].

3951 —— Low Pay: What can Local Authorities Do? 1984. [Low Pay Unit.].

3952 —— No Return to Sweatshops! Government Economic Strategy and the Wages Councils. 1984. [Low Pay Unit.].

3953 POND (CHRIS) *and* WINYARD (STEVE). The Case for a National Minimum Wage. 1982. [Low Pay Unit.].

3954 BOWEY (ANGELA M.), THORPE (RICHARD), *and* HELLIER (PAUL). Payment Systems and Productivity. Basingstoke. 1986.

3955 HOLDEN (K.), PEEL (D. A.), *and* THOMPSON (J. L.). The Economics of Wage Controls. 1987.

3956 MILLER (PAUL W.). 'The Wage Effect of the Occupational Segregation of Women in Britain'. *Econ. J.* 97 (1987), 885–96.

3957 SMAIL (ROBIN). Breadline Wages: Low Pay in Greater Manchester. Lond. 1985.

3958 —— Two Nations: Poverty and Wages in the North. 1985.

3959 BICKERSTAFFE (RODNEY). Privatisation and Low Pay: The Impact of Government Policies. Nottingham. 1984.

3960 BROSNAN (PETER). Cheap Labour: Britain's False Economy. 1987.

3961 MEADE (JAMES EDWARD). Wage-Fixing Revisited. 1985.

3962 NEUBERGER (HENRY). From the Dole Queue to the Sweatshop. 1984. [Low Pay Unit.].

3963 BROWN (JOAN C.). Low Pay and Poverty in the United Kingdom. 1981.

3964 BYRNE (DOMINIC). Making Ends Meet: Working for Low Wages in the Civil Service. 1983.

3965 McNAY (MARIE) *and* POND (CHRIS). Low Pay and Family Poverty. 1980. [Low Pay Unit.].

3966 JONES (RUSSELL). Wages and Employment Policy, 1936–1985. 1987.

3967 MacNEILL (KATE) *and* POND (CHRIS). Britain Can't Afford Low Pay. 1988. [Low Pay Unit.].

4. EMPLOYMENT PENSION SCHEMES

3968 HOSKING (GORDON A.). Pension Schemes and Retirement Benefits. 1956. 3rd edn 1968. 4th edn by K. Muir Mckervey *et al.* 1977.

3969 RHODES (GERALD). Public Sector Pensions. 1965.

3970 CAGAN (PHILIP). The Effect of Pension Plans on Aggregate Savings: Evidence from a Sample Survey. N.Y. 1965.

3971 DIXON (DANIEL). Can You Retire? Some Thoughts about the Individual, Administrative and Economic Aspects of Retirement. Oxf./N.Y. 1968.

3972 PILCH (MICHAEL) *and* WOOD (VICTOR). Pension Schemes. 1960.

3973 —— New Trends in Pensions. 1964.

3974 —— Pension Schemes Practice. 1967.

3975 —— Company Pension Schemes. 1971.

3976 —— Managing Pension Schemes: A Guide to Contemporary Pension Plans and the Social Security Act. Epping. 1974.

3977 WARD (SUE). Pensions: What to Look for in Company Pension Schemes and How to Improve Them. 1981.

3978 The Essential Guide to Pensions: A Workers' Handbook. 1988.

3979 McGOLDRICK (ANN). Equal Treatment in Occupational Pension Schemes: A Research Report. Manch. 1984.

3980 MORGAN (EDWARD VICTOR). Choice in Pensions: The Political Economy of Saving for Retirement. 1984.

3981 FRY (V. C.). The Taxation of Occupational Pension Schemes in the United Kingdom. 1985.

3982 LOWE (JONQUIL). Choose Your Pension: An Independent Guide to Choosing the Best Pension Scheme for You. 1989.

5. INFLATION

3983 EINZIG (PAUL). Inflation. 1952.

3984 CHARLESWORTH (HAROLD KARR). The Economics of Repressed Inflation. 1956.

3985 BROWN (ARTHUR JOSEPH). 'Inflation and the British Economy'. *Econ. J.* 68 (1958), 449–63.

3986 PAISH (FRANK WALTER). 'Inflation in the United Kingdom, 1948–1957'. *Economica* 25 (1958), 94–105.

3987 —— Studies in an Inflationary Economy in the United Kingdom, 1948–1961. 1962.

3988 MacDOUGALL (*Sir* GEORGE DONALD ALISTAIR). 'Inflation in the United Kingdom'. *Econ. Record* 25 (1959), 371–88.

3989 DICKS-MIREAUX (L. A.) *and* DOW (J. C.). 'The Determinants of Wage Inflation: United Kingdom, 1946–1956'. *J. Roy. Stat. Soc.* 122 (1959), [Series A], 145–74.

3990 CHAMPERNOWNE (DAVID GAWEN). 'The Determinants of Wage Inflation: United Kingdom, 1946–1956: A Discussion'. *J. Roy. Stat. Soc.* 122 (1959), [Series A], 174–84.

3991 DICKS-MIREAUX (L. A.). 'The Inter-relationship between Cost and Price Changes, 1946–1959: A Study in Inflation in Post-War Britain'. *Oxf. Econ. Papers* 13 (1961), 267–92.

3992 HINES (ALBERT GREGORIO). 'Trade Unions and Wage Inflation in the United Kingdom 1893–1961'. *Rev. Econ. Studs* 31 (1964), 221–52.

3993 —— 'Wage Inflation in the United Kingdom, 1948–1962: A Disaggregated Study'. *Econ. J.* 79 (1969), 66–89.

3994 KNIGHT (K. G.). 'Strikes and Wage Inflation in British Manufacturing Industry 1950–1968'. *Bull. Oxf. Univ. Inst. Econ. Stats* 34 (1972), 281–94.

3995 CAGAN (PHILIP). 'Inflation and Market Structure, 1967–1973'. *Explor. Econ. Res.* 2 (1975), 203–16.

3996 WILSON (THOMAS). Inflation. Oxf. 1961.

3997 DOBB (MAURICE HERBERT). 'Inflation and all That'. *Marxism Today* 9 (1965), 84–7.

3998 HARVEY (JAMES T.) *and* MCCALLUM (WILLIAM). 'Problems of Inflation'. *Marxism Today* 9 (1965), 126–8.

3999 BALL (R. J.) *and* DOYLE (PETER) *eds.* Inflation. Harmondsworth. 1969.

4000 BALOGH (THOMAS). Labour and Inflation. 1970.

4001 JACKSON (DUDLEY) *et al.* Do Trade Unions Cause Inflation? 1972.

4002 PHELPS (EDMUND STRUTHER). Inflation Policy and Unemployment Theory: The Cost Benefit Approach to Monetary Planning. 1972.

4003 —— Microeconomic Foundations of Employment and Inflation Theory. N.Y. 1970.

4004 JOHNSON (HARRY GORDON). Inflation and the Monetarist Controversy. Amsterdam/Lond. 1972.

4005 JONES (AUBREY). The New Inflation: The Politics of Prices and Incomes. 1973.

4006 LAIDLER (DAVID E. W.) and PURDY (D.). Inflation and Labour Markets. Manch. 1974.

4007 FLEMMING (JOHN STANTON). Inflation. Oxf. 1976.

4008 GRIFFITHS (BRIAN). Inflation: The Price of Prosperity. 1976.

4009 CURWEN (PETER J.). Inflation. 1976.

4010 FOSTER (J.). 'The Redistributive Effect of Inflation on Building Society Shares and Deposits 1961–1974'. *Bull. Econ. Res.* 28 (1976), 66–76.

4011 PARKIN (MICHAEL) and SUMNER (MICHAEL THOMAS). Inflation in the United Kingdom. Manch. 1978.

4012 BOWERS (J. K.) ed. Inflation, Development and Integration; Essays in honour of A. J. Brown. Leeds. 1979.

4013 TREVITHICK (JAMES ANTHONY). Inflation: A Guide to the Crisis in Economics. Harmondsworth. 1977. 2nd edn 1980.

4014 SEERS (DUDLEY). Inflation. Brighton. 1981. [Brighton Inst. Devlpt Studies.].

4015 HAGGER (ALFRED JAMES). Inflation: A Theoretical Survey and Synthesis. 1982.

4016 FEINSTEIN (CHARLES HILLIARD) ed. The Managed Economy: Essays in British Economic Policy since 1929. Oxf. 1983. See chs by Frank Walter Paish, 'Inflation and the Balance of Payments in the U.K., 1952–1967' and R. J. Ball and T. Burns, 'The Inflationary Mechanism in the U.K. Economy'.

4017 WILSON (THOMAS) and MacLENNAN (MALCOLM CAMERON). Inflation, Unemployment and the Market. Oxf. 1984.

4018 KING (JOHN) and WOOKEY (CHARLES). Inflation. 1987. [London Inst. for Fiscal Studies.].

4019 NEVILLE (J. W.) and ARGY (VICTOR). Inflation and Unemployment. 1985.

4020 BECKERMAN (WILFRED) and JENKINSON (T.). 'What Stopped the Inflation? Unemployment or Commodity Prices?'. *Econ. J.* 96 (1986), 39–54.

4021 HORSMAN (GEORGE). Inflation in the 20th Century. Hemel Hempstead. 1988. [See esp. ch. 'The United Kingdom from Wilson to Thatcher'.].

C. NATIONAL INSURANCE, SOCIAL SECURITY, HEALTH, AND SAFETY AT WORK

Material in this section covers topics which refer back to the previous section in part but which are also distinct. The categories which have been identified are themselves separate though, at different stages in the creation of the provisions to which they related, they have been seen as different aspects of the same problem. Their bearing on social and industrial policy, considered subsequently, needs no emphasis.

I. UNEMPLOYMENT AND NATIONAL INSURANCE

4022 MARLEY (FELIX). Unemployment Relief in Great Britain: A Study in State Socialism. 1924.

4023 CREW (ALBERT) with BLACKHAM (R. J.). The Unemployment Insurance Acts, 1920–1927. 1928. New edn 1930.

4024 GIBSON (MARY BARNET). Unemployment Insurance in Great Britain. N.Y. 1931.

4025 HOHMAN (HELEN FISHER). The Development of Social Insurance and Minimum Wage Legislation in Great Britain. Boston, Mass. 1933.

4026 BAKKE (EDWARD WRIGHT). Insurance or Dole? The Adjustment of Unemployment Insurance to Economic and Social Facts in Britain. 1935.

4027 COHEN (PERCY). Unemployment Insurance and Assistance in Britain. 1938.

4028 WILSON (Sir ARNOLD TALBOT) and LEVY (HERMANN JOACHIM). Workmen's Compensation. 2 vols 1939–1941.

4029 —— Industrial Assurance: A Historical and Critical Study. 1937.

4030 TILLYARD (Sir FRANK) and BALL (FRANK NORMAN). Unemployment Insurance in Great Britain, 1911–1948. Leigh-on-Sea. 1949.

4031 PEACOCK (Sir ALAN TURNER). The Economics of National Insurance. 1952.

4032 HOOD (KATHERINE). Room at the Bottom: National Insurance in the Welfare State. 1960.

4033 HAUSER (MARK M.) and BURROWS (PAUL). The Economics of Unemployment Insurance. 1969.

4034 STEWART (J. ANDREW). 'Jubilee of the National Insurance Act'. *Pharm. J.* 135 (1962), 33–5.

4035 DEACON (ALAN). In Search of the Scrounger: The Administration of Unemployment Insurance in Britain, 1920–1931. 1976.

4036 LYNES (TONY ALFRED). National Assistance and National Prosperity. Welwyn. 1962.

4037 MARSH (DAVID CHARLES). National Insurance and Assistance in Britain. 1950.

4038 GILBERT (BENTLEY BRINKERHOFF). The Evolution of National Insurance in Great Britain: The Origins of the Welfare State. 1966.

4039 FULBROOK (JULIAN). Administrative Justice and the Unemployed. 1978.

4040 MESHER (JOHN). Compensation for Unemployment. 1976.

4041 RHYS WILLIAMS (*Sir* BRANDON). Stepping Stones to Independence: National Insurance after 1990. Aberd. 1989.

2. PENSIONS AND BENEFITS

4042 GILLING-SMITH (GORDON DRYDEN). The Complete Guide to Pensions and Superannuation. Harmondsworth. 1967. 2nd edn 1968.

4043 PARTINGTON (MARTIN) *et al. comps.* Welfare Rights: A Bibliography on Law and the Poor 1970–1975. 1976.

4044 WILSON (*Sir* ARNOLD TALBOT) *and* LEVY (HERMANN JOACHIM). Burial Reform and Funeral Costs. 1938.

4045 WILSON (*Sir* ARNOLD TALBOT) *and* McKAY (G. S.). Old Age Pensions: An Historical and Critical Study. 1941.

4046 DAVIES (RHYS JOHN). Widowed Mothers Pensions. 1923.

4047 MINISTRY OF PENSIONS. Pensions for Disablement or Death due to Service in the Forces after 2nd September 1939. 1951. Rev. edn 1956.

4048 FOGARTY (MICHAEL PATRICK). Pensions Where Next? 1976.

4049 —— Under-Governed and Over-Governed. 1962.

4050 U.K. D.H.S.S. Strategy for Pensions: The Future Development of State and Occupational Pensions. 1971.

4051 SHRAGGE (ERIC). Pensions Policy in Britain: A Socialist Analysis. 1984.

4052 REARDON (A. M.). Pensions Guide. 1984.

4053 BENJAMIN (BERNARD). Pensions: The Problems of Today and Tomorrow. 1987.

4054 BACON (W. F.) *et al.* 'The Growth of Pension Rights and their Impact on the National Economy'. *J. Inst. Actuaries* 80 (1954), 141–66.

4055 BISSANTI (ANDREA ANTONIO). 'Considerazioni Geografica sulla Distribuzione della Populazione in eta Pensionabile in Gran Bretagna'. *Boll. Soc. Geog. Ital.* 105 (1968), [Series 9], 587–604.

4056 LISTER (RUTH). As Man and Wife: A Study of the Cohabitation Rule. 1972.

4057 —— Supplementary Benefit Rights. 1974.

4058 U.K. D.H.S.S. SUPPLEMENTARY BENEFITS COMMISSION. Supplementary Benefits Handbook. 1971. [Revised annually.].

4059 —— Cohabitation: The Administration of the Relevant Provisions of the Ministry of Social Security Act 1966 . . . 1971.

4060 U.K. MINISTRY OF SOCIAL SECURITY. Circumstances of Families: Report on an Enquiry by the Ministry of Pensions and National Insurance with the Co-operation of the National Assistance Board, subsequently combined to form the Ministry of Social Security. 1967.

4061 U.K. CENTRAL OFFFICE OF INFORMATION. Social Security in Britain. 1970. 2nd edn 1973.

4062 WALLEY (*Sir* JOHN). Social Security: Another British Failure? 1972.

4063 U.K. COMMITTEE ON ABUSE OF SOCIAL SECURITY BENEFITS. Report. 1973.

4064 U.K. D.H.S.S. Family Benefits and Pensions. 1973. [Pub. annually.].

4065 —— Social Security Statistics. 1972. [Pub. Annually.].

4066 U.K. D.H.S.S. NORTHERN IRELAND. Report of the Supplementary Benefits Commission. Belfast. 1966. [Pub. annually.].

4067 ROSE (MICHAEL EDWARD) *comp.* The English Poor Law, 1780–1930. Newton Abbot. 1971.

4068 DUMSDAY (WILLIAM HENRY) *and* MOSS (JOHN). The Relieving Officers' Handbook: Being a Complete and Practical Guide to the Law Relating to the Powers, Duties and Liabilities of Relieving Officers. 1st pub. 1902. 3rd edn 1923, 7th edn 1938.

4069 EXLEY (C. H.). The Guide to Poor Relief. L/pool. 1932. 4th edn 1935.

4070 DIGBY (ANNE). Pauper Palaces. 1973.

4071 MENCHER (SAMUEL). Poor Law to Poverty Program: Economic Security Policy in Britain and the United States. Pittsburgh, Pa. 1967.

4072 U.K. REGISTER OF FRIENDLY SOCIETIES AND OFFICE OF THE INDUSTRIAL INSURANCE COMMISSIONER. Guide to the Friendly Societies' Act and the Industrial Assurance Acts. 1962.

4073 FULLER (MARGARET DOROTHY). West Country Friendly Societies: An Account of Village Benefit Clubs and their Brass Pole Heads. Lingfield. 1964.

4074 POTTER (WARREN) *and* OLIVER (ROBERT). Fraternally Yours: A History of the Independent Order of Foresters. 1967.

4075 U.K. MINISTRY OF HOUSING AND LOCAL GOVERNMENT. Report of the Committee of Inquiry into the Impact of Rates on Households. 1965.

4076 MEACHER (MOLLY). Rate Rebates: A Study of the Effectiveness of Means Tests. 1972.

4077 U.K. DEPARTMENT OF THE ENVIRONMENT *and* THE WELSH OFFICE. Rate Rebates in England and Wales 1968/69. 1969. [Pub. annually.].

4078 SCOTTISH OFFICE. Rate Rebates in Scotland 1969/70. 1971. [Pub. annually.].

4079 U.K. NATIONAL ASSISTANCE BOARD. Handbook for Newcomers. [Interim Edition.] 1948.

4080 GLENNERSTER (HOWARD). National Assistance: Service or Charity? 1962. [Fabian Society.].

4081 KINCAID (JAMES COLLINS). Poverty and Equality in Britain: A Study of Social Security and Taxation. 1973. Rev. edn Harmondsworth. 1975.

4082 GEORGE (VIC). Social Security and Society. 1973.

4083 ATKINSON (ANTHONY BARNES). Poverty in Britain and the Reform of Social Security. 1969.

4084 HECLO (HUGH). From Relief to Income Maintenance: Modern Social Policy-Making in Britain and Sweden. New Haven, Conn. 1974.

4085 CLARKE (JOHN JOSEPH). Public Assistance: Being the Relevant Sections from 'Social Administration, Including the Poor Laws'. 1934.

4086 CLARKE (JOAN SIMEON). The Assistance Board. 1941.

4087 —— Social Security. 1943.

4088 RATHBONE (ELEANOR FLORENCE). The Case for Family Allowances. Harmondsworth. 1940.

4089 —— The Disinherited Family: A Plea for the Endowment of the Family. 1924. 3rd edn 1927. [Retitled as 'Family Allowances', in 1949 edn with a new ch. by Eva M. Hubback. This edn repr. Bristol 1986, under original title, 'The Disinherited Family'.].

4090 —— The Ethics and Economics of Family Endowment. 1927.

4091 MacNICOL (JOHN). The Movement for Family Allowances, 1918–1945: A Study in Social Policy Development. 1980.

4092 MILLAR (JANE). Poverty and the One Parent Family: The Challenge to Social Policy. Aldershot. 1989.

4093 BROWN (JOAN C.). Family Income Support Part One: Family Income Supplement. 1983.

4094 —— F.I.S. Part Twelve: The Future of Family Income Support. 1987.

4095 RICHARDSON (ANN). F.I.S. Part Four: Widow's Benefits. 1984.

4096 COOPER (STEVEN). F.I.S. Part Five: Health Benefits. 1985.

4097 FIELD (FRANK). F.I.S. Part Six: What Price a Child? A Historical Review of the Relative Cost of Dependants. 1985.

4098 FISHER (ALAN GEORGE BERNARD). Economic Progress and Financial Aspects of Social Security: An International Survey. 1960.

4099 RICHARDSON (JOHN HENRY). Economic and Financial Aspects of Social Security. 1960.

4100 JOSEPH (*Sir* KEITH SINJOHN). A New Strategy for Social Security. 1966.

3. HEALTH INSURANCE, SAFETY AT WORK, AND INDUSTRIAL ARBITRATION

4101 POLLARD (ROBERT SPENCE WATSON). Introducing the National Insurance (Industrial Injuries) Acts, 1946–1953. 1955.

4102 U.K. MINISTRY OF PENSIONS AND NATIONAL INSURANCE. Report of an Enquiry into the Incidence of Incapacity for Work. (1964–1965). [2 parts.].

4103 HOFFMAN (FREDERICK LUDWIG). National Health Insurance and the Friendly Societies . . . Newark, N.J. 1921.

4104 OLIVER (*Sir* THOMAS). Diseases of Occupation, from the Legislative, Social and Medical Points of View. 1908. 3rd rev. edn 1916.

4105 GREENWOOD (MAJOR) [The Younger] *and* TEBB (ALBERT EDWARD). An Inquiry into the Prevalence and Aetiology of Tuberculosis among Industrial Workers. 1919.

4106 GREENWOOD (MAJOR) *and* WOODS (HILDA M.). The Incidence of Industrial Accidents upon Individuals with Special Reference to Multiple Accidents. 1919.

4107 SMITH (MAY), LEIPER (M. A.), *and* GREENWOOD (MAJOR). Sickness Absence and Labour Wastage. 1936.

4108 COLLIS (EDGAR LEIGH) *and* GREENWOOD (MAJOR). Industrial Pneumoconiosis, with Special Reference to Dust-Pthisis. 1919.

4109 —— The Health of Industrial Workers. 1921.

4110 COLLIS (EDGAR LEIGH) *ed.* The Industrial Clinic: A Handbook Dealing with Health in Work. 1920.

4111 EDER (NORMAN R.). National Health Insurance and the Medical Profession in Britain, 1913–1939. N.Y./Lond. 1982.

4112 MEDICAL RESEARCH COUNCIL. Memorandum No. 1: Reactions of Mines Rescue Personnel to Work in Hot Environments. 1957.

4113 HOPE (EDWARD WILLIAM), HANNA (WILLIAM), *and* STALLYBRASS (CLARE OSWALD). Industrial Hygiene and Medicine. 1923.

4114 COLLIE (*Sir* ROBERT JOHN). Workmen's Compensation: Its Medical Aspect. 1933.

4115 LEGGE (*Sir* THOMAS MORRISON). Industrial Maladies. 1934.

4116 VERNON (HORACE MIDDLETON). Road Accidents in War-Time. 1941.

4117 ROSEN (GEORGE). The History of Miners' Diseases: A Medical and Social Interpretation. N.Y. 1943.

4118 TELEKY (LUDWIG). History of Factory and Mine Hygiene. N.Y. 1948.

4119 LEVY (HERMANN). National Health Insurance: A Critical Study. Camb. 1964.

4120 CAMPBELL (DOROTHY ADAMS), RIDILL (WILLIAM JOHN BROWNLOW), *and* MACNALTY (ARTHUR SALUSBURY). Eyes in Industry: A Complete Book on Eyesight Written for Industrial Workers. 1951.

4121 HUNTER (DONALD). The Diseases of Occupations. 1955. 6th edn 1978.

4122 WILLIAMS (JOHN LEWIS). Accidents and Ill-Health at Work. 1960.

4123 EAGGER (ARTHUR AUSTIN). Venture in Industry: The Slough Industrial Health Service, 1947–1963. 1965.

4124 U.K. MINISTRY OF LABOUR, NORTHERN IRELAND. Byssinosis in Flax Workers in Northern Ireland: A Report to the Minister of Labour and National Insurance. Belfast. 1965.

4125 U.K. MINISTRY OF LABOUR. The Appointed Factory Doctor Service: Report by a Sub-Committee of the Industrial Health Advisory Committee. 1966. [Chairman: N. Singleton.]

4126 MCFEELY (MARY DRAKE). Lady Inspectors: The Campaign for a Better Workplace, 1893–1921. Oxf. 1988.

4127 DAVIES (CHARLES NORMAN) *and* DAVIES (P. R.). The Effects of Abnormal Physical Conditions at Work. Edin. 1967.

4128 DAVIES (CHARLES NORMAN) *ed.* Health Conditions in the Ceramic Industry. Oxf. 1969.

4129 LUFFINGHAM (RAYMOND LAURENCE). A New Look at Industrial Medicine. 1967.

4130 BAKER (FRANK), MCEWAN (PETER J. M.), *and* SHELDON (ALAN) *eds.* Industrial Organisations and Health. 2 vols 1969.

4131 SCHILLING (RICHARD SELWYN FRANCIS). Modern Trends in Occupational Health. 1960.

4132 —— Occupational Health Practice. 1973.

4133 U.K. DEPT. OF HEALTH AND PRODUCTIVITY. Asbestos: Health Precautions in Industry. [Health and Safety at Work Pamphlet No.44.] 1970.

4134 U.K. MINISTRY OF LABOUR FACTORY INSPECTORATE. Problems Arising from the use of Asbestos: Memorandum . . . 1967.

4135 U.K. HEALTH AND SAFETY EXECUTIVE. [Advisory Committee on Asbestos] Asbestos: Final Report. 1979, 2 vols.

4136 SELIKOFF (IRVING J.) *et al.* Asbestos and Disease. Lond./N.Y. 1978.

4137 DOLL (RICHARD). Effects on Health of Exposure to Asbestos. 1985.

4138 NICHOLS (THEO) *and* ARMSTRONG (PETE). Safety or Profit: Industrial Accidents and the Conventional Wisdom. Bristol. 1973.

4139 GAUVAIN ([CATHERINE JOAN] SUZETTE) *ed.* Occupational Health: A Guide to Sources of Information. 1974.

4140 BRYAN (*Sir* ANDREW MEIKLE). The Evolution of Health and Safety in Mines. 1975.

4141 GARDNER (WARD) *and* TAYLOR (PETER). Health at Work. 1975.

4142 DEWIS (MALCOLM). The Law on Health and Safety at Work. Plymouth. 1978.

4143 DEWIS (MALCOLM) *and* STRANKS (JEREMY) *eds.* Tolley's Health and Safety at Work Handbook. 1983. 2nd edn 1988.

4144 U.K. HEALTH AND SAFETY AT WORK EXECUTIVE. Some Aspects of the Safety of Nuclear Installations in Great Britain. 1977.

4145 —— Lighting at Work. 1987.

4146 CURRY (N.). Working Conditions in Universities: A Pilot Study. 1978.

4147 U.K. HEALTH AND SAFETY COMMISSION. A Guide to the Health and Safety at Work etc. Act 1974. 1980.

4148 CONSTRUCTION INDUSTRY ADVISORY COMMITTEE. Managing Health and Safety in Construction. 1987.

4149 INDUSTRIAL INJURIES ADVISORY COUNCIL. Bronchitis and Emphysema . . . 1988.

4150 RUBIN (G. R.). 'The Origins of Industrial Tribunals: Munitions Tribunals During the First World War'. *Inst. Law. J.* 6 (1977), 149–64.

4151 MACKENZIE (WILLIAM WARRENDER) *Baron Amulree*. Industrial Arbitration in Great Britain. 1929.

4152 SEYMOUR (JOHN BARTON). The Whitley Councils Scheme. 1932.

4153 SHARP (IAN G.). Industrial Conciliation and Arbitration in Britain. 1950.

4154 CONCANNON (H.). 'The Growth of Arbitration Work in A.C.A.S.'. *Ind. Relns J.* 9 (1978), 12–18.

4155 ARMSTRONG (ERIC GEORGE ABBOT) *and* LUCAS (ROSEMARY E.). Improving Industrial Relations: The Advisory Role of A.C.A.S. 1985.

4156 GINNINGS (ARTHUR T.). Arbitration: A Practical Guide. Aldershot. 1984.

4157 ADVISORY, CONCILIATION AND ARBITRATION SERVICE [ACAS]. Industrial Relations Handbook. 1980.

4158 —— First Annual Report. 1979.

4159 —— The Contract Cleaning Industry: A Report. 1980.

4160 —— The Laundry Wages Council. 1980.

4161 —— Workplace Communications. 1983.

4162 ACAS *and* CENTRAL OFFICE OF INFORMATION. Disciplinary Practice and Procedures in Employment. 1977.

4163 LEWIS (PAUL). 'The Role of A.C.A.S. Conciliators in Unfair Dismissal Cases'. *Ind. Relns J.* 13 (1982), 50–6.

4164 JONES (MICHAEL) *and* DICKENS (LINDA). 'Resolving Industrial Disputes: The Role of A.C.A.S. Conciliation'. *Ind. Relns J.* 14 (1983), 6–17.

4165 MEASURES (J.) *and* NORTON (S.). 'Joint Working Parties: A Case Study of the A.C.A.S. Approach to Improving Industrial Relations'. *Employee Rels J.* 6 (1983), 10–12.

4166 COSMO (GRAHAM). The Role of A.C.A.S.: Conciliation in Equal Pay and Sex Discrimination Cases. Manch. 1985.

4167 BYRE (ANGELA). Human Rights at the Workplace: A Handbook for Industrial Relations Practitioners. 1988.

D. FINANCE

The miscellany of topics gathered in this section is indeed wide. Yet, while some titles in the individual sub-sections also suggest linkages with other subsequent sections—'advertising' is a case in point—'finance' is sufficiently capacious to offer shelter both to the treatment of particular types of financial institution and to broad issues of national finance. The historiography of these sub-sections, however, is at markedly different stages of development. Issues of monetary policy or of public expenditure, to take but two examples, have inevitably held centre stage but have been debated between economists. With rare exceptions, general historians have not ventured into these areas. It is arguable therefore, in these and other respects, whether the material which has been listed constitutes 'history' or whether it constitutes the raw material of history. It is, of course, a problem not restricted to this section or indeed this chapter. In addition, other sub-sections call up other problems. It is only recently, for example, that accounting has begun to attract the attention of 'accounting historians' and what has been achieved represents, one supposes, but a small portion of what might be achieved. Banking history, on the other hand has a lengthier pedigree but in the case of banks, and to some extent building societies and other savings institutions, much of the work published has been directly commissioned by the institutions themselves. It is no criticism of the high standards frequently achieved by the writers of such histories to point out the danger which exists when a particular field of history is largely investigated in this manner. The willingness of institutions to finance such work is indeed to be commended but it can also mean that banking historians write very much from 'inside' and, for example, what might be described as a 'social history' of British banking scarcely exists.

1. ACCOUNTING

4168 PARKER (ROBERT HENRY). British Accountants: A Biographical Sourcebook. 1980.

4169 STACEY (NICHOLAS ANTHONY HOWARD). English Accountancy: A Study in Social and Economic History, 1800–1954. 1954.

4170 CHATFIELD (MICHAEL). A History of Accounting Thought. Hinsdale, Ill. 1974. Repr. N.Y. 1977.

4171 —— An Introduction to Financial Accounting. 1981. Rev. edn 1983.

4172 PRYCE-JONES (JANET E.) *and* PARKER (ROBERT HENRY). Accounting in Scotland: A Historical Biography. 1974. 2nd edn 1976. Repr. 1984.

4173 NOBES (CHRISTOPHER) *and* PARKER (ROBERT HENRY). Comparative International Accounting. Oxf. 1981.

4174 JONES (EDGAR). Accounting and the British Economy 1880–1980: The Evolution of Ernst & Whinney. 1981.

4175 KETTLE (*Sir* RUSSELL). Deloitte and Co. 1845–1956. 1958.

4176 WINSBURY (R.). Thomson McLintock & Co.—The First Hundred Years 1877–1977. 1977.

4177 RICHARDS (ARCHIBALD B.). Touche Ross and Co. 1899–1981: The Origins and Growth of the United Kingdom Firm. 1981.

4178 McDOUGALL (E. H. V.). Fifth Quarter Century: Some Chapters in the History of the Chartered Accountants of Scotland. Edin. 1980.

4179 INSTITUTE OF CHARTERED ACOUNTANTS OF SCOTLAND. A History of the Chartered Accountants of Scotland, from the Earliest Times to 1954. Edin. 1954. Repr. Lond./N.Y. 1984.

4180 KITCHEN (JACK) *and* PARKER (ROBERT HENRY). Accounting Thought and Education: Six English Pioneers. 1980.

4181 ASHWORTH (WILLIAM). Fifty Years: The Story of the Association of Certified and Corporate Accountants, 1904–1954. 1954.

4182 GARRETT (ALEXANDER ADNETT). History of the Society of Incorporated Accountants, 1885–1957. Oxf. 1961.

4183 KITCHEN (JACK). Accounting: A Century of Development. Hull. 1978.

4184 EDWARDS (JOHN RICHARD). Company Legislation and Changing Patterns of Disclosure in British Company Accounts, 1900–1940. 1981.

4185 PARKER (ROBERT HENRY). The Macmillan Dictionary of Accounting. 1984.

4186 —— Men of Account. Exeter. 1977.

4187 —— Management Accounting: An Historical Perspective. Exeter. 1969.

4188 —— Readings in Accounting and Business Research, 1970–1977. 1978.

4189 —— The Study of Accounting History. Exeter. 1980.

4190 —— Papers on Accounting History. N.Y./Lond. 1984.

4191 CARRINGTON (ATHOL SPROTT). Accounting: Concepts, Systems, Applications. 1967.

4192 WALLIS (JOHN WILLIAM). Accounting: A Modern Approach. Maidenhead. 1970.

4193 EVE (JOHN) *and* FORTH (GEOFFREY N.). Accounting: An Insight. 1979.

4194 COULDERY (FREDERICK ALAN JAMES). Accounting Standards Study Book. 1978.

4195 ASHTON (RAYMOND K.). The United Kingdom Financial Accounting Standard: A Descriptive and Financial Approach. Camb. 1983.

4196 INSTITUTE OF CHARTERED ACCOUNTANTS OF ENGLAND AND WALES. Setting Accounting Standards. 1978.

4197 —— The Making of Accounting Standards. 1988.

4198 HOPKINS (LEON). The Hundredth Year [of the Institute of Chartered Accountants]. Plymouth. 1980.

4199 HOWITT (*Sir* HAROLD). History of the Institute of Chartered Accountants in England and Wales 1870–1965. 1966. Repr. N.Y./Lond. 1984.

4200 TANTRAL (PANADDA). Accounting Literature in Non-Accounting Journals: An Annotated Bibliography. N.Y./Lond. 1984.

4201 LEE (THOMAS) *ed.* Transactions of the Chartered Accountants Students' Societies of Edinburgh and Glasgow: A Selection of Writings 1886–1958. N.Y./Lond. 1984.

4202 HERBERT (MIKE). Accounting. 1989.

4203 HINES (TONY). Accounting and Finance. 1989.

4204 CORK (*Sir* KENNETH). Cork on Cork: Sir Kenneth Cork Takes Stock. 1988.

2. INSURANCE

4205 COCKERELL (HUGH ANTHONY LEWIS) *and* GREEN (EDWIN). The British Insurance Business, 1547–1970: An Introduction and Guide to Historical Records in the United Kingdom. 1976.

4206 INSURANCE ANNUAL REPORT. 1975+.

4207 COCKERELL (HUGH ANTHONY LEWIS). Sixty Years of the Chartered Insurance Institute, 1897–1957. 1957.

4208 SUPPLE (BARRY EMMANUEL). The Royal Exchange Assurance: A History of British Insurance, 1720–1970. Camb. 1970.

4209 DICKSON (PETER GEORGE MUIR). The Sun Insurance Office 1710–1960. 1960.

4210 JOHNSTON (JOHN) *and* MURPHY (GEORGE WILLIAM). The Growth of Life Assurance in the United Kingdom since 1880. 1957.

4211 —— 'The Growth of Life Actuaries in the United Kingdom Since 1880'. *Trans. Manch. Stat. Soc.* (1965), 1–76.

4212 WILSON (D. J.). 100 Years of the Association of Average Adjusters, 1869–1969. 1969.

4213 CARTER (E. F. CATO). The Real Business: A Narrative of the Vital Role Developed by Loss Adjusters. 1972.

4214 DOVER (VICTOR). 'Marine Insurance through Two Wars'. *Banker* 29 (1946), 45–9.

4215 FRANCIS (E. V.). London and Lancashire History: The History of the London and Lancashire Insurance Co. Ltd. 1962.

4216 ALLEN (W. GORE). We the Undersigned: A History of the Royal London Insurance Society Ltd. and its Times, 1861–1961. 1961.

4217 GARNETT (RONALD GEORGE). A Century of Co-operative Insurance: The Co-operative Insurance Society, 1867–1967: A Business History. 1968.

4218 DUNNING (JOHN HARRY). Insurance in the Economy. 1971.

4219 RAYNES (HAROLD ERNEST). A History of British Insurance. 1948. 2nd edn 1954.

4220 DODDS (JAMES COLIN). The Investment Behaviour of British Life Insurance Companies. 1979.

4221 HILL (*Sir* NORMAN) *et al.* War and Insurance. 1927.

4222 WITHERS (HARTLEY). Pioneers of British Life Assurance . . . 1951.

4223 SCOTTISH AMICABLE LIFE ASSURANCE SOCIETY. A History of the Scottish Amicable Life Assurance Society 1826–1976. Glasgow. 1976.

4224 FRANKLIN (PETER J.) *and* WOODHEAD (CAROLINE). The U.K. Life Assurance Industry: A Study in Applied Economics. 1980.

4225 DAVIDSON (ANDREW RUTHERFORD). The History of the Faculty of Actuaries in Scotland 1856–1956. Edin. 1956.

4226 INSTITUTE OF ACTUARIES *AND* FACULTY OF ACTUARIES. The Ivanhoe Guide to Actuaries. Oxf. 1989.

4227 CLAYTON (GEORGE). Insurance Company Investment: Principles and Policy. 1965.

4228 —— British Insurance. 1971.

4229 U.K. DEPARTMENT OF COMMERCE (NORTHERN IRELAND). Insurance Companies General Annual Report 1974. Belfast. 1976. [Pub. annually.].

4230 LEWIS (DAVID BENJAMIN) ed. *et al.* Regular Savings Plans: The Handbook for Investment Linked Assurance. 1974. 2nd edn 1976.

4231 BENJAMIN (BERNARD). General Insurance. 1977.

4232 HARRIS (PETER). Estate Planning and Life Assurance. 1977.

4233 LIFE OFFICES ASSOCIATION. Life Assurance in the United Kingdom 1972–1976. 1977.

4234 CUMMINS (J. DAVID). The Investment Activities of Life Insurance Companies. 1977.

4235 U.K. CENTRAL OFFICE OF INFORMATION (Reference Division). Insurance in Britain. 1979.

4236 TREGONING (DAVID) *and* COCKERELL (HUGH ANTHONY LEWIS). Friends for Life: Friends' Provident Life Office, 1832–1982. 1982.

4237 STREET (ERIC). The History of the National Mutual Life Assurance Society 1830–1980. 1980. *Ed.* by Richard Glenn.

4238 WESTALL (OLIVER M.) ed. The Historian and the Business of Insurance. Manch. 1984.

4239 INGRAM (C. A.). Four Score and Four: The Story of the Insurance and Actuarial Society of Glasgow. Glasgow. 1967.

4240 MAGNUSSON (MAMIE). A Length of Days: The Scottish Mutual Assurance Society 1883–1983. 1983.

4241 BROWN (ANTONY). Hazard Unlimited: The Story of Lloyd's of London. 1973. 2nd edn 1978.

4242 HODGSON (GODFREY). Lloyd's of London: A Reputation at Risk. 1984.

4243 COCKERELL (HUGH ANTHONY LEWIS). Lloyd's of London: A Portrait. 1984.

3. 'THE CITY'

4244 COAKLEY (JERRY) *and* HARRIS (LAURENCE). The City of Capital: London's Role as a Financial Centre. 1983.

4245 McRAE (HAMISH) *and* CAIRNCROSS (FRANCES). Capital City: London as a Financial Centre. 1973. New edn 1985. Repr. 1986.

4246 GIBSON-JARVIE (ROBERT). The City of London: A Financial and Commercial History. Camb. 1979. New edn 1984. Rev. 1985.

4247 —— The London Metal Exchange: A Commodity Market. 1976. 2nd edn 1983.

4248 WITHERS (HARTLEY). The Quicksands of the City and a Way through for Investors. 1930.

4249 —— Stocks and Shares. 1910. New edn 1917. 4th edn 1948.

4250 WADE (ARTHUR SHEPERS). Modern Finance and Industry: A Plain Account of the British Financial System. 1926.

4251 REED (MALCOLM CHRISTOPHER). A History of James Capel and Co. 1975.

4252 BARTY-KING (HUGH). The Baltic Exchange. 1977.

4253 MORGAN (EDWARD VICTOR) *and* THOMAS (WILLIAM A.). The Stock Exchange: Its History and Functions. 1979.

4254 MORGAN (EDWARD VICTOR) *and* DUNNING (JOHN HARRY). An Economic Study of the City of London. 1971.

4255 GRANT (ALEXANDER THOMAS KINGDOM). A Study of the Capital Market in Britain from 1919 to 1936. 1937. 2nd edn 1967. [1st pub. under title, 'A Study of the Capital Market in Post-War Britain'.].

4256 READER (WILLIAM JOSEPH). A House in the City: A Study of the City and the Stock Exchange Based on the Records of Foster and Braithwaite 1825–1975. 1979.

4257 THOMAS (WILLIAM ARTHUR). The Finance of British Industry 1918–1976. 1978.

4258 —— The Provincial Stock Exchanges. 1973.

4259 BATES (JAMES). 'Company Finance in the United Kingdom'. *Banker's Mag.* 199 (1965), 337–42.

4260 GREENGRASS (H. W.). The Discount Market in London: Its Organisation and Recent Development. 1930.

4261 FLOWER (RAYMOND) *and* WYNN JONES (MICHAEL). Lloyds of London: An Illustrated History. Newton Abbot. 1974.

4262 BROWN (ANTONY). 300 Years of Lloyds. Croydon. 1984.

4263 KINDLEBERGER (CHARLES POOR). Manias, Panics and Crashes: A History of Financial Crises. 1978.

4264 KINDLEBERGER (CHARLES POOR) *and* LAFFARGUE (JEAN-PIERRE). Financial Crises: Theory, History and Policy. Camb. 1982.

4265 BURTON (HARRY) *and* CORNER (D. C.). Investment and Unit Trusts in Britain and America. 1968.

4266 VERNON (ROBIN ANTHONY) *et al.* Who Owns the Blue Chips? A Study of Shareholding in a Leading Company. 1973.

4267 LIVERPOOL STOCK EXCHANGE. The Centenary Book of the Liverpool Stock Exchange 1836–1936. 1936.

4268 U.K. STOCK EXCHANGE (London). Stock Exchange Fact Book. 1972.

4269 —— Highest and Lowest Prices and Dividends 1940–1949. 1950. [Pub. decennially.].

4270 BRISTON (RICHARD J.) *and* DOBBINS (RICHARD). The Growth and Impact of Institutional Investors: A Report . . . 1978.

4271 U.K. ECONOMICS ADVISORY GROUP. An Economic Study of the City of London. 1971.

4272 WILSON (STEPHEN) *ed.* Alexander Cowan Wilson, 1866–1955: His Finances and His Causes. 1974.

4273 SHEPPARD (DAVID KENT). The Growth of United Kingdom Financial Institutions 1880–1962. 1971.

4274 KELLY (AIDAN). The Stock Exchange. Dublin. 1974.

4275 JENKINS (ALAN). The Stock Exchange Story. 1973.

4276 SHAW (E. R.). The London Money Market. 1975. 3rd edn 1981.

4277 MAKIN (FRANK BRADSHAW). The London Money Market. 1932.

4278 SPALDING (WILLIAM FREDERICK). The London Money Market: A Practical Guide . . . 1922. 6th edn 1938.

4279 MORGAN (EDWARD VICTOR). City Lights: Essays in Financial Institutions and Markets in the City of London. 1979.

4280 IRVING (JOE). The City at Work: A Guide to the Institutions that Make up the City of London and their Roles. 1981.

4281 INGHAM (GEOFFREY). Capitalism Divided?: The City and Industry in British Social Development. 1984.

4282 BANK EDUCATION SERVICE. The City of London and its Markets. 1975. Repr. 1980.

4283 CLARKE (WILLIAM MALPAS). Inside the City: A Guide to London as a Financial Centre. 1979. Rev. edn 1983.

4284 —— How the City of London Works: An Introduction to its Financial Markets. 1986.

4285 COGGAN (PHILIP). The Money Machine: How the City Works. Harmondsworth. 1986.

4286 PENDER (JOHN) *and* WALLACE (PAUL). The Square Mile: A Guide to the New City of London. 1985. Repr. 1986.

4287 CLARKE (MICHAEL). Regulating the City: Competition, Scandal and Reform. Milton Keynes. 1986.

4288 WIDLAKE (BRIAN). In the City. 1986.

4289 WELSH (FRANK). Uneasy City: An Insider's View of the City of London. 1986.

4290 HALL (MAXIMILIAN). The City Revolution: Causes and Consequences. Basingstoke. 1987.

4291 TAYLOR (LINDA KING). The Stock Exchange Press Guide to Investing for Income and Growth. 1987.

4292 JOHNSTON (LUKE). The Key to Making Money in the New Stock Market. 1988.

4293 REID (MARGARET). All Change in the City: The Revolution in Britain's Financial Sector. Basingstoke. 1988.

4294 CUMMINGS (GORDON). Investor's Guide to the Stock Market. 1963. Harmondsworth. 5th edn 1988. [1st pub. under title, 'The Complete Guide to Investment'.].

4295 GALLETLY (GUY). The Big Bang: The Financial Revolution in the City of London and What it Means to You after the Crash. 1989.

4. ADVERTISING

4296 HOLME (BRYAN) *comp.* Advertising: Reflections of a Century. 1982.

4297 NEVETT (TERRY R.). Advertising in Britain: A History. 1982.

4298 ELLIOTT (BLANCHE B.). A History of English Advertising. 1962.

4299 ROBERTS (PETER). Any Colour so Long as it's Black: The First Fifty Years of Automobile Advertising. Colchester. 1988.

4300 DEMPSEY (MIKE) *ed.* Bubbles: Early Advertising Art from A. & F. Pears Ltd. 1978.

4301 —— *Ed.* Pipe Dreams: Early Advertising Art from the Imperial Tobacco Company. 1982.

4302 HENRY (BRIAN) *ed.* British Television Advertising: The First Thirty Years. 1986.

4303 PRICE (JONATHAN). The Best Thing on T.V.: Commercials. Harmondsworth. 1978.

4304 WINSHIP (JANICE). Advertising in Women's Magazines, 1956–1974. Birm. 1980.

4305 MAYLE (PETER). Thirsty Work: Ten Years of Heineken Advertising. 1983.

4306 KALDOR (NICHOLAS) *Baron and* SILVERMAN (RODNEY). A Statistical Analysis of Advertising Expenditure and the Revenue of the Press. Camb. 1948.

4307 COWLING (KEITH), CABLE (JOHN), KELLY (MICHAEL), *and* MCGUINNESS (TONY). Advertising and Economic Behaviour. 1975.

4308 COWLING (KEITH). Optimality in Firms' Advertising Policies: An Empirical Analysis. Coventry. 1972.

4309 HARRIS (RALPH) *and* SELDON (ARTHUR). Advertising and the Public. 1962.

4310 —— Advertising in a Free Society. 1979.

4311 BRITISH CODE OF ADVERTISING PRACTICE COMMITTEE. (Economists Advisory Group) The Economics of Advertising. 1967.

4312 —— The British Code of Advertising Practice. 1962. 3rd edn 1967. 5th edn 1974. Rev. 1977.

4313 FIELD (ERIC). Advertising: The Forgotten Years. 1959.

4314 INSTITUTE OF PRACTITIONERS IN ADVERTISING. Advertising: A General Introduction. 1959. 2nd rev. edn 1967.

4315 DUNN (S. WATSON). Advertising: Its Role in Modern Marketing. 1961.

4316 HANCOCK (ALAN). Advertising. 1965.

4317 SAVAGE (ERIC). Advertising. 1971.

4318 ADVERTISING: AN ANNOTATED BIBLIOGRAPHY, 1972. [Selected by J. Walter Thompson and Co. Ltd.] 1972.

4319 CANNON (TOM). Advertising: The Economic Implications. Leighton Buzzard. 1974.

4320 TELSER (LESTER G.). Advertising and Competition. 1965. [Inst. Econ. Affs.].

4321 ADVERTISING ASSOCIATION. Advertising Expenditure 1948. 1951.

4322 —— Advertising Expenditure 1960–1974. 1976.

4323 JEFKINS (FRANK). Advertising Today. 1971.

4324 —— Advertising Made Simple. 1973. 2nd edn 1977.

4325 —— A Dictionary of Advertising. 1989.

4326 EVANS (WILLIAM ARTHUR). Advertising Today and Tomorrow. 1974.

4327 O'CONNOR (JAMES). The Practice of Advertising. 1978.

4328 LAWSON (RICHARD GRENVILLE). Advertising Law. Plymouth. 1978.

4329 WOOD (JOHN). The Instrument of Advertising. 1978.

4330 WHITE (RODERICK). Advertising: What it is and How to do it. 1980.

4331 DOUGLAS (TORIN). The Complete Guide to Advertising. 1984.

4332 KLEINMAN (PHILIP). The Saatchi and Saatchi Story. 1987.

4333 COHEN (DOROTHY). Advertising. 1988.

4334 KING (SALLY). The Pocket Guide to Advertising. 1989.

5. SAVINGS BANKS

4335 HORNE (H. OLIVER). A History of Savings Banks. 1947.

4336 RADICE (EDWARD ALBERT). Savings in Great Britain, 1922–1935. 1939.

4337 LAWTON (CHARLES). A Guide to the Law of Trustee Savings Banks. 1962.

4338 SAVINGS BANK INSTITUTE. Trustee Savings Bank Legislation and Management. 1977.

4339 TRUSTEE SAVINGS BANK. Report of the Inspection Committee of Trustee Savings Banks for the Year Ended 20th November–80th Annual Report 1970/71. 1972.

4340 HENNESSY (J. M.). Trustee Savings Bank Legislation and Management. 1976.

4341 FAIRLAMB (DAVID) and IRELAND (JENNY). Savings and Co-operative Banking. 1981.

4342 HENDERSON (THOMAS). The Savings Bank of Glasgow: A Short History. Glasgow. 1924.

4343 —— The Savings Bank of Glasgow: One Hundred Years of Thrift. Glasgow. 1936.

4344 CAMPBELL (J. D.). The Savings Bank of Glasgow. Edin. 1986.

4345 KNOX (JAMES). The Triumph of Thrift: The Story of the Savings Bank of Airdrie. Glasgow. 1927.

4346 GLASS (ARCHIBALD). A History of the Greenock Provident Savings Bank, 1815–1976. Greenock. 1976.

4347 HORNE (H. OLIVER). Savings Banks at Kintore and Inverurie: A Short History. Aberd. 1937.

4348 —— Insch and Upper Garioch Savings Bank. Aberd. 1938.

4349 —— Forres Savings Bank 1839–1939. Aberd. 1939.

4350 —— Ellon Savings Bank 1839–1939. Aberd. 1939.

4351 —— Stonehouse Savings Bank, 1838–1938. Aberd. 1939.

4352 MARTIN (DANIEL). A History of the Savings Bank in Carluke, 1815–1965. Carluke. 1965.

4353 HEBDEN (DONALD C.). The Trustee Savings Bank of Yorkshire and Lincoln: The Story of its Formation and of the Six Savings Banks from which it was Constituted. Hull. 1981.

4354 TYRRELL (W.). A History of the Belfast Savings Bank. Belfast. 1946.

6. BUILDING SOCIETIES

4355 BUILDING SOCIETIES YEARBOOK. 1927+.

4356 HODGSON (LEONARD GRUNDY). Building Societies: Their Origin, Methods and Principles. 1929.

4357 LEAVER (JOHN BARKER). Building Societies: Past, Present and Future.

4358 CLEARY (ESMOND JOHN). The Building Society Movement. 1965.

4359 MATTEI-GENTILI (MATTEO). Le Building Society in Gran Bretagna. Milan. 1968.

4360 PRICE (SEYMOUR JAMES). Building Societies: Their Origin and History. 1958.

4361 WOLFENDEN (Sir JOHN FREDERICK). The Purpose and Influence of the British Building Society. 1966.

4362 BODDY (MARTIN). The Building Societies. 1980.

4363 DAVIES (GLYN) with DAVIES (MARTIN J.). Building Societies and their Branches: A Regional Economic Survey. 1981.

4364 MAYES (DAVID G.). The Property Boom: The Effects of Building Society Behaviour on House Prices. 1979.

4365 BUILDING SOCIETIES INSTITUTE RESEARCH GROUP. Insurance in Building Society Practice. 1972.

4366 GREER (RITA) and GREER (RUPERT). Building Societies. 1974. [Fabian Society Research Series, No.319.].

4367 FOSTER (J.). 'The Redistributive Effect of Inflation on Building Society Shares and Deposits, 1961–1974'. *Bull. Econ. Res.* 28 (1976), 67–76.

4368 PRATT (MARK JONES). Building Societies: An Econometric Model. 1980.

4369 BARNES (PAUL). Building Societies: The Myth of Mutuality. 1984.

4370 FULLER (ROY BROADBENT). The Building Societies Acts, 1874–1960. 1961.

4371 BUILDING SOCIETIES ASSOCIATION. Facts about Building Societies. 1981.

4372 —— Studies in Building Society Activity 1974–1979. 1980.

4373 —— The Future Constitution and Power of Building Societies. 1983.

4374 —— Building Societies and the Savings Market. 1983.

4375 —— Understanding Building Societies. 1983.

4376 —— New Legislation for Building Societies. 1984.

4377 BOLEAT (MARK). The Building Societies Association. 1981. 2nd edn 1984.

4378 —— Building Societies: A Descriptive Study. 1981.

4379 —— The Building Society Industry. 1982. 2nd edn 1986.

4380 BUILDING SOCIETIES INSTITUTE. Building Society Branches: Their Development and Organisation. 1951.

4381 —— [International School 1964.] The Influence of Building Societies on the Present and Future Patterns of Society. 1964.

4382 BUTLER (E. C. L.). The Building Societies Institute 1934–1978: An Historical Account. 1980.

4383 FORD (JANET). 'The Role of the Building Society Manager in the Urban Stratification System: Autonomy Versus Constraint'. *Urban Stud.* 12 (1975), 295–302.

4384 PHILLIPS (BRIAN M.). Building Society Finance. 1983.

4385 GOUGH (T. J.). The Economics of Building Societies. 1982.

4386 ASHWORTH (HERBERT). The Building Society Story. 1980.

4387 STEVENS (L.). Ethnic Minorities and Building Society Lending in Leeds . . . Leeds. 1981.

4388 HOBSON (*Sir* OSCAR RUDOLF). A Hundred Years of the Halifax: The History of the Halifax Building Society, 1853–1953. 1953.

4389 CASSELL (MICHAEL). Inside Nationwide: One Hundred Years of Co-operation. 1984.

4390 RITCHIE (BERNIE). The Key to the Door: The Abbey National Story. 1989.

4391 IPSWICH PERMANENT BUILDING SOCIETY. One Hundred Years of Service, 1850–1950: A Brief History . . . 1950.

4392 DAVIES (MARTIN J.). Every Man his own Landlord: A History of Coventry Building Society. Coventry. 1985.

4393 HARVEY (CHARLES E.). 'Old Traditions, New Departures: The Later History of the Bristol and West Building Society'. In Studies in the Business History of Bristol. Charles E. Harvey and Jon Press, *eds*. Bristol. 1988.

4394 PRICE (SEYMOUR J.). From Queen to Queen: The Centenary Story of the Temperance Permanent Building Society, 1854–1954. 1954.

4395 WILLIAMS (P.). 'Building Societies and the Inner City'. *Trans. Inst. Brit. Geog.* 3 (1978), 23–34.

7. BANKS AND BANKING

(a) General Surveys

4396 PRESSNELL (LESLIE SEDDEN) *et al.* A Guide to the Historical Records of British Banking. Aldershot. 1985.

4397 GREGORY (THEODORE EMMANUEL GUGGENHEIM) *ed.* Select Statutes, Documents and Reports Relating to British Banking, 1832–1928. 2 vols 1928. Repr. 1964.

4398 SAYERS (RICHARD SIDNEY). Modern Banking. 1938. 3rd edn 1951. 7th edn 1967.

4399 —— Twentieth Century English Banking. Manch. 1954.

4400 CHANDLER (GEORGE). Four Centuries of Banking. 2 vols 1964. 1968.

4401 GREEN (EDWIN). Banking: An Illustrated History. Oxf. 1989.

4402 —— Debtors to their Profession: A History of the Institute of Bankers, 1879–1979. 1979.

4403 KERR (ANDREW WILLIAM). A History of Banking in Scotland. 3rd edn Lond. 1918. 1st pub. Glasgow. 1884.

4404 CHECKLAND (SYDNEY GEORGE). Scottish Banking: A History, 1695–1973. Glasgow. 1975.

4405 GASKIN (MAXWELL). The Scottish Banks: A Modern Survey. 1965.

4406 TAYLOR (FRANK SALMOND). Banking in Scotland. 1949. 2nd edn 1956.

4407 PRINGLE (ROBIN). A Guide to Banking in Britain. 1973.

4408 GRANT (G. L.). The Standard Catalogue of Provincial Banks and Banknotes. 1977.

4409 CRICK (WILFRID FRANK). A Hundred Years of Joint Stock Banking. 1936.

4410 WADSWORTH (JOHN EDWIN) *ed.* The Banks and the Monetary System in the United Kingdom 1959–1971. 1973.

4411 THOMAS (SAMUEL EVELYN). British Banks and the Finance of Industry. 1931.

4412 WILMOT (JOHN). Labour's Way to Control Banking and Finance. 1935.

4413 CONWAY (LEONARD THOMSON). The International Position of the London Money Market, 1931–1937. Philadelphia, Pa. 1946.

4414 TRUPTIL (ROGER JEAN). British Banks and the London Money Market. 1936.

4415 DAUGHERTY (MARION ROBERTS). The Currency-Banking Controversy. Chicago. 1941.

4416 COPPIETERS (EMMANUEL). English Bank Note Circulation, 1694–1954. The Hague. 1955.

4417 BRENNAN (WILFRID KAYAN). Money, Banks and Banking. Leeds. 1966.

4418 BOLTON (*Sir* GEORGE LEWIS FRENCH). A Banker's World: The Revival of the City, 1957–1970. 1970.

4419 WITHERS (HARTLEY). Should the Banks be Nationalised? 1934.

4420 —— The War and Lombard Street. 1915. 2nd edn 1916.

4421 JONES (G.). 'Lombard Street on the Riviera: The British Clearing Banks and Europe 1900–1960'. *Bus. Hist.* 2 (1982), 186–210.

4422 WILLIAMS (DAVID). 'Montagu Norman and Banking Policy in the 1920s'. *Yorks. Bull. Econ. Soc. Res.* 11 (1959), 38–55.

4423 BOYLE (ANDREW). Montagu Norman, A Biography. 1967.

4424 HARGAVE (JOHN GORDON). Professor Skinner, Alias Montagu Norman. 1939.

4425 EINZIG (PAUL). Montagu Norman: A Study in Financial Statesmanship. 1932.

4426 CLAY (*Sir* HENRY). Lord Norman. 1957.

4427 HAWTREY (*Sir* RALPH GEORGE). A Century of Bank Rate. 1962.

4428 WOOD (WILLIAM WALES). Banker and Customer. Edin./Lond. 1951. 2nd edn 1965.

4429 WADSWORTH (J. E.) *ed.* The Banks and the Monetary System in the U.K. 1959–1971. 1972.

4430 REVELL (JACK ROBERT STEPHEN). Changes in British Banking: The Growth of a Secondary Banking System. 1968.

4431 REID (MARGARET). The Secondary Banking Crisis, 1973–75: Its Causes and Course. 1982.

4432 LANE (PETER). Banks. 1976.

4433 INSTITUTE OF BANKERS. Banks and Society. 1974.

4434 CAPIE (FORREST) *and* WEBBER (ALAN). Bank Deposits and the Quantity of Money in the United Kingdom 1870–1921. 1982.

4435 —— Profits and Profitability in British Banking 1870–1939. 1985.

4436 CAPIE (FORREST). Was the War Loan Conversion a Success?

4437 BANK EDUCATION SERVICE. A History of Banking. 1975.

4438 —— The Clearing System. 1982.

4439 —— The Role of the Banks. 1980.

4440 —— Banks and Overseas Trade. 1980. Repr. 1982.

4441 BANKERS ALMANAC AND YEARBOOK. [Pub. annually since 1845.].

4442 BALL (JOHN) *et al.* Cops and Robbers: An Investigation into Armed Bank Robbery. Harmondsworth. 1979.

4443 BROWN (ROGER V.). Banking in Britain. 1984.

4444 CHANNON (DEREK FRENCH). British Banking Strategy and the International Challenge. 1981.

4445 BARCLAY (CHRISTOPHER). Competition and the Regulation of Banks. Cardiff. 1978.

4446 ECONOMISTS ADVISORY GROUP. The British and German Banking System: A Comparative Study . . . 1981.

4447 SAMPSON (ANTHONY). The Money Lenders. 1981.

4448 MORSE (*Sir* JEREMY). How Banking has Changed. 1982.

4449 GRADY (JOHN) *and* WEALE (MARTIN). British Banking 1960–1985. Basingstoke. 1986.

4450 MORAN (MICHAEL). The Politics of Banking: The Strange Case of Competition and Credit Control. 2nd edn 1986.

4451 MULLINEUX (W.). U.K. Banking After Deregulation. 1987.

4452 MORRIS (TIMOTHY). Innovations in Banking. 1986.

4453 GARDENER (EDWARD P. M.). U.K. Banking Supervision: Evolution, Practice and Issues. 1986.

4454 MARSH (JOHN R.). The Practice of Banking. 1985. 2nd edn 1988.

4455 CHARTERED INSTITUTE OF BANKERS. Bank Strategies for the 1990's. 1987.

4456 COLLINS (MICHAEL). Money and Banking in the U.K.: A History. 1988.

(b) Clearing Banks and Merchant Banking

4457 JONES (GEOFFREY). 'British Overseas Banks in the Middle East, 1920–70: A Study in Multinational Middle Age'. In Multinational Enterprise in Historical Perspective. Alice Teichova, Maurice Lévy-Leboyer and Helga Nussbaum, *eds.* 1986.

4458 NEVIN (EDWARD) *and* DAVIS (E. W.). The London Clearing Banks. 1970.

4459 MATTHEWS (PHILIP W.). The Bankers' Clearing House: What it is and What it does. 1921.

4460 FRAZER (PATRICK). The Clearing Banks: Their Role and Activities. 1983.

4461 COMMITTEE OF LONDON CLEARING BANKS. The London Clearing Banks. 1977.

4462 —— The Banks and Industry: Some Recent Developments. 1981.

4463 CHAPMAN (STANLEY DAVID). The Rise of Merchant Banking. 1984. Repr. 1988.

4464 CHOWN (J. F.). 'Merchant Banks in Britain and the New Europe'. *Moorgate and Wall St.* (Spring 1962), 52–72.

4465 YOUNG (GEORGE KENNEDY). Merchant Banking: Practice and Prospects. 1965.

4466 FERRIS (PAUL). Gentlemen of Fortune: The World's Merchant and Investment Bankers. 1984.

4467 CLAY (CHARLES JOHN JERVIS). Clay and Wheble's Modern Merchant Banking: A Guide to the Workings of the Accepting Houses of the City of London . . . 1976. 2nd rev. edn Camb. 1983.

4468 ELLIS (AYTOUN). Heir of Adventure: The Story of Brown, Shipley and Co. Merchant Bankers 1810–1960. 1960.

4469 MUIR (AUGUSTUS). Blythe, Greene, Jourdain & Co., 1810–1960. 1961.

4470 BRAMSEN (BO) *and* WAIN (KATHLEEN). The Hambros 1779–1979. 1979.

4471 BURK (KATHLEEN). Morgan Grenfell 1838–1988: The Biography of a Merchant Bank. Oxf. 1989.

4472 WILSON (DEREK). Rothschild: A Story of Wealth and Power. 1988.

4473 ROBERTS (RICHARD). A History of Schroders. 1988.

4474 RAW (CHARLES). Slater Walker: An Investigation of a Financial Phenomenon. 1977.

4475 SLATER (JIM). Return to Go: My Autobiography. 1977.

4476 KINROSS (JOHN). Fifty Years in the City: Financing Small Business. 1982.

4477 ATTALI (JACQUES). A Man of Influence: Sir Siegmund Warburg, 1902–82. 1986.

4478 CLARK (RODNEY). Venture Capital in Britain, America and Japan. 1987.

4479 O'SULLIVAN (TIMOTHY). Julian Hodge: A Biography. 1981.

(c) Banks—Individual Histories

4480 SAYERS (RICHARD SIDNEY). The Bank of England, 1819–1944. **3** vols Camb. 1976. Repr. 1986.

4481 SAW (REGINALD C. WYKEHAM). The Bank of England 1694–1944, and its Buildings Past and Present. 1944.

4482 GIUSEPPI (JOHN). The Bank of England: A History from its Foundation in 1694. 1966.

4483 CLAPHAM (*Sir* JOHN HAROLD). The Bank of England. 2 vols Camb. 1944.

4484 STOCKDALE (*Sir* EDMUND). The Bank of England in 1934. 1967.

4485 KING (W. T. C.). 'The Bank of England'. *Econ. Hist. Rev.* 15 (1945), 67–72.

4486 BANK OF ENGLAND. Report for the Year Ended 28th February. 1950. [Pub. annually.].

4487 DAY (ALAN C. L.). 'The Bank of England in the Modern State'. *Public Admin.* 39 (1961), 15–26.

4488 MILLER (DAVID M.). The Bank of England and Treasury Notes, 1694–1970. Newcastle-upon-Tyne. 1970.

4489 GEDDES (PHILIP). Inside the Bank of England. 1987.

4490 FAY (STEPHEN). Portrait of an Old Lady: Turmoil at the Bank of England. 1987.

4491 FULFORD (ROGER THOMAS BALDWIN). Glyn's 1753–1953: Six Generations in Lombard Street. 1953.

4492 TUKE (A. W.) *and* GILLMAN (R. J. H.). Barclays Bank, 1926–1969: Some Recollections. 1972.

4493 BARCLAYS BANK D.C.O. A Banking Centenary: Barclays Bank (Dominion, Colonial and Overseas) 1836–1936. 1936.

4494 CROSSLEY (*Sir* JULIAN) *and* BLANDFORD (JOHN). The D.C.O. Story: A History of Banking in Many Countries, 1925–1971. 1975.

4495 MATTHEWS (PHILIP W.) *comp.* A History of Barclays Bank Ltd. 1926.

4496 GREEN (EDWIN). The Making of a Modern Banking Group: A History of the Midland Banking Group since 1900. 1979.

4497 GREEN (EDWIN) *and* HOLMES (A. R.). Midland: 150 Years of Banking Business. 1986.

4498 SAYERS (RICHARD SIDNEY). Lloyds Bank in the History of English Banking. 1957.

4499 WINTON (J. R.). Lloyds Bank 1918–1969. Oxf. 1982.

4500 MCKEE (ROBERT). Lloyds Bank. Hove. 1982.

4501 LLOYD'S BANK. Lloyd's Bank in the Community. 1982.

4502 WITHERS (HARTLEY). National and Provincial Bank 1833–1933. 1933.

4503 REED (RICHARD). National Westminster Bank: A Short History. 1983.

4504 GREGORY (J. E.). The Westminster Bank through a Century. **2** vols 1936.

4505 BANKING INSURANCE FINANCE UNION. Beyond 1984: A Perspective of the Impact of New Technology and Working Procedure in the National Westminster Bank. 1981.

4506 LEIGHTON-BOYCE (JOHN ALFRED STUART). Smith's the Bankers 1658–1958. 1958.

4507 HENRY (J. A.) *and* SIEPMANN (H. A.) *eds.* The First Hundred Years of the Standard Bank. 1963.

4508 STANDARD CHARTERED BANK LTD. Standard Chartered Bank Ltd.: A Story Brought Up to Date. 1983.

4509 SAYERS (RICHARD SIDNEY). Gilletts in the London Money Market, 1867–1967. Oxf. 1968.

4510 TAYLOR (AUDREY M.). Gilletts: Bankers at Banbury and Oxford. Oxf. 1964.

4511 FLETCHER (G. A.). The Discount Houses in London: Principles, Operations and Change. 1976.

4512 C. HOARE & CO. LTD. Hoare's Bank: A Record 1672–1955. 1932. Rev. edn 1955.

4513 FORBES (R. N.). The History of the Institute of Bankers in Scotland, 1875–1975. Edin. 1975.

4514 MALCOLM (CHARLES ALEXANDER). The British Linen Bank, 1746–1946. Edin. 1950.

4515 —— The Bank of Scotland 1695–1945. Edin. 1945.

4516 REID (JAMES McARTHUR). The History of the Clydesdale Bank 1838–1938. Glasgow. 1938.

4517 MUNN (CHARLES W.). The Clydesdale Bank: The First One Hundred and Fifty Years. Glasgow. 1988.

4518 RAIT (*Sir* ROBERT SANGSTER). The History of the Union Bank of Scotland. 1930.

4519 TAMAKI (NARIO). The Life Cycle of the Union Bank of Scotland 1830–1954. Aberd. 1983.

4520 COMMERCIAL BANK OF SCOTLAND LTD. Our Bank: The Story of the Commercial Bank of Scotland Ltd. 1810–1941. Edin. 1941.

4521 THE NATIONAL BANK OF SCOTLAND LTD. The National Bank of Scotland Ltd. Edin. 1947.

4522 MUNRO (NEIL). The History of the Royal Bank of Scotland 1727–1927. Edin. 1928.

4523 ROYAL BANK OF SCOTLAND. The Royal Bank of Scotland 1727–1977. Edin. 1977.

4524 STEWART (Sir K. D.). The Royal Bank in Glasgow, 1783–1983. Glasgow. 1983.

4525 SIMPSON (NOEL). The Belfast Bank, 1827–1970: 150 Years of Banking in Ireland. Belfast. 1975.

4526 KNOX (WILLIAM JAMES). Decades of the Ulster Bank, 1836–1964. Belfast. 1965.

4527 HALL (FREDERICK GEORGE). A History of the Bank of Ireland. Dublin/Oxf. 1949.

4528 SHARE (BERNARD) ed. Root and Branch: Allied Irish Banks, Yesterday, Today, Tomorrow. Dublin. 1979.

4529 JONES (GEOFFREY). Banking and Oil: The History of the British Bank of the Middle East. Camb. 1987.

4530 MACKENZIE (Sir COMPTON). Realms of Silver: One Hundred Years of Banking in the East. 1954. [The Chartered Bank.].

4531 FRY (RICHARD). Bankers in West Africa: The Story of the Bank of British West Africa Ltd. 1976.

4532 TYSON (G. W.). 100 Years of Banking in Asia and Africa, 1863–1963. 1963. [National and Grindlay's Bank.].

4533 DAVIES (GLYN). National Giro: Modern Money Transfer. 1973.

4534 KIRKMAN (PATRICK). Electronic Funds Transfer Systems: The Revolution in Cashless Banking and Payment Methods. Oxf. 1987.

4535 HANSON (D. G.). Service Banking: The Arrival of the All-Purpose Bank. 1982.

4536 MATATKO (JOHN) and STAFFORD (DAVID). Key Developments in Personal Finance. Oxf. 1985.

4537 LAMB (ANDREW). 'International Banking in London, 1975–85'. Bank of England Q. Bull. 26 (1986), 367–78.

8. MISCELLANY

4538 HUDSON (KENNETH). Pawnbroking, An Aspect of British Social History. 1982.

4539 TEBBUTT (MELANIE). Making Ends Meet: Pawnbroking and Working Class Credit. Leicester, 1983. Lond. 1984.

4540 WEIR (WILLIAM). 'The First One Hundred Years': A Sketch of the History of the Glasgow Pawnbrokers Association. Glasgow. 1951.

4541 MOORBY (RONALD LEONARD) et al. A Century of Trade Marks: A Commentary on the Work and History of the Trade Mark Registry . . . 1976.

4542 ELMHIRST (EDWARD MARS) and DOW (LESLIE). Merchant's Marks. 1959.

4543 KERLY (Sir DUNCAN MACKENZIE) et al. Kerly's Law of Trade Marks and Trade Names. 1st pub. 1894, under the title 'The Law of Trade Marks, Trade-Name, and Merchandising Marks'; 4th edn 1919. 7th edn 1951. 12th edn 1986. [Current eds. Thomas Anthony Blanco White and Robin Jacob.].

9. FINANCE AND MONETARY POLICY

4544 CAPIE (FORREST) and WEBBER (ALAN). A Monetary History of the United Kingdom, 1870–1982. Vol. 1—Data, Sources, Methods. 1985.

4545 GIBSON (A. H.). British Finance, 1914–1921. 1921.

4546 KIRKALDY (ADAM WILLIS) ed. British Finance During and After the War, 1914–1921. 1921.

4547 McVEY (FRANK LEROND). The Financial History of Great Britain, 1914–1918. N.Y. 1918.

4548 ASHTON (THOMAS SOUTHCLIFFE) and SAYERS (RICHARD SIDNEY) eds. Papers in English Monetary History. Oxf. 1983.

4549 LAWSON (WILLIAM RAMAGE). Europe after the World War: A Financial and Economic Survey: vol. 1. Britain. 1921.

4550 MASON (DAVID MARSHALL). Monetary Policy, 1914–1918. 1928.

4551 MAXWELL (DAVID WELLESLEY). The Principal Cause of Unemployment: A Simple Explanation of our Defective Monetary System. 1932.

4552 MORGAN (EDWARD VICTOR). Studies in British Financial Policy, 1914–1925. 1952.

4553 —— 'Funding Policy and the Gilt-Edged Market'. Lloyds Bank Review 66 (1962), 40–53.

4554 ALBJERG (VICTOR L.). 'British Finance, 1914–1939'. Current Hist. 24 (1953), 193–200.

4555 OHRNIAL (A. J. H.) and FOLDES (L. P.). 'Estimates of Marginal Tax Rates for Dividends and Bond Interest in the United Kingdom, 1919–1970'. Economica 42 (1975), 79–91.

4556 STAMP (JOSIAH CHARLES) Baron. The Financial Aftermath of War. 1932.

4557 BALL (R. J.). 'Some Econometric Analyses of the Long-Term Rate of Interest in the United Kingdom, 1921–1961'. Manch. Sch. Econ. Soc. Studs 33 (1965), 45–96.

4558 MOGGRIDGE (DONALD EDWARD). British Monetary Policy, 1924–1931: The Norman Conquest of $4.86. Camb. 1972.

4559 —— 'Financial Crises and Lenders of Last Resort: Policy in the Crises of 1920 and 1929'. *J. Eur. Econ. Hist.* 10 (1981), 47–69.

4560 CLARKE (STEPHEN V. O.). Central Bank Co-operation, 1924–1931. N.Y. 1967.

4561 BENHAM (FREDERICK CHARLES). British Monetary Policy. 1932.

4562 NEVIN (EDWARD THOMAS). Mechanism of Cheap Money: A Study of British Monetary Policy, 1931–1939. Cardiff. 1955.

4563 —— 'The Origins of Cheap Money, 1931–1932'. *Economica* n.s. 20 (1953), 24–37.

4564 LEES (DENNIS SAMUEL). 'Public Departments and Cheap Money, 1932–1938'. *Economica* 22 (1955), 61–80.

4565 MORTON (WALTER ALBERT). British Finance, 1930–1940. Madison, Wisconsin. 1943.

4566 STOLPER (WOLFGANG FREDERICK). 'British Monetary Policy and the Housing Boom'. *Q. J. Econ.* 56 (1941), 108–45.

4567 SAYERS (RICHARD SIDNEY). Financial Policy, 1939–1945. 1956.

4568 CRICK (WILFRID FRANK). Thirty Years of Monetary Change, 1914–1945. 1945.

4569 PAISH (FRANK WALTER). The Post-War Financial Problem and other Essays. 1950.

4570 ILERSIC (ALFRED ROMAN). Government Finance and Fiscal Policy in Post-War Britain. 1955.

4571 BARR (N.). 'Real Rates of Return to Financial Assets since the War'. *Three Banks Rev.* 106 (1975), 23–44.

4572 CHAPMAN (RICHARD A.). 'The Bank Rate Decision of 19 September 1957: A Case Study in Joint Decision Making'. *Public Admin* 43 (1965), 199–213.

4573 ESHAG (EPRIME). From Marshall to Keynes: An Essay on the Monetary Theory of the Cambridge School. Oxf. 1963.

4574 WILSON (JOHN STUART GLADSTONE). Monetary Policy and the Development of Money Markets. 1966.

4575 BAIN (A. D.). The Control of the Money Supply. Harmondsworth. 1970. 3rd edn 1980.

4576 LIPTON (MICHAEL). Assessing Economic Performance. 1968.

4577 LONDON AND CAMBRIDGE ECONOMIC SERVICE. The British Economy: Key Statistics, 1900–1970. 1973.

4578 HOWSON (SUSAN). Domestic Monetary Management in Britain, 1919–1938. Camb. 1975.

4579 HARGREAVES (ERIC LYDE). The National Debt. 1966.

4580 HICKS (*Lady* URSULA KATHLEEN). The Finance of British Government, 1920–1936. 1938.

4581 —— Public Finance. 1954. 3rd edn 1968. [1st pub. under title, 'British Public Finances: Their Structure and Development, 1880–1952'.].

4582 DAVID (WILFRID L.) *ed.* Public Finance, Planning and Economic Development: Essays in honour of Lady Hicks. 1973.

4583 JOHNSON (G. GRIFFITH). The Treasury and Monetary Policy, 1933–1938. 1940.

4584 LIPSON (EPHRAIM). A Planned Economy or Free Enterprise: The Lessons of History. 1944. 2nd edn 1946.

4585 SANDFORD (CEDRIC THOMAS). Economics of Public Finance: An Economic Analysis of Government Expenditure and Revenue in the United Kingdom. Oxf. 1969.

4586 HAYS (SAMUEL). National Income and Expenditure in Britain and O.E.C.D. Countries. 1971.

4587 PEACOCK (*Sir* ALAN TURNER). The Economic Analysis of Government. 1979.

4588 PEACOCK (*Sir* ALAN TURNER) *and* SHAW (G. K.). The Economic Theory of Fiscal Policy. 1971.

4589 PREST (ALAN RICHMOND). Public Finance. 1960. 5th edn 1975.

4590 PREST (ALAN RICHMOND) *and* BARR (N. A.). Public Finance in Theory and Practice. i.e. 6th edn of above, 1979. 7th edn 1985.

4591 PIGOU (ARTHUR CECIL). A Study in Public Finance. 1928. 3rd rev. edn 1947.

4592 JOHNSON (HARRY GORDON) *et al.* Readings in British Monetary Economics. Oxf. 1972.

4593 ROBINSON (LELAND REX). Foreign Credit Facilities in the United Kingdom: A Sketch of Post-War Development and Present Status. N.Y. 1968.

4594 REES (GRAHAM LLOYD). Britain and the Post-War European Payments System. Cardiff. 1963.

4595 JOHNSON (HARRY GORDON). 'Financial and Monetary Problems of the United Kingdom: Their Relation to British Entry into the Common Market'. *J. World Trade Law* 3 (1969), 364–73.

4596 REVELL (JACK ROBERT STEPHEN) *et al.* The Wealth of the Nation: The National Balance Sheet of the United Kingdom, 1957–1961. Camb. 1967.

4597 —— Financial Structure and Government Regulation in the United Kingdom, 1952–1980 [sic]. 1972.

4598 —— The British Financial System. 1973.

4599 LEE (DEREK). Control of the Economy. 1974.

4600 JOHNSON (PETER DAVID). Money and Economic Activity in the Open Economy: The United Kingdom, 1880–1970. 1975.

4601 JOHNSON (CHRISTOPHER). Anatomy of U.K. Finance, 1970–1975. 1976.

4602 WALTERS (*Sir* ALAN ARTHUR). 'Money Multipliers in the United Kingdom, 1880–1962'. *Oxf. Econ. Papers* 18 (1966), 270–83.

4603 ALLAN (C. M.). 'Fiscal Marksmanship, 1951–1963'. *Oxf. Econ. Papers* 17 (1965), 317–27.

4604 KENEN (PETER BAIN). British Monetary Policy and the Balance of Payments, 1951–1957. Camb. Mass. 1960.

4605 COLLINS (E. A.). 'The Price of Financial Control'. *Public Admin* 40 (1962), 289–310.

4606 NEVIN (EDWARD THOMAS). The Problem of the National Debt. Cardiff. 1954.

4607 DRAKATOS (C.). 'Short Term Fluctuations in the Velocity of Circulation of Money in the U.K., 1954–1961'. *Bankers Mag.* 194 (1962), 408–15.

4608 CHALMERS (ERIC BROWNLIE) ed. Monetary Policy in the Sixties: The U.K., the U.S.A. and West Germany. 1968.

4609 —— United Kingdom Monetary Policy. 1968.

4610 CLAYTON (G.). 'British Financial Intermediaries in Theory and Practice'. *Econ. J.* 72 (1962), 869–86.

4611 ARTIS (MICHAEL JOHN). 'Monetary Policy and Financial Intermediaries: The Hire Purchase Financial Houses'. *Bull. Oxf. Univ. Inst. Stats* 25 (1963), 11–46.

4612 —— Foundations of British Monetary Policy. Oxf. 1965.

4613 HIRSCH (FRED). 'Britain's Debts and World Liquidity'. *Banker* 115 (1965), 649–58.

4614 HODJERA (ZORAN). 'Short Term Capital Movements of the United Kingdom, 1963–1967'. *J. Pol. Econ.* 79 (1971), 739–75.

4615 BELL (GEOFFREY L.) and BERMAN (LAWRENCE S.). 'Changes in the Money Supply in the United Kingdom, 1954–1964'. *Economica* 33 (1966), 148–65.

4616 SHEPPARD (D. K.). 'Changes in the Money Supply in the United Kingdom, 1954–1964: A Comment'. *Economica* 35 (1968), 297–302. [Criticism of above article.].

4617 ROWAN (D. C.). 'The Monetary System in the Fifties and Sixties'. *Manch. Sch. Econ. Soc. Studs* 41 (1973), 19–42.

4618 SCHWARTZ (ANNA JACOBSON). 'Monetary Trends in the United States and the United Kingdom, 1878–1970: Selected Findings'. *J. Econ. Hist.* 35 (1975), 138–59.

4619 BROWN (ARTHUR JOSEPH). The Great Inflation, 1939–1951. 1955.

4620 GARDNER (RICHARD NEWTON). Sterling-Dollar Diplomacy. Oxf. 1956. New edn 1969. New enlgd edn N.Y./Guildford. 1980.

4621 ZUPNICK (ELLIOT). Britain's Post-War Dollar Problem. N.Y. 1957.

4622 MASON (SANDRA). The Flow of Funds in Britain. 1976.

4623 LAIDLER (DAVID) and PARKIN (MICHAEL). 'The Demand for Money in the United Kingdom, 1956–1967: Preliminary Estimates'. *Manch. Sch. Econ. Soc. Studs* 38 (1970), 187–208.

4624 WALTERS (Sir ALAN ARTHUR). Money in Boom and Slump: An Empirical Inquiry into British Experience Since the 1880's. 1969.

4625 NORTON (W. E.). 'Debt Management and Monetary Policy in the United Kingdom'. *Econ. J.* 79 (1969), 475–93.

4626 WELHAM (PHILIP JOHN). Monetary Circulation in the United Kingdom: A Statistical Study. Oxf. 1969.

4627 CROOME (DAVID ROBIN) and JOHNSON (HARRY GORDON). Money in Britain, 1959–1969. 1970.

4628 JONSON (P. D.). 'Money and Economic Activity in the Open Economy: The United Kingdom, 1880–1970'. *J. Pol. Econ.* 84 (1976), 979–1012.

4629 HODGMAN (DONALD R.). 'British Techniques of Monetary Policy: A Critical Review'. *J. Money Cred. Bank.* 3 (1971), 760–80.

4630 NOBAY (A. R.). 'The Bank of England, Monetary Policy and Monetary Theory in the United Kingdom, 1951–1971'. *Manch. Sch. Econ. Soc. Studs* 41 (1973), 43–58.

4631 JOSSET (CHRISTOPHER ROBERT). Money in Great Britain and Ireland. 1971.

4632 MILLS (T. C.) and WOOD (GEOFFREY E.). 'Money Substitutes and Monetary Policy in the United Kingdom, 1922–1974'. *Eur. Econ. Rev.* 10 (1977), 19–36.

4633 GRIFFITHS (BRIAN). 'Resource Efficiency, Monetary Policy and the Reform of the U.K. Banking System'. *J. Money Cred. Bank.* 5 (1973), 61–77.

4634 —— 'The Development of Restrictive Practices in the U.K. Monetary System'. *Manch. Sch. Econ. Soc. Studs* 41 (1973), 3–18.

4635 —— 'Two Monetary Enquiries in Great Britain: The Macmillan Report of 1931 and the Radcliffe Committee of 1959'. *J. Money Cred. Bank.* 6 (1974), 101–14.

4636 GRIFFITHS (BRIAN) and WOOD (GEOFFREY E.). Monetarism in the United Kingdom. 1984.

4637 CHALMERS (ERIC BROWNLIE). The Money World: A Guide to Money and Banking in the Age of Inflation. 1974.

4638 GILMOUR (Sir IAN). Britain Can Work. Oxf. 1983. [See esp. chs. on 'The Post-War Years and How Monetarism Captured the Conservatives', 'The Monetarist Diagnosis', and 'The Monetarist Cure'.].

4639 CHAPMAN (RICHARD A.). Decision Making: A Case Study of the Decision to Raise the Bank Rate in December 1957. 1969.

4640 CONGDON (TIM). Monetary Control in Britain. 1982.

4641 POSNER (MICHAEL) ed. Demand Management. 1978.

4642 TEMPERTON (PAUL). A Guide to Monetary Policy. 1986.

4643 WADSWORTH (JOHN EDWIN) ed. The Banks and the Monetary System in the U.K., 1959–1970. 1973.

4644 RICHARDSON (HENRY WARD). 'Fiscal Policy in the 1930s'. ch. in The Managed Economy: Essays in British Economic Policy and Performance since 1929. Ed by Charles Hilliard Feinstein. Oxf. 1983.

4645 BROADBERRY (S. N.). 'Fiscal Policy in Britain in the 1930s'. *Econ. Hist. Rev.* 37 (1984), 95–102.

4646 MIDDLETON (ROGER). 'The Measurement of Fiscal Influence in Britain in the 1930s'. *Econ. Hist. Rev.* 37 (1984), 103–6.

4647 GRANT (A. T. K.). A Study of the Capital Market in Britain from 1919–1936. 1937. 2nd edn 1967.

4648 COTTRELL (P. L.) *and* MOGGRIDGE (DONALD EDWARD) *eds.* Money and Power: Essays in Honour of L. S. Pressnell. 1988.

4649 CLAPHAM (*Sir* JOHN HAROLD) *et al.* Monetary Policy. 1921.

4650 LAVINGTON (FREDERICK). The English Capital Market. 1921.

4651 ELTIS (WALTER A.) *and* SINCLAIR (P. J. N.) *eds.* The Money Supply and the Exchange Rate. Oxf. 1981.

4652 LLEWELLYN (DAVID T.) *et al.* The Framework of U.K. Monetary Policy. 1982.

4653 GOODWIN (R. M.). 'The Supply of Bank Money in England and Wales 1920–1938'. *Oxf. Econ. Papers* 5 (1941), 1–29.

4654 SHAW (G. K.). Fiscal Policy. 1972.

4655 LAWSON (WILLIAM RAMAGE). British War Finance 1914–1915. 1915. 2nd edn 1916.

4656 SPENCER (PETER D.). Financial Innovation Efficiency and Disequilibrium: Problems of Monetary Management in the U.K. 1971–1981. Oxf. 1986.

4657 HOCKLEY (GRAHAM C.). Public Finance: An Introduction. 1970. Rev. edn 1979.

4658 HOUGHTON (R. W.) *ed.* Public Finance. Harmondsworth. 1970.

4659 HEYER (FRITZ). Das Britische Finanzsystem. Jena. 1930.

4660 ASHWORTH (MARK), HILLS (JOHN), *and* MORRIS (NICK). Public Finances in Perspective. 1984.

4661 BROWN (CHARLES VICTOR) *and* JACKSON (P. M.). Public Sector Economics. 1978. 2nd edn 1982.

4662 BALOPOLOUS (ELIAS T.). Fiscal Policy Models of the British Economy. Amsterdam. 1967.

4663 WALLER HILLS (JOHN). The Finance of Government. 1925. 2nd edn rev. and enlgd. 1932.

4664 HILTON YOUNG (E.) *Lord Kennet.* The System of National Finance. 1915. 2nd edn 1924. 3rd edn 1936.

4665 FETTER (FRANK WHITSON) *and* GREGORY (DEREK). Monetary and Financial Policy. Dublin. 1973.

4666 SHORT (JOHN) *and* NICHOLAS (DAVID J.). Money Flow in the United Kingdom Regions. Aldershot. 1981.

10. THE FATE OF STERLING

4667 MEYER (FREDERICK VICTOR). The Functions of Sterling. 1973.

4668 HAWTREY (*Sir* RALPH GEORGE). Towards the Rescue of Sterling. 1954.

4669 —— The Pound at Home and Abroad. 1961.

4670 BROWN (WILLIAM ADAMS). England and the New Gold Standard, 1919–1926. 1929.

4671 FEAVERYEAR (*Sir* ALBERT EDGAR). The Pound Sterling: A History of English Money. 1931. 2nd edn Oxf. 1963.

4672 EINZIG (PAUL). The Tragedy of the Pound. 1932.

4673 —— The Comedy of the Pound. 1933.

4674 PRESSNELL (LESLIE S.). '1925: The Burden of Sterling'. *Econ. Hist. Rev.* 31 (1978), 67–88.

4675 JONES (M. E. F.). 'The Regional Impact of an Overvalued Pound in the 1920s'. *Econ. Hist. Rev.* 38 (1985), 393–401.

4676 MATTHEWS (K. G. P.). 'Was Sterling Overvalued in 1925?'. *Econ. Hist. Rev.* 39 (1986), 572–87.

4677 REDMOND (JOHN). 'Was Sterling Overvalued in 1925?: A Comment'. *Econ. Hist. Rev.* 42 (1989), 87–9.

4678 MATTHEWS (K. G. P.). 'Was Sterling Overvalued in 1925?: A Reply and Further Evidence'. *Econ. Hist. Rev.* 42 (1989), 90–6.

4679 SMITH (LAWRENCE). 'England's Return to the Gold Standard in 1925'. *J. Econ. Bus. Hist.* 4 (1932), 228–58.

4680 MOGGRIDGE (DONALD EDWARD). The Return to Gold, 1925: The Formulation of Economic Policy and and its Critics. Camb. 1969.

4681 MORGAN-WEBB (*Sir* CHARLES). The Rise and Fall of the Gold Standard. 1934.

4682 PEDDIE (JOHN TAYLOR). The Crisis of the Pound. 1932.

4683 POLLARD (SIDNEY) *ed.* The Gold Standard and Employment Policies Between the Wars. 1970.

4684 FURNESS (ERIC LONGFELLOW). British Monetary and Fiscal Policy in Relation to the Operation of the Gold Standard, 1925–1931. 1953.

4685 GIFFORD (JOHN LIDDLE KING). The Devaluation of the Pound. 1934.

4686 WHITAKER (JOHN K.) *and* HUDGINS (MICHAEL W.) *Jnr.* 'The Floating Pound Sterling of the Nineteen Thirties'. *Southern Econ. J.* 43 (1977), 1478–85.

4687 HOWSON (SUSAN). 'The Managed Floating Pound, 1932–1939'. *Banker* 126 (1976), 249–55.

4688 —— 'The Management of Sterling, 1932–1939'. *J. Econ. Hist.* 40 (1980), 53–60.

4689 —— 'Sterling's Managed Float: The Operation of the Exchange Equalisation Account, 1932–1939'. Princeton, N.J. Studies in International Finance, No.46, 1980.

4690 DRUMMOND (IAN M.). The Floating Pound and the Sterling Area 1931–1939. Camb. 1981.

4691 FRASER (HERBERT FREEMAN). Great Britain and the Gold Standard. 1933.

4692 REDMOND (JOHN). 'An Indicator of the Effective Exchange Rate of the Pound in the 1930s'. *Econ. Hist. Rev.* 33 (1980), 83–91.

4693 CAIRNCROSS (*Sir* ALEXANDER KIRKLAND) *and* EICHENGREEN (BARRY). Sterling in Decline: The Devaluations of 1931, 1949, and 1967. Oxf. 1983.

4694 EICHENGREEN (BARRY) *ed.* The Gold Standard in Theory and History. 1985.

4695 CASSEL (KARL GUSTAV). The Downfall of the Gold Standard. Oxf. 1936.

4696 NEWTON (C. C. S.). 'The Sterling Crisis of 1947 and the British Response to the Marshall Plan'. *Econ. Hist. Rev.* 37 (1984), 391–408.

4697 BELL (PHILIP WILKES). The Sterling Area in the Post-War World: Internal Mechanism and Cohesion, 1946–1952. Oxf. 1956.

4698 MEYER (FREDERICK VICTOR). Britain, The Sterling Area and Europe. Camb. 1952.

4699 COWAN (ARTHUR ROBERT). The Sterling Area. 1952.

4700 —— The Problem of Sterling. 1966.

4701 DAY (ALAN CHARLES LYNN). The Future of Sterling. Oxf. 1954.

4702 POLK (JUDD). Sterling: Its Meaning in World Finance. N.Y. 1956.

4703 BACHMANN (HANS) *and* LUTOLF (FRANZ). Die britische Sterling und Devisenkontrolle. Zürich. 1954.

4704 BAREAU (PAUL). The Future of the Sterling System. 1958. [Institute of Econ. Affairs.].

4705 PERKINS (J. O. N.). 'Europe and the Sterling Area'. *Banker* 112 (1962), 306–12.

4706 MCMAHON (CHRISTOPHER WILLIAM). Sterling in the Sixties. 1964.

4707 HIRSCH (FRED). The Pound Sterling: A Polemic. 1965.

4708 BRANDON (HENRY). In the Red: The Struggle for Sterling, 1964–1966. 1966.

4709 PEARCE (D. W.). 'Retrospect on Sterling: The Crises of 1964 and 1965'. *Bankers Mag.* 202 (1966), 337–43.

4710 GRANT (ALEXANDER THOMAS KINGDOM). The Machinery of Finance and the Management of Sterling. 1967.

4711 ARTIS (MICHAEL JOHN). 'Effects of the Devaluation of 1967 on the Current Balance of Payments'. *Econ. J.* 82 (1972), 442–64.

4712 BARKER (TERENCE S.). 'Devaluation and the Rise in U.K. Prices'. *Bull. Oxf. Univ. Inst. Econ. Stats* 30 (1968), 129–41.

4713 STRANGE (SUSAN). 'Sterling and British Policy: A Political View'. *Inl. Affs* 47 (1971), 302–15.

4714 —— Sterling and British Policy: A Political Study of an International Currency in Decline. 1971.

4715 —— The Sterling Problem and the Six. [P.E.P. European Series, No. 4, June 1967.].

4716 MONROE (W. F.). 'Evaluation of Foreign Exchange Market Intervention: The Pound Sterling, 1964–1968'. *Nebraska J. Econ. Bus.* 9 (1970), 25–36.

4717 WILSHER (PETER). The Pound in your Pocket, 1870–1970. 1970.

4718 DAVIS (WILLIAM). Three Years Hard Labour: The Road to Devaluation. 1968.

4719 GRANT (WYN). 'The Politics of the Green Pound, 1974–1979'. *J. Com. Mkt. Studs.* 19 (1981), 313–29.

4720 MACKENZIE (A. D.). The Bank of England Note: A History of its Printing. Camb. 1953.

4721 CRAIG (*Sir* JOHN HERBERT). The Mint: A History of the London Mint from AD 287 to 1948. Camb. 1953.

11. DECIMAL CURRENCY

4722 CRAIG (WALTER LENNOX). Sterling Decimal Coinage: A Colonial Plea for Modernising our Money. 1918.

4723 BRITISH ASSOCIATION FOR THE ADVANCEMENT OF SCIENCE AND THE ASSOCIATION OF BRITISH CHAMBERS OF COMMERCE. Decimal Coinage and the Metric System: Should Britain Change? 1960.

4724 WOOD (DAVID NEVILLE). Decimal Currency for Britain. 1967.

4725 MOORE (N. E. A.). The Decimalisation of Britain's Currency. 1973.

4726 TETHER (C. GORDON). 'Decimal Currency for Britain?'. *Banker* 111 (1961), 805–12.

4727 COMMITTEE OF INQUIRY ON DECIMAL CURRENCY. Minutes and Papers Presented to the Committee. 5 vols 1962–3.

4728 KELLAWAY (F. W.) *ed.* Metrication. Harmondsworth. 1968.

4729 DUNBAR (DAVID STUART). Planning and Pricing for Decimalisation. 1969.

4730 U.K. TREASURY. Report of the Committee of Enquiry on Decimal Currency. 1963.

12. INVESTMENT

4731 BRETHERTON (RUSSELL FREDERICK) *et al.* Public Investment and the Trade Cycle in Great Britain. Oxf./N.Y. 1941.

4732 FEINSTEIN (CHARLES HILLIARD). Domestic Capital Formation in the United Kingdom, 1920–1938. Camb. 1965.

4733 —— Studies in Capital Formation in the United Kingdom 1750–1950. 1988.

4734 HUTTON (JOHN P.). 'Model of Short Term Capital Movements, the Foreign Exchange Market and Official Intervention in the U.K. 1963–1970'. *Rev. Econ. Studs* 44 (1977), 31–41.

4735 GLYN (ANDREW). 'The Stock Market Valuation of British Companies and the Cost of Capital, 1955–1969'. *Oxf. Econ. Papers* 25 (1973), 213–40.

4736 CAULCOTT (T. H.). 'The Control of Public Expenditure'. *Public Admin.* 40 (1962), 267–88.

4737 WILLIAMS (D.). 'The Anatomy of a Crisis: Investment and Output in Britain 1958–1962'. *Banca Naz. Lav. Q. Rev.* 44 (1963), 108–20.

4738 ROWLEY (J. C. R.). 'Fixed Capital Formation in the British Economy, 1956–1965'. *Economica* n.s. 39 (1972), 176–89.

4739 ROZEN (MARVIN E.). 'Investment Control in Post-War Britain, 1945–1955'. *Can. J. Econ. Pol. Sci.* 29 (1963), 185–202.

4740 PAISH (FRANK WALTER). 'Britain's Changing Capacity for Overseas Investment'. *Optima* 12 (1962), 66–71.

4741 NICHOLSON (R. J.). 'Capital Stock, Employment and Output in British Industry, 1948–1964'. *Yorks. Bull. Econ. Soc. Res.* 18 (1966), 65–85.

4742 NEEDLEMAN (LIONEL). 'Growth, Investment and Efficiency in Britain: Some Policy Suggestions'. *Scot. J. Pol. Econ.* 9 (1962), 169–92.

4743 BREWIS (T. N.). 'Selective Credit and Investment Controls in the United Kingdom'. *Can. Pub. Admin* 5 (1962), 89–103.

4744 BROWN (*Sir* ERNEST HENRY PHELPS) *and* WEBBER (BERNARD). 'Accumulation, Productivity and Distribution in the British Economy, 1870–1938'. *Econ. J.* 63 (1953), 263–88.

4745 PANIC (M.). 'Gross Fixed Capital Formation and Economic Growth in the United Kingdom and West Germany, 1954–1964'. *Bull. Oxf. Univ. Inst. Econ. Stats* 29 (1967), 395–406.

4746 GILBERT (J. C.). 'British Investment and Unit Trusts since 1960'. *Yorks. Bull. Econ. Soc. Res.* 17 (1965), 117–29.

4747 JUNANKAR (P. N.). 'The Relationship between Investment and Spare Capacity in the United Kingdom, 1957–1966'. *Economica* 37 (1970), 277–91.

4748 RAW (CHARLES). Slater Walker: An Investigation of a Financial Phenomenon. 1977.

4749 BRECH (MICHAEL) *and* SHARP (MARGARET). Inward Investment: Policy Options for the United Kingdom. 1984.

4750 BUCKLEY (PETER J.), BERKOVA (ZDENKA), *and* NEWBOULD (GERALD D.). Direct Investment in the United Kingdom by Smaller European Firms. 1983.

4751 MINNS (RICHARD) *and* THORNLEY (JENNIFER). State Shareholding: The Role of the Local and Regional Authorities. 1978.

4752 RIPPY (J. FRED). British Investment in Latin America, 1822–1949. Minneapolis, Minn. 1959.

4753 DAVIES (JEFFREY ROWE) *and* HUGHES (S.). Investment in the British Economy. 1980.

4754 DUNNING (JOHN H.). American Investment in British Manufacturing Industry. 1958.

4755 FORSYTH (DAVID J. C.). U.S. Investment in Scotland. N.Y. 1972.

4756 THOMAS (WILLIAM ARTHUR). The Finance of British Industry 1918–1976. 1978.

13. PUBLIC EXPENDITURE

4757 PEACOCK (*Sir* ALAN TURNER) *and* WISEMAN (JACK). The Growth of Public Expenditure in the United Kingdom. Princeton, N.J., 1961. 2nd rev. edn 1967.

4758 PEACOCK (*Sir* ALAN TURNER). 'The Control and Appraisal of Public Investment in the United Kingdom since 1790'. *Finanzarchiv* 22 (1962), 79–91.

4759 PEACOCK (*Sir* ALAN TURNER) *and* ROBERTSON (D. G.) *eds.* Public Expenditure: Appraisal and Control. Edin./Lond. 1963.

4760 SYKES (JOSEPH). British Public Expenditure, 1921–1931. 1933.

4761 VEVERKA (JINDRICH). 'The Growth of Public Expenditure in the United Kingdom since 1950'. *Scot. J. Pol. Econ.* 10 (1963), 111–27.

4762 BARKER (A.). 'The Planning and Control of Public Expenditure'. *Moorgate and Wall St.* (Sept 1964), 25–43.

4763 HOLMANS (A. E.). 'The Growth of Public Expenditure in the United Kingdom since 1950'. *Manch. Sch. Econ. Soc. Studs* 36 (1968), 313–27.

4764 POLLITT (CHRISTOPHER). 'The Public Expenditure Survey, 1961–1972'. *Public Admin* 55 (1977), 127–42.

4765 GROSSMAN (HERSCHEL I.) *and* LUCAS (ROBERT F.). 'Macroeconomic Effects of Productive Public Expenditure'. *Manch. Sch. Econ. Soc. Studs* 42 (1974), 162–70.

4766 PETERS (GEORGE HENRY). Cost-Benefit Analysis and Public Expenditure. 1968.

4767 WALSH (H. G.) *and* WILLIAMS (ALAN). Current Issues in Cost-Benefit Analysis. 1969.

4768 BEGG (H. M.) *et al.* 'Expenditure on Regional Assistance to Industry: 1960/1 and 1973/4'. *Econ. J.* 85 (1975), 884–7.

4769 ELSE (P. K.) *and* MARSHALL (G. P.). 'The Unplanning of Public Expenditure: Recent Problems in Expenditure Planning and the Consequences of Cash Limits'. *Public Admin.* 59 (1981), 253–78.

4770 JONES (ROWAN) *and* PENDLEBURY (MAURICE). Public Sector Accounting. 1984.

4771 GLYNN (JOHN). Public Sector Financial Control and Accounting. Oxf. 1987.

4772 LIKIERMAN (ANDREW). Public Expenditure and the Public Spending Process. Harmondsworth. 1988.

4773 FLEGMANN (VILMA). Public Expenditure and the Select Committees of the House of Commons. Aldershot. 1986.

4774 U.K. TREASURY. The Government's Expenditure Plans 1988/89 and 1990/91. 1988.

14. OVERSEAS TRADE

4775 ATKIN (JOHN). 'Official Regulation of British Overseas Investment, 1914–1931'. *Econ. Hist. Rev.* 23 (1970), 324–35.

4776 KOLZ (ARNO W. F.). 'British Economic Interests in Siberia during the Russian Civil War, 1918–1920'. *J. Mod. Hist.* 48 (1976), 483–91.

4777 CORNER (D. C.). 'Exports and the British Trade Cycle: 1929'. *Manch. Sch. Econ. Soc. Studs* 24 (1956), 124–60.

4778 RICHARDSON (JOHN HENRY). British Economic Foreign Policy. 1936.

4779 KINDLEBERGER (CHARLES P.). 'Foreign Trade and Growth: Lessons from British Experiences since 1913'. *Lloyds Bank Rev.* 65 (1962), 16–28.

4780 BOOER (T. G.). 'Can Britain's Exports Grow?'. *Banker* 112 (1962), 18–22.

4781 PARKINSON (J. R.). 'The Progress of United Kingdom Exports'. *Scot. J. Pol. Econ.* 13 (1966), 5–26.

4782 CLARKE (WILLIAM MALPAS). Britain's Invisible Earnings: The Report of the Committee on Invisible Exports. 1967.

4783 WHITING (DESMOND PERCIVAL). Finance of Foreign Trade and Foreign Exchange. 1968.

4784 MAJOR (ROBIN L.). 'The Competitiveness of British Exports Since Devaluation'. *Nat. Inst. Econ. Rev.* 48 (1969), 31–8.

4785 —— Ed. Britain's Trade and Exchange Rate Policy. 1979.

4786 MATTHEWS (ROBERT C. O.). 'Foreign Trade and British Economic Growth'. *Scot. J. Pol. Econ.* 20 (1973), 195–209.

4787 FLANDERS (M. JUNE). 'The Effects of Devaluation on Exports'. *Bull. Oxf. Univ. Inst. Stats* 25 (1963), 165–93.

4788 DRUMMOND (IAN M.). 'Empire Trade and Russian Trade: Economic Diplomacy in the 1930s'. *Can. J. Econ.* 5 (1972), 35–47.

4789 MACROSTY (HENRY W.). 'The Overseas Trade of the United Kingdom, 1930–1939'. *J. Roy. Stat. Soc.* 103 (1940), 451–90.

4790 GLENNY (M. V.). 'The Anglo-Soviet Trade Agreement, March 1921'. *J. Contemp. Hist.* 5 (1970), 63–82.

4791 MACDOUGALL (G. DONALD A.). 'Britain's Foreign Trade Problem'. *Econ. J.* 57 (1947), 69–113.

4792 BARKER (T. S.) *and* LECOMBERT (J. R. C.). 'The Import Content of Final Expenditures for the United Kingdom, 1954–1972'. *Bull. Oxf. Univ. Inst. Econ. Stats* 32 (1970), 1–17.

4793 SCOTT (MAURICE FITZGERALD). A Study of United Kingdom Imports. Camb. 1963.

4794 MACKAY (D. I.). 'Exporters and Export Markets'. *Scot. J. Pol. Econ.* 11 (1964), 205–17.

4795 WELLS (SIDNEY JOHN). British Export Performance: A Comparative Study. Camb. 1964.

4796 SCHLOTE (WERNER). British Overseas Trade from 1700 to the 1930's. 1952.

4797 REDFORD (ARTHUR). Manchester Merchants and Foreign Trade, vol. 2 1850–1939. 1956.

4798 LOVEDAY (ALEXANDER). Britain and World Trade. 1931.

4799 ANTHONY (VIVIAN STANLEY). Britain's Overseas Trade: The Recent History of British Trade, 1868–1968. 1969. 2nd edn 1971.

4800 ANDERSON (JOHN RICHARD LANE). East of Suez: A Study of Britain's Greatest Trading Enterprise. 1969.

4801 ABRAMS (MARK ALEXANDER) *ed.* Britain and her Export Trade. 1945.

4802 WILLIAMS (LAWRENCE JOHN). Britain and the World Economy, 1919–1970. 1971.

4803 ROBERTSON (*Sir* DENNIS HOLME). Britain in the World's Economy. 1954.

4804 HEMMING (M. F. W.) *et al.* 'A Statistical Summary of the Extent of Import Control in the United Kingdom since the War'. *Rev. Econ. Studs* 26 (1959), 75–109.

4805 —— Studies in Capital Formation in the United Kingdom 1750–1950. 1988.

4806 ROOTH (T. J. T.). 'Limits of Leverage: The Anglo-Danish Trade Agreement of 1933'. *Econ. Hist. Rev.* 37 (1984), 211–28.

4807 MUNRO (JOHN FORBES). Britain in Tropical Africa, 1880–1960: Economic Relationships and Impact. 1984.

4808 CARSE (STEPHEN), WILLIAMSON (JOHN), *and* WOOD (GEOFFREY E.). The Financing Procedures of British Foreign Trade. Camb. 1980.

4809 GULL (EDWARD MANICO). British Economic Interests in the Far East. 1943.

4810 MEYER (FREDERICK VICTOR). United Kingdom Trade with Europe. 1957.

4811 LLOYD (MICHAEL). 'The United Kingdom's Trade and the European Community: 1973 and 1974'. *Contemp. Rev.* 226 (1975), 258–64.

4812 MILLINGTON (A.). The Penetration of E.C. Markets by U.K. Manufacturing Industry. Aldershot. 1988.

4813 DAVIES (P. N.). Trading in West Africa 1840–1920. 1976.

4814 P.E.P. Britain and World Trade. 1947.

4815 SAYERS (RICHARD SIDNEY). The Vicissitudes of an Export Economy: Britain since 1880. Sydney. 1965.

4816 MARRET (*Sir* ROBERT). Latin America: British Trade and Investment. 1973.

4817 SCOTT (MAURICE FITZGERALD). A Study of United Kingdom Imports. Camb. 1963.

4818 COOPER (R. A.), HARTLEY (K.), *and* HARVEY (C. R. M.). Export Performance and the Pressure of Demand. 1970.

4819 U.K. BOARD OF TRADE. Accounts Relating to the Export Trade of the United Kingdom for the Years 1939, 1940 and 1941. 1944.

4820 JENKINS (ROY) *ed.* Britain and the E.E.C. [Proceedings of the Economic Section of the British Assoc. for the Advancement of Science.] 1983.

4821 COHEN (C. D.). The Common Market Ten Years After: An Economic Review of Britain's Membership of the E.E.C. 1973–1983. Oxf. 1983.

4822 ECONOMIST INTELLIGENCE UNIT. Britain and Europe: A Study of the Effects on British Manufacturing Industry of a Free Trade Area and the Common Market. 1957.

4823 WHITING (D. P.). The Finance of Foreign Trade. 1966.

15. TAXATION

4824 KAY (JOHN ALEXANDER) *and* KING (MERVYN A.). The British Tax System. 1978. 4th edn 1986.

4825 ROBINSON (ANN) *and* SANDFORD (CEDRIC THOMAS). Tax-Policy Making in the United Kingdom: A Study of Rationality, Ideology and Politics. 1983.

4826 SANDFORD (CEDRIC THOMAS). Taxing Inheritance and Capital Gains. 1965.

4827 SANDFORD (CEDRIC THOMAS) *et al.* Costs and Benefit of V.A.T. 1981.

4828 SANDFORD (CEDRIC THOMAS), WILLIS (R. J. M.), *and* IRONSIDE (D. J.). An Accessions Tax. 1973.

4829 FIJALKOWSKI-BEREDAY (G. Z.). 'The Equalising Effects of the Death Duties'. *Oxf. Econ. Papers* 2 (1950).

4830 SHIRRAS (GEORGE FINDLAY) *and* ROSTAS (LASZLO). The Burden of British Taxation, 1937/8 and 1941/2. Camb. 1942.

4831 —— Public Policy and the Tax System. 1980.

4832 SHEHAB (FAKHRI). Progressive Taxation: A Study in the Development of the Progressive Principle in the British Income Tax. Oxf. 1953.

4833 STAMP (JOSIAH CHARLES) *Baron*. Taxation during the War. 1932.

4834 —— Wealth and Taxable Capacity. 1922.

4835 —— The Social Significance of Death Duties. 1925.

4836 PINSON (BARRY). Revenue Law, Comprising Income Tax, Surtax and Profit Tax; Estate Duty; Stamp Duties; Tax and Estate Planning. 1962.

4837 CARTER (A. H.). 'The Lesser Evil: Some Aspects of Income Tax Administration in the U.S.A. and the U.K.'. *Public Admin* 40 (1962), 69–89.

4838 STURMEY (S. G.). 'Income Tax and Economic Stability'. *Bankers Mag.* 193 (1962), 302–6.

4839 PREST (ALAN RICHMOND). 'The Sensitivity of the Yield of Personal Income Tax in the United Kingdom'. *Amer. Econ. Rev.* 52 (1962), 346–8.

4840 —— The Taxation of Urban Land. Manch. 1981.

4841 —— The State of Taxation. 1977.

4842 —— Value Added Taxation: The Experience of the United Kingdom. Washington, D.C./Lond. 1980.

4843 CRAWFORD (M.). 'The 1965 Reforms in the British Tax System'. *Moorgate and Wall St.* (1965), 38–57.

4844 WALLEY (JOHN). 'The United Kingdom Tax System, 1968–1970: Some Fixed Point Indicators of its Economic Impact'. *Econometrica* 45 (1977), 1837–58.

4845 —— 'A General Equilibrium Assessment of the 1973 United Kingdom Tax Reform'. *Economica* 42 (1975), 139–61.

4846 DOSSER (DOUGLAS). British Taxation and the Common Market. 1973.

4847 ALLEN (R. D. G.). 'The Economic Effects of the British Value-Added Tax'. *Busin. Econ.* 5 (1973), 24–40.

4848 SMITH (GRAHAM). Something to Declare: 1000 Years of Customs and Excise. 1980.

4849 LEWIS (ALAN). The Psychology of Taxation. Oxf. 1982.

4850 JAMES (SIMON) *and* NOBES (CHRISTOPHER). The Economics of Taxation. Oxf. 1978.

4851 ALLAN (CHARLES M.). The Theory of Taxation. Harmondsworth. 1971.

4852 REDDAWAY (WILLIAM BRYAN) *et al.* Effects of Selective Income Tax: Final Report. Camb. 1973.

4853 HUGHES (GORDON ALEXANDER) *and* HEAL (G. M.). Public Policy and the Tax System. 1980.

4854 BLACK (DUNCAN). The Incidence of Income Taxes. 1939.

4855 FIELD (FRANK), MEACHER (MOLLY), *and* POND (CHRIS). To Him who Hath: A Study of Poverty and Taxation. Harmondsworth. 1977.

4856 ILERSIC (ALFRED ROMAN). The Taxation of Capital Gains. 1962.

4857 U.K. BOARD OF INLAND REVENUE. Capital Gains Tax. 1966.

4858 WILLIS (J. R. M.) *and* HARDWICK (P. J. W.). Tax Expenditures in the United Kingdom. 1978.

4859 SABINE (BASIL ERNEST VYVYAN). A History of Income Tax. 1966.

4860 DEWAR (G. D. H.). V.A.T. 73: An Accountant's Guide to V.A.T. Edin. 1972.

4861 U.K. NATIONAL ECONOMIC DEVELOPMENT OFFICE. Value Added Tax. 1969.

16. LOCAL AUTHORITY FINANCE

4862 SYKES (JOSEPH). A Study in English Local Authority Finance. 1939.

4863 BOYLE (*Sir* LAWRENCE). Equalisation and the Future of Local Government Finance. Edin./Lond. 1966.

4864 HICKS (*Sir* JOHN RICHARD), HICKS (*Lady* URSULA KATHLEEN), *and* LESER (C. E. V.). The Problem of Valuation for Rating. Camb. 1944.

4865 HICKS (*Sir* JOHN RICHARD) *and* HICKS (*Lady* URSULA KATHLEEN). The Incidence of Local Rates in Great Britain. Camb. 1945.

4866 HEPWORTH (NOEL PEERS). The Finance of Local Government. 1970. 6th edn 1980.

4867 BURGESS (TYRRELL) *and* TRAVERS (TONY). Ten Billion Pounds: Whitehall's Takeover of the Town Halls. 1980.

4868 NEWTON (KENNETH). Balancing the Books: Financial Problems for Local Government in Western Europe. 1980.

4869 MARSHALL (ARTHUR HEDLEY). Financial Administration in Local Government. 1960.

4870 MIDWINTER (ARTHUR). The Politics of Local Spending. Edin. 1984.

4871 DRUMMOND (JOSEPH MARGACH). The Finance of Local Government: England and Wales. 1952. [2nd rev. edn 1962, by W. A. C. Kitching.].

4872 FOSTER (CHRISTOPHER DAVID), JACKSON (R. A.), *and* PERLMAN (MORRIS). Local Government Finance in a Unitary State. 1980.

4873 PREST (ALAN RICHMOND). Intergovernmental Financial Relations in the United Kingdom. Canberra. 1978.

4874 HARRIS (RALPH) *and* SELDON (ARTHUR). Pricing or Taxing? 1976. [Evidence invited by the Layfield Cttee, and a Critique of the Report.].

4875 CRIPPS (FRANCIS) *and* GODLEY (WYNNE). Local Government Finance and its Reform: A Critique of the Layfield Committee's Report. 1976.

4876 ELCOCK (HOWARD) *et al.* Budgeting in Local Government: Managing the Margins. Harlow. 1989.

4877 STUDY GROUP OF THE ROYAL INSTITUTE OF PUBLIC ADMINISTRATION. Budgeting in Public Authorities. 1959.

4878 MAYNARD (ALAN K.) *and* KING (DAVID N.). Rates or Prices?: A Study of the Economics of Local Government and its Replacement by the Market. 1972.

4879 INSTITUTE OF MUNICIPAL TREASURERS AND ACCOUNTANTS. Capital Finance of Local and Public Authorities. Camb. 1959.

4880 —— Local Expenditure and Exchequer Grants. 1956.

4881 BUTLER (EAMONN) *and* PIRIE (MADSEN). Economy and Local Government. 1981. [Adam Smith Institute.].

4882 BARKER (WILLIAM). Local Government Statistics. 1965.

4883 TRAVERS (TONY). The Politics of Local Government Finance. 1986.

4884 SMITH (STEPHEN) *and* SQUIRE (DUNCAN). Local Taxes and Local Government. 1987.

17. NATIONAL INCOME

4885 BECKERMAN (WILFRED). An Introduction to National Income Analysis. 1968. Repr. 1972.

4886 BOWLEY (*Sir* ARTHUR LYON) *and* STAMP (JOSIAH CHARLES) *Baron*. The National Income 1924: A Comparative Study of the Income of the U.K., 1911, and 1924. Oxf. 1927.

4887 BOWLEY (*Sir* ARTHUR LYON). Studies in National Income 1924–1938. Camb. 1942.

4888 MEADE (JAMES EDWARD) *and* STONE (*Sir* RICHARD). National Income and Expenditure. 1st pub. 1944. 4th edn 1957.

4889 STONE (*Sir* RICHARD) *and* STONE (GIOVANNA). National Income and Expenditure. 5th rev. edn of above, 1961. 10th edn 1977.

4890 STONE (*Sir* RICHARD). Inland Revenue Report on National Income, 1929. Camb. 1977.

4891 JEFFREYS (JAMES B.) *and* WALTERS (DOROTHY). 'National Income and Expenditure of the United Kingdom, 1870–1952'. *Income and Wealth* [5th series], (1955), 1–40.

4892 FEINSTEIN (CHARLES HILLIARD). National Income, Expenditure and Output of the United Kingdom, 1855–1965. Camb. 1972.

4893 CLARK (COLIN GRANT). National Income, 1924–1931. 1932.

4894 —— National Income and Outlay. 1937.

4895 OXFORD UNIVERSITY AGRICULTURAL ECONOMICS RESEARCH INSTITUTE. Changes in the Economic Pattern. 1960.

4896 THE TIMES. British War Production, 1939–1945: A Record. 1945.

4897 McDONALD (JOHN). 'An Analysis of the Significance of Revisions to Some Quarterly U.K. National Income Time Series'. *J. Roy. Stat. Soc.* (Series A), 138 (1975), 242–56.

4898 LYDALL (HAROLD FRENCH). British Incomes and Savings. 1955.

4899 KING (DAVID). An Introduction to National Income Accounting. 1984.

4900 U.K. REPORT OF THE COMMITTEE ON INVISIBLE EXPORTS. Britain's Invisible Earnings. 1967.

4901 BENEMY (FRANK WILLIAM GEORGESON). Industry, Income and Investment. 1962. Enlgd edn 1970.

18. BUDGETS

4902 MALLET (BERNARD) *and* GEORGE (CYRIL OSWALD). British Budgets. 3 vols 1913–33.

4903 SABINE (BASIL ERNEST VYVYAN). British Budgets in Peace and War, 1932–1945. 1970.

4904 BROTHWELL (J. F.). 'Budget Adjustments with a Consumption Tax'. *Yorks. Bull. Econ. Soc. Res.* 14 (1962), 59–73.

4905 TAIT (ALAN A.). 'Long Term Policy and the British Budget 1962–1963'. *Finanzarchiv* 22 (1963), 298–313.

4906 —— 'British Budgetary Policy, 1963–1964'. *Finanzarchiv* 24 (1965), 84–96.

4907 —— 'British Budgetary Policy 1965–1966: A Sequence of Budgets and the Selective Employment Tax'. *Finanzarchiv* 26 (1967), 78–100.

4908 —— 'International Constraints on Domestic Budgetary Policy: The British Budget 1967'. *Finanzarchiv* 26 (1967), 534–48.

4909 —— 'Political Economy: The British Budget 1971'. *Finanzarchiv* 30 (1972), 489–512.

4910 BOWER (*Sir* FRANK). 'Some Reflections on the Budget'. *Lloyds Bank Rev.* 65 (1962), 29–46.

4911 HIRST (FRANCIS WRIGLEY) *and* ALLEN (JOHN ERNEST). British War Budgets. 1926.

4912 MAURICE (RITA) *ed.* National Accounts Statistics: Sources and Methods. 1968.

4913 BRITTAIN (*Sir* HERBERT). The British Budgetary System. 1959.

4914 STUDY GROUP OF THE ROYAL INSTITUTE OF PUBLIC ADMINISTRATION. Budgeting in Public Authorities. 1959.

4915 WILLIAMS (ALAN). Public Finance and Budget Policy. 1963.

4916 MIDDLETON (ROGER). 'The Constant Employment Budget Balance and British Budgetary Policy, 1929–1939'. *Econ. Hist. Rev.* 34 (1981), 266–86.

4917 HICKS (*Sir* JOHN RICHARD). The Problem of Budgetary Reform. Oxf. 1948.

19. BALANCE OF PAYMENTS

4918 KAHN (ALFRED E.). 'The British Balance of Payments and Problems of Domestic Policy'. *Q. J. Econ.* 61 (1947), 368–96.

4919 CHANG (TSE CHUN). 'The British Balance of Payments, 1924–1933'. *Econ. J.* 57 (1947), 475–503.

4920 NATIONAL INSTITUTE OF ECONOMIC RESEARCH. 'The United Kingdom Balance of Payments'. *Nat. Inst. Econ. Rev.* 13 (1961), 29–37.

4921 BURTON (F. N.) *and* GLAMBOS (P.). 'The Role of Invisible Trade in the United Kingdom Balance of Payments, 1952–1966'. *Nat. Prov. Bank Rev.* 82 (1968), 9–15.

4922 CONAN (A. R.). 'Postscript on the Balance of Payments'. *Bankers Mag.* 182 (1961), 309–13.

4923 —— 'The Balance of Payments Policy in Operation'. *Bankers Mag.* 194 (1962), 315–20.

4924 EGGLESTON (JOHN FRANCIS). Mr. Selwyn Lloyd: the Balance of Payments and the Dollar Reserve. Harrow. 1962.

4925 KLEIN (THOMAS M.). 'The United Kingdom Balance of Payments Accounts'. *Econ. J.* 74 (1964), 946–53.

4926 PAISH (FRANK WALTER). 'Inflation and the Balance of Payments in the United Kingdom, 1952–1967'. *Scot. J. Pol. Econ.* 15 (1964), 946–53.

4927 THIRLWALL (A. P.). 'Another Autopsy on Britain's Balance of Payments: 1958–1967'. *Banca Naz. Lav. Q. Rev.* 94 (1970), 308–25.

4928 CENTRAL STATISTICAL OFFICE. United Kingdom Balance of Payments, 1963–1973. 1974.

4929 FAUSTEN (DIETRICH K.). The Consistency of British Balance of Payments Policies. 1975.

4930 U.K. TREASURY. United Kingdom Balance of Payments, 1946–1949. 1950.

4931 —— United Kingdom Balance of Payments, 1958–1961. 1962.

4932 ROBERTSON (DONALD JAMES) *and* HUNTER (LAURENCE COLVIN) *eds.* The British Balance of Payments. 1966.

4933 MacDOUGALL (*Sir* DONALD). Studies in Political Economy: Vol. 1—The Inter-war Years and the 1940s: vol. 2—International Trade and Domestic Economic Policy. 1975.

4934 BRITTAN (SAMUEL). The Price of Economic Freedom. 1970.

E. INDUSTRY

The items identified in this section have obvious linkages both with general economic history and with finance and, in some cases, could with equal logic have been listed there. However, the initial sub-section highlights both the increasing maturity of 'business history' as a sub-discipline with its own methodologies and techniques, and the wide variety of angles from which 'industry' can be approached. The adoption of a regional emphasis reflects the extent to which it is difficult, and in some cases impossible, to talk generally about the fate of industry on an 'all-British' basis. The success or failure of particular industries can often only be understood in particular social or cultural contexts. Material in this sub-section does therefore range very widely, perhaps too widely, to include 'regional policy' generously interpreted. Such breadth, however, reflects a conviction that statements about British industry do indeed need to be anchored in their local contexts.

Alongside the broad analysis of 'economic decline' has gone some specific attention to alleged failing in 'management' looked at in a broad cultural context. The post-war decades have also seen the emergence of 'business management' as an increasingly influential discipline. The literature in this sub-section reflects material emanating from both concerns, though a reading of the section as a whole makes it apparent that in the actual writing there is very little cross-fertilization between technical exposition of managerial and structural issues on the one hand, and the broad course of social and economic development on the other.

Subsequent sub-sections deal with other relevant specialisms within the field of industrial relations which apply across the board but also with the histories of particular companies and industries. The maturity of modern British business historiography has not been achieved without a good deal of trial and error. It is apparent that some individual business histories have been written by authors familiar with a particular company but who lack any general historical awareness. As has been noted in the case of banking history there is a danger with business history in general that it has been 'commissioned' history to an understandable but not altogether desirable extent. It is hoped that the separate listing of companies in particular industries, when taken together with the general and regional subsections, will enable the reader to approach the problems of the British economy and British industry from related but distinct viewpoints.

The performance of British industry, particularly since the Second World War, cannot be divorced from industrial relations. It is therefore thought appropriate to include here subsections on trade unionism as a whole and on strikes in particular. Naturally, trade unionism must also be looked at in a broader political context and it features elsewhere in the history of the Labour Party. Strikes, together with broad issues of employment/unemployment, can also be approached from directions which are not simply industrial. Conversely, a specialist in industrial relations might not order the material in the way that it has been attempted if this sub-section had been located elsewhere within chapters which concern themselves with law and order and the social structure generally. It should be obvious that linkages with such literature should be pursued in those chapters.

1. BUSINESS HISTORY

4935 SWANN (DENNIS), O₃BRIEN (DENIS P.), MAUNDER (W. PETER J.), and HOWE (W. STEWART). Competition in British Industry: Restrictive Practices Legislation in Theory and Practice. 1974.

4936 LINCOLN (JOHN A.). The Restrictive Society. 1967.

4937 SUPPLE (BARRY E.) ed. Essays in British Business History. Oxf. 1977.

4938 TANN (JENNIFER). The Development of the Factory. 1970.

4939 PRAIS (S. J.). The Evolution of Giant Firms in Britain: A Study of the Growth of Concentration in Manufacturing Industry in Britain, 1909–1970. Camb. 1976.

4940 THOMAS (RAYMOND ELLIOTT). The Government of Business. Deddington. 1976.

4941 DUNNING (JOHN HARRY) and THOMAS (CLIFFORD J.). British Industry: Change and Development in the Twentieth Century. 1961. 2nd edn 1963.

4942 KHALILZADEH-SHIRAZI (J.). 'Market Structure and Price-cost Margins in United Kingdom Manufacturing Industries'. Rev. Econ. Stats 56 (1974), 67–76.

4943 PRAIS (S. J.). 'New Look at the Growth of Industrial Concentration'. Oxf. Econ. Papers 26 (1974), 273–88.

4944 CROSBY (ANDREW C.). Creativity and Performance in Industrial Organization. 1968.

4945 EDWARDS (*Sir* RONALD STANLEY) *and* TOWNSEND (HARRY). Business Enterprise: Its Growth and Organisation. 1958.

4946 —— Eds. Studies in Business Organisation. 1961.

4947 —— Eds. Business Growth. 1966.

4948 SOFER (C.). 'Buying and Selling: A Study in the Sociology of Distribution'. *Sociol. Rev.* 13(2) (1965), 183–207.

4949 WOODWARD (J.). The Saleswoman. 1960.

4950 NEILD (P. G.). 'Financial Planning in British Industry'. *J. Bus. Pol.* ii (1973), 11–18.

4951 NEVIN (EDWARD THOMAS). 'The Cost Structure of British Manufacturing, 1948–1961'. *Econ. J.* lxxiii (1963), 642–59.

4952 NOYES (A.). 'The Industrial Economy of North Staffordshire in the Second World War'. *N. Staffs. J. of Field Studs* xvi (1976), 73–86.

4953 DEAKIN (B. M.) *and* PRATTEN (CLIFFORD F.). Effects of the Temporary Employment Subsidy. Camb. 1982.

4954 WILMORE (ALBERT). Industrial Britain, A Survey. 1930. Rev. edn 1939.

4955 HOFFMANN (ALTHER GUSTAV). British Industry, 1700–1950. 1955.

4956 BALDAMUS (WILHELM). Efficiency and Effort: An Analysis of Industrial Administration. 1961.

4957 WOOLNER (ALFRED HERBERT). Modern Industry in Britain. 1963.

4958 ALLEN (GEORGE CYRIL). British Industries and their Organisation. 1933. 4th edn 1959.

4959 The Structure of Industry in Britain: A Study in Economic Change. 1961.

4960 SILVERMAN (HERBERT ALBERT) *ed.* Studies in Industrial Organisation. 1948.

4961 SELEKMAN (BENJAMIN MORRIS) *and* SELEKMAN (SYLVIA KOPALD). British Industry Today. 1929.

4962 REID (GRAHAM LIVINGSTONE) *and* KALLEN (KEVIN A.). Nationalised Industries. Harmondsworth. 1970.

4963 PRATTEN (CLIFFORD) *et al.* The Economies of Large Scale Production in British Industry: an Introductory Study. 1966.

4964 BARNA (TIBOR). Investment and Growth Policies in British Industrial Firms. Camb. 1962.

4965 BOWN (IAN). Britain's Industrial Survival. 1947.

4966 COLE (GEORGE DOUGLAS HOWARD). British Trade and Industry, Past and Future. 1932.

4967 DOBB (MAURICE HERBERT). Studies in the Development of Capitalism. 1947.

4968 GWENAULT (PAUL HERBERT) *and* JACKSON (JOSEPH MICHAEL). The Control of Monopoly in the United Kingdom. 1960.

4969 PLUMMER (ALFRED). New British Industries in the Twentieth Century. 1937.

4970 BURN (DUNCAN LYALL) *ed.* The Structure of British Industry: A Symposium. 2 vols Camb. 1958.

4971 COMPTON (MAURICE) *and* BOTT (EDWARD HUGH). British Industry: Its Changing Structure in Peace and War. 1940.

4972 MILLER (HARRY). The Way of Enterprise: A Study of the Origins, Problems and Achievements in the Growth of Post-War British Firms. 1963.

4973 ABRAHAM (NEVILLE). Big Business and Government: The New Disorder. 1974.

4974 CARTER (CHARLES) *ed.* Industrial Policy and Innovation. 1981.

4975 COOMBES (DAVID). Representative Government and Economic Power. 1982.

4976 GANZ (GABRIELE). Government and Industry. Abingdon. 1977.

4977 HAGUE (DOUGLAS) *and* WILKINSON (GEOFFREY). The IRC—An Experiment in Industrial Intervention. 1983.

4978 JEWKES (JOHN). Public and Private Enterprise. 1964.

4979 EVELY (RICHARD) *and* LITTLE (IAN MALCOLM DAVID). Concentration in British Industry: An Empirical Study of the Structure of Industrial Production, 1935–1951. Camb. 1960.

4980 JERVIS (FRANK ROBERT JOSEPH). The Evolution of Modern Industry. 1960.

4981 MACLAREN (CHARLES BENJAMIN BRIGHT) *Lord Aberconway.* The Basic Industries of Great Britain: An Historic and Economic Survey. 1927.

4982 MADGE (CHARLES HENRY) *and* TYERMAN (DONALD). Industry After the War. 1943.

4983 MAUNDER (PAMELA ANN). Modern Industry in Britain. 1964.

4984 KUEHN (DOUGLAS). Takeovers and the Theory of the Firm: An Empirical Analysis of the United Kingdom, 1957–1967. 1975.

4985 MACKINTOSH (ATHOLE SPALDING). The Development of Firms: An Empirical Study with Special Reference to the Economic Effects of Taxation. Camb. 1963.

4986 WRIGHT (FRANK JOSEPH). The Evolution of Modern Industrial Organization. 1954. 2nd edn 1957.

4987 COPEMAN (G. H.). Leaders of British Industry: A Study of the Careers of More than a Thousand Public Company Directors. 1955.

4988 HART (P. E.), UPTON (M. A.), *and* WALSHE (G.). Mergers and Concentration in British Industry. Camb. 1973.

4989 GORDON (LINCOLN). The Public Corporation in Great Britain. 1938.

4990 ALLEN (G. C.). Monopoly and Restrictive Practices. 1968.

4991 MENNELL (WILLIAM). Takeover: The Growth of Monopoly in Britain, 1951–1961. 1962.

4992 COWLING (KEITH), STONEMAN (PAUL), CUBBIN (JOHN), *et al.* Mergers and Economic Performance. Camb. 1980.

4993 HANNAH (LESLIE) *and* KAY (J. A.). Concentration in Industry: Theory, Measurement and the U.K. Experience. 1977.

4994 JONES (ROBERT) *and* MARRIOTT (OLIVER). Anatomy of a Merger: A History of G.E.C., A.E.I. and English Electric. 1970.

4995 RIDLEY (T. M.). 'Industrial Production in the United Kingdom, 1900–1953'. *Economica* n.s. xxii (1955), 1–11.

4996 HOFFMAN (W.). 'The Growth of Industrial Production in Great Britain: A Quantitative Study'. *Econ. Hist. Rev.* 2nd ser. ii (1949), 162–80.

4997 THIRLWALL (A. P.). 'Changes in Industrial Composition in the U.K. and U.S. and Labour's Share of the National Income, 1948–1969'. *Bull. Oxf. Univ. Inst. Econ. Soc. Stats* 34 (1972), 373–82.

4998 FLORENCE (PHILIP SARGANT). The Logic of British and American Industry: A Realistic Analysis of Economic Structure and Government. 1953. Rev. edn 1961.

4999 DUNNING (JOHN HARRY). American Investment in British Manufacturing Industry. 1958.

5000 —— The Role of American Investment in the British Economy. 1969.

5001 BUXTON (NEIL K.) *and* ALDCROFT (DEREK H.) *eds.* British Industry between the Wars: Instability and Industrial Development, 1919–1939. 1979.

5002 DRUMMOND (IAN MACDONALD). The Floating Pound and the Sterling Area, 1931–1939. Camb. 1981.

5003 BROWN (ARTHUR JOSEPH). The Great Inflation, 1939–1951. 1955.

5004 BRITTAN (SAMUEL). The Treasury under the Tories, 1951–1964. 1964. Rev. edn 1969.

5005 DONALDSON (PETER). Guide to the British Economy. Harmondsworth. 1965.

5006 DEANE (PHYLLIS MARY) *and* COLE (WILLIAM ALAN). British Economic Growth, 1688–1959: Trends and Structure. Camb. 2nd edn 1967.

5007 DRUMMOND (IAN MACDONALD). British Economic Policy and the Empire, 1919–1939. 1972.

5008 —— Imperial Economic Policy, 1917–1939: Studies in Expansion and Protection. 1974.

5009 DRAKE (KEITH). Britain's Exports and the Balance of Payments. 1970.

5010 DOW (JOHN CHRISTOPHER RODERICK). The Management of the British Economy, 1945–1960. Camb. 1964.

5011 FLORENCE (PHILIP SARGANT). Ownership, Control and Success of Large Companies: An Analysis of English Industrial Structure and Policy, 1939–1951. 1961.

5012 —— Post-war Investment, Location and Size of Plant. Camb. 1962.

5013 WHITE (THOMAS ANTHONY BLANCO). Patents for Inventions and the Registration of Industrial Designs. 1st edn 1947. 3rd edn 1962.

5014 TERRELL (THOMAS). On the Law of Patents. Eleventh Edition by Guy Aldous and others. 1965.

5015 U.K. PATENT OFFICE. Reports of Patent, Design and Trademark Cases. Vol. 62. 1945.

5016 BOEHM (KLAUS) *and* SILBERSTON (AUBREY). The British Patent System. 1. Administration. Camb. 1967.

5017 BROWN (DAVID) *and* HARRISON (MICHAEL J.). A Sociology of Industrialisation: An Introduction. 1978.

5018 INSTITUTE OF PRACTITIONERS IN ADVERTISING. Poster Audience Survey: An Investigation into Poster Campaign Audiences Based on Surveys in Ipswich and the West Midlands Conurbation. 1964.

5019 U.K. 1963. LONDON TRANSPORT BOARD. London Transport Posters, with an Introduction and Notes by Harold F. Hutchison. 1963.

5020 SHERMAN (ALFRED V.). Price Control by any Other Name: The National Board for Prices and Incomes and its Powers. 1965.

5021 SERGEANT (WINSLEY) *and* ROYDHOUSE (ERIC). Prices and Wages Freeze: A Narrative Guide to the Prices and Incomes Act 1966—Together with the Text of the Act. 1966.

5022 U.K. 1967 MINISTRY OF HOUSING AND LOCAL GOVERNMENT. Refuse Storage and Collection: Report of the Working Party on Refuse Collection. 1967.

5023 PRANDY (KENNETH). Professional Employees: A Study of Scientists and Engineers. 1967.

5024 U.K. 1965 TREASURY. Report of a Committee Appointed to Review the Organisation of the Scientific Civil Service. 1965.

5025 U.K. 1961 CIVIL SERVICE COMMISSION. The Scientific Civil Service. 1961.

5026 U.K. 1961 CENSUS. Great Britain: Scientific and Technological Qualifications. 1962.

5027 JACKSON (*Sir* WILLIS). Scientific, Technological and Technical Manpower. Southampton. 1963.

5028 ROYAL SOCIETY OF LONDON. Emigration of Scientists from the United Kingdom: Report. 1963.

5029 LEVER (JEREMY FREDERICK). The Law of Restrictive Practices and Resale Price Maintenance. 1964.

5030 MACDONALD (IAN ALEXANDER). Resale Price Maintenance. Foreword by Sir Derek Walker-Smith. 1964.

5031 RESEARCH INSTITUTE FOR CONSUMER AFFAIRS. Essays and Enquiries. 8. Fair Trading: Protecting Consumers. 1964.

5032 U.K. 1964 REGISTRAR OF RESTRICTIVE TRADING AGREEMENTS, OFFICE OF. Guide to the Registration of Goods Under the Resale Prices Act, 1964. 1964.

5033 YAMEY (BASIL SELIG). Resale Price Maintenance and Shoppers' Choice. 1961. 4th edn 1964. I.E.A. Hobart Papers.

5034 GOODHART (PHILIP). A Nation of Consumers. 1965. C.P.C.

5035 PICKERING (J. F.). Resale Price Maintenance in Practice. 1966.

2. REGIONAL ECONOMIES

(a) General Studies

5036 STAMP (Sir LAURENCE DUDLEY) and BEAVER (STANLEY HENRY). The British Isles: A Geographic and Economic Survey. 1933. 3rd enlgd edn 1962.

5037 HANNINGTON (WALTER). The Problem of Distressed Areas. 1937.

5038 DENNISON (STANLEY RAYMOND). The Location of Industry and the Depressed Areas. 1939.

5039 FOGARTY (MICHAEL PATRICK). Prospects of the Industrial Areas of Great Britain. 1945.

5040 DICKINSON (ROBERT ERIC). City Region and Regionalism: A Geographical Contribution to Human Ecology. 1947.

5041 —— City and Region: A Geographical Interpretation. 1964.

5042 —— Regional Ecology: The Study of Man's Environment. N.Y./Lond. 1970.

5043 —— Regional Concept: The Anglo-American Leaders. 1976.

5044 SELF (PETER JOHN OTTER). Regionalism: A Report to the Fabian Society. 1949.

5045 —— 'Regional Development Incentives'. Pol. Q. 45 (1974), 246–9.

5046 HOWARD (ROBERT SUGDEN). The Movement of Manufacturing Industry in the United Kingdom 1945–1965. 1968. [For the Board of Trade.].

5047 HORNBY (WILLIAM). Factories and Plant. 1958.

5048 KOHAN (CHARLES MENDEL). Works and Buildings. 1952.

5049 WRIGHT (WALTER DAWSON). Life and Commerce in Britain: An Approach to Social Geography. 1952.

5050 DURY (GEORGE HARRY). The British Isles: A Systematic and Regional Geography. 1961. 5th edn 1973.

5051 GOSS (ANTHONY). British Industry and Town Planning. 1962.

5052 LUTTRELL (WILLIAM FOWNES). Factory Location and Industrial Movement: A Study of Recent Experience in Great Britain. 2 vols 1962.

5053 MILLER (EUGENE WILLARD). A Geography of Manufacturing. 1962.

5054 JONES (L. H.). 'Industrial Location and Unemployment'. Contemp. Rev. 203 (1963), 71–6.

5055 BEST (ROBIN H.). 'Recent Changes and Future Prospects of Land Use in England and Wales'. Geog. J. 131 (1965), 1–12.

5056 ARMSTRONG (ALAN) and SILBERSTON (AUBREY). 'Size of Plant, Size of Enterprise and Concentration in British Manufacturing Industry 1935–1958'. J. Roy. Stat. Soc. 128 (1965), 1–12.

5057 HART (Sir WILLIAM). 'The Conurbations and the Regions'. Pol. Q. 37 (1966), 128–38.

5058 HEMMING (M. F. W.). 'The Regional Problem'. Nat. Inst. Econ. Rev. No. 25 (Aug. 1965), 40–57.

5059 WILSON (THOMAS). Policies for Regional Development. Edin. 1964.

5060 STEELE (DAVID). More Power to the Regions. 1964. [Fabian Soc., Young Fabian Group pub.].

5061 SMITH (BRIAN C.). Regionalism in England. 3 vols 1964/5.

5062 CAMERON (GORDON CAMPBELL) and CLARK (BRIAN DRUMMOND). Industrial Movement and the Regional Problem. Edin./Lond. 1966.

5063 CAMERON (GORDON CAMPBELL) and WINGO (LOWDON) eds. Cities, Regions and Public Policy. 1973.

5064 —— The Relevance to the U.S. of British and French Regional Population Strategies. Glasg. 1973.

5065 CULLINGWORTH (JOHN BARRY) and ORR (SARAH CRAIG). Regional and Urban Studies: A Social Science Approach. 1969.

5066 NORTHERN UNIVERSITIES GEOGRAPHICAL SOCIETIES. Regional Planning in Britain: Proceedings [of a Conference]. Hull. 1969.

5067 McCRONE (GAVIN). Regional Policy in Britain. 1969.

5068 U.K. DEPARTMENT OF ECONOMIC AFFAIRS. The Development Areas: A Proposal for a Regional Employment Premium. 1967.

5069 U.K. BOARD OF TRADE. Government Help for Your Business in the Development Areas and Northern Ireland. 1967.

5070 —— What the Development Areas Offer. 1967.

5071 TOWNROE (PETER MICHAEL). Industrial Location and Regional Economic Policy: A Selected Bibliography. Birm. 1968.

5072 —— Industrial Location Decisions: A Study in Management Behaviour. 1971.

5073 LEE (DEREK). Regional Planning and Location of Industry. 1969. 2nd edn 1970. 3rd edn 1980.

5074 CHISHOLM (MICHAEL). Geography and Economics. 1966. 2nd edn 1970.

5075 —— 'Regional Policies for the 1970s'. Geog. J. 140 (1974), 215–44.

5076 CHISHOLM (MICHAEL) and OEPPEN (JIM). The Changing Pattern of Employment: Regional Specialisation and Industrial Localisation in Britain. 1973.

5077 CHISHOLM (MICHAEL) *and* MANNERS (GERALD) *eds.* Spatial Policy Problems of the British Economy. Camb. 1971.

5078 CHISHOLM (MICHAEL) *et al.* Regional Forecasting: Proceedings of the Twenty Second Symposium of the Colston Research Society. 1970. 1971.

5079 U.K. CENTRAL OFFICE OF INFORMATION. Regional Development in Britain. 1967. 3rd edn 1976.

5080 COATES (BRYAN ELLIS) *and* RAWSTRON (ERIC MITCHELL). Regional Variations in Britain: Studies in Economic and Social Geography. 1971. Repr. 1972.

5081 COATES (BRYAN ELLIS), JOHNSTON (RONALD JOHN), *and* KNOX (PAUL LESLIE). Geography and Inequality. Oxf. 1977.

5082 HECHTER (MICHAEL). 'Industrialization and National Development in the British Isles'. *J. Dvlpt Studs* 8 (1972), 155–82.

5083 —— Internal Colonialism: The Celtic Fringe in British National Development, 1536–1966. 1975.

5084 —— 'The Persistence of Regionalism in the British Isles, 1885–1966'. *Amer. J. Sociol.* 79 (1973), 319–42.

5085 MANNERS (GERALD) *et al.* Regional Development in Britain. 1972. 2nd edn Chichester. 1980.

5086 KING (DAVID NEDEN). Financial and Economic Aspects of Regionalism and Separatism. 1973.

5087 SANT (MORGAN EUGENE CYRIL). Industrial Movement and Regional Development: The British Scene. Oxf. 1975.

5088 —— Regional Disparities. 1974.

5089 THIRLWALL (ANTHONY PHILIP). 'Types of Unemployment in the Regions of Great Britain'. *Manch. Sch. Econ. Soc. Stud.* 42 (1974), 325–39.

5090 ROSE (RICHARD) *and* URWIN (DEREK W.). Regional Differentiation and Practical Unity in Western Nations. 1975.

5091 BURROWS (E. MICHAEL) *and* BROWN (ARTHUR JOSEPH). Regional Economic Problems: Comparative Experiences of Some Market Economies. 1977.

5092 BROWN (ARTHUR JOSEPH). 'Surveys of Applied Economics: Regional Economics, with special reference to the United Kingdom'. *Econ. J.* 79 (1969), 759–96.

5093 —— *Et al.* 'Regional Problems and Regional Policy'. *Nat. Inst. Econ. Rev.* No. 46 (Nov. 1968), 42–51.

5094 —— The Framework of Regional Economies in the United Kingdom. 1972.

5095 KENNETT (STEPHEN). Differential Migration between British Labour Markets: Some Policy Implications. 1978.

5096 GUDGIN (GRAHAM). Industrial Location Processes and Regional Employment Growth. Farnborough. 1978.

5097 GLASSON (JOHN). An Introduction to Regional Planning: Concepts, Theory and Practice. 1974. 2nd edn 1978.

5098 GILLINGWATER (DAVID). Regional Planning and Social Change: A Responsive Approach. Farnborough. 1975.

5099 GILLINGWATER (DAVID) *and* HART (DOUGLAS ALLEN) *eds.* The Regional Planning Process. 1978.

5100 BUTTON (KENNETH JOHN) *and* GILLINGWATER (DAVID). Case Studies in Regional Economies. 1976.

5101 NEEDLEMAN (LIONEL) *and* SCOTT (B). 'Regional Problems and Location of Industry Policy in Britain'. *Urban Studs* 1 (1964), 153–73.

5102 MOORE (BARRY) *and* RHODES (JOHN). 'Evaluating the Effects of British Regional Economic Policy'. *Econ. J.* 83 (1975), 87–110.

5103 BEGG (HUGH M.) *et al.* 'Expenditure on Regional Assistance to Industry: 1960/61–1973/74'. *Econ. J.* 85 (1975), 884–7.

5104 RICHARDSON (HARRY WARD). Elements of Regional Policy. Harmondsworth. 1969.

5105 —— Regional Economics: Location Theory, Urban Structure and Regional Change. 1969.

5106 —— *Ed.* Regional Economics: A Reader. 1970.

5107 —— Regional Growth Theory. 1973.

5108 —— Regional and Urban Economics. Harmondsworth. 1978.

5109 BRAZIER (S.) *and* HARRIS (R. J. P.). 'Inter-authority Planning'. *Town Planning Rev.* 46 (1975), 255–65.

5110 DONNISON (DAVID). 'Economics and Politics of the Regions'. *Pol. Q.* 45 (1974), 179–89.

5111 SENIOR (DEREK). 'Organization for Regional Planning'. *Town and Country Planning* 43 (1975), 468–71.

5112 SOLESBURY (WILLIAM). 'Ideas about Structure Plans: Past, Present and Future'. *Town Planning Rev.* 46 (1975), 245–54.

5113 TOWNROE (PETER MICHAEL). 'Branch Plants and Regional Development'. *Town Planning Rev.* 46 (1975), 47–62.

5114 —— *Comp.* Industrial Location and Regional Economic Policy: A Selected Bibliography. Birm. 1968.

5115 STONEY (P. J. M.) *and* PATTERSON (A. T.). A Bibliography of Sources in Regional Industrial Development. L/pool. 1978.

5116 MASON (COLIN M.). Industrial Promotion by Local and Regional Authorities: The Effectiveness of Advertising Material. S/hampton. 1979.

5117 MacLENNAN (DUNCAN) *and* PARR (JOHN B.) *eds.* Regional Policy: Past Experiences and New Directions. Oxf. 1979.

5118 UNIVERSITY OF READING, DEPARTMENT OF ECONOMICS. Discussion Paper in Urban and Regional Economics. Reading. 1979.

5119 LAW (CHRISTOPHER M.). British Regional Development since World War One. Newton Abbot. 1980. Lond. 1981.

5120 THWAITES (ALFRED T.) *et al.* Industrial Innovation and Regional Development: Final Report to the Department of the Environment. 2 vols Newcastle. 1981.

5121 CONFEDERATION OF BRITISH INDUSTRY. The Future of Regional Policy. 1983.

5122 GODDARD (JOHN BURGESS) *and* CHAMPION (ANTHONY GERARD) *eds*. The Urban and Regional Transformation of Britain. 1983.

5123 WRAY (IAN). Re-structuring the Regions: A Framework for Managing Regional Growth and Decline in the 1980's and 1990's. Birm. 1984.

5124 MASSEY (DOREEN BARBARA). Spatial Divisions of Labour: Social Structures and the Geography of Production. 1984.

5125 STOREY (DAVID JOHN) *ed*. Small Firms in Regional Economic Development. Camb. 1985.

5126 BALCHIN (PAUL N.) *and* BULL (GREGORY H.). Regional and Urban Economics. 1987.

5127 DAMESICK (PETER J.) *and* WOOD (PETER ANTHONY). Regional Problems, Problem Regions and Public Policy in the United Kingdom. Oxf. 1987.

5128 LOEBL (HERBERT). Government Factories and the Origins of British Regional Policy 1934–1948. Aldershot. 1988.

See also Regions of the British Isles Series published by Nelson.

5129 SMAILES (ARTHUR ELTRINGHAM). North England. 1960.

5130 O'DELL (ANDREW CHARLES). The Highlands and Islands of Scotland. 1962.

5131 DURY (GEORGE HARRY). The East Midlands and the Peak. 1963.

5132 FREEMAN (THOMAS WALTER) *et al*. Lancashire, Cheshire and the Isle of Man. 1966.

5133 SHORTER (ALFRED HENRY) *et al*. Southwest England. 1969.

5134 WALKER (FRANK). The Bristol Region. 1972.

See also The Industrial Britain Series, published by David and Charles, Newton Abbot.

5135 HOUSE (JOHN WILLIAM). The North East. 1969.

5136 SMITH (DAVID MARSHALL). The North West. 1969.

5137 LEWIS (PETER) *and* JONES (PHILIP N.). The Humberside Region. 1970.

5138 HUMPHREYS (GRAHAM). South Wales. 1972.

5139 WOOD (PETER ANTHONY). The West Midlands. 1976.

5140 TURNOCK (DAVID). The New Scotland. 1979.

(b) English Regional Studies

5141 GILL (CONRAD) *and* BRIGGS (ASA). A History of Birmingham, vol. 2: Borough and City 1865–1938. 1958.

5142 SUTCLIFFE (ANTHONY) *and* SMITH (ROGER). A History of Birmingham, vol. 3: Birmingham 1939–1970. 1974.

5143 BRITISH ASSOCIATION FOR THE ADVANCEMENT OF SCIENCE. Birmingham and its Regional Setting: A Scientific Survey. Birm. 1950. Repr. Wakefield. 1970.

5144 SMITH (BARBARA MARY DIMOND) *et al*. Industrial Relocation in Birmingham: The 'Short' Questionnaire Inquiry. Birm. 1974.

5145 BRITISH ASSOCIATION FOR THE ADVANCEMENT OF SCIENCE. A Scientific Survey of Blackpool and District. 1936.

5146 BRITTON (JOHN NIGEL HASKINGS). Regional Analysis and Economic Geography: A Case Study of Manufacturing in the Bristol Region. 1967.

5147 BRITISH ASSOCIATION FOR THE ADVANCEMENT OF SCIENCE. Bristol and its Adjoining Counties. Bristol. 1955.

5148 —— A Scientific Survey of Cambridge District. Camb. 1938.

5149 —— The Cambridge Region. Camb. 1965.

5150 SYLVESTER (DOROTHY) *and* NULTY (GEOFFREY) *eds*. The Historical Atlas of Cheshire edited for the Local History Committee of the Cheshire Community Council. Chester. 1959.

5151 BULMER (MARTIN) *ed*. Mining and Social Change: Durham County in the Twentieth Century. 1978.

5152 BRITISH ASSOCIATION FOR THE ADVANCEMENT OF SCIENCE. Durham County and City, with Teesside. Durham. 1970.

5153 LEMON (ANTHONY). Postwar Industrial Growth in East Anglian Small Towns: A Study of Migrant Firms, 1945–1970. Oxf. 1975.

5154 U.K. CENTRAL OFFICE OF INFORMATION REFERENCE DIVISION. (The English Regions): East Anglia. 1976.

5155 SANT (MORGAN EUGENE CYRIL) *and* MOSELEY (MALCOLM J.). The Industrial Development of East Anglia. Ipswich. 1977.

5156 U.K. DEPARTMENT OF ECONOMIC AFFAIRS. The East Midlands Study. 1966.

5157 ALDCROFT (DEREK HOWARD). The East Midlands Economy: An Economic and Business Review of the East Midlands Region. 1979.

5158 U.K. MINISTRY OF HOUSING AND LOCAL GOVERNMENT. South Hampshire Study: Report on the Feasibility of Major Urban Growth. 1966.

5159 WRAY (MARGARET), MARKHAM (RICHARD), *and* WATTS (DAVID R.). Location of Industry in Hertfordshire: Planning and Industry in the Post-War Period. Hatfield. 1974.

5160 BRITISH ASSOCIATION FOR THE ADVANCEMENT OF SCIENCE. Handbook to Hull and the East Riding of Yorkshire. Hull/Lond. 1922.

5161 U.K. DEPARTMENT OF ECONOMIC AFFAIRS. Humberside: A Feasibility Study. 1969.

5162 BRITISH ASSOCIATION FOR THE ADVANCEMENT OF SCIENCE. Handbook to Hull and the East Riding of Yorkshire, prepared for the British Association. Hull. 1922.

5163 BIRCH (JACK WILLIAM). The Isle of Man: A Study in Economic Geography. Camb. 1964.

5164 JESSUP (FRANK WILLIAM) *comp.* The History of Kent: A Select Bibliography. Maidstone. 1966.

5165 HULL DEVELOPMENT COMMITTEE. The City and County of Kingston upon Hull. Hull. 1961.

5166 U.K. BOARD OF TRADE. An Industrial Survey of the Lancashire Area. 1932.

5167 BRITISH ASSOCIATION FOR THE ADVANCEMENT OF SCIENCE. Leeds and its Region. Leeds. 1967.

5168 —— A Scientific Survey of Leicester and District. Leics. 1933.

5169 —— Leicester and its Region. Leics. 1972.

5170 —— Handbook to Liverpool and District. Lond. 1923.

5171 HYDE (FRANCIS E.). Liverpool and the Mersey: An Economic History of a Port 1700–1970. 1971.

5172 HARRIS (JOHN RAYMOND) *ed.* Liverpool and Merseyside: Essays in the Economic and Social History of the Port and its Hinterland. 1969.

5173 MARTIN (JOHN EDWARD). Greater London: An Industrial Geography. 1966.

5174 HALL (JOHN MARTIN). London: Metropolis and Region. Oxf. 1976.

5175 ECONOMIST INTELLIGENCE UNIT. A Survey of Factors Governing the Location of Offices in the London Area, prepared for the Location of Offices Bureau. 1964.

5176 BRITISH ASSOCIATION FOR THE ADVANCEMENT OF SCIENCE. Manchester and its Region: A Survey. Manch. 1962.

5177 JONES (DAVID CARADOG). The Social Survey of Merseyside. 3 vols. L/pool. 1934.

5178 —— Handbook of Social Statistics Relating to Merseyside. L/pool. 1936.

5179 —— New Handbook of Social Statistics. L/pool. 1940.

5180 U.K. BOARD OF TRADE. An Industrial Survey of Merseyside. 1932.

5181 BRITISH ASSOCIATION FOR THE ADVANCEMENT OF SCIENCE. A Scientific Survey of Merseyside. L/pool. 1953.

5182 U.K. DEPARTMENT OF ECONOMIC AFFAIRS. The Problems of Merseyside: An Appendix to the North West: A Regional Study. 1965.

5183 PATMORE (JOHN ALLAN) *and* HODGKISS (ALAN GEOFFREY) *eds.* Merseyside in Maps. 1970.

5184 LAWTON (RICHARD) *and* CUNNINGHAM (CATHERINE M.) *eds.* Merseyside Social and Economic Studies. 1971.

5185 MARRINER (SHEILA). The Economic and Social Development of Merseyside. 1982.

5186 ANDERSON (BRUCE LOUIS) *and* STONEY (P. J. M.). Commerce, Industry and Transport: Studies in Economic Change in Merseyside. L/pool. 1983.

5187 BRITISH ASSOCIATION FOR THE ADVANCEMENT OF SCIENCE. Official Handbook to Newcastle and District. Newcastle. 1916.

5188 —— Handbook to Newcastle upon Tyne. Newcastle. 1949.

5189 NORTH EAST LANCASHIRE STRUCTURE PLAN. Summary Report of the Survey Plan. Preston. 1973. [Plus many other individual survey reports of the same year.].

5190 TURNER (GRAHAM). The North Country. 1967.

5191 U.K. DEPARTMENT OF ECONOMIC AFFAIRS. Challenge of the Changing North: A Preliminary Study. 1966.

5192 NORTHERN REGION STRATEGY TEAM. Movement of Manufacturing Industry: The Northern Region, 1961–1973. Newcastle-upon-Tyne. 1976.

5193 —— Rural Development in the Northern Region. Newcastle. 1976.

5194 HOUSE (JOHN WILLIAM) *ed.* Northern Geographical Essays: In Honour of G. H. J. Daysh. Newcastle. 1966.

5195 —— North Eastern England. Newcastle. 1954.

5196 —— Rural North-East England 1951–1961: Report to the Development Commissioners. Newcastle. 1965.

5197 —— People on the Move: The South Tyne in the Sixties: Report to the Minister of Labour. Newcastle. 1965.

5198 HOUSE (JOHN WILLIAM) *and* KNIGHT (ELIZABETH MARY). Migrants of North-East England 1951–1961: Character, Age and Sex. Newcastle. 1965.

5199 U.K. BOARD OF TRADE. An Industrial History Survey of the North East Coast Area. 1932.

5200 —— The North East: A Programme for Regional Development and Growth. 1963.

5201 WILSON (GAIL GRAHAM). Social and Economic Statistics of North East England: Sub-Regional and Local Authority Statistics of Population, Housing, Rateable Values and Employment. Durham. 1966.

5202 BRITISH ASSOCIATION FOR THE ADVANCEMENT OF SCIENCE. A Scientific Survey of North-Eastern England. Newcastle. 1949.

5203 McCORD (NORMAN). North East England: An Economic and Social History. 1979.

5204 U.K. DEPARTMENT OF ECONOMIC AFFAIRS. The North West: A Regional Study. 1968.

5205 U.K. CENTRAL OFFICE OF INFORMATION REFERENCE DIVISION. (The English Regions)—The North West. 1975.

5206 TAYLOR (HUGH A.) *comp.* Northumberland History: A Brief Guide to Records and Aids in Newcastle upon Tyne. Newcastle. 1963.

5207 HOUSE (JOHN WILLIAM). Northumbrian Tweedside: The Rural Problem. Newcastle. 1956.

5208 BRITISH ASSOCIATION FOR THE ADVANCEMENT OF SCIENCE. A Scientific Survey of Nottingham and District. Lond. 1937.

5209 EDWARDS (KENNETH CHARLES) *ed.* Nottingham and its Region. Nottingham. 1966. [For the British Assoc. for the Advancement of Science.].

5210 OSBORNE (RICHARD HORSLEY) *et al.* Geographical Essays in Honour of K. C. Edwards. Nottingham. 1970.

5211 LOWE (HENRY JOHN). Plan for Rural Nottinghamshire. Nottingham. 1966.

5212 HARRIS (R. J. P.). 'Inter-regional Movement of Manufacturing Industry: A Comparative Evaluation of the Findings in the Nottinghamshire–Derbyshire Sub-Region'. *Town Planning Rev.* 45 (1974), 431–43.

5213 BRITISH ASSOCIATION FOR THE ADVANCEMENT OF SCIENCE. The Oxford Region: A Scientific and Historical Survey. 1954.

5214 WHITING (R. C.). The View from Cowley: The Impact of Industrialisation upon Oxford, 1918–1939. Oxf. 1983.

5215 U.K. MINISTRY OF HOUSING AND LOCAL GOVERNMENT. The South East Study, 1961–1981 [*sic*]. 1964.

5216 —— A Strategy for the South East. 1967.

5217 U.K. DEPARTMENT OF ECONOMIC AFFAIRS. A Region with a Future: A Draft Strategy for the South West. 1967.

5218 ASSOCIATED INDUSTRIAL CONSULTANTS LTD. The Economic and Industrial Development of the South West. 1965.

5219 U.K. CENTRAL OFFICE OF INFORMATION. (The English Regions)—The South West. 1978.

5220 BRITISH ASSOCIATION FOR THE ADVANCEMENT OF SCIENCE. A Survey of Southampton and its Region. S/hampton. 1964.

5221 U.K. DEPARTMENT OF ECONOMIC AFFAIRS. The West Midlands: A Regional Study. 1965.

5222 —— The West Midlands: Patterns of Growth: A First Report. 1967.

5223 LOMAS (GRAHAM MAURICE) *and* WOOD (PETER A.). Employment Location in Regional Economic Planning: A Case Study of the West Midlands. 1970.

5224 EVERSLEY (DAVID EDWARD CHARLES) *et al.* The Overspill Problem in the West Midlands. 1958.

5225 —— Population Growth and Planning Policy: An Analysis of Social and Economic Factors Affecting Housing and Employment Location in the West Midlands. 1965.

5226 MAWSON (JOHN) *and* SMITH (BARBARA MARY DIMOND). British Regional and Industrial Policy in the 1970s: A Critical Review with Special Reference to the West Midlands in the 1980s. Birm. 1980.

5227 HEALEY (MICHAEL) *and* CLARK (DAVID). De-industrialisation and Employment Decline in the West Midlands and Coventry. Coventry. 1983.

5228 GROVES (R.). Economic and Social Change in the West Midlands. Birm. 1983.

5229 SPENCER (KEN) *et al.* Crisis in the Industrial Heartland: A Study of the West Midlands. Oxf. 1986.

5230 ELLIS (BRIAN). The West Midlands. Camb. 1987.

5231 ROWLANDS (MARIE BERNADETTE). The West Midlands from AD 1000. 1987.

5232 U.K. DEPARTMENT OF ECONOMIC AFFAIRS. A Review of Yorkshire and Humberside. 1966.

5233 COATES (BRYAN E.) *and* HAY (ALAN M.). 'South Yorkshire County is Born and Analysed'. *Geog. Mag.* 46 (1974), 394–6.

5234 HARTLEY (MARIE) *and* INGILBY (JOAN). Life and Tradition in West Yorkshire. 1976.

5235 BRITISH ASSOCIATION FOR THE ADVANCEMENT OF SCIENCE. Handbook to York. York. 1932.

(c) Scottish Regional Studies

5236 MARWICK (WILLIAM HUTTON). The Economic Development of Scotland. Edin. 1930. [Workers' Educational Association pub.].

5237 —— Scotland in Modern Times: An Outline of Economic and Social Development since the Union of 1707. 1964.

5238 —— 'A Bibliography of Scottish Economic History, 1951–1962'. *Econ. Hist. Rev.* [2nd ser.], 16 (1963), 147–54.

5239 GRANT (ISABEL FRANCES). The Economic History of Scotland. 1934.

5240 OAKLEY (CHARLES ALLEN). Scottish Industry To-day: A Survey of Recent Developments Undertaken for the Scottish Development Council. Edin. 1937.

5241 —— Industrial Map of Scotland. Edin./Lond. 1939.

5242 —— *Ed.* Scottish Industry: An Account of what Scotland Makes and where she Makes it. Edin. 1953.

5243 LESER (CONRAD EMANUEL VICTOR) *and* SILVEY (ANNE H.). 'Scottish Industries During the Inter-war Period'. *Manch. Sch. Econ. Soc. Studs* 18 (1950), 163–74.

5244 LESER (CONRAD EMANUEL VICTOR). Some Aspects of the Industrial Structure of Scotland. Glasg. 1951.

5245 LAMONT (ARCHIBALD). Scotland—The Wealthy Nation: A Scientist's Survey of Scots' Resources. Glasg. 1952.

5246 CAIRNCROSS (*Sir* ALEXANDER KIRKLAND) *ed.* The Scottish Economy: A Statistical Account of Scottish Life. Camb. 1954.

5247 U.K. SCOTTISH HOME DEPARTMENT. Industry and Employment in Scotland, and Scottish Roads Report. Edin. 1959–60.

5248 MURRAY (DAVID). The First Nation in Europe: A Portrait of Scotland and the Scots. 1960.

5249 WILSON (THOMAS) *and* TAYLOR (F. S.). 'Scotland: A Financial and Industrial History'. *Banker* 122 (1962), 242–55.

5250 CHECKLAND (SYDNEY GEORGE). 'Scottish Economic History: Recent Work'. *Economica* 44 (1964), 296–313.

5251 SLAVEN (ANTHONY) *and* ALDCROFT (DEREK HOWARD). Business, Banking and Urban History: Essays in Honour of S. G. Checkland. Edin. 1982.

5252 U.K. SCOTTISH OFFICE. The Scottish Economy, 1965–1970: A Plan for Expansion. Edin. 1966.

5253 —— Development and Growth in Scotland. Edin. 1963/4.

5254 CREDLAND (GEOFFREY DENIS) *et al.* Scotland: The Vital Market. Glasg. 1966.

5255 CREDLAND (GEOFFREY DENIS) *and* MURRAY (GEORGE THURSBY). Scotland: A New Look. 1969.

5256 LEE (M. D.). 'Scottish History Since 1940'. Ch. in Changing Views on British History: Essays on Historical Writing since 1939. *Ed.* by Elizabeth Chapin Furber. Camb, Mass. 1966.

5257 LINKLATER (ERIC). The Survival of Scotland: A Review of Scottish History from Roman Times to the Present Day. 1968.

5258 PATON (HERBERT JAMES). The Claim of Scotland. 1968.

5259 CAMPBELL (ROY HUTCHESON). Scotland since 1707: The Rise of an Industrial Society. Oxf. 1965. Repr. Edin. 1980. 2nd edn Edin. 1985.

5260 CAMERON (GORDON CAMPBELL) *and* REID (GRAHAM LIVINGSTONE). Scottish Economic Planning and the Attraction of Industry. Edin. 1966.

5261 PAYNE (PETER LESTER) *ed.* Studies in Scottish Business History. 1967.

5262 McCRONE (GAVIN). Scotland's Economic Progress, 1951–1960: A Study in Regional Accounting. 1965.

5263 —— Scotland's Future: The Economics of Nationalism. Oxf. 1969.

5264 McINTOSH (IAN GRAHAM) *and* MARSHALL (CHARLES BLYTHE). The Face of Scotland. Oxf. 1966.

5265 DONNACHIE (IAN LOWE) *et al.* Industrial History in Pictures: Scotland. Newton Abbot. 1968.

5266 JOHNSTON (THOMAS LOTHIAN) *et al.* Structure and Growth of the Scottish Economy. 1971.

5267 FORSYTH (DAVID JAMES CAMERON) *and* DOCHERTY (KATHRYN). U.S. Investment in Scotland. 1972.

5268 ROBERTSON (WILLIAM STEWART). Scotland Today: Economic Developments. Edin. 1974.

5269 MOORE (BARRY) *and* RHODES (JOHN). 'Regional Policy and the Scottish Economy'. *Scot. J. Pol. Econ.* 21 (1974), 215–35.

5270 LYTHE (SAMUEL GORDON EDGAR) *and* BUTT (JOHN). An Economic History of Scotland 1100–1939. Glasg. 1975.

5271 LENMAN (BRUCE). An Economic History of Modern Scotland, 1660–1976. 1977.

5272 MITCHISON (ROSALIND). Life in Scotland. 1978.

5273 SCOTT (JOHN) *and* HUGHES (MICHAEL). The Anatomy of Scottish Capital: Scottish Companies and Scottish Capital, 1900–1979. 1980.

5274 PATRICK (JOHN). The Rise of Scotland. 1980.

5275 LYTHE (CHARLOTTE) *and* MAJUMDAR (MADHAVI). The Renaissance of the Scottish Economy? 1982.

5276 INGHAM (KEITH P. D.) *and* LOVE (JAMES). Understanding the Scottish Economy. Oxf. 1983.

5277 HOOD (NEIL) *and* YOUNG (STEPHEN) *eds.* Industry, Policy and the Scottish Economy. Edin. 1984.

5278 SAVILLE (RICHARD) *ed.* The Economic Development of Modern Scotland 1950–1980. Edin. 1985.

5279 U.K. SCOTTISH COUNCIL OF SOCIAL SERVICE. Third Statistical Account of Scotland—The County of Dumbarton. Glasg. 1959. [See also 26 other volumes in the series.].

5280 U.K. CENTRAL OFFICE OF INFORMATION REFERENCE DIVISION—Scotland. 1974.

5281 BRITISH ASSOCIATION FOR THE ADVANCEMENT OF SCIENCE. A Scientific Survey of Aberdeen and District. Aberd. 1934.

5282 SHAW (JAMES EDWARD). Ayrshire, 1745–1950: A Social and Industrial History of the County. Edin. 1953.

5283 BRITISH ASSOCIATION FOR THE ADVANCEMENT OF SCIENCE. A Scientific Survey of Dundee and District. Lond. 1939.

5284 —— Dundee and District. Dundee. 1968.

5285 GRIEVE (ROBERT) *and* ROBERTSON (DONALD JAMES). [Edinburgh] The City and the Region. Edin. 1964.

5286 HERIOT WATT UNIVERSITY. The Esk Valley: A Sub-regional Study of Eastern Midlothian: A Study Carried Out for Midlothian County Council. Edin. 1969.

5287 DONNACHIE (IAN LOWE). The Industrial Archaeology of Galloway. Newton Abbot. 1971.

5288 DONNACHIE (IAN LOWE) *and* MACLEOD (INNES). Old Galloway. Newton Abbot. 1974.

5289 BRITISH ASSOCIATION FOR THE ADVANCEMENT OF SCIENCE. Glasgow: Sketches by various authors. Glasg. 1928.

5290 ABERDEEN UNIVERSITY. (Dept. of Geography) Royal Grampian Country: A Report for the Scottish Tourist Board. Aberd. 1969.

5291 HUNT (DEIRDRIE). The Engineering Industry in the Grampian Region: A Study for the North East Scotland Development Authority. Aberd. 1978.

5292 GRANGEMOUTH/FALKIRK REGIONAL SURVEY AND PLAN. 2 vols Edin. 1968.

5293 LOTHIANS REGIONAL SURVEY AND PLAN. 2 vols Edin./Lond. 1966.

5294 MacDONALD (JOHN RONALD MORETON). 'The Economic Future of the Highlands'. *Quart. Rev.* (Jan. 1920), 153–71.

5295 QUIGLEY (HUGH). The Highlands of Scotland. 1936. 4th edn 1949.

5296 —— A Plan for the Highlands: Proposals for a Highland Development Board. 1936.

5297 THOMSON (DERICK SMITH) *and* GRIMBLE (IAN) *eds.* The Future of the Highlands. 1968.

5298 O'DELL (ANDREW CHARLES) *and* WALTON (KENNETH). The Highlands and Islands of Scotland. 1962.

5299 SIMPSON (D.). 'Investments, Employment and Government Expenditure in the Highlands, 1950–1960'. *Scot. J. Pol. Econ.* 10 (1963), 259–88.

5300 BRITISH ASSOCIATION FOR THE ADVANCEMENT OF SCIENCE. The North East of Scotland. 1963.

5301 —— A Scientific Survey of South Eastern Scotland. Edin. 1951.

5302 BRITISH ASSOCIATION FOR THE ADVANCEMENT OF SCIENCE. The Stirling Region. Stirling. 1974.

5303 CARSTAIRS (ANDREW McLAREN). The Tayside Industrial Population: The Changing Character and Distribution of the Industrial Population in the Tayside Area, 1911–1951. Dundee. 1974.

(d) Welsh Regional Studies

5304 MORGAN (J. VYRYNWY). 'Industrialism in Wales'. *Edin. Rev.* (Jan. 1920), 134–42.

5305 REES (*Sir* JAMES FREDERICK). Studies in Welsh History: Collected Papers, Lectures and Reviews. Cardiff. 1947.

5306 —— The Problem of Wales, and other Essays. Cardiff. 1963.

5307 NATIONAL INDUSTRIAL DEVELOPMENT COUNCIL OF WALES AND MONMOUTHSHIRE LTD. Made in Wales: Where and What to Buy from Wales and Monmouthshire. Cardiff. 1947.

5308 —— Wales and Monmouthshire: An Illustrated Review. Cardiff. 1947.

5309 REES (WILLIAM). An Historical Atlas of Wales from Early to Modern Times. Cardiff. 1951.

5310 BEACHAM (ARTHUR). Industries in Welsh Country Towns. 1951.

5311 SCOTT (PETER). 'The Development of Rural Wales'. *Industrial Wales* 42 (1957), 19–21.

5312 MARTIN (ANNE) *and* LEWIS (JOHN PARRY). Welsh Economic Statistics: A Handbook of Sources. Cardiff. 1953.

5313 MORGAN (EDWARD VICTOR). 'How Serious is Welsh Unemployment?'. *Banker* 108 (1958), 252–6.

5314 —— 'Wales in Recession'. *Banker* 109 (1959), 324–7.

5315 —— 'Progress and Problems in Wales'. *Banker* 116 (1966), 331–5.

5316 THOMAS (TREVOR MORGAN). The Mineral Wealth of Wales and its Exploitation. 1961.

5317 THOMAS (BRINLEY) *ed.* The Welsh Economy: A Study in Expansion. Cardiff. 1962.

5318 THOMAS (ROY). Industry in Rural Wales: Welsh Economic Studies, No. 3. Cardiff. 1966.

5319 NEVIN (EDWARD THOMAS). 'The Growth of the Welsh Economy'. *Trans. Soc. Cymmrod.* (1966), 134–48.

5320 —— *Et al.* The Structure of the Welsh Economy. Cardiff. 1966.

5321 —— The Social Accounts of the Welsh Economy, 1948–1952. Cardiff. 1966.

5322 —— 'The "New" Industrial Revolution in Wales'. *Midland Bank Rev.* (May 1967), 13–19.

5323 THOMAS (B.). 'Economic and Social Planning in Wales'. *J. Town Planning Inst.* 55 (1970).

5324 REES (GRAHAM LLOYD) *et al.* A Survey of the Welsh Economy. 1973.

5325 REVELL (JOHN ROBERT STEPHEN) *and* TOMKINS (CYRIL ROBERT). Personal Wealth and Finance in Wales. 1974.

5326 MOORE (BARRY CHARLES). Regional Policy and the Economy of Wales. 1975.

5327 THOMAS (DAVID) *ed.* Wales: A New Study. Newton Abbot. 1977.

5328 WILLIAMS (GLYN) *ed.* Social and Cultural Change in Contemporary Wales. 1978.

5329 U.K. MINISTRY OF RECONSTRUCTION. Welsh Advisory Council: First Interim Report. 1944.

5330 U.K. WELSH OFFICE. Digest of Welsh Statistics. [Pub. annually.] Cardiff. 1954.

5331 U.K. WELSH OFFICE (WELSH COUNCIL). Industrial Development Policy: An Analysis of the Measures Introduced, March 1972. 1972.

5332 —— Location, Size, Ownership and Control Tables for Welsh Industry. 1973.

5333 —— Report on Water in Wales. 1970.

5334 —— The Steel Industry in Wales. 1974.

5335 —— Unemployment in Wales: A Study. 1973.

5336 —— Wales: Employment and Economy, a Report Submitted by the Welsh Council to the Secretary of State for Wales. Cardiff. 1972.

5337 U.K. CENTRAL OFFICE OF INFORMATION REFERENCE SECTION. Wales. 1983.

5338 WELSH COLLEGE OF ADVANCED TECHNOLOGY. Occupational Survey of Manufacturing Industries in Wales Reports. In 7 vols. Cardiff. 1965/6.

5339 U.K. MINISTRY OF WORKS. The Welsh Slate Industry. 1946.

5340 LEWIS (WILLIAM JOHN). Lead Mining in Wales. 1967.

5341 JENKINS (JOHN GERAINT). The Welsh Woollen Industry. Cardiff. 1969.

5342 —— From Fleece to Fabric: The Technological History of the Welsh Woollen Industry. Llandysul. 1981.

5343 ROBERTS (R. O.). 'The Development and Decline of the Copper and Other Non-Ferrous Metal Industries in South Wales'. *Trans. Soc. Cymmrod.* (1956/7), 78–115.

5344 WILLIAMS (L. J.) *and* BOYNS (T.). 'Occupation in Wales, 1851–1971'. *Bull. Econ. Res.* 29 (1977), 71–83.

5345 SIMPSON (DAVID HUGH). Manufacturing Industry in Wales: Prospects for Employment Growth. Cardiff. 1987.

5346 COUNCIL FOR WALES AND MONMOUTHSHIRE. Report on the Welsh Holiday Industry. 1963.

5347 SADLER (PETER), ARCHER (BRIAN), and OWEN (CHRISTINE). Regional Income Multipliers: The Anglesey Study. Bangor. 1973.

5348 JENNINGS (HILDA). Bryn Mawr: A Study of a Distressed Area. 1934.

5349 JONES (J. E. OWEN). 'A Brief Review of Industry in Caernarvonshire'. *Industrial Wales* 78 (1967), 10–17.

5350 JONES (EMYR). Canrif y Chwarelwyr. Denbigh. 1963.

5351 BRITISH ASSOCIATION FOR THE ADVANCEMENT OF SCIENCE. The Cardiff Region: A Survey. Cardiff. 1960.

5352 JENKINS (JOHN GERAINT). 'Technological Improvement and Social Change in South Cardiganshire'. *Agric. Hist. Rev.* 13 (1965), 94–105.

5353 —— 'Rural Industry in Cardiganshire'. *Ceredigion* 6 (1960), 90–127.

5354 WILLIS (ERIC). An Analysis of Industrial Change within the County Borough of Merthyr Tydfil, 1939–1969. 1972.

5355 BRUNT (BARRY MAYNARD). The Contemporary Economic Problems of Merthyr Tydfil. M. Tydfil. 1972.

5356 EDWARDS (ARTHUR TRYSTAN). Merthyr, Rhondda and the Valleys. 1958.

5357 MID-WALES INDUSTRIAL DEVELOPMENT ASSOCIATION. Development in Mid-Wales: A Review of the M.W.I.D.A. 1957–1959. Aberystwyth. 1960.

5358 WENGER (GWYNIFER CLARE). Mid-Wales: Deprivation or Development: A Study of Patterns of Employment in Selected Communities. Cardiff. 1980.

5359 ALDEN (JEREMY) et al. Regional Development Policies for Rural Wales: Mid-Wales. Cardiff. 1983.

5360 —— Rural Schleswig-Holstein and Mid Wales: A Comparative Study of Regional Development. 1987.

5361 PRITCHARD (D. D.). The Economic Conditions of the Nantlle Valley and Certain Contiguous Areas. 1945.

5362 CAERNARVONSHIRE COUNTY COUNCIL. Hydro-electric Power in North Wales. Caernarfon. 1951.

5363 JONES (R. MERFYN). The North Wales Quarrymen 1874–1922. Cardiff. 1981.

5364 LEWIS (EVAN DAVID). The Rhondda Valleys: A Study in Industrial Development, 1800 to the Present Day. 1969.

5365 CLEARY (ESMOND JOHN) and THOMAS (R. E.). The Economic Consequences of the Severn Bridge and its Associated Motorways. Bath. 1973.

5366 DOBBINS (E. LLOYD). South Wales as the Chief Industrial Centre of the United Kingdom. Cardiff. 1922.

5367 U.K. BOARD OF TRADE. An Industrial Survey of South Wales. 1932.

5368 NATIONAL INDUSTRIAL DEVELOPMENT COUNCIL FOR WALES AND MONMOUTHSHIRE LTD. The Second Industrial Survey of South Wales. 3 vols. Cardiff. 1937.

5369 MARQUAND (HILARY ADAIR). South Wales Needs a Plan. 1936.

5370 MASSEY (PHILIP HUBERT). Industrial South Wales: A Social and Political Survey. 1940.

5371 DAVIES (H. W. E.) and HAGGER (D. F.). 'Recent Industrial Changes in South Wales'. *Advancement of Science* 18 (1961), 65–73.

5372 CONKLING (EDGAR C.). A Geographical Analysis of Diversification in South Wales. Evanston, Ill. 1962.

5373 MANNERS (GERALD) ed. South Wales in the Sixties: Studies in Industrial Geography. Oxf. 1968.

5374 REDDIN (TERENCE). South Wales. 1971.

5375 THOMAS (RUTH). South Wales. Edin. 1977.

5376 TOWN (STEPHEN WILLIAM). After the Mines: Changing Employment Opportunities in a South Wales Valley. Cardiff. 1978.

5377 REES (GARETH) and REES (TERESA L.). Migration, Industrial Structuring and Class Relations: The Case of South Wales. Cardiff. 1981.

5378 BRUTON (MICHAEL J.) and NICHOLSON (DAVID J.). Local Planning in South Wales. Cardiff. 1983.

5379 LOVERING (JOHN). The 'Success' of Bristol and the 'Failure' of South Wales. Cardiff. 1984.

5380 BABER (COLIN) and WILLIAMS (LAWRENCE JOHN) eds. Modern South Wales: Essays in Economic History. Cardiff. 1986.

5381 BRENNAN (THOMAS), COONEY (E. W.), and POLLINS (HAROLD). Social Change in South-West Wales. 1954.

5382 BRENNAN (THOMAS) and COONEY (E. W.). The Social Pattern: A Handbook of Social Statistics of South-West Wales. Swansea. 1950.

5383 BRITISH ASSOCIATION FOR THE ADVANCEMENT OF SCIENCE. Swansea and its Region. Swansea. 1971.

(e) Northern Ireland Regional Studies

5384 FREEMAN (THOMAS WALTER). Ireland's General and Regional Geography. Lond./N.Y. 1950. 4th edn 1969.

5385 ISLES (KEITH SYDNEY) and CUTHBERT (NORMAN). An Economic Survey of Northern Ireland. Belf. 1957.

5386 NORTHERN IRELAND ECONOMIC ADVISORY OFFICE. Northern Ireland, Economic Survey. Belf. 1963.

5387 PARKINSON (JOHN RICHARD). Economic Development in Northern Ireland. Nottingham. 1970.

5388 THOMAS (MORGAN D.) and STEED (GUY P. F.). 'Regional Industrial Change: Northern Ireland'. *Ann. Assoc. Amer. Geog.* 61 (1971), 344–60.

5389 O'NEILL (HELEN B.). Spatial Planning in the Small Economy: A Case Study of Ireland. N.Y./Lond. 1971.

5390 GIBSON (N.). 'Economic Conditions and Policy in Northern Ireland'. *Econ. Soc. Rev.* 4 (1973), 349–64.

5391 MURIE (ALAN S.) *et al.* Regional Policy and the Attraction of Manufacturing Industry in Northern Ireland. 1974.

5392 HARVEY (STEPHEN) *and* REA (DESMOND). The Northern Ireland Economy: With Special Reference to Industrial Development. Newtownabbey. 1982.

5393 U.K. CENTRAL OFFICE OF INFORMATION REFERENCE SECTION. Northern Ireland. 1975. 2nd edn 1979.

5394 SAMS (K. I.) *and* SIMPSON (J. V.). 'A Case Study of a Shipbuilding Redundancy in Northern Ireland'. *Scot. J. Pol. Econ.* 15 (1968), 267–82.

5395 BRITISH ASSOCIATION FOR THE ADVANCEMENT OF SCIENCE. Belfast in its Regional Setting. Belf. 1952.

5396 KENNEDY (LIAM) *and* OLLERENSHAW (PHILIP) *eds.* An Economic History of Ulster 1820–1940. Manch. 1985.

5397 BEACHAM (ARTHUR). 'The Ulster Linen Industry'. *Economica* 11 (1944), 199–209.

(f) *Economics of Urban Areas*

5398 GOODALL (BRIAN). The Economics of Urban Areas. 1972.

5399 BUTTON (KENNETH JOHN). Urban Economics: Theory and Policy. 1976.

5400 —— The Economics of Urban Transport. Farnborough. 1977. Repr. 1978.

5401 HARLOE (MICHAEL) *ed.* Captive Cities: Studies in the Political Economy of Cities and Regions. 1977.

5402 JACOBS (JANE). The Economy of Cities. Lond. 1970. Harmondsworth. 1972.

5403 RICHARDSON (HARRY WARD). The Economics of Urban Size. Farnborough. 1973. Repr. 1975.

5404 —— The New Urban Economics and Alternatives. 1977.

5405 RICHARDSON (HARRY WARD), VIPOND (JOAN), *and* FURBEY (ROBERT). Housing and Urban Spatial Structure: A Case Study. Farnborough. 1975.

5406 LICHFIELD (NATHANIEL). Economics of Planned Development. 1956.

5407 —— Cost–Benefit Analysis in Urban Redevelopment. 1962.

5408 —— Cost–Benefit Analysis in Town Planning: A Case Study of Cambridge. Camb. 1966.

5409 PARKER (HERBERT RONALD). Paying for Urban Development. 1959. [Fabian pamphlet.].

5410 KIRWAN (RICHARD MARTIN) *and* MARTIN (D. B.). The Economics of Urban Residential Renewal and Improvement. 1972. [CES Working Paper 77.].

3. INDUSTRIAL MANAGEMENT

(a) *Management and Managers*

5411 POLLARD (SIDNEY). The Genesis of Modern Management: A Study of the Industrial Revolution in Great Britain. 1963.

5412 JERVIS (FRANK ROBERT JOSEPH). Bosses in British Business: Managers and Management from the Industrial Revolution to the Present Day. 1974.

5413 MUSSON (ALBERT EDWARD). The Growth of British Industry. 1978.

5414 MILLER (HARRY). The Way of Enterprise: A Study of the Origins, Problems and Achievements in the Growth of Post-war British Firms. 1963.

5415 CAMPBELL (ROY HUTCHESON) *and* WILSON (RICHARD GEORGE) *eds.* Entrepreneurship in Britain, 1750–1939. 1975.

5416 WIENER (MARTIN J.). English Culture and the Decline of the Industrial Spirit, 1850–1980. Camb. 1981.

5417 HUNT (P.). 'The Case Study Method in Management Training'. *Management Rev.* 13 (1955), 143–55.

5418 SOFER (CYRIL) *and* HUTTON (GEOFFREY). New Ways in Management Training: A Technical College Develops its Service to Industry. 1958.

5419 CEMACH (HARRY PAUL). Work Study in the Office. 1958.

5420 LEWIS (ROY) *and* STEWART (ROSEMARY). The Boss: The Life and Times of the British Businessman. 1958. Rev. edn 1961.

5421 CLEMENTS (ROGER VICTOR). Managers: A Study of their Careers in Industry. 1958.

5422 ELLIOTT (OSBORN). Men at the Top. 1959.

5423 JENKINS (CLIVE). Power at the Top: A Critical Survey of the Nationalized Industries. 1959.

5424 —— Power Behind the Screen: Ownership and Motivation in British Commercial Television. 1961.

5425 McGIVERING (IAN C.), MATTHEWS (DAVID G. J.), *and* SCOTT (WILLIAM HENRY). Management in Britain: A General Characterization. L/pool. 1960.

5426 SMITH (J. H.). 'Sociology and Management Studies'. *Brit. J. Sociol.* 11 (1960), 103–11.

5427 BURNS (TOM). The Management of Innovation. 1961.

5428 HUMBLETT (J. E.). 'A Comparative Study of Management in Three European Countries: Preliminary Findings'. *Sociol. Rev.* 9 (1961), 351–60.

5429 AARONOVITCH (SAM). The Ruling Class: A Study of British Finance Capital. Lond. 1961. Newport, Conn. 1979.

5430 BARRY (WILLIAM SYDNEY). The Fundamentals of Management. 1963.

5431 —— Managing a Transport Business. 1963.

5432 VICKERS (*Sir* GEOFFREY). The Art of Judgement. 1965.

5433 —— Industry, Human Relations and Mental Health. 1965.

5434 —— Towards a Sociology of Management. 1967.

5435 —— Making Institutions Work. 1973.

5436 DEVERELL (CYRIL SPENCER). Business Administration and Management. 1966.

5437 —— Office Personnel: Organisation and Management. 1966.

5438 —— Management Planning and Control. 1967.

5439 GATER (ANTHONY). Thrusters and Sleepers: A Study in Industrial Management. 1965.

5440 LUPTON (THOMAS). Management and the Social Sciences. 1966. 2nd edn 1970.

5441 THOMASON (G. F.). 'Management Work Roles and Relationships'. *J. Manag. Studs* 4 (1967), 17–30.

5442 PYM (DENIS) *ed.* Industrial Society: Social Sciences in Management. Harmondsworth. 1968.

5443 DRUCKER (PETER FERDINAND). Managing for Results. 1968.

5444 —— The Age of Discontinuity: Guidelines to our Changing Society. 1969.

5445 —— The Effective Executive. 1970.

5446 —— Technology, Management and Society. 1970.

5447 HEBDEN (J. E.), ROSE (M. J.), *and* SCOTT (W. H.). 'Management Structure and Computerization'. *Sociology* 3 (1969), 379–96.

5448 SOFER (CYRIL). Men in Mid-Career: A Study of British Managers and Technical Specialists. Camb. 1970.

5449 KEMPNER (THOMAS), MACMILLAN (KEITH), *and* HAWKINS (KEVIN). Business and Society: Tradition and Change. 1974.

5450 MANT (ALISTAIR). The Rise and Fall of the British Manager. 1977. Rev. edn 1979.

5451 POOLE (MICHAEL) *et al.* Managers in Focus: The British Manager in the Early 1980's. Aldershot. 1981.

5452 CROCKETT (GEOFFREY) *and* ELIAS (PETER). British Managers: A Study of their Education, Training, Mobility and Earnings. Coventry. 1981.

5453 LOCKE (R. R.). The End of the Practical Man: Higher Education and the Institutionalisation of Entrepreneurial Performance in Germany, France and Great Britain 1880–1940. 1984.

5454 SCOTT (J.) *and* GRIFF (C.). Directors of Industry: The British Corporate Network 1904–1976. Camb. 1984.

5455 BRITISH INSTITUTE OF MANAGEMENT. Women Managers: The Future. 1986.

5456 BOWMAN (CLIFF). Strategic Management: Corporate Strategy and Business Policy. 1986.

5457 EDWARDS (PAUL K.). Managing the Factory: A Survey of General Managers. Oxf. 1987.

5458 EATON (JACK) *and* FLETCHER (A.). 'Workers' Participation in Management: A Survey of Post-war Organised Opinion'. *Pol. Q.* 47 (1976), 82–92.

5459 CLARKE (RONALD OLIVER), FATCHETT (DEREK JOHN), *and* ROBERTS (BENJAMIN CHARLES). Workers' Participation in Management in Britain. 1972.

5460 WILSON (WILLIAM). Towards Industrial Democracy in Britain. Manch. 1978.

5461 NORTHCOTT (CLARENCE HUNTER). Personnel Management: Its Scope and Practice. 1946. 4th edn 1960.

5462 INSTITUTE OF PERSONNEL MANAGEMENT. Personnel Management: A Bibliography. 1950. New edn 1962. Rev. edn 1969.

5463 —— Personnel Management 1913–1963: The Growth of Personnel Management and the Development of the Institute. 1967. New edn 1978.

5464 ROGERS (T. G. P.). 'Recent Advances in Personnel Management'. *Pol. Q.* 22 (1956), 260–9.

5465 LUPTON (THOMAS). Industrial Behaviour and Personnel Management. 1964.

5466 MINER (JOHN BURNHAM). Personnel Psychology. 1969.

5467 McFARLAND (DALTON EDWARD) *ed.* Personnel Management: Selected Readings. Harmondsworth. 1971.

5468 ROSE (FRANK WILLIAM). Personnel Management Law. 1972.

5469 BEYNON (HUW) *and* BLACKBURN (ROBERT MARTIN). Perceptions of Work: Variations within a Factory. 1972.

5470 MARKS (WINIFRED ROSE). Politics and Personnel Management: An Outline History, 1960–1976. 1978.

5471 WATSON (TONY J.). The Personnel Managers: A Study in the Sociology of Work and Employment. 1977.

5472 ROBBINS (STEPHEN PAUL). Personnel: The Management of Human Resources. 1978. 2nd edn 1982.

5473 HUNT (JOHN). Managing People at Work: A Manager's Guide to Behaviour in Organisations. 1979. Repr. 1981.

5474 McILWEE (TERRY). Personnel Management in Context: The 1980s. 1982. 2nd edn 1986.

5475 BROWN (IAN M.). Personnel Management in Five Public Services: Its Development and Future. Birm. 1982.

5476 ATTWOOD (MARGARET). Introduction to Personnel Management. 1985.

5477 FRASER (JOHN MUNRO). Human Relations in a Fully Employed Democracy. 1960.

5478 —— Principles and Practice of Supervisory Management. 1967. Repr. 1971.

5479 —— Introduction to Personnel Management. 1971.

5480 BROWN (JAMES ALEXANDER CAMPBELL). The Social Psychology of Industry: Human Relations in the Factory. Harmondsworth. 1954. Repr. 1986.

5481 IVENS (MICHAEL W.) *and* BROADWAY (FRANK) *eds.* Case Studies in Human Relations, Productivity and Organization. 1966.

5482 WILLINGS (DAVID RICHARD). The Human Element in Management. 1968.

5483 HUGHES (ERNEST WILLIAM). Human Relations in Management. Oxf. 1970.

5484 DEEP (SAMUEL DAVID). Human Relations in Management. 1978.

5485 RAE (LESLIE). The Skills of Human Relations Training: A Guide for Managers and Practitioners. Aldershot. 1985.

5486 CORNWALLIS-JONES (ARTHUR THOMAS). Education for Leadership: The International Administrative Staff Colleges, 1948–1984. 1985.

5487 BLANK (STEPHEN). Industry and Government in Britain: The Federation of British Industries in Politics, 1945–1965. Farnborough. 1973.

5488 GRANT (WYN P.) *and* MARSH (DAVID). 'The Confederation of British Industries'. *Pol. Studs* 19 (1971), 403–15.

5489 —— 'The Politics of the C.B.I.: 1974 and after'. *Govt and Opp.* 10 (1975), 90–104.

5490 —— The Confederation of British Industries. 1977.

5491 WILCOX (MICHAEL). The Confederation of British Industry Predecessor Archive. Coventry. 1984.

5492 CONFEDERATION OF BRITISH INDUSTRY. Britain Means Business: The Full Proceedings of the C.B.I. First National Conference. 1977. 1978.

5493 —— Twenty Five Years of 'Ups' and 'Downs'. 1983.

5494 WIGHAM (ERIC LEONARD). The Power to Manage: A History of the Engineering Employers Federation. 1973.

5495 HANNAH (LESLIE). 'Management Innovation and the Rise of the Large-Scale Company in Inter-war Britain'. *Econ. Hist. Rev.* 2nd ser. 27 (1974), 252–70.

5496 —— Engineers, Managers and Politicians: The First Fifteen Years of Nationalized Electricity Supply in Britain. 1982.

5497 TURNER (HERBERT ARTHUR). 'The Donovan Report [Royal Commission Report on Trade Unions and Employers' Associations, 1965–1968]'. *Econ. J.* 79 (1969), 1–10.

5498 RAE (JOHN B.). Harry Ferguson and Henry Ford. Belf. 1980.

5499 WYMER (NORMAN). Harry Ferguson. 1961.

5500 POUND (REGINALD). Selfridge: A Biography. 1960.

5501 KIRBY (MAURICE W.). Men of Business and Politics: The Rise and Fall of the Quaker Pease Dynasty of North-East England 1700–1943. 1984.

5502 BUCKMASTER (OWEN STANLEY) *Viscount*. Roundabout: The Autobiography of Viscount Buckmaster. 1969.

5503 MacFADYEAN (*Sir* ANDREW). Recollected in Tranquillity. 1964.

5504 DAVENPORT-HINES (RICHARD PETER TREADWELL). Dudley Docker: The Life and Times of a Trade Warrior. Camb. 1984.

5505 DE GUINGAND (*Sir* FRANCIS). From Brass Hat to Bowler Hat. 1979.

5506 EDWARDES (*Sir* MICHAEL). Back from the Brink. 1983.

5507 GOLDENBERG (SUSAN). The Thomson Empire: The First Fifty Years. 1985.

(b) Mergers, Monopolies, and Multinationals

5508 LEVY (HERMANN). Monopolies, Cartels and Trusts in British Industry. 1927.

5509 —— The New Industrial System: A Study of the Origin, Forms, Finance and Prospects of Concentration in Industry. 1936.

5510 NATIONAL INDUSTRIAL CONFERENCE BOARD. Mergers in Industry. 1929.

5511 PENROSE (EDITH TILTON). The Theory of the Growth of a Firm. Oxf. 1959.

5512 BERNHARD (RICHARD C.). 'English Law and American Law on Monopolies and Restraints of Trade'. *J. Law Econ.* 3 (1960), 136–45.

5513 MENNELL (WILLIAM). Takeover: The Growth of Monopoly in Britain, 1951–1961. 1962.

5514 ROWLEY (CHARLES KERSHAW). The British Monopolies Commission. 1966.

5515 LEE (DEREK) *et al.* Monopoly. 1968. 2nd edn 1980. *Eds* Christopher Laurence Pass and John Richard Sparkes.

5516 U.K. BOARD OF TRADE. Mergers: A Guide to Board of Trade Practice. 1969.

5517 NEWBOULD (GERALD DAVID). Management and Merger Activity. L/pool. 1970. Repr. 1971.

5518 BLOCK (F.). 'Expanding Capitalism: The British and American Cases'. *Berkeley J. Sociol.* 15 (1970), 138–65.

5519 SINGH (AVTAR). Take-overs. 1971.

5520 MOOS (SIEGFRIED). Aspects of Monopoly and Restrictive Practices Legislation in Relation to Small Firms. 1971.

5521 UTTON (MICHAEL ARTHUR). 'The Effect of Mergers on Concentrations: U.K. Manufacturing Industry, 1954–1965'. *J. Indust. Econ.* 20 (1971/2), 42–58.

5522 —— 'On Measuring the Effects of Industrial Mergers'. *Scot. J. Pol. Econ.* 21 (1973), 13–28.

5523 VERMA (P.). 'Mergers in British Industry, 1949–1966'. *J. Bus. Pol.* 2 (1972), 31–40.

5524 BANNOCK (GRAHAM BERTRAM). The Juggernauts: The Age of the Big Corporation. 1971. Harmondsworth. 1973.

5525 POLANYI (GEORGE). Which Way Monopoly Policy?: Some Questions Raised by Recent Reports of the Monopolies Commission. 1973.

5526 HART (PETER EDWARD) *et al.* Mergers and Concentration in British Industry. Camb. 1973.

5527 HART (PETER EDWARD) *and* CLARKE (ROGER). Concentration in British Industry 1935–1975: A Study of the Growth, Causes and Effects of Concentration in British Manufacturing Industries. Camb. 1980.

5528 HECLO (HUGH) *and* WILDAVSKY (AARON). The Private Government of Public Money. 1974.

5529 WALSHE (GRAHAM). Recent Trends in Monopoly in Great Britain. 1974.

5530 AARONOVITCH (SAM) *and* SAWYER (MALCOLM C.). 'The Concentration of British Manufacturing'. *Lloyds Bank Rev.* 114 (Oct. 1974), 14–23.

5531 SAWYER (MALCOLM C.). 'Concentration in British Manufacturing Industry'. *Oxf. Econ. Papers* 23 (1971), 352–83.

5532 MEEKS (GEOFFREY) *and* WHITTINGTON (GEOFFREY). 'Giant Companies in the United Kingdom, 1948–1969'. *Econ. J.* 85 (1975), 824–43.

5533 PRAIS (SIGBERT JON). The Evolution of Giant Firms in Britain: A Study of the Growth of Concentration in Manufacturing Industry in Britain 1909–1970. Camb. 1976. 2nd edn 1981.

5534 NICHOLSON (HUGH THAYER) *and* PALMER (ERNEST BARRY). Mergers and Associations of Professional Firms. 1965. 3rd rev. edn 1978.

5535 COWLING (KEITH). Monopolies and Mergers Policy: A View on the Green Paper. Warwick. 1978.

5536 —— Monopoly Capitalism. 1982.

5537 PICKERING (JOHN FREDERICK). 'The Abandonment of Major Mergers in the United Kingdom, 1965–1975'. *J. Indust. Econ.* 27 (1978/9), 123–32.

5538 —— The Causes and Consequences of Abandoned Mergers. Manch. 1979.

5539 —— The Implementation of British Competition Policy on Mergers. Manch. 1980.

5540 —— *Et al.* Concentration in British Manufacturing Industry into the 1970s. Manch. 1982.

5541 PICKERING (JOHN FREDERICK) *and* SHELDON (I. M.). International Trade Performance and Concentration in British Industry. Manch. 1982.

5542 MORSE (GEOFFREY). Company Finance, Takeovers and Mergers. 1979.

5543 DUTTON (PATRICIA A.). A Case Study of the G.E.C./A.E.I./English Electrical Mergers. Coventry. 1978.

5544 WILLIAMS (JAMES GEOFFREY). Acquisitions and Mergers. 1980.

5545 WEINBERG (MARK AUBREY), BLANK (MAURICE VICTOR), *and* GREYSTOKE (A. L.). Take-overs and Mergers. 4th edn 1979. 1st pub. in 1963, under the title 'Take-overs and Amalgamations'.

5546 JOHNSTON (*Sir* ALEXANDER). The City Take-over Code. Oxf. 1980.

5547 GOLDBERG (WALTER H.). Mergers: Motives, Modes, Methods. Aldershot. 1983.

5548 WRIGHT (MICHAEL) *and* COYNE (JOHN). Management Buyouts. 1985.

5549 COOKE (TERENCE E.). Mergers and Acquisitions. Oxf. 1986.

5550 MORGAN (EDWARD VICTOR). Monopolies, Mergers and Restrictive Practices: U.K. Competition Policy 1948–1984. Edin. 1987.

5551 FALLON (IVAN) *and* SRODES (JAMES). Takeovers. 1987.

5552 SHAW (RICHARD) *and* SIMPSON (PAUL). The Monopolies Commission and the Market Process: An Examination of the Effectiveness of Public Policy in Selected U.K. Industries. 1989.

5553 FAIRBURN (JAMES A.) *and* KAY (JOHN ANDERSON) *eds.* Mergers and Merger Policy. Oxf. 1989.

5554 STOPFORD (JOHN MORTON). 'Origins of British-based Multinational Manufacturing Enterprises'. *Bus. Hist. Rev.* 48 (1974), 303–35.

5555 STOPFORD (JOHN MORTON) *and* TURNER (LOUIS). Britain and the Multinationals. Chichester. 1985.

5556 HODGES (MICHAEL). Multinational Corporations and National Government: A Case Study of the United Kingdom's Experience, 1964–1970. Farnborough. 1974.

5557 EDWARDS (BOB). Multinational Companies and the Trade Unions. Nottingham. 1977.

5558 FIELDHOUSE (DAVID KENNETH). Unilever Overseas: The Anatomy of a Multinational, 1895–1965. 1978.

5559 MAXCY (GEORGE). The Multinational Motor Industry. 1981.

5560 MAXWELL (STEPHEN) *ed.* Scotland, Multinationals and the Third World. Edin. 1982.

5561 BUCKLEY (PETER J.) *and* CASSON (MARK). The Future of the Multinational Enterprise. 1976.

5562 CASSON (MARK). Alternatives to Multinational Enterprise. 1979.

5563 —— The Firm and the Market: Studies on Multinational Enterprise and the Scope of the Firm. Oxf. 1987.

5564 JONES (GEOFFREY) *ed.* British Multinationals: Origins, Management and Performance. Aldershot. 1986.

5565 YOUNG (STEPHEN), HOOD (NEIL), *and* HAMILL (JAMES). Foreign Multinationals and the British Economy: Impact and Policy. 1988.

4. INDUSTRIAL RELATIONS

(Including Industrial Psychology and Sociology)

5566 WARD (JOHN T.) *and* FRASER (W. HAMISH). Workers and Employers: Documents on Trade Unions and Industrial Relations in Britain Since the 18th Century. 1980.

5567 GOTTSCHALK (ANDREW WILLIAM) *and* WHITTINGHAM (TERENCE GEORGE). British Industrial Relations: An Annotated Bibliography. Nottingham. 1970.

5568 BAIN (GEORGE SAYERS) *and* WOOLVEN (GILLIAN B.). A Bibliography of British Industrial Relations. Camb. 1979.

5569 BAIN (GEORGE SAYERS) *and* BENNETT (JOHN D.). A Bibliography of British Industrial Relations 1971–1979. Camb. 1985.

5570 BENNETT (JOHN D.). 'A Bibliography of Industrial Relations, 1980'. *Brit. J. Ind. Relns* 20 (1982), 377–414.

5571 —— 'A Bibliography of Industrial Relations, 1981'. *Brit. J. Ind. Relns* 21 (1983), 234–64.

5572 BENNETT (JOHN D.) *and* FLETCHER (JOHN). 'Industrial Relations Material in Warwick University Library'. *Ind. Relns J.* 12/1 (1981), 62–6.

5573 SMART (CAROL ROSEMARY) *comp.* Industrial Relations in Britain: A Guide to Sources of Information. 1980.

5574 BURGESS (KEITH). The Origins of British Industrial Relations. 1975.

5575 JACKSON (MICHAEL P.). Industrial Relations: A Textbook. 1977. 3rd edn 1985.

5576 WRIGLEY (CHRIS) *ed.* A History of British Industrial Relations. Vol. 1. Brighton. 1982.

5577 —— The Government and Industrial Relations in Britain 1910–1921. Loughborough. 1979.

5578 CHARLES (RODGER). The Development of Industrial Relations in Britain, 1911–1939: Studies in the Evolution of Collective Bargaining at National and Industrial Level. 1973.

5579 RUBIN (GERRY R.). War, Law and Labour: The Munitions Acts, State Regulation and the Unions, 1915–1921. Oxf. 1987.

5580 HAWKINS (KEVIN H.). British Industrial Relations, 1945–1975. 1976.

See also British Journal of Industrial Relations 1963– and Industrial Relations Journal 1971–.

5581 RAMSAY (*Sir* ALEXANDER). Terms of Industrial Peace. 1917.

5582 —— The Truth about Industry. 1930.

5583 MYERS (CHARLES SAMUEL). Present-Day Applications of Psychology with Special Reference to Industry, Education and Nervous Breakdown. 1918.

5584 —— Mind and Work: The Psychological Factors in Industry and Commerce. 1920.

5585 —— Industrial Psychology in Great Britain. 1926. 2nd edn 1933.

5586 O'DONOVAN (WILLIAM JAMES). 'The War-Time Experiences of Factory Medical Officers and the Position of Factory Medicine under Peace Conditions'. *J. State Medicine* (Aug. 1919), 241–51.

5587 MACASSEY (*Sir* LYNDEN LIVINGSTONE). 'The Industrial Courts Act, 1919'. *J. Comp. Legisl.* 3rd ser. 2 (1920), 72–6.

5588 —— Labour Policy—False and True: A Study in Economic History and Industrial Economics. 1922.

5589 MESS (HENRY ADOLPHUS). Factory Legislation and its Administration. 1926.

5590 McDONALD (G. W.) *and* GOSPEL (HOWARD F.). 'The Mond-Turner Talks 1927–1933: A Study in Industrial Co-operation'. *Hist. J.* 16 (1973), 807–29.

5591 KELSALL (ROGER KEITH) *and* PLAUT (THEODOR). Industrial Relations in the Modern State: An Introductory Survey. 1937.

5592 BENNEY (MARK) *pseud.* [i.e. DEGRAS (HENRY ERNEST)]. Over to Bombers. 1943. [An account of work in an aircraft factory.].

5593 U.K. MINISTRY OF LABOUR AND NATIONAL SERVICE. Industrial Relations Handbook 1944. 1944– ; from 1980 pub. by Advisory, Conciliation and Arbitration Service (A.C.A.S.).

5594 RICHMOND (ANTHONY HENRY). The Human Factor in Industry. 1948.

5595 FOGARTY (MICHAEL PATRICK) *ed.* Further Studies in Industrial Organisation. 1948.

5596 FRANK (WILLIAM FRANCIS). The New Industrial Law. 1950.

5597 —— 'The State and Industrial Arbitration in the United Kingdom'. *Louisiana Law Rev.* 19 (1959), 617–43.

5598 FRANK (WILLIAM FRANCIS) *and* JERVIS (FRANK ROBERT JOSEPH). An Introduction to Industrial Administration. 1962. 2nd rev. edn 1970.

5599 SHARP (IAN GORDON). Industrial Conciliation and Arbitration in Great Britain. 1950.

5600 TURNER (HERBERT ARTHUR). Arbitration: A Study of Industrial Experience. 1952.

5601 —— *Et al.* Labour Relations in the Motor Industry: A Study of Industrial Unrest and an International Comparison. 1967.

5602 —— 'Collective Bargaining and the Eclipse of the Incomes Policy: Retrospect, Prospect and Possibilities'. *Brit. J. Ind. Relns* 8 (1970), 197–212.

5603 BROWN (WILFRID) *Baron.* Some Problems of a Factory: An Analysis of Industrial Institutions. 1953.

5604 —— Bismarck to Bullock: Conversations about Institutions in Politics and Industry in Britain and Germany between Wilfrid Brown and Wolfgang Hirsch-Weber. 1983. Ed. Hans Weiner.

5605 RICHARDSON (JOHN HENRY). An Introduction to the Study of Industrial Relations. 1954.

5606 WRIGHT (FRANK JOSEPH). The Evolution of Modern Industrial Organisation. 1954.

5607 —— The Elements of Modern Industrial Organisation. 1958.

5608 FLANDERS (ALLAN DAVID). The Fawley Productivity Agreements: A Case Study of Management and Collective Bargaining. 1964. 2nd edn 1966.

5609 —— Industrial Relations: What is Wrong with the System? An Essay on its Theory and Failure. 1965.

5610 —— The Future of Voluntarism in Industrial Relations. 1966.

5611 —— Collective Bargaining: Prescription for Change. 1967.

5612 —— *Ed.* Collective Bargaining: Selected Readings. Harmondsworth. 1969.

5613 —— Management and Unions: The Theory and Reform of Industrial Relations. 1970. Repr. 1975.

5614 FLANDERS (ALLAN DAVID) *and* CLEGG (HUGH ARMSTRONG) *eds.* The System of Industrial Relations in Great Britain: Its History, Law and Institutions. Oxf. 1954. 2nd edn 1964.

5615 CLEGG (HUGH ARMSTRONG). The System of Industrial Relations in Great Britain. Oxf. 1970. 3rd edn 1978.

5616 —— The Changing System of Industrial Relations in Great Britain. Oxf. 1979.

5617 —— Industrial Courts Act 1919: Report of a Court of Inquiry into a Dispute Concerning the Operation of Fork Lift Trucks at the Albert Edward Dock, North Shields. 1966.

5618 CLEGG (HUGH ARMSTRONG) *and* ADAMS (REX). The Employers' Challenge: A Study of the National Shipbuilding and Engineering Disputes of 1957. Oxf. 1957.

5619 SPERO (STERLING DENHARD). Labor Relations in British Nationalized Industry. N.Y. 1955.

5620 DERBER (MILTON). 'Labor Relations in British Metalworking'. *Monthly Lab. Rev.* 78 (1955), 403–9.

5621 —— Labor-Management Relations at Plant Level under Industry-Wide Bargaining: A Study of the Engineering (Metalworking) Industry in Birmingham (England). Chicago. 1955.

5622 —— 'Adjustment Problems of a Long Established Industrial Relations System: An Appraisal of British Engineering 1954–1961'. *Quart. Rev. Econ. Bus.* 3 (1963), 37–48.

5623 —— 'Collective Bargaining in Great Britain and the United States'. *Quart. Rev. Econ. Bus.* 8 (1968), 55–66.

5624 LOCKWOOD (DAVID). 'Arbitration and Industrial Conflict'. *Brit. J. Sociol.* 6 (1955), 335–47.

5625 BELBIN (EUNICE). 'The Problems of Industrial Training'. *Brit. Management Rev.* 13 (1955), 165–73.

5626 CALLIES (G.). 'Les Comités d'entreprise en Grande-Bretagne'. *R. Action Pop.* 89 (1955), 723–32.

5627 ROBERTS (BENJAMIN CHARLES). Trade Union Government and Administration in Great Britain. 1956.

5628 —— Industrial Relations: Contemporary Problems and Perspectives. 1962. Rev. edn 1968.

5629 —— 'Employers and Industrial Relations in Britain and America'. *Pol. Q.* 27 (1956), 324–39.

5630 FOGARTY (MICHAEL PATRICK). Personality and Group Relations in Industry. Lond./N.Y. 1956.

5631 —— The Rules of Work. 1963.

5632 SCOTT (WILLIAM HENRY). Technical Change and Industrial Relations. L/pool. 1956.

5633 —— 'The Aims of Industrial Sociology: Some Reflections'. *Brit. J. Sociol.* 10 (1959), 193–203.

5634 —— *Et al.* Coal and Conflict: A Study of Industrial Relations at Collieries. L/pool. 1963.

5635 WYATT (STANLEY) *et al.* A Study of Attitudes to Factory Work. 1956.

5636 ROUTH (GUY). 'The Structure of Collective Bargaining'. *Pol. Q.* 27 (1956), 44–56.

5637 COLE (GEORGE DOUGLAS HOWARD). The Case for Industrial Partnership. 1957.

5638 SHELL (KURT T.). 'Industrial Democracy and the British Labour Movement'. *Pol. Sci. Q.* 72 (1957), 515–39.

5639 BAYLISS (F. J.). 'The Independent Members of British Wages Councils and Boards'. *Brit. J. Sociol.* 8 (1957), 1–24.

5640 FRANKEL (M.). 'Joint Industrial Planning in Great Britain'. *Ind. Relns J.* 11 (1958), 429–45.

5641 HARE (ANTHONY EDWARD CHRISTIAN). The First Principles of Industrial Relations. 1958. 2nd edn 1965.

5642 SMITH (MAY). An Introduction to Industrial Psychology. 1958.

5643 BADGER (ALFRED BOWEN). Man in Employment: The Fundamental Principles of Industrial Relations. 1958. 2nd edn 1966.

5644 JOHNSON (LEONARD GEORGE). The Social Evolution of Industrial Britain: A Study in the Growth of our Industrial Society. L/pool. 1959.

5645 ROBERTS (ROBERT DAVID VALPO) *and* SALLIS (H.). 'Joint Consultations in the Electricity Supply Industry, 1949–1959'. *Public Admin* 37 (1959), 115–33.

5646 —— 'Labor/Management Co-operative Committees in Britain's Electricity Supply Industry'. *Ind. Lab. Relns R.* 12 (1958), 86–103.

5647 SYKES (A. J. M.). 'The Pattern of Industrial Relations'. *Quart. Rev.* 297 (1959), 432–43.

5648 SMITH (J. H.). 'New Ways in Industrial Sociology'. *Brit. J. Sociol.* 10 (1959), 244–52.

5649 PATERSON (THOMAS THOMSON). Glasgow Limited: A Case-study in Industrial War and Peace. Lond/N.Y. 1960.

5650 BESCOBY (JOHN) *and* TURNER (HERBERT ARTHUR). 'An Analysis of Post-War Labour Disputes in the British Car

Manufacturing Firms'. *Manch. Sch. Econ. Soc. Studs* 29 (1961), 133–60.

5651 HANDSAKER (MORRISON) *and* HANDSAKER (MARJORIE L.). 'Arbitration in Great Britain'. *Ind. Relns* 1 (1961), 117–36.

5652 WILKIE (ROY). 'The Ends of Industrial Sociology'. *Sociol. Rev.* 9 (1961), 215–24.

5653 U.K. DEPARTMENT OF SCIENTIFIC AND INDUSTRIAL RESEARCH. Human Sciences Aid to Industry. 1961.

5654 —— Human Sciences in Industry: An Annotated Bibliography. 1964.

5655 WELTON (HARRY). The Necessary Conflict: A Commonsense View of Industrial Relations. 1962.

5656 LUPTON (THOMAS). On the Shop Floor: Two Studies in Workshop Organisation and Output. Oxf. 1963.

5657 ROSS (ARTHUR M.). 'Prosperity and British Industrial Relations'. *Ind. Relns* 2 (1963), 63–94.

5658 MARSH (ARTHUR IVOR). Managers and Shop Stewards. 1963.

5659 —— Industrial Relations in Engineering. Oxf. 1965.

5660 —— Research and Teaching in Industrial Relations: The British Experience. Geneva. 1967.

5661 —— *Et al.* Workplace Industrial Relations in Engineering. 1971.

5662 MARSH (ARTHUR IVOR), HACKMANN (MARIA), *and* MILLER (DOUGLAS). Workplace Industrial Relations in the Engineering Industry in the United Kingdom and the Federal Republic of Germany. Kettering. 1981.

5663 MARSH (ARTHUR IVOR) *and* McCARTHY (WILLIAM EDWARD JOHN) *Baron*. Disputes Procedures in Britain. 1969.

5664 McCARTHY (WILLIAM EDWARD JOHN) *Baron*. The Closed Shop in Britain. Oxf. 1964.

5665 —— The Role of Shop Stewards in British Industrial Relations: A Survey of Existing Information and Research. 1966.

5666 —— Industrial Relations in Britain: A Guide for Management and Unions. 1969.

5667 —— Management by Agreement: An Alternative to the Industrial Relations Act. 1973.

5668 TOPHAM (TONY). ' "Package Deals" et Negociation Collective en Grande-Bretagne'. *Rev. Inl Sociol.* 1 (1964), 540–64.

5669 CHILD (JOHN). 'Quaker Employers and Industrial Relations'. *Sociol. Rev.* 12 (1964), 293–315.

5670 —— Industrial Relations in the British Printing Industry: The Quest for Security. 1967.

5671 OAKLEY (C.), O₃DOHERTY (K.), *and* MORTON (R.). 'The Social Effects of Industrial Changes in Great Britain, the Republic of Ireland and Northern Ireland'. *Administration* (Dublin), 12 (1964), 146–62.

5672 ELDRIDGE (JOHN ERIC THOMAS). 'Plant Bargaining in Steel: North East Case Studies'. *Sociol. Rev.* 13 (1965), 131–47.

5673 —— The Demarcation Dispute in the British Shipbuilding Industry: A Study in the Sociology of Conflict. Geneva. 1967.

5674 —— Industrial Disputes: Essays in the Sociology of Industrial Relations. Lond./N.Y. 1968.

5675 —— Sociology and Industrial Life. 1971.

5676 ELDRIDGE (JOHN ERIC THOMAS) *and* CROMBIE (A. D.). A Sociology of Organisations. 1974.

5677 PARKER (STANLEY ROBERT). A Bibliography of Industrial Sociology, Including the Sociology of Occupations. 1965.

5678 —— *Et al.* The Sociology of Industry. 1967. 4th edn 1981.

5679 —— Effects of the Redundancy Payments Act: A Survey Carried out in 1969 for the Department of Employment. 1971.

5680 —— Workplace Industrial Relations 1972, An Enquiry Carried out on behalf of the Department of Employment. 1974.

5681 BROWN (RICHARD K.). 'Participation, Conflict and Change in Industry'. *Sociol. Rev.* 13 (1965), 273–95.

5682 —— 'Research and Consultancy in Industrial Enterprises: A Review of the Contribution of the Tavistock Institute of Human Relations to the Development of Industrial Sociology'. *Soc.* 1 (1967), 33–60.

5683 OLDFIELD (FREDERICK E.). New Look Industrial Relations. 1966.

5684 CLARKE (MICHAEL). Industrial Relations. 1966. Rev. edn 1974, by Michael Clarke and Patrick Tolfree.

5685 FOX (ALAN). Industrial Sociology and Industrial Relations: An Assessment of the Contribution which Industrial Sociology can make towards Understanding and Resolving some of the Problems Now being Considered by the Royal Commission [Donovan Commission]. 1966.

5686 —— 'Management Ideology and Labour Relations'. *Brit. J. Ind. Relns* 4 (1966), 366–78.

5687 —— A Sociology of Work in Industry. 1971.

5688 —— Socialism and Shop Floor Power. 1978. [Fabian Soc. Res. Ser. No. 338.].

5689 —— History and Heritage: The Social Origins of the British Industrial Relations System. 1985.

5690 FOX (ALAN) *and* FLANDERS (ALLAN DAVID). 'The Reform of Collective Bargaining—From Donovan to Durkheim'. *Brit. J. Ind. Relns* 7 (1969), 151–80.

5691 EDWARDS (*Sir* RONALD STANLEY). An Experiment in Industrial Relations: The Electricity Supply Industry's Status Agreement for Staff. 1967.

5692 EDWARDS (*Sir* RONALD STANLEY) *and* ROBERTS (ROBERT

DAVID VALPO). Status, Productivity and Pay—A Major Experiment: A Study of the Electricity Supply Industry's Agreements and their Outcome, 1961–1971. 1971.

5693 CLACK (GARFIELD). Industrial Relations in a British Car Factory. Camb. 1967.

5694 ROBINSON (OLIVE). 'White-Collar Bargaining: A Case Study in the Private Sector'. *Scot. J. Pol. Econ.* 14 (1967), 256–74.

5695 —— 'Representation of the White-Collar Worker: The Bank Staff Associations in Britain'. *Brit. J. Ind. Relns* 7 (1969), 19–41.

5696 INGHAM (GEOFFREY K.). 'Organizational Size, Orientation to Work and Industrial Behaviour'. *Sociology* 1 (1967), 239–58.

5697 MORTIMER (JAMES EDWARD). Industrial Relations. 1968.

5698 COATES (KENNETH SIDNEY) *and* TOPHAM (ANTHONY). Industrial Democracy in Great Britain. 1968.

5699 —— The Shop Steward's Guide to the Bullock Report. Nottingham. 1977.

5700 COATES (KENNETH SIDNEY). Democracy in the Mines. Nottingham. 1974.

5701 U.K. GOVERNMENT SOCIAL SURVEY DEPARTMENT. Workplace Industrial Relations: An Enquiry Undertaken for the Royal Commission on Trade Unions and Employers Associations [Donovan Commission] in 1966. 1968.

5702 UNIVERSITY OF MICHIGAN, PROGRAM IN INTERNATIONAL BUSINESS. Labor Relations and the Law in the United Kingdom and the United States. Ann Arbor, Michigan. 1968.

5703 CASSON (JOHN). Using Words: Verbal Communications in Industry. 1968.

5704 BLUMBERG (PAUL). Industrial Democracy: The Sociology of Participation. 1968.

5705 ANTHONY (PETER D.) *and* CRICHTON (ANNE). Industrial Relations and the Personnel Specialists. 1969.

5706 ANTHONY (PETER D.). The Conduct of Industrial Relations. 1977.

5707 —— The Ideology of Work. 1977.

5708 GOTTSCHALK (ANDREW WILLIAM) *and* TOWERS (BRIAN). Productivity Bargaining: A Case Study and Simulation Exercise. Nottingham. 1969.

5709 BURNS (TOM) *ed.* Industrial Man: Selected Readings. Harmondsworth. 1969.

5710 GRANT (JEANNE VALERIE) *and* SMITH (G. J.). Personnel Administration and Industrial Relations. Harlow. 1969.

5711 GOODMAN (JOHN FRANCIS BRADSHAW). Shop Stewards in British Industry. N.Y./Maidenhead. 1969. Rev. edn Lond. 1973.

5712 —— *Et al.* Rule Making and Industrial Peace: Industrial Relations in the Footwear Industry. 1977.

5713 DANGERFIELD (CHRISTABEL). Insight into Industry: An Introduction to the Growth of Present Day Conditions of British Industry. 1969.

5714 DANIEL (WILLIAM WENTWORTH). 'Industrial Behaviour and Orientation to Work: A Critique'. *J. Manag. Studs* 6 (1969), 366–75.

5715 —— Workplace Industrial Relations and Technical Change. 1987.

5716 DANIEL (WILLIAM WENTWORTH) *and* McINTOSH (NEIL). The Right to Manage?: A Study of Leadership and Reform in Employee Relations. 1972.

5717 GABARINO (JOSEPH W.). 'Managing Conflict in Industrial Relations: U.S. Experience and Current Issues in Britain'. *Brit. J. Ind. Relns* 7 (1969), 317–35.

5718 —— 'British Experiments with Industrial Relations Reform'. *Ind. Lab. Relns* 26 (1973), 793–804.

5719 GILL (JOHN). 'One Approach to the Teaching of Industrial Relations'. *Brit. J. Ind. Relns* 7 (1969), 265–72.

5720 BARLOW (GRAHAM). 'Some Latent Influences in a Pay-claim: An Examination of a White-Collar Dispute'. *Brit. J. Ind. Relns* 7 (1969), 200–10.

5721 BANKS (R. F.). 'The Reform of British Industrial Relations: The Donovan Report and the Labour Government's Policy Proposals'. *Relations Industr.* 24 (1969), 333–82.

5722 —— 'British Collective Bargaining: The Challenge of the 1970s'. *Rel. Industr.* 26 (1971), 642–91.

5723 KAHN-FREUND (*Sir* OTTO). 'Industrial Relations and the Law: Retrospect and Prospect'. *Brit. J. Ind. Relns* 7 (1969), 241–67.

5724 —— 'Trade Unions, the Law and Society'. *Mod. Law Rev.* 33 (1970), 241–67.

5725 KILROY-SILK (ROBERT). 'The Problem of Industrial Relations'. *Manch. Sch. Econ. Soc. Studs* 3 (1969), 249–57.

5726 ROBERTSON (NORMAN) *and* SAMS (KENNETH IAN). 'Les Relations Professionelles en Grande-Bretagne: Perspectives d'un Nouveau Système'. *A. Econ. Coll.* 57 (1969), 267–90.

5727 NEAL (*Sir* LEONARD F.). Industrial Relations in the 1970s. 1970.

5728 McLEOD (CHARLES). 'All Change': Railway Industrial Relations in the Sixties. 1970.

5729 FLANDERS (ALLAN DAVID). Management and Unions: The Theory and Reform of Industrial Relations. 1970.

5730 PAUL (WILLIAM JAMES) *and* ROBERTSON (KEITH BARRIE). Job Enrichment and Employee Motivation. 1970.

5731 GRANT (RONALD MELVILLE). Industrial Relations. 1970. Rev. edn 1979, by Maureen Woodhall.

5732 BLAIN (ALEXANDER NICHOLAS JOHN) *and* GENNARD (JOHN). 'Industrial Relations Theory: A Critical Review'. *Brit. J. Ind. Relns* 8 (1970), 389–407.

5733 WHITTINGHAM (TERENCE GEORGE), *and* GOTTSCHALK (ANDREW WILLIAM). 'Proposals for Change in the British System of Industrial Relations—An Evaluation'. *J. Ind. Relns* 12 (1970), 52–71.

5734 CARSON (WESLEY GEORGE). 'Some Sociological Aspects of Strict Liability and the Enforcement of Factory Legislation'. *Mod. Law Rev.* 33 (1970), 396–412.

5735 LEWIS (ROY). 'The Legal Enforcibility of Collective Agreements'. *Brit. J. Ind. Relns* 8 (1970), 313–33.

5736 SCOTTISH JOURNAL OF POLITICAL ECONOMY SPECIAL ISSUE. 'Industrial Relations'. 17 (1970), 117–336. [By various authors.].

5737 KESSLER (SIDNEY) *and* WEEKES (BRIAN) *eds.* Conflict at Work: Reshaping Industrial Relations—A Book of Original Essays. 1971.

5738 CAMPBELL (ALAN). The Industrial Relations Act: An Introduction. 1971.

5739 HARVEY (RICHARD JON). Industrial Relations (including the 1971 Industrial Relations Act). 1971.

5740 U.K. DEPARTMENT OF EMPLOYMENT *AND* CENTRAL OFFICE OF INFORMATION. Industrial Relations: A Guide to the Industrial Relations Act. 1971.

5741 CRABTREE (CYRIL). The Industrial Relations Act: A Comprehensive Guide. 1971.

5742 HENDERSON (JOAN). The Industrial Relations Act at Work. 1971.

5743 —— The Industrial Relations Act in the Courts. 1973.

5744 ALLEN (VICTOR LEONARD). The Sociology of Industrial Relations: Studies in Method. 1971.

5745 WILSON (A. T. M.), MITCHELL (JEREMY) *and* CHERNS (ALBERT) *eds.* Social Science Research and Industry. 1971.

5746 FELDMAN (MAURICE PHILIP). Psychology in the Industrial Environment. 1971.

5747 WARR (PETER) *ed.* The Psychology of Work. 1971. 2nd edn 1979.

5748 MINER (JOHN BURNHAM). Personnel and Industrial Relations: A Managerial Approach. 1971.

5749 GEORGE (KENNETH DESMOND) *and* JOLL (CAROLINE). Industrial Organisation: Competition, Growth and Structural Change in Britain. 1971. 3rd edn 1981.

5750 CHARLOT (MONICA). 'La Réforme des Relations du Travail en Grande-Bretagne'. *Projet* 59 (1971), 1090–7.

5751 HAWKINS (KEVIN H.). 'Productivity Bargaining: A Reassessment'. *Ind. Relns J.* 2 (1971), 10–34.

5752 —— The Management of Industrial Relations. Harmondsworth. 1978.

5753 —— Case Studies in Industrial Relations. 1982.

5754 THOMSON (ANDREW W. J.). 'Collective Bargaining under Incomes Legislation: The Case of Britain's Buses'. *Ind. Lab. Relns R.* 24 (1971), 389–406.

5755 LOWNDES (RICHARD). Industrial Relations: A Contemporary Survey. 1972.

5756 ROBERTS (BENJAMIN CHARLES) *et al.* Reluctant Militants: A Study of Industrial Technicians. 1972.

5757 BLAIN (ALEXANDER NICHOLAS JOHN). Pilots and Management: Industrial Relations in the United Kingdom Airlines. 1972.

5758 BALFOUR (CAMPBELL). Industrial Relations in the Common Market. 1972.

5759 AARON (BENJAMIN) *and* WEDDERBURN (KENNETH WILLIAM) *Baron.* Industrial Conflict: A Comparative Legal Survey. 1972.

5760 BULL (GEORGE ANTHONY), HOBDAY (PETER), *and* HAMWAY (JOHN). Industrial Relations: The Boardroom Viewpoint. 1972.

5761 HALL (D. J.). Industrial Relations Problems and the Industrial Relations Act. 1972.

5762 HYMAN (RICHARD). Disputes Procedure in Action: A Study of the Engineering Industry Disputes Procedure in Coventry. 1972.

5763 —— Industrial Relations: A Marxist Introduction. 1975.

5764 HYMAN (RICHARD) *and* BROUGH (IAN). Social Values and Industrial Relations: A Study of Fairness and Equality. Oxf. 1975.

5765 HEFFER (ERIC SAMUEL). The Class Struggle in Parliament: A Socialist View of Industrial Relations. 1973.

5766 CUTHBERT (NORMAN H.) *and* HAWKINS (KEVIN H.) *eds.* Company Industrial Relations Policies: The Management of Industrial Relations in the 1970's. 1973.

5767 DORFMAN (GERALD ALLEN). Wage Politics in Britain, 1945–1967. Ames, Iowa. 1973.

5768 BAGWELL (PHILIP SIDNEY). Industrial Relations. Dublin. 1974.

5769 GOLDTHORPE (JOHN H.). 'Industrial Relations in Great Britain: A Critique of Reformism'. *Pol. and Soc.* 4 (1974), 419–52.

5770 CARSON (WESLEY GEORGE O.) *and* MARTIN (BERNICE). The Development of Factory Legislation: The Sociology of a Law and its Enforcement. 1975.

5771 WEEKES (O) *et al.* Industrial Relations and the Limits of Law: The Industrial Effects of the Industrial Relations Act 1971. Oxf. 1975.

5772 —— The Law and Practice of the Closed Shop. Coventry. 1978.

5773 THOMSON (ANDREW WILLIAM JOHN) *and* ENGLEMAN (STEPHEN ROBERT). The Industrial Relations Act: A Review and Analysis. 1975.

5774 U.K. ADVISORY, CONCILIATION AND ARBITRATION SERVICE. First Annual Report, 1975. 1975.

5775 BELL (J. D. M.). 'The Development of Industrial Relations in Nationalized Industries in Post-war Britain'. *Brit. J. Ind. Relns* 13 (1975), 1–13.

5776 FULCHER (JAMES). 'Industrial Conflict in Britain and Sweden'. *Sociology* 9 (1975), 477–84.

5777 LISCHERON (JOE) *and* WALL (TOBY D.). 'Attitudes Towards Participation Among Local Authority Employees'. *Human Relns* 28 (1975), 499–517.

5778 COOPER (BRUCE M.) *and* BARTLETT (A. F.). Industrial Relations: A Study in Conflict. 1976.

5779 DEGEN (GUNTHER R.). Shop Stewards: Ihre Zentrale Bedeutung für die Gewerkschaftsbewegung in Grossbritannien. Frankfurt. 1976.

5780 THAKUR (MANAB) *and* GILL (DEIRDRIE ROCKINGHAM). Job Evaluation in Practice: A Survey of 213 Organisations in the U.K. 1976.

5781 BOWEN (PETER). Social Control in Industrial Organisations: Industrial Relations and Industrial Sociology: A Strategic and Occupational Study of British Steelmaking. 1976.

5782 HUGHES (JOHN). Industrial Restructuring: Some Manpower Problems. 1976.

5783 HARTMAN (PAUL). 'Industrial Relations in the News Media'. *Indust. Relns J.* 6 (1976), 4–18.

5784 WALKER (KENNETH F.). 'Towards useful Theorising about Industrial Relations'. *Brit. J. Ind. Relns* 15 (1976), 307–16.

5785 CROUCH (COLIN). Class Conflict and the Industrial Relations Crisis: Compromise and Corporatism in the Policies of the British State. Atlantic Highlands, N.J./Lond. 1977.

5786 —— The Politics of Industrial Relations. Manch./Lond. 1979.

5787 OTTAWAY (RICHARD N.) *ed.* Humanising the Work Place: New Proposals and Perspectives. 1977.

5788 NICHOLLS (THEO) *and* BENYON (HUW). Living with Capitalism: Class Relations and the Modern Factory. 1977.

5789 BATSTONE (ERIC), BORASTON (IAN) *and* FRENKEL (STEPHEN). Shop Stewards in Action. Oxf. 1977.

5790 MORAN (MICHAEL). The Politics of Industrial Relations: The Origins, Life and Death of the 1971 Industrial Relations Act. 1977.

5791 HUNT (DENNIS D.). Common Sense Industrial Relations. Newton Abbot. 1977.

5792 GREGORY (DENIS) *ed.* Work Organization: Swedish Experience and British Context. 1978.

5793 LOCKYER (CLIFF J.). Industrial Relations in Britain. Glasg. 1978.

5794 —— Industrial Relations. 1988.

5795 TERRY (MICHAEL). The Emergence of a Lay Elite?: Some Recent Changes in Shop Steward Organisation. Coventry. 1978.

5796 BROWN (WILLIAM), EBSWORTH (ROBERT), *and* TERRY (MICHAEL). Factors Shaping Shop Steward Organisation in Britain. Coventry. 1978.

5797 GILL (COLIN), MORRIS (RICHARD), *and* EATON (JACK). Industrial Relations in the Chemical Industry. Farnborough. 1978.

5798 McCORMICK (BRIAN JOSEPH). Industrial Relations in the Coal Industry. 1979.

5799 LOVELL (JOHN C.) 'Collective Bargaining and the Emergence of National Employer-Organisations in the British Ship-building Industry'. *Inl. Rev. Soc. Hist.* 36 (1991) 59–91.

5800 BROWN (WILLIAM) *Ed.* The Changing Contours of British Industrial Relations. Oxf. 1981.

5801 STEPHENSON (GEOFFREY M.) *and* BROTHERTON (CHRISTOPHER M.) *eds.* Industrial Relations: A Social Psychological Approach. Chich. 1979.

5802 CRONIN (JAMES E.). Industrial Conflict in Modern Britain. 1979.

5803 LOCKYER (JOHN). Industrial Arbitration in Great Britain: Everyman's Guide. 1979.

5804 SINGH (DAVINDER) *and* WILLIAMS (C. GLYN). 'A Model of Collective Bargaining for U.K. and U.S. Manufacturing: A Comparative Study'. *Brit. J. Ind. Relns* 17 (1979), 386–9.

5805 WORTLEY (IAN). Industrial Relations. 1980.

5806 WATSON (TONY J.). Sociology, Work and Industry. 1980. 2nd edn 1987.

5807 KAY (MAURICE). Arbitration. 1980.

5808 SORGE (ARNDT) *and* WARNER (MALCOLM). 'The Context of Industrial Relations in Great Britain and West Germany'. *Ind. Relns J.* 11/1 (1980), 41–9.

5809 MACKIE (KARL) *and* HOOKER (IAN). 'Industrial Relations Law Commentary: Proposed Changes in the Law'. *Ind. Relns J.* 11/2 (1980), 5–12.

5810 MACKIE (KARL). 'Industrial Relations Law Commentary: The Employment Act 1980'. *Ind. Relns J.* 12/1 (1981), 6–10.

5811 —— 'Trends and Developments in Industrial Relations Law: The Employment Act 1988'. *Ind. Relns J.* 19 (1988), 265–71.

5812 BAMBER (GREG). 'Microchips and Industrial Relations'. *Ind. Relns J.* 11/5 (1980), 7–19.

5813 POOLE (MICHAEL). Theories of Trade Unionism: A Sociology of Industrial Relations. 1981.

5814 —— Industrial Relations: Origins and Patterns of National Diversity. 1986.

5815 ARMSTRONG (PETER J.) *et al.* Ideology and Shopfloor Industrial Relations. 1981.

5816 JOHNSTON (THOMAS LOTHIAN). An Introduction to Industrial Relations. Plymouth. 1981. 2nd edn 1985.

5817 HANSON (CHARLES), JACKSON (SHEILA), *and* MILLER (DOUGLAS). The Closed Shop: A Comparative Study in Public Policy and Trade Union Security in Britain, the USA and West Germany. Aldershot. 1982.

5818 STRINATI (DOMINIC). Capitalism, the State and Industrial Relations. 1982.

5819 FROW (EDMUND) *and* FROW (RUTH). Engineering Struggles: Episodes in the Story of the Shop Stewards' Movement. Manch. 1982.

5820 McDERMOTT (PHILIP J.) *and* TAYLOR (MICHAEL). Industrial Organisation and Location. Camb. 1982.

5821 BASNETT (DAVID). The Future of Collective Bargaining. 1982. [Fabian Tract No. 481.].

5822 WILLIAM (PAUL). Fairness, Collective Bargaining and Incomes Policy. Oxf. 1982.

5823 OGDEN (S. G.). 'Bargaining Structure and the Control of Industrial Relations'. *Brit. J. Ind. Relns* 20 (1982), 170–85.

5824 ARMSTRONG (ERIC GEORGE ABBOTT). 'The Conciliatory Negotiation of Change: A Case Study of the Norwich Footwear Arbitration Board, 1909–1980'. *Ind. Relns J.* 13/1 (1982), 43–56.

5825 ARMSTRONG (ERIC GEORGE ABBOTT) *and* LUCAS (ROSEMARY). Improving Industrial Relations: The Advisory Role of A.C.A.S. 1985.

5826 BAIN (GEORGE SAYERS) *ed.* Industrial Relations in Britain. 1983.

5827 THURLEY (KEITH) *and* WOOD (STEPHEN). Industrial Relations and Management Strategy. Camb. 1983.

5828 VINCENT (MIKE). An Introduction to Industrial Relations. 1983.

5829 BRADLEY (KEITH) *and* GELB (ALAN). Worker Capitalism: The New Industrial Relations. 1983.

5830 PARRIS (JOHN). Arbitration: Principles and Practice. 1983.

5831 McGOLDRICK (JAMES). 'Industrial Relations and the Division of Labour in the Shipbuilding Industry since the War'. *Brit. J. Ind. Relns* 21 (1983), 197–220.

5832 WINCHESTER (DAVID). 'Industrial Relations Research in Britain'. *Brit. J. Ind. Relns* 21 (1983), 100–14.

5833 BROWN (WILLY) *and* SISSON (KEITH). 'Industrial Relations: The Next Decade'. *Ind. Relns J.* 14/1 (1983), 9–21.

5834 BRIGHT (DAVID) *et al.* 'The Industrial Relations of Recession'. *Ind. Relns J.* 14/3 (1983), 24–33.

5835 BROAD (GEOFFREY). 'Shop Steward Leadership and the Dynamics of Workplace Industrial Relations'. *Ind. Relns J.* 14/3 (1983), 59–67.

5836 DUNN (STEPHEN) *and* GENNARD (JOHN). The Closed Shop in British Industry. 1984.

5837 WINDMULLER (JOHN P.) *and* GLADSTONE (ALAN) *eds.* Employers' Associations and Industrial Relations: A Comparative Study. Oxf. 1984.

5838 McCARTHY (CHARLES). Elements in a Theory of Industrial Relations. Dublin. 1984.

5839 GINNINGS (ARTHUR T.). Arbitration: A Practical Guide. Aldershot. 1984.

5840 MUNCK (RONNIE). Industrial Sociology: An Introduction: With Northern Ireland Case Studies. Newtownabbey. 1983. 2nd edn 1984.

5841 BREWSTER (CHRIS). Understanding Industrial Relations. 1984.

5842 BLACK (BOYD). 'Industrial Relations in Northern Ireland: A Survey'. *Ind. Relns J.* 15 (1984), 29–36.

5843 FOSH (PATRICIA) *and* LITTLER (CRAIG R.) *eds.* Industrial Relations and the Law in the 1980's: Issues and Future Trends. Aldershot. 1985.

5844 MARSDEN (DAVID) *et al.* The Car Industry: Labour Relations and Industrial Adjustment. 1985.

5845 BUCKLEY (PETER J.) *and* ENDERVILLE (PETER). The Industrial Relations Position of Foreign-Owned Firms in Britain. 1985.

5846 WOOD (*Sir* JOHN). 'Last Offer Arbitration'. *Brit. J. Ind. Relns* 28 (1985), 415–24.

5847 INGHAM (MIKE). 'Industrial Relations in British Local Government'. *Ind. Relns J.* 16/1 (1985), 6–15.

5848 ARTHURS (ALAN). 'Industrial Relations in the Civil Service: Beyond GCHQ'. *Ind. Relns J.* 16/2 (1985), 26–33.

5849 STIRLING (JOHN) *and* BRIDGFORD (JEFF). 'British and French Shipbuilding: The Industrial Relations of Decline'. *Ind. Relns J.* 16/4 (1985), 7–16.

5850 BASSETT (PHILIP). Strike Free: New Industrial Relations in Britain. 1986.

5851 STEWART (MARK B.). Collective Bargaining Arrangements, Closed Shops and Relative Pay. Coventry. 1986.

5852 LEE (ERIC). Dictionary of Arbitration Law and Practice. 1986.

5853 FOWLER (ALAN). Effective Negotiation. 1986.

5854 PALMER (GILL). 'Donovan, the Commission on Industrial Relations and Post-liberal Rationalisation'. *Brit. J. Ind. Relns* 24 (1986), 267–96.

5855 MacINNES (JOHN). Thatcherism at Work: Industrial Relations and Economic Change. Milton Keynes. 1987.

5856 KELLY (JOHN) *et al.* 'Symposium: British Workplace Industrial Relations 1980–1984'. *Brit. J. Ind. Relns* 25 (1987), 275–94.

5857 EVANS (STEPHEN). 'The Use of Injunctions in Industrial Disputes, May 1984–April 1987'. *Brit. J. Ind. Relns* 25 (1987), 419–35.

5858 HUTT (CLIVE). 'The Reporting of Industrial Relations on Breakfast Television'. *Ind. Relns J.* 18 (1987), 90–9.

5859 BEVERIDGE (JOHN) *and* GOODMAN (JOHN). 'The British Universities' Industrial Relations Association: The First 35 Years'. *Brit. J. Ind. Relns* 25 (1988), 155–77.

5860 HUNTER (LAURIE). 'Unemployment and Industrial Relations'. *Brit. J. Ind. Relns* 25 (1988), 203–28.

5. THE LABOUR FORCE

(a) Occupations (General Works); Manpower; Employment Training

5861 GEDDES (*Sir* ERIC CAMPBELL). Mass Production: The Revolution which Changes Everything. 1931.

5862 CLARK (FREDERICK LE GROS) *and* DUNNE (AGNES CLARISSA). Ageing in Industry: An Inquiry Based on Figures Derived from Census Reports into the Problems of Ageing under the Conditions of Modern Industry. 1955.

5863 CLARK (FREDERICK LE GROS). Age and the Working Lives of Men: An Attempt to Reduce the Statistical Evidence to its Practical Shape. 1959.

5864 VICKERS (*Sir* GEOFFREY). 'Incentives of Labour'. *Pol. Q.* 27 (1956), 284–93.

5865 CLEARY (A. J.). 'The Placings Service of the Ministry of Labour'. *Sociol. Rev.* 4 (1956), 191–8.

5866 ARGYLE (MICHAEL), GARDNER (GODFREY), *and* CIOFFI (FRANK). 'The Measurement of Supervisory Methods'. *Human Relns* 10 (1957), 295–313.

5867 BHIDE (M. Y.). 'Vocational Guidance in the United Kingdom'. *J. Voc. Educ. Guid.* 4 (1958), 134–9.

5868 McCORMICK (BRIAN). 'Managerial Unionism in the Coal Industry'. *Brit. J. Sociol.* 11 (1960), 356–69.

5869 DUFFY (NORMAN FRANCIS). 'Occupational Status, Job Satisfaction and Levels of Aspiration'. *Brit. J. Sociol.* 7 (1960), 348–55.

5870 MILLARD (PATRICIA) *comp.* Trade Associations and Professional Bodies of the United Kingdom: A Directory and Classified Index. 1962.

5871 NEILD (ROBERT RALPH). Pricing and Employment in the Trade Cycle: A Study of British Manufacturing Industry, 1950–1961. Camb. 1963.

5872 BROOM (L.) *and* SMITH (J. H.). 'Bridging Occupations'. *Brit. J. Sociol.* 14 (1963), 321–34.

5873 MITCHELL (J. CLYDE). 'Occupational Prestige and the Social System: A Problem in Comparative Sociology'. *Inl J. Comp. Sociol.* 5 (1964), 78–90.

5874 —— 'The Difference in an English and an American Rating of the Prestige of Occupations'. *Brit. J. Sociol.* 15 (1964), 166–73.

5875 ROBERTSON (ANDREW). 'Technological Change, Management and Labour'. *Pol. Q.* 35 (1964), 171–81.

5876 PARKER (S. R.). 'Work and Non-Work in Three Occupations'. *Sociol. Rev.* 13 (1965), 65–75.

5877 PRIESTLEY (BARBARA) *comp.* British Qualifications: A Comprehensive Guide to Educational, Technical, Professional and Academic Qualifications in Britain. 1966.

5878 CUNNISON (SHEILA). Wages and Work Allocation: A Study of Social Relations in a Garment Workshop. 1966.

5879 BRITTENDEN (FREDERICK HENRY). A Guide to the Selective Employment Tax. 1966.

5880 OLDMAN (DAVID) *and* ILLSLEY (RAYMOND). 'Measuring the Status of Occupations'. *Sociol. Rev.* 14 (1966), 53–72.

5881 U.K. CENTRAL OFFICE OF INFORMATION. Labour Relations and Conditions of Work in Britain. 1967.

5882 U.K. MINISTRY OF LABOUR. Occupational Changes, 1951–1961. 1967.

5883 OWEN (JOHN P.) *and* BELZUNG (L. D.). 'Consequences of Voluntary Early Retirement: A Case Study of a New Labour Force Phenomenon'. *Brit. J. Ind. Relns* 5 (1967), 162–89.

5884 CANNON (I. C.). 'Ideology and Occupational Community: A Study of Compositors'. *Sociology* 1 (1967), 165–85.

5885 CHADWICK-JONES (JOHN). 'Shift-working: Physiological Effects and Social Behaviour'. *Brit. J. Ind. Relns* 5 (1967), 237–43.

5886 FRASER (RONALD) *ed.* Work: Twenty Personal Accounts . . . with a Concluding Essay by Raymond Williams. Harmondsworth. 1968.

5887 DUDLEY (NORMAN ALFRED). Work Measurement: Some Research Studies. 1968.

5888 ROBERTS (K.). 'The Entry into Employment: An Approach Towards a General Theory'. *Sociol. Rev.* 16 (1968), 165–84.

5889 SMITH (MICHAEL A.). 'Process Technology and Powerlessness'. *Brit. J. Sociol.* 19 (1968), 76–88.

5890 STACEY (B. G.). 'Inter-generational Occupational Mobility in Britain'. *Occup. Psychol.* 42 (1968), 33–48.

5891 GASSON (RUTH). 'Occupations Chosen by the Sons of Farmers'. *J. Agric. Econ.* 19 (1968), 317–26.

5892 FINNEGAN (JOHN). Industrial Training Management. 1970.

5893 —— The Right People in the Right Jobs. 1973.

5894 MITCHELL (DANIEL J. B.). 'Some Aspects of Labour Mobility and Recent Policy in Britain'. *Brit. J. Ind. Relns* 7 (1969), 353–67.

5895 U.K. OFFICE OF POPULATION CENSUSES AND SURVEYS. Classification of Occupations. 1970.

5896 TIMPERLEY (STUART R.) *and* GREGORY (ALISON M.). 'Some Factors Affecting the Career Choice and Career Perceptions of Sixth Form School Leavers'. *Sociol. Rev.* 19 (1971), 95–114.

5897 WEDDERBURN (DOROTHY) *and* CROMPTON (MARY). Workers' Attitudes and Technology. Camb. 1972.

5898 BURRAGE (MICHAEL). 'The Group Ties of Occupations in Britain and the United States'. *Admin. Sci. Q.* 17 (1972), 240–53.

5899 BOWEY (ANGELA) *and* LUPTON (THOMAS). Job and Pay Comparisons: How to Identify Similar Jobs in Different Companies and Compare their Rates of Pay. Epping. 1973.

5900 BROWN (WILFRID). The Earnings Conflict. 1973.

5901 KUHN (ANNETTE) *et al.* 'An Analysis of Graduate Job Mobility'. *Brit. J. Ind. Relns* 11 (1973), 124–42.

5902 WILLIAMS (WILLIAM MORGAN) *ed.* Occupational Choice: A Selection of Papers from the Sociological Review. 1974.

5903 BAILEY (MARTIN NEIL). 'Wages and Employment under Uncertain Demand'. *Rev. Econ. Studs* 41 (1974), 37–50.

5904 BOSHIER (ROGER) *and* JOHNSON (DEREK). 'Does Conviction Affect Employment Opportunities?'. *Brit. J. Criminology* 14 (1974), 264–8.

5905 O'CLEIREACAIN (CAROL CHAPMAN). 'Labour Market Trends in London and the Rest of the South-East'. *Urban Studs* 11 (1974), 329–39.

5906 DUNKERLEY (DAVID). Occupations and Society. 1975.

5907 EASTWOOD (GERRY). Skilled Labour Shortages in the United Kingdom with Particular Reference to the Engineering Industry. 1976.

5908 WEIR (MARY) *ed.* Job Satisfaction: Challenge and Response in Modern Britain. Glasg. 1976.

5909 SLOANE (PETER JAMES). Changing Patterns of Working Hours. 1976.

5910 SHOWLER (BRIAN). The Public Employment Service. 1976.

5911 BUXTON (NEIL KEITH) *and* McKAY (DONALD IAN) *assisted by* WOOD (C. L.). British Employment Statistics: A Guide to Sources and Methods. Oxf. 1977.

5912 PAYNE (GEOFF). 'Occupational Transition in Advanced Industrial Societies'. *Sociol. Rev.* 25 (1977), 5–39.

5913 JONES (TREVOR W.). 'Occupational Transition in Advanced Industrial Societies: A Reply'. *Sociol. Rev.* 25 (1977), 387–407.

5914 PAYNE (GEOFF). 'Understanding Occupational Transition: A Comment on Jones'. *Sociol. Rev.* 25 (1977), 409–27.

5915 WRAGG (RICHARD) *and* ROBERTSON (JAMES). Post-war Trends in Employment, Productivity, Output, Labour Costs and Prices by Industry in the United Kingdom. 1978.

5916 RICHARDS (PAULINE N.) *comp.* Shift Work: A Selective Annotated Bibliography. 1978.

5917 COXON (ANTHONY P. M.) *and* JONES (CHARLES L.). The Images of Occupational Prestige. 1978.

5918 —— Measurement and Meanings: Techniques and Methods of Studying Occupational Cognition. 1979.

5919 METCALF (DAVID). Low Pay, Occupational Mobility and Minimum Wage Policy in Great Britain. 1980.

5920 SANDERS (CONRAD). The Social Stigma of Occupations: The Lower Grade Worker in Service Organisations. Farnborough. 1981.

5921 NICKIE (CHARLES) *and* BROWN (DAVID). 'Women, Shiftworking and the Sexual Division of Labour'. *Sociol. Rev.* 29 (1981), 685–704.

5922 WOOD (STEPHEN). 'Redundancy and Female Employment'. *Sociol. Rev.* 29 (1981), 649–83.

5923 GREENHALGH (CHRISTINE A.) *and* STEWART (MARK B.). Occupational Status and Mobility of Men and Women. Coventry. 1982.

5924 PORTWOOD (DEREK). 'Careers and Redundancy'. *Sociol. Rev.* 33 (1985), 449–68.

5925 DEX (SHIRLEY). Women's Occupational Mobility: A Lifetime Perspective. 1987.

5926 LABOUR RESEARCH DEPARTMENT. Shift Work and Unsocial Hours: A Negotiators' Guide. 1987.

5927 PERRY (PETER JOHN CHARLES). The Evolution of British Manpower Policy: From the Statute of Artificers 1563 to the Industrial Training Act 1964. Chichester. 1976.

5928 GRIEVES (KEITH). The Politics of Manpower 1914–1918. Manch. 1988.

5929 GOWING (MARGARET M.). 'The Organisation of Manpower in Britain During the Second World War'. *J. Contemp. Hist.* 7 (1972), 147–67.

5930 POLITICAL AND ECONOMIC PLANNING. Manpower: A Series of Studies of the Composition of Britain's Labour Force. 1951.

5931 PARKER (HENRY MICHAEL DENNE). Manpower. 1957.

5932 U.K. DEPARTMENT OF EMPLOYMENT. Manpower Studies Nos. 1–12. 1964–72.

See also Department of Employment, Various 'Manpower Papers'. 1968–78.

5933 ROBERTS (BENJAMIN CHARLES) *and* SMITH (JOHN HAROLD) *eds.* Manpower Policy and Employment Trends. 1966.

5934 GRAY (DANIEL HALE). Manpower Planning: An Approach to the Problem. 1966.

5935 LEWIS (CHARLES G.) *ed.* Manpower Planning: A Bibliography. 1969.

5936 ORGANISATION FOR ECONOMIC CO-OPERATION AND DEVELOPMENT. Manpower Policy in the United Kingdom. Paris/Lond. 1970.

5937 U.K. DEPARTMENT OF EDUCATION AND SCIENCE. Survey of Earnings of Qualified Manpower in England and Wales 1966/67. 1971.

5938 KENNEY (JOHN P.) *and* DONNELLY (EUGENE LAWRENCE). Manpower Training and Development. 1972. 2nd edn 1979.

5939 U.K. CENTRAL OFFICE OF INFORMATION. (Reference Division) Manpower in Britain: The Trade Unions. 1975. 2nd edn 1977.

5940 —— Manpower in Britain: Occupations and Conditions of Work. 1976.

5941 —— Manpower in Britain: Industrial Relations. 1977.

5942 —— Manpower in Britain: The Role of Government. 1978.

5943 —— Manpower in Britain: Industrial Training. 1978.

5944 THAKUR (MANAB). Manpower Planning in Action. 1975.

5945 BRAHAM (JOHN). Practical Manpower Planning. 1975. 2nd edn 1978.

5946 BARTHOLOMEW (DAVID JOHN) ed. Manpower Planning: Selected Readings. Harmondsworth. 1976.

5947 WABE (J. STUART). Manpower Changes in the Engineering Industry. Watford. 1977.

5948 ZIDERMAN (ADRIAN). Manpower Training: Theory and Policy. 1978.

5949 McBEATH (GORDON). Manpower Planning and Control. 1978.

5950 EVANS (ALISTAIR). A Guide to Manpower Information. 1980.

5951 LONG (ANDREW F.) and MERCER (GEOFFREY) eds. Manpower Planning in the National Health Service. Farnborough. 1981.

5952 WALKER (B. J.). The Manpower Services Commission and Youth Training Schemes: A Critical Appraisal. Sheffield. 1986.

5953 LIEPMANN (KATE K.). Apprenticeship: An Enquiry into its Adequacy under Modern Conditions. 1960.

5954 TONKINSON (ERNEST), THOMAS (RAYMOND E.), and HANNAFORD (R. G. MAGNUS). Commercial Apprenticeships. 1962.

5955 BEVERIDGE (ANDREW). Apprenticeship Now: Notes on the Training of Young Entrants to Industry. 1963.

5956 WILLIAMS (Lady GERTRUDE). Apprenticeship in Europe: The Lesson for Britain. 1963.

5957 WELLENS (JOHN). The Training Revolution: From Shopfloor to Boardroom. 1963.

5958 BELBIN (EUNICE) and SERGEAN (ROBERT). Training in the Clothing Industry: A Study of Recruitment Training and Education. 1963.

5959 KING (DAVID). Training within the Organization: A Study of Company Policy and Procedures for the Systematic Training of Operators and Supervisors. 1964.

5960 WHEATLEY (DAVID ERNEST). Apprenticeships in the United Kingdom. Brussels. 1976.

5961 RYRIE (ALEXANDER C.) and WEIR (ALEXANDER DOUGLAS). Getting a Trade: A Study of Apprentices' Experience of Apprenticeship. 1978.

5962 POLLOCK (G. J.) and NICHOLSON (V. M.). Just the Job: The Employment and Training of Young School Leavers: A Summary Report. 1981.

5963 RODERICK (GORDON) and STEPHENS (MICHAEL) eds. The British Malaise: Industrial Performance, Education and Training in Britain Today. 1982.

5964 LEE (GLORIA L.). Skill Seekers: Black Youth, Apprenticeships and Disadvantage. Leicester. 1983.

5965 PEARSON (RICHARD) et al. Education, Training and Employment. Aldershot. 1984.

5966 BERRY (FRANK). Bench, Saw and Plane: A Cotswold Apprenticeship. Andoverford. 1988.

5967 COLLINS (ANTHEA). Non-Specialist Graduates in Industry. 1955.

5968 —— Et al. The Arts Graduate in Industry. 1962.

5969 U.K. POLITICAL AND ECONOMIC PLANNING. Graduate Employment: A Sample Survey. 1956.

5970 RUDD (ERNEST) and HATCH (STEPHEN). Graduate Study and After. 1968.

5971 NATIONAL ADVISORY CENTRE ON CAREERS FOR WOMEN. Training and Employment for the Arts Graduate: An Introduction. 1973. 3rd edn 1980.

5972 PRENTICE (WILLIAM R.). The Employment of Graduates. New Malden. 1976.

5973 BROWN (ALAN) and BOURNER (TOM). 'Initial Employment Experience of Sociology Graduates in the United Kingdom, 1976–1978'. Sociol. Rev. 29 (1981), 339–60.

5974 GOTHARD (W. P.). 'The Brightest and the Best': A Study of Graduates and their Occupational Choices in the 1970s. Duffield. 1982.

5975 MABEY (CHRISTOPHER). Graduates in Industry: A Survey of Changing Graduate Attitudes. Aldershot. 1986.

5976 U.K. MINISTRY OF PENSIONS AND NATIONAL INSURANCE. Report on an Enquiry into the Incidence of Incapacity for Work 1964/65. 2 Pts. 1964, 1965.

5977 U.K. OFFICE OF HEALTH ECONOMICS. Work Lost through Sickness. 1965.

5978 YOUNG (AGNES FREDA). Social Services in British Industry. Lond./N.Y. 1968.

5979 STEIN (BRUNO). Work and Welfare in Britain and the U.S.A. 1976.

5980 SOCIAL SCIENCE RESEARCH COUNCIL. The Social Responsibilities of Business: A Report. 1976.

5981 BRIDGE (BRIAN). Employment Service for the Disadvantaged: A Report to the Personal Social Services Council on Current Needs and Provision, Including a Study of Supported Employment. 1977.

(b) Profits and Productivity; Industrial Democracy

5982 WORSWICK (GEORGE DAVID NORMAN) and TIPPING (DAVID GUY). Profits in the British Economy, 1909–1938. 1967.

5983 HART (PETER EDWARD). Studies in Profit, Business Saving and Investment in the United Kingdom, 1920–1962. 2 vols. 1965, 1968.

5984 APPLEBY (ROBERT). Profitability and Productivity in the United Kingdom, 1954–1964. 1967.

5985 PAISH (F. W.). 'Profits and Dividends: The Next Five Years'. *Banker* 112 (1962), 499–505.

5986 PARKER (JOHN EDGAR SAYCE). 'Profitability and Growth of British Industrial Firms'. *Manch. Sch. Econ. Soc. Studs* 32 (1964), 113–30.

5987 BLACKETT (PATRICK MAYNARD STEWART). Technology, Industry and Economic Growth. S/hampton. 1966.

5988 PANIC (M.). 'The Profitability of British Manufacturing Industry'. *Lloyds Bank Rev.* 109 (July 1973), 17–30.

5989 HAYS (SAMUEL). 'Productivity Bargaining before the War and Now'. *Accountant* 6 (1947), 358–9.

5990 ROSTAS (LAZLO). Comparative Productivity in British and American Industry. Camb. 1948.

5991 U.K. NATIONAL BOARD FOR PRICES AND INCOMES. Productivity Agreements in the Bus Industry. 1967.

5992 INDUSTRIAL SOCIETY. Productivity Agreements: The Process of Negotiating and Communicating. 1967.

5993 STETTNER (NORA). Productivity Bargaining and Industrial Change. Oxf. 1969.

5994 NORTH (DICK TREVOR BROOKE) *and* BUCKINGHAM (GRAEME L.). Productivity Agreements and Wage Systems. 1969.

5995 HUTTON (GRAHAM). Whatever Happened to Productivity? 1980.

5996 WOOD (EDWARD GEOFFREY). Productivity for Profit. Sheffield. 1984.

5997 WALLACE (WILLIAM). Profit-Sharing and Co-partnership. 1920. [Ministry of Labour Report.].

5998 NATIONAL INSTITUTE OF INDUSTRIAL PSYCHOLOGY. Joint Consultation in British Industry: A Report of an Inquiry. Lond./N.Y. 1952.

5999 DITZ (G. W.). Joint Consultation in the British Coal Industry. Ann Arbor, Mich. 1955.

6000 COPEMAN (GEORGE H.). The Challenge of Employee Shareholding: How to Close the Gap between Capital and Labour. 1958.

6001 BANKS (JOSEPH AMBROSE). Industrial Participation: Theory and Practice: A Case Study. L/pool. 1963.

6002 FLANDERS (ALLAN DAVID) *et al.* Experiment in Industrial Democracy: A Study of the John Lewis Partnership. 1968.

6003 COATES (KEN). Can the Workers Run Industry? 1968.

6004 —— *Ed.* The New Worker Co-operatives, with contributions by Tony Benn and others. Nottingham. 1977.

6005 —— Beyond Wage Slavery. Nottingham. 1977.

6006 —— The Right to Useful Work: Planning by the People. Nottingham. 1978.

6007 COATES (KEN) *and* TOPHAM (ANTHONY) *eds.* Industrial Democracy in Great Britain: A Book of Readings and Witnesses for Workers' Control. 1968.

6008 —— The New Unionism: The Case for Workers' Control. 1972.

6009 HENDERSON (JOAN). Effective Joint Consultation. 1965.

6010 LABOUR PARTY. Industrial Democracy: A Discussion Document. 1967.

6011 BRITISH INSTITUTE OF MANAGEMENT. (Occasional Papers). Industrial Democracy: Some Implications for Management: An Exploratory Study. 1968.

6012 WABE (J. STUART). 'Labour Force Participation Rates in the London Metropolitan Region'. *J. Roy. Stat. Soc.* [ser. A], 132 (1969), 245–64.

6013 PATEMAN (CAROLE). Participation and Democratic Theory. Camb. 1970.

6014 TABB (JAI YANAI) *and* GOLDFARB (AMIRA). Workers' Participation in Management: Expectations and Experience. Oxf. 1970.

6015 BUTTERISS (MARGARET). Job Enrichment and Employee Participation: A Study. 1971.

6016 APPLEYARD (JOHN ROLLO) *and* COATES (J. A. C.). Workers' Participation in Western Europe. 1971.

6017 CLARKE (RONALD OLIVER), FATCHETT (DEREK JOHN), *and* ROTHWELL (S. G.). Workers' Participation and Industrial Democracy. 1969.

6018 CLARKE (RONALD OLIVER), FATCHETT (DEREK JOHN), *and* ROBERTS (BENJAMIN CHARLES). Workers' Participation in Management in Britain. 1972.

6019 BOW GROUP. Employee Participation in British Companies: An Examination of all Levels of Employee Participation in Industry. 1973.

6020 GUEST (DAVID E.) *and* FATCHETT (DEREK JOHN). Worker Participation. 1974.

6021 POOLE (MICHAEL). Workers' Participation in Industry. Lond./Boston. 1975. Rev. edn 1978.

6022 —— Towards a New Industrial Democracy: Workers' Participation in Industry. 1986. [Based on the above book].

6023 BULLOCK (ALAN) *Baron.* Report of the Committee of Inquiry on Industrial Democracy. 1977. [HMSO].

6024 DENTON (GEOFFREY). Beyond Bullock: The Economic Implications of Worker Participation in Control and Ownership of Industry. 1977.

6025 HEBDEN (JOHN E.) *and* SHAW (GRAHAM H.). Pathways to Participation. 1977.

6026 SMITH (CYRIL). Industrial Participation. 1977.

6027 INDUSTRIAL PARTICIPATION ASSOCIATION. Industrial Democracy—An Acceptable Solution: A Submission to the Government. 1977.

6028 PACE (DAVID E.) *and* HUNTER (JOHN). Direct Participation in Action: The New Bureaucracy. Farnborough. 1978.

6029 ELLIOTT (JOHN). Conflict or Co-operation? The Growth of Industrial Democracy. 1978. 2nd edn 1984.

6030 WILSON (WILLIAM). Towards Industrial Democracy in Britain. Manch. 1978.

6031 PACE (DAVID). Direct Participation in Action: The New Bureaucracy. Farnborough. 1978.

6032 REILLY (PETER A.). Employee Financial Participation. 1978.

6033 —— Participation, Democracy and Control: Forms of Employee Involvement. 1979.

6034 BELL (D. WALLACE). Industrial Participation. 1979.

6035 MORSE (GEOFFREY) *and* WILLIAMS (DAVID). Profit-Sharing: Legal Aspects of Employee Share Schemes. 1979.

6036 SANDISON (FRANCIS G.). Profit Sharing and other Share Acquisition Schemes. Croydon. 1979.

6037 PETTMAN (BARRY OLIVER). Industrial Democracy: A Selected Bibliography. Bradford. 1979.

6038 HELLER (FRANK). What do the British Want from Participation and Industrial Democracy? 1979.

6039 GREENHILL (RICHARD). Employee Remuneration and Profit Sharing. Camb. 1980.

6040 CRESSEY (PETER) *et al.* Employee Participation in Scottish Industry and Commerce: A Survey of Attitudes and Practices. Glasg. 1980.

6041 —— Participation in the Electronics Sector: The Comco Case Study. Glasg. 1984.

6042 DOWLING (M. J.) *et al.* Employee Participation in Manufacturing Industry: Themes and Implications. Manch. 1981.

6043 —— Employee Participation in Manufacturing Industry: Trade Union Attitudes. Manch. 1981.

6044 —— Employee Participation in Manufacturing Industry: Management Attitudes. Manch. 1981.

6045 EDWARDS (ROBERT). Industrial Democracy. Birm. 1982.

6046 CLUTTERBUCK (RICHARD). Industrial Conflict and Democracy: The Last Chance. 1984.

6047 MacINNES (JOHN). Joint Consultation: A Critical Review of Post-War Experience in Britain. Glasg. 1984.

6048 MARCHINGTON (MICK) *and* ARMSTRONG (ROGER). Joint Consultation Revisited. Glasg. 1985.

6049 WEITZMAN (MARTIN L.). The Case for Profit-Sharing. 1986.

6050 BLANCHFLOWER (D. G.) *and* OSWALD (ANDREW J.). Profit-Sharing: Can it Work? 1986.

6051 STEEL (DAVID). Sharing Profits: The Partnership Path to Economic Recovery. Hebden Bridge. 1986.

6052 BRADLEY (KEITH) *and* ESTRIN (SAUL). Profit Sharing in the Retail Sector: The Relative Performance of the John Lewis Partnership. 1987.

6. NATIONALIZED INDUSTRIES, PUBLIC OWNERSHIP, PLANNING

6053 MACKAY (D. I.). 'Discussion of Public Works Programmes, 1917–1935: Some Remarks on the Labour Movement's Contribution'. *Inl. Rev. Soc. Hist.* xi (1966), 8–17.

6054 LOWE (RODNEY). 'The Erosion of State Intervention in Britain, 1917–1924'. *Econ. Hist. Rev.* xxxi (1978), 270–86.

6055 MOND (ALFRED MORITZ) *Baron Melchett*. Liberalism and Modern Industrial Problems: Trade, Currency, Industry and Unemployment. 1925.

6056 —— Industry and Politics. 1927.

6057 ROBSON (WILLIAM ALEXANDER) *ed.* Public Enterprise: Developments in Social Ownership and Control in Great Britain. 1937.

6058 O'BRIEN (TERENCE HENRY). British Experiments in Public Ownership and Control. 1937.

6059 WALLACE (WILLIAM). Enterprise First: The Relationship of the State to Industry, with Particular Reference to Private Enterprise. 1946.

6060 CHESTER (*Sir* DANIEL NORMAN). The Nationalised Industries: An Analysis of the Statutory Provisions. 1948. 2nd rev. edn 1951.

6061 —— The Nationalisation of British Industry. 1945–1951. 1975.

6062 CRAWFURD (HORACE EVELYN) *and* SHORT (ERNEST HENRY). That's the Way the Money Goes: A Study of the Relations Between British Industry and Taxation. 1951.

6063 NEUMAN (ANDREW MARTIN DE). The Economic Aspects of Nationalisation in Great Britain. Camb. 1952.

6064 FLORENCE (PHILIP SARGANT). Industry and the State. 1957.

6065 WALKER (GILBERT). Economic Planning by Programme and Control in Great Britain. 1957.

6066 KELF-COHEN (REUBEN). Nationalisation in Britain: The End of a Dogma. 1958.

6067 RAMANADHAM (VENKATA VEMURI). Public Enterprise in Britain: Thoughts on Recent Experiences. 1959.

6068 WEINER (HERBERT ELIAS). British Labor and Public Ownership. 1960.

6069 ROBSON (WILLIAM ALEXANDER). Nationalised Industry and Public Ownership. 1960. 2nd edn 1962.

6070 COMYNS-CARR (*Sir* ARTHUR). 'Our Economy and Our Nationalised Industries'. *Contemp. Rev.* ccii (1962), 132–4.

6071 GROVE (JACK WILLIAM). Government and Industry in Great Britain. 1962.

6072 LOW (T.). 'The Select Committee on Nationalised Industries'. *Public Admin.* xl (1962), 1–15.

6073 MERRETT (A. J.) *and* SYKES (A.). 'Financial Control of State Industry'. *Banker* cii (1962), 156–64, 227–33.

6074 ROBSON (WILLIAM ALEXANDER). 'The Political Control of Nationalised Industries in Britain'. In Studies in Political Science. J. S. Bains, *ed.* N.Y. 1961. 291–317.

6075 SHEPHERD (WILLIAM G.). 'British Nationalized Industry: Performance and Policy'. *Yale Econ. Essays* iv (1964), 183–224.

6076 —— Economic Performance under Public Ownership: British Fuel and Power. 1965.

6077 BARRY (E. ELDON). Nationalisation in British Politics: The Historical Background. 1965.

6078 TIVEY (LEONARD JAMES). Nationalization in British Industry. 1966.

6079 POLANYI (GEORGE). Planning in Britain: The Experience of the 1960s. 1967.

6080 JEWKES (JOHN). The New Ordeal by Planning: The Experience of the Forties and the Sixties. 1968.

6081 KELF-COHEN (REUBEN). Twenty Years of Nationalisation: The British Experience. 1969.

6082 SKUSE (ALLEN). Government Intervention and Industrial Policy. 1970.

6083 MOONMAN (ERIC). Reluctant Partnership: A Critical Study of the Relationship Between Government and Industry. 1971.

6084 PRYKE (RICHARD). Public Enterprise in Practice: The British Experience of Nationalization Over Two Decades. 1971.

6085 KELF-COHEN (REUBEN). British Nationalisation, 1945–1973. 1973.

6086 TIVEY (LEONARD JAMES) *ed.* The Nationalized Industries Since 1960: A Book of Readings. 1973.

6087 REED (PETER WILLIAM). The Economics of Public Enterprise. 1973.

6088 HANNAH (LESLIE). The Rise of the Corporate Economy. 1976.

6089 SHANKS (MICHAEL). What Future for 'Neddy'? *Pol. Q.* xxxiii (1962), 348–59.

6090 BROWN (H. P.). 'The National Economic Development Organisation'. *Public Admin.* xli (1963), 239–46.

6091 MITCHELL (JOAN). 'The Functions of the National Economic Development Council'. *Pol. Q.* xxxiv (1963), 354–65.

6092 ROBSON (WILLIAM ALEXANDER) *ed.* Problems of Nationalised Industry. 1952.

6093 THORNHILL (WILLIAM). The Nationalized Industries: An Introduction. 1968.

6094 SHANKS (MICHAEL) *ed.* The Lessons of Public Enterprise. 1963.

6095 TOMLINSON (JIM). The Unequal Struggle? British Socialism and the Capitalist Enterprise. 1982.

6096 TURVEY (RALPH). Economic Analysis and Public Enterprise. 1971.

6097 CHESTER (*Sir* DANIEL NORMAN). 'The Treasury, 1962'. *Public Admin.* xl (1962), 419–26.

6098 —— 'The British Treasury and Economic Planning'. *Indian J. Pub. Admin.* x (1964), 159–71.

6099 BRITTAN (SAMUEL). The Treasury under the Tories, 1951–1964. 1964.

6100 WINCH (DONALD NORMAN). Economics and Policy: A Historical Study. 1969.

6101 HARRISON (ANTHONY J.). The Framework of Economic Activity: The International Economy and the Rise of the State in the Twentieth Century. 1967.

6102 HURWITZ (SAMUEL JUSTIN). State Intervention in Great Britain: A Study of Economic Control and Social Response, 1914–1919. N.Y. 1949.

6103 TAWNEY (RICHARD HENRY). 'The Abolition of Economic Controls, 1918–1921'. *Econ. Hist. Rev.* xiii (1943), 1–30.

6104 LAUTERBACH (ALBERT T.). 'Economic Demobilisation in Great Britain After the First World War'. *Pol. Sci. Q.* lvii (1942), 376–93.

6105 CLINE (PETER K.). 'Re-opening the Case of the Lloyd George Coalition and the Post-War Economic Transition 1918–1919'. *J. Brit. Studs* x (1970), 162–75.

6106 JOHNSON (PAUL BARTON). Land Fit for Heroes: The Planning of British Reconstruction, 1916–1919. 1968.

6107 BAKER (CHARLES WHITING). Government Control and Operation of Industry in Great Britain and the United States During the World War. N.Y. 1921.

6108 DENNISON (STANLEY R.). 'The British Restrictive Trade Practices Act of 1956'. *J. Law Econ.* ii (1959), 64–83.

6109 COTTIS (S. P.). 'Restrictive Practices Legislation: An Industrial View'. *J. Com. Mkt. Studs* i (1962), 29–39.

6110 ALDCROFT (DEREK HOWARD). 'The Effectiveness of Direct Controls in the British Economy, 1946–1950'. *Scot. J. Pol. Econ.* x (1963), 226–42.

6111 YOUNG (STEPHEN) *and* LOWE (ALEXANDRA VIVIEN). Intervention in the Mixed Economy: The Evolution of British Industrial Policy, 1964–1972. 1974.

6112 BROADWAY (FRANK EDWARD). State Intervention in British Industry, 1964–1968. 1969.

6113 SHONFIELD (ANDREW A.). 'The Public Sector Versus Private Sector in Britain'. *Mod. Age* vi (1961), 43–55.

6114 —— 'Economic Planning in Great Britain: Pretense and Reality'. *Mod. Age.* vii (1963), 143–56.

6115 PAISH (FRANK WALTER). 'The Management of the British Economy'. *Lloyds Bank Rev.* lxxvi (1965), 1–17.

6116 HARRIS (NIGEL). Competition and the Corporate Society: British Conservatives, the State and Industry, 1945–1964. 1972.

6117 CLARKE (*Sir* RICHARD WILLIAM BARNES). The Management of the Public Sector of the National Economy. 1964.

6118 STEWART (M.). 'Planning and Persuasion in a Mixed Economy'. *Pol. Q.* xxxv (1964), 148–60.

6119 DEVONS (ELY). Planning in Practice. Camb. 1950.

6120 BRITTAIN (*Sir* HERBERT). 'The Treasury's Responsibilities'. *Public Admin.* xxxix (1961), 1–14.

6121 SCAMMEL (W. M.). 'The Treasury and Stagnation'. *Bankers' Mag.* cxciii (1962), 295–301.

6122 BRITTAN (SAMUEL). Steering the Economy. 1969.

6123 BAILEY (RICHARD). Managing the British Economy: A Guide to Economic Planning in Britain since 1962. 1969.

6124 CHESTER (T. E.). 'The Nationalised Industries in Great Britain'. *Trans. of the 3rd World Congress of Sociology* ii (1956), 49–55.

6125 ARMITAGE (SUSAN). The Politics of Decontrol of Industry: Britain and the United States. 1969.

6126 BLANK (STEPHEN). Industry and Government in Britain: The Federation of British Industries in Politics, 1945–1965. 1973.

6127 CHARLES (RODGER). Development of Industrial Relations in Britain, 1911–1939. 1973.

6128 CLARKE (RONALD OLIVER) *et al.* Workers' Participation in Management in Britain. 1973.

6129 HAWKINS (KEVIN). British Industrial Relations, 1945–1975. 1976.

6130 HICKS (URSULA KATHLEEN) *Lady.* The Finance of British Government, 1920–1936. 1938.

6131 LEWIS (BEN WILLIAM). British Planning and Nationalization. N.Y. 1952.

6132 ROGOW (ARNOLD A.). The Labour Government and British Industry, 1945–1951. 1956.

6133 SHARP (IAN GORDON). Industrial Conciliation and Arbitration in Great Britain. 1950.

6134 SMITH (JOHN H.) *and* CHESTER (T. E.). 'The Distribution of Power in Nationalised Industries'. *Brit. J. Sociol.* ii (1951), 275–93.

6135 SMITH (T. A.). The Politics of the Corporate Economy. 1979.

6136 SKIDELSKY (ROBERT) *ed.* The End of the Keynesian Era: Essays on the Disintegration of the Keynesian Political Economy. 1977.

6137 BUDD (A.). The Politics of Economic Planning. 1978.

6138 LUCAS (ARTHUR FLETCHER). Industrial Reconstruction and the Control of Competition: The British Experiments. 1937.

6139 HOWSON (SUSAN) *and* WINCH (DONALD). The Economic Advisory Council, 1930–1939. 1977.

6140 ALDCROFT (DEREK HOWARD). 'The Development of the Managed Economy Before 1939'. *J. Contemp. Hist.* iv (1969), 117–37.

6141 —— 'The Diminishing Scope of Government Trading, 1946–1954'. *Yorks. Bull. Econ. Soc. Res.* xiv (1962), 23–36.

6142 TREBILCOCK (R. C.). 'A "Special Relationship"—Government, Rearmament and the Cordite Firms'. *Econ. Hist. Rev.* 2nd Ser. xix (1966), 364–79.

6143 TIVEY (LEONARD JAMES). 'The Political Consequences of Economic Planning'. *Law Q. Rev.* xx (1967), 297–314.

6144 PRITCHARD (E. P.). 'The Responsibility of the Nationalized Industries to Parliament'. *Parl. Affs* xvii (1964), 439–49.

6145 DAVIES (ERNEST ALBERT JOHN). National Enterprise: The Development of the Public Corporation. 1946.

6146 ROSE (R.) *et al.* Public Employment in Western Nations. Camb. 1985.

6147 GREENAWAY (D.) *and* SHAW (G. K.) *eds.* Public Choice, Public Finance and Public Policy. Oxf. 1985.

6148 PEACOCK (A.) *and* FORTE (F.) *eds.* Public Expenditure and Government Growth. Oxf. 1985.

7. PARTICULAR INDUSTRIES

6149 BRITISH ALUMINIUM COMPANY. The History of the British Aluminium Company Limited, 1894–1955. 1955.

6150 DRUMMOND (G. GORDON). The Invergordon Smelter: A Case Study in Management. 1977.

6151 STORCK (JOHN) *and* TEAGUE (W. D.). Flour for Man's Bread: A History of Milling. Minneapolis. 1952.

6152 BALL (MIA). The Worshipful Company of Brewers: A Short History. 1977.

6153 HAWKINS (K. H.) *and* PASS (C. L.). The Brewing Industry: A Study in Industrial Organisation and Public Policy. 1979.

6154 MARK (JOHN). 'Change in the Brewing Industry in the Twentieth Century'. In Diet and Health in Modern Britain. Derek S. Oddy and Derek J. Miller, *eds.* 1985. 81–101.

6155 WHITBREAD AND COMPANY. Whitbread's Brewery: Incorporating the Brewer's Art. 1951.

6156 HAWKINS (K. H.). A History of Bass Charrington. Oxf. 1978.

6157 SLATER (NORMAN). A Brewer's Tale: The Story of Greenall Whitley & Co. Ltd. through Two Centuries. 1980.

6158 WILSON (R. G.). Greene King: A Business and a Family History. 1983.

6159 BROWN (JOHN FALCON). Guinness and Hops. 1980.

6160 ELLIS (AYTOUN). Yorkshire Magnet: The Story of John Smith's Tadcaster Brewery. Tadcaster. 1953.

6161 JANES (HENRY HURFORD). Albion Brewery, 1808–1958: The Story of Mann, Crossman and Paulin Ltd. 1959.

6162 —— The Red Barrel: A History of Watney Mann. 1963.

6163 GOURVISH (TERRY R.). Norfolk Beers from English Barley: A History of Steward and Patteson, 1793–1963. Norwich. 1987.

6164 READER (W. J.). Grand Metropolitan: A History, 1962–1987. Oxf. 1988.

6165 TRUMAN HANBURY BUXTON AND COMPANY. Trumans the Brewers (1666–1966): The Story of Truman, Hanbury, Buxton & Co. Ltd, London and Buxton. 1966.

6166 DONNACHIE (IAN L.). A History of the Brewing Industry in Scotland. Edin. 1979.

6167 CORRAN (H. S.). A History of Brewing. Newton Abbot. 1975.

6168 WATTS (H. D.). 'Market Areas and Spatial Rationalization: The British Brewing Industry after 1945'. *Tijd. Econ. Soc. Geog.* lxviii (1977), 224–40.

6169 VAIZEY (JOHN ERNEST) *Baron*. The Brewing Industry, 1886–1951. 1960.

6170 BRIGGS (ASA) *Baron*. Wine for Sale: Victoria Wine and the Liquor Trade, 1860–1984. 1985.

6171 BRUCE (GEORGE). A Wine Day's Work: The London House of Deinhard, 1835–1985. 1985.

6172 WILKINSON (L. P.). Bulmers of Hereford: A Century of Cider-Making. Newton Abbot. 1987.

6173 POWELL (CHRISTOPHER G.). An Economic History of the British Building Industry, 1815–1979. 1980.

6174 RICHARDSON (HARRY WARD) *and* ALDCROFT (DEREK HOWARD). Building in the British Economy Between the Wars. 1968.

6175 A REPORT on Craft Skills in the Building Industry: by a Working Group, Chairman Donald Ensom. 1976.

6176 LEA (*Sir* FREDERICK MEASHAM). Science and Building: A History of the Building Research Station. 1971.

6177 KINGSFORD (P. W.). Builders and Building Workers. 1973.

6178 HILLEBRANDT (PATRICIA M.). Analysis of the British Construction Industry. 1984.

6179 LEWIS (J. PARRY). Building Cycles and Britain's Growth. 1965.

6180 EARLE (J. B. E.). A Century of Road Materials: The History of the Roadstone Division of Tarmac Ltd. Oxf. 1971.

6181 —— Blacktop: A History of the British Flexible Roads Industry. Oxf. 1974.

6182 JENKINS (ALAN). Built on Teamwork. 1980. [A history of Taylor Woodrow.].

6183 WHITE (VALERIE). Wimpey: The First Hundred Years. 1980.

6184 —— Balfour Beattie, 1909–1984. 1984.

6185 COAD (RAY). Laing: The Biography of Sir John W. Laing, CBE, 1879–1978. 1979.

6186 SMYTH (H.). Property Companies and the Construction Industry in Britain. Camb. 1985.

6187 GOODMAN (W. L.). The History of Woodworking Tools. 1964.

6188 —— Woodwork. Oxf. 1962.

6189 ALFORD (B. W. E.) *and* BARKER (T. C.). A History of the Carpenters Company. 1968.

6190 ROSENBERG (NATHAN). 'Government Economic Controls in the British Building Industry, 1945–1949'. *Can. J. Econ. Pol. Sci.* xxiv (1958), 345–54.

6191 —— Economic Planning in the British Building Industry, 1945–1949. Philadelphia, Pa. 1960.

6192 BRAAE (G. P.). 'Investment and Housing in the United Kingdom, 1924–1938'. *Manch. Sch. Econ. Soc. Studs* xxxii (1964), 15–24.

6193 COLCLOUGH (JOHN RICHARD). The Construction Industry of Great Britain. 1965.

6194 BOWLEY (MARIAN). The British Building Industry: Four Studies in Response and Resistance to Change. Camb. 1966.

6195 HARLOW (P. A.). A Decade of Quantity Surveying: Review of the Literature, 1970–1979. 1980.

6196 TOPLISS (C. E.). Demolition. 1982.

6197 KNOWLES (C. C.) *and* PITT (P. H.). A History of Building Regulation in London, 1189–1972, With An Account of the District Surveyors' Association. 1972.

6198 BRACE (HAROLD W.). History of Seed-Crushing in Great Britain. 1960.

6199 BITTING (A. W.). Appetizing or the Art of Canning: Its History and Development. San Francisco. 1937?

6200 CAMPBELL (WILLIAM ALEC). A Century of Chemistry on Tyneside, 1868–1968. Newcastle upon Tyne. 1968.

6201 —— The Chemical Industry. 1971.

6202 GILL (C.), MORRIS (R.), *and* EATON (J.). Industrial Relations in the Chemical Industry. 1978.

6203 BROAD (D. W.). Centennial History of the Liverpool Section, Society of Chemical Industry, 1881–1981. 1981.

6204 CAIRNS (A. C. H.). The Chemical Industry: Its Position in the U.K. Economy. Warrington. 1967.

6205 GOODMAN (J.). The Mond Legacy: A Family Saga. 1982.

6206 READER (WILLIAM JOSEPH). Imperial Chemical Industries: A History. Vol. 1, The Forerunners 1870–1926, 1970; Vol. 2, The First Quarter-Century 1926–1952. 1975.

6207 PETTIGREW (A. M.). The Awakening Giant: Continuity and Change in Imperial Chemical Industries. Oxf. 1985.

6208 HUNTER (LAURENCE C.) *et al.* Labour Problems of Technological Change. 1970.

6209 WILLIAMS (TREVOR ILLTYD). The Chemical Industry: Past and Present. 1953.

6210 SHERWOOD TAYLOR (FRANK). A History of Industrial Chemistry. 1957.

6211 SCHROETER (J.). Discovery of Chlorine and the Beginning of the Chlorine Industry: The Story of Chlorine Down to the Present. *Ciba Rev.* No. 139, 12 (1960).

6212 SCIENCE MUSEUM, LONDON. Books on the Chemical and Allied Industries: A Subject Catalogue of Books in the Science Library. *Comp.* L. R. Day.

6213 ASSOCIATION OF BRITISH CHEMICAL MANUFACTURERS. Report on the Chemical Industry. 1949.

6214 MIALL (STEPHEN). History of the British Chemical Industry. 1931.

6215 MORGAN (*Sir* GILBERT THOMAS) *and* PRATT (DAVID DOIG). British Chemistry Industry: Its Rise and Development. 1938.

6216 BLUM (FRED H.). Work and Community: The Scott Barder Commonwealth and the Quest for a New Social Order. 1968.

6217 HOE (SUSANNA). The Man Who Gave His Company Away: A Biography of Ernest Barder, Founder of the Scott Barder Commonwealth. 1978.

6218 READER (WILLIAM JOSEPH). Fifty Years of Unilever, 1930–1980. 1980.

6219 WILSON (CHARLES HENRY). Unilever 1945–1965: Challenge and Response in the Industrial Revolution. 1968.

6220 FIELDHOUSE (DAVID K.). Unilever Overseas: The Anatomy of a Multinational, 1895–1965. 1978.

6221 COPPING (GEORGE). A Fascinating Story: The History of OCCA, 1918–1968. 1968. [The Oil and Colour Chemists' Association.].

6222 TRAVIS (N. J.) *and* COCKS (E. J.). The Tincal Trail: A History of Borax. 1984.

6223 MORGAN (*Sir* GILBERT THOMAS). Achievements of the British Chemical Industry in the Last 25 Years. 1939.

6224 KAUFFMANN (MORRIS). The First Century of Plastics: Celluloid and its Sequel. 1963.

6225 —— The History of P.V.C.: The Chemical and Industrial Production of Polyvinylchloride. 1969.

6226 HARDIE (DAVID WILLIAM FERGUSON) *and* PRATT (JAMES DAVIDSON). A History of the Modern British Chemical Industry. 1966.

6227 GRANT (WYN), PATERSON (WILLIAM), *and* WHITSON (COLIN). Government and the Chemical Industry: A Comparative Study of Britain and West Germany. Oxf. 1989.

6228 HARDIE (DAVID WILLIAM FERGUSON). 'The Chemical Industry of Merseyside'. *Proc. Chem. Soc.* lii–lvii (1961).

6229 —— A History of the Chemical Industry in Widnes. Liverpool. 1950.

6230 MUSSON (A. E.). Enterprise in Soap and Chemicals: Joseph Crosfield and Sons Ltd., 1815–1965. Manch. 1965.

6231 HABER (LUDWIG FRITZ). The Chemical Industry, 1900–1930: International Growth and Technological Change. Oxf. 1971.

6232 WARREN (KENNETH). Chemical Foundations: The Alkali Industry in Britain to 1926. Oxf. 1980.

6233 WELSH COLLEGE OF ADVANCED TECHNOLOGY. Occupational Survey of Manufacturing Industries in Wales. Report 2: Survey of Chemical and Allied Industries in Wales as at April 1962. Cardiff. 1964.

6234 DINGLEY (CYRIL S.). The Story of B.I.P. 1894–1962. Oldbury. 1963. [British Industrial Plastics.].

6235 LAZELL (H. G.). From Pills to Penicillin: The Beecham Story. 1975.

6236 DONY (JOHN GEORGE). A History of the Straw Hat Industry. Luton. 1942.

6237 WILLS (JOHN). Wilkinson and Riddell Limited, 1851–1951. Birm. 1951.

6238 REDMAYNE (RONALD) *ed.* Ideals in Industry: Being the Story of Montague Burton Ltd., 1900–1950. Leeds. 1950.

6239 TUTE (WARREN). The Grey Top Hat: The Story of Moss Bros. of Covent Garden. 1961.

6240 RYOTT (DAVID). John Barran's of Leeds, 1851–1951. Leeds. 1951.

6241 THOMAS (JOAN). A History of the Leeds Clothing Industry. *Yorks. Bull. Econ. Soc. Res.* Occ. Paper No. 1. (1955).

6242 HALL (PETER GEOFFREY). 'The Location of the Clothing Trades in London, 1861–1951'. *Trans. Inst. Brit. Geog.* xxvii (1960), 155–78.

6243 GULVIN (G.). The Scottish Hosiery and Knitwear Industry 1680–1980. Edin. 1984.

6244 BENSON (JOHN), NEVILLE (ROBERT G.), *and* THOMPSON (CHARLES H.). Bibliography of the British Coal Industry. Oxf. 1981.

6245 KIRBY (MAURICE W.). The British Coalmining Industry, 1870–1946. 1977.

6246 SUPPLE (BARRY). The History of the British Coal Industry. Vol. 4: 1913–1946: The Political Economy of Decline. Oxf. 1987.

6247 ASHWORTH (WILLIAM). The History of the British Coal Industry. Vol. 5: 1946–1982. Oxf. 1986.

6248 LEE (W. A.). Thirty Years in Coal, 1917–1947: A Review of the Coal Mining Industry Under Private Enterprise. 1954.

6249 MANNERS (G.). Coal in Britain. 1981.

6250 MINISTRY OF FUEL AND POWER. Coal Mines Acts, 1887–1949: The Abstract and the General Regulations. 1951.

6251 JEVONS (HERBERT STANLEY). The British Coal Trade. 1915.

6252 HODGES (FRANK). The Nationalisation of the Coal Industry. 1920.

6253 REDMAYNE (*Sir* RICHARD AUGUSTINE STUDDERT). British Coal-Mining Industry during the War. Oxf. 1923.

6254 COLE (GEORGE DOUGLAS HOWARD). Labour in the Coal Mining Industry, 1914–1921. Oxf. 1923.

6255 SHURICK (ADAM THOMAS). The Coal Industry. 1924.

6256 WILLIAMS (D. JEFFREY). Capitalist Combination in the Coal Industry. 1924.

6257 LUBIN (ISADOR) *and* EVERETT (HELEN). The British Coal Dilemma. 1927.

6258 COMYNS-CARR (*Sir* ARTHUR STRETTELL) *and* FORDHAM (WILFRED GURNEY). Recent Mining Legislation, Including the Coal Mines Act, 1930. 1931.

6259 SMART (REGINALD CECIL). The Economics of the Coal Industry. 1930.

6260 NEUMAN (ANDREW MARTIN). Economic Organization of the British Coal Industry. 1934.

6261 WATKINS (HAROLD MOSTYN). Coal and Men: An Economic and Social Study of the British and American Coalfields. 1934.

6262 PLATT (JOHN). British Coal: A Review of the Industry, its Organisation and Management. 1968.

6263 KRIEGER (JOEL). Undermining Capitalism: State Ownership and the Dialectic of Control in the British Coal Industry. Princeton, NJ. 1983.

6264 SINCLAIR (JOHN). Coal-Mining: Organisation and Management. 1957. 2nd edn 1967.

6265 TOMLINSON (ROLFE C.). OR Comes of Age: A Review of the Work of the Operational Research Branch of the National Coal Board 1948–1969. 1971.

6266 SCHUMACHER (E. F.). 'Some Aspects of Coal Board Policy, 1947–1967'. *Econ. Studs.* 4 (1969), 3–29.

6267 DICKIE (JOHN PURCELL). The Coal Problem—A Survey: 1910–1936. 1936.

6268 BUXTON (NEIL K.). 'Entrepreneurial Efficiency in the British Coal Industry between the Wars'. *Econ. Hist. Rev.* xxiii (1970), 476–97.

6269 —— 'Entrepreneurial Efficiency in the British Coal Industry between the Wars: Reconfirmed'. *Econ. Hist. Rev.* xxv (1972), 658–64.

6270 —— 'Avoiding the Pitfalls: Entrepreneurial Efficiency in the Coal Industry Again'. *Econ. Hist. Rev.* xxv (1972), 669–73.

6271 —— The Economic Development of the British Coal Industry: From Industrial Revolution to the Present Day. 1978.

6272 KIRBY (MAURICE W.). 'The Control of Competition in the British Coal-Mining Industry in the Thirties'. *Econ. Hist. Rev.* xxvi (1973), 273–84.

6273 —— 'Entrepreneurial Efficiency in the British Coal Industry between the Wars: A Comment'. *Econ. Hist. Rev.* xxv (1972), 655–7.

6274 —— 'Government Intervention in Industrial Organisation: Coal Mining in the Nineteen Thirties'. *Bus. Hist.* xv (1973), 160–73.

6275 JOHNSON (W.). 'Entrepreneurial Efficiency in the British Coal Industry between the Wars: A Second Comment'. *Econ. Hist. Rev.* xxv (1972), 665–8.

6276 COURT (WILLIAM HENRY BASSANO). 'Problems of the British Coal Industry between the Wars'. *Econ. Hist. Rev.* xv (1945), 1–24.

6277 CHALONER (W. H.). 'The British Miners and the Coal Industry between the Wars'. *History Today* xiv (1964), 418–26.

6278 POLITICAL AND ECONOMIC PLANNING: INDUSTRIES GROUP. Report on the British Coal Industry. 1936.

6279 ROBERTS (PETER GEOFFREY). The Coal Act, 1938. 1938.

6280 JONES (JOHN HARRY) *et al.* The Coal Mining Industry. 1939.

6281 HEINEMANN (MARGOT). Britain's Coal: A Study of the Mining Crisis. 1944.

6282 GRENFELL (DAVID RHYS). Coal. 1947.

6283 CARVEL (JOHN LEES). Fifty Years of Machine Mining Progress, 1899–1949. Motherwell. 1949.

6284 DITZ (GERHARD WILLIAM). British Coal Nationalized. New Haven, Conn. 1951.

6285 LEE (WILLIAM ALEXANDER). Thirty Years in Coal, 1917–1947: A Review of the Coalmining Industry Under Private Enterprise. 1954.

6286 SIMONS (R. B.). 'The British Coal Industry—A Failure of Private Enterprise'. *Historian* xvi (1953), 3–17.

6287 KLEIN (DARYL). Coal Cavalcade. 1950.

6288 MACKENZIE (*Sir* C.). The House of Coalport, 1750–1950. 1951.

6289 COURT (WILLIAM HENRY BASSANO). Coal. 1951.

6290 TOWNSHEND-ROSE (HENRY). The British Coal Industry. 1951.

6291 HAYNES (WILLIAM WARREN). Nationalization in Practice: The British Coal Industry. 1953.

6292 BALDWIN (GEORGE BENEDICT). Beyond Nationalisation: The Labour Problems of British Coal. 1956.

6293 BOWER (*Sir* WILLIAM GUY NOTT) *and* WALKERDINE (REGINALD HUBERT) *eds.* National Coal Board: The First Ten Years. 1956.

6294 NATIONAL COAL BOARD. British Coal: The Rebirth of an Industry, Published on the Completion of the First Ten Years of Public Ownership. 1957.

6295 SINCLAIR (JOHN). Coal Mining Economics. 1957.

6296 YOUNG (A.), LONGDON (H. A.), *and* METCALF (B. L.). 'Post-War Developments in the Coal Mining Industry'. *Proc. Inst. Civil Engineers* 6 (1957), 662–708.

6297 THOMAS (T. M.). 'Recent Trends and Developments in the British Coal Mining Industry'. *Econ. Geog.* 34 (1958), 19–41.

6298 BROWN (MICHAEL BARRATT). 'Determinants of the Structure and Level of Wages in the Coal Mining Industry Since 1956'. *Bull. Oxf. Univ. Inst. Econ. Stats* xxix (1967), 139–70.

6299 CLAYTON (CHERYL ANNE). The Coal Industry and the Iron and Steel Industry of Great Britain Under Nationalization, 1945–1958: An Analytical Study. Sweet Briar, Va. 1965.

6300 FORSTER (CHARLES IAN KENNERLEY). The Changing Balance of Fuel and Power. Manch. 1959.

6301 FARRELL (M. J.) *and* JOLLY (A. R.). 'The Structure of the British Coal Mining Industry in 1955'. *J. Indust. Econ.* xi (1963), 199–216.

6302 HASSON (J. A.). 'Development in the British Coal Industry'. *Land Econ.* iv (1962), 351–62.

6303 BRENNER (M. F.). 'Public Pricing of Natural Resources'. *J. Farm. Econ.* xliv (1962), 35–49.

6304 BAILEY (R.). 'Coal in Britain and Europe: Problems and Solutions'. *Inl Affs* xlii (1966), 432–43.

6305 SIMPSON (EDWARD SMETHURST). Coal and the Power Industries in Postwar Britain. 1966.

6306 PLATT (JOHN). British Coal: A Review of the Industry, its Organisation and Management. 1968.

6307 FORSYTH (DAVID JAMES CAMERON). Studies in the British Coal Industry. Oxf. 1969.

6308 HARDY (L. J.). 'Absenteeism and Attendance in the British Coal-Mining Industry: An Examination of Post-War Trends'. *Brit. J. Indust. Rel.* 6 (1968), 27–**50**.

6309 JENCKS (C. E.). 'Social Status of Coal Miners in Britain Since Nationalisation'. *Amer. J. Econ. Sociol.* 26 (1967), 301–12.

6310 GRIFFIN (ALAN RAMSAY). Coal Mining. 1971.

6311 ROBENS (ALFRED) *Baron*. Ten Year Stint. 1972.

6312 JACKSON (MICHAEL). The Price of Coal. 1974.

6313 BLUNDEN (JOHN RUSSELL). The Mineral Resources of Britain: A Study in Exploitation and Planning. 1975.

6314 BERKOVITCH (ISRAEL). Coal on the Switchback: The Coal Industry Since Nationalisation. 1977.

6315 GRIFFIN (ALAN RAMSAY). The British Coalmining Industry: Retrospect and Prospect. Buxton. 1977.

6316 JONES (P. N.). Colliery Settlement in the South Wales Coalfield, 1850–1926. Hull. 1969.

6317 DUCKHAM (HELEN) *and* DUCKHAM (BARON FREDERICK). Great Pit Disasters: Great Britain to the Present Day. Newton Abbot. 1973.

6318 SELLWOOD (A.) *and* SELLWOOD (M.). Black Avalanche. 1960.

6319 GRIFFIN (ALAN RAMSAY). The Nottinghamshire Miners. 1962.

6320 FRANCIS (HYWEL) *and* SMITH (DAVID). The Fed: A History of the South Wales Miners in the Twentieth Century. 1980.

6321 DUCKHAM (BARON FREDERICK). A History of the Scottish Coal Industry. Newton Abbot. 1970.

6322 McKECHNIE (JAMES) *and* MacGREGOR (MURRAY). A Short History of the Scottish Coal Mining Industry. 1958.

6323 DOWN (C. G.) *and* WARRINGTON (A. J.). The History of the Somerset Coalfield. Newton Abbot. 1971.

6324 MINISTRY OF FUEL AND POWER. South Wales Coalfields: Regional Survey Report. 1946.

6325 METCALFE (JOHN ERNEST). British Mining Fields. 1969.

6326 LERRY (GEORGE G.). The Collieries of Denbighshire: Past and Present. Wrexham. 1946.

6327 JOHNSON (RAYMOND). Mines and Quarries in Britain. 1971.

6328 GRIFFIN (ALAN RAMSAY). Mining in the East Midlands, 1550–1947. 1971.

6329 MOYES (A.). 'Post-War Changes in Coalmining in the West Midlands'. *Geog.* 59 (1974), 111–20.

6330 BENSON (JOHN) *and* NEVILLE (ROBERT G.). Studies in the Yorkshire Coal Industry. 1976.

6331 NATIONAL COAL BOARD: SCOTTISH DIVISION. A Short History of the Scottish Coal-Mining Industry. Edin. 1958.

6332 NORTH (FREDERICK JOHN). Coal and the Coalfields in Wales. Cardiff. 1931.

6333 TOWN (STEPHEN W.). After the Mines: Changing Employment Opportunities in a South Wales Valley. Card. 1978.

6334 SEWEL (JOHN). Colliery Closure and Social Change: A Study of a South Wales Mining Valley. Card. 1975.

6335 FRANCIS (HYWEL) *and* REES (GARETH). 'No Surrender in the Valleys: The 1984–1985 Miners' Strike in South Wales'. *Llafur* 5/2 (1988), 41–71.

6336 BENSON (JOHN) *and* NEVILLE (ROBERT G.). 'A Bibliography of the Coal Industry in Wales'. *Llafur* 2/4 (1979), 78–91.

6337 FRANCIS (HYWEL) *and* HOWELLS (KIM). 'The Politics of Coal in South Wales, 1945–48'. *Llafur* 3 (1981), 74–85.

6338 GARSIDE (W. R.). 'The North-Eastern Coalfield and the Export Trade, 1919–1939'. *Durham Univ. J.* lxii (1969), 1–16.

6339 GOFFEE (R. E.). 'The Butty System and the Kent Coalfield'. *Bull. Soc. Stud. Lab. Hist.* xxxiv (1977), 41–**55**.

6340 GRIFFITHS (I. L.). 'The New Welsh Anthracite Industry'. *Geog.* xlvii (1962), 388–400.

6341 PEACE (K.). 'Some Changes in the Coalmining Industry of Southern Yorkshire, 1951–1971'. *Geog.* lviii (1973), 340–2.

6342 HEPWORTH (R.) *et al*. 'The Effects of Technological Change in the Yorkshire Coalfield, 1960–1965'. *Econ. Studs* 4 (1969), 221–37.

6343 Report of the Tribunal Appointed to Enquire into the Disaster at Aberfan on October 21st, 1966. Cmnd 553. Parliamentary Papers, xxi (1966–7).

6344 McNEIL (JOHN). 'The Fife Coal Industry, 1947–1967: A Study of Changing Trends and their Implications'. *Scot. Geog. Mag.* lxxxix (1973), 81–94, 163–79.

6345 DIACK (WILLIAM). 'The Scottish Mines'. *Scot. Rev.* (Spr. 1920), 16–42.

6346 EZRA (*Sir* DEREK JOSEPH). Coal and Energy: The Need to Exploit the World's Most Abundant Fossil Fuel. 1978.

6347 WILSON (*Sir* HAROLD). New Deal for Coal. 1943. United Kingdom Mineral Statistics. 1973+.

6348 STANIER (PETER). 'The Granite Quarrying Industry in Devon and Cornwall: Part Two 1910–1985'. *Indust. Arch. Rev.* 9 (1986), 7–23.

6349 HUDSON (KENNETH). The History of English China Clays: Fifty Years of Pioneering and Growth. Newton Abbot. 1969.

6350 JOHNSON (PAUL). Gold Fields: A Centenary Portrait. 1987.

6351 HARVEY (CHARLES E.). The Rio Tinto Company: An Economic History of a Leading International Mining Concern, 1873–1951. 1981.

6352 ROWE (DAVID). Lead Manufacturing in Britain: A History. 1983.

6353 MINCHINTON (WALTER E.). The British Tinplate Industry. 1957.

6354 LEWIS (WILLIAM JOHN). Lead Mining in Wales. Cardiff. 1967.

6355 STOKES (ARTHUR HENRY). Lead and Lead Mining in Derbyshire. Sheffield. 1964.

6356 BARTON (D. B.). A Historical Survey of the Mines and Mineral Railways of East Cornwall and West Devon. Truro. 1964.

6357 —— Essays in Cornish Mining History. Vol. 1. Truro. 1968.

6358 HAMILTON JENKIN (A. K.). Mines and Miners of Cornwall. 10 pts. Truro. 1961–5.

6359 RAISTRICK (ARTHUR) *and* JENNINGS (BERNARD). A History of Lead Mining in the Pennines. 1965.

6360 HARTLEY (*Sir* HAROLD). The Contribution of Engineering to the British Economy. 1965.

6361 ROBENS (ALFRED) *Baron*. Engineering and Economic Progress. 1965.

6362 MUIR (C. A.). The History of Baker Perkins. Camb. 1968.

6363 DONNELLY (DESMOND). David Brown's: The Story of a Family Business, 1860–1960. 1960.

6364 ROLT (L. T. C.). The Dowty Story. 1962.

6365 DAVIS (RALPH). Twenty One and a Half Bishop Lane: A History of J. H. Fenner & Co. Ltd., 1861–1961. 1961.

6366 JONES (EDGAR). A History of G.K.N. Vol. 1: Innovation and Enterprise, 1759–1918. 1987.

6367 WILSON (*Sir* CHARLES HENRY). Men and Machines: A History of D. Napier & Son Engineers Ltd., 1808–1958. 1958.

6368 SCOTT (J. D.). Vickers: A History. 1963.

6369 EVANS (HAROLD). Vickers: Against the Odds, 1956–1977. 1978.

6370 NEWMAN (BERNARD). One Hundred Years of Good Company (The Story of Ruston and Hornby), Published on the Occasion of the Ruston Centenary, 1857–1957. Lincoln. 1957.

6371 JANES (HURFORD). Sons of the Forge: The Story of B. & S. Massey Limited, 1861–1961. 1961.

6372 RANSOMES, SIMS & JEFFERIES. Wherever the Sun Shines: 175 Years of Progress by Ransomes. Ipswich. 1965.

6373 GRACE (D. R.) *and* PHILLIPS (D. C.). Ransomes of Ipswich: A History of the Firm and Guide to its Records. Ipswich. 1975.

6374 READER (WILLIAM JOSEPH). The Weir Group: A Centenary History, with a Final Chapter by Viscount Weir, Research by Elizabeth McClure Thomson. 1971.

6375 HUME (JOHN R.) *and* MOSS (MICHAEL S.). Beardmore: The History of a Scottish Industrial Giant. 1979.

6376 BRACEGIRDLE (BRIAN). Engineering in Chester: 200 Years of Progress. Chester. 1966.

6377 BENNETT (STUART). A History of Control Engineering 1800–1930. Stevenage. 1979.

6378 CHURCHILL MACHINE TOOL COMPANY. The Story of the Churchill Machine Tool Co. Ltd.: A History of Precision Grinding: Golden Jubilee, 1906–1956. Broadheath. 1956.

6379 COE (W. E.). The Engineering Industry of the North of Ireland. Newton Abbot. 1969.

6380 HAYS (SAMUEL FRIMMER). The Engineering Industries. 1972.

6381 LINDLEY (ROBERT M.). The Demand for Apprentice Recruits by the Engineering Industry. 1951–1971. Coventry. 1974.

6382 HART (R. A.) *and* MACKAY (D. I.). 'Engineering Earnings in Britain, 1914–1968'. *J. Roy. Stat. Soc.* Ser. A, cxxxviii (1975), 32–50.

6383 CENTRAL ELECTRICITY AUTHORITY. Report and Statement of Accounts. 1947/9–1957.

6384 CENTRAL ELECTRICITY GENERATING BOARD. Annual Report and Accounts. 1958/9+.

6385 ELECTRICITY COUNCIL. Electricity Supply in Great Britain: A Chronology from the Beginnings of the Industry. 1987.

6386 HANNAH (LESLIE). Electricity Before Nationalisation: A Study in the Development of the Electricity Supply Industry in Britain to 1948. 1979.

6387 —— Engineers, Managers and Politicians: The First Fifteen Years of Nationalised Electricity Supply in Britain. 1982.

6388 FERNS (J. L.). 'Electricity Supply and Industrial Archaeology'. *Indust. Arch. Rev.* 17 (1982), 10–18.

6389 BURROUGHES (H. R.). 'Political and Administrative Problems of Development Planning: The Case of the C.E.G.B. and the Supergrid'. *Public Admin* 49 (1974), 131–48.

6390 CARLTON (J.) *and* HEALD (D.). 'Restructuring the Electricity Supply Industry'. *Public Admin Bull.* 29 (1979), 43–60.

6391 ROBINSON (SIDNEY). Seebord: The First Twenty Five Years. 1974.

6392 GORDON (B.). One Hundred Years of Electricity, 1881–1981. 1981.

6393 HINTON (CHRISTOPHER) *Baron*. Heavy Current Electricity in the United Kingdom: History and Development. Oxf. 1979.

6394 KIEVE (JEFFREY). The Electric Telegraph: A Social and Economic History. Newton Abbot. 1973.

6395 EDWARDS (HAROLD RAYMOND). Competition and Monopoly in the British Soap Industry. Oxf. 1962.

6396 BIBBY (JOHN BENJAMIN) *and* BIBBY (C. L.). A Miller's Tale: A History of J. Bibby and Sons Ltd., Liverpool. L/pool. 1978.

6397 GAS COUNCIL. Annual Report and Accounts. 1948/50–1972/3.

6398 CHANDLER (DEAN) *and* LACEY (A. DOUGLAS). The Rise of the Gas Industry in Britain. 1949.

6399 ELTON (ARTHUR). 'The Rise of the Gas Industry in England and France'. *Arch. Hist. Sci.* v (1952), 320–32.

6400 WILLIAMS (TREVOR I.). A History of the British Gas Industry. Oxf. 1981.

6401 PEEBLES (MALCOLM W. H.). Evolution of the Gas Industry. 1980.

6402 FALKUS (MALCOLM). Always under Pressure: A History of North Thames Gas since 1949. 1988.

6403 HUTCHISON (KENNETH). 'Searching for Gas and Oil under the North Sea'. *J. Roy. Soc. Arts* cxiii (1965), 883–903.

6404 —— High Speed Gas: An Autobiography. 1987.

6405 REID (GRAHAM LIVINGSTONE) *et al.* The Nationalised Fuel Industries. 1973.

6406 ASHMORE (OWEN). The Development of Power in Britain. 1967.

6407 CALLOW (CLIVE). Power from the Sea: The Search for North Sea Oil and Gas. 1973.

6408 DIMOCK (MARSHALL EDWARD). British Public Utilities and National Development. 1933.

6409 EVERARD (STIRLING). History of the Gas, Light and Coke Company, 1812–1949. 1949.

6410 HALDANE (THOMAS GRAEME NELSON). The Socialization of the Electrical Supply Industry. 1934.

6411 CHANTLER (P.). The British Gas Industry: An Economic Study. Manch. 1938.

6412 POLITICAL AND ECONOMIC PLANNING. Report on the Gas Industry in Great Britain. 1939.

6413 HARTE (NEGLEY BOYD) *and* PONTING (KENNETH GEORGE) *eds*. Textile History and Economic History: Essays in Honour of Miss Julia de Lacy Mann. Manch. 1973.

6414 TANN (JENNIFER). Gloucestershire Woollen Mills. Newton Abbot. 1967.

6415 GRIERSON (FLORA). The Story of Woodstock Gloves. Woodstock. 1962.

6416 JENKINS (J. GERAINT) *ed.* The Wool Textile Industry in Great Britain. 1972.

6417 BREARLEY (ALAN). The Woollen Industry. 1965.

6418 RAINNIE (GEORGE FRASER) *ed.* The Woollen and Worsted Industry: An Economic Analysis. Oxf. 1965.

6419 COLEMAN (DONALD CUTHBERT). Courtaulds: An Economic and Social History. 3 vols Oxf. 1969–1980.

6420 KNIGHT (ARTHUR). Private Enterprise and Public Intervention: The Courtaulds Experience. 1974.

6421 BEER (EDWIN JOHN). The Beginning of Rayon. Paignton. 1962.

6422 HARD (ARNOLD HENRY). The Story of Rayon and other Synthetic Textiles. 1939.

6423 —— Berisfords, the Ribbon People: Jubilee, 1858–1958. Congleton. 1958.

6424 CROZIER (MARY). An Old Silk Family, 1745–1945: The Brocklehursts of Brocklehurst—Whiston Amalgamated Limited. 1947.

6425 HAFFORD (E. R.) *and* HAFFORD (J. H. P.). Employer and Employed: Ford Ayrton & Co. Ltd.: Silk Spinners with Worker Participation, Leeds and Low Bentham, 1870–1970. 1974.

6426 HAGUE (DOUGLAS C.). The Economics of Man-Made Fibres. 1957.

6427 WOODHOUSE (THOMAS) *and* BRAND (ALEXANDER). A Century's Progress in Jute Manufacture, 1833–1933. Dundee. 1934.

6428 PONTING (KENNETH GEORGE). The Wool Trade: Past and Present. Manch./Lond. 1961.

6429 BARTLETT (J. NEVILLE). Carpeting the Millions: The Growth of Britain's Carpet Industry. Edin. 1978.

6430 PHILPOTT (B. P.). 'Fluctuations in Wool Prices, 1870–1953'. *Yorks. Bull. Econ. Soc. Res.* vii (1955), 1–28.

6431 SIGSWORTH (ERIC MILTON). Black Dyke Mills: A History with Introductory Chapters on the Development of the Worsted Industry in the Nineteenth Century. L/pool. 1958.

6432 BLYTH (H. E.). Through the Eye of a Needle: The Story of the English Sewing Cotton Company. Manch. 1947.

6433 LONGWORTH (J. E.). Oldham Master Cotton Spinners Association Ltd.: Centenary Year. Oldham. 1966.

6434 WELLS (FREDERICK ARTHUR). The British Hosiery Trade: Its History and Organisation. 1935.

6435 —— Hollins and Viyella: A Study in Business History. Newton Abbot. 1968.

6436 —— The British Hosiery and Knitwear Industry: Its History and Organisation. Newton Abbot. 1972.

6437 WARNER (FRANK). The Silk Industry of the United Kingdom: Its Origin and Development. 1921.

6438 STEWART (MARGARET) *and* HUNTER (LESLIE). The Needle is Threaded: 'The History of an Industry'. 1964.

6439 PASOLD (ERIC W.). Ladybird, Ladybird: A Story of Private Enterprise. Manch. 1977.

6440 PLUMMER (ALFRED) *and* EARLY (RICHARD ELLIOTT). The Blanket Makers, 1669–1969: A History of Charles Early and Marriott (Witney) Ltd. 1969.

6441 PLUMMER (ALFRED). The London Weavers' Company, 1600–1970. 1972.

6442 MORTON (JOCELYN). Three Generations in a Family Textile Firm. 1971.

6443 HOWITT (FREDERICK OLIVER). Bibliography of the Technical Literature on Silk. 1947.

6444 FENSHAM (PETER JAMES) *and* HOOPER (DOUGLAS). The Dynamics of a Changing Technology: A Case Study in Textile Manufacturing. 1964.

6445 TIPPETT (LEONARD HENRY CALEB). A Portrait of the Lancashire Textile Industry. 1969.

6446 DUPREE (MARGUERITE) ed. Lancashire and Whitehall: The Diary of Sir Raymond Streat. 2 vols. Manch. 1987.

6447 SINGLETON (JOHN). 'Lancashire's Last Stand: Declining Employment in the British Cotton Industry, 1950–1970'. *Econ. Hist. Rev.* 2nd ser. 39 (1985), 92–107.

6448 LAZONICK (WILLIAM). 'Industrial Organisation and Technological Change: The Decline of the British Cotton Industry'. *Bus. Hist. Rev.* 57 (1983), 195–236.

6449 MILES (CAROLINE). Lancashire Textiles: A Case Study of Industrial Change. Camb. 1968.

6450 SANDBERG (LARS G.). Lancashire in Decline: A Study in Entrepreneurship, Technology and International Trade. Columbus, Ohio. 1974.

6451 RODGERS (H. B.). 'The Changing Geography of the Lancashire Cotton Industry'. *Econ. Geog.* xxxviii (1962), 299–314.

6452 RIVETT (PATRICK). Integrated Planning in the Textile Industry. Manch. 1963.

6453 ROBSON (ROBERT). The Cotton Industry in Britain. 1957.

6454 ORMEROD (A.). 'The Prospects of the British Cotton Industry'. *Yorks. Bull. Econ. Soc. Res.* xv (1963), 3–24.

6455 KEITH (K.). 'Finance and Structural Changes in British Industry with Particular Reference to Cotton'. *Moorgate and Wall St.* (Autumn 1963), 25–37.

6456 BLACKBURN (J. A.). 'The British Cotton Industry in the Common Market'. *Three Banks Rev.* lvi (1962), 3–23.

6457 PIGOTT (STANLEY C.). Hollins: A Study of Industry, 1784–1949. Nottingham. 1949.

6458 BRISCOE (LYNDEN). The Textile and Clothing Industries of the United Kingdom. Manch. 1971.

6459 TIGNOR (ROBERT L.). Egyptian Textiles and British Capital, 1930–1956. Cairo. 1989.

6460 MILES (CAROLINE). 'Protection of the British Textile Industry'. In Public Assistance to Industry: Protection and Subsidies in Britain and Germany. W. M. Carden and Gerhard Fels, eds. 1976. 184–214.

6461 CRAGG (ROWLAND). Anvil and Loom: A Survey of British Industries. 1926.

6462 CRANKSHAW (WILLIAM P.). Report on a Survey of the Welsh Textile Industry. Cardiff. 1927.

6463 FRASER (GRACE LOVAT). Textiles by Britain. 1948.

6464 LOCKWOOD (ERNEST). Colne Valley Folk: The Romance and Enterprise of a Textile Stronghold. 1936.

6465 MARS (PENELOPE A.). 'An Economic Comparison of the Textile Industries in the U.K. and the U.S.A.'. *J. Indust. Econ.* ix (1961), 181–94.

6466 EWING (A. F.). 'Monopoly and Competition in the British Textile Industry'. *J. World Trade Law* iv (1970), 770–90.

6467 GLOVER (FREDERICK J.). 'Government Contracting, Competition and Growth in the Heavy Woollen Industry'. *Econ. Hist. Rev.* xvi (1964), 478–98.

6468 TURNER (W. H. K.). 'Wool Textile Manufacture in Scotland: An Historical Geography'. *Scot. Geog. Mag.* lxxx (1964), 81–9.

6469 BELLAMY (JOYCE M.). 'Cotton Manufacture in Kingston-upon-Hull'. *Business History* iv (1961–62), 91–108.

6470 JEWKES (JOHN). 'The Localisation of the Cotton Industry'. *Econ. Hist. Suppl. of Econ. J.* ii (1930–3), 91–106.

6471 MELLOR (JOHN HANSON) *et al.* A Century of British Fabrics, 1850–1950. Leigh-on-Sea. 1955.

6472 VARLEY (D. E.). A History of the Midland Counties Lace Manufacturers Association, 1915–1958. 1959.

6473 TURNBULL (JOHN GEOFFREY) ed. A History of the Calico Printing Industry of Great Britain. Altrincham. 1951.

6474 HIGGINS (SYDNEY HERBERT). A History of Bleaching. 1924.

6475 DAWE (DONOVAN ARTHUR). Skilbecks: Drysalters, 1650–1950. 1950.

6476 ROWE (FREDERICK MAURICE). Two Lectures on the Development of the Chemistry of Commercial Synthetic Dyes, 1856–1938. 1938.

6477 RICHARDSON (HARRY WARD). 'The Development of the British Dyestuffs Industry Before 1939'. *Scot. J. Pol. Econ.* ix (1962), 110–29.

6478 LAWRIE (LESLIE GORDON). A Bibliography of Dyeing and Textile Printing: Comprising a List of Books from the Sixteenth Century to the Present Time. 1946.

6479 PRITCHARD (JACK). View from a Long Chair. 1984.

6480 KIRKHAM (PAT), MACE (RODNEY), *and* PORTER (JULIA). Furnishing the World: The East London Furniture Trade, 1830–1980. 1987.

6481 OLIVER (JOHN LEONARD). The Development and Structure of the Furniture Industry. 1966.

6482 BARKER (THEODORE CARDWELL). Pilkington Brothers and the Glass Industry. 1960.

6483 —— The Glassmakers Pilkington: The Rise of An International Company, 1826–1976. 1977.

6484 DOUGLAS (R. W.) *and* FRANK (SUSAN). A History of Glassmaking. Henley on Thames. 1972.

6485 DUNCAN (GEORGE SANG). Bibliography of Glass, From the Earliest Records to 1940. 1960.

6486 BRITISH PHONOGRAPH COMMITTEE. The British Record: The Gramaphone Record Industry's Services to the Nation from 1898 to the Present Day. 1959.

6487 LITTLE (BRYAN). David Jones 1862–1962: A Hundred Years of Wholesale Grocery. 1962.

6488 DUNPHY (ELAINE M.). Oil: A Bibliography. Aberd. 1977.

6489 JONES (GEOFFREY). The State and the Emergence of the British Oil Industry. 1981.

6490 MacKAY (D. I.) *and* MacKAY (G. A.). The Political Economy of North Sea Oil. 1975.

6491 NORENG (OYSTEIN). The Oil Industry and Government Strategy in the North Sea. 1980.

6492 CHAPMAN (KEITH). North Sea Oil and Gas: A Geographical Perspective. Newton Abbot. 1976.

6493 HAMILTON (ADRIAN). North Sea Impact: Offshore and the British Economy. 1978.

6494 HANN (DANNY). Government and North Sea Oil. 1986.

6495 ROWLAND (CHRIS) *and* HANN (DANNY). The Economics of North Sea Oil Taxation. 1987.

6496 MATRO (ROBERT) *et al.* The Market for North Sea Crude Oil. Oxf. 1986.

6497 JOHNSON (LUKE). Shell Expro: A History. 1989.

6498 JONES (C. GARETH). 'The British Government and the Oil Companies, 1912–1924: The Search for an Oil Policy'. *Hist. J.* xx (1977), 647–72.

6499 PAYTON-SMITH (DEREK JOSEPH). Oil. 1971.

6500 WATTS (D. G.). 'Milford Haven and its Oil Industry'. *Geog.* lv (1970), 64–72.

6501 WATT (DONALD CAMERON). 'Britain and North Sea Oil: Policies Past and Present'. *Pol. Q.* xlvii (1976), 377–97.

6502 JENKIN (MICHAEL). British Industry and the North Sea: State Intervention in a Developing Industrial Sector. 1981.

6503 WOODLIFFE (J. C.). 'State Participation in the Development of United Kingdom Offshore Petroleum Resources'. *Public Law* (1977), 249–71.

6504 ODELL (PETER R.) *and* ROSING (KENNETH E.). Optimal Development of the North Sea's Oil Fields: A Study in Divergent Government and Company Interests and their Reconciliation. 1976.

6505 LOWE (J. F.). 'Competition in the U.K. Retail Petrol Market, 1960–1973'. *J. Indust. Econ.* xxiv (1976), 203–20.

6506 JOHNSON (H.). 'Oil, Imperial Policy and the Trinidad Disturbances'. *J. Imp. Cwealth Hist.* iv (1976), 29–54.

6507 FRANKEL (P. H.). 'Oil Supplies During the Suez Crisis: On Meeting a Political Emergency'. *J. Indust. Econ.* 6 (2) (1958), 85–100.

6508 DIXON (DONALD F.). 'The Development of the Solus System of Petrol Distribution in the United Kingdom, 1950–1960'. *Economics* xlii (1962), 40–52.

6509 —— 'Petrol Distribution in the United Kingdom, 1900–1950'. *Bus. Hist.* vi (1963), 1–19.

6510 MITCHELL (W. H.) *and* SAWYER (L. A.). Sailing Ship to Supertanker: The Hundred Year Story of British Esso and its Ships. 1988.

6511 DALTON (C. P.). 'The Place of the Petroleum Industry in the U.K.'. *Trans. Manch. Stat. Soc.* (1956–7), 24–5.

6512 ATKINSON (FRED) *and* HALL (STEPHEN). Oil and the British Economy. 1983.

6513 WOODWARD (GUY H.) *and* WOODWARD (GRACE STEELE). The Secret of Sherwood Forest: Oil Production in England During World War II. Norman, Okla. 1973.

6514 STRANGES (ANTHONY N.). 'From Birmingham to Billingham: High Pressure Coal Hydrogenisation in Great Britain'. *Technology & Culture* 26 (1985), 726–57.

6515 SELL (GEORGE) *ed.* The Post-War Expansion of the United Kingdom Petroleum Industry. 1953.

6516 HAYMAN (ROY). The Institute of Fuel: The First 50 Years. 1977.

6517 HEPPLE (PETER) *ed.* The Joint Problems of the Oil and Water Industries. 1967.

6518 —— The Petroleum Industry in the United Kingdom. 1966.

6519 LONGHURST (HENRY CARPENTER). Adventure in Oil: The Story of British Petroleum. 1959.

6520 FERRIER (R. W.). The History of the British Petroleum Company. Vol. 1. The Developing Years, 1901–1932. Camb. 1982.

6521 ANDERSON (J. R. L.). East of Suez: A Study of Britain's Greatest Trading Enterprise. 1969.

6522 WILLIAMS (M. E. W.). 'Choices in Oil Refining: The Case of BP, 1900–1960'. *Bus. Hist.* 26 (1984), 307–28.

6523 ATTERBURY (PAUL) *and* MACKENZIE (JULIA). A Golden Adventure: The First Fifty Years of Ultramar. 1985.

6524 CAIRNS (WILLIAM J.) *and* ROGERS (PATRICK). Onshore Impacts of Offshore Oil. Lond./NJ. 1981.

6525 PETERS (ALAN FREDERICK) *ed.* Impact of Offshore Oil Operations. Barking. 1974.

6526 GASKIN (MAXWELL) *and* MACKAY (D. I.). The Economic Impact of North Sea Oil on Scotland. 1978.

6527 MOORE (ROBERT). The Social Impact of Oil: The Case of Peterhead. 1982.

6528 NICOLSON (JAMES R.). Shetland and Oil. 1975.

6529 HUTCHESON (A.) *and* HOGG (A.). Scotland and Oil. Edin. 1975.

6530 LEWIS (T. M.) *and* MCNICOLL (I. H.). North Sea Oil and Scotland's Economic Prospects. 1978.

6531 MARSHALL (ELIZABETH). Shetland's Oil Era. Lerwick. 1977.

6532 PARSLER (RON) *and* SHAPIRO (DAN) *eds.* The Social Impact of Oil in Scotland. Farnborough. 1980.

6533 BUTTON (JOHN) *ed.* The Shetland Way of Oil. Sandwick. 1976.

6534 ROSIE (GEORGE). The Ludwig Initiative: A Cautionary Tale of North Sea Oil. Edin. 1978.

6535 ALFORD (BERNARD WILLIAM ERNEST). W. D. & H. O. Wills and the Development of the U.K. Tobacco Industry, 1786–1965. 1973.

6536 CORINA (MAURICE). Trust in Tobacco: The Anglo-American Struggle for Power. 1975.

6537 TAYLOR (PETER). Smoke Ring: The Politics of Tobacco. 1984.

6538 DUNHILL (MARY). Our Family Business. 1979.

6539 POPHAM (G. T.). 'Government and Smoking: Policy Making and Pressure Groups'. *Policy & Politics* 9 (1981), 331–43.

6540 HADLEY (GUY). Citizens and Founders: A History of the Worshipful Company of Founders, London 1365–1975. 1976.

6541 COSTER (IAN). The Sharpest Edge in the World: The Story of the Rise of a Great Industry. 1948.

6542 BREARLEY (HARRY). Steel-Makers. 1933.

6543 PAYNE (PETER L.). 'Rationality and Personality: A Study of Mergers in the Scottish Iron and Steel Industry, 1916–1936'. *Bus. Hist.* xix (1977), 162–91.

6544 BUXTON (NEIL K.). 'Efficiency and Organization in Scotland's Iron and Steel Industry during the Interwar Period'. *Econ. Hist. Rev.* 2nd ser. xxix (1976), 107–24.

6545 BURNHAM (THOMAS HALL) *and* HOSKINS (GEORGE OWEN). Iron and Steel in Britain, 1870–1930. 1943.

6546 BROWN (G.) *and* ORFORD (A. L.). The Iron and Steel Industry. 1940.

6547 OWEN (HENRY). Steel: The Facts about Monopoly and Nationalization. 1946.

6548 BURN (DUNCAN LYALL). 'Recent Trends in the History of the Steel Industry'. *Econ. Hist. Rev.* xvii (1947), 95–102.

6549 FIENBURGH (WILFRED) *and* EVELY (RICHARD). Steel is Power: The Case for Nationalisation. 1948.

6550 CARR (JAMES CECIL) *and* TAPLIN (WALTER). History of the British Steel Industry. Camb., Mass. 1962.

6551 GUMBEL (WALTER) *and* POTTER (KENNETH). The Iron and Steel Act, 1949, With General Introduction and Annotations. 1951.

6552 ROEPKE (HOWARD GEORGE). Movements of the British Iron and Steel Industry, 1720–1951. Ill. 1956.

6553 MCEACHERN (DOUG). A Class Against itself: Power and the Nationalisation of the British Steel Industry. Camb. 1980.

6554 MILLER (THOMAS RONALD). The Monkland Tradition. Lond./Edin. 1958.

6555 SARA (E. T.). 'Progress in the United Kingdom Iron and Steel Industry'. *Yorks. Bull. Econ. Soc. Res.* ix (1958), 31–53.

6556 MANNERS (GERALD). The Tinplate and Steel Industries in South West Wales'. *Geog.* xliv (1959). 38–40.

6557 SHONE (*Sir* ROBERT). 'The Economic Development of the United Kingdom Steel Industry'. *J. Roy. Soc. Arts* cix (1961), 595–612.

6558 PRATTEN (C. F.). 'Steel to Nationalise or not to Nationalise'. *Moorgate and Wall St.* (spring 1965), 67–84.

6559 SWANN (D.) *and* MCLACHLAN (D. L.). 'Steel Pricing in A Recession: An Analysis of United Kingdom and ECSC Experience'. *Scot. J. Pol. Econ.* xii (1965), 81–104.

6560 BURN (DUNCAN LYALL). The Economic History of Steelmaking, 1867–1939: A Study in Competition. Camb. 1940.

6561 MCCLOSKEY (D. N.). 'Productivity Change in British Pig Iron, 1870–1939'. *Q. J. Econ.* lxxxii (1968), 281–96.

6562 EDWARDS (KENNETH HARRY REESE). Chronology of the Development of the Iron and Steel Industries of Teesside. Wigan. 1955.

6563 GIBSON (I. F.). The Economic History of the Scottish Iron and Steel Industry. 1955.

6564 DEARDEN (JOHN). Iron and Steel Today. 1956.

6565 BURN (DUNCAN LYALL). The Steel Industry, 1939–1959. Camb. 1961.

6566 TRIPP (BASIL HOWARD). The Joint Iron Council, 1945–1966. 1966.

6567 MURRAY (DAVID). Steel Curtain: A Biography of the British Iron and Steel Industry. 1959.

6568 ERICKSON (CHARLOTTE). British Industrialists: Steel and Hosiery, 1850–1950. Camb. 1959.

6569 ALLEN (JAMES ALBERT). Studies in Innovation in the Steel and Chemical Industries. Manch. 1967.

6570 HOWE (M.). 'The Iron and Steel Board and Steel Pricing, 1953–1967'. Scot. J. Pol. Econ. xv (1968), 43–67.

6571 BRITISH IRON AND STEEL FEDERATION. The Welsh Steel Industry. 1963.

6572 MUSGRAVE (PETER WILLIAM). Technical Change, The Labour Force and Education: A Study of the British and German Iron and Steel Industries, 1860–1964. Oxf. 1967.

6573 KEELING (BERNARD SYDNEY) and WRIGHT (ANTHONY EDGAR GARTSIDE). The Development of the Modern British Steel Industry. 1964.

6574 THORNES (VERNON) and KITTS (ALBERT). Steel: The Commanding Height of the Economy. 1964.

6575 ROSS (GEORGE WILLIAM). The Nationalization of Steel: One Step Forward, Two Steps Back? 1965.

6576 BURK (KATHLEEN). The First Privatisation: The Politicians, the City and the Denationalisation of Steel. 1988.

6577 OVENDEN (KEITH). The Politics of Steel. 1978.

6578 RICHARDSON (JEREMY JOHN). Steel Policy in the U.K.: The Politics of Industrial Decline. Glas. 1983.

6579 ABROMEIT (HEIDRUN). British Steel: An Industry Between the State and Private Sector. Leamington Spa. 1986.

6580 AYLES (JONATHAN). 'Privatisation of the British Steel Corporation'. Fiscal Studs. 9 (1988), 1–25.

6581 YOUNG (STEPHEN). 'The Implementation of Britain's National Steel Strategy at the Local Level'. In The Politics of Steel: Western Europe and the Steel Industry in the Crisis Years, 1974–1984. Y. MENY and V. WRIGHT eds. Berlin. 1986. 369–415.

6582 RUSSELL (B. S.). 'The British Steel Industry'. J. World Trade Law ii (1968), 243–84.

6583 WARREN (KENNETH). 'Recent Changes in the Geographical Location of the British Steel Industry'. Geog. J. cxxxv (1969), 343–64.

6584 GALE (WALTER KEITH VERNON). Iron and Steel. 1969.

6585 WARREN (KENNETH). The British Iron and Steel Sheet Industry Since 1840: An Economic Geography. 1970.

6586 ROWLEY (CHARLES KERSHAW). Steel and Public Policy. 1971.

6587 KEANE (J. P.). 'The British Steel Industry and the European Coal and Steel Community'. Three Banks Rev. civ (1974), 58–72.

6588 PITFIELD (DAVID E.). 'Regional Economic Policy and the Long-run: Innovation and Location in the Iron and Steel Industry'. Bus. Hist. 16 (1974), 160–74.

6589 VAIZEY (JOHN) Baron. The History of British Steel. 1974.

6590 HEAL (DAVID WALTER). The Steel Industry in Post-War Britain. Newton Abbot. 1974.

6591 GALE (WALTER KEITH VERNON). The British Iron and Steel Industry: A Technical History. Newton Abbot. 1967.

6592 —— The Black Country Iron Industry: A Technical History. 1966.

6593 U.K. 1964. MINISTRY OF LABOUR. Report of the Joint Advisory Committee for the Cutlery and Silverware Trades in Sheffield and District. 1964.

6594 ROLT (LIONEL THOMAS CASWELL). Waterloo Ironworks: A History of Taskers of Andover, 1809–1968. 1969.

6595 WILSON (Sir CHARLES H.). A Man and his Times: A Memoir of Sir Ellis Hunter. 1962.

6596 PAYNE (PETER L.). Colvilles and the Scottish Steel Industry. Oxf. 1979.

6597 OWEN (JOHN A.). The History of the Dowlais Ironworks, 1959–1970. Risca. 1977.

6598 LANCASTER (J. Y.) and WATTLEWORTH (D. R.). The Iron and Steel Industry of West Cumberland: An Historical Survey. Workington. 1977.

6599 GIRTIN (THOMAS). The Mark of the Sword: A Narrative History of the Cutler's Company, 1189–1975. 1975.

6600 ANDREWS (PHILIP WALTER SAWFORD) and BRUNNER (ELIZABETH). Capital Development in Steel: A Study of the United Steel Companies Ltd. Oxf. 1951.

6601 LEE (NORMAN) and STUBBS (PETER). The History of Dorman Smith, 1878–1972. 1972.

6602 PEDDIE (RONALD). The United Steel Companies Ltd., 1918–1968. Sheffield. 1969.

6603 BARRACLOUGH (K. C.). Sheffield Steel. Buxton. 1976.

6604 HORSFALL (JOHN). The Iron Masters of Penns., 1720–1970. Kineton. 1971.

6605 BOSWELL (JONATHAN S.). Business Policies in the Making: Three Steel Companies Compared. 1983.

6606 BRYER (R. A.), BRIGNALL (T. J.), and MAUNDEN (A. R.). Accounting for British Steel: A Financial Analysis of the Failure of the British Steel Corporation 1967–80, and Who Was to Blame. 1982.

6607 MILLIGAN (JOHN). The Resilient Pioneers: A History of the Elastic Rail Spike Company and its Associates. Aberdeen. 1975.

6608 DAY (JOHN). Bristol Brass: A History of the Industry. Newton Abbot. 1973.

6609 HULL (DANIEL R.). Casting of Brass and Bronze. Cleveland. 1950.

6610 INMAN (PEGGY). Labour in the Munitions Industries. 1957.

6611 FFOULKES (CHARLES). The Gun-Founders of England. Camb. 1937.

6612 HOGG (OLIVER FREDERICK GILLILAN). The Royal Arsenal: its Background, Origin and Subsequent History. 2 vols 1963.

6613 DIXON (WILLIAM HEPWORTH). The Match Industry: Its Origin and Development. 1925.

6614 READER (WILLIAM JOSEPH). Metal Box: A History. 1976.

6615 WARD-JACKSON (CYRIL HENRY). The 'Cellophane' Story: Origins of a British Industrial Group. Bridgwater. 1977.

6616 WILSON (RONALD ELIOT). Two Hundred Precious Metal Years: A History of the Sheffield Smelting Co. Ltd., 1760–1960. 1960.

6617 COCKS (EDWARD JOHN) *and* WALTERS (BERNHARDT). A History of the Zinc Smelting Industry in Britain. 1968.

6618 PHILLIPS (MARTIN). The Copper Industry in the Port Talbot District. Neath. 1935.

6619 ARMITAGE (FRANK). The British Paint Industry. 1967.

6620 SHORTER (ALFRED H.). Paper Making in the British Isles: A Historical and Geographical Study. Newton Abbot. 1971.

6621 READER (W. J.). Bowater: A History. Camb. 1981.

6622 WEST (CLARENCE J.) *comp.* Bibliography of Pulp and Paper Making, 1900–1928. N.Y. 1929, With Suppls.

6623 KETELBEY (C. D. M.). Tullis Russell. Manch. 1967.

6624 BEVAN (A.). 'The U.K. Potato Crisp Industry, 1960–1972: A Study of New Entry Competition'. *J. Indust. Econ.* xxii (1974), 281–97.

6625 MACHIN (DONALD JOHN). The Changing Structure of the British Pottery Industry, 1935–1968. Keele. 1970.

6626 GAY (PHILIP WILLIAM) *and* SMYTH (ROBERT LESLIE). The British Pottery Industry. 1974.

6627 GODDEN (G. A.). English China. 1985.

6628 EYLES (DESMOND). Royal Doulton, 1815–1965. 1965.

6629 KELLY (A.). The Story of Wedgwood. 1975.

6630 BARTON (R. M.). A History of the China-Clay Industry. Truro. 1966.

6631 PARSONS (R. H.). The Early Days of the Power Station Industry. Camb. 1939.

6632 ROSNER (CHARLES). Printer's Progress: A Comparative Survey of the Craft of Printing, 1851–1951, Dedicated to 100 Years of British Printing by Balding and Mansell, Printers. 1951.

6633 WIBORG (FRANK B.). Printing Ink: A History with a Treatise on Modern Methods of Manufacture and Use. N.Y. 1926.

6634 CLAIR (COLIN). A History of Printing in Britain. 1965.

6635 HANDOVER (P. M.). Printing in London from 1476 to Modern Times. Camb., Mass. 1960.

6636 PYE LIMITED. The Story of Pye. Camb. 1961.

6637 GRANT (WYN P.) *and* MARSH (DAVID). 'Representation of Retail Interests in Britain'. *Pol. Studs* 22 (1974), 168–77.

6638 SHEPHERD (P.) *and* THORPE (D.). Urban Redevelopment and Changes in Retail Structure, 1961–1971. Manch. 1977.

6639 PAYNE (PETER FREDERICK). British Commercial Institutions. 1961. 2nd edn 1964.

6640 JEFFERYS (JAMES BAVINGTON). Retail Trading in Britain, 1850–1950. Camb. 1954.

6641 LEVY (HERMANN JOACHIM). Retail Trade Associations. 1942.

6642 —— Shops of Britain. 1948.

6643 DAVIES (ROSS L.). Urban Change in Britain and the Retail Response. Oxf. 1987.

6644 McCLELLAND (W. G.). Studies in Retailing. Oxf. 1963.

6645 HUDSON (KENNETH). Behind the High Street. 1982.

6646 WARD (T. S.). The Distribution of Consumer Goods: Structure and Performance. Camb. 1973.

6647 BENNISON (D. J.) *and* DAVIES (ROSS L.). The Impact of Town Centre Shopping Schemes in Britain: Their Impact on Traditional Environments. Oxf. 1980.

6648 CORINA (MAURICE). Pile it High, Sell it Cheap: The Authorised Biography of Sir John Cohen. 1971.

6649 MATHIAS (PETER). Retailing Revolution: A History of Multiple Retailing in the Food Trade Based Upon the Allied Suppliers Group of Companies. 1967.

6650 PEEL (D. W.). A Garden in the Sky: The Story of Barkers of Kensington, 1870–1957. 1960.

6651 BENTHAL (ROWAN). My Store of Memories. 1974.

6652 CORINA (MAURICE). From Silks and Oak Counters: Debenhams 1878–1978. 1978.

6653 PICKERING (J. F.). Resale Price Maintenance in Practice. 1966.

6654 TIMPSON (DAVID JOHN). William Timpson Ltd.: A Century of Service, 1865–1965. Manch. 1965.

6655 GUY (CLIFFORD M.). Retail Location and Retail Planning in Britain. Farnborough. 1980.

6656 JONES (ANNA M.). The Rural Industries of England and Wales. 1927.

6657 JENKINS (JOHN GERAINT). Traditional Country Craftsmen. 1965.

6658 ANTHONY (L. J.). Sources of Information on Atomic Energy. Oxf. 1966.

6659 UNITED KINGDOM ATOMIC ENERGY AUTHORITY. Annual Report. 1955+.

6660 —— The Development of Atomic Energy, 1939–1984: Chronology of Events. 1984.

6661 POCOCK (ROWLAND FRANCIS). Nuclear Power: Its Development in the United Kingdom. Old Woking. 1977.

6662 ISARD (WALTER) *and* WHITNEY (VINCENT HEATH). Atomic Power: An Economic and Social Analysis: A Study in

Industrial Location and Regional Economic Development. 1952.

6663 BURN (DUNCAN LYALL). Nuclear Power and the Energy Crisis. 1978.

6664 EVANS (NIGEL) *and* HOPE (CHRIS). Nuclear Power: Features, Cash and Benefits. Camb. 1984.

6665 JONES (PETER LLOYD). The Economics of Nuclear Power Programmes in the United Kingdom. 1984.

6666 HALL (TONY). Nuclear Politics: The History of Nuclear Power in Britain. Harmondsworth. 1986.

6667 PATTERSON (W.). Going Critical: An Unofficial History of British Nuclear Power. 1985.

6668 ELLIOTT (DAVE) *et al.* The Politics of Nuclear Power. 1978.

6669 FOTHERGILL (STEPHEN) *and* MACKERROW (GORDON). The Economics of Nuclear Power. 1988.

6670 PEARCE (D. W.), EDWARDS (LYNNE), *and* BEURET (GEOFF). Decision Making for Energy Futures: A Case Study of the Windscale Inquiry. 1979.

6671 PARKER (ROGER JOCELYN). The Windscale Inquiry. 3 vols 1978.

6672 SIZEWELL B PUBLIC INQUIRY: Report on Applications by the Central Electricity Generating Board for Consent for the Construction of a Pressurized Water Reactor and a Direction that Planning Permission be Deemed Granted for that Development. 8 vols 1987.

6673 O'RIORDAN (TIMOTHY), KEMP (RAY), *and* PURDUE (MICHAEL). Sizewell B: An Anatomy of the Inquiry. 1988.

6674 WILLIAMS (ROGER). The Nuclear Power Decisions: British Policies 1953–78. 1980.

6675 U.K. 1965 ELECTRICITY COUNCIL. The Growth of the British Distribution System: by H. L. Sheppard.

6676 BRIGHT (ARTHUR A.) *Jnr.* The Electric-Lamp Industry: Technological Change and Economic Development from 1800–1947. N.Y. 1949.

6677 CORLEY (THOMAS ANTHONY BUCHANAN). Domestic Electrical Appliances. 1966.

6678 JONES (ROBERT) *and* MARRIOTT (OLIVER). Anatomy of a Merger: A History of G.E.C., A.E.I. and English Electric. 1970.

6679 BAKER (W. J.). A History of the Marconi Company. 1970.

6680 MARTIN (DEREK). Thorn EMI: 50 Years of Radar: 50 Years of Company Involvement with Radar Technology, 1936–1986. 1986.

6681 HENNESSEY (R. A. S.). The Electric Revolution. Newcastle upon Tyne. 1972.

6682 BARTY-KING (HUGH). Light Up the World: The Story of the Success of the Dale Electric Group, 1935–1985. 1985.

6683 O'DEA (WILLIAM T.). The Social History of Lighting. Lond. 1958. N.Y. 1959.

6684 SCOTTISH DEVELOPMENT DEPARTMENT. Electricity in Scotland: Report of the Committee on the Generation and Distribution of Electricity in Scotland [Chairman: C. H. Mackenzie.]. Edin. 1962.

6685 SELF (*Sir* ALBERT HENRY) *and* WATSON (ELIZABETH M.). Electricity Supply in Great Britain: Its Development and Organization. 1952.

8. TRADE UNIONISM

6686 MARSH (ARTHUR IVOR) *and* RYAN (VICTORIA). Historical Directory of British Trade Unions. 3 vols Farnborough. 1980–7.

6687 MARSH (ARTHUR IVOR). Trade Union Handbook: A Guide and Directory to the Structure, Membership, Policy and Personnel of the British Trade Unions. Farnborough. 1979. 3rd edn 1984.

6688 HOBSBAWM (ERIC J.). 'Trade Union Historiography'. *Bull. Soc. Stud. Lab. History* viii (1964), 31–6.

6689 FROW (RUTH), FROW (EDMUND), *and* KATANKA (MICHAEL). The History of British Trade Unions: A Select Bibliography. 1969.

6690 PELLING (HENRY MATHISON). A History of British Trade Unionism. 1963. 4th edn 1987.

6691 HUTT (GEORGE ALLEN). British Trade Unionism: A Short History. 1943. 6th edn 1975.

6692 WILLIAMS (FRANCIS) *Baron.* Magnificent Journey: The Rise of the Trade Unions. 1954.

6693 CLEGG (HUGH ARMSTRONG). History of British Trade Unions Since 1889: vol. II, 1911–1933. 1985.

6694 WIGHAM (ERIC LEONARD). Trade Unions. 1969.

6695 BROWN (KENNETH D.). The English Labour Movement 1700–1951. Dublin. 1982.

6696 PHILLIPS (GORDON ASHTON). 'The Triple Industrial Alliance in 1914'. *Econ. Hist. Rev.* 2nd ser. xxiv (1970), 55–67.

6697 PRIBICEVIC (BRANKO). The Shop Stewards' Movement and Workers' Control, 1910–1922. Oxf. 1959.

6698 HINTON (JAMES). The First Shop Stewards' Movement. 1974.

6699 DOBB (MAURICE HERBERT). Trade Union Experience and Policy, 1914–1918. 1940.

6700 POLLARD (SIDNEY). A History of Labour in Sheffield. L/pool. 1959.

6701 MUSSON (ALBERT EDWARD). Trade Union and Social History. 1974.

6702 ROBERTS (BENJAMIN CHARLES). The Trades Union Congress, 1868–1921. 1958.

6703 LOVELL (JOHN CHRISTOPHER) *and* ROBERTS (BENJAMIN CHARLES). A Short History of the T.U.C. 1968.

6704 BIRCH (JACK ERNEST LIONEL) *ed.* The History of the T.U.C., 1868–1968. 1968.

6705 ALLEN (VICTOR LEONARD). 'The Centenary of the British Trades Union Congress, 1868–1968'. *Soc. Reg.* (1968), 231–52.

6706 MARTIN (ROSS M.). T.U.C.: The Growth of a Pressure Group, 1868–1976. Oxf. 1980.

6707 ALLEN (VICTOR LEONARD). 'The Reorganisation of the Trades Union Congress, 1918–1927'. *Brit. J. Sociol.* xi (1960), 24–43.

6708 GOLDSTEIN (JOSEPH). The Government of a British Trade Union. 1952.

6709 ROSE (ARNOLD MARSHALL). Union Solidarity. 1952.

6710 ALLEN (VICTOR LEONARD). Power in Trade Unions. 1954.

6711 —— Trade Union Leadership. 1957.

6712 —— Militant Trade Unionism. 1966.

6713 RICHTER (IRVING). Political Purpose in Trade Unions. 1973.

6714 MAY (TIMOTHY C.). Trade Unions and Pressure Group Politics. Farnborough. 1975.

6715 COCKBURN (CLAUD FRANCIS). Union Power: The Growth and Challenge in Perspective. 1976.

6716 CLEGG (HUGH ARMSTRONG), KILLICK (A. J.), *and* ADAMS (REX). Trade Union Officers: A Study of Full-Time Officers, Branch Secretaries and Shop Stewards in British Trade-Unions. Camb. Mass./Oxf. 1961.

6717 MARENGO (FRANCO DAMASO). The Code of British Trade Union Behaviour. Farnborough. 1979.

6718 CLINTON (ALAN). The Trade Union Rank and File: Trades Councils in Britain, 1900–1940. Manchester. 1977.

6719 FOSH (PATRICIA). The Active Trade Unionist: A Study of Motivation and Participation at Branch Level. Camb. 1981.

6720 PRITT (DENIS NOWELL). Law, Class and Society: Book 1: Employers, Workers and Trade Unions. 1970.

6721 BORASTON (IAN), CLEGG (HUGH ARMSTRONG), *and* RIMMER (MALCOLM). Workplace and Union: A Study of Local Relationship in Fourteen Unions. 1975.

6722 BAIN (GEORGE SAYERS), COATES (DAVID), *and* ELLIS (VALERIE). Social Stratification and Trade Unionism: A Critique. 1973.

6723 JEFFERYS (JAMES BAVINGTON). Trade Unions in a Labour Britain. 1947.

6724 TRACEY (HERBERT). The British Trade Union Movement. Brussels. 1954.

6725 ROBERTS (BENJAMIN CHARLES). Trade Unions in a Free Society. 1959.

6726 CLEMENTS (RICHARD). Glory Without Power: A Study of Trade Unionism in our Present Society. 1959.

6727 CYRIAX (GEORGE) *and* OAKESHOTT (ROBERT). The Bargainers: A Survey of Modern Trade Unionism. 1960.

6728 BUREAU INTERNATIONAL DU TRAVAIL. La Situation Syndicale au Royaume-Uni. Geneva. 1961.

6729 BEALEY (FRANK) *and* PARKINSON (STEPHEN). Unions in Prosperity. I.E.A. Hobart Paper. 1960.

6730 BOTTOMLEY (ARTHUR). The Use and Abuse of Trade Unions. 1963.

6731 WILLIAMSON (HUGH). The Trade Unions. 1970. 2nd edn 1972.

6732 SMITH (ANTHONY). The Trade Unions. Edin. 1969.

6733 VAN DEN BERGH (TONY). The Trade Unions—What Are They? Oxf. 1970.

6734 GARD (ELIZABETH). British Trade Unions. 1970.

6735 CHARLOT (MONICA). Le syndicalisme en Grande Bretagne. Paris. 1970.

6736 TOMISON (MAUREEN). The English Sickness: The Rise of Trade Union Political Power. 1972.

6737 HUGHES (JOHN DENNIS) *and* POLLINS (HAROLD) *eds.* Trade Unions in Great Britain. Newton Abbot. 1973.

6738 MILLIGAN (STEPHEN). The New Barons: Union Power in the 1970s. 1976.

6739 BROWN (*Sir* ERNEST HENRY PHELPS). The Origins of Trade Union Power. Oxf. 1983.

6740 INSTITUTE OF ECONOMIC AFFAIRS. Trade Unions: Public Goods or Public 'Bads'? 1978.

6741 UNDY (R.), ELLIS (V.), McCARTHY (WILLIAM EDWARD JOHN) *Baron, and* HALMOS (A. M.). Change in Trade Unions: the Development of U.K. Unions Since the 1960's. 1981.

6742 MASON (KEITH). Front Seat. Nottingham. 1981.

6743 MILNE-BAILEY (WALTER). Trade Union Documents. 1929.

6744 ROBERTSON (NORMAN) *and* SAMS (KENNETH IAN) *eds.* British Trade Unionism: Select Documents. 2 vols Oxf./Totowa, N.J. 1972.

6745 HUTT (ROSEMARY). 'Trade Unions as Friendly Societies, 1912–1952'. *Yorks. Bull. Econ. Soc. Res.* 7(1) (1955), 69–87.

6746 BURKITT (B.) *and* BOWERS (D.). 'The Degree of Unionization, 1948–1968'. *Bull. Econ. Res.* xxvi (1974), 79–100.

6747 MAYHEW (K.). 'The Degree of Unionization, 1948–1968: A Comment'. *Bull. Econ. Res.* xxix (1977), 51–3.

6748 BURKITT (B.) *and* BOWERS (D.). 'The Degree of Unionization, 1948–1968: A Reply'. *Bull. Econ. Res.* xxix (1977), 54–6.

6749 BANKS (J. AMBROSE). Trade Unionism. 1974.

6750 WARD (GEORGE). Fort Grunwick. 1977.

6751 DROMEY (JACK) *and* TAYLOR (GRAHAM). Grunwick: The Workers' Story. 1978.

6752 SYKES (E. I.). 'Trade Union Autonomy in Great Britain'. *Univ. Queensland Law J.* 2(4) (1955), 336–48.

6753 —— 'Trade Unionism Today'. *Round Table* (Dec. 1955), 27–37.

6754 WRAY (J. V. C.). 'Les syndicats et les jeunes travailleurs en Grande-Bretagne'. *R. Int. Trav.* 75(4) (1957), 333–48.

6755 STEPHENSON (T. E.). 'The Changing Role of Local Democracy: The Trade Union Branch and its Members'. *Sociol. Rev.* 5(1) (1957), 27–40.

6756 HART (P. E.) *and* BROWN (*Sir* ERNEST HENRY PHELPS). 'The Sizes of Trade-Unions: A Study in the Laws of Aggregation'. *Econ. J.* 67(265) (1957), 1–15.

6757 DAVIES (S. C.). 'Trade Union Rivalry and the Bridlington Agreement'. *Brit. J. Admin Law* (3) (1954), 97–101.

6758 SMITH (E. O.). 'The Trend in Trade Union Amalgamation'. *Loughborough J. Soc. Studs* 3, 17–29, 26–30.

6759 SIMPSON (D. H.). 'An Analysis of the Size of Trade Unions'. *Brit. J. Indust. Rev.* 10(3) (1972), 382–92.

6760 BOYFIELD (R.). 'T.U.C. Machinery for Disputes Between Unions'. *Brit. J. Admin Law* 2(2) (1955), 56–60.

6761 ROBERTSON (DONALD JAMES). 'Trade Unions and Wage Policy'. *Pol. Q.* 2(1) (1956), 17–30.

6762 POLLOCK (G.). 'Employers and Trade Unions'. *Pol. Q.* 27(3) (1956), 237–49.

6763 BELL (J. D. M.). 'Stability of Membership in Trade Unions'. *Scot. J. Pol. Econ.* 1(1) (1954), 49–74.

6764 MITRA (A.). 'The British Trade Union Movement: A Statistical Analysis'. *Ind. Econ. J.* 3(1) (1955), 1–17.

6765 ESTEY (MARTIN S.). 'Trends in Concentration of Union Membership, 1897–1962'. *Q. J. Econ.* 80 (1966). 343–60.

6766 MACK (J. A.). 'Trade Union Leadership'. *Pol. Q.* 27(1) (1956), 71–81.

6767 PRICE (ROBERT J.) *and* BAIN (GEORGE SAYERS). 'Union Growth Revisited: 1948–1974 in Perspective'. *Brit. J. Indust. Rel.* 14 (1976), 339–55.

6768 MURRAY (L.). 'Le Syndicalisme et la Planification en Grande Bretagne'. *A. Econ. Coll.* 51(4) (1963), 555–62.

6769 RENSHAW (PATRICK). 'Trade Unions in America and Britain'. *Quart. Rev.* 638 (1963), 413–22.

6770 PICKARD (D. G.). 'Clerical Workers and the Trade Unions'. *Brit. Management Rev.* 13(2) (1955), 102–20.

6771 KNIGHT (R.). 'Unionism Among Retail Clerks in Post-War Britain'. *Industr. Lab. Relat. R.* 14(4) (1961), 515–27.

6772 HENNESSY (B.). 'Trade Unions and the British Labour Party'. *Amer. Pol. Sci. Rev.* 49(4) (1955), 1050–66.

6773 HARLE (R.). 'The Role of Trade Unions in Increasing Productivity'. *Pol. Q.* 27(1) (1956), 93–100.

6774 FLETCHER (E.). 'Trade Union Reaction to Industrial Change'. *J. Brit. Inst. Management* 1(1) (1957), 25–31.

6775 HUDDLESTON (J.). 'Trade Unions in a Technological Society'. *Contemp. Rev.* 211(1222) (1967), 251–9.

6776 CYRIAX (GEORGE). 'How to Make Trade Unions More Responsible'. *Pol. Q.* 32(4) (1961), 319–27.

6777 BOYD (A.). 'The Social Importance of Trade Unions'. *Contemp. Rev.* 1076 (1955), 120–2.

6778 DONOGHUE (BERNARD) *Baron, and* AKKER (J.). 'Trade Unions in a Changing Society'. *Planning* 29(472) (1963), 173–223.

6779 MARTIN (RODERICK). 'Union Democracy: An Exploratory Framework'. *Sociol.* 2(2) (1968), 205–20.

6780 EDELSTEIN (J. D.), WARNER (M.), *and* COOKE (W. F.). 'The Pattern of Opposition in British and American Unions'. *Sociol.* 4(2) (1970), 145–63.

6781 EDELSTEIN (J. D.). 'Countervailing Powers and the Political Process in the British Mineworkers Union'. *Inl. J. Comp. Sociol.* 8(3–4) (1968), 255–88.

6782 —— 'Democracy in a National Union: The British AEU'. *Indust. Relat.* 4(3) (1965), 105–25.

6783 BROWN (MICHAEL BARRATT). 'The Trade Union Question'. *Pol. Q.* 38(2) (1967), 156–64.

6784 BAIN (GEORGE SAYERS). 'The Growth of White-Collar Unionism in Great Britain'. *Brit. J. Indust. Rel.* 4(3) (1966), 304–35.

6785 BLACKBURN (ROBERT MARTIN) *and* PRANDY (K.). 'White Collar Unionization: A Conceptual Framework'. *Brit. J. Sociol.* 16(2) (1965), 111–21.

6786 COPPS (J. A.). 'The Union in British Socialist Thought'. *Southern Econ. J.* 2(1) (1959), 50–7.

6787 MOGRIDGE (BASIL). 'Les Syndicats Ouvriers de la Grande-Bretagne'. *R. Inst. Sociol.* (3) (1959), 371–409.

6788 SHANKS (MICHAEL). 'Politics and the Trade Unionist'. *Pol. Q.* 30(1) (1959), 44–53.

6789 MCCORMICK (B. J.). 'Trade Union Reaction to Technological Change in the Construction Industry'. *Yorks. Bull. Econ. Soc. Res.* 16(1) (1964), 15–30.

6790 SMITH (N. A.). 'Government Versus Trade Unions in Britain'. *Pol. Q.* 46(29) (1975), 293–303.

6791 CHANDRASEKHAR (B. K.). 'Trade Union Government: Regulation by Registration—A Comparative Study'. *Inl. Comp. Law Q.* 17(1) (1968), 167–82.

6792 HEIDENHEIMER (A. J.). 'Trade Unions, Benefit Systems and Party Mobilization Styles: Horizontal Influences on the British Labour and German Social Democratic Parties'. *Comp. Polit.* 1(3) (1969), 313–42.

6793 ALEXANDER (*Sir* KENNETH J. W.). 'Political Economy of Change'. *Pol. Q.* 46 (1975), 7–24.

6794 —— 'Membership Participation in a Printing Trade Union'. *Sociol. Rev.* 2(2) (1954), 161–8.

6795 JENKINS (CLIVE) *and* SHEERMAN (BARRIE). Collective Bargaining: What You Always Wanted to Know about Trade Unions and Never Dared to Ask. 1977.

6796 JENKINS (CLIVE) *and* MORTIMER (JAMES EDWARD). The Kind of Laws the Unions Ought to Want. Oxf. 1968.

6797 —— British Trade Unions Today. N.Y./Oxf. 1965.

6798 ROBERTSON (ANDREW). The Trade Unions. 1965.

6799 STAGNER (R.) *and* ROSEN (H.). Psychology of Union—Management Relations. 1966.

6800 FLANAGAN (DESMOND). 1869–1969: A Centenary Story of the Co-operative Union of Great Britain and Ireland. 1969.

6801 WARD (JOHN T.) *and* FRASER (W. HAMISH). Workers and Employers. Documents on Trade Unions and Industrial Relations in Britain Since the Eighteenth Century. 1980.

6802 BAIN (GEORGE SAYERS) *and* PRICE (ROBERT). Profiles of Union Growth: A Comparative Statistical Portrait of Eight Countries. Oxf. 1980.

6803 TAPLIN (ERIC). The Dockers' Union: A Study of the National Union of Dock Labourers 1899–1922. 1985.

6804 LOVELL (JOHN). British Trade Unions, 1875–1933. 1977.

6805 HANNINGTON (WALTER). Never on our Knees. 1967.

6806 SCHNEER (JONATHAN). Ben Tillett. 1982.

6807 McCORMICK (BRIAN). 'Managerial Unionism in the Coal Industry'. *Brit. J. Sociol.* 11(4) (1960), 356–69.

6808 WILLIAMS (ROBERT). 'Unity of Command'. *English Rev.* (Jan. 1920), 72–8.

6809 LACEY (T. A.). 'The Political Basis of Trade Unionism'. *Nineteenth Century* (July 1920), 136–43.

6810 FISHER (VICTOR). 'Labour Evolution and Social Revolution'. *Nineteenth Century* (Oct. 1920), 595–606.

6811 SYKES (A. J. M.). 'The Approaching Crisis in the Trade Unions'. *Quart. Rev.* 298(626) (1960), 383–95.

6812 —— 'Trade-Union Workshop Organization in the Printing Industry: The Chapel'. *Human Relns.* 13(1) (1960), 49–65.

6813 ALDERMAN (GEOFFREY). 'The Railway Companies and the Growth of Trade Unionism in the Late Nineteenth and Early Twentieth Centuries'. *Hist. J.* xiv (1971), 129–52.

6814 MOGRIDGE (BASIL). 'Militancy and Inter-Union Rivalries in British Shipping, 1911–1929'. *Inl. Rev. Soc. Hist.* vi (1961), 375–412.

6815 PAYNTER (WILL). British Trade Unions and the Problem of Change. 1970.

6816 ARNOT (ROBERT PAGE). The Miners: Years of Struggle. A History of the Miners' Federation of Great Britain. 1953. [From 1910 onwards.].

6817 —— The Miners: In Crisis and War: A History of the Miners' Federation of Great Britain (from 1930 onwards). 1961.

6818 —— A History of the Scottish Miners from the Earliest Times. 1955.

6819 GARSIDE (WILLIAM REDVERS). The Durham Miners, 1919–1960. 1971.

6820 BAGWELL (PHILIP SIDNEY). The Railwaymen: The History of the National Union of Railwaymen. 1963.

6821 CLEGG (HUGH ARMSTRONG). 'Some Consequences of the Great Strike'. *Trans. Manch. Stat. Soc.* (1954), 1–29.

6822 ALLEN (VICTOR LEONARD). Militant Trade Unionism: A Re-analysis of Industrial Action in an Inflationary Situation. 1966.

6823 ORTON (WILLIAM AYLOTT). Labour in Transition: A Survey of British Industrial History Since 1914. 1921.

6824 BRIGGS (ASA) *and* SAVILLE (JOHN) eds. Essays in Labour History. Vol. 2: 1886–1923. 1971.; Vol. 3. 1918–1939. 1977.

6825 SMITH (DAVID). 'The Struggle against Company Unionism in the South Wales Coalfield, 1926–1939'. *Welsh Hist. Rev.* vi (1973), 354–78.

6826 HARROD (JEFFREY). Trade Union Policy: A Study of British and American Trade Union Activities in Jamaica. 1972.

6827 GONVERTCH (PETER), MARTIN (ANDREW), ROSS (GEORGE), ALLEN (CHRISTOPHER), BORNSTEIN (STEPHEN), *and* MARKOVITS (ANDREI). Unions and Economic Crisis: Britain, West Germany and Sweden. 1984.

6828 REMER (ROBERT). The Blue-Coated Worker: A Sociological Study of Police Unionism. Camb. 1980.

6829 JAMES (LARRY). Power in a Trade Union: The Role of the District Committee of the A.U.E.W. Camb. 1984.

6830 JENKINS (CLARE) *and* SHERMAN (BARRIE). White-Collar Unionism: The Rebellious Salariat. 1979.

6831 DOUGAN (DAVID). The Shipwrights: The History of the Shipconstructors' and Shipwrights' Association, 1882–1963. Newcastle upon Tyne. 1975.

6832 HUGHES (JOHN) *and* POLLINS (HAROLD) eds. Trade Unions in Great Britain. Newton Abbot. 1973.

6833 HYMAN (RICHARD). The Workers' Union. Oxf. 1971.

6834 BEHARRELL (PETER) *and* PHILO (GREG) eds. Trade Unions and the Media. 1977.

6835 HOWE (ELLIS). The British Federation of Master Printers, 1900–1950. 1950.

6836 WEIGHELL (SIDNEY). On the Rails. 1983.

6837 SEGLOW (PETER). Trade Unionism in Britain. Aldershot. 1978.

6838 CORBETT (JOHN). The Birmingham Trades Council, 1866–1966. 1966.

6839 TUCKETT (ANGELA). The Blacksmiths' History. 1974.

6840 HOWE (ELLIS) *and* CHILD (JOHN). The Society of London Bookbinders, 1780–1951. 1952.

6841 MORTIMER (JAMES E.). History of the Boilermakers' Society. Vol. 2. 1906–1939. 1982.

6842 CRAIK (WILLIAM WHITE). Bryn Roberts and the National Union of Public Employees. 1955.

6843 FRENCH (JOHN OLIVER). Plumbers in Unity: History of the Plumbing Trades Union, 1865–1965. 1965.

6844 MORAN (JAMES). Natsopa Seventy-five Years: The National Society of Operative Printers and Assistants, 1889–1964. 1964.

6845 BAGWELL (PHILIP SIDNEY). The Railwaymen: The History of the National Union of Railwaymen. 1963.

6846 —— Vol. 2. The Beeching Era and After. 1982.

6847 PUGH (*Sir* ARTHUR). Men of Steel, By One of them: A Chronicle of Eighty Years of Trade Unionism. 1951.

6848 HUGHES (GORONWY ALUN) *ed.* Men of No Property: Historical Studies of Welsh Trade Unions. Caerwys. 1971.

6849 NEWMAN (J. R.). The N.A.O.P. Heritage: A Short Historical Review of the Growth and Development of the National Association of Operative Plasterers, 1860–1960. Wembley. 1960.

6850 ROWLES (GEORGE E.). The 'Line' is on: A Centenary Souvenir of the London Society of Compositors, 1848–1948. 1948.

6851 HIGENBOTHAM (S.) *comp.* Amalgamated Society of Woodworkers: Our Society's History. 1939.

6852 HUMPHREYS (BETTY VANCE). Clerical Unions in the Civil Service. 1958.

6853 BAIN (GEORGE SAYERS). The Growth of White-Collar Unionism. 1970.

6854 SPOOR (ALEC). White-Collar Union: Sixty Years of NALGO. 1967.

6855 LUMLEY (ROGER). White-Collar Unionism in Britain: A Survey of the Present Position. 1973.

6856 BLACKBURN (ROBERT MARTIN). Union Character and Social Class: A Study of White-Collar Unionism.

6857 LERNER (SHIRLEY WACOWITZ). Breakaway Unions and the Small Trade Union. 1961.

6858 HEPPLE (B. A.) *and* O₃HIGGINS (PAUL). Public Employee Trade Unionism in the United Kingdom: The Legal Framework. Ann Arbor, Mich. 1971.

6859 CLINTON (ALAN). The Post Office Workers: A Trade Union and Social History. 1984.

6860 MULLER (WILLIAM D.). The 'Kept Men'?: The First Century of Trade Union Representation in the British House of Commons, 1874–1975. 1976.

6861 ANDERSON (ALAN). 'The Labour Laws and the Cabinet Legislative Committee of 1926–1927'. *Bull. Soc. Stud. Lab. Hist.* xxiii (1971), 37–54.

6862 DESMARAIS (RALPH H.). 'The British Government's Strike Breaking Organisation and Black Friday'. *J. Contemp. Hist.* vi (1971), 112–27.

6863 RENSHAW (PATRICK). 'Black Friday, 1921'. *History Today* xxi (1971), 416–25.

6864 MARTIN (RODERICK). Communism and the British Trade Unions, 1924–1933: A Study of the National Minority Movement. Oxf. 1969.

6865 MILNE-BAILEY (WALTER). Trade Unions and the State. 1934.

6866 MULLER (WILLIAM D.). 'Trade Union Sponsored Members of Parliament in the Defence Dispute of 1960–1'. *Parl. Aff.* xxiii (1970), 258–76.

6867 MACDONALD (DONALD FARQUHAR). The State and the Trade Unions. 1960. 2nd edn. 1976.

6868 WELTON (HARRY). The Trade Unions, The Employers and the State. 1960.

6869 ALLEN (VICTOR LEONARD). Trade Unions and the Government. 1960.

6870 HARRISON (MARTIN). Trade Unions and the Labour Party Since 1945. 1960.

6871 MACINTYRE (STUART). 'Socialism, the Unions and the Labour Party after 1918'. *Bull. Soc. Stud. Lab. Hist.* xxxi (1975), 101–11.

6872 WARNER (A. W.). British Trade Unionism Under a Labour Government 1945–1951. Ann Arbor, Mich. 1954.

6873 ROGOW (A. A.). 'Labor Relations Under the British Labor Governments'. *Amer. J. Econ. Sociol.* 14(4) (1955), 357–76.

6874 SIMPSON (BILL). Labour, the Unions and the Party: A Study of the Trade Unions and the British Labour Movement. 1973.

6875 DORFMAN (GERALD ALLEN). Wage Politics in Britain, 1945–1967: Government Versus the T.U.C. 1974.

6876 WOOTTON (GRAHAM). Workers, Unions and the State. 1966.

6877 BOUVARD (MARGUERITE). Labor Movements in the Common Market Countries: The Growth of a European Pressure Group. N.Y. 1972.

6878 FOX (ALAN). A History of the National Union of Boot and Shoe Operatives, 1874–1957. Oxf. 1958.

6879 EDWARDS (KATHLEEN LOUISE). The Story of the Civil Service Union. 1975.

6880 JEFFERYS (JAMES B.). The Story of the Engineers, 1800–1945. 1945.

6881 MARSH (ARTHUR IVOR). Industrial Relations in Engineering. Oxf. 1965.

6882 CUTHBERT (NORMAN H.). The Lace Makers' Society: A Study of Trade Unionism in the British Lace Industry 1760–1960. 1960.

6883 MORAN (MICHAEL). The Union of Post Office Workers: A Study in Political Sociology. 1974.

6884 BUNDOCK (CLEMENT JAMES). The Story of the National Union of Printing, Bookbinding and Paper Workers. Oxf. 1959.

6885 GILLESPIE (SARAH C.). A Hundred Years of Progress: The Record of the Scottish Typographical Association, 1853–1952. Glas. 1953.

6886 MUSSON (ALBERT EDWARD) *ed*. The Typographical Association: Origins and History Up to 1949. 1954.

6887 BELOFF (NORA). Freedom Under Foot: The Battle Over the Closed Shop in British Journalism. 1976.

6888 TUCKETT (ANGELA). The Scottish Carter: The History of the Scottish Horse and Motormen's Association, 1898–1964. 1967.

6889 HIKINS (HAROLD R.) *ed*. Building the Union: Studies on the Growth of the Workers' Movement: Merseyside, 1756–1967. L/pool. 1973.

6890 ALLEN (VICTOR LEONARD) *and* WILLIAMS (SHEILA). 'The Growth of Trade Unionism in Banking, 1914–1927'. *Manch. Sch. Econ. Soc. Studs* xxviii (1960), 299–318.

6891 TURNER (HERBERT ARTHUR). Trade Union Growth, Structure and Policy: A Comparative Study of the Cotton Unions. 1962.

6892 BEAN (R.). 'Militancy, Policy Formation and Membership Opposition in the Electrical Trade Union, 1945–1960'. *Pol. Q.* 36 (1965), 181–90.

6893 ELECTRICAL TRADES UNION. The Story of the E.T.U. The Official History of the Electrical Trades Union. Bromley. 1952.

6894 PROCHASKA (ALICE). History of the General Federation of Trade Unions, 1899–1980. 1982.

6895 MARSH (ARTHUR IVOR) *and* SPEIRS (M.). 'The General Federation of Trade Unions, 1945–1970'. *Ind. Rln J.* 2 (1971), 22–34.

6896 CLEGG (HUGH ARMSTRONG). General Union in a Changing Society: A Short History of the National Union of General and Municipal Workers, 1889–1964. Oxf. 1964.

6897 BUNDOCK (CLEMENT JAMES). The National Union of Journalists: A Jubilee History, 1907–1957. 1957.

6898 GRIFFIN (ALAN RAMSAY). The Miners of Nottinghamshire, 1914–1944: A History of the Nottinghamshire Miners' Unions. 1962.

6899 EDWARDS (NESS). History of the South Wales Miners' Federation. 1938.

6900 ALLEN (VICTOR LEONARD). The Militancy of British Miners. Shipley. 1981.

6901 FRANCIS (HYWEL) *and* SMITH (DAVID). The Fed: A History of the South Wales Miners in the Twentieth Century. 1980.

6902 WILLIAMS (J. E.). The Derbyshire Miners. 1962.

6903 MACHIN (FRANK). The Yorkshire Miners: A History. 1958.

6904 BALDWIN (G. B.). 'Structural Reform in the British Miners' Union'. *Q. J. Econ.* lxvii (1953), 576–97.

6905 ARNOT (ROBERT PAGE). The Miners: One Union, One Industry: A History of the National Union of Mineworkers, 1939–1946. 1979.

6906 DORFMAN (GERALD ALLEN). British Trade Unionism Against the Trades Union Congress. 1983.

6907 CLINTON (ALAN). 'Trade Councils During the First World War'. *Inl Rev. Soc. Hist.* xv (1970), 202–34.

6908 JACOBS (JULIUS) *ed*. London Trades Council, 1860–1950. 1950.

6909 CORBETT (JOHN). The Birmingham Trades Council, 1866–1966. 1966.

6910 MCCARTHY (WILLIAM EDWARD JOHN) *Baron*. The Closed Shop in Britain. 1964.

6911 BLACKBURN (ROBIN M.) *and* COCKBURN (ALEXANDER) *eds*. The Incompatibles: Trade Union Militancy and Consensus. Harmondsworth. 1967.

6912 JACKSON (MICHAEL P.). Trade Unions. 1982.

6913 CLARKE (TOM) *and* CLEMENTS (LAWRIE). Trade Unions Under Capitalism. 1978.

6914 ROBERTS (BENJAMIN CHARLES). 'Trade Unions in the Welfare State'. *Pol. Q.* 27 (1956), 6–18.

9. STRIKES

6915 CRONIN (JAMES E.). Industrial Conflict in Modern Britain. 1979.

6916 DURCAN (J. W.), MCCARTHY (WILLIAM EDWARD JOHN) *Baron, and* REDMAN (G. P.). Strikes in Post-War Britain: A Study of Stoppages of Work due to Industrial Disputes, 1948–1973. 1983.

6917 LEESON (ROBERT ARTHUR) *comp*. Strike: A Live History 1887–1971. 1973.

6918 —— United we Stand. An Illustrated Account of Trade Union Emblems. Bath. 1971.

6919 MCCORD (NORMAN). Strikes. Oxf. 1980.

6920 BEYNON (HUW) *ed*. Digging Deeper: Issues in the Miners' Strike. 1985.

6921 OTTEY (ROY). The Strike: An Insider's Story. 1985.

6922 FINE (BEN) *and* MILLAR (ROBERT) *eds*. Policing the Miners' Strike. 1985.

6923 WIGHAM (ERIC LEONARD). Strikes and the Government, 1893–1974. 1976. 2nd edn 1982.

6924 —— What's Wrong with the Unions? Baltimore. 1961.

6925 —— Trade Unions. 1956. 2nd edn 1969.

6926 KIBBLEWHITE (LIZ) *and* RIGBY (ANDREW). Aberdeen in the General Strike. Aberdeen. 1977.

6927 DAVIES (TREVOR). Bolton, May 1926: A Review of the General Strike as it Affected Bolton and District. Bolton. 1976.

6928 KNOWLES (KENNETH GUY JACK CHARLES). Strikes: A Study in Industrial Conflict. Oxf. 1952.

6929 CLEGG (HUGH ARMSTRONG). 'Strikes'. *Pol. Q.* 27(1) (1956), 31–43.

6930 SMITH (C. T. B.). Strikes in Britain: A Research Study of Industrial Stoppages in the United Kingdom. 1978.

6931 GENNARD (JOHN). Financing Strikers. 1977.

6932 DURCAN (J. W.) and MCCARTHY (WILLIAM EDWARD JOHN) Baron. 'The State Subsidy Theory of Strikes: An Examination of Statistical Data for the Period 1956–7'. *Brit. J. Ind. Relns* 12 (1974), 26–47.

6933 HUNTER (LAURENCE COLVIN). 'The State Subsidy Theory of Strikes—A Reconsideration'. *Brit. J. Ind. Relns* 12 (1974), 438–44.

6934 KNIGHT (K. G.). 'Strikes and Wage Inflation in British Manufacturing Industry, 1950–1968'. *Bull. Oxf. Univ. Inst. Econ. Stats* 34 (1972), 281–94.

6935 SLAUGHTER (C.). 'The Strike of Yorkshire Mineworkers in May, 1955'. *Sociol. Rev.* n.s. vi (1958), 241–59.

6936 SILVER (MICHAEL). 'Recent British Strike Trends: A Factual Analysis'. *Brit. J. Ind. Relns* xi (1973), 66–104.

6937 LANE (TONY) and ROBERTS (KENNETH). Strike at Pilkingtons. 1971.

6938 COATES (KEN). Work-ins, Sit-ins and Industrial Democracy. Nottingham. 1981.

6939 HARTLEY (JEAN), KELLY (JOHN), and NICHOLSON (NIGEL). Steel Strike: A Case Study in Industrial Relations. 1983.

6940 KAHN (PEGGY) et al. Picketing: Industrial Disputes, Tactics and the Law. 1983.

6941 SHELLEY (JEFFREY) ed. The General Strike. 1976.

6942 BURNS (EMILE) comp. The General Strike, May 1926: Trades Councils in Action. 1926.

6943 ARNOT (ROBERT PAGE) comp. The General Strike, May 1926: Its Origins and History. 1926.

6944 FARMAN (CHRISTOPHER). The General Strike: May 1926. 1972.

6945 NOEL (GERARD). The Great Lock-Out of 1926. 1976.

6946 MORRIS (MARGARET). The General Strike. Harmondsworth. 1957.

6947 SYMONS (JULIAN). The General Strike. 1957.

6948 RENSHAW (PATRICK). Nine Days in May. 1975.

6949 —— The General Strike. 1975.

6950 PHILLIPS (G. A.). The General Strike: The Politics of Industrial Conflict. 1976.

6951 MCLEAN (JOHN). The 1926 General Strike in North Lanarkshire. 1976. [Communist Party History Group Publication.].

6952 HILLS (R. I.). The General Strike in York, 1926. York. 1980. [Borthwick pamphlet.].

6953 GAMSER (H. G.). 'Interunion Disputes in Great Britain and the United States'. *Industr. Lab. Relns Rev.* 9(1) (1955), 3–23.

6954 PICKHAUS (K.). 'Dockerstreik in Grossbritannien'. *Sozial Polit.* 4 (20) (1972), 55–74.

6955 WEDDERBURN (K. W.) Baron. 'The Right to Threaten Strikes'. *Mod. Law Rev.* 24(5) (1961), 573–91.

6956 GALAMBOS (P.) and EVANS (E. W.). 'Work Stoppages in the United Kingdom, 1951–1964: A Quantitative Study'. *Bull. Oxf. Univ. Inst. Econ. Stats* xxviii (1966), 33–62.

6957 —— 'Work Stoppages in the United Kingdom 1965–1970: A Quantitative Study'. *Bull. Econ. Res.* xxv (1973), 22–42.

6958 EDWARDS (PAUL). 'Britain's Changing Strike Problem'. *Ind. Rlns J.* 13 (1982), 5–20.

6959 EVANS (E. W.) and CREIGH (S. W.) eds. Industrial Conflict in Britain. 1977.

6960 PENCAVEL (JOHN H.). 'An Investigation into Industrial Strike Activity in Britain'. *Economica* n.s. xxxvii (1970), 239–56.

6961 BLUMLER (JAY G.) and EWBANK (A. J.). 'Trade Unionists, the Mass Media and Unofficial Strikes'. *Brit. J. Ind. Relns* 8(1), (1970), 32–54.

6962 GOODMAN (J. F. B.). 'Les Grèves au Royaume-Uni: Statistiques et Tendances Récentes'. *R. Int. Trav.* 95(5) (1967), 512–30.

6963 STIEBER (J.). 'Unauthorized Strikes Under the American and British Industrial Relations Systems'. *Brit. J. Ind. Relns* 6(2) (1968), 232–8.

6964 TURNER (HERBERT ARTHUR). Is Britain Really Strike Prone? A Review of the Incidence, Character and Costs of Industrial Conflict. Camb. 1969.

6965 MCCARTHY (WILLIAM EDWARD JOHN) Baron. 'The Nature of Britain's Strike Problem'. *Brit. J. Ind. Relns* 8(2) (1970), 224–36.

6966 RIDEOUT (R. W.). 'Strikes'. *Curr. Legal Probl.* 23 (1970), 137–55.

6967 —— 'Responsible Self-Government in British Trade Unions'. *Brit. J. Ind. Rlns* 5(1), (1967), 74–86.

6968 —— 'The Content of Trade Union Rules Regulating Admission'. *Brit. J. Ind. Rlns* 4(1), (1966), 77–89.

6969 —— The Right to Membership of a Trade Union. 1963.

6970 FROW (RUTH) and KATANKA (MICHAEL). 'Strikes': A Documentary History. 1971.

6971 DESMARAIS (R.). 'Lloyd George and the Development of the British Government's Strikebreaking Organization'. *Inl Rev. Soc. Hist.* 20(1), (1975), 1–13.

6972 HYMAN (RICHARD). Strikes. 1972. 3rd edn 1984.

10. EMPLOYMENT/UNEMPLOYMENT

6973 KAHN (HILDA RENATE). Repercussions of Redundancy: A Local Survey. 1964.

6974 MUKHERJEE (SANTOSH). Through No Fault of their Own: Systems for Handling Redundancy in Britain, France and Germany. 1973.

6975 —— Unemployment Costs. 1976.

6976 SAMUELS (HARRY) *and* PEARSON (NEVILLE STEWART). Redundancy Payments: An Annotation and Guide to the Redundancy Payments Act, 1965. 1965.

6977 SINFIELD (ADRIAN). The Long-Term Unemployed—Comparative Survey. 1968.

6978 WEDDERBURN (DOROTHY). White-Collar Redundancy: A Case Study. Camb. 1964.

6979 —— Redundancy and the Railwaymen. Camb. 1965.

6980 BAXTER (J. L.). 'Long-Term Unemployment in Great Britain, 1953–1971'. *Bull. Oxf. Univ. Inst. Econ. Stats* xxxiv (1972), 329–44.

6981 BOSANQUET (NICHOLAS) *and* STANDING (GUY). 'Government and Unemployment, 1966–1970: A Study of Policy and Evidence'. *Brit. J. Ind. Relns* x (1972), 180–92.

6982 JONES (MERVYN). Life on the Dole. 1972.

6983 U.K. 1977 DEPARTMENT OF EMPLOYMENT, UNIT FOR MANPOWER STUDIES. Employment in Metropolitan Areas: Project Report. 1977.

6984 —— British Labour Statistics Year Book. Annual.

6985 —— Department of Employment Gazette. Monthly.

6986 SHOWLER (BRIAN). The Public Employment Service. 1976.

6987 ROBERTS (KENNETH). From School to Work: A Study of the Youth Employment Service. 1972.

6988 FIELD (FRANK) *ed.* The Conscript Army: A Study of Britain's Unemployed. 1977.

6989 DANIEL (WILLIAM WENTWORTH) *and* STILGOE (ELIZABETH). The Impact of Employment Protection Laws. 1978.

6990 SWANN (BRENDA AUDREY SWANTON) *and* TURNBULL (MAUREEN). Records of Interest to Social Scientists, 1919–1939: Employment and Unemployment. 1978.

6991 HARRIS (JOSÉ). Unemployment and Politics: A Study of English Social Policy 1886–1914. 1972.

6992 JOINT COMMITTEE ON LABOUR PROBLEMS AFTER THE WAR. The Problem of Demobilisation: A Statement and some Suggestions Including Proposals for the Reform of Employment Exchanges. 1916.

6993 GRAHAM (ALLAN BARNS). Social Problems: Are Our Disabled Sailors and Soldiers to be Properly Provided for by the State? 1916.

6994 HANCOCK (KEITH J.). 'Unemployment and the Economists in the 1920s'. *Economica* n.s. xxvii (1960), 305–21.

6995 —— 'The Reduction of Unemployment as a Problem of Public Policy 1920–1929'. *Econ. H. R.* xv (1962), 328–43.

6996 GRIFFIN (K. B.). 'A Note on Wages, Prices and Unemployment'. *Bull. Oxf. Univ. Inst. Stats* xxiv (1962), 379–85.

6997 BOOTH (A. E.) *and* GLYNN (SEAN). 'Unemployment in the Inter-war Period: A Multiple Problem'. *J. Contemp. Hist.* x (1975), 611–36.

6998 DEACON (A.). 'Labour and the Unemployed: The Administration of Insurance in the Twenties'. *Bull. Soc. Stud. Lab. Hist.* xxxi (1975), 10–11.

6999 MILLER (FREDERIC M.). 'The Unemployment Policy of the National Government, 1931–1936'. *Hist. J.* 19 (1976), 453–76.

7000 MEARA (GWYNNE). Juvenile Unemployment in South Wales. Cardiff. 1936.

7001 GARSIDE (W. R.). 'Juvenile Unemployment and Public Policy Between the Wars'. *Econ. H. R.* 2nd Ser. xxx (1977), 322–39.

7002 TOMLINSON (J. D.). 'Unemployment and Government Policy between the Wars: A Note'. *J. Contemp. Hist.* xiii (1978), 65–78.

7003 HILL (ARTHUR CHENEY CLIFTON) *and* LUBIN (ISADOR). The British Attack on Unemployment. 1934.

7004 BENN (*Sir* ERNEST JOHN PICKSTONE). Unemployment and Work. 1930.

7005 MARSH (LEONARD CHARLES). Health and Unemployment: Some Studies of their Relationships. 1938.

7006 DAVISON (*Sir* RONALD CONWAY). British Unemployment: The Modern Phase Since 1930. 1938.

7007 CARNEY (JAMES JOSEPH). Institutional Change and the Level of Employment: A Study of British Unemployment, 1918–29. Florida. 1956.

7008 BURNS (EVELINE MABEL). British Unemployment Programs, 1920–1938. Washington, D.C. 1941.

7009 CRIPPS (T. F.) *and* TARLING (R. J.). 'Analysis of the Duration of Male Unemployment in Great Britain, 1932–1973'. *Econ. J.* lxxxiv (1974), 289–316.

7010 THOMAS (R. L.) *and* STONEY (P. J. M.). 'Unemployment Dispersion as a Determinant of Wage Inflation in the U.K., 1925–1966'. *Manch. Sch. Econ. Soc. Studs* xxxix (1971), 83–116.

7011 ROSE (ARTHUR GORDON). The Older Unemployed Man in Hull. 1953.

7012 EVANS (ERIC WYN) *and* HARTLEY (KEITH). Employment and Unemployment in the Hull Region, 1951–1968. Hull. 1964.

7013 SMITH (BARBARA MARY DIMOND). Black Country Employment, 1959–1970. An Analysis Based on Employment Exchange Data and Incorporating Comparisons between Inner and Outer Exchanges and between the Black Country and Birmingham and Great Britain. Birm. 1973.

7014 JONES (S.) *and* SMITH (G. P.). Employment and Unemployment in North West Wales. Bangor. 1960.

7015 RUDDY (SHEILA ANN), SMITH (BARBARA MARY DIMOND), *and* CHERRY (GORDON EMANUEL). Employment Problems in a County Town: A Study of Bridgnorth, Shropshire. 1971.

7016 HILL (MICHAEL J.), HARRISON (R. M.), SARGEANT (A. V.), *and* TALBOT (V.). Men out of Work: A Study of Unemployment in Three English Towns. Camb. 1973.

7017 COCKETT (I. E. N.) *comp.* Research Projects of Employment within the London Boroughs 1966–Nov. 1976. Compiled from the Register of Research in the London Boroughs. 2nd edn 1976.

7018 PHILLIPS (GORDON) *and* WHITESIDE (NOEL). Casual Labour: The Unemployment Question in the Port Transport Industry 1880–1970. Oxf. 1985.

7019 GALAMBOS (P.). 'On the Growth of the Employment of Non-manual Workers in the British Manufacturing Industries, 1948–1962'. *Bull. Oxf. Univ. Inst. Stats* xxvi (1964), 369–87.

7020 CRAIG (J.) *et al.* 'Humberside: Employment, Unemployment and Migration: The Evolution of Industrial Structure 1951–1966'. *Yorks. Bull. Econ. Soc. Res.* xxii (1970), 123–42.

7021 LEE (C. H.). British Regional Employment Statistics 1841–1971. Camb. 1979.

7022 MILLER (FREDERIC M.). 'National Assistance or Unemployment Assistance? The British Cabinet and Relief Policy, 1932–33'. *J. Contemp. Hist.* ix (1974), 163–84.

7023 GARSIDE (W. R.). The Measurement of Unemployment: Methods and Sources in Great Britain 1850–1979. Oxf. 1980.

7024 KUZMINOV (I.). 'The Unemployment Problem in Great Britain'. *Int. Aff. (Moscow)* 9 (1956), 47–60.

7025 HANNINGTON (WALTER). Unemployed Struggles, 1919–1936: My Life and Struggles Amongst the Unemployed. 1936. Reprint 1973.

11. MISCELLANEOUS

7026 TREASE (GEORGE EDWARD). Pharmacy in History. 1964.

7027 MATTHEWS (LESLIE G.). History of Pharmacy in Britain. Edin./Lond. 1962.

7028 U.K. 1966 WATER RESOURCES BOARD. Morecambe Bay and Solway Barrages: Report on Desk Studies. 1966.

7029 —— Morecambe Bay Barrage: Desk Study: Report of Consultants. 1966.

7030 —— Solway Barrage: Desk Study: Report of Consultants. 1966.

7031 —— Water Supplies in South East England. 1966.

7032 —— Interim Report on Water Resources in the North. 1967.

7033 ASHBY (ERIC W.) *Baron, and* ANDERSON (MARY). 'Studies in the Politics of Environmental Protection: The Historical Roots of the British Clean Air Act, 1956'. *Interdisc. Sci. Rev.* I (1976), 279–90; 2 (1977), 190–206.

7034 SANDERSON (MICHAEL). 'Research and the Firm in British Industry 1919–39'. *Sci. Stud.* ii (1972), 107–51.

7035 McGOWAN (H.). '1851–1951: A Century of British Industry'. *J. Roy. Soc. Arts* xcix (1951), 235–45.

7036 USHER (ABBOTT PAYSON). 'The Industrialization of Modern Britain'. *Technol. Cult.* ii (1960), 109–27.

7037 LAWRENCE (DEREK W.). 'The Enemy Unseen: The Origins of Submarine Design'. *Hist. Today* xxiv (1974), 534–41.

7038 JENKINS (J. GERAINT). 'Technological Improvement and Social Change in South Cardiganshire'. *Agric. Hist. Rev.* xiii (1965), 94–105.

7039 HUNT (L. B.). 'The Worshipful Company of Goldsmiths'. *Gold. Bull.* xi (1978), 94–104.

7040 HOWELL (TREVOR H.). 'Origins of British Geriatrics'. *Proc. Roy. Soc. Med.* lxix (1976), 445–9.

7041 HOLMYARD (E. J.). 'Priests of Pomona'. *Endeavour* xiii (1954), 3–4.

7042 HOBBS (WILLIAM H.). 'The British Arctic Air Route Expedition'. *Geogr. Rev.* xxii (1932), 684–6.

7043 JONES (FRANCIS AVERY). 'The Norwich Schools of Surgery: The Evolution of Surgery in an English City'. *Ann. Roy. Coll. Surg.* lviii (1976), 203–21.

7044 HACKER (BARTON C.). 'Resistance to Innovation: The British Army and the Case Against Mechanization, 1919–1939'. *Actes xiiie Cong. Int. Hist. Sci.* ii (1971), 225–31.

7045 CROSLEY (A. S.). 'Early Development of the Railless Electric Trolleybus, in Particular its Application in Great Britain and Elsewhere Up to 1924'. *Trans. Newcomen. Soc.* xxxiii (1960–1), 93–111.

7046 TAYLOR (JAMES). 'Cobalt, Madder and Computers—The Society's Changing Scene'. *J. R. Soc. Arts* cxviii (1969), 9–14.

7047 YOUNG (DONALD). 'Brickmaking at Sandleheath, Hampshire'. *Ind. Archaeol. Rev.* vii (1970), 439–42.

7048 WILSON (PAUL W.). 'The Gunpowder Mills of Westmorland and Furness'. *Trans. Newcomen. Soc.* xxxvi (1963–4, publ. 1966), 47–65.

7049 MELLORD (C. M.) *and* CARSWELL (DONALD S. L.). 'Dyes and Dyeing'. *Brit. J. Hist. Sci.* I (1963), 265–79.

7050 MOUNFIELD (P. R.). 'Early Technological Innovation in the British Footwear Industry'. *Ind. Archaeol. Rev.* ii (1978), 129–42.

7051 PIPER (L. P. S.). 'A Short History of the Camborne School of Mines'. *J. Tevithick Soc.* ii (1974), 9–44.

7052 WARREN (KENNETH). 'Locational Problems of the Scottish Iron and Steel Industry since 1760, pt.1'. *Scot. Geog. Mag.* lxxxi (1965), 18–37.

7053 RICHARDS (G. TILGHMAN). The History and Development of Typewriters. Based on the Collection in the Science Museum. 2nd edn 1964.

7054 ADLER (MICHAEL H.). The Writing Machine. 1973.

7055 BEECHING (WILFRED A.). Century of the Typewriter. 1974.

7056 EVANS (ARTHUR F.). The History of the Oil Engine. A Review in Detail of the Development of the Oil Engine from the Year 1680 to the Beginning of the Year 1930. 1932.

7057 CAUNTER (C. F.). The History and Development of Cycles. 1955.

7058 DAVIS (TENNEY L.). The Chemistry of Powder and Explosives. N.Y./Lond. 1941–3.

7059 READ (JOHN). Explosives. Harmondsworth/N.Y. 1942.

7060 AUER (MICHEL). The Illustrated History of the Camera from 1839 to the Present. Trans. and adapted by D. B. Tubbs. Kings Langley. 1976.

7061 FLOWERS (ARTHUR W.). Forty Years of Steam, 1926–1966. Shepperton. 1969.

7062 LAVINGTON (SIMON H.). A History of Manchester Computers. Manchester. 1975.

7063 MACRAE (ROBERT STUART). Winston Churchill's Toyshop. Kineton. 1971.

7064 MIDDLETON (WILLIAM E. KNOWLES). The History of the Barometer. Baltimore. 1964.

7065 —— A History of the Thermometer and its Use in Meteorology. Baltimore. 1966.

7066 MORAN (JAMES). Printing Presses: History and Development from the 15th Century to Modern Times. 1973.

7067 MORTON (HUDSON T.). Anti-friction Bearings. Ann Arbor, Mich. 1954.

7068 ROBINS (F. W.). The Story of the Lamp (and the Candle). 1939.

7069 ROBINSON (STUART). A History of Dyed Textiles: Dyes, Fibres, Painted Bark, Batik, Starch-Resist, Discharge, Tie-Dye, Further Sources for Research. 1969.

7070 —— A History of Printed Textiles: Block, Roller, Screen, Design, Dyes, Fibres, Discharge, Resist, Further Sources for Research. 1969.

7071 BLAND (DAVID). History of Book Illustration. Cleveland. 1958.

7072 —— The Illustration of Books. 3rd edn Lond. 1962.

7073 SACHS (CURT). The History of Musical Instruments. N.Y. 1940.

7074 CLUTTON (CECIL) *and* NILAND (AUSTIN). The British Organ. 1963.

7075 GIBBONS (CHESTER H.). Materials Testing Machines. Pittsburgh. 1935.

7076 HATFIELD (H. STAFFORD). The Inventor and his World. West Drayton. 1948. First publ. Lond. 1933.

7077 GRAY (EDWYN). The Devil's Device: The Story of Robert Whitehead, Inventor of the Torpedo. 1975.

7078 HOGG (IAN V.). A History of Artillery. 1974.

7079 HOGG (O. F. G.). Artillery: Its Origins, Heyday and Decline. 1970.

7080 DICKINSON (HENRY W.). A Short History of the Steam Engine. 1938. Reprint, with new introduction, 1963.

7081 THWING (LEROY). Flickering Flames: A History of Domestic Lighting Through the Ages. Rutland, Vt. 1958.

7082 DODD (KENNETH N.). Computers. 1966.

7083 HARGREAVES (JOHN). Computers and the Changing World: A Theme for the Automation Age. 1967.

7084 MURPHY (BRIAN). The Computer in Society. 1966.

7085 McRAE (THOMAS WATSON). The Impact of Computers on Accounting. 1964.

7086 LEVESON (JOSEPH HARRY) *ed*. Electronic Business Machines. 1959.

7087 BURTON (ALFRED JOSEPH) *and* MILLS (RONALD GERALD). Electronic Computers and their Business Applications. 1960.

7088 BERNSTEIN (JEREMY). The Analytical Engine: Computers—Past, Present and Future. 1965.

7089 HOLLINGDALE (STUART HAVELOCK) *and* TOOTHILL (G. C.). Electronic Computers. Harmondsworth. 1965.

7090 WOOD (TIMOTHY) *et al.* Computers in Britain: A Survey of the Use of Computing Equipment for Data Processing and Process Control in Great Britain. 1967.

7091 THOMAS (SHIRLEY). Computers: Their History, Present Applications and Future. N.Y. 1965.

7092 ROSENBERG (JERRY M.). The Computer Prophets. N.Y. 1969.

7093 RANDELL (BRIAN). The Origins of Digital Computers: A Bibliography. Newcastle upon Tyne. 1972.

7094 MARTIN (JAMES) *and* NORMAN (ADRIAN R. D.). The Computerised Society: An Appraisal of the Impact of Computers on Society over the Next Fifteen Years. 1970.

7095 HAWKES (NIGEL). The Computer Revolution. 1971.

7096 GEORGE (FRANK H.). Computers, Science and Society. 1970.

7097 FLEMING (*Sir* JOHN AMBROSE). Fifty Years of Electricity: The Memories of an Electrical Engineer. 1921.

7098 —— Memories of a Scientific Life. Lond./Edin. 1934.

7099 MACGREGOR-MORRIS (JOHN T.). The Inventor of the Valve: A Biography of Sir Ambrose Fleming. 1954.

7100 TUCKER (DAVID G.). Gisbert Kapp, 1852–1922. First Professor of Electrical Engineering at the University of Birmingham, Appointed 1905, Retired 1919. Birmingham. 1973.

7101 TAYLOR (H. G.). An Experiment in Co-operative Research: An Account of the First Fifty Years of the Electrical Research Association. 1970.

7102 APPLEYARD (ROLLO). The History of the Institution of Electrical Engineers, 1871–1931. 1939.

7103 ALLEN (CECIL JOHN). A Century of Scientific Instrument Making, 1853–1953. 1953.

7104 DISNEY (ALFRED N.), HILL (CYRIL F.), *and* WATSON (W. E.) *eds*. Origin and Development of the Microscope. 1928.

7105 CLAY (REGINALD S.) *and* COURT (THOMAS H.). The History of the Microscope. 1932.

7106 BRADBURY (SAVILE). The Microscope Past and Present. Oxf. 1968. [An abridgement, with some new material, of his Evolution of the microscope. Oxf. 1967.].

7107 TRANSACTIONS OF THE NEWCOMEN SOCIETY for the Study of the History of Engineering and Technology. Vol. 1.

7108 TUBBS (F. R.). 'The East Malling Research Station (1913–1963)'. *Nature* cxcviii (1963), 327–31.

7109 WERSKEY (PAUL GARY). 'The Perennial Dilemma of Science Policy'. *Nature* ccxxxiii (1971), 529–32.

7110 VARCOE (IAN). 'Scientists, Government and Organised Research in Great Britain, 1914–16: The Early History of the Department of Scientific and Industrial Research'. *Minerva* viii (1970), 192–216.

7111 WALKLAND (S. A.) *and* VIG (NORMAN J.). 'Parliament, Science and Technology'. *Tech. Soc.* iv (1967), 40–5.

7112 WATHEN (ROBERT L.). 'Genesis of a Generator . . . The Early History of the Magnetron'. *J. F. I.* cclv (1953), 271–87.

7113 NEIL (HERBERT). 'History of Chromatography'. *Nature* clxvi (1950), 1000–1.

7114 WHITE (WILLIAM C.). 'Evolution of Electronics'. *Electronics* xxv (1952), 98–9.

7115 WHITROW (GERALD JAMES). 'The Limits of the Physical Universe'. *Stud. Gen.* v (1952), 329–37.

7116 —— 'An Analysis of the Evolution of Scientific Method'. *Age Science* (Paris), iii (1970), 255–80.

7117 —— 'Is the Physical Universe A Self-Contained System?'. *Monist* xlvii (1962), 77–93.

7118 WHITTAKER (EDMUND). 'Chance, Freewill and Necessity in the Scientific Conception of the Universe'. *Proc. Phys. Soc.* lv (1943), 459–71.

7119 WIGHTMAN (WILLIAM PERSEHOUSE DELISLE). 'Presidential Address: The Tyranny of Abstractions'. *Br. Jnl Hist. Soc.* vi (1973), 233–46.

7120 WILKINS (A. F.). 'The Story of Radar'. *Research* vi (1953), 434–40.

7121 WILLIAMS (W. T.) *ed.* 'Science in Science Fiction'. *Advmt. Sci.* xxii (1965), 195–207.

7122 WILLSTATTER (RICHARD). 'A Chemist's Retrospects and Perspectives'. *Science* lxxviii (1933), 271–4.

7123 WILSON (ALAN HERRIES). Semiconductors and Metals: An Introduction to the Electron Theory of Metals. Camb. 1939.

7124 WILSON (JOHN C.). 'Twenty Five Years' Change in Television'. *J. Televis. Soc.* 2 (1935), 86–93.

7125 WOLFENDALE (ARNOLD WHITTAKER). The Search for the Neutrino. 1971.

7126 WOLFENDEN (J. H.). 'The Dawn of Hot Atom Chemistry'. *J. Chem. Educ.* xxxii (1955), 276.

7127 WOOLLEY (*Sir* RICHARD). 'The Stars and the Structure of the Galaxy'. *Q. J. Roy. Astr. Soc.* xi (1970), 403–28.

7128 WRIGHT (J. E.). 'The Library of the Institution of Electrical Engineers in London'. *Technology Cult.* ix (1968), 191–6.

7129 YOUNG (A. D.). 'Dr. A. P. Thurston, A Review of his Contributions to Aeronautics'. *Trans. Newcomen. Soc.* xxxviii (1963–6), 107–26.

7130 ZINBERG (DOROTHY). 'The Widening Gap: Attitudes of First Year Students and Staff Towards Chemistry, Science, Careers and Commitment: An Informal Study of the Chemistry Department of an English University'. *Sci. Stud.* (1971), 287–313.

7131 ZUCKERMAN (HARRIET). 'Nobel Laureates in Science: Patterns of Productivity, Collaboration and Authorship'. *Am. Soc. Rev.* xxxii (1967), 391–403.

7132 WHITLEY (RICHARD D.). 'The Operation of Science Journals: Two Case Studies in British Social Science'. *Sociol. Rev.* xviii (1970), 241–58.

7133 —— 'Communication Nets in Science: Status and Citation Patterns in Animal Physiology'. *Sociol. Rev.* xvii (1969), 219–33.

7134 MALIN (S. R. C.). 'British World Magnetic Charts'. *Q. J. Roy. Astr. Soc.* x (1969), 309–16.

7135 HUANG (SU-SHU). 'Jeans' Criterion of Gravitational Instability'. *Sky Telesc.* xxvi (1963), 77–9.

7136 DINGLE (HERBERT). 'Particle and Field Theories of Gravitation'. *Br. J. Phil. Sci.* xviii (1967), 57–64.

7137 BOZORTH (RICHARD M.). 'Magnetism'. *Rev. Mod. Phys.* xix (1947), 29–86.

7138 USHER (ABBOTT PAYSON). A History of Mechanical Inventions. 2nd edn Camb., Mass. 1954.

7139 CRESSY (EDWARD). Discoveries and Inventions of the Twentieth Century. 5th edn by J. G. Crowther. 1966.

7140 JEWKES (JOHN), SAWERS (DAVID), *and* STILLERMAN (RICHARD). The Sources of Invention. 1958. 2nd edn 1969.

7141 ECO (U.) *and* ZORZOLI (G. B.). A Pictorial History of Inventions. 1962.

7142 FAIRLEY (PETER). British Inventions in the 20th Century. Rev. edn 1972.

7143 CLARK (RONALD W.). The Scientific Breakthrough: The Impact of Modern Invention. 1974.

7144 CARDWELL (DONALD S. L.). 'The History of Technology: Now and in the Future'. *Ind. Arch. Rev.* ii (1978), 103–10.

7145 —— 'The Academic Study of the History of Technology'. *Hist. Sci.* vii (1968), 112–24.

7146 BUCHANAN (ROBERT ANGUS). 'The Contribution of Industrial Archaeology to the History of Technology'. *Actes XIIe Cong. Int. Hist. Sci.* 1968. Publ. 1971.

7147 —— Industrial Archaeology: Retrospect and Prospect. *Antiquity* xliv (1970), 281–7.

7148 BUGGE (GUNTHER). 'Some Problems Relating to the History of Science and Technology'. *J. Chem. Educ.* ix (1932), 1567–75.

7149 SHERWOOD TAYLOR (F.). 'The Science Museum, London'. *Endeavour* x (1951), 82–8.

7150 YOUNG (JAMES HARVEY). Patent Medicines: An Early Example of Competitive Marketing. *J. Econ. Hist.* xx (1960), 648–56.

7151 QUIRK (R. N.). 'The Problem of Scientific Manuscripts in Britain'. *Isis* liii (1962), 151–4.

7152 STREAT (*Sir* RAYMOND). 'Manchester and Cotton—Today'. *Ciba Rev.* ii (1962), 2–9.

7153 SPENCER JONES (HAROLD). 'The History of the Marine Chronometer'. *Endeavour* xiv (1955), 212–19.

7154 ROOSEBOOM (MARIA). 'The History of the Microscope'. *Proc. Roy. Microsc. Soc.* ii (1967), 266–93.

7155 PROUDFOOT (W. B.). 'Copying Methods Past and Present'. *Proc. Roy. Instn Gr. Br.* xli (1966), 270–309.

7156 REMILLARD (W. J.). 'The History of Thunder Research'. *Weather* xvi (1961), 245–53.

7157 HALL (A. RUPERT). 'The History of Time'. *Discovery* xxvi (1965), 11–13.

7158 HABER (L. F.). 'Government Intervention at the Frontiers of Science: British Dyestuffs and Synthetic Organic Chemicals, 1914–39'. *Minerva* xl (1973), 79–94.

7159 GOODEN (R. Y.). 'Modern English Silversmithing'. *J. Roy. Soc. Arts* cxiv (1966), 890–903.

7160 GABOR (DENNIS). 'Holography, 1948–1971'. *Science* clxxvii (1972), 299–313.

7161 GROVER (H. W.). 'Reflections on Early X-ray Engineering'. *Br. J. Radiol.* xlvi (1973), 757–61.

7162 LOVINS (AMORY BLOCH). Soft Energy Paths: Towards A Durable Peace. Harmondsworth. 1977.

7163 CARR (DONALD EATON). Energy and the Earth Machine. 1978.

7164 ROBERTS (D. E.) *and* FRISBY (J. H.). The Northampton Gas Undertaking 1823–1949. Leicester. 1980.

7165 LONG (GEOFFREY). Solar Energy: Its Potential Contribution Within the United Kingdom: A Report Prepared for the Department of Energy. 1976.

7166 A.E.R.E. (U.K.) Energy Technology Support Unit. J. Allen and R. A. Bird. The Prospect for the Generation of Electricity from Wind Energy in the United Kingdom: A Report Prepared for the Department of Energy. U.K. Dept. of Energy Papers. No. 21.

7167 LAMB (P. G.). Electricity in Bristol 1863–1948. Bristol. 1981.

7168 HIGHFIELD (JOHN SOMERVILLE). 'The Supply of Electricity'. *Jl Roy. Soc. Arts* (16 May 1919), 408–24.

7169 SWANSON (EDWARD B.). A Century of Oil and Gas in Books: A Descriptive Bibliography. N.Y. 1960.

7170 LEWIS (T. M.) *and* MCNICOLL (IAIN HUGH). North Sea Oil and Scotland's Economic Prospects. 1978.

7171 ROBINSON (COLIN) *and* MORGAN (JON). North Sea Oil in the Future: Economic Analysis and Government Policy. 1978.

7172 HUTCHESON (ALEXANDER MACGREGOR) *and* HOGG (ALEXANDER) *eds.* Scotland and Oil. Edin. 1973. 2nd edn 1975.

7173 COOPER (BRYAN) *and* GASKELL (T. F.). The Adventure of North Sea Oil. 1976.

7174 KLITZ (J. KENNETH). North Sea Oil: Resource Requirements for Development of the U.K. Sector. Oxf. 1984.

7175 MCRAE (THOMAS WATSON). North Sea Oil: Mecca or Mirage? Bradford. 1976.

7176 FISCHER (DAVID W.). North Sea Oil—An Environment Interface. Bergen. 1980.

7177 MILLER (HARRY). The Future of North Sea Gas. 1969.

7178 MORTON (FRANK). Report of the Inquiry into the Safety of Natural Gas as a Fuel. 1970.

7179 HUNTER (LESLIE). Oil. 1961.

7180 BEEBY-THOMPSON (A.). Oil Pioneer: Selected Experiences and Incidents Associated with Sixty Years of World-Wide Petroleum Exploration and Oil Field Development. 1961.

7181 UNITED KINGDOM ATOMIC ENERGY AUTHORITY. Glossary of Atomic Terms. 4th edn 1962.

7182 —— Guide to U.K.A.E.A. Documents. 3rd edn *ed.* by J. Roland Smith. 1963.

7183 —— The Nuclear Energy Industry of the United Kingdom. 2nd edn 1961.

7184 —— The U.K.A.E.A.: Its History and Organisation. 1962.

7185 —— List of Publications Available to the Public. (Monthly) Hansell. Dec. 1955.

7186 —— Scientific and Technical News Service. (ST n.s.).

7187 —— Press Releases. (A E series.).

7188 —— Annual Report, 1955 (Of which a popular version is issued annually entitled 'Atom'.).

7189 —— *Atom*. (Monthly) 1956.

7190 LABOUR PARTY AND TRADES UNION CONGRESS. Fuel and Power: An Immediate Policy. Joint Statement. 1960.

7191 FEDERATION OF BRITISH INDUSTRY. Fuel and Energy Policy. 1963.

7192 GOLDING (E. W.). Power Supplies. 1963. (Overseas Development Institute.).

7193 U.K. COMMONWEALTH ECONOMIC COMMITTEE. Sources of Energy: A Review. 1966.

7194 SIMPSON (EDWARD SMETHURST). Coal and the Power Industries in Post-War Britain. 1966.

7195 LLOYD (BRUCE). Energy Policy. 1968. Young Fabian Group, YFP 16.

7196 FISCHLER (GUIDO). Der britische Energiemarkt und die Atomkraftnutzung. Basel. 1964.

7197 SCOTTISH COUNCIL (DEVELOPMENT AND INDUSTRY). Committee on Natural Resources in Scotland. Natural Resources in Scotland: Symposium at the Royal Society of Edinburgh. 31st October to 2nd November 1960. Edin. 1961.

7198 IMPERIAL METAL INDUSTRIES (KYNOCH). Under Five Flags: The Story of Kynoch Works, Witton, Birmingham, 1862–1962. Birm. 1962.

7199 U.K. 1963 IRON AND STEEL BOARD. Research in the Iron and Steel Industry: Special Report. 1963.

7200 McKECHNIE BROTHERS LIMITED. The McKechnie Story. 1965.

7201 BOLDT (JOSEPH R.). The Winning of Nickel: Its Geology, Mining and Extractive Metallurgy. 1967.

7202 HOWARD-WHITE (FRANK BULLER). Nickel: An Historical Review. 1963.

7203 STRIDE (H. G.). Nickel for Coinage. 1964.

7204 U.K. 1965 MINISTRY OF LABOUR. The Metal Industries: A Study of Occupational Trends in the Metal Manufacturing and Metal Using Industries. 1965.

7205 HESS (ALAN CHARLES). Some British Industries: Their Expansion and Achievements, 1936–1956. 1957.

7206 HODGSON (STUART). The Liberal Policy for Industry. 1928.

7207 WOODWARD (V. H.). 'Economic Policy and the Energy Supply Situation in Britain'. *Busin. Economist* vi (1974), 73–113.

7208 CURRAN (*Sir* SAMUEL C.) *and* CURRAN (JOHN). Energy and Human Needs. Edin. 1979.

7209 EVANS (SIMON CARADOC) *ed.* Energy Options in the United Kingdom. 1975.

7210 LOVELL (ALFRED CHARLES BERNARD). World Power Resources and Social Development. 1945.

7211 AYRES (EUGENE) *and* SCARLOTT (CHARLES A.). Energy Sources—Wealth of the World. N.Y. 1952.

7212 UBBELOHDE (A. R.). Man and Energy. 1954.

7213 THEOBALD (DAVID W.). The Concept of Energy. 1966.

7214 MADDOX (JOHN). Beyond the Energy Crisis. 1975.

7215 CHAPMAN (PETER). Fuel's Paradise: Energy Options for Britain. Harmondsworth. 1975.

7216 SIMON (A. L.). Energy Resources. Oxf. 1975.

7217 McMULLAN (JOHN T.) *et al.* Energy Resources and Supply. 1976.

7218 BAILEY (RICHARD). Energy: The Rude Awakening. 1977.

7219 FOLEY (GERALD). The Energy Question. Harmondsworth. 1976.

7220 COOK (PAULINE LESLEY) *and* SURREY (A. J.). Energy Policy: Strategies for Uncertainty. 1977.

12. ODDMENTS

7221 HILTON (GEORGE WOODMAN). The Truck System, Including A History of the British Truck Acts, 1465–1960. Camb. 1960.

7222 MESS (HENRY ADOLPHUS). Factory Legislation and its Administration 1891–1924. 1926.

7223 FREEDLAND (M. R.). The Contract of Employment. Oxf. 1976.

7224 RICHARDSON (HARRY WARD). 'The New Industries Between the Wars'. *Oxf. Econ. Papers* xiii (1961), 360–84.

7225 PAGE (A. C.). 'State Intervention in the Inter-war Period: The Special Areas Acts, 1934–1937'. *Brit. J. Law Soc.* iii (1976), 175–203.

7226 LINDLEY (R. M.). 'Inter-industry Mobility of Male Employees in Great Britain, 1959–1968'. *J. Roy. Stats Soc.* cxxxix (1976), 56–79.

7227 LITTLE (IAN M. D.) *and* EVELY (R.). 'Some Aspects of the Structure of British Industry, 1935–1951'. *Trans. Man. Stat. Soc.* (1957–8).

7228 HART (P. E.). 'Profits in Non-Manufacturing Industries in the United Kingdom, 1920–1938'. *Scot. J. Pol. Econ.* x (1963), 167–97.

7229 HALL (R.). 'Changes in the Industrial Structure of Britain'. *Lloyds Bank Rev.* lxvii (1963), 1–13.

7230 HAHN (FRANK H.) *and* MATTHEWS (ROBERT C. O.). 'The Theory of Economic Growth: A Survey'. *Econ. J.* lxxiv (1964), 779–902.

7231 HADDY (PAMELA) *and* CURRELL (MELVILLE E.). 'British Inter-industrial Earnings Differentials, 1924–1955'. *Econ. J.* lxviii (1958), 104–11.

7232 GUPTA (S.). 'Input and Output Trends in British Manufacturing Industry, 1948–1954'. *J. Roy. Stat. Soc.* cxxvi (1963), 433–45.

7233 GEORGE (KENNETH D.). 'Changes in British Industrial Concentration 1951–1958'. *J. Indust. Econ.* xv (1967), 200–11.

7234 —— 'The Changing Structure of Competitive Industry'. *Econ. J.* lxxxii (1972), 353–68.

7235 BUXTON (NEIL K.). 'The Role of the "New" Industries in Britain During the 1930s: A Reinterpretation'. *Bus. Hist. Rev.* xlix (1975), 205–22.

7236 SMITH (GEORGE WILLIAM). Britain's Economy: Its Structure and Development. 1963.

7237 JAQUES (ELLIOTT). The Changing Culture of a Factory. 1951.

7238 HOLLOWELL (P. G.). The Lorry Driver. 1968.

7239 WHYTE (WILLIAM HAMILTON). Decasualization of Dock Labour, with Special Reference to the Port of Bristol. Bristol. 1934.

7240 UNIVERSITY OF LIVERPOOL: SOCIAL SCIENCE DEPARTMENT. The Dock Worker: An Analysis of Conditions of Employment in the Port of Manchester. L/pool. 1954.

7241 SHADWELL (ARTHUR). The Problem of Dock Labour. 1920.

7242 TURNER (HERBERT ARTHUR), CLACK (GARFIELD), *and* ROBERTS (GEOFFREY). Labour Relations in the Motor Industry: A Study of Industrial Unrest and an International Comparison. 1967.

7243 PAYNTER (WILL). British Trade Unions and the Problem of Change. 1970.

7244 MORTIMER (JAMES EDWARD). Trade Unions and Technological Change. 1971.

7245 D.S.I.R. Man, Steel and Technical Change. 1957.

7246 —— Automation: A Report on Technical Trends and their Impact on Management and Labour. 1956.

7247 CHRISTENSEN (ERIC). Automation and the Workers. 1968.

7248 SADLER (PHILIP). Social Research on Automation. 1968.

7249 EVANS (*Sir* TREVOR) *and* STEWART (MARGARET). Pathway to Tomorrow: The Impact of Automation on People—A Survey of the International Conference on Automation, Full Employment and a Balanced Economy at Rome in June 1967. 1967.

7250 BENN (ANTHONY NEIL WEDGWOOD). The Social and Political Implications of Automation. 1966.

7251 CHADWICK-JONES (JOHN K.). Automation and Behaviour: A Social Psychological Study. 1969.

7252 BANKS (OLIVE). The Attitudes of Steelworkers to Technical Change. L/pool. 1960.

7253 BALDWIN (GEORGE BENEDICT). Beyond Nationalization: The Labor Problems of British Coal. Camb., Mass. 1955.

7254 HURSTFIELD (JOEL). 'The Control of British Raw Material Supplies, 1919–1939'. *Econ. Hist. Rev.* xiv (1944), 1–31.

7255 —— Control of Raw Materials. 1953.

7256 WILLS (GORDON) *comp.* Sources of U.K. Marketing Information. 1969.

7257 HARGREAVES (ERIC LYDE) *and* GOWING (MARGARET MARY). Civil Industry and Trade. 1952.

7258 MURRAY (GEORGE THURSBY). The United Kingdom: An Economic and Marketing Study. 1964.

4

BRITISH SOCIETY

A section devoted to 'society' is potentially all-embracing. While the literature concerning population is relatively self-contained, the material incorporated into subsequent sub-sections does not fall easily into the categories that have been identified. Inevitably, certain books and articles flow across boundaries. It follows that in this section above all the reader should investigate more than one sub-section in search of relevant items. Also in this section the reader will also find much material listed which represents 'work in progress' or 'interim studies' rather than monographs which represent even an attempt to write a definitive account of a particular problem. Much of this material stems from the rapid expansion of sociological investigation and of sociology as a discipline in the 1960s in particular. It also reflects the fact that 'society' itself has been perceived to be changing at an ever increasing rate. Such changes have had profound consequences for the social structure as a whole and, amongst other things, on marriage, the family, children, and elderly. How 'society' should respond to the adverse effects of these changes has in turn led to an expanded literature on social work and social administration. The considerable changes in the ethnic composition of Britain have likewise produced a substantial literature covering the broad area of 'race relations'. For obvious reasons, too, that literature largely relates to recent decades. Crime, on the other hand, has been a concern of scholars throughout the period.

Marked differences of approach can be found in the literature which has been located. The categories and sub-categories that have been used in this section may not necessarily reflect the organization which would occur to a criminologist or a sociologist. If so, it must be stressed again that the ordering is that of a particular historian according to the general assumptions which have prevailed elsewhere in the volume.

1. POPULATION, MIGRATION, AND IMMIGRATION

7259 TRANTER (NIGEL L.). Population and Society 1750–1940. 1985.

7260 THOMPSON (ERIC JOHN). Demographic Social and Economic Trends for Wards in Greater London. 1972.

7261 CARR-SAUNDERS (Sir ALEXANDER MORRIS) et al. Memorandum on the Present Position and Needs of the Social Sciences with Particular Reference to Population Problems. [With a Covering Letter from the Vice-Chancellor of Liverpool University.]. L/pool. 1936.

7262 BLACKER (CARLOS PATON). 'Sir Alexander Carr-Saunders, 14th January 1886–6th October 1966'. *Pop. Studs* 20 (1967), 365–9.

7263 U.K. ROYAL COMMISSION ON THE DISTRIBUTION OF THE INDUSTRIAL POPULATION REPORT. Cmnd 6153. (Barlow Report) 1940.

7264 U.K. DEPARTMENT OF EMPLOYMENT. Long-Term Population Distribution in Great Britain—A Study. 1971.

7265 REDFORD (ARTHUR). Labour Migration in England. 3rd edn 1976.

7266 HILL (ALFRED BOSTOCK). Internal Migration—And its Effects Upon Death Rates. (MRC Special Report no. 95) 1925.

7267 ROWNTREE (JOHN A.). Internal Migration: A Study of the Frequency of Movement of Migrants. 1957.

7268 JANSEN (CLIFFORD JOHN). Social Aspects of Internal Migration: Research Report. Bath. 1968.

7269 —— Ed. Readings in the Sociology of Migration. Oxf. 1970.

7270 HOUSE (JOHN WILLIAM) and WILLIS (K. G.). Northern Region and Nation: A Short Migration Atlas 1960–1961. Papers on Migration and Mobility in Northern England, No. 4. Newcastle. 1967.

7271 HOUSE (JOHN WILLIAM) et al. Mobility of the Northern Business Manager. Report of the Ministry of Labour. P.M.N.E. No. 8. Newcastle. 1968.

7272 —— Et al. Where Did the School Leavers Go? Report of the Ministry of Labour. P.M.N.E. No. 7. Newcastle. 1968.

7273 HARRIS (AMELIA ISABELLA) assisted by CLAUSEN (ROSEMARY). Government Social Survey. Labour Mobility in Great Britain, 1953–1963: An Enquiry Undertaken for the Ministry of Labour and National Service in 1963. 1966.

7274 U.K. MINISTRY OF HOUSING AND LOCAL GOVERNMENT. Projecting Growth Patterns in Regions—Statistics for Town Planning: Series Three. Population and Households. No. 1. 1970.

7275 FRIEDLANDER (DOV) and ROSHIER (R. J.). Internal Migration in England and Wales 1851–1951. 1966.

7276 HOLLINGSWORTH (THOMAS HENRY). Migration: A Study Based on Scottish Experience between 1939 and 1964. Edin. 1971.

7277 BIRCH (STEPHANIE) and MACMILLAN (BRENDA). Managers on the Move: A Study of British Managerial Mobility. 1971.

7278 NEWPORT and MONMOUTHSHIRE COLLEGE OF TECHNOLOGY. (Department of Business and Managerial Studies) Labour Mobility in Monmouthshire. Newport. 1967.

7279 UNGERSON (CLARE). Moving Home: A Study of the Redevelopment Process in Two London Boroughs. 1971.

7280 UNGERSON (CLARE) and DEAKIN (NICHOLAS). Leaving London: Planned Mobility and the Inner-City. 1977.

7281 SIMMIE (JAMES M.). The Sociology of Internal Migration: A Discussion of Theories and Analysis of a Survey in Southampton County Borough. 1972.

7282 PICKETT (KATHLEEN GORDON) and BOULTON (DAVID K.). Migration and Social Adjustment: Kirkby and Maghall. L/pool. 1974.

7283 JOHNSON (JAMES HENRY) et al. Housing and the Migration of Labour in England and Wales. Farnborough. 1974.

7284 MITCHELL (FANNY HARRIET) and HUNTER (LAURENCE COLVIN). Migration in Scotland 1958–1973. 1976.

7285 U.K. OFFICE OF POPULATION, CENSUSES AND SURVEYS. Population Projections: Area Population Projections by Sex and Age for Standard Regions, Counties and Metropolitan Districts of England 1974–1991.

7286 —— Guide to Census Reports, Great Britain 1801–1966. 1977.

7287 —— Population Trends—1. 1975.

7288 U.K. CENTRAL POLICY REVIEW STAFF. Population and the Social Services Report. 1977.

7289 —— Population Panel Report. Cmnd 5258. 1973.

7290 —— Long Term Population Distribution in Great Britain: A Study. 1971.

7291 U.K. WELSH OFFICE, Planning Services Division. Welsh Population Change 1961–1971. Cardiff. 1975.

7292 U.K. CENSUS 1961.

GREAT BRITAIN: SCIENTIFIC AND TECHNOLOGICAL QUALIFICATIONS. 1962.

ENGLAND AND WALES: HOUSING TABLES. 1964.

ENGLAND AND WALES: AGE, MARITAL CONDITION AND GENERAL TABLES. 1964.

ENGLAND AND WALES: BIRTHPLACE AND NATIONALITY TABLES. 1964.

ENGLAND AND WALES: USUAL RESIDENCE TABLES. 1964.

ENGLAND AND WALES: OCCUPATION, INDUSTRY SOCIO-ECONOMIC GROUPS. 1964.

ENGLAND AND WALES: COMMONWEALTH IMMIGRANTS IN THE CONURBATIONS. 1965.

ENGLAND AND WALES: INDEX OF PLACENAMES. 2 vols 1965.

ENGLAND AND WALES: MIGRATION NATIONAL SUMMARY TABLES. 1965.

ENGLAND AND WALES: FERTILITY TABLES. 1966.

ENGLAND AND WALES: GREATER LONDON TABLES. 1966.

ENGLAND AND WALES: HOUSEHOLD COMPOSITION, NATIONAL SUMMARY TABLES. 1966.

ENGLAND AND WALES: INDUSTRY TABLES. 1966.

ENGLAND AND WALES: SOCIO-ECONOMIC GROUP TABLES. 1966.

ENGLAND AND WALES: WORKPLACE TABLES. 1966.

GREAT BRITAIN: SUMMARY TABLES. 1966.

ENGLAND AND WALES: COUNTY REPORTS. 1962.

ENGLAND AND WALES: POPULATION, DWELLINGS, HOUSEHOLDS. 1962.

N.B. CENSUSES OF POPULATION. REPORTS DECENNIALLY (EXCEPT 1941).

7293 NORTHERN IRELAND CENSUS 1961.

COUNTY REPORTS. Belf. 1963.

FERTILITY REPORT. Belf. 1965.

GENERAL REPORT. Belf. 1965.

7294 U.K. CENSUS 1966.

NORTHERN IRELAND: PRELIMINARY REPORT. Belf. 1966.

ENGLAND AND WALES: COUNTY REPORTS. 1967.

GREAT BRITAIN: SUMMARY TABLES. 1967.

7295 U.K. OFFICE OF POPULATION CENSUSES AND SURVEYS. General Household Survey: An Introductory Report. 1973.

7296 —— People in Britain: A Census Atlas. 1980.

7297 —— 1991 Census of Population. 1988.

7298 COMPTON (PAUL ALWYN). 'Aspects of Intercommunity Population Balance in Northern Ireland'. *Econ. Soc. Rev.* (Dublin) 1 (1970), 455–76.

7299 WILLATS (E. C.) *and* NEWSON (MARION G. C.). 'The Geographical Pattern of Population Changes in England and Wales, 1921–1951'. *Geog. J.* 1953, 431–54.

7300 WELCH (RUTH LILLIAN). Migration Research and Migration in Britain: A Selected Bibliography. 1970.

7301 —— Migration in Britain: Data Sources and Estimation Techniques. Birm. 1971.

7302 U.K. OVERSEAS SETTLEMENT DEPARTMENT. 2. Life Overseas. 1928.

7303 —— 7. Index to Official and Voluntary Agencies in Great Britain and the Overseas Dominions. 1928.

7304 —— 25. Training Centres for Women who Wish to Settle Overseas. 1924.

7305 —— 30. The Empire Overseas. (n.d.)

7306 U.K. ANNUAL REPORT OF THE OVERSEA MIGRATION BOARD. 1953–1954.

7307 ROYAL SOCIETY OF LONDON. Emigration of Scientists from the United Kingdom: Report of a Committee Appointed by the Council of the Royal Society. (Chairman: *Sir* Donald Sutherland) 1963.

7308 THOMAS (BRINLEY). 'The International Circulation of Human Capital'. *Minerva* 5 (1967), 476–506.

7309 GRUBEL (HERBERT G.). 'The Reduction of the Brain Drain: Problems and Policies'. *Minerva* 6 (1968), 541–58.

7310 REED (LAURENCE). Our Export of Intelligence: A Question of National Debilitation. 1968.

7311 CARRIER (NORMAN HENRY) *and* JEFFREY (JAMES R.). External Migration: A Study of the Available Statistics 1850–1950. 1953. (U.K. Registrar General: Studies on Medical and Population Subjects. No. 6.).

7312 EDGAR (J.). 'The Big Rush: Britons Emigrate'. *Soc. Sci.* (Philadelphia) 33 (1958), 160–3.

7313 BROWN (L. B.). 'English Migrants to New Zealand: The Decision to Move'. *Human Relns* 13 (1960), 167–73.

7314 SHEPPERSON (WILBUR STANLEY). British Emigration to North America. 1957.

7315 —— Emigration and Disenchantment: Portraits of Englishmen Repatriated from the United States. Norman, Okla. 1965.

7316 TAYLOR (PHILIP ARTHUR MICHAEL). The Distant Magnet: European Emigration to the USA. Lond./N.Y. 1971.

7317 THOMAS (BRINLEY). Migration and Economic Growth: A Study of Great Britain and the Atlantic Economy. Camb. 2nd edn 1973.

7318 —— Migration and Urban Development: A Reappraisal of British and American Long Cycles. 1972.

7319 RICHMOND (ANTHONY HENRY). 'Return Migration from Canada to Britain'. *Pop. Studs* 22 (1968), 263–71.

7320 APPLEYARD (REGINALD THOMAS). British Emigration to Australia. 1964.

7321 —— 'The Return Movement of U.K. Migrants from Australia'. *Pop. Studs* 15 (1962), 214–25.

7322 RICHARDSON (ALAN). 'Some Psycho-social Characteristics of Satisfied and Dissatisfied British Immigrant Skilled Manual Workers in Western Australia'. *Human Rlns* 10 (1957), 235–48.

7323 —— British Immigrants and Australia: A Psycho-social Inquiry. Canberra. 1974.

7324 —— 'Some Psycho-social Aspects of British Immigration to Australia'. *Brit. J. Sociol.* 10 (1959), 327–37.

7325 —— 'The Assimilation of British Immigrants in Australia'. *Human Rlns* 10 (1957), 157–66.

7326 STONE (JOHN). Colonist or Uitlander? A Study of the British Immigrant in South Africa. Oxf. 1963.

7327 JOHNSTON (P. H. W.). British Emigration to Durban, South Africa: A Sociological Examination of Richardson's Conceptual Framework. Pietermaritzburg. 1970.

7328 PEPPARD (NADINE). 'Migration: Some British and European Comparisons'. *Race* 6 (1964), 100–9.

7329 MUSGROVE (FRANK). The Migratory Elite. 1963.

7330 BLANDY (R.). 'Brain Drains in an Integrating Europe'. *Comp. Educ. Rev.* 12 (1968), 180–93.

7331 BOHNING (WOLF-RUDIGER). The Migration of Workers in the United Kingdom and the European Community. 1972.

7332 JONES (HUW A.). Recent Migration in Northern Scotland: Pattern, Process, Impact. 1982.

7333 JACKSON (JOHN ARCHER) *ed.* Migration. Camb. 1969.

7334 ROBERTSON (D. J.). 'The Migrating Scot'. *Scot. Accountants Mag.* 1953, 301–5.

7335 DONALDSON (GORDON). The Scots Overseas. 1966.

7336 BRANDER (M.). The Emigrant Scots. 1982.

7337 MacKAY (DONALD IAIN). Geographical Mobility and the Brain Drain: A Case Study of Aberdeen University Graduates, 1860–1960. 1969.

7338 CAIRD (JAMES BROWN). 'Migrating Scots'. *Geog. Mag.* 1974. 249–53.

7339 CRAMOND (RONALD DUNCAN) *and* MARSHALL (J. L.). 'Housing and Mobility'. *Scot. J. Pol. Econ.* 11 (1964), 57–84.

7340 DE JONG (GORDON F.). 'Population Redistribution Policies: Alternatives from the Netherlands, Great Britain and Israel'. *Soc. Sci. Q.* 56 (1975), 262–73.

7341 DONNISON (DAVID VERNON). 'The Movements of Households in England'. *J. Roy. Stat. Soc.* (Series A), 124 (1961), 60–80.

7342 HUMPHRYS (GRAHAM). 'No Welcome in the Hillsides'. *Geog. Mag.* 1974. 184–7.

7343 ILLSLEY (RAYMOND), FINLAYSON (A.), *and* THOMPSON (B.). 'The Motivation and Characteristics of Internal Migrants: A Socio-medical Study of Young Migrants in Scotland (*sic*)'. *Millbank Mem. Fund Q.* 41 (1965), 115–44.

7344 JACK (A. B.). 'Inter-Regional Migration in Great Britain: Some Cross-Sectional Evidence'. *Scot. J. Pol. Econ.* 18 (1971), 184–7.

7345 MOINDROT (CLAUDE). 'Les Mouvements de la Population dans la Région de Birmingham'. *Population* 9 (1962), 424–34.

7346 OSBORNE (RICHARD HORSLEY). 'Internal Migration in England and Wales, 1951'. *Advan. & Science* 12 (1956), 317–32.

7347 PICKETT (KATHLEEN GORDON). 'Aspects of Migration in North West England, 1959–1961'. *Town Planning Rev.* 38 (1967), 233–44.

7348 PICKVANCE (CHRISTOPHER GEOFFREY). 'Life-cycle, Housing Tenure and Residential Mobility: A Path Analytical Approach'. *Urban Studs* 11 (1974), 171–88.

7349 SMITH (H. R.). 'The Dispersal of Population from Congested Urban Centres in Scotland'. *Public Admin.* 34 (1956), 125–34.

7350 MacDOUGALL (G. D. A.). 'Inter-war Population Changes in Town and Country'. *J. Roy. Stat. Soc.* 113 (1940), 30–60.

7351 FOX (ALAN). The Milton Plan: An Exercise in Manpower Planning and the Transfer of Production. 1963.

7352 'J.E.T.' 'Migration to and from Monmouthshire'. *Welsh Outlook* (Mar. 1915), 105–9.

7353 POWER (EDWARD RAYMOND ROPER). Population Prospects. Oxf. 1938.

7354 HOGBEN (LANCELOT) *ed.* Political Arithmetic: A Symposium of Population Studies. Lond./N.Y. 1938.

7355 MacCLEARY (GEORGE FREDERICK). The Menace of British Depopulation: Today's Question. 1938.

7356 —— Race Suicide? 1945.

7357 —— The Malthusian Population Theory. 1953.

7358 CADBURY (LAURENCE JOHN). This Question of Population: Europe in 1970. 1945.

7359 GLASS (DAVID VICTOR). Population: Policies and Movements in Europe. Oxf. 1940.

7360 GLASS (DAVID VICTOR) *and* GREBENIK (E.). The Trend and Pattern of Fertility in Great Britain: A Report on the Family census of 1946. 1954.

7361 HUBBACK (EVA MARIAN). The Population of Britain. West Drayton/N.Y. 1947.

7362 —— Population Facts and Policies. 1945.

7363 U.K. ROYAL COMMISSION ON POPULATION. PAPERS. 1954.

7364 NEWSHOLME (HENRY PRATT). The Population Report and the Survival of the Christian Family. 1949.

7365 FORD (J. R.) *and* STEWART (C. M.). 'An Estimate of the Future Population of England and Wales'. *Eugenics Rev.* 52 (1960), 151–60.

7366 HOLMANS (A.). 'Current Population Trends in Britain'. *Scot. J. Pol. Econ.* 11 (1964), 31–56.

7367 HOLLINGSWORTH (THOMAS HENRY). 'The Demography of the British Peerage'. *Pop. Studs* 18 Suppl. Nov. 1964.

7368 —— The Demography of the English Peerage. 1965.

7369 CLARKE (JOHN INNES). 'Rural and Urban Sex Ratios in England and Wales'. *Tijd. Econ. Soc. Geog.* 51 (1960), 29–38.

7370 LASLETT (PETER), EVERSLEY (DAVID EDWARD CHARLES), *and* ARMSTRONG (WALTER ALAN). An Introduction to Historical Demography. *Ed.* by Edward Anthony Wrigley. 1966.

7371 BOWEN (IAN). Economics and Demography. 1976.

7372 CARRIER (NORMAN HENRY). 'An Examination of Generation Fertility in England and Wales'. *Pop. Studs* 9 (1955), 3–23.

7373 MICKLEWRIGHT (F. H. AMPHLETT). 'The Rise and Decline of English Neo-Malthusianism'. *Pop. Studs* 15 (1961), 32–51.

7374 DAVIS (KINGSLEY). 'The Theory of Change and Response in Modern Demographic History'. *Pop. Index* 29 (1963), 345–66.

7375 —— World Population in Transition. Philadelphia. 1945.

7376 OSBORN (FREDERICK) *ed.* Our Crowded Planet: Essays on the Pressure of the Population. 1963.

7377 LEVINE (AARON LAWRENCE). 'Economic Science and Population Theory'. *Pop. Studs* 19 (1965), 139–54.

7378 CASE (ROBERT ALFRED MARTIN) *et al. comps.* The Chester Beatty Research Institute. Serial Bridged Life Tables; England and Wales, 1841–1960. Part 1 (Tables, Preface, and Notes.). 1962.

7379 COX (P. R.). 'The Demographic Characteristics of Britain Today, and their Implications'. *Eugenics Rev.* 59 (1967), 222–31.

7380 —— 'Demographic Development in Great Britain since the Royal Commission on Population'. *Eugenics Rev.* 47 (1955), 21–31.

7381 U.K. ROYAL COMMISSION ON POPULATION. Cmnd Report 7695. 1949, repr. 1953.

7382 UNITED NATIONS ECONOMIC COMMISSION FOR EUROPE. Population Structure in European Countries. N.Y. 1966.

7383 BECHHOFER (FRANK) *ed.* Population Growth and the Brain Drain. Edin. 1969.

7384 DRAKE (MICHAEL) *ed.* Population in Industrialisation. 1969.

7385 —— *Et al.* The Population Explosion: An Interdisciplinary Approach. Bletchley. 1971.

7386 BENJAMIN (BERNARD). The Population Census. 1970.

7387 —— Demographic Analysis. 1969.

7388 —— Social and Economic Factors Affecting Mortality. 1965.

7389 —— Health and Vital Statistics. 1968.

7390 —— *Ed.* Medical Records. 1977.

7391 HARRISON (GEOFFREY AINSWORTH) *and* BOYCE (A. J.) *eds.* Population Structure and Human Variation. Camb. 1977.

7392 TAYLOR (LIONEL ROY) *ed.* The Optimum Population for Britain. Lond./N.Y. 1970.

7393 WILLIAMS (ROBERT MICHAEL). British Population. 1972. 2nd edn 1978.

7394 ISAACS (JULIUS). British Post-war Migration. Camb. 1954.

7395 JOHNSON (STANLEY) *ed.* The Population Problem. Newton Abbot. 1973.

7396 KELSALL (ROGER KEITH). Population. 1967.

7397 COLEMAN (DAVID A.). Demography of Immigrants and Minority Groups in the United Kingdom. 1982.

7398 GLASS (DAVID VICTOR) *and* TAYLOR (PHILIP ARTHUR MARSHALL). Population and Emigration. Dublin. 1976.

7399 GLASS (DAVID VICTOR) *and* EVERSLEY (DAVID EDWARD CHARLES) *eds.* Population in History: Essays in Historical Demography. 1965.

7400 GLASS (DAVID VICTOR) *and* REVELLE (ROGER) *eds.* Population and Social Change. 1972.

7401 GLASS (DAVID VICTOR) *comp.* The Development of Population Statistics: A Collective Reprint of Materials Concerning the History of Census Taking and Vital Registration in England and Wales. Farnborough. 1973.

7402 WRIGLEY (EDWARD ANTHONY). Population and History. Lond./N.Y. 1969.

7403 HAWTHORN (GEOFFREY). Population Policy: A Modern Delusion. 1973.

7404 POPULATION INVESTIGATION COMMITTEE: LONDON SCHOOL OF ECONOMICS. 'Towards a Population Policy for the United Kingdom'. Suppl. to *Pop. Studs* 24 (May 1970).

7405 BROOKS (EDWIN). This Crowded Kingdom: An Essay on Population Pressure in Great Britain. 1973.

7406 CRAIG (JOHN). Population Density and Concentration in Great Britain 1931, 1951 and 1961. 1975.

7407 CRAIG (JOHN) *and* WEBBER (RICHARD). Socioeconomic Classification of Local Authority Areas. 1978.

7408 McKEOWN (THOMAS). The Modern Rise of Population. 1976.

7409 U.K. CENTRAL POLICY REVIEW STAFF. 1977. Population and the Social Services: A Report. 1977.

7410 MITCHISON (ROSALIND). British Population Change since 1860. 1977.

7411 PARSONS (JACK). Population Fallacies. 1977.

7412 LORAINE (JOHN ALEXANDER). Syndromes of the Seventies: Population, Sex and Social Change. 1977.

7413 JACKSON (VALERIE JEAN). Population in the Countryside: Growth and Stagnation in the Cotswolds. 1968.

7414 SCHNEIDER (J. R. L.). 'Local Population Projections in England and Wales'. *Pop. Studs* 10 (1956), 95–114.

7415 OSBORNE (RICHARD HORSLEY). Atlas of Population Change in the East Midland Counties 1951–1961. Nottingham. 1966.

7416 EVERSLEY (DAVID EDWARD CHARLES), JACKSON (VALERIE JEAN) *and* LOMAS (GRAHAM M.), Population Growth and Planning Policy: An Analysis of Social and Economic Factors Affecting Housing and Employment Location in the West Midlands. 1965.

7417 WALKDEN (A. H.). 'The Estimation of Future Numbers of Private Households in England and Wales'. *Pop. Studs* 15 (1961), 174–86.

7418 TRANTER (NIGEL L.). 'Population and Social Structure in a Bedfordshire Parish: The Cardington Listing of Inhabitants'. *Pop. Studs* 21 (1967), 261–82.

7419 HABAKKUK (*Sir* HROTHGAR JOHN). Population Growth and Economic Development Since 1750. Leicester. 1971.

7420 HOLE (WINIFRED VERE) *and* POUNTNEY (MELVILLE TREVOR). Trends in Population, Housing and Occupancy Rates 1861–1961. 1971.

7421 GOODY (JOHN RANKINE). Production and Reproduction: A Comparative Study of the Domestic Domain. Camb. 1976.

7422 PARKES (*Sir* ALAN STERLING) *et al. eds.* Towards a Population Policy for the United Kingdom. Suppl. to *Pop. Studs* 24 (May 1970).

7423 U.K. MINISTRY OF HOUSING AND LOCAL GOVERNMENT. Depopulation in Mid-Wales. 1964.

7424 RICHARDS (HAMISH) *ed.* Population. Factor Movements and Economic Development: Studies Presented to Brinley Thomas. 1976.

7425 BARKER (THEODORE CARDWELL) *and* DRAKE (MICHAEL) *eds.* Population and Society, 1850–1980. N.Y. 1982.

7426 SCOTLAND: DEPARTMENT OF HEALTH. Depopulation and Rural Life in Scotland: A Summary Report by Bertram Hutchinson of Three Enquiries for the Department of Health for Scotland. Repr 1963.

7427 MAXWELL (JAMES). Social Implications of the 1947 Scottish Mental Survey. 1953.

7428 THOMSON (G. H.). The Trend of Scottish Intelligence. 1949.

7429 SCOTTISH COUNCIL FOR RESEARCH IN EDUCATION. Mental Survey Committee. Educational and other Aspects of the 1947 Scottish Mental Survey. 1958.

7430 FLINN (MICHAEL WALTER) et al. Scottish Population History from the 17th Century to the 1930s. Camb. 1977.

7431 McKEOWN (THOMAS), RECORD (R. G.), and TURNER (R. D.). 'An Interpretation of the Decline of Mortality in England and Wales during the Twentieth Century'. *Pop. Studs* 29 (1975), 391–422.

7432 WINTER (JAY MURRAY). 'Some Aspects of the Demographic Consequences of the First World War in Britain'. *Pop. Studs* 30 (1976), 539–52.

7433 —— 'Britain's "Lost Generation" of the First World War'. *Pop. Studs* 31 (1977), 449–66.

7434 —— 'Unemployment, Nutrition and Infant Mortality in Britain' 1920–1950'. In The Working Class in Modern British History: Essays in Honour of Henry Pelling. Jay Murray Winter, *ed.* Camb. 1983.

7435 HIORNS (R. W.) *ed.* Demographic Patterns in Developed Societies. 1980.

7436 ERMISCH (J. F.). 'Economic Opportunities, Marriage Squeezes, and the Propensity to Marry: An Economic Analysis of Period Marriage Rates in England and Wales'. *Pop. Studs* 35 (1981), 347–56.

7437 KOZLOV (V. I.). 'Etnorasovye izmeneniya v sostave naseleniya Velikobritanii'. ('Ethnic and Racial Changes in the Population of Great Britain'). *Sovetskaya Etnografiya* 4 (1980), 40–56.

7438 MARR (W. L.). 'The United Kingdom's International Migration in the Inter-war Period: Theoretical Considerations and Empirical Testing'. *Pop. Studs* 31 (1977), 571–80.

7439 CHAMPION (A. G.). Changing Places: Britain's Demographic, Economic and Social Complexion. 1987.

7440 U.K. OFFICE OF POPULATION, CENSUSES AND SURVEYS. Census 1981. 1984.

7441 —— Guide to Census Reports, Great Britain 1801–1966.

7442 —— 1991 Census of Population: User Consultation. 1988.

2. MORTALITY, BIRTH RATE, AND BIRTH CONTROL

(a) Mortality

7443 CAMPBELL (*Dame* JANET MARY). Maternal Mortality. 1924.

7444 —— Infant Mortality: International Inquiry of the Health Organisation of the League of Nations, English Section. 1929.

7445 CAMPBELL (*Dame* JANET MARY) et al. High Maternal Mortality in Certain Areas. Reports. 1932.

7446 U.K. GENERAL REGISTER OFFICE. The Registrar-General's Decennial Supplement, England and Wales. 1951. Occupation Mortality. Part One 1954.

7447 Decennial Supplement for 1961. Occupation Mortality. 1970.

7448 U.K. GENERAL REGISTER OFFICE. Regional and Social Factors in Infant Mortality. By C. C. Spicer and L. Lipworth. 1966.

7449 Social and Biological Factors in Infant Mortality. 1959.

7450 U.K. MINISTRY OF HEALTH. Report on Confidential Enquiries into Maternal Deaths in England and Wales 1958–1960. By *Sir* Arnold L. Walker et al. 1963.

7451 —— Report on Confidential Enquiries into Maternal Deaths in England and Wales 1961–1963. By *Sir* Arnold L. Walker et al. 1966.

7452 —— Report on Confidential Enquiries into Maternal Deaths in Northern Ireland 1960–1963. By H. L. Hardy Greer et al. Belf. 1965.

7453 DODGE (DAVID LAWRENCE) and MARTIN (WALTER T.). Social Stress and Chronic Illness: Mortality Patterns in Industrial Society. 1970.

7454 BUTLER (NEVILLE ROY) and BONHAM (DENNIS GEOFFREY). Perinatal Mortality: The First Report of the 1958 Perinatal Mortality Survey, Under the Auspices of the National Birthday Trust Fund. 1963.

7455 CAMPBELL (J.). Changes in Mortality Trends: England and Wales 1931–1961: A Study of Trends in the Death Rates in England and Wales Analysed by Sex, Age and Cause of Death, as Part of a Survey of Trends in the United States and other Countries. Washington. 1965.

7456 HEADY (J. A.) and HEASMAN (MICHAEL ANTHONY). Social and Biological Factors in Infant Mortality. 1959.

7457 HOWE (GEORGE MELVYN). National Atlas of Disease Mortality in the United Kingdom: Prepared on Behalf of the Royal Geographical Society. 1963. Rev. edn 1970.

7458 GLASS (DAVID VICTOR). 'Some Indications of Differences between Urban and Rural Mortality in England and Wales and Scotland'. *Pop. Studs* 17 (1964), 263–8.

7459 GRIFFITH (M.). 'A Geographical Study of Mortality in an Urban Area'. *Urban Studs* 5. 8 (1971), 111–20.

7460 HAIR (P. E. H.). 'Deaths from Violence in Britain: A Tentative Secular Survey'. *Pop. Studs* 24 (1971), 59–70.

7461 LOGAN (WILLIAM PHILIP DOWIE). 'Mortality in the London Fog Incident, 1952'. *Lancet* 332 (1953), 336–8.

7462 —— 'Mortality in England and Wales from 1848–1947'. *Pop. Studs* 4 (1950), 132–78.

7463 —— 'Social Class Variations in Mortality'. *Brit. J. Prev. Soc. Med.* 8 (1954), 128–37.

7464 LOGAN (WILLIAM PHILIP DOWIE) *and* BENJAMIN (B.). Tuberculosis Statistics for England and Wales, 1938–1955: An Analysis of Trends and Geographical Distribution. 1957.

7465 PRESTON (S. H.). 'An International Comparison of Excessive Adult Mortality'. *Pop. Studs* 24 (1970), 1–20.

7466 SILCOCK (H.). 'The Comparison of Occupational Mortality Rates'. *Pop. Studs* 13 (1959), 183–92.

7467 MARMOT (G.). Immigrant Mortality in England and Wales, 1970–1978: Cause of Death by Country of Birth. [HMSO. 1984.].

7468 SCOTTISH HOME AND HEALTH DEPARTMENT. A Report and Enquiry into Maternal Deaths in Scotland, 1965–1971. By John Dunlop. Edin. HMSO. 1974.

7469 McAVINCHY (IAN D.). Unemployment and Mortality: Some Aspects of the Scottish Case 1950–1978. Aberd. 1982.

7470 GENERAL REGISTER OFFICE SCOTLAND. Occupational Mortality, 1969–1973. Edin. 1981.

7471 McKEOWN (THOMAS). 'Fertility, Mortality and the Causes of Death'. *Pop. Studs* 32 (1978), 535–42.

7472 PAMUK (ELSIE M.). 'Social Class Inequality in Mortality from 1921 to 1972 in England and Wales'. *Pop. Studs* 39 (1985), 17–32.

7473 WOODS (R. I.), WATTERSON (P. A.), *and* WOODWARD (J. H.). 'The Causes of Rapid Mortality Decline in England and Wales 1861–1921'. *Pop. Studs* 42 (1988), 343–66.

7474 WILLIAMSON (J. G.). 'British Mortality and the Value of Life 1781–1931'. *Pop. Studs* 39 (1984), 157–72.

(b) Birth Rate and Birth Control

7475 BROWN (J. W.), GREENWOOD (MAJOR), *and* WOOD (FRANCES). 'The Fertility of the English Middle Classes: A Statistical Study'. *Eugenics Rev.* (Oct. 1920), 158–211.

7476 CHARLES (ENID). The Effects of Present Trends in Fertility and Mortality upon the Future Population of England and Wales and upon its Age Composition. (Royal Economic Society Memorandum 55.) 1935.

7477 —— The Practice of Birth Control: An Analysis of Birth-control Experiences of Nine Hundred Women. 1932.

7478 —— The Twilight of Parenthood: A Biological Study of the Decline of the Population Growth. 1934.

7479 —— The Menace of Underpopulation. 1936.

7480 FISHER (*Sir* RONALD A.). 'Positive Eugenics'. *Eugenics Rev.* (Oct. 1917), 206–12.

7481 TITMUSS (RICHARD MORRIS) *and* TITMUSS (KATHLEEN). Parents' Revolt: A Study of the Declining Birthrate in Acquisitive Societies. 1942.

7482 ROYAL COLLEGE OF OBSTETRICS AND GYNAECOLOGISTS AND POPULATION INVESTIGATION JOINT COMMITTEE. Maternity in Great Britain: A Survey of Social and Economic Aspects of Pregnancy. 1948.

7483 BERENT (JERZY). 'Fertility and Social Mobility'. *Pop. Studs* 5 (1952), 244–60.

7484 SCOTT (W.). 'Fertility and Social Mobility among Teachers'. *Pop. Studs* 11 (1958), 251–60.

7485 EVERSLEY (DAVID EDWARD CHARLES). Social Theories of Fertility and the Malthusian Debate. Oxf. 1959.

7486 WRONG (DENNIS HUME). 'Class Fertility Differences in England and Wales'. *Millbank Mem. Fund Q.* 38 (1960), 37–47.

7487 COX (PETER). Demography. 1950. 5th edn 1976.

7488 SILVER (MORRIS). 'Births, Marriages and Income Fluctuations in the United Kingdom and Japan'. *Econ. Dvlpt Cult. Change* 14 (1966), 302–15.

7489 CARLSSON (GOSTA). 'The Decline of Fertility: Innovation or Adjustment Process?'. *Pop. Studs* 20 (1966), 149–74.

7490 CHOU (RU-CHI) *and* BROWN (SUSANNAH). 'A Comparison of the Size of Families of Roman Catholics and Non-Catholics in Great Britain'. *Pop. Studs* 22 (1968), 51–60.

7491 SIMON (JULIAN LINCOLN). 'The Effect of Income on Fertility'. *Pop. Studs* 23 (1969), 327–42.

7492 WOOLF (MYRA). Family Intentions. 1971.

7493 WOOLF (MYRA) *and* PEGDEN (SUE). Families Five Years on. 1976.

7494 FARID (S. M.). 'On The Pattern of Cohort Fertility'. *Pop. Studs* 27 (1973), 159–68.

7495 HALL (RAY). 'Recent Changes in the Birthrate of England and Wales'. *Geog.* 60 (1975), 300–3.

7496 BUSFIELD (JOAN) *and* PADDON (MICHAEL). Thinking About Children: Sociology and Fertility in Post-War England. Camb. 1977.

7497 PRAIS (SIGBERT JON) *and* SCMOOL (MARLENA). 'The Fertility of Jewish Families in Britain, 1971'. *Jew. J. Sociol.* 15 (1973).

7498 LESER (CONRAD EMANUEL VICTOR). 'Fertility Changes in Scottish Cities and Countries (sic)'. *Scot. J. Pol. Econ.* 3 (1956), 83–91.

7499 TEPER (SUSAN). Patterns of Fertility in Greater London: A Comparative Study: Population Trends Project Supported in the Department of Statistics, London School of Economics, by the Greater London Council (Research Intelligence Unit.). 1968.

7500 TAYLOR (WALLIS). 'Comparative Fertility in the Local Government Areas of England and Wales, 1951'. *Brit. J. Prev. Soc. Med.* 8 (1954), 176–7.

7501 BLACKER (CARLOS PATON). 'Family Planning and Eugenic Movements in the Mid-Twentieth Century'. *Eugenics Rev.* 47 (1956), 225–33.

7502 ROWNTREE (GRISELDA) *and* PIERCE (RACHEL M.). 'Birth Control in Britain'. *Pop. Studs* Pt. One 15, 1 (1961), 3–31. Pt. Two 15, 2 (1961), 121–60.

7503 LANGFORD (C. M.). Birth Control Practice and Marital Fertility in Great Britain: A Report on a Survey Carried Out in 1967–1968. 1976.

7504 RIDKER (RONALD G.). 'Desired Family Size and the Efficacy of Current Family Planning Programmes'. *Pop. Studs* 22 (1969), 279–84.

7505 GLASS (DAVID VICTOR). 'Family Planning Programmes and Action in Western Europe'. *Pop. Studs* 19 (1966), 221–38.

7506 MEDAWAR (JEAN) *and* PIKE (DAVID) *eds.* Family Planning. Harmondsworth. 1971.

7507 PEEL (JOHN) *and* CARR (GRISELDA). Contraception and Family Design: A Study of Birth Planning in Contemporary Society. Edin. 1975.

7508 JEGER (LENA MAY). Illegitimate Children and their Parents. 1951.

7509 —— 'The Politics of Family Planning'. *Pol. Q.* 33 (1962), 48–58.

7510 DOWSE (ROBERT EDWARD) *and* PEEL (JOHN). 'The Politics of Birth Control'. *Pop. Studs* 13 (1965), 179–97.

7511 PEEL (JOHN). 'The Hull Family Survey. Pt. One, The Survey Couples, 1966'. *J. Biosoc. Sci.* 2 (1970), 45–70. Pt. Two, 'Family Planning in the First Five Years of Marriage'. *J. Biosoc. Sci.* 4 (1972), 333–46.

7512 HAREWOOD (JACK). 'Changes in the Use of Birth Control Methods'. *Pop. Studs* 27 (1973), 33–57.

7513 ADAMS (PAUL) *et al.* Children's Rights: Towards the Liberation of the Child. 1971.

7514 DRAPER (ELIZABETH). Birth Control in the Modern World: The Role of the Individual in Population Control. 1965.

7515 FRYER (PETER). The Birth Controllers. 1965.

7516 BRIANT (KEITH RUTHERFORD). Marie Stopes: A Biography. 1962.

7517 HALL (RUTH). Marie Stopes: A Biography. 1977.

7518 WEEKS (JEFFRY). Sex, Politics and Society: The Regulation of Sexuality since 1800. 1981.

7519 LETHARD (AUDREY). The Fight for Family Planning: The Development of Family Planning Services in Britain 1921–1974. 1980.

7520 AITKEN-SWAN (JEAN). Fertility Control and the Medical Profession. 1977.

7521 HAWTHORN (GEOFFREY). The Sociology of Fertility. 1970.

7522 THOMPSON (BARBARA). 'Problems of Abortion in Britain: Aberdeen, A Case Study'. *Pop. Studs* 31 (1977), 143–52.

7523 BONE (MARGARET). Family Planning in Scotland in 1982: A Survey Carried out on Behalf of the Scottish Home and Health Department. 1985.

7524 COWARD (JOHN). 'Recent Characteristics of Roman Catholic Fertility in Northern and Southern Ireland'. *Pop. Studs* 34 (1980), 31–44.

7525 MAIRE NI BHROLCHAIN. 'Period Parity Progression Ratios and Birth Intervals in England and Wales 1941–1971: A Synthetic Life Table Analysis'. *Pop. Studs* 41 (1987), 103–25.

3. SOCIAL CHANGE

7526 WESTERGAARD (JOHN HARALD). Modern British Society: A Bibliography. 1974.

7527 CHALONER (WILLIAM HENRY) *and* RICHARDSON (R. C.) *comp.* British Economic and Social History: A Bibliographical Guide. Manch. 1976. 2nd edn Manch. 1984.

7528 CAMPBELL (ROY HUTCHESON) *and* DOW (J. B. A.). A Source Book of Scottish Economic and Social History. Oxf. 1968.

7529 COLE (GEORGE DOUGLAS HOWARD) *and* POSTGATE (RAYMOND). The Common People, 1746–1938. 1938. 4th edn [to 1946] 1949.

7530 MACIVER (ROBERT MORRISON) *and* PAGE (CHARLES HUNT). Society: An Introductory Analysis. 1949.

7531 BARKER (THEODORE) *ed.* The Long March of the Common Man. 1750–1960. Harmondsworth. 1978. [Originally published in London 1975. Translation into book form of the second half of the similarly titled BBC Radio 4 series.].

7532 CALDER (ANGUS) *and* SHERIDAN (DOROTHY) *eds.* Speak for Yourself: A Mass-Observation Anthology, 1937–1949. Oxf. 1985.

7533 CALDER (ANGUS). The People's War: Britain, 1939–1945. 1969.

7534 MOSLEY (LEONARD). Backs to the Wall: London Under Fire, 1939–45. 1971.

7535 LONGMATE (NORMAN). The Way We Lived Then: A History of Everyday Life during the Second World War. 1971.

7536 ADDISON (PAUL). Now the War is over: A Social History of Britain from 1945 to 1951. 1985.

7537 MARWICK (ARTHUR). The Deluge: British Society and the First World War. Harmondsworth 1967.

7538 —— Britain in the Century of Total War: War, Peace and Social Change, 1900–1967. 1968.

7539 —— Social Change in Britain: 1920–1970. 1970.

7540 —— The Explosion of British Society 1914–1962. 1963.

7541 —— Between Two Wars. Milton Keynes. 1973.

7542 —— The Home Front: The British and the Second World War. 1976.

7543 —— War and Social Change in the Twentieth Century: A Comparative Study of Britain, France, Germany, Russia and the United States. 1974.

7544 —— British Society Since 1945. Harmondsworth. 1982.

7545 —— Britain in Our Century: Images and Controversies. 1984.

7546 MONTGOMERY (JOHN). The Twenties, an Informal Social History. N.Y./Lond. 1957.

7547 —— The Fifties. 1965.

7548 MASTERMAN (CHARLES FREDERICK GURNEY). England after the War. A Study. 1922.

7549 U.K. MINISTRY OF PROPAGANDA. After Twelve Months of War. [By Charles Masterman.]. 1915.

7550 WORSFIELD (W. BASIL). The War and Social Reform. 1919.

7551 PLAYNE (CAROLINE E.). Society at War, 1914–1916. 1931.

7552 —— Britain Holds On, 1917–1918. 1933.

7553 GREENWOOD (GEORGE ARTHUR). England To-day: A Social Study. 1922. Rev. edn 1926.

7554 BLYTHE (RONALD). The Age of Illusion: England in the Twenties and Thirties, 1919–1940. 1963.

7555 MUGGERIDGE (MALCOLM). The Thirties: 1930–1940 in Great Britain. 1940.

7556 —— The Sun Never Sets: The Story of England in the Nineteen-Thirties. N.Y. 1940.

7557 GRAVES (ROBERT) and HODGE (ALAN). The Long Weekend: A Social History of Great Britain, 1918–1939. 1940.

7558 BÉDARIDA (FRANÇOIS). A Social History of England, 1851–1975. 1979.

7559 GLYNN (SEAN) and OXBURROW (JOHN). Inter-war Britain: A Social and Economic History. 1976.

7560 OGILVIE (VIVIAN). Our Times: A Social History, 1912–1952. 1953.

7561 ROEBUCK (JANET). The Making of Modern English Society from 1850. 1973.

7562 RATHBONE (JESSIE). The Curious Years: History, Recent and Remote. Oxf. 1927.

7563 BARKER (Sir ERNEST). Britain and the British People. 1942. 2nd edn 1955.

7564 —— Ed. The Character of England. Oxf. 1947.

7565 —— National Character and the Factors in its Formation. 1927.

7566 STEVENSON (JOHN). Social Conditions in Britain Between the Wars. Harmondsworth. 1977.

7567 —— British Society 1914–1945. Harmondsworth. 1984.

7568 STEVENSON (JOHN) and COOK (CHRIS). The Slump: Society and Politics during the Depression. 1977.

7569 —— Comps. Longman Atlas of Modern British History: A Visual Guide to British Society and Politics, 1700–1970. 1978.

7570 JENNINGS (HUMPHRY) and MADGE (CHARLES) eds. May the Twelfth. [Mass Observation Day Surveys 1937.]. 1937.

7571 SHERIDAN (D.). 'Mass Observing the British'. Hist. Today 34 (1984), 42–6.

7572 JENNINGS (HILDA). Societies in the Making: A Study of Development and Redevelopment within a County Borough. 1962.

7573 MANNHEIM (KARL). Man and Society in an Age of Reconstruction: Studies in Modern Social Structure. With a Bibliographical Guide to the Study of Modern Society. 1940.

7574 ABRAMS (MARK). The Condition of the British People, 1911–1945: A Study Prepared for the Fabian Society. 1945.

7575 HOPKINS (HARRY). The New Look: A Social History of the Forties and Fifties in Britain. 1963.

7576 SISSONS (MICHAEL) and FRENCH (PHILIP) eds. Age of Austerity. 1963. [Essays on Postwar Britain.].

7577 SPINLEY (BETTY MARTHA). The Deprived and the Privileged: Personality Development in English Society. 1953.

7578 RESEARCH SERVICES LIMITED. Britain Today: Her International Affiliation; Her Standing in the World, Her Daily Newspapers: A Study of the Opinions of People Listed in Who's Who. 1963.

7579 MOORHOUSE (GEOFFREY). Britain in the Sixties: The Other England. Harmondsworth. 1964.

7580 U.K. CENTRAL STATISTICAL OFFICE. Social Trends. [Published annually since 1970.].

7581 RADCLIFFE (CYRIL JOHN). Viscount Radcliffe. The Dissolving Society: Oration Delivered at the London School of Economics and Political Science. 1966.

7582 ANNAN (NOËL GILROY). Baron Annan. The Disintegration of an Old Culture. Oxf. 1965.

7583 LUSTY (MARGARET). The Foundations of Our Society. 1966.

7584 HALSEY (ALBERT H.). Trends in British Society since 1900: A Guide to the Changing Social Structures of Britain. 1972. 2nd edn 1974.

7585 —— Change in British Society. 1978. 2nd edn Oxf. 1981.

7586 JOHNS (EDWARD ALISTAIR). The Social Structure of Modern Britain. 1965. 2nd edn Oxf. 1972. 3rd edn Oxf. 1979.

7587 LASLETT (PETER). The World We Have Lost. 1965.

7588 KLEIN (JOSEPHINE). Samples from English Cultures. 2 vols 1965.

7589 U.K. CENTRAL OFFICE OF INFORMATION. Regional Trends. No. 24. 1989. [Published annually HMSO.].

7590 WILLIAMS (RAYMOND HENRY). Culture and Society, 1780–1950. 1951.

7591 BRIGGS (ASA). They Saw it Happen: IV. An Anthology of Eye-Witness Accounts of Events in British History, 1897–1940. 1960. 2nd edn 1972.

7592 —— 'Social History 1900–1945'. Ch. in 'The Economic History of Britain Since 1700' by Roderick Floud and Donald McCloskey eds. [Vol. 2 1860 to the 1970's.]. 1981.

7593 —— A Social History of England. 1983. 2nd edn 1987.

7594 SCOTT (J. D.). Life in Britain. 1956.

7595 BROMHEAD (PETER). Life in Modern Britain. 1962.

7596 CARSTAIRS (GEORGE MORRISON). This Island Now: The Surge of Social Change in the Twentieth Century. 1962.

7597 GUSFIELD (JOSEPHINE R.). ed. Protest, Reform and Revolt: A Reader in Social Movements. N.Y./Chichester. 1970.

7598 READ (Sir HERBERT EDWARD). To Hell with Culture and other Essays on Art and Society. 1963.

7599 WOOTTON (BARBARA FRANCES). Baroness Wootton. Contemporary Britain: Three Lectures. 1971.

7600 BUTTERWORTH (ERIC) and WEIR (DAVID) eds. The Sociology of Modern Britain: An Introductory Reader. 1970. Repr. 1971.

7601 —— Eds. Social Problems of Modern Britain. 1972.

7602 BUTTERWORTH (ERIC), WEIR (DAVID), and HOLMAN (ROBERT). Social Welfare in Modern Britain. 1975.

7603 CUNNINGHAM (GEORGE) ed. Britain and the World in the Seventies: A Collection of Fabian Essays. 1970.

7604 HAMILTON (M. B.) and ROBERTSON (K. G.) eds. Britain's Crisis in Sociological Perspective. Reading. 1976.

7605 AMIS (KINGSLEY). Harold's Years: Impressions from the New Statesman and the Spectator. 1977.

7606 COLMER (JOHN). Coleridge to Catch 22: Images of Society. 1978.

7607 BEESON (TREVOR). Britain Today and Tomorrow. 1978.

7608 BUCHANAN (COLIN). The State of Britain. 1972.

7609 SAMPSON (ANTHONY). The New Anatomy of Britain. 1973.

7610 NOBLE (TREVOR). Modern Britain: Structure and Change. 1975.

7611 TRIBE (DAVID). The Rise of the Mediocracy. 1975.

7612 MEDLIK (SLAVOJ). Britain: Workshop or Service Centre to the World? Guildford. 1977.

7613 HOPKINS (ERIC). A Social History of the English Working Classes 1815–1945. 1979.

7614 FURTH (CHARLES). Life since 1900. 1966.

7615 FLINN (MICHAEL WALTER). An Economic and Social History of Britain since 1700. 1963. Repr. 1973.

7616 FLINN (MICHAEL WALTER) and SMOUT (THOMAS CHRISTO-PHER) eds. Essays in Social History. 1974.

7617 SMOUT (THOMAS CHRISTOPHER) ed. The Search for Wealth and Stability: Essays in Economic and Social History presented to M. W. Flinn. 1979.

7618 RYDER (JUDITH) and SILVER (HAROLD). Modern English Society: History and Structure, 1850–1970. 1970. 2nd edn 1977.

7619 HARTWELL (RONALD MAXWELL) and BREACH (ROBERT WAL-TER) eds. British Economy and Society, 1870–1970: Documents, Descriptions, Statistics. 1972.

7620 ASHLEY (MAURICE). The People of England: A Short Social and Economic History. 1984.

7621 CRONIN (JAMES E.). Labour and Society in Britain 1918–1979. 1984.

4. THE STATUS OF WOMEN

7622 CRAWFORD (ANNE) et al. eds. The Europa Biographical Dictionary of British Women. 1983.

7623 DARTER (PAT). The Women's Movement. 1983.

7624 AMOS (VALERIE). 'Black Women in Britain: A Bibliographical Essay'. Sage Race Relations Abstracts. 7 (1982), 1–11.

7625 COWLEY (RUTH). What About Women? Information Sources for Women's Studies. 1986.

7626 RITCHIE (M.). Women's Studies: A Checklist of Bibliographies. 1980.

7627 FREY (LINDA), FREY (MARRSHA), and SCHNEIDER (JOANNA) eds. Women in Western European History: A Select Chronological and Topical Bibliography: The Nineteenth and Twentieth Centuries. Westport, Conn. 1984.

7628 GILBERT (VICTOR F.) and TATLA (DARSHAN SINGH). Women's Studies: A Bibliography of Dissertations 1870–1982. 1985.

7629 ROWBOTHAM (SHEILA) comp. Women's Liberation and Revolution: A Bibliography. 2nd edn Bristol. 1973.

7630 —— A New World For Women: Stella Browne: Socialist Feminist. 1977.

7631 —— Women, Resistance and Revolution: A History of Women and Revolution in the Modern World. 1972.

7632 —— Women's Consciousness, Man's World. Harmondsworth. 1973.

7633 —— Hidden from History: 300 Years of Women's Oppression and the Fight against it. 1973. 3rd edn 1977.

7634 —— The Past Before Us: Feminism in Action since the 1960s. 1989.

7635 HEWINS (ANGELA) ed. Mary, after the Queen: Memories of a Working Girl. 1983.

7636 BOUCHER (DAVID). The Movement for Women's Liberation in Britain and the USA. 1983.

7637 LEWIS (JANE) ed. Labour and Love: Women's Experiences of Home and Family, 1850–1940. 1986.

7638 ROBERTS (ELIZABETH). A Women's Place: An Oral History of Working-Class Women 1890–1940. 1984.

7639 —— Women's Work 1840–1940. Basingstoke. 1988.

7640 SMITH (ANNE). Women Remember: An Oral History. 1986.

7641 DYHOUSE (CAROL). Feminism and the Family in England, 1880–1930. 1989.

7642 SMITH (HAROLD L.) ed. British Feminism in the Twentieth Century. Aldershot. 1989.

7643 PENNINGTON (SHELLEY) and WESTOVER (BELINDA). A Hidden Workforce. Women Homeworkers in Britain, 1850–1985. 1989.

7644 ALLEN (SHEILA) and WOLKOWITZ (CAROL). Homeworking: Myths and Realities. 1987.

7645 JOHN (ANGELA V.). Unequal Opportunities: Women's Employment in England, 1800–1918. 1985.

7646 DAVIDOFF (LEONORE) and WESTOVER (BELINDA) eds. Our Work, Our Lives, Our Words. 1986.

7647 MARWICK (ARTHUR). Women at War, 1914–1918. 1977.

7648 MANGAN (J. A.) and PARK (ROBERTA J.) eds. From 'Fair Sex' to Feminism: Sport and the Socialisation of Women in the Industrial and Post-Industrial Eras. 1987.

7649 WILSON (ELIZABETH). Only Halfway to Paradise: Women in Post-War Britain, 1945–1968. 1981.

7650 CO-OPERATIVE WOMEN'S GUILD. Maternity: Letters from Working-Women. 1915.

7651 GRANT (I.). National Council of Women of Great Britain: The First Sixty Years, 1895–1955. 1955.

7652 HALL (DOROTHY V.). Making Things Happen: History of the National Federation of Business and Professional Women's Clubs of Great Britain and Northern Ireland. 1963.

7653 JARMAN (BETTY). The Lively-Minded Women: The First Twenty Years of the National Housewives Register. 1981.

7654 GOODENOUGH (S.). Jam and Jerusalem: A History of the Women's Institution. 1977.

7655 SCHARLIEB (Dame MARY DACOMB). The Seven Ages of Women. 1915.

7656 —— The Welfare of the Expectant Mother. 1919.

7657 —— Reminiscences. 1924.

7658 GOLLANCZ (VICTOR) ed. The Making of Women: Oxford Essays. 1917.

7659 FAWCETT (MILLICENT GARRETT). What I Remember. 1924.

7660 —— The Women's Victory—and after: Personal Reminiscences 1911–1918. 1920.

7661 CREIGHTON (LOUISE). 'Women Police'. *Fort. Rev.* July 1920, 109–17.

7662 ERNLE *Lord*. 'Women's Land Army'. *Nineteenth Century* (Jan. 1920), 1–16.

7663 HARTLEY (W. FREDA). 'The Farewell Rally of the Women's Land Army and a Retrospect'. *J. Min. Agric.* (Mar. 1920), 1205–12.

7664 PARSONS (*Lady* KATHERINE). 'Women's Work in Engineering and Shipbuilding during the War'. *Trans NE Coast Inst. Eng. Shipbuilders* 35 (1918–1919), 227–36.

7665 ANDERSON (*Dame* ADELAIDE MARY). Women in the Factory, 1893 to 1921. 1922.

7666 NADIA (A. R.). The Ethics of Feminism: A Study of the Revolt of Women. 1923.

7667 REISS (ERNA). Rights and Duties of Englishwomen: A Study in Law and Public Opinion. Manch. 1934.

7668 COSTELLOE (Later STRACHEY) (RACHEL/RAY). Careers and Openings for Women: A Survey of Women's Employment and a Guide for those Seeking Work. 1935. 2nd edn 1937.

7669 —— 'The Cause': A Short History of the Women's Movement in Great Britain. 1928.

7670 —— *Ed.* Our Freedom and its Results. By Five Women: Eleanor Rathbone, Erna Reiss, Ray Strachey, Alison Neilans, Mary Agnes Hamilton. 1936.

7671 —— Women's Suffrage and Women's Service: The History of the London and National Society for Women's Service. 1927.

7672 SMITH (HAROLD L.). 'Sex Versus Class: British Feminists and the Labour Movement 1919–1929'. *Historian* 47 (1984–85), 19–37.

7673 —— 'The Woman-Power Problem in Britain during the Second World War'. *J. Mod. Hist.* 53 (1981), 652–72.

7674 ZWEIG (FERDYNAND). Women's Life and Labour. 1952.

7675 FRY (SARA MARGERY). The Single Woman. 1953.

7676 SUMMERFIELD (PENNY). Women Workers in the Second World War: Production and Patriarchy in Conflict. 1984.

7677 HARRIS (EVELYN MARJORIE). Married Women in Industry. 1954.

7678 HUBBACK (JUDITH). Wives Who Went to College. 1957.

7679 —— 'The Fertility of Graduate Women'. *Eugenics Rev.* 47 (1955), 107–13.

7680 BRITTAIN (VERA). The Women at Oxford: A Fragment of History. 1960.

7681 —— Lady into Woman: A History of Women from Victoria to Elizabeth II. 1953.

7682 ILLSLEY (RAYMOND) and THOMPSON (B.). 'Women from Broken Homes'. *Sociol. Rev.* 9 (1961), 27–54.

7683 JEPHCOTT (AGNES PEARL), SEEAR (NANCY) *Baroness, and* SMITH (JOHN HAROLD). Married Women Working. 1962.

7684 CLARK (FREDERICK LE GROS). Women, Work and Age: To Study the Employment of Working Women Throughout their Middle Lives. 1962.

7685 O'DONOVAN (K.). Sexual Divisions in Law. 1985.

7686 REID (I.) *and* WORMALD (E.) *eds.* Sex Differences in Britain. 1982.

7687 NATIONAL FEDERATION OF BUSINESS AND PROFESSIONAL WOMEN'S CLUBS OF GREAT BRITAIN AND NORTHERN IRELAND. The Changing Pattern: Report on the Training of Older Women. 1966.

7688 YUDKIN (SOLOMON SIMON) *and* HOLME (ANTHEA). Working Mothers and their Children: A Study for the Council for Children's Welfare. 1963.

7689 CLARK (FREDERICK LE GROS). The Economic Rights of Women. L/pool. 1963.

7690 McKINLEY (DONALD GILBERT). Social Class and Family Life. 1964.

7691 HERON (LIZ) *ed.* Truth, Dare or Promise: Girls Growing Up in the Fifties. 1985.

7692 DIX (CAROL). Say I'm Sorry to Mother: Growing Up in the Sixties. 1978.

7693 HUNT (FELICITY). Lessons for Life: The Schooling of Girls and Women, 1850–1950. 1987.

7694 ACKWORTH (EVELYN). The New Matriarchy. 1965.

7695 WILLIAMS (GERTRUDE *Lady*). The Changing Pattern of Women's Employment. L/pool. 1965.

7696 —— The Marriage Rate and Women's Employment. 1967.

7697 KLEIN (VIOLA). Britain's Married Women Workers. 1965.

7698 —— Women Workers: Working Hours and Services. Paris. 1965. OECD.

7699 —— Employing Married Women. (Institute of Personnel Management) 1961.

7700 —— The Feminine Character: History of an Ideology. 1946.

7701 —— Working Wives: A Survey of Facts and Opinions Concerning the Gainful Employment of Married Women in Britain. 1960.

7702 MITCHELL (DAVID). Women on the Warpath: The Story of the Women of the First World War. 1966.

7703 OLDFIELD (SYBIL). Women Against the Iron Fist: Alternatives to Militarism, 1900–1989. 1989.

7704 CONDELL (DIANA) *and* LIDDIARD (JEAN). Working for Victory? Images of Women in the First World War, 1914–18. 1987. [A photographic collection.].

7705 BRAYBON (GAIL). Women Workers in the First World War. 1981.

7706 LONDON SCHOOL OF ECONOMICS AND POLITICAL SCIENCE. Woman, Wife and Worker. 1968.

7707 MacCARTHY (FIONA). Work for Married Women. 1966.

7708 KAMM (JOSEPHINE). Rapiers and Battleaxes: The Women's Movement and its Aftermath. 1966.

7709 GAVRON (HANNAH). The Captive Wife: Conflicts of Housebound Mothers. 1966.

7710 —— Bibliography on Women Workers, 1861–1965. Geneva. 1970.

7711 ARREGGER (CONSTANCE E.) *ed.* Graduate Women at Work: A Study by a Working Party of the British Federation of University Women. Newcastle. 1966.

7712 WALTON (RONALD G.). Women in Social Work. 1975.

7713 POLITICAL AND ECONOMIC PLANNING. Women and Top Jobs: An Interim Report. By Michael Patrick Fogarty *et al.* 1967.

7714 FOGARTY (MICHAEL PATRICK), ALLEN (M. J.), ALLEN (ISOBEL), *and* WALTERS (P.). Women in Top Jobs: Four Studies in Achievement. 1971.

7715 FOGARTY (MICHAEL PATRICK), RAPOPORT (RHONA), *and* RAPOPORT (ROBERT NORMAN). Sex, Career and Family: Including an International Review of Women's Roles. 1971.

7716 FOGARTY (MICHAEL PATRICK). Women in Top Jobs 1968–1979. 1981.

7717 McNALLY (FIONA). Women for Hire: A Study of the Female Office Worker. 1979.

7718 MARTIN (RODERICK) *and* WALLACE (JUDITH). Working Women in Recession: Employment, Redundancy and Unemployment. Oxf. 1984.

7719 RAPOPORT (RHONA) *and* RAPOPORT (ROBERT NORMAN). Dual Career Families. Harmondsworth. 1971.

7720 GAUDART (D. J.). Social Situation of Women in Europe: The Effects of the Opportunities of General and Vocational Training on the Social Position of Women. Strasbourg. 1971.

7721 MITCHELL (JULIET). Women's Estate. Harmondsworth. 1971.

7722 —— Women and Equality. Cape Town. 1975.

7723 GLENDINNING (CAROLINE) *and* MILLER (JANE) *eds.* Women and Poverty in Britain. Brighton. 1987.

7724 MESSENGER (ROSALIND). The Doors of Opportunity: A Biography of Dame Caroline Haslett, D.B.E. Companion I.E.E. 1967.

7725 STACK (PRUNELLA). Movement is Life: The Autobiography of Prunella Stack. 1973.

7726 BRYAN (BEVERLEY), DADZIE (STELLA), *and* SCAFE (SUZANNE). The Heart of the Race: Black Women's Lives in Britain. 1985.

7727 DIXEY (R.). 'It's a Great Feeling When You Win: Women and Bingo'. *Leisure Studs* 6 (1987), 199–214.

7728 WILSON (PATRICK). Murderess: A Study of the Women Executed in Britain Since 1823. 1971.

7729 DAVIES (JEAN) *and* GOODMAN (NANCY). Girl Offenders aged Seventeen to Twenty Years. 1972.

7730 SULLIVAN (K.). Girls Who Go Wrong. 1956.

7731 LOCK (JOAN). The British Policewoman: Her Story. 1979.

7732 SMITH (ANN D.). Women in Prisons: A Study in Penal Methods. 1962.

7733 FIELD (XENIA). Under Lock and Key: A Study of Women in Prison. 1963.

7734 HENRY (JOAN). Who Lie in Gaol. 1952.

7735 JOHNSTON (ROSIE). Inside Out. 1989.

7736 DEEM (ROSEMARY). Women and Schooling. 1978.

7737 —— Ed. Schooling for Women's Work. 1980.

7738 FLETCHER (SHEILA). Women First: The Female Tradition in English Physical Education, 1880–1980. 1984.

7739 BECKETT (WENDY). Contemporary Women Artists. 1987.

7740 CROSLAND (MARGARET). Beyond the Lighthouse: English Women Novelists in the Twentieth Century. 1987.

7741 LEWENHAK (SHEILA). 'Women in the Leadership of the Scottish Trades Unions, 1897–1970'. Scot. Lab. Hist. Soc. 7 (1973), 3–23.

7742 GLASGOW WOMEN'S GROUP. Uncharted Lives: Extracts from Scottish Women's Experiences, 1850–1982. Glas. 1983.

7743 FAIRWEATHER (E.), MCDONOUGH (R.), and MCFADYEAN (H.). Only the Rivers Run Free: Northern Ireland: The Women's War. 1984.

7744 LEWIS (JANE). Women in England 1870–1950: Sexual Divisions and Social Change. Brighton. 1984.

7745 MARSHALL (R. K.). Virgins and Viragos: A History of Women in Scotland 1080–1980. 1983.

7746 DEUTSCH (RICHARD R.). Mairead Corrigan, Betty Williams: Two Women Who Ignored Danger in Campaigning for Peace in Northern Ireland. Woodbury, N.Y. 1977.

7747 LIND (MARY ANN). The Compassionate Memsahibs: Welfare Activities of British Women in India, 1900–1947. 1988.

7748 HOLDEN (PAT). Women Administrative Officers in Colonial Africa, 1944–1960. Rhodes House Library, Oxf. 1985.

7749 CALLAWAY (HELEN). Gender, Culture and Empire: European Woman in Colonial Nigeria. 1987.

7750 SEDDON (VICKY) ed. The Cutting Edge: Women and the Pit Strike. 1987.

7751 BOSTON (SARAH). Women Workers and the Trade Unions, 1980. 2nd edn 1987.

7752 LEWENHAK (SHEILA). Women and Trade Unions: An Outline History of Women in the British Trade Union Movement. 1977.

7753 SOLDEN (NORBERT C.). Women in British Trade Unions, 1874–1976. Dublin. 1978.

7754 DRAKE (BARBARA). Women in Trade Unions. 1984.

7755 OAKLEY (ANN). Sex, Gender and Society. 1972.

7756 —— The Sociology of Housework. 1974.

7757 —— Housewife. Harmondsworth. 1976.

7758 —— Becoming a Mother. Oxf. 1979.

7759 —— Women Confined: Towards a Sociology of Childbirth. Oxf. 1980.

7760 —— Subject Women. Oxf. 1980.

7761 —— Taking it Like a Woman. 1984.

7762 —— What is Feminism? Oxf. 1986.

7763 RILEY (DENISE). 'Am I That Name?': Feminism and the Category of 'Women' in History. Basingstoke. 1988.

7764 JAMES (MARGARET) ed. The Emancipation of Women in Great Britain. 1972.

7765 ALEXANDER (SALLY) ed. Women's Fabian Tracts. 1988.

7766 COLTON (MARY). Fair and Equal. 1974.

7767 HEWITT (PATRICIA) ed. Danger! Women at Work. [Report of a Conference organized by the National Council for Civil Liberties on 11 February 1974.]. 1974.

7768 ANDERSON (GREGORY) ed. The White Blouse Revolution: Female Office Workers Since 1870. Manch. 1988.

7769 ALLEN (SANDRA), SANDERS (LEE), and WALLIS (JAN) eds. Conditions of Illusion: Papers from the Women's Movement. Leeds. 1974.

7770 COOK (ALICE HANSON). The Working Mother: A Survey of Problems and Programmes in Nine Countries. Ithaca, N.Y. 1975.

7771 Royal Commission on Equal Pay, 1944–1946: Report. Cmnd 6937. Parliamentary Papers, xi (1945–6).

7772 JOSEPH (G.). Women at Work: The British Experience. Deddington. 1983.

7773 JOSHI (HEATHER), LAYARD (RICHARD), and OWEN (SUSAN). Female Labour Supply in Post-War Britain: A Cohort Approach. Centre for Labour Economics, London School of Economics. 1981.

7774 GALES (K.) and MARKS (P.). 'Twentieth Century Trends in the Work of Women in England and Wales'. Roy. Stats. Soc. Series A 1937 (1974), 60–74.

7775 JAMES (E.). 'Women at Work in Twentieth Century Britain: The Changing Structure of Female Employment'. Man. Sch. Econ. Soc. Studs 30 (1962), 283–300.

7776 DAVIES (ROSS). Women at Work. 1975.

7777 U.K. EQUAL OPPORTUNITIES COMMISSION. Women and Low Incomes: A Report based on Evidence to the Royal Commission on Income Distribution and Wealth. 1977.

7778 —— Annual Report. 1976+.

7779 COUSSINS (JEAN). The Equality Report: One Year of the Equal Pay Act, the Sex Discrimination Act, the Equal Opportunities Commission. 1976.

7780 CREIGHTON (W. B.). Working Women and the Law. 1979.

7781 PANNICK (DAVID). Sex Discrimination Law. Oxf. 1985.

7782 HEPPLE (B. A.). Equal Pay and the Industrial Tribunals. 1984.

7783 RUBENSTEIN (M.). Equal Pay for Work of Equal Value. 1984.

7784 POTTER (ALLEN M.). 'The Equal Pay Campaign Committee'. *Pol. Studs* (1957), 49–64.

7785 MEPHAM (GEORGE JAMES). Problems of Equal Pay. 1969.

7786 U.K. DEPARTMENT OF EMPLOYMENT. Equal Pay: A Guide to the Equal Pay Act 1970. 1970.

7787 HUNT (AUDREY) ed. Women and Paid Work: Issues of Equality. 1988.

7788 CHIPLIN (BRIAN) *and* SLOANE (PETER JAMES). Sex Discrimination in the Labour Market. 1976.

7789 CHIPLIN (BRIAN) *and* SLOANE (PETER JAMES). 'Sexual Discrimination in the Labour Market'. *Brit. Ind. Relns* 12 (1974), 371–402.

7790 ZABALZA (A.) *and* TZANNOTOS (Z.). Women and Equal Pay: The Effects of Legislation on Female Employment and Wages in Britain. 1985.

7791 MEEHAN (ELIZABETH). Women's Rights at Work: Campaigns and Policy in Britain and the United States. 1984.

7792 LISTER (RUTH) *and* WILSON (LEO). The Unequal Breadwinner: A New Perspective on Women and Social Security. 1976.

7793 BARKER (DIANA LEONARD) *and* ALLEN (SHEILA) *eds.* Sexual Divisions and Society: Process and Change. 1976.

7794 —— *Eds.* Dependence and Exploitation in Work and Marriage. 1976.

7795 BANKS (OLIVE). Faces of Feminism: A Study of Feminism as a Social Movement. 1981. Rev. edn 1986.

7796 HERON (LIZ). Changes of Heart: Reflections on Women's Independence. 1986.

7797 COOTE (ANNA) *and* CAMPBELL (BEATRIX). Sweet Freedom. Oxf. 1987.

7798 NEUSTATTER (ANGELA). Hyenas in Petticoats: A Look at Twenty Years of Feminism. Harmondsworth. 1989.

7799 MITCHELL (JULIET) *and* OAKLEY (ANN) *eds.* Essays on Women. Harmondsworth. 1976.

7800 BRADLEY (HARRIET). Men's Work, Women's Work: A History of the Sex-Typing of Jobs in Britain. Camb. 1989.

7801 GILL (DEREK). Illegitimacy, Sexuality and the Status of Women. Oxf. 1977.

7802 CANTOR (MILTON) *and* LAURIE (BRUCE) *eds.* Class, Sex and the Woman Worker. 1977.

7803 COLLINS (WENDY), FRIEDMAN (ELLEN), *and* PIVOT (AGNES). Women. 1978.

7804 HAMILTON (ROBERTA). The Liberation of Women: A Study of Patriarchy and Capitalism. 1978.

7805 WEIR (ANGELA) *and* WILSON (ELIZABETH). 'The British Women's Movement'. *New Left Rev.* 148 (1984), 74–103.

7806 WHEELER-BENNETT (JOAN) *in collaboration with* MUSGRAVE (BEATRICE) *and* HERSON (ZOE). Women at the Top: Achievement and Family Life. 1977.

7807 MACKIE (LINDSAY) *and* PATULLO (POLLY). Women at Work. 1977.

7808 HEATH (GRAHAM). The Illusory Freedom: The Intellectual Origins and Social Consequences of the Sexual 'Revolution'. 1978.

7809 ROWBOTHAM (SHEILA) *and* McCRINDLE (JEAN). Dutiful Daughters: Women Talk about their Lives. 1977.

7810 BIRMINGHAM UNIVERSITY CENTRE FOR CONTEMPORARY CULTURAL STUDIES. (Women's Studies Group). Women Take Issue: Aspects of Women's Subordination. 1978.

7811 COXHEAD (ELIZABETH). Women in the Professions. 1961.

7812 PEARSON (SYLVIA). Mothers at Work. 1964.

7813 SEEAR (BEATRICE NANCY) *Baroness Seear. et al.* A Career for Women in Industry? Edin. 1964.

7814 GREENWOOD (JOHN A.). Some Problems in the Implementation of an Equal Pay Policy. 1969.

7815 CHAFETZ (JANET SALTZMAN) *and* POLK (BARBARA BOVEE). 'Room at the Top: Social Recognition of British and American Females Over Time'. *Soc. Sci. Q.* 54 (1974), 843–53.

7816 COLE (MARGARET). 'The Woman's Vote: What has it Achieved?' *Pol. Q.* 33 (1962), 74–83.

7817 DUNNING (JOHN H.). 'Employment for Women in the Development Areas 1939–1951'. *Man. Sch. Econ. Soc. Studs* 21 (1953), 271–7.

7818 JAMES (EDWARD). 'Women at Work in Twentieth Century Britain'. *Man. Sch. Econ. Soc. Studs* 30 (1962), 283–300.

7819 KELSALL (ROGER KEITH) *and* MITCHELL (SHEILA). 'Married Women and Employment in England and Wales'. *Pop. Studs* 13 (1959), 19–33.

7820 LESER (CONRAD EMANUEL VICTOR). 'The Supply of Women for Gainful Work in Britain'. *Pop. Studs* 9 (1955), 142–7.

7821 McGREGOR (OLIVER ROSS). 'Equality, Sexual Values and Permissive Legislation: The English Experience'. *J. Social Policy* 1 (1972), 44–59.

7822 PINDER (PAULINE). 'Women at Work'. *Planning* 512 (1968), 528–653.

7823 —— Women at Work. 1969.

7824 RAPOPORT (RHONA) *and* RAPOPORT (ROBERT NORMAN). 'Early and Later Experiences as Determinants of Adult Behaviour: Married Women's Family and Career Patterns'. *Brit. J. Sociol.* 22 (1971), 16–30.

7825 RODGERS (HARRY BRIAN). 'Women and Work in New and Expanding Towns'. *Town and Country Planning* 37 (1969), 23–7.

7826 THOMPSON (BARBARA) *and* FINLAYSON (ANGELA). 'Married Women who Work in Early Motherhood'. *Brit. J. Sociol.* 14 (1963), 150–68.

7827 VALLANCE (ELIZABETH). 'Equality for Women: A Note on the White Paper'. *Pol. Q.* 46 (1975), 201–6.

7828 —— Women in the House: A Study of Women Members of Parliament. 1979.

7829 VALLANCE (ELIZABETH), BARON (CHRISTINA), *and* BROMHEAD (EVELYN). Fair Shares in Parliament: Or, How to Elect More Women MPs. 1981.

7830 STOBHAUGH (B. P.). Women and Parliament 1918–1970. N.Y. 1978.

7831 PHILLIPS (M.). The Divided House: Women at Westminster. 1980.

7832 BRISTOW (S. E.). 'Women Councillors: An Explanation of the Under-representation of Women in Local Government'. *Local Gvt. Studs* 6 (1980), 73–90.

7833 HILLS (J.). 'Women Local Councillors: A Reply to Bristow'. *Local Gvt. Studs* 8 (1982), 61–71.

7834 RASMUSSEN (JORGEN S.). 'Women's Role in British Politics: Impediments to Parliamentary Candidature'. *Parl. Affs.* 36 (1983), 300–15.

7835 ABDELA (LESLEY). Women with X Appeal: Women Politicians in Britain Today. 1989.

7836 U.K. EQUAL OPPORTUNITIES COMMISSION. Women and Men in Great Britain: A Research Profile. 1988.

7837 SPRING-RICE (MARGERY). Working-class Wives: Their Health and Conditions. 2nd edn 1981.

7838 KENNA (CHARMIAN). No Time for Women: Exploring Women's Health in the 1930s and Today. 1985.

7839 SHOWALTER (ELAINE). The Female Malady: Women, Madness and English Culture, 1830–1980. N.Y. 1985.

7840 MOSCUCCI (ORNELLA). The Science of Woman: Gynaecology and Gender in England, 1800–1929. Camb. 1990.

7841 PAHL (J.). A Refuge for Battered Women: A Study of the Role of a Woman's Centre. 1978.

7842 ADAM (RUTH). A Woman's Place, 1910–75. 1976.

7843 RILEY (DENISE). 'The Free Mothers: Pronatalism and Working Women in Industry at the End of the Last War in Britain'. *Hist. Workshop* 11 (1981), 59–119.

7844 HUTTER (BRIDGET) *and* WILLIAMS (GILLIAN) *eds.* Controlling Women: The Normal and the Deviant. 1980.

7845 PHILLIPS (ANNE). Hidden Hands: Women and Economic Policies. 1983.

7846 BRAILEY (MARY J.). Women's Access to Council Housing. Glasg. 1986.

7847 BREAKWELL (GLYNIS MARIE). Young Women in 'Gender-Atypical' Jobs: The Case of Trainee Technicians in the Engineering Industry. (London Department of Employment) 1987.

7848 GALLAGHER (MARGARET). Unequal Opportunities: The Case of Women and the Media. Paris. 1981.

7849 STACEY (MARGARET). Women, Power and Politics. 1981.

7850 YOUNG (JAMES D.). Women and Popular Struggles: A History of British Working Class Women, 1560–1984. Edin. 1984.

7851 CAMPBELL (BEATRIX). The Iron Ladies: Why do Women Vote Tory? 1987.

7852 MIDDLETON (LUCY). Women in the Labour Movement: The British Experience. 1977.

7853 RANDALL (VICKY). Women in Politics. 1982.

7854 O₃NEILL (WILLIAM). The Woman Movement: Feminism in the United States and in England. 1969.

7855 PLATT (BERYL CATHERINE). *Baroness Platt.* Women in Technology. Guildford. 1984.

7856 SILVERSTONE (ROSALIE) *and* WARD (AUDREY). Careers of Professional Women. 1980.

7857 ALDRED (CHRIS). Women at Work. 1981.

7858 HAMILTON (MARY AGNES). Women at Work: A Brief Introduction to Trade Unionism for Women. 1941.

7859 BOSTON (SARAH). Women Workers and the Trade Union Movement. 1980.

7860 GREER (GERMAINE). The Female Eunuch. 1970.

7861 Sex and Destiny: The Politics of Human Fertility. 1984.

7862 SOLDON (NORBERT C.). Women in British Trade Unions 1874–1976. Dublin. 1978.

7863 PHILLIPS (ANNE). Feminism and Equality. 1987.

7864 CARTER (APRIL). The Politics of Women's Rights. 1988.

7865 DALE (JENNIFER). Feminists and State Welfare. 1986.

7866 FERGUSON (MARJORIE). Forever Feminine: Women's Magazines and the Cult of Femininity. 1983.

7867 HARRIS (SARAH). Women in Twentieth Century Britain. 1989.

7868 WIMPERIS (VIRGINIA). The Unmarried Mother and Her Child. 1960.

7869 NICHOLSON (GILL). Mother and Baby Homes: A Survey of Homes for Unmarried Mothers. 1968.

7870 YELLOLY (MARGARET A.). 'Factors Relating to an Adoption Decision by Mothers of Illegitimate Infants'. *Sociol. Rev.* 13 (1965), 5–14.

7871 MACKAY (ANN), WILDING (PAUL), *and* GEORGE (VICTOR). 'Stereotypes of Male and Female Roles and their Influence on People's Attitudes to One Parent Families'. *Sociol. Rev.* 20 (1972), 79–92.

7872 STREATHER (JANE). Social Insecurity: Single Mothers on Benefit. 1974.

7873 HOPKINSON (ANGELA). Single Mothers: The First Year: A Scottish Study of Mothers Bringing up Children on their Own. (Scottish Council for Single Parents) Edin. 1976.

7874 MARSDEN (DENNIS). Mothers Alone: Poverty and the Fatherless Family. 1969.

7875 Abortion Statistics. 1974+ Annual.

7876 HINDELL (KEITH) *and* SIMMS (MADELEINE). Abortion Law Reformed. 1971.

7877 —— Abortion and Contraception: A Study of Patient's Attitudes. 1972.

7878 FERRIS (PAUL). The Nameless: Abortion in Britain Today. 1966.

7879 MARSH (DAVID) *and* CHAMBERS (JOANNA). Abortion Politics. 1981.

7880 BROOKES (BARBARA). Abortion in Britain, 1900–1967. 1988.

7881 HORDEN (ANTHONY). Legal Abortion: The English Experience. Oxf. 1971.

7882 HOROBIN (GORDON) *ed.* Experience with Abortion: A Case Study of North-East Scotland. 1973.

7883 U.K. REPORT ON THE COMMITTEE ON THE WORKING OF THE ABORTION ACT. (The Lane Committee) 1974.

7884 GREENWOOD (VICTORIA) *and* YOUNG (JOCK). Abortion on Demand. 1976.

7885 GOODHART (C. B.). 'On the Incidence of Illegal Abortion'. *Pop. Studs* 27 (1973), 207–33.

7886 JAMES (WILLIAM H.). 'The Incidence of Illegal Abortion'. *Pop. Studs* 25 (1971), 327–39.

7887 PEARSON (J. E.). 'Pilot Study of Single Women Requesting a Legal Abortion'. *J. Biosoc. Sci.* 3 (1971), 417–48.

7888 SIMMS (MADELEINE). 'Abortion Law and Medical Freedom'. *Brit. J. Criminol.* 22 (1971), 118–31.

7889 —— 'Abortion Act after Three Years'. *Pol. Q.* 42 (1971), 269–86.

5. SOCIOLOGY, SOCIAL SCIENCE, AND MODERN BRITISH SOCIETY

7890 MACIVER (ROBERT MORRISON). The Elements of Social Science. 1921. 9th edn 1949.

7891 HOBSON (JOHN ATKINSON). Free-thought in the Social Sciences. 1926.

7892 BARNES (HARRY ELMER). An Introduction to the History of Sociology. Chicago, Ill. 1948. Abridged Chicago 1966.

7893 —— Society in Transition: Problems of a Changing Age. N.Y. 1945.

7894 —— *Ed.* The History and Prospects of the Social Sciences. N.Y. 1925.

7895 MOORE (ELDON). 'Social Progress and Social Decline'. *Eugenics Rev.* 1926, 124–7.

7896 MERTON (ROBERT KING) *et al. eds.* Sociology Today: Problems and Prospects. N.Y. Repr. 1960.

7897 —— Social Theory and Social Structure: Toward the Codification of Theory and Research. Glencoe, Ill. 1951.

7898 —— Social Theory and Social Structure. Rev. and Extended Repr. Glencoe, 1964.

7899 WHITLEY (RICHARD) *ed.* Social Processes of Scientific Development. 1974.

7900 —— 'The Operation of Science Journals: Two Case Studies in British Social Science'. *Sociol. Rev.* 18 (1970), 241–58.

7901 SILBERMAN (LEO). Analysis of Society. 1951.

7902 MADGE (JOHN HYLTON). The Tools of Social Science. 1953.

7903 —— The Origins of Scientific Sociology. N.Y. 1962.

7904 —— *Et al.* Workbook for 'People in Towns': A Course of Twenty Radio Programmes on Urban Sociology. (BBC Series) 1968.

7905 —— 'Obituary John Madge (1914–1968)'. *Sociol.* 3 (1969), 110.

7906 WHITELEY (DENYS EDWARD HUGH) *and* MARTIN (RODERICK) *eds.* Sociology, Theology and Conflict. Oxf. 1969.

7907 HOBSBAWM (ERIC J.). 'From Social History to the History of Society'. *Daedalus* 100 (1971), 20–45.

7908 SKLAIR (LESLIE). The Sociology of Progress. 1970.

7909 —— Organised Knowledge: A Sociological View of Science and Technology. St Albans. 1973.

7910 MADGE (CHARLES HENRY). Society in the Mind: Elements of Social Eidos. 1964.

7911 BARRY (BRIAN). Sociologists, Economists and Democracy. 1970.

7912 MARSH (DAVID CHARLES) *ed.* The Social Sciences: An Outline for the Intending Student. 1965.

7913 —— The Changing Social Structure of England and Wales, 1871–1951. 1958. Rev. edn to 1961. 1965.

7914 NELSON (GEOFFREY K.). 'Social Science and the British Association'. *Soc. Sci. Info.* 14 (1975), 235–55.

7915 TROMPF (G. W.). 'Social Science in Historical Perspective'. *Phil. Soc. Sci.* 7 (1977), 113–38.

7916 FRASER DARLING (*Sir* FRANK). 'The Ecological Approach to the Social Sciences'. *Amer. Scientist* 39 (1951), 244–54.

7917 THERBORN (GORAN). Science, Class and Society: On the Formation of Sociology and Historical Materialism. 1976.

7918 HALE (BARBARA M.). The Subject Bibliography of the Social Sciences and Humanities. Oxf./N.Y. 1970.

7919 BILBOUL (ROGER R.) *ed.* Retrospective Index to Theses of Great Britain and Ireland, 1716–1950. Vol. 1 Social Sciences and Humanities and addenda to 1971. Santa Barbara. 1975.

7920 BURRINGTON (GILLIAN A.). How to Find Out About the Social Sciences. Oxf. 1973.

7921 BRITTAIN (JOHN MICHAEL) *and* ROBERTS (STEPHEN ANDREW) *eds.* Inventory of Information Resumés in the Social Sciences. Farnborough. 1975.

7922 BELSON (WILLIAM ALBERT). Bibliography of Methods of Social and Business Research. 1973.

7923 URRY (JOHN) *and* WAKEFORD (JOHN) *eds.* Power in Britain: Sociological Readings. 1973.

7924 LONG (NORMAN). An Introduction to the Sociology of Rural Development. 1971.

7925 BANKS (JOSEPH AMBROSE), HALSEY (ALBERT HENRY), *and* SCOTT (W. H.). 'Sociological Aspects of Technical Change in a Steel Plant'. *Transactions of the Third World Congress of Sociology* 2 (1956), 86–96.

7926 LASLETT (PETER) *and* RUNCIMAN (WALTER GARRISON) *eds.* Philosophy, Politics and Society. Second Series. Oxf. 1962.

7927 WOOTTON (BARBARA FRANCES) *Baroness Wootton.* Testament for Social Science: An Essay in the Application of Scientific Method to Human Problems. 1950.

7928 —— The Future of the Social Sciences: The Second Annual Lecture of the Research Students' Association, Delivered at Canberra on 18 October, 1961. Canberra. 1962.

7929 WOOTTON (BARBARA FRANCES) *asstd by* SEAL (VERA G.) *and* CHAMBERS (ROSALIND). Social Science and Social Pathology. 1959.

7930 ROSE (ARNOLD MARSHALL). Theory and Method in the Social Sciences. Minnesota/Oxf. 1954.

7931 —— Human Behaviour and Social Processes: An Interactionist Approach. 1962.

7932 LEWIS (PETER RONALD). The Literature of the Social Sciences: An Introductory Survey and Guide. 1960.

7933 GOULD (SAMUEL JULIUS) *ed.* Penguin Survey of the Social Sciences. 1965.

7934 —— Penguin Social Sciences Survey, 1968. 1968.

7935 GOULD (SAMUEL JULIUS) and KOLB (WILLIAM L.) *eds.* Dictionary of the Social Sciences. 1964.

7936 MACKENZIE (NORMAN) *ed.* A Guide to the Social Sciences. 1966.

7937 CHERNS (ALBERT BERNARD). 'The Problems Facing the Social Science Research Council during its First Year of Existence'. *Soc. Sci. Info.* 6 (1967), 199–205.

7938 —— 'Organised Social Science Research in Great Britain'. *Soc. Sci. Info.* 2,1 (1963), 66–81 and 2,2 (1963), 93–112.

7939 —— *Et al.* 'Research in Universities, Independent Institutes and Government Departments: Eleven Contributions to a Discussion'. *Soc. Sci. Info.* 6 (1967), 247–87.

7940 THOMPSON (DENNIS FRANK). The Democratic Citizen: Social Science and Democratic Theory in the Twentieth Century. Camb. 1970.

7941 SWANN (BRENDA) *and* TURNBULL (MAUREEN). Records of Interest to Social Scientists, 1919–1939: Introduction. 1971.

7942 ROBSON (WILLIAM ALEXANDER) *ed.* Man and the Social Sciences: Twelve Lectures Delivered at the London School of Economics and Political Science, Tracing the Development of the Social Sciences during the Present Century. 1972.

7943 WESTOBY (ADAM) *et al.* Social Scientists at Work. Guildford. 1976.

7944 COTGROVE (STEPHEN). The Science of Society: An Introduction to Sociology. 1967. Rev. edn 1972, 3rd edn 1975, 4th edn 1978.

7945 —— The Sociology of Science and Technology. Bath. 1967.

7946 COTGROVE (STEPHEN) *and* BOX (STEVEN). Science, Industry and Society: Studies in the Sociology of Science. 1970.

7947 FYVEL (TOSCO RAPHAEL) *and* FYVEL (RAPHAEL JOSEPH) *eds.* The Future of Sociology. 1964.

7948 ROBERTS (NORMAN) *ed.* Use of Social Sciences Literature. 1977.

7949 FARQUHARSON (DOROTHEA). 'Dissolution of the Institute of Sociology'. *Sociol. Rev.* 3 (1955), 165–73.

7950 BECKER (HOWARD) *and* BOSKOFF (ALVIN) *eds.* Modern Sociological Theory in Continuity and Change. N.Y. 1957. See chapter by Walter Sprott 'Sociology in Britain: Preoccupations'.

7951 SPROTT (WALTER JOHN HERBERT). Social Psychology. 1952.

7952 —— Sociology. 1949. 2nd edn 1957. Repr. 1964.

7953 —— Science and Social Action. 1954.

7954 —— Human Groups. 1958.

7955 —— Sociology and the Seven Dials. 1962.

7956 —— 'Principia Sociologica'. *Brit. J. Sociol.* 14 (1963), 307–20.

7957 —— Making Good Citizens—The Process of Socialization. Sheffield. 1964.

7958 MUMFORD (LEWIS). 'Sociology and its Prospects in Great Britain'. *Athenaeum* 10 Dec. 1920, 815–16.

7959 CULLINGWORTH (JOHN BARRY). The Politics of Research. Birm. 1969.

7960 GLASS (DAVID VICTOR). 'The Application of Social Research'. *Brit. J. Sociol.* 1 (1953), 17–30.

7961 FLETCHER (RONALD). 'The British Sociological Association Conference 1957'. *Brit. J. Sociol.* 8 (1957), 95–6. (The theme was 'Sociology in Retrospect and Prospect'.).

7962 MACRAE (DONALD G.). 'Social Theory: Retrospect and Prospect'. *Brit. J. Sociol.* 8 (1957), 97–105.

7963 MANNHEIM (KARL). Systematic Sociology: An Introduction to the Study of Society. 1957.

7964 MARSHALL (THOMAS HUMPHREY). 'Sociology and Social Pathology'. *Brit. J. Sociol.* 11 (1960), 82–6.

7965 —— Sociology at the Crossroads. 1963.

7966 —— Social Policy. 1965.

7967 —— Social Policy in the Twentieth Century. 1967. 2nd edn of above. 3rd rev. edn 1970. 4th rev. edn 1975.

7968 SMITH (JOHN HAROLD). The University Teaching of the Social Sciences: Industrial Sociology. Paris. 1961.

7969 —— Industrial Sociology. 1962.

7970 BOTTOMORE (THOMAS BURTON). Sociology: A Guide to Problems and Literature. 1962.

7971 —— 'La Sociologie Anglaise Contemporaine'. *C. Int. Sociol.* 18 (1955), 175–89.

7972 WELFORD (ALAN TRAFFORD) *et al. eds.* Society: Problems and Methods of Study. 1962.

7973 TAVISTOCK INSTITUTE OF HUMAN RELATIONS. Tavistock Pamphlets No. 7. Social Research and a National Policy for Science. 1964.

7974 ACTON SOCIETY TRUST. The Acton Society Trust: Its Aims, Work and Publications. 1965.

7975 LITTLE (A.). 'Sociology in Britain since 1945'. *Info. Sci. Soc.* (1963), 64–92.

7976 DE KADT (EMANUEL J.). 'Research Note: Sociology Graduate Students at the L.S.E.'. *Brit. J. Sociol.* 14 (1963), 270–80.

7977 WILLIAMS (WILLIAM MORGAN). Sociology, the Proper Study. Swansea. 1964.

7978 GREEN (BRYAN SIDNEY RICHARD) *and* JOHNS (EDWARD ALLISTER). An Introduction to Sociology. 1966.

7979 HALLORAN (JAMES DERMOT) *and* BROTHERS (JOAN) *eds.* The Uses of Sociology. 1966.

7980 BURNS (TOM). Sociological Explanation. Edin. 1966.

7981 BURNS (TOM) *and* SAUL (SAMUEL BERRICK) *eds.* Social Theory and Economic Change. 1967.

7982 LAWRENCE (JOHN RAYMOND) *ed.* Operational Research and the Social Sciences. 1966.

7983 EISERMANN (G.) *ed.* Die Gegenwärtige Situation der Soziologie. Stuttgart. 1967. See chapter by Viola Klein 'Der Gegenwärtige Situation der Soziologie in Gross Britannien'.

7984 FARMER (MARY E.). 'The Positivist Movement and the Development of English Sociology'. *Sociol. Rev.* 15 (1967), 5–20.

7985 CARTER (MICHAEL PERCY). 'Report on a Survey of Sociological Research in Britain'. *Sociol.Rev.* 16 (1968), 5–40.

7986 GOLDTHORPE (JOHN ERNEST). An Introduction to Sociology. Camb. 1968.

7987 MITCHELL (GEOFFREY DUNCAN). A Hundred Years of Sociology. 1968.

7988 —— *Ed.* A Dictionary of Sociology. 1968.

7989 —— Sociology: The Study of Social Systems. 1959.

7990 —— Sociological Questions. Exeter. 1969.

7991 —— *Et al.* Neighbourhood and Community: An Enquiry into Social Relationships on Housing Estates in Liverpool and Sheffield. L/pool. 1954.

7992 HALLIDAY (RICHARD JOHN). 'The Sociological Movement, the Sociological Society and the Genesis of Academic Sociology in Britain'. *Sociol. Rev.* 16 (1968), 377–98.

7993 SIMON (RITA JAMES). 'A Comment on Sociological Research and Interest in Britain and the United States'. *Sociol. Rev.* 17 (1969), 5–10.

7994 STACEY (MARGARET) *ed.* Comparability in Social Research. 1969.

7995 RAISON (TIMOTHY). The Founding Fathers of Social Science. A Series from *New Society.* Harmondsworth. 1969.

7996 BANKS (JOSEPH AMBROSE) *ed.* Studies in British Society. 1969.

7997 KRAUSZ (ERNEST). Sociology in Britain: A Survey of Research. 1969.

7998 RUNCIMAN (WALTER GARRISON). Sociology in its Place, and other Essays. Camb. 1970.

7999 MUSGRAVE (PETER WILLIAM) *ed.* Sociology, History and Education. 1970.

8000 —— The Sociology of Education. 1965. Repr. 1968.

8001 JARY (DAVID) *and* PHILLIPS (JOHN). 'The Philosophical Critique of a Scientific Sociology: Some Remarks on Bryant's Defence'. *Brit. J. Sociol.* 22 (1971), 183–92.

8002 THOMPSON (KENNETH) *and* TUNSTALL (JEREMY). Sociological Perspectives: Selected Readings. Harmondsworth. 1971.

8003 OROMANER (MARK JAY). 'Comparison of Influentials in Contemporary American and British Sociology: A Study in the Internationalization of Sociology'. *Brit. J. Sociol.* 21 (1970), 324–32.

8004 FLETCHER (RONALD) *ed.* The Making of Sociology: A Study of Social Theory. In 2 vols; Vol. 1. Beginnings and Foundations. Vol. 2. Developments. 1971.

8005 —— *Ed.* The Science of Society and the Unity of Mankind. (A Memorial Volume for Morris Ginsberg from the British Sociological Association.). 1974.

8006 MACRAE (DONALD G.). 'Morris Ginsberg: Five Memorial Addresses'. *Jew. J. Sociol.* 13 (1971), 5–16.

8007 MACRAE (DONALD G.) *and* MARSHALL (THOMAS HUMPHREY). 'Morris Ginsberg, MA, D.Litt, and FBA, 1889–1970'. *Brit. J. Sociol.* 21 (1970), 357–61.

8008 GINER (SALVADOR). Sociology. 1972.

8009 WORSLEY (PETER). Problems of Modern Society: A Sociological Perspective. Harmondsworth. 1972.

8010 —— *Ed.* Modern Sociology: Introductory Readings; Selected Readings. Harmondsworth. 1970. Repr. 1974.

8011 HALMOS (PAUL) *ed.* The Teaching of Sociology to Students of Education and Social Work. Keele. 1961.

8012 —— Sociology and Medicine. Keele. 1962.

8013 —— *Ed.* Moral Issues in the Training of Teachers and Social Workers. Keele. 1960.

8014 —— Sociological Studies in Economics and Administration. Keele. 1969.

8015 —— The Sociology of Sociology. Keele. 1970.

8016 —— The Sociology of Mass-Media Communicators. Keele. 1969.

8017 —— The Personal Service Society. 1970.

8018 —— *Ed.* The Sociology of Science. Keele. 1972.

8019 —— *Ed.* Professionalisation and Social Change. Keele. 1973.

8020 —— The Personal and Political: Social Work and Political Action. 1978.

8021 —— *Et al.* Introduction to Welfare: Concepts and History. Milton Keynes. 1978.

8022 HINDESS (BARRY). The Use of Official Statistics in Sociology: A Critique of Positivism and Ethnomethodology. 1973.

8023 —— Philosophy and Methodology in the Social Sciences. Hassocks. 1977.

8024 REX (JOHN ARDENNE) *ed.* Approaches to Sociology: An Introduction to Major Trends in British Sociology. 1974.

8025 TOWNSEND (PETER). Sociology and Social Policy. 1975.

8026 BERGER (PETER LUDWIG) *and* BERGER (BRIGITTE). Sociology: A Biographical Approach. Rev. edn Harmondsworth. 1976.

8027 BERGER (PETER LUDWIG). Invitation to Sociology: A Humanistic Perspective. Harmondsworth. 1966. Repr. 1969.

8028 BRYANT (CHRISTOPHER GORDON ALISTAIR). Sociology in Action: A Critique of Selected Conceptions of the Social Role of the Sociologist. 1976.

8029 HAWTHORN (GEOFFREY). Enlightenment and Despair: A History of Sociology. Camb. 1976.

8030 THORNS (DAVID CHRISTOPHER). New Directions in Sociology. Newton Abbot. 1976.

8031 PLATT (JENNIFER). Realities of Social Research: An Empirical Study of British Sociologists. 1976.

8032 —— Social Research in Bethnal Green: An Evaluation of the Work of the Institute of Community Studies. 1971.

8033 HOWARTH-WILLIAMS (MARTIN). R. D. Laing: His Work and its Relevance to Sociology. 1977.

8034 BELL (COLIN) *and* ENGEL (SOLOMON). Inside the Whale: The Personal Accounts of Social Research. 1978.

8035 O'NEILL (JOHN). Sociology as a Skin Trade: Essays towards a Reflective Sociology. 1972.

8036 MORGAN (D. H. J.). 'The British Association Scandal: The Effect of Publicity on a Sociological Investigation'. *Sociol. Rev.* 20 (1972), 185–206.

8037 HOBHOUSE (LEONARD TRELAWNEY). Sociology and Philosophy: A Centenary Collection of Essays and Articles. 1966.

8038 RYAN (ALAN). The Philosophy of the Social Sciences. Lond./N.Y. 1970.

8039 —— *Ed.* The Philosophy of Social Explanation. 1973.

8040 COLFAX (JOHN DAVID) *and* ROACH (JACK LESLIE) *eds.* Radical Sociology. 1971.

8041 SERGEANT (GRAHAM). A Textbook of Sociology. 1971. 2nd edn Basingstoke. 1979.

8042 —— A Statistical Sourcebook for Sociologists. 1972.

8043 MYRDAL (GUNNAR). 'How Scientific are the Social Services?'. *J. Soc. Issues* 28 (1972), 151–70.

8044 NISBET (ROBERT ALEXANDER). The Sociological Tradition. 1970.

8045 —— Sociology as an Art Form. N.Y. 1970.

8046 —— Tradition and Revolt: Historical and Sociological Essays. N.Y. 1968.

8047 —— The Social Bond: An Introduction to the Study of Society. N.Y. 1970.

8048 —— Social Change and History: Aspects of the Western Theory of Development. N.Y. 1969.

8049 —— The Social Philosophers: Community and Conflict in Western Thought. 1974.

8050 —— Twilight of Authority. 1976.

8051 ABRAHAM (JOSEPH HAYIM). The Origins and Growth of Sociology. Harmondsworth. 1973.

8052 —— Sociology. 1967.

8053 ABRAMS (PHILIP) *et al.* Communes, Sociology and Society. Camb. 1976.

8054 ALLEN (SHEILA). Sociology in a Technological University. Bradford. 1974.

8055 BARKER (PAUL). The Social Sciences Today. 1975.

8056 MORGAN (DAVID). 'British Social Theory: Review Article'. *Sociol.* 9 (1975), 119–24.

8057 SMITH (CYRIL S.). 'Employment of Sociologists in Research Occupations in Britain in 1973'. *Sociol.* 9 (1975), 309–16.

8058 SICARD (GERALD L.) *and* WEINBERGER (PHILIP) *eds.* Sociology for our Times. Glenview, Ill. 1977.

8059 REID (IVAN). Sociological Perspectives on School and Education. 1978.

8060 MANN (PETER HENRY). An Approach to Urban Sociology. Lond./N.Y. 1965.

8061 MELLOR (ROSEMARY). 'Urban Sociology in an Urban Society'. *Brit. J. Sociol.* 26 (1975), 276–93.

8062 NOBLE (TREVOR). 'Sociology and Literature'. *Brit. J. Sociol.* 27 (1976), 211–24.

8063 LUPTON (THOMAS). Management and the Social Sciences: An Essay. 1966.

8064 BANKS (JOSEPH AMBROSE). Sociology as a Vocation. 1971.

8065 —— The Sociology of Social Movements. 1972.

8066 U.K. SOCIAL SERVICE RESEARCH COUNCIL. Reviews of Current Research. 3. Research in Social Anthropology. 1968.

8067 FORTES (MEYER). Kinship and Social Order: The Legacy of Lewis Henry Morgan. 1970.

8068 ROBERTSON (JAMES HUGH). The Same Alternative: Signposts to a Self-fulfilling Future. 1978.

8069 HALSEY (ALBERT HENRY) *ed.* Traditions of Social Policy: Essays in Honour of Violet Butler. Oxf. 1976.

8070 BOARDMAN (PHILIP). Patrick Geddes: Maker of the Future. Chapel Hill, N.C. 1944.

8071 —— The Worlds of Patrick Geddes: Biologist, Town Planner, Re-educator, Peace Warrior. 1978.

8072 TYRWHITT (JACQUELINE) *ed.* Patrick Geddes in India. 1947.

8073 MAIRET (PHILLIPE). Pioneer of Sociology: The Life and Letters of Patrick Geddes. 1957.

8074 KITCHEN (PADDY). A Most Unsettling Person: An Introduction to the Ideas and Life of Patrick Geddes. 1975.

8075 BRIGGS (ASA). Social Thought and Social Action: A Study of the Work of Seebohm Rowntree, 1871–1954. 1961.

8076 STEDMAN JONES (GARETH). 'From Historical Sociology to Theoretical History'. *Brit. J. Sociol.* 27 (1976), 295–306.

8077 ROTH (GUENTHER). 'History and Sociology in the Work of Max Weber'. *Brit. J. Sociol.* 27 (1976), 306–18.

8078 THOMPSON (E. P.). 'On History, Sociology and Historical Relevance'. *Brit. J. Sociol.* 27 (1976), 387–402.

8079 SMITH (ANTHONY DAVID). 'The Diffusion of Nationalism: Some Historical and Sociological Perspectives'. *Brit. J. Sociol.* 29 (1978), 234–48.

8080 SMITH (ANTHONY DOUGLAS). Social Change: Social Theory and Historical Processes. 1976.

8081 BOCOCK (ROBERT). 'British Sociologists and Freud: A Sociological Analysis of the Absence of a Relationship'. *Brit. J. Sociol.* 32 (1981), 346–81.

8082 SCRUTON (ROGER). 'Notes on the Sociology of War'. *Brit. J. Sociol.* 38 (1987), 295–309.

8083 MURPHY (JOHN W.). 'Making Sense of Post-modern Sociology'. *Brit. J. Sociol.* 39 (1988), 600–18.

8084 ELDRIDGE (JOHN ERIC THOMAS). Recent British Sociology. 1980.

8085 JONES (GRETA). Social Darwinism and English Thought: The Interaction between Biological and Social Theory. Brighton. 1980.

8086 BULMER (MARTIN). Essays on the History of British Sociological Research. Camb. 1985.

8087 INGLIS (FRED). Radical Earnestness: English Social Theory 1880–1980. Oxf. 1982.

8088 SWINGEWOOD (ALAN). A Short History of Sociological Thought. 1984.

8089 SMITH (ARTHUR). Foundations of Sociology. Rochdale. 1974.

8090 SZACKI (JERZI). History of Sociological Thought. 1979.

8091 EASTHOPE (GARY). A History of Social Research Methods. 1974.

8092 BURKE (PETER). Sociology and History. 1980.

8093 HARALAMBOS (MICHAEL). Sociology: Themes and Perspectives. Slough. 1980.

8094 POTTER (DAVID). Society and the Social Sciences: An Introduction. 1981.

8095 ALEXANDER (JEFFREY C.). Sociological Theory since 1945. 1987.

6. CHILDREN AND CHILDHOOD

8096 ADAMSON (G.). 'Should Foster Mums be Paid?'. *New Society* 22 (22 Aug. 1968), 268–9.

8097 —— The Care Takers. 1973.

8098 ARMISTEAD (NIGEL). Data for 1975 Report on Children's Day Care Facilities in London. 1976.

8099 BARKLEY (JOHN MONTEITH). The Presbyterian Orphan Society, 1866–1966. Belf. 1966.

8100 BELSON (WILLIAM ALBERT). The Impact of Television: Methods and Findings in Programme Research. 1967. Repr. 1968.

8101 BERG (LEILA). Look at Kids. Harmondsworth. 1972.

8102 BERRY (JULIET). Social Work with Children. 1972.

8103 BOAS (GEORGE). The Cult of Childhood. 1966.

8104 BOSS (PETER). Exploration into Childcare. 1971.

8105 BOWLBY (EDWARD JOHN MOSTYN). Childcare and the Growth of Love. (*Abr.* and *ed.* by Margery Fry). 1953. New edn and two new chs. by Mary Ainsworth. Harmondsworth. 1965.

8106 —— Attachment and Loss. In three vols; Vol. 1 1969, Vol. 2 1973, Vol. 3 1980.

8107 BOWLEY (AGATHA HILLIAM). A Study of the Factors Influencing the General Development of the Child during the Pre-school Years by Means of Record Forms. Camb. 1942.

8108 —— Psychological Aspects of Child Care. L/pool. 1949.

8109 —— Child Care. 1951.

8110 —— *Ed.* The Psychological Care of the Child in Hospital. 1961.

8111 BOWLEY (AGATHA HILLIAM) *and* TOWNROE (M.) *eds.* The Spiritual Development of the Child. 1953.

8112 BRAMALL (MARGARET), ROWE (JANE), *and* JENKINS (RACHEL). Adoption and Fostering: Papers. Birm. 1973.

8113 BRANCH (MARGARET) *and* CASH (AUBREY). Gifted Children: Recognising and Developing Exceptional Ability. 1966.

8114 BRILL (KENNETH) *and* THOMAS (RUTH). Children in Homes. 1964.

8115 BRITISH NATIONAL CONFERENCE ON SOCIAL WELFARE. Children and Young People: A Guide to Studies for the British National Conference on Social Welfare at the University of Edinburgh. Aug. 11–15, 1957. 1956.

8116 BRITTON (CLARE). Child Care and Social Work: A Collection of Papers Written between 1954 and 1963. Welwyn. 1964.

8117 BYNNER (JOHN MORGAN). The Young Smoker: A Study of Smoking Among Schoolboys Carried Out for the Ministry of Health. 1969.

8118 U.K. THE SCOTTISH EDUCATION DEPARTMENT. The Child Care Service at Work. *Ed.* 1963. By Tom Burns and Susan Sinclair. Published by The Scottish Advisory Council on Child Care.

8119 BURNETT (JOHN). 'Autobiographies of Childhood: The Experience of Education.' *History Today* 32 (1982), 8–15.

8120 —— Destiny Obscure: Autobiographies of Childhood, Education and Family from the 1820's to the 1920's. 1982.

8121 BURLINGHAM (DOROTHY) *and* FREUD (ANNA). Infants without Families: The Case For and Against Residential Nurseries. 1944. Repr. 1947.

8122 —— Staffing of Local Authority Children's Departments: A Report by the Scottish Advisory Council on Child Care. Edin. 1963.

8123 BURPITT (HARRY REGINALD). 'The Provision of Occupations for Children Out of School Hours.' *Child* (Mar. 1920), 246–9.

8124 BURTON (LINDY). The Family Life of Sick Children: A Study of Families Coping with Chronic Childhood Disease. 1975.

8125 —— Care for the Child Facing Death. 1974.

8126 —— Vulnerable Children: Three Studies of Children in Conflict. 1968.

8127 CADOGAN (MARY). You're a Brick Angela!: A New Look at Girls' Fiction from 1839 to 1975. 1976.

8128 CAMPBELL (BEATRIX). Unofficial Secrets: Child Sex Abuse: The Cleveland Case. 1988.

8129 CAMERON (HECTOR CHARLES). Diet and Disease in Infancy. 1915.

8130 —— Diseases of Children. 1926.

8131 —— The Nervous Child. 1919. 5th edn 1946.

8132 —— The Nervous Child and School. 1933.

8133 —— 'Maternity and Child Welfare Work.' *Lancet* (24 Apr. 1920), 901–3.

8134 CAMPAIGN FOR THE CARE OF THE DEPRIVED CHILD. Justice for Children: The Scottish System and its Application to Ireland. Dublin. 1974.

8135 CARLEBACH (JULIUS). Caring for Children in Trouble. 1970.

8136 U.K. CENTRAL OFFICE OF INFORMATION. Children in Britain. 2nd edn 1962. 3rd edn 1965. 6th edn 1976.

8137 CHESSER (EUSTACE). Cruelty to Children. 1951.

8138 CHILDREN AND SOCIETY. Special Issue 'Lessons of Cleveland'. 2 (1988).

8139 CHURCH OF ENGLAND. National Assembly Board for Social Responsibility. Fatherless by Law? The Law and the Welfare of Children Designated Illegitimate. 1966.

8140 CLAYPON (JANET ELIZABETH LANE). The Child Welfare Movement. 1920.

8141 —— Hygiene of Women and Children. 1921.

8142 —— Maternity and Child Welfare. Pt. 1: A Memorandum on Health Visiting. Pt. 2: An Extract from the Third Report on Infant Mortality by the Medical Officer of the Board, Sir A. Newsholme. 1914.

8143 —— Milk and its Hygienic Relations. 1916. [MRC].

8144 CLEGG (*Sir* ALEXANDER BRADSHAW) *and* MEGSON (BARBARA) Children in Distress. Harmondsworth. 1968.

8145 COLLIS (ARTHUR T.) *and* POOLE (VERA E.). These our Children: An Account of the Home Life and Social Environment of Children in an Industrial Slum District. 1950.

8146 COOPER (CHRISTINE). The Illegitimate Child. 1955.

8147 COOPER (JOAN D.). Patterns of Family Placement: Current Issues in Fostering and Adoption. 1978.

8148 CREECH-JONES (VIOLET). 'Select Committee on Estimates: Report on Child Care.' *Howard J.* 8 (1953), 271–2.

8149 CRELLIN (EILEEN) *et al.* Born Illegitimate: Social and Educational Implications. Slough. 1971. [Report by the National Children's Bureau.]

8150 CROSBY (TRAVIS L.). The Impact of Civilian Evacuation in the Second World War. 1986.

8151 CRUICKSHANK (MARJORIE). Children and Industry. Manch. 1981.

8152 DAVIDSON (AUDREY) *and* FAY (JUDITH). Phantasy [*sic*] in Childhood. 1952.

8153 DAVIE (RONALD BUTLER NEVILLE). Children and Families with Special Needs. Cardiff. 1975.

8154 DAVIES (SIDNEY HERBERT). 'The Health Factor in Education.' *Child* (Nov. 1920), 33–45.

8155 'On Offspring: By A Parent.' *Englishwoman* (Jan. 1920), 45–51.

8156 DENNEY (ANTHONY). Children in Need. 1966.

8157 DINNAGE (ROSEMARY) *and* PRINGLE (MIA LILY KELLMER). Foster Home Care: Facts and Fallacies: A Review of Research in the United States, Western Europe, Israel and Great Britain between 1948 and 1966. 1967.

8158 —— Residential Home Care: (Rest of title as above.) 1967.

8159 DOCKAR-DRYSDALE (BARBARA). Therapy in Children: Collected Papers. 1969. Repr. 1970.

8160 DONNISON (DAVID VERNON) *and* STEWART (MARY). The Child and the Social Services. 1958. Fabian Society.

8161 DONNISON (DAVID VERNON). The Neglected Child and the Social Services: A Study of the Work Done in Manchester and Salford by Social Services of all Kinds for 118 Families whose Children Came into Public Care. Manch. 1954.

8162 —— *Ed.* A Pattern of Disadvantage: A Commentary on 'From Birth to Seven'. Slough. 1972.

8163 DOUGLAS (JAMES WILLIAM BRUCE). The Home and the School: A Study of Ability and Attainment in the Primary School. 1966.

8164 —— 'Broken Families and Child Behaviour'. *J. Roy. Coll. Physicians* 4 (1970)

8165 DOUGLAS (JAMES WILLIAM BRUCE) *and* BLOMFIELD (J. M.). Children Under Five: The Results of a National Survey. 1958.

8166 DREIKURS (R.). 'The War between the Generations.' *Brit. J. Soc. Psychiatry Com. Health* 4 (1970–1), 31–9.

8167 DUKES (ETHEL) *and* HAY (MARGARET). Children of Today and Tomorrow. 1949.

8168 EDMUNDS (VINCENT) *and* SCORER (CHARLES GORDON) *eds.* Medical Ethics: A Christian View. 1966. Ch. by Vincent Edmunds 'Child Development, Mental Deficiency and Child Delinquency'.

8169 ELLISON (MARY). The Deprived Child and Adoption. 1963.

8170 ERICKSON (ERIC HOMBURGER). Childhood and Society. 1953. 2nd rev. edn N.Y. 1963. Harmondsworth. 1965.

8171 EVANS (P. A.). A Hard Day's Night: The Problem of the Residential Child Care Worker. 1969.

8172 FANSHEL (D.). Foster-Parenthood: A Role Analysis. 1966.

8173 FERGUSON (THOMAS). Children in Care and After. 1966.

8174 FLINT (BETTY M.). The Child and the Institution: A Study of Deprivation and Recovery. 1967.

8175 FORD (DONALD). The Deprived Child and the Community. 1955.

8176 FOX (JOSEPH TYLOR). 'The Care of the Epileptic Child'. *Child* (1920), 492–4.

8177 FREEMAN (MICHAEL DAVID ALAN). The Rights and Wrongs of Children. 1983.

8178 FREEMAN (KATHLEEN). If any Man Build: The History of the Save the Children Fund. 1965.

8179 FREUD (ANNA). Infants without Families and Reports on the Hampstead Nurseries. 1974.

8180 FULLER (EDWARD). The Rights of the Child: A Chapter in Social History. 1951.

8181 —— Child Welfare in England, with Special Reference to the Family. 1954. [Compiled for the World Congress on Child Welfare, Zagreb, 1954.].

8182 FRY (SARA MARGERY). The Ancestral Child. 1940.

8183 —— Children as Citizens. 1950. [National Children's Home.].

8184 GAFFIKIN (PRUDENCE). 'A Scheme for the Study of Nature and Nutrition in Relation to Child Welfare'. *Child* (June 1920), 389–92.

8185 GAMMIE (ALEXANDER). William Quarrier and the Story of the Orphan Homes of Scotland. 1936.

8186 GATHORNE-HARDY (JONATHAN). The Rise and Fall of the British Nanny. 1972.

8187 GEACH (BOB). The Rights of Children. Oxf. 1986.

8188 GEORGE (J. T. A.) *et al.* 'An Examination of the Work of Local Authority Child Welfare Clinics'. *Lancet* (1953), 88–92.

8189 GEORGE (VICTOR). Foster Care: Theory and Practice. 1970.

8190 GIBBS (MARY ANN). The Years of the Nannies. 1960.

8191 GIRDLESTONE (GATHORNE ROBERT). 'The Care of Crippled Children'. *Brit. Med. J.* (22 May 1920), 697–700.

8192 —— A Description of the National Scheme for the Welfare of Crippled Children. 1923.

8193 —— The Care and Cure of Crippled Children: The Scheme of the Central Committee for the Care of Cripples. Bristol. 1925.

8194 GOODACRE (IRIS). Adoption Policy and Practice: A Study. 1966.

8195 GRAHAM-DIXON (S.). Never Darken My Door: Working for Single Parents and their Children 1918–1978: National Council for One Parent Families. 1981.

8196 GRAY (P. G. C.) *and* PARR (ELIZABETH A.). Children in Care and the Recruitment of Foster Parents. 1957. [UK Social Survey.].

8197 GREENBERG (BRADLEY S.). 'British Children and Television Violence'. *Pub. Op. Q.* 38 (1974/5), 531–47.

8198 GREENWOOD (GEORGE ARTHUR). 'The Era of the Child: "A New Mind and a New Earth in a Single Generation"'. *World's Work* (Sept. 1920), 336–9.

8199 GREIG (JAMES WILLIAM). 'On the Guardianship, Maintenance and Education of Infants'. *Child* (Oct. 1920), 12–13.

8200 —— 'Training of the Schoolgirl in Infant Care'. *Child-Study* (July 1920), 9–11.

8201 GREY (ELEANOR) *and* BLUNDEN (RONALD M.). A Survey of Adoption in Great Britain. 1971.

8202 HALLORAN (JAMES DERMOT). The Effects of Mass Communication with Special Reference to Television: A Survey. Leics. 1964.

8203 —— Ed. The Effects of Television. 1970.

8204 HANDLER (JOEL F.). 'The Coercive Children's Officers'. *New Society* 12 (3 Oct. 1965), 485–7.

8205 HARRISON (PAUL). 'The Children Act Under Attack'. *New Society* 32 (12 Jun. 1975), 642–4.

8206 HEALTH VISITOR. 'Child Health and Education in the Seventies: A National Study in England, Scotland and Wales of all Children Born 5–11th April 1970'. *Health Visitor* 48 (1975).

8207 HEDDLE (A.). Forty Five Years: A History of the Woolwich and District Invalid Children's Aid Association, 1892–1937. Woolwich. 1937.

8208 WOOLWICH AND DISTRICT INVALID CHILDREN'S AID ASSOCI-ATION. Annual Report for Year Ending Dec. 31 1928. Woolwich. 1929.

8209 —— Annual Report 1936. Woolwich. 1937.

8210 HEIMAN (MARCEL) ed. Psychoanalysis and Social Work. 1953. Ch. by A. P. Fabian, 'The Contribution of Psychoanalysis to Child Guidance in Art'.

8211 HENDERSON (J. L.). 'The Evolution of Child Care'. *Lancet* (1953), 261–6.

8212 HENRIQUES (*Sir* BASIL LUCAS QUIXANO). The Homemenders: The Prevention of Unhappiness in Children. 1955.

8213 —— The Indiscretions of a Magistrate: Thoughts on the Work of the Juvenile Court. 1950.

8214 HEYWOOD (JEAN SCHOFIELD). Children in Care: The Development of the Service for the Deprived Child. 1st edn 1959. 2nd edn 1965. 3rd rev. edn 1978.

8215 —— An Introduction to Teaching Casework Skills. 1964.

8216 —— Casework and Pastoral Care. 1967.

8217 —— 'Recent Developments in the Structure and Practice of Child Care'. *Soc. and Econ. Admin.* 4, (1970), 60–2.

8218 HIMMELWEIT (HILDE T.), OPPENHEIM (A. N.), *and* VINCE (PAMELA). Television and the Child. 1958.

8219 HITCHMAN (JANET). They Carried the Sword. 1966.

8220 HOLDEN (ALAN S.). Children in Care. 1st edn 1982. 2nd edn 1985.

8221 HOLGATE (EILEEN). *ed.* Communicating with Children: Collected Papers. 1972.

8222 HOLMAN (ROBERT). Trading in Children: A Study of Private Fostering. 1973.

8223 —— 'The Place of Fostering in Social Work'. *Brit. J. Social Work* 5, (1975), 3–29.

8224 HOLMES (G. V.). The Likes of Us. [An account of the author's life as a child in one of Dr Barnardo's Homes.]. 1968.

8225 HOPKINSON (*Sir* ALFRED). 'Adoption'. *J. Contemp. Legisl.* (3rd Ser.) 2 (1920), 3–9.

8226 —— 'Wife Desertion and Adoption of Children'. *Poor Law Mag.* (Sept. 1920), 267–73.

8227 HUMPHRIES (STEPHEN). Hooligans or Rebels? An Oral History of Working Class Children and Youth, 1889–1939. Oxf. 1981.

8228 HUMPHREY (MICHAEL). The Hostage Seekers: A Study of Childless and Adopting Couples. 1969.

8229 JACKA (ALAN A.). Adoption in Brief: Research and Other Literature in the United States, Canada and Great Britain, 1966–1972, An Annotated Bibliography. Slough. 1973.

8230 JOBLING (MEGAN) *et al.* Helping the Handicapped Child. Slough. 1975. [Based on work done by the National Children's Bureau.].

8231 JOHNSON (RUTH). Old Road: A Lancashire Childhood, 1912–1926. [Recalled by Ruth Johnson and Compiled and Written by Alfred Body.]. Manch. 1974.

8232 KAHAN (BARBARA). Growing up in Care. Oxf. 1979.

8233 KAMMERER (GLADYS MARIE). British and American Child Welfare Services: A Comparative Study in Administration. Detroit. 1962.

8234 KASTELL (JEAN). Casework in Childcare. 1962.

8235 KIMMINS (CHARLES WILLIAM). The Child in the Changing Home. 1926.

8236 —— Ed. The Mental and Physical Welfare of the Child. 1927.

8237 —— The Child's Attitude to Life: A Study of Children's Stories. 1926.

8238 —— Children's Dreams. 1920.

8239 —— Children's Dreams: An Unexplored Land. 1937.

8240 KIMMINS (CHARLES WILLIAM) *and* RENNIE (BELLE). The Triumph of the Dalton Plan. 1932.

8241 KIMMINS (MRS CHARLES WILLIAM). 'Orthopedic Hospital Schools'. *Child* (Aug. 1920), 485–91.

8242 KING (ROY DAVID), RAYNES (NORMA V.), *and* TIZARD (JACK). Patterns of Residential Care: Sociological Studies in Institutions for Handicapped Children. 1971.

8243 KING-HALL (MAGDALEN). The Story of the Nursery. 1958.

8244 KORNITZER (MARGARET). Adoption and Family Life. 1968.

8245 LANE-CLAYPON (JANET ELIZABETH). 'The Privileges of Organisation and Administration in Child Welfare Work'. *J. State Medicine* (Feb 1917), 33–40.

8246 LAWSON (JOAN). Children in Jeopardy: The Life of a Child Care Officer. 1965.

8247 LENNHOFF (FREDERICK GEORGE). Exceptional Children: Residential Treatment of Emotionally Disturbed Boys at Shotton Hall. 1st edn 1960. 2nd edn 1966.

8248 LEWIS (HILDA NORTH). Deprived Children: The Mersham Experiment: A Social and Clinical Study. 1954.

8249 LYNN (R.) *and* GORDON (I. E.). 'Maternal Attitudes to Child Socialization: Some Social and National Differences'. *Brit. J. Soc. Clin. Psychol.* 1 (1962), 52–5.

8250 MANN (PAMELA). Children in Care Revisited. 1984.

8251 MARCH (NORAH HELENA). 'Eugenic Aspects of National Baby Week'. *Eugenics. Rev.* (July 1917), 95–108.

8252 MENCHER (S.). 'Factors Affecting the Relationship of the Voluntary and Statutory Child-Care Services in England'. *Soc. Serv. Rev.* 32 (1958), 24–32.

8253 MERSHAM CHILDREN'S RECEPTION CENTRE. Interim Report. 1948.

8254 MACKENZIE (LESLIE *Lady*). 'The Social Care of the Child'. *J. State. Med.* (Oct. 1919), 306–11.

8255 MACLAY (DAVID THOMSON). Treatment for Children: The Work of a Child Guidance Clinic. 1970.

8256 MacLENNAN (EMMA). Child Labour in London. 1982.

8257 —— Working Children. 1985.

8258 McNAIR (HENRY S.). A Survey of Children in Residential Schools for the Maladjusted in Scotland. 1969.

8259 McWHINNIE (ALEXINA MARY). Adopted Children: How they Grow Up: A Study of their Adjustment as Adults. 1967.

8260 MARCH (NORAH HELENA). Towards Racial Health: A Handbook on the Training of Boys and Girls. 1915. 3rd edn 1918.

8261 MEERING (AGNES BROWNLIE). A Handbook for Nursery Nurses. 1947. 2nd edn 1953.

8262 MIDDLETON (NIGEL GORDON). When Family Failed: The Treatment of Children in the Care of the Community during the First Half of the Twentieth Century. 1971.

8263 MILLER (GORDON WESLEY). Educational Opportunity and the Home. 1971.

8264 MITCHELL (ANNE K.). Children in the Middle: Living Through Divorce. 1985.

8265 MITCHELL (M.). 'The Effects of Unemployment on the Social Condition of Women and Children in the 1930's'. *Hist. Workshop* 19 (1985), 105–27.

8266 MUSGRAVE (P. W.). 'How Children Use Television.' *New Society* 13 (20 Feb. 1969), 277–8.

8267 NATIONAL BUREAU FOR CO-OPERATION IN CHILD CARE. Annual Report. 1963/4 onwards.

8268 —— (Proceedings of the First Annual Conference). Investment in Children: A Symposium on Positive Child Care and Constructive Education. *Ed.* by Mia Pringle. 1963.

8269 NATIONAL CHILDREN3S BUREAU. (Information Service). Spotlight on Physical and Mental Assessment. By Jessie Parfit. 1971.

8270 —— Spotlight on Services for the Young Handicapped Child. By Jessie Parfit. 1972.

8271 —— Spotlight on Groupwork with Parents in Special Circumstances. By Jessie Parfit. 1973.

8272 —— Spotlight on Sources of Information About Children. With major contributions from Keith Howes, Jessie Parfit, and Megan Jobling. 1974.

8273 —— Handicapped School-leavers: Their Further Education, Training and Employment. By Linda Tuckey, Jessie Parfit, and Bob Tuckey. Slough. 1974.

8274 —— The Child with Cerebral Palsy. By Doria Pelling. 1973.

8275 —— The Child with a Chronic Medical Problem. By Doria Pelling. 1973.

8276 —— The Child with Asthma. By Doria Pelling. 1975.

8277 —— Growing Up in a One Parent Family. By Elsa Ferri. Slough. 1976.

8278 —— Disadvantaged Families and Playgroups. By Elsa Ferri and Rosalind Niblett. Slough. 1977.

8279 —— Coping Alone. By Elsa Ferri and Hilary Robinson. 1976.

8280 —— Growing Up in Great Britain: Papers from the National Child Development Study. By Kenneth Fogelman. 1983.

8281 —— Who Cares? Young People in Care Speak Out. 1977.

8282 —— Inequalities and Childhood: The Proceedings of a Conference held on 26 April 1985 at Queen's Hall, Edinburgh. Edin. 1985.

8283 —— Warnock Seven Years on: A Scottish Perspective. Glasgow. 1986.

8284 NATIONAL CHILD DEVELOPMENT STUDY. 1958 Cohort. 11,000 seven-year-olds: First Report of the NCDS—1958 Cohort—Submitted to the Central Advisory Committee for Education (England), April 1966.

8285 —— From Birth to Seven: The Second Report of the NCDS—1958 Cohort—with Full Statistical Appendix by Ronald Davie *et al.* 1972.

8286 —— Britain's Sixteen-Year-Olds: Preliminary Findings from the Third Follow-Up of the NCDS—1958 Cohort. *Ed.* by Ken Fogelman, *appendix* by Harvey Goldstein. 1976.

8287 NEWSON (JOHN) *and* NEWSON (ELIZABETH). Four Years Old in an Urban Community. 1968.

8288 —— Perspectives on School at Seven Years Old. 1977.

8289 —— Seven Years Old in the Home Environment. 1976.

8290 —— Infant Care in an Urban Community. 1963.

8291 Patterns of Infant Care in an Urban Community. 1963. 2nd edn Harmondsworth. 1972.

8292 NOBLE (GRANT). Children in Front of the Small Screen. 1975.

8293 OLIVER (Sir THOMAS) Foreword to—The Health of the Child of School Age. [By various authors.]. 1927.

8294 OPIE (IONA) and OPIE (PETER). Children's Games in Street and Playground: Chasing, Catching, Seeking, Hunting, Racing, Duelling, Exerting, Daring, Guessing, Acting, Pretending. Oxf. 1969.

8295 —— The Language and Lore of Children. Oxf. 1960.

8296 OSBORN (A. F.) et al. The Social Life of Britain's Five Year Olds: A Report of the Child Health and Education Study. 1984.

8297 OWEN JONES (EVAN). 'Those who Cease to Foster'. Brit. J. Social Work 5 (1975), 31–41.

8298 PACKMAN (JEAN). Childcare: Needs and Numbers. 1968 [with Editorial Assistance from R. A. Parker.]. 1968.

8299 —— The Child's Generation: Child Care Policy from Curtis to Houghton. Oxf. 1975.

8300 —— Who Needs Care? Social Work Decisions about Children. Oxf. 1986.

8301 PARKER (ROY ALFRED). Decisions in Child Care: A Study of Prediction in Fostering. 1966.

8302 PARRY-EDWARDS (E. L.). 'The Next Generation—A Welsh County Record of Maternity and Child Welfare'. Welsh Outlook (May 1918), 145–8.

8303 PAYLEY (J.) and THORPE (R.). Children: Handle with Care: A Critical Analysis of the Development of Intermediate Treatment. Leicester. 1974.

8304 PARFIT (JESSIE). The Community's Children: Long-Term Substitute Care: A Guide for the Intelligent Layman. Lond./N.Y. 1967.

8305 PAVENSTEDT (ELEANOR) ed. The Drifters: Children of Disorganised Lower-Class Families. 1967.

8306 PINCHBECK (IVY) and HEWITT (MARGARET). Children in English Society: Vol. 2. From the 18th Century to the Children's Act 1948. 1974.

8307 POWLINSON (CHARLES F.). 'Exhibit Posters on Child Welfare Work'. Child (Jan. 1920), 156–9.

8308 PRIESTLEY (PHILIP) et al. Justice for Juveniles: The 1969 Children and Young Persons Act: A Case for Reform? 1977.

8309 PRINGLE (MIA LILY KELLMER) and others. Eds. Directory of Voluntary Organisations Concerned with Children. 1969.

8310 —— The Needs of Children: A Personal Perspective. 1974. [Prepared for the DHSS.].

8311 —— 'Better Adoption'. New Society 11 (Sept. 1972), 207.

8312 —— Caring for Children: A Symposium on Co-operation in Childcare. N.Y./Lond. 1969.

8313 —— The Emotional and Social Adjustment of Blind Children. Slough. 1964.

8314 —— Investment in Children. Exeter. 1982.

8315 —— Et al. Putting Children First. 1987.

8316 PRITCHARD (ERIC LAW). The Infant, Nutrition and Management. 1914.

8317 —— The Physiological Feeding of Infants. 2nd edn 1904. 3rd edn 1909. 4th edn 1919. Rev. edn 1922.

8318 —— The New-born Baby. 1934.

8319 —— The Infant: A Handbook of Modern Treatment. 1938.

8320 PROSSER (HILARY). Perspectives on Residential Care: An Annotated Bibliography: Research and other Literature in the United States and Great Britain 1966–1974. Windsor. 1976.

8321 PUGH (ELIZABETH). Social Work in Child Care. 1968.

8322 RAVERAT (GWEN). Period Piece: A Cambridge Childhood. 1952.

8323 RENNIE (JANE). 'The Recreational Needs of Adolescence'. Child (Jul. 1920), 1–5.

8324 ROBINS (DAVID) and COHEN (PHILIP). Knuckle Sandwich: Growing Up in the Working Class City. Harmondsworth. 1978. [Also in Juvenile Crime Section.].

8325 RODAWAY (ANGELA). A London Childhood. New edn 1985.

8326 ROGERS (RICK). Crowther to Warnock: How Fourteen Reports Tried to Change Children's Lives. 1980.

8327 ROWE (JANE). Parents, Children and Adoption: A Handbook for Adoption Workers. 1966.

8328 —— Yours by Choice: A Guide for Adoptive Parents. Rev. edn 1969.

8329 ROWE (JANE) and LAMBERT (LYDIA). Children who Wait: A Study of Children Needing Substitute Families. 1973.

8330 RUDOLPH (MILDRED DE MONTJOIE). Everybody's Children: The Story of the Church of England's Children's Society, 1921–48. 1950.

8331 RUSSELL (ROBERT). 'Are Maternity and Child Welfare Schemes Proceeding on Right Lines?' Trans. Inc. Sanitary Assn. Scotland 20, (1919), 17–44.

8332 RUTTER (MICHAEL) et al. Education, Health and Behaviour. 1970.

8333 —— Psychiatric Study. 1966. Repr. 1973.

8334 —— Helping Troubled Children. Harmondsworth. 1975.

8335 —— Ed. Infant Autism: Concepts, Characteristics and Treatment. 1970.

8336 —— Maternal Deprivation Reassessed. Harmondsworth. 1972. Repr. 1973.

8337 —— Et al. A Neuropsychiatric Study in Childhood. 1970.

8338 —— Changing Youth in a Changing Society: Patterns of Adolescent Development. 1979.

8339 —— Fifteen Thousand Hours: Secondary Schools and their Effects on Children. 1979.

8340 —— Stress, Coping and Development in Children. N.Y./Lond. 1983.

8341 —— Depression in Young People: Developmental and Clinical Perspectives. N.Y./Lond. 1986.

8342 RUTTER (MICHAEL) *and* HERSOV (LIONEL) *eds.* Child Psychiatry: Modern Approaches. Oxf. 1976.

8343 RUTTER (MICHAEL) *and* MARTIN (J. A. M.). The Child with Delayed Speech. 1972.

8344 RUTTER (MICHAEL) *and* MADGE (NICOLA). Cycles of Disadvantage: A Review of Research. 1976.

8345 SCHAFFER (HEINZ RUDOLPH) *and* SCHAFFER (EVELYN B.). Child Care and the Family: A Study of Short Term Admission to Care. 1968.

8346 SCHARLIEB (*Dame* MARY DACOMB). Maternity and Infancy. 1926.

8347 —— The Psychology of Childhood. 1927.

8348 —— The Hope of the Future: The Management of Children in Health and Disease. 1916.

8349 —— 'Save the Children'. *Eugenics Rev.*, (Jul. 1917), 109–16.

8350 SCURFIELD (HAROLD). Infant and Young Child Welfare. 1919.

8351 SCHORR (ALVIN LOUIS). Children and Decent People. 1975.

8352 SCOTT (L. P.). Growing Up in Shoreditch. 1938.

8353 SEABROOK (JEREMY). Working-Class Childhood. 1982.

8354 SEGAL (CHARLES SOLOMON). Penn'orth of Chips: Backward Children in the Making. 1939.

8355 —— Backward Children in the Making. 1949.

8356 SEGAL (STANLEY SOLOMON). From Care to Education. 1972.

8357 SHIELDS (JAMES BOWIE). The Gifted Child. 1968.

8358 SKODAK (M.) *and* SKEELS (H. M.). 'A Final Follow-up Study of One Hundred Adopted Children'. *J. Genetic Psychol.* 75 (1949), 85–125.

8359 SNOWDEN (ETHEL) *Viscountess.* British Students of Child Welfare, Tested by the 'Declaration of Geneva'. 1926. (Shaftesbury Society and Ragged School Union. Shaftesbury Lecture No. 6.).

8360 SPINLEY (BETTY MARTHA). The Deprived Child and the Privileged: Personality Development in English Society. 1953.

8361 SHANKLAND-COX PARTNERSHIP AND INSTITUTE OF COMMUNITY STUDIES. Inner Area Study: Lambeth: The Groveway Project: An Experiment in Salaried Childminding. 1977.

8362 STEWART (WILLIAM FREDERICK ROY). Children in Flats: A Family Study. 1970.

8363 STONE (MAUREEN). The Education of the Black Child in Britain: The Myth of Multi-racial Education. 1981.

8364 STROUD (JOHN) *ed.* Services for Children and their Families: Aspects of Childcare for Social Workers. Oxf. 1973.

8365 —— An Introduction to the Child Care Service. 1965. Repr. 1966.

8366 —— Thirteen Penny Stamps: The Story of the Church of England Children's Society (Waifs and Strays) from 1881 to the 1970's. 1971.

8367 THOMAS (MAURICE W.). Young People in Industry, 1750–1945. 1945.

8368 THOMPSON (OWEN). 'Some Points and Practice in the law of Infants'. *Law Times* (18 Dec. 1920), 377–8.

8369 TIMMS (NOEL). Casework in the Child Care Service. 1962.

8370 —— *Ed.* The Receiving End: Consumer Accounts of Social Help for Children. 1973.

8371 TIZARD (BARBARA). Adoption: A Second Chance. 1977.

8372 TIZARD (JACK), MOSS (PETER), *and* PERRY (JANE). All our Children: Pre-School Services in a Changing Society. 1976.

8373 TOD (ROBERT JAMES NIEBOHR) *ed.* Social Work in Foster Care: Collected Papers. 1971.

8374 Disturbed Children. 1968.

8375 *Ed.* Children in Care. 1968.

8376 *Ed.* Social Work in Adoption: Collected Papers. 1971.

8377 TRASLER (GORDON). In Place of Parents: A Study of Foster Care. Lond./N.Y. 1960.

8378 TRISELOTIS (JOHN). Hard to Place: The Outcome of Adoption and Residential Care. 1984.

8379 TANSLEY (ALBERT EDWARD) *and* GUILDFORD (RONALD). The Education of Slow Learning Children. 1960.

8380 TURNER (J. NEVILLE). Improving the Lot of Children Born Outside Marriage: A Comparison of Three Recent Reforms: England, New Zealand and West Germany. 1973. (National Council for One Parent Families.).

U.K. GOVERNMENT LEGISLATION ON CHILDREN

8381 U.K. DEPT. OF ENVIRONMENT. Children at Play. 1973.

8382 U.K. The Children Act. 1948.

8383 U.K. Report of the Care of Children Committee. Cmnd 6922. (Curtis) 1946.

8384 U.K. HOME OFFICE. Children and Young Persons. (Ingelby Report) Cmnd 1191. 1964.

8385 U.K. Report of the Committee on Children and Young Persons (Scotland). (Kilbrandon) Cmnd 2306. 1964.

8386 U.K. HOME OFFICE. Children in Care in England and Wales. Cmnd 3204. 1966.

8387 U.K. The Children and Young Persons Act 1963. 1969.

8388 U.K. DHSS. Youth Treatment Centres: A New Form of Provision for Severely Disturbed Children. 1971.

8389 U.K. DHSS. Intermediate Treatment. A Guide for the Regional Planning of New Forms of Treatment for Children in Trouble. 1972.

8390 U.K. DHSS. Report of the Committee of Inquiry into the Care and Supervision Provided in Relation to Maria Colwell. 1974.

8391 U.K. PARLIAMENTARY GROUP VIDEO INQUIRY. Video Violence and Children: Part One—Children's Viewing Patterns in England and Wales. By Clifford Hill. 1983.

8392 U.K. HOUSE OF COMMONS SOCIAL SERVICES COMMITTEE. Children in Care: Second Report of the Social Service Committee, Session 1983/4. 1984.

8393 U.K. DHSS. Report of the Inquiry into Child Abuse in Cleveland, 1987. Elizabeth Butler Sloss. 1988.

8394 VARMA (VED PRAKASH) ed. Stresses in Children. 1973. Repr. 1974.

8395 WAGNER (GILLIAN). Children of the Empire. 1982.

8396 WAKEFORD (JOHN). 'Fostering—A Sociological Perspective'. *Brit. J. Sociol.* 14 (1963), 335–46.

8397 WOLFF (SULA). Children under Stress. Rev. edn Harmondsworth. 1973. Repr. 1976.

8398 WEDGE (PETER) and PROSSER (HILARY). Born to Fail. 1973. Repr. 1974. [Follow up of National Child Development Study].

8399 WILKINSON (GEORGE STEPHEN). Legal Aspects of Illegitimacy. 1965.

8400 WILSON (A.). 'Recent Developments in Social Work'. *Inl. J. Offend. Therapy* 18 (1974), 247–59.

8401 WILSON (ANNE). Mixed Race Children: A Study of Identity. 1987.

8402 WILSON (HARRIET). Parents and Children in the Inner City. 1978.

8403 WHITMORE (KINGSLEY). The Contribution of Child Guidance to the Community. 1974.

8404 WILLIAMSON (DAVID). Lord Shaftesbury's Legacy: A Record of Eighty Years' Service by the Shaftesbury Society and Ragged School Union, 1824–1924. 1924.

8405 —— Ninety . . . not out: A Record of Ninety Years Child Welfare Work of the Shaftesbury Society and Ragged School Union. 1934.

8406 WINNICOTT (CLARE). Child Care and Social Work: A Collection of Papers Written between 1954 and 1963. Welwyn. 1964.

8407 YOUNGHUSBAND (EILEEN) Living with Handicap: The Report of a Working Party on Children with Special Needs. 1970. [National Bureau for Co-operation in Child Care].

7. YOUTH

8408 THE NATIONAL YOUTH BUREAU. Bibliography of Youth Social Work. Leics. 1974.

8409 GOTTLIEB (DAVID) and REEVES (JON). Adolescent Behaviour in Urban Areas: A Bibliographic Review and Discussion of the Literature. 1963.

8410 DERRICK (DEBORAH). Selected and Annotated Bibliography of Youth, Youth Work, and the Provision for Youth. 1977.

8411 RICHMOND (KENNETH). 'Adolescence and Neurosis'. *Child* (May 1920), 364–79.

8412 FERGUSON (THOMAS) and CUNNISON (JAMES). In their Early Twenties: A Study of Glasgow Youth. Glas. 1956.

8413 —— The Young Wage Earner: A Study of Glasgow Boys. 1951.

8414 —— 'The Impact of National Service'. *Brit. J. Sociol.* 10 (1959), 283–90.

8415 LUSH (ARCHIBALD JAMES). The Young Adult. Cardiff. 1964.

8416 EPPEL (EMANUEL MONTAGUE) and EPPEL (MAY). 'A Pioneer Investigation of the Needs, Interests, and Attitudes of 380 Young Workers attending a County College'. *Brit. J. Educ. Psychol.* 1953. 29–44, 87–96.

8417 BRYDEN (RONALD). 'Generation in Exodus'. *Pol. Q.* 26 (1955), 286–96.

8418 BARKER (DIANA). 'Young People and their Homes: Spoiling and "Keeping Close" in a South Wales Town'. *Sociol. Rev.* 20 (1972), 569–90.

8419 ABRAMS (PHILIP) and LITTLE (ALAN). 'The Young Voter in British Politics'. *Brit. J. Sociol.* 16 (1965), 95–109.

8420 —— 'The Young Activist in British Politics'. *Brit. J. Sociol.* 16 (1965), 315–33.

8421 BROWN (R. L.) and O₃LEARY (M.). 'Pop Music in an English Secondary School System'. *Amer. Behavioral Scientist* Jan./Feb. 1970.

8422 LAYTON-HENRY (ZIG). 'Labour's Militant Youth'. *Pol. Q.* 45 (1974), 418–25.

8423 BREN (MARY WINIFRED JOSEPHINE MACALISTER). Youth and Youth Groups. 1957. 2nd edn rev. by Joan Matthews, 1968.

8424 JEPHCOTT (AGNES PEARL). 'Going out to Work: A Note on the Adolescent Girl in Britain'. *Inl. J. Soc. Work* 18 (1957), 12–16.

8425 —— Girls Growing Up. 1942.

8426 —— Rising Twenty. 1948.

8427 HEMMING (JAMES). Problems of Adolescent Girls. 1960. 2nd edn 1967.

8428 JOSEPH (JOYCE). 'Research Note: Attitudes of 600 Adolescent Girls to Work and Marriage'. *Brit. J. Sociol.* 12 (1961), 176–81.

8429 WILMOTT (PETER). Adolescent Boys in East London. 1966.

8430 BELSON (WILLIAM). Television Violence and Adolescent Boys. 1978.

8431 FLEMING (CHARLOTTE MARY). Adolescence, its Social Psychology: With an Introduction to Recent Findings from the Fields of Anthropology, Physiology, Medicine, Psychometrics and Sociometry. 2nd rev. edn 1963.

8432 GOTTLIEB (DAVID), REEVES (JON), *and* TEN HOUTON (WARREN D.). The Emergence of Youth Societies: A Cross Cultural Approach. 1966.

8433 WILKINSON (PAUL). 'English Youth Movements, 1908–30.' *J. Contemp. Hist.* 4 (1969), 3–23.

8434 MUSGROVE (PETER WILLIAM). Youth and the Social Order. 1964.

8435 —— The Family, Education and Society. 1966.

8436 CARTER (MICHAEL PERCY). Home, School and Work: A Study of the Education and Employment of Young People in Britain. Oxf. 1962.

8437 —— Education, Employment and Leisure: A Study of Ordinary Young People. Oxf. 1963.

8438 —— Into Work. Harmondsworth. 1966.

8439 JUPP (JAMES). 'The Discontents of Youth'. *Pol. Q.* 40 (1969), 411–18.

8440 KEELE (E. TERESA), RIDDELL (D. S.), *and* GREEN (B. S. R.). 'Youth and Work: Problems and Perspectives'. *Sociol. R.* 14 (1966), 117–37.

8441 LESSE (L.). 'Our Current Youth in Relation to the Basic Determinants and Trends of our Future Society'. *Brit. J. Soc. Psychiatry Community Health* 14 (1970/1), 16–27.

8442 MARWICK (ARTHUR J. B.). 'Youth in Britain, 1920–1960: Detachment and Commitment'. In 'Generations in Conflict' by Walter Laqueur and G. Mosse *eds.* Special Issue of *J. Contemp. Hist.* 5 (1970).

8443 MAYS (JOHN BARRON). Growing Up in the City: A Study of Juvenile Delinquency in an Urban Neighbourhood. L/pool. 1954. [Also in Juvenile Crime Section.].

8444 —— The Young Pretenders: A Study of Teenage Culture in Contemporary Society. 1965. 2nd edn 1969.

8445 LOGAN (R. F. L.) *and* GOLDBERG (E. M.). 'Rising Eighteen in a London Suburb: Some Aspects of the Life and Health of Young Men'. *Brit. J. Sociol.* 4 (1953), 323–45.

8446 MILSON (FRED). 'Social Origins and Full-Time Youth Leaders'. *Sociol. Rev.* 14 (1966), 197–200.

8447 MURDOCK (GRAHAM) *and* PHELPS (GUY). 'Youth Culture and the School Revisited'. *Brit. J. Sociol.* 23 (1972), 478–82.

8448 OPPENHEIM (A. N.). 'Social Status and Clique Formation Among Grammar School Boys'. *Brit. J. Sociol.* 6 (1955), 228–45.

8449 SUGARMAN (BARRY). 'Involvement in Youth Culture, Academic Achievement and Conformity in School: An Empirical Study of London Schoolboys'. *Brit. J. Sociol.* 18 (1967), 151–65.

8450 —— 'Social Norms in Teenage Boys' Peer Groups'. *Human Relns* Feb. 1968.

8451 BULMAN (INGA), CRAFT (MAURICE), *and* MILSON (FRED) *eds.* Youth Service and Inter-professional Studies. Oxf. 1970.

8452 BLACKLER (ROSAMUNDE). Fifteen Plus: School Leavers and the Outside World. 1970.

8453 BAZALGETTE (JOHN). Freedom, Authority and the Young Adult: A Report to the Department of Education and Science on the Young Adult Project: In Particular Examining how the Resources of Adults are Used by Young People as they Take up Full Adult Roles in Society. 1971.

8454 CAPES (MARY) *et al.* Stress in Youth: A Five Year Study of the Psychiatric Treatment, Schooling and Care of 150 Adolescents. 1971.

8455 POLK (KENNETH) *and* PINK (WILLIAM). 'Youth Culture and the School: A Replication'. *Brit. J. Sociol.* 22 (1971), 160–71.

8456 CARNEGIE UNITED KINGDOM TRUST. The Carnegie Bursary Scheme for the Training of Young Leaders. A Report. Dunfermline. 1943.

8457 SMITH (DAVID M.). 'An Exploratory Study of Adults' Attitudes Towards Adolescence'. *Sociol. R.* 19 (1971), 233–40.

8458 ASHTON (D. N.) *and* FIELD (DAVID). Young Workers. 1976.

8459 COLE (LUELLA WINIFRED) *and* HALL (IRMA NELSON). Psychology of Adolescence. 1936. 7th edn 1970.

8460 COOKE (DOUGLAS) *ed.* Youth Organisations of Great Britain: With a Foreword by the Countess of Albemarle. 1962.

8461 COX (DEREK MAURICE). The Community Approach to Youth Work in East London. 1970.

8462 DANIEL (SUSIE) *and* McGUIRE (P.) *eds.* The Painthouse: Words from an East End Gang. Harmondsworth. 1972.

8463 DAVIES (BERNARD DAVID) *and* GIBSON (ALAN). The Social Education of the Adolescent. 1967.

8464 DUCROCQ (P.) *and* VALDIN-GUILLOU (A.). Youth in Contemporary Britain. Paris. 1970.

8465 EMMETT (ISABEL). Youth and Leisure in an Urban Sprawl. Manch. 1971.

8466 EPPEL (EMANUEL MONTAGUE) *and* EPPEL (MAY). Adolescents and Morality: A Study of Some Moral Values and Dilemmas of Working Adolescents in the Context of a Changing Climate of Opinion. 1966.

8467 —— 'Connotations of Morality: The Views of Some Adults on the Standards and Behaviour of Adolescents'. *Brit. J. Sociol.* 12 (1962), 243–63.

8468 EVANS (WINIFRED MAY). Young People in Society. Oxf. 1965.

8469 GOETSCHIUS (GEORGE W.) *and* TASH (JOAN M.). Working with Unattached Youth. 1967.

8470 GOLDMAN (RONALD). Angry Adolescents. 1969.

8471 HADLEY (ROGER), WEBB (ADRIAN), *and* FARRELL (CHRISTINE). Across the Generations: Old People and Young Volunteers. 1975.

8472 HALE (SUSAN). The Idle Hill: A Prospect for Young Workers in a Rural Area. 1971.

8473 HEGINBOTHAM (HERBERT). The Youth Employment Service. 1951.

8474 LEIGH (JOHN). Young People and Leisure. 1971.

8475 JORDAN (GEORGE WILLIAM) *and* FISHER (ELSIE MAUDE). Self-Portrait of Youth: Or, the Urban Adolescent. 1955.

8476 LAURIE (PETER). The Teenage Revolution. 1965.

8477 LAYCOCK (ARTHUR LESLIE). Adolescence and Social Work. 1970.

8478 LEICESTER (JAMES H.) *and* FARNDALE (WILLIAM ARTHUR JAMES) *eds.* Trends in the Services for Youth. Oxf. 1967.

8479 MANNERS (ELIZABETH). The Vulnerable Generation. 1971.

8480 MILLER (DEREK). The Age between: Adolescents in a Disturbed Society. 1969.

8481 MEASHAM (DONALD CHARLES) *ed.* Fourteen: Autobiography of an Age-group. Camb. 1965.

8482 MILLS (RICHARD). Young Outsiders: A Study of Alternative Communities. 1973.

8483 MILSON (FRED). Youth in a Changing Society. 1972.

8484 PARKER (HOWARD JOHN). View from the Boys: A Sociology of Down-town Adolescents. Newton Abbot. 1974.

8485 PATRICK (JAMES). A Glasgow Gang Observed. 1973. (Also in Juvenile Crime Section.).

8486 PEEL (EDWINA ARTHUR). The Nature of Adolescent Judgement. 1971.

8487 PRINCE (GORDON STEWART). Teenagers Today. 1968.

8488 SCHOFIELD (MICHAEL) *et al.* The Sexual Behaviour of Young People. 1965.

8489 —— The Sexual Behaviour of Young Adults. 1973.

8490 —— Promiscuity. 1976.

8491 SMITH (CYRIL STANLEY). Adolescence: An Introduction to the Problem of Order and the Opportunities for Continuity Presented by Adolescence in Britain. 1968.

8492 THOMAS (ROGER). Looking Forward to Work: A Report on the Follow-up Survey of Fifteen and Sixteen Year Old Boy School-leavers, Carried out by the Social Survey Division of the Office of Population Censuses and Surveys on Behalf of the Central Youth Employment Executive. 1974.

8493 TIMMS (NOEL). Rootless in the City. 1968.

8494 VENESS (THELMA). School Leavers: Their Aspirations and Expectations. 1962.

8495 WILKINS (LESLIE THOMAS). The Adolescents in Britain. 1956.

8496 WILMOTT (PETER). Adolescent Boys of East London. 1966. Rev. edn Harmondsworth. 1969.

8497 WILLS (DAVID). A Place Like Home: A Hostel for Disturbed Adolescents. 1971.

8498 U.K. MINISTRY OF EDUCATION. The Training of Part-time Youth Leaders and Assistants. [Report of a working party appointed by the Minister of Education in July 1961, chaired by G. S. Bessey]. 1962.

8499 U.K. DEPARTMENT OF EDUCATION AND SCIENCE. A Second Report on the Training of Part-time Youth Leaders and Assistants. [Report of the Review Committee of the Youth Service Development Council, chaired by the Countess of Albemarle]. 1966.

8500 —— The Youth Service in England and Wales. (The Albemarle Report) 1960. CMD 929.

8501 LONDON REGIONAL ADVISORY COUNCIL FOR YOUTH EMPLOYMENT. A Guide to Employment for Boys and Girls in Greater London. 1938.

8502 —— Memorandum on the Problem of Post-War Entry of Juveniles into Employment. 1942.

8503 U.K. BOARD OF EDUCATION YOUTH ADVISORY COUNCIL. The Youth Service After the War. 1943.

8504 —— The Purpose and Content of the Youth Service: A Report. 1945.

8505 —— The Youth Service Scheme in Scotland. *Ed.* 1944.

8506 U.K. SOCIAL SURVEY. The Adolescent in Great Britain: A Report on a Nation-wide Survey of Young Persons between 15–19 Years of Age Carried out in 1950 by the Social Survey. Leslie Thomas Wilkins. 1955.

8507 U.K. OFFICE OF POPULATION, CENSUSES AND SURVEYS. Young People's Employment Study: Preliminary Report No. 1—1973. No. 2—1974.

8508 SPRINGHALL (JOHN). Youth, Empire and Society: British Youth Movements, 1883–1940. 1977.

8509 —— Coming of Age: Adolescence in Great Britain 1860–1960. Dublin. 1985.

8510 SPRINGHALL (JOHN), FRASER (BRIAN), *and* HOARE (MICHAEL). Sure and Stedfast: A History of the Boys' Brigade, 1883–1983. Lond./Glasg. 1983.

8511 GIBBON (FREDERICK P.). William A. Smith of the Boys' Brigade. 1934.

8512 PEACOCK (ROGER S.). Pioneer of Boyhood: Story of Sir W. A. Smith. 1954.

8513 HALDANE (RICHARD BURDON) *Viscount.* 'The Future of the Boys' Brigade Organisation and the Cadet Movement'. *Proc. Roy. Phil. Soc. Glasgow* (1917–1918), 1–9.

8514 BUNT (SIDNEY). Jewish Youth in Britain: Past, Present and Future. 1975.

8515 COLLIS (HENRY), HURLL (FRED) *and* HAZLEWOOD (REX). B-P's Scouts: An Official History of the Boy Scouts Association. 1961.

8516 ROWALLAN (THOMAS GODFREY POLSON CORBETT) *Baron*. Autobiography. Ed. 1976.

8517 MORSE (MARY). The Unattached: A Report of the Three-Year Project Carried out by the National Association of Youth Clubs. (With an Introduction by Robert Beloe). Harmondsworth. 1965.

8518 MATTHEWS (JOAN ETHEL). Working with Youth Groups. 1966.

8519 KUENSTLER (PETER HAROLD KEITH). Gangs, Groups and Clubs. 1960.

8520 —— Voluntary Youth Leaders. 1953.

8521 HAYWOOD (HAROLD). A Role for Voluntary Youth Work. 1968.

8522 GILLETT (ARTHUR). One Million Volunteers: The Story of the Volunteer Youth Service. Harmondsworth. 1968.

8523 DAWES (FRANK). A Cry from the Streets: The Boys' Club Movement in Britain from the 1850's to the Present Day. 1975.

8524 LEWIS (GEORGE H.). 'The Structure of Support in Social Movements: An Analysis of Organisation and Resource Mobilisation in the Youth Contra-Culture'. *Brit. J. Sociol.* 27 (1976), 184–96.

8525 SMITH (DAVID M.). 'New Movements in the Sociology of Youth: A Critique'. *Brit. J. Sociol.* 32 (1981), 239–51.

8526 BELL (DESMOND). 'Acts of Union: Youth Sub-Culture and Ethnic Identity amongst Protestants in Northern Ireland'. *Brit. J. Sociol.* 38 (1987), 158–83.

8527 CASHMORE (ERNEST). No Future: Youth and Society. 1984.

8528 HALL (STUART) *et al.* Resistance through Rituals: Youth Sub-Cultures in Post-War Britain. 1976.

8529 HUDSON (KENNETH). A Dictionary of the Teenage Revolution and its Aftermath. 1983.

8530 JONES (SIMON). Black Culture, White Youth and the Reggae Tradition from JA. to U.K. Basingstoke. 1988.

8531 MARSLAND (DAVID). Education and Youth. 1987.

8532 MORGAN (A. E.). Young Citizen. Harmondsworth. 1943.

8533 ROBERTS (KENNETH). Youth and Leisure. 1983.

8534 TAPPER (TED). Young People and Society. 1971.

8535 WILSON (BRYAN RONALD). The Social Context of the Youth Problem. 1965.

8536 U.K. YOUTH SERVICE DEVELOPMENT COUNCIL. Youth and Community Work in the 1970's. 1969.

8537 U.K. DHSS. Adolescent Drinking: A Survey Carried out on Behalf of the DHSS. By Alan Marsh. 1986.

8538 PLANT (MARTIN A.). Alcohol, Drugs and School-Leavers. 1985.

8539 BRAKE (MIKE). The Sociology of Youth Culture and Sub-cultures. 1979.

8540 HEBDIDGE (DICK). Subculture: The Meaning of Style. 1979.

8541 WALKER (TINA). Biding Time: Reflections of Unemployed Young People in Kirkcaldy. 1982.

8542 SAWARD (MICHAEL). Christian Youth Groups. 1965.

8543 CAMERON (JOHN S.). Solvent Abuse: A Guide for the Carer. 1988.

8544 O'CONNOR (DENIS). Glue Sniffing and Volatile Substance Abuse. Aldershot. 1983.

8545 YOUTHAID. The Youth Opportunities Programme: Making it Work. 1978.

8546 CHAPMAN (PAUL G.). The Youth Training Scheme in the U.K. Aldershot. 1987.

8547 KEEP (EWART). Designing the Stable Door: A Study of How the Youth Training Scheme was Planned. Warwick. 1986.

8548 GRAY (DUNCAN) *and* KING (SUZANNE). The Youth Training Scheme: The First Three Years. Sheffield. 1986. Manpower Services Commission.

8549 CRAIG (RACHEL). The Youth Training Scheme: A Study of Non-Participants and Early Leavers. Sheffield. 1986.

8550 FINN (DAN). Training without Jobs: New Deals and Broken Promises: From Raising the School Leaving Age to the Youth Training Scheme. Basingstoke. 1987.

8. MIDDLE AGE

8551 WALLIS (JACK HAROLD). The Challenge of Middle Age. 1962.

8552 CHESSER (EUSTACE). Challenge of the Middle Years. 1964.

8553 SODDY (KENNETH) *with* KIDSON (MARY C.). Men in Middle Life. 1967.

8554 OGILVIE (*Sir* HENEAGE) *ed.* Fifty: An Approach to the Problems of Middle Age. 1962.

8555 U.K. CENTRE FOR STUDIES IN SOCIAL POLICY. Forty to Sixty: How We Waste the Middle Aged. 1975.

9. THE ELDERLY

8556 WILLIAMS (LEONARD LLEWELYN BULKELEY). Middle Age and Old Age. 1925.

8557 FRY (SARA MARGERY). Old Age Looks at Itself. 1955.

8558 TOWNSEND (PETER BRERETON). The Family Life of Old People: An Inquiry in East London. 1957.

8559 —— The Development of Home and Welfare Services for Old People, 1946–1960. Leics. 1961.

8560 —— The Last Refuge: A Survey of Residential Institutions and Homes for the Aged in England and Wales. 1962.

8561 TOWNSEND (PETER BRERETON) *and* REES (B.). The Personal Family and Social Circumstances of Old People: Report of an Investigation Carried Out in England in 1959 to Pilot a Future Cross-National Survey of Old Age. 1959.

8562 U.K. SOCIAL SURVEY. Older People and their Employment: Commentary on a Sample Survey Made in Britain in the 1950's. By Louis Moss. 1955.

8563 NATIONAL OLD PEOPLE3S WELFARE COUNCIL. Employment and Workshops for the Elderly. New edn 1963.

8564 SHENFIELD (BARBARA ESTELLE). Social Policies for Old Age: A Review of Social Provisions for Old Age in Great Britain. 1957.

8565 U.K. MINISTRY OF PENSIONS AND NATIONAL INSURANCE. Provision for Old Age: The Future Development of the National Insurance Scheme. 1958.

8566 WELFORD (A. T.). Ageing and Human Skill. 1958.

8567 CARPENTER (N.). Programs for Older People in Great Britain. Buffalo. 1959.

8568 SLACK (KATHLEEN MARY). Councils, Committees and Concern for the Old. Welwyn. 1960.

8569 —— Old People and London Government: A Study of Change, 1958–1970. 1970.

8570 ROBERTS (NESTA). Not in Perfect Mind: The Care of Mentally Frail Old People. 1961.

8571 HERON (ALISTAIR) *and* CHOWN (SHEILA M.). Ageing and Semi-skilled: A Survey in Manufacturing Industry on Merseyside. 1961.

8572 HILL (MARGARET NEVILLE). An Approach to Old Age and its Problems. Ed. 1961.

8573 U.K. MINISTRY OF HEALTH. Residential Accommodation for Elderly People. 1962.

8574 CHURCH OF ENGLAND. (Church Information Office) Homes for Old People: A Church of England Guide to Helping with Accommodation and other Practical Problems. 1965.

8575 COLE (DOROTHY) *and* UTTING (J. E. G.). The Economic Circumstances of Old People. Welwyn. 1962.

8576 RHODES (GERALD). Public Sector Pensions. 1965.

8577 HOSKING (GORDON ALBERT). Pension Schemes and Retirement Benefits. 3rd edn 1968.

8578 HAYNES (K. J.) *and* RAVEN (J.). The Living Pattern of Some Old People. Garston. 1966.

8579 MILLER (HERBERT CROSSLEY). The Ageing Countryman: A Socio-Medical Report on Old Age in a Country Practice. 1963.

8580 SNELLGROVE (DOUGLAS ROSEBERY). Elderly Housebound: A Report on Elderly People who are Incapacitated. Luton. 1963.

8581 ARKLEY (JOYCE). The Over-Sixties. A Survey of Social Problems and Unmet Needs among a Sample of Men and Women Aged about Sixty or over. 1964.

8582 BROCKINGTON (COLIN FRASER) *and* LEMPERT (SUSANNE MARTINA). The Social Needs of the over-80's: The Stockport Survey. Manch. 1966.

8583 EDINBURGH ROYAL COLLEGE OF PHYSICIANS. (Publications—No. 22). The Care of the Elderly in Scotland. Edin. 1963.

8584 RICHARDSON (IAN MILNE). Age and Need: A Study of Older People in North-East Scotland. Edin. 1964.

8585 TOWNSEND (PETER BRERETON) *and* WEDDERBURN (DOROTHY). The Aged in the Welfare State: The Interim Report of A Survey of Persons Aged 65 and over in Britain, 1962 and 1963. 1965.

8586 HOBMAN (DAVID). The Social Challenge of Ageing. 1978.

8587 TUNSTALL (JEREMY). Old and Alone: A Sociological Study of Old People. 1966.

8588 CLARK (FREDERICK LE GROS). Work, Age and Leisure: Causes and Consequences of the Shortened Working Life. 1966.

8589 BRACEY (HOWARD EDWIN). In Retirement: Pensioners in Great Britain and the United States. 1966.

8590 STEER (HERBERT PHILIP). Caring for the Elderly. 1966.

8591 HERON (ALISTAIR) *and* CHOWN (SHEILA). The Home Help Service in England and Wales. 1968.

8592 HUNT (AUDREY). The Elderly at Home: A Survey Carried Out on Behalf of the Department of Health and Social Security. 1978.

8593 HARRIS (AMELIA ISABELLA) *asstd by* CLAUSEN (ROSEMARY). Social Welfare for the Elderly: A Study in Thirteen Local Authority Areas in England, Wales and Scotland: Vols 1. and 2. 1968.

8594 SHANAS (ETHEL) *et al.* Old People in Three Industrial Societies. 1968.

8595 SUMMER (G.) *and* SMITH (R.). Planning Local Authority Services for the Elderly. 1969.

8596 AGATE (JOHN) *and* MEACHER (MICHAEL). The Care of the Aged. 1969.

8597 AGATE (JOHN). Geriatrics for Nurses and Social Workers. 1972.

8598 —— *Ed.* Medicine in Old Age. 1966.

8599 WHITEHEAD (JOHN ANTHONY). In the Service of Old Age: The Welfare of Psychogeriatric Patients. 1970.

8600 GOLDBERG (ELSA MATHILDE) *et al.* Helping the Aged: A Field Experiment in Social Work. 1970.

8601 SHAW (JACK). On our Conscience: The Plight of the Elderly. Harm. 1971.

8602 SCAMMELS (BRIAN). The Administration of Health and Welfare Services: A Study of the Provision of Care for Elderly People. Manch. 1971.

8603 DAVIES (BLEDDYN PRICE) *et al.* Variations in Services for the Aged: A Causal Analysis. 1971.

8604 WAGER (R.). Care of the Elderly: An Exercise in Cost–Benefit Analysis Commissioned by Essex County Council. 1972.

8605 ISAACS (BERNARD) et al. Survival of the Unfittest: A Study of Geriatric Patients in Glasgow. 1972.

8606 CHEESMAN (DAVID) et al. Neighbourhood Care and Old People: A Community Development Project. 1972.

8607 BOLDY (DUNCAN) et al. The Elderly in Grouped Dwellings: A Profile. Exeter. 1973.

8608 GREGORY (PETER). Telephones for the Elderly. 1973.

8609 GREGORY (PETER) and YOUNG (MICHAEL). Lifeline Telephone Service for the Elderly: An Account of a Pilot Project in Hull. 1972.

8610 CHISOLM (CECIL). The £.s.d. of Retirement. 1958.

8611 —— Retire and Enjoy It. 1954.

8612 —— Retire into the Sun: A Survey of Some Possibilities in Nine Paradises. 1961.

8613 WILSON (THOMAS) Ed. Pensions, Inflation and Growth: A Comparative Study of the Elderly in the Welfare State. 1974.

8614 GORDIN (IAN R.). The Retirement Industry in the South West: A Survey of its Size, Distribution and Economic Aspects. Bristol. 1975.

8615 BREARLEY (CHRISTOPHER PAUL). Social Work, Ageing and Society. 1975.

8616 HAZELL (KENNETH). Social and Medical Problems of the Elderly. 4th edn 1976.

8617 BUTCHER (HUGH) and CROSBIE (DAVID). Pensioned Off: A Study of Elderly People in Cleator Moor. Heslington. 1977.

8618 KARN (VALERIE A.). Retiring to the Seaside. 1977.

8619 U.K. CENTRAL OFFICE OF INFORMATION. Care of the Elderly in Britain. (IRP 121.) 2nd edn 1977.

8620 WICKS (MALCOLM). Old and Cold: Hypothermia and Social Policy. 1978.

8621 NATIONAL OLD PEOPLE'S WELFARE COUNCIL. Age is Opportunity: A Handbook of Historical and Social Development Concerning the Care of the Elderly in the United Kingdom, with Information about Practical Schemes and with some Reference to Development Overseas. 1961.

8622 COLEMAN (P. G.). 'Social Gerontology in England, Scotland and Wales: A Review of Recent and Current Research'. Gerontologist 15 (1975), 219–29.

8623 CRAWFORD (M. P.). 'Retirement and Role Playing'. Sociol. 6 (1972), 217–36.

8624 GARSIDE (R. F.), KAY (D. W.), and ROTH (M.). 'Old Age Mental Disorders in Newcastle-upon-Tyne: A Factorial Study of Medical Psychiatric and Social Characteristics'. Brit. J. Psychiatry 3 (1965), 939–46.

8625 LIPMAN (A.). 'Old People's Homes: Siting and Neighbourhood Integration'. Sociol. Rev. 15 (1967), 323–38.

8626 MARTIN (J.) and DORAN (A.). 'Evidence Concerning the Relationship between Health and Retirement'. Sociol. Rev. 14 (1966), 327–43.

8627 RUCK (SYDNEY KENNETH). 'A Policy for Old Age'. Pol. Q. 31 (1960), 120–31.

8628 SIMONDS (W. H.) and STEWART (A.). 'Old People Living in Dorset: A Socio-medical Survey of Private Households'. Brit. J. Prev. Soc. Med. 8 (1954), 139–46.

8629 SYKES (A. J. M.). 'The Problem of Status in Old Age'. Quart. Rev. 298 (1960), 278–89.

8630 YOUNG (M.) and GEERTZ (H.). 'Old Age in London and San Francisco: Some Families Compared'. Brit. J. Sociol. 12 (1961), 124–41.

8631 TINKER (ANTHEA). The Elderly in Modern Society. 1981.

8632 PYKE (MAGNUS). Long Life: Expectations for Old Age. 1980.

8633 FENTON (STEVE). Ageing Minorities: Black People as they Grow Old in Britain. 1987.

8634 PYKE-LEES (CELIA). Elderly Ethnic Minorities. Mitcham. 1974.

8635 CARVER (VIDA) and LIDDIARD (PENNY). An Ageing Population. Sevenoaks. 1978.

8636 BOSANQUET (NICHOLAS). New Deal for the Elderly. 1975.

8637 BOOTH (TIMOTHY A.). Home Truths: Old People's Homes and the Outcome of Care. Aldershot. 1985.

8638 MEACHER (MICHAEL). Taken for a Ride: Special Residential Homes for Confused Old People: A Study of Separatism in Social Policy. Harlow. 1972.

8639 WILLCOCKS (DIANE M.). Private Lives in Public Places: A Research Based Critique of Residential Life in Local Authority Old People's Homes. 1987.

8640 CREEDY (JOHN). State Pensions in Britain. Camb. 1982.

8641 U.K. DHSS. A Happier Old Age: A Discussion Document on Elderly People in our Society. 1978.

8642 MEANS (ROBIN). The Development of Welfare Services for Elderly People. 1985.

8643 BROWN (PAT). The Other Side of Growing Older. 1982.

8644 WELLS (NICHOLAS). The Ageing Population: Burden or Challenge? Basingstoke. 1988.

8645 FOGARTY (MICHAEL PATRICK). Retirement Age and Retirement Costs. 1980.

8646 —— Retirement Policy: The Next Fifty Years. 1982.

8647 TAYLOR (HEDLEY). Growing Old Together: Elderly Owner-Occupiers and their Housing. 1986.

8648 BRITISH MEDICAL ASSOCIATION. All our Tomorrows: Growing Old in Britain. 1986.

8649 WARREN (LINDA). Older Women and Feminist Social Work. Coventry. 1985.

10. SOCIAL POLICY, SOCIAL WELFARE, AND SOCIAL WORK

8650 BESSELL (ROBERT). Introduction to Social Work. 1970.

8651 PLANT (RAYMOND). Social and Moral Theory in Casework. 1970.

8652 BATTEN (THOMAS REGINALD) *and* BATTEN (MADGE). The Human Factor in Casework. Lond./N.Y. 1970.

8653 THOMPSON (SHEILA) *and* KAHN (JACK). The Group Process as a Helping Technique. Oxf./N.Y. 1970.

8654 WOOTTON (BARBARA) *Baroness*. 'The Image of the Social Worker'. *Brit. J. Sociol.* 11 (1960), 373–85.

8655 WILTSE (K. T.). 'Social Casework and Public Assistance'. *Soc. Serv. R.* 32 (1958), 41–50.

8656 WARD (PATRICK) *and* BAKER (MARGARET). Social Worker. 1969.

8657 NOKES (PETER L.). The Professional Task in Welfare Practice. 1967.

8658 DAVIES (BERNARD DAVID). The Use of Groups in Social Work Practice. 1975.

8659 KUENSTLER (PETER HAROLD KEITH) *ed.* Social Group Work in Great Britain. 1955.

8660 —— Spontaneous Youth Groups. 1955.

8661 —— Community Organisations in Great Britain. 1961.

8662 CAVENAGH (WINIFRED ELIZABETH). Four Decades of Students in Social Work. Birm. 1956.

8663 YOUNGHUSBAND (*Dame* EILEEN LOUISE). 'Trends in Social Work Education'. *Social Work* 18 (1956), 241–56.

8664 —— 'Social Work Education in the World Today'. *Social Work* 13 (1956), 159–67.

8665 —— 'Social Work in Public and Voluntary Agencies.' *Social Work* 17 (1960), 2–5.

8666 —— New Developments in Casework. 1966.

8667 —— Social Work and Social Change. 1964.

8668 —— Readings in Social Work. 1965.

8669 —— Social Work and Social Values. 1967.

8670 —— Social Work in Britain, 1950–1975: A Follow-up Study. 2 vols 1978.

8671 —— (Chairman). Study Group on Training for Community Work. 1968.

8672 —— (Vice-Chairman). Current Issues in Community Work: A Study by the Community Work Group. 1973. [Chaired by Edward Boyle, *Baron*.].

8673 —— Working Party on Social Workers in the Local Authority Health and Welfare Services. 1959.

8674 —— Community Work and Social Change. Harlow. 1968.

8675 —— The Newest Profession: A Short History of Social Work. Sutton. 1981.

8676 JONES (KATHLEEN). Eileen Younghusband: A Biography. 1984.

8677 —— Health and Social Services Merry Go-Round. 1973.

8678 —— Mental Health and Social Policy. 1978.

8679 BENDER (MICHAEL PHILIP). Community Psychology. 1976. [Psychiatric Social Work.].

8680 TUXFORD (J.) *and* DENNIS (N.). 'Research and Social Work'. *Social Work* 15 (1958), 460–62.

8681 BAILEY (M. B.). 'Community Orientations Towards Social Casework'. *Social Work* 4 (1959), 60–7.

8682 KENDALL (K. A.). 'New Dimensions in Casework and Group Work Practice, Implications for Professional Education'. *Social Work* 4 (1954), 49–57.

8683 MEEK (E. G.). 'Social and Cultural Factors in Casework Diagnosis'. *Social Work* 4 (1959), 15–27.

8684 WIDEM (P.). 'Social Casework in a British Day Hospital'. *Social Work* 4 (1959), 98–104.

8685 U.S. EDUCATIONAL COMMISSION IN THE U.K. Some Impressions of Social Services in Great Britain by an American Social Work Team. 1956.

8686 LEVINE (E. E.). 'Renaissance in British Casework'. *Social Work* 13 (1956), 187–94.

8687 SETH-SMITH (J.). 'The New Look in Family Casework'. *Social Work* 15 (1958), 447–51.

8688 KEENLEYSIDE (M.). 'Development in Casework Method'. *Social Work* 15 (1958), 516–21.

8689 CUNLIFFE (M. A.). 'The Use of Supervision in Casework Practice'. *Social Work* 15 (1958), 408–13.

8690 HALMOS (PAUL) *ed.* Moral Issues in the Training of Teachers and Social Workers. Keele. 1960.

8691 COLLIS (A.). 'Social Work. A Current Assessment of Training and Related Topics'. *Social Work* 18 (1961), 5–9.

8692 DAVISON (EVELYN HOPE). 'The Southampton Generic Course'. *Social Work* 18 (161), 10–12.

8693 TIMMS (NOEL). 'Knowledge, Opinion and the Social Services'. *Sociol. Rev.* 9 (1961), 361–5.

8694 —— 'On Wootton's Image of the Social Worker'. *Social Work* 18 (1961), 17–21.

8695 —— A Sociological Approach to Social Problems. 1967.

8696 —— Social Casework: Principles and Practice. 1964. 2nd edn 1966.

8697 —— Recording in Social Work. 1972.

8698 —— Social Work: An Outline for the Intending Student. 1970.

8699 —— The Language of Social Casework. 1968.

8700 —— Social Welfare: Why and How? 1980.

8701 —— Social Work Values: An Enquiry. 1983.

8702 TIMMS (NOEL) *and* TIMMS (RITA). Perspectives in Social Work. 1977.

8703 TIMMS (NOEL) *and* WATSON (DAVID) *eds.* Talking about Welfare: Readings in Philosophy and Social Policy. 1976.

8704 —— *Eds.* Philosophy in Social Work. 1978.

8705 CURTIS (HELENE) *and* HOWELL (CATHERINE). Part-time Social Work: A Study of Opportunities for the Employment of Trained Social Workers. 1965. [NCSS.].

8706 DAVISON (EVELYN HOPE). Social Casework: A Basic Textbook for Students of Casework and for Administrators in the Social Services. 1965.

8707 SETH-SMITH (J.). 'Modern Trends in Social Work—the Family Casework'. *Social Work* 17 (1960), 61–72.

8708 OWENS (JOAN LLEWELLYN). Careers in Social Work. 1965.

8709 SCOTLAND. 1963. Staffing of Local Authority Children's Departments: A Report. Edin. 1963.

8710 BROWN (SIBIL CLEMENT). The Field Training of Social Workers: A Survey. 1966.

8711 BROWN (SIBIL CLEMENT) *and* ASHDOWN (MARGARET). Social Services and Mental Health: An Essay in Psychiatric Social Workers. 1953.

8712 ROGERS (BARBARA N.). A Follow-up Study of Social Administration Students of Manchester University 1940–1960: Their Further Training and Subsequent Careers, with Particular Reference to the Contribution Made by the Married Woman to Social Work. Manch. 1963.

8713 JONES (HOWARD) *ed.* Towards a New Social Work. 1975.

8714 —— The Residential Community: A Setting for Social Work. 1979.

8715 HANCOCK (ALAN) *and* WILLMOTT (PHYLLIS) *eds.* The Social Workers. 1965.

8716 BELL (KATHLEEN M.). 'The Development of Community Care'. *Public. Admin.* 43 (1965), 419–35.

8717 GOLDBERG (ELSA MATHILDE). Welfare in the Community: Talks on Social Work to Welfare Officers. 1966. [NCSS.].

8718 COUNCIL FOR CHILDREN'S WELFARE. A Family Service and a Family Court. 1966.

8719 PETTES (DOROTHY ELIZABETH). Supervision in Social Work: A Method of Student Training and Staff Development. 1967.

8720 DAY (PETER RUSSELL). Communication in Social Work. Oxf. 1972.

8721 JEHU (DEREK) *et al.* Behaviour Modification and Social Work. 1972.

8722 DHSS. Social Service Teams: The Practitioner's View. 1978.

8723 COLLIS (A.). 'Casework in a Statutory and Voluntary Setting'. *Social Work* 15 (1958), 451–60.

8724 COOPER (R.). 'Trends in Medical Social Work in the United Kingdom and the United States'. *Soc. Serv. Rev.* 32 (1958), 387–99.

8725 COYLE (G.). 'Some Principles and Methods in Social Work Education'. *Social Work* 13 (1958), 413–22.

8726 HAYNES (*Sir* GEORGE E.). 'Social Work in the Sixties'. *Soc. Serv. Q.* 35 (1961–62), 97–100.

8727 NEWMAN (E. L.). 'An American Looks at British Social Service'. *Soc. Serv. Q.* 35 (1961–2), 14–19.

8728 STANDING CONFERENCE OF COUNCILS OF SOCIAL SERVICE. Social Work in the 1960's: Report of a Conference. 1962.

8729 —— Community Services for Health and Welfare Cooperation Between Local Authorities and Voluntary Organisations: Report of a Conference. 1963.

8730 —— Working in the Community: Report of a Conference . . . 1964.

8731 SMITH (MARJORIE JEAN), Introduction by TITMUSS (RICHARD M.). Professional Education for Social Work in Britain: An Historical Account. 1965.

8732 RODGERS (BARBARA N.) *and* DIXON (JULIA). Portrait of Social Work: A Study of Social Services in a Northern Town. Oxf. 1960.

8733 RODGERS (BARBARA N.) *and* STEVENSON (JUNE). A New Portrait of Social Work: A Study of Social Services in a Northern Town from Younghusband to Seebohm. 1973.

8734 MOFFETT (JONATHAN). Concepts in Casework Treatment. 1968.

8735 FORDER (ANTHONY). Concepts in Social Administration: A Framework for Analysis. 1974.

8736 —— Theories of Welfare. 1984.

8737 FORDER (ANTHONY) *and* KAY (SHEILA). 'Recent Developments in Social Work'. *Soc. Econ. Admin.* 3 (1969), 75–105.

8738 HALL (MARY PENELOPE). The Church in Social Work: A Study of Moral Welfare Work Undertaken by the Church of England. 1965.

8739 —— The Social Services of Modern England. 1952.

8740 HALL (MARY PENELOPE) *and* FORDER (ANTHONY). Penelope Hall's Social Services of England and Wales. New edn 1969, 10th edn 1983.

8741 MAYER (JOHN E.) *and* TIMMS (NOEL). The Client Speaks. 1970.

8742 STEVENSON (OLIVE). Claimant or Client?: A Social Worker's View of the Supplementary Benefits Commission. 1973.

8743 SAINSBURY (ERIC). Social Diagnosis in Casework. 1970.

8744 —— Social Work with Families. 1973.

8745 —— The Personal Social Services. 1977.

8746 WALKER (REA), GOLDBERG (ELSA MATHILDE), *and* FRUIN (DAVID JOHN). Social Workers and their Workloads in Northern Ireland Welfare Departments. 1972.

8747 BRYANT (RICHARD). 'Professionals in the Firing Line'. *Brit. J. Social Work* 3 (1973), 161–74.

8748 —— Change and Conflict: A Study of Community Work in Glasgow. Aberd. 1982.

8749 BRYANT (RICHARD) *and* BRADSHAW (JONATHAN). Welfare Rights and Social Action: The York Experiment. 1972. [Child Poverty Action Group.].

8750 FARBER (RUTH). 'Informal View of British Social Work Agencies'. *Soc. Casework* 55 (1974), 263–70.

8751 SEED (PHILIP). The Expansion of Social Work in Britain. 1973.

8752 SHAW (JOHN). The Self in Social Work. 1974.

8753 PATTERSON (W. J.). Social Work's Theory of Man: A New Profession's Philosophical Anthropology. Coleraine. 1975.

8754 MCDERMOTT (F. E.) *ed.* Self-Determination in Social Work: A Collection of Essays. 1975.

8755 BRAKE (MIKE) *and* BAILEY (ROY) *eds.* Radical Social Work and Practice. 1980.

8756 STROUD (JOHN). In the Care of the Council: Social Workers and their World. 1975.

8757 BALDOCK (PETER). Community Work and Social Work. 1974.

8758 WALTON (RONALD GORDON). Women in Social Work. 1975.

8759 BUTRYM (ZOFIA TERESA). The Nature of Social Work. 1976.

8760 MAYO (MARJORIE) *et al. eds.* Women in the Community. 1977.

8761 GREGORY (J.). 'Social Justice'. *Social Work Today* 6 (1975).

8762 CHEETHAM (JULIET). Social Work with Immigrants. 1972.

8763 —— Social Work Services for Ethnic Minorities in Britain and the USA. Oxf. 1981.

8764 CHEETHAM (JULIET) *et al.* Social and Community Work in a Multicultural Society. 1981.

8765 TRISELIOTIS (JOHN PAUL). Social Work with Coloured Immigrants and their Families. 1972.

8766 ELY (PETER). Social Work in a Multi-racial Society. Aldershot. 1987.

8767 NATIONAL INSTITUTE FOR SOCIAL WORK. Social Workers: Their Role and Tasks. 1982.

8768 BREARLEY (C. PAUL). Risk and Social Work. 1982.

8769 WILLIAMS (JULIETTE EVANGELINE RHYS). Something to Look Forward to: A Suggestion for a New Social Contract. 1943.

8770 —— Proposals for Simplifying and Reducing Income Tax, also Making Provision for Family Allowances and Social Security in a Draft Post-War Budget. 1945.

8771 —— Taxation and Incentive. 1953.

8772 ZWEIG (FERDYNAND). The Planning of Free Societies. 1942.

8773 ABRAMS (MARK). Social Surveys and Social Action. 1951.

8774 MYRDAL (GUNNAR). 'The Relation Between Social Theory and Social Policy'. *Brit. J. Sociol.* 4 (1953), 210–42.

8775 ARCHER (PETER) *ed.* Social Welfare and the Citizen. Harmonds-worth. 1957.

8776 MacGREGOR (OLIVER ROSS) *Baron.* 'Social Facts and Social Conscience'. *Twentieth Century* 167 (1960), 389–96.

8777 BREMME (G.). Freiheit und sozialer Sicherheit. Motive und Prinzipien sozialer Sicherung dargestellt in England und Frankreich. Stuttgart. 1961.

8778 LASLETT (PETER), SKINNER (QUENTIN), *and* RUNCIMAN (WALTER GARRISON) *eds.* Philosophy, Politics and Society. (Second Series.). Oxf. 1962.

8779 FORD (PERCY). Social Theory and Social Practice: An Exploration of Experience. 1968.

8780 RUNCIMAN (WALTER GARRISON). Relative Deprivation and Social Justice: A Study of Attitudes to Social Inequality in 20th Century England. 1966.

8781 —— Social Science and Political Theory. 1963. 2nd edn 1969.

8782 —— A Treatise on Social Theory. 1983.

8783 ASHTON (ELWYN THOMAS). Social Work and the Social Sciences. Bala, Gwynedd. 1966.

8784 LEONARD (PETER). Sociology in Social Work. 1966.

8785 —— 'The Application of Sociological Analysis to Social Work Training'. *Brit. J. Sociol.* 19 (1968), 375–84.

8786 GINSBERG (MORRIS). On Justice in Society. 1963.

8787 SINFIELD (ADRIAN). Which Way for Social Work? 1969. [Fabian Tract 393.].

8788 HERAUD (BRIAN JEREMY). Sociology and Social Work: Perspectives and Problems. Oxf. 1970.

8789 WIENER (R. S. P.) *and* BAYLEY (J. C. R.). 'The Administration and Evaluation of Research Units and Projects'. *Brit. J. Sociol.* 22 (1971), 193–9.

8790 SOCIOLOGICAL REVIEW SPECIAL ISSUE. 'Aspects of the Sociology of Social Welfare'. *Sociol. Rev.* 21 (1973), 536–612.

8791 COLE (GEORGE DOUGLAS HOWARD). 'Sociology and Social Policy'. *Brit. J. Sociol.* 8 (1957), 158–71.

8792 —— The Next Ten Years in British Social and Economic Policy. 1929.

8793 —— British Social Services. 1959.

8794 SMITH (GILBERT). Social Work and the Sociology of Organisations. 1970. Rev. edn 1979.

8795 LEES (RAY). Politics and Social Work. 1972.

8796 HONDERICH (TED) *ed.* Social Ends and Political Means. 1976.

8797 GEORGE (VICTOR) *and* WILDING (PAUL). Ideology and Social Welfare. 1976. Rev. edn 1985.

8798 DIGBY (ANNE). British Welfare Policy: Workhouse to Workforce. 1989.

8799 GEORGE (VICTOR). Social Security and Society. 1973.

8800 SMITH (DAVID MARSHALL). Human Geography: A Welfare Approach. 1977.

8801 WEALE (ALBERT). Equality and Social Policy. 1978.

8802 —— Political Theory and Social Policy. 1983.

8803 JAQUES (ELLIOTT). 'The Science of Society'. *Human Relns* 19 (1966), 125–37.

8804 HALMOS (PAUL). The Personal and the Political: Social Work and Political Action. 1978.

8805 —— The Personal Service Society. 1970.

8806 GRIMOND (JOSEPH). The Common Welfare. 1978.

8807 JONES (KATHLEEN) *et al.* Issues in Social Policy. 1978.

8808 —— *Ed.* Yearbook of Social Policy in Britain—1971. 1972. (Yearbooks published annually from 1971 under various editors.).

8809 BRENTON (MARIA) *and* UNGERSON (CLAIRE). Yearbook of Social Policy in Britain, 1987–88. 1988. [Most recent volume in series.].

8810 JONES (CATHERINE). Patterns of Social Policy: An Introduction to Comparative Analysis. 1985.

8811 KING (JOAN FAYE SENDALL). New Thinking for Changing Needs. 1963.

8812 DONNISON (DAVID VERNON). The Child and the Social Services. 1958. [Fabian Society Research Series No. 196.].

8813 —— Health, Welfare and Democracy in Greater London. 1962.

8814 —— *Et al.* Social Policy and Administration: Studies in the Development of Social Service at the Local Level. 1965.

8815 —— An Approach to Social Policy. Dublin. 1975.

8816 —— *Et al. eds.* Social Policy and Administration Revisited: Studies in the Development of Social Service at the Local Level. 1975.

8817 CHERNS (ALBERT B.), SINCLAIR (R.), *and* JENKINS (W.) *eds.* Social Science and Government: Policies and Problems. 1972.

8818 BUTTERWORTH (ERIC) *and* HOLMAN (ROBERT) *eds.* Social Welfare in Modern Britain. 1975.

8819 BULMER (MARTIN) *ed.* Social Policy Research. 1978.

8820 —— Social Science and Social Policy. 1986.

8821 BROWN (MARTIN JAMES) *ed.* Social Issues and the Social Services. 1974.

8822 WATSON (GEORGE) *ed.* The Unservile State: Essays in Liberty and Welfare. 1957.

8823 ROBSON (WILLIAM ALEXANDER) *and* CRICK (BERNARD) *eds.* The Future of the Social Services. Harmondsworth. 1970.

8824 MARSHALL (THOMAS HUMPHREY). Social Policy. 1965.

8825 —— Social Policy in the Twentieth Century. 2nd rev. edn of above, 1967. 5th rev. edn 1985.

8826 TITMUSS (RICHARD MORRIS). The Gift Relationship: From Human Blood to Social Policy. 1970.

8827 —— Problems of Social Policy. 1950.

8828 —— The Social Division of Welfare. Liverpool. 1956.

8829 —— Commitment to Welfare. 1968. 2nd edn 1976.

8830 —— The Irresponsible Society. 1960.

8831 TITMUSS (RICHARD MORRIS), ABEL-SMITH (BRIAN), *and* TITMUSS (KAY) *eds.* Social Policy: An Introduction. 1974.

8832 WEBB (ADRIAN). Planning, Need and Scarcity: Essays on the Personal Social Services. 1986.

8833 CULYER (ANTHONY JOHN). The Economics of Social Policy. 1973.

8834 —— The Political Economy of Social Policy. 1st edn 1973. New edn Oxf. 1980.

8835 HILL (MICHAEL J.). Analysing Social Policy. Oxf. 1986.

8836 LEE (PHIL). Welfare Theory and Social Policy: Reform or Revolution? 1988.

8837 PAYNE (DOUGLAS). A Study of Job Satisfaction in Social Work. Edin. 1984.

8838 LESTER (MURIEL). It Occurred to Me. 1937. [Autobiography of a Social and Religious Worker.].

8839 DARVILL (GILES). Preparing for Community Social Work. 1983.

8840 FALK (NICHOLAS). Planning the Social Services. Farnborough. 1978.

8841 BAILEY (ROY) *and* YOUNG (JOCK) *eds.* Contemporary Social Problems in Britain. Farnborough. 1973.

8842 PACKMAN (JEAN). Who Needs Care?: Social Work Decisions about Children. Oxf. 1986.

8843 BARCLAY (PETER M.). Social Workers: Their Role and Tasks. The Report of a Working Party. 1982. [National Institute for Social Work.].

8844 COOPER (JOAN). The Creation of the British Personal Social Services 1962–1974. 1983.

8845 MacNICOL (JOHN). The Movement for Family Allowances, 1918–45: A Study on Social Policy Development. 1980.

8846 JONES (GRETA). 'Eugenics and Social Policy between the Wars'. *Hist. J.* 25 (1982), 717–28.

8847 REISMAN (DAVID). State and Welfare: Tawney, Galbraith and Adam Smith. 1982.

8848 —— Richard Titmuss: Welfare and Society. 1977.

8849 CROWTHER (M. ANNE). British Social Policy, 1914–1939. Basingstoke. 1988.

8850 —— The Workhouse System 1834–1929: The History of an English Social Institution. 1981.

8851 SHONFIELD (*Sir* ANDREW) *and* SHAW (STELLA) *eds.* Social Indicators and Social Policy. 1972.

8852 SHONFIELD (*Sir* ANDREW). The Social Sciences in the Great Debate on Science Policy. 1973. [Repr. from *Minerva* 10 (1972), 426–38.].

8853 WILLIAMS (GERTRUDE *Lady*) *ed.* Caring for People: Staffing Residential Homes. 1967.

8854 HALL (PHOEBE), LAND (HILARY), *and* WEBB (ADRIAN). Change, Choice and Conflict in Social Policy. 1975.

8855 HALL (PHOEBE). Reforming the Welfare: The Politics of Change in the Personal Social Services. 1976.

8856 GILBERT (BENTLEY BRINKERHOFF). British Social Policy 1914–1939. 1970.

8857 FERGUSON (SHEILA) *and* FITZGERALD (HILDE). Studies in the Social Services. 1954.

8858 BRITISH NATIONAL CONFERENCE ON SOCIAL WELFARE 1964. Communities and Social Change: Implications for Social Welfare: Introductory Survey for the . . . Conference, etc. 1963.

8859 —— Report of the Fifth Conference, etc. 1964.

8860 WEINBERGER (PAUL ERIC). Perspectives on Social Welfare: An Introductory Anthology. 1969.

8861 BEALES (HUGH LANCELOT). The Making of Social Policy. 1945.

8862 MORRIS (*Sir* PHILIP ROBERT). Welfare and Responsibility. 1953.

8863 ESSEX WELFARE COMMITTEE. Welfare Services in Essex, 1957–1965: A Report Submitted to the Welfare Committee of the County Council of Essex by the County Welfare Officer, W. E. Boyce. Chelmsford. 1965.

8864 EUROPEAN JOURNAL OF SOCIOLOGY. [Archives Européennes de Sociologie.]. Special Issue on 'Welfare State'. 2 pt. 3 (1961), 185–300.

8865 FARNDALE (WILLIAM ARTHUR JAMES) *ed.* Trends in Social Welfare. Oxf. 1965.

8866 NATIONAL COUNCIL OF SOCIAL SERVICE. Public Social Services: Handbook of Information. 1964. 12th edn.

8867 —— Councils of Social Service: A Handbook. 1963.

8868 —— Dictionary of Social Services: Policy and Practice. 1972. 2nd edn 1977.

8869 —— Welfare State and Welfare Society: A Guide to Studies for the Sixth British National Conference on Social Welfare, April 1967. 1965.

8870 BRISTOL DEVELOPMENT DEPARTMENT. The Story of Social Welfare in Bristol, 1696–1948. Bristol. 1950.

8871 BOURDILLON (ANNE FRANCES CLAUDINE) *ed.* A Survey of the Social Services in the Oxford District. 2 vols Oxf. 1938 and 1940.

8872 FAIRWEATHER (GEORGE WILLIAM) *and* TURUATZKY (LOUIS G.). Experimental Methods for Social Policy Research Oxf. 1977.

8873 ROOKE (PATRICK JOHN). The Growth of the Social Services. 1968.

8874 BAUGH (WILLIAM ELLIS). Introduction to the Social Services. 3rd edn 1977.

8875 CLARKE (JOHN JOSEPH). Social Welfare. 1953. [An Abridgement.].

8876 SIMEY (THOMAS SPENSLEY). Social Science and Social Purpose. 1968.

8877 HALL (ANTHONY STEWART). The Point of Entry: A Study of Client Reception in the Social Services. 1974.

8878 WALTON (RONALD G.) *and* ELLIOTT (DOREEN). Residential Care: A Reader in Current Theory and Practice. Oxf. 1980.

8879 HUSTWIT (JANE) *and* WEBLEY (MAUREEN) *comp.* Information in Social Welfare: A Study of Resources. 1977.

8880 MORRISH (ROBERT). Towards a Caring Society: The Report of a US Study Team on its Visit to England, Scotland and Wales to Observe the Work of Local Authority Social Services, with Implications Noted for the United States. N.Y. 1974.

8881 JOHNSON (A.). 'Some Guides to Understanding the British Social Services'. *Soc. Serv. Rev.* 29 (1955), 351–7.

8882 WILLMOTT (PHYLLIS). Consumer's Guide to the British Social Services. Harmondsworth. 1967.

8883 YOUNG (AGNES FREDA). Social Services in British Industry. 1968.

8884 ENGLISH (JOHN) *and* MARTIN (F. M.) *eds.* Social Services in Scotland. Edin. 1979. 2nd edn 1983.

8885 DARBY (JOHN) *and* WILLIAMSON (ARTHUR). *eds.* Violence and the Social Services in Northern Ireland. 1978.

8886 TAYLOR-GOODBY (PETER) *and* DALE (JENNIFER). Social Theory and Social Welfare. 1987.

8887 EYDEN (JOAN LILY MARY). Social Policy in Action. 1969.

8888 BRITISH ASSOCIATION OF SOCIAL WORKERS. Research and Social Work. 1970.

8889 CARRIER (JOHN) *and* KENDALL (IAN). 'Social Policy and Social Change—Explanations of the Development of Social Policy'. *J. Social Policy* 2 (1973), 209–24.

8890 FRANCIS (CONSTANCE). The Welfare of the Needy. 1971.

8891 MARTIN (ERNEST WALTER) *ed.* Comparative Development in Social Welfare. 1972.

8892 LISTER (RUTH). National Welfare Benefits Handbook. 1972. 8th edn 1978.

8893 —— Supplementary Benefit Rights. 1974.

8894 —— Social Assistance: The Real Challenge. 1978.

8895 —— Welfare Benefits. 1980.

8896 WARHAM (JOYCE). Social Policy in Context. 1970.

8897 —— An Introduction to Administration for Social Workers. 1967.

8898 —— The Organisational Context of Social Work.

8899 EASTHOPE (GARY). A History of Social Research Methods. 1974.

8900 STEIN (BRUNO). Work and Welfare in Britain and the USA. 1976.

8901 STEIN (BRUNO) *and* MILLER (S. M.) *eds.* Incentives and Planning in Social Policy. Chicago. 1973.

8902 MEANS (ROBIN). Social Work and the 'Undeserving Poor'. Birm. 1977.

8903 COULSHED (VERONICA). Social Work Practice: An Introduction. Basingstoke. 1988.

8904 DAVIES (MARTIN). The Essential Social Worker. 1981.

8905 HOWE (DAVID). An Introduction to Social Work: Theory Making Sense in Practice. Aldershot. 1987.

8906 REES (STUART). Verdicts on Social Work. 1982.

8907 WROE (ASHLEY). Social Work, Child Abuse and the Press. Norwich. 1986. [Social Work Monographs No. 66.].

8908 FRY (ANNE). Media Matters: Social Work, the Press and Broadcasting. 1987.

8909 FITZGERALD (MIKE) *et al. eds.* Welfare in Action. 1977.

8910 ROSE (HILARY). Social Welfare in the Inner City. Bradford. 1977.

8911 TAYLOR (ROBERT). Labour and the Social Contract. 1978. [Fabian Tract No. 458.].

8912 CROSSMAN (RICHARD HOWARD STAFFORD). Paying for the Social Services. 1969. [Fabian Tract No. 399.].

8913 MARSH (DAVID CHARLES) *ed.* Introducing Social Policy. 1979.

8914 TOWNSEND (PETER) *and* BOSANQUET (NICHOLAS). Labour and Equality: A Study in Social Policy, 1964–1970. 1972.

8915 TOWNSEND (PETER). The Social Minority. 1973.

8916 SANDFORD (CEDRIC), POND (CHRIS), *and* WALKER (ALBERT). Taxation and Social Policy. 1980.

8917 THANE (PAT) *ed.* The Origins of British Social Policy. 1978. [Essays Presented to a Conference on the History of British Social Policy 1870–1945, held at Manchester University in 1976.].

8918 HOHMAN (HELEN FISHER). The Development of Social Insurance and Minimum Wage Legislation in Great Britain. Boston, Mass. 1933.

8919 UNITED KINGDOM CENTRAL OFFICE OF INFORMATION. Social Services in Britain. 11th edn 1977.

8920 U.K. DHSS. Annual Report.

8921 —— Annual Report on Departmental Research and Development.

8922 —— A Guide to Health and Social Security Statistics. [Monthly.].

8923 —— Studies on Community Health and Personal Social Services. [Annually.].

8924 —— Health and Personal Social Service Statistics for England, (With Summary Tables for Great Britain) [Annually.].

8925 —— Social Security Statistics.

8926 U.K. SOCIAL WORK SERVICES AND SCOTTISH EDUCATION DEPT. Scottish Social Work Statistics. 1972.

8927 U.K. SCOTTISH EDUCATION DEPT. Social Work and the Community: Proposals for Reorganising Local Authority Services in Scotland. Edin. 1966.

8928 JONES (JOHN HARRY). Social Reconstruction: A Proposal. Glasgow. 1917.

8929 —— Social Economics. 1920.

8930 LITTLE (IAN MALCOLM DAVID). A Critique of Welfare Economics. Oxf. 1950. 2nd edn 1957.

8931 HILL (DAVID) *ed.* The Burden on the Community. 1962.

8932 LEES (DENNIS SAMUEL) *et al.* Freedom or Free-For-All? Essays in Welfare, Trade and Choice. 2nd edn 1965.

8933 SELDON (ARTHUR). Taxation and Welfare: A Report on Private Opinion and Public Policy. 1967.

8934 SELDON (ARTHUR) *and* GRAY (HAMISH). Universal or Selective Social Benefits? 1967.

8935 RIMLINGER (GASTON VICTOR). 'Welfare Policy and Economic Development'. *J. Econ. Hist.* 26 (1966), 556–71.

8936 HOUGHTON (DOUGLAS) *Baron.* Paying for the Social Services. 1967.

8937 POLITICAL QUARTERLY. 49 (1969), Special Issue on the Future of the Social Services.

8938 ABEL-SMITH (BRIAN). 'Public Expenditure on the Social Services'. *Social Trends* No. 1 (Central Statistical Office), 1970.

8939 MILLS (JOHN). Growth and Welfare: A New Policy for Britain. 1972.

8940 HEIDENHEIMER (ARNOLD J.). 'The Politics of Public Education, Health and Welfare in the USA and Western Europe: How Growth and Reform Potentials Have Differed'. *Brit. J. Pol. Sci.* 3 (1973), 315–40.

8941 WITTMAN (M.). 'Social Work Manpower for Mental Health Services in England'. *Soc. Serv. Rev.* 48 (1974), 531–8.

8942 GALES (KATHLEEN) *and* WRIGHT (REGINALD CHARLES). A Survey of Manpower Demand Forecasts for the Social Services. 1967.

8943 CENTRE FOR STUDIES IN SOCIAL POLICY. Social Policy and Public Expenditure. 1975. Written by Rudolf Klein.

8944 KLEIN (RUDOLF) *et al.* Social Policy and Public Expenditure: An Interpretative Essay. 1974.

8945 —— Constraints and Choices, A Commentary on the Public Expenditure White Paper. 1976.

8946 KLEIN (RUDOLF) *and* HALL (PHOEBE). Caring for Quality in the Caring Services. 1974. [NCSS.].

8947 BOHM (PETER). Social Efficiency: A Concise Introduction to Welfare Economics. 1974.

8948 CULYER (ANTHONY JOHN) ed. Economic Policies and Social Goals: Aspects of Public Choice. 1974.

8949 —— The Economics of Social Policy. 1973.

8950 WILLIAMS (ALAN) and ANDERSON (ROBERT). Efficiency in the Social Services. Oxf. 1975.

8951 GLENNERSTER (HOWARD). Social Science Budgets and Social Policy: British and American Experience. 1975.

8952 BUXTON (MARTIN). Social Policy and Public Expenditure: Constraints and Choices. 1976.

8953 BUXTON (MARTIN) and CRAVEN (EDWARD) eds. The Uncertain Future: Demographic Change and Social Policy. 1976.

8954 CRAVEN (EDWARD). Regional Devolution and Social Policy. 1975.

8955 CHEUNG (STEVEN N. S.). The Myth of Social Cost: A Critique of Welfare Economics and their Implications for Public Policy. 1978.

8956 ROBERTSON (JAMES HUGH). Profit or People?: The New Social Role of Money. 1974.

8957 —— Power, Money and Sex: Towards a New Social Balance. 1976.

8958 JUDGE (KEN). Rationing Social Services: A Study of Resource Allocation and the Personal Social Services. 1978.

8959 KIRBY (ANDREW). Education, Health and Housing: An Empirical Investigation of Resource Accessibility. 1979.

8960 RUTTER (ERNEST GEORGE) and OTTAWAY (KATHLEEN). Sick Pay. 1967.

8961 GLASTONBURY (BRYAN). Managing People in the Personal Social Services. Chichester. 1987.

8962 FINEMAN (STEPHEN). Social Work Stress and Intervention. Aldershot. 1985.

8963 MISHRA (RAMESH). Society and Social Policy: Theories and Practice of Welfare. 1977. 2nd edn 1981.

8964 PINKER (ROBERT). Social Theory and Social Policy. 1971.

8965 JORDAN (WILLIAM). Rethinking Welfare. N.Y./Oxf. 1987.

8966 MANNING (NICK). Social Problems and Welfare Ideology. Aldershot. 1986.

8967 FOSTER (PEGGY). Access to Welfare: An Introduction to Welfare Rationing. 1983.

11. POVERTY AND THE WELFARE STATE

8968 SMITH (NEVILLE JOHN). Poverty in England, 1601–1932. Newton Abbot. 1972.

8969 DONNACHIE (IAN). Poverty and Social Policy 1885–1950. Oxf. 1974.

8970 WILLIAMS (GERTRUDE Lady). The Price of Social Security. 1944.

8971 —— The Coming of the Welfare State. 1967.

8972 GABOR (ANDRE). 'The Economics of the Welfare State in Britain'. Advancement of Science 16 (1960), 157–64.

8973 MARSHALL (THOMAS HUMPHRY). 'The Welfare State: A Sociological Interpretation'. Arch. Eur. Sociol. 2 (1961), 284–300.

8974 BRIGGS (ASA) Baron 'The Welfare State in Historical Perspective'. Archiv. Eur. Sociol. 2 (1961), 221–59.

8975 FOGARTY (MICHAEL PATRICK). 'Tendences Nouvelles du "Welfare State"'. Vie Econ. Soc. 33/1 (1962), 1–14, 33/2 (1962), 93–110.

8976 BARKER (Sir ERNEST). The Development of Public Services in Western Europe, 1660–1930. 1944.

8977 BRUCE (MAURICE). The Rise of the Welfare State: English Social Policy, 1601–1971. 1973.

8978 —— The Coming of the Welfare State. 1961, 4th edn 1968.

8979 JOHNSON (PAUL BARTON). Land Fit for Heroes: The Planning of British Reconstruction, 1916–1919. Chicago/Lond. 1968.

8980 LIVERPOOL COUNCIL OF SOCIAL SERVICE. Social Reconstruction in Liverpool: An Introductory Memorandum. Liverpool. 1919.

8981 SMITH (CYRIL STANLEY). People in Need and other Essays: A Study of Contemporary Social Needs and of their Relation to the Welfare State. 1957.

8982 WOODROOFE (KATHLEEN). From Charity to Social Work in England and the United States. 1962.

8983 KRIEGER (LEONARD). 'The Idea of the Welfare State in Britain and the United States'. J. Hist. Ideas 24 (1963), 553–68.

8984 TITMUSS (RICHARD MORRIS). Poverty and Population: A Factual Study of Contemporary Social Waste. 1938.

8985 —— Essays on the 'Welfare State'. 1958. 2nd edn 1963, 3rd edn 1976.

8986 —— Choice and the 'Welfare State'. 1967. [Fabian Tract No.370.].

8987 FRASER (DEREK). The Evolution of the Welfare State: A History of Social Policy since the Industrial Revolution. 1973. 2nd edn 1983.

8988 GILBERT (BENTLEY BRINKERHOFF). The Evolution of National Insurance in Great Britain: The Origins of the Welfare State. 1966.

8989 MARSH (DAVID CHARLES). The Future of the Welfare State. Harm. 1964.

8990 —— The Welfare State. 1970.

8991 MARTIN (IAN). From Workhouse to Welfare: The Founding of the Welfare State. Harmondsworth. 1971.

8992 ASHFORD (DOUGLAS E.). The Emergence of the Welfare State. Oxf. 1986.

8993 GOODIN (ROBERT E.). Not only the Poor: The Middle Classes and the Welfare State. 1987.

8994 TURNER (ERNEST SACKVILLE). Roads to Ruin: The Shocking History of Social Reform. Harmondsworth. 1966.

8995 PIKE (EDGAR ROYSTON). Pioneers of Social Change. 1963.

8996 SCHOTTLAND (CHARLES IRWIN) *ed.* The Welfare State: Selected Essays. N.Y./Lond. 1967.

8997 GREGG (PAULINE). The Welfare State: An Economic and Social History of Great Britain, 1945 to Present Day. 1967.

8998 ROBSON (WILLIAM ALEXANDER). The Welfare State. 1957.

8999 —— Welfare State and Welfare Society: Illusion and Reality. 1976.

9000 WOOTTON (BARBARA) *Baroness.* 'Is There a Welfare State? A Review of Recent Social Change in Britain'. *Pol. Sci. Q.* 78 (1963), 179–97.

9001 MARSHALL (THOMAS HUMPHREY). 'The Right to Welfare'. *Sociol. Rev.* 13 (1965), 261–72.

9002 BIRCH (REGINALD CHARLES). The Shaping of the Welfare State. 1974.

9003 COLEMAN (PETER W.). Catholics and the Welfare State. 1977.

9004 WILSON (THOMAS) *and* WILSON (DOROTHY J.). The Political Economy of the Welfare State. 1982.

9005 WILSON (ELIZABETH). Women and the Welfare State. 1977.

9006 HAY (JAMES ROY) *ed.* The Development of the British Welfare State 1880–1975. 1978.

9007 WEBB (ADRIAN) *and* WISTOW (GERALD). Whither State Welfare?: Policy Implementation in the Personal Social Services 1979–1980. 1982.

9008 WALLEY (*Sir* JOHN). Social Security: Another British Failure? 1972.

9009 GOLDING (PETER) *and* MIDDLETON (SUE). Images of Welfare: Press and Public Attitudes to Poverty. Oxf. 1983.

9010 LE GRAND (JULIEN) *and* ROBINSON (RAY) *eds.* Privatisation and the Welfare State. 1984.

9011 SLEEMAN (JOHN FREDERICK). The Welfare State: Its Aims, Benefits and Costs. 1973.

9012 MYRDAL (GUNNAR). Beyond the Welfare State. 1960.

9013 NEILL (DESMOND GORMAN). The Unfinished Business of the Welfare State. Belfast. 1958.

9014 CLARK (COLIN GRANT). Poverty before Politics: A Proposal for Reverse Income Tax. 1977. [Institute of Economic Affairs.].

9015 TOWNSEND (PETER). 'The Meaning of Poverty'. *Brit. J. Sociol.* 13 (1962), 210–27.

9016 —— Poverty in the United Kingdom. 1979. Based on a National Survey 1968/9.

9017 ROWNTREE (BENJAMIN SEEBOHM). Poverty and Progress: A Social Survey of York. 1941.

9018 —— Poverty and the Welfare State: A Third Social Survey of York Dealing only with Economic Questions. 1951.

9019 BRIGGS (ASA) *Baron.* Social Thought and Social Action: A Study of the Work of Seebohm Rowntree, 1871–1954. 1961.

9020 BOWLEY (*Sir* ARTHUR LYON) *and* HURST (ALEXANDER ROBERT BURNETT). Livelihood and Poverty: A Study in the Economic Conditions of Working Class Households in Northampton, Warrington, Stanley and Reading. With an Introduction by R. H. Tawney. 1915.

9021 BOWLEY (*Sir* ARTHUR LYON) *and* HOGG (MARGARET H.). Has Poverty Diminished? A Sequel to 'Livelihood and Poverty'. 1925.

9022 MESS (HENRY ADOLPHUS). The Facts of Poverty. 1920.

9023 JONES (DAVID CARADOG). Merseyside: The Relief of the Poor. Liverpool. 1936.

9024 JONES (DAVID CARADOG) *and* WYATT (THOMAS WILLIAM). Post-War Poverty and Unemployment can be Prevented. 1940.

9025 BEVERIDGE (WILLIAM HENRY) *Baron.* Social Insurance and Allied Services: Report. 2 vols 1942. cmnd 6404, 6405.

9026 —— The Beveridge Report in Brief: Social Insurance and Allied Services. 1942. [HMSO.].

9027 —— Pillars of Security. 1943.

9028 —— Full Employment in a Free Society. 1944.

9029 —— Beveridge on Beveridge. Recent Speeches *ed.* by Joan Simeon Clarke. 1944.

9030 HILTON (JOHN). Rich Man, Poor Man. [With a Foreword by William Beveridge.]. 1944.

9031 LABOUR RESEARCH DEPARTMENT. Beveridge Report: what it Means: A Brief and Clear Analysis Showing how it Affects Various Sections, What Changes it Proposes, its Financial Basis, etc. etc. 1943.

9032 COLE (GEORGE DOUGLAS HOWARD). Beveridge Explained: What the Beveridge Report on Social Security Means. 1942. [New Statesman Pamphlet.].

9033 POLLARD (ROBERT SPENCE WATSON). Beveridge in Brief. 1943. [Society of Friends Publication.].

9034 NISBET (JAMES WALKER). The Beveridge Plan. 1943. [Society of Individuals.].

9035 STEWART (MAXWELL SLUTZ). The Beveridge Plan. N.Y. 1943.

9036 SAXTON (CLIFFORD CLIVE). The Beveridge Report Criticised. 1943.

9037 SINGER (HANS WOLFGANG). Can We Afford Beveridge? 1943. [Fabian Research Series No.72.].

9038 BEVERIDGE (JANET). Beveridge and his Plan. 1954.

9039 MOOS (SIEGFRIED). A Pioneer of Social Advance: William Henry Beveridge, 1879–1963. Durham. 1963. [Dept. of Social Science, Durham University.].

9040 KEYNES (JOHN MAYNARD) *Baron.* 'A Reply to Sir William Beveridge' in 'Essays in the Economics of Socialism and Capitalism' *ed.* by Robert Smyth. 1964.

9041 HARRIS (JOSÉ). 'The Social Thought of William Beveridge'. *Bull. Soc. Stud. Lab. Hist.* 31 (1975), 8–10.

9042 —— William Beveridge: A Biography. Oxf. 1977.

9043 MAIR (PHILIP BEVERIDGE). 'Shared Enthusiasm': William Beveridge. 1982.

9044 ASHLEY (PETER). Social Security after Beveridge. 1984.

9045 SMITH (STIRLING). Burying Beveridge: Conservatives and Social Security Reform. 1985.

9046 WILLIAMS (KAREL). A Beveridge Reader. 1987.

9047 DE SCHWEINITZ (KARL). England's Road to Social Security: From 'The Statute of Laborers' to the 'Beveridge Report' of 1942. N.Y. 1961.

9048 CULYER (ANTHONY JOHN). Keynes, Beveridge and Beyond. 1986.

9049 GEORGE (VICTOR). Social Security: Beveridge and After. 1968.

9050 —— Social Security and Society. 1973.

9051 ZWEIG (FERDYNAND). Labour, Life and Poverty. 1949.

9052 MORGAN (JOHN S.). 'The Break-up of the Poor Law in Britain, 1907–47: An Historical Footnote'. *Canadian J. Pol. Sci.* 14 (1948), 209–19.

9053 MISHAN (EZRA J.). 'A Survey of Welfare Economics, 1939–1951'. *Econ. J.* 70 (1960), 197–265.

9054 CASSEN (R. H.) *and* GERVASI (SEAN D.). 'Social Priorities and Economic Policy'. *Pol. Q.* 35 (1964), 131–47.

9055 ROWLEY (CHARLES KERSHAW) *and* PEACOCK (ALAN TURNER). Welfare Economics: A Liberal Restatement. 1975.

9056 WILSON (HARRIET). Poverty in Britain Today. 1964.

9057 ABEL-SMITH (BRIAN) *and* TOWNSEND (PETER BRERETON). The Poor and the Poorest: A New Analysis of the Ministry of Labour's Family Expenditure Surveys of 1953–54 and 1960. 1965.

9058 ABEL-SMITH (BRIAN). Child Poverty. 1976.

9059 BALOGH (THOMAS) *Baron.* The Economics of Poverty: Essays. Lond./N.Y. 1966.

9060 RUNCIMAN (WALTER GARRISON). Relative Deprivation and Social Justice: A Study of Attitudes to Social Inequality in Twentieth Century England. 1966.

9061 RAYNES (HAROLD ERNEST). Social Security in Britain: A History. 1967.

9062 SOCIAL SCIENCE RESEARCH COUNCIL COMMITTEE. Research on Poverty. 1968.

9063 RODGERS (BRIAN). The Battle Against Poverty. 2 vols. 1968. 1969.

9064 MARSDEN (DENNIS). Mothers Alone: Poverty and the Fatherless Family. 1969.

9065 ATKINSON (ANTHONY BARNES). Poverty in Britain and the Reform of Social Security. Camb. 1969.

9066 BAGLEY (CHRISTOPHER). The Cost of a Child: Problems in the Relief and Measurement of Poverty. 1969.

9067 CHRISTOPHER (ANTHONY) *and* POLANYI (RICHARD) *et al.* Policy for Poverty. 1970.

9068 COATES (KEN) *and* SILBURN (RICHARD). Poverty: The Forgotten Englishman. Harmondsworth. 1970.

9069 —— Poverty, Deprivation and Morale in a Nottingham Community: St. Ann's: A Report of the Preliminary Findings of the St. Ann's Study Group. Nott. 1967.

9070 BULL (DAVID) *ed.* Family Poverty: Programmes for the Seventies. 1971. 2nd edn 1973.

9071 BOYSON (RHODES) *ed.* Down with the Poor. 1971.

9072 WEDDERBURN (DOROTHY). 'Poverty in Britain Today: The Evidence'. *Sociol. Rev.* 10 (1962), 257–80.

9073 —— *Ed.* Poverty, Inequality and Class Structure. 1974.

9074 WEBB (ADRIAN LEONARD) *and* SIEVE (JACK E. B.). Income Distribution and the Welfare State. 1971.

9075 JACKSON (DUDLEY). Poverty. 1972.

9076 ROACH (JACK LESLIE) *and* ROACH (JANET K.). Poverty. Harmondsworth. 1972.

9077 LEVITT (IAN). Poverty in Scotland 1890–1948. Edin. 1988.

9078 LEFCOWITZ (MYRON J.). Poverty and Health: A Re-Examination. 1973.

9079 HOLMAN (ROBERT). Poverty: Explanations of Social Deprivation. 1978.

9080 —— *Ed.* Socially Deprived Families in Britain. 1970.

9081 YOUNG (MICHAEL) *ed.* Poverty Report 1974: A Review of Policies and Problems in the Last Year. 1974.

9082 —— Poverty Report 1975 etc. 1975.

9083 JORDAN (WILLIAM). Poor Parents: Social Policy and the Cycle of Deprivation. 1974.

9084 —— Paupers: The Making of the New Claiming Class. 1973.

9085 CLARK (GEORGE). Whatever Happened to the Welfare State? A Working Note on Social Problems and Poverty in Great Britain in the Early 1970's. 1974.

9086 WILLMOTT (PETER) *ed.* Sharing Inflation? Poverty Report. 1976.

9087 CLIFF (SHEILA) *and* FIELD (FRANK). 'I Dread to Think about Christmas': A Study of Poor Families in 1976. 1976.

9088 BERTHOUD (RICHARD). The Disadvantages of Inequality: A Study of Social Deprivation: A PEP Report. 1976.

9089 —— The Examination of Social Security. 1985.

9090 —— Family Income Support. 1985.

9091 BERTHOUD (RICHARD), BROWN (JOAN C.) *with* COOPER (STEVEN). Poverty and the Development of Anti-poverty Policy in the United Kingdom. 1981.

9092 TOPPING (PHILIP R.) *and* SMITH (GEORGE ANTHONY NOEL). Government against Poverty? Liverpool Community Development Project, 1970–1975. Oxf. 1977.

9093 FIEGEHEN (GUY C.), LANSLEY (P. STEWART), *and* SMITH (ANTHONY DOUGLAS). Poverty and Progress in Britain , 1953–1973: A Statistical Study of Low Income Households, their Numbers, Types and Expenditure Patterns. Camb. 1977.

9094 FIELD (FRANK), MEACHER (MOLLY), *and* POND (CHRIS). To Him who Hath: A Study of Poverty and Taxation. Harmondsworth. 1977.

9095 FIELD (FRANK). Poverty: The Facts. 1975.

9096 —— Inequality in Britain: Freedom, Welfare and the State. 1981.

9097 —— Poverty and Politics: The Inside Story of the Child Poverty Action Groups' Campaigns in the 1970's. 1982.

9098 —— Family Income Support. 1985.

9099 NORRIS (GEOFF). Poverty: The Facts in Scotland. 1977.

9100 DISCUSSION PAPERS IN SOCIAL RESEARCH, UNIVERSITY OF GLASGOW. No. 17. Poverty in Scotland: An Analysis of Official Statistics. Glas. 1977.

9101 MURPHY (MICHAEL JOSEPH). Poverty in Cambridgeshire. Camb. 1978.

9102 LAYARD (RICHARD), PIACHAUD (D.), STEWART (MICHAEL), *et al.* The Causes of Poverty. 1978.

9103 HIGGINS (JOAN). The Poverty Business: Britain and America. Oxf. 1978.

9104 FINNEGAN (FRANCES). Poverty and Social Policy: An Historical Study of Batley. Heslington. 1978.

9105 —— Poverty and Prostitution. 1979.

9106 WALKER (ALAN). Rural Poverty: Poverty, Deprivation and Planning in Rural Areas. 1978.

9107 COOPER (STEVEN). Rural Poverty in the United Kingdom. 1981.

9108 MACK (JOANNA) *and* LANSLEY (STEWART). Poor Britain. 1985.

9109 DONNISON (DAVID VERNON). The Politics of Poverty. Oxf. 1982.

9110 CAMPBELL (BEATRIX). Wigan Pier Revisited: Poverty and Politics in the 80's. 1984.

9111 BECKERMAN (WILFRED). Poverty and Social Security in Britain since 1961. Oxf. 1982.

9112 HEMMING (RICHARD). Poverty and Incentives: The Economics of Social Security. Oxf. 1984.

9113 WHITELEY (PAUL). Pressure for the Poor: The Poverty Lobby and Policy Making. 1987.

12. CHARITIES AND VOLUNTARY WORK

9114 Charities Digest. 1882+.

9115 Voluntary Social Service: A Directory of National Organisations. 1928+.

9116 Annual Report of the Chief Registrar of Friendly Societies, 1894–1974. Continued as: Annual Report of the Certification Officer.

9117 MELLOR (HUGH). The Role of Voluntary Organisations in Social Welfare. 1985.

9118 SMITH (*Sir* HUBERT LLEWELLYN). The Borderland Between Public and Voluntary Action in the Social Services. 1937.

9119 MESS (HENRY ADOLPHUS) *et al.* Voluntary Social Services Since 1918. 1948.

9120 PROCHASKA (FRANK). The Voluntary Impulse: Philanthropy in Modern Britain. 1988.

9121 U.K. NATIONAL COUNCIL OF SOCIAL SERVICE. The Voluntary Worker in the Social Services. 1969.

9122 GAMMIE (ALEXANDER). In Glasgow's Underworld: The Social Work of the Salvation Army. 1942.

9123 CROSSLEY (B.) *and* DENMARK (J. C.). 'Community Care: A Study of the Psychiatric Morbidity of a Salvation Army Hospital'. *Brit. J. Sociol.* 20 (1969), 443–9.

9124 LIPMAN (VIVIAN DAVID). A Century of Social Service, 1859–1959: The Jewish Board of Guardians. 1959.

9125 LOW'S Handbook to the Charities of London . . . 1969–70. [133rd year of publication, revised according to the latest reports.]. 1970.

9126 ROBERTSON (WILLIAM). Welfare in Trust: A History of the Carnegie United Kingdom Trust 1913–1963. Dunfermline. 1964.

9127 PHILLIPS (MARION). Women and the Miner's Lock-Out: The Story of the Women's Committee for the Relief of the Miner's Wives and Children. 1927.

9128 MAUDE (*Sir* EVELYN JOHN). The Story of the Royal United Kingdom Beneficent Association 1863–1963. 1963.

9129 POTTER (WARREN) *and* OLIVER (ROBERT). Fraternally Yours: A History of the Independent Order of Foresters. 1967.

9130 U.K. REGISTRY OF FRIENDLY SOCIETIES AND OFFICE OF THE INDEPENDENT ASSURANCE COMMISSIONER. Guide to the Friendly Societies Act and the Industrial Assurance Acts. 1962.

9131 FULLER (MARGARET DOROTHY). 'West Country Friendly Societies': An Account of Village Benefit Clubs and their Brass Pole Heads. Lingfield. 1964.

9132 BATTERSEA UNITED CHARITIES. The Battersea United Charities, 1641–1966. 1966.

9133 POOLE (HERBERT REGINALD). The Liverpool Council of Social Service 1909–1954. Liverpool. 1960.

9134 RUCK (SYDNEY KENNETH). London Government and the Welfare Services. 1963.

9135 BRIGGS (ASA) *Baron and* MACARTNEY (ANNE). Toynbee Hall: the First Hundred Years. 1984.

9136 BOURDILLON (ANNE FRANCES CLAUDINE). Voluntary Social Services: Their Place in the Modern State. 1945.

9137 TUDOR (OWEN DAVIES). On Charities. 1st edn 1929. 7th edn 1984. By MAURICE (SPENCER G.) *et al.*

9138 CLEARY (JOHN MARTIN). Catholic Social Action in Britain, 1909–1959: A History of the Catholic Social Guild. Oxf. 1961.

9139 ROOFF (MADELINE). Voluntary Societies and Social Policy. 1957.

9140 —— A Hundred Years of Family Welfare: A Study of the Family Welfare Association [formerly Charity Organisation Society]. 1869–1969. 1972.

9141 U.K. REPORT OF THE WOLFENDEN COMMITTEE. The Future of Voluntary Organisations. 1978.

9142 U.K. NATIONAL COUNCIL OF SOCIAL SERVICE. Charitable Fund-Raising: A Report of a Working Party . . . 1969.

9143 —— Charities Aid Fund: Directory of Grant-Making Trusts. 1968.

9144 U.K. WOMEN'S VOLUNTARY SERVICES. Report on 25 Years Work, WVS Civil Defence, 1938–1963. 1963.

9145 MORRIS (MARY *Lady*). *asstd by* DALBY (G. R.). Social Enterprise: A Study of the Activities of Voluntary Societies and Voluntary Workers in an Industrial Town. 1962. [National Council of Social Services.].

9146 MORRIS (MARY *Lady*). Voluntary Work in the Welfare State. 1969.

9147 —— A Study of Halifax concerned with the Recruitment, Training and Deployment of Volunteers in the Social Services. 1965. [NCSS.].

9148 RUSSELL (WILFRID). New Lives for Old: The Story of the Cheshire Homes . . . 1963. Rev. edn 1980.

9149 RYDER (SUE). Child of My Love: An Autobiography. 1986.

9150 FINCH (J.) *and* GROVES (D.). Labour of Love: Women, Work and Caring. 1983.

9151 OWEN (DAVID EDWARD). English Philanthropy, 1660–1960. Camb., Mass. 1965.

9152 VARAH (EDWARD CHAD). The Samaritans: To Help those Tempted to Suicide or Despair . . . 1965. 2nd edn 1987.

9153 WADDILOVE (LEWIS E.). Private Philanthropy and Public Welfare: The Joseph Rowntree Memorial Trust 1954–1979. 1983.

9154 CLARK (R. W.). A Biography of the Nuffield Foundation. 1972.

9155 GRAHAM-DIXON (SUE). Never Darken My Door: Working for Single Parents and their Children, 1918–1978. 1978.

9156 ROMANYSHYN (JOHN M.). Social Welfare: Charity to Justice. N.Y. 1971.

9157 TANNAHILL (JOHN ALLAN). European Volunteer Workers in Britain. Manch. 1958.

9158 WAINWRIGHT (DAVID). The Volunteers: The Story of Overseas Voluntary Service. 1965.

9159 ADAMS (M. E.). Voluntary Service Overseas—The Story of the First Ten Years. 1968.

9160 DICKSON (NORA). A World Elsewhere: Voluntary Service Overseas. 1964.

9161 ROBERTS (GLYN). Volunteers in Africa and Asia: A Field Study. 1965.

9162 SCHUSTER (*Sir* GEORGE). Private Work and Public Causes: A Personal Record, 1881–1935. 1979.

9163 U.K. MINISTRY OF OVERSEAS DEVELOPMENT. The Young Volunteer. 1965.

9164 —— The Work of the Ministry of Overseas Development. 1965. [British Aid for Overseas Development Factsheet No. 1, rev. edn.].

9165 —— U.K. Figures on Aid. (Factsheet No. 2, rev. edn 1965.).

9166 —— Overseas Appointments. (Factsheet No. 4, 1965.).

9167 —— Training in Britain. (Factsheet No. 5, rev. edn 1966.).

9168 —— Helping Universities Overseas . . . (1965).

9169 U.K. COLONIAL OFFICE. Commonwealth Development Act, 1963. 1963.

9170 U.K. DEPARTMENT OF TECHNICAL CO-OPERATION AND THE CENTRAL OFFICE OF INFORMATION. Department of Technical Co-operation. 1962.

9171 CONSERVATIVE POLITICAL CENTRE. (Publications). No. 293. Service Overseas: The Young Idea. 1963.

9172 U.K. DEPARTMENT OF TECHNICAL CO-OPERATION. New Work and Ideas in the Field of Technical Co-operation: . . . the Henry Morley Lecture to the Royal Society of Arts. . . . by *Sir* Andrew Cohen. 1963.

9173 U.K. DEPARTMENT OF TECHNICAL CO-OPERATION. Report of a Committee on Training in Public Administration for Overseas Countries. [Chaired by *Lord* Bridges.]. 1963.

9174 OVERSEAS DEVELOPMENT INSTITUTE. British Aid 4: Technical Assistance: A Factual Survey of Britain's Aid to Overseas Development through Technical Assistance. 1964.

9175 U.K. CENTRAL OFFICE OF INFORMATION. British Aid to Developing Nations. By BARKER (DUDLEY). [Shorter version of 'Aid to Developing Countries', Cmnd 2147.]. 1964.

9176 —— Britain and the Developing Countries: Overseas Aid: A Brief Survey. 5th edn 1978. [Cen. Office of Information Pamphlet, No. 77.].

9177 —— Financial and Technical Aid from Britain. 1964.

9178 —— Britain and the Developing Countries: Economic Aid: A Brief Survey. 1966.

9179 VELIZ (C.). 'Britain and the Underdeveloped World' in 'Labour's New Frontiers' *ed.* by Peter Hall. 1964.

9180 WILLIAMS (PETER) *and* MOYES (ADRIAN). Not by Government Alone: The Role of British Non-Government Organisations in the Development Decade. 1964.

9181 —— Aid in the Commonwealth. 1965.

9182 LONGBOTTOM (CHARLES). 'Britain and the Underdeveloped World' in 'The Conservative Opportunity: Fifteen . . . Essays on Tomorrow's Toryism' by the Bow Group. 1965.

9183 BRITISH COUNCIL OF CHURCHES *AND* THE CONFERENCE OF BRITISH MISSIONARY SOCIETIES. World Poverty and British Responsibility. 1966.

9184 TAYLOR (DON). 'No Cutbacks on the Horizon'. *Far Eastern Econ. Rev.* 86, No. 46 (Nov. 22 1974), p. 9 of Special Supplement, 'Britain in Asia '74'. 3–30.

9185 LITTLE (IAN MALCOLM DAVID) *and* CLIFFORD (JULIET MARY). International Aid: A Discussion of the Flow of Public Resources from Rich to Poor Countries, with Particular Reference to British Policy. 1965.

9186 BURCH (DAVID). Overseas Aid and the Transfer of Technology. Aldershot. 1987.

9187 MOSLEY (PAUL). Overseas Aid: Its Defence and Reform. Brighton. 1987.

9188 U.K. OVERSEAS DEVELOPMENT ADMINISTRATION. Overseas Development and Aid: A Guide to Sources of Information and Material. 1986.

9189 CASSEN (ROBERT). Does Aid Work? Report to an Intergovernmental Task Force. Oxf. 1986.

9190 SINGER (HANS WOLFGANG). Food Aid: The Challenge and the Opportunity. Oxf. 1987.

9191 LESTER (JOAN) *and* WARD (DAVID). Beyond Band Aid: Charity is not Enough. 1987. [Fabian Society.].

9192 HILMORE (PETER). Live Aid. 1985.

9193 JONES (MERVYN). Two Ears of Corn: Oxfam in Action. 1965.

9194 WHITAKER (BEN). A Bridge of People: A Personal View of Oxfam's First Forty Years. 1983.

9195 —— The Foundations: An Anatomy of Philanthropy and Society. 1974.

9196 FREEMAN (KATHLEEN). If any Man Build: The History of the Save the Children Fund. 1965.

9197 FULLER (EDWARD). The Right of the Child: A Chapter in Social History. 1951. [Save the Children Fund History.].

9198 THURNLEY (JEAN). Some Voluntary Work in the North West: the Guide . . . Wilmslow. 1966.

9199 EVANS (STANLEY GEORGE). The Church in the Backstreets. 1962.

9200 HEASMAN (KATHLEEN). Christians and Social Work. 1965.

9201 CHURCH OF ENGLAND COUNCIL FOR SOCIAL WORK. Annual Report. London 1939–1959, 1st—20th reports.

9202 HEYWOOD (JEAN SCHOFIELD). Casework and Pastoral Care. 1967.

9203 CHURCH OF ENGLAND COMMITTEE FOR DIOCESAN MORAL AND SOCIAL WELFARE COUNCILS. A Directory of Social and Moral Welfare Work. 1969.

9204 CHURCH OF ENGLAND COMMITTEE OF SOCIAL SERVICES. Directory of Church of England Social Services. 1972, annually until 1980.

9205 AVES (GERALDINE MAITLAND). The Voluntary Worker in the Social Services. [The Report of a Committee.].1969.

9206 BRASNETT (MARGARET). Voluntary Social Action: A History of the National Council of Social Service, 1919–1969. 1969.

9207 McKEE (CHRISTINE D.). Charitable Organisations. Birm. 1974.

9208 MURRAY (GEORGE JOHN). Voluntary Organisations and Social Welfare: An Administrator's Impressions. Edin. 1969.

9209 LANSLEY (JOHN). Voluntary Organisations Facing Change: The Report of a Project to Help Councils for Voluntary Service Respond to Local Government Reorganisation. 1976.

9210 NEWTON (KENNETH) *and* MORRIS (D. S.). 'British Interest Group Theory Re-examined: The Politics of Four Thousand Voluntary Organisations in a British City'. *Comp. Pol.* 7 (1975), 577–95

9211 NIGHTINGALE (BENEDICT). Charities. 1973.

9212 HOLME (ANTHEA) *and* MAIZELS (JOAN). Social Workers and Volunteers. 1978.

9213 LOVE (BRIAN). Would You Care to Make a Contribution? [Fundraising 1870–1978.]. 1978.

9214 CLARK-KENNEDY (ARCHIBALD EDMUND). The London: A Study in the Voluntary Hospital System. [Vol. 2 The Second Hundred Years, 1840–1948.]. 1963.

9215 —— London Pride: The Story of a Voluntary Hospital. 1979.

9216 NEWELL (PHILIP). Greenwich Hospital: A Royal Foundation, 1692–1983. 1984.

9217 BRENTON (MARIA). The Voluntary Sector in British Social Services. 1985.

9218 BIRRELL (WILLIAM DEREK). Voluntary Organisations in the United Kingdom and their Role in Combatting Poverty. Coleraine. 1980.

9219 HANDY (CHARLES B.). Understanding Voluntary Organisations. Harmondsworth. 1988.

9220 U.K. NATIONAL COUNCIL FOR VOLUNTARY ORGANISATIONS. The Voluntary Agencies Directory. 11th edn 1989. [First published in 1928 by the National Council of Social

Service under the title 'Voluntary Social Services Handbook and Directory'.].

9221 U.K. SCOTTISH COUNCIL FOR VOLUNTARY ORGANISATIONS. Directory of National Voluntary Organisations for Scotland. 7th edn 1987.

9222 U.K. WALES COUNCIL FOR VOLUNTARY ACTION. The Wales Funding Handbook for Community and Voluntary Organisations. Caerphilly. 1988.

9223 U.K. CHARITIES DATA SERVICES. The Handbook of Charities 1987–1988. 1988.

9224 U.K. CHARITIES AID FOUNDATION. The Give as You Earn Directory of Charities. 1988.

9225 U.K. NATIONAL COUNCIL FOR VOLUNTARY ORGANISATIONS. Charity and Change Norms, Beliefs and Effectiveness—A Profile of the Voluntary Sector. 1983. [By David Gerard.].

9226 GERARD (DAVID). Charities in Britain: Conservatism or Change? 1983.

9227 GLADSTONE (FRANCIS J.). Charity, Law and Social Justice. 1982.

9228 HALL (A. RUPERT). Physic and Philanthropy: A History of the Wellcome Trust 1936–1986. Camb. 1986.

9229 TOMPSON (RICHARD STEVENS). The Charity Commission and the Age of Reform. 1979.

9230 SUGDEN (ROBERT). Who Cares? An Economic and Ethical Analysis of Private Charity and the Welfare State. 1983.

13. SOCIAL ADMINISTRATION

9231 FORDER (ANTHONY). Social Casework and Administration. 1966.

9232 —— Concepts in Social Administration: A Framework for Analysis. 1974.

9233 WEBB (ADRIAN). 'Social Service Administration: Principles and Practices'. *Public Admin.* 49 (1971), 321–39.

9234 RODGERS (BARBARA NOEL), GREVE (JOHN), *and* MORGAN (JOHN S.). Comparative Social Administration. 1968.

9235 BRUNEL INSTITUTE OF ORGANIZATION AND SOCIAL STUDIES. Organising some Social Service Departments. 1980. [By David Billis.].

9236 BLACKSTONE (TESSA ANNE VOSPER) *Baroness.* Social Policy and Administration: A Bibliography. 1975.

9237 JOINT UNIVERSITY COUNCIL FOR SOCIAL AND PUBLIC ADMINISTRATION. Bibliography of Social Work and Administration: A Classified List of Articles from Selected Periodicals: 1930–1952. [*Comp.* by F. Birkett.]. 1954.

9238 LOCHHEAD (ANDREW VAN SYLKE) *ed.* A Reader in Social Administration. 1968.

9239 CLARKE (JOHN JOSEPH). Social Administration, Including the Poor Laws. 1922. 2nd edn 1935. 4th edn 1946.

9240 SIMEY (THOMAS SPENSLEY) *Baron.* Principles of Social Administration. 1937.

9241 SLACK (KATHLEEN MARY). Social Administration and the Citizen. 1966.

9242 MARSH (DAVID CHARLES) *ed.* An Introduction to the Study of Social Administration. 1965.

9243 ASSOCIATION OF SOCIAL WORKERS OF GREAT BRITAIN. (education Sub-Committee). New Thinking About Administration. . . . 1966.

9244 BROWN (MURIEL). Introduction to Social Administration in Britain. Rev. edn 1971. 6th edn 1985.

9245 BIRRELL (WILLIAM DEREK) *et al. eds.* Social Administration: Readings in Applied Social Science. Harmondsworth. 1973.

9246 BROWN (RONALD GORDON SCLATER). The Management of Welfare: A Study of British Social Service Administration. 1975.

9247 —— The Administrative Process in Britain. 1970. 2nd edn 1979. [Later edn by Ronald Brown and D. R. Steel.].

9248 HALL (ANTHONY STEWART) *and* ALGIE (JIMMY). A Management Game for Social Services. 1974.

9249 GATHERER (ALEXANDER). Management and the Health Services. Oxf. 1971.

9250 MASSAM (BRYAN). Location and Space in Social Administration. 1975.

9251 HALLET (CHRISTINE). The Personal Social Services in Local Government. 1982.

9252 BOOTH (TIMOTHY A.). Planning for Welfare: Social Policy and the Expenditure Process. Oxf. 1979.

9253 GORTNER (HAROLD F.). Administration in the Public Sector. N.Y./Lond. 1977.

9254 ABEL-SMITH (BRIAN). The Hospitals, 1800–1948: A Study in Social Administration in England and Wales. 1964.

9255 OCCASIONAL PAPERS IN SOCIAL ADMINISTRATION. 1961–1987. [Various authors, covering a variety of topics.].

9256 HILL (MICHAEL J.). The Sociology of Public Administration. 1972.

14. LOCAL COMMUNITIES AND COMMUNITY CONCERNS

9257 THOROLD (HENRY KARSLAKE) *and* FANNON (D. G.). Community Centres: Some Service Experiences. 1945.

9258 AITKEN (H. H.). Northumberland Village Halls. Newcastle-upon Tyne. 1959.

9259 U.K. MINISTRY OF HOUSING AND LOCAL GOVERNMENT. WELSH OFFICE. The Needs of New Communities: A Report on Social Provision in New and Expanding Communities, Prepared by a Sub-Committee of the

Central Housing Advisory Committee. [Chairman: J. B. Cullingworth.]. 1967.

9260 STANDING CONFERENCE OF SOCIAL SERVICE. New Approaches to Community Work: Report. 1967.

9261 BANKS (JOHN) *et al.* Community Action: Arguments. [Fabian Tracts No. 400, *ed.* by Ann Lapping.]. 1970.

9262 ADENEY (MARTIN). Community Action: Four Examples. 1971.

9263 TOWNSEND (PETER) *et al.* The Fifth Social Service: A Critical Analysis of the Seebohm Proposals. [Nine Fabian Essays.]. 1970.

9264 U.K. HOME OFFICE COMMUNITY DEVELOPMENT PROJECT. (Information and Intelligence Unit.). The National Community Development Project: Interim Report. 1973.

9265 —— (Information and Intelligence Unit). Inter-Project Report. 1974.

9266 —— Forward Plan, 1975–76. 1975.

9267 —— Action-Research in Community Development. 1975. [By Ray Lees and George Smith.].

9268 —— The Costs of Industrial Change. 1977.

9269 —— Cutting the Welfare State: Who Profits? 1976.

9270 —— Limits of the Law. 1977.

9271 —— The Poverty of the Improvement Programme. 1975.

9272 —— Profits against Houses. 1976.

9273 —— Rates of Decline: An Unacceptable Base of Public Finance. 1975.

9274 —— Whatever Happened to Council Housing ? A Report. . . . 1976.

9275 —— Workers and the Industry Bill: Time for a Rank and File Response. 1975.

9276 LONEY (MARTIN). Community against Government: The British Community Development Project, 1968–1978: A Study of Government Impotence. 1983.

9277 TOPPING (PHILIP R.) *and* SMITH (GEORGE ANTHONY NOEL). Government against Poverty?: Liverpool Community Development Project 1970–1975. Oxf. 1977.

9278 ENGLISH (JOHN). Ferguslie Park: Profile of a Deprived Community. Glasg. 1974. [Based on work done by the Paisley Community Development Project.].

9279 —— A Profile of Ferguslie Park. Paisley. 1978.

9280 MACKAY (ALEX). Social Indicators for Urban Sub-Areas: The Use of Administrative Records in the Paisley Community Development Project. Glasg. 1974.

9281 DAVIS (ALAN) *et al.* The Management of Deprivation: Final Report of Southwark Community Development Project. 1976.

9282 COVENTRY COMMUNITY DEVELOPMENT PROJECT. CDP Final Report: Part One: Coventry and Hillfields. 1975.

9283 —— CDP Final Report: Part Two: Background Working Papers. 1975.

9284 —— School Life and Working Life: A Report Carried out for the Home Office CDP in Coventry, 1971–1975. 1975. [By John Bazalgette.].

9285 —— (Inter-Project Editorial Team). Gilding the Ghetto: The State and the Poverty Experiments. 1977.

9286 COMMUNITY DEVELOPMENT PROGRAMME, POLITICAL ECONOMY COLLECTIVE, NEWCASTLE-UPON-TYNE. Back-Street Factory. 1980. [By Peter Morris.].

9287 —— From Rags to Ruins: Batley, Woollen Textiles and Industrial Change. 1980. [By Nigel Moor and Paul Waddington.].

9288 —— Housing Action?: The Myth of Area Improvement. 1982. [By Angela Birthill and Steven Taylor.].

9289 NORTH TYNESIDE COMMUNITY DEVLOPMENT PROJECT. North Shields: Living with Industrial Change. 1978.

9290 —— North Shields: Organisation for Change in a Working Class Area. 1978.

9291 —— North Shields: Women's Work. 1978.

9292 —— North Shields: Working Class Politics and Housing, 1900–1977. 1978.

9293 GLAMORGAN-GLYNCORRWG COMMUNITY DEVELOPMENT PROJECT. Transport and the Younger Unemployed. Port Talbot. 1973.

9294 —— State of the Community Report: Community Health and Welfare. 1972.

9295 —— Job Getting and Holding Capacities. 1972.

9296 UPPER AFAN COMMUNITY DEVELOPMENT PROJECT. Upper Afan CDP: Final Report to Sponsors. Cardiff. 1977. [By Richard Penn and Jeremy Alden.].

9297 COMMUNITY DEVELOPMENT WORKING GROUP. 'The British National Community Development Project'. *Community Development J.* 9 (1974), 162–86.

9298 McGRATH (MORAG). Batley East and West: A Community Development Project Survey. York. 1976.

9299 HENDERSON (PAUL). Community Work and the Local Authority: A Case Study of the Batley Community Development Project. Manch. 1978.

9300 SHENTON (NEIL) *and* COLLIS (PAT). Neighbourhood Information and Advice Centres: Oldham Community Development Project. 1978.

9301 BIRMINGHAM COMMUNITY DEVELOPMENT PROJECT. (Final Reports No. 1—The Transport Industry.). Driven on Wheels. 1977.

9302 —— (Final Reports No. 2—Employment.). The Scrapheap. 1977.

9303 —— (Final Reports No. 3—Immigration and the State.). People in Paper Chains. 1977.

9304 —— (Final Reports No. 4—Young Workers.). Youth on the Dole. 1977.

9305 —— (Final Reports No. 5—Housing.). Leasehold Loophole. 1977.

9306 BIRMINGHAM COMMUNITY CLUB. Community Club Birmingham, 1916–1955: A Short Account of an Effort in Friendliness. 1955.

9307 MILTON (ROGER) *and* MORRISON (ELIZABETH). A Community Project in Notting Dale. 1972.

9308 PEARSE (INNES H.) *and* CROCKER (LUCY H.). The Peckham Experiment: A Study in the Living Structure of Society. 1943. [Pioneer Health Centre.].

9309 NATIONAL FEDERATION OF COMMUNITY ASSOCIATIONS. Creative Living: The Work and Purposes of Community Associations. 1964. [Community Associations New Series No. 1.].

9310 NATIONAL COUNCIL OF SOCIAL SERVICE. (Community Centres and Associations Committee). New Housing Estates and their Problems. 4th edn rev. and enlgd 1937.

9311 —— Community Centres and Associations. 1937.

9312 —— Community Centres and Associations Conference. [1943.]. Report of Speeches Delivered . . . 1943.

9313 —— Community Organisation—An Introduction. 1962.

9314 —— Community Organisation: Work in Progress. 1965.

9315 YOUNG (TERENCE). Beacontree and Dagenham: The Story of the Growth of a Housing Estate. 1934. [A Report for the Pilgrim Trust.].

9316 WILLMOTT (PETER). The Evolution of a Community: A Study of Dagenham after Forty Years. 1963.

9317 —— Whatever's Happening to London?: An Analysis of Changes in Population Structure and their Effects on Community Life. 1975. [London Council of Social Service.].

9318 —— The Debate about Community: Papers from a Seminar on 'Community Social Policy'. 1986.

9319 —— Friendship Networks and Social Support 1987. [London Policy Studies Inst.].

9320 —— Local Government Decentralisation and Community. 1987. [Lond. Policy Studs Inst. Discussion Paper No.18.].

9321 —— Planning and the Community. 1987. [Discussion paper No. 17.].

9322 WILLMOTT (PETER) *with* THOMAS (DAVID). Community in Social Policy. 1984.

9323 WILLMOTT (PHYLLIS). Lambeth, Inner Area Study. 1977.

9324 WILLIAMS (W.). Population Problems of New Estates, with Special Reference to Norris Green. Liverpool. 1939.

9325 DURANT (RUTH). Watling: A Survey of Social Life on a New Housing Estate. 1939.

[See *Mental Health Section* for HARE *and* SHAW, 'Mental Health on a Housing Estate'; SPENCER (J.) *et al.* 'Stress and Release on an Urban Estate'; TAYLOR *Lord and* CHAVE, 'Mental Health and Environment'.].

9326 GLASS (RUTH) *ed.* The Social Background of a Plan: A Study of Middlesbrough. 1948.

9327 BROADY (MAURICE) *ed.* Marginal Regions: Essays on Social Planning. 1973.

9328 —— Planning for People: Essays on the Social Context of Planning. 1968.

9329 MESS (HENRY ADOLPHUS). Industrial Tyneside: A Social Survey Made for the Bureau of Social Research for Tyneside. 1928.

9330 WHITE (LEONARD EDWARD). Community or Chaos: Housing Estates and their Social Problems. 1950.

9331 —— Small Towns: Their Social and Community Problems. 1951.

9332 —— New Towns: Their Challenge and Opportunity. 1951.

9333 DUNCAN (OTIS DUDLEY) *and* REISS (ALBERT JOHN). Social Characteristics of Urban and Rural Communities. 1950. 2nd edn 1956.

9334 MACIVER (ROBERT MORRISON). Community: A Sociological Study. Being an Attempt to Set Out the Nature and Fundamental Laws of Social Life. 1917.

9335 LIVERPOOL UNIVERSITY, DEPT. OF SOCIAL SCIENCE. Social Aspects of a Town Development Plan: A Study of the County Borough of Dudley. Liverpool. 1951.

9336 KERR (MADELINE). The People of Ship Street [Liverpool.]. Lond./N.Y. 1958.

9337 NORMAN (FRANK). Stand on Me: A True Story of Soho. 1960.

9338 NORRIS (JUNE). Human Aspects of Redevelopment. Birm. 1960.

9339 NICHOLSON (JOHN HENRY). New Communities in Britain. 1961. [NCSS.].

9340 VEREKER (CHARLES) *et al.* Urban Redevelopment and Social Change: A Study of Social Conditions in Central Liverpool, 1955–1956. Liverpool. 1961.

9341 KUENSTLER (PETER HAROLD KEITH) *ed.* Community Organisation in Great Britain. 1961.

9342 BRITISH NATIONAL CONFERENCE ON SOCIAL WELFARE 1964. Communities and Social Change: Implications for Social Welfare: A Guide to Studies for the Conference. 1964.

9343 MITCHELL (G. DUNCAN) *et al.* Neighbourhood and Community: An Enquiry into Social Relationships on Housing Estates in Liverpool and Sheffield. Liverpool. 1955.

9344 THOMPSON (GEORGE FREDERICK). Community Development in Urban Areas. 1961.

9345 —— The Professional Approach to Community Work. 1969.

9346 JENNINGS (HILDA). Societies in the Making: A Study of Development and Redevelopment within a County Borough. [Bristol.]. 1962.

9347 WILSON (ROGER COWAN). Difficult Housing Estates. 1963.

9348 JEPHCOTT (AGNES PEARL). A Troubled Area: Notes on Notting Hill. 1964.

9349 BRACEY (HOWARD EDWIN). Neighbours: On New Estates and Subdivisions in England and the USA. 1964.

9350 CRICHTON (RUTH MORLEY). Commuter's Village: A Study of Community and Commuters in the Berkshire Village of Stratfield Mortimer. Dawlish. 1964.

9351 ELIAS (NORBERT) *and* SCOTSON (JOHN L.). The Established and the Outsiders: A Sociological Enquiry into Community Problems. 1965.

9352 CHINGFORD COMMUNITY ASSOCIATION. Chingford Community Association, 1940–1965. [*Ed.* by David Pigott.]. Chingford. 1965.

9353 MORLEY (KENNETH C.). Social Activity and Social Enterprise: A Study of the Present Condition and Future Role of Voluntary Social Organisations in the Designated New Town of Redditch. Redditch. 1966.

9354 —— 'Social Participation and Social Enterprise in Redditch (England)'. *Comm. Devlpt. J.* 3 (1968), 4–9.

9355 LOMAS (GRAHAM M.) *ed.* Social Aspects of Urban Development: United Kingdom Report on the Social Welfare Implications of Urban Development. . . . 1966. [NCSS.].

9356 FRANKENBERG (RONALD). Communities in Britain: Social Life in Town and Country. Harmondsworth. 1966. Repr. 1969.

9357 CULLINGWORTH (JOHN BARRY) *et al.* The Needs of New Communities. 1967.

9358 —— 'The Swindon Social Survey: A Second Report on the Social Implications of Overspill'. *Sociol. Rev.* 9 (1961), 150–66.

9359 HAMPTON (WILLIAM A.). Democracy and Community: A Study of Politics in Sheffield. Lond./N.Y. 1970.

9360 RESEARCH SERVICES LIMITED. Community Survey: Scotland; Prepared for the Government Social Survey. Edin. 1969. [Scottish Royal Comm. on Local Govt in Scotland, 1966.].

9361 —— Community Attitudes Survey: England; Prepared for the Government Social Survey. [UK Royal Comm. on Local Govt in England.]. 1969.

9362 HILL (DILYS M.). Participating in Local Affairs. Harmondsworth. 1970.

9363 PLATT (JENNIFER). Social Research in Bethnal Green: An Evaluation of the Work of the Institute of Community Studies. 1971.

9364 SPYER (GEOFFREY). Architect and Community: Environmental Design in an Urban Society. 1971.

9365 BELL (COLIN) *and* NEWBY (HOWARD). Community Studies: An Introduction to the Sociology of the Local Community. 1971.

9366 —— *Eds.* The Sociology of Community: A Selection of Readings. 1974.

9367 CAREY (LYNETTE) *and* MAPES (ROY). The Sociology of Planning: A Study of Social Activity on New Housing Estates. 1972.

9368 THORNS (DAVID CHRISTOPHER). The Quest for Community: Social Aspects of Residential Growth. 1976.

9369 ROWLAND (JON). Community Decay. Harmondsworth. 1973.

9370 SCHERER (JACQUELINE). Contemporary Community: Sociological Illusion or Reality? 1974.

9371 MAYO (MARJORIE). Community Development and Urban Deprivation. 1974. [NCSS.].

9372 MAYO (MARJORIE) *and* JONES (DAVID) *eds.* Community. 1974.

9373 —— *Eds.* Community Work. 1975.

9374 MAYO (MARJORIE), CRAIG (GARY), *and* SHARMAN (DICK) *eds.* Jobs and Community Action. 1979.

9375 THOMAS (DAVID N.). Organising for Social Change: A Study in the Theory and Practice of Community Work. 1976.

9376 —— The Making of Community Work. 1983.

9377 —— *and* WARBURTON (R. WILLIAM). Community Workers in a Social Services Department: A Case Study. 1977.

9378 —— *and* BRISCOE (CATHERINE) *eds.* Community Work: Learning and Supervision. 1977.

9379 BATLEY (RICHARD). The Neighbourhood Scheme: Cases of Central Government Intervention in Local Deprivation. 1976.

9380 —— *Et al.* An Evaluation of Two Neighbourhood Schemes in Liverpool and Teesside. Leeds. 1975.

9381 GUSFIELD (JOSEPHINE R.). Community: A Critical Response. Oxf. 1975.

9382 EDWARDS (JOHN R.) *et al.* Social Patterns in Birmingham, 1966: A Reference Manual. Birm. 1970.

9383 DUNCAN (THOMAS LINDSAY CAMERON) *et al.* The Kings Heath Study: Report of an Exploratory Survey of Attitudes to House and Neighbourhood Improvement in an Older Part of Birmingham. 1971.

9384 TWELVETREES (ALAN CLYDE). Community Associations and Centres: A Comparative Study. Oxf. 1976.

9385 BUTTON (JOHN) *ed.* The Shetland Way of Oil: Reactions of a Small Community to Big Business. Sandwick, Shetland. 1976.

9386 O'MALLEY (JAN). The Politics of Community Action: A Decade of Struggle in Notting Hill. Nottingham. 1977.

9387 NORTON (MICHAEL). Community. [The Dictionary of Social Change. Vol. 2.]. 1977.

9388 GLASSER (RALPH). The Net and the Quest: Patterns of Community and Housing: How they can Survive Progress. 1977.

9389 BOLSTERLI (MARGARET JONES). The Early Community at Bedford Park: 'Corporate Happiness' in the First Garden Suburb. 1977.

9390 MEADOWS (DANIEL). Nattering in Paradise: A Word from the Suburbs. 1988.

9391 EDWARDS (A. M.). The Design of Suburbia: A Critical Study of Environmental History. 1981.

9392 BURTON (FRANK PATRICK). The Politics of Legitimacy: Struggles in a Belfast Community. 1978.

9393 PEOPLE'S AUTOBIOGRAPHY OF HACKNEY ASSOCIATION. The Island: The Life and Death of an East London Community 1870–1970. 1979.

9394 COWLEY (JOHN) et al. Community or Class Struggle. 1977.

9395 BRACEY (HOWARD EDWIN). Social Provision in Rural Wiltshire. 1952.

9396 CLARKE (RAYMOND THURSTON) ed. Working with Communities: A Study of Community Work in Great Britain, Based upon a Conference Sponsored by the Society of Neighbourhood Workers . . . 1963.

9397 BATTEN (THOMAS REGINALD). The Non-Directive Approach in Group and Community Work. 1967.

9398 —— Training for Community Development: A Critical Study of Method. 1962.

9399 —— The Human Factor in Community Work. 1965.

9400 GOETSCHIUS (GEORGE W.). Working with Community Groups: Using Community Development as a Method of Social Work. 1969.

9401 HORROCKS (MERYL). Social Development in the New Communities. Birm. 1974.

9402 GLASTONBURY (BRYAN) et al. 'Community Perceptions and Personal Social Services'. Policy and Politics 1 (1973), 191–212.

9403 CRANFORTH (JOHN) et al. Working in the Community. Nottingham. 1975. [Nottingham University, Dept. of Applied Social Science. Social Work Studies No. 1.].

9404 LOCHHEAD (ANDREW VAN SYLKE). 'Current Issues in Community Work: A Review Article'. Comm. Dvlpt. J. 9 (1974), 11–16.

9405 KIRKPATRICK (D. G.). 'How Close is American to British Community Development?: Some Impressions'. Comm. Dvlpt. J. 9 (1974), 108–16.

9406 ELSE (R.). 'Corporate Planning and Community Work in Britain'. Comm. Dvlpt. J. 10 (1975), 30–7.

9407 ARMSTRONG (R.) and DAVIES (C. T.). 'Educational Elements in Community Work in Britain'. Comm. Dvlpt. J. 10 (1975), 155–61.

9408 TILLEY (J.). 'Local Government Councillors and Community Work'. Comm. Dvlpt. J. 10 (1975), 89–94.

9409 JAMES (D. E.). 'University Involvement in Community Development'. Comm. Dvlpt. J. 9 (1974), 203–5.

9410 BARKE (MIKE). Social Change in Benwell, Written in . . . Conjunc-tion with Benwell Community Project. Newcastle-upon-Tyne. 1977.

9411 BENWELL IDEAS GROUP. Four Big Years: The History of Benwell's Independent Funding Organisation 1973–1977. Newcastle upon-Tyne. 1977.

9412 BAKER (JOHN). The Neighbourhood Advice Centre: A Community Project in Camden. 1973. [Assoc. for Neighbourhood Councils.].

9413 SNAITH (JILL). An Information Service in a Deprived Housing Estate. Glasg. 1976.

9414 BUTCHER (HUGH) et al. Information and Action Services for Rural Areas: A Study in West Cumbria. York. 1976.

9415 COMMUNITY WORK GROUP. Current Issues in Community Work. 1973.

9416 BARRESI (C. M.) and LINDQUIST (J. H.). 'The Urban Community: Attitudes Towards Neighbourhood and Urban Renewal'. Urban-Aff. Q. (1970), 278–90.

9417 BRYANT (DAVID) and KNOWLES (DICK). 'Social Contacts on the Hyde Park Estate, Sheffield'. Town Planning Rev. 45 (1974), 207–14.

9418 DENNIS (NORMAN). 'The Popularity of the Neighbourhood Community Idea'. Sociol. Rev. 6 (1958), 191–206.

9419 DICKIE (M. A. M.). 'Community Development in Scotland'. Comm. Dvlpt. J. 3 (1968), 175–83.

9420 FLYNN (M.), FLYNN (P.), and MELLOR (N.). 'Social Malaise Research: A Study in Liverpool'. Social Trends No. 3, 1972. [Central Statistical Office.].

9421 HANCOCK (THOMAS). 'Crisis and Community Structure'. Town and Country Planning 43 (1975), 375–78.

9422 HOLE (WINIFRED VERE). 'Social Effects of Planned Rehousing'. Town Planning Rev. 30 (1959), 161–73.

9423 HOROBIN (GORDON W.). 'Community and Occupation in the Hull Fishing Industry'. Brit. J. Sociol. 8 (1957), 343–56.

9424 WILKINSON (R.) and MERRY (D. M.). 'A Statistical Analysis of Attitudes to Moving: A Survey of Slum Clearances in Leeds'. Urban Studies 2 (1965), 1–14.

9425 NEILL (D. G.). 'Housing and the Social Aspects of Town and Country Planning in Northern Ireland'. Administration (Dublin), 2 (1954), 49–60.

9426 YOUNG (TIM). Community Technical Aid: A Directory of Technical Aid Centres Serving Community Groups in London. 1984.

9427 LOVELL (GEORGE). The Church and Community Development. 1972.

9428 JACKSON (HILARY). Unlocking Community Resources: Four Experimental Government Small Grant Schemes. 1986. [Home Office Research and Planning Unit Paper 18.].

9429 VEAL (A. J.). New Communities in the UK: A Classified Bibliography. Birm. 1973.

9430 VEAL (A. J.) *and* MURPHY (B. J.). Community use of Community Schools at the Primary Level: Two Case Studies in Walsall. 1968. [Sports Council Research Working papers, No. 5.].

9431 GOVAN AREA RESOURCE CENTRE. Resources for Community Action: Final Report of Govan Area Resource Centre. 1980. [European Programme of Pilot Schemes and Studies to Combat Poverty.].

9432 SCOTTISH COUNCIL OF SOCIAL SERVICE. Community Councils. Edin. 1973. [By Andrew Rowe.].

9433 HART (DAVID W.). A Review of Community Councils in Scotland, 1983–1984. Edin. 1986.

9434 NICHOLSON (SIMON). Community Participation in City Decision Making. Milton Keynes. 1973.

9435 PARKER (TONY). The People of Providence: A Housing Estate and some of its Inhabitants. 1983. [London Housing Estate.].

9436 BALL (COLIN). What the Neighbours Say: A Report on a Study of Neighbours. Berkhamstead. 1982.

15. CLASS AND STATUS

9437 ABRAMSON (PAUL R.). 'Social Class and Political Change in Western Europe: A Cross-National Longitudinal Analysis'. *Comp. Pol. Studs.* 4 (1971), 131–56.

9438 —— 'Il Nuovo Ruolo delle Classi in Europa'. *Riv. Ital. Sci. Pol.* 1 (1971), 595–628.

9439 —— 'Social Mobility and Political Attitudes: A Study of Intergenerational Mobility among Young British Men'. *Comp. Pol.* 3 (1971), 403–28.

9440 HARRISON (GEOFFREY AINSWORTH) *et al.* 'Social Class and Marriage Patterns in Some Oxfordshire Populations'. *J. Biosoc. Sci.* 3 (1971), 1–12.

9441 —— Population Structure and Human Variation. Camb. 1977.

9442 HARRISON (GEOFFREY AINSWORTH) *and* BOYCE (ANTHONY JOHN) *eds.* The Structure of Human Populations. Oxf. 1972.

9443 JAMES (W. H.). 'Social Class and Season of Birth'. *J. Biosoc. Sci.* 3 (1971), 309–20.

9444 MYERS (F. E.). 'Social Class and Political Change in Western Industrial Systems'. *Comp. Pol.* 2 (1970), 389–412.

9445 GOLDTHORPE (JOHN HARRY). 'Class, Status and Party in Modern Britain'. *Arch. Eur. Sociol.* 13 (1972), 342–72.

9446 GOLDTHORPE (JOHN HARRY) *and* LOCKWOOD (D.). 'Affluence and the British Class Structure'. *Sociol. R.* 11 (1963), 143–64.

9447 WEINBERG (AUBREY) *and* LYONS (FRANK). 'Class Theory and Practice'. *Brit. J. Sociol.* 23 (1972), 51–65.

9448 JESSOP (BOB). Social Order, Reform and Revolution: A Power, Exchange and Institutionalisation Perspective. 1972.

9449 HILLER (PETER). 'Social Reality and Social Stratification'. *Sociol. Rev.* 21 (1973), 77–99.

9450 ALLEN (SHEILA). 'Class, Culture and Generation'. *Sociol. Rev.* 21 (1973), 437–46.

9451 MOORHOUSE (H. F.) *and* CHAMBERLAIN (C. W.). 'Lower Class Attitudes to Property: Aspects of the Counter Ideology'. *Sociol.* 8 (1974), 387–405.

9452 GOODCHILD (BARRY). 'Class Differences in Environmental Perception: An Exploratory Study'. *Urban Studs* 11 (1974), 157–69.

9453 GIBSON (COLIN). 'Association Between Divorce and Social Class in England and Wales'. *Brit. J. Sociol.* 25 (1974), 79–93.

9454 ANDREWS (WILLIAM G.). 'Social Change and Electoral Politics in Britain: A Case Study of Basingstoke, 1964 and 1974'. *Pol. Studs* 22 (1974), 324–36.

9455 TREIMAN (DONALD J.) *and* TERRELL (KERMIT). 'The Process of Status Attainment in the United States and Great Britain'. *Amer. J. Sociol.* 81 (1975), 563–83.

9456 KERCKHOFF (ALAN C.). 'Patterns of Educational Attainment in Great Britain'. *Amer. J. Sociol.* 80 (1975), 1428–37.

9457 BURNS (TOM R.) *and* BUCKLEY (WALTER) *eds.* Power and Control: Social Structures and their Transformation. 1976.

9458 ROBERTSON (JAMES HUGH). Power, Money and Sex: Towards a New Social Balance. 1976.

9459 —— Profit or People? The New Social Role of Money. 1974.

9460 SMITH (ANTHONY DOUGLAS). Social Change: Social Theory and Historical Processes. 1976.

9461 MARWICK (ARTHUR J. B.). Class: Image and Reality in Britain, France and the USA since 1930. 1980.

9462 —— Class in the Twentieth Century. Brighton. 1986.

9463 VAN DEN HAAG (ERNEST). 'Snobbery'. *Brit. J. Sociol.* 7 (1956), 212–16.

9464 PRAIS (SIGBERT JON). 'Measuring Social Mobility'. *J. Roy. Stat. Soc.* 118 (1955), 56–66.

9465 —— 'The Formal Theory of Social Mobility'. *Pop. Studs* 9 (1955), 72–81.

9466 CULYER (ANTHONY JOHN) *et al.* 'Social Indicators: Health'. *Social Trends* No. 2 (1971). [Central Statistical Office.].

9467 MARSH (DAVID CHARLES). The Changing Social Structure of England and Wales, 1871–1951. 1958. Rev. edn covering '1871 to 1961' 1965.

9468 ADCOCK (CYRIL J.) *and* BROWN (L. B.). 'Social Class and the Ranking of Occupations'. *Brit. J. Sociol.* 8 (1957), 26–32.

9469 SIMPSON (RICHARD L.). 'A Note on Status, Mobility, and Anomie'. *Brit. J. Sociol.* 11 (1960), 370–2.

9470 WILLIAMS (JAC L.). 'Some Social Consequences of Grammar School Education in a Rural Area of Wales'. *Brit. J. Sociol.* 10 (1959), 125–8.

9471 SAMUEL (R.). 'Classi e Coscienza di Classe'. *Pass. Pres.* 13 (1960), 1685–1703. [Classes and Class Consciousness.].

9472 REES (MERLYN). 'The Social Setting'. *Pol. Q.* 31 (1960), 285–99. [British Social Structure and the Labour Party.].

9473 ABRAMS (MARK ALEXANDER). Education, Social Class and Reading of Newspapers and Magazines. 1966.

9474 —— 'Social Class and British Politics'. *Pub. Op. Q.* 25 (1961), 342–51.

9475 PLOWMAN (D. E. G.), MINCHINTON (WALTER E.), *and* STACEY (MARGARET). 'Local Social Status in England and Wales'. *Sociol. Rev.* 10 (1962), 161–202.

9476 FLETCHER (RONALD). 'Social Changes in Britain'. *Pol. Q.* 34 (1963), 399–410.

9477 —— Human Needs and Social Order. 1965. [A Series of Radio Talks.].

9478 —— Britain in the Sixties: The Family and Marriage. An Analysis and Moral Assessment. 1962.

9479 LITTLE (ALAN) *and* WESTERGAARD (JOHN HARALD). 'The Trend of Class Differentials in Educational Opportunity in England and Wales'. *Brit. J. Sociol.* 15 (1964), 301–16.

9480 BERNSTEIN (BASIL). 'Social Class, Speech Systems and Psychotherapy'. *Brit. J. Sociol.* 15 (1964), 54–64.

9481 —— 'Some Sociological Determinants of Perception'. *Brit. J. Sociol.* 9 (1958), 159–74.

9482 —— 'Language and Social Class'. *Brit. J. Sociol.* 11 (1960), 271–6.

9483 BERNSTEIN (BASIL) *and* HENDERSON (DOROTHY). 'Social Class Difference: The Relevance of Language to Socialization'. *Sociol.* 3 (1969), 1–20.

9484 BERNSTEIN (BASIL) *and* YOUNG (DOUGLAS). 'Social Class Differences in Conceptions of the Uses of Toys'. *Sociol.* 1 (1967), 131–40.

9485 RUNCIMAN (WALTER GARRISON). '"Embourgeoisement", Self-rated Class and Party Preference'. *Sociol. Rev.* 12 (1964), 137–54.

9486 —— Relative Deprivation and Social Justice: A Study of Attitudes Towards Social Inequality in 20th Century England. 1966.

9487 PICKETTJOHNS (EDWARD ALLISTER). The Social Structure of Modern Britain. N.Y./Oxf. 1965.

9488 ROSE (RICHARD). 'Classes Sociales et Partis Politiques en Grande Bretagne dans une Perspective Historique'. *Rev. Fran. Sociol.* 7 (1966), 636–62.

9489 KAHAN (MICHAEL), BUTLER (DAVID), *and* STOKES (DONALD). 'On the Analytical Division of Social Class'. *Brit. J. Sociol.* 17 (1966), 122–32.

9490 EMMET (DOROTHY MARY). Rules, Roles and Relations. 1966.

9491 SUGARMAN (B. N.). 'Social Class and Values as Related to Achievement and Conduct in School'. *Sociol. Rev.* 14 (1966), 287–301.

9492 SWIFT (D. F.). 'Social Class, Mobility-Ideology and Eleven Plus Success'. *Brit. J. Sociol.* 18 (1967), 165–86.

9493 STRONGMAN (KENNETH T.) *and* WOOSLEY (JANET). 'Stereotypical Reactions to Regional Accents'. *Brit. J. Social and Clinical Psychology* 6 (1967), 164–7.

9494 HOROBIN (GORDON W.), OLDMAN (DAVID), *and* BYTHEWAY (BILL). 'The Social Differentiation of Ability'. *Sociol.* 1 (1967), 113–29.

9495 SEABROOK (JEREMY). The Unprivileged. 1967.

9496 HALL (C. B.) *and* SMITH (R. A.). 'Socio-economic Patterns of England and Wales'. *Urban Studs.* 5 (1968), 59–66.

9497 BERNARD (T. L.). 'Implications of Social Class Factors in Contemporary English Secondary Education'. *Ind. Sociol. B.* 6 (1969), 104–6.

9498 WILLMOTT (PETER). 'Tendences de la Société Anglaise'. *Anal. et Previs.* 9 (1970), 279–94.

9499 HUNT (ALAN). 'Class Structure in Britain Today'. *Marxism Today* 14 (1970), 167–72.

9500 —— Class and Class Structure. 1977.

9501 EPSTEIN (LEON D.). 'British Class Consciousness and the Labour Party'. *J. Brit. Studs* 2 (1962), 136–60

9502 RUBINSTEIN (W. D.). 'Wealth, Elites and the Class Structure of Modern Britain'. *Past and Present* 76 (1977), 9–126.

9503 HIMMELWEIT (H. T.), HALSEY (ALBERT HENRY), *and* OPPENHEIM (A. N.). 'The Views of Adolescents on Some Aspects of Social Class Structure'. *Brit. J. Sociol.* 3 (1952), 148–72.

9504 CLEMENTS (E. M. B.) *and* PICKETT (KATHLEEN GORDON). 'Bodyweight of Men Related to Structure, Age and Social Status' and 'Chest Girth of Men Related to Structure, Age, Bodyweight and Social Status'. *Brit. J. Prev. Soc. Med.* 8 (1954), 99–116.

9505 CHINOY (ELY). 'Social Stratification: Theory and Synthesis'. *Brit. J. Sociol.* 8 (1957), 370–7.

9506 GINSBERG (MORRIS). 'Social Change'. *Brit. J. Sociol.* 9 (1958), 205–29.

9507 WITKIN (ROBERT W.). 'Social Class Influence on the Amount and Type of Positive Evaluation of School Lessons'. *Sociol.* 5 (1971), 169–89.

9508 TAYLOR (GEORGE) *and* AYRES (N.). Born and Bred Unequal. 1969.

9509 POWER (EDWARD RAYMOND ROPER). The Social Structure of an English Country Town. 1937.

9510 JACKSON (JOHN ARCHER) ed. Social Stratification. Camb. 1948.

9511 MARSHALL (THOMAS HUMPHREY). Citizenship and Social Class, and other Essays. Camb. 1950.

9512 —— 'General Surveys of Changes in Stratification in the Twentieth Century', in *Transactions of the Third World Congress of Sociology*, vol. 3 (1956).

9513 PEAR (TOM HATHERLEY). English Social Differences. 1955.

9514 —— Personality, Appearance and Speech. 1957.

9515 CHAPMAN (DENNIS). People and Their Homes. 1950.

9516 —— The Home and Social Status. 1955.

9517 COLE (GEORGE DOUGLAS HOWARD). Studies in Class Structure. 1955.

9518 MACRAE (DONALD GUNN). 'Social Stratification: A Trend: Report and Bibliography'. *Current Sociol.* 2 (1953–4), 7–31.

9519 —— Ideology and Society: Papers in Sociology and Politics. 1961.

9520 FLOUD (JEAN E.) *et al.* Social Class and Educational Opportunity. 1956.

9521 FLOUD (JEAN E.), HALSEY (ALBERT HENRY), *and* ANDERSON (CHARLES ARNOLD) eds. Education, Economy and Society: A Reader in the Sociology of Education. 1961.

9522 LOCKWOOD (DAVID). The Black-Coated Worker: A Study in Class Consciousness. 1958.

9523 YOUNG (MICHAEL). The Rise of the Meritocracy, 1870–2033 [sic]: An Essay on Education and Equality. 1958.

9524 DAHRENDORF (RALF). Class and Conflict in an Industrial Society. 1959.

9525 —— Inequality, Hope and Progress. Liverpool. 1976.

9526 WILLIAMS (RAYMOND). The Long Revolution. 1961. Pbk. 1965. repr. 1984.

9527 ROBBINS (LIONEL CHARLES) *Baron.* Liberty and Equality. 1977.

9528 DAVENPORT (NICHOLAS). The Split Society. 1964.

9529 MUSGROVE (FRANK). The Migratory Elite. 1963.

9530 OSSOWSKI (STANISLAW). Class Structure in the Social Consciousness. 1963.

9531 BARBER (EDWARD) *and* BARBER (ELINOR GELLERT) eds. European Social Class: Stability and Change. N.Y. 1965.

9532 MONTAGUE (JOEL BENJAMIN). Class and Nationality: English and American Studies. 1963.

9533 MACLAREN (ARCHIBALD ALLAN) *ed.* Social Class in Scotland: Past and Present. Edin. 1976.

9534 McKINLEY (DONALD GILBERT). Social Class and Family Life. 1964.

9535 HALMOS (PAUL) *ed.* The Development of Industrial Societies. 1964.

9536 FREEDMAN (MAURICE) *ed.* Social Organisation: Essays Presented to Raymond Firth. 1967.

9537 COLLISON (PETER CHEESEBOROUGH). The Cutteslowe Walls: A Study in Social Class. 1963.

9538 MABEY (RICHARD) *ed.* Class: A Symposium. 1966.

9539 MILLAR (ROBERT). The New Classes. 1966.

9540 BOTTOMORE (THOMAS BURTON). Classes in Modern Society. 1955, repr. 1966.

9541 FORD (JULIENNE). Social Class and the Comprehensive School. 1969.

9542 DAVIES (IOAN). Social Mobility and Political Change. 1970.

9543 CRAFT (MAURICE) *ed.* Family, Class and Education: A Reader. 1970.

9544 BRANDIS (WALTER) *and* HENDERSON (DOROTHY). Social Class, Language and Communication. 1970.

9545 GLASER (BARNEY GALLAND) *and* STRAUSS (ANSELM L.). Status Passage. 1971.

9546 GINER (SALVADOR) *and* SCOTCHFORD ARCHER (MARGARET) eds. Contemporary Europe: Class, Status and Power. [See ch. by David Martin and Colin Crouch 'Class and Status in Modern Britain'.]. 1971.

9547 GIDDENS (ANTHONY). The Class Structure of the Advanced Societies. 1973. 2nd edn 1981.

9548 GIDDENS (ANTHONY) *and* MACKENZIE (GAVIN) eds. Social Class and the Division of Labour: Essays in Honour of Ilya Neustadt. Camb. 1982.

9549 GILES (HOWARD) *and* POWESLAND (PETER F.). Speech Style and Social Evaluation. 1975.

9550 CROMPTON (ROSEMARY) *and* GUBBAY (JON). Economy and Class Structure. 1977.

9551 COXON (ANTHONY PETER MACMILLAN) *and* JONES (CHARLES L.). The Images of Occupational Prestige. 1978.

9552 GOLDTHORPE (JOHN HARRY) *and* HOPE (KEITH). The Social Grading of Occupations: A New Approach and Scale. Oxf. 1974.

9553 HOPE (KEITH) *ed.* The Analysis of Social Mobility: Methods and Approaches. Oxf. 1972.

9554 HALSEY (ALBERT HENRY). Change in British Society. Oxf. 1978.

9555 —— *Ed.* Trends in British Society Since 1900: A Guide to the Changing Social Structure of Britain. 1972.

9556 —— 'Social Mobility in Britain: A Review'. *Sociol. Rev.* 2 (1954), 169–77.

9557 LAWTON (DENIS). Class, Structure and the Curriculum. 1975.

9558 —— Social Change, Educational Theory and Curriculum Planning. 1973.

9559 —— Education and Social Justice. 1977.

9560 ENTWISTLE (HOWARD). Class, Culture and Education. 1978.

9561 CROUCH (COLIN) *and* PIZZURNO (ALESSANDRO) *eds.* The Resurgence of Class Conflict in Western Europe since 1968. 1978.

9562 WRIGHT (ERIC OLIN). Class, Crisis and the State. 1978.

9563 —— Classes. 1985.

9564 WILSON (JOHN BOYD). Equality. 1966.

9565 OWEN (CAROL). Social Stratification. 1968.

9566 FABIAN SOCIETY. Labour and Inequality. 1972.

9567 POLANYI (GEORGE) *and* WOOD (JOHN B.). How Much Inequality? An Inquiry into the 'Evidence'. 1974.

9568 WESTERGAARD (JOHN HARALD) *and* RESLER (HENRIETTA). Class in a Capitalist Society: A Study of Contemporary Britain. 1975.

9569 LANE (DAVID). The End of Inequality? Stratification Under State Socialism. Harmondsworth. 1971.

9570 LITTLEJOHN (JAMES). Social Stratification: An Introduction. 1972.

9571 PARKIN (FRANK). Class, Inequality and Political Order: Social Stratification in Capitalist and Communist Societies. 1st edn 1971. Pbk. 1972.

9572 —— *Ed.* The Social Analysis of Class Structure. 1974.

9573 REES (JOHN COLLWYN). Equality. 1971.

9574 WEDDERBURN (DOROTHY) *ed.* Poverty, Inequality and Class Structure. Camb. 1974.

9575 KELSALL (ROGER KEITH) *and* KELSALL (HELEN MARTIN). Stratification: An Essay on Class and Inequality. 1974.

9576 REID (IVAN). Social Class and Differences in Britain: A Sourcebook. 1977.

9577 BAUMAN (ZYGMUNT). Between Class and Elite: the Evolution of the Labour Movement, A Sociological Study. Manch. 1972.

9578 RICHARDSON (CHARLES JAMES). Contemporary Social Mobility. 1977.

9579 ROBERTS (KENNETH) *et al.* The Fragmentary Class Structure. 1977.

9580 SCASE (RICHARD) *ed.* Industrial Society: Class, Cleavage and Control. 1977.

9581 —— Social Democracy in Capitalist Society: Working Class Politics in Britain and Sweden. 1977.

9582 CALVERT (PETER). The Concept of Class. 1982.

9583 KAELBLE (HARTMUT). Historical Research on Social Mobility: Western Europe and the USA in the 19th and 20th Centuries. 1981.

9584 ASHBY (A. W.) *and* MORGAN JONES (J.). 'The Social Origins of Farmers in Wales'. *Sociol. Rev.* [Old Series], 18 (1926), 131–8.

9585 GLASS (DAVID VICTOR) *ed.* Social Mobility in Britain. 1954.

9586 BERENT (JERZY). 'Fertility and Social Mobility'. *Pop. Studs* 5 (1952), 244–60.

9587 BENJAMIN (BERNARD). 'Inter-generation Differences in Occupation: A Sample Comparison in England and Wales of Census and Birth Registration Records'. *Pop. Studs* 11 (1958), 262–8.

9588 STEPHENSON (RICHARD M.). 'Stratification, Education and Occupational Orientation: A Parallel Study and Overview'. *Brit. J. Sociol.* 9 (1958), 42–52.

9589 YOUNG (MICHAEL) *and* GIBSON (JOHN). 'In Search of an Explanation of Social Mobility'. *Brit. J. Stat. Psychol.* 16 (1963), 27–35.

9590 ABBOTT (JOAN). 'The Concept of Mobility'. *Sociol. Rev.* 14 (1966), 153–61.

9591 TURNER (RALPH H.). 'Life Situation and Subculture: A Comparison of Merited Prestige Judgements by Three Occupational Classes in Britain'. *Brit. J. Sociol.* 9 (1958), 299–320.

9592 —— 'Acceptance of Irregular Mobility in Britain and the United States'. *Sociometry* 29 (1966), 334–52.

9593 GIBSON (JOHN). 'Biological Aspects of a High Socio-economic Group'. *J. Biosoc. Sci.* 2 (1970), 1–16.

9594 GIBSON (JOHN) *and* MASCIE-TAYLOR (C. G. NICHOLAS). 'Biological Aspects of a High Socio-economic Group II: IQ Components and Social Mobility'. *J. Biosoc. Sci.* 5 (1973), 17–30.

9595 STEWART (ANDREW), PRANDY (KENNETH), *and* BLACKBURN (ROBERT MARTIN). Social Stratification and Occupations. 1980.

9596 BLACKBURN (ROBERT MARTIN). Union Character and Social Class: A Study of White-Collar Unionism. 1967.

9597 THOMPSON (PATRICIA G.). 'Some Factors in Upward Social Mobility in England'. *Sociol. Soc. Res.* 55 (1971), 181–90.

9598 TOOMEY (D. M.). 'Ambition, Occupational Values and School Organisation'. *Inl. J. Comp. Sociol.* 12 (1971), 192–9.

9599 NOBLE (TREVOR). 'Social Mobility and Class Relations in Britain'. *Brit. J. Sociol.* 23 (1972), 422–36.

9600 —— 'Intergenerational Mobility in Britain: A Criticism of the Counter-balance Theory'. *Sociol.* 8 (1974), 475–83.

9601 KRAUSZ (ERNEST). 'Factors of Social Mobility in a British Minority Group'. *Brit. J. Sociol.* 23 (1972), 275–86.

9602 WEBB (BARBARA) *and* WILLIAMS (W. M.). 'Mobility of General Practitioners during the First Few Years in General Practice'. *Sociol. Rev.* 20 (1972), 591–600.

9603 RIDGE (JOHN MICHAEL) *ed.* Mobility in Britain Reconsidered. 1974.

9604 HEATH (ANTHONY). Social Mobility. 1981.

9605 ABBOTT (PAMELA). Women and Social Class. 1987.

9606 TRUDGILL (PETER). The Social Differentiation of English in Norwich. 1974. [Dialects and Social Classes.].

9607 BAIN (GEORGE SAYERS), COATES (DAVID), *and* ELLIS (VALERIE). Social Stratification and Trade Unionism: A Critique. 1973.

9608 NEWBY (HOWARD). Property, Paternalism and Power: Class Control in Rural England. 1978.

9609 HOGGART (KEITH). Politics, Geography and Social Stratification. 1986.

9610 KELLEY (JONATHAN). The Decline of Class Revisited: Class and Party in England, 1964–1979. Glasg. 1985.

9611 MARSHALL (GORDON). Social Class in Modern Britain. 1988.

9612 MUSGROVE (FRANK). School and the Social Order. Chichester. 1979.

9613 ROGERS (RICK). Education and Social Class. 1986.

9614 THRIFT (NIGEL). Class and Space: The Making of Urban Society. 1987.

9615 RENTOUL (JOHN). The Rich Get Richer: The Growth of Inequality in Britain in the 1980's. 1987.

9616 WAITES (BERNARD A.). 'The Effect of the First World War on Class and Status in England, 1910–1920'. *J. Contemp. Hist.* 11 (1976), 27–48.

9617 —— A Class Society at War: England, 1914–1918. Leamington Spa. 1987.

9618 TURNER (BRYAN S.). Social Stratification. Milton Keynes. 1988.

16. THE WORKING CLASSES

9619 COLE (GEORGE DOUGLAS HOWARD). A Short History of the British Working Class Movement 1789–1927. 1930. New edn covering 1789–1947. 1948.

9620 HUTT (GEORGE ALLEN). The Condition of the Working Class in Great Britain. 1933.

9621 —— The Post War History of the British Working Class. 1937.

9622 LAMBERT (RICHARD STANTON) *and* BEALES (HUGH L.) *eds.* Memoirs of the Unemployed. 1934.

9623 RICE (MARGERY SPRING). Working Class Wives. Harmondsworth. 1939.

9624 ORWELL (GEORGE). The Road to Wigan Pier. 1937.

9625 POSTGATE (RAYMOND WILLIAM). A Pocket History of the British Working Class. 2nd edn 1942. 3rd edn 1964. [1st pub. under the title 'A Pocket History of the British Workers to 1919'.]. 1937.

9626 MAP (KURT). The British Economy and the Working Class 1946–1958: An Analysis of Post War Capitalism. 1957. 2nd rev. edn 1959.

9627 GOLDTHORPE (JOHN HARRY) *et al.* The Affluent Worker: Political Attitudes and Behaviour. 1968.

9628 BAXTER (R.). 'The Working Class and Labour Politics'. *Pol. Studs* 20 (1972), 97–107.

9629 JOHNSON (PAUL). Saving and Spending: The Working Class Economy in Britain 1870–1939. Oxf. 1985.

9630 WINTER (JAY) *ed.* The Working Class in Modern English History: Essays in Honour of Henry Pelling. Camb. 1983.

9631 JONES (*Sir* EDGAR R.). Toilers of the Hills: An Historical Record of those who Worked Through More Than a Century on Iron, Steel, and Tin Plate among the Welsh Hills and Valleys. Pontypool. 1959.

9632 CHALONER (WILLIAM HENRY). 'The British Miners and the Coal Industry Between the Wars'. *Hist. Today* 14 (1964), 418–21.

9633 McGEOWN (PATRICK). Heat the Furnace Seven Times More: An Autobiography. 1967.

9634 ZWEIG (FERDYNAND). Men in the Pits. 1948.

9635 —— The British Worker. Harmondsworth. 1948.

9636 —— The Worker in an Affluent Society: Family Life and Industry. 1961.

9637 DENNIS (NORMAN), HENRIQUES (LOUIS FERNANDO), *and* SLAUGHTER (CLIFFORD). Coal is Our Life: An Analysis of a Yorkshire Mining Community. 1956.

9638 McCUTCHEON (JOHN ELLIOTT). Troubled Scenes: The Story of a Pit and its People. Seaham. 1955.

9639 SAMUEL (RAPHAEL) *ed.* Miners, Quarrymen and Saltworkers. 1977.

9640 MOFFAT (ABE). My Life with the Miners. 1965.

9641 DOUGLAS (DAVID). Pit Life in County Durham: Rank and File Movements and Workers Control. Oxf. History Workshop. 1972.

9642 JENCKS (C. E.). 'Social Status of Coal Miners in Britain Since Nationalisation'. *Amer. J. Econ. Sociol.* 26 (1967), 310–12.

9643 HOUSE (JOHN WILLIAM). Pit Closure and the Community: Report to the Minister of Labour, Newcastle-upon-Tyne. 1967.

9644 SEWEL (JOHN). Colliery Closure and Social Change: A Study of a South Wales Mining Valley. Cardiff. 1975.

9645 HOWARTH (KEN). Dark Days: Memoirs and Reminiscences of the Lancashire and Cheshire Coalmining Industry up to Nationalisation. Manch. 1979.

9646 BULMER (MARTIN I. A.). 'Sociological Models of the Mining Community'. *Sociol. Rev.* 23 (1973), 61–92.

9647 —— Studies in Working Class Imagery. 1974.

9648 —— Working Class Images of Society. 1975.

9649 WILLIAMS (JAMES ECCLES). The Derbyshire Miners: A Study in Industrial and Social History. 1962.

9650 ARNOT (R. PAGE). A History of the Scottish Miners from the Earliest Times. 1955.

9651 CHALLINOR (RAYMOND). The Lancashire and Cheshire Miners. Newcastle-upon-Tyne. 1972.

9652 EVANS (E. W.). The Miners of South Wales. 1961.

9653 BRENNAN (TOM) *et al*. Social Change in South-West Wales. 1954.

9654 TUNSTALL (JEREMY). The Fishermen. 1962.

9655 THOMPSON (PAUL). Living the Fishing. 1983.

9656 STERN (WALTER MARCEL). The Porters of London. 1960.

9657 GORDON (CECIL), EMERSON (A. R.), *and* PUGH (D. S.). 'The Age Distribution of an Industrial Group [Scottish Railwaymen.]'. *Pop. Studs* 12 (1959), 223–39.

9658 JACKSON (BRIAN). Working Class Community: Some General Notions Raised by a Series of Studies in Northern England. 1968.

9659 DUFFY (NORMAN FRANCIS) *ed*. The Sociology of the Blue Collar Worker. 1969.

9660 LIVERPOOL UNIVERSITY SOCIAL SCIENCE DEPT. The Dock Worker. L/pool. 1954.

9661 PHILLIPS (GORDON). Casual Labour: The Unemployment Question in the Port Transport Industry, 1880–1970. Oxf. 1985.

9662 BROWN (RICHARD) *and* BRANNEN (PETER). 'Social Relations and Social Perspectives among Shipbuilding Workers: A Preliminary Statement'. *Sociol.* 4 (1970), 71–84 and 197–211.

9663 BROWN (RICHARD), BRANNEN (PETER), COUSINS (JAMES M.), *and* SAMPHIER (M.). 'The Contours of Solidarity: Social Stratification and Industrial Relations in Shipbuilding'. *Brit. J. Ind. Relns* 10 (1972), 12–41.

9664 REID (JAMES). Reflections of a Clyde-Built Man. 1976.

9665 DASH (JACK). Good Morning Brothers! 1969.

9666 HOLLOWELL (PETER GILBERT). The Lorry Driver. 1968.

9667 BELL (JAMES H.). The Sewermen at Work: Report of the Investigation into the Health and Conditions of Work of Glasgow Sewermen. Glasg. 1952.

9668 ROBINSON (OLIVE) *and* WALLACE (JOHN). Pay and Employment in Retailing. Farnborough. 1976.

9669 JONES (GARETH STEDMAN). Languages of Class: Studies in English Working Class History, 1832–1932. Camb. 1983.

9670 JONES (GARETH STEDMAN) *and* CROMPTON (ROSEMARY). White-Collar Proletariat: Deskilling and Gender in Clerical Work. 1984.

9671 DALE (JOHN RODNEY). The Clerk in Industry. L/pool. 1962.

9672 PRANDY (KENNETH). White Collar Work. 1982.

9673 ARMSTRONG (PETER). White Collar Workers, Trade Unions and Class. 1986.

9674 HOGGART (RICHARD). The Uses of Literacy: Aspects of Working Class Life, with Special Reference to Publications and Entertainments. 1957.

9675 DAHRENDORF (RALF). 'La Situation de la Classe Ouvrière en Angleterre'. *Rev. Social.* 88 (1955), 78–82, 89 (1955), 153–66.

9676 MILLER (S. M.) *and* REISMAN (FRANK). 'The Working Class Subculture'. *Soc. Probs* 9 (1961), 86–97.

9677 NAIRN (TOM). 'The English Working Class'. *New Left Rev.* 24 (1964), 43–57.

9678 ROSE (GORDON). The Working Class. 1968.

9679 MACKENZIE (G.). 'The Class Situation of Manual Workers: The United States and Britain: A Review Article'. *Brit. J. Sociol.* 21 (1970), 333–42.

9680 GOLDTHORPE (JOHN HARRY) *et al*. 'The Affluent Worker and the Thesis of "Embourgoisement": Some Preliminary Research Findings'. *Sociol.* 1 (1967), 11–31.

9681 KEMENY (PAUL JAMES). 'The Affluent Worker Project: Some Criticisms and a Derivative Study'. *Sociol. Rev.* 14 (1966), 249–67.

9682 LOCKWOOD (DAVID). 'Sources of Variation in Working Class Images of Society'. *Sociol. Rev.* 20 (1972), 373–89.

9683 NORDLINGER (ERIC A.). The Working Class Tories: Authority, Deference and Stable Democracy. 1967.

9684 PARKIN (FRANK). 'Working Class Conservatives: A Theory of Political Deviance'. *Brit. J. Sociol.* 18 (1967), 276–90.

9685 McKENZIE (ROBERT THRELFORD) *and* SILVER (ALLAN). Angels in Marble: Working Class Conservatism in Urban England. 1968.

9686 HOBSBAWM (ERIC J.). Labouring Men: Studies in the History of Labour. 1964.

9687 HINDESS (BARRY). The Decline of Working Class Politics. 1971.

9688 HILL (JOHN MICHAEL MEATH). The Seafaring Career: A Study . . . 1972.

9689 JONES (MERVYN). Life on the Dole. 1972.

9690 GOULD (TONY) *and* KENYON (JOE). Stories from the Dole Queue. 1972.

9691 CHAMBERLAIN (C. W.) *and* MOORHOUSE (H. F.). 'Lower Class Attitudes Towards the British Political System'. *Sociol. Rev.* 22 (1974), 503–25.

9692 MOORHOUSE (H. F.). 'The Political Incorporation of the British Working Class: An Interpretation'. *Sociol.* 7 (1973), 341–59.

9693 MANN (MICHAEL). Consciousness and Action among the Western Working Class. 1973.

9694 HILL (MICHAEL J.) *et al*. Men out of Work: A Study of Unemployment in Three English Towns. Camb. 1973.

9695 LOVETT (TOM). Adult Education, Community Development and the Working Class. 1975.

9696 WILLIS (PAUL E.). Learning to Labour: How Working Class Kids get Working Class Jobs. Farnborough. 1977.

9697 COLLS (ROBERT M.). The Collier's Rant: Song and Culture in the Industrial Village. 1977.

9698 DANIEL (WILLIAM WENTWORTH). Where are they Now? A Follow Up Study of the Unemployed. 1977.

9699 FIELD (FRANK). The Conscript Army: A Study of Britain's Unemployed. 1977.

9700 GALLIE (DUNCAN). In Search of the New Working Class: Automation and Social Integration within the Capitalist Enterprise. Camb. 1978.

9701 HUGGETT (FRANK EDWARD). Life Below Stairs: Domestic Servants in England from Victorian Times. 1977.

9702 DEWEY (P. E.). 'Agricultural Labour Supply in England and Wales during the First World War'. *Econ. Hist. Rev.* 52 (1975), 100–12.

9703 PARKER (TONY). The Plough Boy. 1965.

9704 GOODLAND (N. L.). 'Farm Workers—Past and Present'. *Quart. Rev.* 1961, 84–96.

9705 NEWBY (HOWARD). 'Agricultural Workers in the Class Structure'. *Sociol. Rev.* 20 (1972), 413–39.

9706 NEWBY (HOWARD) *and* BELL (COLIN). 'The Sources of Variation in Agricultural Workers' Images of Society'. *Sociol. Rev.* 21 (1973), 231–53.

[Above two articles criticized in 'Agricultural Workers in the Class Structure: A Critical Note' by Ian Carter. *Sociol. Rev.* 22 (1974), 271–8.].

[Reply by Newby, 'Deference and the Agricultural Worker'. *Sociol. Rev.* 23 (1975), 51–60.].

9707 NEWBY (HOWARD). The Deferential Worker: A Study of Farm-workers in East Anglia. 1977.

9708 HOWKINS (ALUN). Poor Labouring Men: Rural Radicalism in Norfolk, 1872–1923. 1985.

9709 ARMSTRONG (ALAN). Farmworkers: A Social and Economic History 1770–1980. 1988.

9710 WINYARD (STEVE). Poor Farmworkers, Rich Farms. 1986.

9711 CANNON (ISIDORE CYRIL). 'Ideology and Occupational Community: A Study of Compositors'. *Sociol.* 1 (1967), 165–85.

9712 INEICHEN (BERNARD). 'Home Ownership and Manual Workers' Lifestyles'. *Sociol. Rev.* 20 (1972), 391–412.

9713 NICHOLS (THEO). 'Labourism and Class Consciousness: The Class Ideology of Some Northern Foremen'. *Sociol. Rev.* 22 (1974), 483–502.

9714 SADLER (PHILIP). 'Sociological Aspects of Skill'. *Brit. J. Ind. Relns* 8 (1970), 22–31.

9715 SYKES (A. J. M.). 'Navvies: Their Work Attitudes'. *Sociol.* 3 (1969), 21–35.

9716 —— 'Navvies: Their Social Relations'. *Sociol.* 3 (1969), 157–72.

17. THE MIDDLE CLASSES

9717 MASTERMAN (CHARLES FREDERICK GURNEY). 'The Collapse of the Middle Class'. *New World* (May 1920), 305–14.

9718 LEWIS (ROY) *and* MAUDE (ANGUS). The English Middle Classes. 1949.

9719 BONHAM (JOHN). The Middle Class Vote. 1954.

9720 BONHAM (JOHN) *and* MARTIN (FREDERICK M.). 'Two Studies in the Middle Class Vote'. *Brit. J. Sociol.* 3 (1952), 222–41.

9721 KELSALL (ROGER KEITH) *et al.* 'The New Middle Class in the Power Structure of Great Britain'. *Transactions of the Third World Congress of Sociology*, 5 (1956), 320–9.

9722 SCHULTZ (T.). 'Middle Class Families in France and in England'. *Bull. Oxf. Univ. Inst. Stat.* 20 (1958), 357–72.

9723 BELL (COLIN). Middle Class Families: Social and Geographical Mobility. 1969.

9724 —— 'Mobility and the Middle Class Extended Family'. *Sociol.* 2 (1968), 173–84.

9725 RAYNOR (JOHN). The Middle Class. 1969. [2nd edn 1981. with Roger King.].

9726 RALLINGS (COLIN S.). 'Two Types of Middle-Class Labour Voter?'. *Brit. J. Pol. Sci.* 5 (1975), 107–12.

9727 SCASE (RICHARD) *and* GOFFEE (ROBERT). The Entrepreneurial Middle Class. 1982.

9728 BRADLEY (IAN). The English Middle Classes are Alive and Kicking. 1982.

9729 PAHL (JANKE MARY) *and* PAHL (RAYMOND EDWARD). Managers and their Wives: A Study of Career and Family Relationships in the Middle Class. 1971.

9730 KING (ROGER) *and* NUGENT (NEILL). Respectable Rebels: Middle Class Campaigns in Britain in the 1970s. 1979.

9731 PARKIN (FRANK). Middle Class Radicalism: The Social Bases of the British Campaign for Nuclear Disarmament. Manch. 1968.

9732 HUTBER (PATRICK). The Decline and Fall of the Middle Class: And How it Can Fight Back. 1976.

9733 PAYNE (GEOFF). 'Typologies of Middle Class Mobility'. *Sociol.* 7 (1973), 417–28.

9734 ABERCROMBIE (NICHOLAS). Capital, Labour and the Middle Classes. 1983.

9735 GARRARD (JOHN), JARY (DAVID), GOLDSMITH (MICHAEL), *and* OLDFIELD (ADRIAN) *eds.* The Middle Class in Politics. Farnborough. 1978.

9736 READER (W. J.). The Middle Classes. 1972.

9737 SIMPSON (MICHAEL ANTHONY) *and* LLOYD (TERENCE HENRY) *eds.* Middle Class Housing in Britain. 1977.

18. THE UPPER CLASSES

9738 SCOTT (JOHN). The Upper Classes: Property and Privilege. 1982.

9739 MINGAY (GORDON EDMUND). The Gentry: The Rise and Fall of a Ruling Class. 1976.

9740 PERROTT (ROY). The Aristocrats: A Portrait of Britain's Nobility and their Way of Life Today. 1968.

9741 WINGFIELD-STRATFORD (ESMÉ). The Squire and his Relations. 1956.

9742 MITFORD (NANCY). Noblesse Oblige: An Inquiry into the Identifiable Characteristics of the English Aristocracy. N.Y. 1956.

9743 —— 'Die Englische Aristokratie'. *Monat.* 9 (1956), 40–9.

9744 LAMBERT (ANGELA). Unquiet Souls: The Indian Summer of the British Aristocracy 1880–1918. 1984.

9745 BUSH (MICHAEL LACCOHEE). The English Aristocracy. Manch. 1984.

9746 BRIDGEMAN (HARRIET) *and* DRURY (ELIZABETH) *eds.* Society Scandals. Newton Abbot. 1977.

9747 BARRON (ANDREW). Gossip: A History of High Society from 1920 to 1970. 1978.

9748 MASON (PHILIP). The English Gentleman: The Rise and Fall of an Ideal. 1982.

9749 SPROULE (ANNA). The Social Calender. Poole. 1978.

9750 GUTTSMAN (WILHELM LEO). The English Ruling Class. 1969.

9751 —— The British Political Elite. 1963.

9752 —— 'Social Stratification and Political Elite'. *Brit. J. Sociol.* 11 (1960), 137–50.

9753 DAVIDOFF (LEONORE). The Best Circles: Society, Etiquette and the Season. 1974.

9754 RUBINSTEIN (W. D.). Men of Property: The Very Wealthy in Britain Since the Industrial Revolution. 1981.

9755 CORNFORD (JAMES PETERS). British Elites 1870–1950. Milton Keynes. 1974.

9756 AARONOVITCH (SAM). The Ruling Class: A Study of British Finance Capital. 1961.

9757 —— Monopoly: A Study of British Monopoly Capitalism. 1955.

9758 NAIRN (TOM). 'The British Political Elite'. *New Left Rev.* 23 (1964), 19–25.

9759 BLOOMFIELD (PAUL). Uncommon People: A Study of England's Elite. 1955.

9760 BOTTOMORE (THOMAS BURTON). Elites and Society. 1964.

9761 WILKINSON (RUPERT). The Prefects: British Leadership and the Public School Tradition: A Comprehensive Study in the Making of Rulers. 1964.

9762 —— Governing Elites: Studies in Training and Selection. N.Y. 1969.

9763 THOENES (PIET). The Elite in the Welfare State. 1966.

9764 CLEGG (STEWART). Power, Rule and Domination: A Critical and Empirical Understanding of Power in Sociological Theory and Organization Life. 1972.

9765 GIDDENS (ANTHONY). 'Elites in the British Class Structure'. *Sociol. Rev.* 3 (1972), 345–72.

19. PROFESSIONAL OCCUPATIONS

9766 CARR-SAUNDERS (*Sir* ALEXANDER MORRIS) *and* WILSON (PAUL ALEXANDER). The Professions. Oxf. 1933.

9767 LEWIS (ROY) *and* MAUDE (ANGUS EDMUND UPTON). *Baron.* Professional People. 1952.

9768 LEES (DENNIS SAMUEL). Economic Consequences of the Professions. 1966.

9769 HICKSON (D. J.) *and* THOMAS (M. W.). 'Professionalisation in Britain: A Preliminary Measure'. *Sociol.* 3 (1969), 37–53.

9770 JACKSON (JOHN ARCHER) *ed.* Professions and Professionalization. Camb. 1970.

9771 MILLERSON (GEOFFREY LEONARD). The Qualifying Associations: A Study in Professionalization. 1964.

9772 JOHNSON (TERENCE JAMES). Professionals and Power. 1972.

9773 ELLIOTT (PHILIP). The Sociology of the Professions. 1972.

9774 LANSBURY (RUSSELL). 'Careers, Work and Leisure among the New Professionals'. *Sociol. Rev.* 22 (1974), 385–400.

9775 HUDSON (KENNETH). The Jargon of the Professionals. 1978.

9776 BERTHOUD (RICHARD). Unemployed Professionals and Executives. 1979.

9777 WILSON (AUBREY). The Marketing of Professional Services. Maidenhead/London. 1972.

9778 KLINGENDER (FRANCIS DONALD). The Condition of Clerical Labour in Britain. 1935.

9779 NIVEN (MARY MARGARET). Personnel Management 1913–1963: The Growth of Personnel Management and the Development of the Institute [of Personnel Management]. 1967.

9780 SISSON (KEITH) *ed.* Personnel Management in Britain. Oxf. 1989.

9781 ANTHONY (PETER) *and* CRICHTON (ANNE). Industrial Relations and the Personnel Specialists. 1969.

9782 MACKAY (LESLEY) *and* TORRINGTON (DEREK). The Changing Nature of Personnel Management. 1986.

9783 TUNSTALL (JEREMY). The Advertising Man in London Advertising Agencies. 1964.

9784 WALKER (NIGEL). Morale in the Civil Service: A Study of the Desk Worker. Edin. 1961.

9785 JEREMY (DAVID J.) *ed.* Dictionary of Business Biography: A Biographical Dictionary of Business Leaders Active in the Period 1860–1950. 5 vols 1984–6.

9786 SLAVEN (ANTHONY) *and* CHECKLAND (SYDNEY G.) *eds.* Dictionary of Scottish Business Biography, 1860–1960. 2 vols Aberd. 1985–6.

9787 SCOTT (JOHN) *and* GRIFF (CATHERINE). Directors of Industry: The British Corporate Network, 1904–76. Camb. 1984.

9788 JEREMY (DAVID J.). 'Anatomy of the British Business Elite, 1860–1980'. *Bus. Hist.* 26 (1984), 3–23.

9789 LEWIS (ROY) *and* STEWART (ROSEMARY). The Boss: The Life and Times of the British Business Man. 1958.

9790 GATER (ANTHONY) *et al.* Thrusters and Sleepers: A Study in Industrial Management. A PEP Report. 1965.

9791 SOFER (CYRIL). Men in Mid-Career: A Study of British Managers and Technical Specialists. Camb. 1970.

9792 TISDALL (PATRICIA). Agents of Change: The Development and Practice of Management Consultancy. 1982.

9793 WHEATCROFT (MILDRED). The Revolution in British Management Education. 1970.

9794 MANT (ALISTAIR). The Rise and Fall of the British Manager. 1977.

9795 JERVIS (FRANK ROBERT JOSEPH). Bosses in British Business: Management from the Industrial Revolution to the Present Day. 1974.

9796 COPEMAN (GEORGE). Leaders of British Industry: A Study of the Careers of More than a Thousand Public Company Directors. 1955.

9797 CREW (ALBERT). The Profession of an Accountant . . . 1925.

9798 —— The Profession of a Secretary . . . Camb. 1942.

9799 DALE (JOHN RODNEY). The Clerk in Industry: A Survey of the Occupational Experience, Status, Education and Vocational Training of a Group of Male Clerks Employed by Industrial Companies. L/pool. 1962.

9800 FINDLATER (RICHARD). What are Writers Worth? A Survey of Authorship Prepared . . . for the Society of Authors. 1963.

9801 BONHAM-CARTER (VICTOR). Authors by Profession: Vol. 2 From the Copyright Act 1911 until the End of 1981. 1984.

9802 EHRLICH (CYRIL). The Music Profession in Britain since the Eighteenth Century: A Social History. Oxf. 1985.

9803 SYKES (A. J. M.). 'Some Differences in the Attitudes of Clerical and Manual Workers'. *Sociol. Rev.* 13 (1965), 297–310.

9804 CLARK (DAVID GEORGE). The Industrial Manager: His Background and Career Pattern. 1966.

9805 SOFER (CYRIL). Men in Mid-Career: A Study of British Managers and Technical Specialists. Camb. 1970.

9806 THOMPSON (FRANCIS MICHAEL LONGSTRETH). Chartered Surveyors: The Growth of a Profession. 1968.

9807 PRANDY (KENNETH). Professional Employees: A Study of Scientists and Engineers. 1965.

9808 RICHARDSON (V. A.). 'A Measurement of Demand for Professional Engineers'. *Brit. J. Ind. Relns* 7 (1969), 52–70.

9809 WALKER (DEREK). The Great Engineers: The Art of British Engineers 1837–1987. 1987.

9810 WILLIAMS (TREVOR I.). A Biographical Dictionary of Scientists. 1969.

9811 BENTWICH (NORMAN). The Rescue and Achievement of Refugee Scholars: The Story of Displaced Scholars and Scientists 1933–1952. The Hague. 1953. [Largely British-based research.].

9812 RICHTER (MELVIN). 'Intellectual and Class Alienation: Oxford Idealist Diagnoses and Prescriptions'. *Arch. Eur. Sociol.* 7 (1966), 1–26.

9813 ZANDER (MICHAEL). Lawyers and the Public Interest. 1968.

9814 PHILLIPS (ALFRED). The Lawyer and Society. Glasg. 1987.

9815 GOWER (L. C. B.) *and* PRICE (LEOLIN). 'The Profession and Practice of Law in England and America'. *Mod. Law Rev.* 20 (1957), 317–46.

9816 WEBSTER (ROBIN MACLEAN). Professional Ethics and Practices for Scottish Solicitors. Edin. 1976. 2nd edn 1984.

9817 DINGWALL (ROBERT) *and* LEWIS (PHILIP). The Sociology of the Professions: Lawyers, Doctors and Others. 1983.

9818 McCORMICK (JAMES). The Doctor: Father-Figure or Plumber? 1979.

9819 McGREGOR (ROBERT MURDOCH). The Work of a Family Doctor. Edin. 1969.

9820 GIBSON (R.). The Family Doctor: His Life and History. 1981.

9821 GOULD (DONALD). The Black and White Medical Show: How Doctors Serve and Fail their Customers. 1985.

9822 MENZIES (CAMPBELL J.). From a Trade to a Profession: Byways in Dental History. 1958.

9823 WILSON (KENNETH). The Story of Dentistry. Ilfracombe. 1985.

9824 PATTISON (IAIN). The British Veterinary Profession, 1791–1948. 1984.

9825 ROYAL COLLEGE OF VETERINARY SURGEONS. A Career as a Veterinary Surgeon. 5th edn 1988.

9826 U.K. INSTITUTE OF CHARTERED ACCOUNTANTS IN ENGLAND AND WALES. The History of the Institute . . . 1880–1965. 1966.

9827 U.K. INSTITUTE OF CHARTERED ACCOUNTANTS OF SCOTLAND. A History of the Chartered Accountants of Scotland from the Earliest Times to 1954. Edin. 1954.

9828 HASTINGS (ANTHONY) *and* HINNINGS (C. R.). 'Role Relations and Value Adaptation: A Study of the Professional Accountant in Industry'. *Sociol.* 4 (1970), 353–66.

9829 POCKSON (JONATHAN R. H. H.). Accountants' Professional Negligence: Developments in Legal Liability. 1982.

9830 LIPMAN (ALAN). 'Architectural Education and the Social Commitments of Contemporary British Architecture'. *Sociol. Rev.* 18 (1970), 5–27.

9831 BEN-DAVID (JOSEPH). 'Professions in the Class System of Present Day Societies'. *Current Sociol.* 12 (1963/4), 247–330. [Lengthy report divided into 3 chs.].

9832 BOX (STEVEN) *and* COTGROVE (STEPHEN). 'Scientific Identity, Occupational Selection and Role Strain'. *Brit. J. Sociol.* 17 (1966), 20–8.

9833 COATS (A. W.) *and* COATS (S. E.). 'The Changing Social Composition of the Royal Economic Society 1890–1960 and the Professionalisation of British Economics'. *Brit. J. Sociol.* 24 (1973), 165–87.

9834 COLLISON (PETER) *and* MILLEN (JAMES). 'University Chancellors, Vice-Chancellors and College Principals: A Social Profile'. *Sociol.* 3 (1969), 77–109.

9835 TROW (MARTIN A.) *and* HALSEY (ALBERT HENRY). The British Academics. 1971.

9836 —— 'British Academics and the Professorship'. *Sociol.* 3 (1969), 321–39.

9837 WILLIAMS (GARETH), BLACKSTONE (TESSA), *and* METCALF (DAVID). The Academic Labour Market: Economic and Social Aspects of a Profession. 1974.

9838 ELIAS (NORBERT). 'Studies in the Genesis of the Naval Profession'. *Brit. J. Sociol.* 1 (1950), 291–309.

9839 MANZER (RONALD ALEXANDER). Teachers and Politics. Manch. 1970.

9840 KELSALL (ROGER KEITH) *and* KELSALL (HELEN). The School Teacher in England and the United States: The Findings of Empirical Research. Oxf. 1969.

9841 COLLINS (M.). Women Graduates and the Teaching Profession. Manch. 1964. [British Federation of University Women.].

9842 ROY (W.). 'Membership Participation in the National Union of Teachers'. *Brit. J. Ind. Relns* 2 (1964), 189–208.

9843 TROPP (ASHER). The School Teachers. 1957.

9844 BARON (G.). 'The Teachers' Registration Movement'. *Brit. J. Educ. Studs* 2 (1954), 133–44.

9845 TUDOPE (WILLIAM B.). 'Motives for the Choice of the Teaching Profession by Training College Students'. *Brit. J. Educ. Psychol.* 14 (1944), 129–41.

9846 MUSGROVE (FRANK) *and* TAYLOR (PHILIP HAMPSON). Society and the Teacher's Role. 1969.

9847 GOSDEN (PETER HENRY JOHN HEATHER). The Evolution of a Profession: A Study of the Contribution of Teachers' Associations to the Development of School Teaching as a Professional Occupation. 1972.

9848 DENT (HAROLD COLLET). The Training of Teachers in England and Wales, 1800–1975. 1977.

9849 RUSK (ROBERT H.). The Training of Teachers in Scotland: A Historical Overview. Edin. 1928.

9850 CRUICKSHANK (MARJORIE). A History of the Training of Teachers in Scotland. 1970.

9851 KIRK (GORDON). Teacher Education and Professional Development. Edin. 1988.

20. STUDENTS

9852 SELECT COMMITTEE ON EDUCATION AND SCIENCE. Student Relations. HC Paper 449. Parliamentary Papers, vii–x (1968–9).

9853 MARWICK (ARTHUR J. B.). 'Youth in Britain, 1920–1960: Detachment and Commitment'. *J. Contemp. Hist.* 5 (1970), 37–51.

9854 ABBOTT (JOAN). Student Life in a Class Society. Oxf. 1971.

9855 —— 'Students' Class in Three Northern Universities'. *Brit. J. Sociol.* 16 (1965), 206–20.

9856 KLINGENDER (FRANCIS DONALD). 'Changing Patterns of University Recruitment in England'. *Univ. Q.* 9 (1955), 168–76.

9857 ZWEIG (FERDYNAND). The Student in the Age of Anxiety: A Survey of Oxford and Manchester Students. 1963.

9858 ALBROW (MARTIN C.). 'The Influence of Accommodation upon 64 Reading University Students'. *Brit. J. Sociol.* 17 (1966), 403–18.

9859 COCKBURN (ALEXANDER) *and* BLACKBURN (ROBIN) *eds.* Student Problems, Diagnosis, Action. Harmondsworth. 1969.

9860 WILSON (BRYAN RONALD). The Youth Culture and the Universities. 1970.

9861 ROTHMAN (STANLEY) *and* LICHTER (ROBERT). Roots of Radicalism: Jews, Christians and the New Left. Oxf. 1983.

9862 ASHBY (ERIC) *Baron and* ANDERSON (MARY). The Rise of the Student Estate in Britain. Camb., Mass./London. 1970.

9863 ROOKE (M. A.). Anarchy and Apathy: Student Unrest 1968–1970. 1971.

9864 SEARLE (J. R.). The Campus War. Harmondsworth. 1972.

9865 CROUCH (COLIN). The Student Revolt. 1970.

9866 JACKS (KEITH), COX (CAROLINE), *and* MARKS (JOHN). Rape of Reason: The Corruption of the Polytechnic of North London. 1975.

9867 HORNSEY COLLEGE OF ART. The Hornsey Affair. Harmondsworth. 1969.

9868 CAMPBELL (HILARY). 'Students and University Teachers: A Case Study of Informal Pressures'. *Sociol.* 5 (1971), 191–205.

9869 MOTT (J.) *and* GOLDIE (M.). 'The Social Characteristics of Militant and Anti-militant Students'. *Univ. Q.* 26 (1971), 28–40.

9870 MUSGROVE (FRANK). 'Social Class and Levels of Aspiration in a Technological University'. *Sociol. Rev.* 15 (1967), 311–22.

9871 ASHLEY (B.) *et al.* 'A Sociological Analysis of Students' Reasons for Becoming Teachers'. *Sociol. Rev.* 18 (1970), 53–69.

9872 RUDD (ERNEST) *and* HATCH (STEPHEN). Graduate Study and After. 1968.

9873 RUDD (ERNEST) *and* SIMPSON (RENATE). The Highest Education: A Study of Graduate Education in Britain. 1975.

9874 RUDD (ERNEST). A New Look at Postgraduate Failure. Surrey. 1985.

9875 LYNN (RICHARD). The Universities and the Business Community. 1969.

9876 HOUSE (JOHN WILLIAM) *and* THOMAS (A. D.). Northern Graduates of '64: Braindrain or Brainbank? Newcastle-upon-Tyne. 1968.

9877 CRAIG (CHRISTINE). The Employment of Cambridge Graduates. Camb. 1963.

9878 WEBB (DAVID). 'Some Factors Associated with the Employment of Sociology Graduates in the Field of Social Work'. *Sociol. Rev.* 21 (1973), 599–612.

9879 JACKS (DIGBY). Student Politics and Higher Education. 1975.

9880 U.K. POLITICAL AND ECONOMIC PLANNING. Colonial Students in Great Britain: A Report. 1955.

9881 U.K. BRITISH COUNCIL. How to Live in Britain: A Handbook for Students from Overseas. 11th edn 1964.

9882 WILLIAMS (PETER). The Overseas Student Question: Studies for a Policy. 1981.

9883 BUSH (PETER). Undergraduate Income and Expenditure. 1979.

9884 ENTWISTLE (N. J.). Degrees of Excellence: The Academic Achievement Game. 1977.

9885 BRENNAN (JOHN). Employment of Graduates from Ethnic Minorities: A Research Report. 1987.

9886 SEN (AMYA). Problems of Overseas Students and Nurses. Slough. 1970.

9887 COHEN (R. A.) *and* DAVIES (ANNE H.). One Hundred Years: A History of the University of Birmingham Dental Students' Society [1886–1986]. Birm. 1986.

9888 McWILLIAMS-TULLBERG (RITA). Women at Cambridge: A Men's University—Though of a Mixed Type. 1975.

9889 PEARSON (RICHARD) *and* PIKE (GEOFF). Graduate Supply and Demand into the 1990's. Brighton. 1988.

21. SOCIAL BEHAVIOUR AND CUSTOMS

9890 TOYNBEE (ARNOLD JOSEPH). Change and Habit: The Challenge of our Time. 1966.

9891 LESSING (DORIS). In Pursuit of the English: A Documentary. 1960. 2nd edn 1977.

9892 WILSON (*Sir* ARNOLD TALBOT) *and* MacEWAN (JOHN HELIAS FINNIE). Gallantry: Its Public Recognition and Reward, in Peace and in War, at Home and Abroad. 1939.

9893 LANDSBERG (STEPHEN E.). 'Taste Change in the United Kingdom, 1900–1955'. *J. Pol. Econ.* 89 (1981), 92–104.

9894 FRYER (PETER). Mrs Grundy: Studies in English Prudery. 1963.

9895 —— Private Case—Public Scandal. 1966.

9896 LORD DENNING'S REPORT. Cmnd 2152. Parliamentary Papers, xxiv (1962–3). [The Profumo Affair.].

9897 IRVING (CLIVE) *et al.* Scandal '63: A Study of the Profumo Affair. 1963.

9898 YOUNG (WAYLAND HILTON) *Baron Kennet.* The Profumo Affair: Aspects of Conservatism. Harmondsworth. 1963.

9899 WARD (STEPHEN). Stephen Ward Speaks: Conversations with Warwick Chalton: Judge Gerald Sparrow Sums up the Profumo Affair. 1963.

9900 KEELER (CHRISTINE). Scandal! 1989.

9901 SUMMERS (ANTHONY). Honey Trap: The Secret World of Stephen Ward. 1987.

9902 KENNEDY (LUDOVIC). The Trial of Stephen Ward. 1964.

9903 KNIGHTLEY (PHILLIP) *and* KENNEDY (CAROLINE). An Affair of State: The Profumo Case and the Framing of Stephen Ward. 1987.

9904 CRAWFORD (IAIN). The Profumo Affair. 1963.

9905 KNIGHTLEY (PHILLIP). An Affair of State: The Profumo Case and the Framing of Stephen Ward. 1987.

9906 LINKLATER (MAGNUS). Not with Honour: The Inside Story of the Westland Scandal. 1986.

9907 CHRISTIAN (ROY). The 'Country Life' Book of Old English Customs. 1966.

9908 —— Old English Customs. Newton Abbot. 1972.

9909 PINE (LESLIE GILBERT). Tradition and Custom in Modern Britain. 1967.

9910 BANKS (MARY MacLEOD). British Calendar Customs. Vol. 1 -1937. Vol. 2 -1939. Vol. 3 -1941.

9911 HENREY (ROBERT). Mrs Bloomsbury Fair. 1955.

9912 PEEL (C. S.). 'Domestic Life in England To-day'. *North Amer. Rev.* Feb. 1920, 203–11.

9913 MITCHELL (BASIL). Law, Morality and Religion in a Secular Society. 1967.

9914 BRITISH BROADCASTING CORPORATION. [Audience Research Depart-ment.] The People's Activities: Statistics of what People are doing Half-Hour by Half-Hour from Six-thirty am until Midnight. 1965.

9915 BOCOCK (ROBERT). Ritual in Industrial Society: A Sociological Analysis of Ritualism in Modern England. 1974.

9916 GIROUARD (MARK). The Return to Camelot: Chivalry and the English Gentleman. New Haven, Conn./Lond. 1971. [20th Century.].

9917 WAITES (BERNARD A.). Popular Culture Past and Present: A Reader. 1982.

22. MARRIAGE, DIVORCE, AND FAMILY LIFE

9918 U.K. OFFICE OF POPULATION CENSUSES AND SURVEYS. Marriage and Divorce Statistics. 1974+

9919 SELL (K. D.) and SELL (B. H.) eds. Divorce in the United States, Canada and Great Britain: A Guide to Information Sources. 1978.

9920 ROYAL COMMISSION ON MARRIAGE AND DIVORCE. 1951–55. Cmnd 9678. Parliamentary Papers, xxii (1955–6). [Chairman Lord Morton of Henryton.].

9921 ARCHBISHOP'S COMMISSION ON THE CHRISTIAN DOCTRINE OF MARRIAGE. Marriage, Divorce and the Church: The Report of a Commission Appointed by the Archbishop of Canterbury to Prepare a Statement on the Christian Doctrine of Marriage. 1971. [Chairman Professor H. Root.].

9922 ALDOUS (JOAN) and HILL (REUBEN). International Bibliography of Research in Marriage and the Family, 1900–1964. 1968.

9923 BOTT (ELIZABETH). Family and Social Network. 1957. 2nd edn 1971.

9924 FAMILY PLANNING ASSOCIATION. [Working Party.] Family Planning in the Sixties: A Report. 1963.

9925 CARTWRIGHT (MARY). How Many Children? 1976.

9926 —— Parents and Family Planning Services. 1970.

9927 —— Recent Trends in Family Planning and Contraception. 1978.

9928 CARTWRIGHT (MARY) and WILKINS (WARWICK). Changes in Family Building Plans: A Follow up Study to 'How Many Children?'. (1976).

9929 MARCHANT (Sir JAMES) ed. Medical Views on Birth Control. 1926.

9930 U.K. DHSS. Family Planning Services in England and Wales: A Report Carried out on behalf of the DHSS. 1973.

9931 U.K. DHSS SOCIAL SURVEY DIVISION. (New Series), 1055. The Family Planning Services: Changes and Effects: A Survey . . . 1978.

9932 —— Family Planning Services in England and Wales. 1973.

9933 —— Family Planning in Scotland in 1982 . . . 1985.

9934 RAPOPORT (RHONA) et al. Fathers, Mothers and Others: Towards New Alliances. 1977.

9935 RAPOPORT (RHONA) and RAPOPORT (ROBERT) eds. Working Couples. 1978.

9936 RAPOPORT (ROBERT) et al. Families in Britain. 1982.

9937 RAPOPORT (R.) and SIERAKOWSKI (M.). Recent Social Trends in Family and Work in Britain. 1982.

9938 RIMMER (L.) and POPAY (J.). Employment Trends and the Family Study. 1982.

9939 COLEMAN (D. A.). 'Recent Trends in Marriage and Divorce in Britain and Europe'. In 'Demographic Patterns in Developed Societies'. Ed. by R. W. Hiorns. 1980.

9940 SCHOEN (R.) and BAJ (J.). 'Twentieth Century Cohort Marriage and Divorce in England and Wales'. Pop. Studs 38 (1984), 439–50.

9941 HUNT (AUDREY), FOX (JUDITH), and MORGAN (MARGARET). Families and their Needs, with Particular Reference to One-Parent Families. 2 vols 1973.

9942 GEORGE (VICTOR) and WILDING (PAUL). Motherless Families. 1972.

9943 BARBER (DOLAN). One-Parent Families. 1978.

9944 CHEETHAM (JULIET). Unwanted Pregnancy and Counselling. 1977.

9945 CALLAN (HILARY) and ARDENER (SHIRLEY) eds. The Incorporated Wife. 1984.

9946 WYNN (MARGARET). Fatherless Families . . . 1964.

9947 FERRI (ELSA). Growing up in a One-Parent Family: A Long-term Study of Child Development. Slough. 1978.

9948 MARSDEN (DENNIS). Mothers Alone: Poverty and the Fatherless Family. 1969.

9949 BLAKE (PAMELA). The Plight of One-Parent Families. 1972.

9950 MILLER (JANE). Poverty and the One-Parent Family. Aldershot. 1989.

9951 COOTE (ANNA). Battered Women and the Law. 1978.

9952 PAHL (JANICE MARY). A Refuge for Battered Women: A Study of the Role of a Woman's Centre. 1978.

9953 GILES-SIMS (JEAN). Wife Battering: A Systems Theory Approach. N.Y./Lond. 1983.

9954 EEKELAAR (JOHN M.) and KATZ (SANFORD M.) eds. Family Violence: An International and Interdisciplinary Study. Toronto. 1978.

9955 EEKELAAR (JOHN M.). Family Law and Social Policy. 1978.

9956 —— Family Security and Family Breakdown. Harmondsworth. 1971.

9957 —— Et al. Custody after Divorce: The Disposition of Custody in Divorce Cases in Great Britain. Oxf. 1977.

9958 BAHER (EDWINA). At Risk: An Account of the Battered Child Research Department, NSPCC. 1976.

9959 SMITH (SELWYN MICHAEL). The Battered Child Syndrome. 1975.

9960 RENVOIZE (JEAN). Children in Danger: The Causes and Prevention of Baby Battering. 1974.

9961 STURGESS (JANET) *and* HEAL (KEVIN). Non-Accidental Injury to Children Under the Age of Seventeen. 1975.

9962 MARTIN (JOHN POWELL). Violence and the Family. Chich./N.Y. 1978.

9963 HAJNAL (JOHN). 'Age at Marriage and Proportions Marrying'. *Pop. Studs* 7 (1953), 11–136.

9964 PINCUS (LILY) *ed.* Marriage: Studies in Emotional Conflict and Growth. 1960.

9965 MOBEY (J.). 'Marriage Counselling and Family Life Education in England'. *Marriage and Family Living* 23 (1961), 146–54.

9966 HALMOS (PAUL). The Faith of the Counsellors. 1965. [Marriage Guidance.].

9967 COLE (MARGARET). Marriage Past and Present. 1939.

9968 PIERCE (RACHEL M.). 'Marriage in the Fifties'. *Sociol. Rev.* 11 (1963), 215–40.

9969 WALKER (KENNETH MacFARLANE) *and* WHITNEY (OWEN). The Family and Marriage in a Changing World. 1965.

9970 DOMINIAN (JACK). Marriage in Britain, 1945–1980. 1980.

9971 GILLIS (JOHN R.). For Better, for Worse: British Marriages, 1600 to the Present. N.Y./Oxf. 1986.

9972 WOLFRAM (SYBIL). In-Laws and Out-Laws: Kinship and Marriage in England. 1987.

9973 STAFFORD (ANN). The Age of Consent. 1964.

9974 WRIGHT (HELENA). Sex and Society. 1966.

9975 GIBSON (COLIN). 'The Association Between Divorce and Social Class in England and Wales'. *Brit. J. Sociol.* 25 (1974), 74–93.

9976 COALE (ANSLEY J.). 'Age Patterns of Marriage'. *Pop. Studs.* 25 (1971), 193–214.

9977 KELSALL (ROGER KEITH) *et al.* 'Marriage and Family-Building Patterns of University Graduates'. *J. Biosoc. Sci.* 3 (1971), 281–87.

9978 CHESTER (ROBERT). 'Contemporary Trends in the Stability of English Marriage'. *J. Biosoc. Sci.* 3 (1971), 389–402.

9979 EDGELL (STEPHEN). 'Marriage and the Concept of Companionship'. *Brit. J. Sociol.* 23 (1972), 452–61.

9980 PRAIS (SIGBERT JON) *and* SCHMOOL (MAURICE). 'Synagogue Marriages in Great Britain, 1966–1968'. *Jew. J. Sociol.* (1970), 21–8.

9981 MILLER (E.). 'Divorce and the Family Structure'. *Twentieth Century* (1955), 417–24.

9982 McGREGOR (OLIVER ROSS). Divorce in England: A Centenary Study. 1957.

9983 McGREGOR (OLIVER ROSS) *et al.* Separated Spouses: A Study of the Matrimonial Jurisdiction of Magistrates' Courts. 1970.

9984 —— Family Breakdown and Social Policy. 1974.

9985 —— 'The Stability of the Family in the Welfare State'. *Pol. Q.* 12 (1960), 132–41.

9986 —— 'Some Research Possibilities and Historical Materials for Family and Kinship Study in Britain'. *Brit. J. Sociol.* 12 (1961), 310–17.

9987 CARRIER (NORMAN HENRY) *and* ROWNTREE (GRISELDA). 'The Resort to Divorce in England and Wales, 1858–1957'. *Pop. Studs* 11 (1958), 188–233.

9988 POLLARD (ROBERT SPENCE WATSON). The Problem of Divorce. 1958.

9989 —— Family Problems and the Law. 1959.

9990 THORNES (BARBARA) *and* COLLARD (JEAN). Who Divorces? 1979.

9991 ROWNTREE (GRISELDA). 'Some Aspects of Marriage Breakdown in Britain during the Last Thirty Years'. *Pop. Studs* 18 (1963), 147–64.

9992 —— 'Early Childhood in Broken Families'. *Pop. Studs* 8 (1955), 247–63.

9993 RHEINSTEIN (MAX). Marriage Stability, Divorce and the Law. Chicago/Lond. 1972.

9994 LEE (BANG HA). Divorce Law Reform in England. 1974.

9995 TOLSTOY (DIMITRY). The Law and Practice of Divorce and Matrimonial Causes, Including Proceedings in Magistrates' Courts. 1946. 7th edn 1971.

9996 RAYDEN (WILLIAM). Practice and Law of Divorce. 11th edn 1971.

9997 MORRIS (DAVID). The End of Marriage. 1971.

9998 HART (NICKY). When Marriage Ends: A Study in Status Passage. 1976.

9999 U.K. ROYAL COMMISSION ON MARRIAGE AND DIVORCE. Report 1951–1955. 1956.

10000 —— Minutes of Evidence, Appendix and Index, 1952–1956. 1956.

10001 HUNT (MORTON MAGILL). The World of the Formerly Married. 1968.

10002 NICHOLS (DAVID IAN). Marriage, Divorce and the Family in Scotland. Edin. 1976. 3rd rev. edn 1978.

10003 PARKINSON (LISA). Separation, Divorce and Families. Basingstoke. 1987.

10004 GRANT (HUBERT BRIAN). Marriage, Separation and Divorce. 1946. 2nd edn 1948.

10005 PERKINS (DUDLEY). Husbands and Wives: A Survey of Recent Changes in the Law. 1962.

10006 ROSEN (LIONEL). Matrimonial Offences with Particular Reference to the Magistrates' Courts. 1962. 2nd edn 1965.

10007 PUGH (LESLIE MERVYN) *and* ROYDHOUSE (ERIC). Matrimonial Proceedings Before Magistrates. 1961. 2nd edn 1966.

10008 ARCHBISHOP OF CANTERBURY'S GROUP ON THE DIVORCE LAW. Putting Asunder . . . [Mortimer Report.]. 1966.

10009 LAW REFORM COMMISSION. Putting Asunder: A Divorce Law for Contemporary Society. 1966.

10010 SMOUT (T. C.). 'Scottish Marriage, Regular and Irregular, 1500–1940' in Marriage and Society: Studies in the Social History of Marriage, by Brian R. Outhwaite. 1981.

10011 MOUNT (FERDINAND). The Subversive Family: An Alternative History of Love and Marriage. 1982.

10012 CHESTER (ROBERT) and PEEL (JOHN) eds. Equalities and Inequalities of Family Life. 1977.

10013 PUXON (CATHERINE MARGARET). The Family and the Law: The Laws of Marriage, Separation and Divorce. Harmondsworth. 1963.

10014 WEBB (PHILIP RICHARD HYLTON) and BEVAN (HUGH). Source Book of Family Law. 1964.

10015 JOHNSON (EDWARD LEA). Family Law. 1965.

10016 BROMLEY (PETER MANN). Family Law. 1957. 7th edn 1987.

10017 HALL (JOHN CHALLICE). Sources of Family Law. Camb. 1966.

10018 BARKER (Sir ERNEST). Reflections on Family Life. 1947.

10019 —— Mothers and Sons in War-time and other Pieces. 1915. New and enlgd edn 1918.

10020 BOWLEY (AGATHA HILLIAM). The Problems of Family Life: An Environmental Study. 1946. 2nd edn 1948.

10021 MARCHANT (Sir JAMES) ed. Rebuilding Family Life in the Postwar World: An Enquiry with Recommendations. 1945.

10022 FIRTH (Sir RAYMOND WILLIAM). Two Studies on Kinship in London. 1956.

10023 —— 'Family and Kin Ties in Britain and their Social Implications: Introduction'. Brit. J. Sociol. 12 (1961), 305 -10.

10024 —— Et al. Families and their Relatives: Kinship in a Middle-Class Sector of London: An Anthropological Study . . . 1969.

10025 GLASS (RUTH) and DAVIDSON (F. G.). 'Household Structure and Housing Needs'. Pop. Studs 4 (1951), 395–420.

10026 BALDAMUS (W.) and TIMMS (NOEL). 'The Problem Family: A Sociological Approach'. Brit. J. Sociol. 6 (1955), 318–27.

10027 SLATER (ELIOT TREVOR OAKESHOTT) and WOODSIDE (MOXA). Patterns of Marriage: A Study of Marriage Relationships in the Urban Working Classes. 1955.

10028 SHAW (LULIE A.). 'Impressions of Family Life in a London Suburb'. Sociol. Rev. 2 (1954), 179–94.

10029 MOGEY (JOHN MacFARLANE). 'Changes in Family Life Experienced by English Workers Moving from Slums to Housing Estates'. J. Marr. Fam. Liv. 17 (1955), 123–8.

10030 —— Family and Neighbourhood: Two Studies in Oxford. 1956.

10031 —— Ed. Sociology of Marriage and Family Behaviour, 1957–1968, A Trend Report and Bibliography. The Hague. 1971.

10032 WILLOUGHBY (G.). 'The Working Class Family in England'. Transactions of the Third World Congress of Sociology 4 (1956), 155–60.

10033 YOUNG (MICHAEL D.) and WILLMOTT (PETER). Family and Kinship in East London. 1957.

10034 —— Family and Class in a London Suburb. 1960.

10035 —— The Symmetrical Family: A Study of Work and Leisure in a London Region. 1973.

10036 WILLMOTT (PETER). 'Kinship and Social Legislation'. Brit. J. Sociol. 9 (1958), 126–41.

10037 LAND (HILARY). Large Families in London: A Study of 86 Families. 1969.

10038 BOTT (ELIZABETH J.). Family and Social Network: Roles, Norms and External Relationships in Ordinary Urban Families. 1957. 2nd edn 1971.

10039 SCOTT (JOHN ALEXANDER). Problem Families in London. 1958.

10040 MARRIS (PETER). Widows and their Families. 1956.

10041 FINN (WALTER HENRY) ed. Family Therapy in Social Work: A Collection of Papers. 1974.

10042 U.K. POLITICAL ECONOMIC PLANNING. Family Needs and the Social Services. 1961.

10043 LOUDON (J. B.). 'Kinship and Crisis in South Wales'. Brit. J. Sociol. 12 (1961), 333–51.

10044 ROSSER (COLIN) and HARRIS (CHRISTOPHER C.). 'Relationships through Marriage in a Welsh Urban Area'. Sociol. Rev. 9 (1961), 293–321.

10045 —— The Family and Social Change: A Study of Family and Kinship in a South Wales Town. 1965.

10046 LANCASTER (LORRAINE). 'Some Conceptual Problems in the Study of Family and Kin Ties in the British Isles'. Brit. J. Sociol. 12 (1961), 317–33.

10047 FLETCHER (RONALD). Britain in the Sixties: The Family and Marriage, an Analysis and Moral Assessment. Harmondsworth. 1962. [Republished as 'The Family and Marriage in Britain: An Analysis and Moral Assessment'. 1966. 3rd edn 1973.].

10048 —— The Shaking of the Foundations: Family and Society. 1988.

10049 SHORTER (EDWARD). The Making of the Modern Family. 1977.

10050 MCKEE (LORNA) and O'BRIEN (MARGARET). The Father Figure. 1982.

10051 GITTINS (DIANA). Fair Sex: Family Size and Structure 1900–1939. 1982.

10052 —— The Family in Question. 1985.

10053 BRANNEN (JULIA). Give and Take in Families: Studies in Resource Distribution. 1987.

10054 HENWOOD (MELANIE). Inside the Family: The Changing Roles of Men and Women. 1987.

10055 U.K. BRITISH FAMILY RESEARCH COMMITTEE. Families in Britain. 1982.

10056 U.K. OFFICE OF POPULATION CENSUSES AND SURVEYS. (Social Survey Division) Families Five Years On. 1976.

10057 —— Family Formation 1976. . . . 1979.

10058 —— Family Expenditure Survey . . . 1980.

10059 DONNISON (DAVID VERNON) *et al.* The Ingelby Report: Three Critical Essays. 1962.

10060 OXFORD UNIVERSITY DEPARTMENT OF SOCIAL AND ADMINISTRATIVE STUDIES. (New Barnett Papers, No. 1) The Family in Modern Society. 1964.

10061 PHILP (ALBERT FREDERIC). Family Failure: A Study of 129 Families with Multiple Problems. 1963.

10062 PHILP (ALBERT FREDERIC) *and* TIMMS (NOEL). The Problem of the 'Problem Family': A Critical Review of the Literature Concerning the 'Problem Family' and its Treatment. 1957.

10063 DAVIES (CLARICE STELLA). North Country Bred: A Working Class Family Chronicle . . . (with an Introduction by PERKIN (HAROLD). 1964.

10064 U.K. COUNCIL FOR CHILDREN'S WELFARE. A Family Service and a Family Court. 1965.

10065 HUBERT (JANE). 'Kinship and Geographical Mobility in a Sample from a London Middle-Class Area'. *Int. J. Comp. Sociol.* 6 (1963), 61–80.

10066 STERN (HANS HEINRICH). Parent Education: An International Survey. Hull. 1960.

10067 TOWNSEND (PETER BRERETON). The Family of Three Generations in Britain, the United States and Denmark. 1963.

10068 LAWSON (WILLIAM). Family Handbook. Oxf. 2nd edn 1963.

10069 BASKERVILLE (DORIS RENWICK). Behavioural Patterns of Families in a London Borough: A Study of Marital and Parental Roles. 1963.

10070 JACKSON (JOSEPH M.). Family Income. Oxf. 1964.

10071 RYLE (ANTHONY). Neurosis in the Ordinary Family: A Psychiatric Survey. 1967.

10072 HOWELLS (JOHN GWILYM). Family Psychiatry. Edin. 1963.

10073 McKIE (ERIC). Venture in Faith: The Story of the Establishment of the Liverpool Family Service Unit and the Development of the Work with Problem Families. L/pool. 1963.

10074 LEISSNER (ARYEH). Family Advice Services: An Exploratory Study of a Sample of such Services Organised by Children's Departments in England. 1967.

10075 —— *Et al.* Advice, Guidance and Assistance: A Study of Seven Family Advice Centres. 1971.

10076 HASTINGS (SOMERVILLE) *and* JAY (PEGGY). The Family and the Social Services. 1965.

10077 FOX (ROBIN). Kinship and Marriage: An Anthropological Perspective. Harmondsworth. 1967.

10078 LOMAS (PETER) *ed.* The Predicament of the Family: A Psycho-analytical Symposium. 1967.

10079 MUSGROVE (FRANK). The Family, Education and Society. 1966.

10080 WINNICOTT (DONALD WOODS). The Child, the Family and the Outside World. 1964.

10081 —— The Family and Individual Development. 1968.

10082 TURNER (CHRISTOPHER). Family and Kinship in Modern Britain: An Introduction. 1969.

10083 BREMNER (MARJORIE K.). Dependency and the Family: A Psychological Study in Preferences Between Family and Official Decision Making. 1968.

10084 TOOMEY (DEREK M.). 'Home Centred Working-Class Parents' Attitudes towards their Sons' Education and Careers'. *Sociol.* 3 (1969), 299–320.

10085 PLATT (JENNIFER). 'Some Problems in Measuring the Jointness of Conjugal Role-Relationships'. *Sociol.* 3 (1969), 287–97.

10086 WIMBERLEY (H.). 'Conjugal Role Organisation and Social Networks in England and Japan'. *J. Marr. Fam. Liv.* 35 (1973), 125–30.

10087 NOBLE (TREVOR). 'Family Breakdown and Social Networks'. *Brit. J. Sociol.* 21 (1970), 135–50.

10088 HARRIS (CHRISTOPHER C.) *ed.* Readings in Kinship in Urban Society. Oxf. 1970.

10089 —— The Family: An Introduction. 1969.

10090 FINCH (JANET). Married to the Job: Wives' Incorporation in Men's Work. 1983.

10091 FARMER (MARY). The Family. 1970. 2nd edn 1979.

10092 CRAFT (MAURICE) *ed.* Family, Class and Education: A Reader. 1970.

10093 HEYWOOD (JEAN SCHOFIELD) *and* ALLEN (BARBARA K.). Financial Help in Social Work: A Study of Preventative Work with Families under the Children and Young Persons Act, 1963. Manch. 1971.

10094 ANDERSON (MICHAEL) *ed.* The Sociology of the Family: Selected Readings. Harmondsworth. 1971.

10095 ORFORD (TIM) *and* HARWIN (JUDITH). Alcohol and the Family. 1982.

10096 BARNES (G. M.) *and* AUGUSTINO (D. K.) *eds.* Alcohol and the Family: A Comprehensive Bibliography. 1987.

10097 COOPER (DAVID GRAHAM). The Death of the Family. 1971.

10098 KENNET (K. C.) *and* CROPLEY (A. J.). 'Intelligence, Family Size and Socio-economic Status'. *J. Biosoc. Sci.* 3 (1970), 227–36.

10099 GOLDRING (PATRICK). The Friend of the Family: The Work of Family Service Units. Newton Abbot. 1973.

10100 JORDAN (WILLIAM). The Social Worker in Family Situations. 1972.

10101 GORER (GEOFFREY). Sex and Marriage in England Today: A Study of the Views and Experience of the under 45s. 1971.

10102 U.K. DHSS. The Family in Society, Preparation for Parenthood. 1974.

10103 SMITH (DONALD M.) ed. Families and Groups: A Unit at Work: A Description and Analysis of Work with Families, Groups and the Neighbourhood, Undertaken at the East London Family Service Unit. 1974.

10104 MARSDEN (DENNIS). Some Unemployed Men and their Families: An Exploration of the Social Contract between Society and Worker. 1975.

10105 ZARETSKY (ELI). Capitalism, the Family and Personal Life. 1976.

10106 MORONEY (ROBERT M.). The Family and the State: Considerations for Social Policy. 1976.

10107 CORBIN (MARIE) ed. The Couple. Harmondsworth. 1976.

10108 WILSON (HARRIET), HERBERT (G. W.), *and* WILSON (JOHN VEIT). Parents and Children in the Inner City. 1978.

23. UNCLASSIFIED

10109 MACKENZIE (DONALD). Statistics in Britain 1865–1930: The Social Construction of Scientific Knowledge. Edin. 1981.

10110 GORER (GEOFFREY). Death, Grief and Mourning in Contemporary Britain. 1965.

10111 SHUTTLEWORTH (ALAN). Two Working Papers in Cultural Studies. Birm. 1966.

10112 BIRMINGHAM UNIVERSITY CENTRE FOR CONTEMPORARY CULTURAL STUDIES. First Report. Birm. 1964.

10113 LAWTON (RICHARD) *and* CUNNINGHAM (CATHERINE M.). Merseyside Social and Economic Studies. 1970.

10114 U.K. SCOTTISH COUNCIL OF SOCIAL SERVICE. (Third Statistical Account of Scotland). The Stewartry of Kirkcudbright. [*Ed.* by John Laird and D. G. Ramsay.]. Glasg. 1965.

10115 —— The County of Wigtown. [*Ed.* by M. C. Arnott.]. Glasg. 1965.

10116 —— The County of Angus. [*Ed.* by William Illsley.]. 1977.

10117 —— The City of Dundee. [*Ed.* by J. M. Jackson.]. 1979.

10118 —— The Counties of Perth and Kinross. [*Ed.* by David Taylor.]. 1979.

10119 RENNIE (JAMES ALAN). The Scottish People, their Clans, Families and Origins. 1960.

10120 PHILLIPS (MARGARET). Small Social Groups in England. 1965.

10121 EGERTON (FRANK N.). 'A Bibliographical Guide to the History of General Ecology and Popular Ecology'. *Hist. Science* 15 (1977), 189–215.

10122 KROGMAN (WILTON MARION). 'Fifty Years of Physical Anthropology: The Men, the Material, the Concepts, the Methods'. *Ann. Rev. Anthrop.* 5 (1976), 1–14.

10123 DARNELL (REGINA). 'History of Anthropology in Historical Perspective'. *Ann. Rev. Anthrop.* 6 (1977), 399–417.

10124 FORTES (MEYER). Kinship and the Social Order: The Legacy of Lewis Henry Morgan. 1970. [Social Anthropology.].

10125 GLUCKMANN (HERMAN MAY). Closed Systems and Open Minds: The Limits of Naivety in Social Anthropology. Edin. 1964.

10126 LITTLE (KENNETH LINDSAY). 'Department of Social Anthropology, the University of Edinburgh'. *Sociol. Rev.* 8 (1960), 255–66.

10127 —— Social Anthropology in Modern Life. Edin. 1965.

24. CRIME, CRIMINALS, AND CRIMINOLOGY

(a) General

10128 CAMBRIDGE INSTITUTE OF CRIMINOLOGY. Bibliographical Series. Camb. 1966.

10129 HOOD (ROGER GRAHAME) ed. Crime, Criminology and Public Policy: Essays in Honour of Sir Leon Radzinowicz. 1974.

10130 HOOD (ROGER GRAHAME) *and* SPARKS (RICHARD). Key Issues in Criminology. 1970.

10131 RADZINOWICZ (*Sir* LEON) *and* KING (JOAN). The Growth of Crime: The International Experience. 1977.

10132 RADZINOWICZ (*Sir* LEON). Ideology and Crime: A Study of Crime in its Social and Historical Context. 1966.

10133 —— In Search of Criminology. Camb., Mass./Lond. 1962.

10134 MANNHEIM (HERMANN). Social Aspects of Crime in England between the Wars. 1940.

10135 —— Group Problems in Crime and Punishment and other Studies in Criminology and Criminal Law. 1955.

10136 —— Comparative Criminology. 2 vols 1965.

10137 LOPEZ-REY Y ARROJO (MANUEL). Crime: An Analytical Appraisal. 1970.

10138 WHITAKER (BENJAMIN CHARLES GEORGE). Crime and Society. 1967.

10139 BORRELL (CLIVE) *and* CASHINELLA (BRIAN). Crime in Britain Today. 1975.

10140 WEBB (THOMAS DUNCAN). Deadline for Crime. 1955.

10141 —— Line-Up for Crime. 1956.

10142 —— Crime is my Business. 1956.

10143 TROTTER (SALLIE WALLACE BROWN). No Easy Road: A Study of the Theories and Problems Involved in the Rehabilitation of the Offender. 1967.

10144 TRASLER (GORDON). The Explanation of Criminality. 1962.

10145 TAYLOR (IAN), WALTON (PAUL), *and* YOUNG (JOCK) *eds.* Critical Criminology. 1975.

10146 —— The New Criminology: For a Social Theory of Deviance. 1973.

10147 WILLIAMS (FRANK P.). Criminological Theory. Englewood Cliffs, NJ./Lond. 1989.

10148 TAYLOR (IAN) *and* TAYLOR (LAURIE) *eds.* Politics and Deviance. Harmondsworth. 1973.

10149 TAYLOR (LAURIE). Deviance and Society. 1971.

10150 TAYLOR (LAURIE) *and* ROBERTSON (ROLAND). Deviance, Crime and Socio-legal Control: Comparative Perspectives. 1973.

10151 TAYLOR (LAURIE), MORRIS (ALISON) *and* DOWNES (DAVID). Signs of Trouble: Aspects of Delinquency. 1976.

10152 NORTON (PHILIP). Law and Order and British Politics. Aldershot. 1984.

10153 SMITH (PETER GLADSTONE). The Crime Explosion. 1970.

10154 SMITH (MAURICE HAMBLIN). The Psychology of the Criminal. 1922.

10155 PRINS (HERSCHEL ALBERT). Criminal Behaviour: An Introduction to its Study and Treatment. 1973.

10156 MORRISH (REGINALD). The Police and Crime Detection Today. 2nd edn 1955.

10157 MORRIS (TERENCE PATRICK). The Criminal Area: A Study in Social Ecology. 1958.

10158 MORGAN (PATRICIA). Delinquent Fantasies. 1978.

10159 LAMBERT (JOHN RICHARD). Crime, Police and Race Relations: A Study in Birmingham. 1970.

10160 JACKSON (ROBERT LOUIS). Occupied with Crime. 1967.

10161 —— *Ed.* Twentieth Century Interpretations of Crime and Punishment: A Collection of Critical Essays. Englewood Cliffs. 1976.

10162 ROCK (PAUL ELLIOT). 'Sociology of Deviancy and Conceptions of Moral Order'. *Brit. J. Criminol.* 14 (1975), 139–49.

10163 KOHLER (K. H.). 'Parental Deprivation, Family Background and Female Delinquency'. *Brit. J. Psychiatry* 118 (1971), 319–27.

10164 LITTLE (ALAN). 'The Prevalence of Recorded Delinquency and Recidivism in England and Wales'. *Amer. Sociol. Rev.* 30 (1965), 210–63.

10165 BOX (STEVEN). 'New Criminology: For a Social Theory of Deviance' by I. Taylor *and others*: Review Article *Sociol.* 8 (1974), 317–22.

10166 BOX (STEVEN) *and* FORD (JULIENNE). 'The Facts don't Fit: On the Relationship between Social Class and Criminal Behaviour'. *Sociol. Rev.* 19 (1971), 31–52.

10167 GIBBS (D. N.). 'The National Serviceman and Military Delinquency'. *Sociol. Rev.* 5 (1957), 255–63.

10168 MILLUM (TREVOR). Working Papers in Cultural Studies (3 vols in 1). Birm. 1972.

10169 FAIRHEAD (SUZAN). Persistent Petty Offenders. 1981.

10170 MOORE (COLIN) *and* BROWN (JOHN). Community Versus Crime. 1981.

10171 WOOTTON (BARBARA FRANCES) *Baroness.* Crime and the Criminal Law: Reflections of a Magistrate and Social Scientist. 1968.

10172 —— Crime and Penal Policy: Reflections on Fifty Years' Experience. 1978.

10173 WOOTTON (BARBARA FRANCES) with SEAL (VERA G.) *and* CHAMBERS (ROSALIND). Social Science and Social Pathology. 1959.

10174 HIBBERT (CHRISTOPHER). The Roots of Evil: A Social History of Crime and Punishment. Harmondsworth. 1966.

10175 GRYGIER (TADEUSZ) *et al. eds.* Criminology in Transition: Essays in Honour of Hermann Mannheim. 1965.

10176 GODWIN (GEORGE). Crime and Social Action. 1956.

10177 McCLINTOCK (FREDERICK HEMMING) *et al.* Crimes of Violence: An Enquiry by the Cambridge Institute of Criminology . . . 1963.

10178 —— Crimes Against the Person. Manch. 1963.

10179 McCLINTOCK (FREDERICK HEMMING) *and* GIBSON (EVELYN). Robbery in London: An Enquiry. 1961.

10180 McCLINTOCK (FREDERICK HEMMING) *and* AVISON (NEVILLE HOWARD). Crime in England and Wales. 1968.

10181 ARNOTT (ALISON JUNE ELPHINSTONE) *and* DUNCAN (JUDITH ANNE). The Scottish Criminal. Edin. 1970.

10182 GLOVER (EDWARD). The Roots of Crime. 1960.

10183 SHIELDS (JOHN VEYSIE MONTGOMERY) *and* DUNCAN (JUDITH ANNE). The State of Crime in Scotland. 1964.

10184 EYSENCK (HANS JURGEN). Crime and Personality. 3rd edn 1977.

10185 CRESSEY (DONALD RAY). Criminal Organization: Its Elementary Forms. 1972.

10186 BOX (STEVEN). Deviance, Reality and Society. 1971.

10187 BALL (D. B.). Crime in our Time. 1962.

10188 BALDWIN (JOHN), BOTTOMS (ANTHONY EDWARD), *with* WALKER (MONICA). The Urban Criminal: A Study in Sheffield. 1976.

10189 BALDWIN (JOHN) *and* BOTTOMLEY (ALLAN KEITH) *eds.* Criminal Justice: Selected Readings. 1978.

10190 MARTIN (JOHN POWELL) *and* WEBSTER (DOUGLAS). The Social Consequences of Conviction. 1971.

10191 MAYO (PATRICIA ELTON). The Making of a Criminal: A Comparative Study of Two Delinquency Areas. 1969.

10192 —— MAYS (JOHN BARRON). Crime and the Social Structure. 1963.

10193 —— Crime and its Treatment. 1970.

10194 DOWNES (DAVID) *and* ROCK (PAUL ELLIOT). 'Social Reaction to Deviance and its Effects on Crime and Criminal Careers'. *Brit. J. Sociol.* 22 (1971), 351–64.

10195 GRUNHUT (MAX). 'Progress in Criminal Statistics: Comments on Criminal Statistics, England and Wales, 1953'. *Howard J.* 9 (1955), 146–52.

(The Journal has a similar commentary by others on the criminal statistics annually).

10196 HEIDENSOHN (FRANCES). 'The Deviance of Women: A Critique and an Inquiry'. *Brit. J. Sociol.* 19 (1968), 160–75.

10197 —— 'The Able Criminal'. *Brit. J. Criminol.* 12 (1972), 44–54.

10198 ROSE (GORDON ARTHUR). 'Trends in the Development of Criminology in Britain'. *Brit. J. Sociol.* 9 (1958), 53–65.

10199 SCOTT (PETER D.). 'Gangs and Delinquent Groups in London'. *Brit. J. Delinquency* 7 (1956), 4–25.

10200 BELSON (WILLIAM ALBERT). Juvenile Theft: Its Causal Factors. 1975.

10201 PRATT (MICHAEL). Mugging as a Social Problem. 1980.

10202 HAMMOND (WILLIAM HOBSON) *and* CHAYEN (EDNA). Persistent Criminals: A Study of all Criminals Liable to Preventative Detention in 1956. 1963.

10203 HOME OFFICE RESEARCH UNIT. Report No. 11: Studies of Female Offenders. 1967.

10204 U.K. HOME OFFICE. The War Against Crime in England and Wales, 1959–1964. Cmnd 2296. 1964.

10205 —— Research Bulletin. Semi-annually from spring 1975.

10206 CENTRAL OFFICE OF INFORMATION. The Treatment of Offenders in Britain. 2nd edn 1964.

10207 WEATHERHEAD (ALAN DOUGLAS) *and* ROBINSON (BRETT MALLON). Firearms in Crime: A Home Office Statistical Division Report on Indictable Offences Involving Firearms in England and Wales. 1970.

10208 OXFORD UNIVERSITY PENAL RESEARCH UNIT. Occasional Papers No.1 The Violent Offender: Reality or Illusion? Oxf. 1970.

10209 U.K. HOME OFFICE. The Adult Offender. Cmnd 2852. 1965.

10210 KEENE (DAVID) *et al.* The Adult Criminal 1967.

10211 U.K. REPORT of the Departmental Committee on Criminal Statistics. (Perks Committee) Cmnd 3448 1968.

10212 ROCK (PAUL ELLIOT). 'Observation on Debt Collection'. *Brit. J. Sociology* 19 (1968), 176–90.

10213 CHAPPELL (D.) *and* WALSH (M.). 'No Questions Asked: A Consideration of the Criminal Crime of Receiving'. *Crime and Delinquency* 20, 157–68.

10214 CHAPMAN (DENNIS). Sociology and the Stereotype of the Criminal. 1968.

10215 BREED (BRYAN). White Collar Bird. 1979.

10216 FORDHAM (PETA). Inside the Underworld. 1972.

10217 FLETCHER (JOHN WILLIAM). A Measure to Society. 1972.

10218 FLETCHER (GEOFFREY SCOWLAND). Down Among the Meths Men. 1966.

10219 WILLETTS (PHOEBE). Invisible Bars. 1965.

10220 IANNI (FRANCIS A.) *and* REUSS-IANNI (ELIZABETH). A Family Business: Kinship and Social Control in Organised Crime. 1972.

10221 HOYLES (JAMES ARTHUR). The Church and the Criminal. 1963.

10222 PROBYN (WALTER). Angelface: The Making of a Criminal. 1977.

10223 WALSH (D. P.). Shoplifting: Controlling a Major Crime. 1978.

10224 SPENSER (JAMES). Limey Breaks In. 1936.

10225 GOODMAN (DERICK). Crime of Passion. 1958.

10226 GIBBENS (TREVOR CHARLES NOEL) *and* PRINCE (JOYCE). Shoplifting. 1962.

10227 FABIAN (ROBERT). The Anatomy of Crime. 1970.

10228 WOLPIN (KENNETH I.). 'An Economic Analysis of Crime and Punishment in England and Wales, 1894–1967'. *J. Pol. Econ.* 86 (1978), 815–40.

10229 RADZINOWICZ (*Sir* LEON). 'Changing Attitudes Towards Crime and Punishment'. *Law Q. Rev.* 75 (1959), 381–400.

10230 WALKER (NIGEL). 'The Habitual Criminal: An Administrative Problem'. *Public Admin.* 41 (1963), 265–80.

10231 PARKER (TONY). The Unknown Citizen. Harmondsworth. 1966.

10232 WILLIAMS (FRANK). No Fixed Address: Life on the Run for the Great Train Robbers. 1973.

10233 READ (PIERS PAUL). The Train Robbers. 1978.

10234 WILLETT (TERENCE CHARLES). Criminals on the Road: A Study of Serious Motoring Offences and Those who Commit Them. 1964.

10235 —— Drivers After Sentence. 1973.

10236 BALL (JOAN), CHESTER (LEWIS), *and* PERROTT (ROY). Cops and Robbers: An Investigation into Armed Bank Robbery. 1978.

10237 CARR-HILL (ROY) *and* STERN (NICHOLAS HERBERT). Crime: The Police and Criminal Statistics. 1979.

10238 FITZGERALD (MIKE). Crime and Society: Readings in History and Theory. 1981.

10239 BOTTOMLEY (ALLAN KEITH). Criminal Justice: Selected Readings. 1978.

10240 —— Criminology in Focus: Past Trends and Future Prospects. 1979.

10241 BOTTOMLEY (ALLAN KEITH) *and* COLEMAN (C.). Understanding Crime Rates. 1981.

10242 WILKINS (LESLIE THOMAS). Consumerist Criminology. 1984.

10243 MCCONVILLE (MICHAEL) *and* BALDWIN (JOHN). 'The Role of Interrogation in Crime Discovery and Conviction'. *Brit. J. Criminol.* 22 (1982), 165–75.

10244 SMITH (SUSAN J.). 'Crime in the News'. *Brit. J. Criminol.* 24 (1984), 289–95.

10245 MAYHEW (PAT) *and* SMITH (LORNA J. F.). 'Crime in England and Wales and Scotland: A British Crime Survey Comparison'. *Brit. J. Criminol.* 25 (1985), 148–59.

10246 GLICKMAN (M. J. A.). From Crime to Rehabilitation. Aldershot. 1983.

10247 SMITH (J. A.). 'The Scottish Criminal System: Some Distinctive Features'. *Howard J.* 9 (3) (1956), 209–14.

10248 HENDERSON (*Sir* DAVID KENNEDY). Society and Criminal Conduct. Edin. 1955.

10249 KLARE (HUGH JOHN) ed. Changing Concepts of Crime and its Treatment. N.Y./Oxf. 1966.

10250 —— Delinquency, Social Support and Control Systems. 1966.

10251 —— Anatomy of Prison. 1960.

10252 —— People in Prison. 1973.

10253 KLARE (HUGH JOHN) *and* HAXBY (DAVID) eds. Frontiers of Criminology: Summary of the Proceedings. N.Y./Oxf. 1967.

10254 JONES (HOWARD). Crime in a Changing Society. Harmondsworth. 1965.

10255 —— Prison Reform Now. 1959. Fabian Society.

10256 —— Reluctant Rebels: Re-education and Group Process in a Residential Community. 1960.

10257 —— Crime and the Penal System. A Textbook of Criminology. 1956. 2nd edn 1962. 3rd edn 1965.

10258 —— The Residential Community: A Setting for Social Work. 1979.

10259 CHARMAN (DENNIS). Sociology and the Stereotype of the Criminal. 1968.

10260 CLAYTON (TOM). Men in Prison. 1970.

10261 HOWARD LEAGUE FOR PENAL REFORM. The Howard Journal of Penology and Crime Prevention 1921–1975 Cumulative Index .Oxf. 1979.

10262 ALLERIDGE (PATRICIA). 'Criminal Insanity: Bethlem to Broadmoor'. *Proc. Roy. Soc. Med.* 67 (1974), 897–904.

10263 FITZGERALD (MIKE), MCLENNAN (GREGOR), *and* DAWSON (JENNY). Crime and Society: Readings in History and Theory. 1981.

10264 CRESSEY (DONALD). Criminal Organisation: Its Elementary Form. 1972.

10265 STEVENS (PHILIP) *and* WILLIS (CAROLE). Race, Crime and Arrests. 1979.

10266 CARSON (W. G.) *and* WILES (PAUL) eds. Delinquency in Britain: Sociological Readings. 1971.

10267 WILES (PAUL). The Sociology of Crime and Delinquency in Britain. Vol. 2 The New Criminologies. 1976.

10268 SMITHIES (EDWARD). Crime in Wartime Britain: A Social History of Crime in World War Two. 1982.

10269 CHAMBERS (GERRY) *and* TOMBS (JACQUELINE) eds. The British Crime Survey: Scotland. Edin. 1984.

10270 HALL (STUART MCPHAIL) *et al.* Policing the Crisis: Mugging, the State and Law and Order. 1978.

10271 OUGHTON (FREDERICK). Fraud and White Collar Crime. 1971.

10272 HEPWORTH (MIKE). Blackmail: Publicity and Secrecy in Everyday Life. 1975.

10273 CONNELL (JON) *and* SUTHERLAND (DOUGLAS). Fraud: The Amazing Case of Doctor Savundra. 1978.

10274 BENNEY (MARK). Low Company: Describing the Evolution of a Burglar. 1936.

10275 HENRY (STUART). The Hidden Economy: The Context and Control of Borderline Crime. 1978.

10276 BURROWS (JOHN) *and* TARLING (ROGER). 'The Investigation of Crime in England and Wales'. *Brit. J. Criminol.* 27 (1987), 229–51.

10277 KINSEY (RICHARD). Losing the Fight against Crime. Oxf. 1986.

10278 WALKER (MONICA). Crime. Oxf. 1981.

10279 MATTHEWS (ROGER) *and* YOUNG (JOCK). Confronting Crime. 1986.

10280 BRAITHWAITE (JOHN). Crime, Shame and Re-integration. Camb. 1989.

10281 HEIDENSOHN (FRANCES). Crime and Society. Basingstoke. 1989.

(b) The Courts

10282 WALKER (PETER NORMAN). The Courts of Law: A Guide to their History and Working. Newton Abbot. 1970.

10283 ARCHER (PETER KINGSLEY). The Queen's Courts. 1956.

10284 HANBURY (HAROLD GREVILLE). The English Courts of Law. 1944. 2nd edn 1953. 4th edn 1967. Prepared by D. Yardley.

10285 MAXWELL (LESLIE F.). A Bibliography of English Law from 1801 to June 1932. 1933.

10286 CHLORDS (ALEXANDER GEORGE) ed. A Bibliographical Guide to the Law of the United Kingdom, the Channel Islands and the Isle of Man. 1956. 2nd edn 1973.

10287 CUMMING (Sir JOHN GUEST). A Contribution Towards a Bibliography Dealing with Crime and Cognate Subjects. [Receiver for Metropolitan Police District.] 3rd edn 1935.

10288 HEWITT (WILLIAM H.). A Bibliography of Police Administration, Public Safety and Criminology, to July 1 1965. Springfield, Ill. 1967.

10289 SCOTT (Sir HAROLD RICHARD). The Concise Encyclopedia of Crime and Criminals. Lond./N.Y. 1961.

10290 RADZINOWICZ (Sir LEON). A History of English Criminal Law and its Administration, from 1750. Four vols from 1948.

10291 GREENWOOD (MAJOR), MARTIN (W. J.) and RUSSELL (W. T.). 'Deaths by Violence, 1837–1937'. Roy. Stat. Soc. J. 1941. 146–63.

10292 RADZINOWICZ (Sir LEON) and HOOD (ROGER GRAHAME). Criminology and the Administration of Criminal Justice: A Bibliography. 1976.

10293 STEVENS (ROBERT). 'The Role of a Final Appeal Court in a Democracy: The House of Lords Today'. Mod. Law Rev. 28 (1965), 509–39.

10294 BLOM-COOPER (LOUIS JACQUES) and DREWRY (GAVIN). Final Appeal: A Study of the House of Lords in its Judicial Capacity, Oxf. 1972.

10295 —— Eds. Law and Morality. 1976.

10296 MORRISON (ARTHUR CECIL LOCKWOOD) and HUGHES (EDWARD) eds. The Criminal Justice Act 1948. 2nd edn 1952.

10297 NAPIER (BRIAN). 'Judicial Attitudes Towards the Employment Relationship: Some Recent Developments'. Ind. Law J. 6 (1977), 1–18.

10298 DEVLIN (PATRICK) Baron. Trial by Jury. 1956.

10299 —— Law and Morals. Birm. 1961.

10300 —— Samples of Lawmaking. 1962.

10301 —— The Enforcement of Morals. 1965.

10302 —— What's Wrong with the Law. 1970.

10303 —— The Judge. Oxf. 1979.

10304 SCOTTISH HOME AND HEALTH DEPARTMENT. Use of Short Sentences of Imprisonment by the Courts. Report of a Committee of the Scottish Advisory Council on the Treatment of Offenders. 1960.

10305 McCONVILLE (MICHAEL) and BALDWIN (JOHN). Courts, Prosecution and Conviction. 1981.

10306 —— Confessions in Crown Court Trials. 1980.

10307 —— Jury Trials. Oxf. 1979.

10308 —— Negotiated Justice: Pressures to Plead Guilty. 1977.

10309 —— 'Juries, Foremen and Verdicts'. Brit. J. Criminol. 20 (1980), 35–44.

10310 ASHWORTH (ANDREW). The English Sentencing System. 3rd edn 1981.

10311 —— Sentencing and Penal Policy. 1983.

10312 —— Sentencing in the Crown Court. Oxf. 1984.

10313 BOTTOMLEY (ALLAN KEITH). Decisions in the Penal Process. 1973.

10314 ROCK (PAUL ELLIOT). Making People Pay. 1973.

10315 MELVIN (MICHAEL). Pre-trial Bail and Custody in the Scottish Sheriff Courts. Edin. 197.

10316 TENNANT (T. GAVIN). 'The Use of Remand on Bail or in Custody by the London Juvenile Courts: A Comparative Study'. Brit. J. Criminol. 11 (1972), 80–5.

10317 BOTTOMLEY (ALLAN KEITH) and DELL (SUSANNE). 'Bail Procedures in Magistrates' Courts'. Brit. J. Criminol. 15 (1975), 81–7.

10318 DAVIES (CLIVE). 'Pre-Trial Imprisonment: A Liverpool Study'. Brit. J. Criminol. 11 (1971), 32–48.

10319 TUTT (NORMAN). Care or Custody: Community Houses and the Treatment of Delinquency. 1974.

10320 —— Alternative Strategies for Coping with Crime. Oxf. 1978.

10321 KING (MICHAEL) and JACKSON (CHRISTINE). Bail or Custody. 1971.

10322 DOBIE (WILLIAM JARDINE). Law and Practice of the Sheriff Courts in Scotland. Collieston. 1986.

10323 WALKER (DAVID MAXWELL). Scottish Courts and Tribunals. Glasg. 2nd edn 1972. 3rd edn 1975.

(c) Punishment and the Penal System

10324 WALKER (NIGEL DAVID). Crime and Punishment in Britain. Edin. 1965.

10325 PLAYFAIR (GILES WILLIAM) and SINGTON (DERRICK). Crime, Punishment and Cure. 1965.

10326 —— The Offenders: The Case against Legal Vengeance. 1957.

10327 —— The Offenders: Society and the Atrocious Crime. 1957.

10328 HINDE (RICHARD STANDISH ELPHINSTONE). The British Penal System 1773–1950. 1951.

10329 HALMOS (PAUL) ed. Sociological Studies in the British Penal System. Keele. 1965.

10330 BOTTOMLEY (ALLAN KEITH). Prison Before Trial: A Study of Remand Decisions in Magistrates' Courts. 1970.

10331 BABINGTON (ANTHONY). The Power to Silence: A History of Punishment in Britain. 1968.

10332 CALLARD (P.). 'Punishment by the State, Its Motives and Form'. *Brit. J. Delinquency* 10 (1959), 36–45.

10333 EDWARDS (JOHN LLEWELYN JONES). 'A New Doctrine in Criminal Punishment'. *Law Q. Rev.* 72, 285 (1956), 117–22.

10334 GARDINER (GERALD). 'The Purpose of Criminal Punishment'. *Mod. Law Rev.* 21, 2, 117–28; 21, 3, 221–35 (1958).

10335 GARLAND (DAVID). Punishment and Welfare: A History of Penal Strategies. Aldershot. 1985.

(d) Prisons, Prisoners, and Prison Officers

10336 WEBB (SIDNEY JAMES) *Baron* Passfield *and* WEBB (BEATRICE). English Prisons under Local Government. 1922.

10337 HOBHOUSE (STEPHEN) *and* BROCKWAY (ARCHIBALD FENNER) *Baron Brockway*. English Prisons To-day: Being the Report of the Prison System Enquiry Committee. 1922.

10338 HOOD (ROGER GRAHAME). 'Social Work in Prison'. *Brit. J. Criminol.* 15 (1975), 227–80.

10339 EDWARDS (ANNE). 'Inmate Adaptations and Socialization in the Prison'. *Sociol.* 4 (1970), 213–25.

10340 BLAXALL (ARTHUR). Suspended Sentence. 1965.

10341 MORRIS (TERENCE PATRICK) *and* MORRIS (PATRICIA). 'The Experience of Imprisonment'. *Brit. J. Criminol.* 2 (1962) 337–60.

10342 MATHIESEN (THOMAS). 'The Sociology of Prisons: Problems for Future Research'. *Brit. J. Sociol.* 17 (1966), 360–79.

10343 KLARE (HUGH JOHN). 'Prison Reform—Retrospect and Prospect'. *Howard J.* 9 (1957), 328–37.

10344 KELLEY (JOANNA). 'Askham Grange—Open Prison for Women'. *Howard J.* 9 (1955), 124–30.

10345 BENSON (C.). 'Report of the Commissioner of Prisons, 1953'. *Howard J.* 9 (1955), 142–6.

10346 BANKS (C.) *et al.* 'Public Attitudes to Crime and the Penal System'. *Brit. J. Criminol.* 15 (1975), 64–6.

10347 VIDLER (JOHN) *and* WOLFF (MICHAEL). If Freedom Fail. 1964.

10348 TURNER (MERFYN LLOYD). A Pretty Sort of Prison. 1964.

10349 RHODES (ALBERT JOHN). Dartmoor Prison: A Record of 126 Years of Prisoner of War and Convict Life, 1806–1932. 1933.

10350 TULLET (TOM). Inside Dartmoor. 1966.

10351 THOMAS (JAMES EDWARD). The English Prison Officer Since 1850: A Study in Conflict. 1972.

10352 SPARKS (RICHARD FRANKLIN). Local Prisons: The Crisis in the English Penal System. 1971.

10353 MORRIS (TERENCE) *and* MORRIS (PAULINE). Pentonville: A Sociological Study of an English prison. 1963.

10354 MORRIS (PAULINE). Prisoners and their Families. 1965.

10355 —— Put Away. 1969.

10356 MIKES (H. GEORGE). Come to Prison. 1957.

10357 NORMAN (FRANK). Lock 'em Up and Count 'em: Reform of the Penal System. 1970.

10358 McCONVILLE (SEAN). The Use of Imprisonment: Essays in the Changing State of English Penal Policy. 1975.

10359 MACARTNEY (WILFRID). Walls Have Mouths: A Record of Ten Year's Penal Servitude. 1936.

10360 KELLEY (JOANNA). When the Gates Shut. 1967.

10361 JONES (HOWARD) *ed.* Society against Crime: Penal Practice in Modern Britain. Harmondsworth. 1981.

10362 HOWARD (DEREK LIONEL). The English Prisons: Their Past and Future. 1960.

10363 —— The Education of Offenders: A Select Bibliography. Camb. 1971.

10364 JONES (ENID HUWS). Margery Fry: The Essential Amateur. Oxf. 1966.

10365 HIGNETT (NORMAN HOWARTH). Portrait in Grey, being a Full Length Portrait of Prison Conditions and Administration, and of the Philosophy which Supports Them . . . 1956.

10366 FITZGERALD (MIKE). Prisoners in Revolt. Harmondsworth. 1977.

10367 FITZGERALD (MIKE) *and* SIM (JOE). British Prisons. Oxf. 1979. 2nd edn 1982.

10368 JONES (HOWARD) *and* CORNES (PAUL) with STOCKFORD (RICHARD). Open Prisons. 1977.

10369 MURRAY (ANNE). Reforming Scotland's Prisons. A Task for the Assembly. Glasg. 1979.

10370 DITCHFIELD (JOHN). Grievance Procedures in Prisons: A Study of Prisoners' Applications and Petitions. 1986.

10371 SCOTTISH HOME AND HEALTH DEPARTMENT. Prisons in Scotland. (1959 report.) Edin. 1960.

10372 —— Prisons in Scotland (1962 report.) Edin. 1963.

10373 —— Organisation of After-Care in Scotland. Report of a Committee of the Scottish Advisory Council on the Treatment of Offenders. Edin. 1963.

10374 —— The Extension of Compulsory After-Care to Additional Categories of Inmates and Prisoners. Report of a Committee of the Scottish Advisory Council on the Treatment of Offenders. Edin. 1961.

10375 —— Use of Short Sentences of Imprisonment by the Courts. Report of a Committee of the Scottish Advisory Council on the Treatment of Offenders. Edin. 1960.

10376 FIELD (XENIA). Under Lock and Key: A Study of Women in Prison. 1960.

10377 EMERY (FREDERICK EDMUND). Freedom and Justice Within Walls: The Bristol Prison Experiment. 1970.

10378 GREW (BENJAMIN DIXON). Prisoner Governor. 1958.

10379 EVANS (PETER). Prison Crisis. 1980.

10380 CREW (ALBERT). London Prisons of Today and Yesterday: Plain Facts and Coloured Impressions. 1933.

10381 BEAN (PHILIP). Rehabilitation and Deviance. 1976.

10382 —— Punishment: A Philosophical and Criminological Inquiry. Oxf. 1981.

10383 CROSS (ALFRED RUPERT NEALE). Punishment, Prison and the Public: An Assessment of Penal Reform in 20th Century England by an Armchair Penologist. 1971.

10384 RUTHERFORD (ANDREW). Prison and the Reductionist Challenge. 1984.

10385 COHEN (STANLEY) *and* TAYLOR (LAURIE). Psychological Survival: The Experience of Long-Term Imprisonment. Harmondsworth. 1972.

10386 CLAYTON (GEROLD FANCOURT). The Wall is Strong. 1958.

10387 CARTER (*Lady* MARY). A Living Soul in Holloway. 1938.

10388 BISHOP (GERTRUDE MURIEL FENNELL). They all Come Out. 1965.

10389 ANDRY (ROBERT GEORGE). The Short-Term Prisoner: A Study in Forensic Psychology. 1963.

10390 —— Delinquency and Parental Pathology: A Study in Forensic and Clinical Psychology. 1960. Rev. edn 1971.

10391 SHORT (RENÉE). The Case of the Long-term Prisoner. 1979.

10392 BLOM-COOPER (LOUIS JACQUES) *ed.* Progress in Penal Reform. Oxf. 1974.

10393 RYAN (MICK). The Acceptable Pressure Group: Inequality in the Penal Lobby: A Case Study of the Howard League and R. A. P. Farnborough. 1978.

10394 BRANDON (RUTH) *and* DAVIES (CHRISTIE). Wrongful Imprisonment: Mistaken Convictions and their Consequences. 1973.

10395 BOTTOMLEY (ALLAN KEITH). Decisions in the Penal Process. 1974.

10396 GARLAND (DAVID) *and* YOUNG (PETER). The Power to Punish 1983.

10397 ATHOLL (JUSTIN). Prison on the Moor: The Story of Dartmoor Prison. 1953.

10398 WADDINGTON (P. A. J.). The Training of Prison Governors. 1983.

10399 HINDE (RICHARD STANDISH ELPHINSTONE). The British Penal System, 1773–1950. 1951.

10400 HALL-WILLIAMS (JOHN ERYLE). The English Penal System in Transition. 1970.

10401 —— Changing Prisons. 1975.

10402 JONES (HOWARD). 'The Prisons in 1960'. *Brit. J. Criminol.* 2 (1962), 393–5.

10403 FOX (*Sir* LIONEL WREAY). The English prisons and Borstal Systems. 1952.

10404 —— The Modern English Prison. 1934.

10405 FRY (SARA MARGERY). The Future Treatment of the Adult Offender. 1944.

10406 KING (ROY DAVID) *and* MORGAN (RODNEY) *with* MARTIN (JOHN POWELL) *and* THOMAS (JAMES EDWARD). The Future of the Prison System. Farnborough. 1980.

10407 KING (ROY DAVID) *and* ELLIOT (KENNETH). Albany: Birth of a Prison—End of an Era. 1977.

10408 KING (ROY DAVID) *and* MORGAN (RODNEY). A Taste of Prison: Custodial Conditions for Trial and Remand Prisoners. 1976.

10409 DAVIES (MARTIN). Prisoners of Society: Attitudes and After-Care. 1974.

10410 PARKER (TONY). Five Women. 1965.

10411 —— A Man of Good Abilities. 1967.

10412 —— The Frying Pan: A Prison and its Prisoners. 1970.

10413 PATERSON (*Sir* ALEXANDER). Paterson on Prisons: Being the Collected Papers of Sir Alexander Paterson. Edited with an Introduction by S. Kenneth Ruck. 1951.

10414 SMITH (KATHLEEN JOAN). A Cure for Crime: The Case of the Self-determinate Prison Sentence. 1965.

10415 SMITH (L. W. MERROW). Prison Screw. 1962.

10416 U.K. The Regime for Long-term Prisoners in Conditions of Maximum Security—Report of the Advisory Council on the Penal System. (The Radzinowicz Report.). 1968.

10417 U.K. Report of the Inquiry into Prison Escapes and Security. (The Mountbatten Report.) Cmnd 3175. 1966.

10418 U.K. People in Prison. Cmnd 4214. 1969.

10419 U.K. ROYAL COMMISSION. On the Penal System in England and Wales. 1964.

10420 U.K. ROYAL COMMISSION. Written Evidence from Government Departments, Miscellaneous Bodies and Individual Witnesses. 1967.

10421 U.K. ROYAL COMMISSION. Minutes of Evidence Taken. 1967.

10422 U.K. HOME OFFICE. The Organisation of the Prison Medical Service: Report of the Working Party. 1964.

10423 U.K. Penal Practice in a Changing Society. Cmnd 645. 1959.

10424 U.K. HOME OFFICE. Report on the Work of the Prison Department. [Pub. annually.].

10425 —— Prisons and Borstals. Statements of Policy and Practice in the Administration of Prison and Borstal Institutions in England and Wales. Rev. edn 1960.

10426 —— Report of the Parole Board. [Pub. annually.].

10427 —— People in Prison. Cmnd 4217. 1969.

10428 —— Prisons and the Prisoner. 1977.

10429 WRIGHT (MARTIN). Making Good: Prisons, Punishment and Beyond. 1982.

10430 WOLFF (MICHAEL). Prison: The Penal Institutions of Britain: Prisons, Borstals, Detention Centres, Approved Schools and Remand Homes. 1967.

10431 WINFIELD (*Sir* PERCY HENRY) *ed.* Penal Reform in England 1940. 2nd edn 1946.

10432 WICKS (H. W.). The Prisoner Speaks. n.d.

10433 WARD (DAVID) *and* KASSENBAUM (GENE). Women's Prisons: Sex and Social Structure. 1966.

10434 BEDFORD (ALAN). 'Women and Parole'. *Brit. J. Criminol.* 14 (1974), 106–17.

10435 GRANT (WILLIAM RUSSELL). Principles of Rehabilitation. Edin. 1963.

10436 CARLEN (PAT). Women's Imprisonment: A Study in Social Control. 1983.

10437 SMITH (ANNE DOROTHEA). Women in Prison: A Study in Penal Methods. 1962.

10438 PARTRIDGE (RALPH). Broadmoor: A History of Criminal Lunacy and its Problems. 1953.

10439 PLAYFAIR (GILES). The Punitive Obsession: An Unvarnished History of the English Prison System. 1971.

10440 ROSE (ARTHUR GORDON). The Struggle for Penal Reform. 1961.

10441 BONE (EDITH). Seven Years Solitary. 1966.

10442 MOTT (JOY). Adult Prisons and Prisoners in England and Wales 1970–1982. 1985.

10443 MELOSSI (DARIO). The Prison and the Factory: Origins of the Penitentiary System. 1981.

10444 GARLAND (DAVID). Punishment and Welfare: A History of Penal Strategies. Aldershot. 1985.

10445 LEGGE (KAREN). 'Work in Prison: The Process of Inversion'. *Brit. J. Criminol.* 18 (1978), 6–22.

10446 STOCKDALE (ERIC). 'A Short History of Prison Inspection in England'. *Brit. J. Criminol.* 23 (1983), 209–28.

10447 McGURK (BARRY) *and* McGURK (RAE). 'Personality Types Among Prisoners and Prison Officers'. *Brit. J. Criminol.* 19 (1979), 31–49.

10448 LAYCOCK (GLORIA). 'Behaviour Modifications in Prisons'. *Brit. J. Criminol.* 19 (1979), 400–15.

10449 FREEMAN (JOHN). Prisons Past and Future. 1978.

10450 WILKINS (LESLIE THOMAS). The Evaluation of Penal Measures. N.Y. 1969.

10451 ROTNER (SHEILA). 'Design for a Women's Prison'. *Howard J.* 11, 2 (1963), 134–44.

10452 JONES (HOWARD). 'Prison Officers as Therapists'. *Howard J.* 12, 1 (1966), 34–41.

10453 HEIDENSOHN (FRANCES). 'Prisons for Women'. *Howard J.* 12, 4 (1969), 281–88.

10454 THOMAS (JAMES EDWARD). 'Hull '76: Observations on the Inquiries into the Prison Riot'. *Howard J.* 16, 3 (1978), 123–33.

10455 KING (ROY DAVID). 'Industrial Relations in the Prison Service'. *Howard J.* 21, 2 (1982), 71–5.

10456 KING (ROY DAVID) *and* MORGAN (RODNEY). 'The Prison System: Prospects for Change'. *Howard J.* 21, 2 (1982), 94–104.

10457 SMITH (DAVID). Life-sentence Prisoners. 1979. HMSO

10458 —— *Et al.* Reducing the Prison Population: An Exploratory Study in Hampshire. H.O. 1984.

10459 SMITH (DAVID), AUSTIN (CLAIRE) *and* DICHFIELD (JOHN). Board of Visitor Adjudications H.O. 1981.

10460 BORNA (SHAHEEN). 'Free Enterprise Goes to Prison'. *Brit. J. Criminol.* 26 (1986), 321–34.

10461 WEST (DONALD JAMES). The Habitual Prisoner. 1963.

(e) Probation and After-Care

10462 JARVIS (FREDERICK VICTOR). Advise, Assist and Befriend: A History of the Probation and After-Care Service. 1972.

10463 WALKER (HILARY) *and* BEAUMONT (BILL). Probation Work: Critical Theory and Socialist Practice. Oxf. 1981.

10464 SOOTHILL (KEITH). The Prisoner's Release: A Study in the Employment of Ex-prisoners. 1974.

10465 SIMON (FRANCES HAMILTON). Prediction Methods in Criminology: Including a Prediction Study of Young Men on Probation. 1971.

10466 SINCLAIR (IAN). Hostels for Probationers. 1971.

10467 SILBERMAN (IAN) *et al.* Explorations in After-care: Home Office Research Studies No. 9. 1971.

10468 PARSLOE (PHYLLIDA). The Work of the Probation and After-Care Officer. 1967.

10469 MONGER (MARK). Casework in After-Care. 1967.

10470 —— Casework in Probation. 1972.

10471 KING (JOAN FAYE SENDALL) *ed.* The Probation and After-care Service 1970. 3rd edn of The Probation Service.

10472 HAXBY (DAVID). Probation: A Changing Service. 1978.

10473 GLOVER (ELIZABETH REAVELEY). Probation and Re-education. 2nd edn 1956.

10474 DE-LA-NOY (MICHAEL). Young Once Only: A Study of Boys on Probation. 1965.

10475 DE'ATH (WILFRID) *ed.* Just Me and Nobody Else. 1966.

10476 DAVIES (MARTIN). Probationers in their Social Environment: A Study of Male Probationers Aged

17–20, Together with an Analysis of those Reconvicted within Twelve Months. 1969.

10477 —— Financial Penalties and Probation. 1970 H.O.R. STUDS. 5.

10478 CAMBRIDGE DEPARTMENT OF CRIMINAL SCIENCE. The Results of Probation. 1958.

10479 BOCHEL (DOROTHY). Probation and After-care: Its Development in England and Wales. Edin. 1976.

10480 BARR (HUGH). Volunteers in Prison After-Care: The Report of the Teamwork Associates. 1971.

10481 Probation Research: A Study of Group Work in the Probation Service. 1966. HMSO

10482 BARR (HUGH) and O₃LEARY (E.). Trends and Regional Comparisons in Probation. 1966.

10483 NEEDHAM (ROBERT). 'Probation Politics'. *Brit. J. Criminol.* 7 (1967), 77–82.

10484 MORTON (H. M.). 'The Trained Social Worker and After-care'. *Howard J.* 9, 1 (1954), 47–51.

10485 DAUNTON-FEAR (MARY). 'Social Inquiry Reports: Comprehensive and Reliable?' *Brit. J. Criminol.* 15 (1975), 128–39.

10486 U.K. HOME OFFICE. Probation and After-Care. Department Report., 1962–3. [HMSO.] Report on the Work of the Probation and After-care Service. Cmnd 5158. 1972.

10487 SCOTLAND 1966 Probation Hostels in Scotland: Final Report by the Scottish Probation Advisory and Training Council. Edin. 1966.

10488 U.K. HOME OFFICE. Residential Provision for Homeless Discharged Offenders. 1966.

10489 SMITH (CYRIL) et al. The Wincroft Youth Project. 1972.

10490 U.K. FIRST REPORT OF THE EXPENDITURE COMMITTEE. Probation and After-Care. 1972.

10491 U.K. HOME OFFICE. The Probation and After-Care Service in a Changing Society. 1976.

10492 WEST (DONALD JAMES) ed. The Future of Parole: Commentaries on Systems in Britain and the USA. 1972.

10493 YOUNG (WARREN). Community Service Orders. 1979.

10494 WILKINS (LESLIE THOMAS) and CARTER (ROBERT). Probation and Parole: Selected Readings. N.Y./Chichester. 1970.

10495 PEASE (KEN). Community Service Orders. 1975.

10496 PRINS (HERSCHEL ALBERT). 'Probation and After-Care'. *Howard J.* 13, 1 (1970), 47–57.

10497 McWILLIAMS (WILLIAM). 'The Mission Transformed: Professionalisation of Probation between the Wars'. *Howard J.* 24, 4 (1985), 257–74.

10498 LEESON (CECIL). The Probation System. 1914.

(f) Young Offenders, Borstals, and Delinquency

10499 HAWKINS (KEITH) and WRIGHT (MARTIN) Comp. Deprivation of Liberty for Young Offenders: A Select Bibliography on Approved Schools, Attendance Centres, Borstals, Detention Centres and Remand Homes, 1940–1965. Camb. 1967.

10500 GOLDBERG (MARY). 'Confrontation Groups in a Girls' Approved School'. *Brit. J. Criminol.* 14 (1974), 132–8.

10501 WILLS (WILLIAM DAVID). The Hawkspar Experiment: An Informal Account of the Training of Adolescents. 1941. 2nd edn 1967.

10502 —— Common Sense About Young Offenders. 1962.

10503 —— Throw Away thy Rod. 1960.

10504 —— A Place Like Home: A Hostel for Disturbed Adolescents. 1970.

10505 —— Spare the Child: The Story of an Experimental Approved School. Harmondsworth. 1971.

10506 ROSE (ARTHUR GORDON). Schools for Young Offenders. 1967.

10507 —— 500 Borstal Boys. Oxf. 1954.

10508 RICHARDSON (HELEN JANE). Adolescent Girls in Approved Schools. 1969.

10509 MILLHAM (SPENCER), BULLOCK (ROGER), and CHERRETT (PAUL). After Grace—Teeth: A Comparative Study of the Residential Experiment of Boys and Approved Schools. 1975.

10510 JOYCE (CYRIL ALFRED). By Courtesy of the Criminal: The Human Approach to the Treatment of Crime. 1955.

10511 —— Fair Play. 1958.

10512 JOYCE (CYRIL ALFRED) and LONGLAND (Sir JOHN LAURENCE). Education and Delinquency. 1956.

10513 WARD (RICHARD HERON). The Hidden Boy: The Work of C. A. Joyce as Headmaster of an Approved School. 1962.

10514 GILL (OWEN). Whitegate: An Approved School in Transition. L/pool. 1974.

10515 —— 'Residential Treatment for Young Offenders: The Boys' Perspectives'. *Brit. J. Criminol.* 14 (1974), 318–35.

10516 FOX (LIONEL WRAY). The English Prison Systems: An Account of the Prison and Borstal System in England and Wales after the Criminal Justice Act 1948, with an Historical Introduction and an Examination of the Principles of Imprisonment as Legal Punishment. 1952.

10517 DUNLOP (ANNE) and McCABE (SARAH). Young Men in Detention Centres. 1965.

10518 BARMAN (S.). The English Borstal System. 1934.

10519 SCOTLAND 1962. Custodial Training for Young Offenders: Report of a Committee of the Scottish

Advisory Council on the Treatment of Offenders. Edin. 1962.

10520 U.K. HOME OFFICE. Detention Centres: Report of the Advisory Council on the Penal System. 1970.

10521 FISHER (ROBERT). The Assessment of the Effects on English Borstal Boys of Different Correctional Training and Treatment Programmes. 1967.

10522 ADAMS (R. H.). Club Life and the Approved School Boy. 1954.

10523 STRATTA (ERICA). The Education of Borstal Boys. 1970.

10524 LOWSON (DAVID MURRAY). City Lads in Borstal: A Study Based on 100 Lads Discharged to Addresses in Liverpool. L/pool. 1970.

10525 HOOD (ROGER GRAHAME). Borstal Re-assessed. 1965.

10526 —— Homeless Borstal Boys: A Study of their After-Care and After-Conduct. 1966.

10527 —— The Research Potential of the Case Records of Approved School Boys: A Detailed Study of the Information Available in the Records of Boys at an Approved School Classifying Centre. 1963.

10528 GORE (ELIZABETH). The Better Fight: The Story of Dame Lilian Barker. 1975.

10529 GIBBENS (TREVOR CHARLES NOEL). Psychiatric Studies of Borstal Lads. 1963.

10530 FARRINGTON (DAVID) *et al.* 'Unemployment, School Leaving and Crime'. *Brit. J. Criminol.* 26 (1986), 335–56.

10531 PRATT (JOHN). 'Diversion from the Juvenile Court'. *Brit. J. Criminol.* 26 (1986), 212–33.

10532 HUFF (GRAHAM) *and* COLLISON (FRANCES). 'Young Offenders, Gambling and Video Game Playing'. *Brit. J. Criminol.* 27 (1987), 401–10.

10533 MORRIS (ALISON). Understanding Juvenile Justice. 1987.

10534 HALL (STUART). Resistance Through Rituals: Youth Sub-cultures in Post-War Britain. 1976.

10535 WALKER (MONICA). 'The Court Disposal of Young Males, by Race, in London in 1983'. *Brit. J. Criminol.* 28 (1988), 441–60.

10536 EYSENCK (SYBIL B. G.) *and* EYSENCK (HANS J.). 'Personality and Recidivism in Borstal Boys'. *Brit. J. Criminol.* 14 (1974), 385–7.

10537 CROOKES (T. G.). 'Burgess "H" Score in Psychiatric Patients'. *Brit. J. Criminol.* 14 (1974), 273–5.

10538 SMITH (DAVID ELLIOTT). 'Relationships between the Eysenck and Personality Inventories'. *Brit. J. Criminol.* 14 (1974), 376–84.

10539 COCKETT (R.). 'Borstal Training: A Follow-up Study'. *Brit. J. Criminol.* 7 (1967), 150–83.

10540 BRADLEY (R. L.). 'The English Borstal System'. *J. Corr. Wk.* 4 (1957), 29–34.

10541 SCOTLAND 1960. Custodial Sentences for Young Offenders: Report. Edin. 1960.

10542 U.K. Advisory Council on the Employment of Prisoners. Work and Vocational Training in Borstals. England and Wales Report. 1962.

10543 FRANKLIN (MARJORIE E.) *ed.* Camp: An Epitome of Experiences at Hawkspur Camp 1936–1940 . . . 1966.

10544 U.K. HOME OFFICE. Directory of Approved Schools, Remand Homes and Special Reception Centres in England and Wales. 1965.

10545 HOBKIRK (E. I. W.). The Training of Girls in the Scottish Borstal System. 1961.

10546 BURT (CYRIL L.). 'The Delinquent Child'. *Child Ag.* (1926), 321–32.

10547 BAGHOT (JOHN HENRY). Juvenile Delinquency: A Comparative Study of the Position in Liverpool and in England and Wales. 1941.

10548 —— Punitive Detention: An Inquiry into the Results of Treatment (Under Section 54 of the Children and Young Persons Act 1939) of Juvenile Delinquents in Liverpool During the Years 1940, 1941, and 1942. 1944.

10549 CARR-SAUNDERS (*Sir* ARTHUR M.), MANNHEIM (HERMANN), *and* RHODES (E. C.). Young Offenders: An Enquiry into Juvenile Delinquency. Camb. 1944.

10550 BOWLBY (EDWARD JOHN MOSTYN). Forty-Four Juvenile Thieves: Their Characters and Home Life. 1946.

10551 MANNHEIM (HERMANN). Juvenile Delinquency in an English Middletown. 1948.

10552 MANNHEIM (HERMANN) *and* WILKINS (LESLIE THOMAS). Prediction Methods in Relation to Borstal Training. 1955.

10553 FERGUSON (THOMAS). The Young Delinquent in his Social Setting: A Glasgow Case study. Oxf. 1952.

10554 JEPHCOTT (AGNES PEARL) *and* CARTER (MICHAEL PERCY). The Social Background of Delinquency. Nottingham. 1954.

10555 GRUNHUT (MAX). Penal Reform. 1948.

10556 —— Juvenile Offenders Before the Courts. Oxf. 1956.

10557 RITCHIE (MARGARET) *and* MACK (JOHN ANDERSON). Police Warnings. Glasg. 1974.

10558 FINE (BENJAMIN). 1,000,000 Delinquents. 1956.

10559 COHEN (ALBERT KIRCIDEL). Delinquent Boys: The Culture of the Gang. 1956.

10560 FORD (DONALD). The Delinquent Child and the Community. 1957.

10561 —— The Deprived Child and the Community. 1955.

10562 MACK (JOHN ANDERSON). Delinquency and the Changing Social Pattern. 1957.

10563 —— Family and Community: A Private Report to the Carnegie United Kingdom Trust Arising out of a

Review of Activities Concerned with Juvenile Delinquency. Glasg. 1953.

10564 TRENAMAN (JOSEPH). Out of Step: A Study of Young Delinquent Soldiers in Wartime: Their Offences, their Background, and their Treatment under an Army Experiment. 1952.

10565 BRENNAN (TOM). 'Cheerful Delinquents and Grey Scrabblers: An Hypothesis on Problem Behaviour'. *Scot. J. Pol. Econ.* 6 (1959), 13–32.

10566 PAGE (I.). 'Hostels for Educationally Sub-Normal Adolescents'. *Soc. Wk.* 18 (1961), 22–5.

10567 WILKINS (LESLIE THOMAS). Delinquent Generations: Studies in the Causes of Delinquency and the Treatment of Offenders. 1960.

10568 FYVEL (TOSCO RAPHAEL). Troublemakers: Rebellious Youth in an Affluent Society. N.Y. 1962.

10569 —— The Insecure Offenders: Rebellious Youth in the Welfare State. 1961. Rev. edn Harmondsworth. 1963.

10570 OSBOROUGH (NIAL). 'Police Discretion not to Prosecute Juveniles'. *Mod. Law Rev.* 28 (1965), 421–31.

10571 SCOTT (PETER D.). 'Juvenile Courts—the Juvenile's Point of View'. *Brit. J. Delinquency* 9 (1959), 200–11.

10572 GIBBENS (TREVOR CHARLES NOEL) *with* MARRIAGE (A.) *and* WALKER (A.). Psychiatric Studies of Borstal Lads. 1963.

10573 GIBBENS (TREVOR CHARLES NOEL) *and* AHRENFELDT (ROBERT HENRY) *eds.* Cultural Factors in Delinquency. 1966.

10574 —— *Et al.* Medical Remands in the Criminal Court. Oxf. 1977.

10575 GIBBS (JACK P.). 'Conceptions of Deviant Behaviour: The Old and the New'. *Pacific Sociol. Rev.* 9 (1966), 9–14.

10576 —— 'Crime, Unemployment and Status Integration'. *Brit. J. Criminol.* 6 (1966), 47–58.

10577 STOKES (SEWELL). Our Dear Delinquents. 1965.

10578 SARGENT (WILLIAM EWART) *ed.* Adolescent Problems: Their Nature and Understanding. 1964.

10579 WIENDER (R. S. P.). Drugs and Schoolchildren. 1970.

10580 WALTER (J. A.). Sent Away: A Study of Young Offenders in Court. Farnborough. 1978.

10581 MAYS (JOHN BARRON). Growing Up in the City: A Study of Juvenile Delinquency in an Urban Neighbourhood. L/pool. 1954. 3rd rev. edn 1964.

10582 —— *Ed.* Juvenile Delinquency, the Family and the Social Group: A Reader. 1972.

10583 —— On the Threshold of Delinquency. L/pool. 1959.

10584 MILLER (DEREK). Growth to Freedom: The Psychological Treatment of the Delinquent Youth . . . 1964.

10585 PATCHETT (KENNETH WILLIAM) *and* MACLEAN (J. D.). 'Decision-making in Juvenile Cases'. *Criminal Law Rev.* (1965), 699.

10586 HUTCHESON (B. R.) *et al.* 'A Prognostic (predictive) Classification of Juvenile Court First Offenders Based on a Follow Up Study'. *Brit. J. Criminol.* 6 (1966), 354–63.

10587 STOTT (DENIS HERBERT). 'Delinquency and Cultural Stress'. *Brit. J. Soc. Clin. Psychol.* 1 (1962), 182–91.

10588 —— 'The Prediction of Delinquency from Non-Delinquent Behaviour'. *Brit. J. Delinq.* 10 (1962), 1–16.

10589 —— 'Delinquency, Maladjustment and Unfavourable Ecology'. *Brit. J. Psychol.* 51 (1960), 157–70.

10590 FARRINGTON (DAVID PHILIP), OSBORN (S. G.), *and* WEST (DONALD JAMES). 'The Persistence of Labelling Effects'. *Brit. J. Criminol.* 18 (1978), 277–84.

10591 McCLINTOCK (FREDERICK HEMMINGS). Attendance Centres. 1961.

10592 DUNLOP (ANNE B.) *and* MCCABE (SARAH). Young Women in Detention Centres. 1965.

10593 BALDWIN (JOHN). 'Delinquent Schools in Tower Hamlets: A Critique'. *Brit. J. Criminol.* 13 (1972), 399–402.

10594 BELSON (WILLIAM ALBERT). 'The Extent of Stealing by London Boys'. *Advancement of Science* 25 (1968), 171–84.

10595 WALKER (NIGEL). Adolescent Maladjustment. 1963.

10596 WILSON (HARRIET L.). Delinquency and Child Neglect. 1962.

10597 WHITELEY (STUART), BRIGGS (DENNIS), *and* TURNER (MERFYN). Dealing with Delinquents. 1972.

10598 BAGLEY (CHRISTOPHER). Dealing with Delinquents. 1972.

10599 DOUGLAS (JAMES WILLIAM BRUCE) *et al.* 'Delinquency and Social Class'. *Brit. J. Criminol.* 6 (1966).

10600 LITTLE (W. R.) *and* NTSEKHE (V. R.). 'Social Class Backgrounds of Young Offenders from London'. *Brit. J. Criminol.* 10 (1959), 130–5.

10601 McDONALD (MARY LYNN). Social Class and Delinquency. 1969.

10602 MARSHALL (TONY) *and* MASON (ALAN). 'A Framework for the Analysis of Juvenile Delinquency Causation'. *Brit. J. Sociol.* 19 (1968), 130–42.

10603 RUTTER (MICHAEL) *and* GILLER (HENRY). Juvenile Delinquency: Trends and Perspectives. Harmondsworth. 1983.

10604 DOWNES (DAVID MALCOLM) *and* ROCK (PAUL ELLIOT). Deviant Interpretations. Oxf. 1979.

10605 —— The Delinquent Solution: A Study in Subcultural Theory. 1966.

10606 SHAW (OTTO LESLIE). Maladjusted Boys. 1965.

10607 —— Youth in Crisis: A Radical Approach to Delinquency. 1966.

10608 —— Prisoners of the Mind. 1969.

10609 BISS (PETER). Social Policy and the Young Delinquent. 1967.

10610 WEST (DONALD JAMES). Present Conduct and Future Delinquency: First Report of the Cambridge Study in Delinquent Development. 1969.

10611 WEST (DONALD JAMES) *and* FARRINGTON (DAVID PHILIP). Who Becomes Delinquent?: Second Report of the Cambridge Study in Delinquent Development. 1973.

10612 —— The Delinquent Way of Life: Third Report of the Cambridge Study in Delinquent Development. 1977.

10613 BEERMAN (RENÉ). 'Juvenile Delinquency in Great Britain and the USSR'. *Coexistence* 3 (1966), 249–60.

10614 —— Delinquency: Its Roots, Causes and Prospects. 1982.

10615 PEARCE (JOHN DALZIEL WYNDHAM). Juvenile Delinquency: A Short Text-Book on the Medical Aspects of Juvenile Delinquency. 1952.

10616 WEST (DONALD JAMES). The Young Offender. 1967.

10617 —— The Habitual Offender. 1963.

10618 PATRICK (JAMES). A Glasgow Gang Observed. 1973.

10619 COHEN (STANLEY). 'The Teddy Boys'. In 'The Age of Affluence, 1951–1964' by Vernon Bogdanor and Robert Skidelsky. 1970.

10620 PHILLIPSON (MICHAEL). Sociological Aspects of Crime and Delinquency. 1971.

10621 COWIE (JOHN), COWIE (VALERIE), *and* SLATER (ELIOT). Delinquency in Girls. 1971.

10622 CARSON (WESLEY GEORGE) *and* WILES (PAUL). Crime and Delinquency in Britain: Sociological Readings. 1971.

10623 —— Later edition with the title 'The Sociology of Crime and Delinquency in Britain'. Vol. 1 'The British Tradition'. 1976. Vol. 2 'The New Criminologies'. 1976.

10624 DAVIES (JEAN). Girl Offenders Aged 17 to 20 Years. 1972.

10625 BOTTOMS (ANTHONY EDWARD) *and* McCLINTOCK (FREDERICK HEMMINGS). Criminals Coming of Age: A Study of Institutional Adaptation in the Treatment of Adolescent Offenders. 1973.

10626 COHEN (STANLEY) *and* YOUNG (JOCK). The Manufacture of News: Social Problems, Deviance and the Mass Media. 1973.

10627 GATH (DENNIS) *et al.* Child Guidance and Delinquency in a London Borough. 1977.

10628 BLACKMORE (JOHN). 'Relationship Between Self-Reported Delinquency and Official Convictions among Adolescent Boys'. *Brit. J. Criminol.* 14 (1974), 376–84.

10629 COHEN (STANLEY) *ed.* Images of Deviance. Harmondsworth. 1971.

10630 —— Folk Devils and Moral Panics: The Creation of the Mods and Rockers. 1972. 2nd edn 1980.

10631 BOTTOMS (ANTHONY EDWARD). 'Delinquency among Immigrants'. *Race* 8 (1967), 357–83.

10632 BATTA (I.D.) *et al.* 'Study of Juvenile Delinquency amongst Asians and Half-Asians: A Comparative Study in a Northern Town, Based on Official Statistics'. *Brit. J. Criminol.* 15 (1975), 34–42.

10633 BELSON (WILLIAM ALBERT). Juvenile Theft: The Causal Factors. 1975.

10634 MORRIS (ALISON), GILLER (HENRY), GILLER (ELIZABETH), *and* GEACH (HUGH). Justice for Children. 1980.

10635 DOUGLAS (JAMES WILLIAM BRUCE) *et al.* 'Delinquency and Social Class'. *Brit. J. Criminol.* 6 (1966), 294–302.

10636 GLATT (MAX MEIER). 'Alcoholism, Crime and Juvenile Delinquency'. *Brit. J. Delinquency.* 9 (1958), 84–93.

10637 PALMAI (G.) *et al.* 'Social Class and the Young Offender'. *Brit. J. Psychiatry* 113 (1967), 1072–82.

10638 POLSKY (HOWARD W.). 'Changing Delinquent Subcultures: A Social-psychological Approach'. *Soc. Wk.* 4 (1959), 3–16.

10639 GOLDSMITH (A. O.). 'Challenges of Delinquency Casework Treatment'. *Soc. Wk.* 4 (1959), 14–20.

10640 POWER (MICHAEL JOHN) *et al.* 'Neighbourhood, School and Juveniles Before the Courts'. *Brit. J. Criminol.* 12 (1972), 111–32.

10641 WALLIS (C. P.) *and* MALIPHANT (RODNEY). 'Delinquent Areas in the County of London: Ecological Factors'. *Brit. J. Criminol.* 7 (1967), 250–84.

10642 WARDROP (KEITH R. H.). 'Delinquent Teenage Types'. *Brit. J. Criminol.* 7 (1967), 371–80.

10643 MORRIS (ALISON). Providing Criminal Justice for Children. 1983.

10644 PARKER (HOWARD), CASBURN (MAGGIE), *and* TURNBULL (DAVID). Receiving Juvenile Justice. Oxf. 1981.

10645 MARTIN (FREDERICK MORRIS) *and* MURRAY (KATHLEEN) *eds.* The Scottish Juvenile Justice System. Edin. 1982.

10646 DOWNES (DAVID MALCOLM). Delinquent Subcultures in East London. 1964.

10647 —— The Delinquent Solution: A Study in Subcultural Theory. 1966.

10648 LITTLE (A.). 'The Prevalence of Recorded Delinquency and Recidivism in England and Wales'. *Amer. Sociol. Rev.* 30 (1965), 260–3.

10649 —— 'Penal Theory, Penal Reform and Borstal Practice'. *Brit. J. Criminol.* 3 (1963), 257–75.

10650 CAVENAGH (WINIFRED ELIZABETH). The Child and the Court. 1959.

10651 —— *Et al.* The Problem Family. 1958.

10652 BURNS (CHARLES C.). Maladjusted Children. 1955.

10653 VODOPIVEC (KATJA). Maladjusted Youth: An Experiment in Rehabilitation. Farnborough. 1974.

10654 HOOD (ROGER GRAHAME) *and* SPARKS (RICHARD FRANKLIN) *eds.* Community Homes and the Approved School System. Papers Presented to the Cropwood Round Table Conference, Cambridge Institute of Criminology. 1979.

10655 —— *Eds.* The Residential Treatment of Disturbed and Delinquent Boys. Papers Presented to the Cropwood Round Table Conference, Cambridge Institute of Criminology. 1968.

10656 SCOTTISH ADVISORY COUNCIL on the TREATMENT and REHABILITATION of OFFENDERS—Approved Schools. Edin. 1947.

10657 SCOTTISH HOME DEPARTMENT. Custodial Sentences for Young Offenders. Report of a Committee of the Scottish Advisory Council on the Treatment of Offenders. 1960.

10658 MUNCIE (JOHN). The Trouble with Kids Today. 1984.

10659 CAMPBELL (ANNE). Girl Delinquents. Oxf. 1981.

10660 WARD (COLIN). Vandalism. 1973.

10661 CLARKE (R. V. G.). Tackling Vandalism. 1978.

10662 MARTIN (FREDERICK MORRIS). Children Out of Court. Edin. 1981.

10663 WILKINS (LESLIE THOMAS). Delinquent Generations. 1960.

10664 HUMPHRIES (STEVE). Hooligans or Rebels? Oxf. 1981.

10665 PEARSON (GEOFFREY). Hooligan: A History of Respectable Fears. 1983.

10666 MARSH (PETER). Aggro: The Illusion of Violence. 1978.

10667 ROBINS (DAVID) *and* COHEN (PHILIP). Knuckle Sandwich: Growing Up in the Working Class City. 1978.

10668 MARTIN (FREDERICK MORRIS) *and* MURRAY (KATHLEEN). Children's Hearings. Edin. 1976.

10669 COCKETT (R.). Drug Abuse and Personality in Young Offenders. 1971.

10670 VELARDE (ALBERT). 'Do Delinquents Really Drift?' *Brit. J. Criminol.* 18 (1978), 23–39.

10671 FISCHER (C. J.) *and* MAWBY (ROB). 'Juvenile Delinquency and Police Discretion in an Inner-City Area'. *Brit. J. Criminol.* 22 (1982), 63–75.

10672 MORASH (MERRY). 'Gangs, Groups and Delinquency'. *Brit. J. Criminol.* 23 (1983), 309–31.

10673 GIBBENS (TREVOR CHARLES NOEL). 'Borstal Boys After 25 Years'. *Brit. J. Criminol.* 24 (1984), 44–62.

10674 LANDAU (SIMHA F.). 'Juveniles and the Police'. *Brit. J. Criminol.* 21 (1981), 27–46.

10675 TRIVIZAS (EUGENE). 'Offences and Offenders in Football Crowd Disorders'. *Brit. J. Criminol.* 20 (1980), 276–88.

10676 —— 'Sentencing the "Football Hooligan"'. *Brit. J. Criminol.* 21 (1981), 342–9.

10677 —— 'Disturbances Associated with Football Matches: Types of Incidents and Selection of Charges'. *Brit. J. Criminol.* 24 (1984), 361–83.

10678 WALKER (ANNELISE). 'Delinquent and Maladjusted Girls'. *Howard J.* 11 (1962), 22–36.

10679 BARBOUR (ROBERT F.). 'The Young Offenders'. *Howard J.* 11 (1962), 41–6.

10680 MAY (MARGARET). 'Delinquent and Maladjusted Girls'. *Howard J.* 11,2 (1963), 145–8.

10681 COHEN (STANLEY). 'Mods, Rockers and the Rest'. *Howard J.* 12 (1967), 121–30.

10682 CRAFT (MICHAEL). 'The Treatment of Adolescents with Personality Disorders'. *Howard J.* 11 (1963), 47–57.

10683 HOLLOWAY (VERNON). 'Institutional Treatment of Young Offenders'. *Howard J.* 12 (1969), 270–80.

10684 EVANS (DAVID JOHN). Geographical Perspectives on Juvenile Delinquency. Farnborough. 1980.

(g) Police

10685 SOLMES (ALWYN). The English Policeman 1871–1941. 1935.

10686 THOMSON (*Sir* BASIL HOME). The Scene Changes. 1937.

10687 JUDGE (ANTHONY). A Source Book of Police. 1976.

10688 HART (JENNIFER MARGARET MURRAY). The British Police. 1951.

10689 HOWARD (GEORGE). Guardians of the Queen's Peace: The Development and Work of Britain's Police. 1953.

10690 REITH (CHARLES). A New Study of Police History. Edin. 1956.

10691 U.K. ROYAL COMMISSION ON THE POLICE. Final Report. Cmnd 1728. 1962.

10692 POLLARD (DAVID W.). 'The Police Act 1964'. *Public Law* (spring 1966), 35–64.

10693 WHITAKER (BENJAMIN CHARLES GEORGE). The Police. 1964.

10694 PULLING (CHARLES ROBERT DRUCE). Mr Punch and the Police. 1964.

10695 HEARN (CYRIL VICTOR). A Duty to the Public: A Frank Assessment of Today's Police Force. 1965.

10696 MINTO (GEORGE ARCHIBLAD). The Thin Blue Line. 1965.

10697 CRITCHLEY (THOMAS ALAN). A History of Police in England and Wales, 1900–1966. 1967.

10698 —— The Conquest of Violence: Order and Liberty in Britain. 1970.

10699 MARTIN (JOHN POWELL) *and* WILSON (GAIL). The Police: A Study in Manpower: The Evolution of the Service in England and Wales, 1825–1965. 1969.

10700 FOWLER (PETER NORMAN). Police in the Seventies. 1970.

10701 EVANS (PETER C. C.). The Police Revolution. 1974.

10702 WILCOX (A. F.). 'Police 1964–1973'. *Crim. Law Rev.* (1974), 144–57.

10703 PURCELL (WILLIAM ERNEST). British Police in a Changing Society. 1974.

10704 MORTER (PETER). The Police. 1976.

10705 HOLDAWAY (SIMON) ed. The British Police. 1979.

10706 —— Inside the British Police: A Force at Work. 1983.

10707 MANNING (PETER KIRBY). Police Work: The Social Organisation of Policing. 1977.

10708 REYNOLDS (GERALD WILLIAM) and JUDGE (ANTHONY). The Night the Police went on Strike. 1968.

10709 WHITTLE (PETER). Dark Blue for Courage: With Contributory Articles by . . . Kelwyn Cosway and others. Maidstone. 1966.

10710 HAIN (PETER) ed. Policing the Police. 1979.

10711 BROGDEN (MICHAEL). The Police: Autonomy and Consent. 1982.

10712 MANWARING-WHITE (SARAH). The Policing Revolution: Police Technology, Democracy and Liberty. Brighton. 1983.

10713 BROWN (JOHN). Policing by Multi-racial Consent: The Handsworth Experiment. 1982.

10714 MARK (*Sir* ROBERT). Policing a Perplexed Society. 1977.

10715 —— In the Office of Constable. 1978.

10716 JACKSON (*Sir* RICHARD) Occupied with Crime. 1967.

10717 BROWNLIE (ALISTAIR R.) ed. Crime Investigation: Art or Science? Edin./Lond. 1984.

10718 JUDGE (ANTHONY). A Man Apart: The British Policeman and his Job. 1972.

10719 —— The First Fifty Years. [Police Federation.] 1969.

10720 MARSHALL (GEOFFREY). Police and Government: The Status and the Accountability of the English Constable. 1965.

10721 BALDWIN (ROBERT) and KINSEY (RICHARD). Police Powers and Politics. 1982.

10722 BOX (STEVEN) and RUSSELL (K.). 'Politics of Accountability: Disarming Complaints Against the Police'. *Sociol. Rev.* 23 (1945), 315–46.

10723 BROWN (JOHN) and HOWES (GRAHAM). The Police and the Community. 1964.

10724 FOWLER (PETER NORMAN). After the Riots: The Police in Europe. 1979.

10725 CLARKE (C. F. O.) ed. Police/Community Relations: Report of a Conference . . . Ditchley Park. 1970.

10726 ROLPH (CECIL HEWITT) comp. The Police and the Public. 1962.

10727 TOBIAS (JOHN JACOB). 'Police and Public in the United Kingdom'. *J. Contemp. Hist.* 7 (1972), 201–19.

10728 CAIN (MAUREEN ELIZABETH). Society and the Policeman's Role. 1973.

10729 BELSON (WILLIAM ALBERT). The Public and the Police. 1975.

10730 FRIEDLANDER (CECIL PAUL) and MITCHELL (EDWARD). The Police: Servants or Masters? 1974.

10731 ALDERSON (JOHN COTTINGHAM). 'The Role of the Police in Society'. *J. Roy. United Services Institute for Defence Studies* cxviii (1973), 18–24.

10732 ALDERSON (JOHN COTTINGHAM) and STEAD (PHILIP JOHN). The Police We Deserve. 1973.

10733 ACKROYD (CAROL), MARGOLIS (KAREN), ROSENHEAD (JONATHAN) and SHALLICE (TIM). The Technology of Police Control. Harmondsworth. 1977. 2nd edn London. 1980.

10734 BOWES (STUART). The Police and Civil Liberties. 1966.

10735 BUNYAN (TONY). The History and Practice of the Political Police in Britain. 1976.

10736 POPE (DAVID WATTS) and WEINDER (NORMAN L.) eds. Modern Policing. 1981.

10737 HEWITT (WILLIAM H.). British Police Administration. Springfield, Ill. 1965.

10738 CONLIN (JAMES). Local and Central Government: Police Administration. 1967.

10739 U.K. HOME OFFICE. Report of a Working Party on Police Cadets. 1965.

10740 U.K. HOME OFFICE. Police Manpower, Equipment and Efficiency Reports. 1967.

10741 U.K. HOME OFFICE. The Recruitment of People with Higher Educational Qualifications into the Police Service. 1967.

10742 MARTIENSSEN (ANTHONY KENNETH). Crime and the Police. 1951.

10743 WILLIAMS (DAVID GLYNDWR TUDOR). Keeping the Peace: The Police and Public Order. 1967.

10744 —— 'The Police and Law Enforcement'. *Crim. Law Rev.* (1968), 351–62.

10745 SPEED (PETER FREDERICK). Police and Prisons. 1968.

10746 STEER (DAVID). Police Cautions—A Study in the Exercise of Police Discretion. Oxf. 1970.

10747 MORIARTY (CECIL CHARLES HUDSON). Police Procedure and Administration. 1930. 6th edn 1955.

10748 MARTIN (JOHN POWELL) and WILSON (GAIL). The Police: A Study in Manpower: The Evolution of the Service in England and Wales. 1969.

10749 DILMOT (GEORGE). Scotland Yard: Its History and Organisation, 1829–1929. 1929.

10750 MOYLAN (*Sir* JOHN FITZGERALD). Scotland Yard and the Metropolitan Police. Whitehall Series. 1929. Rev. edn 1934.

10751 FALLON (THOMAS). The River Police: The Story of Scotland Yard's Little Ships. 1956.

10752 BROWNE (DOUGLAS GORDON). The Rise of Scotland Yard: A History of the Metropolitan Police. 1956.

10753 SCOTT (*Sir* HAROLD RICHARD). Scotland Yard. 1957.

10754 SCOTT (*Sir* HAROLD RICHARD) *and* PEARCE (PHILIPPA). From Inside Scotland Yard. 1963.

10755 HOWE (*Sir* RONALD MARTIN). The Story of Scotland Yard: A History of the C.I.D. from the Earliest Times to the Present Day. 1965.

10756 LAURIE (PETER). Scotland Yard: A Personal Inquiry. 1970.

10757 COX (BARRY), SHIRLEY (JOHN), *and* SHORT (MARTIN). The Fall of Scotland Yard. Harmondsworth. 1977.

10758 MITCHELL (D. J. B.). 'The Constitutional Position of the Police in Scotland'. *Juridical Rev.* (1962), 1–20.

10759 JONES (JAMES OWAIN). The History of the Caernarvonshire Constabulary 1856–1950. Caernarvon. 1963.

10760 BETH (RONALD). The Specials: History of the Special Constabulary in England, Wales and Scotland. 1961.

10761 SILLITOE (*Sir* PERCY). Cloak without Dagger. 1955.

10762 HEZLET (*Sir* ARTHUR). The 'B' Specials: A History of the Ulster Special Constabulary. 1972.

10763 GRANT (DOUGLAS). The Thin Blue Line: A History of the City of Glasgow Police. 1973.

10764 MATHEW (*Sir* THEOBALD). The Office and Duties of the Director of Public Prosecutions. 1950.

10765 ANDREWS (ALLEN). The Prosecutor: The Life of M. P. Pugh, Prosecuting Solicitor and Agent for the Director of Public Prosecutions. 1968.

10766 REINER (ROBERT). The Politics of the Police. 1984.

10767 STEAD (PHILIP JOHN). The Police of Britain. 1985.

10768 FINE (BEN). *Ed.* Policing the Miner's Strike. 1985.

10769 GEARY (ROGER). Policing Industrial Disputes: 1893 to 1985. Camb. 1985.

10770 DRAPER (HILARY). Private Police. 1978.

10771 SOUTH (NIGEL). Policing for Profit: The Private Security Sector. 1988.

10772 GORDON (PAUL). Policing Scotland. Glasg. 1980.

10773 HEAL (KEVIN). 'The Police, the Public and the Prevention of Crime'. *Howard J.* 22 (1981), 91–100.

10774 BALDWIN (JOHN) *and* LENG (ROGER). 'Police Powers and the Citizen'. *Howard J.* 23 (1984), 88–98.

10775 LAYCOCK (GLORIA) *and* TARLING (ROGER). 'Police Force Cautioning: Policy and Practice'. *Howard J.* 24 (1985), 81–92.

10776 BROGDEN (MIKE). 'The Emergence of the Police: The Colonial Dimension'. *Brit. J. Criminol.* 27 (1987), 4–14.

10777 CHATERTON (MICHAEL). 'Assessing Police Effectiveness—Future Prospects'. *Brit. J. Criminol.* 27 (1987), 80–6.

10778 MORGAN (RODNEY). 'Police Accountability: Developing the Local Infrastructure'. *Brit. J. Criminol.* 27 (1987), 87–96.

10779 SIMEY (MARGARET). Democracy Rediscovered: A Study in Police Accountability. 1988.

10780 CLAYTON (RICHARD). Civil Action Against the Police. 1987.

10781 FITZGERALD (MIKE). Stranger on the Line: The Secret History of Phone Tapping. 1987.

10782 LONDON DEPARTMENT OF TRANSPORT. Crime on the London Underground. 1986.

10783 SMALL (STEPHEN). Police and People in London. 1983.

10784 AINSWORTH (PETER). Police Work. 1987.

10785 ASCOLI (DAVID). The Queen's Peace. The Origins and Development of the Metropolitan Police 1829–1979. 1979.

10786 TANCRED (EDITH). Women Police. 1951.

10787 PRINCE (MICHAEL). God's Cop: The Biography of James Anderton. 1988.

10788 STALKER (JOHN). Stalker. 1988.

(h) Murder

10789 GILLIES (HUNTER). 'Murder in the West of Scotland'. *Brit. J. Psychiatry* 3 (1965), 1087–94.

10790 HOLLIS (MAURICE CHRISTOPHER). The Homicide Act: With a Foreword by Gerald Gardiner. 1964.

10791 MORRIS (TERENCE PATRICK) *and* BLOM-COOPER (LOUIS JACQUES). A Calendar of Murder: Criminal Homicide in England Since 1957.

10792 WEST (DONALD JAMES). Murder Followed by Suicide: An Inquiry . . . 1965.

10793 LEGAL RESEARCH UNIT. Criminal Homicide in England and Wales, 1957–1968. 1969.

10794 JOHNSON (PAMELA HANSFORD). On Iniquity: Some Personal Reflections Arising out of the Moors Murder Trial. 1967.

10795 HUGGETT (RENÉE) *and* BERRY (PAUL). Daughters of Cain: The Story of Eight Women Executed Since Edith Thompson in 1923. 1956.

10796 GIBSON (EVELYN) *and* KLEIN (SYDNEY). Murder, 1957 to 1968: A Home Office Statistical Division Report on Murder in England and Wales (with an annex by the Scottish Home and Health Department on Murder in Scotland). 1969.

10797 FIRMIN (STANLEY). Murderers in Our Midst. 1965.

10798 NEUSTATTER (W. LINDESEY). The Mind of the Murderer. 1957.

10799 CAMP (JOHN). One Hundred Years of Medical Murder. 1982.

10800 DELL (SUSANNE). Murder into Manslaughter. The Diminished Responsibility Defence in Practice. Oxf. 1984.

10801 HEWLINGS (DAVID). 'The Treatment of Murderers'. *Howard J.* 13 (1971), 96–106.

(i) Suicide

10802 STENGEL (ERWIN) *and* COOK (NANCY GWENDOLYN). Attempted Suicide: Its Social Significance and Effects. 1958.

10803 STENGEL (ERWIN). Suicide and Attempted Suicide. Harmondsworth. 1964.

10804 MAXWELL-ATKINSON (J.). 'Suicide, Status Integration and Pseudo-Science'. *Sociology* 7 (1973), 437–45.

10805 —— 'On the Sociology of Suicide'. *Sociol. Rev.* 16 (1968), 83–92.

10806 —— Discovering Suicide. 1978.

10807 BAGLEY (CHRISTOPHER) *and* GREEN (STEVEN). '"Black Suicide": A Report of 25 English Cases and Controls'. *J. Soc. Psychol.* 86 (1972), 175–9.

10808 McCORMICK (GEORGE DONALD KING). The Unseen Killer: A Study of Suicide, its History, Causes and Cures. 1964.

10809 GIDDENS (ANTHONY) ed. The Sociology of Suicide: A Selection of Readings. 1971.

10810 ST JOHN-STEVAS (NORMAN HENRY ANTHONY). The Right to Life. 1963.

10811 KOBLER (ARTHUR L.) *and* STOLAND (EZRA). The End of Hope: A Sociological-Clinical Study of Suicide. 1964.

10812 HILLMAN (JAMES). Suicide and the Soul. 1964.

10813 ALVAREZ (ALFRED). The Savage God: A Study of Suicide. 1972.

10814 BALFOUR SCLARE (A.) *and* HAMILTON (C. M.). 'Attempted Suicide in Glasgow'. *Brit. J. Psychiatry* 109 (462) (1963), 609–15.

10815 SAINSBURY (PETER). Suicide in London: An Ecological Study. 1955.

10816 BIRTCHNELL (JOHN) *and* ALAREON (JOSÉ). 'Depression and Attempted Suicide: A Study of 91 Cases Seen in a Casualty Department'. *B. J. Psychiatry* 118 (544) (1971), 289–96.

10817 CRESSWELL (PETER). 'Interpretations of "Suicide"'. *Brit. J. Sociol.* 23 (2) (1972), 133–45.

10818 SEAGER (CHARLES PHILIP) *and* FLOOD (R. ANTHONY). 'Suicide in Bristol'. *Brit. J. Psychiatry* 3 (479) (1965), 919–32.

10819 CHESSER (EUSTACE). Living with Suicide. 1967.

10820 HAIM (ANDRE). Adolescent Suicide. 1974.

10821 HENDIN (HERBERT). Black Suicide. 1970.

10822 McCULLOCH (WALLACE). Suicidal Behaviour. Oxf. 1972.

10823 FARRIER (RICHARD) *and* HIRSCH (STEVEN). The Suicide Syndrome. 1980.

(j) Drugs

10824 U.K. ADVISORY COMMITTEE ON DRUG DEPENDENCE. Report on Cannabis. 1968.

10825 GLATT (MAX MEIER) *et al.* The Drug Scene in Great Britain. 1967.

10826 —— Ed. Drug Dependence: Current Problems and Issues. Lancaster. 1977.

10827 —— A Guide to Addiction and its Treatment. Lancaster. 1974.

10828 BEAN (PHILIP). The Social Control of Drugs. 1974.

10829 HENRY (B. C.). 'Helping Women Addicts at the Coke Hill, England'. *Inl. J. Offend. Therapy* 18 (1974), 68–76.

10830 TEFF (HARVEY). Drugs, Society and the Law. Farnborough. 1975.

10831 BAKALAR (JAMES B.). Drug Control in a Free Society. Camb. 1984.

10832 YOUNG (JOCK). The Drugtakers: The Social Meaning of Drug Use. 1971.

10833 EDWARDS (GRIFFITH) *and* BUSCH (CAROL). Drug Problems in Britain. A Review of Ten Years. 1981.

10834 INGLIS (BRIAN). The Forbidden Game. A Social History of Drugs. 1975.

10835 LORD (RICHARD). Controlled Drugs: Law and Practice. 1984.

10836 LYDIATE (P. W. H.). The Law Relating to the Misuse of Drugs. 1977.

10837 GIBBENS (TREVOR CHARLES NOEL). 'The Misuse of Drugs'. *Howard J.* 11 (1965), 257–61.

10838 WILKINS (LESLIE THOMAS). 'A Behavioural Theory of Drug Taking'. *Howard J.* 11 (1965), 262–73.

10839 MACGREGOR (SUSANNE). Drugs and British Society: Responses to a Social Problem in the 1980's. 1989.

(k) Sexual Offences

10840 CAMBRIDGE UNIVERSITY DEPARTMENT OF CRIMINAL SCIENCE. Sexual Offences: A Report. 1957.

10841 CHURCH OF ENGLAND MORAL WELFARE COUNCIL. Sexual Offenders and Social Punishment. 1956.

10842 BLOM-COOPER (LOUIS JACQUES). 'Prostitution: A Socio-legal Comment on the Case of Dr Ward'. *Brit. J. Sociol.* 15 (1964), 65–71.

10843 MARSHALL (HONOR). Twilight London: A Study in Degradation. 1971.

10844 HINES (N.). Lost Girls. 1955.

10845 HALL (GLADYS MARY). Prostitution: A Survey and a Challenge. 1933.

10846 GOSLING (JOHN) *and* WARNER (DOUGLAS). The Shame of a City: An Inquiry into the Vice of London. 1960. Repr. 1963.

10847 ROLPH (CECIL HEWITT) *ed.* Women of the Streets: A Sociological Study of the Common Prostitute. 1955.

10848 HALL (JEAN GRAHAM). 'The Prostitute and the Law'. *Brit. J. Delinquency* 9 (1959), 174–81.

10849 MCINTOSH (MARY). 'Vagrancy and Street Offences'. *Brit. J. Criminol.* 15 (1975), 280–4.

10850 ROWSE (ALFRED LESLIE). Homosexuals in History. A Study of Ambivalence in Society, Literature and the Arts. 1977.

10851 CRANE (PAUL). Gays and the Law. 1982.

10852 NEUSTATTER (W. LINDESEY). 'Homosexuality'. *Howard J.* 10 (1958), 18–25.

10853 SANDFORD (JEREMY). Prostitutes: Portraits of People in the Sexploitation Business. 1975.

10854 GIBBENS (TREVOR CHARLES NOEL). 'Prostitution'. *Howard Journal* 10 (1958), 25–9.

10855 WEST (DONALD JAMES). Homosexuality. 1955.

10856 —— Homosexuality Re-examined. 4th edn 1975.

10857 BRODSKY (SAMUEL L.). 'Understanding and Treating Sexual Offenders'. *Howard J.* 19 (1982), 71–5.

10858 SCHOFIELD (MICHAEL G.). A Minority: A Report on the Life of a Male Homosexual in Great Britain. 1960.

10859 —— Sociological Aspects of Homosexuality: A Comparative Study of Three Types of Homosexuals. 1965.

10860 CHESSER (EUSTACE). Live and Let Live: The Moral of the Wolfenden Report. 1958.

10861 MAGEE (BRYAN EDGAR). One in Twenty: A Study of Homosexuality in Men and Women. 1966.

10862 MORLAND (NIGEL). An Outline of Sexual Criminology. Oxf. 1966.

10863 HENRIQUES (FERNANDO). Prostitution and Society. 2 vols 1966.

10864 GINSBERG (MORRIS). 'Enforcement of Morals'. *Brit. J. Sociol.* 12 (1961), 65–8.

10865 RUITENBEEK (HENDRIK MARINUS) *ed.* Homosexuality: A Changing Picture. 1973.

10866 HOMOSEXUAL LAW REFORM SOCIETY. Memorandum 1965.

10867 —— Homosexuality: The Law in Action. 1969.

10868 HALL (RUTH E.). Ask Any Woman: A London Inquiry into Rape and Sexual Assault. Bristol. 1985.

10869 HARPER (ROSS). The Glasgow Rape Case. 1983.

10870 BLAIR (IAN). Investigating Rape: A New Approach for Police. 1985.

(*l*) *Miscellany*

10871 KETTLE (MARTIN). Uprising! The Police, the People and the Riots in Britain's Cities. 1982.

10872 JOSHUA (HARRIS). To Ride the Storm: The 1980 Bristol 'Riots' and the State. 1983.

10873 COOPER (PAUL). 'Competing Explanations of the Merseyside Riots'. *Brit. J. Criminol.* 25 (1985), 60–9.

10874 HEIDENSOHN (FRANCES). Women and Crime. 1985.

10875 PRICE (JEAN) *and* GOODMAN (NANCY). Studies of Women Offenders. 1967.

10876 SMART (CAROL). Crime and Criminology: A Feminist Critique. 1977.

10877 EDWARDS (SUSAN M.). Women on Trial. Manch. 1984.

10878 GLATT (MAX MEIER) *et al.* The Alcoholic and the Help he Needs. 2nd edn 1972.

10879 WILLIAMS (GWYLMOR PRYS). High Spirited Years: A Regional Analysis of Two Periods, 1954 to 1958 and 1961 to 1964, when Convictions for Drunkenness in England and Wales Rose and Fell to an Unusual Extent. 1966.

10880 —— Decade of Drunkenness: A Summary of Official Statistics of Pedestrian and Motorised Offences for the Ten Years before the Coming into Effect, from 1964 Onwards, of Changes in the Licensing and Traffic Regulations. 1965.

10881 BURNETT (GORDON B.). 'The Habitual Drunkenness Offender'. *Brit. J. Criminol.* 19 (1979), 158–63.

10882 CLAYTON (THOMAS). The Protectors: The Inside Story of Britain's Private Security Forces. 1967.

10883 MCCLINTOCK (FREDERICK HEMMING) *and* WILES (PAUL). The Security Industry in the United Kingdom. 1971.

10884 WILSON (H. H.) *and* GLICKMAN (HARVEY). The Problem of Internal Security in Great Britain 1948–1953. N.Y. 1954.

10885 SPEARING (A.). 'George Blake versus Two Home Secretaries'. *Contemp. Rev.* 1967, 169–70.

10886 TREVOR-ROPER (HUGH). The Philby Affair: Espionage, Treason and Secret Service. 1968.

25. RACE RELATIONS

(*a*) *General*

10887 GILBERT (VICTOR F.) *and* TATLA (DARSHAN SINGH). Immigrants, Minorities and Race Relations: A Bibliography of Theses and Dissertations Presented at British and Irish Universities, 1900–1981. 1984.

10888 RADICAL STATISTICS RACE GROUP. Britain: Black Population. 1980.

10889 AKINSANYA (J.) *and* DADA (L.). A Bibliography of Race and Race Relations. 1984.

10890 LAYTON-HENRY (ZIG). Race and Politics in Britain: A Select Bibliography. 1979.

10891 BEN-TOVIN (GIDEON) *and* GABRIEL (JOHN). 'The Politics of Race in Britain, 1962–1970: A Review of the Major Trends and of the Recent Literature'. *Sage Race Relations Abstracts* 4/4 (1979), 1–56.

10892 LITTLE (KENNETH LINDSAY). Negroes in Britain: A Study of Racial Relations in English Society. 1948. Rev. edn 1972.

10893 —— Colour and Commonsense. [Fabian Society. Foreword by MANLEY (NORMAN).]. 1958.

10894 —— Race and Society. 1966.

10895 —— 'Loudon Square: A Community Survey 1'. *Sociol. Rev.* 34 (Jan.—Apr. 1942), 12–33.

10896 —— 'Loudon Square: A Community Survey 2'. *Sociol. Rev.* 34 (Jul.—Oct. 1942), 119–46.

10897 —— 'The Coloured Folk of Cardiff—A Challenge to Reconstruction'. *New Statesman* 24 No. 617 (19 Dec., 1942), 406.

10898 —— 'The Position of Coloured People in Britain'. *Phylon* 15 (1954).

10899 STRACHEY (JOHN). 'Racial Equality (The Key to a Successful World Policy for Britain)'. *Twentieth Century* 153 (1953), 7–12.

10900 AMERY (JULIAN). Reply to Above. *Twentieth Century* 153 (1953), 87–92.

10901 COLLINS (SYDNEY F.). Coloured Minorities in Britain: Studies in British Race Relations, Based on African, West Indian, and Asiatic Immigrants. 1957.

10902 —— 'The British-Born Coloured'. *Sociol. Rev.* 3 (1955), 77–92.

10903 —— 'The Moslem Family in Britain'. *Soc. Econ. Studs* 4 (1955), 326–37.

10904 PILKINGTON (EDWARD). Beyond the Mother Country: West Indians and the Notting Hill White Riots. 1988.

10905 GITTLER (JOSEPH BERTRAM) *ed.* Review of Sociology. Analysis of a Decade. N.Y. 1957. See chapter by W. L. Warner 'The Study of Social Stratification' and chapter by R. M. Williams 'Racial and Cultural Relations'.

10906 —— *Ed.* Understanding Minority Groups. 1956. [See his own chapter 'Understanding Minority Groups' and chapter by W. A. R. Leys 'The Philosophical and Ethical Aspects of Group Relations'.].

10907 HOROBIN (GORDON W.). 'Adjustment and Assimilation: The Displaced Person'. *Sociol. Rev.* 5 (1957), 239–52.

10908 SENIOR (CLARENCE). 'Race Relations and Labour Supply in Great Britain'. *Social Problems* 4 (1957), 302–14.

10909 NDEM (E. B.). 'The Status of Coloured People in Britain'. *Phylon* 18 (1957) 82–7.

10910 HAUSER (PHILIP MORRIS) *ed.* Population and World Politics. 1958. See chapter by D. S. Thomas 'International Migration'.

10911 RACE RELATIONS IN BRITAIN. *Round Table* 193: 29–36. 1958.

10912 WICKENDEN (JAMES). Colour in Britain. Oxf. 1958. [IRR].

10913 BANTON (MICHAEL PARKER). The Coloured Quarter: Negro Immigrants in an English City. 1955.

10914 —— White and Coloured: The Behaviour of British People towards Coloured Immigrants. 1959.

10915 —— Race Relations. 1967.

10916 —— The Idea of Race. 1977.

10917 —— Rational Choice: A Theory of Racial and Ethnic Relations. Bristol. 1977.

10918 —— The Race Concept. Newton Abbot. 1975.

10919 —— Racial Minorities. 1972.

10920 —— 'Sociology and Race Relations'. *Race* 1 (1959), 3–14.

10921 —— Racial and Ethnic Competition. Camb. 1983.

10922 —— 'Optimism and Pessimism about Racial Relations'. *Patterns of Prejudice* 22 (1988), 3–13.

10923 DEIGHTON (HERBERT STANLEY). 'History and the Study of Race Relations'. *Race* 1 (1959), 15–25.

10924 FREEDMAN (MAURICE). 'The Relations of Race: A Review of New Writing'. *Brit. J. Sociol.* 11 (1960), 74–81.

10925 SYMPOSIUM ON RACE AND RACE RELATIONS. Man, Race and Darwin; Papers Read at a Joint Conference of the Royal Anthropological Institute of Great Britain and Ireland, and the Institute of Race Relations—With an Introduction and Epilogue by Philip Mason. Lond./N.Y. 1960.

10926 LEE (F. E.). 'Racial Patterns in a British City: An Institutional Approach'. *Phylon* 21 (1960), 40–50.

10927 —— 'Social Controls in British Race Relations'. *Sociol. Soc. Res.* 44 (1960), 326–34.

10928 WAUGHRAY (VERNON). Race Relations in Great Britain. 1961. [Peace News Pamphlet.].

10929 MASON (PHILIP). Christianity and Race. 1956.

10930 —— Common Sense about Race. 1961.

10931 —— Prospero's Magic: Some Thoughts on Class and Race. 1962.

10932 —— Race Relations: A Field Study Comes of Age. 1968.

10933 —— Race Relations. 1970.

10934 —— Patterns of Dominance. 1970.

10935 —— How People Differ: An Introduction to Race Relations. 1971.

10936 HOLTON (J. E.). 'The Status of the Coloured in Britain'. *Phylon* 22 (1961), 31–40.

10937 PRICE (C. A.) *and* ZUBRZYCKI (J.). 'The Use of Inter-Marriage Statistics as an Index of Assimilation'. *Pop. Studs* 16 (1962), 58–69.

10938 GLASS (RUTH). Insider-Outsiders: The Position of Minorities. Fifth World Congress of Sociology. Vol. 3 1964.

10939 THOMPSON (RICHARD). Race and Sport. 1964.

10940 DEAKIN (NICHOLAS). 'Harold Macmillan and the Control of Commonwealth Immigration' *New Community* 4, (1975) 91–4.

10941 —— ed. Colour and the British Electorate, 1964: Six Case Studies. 1965.

10942 HOOPER (RICHARD) ed. Colour in Britain . . . Based on a BBC Radio Series. 1965.

10943 HUNTER (GUY) ed. Industrialisation and Race Relations: A Symposium. 1965.

10944 INGRAM (DEREK). Commonwealth for a Colour-Blind World. 1965.

10945 GARDINER (ROBERT). A World of Peoples. 1966. [BBC Reith Lectures 1965.].

10946 MORLEY (JOHN). 'Can White Management Cope with Coloured Workers?' *Business* 96 (1966), 39–45.

10947 ISHERWOOD (HENRY BURTON). Racial Integration: The Rising Tide of Colour. 1966.

10948 —— Racial Contours: The Factor of Race in Human Survival. Douglas. 1965.

10949 CHATER (ANTHONY). Race Relations in Britain. 1966.

10950 BURNEY (ELIZABETH). Black in a White World. 1968.

10951 HILL (CLIFFORD STANLEY) *and* MATHEWS (DAVID) eds. Race: A Christian Symposium. 1968.

10952 FREYRE (GILBERTO DE MELLO). The Racial Factor in Contemporary Politics. 1966.

10953 GRIFFITHS (PETER). A Question of Colour. 1966.

10954 BUSSEY (ELLEN M.). 'Coloured Minorities and Present British Policies'. *Monthly Lab. Rev.* 89 (1966), 1111–15.

10955 BENNETT (A.). 'Training and Selection of Nurses from Commonwealth Countries'. *Midwife and Health Visitor* 2 (1966), 333–6.

10956 KNOX (DAVID). 'Britain's Black Powerhouse: Michael X'. *Life* 153 (1967), 8–17.

10957 BROCKWAY (ARCHIBALD FENNER) *Baron Brockway*. This Shrinking Explosive World: A Study of Race Relations. 1967.

10958 LEWIN (JULIUS) comp. The Struggle for Racial Equality. 1967.

10959 GRIGG (MARY). The White Question. 1967.

10960 DESCLOITRES (ROBERT). Les Travailleurs Étrangers, leur Adaptation au Travail Industriel et à la Vie Urbaine. Paris/Lond. 1967.

10961 LABOUR PARTY. REPORT OF A WORKING PARTY ON RACE RELATIONS. 1967.

10962 FABIAN SOCIETY. Politics for Racial Equality. 1967.

10963 RAYNOR (LOIS). 'Agency Adoptions of Non-White Children in the United Kingdom: A Quantitative Study'. *Race* 10 (1968), 153–62.

10964 HEGINBOTHAM (HERBERT). 'Young Immigrants and Work'. *IRR Newsletter* 1 (1967), 215–17.

10965 JONES (KIT). 'Immigrants and the Social Services'. *Nat. Inst. Econ. Rev.* No. 41 (Aug 1967), 28–35.

10966 COHEN (BRIAN) *and* JENNER (PETER). 'The Employment of Immigrants: A Case Study within the Wool Industry'. *Race* 10 (1968), 41–56.

10967 ADAMS (WALTER), REX (JOHN), DEAKIN (NICHOLAS), CALVOCORESSI (PETER), PATTERSON (SHEILA), MARSHALL (ROY), *and* IGNOTUS (PAUL). 'Foreigners in Britain'. *Pol. Q.* 39 (1968), 1–93.

10968 MALIK (MICHAEL ABDUL). From Michael de Freitas to Michael X. 1968.

10969 KUNZ (PHILIP R.). 'Immigrants and Socialization: A New Look'. *Sociol. Rev.* 16 (1968), 363–76.

10970 NEWMAN (JEREMIAH). Race: Migration and Immigration. 1968.

10971 HEPPLE (ALEXANDER). Race, Jobs and the Law in Britain. 1968. 2nd edn Harmondsworth 1970.

10972 —— Business and Employment. 1. Race Relations (Conference Paper), 1967.

10973 —— The Position of Coloured Workers in British Industry. CRE 1967.

10974 BARTLETT (VERNON OLDFIELD). The Colour of their Skin. 1969.

10975 HERNTON (CALVIN C.). Sex and Racism. 1969.

10976 RODNEY (WALTER). The Groundings with my Brothers . . . 1969.

10977 ROSE (E. JAMES B.) *et al.* Colour and Citizenship: A Report on British Race Relations. 1969. [IRR].

10978 PATTERSON (SHEILA). 'Race Relations in Birmingham'. *IRR Newsletter* (Oct. 1961 Suppl.).

10979 —— Immigrants in London: Report of a Study Group Set up by the London Council of Social Service. 1963.

10980 —— Dark Strangers: A Sociological Study of the Absorption of a Recent West Indian Migrant Group in Brixton, South London. 1963.

10981 —— Immigrants in Industry. 1968.

10982 —— Immigration and Race Relations in Britain 1960–1967. 1969.

10983 LA PRESLÉ (A. DE). 'Racisme et Libertés Publiques en Angleterre'. *Esprit* 37 (1969), 1117–33.

10984 EVERSLEY (DAVID EDWARD CHARLES) *and* SUKDEO (FRED). The Dependants of the Coloured Commonwealth Population of England and Wales. 1969.

10985 STREET (HARRY) *et al.* Report on Anti-discrimination Legislation. Sponsored by the Race Relations Board and the National Committee for Commonwealth Immigrants. 1967.

10986 RICHMOND (ANTHONY HENRY). 'Housing and Racial Attitudes in Bristol'. *Race* 12 (1970), 49–59.

10987 —— 'The Significance of a Multi-Racial Commonwealth'. *Phylon* 16 (1955), 380–6.

10988 —— 'Tendances Récentes de la Recherche en Matière de Relations Raciales: Grande Bretagne'. *B. Int. Sci. Soc.* 10 (1958), 400–30.

10989 —— 'Sociological and Psychological Explanations of Racial Prejudice'. *Pacific Sociol. Rev.* 4 (1961), 63–9.

10990 —— 'Immigration as a Social Process: The Case of the Coloured Colonials in the United Kingdom'. *Soc. Econ. Stud.* 5 (1956), 185–201.

10991 —— 'Teaching Race Questions in Schools'. *Phylon* 17 (1956), 239–49.

10992 HOROWITZ (DANIEL). 'The British Conservatives and the Racial Issue in the Debate on Decolonization'. *Race* 12 (1970), 169–88.

10993 DEAKIN (NICHOLAS) with COHEN (BRIAN) *and* MCNEAL (JULIA). Colour, Citizenship and British Society. 1970.

10994 COUSINS (FRANK). 'Race Relations in Employment in the United Kingdom'. *Inl. Lab. Rev.* 102 (1970), 1–13.

10995 HILL (DAVID). 'The Attitudes of West Indian and English Adolescents in Britain'. *Race* 11 (1970), 313–22.

10996 WELLS (ALAN F.). Social Institutions. 1970.

10997 MAIR (LUCY). Anthropology and Social Change. Lond./N.Y. 1969.

10998 CALLAN (HILARY). Ethnology and Society: Towards an Anthropological View. Oxf. 1970.

10999 COMMUNITY. Journal of the UK COMMUNITY RELATIONS COMMISSION Jan. 1970–Apr. 1971. Ceased publication. See NEW COMMUNITY published from 1972 onwards.

11000 MORRISH (IVOR). The Background of Immigrant Children. 1971.

11001 KRAUSZ (ERNEST). Ethnic Minorities in Britain. 1971.

11002 DAVIES (P.) *and* NEWTON (KENNETH). 'The Social Patterns of Immigrant Areas'. *Race* 14 (1972), 43–57.

11003 JENKINS (SIMON). Here to Live: A Study of English Race Relations in an English Town. 1971.

11004 ABBOTT (SIMON). 'Race Studies in Britain'. *Inform. Sci. Soc.* 10 (1971), 91–101.

11005 U.K. HOUSE OF COMMONS SELECT COMMITTEE ON RACE RELATIONS AND IMMIGRATION SESSION 1970–1971. Includes 'Housing and Race Relations' by Nicholas Deakin and Clare Ungerson. In vol. 3 House of Commons Paper 508. [1971 HMSO.].

11006 —— Control of Commonwealth Immigration: An Analysis of the Evidence Taken by the Select Committee on Race Relations and Immigration 1969–1970 by Arthur Bottomley and George Sinclair. (Published by the Runnymede Trust 1970.).

11007 DEAKIN (NICHOLAS). 'Survey of Race Relations in Britain'. *Ethnics* 1 (1971), 75–90.

11008 —— 'Racial Integration and Whitehall: A Plan for Reorganisation'. *Pol. Q.* 39 (1968), 415–26.

11009 LEWIS (G. K.). 'An Introductory Note to the Study of Race Relations in Great Britain'. *Carib. Studs* 11 (1971), 5–29.

11010 —— 'Protest among the Immigrants'. *Pol. Q.* 40 (1969), 426–35.

11011 HILL (MICHAEL JAMES) *and* ISSACHAROFF (RUTH MIRYAM). Community Action and Race Relations: A Study of Community Relations Committees in Britain. 1971.

11012 HIRO (DILIP). Black British, White British. 1973.

11013 —— The Indian Family in Britain. 1967.

11014 —— 'Three Generations of Tiger Bay'. *New Society* 10 (1967), 385–87.

11015 GOLDSWORTHY (DAVID). Colonial Issues in British Politics, 1945–1961. 1971.

11016 BLOOM (LEONARD). The Social Psychology of Race Relations. 1971.

11017 HUMPHRY (DEREK), *With Commentary by* JOHN (GUS). Police Power and Black People. 1972.

11018 HARTMANN (PAUL) *and* HUSBAND (CHARLES). 'A British Scale for Measuring White Attitudes to Coloured People'. *Race* 14 (1972–3), 195–204.

11019 BAXTER (PAUL) *and* SANSOM (BASIL) *eds.* Race and Social Difference. Harmondsworth. 1972.

11020 RUNCIMAN (WALTER GARRISON). 'Race and Social Stratification'. *Race* 13 (1972), 497–509.

11021 LOMAS (GLENYS BARBARA GILLIAN). Census 1971: The Coloured Population of Great Britain: Preliminary Report. 1973. [Runnymede Trust.].

11022 SCOBIE (EDWARD). Black Britannia: A History of Blacks in Britain. Chicago. 1972.

11023 REX (JOHN). 'The Future of Race Relations Research in Britain: Sociological Research and the Politics of Racial Justice'. *Race* 14 (1973), 481–8.

11024 —— 'The Concept of Housing Class and the Sociology of Race Relations'. *Race* 12 (1971), 293–301.

11025 —— 'The Future of Black Culture and Politics in Britain'. *New Community* 7 (1978), 225–32.

11026 —— Colonial Immigrants in a British City. 1979.

11027 SIVANANDAN (A.). 'Race, Class and Power: An Outline for Study'. *Race* 14 (1973), 383–91.

11028 —— 'Race, Class and the State: The Black Experience in Britain'. *Race and Class* 16 (1976), 347–68.

11029 —— A Different Hunger: Writings on Black Resistance. 1982.

11030 TOWNSEND (PETER). The Social Minority. 1973.

11031 RICHMOND (ANTHONY HENRY). The Colour Problem: A Study of Race Relations. Harmondsworth. 1955.

11032 —— Readings in Race and Ethnic Relations. Oxf./N.Y. 1972.

11033 U.K. HOME OFFICE. Police/Immigrant Relations in England and Wales. Cmnd 5438. 1973.

11034 BOSANQUET (NICHOLAS). Race and Employment in Britain: A Report. 1973. [A Runnymede Trust Publication.].

11035 WALVIN (JAMES). Black and White: The Negro and English Society 1555–1945. 1973.

11036 —— Passage to Britain. 1984.

11037 KATZNELSON (IRA). Black Men and White Cities: Race Politics and Migration in the United States 1900–1930, and Britain 1948–1968. 1973. [Institute of Race Relations Publication.].

11038 BRIDGES (LEE). 'Race Relations Research: From Colonialism to Neo-Colonialism? Some Random Thoughts'. *Race* 14 (1973), 331–41.

11039 BAGLEY (CHRISTOPHER). 'Race Relations and the Press: An Empirical Analysis'. *Race* 15 (1973), 59–89.

11040 COMMUNITY RELATIONS COMMISSION. Unemployment and Homelessness. 1974.

11041 —— 'Some of my Best Friends . . .': A Report on Race Relations Attitudes. 1976.

11042 —— Housing in Multi-racial Areas: Prepared by a Working Party of Housing Directors. 1976.

11043 —— Black Employees: Job Levels and Discrimination. 1976.

11044 LERUEZ (JACQUES). 'Actualité du Problème Ethnique en Grande Bretagne'. *R. Franc. Sci. Polit.* 23 (1974), 1080–90.

11045 HUMPHRY (DEREK) *and* WARD (MICHAEL). Passports and Politics. Harmondsworth. 1974.

11046 GEISS (IMMANUEL). The Pan-African Movement. 1974.

11047 WOOD (SUSANNE). 'The Coloured Population of Great Britain'. *Pol. Q.* 45 (1974), 251.

11048 HECHTER (MICHAEL). 'Political Economy of Ethnic Change'. *Amer. J. Sociol.* 79 (1974), 1151–78.

11049 MONCK (ELIZABETH MARY) *and* LOMAS (GLENYS BARBARA GILLIAN). The Employment and Socio-economic Conditions of the Coloured Population. 1975.

11050 YUDKIN (SOLOMON SIMON). The Health and Welfare of the Immigrant Child. 1967.

11051 ASSOCIATION OF MULTI-RACIAL PLAYGROUPS. Occasional Papers, No. 1. Action in the Priority Areas: A Note on the Aims and Workings of the Association of Multi-racial Playgroups. Camb. 1969.

11052 —— No. 2. Work in the Midlands. Camb. 1969.

11053 COMMUNITY RELATIONS COMMISSION. Caring for the Under-Fives in a Multi-Racial Society. 1977.

11054 KOHLER (DAVID F.). Ethnic Minorities in Britain: Statistical Data. 6th edn 1976. [Community Relations Commission.].

11055 BUNKER (GORDON) *and* CARRIER (JOHN WOLFE) *eds*. Race and Ethnic Relations: Sociological Readings. 1976.

11056 BIDWELL (SIDNEY). Red, White and Black: Race Relations in Britain. 1976.

11057 WATSON (JAMES LEE) *ed*. Between Two Cultures: Migrants and Minorities in Britain. Oxf. 1977.

11058 U.K. CENTRAL OFFICE OF INFORMATION. Race Relations in Britain. 2nd edn 1977.

11059 —— Immigration into Britain. Rev. edn 1977.

11060 COMMUNITY RELATIONS COMMISSION. Evidence to the Royal Commission on the National Health Service. 1977.

11061 —— The Multi-Racial Community: A Guide for Local Councillors. 1977.

11062 —— Urban Deprivation, Racial Inequality and Social Policy. 1977. Repr. 1978.

11063 —— Meeting their Needs: An Account of Language Tuition Schemes for Ethnic Minority Women. By Michael Mobos. 1977.

11064 —— The Views of Social Workers in Multi-Racial Areas. 1977.

11065 —— [Youth and Community Section.] Seen but Not Served: Black Youth and the Youth Service. 1977.

11066 CROSS (CRISPIN). Ethnic Minorities in the Inner City: The Ethnic Dimension in Urban Deprivation in England. 1978.

11067 D₃ABEYDEEN (DAVID). The Black Presence in English Literature. Manch. 1985.

11068 POLLINS (HAROLD). 'Coloured People in Post-War English Literature'. *Race* 1 (1960), 3–13.

11069 —— 'The West Indian Comes to England'. *Soc. Wk.* 17 (1960), 34–7.

11070 DUMMETT (ANN). Citizenship and Nationality. 1976.

11071 WALLMAN (SANDRA). Ethnicity at Work. 1979.

11072 GILROY (PAUL). 'Managing the "Under-Class": A Further Note on the Sociology of Race Relations in Britain'. *Race and Class* 22 (1980), 47–62.

11073 HUSBANDS (CHRISTOPHER TEMPLE). 'Race' in Britain: Continuity and Change. 1987.

11074 FIELD (S.). Ethnic Minorities in Britain: A Study of Trends in their Position Since 1961. 1981.

11075 FYLE (NIGEL) *and* POWER (CHRISTOPHER). Black Settlers in Britain 1555–1958. 1981.

11076 HISTORY TODAY. Special Issue on 'The History of Blacks in Britain'. 31 (Sept. 1981).

11077 JOSHUA (HARRIS). To Ride the Storm: The 1980 Bristol 'Riot' and the State. 1983.

11078 FRYER (PETER). Staying Power: The History of Black People in Britain. 1984.

11079 —— Black People in the British Empire: An Introduction. 1988.

11080 MULLARD (CHRIS). Black Britain. 1977.

11081 JACOBS (BRIAN D.). Racism in Britain. 1988.

11082 GLAZER (NATHAN) and YOUNG (KEN) eds. Ethnic Pluralism and Public Policy: Achieving Equality in the United States and Britain. 1983.

11083 LUNN (KENNETH). Hosts, Immigrants and Minorities. Folkestone. 1980.

11084 —— Ed. Race and Labour in Twentieth Century Britain. 1985.

11085 RAMDIN (ROGER). The Making of the Black Working Class in Britain. 1987.

11086 LOTZ (RAINER) and PEGG (IAN). Under the Imperial Carpet. 1987.

11087 BANTON (MICHAEL). 'The Beginning and the End of the Racial Issue in British Politics'. *Policy & Politics* 15 (1987), 39–47.

11088 JACOBS (BRIAN D.). Black Politics and Urban Crisis in Britain. Camb. 1986.

11089 CENTRE FOR CONTEMPORARY CULTURAL STUDIES. The Empire Strikes Back: Race and Racism in 70s Britain. 1982.

11090 RICH (PAUL). Race and Empire in British Politics. Camb. 1986.

11091 —— Race, Government and Politics in Britain. Basingstoke. 1986.

(b) Race Relations and Government Legislation

11092 Control of Immigration Statistics, United Kingdom. 1980+. Annual.

11093 BEVAN (VAUGHAN). The Development of British Immigration Law. 1986.

11094 LESTER (ANTHONY). Citizens without Status. 1972.

11095 POULTER (S. M.). English Law and Ethnic Minority Customs. 1986.

11096 LIU (W. H.). 'The Evolution of Commonwealth Citizenship and U.K. Statutory Control Over Commonwealth Immigration'. *New Community* 5 (1977), 426–47.

11097 COLYER (WILLIAM THOMAS). The Workers Passport: A Study of the Legal Restrictions on Migrant Workers: Prepared by the Labour Defence Council. 1928.

11098 DEAN (D. W.). 'Coping with Coloured Immigration: The Cold War and Colonial Policy, The Labour Government and Black Communities in Great Britain, 1945–51'. *Immigrants and Minorities* 6 (1987), 305–34.

11099 CARTER (BOB), HARRIS (CLIVE), and JOSHI (SHIRLEY). 'The 1951–55 Conservative Government and the Racialisation of Black Immigration'. *Immigrants and Minorities* 6 (1987), 335–47.

11100 HINDELL (KEITH). 'The Genesis of the Race Relations Bill'. *Pol. Q.* 36 (1965), 390–405.

11101 BONFIELD (ARTHUR EARL). 'The Role of Legislation in Eliminating Racial Discrimination'. *Race* 7 (1965), 107–22.

11102 DAVIS (P. A.). A Sledgehammer to Crack a Nut: An Examination of the Race Relations Bill. 1965.

11103 U.K. HOME OFFICE. Commonwealth Immigrants Act 1962. Instructions to Immigration Officers. Cmnd 1716. 1962. Superseded by Cmnd 3064. 1966.

11104 —— Admission of Commonwealth Citizens to the United Kingdom. 1967.

11105 —— Immigration Appeals: Report of the Committee. Cmnd 3387. Parliamentary Papers, xxxvi (1966–7).

11106 GORDON (P.). Policing Immigration: Britain's Internal Controls. 1985.

11107 MOORE (ROBERT) and WALLACE (TINA). Slamming the Door: The Administration of Immigration Control. 1975.

11108 STOREY (H.). 'United Kingdom Immigration Controls and the Welfare State'. *J. Soc. Welfare Law* (1984), 14–28.

11109 LESTER (ANTHONY). 'Fair Employment Practices: The Government's Role'. *IRR Newsletter* (May 1966), 11–14.

11110 POLITICAL AND ECONOMIC PLANNING. Anti-discrimination Legislation. [Street Report.] 1967.

11111 NANDY (DIPAK). 'Discrimination and the Law'. *Lab. Monthly* (Jan. 1967).

11112 —— 'Immigration: The Great Betrayal'. *Views* 10 (1966), 8–18.

11113 U.K. RACE RELATIONS BOARD. Discrimination and You. 1967.

11114 —— Explaining the Race Relations Act. 1965. 1967.

11115 —— A Guide to the Race Relations Act. 1967.

11116 —— Annual Reports.

11117 BONHAM-CARTER (MARK). 'Legislation and the Race Relations Board'. *IRR Newsletter* No. 4 (1967).

11118 STEEL (DAVID). No Entry: The Background and Implications of the Commonwealth Immigrants Act 1968. 1969.

11119 MARSHALL (ROY). 'The Law and Race Relations'. *Polit. Q.* 39 (1968), 70–82.

11120 U.K. SELECT COMMITTEE ON RACE RELATIONS AND IMMIGRATION. (House of Commons Session 1968–1969.). The Problems of Coloured School-leavers, Vol. 1— Report. 1969.

11121 MACDONALD (IAN ALEXANDER). Race Relations and Immigration Law. 1969.

11122 —— The New Immigration Law. 1972.

11123 —— Race Relations: The New Law. 1977.

11124 —— Immigration Law and Practice in the United Kingdom. 1983.

11125 AGEE-HOSENBALL DEFENCE COMMITTEE. Scrap the Act: Empire and Immigration: A Historical Background to the 1971 Immigration Act. 1976.

11126 LESTER (ANTHONY) and BIDMAN (GEOFFREY). Race and Law. Harmondsworth. 1972.

11127 COMMISSION FOR RACIAL EQUALITY. A Guide to the New Race Relations Act 1976: Employment. 1976.

11128 —— Your Rights to Equal Treatment under the New Race Relations Act 1976: Employment. 1976.

11129 THORNBERRY (CEDRIC). The Stranger at the Gate: A Study of the Law on Aliens and Commonwealth Citizens. 1964. (Fabian Soc. Res. Series No. 243.).

11130 —— 'Commitment or Withdrawal? The Place of Law in Race Relations in Britain'. Race 7 (1965), 73–85.

11131 —— 'Discretion and Appeal in British Immigrant Law'. IRR Newsletter (Nov. 1965).

11132 ROSE (HANNAH). 'The Immigration Act, 1970: A Case Study in the Work of Parliament'. Parl. Affs. 26 (1972–3), 69–91.

11133 —— 'The Politics of Migration after the 1971 Act'. Pol. Q. 44 (1973), 183–96.

11134 NORTON (PHILIP). 'Intra-Party Dissent in the House of Commons: A Case Study: The Immigration Rules, 1972'. Parl. Affs 29 (1976), 404–20.

11135 FRANSMAN (L.). British Nationality Law and the 1981 Act. 1982.

11136 SONDHI (RANJIT). Divided Families: British Immigration Control in the Indian Sub-Continent. 1987.

11137 LAYTON-HENRY (ZIG). The Politics of Race in Britain. 1984.

11138 NANDY (DIPAK). The Politics of Race Relations. 1980.

11139 SHAW (JOHN W.), NORDLIE (PETER G.), and SHAPIRO (RICHARD M.). Strategies for Improving Race Relations: The Anglo-American Experience. Manch. 1987.

11140 SOLOMOS (JOHN). Black Youth, Racism and the State: The Politics of Ideology and Policy. Camb. 1988.

11141 BANTON (MICHAEL). Promoting Racial Harmony. Camb. 1985.

11142 JENKINS (RICHARD) and SOLOMOS (JOHN) eds. Racism and Equal Opportunity Policies in the 1980s. Camb. 1987.

11143 LAYTON-HENRY (ZIG) and RICH (PAUL B.). Race, Government and Politics in Britain. 1986.

(c) Racism, Prejudice, and Racial Disadvantage

11144 MUDGE (G. P.). 'The Menace to the English Race and to the Traditions of Present-day Immigration and Emigration'. Eugenics Rev. (Jan. 1920), 202–12. [Criticism of this, Eugenics Rev. (Apr. 1920), 38–40.].

11145 MAYKOVITCH (MINAKO KUROKAWA). 'Changes in Racial Stereotypes Among College Students'. B. J. Psychiatry 6 (1972), 126–33.

11146 HUXLEY (Sir JULIAN SORRELL) and HADDOW (ALFRED CORT). We Europeans: A Survey of Racial Problems. 1935.

11147 HUXLEY (Sir JULIAN SORRELL). 'Race' in Europe. Oxf. 1939.

11148 HOFSTETTER (P.). 'Le Problème Noir en Grande Bretagne'. Def. Occident 23 (1955), 54–61.

11149 DRAKE (ST CLAIR). 'The "Colour Problem" in Britain: A Study of Social Definitions'. Sociol. Rev. 3 (1955), 197–217.

11150 NORTHCOTT (CECIL). 'The Colour Problem in Britain'. Contemp. Rev. 1957, 91–3.

11151 BIBBY (HAROLD CYRIL). Race, Prejudice and Education. 1959.

11152 MASON (PHILIP). 'An Approach to Race Relations'. Race 1 (1959), 41–52.

11153 —— 'The Colour Problem in Britain as [sic] Affects Africa and the Commonwealth'. Af. Affs. 231 (1959), 367–79.

11154 ADINARAYAN (SAMUEL PUNDIPEDDI). The Case for Colour: An Analysis of the Causes, Manifestations and Effects of Colour Prejudices. A Survey of Remedial Measures and Some Suggestions for a Cure. 1965.

11155 ELIAS (NORBERT) and SCOTSON (JOHN L.). The Established and the Outsiders: A Sociological Enquiry into Community Problems. 1965.

11156 PREM (DHANI R.). The Parliamentary Lepers: A History of Colour Prejudice in Britain. Aligarh. 1965.

11157 LASK (M.). 'Racial Attitudes in General Practice'. Med. World 113 (1965), 10–15.

11158 SILBERMAN (CHARLES ELIOT). Crisis in Black and White. 1965.

11159 HILL (CLIFFORD STANLEY). How Colour Prejudiced is Britain? 1965.

11160 —— Immigration and Integration: A Study of the Settlement of Coloured Minorities in Britain. 1970.

11161 POLITICAL AND ECONOMIC PLANNING RESEARCH SERVICES LIMITED. Racial Discrimination. 1967. [A PEP Report Sponsored by the Race Relations Board and the National Committee for Commonwealth Immigrants; Research by Research Services Ltd.].

11162 HUNT (J.). 'Race Relations in Britain'. Patterns of Prejudice 1 (1967), 8–11.

11163 WILLIAMSON (J.). 'Threat of Racialism in Britain'. *Polit. Affs* 45 (1966), 34–42.

11164 DANIEL (WILLIAM WENTWORTH). Racial Discrimination in England: Based on the PEP Report. Harmondsworth. 1968.

11165 KIERNAN (VICTOR GORDON). The Lords of Human Kind: European Attitudes towards the Outside World in the Imperial Age. 1969.

11166 ZUBAIDA (SAMI) *ed.* Race and Racialism. (Selected Contributions from the Annual Conference of the British Sociological Association.). 1969.

11167 JOWELL (ROGER) *and* PRESCOTT-CLARKE (PATRICIA). 'Racial Discrimination and White Collar Workers in Britain'. *Race* 11 (1970), 397–417.

11168 ABBOTT (SIMON). The Prevention of Racial Discrimination in Britain. 1971.

11169 JOHN (GUS) *and* HUMPHRY (DEREK). Because they're Black. Harmondsworth. 1972.

11170 HEINEMAN (BENJAMIN WALTER). The Politics of the Powerless: A Study of the Campaign against Racial Discrimination. 1972.

11171 BAGLEY (CHRISTOPHER). Social Structure and Prejudice in Five English Boroughs. (A Report Prepared for the IRR Survey of Race Relations in Britain.). 1972.

11172 CHARLOT (MONICA) *ed.* Naissance d'un Problème Racial: Minorités de Couleur en Grande Bretagne. Paris. 1972.

11173 GARNER (JOHN FRANCIS). 'Racial Restrictive Covenants in England and the United States'. *Mod. Law Rev.* 35 (1972), 478–88.

11174 COLMAN (ANDREW M.). 'Scientific Racism and the Evidence on Race and Intelligence'. *Race* 14 (1972), 137–53.

11175 DUMMETT (ANN). A Portrait of English Racism. Harmondsworth. 1973.

11176 HARTMANN (PAUL) *and* HUSBAND (CHARLES). Racism and the Mass Media: A Study of the Mass Media in the Formation of White Beliefs and Attitudes in Britain. 1974.

11177 SMITH (DAVID JOHN). Racial Disadvantage in Employment. 1974.

11178 —— The Facts of Racial Disadvantage: A National Survey. 1976.

11179 —— Racial Disadvantage in Britain: The PEP Report. Harmondsworth. 1977.

11180 MOORE (ROBERT SAMUEL). Racism and Black Resistance in Britain. 1975.

11181 HOLMES (COLIN). 'Violence and Race Relations in Britain, 1953–1968'. *Phylon* 36 (1975), 113–24.

11182 ELKIN (STEPHEN L.) *and* PANNING (WILLIAM H.). 'Structural Effects and Individual Attitudes: Racial Prejudice in English Cities'. *Pub. Op. Q.* 39 (1975), 159–77.

11183 MADGE (NIC). Racial Discrimination: NCCL's Comments on the White Paper. 1975.

11184 BERREMAN (GERALD D.). 'Race, Caste and other Invidious Distinctions in Social Stratification'. *Race* 13 (1972), 385–414.

11185 STUDLAR (DONLEY T.). 'British Public Opinion, Colour Issues and Enoch Powell: A Longitudinal Analysis'. *Brit. J. Pol. Sci.* 4 (1974), 371–81.

11186 FOOT (PAUL). The Rise of Enoch Powell: An Examination of Enoch Powell's Attitude to Immigration and Race. 1969.

11187 HOOGVELT (ANKIE M.). 'Ethnocentrism, Authoritarianism and Powellism'. *Race* 11 (1969), 1–12.

11188 BARNETT (A.S.), PICKVANCE (CHRISTOPHER GEOFFREY), *and* WARD (ROBIN HARWOOD). 'Some Factors Underlying Racial Discrimination in Housing'. *Race* 12 (1970), 75–87.

11189 MILES (ROBERT) *and* PHIZACKLEA (ANNIE) *eds.* Racism and Political Action in Britain. 1979.

11190 MILES (ROBERT). The TUC, Black Workers and New Commonwealth Immigration, 1954–1973. Bristol. 1977. Working Papers on Ethnic Relations No. 6.

11191 —— Labour and Racism. 1980.

11192 —— Racism and Migrant Labour. 1982.

11193 —— The Relative Autonomy of Ideology: Racism and the Migration of Labour to Britain since 1945. Paris. 1985.

11194 —— 'The Riots of 1958: The Ideological Construction of "Race Relations" as a Political Issue in Britain'. *Immigrants and Minorities* 3 (1984), 252–75.

11195 MILES (ROBERT) *and* PHIZACKLEA (ANNIE). White Man's Country: Racism and British Politics. 1984.

11196 EDGAR (DAVID). 'Racism, Fascism and the Politics of the National Front'. *Race and Class* 19 (1977), 111–32.

11197 BILLIG (MICHAEL). 'Patterns of Racism: Interviews with National Front Members'. *Race and Class* 20 (1978), 161–80.

11198 BAGLEY (CHRISTOPHER). Racial Prejudice. Farnborough. 1979.

11199 FREEMAN (GARY P.). Immigrant Labour and Racial Conflict in Industrial Societies: The French and the British Experience 1945–1975. Princeton, N.J. 1979.

11200 SMITH (GRAHAM A.). 'Jim Crow on the Home Front 1942–1945'. *New Community* 8 (1980), 317–28.

11201 FLINT (J.). 'Scandal at the Bristol Hotel: Some Thoughts on Racial Discrimination in Britain and West Africa and its Relationship to the Planning of Decolonisation, 1939–1947'. *J. Imp. Cwealth Hist.* 12 (1983–4), 74–93.

11202 RICH (PAUL B.). 'Philanthropic Racism in Britain: The Liverpool Universal Settlement, the Anti-Slavery Society and the Question of "Half-caste"

Children 1919–1951'. *Immigrants and Minorities* 3 (1984), 30–48.

11203 —— 'Doctrines of Racial Segregation in Britain 1900–1944'. *New Community* 12 (winter 1984–5), 75–86.

11204 BRIDGES (LEE) *and* FEKETE (LIZ). 'Victims, the "Urban Jungle" and the New Racism'. *Race and Class* 27 (1985), 63–87.

11205 KUSHNER (TONY) *and* LUNN (KENNETH). Traditions of Intolerance: Historical Perspectives on Fascism and Race Discourse in Britain. Manch. 1989.

(d) Nationalities

(i) Asian Communities

11206 VISRAN (ROZINA). Ayahs, Lascars and Princes: Indians in Britain 1700–1947. 1986.

11207 KARN (VALERIE). 'Property Values amongst Indians and Pakistanis in a Yorkshire Town'. *Race* 10 (1969), 269–84.

11208 EAMES (E.) *and* ROBBOY (H.). 'Not Welcome: The Punjabi Visitor and British Officialdom'. *Int. J. Cont. Sociol.* 9 (1972), 44–55.

11209 DAHYA (BADR). 'Pakistanis in Britain: Transients or Settlers?'. *Race* 14 (1973), 241–77.

11210 —— 'Yemenis in Britain: An Arab Migrant Community'. *Race* 6 (1965), 177–90.

11211 PEARL (DAVID). 'Muslim Marriages in English Law'. *Camb. Law J.* 30 (Apr. 1972), 120–43.

11212 HUNTER (KATHLEEN). History of Pakistanis in Britain. 1962.

11213 AURORA (GURDIP SINGH). The New Frontiersmen: A Sociological Study of Indian Immigrants in the United Kingdom. Bombay. 1967.

11214 —— 'Process of Social Adjustment of Indian Immigrants in Britain'. *Sociol. B.* (Bombay), 14 (1965), 39–49.

11215 MARSH (PETER). The Anatomy of a Strike: Unions, Employers and Punjabi Workers in a Southall Factory. 1968. [IRR Special Series].

11216 SHARMA (URSULA). Rampal and his Family. 1971.

11217 JAMES (ALAN). Sikh Children in Britain. 1973. (IRR).

11218 DE WITT (JOHN J.). Indian Workers' Associations in Britain. 1969. [IRR Survey of Race Relations in Britain.].

11219 DESAI (RASHMI). Indian Immigrants in Britain. 1963. (IRR).

11220 PAREKH (PRAMILA) *and* PAREKH (BHIKHU). Cultural Conflict and the Asian Family: Report of a Conference Organised by the National Association of Indian Youth (in Leicester in 1975). 1976.

11221 TINKER (HUGH). The Banyan Tree: Overseas Immigrants from Pakistan and Bangladesh. Oxf. 1977.

11222 JEFFREY (PATRICIA). Migrants and Refugees: Muslim and Christian Pakistani Families in Bristol. Camb. 1976.

11223 BUTTERWORTH (ERIC). Immigrants in West Yorkshire: Social Conditions and the Lives of Pakistanis, Indians and West Indians. 1967.

11224 JAHODA (GUSTAV), THOMSON (S. S.), *and* BHATT (S.). 'Ethnic Identity and Preferences Among Asian Immigrant Children in Glasgow: A Replicated Study'. *Eur. J. Soc. Psychol.* 2 (1972), 19–32.

11225 DICKINSON (LESLIE) *et al.* The Immigrant School Leaver: A Study of Pakistani Pupils in Glasgow. Slough. 1975.

11226 AHMED (N.). 'Race Relations in Britain'. *Pakistan Horizon* 21 (1968), 108–15.

11227 ROMIJN (JAN). Tabu: Ugandan Asians: The Old, the Weak, the Vulnerable. A Report on . . . Work with the Elderly and Handicapped Among the Ugandan Asian Evacuees in London . . . 1976.

11228 WANDSWORTH COUNCIL FOR COMMUNITY RELATIONS. Ugandan Resettlement Unit. Ugandan Asians in Wandsworth: A Report Produced for Sir Charles Cunningham, Chairman of the Ugandan Resettlement Board. 1973.

11229 MAMDANI (MAHMOOD). From Citizen to Refugee: Ugandan Asians come to Britain. 1973.

11230 WILSON (AMRIT). 'A Burning Fever: The Isolation of Asian Women in Britain'. *Race and Class* 20 (1978), 129–42.

11231 MUHAMED (ANWAR). The Myth of Return: Pakistanis in Britain. 1979.

11232 WERBNER (PRIMA). 'Avoiding the Ghetto: Pakistani Migrants and Settlement Shifts in Manchester'. *New Community* 7 (1979), 376–85.

11233 —— 'From Rags to Riches: Manchester Pakistanis in the Textile Trade'. *New Community* 8 (1980), 84–95.

11234 ROBINSON (V.). 'Correlates of Asian Immigration, 1959–74'. *New Community* 8 (1980), 115–22.

(ii) Afro-Caribbeans

11235 SUTTEN (H. M. A.). 'West Indians, Britain's New Coloured Citizens'. *Crisis* 68 (1961), 481–8.

11236 BAYLISS (F. J.) *and* COATES (J. B.). 'West Indians at Work in Nottingham'. *Race* 7 (1965), 157–66.

11237 WATSON (ARNOLD R.). West Indian Workers in Britain. 1942.

11238 CONSTANTINE (*Sir* LEARY NICHOLAS). Colour Bar. 1954.

11239 RICHMOND (ANTHONY HENRY). Colour Prejudice in Britain: A Study of West Indian Workers in Liverpool, 1944–51. 1954.

11240 MAUNDER (W. F.). 'The New Jamaican Immigration'. *Soc. Econ. Studs* 4 (1955), 38–60.

11241 ROBERTS (GEORGE W.). 'Emigration from the Island of Barbados'. *Soc. Econ. Studs* 4 (1955), 245–88.

11242 SENIOR (CLARENCE) *and* MANLEY (DOUGLAS). The West Indian in Britain. 1956. Ed. by Norman Mackenzie. Fabian Society.

11243 BERTRAM (GEORGE COLIN LAWDER). West Indian Immigration. 1958. Eugenics Society Pamphlet.

11244 FAMILY PLANNING ASSOCIATION. The West Indian Comes to England. 1960. A Report Prepared for the Trustees of the London Parochial Charities by the FPA. Ed. by J. Ruck.

11245 BRAITHWAITE (EUSTACE EDWARD RICARDO). Paid Servant. 1962.

11246 —— To Sir, with Love. 1959. Reminiscences of a Black Teacher in London.

11247 MADDOX (H.). 'The Assimilation of Negroes in a Dockland Area in Britain'. *Sociol. Rev.* 8 (1960), 5–15.

11248 GLASS (RUTH) asstd by POLLINS (HAROLD). Newcomers: The West Indians in London. 1960.

11249 MILSON (FREDERICK WILLIAM) *et al.* Operation Integration. . . . An Enquiry into the Experience of West Indians Living in Birmingham with Particular Reference to Children and Young People . . . 1961.

11250 HILL (CLIFFORD STANLEY). West Indian Migrants and the London Churches. 1963.

11251 DAVISON (ROBERT BARRY). West Indian Migrants: Social and Economic Facts of Migration from the West Indies. 1962.

11252 —— Commonwealth Immigrants. 1964.

11253 —— Black British: Immigrants to England. 1966. (IRR).

11254 KIEV (ARI). 'Beliefs and Delusions of West Indian Immigrants to London'. *Brit. J. Psychiatry* 109 (1963), 356–63.

11255 COLLINS (WALLACE BARRYMORE). Jamaican Migrant. 1965.

11256 CALLEY (MALCOLM J. C.). God's People: West Indian Pentecostal Sects in England. 1965.

11257 HINDS (DONALD). Journey to an Illusion: The West Indians in Britain. 1966.

11258 PEACH (CERI). 'West Indian Migration to Britain'. *Inl. Migration R.* 1 (1967), 34–44.

11259 —— West Indian Migration to Britain: A Social Geography. 1968. [IRR].

11260 —— 'West Indian Migration to Britain: The Economic Factors'. *Race* 7 (1965), 31–46.

11261 FITZHERBERT (KATRIN). West Indian Children in London. 1967.

11262 MARSH (ALAN). 'Awareness of Racial Differences in West Indian and British Children'. *Race* 11 (1970), 289–302.

11263 HOOD (CATRIONA) *et al.* Children of West Indian Immigrants: A Study of One-Year-Olds in Paddington. 1970. [IRR Special Series.].

11264 BONHOMME (SAMUEL). Enoch Powell and West Indian Immigrants. 1971.

11265 STACEY (TOM). Immigration and Enoch Powell. 1970.

11266 LOWENTHAL (DAVID). West Indian Societies. Lond./N.Y. 1972.

11267 RUTTER (MICHAEL) *et al.* 'Children of West Indian Immigrants: 1. Rates of Behavioural Deviance and Psychiatric Disorder'. *J. Child Psychol. & Psychiatry* 15 (1974), 241–62.

11268 —— 'Children of West Indian Immigrants: 3. Home Circum-stances and Family Patterns'. *J. Child Psychol. & Psychiatry* 16 (1975), 105–23.

11269 MILES (ROBERT). Between Two Cultures?: The Case of Rastafarianism. Bristol. 1978. Working Papers on Ethnic Relations.

11270 ALLEN (SHEILA). New Minorities, Old Conflicts: Asian and West Indian Migrants in Great Britain. N.Y. 1971.

11271 LEACH (BRIDGET). 'Postal Screening for a Minority Group: Young West Indians in Leeds'. *Urban Studs* 12 (1975), 285–94.

11272 CAMPBELL (HORACE). 'Rastafari: Culture of Resistance'. *Race and Class* 22 (1980), 1–22.

11273 PEACH (CERI). 'British Unemployment Cycles and West Indian Immigration, 1955–74'. *New Community* 7 (1979), 40–4.

(iii) Jews (See also JUDAISM)

11274 RATHBONE (ELEANOR FLORENCE). Falsehoods and Facts about the Jews. 1944.

11275 ROTH (CECIL). Magna Biblioteca Anglo-Judaica: A Bibliographical Guide to Anglo-Jewish History. New edn revised and enlarged 1937.

11276 —— A History of the Jews in England. Oxf. 3rd edn 1964.

11277 LEHMANN (RUTH PAULINE) ed. Nova Bibliotheca Anglo-Judaica: A Bibliographical Guide to Anglo-Jewish History 1937–1960. 1961.

11278 LEHMAN (RUTH PAULINE). Anglo-Jewish bibliography, 1937–1970. 1973.

11279 SHAFTELSEY (JOHN M.) ed. Remember the Days: Essays on Anglo-Jewish History Presented to Cecil Roth by Members of the Council of the Jewish Historical Society of England. 1966.

11280 LIPMAN (VIVIAN DAVID) ed. Three Centuries of Anglo-Jewish History: A Volume of Essays. 1961.

11281 —— A Century of Social Service 1859–1959: The Jewish Board of Guardians. 1959.

11282 —— A Social History of the Jews in England 1850–1950. 1954.

11283 JEWISH CHRONICLE. Special Supplements to Celebrate the Tercentenary of the Resettlement of the Jews in the British Isles 1656–1956.

11284 FREEDMAN (MAURICE) *ed.* A Minority in Britain: Social Studies of the Anglo-Jewish Community. 1955.

11285 CESARANI (DAVID) *ed.* The Making of Modern Anglo-Jewry. 1989.

11286 FISCH (HAROLD). The Dual Image: The Study of the Figure of the Jew in English Literature. 1959.

11287 ELMAN (PETER). The Jewish Marriage. 1968.

11288 BERMANT (CHAIM). The Cousin-Hood: The Anglo-Jewish Gentry. 1971.

11289 —— Troubled Eden: An Anatomy of British Jewry. 1969.

11290 BARNETT (ARTHUR). The Western Synagogue through Two Centuries 1761–1961. 1961.

11291 ARIS (STEPHEN). The Jews in Business. 1970.

11292 WASSERSTEIN (BERNARD). 'Jewish Identification Among Students at Oxford'. *Jew. J. Sociol.* 13 (1971), 135–52.

11293 STEINBERG (B.). 'Jewish Education in Great Britain during World War'. *Jew. Soc. Stud.* 29 (1967), 27–63.

11294 SCHMOOL (MARLENA). 'Register of Social Research on Anglo-Jewry, 1968–1971'. *Jew. J. Sociol.* 13 (1971), 189–96.

11295 PRAIS (SIGBERT JON) *and* SCHMOOL (MARLENA). 'The Size and Structure of the Anglo-Jewish Population 1960–1965'. *Jew. J. Sociol.* 10 (1968), 5–34.

11296 LIPMAN (VIVIAN DAVID). 'Trends in Anglo-Jewish Occupations'. *Jew. J. Sociol.* 2 (1960), 202–18.

11297 GARRARD (JOHN ADRIAN). 'Parallels of Protest: English Reactions to Jewish and Commonwealth Immigration'. *Race* 9 (1967), 47–66.

11298 BENTWICH (NORMAN). 'The Social Transformation of Anglo-Jewry 1883–1960'. *Jew. J. Sociol.* 2 (1960), 16–24.

11299 BROTZ (HOWARD). 'The Position of the Jews in English Society'. *Jew. J. Sociol.* 1 (1960), 94–112.

11300 FISHER (SAMUEL) *Baron Fisher of Camden.* Brodetsky: Leader of the Anglo-Jewish Community. Leeds. 1976.

11301 ROCKER (RUDOLPH). The London Years: Translated by Joseph Leftwich. (An Abridgement from the Memoirs of R. Rocker.). 1957.

11302 —— Nationalism and Culture. Los Angeles. 1937.

11303 LONDON COMMITTEE OF DEPUTIES OF THE BRITISH JEWS. Annual Report. 1939.

11304 JAKOBOVITS (IMMANUEL). Journal of a Rabbi. 1967.

11305 GOULD (JULIUS) *and* ESH (SAUL) *eds.* Jewish Life in Modern Britain: Papers and Proceedings of a Conference . . . held on . . . 2nd April 1962. 1964.

11306 GERSHON (KAREN). We Came as Children: A Collective Autobiography. 1966.

11307 STEIN (LEONARD). Weizmann and England . . . 1964.

11308 WILLIAMS (KEITH). Britons Awake! . . . Pt. 2. Straight Shooting. Kingsbridge. 1940.

11309 COUNCIL OF CHRISTIANS AND JEWS. Annual Report 1960.

11310 —— The Corner of the Earth: Souvenir of an Anglo-Jewish Exhibition in the Undercroft of Westminster Abbey in the 900th Anniversary Year. 1966.

11311 PARKES (JAMES WILLIAM). A History of the Jewish People. 1962.

11312 WASSERSTEIN (BERNARD). Britain and the Jews of Europe, 1939–1945. 1979.

11313 HARRIS (SYDNEY). 'The Identity of Jews in an English City'. *Jew. J. Sociol.* 14 (1972), 63–84.

11314 KRAUSZ (ERNEST). 'An Anglo-Jewish Community: Leeds'. *Jew. J. Sociol.* 3 (1961), 88–106.

11315 —— Leeds Jewry: Its History and Social Structure . . . With an Introduction by Julius Gould. Camb. 1964.

11316 —— A Sociological Field Study of Jewish Suburban Life in Edgware 1962–63. With Special Reference to Minority Identification. 1965.

11317 GOLDBERG (PERCY SELVIN). The Manchester Congregation of British Jews 1857–1957. Manch. 1957.

11318 KOSMIN (BARRY A.) *et al.* Steel City Jews: A Study of Ethnicity and Social Mobility in the Jewish Population of the City of Sheffield, South Yorkshire. 1976.

11319 —— 'Exclusion and Opportunity: Traditions of Work Amongst British Jews'. In 'Discrimination and Disadvantage in Employment: The Experience of Black Workers' by Peter Braham *et al.* 1981.

11320 KOSMIN (BARRY A.) *and* GRIZZARD (NIGEL). Jews in an Inner London Borough: A Study of the Jewish Population of Hackney based on the 1971 Census. 1975.

11321 LEVY (ABRAHAM). History of the Sunderland Jewish Community. 1956.

11322 BERGHAHN (MARION). German-Jewish Refugees in England: The Ambiguities of Assimilation. 1984.

11323 ALDERMAN (GEOFFREY). The Jewish Community in British Politics. 1983.

11324 —— The Jewish Vote in Great Britain Since 1945. Glasg. 1980.

11325 —— London Jewry and London Politics, 1889–1986. 1989.

11326 —— 'Anglo-Jewry: The Politics of an Image'. *Parlt. Affs.* 37 (1984), 160–82.

11327 GRUNFELD (J.). Shefford: The Story of a Jewish School Community in Evacuation, 1939–1945. 1980.

11328 POLLINS (HAROLD). Economic History of the Jews in England. 1982.

11329 —— 'The Jews'. *History Today* (July 1985), 8–14.

11330 BURMAN (R.). 'The Jewish Woman as Breadwinner: The Changing Value of Women's Work in a Manchester Immigrant Community'. *Oral Hist.* 10 (1982), 27–39.

11331 BILD (IAN). The Jews in Britain. 1984.

(iv) Anti-Semitism

11332 ROBB (JAMES HARDING). Working Class Anti-Semite: A Psychological Study in a London Borough. 1955.

11333 PARKES (JAMES WILLIAM). The Conflict of the Church and the Synagogue: A Study in the Origins of Anti-Semitism. 1934.

11334 —— The Jewish Question. 1941.

11335 —— The Emergence of the Jewish Problem 1878–1939. 1946.

11336 LAZARE (BERNARD). Antisemitism: Its History and Causes. 1967.

11337 MANDLE (WILLIAM FREDERICK). Anti-Semitism and the British Union of Fascists. 1968.

11338 HOLMES (COLIN) *ed.* Anti-Semitism in British Society, 1876–1939. 1979.

11339 WALTON (D.). 'George Orwell and Antisemitism'. *Patterns of Prejudice* 16 (1982), 19–34.

11340 BREWER (J. D.). 'The British Union of Fascists and Antisemitism in Birmingham'. *Midland Hist.* 9 (1984), 109–22.

(v) Gypsies

11341 FITZGERALD (BRIAN VESEY). Gypsies of Britain: An Introduction to their History. 1944.

11342 DODDS (NORMAN NOEL). Gypsies, Didikois and other Travellers. 1966.

11343 U.K. SOCIOLOGICAL RESEARCH SECTION. MINISTRY OF HOUSING AND LOCAL GOVERNMENT. Gypsies and other Travellers. 1967.

11344 GENTLEMAN (HUGH) *and* SWIFT (SUSAN). Scotland's Travelling People: Problems and Solutions: A Report of the Study of a Minority Group within Scotland's Population, with Recommendations as to the Possible Solutions to these Problems . . . Edin. 1971.

11345 ACTON (THOMAS ALAN) *ed.* Current Changes Amongst British Gypsies and their Place in International Patterns of Development. 1971.

11346 —— Gypsy Politics and Social Change: The Development of Ethnic Ideology and Pressure Politics among British Gypsies from Victorian Reformism to Romany Nationalism. 1974.

11347 ADAMS (BARBARA). Gypsies and Government Policy in England: A Study of the Travellers' Way of Life in Relation to the Policies and Practices of Central and Local Government. 1975.

11348 WATERSON (MARY). Gypsy Family. 1978.

11349 PUXON (GRATTAN). On the Road: . . . to Minnie Rose Smith, a Gypsy who Died of Bronchial Pneumonia, Aged Three Months. 1968. [NCCL].

11350 SANDFORD (JEREMY). Gypsies. 1973.

11351 WORCESTERSHIRE COUNTY COUNCIL. Working Party on Gypsies—Report. Worcester. 1966.

11352 OKLEY (JUDITH). The Traveller-Gypsies. Camb. 1983.

11353 BINNS (DENIS). A Gypsy Bibliography. Manch. 1982.

11354 CRIPPS (JOHN). Accommodation for Gypsies: A Report on the Working of the Caravan Sites Act, 1968, Presented to the Secretary of State for the Environment, December 1976. 1977.

11355 SIBLEY (D.). Outsiders in Urban Societies. Oxf. 1981.

11356 ELCOCK (HOWARD). 'Politicians, Organisations and the Public—The Provision of Gypsy Sites'. *Local Govt. Studs* 5 (1979), 43–54.

11357 HARVEY (DENIS). The Gypsies: Waggon-Time and After. 1979.

(vi) Irish

11358 DOOLEY (PAT). The Irish in Britain. 1943.

11359 JACKSON (JOHN ARCHER). 'The Irish'. Chapter in 'London: Aspects of Change' by Ruth Glass *et al.* 1964.

11360 —— The Irish in Britain. 1963.

11361 —— 'The Irish in Britain'. *Sociol. R.* 10 (1962), 5–16.

11362 —— 'The Irish in Britain'. In P. J. Drudy *ed.* Ireland and Britain Since 1922. Camb. 1986. 125–38.

11363 O'CONNOR (KEVIN). The Irish in Britain. 1972.

11364 MACAMLAIGH (DONALL). An Irish Navvy: The Diary of an Exile. Translated from the Irish by Valentina Iremonger. 1964.

11365 CURTIS (LIZ). Nothing But the Same Old Story: The Roots of Anti-Irish Racism. 1984.

11366 ULAH (PHILIP). 'Second Generation Irish Youth: Identity and Ethnicity'. *New Community* 12 (1985), 310–20.

11367 HARTIGAN (MAUREEN), HICKMAN (MARY), *and* LYNCH (ANGELA), The History of the Irish in Britain: A Bibliography. 1986.

11368 DRUDY (P. J.). 'Migration between Ireland and Britain Since Independence'. In P. J. Drudy *ed.* Ireland and Britain Since 1922. Camb. 1986. 107–23.

11369 KIRWIN (F. X.) *and* NAIRN (A. G.). 'Migrant Employment and the Recession—The Case of the Irish in Britain'. *Inl. Migration Rev.* 17 (1983–4). 672–81.

11370 CONNOR (TOM). Irish Youth in London Survey. 1985.

(vii) Poles

11371 ZUBRZYCKI (JERZY). Polish Immigrants in Britain: A Study of Adjustment. The Hague. 1956.

11372 PATTERSON (SHEILA). 'The Polish Exile Community in Britain'. *Polish. Rev.* 6 (1961), 69–97.

11373 STRONNICTWO (NAROLOWE). Centralny zjazd Delegatow, 2/1/1961. Drugi Centralny zjazd . . . odbyty w Londynie w Driach 19–22 Maja 1961: Obrady, Uchwaly, Przemowienia. London. 1962.

11374 TEMKINOWA (HANNA). Gromndy Ludu Polskiego: Zarys Ideologii. Warsaw. 1962.

11375 POLISH-CATHOLIC MISSION IN LONDON 1894–1944. [Summary in English.]. 1945.

11376 SWORD (KEITH R.). '"Their Prospects Will Not be Bright": British Responses to the Problem of the Polish "Recalcitrants", 1946–49'. *Jnl Contemp. Hist.* 21 (1986), 367–90.

(viii) Chinese

11377 NG (KWEE CHOO). The Chinese in London. 1968.

11378 BROADY (MAURICE). 'The Sociological Adjustment of Chinese Immigrants in Liverpool'. *Sociol. Rev.* 3 (1955), 65–75.

11379 —— 'The Chinese in Great Britain'. In M. H. Fried *ed.* Colloquium on Overseas Chinese. 1958.

11380 MACLEOD (ALEXANDER). 'London Magnet'. *Far East Econ. Rev.* 83, (1974), 24.

11381 JONES (DOUGLAS). 'The Chinese in Britain: Origins and Development of a Community'. *New Community* 7 (1979), 397–401.

11382 —— 'Chinese Schools in Britain: A Minority Response to its Own Needs'. *Trends in Educ.* (1980), 15–18.

11383 Second Report from the Home Affairs Committee: Chinese Community in Britain. 3 vols HC Paper 102, Parliamentary Papers, 1984–5.

11384 SHANG (ANTHONY). The Chinese in Britain. 1984.

(ix) Italians

11385 CHADWICK-JONES (J. K.). 'Italian Workers in a British Factory: A Study of Informal Selection and Training'. *Race* 6 (1965), 191–8.

11386 MARIN (U.). Italiani in Gran Bretagna. Rome. 1975.

11387 KING (R.). 'Italian Migration to Great Britain'. *Geog.* 62 (1977), 176–86.

11388 GARIGUE (P.) *and* FIRTH (R. W.). 'Kinship and Organisation of Italians in London'. In R. W. Firth *ed.* Two Studies of Kinship in London. 1956. 65–93.

(x) Cypriots

11389 GEORGE (VIC). 'The Assimilation of Cypriot Immigrants in London'. *Eugenics Rev.* 58 (1966), 188–92.

(xi) Maltese

11390 DENCH (G.). Maltese in London: A Case Study in the Erosion of Ethnic Consciousness. 1975.

(xii) Vietnamese

11391 JONES (P. R.). Vietnamese Refugees: A Study of Their Reception and Resettlement in the United Kingdom. 1982.

11392 Refugees and Asylum with Special Reference to the Vietnamese. 1985.

11393 SOMERSET (FELICITY). 'Vietnamese Refugees in Britain: Resettlement Experiences'. *New Community* 10 (1983), 454–63.

(xiii) General

11394 WILSON (FRANCESCA M.). They Came as Strangers: The Story of Refugees to Great Britain. 1959.

11395 BULBRING (MAUD). 'Post-War Refugees in Great Britain'. *Pop. Studs* 8 (1954), 99–112.

(e) Immigration

11396 INSTITUTE OF RACE RELATIONS. GRIFFITH (JOHN ANEURIN GREY) *et al.* Coloured Immigrants in Britain. 1960.

11397 HUXLEY (ELSPETH). Back Street New Worlds: A Look at Immigrants in Britain. 1964.

11398 ELTON (GODFREY) *Baron Elton.* The Unarmed Invasion: A Survey of Afro-Asian Immigration. 1965.

11399 MOINDROT (CLAUDE). 'Les Vagues d'immigration en Grande Bretagne'. *Population* 20 (1965), 633–50.

11400 MOINDROT (CLAUDE) *and* SAUVY (ALFRED). 'Le Renversement du Courant d'immigration Séculaire: 1. Considérations Générales et Perspectives pour l'ensemble Europe-Mediterranée. 2. Application à l'Angleterre'. *Population* 17 (1962), 51–64.

11401 GWYNN (J. B.). 'Some Economic Aspects of Immigration'. *IRR Newsletter* (March 1965), 13–16.

11402 THOMAS (BRINLEY). The Economics of the Immigration White Paper. 1966. [IRR].

11403 —— 'The International Circulation of Human Capital'. *Minerva* 5 (1967), 479–506.

11404 FOOT (PAUL). Immigration and Race in British Politics. 1965.

11405 ROSE (E. JAMES B.). 'The Problems of Immigration and Integration'. *Cwealth J.* 8 (1975), 225–30.

11406 PANNELL (NORMAN ALFRED) *and* BROCKWAY (ARCHIBALD FENNER) *Baron.* Immigration: What is the Answer? Two Opposing Views. 1965.

11407 WOLSTENHOLME (GORDON ETHELBERT WARD) *and* O'CONNOR (MAEVE) *eds.* Immigration: Medical and Social Aspects. 1966.

11408 MISHAN (EZRA JOSHUA) *and* NEEDLEMAN (LIONEL). 'Immigration: Some Economic Effects'. *Lloyds Bank Rev.* 81 (1966), 34–46.

11409 —— 'Immigration: Excess Aggregate Demand and the Balance of Payments'. *Economica* (May 1966), 129–47.

11410 JENNER (PETER J.) *and* COHEN (BRIAN). 'Economic Effects of Immigration'. *IRR Newsletter* (Nov./Dec. 1966), 28–34. [Criticism of above article.].

11411 NEEDLEMAN (LIONEL). Reply to Criticism. *IRR Newsletter* (Feb. 1967), 16–20.

11412 PEACH (CERI). West Indian Migration: A Social Geography. 1968.

11413 NIKOLINAKOS (MARIOS). 'Notes on an Economic Theory of Racism'. *Race* 14 (1973), 365–81.

11414 RUNCIMAN (WALTER GARRISON) *and* BAGLEY (CHRISTOPHER). 'Status Consistency, Relative Deprivation and Attitudes to Immigrants'. *Sociol.* 3 (1969), 359–75.

11415 JUPP (JAMES). 'Immigrants Involvement in British and Australian Politics'. *Race* 10 (1969), 323–40.

11416 THOMAS (C. J.). 'Projections of the Growth of the Coloured Immigrant Population of England and Wales'. *J. Biosoc. Sci.* 2 (1970), 265–82.

11417 JONES (K.) *and* SMITH (A. D.). The Economic Impact of Commonwealth Immigration. Camb. 1970.

11418 THAKUR (MANAB). Industry as Seen by Immigrant Workers: A Summary of Research Findings from a Textile Mill. (Ed. by Robert Whymant for Runnymede Trust Industrial Unit.). 1970.

11419 WILD (RAYMOND) *and* RIDGEWAY (CHRISTOPHER). 'The Job Expectations of Immigrant Workers'. *Race* 11 (1970), 323–34.

11420 LIVI-BACCI (MASSIMO) *and* HAGMANN (H. M.). Report on the Demographic and Social Pattern of Migrants in Europe, Especially with Regard to International Migrations. Strasbourg. 1971.

11421 BLAKE (JOHN). 'The Planner and Immigration'. *Town and Country Planning* 40 (Nov. 1972), 513–15.

11422 CASTLES (STEPHEN) *and* KOSACK (GODULA). Immigrant Workers and Class Structure in Western Europe. 1973. [IRR].

11423 KLAASEN (LEO HENDRIK) *and* DREWE (PAUL). Migration Policy in Europe: A Comparative Study. Farnborough/Lexington. 1973.

11424 ALLEN (SHEILA) *et al.* Work, Race and Immigration. Bradford. 1977.

11425 —— Unions and Immigrant Workers: How They See Each Other. 1970.

11426 JONES (CATHERINE JOY). Immigration and Social Policy in Britain. 1977.

11427 DEMUTH (CLARE). Immigration: A Brief Guide to the Numbers Game. 1978. [Runnymede Trust Briefing Papers No. 1.].

11428 EVERSLEY (DAVID CHARLES). A Question of Numbers? 1973.

11429 JOINT COUNCIL FOR THE WELFARE OF IMMIGRANTS. The Numbers Game . . . Evidence to the Select Committee on Race Relations and Immigration. 1977.

11430 KOHLER (DAVID F.). Immigration and Race Relations. 1977. [Liberal Publication Dept. Study Papers No. 7.].

11431 HOLMES (COLIN) *ed.* Immigrants and Minorities in British Society. 1978.

11432 —— 'Immigration into Britain: The Myth of Fairness: Racial Violence in Britain'. *History Today* 35/10 (1985), 41–5.

11433 —— John Bull's Island: Immigration and British Society 1871–1971. Basingstoke. 1988.

11434 PORMINDER (BHACHU). Twice Migrants: East African Sikh Settlers in Great Britain. 1985.

11435 WILSON (C.), COLLARD (D.), *and* HITT (W. H.). Economic Issues in Immigration—An Exploration of the Liberal Approach to Public Policy on Immigration. 1970.

11436 COLLISON (PETER). 'Immigrants and Residence'. *Sociol.* 1 (1967), 277–92.

11437 GISH (OSCAR). 'Color and Skill: British Immigration 1955–1968'. *Inl. Migr. Rev.* 3 (1968), 19–37.

11438 JONES (FRANK E.) *and* LAMBERT (WALKER E.). 'Some Situational Influences on Attitudes Toward Immigrants'. *Brit. J. Sociol.* 18 (1967), 408–24.

11439 LAYTON-HENRY (ZIG). 'Immigration into Britain: The New Commonwealth Migrants, 1945–1962'. *History Today* 35/12 (1985), 27–32.

11440 HOCH (P. K.). 'Immigration into Britain: No Utopia: Refugee Scholars in Britain'. *History Today* 35/11 (1985), 53–6.

11441 COMMISSION FOR RACIAL EQUALITY. Immigrant Control Procedures: Report of a Formal Investigation. 1985.

11442 GORDON (PAUL). British Immigration Control: A Brief Guide. 1985.

11443 RICHMOND (ANTHONY HENRY). Immigration and Ethnic Conflict. Basingstoke. 1988.

(f) Regional Studies

(i) London

11444 GLASS (RUTH) *et al.* London: Aspects of Change . . . 1967.

11445 HYNDMAN (A.). 'The Welfare of Coloured People in London'. *Soc. Wk.* 15 (1958), 492–8.

11446 JEPHCOTT (AGNES PEARL). A Troubled Area: Notes on Notting Hill. 1964.

11447 ALYSON-SMITH (K.). 'A Study of Immigrant Group Relations in North London'. *Race* 9 (1968), 467–76.

11448 KAWWA (TASIR). 'Three Sociometric Studies of Ethnic Relations in London Schools'. *Race* 10 (1968), 173–80.

11449 LITTLE (ALAN), MABEY (CHRISTINE), *and* WHITAKER (GRAHAM). 'The Education of Immigrant Pupils in Inner London Primary Schools'. *Race* 9 (1968), 439–52.

11450 LAISHLEY (JENNY). 'Skin Colour Awareness and Preference in London Nursery-school Children'. *Race* 13 (1971), 47–64.

11451 SHAH (SAMIR). Immigrants and Employment in the Clothing Industry: The Rag Trade in London's East End. 1975.

11452 BROOKS (DENNIS). Race and Labour in London Transport. 1975. [IRR and the Action Society Trust.].

11453 LEE (TREVOR ROSS). Race and Residence: The Concentration and Dispersal of Immigrants in London. Oxf. 1977.

(ii) Birmingham

11454 BIRMINGHAM PLANET. Smethwick Survey. Issues of 3–17 June 1965. Nos 92–4, 3 parts.

11455 LENTON (JOHN), BUDGEN (NICHOLAS), *and* CLARKE (KENNETH). Immigration, Race and Politics: A Birmingham View. 1966.

11456 JONES (PHILIP NICHOLAS). The Segregation of Immigrant Communities in the City of Birmingham, 1961. Hull. 1967.

11457 REX (JOHN) *and* MOORE (ROBERT) *with the assistance of* SHUTTLEWORTH (ALAN) *and* WILLIAMS (JENNIFER). Race, Community and Conflict: A Study of Sparkbrook. 1967.

11458 BEETHAM (DAVID). Immigrant School Leavers and the Youth Employment Service in Birmingham. 1967. [IRR Special Series.].

11459 —— Transport and Turbans: A Comparative Study in Local Politics. 1970.

11460 LAMBERT (JOHN). Crime, Police and Race Relations: A Study in Birmingham. 1970.

(iii) Manchester

11461 REID (JANET). 'Employment of Negroes in Manchester'. *Sociol. Rev.* 4 (1956), 191–8.

11462 WERBNER (PRIMA). 'Avoiding the Ghetto: Pakistani Migrants and Settlement Shifts in Manchester'. *New Community* 7 (1979), 376–85.

(iv) Liverpool

11463 RICHMOND (ANTHONY HENRY). Colour Prejudice in Britain: A Study of West Indian Workers in Liverpool, 1941–1951. 1954.

11464 MAY (ROY) *and* COHEN (ROBIN). 'The Interaction Between Race and Colonialism: A Case Study of the Liverpool Race Riots of 1919'. *Race and Class* 16 (1974), 111–26.

11465 JULIENNE (L.). Charles Wootton: The 1919 Race Riots in Liverpool. L/pool. 1979.

11466 LAW (IAN). A History of Race and Racism in Liverpool. L/pool. 1981.

(v) Cardiff and South Wales

11467 LITTLE (KENNETH LINDSAY). 'Loudon Square—A Community Survey I'. *Soc. Rev.* 34 (Jan.–Apr. 1942), 12–33.

11468 'Loudon Square—A Community Survey II'. *Soc. Rev.* 34 (Jul.–Oct. 1942), 119–46.

11469 EVANS (NEIL). 'The South Wales Race Riots of 1919'. *Llafur* 3 (1980), 5–29.

11470 —— 'The South Wales Race Riots of 1919: A Documentary Postscript'. *Llafur* 6 (1983), 76–87.

11471 —— 'Regulating the Reserve Army: Arabs, Blacks and the Local State in Cardiff, 1919–1945'. Ch. in 'Race and Labour in Twentieth-Century History' *ed.* by Kenneth Lunn. 1985.

(vi) Miscellaneous Areas

11472 RIMMER (MALCOLM). Race and Industrial Conflict: A Study in a Group of Midland Foundries. 1972.

11473 WRIGHT (PETER L.). The Coloured Worker in British Industry, with Special Reference to the Midlands and North of England. 1968.

11474 AVISON (E.). 'Immigrants in a Small Borough'. (Bedford) *IRR Newsletter* (Oct. 1965), 11–15.

11475 BELL (R.). 'Smethwick'. (Staffordshire) *IRR Newsletter* (Sept. 1966).

11476 ROWLEY (GWYN) *and* TIPPLE (GRAHAM). 'Coloured Immigrants Within the City: An Analysis of Housing and Travel Preferences'. *Urban Stud.* 11 (1974), 81–9.

11477 KATZNELSON (IRA). 'The Policy of Racial Buffering in Nottingham, 1954–1968'. *Race* 11 (1970), 431–46.

11478 LAWRENCE (DANIEL). Black Migrants and White Natives: A Study of Race Relations in Nottingham. Camb. 1974.

11479 ISRAEL (WILLIAM H.). Colour and Community: A Study of Coloured Immigrants and Race Relations in an Industrial Town. [Slough. 1964. Slough Council of Social Service.].

11480 GUMMER (JOHN) *and* GUMMER (JOHN SELWYN). When the Coloured People Come. 1966. [Sikhs in Gravesend.].

11481 RICHMOND (ANTHONY HENRY) *et al.* Immigration and Race Relations in an English Town: A Study in Bristol. 1973. [IRR.].

11482 GREEN (JEFFRY P.). '"Beef Pie with a Suet Crust": A Black Childhood in Wigan, 1906–1920'. *New Community* 11 (1984), 291–8.

11483 BROOKS (DENNIS). Black Employment in the Black Country: A Study of Walsall. 1975. [Runnymede Trust.].

11484 BYRNE (DAVID). 'The 1930 "Arab Riot" in South Shields: A Race Riot that Never was'. *Race and Class* 18 (1977), 261–76.

11485 TURNER (IAN). ' "Spot of Bother"—Civil Disorder in the North-East between the Wars'. *J. N. E. Lab. Hist.* No. 18 (1984), 40–7.

11486 BAKER (PETER). Attitudes to Coloured People in Glasgow. Glasg. 1970.

11487 JENKINSON (JACQUELINE). 'The Glasgow Race Disturbances of 1919'. Ch. in Race and Labour in Twentieth-Century Britain. *Ed.* by Kenneth Lunn. 1985.

11488 —— 'The Black Community of Salford and Hull 1919–1921'. *Immigrants and Minorities* 7 (1988).

11489 BROWN (JOHN). The Unmelting Pot: An English Town and its Immigrants. 1970. [This book refers to Bedford.].

(g) Housing

11490 DUNCAN (S. S.). Housing Disadvantage and Residential Mobility: Immigrants and Institutions in a Northern Town. Brighton. 1977.

11491 BURNEY (ELIZABETH). Housing on Trial: A Study of Immigrants and Local Government. 1967.

11492 DUKE (CHRISTOPHER). Colour and Rehousing: A Study of Redevelopment in Leeds. 1970. [IRR].

11493 BUSH (MARTHA) *comp.* Immigrant Housing. 1976. [London GLC Research Library. Research Bibliographies No. 74.].

11494 McKAY (DAVID H.). Housing and Race in Industrial Society: Civil Rights and Urban Policy in Britain and the United States. 1977.

11495 SMITH (DAVID JOHN) *and* WHALLEY (ANNE). Racial Minorities and Public Housing. 1975. [PEP Broadsheet, No.556.].

(h) Students

11496 SINGH (AMAL KUMAR). Indian Students in Britain: A Survey of their Adjustment and Attitudes. Bombay. 1963.

11497 CAREY (ALEXANDER TIMOTHY). Colonial Students: A Study of the Social Adaptation of Colonial Students in London. 1956.

11498 POLITICAL AND ECONOMIC PLANNING. New Commonwealth Students in Britain: With Special Reference to Students from East Africa. 1965.

11499 —— Colonial Students in Britain. 1955.

11500 TAJFEL (HENRI) *and* DAWSON (JOHN LEWIS) *eds.* Disappointed Ghosts: Essays by African, Asian and West Indian Students. 1965. [IRR].

11501 TAJFEL (HENRI). 'Pregiudizi di Colore in Gran Bretagna: L'Esperienza degli Studenti d'Africa, d'Asia e delle Indie Occidentali'. *Riv. Sociol.* 4 (1966), 53–82.

11502 LONDON CONFERENCE ON OVERSEAS STUDENTS STANDING COMMITTEE. Overseas Students in Britain: A Handbook. Rev. edn 1962.

11503 LIVINGSTONE (ARTHUR STANLEY). The International Student. 1964.

11504 BURNS (DONALD GEORGE). Travelling Scholars: An Enquiry into the Adjustment and Attitudes of Overseas Students Holding Commonwealth Bursaries in England and Wales. Slough. 1965.

11505 U.K. MINISTRY OF OVERSEAS DEVELOPMENT. Training in Britain. 1965. Rev. edn 1966.

11506 BRITISH COUNCIL FOR OVERSEAS STUDENTS IN BRITAIN. A Handbook for All who are Interested in the Welfare of Overseas Students. Rev. edn 1966.

11507 BANHAM (MARTIN). 'The Nigerian Student in Britain'. *Univ. Q.* 12 (1958), 363–6.

11508 ANIMASHAWUN (G. K.). 'African Students in Britain'. *Race* 5 (1963), 38–47.

11509 MacFARLANE (RONALD). 'The Welfare of Commonwealth Students'. *Univ. Q.* 12 (1958), 360–3.

11510 —— 'Overseas Students in British Universities 1957–1958'. *Univ. Q.* 12 (1958), 366–70.

11511 BOTTING (JOSEPH HENRY ALFRED). 'Studenti Africani a Londra'. *Nigrizia* 82 (1964), 24–36.

(i) Autobiographies

11512 LO BOGOLA. An African Savage's Own Story. 1930.

11513 MARKE (ERNEST). Old Man Trouble. 1974.

11514 JINGOES (JASON). A Chief is a Chief by the People. (The Autobiography of Stimela Jason Jingoes Recorded and Compiled by John and Cassandra Perry.). 1975.

11515 McKAY (CLAUDE). A Long Way from Home: An Autobiography. N.Y. 1970.

See also Wayne Cooper *and* Robert Reinders, 'A Black Briton Comes "Home": Claude McKay in England, 1920'. *Race* 9 (1967), 67–85.

(j) Bibliographies

11516 SIVANANDAN (A.) *comp.* Coloured Immigrants in Britain: A Select Bibliography Based on the Holdings of the Library of the Institute of Race Relations. 1965. 2nd edn 1967. [IRR].

11517 SIVANANDAN (A.) *and* SCRUTTON (M.) *comps.* Register of Research on Commonwealth Immigrants in Britain. 1967.

11518 RUNNYMEDE TRUST. Briefing Papers. No. 6. Ethnic Minorities in Britain: A Select Bibliography. 1977.

11519 CAMPBELL-PLATT (K.). Ethnic Minorities in Society: A Reference Guide. 1976.

11520 GRAYSHON (MATTHEW CLIFFORD) *and* HOUGHTON (VINCENT PAUL) *comps.* Initial Bibliography of Immigration and Race. Nottingham. 1966.

11521 COMMUNITY RELATIONS COMMISSION. Race Relations in Britain: A Select Bibliography with Emphasis on Commonwealth Immigrants. 1969.

11522 MADAN (RAJ). Coloured Minorities in Great Britain: A Comprehensive Bibliography. Westport, Conn. 1979.

11523 GORDON (PAUL) *and* KLUG (FRANCESCA). Racism and Discrimination in Britain: A Select Bibliography 1970–1983. 1984.

11524 CASHMORE (ERNEST). Dictionary of Race and Ethnic Relations. 1984.

11525 GILBERT (VICTOR F.). 'Race and Labour in Britain: A Bibliography'. Ch. in 'Race and Labour in Twentieth-Century Britain' by Kenneth Lunn. 1985.

5

RELIGION AND THE CHURCHES

The assumptions which could still legitimately underpin a bibliography of British religion as of 1914 can scarcely be maintained seventy-five years later. The weakened position of the churches, sometimes seen as the consequence of 'secularization', and the advent of adherents of other world religions in substantial numbers in recent decades, makes the consistent ordering of the literature particularly difficult. The scholarly study of non-Christian religions in Britain remains as yet relatively underdeveloped: the bulk of the scholarship relates to Christianity in the various ecclesiastical families to be found in the United Kingdom. The bibliography therefore retains that emphasis. It has long been the case, however, that the broad confessional groupings have different strengths within the countries of the United Kingdom and that religious differences, however 'secularized' they may have become, have been important markers of identity in England, Northern Ireland, Scotland, and Wales. It may be noted, in this connection, how little substantial work there appears to be on Roman Catholicism in Northern Ireland—and there are other transparent gaps. Therefore, while it would have been possible to organize the sub-sections on an entirely confessional basis, a compromise has been made and confessional categories appear within national sub-sections. Such arrangements cannot be without exceptions since there are even a few books which do in fact attempt to tackle religion on a 'British' basis. In the initial sub-sections, also, an attempt has been made to collate material which assesses the social and political impact of the churches though in some cases the items might have appeared within the 'politics' section. Works relating to the missionary activities of British churches overseas have been kept to a minimum. Most of the literature which has been arranged can be classified as 'ecclesiastical history' but a sub-section notes the important contribution made by sociologists of religion in recent decades.

1. GENERAL

11526 INTERNATIONAL BIBLIOGRAPHY OF THE HISTORY OF RELIGIONS For the Year 1952+. Leiden. 1954+. Annual.

11527 CHADWICK (*Sir* WILLIAM OWEN). The History of the Church: A Select Bibliography. Hist. Assoc. Helps for Students 66. 1962. Rev. edn 1966.

11528 REVUE D₃HISTOIRE ECCLÉSIASTIQUE. Louvain. 1900+. Quart.

11529 CROSS (FRANK LESLIE) *and* LIVINGSTONE (ELIZABETH ANNE) *eds.* The Oxford Dictionary of the Christian Church. 1957. 2nd edn 1974.

11530 PETERSEN (PAUL D.) *and* FRASER (RUTH F.). Religion and Politics: A Bibliography Selected from the Atlas Religious Database. Rev. edn Chicago. 1984.

11531 R.C.H.M. Guides to Sources for British History 6: Papers of British Churchmen 1780–1940. 1987.

11532 CHURCH OF ENGLAND OFFICIAL YEARBOOK. 1885+. Annual.

11533 CROCKFORD'S CLERICAL DIRECTORY. 1858+.

11534 CHURCH COMMISSIONERS FOR ENGLAND ANNUAL REPORT. 1949+.

11535 FACTS AND FIGURES ABOUT THE CHURCH OF ENGLAND. *Ed.* by R. F. Neuss. 1959–65.

11536 HISTORICAL MAGAZINE OF THE PROTESTANT EPISCOPALIAN CHURCH. 1966+.

11537 JOURNAL OF ECCLESIASTICAL HISTORY. Camb. 1+. 1950+.

11538 JOURNAL OF RELIGIOUS HISTORY. Sydney. 1960–1+.

11539 CHURCH HISTORY. Chicago. 1932+.

11540 JOURNAL OF THEOLOGICAL STUDIES. 1899+.

11541 STUDIES IN CHURCH HISTORY.

11542 HIBBERT JOURNAL.

11543 THE MODERN CHURCHMAN.

11544 THE HARVARD THEOLOGICAL REVIEW.

11545 GAY (JOHN DENNIS). The Geography of Religion in England. 1971.

11546 CURRIE (ROBERT), GILBERT (ALAN D.), *and* HORSLEY (LEE). Churches and Churchgoers: Patterns of Church Growth in the British Isles Since 1700. Oxf. 1977.

11547 BRIERLEY (PETER). U.K. Christian Handbook—1983+.

11548 CENTRAL BOARD OF FINANCE OF THE CHURCH OF ENGLAND. Church Statistics: Some Facts and Figures about the Church of England. 1985.

11549 KENT (JOHN HENRY SOMERSET). 'The Study of Modern Ecclesiastical History Since 1930'. In J. Daniélou *et al.* The Pelican Guide to Modern Theology. Vol. 2 Historical Theology. Harmondsworth. 1969.

11550 ROBBINS (KEITH GILBERT). 'Institutions and Illusions: The Dilemma of the Modern Ecclesiastical Historian'. Studies in Church History. Vol. 11. 1975. 355–65.

11551 OWEN (DOROTHY MARY). The Records of the Established Church in England, Excluding Parochial Records. British Records Assoc. 1970.

11552 KITCHING (CHRISTOPHER J.). The Central Records of the Church of England: A Report and Survey. 1976.

11553 SMYTHE (PAUL RODNEY). A Bibliography of Anglican Modernism. Camb. 1947.

2. HISTORIES

11554 LATOURETTE (KENNETH SCOTT). Christianity in a Revolutionary Age: A History of Christianity in the Nineteenth and Twentieth Centuries. 4 vols. N.Y. 1953–61.

11555 VIDLER (ALEXANDER ROPER). The Church in an Age of Revolution: 1789 to the Present Day. Harmondsworth. 1962.

11556 SPINKS (GEORGE STEPHENS) *et al.* Religion in Britain Since 1900. 1952.

11557 HASTINGS (ADRIAN). A History of English Christianity 1920–1985. 1986.

11558 WORRALL (B. G.). The Making of the Modern Church: Christianity in England Since 1800. 1988.

11559 MCLEOD (HUGH). Religion and the People of Western Europe, 1789–1970. 1981.

11560 PERMAN (DAVID). Change and the Churches. 1977.

11561 BADHAM (PAUL) *ed.* Religion, State and Society in Modern Britain. Lampeter. 1989.

11562 GILBERT (ALAN D.). Religion and Society in Industrial England. 1976.

11563 —— The Making of Post-Christian Britain. 1980.

11564 COWLING (MAURICE JOHN). Religion and Public Doctrine in Modern England. Vol. 1. Camb. 1980. Vol. 2. Camb. 1985.

11565 BENNETT (GARETH VAUGHAN) *and* WALSH (JOHN DIXON) *eds.* Essays in Modern English Church History, in Memory of Norman Sykes. 1966.

11566 JAMES (EDWIN OLIVER). A History of Christianity in England. 1949.

11567 MOORMAN (JOHN RICHARD HUMPIDGE). A History of the Church in England. 1953. Rev. edn 1973.

11568 OLLARD (SIDNEY LESLIE) *et al.* Dictionary of English Church History. 1912. 3rd edn 1948.

11569 CLARK (GEORGE SIDNEY ROBERTS KITSON). The English Inheritance: An Historical Essay. 1950.

11570 PEPLER (CONRAD). The English Religious Heritage. 1958.

11571 SYKES (NORMAN). The English Religious Tradition. 1953.

11572 MALDEN (RICHARD HENRY). The English Church and Nation. 1952.

11573 SMYTH (CHARLES HUGH EGERTON). The Church and the Nation: Six Studies in the Anglican Tradition. 1962.

11574 WILLIAMS (ALWYN TERRELL PETRE). The Anglican Tradition in the Life of England. 1947.

11575 HARVEY (GEORGE LEONARD HUNTON). The Church and the Twentieth Century. 1936.

11576 NORMAN (EDWARD ROBERT). Church and Society in England, 1770–1970. 1976.

11577 HABGOOD (JOHN). Church and Nation in a Secular Age. 1983.

11578 JENKINS (DANIEL THOMAS). The British: Their Identity and their Religion. 1975.

11579 THOMAS (TERENCE). The British: Their Religious Beliefs and Practices 1800–1986. Lond./N.Y. 1988.

11580 ROBBINS (KEITH GILBERT). 'Religion and Identity in Modern British History'. Studies in Church History. Vol. 18 465–87.

11581 DAVIES (RUPERT ERIC). The Church in Our Times: An Ecumenical History from a British Perspective. 1979.

11582 —— *Ed.* The Testing of the Churches 1932–1982. 1982.

11583 JEFFERSON (PHILIP CLARKE) *ed.* The Church in the 60s. 1962.

11584 SLACK (KENNETH). The British Churches Today. 1961. 2nd edn 1970.

11585 MICKLEM (CARYL). 'Is Britain Still Christian?'. *Religion in Life* xxxiv (1965), 605–7.

11586 NORTHCOTT (WILLIAM CECIL). 'Decade of Change in the Churches'. *Contemp. Rev.* ccxviii 292–6.

11587 COX (JEFFREY). The English Churches in a Secular Society: Lambeth 1870–1930. N.Y. 1982.

11588 RANSON (S.), BRYMAN (A.), *and* HININGS (B.). Clergy, Ministers and Priests. 1977.

3. THE CHURCH OF ENGLAND

11589 MOORE (E. GARTH) *and* BRIDEN (TIMOTHY). Moore's Introduction to English Canon Law. 1985.

11590 HEADLAM (ARTHUR CAYLEY). The Church of England. 1924. 2nd edn 1925.

11591 JOHNSON (HUMPHREY JOHN THEWLIS). Anglicanism in Transition. 1938.

11592 —— 'Tendencies in the Church of England: Some Recent Views'. *Dublin Rev.* (Autumn 1947), 73–85.

11593 —— 'Anglicanism in the 20th Century: 4. The Church of England and Other Denominations'. *Clergy Rev.* n.s. xl (1955), 65–78.

11594 NEILL (STEPHEN CHARLES). Anglicanism. 1958. 3rd edn 1965.

11595 WAND (JOHN WILLIAM CHARLES). Anglicanism in History and Today. 1961.

11596 MAYFIELD (GUY). The Church of England: Its Members and its Business. 1963.

11597 BAYNE (STEPHEN FIELDING). An Anglican Turning Point: Documents and Interpretations. 1964.

11598 LLOYD (ROGER BRADSHAIGH). The Church of England, 1900–1965. 1966.

11599 HUNTER (LESLIE STANNARD) *ed.* The English Church: A New Look. 1966.

11600 BEESON (TREVOR RANDALL). The Church of England in Crisis. 1973.

11601 MOORE (CHARLES), WILSON (A. N.), *and* STAMP (GAVIN). The Church in Crisis: A Critical Assessment of the Current State of the Church of England. 1986.

11602 WELSBY (PAUL A.). A History of the Church of England 1945–1980. Oxf. 1984.

11603 STAPLES (PETER). The Church of England 1961–1980. Leiden/Utrecht. 1981.

11604 FLINDALL (ROY PHILIP). The Church of England, 1815–1948: A Documentary History. 1972.

11605 HARRISON (D. E. W.) *and* SANSOM (MICHAEL C.). Worship in the Church of England. 1982.

11606 CUMING (GEOFFREY JOHN). A History of Anglican Liturgy. 1969. 2nd edn 1982.

11607 ADDLESHAW (GEORGE WILLIAM OUTRAM) *and* ETCHELLS (FREDERICK). The Architectural Setting of Anglican Worship: An Inquiry into the Arrangements for Public Worship in the Church of England from the Reformation to the Present Day. 1948. 2nd edn 1956.

11608 JAGGER (PETER JOHN). Christian Initiation, 1552–1969: Rites of Baptism and Confirmation since the Reformation Period. 1970.

11609 BRADSHAW (PAUL FREDERICK). The Anglican Ordinal: Its History and Development from the Reformation to the Present Day. 1971.

11610 SCOTT (JUDITH G.). 'Ecclesiological Influences in England, 1846–1963'. *Scot. Ecclesiol. Soc. Trans.* xv (1965), 29–32.

11611 THOMPSON (KENNETH ALFRED). Bureaucracy and Church Reform: The Organizational Response of the Church of England to Social Change, 1800–1965. Oxf. 1970.

11612 NICHOLLS (DAVID). Church and State in Britain Since 1820. 1969.

11613 WICKHAM (EDWARD RALPH). Church and People in an Industrial City. 1957.

11614 WALTON (MARY). A History of the Diocese of Sheffield, 1914–1979. Sheffield. 1981.

11615 PICKERING (WILLIAM STUART FREDERICK) *ed.* A Social History of the Diocese of Newcastle. 1981.

11616 WINNETT (ARTHUR ROBERT). Attempt Great Things: The Diocese of Guildford, 1927–1977. Guildford. 1977.

11617 DENNY (BARBARA). King's Bishop: The Lords Spiritual of London. 1985.

11618 JAGGER (PETER JOHN). A History of the Parish and People Movement. Leighton Buzzard. 1977.

11619 SOUTHCOTT (ERNEST WILLIAM). The Parish Comes Alive. 1957.

11620 GRAY (DONALD). Earth and Altar. The Evolution of the Parish Communion in the Church of England to 1945. 1986.

11621 THOMPSON (DAVID MICHAEL). 'The Politics of the Enabling Act (1919)'. Studies in Church History. Vol. 12 1975. 383–92.

11622 ZIMMERMAN (J. D.). 'A Chapter in English Church Reform: The Enabling Act of 1919'. *Hist. Mag. Prot. Episc. Ch.* xvi (1977), 215–25.

11623 WHITE (GAVIN DONALD). 'The Hectic Night: The Prayer Book Debate, 1927 and 1928'. *Theology* lxxvii (1974), 639–46.

11624 —— ' "No-one is Free from Parliament": The Worship and Doctrine Measure in Parliament 1974'. In 'Religion and National Identity'. Studies in Church History. Vol. 18 by Stuart Mews. Oxf. 1982. 557–65.

11625 AMOS (CHARLES WILLIAM HALE) *ed.* Call to Action in Defence of Church and State in England, 1933–35. 1936.

11626 GARBETT (CYRIL FORSTER). Church and State in England. 1949.

11627 LAUNDY (PHILIP ALAN CHARLES). 'Parliament and the Church'. *Parl. Affs* xii (1959), 445–60.

11628 HEUBEL (E. J.). 'Church and State in England: The Price of Establishment'. *Western Pol. Q.* xviii (1965), 646–65.

11629 HINCHLIFF (PETER BINGHAM). The One-Sided Reciprocity: A Study in the Modification of the Establishment. 1966.

11630 NORTHCOTT (WILLIAM CECIL). 'Church and State in England'. *Quart. Rev.* cccv (1967), 273–82.

11631 TURNER (HENRY JOHN MANSFIELD). 'Is Establishment Defensible Today?'. *Theology* lxxii (1969), 356–60.

11632 DREWRY (GAVIN) *and* BROCK (JENNY). 'Prelates in Parliament'. *Parl. Affs* xxiv (1971), 220–50.

11633 PAUL (LESLIE ALLEN). 'The Legal Straitjacket of the Church of England'. *Contemp. Rev.* ccxx (1972), 242–8.

11634 MEDHURST (KENNETH N.) *and* MOYSER (GEORGE H.). Church and Politics in a Secular Age. Oxf. 1988.

11635 MOYSER (GEORGE H.) *ed.* Church and Politics Today. Edin. 1985.

11636 LAMBETH PALACE. The Lambeth Conferences 1867–1948. The Reports of the 1920, 1930 and 1948 Conferences, with Selected Resolutions from the Conferences of 1867, 1878, 1888, 1897 and 1908. 1948.

11637 SMETHURST (ARTHUR FREDERICK) *ed.* Acts of the Convocations of Canterbury and York together with Certain Other Resolutions, Passed since the Reform of the Convocations in 1921. 1948.

11638 STEPHENSON (ALAN MALCOLM GEORGE). Anglicanism and the Lambeth Conference. 1978.

11639 LAMBETH PALACE. The Lambeth Conference. 1958, 1968, 1978, 1988.

11640 EDWARDS (DAVID LAWRENCE). '101 years of the Lambeth Conference'. *Church Q. Rev.* i (1968), 21–35.

11641 STEWART (HERBERT LESLIE). A Century of Anglo-Catholicism. 1929.

11642 SIMPSON (WILLIAM JOHN SPARROW). History of the Anglo-Catholic Revival from 1845. 1932.

11643 MOSS (CLAUDE BEAUFORT). Anglo-Catholicism at the Crossroads. 1932.

11644 The Orthodox Revival, 1833–1933: Six Lectures on the Oxford Movement. 1933.

11645 MAY (JAMES LEWIS). The Oxford Movement: Its History and its Future, a Layman's Estimate. 1933.

11646 LESLIE (*Sir* JOHN RANDOLPH SHANE). The Oxford Movement, 1833–1933. 1933.

11647 KNOX (WILFRID LAWRENCE). The Catholic Movement in the Church of England. 1932.

11648 SIMPSON (WILLIAM JOHN SPARROW). The Contribution of Cambridge to the Anglo-Catholic Revival. 1934.

11649 KELWAY (ALBERT CLIFTON). The Story of the Catholic Revival, 1833–1933. 1933.

11650 CECIL (HUGH RICHARD HEATHCOTE) *Baron Quickswood, et al.* Anglo-Catholicism Today. 1934.

11651 WILKINSON (JOHN DONALD) *ed.* Catholic Anglicans Today. 1968.

11652 PENHALE (FRANCIS). The Anglican Church Today: Catholics in Crisis. 1986.

11653 PICKERING (WILLIAM STUART FREDERICK). Anglo-Catholicism: A Study in Religious Ambiguity. 1989.

11654 BALLEINE (GEORGE REGINALD). A History of the Evangelical Party in the Church of England. 1933. 3rd edn 1951.

11655 POOLE-CONNER (EDWARD JOSHUA). Evangelicalism in England. 1951.

11656 MANWARING (RANDLE). The Heart of this People: An Outline of the Protestant Tradition in England Since 1900. 1954.

11657 CAPON (JOHN). And Then There Was Light . . . The Story of the Nationwide Festival of Light. 1972.

11658 KING (JOHN CHARLES) *ed.* Evangelicals Today: 13 Stock-Taking Essays. 1973.

11659 MANWARING (RANDLE). From Controversy to Co-existence: Evangelicals in the Church of England 1914–1980. Camb. 1985.

11660 BEBBINGTON (DAVID WILLIAM). Evangelicalism in Modern Britain. A History from the 1730s to the 1980s. 1989.

11661 POLLOCK (JOHN CHARLES). A Cambridge Movement. 1953.

11662 JOHNSON (DOUGLAS). Contending for the Faith: A History of the Evangelical Movement in the Universities and Colleges. Leicester. 1979.

11663 BARCLAY (OLIVER R.). Whatever Happened to the Jesus Lane Lot? Leicester. 1977.

11664 COGGAN (FREDERICK DONALD) *ed.* Christ and the Colleges: A History of the Inter-varsity Fellowship. 1934.

11665 TATLOW (TISSINGTON). The Story of the Student Christian Movement. 1933.

11666 MCCAUGHEY (J. D.). Christian Obedience in the University: Studies in the Life of the Student Christian Movement of Great Britain, 1930–1950. 1958.

11667 ANSON (PETER FREDERICK). The Call of the Cloister: Religious Communities and Kindred Bodies in the Anglican Communion. 1955.

11668 WILLIAMS (BARRIE). The Franciscan Revival in the Anglican Communion. 1982.

11669 HEENEY (BRIAN). The Women's Movement in the Church of England 1850–1930. Oxf. 1988.

11670 CHAPMAN (JENNIFER). The Last Bastion. 1989.

11671 DOWELL (SUSAN) and HURCOMBE (LINDA). Dispossessed Daughters of Eve. 1981.

11672 ALDRIDGE (ALAN). 'In the Absence of a Minister: Structures of Subordination in the Role of the Deaconess in the Church of England'. *Sociol.* 21 (1987), 377–92.

11673 MALMGREEN (GAIL) ed. Religion in the Lives of English Women, 1760–1930. 1986.

11674 JOHNSON (DALE A.). Women in English Religion 1700–1925. N.Y. 1923.

11675 PARKER (OLIVE). For the Family's Sake: A History of the Mothers Union, 1876–1976. 1976.

11676 EDWARDS (DAVID LAWRENCE). Leaders of the Church of England, 1828–1944. 1971. Rev. edn 1978.

11677 TOWLER (ROBERT) and COXON (ANTHONY P. M.). The Fate of the Anglican Clergy: A Sociological Study. 1979.

11678 RUSSELL (ANTHONY JOHN). The Clerical Profession. 1980.

11679 PAUL (LESLIE). The Deployment and Payment of the Clergy. 1964.

11680 —— A Church by Daylight: A Reappraisement of the Church of England and its Future. 1973.

11681 MORGAN (D. H. J.). 'The Social and Educational Background of Anglican Bishops—Continuities and Changes'. *Brit. J. Sociol.* xx (1969), 295–310.

11682 LONGFORD (FRANK) *Earl.* The Bishops: A Study of Leaders in the Church Today. 1986.

11683 PATON (DAVID MACDONALD). Reform of the Ministry: A Study in the Work of Roland Allen. 1968.

11684 McDOWELL (ROBERT BRENDAN). 'The Anglican Episcopate, 1780–1945'. *Theology* (June 1947), 202–9.

11685 MEDHURST (KENNETH N.) and MOYSER (GEORGE). 'Studying a Religious Elite: The Case of the Anglican Episcopate'. In Research Methods for Elite Studies. *Ed.* by George Moyser and M. Wagstaffe. 1987.

11686 THOMPSON (KENNETH ALFRED). 'The Church of England Bishops as an Elite'. In Elites and Power in British Society. *Ed.* by P. Stanworth and Anthony Giddens. Camb. 1974.

11687 RILEY (HAROLD) and GRAHAM (R. J.) *eds.* Acts of the Convocations of Canterbury and York, 1921–1970. 1971.

Archbishops of Canterbury and York

11688 CARPENTER (EDWARD FREDERICK). Cantuar: The Archbishops in their Office. 1971. Rev. edn 1988.

11689 COGGAN. Donald Coggan: Servant of Christ. By Margaret Pawley. 1987.

11690 DAVIDSON. Randall Davidson, Archbishop of Canterbury. By George Kennedy Allen Bell. 2 vols. 1935. 3rd edn 1952.

11691 HERBERT (CHARLES). Twenty-Five Years as Archbishop of Canterbury: A Biography of Archbishop Davidson. 1929.

11692 DARK (SIDNEY). Archbishop Davidson and the English Church. 1929.

11693 MOORMAN (JOHN RICHARD HUMPIDGE). 'Archbishop Davidson and the Church'. *Theology* lix (1956), 269–75.

11694 FISHER. Fisher of Lambeth: A Portrait from Life. By William Ernest Purcell. 1969.

11695 —— The Archbishop Speaks. *Ed.* by Edward Carpenter. 1958.

11696 GARBETT. Cyril Forster Garbett: Archbishop of York. By Charles Hugh Egerton Smyth. 1959.

11697 —— In an Age of Revolution. 1952.

11698 HABGOOD. Living with Paradox: John Habgood, Archbishop of York. By John Stuart Peart t-Binns. 1987.

11699 LANG. Cosmo Gordon Lang. By John Gilbert Lockhart. 1949.

11700 RAMSEY. Michael Ramsey: A Life. By William Owen Chadwick. 1989.

11701 RUNCIE. Runcie: The Making of an Archbishop. By Margaret Duggan. 1983.

11702 —— Robert Runcie. By Adrian Hastings. 1990.

11703 TEMPLE. William Temple. By Frederic Athelwold Iremonger. 1948.

11704 —— William Temple: An Estimate and an Appreciation. By Walter Robert Matthews, *et al.* 1946.

11705 William Temple, 1882–1944. By Ralph Stanley Dean. 1947.

11706 'William Temple, Archbishop of Canterbury'. By David Grant Walker. *Church Q. Rev.* clxi (1960), 479–99.

11707 William Temple: Twentieth Century Christian. By Joseph Francis Fletcher. N.Y. 1963.

11708 'The Limitations of William Temple'. By Alexander Roper Vidler. *Theology* lxxix (1976), 36–41.

11709 William Temple, an Archbishop for all Seasons. By Charles W. Lowry. Washington. 1982.

11710 TEMPLE (FREDERICK STEPHEN) ed. William Temple: Some Lambeth Letters, 1942–1944. 1963.

11711 TEMPLE (WILLIAM). Christianity and Social Order. Harmondsworth. 1942.

11712 CRAIG (ROBERT S.). Social Concern in the Thought of William Temple. 1963.

11713 CARMICHAEL (JOHN DAVID) and GOODWIN (HAROLD SIDNEY). William Temple's Political Legacy: A Critical Assessment. 1963.

11714 SUGGATE (ALAN M.). William Temple and Christian Social Ethics Today. Edin. 1987.

Diocesan Bishops

11715 BARDSLEY. Cyril Bardsley, Evangelist. By Joan Bayldon. 1942.

11716 BARDSLEY. Cuthbert Bardsley, Bishop, Evangelist, Pastor. By Frederick Donald Coggan. 1989.

11717 BARNES (*Sir* [ERNEST] JOHN [WARD]). Ahead of his Age: Bishop Barnes of Birmingham. 1979.

11718 BARRY (FRANK RUSSELL). Period of My Life. 1970.

11719 —— F. R. B.: A Portrait of Bishop Russell Barry. By Frank H. West. Bramcote. 1980.

11720 BELL. George Bell, Bishop of Chichester. By Ronald Claud Dudley Jasper. 1967.

11721 —— George Bell. By Kenneth Slack. 1971.

11722 —— I Seek My Brethren: Bishop George Bell and the German Churches. By Ernest Gordon Rupp. 1975.

11723 —— Unity and Compassion: Moral Issues in the Life and Thought of George K. A. Bell. By Jaakko Rusama. Helsinki. 1986.

11724 BLUNT. Blunt. By John Stuart Peart-Binns. Bradford. 1969.

11725 BURGE. Discourses and Letters of Hubert Murray Burge, D.D., K.C.V.O., Bishop of Southwark, 1911–1919, Bishop of Oxford, 1919–1925. *Ed.* with a memoir by Percy Cuthbert Quilter, *Baron Charnwood*. 1930.

11726 BURROUGHS. Arthur Burroughs. By H. G. Mulliner. 1936.

11727 BURROWS. Winfrid Burrows, 1858–1929: Bishop of Truro, 1912–1919, Bishop of Chichester, 1919–1929. By his daughter Mary Moore. 1932.

11728 CHAVASSE. Francis James Chavasse, Bishop of Liverpool. By John Bennett Lancelot. Oxf. 1929.

11729 —— The Chavasse Twins. By John Selwyn Gummer. 1963.

11730 DE CANDOLE. Bishop Henry de Candole: His Life and Times, 1895–1971. By Peter John Jagger. Leighton Buzzard. 1975.

11731 FLEMING. Friend for Life: A Portrait of Lancelot Fleming. By David Lindsay. 1981.

11732 GORE. The Life of Charles Gore, A Great Englishman. By George Leonard Prestige. 1935.

11733 —— James Anderson Carpenter. Gore: A Study in Liberal Catholic Thought. 1960.

11734 —— Albert Mansbridge. Edward Stuart Talbot and Charles Gore. 1935.

11735 GORTON. Neville Gorton, Bishop of Coventry, 1943–1955. By Francis Walter Moyle. 1957.

11736 —— HAIGH. Mervyn Haigh. By Frank Russell Barry. 1964.

11737 HEADLAM. Arthur Cayley Headlam: Life and Letters of a Bishop. By Ronald Claud Dudley Jasper. 1960.

11738 HICKS. The Life an Edward Lee Hicks, Bishop of Lincoln, 1910–1919. By John Henry Fowler. 1922.

11739 HENSON. Hensley Henson. By Sir William Owen Chadwick. Oxf. 1983.

11740 —— Herbert Hensley Henson, Retrospect of an Unimportant Life. 3 vols. 1942–50.

11741 'Herbert Hensley Henson, 1863–1947'. *Durham Univ. J.* lii (1960) David Walker.

11742 —— Letters of Herbert Hensley Henson. *Ed.* by E. F. Braley. 1950.

11743 —— More Letters of Herbert Hensley Henson. *Ed.* by E. F. Braley. 1954.

11744 HOSKYNS. Sir Edwyn Hoskyns, Bishop of Southwell, 1904–1925. By Edward Gordon Selwyn. 1926.

11745 HUDDLESTON. Trevor Huddleston: Essays on his Life and Work. *Ed.* by Deborah Duncan Honoré. 1988.

11746 HUNKIN. Cornish Bishop [J. W. Hunkin]. By John Stuart Peart-Binns. 1977.

11747 HUNTER. Strategist for the Spirit: Leslie Hunter, Bishop of Sheffield. *Ed.* by Gordon Hewitt. 1985.

11748 KIRK. Life and Letters of Kenneth Escott Kirk, Bishop of Oxford, 1937–1954. By Eric Waldram Kemp. 1959.

11749 KNOX. Reminiscences of an Octogenarian, 1847–1934. By Edmund Arbuthnott Knox. 1935.

11750 LEONARD. Graham Leonard: Bishop of London. By John Stuart Peart-Binns. 1988.

11751 MOULE. Handley Carr Glyn Moule, Bishop of Durham, 1901–20: A Biography. By John Battersby Harford and Frederick Charles Macdonald. 1922.

11752 PAGET. Henry Luke Paget: Portrait and Frame. By Elma Katie Paget. 1939.

11753 POLLOCK. A Twentieth-Century Bishop: Recollections and Reflections. By Bertram Pollock. 1944.

11754 RAMSEY. Ian Ramsey, Bishop of Durham: A Memoir. By David Lawrence Edwards. Oxf. 1973.

11755 REEVES. Ambrose Reeves. By John Stuart Peart-Binns. 1973.

11756 ROBINSON. A Life of Bishop John A. T. Robinson: Scholar, Pastor, Prophet. By Eric James. 1987.

11757 STOCKWOOD. Chanctonbury Ring: An Autobiography. By Mervyn Stockwood. 1982.

11758 STRONG. T. B. Strong: Bishop, Musician, Dean, Vice-Chancellor. By Harold Anson. 1949.

11759 TALBOT. Edward Stuart Talbot, 1844–1934. By Gwendolen Stephenson. 1936.

11760 TALBOT. Neville Stuart Talbot, 1879–1943: A Memoir. By Frank Herbert Brabant. 1949.

11761 TREACY. Eric Treacy. By John Stuart Peart-Binns. 1980.

11762 WAND. Changeful Page: An Autobiography. By William Wand. 1965.

11763 —— Wand of London. By John Stuart Peart-Binns. 1987.

11764 WILLIAMS. Defender of the Church of England: The Life of Bishop R. R. Williams. By John Stuart Peart-Binns. 1984.

11765 WILSON. John Leonard Wilson, Confessor for the Faith. By Roy McKay. 1973.

11766 WINNINGTON-INGRAM. Winnington-Ingram: A Biography of Arthur Foley Winnington-Ingram. Bishop of London, 1901–1939. By Spencer Cecil Carpenter. 1949.

11767 WINNINGTON-INGRAM (ARTHUR FOLEY). Fifty Years Work in London, 1889–1939. 1940.

11768 —— Twenty Five Years as Bishop of London: A Biography of Bishop Winnington-Ingram. By Charles Herbert. 1926.

11769 WOODS. The Life of Edward Woods. By Oliver Stratford Tomkins. 1957.

11770 WOODS. Robin Woods, an Autobiography. 1986.

11771 WOODS. Theodore, Bishop of Winchester. By Edward Sydney Woods and Frederick Brodie MacNutt. 1933.

Other prominent members of the Church of England.

11772 ANDREWS. Canon's Folly. By Leonard Martin Andrews. 1974.

11773 BAILLIE. My First Eighty Years. By Albert Victor Baillie. 1951.

11774 BRUCE. The Last of the Eccentrics: A Life of Rosslyn Bruce. By Verity Anderson. 1972.

11775 CARLILE. Wilson Carlile, the Laughing Cavalier of Christ. By Sidney Dark. 1944.

11776 CLARKE. Unfinished Conflict: An Autobiography. By Oliver Fielding Clarke. 1971.

11777 COLLINS. Faith Under Fire. By Lewis John Collins. 1966.

11778 DAVIES (DAVID RICHARD). In Search of Myself. 1961.

11779 DEARMER. The Life of Percy Dearmer. By his wife Nancy Dearmer. 1940.

11780 DUNCAN-JONES. Duncan-Jones of Chichester. By Spencer Cecil Carpenter. 1956.

11781 FARRER. A Hawk Among Sparrows: A Biography of Austin Farrer. By Philip Curtis. 1985.

11782 GREEN. Canon Peter Green: A Biography of a Great Parish Priest. By H. E. Sheen. 1965.

11783 GROSER. John Groser: East End Priest. *Ed.* by Kenneth Brill. 1971.

11784 GRUBB. Crypts of Power: An Autobiography. By Sir Kenneth Grubb. 1971.

11785 HARTHILL. Joyful Servant: The Ministry of Percy Harthill. By A. M. D. Ashley. 1967.

11786 HOLLAND. Henry Scott Holland . . . Memoir and Letters. *Ed.* by Stephen Paget. 1921.

11787 INGE. Dean Inge. By Adam Fox. 1960.

11788 —— William Ralph Inge. Diary of a Dean: St Paul's, 1911–1934. 1949.

11789 —— Outspoken Essays. 1919 and 1923.

11790 —— Robert M. Helm. The Gloomy Dean: The Thought of William Ralph Inge. Winston-Salem, N.C. 1962.

11791 JELLICOE. Basil Jellicoe. By Kenneth Ingram. 1936.

11792 JENKINSON. This Turbulent Priest: The Story of Charles Jenkinson, Parish Priest and Housing Reformer. 1952.

11793 JENNINGS. Men of the Lanes: The Autobiography of the Tramps' Parson. By Frank Jennings. 1958.

11794 JOHNSON. Searching for Light: An Autobiography. By Hewlett Johnson. 1968.

11795 —— Hewlett Johnson, Priest, Prophet and Man of Action. By Clive Hancock. 1944.

11796 —— The Red Dean: The Life and Riddle of Dr Hewlett Johnson, Born 1874, Died 1966, Dean of Canterbury 1931 to 1963. By Robert Hughes. Worthing. 1987.

11797 KELLY. Herbert Kelly: No Pious Person. *Ed.* by George Every. 1960.

11798 KNOX. The Knox Brothers: Edmund ('Evoe') 1881–1971, Dillwyn (1883–1943), Wilfred (1886–1950), Ronald (1888–1957). 1977.

11799 LAMPE. G. W. H. Lampe. *Ed.* by Charles F. D. Moule.

11800 MATTHEWS. Memoirs and Meanings. By Walter Robert Matthews.

11801 MILNER-WHITE. Eric Milner-White, 1884–1963. By Philip Norris Pare and Donald Bertram Harris. 1965.

11802 PATEY. My Liverpool Life. By Edward H. Patey. 1983.

11803 PHILLIPS. The Price of Success. By J. B. Phillips. 1984.

11804 RASHDALL. The Life of Hastings Rashdall. By Percy Ewing Matheson. 1928.

11805 RAVEN. Charles Raven. By Frederick William Dillistone. 1975.

11806 —— C. E. Raven. Musings and Memories. 1931.

11807 RECKITT. As it Happened: An Autobiography. By Maurice Bennington Reckitt. 1941.

11808 ROYDEN. Maude Royden. By Sheila Fletcher. Oxf. 1989.

11809 SHEPPARD. Dick Sheppard: A Biography. By Carolyn Scott. 1977.

11810 Richard Ellis Roberts. H. R. L. Sheppard: Life and Letters. 1942.

11811 Charles Henry Selfe Matthews. Dick Sheppard: Man of Peace. 1948.

11812 STACEY. Who Cares? By Nicolas David Stacey. 1971.

11813 STONE. Darwell Stone. By Frank Leslie Cross. 1943.

11814 STORR. Vernon Faithfull Storr: A Memoir. By George Herbert Harris. 1943.

11815 SULLIVAN. Watch How You Go: An Autobiography. By Martin Gloster Sullivan. 1975.

11816 VIDLER. Scenes from a Clerical Life. By Alexander Roper Vidler. 1977.

11817 WAITE. Terry Waite: Man with a Mission. By Trevor Barnes. 1987.

11818 WARREN. Into all the World: A Biography of Max Warren. By Frederick William Dillistone. 1980.

11819 —— Crowded Canvas: Some Experiences of a Lifetime. 1974.

11820 WATSON. You are My God. By David Watson. 1982.

11821 —— David Watson: A Portrait by his Friends. *Ed.* by Edward England. 1985.

11822 WILLIAMS. Some Day I'll Find You: An Autobiography. By Harry A. Williams. 1982.

11823 WILLIAMSON. Father Joe: The Autobiography of Joseph Williamson of Poplar and Stepney. By Joseph Williamson. 1963.

4. SOCIAL QUESTIONS

11824 WAGNER (DONALD O.). The Church of England and Social Reform Since 1854. N.Y. 1930.

11825 RECKITT (MAURICE BENINGTON). Faith and Society: A Study of the Structure, Outlook and Opportunity of the Christian Social Movement in Great Britain and the U.S.A. 1932.

11826 —— *Ed.* Prospect for Christianity: Essays in Catholic Social Reconstruction. 1945.

11827 —— Maurice to Temple: A Century of the Social Movement in the Church of England (1846–1946). 1947.

11828 —— P. E. T. Widdrington, A Study in Vocation and Versatility. 1961.

11829 —— *Ed.* For Christ and the People: Studies of Four Socialist Priests and Prophets of the Church of England Between 1870 and 1930. 1968.

11830 LEWIS (JOHN) *et al.* Christianity and the Social Revolution. 1936.

11831 OLIVER (JOHN KEITH). The Church and Social Order: Social Thought in the Church of England, 1918–1939. 1968.

11832 GILL (ROBIN). Theology and Social Structure. 1977.

11833 HALL (M. PENELOPE) *and* HOWES (ISMENE V.). The Church in Social Work: A Study of Moral Welfare Work Undertaken by the Church of England. 1965.

11834 GROVES (REGINALD). Conrad Noel and the Thaxted Movement: An Adventure in Christian Socialism. 1967.

11835 BRAND (MARY VIVIAN). The Social Catholic Movement in England, 1920–1955. N.Y. 1963.

11836 CLEARY (JOHN MARTIN). Catholic Social Action in Britain, 1909–1959: A History of the Catholic Social Guild. Oxf. 1961.

11837 PRESTON (RONALD HAYDN). Church and Society in the Late Twentieth Century: The Economic and Political Task. 1983.

11838 STUDDERT-KENNEDY (WILLIAM GERALD). Dog-Collar Democracy. The Industrial Christian Fellowship, 1919–1929. 1982.

11839 —— '"Woodbine Willie": Religion and Politics After the Great War'. *Hist. Today* 36/12 (1986), 40–5.

11840 JEREMY (DAVID J.) ed. Business and Religion in Britain. Aldershot. 1988.

11841 COMAN (PETER). Catholics and the Welfare State.

11842 HOWELL-THOMAS (DOROTHY). Mutual Understanding: The Social Services and Christian Belief. 1974.

11843 CAMPBELL (ROY HUTCHESON). 'The Church and Social Reform'. *Scot. J. Pol. Econ.* viii (1961), 137–47.

11844 CHURCH OF ENGLAND. Faith in the City: A Call for Action by Church and Nation. Richard O'Brien, Chmn. 1985.

11845 BINNEY (MARCUS) *and* BURMAN (P.) *eds.* Change and Decay: The Future of Our Churches. 1977.

11846 AHERN (GEOFFREY) *and* DAVIE (GRACE). Inner City God: The Nature of Belief in the Inner City. 1987.

11847 SHEPPARD (DAVID). Built as a City. 1974.

11848 —— Bias to the Poor. 1983.

11849 SHEPPARD (DAVID) *and* WORLOCK (DEREK). Better Together: Christian Partnership in a Hurt City. 1988.

11850 FORRESTER (DUNCAN B.). Christianity and the Future of Welfare. 1985.

5. POLITICS

11851 WILKINSON (ALAN). Dissent or Conform? War, Peace and the English Churches 1900–1945. 1986.

11852 —— The Church of England and the First World War. 1978.

11853 MARRIN (ALBERT). The Last Crusade: The Church of England in the First World War. Durham, N.C. 1974.

11854 TAYLOR (BRIAN). 'The Cowley Fathers and the First World War'. Studies in Church History. Vol. 20 (1983), 383–90.

11855 CLEMENTS (KEITH WINSTON). 'Baptists and the Outbreak of the First World War'. *Baptist Q.* xxvi (1975), 74–92.

11856 HENRY (S. D.). 'Scottish Baptists and the First World War'. *Baptist Q.* xxxi (1985), 52–65.

11857 MEWS (STUART PAUL). 'Neo-Orthodoxy, Liberalism and War: Karl Barth, P. T. Forsyth and John Oman, 1914–1918'. Studies in Church History. Vol. 14 (1977), 361–76.

11858 THOMPSON (DAVID MICHAEL). 'War, the Nation, and the Kingdom of God: The Origins of the National Mission of Repentance and Hope, 1915–16'. Studies in Church History. Vol. 20 (1983), 337–50.

11859 MEWS (STUART PAUL). 'Urban Problems and Rural Solutions: Drink and Disestablishment in the First World War'. Studies in Church History. Vol. 16 (1979), 449–76.

11860 MOYNIHAN (MICHAEL). God on Our Side: The British Padre in the First World War. 1983.

11861 ROBBINS (KEITH GILBERT). 'Free Churchmen and the Twenty Years' Crisis: 1919–1939'. *Baptist Q.* xxvii (1978), 346–57.

11862 —— 'Church and Politics: Dorothy Buxton and the German Church Struggle'. Studies in Church History. Vol. 12 (1975), 419–33.

11863 BENTLEY (JAMES). 'British and German High Churchmen in the Struggle Against Hitler'. *J. Eccles Hist.* xxiii (1972), 233–49.

11864 ROBBINS (KEITH GILBERT). 'Martin Niemöller: The German Church Struggle and English Opinion'. *J. Eccles. Hist.* xxi (1970), 149–70.

11865 MEWS (STUART PAUL). 'The Sword of the Spirit: A Catholic Cultural Crusade of 1940'. Studies in Church History. Vol. 20 The Church and War. *Ed.* by William Sheils. Oxf. 1983. 409–30.

11866 ROBBINS (KEITH GILBERT). 'Britain, 1940 and "Christian Civilization"'. In History, Society and the Churches: Essays in Honour of Owen Chadwick. *Ed.* by Derek Beales and Geoffrey Best. Camb. (1985), 279–99.

11867 WHITE (GAVIN DONALD). 'The Fall of France'. Studies in Church History. Vol. 20 (1983), 431–41.

11868 MACHIN (GEORGE IAN THOM). Politics and the Churches in Great Britain 1869 to 1921. Oxf. 1987.

6. DOCTRINE

11869 RAMSEY (ARTHUR MICHAEL). From Gore to Temple: The Development of Anglican Theology between 1889 and 1939. 1960.

11870 VIDLER (ALEXANDER ROPER). Twentieth Century Defenders of the Faith. 1965.

11871 CLEMENTS (KEITH WINSTON). Lovers of Discord: Twentieth-Century Theological Controversies in England. 1988.

11872 ROBINSON (JOHN ARTHUR THOMAS). Honest to God. 1963.

11873 EDWARDS (DAVID LAWRENCE) *ed.* The Honest to God Debate. 1963.

11874 JAMES (ERIC A.) *ed.* God's Truth: Essays to Commemorate the Twenty Fifth Anniversary of the Publication of Honest to God. 1988.

11875 PAGE (ROBERT JEFFRESS). New Directions in Anglican Theology: A Survey from Temple to Robinson. 1965.

11876 MOZLEY (JOHN KENNETH). Some Tendencies in British Theology from the Publication of 'Lux Mundi' to the Present Day. 1951.

11877 DAVIES (RUPERT ERIC). Religious Authority in an Age of Doubt. 1968.

11878 MAJOR (HENRY DEWSBURY ALVES). English Modernism: Its Origins, Methods, Aims. 1927.

11879 STEPHENSON (ALAN MALCOLM GEORGE). The Rise and Decline of English Modernism. 1984.

11880 WOOD (HERBERT GEORGE). Belief and Unbelief Since 1850. Camb. 1955.

11881 —— Living Issues in Religious Thought from George Fox to Bertrand Russell. 1924.

11882 WARD (BARBARA). Faith and Freedom: A Study of Western Society. 1964.

11883 SYKES (STEPHEN W.) *ed.* England and Germany: Studies in Theological Diplomacy. Frankfurt am Main/Berne. 1982.

11884 MASCALL (ERIC L.). 'Anglican Dogmatic Theology, 1939–1960: A Survey and a Retrospect'. *Theology* 63 (Jan. 1960), 1–7.

11885 GALLOWAY (ALLAN DOUGLAS). Faith in a Changing Culture. 1967.

11886 ROBINSON (JOHN ARTHUR THOMAS). 'But that I can't Believe!'. 1967.

11887 EDWARDS (DAVID LAWRENCE). Religion and Change. 1969.

11888 WEATHERHEAD (LESLIE DIXON). The Christian Agnostic. 1965.

11889 PICKERING (WILLIAM STUART FREDERICK). 'Persistence of Rites of Passage: Towards an Explanation'. *Brit. J. Sociol.* 25 (1974), 63–78.

11890 BUDD (SUSAN). Varieties of Unbelief: Atheists and Agnostics in English Society 1850–1960. 1977.

11891 WICKER (BRIAN). 'The New Left: Christians and Agnostics'. *New Blackfriars* xlviii (1967), 198–204.

11892 —— 'Atheism and the Avant-Garde'. *New Blackfriars* li (1970), 527–35.

11893 BLACKHAM (HAROLD JOHN) *et al.* Living as a Humanist. 1950.

11894 —— Religion in a Modern Society. 1966.

11895 BLUM (FRED HERMAN). Ethics of Industrial Man: An Empirical Study of Religious Awareness and the Experience of Society. 1970.

11896 HERRICK (J.). Vision and Realism: A Hundred Years of *The Freethinker*. 1982.

7. THEOLOGICAL EDUCATION

11897 ROBINSON (JOHN ARTHUR THOMAS). 'The Teaching of Theology for the Ministry'. *Theology* 61 (1958), 486–95.

11898 GUNDRY (DUDLEY WILLIAM). 'The Church, the Universities and Theological Studies'. *Church Q. Rev.* (April 1947), 1–16.

11899 —— 'University Theology in a Technological Age'. *Church Q. Rev.* (October 1958), 488–98.

11900 FROST (STANLEY B.). 'Selection and Training of Candidates for the Ministry: Postgraduate Theological Training'. *Expository Times* lxxiv (1963), 112–14.

11901 DYSON (ANTHONY OAKLEY). 'The Church's Educational Institutions: Some Theological Institutions'. *Theology* lxxx (1977), 273–9.

11902 CHAMPION (LEONARD GEORGE). 'Reflections Upon the Present Curriculum of Theological Colleges'. *Baptist Q.* xix (1962), 270–6.

11903 BATTEN (MOLLIE). 'Theological Education'. *Theology* lxviii (1965), 25–31.

11904 MCINTYRE (JOHN). 'The Structure of Theological Education'. *Expository Times* Vol. 70 (April 1959), 210–15.

11905 ELMSLIE (WILLIAM ALEXANDER LESLIE). Westminster College, Cambridge: An Account of its History, 1899–1949. 1949.

11906 BROWN (KENNETH D.). A Social History of the Nonconformist Ministry in England and Wales 1800–1930. Oxf. 1988.

11907 CLIFF (P. B.). The Rise and Development of the Sunday School Movement in England, 1780 to 1980. Redhill. 1986.

11908 BULLOCK (FREDERICK WILLIAM BAGSHAWE). A History of Training for the Ministry of the Church of England in England and Wales from 1875 to 1974. 1976.

11909 —— The History of Ridley Hall, Cambridge. Vol. 2 1908–1951. 1953.

11910 CHADWICK (WILLIAM OWEN). The Founding of Cuddesdon. Oxf. 1954.

11911 HEISER (FRANCIS BERNHARD). The Story of St Aidan's College, Birkenhead, 1847–1947. Chester. 1947.

11912 DAVIES (GEORGE COLLISS BOARDMAN). Men for the Ministry: The History of the London College of Divinity. 1963.

11913 MOSS (BASIL STANLEY). Clergy Training Today. 1964.

11914 STEPHENSON (ALAN MALCOLM GEORGE). 'Ripon Hall, 1897–1964'. *Theology* lxvii (1964), 305–10.

8. THE BIBLE, PREACHING, MUSIC

11915 ROE (JAMES MOULTON). A History of the British and Foreign Bible Society, 1905–1954. 1965.

11916 BRUCE (FREDERICK FYVIE). The English Bible: A History of Translations. 1961. Rev. edn 1970.

11917 HARRISON (FREDERICK). The Bible in Britain. 1949.

11918 MACPHAIL (*Sir* ANDREW). The Bible in Scotland. 1931.

11919 NEILL (STEPHEN CHARLES). The Interpretation of the New Testament, 1861–1961. 1964. 2nd edn 1861–1986 by Thomas Wright. 1988.

11920 DAVIES (DANIEL HORTON MARLAIS). Worship and Theology in England. Vol. 5 The Ecumenical Century, 1900–1965. Oxf. 1965.

11921 —— Varieties of English Preaching, 1900–1960. 1963.

11922 LONG (KENNETH ROY). The Music of the English Church. 1972.

11923 HAYDEN (A. J.) *and* NEWTON (R. F.) *eds.* British Hymn Writers and Composers: A Check List Giving their Dates and Places of Birth and Death. 1977.

11924 ROUTLEY (ERIK REGINALD). The Music of Christian Hymnody: A Study of the Development of the Hymn Tune Since the Reformation, with Special Reference to English Protestantism. 1957.

11925 —— The English Carol. 1958.

11926 CLARKE (WILLIAM KEMP LOWTHER). A Hundred Years of Hymns Ancient and Modern. 1960.

11927 MARTIN (HUGH) *ed.* The Baptist Hymn Book Companion. 1962.

11928 PARRY (KENNETH LLOYD) *ed.* Companion to Congregational Praise. 1953. Suppl. 1960.

11929 MOFFATT (JAMES). Handbook to the Church Hymnary. 1927.

11930 BARKLEY (JOHN MONTEITH) *ed.* Handbook to Church Hymnary. 3rd edn 1979.

11931 DEARMER (PERCY). Songs of Praise Discussed. Oxf. 1933.

9. ROMAN CATHOLICISM IN ENGLAND AND WALES

11932 THE CATHOLIC DIRECTORY OF ENGLAND AND WALES. 1839+.

11933 CATHOLIC ARCHIVES. 1980.

11934 LOUGHRAN (MARY MALACHY). Catholics in England between 1918 and 1945. Philadelphia, Pa. 1954.

11935 GARDNER (GEORGE LAWRENCE HARTER). English Catholicism in the Present Day. 1920.

11936 GWYNN (DENIS ROLLESTON). A Hundred Years of Catholic Emancipation, 1829–1929. 1929.

11937 MATHEW (DAVID). Catholicism in England. 1936. 3rd edn 1955.

11938 O'CONNOR (JOHN JOSEPH). Catholic Revival in England. N.Y. 1942.

11939 BECK (GEORGE ANDREW). The English Catholics, 1850–1950: Essays to Commemorate the Centenary of the Restoration of the Hierarchy of England and Wales. 1950.

11940 WATKIN (EDWARD INGRAM). Roman Catholicism in England from the Reformation to 1950. 1957.

11941 WARD (CONOR). 'English Catholics in Transition'. *Month* xxxiii (1965), 31–5.

11942 REYNOLDS (ERNEST EDWIN). The Roman Catholic Church in England and Wales: A Short History. 1973.

11943 NORMAN (EDWARD ROBERT). Roman Catholicism in England from the Elizabethan Settlement to the Second Vatican Council. Oxf. 1985.

11944 HASTINGS (ADRIAN) ed. Bishops and Writers: Aspects of the Evolution of Modern English Catholicism. Wheathampstead. 1977.

11945 GRADY (F. J.). 'The Exclusion of Catholics from the Lord Chancellorship, 1673–1954'. *Recusant History* viii (1965), 166–74.

11946 HOLLIS (MAURICE CHRISTOPHER). Social Evolution in Modern English Catholicism. 1953.

11947 HOLMES (J. DEREK). 'English Catholicism from Hinsley to Heenan'. *Clergy Rev.* 62 (1977), 44–54.

11948 HICKEY (JOHN VINCENT). Urban Catholics: Urban Catholicism in England and Wales from 1829 to the Present Day. 1967.

11949 O₃DONOVAN (PATRICK). 'Catholicism and Class in England'. *Twentieth Century* cxxiii (1965), 52–7.

11950 HORNSBY-SMITH (MICHAEL P.). Roman Catholics in England: Studies in Social Structure since the Second World War. Camb. 1987.

11951 SCOTT (GEORGE EDWIN). The R.C.s: A Report on Roman Catholics in Britain Today. 1967.

11952 WARD (CONOR). 'The Catholic Family as a Minority Group'. *Blackfriars* xliii (1962), 527–33.

11953 SPENCER (ANTHONY ERNEST CHARLES WINCHCOMBE). 'The Catholic Community as a British Melting Pot'. *New Community* ii (1973), 125–31.

11954 —— 'Demography of Catholicism'. *Month* ccxxxvi (1975), 100–5.

11955 —— 'The Newman Demographic Survey, 1953–1962'. *Wiseman Rev.* ccccxcii (1962), 139–54.

11956 —— 'The Demography and Sociology of the Catholic Community in England and Wales'. In The Committed Church. *Ed.* by Laurence Bright and Simon Clements. 1966.

11957 ARCHER (ANTHONY). 'The Passing of the "Simple Faithful"'. *New Blackfriars* lvi (1975), 196–204.

11958 CARSON (R. L.). 'Multiplication Tables: The Progress of Catholicism in England and Wales, 1702–1949'. *Clergy Rev.* xxxii (1949), 21–30.

11959 MILLIKEN (ERNEST KENNETH). English Monasticism Yesterday and Today. 1967.

11960 ANSON (PETER FREDERICK). The Religious Orders and Congregations of Great Britain and Ireland. Worcester. 1949.

11961 GUMBLEY (WALTER). 'The English Dominicans from 1555 to 1950'. *Dominican Studs* v (1952), 103–33.

11962 SUTCLIFFE (EDMUND FELIX). Bibliography of the English Province of the Society of Jesus, 1773–1953. 1957.

11963 BASSET (BERNARD). The English Jesuits from Campion to Martindale. 1967.

11964 MILBURN (DAVID). A History of Ushaw College: A Study of the Origin, Foundation and Development of an English Catholic Seminary. Durham. 1964.

11965 SWEENEY (GARRETT). St Edmund's House, Cambridge: The First Eighty Years. Camb. 1980.

11966 WILKINS (J.). 'The English Catholic Press'. *Month* ccxxxvi (1975), 114–17.

11967 WILLIAMS (MICHAEL). The Venerable English College, Rome: A History 1539–1979. 1979.

11968 VIDLER (ALEXANDER ROPER). The Modernist Movement in the Roman Church: Its Origins and Outcome. Camb. 1934.

11969 —— A Variety of Catholic Modernists. Camb. 1970.

11970 —— 'Abortive Renaissance: Catholic Modernists in Sussex'. *Studs in Church Hist.* Vol. 14 (1977), 377–92.

11971 CLEMENTS (SIMON) *and* LAWLOR (MONICA). The McCabe Affair: Evidence and Comment. 1967.

11972 DAVIS (CHARLES). A Question of Conscience. 1967.

11973 LASH (NICHOLAS LANGRISHE ALLEYNE). 'English Catholic Theology: Ten Years on'. *Month* viii (1975), 286–9.

11974 KENNY (ANTHONY JOHN PATRICK). A Path from Rome: An Autobiography. 1985.

11975 ARCHER (ANTHONY). The Two Catholic Churches: A Study in Oppression. 1986.

11976 CRICHTON (J. D.), WINSTONE (H. E.), *and* AINSLIE (J. R.) eds. English Catholic Worship: Liturgical Renewal in England Since 1900. 1979.

11977 WALSH (MICHAEL J.). 'Ecumenism in Wartime Britain: The Sword of the Spirit and Religion and Life, 1940–1945'. *Heythrop Journal* 23 (July 1982).

11978 —— From Sword to Ploughshare. 1980.

11979 BERKELEY (HUMPHREY JOHN). 'Catholics in English Politics'. *Wiseman Rev.* ccccxciv (1962), 300–8.

11980 GUMBLEY (WALTER) comp. Obituary Notices of the English Dominicans, 1555–1952. 1955.

11981 VON HÜGEL. Baron Friedrich von Hügel and the Modernist Crisis in England. By Lawrence F. Barmann. Camb. 1972.

11982 —— The Life of Baron von Hügel. By Michael de la Bedoyère. 1951.

11983 —— The Spirituality of Friedrich von Hügel. By Joseph P. Whelan. 1971.

11984 —— Baron Friedrich von Hügel: Selected Letters, 1896–1924. *Ed.* by Bernard Holland. 1927.

11985 —— Letters from Baron Friedrich von Hügel to a Niece. *Ed.* by Gwendolen Maud Greene. 1928.

11986 —— Two Witnesses: A Personal Recollection of Hubert Parry and Friedrich von Hügel. 1930.

11987 HUGHES (ANSELM). The Rivers of the Flood: A Personal Account of the Catholic Revival in England in the Twentieth Century. 1961.

11988 WALL (BERNARD). Headlong into Change: An Autobiography and a Memoir of Ideas Since the Thirties. 1969.

11989 CLIFTON (MICHAEL). Amigo: Friend of the Poor. Bishop of Southwark, 1904–1949. 1987.

11990 HEENAN (JOHN CARMEL). Cardinal Hinsley. 1944.

11991 —— Not the Whole Truth. 1971.

11992 —— A Crown of Thorns: An Autobiography, 1951–1963. 1974.

11993 CASTLE (TONY). Basil Hume: A Portrait. 1986.

11994 HURN (DAVID ABNER). Archbishop Roberts, S.J.: His Life and Writings. 1966.

11995 CARAMAN (PHILIP). C. C. Martindale: A Biography. 1967.

11996 ORCHARD (WILLIAM EDWIN). From Faith to Faith: An Autobiography of Religious Development. 1933.

10. The Free Churches

11997 DAVIE (DONALD [ALFRED]). A Gathered Church: The Literature of the English Dissenting Interest, 1700–1930. 1978.

11998 YOUNG ([CHARLES] KENNETH). Chapel: The Joyous Days and Prayerful Nights of the Non-Conformists in their Hey-Day, circa 1850–1950. 1972.

11999 JORDAN (EDWARD KENNETH HENRY). Free Church Unity: A History of the Free Church Council Movement, 1896–1941. 1956.

12000 HEALEY (FRANCIS GEORGE). Rooted in Faith: Three Centuries of Nonconformity, 1662–1962. 1961.

12001 NUTTALL (GEOFFREY FILLINGHAM) *and* CHADWICK (WILLIAM OWEN) *eds.* From Uniformity to Unity, 1662–1962. 1962.

12002 WILKINSON (JOHN THOMAS). 1662—and After: Three Centuries of English Nonconformity. 1962.

12003 GRANT (JOHN WEBSTER). Free Churchmanship in England, 1870–1940, with Special Reference to Congregationalism. 1955.

12004 PEEL (ALBERT). The Free Churches, 1903–1926. 1927.

12005 DAVIES (HORTON). The English Free Churches. 1952. 2nd edn 1963.

12006 SHAKESPEARE (JOHN HOWARD). The Churches at the Crossroads: A Study in Church Unity. 1918.

12007 ROUTLEY (ERIK REGINALD). English Religious Dissent. 1960.

12008 DRIVER (CHRISTOPHER). A Future for the Free Churches? 1962.

12009 SANGSTER (PAUL). A History of the Free Churches. 1983.

12010 BRAKE (GEORGE THOMPSON). Inside the Free Churches. 1964.

12011 PAYNE (ERNEST ALEXANDER). The Free Church Tradition in the Life of England. 1944.

12012 —— Free Churchmen Unrepentant and Repentant and Other Papers. 1965.

12013 BINFIELD (JOHN CLYDE GOODFELLOW). So Down to Prayers: Studies in English Nonconformity, 1780–1920. 1977.

12014 KOSS (STEPHEN EDWARD). Nonconformity in Modern British Politics. 1975.

12015 MACKINTOSH (WILLIAM HORATIUS). Disestablishment and Liberation: The Movement for the Separation of the Anglican Church from State Control. 1972.

12016 TOWNSEND (HENRY). The Claims of the Free Churches. 1949.

(a) Baptists

12017 THE BAPTIST UNION DIRECTORY. 1862+.

12018 CLEMENTS (KEITH WINSTON) *ed.* Baptists in the Twentieth Century. 1983.

12019 BROWN (KENNETH D.). 'Patterns of Baptist Ministry in the Twentieth Century'. *Baptist Q.* 33 (1989), 81–93.

12020 CLIPSHAM (ERNEST F.). 'The Baptist Historical Society: Sixty Years Achievement'. *Baptist Q.* 22 (1968), 339–51.

12021 WHITLEY (WILLIAM THOMAS). A History of British Baptists. 1923. 2nd edn 1932.

12022 ROBINSON (HENRY WHEELER) *and* RUSHBROOKE (JAMES HENRY). Baptists in Britain. 1937.

12023 UNDERWOOD (ALFRED CLAIR). A History of the English Baptists. 1947.

12024 PAYNE (ERNEST ALEXANDER). The Baptist Union: A Short History. 1959.

12025 HIMBURY (DAVID MERVYN). British Baptists: A Short History. 1962.

12026 WHITLEY (WILLIAM THOMAS). Calvinism and Evangelism in England, Especially in Baptist Circles. 1933.

12027 CARLILE. My Life's Little Day. By John Charles Carlile. 1935.

12028 BLACK. Robert Wilson Black. By Henry Townsend. 1954.

12029 PAYNE. To be a Pilgrim: A Memoir of Ernest A. Payne. By William Morris Schumm West. 1983.

12030 RUSHBROOKE. James Henry Rushbrooke, 1870–1947: A Baptist Greatheart. By Ernest Alexander Payne. 1954.

12031 GOULD. Sir Alfred Pearce Gould. By Charles Thomas Le Quesne. 1946.

12032 CHAMBERS (RALPH FREDERICK). The Strict Baptist Chapels of England. 1955.

12033 TOON (PETER). 'English Strict Baptists'. *Baptist* Q. xxi (1965), 30–6.

12034 SUMMERS (J. E.). 'Strict Baptists in the 1970s'. *Baptist Q.* xxiv (1972), 225–9.

12035 SELLERS (IAN) *ed.* Our Heritage: The Baptists of Yorkshire, Lancashire and Cheshire, 1647–1987. Leeds. 1987.

12036 PARSONS (KENNETH A. C.) *ed.* St Andrew's Street Baptist Church, Cambridge: Three Historical Lectures Given on the 250th Anniversary of the Foundation of the Church. Camb. 1971.

12037 BINFIELD (JOHN CLYDE GOODFELLOW). Pastors and People: The Biography of a Baptist Church: Queen's Road, Coventry. Coventry. 1984.

12038 JOHNSON (W. C.). Encounter in London: The Story of the London Baptist Association, 1865–1965. 1965.

12039 BRIGGS (JOHN H. Y.). 'She-Preachers, Widows and Other Women: The Feminine Dimension in Baptist Life since 1600'. *Baptist Q.* xxxi (July 1986), 337–52.

12040 LEHMAN (EDWARD). 'Reactions to Women in Ministry: A Survey of English Baptist Church Members'. *Baptist Q.* xxxi (July 1986), 302–19.

12041 BARRETT (JOHN OLIVER). Rawdon College (Northern Baptist Education Society) 1804–1954: A Short History. 1954.

12042 HIMBURY (DAVID MERVYN). The South Wales Baptist College, 1807–1957. Cardiff. 1957.

12043 MOON (NORMAN SYDNEY). Education for Ministry: Bristol Baptist College, 1679–1979. Bristol. 1979.

(b) Congregationalists and United Reformed Church

12044 CONGREGATIONAL YEAR BOOK. 1846+.

12045 UNITED REFORMED CHURCH YEAR BOOK. 1973+.

12046 PEEL (ALBERT). A Brief History of English Congregationalism. 1953.

12047 —— These Hundred Years: A History of the Congregational Union of England and Wales. 1931.

12048 JONES (ROBERT TUDUR). Congregationalism in England, 1662–1962. 1962.

12049 ROUTLEY (ERIK). The Story of Congregationalism. 1961.

12050 TAYLOR (J. H.). L.C.U. Story 1873–1972. 1972.

12051 CLEAVES (R. W.). Congregationalism 1960–1976: The Story of the Federation. Swansea. 1977.

12052 MacARTHUR (ARTHUR). 'The Background to the Formation of the United Reformed Church (Presbyterian and Congregational) in England and Wales in 1972'. *J. Unit. Reformed Ch. Hist. Soc.* 4 (1987), 3–22.

12053 KAYE (ELAINE). The History of the King's Weigh House. 1968.

12054 CLARE (ALBERT). The City Temple, 1640–1940. 1940.

12055 ROBBINS (KEITH GILBERT). 'The Spiritual Pilgrimage of the Rev. R. J. Campbell'. *J. Eccles. Hist.* 30 (1979), 261–76.

12056 RICHARDS (EDITH RYLEY). Private View of a Public Man: The Life of Leyton Richards. 1950.

12057 PORRITT (ARTHUR). J. D. Jones of Bournemouth. 1942.

12058 DILLISTONE (FREDERICK WILLIAM). C. H. Dodd: Interpreter of the New Testament. 1977.

12059 MICKLEM (NATHANIEL). The Box and the Puppets. 1957.

12060 GOODALL (NORMAN). 'Nathaniel Micklem'. *J. Unit. Reformed Ch. Hist. Soc.* l(10), (Oct. 1977), 286–95.

12061 GARVIE (ALFRED ERNEST). Memories and Meanings of my Life. 1938.

12062 KAYE (ELAINE). C. J. Cadoux: Theologian, Scholar and Pacifist. Edin. 1988.

(c) Methodism

12063 MINUTES AND YEARBOOK OF THE METHODIST CONFERENCE. 1932+.

12064 GARLICK (KENNETH BENJAMIN). Garlick's Methodist Registry. 1983.

12065 PROCEEDINGS OF THE WESLEY HISTORICAL SOCIETY. 1893+.

12066 DAVIES (RUPERT ERIC), GEORGE (A. RAYMOND), *and* RUPP ([ERNEST] GORDON). A History of the Methodist Church in Great Britain. Vols 3 and 4. 1983, 1987.

12067 EAYRS (GEORGE). British Methodism: A Handbook and Short History. 1920.

12068 BRASH (WILLIAM BARDSLEY). Methodism. 1928.

12069 PARKINSON (GEORGE ANTHONY). The People Called Methodists: A Short Survey of the History of the Methodist Church. 1937.

12070 CARTER (HENRY). The Methodist Heritage. 1951.

12071 DAVEY (CYRIL JAMES). The March of Methodism. 1951.

12072 —— The Methodist Story. 1955.

12073 DAVIES (RUPERT ERIC). Methodism. Harmondsworth. 1963. 2nd edn 1985.

12074 KISSACK (REGINALD). Church or No Church? A Study of the Development of the Concept of Church in British Methodism. 1964.

12075 CURRIE (ROBERT). Methodism Divided: A Study in the Sociology of Ecumenicalism. 1968.

12076 KENT (JOHN HENRY SOMERSET). The Age of Disunity. 1966.

12077 —— 'The Methodist Union in England, 1932'. In Institutionalism and Church Unity. Ed. by Nils Ehrenstrom and Walter Moelder. 1963. 195–220.

12078 GEORGE (A. RAYMOND). 'The Changing Face of Methodism: 1. The Methodist Service Book'. Proc. Wes. Hist. Soc. 41 (1977–8), 65–2.

12079 DOLBY (GEORGE W.). 'The Changing Face of Methodism: 2. The Methodist Church Act, 1976'. Proc. Wes. Hist. Soc. 41 (1977–8), 97–103.

12080 WYCHERLEY (RICHARD NEWMAN). The Pageantry of Methodist Union: Being a Pictorial Record of Events Leading up to and Consummating in the Historic Uniting Conference of 1932. 1936.

12081 RACK (HENRY D.). The Future of John Wesley's Methodism. 1965.

12082 TURNER (JOHN MUNSEY). Conflict and Reconciliation: Studies in Methodism and Ecumenism in England, 1740–1982. 1985.

12083 BRAKE (GEORGE THOMPSON). Policy and Politics in British Methodism, 1932–1982. 1984.

12084 PERKINS (ERNEST BENSON). So Appointed: An Autobiography. 1964.

12085 WAKEFIELD (GORDON STEVENS). Robert Newton Flew, 1886–1962. 1971.

12086 LIDGETT (JOHN SCOTT). My Guided Life. 1936.

12087 DAVIES (RUPERT ERIC) ed. John Scott Lidgett: A Symposium. 1957.

12088 MAITLAND ([GEORGE BAKER] CHRISTOPHER). Dr Leslie Weatherhead of the City Temple. 1960.

12089 WEATHERHEAD (A. KINGSLEY). Leslie Weatherhead: A Personal Portrait. 1975.

12090 PURCELL (WILLIAM ERNEST). Portrait of Soper: A Biography of the Reverend the Lord Soper of Kingsway. Oxf. 1972. 2nd edn 1983.

12091 THOMPSON (DOUGLAS WEDDELL). Donald Soper. 1971.

12092 SOPER (DONALD OLIVER). Calling for Action: An Autobiographical Enquiry. 1984.

12093 WILKINSON (JOHN T.). Arthur Samuel Peake. 1971.

12094 NEWALL (ROY NORMAN). Methodist Preacher and Statesman: Eric W. Baker, 1899–1973. 1984.

12095 URWIN (EVELYN CLIFFORD). Henry Carter, C.B.E. 1955.

12096 SANGSTER (PAUL). Dr Sangster. 1962.

12097 NEWTON (JOHN ANTHONY). A Man for all Churches: Marcus Ward, 1906–1978. 1984.

12098 FIELD (CLIVE D.). 'The Social Structure of English Methodism: Eighteenth–Twentieth Centuries'. Brit. J. Sociol. xxviii (1977), 199–225.

12099 —— 'A Sociological Profile of English Methodism, 1900–1932'. Oral Hist. iv (1976), 73–95.

12100 EDWARDS (MALDWYN LLOYD). Methodism and England: A Study of Methodism in its Social and Political Aspects, 1850–1932. 1943.

12101 WEARMOUTH (ROBERT FEATHERSTONE). Methodism and the Trade Unions. 1959.

12102 —— The Social and Political Influence of Methodism in the Twentieth Century. 1957.

12103 TURNER (JOHN MUNSEY). 'Robert Featherstone Wearmouth, (1882–1963). Methodist Historian'. Proc. Wes. Hist. Soc. 43 (1982), 111–16.

12104 WAKEFIELD (GORDON STEVENS). Methodist Devotion: The Spiritual Life in the Methodist Tradition, 1791–1945. 1966.

12105 THOMAS (J. A.). 'Liturgy and Architecture, 1932–1960: Methodist Influence and Ideas'. Proc. Wes. Hist. Soc. xl (1976), 106–13.

12106 CUMBERS (FRANK HENRY). The Book Room: The Story of the Methodist Publishing House and Epworth Press. 1956.

12107 BRASH (WILLIAM BARDSLEY). The Story of Our Colleges, 1835–1935: A Centenary Record of Ministerial Training in the Methodist Church. 1935.

12108 SAILES (GEORGE W.). At the Centre: The Story of Methodism's Central Missions. 1970.

12109 COOPER (W. B.). Methodism in Portsmouth, 1750–1932. Portsmouth. 1973.

12110 BURGESS (J.). A History of Cumbrian Methodism. Kendal. 1980.

12111 SHAW (THOMAS). A History of Cornish Methodism. Truro. 1967.

12112 WHITE (G. W.). A Half-Century of Cornish Methodism, 1925–1975. 1975.

(d) Smaller Free Churches

Unitarianism

12113 MCLACHLAN (HERBERT). Essays and Addresses. Manch. 1950.

12114 HOLT (RAYMOND VINCENT). The Unitarian Contribution to Social Progress in England. 1938. 2nd edn 1952.

12115 HAGUE (GRAHAM) and HAGUE (JUDY). The Unitarian Heritage: An Architectural Survey of Chapels and Churches in the Unitarian Tradition in the British Isles. Sheffield. 1986.

12116 BOLAM (CHARLES GORDON) et al. The English Presbyterians: From Elizabethan Puritanism to Modern Unitarianism. 1968.

Nazarenes

12117 FORD (JACK). In the Steps of John Wesley: The Church of the Nazarene in Britain. Kansas City. 1968.

Churches of Christ

12118 YEARBOOK OF THE CHURCHES OF CHRIST IN GREAT BRITAIN AND IRELAND, 1846–1981.

12119 THOMPSON (DAVID MICHAEL). 'Let Sects and Parties Fall': A Short History of the Association of the Churches of Christ in Great Britain and Ireland. Birm. 1980.

12120 GRAY (JAMES) *ed.* W. R., The Man and His Work: A Brief Account of the Life and Work of William Robinson, M.A., B.Sc., D. D., 1888–1963. Birm. 1978.

Presbyterians

12121 ROSS (J. M.) *comp.* The Presbyterian Church of England: Index to the Proceedings of the General Assembly, 1921–1972. 1973.

12122 DARLING (J. T.). 'Presbyterian Church of England Records'. *Archives* v (1961), 6.

12123 MOFFAT (JAMES). The Presbyterian Churches. 1928.

12124 KELLEY (LILLIAN WINIFRED). Some Sources of English Presbyterian History. 1950.

Salvation Army

12125 SALVATION ARMY YEARBOOK. 1906..

12126 SANDALL (ROBERT). The History of the Salvation Army. 1947. Vols 4 and 5 by Archibald Wiggins and Vols 6 and 7 by Frederick Coutts. 1963.

12127 WATSON (BERNARD). A Hundred Years of War: The Salvation Army, 1865–1965. 1965.

12128 COUTTS (JOHN). The Salvationists. 1978.

City Mission

12129 READ (GORDON) *and* JEBSON (DAVID). A Voice in the City: Liverpool City Mission. 1979.

Others

12130 HOLLENWEGER (WALTER). The Pentecostals. 1972.

12131 HOCKEN (PETER). Streams of Renewal: The Origins and Early Development of the Charismatic Movement in Great Britain. Exeter. 1986.

12132 WALKER (ANDREW). Restoring the Kingdom: The Radical Christianity of the House Church Movement. 1985.

12133 MARTIN (DAVID) *and* MULLEN (PETER) *eds.* Strange Gifts? A Guide to Charismatic Renewal. Oxf. 1984.

12134 GUNSTONE (JOHN). Pentecostal Anglicans. 1982.

(e) Quakers

12135 MINUTES AND PROCEEDINGS OF THE LONDON YEARLY MEETING OF THE SOCIETY OF FRIENDS. 1857+.

12136 WILSON (GLADYS). Quaker Worship: An Introductory Historical Study of the English Friends' Meeting. 1952.

12137 BRINTON (HOWARD HAINES). Friends for 300 Years. 1953.

12138 VIPONT (ELFRIDA) *pseud.* The Story of Quakerism, 1652–1952. 1954. 2nd edn 1960.

12139 PUNSHON (JOHN). Portrait in Grey: A Short History of the Quakers. 1984.

12140 BAILY (LESLIE WILLIAM ALFRED). Craftsman and Quaker, the Story of James T. Baily, 1876–1957. 1959.

12141 HUGHES (WILLIAM RAVENSCROFT). Indomitable Friend: The Life of Corder Catchpool, 1883–1952. 1956. 2nd edn 1964.

12142 FOX (HUBERT) *ed.* Marion Fox, Quaker: A Selection of Her Letters. 1951.

12143 DUDLEY (JAMES). The Life of Edward Grubb, 1854–1939: A Spiritual Pilgrimage. 1946.

12144 BARTLETT (PERCY). Barrow Cadbury: A Memoir. 1960.

12145 WOOD (HERBERT GEORGE). Henry T. Hodgkin: A Memoir. 1937.

12146 VERNON (ANNE). A Quaker Businessman: The Life of Joseph Rowntree, 1836–1925. 1958.

12147 FREEMAN (RUTH). Quakers and Peace. 1947.

12148 HIRST (MARGARET E.). The Quakers in Peace and War. 1923.

12149 FRY (JOAN MARY). Friends Lend a Hand in Alleviating Unemployment: The Story of a Social Experiment Extending Over 20 Years, 1926–1946. 1947.

12150 WILSON (ROGER COWAN). Quaker Relief: An Account of the Relief Work of the Society of Friends, 1940–1948. 1952.

12151 MILLIGAN (EDWARD H.). The Past is Prologue: 100 Years of Quaker Overseas Work, 1868–1968. 1968.

12152 DAVIS (ROBERT) *ed.* Woodbrooke, 1903–1953: A Brief History of a Quaker Experiment in Religious Education. 1953.

12153 LOUKES (HAROLD). Friends and their Children: A Study in Quaker Education. 1958.

11. IRELAND

(a) General

12154 HICKEY (JOHN VINCENT). Religion and the Northern Ireland Problem. Dublin and Totowa, N.J. 1984.

12155 WALSH (B. M.), GEARY (R. C.), *and* HUGHES (J. G.). Religion and Demographic Behaviour . . . Dublin. 1970.

12156 COMPTON (PAUL A.) *and* POWER (JOHN P.). 'Estimates of the Religious Composition of Northern Ireland Local Government Districts in 1981 and Change in the Geographical Pattern of Religious Composition Between 1971 and 1981'. *Econ. Soc. Rev.* 17 (1986), 87–195.

12157 BOYD (ANDREW). Holy War in Belfast. Tralee. 2nd edn 1970.

12158 MAWHINNEY (BRIAN STANLEY) *and* WELLS (RONALD). Conflict and Christianity in Northern Ireland. 1975.

12159 EDWARDS (OWEN DUDLEY). The Sins of the Fathers: Roots of Conflict in Northern Ireland. Dublin. 1970.

12160 BARRITT (DENIS PHILLIPS) *and* BOOTH (ARTHUR). Orange and Green: A Quaker Study of Community Relations in Northern Ireland. Sedbergh. 3rd edn 1972.

12161 BARRITT (DENIS PHILLIPS) *and* CARTER (CHARLES FREDERICK). The Northern Ireland Problem: A Study in Group Relations. 1962. 2nd edn 1972.

12162 MILLER (DAVID WILLIAM). Church, State and Nation in Ireland, 1898–1921. Dublin. 1973.

12163 LARKIN (EMMET). 'Church, State and Nation in Modern Ireland'. *Amer. Hist. Rev.* lxxx (1975), 1244–76.

12164 HELMICK (RAYMOND C.). 'Church Structure and Violence in Northern Ireland'. *Month* x (1977), 273–6.

12165 ROCHE (D. J.), BIRRELL (DEREK), *and* GREER (J. I.). 'A Socio-Political Opinion Profile of Clergymen in Northern Ireland'. *Soc. Studs* 4 (1975), 143–51.

12166 WILSON (DESMOND). 'The Churches and Violence in Ireland'. *Month* x (1977), 41–5.

12167 EASTHOPE (GARY). 'Religious War in Northern Ireland'. *Sociol. Rev.* x (1976), 427–50.

12168 GANNON (JACK). Catholic Political Culture and the Constitution of Ireland. Belf. 1972.

12169 GALLAGHER (ERIC). 'The Irish Churches 1968–1983'. *Month* 245 (1983), 271–9.

12170 GALLAGHER (ERIC) *and* WORRALL (STANLEY). Christians in Ulster 1968–1980. Oxf. 1982.

12171 AKENSON (DONALD HARMAN). Education and Enmity: The Control of Schooling in Northern Ireland, 1920–50. Newton Abbot. 1973.

(b) Presbyterianism

12172 BROOKE (PETER). Ulster Presbyterianism. The Historical Perspective 1610–1970. Dublin and N.Y. 1987.

12173 BARKLEY (JOHN MONTEITH). A Short History of the Presbyterian Church in Ireland. Belf. 1960.

12174 —— 'The Presbyterian Church in Ireland and the Government of Ireland Act 1920'. *Studs in Church Hist* Vol. 12 (1975), 393–404.

12175 BAILIE (W. D.) *ed.* A History of Congregations in the Presbyterian Church in Ireland 1610–1982. Belf. 1982.

12176 ALLEN (ROBERT). The Presbyterian College, Belfast, 1853–1953. Belf. 1954.

12177 GALLAGHER (TOM). 'Religion, Reaction and Revolt in Northern Ireland: The Impact of Paisleyism in Ulster'. *J. Church State* 23 (1981), 423–44.

12178 BARKLEY (JOHN MONTEITH). 'Presbyterian-Roman Catholic Relations in Ireland (1780–1975)'. *Month* 2nd ser. 14 (1981), 221–9.

(c) Church of Ireland

12179 THE IRISH CHURCH DIRECTORY AND YEARBOOK. 1862+.

12180 PATTON (HENRY EDMUND). Fifty years of Disestablishment: A Sketch of the History of the Church of Ireland, 1869–1920. Dublin. 1922.

12181 HURLEY (MICHAEL) *ed.* Irish Anglicanism, 1869–1969: Essays on the Role of Anglicanism in Irish Life Presented to the Church of Ireland on the Occasion of the Centenary of its Disestablishment. Dublin. 1970.

12182 McDOWELL (ROBERT BRENDAN). The Church of Ireland, 1869–1969. 1975.

(d) Methodism

12183 JEFFERY (FREDERICK). Irish Methodism: An Historical Account of its Traditions, Theology and Influence. Belf. 1964.

12184 COLE (RICHARD LEE). One Methodist Church, 1860–1960: Vol. 4 of the History of Methodism in Ireland. Belf. 1960.

12185 McCREA (ALEXANDER) *ed.* Irish Methodism in the Twentieth Century. Belf. 1931.

(e) Roman Catholicism

12186 ROGERS (PATRICK). St Peter's Pro-Cathedral, Belfast, 1866–1966. Belf. 1967.

12. SCOTLAND

(a) General

12187 BROWN (CALLUM G.). The Social History of Religion in Scotland Since 1730. 1987.

(b) Presbyterianism

12188 CHURCH OF SCOTLAND YEARBOOK. 1930..

12189 LAMB (JOHN ALEXANDER) *ed.* Fasti Ecclesiae Scoticanae: The Succession of Ministers in the Church of Scotland Since the Reformation. Vol. 9. Ministers of the Church from the Union of the Church, 2 October 1929 to 31 December 1954. Edin. 1961.

12190 COX (JAMES T.) *and* MACDONALD (D. F. N.). Practice and Procedure in the Church of Scotland. Edin. 1976.

12191 HENDERSON (GEORGE DAVID). The Claims of the Church of Scotland. 1951.

12192 —— The Scottish Ruling Elder. 1935.

12193 LOUDEN (R. STUART). The True Face of the Kirk. An Examination of the Ethos and Traditions of the Church of Scotland. Oxf. 1963.

12194 MECHIE (STEWART). The Office of Lord High Commissioner. Edin. 1957.

12195 BURLEIGH (JOHN HENDERSON SEAFORTH). A Church History of Scotland. 1960.

12196 FLEMING (JOHN ROBERT). A History of the Church in Scotland, 1843–1929. 2 vols. Edin. 1927–33.

12197 HENDERSON (GEORGE DAVID). Presbyterianism. Aberd. 1955.

12198 —— Church and Ministry: A Study in Scottish Experience. 1951.

12199 BURNET (GEORGE BAIN). The Holy Communion in the Reformed Church in Scotland, 1560–1960. 1960.

12200 FORRESTER (DUNCAN B.) *and* MURRAY (DOUGLAS M.) *eds.* Studies in the History of Worship in Scotland. Edin. 1984.

12201 MAXWELL (WILLIAM DELBERT). A History of Worship in the Church of Scotland. 1955.

12202 SHAW (DUNCAN) *ed.* Reformation and Revolution. Edin. 1967.

12203 CLARK (IVO MACNAUGHTON). A History of Church Discipline in Scotland. Aberd. 1929.

12204 SJÖLINDER (ROLF). Presbyterian Reunion in Scotland, 1907–1921: Its Background and Development. Trans. by Eric J. Sharpe. Stockholm. 1962.

12205 WHITE (GAVIN DONALD). 'Whose are the Teinds? The Scottish Union of 1929'. In The Church and Wealth. *Ed.* by William Sheils and Diana Wood. Oxf. 1987. 383–92.

12206 SMALL (MABEL). Growing together: Some Aspects of the Ecumenical Movement in Scotland, 1924–1964. Edin. 1975.

12207 HENDERSON (IAN). Power without Glory: A Study of Ecumenical Politics. 1967.

12208 BLACK (CHARLES STEWART). The Scottish Church: A Short Study in Ecclesiastical History. Glasgow. 1952.

12209 BARBOUR (GEORGE FREELAND). Church and Nation in Scotland Today. 1930.

12210 DONALDSON (GORDON). Scotland, Church and Nation through Six Centuries. 1960. 2nd edn Edin. 1972.

12211 REID (JAMES MACARTHUR). Kirk and Nation: The Story of the Reformed Church of Scotland. 1960.

12212 BLACK (WILLIAM GEORGE). The Parochial Ecclesiastical Law of Scotland as Modified by the Church of Scotland Acts, 1921 and 1925. Edin. 1928.

12213 CHEYNE (ALEXANDER C.). The Transforming of the Kirk: Victorian Scotland's Religious Revolution. Edin. 1983.

12214 SEFTON (HENRY R.). 'The Church of Scotland and Scottish Nationhood'. In Religion and National Identity. Studies in Church History. Vol. 18 *ed.* by Stuart Mews. Oxf. 1982. 465–87.

12215 LYALL (FRANCIS). Of Presbyters and Kings: Church and State in the Law of Scotland. Aberd. 1980.

12216 SISSONS (P. L.). The Social Significance of Church Membership in the Burgh of Falkirk. Edin. 1960.

12217 KENNEDY (J.), SMITH (C. A.), *and* FRASER (J. M.). The Place of Women in the Church. Edin. 1959.

12218 CAMERON (LEWIS LEGERTWOOD LEGG). The Challenge of Need: A History of Social Service by the Church of Scotland, 1869–1969. Edin. 1971.

12219 —— A Badge to be Proud of: A History of the Church of Scotland Huts and Canteens. Edin. 1972.

12220 MACGREGOR (MALCOLM BLAIR). Towards Scotland's Social Good: A Hundred Years of Temperance Work in the Church of Scotland. Edin. c.1950.

12221 WATT (HUGH). New College, Edinburgh: A Centenary History. Edin. & Lond. 1946.

12222 MECHIE (STEWART). Trinity College, Glasgow, 1856–1956. Glasgow. 1956.

12223 HERRON (ANDREW). Kirk by Divine Right: Church and State: Peaceful Co-Existence. Edin. 1985.

12224 FERGUSON (RON). Chasing the Wild Goose. 1988. [The Iona Community.].

12225 RAWLINS (CLIVE L.). William Barclay: The Authorised Biography. Exeter. 1984.

12226 WHITLEY (HENRY CHARLES). Laughter in Heaven. 1962.

12227 WARR (*Sir* CHARLES LAING). The Glimmering Landscape, an Autobiography. 1960.

12228 MUIR (AUGUSTUS). John White, C.H., D.D., LL.D. 1958.

12229 GORDON (E. OLGA M. HUNTLY). The Minister's Wife. 1978.

12230 FALCONER (RONALD). The Kilt Beneath My Cassock. Edin. 1978.

12231 MAXWELL-ARNOT (M.). 'Social Change and the Church of Scotland'. In A Sociological Yearbook of Religion in Britain. *Ed.* by Michael Hill. 1974.

12232 CAMERON (GEORGE G.). The Scots Kirk in London. Oxf. 1979.

12233 GILBERT (HEATHER). As a Tale is Told: A Church of Scotland Parish 1913–54. Aberd. 1983.

12234 WRIGHT (RONALD SELBY) *ed.* Fathers of the Kirk: Some Leaders of the Church in Scotland from the Reformation to the Reunion. 1960.

12235 —— Another Home. 1980.

12236 HEWAT (ELIZABETH GLENDINNING KIRKWOOD). Vision and Achievement, 1796–1956: A History of the Foreign Missions of the Churches United in the Church of Scotland. 1960.

12237 McINTYRE (JOHN). 'Current Theology: Scotland'. *Relig. in Life* xxxvii (1968), 180–90.

12238 SHORT (L. B.). 'The Challenge to Scottish Calvinism'. *Hibbert J.* lxii (1963), 27–31.

12239 SELL (ALAN P. F.). Defending and Declaring the Faith: Some Scottish Examples 1860–1920. Exeter. 1987.

12240 WOLFE (J. N.) *and* PICKFORD (M.). The Church of Scotland: An Economic Survey. 1980.

12241 HIGHET (JOHN). The Churches in Scotland Today: A Survey of their Principles, Strength, Work and Statements. Glasgow. 1950.

12242 —— The Scottish Churches: A Review of their State 400 Years after the Reformation. 1960.

12243 —— 'Churchgoing in Scotland'. *New Society* (26.12.1963), 13–14.

12244 BRIERLEY (PETER) *ed.* Prospects for Scotland: Report of the 1984 Census of the Churches. 1985.

12245 NORTHCOTT (WILLIAM CECIL). 'Scotland's New Style Sabbath'. *Contemp. Rev.* ccvii (1965), 86–90.

12246 BRUCE (STEVE). No Pope of Rome: Anti-Catholicism in Modern Scotland. Edin. 1985.

12247 GALLAGHER (THOMAS). 'Protestant Extremism in Urban Scotland 1930–1939: Its Growth and Contraction'. *Scot. Hist. Rev.* 64 (1985), 143–67.

12248 —— Glasgow: The Uneasy Peace: Religious Tension in Modern Scotland. Manch. 1987.

12249 —— Edinburgh Divided: John Cormack and No Popery in the 1930s. Edin. 1987.

12250 BARR (JAMES). The Scottish Church Question. 1920.

12251 —— The United Free Church of Scotland. 1934.

12252 HANDBOOK OF THE UNITED FREE PRESBYTERIAN CHURCH OF SCOTLAND. 1931+.

12253 REITH (GEORGE MURRAY). Reminiscences of the United Free Church General Assembly, 1900–1929. 1933.

12254 FREE PRESBYTERIAN CHURCH OF SCOTLAND. A History of the Free Presbyterian Church of Scotland. Inverness. 1965.

(c) Non-Presbyterian Protestants

12255 ESCOTT (HARRY). A History of Scottish Congregationalism. Glasgow. 1960.

12256 YUILLE (GEORGE) *ed.* History of the Baptists in Scotland from Pre-Reformation Times. Glasgow. 1926.

12257 MURRAY (DEREK BOYD). The First Hundred Years: The Baptist Union of Scotland. Glasgow. 1969.

12258 BEBBINGTON (DAVID WILLIAM) *ed.* The Baptists in Scotland: A History. Glasgow. 1988.

12259 BRUCE (STEVE). 'Ideology and Isolation: A Failed Scots Protestant Movement'. *Archives de Sciences Sociales des Religions* 56 (1983), 147–59.

12260 SWIFT (WESLEY FRANK). Methodism in Scotland. 1947.

12261 BURNET (GEORGE BAIN). The Story of Quakerism in Scotland, 1650–1850. With an Epilogue of the Period 1850–1950 by William Hutton Marwick. 1952.

12262 MACWHIRTER (ARCHIBALD). 'Unitarianism in Scotland'. *Records Scot. Church Hist. Soc.* xiii (1957–9), 101–43.

(d) Episcopalianism

12263 SCOTTISH EPISCOPAL CHURCH YEARBOOK. 1892+.

12264 COWAN (IAN BORTHWICK) *and* ERVIN (SPENCER). The Scottish Episcopal Church: The Ecclesiastical History and Polity. Ambler, Pa. 1966.

12265 GOLDIE (FREDERICK). A Short History of the Episcopal Church in Scotland from the Reformation to the Present Time. 1951.

12266 HOLTBY (ROBERT TINSLEY). Eric Graham, 1888–1964. 1967.

12267 WHITE (GAVIN DONALD). 'Ideals in Urban Mission: Episcopalians in Twentieth-Century Glasgow'. Studies in Church History. Vol. 16. 1979. 441–8.

12268 TIBBATTS (GEORGE). John How: A Cambridge Don, Parish Priest, Scottish Primus: A Biography. Oxf. 1983.

(e) Roman Catholicism

12269 McROBERTS (DAVID) *ed.* Modern Scottish Catholicism, 1878–1978. 1979.

12270 DARRAGH (JAMES). The Catholic Hierarchy of Scotland. A Biographical List, 1653–1985. Glasgow. 1986.

12271 ANSON (PETER FREDERICK). The Catholic Church in Modern Scotland, 1560–1937. 1937.

12272 MACKENZIE (*Sir* COMPTON). Catholicism and Scotland. 1936. Repr. 1971.

12273 SCOTT-MONCRIEFF (GEORGE). The Mirror and the Cross: Scotland and the Catholic Faith. 1960.

12274 MACLEAN (DONALD). The Counter-Reformation in Scotland, 1560–1930. 1931.

12275 GORDON (ANDREW MACDONALD). Scottish Catholics and the Reformation, 1500–1956. Glasgow. 1956.

12276 ASPINWALL (BERNARD). 'Broadfield Revisited: Some Scottish Catholic Responses to Wealth 1918–40'. In The Church and Wealth. *Ed.* by William Sheils and Diana Wood. Oxf. 1987. 393–406.

12277 —— 'Popery in Scotland: Image and Reality, 1820–1920'. *Records Scot. Church Hist. Soc.* (1986), 235–57.

12278 McCAFFREY (JOHN FRANCIS). 'Roman Catholics in Scotland in the 19th and 20th Centuries'. *Records Scot. Church Hist. Soc.* xxi (1983), 275–300.

13. WALES

12279 BELL (PHILIP MICHAEL HETT). Disestablishment in Ireland and Wales. 1969.

12280 JAMES (JOHN WILLIAMS). A Church History of Wales. Ilfracombe. 1945.

12281 EDWARDS. Memories. By Alfred George Edwards, Archbishop of Wales. 1927.

12282 OWEN. The Later Life of Bishop Owen: A Son of Lleyn. By Eluned Elizabeth Owen. Llandyssul. 1961.

12283 JONES. John Bangor, The People's Bishop: The Life and Work of John Charles Jones, Bishop of Bangor, 1949–56. 1962.

12284 HARTWELL-JONES. A Celt Looks at the World. By Griffith Hartwell-Jones. *Ed.* by Wyn Griffith. Cardiff. 1946.

12285 WALKER (DAVID GRANT) *ed.* A History of the Church in Wales. Penarth. 1977.

12286 GREEN (CHARLES ALFRED HOWELL). The Setting of the Constitution of the Church in Wales. 1937.

12287 WILLIAMSON (EDWARD WILLIAM). 'The Church in Wales'. *Theology* li (1948), 123–33.

12288 PRICE (D. T. WILLIAM). 'The Contribution of St. David's College, Lampeter to the Church in Wales, 1920–71'. *J. Welsh Eccl. Hist.* 1 (1984), 63–83.

12289 MORGAN (KENNETH OWEN). Freedom or Sacrilege? A History of the Campaign for Welsh Disestablishment. Penarth. 1966.

12290 JONES (ANTHONY). Welsh Chapels. Cardiff. 1984.

12291 ROBERTS (BRYNLEY). 'Welsh Nonconformist Archives'. *J. Welsh Eccl. Hist.* 3 (1986), 61–72.

12292 REES (DAVID BEN). Chapels in the Valley: A Study in the Sociology of Welsh Nonconformity. Upton. 1975.

12293 JONES (VIVIAN) *ed.* The Church in a Mobile Society: A Survey of the Zone of Industrial South West Wales. Llandybie. 1969.

12294 HARRIS (C. C.). 'Church, Chapels and the Welsh'. *New Society* (21.2.1963), 18–19.

12295 BRIERLEY (PETER) *ed.* Prospects for Wales: Report of the 1982 Census of the Churches. 1983.

12296 ROBERTS (JOHN). The Calvinistic Methodism of Wales. Caernarvon. 1934.

12297 WILLIAMS (MORGAN WATCYN). Creative Fellowship: An Outline of the History of Calvinistic Methodism in Wales. Caernarvon. 1935.

12298 BASSETT (THOMAS MYRFYN). The Welsh Baptists. Swansea. 1977.

12299 HIMBURY (D. MERVYN). The South Wales Baptist College, 1807–1957. Cardiff. 1957.

12300 RICHARDS (DANIEL). Honest to Self. Ammanford. 1971.

12301 ATTWATER (DONALD). The Catholic Church in Modern Wales: A Record of the Past Century. 1935.

12302 DANIEL (JOHN). 'Welsh Opinion: Ecumenical Developments'. *Blackfriars* xlii (1961), 270–3.

14. ECUMENISM

12303 HACHEY (THOMAS E.). 'The Archbishop of Canterbury's Visit to Palestine: An Issue in Anglo-Vatican Relations in 1931'. *Church Hist.* xli (1972), 198–207.

12304 GREAVES (ROBERT WILLIAM). 'Church and Chapel: The Historical Background of Home Reunion, 1559–1952'. *Church Q. Rev.* cliii (1952), 452–69.

12305 PICKERING (WILLIAM STUART FREDERICK) *ed.* Anglican-Methodist Relations: Some Institutional Factors. 1961.

12306 CONVERSATIONS between the Church of England and the Methodist Church: A Report to the Archbishops of Canterbury and York and the Conference of the Methodist Church. 1963.

12307 CLARK (DAVID BERNARD). A Survey of Anglicans and Methodists in Four Towns. 1965.

12308 GILLION (FREDERICK ARTHUR). 'An Attempt towards Church Unity: Anglicans and Methodists in England Propose a First Step'. *Contemp. Rev.* ccxv (1969), 113–18.

12309 BROWN (LESLIE WILFRED) *et al.* 'Anglican–Methodist Unity—a Symposium'. *Church Q. Rev.* i (1968), 98–136.

12310 TURNER (JOHN MUNSEY). Conflict and Reconciliation: Studies in Methodism and Ecumenism in England 1740–1982. 1985.

12311 BACKUS (J. H.). 'Archbishop Temple and the Orthodox: A Note on the Preparations for the Joint Doctrinal Commission of 1931'. *Eastern Churches Rev.* vi (1974), 181–8.

12312 WOOD (CHARLES LINDLEY) *Viscount Halifax, ed.* The Conversations at Malines, 1921–1925: Original Documents. 1930.

12313 LAHEY (R. J.). 'The Origins and Approach of the Malines Conversations'. *Church Hist.* (Sept. 1974), 1–19.

12314 WARD (ARTHUR MARCUS). The Churches Move together: A Brief Account of the Ecumenical Movement from the Edinburgh Conference of 1910. Redhill. 1968.

12315 BELL (GEORGE KENNEDY ALLEN) *ed.* Documents on Christian Unity. 2 vols 1948–55.

12316 ROUSE (RUTH) *and* NEILL (STEPHEN CHARLES) *eds.* A History of the Ecumenical Movement, 1517–1948. 1948. 2nd edn 1968.

12317 FEY (HAROLD EDWARD) *ed.* Ecumenical Advance: A History of the Ecumenical Movement, 1948–1968. 1970.

12318 GOODALL (NORMAN). The Ecumenical Movement: What it is and what it Does. 1961. 2nd edn. 1964.

12319 —— Ecumenical Progress: A Decade of Change in the Ecumenical Movement, 1961–1971. 1972.

12320 —— Second Fiddle: Recollections and Reflections. 1979.

12321 TILL (BARRY DORN). The Churches Search for Unity. Harmondsworth. 1972.

12322 DAVIES (RUPERT ERIC). The Church in Our Times: An Ecumenical History from a British Perspective. 1979.

12323 OLDHAM (JOSEPH HOULDSWORTH). The Churches Survey their Task: The Report of the Conference at Oxford, July 1937, on Church, Community and State. 1937.

12324 THOMPSON (DAVID MICHAEL). 'Theological and Sociological Approaches to the Motivation of the Ecumenical Movement'. Studies in Church History. Vol. 15 1978. 467–80.

12325 EDWARDS (ROWLAND ALEXANDER). Church and Chapel: A Study of the Problem of Reunion in the Light of History. 1952.

12326 SYKES (NORMAN). 'Anglican–Presbyterian Relations'. Mod. Churchman n.s. vol.1 (Jan. 1958), 159–63.

12327 MOORMAN (JOHN RICHARD HUMPIDGE). Vatican Observed: An Anglican Impression of Vatican II. 1967.

12328 PAWLEY (BERNARD CLINTON). The Second Vatican Council: Studies by Eight Anglican Observers. 1967.

12329 PAWLEY (BERNARD CLINTON) and PAWLEY (MARGARET). Rome and Canterbury through Four Centuries: A Study of the Relations between the Church of Rome and the Anglican Churches, 1530–1973. 1974.

12330 STACPOOLE (ALBERIC). 'Ecumenism on the Eve of the Council: Anglican/Roman Catholic Relations'. Clergy Rev. (1984), 300–6, 333–8.

12331 —— 'Anglican/Roman Catholic Relations after the Council 1965–1970'. Clergy Rev. (1985), 55–62, 91–8.

12332 COVENTRY (JOHN SETON). 'Ecumenism in England since the Council'. Month ccxxxvi (1975), 74–8.

12333 CLARK (ALAN) and DAVEY (COLIN) eds. Anglican/Roman Catholic Dialogue. 1974.

12334 AVELING (JOHN C. H.), LOADES (DAVID M.), and McADOO (HENRY R.). Rome and the Anglicans. 1982.

12335 MONTEFIORE (HUGH). So Near and yet so Far: Rome, Canterbury and ARCIC. 1986.

12336 STEWART (RICHARD LOUIS). Anglicans and Roman Catholics. 1977.

12337 HUELIN (GORDON). Old Catholics and Anglicans 1931–1981. Oxf. 1983.

12338 MacARTHUR (ARTHUR). 'The Background to the Formation of the United Reformed Church (Presbyterian and Congregational) in England and Wales in 1972'. J. United Reformed Church Hist. Soc. 4(1) (October 1987), 3–21.

12339 PAYNE (ERNEST ALEXANDER). 'Baptists and the Ecumenical Movement'. Baptist Q. xviii (1960), 258–67.

12340 ST JOHN (HENRY). 'Ecumenical Survey–Anglo Catholic Hopes'. Blackfriars xlii (1961), 220–2.

12341 QUINN (JAMES). 'Christian Unity in Scotland'. Month xxx (1963), 291–4.

12342 NEILL (STEPHEN CHARLES). Towards Church Union, 1937–1952. 1952.

12343 MACQUARRIE (JOHN). Christian Unity and Christian Diversity. 1975.

12344 GOOD (JAMES). The Church of England and the Ecumenical Movement. 1961.

12345 Unity Begins at Home: A Report from the First British Conference on Faith and Order. Nottingham. 1964.

12346 PAYNE (ERNEST ALEXANDER). Thirty Years of the British Council of Churches 1942–1972. 1972.

12347 EDWARDS (DAVID LAWRENCE). The British Churches Turn to the Future. 1973.

12348 WOOLLCOMBE (KENNETH J.). The Failure of the English Covenant. 1983.

12349 COVENTRY (JOHN SETON). Reconciling. 1985.

12350 MATTHEWS (JOHN). The Unity Scene. 1986.

12351 BABINGTON SMITH (CONSTANCE). Iulia de Beausobre: A Russian Christian in the West. 1983.

15. MISSIONS

12352 INTERNATIONAL REVIEW OF MISSIONS. 1911–1969. 1969+.

12353 NEILL (STEPHEN CHARLES) et al. eds. Concise Dictionary of the Christian World Missions. 1970.

12354 HOGG (WILLIAM RICHEY). Ecumenical Foundations: A History of the International Missionary Council and its Nineteenth-Century Background. N.Y. 1952.

12355 MOORHOUSE (GEOFFREY). The Missionaries. 1973.

12356 ROE (JAMES MOULTON). A History of the British and Foreign Bible Society, 1905–1954. 1965.

12357 THOMPSON (HENRY PAGET). Into all Lands: The History of the Society for the Propagation of the Gospel in Foreign Parts, 1701–1950. 1951.

12358 CLARKE (WILLIAM KEMP LOWTHER). A History of the S.P.C.K. 1959.

12359 HEWITT (GEORGE HENRY GORDON). The Problems of Success: A History of the Church Missionary Society, 1910–42.

12360 GOODALL (NORMAN). A History of the London Missionary Society, 1895–1945. 1954.

12361 LORD (FRED TOWNLEY). Achievement: A Short History of the Baptist Missionary Society, 1792–1942. [1942.].

12362 BAND (EDWARD). Working His Purpose Out: The History of the English Presbyterian Mission, 1847–1947. 1948.

12363 HILLIARD (DAVID). God's Gentlemen: A History of the Melanesian Mission, 1849–1942. St Lucia, Queensland. 1978.

12364 PATON (DAVID M.). R.O.: The Life and Times of Bishop Ronald Hall of Hong Kong. Hong Kong. 1985.

12365 LATOURETTE (KENNETH SCOTT). A History of the Expansion of Christianity. 7 vols. 1937–45.

12366 WARREN (MAX ALEXANDER CUNNINGHAM). The Missionary Movement from Britain in Modern History. 1965.

12367 NEILL (STEPHEN CHARLES). A History of Christian Missions. 1965.

12368 WILLIAMSON (HENRY RAYMOND). British Baptists in China 1845–1952. 1957.

12369 HASTINGS (ADRIAN). Church and Mission in Modern Africa. 1967.

12370 GROVES (CHARLES PELHAM). The Planting of Christianity in Africa. Vol. 4: 1914–1954. 1964.

12371 HARDYMAN (J. T.) *and* ORCHARD (R. K.). Two Minutes from Sloane Square: A Brief History of the Conference of Missionary Societies in Great Britain and Ireland, 1912–1977. 1977.

12372 TEMU (A. J.). British Protestant Missions. 1972.

12373 WARD (W. E. F.). Fraser of Trinity and Achimota. Accra. 1965.

12374 THOMSON (D. P.). Eric H. Liddell: Athlete and Missionary, Crieff. 1971.

12375 JACKSON (ELEANOR M.). Red Tape and the Gospel: A Study of the Significance of the Ecumenical Missionary Struggle of William Paton (1886–1943). Birmingham. 1980.

12376 NEWBIGIN (LESSLIE). Unfinished Agenda: An Autobiography. 1985.

12377 JARRETT-KERR (MARTIN). Patterns of Christian Acceptance: Individual Response to the Missionary Impact 1550–1950. 1972.

16. SOCIOLOGY OF RELIGION

12378 WILSON (BRYAN RONALD). Sects and Society: A Sociological Study of Three Religious Groups in Britain. 1961.

12379 —— Patterns of Sectarianism: Organisation and Ideology in Social and Religious Movements. 1967.

12380 —— 'Becoming a Sectarian: Motivation and Commitment'. In Religious Motivation: Biographical and Sociological Problems for the Church Historian. *Studs in Church Hist.* Vol. 15. *Ed.* by Derek Baker. 1978. 481–506.

12381 ARGYLE (MICHAEL). Religious Behaviour. 1958.

12382 MARTIN (DAVID ALFRED). A Sociology of English Religion. 1967.

12383 —— The Religious and the Secular: Studies in Secularization. 1969.

12384 —— A General Theory of Secularization. Oxf. 1978.

12385 MOORE (ROBERT). Pitmen, Preachers and Politics: The Effects of Methodism in a Durham Mining Community. Camb. 1974.

12386 TOWLER (ROBERT). The Need for Certainty: A Sociological Study of Conventional Religion. 1984.

12387 LYON (D.). The Steeple's Shadow. 1985.

12388 HILL (MICHAEL). A Sociology of Religion. 1973.

12389 PRATT (VERNON). Religion and Secularisation. 1970.

12390 MARTIN (DAVID ALFRED) *ed.*, followed by Michael Hill *ed.* Sociological Yearbook of Religion in Britain. Annual. 1968–75.

12391 INGLIS (BRIAN). Private Conscience–Public Morality. 1964.

12392 WHITELEY (CHARLES HENRY) *and* WHITELEY (WINIFRED MAY). The Permissive Morality. 1964.

12393 MACINTYRE (ALASDAIR CHALMERS). Secularization and Moral Change. 1967.

12394 KNOOP (DOUGLAS) *and* JONES (GWILYM PEREDUR). The Genesis of Freemasonry.

12395 WILSON (J.). 'British Israelism'. *Sociol. Rev.* 16(I) (1968), 41–57.

12396 NIVEN (CHARLES DAVID). History of the Humane Movement. 1967.

17. MORAL RE-ARMAMENT

12397 HOWARD (PETER). Britain and the Beast. 1963.

12398 BEBBINGTON (DAVID WILLIAM). 'The Oxford Group Movement Between the Wars'. In Voluntary Religion. *Ed.* by William Sheils. Oxf. 1986.

12399 HENSON (HERBERT HENSLEY). The Oxford Groups. 1933.

12400 GORDON (ANNE WOLRIGE). Peter Howard: Life and Letters. 1969.

12401 WILLIAMSON (GEOFFREY). Inside Buchmanism: An Independent Inquiry into the Oxford Group Movement and Moral Rearmament. 1955.

12402 DRIBERG (THOMAS EDWARD NEIL). The Mystery of Moral Rearmament: A Study of Frank Buchman and His Movement. 1964.

12403 CLARK (WALTER HOUSTON). The Oxford Group: Its History and Significance. N.Y. 1951.

12404 LEAN (GARTH). Frank Buchman: A Life. 1985.

12405 BUCHMAN (FRANK NATHAN DANIEL). Remaking the World. 1947.

12406 CROSSMAN (RICHARD HOWARD STAFFORD) *ed.* Oxford and the Groups. Oxf. 1934.

18. JUDAISM (SEE ALSO JEWS)

12407 THE JEWISH YEARBOOK. 1896+.

12408 GARNER (LLOYD P.). 'A Quarter Century of Anglo-Jewish Historiography'. *Jewish Soc. Studs* 48 (1986), 105–26.

12409 ROTH (CECIL). A History of the Jews in England. Oxf. 1941. 3rd edn 1964.

12410 LIPMAN (VIVIAN DAVID). Social History of the Jews in England, 1850–1950. 1954.

12411 ROTH (CECIL). Essays and Portraits in Anglo-Jewish History. Phila. 1962.

12412 ARIS (STEPHEN). The Jews in Business. 1971.

12413 FREEDMAN (MAURICE) ed. A Minority in Britain: Social Studies of the Anglo-Jewish Community. 1955.

12414 LEVIN (SALMOND S.) ed. A Century of Anglo-Jewish Life, 1870–1970. 1970.

12415 ZIONIST FEDERATION OF GREAT BRITAIN AND IRELAND. Aspects of Anglo-Jewish Life, 1856–1956: A Tercentenary Brochure. 1956.

12416 COHEN (S. A.). English Zionists and British Jews: The Communal Politics of Anglo-Jewry, 1895–1920. 1982.

12417 BROOK (STEPHEN). The Club: The Jews of Modern Britain. 1989.

12418 LIPMAN (S. L.) and LIPMAN (VIVIAN DAVID) eds. Jewish Life in Britain, 1962–1977. 1981.

12419 WATERMAN (STANLEY) and KOSMIN (BARRY). British Jewry in the Eighties: A Statistical and Geographical Study. 1986.

12420 NEWMAN (AUBREY NORRIS). The Board of Deputies of British Jews, 1760–1985: A Brief Survey. 1987.

12421 SEBAG-MONTEFIORE (RUTH). A Family Patchwork: Five Generations of an Anglo-Jewish Family. 1987.

12422 SIMPSON (WILLIAM W.). 'Jewish-Christian Relations Since the Inception of the Council of Christians and Jews'. *Trans. Jewish Hist. Soc. Eng.* 28 (1981–2), 89–101.

12423 GOULD (SAMUEL JULIUS) and ESH (SAUL) eds. Jewish Life in Modern Britain. 1964.

12424 HOMA (BERNARD). Orthodoxy in Anglo-Jewry, 1880–1940. 1969.

12425 HYAMSON (ALBERT MONTEFIORE). The Sephardim of England: A History of the Spanish and Portuguese Jewish Community, 1492–1951. 1951.

12426 ROTH (CECIL). The Great Synagogue, London, 1690–1940. 1950.

12427 BARNETT (ARTHUR). The Western Synagogue Through Two Centuries (1761–1961). 1961.

12428 NEWMAN (AUBREY NORRIS). The United Synagogue, 1870–1970. 1977.

12429 APPLE (RAYMOND). The Hampstead Synagogue, 1892–1967. 1967.

12430 PRAIS (S. J.). 'Synagogue Statistics and the Jewish Population of Great Britain, 1900–1970'. *Jew. J. Sociol.* 14 (1972), 215–78.

12431 JAKOBOVITZ (IMMANUEL). If Only my People . . . Zionism in My Life. 1984.

12432 EMDEN (PAUL HERMAN). Jews of Britain: A Series of Biographies. 1944.

12433 COHEN (ISRAEL). A Jewish Pilgrimage: The Autobiography of Israel Cohen. 1956.

12434 WEIZMANN (CHAIM). Trial and Error: The Autobiography of Chaim Weizmann. 1949.

12435 CARDOZO (DAVID ABRAHAM JESSURUN). Think and Thank: The Montefiore Synagogue and College, Ramsgate, 1833–1933. 1933.

12436 HYAMSON (ALBERT MONTEFIORE). Jews' College, London, 1855–1955. 1955.

12437 PANETH (PHILIPP). The Guardian of the Law: The Chief Rabbi, Dr J. H. Hertz. 1943.

12438 KRAUSZ (ERNEST). Leeds Jewry: Its History and Social Structure. Camb. 1964.

12439 GOLDBERG (PERCY SELVIN). The Manchester Congregation of British Jews, 1857–1957. Manch. 1957.

12440 KRAUSZ (A.). Sheffield Jewry: Commentary on a Community. Raimat-Gau. 1980.

12441 OLSOVER (L.). The Jewish Communities of North-East England, 1755–1980. Gateshead. 1981.

12442 KRAUSZ (ERNEST). 'Occupation and Social Advancement in Anglo-Jewry'. *Jew. J. Sociol.* 4(1) (1962), 82–9.

19. AFRO-CARIBBEAN MOVEMENTS

12443 VINE (RAYMOND DOUGLAS) ed. A Century of Adventism in the British Isles. 1974.

12444 HILL (CLIFFORD STANLEY HORACE). West Indian Migrants and the London Churches. 1963.

12445 CLARKE (P.). Black Paradise: The Rastafarian Movement. Wellingborough. 1986.

12446 CASHMORE (ERNEST). Rastaman: The Rastafarian Movement in England. 1979.

12447 HILL (CLIFFORD STANLEY HORACE). Black Churches: West Indian and African Sects in Britain. 1971.

12448 '—— From Church to Sect: West Indian Religious Sect Development in Britain'. *J. Sci. Stud. Rel.* x (1971), 114–23.

12449 CALLEY (MALCOLM J. C.). God's People: West Indian Pentecostal Sects in England. 1965.

20. MISCELLANEOUS

12450 LINDEBOOM (JOHANNES). Austin Friars: History of the Dutch Reformed Church in London, 1550–1950. The Hague. 1950.

12451 DEMPSEY (WILLIAM S.). The Story of the Catholic Church in the Isle of Man. 1958.

12452 NEWMAN-NORTON (SERAPHIM). The Time of Silence: A History of the Catholic Apostolic Church, 1901–1971. Leicester. 3rd edn 1975.

12453 MacKAY (JOHNSTON R.). 'The Impact of American Religion on Great Britain'. *Expository Times* (Oct. 1959), 19–21.

12454 BRADEN (CHARLES SAMUEL). Christian Science Today: Power, Policy, Practice. 1959.

21. NON-CHRISTIAN RELIGIONS

12455 JODY (DANIELE) *and* NIELSEN (JORGEN). Muslims in Britain: An Annotated Bibliography, 1960–1984. Coventry. 1985.

12456 MAHMOUD-HARRIS (MARIYAM). World Religions in Britain: A Series of Study Pamphlets Designed to Help the Ordinary Reader's Understanding of Some Non-Christian Faiths Practised in Britain. 1974.

12457 SHUKLA (HARI). 'Living in a Multi-cultural Society: The Hindu Community in Britain'. *Expository Times* lxxxix (1977), 37–40.

12458 BROWN (DAVID). A New Threshold: Guidelines for the Churches in their Relations with Muslim Communities. 1976.

12459 BUTTERWORTH (ERIC). A Muslim Community in Britain. 1967.

12460 NATIONAL SPIRITUAL ASSEMBLY OF THE BAHA₃IS OF THE BRITISH ISLES. The Centenary of a World Faith: The History of the Baha'i Faith in the British Isles. 1944.

12461 PERKINS (M.) *and* HAINSWORTH (P.). The Baha'i Faith. 1980.

12462 OLIVER (IAN P.). Buddhism in Britain. 1979.

12463 HUMPHREYS (TRAVERS CHRISTMAS). The Development of Buddhism in England. 1937.

12464 —— Sixty Years of Buddhism in England (1907–1967): A History and Survey. 1968.

12465 HELWEG (ARTHUR WESLEY). Sikhs in England: The Development of a Migrant Community. 2nd edn 1986.

12466 HARBHAJAN (SINGH JANJUA). Sikh Temples in the U.K. and the People Behind their Management. 1976.

12467 BURGHART (RICHARD) *ed.* Hinduism in Great Britain: The Perpetuation of Religion in an Alien Cultural Milieu. 1987.

12468 BRIDGER (PETER A.). A Hindu Family in Great Britain. 1969.

6

EXTERNAL RELATIONS

A. THE BRITISH EMPIRE/COMMONWEALTH

The general problems posed for the ordering of a bibliography by the very considerable changes that have taken place during the period in British relations with the external world have already been alluded to in the initial introduction. They are compounded by the fact that within the imperial context there is sometimes no clear division between 'internal' and 'external'. Indeed, at least during the period of the British Empire/British Commonwealth, there was a sense in which all imperial affairs were 'internal'. No such comprehensive conception has been attempted here. Readers seeking detailed guidance on the internal developments within overseas territories during British rule will in general have to look elsewhere. The titles that have been included have been chosen because in certain respects they contain important material on particular aspects of the British connection. It is recognized, however, that individual items conspire against this general intention.

1. GENERAL

12469 THE CAMBRIDGE HISTORY OF THE BRITISH EMPIRE. Vol. III. The Empire—Commonwealth, 1870–1919. Camb.

12470 COOK (CHRIS) *and* PAXTON (JOHN). Commonwealth Political Facts. 1979.

12471 LIVINGSTON (WILLIAM SAMUEL) ed. Federalism in the Commonwealth: A Bibliographical Commentary. 1963.

12472 WIGHT (MARTIN). The Development of the Legislative Council, 1606–1945. 1946.

12473 McINTYRE (WILLIAM DAVID). Colonies into Commonwealth. 1966.

12474 —— The Commonwealth of Nations: Origins and Impact, 1869–1971. Minneapolis. 1977.

12475 PORTER (BERNARD). The Lion's Share: A Short History of British Imperialism, 1850–1970. 1975. 2nd edn 1984. Standard text.

12476 BETTS (RAYMOND F.). Uncertain Dimensions: Western Overseas Empires in the Twentieth Century. Minneapolis/Oxf. 1985.

12477 HALL (HESSEL DUNCAN). Commonwealth: A History of the British Commonwealth of Nations. 1971. Fruit of a long commonwealth involvement.

12478 CROSS (COLIN). The British Empire. 1972.

12479 JUDD (DENIS O.) *and* SLINN (PETER). The Evolution of the Modern Commonwealth, 1902–80. 1982.

12480 KIERNAN (VICTOR GORDON). European Empires from Conquest to Collapse, 1815–1960. Leicester. 1982.

12481 FIELDHOUSE (DAVID KENNETH). Colonialism 1870–1945: An Introduction. 1981.

12482 GRIFFITHS (*Sir* PERCIVAL JOSEPH). Empire into Commonwealth. 1969.

12483 WATSON (JACK BRIERLEY). Empire to Commonwealth, 1919 to 1970. 1971.

12484 GORDON (DONALD CRAIGIE). The Moment of Power: Britain's Imperial Epoch. Englewood Cliffs N.J. 1970.

12485 WIENER (JOEL H.) ed. Great Britain: Foreign Policy and the Span of Empire, 1689–1971: A Documentary History. 4 vols N.Y. 1972.

12486 CUMPSTON (INA MARY). The Growth of the British Commonwealth, 1880–1932. 1973.

12487 PORTER (ANDREW N.) *and* STOCKWELL (A. J.) *eds.* British Imperial Policy and Decolonization, 1938–64. Vol. 1 1938–51. 1987. Good doc. collections.

12488 ROBINSON (KENNETH ERNEST) *and* MADDEN (ALBERT FREDERICK) *eds.* Essays in Imperial Government Presented to Margery Perham. 1963.

12489 MADDEN (ALBERT FREDERICK) *and* FIELDHOUSE (DAVID KENNETH). Oxford and the Idea of the Commonwealth: Essays Presented to Sir Edgar Williams. 1982.

12490 ROBINSON (E. AUSTIN). Fifty Years of Commonwealth Economic Development. Camb. 1972.

12491 MEREDITH (D.). 'The British Government and Colonial Economic Policy, 1919–1939'. *Econ. Hist. Rev.* xxviii (1975), 484–99.

12492 LEE (J. MICHAEL) *and* PETTER (M.). The Colonial Office, War, and Redevelopment Policy. 1982

12493 —— 'Forward Thinking and War: The Colonial Office During the 1940s'. *J. Imp. Cwealth Hist.* vi (1977), 64–79.

12494 PERHAM (*Dame* MARGERY FREDA). Lugard: The Years of Authority, 1898–1945: The Second Part of the Life of Frederick Dealtry Lugard. 1960.

12495 BRADLEY (*Sir* KENNETH GRANVILLE). The Diary of a District Officer. 1943. 4th edn 1966.

12496 —— The Colonial Service as a Career. 1950.

12497 —— Once a District Officer. 1966.

12498 CLIFFORD (*Hon. Sir* BEDE EDMUND HUGH). Proconsul. 1964.

12499 GAILEY (H. A.). Clifford: Imperial Consul. 1982.

12500 JEFFERIES (*Sir* CHARLES JOSEPH). The Colonial Empire and its Civil Service. Camb. 1938.

12501 HALL (HENRY L.). The Colonial Office: A History. 1937.

12502 JEFFERIES (*Sir* CHARLES JOSEPH). Whitehall and the Colonial Service: An Administrative Memoir, 1939–1956. 1972.

12503 PURCELL (VICTOR). The Memoirs of a Malayan Official. 1965.

12504 FOOT (HUGH MACKINTOSH) *Baron Caradon.* A Start in Freedom. 1964.

12505 ROONEY (D.). Sir Charles Arden-Clarke. 1982.

12506 CROSS (JOHN ARTHUR). Whitehall and the Commonwealth: British Departmental Organisation for Commonwealth Relations, 1900–1966. 1967.

12507 PARKINSON (*Sir* ARTHUR CHARLES COSMO). The Colonial Office from Within, 1909–1945. 1947.

12508 BURNS (*Sir* ALAN CUTHBERT). Colonial Civil Servant. 1949.

12509 FURSE (*Sir* RALPH DOLIGNON). Aucuparius: Recollections of a Recruiting Officer. 1962.

12510 HEUSSLER (ROBERT). Yesterday's Rulers: The Making of the British Colonial Service. 1963.

12511 REESE (TREVOR RICHARD). The History of the Royal Commonwealth Society, 1868–1968. 1968.

12512 The Merger of the Foreign Office and the Commonwealth Office. 1968. HMSO.

12513 KIRK-GREENE (A. H. M.). 'The Progress of Pro-consuls: Advancement and Migration Among the Colonial Governors of British African Territories, 1900–1965'. *J. Imp. Cwealth Hist.* 7 (1979), 180–212.

12514 TOYNBEE (ARNOLD JOSEPH) *ed.* The Conduct of British Empire Foreign Relations Since the Peace Settlement. 1928.

12515 LOUIS (WILLIAM ROGER). 'Great Britain and the African Peace Settlement of 1919'. *Amer. Hist. Rev.* lxxi (1966), 875–92.

12516 —— 'The United Kingdom and the Beginning of the Mandates System, 1919–1922'. *Inl. Organisation* xxiii (1969), 73–96.

12517 CARTER (GWENDOLEN MARGARET). The British Commonwealth and International Security: The Role of the Dominions, 1919–1939. Westport, Conn. 1971.

12518 MANSERGH (PHILIP NICHOLAS SETON). 'Britain and the Dominions: Consultation and Cooperation in Foreign Policy'. *India Q.* iv (1948), 3–12.

12519 MEYERS (REINHARD). 'Britain, Europe and the Dominions in the 1930s: Some Aspects of British, European and Commonwealth Policies'. *Aust. J. Pol. Hist.* xxii (1976), 36–50.

12520 STEBBING (JOHN). 'Commonwealth Consultation in External Affairs: Ups and Downs Over 74 years'. *Cwealth J.* v (1962), 23–5.

12521 INGRAM (DEREK). 'Ten Turbulent Years: The Commonwealth Secretariat at Work'. *Round Table* cclviii (1975), 138–48.

12522 SMITH (ARNOLD) *with* SANGER (CLYDE). Stitches in Time: The Commonwealth and World Politics. Don Mills 1981.

12523 PAPADOPOULOS (ANDRESTINOS N.). Multilateral Diplomacy Within the Commonwealth. The Hague. 1982.

12524 WIGHT (MARTIN). 'Is the Commonwealth a Non-Hobbesian Institution?'. *J. Cwealth Comp. Pol.* 16 (1978), 119–33.

12525 BELOFF (MAX) *Baron.* Imperial Sunset: Britain's Liberal Empire, 1897–1921. 1969.

12526 GROOM (A. J. R.) *ed.* The Commonwealth in the 1980s. 1984.

12527 MACKENZIE (JOHN). Propaganda and Empire: The Manipulation of British Public Opinion 1880–1960. Manchester. 1984.

12528 —— *Ed.* Imperialism and Popular Culture. Manchester. 1985.

12529 LUCAS (*Sir* CHARLES PRESTWOOD). The British Empire. 1916. An administrator's perspective.

12530 MILLS (JOHN SAXON). The Future of the Empire. 1918. Inspired Journalism.

12531 HALL (HESSEL DUNCAN). The British Commonwealth of Nations: A Study of its Past and Future Development. 1920.

12532 —— Mandates, Dependencies and Trusteeship. 1948.

12533 ROBINSON (KENNETH ERNEST). The Dilemmas of Trusteeship; Aspects of British Colonial Policy between the Wars. 1965. First-rate, first-hand reflections.

12534 HALL (HESSEL DUNCAN). 'The Genesis of the Balfour Declaration of 1926'. *J. Comm. Pol. Studs* i (1961–1963), 169–93.

12535 WIGLEY (PHILIP G.) *and* HILLMER (NORMAN). 'Defining the First British Commonwealth: The Hankey Memorandum and the 1926 Imperial Conference'. *J. Imp. Cwealth Hist.* 8 (1979), 105–16.

12536 DRUMMOND (IAN M.). British Economic Policy and the Empire, 1919–1939. 1972. Text and documents.

12537 LOWELL (ABBOTT LAWRENCE) *and* HALL (HESSEL DUNCAN). The British Commonwealth of Nations. 1927. An American-Australian Combination.

12538 EGERTON (HUGH EDWARD). British Colonial Policy in the Twentieth Century. 1922. A view from Oxford.

12539 McINNES (C. M.). The British Commonwealth and its Unsolved Problems. 1925. Reflections of a blind Canadian exile.

12540 BROCK (WILLIAM RANULF). Britain and the Dominions. Camb. 1951

12541 ELLIOTT (WILLIAM YANDELL). The New British Empire. N.Y. 1932.

12542 FULLER (JOHN FREDERIC CHARLES). Empire Unity and Defence. Bristol. 1934.

12543 DARWIN (JOHN G.). 'Imperialism in Decline: Tendencies in British Imperial Policy between the Wars'. *Hist. J.* 23 (1980), 647–79.

12544 STOYE (JOHANNES). The British Empire: Its Structure and its Problems. 1936. A German view.

12545 SCHILLER (F. C. S.). The Future of the British Empire After Ten Years. 1936. A philosophical glimpse.

12546 SPENDER (JOHN ALFRED). Great Britain, Empire and Commonwealth 1886–1935. 1936. Silver Jubilee performance.

12547 COOK (E. THOMAS) *ed.* The Empire and the World. 1937.

12548 HODSON (HENRY VINCENT) *ed.* The British Commonwealth and the Future. 1939. All may not be for the best.

12549 HODSON (HENRY VINCENT). The British Empire. 1939.

12550 NEWTON (ARTHUR PERCIVAL). A Hundred Years of the British Empire. 1940.

12551 TURNER (W. J.) *ed.* The British Commonwealth and Empire. 1943.

12552 ELLIOTT (WILLIAM YANDELL) *and* HALL (HESSEL DUNCAN) *eds.* The British Commonwealth at War. 1943.

12553 WALKER (ERIC ANDERSON). The British Empire, its Structure and Spirit. 1943. 2nd edn Camb. 1953.

12554 BARKER (*Sir* ERNEST). The Ideas and Ideals of the British Empire. Camb. 1941.

12555 ELTON (GODFREY) *Baron Elton*. Imperial Commonwealth. 1945.

12556 FROST (RICHARD). The British Commonwealth and the World. 1945. British wartime imperial enthusiasm.

12557 KNAPLUND (PAUL). The British Empire 1815–1939. 1941. American endorsement.

12558 MORGAN (DAVID JOHN). The Official History of Colonial Development. 1980. 4 vols. 1. The Origins of British Aid Policy 1924–1945. 2. Developing British Colonial Resources 1945–1951. 3. A Re-assessment of British Aid Policy 1951–1955. 4. Changes in British Aid Policy, 1951–1970. Solid and sober.

12559 HALL (NOEL E.). 'Colonial Development and Welfare: The Emergence of a New British Policy'. *London Q. World Affs* xii (1946), 129–34.

12560 WILLIAMSON (C.). 'Britain's New Colonial Policy, 1940–1951'. *South Atl. Q.* li (1952), 366–73.

12561 HALL (HESSEL DUNCAN). Mandates, Dependencies and Trusteeship. 1948. Informed contemporary assessments.

12562 FROST (RICHARD) *ed.* The British Commonwealth and World Society. 1947.

12563 HODSON (HENRY VINCENT). Twentieth Century Empire. 1948.

12564 CARRINGTON (CHARLES EDMUND). The British Overseas: Exploits of a Nation of Shopkeepers. Camb. 1950. 2nd edn 2 vols 1968. 'Exploits' predominate.

12565 DUTT (RAJANI PALME). Britain's Crisis of Empire. 1949.

12566 —— The Crisis of Britain and the British Empire. 1957. Exploitation predominates.

12567 HINDEN (RITA). Empire and After: A Study of British Imperial Attitudes. 1949.

12568 GOLDSWORTHY (DAVID J.). Colonial Issues in British Politics, 1945–1961: From 'Colonial Development' to 'Wind of Change'. 1971. A useful evaluation.

12569 THORNTON (ARCHIBALD PATON). The Imperial Idea and its Enemies. 1959. 2nd edn 1985.

12570 —— For the File on the Empire. 1968. Incisive studies.

12571 MARTEL (GORDON) *ed.* Studies in British Imperial History: Essays in Honour of A. P. Thornton. 1986.

12572 KIERNAN (VICTOR GORDON). 'Labour and Imperialism'. *Bull. Soc. Stud. Lab. Hist.* xxxi (1975), 96–101.

12573 SPEERS (PETER C.). 'Colonial Policy of the British Labour Party'. *Soc. Res.* xv (1948), 304–26.

12574 HANCOCK (*Sir* WILLIAM KEITH). Survey of British Commonwealth Affairs. 2 vols 1937–42.

12575 MANSERGH (PHILIP NICHOLAS SETON). Survey of British Commonwealth Affairs: Problems of Wartime Co-operation and Postwar Change, 1939–1952. 1958. Authoritative. He also published a selection of essays entitled 'The Commonwealth and the Nations'. 1948.

12576 —— *ed.* Documents and Speeches on British Commonwealth Affairs: Problems of External Policy, 1931–1939. 1952.

12577 MILLER (JOHN DONALD BRUCE). Survey of Commonwealth Affairs: Problems of Expansion and Attrition, 1953–1969. 1974.

12578 CASEY (RICHARD GARDINER) *Baron.* The Future of the Commonwealth. 1963.

12579 COWEN (*Sir* ZELMAN). The British Commonwealth of Nations in a Changing World. Evanston. 1965. Australian commentaries.

12580 WISEMAN (H. VICTOR). Britain and the Commonwealth. 1965.

12581 INGRAM (DEREK). Commonwealth for a Colour-Blind World. 1965.

12582 TAYLOR (DON). The Years of Challenge: The Commonwealth and the British Empire, 1945–1958. 1959.

12583 BRADLEY (*Sir* KENNETH GRANVILLE), *ed.* The Living Commonwealth. 1961.

12584 HAMILTON (WILLIAM BASKERVILLE), ROBINSON (KENNETH ERNEST), and GOODWIN (CRAUFORD DAVID WYCLIFFE). A Decade of the Commonwealth, 1955–1964. Durham, N.C. 1966. Mingled apologetics and analysis.

12585 KIRKMAN (WILLIAM PATRICK). Unscrambling an Empire: A Critique of British Colonial Policy, 1956–1966. 1966. A view from within the Colonial Service.

12586 CROSS (COLIN). The Fall of the British Empire, 1918–1968. 1968.

12587 WOODCOCK (GEORGE). Who Killed the British Empire? 1974.

12588 TOWNSEND (PETER). The Last Emperor: Decline and Fall of the British Empire. 1973. Poses preliminary questions and supplies early answers.

12589 MORRIS (JAN). Farewell the Trumpets: An Imperial Retreat. 1978. Evocative.

12590 LAPPING (BRIAN). End of Empire. 1985. Television-originated.

12591 GALLAGHER (JOHN) *and* SEAL (ANIL) *ed.* The Decline, Revival and Fall of the British Empire. Camb. 1982. Takes a longer review, as do Gerald Sandford Graham,

Tides of Empire. 1972, and John Edward Bowle, The Imperial Achievement: The Rise and Transformation of the British Empire. 1974.

12592 DARWIN (JOHN G.). Britain and Decolonisation 1945–65. 1985.

12593 HOLLAND (ROBERT F.). European Decolonization 1918–81. 1985.

12594 CHAMBERLAIN (MURIEL EVELYN). Decolonization: The Fall of the European Empires. Oxf. 1985. Useful introductory studies.

12595 KAHLER (MILES). Decolonization in Britain and France: the Domestic Consequences of International Relations. Princeton, NJ. 1984.

12596 SMITH (T.). 'A Comparative Study of French and British Decolonization'. *Comparative Studs in Society and Hist.* 20 (1978), 70–102.

12597 HOROWITZ (DAN). 'The British Conservatives and the Racial Issue in the Debate on Decolonization'. *Race* xii (1970), 169–87.

12598 LOUIS (WILLIAM ROGER). Imperialism at Bay: The United States and the Decolonization of the British Empire. Oxf. 1977. Full.

12599 LOW (D. ANTHONY). The Contraction of England. Camb. 1985: 'The Contraction of England: National Decline and the Loss of Empire' B. R. Tomlinson. *J. Imp. Cwealth. Hist.* 11 (1982), 58–72.

2. THE 'OLD DOMINIONS'

(a) Australia

12600 KEPARS (I.). Australia. 1984. [Bibliography.].

12601 REESE (TREVOR R.). Australia in the Twentieth Century: A Short Political Guide. 1964.

12602 WARD (RUSSELL). A Nation for a Continent: The History of Australia 1901–1975. 1977.

12603 WILSON (*Sir* CHARLES H.). Australia 1788–1988: The Creation of a Nation. 1988.

12604 MILLER (J. D. B.). Australian Government and Politics. 1954. 2nd edn 1959.

12605 MEANEY (NEVILLE). Australia and the World: A Documentary History from the 1870s to the 1970s. Melbourne. 1985.

12606 STARGARDT (A. W.). Australia's Asian Policies: The History of a Debate 1839–1972. Hamburg/Wiesbaden. 1977.

12607 MILLER (J. D. BRUCE) *ed.* Australians and British: Social and Political Connections. 1987.

12608 MADDEN (A. FREDERICK) *and* MORRIS-JONES (W. H.) *eds.* Australia and Britain: Studies in Changing Relationships. 1980.

12609 MILLAR (T. B.) *ed.* The Australian Contribution to Britain. 1988.

12610 HALL (HENRY L.). Australia and England: A Study in Imperial Relations. 1934.

12611 DIGNAN (D. K.). 'Australia and British Relations with Japan, 1914–1921'. *Austral. Outlook* xxi (1967), 135–50.

12612 FITZHARDINGE (L. F.). 'Australia, Japan and Great Britain, 1914–1918: A Study in Triangular Diplomacy'. *Hist. Studs* xiv (1970), 250–9.

12613 SNELLING (R. C.). 'Peacemaking 1919: Australia, New Zealand and the British Empire Delegation at Versailles'. *J. Imp. Cwealth Hist.* 4 (1976), 15–28.

12614 SALES (PETER M.). 'W. M. Hughes and the Chanak Crisis of 1922'. *Austral. J. Pol. Hist.* xvii (1971), 392–405.

12615 MEGAW (M. R.). 'Australia and the Anglo-American Trade Agreement 1938'. *J. Imp. Cwealth Hist.* 3 (1975), 191–211.

12616 WATT (*Sir* ALAN). The Evolution of Australia's Foreign Policy 1938–1965. Camb. 1967.

12617 —— Australian Defence Policy 1951–1963: Major International Aspects. Canberra. 1963.

12618 GRANT (BRUCE). The Crisis of Loyalty: A Study of Australian Foreign Policy. Sydney. 1972.

12619 RICHARDS (PETER G.). Prime Ministers and Diplomats: The Making of Australian Foreign Policy 1901–1949. Oxf. 1983.

12620 RENOUF (ALAN). Let Justice be Done: The Foreign Policy of Dr. H. V. Evatt. St Lucia, Queensland. 1983.

12621 ARNOLD (LORNA). A Very Special Relationship. British Atomic Weapons Trials in Australia. 1987.

12622 HAZELHURST (CAMERON). Menzies Observed. Sydney. 1979.

12623 HASLUCK (*Sir* PAUL). Sir Robert Menzies. Melbourne. 1980.

12624 BUNTING (*Sir* JOHN). R. G. Menzies: A Portrait. 1988.

12625 PERKINS (KEVIN). Menzies, The Last of the Queen's Men. Sydney. 1968.

12626 MENZIES (*Sir* ROBERT GORDON). Afternoon Light: Some Memories of Men and Events. 1967.

12627 —— The Measure of the Years. 1970.

12628 DAY (D.). Menzies and Churchill at War. 1986.

12629 CASEY (RICHARD GARDINER) *Baron*. Personal Experience, 1939–1946. 1962.

12630 —— Friends and Neighbours: Australia and the World. Melbourne. 1954.

12631 MILLAR (T. B.) *ed*. Australian Foreign Minister: The Diaries of R. G. Casey 1951–1960. 1972.

12632 HUDSON (W. J.). Casey. Oxf. 1986.

12633 MILLAR (T. B.). Australia's Foreign Policy. Sydney. 1968.

12634 HASLUCK (*Sir* PAUL). Mucking About. Melbourne. 1977.

12635 PERKINS (JAMES OLIVER NEWTON). Britain and Australia: Economic Relationships in the 1950s. Melbourne. 1962.

12636 MILLER (J. D. BRUCE). The EEC and Australia. 1976.

12637 GELBER (HARRY GREGOR). Australia, Britain and the EEC 1961 to 1963. Oxf. 1966.

12638 CRAWFORD (JOHN G.), *with* ANDERSON (NANCY) *and* MORRIS (MARGARET G. N.) *eds*. Australian Trade Policy 1942–1966. 1968.

12639 WARHURST (JOHN). 'The Australia-Britain Relationship: The Future of Australia's Political Relationship to Britain'. *J. Cwealth Comp. Pol.* 24 (1986), 35–47.

(b) Canada

12640 GRENATSTEIN (J. L.) *and* STEVENS (PAUL). Canada Since 1867: A Bibliographical Guide. Toronto. 1974.

12641 BOTHWELL (ROBERT), DRUMMOND (IAN), *and* ENGLISH (JOHN). Canada since 1945: Power, Politics and Provincialism. Toronto. 1981.

12642 CREIGHTON (DONALD). The Forked Road: Canada 1939–1957. Toronto. 1976

12643 DEWITT (DAVID B.) *and* KIRTON (JOHN J.). Canada as a Principal Power: A Study in Foreign Policy and International Relations. Toronto. 1983.

12644 STACEY (C. P.). Canada and the Age of Conflict: A History of Canadian External Policies. Vol. 2 Toronto. 1981.

12645 KIRK-GREENE (ANTHONY H. M.). 'The Governors-General of Canada 1867–1952: A Collective Profile'. *J. Can. Studs* 13 (1978), 35–57.

12646 Canada in London: An Unofficial Glimpse of Canada's Sixteen High Commissioners 1880–1980. 1980.

12647 GRAHAM (GERALD SANDFORD). Britain and Canada. 1943.

12648 WIGLEY (PHILIP G.). Canada and the Transition to Commonwealth: British-Canadian Relations, 1917–1926. Camb. 1977.

12649 CARLAND (JOHN M.). 'Shadow and Substance: Mackenzie King's Perceptions of British Intentions at the 1923 Imperial Conference'. In 'Studies in British Imperial History: Essays in Honour of A. P. Thornton'. *Ed.* by Gordon Martel. 1986, 178–200.

12650 KIRK-GREENE (ANTHONY H. M.). 'Taking Canada into Partnership in the "White Man's Burden": The British Colonial Service and the Dominions Selection Scheme of 1923'. *Can. J. Afr. Studs* 15 (1981), 33–54.

12651 BOYCE (ROBERT). 'Insects and International Relations: Canada, France, and British Agricultural Sanitary Import Restrictions between the Wars'. *Inl Hist. Rev.* (1987), 1–27.

12652 CUNNINGHAM (W. B.) *ed*. Canada, the Commonwealth and the Common Market. Montreal. 1962.

12653 HOLMES (JOHN W.). The Better Part of Valor: Essays on Canadian Diplomacy. Toronto. 1970.

12654 LYON (PETER) ed. Britain and Canada: Survey of a Changing Relationship since 1945. 1976.

12655 BREEN (D. H.). 'Anglo-American Rivalry and the Evolution of Canadian Petroleum Policy to 1930'. *Can. Hist. Rev.* 62 (1981), 283–303.

12656 HOLLAND (ROBERT F.). 'The End of an Imperial Economy: Anglo-Canadian Disengagement in the 1930s'. *J. Imp. Cwealth Hist.* 11 (1983), 159–74.

12657 DAVIS (J.). 'ATFERO: The Atlantic Ferry Organisation'. *J. Contemp. Hist.* 20 (1985), 71–97.

12658 MCEVOY (F. J.). 'Canada, Ireland and the Commonwealth: The Declaration of the Irish Republic, 1948–9'. *Irish. Hist. Studs* 24 (1985), 506–27.

12659 DILKS (DAVID N.). Three Visitors to Canada: Stanley Baldwin, Neville Chamberlain and Winston Churchill. 1985.

12660 —— 'The Great Dominion: Churchill's Farewell Visits to Canada 1952 and 1954'. *Can. Jnl Hist./Annales Can. d'Hist.* 23 (1988), 49–72.

12661 PICKERSGILL (J. W.) and FOSTER (D. F.). The Mackenzie King Record. 4 vols. Toronto. 1963–76.

12662 PEARSON (LESTER BOWLES). Memoirs Vol. I: 1897–1948: Through Diplomacy to Politics. 1973.

12663 —— Memoirs Vol. II: 1948–1957: The International Years. 1974.

12664 DIEFENBAKER (JOHN). One Canada: Memoirs of the Right Honourable John Diefenbaker Vol. I: The Crusading Years 1895–1956. Toronto. 1975.

12665 —— Vol. II: The Years of Achievement 1957–1962. 1976.

12666 —— Vol. III: The Tumultuous Years. 1977.

12667 RADWANSKI (GEORGE). Trudeau. 1979.

(c) New Zealand

12668 GROVER (R. F.). New Zealand. Oxf. 1980. [Bibliography.].

12669 SINCLAIR (KEITH). A History of New Zealand. 2nd edn Harmondsworth. 1969.

12670 New Zealand Foreign Policy: Statements and Documents 1943–1957. Wellington. 1972.

12671 KENNAWAY (RICHARD). New Zealand Foreign Policy 1951–1971. 1972.

12672 MCINTOSH (A.) et al. New Zealand in World Affairs. Vol. I 1977. [Covers 1930–1960.].

12673 LODGE (JULIET). The European Community and New Zealand. 1982.

3. AFRICA

(a) General

12674 KIRKWOOD (KENNETH). Britain and Africa. 1965.

12675 CROWDER (MICHAEL) ed. The Cambridge History of Africa.

12676 GANN (LEWIS H.) and DUIGNAN (PETER) eds. Colonialism in Africa 1870–1960. 5 vols Camb. 1969–75.

12677 MCEWAN (P. J. M.) ed. Twentieth Century Africa. Oxf. 1968.

12678 CLAYTON (ANTHONY) and KILLINGRAY (DAVID). Khaki and Blue: The Military Police in British Colonial Africa. Oxf. 1989.

12679 COHEN (Sir ANDREW BENJAMIN). British Policy in Changing Africa. 1959.

12680 BRADLEY (Sir KENNETH GRANVILLE). Britain's Purpose in Africa. 1959.

12681 PERHAM (Dame MARGERY FREDA). Colonial Sequence, 1930–1949: A Chronological Commentary upon British Colonial Policy, Especially in Africa. 1967.

12682 —— Colonial Sequence, 1949–1969: A Chronological Commentary upon British Colonial Policy, Especially in Africa. 1970.

12683 —— The Colonial Reckoning: The End of Imperial Rule in Africa in the Light of British Experience. 1977.

12684 ROBINSON (KENNETH) and MADDEN (A. FREDERICK). Essays in Imperial Government Presented to Margery Perham. Oxf. 1963.

12685 ALLEN (CHARLES) ed. Tales from the Dark Continent: Images of British Colonial Africa in the Twentieth Century. 1979.

12686 MUNRO (JOHN STABLES FORBES). Britain in Tropical Africa, 1880–1960: Economic Relationships and Impact. 1984.

12687 HETHERINGTON (P.). British Paternalism and Africa, 1920–1940. 1978.

12688 PADMORE (GEORGE). Africa: Britain's Third Empire. 1949.

12689 HOOKER (JAMES R.). Black Revolutionary: George Padmore's Path from Communism to Pan-Africanism. 1967.

12690 PEARCE (R. D.). The Turning Point in Africa: British Colonial Policy, 1938–1948. 1982.

12691 —— 'The Colonial Office and Planned Decolonisation in Africa'. *Afr. Affs* 83 (1984), 77–94.

12692 FLINT (JOHN E.). 'The Failure of Planned Decolonisation in British Africa'. *Afr. Affs* 82 (1983), 389–412.

12693 HYAM (RONALD). 'Africa and the Labour Government 1945–1951'. *J. Imp. Cwealth Hist.* 16 (1988), 148–72.

12694 BROCKWAY (ARCHIBALD FENNER). African Journeys. 1955.

12695 CELL (JOHN W.). 'On the Eve of Decolonisation: The Colonial Office's Plans for the Transfer of Power in Africa'. *J. Imp. Cwealth Hist.* 8 (1980), 235–57.

12696 PEARCE (R. D.). 'The Colonial Office in 1947 and the Transfer of Power; An Addendum to John Cell'. *J. Imp. Cwealth Hist.* 10 (1982), 211–15.

12697 GIFFORD (PROSSER) *and* LOUIS (WILLIAM ROGER) *eds.* The Transfer of Power in Africa: Decolonization 1940–1960. New Haven, Conn. 1982.

12698 ARMOUR (CHARLES). 'The BBC and the Development of Broadcasting in British Colonial Africa 1946–1956'. *Afr. Affs* 83 (1984), 359–402.

12699 KILLINGRAY (DAVID) *and* RATHBONE (RICHARD) *eds.* Africa and the Second World War. 1987.

12700 SMYTH (R.). 'Britain's African Colonies and British Propaganda during the Second World War'. *J. Imp. Cwealth Studs* 14 (1985), 65–82.

12701 OVENDALE (RITCHIE). The English-Speaking Alliance: Britain, the United States, the Dominions and the Cold War, 1945–1951. 1985.

12702 HOROWITZ (DAN). 'Attitudes of British Conservatives towards Decolonisation in Africa'. *Afr. Affs* 59 (1970), 9–26.

12703 KIRK-GREENE (ANTHONY H. M.). A Biographical Dictionary of the British Colonial Governor. Vol. I: Africa. Brighton. 1980.

12704 —— *Ed.* Africa in the Colonial Period III: The Transfer of Power: The Colonial Administrator in the Age of Decolonisation. Oxf. 1979.

12705 GANN (LEWIS H.) *and* DUIGNAN (PETER) *eds.* African Proconsuls: European Governors in Africa. 1978.

12706 CLAYTON (ANTHONY) *and* KILLINGRAY (DAVID). Khaki and Blue: The Military Police in British Colonial Africa. Oxf. 1989.

12707 BANGURA (Y.). Britain and Commonwealth Africa: The Politics of Economic Relationships. Manch. 1983.

(b) High Commission Territories

12708 HYAM (RONALD). 'The Politics of Partition in Southern Africa, 1908–1961'. In 'Reappraisals in British Imperial History' by Ronald Hyam and Ged Martin. 1975.

12709 SPENCE (JOHN E.). 'British Policy Towards the High Commission Territories'. *J. Mod. Afr. Studs* 2 (1964) 221–46.

12710 —— Lesotho: The Politics of Independence. Oxf. 1968.

12711 WILLETT (SHELAGH M.) *and* AMBROSE (DAVID). Lesotho. Oxf. 1980. [Bibliography.].

12712 DOXEY (G. V.). The High Commission Territories and South Africa. Oxf. 1963.

12713 HYAM (RONALD). 'The Political Consequences of Seretse Khama: Britain, the Bangwato and South Africa 1948–1952'. *Hist. J.* 29 (1986), 921–47.

(c) South Africa

12714 OVENDALE (RITCHIE). 'The South African Policy of the British Labour Government 1947–1951'. *Inl. Affs* 59 (1982–1983), 41–58.

12715 AUSTIN (DENNIS). Britain and South Africa. 1966.

12716 BERRIDGE (GEOFFREY). Economic Power in Anglo-South African Diplomacy: Simonstown, Sharpeville and after. 1981.

12717 FIRST (RUTH), STEELE (JONATHAN), *and* GURNEY (CHRISTABEL). The South African Connection: Western Investment in Apartheid. 1972.

12718 GEYSER (OTTO). Watershed for South Africa: London, 1961. Cape Town. 1983.

12719 MILLER (J. D. BRUCE). 'South Africa's Departure'. *J. Cwealth Pol. Studs* 1 (1961–63), 56–84.

12720 HAYES (FRANK). 'South Africa's Departure from the Commonwealth 1960–1961'. *Inl Hist. Rev.* 2 (1980), 453–84.

12721 WOOD (J. R. T.). 'The Roles of Diefenbaker, Macmillan and Verwoerd in the Withdrawal of South Africa from the Commonwealth'. *J. Contemp. Afr. Studs* 6 (1987), 153–82.

12722 BARBER (JAMES). The Uneasy Relationship: Britain and South Africa. 1983.

12723 HANCOCK (*Sir* WILLIAM KEITH). Smuts: The Fields of Force, 1919–1950. 1968.

12724 HANCOCK (*Sir* WILLIAM KEITH) *and* VAN DER POEL (JEAN). Selections from the Smuts Papers. 1966.

12725 INGHAM (KENNETH). Jan Christian Smuts: The Conscience of a South African. 1986.

12726 SMUTS (JAN CHRISTIAN). Jan Christian Smuts. 1952. [A biography by his son.].

(d) West Africa

(i) General

12727 AJAYI (J. F. A.) *and* CROWDER (MICHAEL) *eds.* History of West Africa. 2 volumes.

12728 CARY (ARTHUR JOYCE LUNEL). Britain and West Africa. 1947.

12729 CROWDER (MICHAEL). West Africa under Colonial Rule. 1968.

12730 HILLIARD (FRANK H.). A Short History of Education in British West Africa. 1957.

12731 AYODELE (J.). Pan-Africanism and Nationalism in West Africa, 1900–1945. Oxf. 1973.

12732 AUSTIN (DENNIS). West Africa and the Commonwealth. Harmondsworth. 1957.

12733 HOPKINS (A. G.). An Economic History of West Africa. 1973.

12734 HARGREAVES (JOHN D.). The End of Colonial Rule in West Africa: Essays in Contemporary History. 1979.

12735 FLINT (JOHN E.). 'Scandal at the Bristol Hotel: Some Thoughts on Racial Discrimination in Britain and West Africa and its Relationship to the Planning of Decolonisation 1939–1947'. *J. Imp. Cwealth Hist.* 12 (1983), 74–93.

(ii) Ghana

12736 JOHNSON (ALBERT F.) *comp.* A Bibliography of Ghana 1930–1961. 1964.

12737 KAY (G. B.) *ed.* The Political Economy of Colonialism in Ghana: A Collection of Documents and Statistics 1900–1960. Camb. 1972.

12738 APTER (DAVID E.). Ghana in Transition. Princeton. 1955. 2nd edn 1972.

12739 METCALFE (GEORGE EDGAR) *comp.* Great Britain and Ghana: Documents of Ghana History, 1807–1957. 1964.

12740 BOURRET (FLORENCE MABEL). Ghana—The Road to Independence 1919–1957. 2nd edn. Oxf. 1960.

12741 REDMAYNE (P. B.). Gold Coast to Ghana. 1957.

12742 GHANA. Survey of the Gold Coast on the Eve of Independence. R.I.I.A. 1957.

12743 ARDEN-CLARKE (*Sir* CHARLES). 'Gold Coast into Ghana: Some Problems of Transition'. *Inl. Affs.* 34 (1958), 49–56.

12744 WIGHT (MARTIN). The Gold Coast Legislative Council. 1947.

12745 RATHBONE (RICHARD). 'The Government of the Gold Coast after the Second World War'. *Afr. Affs* 67 (1968), 209–18.

12746 CROOK (RICHARD C.). 'Decolonisation, the Colonial State and Chieftaincy in the Gold Coast'. *Afr. Affs* 85 (1986), 75–105.

12747 AUSTIN (DENNIS). Politics in Ghana 1946–1960. Oxf. 1970.

12748 KIMBLE (DAVID). A Political History of Ghana: The Rise of Gold Coast Nationalism, 1850–1928. Oxf. 1963.

12749 ROONEY (DAVID). Kwame Nkrumah: A Political Kingdom in the Third World. 1988.

12750 NKRUMAH (KWAME). The Autobiography of Kwame Nkrumah. 1967.

12751 BING (GEOFFREY H. C.). Reap the Whirlwind: An Account of Kwame Nkrumah's Ghana from 1950 to 1966. 1968.

12752 MILBURN (JOSEPHINE F.). British Business and Ghanaian Independence. 1978.

(iii) Nigeria

12753 AGUOLU (C. C.). Nigeria: A Comprehensive Bibliography in the Humanities and Social Sciences 1900–1971. Boston, Mass. 1973.

12754 CROWDER (MICHAEL). The Story of Nigeria. 4th edn 1978.

12755 NICOLSON (I. F.). The Administration of Nigeria 1900–1960: Men, Methods and Myths. Oxf. 1969.

12756 KIRK-GREENE (ANTHONY H. M.) *ed.* The Principles of Native Administration in Nigeria: Select Documents 1900–1947. 1965.

12757 WHITAKER (C. S.). The Politics of Tradition: Continuity and Change in Northern Nigeria 1946–1966. 1970.

12758 HEUSSLER (ROBERT V.). The British in Northern Nigeria. 1968.

12759 HARRIS (P. J.). Local Government in Southern Nigeria. Camb. 1957.

12760 WHITE (JEREMY). Central Administration in Nigeria 1914–1948: The Problem of Polarity. 1981.

12761 OLUSANYA (G. O.). The Second World War and Politics in Nigeria 1939–1953. 1973.

12762 POST (K. W. J.) *and* JENKINS (G. D.). The Price of Liberty: Personality and Politics in Colonial Nigeria. Camb. 1973.

12763 PEARCE (R. D.). 'Government, Nationalists and Constitutions in Nigeria 1935–1951'. *J. Imp. Cwealth Hist.* 9 (1981), 289–307.

12764 CALLAWAY (HELEN). Gender, Culture and Empire: European Women in Colonial Nigeria. 1987.

12765 LEITH-ROSS (SYLVIA). Stepping Stones; Memoirs of Colonial Nigeria 1907–1960. 1983.

12766 BELLO (*Sir* AHMADU). My Life. Camb. 1962.

12767 AZIKWE (NNAMDI). My Odyssey: An Autobiography. 1971.

12768 LEWIS (ROY). 'Britain and Biafra: A Commonwealth Civil War'. *Round Table* 239 (1970), 241–8.

(iv) Sierra Leone

12769 FYFE (CHRISTOPHER). A History of Sierra Leone. 1962.

12770 CARTWRIGHT (JOHN F.). Politics in Sierra Leone 1947–67. Toronto. 1970.

(v) The Gambia

12771 GAMBLE (DAVID P.). The Gambia. Oxf. 1988. [Bibliography.].

12772 GAILEY (H. A.). A History of the Gambia. 1964.

(vi) British Cameroons

12773 DELANCEY (MARK) *and* SCHROEDER (PETER J.). Cameroon. Oxf. 1986. [Bibliography.].

12774 LEVINE (VICTOR). The Cameroons from Mandate to Independence. Berkeley, Ca. 1964.

(e) Central Africa

(i) Northern Rhodesia/Zambia

12775 GANN (LEWIS HENRY). A History of Northern Rhodesia: Early Days to 1953. 1964.

12776 ROTBERG (ROBERT IRWIN). The Rise of Nationalism in Central Africa: The Making of Malawi and Zambia, 1873–1964. Camb., Mass. 1965.

12777 MACPHERSON (FERGUS). Anatomy of a Conquest: The British Occupation of Zambia, 1884–1924. 1981.

12778 SHEPPERSON (GEORGE ALLCOT) and PRICE (THOMAS). Independent African: John Chilembwe and the Origins, Setting and Significance of the Nyasaland Native Rising in 1915. Edin. 1958.

12779 EEBELO (H. S.). Reaction to Colonialism: A Prelude to the Politics of Independence in Northern Zambia, 1893–1939. Manchester. 1971.

12780 MULFORD (DAVID C.). Zambia: the Politics of Independence, 1957–1964. Oxf. 1967.

(ii) Central African Federation

12781 ROTBERG (R. I.). 'The Federation Movement in British East and Central Africa 1889–1953'. *J. Cwealth Pol. Studs* 2 (1963–4), 141–60.

12782 HYAM (RONALD). 'The Geopolitical Origins of the Central African Federation: Britain, Rhodesia and South Africa, 1948–1953'. *Hist. J.* 30 (1987), 145–72.

12783 WELENSKY (*Sir* ROY). 4000 days: The Life and Death of the Federation of Rhodesia and Nyasaland. 1964.

12784 WOOD (J. R. T.). The Welensky Papers: A History of the Federation of Rhodesia and Nyasaland. Durban. 1983.

12785 TAYLOR (D.). The Rhodesian: The Life of Sir Roy Welensky. 1955.

12786 ALPORT (CUTHBERT J. M.) *Baron*. The Sudden Assignment: Central Africa 1961–1963. 1965.

12787 FRANKLIN (HARRY). Unholy Wedlock: The Failure of the Central African Federation. 1963.

12788 KEATLEY (PATRICK). The Politics of Partnership. Harmondsworth. 1963.

12789 THOMAS (GILBERT). A Biography of Jay (John Jestyn) The Rt Hon. Lord Llewellin of Upton. 1961.

(iii) Southern Rhodesia/Zimbabwe

12790 WINDRICH (ELAINE). The Rhodesia Problem: A Documentary Record 1923–1973. 1975.

12791 BAUMHOGGER (GOSWIN). The Struggle for Independence: Documents on the Recent Development of Zimbabwe 1975–1980. 7 vols. Hamburg. 1984.

12792 GANN (LEWIS H.). A History of Southern Rhodesia to 1953. 1965.

12793 BLAKE (ROBERT) *Baron*. A History of Rhodesia. Lond. 1977.

12794 VERRIER (ANTHONY). The Road to Zimbabwe 1890 to 1980. 1985.

12795 LONEY (MARTIN). Rhodesia: White Racism and Imperial Response. Harmondsworth. 1975.

12796 HODDER-WILLIAMS (RICHARD). White Farmers in Rhodesia, 1890–1965. 1984.

12797 LEYS (COLIN). European Politics in Southern Rhodesia. Oxf. 1961.

12798 HENDERSON (IAN). 'White Populism in Southern Rhodesia'. *Comp. Studs Soc. Hist.* 14 (1972), 387–99.

12799 MTSHALI (B. V.). Rhodesia: Background to Conflict. 1967.

12800 MacFARLANE (L. J.). 'Justifying Rebellion: Black and White Nationalism in Rhodesia'. *J. Cwealth Pol Studs* 6 (1968), 54–79.

12801 HUDSON (MILES). Triumph or Tragedy?: Rhodesia to Zimbabwe. 1982.

12802 CAUTE (DAVID). Under the Skin: The Death of White Rhodesia. Harmondsworth. 1982.

12803 HANCOCK (I.). White Liberals, Moderates and Radicals in Rhodesia 1953–1980. 1984.

12804 WINDRICH (ELAINE). Britain and the Politics of Rhodesian Independence. 1978.

12805 GOOD (ROBERT). UDI: The International Politics of the Rhodesian Rebellion. 1973.

12806 MARTIN (DAVID) *and* JOHNSON (PHYLLIS). The Struggle for Zimbabwe: The Chimurenga War. Harare. 1981.

12807 SOUTHERN RHODESIA: Constitutional Conference Held at Lancaster House, London September–December 1979. Cmnd 7802. Parliamentary Papers (1979–80).

12808 DAVIDOW (JEFFREY). A Peace in Southern Africa. The Lancaster House Conference on Rhodesia, 1979. 1984.

12809 WISEMAN (HARRY) *and* TAYLOR (ALASTAIR M.). From Rhodesia to Zimbabwe: The Politics of Transition. Oxf. 1981.

12810 MORRIS-JONES (W. H.) *and* AUSTIN (DENNIS) *eds*. From Rhodesia to Zimbabwe: Behind and Beyond Lancaster House. 1980.

12811 BINGHAM (T. H.) *and* GRAY (S. M.). Report on the Supply of Petroleum and Petroleum Products to Rhodesia. 1978.

12812 WILLIAMS (M.) *and* PARSONAGE (M.). 'Britain and Rhodesia: The Economic Background to Sanctions'. *World Today* xxix (1973), 379–88.

12813 AUSTIN (DENNIS). 'Sanctions and Rhodesia'. *World Today* xxii (1966), 106–13.

12814 CHANDRASEKHAR (P.). 'The Rhodesian Crisis and the Use of Force'. *Africa Q.* vi (1967), 285–96.

12815 LIBBY (R. T.). 'Anglo-American Diplomacy and the Rhodesian Settlement: A Loss of Impetus'. *Orbis* xxiii (1979), 185–211.

(f) East Africa

(i) General

12816 MACPHERSON (FERGUS). 'Future of East Africa 1939–1948: A Case Study of the "Official Mind of Imperialism"'. *J. Imp. Cwealth Hist.* 10 (1981), 67–88.

12817 LONSDALE (JOHN). 'Some Origins of Nationalism in East Africa'. *J. Afr. Hist.* 9 (1968), 119–46.

12818 HUXLEY (ELSPETH). The Sorcerer's Apprentice: A Journey through East Africa. 1948.

12819 BECK (ANN). 'Colonial Policy and Education in British East Africa'. *J. Brit. Studs* 5 (1966), 115–38.

(ii) Kenya

12820 WEBSTER (JOHN B.) *et al.* A Bibliography on Kenya. Syracuse. 1967.

12821 COLLISON (ROBERT L.). Kenya. 1982.

12822 BENNETT (GEORGE). Kenya: A Political History: The Colonial Period. Oxf. 1963.

12823 MacPHEE (MARSHALL). Kenya. N.Y. 1968.

12824 GRIGG (EDWARD) *Lord Altrincham.* Kenya's Opportunity: Memories, Hopes and Ideas. 1955.

12825 FROST (RICHARD). Race against Time: Human Relations and Politics in Kenya before Independence. 1978.

12826 WYLIE (D.). 'Confrontation over Kenya: The Colonial Office and its Critics, 1918–1940'. *J. Afr. Hist.* xviii (1977), 427–47.

12827 LEYS (NORMAN). By Kenya Possessed: The Correspondence of Norman Leys and J. H. Oldham. 1918–1926. Chicago. 1976.

12828 RAWCLIFFE (D. H.). The Struggle for Kenya. 1954.

12829 BENNETT (GEORGE) *and* ROSBERG (C. G.). The Kenyatta Election: Kenya 1960–1961. Oxf. 1961.

12830 PORTER (ANDREW N.). 'Iain Macleod, Decolonization in Kenya and Tradition in British Colonial Policy'. *J. Contemp. Hist.* 2 (1975/6), 37–59.

12831 DOUGLAS-HOME (CHARLES). Evelyn Baring: The Last Proconsul. 1978.

12832 THROUP (DAVID). Economic and Social Origins of Mau Mau 1945–1953. Nairobi. 1987.

12833 WASSERMAN (GARY B.). The Politics of Decolonization: Kenya Europeans and the Land Issue 1960–1965. Camb. 1976.

12834 MOSLEY (PAUL). The Settler Economies: Studies in the Economic History of Kenya and Southern Rhodesia. Camb. 1983.

12835 FORAN (W. R.). The Kenya Police 1887–1960. 1962.

12836 CLAYTON (ANTHONY) *and* SAVAGE (DONALD C.). Government and Labour in Kenya 1895–1963. 1974.

12837 CALVOCORESSI (PETER). 'The Lure of the Horizon: Aspects of British Foreign Policy with Particular Reference to Africa and Asia'. *Afr. Affs* lxiv (1965), 191–201.

12838 WOLFF (R. D.). The Economics of Colonialism: Britain and Kenya; 1870–1930. New Haven, Conn. 1974.

(iii) Uganda

12839 KAVUMA (P.). Crisis in Buganda 1953–1955: The Story of the Exile and Return of the Kabaka Mutesa II. 1979.

12840 JORGENSEN (J. J.). Uganda: A Modern History. 1981.

(iv) Tanganyika/Zanzibar/Tanzania

12841 MCCARTHY (D. M. P.). Colonial Bureaucracy and Creating Underdevelopment in Tanganyika 1919–1940. Iowa. 1982.

12842 ILIFFE (JOHN). A Modern History of Tanganyika. Camb. 1979.

12843 KANIKI (M. H. Y.). Tanzania under Colonial Rule. 1980.

12844 PRATT (C.). The Critical Phase in Tanzania 1945–1968: Nyerere and the Emergence of a Socialist Strategy. Camb. 1976.

12845 AYANY (S. G.). A History of Zanzibar. Nairobi. 1970. Concentrates on constitutional developments 1934–64.

(v) British Somaliland/Somalia

12846 LEWIS (IOAN M.). The Modern History of Somaliland: from Nation to State. 1965. 2nd edn as A Modern History of Somalia. 1979.

4. MEDITERRANEAN

(a) Gibraltar

12847 SHIELDS (Graham J.). Gibraltar. 1987.

12848 ABBOTT (WILBUR CORTEZ). An Introduction to the Documents Relating to the International Status of Gibraltar, 1704–1934. N.Y. 1934.

12849 GARRATT (GEOFFREY THEODORE). Gibraltar and the Mediterranean. 1939.

12850 STEWART (JOHN D.). Gibraltar the Keystone. 1967.

12851 FAWCETT (J. E. S.). 'Gibraltar: The Legal Issues'. *Inl Affs* 43 (1967), 236–51.

12852 LANCASTER (THOMAS D.) *and* TAULBEE (JAMES L.). 'Britain, Spain and the Gibraltar Question'. *J. Cwealth Comp. Pol.* 22 (1985), 251–66.

12853 HILLS (GEORGE). Rock of Contention: A History of Gibraltar. 1974.

12854 JACKSON (*Sir* WILLIAM G. F.). The Rock of Gibraltar. 1988.

(b) Malta

12855 THACKRAH (JOHN RICHARD). Malta. 1985.

12856 SMITH (PETER C.). Pedestal: The Malta Convoy of August 1942. 1987.

12857 DOBBIE (S.). Faith and Fortitude: The Life and Work of General Sir William Dobbie. Gillingham. 1979.

12858 Malta Round Table Conference 1955: Report. Cmnd 9657. Parliamentary Papers (1955–6).

12859 DOBIE (EDITH). Malta's Road to Independence. Oklahoma. 1967.

12860 AUSTIN (DENNIS). Malta and the End of Empire. 1971.

(c) Cyprus

12861 KITROMILIDES (PASHALIS) *and* EVRIADES (MARIOS L.). Cyprus. 1982.

12862 REDDAWAY (JOHN). Burdened with Cyprus: The British Connection. 1987.

12863 GEORGHALLIDES (G. S.). 'The Management of Public Records under the British Colonial Administration in Cyprus'. *Inl Hist. Rev.* 7 (1985), 622–9.

12864 ROSENBAUM (NAOMI). 'Success in Foreign Policy: The British in Cyprus, 1878–1960'. *Can. J. Pol. Sci.* iii (1970), 605–27.

12865 LERODIOKONOS (LEONTIOS). The Cyprus Question. Stockholm. 1971.

12866 CRAMSHAW (NANCY). The Cyprus Revolt: An Account of the Struggle for Union with Greece. 1978.

12867 MAYES (STANLEY). Makarios. A Biography. 1981.

12868 FOLEY (CHARLES) *ed.* The Memoirs of General Grivas. 1964.

12869 FOOT (SYLVIA). Emergency Exit. 1960.

12870 HARBOTTLE (MICHAEL). The Impartial Soldier. Oxf. 1970.

12871 CYPRUS: The Dispute and the Settlement. R.I.I.A. 1959.

5. THE PACIFIC

(a) General

12872 DICKSON (DIANE) *and* DOSSOR (CAROL). World Catalogue of Theses on the Pacific Islands. Canberra. 1970.

12873 HUGHES (ROGER) *comp.* Oceania: A Basic Annotated Bibliography. 1977.

12874 FRY (GERALD W.) *and* MAURICIO (RUFINO). Pacific Basin and Oceania. Oxf. 1988.

12875 COATES (A.). Western Pacific Islands. 1971.

12876 GRATTAN (HARTLEY C.). The South-West Pacific: A Modern History. Vol. 2: The South-West Pacific since 1900. Ann Arbor, Mich. 1963.

12877 BROOKFIELD (H. C.). Colonialism, Development and Independence—The Case of the Melanesian Islands in the South Pacific. Camb. 1973.

12878 BELSHAW (CYRIL S.). Island Administration in the South West Pacific. 1950.

(b) Fiji

12879 SNOW (PHILIP A.). A Bibliography of Fiji, Tonga and Rotuma. Canberra. 1969.

12880 SPATE (OSKAR HERMANN KHRISTIAN). The Fijian People: Economic Problems and Prospects: A Report. Suva Fiji. 1959.

12881 BURNS (*Sir* ALAN). Fiji. 1963.

12882 ROTH (G. K.). Fijian Way of Life. 1953. 2nd edn Oxf. 1973.

12883 BAIN (KENNETH). Treason at 10: Fiji at the Crossroads. 1989.

(c) The Gilbert and Ellice Islands (Kiribati and Tuvalu) and Nauru

12884 MACDONALD (BARRIE). Cinderellas of the Empire. Towards a History of Kiribati and Tuvalu. Canberra. 1982.

12885 WILLIAMS (MASLYN) *and* MACDONALD (BARRIE). The Phosphaters: A History of the British Phosphate Commissioners and the Christmas Island Phosphate Commission. Melbourne. 1985.

12886 VIVIANI (NANCY). Nauru: Phosphate and Political Progress. Canberra. 1970.

(d) New Hebrides/Vanuatu

12887 LINI (WALTER). Beyond Pandemonium: From the New Hebrides to Vanuatu. Wellington. 1980.

12888 PLANT (CHRIS) *ed.* New Hebrides: The Road to Independence. Suva Fiji. 1977.

12889 BEASANT (JOHN). The Santo Rebellion: An Imperial Reckoning. 1984.

12890 SHEARS (RICHARD). The Coconut War: The Crisis on Espiritu Santo. 1980.

(e) Pitcairn Island

12891 NICOLSON (ROBERT). The Pitcairners. Sydney. 1966.

12892 BALL (IAN M.). Pitcairn: Children of the Bounty. 1973.

(f) Western Samoa

12893 MCKAY (C. G. R.). Samoana: A Personal Story of the Samoan Islands. Wellington New Zealand. 1968.

12894 DAVIDSON (J. W.). Samoa Mo Samoa: The Emergence of the Independent State of Western Samoa. Melbourne. 1967.

(g) Solomon Islands

12895 KENT (JANET). The Solomon Islands. Newton Abbot. 1972.

(h) Tonga

12896 LATUKEFU (SIONE). The Tongan Constitution: A Brief History to Celebrate its Centenary. Nuku'alofa. 1975.

6. SOUTH-EAST ASIA

(a) Malaya/Malaysia

12897 HEUSSLER (ROBERT) *ed.* British Malaya: A Bibliographical and Biographical Compendium. N.Y. 1981.

12898 CHEESEMAN (H. R.) *comp.* Bibliography of Malaya: Being a Classified List of Books Wholly or Partly in English Relating to the Federation of Malaya and Singapore. 1959.

12899 ALLEN (J. DE V.), STOCKWELL (A. J.), *and* WRIGHT (L. R.) *eds.* A Collection of Treaties and Other Documents Affecting the States of Malaysia 1761–1963. 2 vols 1981.

12900 BASTIN (JOHN STURGUS) *and* WINKS (ROBIN WILLIAM) *comps.* Malaysia: Selected Historical Readings. Kuala Lumpur. 1966.

12901 STOCKWELL (A. J.). 'The Historiography of Malaysia: Recent Writings in English on the History of the Area Since 1874'. *J. Imp. Cwealth Hist.* 5 (1976), 82–110.

12902 MIDDLEBROOK (S. M.) *and* PINNICK (A. W.). How Malaya is Governed. 1949.

12903 MILLS (LENNOX ALGERNON). Malaya: A Political and Economic Appraisal. 1958.

12904 TILMAN (ROBERT O.). Bureaucratic Transition in Malaya. Durham, N.C. 1964.

12905 ONGKILI (JAMES P.). Nation-Building in Malaysia 1946–1974. Oxf. 1985.

12906 GULLICK (J. M.). Malaya. 1963.

12907 TREGONNING (KENNEDY GORDON PHILLIP). A History of Modern Malaya. Singapore. 1964.

12908 GUNGWU (WANG) *ed.* Malaysia: A Survey. 1964.

12909 PURCELL (VICTOR WILLIAM WILLIAMS SAUNDERS). Malaysia. 1965.

12910 WINSTEDT (*Sir* RICHARD OLOF). Britain and Malaya, 1786–1941. 1944.

12911 RYAN (NEIL JOSEPH). The Making of Modern Malaysia. Kuala Lumpur. 3rd edn 1967.

12912 RAHMAN (TUNKU ABDUL). Malaysia, the Road to Independence. Petaling Jaya. 1985.

12913 KHONG (KIM HOONG). Merdeka! British Rule and the Struggle for Independence in Malaya 1945–1957. Petaling Jaya. 1984.

12914 HAWKINS (D. C.). 'Britain and Malaysia—Another View: Was the Decision to Withdraw Entirely Voluntary or was Britain Pushed a Little?'. *Asian Survey* 9 (1969), 546–62.

12915 JACKSON (JAMES CHARLES). Planters and Speculators: Chinese and European Agricultural Enterprises in Malaya, 1786–1921. 1968.

12916 PURCELL (VICTOR WILLIAM WILLIAMS SAUNDERS). The Chinese in Malaya. 1948.

12917 SANDHU (KERNIAL SINGH). Indians in Malaya: Some Aspects of their Immigration and Settlement (1786–1957). Camb. 1969.

12918 MOORE (DONALD) *and* MOORE (JOANNA). The First 150 Years of Singapore. Singapore. 1969.

12919 HEUSSLER (ROBERT). British Rule in Malaya: The Malayan Civil Service and its Predecessors, 1867–1942. Oxf. 1981.

12920 —— Completing a Stewardship: The Malayan Civil Service 1942–1957. Westport, Conn. 1983.

12921 GILMOUR (ANDREW). An Eastern Cadet's Anecdotage. Singapore. 1974.

12922 LOCKE (ARTHUR). The Tigers of Trengganu. 1954.

12923 NEILL (J. D. H.). Elegant Flower. 1956.

12924 SHEPPARD (MUBIN). Taman Budiman: Memoirs of an Unorthodox Civil Servant. Kuala Lumpur. 1979.

12925 BRIDGES (B.). 'Britain and Japanese Espionage in Pre-War Malaya: the Shinozaki Case'. *J. Contemp. Hist.* 21 (1986), 391–411.

12926 MONTGOMERY (B.). Shenton of Singapore: Governor and Prisoner of War. 1984.

12927 KENNEDY (JOSEPH). British Civilians and the Japanese War in Malaya and Singapore, 1941–45. 1987.

12928 RUDNER (MARTIN). 'The Organisation of the British Military Administration in Malaya 1946–1948'. *J. Southeast Asian Hist.* 9 (1968), 95–106.

12929 CLUTTERBUCK (RICHARD). Riot and Revolution in Singapore and Malaya, 1945–1963. 1973.

12930 CLOAKE (J.). Templer, Tiger of Malaya: The Life of Field Marshal Sir Gerald Templer. 1985.

12931 SHORT (ANTHONY). The Communist Insurrection in Malaya, 1948–60. 1975.

12932 STOCKWELL (A. J.). British Policy and Malay Politics During the Malayan Union Experiment, 1942–48. Kuala Lumpur. 1979.

12933 —— 'British Imperial Policy and De-colonisation in Malaya 1942–1952'. *J. Imp. Cwealth Hist.* 13 (1984), 68–87.

12934 TURNBULL (C. M.). 'British Planning for Post-War Malaya'. *J. South East Asian Studs* (1974), 239–54.

12935 MALAYSIA: Agreement Concluded Between the United Kingdom of Great Britain and Northern Ireland, the Federation of Malaya, North Borneo, Sarawak and Singapore. Cmnd 2094, Parliamentary Papers xxxviii (1962–3).

12936 SMITH (T. E.). The Background to Malaysia. Oxf. 1963.

12937 LIEFER (MICHAEL). 'Anglo-American Differences Over Malaysia'. *World Today* 20 (1964), 156–67.

12938 HANNA (W. A.). The Formation of Malaysia. N.Y. 1964.

12939 TILMAN (ROBERT O.). 'Malaysia: Problems of Federation'. *Western Pol. Q.* 16 (1963).

12940 ALLEN (*Sir* RICHARD). Malaysia: Prospect and Retrospect: The Impact and Aftermath of Colonial Rule. Oxf. 1968.

12941 CHIN (K. W.). The Defence of Malaysia and Singapore: The Transformation of a Security System, 1957–1971. Camb. 1983.

12942 LIEFER (MICHAEL). 'Anglo-Malaysian Alienation'. *Round Table* 285 (1983), 56–63.

12943 KERSHAW (ROGER). 'Anglo-Malaysian Relations: Old Roles Versus New Rules'. *Inl. Affs.* 59 (1983), 629–44.

(b) Sarawak

12944 RUNCIMAN (*Sir* STEVEN *i.e. Sir* JAMES COCHRAN STEVENSON). The White Rajahs: The History of Sarawak from 1841 to 1946. Camb. 1960.

12945 PRINGLE (ROBERT). Rajahs and Rebels: The Ibans of Sarawak Under Brooke Rule, 1841–1941. 1970.

12946 REECE (R. H. W.). The Name of Brooke: The End of White Rajah Rule in Sarawak. Oxf. 1982.

12947 Report of the Commission of Enquiry, North Borneo and Sarawak 1962. Cmnd 1794, Parliamentary Papers xi (1961–2).

(c) Brunei

12948 KRAUSSE (SYLVIA C. E.) *and* KRAUSSE (GERALD H.). Brunei. Oxf. 1988.

12949 TARLING (NICHOLAS). Britain, the Brookes and Brunei. Kuala Lumpur. 1971.

12950 HORTON (A. V. M.). The British Residency in Brunei 1906–1959. Hull. 1984.

12951 HAMZAH (B. A.). 'Oil and Independence in Brunei: A Perspective'. *Southeast Asian Affs* (1981), 93–102.

12952 CROSBIE (A. J.). 'Brunei in Transition'. *Southeast Asian Affs* (1981), 75–92.

(d) North Borneo/Sabah

12953 BAKER (M. H.). Sabah: The First Ten Years as a Colony 1946–1956. 2nd edn Singapore. 1965.

12954 TREGONNING (KENNEDY GORDON PHILLIP). North Borneo. 1960.

12955 —— A History of Modern Sabah (North Borneo). 1881–1963. 1965.

12956 SULLIVAN (ANWAR) *and* LEONG (CECILIA) *eds.* Commemorative History of Sabah 1881–1981. Kota Kinabalu. 1981.

(e) Singapore

12957 QUAH (STELLA R.) *and* QUAH (J. S. T.). Singapore. Oxf. 1988.

12958 LEE (EDWIN). 'The Historiography of Singapore'. In Singapore Studies: Critical Surveys of the Humanities and Social Sciences *ed.* by B. K. Kapur. Singapore. 1986. 1–32.

12959 TURNBULL (C. M.). A History of Singapore 1819–1975. Oxf. 1977.

12960 SCHONENBERGER (TONI). Der britische Rückzug aus Singapore 1945–1976. Zürich. 1981.

12961 WAH (YEO KIM). Political Development in Singapore 1945–1955. Singapore. 1963.

12962 BELLOWS (THOMAS J.). The People's Action Party of Singapore: Emergence of a Dominant Party System. New Haven, Conn. 1970.

12963 CHEE (CHAN HENG). A Sensation of Independence: A Political Biography of David Marshall. Oxf. 1984.

12964 MINCHIN (JAMES). No Man is an Island: A Study of Singapore's Lee Kuan Yew. 1986.

12965 JOSEY (ALEX). Lee Kuan Yew and the Commonwealth. Singapore. 1969.

(f) Hong Kong

12966 ENDACOTT (GEORGE BEER) *comp.* An Eastern Entrepôt: A Collection of Documents Illustrating the History of Hong Kong. Hong Kong. 1964.

12967 —— A History of Hong Kong. 1958.

12968 —— Government and People in Hong Kong, 1841–1962: A Constitutional History. Hong Kong. 1964.

12969 INGRAMS (HAROLD). Hong Kong. 1952.

12970 COLLINS (*Sir* CHARLES HENRY). Public Administration in Hong Kong. 1952.

12971 RIDE (E.). BAAG: Hong Kong Resistance 1942–1945. Oxf. 1981.

12972 MINERS (N. J.). Government and Politics of Hong Kong. Oxf. 1982.

12973 —— 'Plans for Constitutional Reform in Hong Kong 1946–52'. *China Q.* 107 (1986), 463–82.

12974 PODMORE (DAVID). 'Localisation in the Hong Kong Government Service 1948–1968'. *J. Cwealth Pol. Studs* 9 (1971), 36–51.

12975 HARRIS (PETER). Hong Kong: A Study in Bureaucratic Politics. 2nd edn 1980.

12976 —— 'Hong Kong Confronts 1997: An Assessment of the Sino–British Agreement'. *Pacific Affs.* 59 (1986).

12977 CHANG (JOSEPH Y. S.) *ed.* Hong Kong in the 1980s. Hong Kong. 1982.

12978 —— *Ed.* Hong Kong in Transition. Oxf. 1987.

12979 —— 'A Draft Agreement Between the Government of the United Kingdom of Great Britain and Northern Ireland and the Government of the People's Republic of China on the Future of Hong Kong'. *Asian J. Pub. Admin.* 6 (1984), 193–226. [The agreement is printed in full and discussed in this article.].

12980 KELLY (IAN). Hong Kong: A Political–Geographical Analysis. 1987.

(g) Ceylon/Sri Lanka

12981 SAMERAWEERA (VIJAYA). Sri Lanka. Oxf. 1987.

12982 DE SILVA (K. M.) ed. History of Ceylon vol. iii: From the Beginning of the Nineteenth Century to 1948. Colombo. 1973.

12983 LUDOWYCK (E. F. C.). The Modern History of Ceylon. 1966.

12984 JENNINGS (Sir W. IVOR). Nationalism and Political Development in Ceylon. N.Y. 1950.

12985 COLLINS (Sir CHARLES). Public Administration in Ceylon. 1952.

12986 JEFFERIES (Sir CHARLES). Ceylon—The Path to Independence. 1962.

12987 —— 'O.E.G.': A Biography of Sir Oliver Ernest Goanetilleke. 1969.

12988 KOTELAWALA (Sir JOHN). An Asian Prime Minister's Story. 1956.

12989 JACOB (LUCY M.). Sri Lanka: From Dominion to Republic: A Study of the Changing Relations with the United Kingdom. Delhi. 1973.

7 · WEST INDIES

(a) General

12990 GRIEB (KENNETH J.) ed. Research Guide to Central America and the Caribbean. Madison, Wis. 1985.

12991 LUX (WILLIAM). Historical Dictionary of the British Caribbean. 1975.

12992 Constitutional Development of the West Indies 1922–1968: A Selection from Major Documents. 1975.

12993 ROBERTS (AUDREY) comp. Bibliography of Commissions of Enquiry and Other Government-Sponsored Reports on the Commonwealth Caribbean 1900–1975. Madison, Wis. 1985.

12994 JORDAN (ALMA) and COMMISSIONG (BARBARA). The English-Speaking Caribbean: A Bibliography of Bibliographies. 1984.

12995 CARIBBEAN COMMISSION. Current Caribbean Bibliography, 1951+. [Annual].

12996 Bibliography of the English-Speaking Caribbean, 1979+. [Annual].

12997 COMITAS (LAMBROS). The Complete Caribbeana 1900–1975: A Topical Bibliography. Seattle. 1977.

12998 ZUBATSKY (DAVID S.) comp. Doctoral Dissertations in History and the Social Sciences in Latin America and the Caribbean Accepted by Universities in the United Kingdom 1920–1972. 1973.

12999 British Dependencies in the Caribbean and North Atlantic 1939–1952. Cmnd 8575, Parliamentary Papers xxiv (1951–2).

13000 Developments Towards Self-Government in the Caribbean: A Symposium Held under the Auspices of the Netherlands Universities Foundation for International Co-operation at The Hague, September 1954.

13001 BURNS (Sir ALAN). The History of the British West Indies. 1954. 2nd edn 1965.

13002 PROUDFOOT (MARY). Britain and the United States in the Caribbean. 1954.

13003 ROYAL INSTITUTE OF INTERNATIONAL AFFAIRS. The British Caribbean: A Brief Political and Economic Survey. 1957.

13004 SIRES (RONALD VERNON). 'Government in the British West Indies: An Historical Outline'. Soc. Econ. Studs 6 (1957), 108–32.

13005 WALLACE (ELIZABETH). The British Caribbean from the Decline of Colonialism to the End of Federation. Toronto. 1977.

13006 MACMILLAN (W. M.). The Road to Self-Rule: A Study in Colonial Evolution. N.Y. 1960.

13007 MITCHELL (Sir HAROLD). Europe in the Caribbean: The Policies of Great Britain, France and the Netherlands towards their West Indian Territories in the Twentieth Century. 1963.

13008 AYEARST (MORLEY). The British West Indies: The Search for Self-Government. 1960.

13009 PROCTOR (JESSE HARRIS). 'British West Indies Society and Government in Transition 1920–1960'. Soc. Econ. Studs 11 (1962), 273–304.

13010 TINKER (HUGH). 'British Policy towards the Separate Indian Identity in the Caribbean 1920–1950'. In 'East Indians in the Caribbean: Colonialism and the Struggle for Identity'. Ed. by Bridget Brereton and Winston Deokeran. Liechtenstein. 1981. 33–48.

13011 LEWIS (GORDON K.). 'The Social Legacy of British Colonialism in the Caribbean'. New World Q. 3 (1967), 13–32.

13012 SHERLOCK (PHILIP). West Indies. 1966.

13013 BELL (WENDELL) ed. The Democratic Revolution in the West Indies. Camb., Mass. 1967.

13014 LEWIS (GORDON K.). The Growth of the Modern West Indies. 1968.

13015 WILLIAMS (ERIC EUSTACE). Britain and the West Indies. 1969.

13016 FREYMOND (JEAN F.). Political Integration in the Commonwealth Caribbean: A Survey of Recent Attempts with Special Reference to the Associated States (1967–1974). Geneva. 1980.

13017 BLACKBURNE (KENNETH). 'Changing Patterns of Caribbean International Relations: Britain and the "British" Caribbean'. In 'The Restless Caribbean: Changing Patterns of International Relations'. *Ed.* by Richard Millet and Will Marvin. N.Y. 1979. 204–18.

13018 STONE (CAROL) *and* PAGE (HENRY) eds. The Newer Caribbean: Decolonisation, Democracy and Development, Philadelphia. 1983.

(b) Bahamas

13019 ALBERY (PAUL). The Story of the Bahamas. 1975.

13020 HUGHES (COLIN A.). Race and Politics in the Bahamas. St Lucia, Queensland. 1981.

(c) Belize/British Honduras

13021 WOODWARD (RALPH LEE). Belize. 1980.

13022 MINKEL (CLARENCE) *and* ALDERMAN (RALPH). A Bibliography of British Honduras 1900–1970. East Lansing, Mich. 1970.

13023 GRUNEWALD (DONALD). 'The Anglo-Guatemalan Dispute Over the Colony of Belize (British Honduras)'. *J. Lat. Amer. Studs* 11 (1979), 343–71. [The dispute up to 1949.].

13024 CAIYER (STEPHEN L.). British Honduras: Past and Present. 1951.

13025 BRITISH HONDURAS: Report of an Inquiry Held by Sir Reginald Sharpe QC into Allegations of Contacts between the People's United Party and Guatemala. Cmnd 9139, Parliamentary Papers x (1953–1954).

13026 BIANCHI (WILLIAM J.). Belize: The Controversy Between Guatemala and Great Britain over the Territory of British Honduras in Central America. N.Y. 1959.

13027 WADDELL (DAVID ALAN GILMOUR). British Honduras: An Historical and Contemporary Survey. Oxf. 1961.

13028 GREG (A. R.). British Honduras. 1968.

13029 DOBSON (N.). A History of Belize. 1973.

13030 GRANT (CEDRIC H.). The Making of Modern Belize: Politics, Society and British Colonialism in Central America. Camb. 1976.

13031 MENON (P. K.). 'The Anglo-Guatemalan Territorial Dispute over the Colony of Belize (British Honduras)'. *J. Lat. Amer. Studs* 11 (1979), 343–71.

13032 SETZEKORN (WILLIAM DAVID). Formerly British Honduras: A Profile of the New Nation of Belize. 2nd edn Ohio. 1981.

13033 THORNDIKE (TONY). 'Belizean Political Parties: The Independence Crisis and After'. *J. Cwealth Comp. Pol.* 21 (1983), 195–211.

13034 CALVERT (PETER). Guatemala. 1965.

(d) British Guiana/Guyana

13035 CHAMBERS (FRANCES). Guyana. Oxf. 1988.

13036 SIRES (RONALD VERNON). 'British Guiana: The Suspension of the Constitution'. *Pol. Q.* 25 (1954), 554–69.

13037 SWAN (M.). British Guiana. 1957.

13038 YOUNG (ALLAN). The Approach to Local Self-Government in British Guiana. 1958.

13039 RAWLINS (RANDOLPH). 'What Really Happened in British Guiana'. *J. Inter-Amer. Studs* 5 (1963), 140–7.

13040 SANDERS (ANDREW). 'British Colonial Policy and the Role of the Amerindians in the Politics of the Nationalist Period in British Guiana'. *Soc. Econ. Studs* 36/3 (1987), 77–98.

13041 SIMMS (PETER). Trouble in Guyana: An Account of People, Personalities as they were in British Guiana. 1966.

13042 JAGAN (CHEDDI). The West on Trial: My Fight for Guyana's Freedom. 1966.

13043 WOUK (JONATHAN). 'British Guiana: A Case Study in British Colonial and Foreign Policy'. *Pol. Scientist* 3 (1967), 41–59.

13044 INCE (BASIL A.). Decolonization and Conflict in the United Nations: Guyana's Struggle for Independence, Camb., Mass. 1974.

13045 SPINNER (THOMAS J.). A Political and Social History of Guyana 1945–1983. 1986.

13046 BURROWES (REYNOLD A.). The Wild Coast: An Account of Politics in Guyana. Camb., Mass. 1984.

(e) Cayman Islands

13047 WILLIAMS (NEVILLE). A History of the Cayman Islands. Georgetown, Grand Cayman. 1970.

(f) Jamaica

13048 INGRAM (KENNETH E.). Jamaica. Oxf. 1984.

13049 ABRAHAMS (P.). Jamaica. 1957.

13050 BLACK (CLINTON V.). History of Jamaica. 1979. Up to independence in 1962.

13051 GLASSNER (MARTIN IRA). 'The Foreign Relations of Jamaica and Trinidad and Tobago 1960–1965'. *Carib. Studs* 10 (1970), 116–53.

13052 EATON (GEORGE E.). Alexander Bustamente and Modern Jamaica. Kingston. 1975.

13053 SHERLOCK (PHILIP). Norman Manley. 1980.

13054 NETTLEFORD (REX). 'Manley and the Politics of Jamaica—towards an Analysis of Political Change in Jamaica 1938–1968'. *Soc. Pol. Studs* 20 (1981), 1–72.

13055 NETTLEFORD (REX) ed. Norman Washington Manley and the New Jamaica: Selected Speeches and Writings 1938–1968. 1971.

13056 —— *Ed.* Jamaica in Independence: Essays on the Early Years. Kingston. 1989.

(g) Leeward Islands

13057 A Guide to Records in the Leeward Islands. Oxf. 1965.

(i) Antigua and Barbuda

13058 CALLENDER (JEAN A.) *and* WILKINSON (AUDINE C.). 'The Road to Independence: Antigua and Barbuda—A Select Bibliography'. *Bull. Eastern Caribb. Affs* 7 (1981), 50–8.

(ii) St Kitts-Nevis and Anguilla

13059 WOODING (HUGH) *ed.* Report of the Commission of Inquiry Appointed by the Governments of the United Kingdom and St. Christopher-Nevis-Anguilla to Examine the Anguilla Problem. 1970.

13060 INCE (BASIL). 'The Diplomacy of New States: The Commonwealth Caribbean and the Case of Anguilla'. *S. Atlantic Q.* 69 (1970), 382–96.

13061 ABBOT (GEORGE C.). 'Political Disintegration: The Lessons of Anguilla'. *Gvt Opp.* 6 (1971), 58–74.

(iii) British Virgin Islands

13062 DOOKHAN (ISAAC). A History of the British Virgin Islands 1672–1970. Kingston, Jamaica. 1975.

(h) Trinidad and Tobago

13063 CHAMBERS (FRANCES). Trinidad and Tobago. Oxf. 1980.

13064 CRAIG (H.). The Legislative Council of Trinidad and Tobago. 1952.

13065 SPACKMAN (ANN). 'Constitutional Development in Trinidad and Tobago'. *Soc. Econ. Studs* 14 (1965), 283–320.

13066 WILLIAMS (ERIC EUSTACE). History of the People of Trinidad and Tobago. 1964.

13067 OXAAL (IVAR). Black Intellectuals Come to Power: The Rise of Creole Nationalism in Trinidad and Tobago. Camb., Mass. 1968.

13068 JAMES (C. R. L.). At the Rendezvous of History. 1984.

13069 WOODSTOCK (HENRY ILES). A History of Tobago. 1971.

13070 RYAN (SELWYN D.). Race and Nationalism in Trinidad and Tobago: A Study of Decolonisation in a Multiracial Society. Toronto. 1972.

13071 DEOSARAN (RAMESH). Eric Williams: The Man, His Ideas and His Politics. Port of Spain. 1981.

13072 WILLIAMS (ERIC EUSTACE). Inward Hunger: The Education of a Prime Minister. 1969.

(i) Windward Islands

13073 BAKER (EDWARD CECIL). A Guide to Records in the Windward Islands. Oxf. 1968.

(i) Barbados

13074 CHANDLER (M. J.). A Guide to Records in Barbados. Oxf. 1965.

13075 POTTER (ROBERT B.) *and* DANN (GRAHAM M. S.). Barbados. Oxf. 1987.

13076 LEWIS (GORDON K.). 'Struggle for Freedom (A Story of Contemporary Barbados)'. *New World Q.* 3 (1966), 14–29.

13077 SPRINGER (HUGH W.). 'Barbados as a Sovereign State'. *J. Roy. Soc. Arts* 115 (1965), 283–320.

13078 HOYOS (F. A.). Barbados: A History from the Amerindians to Independence. 1979.

(ii) Dominica

13079 MYERS (ROBERT A.). Dominica. Oxf. 1987.

(iii) Grenada

13080 PAYNE (ANTHONY), SUTTON (PAUL), *and* THORNDIKE (TONY). Grenada: Revolution and Invasion. 1984.

13081 SANDFORD (GREGORY) *and* VIGILANTE (RICHARD). Grenada: The Untold Story. 1984.

13082 GILMORE (WILLIAM C.). The Grenada Intervention: Analysis and Documentation. 1984.

13083 O'SHAUGHNESSY (HUGH). Grenada: Revolution, Invasion and Aftermath. 1984.

13084 SEABURY (PAUL) *and* McDOUGALL (WALTER A.). The Grenada Papers. San Francisco, Ca. 1984.

13085 EMMANUEL (PATRICK). Crown Colony Politics in Grenada 1917–1951. Kingston, Jamaica. 1978.

13086 CROZIER (BRIAN) *ed.* The Grenada Documents. 1987.

13087 DAVIDSON (SCOTT). Grenada: A Study in Politics and the Limits of International Law. Aldershot. 1987.

13088 LEWIS (GORDON). Grenada: The Jewel Despoiled. Baltimore. 1987.

(iv) St Lucia

13089 BREEN (HENRY H.). St Lucia: Historical, Statistical and Descriptive. 1970.

(v) St. Vincent and the Grenadines

13090 SHEPHERD (CHARLES). A Historical Account of the Island of St. Vincent. 1971.

(j) West Indian Federation

13091 STEPHENSON (YVONNE) *comp.* A Bibliography of the West Indian Federation. Georgetown, Guyana. 1972.

13092 WILLIAMS (ERIC EUSTACE) *ed.* 'The Historical Background of the British West Indies Federation: Select Documents'. *Carib. Hist. Rev.* 3–4 (1954), 13–69.

13093 STOCKDALE (FRANK A.). 'The Work of the Caribbean Commission'. *Inl Affs* 23 (1947), 213–20.

13094 FOOTE (BERNARD L.). The Caribbean Commission: Background of Co-operation in the West Indies. Columbia, S. C. 1951.

13095 PROCTOR (JESSE HARRIS). 'The Development of the Idea of Federation of the British Caribbean Territories'. *Revista de Historia de America* 30 (1955), 61–105.

13096 —— *Ed.* 'Britain's Pro-Federation Policy in the Caribbean: An Inquiry into Motivation'. *Can. J. Econ. Pol. Sci.* 22 (1956), 319–57.

13097 SCHNEIDER (FRED D.). 'British Policy in West Indian Federation'. *World Affs Q.* 28 (1957), 49–65.

13098 LEWIS (GORDON K.). 'The British Caribbean Federation: The West Indian Background'. *Pol. Q.* 28 (1957).

13099 HUGHES (COLIN A.). 'Experiment towards Closer Union in the British West Indies'. *J. Negro Hist.* 43 (1958), 85–104.

13100 RAMPHAL (SHRIDATH). 'The West Indies—Constitutional Background to Federation'. *Public Law* (1959), 128–51.

13101 LOWENTHAL (DAVID) *ed.* West Indian Federation: Perspectives on a New Nation. N.Y. 1961.

13102 WALLACE (ELIZABETH). 'The West Indian Federation: Decline and Fall'. *Inl J.* 17 (1962), 269–88.

13103 MORDECAI (JOHN). The West Indies: The Federal Negotiations. 1968.

8. INDIAN SUB-CONTINENT

(a) India

13104 WILSON (PATRICK) *ed.* Government and Politics of India and Pakistan 1885–1955: A Bibliography of Works in Western Languages. Berkeley, Calif. 1956.

13105 LANCASTER (JOAN C.). A Guide to Lists and Catalogues of the India Office Records. 1966.

13106 SIMS (JOHN) *comp.* A List and Index of Parliamentary Papers Relating to India 1908–1947. 1981.

13107 CHAMBERLAIN (MURIEL EVELYN). Britain and India. 1974.

13108 ZINKIN (MAURICE) *and* ZINKIN (TAYA). Britain and India: Requiem for Empire. 1964.

13109 BROWN (JUDITH M.). Modern India: The Origins of an Asian Democracy. Oxf. 1985.

13110 WOLPERT (S. A.). A New History of India. Oxf. 2nd edn 1982.

13111 SARKAR (S.). Modern India, 1885–1947. 1987.

13112 KUMAR (D.) *ed.* The Cambridge Economic History of India. Vol. 2: *c.*1757–*c.*1970. Camb. 1983.

13113 PHILIPS (CYRIL H.) *and* PANDEY (BISHWA NATH) *eds.* The Evolution of Modern India and Pakistan 1858 to 1947. Select Documents. 1962.

13114 PANDEY (BISHWA NATH) *ed.* The Indian Nationalist Movement 1885–1947. Select Documents. 1979.

13115 SINGH (A. K. J.) *comp.* Gandhi and Civil Disobedience: Documents in the India Office Records 1922–1946. 1980.

13116 O'DWYER (*Sir* MAURICE) *and* APPADORAI (A.) *eds.* Speeches and Documents on the Indian Constitution 1925–1947. 2 vols Oxf. 1957.

13117 GREENBERGER (ALLEN JAY). The British Image of India: A Study in the Literature of Imperialism, 1880–1960. 1969.

13118 BALLHATCHET (K.). Race, Sex and Class under the Raj: Imperial Attitudes and Policies and their Critics 1793–1905. 1980.

13119 GRIFFITHS (*Sir* PERCIVAL JOSEPH). The British in India. 1946.

13120 —— The British Impact on India. 1952.

13121 HUNT (ROLAND) *and* HARRISON (JOHN). The District Officer in India 1930–1947. 1980.

13122 POTTER (DAVID C.). India's Political Administrators, 1919–1983. Oxf. 1986.

13123 'Manpower Shortage and the End of Colonialism: The Case of the Indian Civil Service'. *Mod. Asian Studs* 77 (1975).

13124 BEAGLEHOLE (T. H.). 'From Rulers to Servants: The I.C.S. and the British Demission of Power in India'. *Mod. Asian Studs* 11 (1977).

13125 HARDINGE (CHARLES) *comp.* My Indian Years 1910–1916. 1948.

13126 ELLINWOOD (DEWITT C.) *and* PRADHAN (S. D.) *eds.* India and World War I. New Delhi. 1978.

13127 FRASER (THOMAS G.). 'India in Anglo-Japanese Relations during the First World War'. *History* lxiii (1978), 366–84.

13128 ROBB (PETER G.). The Government of India and Reform: Policies towards Politics and the Constitution. Oxf. 1976.

13129 —— 'The British Cabinet and Indian Reform, 1917–1919'. *J. Imp. Cwealth Hist.* iv (1976), 318–34.

13130 WALEY (*Sir* SIGISMUND DAVID). Edwin Montagu: A Memoir and an Account of His Visits to India. 1964.

13131 MONTAGU (EDWIN S.). An Indian Diary. 1930.

13132 ODDIE (G.). 'Some British Attitudes towards Reform and Repression in India, 1917–1920'. *Aust. J. Pol. Hist.* xix (1973), 224–40.

13133 RUMBOLD (*Sir* ANTHONY). Watershed in India, 1914–1922. 1979.

13134 AHMED (MESBAHUDDIN). The British Labour Party and the Indian Independence Movement 1917–1939. 1987.

13135 LEVE (H. J.). Britisch Indien-Politik 1926–1932: Motive, Methoden und Misserfolg imperialer Politik am Vorabend der Dekolonisation. Wiesbaden. 1981.

13136 BROWN (JUDITH M.). Gandhi's Rise to Power: Indian Politics 1915–1922. Camb. 1972.

13137 —— Gandhi and Civil Disobedience: The Mahatma in Indian Politics 1928–1934. Camb. 1977.

13138 —— Gandhi. London and New Haven, Conn. 1989.

13139 COPLEY (A. R. H.). Gandhi Against the Tide. Oxf. 1987.

13140 EDWARDES (MICHAEL). The Myth of the Mahatma: Gandhi, the British and the Raj. 1986.

13141 GOPAL (SARVEPALLI). The Viceroyalty of Lord Irwin 1926–1931. Oxf. 1957.

13142 MOORE (ROBIN JAMES). The Crisis of Indian Unity 1917–1940. Oxf. 1974.

13143 KLEIN (IRA). 'British Imperialism in Decline: Tibet 1914–1921'. *Historian* xxxiv (1971), 100–15.

13144 PEELE (GILLIAN). 'Revolt over India'. In 'The Politics of Reappraisal, 1918–1939'. *Ed.* by Gillian Peele and Chris Cook. 1975. 114–45.

13145 FULLER (JOHN FREDERIC CHARLES). India in Revolt. 1931.

13146 GHOSH (S. C.). 'Pressure and Privilege: The Manchester Chamber of Commerce and the Indian Problem, 1930–1934'. *Parl. Affs* xviii (1965), 201–25.

13147 TOMLINSON (BRIAN R.). 'Britain and the Indian Currency Crisis, 1930–1932'. *Econ. Hist. Rev.* 2nd ser. 32 (1979), 88–99.

13148 —— The Political Economy of the Raj, 1914–1947: The Economics of Decolonisation in India. 1979.

13149 BROWN (JUDITH M.). 'Imperial Façade: Some Constraints upon and Contradictions in the British Position in India, 1919–1935'. *Trans. Roy. Hist. Soc.* xxvi (1976), 32–52.

13150 TOMLINSON (BRIAN R.). The Indian National Congress and the Raj 1929–1942. The Penultimate Phase. 1976.

13151 LOW (DONALD ANTHONY) *ed.* Congress and the Raj. Facets of the Indian Struggle. 1917–1947. 1978.

13152 BRIDGE (CARL). Holding India to the Empire: The British Conservative Party and the 1935 Constitution. 1987.

13153 —— 'Conservatism and Indian reform (1929–1939): Towards a Prerequisites Model in Imperial Constitution-Making'. *J. Imp. Cwealth Hist.* vi (1978), 281–99.

13154 GHOSH (S. C.). 'Decision-Making and Power in the British Conservative Party: A Case Study of the Indian Problem, 1929–34'. *Pol. Studs* xiii (1965), 198–212.

13155 VEERATHAPPA (K.). The British Conservative Party and Indian Independence 1930–1947. New Delhi. 1976.

13156 PHILIPS (CYRIL H.) *and* WAINWRIGHT (MARY DOREEN) *eds.* The Partition of British India. Policies and Perspectives 1935–1947. 1970.

13157 RIZVI (GOWHER). Linlithgow and India: A Study of British Policy and the Political Impasse in India, 1936–1943. 1979.

13158 ASHTON (STEPHEN R.). British Policy towards the Indian States, 1905–1939. 1982.

13159 AZIZ (K. K.). Britain and Muslim India. 1963.

13160 MANSERGH (PHILIP NICHOLAS SETON) *et al.* Constitutional Relations Between Britain and India: The Transfer of Power, 1942–1947. 7 vols 1970–7.

13161 MOON (*Sir* PENDEREL). Wavell: The Viceroy's Journal. 1973.

13162 THORNTON (ARCHIBALD PATON). 'With Wavell on to Simla and Beyond'. *J. Imp. Cwealth Hist.* 8 (1979), 175–85.

13163 CHAN (K. C.). 'Britain's Reaction to Chiang Kai-Shek's Visit to India, February 1942'. *Austral. J. Pol. Hist.* xxi (1975), 52–61.

13164 MOORE (ROBIN JAMES). Churchill, Cripps and India, 1939–1945. Oxf. 1979.

13165 DENNIS (PETER). Troubled Days of Peace: Mountbatten and the South-East Asia Command, 1941–1946. Manch. 1987.

13166 LUMBY (E. W. R.). The Transfer of Power in India 1945–1947. 1954.

13167 MENON (V. P.). The Transfer of Power in India 1939–1947. 1957.

13168 MOSLEY (LEONARD). The Last Days of the British Raj. 1961.

13169 MOON (*Sir* PENDEREL). Divide and Quit. 1962.

13170 EDWARDES (MICHAEL). The Last Years of British India. 1963.

13171 TINKER (HUGH). Experiment with Freedom: India and Pakistan 1947. Oxf. 1967.

13172 PANDEY (BISHWA NATH). The Break-up of British India. 1969.

13173 HODSON (HENRY VINCENT). The Great Divide: Britain, India, Pakistan. 1969. 2nd edn 1985.

13174 FRASER (THOMAS G.). Partition in Ireland, India and Palestine: Theory and Practice. 1984.

13175 SINGH (ANITA INDER). The Origins of the Partition of India, 1936–1947. Oxf. 1987.

13176 —— 'Imperial Defence and the Transfer of Power in India, 1946–1947'. *Inl Hist. Rev.* 4 (1982), 568–88.

13177 —— 'Keeping India in the Commonwealth: British Political and Military Aims, 1947–1949'. *J. Contemp. Hist.* 20 (1985), 469–81.

13178 KRISHAN (Y.). 'Mountbatten and the Partition of India'. *Hist.* 68 (1983), 22–38.

13179 TALBOT, (IAN A.). 'Mountbatten and the Partition of India: A Rejoinder'. *Hist.* 69 (1984), 29–35.

13180 CAMPBELL-JOHNSON (ALAN). Mission with Mountbatten. 1951. 2nd edn 1972.

13181 —— 'Reflections on the Transfer of Power'. *Asiatic Review* 48 (1952), 163–82.

13182 MOORE (ROBIN JAMES). Escape from Empire: The Attlee Government and the Indian Problem. Oxf. 1983.

13183 TREVELYAN (HUMPHREY) *Baron.* The India We Left: Charles Trevelyan, 1826–1865; Humphrey Trevelyan, 1929–1947. 1972.

13184 COLLINS (LARRY) *and* LAPIERRE (DOMINIQUE). Mountbatten and Independent India 16 August 1947–18 June 1948. New Delhi. 1984.

13185 SINGH (ANITA INDER). 'Post-Imperial British Attitudes to India: The Military Aspect 1947–1951'. *Round Table* 296 (1985), 360–75.

13186 GRIGG (JOHN). 'Aftermath of Empire: Britain and India Since Independence'. *Encounter* xxxviii (1972), 8–15.

13187 TOMLINSON (BRIAN R.). 'Indo-British Relations in the Post-Colonial Era: The Sterling Balances Negotiations, 1947–1949'. *J. Imp. Cwealth Hist.* 13 (1985), 142–62.

13188 GUPTA (R. L.). Conflict and Harmony: Indo-British Relations: A New Perspective. New Delhi. 1976.

13189 BAROOAH (D. P.). Indo-British Relations 1950–1960. New Delhi. 1977.

13190 LIPTON (MICHAEL) *and* FIRN (JOHN). The Erosion of a Relationship: India and Britain Since 1960. 1975.

13191 BANERJI (ARUN KUMAR). India and Britain 1947–68: The Evolution of Post-Colonial Relations. Calcutta. 1977.

(b) Pakistan

13192 AZIZ (K. K.). The Making of Pakistan. 1967.

13193 —— Britain and Pakistan: A Study of British Attitudes towards the East Pakistan Crisis of 1971. Islamabad. 1974.

13194 QURESHI (M. ASLAM). Anglo-Pakistan Relations, 1947–1976. Lahore. 1976.

(c) Indian Ocean

13195 GOTTHOLD (J. J.) *and* GOTTHOLD (D. W.). Indian Ocean. Oxf. 1988. [Bibliography.].

13196 BHASIN (V. K.). Superpower Rivalry in the Indian Ocean. New Delhi. 1981.

13197 WATT (DONALD CAMERON). 'Britain and the Indian Ocean: Diplomacy Before Defence'. *Pol. Q.* xliii (1971), 306–15.

13198 ROUCEK (J. S.). 'Britain's Retreat from Aden and East of Suez'. *Politics* xxxiii (1968), 414–26.

13199 LEWIN (TERENCE). 'The Indian Ocean and Beyond: British Interests'. *Asian Affairs* 9 (1978), 247–59.

(d) Burma

13200 GRIFFIN (A.). A Brief Guide to the Sources for the Study of Burma in the India Office Records. 1979.

13201 HTIN AUNG (MAUNG). The Stricken Peacock: Anglo-Burmese Relations 1752–1948. The Hague. 1965.

13202 DONNISON (F. S. V.). Burma. 1970.

13203 TINKER (HUGH) *ed.* Constitutional Relations between Britain and Burma: Burma: The Struggle for Independence 1944–1948: Documents from Official and Private Sources. 2 vols 1983–4.

13204 COLLIS (MAURICE). Last and First in Burma 1941–1948. 1956.

13205 TARLING (NICHOLAS). 'Lord Mountbatten and the Return of Civil Government to Burma'. *J. Imp. Cwealth Hist.* 11 (1983), 197–226.

13206 ALLEN (LOUIS). 'Transfer of Power in Burma'. *J. Imp. Cwealth Hist.* 13 (1985), 185–94.

B. FOREIGN RELATIONS (OUTSIDE THE EMPIRE/COMMONWEALTH)

Relations with foreign powers are also intrinsically difficult to order bibliographically. The initial sections deal substantially with works on foreign policy in general and also on the mechanisms and structures involved. The well-established disposition on the part of diplomats to write memoirs is reflected in an ample selection of the genre. Some of this material naturally relates both to the conduct of 'foreign' and 'Commonwealth' policy.

Thereafter, however, difficulties begin and it has proved impossible to order the material in a fashion which both meets the needs of a reader seeking literature on particular periods, perhaps decades, of foreign policy and the needs of a reader seeking literature on relations with a particular country across the period as a whole. What has emerged is a compromise which groups material into sub-sections which are largely chronologically ordered but which do in addition identify particular countries. It is apparent, for reasons which need little elaboration, that scholars have been attracted to particular topics at the expense of others—'Appeasement' is one obvious example. Hence, some sub-sections are dense while others are comparatively light. In addition, students of international history will recognize that there is a certain artificiality in attempting to group material on a bilateral basis. Many books and articles are properly multilateral in their approach and content. Their attribution to one country's sub-section rather than another can therefore be somewhat arbitrary. Readers should keep this point firmly in mind.

Some attempt has been made to include sub-sections which have material on public attitudes to external relations. Hence the inclusion, for example, of material on the Labour Party and foreign policy. That topic has been written about quite extensively, perhaps too extensively when one notes how few other studies exist on the attitudes of other political parties or organizations. However, a sub-section does deal at some length with 'pacifism' in all its varied manifestations and, in addition, with the emergence and functioning of the League of Nations and the United Nations. Mention of 'pacifism' makes it useful also to refer to war. The position of 'diplomacy in wartime' is as difficult as its conduct. Foreign policy in the First World War has a sub-section, but external relations during the Second World War are considered within the context of the section on the Second World War itself.

Notwithstanding the fact that old-style diplomatic history is frequently supposed to be dead, the reader will be struck not only by the density of material, at least on certain themes, but also by the patchy attention to less 'central' ones. It will also be noted, however, that scholarly attention tends to shift from topic to topic largely as new public documentation becomes available for investigation. It follows that archivally based studies of post-1945 external policy were only beginning to appear in some depth as this bibliography was concluded. It may be confidently asserted that many more will appear with successive releases of documents under the thirty-year rule for British public archives. Even so, many items relating to both the period before 1945 and subsequently have continued to be listed because even though 'superseded' by works with greater access to documents they do have a historiographical significance in their own right.

1. FOREIGN POLICY: GENERAL SURVEYS

13207 WEIGALL (DAVID). Britain and the World 1815–1986: A Dictionary of International Relations. 1987.

13208 WILLERT (Sir ARTHUR). Aspects of British Foreign Policy. 1928.

13209 —— The Frontiers of England. 1935.

13210 EDWARDS (WILLIAM). British Foreign Policy from 1815 to 1933. 1934.

13211 REYNOLDS (PHILIP ALAN). British Foreign Policy in the Inter-War Years. 1954.

13212 STRANG (WILLIAM) Baron. Britain in World Affairs. 1961.

13213 NORTHEDGE (FREDERICK SAMUEL). The Troubled Giant: Britain among the Great Powers, 1916–1939. 1966.

13214 WEBSTER (Sir CHARLES KINGSLEY) et al. United Kingdom Policy: Foreign, Strategic, Economic: Appreciations by Sir Charles Webster and others. 1950.

13215 SIDEY (PHILIP JOHN). Britain in the World. 1966.

13216 BULLOCK (ALAN LOUIS CHARLES) Baron. Great Britain in the World of the Twentieth Century. 1952.

13217 FRANKS (OLIVER SHEWELL) Baron. Britain and the Tide of World Affairs. 1954.

13218 FOOT (MICHAEL RICHARD DANIELL). British Foreign Policy Since 1898. 1956.

13219 TAYLOR (ALAN JOHN PERCIVALE). The Troublemakers: Dissent Over Foreign Policy, 1792–1939. 1957.

13220 BRANSTON (URSULA). Some Reflections on British Foreign Policy. 1959.

13221 ROTHSTEIN (ANDREW). British Foreign Policy and its Critics, 1830–1950. 1969.

13222 CRISP (DOROTHY). The Dominance of England. 1960.

13223 HAIGH (AUSTIN ANTHONY FRANCIS). Congress of Vienna to Common Market: An Outline of British Foreign Policy, 1815–1972. 1973.

13224 HAYES (PAUL MARTIN). Modern British Foreign Policy: the Twentieth Century, 1880–1939. 1978.

13225 MEDLICOTT (WILLIAM NORTON). British Foreign Policy Since Versailles. 1940. New edn British Foreign Policy 1919–1963. 1963.

13226 WOODHOUSE (CHRISTOPHER MONTAGUE). British Foreign Policy Since the Second World War. 1961.

13227 YOUNGER (*Sir* KENNETH GILMOUR). The Changing Aims of British Foreign Policy. 1958.

13228 —— Changing Perspectives in British Foreign Policy. 1964.

13229 MANDER (JOHN GEOFFREY GRYLES). Great Britain or Little England? 1963.

13230 MACLEAN (DONALD DUART). British Foreign Policy: The Years Since Suez, 1956–1968. 1970.

13231 NORTHEDGE (FREDERICK SAMUEL) *ed*. The Foreign Policies of the Powers. 1968.

13232 HUGO (GRANT). Britain in Tomorrow's World: Principles of Foreign Policy. 1969.

13233 BELOFF (MAX). The Future of British Foreign Policy. 1969.

13234 RICHARDSON (PAUL). Britain, Europe and the Modern World 1918–1968. Camb. 1970.

13235 BAILEY (MAURICE HOWARD). Britain and World Affairs in the Twentieth Century. Edin. 1971.

13236 BARNETT (CORRELLI DOUGLAS). The Collapse of British Power. 1972.

13237 MARCHAM (ANTHONY JAMES). Foreign Policy. 1973.

13238 BELOFF (NORA). Transit of Britain: A Report on Britain's Changing Role in the Post-War World. 1973.

13239 NORTHEDGE (FREDERICK SAMUEL). Descent from Power: British Foreign Policy 1945–1973. 1974.

13240 JONES (ROY ELLIOTT). The Changing Structure of British Foreign Policy. 1974.

13241 FRANKEL (JOSEPH). British Foreign Policy 1945–1973. Oxf. 1975.

13242 HEATER (DEREK BENJAMIN). Britain and the Outside World. 1976.

13243 DILKS (DAVID N.) *ed*. Retreat from Power: Studies in Britain's Foreign Policy of the Twentieth Century. 2 vols 1981.

13244 PORTER (BERNARD). Britain, Europe and the World, 1850–1982: Delusions of Grandeur. 1983. 2nd edn (to 1986) 1987.

13245 VERRIER (ANTHONY). Through the Looking Glass: British Foreign Policy in the Age of Illusions. 1983.

13246 TARLING (NICHOLAS). The Sun Never Sets: An Historical Essay on Britain and its Place in the World. 1987.

13247 BARTLETT (CHRISTOPHER J.). British Foreign Policy in the Twentieth Century. 1989.

2. DIPLOMATS AND DIPLOMACY

13248 NIGHTINGALE (ROBERT T.). The Personnel of the British Foreign Office and Diplomatic Service, 1851–1921. Fabian Tract no. 232. 1930.

13249 ZAMETICA (JOHN) *ed*. British Officials and British Foreign Policy 1945–1950. Leicester. 1990.

13250 BAILEY. Mission to Tashkent. By Frederick Marshman Bailey. 1946.

13251 BALFOUR. Not Too Correct an Aureole: The Recollections of a Diplomat. By Sir John Balfour 1983.

13252 BUCHANAN. My Mission to Russia and other Diplomatic Memories. By Sir George William Buchanan. 2 vols 1923.

13253 BULLARD. The Camels Must Go. By Sir Reader William Bullard. 1961.

13254 BUSK. The Craft of Diplomacy. By Sir Douglas Laird Busk. 1967.

13255 BUTLER. Confident Morning. By Sir Harold Beresford Butler. 1950.

13256 CADOGAN. The Diaries of Sir Alexander Cadogan, 1938–1945. Ed. by David N. Dilks. 1971.

13257 CAMPBELL. Of True Experience. By Sir Gerald Campbell. 1949.

13258 COLLIER. Flight from Conflict. By Sir Laurence Collier. 1944.

13259 CRAIGIE. Behind the Japanese Mask. By Sir Robert Leslie Craigie. 1946.

13260 CROSBY. Siam: The Crossroads. By Sir Josiah Crosby. 1945.

13261 D'ABERNON. Diary of an Ambassador. By Edgar Vincent d'Abernon, Viscount d'Abernon. 3 vols 1929–31.

13262 —— Red Cross and Berlin Embassy, 1915–1926. By Viscountess d'Abernon. 1946.

13263 DIXON. Double Diploma: The Life of Sir Pierson Dixon, Don and Diplomat. By Piers Dixon. 1968.

13264 EWART-BRIGGS. Pay, Pack and Follow: Memoirs. By Jane Ewart-Biggs. 1984.

13265 FRY. As Luck would have it. A Memoir. By Sir Leslie Fry. Chichester. 1978.

13266 GLADWYN. Memoirs. By Hubert Miles Gladwyn Jebb, Baron Gladwyn. 1972.

13267 GORE-BOOTH. With Great Truth and Respect. By Lord Gore-Booth. 1974.

13268 GRAFFTEY-SMITH. Bright Levant. By Sir Laurence Baton Grafftey-Smith. 1970.

13269 GREGORY. On the Edge of Diplomacy: Rambles and Reflections, 1902–1928. By John Duncan Gregory. 1929.

13270 HARDINGE. Old Diplomacy. By Charles Hardinge, Baron Hardinge of Penshurst. 1947.

13271 HARVEY. Diplomatic Diaries of Oliver Harvey, 1937–1940. Ed. by John Harvey. 1970.

13272 —— War Diaries of Oliver Harvey, 1941–1945. *Ed.* by John Harvey. 1978.

13273 HAYTER. The Kremlin and the Embassy. By Sir William Hayter. 1966.

13274 —— A Double Life: The Memoirs of Sir William Hayter. 1974.

13275 HENDERSON. Failure of a Mission: Berlin 1937–1939. By Sir Nevile Meyrick Henderson. 1940.

13276 —— Water Under the Bridges. By Sir Nevile Meyrick Henderson. 1945.

13277 HENDERSON. The Private Office: A Personal View of Five Foreign Secretaries and of Government from the Inside. By Sir Nicholas Henderson. 1984.

13278 HEWLETT. Forty Years in China. By Sir William Meyrick Hewlett. 1943.

13279 HOARE. Ambassador on Special Mission. By Samuel John Gurney Hoare, Baron Templewood. 1946.

13280 HOHLER. Diplomatic Petrel. By Sir Thomas Beaumont Hohler. 1942.

13281 HOWARD. Theatre of Life. By Esmé William Howard, Baron Howard of Penrith. 1936.

13282 HUNT. On the Spot: An Ambassador Remembers. By Sir David Wathen Stather Hunt. 1975.

13283 JACKSON. Concorde Diplomacy: The Ambassador's Role in the World Today. By Sir Geoffrey Jackson. 1981.

13284 KELLY. The Ruling Few. By Sir David Victor Kelly. 1952.

13285 KILLEARN. The Killearn Diaries, 1934–1946. *Ed.* by Trefor Ellis Evans. 1972.

13286 KIRKBRIDE. A Crackle of Thorns: Experiences in the Middle East. By Sir Alec Seath Kirkbride. 1956.

13287 KIRKPATRICK. The Inner Circle. By Sir Ivone Kirkpatrick. 1959.

13288 KNATCHBULL-HUGESSEN. Diplomat in Peace and War. By Sir Hugh Montgomery Knatchbull-Hugessen. 1949.

13289 LAWFORD. Bound for Diplomacy. By Valentine George Lawford. 1963.

13290 LEEPER. When Greek Meets Greek. By Sir Reginald Wildig Allen Leeper. 1950.

13291 LINDLEY. A Diplomat Off Duty. By Sir Francis Oswald Lindley. 1928.

13292 LOMAX. The Diplomatic Smuggler. By Sir John Garnett Lomax. 1965.

13293 MOTT-RADCLYFFE. Foreign Body in the Eye: A Memoir of the Foreign Service. 1975.

13294 O'MALLEY. The Phantom Caravan. By Sir Owen St Clair O'Malley. 1954.

13295 —— Permission to Resign. Goings-on in the Corridors of Power. By Ann Bridge, Lady O'Malley. 1971.

13296 ONSLOW. Sixty Three years: Diplomacy, the Great War and Politics, with Notes on Travel, Sport and other Things. By Richard William Alan Onslow, Earl of Onslow. 1944.

13297 PARROTT. The Tightrope. By Sir Cecil Parrott. 1975.

13298 —— The Serpent and the Nightingale. By Sir Cecil Parrott. 1978.

13299 PARSONS. The Pride and the Fall: Iran 1974–1979. 1984. By Sir Anthony Parsons. 1984.

13300 PETERSON. Both Sides of the Curtain. By Sir Maurice Drummond Peterson. 1950.

13301 PECK. Dublin from Downing Street. By Sir John Peck. 1978.

13302 RANDALL. Vatican Assignment. By Sir Alec Walter George Randall. 1956.

13303 RENDEL. The Sword and the Olive: Recollections of Diplomacy and the Foreign Service, 1913–1954. By Sir George William Rendel. 1957.

13304 RENNELL. Social and Diplomatic Memoirs: Third Series 1902–1919. By James Rennell Rodd, Baron Rennell. 1925.

13305 RYAN. The Last of the Dragomans. By Sir Andrew Ryan. 1951.

13306 SCOTT. Ambassador in Black and White: Thirty Years of Changing Africa. By Sir David Scott. 1981.

13307 SELBY. Diplomatic Twilight, 1930–1940. By Sir Walford Harmood Montague Selby. 1953.

13308 SKRINE. World War in Iran. By Sir Clarmont Percival Skrine. 1962.

13309 SPRING RICE. The Letters and Friendships of Sir Cecil Spring Rice: A Record. *Ed.* by Stephen Lucius Gwynn. 2 vols 1929.

13310 STORRS. Orientations. By Sir Ronald Storrs. 1937.

13311 STRANG. Home and Abroad. By William Strang, Baron Strang. 1956.

13312 THOMPSON. Front Line Diplomat. By Sir Geoffrey Harington Thompson. 1959.

13313 TILLEY. London to Tokyo. By Sir John Anthony Cecil Tilley. 1942.

13314 TREVELYAN. Worlds Apart: China 1953–1955: Soviet Union 1962–1965. 1971. By Sir Humphrey Trevelyan.

13315 —— Public and Private. By Sir Humphrey Trevelyan, Baron Trevelyan. 1980.

13316 VANSITTART. The Mist Procession. By Robert Gilbert Vansittart, Baron Vansittart. 1958.

13317 —— Black Record. By Robert Gilbert Vansittart, Baron Vansittart. 1941.

Polemical pieces by the same author should be noted: Lessons of my Life. 1943; Bones of Contention. 1945; Events and Shadows. 1947; Even Now. 1949.

13318 WELLESLEY. Diplomacy in Fetters. By Sir Victor Wellesley. 1944.

13319 WILLERT. Washington and Other Memories. By Sir Arthur Willert. Boston, Mass. 1972.

13320 BERTIE. Bertie of Thame: Edwardian Ambassador. By Keith Hamilton. 1990.

13321 HOWARD. Esmé Howard: A Diplomatic Biography. By Brian J. C. McKercher. Camb. 1989.

13322 SATOW (Sir ERNEST MASON). A Guide to Diplomatic Practice. 2 vols 1917.

13323 NICOLSON (Sir HAROLD GEORGE). The Evolution of Diplomatic Method. 1954.

13324 WEBSTER (Sir CHARLES KINGSLEY). The Art and Practice of Diplomacy. 1961.

13325 STRANG (WILLIAM) Baron. The Diplomatic Career. 1962.

13326 THE FOREIGN OFFICE LIST. Annual.

13327 TILLEY (Sir JOHN ANTHONY CECIL) and GASELEE (STEPHEN). The Foreign Office. Whitehall Series. 1933.

13328 STRANG (WILLIAM) Baron. The Foreign Office. New Whitehall Series. 1955.

13329 ASHTON-GWATKIN (FRANK TRELAWNY ARTHUR). The British Foreign Service: A Discussion of the Development and Function of the British Foreign Service. 1950.

13330 CRAIG (GORDON ALEXANDER) and GILBERT (FELIX) eds. The Diplomats, 1919–1939. 1953.

13331 CONNELL ([JOHN HENRY ROBERTSON) JOHN). The 'Office': A Study of British Foreign Policy and its Makers, 1919–1951. 1958.

13332 MOORHOUSE (GEOFFREY). The Diplomats: The Foreign Office Today. 1977.

13333 TREVELYAN (HUMPHREY). Diplomatic Channels. 1973.

13334 CROMWELL (VALERIE). 'The Foreign and Commonwealth Office' in 'The Times Survey of Foreign Ministries of the World'. Ed. by Zara Steiner. 1982.

13335 JENKINS (SIMON) and SLOMAN (ANNE). With Respect, Ambassador: An Inquiry into the Foreign Office. 1985.

13336 BULLEN (ROGER) ed. The Foreign Office 1782–1982. 1984.

13337 LARNER (CHRISTINA J.). 'The Amalgamation of the Diplomatic Service with the Foreign Office'. J. Contemp. Hist. vii (1972), 107–26.

13338 WARMAN (ROBERTA M.). 'The Erosion of Foreign Office Influence in the Making of Foreign Policy, 1916–1918'. Hist. J. xv (1972), 133–59.

13339 SHARP (ALAN J.). 'The Foreign Office in Eclipse, 1919–1922'. Hist. 61 (1976), 198–218.

13340 STEINER (ZARA SHAKOW) and DOCKRILL (MICHAEL L.). 'The Foreign Office Reforms, 1919–1921'. Hist. J. xvii (1974), 131–56.

13341 BOADLE (DONALD GRAEME). 'The Formation of the Foreign Office Economic Relations Section, 1930–1937'. Hist. J. xx (1977), 919–36.

13342 KENNEDY (AUBREY LEO). 'Reorganisation of the Foreign Office'. Q. Rev. 283 (1945), 397–412.

13343 PONSONBY (ARTHUR AUGUSTUS WILLIAM HENRY) Baron. Democracy and Diplomacy: A Plea for Popular Control of Foreign Policy. 1915.

13344 SCHRODER (KARSTEN). Parlament und Aussenpolitik in England 1911–1914. Göttingen. 1974.

13345 LANGFORD (RICHARD VICTOR). British Foreign Policy: its Formulation in Recent Years. Washington, DC. 1942.

13346 RICHARDSON (JOHN HENRY). British Economic Foreign Policy. 1936.

13347 STRANG (WILLIAM) Baron. 'The Formation and Control of Foreign Policy'. Dur. Univ. J. xviii (1957), 98–108.

13348 LAWFORD (VALENTINE GEORGE). 'Inside the Foreign Office: Halifax, Eden, Bevin'. Atlantic Monthly ccv (1960), 45–54.

13349 WATT (DONALD CAMERON). 'Divided Control of British Foreign Policy: Danger or Necessity?'. Pol. Q. xxxiii (1962), 370–8.

13350 —— 'Foreign Affairs, the Public Interest and the Right to Know'. Pol. Q. xxxiv (1963), 121–36.

13351 —— Personalities and Policies: Studies in the Formulation of British Foreign Policy in the Twentieth Century. 1965.

13352 —— 'The Home Civil Service and the New Diplomacy'. Pol. Q. xxxviii (1967), 283–9.

13353 BELOFF (MAX) Baron. 'The Projection of Britain Abroad'. Inl Affs xli (1965), 478–89.

13354 BANKS (MICHAEL). 'Professionalism in the Conduct of Foreign Policy'. Inl Affs xliv (1968), 720–34.

13355 BISHOP (DONALD GORDON). The Administration of Britain's Foreign Relations. 1961.

13356 RICHARDS (PETER GODFREY). Parliament and Foreign Affairs. 1967.

13357 VITAL (DAVID). The Making of British Foreign Policy. 1968.

13358 —— 'The Making of British Foreign Policy'. Pol. Q. xxxix (1968), 255–68.

13359 LEIFER (MICHAEL) ed. Constraints and Adjustments in British Foreign Policy. 1972.

13360 BOARDMAN (ROBERT) and GROOM (ARTHUR JOHN RICHARD) eds. The Management of Britain's External Relations. 1973.

13361 WALLACE (WILLIAM J. L.). The Foreign Policy Process in Britain. 1976.

13362 Report of the Review Committee on Overseas Representation 1968–1969. Cmnd 4107. Parliamentary Papers (1968–9).

13363 COHEN (YOEL). Media Diplomacy: The Foreign Office in the Mass Communications Age. 1986.

3. DIPLOMACY/FOREIGN POLICY IN THE FIRST WORLD WAR

13364 GUINN (PAUL). British Strategy and Politics, 1914–1918. Oxf. 1965.

13365 STEVENSON (DAVID). The First World War and International Politics. Oxf. 1988.

13366 ROBBINS (KEITH GILBERT). The First World War. Oxf. 1984.

13367 ROTHWELL (VICTOR HOWARD). British War Aims and Peace Diplomacy, 1914–1918. Oxf. 1971.

13368 HUNT (B.) *and* PRESTON (ADRIAN) *eds*. War Aims and Strategic Policy in the Great War, 1914–1918. 1977.

13369 FRENCH (DAVID). British Strategy and War Aims 1914–1916. 1986.

13370 GALBRAITH (JOHN S.). 'British War Aims in World War I: A Commentary on "Statesmanship"'. *J. Imp. Cwealth Hist.* 13 (1984), 25–45.

13371 HALPERN (PAUL G.). 'The Anglo-French-Italian Naval Convention of 1915'. *Hist. J.* xiii (1970), 106–29.

13372 LOWE (CEDRIC J.). 'Britain and Italian Intervention, 1914–1915'. *Hist. J.* xii (1969), 533–48.

13373 BRAND (CARL F.). 'British Labour and the International during the Great War'. *J. Mod. Hist.* viii (1936), 40–63.

13374 KIRBY (DAVID). 'International Socialism and the Question of Peace: The Stockholm Conference of 1917'. *Hist. J.* 25 (1982), 709–16.

13375 MEYNELL (H.). 'The Stockholm Conference of 1917'. *Inl Rev. Soc. Hist.* 5 (1960), 1–25, 202–25.

13376 WINTER (JAY M.). 'Arthur Henderson, the Russian Revolution, and the Reconstruction of the Labour Party'. *Hist. J.* 15 (1972), 753–73.

13377 FARRAR (L. L.). Divide and Conquer: German Efforts to Conclude a Separate Peace, 1914–1918. N.Y. 1978.

13378 —— 'Opening to the West: German Efforts to Conclude a Separate Peace with England, July 1917–March 1918'. *Can. J. Hist.* x (1975), 73–90.

13379 FEST (WILFRIED B.). 'British War Aims and German Peace Feelers during the First World War (December 1916–November 1918)'. *Hist. J.* xv (1972), 285–308.

13380 WOODWARD (DAVID R.). 'David Lloyd George, a Negotiated Peace with Germany, and the Kuhlmann Peace Kite of September 1917'. *Can. J. Hist.* vi (1971), 75–93.

13381 JAFFE (LORNA S.). The Decision to Disarm Germany: British Policy towards Post-War German Disarmament, 1914–1919. 1985.

13382 LOUIS (WILLIAM ROGER). Great Britain and Germany's Lost Colonies, 1914–1919. Oxf. 1967.

13383 NELSON (HAROLD I.). Land and Power: British and Allied Policy on Germany's Frontiers, 1916–1919. 1963.

13384 KURTZ (HAROLD). 'The Lansdowne Letter'. *Hist. Today* xviii (1968), 85–92.

13385 ROBBINS (KEITH GILBERT). 'British Diplomacy and Bulgaria, 1914–1915'. *Slav. E. Eur. Rev.* xlix. (1971), 560–85.

13386 LOWE (CEDRIC J.). 'The Failure of British Policy in the Balkans, 1914–1916'. *Can. J. Hist.* iv (1969), 73–100.

13387 DUTTON (DAVID J.). 'The Deposition of King Constantine of Greece, June 1917: An Episode in Anglo-French Diplomacy'. *Can. J. Hist.* 12 (1978), 325–45.

13388 HIRSHFIELD (CLAIRE). 'In Search of Mrs Ryder: British Women in Serbia during the Great War'. *East. European Q.* 20 (1986), 387–407.

13389 VINCENT-SMITH (JOHN). 'Britain, Portugal and the First World War 1914–1916'. *Eur. Studs Rev.* iv (1974), 207–38.

13390 CALDER (KENNETH J.). Britain and the Origins of the New Europe, 1914–1918. Camb. 1976.

13391 GOTTLIEB (WOLFRAM WILHELM). Studies in Secret Diplomacy during the First World War. 1957.

13392 HANAK (HARRY). Great Britain and Austria-Hungary during the First World War: A Study in the Formation of Public Opinion. 1962.

13393 —— 'The Government, the Foreign Office and Austria-Hungary, 1914–1918'. *Slav. E. Eur. Rev.* xlvii (1969), 161–97.

13394 SETON-WATSON (HUGH) *and* SETON-WATSON (CHRISTOPHER). The Making of a New Europe: R. W. Seton-Watson and the Last Years of Austria-Hungary. 1981.

13395 CALLCOTT (W. R.). 'The Last War Aim: British Opinion and the Decision for Czechoslovak Independence. 1914–1919'. *Hist. J.* 27 (1984), 979–89.

13396 KENT (MARIAN). 'Great Britain and the End of the Ottoman Empire 1900–1923'. In 'The Great Powers and the End of the Ottoman Empire'. By Marian Kent. 1984.

13397 FOWLER (WILTON B.). British-American Relations, 1917–1918: The Role of Sir William Wiseman. Princeton, NJ. 1969.

13398 MARTIN (LAURENCE W.). Peace without Victory: Woodrow Wilson and the British Liberals. New Haven, Conn. 1958.

13399 COOPER (J. M.) *Jnr*. 'The Command of Gold Reversed: American Loans to Britain, 1915–1917'. *Pac. Hist. Rev.* 45/2 (1976), 209–30.

13400 —— 'The British Response to the House–Grey Memorandum: New Evidence and New Questions'. *J. Amer. Hist.* 59/4 (1973), 958–71.

13401 KERNEK (STERLING J.). 'The British Government's Reaction to President Wilson's "Peace" Note of December 1916'. *Hist. J.* 13 (1970), 721–66.

13402 —— 'Distractions of Peace during War: The Lloyd George Government's Reactions to President Wilson, December 1916–November 1918'. *Trans. Amer. Phil. Soc.* 65 (1975), 1–117.

13403 BURK (KATHLEEN). Britain, America, and the Sinews of War, 1914–1918. Boston, Mass. and London. 1985.

13404 —— 'Great Britain in the United States, 1917–1918: The Turning Point'. *Inl Hist. Rev.* 1/2 (1979), 228–45.

13405 —— 'The Diplomacy of Finance: British Financial Missions to the United States 1914–1918'. *Hist. J.* 22 (1979), 351–72.

13406 —— 'The Mobilization of Anglo-American Finance During World War I'. In 'Mobilization for Total War: The Canadian, American and British Experience, 1914–1918, 1939–1945'. *Ed.* by F. Dreiziger. Waterloo, Ontario. 1981.

13407 DUTTON (DAVID J.). 'The Calais Conference of December 1915'. *Hist. J.* 21 (1978), 143–56.

13408 HARTLEY (STEPHEN). The Irish Question as a Problem in British Foreign Policy 1914–1918. 1987.

13409 NEILSON (KEITH). Strategy and Supply: The Anglo-Russian Alliance, 1914–17. 1984.

13410 —— ' "Joy Rides"? British Intelligence and Propaganda in Russia, 1914–1917'. *Hist. J.* 24 (1981), 885–906.

13411 KOCH (HANS-JOACHIM WERNER). 'Das britische Russlandbild im Spiegel der britischen Propaganda 1914–1918'. *Zeitschrift für Politik* 27 (1980), 71–96.

13412 SMITH (C. J.). 'Great Britain and the 1914–1915 Straits Agreement with Russia: The British Promise of November 1914'. *Amer. Hist. Rev.* 70 (1965), 51–69.

13413 LYYTINEN (EINO). Finland in British Politics during the First World War. Helsinki. 1980.

13414 KAARSTED (T.). Great Britain and Denmark 1914–1920. Odense. 1979.

13415 HACHEY (THOMAS E.) *ed.* Anglo-Vatican Relations 1914–1919. Boston, Mass. 1972.

13416 BUNSELMAYER (ROBERT E.). The Cost of the War, 1914–1919: British Economic War Aims and the Origins of Reparations. Hamden, NJ. 1975.

13417 SCHMIDT (HEIDE-IRENE). 'Wirtschaftliche Kriegsziele Englands und interallierte Kooperation. Die Pariser Wirtschaftskonferenz 1916'. *Mil. Mitt.* 29 (1981), 37–54.

13418 MCDERMOTT (J.). 'Total War and the Merchant State: Aspects of British Economic Warfare Against Germany, 1914–1916'. *Can. J. Hist.* 21 (1986), 61–7.

4. PEACEMAKING 1919

13419 ELCOCK (HOWARD). Portrait of a Decision: The Council of Four and the Treaty of Versailles. 1972.

13420 DOCKRILL (MICHAEL L.) *and* GOOLD (J. DOUGLAS). Peace Without Promise: Britain and the Peace Conferences, 1919–1923. 1981.

13421 GRUNER (W. D.). 'Friedenssicherung und Politisch-soziales System: Grossbritannien auf der Pariser Friedenskonferenzen 1919'. In L'Europe de Versailles, 1918–1923: Bilan, Perspectives et Controverses. Geneva. 1979.

13422 SCHMIDT (GUSTAV). 'Politische Tradition und Wirtschafliche Faktoren in der britischen Friedensstrategie 1918/19'. *Vierteljahreshefte für Zeitgeschichte* 29 (1981), 131–88.

13423 NICOLSON (*Sir* HAROLD GEORGE). Peacemaking 1919: Being Reminiscences of the Paris Peace Conference. 1933.

13424 NORTHEDGE (FREDERICK S.). '1917–1919: The Implications for Britain'. *J. Contemp. Hist.* 3 (1968), 191–209.

13425 BEADON (ROGER HAMMET). Some Memories of the Peace Conference. 1933.

13426 TEMPERLEY (HAROLD NEVILLE VAZEILLE) *ed.* History of the Peace Conference of Paris. 6 vols 1920–4.

13427 HANKEY (MAURICE PASCAL ALERS) *Baron.* The Supreme Control at the Paris Peace Conference, 1919: A Commentary. 1963.

13428 TILLMAN (SETH P.). Anglo-American Relations at the Paris Peace Conference of 1919. Princeton, NJ. 1961.

13429 EGERTON (GEORGE W.). 'Britain and the "Great Betrayal": Anglo-American Relations and the Struggle for United States Ratification of the Treaty of Versailles'. *Hist. J.* 21 (1978), 885–911.

13430 BOOTHE (L. E.). 'A Fettered Envoy: Lord Grey's Mission to the United States 1919–1920'. *Rev. Pol.* 33 (1971), 78–94.

13431 MCCALLUM (RONALD BUCHANAN). Public Opinion and the Last Peace. 1944.

5. PEACE MOVEMENTS, THE LEAGUE OF NATIONS, AND THE UNITED NATIONS

13432 LLOYD (LORNA) *and* SIMS (NICHOLAS A.). British Writing on Disarmament from 1914 to 1978: A Bibliography. 1979.

13433 JOSEPHSON (HAROLD) *ed. et al.* Biographical Dictionary of Modern Peace Leaders. Westport, Conn. 1985.

13434 INGRAM (ARCHIBALD KENNETH). Fifty Years of the National Peace Council: A Short History. 1958.

13435 WALLIS (JILL). Valiant for Peace: A History of the Fellowship of Reconciliation 1914 to 1989. 1991.

13436 MOOREHEAD (CAROLINE). Troublesome People: Enemies of War, 1916–1986. 1987.

13437 HINTON (JAMES). Protests and Visions: Peace Politics in Twentieth Century Britain. 1989.

13438 TAYLOR (RICHARD K.) *and* YOUNG (NIGEL) eds. Campaigning for Peace: British Peace Movements in the Twentieth Century. Manch. 1987.

13439 BUSSEY (GERTRUDE) *and* TIMS (MARGARET). Women's International League for Peace and Freedom 1915–1965. 1965.

13440 HARFORD (BARBARA) *and* HOPKINS (SARAH) eds. Greenham Common; Women at the Wire. 1985.

13441 THOMPSON (DOROTHY) ed. Over our Dead Bodies: Women against the Bomb. 1983.

13442 MORGAN (KENNETH OWEN). 'Peace Movements in Wales 1899–1945'. *Welsh Hist. Rev.* 10 (1981), 398–430.

13443 CROSBY (GERDA RICHARDS). Disarmament and Peace in British Politics, 1914–1919. Camb., Mass. 1957.

13444 ROBBINS (KEITH GILBERT). The Abolition of War: The British 'Peace Movement', 1914–1919. Cardiff. 1976.

13445 CARSTEN (FRANCIS L.). War Against War: British and German Radical Movements in the First World War. 1982.

13446 SCHRAMM (GOTTFRIED). 'Minderheiten gegen den Krieg. Motive und Kampfformen 1914–1918 am Beispiel Grossbritanniens und seines Empire'. *Geschichte und Gesellschaft* 6 (1980), 164–88.

13447 RITTER (GERHARD A.). 'Friedensbewegung in Grossbritannien 1914–1918/19: The Union of Democratic Control und ihr Kampf um eine gerechte Friedensordnung'. *Archiv für Sozialgeschichte* 22 (1982), 403–71.

13448 TIMMERMANN (HEINRICH). Friedensbewegung in den Vereinigten Staaten von Amerika und in Grossbritannien während des Ersten Weltkrieges. Frankfurt a. M. 1978.

13449 BELL (JULIAN) ed. We Did Not Fight: 1914–1918. Experiences of War Resisters. 1935.

13450 WELLER (K.). 'Don't be a Soldier!': The Radical Anti-War Movement in North London, 1914–1918. 1985.

13451 PEACOCK (ALFRED J.). 'Conscience and Politics in York 1914–18'. *York Historian* 5 (1984), 39–50.

13452 KENNEDY (THOMAS C.). The Hound of Conscience: A History of the No-Conscription Fellowship, 1914–1919. Fayetteville, Ark. 1981.

13453 —— 'Public Opinion and the Conscientious Objector, 1915–1919'. *J. Brit. Studs* xii (1973), 105–19.

13454 MOR-O'BRIEN (ANTHONY). ' "Conchie": Emrys Hughes and the First World War'. *Welsh Hist. Rev.* 13 (1987), 328–52.

13455 BOULTON (DAVID). Objection Overruled. 1967.

13456 GRAHAM (JOHN W.). Conscription and Conscience: A History 1916–1919. 1922.

13457 CAIN (EDWARD R.). 'Conscientious Objection in France, Britain and the United States'. *Comp. Pol.* 2 (1970), 274–307.

13458 RAE (JOHN). Conscience and Politics: The British Government and the Conscientious Objector to Military Service 1916–1919. 1970.

13459 HAYES (DENIS). Conscription Conflict: The Conflict of Ideas in the Struggle for and against Military Conscription in Britain between 1901 and 1939. 1949.

13460 VELLACOTT (JO). Bertrand Russell and the Pacifists in the First World War. Brighton. 1980.

13461 SWANWICK (HELENA M.). Builders of Peace: Being Ten Years' History of the Union of Democratic Control. 1924.

13462 SWARTZ (MARVIN). The Union of Democratic Control in British Politics during the First World War. Oxf. 1971.

13463 PAUL (J. B.). 'The Union of Democratic Control'. *Austral. Outlook* 26 (August 1972), 222–32.

13464 MILLER (J. D. BRUCE). Norman Angell and the Futility of War. 1986.

13465 ANGELL (*Sir* NORMAN). After All: The Autobiography of Norman Angell. 1951.

13466 BISCEGLIA (LOUIS R.). 'Norman Angell and the "Pacifist Muddle"'. *Bull. Inst. Hist. Res.* xlv (1972), 104–21.

13467 —— 'The Politics of a Peace Prize'. *J. Contemp. Hist.* vii (1972), 263–73.

13468 WEINROTH (HOWARD). 'Peace by Negotiation and the British Anti-War Movement, 1914–1918'. *Can. J. Hist.* x (1975), 369–92.

13469 MURRAY (GILBERT). The League of Nations Movement: Some Recollections of the Early Days. 1955.

13470 EGERTON (GEORGE W.). Great Britain and the Creation of the League of Nations: Strategy, Politics and International Organization. Chapel Hill, NC 1978.

13471 —— 'The Lloyd George Government and the Creation of the League of Nations'. *Amer. Hist. Rev.* lxxix (1974), 419–44.

13472 WINKLER (HENRY RALPH). The League of Nations Movement in Great Britain. New Brunswick, NJ 1952.

13473 DANKELMANN (O.). 'Zur Geschichte und Funktion britischer Sozial-Reformistischen Völkerbundkonzeptionen 1916 bis 1919'. *Zeitschrift für Geschichtswissenschaft* 27 (1979), 32–45.

13474 STROMBERG (ROLAND N.). 'Uncertainties and Obscurities about the League of Nations'. *J. Contemp. Hist.* ix (1974), 153–76.

13475 DUBIN (MARTIN DAVID). 'Toward the Concept of Collective Security: The Bryce Group's "Proposals for the Avoidance of War", 1914–1917'. *Inl Organisation* xxiv (1970), 288–318.

13476 ROBBINS (KEITH GILBERT). 'Lord Bryce and the First World War'. *Hist. J.* x (1967), 255–77.

13477 WILSON (TREVOR). 'Lord Bryce's Investigation into Alleged German Atrocities in Belgium, 1914–15'. *J. Contemp. Hist.* 14 (1979), 369–83.

13478 BARROS (JAMES). Office Without Power: Secretary-General Sir Eric Drummond, 1919–1933. 1979.

13479 ZILLIACUS (KONNI). The League of Nations Today: Its Growth, Record and Relation to British Foreign Policy. 1923.

13480 WEBSTER (*Sir* CHARLES KINGSLEY). The League of Nations in Theory and Practice. 1933.

13481 NOEL-BAKER (PHILIP J.). The League of Nations at Work. 1926.

13482 MOST (ECKHARD). Grossbritannien und der Völkerbund: Studien zur Politik der Friedenssicherung, 1925–1934. Frankfurt a. M. 1981.

13483 YEARWOOD (P. J.). ' "Consistently with Honour": Great Britain, the League of Nations and the Corfu Crisis of 1923'. *J. Contemp. Hist.* 21 (1986), 559–79.

13484 BECK (PETER J.). 'From the Geneva Protocol to the Greco-Bulgarian Dispute: The Development of the Baldwin Government's Policy towards the Peace-Keeping Role of the League of Nations, 1924–1925'. *Brit. J. Inl Studs* (1980), 52–68.

13485 CARLTON (DAVID). 'Great Britain and the League Council Crisis of 1926'. *Hist. J.* xi (1968), 354–64.

13486 —— 'Disarmament with Guarantees: Lord Cecil 1922–1927'. *Disarmt Arms Control* iii (1965), 573–98.

13487 CHAPUT (ROLLAND A.). Disarmament in British Foreign Policy. 1935.

13488 TEMPERLEY (ARTHUR CECIL). The Whispering Gallery of Europe. 1938.

13489 CARLTON (DAVID). 'Great Britain and the Coolidge Naval Disarmament Conference of 1927'. *Pol. Sci. Q* lxxxiii (1968), 573–98.

13490 —— 'The Anglo-French Compromise on Arms Limitation, 1928'. *J. Brit. Studs* viii (1969), 141–62.

13491 —— 'The Problem of Civil Aviation in British Disarmament Policy, 1919–1934'. *J. Roy. United Services Inst.* 111 (1966), 307–16.

13492 NOEL-BAKER (PHILIP J.). The First World Disarmament Conference, 1932–1933 and Why it Failed. 1979.

13493 SHARMA (SHIVA KUMAR). Der Völkerbund und die Grossmächte: ein Beitrag zur Geschichte der Völkerbundspolitik Grossbritanniens, Frankreichs und Deutschlands, 1929–1933. Frankfurt a. M. 1978.

13494 BIRN (DONALD S.). The League of Nations Union. Oxf. 1981.

13495 —— 'The League of Nations Union and Collective Security'. *J. Contemp. Hist.* 9 (1974), 131–59.

13496 BRAMSTED (ERNEST K.). 'Apostles of Collective Security: The L.N.U. and its Functions'. *Austral. J. Pol. Hist.* 13 (1967), 347–64.

13497 RAFFO (PETER). 'The League of Nations Philosophy of Lord Robert Cecil'. *Austral. J. Pol. Hist.* 20 (1974), 186–96.

13498 THOMPSON (J. A.). 'Lord Cecil and the Pacifists of the League of Nations Union'. *Hist. J.* 20 (1977), 949–59.

13499 —— 'Lord Cecil and the Historians'. *Hist. J.* 24 (1981), 709–15.

13500 SPEAR (SHELDON). 'Pacifist Radicalism in the Postwar British Labour Party: The Case of E. D. Morel, 1919–1924'. *Inl Rev. Soc. Hist.* 23 (1978), 193–223.

13501 STANNAGE (C. T.). 'The East Fulham By-Election: 25 October 1933'. *Hist. J.* xiv (1971), 165–200.

13502 LIVINGSTONE (ADELAIDE LORD) *Dame, and* JOHNSON (MARJORIE SCOTT). The Peace Ballot: The Official History. 1935.

13503 THOMPSON (J. A.). 'The Peace Ballot of 1935: The Welsh Campaign'. *Welsh Hist. Rev.* 11 (1983), 388–99.

13504 —— 'The Peace Ballot and the Public'. *Albion* 13 (1981), 380–92.

13505 —— 'The "Peace Ballot" and the "Rainbow" Controversy'. *J. Brit. Studs* 20 (1981), 150–70.

13506 CEADEL (MARTIN). 'The First British Referendum: The Peace Ballot, 1934–5'. *Eng. Hist. Rev.* 95 (1980), 810–39.

13507 KYBA (P.). Covenants without the Sword: Public Opinion and British Defence Policy, 1931–1935. 1985.

13508 PUGH (MICHAEL). 'Pacifism and Politics in Britain, 1931–1935'. *Hist. J.* 23 (1980), 641–56.

13509 CEADEL (MARTIN). 'The "King and Country" Debate, 1933: Student Politics, Pacifism and the Dictators'. *Hist. J.* 22 (1979), 397–422.

13510 LUKOWITZ (DAVID C.). 'British Pacifists and Appeasement: The Peace Pledge Union'. *J. Contemp. Hist.* ix (1974), 115–27.

13511 —— 'George Lansbury's Peace Missions to Hitler and Mussolini in 1937'. *Can. J. Hist.* 15 (1980), 67–82.

13512 LANSBURY (GEORGE). My Quest for Peace. 1938.

13513 MORRISON (SYBIL). I Renounce War: The Story of the Peace Pledge Union. 1962.

13514 MARTIN (DAVID ALFRED). Pacifism: An Historical and Sociological Study. 1965.

13515 CEADEL (MARTIN). Pacifism in Britain 1914–1945: The Defining of a Faith. Oxf. 1980.

13516 BIALER (URI). The Shadow of the Bomb: The Fear of Air Attack and British Politics, 1932–1939. 1980.

13517 —— 'Humanization of Air Warfare in British Foreign Policy on the Eve of the Second World War'. *J. Contemp. Hist.* xiii (1978), 79–96.

13518 HAYES (DENIS). Challenge of Conscience: The Story of the Conscientious Objectors of 1939–45. 1949.

13519 REMPEL (RICHARD A.). 'The Dilemmas of British Pacifists During World War II'. *J. Mod. Hist.* 19 (1978), 1–9.

13520 BARKER (RACHEL). Conscience, Government and War: Conscientious Objection in Great Britain 1939–1945. 1982.

13521 PARTRIDGE (FRANCES). A Pacifist's War. 1978.

13522 —— Everything to Lose: Diaries 1945–1960. 1985.

13523 BLISHEN (EDWARD). A Cack-Handed War. 1972.

13524 SPRING (ERNEST). 'Conchie'. The Wartime Experiences of a Conscientious Objector. 1975.

13525 FIELD (G. C.). Pacifism and Conscientious Objection. Camb. 1945.

13526 DRIVER (CHRISTOPHER). The Disarmers: A Study in Protest. 1964.

13527 PARKIN (FRANK). Middle Class Radicalism: The Social Bases of the British Campaign for Nuclear Disarmament. Manch. 1968.

13528 MATTAUSCH (JOHN). A Commitment to Campaign: A Sociological Study of CND. Manch. 1989.

13529 TAYLOR (RICHARD K.) *and* PRITCHARD (COLIN). The Protest Makers: The British Nuclear Disarmament Movement of 1958–1965: Twenty Years On. Oxf. 1980.

13530 BYRNE (PAUL). The Campaign for Nuclear Disarmament. 1988.

13531 MINMAN (JOHN) *and* BOLSOVER (PHILIP) *eds*. The CND Story: The First 25 Years of CND in the Words of the People Involved. 1983.

13532 BRANDON (RUTH). The Burning Question: The Anti-Nuclear Movement Since 1945. 1987.

13533 TAYLOR (RICHARD K.). Against the Bomb: The British Peace Movement 1958–1965. Oxf. 1988.

13534 SABIN (PHILIP A. G.). The Third World War Scare in Britain: A Critical Analysis. 1986.

13535 JONES (GRETA). 'The Mushroomed-Shaped Cloud: British Scientists' Opposition to Nuclear Weapons Policy 1945–1957'. *Annals of Science* 43 (1986), 1–26.

13536 REYNOLDS (PHILIP ALAN) *and* HUGHES (EMMOT J.) *eds*. The Historian as Diplomat: Charles Kingsley Webster and the United Nations, 1939–1946. 1976.

13537 HUGHES (EMMOT J.). 'Winston Churchill and the Formation of the United Nations Organisation'. *J. Contemp. Hist.* 9 (1974), 177–94.

13538 GOODWIN (GEOFFREY LAWRENCE). Britain and the United Nations. 1958.

13539 NUTTING (*Sir* (HAROLD) ANTHONY). Disarmament: An Outline of the Negotiations. Oxf. 1959.

13540 FREEMAN (J. P. G.). Britain's Nuclear Arms Control Policy in the Context of Anglo-American Relations 1957–1968. 1986.

13541 DIVINE (ROBERT A.). Blowing in the Wind: The Nuclear Test Ban Debate 1954–1960. Oxf. 1978.

13542 WRIGHT (*Sir* MICHAEL). Disarm and Verify: An Explanation of the Central Difficulties and of National Policies. 1964.

13543 GWYNNE-JONES (ALUN) *Lord Chalfont, et al.* Disarmament: Nuclear Swords or Unilateral Ploughshares. 1987.

6. THE LABOUR PARTY AND FOREIGN POLICY

13544 DOWSE (ROBERT E.). 'The Independent Labour Party and Foreign Policy, 1918–1923'. *Inl Rev. Soc. Hist.* vii (1962), 33–46.

13545 SACKS (BENJAMIN). 'The Independent Labour Party and World War Peace Objectives'. *Pac. Hist. Rev.* v (1936), 161–73.

13546 SKOP (ARTHUR L.). 'The British Labour Party and the German Revolution, November 1918–January 1919'. *Eur. Studs Rev.* 5 (1975), 277–97.

13547 SPEAR (S.). 'Pacifist Radicalism in the Post-War British Labour Party: The Case of E. D. Morel, 1919–1924'. *Inl Rev. Soc. Hist.* xxii (1978), 193–223.

13548 WINKLER (HENRY R.). 'The Emergence of a Labour Foreign Policy in Great Britain, 1918–1929'. *J. Mod. Hist.* xxviii (1956), 247–58.

13549 HENDERSON (ARTHUR). Labour and Foreign Affairs. 1922.

13550 GLASGOW (GEORGE). MacDonald as Diplomatist: The Foreign Policy of the First Labour Government in Great Britain. 1924.

13551 KESERICH (CHARLES). 'The British Labour Press and Italian Fascism, 1922–1925'. *J. Contemp. Hist.* 10 (1975), 579–90.

13552 CARLTON (DAVID). MacDonald Versus Henderson: The Foreign Policy of the Second Labour Government. 1970.

13553 MacDONALD (JAMES RAMSAY). The Foreign Policy of the Labour Party. 1923.

13554 ROBBINS (KEITH GILBERT). 'Labour Foreign Policy and International Socialism: Ramsay MacDonald and the League of Nations'. In 'L'Internazionale Operaia e Socialista tra le due Guerre'. By Enzo Collotti. Milan. (1985), 105–33.

13555 MADDOX (WILLIAM PERCY). Foreign Relations in British Labour Politics, 1900–1924. Camb., Mass. 1934.

13556 MILLER (KENNETH EUGENE). Socialism and Foreign Policy: Theory and Practice in Britain to 1931. The Hague. 1967.

13557 TUCKER (WILLIAM RAYBURN). The Attitude of the British Labour Party towards European and Collective Security Problems, 1920–1939. Geneva. 1950.

13558 —— 'British Labor and Revision of the Peace Settlement, 1920–1925'. *Southwestern Soc. Sci. Q.* 41 (1960), 136–49.

13559 KRIEGER (WOLFGANG). Labour Party und Weimarer Republik. Ein Beitrag zur Aussenpolitik der britischen Arbeiterbewegung zwischen Programmatik und Parteitaktik (1918–1924). Bonn. 1978.

13560 BURCHARD (JOSEPH RANDALL). The British Labour Movement in European Politics, 1933–1939. Chicago, Ill.. 1945.

13561 GORNY (JOSEPH). The British Labour Movement and Zionism 1917–1948. 1983.

13562 NAYLOR (JOHN FRANCIS). Labour's International Policy: The Labour Party in the 1930s. 1969.

13563 FYRTH (J.) *ed.* Britain, Fascism and the Popular Front. 1985.

13564 NEW FABIAN RESEARCH BUREAU. The Road to War, Being an Analysis of the National Government's Foreign Policy. 1937.

13565 BURRIDGE (TREVOR DAVID). British Labour and Hitler's War. 1976.

13566 WINDRICH (ELAINE). British Labour's Foreign Policy. Stanford, Calif. 1952.

13567 MEEHAN (EUGENE JOHN). The British Left Wing and Foreign Policy: A Study of the Influence of Ideology. New Brunswick, NJ. 1960.

13568 GORDON (MICHAEL R.). Conflict and Consensus in Labour's Foreign Policy, 1914–1965. Stanford, Calif. 1969.

13569 GRANTHAM (J. T.). 'Hugh Dalton and the International Post-War Settlement: Labour Party Foreign Policy Formulation, 1943–1944'. *J. Contemp. Hist.* 14 (1979), 713–29

13570 BURRIDGE (TREVOR DAVID). 'Barnacles and Trouble Makers: Labour's Left Wing and British Foreign Policy 1939–1945'. *Can. J. Hist.* 16 (1981), 1–25.

13571 NEWMAN (MICHAEL). 'British Socialists and the Question of European Unity, 1939–1945'. *Eur. Studs Rev.* 10 (1980), 75–100.

13572 WEILER (PETER). British Labour and the Cold War. Stanford, Calif. 1988.

13573 —— 'British Labour and the Cold War: The London Dock Strike of 1949'. In 'Social Conflict and the Political Order in Modern Britain.' *Ed.* by James Cronin and Jonathan Schneer. 1982.

13574 RIEDEL (H.). 'Labour Party und EWG: zum Antrag Grossbritanniens auf Mitgliedschaft in der EWG in der Zweiten Hälfte der Sechziger Jahre'. *Zeitschrift für Geschichtswissenschaft* 27 (1979), 32–45.

7. POLICY TOWARDS EAST ASIA

(a) General

13575 LOWE (PETER). Britain in the Far East: A Survey from 1918 to the Present. 1981.

13576 ACLAND (*Sir* FRANCIS DYKE). Japan Must be Stopped. 1937.

13577 ROYAL INSTITUTE OF INTERNATIONAL AFFAIRS. British Far Eastern Policy. 1939.

13578 GULL (EDWARD MANICO). British Economic Interests in the Far East. 1943.

13579 WINT (GUY). The British in Asia. N.Y. 1954.

13580 HUBBARD (GILBERT E.). British Far Eastern Policy. N.Y. 1943.

13581 TROTTER (ANN). Britain and East Asia, 1933–1937. 1975.

13582 LOUIS (WILLIAM ROGER). British Strategy in the Far East, 1919–1939. Oxf. 1971.

(b) Japan

13583 MUTO (CHOZO). A Short History of Anglo-Japanese Relations. Tokyo. 1936.

13584 HARGREAVES (JOHN D.). 'The Anglo-Japanese Alliance, 1902–1952'. *History Today* ii (1952), 252–8.

13585 NISH (IAN HILL). Alliance in Decline: A Study in Anglo-Japanese Relations, 1908–1923. 1972.

13586 LOWE (PETER). 'Great Britain, Japan and the Fall of Yuan Shih-k'ai 1915–1916'. *Hist. J.* xiii (1970), 706–20.

13587 ROTHWELL (VICTOR H.). 'The British Government and Japanese Military Assistance, 1914–1918'. *Hist.* lvi (1971), 35–45.

13588 KLEIN (IRA D.). 'Whitehall, Washington and the Anglo-Japanese Alliance, 1919–1921'. *Pac. Hist. Rev.* 41 (1972), 460–83.

13589 SMITH (DENNIS). 'The Royal Navy and Japan in the Aftermath of the Washington Conference, 1922–1926'. *Procs. Brit. Assoc. Jap. Studs* 3 (1978), 69–86.

13590 McKERCHER (B. J. C.). 'A Sane and Sensible Diplomacy: Austen Chamberlain, Japan and the Naval Balance of Power in the Pacific Ocean, 1924–1929'. *Can. J. Hist.* 21 (1986), 187–213.

13591 KENNEDY (MALCOLM DUNCAN). The Estrangement of Great Britain and Japan, 1917–1935. Manch. 1969.

13592 NISH (IAN HILL) *ed.* Anglo-Japanese Alienation, 1919–52: Papers of the Anglo-Japanese Conference on the History of the Second World War. Camb. 1982.

13593 THORNE (CHRISTOPHER GUY). The Limits of Foreign Policy: The West, the League and the Manchurian Crisis, 1931–1933. 1972.

13594 —— 'The Shanghai Crisis of 1932: The Basis of British Policy'. *Amer. Hist. Rev.* 75 (1970), 1616–39.

13595 BASSETT (REGINALD). Democracy and Foreign Policy: A Case History, the Sino-Japanese Dispute, 1931–1933. 1952.

13596 MacCORDOCK (R. STANLEY). British Far Eastern Policy. N.Y. 1931.

13597 LYTTON *Lord*. 'The Problem of Manchuria'. *Inl Affs* 11 (1932), 737–56.

13598 —— The League, the Far East and Ourselves. 1934.

13599 HECHT (ROBERT A.). 'Great Britain and the Stimson Note of January 7, 1932'. *Pac. Hist. Rev.* xxxviii (1969), 177–91.

13600 TROTTER (ANN). 'Tentative Steps for an Anglo-Japanese Rapprochement in 1934'. *Mod. Asian Studs* viii (1974), 59–83.

13601 ROTHWELL (VICTOR H.). 'The Mission of Sir Frederick Leith-Ross to the Far East, 1935–1936'. *Hist. J.* xviii (1975), 147–69.

13602 HAGGIE (PAUL). Britannia at Bay: The Defence of the British Empire against Japan 1931–1941. Oxf. 1981.

13603 OLU AGBI (S.). 'The British Foreign Office and the Roosevelt–Hugessen Bid to Stabilise Asia and the Pacific in 1937'. *Austral. J. Pol. Hist.* 26 (1980), 85–95.

13604 —— 'The Foreign Office and Yoshida's Bid for Rapprochement with Britain in 1936–1937: A Critical Reconsideration of the Anglo–Japanese Conversations'. *Hist. J.* 21 (1978), 173–9.

13605 LEE (BRADFORD A.). Britain and the Sino-Japanese War, 1937–1939. 1973.

13606 LOWE (PETER). Great Britain and the Origins of the Pacific War. 1977.

13607 —— 'Great Britain and the Coming of the Pacific War, 1939–1941'. *Trans. Roy. Hist. Soc.* xxiv (1974), 43–62

13608 —— 'The Dilemmas of an Ambassador: Sir Robert Craigie in Tokyo, 1937–1941'. *Procs Brit. Assoc. Jap. Studs* 2 (1977), 34–56.

13609 SHAI (ARON). Origins of the War in the East: Britain, China and Japan, 1937–1939. 1976.

13610 PRITCHARD (R. JOHN). 'The Far East as an Influence on the Chamberlain Government's Pre-War European Policies'. *Millennium* ii (1974), 7–23.

13611 TABOULET (GEORGES). 'La France et l'Angleterre Face au Conflit Sino-Japonais, 1937–1939'. *Rev. d'Hist. Dipl.* 88 (1974), 112–44.

13612 MEGAW (M. R.). 'The Scramble for the Pacific: Anglo-United States Rivalry in the 1930s'. *Hist. Studs* 17 (1977), 458–73.

13613 THORNE (CHRISTOPHER GUY). 'Chatham House, Whitehall and Far Eastern Issues: 1941–1945'. *Inl Affs* liv (1978), 1–29.

13614 BUCKLEY (ROGER). 'Britain and the Emperor: The Foreign Office and Constitutional Reform in Japan, 1945–1946'. *Mod. Asian Studs* xii (1978), 553–71.

13615 —— Occupation Diplomacy: Britain, the United States and Japan, 1945–1952. Camb. 1982.

13616 —— 'Joining the Club: The Japanese Question and Anglo-American Peace Diplomacy 1950–1951'. *Mod. Asian Studs* 19 (1985), 299–319.

13617 SCHONBERGER (H.). 'Peacemaking in Asia: the United States, Great Britain, and the Japanese Decision to Recognize Nationalist China, 1951–1952'. *Dipl. Hist.* 10 (1986), 59–73.

13618 CUDLIPP (R.). 'One Man's Thoughts on Anglo-Japanese Relations'. *Pac. Community* 1 (1970), 651–63.

13619 FITZSIMONS (M. A.). 'British Foreign Policy and Southern and Far Eastern Asia'. *Rev. Pol.* xxiv (1962), 109–42.

13620 BRACKMAN (ARNOLD C.). The Other Nuremberg: The Untold Story of the Tokyo War Crimes Trials. 1989.

(c) China

13621 PRATT (*Sir* JOHN T.). China and Britain. 1944.

13622 LUARD (DAVID EVAN TRANT). Britain and China. 1962.

13623 DEAN (BRITTEN). 'British Informal Empire: The Case of China'. *J. Cwealth Comp. Pol.* xiv (1976).

13624 GOWEN (ROBERT JOSEPH). 'Great Britain and the Twenty One Demands of 1915: Co-operation Versus Effacement'. *J. Mod. Hist.* xliii (1971), 76–106.

13625 MEGGINSON (WILLIAM JAMES). Britain's Response to Chinese Nationalism, 1925–1927: The Foreign Office Search for a New Policy. 1973.

13626 WANG (C.). Endphase des britischen Kolonialismus in China. Eine Untersuchung zur Rolle der Offentlichen Meinung in Grossbritannien als Reaktion und Einfluss Grosse Britischer Aussenpolitik Gegenüber China während der Nationalen Revolution, 1922–1928. Frankfurt a. M. 1982.

13627 CLIFFORD (NICHOLAS ROWLAND). Retreat from China. 1967.

13628 FRIEDMAN (IRVINE SIGMUND). British Relations with China: 1931–1939. N.Y. 1940.

13629 ENDICOTT (STEPHEN LYON). Diplomacy and Enterprise: British China Policy, 1933–1937. 1975.

13630 OSTERHAMMEL (J.). Britischer Imperialismus im Fernen Osten: Strukturen der Durchdringung und einheimischer Widerstand auf dem Chinesischen Markt, 1932–1937. Bochum. 1983.

13631 SHAI (ARON). Britain and China, 1941–1947: Imperial Momentum. 1984.

13632 PORTER (BRIAN ERNEST). Britain and the Rise of Communist China: A Study of British Attitudes, 1945–1954. 1967.

13633 OVENDALE (RITCHIE). 'Britain, the United States and the Recognition of Communist China'. *Hist. J.* 26 (1983), 139–58.

13634 WOLF (DAVID C.). 'To Secure a Convenience: Britain Recognises China 1950'. *J. Contemp. Hist.* 18 2 (April 1983), 299–326.

13635 BARBER (NOEL). The Fall of Shanghai: The Communist Takeover in 1949. 1979.

13636 MITCHELL (G. E.). 'China and Britain: Their Commercial and Industrial Relations'. *J. Roy. Central Asian Soc.* 49 (1952), 246–58.

13637 BOARDMAN (ROBERT). Britain and the People's Republic of China, 1949–1974. 1976.

13638 MARTIN (EDWIN W.). Divided Counsel: The Anglo-American Response to Communist Victory in China. Lexington, Kentucky. 1986.

13639 JAIN (JAGDISH PRASAD). China in World Politics: A Study of Sino-British Relations, 1949–1975. 1977.

13640 WESLEY-SMITH (PETER). Unequal Treaty, 1897–1997: China, Great Britain and Hong Kong's New Territories. 1980.

13641 SHAI (ARON). 'Britain, China and the End of Empire'. *J. Contemp. Hist.* 15 (1980), 287–97.

13642 —— 'Imperialism Imprisoned: The Closure of British Firms in the People's Republic of China'. *Eng. Hist. Rev.* civ (1989), 88–109.

8. POLICY TOWARDS GERMANY IN THE 1920S

13643 NICOLSON (*Sir* HAROLD GEORGE). Curzon: The Last Phase, 1919–1925: A Study in Post-War Diplomacy. 1934.

13644 MARKS (SALLY). The Illusion of Peace: International Relations in Europe, 1918–1973. 1975. N.Y. 1976.

13645 ORDE (ANNE W.). Great Britain and International Security, 1920–1926. 1978.

13646 CARSTEN (FRANCIS L.). Britain and the Weimar Republic: The British Documents. 1984.

13647 ZWEHL (KONRAD von). Die Deutschlandpolitik Englands von 1922–1924. Augsburg. 1974.

13648 WILLIAMSON (D. G.). 'Cologne and the British'. *Hist. Today* xxvii (1977), 695–702.

13649 SHARP (A.). 'Britain and the Channel Tunnel, 1919–1920'. *Austral. J. Pol. Hist.* 25 (1979), 210–15.

13650 FINK (CAROLE). The Genoa Conference: European Diplomacy 1921–1922. Chapel Hill, NC and London. 1984.

13651 WHITE (STEPHEN LEONARD). The Origins of Detente: The Genoa Conference and Soviet-Western Relations, 1921–1922. Camb. 1985.

13652 CASSELS (ALAN). 'Repairing the Entente Cordiale and the New Diplomacy'. *Hist. J.* 23 (1980), 233–45.

13653 FOX (JOHN P.). 'Britain and the Inter-Allied Military Commission of Control'. *J. Contemp. Hist.* iv (1969), 143–64.

13654 DOHRMANN (BERND). Die Englische Europapolitik in der Wirtschaftskrise 1921–1923. Zur Interdependenz von Wirtschaftsinteressen und Aussenpolitik. Munich. 1980.

13655 JACOBSON (JON). Locarno Diplomacy: Germany and the West 1925–1929. Princeton, NJ. 1972.

13656 BERBER (FRITZ J.) *ed.* Locarno: A Collection of Documents. 1936.

13657 JOHNSON (DOUGLAS W. J.). 'Austen Chamberlain and the Locarno Agreements'. *Univ. Birm. Hist. J.* viii (1961), 62–81.

13658 CROWE (SYBIL EYRE). 'Sir Eyre Crowe and the Locarno Pact'. *Eng. Hist. Rev.* lxxxvii (1972), 49–74.

13659 URBANITSCH (PETER). Grossbritannien und die Verträge von Locarno. Vienna. 1968.

13660 STEED (HENRY WICKHAM). 'Locarno and British Interests'. *J. Brit. Inst. Inl Affs* 4 (1925), 286–99.

13661 DENT (PHILIP). 'The d'Abernon Papers: Origins of "Appeasement"'. *Brit. Mus. Q.* xxxvii (1973), 103–7.

13662 RECKER (M. L.). England und der Donauraum 1919–1929. Stuttgart. 1976.

9. POLICY TOWARDS GERMANY IN THE 1930S

13663 NEWMAN (MICHAEL). 'Britain and the German-Austrian Customs Union Proposal of 1931'. *Eur. Studs Rev.* 6 (1976), 449–72.

13664 WATT (DONALD CAMERON). 'The Anglo-German Naval Agreement of 1935: An Interim Judgement'. *J. Mod. Hist.* 28 (1956), 155–75.

13665 OLLA (PAOLA BRUNDO). Le Origini Diplomatiche Dell'acordo Navale Anglo-Tedesco del Giugno 1935. Milan. 1974.

13666 HARASZTI (EVA H.). Treaty-Breakers or 'Realpolitiker': The Anglo-German Naval Agreement of June 1935. Boppard/R. 1974.

13667 DULFFER (JOST). 'Das Deutsch-Englische Flottenabkommen vom 18 Juni 1935'. *Marine-Rundschau* 69 (1972), 641–59.

13668 HALL (HINES H.). 'The Foreign Policy-Making Process in Britain, 1934–1935 and the Origins of the Anglo-German Naval Agreement'. *Hist. J.* 19 (1976), 477–99.

13669 HILL (C. J.). 'Great Britain and the Saar Plebiscite of 13 January 1935'. *J. Contemp. Hist.* ix (1974), 121–42.

13670 TROTTER (A.). 'MacDonald in Geneva in March 1933: A Study in Britain's European Policy'. *Scand. Hist. J.* 1 (1976), 293–312.

13671 EMMERSON (JAMES THOMAS). The Rhineland Crisis, 7 March 1936: A Study in Multilateral Diplomacy. 1977.

13672 HARASZTI (EVA H.). The Invaders: Hitler Occupies the Rhineland. Budapest. 1983.

13673 MEYERS (REINHARD). 'Sicherheit und Gleichgewicht: Das britische Kabinett und die Remilitarisierung des Rheinlandes 1936'. *Rheinische Vierteljahresblätter* 38 (1974), 406–49.

13674 GRANZOW (BRIGITTE). A Mirror of Nazism: British Opinion and the Emergence of Hitler, 1929–1933. 1964.

13675 GANNON (FRANKLIN REID). The British Press and Germany, 1936–1939. Oxf. 1971.

13676 GOLDMAN (AARON). 'Stephen King-Hall and the German Newsletter Controversy of 1939'. *Can. J. Hist.* x (1975), 209–29.

13677 MORRIS (A. J. ANTHONY). 'The Birmingham Post and Anglo-German Relations, 1933–1935'. *Univ. Birm. Hist. J.* xi (1969).

13678 LEVENTHAL (F. M.). 'Towards Revision and Reconciliation: H. N. Brailsford and Germany, 1914–1939'. In 'Essays in Labour History, 1918–1939' by Asa Briggs and John Saville. 1977. 163–89.

13679 BARNES (JAMES J.) *and* BARNES (PATRICIA P.). Hitler's *Mein Kampf* in Britain & America: A Publishing History. Camb. 1980.

13680 POWERS (R. H.). 'Winston Churchill's Parliamentary Commentary on British Foreign Policy, 1935–1938'. *J. Mod. Hist.* xxvi (1954), 179–82.

13681 KENNEY (M. L.). 'The Role of the House of Commons in British Policy during the 1937–1938 Session'. In 'Essays in Honor of Conyers Read'. Ed. by Norton Downs. Chicago, Ill. (1953), 138–85.

13682 SYKES (CHRISTOPHER HUGH). Troubled Loyalty: A Biography of Adam von Trott zu Solz. 1968.

13683 MACDONAGH (GILES). A Good German: Adam von Trott zu Solz. 1989.

13684 YOUNG (ARTHUR PRIMROSE). The 'X' Documents: The Secret History of Foreign Office Contacts with German Resistance, 1937–1939. 1974.

13685 ASTOR (DAVID). 'Why the Revolt against Hitler Was Ignored: On the British Reluctance to Deal with German Anti-Nazis'. *Encounter* xxxii (1969), 3–13.

13686 SCHMIDT (GUSTAV). England in der Krise. Grundzüge und Grundlagen der britischen Appeasement-Politik (1930–1937). Opladen. 1981.

13687 MACDONALD (CALLUM A.). 'Economic Appeasement and the German 'Moderates' 1937–1939: An Introductory Essay'. *Past and Present* lvi (1972), 105–35.

13688 FORBES (NEIL). 'London Banks, the German Standstill Agreements, and "Economic Appeasement" in the 1930s'. *Econ. Hist. Rev.* 2nd ser. 40 (1987), 571–87.

13689 WINKEL (H.). 'Boykott und Gegenboykott: zu den deutsch-englischen Handelsbeziehungen im Jahre 1933'.: R.A.C. Parker. 'Dr Schacht und die Briten: Auswirkungen von Schachts Paris-Reise im August 1936'. In 'Preussen, Deutschland und der Westen'. *Ed.* by H. Bodensieck. Göttingen. 1980.

13690 ZILLIACUS (KONNI). Inquest on Peace: An Analysis of the National Government's Foreign Policy. 1935.

13691 KENNEDY (AUBREY LEO). Britain Faces Germany. 1936.

13692 HILLSON (NORMAN). I speak of Germany: A Plea for Anglo-German Friendship. 1937.

13693 SCANLON (JOHN). Very Foreign Affairs. 1938.

13694 LENTIN (ANTHONY). Lloyd George, Woodrow Wilson and the Guilt of Germany: An Essay in the Pre-History of Appeasement. Leicester. 1984.

13695 HENKE (JOSEF). England in Hitlers Politischem Kalkül, 1935–1939. Boppard/R. 1973.

13696 COWLING (MAURICE JOHN). The Impact of Hitler. Camb. 1975.

13697 HAUSER (OSWALD). England und das Dritte Reich: Eine Dokumentierte Geschichte der English-Deutschen Beziehungen von 1933 bis 1939 auf Grund Unveröffentlicher Akten aus dem britischen Staatsarchiv. 2 vols Stuttgart. 1972–82.

13698 SETON-WATSON (ROBERT WILLIAM). Britain and the Dictators: A Survey of Post-War British Policy. Camb. 1938.

13699 NAMIER (*Sir* LEWIS BERNSTEIN). In the Margin of History. 1939: Conflicts: Studies in Contemporary History. 1942: Diplomatic Prelude, 1938–1939. 1948: Europe in Decay: A Study in Disintegration, 1936–1940. 1950: In the Nazi Era. 1952: Personalities and Powers. 1955.

13700 GILBERT (MARTIN JOHN). Britain and Germany Between the Wars. 1964.

13701 COLVIN (IAN DUNCAN). The Chamberlain Cabinet: How the Meetings in 10 Downing Street, 1937–1939, led to the Second World War. 1971.

13702 MIDDLEMAS (ROBERT KEITH). Diplomacy of Illusion: The British Government and Germany, 1937–1939. 1972.

13703 MEDLICOTT (WILLIAM NORTON). Britain and Germany: The Search for Agreement, 1930–1937. 1969.

13704 GEORGE (MARGARET). The Hollow Men: An Examination of British Foreign Policy between the Years 1933 and 1939. 1967.

13705 EINZIG (PAUL). Appeasement before, during and after the War. 1941.

13706 NAGLE (THOMAS WHEELER). A Study of British Public Opinion and the European Appeasement Policy, 1933–1939. Wiesbaden. 1957.

13707 FURNIA (ARTHUR HOMER). The Diplomacy of Appeasement: Anglo-French Relations and the Prelude to World War II, 1931–1938. Washington, DC. 1960.

13708 ROWSE (ALFRED LESLIE). All Souls and Appeasement. 1961.

13709 GILBERT (MARTIN JOHN) *and* GOTT (RICHARD WILLOUGHBY). The Appeasers. 1963.

13710 ROWSE (ALFED LESLIE). Appeasement: A Study in Political Decline, 1933–1934. 1963.

13711 WATT (DONALD CAMERON). 'Appeasement: The Rise of a Revisionist School?'. *Pol. Q.* xxxvi (1965), 191–213.

13712 GILBERT (MARTIN JOHN). The Roots of Appeasement. 1966.

13713 ROCK (WILLIAM RAY). Appeasement on Trial: British Foreign Policy and its Critics, 1938–1939. Hamden, Conn. 1966.

13714 ROCK (WILLIAM RAY). British Appeasement in the 1930s. 1977.

13715 ROBBINS (KEITH GILBERT). 'Appeasement: New Tasks for the Historian'. *Inl Affs.* xlviii (1972), 625–30.

13716 ROBBINS (KEITH GILBERT). Appeasement. Oxf. 1988.

13717 DILKS (DAVID N.). 'Appeasement Revisited'. *Univ. Leeds Rev.* xv (1972), 28–56.

13718 —— ' "We Must Hope for the Best and Prepare for the Worst": The Prime Minister, the Cabinet and Hitler's Germany, 1937–1939'. *Proc. Brit. Acad.* lxxiii (1987), 309–52.

13719 THOMPSON (NEVILLE). The Anti-Appeasers: Conservative Opposition to Appeasement in the Thirties. Oxf. 1971.

13720 OVENDALE (RITCHIE). Appeasement and the English-Speaking World: Britain, the United States, the Dominions and the Policy of 'Appeasement'. 1937–1939. Cardiff. 1975.

13721 CROZIER (ANDREW JOSEPH). Appeasement and Germany's Last Bid for Colonies. 1988.

13722 MOMMSEN (WOLFGANG J.) *and* KETTENACKER (LOTHAR) *eds.* The Fascist Challenge and the Policy of Appeasement. 1983.

13723 HAUSER (OSWALD). 'The year 1937: The Decisive Turning-Point in British-German Relations'. *Hist. Studs* x (1976), 132–46.

13724 SCHWOERER (LOUIS G.). 'Lord Halifax's Visit to Germany, November 1937'. *The Historian* xxxii (1970), 353–75.

13725 ORDE (ANNE W.). 'Grossbritannien und die Selbständigkeit Österreichs 1918–1938'. *Vierteljahreshefte für Zeitgeschichte* 28 (1980), 224–47.

13726 WEINBERG (GERHARD L.). 'The May Crisis, 1938'. *J. Mod. Hist.* xxix (1957), 213–25.

13727 WALLACE (WILLIAM V.). 'The Making of the May Crisis of 1938'. *Slav. E. Eur. Rev.* 41 (1963), 368–90.

13728 WATT (DONALD CAMERON). 'The May Crisis of 1938: A Rejoinder to Mr Wallace'. *Slav. E. Eur. Rev.* 44 (1966), 475–80.

13729 WALLACE (WILLIAM V.). 'A Reply to Mr Watt'. *Slav. E. Eur. Rev.* 44 (1966), 480–6.

13730 FRANKE (REINER). 'Die Tschechoslowakei in der Politischen Meinung Englands, 1918–1938'. In 'Die demokratisch-parlamentarische Struktur der ersten Tschechoslowakischen Republik'. *Ed.* by Karl Bosl. Munich. 1975.

13731 BRUEGEL (JOHANN WOLFGANG). Czechoslovakia Before Munich; The German Minority Problem and British Appeasement Policy. Camb. 1973.

13732 —— Tschechen und Deutsche 1918–1938. Munich. 1967.

13733 —— 'Der Runciman Bericht'. *Vierteljahreshefte für Zeitgeschichte* 26 (1978), 652–9.

13734 AULACH (HARINDAR). 'Britain and the Sudeten Issue, 1938: The Evolution of a Policy'. *J. Contemp. Hist.* 18 (1983), 233–59.

13735 —— 'The British View of the Czechs in the Era before the Munich Crisis'. *Slav. E. Eur. Rev.* 57 (1979), 56–70.

13736 CROZIER (ANDREW JOSEPH). 'Prelude to Munich: British Foreign Policy and Germany, 1935–1938'. *Eur. Studs Rev.* 6 (1976), 357–81.

13737 HADLEY (WILLIAM WAITE). Munich: Before and After. 1944.

13738 WHEELER-BENNETT (*Sir* JOHN WHEELER). Munich: Prologue to Tragedy. 1948.

13739 ROTHSTEIN (ANDREW). The Munich Conspiracy. 1958.

13740 EUBANK (WEAVER KEITH). Munich. Oklahoma. 1963.

13741 LAMMERS (DONALD NED). Explaining Munich: The Search for Motive in British Policy. Stanford, Calif. 1966.

13742 ROBBINS (KEITH GILBERT). Munich 1938. 1968.

13743 —— 'Konrad Henlein, the Sudeten Question and British Foreign Policy'. *Hist. J.* xii (1969), 674–97.

13744 MURRAY (WILLIAMSON). 'Munich 1938: The Military Confrontation'. *J. Strat. Studs* 2 (1979), 282–302.

13745 NEWMAN (MICHAEL). 'The Origins of Munich: British Policy in Danubian Europe, 1933–1937'. *Hist. J.* 21 (1978), 371–86.

13746 TAYLOR (TELFORD). Munich: The Price of Peace. 1979.

13747 TEICHOVA (ALICE). An Economic Background to Munich: International Business and Czechoslovakia, 1918–1938. Camb. 1974.

13748 BRUCE (MAURICE). British Foreign Policy: Isolation or Intervention? 1938.

13749 BROOKS (COLLIN). Can Chamberlain Save Britain?: The Lesson of Munich. 1938.

13750 SETON-WATSON (ROBERT WILLIAM). After Munich. 1939.

13751 FITZSIMONS (MATTHEW A.). 'The Masque of Uncertainty: Britain and Munich'. *Rev. Pol.* xii (1950), 489–505.

13752 WEBSTER (*Sir* CHARLES KINGSLEY). 'Munich Reconsidered: A Survey of British Policy'. *Inl Affs.* xxxvii (1961), 137–53.

13753 SCHROEDER (P. W.). 'Munich and the British Tradition'. *Hist. J.* xix (1976), 223–43.

13754 HARASZTI (EVA H.). 'Three Documents Concerning Great Britain's Policy in East-Central Europe in the Period After the Munich Agreement'. *Acta Hist. Acad. Sci. Hung.* xxii (1976), 139–75.

13755 LAMMERS (DONALD NED). 'From Whitehall after Munich: The Foreign Office and the Future Course of British Policy'. *Hist. J.* xvi (1973), 831–56.

13756 DOUGLAS (ROY). In the Year of Munich. 1977.

13757 ZILLIACUS (KONNI). Why We are Losing the Peace: The National Government's Foreign Policy. 1939.

13758 BLYTON (WILLIAM JOSEPH). Anglo-German Future. 1939.

13759 SALTER (JAMES ARTHUR) *Baron Salter*. Security: Can We Retrieve it? 1939.

13760 KEANE (RICHARD). Germany—what Next? An Examination of the German Menace in so far as it Affects Great Britain. 1939.

13761 KENNEDY (JOHN FITZGERALD). Why England Slept. 1940.

13762 KETTENACKER (LOTHAR). 'Die Diplomatie der Ohnmacht: Die gescheiterte Friedensstrategie in der britischen Regierung vor Ausbruch des zweiten Weltkrieges'. In Sommer 1939: Die Grossmächte und der Europäische Krieg. *Ed.* by Wolfgang Benz and Hermann Graml. Stuttgart. 1979.

13763 WATT (DONALD CAMERON). 'Anglo-German Naval Negotiations on the Eve of the Second World War'. *J. Roy. Unit. Serv. Inst.* (May and August 1958), 201–7, 384–91.

13764 —— How War Came: The Immediate Origins of the Second World War 1938–1939. 1989.

13765 THORNE (CHRISTOPHER GUY). The Approach of War, 1938–1939. 1967.

13766 FLEMING (NICHOLAS). August 1939: The Last Days of Peace. 1979.

13767 DOUGLAS (ROY). The Advent of War, 1939–1940. 1978.

13768 —— Ed. 1939: A Retrospect Forty Years After. 1983.

13769 ASTER (SIDNEY). 1939: The Making of the Second World War. 1973.

13770 TAYLOR (ALAN JOHN PERCIVALE). The Origins of the Second World War. 1961. Rev. edn 1963.

13771 MARTEL (GORDON) ed. The Origins of the Second World War Reconsidered: The A. J. P. Taylor Debate After Twenty-Five Years. 1986.

13772 ROBERTSON (ESMONDE MANNING) ed. The Origins of the Second World War. 1971.

13773 PARKINSON (ROGER). Peace for our Time: Munich to Dunkirk, the Inside Story. 1971.

10. POLICY TOWARDS ITALY 1920–1939

13774 BOSWORTH (RICHARD J. B.). 'The British Press, the Conservatives and Mussolini, 1920–1934'. *J. Contemp. Hist.* v (1970), 163–82.

13775 EDWARDS (PETER G.). 'The Foreign Office and Fascism, 1914–1929'. *J. Contemp. Hist.* v (1970), 153–61.

13776 —— 'The Austen Chamberlain–Mussolini Meetings'. *Hist. J.* xiv (1971), 153–64.

13777 —— 'Britain, Fascist Italy and Ethiopia, 1925–1928'. *Eur. Studs Rev.* iv (1974), 359–74.

13778 —— 'Britain, Mussolini and the "Locarno–Geneva" System'. *Eur. Studs Rev.* 10 (1980), 1–16.

13779 ROBERTSON (JAMES C.). 'British Policy in East Africa, March 1891 to May 1935'. *Eng. Hist. Rev.* xciii (1978).

13780 —— 'The Origins of British Opposition to Mussolini over Ethiopia'. *J. Brit. Studs* ix (1969), 122–42.

13781 ROWAN-ROBINSON (HENRY). England, Italy, Abyssinia. 1935.

13782 HARDIE (FRANK). The Abyssinian Crisis. 1974.

13783 BARROS (JAMES). Britain, Greece and the Politics of Sanctions: Ethiopia, 1935–36. 1982.

13784 WALEY (DANIEL P.). British Public Opinion and the Abyssinian War, 1935–1936. 1975.

13785 GOLDMAN (AARON). 'Sir Robert Vansittart's Search for Italian Co-operation Against Hitler, 1933–1936'. *J. Contemp. Hist.* ix (1974), 93–130.

13786 TOSCANO (MARIO). 'Eden's Mission to Rome on the Eve of the Italo-Ethiopian Conflict'. In 'Studies in Diplomatic History and Historiography in Honour of G. P. Gooch'. *Ed.* by A. O. Sarkissian. 1961. 126–52.

13787 CARLTON (DAVID). 'The Dominions and British Policy in the Abyssinian crisis'. *J. Imp. Cwealth Hist.* i (1972), 59–77.

13788 ROBERTSON (JAMES C.). 'The Hoare-Laval Plan'. *J. Contemp. Hist.* x (1975), 433–64.

13789 PRESSEISEN (ERNST L.). 'Foreign Policy and British Public Opinion: The Hoare-Laval Pact of 1935'. *World Affs Q.* xxix (1958), 256–77.

13790 PARKER (R. A. C.). 'Great Britain, France and the Ethiopian Crisis 1935–1936'. *Eng. Hist. Rev.* lxxxix (1974), 293–332.

13791 POST (GAINES). 'The Machinery of British Policy in the Ethiopian Crisis'. *Inl Hist. Rev.* 1 (1979), 522–41.

13792 MARDER (ARTHUR J.). 'The Royal Navy and the Ethiopian Crisis of 1935–1936'. *Amer. Hist. Rev.* 75 (1970), 1327–50.

13793 QUARTARARO (ROSARIA). 'Imperial Defence in the Mediterranean on the Eve of the Ethiopian Crisis'. *Hist. J.* 20 (1977), 185–220.

13794 STAFFORD (PAUL). 'The Chamberlain–Halifax Visit to Rome: A Reappraisal'. *Eng. Hist. Rev.* 98 (1983), 81–100.

13795 GRETTON (PETER). 'The Nyon Conference: The Naval Aspect'. *Eng. Hist. Rev.* xc (1975), 103–12.

11. POLICY TOWARDS THE MIDDLE EAST

General

13796 HUREWITZ (JACOB COLEMAN). Diplomacy in the Near and Middle East: A Documentary Record, 1535–1956. 2 vols Princeton, NJ. 1956.

13797 FRASER (THOMAS G.) *ed.* The Middle East 1914–1979. 1980. [Documents.].

13798 OLSON (WILLIAM JOSEPH). Britain's Elusive Empire in the Middle East, 1900–1921: An Annotated Bibliography. N.Y. 1982.

13799 ANDERSON (MATTHEW SMITH). The Eastern Question, 1774–1923: A Study in International Relations. 1966.

13800 BULLARD (*Sir* READER WILLIAM). Britain and the Middle East from Earliest Times. 2nd edn 1964.

13801 FITZSIMONS (MATTHEW ANTHONY). Empire by Treaty: Britain and the Middle East in the Twentieth Century. 1965.

13802 MARLOWE (JOHN). Arab Nationalism and British Imperialism: A Study in Power Politics. 1961.

13803 MONROE (ELIZABETH). Britain's Moment in the Middle East, 1914–1956. 1963. 2nd edn 1981.

13804 LOUIS (WILLIAM ROGER). The British Empire in the Middle East 1945–1951: Arab Nationalism, the United States and Postwar Imperialism. 1985.

13805 SEARIGHT (SARAH). The British in the Middle East. 1969.

13806 STORRS (*Sir* RONALD HENRY AMHERST). Great Britain in the Near and Middle East. Nottingham. 1932.

13807 HOURANI (ALBERT H.). Britain and the Arab World. 1945.

13808 SETON-WILLIAMS (M. V.). Britain and the Arab States: A Survey of Anglo-Arab Relations, 1920–1948. 1948.

13809 GLUBB (*Sir* JOHN BAGOT). Britain and the Arabs: A Study of Fifty Years, 1908–1958. 1959.

13810 LUNT (J.). Glubb Pasha. 1984.

13811 RUBIN (B.). The Great Powers in the Middle East: The Road to the Cold War. 1980.

13812 LESLIE (*Sir* JOHN RANDOLPH SHANE). Mark Sykes: His Life and Letters. 1923.

13813 RIDLEY (MAURICE ROY). Gertrude Bell. 1941.

13814 WINSTONE (H. V. F.). Gertrude Bell. 1978.

13815 LAWRENCE (THOMAS EDWARD). Seven Pillars of Wisdom: A Triumph. 1925.

13816 LIDDELL HART (*Sir* BASIL HENRY). 'T. E. Lawrence': In Arabia and After. 1934.

13817 REID (BRIAN HOLDEN). 'T. E. Lawrence and Liddell Hart'. *Hist.* 70 (1985), 218–31.

13818 ALDINGTON (RICHARD). Lawrence of Arabia: A Biographical Enquiry. 1955.

13819 KNIGHTLEY (PHILLIP) *and* SIMPSON (COLIN). The Secret Lives of Lawrence of Arabia. 1969.

13820 BRENT (PETER). T. E. Lawrence. 1975.

13821 HELLER (JOSEPH). British Policy towards the Ottoman Empire, 1908–1914. 1983.

13822 KEDOURIE (ELIE). England and the Middle East: The Destruction of the Ottoman Empire, 1914–1921. 1956. 2nd edn Hassocks. 1978.

13823 SMITH (KENNETH B.). A Geopolitical Survey of British Policy in the Arab Lands of the Middle East, 1869–1947. Washington. 1948.

13824 BUSTANI (EMILE). 'The Arab World and Britain'. *Inl Affs* (1959), 427–37.

13825 TOYNBEE (ARNOLD JOSEPH). 'Britain and the Arabs: The Need for a New Start'. *Inl Affs* xl (1964), 638–46.

13826 BARBOUR (NEVILL). 'England and the Arabs'. *Roy. J. Cent. Asian Soc.* ii (1965), 102–15.

13827 KELLY (JOHN BARRETT). Arabia, the Gulf and the West. 1980.

13828 BUSCH (BRITON COOPER). Britain, India and the Arabs, 1914–1921. Berkeley, Calif. 1971.

13829 KLIEMAN (AARON S.). Foundations of British Policy in the Arab World: The Cairo Conference of 1921. 1970.

13830 DARWIN (JOHN G.). Britain, Egypt and the Middle East: Imperial Policy in the Aftermath of War, 1918–1922. 1981.

13831 CUMMING (HENRY HARFORD). Franco-British Rivalry in the Post-War Near East. 1938.

13832 NEVAKIVI (JUKKA). Britain, France and the Arab Middle East, 1914–1920. 1969.

13833 WILLIAMS (ANN). Britain and France in the Middle East and North Africa, 1914–1967. 1968.

Ottoman Empire/Turkey

13834 MEJCHER (HELMUT). 'British Middle East Policy 1917–1921: The Inter-Departmental Level'. *J. Contemp. Hist.* viii (1973), 81–101.

13835 MACFIE (A. L.). 'The British Decision Regarding the Future of Constantinople (November 1918–January 1920)'. *Hist. J.* 18 (1975), 391–400.

13836 WALDER (ALAN DAVID). The Chanak Affair. 1969.

13837 DARWIN (JOHN G.). 'The Chanak Crisis and the British Cabinet'. *Hist.* 65 (1980), 32–48.

13838 CAREW (KARL G.). 'Great Britain and the Greco-Turkish War, 1921–1922'. *Historian* 35 (1973), 256–70.

13839 MONTGOMERY (A. E.). 'Lloyd George and the Greek question, 1918–1922'. In 'Lloyd George: Twelve Essays'. *Ed.* by Alan Taylor. 1971.

13840 FINEFROCK (MICHAEL M.). 'Ataturk, Lloyd George, and the Megali Idea: Cause and Consequence of the Greek Plan to Seize Constantinople from the Allies, June–August 1922'. *J. Mod. Hist.* 52 (1980), D.1047.

13841 EVANS (STEPHEN F.). The Slow Rapprochement: Britain and Turkey in the Age of Kemal Ataturk, 1919–1938. Beverley. 1982.

13842 ZHIVKOVA (LUDMILA). Anglo-Turkish Relations, 1933–1939. 1976.

13843 HALE (W.) *and* BAGIS (A. I.) *eds.* Four Centuries of Turco-British Relations: Studies in Diplomatic, Economic and Cultural Affairs. Beverley. 1984.

13844 WEBER (F. G.). The Evasive Neutral: Germany, Britain and the Quest for a Turkish Alliance in the Second World War. 1979.

The Armenian Question

13845 NASSIBIAN (AKABY). Britain and the Armenian Question, 1915–1923. 1984.

13846 ARSLANIAN (ARTIN H.). 'British Wartime Pledges, 1917–1918: The Armenian Case'. *J. Contemp. Hist.* xiii (1978), 517–30.

13847 OKE (MIM KEMAL). The Armenian Question, 1914–1923. Nicosia. 1988.

Afghanistan

13848 ADAMEC (LUDWIG). Afghanistan's Foreign Affairs to the Mid-Twentieth century: Relations with the USSR, Germany and Britain. Tucson, Ariz. 1974.

Turkestan

13849 MORRIS (L. P.). 'British Secret Missions in Turkestan, 1918–1919'. *J. Contemp. Hist.* xii (1977), 363–79.

Persia/Iran

13850 NAVABPOUR (REZA). Iran. Oxf. 1900.

13851 WRIGHT (*Sir* DENIS). The English amongst the Persians during the Qajar Period, 1787–1921. 1977.

13852 AHMAD (ISHTIAR). Anglo-Iranian Relations 1905–1919. Bombay. 1974.

13853 OLSON (WILLIAM). Anglo-Iranian Relations during World War I. 1984.

13854 STANWOOD (F.). 'Revolution and the "Old Reactionary Policy": Britain in Persia, 1917'. *J. Imp. Cwealth Hist.* 6 (1978), 144–65.

13855 ZURRER (WERNER). Persien zwischen England und Russland 1918–1925: Grossmächteinflüsse und nationaler Wiederaufstieg am Beispiel des Iran. Berne. 1978.

13856 BECK (PETER J.). 'The Anglo-Persian Oil Dispute, 1932–1933'. *J. Contemp. Hist.* ix (1974), 123–51.

13857 CENTRAL OFFICE OF INFORMATION. Paiforce: The Official History of the Persia and Iraq Command 1941–1946. 1948.

13858 ELWELL-SUTTON (L. P.). Persian Oil: A Study in Power Politics. 1955.

13859 AZIMI (FAKHREDDIN). Iran: The Crisis of Democracy 1941–1953. 1988.

13860 SHWADRAN (BENJAMIN). 'The Anglo-Iranian Oil Dispute 1948–53'. *Middle East. Affs* 5 (1954), 193–231.

13861 LOUIS (WILLIAM ROGER) *and* BILL (JAMES A.) *eds.* Mussaddiq, Iranian Nationalism and Oil. 1988.

13862 FORD (A. W.). The Anglo-Iranian Oil Dispute of 1951–1952: A Study of the Rule of Law in the Relations of States. Camb. 1954.

Aden

13863 SMITH (G. REX). The Yemens. Oxf. 1984.

13864 BIDWELL (ROBIN). The Two Yemens. 1983.

13865 LEDGER (DAVID). Shifting Sands: The British in South Arabia. 1983.

13866 MONROE (ELIZABETH). 'Kuwait and Aden: A Contrast in British Policies'. *Mid. East J.* xviii (1964), 63–74.

13867 SICHERMAN (HARVEY). Aden and British Strategy, 1839–1968. Philadelphia, PA. 1972.

13868 REILLY (*Sir* BERNARD). Aden and the Yemen. 1960.

13869 HICKINBOTHAM (*Sir* TOM). Aden. 1958.

13870 KING (GILLIAN). Imperial Outpost—Aden: Its Place in British Strategic Policy. Oxf. 1964.

13871 JOHNSTON (CHARLES HEPBURN). The View from Steamer Point: Being an Account of Three Years in Aden. 1964.

13872 TREVASKIS (*Sir* KENNEDY). Shades of Amber: A South Arabian Episode. 1968.

13873 GAVIN (R. J.). Aden under British Rule 1839–1967. 1975.

13874 PAGET (JULIAN). Last Post: Aden 1964–1967. 1969.

13875 LITTLE (TOM). South Arabia: Arena of Conflict. 1968.

12. POLICY TOWARDS NORTHERN EUROPE

13876 ANDERSON (EDGAR). 'British Policy toward the Baltic States, 1918–1920'. *J. Cent. Eur. Affs* xix (1959), 276–89.

13877 HOVI (O.). The Baltic Area in British Policy, 1918–1921; Vol. I: From the Compiègne Armistice to the Implementation of the Versailles Treaty, 11. 11. 1918–20. 1. 1920. Helsinki. 1980.

13878 PAASDIVIRTA (JOHANI). The Victors in World War I and Finland: Finland's Relations with the British, French and United States Governments in 1918–1919. Helsinki. 1965.

13879 MUNCH-PETERSEN (THOMAS). 'Great Britain and the Revision of the Aland Convention, 1938–1939'. *Scandia* xli (1975), 67–86.

13880 BÉDARIDA (FRANÇOIS). 'France, Britain and the Nordic Countries'. *Scand. J. Hist.* 2 (1977), 7–27.

13881 BAYER (J. A.). 'British Policy towards the Russian-Finnish Winter War 1939–1940'. *Can. J. Hist.* 16 (1981), 27–65.

13882 PARKER (R. A. C.). 'Britain, France and Scandinavia, 1939–1940'. *Hist.* lxi (1976), 369–87.

13883 DILKS (DAVID N.). 'Great Powers and Scandinavia in the "Phoney War"'. *Scand. J. Hist.* 2 (1977), 29–51.

13884 LUDLOW (PETER WOODS). 'Britain and Northern Europe, 1940–1945'. *Scand. J. Hist.* 4 (1979), 123–62.

13885 BRANDELL (ULF). 'Sweden Versus Great Britain and the Soviet Union during the Second World War'. *Contemp. Rev.* 238 (1981), No. 1381, 63–8.

13886 BARCLAY (GLEN ST JOHN). 'Background to EFTA: An Episode in Anglo-Scandinavian Relations'. *Austral. J. Pol. Hist.* xi (1965), 185–97.

13887 ARCHER (T. C.). 'Britain and Scandinavia: Their Relations within EFTA, 1960–1968'. *Co-op. Conflict* xi (1976), 1–23.

13. POLICY TOWARDS POLAND 1919–1945

13888 DAVIES (IVOR NORMAN RICHARD). 'Sir Maurice Hankey and the Inter-Allied Mission to Poland, July–August 1920'. *Hist. J.* 15 (1972), 553–61.

13889 —— 'Lloyd George and Poland, 1919 to 1920'. *J. Contemp. Hist.* vi (1971), 132–54.

13890 ELCOCK (HOWARD J.). 'Britain and the Russo-Polish Frontier, 1919–1921'. *Hist. J.* xii (1969), 137–54.

13891 HARRINGTON (J. F.). 'The Third Polish Uprising in Upper Silesia, 1921: A Case Study in Anglo-French Relations'. *New Rev. East Eur. Hist.* xiv (1974), 78–92.

13892 GAJDA (PATRICIA A.). Postscript to Victory: British Policy and the German–Polish Borderland, 1919–1925. Washington DC, 1982.

13893 CIENCIALA (ANNA M.). Poland and the Western Powers, 1938–1939: A Study in the Interdependence of Eastern and Western Europe. 1968.

13894 PRAZMOWSKA (ANITA J.). Britain, Poland and the Eastern Front, 1939. Camb. 1987.

13895 —— 'War over Danzig? The Dilemma of Anglo-Polish Relations in the Months Preceding the Outbreak of the Second World War'. *Hist. J.* 26 (1983), 177–83.

13896 —— 'Poland's Foreign Policy: September 1938–September 1939'. *Hist. J.* 29 (1986), 853–73.

13897 —— 'The Eastern Front and the British Guarantee to Poland of March 1939'. *Eur. Hist. Q. Rev.* 14 (1984), 183–209.

13898 WILLIAMS (THOMAS DESMOND). 'Negotiations Leading to the Anglo-Polish Agreement of 31 March 1939'. *Hist. Studs* x (1956), 59–93; 156–92.

13899 ROCK (WILLIAM RAY). 'British Guarantee to Poland, March 1939: A Problem in Diplomatic Decision-Making'. *Atlantic Q.* lxv (1966), 229–40.

13900 NEWMAN (SIMON). March 1939, the British Guarantee to Poland: A Study in the Continuity of British Foreign Policy. Oxf. 1976.

13901 WEHNER (GERD). Grossbritannien und Polen 1938–1939: Die britische Polen-Politik zwischen München und dem Ausbruch des Zweiten Weltkrieges. Frankfurt a. M. 1982.

13902 UMIASTOWSKI (ROMAN). Poland, Russia and Great Britain, 1941–1945. 1946.

13903 KACEWICZ (GEORGE V.). Great Britain, the Soviet Union and the Polish Government in Exile (1939–1945). The Hague. 1979.

13904 JEDRZEJEWICZ (WACLAW) ed. Poland in the British Parliament 1939–1945. 3 vols 1946–1962.

13905 PISZCZKOWSKI (T.). Anglia a Polska 1914–1939: w swietle dokumentow Brytyskich. 1975.

13906 NUREK (M.). 'Great Britain and Poland from June 1940 to July 1941'. *Aberd. Univ. Rev.* 48 (1980), 248–58.

13907 POLONSKY (ANTONY B.). 'Polish Failure in Wartime London: Attempts to Forge a European Alliance, 1940–1944'. *Inl Hist. Rev.* 7 (1985), 576–91.

13908 RYAN (H. B.). 'Anglo-American Relations during the Polish Crisis in 1945: A Study of British Efforts to Shape American Policy toward the Soviet Union'. *Austral. J. Pol. Hist.* 30 (1984), 69–84.

14. POLICY TOWARDS THE SOVIET UNION 1917–1945

13909 COATES (WILLIAM PEYTON) *and* COATES (ZELDA K.). A History of Anglo-Soviet Relations. 2 vols 1945. 1958.

13910 KLINGENDER (F. D.). Russia—Britain's Ally, 1812–1942. 1942.

13911 MARRIOTT (*Sir* JOHN ARTHUR RANSOME). Anglo-Russian Relations, 1689–1943. 1944.

13912 MIDDLETON (KENNETH WILLIAM BRUCE). Britain and Russia: An Historical Essay. 1947.

13913 STACEY (FRANCIS WILLIAM). Britain and Russia from the Crimean to the Second World War. 1969.

13914 ARNOT (ROBERT PAGE). The Impact of the Russian Revolution in Britain. 1967.

13915 NORTHEDGE (FREDERICK SAMUEL) *and* WELLS (AUDREY). Britain and Soviet Communism: The Impact of a Revolution. 1982.

13916 HOARE (SAMUEL JOHN GURNEY) *Baron Templewood*. The Fourth Seal: The End of a Russian Chapter. 1930.

13917 GRAUBARD (STEPHEN RICHARDS). British Labour and the Russian Revolution, 1917–1924. 1956.

13918 FISCHER (LOUIS). 'British Labour and the Soviets'. *For. Affs* viii (1930), 260–73.

13919 COATES (WILLIAM PEYTON) *and* COATES (ZELDA KAHAN). Armed Intervention in Russia, 1918–1922. 1935.

13920 KLUKE (PAUL). 'Winston Churchill und die allierte Intervention im revolutionären Russland'. In 'Innen— und Aussenpolitik: Primat oder Independenz?'. By U. Altermatt *et al.* Berne/Stuttgart. 1980.

13921 KETTLE (MICHAEL). Russia and the Allies, 1917–1920. Vol. I The Allies and the Russian Collapse: March 1917–March 1918. 1979.

13922 SILVERLIGHT (JOHN). The Victor's Dilemma: Allied Intervention in the Russian Civil War. 1970.

13923 ULLMAN (RICHARD HENRY). Anglo-Soviet Relations, 1917–1921. 3 vols 1961–1972.

13924 BRADLEY (JOHN F. N.). Allied Intervention in Russia, 1917–1920. N.Y. 1968.

13925 ROTHSTEIN (ANDREW). When Britain Invaded Soviet Russia: The Consul who Rebelled. 1979.

13926 WHITE (STEPHEN LEONARD). Britain and the Bolshevik Revolution: A Study in the Politics of Diplomacy, 1920–1924. 1979.

13927 —— '"Anti-Bolshevik Control Officers" and British Foreign Policy, 1918–1920'. *Co-Existence* 13/2 (1976), 144–56.

13928 FRY (MICHAEL G.). 'Britain, the Allies and the Problem of Russia, 1918–1919'. *Can. J. Hist.* 2 (1967), 62–84.

13929 DEBO (RICHARD K.). 'Lloyd George and the Copenhagen Conference of 1919–20: The Initiation of Anglo-Soviet Negotiations'. *Hist. J.* 24 (1981), 429–41.

13930 DURHAM (M.). 'British Revolutionaries and the Suppression of the Left in Lenin's Russia, 1918–1924'. *J. Contemp. Hist.* 20 (1985), 203–19.

13931 MacFARLANE (LESLIE J.). 'Hands off Russia: British Labour and the Russo-Polish War, 1920'. *Past and Present* xxxviii (1967), 126–52.

13932 ANDREW (CHRISTOPHER M.). 'The British Secret Service and Anglo-Soviet Relations; Part 1: From the Trade Negotiations to the Zinoviev Letter'. *Hist. J.* xx (1977), 673–706.

13933 —— 'British Intelligence and the Breach with Russia in 1927'. *Hist. J.* xxv (1982), 957–64.

13934 GORODETSKY (GABRIEL). The Precarious Truce: Anglo-Soviet Relations, 1924–1927. Camb. 1977.

13935 CHESTER (LEWIS) *et al.* The Zinoviev Letter. 1967.

13936 WARTH (ROBERT D.). 'The Mystery of the Zinoviev Letter'. *S. Atlantic. Q.* xlix (195), 441–53.

13937 CROWE (SYBIL EYRE). 'The Zinoviev Letter: A Reappraisal'. *J. Contemp. Hist.* x (1975), 407–32.

13938 CARR (EDWARD HALLETT). 'The Zinoviev Letter'. *Hist. J.* 22 (1979), 209–10.

13939 ANDREW (CHRISTOPHER M.). 'More on the Zinoviev Letter'. *Hist. J.* 22 (1979), 211–14.

13940 CALHOUN (DANIEL FAIRCHILD). The United Front: The TUC and the Russians, 1923–1928. 1976.

13941 SCHINNESS (ROGER). 'The Conservative Party and Anglo-Soviet Relations, 1925–1927'. *Eur. Studs Rev.* vii (1977), 393–409.

13942 FLORY (HARRIETTE). 'The Arcos Raid and the Rupture of Anglo-Soviet Relations, 1927'. *J. Contemp. Hist.* xxii (1977), 707–23.

13943 LAMMERS (DONALD NED). British Foreign Policy, 1919–1934: The Problem of Soviet Russia. Stanford, Calif. 1960.

13944 —— 'The Second Labour Government and the Restoration of Relations with Soviet Russia (1929)'. *Bull. Inst. Hist. Res.* xxxvii (1964), 60–72.

13945 —— 'The Engineers' Trial (Moscow, 1933) and Anglo-Soviet Relations'. *S. Atlantic Q.* 62 (1963), 256–67.

13946 —— 'Britain, Russia and the Revival of Entente Diplomacy, 1934'. *J. Brit. Studs* 6 (1967), 99–123.

13947 ROCK (WILLIAM RAY). 'Grand Alliance or Daisy Chain: British Opinion and Policy towards Russia, April–August 1939'. In 'Power, Public Opinion and Diplomacy: Essays in Honor of Eber Malcolm Carroll'. *Ed.* by L. P. Wallace. Durham, NC (1959), 297–337.

13948 DELI (P.). 'The Image of the Russian Purges in the *Daily Herald* and the *New Statesman*'. *J. Contemp. Hist.* 20 (1985), 203–19.

13949 MANNE (ROBERT). 'The British Decision for Alliance with Russia, May 1939'. *J. Contemp. Hist.* ix (1974), 3–26.

13950 —— 'The Foreign Office and the Failure of Anglo-Soviet Rapprochement'. *J. Contemp. Hist.* 16 (1981), 725–55.

13951 —— 'Some British Light on the Nazi-Soviet Pact'. *Eur. Studs Rev.* 11 (1981), 83–101.

13952 NIEDHART (GOTTFRIED). Grossbritannien und die Sowjetunion 1934–1939: Studien zur britischen Politik der Friedenssicherung zwischen den beiden Weltkriegen. Munich. 1972.

13953 PANKRASHOVA (M.) *and* SIPOLS (V. Y.). Why War was not Prevented: A Documentary Review of the Soviet–British–French Talks in Moscow, 1939. Moscow. 1970.

13954 KITCHEN (MARTIN). British Policy towards the Soviet Union during the Second World War. Basingstoke. 1986.

13955 —— 'Winston Churchill and the Soviet Union during the Second World War'. *Hist. J.* 30 (1987), 415–36.

13956 ROSS (K. GRAHAM) *ed.* The Foreign Office and the Kremlin: British Documents on Anglo-Soviet Relations, 1941–1945. Camb. 1984.

13957 —— 'Foreign Office Attitudes to the Soviet Union 1941–5'. *J. Contemp. Hist.* 16 (1981), 521–40.

13958 HANAK (HARRY). 'Stafford Cripps as British Ambassador in Moscow, May 1940 to June 1941'. *Eng. Hist. Rev.* xciv (1979), 48–70.

13959 GORODETSKY (GABRIEL). Stafford Cripps' Mission to Moscow, 1940–42. Camb. 1984.

13960 —— 'The Hess Affair and Anglo-Soviet Relations on the Eve of Barbarossa'. *Eng. Hist. Rev.* 101 (1986), 405–20.

13961 —— 'Churchill's Warning to Stalin: A Reappraisal'. *Hist. J.* 29 (1986), 979–90.

13962 LANGER (J. D.). 'The Harriman-Beaverbrook Mission and the Debate Over Unconditional Aid for the Soviet Union, 1942'. *J. Contemp. Hist.* 14 (1979), 535–55.

13963 KIMBALL (WARREN F.). 'Naked Versus Right: Roosevelt, Churchill and Eastern Europe from Tolstoy to Yalta—and a Little Beyond'. *Dipl. Hist.* 9 (1985), 1–24.

13964 BEAUMONT (JOAN). Comrades in Arms: British Aid to Russia, 1941–1945. 1980.

13965 HOLDICH (PATRICK G. H.). 'A Policy of Percentages? British Policy and the Balkans After the Moscow Conference of October 1944'. *Inl Hist. Rev.* 9 (1987), 28–47.

13966 RESIS (A.). 'The Churchill–Stalin Secret "Percentages" Agreement on the Balkans, Moscow, October 1944'. *Amer. Hist. Rev.* 83 (1978), 368–87.

13967 BETHELL (NICHOLAS) *Baron.* The Last Secret: Forcible Repatriation to Russia, 1944–1947. 1974.

13968 TOLSTOY (NIKOLAI). The Minister and the Massacres. 1986.

13969 KNIGHT (ROBERT). 'Harold Macmillan and the Cossacks: Was There a Klagenfurt Conspiracy?'. *Intelligence and National Security* 1 (1986), 234–54.

13970 BEAUMONT (JOAN). 'Trade, Strategy and Foreign Policy in Conflict: The Rolls Royce Affair 1946–1947'. *Inl Hist. Rev.* 2 (1980), 602–18.

13971 BOYLE (PETER J.). 'The British Foreign Office View of Soviet-American Relations 1945–1946'. *Dipl. Hist.* 3 (1979), 307–20.

Eastern Europe

13972 MAX (S. M.). 'Cold War on the Danube: The Belgrade Conference of 1948 and Anglo-American Effort to Reinternationalize the River'. *Dipl. Hist.* 7 (1987), 48–72.

13973 —— The United States, Great Britain and the Sovietization of Hungary, 1945–1948. N.Y. 1985.

13974 HEUSER (BEATRICE). Western Containment Policies in the Cold War: The Yugoslav Case 1948–1953. 1989.

13975 BETHELL (NICHOLAS) *Baron.* The Great Betrayal: The Untold Story of Kim Philby's Biggest Coup. 1984. [Albania.].

15. POLICY TOWARDS SPAIN AND PORTUGAL 1919–1951

13976 MCKERCHER (B. J. C.). '"A Dose of Fascismo": Esmé Howard in Spain, 1919–1924'. *Inl Hist. Rev.* 9 (1987), 555–85.

13977 THOMAS (HUGH SWYNNERTON) *Baron.* The Spanish Civil War. 1960. Rev. edn 1976.

13978 LITTLE (D.). Malevolent Neutrality: The United States, Great Britain, and the Origins of the Spanish Civil War. 1985.

13979 WATKINS (KENNETH WILLIAM). Britain Divided: The Effect of the Spanish Civil War on British Public Opinion. 1963.

13980 KLEINE-AHLBRANDT (WILLIAM LAIRD). The Policy of Simmering: A Study of British Policy during the Spanish Civil War, 1936–1939. The Hague. 1962.

13981 CARLTON (DAVID). 'Eden, Blum and the Origins of Non-Intervention'. *J. Contemp. Hist.* 6 (1971), 40–55.

13982 STONE (GLYN A.). 'Britain, Non-Intervention and the Spanish Civil War'. *Eur. Studs Rev.* ix (1979), 129–50.

13983 EDWARDS (JILL). The British Government and the Spanish Civil War 1936–1939. 1979.

13984 BEEVOR (ANTHONY). The Spanish Civil War. 1982.

13985 LUNN (*Sir* ARNOLD). '"A Most Passionate War": Some Reflections on a Left-Wing View of the Spanish Civil War'. *Month* xxvi (1961), 80–95.

13986 —— 'British Reactions to the Spanish Civil War'. *Month* xxx (1963), 145–51.

13987 FLINT (JAMES). '"Must God Go Fascist?": English Catholic Opinion and the Spanish Civil War'. *Church Hist.* 56 (1987), 364–74.

13988 FRANCIS (HYWEL). Miners Against Fascism: Wales and the Spanish Civil War. 1984.

13989 —— 'Welsh Miners and the Spanish Civil War'. *J. Contemp. Hist.* v (1970), 178.

13990 ALEXANDER (B.). British Volunteers for Liberty: Spain 1936–1939. 1982.

13991 FLEAY (C.) *and* SANDERS (M. L.). 'The Labour Spain Committee: Labour Party Policy and the Spanish Civil War'. *Hist. J.* 28 (1985), 187–97.

13992 GONZALEZ ARNAO (MARIANO). 'El Batallon Britanico en la Guerra Civil Espanola'. *Historia* 16 126 (1986), 19–26.

13993 FYRTH (J.). The Signal was Spain: The Aid Spain Movement in Britain, 1936–39. 1986.

13994 ALPERT (M.). 'Humanitarianism and Politics in the British Response to the Spanish Civil War, 1936–9'. *Eur. Hist. Q.* 14 (1984), 423–40.

13995 SMYTH (D.). Diplomacy and Strategy of Survival: British Policy and Franco's Spain, 1940–1. Camb. 1986.

13996 JWAIDEH (ALICE REID). The Policy of the United Kingdom towards Spain from the End of World War II until the British Elections of 1951. Washington, DC. 1952.

13997 STONE (GLYN A.). 'The Official British Attitude to the Anglo-Portuguese Alliance, 1910–1945'. *J. Contemp. Hist.* x (1975), 729–46.

16. POLICY TOWARDS THE UNITED STATES

13998 ALLEN (HARRY CRANBROOK). Great Britain and the United States: A History of Anglo-American Relations (1783–1952). 1954. Rev. edn of Pt. 1 published as The Anglo-American Relationship Since 1783. 1959.

13999 ALLEN (HARRY CRANBROOK) *and* THOMPSON (ROGER) *eds.* Contrast and Connection: Bicentennial Essays in American History. 1976.

14000 CLARK (WILLIAM DONALDSON). Less than Kin: A Study of Anglo-American Relations. 1957.

14001 NICHOLAS (HERBERT GEORGE). Britain and the United States. 1954.

14002 —— The United States and Britain. 1975.

14003 BREBNER (JOHN BARTLET). North American Triangle: the Interplay of Canada, the United States and Great Britain. New Haven, Conn. 1945.

14004 WALZ (KENNETH N.). Foreign Policy and Democratic Politics: The American and British Experience. Boston, Mass. 1967.

14005 WATT (DONALD CAMERON). Succeeding John Bull: America in Britain's Place, 1900–1975. Camb. 1984.

14006 GELBER (LIONEL). America in Britain's Place. 1961.

14007 COLLIER (BASIL). Barren Victories: Versailles to Suez (1918–1956). 1964.

14008 —— The Lion and the Eagle: British and American Strategy, 1900–1950. 1972.

14009 RUSSETT (BRUCE MARTIN). Community and Contention: Britain and America in the Twentieth Century. Camb., Mass. 1963.

14010 PELLING (HENRY MATHISON). America and the British Left: From Bright to Bevan. 1956.

14011 LEUCHTENBURG (W. E.), QUINTON (ANTHONY), BALL (GEORGE W.), *and* OWEN (DAVID). Britain and the United States: Four Views to Mark the Silver Jubilee. 1979.

14012 DIMBLEBY (DAVID) *and* REYNOLDS (DAVID). An Ocean Apart. 1988.

14013 KLEIN (IRA). 'Whitehall, Washington and the Anglo-Japanese Alliance, 1919–1921'. *Pac. Hist. Rev.* xli (1972), 460–83.

14014 FRY (MICHAEL GRAHAM). 'The North Atlantic Triangle and the Abrogation of the Anglo-Japanese Alliance'. *J. Mod. Hist.* xxxix (1967), 46–64.

14015 —— Illusions of Security: North Atlantic Diplomacy, 1918–1922. Toronto. 1972.

14016 DAYER (ROBERTA ALBERT). 'The British War Debts to the United States and the Anglo-Japanese Alliance, 1920–1923'. *Pac. Hist. Rev.* 45, 1976.

14017 WARD (ALAN JOSEPH). Ireland and Anglo-American Relations, 1899–1921. 1969.

14018 WHELPLEY (JAMES DAVENPORT). British–American Relations. 1924.

14019 DAVENPORT (ERNEST HAROLD) *and* COOKE (SIDNEY RUSSELL). The Oil Trusts and Anglo-American Relations. 1923.

14020 HOGAN (MICHAEL J.). Informal Entente: The Private Structure of Cooperation in Anglo-American Economic Diplomacy, 1918–1928. Columbia, Miss. 1977.

14021 —— 'Informal Entente: Public Policy and Private Management in Anglo-American Petroleum Affairs, 1918–1924'. *Bus. Hist. Rev.* xlviii (1974), 187–205.

14022 MCKERCHER (B. J. C.). The Second Baldwin Government and the United States, 1924–1929: Attitudes and Diplomacy. Camb. 1984.

14023 RHODES (BENJAMIN D.). 'British Diplomacy and the Silent Oracle of Vermont, 1923–1929'. *Vermont History* 50 (1982), 69–79.

14024 MEGAW (M. RUTH). 'The Scramble for the Pacific: Anglo-United States Rivalry in the 1930s'. *Hist. Studs* xvii (1977), 458–73.

14025 WHEELER (GERALD E.). 'Isolated Japan: Anglo-American Diplomatic Cooperation, 1927–1936'. *Pac. Hist. Rev.* xxx (1961), 165–78.

14026 PRATT (LAWRENCE). 'The Anglo-American Naval Conversations on the Far East of January 1938'. *Inl Affs.* xlvii (1971), 745–63.

14027 WEINBERGER (J. M.). 'The British on Borah: Foreign Office and Embassy Attitudes towards Idaho's Senior Senator, 1935–1940'. *Idaho Yesterdays* 25/3 (1981), 2–14.

14028 SCHATZ (ARTHUR W.). 'The Anglo-American Trade Agreements and Cordell Hull's Search for Peace, 1936–1938'. *J. Amer. Hist.* 57 (1970).

14029 PARKER (R. ALISTAIR C.). 'Pound Sterling, the American Treasury and British Preparations for War, 1938–1939'. *Eng. Hist. Rev.* 98 (1983), 261–79.

14030 REYNOLDS (DAVID J.). The Creation of the Anglo-American Alliance, 1937–1941: A Study in Competitive Cooperation. 1981.

14031 —— 'Lord Lothian and Anglo-American Relations 1939–1940'. *Trans. Amer. Phil. Soc.* 73 (1983).

14032 JEFFREYS-JONES (RHODRI). 'Review Article: The Inestimable Advantage of not being English: Lord Lothian's American Ambassadorship, 1939–1940'. *Scot. Hist. Rev.* 63 (1984), 105–10.

14033 REYNOLDS (DAVID J.). 'Roosevelt, the British Left, and the Appointment of John G. Winant as United States Ambassador to Britain in 1941'. *Inl Hist. Rev.* 4 (1982), 393–413.

14034 —— 'Competitive Co-operation: Anglo-American Relations in World War Two'. *Hist. J.* 23 (1980), 233–45.

14035 STOFF (MICHAEL B.). 'The Anglo-American Oil Agreement and the War-time Search for Foreign Policy'. *Bus. Hist. Rev.* 55 (1981), 59–74.

14036 RHODES (BENJAMIN D.). 'The British Royal Visit of 1939 and the "Psychological Approach" to the United States'. *Dipl. Hist.* 2 (1978).

14037 HAGLUND (DAVID G.). 'George C. Marshall and the Question of Military Aid to England, May–June 1940'. *J. Contemp. Hist.* 15 (1980), 745–60.

14038 LASH (JOSEPH P.). Roosevelt and Churchill, 1939–1941: The Partnership that Saved the West. N.Y. 1976.

14039 KIMBALL (WARREN F.) ed. Churchill and Roosevelt: The Complete Correspondence. 3 vols. Princeton, NJ. 1984.

14040 LOEWENHEIM (FRANCIS L.) et al. eds. Roosevelt and Churchill: Their Secret Wartime Correspondence. N.Y. 1975.

14041 HACHEY (THOMAS E.) ed. Confidential Dispatches: Analyses of America by the British Ambassador, 1939–1945. Evanston, Ill. 1974.

14042 NICHOLAS (HERBERT GEORGE) ed. Washington Despatches: Weekly Political Reports from the British Embassy. 1981.

14043 BERLIN (*Sir* ISAIAH). Personal Impressions. *Ed.* by Henry Hardy. 1981.

14044 LEUTZE (JAMES R.). 'The Secret of the Churchill-Roosevelt Correspondence: September 1939–May 1940'. *J. Contemp. Hist.* x (1975), 465–91.

14045 THORNE (CHRISTOPHER GUY). Allies of a Kind: The United States, Great Britain and the War against Japan, 1941–1945. 1978.

14046 McNEILL (WILLIAM HARDY). America, Britain and Russia, their Cooperation and Conflict, 1941–1946. 1953.

14047 WILSON (THEODORE ALLEN). The First Summit: Roosevelt and Churchill at Placentia Bay 1941. 1970.

14048 HARBUTT (FRASER). 'Churchill, Hopkins, and the "Other" Americans: An Alternative Perspective on Anglo-American Relations, 1941–1945'. *Inl. Hist. Rev.* 8 (1986), 236–62.

14049 KIMBALL (WARREN F.). The Most Unsordid Act: Lend-Lease, 1939–1941. Baltimore, Md. 1969.

14050 —— 'Beggar My Neighbour: America and the British Interim Finance Crisis, 1940–1941'. *J. Econ. Hist.* 29 (1969).

14051 —— 'The Temptation of British Opulence, 1937–1942'. *Pol. Sci. Q.* 86 (1971).

14052 GOODHART (PHILIP CARTER). Fifty Ships that Saved the World: The Foundations of the Anglo-American Alliance. 1965.

14053 POLLOCK (F. E.). 'Roosevelt, the Ogdensburg Agreement, and the British Fleet: All Done with Mirrors'. *Dipl. Hist.* 5 (1981), 203–19.

14054 CLARKE (*Sir* RICHARD). Anglo-American Collaboration in War and Peace, 1942–1949. Oxf. 1982.

14055 BAGWELL (PHILIP SIDNEY) *and* MINGAY (GORDON EDMUND). Britain and America, 1850–1939: A Study of Economic Change. 1970.

14056 QUINLAN (PAUL D.). Clash Over Romania: British and American Policies Toward Romania 1938–1947. Los Angeles, Calif. 1977.

14057 LA FEBER (W.). 'Roosevelt, Churchill and Indo-China: 1942–1945'. *Amer. Hist. Rev.* lxxx (1975), 1277–95.

14058 MARCUS (H. G.). Ethiopia, Great Britain and the United States 1941–1974: The Politics of Empire. Berkeley, Calif./London. 1983.

14059 FOX (WILLIAM THORNTON RICKERT). Anglo-American Relations in the Post-War World. New Haven, Conn. 1943.

14060 BERNSTEIN (BARTON J.). 'Uneasy Alliance: Roosevelt, Churchill and the Atomic Bomb, 1940–1945'. *Western Pol. Q.* xxix (1976), 202–30.

14061 ALLEN (ROY G. D.). 'Mutual Aid between the U.S. and the British Empire, 1941–1945'. *J. Roy. Stat. Soc.* cix (1946).

14062 HATHAWAY (R. M.). Ambiguous Partnership: Britain and America, 1944–1947. N.Y./Guildford. 1981.

14063 SHORT (K. R. M.). '"The White Cliffs of Dover": Promoting Anglo-American Alliance in World War II'. *Hist. J. Film Tele.* 2 (1982), 3–25.

14064 ROBERTS (HENRY LITHGOW) *and* WILSON (PAUL ALEXANDER). Britain and the United States: Problems in Co-operation. 1953.

14065 CONANT (JAMES BRYANT). Anglo-American Relations in the Atomic Age. 1952.

14066 EPSTEIN (LEON D.). Britain—Uneasy Ally. 1954.

14067 BIGGS-DAVISON (*Sir* JOHN). The Uncertain Ally. 1957.

14068 CROSSMAN (RICHARD H. S.). 'The Rift in Anglo-American Relations'. *For. Affs* 35, 1957.

14069 MANDERSON-JONES (RONALD BRANDIS). The Special Relationship: Anglo-American Relations and Western Unity, 1947–1956. 1972.

14070 MACINNIS (EDGAR WARDWELL). The Atlantic Triangle and the Cold War. Toronto. 1969.

14071 ALLEN (HARRY CRANBROOK). The Anglo-American Predicament: The British Commonwealth, the United States and European Unity. 1960.

14072 —— 'The Anglo-American Relationship in the Sixties'. *Inl Affs* xxxviii (1963), 37–48.

14073 BROGAN (*Sir* DENIS WILLIAM). 'Anglo-American Relations, Retrospect and Prospect'. *Yale Rev.* li (1961), 11–22.

14074 EDMONDS (ROBIN). Setting the Mould: The United States and Britain 1945–1950. Oxf. 1986.

14075 BEST (RICHARD A.). 'Co-operation with Like-Minded People': British Influence on American Security Policy 1945–1949. 1986.

14076 BOYLE (PETER G.). 'Britain, America and the Transition from Economic to Military Assistance, 1948–1951'. *J. Contemp. Hist.* 22 (1987), 521–38.

14077 —— 'The British Foreign Office and America's Foreign Policy 1947–1948'. *J. Amer. Studs* 16 (1982), 373–89.

14078 DAWSON (RAYMOND) *and* ROSECRANCE (RICHARD). 'Theory and Reality in the Anglo-American Alliance'. *World Pol.* xix (1966), 21–51.

14079 BELL (CORAL). The Debatable Alliance: An Essay in Anglo-American Relations. 1964.

14080 NEUSTADT (RICHARD E.). Alliance Politics. N.Y. 1970.

14081 TURNER (ARTHUR CAMPBELL). The Unique Partnership: Britain and the United States. N.Y. 1971.

14082 BUCHAN (ALASTAIR). 'Mothers and Daughters (or Greeks and Romans)'. *For. Affs* 54 (1976), 645–69.

14083 MACDONALD (IAN S.) *ed.* Anglo-American Relations Since the Second World War. Newton Abbot and N.Y. 1974. [A collection of documents.].

14084 LOUIS (WILLIAM ROGER) *and* BULL (HEDLEY) *eds.* The Special Relationship: Anglo-American Relations Since 1945. Oxf. 1986.

14085 BELOFF (MAX) *Baron.* 'The Special Relationship: An Anglo-American Myth'. In 'A Century of Conflict, 1850–1950'. *Ed.* by Martin Gilbert. (1966), 151–71.

14086 REYNOLDS (DAVID J.). 'A "Special Relationship"? America, Britain and the International Order Since World War Two'. *Inl Affs* 62 (1985–1986), 1–20.

14087 'Re-thinking Anglo-American Relations'. *Inl Affs* 65 (1988–1989), 89–111.

14088 GRAYLING (CHRISTOPHER) *and* LANGDON (CHRISTOPHER). Just Another Star? Anglo-American Relations since 1945. 1988.

14089 MALLALIEU (WILLIAM C.). British Reconstruction and American Policy, 1945–1955. N.Y. 1956.

14090 GARDNER (RICHARD N.). Sterling–Dollar Diplomacy. Oxf. 1956.

14091 —— Sterling–Dollar Diplomacy in Current Perspective. N.Y. 1980.

14092 NUNNERLEY (DAVID). President Kennedy and Britain. 1972.

14093 CYR (ANTHONY). British Foreign Policy and the Atlantic Area: The Techniques of Accommodation. 1979.

14094 MCCAULEY (MARTIN). The Origins of the Cold War. 1983. [A collection of documents.].

14095 FLEMING (D. P.). The Cold War and its Origins 1917–1960. N.Y. 1961.

14096 LUARD (D. EVAN T.) *ed.* The Cold War: A Reappraisal. 1964.

14097 GADDIS (JOHN LEWIS). The United States and the Origins of the Cold War 1941–1947. N.Y. 1972.

14098 —— 'The Emerging Post-Revisionist Synthesis and the Origins of the Cold War'. *Dipl. Hist.* 7 (1983), 171–90.

14099 DOUGLAS (ROY). From War to Cold War 1942–1948. 1981.

14100 REYNOLDS (DAVID J.). 'The Origins of the Cold War: The European Dimension 1944–1951'. *Hist. J.* 28 (1985), 497–515.

14101 THOMAS (HUGH) *Baron.* Armed Truce: The Beginnings of the Cold War 1945–1946. 1986.

14102 DOCKRILL (MICHAEL). The Cold War 1945–1963. 1988.

14103 ARONSON (LAWRENCE) *and* KITCHEN (MARTIN). The Origins of the Cold War: A Comparative Perspective: American, British and Canadian Relations with the Soviet Union 1941–1948. 1988.

14104 DEIGHTON (ANNE) *ed.* Britain and the Cold War. 1989.

14105 HARBUTT (FRASER J.). The Iron Curtain: Churchill, America and the Origins of the Cold War. Oxf. 1986.

14106 RYAN (HENRY B.). The Vision of Anglo-America: The US–UK Alliance and the Emerging Cold War, 1943–1946. Camb. 1987.

14107 —— 'A New Look at Churchill's "Iron Curtain" Speech'. *Hist. J.* 22 (1979), 895–920.

14108 ANDERSON (TERRY H.). The United States, Great Britain and the Cold War 1944–1947. Columbia and London. 1981.

14109 YOUNG (JOHN WILSON). 'Churchill, the Russians and the Western Alliance: The Three-Power Conference at Bermuda, December 1953'. *Eng. Hist. Rev.* 101 (1986), 889–912.

14110 FISH (M. S.). 'After Stalin's Death: The Anglo-American Debate Over a New Cold War'. *Dipl. Hist.* 10 (1986), 333–55.

17. POLICY TOWARDS THE VATICAN

14111 RANDALL (*Sir* ALEC W. G.). Vatican Assignment. 1956.

14112 —— 'British Diplomatic Representation at the Holy See'. *Black.* xxxvii (1956), 356–63.

14113 GRAHAM (ROBERT A.). 'Vatican Radio Between London and Berlin, 1940–41'. *Month* ccxxxvii (1976), 25–30.

14114 CONWAY (JOHN S.). 'The Vatican, Great Britain and Relations with Germany, 1938–1940'. *Hist. J.* 16 (1973), 147–67.

14115 LUDLOW (PETER WOODS). 'Papst Pius XII, die britische Regierung und die Deutsche Opposition im Winter 1939–40'. *Vierteljahreshefte für Zeitgeschichte* (1974).

14116 CHADWICK (WILLIAM OWEN). Britain and the Vatican during the Second World War. Camb. 1986.

14117 MOLONEY (T.). Westminster, Whitehall and the Vatican: The Role of Cardinal Hinsley, 1935–43. 1985.

18. POLICY TOWARDS WESTERN EUROPE SINCE 1945

14118 HENNESSY (JAMES). Britain and Europe since 1945: A Bibliographical Guide. Brighton. 1973. [An annually updated guide to the microfilm collection of the same title published by Harvester.].

14119 BOTTCHER (WINFRIED), JANSEN (JÜRGEN), *and* WELSCH (FRIEDRICH) eds. Britische Europaideen 1940–1970: Eine Bibliographie. Düsseldorf. 1971.

14120 LIPGENS (WALTER). A History of European Integration. Vol. 1 1945–1947. Oxf. 1982.

14121 HUSLER (ANGELO). Contribution à l'étude de l'élaboration de la Politique Etrangère Britannique, 1945–1956. Paris. 1961.

14122 REYNOLDS (DAVID). 'Britain and the New Europe: The Search for Identity Since 1940'. *Hist. J.* 31 (1988), 223–39.

14123 YOUNG (JOHN WILSON). Britain, France and the Unity of Europe, 1945–1951. Leicester. 1984.

14124 OVENDALE (RITCHIE) *ed.* The Foreign Policies of the British Labour Governments, 1945–1951. Leicester. 1984.

14125 WARNER (GEOFFREY). 'Die britische Labour-Regierung und die Einheit Westeuropas 1948–1951'. *Vierteljahreshefte für Zeit-geschichte* 28 (1980), 310–30.

14126 BAILEY (THOMAS ANDREW). The Marshall Plan Summer. Stanford, Calif. 1977.

14127 HOGAN (MICHAEL J.). The Marshall Plan: America, Britain and the Reconstruction of Western Europe, 1947–1952. Camb. 1987.

14128 PELLING (HENRY MATHISON). Britain and the Marshall Plan. 1988.

14129 BURK (KATHLEEN). 'Britain and the Marshall Plan'. In 'Warfare, Diplomacy and Politics: Essays in Honour of A. J. P. Taylor'. *Ed.* by Chris Wrigley. (1986), 210–30.

14130 NEWTON (SCOTT). 'The Sterling Crisis of 1947 and the British Response to the Marshall Plan'. *Econ. Hist. Rev.* 2nd ser. 37 (1984), 391–408.

14131 CROMWELL (WILLIAM C.). 'The Marshall Plan, Britain and the Cold War'. *Rev. Inl Studs* 8 (1982), 233–49.

14132 EISEN (JANET). Anglo-Dutch Relations and European Unity, 1940–1948. Hull. 1980.

14133 GRANTHAM (J. T.). 'British Labour and the Hague "Congress of Europe": National Sovereignty Defended'. *Hist. J.* 24 (1981), 443–52.

14134 VAN DORSTEN (JAN ADRIANUA) *ed.* Ten Studies in Anglo-Dutch Relations. Leiden. 1974.

14135 KOLLING (MIRJAM). Führungsmacht in Westeuropa? Grossbritanniens Anspruch und Scheitern, 1944–1950. Berlin (E.) 1984.

14136 —— 'Grossbritanniens Westeuropapolitik 1944–1947 und die Stabilisierung der bürgerlichen Herrschaft in Frankreich'. *Jahrbuch für Geschichte* 30 (1984), 179–203.

14137 SHLAIM (AVI). Britain and the Origins of European Unity 1945–1951. Reading. 1978.

14138 YOUNG (JOHN W.). Britain, France and the Unity of Europe 1945–1951. Leicester. 1984.

14139 MELISSEN (JAN) *and* ZEEMAN (BERT). 'Britain and Western Europe 1945–1951: Opportunities Lost'. *Inl Affs* 63 (1986–1987), 81–95.

14140 NEWTON (SCOTT). 'The 1949 Sterling Crisis and British Policy towards European Integration'. *Rev. Inl. Studs* 11 (1985), 169–82.

14141 SAHM (ULRICH). 'Britain and Europe 1950'. *Inl Affs* xllll (1967), 12–24.

14142 YOUNGER (*Sir* KENNETH GILMOUR). 'Britain and Europe, 1950: A Comment'. *Inl Affs* xliii (1967), 25–8.

14143 DIEBOLD (WILLIAM). The Schuman Plan: A Study in Economic Co-operation 1950–1959. N.Y. 1959.

14144 MOON (JEREMY). European Integration in British Politics 1950–1963: A Study of Issue Change. Aldershot. 1985.

14145 YOUNG (JOHN WILSON). 'Churchill's "No" to Europe: The Rejection of European Union by Churchill's Post-War Government, 1951–1952'. *Hist. J.* 28 (1985), 923–37.

14146 CHATHAM HOUSE STUDY GROUP. Britain in Western Europe: WEU and the Atlantic Alliance. 1956.

14147 FOGARTY (MICHAEL P.). 'Britain and Europe Since 1945'. *Rev. Pol.* 19 (1957), 90–105.

14148 WOODHOUSE (C. MONTAGUE). 'Great Britain's European Policy Since the Second World War'. *Inl Jnl* 12 (1957), 300–8.

14149 WATT (DONALD CAMERON). 'Grossbritannien und Europa, 1951–1959: Die Jahre konservativer Regierung'. *Vierteljahreshefte für Zeitgeschichte* 28 (1980), 389–409.

14150 PRYCE (ROY). 'Britain's Failure in Europe'. *Twentieth Century* (Sept. 1959), 131–41.

14151 NUTTING (Sir ANTHONY). Europe Will Not Wait. 1960.

14152 CAMPS (MIRIAM). Britain and the European Community, 1955–1963. 1964.

14153 —— 'Britain and the European Crisis'. *Inl Affs* xliii (1966), 45–54.

14154 ABRAMS (MARK). 'British Elite Attitudes and the European Common Market'. *Pub. Op. Q.* 29 (1965), 236–46.

14155 MACKINTOSH (JOHN PITCAIRN). 'Britain in Europe: Historical Perspective and Contemporary Reality'. *Inl Affs* xlv (1969).

14156 SHARP (PAUL). 'The Rise of the European Community in the Foreign Policy of British Governments 1961–1971'. *Millennium: Journal of International Studies* 11 (1982), 155–71.

14157 BELOFF (NORA). The General Says No: Britain's Exclusion from Europe. Harmondsworth. 1963.

14158 KITZINGER (UWE WEBSTER). 'Britain and the Common Market: The State of the Debate'. *World Today* xvii (1961), 233–54.

14159 BUTT (RONALD). 'The Common Market and Conservative Party Politics 1961–1962'. *Gvt. and Opp.* 2 (1967), 372–86.

14160 DIEBOLD (WILLIAM). 'Britain, the Six and the World Economy'. *For. Affs* xl (1962), 407–18.

14161 BALOGH (THOMAS) Baron. 'Post-War Britain and the Common Market'. *New Left Rev.* xvi (1962), 21–30.

14162 LIEBER (ROBERT J.). British Politics and European Unity: Parties, Elites and Pressure Groups. 1970.

14163 —— 'Interest Groups and Political Integration: British Entry into Europe'. *Amer. Pol. Sci. Rev.* lxvi (1972), 53–67.

14164 MALLY (GERHARD). Britain and European Unity. 1966.

14165 MIDDLETON (DREW). The Supreme Choice: Britain and the European Community. 1963.

14166 PINDER (JOHN). Britain and the Common Market. 1961.

14167 CRAWFORD (J. G.). 'Britain, Australia and the Common Market'. *Austral. Outlook* xv (1961), 221–39.

14168 SWIFT (WILLIAM J.) ed. Great Britain and the Common Market, 1957–1969. N.Y. 1970.

14169 VAN DER STOEL (M.). The British Application for Membership of the European Communities 1963–1968. Paris. 1968.

14170 Selected Documents Relating to Problems of Security and Co-operation in Europe 1954–1977. 1977.

14171 FREY (CYNTHIA W.). 'Meaning Business: The British Application to Join the Common Market, November 1966–October 1967'. *J. Com. Mkt Studs* 6 (1983), 197–230.

14172 GERBET (P.) ed. 'La Candidature de la Grande Bretagne aux Communautés Européennes 1967–1968: Les Données de la Problème' *Revue Française de Science Politique* 18 (1968), 861–1002.

14173 CARTER (WILLIAM HORSFALL). Speaking European: The Anglo-Continental Cleavage. 1966.

14174 GELBER (LIONEL MORRIS). The Alliance of Necessity: Britain's Crisis, the New Europe and American Interests. 1967.

14175 GARRAN (PETER). 'Britain and Europe: Past, Present and Future'. *Austral. Outlook* xxiv (1970), 70–80.

14176 STEWART (MICHAEL). 'Britain, Europe and the Alliance'. *For. Affs* 48 (1970), 648–59.

14177 EVANS (DOUGLAS) ed. Destiny or Delusion: Britain and the Common Market. 1971.

14178 YOUNGER (Sir KENNETH GILMOUR). 'Britain in Europe: The Impact on Foreign Policy'. *Inl Affs* xlviii (1972), 579–92.

14179 WALLACE (WILLIAM J. L.). 'British External Relations and the European Community: The Changing Context of Foreign Policy Making'. *J. Common Market Studs* xii (1973), 28–52.

14180 KITZINGER (UWE WEBSTER). Diplomacy and Persuasion: How Britain Joined the Common Market. 1973.

14181 LODGE (JULIET). 'New Zealand, Britain and the E.E.C. in the 1970s'. *Austral. Outlook* xxix (1975), 287–99.

14182 EVANS (DOUGLAS). While Britain Slept: The Selling of the Common Market. 1975.

14183 JOWELL (ROGER) and HOINVILLE (GERALD) eds. Britain into Europe: Public Opinion and the E.E.C. 1961–1975. 1976.

14184 MARX (ROLAND). Le problème du Commonwealth dans les choix européens de la Grande-Bretagne de 1948 à 1975'. *Relations Internationales* 55 (1988), 361–76.

14185 TWITCHETT (K. J.). 'Britain and Community Europe, 1973–1979'. *Inl Rels* 6 (1979), 698–714.

14186 DUNSCH (JÜRGEN). Die 'Europapolitik' der britischen Labour Party 1970–1975. Innerparteiliche Meinungbildung und Parteioffizielle Konzeption. Bad Honnef. 1978.

14187 JANSEN (JÜRGEN). Britische Konservative und Europa. Debattenaussage im Unterhaus zur Westeuropäischen Integration 1945–1972. Baden-Baden. 1978.

14188 CHARLOT (MONICA) *and* SERGEANT (JEAN-CLAUDE). Britain and Europe since 1945. Paris. 1986.

14189 SAINSBURY (KEITH). 'British Policy and German Unity at the End of the Second World War'. *Eng. Hist. Rev.* 94 (1979), 786–804.

14190 BALFOUR (MICHAEL LEONARD GRAHAM) *and* MAIR (JOHN). Four Power Control in Germany and Austria 1945–1946. Oxf. 1956.

14191 FARQUHARSON (JOHN). The Western Allies and the Politics of Food: Agrarian Management in Post-War Germany. Leamington Spa. 1985.

14192 —— 'Land Reform in the British Zone 1945–1947'. *Ger. Hist.* 6 (1988), 35–56.

14193 CARDEN (ROBERT W.). 'Before Bizonia: Britain's Economic Dilemma in Germany, 1945–1946'. *J. Contemp. Hist.* 14 (1979), 535–55.

14194 YOUNG (JOHN W.). 'The Foreign Office, the French and the Post-War Division of Germany'. *Rev. Inl Studs* 12 (1986), 223–34.

14195 CAIRNCROSS (*Sir* ALEXANDER KIRKLAND). The Price of War. British Policy on German Reparations 1941–1949. Oxf. 1986.

14196 —— A Country to Play with: Level-of-Industry Negotiations in Berlin, 1945–1946. Gerrards Cross. 1987.

14197 TURNER (IAN). 'Great Britain and the Post-War German Currency Reform'. *Hist. J.* 30 (1987), 685–708.

14198 GREENWOOD (SEAN). 'Bevin, the Ruhr and the Division of Germany: August 1945/December 1946'. *Hist. J.* 29 (1986), 203–12.

14199 FOSCHEPOTH (JOSEF). 'British Interest in the Division of Germany after the Second World War'. *J. Contemp. Hist.* 21 (1986), 391–411.

14200 FARQUHARSON (JOHN). '"Emotional but Influential": Victor Gollancz, Richard Stokes and the British Zone in Germany: 1945–1949'. *J. Contemp. Hist.* 22 (1987), 501–19.

14201 GOLLANCZ (VICTOR). Our Threatened Values. 1946.

14202 —— In Darkest Germany. 1947.

14203 REUSCH (ULRICH). Deutsches Berufsbeamtentum und britische Besatzung: Planung und Politik 1943–1947. Stuttgart. 1985.

14204 DE ZAYAS (ALFRED M.). Nemesis at Potsdam: the Anglo-Americans and the Expulsion of the Germans: Background, Execution, Consequences. 1977.

14205 JÜRGENSEN (KURT). 'British Occupation Policy After 1945 and the Problems of "Re-educating Germany"'. *Hist.* 68 (1983), 225–44.

14206 SCHNEIDER (U.). 'Grundzüge britischer Deutschland— und Besatzungspolitik'. *Zeitgeschichte* 9 (1981/2), 73–89.

14207 —— 'Zur Deutschland—und Besatzungspolitik Grossbritanniens im Rahmen der Vier-Mächtekontrolle Deutschlands vom Kriegsende bis Herbst 1945. Dokumentation'. *Mil. Mit.* 31 (1982), 77–102.

14208 —— 'Niedersachsen unter Britischer Besatzung. 1945'. *Niedersächsisches Jahrbuch für Landesgeschichte* 54 (1982), 251–319.

14209 STEINIGER (ROLF). 'Grossbritannien und die Ruhr'. In Zwischen Ruhrkontrolle und Mitbestimmung. *Ed.* by W. Frost. Cologne (1983), 9–63.

14210 —— 'Wie die Teilung Deutschlands verhindert wer den sollte: Der Robertson-Plan aus dem Jahre 1948'. *Mil. Mit.* 33 (1983), 49–89.

14211 —— 'Die Rhein-Ruhr Frage im Kontext britischer Deutschlandspolitik 1945/46'. In 'Politische Weichenstellungen im Nachkriegsdeutschland 1945–1953'. By H. A. Winkler. Göttingen. 1979. 111–66.

14212 RUDZIO (W.). 'Grossbritannien als Sozialistische Besatzungsmacht in Deutschland: Aspekte des deutsch-britischen Verhältnisses 1945–1948'. In 'Studien zur Geschichte Englands und der deutsch–britischen Beziehungen'. *Ed.* by Lothar Kettenacker, Manfred Schlencke, and H. Seier. Munich. 1981.

14213 FOSCHEPOTH (JOSEF) *and* STEINIGER (ROLF) eds. Die britische Deutschland—und Besatzungspolitik 1945–1949, Paderborn. 1985.

14214 SCHARF (CLAUS) *and* SCHRODER (HANS-JÜRGEN) eds. Die Deutschlandspolitik Grossbritanniens und die Britische Zone 1945–1949. Wiesbaden. 1979.

14215 KAISER (KARL) *and* MORGAN (ROGER) eds. Britain and West Germany: Changing Societies and the Future of Foreign Policy. Oxf. 1971.

14216 WATT (DONALD CAMERON). Britain Looks to Germany: British Opinion and Policy towards Germany Since 1945. 1965.

14217 von HERWATH (HANS). 'Anglo-German Relations: A German View'. *Inl Affs* xxxix (1963), 511–20.

14218 STEEL (Sir CHRISTOPHER). 'Anglo-German Relations: A British View'. *Inl Affs* xxxix (1963), 521–32.

14219 ROSE (SAUL). 'The Labour Party and German Rearmament: A View from Transport House'. *Pol. Studs* xiv (1966), 133–42.

14220 WATT (DONALD CAMERON). 'Königswinter, 1965'. *Quart. Rev.* ccciii (1965), 433–43.

14221 HEYWOOD (ROBERT W.). 'London, Bonn, the Königswinter Conferences and the Problem of European Integration'. *J. Contemp. Hist.* x (1975), 131–55.

14222 UHLIG (R.). 'Königswinter—Symbol deutsch-britischer Ver-ständnis nach dem Zweiten Weltkrieg'. In 'Geschichte und Gegenwart'. *Ed.* by H. Boockmann. 1980. 491–529.

14223 VON IMHOFF (CHRISTOPH). Zwanzig Jahre Königswinter: deutsch-englisches Gespräch 1949–1969. Düsseldorf. 1969.

14224 GÉRAUD (ANDRÉ). 'Rise and Fall of the Anglo-French Entente'. *For. Affs* 32 (1954), 374–87.

14225 PICKLES (DOROTHY). The Uneasy Entente: French Foreign Policy and Franco-British Misunderstandings. Oxf. 1966.

14226 BARMAN (THOMAS). 'Britain and France, 1967'. *Inl Affs* xliii (1967), 29–38.

14227 —— 'Britain, France and West Germany'. *Inl Affs* xlvi (1970), 269–79.

14228 THOMSON (DAVID). 'General de Gaulle and the Anglo-Saxons'. *Inl Affs* xli (1965), 11–21.

14229 —— 'President de Gaulle and the Mésentente Cordiale'. *Inl J.* 23 (1968), 211–20.

14230 KERSAUDY (FRANÇOIS). Churchill and de Gaulle. 1981.

14231 NEWHOUSE (JOHN). De Gaulle and the Anglo-Saxons. N.Y. 1970.

14232 YOUNG (JOHN W.). 'The Foreign Office and the Departure of General de Gaulle, June 1945–January 1946'. *Hist. J.* 25 (1982), 209–16.

14233 SCEATS (R.). 'The Evolution of Anglo-French Relations'. *Ybook World Affs* xxviii (1974), 76–89.

14234 BILAINKIN (GEORGE). 'France Despairs for British Ally'. *Contemp. Rev.* ccxiv (1969), 306–12.

14235 GENESTE (M. E.). 'Britain, France and the Defence of Europe'. *Orbis* xiii (1969), 170–86.

19. POLICY TOWARDS FRANCE 1919–1942

14236 GAVIN (CATHERINE IRVINE). Britain and France: A Study of 20th Century Relations. 1941.

14237 ALBRECHT-CARRIÉ (RENÉ). Britain and France: Adaptations to a Changing Context of Power. N.Y. 1970.

14238 CHIARI (JOSEPH). Britain and France, the Unruly Twins. 1971.

14239 OSGOOD (S. M.). 'Le Mythe de 'la Perfide Albion' en France, 1919–1940'. *Cahiers d'histoire* 20 (1975), 5–20.

14240 WAITES (NEVILLE) ed. Troubled Neighbours: Franco-British Relations in the Twentieth Century. 1971.

14241 CAIRNS (JOHN C.). 'A Nation of Shopkeepers in Search of a Suitable France: 1919–1940'. *Amer. Hist. Rev.* 79 (1974), 710–43.

14242 C.N.R.S. Les Relations Franco-Britanniques de 1935 à 1939. Paris. 1975.

14243 JOHNSON (DOUGLAS), CROUZET (FRANÇOIS), *and* BÉDARIDA (FRANÇOIS). Britain and France: Ten Centuries. 1980.

14244 GOOLD (J. DOUGLAS). 'Lord Hardinge as Ambassador to France, and the Anglo-French Dilemma over Germany and the Near East, 1920–1922'. *Hist. J.* 21 (1978), 913–37.

14245 WILLIAMSON (DAVID G.). 'Great Britain and the Ruhr Crisis 1923–1924'. *Brit. J. Inl Studs* 3 (1977), 70–91.

14246 FRITZ (STEPHEN E.). 'La Politique de la Ruhr and Lloyd George's Conference Diplomacy: The Tragedy of Anglo-French Relations 1919–1923'. *Proc. Western Soc. Fr. Hist.* 3 (1975), 566–82.

14247 HALL (HINES H.). 'Lloyd George, Briand and the Failure of the Anglo-French Entente'. *J. Mod. Hist.* 50 (1978).

14248 MARKS (SALLY). 'Ménage à Trois: The Negotiations for an Anglo-French-Belgian Alliance in 1922'. *Inl Hist. Rev.* 4 (1982), 524–52.

14249 CASSELS (ALAN). 'Repairing the *Entente Cordiale* and the New Diplomacy'. *Hist. J.* 23 (1980), 133–53.

14250 SELSAM (JOHN PAUL). The Attempts to Form an Anglo-French Alliance, 1919–1924. Philadelphia, Pa. 1936.

14251 PINON (RENÉ). L'avenir de l'entente Franco-Anglaise. Paris. 1924.

14252 RUINE (JOAN JANE). Anglo-French Diplomatic Relations, 1923–1936. Washington, DC. 1949.

14253 SCHUKER (STEPHEN A.). The End of French Predominance in Europe: The Financial Crisis of 1924 and the Adoption of the Dawes Plan. Chapel Hill, N.C. 1976.

14254 HARDEN (MAXIMILIAN FELIX ERNST). Germany, France and England. 1924.

14255 CAMBON (PIERRE PAUL). Correspondence, 1870–1924. 3 vols Paris. 1940–6.

14256 BARDANNE (JEAN). Perfide Albion: An Examination of British Foreign Policy in Relation to France and Germany After the European War. Paris. 1933.

14257 BOYCE (ROBERT W.). 'Britain's First "No" to Europe: Britain and the Briand Plan, 1929–1930. *Eur. Studs Rev.* 10 (1980), 17–45.

14258 ROSTOW (NICHOLAS). Anglo-French Relations, 1934–1936. 1984.

14259 JORDAN (WILLIAM MARK). Great Britain, France and the German Problem, 1918–1939. 1943.

14260 WOLFERS (ARNOLD). Britain and France between Two World Wars: Conflicting Strategies of Peace since Versailles. N.Y. 1940.

14261 PARKER (R. A. C.). 'Anglo-French Conversations, April and September 1938'. In C.N.R.S. Les Relations Franco-Allemandes, 1933–1939. Paris. 1976.

14262 McCALLUM (RONALD BUCHANAN). England and France, 1939–1943. 1944.

14263 MACDONALD (CALLUM A.). 'Britain, France and the April Crisis of 1939'. *Eur. Studs Rev.* 2 (1972), 151–69.

14264 BELL (PHILIP MICHAEL HETT). A Certain Eventuality: Britain and the Fall of France. Farnborough. 1974.

14265 GATES (ELEANOR M.). End of the Affair: The Collapse of the Anglo-French Alliance, 1939–1940. Berkeley, Calif. 1981.

14266 THOMSON (DAVID). The Proposal for Anglo-French Union in 1940. Oxf. 1966.

14267 CAIRNS (JOHN C.). 'Great Britain and the Fall of France: A Study in Allied Disunity'. *J. Mod. Hist.* xxvii (1955), 365–409.

14268 JOHNSON (DOUGLAS W. J.). 'Britain and France in 1940'. *Trans. Roy. Hist. Soc.* xxii (1972), 141–57.

14269 SHLAIM (AVI). 'Prelude to Downfall: The British Offer to France, June 1940'. *J. Contemp. Hist.* ix (1974), 27–63.

14270 DILKS (DAVID N.). 'The Twilight War and the Fall of France: Chamberlain and Churchill in 1940'. *Trans. Roy. Hist. Soc.* xxviii (1978), 61–86.

14271 C.N.R.S. Français et Britanniques dans le Drôle de Guerre. Paris. 1979.

14272 BÉDARIDA (FRANÇOIS). La Stratégie Secrète de la Drôle de Guerre: Le Conseil Suprême Interallié, Septembre 1939–Avril 1940. Paris. 1979.

14273 OSGOOD (S. M.). 'Anglophobia and Other Vichy Obsessions'. *Wiener Lib. Bull.* xxii (1968), 13–18.

14274 FUNK (ARTHUR LAYTON). 'Negotiating the "Deal with Darlan"'. *J. Contemp. Hist.* 8 (1973), 81–117.

14275 MELKO (ROBERT L.). 'Darlan between Britain and Germany, 1940–1941'. *J. Contemp. Hist.* 8 (1973), 57–80.

14276 THOMAS (R. T.). Britain and Vichy: The Dilemma of Anglo-French Relations, 1940–1942. 1979.

20. POLICY TOWARDS PALESTINE/ISRAEL

(a) General

14277 JONES (PHILIP) *comp.* Britain and Palestine, 1914–1948: Archival Sources for the History of the British Mandate. 1979.

14278 CAPLAN (NEIL). Futile Diplomacy. Vol. 1: Early Arab-Zionist Negotiation Attempts 1913–1931. 1983. Vol. 2. Arab–Zionist Negotiations and the End of the Mandate. 1986.

14279 SNYDER (ESTHER M.). Israel. Oxf. 1985.

14280 ROYAL INSTITUTE OF INTERNATIONAL AFFAIRS. Great Britain and Palestine, 1915–1945. 1946.

14281 SYKES (CHRISTOPHER HUGH). Crossroads to Israel. 1965.

14282 KOESTLER (ARTHUR). Promise and Fulfilment: Palestine, 1917–1949. 1949.

14283 GORNY (JOSEPH). The British Labour Movement and Zionism 1917–1948. 1983.

14284 FRIEDMAN (ISAIAH). The Question of Palestine, 1918: British–Jewish–Arab Relations. 1973.

14285 KEDOURIE (ELIE). In the Anglo-Arab Labyrinth: The McMahon–Husayn Correspondence and its Interpretations, 1914–1939. Camb. 1976.

14286 TIBAWI (ABDUL LATIF). Anglo-Arab Relations and the Question of Palestine, 1914–1921. 1977.

14287 HARDIE (F.) *and* HERRMAN (I.). Britain and Zion: The Fateful Entanglement. Belf. 1980.

14288 TAYLOR (ALAN R.). Prelude to Israel: An Analysis of Zionist Diplomacy 1897–1947. 1961.

14289 STEIN (LEONARD). The Balfour Declaration. 1961.

14290 VERÉTÉ (MAYIR). 'The Balfour Declaration and its Makers'. *Mid. East. Studs* vi (1970), 48–76.

14291 CAPLAN (NEIL). 'Britain, Zionism and the Arabs, 1917–1925'. *Wiener Lib. Bull.* xxxi (1978), 4–17.

14292 INGRAMS (DOREEN) *comp.* Palestine Papers, 1917–1922: Seeds of Conflict. 1972.

14293 MCTAGUE (J. J.). 'Zionist–British Negotiations Over the Draft Mandate for Palestine, 1920'. *Jewish Soc. Studs* 42/3–4 (1980), 81–92.

14294 ESCO FOUNDATION FOR PALESTINE. Inc. Palestine: A Study of Jewish, Arab and British Policies. 2 vols New Haven, Conn. 1947.

14295 ROSE (NORMAN ANTHONY). The Gentile Zionists: A Study in Anglo-Zionist Diplomacy, 1929–1939. 1973.

14296 HYAMSON (A. M.). Palestine Under the Mandate 1920–1948. 1950.

14297 MARLOWE (JOHN). The Seat of Pilate: An Account of the Palestine Mandate. 1962.

14298 BETHELL (NICHOLAS) *Baron.* The Palestine Triangle: The Struggle between the British, the Jews and the Arabs. 1979.

14299 MOSSEK (M.). Palestine Immigration Policy under Sir Herbert Samuel: British, Zionist and Arab Attitudes. 1978.

14300 KEDOURIE (ELIE). 'Sir Herbert Samuel and the Government of Palestine'. *Mid. East Studs* 5 (1969), 44–68.

14301 KENT (MARIAN) Moguls and Mandarins: Oil Imperialism and the Middle East in British Foreign Policy 1900–1940. 1993.

14302 WASSERSTEIN (BERNARD). 'Herbert Samuel and the Palestine Problem'. *Eng. Hist. Rev.* xci (1976), 753–75.

14303 —— The British in Palestine: The Mandatory Government and the Arab–Jewish Conflict, 1917–1929. 1978.

14304 SIDEBOTHAM (HERBERT). British Policy and the Palestine Mandate. 1929.

14305 —— Great Britain and Palestine. 1937.

14306 BENTWICH (NORMAN DE MATTOS). England in Palestine. 1932.

14307 —— My 77 Years: An Account of My Life and Times 1883–1960. 1962.

14308 BENTWICH (NORMAN DE MATTOS) *and* BENTWICH (HELEN). Mandate Memories 1918–1948. 1965.

14309 ROSE (NORMAN ANTHONY). 'Arab Rulers and Palestine, 1936: The British Reaction'. *J. Mod. Hist.* xliv (1972), 213–31.

14310 —— *Ed.* Baffy: The Diaries of Blanche Dugdale 1936–1947. 1973.

14311 —— Lewis Namier and Zionism. Oxf. 1980.

14312 COHEN (MICHAEL J.). 'Sir Arthur Wauchope, the Army and the Rebellion in Palestine, 1936'. *Mid. East. Studs* ix (1973), 19–34.

14313 —— 'British Strategy and the Palestine Question, 1936–1939'. *J. Contemp. Hist.* vii (1972), 157–83.

14314 KLIEMAN (AARON S.). 'The Divisiveness of Palestine: Foreign Office Versus Colonial Office on the Issue of Partition, 1937'. *Hist. J.* 22 (1979), 423–41.

14315 ROSE (NORMAN ANTHONY). 'The Debate on Partition, 1937–1938: The Anglo–Zionist Aspect, 1. The Proposal'. *Mid. East. Studs* vi (1970), 297–318.

14316 —— 'The Debate on Partition, 1937–38: The Anglo–Zionist Aspect, 2. The Withdrawal'. *Mid. East. Studs* vii (1971), 3–24.

14317 —— 'Palestine's Role in Britain's Imperial Defence: An Aspect of Zionist Diplomacy, 1938–1939'. *Wiener Lib. Bull.* xxii (1968), 32–5.

14318 —— 'The Moyne Assassination, November 1944: A Political Analysis'. *Mid. East. Studs* 15 (1979), 358–73.

14319 BOWDEN (TOM). The Breakdown of Public Security: The Case of Ireland 1916–1921 and Palestine 1936–1939. 1977.

14320 ZWEIG (RONALD W.). Britain and Palestine during the Second World War. Woodbridge. 1986.

14321 KATZBURG (NATHANIEL). From Partition to White Paper: British Policy in Palestine, 1936–1940. Jerusalem. 1940.

14322 FRIESEL (EVYTAR). The British, Zionism and Palestine: Perceptions and Policies during the Mandate Period. 1986.

14323 COHEN (MICHAEL J.). Palestine, Retreat from the Mandate: The Making of British Policy, 1936–1945. 1978.

14324 —— Churchill and the Jews. 1985.

14325 —— Origins and Evolution of the Arab–Zionist Conflict. Berkeley, Calif. 1987.

14326 —— 'Appeasement in the Middle East: The British White Paper on Palestine, May 1939'. *Hist. J.* xvi (1973), 571–96.

14327 —— 'The British White Paper on Palestine, May 1939: Part II, the Testing of a Policy, 1942–1945'. *Hist. J.* xix (1976), 727–57.

14328 —— 'Why Britain Left: The End of the Mandate'. *Wiener Lib. Bull.* xxxi (1978), 74–86.

14329 —— 'American Influence on British Policy in the Middle East During World War Two: First Attempts at Co-ordinating Allied Policy on Palestine'. *Amer. Jewish Hist. Q.* lxvii (1977), 50–70.

14330 —— 'The Genesis of the Anglo-American Committee on Palestine, November 1945: A Case Study on the Assertion of American Hegemony'. *Hist. J.* 22 (1979), 185–207.

14331 DINNERSTEIN (L.). 'America, Britain and Palestine: The Anglo-American Committee of Enquiry'. *Dipl. Hist.* 6 (1982), 283–301.

14332 ZWEIG (RONALD W.). 'The Political Uses of Military Intelligence: Evaluating the Threat of a Jewish Revolt against Britain during the Second World War'. In 'Diplomacy and Intelligence during the Second World War: Essays in Honour of F. H. Hinsley'. *Ed.* by Richard Langhorne. Camb. 1985.

14333 COHEN (GAVRIEL). Churchill and Palestine, 1939–1942. Jerusalem. 1976.

14334 —— The British Cabinet and the Question of Palestine, April–July 1943. Tel Aviv. 1976.

14335 HARON (M. J.). Palestine and the Anglo-American Connection, 1945–1950. N.Y. 1986.

14336 —— 'Note: United States–British Collaboration on Illegal Immigration to Palestine, 1945–1947'. *Jewish Social Studs* 42/2 (1980), 177–82.

14337 KIMCHE (JON) *and* KIMCHE (DAVID). The Secret Roads: The 'Illegal' Migration of a People 1938–1948. 1954.

14338 NACHMANI (AMIKAM). Great Power Discord in Palestine: The Anglo-American Committee of Inquiry into the Problems of European Jewry and Palestine 1945–1946. 1987.

14339 —— '"It is a Matter of Getting the Mixture Right": Britain's Post-War Relations with America in the Middle East'. *J. Contemp. Hist.* 18 (1983), 117–40.

14340 PODET (ALLEN HOWARD). The Success and Failure of the Anglo-American Committee of Inquiry 1945–1946: Last Chance in Palestine. Lewiston, N.Y. 1986.

14341 COHEN (MICHAEL J.). Palestine and the Great Powers 1945–1948. Princeton, NJ. 1982.

14342 LOUIS (WILLIAM ROGER) and STOOKEY (ROBERT W.) eds. The End of the Palestine Mandate. 1986.

14343 OVENDALE (RITCHIE). 'The Palestine Policy of the British Labour Government 1945–1946'. *Inl Affs* 55 (1979), 409–31.

14344 —— 'The Palestine Policy of the British Labour Government 1947: The Decision to Withdraw'. *Inl Affs* 56 (1980), 73–93.

14345 CROSSMAN (RICHARD H. S.). Palestine Mission: A Personal Record. 1947.

14346 LOUIS (WILLIAM ROGER). 'British Imperialism and the Partitions of India and Palestine'. In 'Warfare, Diplomacy and Politics: Essays in Honour of A. J. P. Taylor'. *Ed.* by Chris Wrigley (1986), 189–209.

14347 —— 'Sir Alan Cunningham and the End of British Rule in Palestine'. *J. Imp. Cwealth Hist.* 16 (1988), 128–47.

14348 CUNNINGHAM (Sir ALAN). 'Palestine: The Last Days of the Mandate'. *Inl Affs* 24 (1948), 481–90.

14349 JONES (MARTIN). Failure in Palestine: Britain and United States Policy After the Second World War. 1985.

14350 OVENDALE (RITCHIE). Britain, the United States and the End of the Palestine Mandate 1942–1948. 1989.

14351 KIMCHE (JON) and KIMCHE (DAVID). Both Sides of the Hill: Britain and the Palestine War. 1960.

14352 SHLAIM (AVI). Collusion across the Jordan: King Abdullah, the Zionist Movement and the Partition of Palestine. Oxf. 1988.

14353 WILSON (MARY C.). King Abdullah, Britain and the Making of Jordan. Camb. 1990.

14354 JESSE (RICHARD L.). 'Great Britain and Abdullah's Plan to Partition Palestine: A Natural Sorting Out'. *Mid. East. Studs* 22 (1986), 505–21.

14355 —— 'Britain and the Anglo-Israeli War of 1948'. *J. Palestine Studs* 16/4 (1987), 50–76.

14356 HELLER (JOSEPH). 'Failure of a Mission: Count Bernadotte and Palestine 1948'. *J. Contemp. Hist.* 14 (1979), 515–34.

14357 GAZIT (MORDECAI). 'American and British Diplomacy and the Bernadotte Mission'. *Hist. J.* 29 (1986), 677–96.

14358 PAPPE (ILAN). Britain and the Arab–Israeli Conflict 1948–1951. 1988.

14359 WILSON (JAMES HAROLD). The Chariot of Israel: Britain, America and the State of Israel. 1981.

14350 CROSSMAN (RICHARD H. S.). A Nation Reborn: The Israel of Weizmann, Bevin and Ben-Gurion. 1960.

(b) The Suez Crisis 1956

14361 FARNIE (D. A.). East and West of Suez: The Suez Canal in History, 1854–1958. Oxf. 1961.

14362 SCHONFIELD (HUGH J.). The Suez Canal in Peace and War 1868–1969. Rev. edn 1969.

14363 WATT (DONALD CAMERON). Britain and the Suez Canal. 1956.

14364 —— Documents on the Suez Crisis 26 July to 6 November 1956. Oxf. 1957.

14365 LAUTERPACHT (E.) ed. The Suez Canal Settlement: A Selection of Documents Relating to the Clearance of the Suez Canal and the Settlement of Disputes between the United Kingdom, France and the United Arab Republic, October 1956–March 1959. 1960.

14366 BOWIE (R. R.). Suez 1956. Oxf. 1974. [A legal study.].

14367 JOHNSON (PAUL). The Suez War. 1957.

14368 WINT (GUY) and CALVOCORESSI (PETER). Middle East Crisis. Harmondsworth. 1957.

14369 ADAMS (MICHAEL). Suez and After: Year of Crisis. 1958.

14370 EPSTEIN (LEON DAVID). British Politics in the Suez Crisis. 1964.

14371 BARKER (A. J.). Suez: The Seven Day War. 1964.

14372 EAYRS (JAMES GEORGE) ed. The Commonwealth and Suez: A Documentary Survey. 1964.

14373 ROBERTSON (TERENCE). Crisis: The Inside Story of the Suez Conspiracy. 1965.

14374 THOMAS (HUGH SWYNNERTON) Baron. The Suez Affair. 1967. 3rd edn 1986.

14375 MONCRIEFF (ANTHONY) ed. Suez—Ten Years After. 1967.

14376 NUTTING (Sir HAROLD ANTHONY). No End of a Lesson: The Story of Suez. 1967.

14377 KERR (MALCOLM H.). 'Coming to Terms with Nasser: Attempts and Failures'. *Inl Affs* xliii (1967), 65–84.

14378 LOVE (ISRAEL KENNETT). Suez: The Twice Fought War. 1970.

14379 BRADDON (RUSSELL). Suez: Splitting of a Nation. 1973.

14380 ZHIGALOV (I. I.). 'The Problem of Great Britain's Participation in the 1956 Suez Crisis and its Reflection in Historical Literature'. *Voprosy Istorii* v (1976), 66–83.

14381 WARNER (GEOFFREY). ' "Collusion" and the Suez Crisis of 1956'. *Inl Affs* lv (1979), 226–39.

14382 LLOYD (SELWYN). Suez 1956: A Personal Account. 1978.

14383 FULLICK (ROY) and POWELL (GEOFFREY). Suez: The Double War. 1979.

14384 SHUCKBURGH (Sir EVELYN). Descent to Suez: Diaries 1951–1956. 1986.

14385 JAMES (ROBERT RHODES). 'Anthony Eden and the Suez Crisis'. *Hist. Today* 36 (1986), 8–15.

14386 NEGRINE (R.). 'The Press and the Suez Crisis: A Myth Re-examined'. *Hist. J.* 25 (1982), 975–83.

14387 GORST (ANTHONY). 'Suez 1956: A Consumer's Guide to Papers at the Public Record Office'. *Contemp. Record* 1 (1987), 9–11.

14388 CARLTON (DAVID). Britain and the Suez Crisis. Oxf. 1988.

14389 GORST (ANTHONY) and LUCAS (W. SCOTT). 'Suez 1956: Strategy and the Diplomatic Process'. *J. Strat. Studs* 11 (1988), 391–436.

14390 LOUIS (WILLIAM ROGER) and OWEN (ROGER) eds. Suez 1956: The Crisis and its Consequences. Oxf. 1989.

14391 TROEN (ILAN) and SHEMESH (MOSHE). The Suez–Sinai Crisis: A Retrospective. 1990.

14392 JOHNMAN (LEWIS). 'Defending the Pound: The Economics of the Suez Crisis 1956'. In 'Postwar Britain 1945–1964: Themes and Perspectives'. *Ed.* by Tony Gorst, Lewis Johnman, and W. Lucas. 1989.

(c) Egypt

14393 MAKAR (RAGAI N.). Egypt. Oxf. 1988.

14394 WARBURG (GABRIEL R.). 'The Sinai Peninsula Borders 1906–1947'. *J. Contemp. Hist.* 14 (1979), 677–92.

14395 MARLOWE (JOHN). A History of Modern Egypt and Anglo-Egyptian Relations, 1800–1956. 2nd edn 1965.

14396 HOLT (PETER MALCOLM). Egypt and the Fertile Crescent, 1516–1922: A Political History. 1966.

14397 VATIKIOTIS (PANAYIOTIS JERASIMOF). The Modern History of Egypt. 1969.

14398 ROYAL INSTITUTE OF INTERNATIONAL AFFAIRS. Great Britain and Egypt, 1914–1951. 1936. New edn 1952.

14399 WILSON (KEITH M.) ed. Imperialism and Nationalism in the Middle East: The Anglo-Egyptian Experience, 1882–1982. 1983.

14400 MANSFIELD (PETER). The British in Egypt. 1971.

14401 EVANS (TREFOR E.) ed. The Killearn Diaries 1934–1946: The Diplomatic and Personal Record of Lord Killearn, Sir Miles Lampson, High Commissioner and Ambassador to Egypt. 1972.

14402 —— Mission to Egypt 1934–1946: Lord Killearn, High Commissioner and Ambassador. Cardiff. 1971.

14403 BISHKU (M. B.). 'The British Press and the Future of Egypt, 1919–1922'. *Inl Hist. Rev.* 8 (1986), 604–12.

14404 GALLAGHER (NANCY E.). 'Anglo-American Rivalry and the Establishment of a Medical Research Institute in Egypt, 1942–1948'. *Inl Hist. Rev.* 9 (1987), 291–8.

14405 HAHN (PETER L.). 'The Anglo-Egyptian Negotiations 1950–1952'. *Mid. East. Affs* 3 (1952), 213–32.

14406 —— 'Containment and Egyptian Nationalism: The Unsuccessful Effort to Establish the Middle East Command 1950–1953'. *Dipl. Hist.* 11 (1987), 23–40.

14407 SELAK (C. B.). 'The Suez Canal Base Agreement of 1954: Its Background and Implications'. *Amer. J. Inl Law* 49 (1955), 487–505.

14408 TIGNOR (ROBERT L.). 'Decolonization and Business: The Case of Egypt'. *J. Mod. Hist.* 59 (1987), 479–505.

(d) Sudan

14409 HILL (RICHARD LESLIE). A Bibliography of the Anglo-Egyptian Sudan, from the Earliest Times to 1937. 1939. Supplemented by A Bibliography of the Sudan, 1938–1958. By Abdel Rahman El Nasric. Oxf. 1962.

14410 —— A Biographical Dictionary of the Sudan. 2nd edn 1967.

14411 DALY (M. W.) ed. Modernization in the Sudan: Essays in Honor of Richard Hill. N.Y. 1985.

14412 ABBAS (MEKKI). The Sudan Question: The Dispute over the Anglo-Egyptian Condominium 1884–1951. 1952.

14413 FABUNMI (L. A.). The Sudan in Anglo-Egyptian Relations: A Case Study in Power Politics 1800–1956. 1960.

14414 HOLT (PETER M.). A Modern History of the Sudan from the Funf Sultanate to the Present Day. 1961.

14415 AL-RAHMAN (MUDDATHIR 2ABD). Imperialism and Nationalism in the Sudan: A Study in Constitutional and Political Development. Oxf. 1969.

14416 WOODWARD (PETER). Condominium and Sudanese Nationalism. 1979.

14417 COLLINS (ROBERT O.) and DENG (FRANCIS M.) eds. The British in the Sudan 1898–1956. 1984.

14418 HENDERSON (K. D. D.). Sudan Republic. 1965.

14419 —— Set Under Authority. Castle Cary. 1987.

14420 SABRY (H. Z.). Sovereignty for Sudan. 1982.

14421 MacMICHAEL (Sir HAROLD). The Sudan. 1954.

14422 —— Sudan Political Service, 1899–1956. Oxf. N.d.

14423 DUNCAN (J. S. R.). The Sudan: A Record of Achievement. 1952.

14424 —— Sudan's Path to Independence. Edin. 1957.

14425 JACKSON (H. C.). Behind the Modern Sudan. 1955.

14426 BELL (G.) and DEE (B. D.). Sudan Political Service, 1899–1956. Oxf. 1958.

14427 COLLINS (ROBERT O.). Shadows in the Grass: Britain in the Southern Sudan, 1918–1956. New Haven, Conn. 1983.

14428 BESHIR (MOHAMMED OMER). The Southern Sudan: Background to Conflict. 1968.

14429 —— Educational Development in the Sudan 1898–1956. Oxf. 1969.

14430 —— Revolution and Nationalism in the Sudan. 1974.

7

WAR AND THE ARMED SERVICES

To cope, organizationally, with both the conduct, course, and consequences of war and also with the respective roles of particular armed services presents difficulties. It is obvious that in some operations one service rather than another will be dominant. There is the additional task of ensuring that the major and at least some minor theatres of war are adequately covered and the relevant literature accessible to the reader. At the same time the role of particular commanders and units is best considered in an operational context. The strategy that has been adopted in this section cannot eliminate some elements of inconsistency. However, the categories within the initial sub-sections attempt an adequate coverage of the two major wars—bearing in mind that bibliographies of both wars do exist and that our task is not to replicate them but to try, so far as possible, to keep in mind that it is 'Britain at war' that is our concern, however much it may also be necessary to have an understanding of both wars as a whole for Britain's particular contribution to be placed in proper context.

The sub-sections that follow deal, in sequence, with the three services in categories which range from literature on structure and personnel to some material on particular operations. There is one sub-section on 'intelligence' which has a wider reach than the two world wars. A final section refers specifically to post-1945 activities, though there is also material in some of the general histories of the individual services which have been listed earlier.

A. THE FIRST WORLD WAR

1. GENERAL (DOMESTIC)

14431 ENSER (A. G. S.). A Subject Bibliography of the First World War: Books in English 1914–1978. Aldershot. 1979.

14432 BAYLISS (G. M.). Bibliographic Guide to the Two World Wars: An Annotated Survey of English-Language Reference Materials. 1977.

14433 CARNEGIE ENDOWMENT FOR INTERNATIONAL PEACE. Economic and Social History of the World War.

14434 POUND (REGINALD). The Lost Generation. 1964.

14435 WOODWARD (*Sir* ERNEST LLEWELLYN). Great Britain and the War of 1914–1918. 1967.

14436 TURNER (JOHN ANDREW). Britain and the First World War. 1988.

14437 —— British Politics in the Great War: Competition and Conflict, 1915–1918. 1991.

14438 ROWE (THOMAS) *ed.* Gathering Moss. A memoir of Owen Tweedy. 1967.

14439 BURK (KATHLEEN). *ed.* War and the State, 1914–19. 1982.

14440 FRENCH (DAVID). British Economic and Strategic Planning 1905–15. 1982.

14441 —— British Strategy and War Aims 1914–16. 1986.

14442 PONSONBY (ARTHUR AUGUSTUS WILLIAM) *Baron Ponsonby.* Falsehood in Wartime. 1928.

14443 MURDOCH (BRIAN). Fighting Songs and Warring Words: Popular Lyrics of Two World Wars. 1990.

14444 GIROUARD (MARK). The Return to Camelot. New Haven./Lond. 1981.

14445 LIDDLE (PETER H.) *ed.* Home Fires & Foreign Fields: British Social and Military Experience in the First World War. 1985.

14446 READER (W. J.). 'At Duty's Call': A Study in Obsolete Patriotism. Manch. 1988.

14447 BECKETT (IAN) *and* SIMPSON (KEITH). A Nation at Arms: A Social Study of the British Army in the First World War. Manch. 1985.

14448 JACKSON (ROBERT) . The Prisoners 1914–18. 1989.

14449 MUNSON (JAMES) *ed.* Echoes of the Great War: The Diary of the Rev. Andrew Clark 1914–1919. Oxf. 1985. [An Essex rector].

2. GENERAL (FIGHTING)

14450 ALLEN (GEORGE HENRY) *et al.* The Great War. 5 vols Philadelphia, Pa. 1915–21.

14451 CRUTTWELL (CHARLES ROBERT MOWBRAY FRASER). A History of the Great War, 1914–1918. Oxf. 1934.

14452 FALLS (CYRIL BENTHAM). The First World War. 1960.

14453 KING-HALL (STEPHEN). History of the War. 2 vols 1939.

14454 HART (BASIL HENRY LIDDELL). The Real War, 1914–1918. 1930.

14455 —— A History of the World War 1914–1918. 1930. 2nd edn 1934.

14456 BROPHY (JOHN). The Five Years: A Conspectus of the Great War. 1936.

14457 McENTEE (GIRARD LINDSLEY). Military History of the World War. N.Y. 1937.

14458 EDMONDS (*Sir* JAMES EDWARD). A Short History of World War I. 1951.

14459 FALLS (CYRIL BENTHAM). A Hundred Years of War. 1953.

14460 TAYLOR (ALAN JOHN PERCIVALE). The First World War: An Illustrated History. 1963.

14461 DOYLE (*Sir* ARTHUR CONAN). The British Campaign in Europe, 1914–1918. 1928.

14462 GREEN (HOWARD). The British Army in the First World War. 1968.

14463 HUGUET (VICTOR JACQUES MARIE). Britain and the War: A French Indictment. 1928.

14464 KEEGAN (JOHN). The Face of Battle. 1976

14465 ROBBINS (KEITH GILBERT). The First World War. Oxf. 1984.

3. THE EXPERIENCE OF SOLDIERS

14466 AITKEN (ALEXANDER CRAIG). Gallipoli to the Somme. 1963.

14467 BARTLETT (ELLIS ASHMEAD). Some of My Experiences in the Great War. 1918.

14468 BELL (DOUGLAS HERBERT). A Soldier's Diary of the Great War. Intro. by Henry Williamson. 1929.

14469 BLUNDEN (EDMUND CHARLES). Undertones of War. 1928. New edn 1956.

14470 —— War Poets 1914–1918. 1958.

14471 BROPHY (JOHN) *and* PARTRIDGE (ERIC HONEYWOOD). Songs and Slang of the British Soldier: 1914–1918. 1930. 3rd rev. edn 1931.

14472 —— The Long Trail. 1965. [A rewritten version of the above book.].

14473 CARRINGTON (CHARLES EDMUND). Soldiers from the Wars Returning. 1965.

14474 —— As EDMONDS (CHARLES). A Subaltern's War: Being a Memoir of the Great War from the Point of View of a Romantic Young Man. 3rd rev. edn 1929.

14475 CLARK (ALAN). The Donkeys. 1961.

14476 CROZIER (FRANK PERCY). A Brass Hat in No Man's Land. 1930.

14477 FUSSELL (PAUL). The Great War and Modern Memory. 1975.

14478 GRAVES (ROBERT). Goodbye to All That. 1930.

14479 HAY (IAN). Arms and the Men. 1977.

14480 HITCHCOCK (FRANCIS CLERE). 'Stand To': A Diary of the Trenches, 1915–1918. 1937.

14481 HOULIHAN (MICHAEL). World War I Trench Warfare. 1974.

14482 LLOYD (A.). The War in the Trenches. 1975.

14483 MASEFIELD (JOHN). The Old Front Line. 1917.

14484 MOYNIHAN (MICHAEL) *ed.* A Place Called Armageddon: Letters From the Great War. Newton Abbot. 1975.

14485 —— Greater Love: Letters Home 1914–1918. 1980.

14486 PARKER (ERNEST WALTER). Into Battle, 1914–1918. 1964.

14487 SASSOON (SIEGFRIED). Memoirs of an Infantry Officer. 1930.

14488 WADE (AUBREY). Gunner on the Western Front. 1936. 2nd edn 1959.

14489 WINTER (DENIS). Death's Men: Soldiers of the Great War. 1978.

The Near East

14490 LAWRENCE (THOMAS EDWARD). Revolt in the Desert. 1927.

14491 —— Seven Pillars of Wisdom: A Triumph. 1935.

14492 LOCK (H. O.). With the British Army in the Holy Land. 1919.

14493 MacMUNN (GEORGE) *and* FALLS (CYRIL B.). Egypt and Palestine. 2 vols 1928–30. [Official history, First World War.].

14494 MASSEY (WILLIAM THOMAS). The Desert Campaigns. 1918.

14495 —— How Jerusalem was Won. 1919.

14496 —— Allenby's Final Triumph. 1920.

14497 WAVELL (ARCHIBALD PERCIVAL) *Earl.* Allenby: A Study in Greatness. 1940.

14498 —— Allenby in Egypt. 1943.

14499 —— The Palestine Campaigns. 1928. Rev. edn 1931.

4. MILITARY COMMANDERS

14500 GARDNER (ROBERT BRIAN). Allenby. 1965.

14501 CARL (ERNST). One Against England: The Death of Lord Kitchener and the Plot Against the British Fleet. 1935.

14502 FRENCH (EDWARD GERALD). The Life of Field Marshal Sir John French, First Earl of Ypres. 1931.

14503 DAVIDSON (*Sir* JOHN). Haig, Master of the Field. 1953.

14504 SIXSMITH (E. K. G.). Douglas Haig. 1976.

14505 BLAKE (ROBERT NORMAN WILLIAM) *Baron, ed.* The Private Papers of Douglas Haig, 1914–1919. 1952.

14506 BORASTON (JOHN HERBERT) *ed.* Sir Douglas Haig's Despatches. December 1915–April 1919. 1919.

14507 COOPER (ALFRED DUFF). Haig. Vol. 1 1935. Vol. 2 1936.

14508 TERRAINE (JOHN). Douglas Haig, the Educated Soldier. 1963.

14509 IRONSIDE (EDMUND OSLAC) *Baron, ed.* High Road to Command: the Diaries of Major General Sir Edmund Ironside, 1920–1922. 1972.

14510 CASSAR (GEORGE H.). Kitchener, Architect of Victory. 1977.

14511 McCORMICK (GEORGE DONALD KING). The Mystery of Lord Kitchener's Death. 1959.

14512 HYDE (HARFORD MONTGOMERY). Solitary in the Ranks: Lawrence of Arabia as Airman and Private Soldier. 1977.

14513 STEWART (D.). T. E. Lawrence. 1977.

14514 MACK (J. E.). A Prince of Our Disorder: The Life of T. E. Lawrence. 1976.

14515 ALDINGTON (RICHARD). Lawrence of Arabia. 1955.

14516 KNIGHTLEY (PHILLIP). Lawrence of Arabia. 1976.

14517 HANNAH (W. H.). Bobs: Kipling's General: Life of Field Marshal Earl Roberts of Kandahar, V.C. 1972.

14518 BONHAM-CARTER (VICTOR). Soldier True: The Life and Times of Field-Marshal Sir William Robertson, 1860–1933. 1963.

14519 ROBERTSON (WILLIAM ROBERT). Soldiers and Statesmen, 1914–1918. 1926.

14520 CALLWELL (*Sir* CHARLES EDWARD). Field Marshal Sir Henry Wilson: His Life and Diaries. 2 vols 1927.

14521 ASH (BERNARD). The Lost Dictator. A Biography of Field-Marshal Sir Henry Wilson. 1968.

5. AFRICA

14522 BUCHANAN (ANGUS). Three Years of War in East Africa. 1919.

14523 DANE (EDMUND). British Campaigns in Africa and the Pacific, 1914–1918. 1919.

14524 HORDERN (CHARLES). East Africa. Vol. 1, August 1914–September 1916 (incomplete). 1941. [Official history, First World War.].

14525 WYNN (ALFRED HEARST WYNN ELIAS). Ambush. 1937. [Reminiscences of the East African campaigns].

14526 MILLER (CHARLES). Battle for the Bundu. The First World War in East Africa. 1974.

14527 MOBERLY (FREDERICK J.). Togoland and the Cameroons, 1914–1916. 1931. [Official History, First World War].

14528 RAYNER (W. S.) *and* O'SHAUGHNESSY (W. W.). How Botha and Smuts Conquered German South West Africa. 1916.

14529 THORNHILL (CHRISTOPHER J.). Taking Tanganyika: Experiences of an Intelligence Officer, 1914–1918. 1937.

14530 McLAUGHLIN (PETER). Ragtime Soldiers: The Rhodesian Experience in the First World War. Bulawayo. 1980.

14531 OSUNTOKUA (A.). Nigeria and the First World War. 1979.

6. THE BALKANS

14532 PALMER (ALAN). The Gardeners of Salonika. 1965.

14533 FALLS (CYRIL BENTHAM). Macedonia. 2 Vols 1933–35. [Official history, First World War.].

14534 PRICE (GEORGE WARD). The Story of the Salonika Army. 1917.

7. THE DARDANELLES

14535 LIDDLE (PETER). Men of Gallipoli: The Dardanelles and Gallipoli Experience, August 1914 to January 1916. 1976.

14536 —— *Ed.* Gallipoli 1915: Pens, Pencils and Cameras at War. Oxf. 1985.

14537 BARTLETT (ELLIS ASHMEAD). Ashmead Bartlett's Despatches from the Dardanelles. 1916.

14538 —— The Uncensored Dardanelles. 1928.

14539 BRODIE (CHARLES GORDON). Forlorn Hope, 1915: The Submarine Passage of the Dardanelles. 1956.

14540 BUSH (ERIC WHEELER). Gallipoli. 1975.

14541 CALLWELL (*Sir* CHARLES EDWARD). The Dardanelles. 1919.

14542 CHATTERTON (EDWARD KEBLE). Dardanelles Dilemma: The Story of Naval Operations. 1935.

14543 DELAGE (EDMOND). The Tragedy of the Dardanelles. 1932.

14544 HAMILTON (IAN). Gallipoli Diary. 2 vols 1920.

14545 HOYT (E. P.). Disaster at the Dardanelles, 1915. 1976.

14546 JAMES (ROBERT RHODES). Gallipoli. 1965.

14547 KEARSEY (ALEXANDER HORACE CYRIL). Notes and Comments on the Dardanelles Campaign. Aldershot. 1934.

14548 KEYES (*Sir* ROGER JOHN BROWNLOW). The Naval Memoirs of Admiral of the Fleet Sir Roger Keyes: 1) The Narrow Seas to the Dardanelles, 1910–1915. 2) Scapa Flow to the Dover Straits, 1916–1918. 2 vols 1934–5.

14549 —— The Fight for Gallipoli. 1941.

14550 MOOREHEAD (ALAN). Gallipoli. 1956.

14551 NEVINSON (HENRY WOODD). The Dardanelles Campaign. 1918.

14552 PATTERSON (J. H.). With the Zionists in Gallipoli. 1916.

14553 PHILLIPSON (C.) *and* BUXTON (NOEL). The Question of the Bosphorus and the Dardanelles. 1917.

14554 SHANKLAND (PETER) *and* HUNTER (ANTHONY). Dardanelles Patrol. 1964.

14555 WESTER-WEMYSS (R. E.). The Navy in the Dardanelles Campaign. 1924.

8. THE ITALIAN FRONT

14556 EDMONDS (*Sir* JAMES EDWARD) *et al.* Italy, 1915–1919. 1949. [Official history, First World War.].

9. MESOPOTAMIA/TRANSCASPIA

14557 ELLIS (CHARLES HOWARD). The Transcaspian Episode. 1918–1919. 1963.

14558 BARKER (ARTHUR JAMES). The Neglected War: Mesopotamia, 1914–1918. 1967.

14559 BLACKLEDGE (WILLIAM JAMES). The Legion of Marching Madmen. 1936.

14560 BURNE (ALFRED HIGGINS). Mesopotamia, the Last Phase. 1936.

14561 CATO (CONRAD). The Navy in Mesopotamia, 1914–1917. 1917.

14562 DANE (EDMUND). British Campaigns in the Nearer East, 1914–1918. 2 vols 1919.

14563 KEARSEY (ALEXANDER HORACE CYRIL). A Study of the Strategy and Tactics of the Mesopotamian Campaign, 1914–1917. Aldershot. 1934.

14564 MILLAR (RONALD). Death of an Army: The Siege of Kut, 1915–1916. Boston, Mass. 1969.

14565 MOBERLY (FREDERICK J.). Mesopotamia. 4 vols 1923–27. [Official history, First World War.].

14566 TOWNSHEND (*Sir* CHARLES VERE-FERRERS). My Campaign in Mesopotamia. 1920.

10. THE RUSSIAN FRONT

14567 COATES (WILLIAM PEYTON) *and* COATES (ZELDA KAHAN). Armed Intervention in Russia 1918–1922. 1935.

14568 BRADLEY (JOHN FRANCIS NEJEZ). Allied Intervention in Russia. 1968.

14569 HALLIDAY (ERNEST MILTON). The Ignorant Armies: The Anglo-American Archangel Expedition, 1918–1919.

14570 IRONSIDE (W. EDMUND) *Baron*. Archangel, 1918–1919. 1953.

14571 MAYNARD (*Sir* CHARLES CLARKSON MARTIN). The Murmansk Venture. 1928.

11. THE WESTERN FRONT

14572 TRAVERS (TIM). The Killing Ground: The British Army, the Western Front and the Emergence of Warfare, 1900–1918. 1987.

14573 TERRAINE (JOHN). The Western Front, 1914–1918. 1964.

14574 SPEARS (*Sir* EDWARD LOUIS). Liaison, 1914. A Narrative of the Great Retreat. 1930.

14575 ASPREY (ROBERT BROWN). The First Battle of the Marne. 1962.

14576 WHITTON (FREDERICK ERNEST). The Marne Campaign. 1917.

14577 WOLFF (LEON). In Flanders Fields: The 1917 Campaign. 1959.

14578 WOOD (HERBERT FAIRLIE). Vimy! 1972.

14579 BLAXLAND (WILLIAM GREGORY). Amiens: 1918. 1968.

14580 CAREW (TIM). Wipers. 1974.

14581 EDMONDS (JAMES EDWARD). France and Belgium. 14 vols 1922–49. [Official history, First World War.].

14582 FARRAR-HOCKLEY (ANTHONY HERITAGE). The Somme. 1964.

14583 GARDNER (ROBERT BRIAN). The Big Push: A Portrait of the Battle of the Somme. 1961.

14584 GILES (JOHN). The Ypres Salient. 1970.

14585 —— The Somme: Then and Now. Folkestone. 1977.

14586 GORDON (GEORGE STUART). Mons and the Retreat: The Operations of the British Army in the Present War. 1918.

14587 HAMILTON (ERNEST WILLIAM *Lord*). The First Seven Divisions: Being a Detailed Account of the Fighting from Mons to Ypres. 1916.

14588 HORNE (ALISTAIR). Death of a Generation: From Neuve Chapelle to Verdun and the Somme. 1970.

14589 KEARSEY (ALEXANDER HORACE CYRIL). The Battle of Amiens 1918, and Operations 8th Aug.–3rd Sept. 1918: The Turn of the Tide on the Western Front. Aldershot. 1950.

14590 MCKEE (ALEXANDER). Vimy Ridge. 1966.

14591 MIDDLEBROOK (MARTIN). The First Day on the Somme, 1st July 1916. 1971.

14592 TERRAINE (JOHN) *ed.* General Jack's Diary 1914–1918. 1964.

14593 —— Mons, the Retreat to Victory. 1960.

14594 —— The Road to Passchendaele, the Flanders Offensive of 1917: A Study in Inevitability. 1977.

14595 TYNG (SEWELL T.). The Campaign of the Marne, 1914. 1935.

14596 PITT (BARRIE WILLIAM). 1918: The Last Act. 1962.

14597 BARCLAY (CYRIL NELSON). Armistice 1918. 1968.

14598 FALLS (CYRIL BENTHAM). Armageddon, 1918. 1964.

14599 ROBINSON (*Sir* HARRY PERRY). The Turning Point: The Battle of the Somme. 1917.

14600 ROGERSON (SIDNEY). The Last Off the Ebb. 1937.

14601 GOUGH (*Sir* HUBERT DE LA POER). The Fifth Army. 1931.

14602 —— The March Retreat. 1934.

14603 FARRAR-HOCKLEY (ANTHONY). Death of an Army. 1967.

12. BLOCKADE

14604 BELL (ARCHIBALD COLQUHOUN). A History of the Blockade of Germany and of the Countries Associated with Her in the Great War: Austria-Hungary, Bulgaria and Turkey, 1914–1918. 1937.

14605 CHATTERTON (EDWARD KEBLE). The Big Blockade. 1932.

14606 GUICHARD (LOUIS). The Naval Blockade, 1914–1918. 1930.

14607 SINEY (MARION C.). The Allied Blockade of Germany, 1914–1916. Ann Arbor, Mich. 1957.

13. MEDICAL SERVICES

14608 CLARK-KENNEDY (ARCHIBALD EDMUND). Edith Cavell: Pioneer and Patriot. 1965.

14609 PIGGOTT (JULIET). Queen Alexandria's Royal Army Nursing Corps. 1975.

14610 PLUMRIDGE (JOHN HENRY). Hospital Ships and Ambulance Trains. 1975.

14. THE INDIAN ARMY

14611 ELLIOTT (JAMES GORDON). The Frontier, 1839–1947. 1970.

14612 INCHBALD (G.). Camels and Others: The Imperial Camel Corps in World War I. 1968.

14613 SANDES (E. W. C.). The Military Engineer in India. 2 vols Chatham. 1933–5.

15. INTELLIGENCE

14614 LINDAU (HENRY). All's Fair: The Story of the British Secret Service Behind the German Lines. N.Y. 1934.

16. PHOTOGRAPHY

14615 HUTCHINSON (WALTER VICTOR) *ed.* Hutchinson's Pictorial History of the War. 1939.

14616 BEAN (CHARLES EDWARD WOODROW) *and* GULLET (*Sir* HENRY SOMER) *eds.* Photographic Record of the War: Reproductions of Pictures Taken by the Australian Official Photographers. Sydney. 1923.

14617 CARMICHAEL (JANE). First World War Photographers. 1989.

17. AIR POWER

14618 COOPER (MALCOLM). The Birth of Independent Air Power: British Air Policy in the First World War. 1986.

14619 CHAMIER (JOHN ADRIAN). The Birth of the Royal Air Force: The Early History and Experiences of the Flying Services. 1943.

14620 CUNEO (JOHN ROBERT). The Air Weapon, 1914–1916. Harrisburg, Pa. 1947.

14621 REYNOLDS (QUENTIN JAMES). They Fought for the Sky: The Story of the First War in the Air. 1958.

14622 MACMILLAN (NORMAN). Offensive Patrol: The Story of the RNAS, RFC and RAF in Italy, 1917–1918. 1973.

14623 COLE (CHRISTOPHER) *ed.* Royal Flying Corps, 1915–1916. 1969.

14624 —— Royal Air Force, 1918. 1968.

14625 —— McCudden, V.C. 1967.

14626 LEWIS (GWILYM HUGH). Wings Over the Somme, 1916-1918. 1976.

14627 MCKEE (ALEXANDER). The Friendless Sky: The Story of Air Combat in World War I. 1962.

14628 TURNER (C. C.). The Struggle in the Air, 1914–1918. 1919.

14629 SHORES (CHRISTOPHER). Fighter Aces. 1975.

14630 MUNSON (KENNETH GEORGE). Fighters, Attack and Training Aircraft 1914–1919. 1968.

14631 —— Bombers, Patrol and Reconnaissance Aircraft 1914–1919. 1968.

14632 —— Aircraft of World War I. 1967.

14633 JOYNSON-HICKS (W.) *Viscount Brentford*. The Command of the Air. 1916.

14634 LAMBERTON (WILLIAM MELVILLE). Reconnaissance and Bomber Aircraft of the 1914–1918 war. 1962.

14635 THETFORD (OWEN G.) *and* RIDING (E. J.). Aircraft of the 1914–1918 War. Leicester. 1946.

14636 MORRIS (ALAN). The Balloonatics. 1970.

14637 FYFE (GEORGE). From Box-Kites to Bombers. 1936.

14638 —— Sopwith Camel: King of Combat. Falmouth. 1978.

14639 BRIDGMAN (LEONARD). The Clouds Remember: The Aeroplanes of World War I. 1972.

14640 BRUCE (JOHN McINTOSH). British Aeroplanes, 1914–1918. 1957.

14641 BARTLETT (CHARLES P.). Bomber Pilot, 1916-1918. *Ed.* by Chaz Bowyer. 1974.

14642 KING (HORACE FREDERICK). Armament of British Aircraft, 1909–1939. 1971.

14643 HIGHAM (ROBIN). The British Rigid Airship, 1908–1931: A Study in Weapons Policy. 1961.

14644 ASHMORE (EDWARD BAILEY). Air Defence. 1929.

18. TRANSPORT

14645 DAVIES (WILLIAM JAMES KEITH). Light Railways of the First World War: A History of Tactical Rail Communications on the British Fronts 1914–18. Newton Abbot. 1967.

14646 HENNIKER (ALAN MAJOR). Transportation on the Western Front, 1914–1918. 1937.

19. NAVAL OPERATIONS

First World War

14647 WARNER (OLIVER MARTIN WILSON). Battle Honours of the Royal Navy. 1956.

Jutland

14648 FROTHINGHAM (THOMAS GODDARD). A True Account of the Battle of Jutland, May 31, 1916. Camb., Mass. 1920.

14649 FAWCETT (HAROLD WILLIAM) *and* HOOPER (GEOFFREY WILLIAM WINSMORE). The Fighting at Jutland. Glasgow. 1921.

14650 BACON (*Sir* REGINALD HUGH SPENCER). The Jutland Scandal. 1925.

14651 GIBSON (LANGHORNE) *and* HARPER (JOHN ERNEST TROYTE). The Riddle of Jutland. 1934.

14652 MACINTYRE (DONALD) . Jutland. 1957.

14653 HOUGH (RICHARD). The Battle of Jutland. 1964.

14654 BENNETT (GEOFFREY MARTIN). The Battle of Jutland. 1964.

14655 IRVING (JOHN). The Smoke Screen of Jutland. 1966.

14656 OAKESHOTT (EDWARD). The Blindfold Game: 'The Day' at Jutland. Oxf. 1969.

14657 COSTELLO (JOHN) *and* HUGHES (T.). Jutland, 1916. 1976.

Zeebrugge

14658 CARPENTER (ALFRED FRANCIS BLAKENEY). The Blocking of Zeebrugge. 1922.

14659 PITT (BARRIE). Zeebrugge: St George's Day 1918. 1958.

14660 WARNER (PHILIP). The Zeebrugge Raid. 1978.

Lusitania

14661 SIMPSON (COLIN). Lusitania. 1972.

14662 BAILEY (THOMAS ANDREW) *and* RYAN (PAUL B.). The Lusitania Disaster: An Episode in Modern Warfare and Diplomacy. N.Y. 1975.

South Atlantic

14663 BINGHAM (BARRY). Falklands. Jutland and the Bight. 1919.

14664 SPENCER-COOPER (H. E. H.). The Battle of the Falkland Islands. 1919.

14665 HIRST (LLOYD). Coronel and After. 1934.

14666 PITT (BARRIE WILLIAM). Coronel and Falkland. 1960.

14667 BENNETT (GEOFFREY MARTIN). Coronel and the Falklands. 1962.

General

14668 LUMBY (E. W. R.) *ed.* Papers Relating to Naval Policy and Operations in the Mediterranean 1912–1914. 1971.

14669 MARDER (ARTHUR JACOB). From the Dreadnought to Scapa Flow: The Royal Navy in the Fisher Era, 1904–1919. 5 vols. 1961–70.

14670 —— From the Dardanelles to Oran: Studies of the Royal Navy in War and Peace, 1915–1940. 1974.

14671 LEYLAND (JOHN). The Achievement of the British Navy in the World War. 1917. Rev. edn 1918.

14672 HURD (ARCHIBALD SPICER). The British Fleet in the Great War. 1918.

14673 FROTHINGHAM (THOMAS GODDARD). The Naval History of the World War. 3 vols Camb., Mass. 1924–26.

14674 CORBETT (*Sir* JULIAN STAFFORD) *and* NEWBOLT (*Sir* HENRY). History of the Great War: Naval Operations. 5 vols 1920–1931. Vol. 3. Rev. edn 1940. [Official history First World War.].

14675 BENNETT (GEOFFREY MARTIN). Naval Battles of the First World War. 1968.

14676 —— Cowan's War: The Story of British Naval Operations in the Baltic, 1918–1920. 1964.

14677 HOWARTH (DAVID). Sovereign of the Seas: The Story of British Sea Power. 1974.

14678 MIDDLEMAS (ROBERT KEITH). Command the Far Seas: A Naval Campaign of the First World War. 1961.

14679 BACON (*Sir* REGINALD HUGH SPENCER). The Dover Patrol, 1915–1917. 2 vols 1919.

14680 USBORNE (CECIL VIVIAN). Smoke on the Horizon: Mediterranean Fighting, 1914–1918. 1933.

14681 ALEXANDER (ROY). The Cruise of the Raider 'Wolf'. 1939.

14682 SHANKLAND (PETER). The Phantom Flotilla: The Story of the Naval Africa Expedition 1915–1916. 1968.

14683 CHATTERTON (EDWARD KEBLE). Q-Ships and Their Story. 1922.

14684 —— The Sea Raiders. 1931.

The Navy in East Asia

14685 BRICE (MARTIN HUBERT). The Royal Navy and the Sino-Japanese Incident 1937–41. 1973.

14686 HAGGIE (PAUL). Britannia at Bay: The Defence of the British Empire Against Japan 1931–1941. Oxf. 1981.

14687 McINTYRE (W. DAVID). The Rise and Fall of the Singapore Naval Base, 1919–42. 1979.

14688 NEIDPATH (JAMES). The Singapore Naval Base and the Defence of Britain's Eastern Empire 1919–41. Oxf. 1981.

14689 MARDER (ARTHUR JACOB). Old Friends, New Enemies: The Royal Navy and the Imperial Japanese Navy, 1936–41. Oxf. 1981.

14690 CHATTERTON (EDWARD KEBLE) *and* EDWARDS (KENNETH). Britain at War: The Royal Navy and Allies. 5 vols 1947.

14691 HARDY (ALFRED CECIL). Everyman's History of the Sea War. 3 vols 1948.

14692 PHILLIPS (CECIL ERNEST LUCAS). Escape of the 'Amethyst'. 1958.

14693 EARL (LAWRENCE). Yangtse Incident: The Story of H.M.S. Amethyst, April 20, 1949 to July 31, 1949. 1952.

20. WOMEN AND THE FIRST WORLD WAR

14694 MARWICK (ARTHUR J. B.). Women at War, 1914–1918. 1977.

14695 MITCHELL (DAVID). Women on the Warpath: The Story of the Women of the First World War. 1966.

21. OPERATIONS: IRELAND

14696 BENNETT (RICHARD LAWRENCE). The Black and Tans. 1959.

14697 HOLT (EDGAR). Protest in Arms: The Irish Troubles, 1916-1923. 1960.

14698 TOWNSHEND (CHARLES). The British Campaign in Ireland, 1919–1921: The Development of Political and Military Policies. 1975.

B. THE SECOND WORLD WAR

1. GENERAL

14699 BEST (GEOFFREY FRANCIS ARTHUR) *and* WHEATCROFT (ANDREW). War, Economy and the Military Mind. 1976.

14700 BOND (BRIAN JAMES) *and* ROY (IAN) *eds*. War and Society: A Yearbook of Military History. 1975.

14701 GILBERT (MARTIN). Auschwitz and the Allies. 1981.

14702 BURNE (ALFRED HIGGINS). Strategy as Exemplified in the Second World War. A Strategical Examination of the Land Operations. Camb. 1946.

14703 CALVOCORESSI (PETER) *and* WINT (GUY). Total War: Causes and Courses of the Second World War. 1972.

14704 CHURCHILL (WINSTON LEONARD SPENCER). The Second World War. 6 vols 1948–53.

14705 COLLIER (BASIL). A Short History of the Second World War. 1967.

14706 FULLER (JOHN FREDERIC CHARLES). The Second World War, 1939–1945: A Strategical and Tactical History. 1948.

14707 HASLUCK (EUGENE LEWIS). The Second World War. 1948.

14708 HART (BASIL HENRY LIDDELL). History of the Second World War. 1970.

2. RE-ARMAMENT IN THE 1930S

14709 SHAY (ROBERT PAUL). British Rearmament in the Thirties: Politics and Profits. 1977.

14710 COGHLAN (F.). 'Armaments, Economic Policy and Appeasement: Background to British Foreign Policy 1931–1937.' *Hist.* lvii (1972), 205–16.

14711 DUNBABIN (JOHN P. D.). 'British Rearmament in the 1930s: A Chronology and a Review.' *Hist. J.* xviii (1975), 587–609.

14712 PARKER (R. A. C.). 'Economics, Rearmament and Foreign Policy: The United Kingdom before 1939—A Preliminary Study.' *J. Contemp. Hist.* x (1975), 637–47.

14713 PEDEN (GEORGE C.). 'Warren Fisher and British Rearmament Against Germany.' *Eng. Hist. Rev.* xciv (1979), 29–48.

14714 SMITH (MALCOLM S.). 'Rearmament and Deterrence in Britain in the 1930s.' *J. Strat. Studs* i (1978), 313–38.

14715 —— 'The Royal Air Force, Air Power and British Foreign Policy, 1932–1937.' *J. Contemp. Hist.* xii (1977), 153–74.

14716 DENNIS (PETER). Decision by Default: Peacetime Conscription and British Defence, 1919–1939. 1972.

3. OFFICIAL HISTORIES

14717 GIBBS (NORMAN HENRY). Grand Strategy. Vol. I. Rearmament Policy. 1976.

14718 HOWARD (MICHAEL ELIOT). The Mediterranean Strategy in the Second World War. 1968.

14719 —— August 1942–August 1943. 1972. [Official history, Second World War: Grand strategy.].

14720 BUTLER (*Sir* JAMES RAMSAY MONTAGU). September 1939–June 1941. 1957. [Official history, Second World War: Grand Strategy].

14721 GWYER (J. M. A.) *and* BUTLER (*Sir* JAMES RAMSAY MONTAGU). June 1941–August 1942. 1964. [Official History, Second World War: Grand strategy.].

14722 EHRMAN (JOHN). August 1943–August 1945. 1956. [Official history, Second World War: Grand strategy.].

14723 MEDLICOTT (W. NORTON). The Economic Blockade. 2 vols. 1952 and 1959.

14724 O'BRIEN (TERENCE H.). Civil Defence. 1955.

14725 COLLIER (BASIL). The Defence of the United Kingdom. 1957. [Official History, Second World War: Campaigns].

14726 ELLIS (LIONEL FREDERIC). France and Flanders, 1939–1940. 1953. [Official history, Second World War: Campaigns.].

14727 *et al.* Victory in the West. 2 vols 1962. [Official history, Second World War: Campaigns.].

14728 PLAYFAIR (IAN STANLEY ORD) *et al.* The Mediterranean and Middle East. 5 vols 1954–1973. [Official history, Second World War: Campaigns.].

4. MILITARY THEORISTS

14729 HIGHAM (ROBIN DAVID STEWART). The Military Intellectuals in Britain 1918–1939. New Brunswick, NJ. 1966.

14730 LUVAAS (JAY). The Education of an Army: British Military Thought 1815–1940. 1965.

14731 FULLER (JOHN FREDERIC CHARLES). On Future Warfare. 1928.

14732 —— Memoirs of an Unconventional Soldier. 1936.

14733 —— Towards Armageddon: The Defence Problem and its Solution. 1937.

14734 TRYTHALL (ANTHONY JOHN). 'Boney' Fuller: The Intellectual General 1878–1966. 1977.

14735 REID (BRIAN HOLDEN). J. F. C. Fuller: Military Thinker. 1987.

14736 LIDDELL HART (BASIL HENRY). Reputations. 1928.

14737 —— Deterrence and Defence. 1960.

14738 —— Memoirs. 2 vols 1965– .

14739 BOND (BRIAN J.). Liddell Hart: A Study of His Military Thought. 1977.

14740 MEARSHEIMER (JOHN J.). Liddell Hart and the Weight of History. 1988.

5. GENERALS

14741 PITT (BARRIE). Churchill and the Generals. 1981.

14742 CARVER (MICHAEL) *Baron ed.* The War Lords: Military Commanders of the Twentieth Century. 1976.

14743 BARCLAY (CYRIL NELSON). On their Shoulders. British Generalship in the Lean Years, 1939–1942. 1964.

14744 IRVING (DAVID). The War Between the Generals. 1981.

14745 BARNETT (CORRELLI DOUGLAS). The Desert Generals. 1960.

14746 LEASOR (JAMES). War at the Top. 1959.

14747 LINDSAY (OLIVER) *ed.* A Guard's General: The Memoirs of Sir Allan Adair. 1986.

14748 FRASER (*Sir* DAVID). Alanbrooke. 1982.

14749 BRYANT (*Sir* ARTHUR). The Turn of the Tide 1939–1943: A Study Based on the Diaries and Autobiographical Notes of Field Marshal the Viscount Alanbrooke. 1957.

14750 —— Triumph in the West, 1943–1946: A Study Based on the Diaries and . . . Alanbrooke. 1959.

14751 HILLSON (N.). Alexander of Tunis: A Biographical Portrait. 1952.

14752 NICOLSON (NIGEL). Alex: The Life of Field Marshal Earl Alexander of Tunis. 1973.

14753 JACKSON (WILLIAM GODFREY FOTHERGILL). Alexander of Tunis: As Military Commander. 1971.

14754 CONNELL (JOHN HENRY ROBERTSON). Auchinleck. 1959.

14755 WARNER (PHILIP). Auchinleck—The Lonely Soldier. 1981.

14756 PARKINSON (ROGER). The Auk: Auchinleck, Victor at Alamein. 1977.

14757 CARVER (MICHAEL) *Baron.* Out of Step: The Memoirs of Field Marshal Lord Carver. 1989.

14758 FERGUSSON (*Sir* BERNARD). The Trumpet in the Hall 1930–1958. 1970.

14759 DE GUINGAND (*Sir* FRANCIS WILFRED). Operation Victory. 1947.

14760 COLVILLE (*Sir* JOHN RUPERT). Man of Valour: The . . . of Field Marshal the Viscount Gort. 1972.

14761 GALE (*Sir* RICHARD NELSON). Call to Arms. 1968.

14762 CARVER (MICHAEL) *Baron*. Harding of Petherton: Field Marshal. 1978.

14763 MACLEOD (RODERICK) *and* KELLY (DENIS) *eds*. The Ironside Diaries 1937–1940. 1962.

14764 ISMAY (HASTINGS LIONEL) *Baron*. The Memoirs of General Lord Ismay. 1960.

14765 WINGATE (*Sir* RONALD). Lord Ismay: A Biography. 1970.

14766 RYDER (ROWLAND). Oliver Leese. 1987.

14767 MONTGOMERY (BERNARD LAW). The Memoirs of Field Marshal the Viscount Montgomery of Alamein, K.G. 1958.

14768 MOOREHEAD (ALAN). Montgomery, A Biography. 1946.

14769 HAMILTON (NIGEL). Monty: The Making of a General, 1887–1942. 1981.

14770 —— Monty: Master of the Battlefield, 1942–1944. 1983.

14771 —— Monty: The Field Marshal, 1944–1976. 1986.

14772 CHALFONT (ALUN GWYNNE JONES) *Baron*. Montgomery of Alamein. 1976.

14773 LEWIN (RONALD). Montgomery as Military Commander. 1971.

14774 LAMB (RICHARD). Montgomery in Europe, 1943–45. 1983.

14775 NEAME (*Sir* PHILIP). Playing with Strife: The Autobiography of a Soldier. 1947.

14776 BARCLAY (CYRIL NELSON). Against Great Odds— Including Extracts from the Personal Account of . . . General Sir Richard N. O'Connor. 1955.

14777 POWNALL (HENRY). Chief of Staff: The Diaries of Lieutenant General Sir Henry Pownall, 1. 1933–1940. *Ed.* by Brian Bond. 1973.

14778 PYMAN (*Sir* HAROLD E.). Call to Arms. 1971.

14779 RICHARDSON (CHARLES). Flashback: A Soldier's Story. 1985.

14780 LEWIN (RONALD). Slim, the Standardbearer: A Biography of Field-Marshal the Viscount Slim. 1976.

14781 SLIM (WILLIAM). Defeat into Victory. 1956.

14782 EVANS (*Sir* GEOFFREY). Slim as Military Commander. 1969.

14783 CONNELL (JOHN HENRY ROBERTSON). Wavell, Soldier and Scholar to June 1941. 1964.

14784 COLLINS (ROBERT JOHN). Lord Wavell, 1883–1941: A Military Biography. 1947.

14785 FERGUSSON (BERNARD). Wavell: Portrait of a Soldier. 1961.

14786 LEWIN (RONALD). The Chief: Field Marshal Lord Wavell, Commander-in-Chief, Viceroy, 1939–1947. 1980.

14787 WOOLLCOMBE (ROBERT). The Campaigns of Wavell, 1939–1943. 1959.

14788 SMYTH (*Sir* JOHN). Bolo Whistler: The Life of General Sir Lashmer Whistler. 1967.

14789 WILSON (HENRY MAITLAND) *Baron*. Eight Years Overseas, 1939–1947. 1950.

14790 BURCHETT (WILFRED GRAHAM). Wingate's Phantom Army. 1946.

14791 SYKES (CHRISTOPHER). Orde Wingate. 1959.

14792 TULLOCH (DEREK). Wingate in Peace and War. 1972.

14793 DOBBIE (S.). Faith and Fortitude: The Life and Work of General Sir William Dobbie. Gillingham. 1979.

6. THE BATTLE OF THE ATLANTIC

14794 CHATTERTON (EDWARD KEBLE). Fighting the U-Boats. 1942.

14795 —— Beating the U-boats. 1943.

14796 COSTELLO (JOHN) *and* HUGHES (T.). The Battle of the Atlantic. 1977.

14797 MACINTYRE (DONALD GEORGE FREDERICK WYVILLE). The Battle of the Atlantic. 1961.

14798 TERRELL (EDWARD). Admiralty Brief: The Story of Inventions that Contributed to Victory in the Battle of the Atlantic. 1958.

14799 WATTS (A. J.). The U-Boat Hunters. 1976.

7. THE BATTLE OF BRITAIN 1940

14800 ALLEN (HUBERT RAYMOND). Battle of Britain. The Recollections of H. R. 'Dizzy' Allen, D.F.C. 1973.

14801 BARCLAY (GLEN ST JOHN). Their Finest Hour. 1977.

14802 BISHOP (EDWARD BARRY). The Battle of Britain. 1960.

14803 CLARK (RONALD WILLIAM). Battle for Britain: Sixteen Weeks that Changed the Course of History. 1965.

14804 COLLIER (BASIL). The Battle of Britain. 1962.

14805 COLLYER (DAVID G.). Battle of Britain Diary: July–September 1940. Deal. 1980.

14806 DEIGHTON (LEN). Battle of Britain. 1980.

14807 —— Fighter: The True Story of the Battle of Britain. 1977.

14808 GREEN (WILLIAM). Aircraft of the Battle of Britain. 1969.

14809 McKEE (ALEXANDER). Strike from the Sky: The Story of the Battle of Britain. 1960.

14810 MASON (FRANCIS KENNETH). Battle over Britain. 1969.

14811 MOSLEY (LEONARD). Battle of Britain. Alexandria, Va. 1977.

14812 PARKINSON (ROGER). Dawn on Our Darkness: The Summer of 1940. 1977.

14813 PRICE (ALFRED). Battle of Britain: The Hardest Day, 18 August 1940. 1979.

14814 VAN ISHOVEN (ARMAND). The Luftwaffe in the Battle of Britain. 1980.

14815 WRIGHT (ROBERT). Dowding and the Battle of Britain. 1969.

14816 WOOD (DEREK) *and* DEMPSTER (DEREK DAVID). The Narrow Margin: The Battle of Britain and the Rise of Air Power, 1930–1940. 1961.

14817 WOOD (DEREK) *comp.* Target England; an Illustrated History of the Battle of Britain. 1980.

8. AIR ÐEFENCE

14818 PILE (*Sir* FREDERICK ALFRED). Ack Ack. 1949.

14819 —— Ack-Ack: Britain's Defence Against Air Attack During the Second World War. 1956.

9. THE DAKAR EXPEDITION

14820 MARDER (ARTHUR JACOB). Operation 'Menace': The Dakar Expedition and the Dudley North Affair. 1976.

14821 WILLIAMS (JOHN). The Guns of Dakar. September 1940. 1976.

14822 PLIMMER (CHARLOTTE) *and* PLIMMER (DENIS). A Matter of Expediency: The Jettisoning of Admiral Sir Dudley North. 1978.

10. THE DIEPPE RAID 1942

14823 ATKIN (RONALD). Dieppe 1942. The Jubilee Disaster. 1980.

14824 FRANKS (NORMAN L. R.). The Greatest Air Battle. Dieppe 19th August 1942. 1979.

14825 LEASOR (JAMES). Green Beach. 1975.

14826 MAGUIRE (ERIC). Dieppe, August 19. 1963.

14827 MORDAL (JACQUES). Dieppe: The Dawn of Decision. 1963.

14828 ROBERTSON (TERENCE). Dieppe: The Shame and the Glory. 1963.

14829 THOMPSON (REGINALD WILLIAM). Dieppe at Dawn: The Story of the Dieppe Raid. 1956.

14830 MELLOR (JOHN). Forgotten Heroes: The Canadians at Dieppe. 1975.

11. DUNKIRK EVACUATION 1940

14831 TURNBULL (PATRICK). Dunkirk: Anatomy of Disaster. Lond. 1978. N.Y. 1980.

14832 SPEARS (*Sir* EDWARD LOUIS). Assignment to Catastrophe. Vol. 1 Prelude to Dunkirk. Vol. 2 The Fall of France. 1954.

14833 SMYTH (*Sir* JOHN GEORGE). Before the Dawn: A Story of Two Historic Retreats. 1957.

14834 NEAVE (AIREY). The Flames of Calais: A Soldier's Battle, 1940. 1972.

14835 MASEFIELD (JOHN). The Nine Days Wonder. 1941. Repr. 1972.

14836 LORD (WALTER). The Miracle of Dunkirk. N.Y. 1982.

14837 JACKSON (ROBERT). Dunkirk: The British Evacuation 1940. 1976.

14838 HARRIS (JOHN). Dunkirk. The Storms of War. Newton Abbot. 1980.

14839 HARMAN (NICHOLAS). Dunkirk. The Necessary Myth. 1980.

14840 DRAPER (THEODORE). The Six Weeks War: France, May 10–June 25, 1940. 1946.

14841 DIVINE (DAVID). The Nine Days of Dunkirk. 1959.

14842 COLLIER (RICHARD HUGHESON). The Sands of Dunkirk. 1961.

14843 BUTLER (EWAN) *and* BRADFORD (J. SELBY). The Story of Dunkirk. 1955.

14844 BLAXLAND (WILLIAM GREGORY). Destination Dunkirk: The Story of Gort's Army. 1973.

14845 BARKER (ARTHUR JAMES). Dunkirk: The Great Escape. 1977.

14846 LONGMATE (NORMAN). If Britain had Fallen. 1975.

14847 MACKESY (KENNETH). Invasion: The German Invasion of England, July 1940. 1980.

12. WAR IN GREECE

14848 HAMMOND (NICHOLAS). Venture into Greece: With the Guerillas, 1943–44. 1983.

14849 MAULE (HENRY). Scobie, Hero of Greece: The British Campaign, 1944–45. 1975.

14850 TURNER (DON). Kircakos: A British Partisan in Wartime Greece. 1982.

14851 WOODHOUSE (C. M.). The Struggle for Greece, 1941–1945. 1976.

14852 BUCKLEY (CHRISTOPHER). Greece and Crete, 1941. 1945.

14853 CLARK (ALAN). The Fall of Crete. 1962.

14854 HECKSTALL-SMITH (ANTHONY) *and* BAILLIE-GROHMAN (HAROLD TOM). Greek Tragedy. 1961.

14855 PACK (STANLEY WALTER CROUCHER). The Battle for Crete. 1973.

14856 SIMPSON (TONY). Operation Mercury: The Battle for Crete 1941. 1981.

14857 SPENCER (J. H.). The Battle for Crete. 1962.

14858 STEWART (I. McD. G.). The Struggle for Crete 20 May–1 June 1941. A Story of Lost Opportunity. 1966.

14859 THOMAS (DAVID ARTHUR). Crete 1941. The Battle at Sea. 1972.

13. THE WAR IN ITALY

14860 BLUMENSON (MARTIN). Anzio: The Gamble that Failed. Philadelphia, Pa. 1963.

14861 BÖHMLER (RUDOLF). Monte Cassino. 1964.

14862 BUCKLEY (CHRISTOPHER). Road to Rome. 1945.

14863 CONNELL (CHARLES). Monte Cassino: The Historic Battle. 1963.

14864 COX (Sir GEOFFREY). The Road to Trieste. 1947.

14865 —— The Race for Trieste. 1977.

14866 DORLING (HENRY TAPRELL). Western Mediterranean 1942–1945. 1947.

14867 LINKLATER (ERIC ROBERT RUSSELL). The Campaign in Italy. 1951.

14868 MELLING (LEONARD). With the Eighth in Italy. 1955.

14869 NEWBY (ERIC). Love and War in the Appennines. 1971.

14870 ORGILL (DOUGLAS). The Gothic Line. The Autumn Campaign in Italy 1944. 1967.

14871 PACK (S. W. C.). Operation 'Husky': The Allied Invasion of Sicily. 1977.

14872 PIEKALKIEWICZ (JANUSZ). Cassino: Anatomy of the Battle. 1980.

14873 POND (HUGH). Salerno. 1961.

14874 —— Sicily. 1962.

14875 SHEPPERD (G. A.). The Italian Campaign, 1943–1945: A Political and Military Re-assessment. 1968.

14876 SMITH (E. D.). The Battles for Cassino. 1975.

14877 TREVELYAN (RALEIGH). The Fortress: A Diary of Anzio and After. 1956.

14878 —— Rome '44. The Battle for the Eternal City. 1981.

14879 LEWIS (NORMAN). Naples 1944. 1978.

14880 VAUGHAN-THOMAS (WYNFORD). Anzio. 1961.

14881 VERNEY (PETER). Anzio 1944: An Unexpected Fury. 1978.

14. WAR IN THE LEVANT

14882 MOCKLER (A.). Our Enemies The French: Being an Account of the War Fought between the French and the British, Syria 1941. 1976.

14883 WARNER (GEOFFREY). Iraq and Syria 1941. 1974.

15. WAR IN THE MEDITERRANEAN

14884 MACINTYRE (DONALD GEORGE FREDERICK WYVILLE). The Battle for the Mediterranean. 1975.

14885 ADMIRALTY. East of Malta, West of Suez: The Admiralty Account of the Naval War in the Eastern Mediterranean, September 1939 to March 1941. 1943.

14886 —— The Mediterranean Fleet, Greece to Tripoli: The Admiralty Account of Naval Operations, April 1941 to January 1943. 1944.

14887 LANGMAID (ROWLAND JOHN ROBB). 'The Med': The Royal Navy in the Mediterranean, 1939–1945. 1948.

16. WAR IN NORTH AFRICA

14888 BARKER (ARTHUR JAMES). Eritrea 1941. 1966.

14889 BLAXLAND (WILLIAM GREGORY). The Plain Cook and the Great Showman: The First and Eighth Armies in North Africa. 1977.

14890 BLUMENSON (MARTIN). Kasserine Pass. Boston, Mass. 1967.

14891 BRADDOCK (DAVID WILSON). The Campaigns in Egypt and Libya, 1940–1942. 1964.

14892 CARVER (RICHARD MICHAEL POWER) Baron. El Alamein. 1962.

14893 DUPUY (TREVOR NEVITT). Land Battles: North Africa, Sicily and Italy. 1964.

14894 FARRAR-HOCKLEY (ANTHONY). The War in the Desert. 1969.

14895 FORTY (GEORGE). Desert Rats at War. 1977.

14896 HECKSTALL-SMITH (ANTHONY). Tobruk. 1959.

14897 HOLDEN (MATTHEW). The Desert Rats. 1973.

14898 MACKSEY (KENNETH). Crucible of Power. The Fight For Tunisia 1942–1943. 1969.

14899 MAJDALANY (FRED). The Battle of El Alamein. 1965.

14900 MOOREHEAD (ALAN McCRAE). African Trilogy. 1959.

14901 JACKSON (WILLIAM G. F.). The North African Campaign, 1940–1943. 1975.

14902 PACK (STANLEY WALTER CROUCHER). Invasion North Africa, 1942. 1978.

14903 PHILLIPS (CECIL ERNEST LUCAS). Alamein. 1962.

14904 PITT (BARRIE). The Crucible of War: Year of Alamein. 1982.

14905 POPE (DUDLEY). Flag 4: The Battle of Coastal Forces in the Mediterranean. 1954.

14906 SAINSBURY (KEITH). The North African Landings, 1942: A Strategic Decision. 1976.

14907 SMITH (PETER CHARLES). War in the Aegean. 1974.

14908 STRAWSON (JOHN). The Battle for North Africa. 1969.

14909 —— El Alamein: Desert Victory. 1981.

14910 TUKER (*Sir* FRANCIS IVAN SIMMS). Approach to Battle: A Commentary, Eighth Army, November 1941 to May 1943. 1963.

14911 VERNEY (G. L.). The Desert Rats: The History of the 7th Armoured Division, 1938–1945. 1954.

14912 WARNER (PHILIP). Alamein. 1979.

17. WAR IN SCANDINAVIA

14913 ASH (BERNARD). Norway, 1940. 1964.

14914 BROOKES (EWART STANLEY). Prologue to a War: The Navy's Part in the Narvik Campaign. 1977.

14915 DERRY (THOMAS KINGSTON). The Campaign in Norway. 1952. [Official history, Second World War: Campaigns.].

14916 DICKENS (PETER). Narvik: Battles in the Fjords. 1974.

14917 MACINTYRE (DONALD GEORGE FREDERICK WYVILLE). Narvik. 1959.

14918 MOULTON (JAMES LOUIS). The Norwegian Campaign of 1940. 1966.

14919 MUNCH-PETERSEN (THOMAS). The Strategy of Phoney War. Britain, Sweden and the Iron-Ore Question 1939–1940. Stockholm. 1981.

14920 BUCKLEY (CHRISTOPHER). Norway. The Commandos' Dieppe. 1951.

14921 SCHOFIELD (STEPHEN). Musketoon: Commando Raid, Glomfjord 1942. 1964.

18. THE 'SECOND FRONT'

14922 DUNN (WALTER SCOTT). Second Front Now 1943. Alabama. 1980.

14923 GRIGG (JOHN). 1943: The Victory that Never was. 1980.

19. WAR IN SOUTH-EAST ASIA

14924 PHILLIPS (CECIL ERNEST LUCAS). The Greatest Raid of all. 1958.

14925 —— The Raiders of Arakan. 1973.

14926 MORAN (JACK WILLIAM GRACE). Spearhead in Malaya. 1959.

14927 GILCHRIST (*Sir* ANDREW). Bangkok: Top Secret. 1970.

14928 CAREW (TIM). The Vanished Army. 1964.

14929 —— The Longest Retreat: The Burma Campaign, 1942. 1969.

14930 CALVERT (MICHAEL). Chindits: Long Range Penetration. 1974.

14931 —— Prisoners of Hope. 1952.

14932 TRENOWDEN (IAN). Operations Most Secret: S.O.E., the Malayan Theatre. 1978.

14933 CAMPBELL (ARTHUR FRASER). Jungle Green. Boston. 1953.

14934 —— The Siege: A Story from Kohima. 1956.

14935 MCKELVIE (ROY). The War in Burma. 1948.

20. WAR IN SOUTH-EAST EUROPE

14936 AUTY (PHYLLIS) *and* CLOGG (RICHARD). British Policy in South-East Europe in the Second World War. 1976.

14937 —— British Policy towards Wartime Resistance in Yugoslavia and Greece. 1975.

14938 DAVIES (EDMUND FRANK). Illyrian Adventure: The Story of the British Military Mission to Enemy-Occupied Albania, 1943–44. 1952.

14939 DEAKIN (FREDERICK WILLIAM DAMPIER). The Embattled Mountain. 1971.

21. VICTORY IN EUROPE

14940 COOPER (JOHN ST JOHN). Invasion! The D-Day Story, June 6, 1944. 1954.

14941 LONGMATE (NORMAN). When we Won the War: The Story of Victory in Europe 1945. 1977.

14942 BLUMENSON (MARTIN). Liberation. Alexandria, Va. 1978.

14943 BOTTING (DOUGLAS S.). The Second Front. Alexandria, Va. 1978.

14944 BELCHEM (DAVID). Victory in Normandy. 1981.

14945 KEEGAN (JOHN). Six Armies in Normandy. 1982.

14946 JACKSON (WILLIAM G. F.). Overlord, Normandy 1944. 1978.

14947 CROOKENDEN (N.). Dropzone Normandy: The Story of the American and British Airborne Assault on D-Day 1944. 1976.

14948 WARNER (PHILIP). The D-Day Landings. 1980.

14949 HARRISON (MICHAEL). Mulberry: The Return in Triumph. 1965.

14950 FARRAR-HOCKLEY (ANTHONY). Airborne Carpet: Operation Market Garden. 1970.

14951 HETHERINGTON (JOHN). Air-Borne Invasion. 1971.

14952 HOWARTH (DAVID). Dawn of D-Day. 1959.

14953 HIBBERT (CHRISTOPHER). The Battle of Arnhem. 1962.

14954 FROST (JOHN). A Drop too Many. 1982.

14955 RYAN (CORNELIUS). A Bridge too Far. 1974.

14956 HARTCUP (GUY). Code Name Mulberry. The Planning, Building and Operation of the Mulberry Harbours. Newton Abbot. 1977.

14957 HORROCKS (*Sir* BRIAN) *with* BELFIELD (EVERSLEY) *and* ESSAME (H.). Corps Commander. 1977.

14958 McKEE (ALEXANDER). The Race for the Rhine Bridges. 1971.

14959 —— Caen: Anvil of History. 1964.

14960 MASON (DAVID). Raid on St. Nazaire. 1970.

14961 MAULE (HENRY). Caen: The Brutal Battle and Break-Out for Normandy. Newton Abbot. 1976.

14962 MERRIAM (ROBERT E.). The Battle of the Ardennes. 1958.

14963 MICHIE (A. A.). The Invasion of Europe: The Story behind D-Day. 1965.

14964 NORTH (JOHN). North-West Europe, 1944–1945: The Achievement of 21st Army Group. 1953.

14965 STAFFORD (DAVID). Britain and European Resistance 1940–1945. A Survey of the Special Operations Executive with Documents. 1980.

14966 STRAWSON (JOHN). The Battle for the Ardennes. 1972.

14967 THOMPSON (REGINALD WILLIAM). The Battle for the Rhineland. 1958.

14968 —— The Eighty-Five Days. The Story of the Battle of the Scheldt. 1957.

14969 —— Spearhead of Invasion: D-Day. 1968.

14970 TOLAND (JOHN). Battle: The Story of the Bulge. 1960.

14971 TUGWELL (MAURICE). Arnhem: A Case Study. 1975.

14972 TURNER (JOHN FRAYN). Invasion '44: The Full Story of D-Day. 1959.

14973 URQUHART (ROBERT ELLIOTT). Arnhem. 1958.

14974 WHITING (CHARLES). Battle of the Ruhr Pocket. 1972.

14975 WILMOT (CHESTER). The Struggle for Europe. 1952.

22. THE R.A.F.

14976 CHARLTON (LIONEL EVELYN OSWALD). Britain at War: the Royal Air Force and U.S.A.A.F. 5 vols. 1947.

14977 MACMILLAN (NORMAN). The Royal Air Force in the World War. Vol 1. 1939–1940, Aftermath of the War, Prelude to the Blitzkrieg, the Campaign in Norway. 1942.

14978 —— Tales of Two Air Wars. 1963.

14979 COLLIER (BASIL). A History of Air Power. 1974.

14980 HIGGIN (G. W.). The Relationship of Social Status and Rank in the R.A.F. 1952.

14981 CHALMERS (WILLIAM SCOTT). Max Horton and the Western Approaches. 1954.

14982 BOLITHO (HENRY HECTOR). Task for Coastal Command: The Story of the Battle of the South West Approaches. 1946.

14983 BOLITHO (HENRY HECTOR). Command Performance: The Authentic Story of the Last Battle of Coastal Command, R.A.F. N.Y. 1946.

14984 ADMIRALTY. Fleet Air Arm. 1943.

14985 KILLEN (JOHN). A History of Marine Aviation, 1911–1968. 1968.

14986 MOORE (JOHN CECIL). The Fleet Air Arm: A Short Account of its History and Achievements. 1943.

14987 CAMERON (IAN). Wings of Morning: The Story of the Fleet Air Arm in the Second World War. 1962.

14988 BEAUMAN (KATHARINE BENTLEY). Partners in Blue: The Story of Women's Service with the Royal Air Force. 1972.

14989 —— Wings on Her Shoulders. 1943.

14990 MONKS (NOEL). Squadrons Up! A First Hand History of the R.A.F. N.Y. 1941.

14991 WYKEHAM (*Sir* PETER GUY). Fighter Command: A Study of Air Defence, 1914–1960. 1960.

14992 BULLMORE (FRANCIS TRESILLIAN KING). The Dark Haven. 1956.

14993 MUSGROVE (G.). Pathfinder Force: A History of 8 Group. 1976.

14994 BOWYER (CHAZ). Path Finders at War. 1977.

14995 GRINNELL-MILNE (DUNCAN WILLIAM). Wind in the Wires. 1957.

14996 JOUBERT DE LA FERTÉ (*Sir* PHILIP BENNET). Rocket. 1957.

14997 —— Birds and Fishes: The Story Of Coastal Command. 1960.

14998 —— The Forgotten Ones: The Story of the Ground Crews. 1961.

14999 KING (ALISON). Golden Wings: The Story of Some of The Women Ferry Pilots of the Air Transport Auxiliary. 1956.

15000 LAWRENCE (W. J.). No. 5 Bomber Group R.A.F., 1939–1945. 1951.

15001 MEAD (PETER W.). Soldiers in the Air. 1967.

15002 MORRIS (ALAN). First of the Many: The Story of Independent Force, R.A.F. 1968.

15003 MOYES (PHILIP JOHN RICHARD). Bomber Squadrons of the R.A.F. and their Aircraft. 1964.

15004 HARRISON (DERRICK INSKIP). These Men are Dangerous: The Special Air Service at War. 1957.

15005 WARNER (PHILIP). The Special Air Service. 1971.

15006 MASTERS (DAVID). 'So Few': The Immortal Record of the Royal Air Force. 1956.

15007 CHATTERTON (GEORGE JAMES STEWART). The Wings of Pegasus. 1962.

15008 CARNE (DAPHNE). The Eyes of the Few. 1960.

15009 GOULDING (JAMES) *and* MOYES (PHILIP J. R.). R.A.F. Bomber Command and its Aircraft 1936-1940. 1975.

15010 GREGORY (BARRY). British Airborne Troops, 1940–1945. 1974.

23. THE NAVY

15011 JAMES (*Sir* WILLIAM MILBOURNE). The British Navies in the Second World War. 1946.

15012 SMITH (PETER). Action: Three Studies of the Naval War in the Mediterranean Theatre during 1940. 1980.

15013 WINTON (JOHN). Air Power at Sea, 1939–45. 1976.

15014 TURNER (L. C. F.) *et al.* War in the Southern Oceans, 1939–1945. Oxf. 1961.

15015 KEMP (PETER). Victory at Sea, 1939–1945. 1957.

15016 ROSKILL (STEPHEN WENTWORTH). The Navy at War, 1939–1945. 1960.

15017 —— The War at Sea, 1939–1945. 3 vols. 1954–1961. [Official history, Second World War: Campaigns].

15018 THOMAS (DAVID ARTHUR). With Ensigns Flying: The Story of H.M. Destroyers at War, 1939–1945. 1958.

15019 SMITH (PETER CHARLES). The Great Ships Pass: British Battleships at War, 1939–1945. 1977.

15020 NORTH (ARTHUR JOHN DAY). Royal Naval Coastal Forces, 1939–1945. New Malden. 1972.

15021 MIDDLEBROOK (MARTIN) *and* MAHONEY (PATRICK). Battleship: The Loss of the Prince of Wales and the Repulse. 1977.

15022 SMITH (PETER CHARLES). Task Force 57: The British Pacific Fleet, 1944–1945. 1969.

15023 WINTON (JOHN). The Forgotten Fleet. 1969.

15024 JAMESON (*Sir* WILLIAM SCARLETT). Ark Royal, 1939–1941. 1957.

15025 APPS (MICHAEL). The Four 'Ark Royals'. 1976.

15026 BRADFORD (ERNLE DUSGATE SELBY). The Mighty 'Hood'. 1959.

15027 HOYT (EDWIN PALMER). The Life and Death of H.M.S. Hood. 1977.

15028 PHILLIPS (CECIL ERNEST LUCAS). Cockleshell Heroes. 1956.

15029 ROSKILL (STEPHEN WENTWORTH). H.M.S. Warspite: The Story of a Famous Battleship. 1957.

15030 ASH (BERNARD). Someone Had Blundered: The Story of the 'Repulse' and the 'Prince of Wales'. 1960.

15031 BENNETT (GEOFFREY MARTIN). The Loss of the 'Prince of Wales' and 'Repulse'. 1973.

15032 HOUGH (RICHARD ALEXANDER). The Hunting of Force Z: The Brief, Controversial Life of the Modern Battleship, and its Tragic Close with the Destruction of 'Prince of Wales' and 'Repulse'. 1963.

15033 SMITH (PETER CHARLES). Fighting Flotilla: H.M.S. Laforey and her Sister Ships. 1976.

15034 POPE (D.). The Battle of the River Plate. 1956.

15035 GRENFELL (RUSSELL). The Bismarck Episode. 1948.

15036 BENNETT (GEOFFREY MARTIN). Battle of the River Plate. 1972.

15037 SNYDER (G. S.). The 'Royal Oak' Disaster. 1976.

15038 GARDNER (LESLIE). The Royal Oak Courts Martial. Edin. 1956.

15039 MARCH (EDGAR J.). British Destroyers: A History of Development, 1892–1953. 1966.

15040 BROWN (J. D.). Carrier Operations in World War II. 1968.

24. BRITISH PRISONERS OF WAR

15041 ROMILLY (GILES) *and* ALEXANDER (MICHAEL). Privileged Nightmare. 1954.

15042 MANSEL (JOHN). The Mansel Diaries: The Diaries of Captain John Mansel, P.O.W., and Camp Forger in Germany, 1940–45. 1977.

15043 DUGGAN (MARGARET) *ed.* Padre in Colditz. The Diary of J. Ellison Platt MBE. 1978.

15044 REID (P. R.). The Colditz Story. 1952.

15045 —— The Latter Days. 1953

15046 LOVELL (TERRY). Camera in Colditz. 1982.

15047 WILLIAMS (ERIC). The Wooden Horse. 1949.

25. DETENTION IN BRITAIN

15048 STENT (RONALD). A Bespattered Page? The Internment of His Majesty's 'Most Loyal Enemy Aliens'. 1980.

15049 GILLMAN (PETER) *and* GILLMAN (LENI). 'Collar the Lot': How Britain Interned and Expelled its Wartime Refugees. 1980.

15050 LAFITTE (FRANÇOIS). The Internment of Allies. 1940.

15051 GOLDMAN (AARON L.). 'Defence Regulation 18B: Emergency Internment of Aliens and Political Dissenters in Great Britain during World War II'. *J. Brit. Studs* xii (1973), 120–36.

15052 FAULK (HENRY). The Re-education of German Prisoners of War in Britain 1945–1948. 1977.

15053 GLEES (ANTHONY). Exile Politics during the Second World War: The German Social Democrats in Britain. Oxf. 1982.

15054 KOCHAN (MIRIAM). Prisoners of England. 1980.

15055 SULLIVAN (MATTHEW BARRY). Thresholds of Peace. Four Hundred Thousand German Prisoners and the People of Britain 1944–1948. 1979.

26. WAR IN ASIA

15056 VOIGT (JOHANNES H.). Indien im Zweiten Weltkrieg. Stuttgart. 1978.

15057 COLLIS (MAURICE STEWART). Last and First in Burma, 1941–1948. 1956.

15058 CALLAHAN (RAYMOND). Burma, 1942–1945. 1978.

15059 KIRBY (STANLEY WOODBURN) *et al.* The War against Japan. 5 vols. 1957–1969. [Official history, Second World War: Campaigns.].

15060 PERCIVAL (A. E.). The War in Malaya. 1949.

15061 MORRISON (IAN). Malayan Postscript. 1942.

15062 FERGUSSON (BERNARD EDWARD). Beyond the Chindwin. 1955.

15063 FRIEND (JOHN FRANCIS). The Long Trek. 1957.

15064 ROLO (CHARLES J.). Wingate's Raiders. 1944.

15065 BIDWELL (SHELFORD). The Chindit War: The Campaign in Burma 1944. 1979.

15066 FERGUSON (EDWARD). Desperate Siege: The Battle of Hong Kong. Toronto. 1980.

15067 FALK (STANLEY LAWRENCE). Seventy Days to Singapore: The Malayan Campaign 1941–1942. 1975.

15068 GRENFELL (RUSSELL). Main Fleet to Singapore. 1951.

15069 GLOVER (EDWIN MAURICE). The 70 Days: The Story of the Japanese Campaign in British Malaya. 1946.

15070 ALLEN (LOUIS). Singapore 1941–42. 1977.

15071 ATTIWILL (KENNETH). The Singapore Story. 1959.

15072 BARBER (JOHN LYSBERG NOEL). Sinister Twilight: The Fall and Rise Again of Singapore. 1968.

15073 CALLAHAN (RAYMOND). The Worst Disaster: The Fall of Singapore. Newark, NJ. 1977.

15074 HOLMES (RICHARD) *and* KEMP (ANTHONY). The Bitter End. Chichester. 1982.

15075 OWEN (FRANK). The Fall of Singapore. 1960.

15076 SIMSON (IVAN). Singapore: Too Little, too Late. 1970.

15077 SMYTH (*Sir* JOHN GEORGE). Percival and the Tragedy of Singapore. 1971.

15078 WOODBURN (STANLEY WOODBURN). Singapore: The Chain of Disaster. 1971.

27. SPECIAL OPERATIONS

15079 HUNT (*Sir* DAVID). A Don at War. 1966.

15080 BOYLE (ANDREW). The Climate of Treason: Five Who Spied for Russia. 1979.

15081 HOWARTH (PATRICK). Under Cover: The Men and Women of the Special Operations Executive. 1980.

15082 BADEN-POWELL (DOROTHY). Operation Jupiter: S.O.E.'s Secret War in Norway. 1982.

15083 BEEVOR (J. G.). S.O.E. Recollections and Reflections, 1940–1945. 1981.

15084 CRUICKSHANK (CHARLES). S.O.E. in the Far East: Special Operations Executive. 1983.

15085 DAVIDSON (BASIL). Special Operations Europe: Scenes from the Anti-Nazi War. 1980.

15086 DODDS-PARKER (*Sir* DOUGLAS). Setting Europe Ablaze. 1983.

15087 FULLER (JEAN OVERTON). The German Penetration of S.O.E.: France 1941–1944. 1975.

15088 WEST (NIGEL). MI5: British Security Operations, 1909–45. 1981.

28. EVACUATION

15089 JOHNSON (B. S.) *ed.* The Evacuees. 1968.

15090 FIGES (EVA). Little Eden: A Child at War. 1978.

15091 LONGMATE (NORMAN). The Home Front: An Anthology of Personal Experiences 1938–1945. 1981.

15092 JOHNSON (DEREK E.). Exodus of Children. Clacton-on-Sea. 1985.

15093 BARKER (RALPH). The Children of the Benares. 1987. [The ill-fated evacuee ship.].

15094 INGLIS (RUTH). The Children's War: Evacuation 1939–1945. 1989.

29. DECEPTION

15095 CRUICKSHANK (CHARLES GREIG). Deception in World War II. Oxf. 1979.

15096 WHEATLEY (DENNIS). The Deception Planners: My Secret War. 1980.

15097 BARKAS (GEOFFREY). The Camouflage Story (from Aintree to Alamein). 1952.

15098 KENYON (JAMES). The Fourth Arm. 1948.

15099 CRUICKSHANK (CHARLES GREIG). The Fourth Arm: Psychological Warfare 1938–45. 1977.

15100 RICHARDSON (FRANK). Fighting Spirit: A Study of Psychological Factors in War. 1978.

15101 BALFOUR (MICHAEL L. G.). Propaganda in War, 1939–1945: Organizations, Policies and Publics in Britain and Germany. 1979.

15102 HOWE (ELLIS). The Black Game: British Subversive Operations against Germany during the Second World War. 1982.

15103 ZEMAN (ZBYNEK). Selling the War: Art and Propaganda in World War II. 1978.

15104 SPROAT (IAIN). Wodehouse at War. New Haven, Conn. 1981.

15105 SHORT (K. R. M.) *ed.* Film and Radio Propaganda in World War II. 1983.

15106 AUCKLAND (R. G.). Catalogue of British 'Black' Propaganda to Germany. 1941–45. St Albans. 1977.

15107 BENNETT (JEREMY). British Broadcasting and the Danish Resistance Movement, 1940–1945. Camb. 1966.

30. ELECTRONIC WARFARE

15108 JONES (REGINALD V.). The Wizard War: British Scientific Intelligence, 1939–1945. N.Y. 1978.

15109 MILLAR (GEORGE). The Bruneval Raid: Flashpoint of the Radar War. 1974.

15110 ROWE (A. P.). One Story of Radar. 1948.

15111 SAYER (A. P.). Army Radar. 1950.

15112 WATSON-WATT (Sir ROBERT ALEXANDER). Three Steps to Victory: A Personal Account by Radar's Greatest Pioneer. 1957.

15113 HILL (ROBERT). The Great Coup. 1977.

15114 BURNS (RUSSELL W.). The History of Radar Development to 1945. 1989.

15115 HOWARD-WILLIAMS (JEREMY N.). Night Intruder: A Personal Account of the Radar War Between the RAF and Luftwaffe Night-fighter Forces. Newton Abbot. 1976.

15116 FORD (BRIAN JOHN). Allied Secret Weapons: The War of Science. 1970.

15117 HARTCUP (GUY). The Challenge of War: Scientific and Engineering Contributions to World War Two. 1970.

15118 PRICE (ALFRED). Instruments of Darkness: The History of Electronic Warfare. 1967. Rev. edn 1977.

15119 POSTAN (M. M.) et al. Design and Development of Weapons. 1964.

15120 PHELAN (KEIREN) . Fast Attack Craft: The Evolution of Design and Tactics. 1977.

15121 NAYLER (J. L.) and OWER (E.). Aviation: Its Technical Development. 1965.

31. CONVOYS AND MERCHANT SHIPPING

15122 ELLIOTT (PETER). Allied Escort Ships of World War II: A Complete Survey. 1977.

15123 BLOND (GEORGES). Ordeal Below Zero: The Heroic Story of the Arctic Convoys in World War II. 1956.

15124 CAMERON (IAN). Red Duster, White Ensign: The Story of the Malta Convoys. 1959.

15125 ADMIRALTY. Merchantmen at War: The Official Story of the Merchant Navy, 1939–1944. 1944.

15126 AGAR (AUGUSTUS). Baltic Episode. A Classic of Secret Service in Russian Waters. 1963.

15127 BROOKES (EWART STANLEY). The Gates of Hell. 1960.

15128 CAMPBELL (Sir IAN) and MACINTYRE (DONALD). The Kola Run: A Record of Arctic Convoys, 1941–1945. 1958.

15129 IRVING (DAVID). The Destruction of Convoy PQ.17. 1968.

15130 MIDDLEBROOK (MARTIN). Convoy: The Battle for Convoys SC.122 and HX.229. 1976.

15131 POOLMAN (KENNETH). Escort Carrier, 1941–1945: An Account of British Escort Carriers in Trade Protection. Shepperton. 1972.

15132 ROSKILL (STEPHEN WENTWORTH). A Merchant Fleet at War. Alfred Holt & Co. 1939–1945. 1962.

15133 COWDEN (JAMES E.). The Price of Peace: Elder Dempster, 1939–1945. Liverpool. 1981.

15134 HAY (DODDY). War Under the Red Ensign: The Merchant Navy, 1939–45. 1982.

15135 RUTTER (OWEN). Red Ensign: A History of Convoy. 1942.

15136 EASTON (ALAN). 50 North: An Atlantic Battleground. 1963.

15137 SCHOFIELD (BRIAN BETHAM). The Russian Convoys. 1964.

32. CIVIL DEFENCE

15138 MORRISON (FRANK). War on Great Cities: A Study of the Facts. 1937.

15139 O'BRIEN (T. H.). Civil Defence. 1955.

15140 HODGSON (ROBIN) and BANKS (ROBERT). Britain's Home Defence Gamble. London. 1978.

15141 THOMPSON (EDWARD P.). Protest and Survive. 1980.

15142 GREENE (OWEN) et al. London after the Bomb: What a Nuclear Attack Really Means. 1982

15143 CAMPBELL (DUNCAN). War Plan U.K. 1983.

15144 VALE (LAWRENCE J.). The Limits of Civil Defence in the USA, Switzerland, Britain and the Soviet Union: The Evolution of Policies since 1945. 1987. [The discussion of Britain can be found on 123–51.].

33. HOME GUARD

15145 WINTLE (F.) and SMITH (N.). The Plymouth Blitz. Bodmin. 1981.

15146 GRAVES (CHARLES). The Home Guard of Britain. 1943.

15147 BROPHY (JOHN). Britain's Home Guard. 1945.

15148 —— Advanced Training for the Home Guard. 1941.

15149 GULVIN (K. R.). Kent Home Guard: A History. Rochester. 1980.

15150 BLAKE (JOHN WILLIAM). Northern Ireland in the Second World War. Belfast. 1956.

15151 FAWKES (RICHARD). Fighting for a Laugh. Entertaining British and American Armed Forces, 1939–1946. 1978.

15152 HUGGETT (FRANK). Goodnight Sweetheart: Songs and Memories of the Second World War. 1979.

15153 HUGHES (JOHN G.). The Greasepaint War: Show Business, 1939–45. 1976.

15154 LEITCH (MICHAEL) ed. Great Songs of World War II: The Home Front in Pictures. 1975.

15155 TURNER (ERNEST S.). The Phoney War on the Home Front. 1961.

15156 LONGMATE (NORMAN). Air Raid. The Bombing of Coventry, 1940. 1976.

15157 ROBBINS (GORDON). Fleet Street Blitzkrieg Diary. 1944.

15158 FARSON (N.). Bomber's Moon. London in the Blitzkrieg. 1941.

15159 KESSLER (L.). The Great York Air Raid. 1979.

15160 JOHNSON (B. S.) ed. The Evacuees. 1968.

15161 GRUNFELD (JUDITH). Shefford: The Story of a Jewish School Community in Evacuation, 1939–1945. 1980.

15162 JOHNSON (DAVID). The City Ablaze. The Second Great Fire of London, 29 December 1940. 1980.

15163 MOSLEY (LEONARD). Backs to the Wall. London Under Fire. 1939–45. 1971.

15164 GRANT (IAN) and MADDREN (NICHOLAS). The City at War. 1975.

15165 PERRY (COLIN). Boy in the Blitz. 1972.

15166 COLLIER (R.). The City that Wouldn't Die. 1959.

15167 RITCHIE (C.). The Siren Years: Undiplomatic Diaries, 1937–1945. 1975.

15168 MILBURN (CLARA E.). Mrs Milburn's Diaries: An Englishwoman's Day-to-Day Reflections, 1939–1945. 1979.

15169 ROUBICZEK (PAUL). Across the Abyss: Diary Entries for the Year 1939–1940. 1982.

34. THE HOME FRONT

15170 MCKENZIE (A. W.). The Treatment of Enemy Property in the United Kingdom during and After the Second World War. Chislehurst. 1981.

15171 MINNS (R.). Bombers and Mash: The Domestic Front 1939–45. 1980.

15172 CHAMBERLIN (E. R.). Life in Wartime Britain. 1972.

15173 MARWICK (ARTHUR J. B.). The Home Front: The British and the Second World War. 1976.

15174 BRIGGS (SUSAN). The Home Front: War Years in Britain, 1939–1945. 1975.

15175 HODGSON (VERA). Few Eggs and No Oranges: A Diary Showing how People in London and Birmingham Lived through the War Years, 1940–45. 1976.

15176 JOHNSON (DEREK E.). East Anglia at War, 1939–1945. 1978.

15177 MOYNIHAN (MICHAEL H.). People at War 1939–1945. Newton Abbot. 1974.

15178 MURPHY (JOHN). Dorset at War. Sherborne. 1979.

15179 REILLY (ROBIN). The Sixth Floor. 1969.

15180 LAQUEUR (WALTER). The Terrible Secret. An Investigation into the Suppression of Information about Hitler's 'Final Solution'. 1980.

15181 TEISSIER DU CROS (JANET) . Divided Loyalties. 1962.

15182 WHEELER (MARK C.). Britain and the War for Yugoslavia, 1940–1943. 1980.

15183 BAILLIE-STEWART (NORMAN). The Officer in the Tower [as told to John Murdoch]. 1967.

15184 ALLINGHAM (MARGERY). The Oaken Heart. 1941. Repub. 1959.

15185 NICOLSON (HAROLD). Friday Mornings 1941–1944. 1944.

15186 WASSERSTEIN (BERNARD). Britain and the Jews of Europe 1939–1945. Oxf. 1979.

15187 BIGLAND (EILEEN). The Riddle of the Kremlin. 1940.

15188 ATTIWILL (KENNETH). The Rising Sunset. 1957.

15189 LAQUEUR (WALTER) ed. The Second World War. Essays in Military and Political History. 1982.

15190 ST JOHN (JOHN) . To the War with Waugh. 1974.

35. INTELLIGENCE

15191 ZUCKERMAN (S.). Scientists and War. 1966.

15192 BADEN-POWELL (DOROTHY). Operation Jupiter. S.O.E.'s Secret War in Norway. 1982.

15193 COOKRIDGE (E. H.). Inside S.O.E. The Story of Special Operations in Western Europe, 1940–45. 1966.

15194 HYDE (HARFORD MONTGOMERY). The Quiet Canadian. The Secret Service Story of Sir William Stephenson. 1962.

15195 JOHNSON (S.). Agents Extraordinary. 1975.

15196 JOHNSTON (BRIAN). The Secret War. 1982.

15197 JONES (R. V.). Most Secret War. 1978.

15198 STRONG (Sir KENNETH). Intelligence at the Top. 1968.

15199 WELCHMAN (GORDON). The Hut Six Story. The Breaking of the Enigma Codes. N.Y. 1982.

15200 BABINGTON SMITH (CONSTANCE). Evidence in Camera: The Story of Photographic Intelligence in World War II. 1958.

15201 GLEESON (J.). They Feared No Evil: The Women Agents of Britain's Secret Armies 1939–1945. 1976.

15202 PAWLE (SHAFTO GERALD STRACHAN). The Secret War, 1939–1945. 1956.

15203 IRVING (DAVID). The Virus House. 1967.

36. SCIENCE

15204 LONGMATE (N.). The Doodlebugs: The Story of the Flying Bombs. 1981.

15205 YOUNG (RICHARD A.). The Flying Bomb. 1978.

15206 MORPURGO (J. E.). Barnes Wallis. A Biography. 1972. Upd edn 1981.

15207 CLARK (RONALD WILLIAM). The Birth of the Bomb: The Untold Story of Britain's Part in the Weapon that Changed the World. 1961.

15208 —— The Rise of the Boffins. 1962.

15209 CLARKE (ROBIN). The Science of War and Peace. 1971.

37. PROPAGANDA (AND IN THE FIRST WORLD WAR)

15210 SANDERS (MICHAEL L.) and TAYLOR (PHILIP M.). British Propaganda During the First World War, 1914–1918. 1982.

15211 SANDERS (MICHAEL L.). 'Wellington House and British Propaganda During the First World War'. Hist. J. 18 (1975), 119–46.

15212 HACHEY (THOMAS E.). 'British War Propaganda and American Catholics, 1918'. Cath. Hist. Rev. 61 (1975), 48–66.

15213 MARQUIS (A. G.). 'Words as Weapons: Propaganda in Britain and Germany during the First World War'. J. Contemp. Hist. 13 (1978), 467–98.

15214 HASTE (CATE). Keep the Home Fires Burning: Propaganda in the First World War. 1977.

15215 BUITENHUIS (PETER). The Great War of Words: Literature as Propaganda 1914–18 and after. Vancouver. 1987. Lond. 1989.

15216 WIEGAND (W. A.). 'British Propaganda in American Public Libraries 1914–1917'. J. Lib. Hist. 18 (1983), 237–54.

15217 COLE (C. R.). 'The Conflict Within: Sir Stephen Tallents and Planning Propaganda Overseas before the Second World War'. Albion 14 (1982). 50–71.

15218 ADAMTHWAITE (ANTHONY). 'The British Government and the Media, 1937–1938'. J. Contemp. Hist. 18 (1983), 281–97.

15219 BLACK (J. B.). Organising the Propaganda Instrument: The British Experience. The Hague. 1975.

15220 BALFOUR (MICHAEL). Propaganda in War, 1939–1945: Organization, Policies and Publics in Britain and Germany. 1979.

15221 CRUICKSHANK (C. G.). The Fourth Arm: Psychological Warfare 1938–1945. 1977.

15222 TAYLOR (PHILIP M.). The Projection of Britain: British Overseas Publicity and Propaganda, 1919–1939. Camb. 1981.

15223 —— '"If War Should Come": Preparing the Fifth Arm for Total War, 1935–1939'. J. Contemp. Hist. 16 (1981), 27–51.

15224 PRONAY (NICHOLAS) and SPRING (D. W.). Propaganda, Politics and Film. 1982.

C. THE ROYAL NAVY

I. GENERAL

15225 The Navy List. 1814+. [Annual.].

15226 MINISTRY OF DEFENCE. Author and Subject Catalogues of the Royal Navy. 5 vols. 1967.

15227 ALBION (ROBERT GREENHALGH). Naval and Maritime History: An Annotated Bibliography. 4th edn Newton Abbot. 1973.

15228 CENTER FOR NAVAL ANALYSES. Naval Abstracts. Arlington, Va. 1977+ [Quarterly.].

15229 LEWIS (MICHAEL ARTHUR). The Navy of Britain: A Historical Portrait. 1948.

15230 —— The History of the British Navy. Harmondsworth. 1957.

15231 CALLENDER (Sir GEOFFREY ARTHUR ROMAINE) and HINSLEY (Sir FRANCIS HENRY). The Naval Side of British History, 1485–1945. 1924. New edn 1952.

15232 HINSLEY (Sir FRANCIS HENRY). Command of the Sea: The Naval Side of British History from 1918 to the End of the Second World War. 1950.

15233 KEMP (PETER). History of the Royal Navy. 1969.

15234 GLADSTONE (ERSKINE WILLIAM). The Royal Navy. Oxf. 1958.

15235 DREYER (Sir CHARLES). The Sea Heritage: A Study of Maritime Warfare. 1955.

15236 GARBUTT (PAUL ELFORD). Naval Challenge: The Story of Britain's Post-War Fleet. 1961.

15237 SCHOFIELD (BRIAN BETHAM). British Sea Power: Naval Policy in the Twentieth Century. 1967.

15238 OWEN (CHARLES). No More Heroes: The Royal Navy in the Twentieth Century: Anatomy of a Legend. 1975.

15239 WARNER (OLIVER MARTIN WILSON). The British Navy: A Concise History. 1975.

15240 HAMPSHIRE (A. CECIL). The Royal Navy: Its Transition to the Nuclear Age. 1975.

15241 KENNEDY (PAUL M.). The Rise and Fall of British Naval Mastery. 1976. New edn 1983.

15242 WETTEN (DESMOND). The Decline of British Seapower. 1982.

15243 SPEED (KEITH). Sea Change: The Battle for the Falklands and the Future of Britain's Navy. 1982.

15244 HUMBLE (RICHARD). The Rise and Fall of the British Navy. 1986.

15245 PRESTON (ANTHONY) ed. History of the Royal Navy in the 20th Century. 1987.

2. ADMIRALS

15246 RANFT (B. MCL.). The Beatty Papers: Selections from the Private and Official Correspondence of Admiral of the Fleet Earl Beatty. 1989.

15247 RAWSON (GEOFFREY). Beatty. 1930. New edn 1936.

15248 CHALMERS (WILLIAM SCOTT). The Life and Letters of David, Earl Beatty. 1951.

15249 ROSKILL (STEPHEN WENTWORTH). Admiral of the Fleet Earl Beatty: The Last Naval Hero. 1980.

15250 CUNNINGHAM OF HYNDHOPE. A Sailor's Odyssey. 1951.

15251 WARNER (OLIVER). Cunningham of Hyndhope: Admiral of the Fleet. 1967.

15252 BACON (Sir REGINALD HUGH SPENCER). The Life of Lord Fisher of Kilverstone. 1929.

15253 MARDER (ARTHUR JACOB) ed. Fear God and Dread Nought: The Correspondence of Admiral of the Fleet Lord Fisher of Kilverstone. 3 vols 1952–9.

15254 KEMP (PETER) ed. The Papers of Admiral Sir John Fisher. 2 vols 1960–4.

15255 HOUGH (RICHARD). First Sea Lord: An Authorised Biography of Admiral Lord Fisher. 1969.

15256 MACKAY (RUDDOCK F.). Fisher of Kilverstone. Oxf. 1974.

15257 HUMBLE (RICHARD). Fraser of North Cape: The Life of Admiral of the Fleet Lord Fraser (1881–1981). 1983.

15258 BENNETT (GEOFFREY MARTIN). Charlie B: A Biography of Admiral Lord Beresford of Metemmeh and Curraghmore, G.C.B., G.C.V.O., LL.D., D.C.L. 1968.

15259 JAMES (Sir WILLIAM). The Portsmouth Letters. 1946.

15260 JELLICOE (JOHN RUSHWORTH) Earl. The Grand Fleet 1914–1916. 1919.

15261 —— The Crisis of the Naval War. 1920.

15262 —— The Submarine Peril: The Admiralty Policy of 1917. 1934.

15263 BACON (Sir REGINALD HUGH SPENCER). The Life of John Rushworth, Earl Jellicoe. 1936.

15264 ALTHAM (EDWARD). Jellicoe. 1938.

15265 PATTERSON (A. TEMPLE). Jellicoe. 1969.

15266 —— Ed. The Jellicoe Papers. 2 vols 1966–8.

15267 ASPINALL-OGLANDER (CECIL FABER). Roger Keyes: Being the Biography of Admiral of the Fleet Lord Keyes of Zeebrugge and Dover. 1951.

15268 HALPERN (PAUL G.). The Keyes Papers: Selections from the Private and Official Correspondence of Admiral of the Fleet Baron Keyes of Zeebrugge. Vol. I 1914–1918. 1979. Vol. II 1919–1938. 1980. Vol. III 1939–1945. 1981.

15269 WARNER (OLIVER). Admiral of the Fleet: The Life of Sir Charles Lambe. 1969.

15270 ZIEGLER (PHILIP). Mountbatten; The Official Life. 1985.

15271 —— Ed. Personal Diary of Admiral the Lord Louis Mountbatten, Supreme Allied Commander, South East Asia, 1943–1946. 1988.

15272 —— Ed. From Shore to Shore: The Final Volume of Lord Mountbatten's Diaries. 1989. [1953–79].

15273 BROWN (DAVID). 'Mountbatten as First Sea Lord'. *Jnl Roy. United Services Inst. Def. Stud.* 131 (1986), 63–8.

15274 TERRAINE (JOHN). The Life and Times of Lord Mountbatten. 1970.

15275 HOUGH (RICHARD). Mountbatten: Hero of our Time. 1981.

15276 SMITH (CHARLES). Fifty Years with Mountbatten. [His butler and valet.].

15277 EVANS (WILLIAM). My Mountbatten Years: In the Service of Lord Louis. 1989.

15278 MARDER (ARTHUR JACOB). Portrait of an Admiral: The Life and Papers of Sir Herbert Richmond. 1952.

15279 HUNT (B. D.). Sailor-Scholar: Admiral Sir Herbert Richmond 1871–1946. Waterloo. 1982.

15280 PATTERSON (A. TEMPLE). Tyrwhitt of the Harwich Force: The Life of Admiral of the Fleet Sir Reginald Tyrwhitt. 1973.

15281 VIAN (Sir PHILIP) Admiral. Action this Day: A War Memoir. 1960.

15282 WESTER WEMYSS (VICTORIA Lady). Life and Letters of Lord Wester Wemyss G.C.B., C.M.G., M.V.O. Admiral of the Fleet. 1935.

3. PROFILES

15283 SCHOFIELD (BRIAN BETHAM). The Royal Navy Today. 1960

15284 BARKER (DENNIS). Ruling the Waves: An Unofficial Portrait of the Royal Navy. 1986.

15285 SCHURMAN (DONALD). The Education of a Navy. 1965.

15286 LEWIS (MICHAEL ARTHUR) . England's Sea Officers: The Story of the Naval Profession. 1939.

15287 GRUSKY (OSCAR). 'Career Patterns and Characteristics of British Naval Officers'. *Brit. Jnl Sociol.* 26 (1975), 35–51.

15288 MACINTYRE (DONALD GEORGE FREDERICK WYVILLE). Fighting Ships and Seamen. 1963.

15289 GRENFELL (RUSSELL). The Men who Defend us. 1938. [Scales of pay and terms of service in the fighting forces].

15290 EDWARD (A. T.). British Bluejacket, 1915–1940. 1940.

15291 LAFFIN (JOHN). Jack Tar: The Story of the British Sailor. 1969.

15292 GARRETT (RICHARD). The British Sailor. 1974.

15293 EREIRA (ALAN). The Invergordon Mutiny. 1981.

15294 CAREW (ANTHONY). The Lower Deck of the Royal Navy 1900–39: The Invergordon Mutiny in Perspective. Man. 1981.

15295 DUNCAN (BARRY). Invergordon '31: How the Men of the RN Struck and Won. Southampton. 1976.

15296 EDWARDS (KENNETH). The Mutiny at Invergordon. 1937.

15297 DIVINE (DAVID). Mutiny at Invergordon. 1970.

15298 WINCOTT (LEN). Invergordon Mutineer. 1974.

15299 DWYER (DENIS JOHN). A History of the Royal Naval Barracks, Portsmouth. Portsmouth. 1961.

15300 BRIDGES (ANTONY). Scapa Ferry. 1957.

15301 COUSINS (GEOFFREY). The Story of Scapa Flow. 1965.

15302 BROWN (MALCOLM) *and* MEEHAN (PATRICIA). Scapa Flow. 1968.

15303 RUGE (FRIEDRICH). Scapa Flow 1919. Das Ende der Deutschen Flotte. Oldenbourg/Hamburg. 1969.

4. MEMOIRS

15304 AGAR (AUGUSTUS). Footprints in the Sea. 1961.

15305 —— Showing the Flag. 1962.

15306 BACON (*Sir* REGINALD HUGH SPENCER). From 1900 Onward. 1939.

15307 BONE (*Sir* DAVID WILLIAM). Landfall at Sunset: The Life of a Contented Sailor. 1955.

15308 BULL (PETER CECIL). To Sea in a Sieve. 1956.

15309 DEWAR (KENNETH GILBERT BALMAIN). The Navy from Within. 1939.

15310 GARDINER (LESLIE). The 'Royal Oak' Courts Martial. 1965. [Capt. K. G. B. Dewar and Cmdr. H. M. Daniel.].

15311 FREMANTLE (*Sir* SYDNEY ROBERT). My Naval Career, 1880–1928. 1949.

15312 HILL (R.). Destroyer Captain. 1975.

15313 JAMES (*Sir* WILLIAM MILBOURNE). Blue Water and Green Fields. 1939.

15314 KENNEDY (LUDOVIC). Sub-Lieutenant: A Personal Record of the War at Sea. 1942.

15315 USBORNE (CECIL VIVIAN). Blast and Counterblast: A Naval Impression of the War. 1935.

15316 WALKER (*Sir* CHARLES). Thirty-Four Years in the Admiralty. 1934.

5. OTHER SERVICES

15317 DRUMMOND (JOHN DORMAN). Blue for a Girl: The Story of the W.R.N.S. 1960.

15318 MASON (URSULA STUART). The Wrens 1917–77: A History of the Women's Royal Naval Service. 1977.

15319 FLETCHER (M. H.). The WRNS: A History of the Women's Royal Naval Service. 1989.

15320 SMITH (PETER CHARLES). Per Mare per Terram: A History of the Royal Marines. St Ives. 1974.

15321 NEILLANDS (ROBIN). By Sea and Land: The Royal Marine Commandos: A History 1942–1982. 1987.

15322 LOCKHART (*Sir* ROBERT BRUCE). The Marines were There; The Story of the Royal Marines in the Second World War. 1950.

15323 KERR (J. LENNOX) *and* GRENVILLE (WILFRED). The RNVR. 1957.

15324 WARNER (PHILIP). The SBS—Special Boat Squadron. 1983.

15325 LADD (JAMES D.). The Invisible Raiders: The History of the SBS from World War Two to the Present. 1983.

15326 COULTER (JACK LEONARD SAGAR) *ed.* The Royal Naval Medical Services. 2 vols. 1954–6.

15327 CLARK (GREGORY). 'Doc': 100 Year History of the Sick Berth Branch. 1984.

15328 ELLIS (HERBERT). Hippocrates RN. 1988.

15329 BIGLAND (EILEEN). The Story of the W.R.N.S. 1946.

15330 MASON (URSULA STUART). The Wrens, 1917–1977: A History of the Women's Royal Naval Service. Reading. 1977.

6. NAVAL POLICY AND STRATEGY

15331 BYWATER (HECTOR CHARLES). Navies and Nations: A Review of Naval Developments since the Great War. 1927.

15332 TRASK (DAVID F.). Captains and Cabinets: Anglo-American Naval Relations, 1917–1918. Columbia, Missouri. 1972.

15333 ROSKILL (STEPHEN WENTWORTH). Naval Policy between the Wars. I. The Period of Anglo-American

Antagonism 1919–1929. 1968. 2. The Period of Reluctant Rearmament 1930–1939. 1976.

15334 ACKWORTH (BERNARD). The Navies of Today and Tomorrow. 1930.

15335 HURD (Sir ARCHIBALD SPICER). The Eclipse of British Sea Power: An Increasing Peril. 1933.

15336 RICHMOND (HERBERT). Sea Power in the Modern World. 1934.

15337 BELL (ARCHIBALD COLQUHOUN). Sea Power and the Next War. 1938.

15338 CRESWELL (JOHN). Naval Warfare: An Introductory Study. 1936. 2nd edn 1942.

15339 BACON (REGINALD HUGH SPENCER) and MCMURTRIE (FRANCIS EDWIN). Modern Naval Strategy. 1940.

15340 RICHMOND (Sir HERBERT). Statesmen and Seapower. Oxf. 1946.

15341 ROSKILL (STEPHEN WENTWORTH). The Strategy of Sea Power: Its Development and Application. 1962.

7. Ships

15342 COLLEDGE (JAMES JOSEPH). Ships of the Royal Navy: An Historical Index. 2 vols Newton Abbot. 1969. [Vol. 1 updated 1987.].

15343 LENTON (HENRY TREVOR). Warships of the British and Commonwealth Navies. 1969. 3rd edn 1971. [Formerly British Warships which reached its 7th edn in 1964.].

15344 ARCHIBALD (EDWARD HUNTER HOLMES). The Metal Fighting Ship in the Royal Navy, 1860–1970. 1971.

15345 RANFT (BRYAN) ed. Technical Change and British Naval Policy, 1860–1939. 1977.

15346 DUNN (LAURENCE). British Warships. 1962.

15347 FOLEY (CEDRIC JOHN). The Boilerplate War. 1963.

15348 HOUGH (RICHARD). Dreadnought: A History of the Modern Battleship. 1968. Rev. edn 1975.

15349 BLUNDELL (WALTER DEREK GEORGE). Royal Navy Battleships, 1895–1946. 1973.

15350 BROWNE (DOUGLAS GORDON). The Floating Bulwark: The Story of the Fighting Ship: 1514–1942. 1963.

15351 DOLBY (JAMES) . The Steel Navy: A History in Silhouette, 1860–1962. 1962.

15352 STEPHEN (G. M.). British Warship Design since 1906. 1985.

15353 DITTMAR (FREDERICK JAMES). British Warships, 1914–1919. 1972.

15354 LENTON (HENRY TREVOR) and COLLEDGE (JAMES JOSEPH). Warships of World War Two. 1964.

15355 BLUNDELL (WALTER DEREK GEORGE). Royal Navy Warships 1939–1945. 1971.

15356 SMITH (PETER C.). The Great Ships Pass: British Battleships at War, 1939–1945. 1977.

15357 BLACKMAN (RAYMOND VICTOR BERNARD). Ships of the Royal Navy. 1973.

15358 YOUNG (J.). A Dictionary of Ships of the Royal Navy of the Second World War. Camb. 1975.

15359 RAVEN (ALAN). British Battleships of World War: The Development and Technical History of the Royal Navy's Battleships and Battlecruisers from 1911 to 1946. 1976.

15360 PARKES (OSCAR). British Battleships: 'Warrior' 1860 to 'Vanguard' 1950: A History of Design, Construction and Armament. 1957.

15361 PEARS (RANDOLPH). British Battleships, 1892–1957: The Great Days of the Fleets. 1957.

15362 LENTON (HENRY TREVOR). British Battleships and Aircraft Carriers. 1972.

15363 —— British Fleet and Escort Destroyers. 2 vols. 1970.

15364 —— British Cruisers. 1973.

15365 —— British Submarines. 1972.

15366 CARR (WILLIAM GUY). By Guess and by God: The Story of the British Submarines in the War. 1930.

15367 JONES (T. M.). Watchdogs of the Deep: Life in a Submarine during the Great War. Sydney. 1935.

15368 DRUMMOND (JOHN DORMAN). H.M. U-boat. 1960.

15369 ELLACOTT (SAMUEL ERNEST). Ships under the Sea. 1961.

15370 GRAY (EDWYN). A Damned Un-English Weapon: The Story of British Submarine Warfare 1914–1918. 1971.

15371 MARS (ALASTAIR). British Submarines at War, 1939–1945. 1971.

15372 THOMAS (DAVID ARTHUR). Submarine Victory: The Story of British Submarines in World War Two. 1961.

15373 WHITESTONE (NICHOLAS). The Submarine: The Ultimate Weapon. 1973.

15374 HART (SYDNEY). Discharged Dead: A True Story of Britain's Submarines at War. 1958.

15375 LIPSCOMBE (FRANK WOODGATE). The British Submarine. 1954.

15376 HEZLET (Sir ARTHUR RICHARD). The Submarine and Sea Power. 1967.

15377 TURNER (JOHN FRAYN). Periscope Patrol: The Saga of Malta Submarines. 1957.

15378 WHITEHOUSE (ARTHUR GEORGE JOSEPH). Subs and Submariners. 1963.

15379 EVERITT (DON). The K Boats: A Dramatic First Report on the Navy's Most Calamitous Submarines. 1963.

15380 WARREN (CHARLES ESME THORNTON) and BENSON (JAMES). 'The Admiralty Regrets. . . .': The Story of His Majesty's Submarines 'Thetis' and 'Thunderbolt'. 1958.

15381 —— Above Us the Waves: The Story of Midget Submarines and Human Torpedoes. 1953.

15382 KEMP (PETER). H.M. Destroyers. 1956,

15383 MANNING (THOMAS DAVID). The British Destroyer. 1961.

15384 MARCH (EDGAR JAMES). British Destroyers: A History of Development 1892–1953. 1967.

15385 BRUCE (MARTIN HUBERT). The Tribals: Biography of a Destroyer Class. 1971.

15386 BROOKES (EWART STANLEY). Destroyer. 1962. New edn 1973.

15387 PRESTON (ANTHONY). 'V and W' Class Destroyers, 1917–1945. 1971.

15388 COCKER (M.). Destroyers of the Royal Navy 1893–1981. 1981.

15389 POOLE (SYDNEY LEONARD). Cruiser: A History of the British Cruiser from 1889 to 1960. 1970.

15390 BYWATER (HECTOR CHARLES). Cruisers in Battle. 1939.

15391 MACINTYRE (DONALD GEORGE FREDERICK WYVILLE). Aircraft Carriers. 1968.

15392 BLUNDELL (WALTER DEREK GEORGE). British Aircraft Carriers. Hemel Hempstead. 1969.

15393 CLEMENTS (J. A.). 'Royal Navy Ship-Based Air Defence 1939–1984'. *Jnl Roy. United Services Inst. Def. Studs* 129 (1984), 19–24.

15394 DORLING (HENRY TAPRELL). Swept Channels: Being an Account of the Work of the Minesweepers in the Great War. 1935.

15395 COWIE (JOHN STEWART). Mines, Minelayers and Minelaying. 1949.

15396 TURNER (JOHN FRAYN). Service Most Silent: The Navy's Fight against Enemy Mines. 1955.

15397 BROOKES (EWART STANLEY). Glory Passed Them By. 1958. [Minesweeping during the Second World War].

15398 HARDY (H.). The Minesweepers' Victory. 1976.

15399 ROGERS (HUGH CUTHBERT BASSETT). Troopships and Their History. 1963.

15400 COOPER (BRYAN). The Battle of the Torpedo Boats. 1970.

15401 GRANVILLE (WILFRED) *and* KELLY (ROBIN ARTHUR). Inshore Heroes: The Story of H.M. Motor Launches in Two World Wars. 1961.

15402 HAMPSHIRE (ARTHUR CECIL). Lilliput Fleet: The Story of the Royal Naval Patrol Service. 1957.

15403 WALDRON (THOMAS JOHN). The Frogmen: The Story of the Wartime Underwater Operations. 1970.

15404 WRIGHT (BRUCE STANLEY). The Frogmen of Burma: The Story of the Sea Reconnaissance Unit. 1970.

15405 LUND (PAUL). Trawlers go to War. 1972.

15406 —— The War of the Landing Craft. 1976.

15407 BONE (*Sir* DAVID WILLIAM). Merchantmen-at-Arms. 1919.

15408 —— Merchantmen Rearmed. 1949.

15409 HILL (J. R.). British Sea Power in the 1980s. 1985.

8. THE ROYAL MARINES

15410 ADMIRALTY. The Royal Marines: The Admiralty Account of Their Achievement, 1939–1943. 1944.

15411 GROVER (GEORGE WALTER MONTAGUE). A Short History of the Royal Marines. 1948. 2nd rev. edn Aldershot 1960.

15412 MOULTON (JAMES LOUIS). The Royal Marines. 1972.

15413 PRINGLE (PATRICK). Fighting Marines. 1966.

15414 JERROLD (DOUGLAS). The Royal Naval Division. 1923.

15415 LADD (JAMES DAVID). Assault from the Sea, 1939–1945: The Craft, the Landings, the Men. Newton Abbot. 1976.

9. NAVAL AVIATION

15416 THETFORD (OWEN GORDON). British Naval Aircraft, 1912–1958. 1958.

15417 HURREN (B. J.). Perchance: A Short History of British Naval Aviation. 1949.

15418 MACINTYRE (DONALD GEORGE FREDERICK WYVILLE). Wings of Neptune: The Story of Naval Aviation. 1963.

15419 GARDNER (RICHARD ERIC). The Flying Navy. 1971.

15420 RAWLINGS (JOHN DUNSTAN RICHARD). Pictorial History of the Fleet Air Arm. 1973.

15421 HOARE (JOHN). Tumult in the Clouds: A Story of the Fleet Air Arm. 1976.

15422 WINTON (JOHN). Air Power at Sea, 1939–1945. 1976.

15423 —— Find, Fix and Strike: The Fleet Air Arm at War, 1939–45. 1980.

15424 GREEN (DENNIS WILLIAM). Flying Boats. 1962.

10. NAVAL INTELLIGENCE

15425 BEESLEY (PATRICK). Very Special Intelligence: The Story of the Admiralty's Operational Intelligence Centre, 1939–1945. 1977.

15426 DEACON (RICHARD). The Silent War: A History of Western Naval Intelligence. Newton Abbot. 1978.

15427 McLACHLAN (DONALD). Room 39: Naval Intelligence in Action 1939–1945. 1968.

D. THE BRITISH ARMY

1. GENERAL

15428 SHEPPARD (ERIC WILLIAMS). A Short History of the British Army. 1926. 4th edn 1950.

15429 BARNETT (CORRELLI DOUGLAS). Britain and Her Army, 1509–1970: A Political and Social Survey. 1970.

15430 HASWELL (JOCK). The British Army: A Concise History. 1975.

15431 BARTHOP (M.). The Armies of Britain, 1485–1980. 1980.

15432 WYLIE (JAMES H.). The Influence of British Arms. 1984. [Military aspects of decolonization, 1956–82].

15433 CLIVE (LEWIS). The People's Army. 1938.

15434 DEWING (RICHARD HENRY). The Army. 1938.

15435 DE WATTEVILLE (HERMAN GASTON). The British Soldier: His Daily Life from Tudor to Modern Times. 1954.

15436 FRENCH (EDWARD GERALD). Goodbye to Boot and Saddle, or, the Tragic Passing of British Cavalry. 1951.

15437 ROGERS (HUGH CUTHBERT BASSET). The Mounted Troops of the British Army, 1066-1945. 1959.

15438 ARMY LEAGUE. The British Army in the Nuclear Age. 1959.

15439 GLADSTONE (ERSKINE WILLIAM). The Army. Oxf. 1961.

15440 BURGESS (ALFRED ROBERT PAUL). The True Book about the British Army. 1960.

15441 YOUNG (PETER). The British Army. 1967.

15442 DIETZ (PETER) ed. Garrison: The British Military Towns. 1986.

15443 MACKENZIE (JOHN M.) ed. Popular Imperialism and the Military 1850–1950. Manch. 1992.

15444 FOOT (MICHAEL RICHARD DANIELL). Men in Uniform: Military Manpower in Modern Industrial Societies. 1961.

15445 SHEPPARD (ERIC WILLIAM). Britain at War: The Army, British and Allies. 5 vols. 1946.

15446 BLAXLAND (WILLIAM GREGORY). The Regiments Depart: A History of the British Army, 1945–1970. 1971.

15447 BABINGTON (ANTHONY). Military Intervention in Britain: From the Gordon Riots to the Gibraltar Incident. 1990.

2. THE BRITISH SOLDIER

15448 ENGLANDER (DAVID) and MASON (TONY). War and Politics: The Experiences of the Serviceman in the Two World Wars. 1985. [A study which embraces all three services.].

15449 BROWNE (DOUGLAS GORDON). Private Thomas Atkins; A History of the British Soldier from 1840 to 1940. 1940.

15450 HAY (I.). The British Infantrymen: An Informal History. 1943.

15451 HOLDEN (MATTHEW). The British Soldier. 1974.

15452 FITZROY (OLIVIA). Men of Valour. Liverpool. 1961.

15453 LAFFIN (JOHN). Tommy Atkins: The Story of the English Soldier. 1966.

15454 AIKEN (ALEX). Courage Past: A Duty Done. Glasgow. 1971.

15455 HOCKEY (JOHN). Squaddies: Portrait of a Subculture. 1986.

15456 COLE (HOWARD NORMAN). The Story of Catterick Camp 1915–1972. Catterick. 1972.

15457 BURNE (ALFRED HIGGINS). The Woolwich Mess. 1954. 2nd edn 1971.

15458 WADGE (D. COLLETT) ed. Women in Uniform. 1947.

15459 BATERRY (ROY). Women in Khaki: The Story of the British Woman Soldier. 1988.

15460 BIDWELL (REGINALD GEORGE SHELFORD). The Women's Royal Army Corps. 1977.

15461 FIELD (VERONICA). On the Strength: The Story of the British Army Wife. 1974.

15462 POPHAM (HUGH). FANY: The Story of the Women's Transport Services 1907–1984. 1984.

15463 SELLWOOD (ARTHUR VICTOR). The Saturday Night Soldiers: The Stirring Story of the Territorial Army. 1966.

15464 TURNER (E. S.). Gallant Gentlemen: A Portrait of the British Officer, 1660–1956. 1956.

15465 DOWNES (CATHY). Special Trust and Confidence: The Making of an Officer. 1991. [A study of recruitment, selection, education and training for officers in all the services based around Sandhurst, Dartmouth, Cranwell, and Lympstone.].

15466 HAGGARD (Sir RIDER). The After-War Settlement and Employment of Ex-service Men in the Overseas Dominions. 1916

15467 WOOTTON (J. GRAHAM). The Politics of Influence: British Ex-Servicemen, Cabinet Decisions and Cultural Change 1917-57. 1963.

15468 —— Official History of the British Legion. 1956.

15469 BROWN (ANTONY). Red for Remembrance: The British Legion 1921-1971. 1971.

3. ORGANIZATIONAL STRUCTURE

15470 MILLET (ALLAN) and MURRAY (WILLIAMSON) eds. Military Effectiveness. Vol. 1 The First World War. Vol. 2 The Interwar Period. Vol. 3 The Second World War. 1988.

[Evaluates and compares the performance of the military institutions of France, Germany, Russia, the USA, Great Britain, Japan, and Italy.].

15471 PULESTON (WILLIAM DILWORTH). High Command in the World War. N.Y. 1934.

15472 HANKEY (MAURICE) *Baron.* The Supreme Command, 1914–1918. 2 vols 1961.

15473 MAURICE (*Sir* FREDERICK BARTON). Lessons of Allied Cooperation: Naval, Military and Air, 1914–1918. 1942.

15474 JOHNSON (FRANKLYN ARTHUR). Defence by Committee: The British Committee of Imperial Defence, 1885–1959. 1960.

15475 HOWARD (MICHAEL). Central Organisation for Defence. 1970.

15476 KEYES (ROGER JOHN BROWNLOW). Amphibious Warfare and Combined Operations. Camb. 1943.

15477 CRESWELL (JOHN). Generals and Admirals: The Story of Amphibious Command. 1952.

15478 FERGUSSON (*Sir* BERNARD). The Watery Maze: The Story of Combined Operations. 1961.

15479 LINDSELL (*Sir* WILFRED GORDON). Military Organisation and Administration. 1957.

15480 CHARTERIS (JOHN). At G.H.Q. 1931.

15481 HILLS (REGINALD JOHN TAYLOR). Phantom was there. 1951.[A history of the G.H.Q. Liaison Regiment 1939–45].

4. WEAPONRY

15482 BIDWELL (SHELFORD) *and* GRAHAM (DOMINICK). Fire-Power: British Army Weapons and Theories of War, 1904–1945. 1985.

15483 BARKER (ARTHUR JAMES). British and American Infantry Weapons of World War II. 1969.

15484 CONNIFORD (MICHAEL PETER). British Light Military Trucks, 1939–1945. 1976.

15485 HOGG (IAN VERNON). Military Smallarms of the Twentieth Century. 1973.

15486 —— Military Pistols and Revolvers: The Handguns of the Two World Wars. 1970.

15487 —— A History of Artillery. 1974.

15488 —— British Artillery Weapons and Ammunition, 1914–1918. 1972.

15489 SKENTELBERY (N.). Arrows to Atom Bombs: A History of the Ordnance Board. 1975.

15490 HOGG (OLIVER FREDERICK GILLILAN). The Royal Arsenal: Its Background, Origin and Subsequent History. 2 vols 1963.

15491 FARMER (HENRY GEORGE). History of the Royal Artillery Band, 1762–1953. 1955.

15492 BATCHELOR (JOHN). Artillery. 1972.

15493 SETON-HUTCHINSON (GRAHAM). Machine Guns. 1938.

15494 WHITE (BRIAN TERENCE). British Armoured Cars, 1914–1945. 1964.

15495 CROW (DUNCAN). British A.F.V.s [Armoured Fighting Vehicles] 1919–1940. Windsor. 1970.

15496 —— British and Commonwealth A.F.V.s 1940–1946. Windsor. 1971.

15497 WILKINSON-LATHAM (JOHN). British Cut and Thrust Weapons. 1971.

15498 YOUNG (PETER). The Machinery of War: An Illustrated History of Weapons. 1973.

15499 BURRELL (BRIAN). Combat Weapons: Hand Guns and Shoulder-arms of World War II. 1973.

15500 CONNIFORD (MICHAEL PETER). A Summary of the Transport used by the British Army 1939–1945. 1969.

15501 CHINN (GEORGE MORGAN). The Machine Gun. Washington, D.C. 1951.

15502 ROGERS (HUGH CUTHBERT BASSET). Weapons of the British Soldier. 1961.

15503 BROOKES (KENNETH). Battle Thunder: The Story of Britain's Artillery. Reading. 1973.

15504 HUTCHISON (GRAHAM SETON). Machine Guns: Their History and Tactical Employment. 1938.

15505 KEMP (NORMAN). The Devices of War. 1956.

15506 SMITH (R. E.). British Army Vehicles and Equipment. 2 vols 1964.

15507 FOLEY (CEDRIC JOHN). ABC of British Army Vehicles, Armoured Cars, Tanks and Guns. 1955.

15508 HACKER (BARTON C.). The Military and the Machine. Chicago. 1967.

15509 HODGES (PETER). British Military Markings 1939–1945. 1971.

15510 HOBART (FRANK WILLIAM ARTHUR). Pictorial History of the Machine Gun. 1971.

15511 HARTLEY (ARTHUR BAMFORD). Unexploded Bomb: A History of Bomb Disposal. 1958.

15512 WEEKS (JOHN). Men Against Tanks: A History of Anti-Tank Warfare. 1975.

15513 —— Infantry Weapons. 1972.

15514 PUGH (STEVENSON). Fighting Vehicles and Weapons of the Modern British Army. 1962.

15515 SWEETING (ROBERT CLIFFORD). Modern Infantry Weapons and Training in their Use. 1962.

15516 BROWNE (DOUGLAS GORDON). The Tank in Action. Edin. 1920.

15517 CHAMBERLAIN (PETER). Modern British Tanks and Fighting Equipment. 1970.

15518 —— British and American Tanks of World War II. 1969.

15519 —— The Churchill Tank: The Story of Britain's Most Famous Tank, 1939–1965. 1971.

15520 —— Tanks of World War I: British and German. 1969.

15521 PERRETT (BRYAN). The Matilda. 1973.

15522 COOPER (BRYAN). Tank Battles of World War I. 1974.

15523 CRISP (ROBERT). Brazen Chariots: An Account of Tank Warfare in the Western Desert, November–December 1941. 1959.

15524 EVEREST (J. H.). The First Battle of the Tanks, Cambrai, November 20th 1917. 1942.

15525 FULLER (JOHN FREDERIC CHARLES). Tanks in the Great War, 1914–1918. 1920.

15526 LEWIN (RONALD). Man of Armour: A Study of Lieut-General Vyvyan Pope and the Development of Armoured Warfare. 1976.

15527 MACKSEY (KENNETH JOHN) . Tank Force: Allied Armour in the Second World War. 1970.

15528 MARTEL (GIFFARD LE QUESNE). In the Wake of the Tank: The First Fifteen Years of Mechanisation in the British Army. 1931.

15529 PERRETT (BRYAN). Tank Tracks to Rangoon: The Story of British Armour in Burma. 1978.

15530 —— The Valentine in North Africa, 1942–1943. Shepperton. 1972.

15531 —— Through Mud and Blood: Infantry-Tank Operations in World War II. 1975.

15532 ROLLS (S. C.). Steel Chariots in the Desert. 1937.

15533 STANHOPE-PALMER (R.). Tank Trap 1940, or, No Battle in Britain. Ilfracombe. 1976.

15534 SUETER (Sir MURRAY FRASER). The Evolution of the Tank. 1937.

15535 SWINTON (Sir ERNEST DUNLOP). Eyewitness: Being Personal Reminiscences of Certain Phases of the Great War, Including the Genesis of the Tank. 1932.

15536 WHITE (BRIAN TERENCE). British Tanks, 1915–1945. 1963.

15537 WHITEHOUSE (ARTHUR GEORGE JOSEPH). Tank: The Battles they Fought, and the Men who Drove them—from Flanders to Korea. 1961.

15538 OGORKIEWICZ (R. M.). 'Fifty Years of British Tanks'. *Roy. United Services Inst. Jnl* 110 (1965), 254–61.

5. REGIMENTS
(a) General

15539 WHITE (A. S.) *comp.* A Bibliography of Regimental Histories of the British Army. 1965.

15540 WICKES (HENRY LEONARD). Regiments of Foot: A Historical Record of all the Foot Regiments of the British Army. Reading. 1974.

15541 WARNER (PHILIP). Stories of Famous Regiments. 1975.

15542 PAGET (Sir J.). The Story of the Guards. 1976.

15543 TALBOT-BOOTH (E. C.). The British Army: Its History, Customs, Traditions and Uniforms. 1937.

15544 BARNES (ROBERT MONEY). A History of the Regiments and Uniforms of the British Army. 1950.

15545 —— Military Uniforms of Britain and the Empire, 1742 to the Present Time. 1960.

15546 LAWSON (CECIL C. P.). A History of the Uniforms of the British Army. 2 vols. 1940–42.

15547 SMITHERMAN (PHILIP HENRY). Infantry Uniforms of the British Army. 3 vols 1970.

15548 EDWARDS (THOMAS JOSEPH). Military Customs. Aldershot. 1947. 5th edn 1961.

15549 GORDON (LAURENCE LEE). Military Origins. 1971.

15550 TURNER (JOHN FRAYN). V.C.'s of the Army, 1939–1951. 1962.

(b) Irish Regiments

15551 MACDONAGH (MICHAEL). The Irish at the Front. 1916.

15552 —— The Irish on the Somme. 1917.

15553 HARRIS (HENRY). The Irish Regiments in the First World War. Cork. 1968.

15554 EVANS (ROGER). The Story of the Fifth Royal Inniskilling Dragoon Guards. Aldershot. 1951.

15555 FOX (Sir FRANK) . The Royal Inniskilling Fusiliers in the World War. 1928.

15556 CUNLIFFE (MARCUS FALKNER). The Royal Irish Fusiliers, 1793–1950. 1952.

15557 HARRIS (HENRY). The Royal Irish Fusiliers. 1972.

15558 KIPLING (RUDYARD) *ed.* The Irish Guards in the Great War. 2 vols 1923.

15559 FITZGERALD (DESMOND J. L.). History of the Irish Guards in the Second World War. Aldershot. 1949.

15560 VERNEY (PETER). The Micks: The Story of the Irish Guards. 1970.

15561 FITZROY (OLIVIA). Men of Valour: The History of the VII King's Royal Irish Hussars. Vol. 3 1927–58. 1961.

15562 CORBALLY (MARCUS JOSEPH PATRICK MATTHEW). The Royal Ulster Rifles, 1793–1957. Glasgow. 1960.

(c) Scottish Regiments

15563 PAUL (WILLIAM PRATT). The Highland Regiments: Tigers in Tartan. Aberd. 1971.

15564 —— The Lowland Regiments: Lions Rampant. Aberd. 1972.

15565 MacECHERN (DUGALD). The Sword of the North: Highland Memories of the Great War. Inverness. 1923.

15566 MACLENNAN (J.). Scots of the Line. 1953.

15567 MALCOLM (G. I.). Argyllshire Highlanders, 1860–1960. Glasgow. 1960.

15568 ANDERSON (ROBERT CHARLES BECKETT). History of the Argyll and Sutherland Highlanders, 1st Battalion, 1909–1939. Edin. 1954. 1939–1954. Edin. 1956.

15569 WAUCHOPE (ARTHUR GRENFELL). A History of the Black Watch (Royal Highlanders) in the Great War. 3 vols. 1925–26.

15570 WHITEHEAD (A. P.) *ed.* The 1st Battalion Tyneside Scottish: The Black Watch—Royal Highland Regiment. Perth. 1947.

15571 GRANT (CHARLES). The Black Watch. Reading. 1971.

15572 LINKLATER (ERIC ROBERT RUSSELL) *and* LINKLATER (A.). The Black Watch: The History of the Royal Highland Regiment. 1977.

15573 HUNTER (THOMAS). Officers of the Black Watch, 1725–1937. Perth. 1937.

15574 MCMICKING (NEIL). Officers of the Black Watch, 1752–1952. Rev. edn 1952.

15575 GUNNING (HUGH). Borderers in Battle. Berwick-upon-Tweed. 1948.

15576 SUTHERLAND (DOUGLAS). Tried and Valiant: The History of the Border Regiment, the 34th and 55th Regiments of Foot, 1702–1959. 1972.

15577 GILLON (STAIR A.). The K.O.S.B. in the Great War. 1930.

15578 MARTIN (DAVID) *ed.* The Fifth Battalion, The Cameronians (Scottish Rifles). 1914–1919. Glasgow. 1936.

15579 MCEWEN (JOHN HELIAS FINNIE). The Fifth Camerons. Edin. 1938.

15580 STORY (HENRY HARLE). History of the Cameronians (Scottish Rifles). Vol. 2 1910–1933. 1957.

15581 BARCLAY (CYRIL NELSON). History of the Cameronians (Scottish Rifles). Vol. 3 1933–1946. 1949.

15582 BAYNES (JOHN). History of the Cameronians (Scottish Rifles): vol. 4 The Close of Empire, 1948–1968. 1971.

15583 Historical Records of the Queen's Own Cameron Highlanders: vol. 7 1949–61. Edin. 1962.

15584 SELLAR (R. J. B.). The Fife and Forfar Yeomanry, 1919–1956. Edin. 1960.

15585 MILES (WILFRID). The Gordon Highlanders, 1919–1945. 1961.

15586 SINCLAIR-STEVENSON (CHRISTOPHER). The Gordon Highlanders. 1968.

15587 —— The Life of a Regiment: The History of the Gordon Highlanders, vol. vi 1945–1970. 1974.

15588 PETRE (FRANCIS LORAINE) *et al.* The Scots Guards in the Great War, 1914–1918. 1925.

15589 ERSKINE (DAVID HERVEY) *comp.* The Scots Guards, 1919–1955. 1956.

15590 EWING (JOHN). The Royal Scots 1914–1919. 2 vols. Edin. 1925.

15591 MUIR (AUGUSTUS). The First of Foot: The History of the Royal Scots. Edin. 1961.

15592 BRANDER (A. MICHAEL). The Royal Scots (The Royal Regiment). 1976.

15593 KEMP (J. C.). The History of the Royal Scots Fusiliers, 1919–1959. Glasgow. 1963.

15594 CARVER (RICHARD MICHAEL POWER). Second to None: The Royal Scots Greys, 1919–1945. Glasgow. 1954.

15595 BLACKLOCK (MICHAEL). The Royal Scots Greys (The 2nd Dragoons). 1971.

15596 HARDY (SYDNEY JAMES) *et al.* History of the Royal Scots Greys (The Second Dragoons). August 1914–March 1919. 1928.

(d) English Regiments

15597 BARTHOP (MICHAEL). Crater to the Creggan: A History of the Royal Anglian Regiment, 1964–1974. 1976.

15598 MURLAND (J. R. W.). The Royal Armoured Corps. 1943.

15599 OWEN (FRANK) *and* ATKINS (H. W.). The Royal Armoured Corps. 1945.

15600 MACKSEY (KENNETH). A History of the Royal Armoured Corps, 1914–1975. 1983.

15601 MASTERS (DAVID). With Pennants Flying: The Immortal Deeds of the Royal Armoured Corps. 1943. Rev. edn 1957.

15602 JOLLY (ALAN). Blue Flash: The Story of an Armoured Regiment. 1952.

15603 BIDWELL (REGINALD GEORGE SHELFORD). Gunners at War: A Tactical Study of the Royal Artillery in the Twentieth Century. 1970. Rev. edn 1972.

15604 BLIGHT (GORDON). The History of the Royal Berkshire Regiment (Princess Charlotte of Wales), 1920–1947. 1953.

15605 WINGFIELD (A. J.). The Bolton Artillery: A History, 1860–1975. Bolton. 1976.

15606 VERDIN (*Sir* RICHARD). The Cheshire (Earl of Chester's) Yeomanry, 1898–1967: The Last Regiment to Fight on Horses. Chester. 1971.

15607 GRANT (CHARLES). The Coldstream Guards. 1971.

15608 STADDEN (CHARLES). Coldstream Guards—Dress and Appointments, 1658–1972. New Malden. 1973.

15609 ROSS OF BLADENSBURG (*Sir* JOHN). The Coldstream Guards, 1914–1918. 3 vols. Oxf. 1928.

15610 HOWARD (MICHAEL ELIOT) *and* SPARROW (JOHN) . The Coldstream Guards, 1920–1946. 1951.

15611 CRICHTON (RICHARD). The Coldstream Guards, 1946–1970. 1972.

15612 QUILTER (DAVID C.). No Dishonourable Name: The 2nd and 3rd Battalions, Coldstream Guards, 1939–1946. 1972.

15613 ATKINSON (CHRISTOPHER THOMAS). The Devonshire Regiment, 1914–1918. Exeter. 1926.

15614 TAYLOR (J.). The Devons: A History of the Devonshire Regiment, 1685–1945. Bristol. 1951.

15615 ATKINSON (CHRISTOPHER THOMAS). The Dorsetshire Regiment. 2 vols. Oxf. 1947.

15616 POPHAM (HUGH). The Dorset Regiment: The 39th/54th Regiment of Foot. 1970.

15617 ATKINSON (CHRISTOPHER THOMAS). History of the Royal Dragoons, 1661–1934. Glasgow. 1934.

15618 BEDDINGTON (WILLIAM RICHARD). A History of the Queen's Bays (The 2nd Dragoon Guards). 1929–1945. Winchester. 1954.

15619 BIRT (WILLIAM RAYMOND). XXII Dragoons, 1760–1945: The Story of a Regiment. Aldershot. 1950.

15620 HILLS (REGINALD JOHN TAYLOR). The Royal Dragoons. 1972.

15621 PITT-RIVERS (J. A.). The Story of the Royal Dragoons, 1938–1945. 1956.

15622 WOOZLEY (A. D.) ed. History of the King's Dragoon Guards, 1938–1945. 1950.

15623 BARCLAY (CYRIL NELSON). History of the Duke of Wellington's Regiment, 1919–1952. 1953.

15624 LUNT (JAMES). The Duke of Wellington's Regiment. 1971.

15625 RISSIK (DAVID). The D.L.I.: The History of the Durham Light Infantry, 1939–1945. Durham. 1953.

15626 WARD (STEPHEN GEORGE PEREGRINE). Faithful: The Story of the Durham Light Infantry. 1963.

15627 MOORE (W.). The Durham Light Infantry. 1975.

15628 BOYD (D.). Royal Engineers. 1975.

15629 GRIEVE (W. GRANT) and NEWMAN (BERNARD). Tunnellers: The Story of the Tunnelling Companies, Royal Engineers during the World War. 1936.

15630 SANDES (E. W. C.). The Royal Engineers in Egypt and the Sudan. Chatham. 1937.

15631 MARTIN (T. A.). The Essex Regiment, 1929–1950. Brentwood. 1952.

15632 O'NEILL (HERBERT CHARLES). The Royal Fusiliers in the Great War. 1922.

15633 PARKINSON (C. NORTHCOTE). Always a Fusilier. 1949.

15634 FOSS (MICHAEL). The Royal Fusiliers. 1967.

15635 PAGAN (A. W.). Infantry: An Account of the 1st Gloucestershire Regiment during the War, 1914–1918. 2 vols. Aldershot. 1951.

15636 DANIELL (DAVID SCOTT). Cap of Honour: The Story of the Gloucestershire Regiment (The 28th/61st Foot). 1694–1975. 1975.

15637 CAREW (TIM). The Glorious Glosters: A Short History of the Gloucestershire Regiment 1945–1970. 1970.

15638 FOX (Sir FRANK). The History of the Royal Gloucestershire Hussars Yeomanry, 1898–1922. 1923.

15639 WYLLY (HAROLD CARMICHAEL). The Green Howards in the Great War, 1914–1918. Richmond. 1926.

15640 SYNGE (WILLIAM ALFRED THACKERAY). The Story of the Green Howards, 1939–1945. Richmond. 1952.

15641 MARTIN (FREDERICK). History of the Grenadier Guards, 1656–1949. Aldershot. 1951.

15642 PONSONBY (Sir FREDERICK) . The Grenadier Guards in the Great War, 1914–1918. 3 vols 1920.

15643 NICOLSON (NIGEL) and FORBES (PATRICK). The Grenadier Guards in the War of 1939–1945. 2 vols 1949.

15644 WHITWORTH (REGINALD HENRY). The Grenadier Guards. 1974.

15645 SMITH (ERIC DAVID). East of Kathmandu: The Story of the 7th Duke of Edinburgh's Own Gurkha Rifles. Vol. 2 1948–1973. 1976.

15646 JAMES (HAROLD DOUGLAS) and SMALL (DENIS SHEIL). A Pride of Gurkhas: The 2nd King Edward VII's Own Goorkhas (The Sirmoor Rifles). 1948–1971. 1975.

15647 ATKINSON (CHRISTOPHER THOMAS). The Royal Hampshire Regiment. Vol. 2 1914–1918. Winchester. 1952.

15648 DANIELL (DAVID SCOTT). Regimental History: The Royal Hampshire Regiment: Vol. 3 1918–54. Aldershot. 1955.

15649 WALKER (G. G.). The Honourable Artillery Company, 1537–1947. Aldershot. 2nd edn 1954.

15650 JOHNSON (R. F.). Regimental Fire: The Honourable Artillery Company in World War 2. 1958.

15651 BIDWELL (REGINALD GEORGE SHELFORD). The Royal Horse Artillery. 1973.

15652 WYNDHAM (HUMPHREY). The Household Cavalry at War. Aldershot. 1952.

15653 ORDE (RODEN POWLETT GRAVES). The Household Cavalry at War. Aldershot. 1953.

15654 MANSER (ROY). The Household Cavalry Regiment. 1975.

15655 BRADDON (RUSSELL READING). All the Queen's Men: The Household Cavalry and the Brigade of Guards. 1977.

15656 WILLCOX (WALTER TEMPLE). The 3rd (King's Own) Hussars in the Great War, 1914–1919. 1925.

15657 BOLITHO (HENRY HECTOR). The Galloping Third: The Story of the 3rd King's Own Hussars. 1963.

15658 EDWARDS (THOMAS JOSEPH). A Short History of the 4th Queen's Own Hussars. Canterbury. 1935.

15659 DANIELL (DAVID SCOTT). 4th Hussars: The Story of the 4th Queen's Own Hussars, 1685–1958. Aldershot. 1959.

15660 EVANS (ROGER). The Years Between: The Story of the 7th Queen's Own Hussars, 1911–1937. Aldershot. 1965.

15661 BRERETON (JOHN MAURICE). The 7th Queen's Hussars. 1975.

15662 DAVY (GEORGE MARK OSWALD). The Seventh and Three Enemies. Camb. 1953.

15663 LUMLEY (L. R.). History of the Eleventh Hussars, 1908–1934. 1936.

15664 CLARKE (DUDLEY WRANGEL). The Eleventh at War: Being the Story of the XIth Hussars through the Years, 1934–1945. 1952.

15665 DURAND (*Sir* HENRY MORTIMER). The 13th Hussars in the Great War. Edin. 1921.

15666 MILLER (C. H.). History of the 13th/18th Royal Hussars, Queen Mary's Own, 1922–1947. 1949.

15667 OATTS (LEWIS BALFOUR). Emperor's Chambermaids: The Story of 14th/20th King's Hussars. 1973.

15668 COURAGE (G.). The History of 15/19 the King's Royal Hussars 1939–1945. Aldershot. 1949.

15669 BLAXLAND (WILLIAM GREGORY). The Farewell Years: The Final Historical Records of the Buffs, Royal East Kent Regiment, 1948–1967. Canterbury. 1967.

15670 —— The Buffs: Royal East Kent Regiment, the 3rd Regiment of Foot. 1972.

15671 —— The Queen's Own Buffs, the Royal East Kent Regiment, 3rd, 50th and 97th Foot. Canterbury. 1974.

15672 ATKINSON (CHRISTOPHER THOMAS). The Queen's Own Royal West Kent Regiment, 1914–1919. 1924.

15673 CLARKE (EDWARD BRIAN STANLEY) *and* TILLOTT (ALAN THEODORE). From Kent to Kohima: Being the History of the 4th Battalion, the Queen's Own Royal West Kent Regiment, 1939–1947. Aldershot. 1951.

15674 CHAPLIN (HOWARD DOUGLAS). The Queen's Own Royal West Kent Regiment, 1951–1961. Maidstone. 1964.

15675 HOLLOWAY (ROGER). The Queen's Own Royal West Kent Regiment: The Dirty Half-Hundred. 1973.

15676 LEGGE-BOURKE (*Sir* EDWARD ALEXANDER HENRY). The King's Guards: Horse and Foot. 1951.

15677 —— The Queen's Guards: Horse and Foot. 1965.

15678 BURKE-GAFFNEY (JOHN JOSEPH). The Story of the King's Regiment, 1914–1948. Formby. 1954.

15679 BIGWOOD (GEORGE). The Lancashire Fighting Territorials. 1916.

15680 SURTEES (GEORGE). A Short History of the XXth Lancashire Fusiliers. 1955.

15681 RAY (CYRIL). Regiment of the Line: The Story of the 20th Lancashire Fusiliers. 1963.

15682 DEAN (CHARLES GRAHAM TROUGHTON). The Loyal Regiment: North Lancashire, 1919–1953. Preston. 1955.

15683 MULLALY (BRIAN REGINALD). The South Lancashire Regiment: The Prince of Wales's Volunteers. Bristol. 1955.

15684 WHALLEY-KELLY (JOSEPH HERBERT). 'Ich dien': The Prince of Wales's Volunteers (South Lancashire) 1914–1934. Aldershot. 1935.

15685 SHEPPARD (ERIC WILLIAM). The Ninth Queen's Royal Lancers, 1715–1936. Aldershot. 1939.

15686 BRIGHT (JOAN) *ed.* The Ninth Queen's Royal Lancers, 1936–1945: The Story of an Armoured Regiment in Battle. Aldershot. 1951.

15687 STEWART (P. T.). The History of the XII Royal Lancers (Prince of Wales's). 1950.

15688 BARCLAY (CYRIL NELSON). History of the 16th/5th: The Queen's Royal Lancers, 1925–61. Aldershot. 1963.

15689 FFRENCH-BLAKE (RICHARD LIFFORD VALENTINE). A History of the 17th/21st Lancers, 1922–59. 1962.

15690 POCOCK (JOHN GRAHAME). The Spirit of a Regiment: Being the History of the 19th King George V's Own Lancers. 1921–1947. 1962.

15691 UNDERHILL (WILLIAM ERNEST) *ed.* The Royal Leicestershire Regiment, 17th Foot: A History of the Years 1928 to 1956. South Wigston. 1958.

15692 HILLS (REGINALD JOHN TAYLOR). The Life Guards. 1971.

15693 GATES (LIONEL CHASEMORE) *comp.* The History of the Tenth Foot, 1919–1950. [The Royal Lincolnshire Regiment.]. 1953.

15694 BAILEY (OLIVER F.) *and* HOLLIER (HAROLD M.). 'The Kensingtons': 13th London Regiment. 1936.

15695 DURAND (ALGERNON THOMAS MARION) *and* HASTINGS (ROBERT HOOD WILLIAM STEWART). The London Rifle Brigade, 1919–1950. Aldershot. 1952.

15696 BARCLAY (CYRIL NELSON) *ed.* The London Scottish in the Second World War, 1939–1945. 1952.

15697 BELL (ARCHIBALD COLQUHOUN). History of the Manchester Regiment. Vol. 3 1st and 2nd Battalions, 1922–1948. Altrincham. 1954.

15698 KEMP (PETER). The Middlesex Regiment (Duke of Cambridge's Own). 1919–1952. Aldershot. 1956.

15699 BLAXLAND (WILLIAM GREGORY). The Middlesex Regiment. 1977.

15700 KEMP (PETER). History of the Royal Norfolk Regiment, Vol. 3 1919–1951. Norwich. 1953.

15701 CAREW (TIM). The Royal Norfolk Regiment. 1967.

15702 JERVOIS (W. J.). The History of the Northamptonshire Regiment: 1934–1948. Northampton. 1953.

15703 BARTHOP (MICHAEL). The Northamptonshire Regiment. 1974.

15704 BARCLAY (CYRIL NELSON). The History of the Royal Northumberland Fusiliers in the Second World War. 1952.

15705 BRIGHT (JOAN). History of the Northumberland Hussars Yeomanry, 1924–1949. 1949.

15706 NEWNHAM (MAURICE). Prelude to Glory: The Story of the Creation of Britain's Parachute Army. 1947.

15707 SAUNDERS (HILARY AIDAN ST GEORGE). The Red Beret: The Story of the Parachute Regiment at War, 1940–1945. 1950.

15708 BRAMMALL (RONALD). The Tenth: A Record of Service of the 10th Battalion, The Parachute Regiment, 1942–1945 and the 10th Battalion, The Parachute Regiment (T. A.). 1947–1965. Ipswich. 1965.

15709 NORTON (GEOFFREY GORDON). The Red Devils: The Story of Britain's Airborne Forces. 1971.

15710 THOMPSON (JULIAN). Ready for Anything: The Parachute Regiment, 1940–1982. 1989.

15711 FOSTER (R. C. G.). History of the Queen's Royal Regiment. Vol. 8 1924–48. 1953. Vol. 9 1961.

15712 BERKELEY (REGINALD CHEYNE) and SEYMOUR (WILLIAM WALTER). The History of the Rifle Brigade in the War of 1914–1918. 2 vols 1927.

15713 BRYANT (Sir ARTHUR WYNNE MORGAN). Jackets of Green: A Study of the History, Philosophy and Character of the Rifle Brigade. 1972.

15714 WILKINSON-LATHAM (C.). The Royal Green Jackets. 1975.

15715 HARBEY (B.). The Rifle Brigade. 1975.

15716 LINDSAY (THOMAS MARTIN). Sherwood Rangers. 1952.

15717 BARCLAY (CYRIL NELSON). The History of the Sherwood Foresters (Nottinghamshire and Derbyshire Regiment). 1919–1957. 1959.

15718 GLADSTONE (ERSKINE WILLIAM). The Shropshire Yeomanry, 1795–1945: The Story of a Volunteer Cavalry Regiment. Manch. 1953.

15719 KEMP (PETER). The History of the 4th Battalion, King's Shropshire Light Infantry, 1745–1945. Shrewsbury. 1955.

15720 WHITEHEAD (KENNETH). History of the Somerset Light Infantry (Prince Albert's). 1946–1960. Taunton. 1961.

15721 WARNER (PHILIP). The Special Air Service. 1972.

15722 SEYMOUR (WILLIAM). British Special Forces. 1985.

15723 GERAGHTY (TONY). Who Dares Wins: The Story of the Special Air Service, 1950–1980. 1980.

15724 COWLES (VIRGINIA). The Phantom Major: The Story of David Stirling and the S. A. S. Regiment. 1958.

15725 KENNEDY (MICHAEL PAUL). Soldier 'I': SAS. 1989.

15726 COOK (HUGH). The North Staffordshire Regiment. 1970.

15727 NICHOLSON (WALTER NORRIS). The Suffolk Regiment, 1928–1946. Ipswich. 1948.

15728 MOIR (GUTHRIE). The Suffolk Regiment. 1969.

15729 DANIELL (DAVID SCOTT). History of the East Surrey Regiment, 1920–1952. 1957.

15730 LANGLEY (MICHAEL). The East Surrey Regiment (The 31st and 70th Regiments of Foot). 1972.

15731 AINSWORTH (JOHN FRANCIS). The Royal Sussex Regiment, 1701–1966. Derby. 1972.

15732 WILLIAMS-ELLIS (BERTRAM CLOUGH) and WILLIAMS-ELLIS (MARY ANABEL NASSAU). The Tank Corps. 1919.

15733 WILSON (GEORGE MURRAY) ed. Fighting Tanks: An Account of the Royal Tank Corps in Action, 1916–1921. 1929.

15734 FORBES (PATRICK). 6th Guards Tank Brigade. 1946.

15735 LIDDELL HART (Sir BASIL HENRY). The Tanks: The History of the Royal Tank Regiment and its Predecessors. 2 vols. 1959.

15736 MACKSEY (KENNETH). The Tanks: A History of the Royal Tank Regiment, 1945–1975. 1979.

15737 CUNLIFFE (MARCUS FALKNER). History of the Royal Warwickshire Regiment, 1919–1955. 1956.

15738 BAKER (PAUL). Yeoman, Yeoman: The Warwickshire Yeomanry, 1920–1956. Birmingham. 1971.

15739 PITTS (P. W.). Royal Wilts: The History of the Royal Wiltshire Yeomanry, 1920–1945. Burrup. 1946.

15740 PARSONS (ANTHONY DALLIN) et al. The Maroon Square: A History of the 4th Battalion, the Wiltshire Regiment in North-West Europe, 1939–1946. 1955.

15741 BIRDWOOD (CHRISTOPHER BROMHEAD) Baron. The Worcestershire Regiment, 1922–1950. Aldershot. 1952.

15742 GUTTERY (DAVID REGINALD). The Queen's Own Worcestershire Hussars, 1922–1956. Stourbridge. 1958.

15743 SHEFFIELD (O. F.). The York and Lancaster Regiment, 1919–1953. Aldershot. 1956.

15744 BOND (REGINALD COPLESTON). History of the King's Own Yorkshire Light Infantry in the Great War, 1914–1918. 1929.

15745 HINGSTON (W.). Never Give Up: The History of the King's Own Yorkshire Light Infantry, 1919–1942. Fulford, York. 1950.

15746 ELLENBERGER (GEORGE FOTHERGILL). History of the King's Own Yorkshire Light Infantry, 1939–1948. Aldershot. 1961.

15747 NIGHTINGALE (P. R.). A History of the East Yorkshire Regiment in the War of 1939–1945. 1952.

15748 BARKER (ARTHUR JAMES). The East Yorkshire Regiment. 1971.

15749 SANDES (EDWARD WARREN CAULFIELD). From Pyramid to Pagoda: The Story of the West Yorkshire Regiment in the War 1939–1945 and Afterwards. York. 1952.

(e) Welsh Regiments

15750 ATKINSON (CHRISTOPHER THOMAS). The History of the South Wales Borderers 1914–1918. 1931.

15751 —— The South Wales Borderers, 24th Foot, 1689–1937. 1937.

15752 BRETT (GEORGE ALBERT) *et al.* History of the South Wales Borderers and the Monmouthshire Regiment, 1937–1952. 5 vols. Pontypool. 1953–56.

15753 ADAMS (JACK). The South Wales Borderers. 1968.

15754 WILKINSON-LATHAM (C.). The South Wales Borderers. Reading. 1975.

15755 KEMP (PETER) *and* GRAVES (JOHN). The Red Dragon: The Story of the Welsh Fusiliers, 1919–1945. Aldershot. 1960.

15756 DE COURCY (JOHN). The History of the Welsh Regiment, 1919–1951. Cardiff. 1952.

15757 BARCLAY (CYRIL NELSON). The History of the 53rd (Welsh) Division in the Second World War. 1956.

15758 WARD (CHARLES HUMBLE DUDLEY). History of the Welsh Guards. 1920.

15759 —— The Welsh Regiment of Foot Guards, 1915–1918. 1936.

15760 ELLIS (LIONEL FREDERIC). Welsh Guards at War. 1946.

(*f*) Auxiliary Corps

15761 LOVEGROVE (P.). Not Least in the Crusade: A Short History of the Royal Army Medical Corps. Aldershot. 1951.

15762 CROZIER (STEPHEN FORSTER). The History of the Corps of Royal Military Police. Aldershot. 1951.

15763 LOVELL-KNIGHT (A. V.). The Story of the Royal Military Police. 1977.

15764 PIGGOTT (J.). Queen Alexandra's Royal Army Nursing Corps. 1975.

15765 SMYTH (*Sir* JOHN). The Will to Live: The Story of Dame Margot Turner, D.B.E., R.R.C. 1970. [Matron-in-Chief and Brigadier of Queen Alexandra's R. A. N. C.].

15766 WINSLOW (T. E.). Forewarned is Forearmed: A History of the Royal Observer Corps. 1948.

15767 WOOD (DEREK). Attack Warning Red: The Royal Observer Corps and the Defence of Britain, 1925–1975. 1976.

15768 OLDFIELD (E. A. L.). History of the Army Physical Training Corps. Aldershot. 1955.

15769 RHODES-WOOD (E. H.). A War History of the Royal Pioneer Corps, 1939–1945. Aldershot. 1960.

15770 BEADON (ROGER HAMMET). The Royal Army Service Corps. Camb. 1931.

15771 CLABBY (JOHN). The History of the Royal Army Veterinary Corps, 1919–1961. 1963.

6. EDUCATION: THE ARMED FORCES

15772 SMYTH (*Sir* JOHN). Sandhurst: The History of the Royal Military Academy, Woolwich; The Royal Military College, Sandhurst; and the Royal Military Academy, Sandhurst, 1741–1961. 1961.

15773 THOMAS (HUGH SWYNNERTON) *Baron.* The Story of Sandhurst. 1961.

15774 BOND (BRIAN J.). 'Educational Changes at R. M. A. Sandhurst 1966-1983'. *Militarhistorisk Tidskrift* 187 (1983), 33–43.

15775 YOUNG (FREDERICK WALTER). The Story of the Staff College 1858–1958. Camberley. 1958.

15776 WHITE (ARCHIE CECIL THOMAS). The Story of Army Education, 1643–1963. 1963.

15777 PACK (S. W. C.). Britannia at Dartmouth: The Story of HMS Britannia and the Britannia Royal Naval College. 1966.

15778 SUMMERS (DAVID LEWIS). HMS Ganges 1866-1966: One Hundred Years of Training Boys for the Royal Navy. 1966.

15779 HASLEM (E. B.). The History of the Royal Air Force, Cranwell. 1983.

E. THE ROYAL AIR FORCE

15780 The Air Force List. 1949+. [Annual.].

1. GENERAL

15781 MINISTRY OF DEFENCE, ADASTRA LIBRARY. Bibliography of the Royal Air Force. 1977.

15782 WORCESTER (RICHARD). The Roots of British Air Policy. 1966.

15783 SIMS (CHARLES). The Royal Air Force: The First Fifty Years. 1968.

15784 TREVENEN (JAMES). The Royal Air Force: The Past Thirty Years. 1976.

15785 BOWYER (CHAZ). The History of the RAF. 1977.

15786 RAWLINGS (J. D. R.). The History of the Royal Air Force. 1984.

15787 TAYLOR (JOHN W. R.) *and* MOYES (PHILIP J. R.). Pictorial History of the RAF. 3 vols 1969.

15788 HARRISON (B.). The RAF: A Pictorial History. 1978.

15789 FLACK (JEREMY). Today's Royal Air Force in Colour. 1987.

15790 POLLARD (A. O.). The Royal Air Force, a Concise History. 1934. Rev. edn 1939.

15791 RALEIGH (WALTER ALEXANDER) *and* JONES (H. A.). The War in the Air. 6 vols. Oxf. 1922–37.

15792 SMITH (NORMAN DAVID). The Royal Air Force. Oxf. 1963.

15793 GOSSAGE (*Sir* ERNEST LESLIE) . The Royal Air Force. 1937.

15794 STEWART (OLIVER). The Story of Air Warfare. 1958.

2 . THE ROYAL AIR FORCE

15795 DEAN (*Sir* MAURICE). The Royal Air Force and Two World Wars. 1979.

15796 OVERY (R. J.). The Air War 1939–1945. 1980.

15797 SAUNDERS (HILARY AIDAN ST GEORGE). Per ardua. The Rise of British Air Power, 1911–1939. 1944.

15798 BARING (MAURICE). R.F.C.H.Q. 1920. New edn Edin. 1968.

15799 CHANT (CHRIS). The Illustrated History of the Air Forces of World War I and World War II. 1979.

15800 JOHNSON (JAMES EDGAR). Full Circle: The Story of Air Fighting. 1964.

15801 JOUBERT DE LA FERTÉ (*Sir* PHILIP BENNET). The Third Service, the Story Behind the Royal Air Force. 1955.

15802 KIERNAN (REGINALD HUGH). The First War in the Air. 1934.

15803 NORRIS (GEOFFREY). The Royal Flying Corps: A History. 1965.

15804 PHILPOTT (BRYAN). Challenge in the Air. 1971.

15805 POWERS (B. D.). Strategy Without Slide Rule: British Air Strategy, 1914–1939. 1976.

15806 SPAIGHT (JAMES MOLONY). The Beginnings of Organised Air Power: A Historical Study. 1927.

15807 THOMPSON (*Sir* ROBERT). The Royal Flying Corps (per ardua ad astra). 1968.

15808 RICHARDS (DENIS) *and* SAUNDERS (HILARY ST. GEORGE). The Royal Air Force, 1939–1945. 3 vols. 1953–54. [Official history, Second World War: Campaigns.].

15809 —— The Royal Air Force 1939–1945. Vol. 2. The Fight Avails. Rev. edn 1975. Vol. 3. The Fight is Won. Rev. edn 1975.

15810 TUGWELL (MAURICE). Airborne to Battle: A History of Airborne Warfare, 1918–1971. 1971.

15811 JAMES (A. E. T.). The Royal Air Force: The Past 30 Years. 1976.

15812 HALLEY (JAMES J.). Famous Maritime Squadrons of the R.A.F. Windsor. 1973.

15813 —— Famous Fighter Squadrons of the R.A.F. Windsor. 1971.

15814 SIMS (EDWARD HOWELL). Fighter Tactics and Strategy, 1914–1970. 1972.

15815 GOULDING (JAMES). Camouflage and Markings: R.A.F. Fighter Command, Northern Europe, 1936-1945. 1971.

15816 PRICE (ALFRED). Aircraft Versus Submarine: The Evolution of the Anti-Submarine Aircraft, 1912 to 1972. 1973.

15817 TAYLOR (JOHN WILLIAM RANSOM). C.F.S.: Birthplace of Air Power. 1958.

15818 MATHEWS (V. L.). Blue Tapestry. 1948.

15819 OWEN (R. FENWICK). The Desert Air Force. 1948.

3 . AIRCRAFT

15820 THETFORD (OWEN). Aircraft of the Royal Air Force Since 1918. 1968.

15821 LEWIS (PETER). The British Fighter Since 1912: Fifty Years of Design and Development. 2nd edn 1965.

15822 —— The British Bomber Since 1914: Sixty-Five Years of Change and Development. 3rd edn 1980.

15823 OLIVER (DAVID). British Combat Aircraft Since 1918.

15824 MUNSON (KENNETH GEORGE). Fighters Between the Wars, 1919–1939, Including Attack and Training Aircraft. 1969.

15825 HARKER (RONALD W.). Rolls-Royce from the Wings: Military Aviation, 1925–1971. Oxf. 1976.

15826 BATCHELOR (JOHN H.) *and* COOPER (BRYAN). Fighter. A History of Fighter Aircraft. 1973.

15827 LLOYD (JOHN PHILLIP). R.A.F. Aircraft of World War II. 1959.

15828 MASON (FRANCIS K.). The Hawker Hurricane. 1987.

15829 BISHOP (EDWARD BARRY). The Wooden Wonder: The Story of the De Havilland Mosquito. 1959. New edn 1972.

15830 BARKER (RALPH HAMMOND). The Hurricats. 1978.

15831 KEITH (CLAUDE HILTON). I Hold My Aim: The Story of How the Royal Air Force was Armed for War. 1946.

15832 MUNSON (KENNETH GEORGE). Fighters, Attack and Training Aircraft 1939–1945. 1969.

15833 BOWYER (CHAZ) *ed.* Hurricane at War. 1974.

15834 —— Mosquito at War. 1973.

15835 SHARP (CECIL M.) *and* BOWYER (MICHAEL. J. F.). Mosquito. 1971.

15836 MUNSON (KENNETH GEORGE). Aircraft of World War Two. 1962.

15837 —— Bombers between the Wars, 1919–1939. 1970.

15838 —— Bombers, Patrol and Transport Aircraft, 1939–1945. 1969.

15839 WHEELER (ALLEN HENRY). That Nothing Failed Them: Testing Aeroplanes in War. 1963.

15840 WALLACE (GRAHAM). The Guns of the Royal Air Force, 1939–1945. 1972.

15841 HURREN (BERNARD JOHN). The Swordfish Saga: Story of the Fairey Swordfish Torpedo Bomber. Hayes. 1946.

15842 GARBETT (MIKE). The Lancaster at War. 1971.

15843 TUBBS (DOUGLAS BURNELL). Lancaster Bomber. 1972.

15844 WILLSON (G. B.). Birth of a Spitfire: The Story of Beaverbrook's Ministry and its First 10,000,000. 1941.

15845 ROBERTSON (BRUCE). Spitfire: The Story of a Famous Fighter. 1960.

15846 VADER (JOHN). Spitfire. 1970.

15847 PRICE (ALFRED). Spitfire, a Documentary History. 1977.

15848 —— The Spitfire Story. 1982.

15849 QUILL (JEFFREY) Spitfire: A Test Pilot's Story. 1983.

15850 GALLICO (PAUL WILLIAM). The Hurricane Story. 1959.

15851 MASON (FRANCIS KENNETH). Hawker Aircraft Since 1920. 1961.

15852 —— The Hawker Hurricane. 1962.

15853 HARDY (M. J.) Mosquito Victory. Newton Abbot. 1977.

15854 POOLMAN (KENNETH). Flying Boat: The Story of the 'Sunderland'. 1962.

15855 —— The Catafighters and Merchant Aircraft Carriers. 1970.

15856 POPHAM (HUGH). Into Wind: A History of British Naval Flying. 1970.

15857 GREY (C. G.). Sea-Flyers. 1942.

15858 JONES (GEOFFREY PATRICK). Raider: The Halifax and its Flyers. 1978.

15859 SMITH (PETER CHARLES). The Story of the Torpedo Bomber. 1974.

15860 THETFORD (OWEN GORDON). Aircraft of the Royal Air Force, 1918–1957. 1957. 3rd. edn 1962.

15861 TURNER (J. F.). British Aircraft of World War II. 1975.

15862 BOWYER (MICHAEL JOHN FREDERICK). Bombing Colours: R.A.F. Bombers, Their Marking and Operations, 1937–1973. Camb. 1973.

15863 —— Fighting Colours: R.A.F. Fighting Camouflage and Markings, 1937–1969. 1969. 2nd edn Camb. 1975.

15864 ROBERTSON (BRUCE). British Military Aircraft Serials, 1912–1963. 1964.

15865 —— Bombing Colours: British Bomber Camouflage and Markings, 1914–1937. 1972.

15866 —— Aircraft Camouflage and Markings, 1907–1954. 1956.

15867 GREEN (DENNIS WILLIAM). Famous Fighters of the Second World War. 1957.

15868 —— Famous Bombers of the Second World War. 1959.

15869 —— Aircraft of the Battle of Britain. 1969.

15870 GUNSTON (BILL). Early Supersonic Fighters of the West. 1976.

15871 —— Bombers of the West. 1973.

15872 MUNSON (KENNETH GEORGE). Bombers in Service: Patrol and Transport Aircraft Since 1960. 1972.

15873 ANDERTON (DAVID A.). Jet Fighters and Bombers. 1976.

15874 MOYES (PHILIP JOHN RICHARD). RAF Jet Fighter Flypast. Shepperton. 1972.

15875 TAYLOR (JOHN WILLIAM RANSOM). Modern Combat Aircraft. 1976.

15876 SHACKLADY (EDWARD). The Gloster Meteor. 1962.

15877 ALLWARD (MAURICE). Gloster Javelin. 1983.

15878 BIRTLES (PHILIP). De Havilland Vampire, Venom and Sea Vixen. 1986.

15879 JACKSON (ROBERT). Avro Vulcan. 1985.

15880 DAVIES (S. D.). 'The History of the Avro Vulcan'. *Jnl Roy. Aeronautical Soc.* 74 (1970), 350–64.

15881 ALLWARD (MAURICE). Buccaneer. 1981.

15882 JACKSON (ROBERT). The V-Bombers. 1981.

15883 GORDON (ANDREW). Handley Page Victor. 1988.

15884 STURIVANT (RAY). The History of Britain's Military Training Aircraft. 1987.

15885 EVERETT-HEATH (JOHN). British Military Helicopters. 1986.

15886 CUMMING (MICHAEL). The Powerless Ones: Gliding in Peace and War. 1966.

15887 HASTINGS (STEPHEN). Murder of the TSR-2. 1966.

15888 WILLIAMS (GEOFFREY), GREGORY (FRANK), *and* SIMPSON (JOHN). Crisis in Procurement: A Case Study of the TSR-2. 1969.

4. AIRMEN

15889 BRICKHILL (PAUL). The Dambusters. 1951.

15890 —— Reach for the Sky. The Story of Douglas Bader. 1954.

15891 BAKER (EDGAR CHARLES RICHARD). The Fighter Aces of the R.A.F., 1939–1945. 1962.

15892 —— Pattle-Supreme Fighter in the Air. 1965.

15893 BOWYER (CHAZ). Guns in the Sky: The Air Gunners of World War II. 1981.

15894 BOYLE (ANDREW). No Passing Glory. The Full and Authentic Biography of Group Captain Cheshire. 1955.

15895 WHEELER (ALLEN HENRY). Flying Between the Wars. 1972.

15896 COMEAU (MARCEL GERARD). Operation Mercury: An Airman in the Battle of Crete. 1961.

15897 DICKSON (LOVAT). Richard Hillary. 1951.

15898 BADER (*Sir* DOUGLAS ROBERT STEWART). Fight for the Sky. 1973.

15899 RICHEY (PAUL). Fighter Pilot: A personal record of the Campaign in France 1939–1940. 1980.

15900 DEERE (ALAN C.). Nine Lives. 1959.

15901 CURTIS (LETTICE). The Forgotten Pilots: A Story of the Air Transport Auxiliary, 1939–1945. 1971.

15902 BARKER (RALPH HAMMOND). Down in the Drink: True Stories of the Goldfish Club. 1955.

15903 MIDDLETON (D. H.). Test Pilots: The Story of British Test Flying 1903–1984. 1984.

15904 PREST (ROBERT). F4 Phantom: A Pilot's Story. 1979.

5. SUPPORT SERVICES

15905 REXFORD-WELCH (SAMUEL CUTHBERT) *ed.* The Royal Air Force Medical Services. 3 vols 1955–1958.

15906 COLE (HOWARD NORMAN). On Wings of Healing: The Story of the Airborne Medical Services, 1940–1960. Edin. 1963.

15907 BISHOP (EDWARD BARRY). The Debt We Owe: The Royal Air Force Benevolent Fund, 1919–1969. 1969. 2nd edn. [to 1979] 1979.

15908 WEEKS (JOHN). Airborne Equipment: A History of its Development. Newton Abbot. 1976.

6. FORMATIONS: FIRST AND SECOND WORLD WARS

15909 BOWYER (CHAZ) . Fighter Command 1936-1963. 1980.

15910 WYKEHAM (PETER). Fighter Command: A Study of Air Defence 1914–60. 1960.

15911 JOUBERT DE LA FERTÉ (PHILIP). Birds and Fishes: The Story of Coastal Command. 1960.

15912 MILLINGTON (EDWARD GEOFFREY LYALL). The Unseen Eye. 1961. [Fighter reconnaisance in World War II.].

15913 WHITTLE (PETER) *and* BORISSOW (MICHAEL). Angels Without Wings: The Dramatic Inside Stories of the R.A.F. Search and Rescue Squadrons. Maidstone. 1966.

15914 BROWN (DAVID). Carrier Air Groups. 1972.

15915 BURGE (CYRIL GORDON). The Annals of 100 Squadron. 1919.

15916 PATTINSON (*Sir* LAWRENCE ARTHUR). History of 99 Squadron Independent Force, Royal Air Force, March 1918–November 1918. Camb. 1920.

15917 HARVEY (WILLIAM FREDERICK JAMES). 'Pi' in the Sky: A History of No. 22 Squadron, Royal Flying Corps and R.A.F. in the War of 1914–1918. Leicester. 1971.

15918 HALLEY (JAMES J.). Royal Air Force Unit Histories. 2 vols. Saffron Walden. 1969.

15919 LEWIS (PETER). Squadron Histories: RFC, RNAS and RAF 1912–59. 1959.

15920 HUNT (J. LESLIE). Twenty-One Squadrons: History of the Royal Auxiliary Air Force 1925–1957. 1973.

15921 AIR TRAINING CORPS. Twenty-First Birthday 1941–62. 1962.

15922 MASON (TIMOTHY). Leads the Field: The History of No. 12 Squadron, Royal Air Force. 1960.

15923 BOWYER (CHAZ). The Flying Elephants: A History of No.27 Squadron, Royal Flying Corps, Royal Air Force 1915–1969. 1972.

15924 BEEDLE (JAMES). 43 Squadron Royal Flying Corps, Royal Air Force: The History of the Fighting Cocks, 1916-1966. 1966.

15925 JONES (JAMES IRA THOMAS). Tiger Squadron: The Story of 74 Squadron, R.A.F in Two World Wars. 1954.

15926 MARR (DOUGLAS STUART BALFOUR). 208 Squadron History. 1967.

15927 MOULSON (THOMAS JAMES). The Flying Sword: The Story of 601 Squadron. 1964.

15928 SHAW (MICHAEL). Twice Vertical: The History of No. 1 (Fighter) Squadron, R.A.F. 1971.

15929 TICKELL (JERRARD). Moon Squadron. Maidstone. 1973.

15930 TIDY (DOUGLAS). I Fear No Man: The Story of No. 74 (Fighter) Squadron. 1972.

15931 ZIEGLER (FRANK). The Story of 609 Squadron: Under the White Rose. 1971.

15932 SUTTON (HAROLD THOMAS). Raiders Approach! The Fighting Tradition of the Royal Air Force Station Hornchurch. 1956.

15933 SETH (RONALD SYDNEY). Lion with Blue Wings: The Story of the Glider Pilot Regiment, 1942–1945. 1955.

15934 WALLACE (GRAHAM). R.A.F. Biggin Hill. 1957.

15935 KINSEY (GORDON). Martlesham Heath: The Story of the Royal Air Force Station 1917–1973. 1975.

15936 BOWYER (MICHAEL JOHN FREDERICK). Action Stations: Military Airfields of East Anglia. Camb. 1979.

15937 HALPENNY (BRUCE BARRYMORE). Action Stations: Military Airfields of Greater London. Camb. 1984.

15938 Group RAF: A Complete History, 1936–1945. 1974.

7. AIR OPERATIONS

15939 AIR MINISTRY. R.A.F. Middle East: The Official Story of Air Operations in the Middle East from February 1942 to January 1943. 1945.

15940 SHORES (CHRISTOPHER FRANCIS). Fighters Over the Desert: The Air Battles in the Western Desert, June 1940 to December 1942. 1969.

15941 JACKSON (ROBERT). The Air War Over France: May-June 1940. 1974.

15942 WISDOM (THOMAS HENRY). Triumph Over Tunisia, Being the Story of the Part of the R.A.F. in the African Victory. 1944.

15943 —— Wings Over Olympus: The Story of the R.A.F. in Libya and Greece. 1942.

15944 RUSSELL (WILFRID WILLIAM). Forgotten Skies: The Story of the Air Force in India and Burma. 1946.

15945 GUEDALLA (PHILIP). Middle East, 1940–1942: A Study in Air Power. 1944.

15946 GRIFFITH (HUBERT FREELING). R.A.F. in Russia. 1942.

15947 GARNETT (DAVID). War in the Air, September 1939 to May 1941. 1941.

15948 MACDONALD (CHARLES BROWN). By Air to Battle. 1970.

15949 LEE (*Sir* DAVID). Eastward: A History of the Royal Air Force in the Far East 1945–1972. 1984.

15950 —— Flight from the Middle East: A History of the Royal Air Force in the Arabian Peninsula and Adjacent Territories 1945–1972. 1980.

15951 —— Wings in the Sun: A History of the Royal Air Force in the Mediterranean 1945–1986. 1989.

15952 AIR MINISTRY. The Origins and Development of Operational Research in the Royal Air Force. 1963.

15953 BOWYER (MICHAEL JOHN FREDERICK). Wartime Military Airfields of East Anglia, 1939–1945. Camb. 1979.

8. COMMANDERS

15954 CAMERON (NEIL) *Baron*. In the Midst of Things: The Autobiography of Lord Cameron of Dalhousie: Marshal of the Royal Air Force. 1986.

15955 DOUGLAS (WILLIAM SHOLTO) *Baron*. Years of Command. 1966.

15956 COLLIER (JOHN BASIL). Leader of the Few: The Authorised Biography of Air Chief Marshal the Lord Dowding of Bentley Priory. 1967.

15957 WRIGHT (ROBERT). Dowding and the Battle of Britain. 1969.

15958 GODDARD (*Sir* VICTOR). Skies to Dunkirk: A Personal Memoir. 1982.

15959 HILL (PRUDENCE). To Know the Sky: The Life of Air Chief Marshal Sir Roderic Hill. 1962.

15960 ORANGE (VINCENT). A Biography of Air Chief Marshal Sir Keith Park. 1984.

15961 RICHARDS (DENIS). Portal of Hungerford: The Life of Marshal of the Royal Air Force, Viscount Portal of Hungerford. 1978. 1977.

15962 SLESSOR (*Sir* JOHN COTESWORTH). The Central Blue. 1956.

15963 —— These Remain. A Personal Anthology, Memoirs of Flying, Fighting and Field Sports. 1969.

15964 TEDDER (ARTHUR) *Lord*. With Prejudice. 1947.

15965 OWEN (R.). Tedder. 1952.

15966 BOYLE (ANDREW). Trenchard. 1962.

15967 ALLEN (HUBERT RAYMOND). The Legacy of Lord Trenchard. 1972.

9. BOMBING

15968 BARKER (RALPH HAMMOND). The Ship-Busters: The Story of R.A.F. Torpedo Bombers. 1957.

15969 —— Strike Hard, Strike Sure: Epics of the Bombers. 1963.

15970 —— The Thousand Plan. 1965.

15971 —— The Blockade Busters. 1976.

15972 FRANKLAND (NOBLE). The Bombing Offensive Against Germany: Outlines and Perspectives. 1965.

15973 BROOKES (ANDREW). Bomber Squadron at War. 1983.

15974 HARRIS (ARTHUR). Bomber Offensive. 1947.

15975 IRVING (DAVID). The Destruction of Dresden. 1963.

15976 JACKSON (ROBERT). Storm from the Skies: The Strategic Bombing Offensive, 1943–1945. 1974.

15977 —— Before the Storm: The Story of Royal Air Force Bomber Command, 1939–1942. 1972.

15978 JONES (NEVILLE). The Origins of Strategic Bombing: A Study of the Development of British Air Strategic Thought and Practice up to 1918. 1973.

15979 SAWARD (DUDLEY). The Bomber's Eye. 1959.

15980 SAUNDBY (*Sir* ROBERT). Air Bombardment: The Story of its Development. 1961.

15981 WEBSTER (CHARLES) *and* FRANKLAND (NOBLE). The Strategic Air Offensive. 4 vols 1961. [Official history, Second World War: Campaigns.].

15982 VERRIER (ANTHONY). The Bomber Offensive. 1968. Rev. edn 1974.

15983 HASTINGS (MAX). Bomber Command. 1979.

15984 LONGMATE (NORMAN). The Bombers; The R.A.F. Offensive Against Germany, 1939–1945. 1983.

15985 MOYES (PHILIP J. R.). Royal Air Force Bombers of World War II. 3 vols Chalfont St. Giles.

15986 MIDDLEBROOK (MARTIN). The Battle for Hamburg: Allied Bomber Forces Against a German City in 1943. 1980.

10. AIR POLICY

15987 TURNER (C. C.). Britain's Air Peril: The Danger of Neglect, Together with Considerations on the Role of an Air Force. 1933.

15988 KINGSTON-MCCLOUGHRY (E. J.). Winged Warfare: Air Problems of Peace and War. 1936.

15989 HYDE (HARFORD MONTGOMERY). British Air Policy Between the Wars, 1918–1939. 1976.

15990 TEDDER (ARTHUR) *Baron*. Air Power in War. 1948.

15991 SLESSOR (*Sir* JOHN). 'The Place of the Bomber in British Strategy'. *Inl Aff.* 29 (1953), 302–7.

15992 BUSHBY (JOHN). Air Defence of Great Britain. 1973.

F. INTELLIGENCE

1. GENERAL

15993 SMITH (MYRON J.) *Jnr.* The Secret Wars: A Guide to Sources in English. I: Intelligence, Propaganda and Psychological Warfare, Resistance Movements and Secret Operations, 1939–1945. II: Intelligence, Propaganda and Psychological Warfare, Covert Operations 1945–1980. Oxf. 1981.

15994 CLINE (MARJORIE W.), CHRISTIANSEN (CARLA E.), *and* FONTAINE (JUDITH M.). Scholar's Guide to Intelligence Literature. Frederick, Maryland. 1983.

15995 PORTER (BERNARD). Plots and Paranoia: A History of Political Espionage in Britain, 1790–1988. 1989.

15996 ANDREW (CHRISTOPHER) *and* NOAKES (JEREMY) *eds.* Intelligence and International Relations 1900–1945. Exeter. 1987.

15997 ANDREW (CHRISTOPHER) *and* DILKS (DAVID N.). 'The Missing Dimension': Governments and the Intelligence Communities in the Twentieth Century. 1984.

15998 ANDREW (CHRISTOPHER M.). Secret Service: The Making of the British Intelligence Community. 1985.

15999 DEACON (RICHARD). A History of the British Secret Services. 1969.

16000 McCORMICK (DONALD). A History of the British Secret Service. NY. 1970.

16001 SHIPLEY (PETER). Hostile Action: The KGB and Secret Service Operations in Britain. 1989.

16002 GLEES (ANTHONY). The Secrets of the Service: British Intelligence and Communist Subversion 1939–51. 1987.

16003 GRUNBAUM (WERNER F.). 'The British Security Program 1948–1958'. *Western Pol. Q.* 13 (1960), 264–79.

16004 WEST (NIGEL). The Friends: Britain's Post-War Intelligence Operations. 1988.

16005 HENNESSY (PETER) *and* BROWNFIELD (GAIL). 'Britain's Cold War Security Purge: The Origins of Positive Vetting'. *Hist. J.* 25 (1982), 965–73.

16006 BLOCH (J.) *and* FITZGERALD (PATRICK). British Intelligence and Covert Action: Africa, Middle East and Europe since 1945. 1983.

16007 ALDRICH (RICHARD) *ed.* British Intelligence, Strategy and the Cold War, 1945–1951. 1991.

16008 RICHELSON (JEFFREY T.) *and* BALL (DESMOND). The Ties that Bind: Intelligence Co-operation in UK/USA Countries–The United Kingdom, The United States of America, Canada, Australia and New Zealand. 1985.

16009 ANDREW (CHRISTOPHER M.). 'Whitehall, Washington and the Intelligence Services'. *Inl Affs* 53 (1977), 390–404.

2. MI6

16010 BROWN (ANTHONY CAVE). The Secret Servant: The Life of Sir Stewart Menzies, Churchill's Spymaster. 1987.

16011 BOWER (TOM). The Red Web: MI6 and the KGB Master Group. 1989.

3. MI5

16012 DEACON (RICHARD). 'C': A Biography of Sir Maurice Oldfield, Head of MI6. 1985.

16013 BULLOCH (JOHN). MI5: The Origin and History of the British Counter-Espionage Service. 1963.

16014 WEST (NIGEL). A Matter of Trust: MI5 1945–72. 1982.

16015 SILLITOE (*Sir* PERCY). Cloak and Dagger. 1955.

16016 COCKERILL (A. W.). Sir Percy Sillitoe. 1975.

16017 CAVENDISH (ANTHONY). Inside Intelligence. 1987.

16018 SCOTLAND (ALEXANDER). The London Cage. 1957.

4. GCHQ

16019 BAMFORD (JAMES). The Puzzle Palace: America's National Security Agency and its Special Relationship with Britain's GCHQ. 1982.

16020 WEST (NIGEL). GCHQ: The Secret Wireless War 1900–1986. 1986.

5. UNIVERSITIES

16021 SINCLAIR (ANDREW). The Red and the Blue: Intelligence, Treason and the Universities. 1986.

16022 ANDREW (CHRISTOPHER M.). 'F. H. Hinsley and the Cambridge Moles: Two Patterns of Intelligence Recruitment'. In Diplomacy and Intelligence during the Second World War: Essays in Honour of F. H. Hinsley, *ed.* by Richard Langhorne. Camb. 1985.

16023 McCORMICK (DONALD). The British Connection: Russia's Manipulation of British Individuals and Institutions. 1979.

6. INDIVIDUALS

16024 SPIRO (EDWARD). Shadow of a Spy: The Complete Dossier on George Blake. 1967.

16025 COOKRIDGE (EDWARD H.). George Blake: Double Agent. 1970.

16026 HYDE (HARFORD MONTGOMERY). George Blake Superspy. 1987.

16027 BOURKE (SEAN). The Springing of George Blake. 1970.

16028 RANDLE (MICHAEL) and POTTLE (PATRICK). The Blake Escape. 1989.

16029 BOYLE (ANDREW). The Climate of Treason: Five who Spied for Russia. 1973.

16030 PENROSE (BARRIE) and FREEMAN (SIMON). Conspiracy of Silence: The Secret Life of Anthony Blunt. St Albans. 1986.

16031 COSTELLO (JOHN). Mask of Treachery. 1988.

16032 SUTHERLAND (DOUGLAS). The Fourth Man. 1980.

16033 BULLOCH (JOHN). Akin to Treason. 1966.

16034 CONNOLLY (CYRIL). The Missing Diplomats. 1952.

16035 PURDY (ANTHONY) and SUTHERLAND (DOUGLAS). Burgess and Maclean. 1963.

16036 DRIBERG (TOM). Guy Burgess: A Portrait with Background. 1956.

16037 HOARE (GEOFFREY). The Missing Macleans. 1955.

16038 CECIL (ROBERT). A Divided Life: A Biography of Donald Maclean. 1988.

16039 HENNESSY (PETER) and TOWNSEND (K.). 'The Documentary Spoor of Burgess and Maclean'. *Intelligence and National Security* 2 (1987), 291–301.

16040 FISHER (JOHN). Burgess and Maclean: A New Look at the Foreign Office Spies. 1977.

16041 HUTTON (BERNARD J.). Frogman Spy: The Incredible Case of Commander Crabb. 1960.

16042 HYDE (HARFORD MONTGOMERY). The Atom Bomb Spies. 1980.

16043 MOSS (NORMAN). Klaus Fuchs, the Man who Stole the Atom Bomb. St Albans. 1987.

16044 WILLIAMS (ROBERT C.). Klaus Fuchs: Atom Spy. Camb., Mass. 1988.

16045 LONSDALE (GORDON). Spy: Twenty Years of Secret Service. 1965.

16046 BULLOCH (JOHN) and MILLER (HENRY). Spy Ring: The Full Story of the Naval Secrets Case. 1961.

16047 COOKRIDGE (EDWARD H.). The Third Man: The Truth about 'Kim' Philby, Double Agent. 1968.

16048 PHILBY (ELEANOR). The Spy I Loved. 1968.

16049 SPIRO (EDWARD). The Third Man. 1968.

16050 TREVOR-ROPER, HUGH REDWALD [LORD DACRE]. The Philby Affair. 1968.

16051 PHILBY (HAROLD A. R. 'KIM'). My Silent War. 1968.

16052 SEALE (PATRICK) and McCONVILLE (MAUREEN). Philby: The Long Road to Moscow. 1973.

16053 PAGE (BRUCE), LEITCH (DAVID), and KNIGHTLEY (PHILLIP). Philby: The Spy who Betrayed a Generation. 2nd edn 1977.

16054 KNIGHTLEY (PHILLIP). Philby: The Life and Views of the KGB Masterspy. 1988.

16055 Report of the Tribunal Appointed to Inquire into the Vassall Case. Cmnds 1871 and 2009, Parliamentary Papers xxiv (1962–3).

16056 FAIRFIELD (CECILY I.). The Vassall Affair. 1963.

16057 VASSALL (WILLIAM J. C.). Vassall: The Autobiography of a Spy. 1975.

16058 WRIGHT (PETER). Spycatcher: The Candid Autobiography of a Senior Intelligence Officer. NY. 1987.

16059 TURNBULL (MALCOLM). The Spycatcher Trial. 1988.

16060 WYNNE (GREVILLE). The Man from Moscow: The Story of Wynne and Penkovsky. 1967.

16061 PINCHER (CHAPMAN). Inside Story: A Documentary of the Pursuit of Power. 1978.

16062 —— Their Trade is Treachery. 1981.

16063 —— Too Secret Too Long. 1984.

16064 —— The Secret Offensive: Active Measures: A Saga of Deception, Disinformation, Subversion, Terrorism, Sabotage and Assassination. 1985.

16065 FITZGERALD (PATRICK) and LEOPOLD (MARK). Strangers on the Line: The Secret History of Phone-Tapping. 1987.

G. POST-1945

1. NATIONAL SERVICE

16066 CHAMBERS (PETER) *and* LAUDRETH (AMY). Called Up: The Personal Experience of Sixteen National Servicemen. 1955.

16067 BAXTER (DAVID). Two Years To Do. 1959.

16068 IONS (EDMUND). A Call to Arms: Interlude with the Military. Newton Abbot. 1972.

16069 JOHNSON (B. S.) *ed.* All Bull: The National Servicemen. 1973.

16070 FORTY (GEORGE). Called Up: A National Service Scrapbook. 1980.

16071 MYERS (FRANK). 'Conscription and the Politics of Military Strategy in the Attlee Government'. *J. Strat. Studs* 7 (1984), 55–73.

16072 ROYLE (TREVOR). The Best Years of Their Lives: The National Service Experience 1945–63. 1986.

16073 WHITELEY (GERALD). 'The British Experience with Peacetime Conscription'. *Army Q.* 117 (1987), 318–29.

2. OPERATIONS

(a) The Falklands Campaign

16074 The Falklands Campaign: A Digest of Debates in the House of Commons 2 April to 15 June 1982. 1982.

16075 Falkland Islands Review: Report of a Committee of Privy Councillors. Cmnd 8787, Parliamentary Papers (1982–3).

16076 DILLON (G. M.). The Falklands, Politics and War. 1988.

16077 DALYELL (TAM). One Man's Falklands. 1982.

16078 Third Report of the House of Commons Foreign Affairs Committee. Events of the Weekend of 1st and 2nd May 1982. HC Paper 11, Parliamentary Papers (1984–5).

16079 FREEDMAN (LAWRENCE) *and* GAMBA-STONEHOUSE (VIRGINIA). Signals of War: The Falklands Conflict of 1982. 1990.

16080 FREEDMAN (LAWRENCE). 'Bridgehead Revisited: The Literature of the Falklands'. *Inl Affs* 59 (1983). 445–52.

16081 —— Britain and the Falklands War. Oxf. 1988.

16082 GAMBA-STONEHOUSE (VIRGINIA). The Falklands/Malvinas War: A Model for North–South Crisis Prevention. 1987.

16083 MORO (RUBEN O.). The History of the South Atlantic Conflict: The War for the Malvinas. Westport, Conn. 1989.

16084 BECK (PETER J.). 'The Anglo-Argentine Dispute over the Title to the Falkland Islands: Changing British Perceptions on Sovereignty since 1910'. *Millennium:* 12 (1983), 6–24.

16085 —— The Falklands War: The Official History. 1983. [The Argentinian and British official communiqués in parallel.].

16086 —— 'The South Atlantic Crisis: Background, Consequences, Documentation'. *United States Dept of State Bull.* 82/2067 (1982), 78–90.

16087 FOWLER (W.). The Battle for the Falklands: Land Forces. 1982.

16088 ENGLISH (A.) *and* WELLS (A.). The Battle for the Falklands: Naval Forces. 1982.

16089 BROWN (DAVID). The Royal Navy and the Falklands War. 1988.

16090 PRESTON (ANTHONY). Sea Combat off the Falklands: The Lessons that Must be Learned. 1982.

16091 BRAYBROOK (R.). The Battle for the Falklands: Air Forces. 1982.

16092 ETHELL (JEFFREY) *and* PRICE (ALFRED). Air War South Atlantic. 1983.

16093 BURDEN (RODNEY), DRAPER (MICHAEL), ROUGH (DOUGLAS), SMITH (COLIN), *and* WILTON (DAVID). Falklands: The Air War. 1986.

16094 ADAMS (VALERIE). 'Logistics Support for the Falklands Campaign'. *J. Roy. Unit. Serv. Inst. Def. Studs* 129 (1984), 43–9.

16095 FREEDMAN (LAWRENCE) . 'Intelligence Operations in the Falklands'. *Intelligence and National Security* 2 (1986), 309–35.

16096 CHARLTON (MICHAEL). The Little Platoon: Diplomacy and the Falklands Dispute. Oxf. 1989.

16097 PARSONS (*Sir* ANTHONY). 'The Falklands Crisis in the United Nations 31 March–14 June 1982'. *Inl Affs* (1983), 169–78.

16098 HENDERSON (*Sir* NICHOLAS). 'America and the Falklands: Case Study in the Behaviour of an Ally'. *Economist* 12/11/1983, 49–60.

16099 MACDONALD (HUGH). 'Britain and the Falklands War: The Lessons of Interdependence'. *Millennium* 12 (1983), 176–88.

16100 TINKER (HUGH). 'The Falklands after Three Years'. *Round Table* 296 (1985), 339–44.

16101 CALVERT (PETER). The Falklands Crisis. 1982.

16102 HASTINGS (MAX) *and* JENKINS (SIMON). The Battle for the Falklands. 1983.

16103 MIDDLEBROOK (MARTIN). Task Force: The South Atlantic 1982. Harmondsworth. 1987.

16104 SUNDAY TIMES INSIGHT TEAM. The Falklands War: The Full Story. 1982.

16105 BISHOP (PATRICK) and WITHEROW (JOHN). The Winter War: The Falklands. 1982.

16106 HANRAHAN (BRIAN) and FOX (ROBERT). 'I Counted Them All Out and I Counted Them All Back': The Battle for the Falklands. 1982.

16107 FOX (ROBERT). Eyewitness Falklands: A Personal Account of the Falklands Campaign. 1982.

16108 COLLIER (SIMON). 'The First Falklands War: Argentine Attitudes'. *Inl Affs* 59 (1983), 459–64.

16109 WYNIA (GARY W.). Argentina: Illusions and Realities. 1986.

16110 MIDDLEBROOK (MARTIN). The Fight for the 'Malvinas': The Argentine Forces in the Falklands War. 1988.

16111 BURNS (JIMMY). The Land that Lost its Heroes: The Falklands, the Postwar and Alfonsin. 1987.

16112 WOODWARD (J.) and MOORE (JOHN). 'The Falklands Experience'. *J. Roy. United Services Inst. Def. Studs* 128 (1983), 25–32.

16113 RISE (DESMOND) and GAVSTON (ARTHUR). The Sinking of the Belgrano. 1984.

16114 THOMPSON (JULIAN). No Picnic. 1985.

16115 LAWRENCE (JOHN) and LAWRENCE (ROBERT). When the Fighting is Over: A Personal Story of the Battle for Tumbledown Mountain and its Aftermath. 1988.

16116 JOLLY (RICK). The Red and Green Life Machine: Diary of the Falklands Field Hospital. 1983.

16117 TINKER (DAVID). A Message from the Falklands. 1982.

16118 VAUX (NICK). March to the South Atlantic. 1986.

16119 BILTON (MICHAEL) and KOSMINSKY (PETER). Speaking Out: Untold Stories from the Falklands War. 1989.

16120 SMITH (JOHN). 74 Days: An Islander's Diary of the Falklands Occupation. 1984.

16121 ADAMS (VALERIE). The Media and the Falklands Campaign. 1986.

16122 GLASGOW UNIVERSITY MEDIA GROUP. War and Peace News, Milton Keynes. 1985.

16123 HARRIS (ROBERT). Gotcha: The Media, the Government and the Falklands Crisis. 1983.

(b) Korea

16124 MACFARLAND (KEITH). The Korean War: An Annotated Bibliography. 1986.

16125 LINKLATER (ERIC). Our Men in Korea. 1952.

16126 MALCOLM (G. I.). The Argylls in Korea. Edin. 1952.

16127 BARKER (ARTHUR JAMES). Fortune Favours the Brave: The Hook, Korea, 1953. 1974.

16128 BARCLAY (CYRIL NELSON). The First Commonwealth Division: The Story of the British Commonwealth Land Forces in Korea 1950–1953. Aldershot. 1954.

16129 THOMAS (R. C. W.). The War in Korea, 1950–1953. Aldershot. 1954.

16130 HOLLES (ROBERT OWEN). Now Thrive The Armourers: A Story of Action with the Gloucesters in Korea. 1955.

16131 FARRAR-HOCKLEY (ANTHONY). The Edge of the Sword. 1954.

16132 GASTON (P.). Thirty-Eighth Parallel: The British in Korea. Glasgow. 1976.

16133 CUNNINGHAM-BOOTHE (ASHLEY) and FARRAR (PETER) eds. British Forces in the Korean War. 1988.

16134 GREY (JEFFREY). The Commonwealth Armies and the Korean War: An Alliance Study. Manch. 1988.

16135 JACKSON (ROBERT). Air War Over Korea. 1973.

16136 THOMPSON (REGINALD WILLIAM). Cry Korea. 1956.

16137 LOWE (PETER). The Origins of the Korean War. 1986.

16138 CUMINGS (BRUCE). The Origins of the Korean War. Princeton, NJ. 1981.

16139 REES (DAVID BERNARD). Korea: The Limited War. 1964.

16140 CAREW (TIM). The Korean War. 1967.

16141 MACDONALD (CALLUM A.). Korea: The War Before Vietnam. 1986.

16142 HASTINGS (MAX). The Korean War. 1987.

16143 HALLIDAY (JOHN) and CUMINGS (BRUCE). Korea: The Unknown War. N.Y. 1988.

16144 COTTON (JAMES) and NEARY (IAN) eds. The Korean War in History. Manch. 1989.

16145 DOCKRILL (MICHAEL L.). 'The Foreign Office, Anglo-American Relations and the Korean War June 1950–June 1951'. *Inl Affs* 62 (1986), 459–76.

16146 REE (YONG-YIL). 'Special Relationship at War: The Anglo-American Relationship during the Korean War'. *J. Strat. Studs* 7 (1984), 301–17.

16147 STUECK (WILLIAM). 'The Limits of Influence: British Policy and American Expansion of the War in Korea'. *Pac. Hist. Rev.* 55 (1986), 65–95.

16148 FARRAR (PETER N.). 'Britain's Proposal for a Buffer Zone South of the Yalu in November 1950: Was it a Neglected Opportunity to End the Fighting in Korea?'. *J. Contemp. Hist.* 18 (1983), 327–51.

16149 FOOT (R. J.). 'Anglo-American Relations in the Korean Crisis: The British Effort to Avert an Expanded War, December 1950–January 1951'. *Dipl. Hist.* 10 (1986), 59–73.

(c) Malaya

16150 PURCELL (VICTOR). Malaya: Communist or Free? 1954.

16151 MILLER (HENRY). Menace in Malaya. 1954.

16152 PYE (LUCIAN W.). Guerrilla Communism in Malaya. 1956.

16153 O'BALLANCE (EDGAR). Malaya: The Communist Insurgent War 1948–1960. 1966.

16154 BARBER (NOEL). The War of the Running Dogs: How Malaya Defeated the Communist Guerrillas 1948–60. 1971.

16155 CLUTTERBUCK (RICHARD). The Long, Long War: The Emergency in Malaya 1948–1960. 1967.

16156 MILLER (HARRY). Jungle War in Malaya: The Campaign Against Communism 1948–60. 1972.

16157 SHORT (ANTHONY). The Communist Insurrection in Malaya 1948–1960. 1975.

16158 MOCKAITIS (THOMAS R.). British Counterinsurgency 1919–60. 1990. [Sees the war in Malaya as the culmination of half a century of experience.].

16159 THOMPSON (ROBERT). Defeating Communist Insurgency: Experience from Malaya and Vietnam. 1978.

16160 SMITH (E. D.). Counter-Insurgency Operations: Malaya and Borneo. 1985.

16161 CLOAKE (JOHN). Templer: Tiger of Malaya: The Life of Field Marshal Sir Gerald Templer. 1985.

16162 POCOCK (TOM). Fighting General: The Public and Private Campaigns of General Sir Walter Walker. 1973.

16163 SHORRICK (N.). Lion in the Sky: The Story of Seletar and the Royal Air Force in Singapore. Singapore. 1968.

16164 CROCKETT (ANTHONY JOHN SINCLAIR). Green Beret, Red Star: The Story of Two Years' Struggle Against the Maylayan [sic] Terrorist. 1958.

16165 OLDFIELD (J. B.). The Green Howards in Malaya (1949–1952): The Story of a Post-War Tour of Duty by a Battalion of the Line. Aldershot. 1953.

16166 MEIRS (RICHARD CAPEL HAMMER). Shoot to Kill. 1959.

16167 CRAWFORD (OLIVER). The Door Marked Malaya. 1958.

3. SUBVERSION AND COUNTER-INSURGENCY

16168 OSANKA (FRANKLIN MARK). Modern Guerrilla Warfare. N.Y. 1962.

16169 PAGET (JULIAN). Counter-Insurgency Campaigning. 1967.

16170 KITSON (FRANK). Gangs and Counter-Gangs. 1960.

16171 —— Bunch of Five. 1977.

16172 —— Low Intensity Operations: Subversion, Insurgency, Peace-keeping. 1971.

16173 BELL (J. BOWYER). On Revolt: Strategies of National Liberation. Harvard. 1976.

16174 CLUTTERBUCK (RICHARD). Guerrillas and Terrorists. 1977.

16175 DEWAR (M.). Brush Fire Wars: Minor Campaigns of the British Army Since 1945. 1984.

16176 TOWNSHEND (CHARLES). Britain's Civil Wars: Counter-Insurgency in the Twentieth Century. 1986.

16177 JAMES (LAWRENCE). Imperial Rearguard: Wars of Empire, 1918–1985. 1988.

16178 ALLEN (CHARLES). The Savage Wars of Peace. 1989.

4. BRITISH ARMY ON THE RHINE

16179 LEE (GORDON). The Half-Forgotten Army: The British Forces in Germany. 1971.

16180 GARNETT (JOHN C.). 'BAOR and NATO'. *Inl Affs* 46 (1970), 670–81.

8

TRANSPORT

The categories employed in this section have not proved very troublesome. The initial sub-sections include material on general aspects of transport. The considerable number of items which refer in one way or another to 'the traffic problem' is largely a reflection of the use of the motor car. The literature includes both discussions of national policy and evaluations of local problems. The material provides the basis for assessments of the impact of transport changes on twentieth-century British society but few such assessments have been noted. Transport economists and historians have commendably built up a body of information but have rarely strayed beyond that which they conceive to be their technical sphere. General historians have rarely reflected on the implications of the material which has now been assembled.

The subsequent sub-sections focus on particular modes of transport—shipping (including inland waterways), railways, roads (all kinds of vehicles), and air. It has been found appropriate to include in these categories the respective construction industries. The decline of the railway has been accompanied by a passion for local railway history. A considerable selection has been made, but there are more publications to be found. In contrast there is a paucity of material on the growth of civil aviation inside Britain and its local domestic consequences.

I. GENERAL HISTORY AND ECONOMICS, TRAFFIC AND COMMUTING, LOCAL TRANSPORT STUDIES, THE CHANNEL TUNNEL, MISCELLANY

16181 ALDCROFT (DEREK HOWARD). British Transport since 1914. 1975.

16182 —— Studies in British Transport History, 1870–1970. Newton Abbot. 1974.

16183 —— 'A New Chapter in 20th Century History: The Transport Revolution'. *J. Transport Hist.* n.s., 3 (1975/6), 217–40.

16184 ALDCROFT (DEREK HOWARD) *and* DYOS (HAROLD JAMES). British Transport: An Economic Survey from the 17th Century to the 20th Century. Leics. 1969. Harmondsworth. 1974.

16185 ALDCROFT (DEREK HOWARD) *and* MORT (DEREK). Rail Transport and Sea Transport. Oxf. 1981. [Reviews of Statistical Sources Series.].

16186 BAXTER (RON) *and* PHILLIPS (CELIA M.). Ports and Inland Waterways and Civil Aviation. Oxf. 1979. [Rev. Stat. Sources Ser.].

16187 MUNBY (DENYS LAWRENCE) *and* WATSON (ANTHONY HERIOT). Road Passenger Transport and Road Goods Transport. Oxf. 1978. [Rev. Stat. Sources Ser.].

16188 MUNBY (DENYS LAWRENCE) *ed.* Inland Transport Statistics, Great Britain 1900–1970: vol. I: Railways, Public Road Passenger Transport, London Transport. Oxf. 1978.

16189 KIRKALDY (ADAM WILLIS) *and* EVANS (ALFRED DUDLEY). The History and Economics of Transport. 1915. 6th edn 1946.

16190 GEORGIANO (GEORGE NICOLAS) *ed.* A History of Transport. 1972.

16191 THOMSON (ANDREW WILLIAM JOHN) *and* HUNTER (LAURENCE COLVIN). The Nationalised Transport Industries. 1973.

16192 BAGWELL (PHILIP SIDNEY). The Transport Revolution from 1770. 1974.

16193 —— End of the Line?: The Fate of Public Transport under Thatcher. 1984.

16194 BLACKWOOD (ALAN). Transport in History. Hove. 1984.

16195 WILKINS (FRANCES). Transport and Travel from 1930 to the 1980s. 1985.

16196 MALTBY (D.) *and* WHITE (HENRY PATRICK). Transport in the United Kingdom. 1982.

16197 WHITE (HENRY PATRICK). Transport Geography. 1983.

16198 OTTLEY (GEORGE) *comp.* A Guide to the Transport History Collection in Leicester University Library. Leics. 1981.

16199 SAVAGE (CHRISTOPHER IVOR). Inland Transport. 1957. Repr. 1967. [History of the Second World War, U.K. Civil Series.].

16200 An Economic History of Transport. 1959. Rev. 1961. 2nd edn 1966.

16201 BARKER (THEODORE CARDWELL) *and* SAVAGE (CHRISTOPHER IVOR). An Economic History of Transport in Britain. 3rd rev. edn of above, 1974.

16202 JACKMAN (WILLIAM T.). The Development of Transport in Modern England. 2 vols 1916. 2nd rev. edn 1962. 3rd edn 1966.

16203 —— Economic Principles of Transportation. Toronto. 1926. 2nd edn 1935.

16204 BONAVIA (MICHAEL ROBERT). The Economics of Transport. 1936. Rev. edn 1954.

16205 —— The Nationalisation of Britain's Transport: The Early History of the British Transport Commission, 1948–53. 1987.

16206 JOHNSTON (L. C.). 'Historical Records of the British Transport Commission'. *J. Transport Hist.* 1 (1953/54), 82–96.

16207 —— 'British Transport Commission Archives: Work since 1953'. *J. Transport Hist.* 5 (1961/2), 159–81.

16208 ALLEN (*Sir* PETER). Transport Pioneers of the Twentieth Century. Camb. 1981.

16209 BALDWIN (NICHOLAS). 'Research in Transport History: The International Transport Workers' Federation Archive'. *J. Transport Hist.* 3rd ser. 7 (1986/7), 61–6.

16210 BOND (MAURICE). 'Materials for Transport History amongst Records of Parliament'. *J. Transport Hist.* 4 (1959/60), 37–52.

16211 DYOS (HAROLD JAMES). 'Transport History in University Theses'. *J. Transport Hist.* 4 (1959/60), 161–73.

16212 BUTT (JOHN). 'Achievement and Prospect: Transport History in the 1970s and 1980s'. *J. Transport Hist.* 3rd ser. 2 (1981), 1–24.

16213 CHALONER (WILLIAM HENRY) *and* RATCLIFFE (BARRIE M.). Trade and Transport: Essays in Economic History in Honour of T. S. Willan. Manch. 1977.

16214 RIDLEY (ANTHONY). An Illustrated History of Transport. Lond./N.Y. 1969.

16215 JOURNAL OF TRANSPORT HISTORY 1953/4. [New series from 1971/2, 3rd ser. from 1980/1.].

16216 TRANSPORT HISTORY 1968–1981.

16217 TRANSPORT 1980+.

16218 JOURNAL OF TRANSPORT ECONOMICS AND POLICY 1967+.

16219 GWILLIAM (KENNETH MASON). Transport and Public Policy. 1964.

16220 GWILLIAM (KENNETH MASON) *and* MACKIE (PETER JOHN). Economics and Transport Policy. 1975.

16221 BUCHANAN (COLIN DOUGLAS). Transport and the Community. 1964.

16222 HIBBS (JOHN ALFRED BLYTH). Transport for Passengers: A Study in Enterprise without Licence. 1963.

16223 —— Transport Studies: An Introduction. 1970.

16224 FOSTER (CHRISTOPHER DAVID). The Transport Problem. 1963.

16225 CHARLESWORTH (GEORGE). A History of the Transport and Road Research Laboratory 1933–1983. Aldershot. 1987.

16226 DEAKIN (BRIAN MEASURES) *and* SEAWARD (THELMA). Productivity in Transport: A Study of Employment, Capital, Output, Productivity, and Technical Change. 1969.

16227 SHARP (CLIFFORD HENRY). Transport Economics. 1973.

16228 —— The Problem of Transport. Oxf. 1965.

16229 BELL (J. GRAHAM) *et al.* The Business of Transport. Plymouth. 1984.

16230 SHARP (CLIFFORD HENRY) *and* JENNINGS (TONY). Transport and the Environment. Leics. 1976.

16231 HUTCHINS (JOHN GREENWOOD BROWN). Transportation and the Environment. 1977.

16232 HAMER (MICK). Getting Nowhere Fast. 1976. [Friends of the Earth.].

16233 CRESSWELL (ROY) *ed.* Passenger Transport and the Environment. 1977.

16234 BANISTER (DAVID). Travel and Energy Use in Great Britain 1969 to 1979: Trends and Options. Manch. 1982.

16235 ULLERTON (BRIAN). The Development of British Transport Networks. 1975.

16236 EYLES (DAVID R.). Road Traffic and Environment. 1969.

16237 —— Road Traffic and Urban Environment in Inner London. 1970.

16238 BOVILL (D. I. N.). Peak Hour and Directional Factors. 1970.

16239 BAKER (EDWARD RONALD) and DODGE (FREDERICK BRIAN). Road Traffic Law Summary. 1946. 7th edn 1980.

16240 PLOWDEN (STEPHEN). Taming Traffic. 1980.

16241 —— Transport Reform: Changing the Rules. 1985.

16242 BRODIE (MARY). Traffic Generation. 1978.

16243 ESSEX COUNTY COUNCIL. Land Use/Transportation Study: Brentwood. Chelmsford. 1967.

16244 —— Land Use/Transportation Study: Colchester. Chelmsford. 1967.

16245 BLUNDEN (WILLIAM ROSS). The Land Use/Transport System. Oxf. 1971.

16246 LIBERAL PARTY TRANSPORT COMMITTEE. Transport: A Report by a Committee under the Chairmanship of Mr. Arthur Holt. M.P. 1962.

16247 U.K. MINISTRY OF TRANSPORT. Rural Transport Surveys: Report of Preliminary Results. 1963.

16248 —— The Transport Needs of Britain in the Next Twenty Years: Report. 1963.

16249 —— Passenger Transport in Great Britain. [Pub. annually, 1962+.].

16250 —— Highland Transport Enquiry Report. 1963.

16251 NATIONAL COUNCIL ON INLAND TRANSPORT. A Future Policy for Britain's Transport. 1964.

16252 WALKER (PETER R. J.). The Future of Transport in Britain. 1964.

16253 RADICE (JONATHAN). Transport. 1965.

16254 LAMBERT (CLAIRE M.) comp. Transport Policy Consultation Document, 1976: Responses to the Government's Transport Policy Consultation Document: A Select List of Material. 1977. [Dept. of Employment.].

16255 LABOUR PARTY CAMPAIGN HANDBOOK. Transport. 1978.

16256 BARKE (MICHAEL). Transport and Trade. Edin. 1986.

16257 NASH (CHRISTOPHER ALFRED). The Economics of Public Transport. 1982.

16258 CHARTERED INSTITUTE OF TRANSPORT. Consumers in Transport. 1981.

16259 ADAMS (JOHN). Transport Planning: Vision and Practice. 1981.

16260 COOPER (BARRY). Transport Planning and Practice, a Review. Cardiff. 1981.

16261 SIMPSON (BARRY JOHN). Planning and Public Transport in Great Britain, France and W. Germany. Harlow. 1987.

16262 WHITE (PETER R.). Public Transport: Its Management and Operation. Pub. in 1976 as 'Planning for Public Transport'. 2nd edn 1986.

16263 PLANNING AND TRANSPORT RESEARCH COMPUTATION. Public Transport Planning and Operations. 1986.

16264 INSTITUTE OF BRITISH GEOGRAPHERS. (Transport Geography Study Group). Public Issues in Transport. Keele. 1983.

16265 SMITH (GAVIN). Getting Around: Transport Today and Tomorrow. 1984.

16266 WISTRICH (ENID). The Politics of Transport. 1983.

16267 SCHUMER (LESLIE ARTHUR). Elements of Transport. Sydney/Lond. 1974.

16268 STUBBS (PETER C.) et al. Transport Economics. 1980. Rev. edn 1984.

16269 HARRISON (ANTHONY JOHN) and GRETTON (JOHN). Transport U.K. 1985: An Economic and Social Policy Audit. Newbury. 1985.

16270 SALFORD TRANSPORT GEOGRAPHY GROUP. Implications of the 1985 Transport Bill . . . Salford. 1985.

16271 O'SULLIVAN (PATRICK). Transport Policy: Geographical, Economic and Planning Aspects. 1980.

16272 ROAD PASSENGER TRANSPORT DIRECTORY FOR THE BRITISH ISLES AND WESTERN EUROPE. [Annually, 1970+.].

16273 BANNISTER (DAVID). Transport Mobility and Deprivation in Inter-Urban Areas. Farnborough. 1980.

16274 LIEPMANN (KATE K.). The Journey to Work. 1944.

16275 WILSON (FRANK RICHARD). Journey to Work: Modal Split; A Study in Transportation. 1967.

16276 LAWTON (R.). 'The Daily Journey to Work in England and Wales'. Town Planning Rev. 29 (1959), 241–57.

16277 WESTERGAARD (JOHN H.). 'Journeys to Work in the London Region'. Town Planning Rev. 28 (1957/58), 37–62.

16278 DANIELS (PETER WALTERS). Office Location and the Journey to Work: A Comparative Study of Five Urban Areas. Farnborough. 1980.

16279 CITY OF WESTMINSTER CHAMBER OF COMMERCE. Travelling to Work: Report of a Working Party. 1980.

16280 FRYER (J. A.) comp. Travel to Work in Greater London: Selected Results from the 1971 Census. 1978.

16281 WEBSTER (F. V.). Urban Passenger Transport: Some Trends and Prospects. Crowthorne. 1977.

16282 —— A Theoretical Estimate of London Car Commuters Transferring to Bus Travel. Crowthorne. 1968.

16283 LEIGH (ROGER). The Journey to Work in Central London, 1921–1951: A Geographical Analysis. 1968.

16284 THOMAS (RAY). Commuting Flows and the Growth of London's New Towns 1951–1971. Milton Keynes. 1977.

16285 STANNARD (CAROL). London's Workers: Changes in the Distribution of Residence 1961–1966. 1970.

16286 HONDELINK (ENGELBERT RUTGERUS). Suburban Passenger Services: A Paper on 'Commuter Traffic'. Northwood. 1964.

16287 SAFAVI (H. A.) *and* STANNARD (ROBERT B.). Rail Commuting to Central London. 1970.

16288 HERMON (CELIA). Commuters' Pastimes. Bognor Regis. 1980.

16289 LOCATION OF OFFICES BUREAU [Research Papers No.1]. White Collar Commuters: A Second Survey: An Inter-Regional Comparison of the Community and Working Conditions of Office Workers. 1967.

16290 FULLERTON (BRIAN) *and* BULLOCK (M.). Accessibility to Employment in the Northern Region Report. Newcastle upon Tyne. 1968.

16291 STONE (H. W. D.). The Principles of Urban Traffic. 1917.

16292 THOMSON (J. MICHAEL). Great Cities and their Traffic. 1977.

16293 RICHARDS (BRIAN). New Movement in Cities. 1966.

16294 SLEEMAN (JOHN). 'The Rise and Decline of Municipal Transport'. *Scot. J. Pol. Econ.* 9 (1962), 46–64.

16295 MACKIE (PETER J.). 'The New Grants System for Local Transport—The First Five Years'. *Public Admin* 58 (1980), 187–206.

16296 SMITH (J. M. A.). 'The Impact of the Motor Car on Public Transport'. *J. Inst. Transport* 29 (1961), 41–8.

16297 WATERS (BRIAN). Get our Cities Moving. 1967.

16298 HANLON (PATRICK). Road Traffic. Chichester. 1981.

16299 SMITH (HAROLD STANLEY VIAN). The Transport Act 1953: An Explanation for the Transport User and Operator. 1953.

16300 HENSHER (DAVID A.) *ed.* Urban Transport Economics. Camb. 1977.

16301 BUTTON (KENNETH JOHN). The Economics of Urban Transport. Farnborough. 1977.

16302 JONES (IAN SHORE). Urban Transport Appraisal. 1977.

16303 HUTCHINS (KENNETH RICHARD). Urban Transport: Public or Private? 1967.

16304 BEESLEY (MICHAEL E.). Urban Transport: Studies in Economic Policy. 1973.

16305 GRANT (JOHN). The Politics of Urban Transport Planning. 1977.

16306 GREY (ALEXANDER). Urban Fares Policy. Farnborough. 1975.

16307 BONSALL (PETER) *et al. eds.* Urban Transportation Planning: Current Themes and Future Prospects. Tunbridge Wells. 1977.

16308 POTTER (STEPHEN). Transport and the New Towns. Milton Keynes. 1976.

16309 —— Transport Planning in the Urban Cities. Milton Keynes. 1981.

16310 COLIN BUCHANAN AND PARTNERS. The Conurbations: A Study. 1969.

16311 THOMAS (DAVID ST JOHN). The Rural Transport Problem. 1963.

16312 MOSELEY (MALCOLM J.). Rural Transport and Accessibility. Norwich. 1977.

16313 WARBURTON (S.) *and* TROWER-FOYAN (M.). Public Transport in Rural Areas: The Increasing Role of Central and Local Government. Newcastle upon Tyne. 1981.

16314 INSTITUTE OF BRITISH GEOGRAPHERS. (Rural Geography Study Group). Rural Accessibility and Mobility. Lampeter. 1985.

16315 SCOTTISH ASSOCIATION FOR PUBLIC TRANSPORT. Public Transport in Rural Scotland. Glasgow. 1973.

16316 BARKER (THEODORE CARDWELL) *and* ROBBINS (RICHARD MICHAEL). A History of London Transport: Passenger Travel and the Development of the Metropolis, Vol. 2—'The 20th Century to 1970'. vol. 2 1974. 1st vol. 1963.

16317 BARMAN (CHRISTIAN). The Man who Built London Transport: A Biography of Frank Pick. Newton Abbot. 1979.

16318 FORTY (A.). 'Lorenzo of the Underground [Frank Pick]'. *London J.* 5 (1979), 113–19.

16319 LONDON TRANSPORT EXECUTIVE. Comments on Transport Policy: A Consultation Document. 1976.

16320 HART (DOUGLAS ALLEN). Strategic Planning in London: The Rise and Fall of the Primary Road Network. Oxf. 1967.

16321 GREATER LONDON COUNCIL. Greater London Transportation Survey. 1976.

16322 —— Greater London Transport: A Plan for Action 1976/77. 1976.

16323 GOLDRICK (MICHAEL KEVIN D'ARCY). The Administration of Transportation in Greater London. 1967.

16324 COLLINS (MICHAEL FRANK) *and* PHAROAH (TIMOTHY MARTIN). Transport Organisation in a Great City: The Case of London. 1975.

16325 LAZARUS (DAVID). Freeing London's Gluepot. 1967.

16326 POLLINS (HAROLD). 'Transport Lines and Social Divisions'. Ch. in GLASS (RUTH) *et al.* London: Aspects of Change. 1964.

16327 LONDON L.C.C. and G.L.C. London Traffic Survey. 2 vols 1964, 1966.

16328 GARBUTT (PAUL ELFORD). London Transport and the Politicians. 1985.

16329 BROOKS (DENNIS). Race and Labour in London Transport. 1975.

16330 JENSON (ALEC G.). Birmingham Transport vol. 1. Birm. 1980.

16331 ABELL (PAUL HENRY). Transport and Industry in Greater Manchester. Barnsley. 1978.

16332 JOYCE (J.). Roads, Rails and Ferries of Liverpool 1900–1950. 1983.

16333 JONES (A. E.). Roads and Rails of West Yorkshire, 1890–1950. 1984.

16334 GLENN (D. F.). Roads, Rails and Ferries of the Solent Area, 1919–1969. 1980.

16335 SPEAKMAN (JOHN). Transport in Yorkshire. 1969.

16336 GLASGOW CORPORATION. Greater Glasgow Transportation Studies, vol. 1—Current Travel Patterns in the Greater Glasgow Area. Glasgow. 1967.

16337 BRITISH TRANSPORT COMMISSION. Passenger Transport in Glasgow and District. 1951.

16338 MILLAR (ALAN). British Passenger Transport Executives—1: Strathclyde. 1985.

16339 WRAGG (RICHARD) and REES (GRAHAM L.). A Study of the Passenger Transport Needs of Urban Wales, prepared for the Welsh Council. Cardiff. 1977.

16340 BLOCK (GEOFFREY DAVID MAURICE). Transport in Wales. 1964.

16341 MORGAN (R. H.). 'The Development of an Urban Transport System: The Case of Cardiff'. *Welsh Hist. Rev.* 13 (1986), 178–93.

16342 THOMAS (DAVID BERNARD). Trains and Buses of Newport, 1845 to 1981. Newport. 1982.

16343 GREER (P. EUGENE). Road versus Rail: Documents on the History of Public Transport in Northern Ireland 1921–1948. Belf. 1982.

16344 GINNS (MICHAEL) and OSBORNE (ERIC N.). Transport in Jersey: An Historical Survey of Public Transport Facilities by Rail and Road in the Island of Jersey 1788–1961. 1961.

16345 HALL (C. C.). Sheffield Transport. Glossop. 1977.

16346 LEICESTER CITY MUSEUM and ART GALLERY. Public Transport in Leicester, 1874–1961. Leics. 1962.

16347 TAYLOR (M. A.). Studies of Travel in Gloucester, Northampton and Reading. Crowthorne. 1968.

16348 DURHAM COUNTY COUNCIL. Durham City: An Interim Traffic Management Study. Durham. 1969.

16349 GRIME (ERIC KEITH). Recent Developments in the Transport Network and the Growth of Population in South East Buckinghamshire. 1965.

16350 OXFORD CITY COUNCIL. Oxford Traffic Survey. In 2 pts. Oxf. 1957, 1959.

16351 EDWARDS (BARRY K.) and SIMPSON (J. G.). Derby City Transport Route History, 1840–1982. Bromley. 1983.

16352 ATTRIDGE (JOHN). Rotherham Transport History. Hendon. 1984.

16353 WILDSMITH (OSMOND). A History of Wolverhampton Transport. Birm. 1987.

16354 HEANOR AND DISTRICT HISTORICAL SOCIETY. Two Centuries of Transport in the Heanor [Derbyshire] Area. Ilkeston. 1978. Repr. 1984.

16355 WATTS (ERIC). Fares Please: The History of Passenger Transport in Portsmouth. Horndean. 1987.

16356 PRICE (ROBERT). Transport and Communications [in Horsforth, Yorkshire]. Horsforth. 1985.

16357 DAVIES (G. A.). The Channel Tunnel. Coventry. 1973. [A bibliography.].

16358 WATSON (A. H.). 'The Channel Tunnel: Investment Appraisals'. *Public Admin* 45 (1967), 1–21.

16359 KENT PLANNING DEPARTMENT. The Channel Tunnel: A Discussion of Terminal Requirements of the British Side and Possible Locations of Terminal Facilities in Kent. Maidstone. 1968.

16360 HUNT (D.). 'The Channel Tunnel Enters the First Phase'. *New Scientist* 49 (1971), 238–9.

16361 JONES (B.) ed. The Channel Tunnel and Beyond. 1987.

16362 HAINING (PETER). Eurotunnel: An Illustrated History of the Channel Tunnel Scheme. 1972.

16363 HENDERSON (*Sir* NICHOLAS). Channels and Tunnels: Reflections on Britain and Abroad. 1987.

16364 BONAVIA (MICHAEL ROBERT). The Channel Tunnel Story. Newton Abbot. 1979. 2nd edn 1987.

16365 HOWIE (WILL) and CHRIMES (MIKE) eds. Thames Tunnel to Channel Tunnel: 150 Years of Civil Engineering. 1987.

16366 BRITISH TOURIST AUTHORITY. The Channel Tunnel: An Opportunity and a Challenge for British Tourism. 1988.

16367 TURNBULL (GERALD L.). Traffic and Transport: An Economic History of Pickfords. 1979.

16368 ORTON (IAN). An Illustrated History of Mobile Library Services in the United Kingdom. Sudbury. 1980.

16369 CAMPBELL (GINA) and MEECH (MICHAEL). Bluebirds: The Story of the Campbell Dynasty. 1988.

16370 GARVEY (JUDE). A Guide to the Transport Museums of Britain. 1982.

2. CANALS AND INLAND WATERWAYS

16371 EDWARDS (L. A.) comp. Inland Waterways of Great Britain and Ireland. 1972.

16372 BRITISH WATERWAYS BOARD. Annual Report and Accounts. 1963+.

16373 HADFIELD ([ELLIS] CHARLES [RAYMOND]). British Canals: An Illustrated History. Lond. 1950. 2nd edn 1959. 7th rev. edn Newton Abbot. 1985.

16374 —— 'Sources for the History of British Canals'. *J. Transport Hist.* 2 (1955/56), 80–100.

16375 —— Introducing Canals: A Guide to British Waterways Today. 1955.

16376 —— Canals and Waterways. Newton Abbot. 1966.

16377 —— World Canals: Inland Navigation Past and Present. 2nd edn 1986. 1st pub. Oxf. 1964, under title 'Canals of the World'.

16378 BALDWIN (MARK) *and* BURTON (ANTHONY) *eds.* Canals: A New Look: Essays in Honour of Charles Hadfield. Chichester. 1984.

16379 BALDWIN (MARK). Canal Books: A Guide to the Literature of the Waterways. 1984.

16380 McKNIGHT (HUGH) *comp.* A Source Book of Canals: Locks and Canal Boats. 1974.

16381 WARE (MICHAEL E.). Canals and Waterways. Princes Risborough. 1987.

16382 GLADWIN (DAVID DANIEL FRANCIS). The Canals of Britain. 1973.

16383 DARWIN (ANDREW). Canals and Rivers of Britain. 1976.

16384 BODY (ALFRED HARRIS). Canals and Waterways. 1969.

16385 BRAITHWAITE (LEWIS). Canals in Towns. 1976.

16386 SQUIRES (ROGER W.). Canals Revived: The Story of the Waterways Restoration Movement. Bradford. 1979.

16387 PORTEOUS (J. DOUGLAS). Canal Ports: The Urban Achievement of the Canal Age. 1977.

16388 SHERWOOD (K. B.). 'The Canal Boatmen's Strike of 1923'. *J. Transport Hist.* 3rd. ser. 7 (1986/7), 61–79.

16389 CORNISH (MARGARET). Troubled Waters: Memoirs of a Canal Boatwoman. 1987.

16390 SMITH (DONALD JOHN). The Horse and the Cut: The Story of the Canal Horses of Britain. Camb. 1982.

16391 EYRE (FRANK) *and* HADFIELD ([ELLIS] CHARLES [RAYMOND]). English Rivers and Canals. 1945.

16392 GLADWIN (DAVID DANIEL FRANCIS) *and* WHITE (JOYCE MARIAN). English Canals. Lingfield. 1967.

16393 de MARÉ (ERIC SAMUEL). The Canals of England. 1950.

16394 LINDSAY (JEAN). The Canals of Scotland. Newton Abbot. 1968.

16395 WRIGHT (IAN L.). Canals in Wales. Truro. 1977.

16396 GLADWIN (DAVID DANIEL FRANCIS). The Canals of the Welsh Valleys and their Tramroads. Lingfield. 1975.

16397 McCUTCHEON (WILLIAM ALAN). The Canals of the North of Ireland. Dawlish. 1965.

16398 HADFIELD ([ELLIS] CHARLES [RAYMOND]). The Canals of Southern England. 1955.

16399 —— The Canals of South West England. Newton Abbot. 1967. 2nd edn 1985.

16400 —— The Canals of South and Southeast England. Newton Abbot. 1969.

16401 —— The Canals of the East Midlands. Newton Abbot. 1966. 2nd edn 1970.

16402 —— The Canals of the West Midlands. Newton Abbot. 1966.

16403 —— The Canals of South Wales and the Border. Cardiff. 1960. 2nd edn Newton Abbot. 1967.

16404 —— The Canals of Yorkshire and North East England. Newton Abbot. 2 vols 1972, 1973.

16405 HADFIELD ([ELLIS] CHARLES [RAYMOND]) *and* BIDDLE (JOHN). The Canals of North West England. 2 vols 1970.

16406 BOYES (JOHN) *and* RUSSELL (RONALD). The Canals of East England. Newton Abbot. 1977.

16407 OWEN (DAVID ELYSTAN). Canals to Manchester. Manch. 1977.

16408 —— The Manchester Ship Canal. Manch. 1983.

16409 FARNIE (DOUGLAS ANTHONY). The Manchester Ship Canal and the Rise of the Port of Manchester, 1894–1975. Manch. 1980.

16410 MAKEPEACE (CHRIS). The Manchester Ship Canal: A Short History. Hendon. 1983.

16411 HODSON (PATRICIA M.). The Manchester Ship Canal: A Guide to Historical Sources. Manch. 1985.

16412 GRANT (RODERICK). The Great Canal. [Manchester Ship Canal.]. 1978.

16413 CLEW (KENNETH R.). The Kennet and Avon Canal. 2nd edn 1973.

16414 LINDSAY (JEAN). The Trent and Mersey Canal. Newton Abbot. 1979.

16415 LEAD (PETER) *comp.* The Trent and Mersey Canal. Ashbourne. 1980.

16416 WILSON (EDWARD A.). The Ellesmere and Llangollen Canal: An Historical Background. 1977.

16417 WATSON (K.). Thames and Medway Canal: A Study of Recreational Potential. Gravesend. 1976.

16418 'OLD UNION' CANALS' SOCIETY. The 'Old Union' Canals of Leicester and Northamptonshire. 1982.

16419 MALET (HUGH). Coal, Cotton and Canals: Three Studies in Local Canal History. Swinton. 1981.

16420 CORNWALL COUNTY AND DIOCESAN RECORD OFFICE. Handlist of Records: Turnpike Roads, Canals, Ferries. Truro. 1983.

16421 FAULKNER (ALAN HENDERSON). The Warwick Canals. Oakham. 1985.

16422 GOULD (ROBERT) *comp.* Canals in Derbyshire: A Bibliography. Matlock. 1979.

16423 CARTER (PAUL) *ed.* Forth and Clyde Canal Guidebook. Glasgow. 1985.

16424 BOWMAN (A. IAN). Swifts and Queens: Passenger Transport on the Forth and Clyde Canal. Glasgow. 1984.

16425 PEARSON (D.). 'The Aberdeenshire Canal: A Description and Interpretation of its Remains'. *Aberd. Univ. Rev.* 51 (1986), 285–306.

16426 BLAIR (MAY). Once Upon the Lagan: The Story of the Lagan Canal. Belf. 1981.

16427 BURTON (ANTHONY). The Waterways of Britain: A Guide to the Canals and Rivers of England, Scotland and Wales. 1983.

16428 GLADWIN (DAVID DANIEL FRANCIS). British Waterways: An Ilustrated History. 1977.

16429 SHERRINGTON (CHARLES ELY ROSE). A Hundred Years of Inland Transport, 1830–1933. 1934.

16430 ROLT (LIONEL THOMAS CASWELL). The Inland Waterways of England. 1950. Repr. 1979.

16431 —— Inland Waterways. 1958.

16432 —— Navigable Waterways. 1969, 1973. Rev. edn Harmonds-worth. 1985.

16433 HADFIELD ([ELLIS] CHARLES [RAYMOND]). Introducing Inland Waterways. Newton Abbot. 1973.

16434 HADFIELD ([ELLIS] CHARLES [RAYMOND]) *and* NORRIS (JOHN). Waterways to Stratford. 1962. 2nd edn 1968.

16435 MILNE (ALISTAIR MURRAY). The Economics of Inland Transport. 1955. 2nd edn 1963, by John Critchley Laight.

16436 SAVAGE (CHRISTOPHER IVOR). Inland Transport. 1957.

16437 CALVERT (ROGER). Inland Waterways of Britain. 1963.

16438 McKNIGHT (HUGH). The Shell Book of Inland Waterways. Newton Abbot. 1975. 2nd edn 1981.

16439 —— Waterways Postcards 1900–1930. Shepperton. 1983.

16440 LLOYDS REGISTER OF SHIPPING. Rules and Regulations for the Classification of Inland Waterways Ships. 1980.

16441 EDWARDS (LEWIS ARTHUR). Inland Waterways of Great Britain. 1951. 2nd edn 1962. 6th rev. edn 1985.

16442 BALDWIN (MARK) *ed.* British Freight Waterways Today and Tomorrow. 1980.

16443 BIDDLE (GORDON). Lancashire Waterways. Clapham, North Yorkshire. 1980.

16444 VINE (PAUL ASHLEY LAURENCE). London's Lost Route to the Sea: An Historical Account of the Inland Navigations which Linked the Thames to the English Channel. Dawlish. 1965.

16445 U.K. BRITISH WATERWAYS BOARD. The Future of Waterways: Interim Report of the Board. 1964.

16446 —— The Facts about the Waterways. 1965.

16447 INLAND WATERWAYS ASSOCIATION. (Development Committee). New Waterways: Interim Report. 1965.

16448 —— Annual Report 1979–80.

16449 AICKMAN (ROBERT). The River Runs Uphill: A Story of Success and Failure. Burton-on-Trent. 1986. [History of the Inland Waterways Assoc.].

See also BAXTER (RON ERIC). Ports and Inland Waterways/Civil Aviation. Oxf. 1979. Reviews of Statistical Sources Series, cited above in Transport (General) section.

3. SHIPPING

(a) Reference and General Shipping Works

16450 MATHIAS (PETER) *and* PEARSALL (H. W. A.) *eds.* Shipping: A Survey of Historical Records. Newton Abbot. 1971.

16451 JARVIS (RUPERT C.). 'Sources for the History of Ships and Shipping'. *J. Transport Hist.* 3 (1957/8), 212–34.

16452 ALBION (ROBERT GREENHALGH). Maritime and Naval History. An Annotated Bibliography. Camb. MA. 1951. 3rd edn 1st Supplements, 1963–1965. Mystic, Conn. 1966.

16453 U.K. BRITISH TRANSPORT COMMISSION. British Transport Commission Historical Records: Canal, Dock, Harbour, Navigation and Steamship Companies. 1977.

16454 MARITIME LIBRARIANS' ASSOCIATION. Marine Transport: A Guide to Libraries and Sources of Information in Great Britain. 1982.

16455 RANFT (BRYAN). Ironclad to Trident: 100 Years of Defence Commentary: Brassey's 1886–1986: Centenary Volume of Brassey's Naval Annual. 1986.

See also BRASSEY₃S NAVAL ANNUAL 1886—*E.g.* 'Standing of the World's Merchant Fleets'. 1920/1. 177–81, and Sir J. P. Maclay, 'Control and De-control of [British] Shipping'. 1920/1. 39–141.

16456 KIRKALDY (ADAM WILLIS). British Shipping: Its History, Organisation and Importance. 1914. Repr. 1970.

16457 FISHER (STEPHEN). British Shipping and Seamen, 1630–1960: Some Studies. Exeter. 1984.

16458 LANE (TONY). Grey Dawn Breaking: British Merchant Seafarers in the Late Twentieth Century. Manch. 1986.

16459 STURMEY (STANLEY GEORGE). British Shipping and World Competition. 1962.

16460 BRANCH (ALAN EDWARD). Elements of Shipping. 1964. 5th edn 1981.

16461 —— Dictionary of Shipping/International Trade Terms and Abbreviations. 1976. 2nd edn 1982.

16462 SIMPER (ROBERT). Britain's Maritime Heritage. Newton Abbot. 1982.

16463 COLVIN (MICHAEL) *and* MARKS (JONATHAN). British Shipping: The Right Course. 1984.

16464 RANKEN (MICHAEL BRUCE FERNIE). British Shipping in the 1990s. Guildford. 1981.

16465 BURLEY (KEVIN). British Shipping and Australia, 1920–1939. Camb. 1968.

16466 U.K. MINISTRY OF TRANSPORT. Committee of Inquiry into Shipping Services to Northern Ireland. 1963.

16467 LLOYD'S REGISTER OF SHIPPING. Annual Report.

16468 GENERAL COUNCIL OF BRITISH SHIPPING. Annual Report.

16469 ALDCROFT (DEREK HOWARD). 'The Eclipse of English Coastal Shipping, 1913–1921'. *J. Transport Hist.* 6 (1963/4), 24–38.

16470 —— 'The Decontrol of British Shipping and Railways after the First World War'. *J. Transport Hist.* 5 (1961/2), 89–104.

16471 FAYLE (CHARLES EDWIN). The War and the Shipping Industry. 1927.

16472 U.K. ADMIRALTY. British Vessels Lost at Sea 1917–1918. Repr. Camb. 1970. 1st pub. as House of Commons Papers, Aug. 1919.

16473 GOTO (S.). 'Daiichiji Taisen to Igirisu Kaigun Gyofuteiki Sengyokai no Shihon Chikuseki o Chusin ni'. ['World War One and the British Shipping Industry'.]. *Shakaikeizaishigaku* [*Socio-Economic History* (Japan)] 46 (1980), 77–113.

16474 CHANDLER (GEORGE). Liverpool Shipping: A Short History. 1960.

16475 ULYATT (MICHAEL E.) *and* PAGET-TOMLINSON (EDWARD W.). Humber Shipping: A Pictorial History. Clapham, N. Yorkshire. 1979.

16476 STAMMERS (MICHAEL K.). West Coast Shipping. Aylesbury. 1976. 2nd edn 1983.

16477 JOYE (GILL) *ed.* Southampton's Ships: An Index to Periodical References. S/hampton. 1978.

16478 COLLARD (JOHN A.). A Maritime History of Rye. Rye. 1978.

16479 FISHER (STEPHEN) *ed.* West Country Maritime and Social History: Some Essays. Exeter. 1980.

16480 DONALDSON (GORDON). Northwards by Sea. [History of Shipping in Scotland.]. Edin. 1966. Rev. 1978.

16481 RIDDELL (JOHN F.). The Clyde: An Illustrated History of the River and its Shipping. 1988.

16482 EAMES (ALED). Ships and Seamen of Anglesey, 1558–1918: Studies in Maritime and Local History. 1981.

16483 NATIONAL MUSEUM OF WALES. The Maritime History of Dyfed. Cardiff. 1982.

16484 JENKINS (JOHN GERAINT). Maritime Heritage: The Ships and Seamen of Ceredigion. Llandysul. 1982.

16485 COURSE (ALFRED GEORGE). The Merchant Navy: A Social History. 1963.

16486 HOPE (RONALD). The Merchant Navy. 1980.

16487 DOUGHTY (MARTIN). Merchant Shipping and War: A Study of Defence Planning in 20th Century Britain. 1982.

16488 BEHRENS (CATHERINE BETTY ABIGAIL). Merchant Shipping and the Demands of War. 1955. Repr. 1978.

16489 MARSHALL (MICHAEL). Ocean Traders: A History of Merchant Shipping from the Portuguese Discoveries to the Present Day. 1989.

16490 BRITISH MARITIME LEAGUE. British Merchant Shipping: An Examination of the Causes of Decline in the British Merchant Fleet since 1975. 1984.

16491 STANTON (LOUIS FRANÇOIS HONORÉ). A Guide to the Merchant Shipping Acts. 2 vols Glasgow. 1976, 1980.

16492 JANE'S MERCHANT SHIPPING REVIEW 1983.

16493 LANGLEY (MARTIN) *and* SMALL (EDWINA). Merchant Shipping at Plymouth. Exeter. 1987.

16494 GRIPAIOS (HECTOR). Tramp Shipping. N.Y./Lond. 1959.

16495 PHILLIPS-BIRT (DOUGLAS). A History of Seamanship. 1971.

16496 CLANCY (ROGER). Ships, Ports and Pilots: A History of the Piloting Profession. Jefferson, N.C./Lond. 1984.

16497 SULLIVAN (DICK). Old Ships, Boats and Maritime Museums. 1978.

16498 ROWLAND (KEITH T.). Steam at Sea: A History of Steam Navigation. Newton Abbot. 1970.

16499 SMITH (EDGAR C.). 'The Centenary of Steam Navigation'. *Trans. Newcomen Soc.* 18 (1937/38), 129–68.

16500 —— A Short History of Naval and Maritime Engineering. Camb. 1938.

16501 —— 'The Centenary of Naval Engineering'. *Trans. Newcomen Soc.* 2 (1921/2), 88–114.

16502 GUTHRIE (JOHN). A History of Marine Engineering. 1971.

16503 BARNABY (KENNETH C.). The Institution of Naval Architects 1860–1960. 1960.

16504 LARN (RICHARD). Shipwrecks of Great Britain and Ireland. Newton Abbot. 1981.

16505 —— Devon Shipwrecks. Newton Abbot. 1974. Lond. 1977.

16506 LARN (RICHARD) *and* CARTER (CLIVE). Cornish Shipwrecks. 2 vols Newton Abbot. 1967, 1970. Lond. 1978.

16507 MARSDEN (PETER). The Historic Shipwrecks of South East England. Norwich. 1987.

16508 BURNETT (DAVID). Dorset Shipwrecks. Wimborne. 1982.

16509 BENNETT (TOM). Welsh Shipwrecks. 2 vols Haverfordwest. 1982. Newport. 1987.

16510 JONES (IVOR WYNNE). Shipwrecks of North Wales. Newton Abbot. 1973. Lond. 1978. 3rd rev. edn Newton Abbot. 1986.

16511 REES (P. H.). Gower Shipwrecks. Swansea. 1978.

16512 SKIDMORE (IAN). Anglesey and Lleyn Shipwrecks. Swansea. 1979.

16513 GODDARD (TED). Pembrokeshire Shipwrecks. Swansea. 1983.

16514 WILSON (IAN). Shipwrecks of the Ulster Coast. Coleraine. 1979.

16515 BARNABY (KENNETH CLOVES). Some Ship Disasters and their Causes. 1968.

16516 WEBB (WILLIAM). Coastguard! An Official History of H.M. Coastguard. 1976.

16517 SCARLETT (BERNARD). Shipminder: The Story of H.M. Coastguard. 1971.

16518 MARTIN (NANCY). Search and Rescue: The Story of the Coastguard Service. Newton Abbot. 1974.

(b) Shipping Lines, Shipowners, Types of Ship

16519 BUCHANAN (D. S.). Merchant Shipping: A Guide to Government Publications. 1975.

16520 CALVERT (J.) *and* MCCONVILLE (J.). The Shipping Industry: Statistical Sources. 1983.

16521 BRITISH SHIPPING REVIEW. 1978+.

16522 BLAKE (GEORGE). Lloyds' Register of Shipping, 1760–1960. 1960.

16523 —— Committee of Enquiry into Shipping: Report. Cmnd 4337, Parliamentary Papers, xxvii 1969–70. [Chairman: *Viscount* Rochdale.].

16524 —— Decline in the UK Registered Merchant Fleet. HC Paper 94, Parliamentary Papers, 1986–7. [Chairman : Gordon T. Bagler.].

16525 JOHN (A. H.). A Liverpool Merchant House: Being the History of Alfred Booth and Company, 1863–1958. 1959.

16526 HYDE (FRANCIS E.). Cunard and the North Atlantic, 1840–1973: A History of Shipping and Financial Management. 1975.

16527 MAXTONE-GRAHAM (JOHN). Cunard: 150 Glorious Years. Newton Abbot. 1989.

16528 MITCHELL (WILLIAM HARRY). The Cunard Line: A Post-War History, 1945–1974. Deal. 1975.

16529 JOHNSON (HOWARD). The Cunard Story. 1987.

16530 SHIPBUILDER AND MARINE ENGINE-BUILDER. Queen Mary, the Cunard White Star Quadruple-Screw North Atlantic Liner . . . 1st pub. 1936. Repr. N.Y. 1979.

16531 PADFIELD (PETER). Beneath the House Flag of the P & O [Peninsular and Oriental Steam Navigation Company.]. 1981.

16532 HOWARTH (DAVID). The Story of P & O: The Peninsular and Orient Steamship Navigation Company. 1986.

16533 McCART (NEIL). 20th Century Passenger Ships of the P & O. Wellingborough. 1985.

16534 ROBSON (STEPHEN). P & O in the Falklands: A Pictorial Record, 5 April–25 September 1982. 1982.

16535 BUSHELL (THOMAS ALEXANDER). 'Royal Mail': A Centenary History of the Royal Mail Line 1839–1939. 1939.

16536 —— Eight Bells: The Royal Mail Lines War Story, 1939–1945. 1950.

16537 GREEN (EDWIN) *and* MOSS (MICHAEL STANLEY). A Business of National Importance: The Royal Mail Shipping Group, 1902–1937. 1982.

16538 MURRAY (MARISCHAL). Union Castle Chronicle, 1853–1953. 1953.

16539 MITCHELL (WILLIAM HARRY) *and* SAWYER (L. A.). The Cape Run: The Story of the Union Castle Service to South Africa. Lavenham. 1984.

16540 —— Sailing Ship to Supertanker: The 100 Year Story of British Esso and its Ships. Lavenham. 1987.

16541 MORRIS (CHARLES F.). Origins, Orient and 'Oriana' [History of the Orient Line.]. Brighton. 1980.

16542 McCART (NEIL). Passenger Ships of the Orient Line. Wellingborough. 1987.

16543 TAYLOR (JAMES ARNOLD). Ellermans: A Wealth of Shipping. 1976.

16544 VAMPLEW (WRAY). Salvesen of Leith. Edin. 1975.

16545 SOMNER (GRAEME). From 70 North to 70 South: A History of the Christian Salvesen Fleet. Edin. 1984.

16546 LONG (A.) *and* LONG (R.). A Shipping Venture: Turnbull Scott & Company, 1872–1972. 1973.

16547 HYDE (FRANCIS EDWIN). Shipping Enterprise and Management, 1830–1939: Harrisons of Liverpool. L/pool. 1967.

16548 SMYTH (HAZEL P.). The B & I Line: A History of the British and Irish Steam Packet Company. Dublin. 1984.

16549 MacARTHUR (IAN C.). The Caledonian Steam Packet Company. Glasgow. 1971.

16550 HUME (JOHN ROBERT) *and* MOSS (MICHAEL STANLEY). A Bed of Sails: The History of P. MacCallum and Sons Ltd., 1781–1981: A Study in Survival. Greenock. 1981.

16551 McLELLAN (R. S.). Anchor Line, 1856–1956. Glasgow. 1956.

16552 ORBELL (JOHN) *with* GREEN (EDWIN) *and* MOSS (MICHAEL STANLEY). From Cape to Cape: The History of the Lyle Shipping Company. Edin. 1978.

16553 KEIR (DAVID). The Bowring Story. 1962.

16554 BLAKE (GEORGE). Gellatly's 1862–1962: A Short History of the Firm. 1962.

16555 —— The Ben Line: The History of Wm. Thomson & Co. of Leith and Edinburgh and of the Ships Owned and Managed by them, 1825–1955. 1956.

16556 DAVIES (P. N.). The Trade Makers: Elder Dempster in West Africa, 1852–1972. 1973.

16557 HOPE (IAN). The Campbells of Kilmun: Shipowners 1853–1980. Johnstone. 1981.

16558 FINCH (ROGER). A Cross in the Topsail: An Account of the Shipping Interests of R. & W. Paul Ltd., Ipswich. Ipswich. 1979.

16559 GIBBS (JOHN MOREL). Morel's of Cardiff: The History of a Family Shipping Firm. Cardiff. 1982.

16560 HEATON (PAUL MICHAEL). The Abbey Line: History of a Cardiff Shipping Venture. Pontypool. 1983.

16561 —— The Reardon Smith Line: History of a South Wales Shipping Venture. Pontypool. 1984.

16562 HOLLET (DAVE). From Cumberland to Cape Horn: The Complete History of the Sailing Fleet of Thomas and John Brocklebank of Whitehaven and Liverpool . . . 1984.

16563 BRITISH AND COMMONWEALTH SHIPPING COMPANY LTD. Annual Report 1977–8.

16564 POWELL (LESLIE HUGHES). The Shipping Federation: A History of the First Sixty Years, 1890–1950. 1950.

16565 MARX (DANIEL) *Jnr*. International Shipping: A Study of Industrial Self-Regulation by Shipping Conferences. Princeton, N.J. 1953.

16566 BEAN (RON). 'Liverpool Shipping Employers and the Anti-Communist Activities of J. M. Hughes, 1920–1925'. *Bull. Soc. Stud. Lab. Hist.* 34 (1977), 22–6.

16567 DAVIES (PETER NEVILLE). Henry Tyrer: A Liverpool Shipping Agent and his Enterprise 1879–1979. 1979.

16568 —— Sir Alfred Jones: Shipping Entrepreneur par Excellence. 1978.

16569 EMMONS (FREDERICK). The Atlantic Liners 1925–70. Newton Abbot. 1972.

16570 MILLER (WILLIAM HENRY). The Last Atlantic Liners. 1985.

16571 —— Transatlantic Liners 1945–1980. Newton Abbot. 1981.

16572 —— Transatlantic Liners at War: The Story of the Queens. Newton Abbot. 1985.

16573 —— Famous Ocean Liners: The Story of Passenger Shipping from the Turn of the Century to the Present Day. Wellingborough. 1987.

16574 —— British Ocean Liners: A Twilight Era, 1960–1985. Wellingborough. 1985.

16575 —— Liner: 50 Years of Passenger Ship Photographs. Wellingborough. 1986.

16576 SEDGWICK (S.) *and* SPRAKE (R. F.). London and Overseas Freighters Limited, 1949–1977: A Shore History. 1977.

16577 COLEMAN (TERRY). The Liners: A History of the North Atlantic Crossing. 1976. Harmondsworth. 1977.

16578 BONSOR (NOEL REGINALD PIXELLE). North Atlantic Story. Prescot. 1955. Rev. and expanded, vol. 1 Newton Abbot. 1975. Vols 2–5, Jersey. 1978–80.

16579 BARRATT (REX). The Hey-Day of the Great Atlantic Liners. Redruth. 1983.

16580 GIBBS (CHARLES ROBERT VERNON). British Passenger Liners of the Five Oceans: A Record of the British Passenger Lines and their Liners from 1838 to the Present Day. 1963.

16581 PHILLIPS-BIRT (DOUGLAS). When Luxury went to Sea. Newton Abbot. 1971.

16582 HUTCHINGS (DAVID F.). The Q.E. 2: A Ship for all Seasons. Southampton. 1988.

16583 WARWICK (RONALD W.) *and* FLAYHART (WILLIAM H.). The Q.E.2. N.Y./Lond. 1985.

16584 WATSON (MILTON E.). Flagships of the Line: A Celebration of the World's Three Funnel Liners. Wellingborough. 1988.

16585 WILLIAMS (DAVID LLOYD) *and* de KERBRECH (RICHARD P.). Damned by Destiny: A Complete Account of all the World's Projects for Passenger Liners which never Entered Service. Brighton. 1982.

16586 WHALE (DEREK). The Liners of Liverpool. Birkenhead. 1988.

16587 HILTON (GEORGE WOODMAN) *et al.* The Illustrated History of Paddle Steamers. Lausanne/Camb. 1977.

16588 COX (BERNARD). Paddle Steamers. Poole. 1979.

16589 SPRATT (HEREWARD PHILIP). Transatlantic Paddle Steamers. Glasgow. 1951. Repr. 1967, 1981.

16590 PATERSON (ALAN JAMES STUART). Classic Scottish Paddle Steamers. Newton Abbot. 1982.

16591 DAVIES (KENNETH). The Clyde Passenger Steamers. Ayr. 1980.

16592 GREENWAY (AMBROSE). A Century of North Sea Passenger Steamers. 1986.

16593 DIX (FRANK L.). Royal River Highway: A History of Passenger Boats and Services on the River Thames. Newton Abbot. 1985.

16594 CLAMMER (RICHARD) *and* KITTRIDGE (ALAN). Passenger Ships of the River Dart and Kingsbridge Estuary. Chatham. 1987.

16595 KITTRIDGE (ALAN). Passenger Steamers of the River Tamar. Truro. 1984.

16596 CRAIG (ROBIN). Steam Tramps and Cargo Liners 1850–1950. 1980.

16597 GREENHILL (BASIL JACK). The Merchant Schooners. 1870–1940. 2 vols 1951, 1957. New and rev. edn Newton Abbot. 1968.

16598 WHITE (E. W.). British Fishing Boats and Coastal Craft. 2 vols 1950, 1952. [HMSO.].

16599 GILL (ALEC). Lost Trawlers of Hull: 900 Losses between 1835 and 1987. Beverley. 1989.

16600 NICOLSON (JAMES ROBERT). Shetland's Fishing Vessels. Lerwick. 1981.

16601 SAWYER (L. A.) *and* MITCHELL (WILLIAM HARRY). Tankers. 1967.

16602 BAKER (WILLIAM AVERY). From Paddle Steamer to Nuclear Ship: A History of the Engine-Powered Vessel. 1965.

16603 FLETCHER (MAX E.). 'From Coal to Oil in British Shipping'. *J. Transport Hist.* n.s. 3 (1975), 1–19.

(c) Shipbuilding

16604 RITCHIE (L. A.) *comp*. Modern British Shipbuilding: A Guide to Historical Records. 1980.

16605 BLAKE (GEORGE). British Ships and Shipbuilders. 1946.

16606 JONES (LESLIE). Shipbuilding in Britain, mainly between the two World Wars. Cardiff. 1957.

16607 SLAVEN (ANTHONY). 'British Shipbuilders: Market Trends and Order Book Patterns between the Wars'. *J. Transport Hist.* 3rd ser. 3 (1982), 37–62.

16608 PARKINSON (JOHN RICHARD). The Economics of Shipbuilding in the United Kingdom. Camb. 1960.

16609 —— 'The Financial Prospects of Shipbuilding after Geddes'. *J. Indust. Econ.* 17 (1968), 1–17.

16610 —— 'Shipbuilding'. Ch. in British Industry between the Wars. *Eds.* Neil Keith Buxton and Derek Howard Aldcroft. 1979.

16611 —— Shipbuilding Enquiry Committee Report. 1965–6. Cmnd 2937, Parliamentary Papers, vii, 1965–6. [Chairman: *Sir* Reay Geddes.].

16612 HEAL (DAVID WALTER) *and* SLAVEN (ANTHONY). Iron and Steel; Shipbuilding. [Reviews of UK Statistical Sources Series.]. Oxf. 1984.

16613 HOGWOOD (BRIAN W.). Government and Shipbuilding: The Politics of Industrial Change. Farnborough. 1979.

16614 RIDDLE (IAN). Shipbuilding Credit. Cardiff. 1983.

16615 MOSS (MICHAEL STANLEY) *and* HUME (JOHN ROBERT). Workshop of the Empire: Engineering and Shipbuilding in the West of Scotland. 1977.

16616 —— Clyde Shipbuilding from Old Photographs. 1975.

16617 BUXTON (NEIL KEITH). 'The Scottish Shipbuilding Industry between the Wars: A Comparative Study'. *Bus. Hist.* 10 (1968), 101–20.

16618 ROBERTSON (A. J.). 'Clydeside Revisited: A Reconsideration of the Clyde Shipbuilding Industry, 1919–1938'. Ch. in Trade and Transport: Essays in Economic History in Honour of T. S. Willan. *Ed.* by William Henry Chaloner and Barrie M. Ratcliffe. Manch. 1977.

16619 WALKER (FRED M.). Song of the Clyde: A History of Clyde shipbuilding. Camb. 1984.

16620 CASTLE (COLIN M.). Better by Yards. Erskine. 1988. [Clyde Shipbuilding.].

16621 BROADWAY (FRANK). Upper Clyde Shipbuilders: A Study of Government Intervention in Industry. 1976.

16622 MCGILL (J.). Crisis on the Clyde: The Story of Upper Clyde Shipbuilders. 1973.

16623 FOSTER (JOHN). The Politics of the U.C.S. Work-in. 1986.

16624 REID (JIMMY). Reflections of a Clydebuilt Man. 1976.

16625 BOWMAN (A. IAN). Kirkintilloch Shipbuilding. Glasgow. 1983.

16626 DOUGAN (DAVID). The History of North East Shipbuilding. 1968.

16627 FLAGG (AMY C.). Notes on the History of Shipbuilding in South Shields 1746–1946. S. Shields. 1979.

16628 ELSON (PETER). Tyneside Shipbuilding 1920–1960: A Personal Selection of Photographs. Newcastle-upon-Tyne. 1986.

16629 WARD-JACKSON (CYRIL HENRY). Ships and Shipbuilders of a West Country Seaport: Fowey 1786–1939. Truro. 1976.

16630 GRANT (*Sir* ALLEN JOHN). Steel and Ships: The History of John Brown's. 1950.

16631 ALEXANDER (KENNETH JOHN WILSON) *and* JENKINS (C. L.). Fairfields: A Study of Industrial Change. 1970.

16632 HOUSTON (JAMES DOBBIE). The Fairfields Project. Glasgow. 1968.

16633 PAULDEN (SYDNEY MAURICE) *and* HAWKINS (BILL). Whatever Happened at Fairfields? 1969.

16634 MOSS (MICHAEL STANLEY) *and* HUME (JOHN ROBERT). Shipbuilders to the World: 125 Years of Harland & Wolff, Belfast, 1861–1986. Belf. 1986.

16635 BARNABY (KENNETH CLOVES). 100 Years of Specialised Shipbuilding and Engineering: John I. Thorneycroft Centenary. 1964.

16636 DU CANE (PETER). An Engineer of Sorts. 1971.

16637 McGOLDRICK (JAMES). 'Industrial Relations and the Division of Labour in the Shipbuilding Industry since the War'. *Brit. J. Indust. Relns* 21 (1983), 197–220.

16638 CAMERON (GORDON C.). 'Post-War Strikes in the North-East Shipbuilding and Ship-Repairing Industry, 1946–1961'. *Brit. J. Indust. Relns* 2 (1964), 1–22.

16639 CLARKE (JOHN FINBAR). Power on Land and Sea: 160 Years of Industrial Enterprise on Tyneside: A History of R. & W. Hawthorn Leslie & Co. Ltd, Engineers and Shipbuilders. Wallsend. 1979.

16640 DENNY (WILLIAM) & Bros. William Denny and Brothers Ltd., Leven Shipyard, Dumbarton, 1844–1932. 1932.

16641 GOODEY (CHARLES). The First Hundred Years: The Story of Richards Shipbuilders. Ipswich. 1976.

16642 REID (JAMES MACARTHUR). James Lithgow: Master of Work 1883–1952. 1964.

16643 HUME (JOHN ROBERT) *and* MOSS (MICHAEL STANLEY). Beardmore: The History of a Scottish Industrial Giant. 1979.

(d) Ports, Docks, and Harbours

16644 BRITISH TRANSPORT DOCKS BOARD. Annual Report and Accounts, 1963–81.

16645 STATISTICAL ABSTRACT OF THE UK PORTS INDUSTRY. 1982+.

16646 OWEN (*Sir* DAVID JOHN). The Origin and Development of the Ports of the United Kingdom. 1939.

16647 BIRD (JAMES HAROLD). The Major Seaports of the United Kingdom. 1963.

16648 REES (HENRY). British Ports and Shipping. 1958.

16649 FORD (PERCY) *and* BOUND (JOHN ALEXANDER). Coastwise Shipping and the Small Ports. Oxf. 1951.

16650 JARVIS (RUPERT C.). 'Sources for the History of Ports'. *J. Transport Hist.* 3 (1957/8), 76–93.

16651 HEATHCOTE (K. A.). 'The Ports of Great Britain'. Ch. in World Shipping in the 1990s. Michael Bruce Fernie Ranken, ed. Guildford. 1981.

16652 WILSON (G. K.). 'Planning: Lessons from the Ports'. *Public Admin* 61 (1983), 266–81.

16653 TAKEL (R. E.). Industrial Port Development: With Case Studies from South Wales and Elsewhere. 1974.

16654 HILLING (D.). 'The Restructuring of the Severn Estuary Ports'. In Seaport Systems and Spatial Change: Technology, Industry and Development Strategies. B. S. Hoyle and D. Hilling, eds. 1984.

16655 JACKSON (GORDON). The History and Archaeology of Ports. Tadworth. 1983.

16656 CARGILL (GAVIN). Blockade '75: The Story of the Fishermen's Blockade of the Ports. Glasgow. 1976.

16657 RITCHIE-NOAKES (NANCY). Old Docks. Princes Risborough. 1987.

16658 Committee of Enquiry into Certain Matters concerning the Port Transport Industry: First Report, Cmnd 2523, Parliamentary Papers, xxi (1964–5). Final Report, Cmnd 2734, Parliamentary Papers, xxi (1964–5). The Committee was chaired by Lord Devlin.

16659 MELLISH (MICHAEL). The Docks after Devlin. 1972.

16660 WILSON (DAVID F.). Dockers: The Impact of Industrial Change. 1972.

16661 ORAM (R. B.). The Dockers' Tragedy. 1987.

16662 HILL (STEPHEN). The Dockers: Class and Tradition in London. 1976.

16663 UNIVERSITY OF LIVERPOOL (Social Research Series). The Dock Worker: An Analysis of Conditions of Employment in the Port of Manchester. L/pool. 1954.

16664 DOUGLAS (R. P. A.). An Outline of the Law Relating to Harbours in Great Britain Managed under Statutory Powers. 1979.

16665 HAYMAN (BERNARD). Harbour Seamanship. Oxf. 1986.

16666 SAUNDERCOCK (VICTOR G.). Harbour Vessels. Colebrook. 1985.

16667 MORRIS (RUTH) *and* MORRIS (FRANK). Scottish Harbours: The Harbours of Mainland Scotland. 1983.

16668 BRITISH PORTS ASSOCIATION. Annual Report 1980–1984. (1981–5). [Contd. as Annual Report and Accounts, 1985.].

16669 —— Annual Statistical Abstract of the United Kingdom Ports Industry 1982. 1982.

16670 ASSOCIATED BRITISH PORTS. Guide to the Nineteen Ports. 1984. 1984.

16671 TURNER (JOHN RAYMOND). Scotland's North Sea Gateway: Aberdeen Harbour AD 1136–1986. Aberd. 1986.

16672 LEVY (CATRIONA). Ardrossan Harbour 1805–1970: A Short History. Glasgow. 1988.

16673 AYR AND TROON—Official Ports Handbook. 1983.

16674 OWEN (*Sir* DAVID JOHN). A Short History of the Port of Belfast. 1917.

16675 MURLESS (BRIAN J.). Bridgewater Docks and the River Parrett. Somerset. 1983.

16676 NEALE (WILFRID GROVES). The Tides of War and the Port of Bristol 1914–1918. Bristol. 1976.

16677 WHITNEY (CHARLES E.). Discovering the Cinque Ports. Princes Risborough. 1978.

16678 HILLIER (CAROLINE). The Bulwark Shore: Thanet and the Cinque Ports. 1980.

16679 BRENTNALL (MARGARET). The Cinque Ports and Romney Marsh. 1972. New enlgd edn 1980.

16680 GREEN (IVAN). The Book of the Cinque Ports: Their Origin, Development and Decline. Buckingham. 1984.

16681 PEARSE (RICHARD). The Ports and Harbours of Cornwall: An Introduction to the Study of Eight Hundred Years of Maritime Affairs. St Austell. 1963.

16682 WREN (WILFRID JOHN). Ports of the Eastern Counties. Lavenham. 1976.

16683 WALLACE (G. J.). 'Felixstowe: Britain's Little Big Port'. *Geog.* 60 (1975), 209–13.

16684 GWILLIAM (KENNETH MASON). A Pilot Study of the Haven Ports of Harwich, Felixstowe and Ipswich. 1967.

16685 FLEETWOOD PORT. Handbook 1984.

16686 STIMPSON (MICHAEL). The History of Gloucester Docks and its Associated Canals and Railways. 1980.

16687 CONWAY-JONES (HUGH). Gloucester Docks: An Illustrated History. Gloucs. 1984.

16688 BRITISH TRANSPORT DOCKS BOARD. The Ports of Grimsby and Immingham 1981. Grimsby. 1981.

16689 HITCHMAN (HARRY G.) *and* DRIVER (PHILIP). Harwich: A Nautical History. 1984.

16690 HUGHES (DAVID LLOYD) *and* WILLIAMS (DOROTHY MARY). Holyhead: The Story of a Port. 1967.

16691 BRITISH TRANSPORT DOCKS BOARD HULL. Official Guide 1982. Gloucester. 1982.

16692 BEAN (RON). 'The Port of Liverpool: Employers and Industrial Relations, 1919–1939'. Ch. in Commerce, Industry and Transport: Studies in Economic Change on Merseyside. Bruce Louis Anderson and P. J. M. Stoney, eds. L/pool. 1983.

16693 MOUNTFIELD (STUART). Western Gateway: A History of the Mersey Docks and Harbour Board. L/pool. 1965.

16694 HYDE (FRANCIS EDWIN). Liverpool and the Mersey: An Economic History of a Port, 1700–1970. Newton Abbot. 1971.

16695 RITCHIE-NOAKES (NANCY). Liverpool's Historic Waterfront: The World's First Mercantile Dock System. 1984.

16696 MERSEY PORTS. Handbook 1983/4—Downham Market. 1983.

16697 GREEVES (IVAN S.). London Docks 1800–1980: A Civil Engineering History. 1980.

16698 BATES (LEONARD MAURICE). The Thames on Fire: The Battle of London River 1939–1945. Lavenham. 1985.

16699 CLEGG (WILLIAM PAUL). Docks and Ports: 2. London. 1987.

16700 OWEN (*Sir* DAVID JOHN). The Port of London, Yesterday and Today. 1927.

16701 —— Liquid History: To Commemorate Fifty Years of the Port of London Authority, 1909–1959. 1960.

16702 CONNOLLY (D. J.). 'Social Repercussions of New Cargo Handling Methods in the Port of London'. *Int. Lab. Rev.* 105 (1972), 543–68.

16703 U.K. PORT OF LONDON AUTHORITY. The Port of London: Official Handbook of the. Authority. 1963.

16704 —— Notes on the Port of London. 1966.

16705 —— The History and Development of the Port of London Authority. 1967.

16706 LANGLEY (MARTIN). Milbay Docks. Exeter. 1987.

16707 MOODY (BERT). 150 Years of Southampton Docks. S/hampton. 1988.

16708 WILLIAMS (DAVID LLOYD). Docks and Ports: 1 Southampton. 1984.

16709 JEFFERS (W.). 'The South Wales Ports'. *Industrial Wales* 41 (1957), 40–4.

16710 HALLETT (GRAHAM). Maritime Industry and Port Development in South Wales. Cardiff. 1970.

16711 HARRIS (EDWARD). Swansea: Its Port and Trade and their Development. Cardiff. 1934.

16712 JONES (WILLIAM HENRY). History of the Port of Swansea. Carmarthen. 1922.

16713 TEES AND HARTLEPOOL PORTS. Handbook 1983/4—Downham Market. 1984.

16714 TRUMP (HAROLD JAMES). Teignmouth: A Maritime History. Chichester. 1976. 2nd edn 1986.

4. RAILWAYS

(a) Reference and General Works

16715 CLINKER (CHARLES RALPH). Railway History: A Handlist of the Principal Sources of Original Material, with notes and guidance on its use. Padstow. 1969.

16716 OTTLEY (GEORGE) *comp.* A Bibliography of British Railway History. 1965. 2nd edn 1983.

16717 —— Railway History: A Guide to 61 Collections in Libraries and Archives in Great Britain. [Subject guides to library resources.]. 1973.

16718 WARDLE (D. B.). 'Sources for the History of Railways at the Public Record Office'. *J. Transport Hist.* 2 (1955/6), 214–34.

16719 ELLIS (CUTHBERT HAMILTON). British Railway History vol. 2 1877–1947. 1959.

16720 PERKIN (HAROLD J.). The Age of the Railway. Newton Abbot. 1970. Repr. 1971.

16721 SIMMONS (JACK). The Railways of Britain: An Historical Introduction. 1961. 2nd edn 1968. 3rd edn 1986.

16722 TURNER (PHYLLIS MARY). Transport History: Railways. Manch. 1981.

16723 POLLINS (HAROLD). Britain's Railways: An Industrial History. Totowa, NJ. 1971.

16724 O'BRIEN (PATRICK). The New Economic History of the Railways. 1977.

16725 ALDCROFT (DEREK HOWARD). British Railways in Transition: The Economic Problems of Britain's Railways since 1914. 1968.

16726 —— 'The Railways and Economic Growth: A Review Article'. *J. Transport Hist.* n.s. 1 (1973), 238–48.

16727 FREEMAN (MICHAEL) *and* ALDCROFT (DEREK HOWARD). The Atlas of British Railway History. 1985.

16728 NOCK (OSWALD STEVENS). 150 Years of Main Line Railways. Newton Abbot. 1980.

16729 JONES (EDGAR). The Penguin Guide to the Railways of Great Britain. Harmondsworth. 1981.

16730 ALLEN (GEOFFREY FREEMAN). Railways of the Twentieth Century. 1983.

16731 ALLEN (GEOFFREY FREEMAN) *and* WHITEHOUSE (PATRICK BRUCE). The Illustrated History of Britain's Railways. 1981.

16732 MCKENNA (FRANK). The Railway Workers, 1840–1970. 1980.

16733 BAGWELL (PHILIP SIDNEY). The Railwaymen: The History of the National Union of Railwaymen. 2 vols 1963, 1982.

16734 —— The Railway Clearing House and the British Economy 1842–1922. 1968.

16735 JOBY (R. S.). The Railwaymen. Newton Abbot. 1984.

16736 DAVEY (RICHARD). My Life on the Footplate. 1974.

16737 CUMMINGS (JOHN MORRISON). Railway Motor Buses and Bus Services in the British Isles, vol. 2, 1902–1933. Oxf. 1980.

16738 HAMILTON (JAMES ALAN BOUSFIELD). Britain's Railways in World War One. 1967.

16739 THOMAS (JOHN). Gretna, Britain's Worst Railway Disaster. 1915. Newton Abbot. 1969.

16740 SMITH (DONALD J. M.). 'The Gretna Train Smash'. *Transport Hist.* 12 (1981), 65–7.

16741 HAMILTON (JAMES ALAN BOUSFIELD). Railway Accidents of the 20th Century. 1967.

16742 NATIONAL GUILDS LEAGUE. Workers' Control on the Railways. 1921.

16743 SIMNETT (WILLIAM EDWARD). Railway Amalgamation in Great Britain. 1923.

16744 SHERRINGTON (CHARLES ELY ROSE). The Economics of Rail Transport in Great Britain. 2 vols 1928.

16745 KIDD (HOWARD C.). A New Era for British Railways. 1929.

16746 MARSHALL (CHARLES FREDERICK DENDY). One Hundred Years of Railways: From Liverpool and Manchester to London Midland and Scottish. 1930.

16747 UNWIN (PETER). Travelling by Train in the 20's and 30's. 1981.

16748 THOMAS (DAVID ST JOHN) *and* WHITEHOUSE (PATRICK). The Great Days of the County Railway. Newton Abbot. 1986.

16749 GARBUTT (PAUL ELFORD). A Survey of Railway Development and Practice. 1938.

16750 BONAVIA (MICHAEL ROBERT). Railway Policy between the Wars. Manch. 1981.

16751 COMMUNIST RAILWAY WORKERS. How to End Muddle on the Railways. 1944.

16752 TATFORD (BARRINGTON). The Story of British Railways. 1945.

16753 BELL (ROBERT). A History of the British Railways during the War, 1939–1945. 1946.

16754 DARWIN (BERNARD RICHARD MEIRION). War on the Line. 1946.

16755 CRUMP (NORMAN EASEDALE). By Rail to Victory. 1947.

16756 KALLA-BISHOP (PETER MICHAEL). Locomotives at War: Army Railway Reminiscences of the Second World War. Truro. 1980.

16757 WESTWOOD (JOHN). Railways at War. 1980.

16758 KENNET (H. JOHN). British Railways and Economic Recovery: A Sociological Study of the Transport Problem. 1949.

16759 NOCK (OSWALD STEVENS). Railways of Britain, Past and Present. 1948. 2nd rev. edn 1962.

16760 —— British Trains, Past and Present. 1951.

16761 —— Scottish Railways. 1950. Rev. edn 1961.

16762 —— British Railways in Action. 1956.

16763 —— Railways in the Transition from Steam, 1950–1965. 1974.

16764 —— Historic Railway Disasters. 1966. 3rd edn 1983.

16765 —— British Railway Signalling: A Survey of Fifty Years Progress. 1969.

16766 —— Railway Signalling: A Treatise on Recent Practice of British Railways. 1980. Repr. 1985.

16767 —— Speed Records on Britain's Railways. Newton Abbot. 1971. Lond. 1972.

16768 ALLEN (CECIL JOHN). Railways of Britain. 1958.

16769 RAILWAY CONVERSIONS LEAGUE. Memorandum on the future of British railways; being an outline of arguments for the conversion into a system of reserved motorways. Guildford. 1960.

16770 AHERN (TOM). The Railways and the People: An Appeal to Passengers and Workers. 1962. [Communist Party publication.].

16771 ROBBINS (MICHAEL). The Railway Age. 1962.

16772 HAMMOND (REGINALD CHARLES HOLT). Railways Tomorrow: a Story of Railway Transport Problems, with Special Emphasis on the Modernisation Plan for British Railways. 1963.

16773 —— Railways in the New Air Age. 1964.

16774 DANIELS (GERALD) *and* DENCH (LESLIE ALAN) *comps*. Passengers No More, 1952–1962: Closures of Stations and Branch Lines. Brighton. 1962.

16775 HONDELINK (ENGELBERT RUTGERUS). Stopping Tracks. 1963. [Great Central Association.].

16776 —— Review of Dr. Beeching's Report. 1965.

16777 DAVIES (WILLIAM JAMES KEITH). Light Railways: Their Rise and Decline. 1964.

16778 PEARSON (ARTHUR JAMES). The Railways and the Nation. 1964.

16779 CALVERT (ROGER). The Future of Britain's Railways. 1965.

16780 ALLEN (GEOFFREY FREEMAN). British Rail after Beeching. 1966.

16781 HUXLEY (GEORGE). The Plight of the Railways. Belf. 1966.

16782 MCLEOD (CHARLES). All Change: Railway Industrial Relations in the 1960s. 1970.

16783 JONES (C. D.). 'The Performance of British Railways, 1962–1968'. *J. Transport Econ. Policy* 4 (1970), 162–70.

16784 PRYKE (RICHARD WALLIS SPEAIGHT) *and* DODGSON (JOHN S.). The Rail Problem. 1975.

16785 WHITEHOUSE (PATRICK BRUCE) *ed*. Britain's Main Line Railways. 1977.

16786 GAMMELL (CHRISTOPHER JOHN). The Branch Line Age: The Minor Railways of the British Isles in Memoriam and Retrospect. Ashbourne. 1979.

16787 JOY (STEWART). The Train that Ran Away: A Business History of Britain's Railways, 1948–1968. 1973.

16788 GOURVISH (TERENCE RICHARD). British Railways, 1948–1973: A Business History. Camb. 1987.

16789 HARRIS (JOHN) *and* WILLIAMS (GLYN). Corporate Management and Financial Planning: The British Rail Experience. 1980.

16790 BONAVIA (MICHAEL ROBERT). British Rail: The First 25 Years. Newton Abbot. 1981.

16791 HARESNAPE (BRIAN). British Rail 1948–1983: A Journey by Design. Shepperton. 1979. 2nd edn 1983.

16792 RICHARDS (JEFFREY) *and* MacKENZIE (JOHN). The Railway Station: A Social History. 1986.

16793 ROSS (DONALD J.). New Street Remembered: The Story of Birmingham's New Street Railway Station, 1854–1967. 1984.

16794 SMITH (DAVID). The Railway and its Passengers: A Social History. Newton Abbot. 1988.

16795 DYER (MALCOLM) *comp.* A History of British Railways Diesel and Electric Locomotive Liveries. Sutton Coldfield. 1979.

16796 CARTER (ERNEST FRANK). Britain's Railway Liveries: Colours, Crests and Linings, 1825–1948. 1952.

16797 TALBOT (EDWARD). The Locomotive Names of British Railways: Their Origins and Meanings. Stafford. 1982.

16798 ELLIS (CUTHBERT HAMILTON). The Flying Scotsman 1862–1962: Portrait of a Train. 1962.

16799 —— Royal Journey: A Retrospect of Royal Trains in the British Isles. 1953. Rev. edn 1960.

16800 WALTERS (DAVID). British Railway Bridges. 1963.

16801 WOODHAMS (JOHN). Funicular Railways. Aylesbury. 1989.

16802 SILVESTER (REGINALD). Official Railway Postcards of the British Isles. Chippenham. 1981.

16803 WEIGHELL (SIDNEY). On the Rails. 1983.

16804 ST AUBIN DE TERAN (LISA). Off the Rails: Memoirs of a Train Addict. 1989.

16805 BURKE (M.). Signalman. Truro. 1982.

16806 VAUGHAN (ADRIAN). Signalman's Morning. 1981.

16807 —— Signalman's Twilight. 1983.

16808 —— Signalman's Nightmare. 1987.

See also THOMAS (DAVID ST JOHN) *and* CLINKER (CHARLES RALPH) *eds.* A Regional History of the Railways of Great Britain, series now includes:

16809 THOMAS (DAVID ST JOHN). The West Country. 1960. 4th edn Newton Abbot. 1973. 6th edn 1988. Vol. 1.

16810 WHITE (HENRY PATRICK). Southern England. 1961. 3rd edn Newton Abbot. 1972. 6th edn 1987. Vol. 2.

16811 —— Greater London. 1963. 5th edn Newton Abbot. 1987. Vol. 3.

16812 HOOLE (KENNETH). North East England. 1965. 5th edn Newton Abbot. 1986. Vol. 4.

16813 DONALDSON (GORDON IAN). The Eastern Counties. Newton Abbot. 1968. 2nd edn 1977. Vol. 5.

16814 THOMAS (JOHN). Scotland: The Lowlands and the Borders. Newton Abbot. 1971. 2nd rev. and enlgd edn 1984. By Alan J. S. Paterson. Vol. 6.

16815 CHRISTIANSEN (REX). The West Midlands. Newton Abbot. 1973. 2nd rev. edn 1986. Vol. 7.

16816 JOY (DAVID). South and West Yorkshire: The Industrial West Riding. Newton Abbot. 1975. 2nd rev. edn 1984. Vol. 8.

16817 LELEUX (ROBIN). The East Midlands. 1976. 2nd rev. edn 1984. Vol. 9.

16818 HOLT (GEOFFREY OGDEN). The North West. Newton Abbot. 1978. 2nd edn 1986. Vol. 10.

16819 BAUGHAN (PETER E.). North and Mid Wales. Newton Abbot. 1980. Vol. 11.

16820 BARRIE (DEREK STIVEN). South Wales. Newton Abbot. 1980. Vol. 12.

16821 CHRISTIANSEN (REX). Thames and Severn. Newton Abbot. 1981. Vol. 13.

16822 JOY (DAVID). The Lake Counties. Newton Abbot. 1983. Vol. 14.

16823 THOMAS (JOHN) *and* TURNOCK (DAVID). The North of Scotland. Newton Abbot. 1989. Vol. 15.

See also Oakwood Library of Railway History, 58 volumes with reprints, pub. 1937–80.

16824 U.K. BRITISH RAILWAYS SOUTHERN REGION. Want to Run a Railway? 1962.

16825 U.K. BRITISH TRANSPORT COMMISSION. British Railways Progress. 1962.

16826 HARDY (RICHARD HARRY NORMAN). Beeching: Champion of the Railway? 1989.

16827 ELLIOT (*Sir* JOHN). On and Off the Rails. 1982.

16828 FIENNES (GERALD). I Tried to Run a Railway. 1967.

16829 PARKER (*Sir* PETER). For Starters: The Business of Life. 1989.

16830 U.K. BRITISH RAILWAYS BOARD. The Re-shaping of British Railways. 1963. [BEECHING REPORT.].

16831 —— The Development of the Major Trunk Routes. 1965.

16832 —— A Study of the Relative True Costs of Rail and Road Freight Transport over Trunk Routes. 1964.

16833 SCOTTISH RAILWAY DEVELOPMENT ASSOCIATION. Scottish Railways: The Next Five Years. St Andrews. 1964.

16834 NATIONAL STANDING JOINT COUNCIL ON ROAD and RAIL TRAFFIC PROBLEMS. The Road and Rail Crisis: Memorandum to the Prime Minister. 1962.

(b) Company and Station Histories; Underground Railways

16835 CARTER (ERNEST FRANK). An Historical Geography of the Railways of the British Isles. 1959.

16836 CROMPTON (W. G.). '"Efficient and Economical Policy?": The Performance of the Railway Companies 1922–1933'. *Business Hist.* 27 (1985), 222–37.

16837 GREENLEAF (HORACE). Britain's Big Four: The Story of the London, Midland and Scottish, London and North Eastern, Great Western, and Southern Railways. 1948.

16838 ELLIS (CUTHBERT HAMILTON). Four Main Lines. 1950.

16839 BONAVIA (MICHAEL ROBERT). The Four Great Railways. Newton Abbot. 1980.

16840 WHITELEY (JOHN STUART) *and* MORRISON (GAVIN STUART). The Big Four Remembered. Sparkford. 1989.

16841 NOCK (OSWALD STEVENS). The Caledonian Railway. 1962. 2nd edn 1973.

16842 ALLEN (CECIL JOHN). The Great Eastern Railway. 1955. 5th edn 1968.

16843 SHARMAN (MIKE). The Great Eastern Railway. Headington. 1987.

16844 PHILLIPS (CHARLES). The Great Eastern since 1900. 1985.

16845 GRINLING (CHARLES HERBERT). The History of the Great Northern Railway 1843–1922; with Supplementary Chapters by H. V. Borley and Cuthbert Hamilton Ellis. 1903. Rev. 1966.

16846 ALLEN (CECIL JOHN). The Great Northern. 1961.

16847 NOCK (OSWALD STEVENS). The Great Northern Railway. 1958. Repr. 1979.

16848 WROTTESLEY (JOHN). The Great Northern Railway vol. 3—The 20th Century to Grouping. 1981.

16849 THROWER (W. RAYNER). The Great Northern Main Line. Trowbridge. 1984.

16850 ARNOLD (ROBERT MCCULLOCH). The Golden Years of the Great Northern Railway [Ireland], Part One. Belf. 1976. Repr. 1979.

16851 —— The Golden Years of the Great Northern Railway Part Two—Newry, Armagh, Clones. Belf. 1980.

16852 MacDERMOT (EDWARD TERENCE) *et al.* History of the Great Western Railway. 1927. Rev. edn 3 vols 1964–7. Repr. 1982.

16853 NOCK (OSWALD STEVENS). The Great Western Railway in the 20th Century. 1964.

16854 —— The Great Western Railway: An Appreciation. 1951.

16855 —— *Ed.* The Great Western. 1975.

16856 ALLEN (CECIL JOHN). The Great Western. 1962.

16857 —— Salute to the Great Western. 1970.

16858 BOOKER (FRANK). The Great Western Railway, a New History. Newton Abbot. 1977.

16859 SEMMENS (PETER). A History of the Great Western Railway. 3 vols 1985.

16860 WHITEHOUSE (PATRICK BRUCE) *and* THOMAS (DAVID ST JOHN). The Great Western Railway: 150 Glorious Years. Newton Abbot. 1984.

16861 PRYTHERCH (RAYMOND JOHN). The Great Western Railway and other Services in the West Country and South Wales: A Bibliography of British Books Published 1950–1969. Leeds. 1980.

16862 GRAFTON (PETER). Men of the Great Western. 1979.

16863 BECK (KEITH M.). The Greatness of the Great Western. 1984.

16864 FAIRCLOUGH (TONY) *and* WILLS (ALAN). Great Western Steam through the Years. Truro. 1977.

16865 HARRIS (MICHAEL LOUIS JOHN). Great Western Coaches from 1890. Newton Abbot. 1966. 3rd edn 1985.

16866 CHANNON (GEOFFREY). 'The Great Western Railway under the British Railways Act of 1921'. *Business Hist. Rev.* 55 (1981), 188–216.

16867 PARR (H. W.). The Great Western Railway in Devon. Dawlish. 1965.

16868 LUCKING (JOHN HORACE). The Great Western at Weymouth: A Railway and Shipping History. Newton Abbot. 1971.

16869 WILSON (ROGER BURDETT). Go Great Western: A History of Great Western Railway Publicity. Newton Abbot. 1970.

16870 HEYES (ALAN). London Midland Steam: The Closing Years. 1980.

16871 BAKER (MICHAEL). The Changing London Midland Scene 1948–1983. 1983.

16872 HARESNAPE (BRIAN). The London Midland and Scottish Railway. 1983.

16873 ELLIS (CUTHBERT HAMILTON). London Midland and Scottish: A Railway in Retrospect. 1970.

16874 ALLEN (CECIL JOHN). Salute to the London Midland and Scottish. 1972.

16875 NOCK (OSWALD STEVENS). A History of the L.M.S. 3 vols 1982, 1983.

16876 —— Britain's New Railways: Electrification of the London-Midland Main Lines. 1965.

16877 —— The Royal Scots and the Patriots of the L.M.S. Newton Abbot. 1978.

16878 WHITEHOUSE (PATRICK BRUCE) *and* THOMAS (DAVID ST JOHN). L.M.S. 150: The London Midland and Scottish Railway: A Century and a Half of Progress. Newton Abbot. 1987.

16879 —— The London Midland and Scottish in the West Midlands. Poole. 1984.

16880 GAMMELL (CHRISTOPHER JOHN). L.M.S. Branch Lines 1945–1965. Oxf. 1980.

16881 KEELEY (RAYMOND). Memoirs of L.M.S. Steam. 1982.

16882 ESSERY (ROBERT) *and* JENKINSON (DAVID). An Illustrated History of L.M.S. Coaches, 1923–1957. 1969. Rev. edn Oxf. 1977.

16883 —— An Illustrated History of L.M.S. Locomotives. Oxf. 1981.

16884 ROSE (R. ERIC). The L.M.S. and the L.N.E.R. in Manchester. 1987.

16885 BONAVIA (MICHAEL ROBERT). A History of the L.N.E.R. 2 vols 1982.

16886 BELL (ROBERT) *and* ARKLE (E. W.). 'The London and North Eastern Railway [1922–1948]'. *J. Transport Hist.* 5 (1962), 133–45.

16887 BUTTERFIELD (PETER). 'Grouping, Pooling, and Competition: The Passenger Policy of the London and North Eastern Railway 1929–1939'. *J. Transport Hist.* 3rd ser. 7 (1986/87), 21–46.

16888 HAY (PETER) *comp.* Pre-Grouping Trains on British Railways: The L.N.E.R. Companies. Poole. 1984.

16889 ALLEN (CECIL JOHN). The London and North Eastern Railway. 1962.

16890 NOCK (OSWALD STEVENS). The London and North Western Railway. 1960.

16891 —— The London and South Western Railway. 1966.

16892 ARTELL (ROBERT). The London and South Western Railway. 1984.

16893 HARDINGHAM (ROGER). Celebrating 150 Years of the London and South Western Railway. S/hampton. 1988.

16894 NOCK (OSWALD STEVENS). The Midland Compounds. Dawlish. 1964.

16895 ELLIS (CUTHBERT HAMILTON). The Midland Railway. 1953. 2nd edn 1955. 3rd edn 1966.

16896 WHITEHEAD (ALAN). The Midland in the 1930s. 1982.

16897 ESSERY (ROBERT). An Illustrated History of Midland Wagons. Oxf. 1980.

16898 MILNER (CHRIS). The Midland Mainline Today. 1986.

16899 RADFORD (JOHN BRIAN). Midland through the Peak: A Pictorial History of the Midland Railway Mainline Routes between Derby and Manchester. 1988.

16900 CLARK (RONALD H.). A Short History of the Midland and Great Northern Joint Railway. Norwich. 1967.

16901 WROTTESLEY (JOHN). The Midland and Great Northern Joint Railway. Newton Abbot. 1970. 2nd edn 1981.

16902 RHODES (JOHN). The Midland and Great Northern Joint Railway. 1982.

16903 ELLIS (CUTHBERT HAMILTON). The North British Railway. 1955. 2nd edn 1959.

16904 JONES (CHARLES MARK JENKIN). The North Eastern Railway: A Centenary Story. York. 1954.

16905 ALLEN (CECIL JOHN). The North Eastern Railway. 1964. 2nd edn 1974.

16906 TOMLINSON (WILLIAM WEAVER). Tomlinson's North Eastern Railway: Its Rise and Development. 1915. New edn Newton Abbot. 1967.

16907 HOOLE (KENNETH). North Eastern Branch Lines since 1925. 1978.

16908 —— North Eastern Railway Buses, Lorries and Autocars. Knaresborough. 1969.

16909 NOCK (OSWALD STEVENS). North Western, A Saga of the Premier Line of Great Britain, 1846–1922. 1968.

16910 MARSHALL (CHAPMAN FREDERICK DENDY). A History of the Southern Railway. 1936. 2nd edn by Roger Wakely Kidner. 2 vols 1963.

16911 MOODY (GEORGE THOMAS). Southern Electric 1909–1979: The History of the World's Largest Suburban Electrified System. 1957. 3rd edn 1960. 5th rev. edn 1979.

16912 ALLEN (CECIL JOHN). Salute to the Southern. 1974.

16913 WHITELEY (JOHN STUART) *and* MORRISON (GAVIN WEDDERBURN). The Southern Remembered. Oxf. 1980.

16914 KLAPPER (CHARLES FREDERICK). Sir Herbert Walker's Southern Railway. 1973.

16915 BODY (GEOFFREY). Railways of the Southern Region. Camb. 1984.

16916 ALLEN (GEOFFREY FREEMAN). The Southern since 1948. Shepperton. 1987.

16917 MARSDEN (COLIN C.). Southern Electric Multiple Units at Work 1948–1973. 1983.

16918 GOUGH (TERRY). The Southern in Kent and Sussex. Poole. 1984.

16919 ELLIS (CUTHBERT HAMILTON). The South Western Railway, its mechanical history and background, 1838–1932. 1956.

16920 HUDSON (GRAHAM S.). The Aberford Railway and the History of the Garforth Collieries. Newton Abbot. 1971.

16921 BLAKEY (MICHAEL) *and* COCKMAN (FREDERICK GEORGE). The Story of Bedfordshire Railways. Bedford. 1983.

16922 THOMAS (JOHN). The Callander and Oban Railway. Newton Abbot. 1966.

16923 ELLIS (PETER). The 150th Anniversary of the Opening of the Canterbury and Whitstable Railway: A Pioneer Line and the Area it Served. 1983.

16924 SPRINKS (NEIL). The Railways of Central and West Wales. Weston-super-Mare. 1987.

16925 HARMAN (REGINALD GORDON). The Conway Valley Railway—Branch Line Handbooks. Teddington. 1963.

16926 CLINKER (CHARLES RALPH). The Railways of Cornwall, 1809–1963. Dawlish. 1963.

16927 STENGELHOFEN (JOHN). Cornwall's Railway Heritage. Truro. 1988.

16928 MAGGS (COLIN GORDON). Railways of the Cotswolds. Cheltenham. 1981.

16929 LUCKING (JOHN HORACE). Dorset Railways. Wimborne. 1982.

16930 HOOLE (KENNETH). The East Coast Main Line since 1925. 1977.

16931 NEVE (ERIC). The East Coast from King's Cross. 1983.

16932 GOODE (CHARLES TONY). The Railways of East Yorkshire. Salisbury. 1981.

16933 WOOD (ROBERT GEORGE ERNEST). Railways in Essex [until 1923.]. Chelmsford. 1978.

16934 HIGHET (CAMPBELL). The Glasgow and South-Western Railway. Lingfield. 1965.

16935 HOUSEHOLD (HUMPHREY). Gloucestershire Railways in the 20th Century. Gloucester. 1984.

16936 WILSON (FRANK). Railways in Guernsey, with special reference to the German Steam Railways. St Peter Port. 1972.

16937 WILLIAMS (G. H.). Railways in Gwynedd. 1979.

16938 ROBERTSON (KEVIN) *and* OPITZ (LESLIE). Hampshire Railways Remembered. Newbury. 1988.

16939 HARMAN (REGINALD GORDON). The Hayling Island Railway. [Branch Line Handbooks.]. Teddington. 1963.

16940 NOCK (OSWALD STEVENS). The Highland Railway. 1965. Repr. 1973.

16941 VALLANCE (HUGH AYMER). The History of the Highland Railway. 1938. Rev. and extnd 1963.

16942 —— The Great North of Scotland Railway. Dawlish. 1965.

16943 COCKMAN (FREDERICK GEORGE). The Railways of Hertfordshire. Hertford. 1981.

16944 HARMAN (REGINALD GORDON). Railways in the Isle of Sheppey. [Branch Line Handbooks.]. Teddington. 1962.

16945 PAYNE (PETER). Isle of Wight Railways Remembered. Poole. 1984.

16946 DYER (B. R.). Kent Railways. St Ives. 1977.

16947 LYNE (R. M.). Military Railways in Kent. Rochester. 1983.

16948 OPITZ (LESLIE). Kent Railways Remembered. Newbury. 1988.

16949 JOY (DAVID). Railways in Lancashire. Clapham, N. Yorkshire. 1975. 2nd edn 1978.

16950 MARSHALL (JOHN). The Lancashire and Yorkshire Railway. 3 vols. Newton Abbot. 1969–72.

16951 MASON (ERIC). The Lancashire and Yorkshire Railway in the 20th Century. 2nd edn 1975.

16952 NOCK (OSWALD STEVENS). The Lancashire and Yorkshire Railway: A Concise History. 1969.

16953 BOTWELL (HAROLD D.). Over Shap to Carlisle: The Lancaster and Carlisle Railway in the 20th Century. 1983.

16954 SQUIRES (STUART E.). The Lost Railways of Lincolnshire. Ware. 1988.

16955 DENDY MARSHALL (CHAPMAN FREDERICK). Centenary History of the Liverpool and Manchester Railway. 1930.

16956 HOLT (GEOFFREY OGDEN). A Short History of the Liverpool and Manchester Railway. 2nd edn Caterham. 1965.

16957 BOX (CHARLES EDWARD). Liverpool Overhead Railway 1893–1956. 1959.

16958 GRAHAM (JOHN W.). Seventeen Stations to Dingle: The Liverpool Overhead Railway Remembered. Birkenhead. 1982.

16959 JACKSON (ALAN ARTHUR). London's Local Railways. Newton Abbot. 1978.

16960 COURSE (EDWIN ALFRED). London Railways. 1962.

16961 KLAPPER (CHARLES FREDERICK). Roads and Rails of London, 1900–1933. 1976.

16962 ATKINSON (FRANCIS GASTON BRYANT) *and* ADAMS (BRIAN WARREN). London's North Western Electric: A Jubilee History. St Alban's. 1962.

16963 LEE (CHARLES EDWARD). The Metropolitan District Railway. Lingfield. 1956.

16964 LASCELLES (THOMAS SPOONER). The City and South London Railway. Lingfield. 1955.

16965 ELLIS (CUTHBERT HAMILTON). The London, Brighton and South Coast Railway from 1839 to 1922. 1960.

16966 GRAY (ADRIAN). The London to Brighton Line 1841–1977. Blandford. 1977.

16967 BAKER (MICHAEL). London to Brighton: 150 Years of Britain's Premier Holiday Line. Wellingborough. 1989.

16968 GOULD (DAVID). The London and Birmingham Railway Fifty Years On. Newton Abbot. 1979.

16969 THORPE (DON). Railways of the Manchester Ship Canal. Poole. 1984.

16970 MORRIS (JOHN). The Railways of Pembrokeshire. Tenby. 1981.

16971 DANE (R. A.). The Railways of Peterborough. Peterborough. 1978.

16972 MORRISS (RICHARD K.). Railways of Shropshire: A Brief History. Shrewsbury. 1983.

16973 MADGE (ROBIN). Somerset Railways. Wimborne. 1984.

16974 SPRINKS (NEIL) *and* YOCKNEY (JOHN) *eds*. The Railways of South East Wales. Cardiff. 1985.

16975 JONES (PHILIP N.). 'Workmen's Trains in the South Wales Coalfield 1870–1926'. *Transport Hist.* 3 (1970), 21–35.

16976 SMITH (DAVID L.). The Little Railways of South West Scotland. Newton Abbot. 1969.

16977 OWEN-JONES (STUART). Railways of Wales. Cardiff. 1981.

16978 WILLIAMS (HERBERT). Railways in Wales. Swansea. 1981.

16979 KIDNER (ROGER WAKELY). The Waterloo-Southampton Line. Trowbridge. 1984.

16980 BAKER (MICHAEL). The Waterloo to Weymouth Line. Wellingborough. 1987.

16981 SIVITER (ROGER). Waverley: Portrait of a Famous Route. S/hampton. 1988.

16982 LESLIE (ROBERT HENDERSON). Steam on the Waverley Route. Truro. 1978.

16983 PEACOCK (BILL). Waverley Route Reflections. Hawick. 1983.

16984 LEE (CHARLES EDWARD). The Welsh Highland Railway. Dawlish. 1965.

16985 WELSH HIGHLAND LIGHT RAILWAY. More about the Welsh Highland Light Railway. Newton Abbot. 1966.

16986 THOMAS (JOHN). The West Highland Railway. Dawlish. 1965.

16987 HAIGH (ALAN) *and* JOY (DAVID). Yorkshire Railways: Including Cleveland and Humberside. Clapham, N. Yorkshire. 1980.

16988 BIDDLE (GORDON). Great Railway Stations of Britain: Their Architecture, Growth and Development. Newton Abbot. 1986.

16989 JOHNSTON (COLIN) *and* HUME (JOHN ROBERT). Glasgow Stations. Newton Abbot. 1979.

16990 BETJEMAN (JOHN). London's Historic Railway Stations. 1972. Repr. 1978.

16991 RESEARCH INSTITUTE FOR CONSUMER AFFAIRS. Essays and Enquiries—3—London Stations: A Users' Assessment. 1963.

16992 HOOLE (KENNETH). Railway Stations in the North East. Newton Abbot. 1985.

16993 BIDDLE (GORDON). Railway Stations in the North West. Clapham, N. Yorkshire. 1981.

16994 THROWER (W. RAYNER). Kings Cross in the Twenties. Tarrant Hinton. 1978.

16995 SMITH (DONALD JOHN). New Street Remembered: The Story of Birmingham's New Street Railway Station 1854–1967. Birm. 1984.

16996 SIMMONS (JACK). St. Pancras Station. 1968.

16997 HARRISON (DEREK). Salute to Snow Hill: The Rise and Fall of Birmingham's Snow Hill Railway Station, 1852–1977. Birm. 1978.

16998 MARSDEN (COLIN J.) *comp.* This is Waterloo. 1981.

16999 NOCK (OSWALD STEVENS). Underground Railways of the World. 1973.

17000 JACKSON (ALAN ARTHUR) *and* CROOME (DESMOND FELIX). Rails through the Clay: A History of London's Tube Railways. 1962.

17001 DAY (JOHN R.). The Story of the London Underground. 1963.

17002 DOUGLAS (HUGH). The Underground Story. 1963.

17003 GARBUTT (PAUL ELFORD). How the Underground Works. 1967.

17004 HOWSON (HENRY F.). London's Underground. 1967. 2nd edn 1981.

17005 SIMMONS (JACK). 'The Pattern of Tube Railways in London'. *J. Transport Hist.* 7 (1965/6), 234–44.

17006 GREEN (OLIVER). The London Underground: An Illustrated History. Shepperton. 1987.

17007 PENNICK (NIGEL). London's Early Tube Railways. Camb. 1988.

17008 LEE (CHARLES EDWARD). [London Transport Board.]. Sixty Years of the Bakerloo. 1966.

17009 —— The Bakerloo Line. 1974.

17010 —— Seventy Years of the Central. 1970.

17011 —— The Central Line. 1974.

17012 —— The Metropolitan Line. 1972. Repr. 1973.

17013 —— Sixty Years of the Northern. 1967.

17014 —— The Northern Line. 1973.

17015 —— Sixty Years of the Piccadilly. 1966.

17016 —— The Piccadilly Line. 1973.

17017 HORNE (M. A. C.). The Central Line. 1987.

17018 —— The Northern Line: A Short History. 1987.

17019 —— The Victoria Line: A Short History. 1988.

17020 INSTITUTION OF MECHANICAL ENGINEERS. (Environmental Engineering Group). The King's Cross Underground Fire. 1989.

17021 THOMSON (DAVID LAWRIE) *and* SINCLAIR (DAVID EDWIN). The Glasgow Subway. Glasgow. 1964.

17022 KELLY (PAUL J.) *and* WILSHER (M. J. D.). Glasgow Subway 1896–1977. 1979.

17023 GRAHAM (JOHN W.). The Line beneath the Liners: 100 Years of Mersey Railway Sights and Sounds. Birkenhead. 1983.

(c) Steam Railways, Railway Construction, Traction Engines

17024 DE GOLYER (EVERETT L.) *Jnr.* 'The Steam Locomotive: A Selective Bibliography'. In A Garland for Jake Zeitlin. *Ed.* J. M. Edelstein. Los Angeles, Calif. 1967.

17025 CLAY (JOHN F.) *ed.* Essays in Steam: An Anthology of Articles from the Journal of the Stephenson Locomotive Society. 1970.

17026 AHRONS (ERNEST L.). The British Steam Railway Locomotive 1825–1925. 1927.

17027 SNELL (JOHN BERNARD). Britain's Railways under Steam. 1965. 2nd rev. edn 1977.

17028 AWDREY (WILBERT) *and* COOK (CHRIS) *eds.* A Guide to the Steam Railways of Britain. 1979.

17029 HOLLINGSWORTH (JOHN BRIAN). The Illustrated Encyclopaedia of the World's Steam Passenger Locomotives from the 1820s to the Present Day. 1982.

17030 GARRATT (COLIN). The Last Days of British Steam Railways. Wellingborough. 1985.

17031 RANSOME-WALLACE (P.). The Last Steam Locomotives of British Railways. 1974.

17032 NOCK (OSWALD STEVENS). O. S. Nock's Encyclopaedia of British Steam Railways and Locomotives. Poole. 1983.

17033 —— Steam Locomotives: The Unfinished Story of Steam Locomotives and Steam Locomotive Men on the Railways of Great Britain. 1957.

17034 —— British Steam Railways. 1961.

17035 —— Railways at the Zenith of Steam, 1920–1940. 1970.

17036 —— The British Steam Railway Locomotive 1925–1965. 1966.

17037 —— The Last Years of British Railways Steam: Reflections of Ten Years after. Newton Abbot. 1978.

17038 —— The Golden Age of Steam: A Critical and Nostalgic Memory of the Last 20 Years before Grouping on the Railways of Great Britain. 1973.

17039 —— L.M.S. Steam. Newton Abbot. 1971.

17040 —— L.N.E.R. Steam. Newton Abbot. 1969. Repr. 1971.

17041 —— Southern Steam. Newton Abbot. 1966. Lond. 1972.

17042 REED (BRIAN). 150 Years of British Steam Locomotives. Newton Abbot. 1975.

17043 BRUTTON (E. D.). British Steam, 1948–1955. 1977.

17044 JONES (KEVIN P.). Steam Locomotive Development: An Analytical Guide to the Literature on British Steam Locomotive Development, 1923–1962. 1969.

17045 HEAVYSIDE (G. TOM). Steam Renaissance: The Decline and Rise of Steam. Newton Abbot. 1984.

17046 CASSERLEY (HENRY CECIL). Welsh Railways in the Heyday of Steam. Truro. 1979.

17047 STEPHEN (R. D.). Steam Supreme: Recollections of Scottish Railways in the 1920s. Truro. 1981.

17048 ROBERTSON (KEVIN). The Last Days of Steam around London. Gloucester. 1988.

17049 ADLEY (ROBERT). Covering My Tracks: Recollections of the Last Years of Steam. Wellingborough. 1988.

17050 BLOOM (ALAN). Steam Engines at Bessingham: The Story of a Live Steam Museum. 1970.

17051 COOPER (BASIL KNOWLAN). Electric Trains in Britain. 1979.

17052 HAUT (F. J. G.). The History of the Electric Locomotive. 1969.

17053 GLOVER (GRAHAM). British Locomotive Design, 1825–1960. 1967.

17054 NOCK (OSWALD STEVENS). British Locomotives at Work. 1947.

17055 —— British Steam Locomotives at Work. 1967.

17056 —— Steam Locomotive: A Retrospect of the Work of Eight Great Locomotive Engineers. 1955. Repr. 1958.

17057 —— British Locomotives of the 20th Century. 2 vols. Camb. 1983/4.

17058 —— The Railway Engineers. 1955.

17059 —— Rocket 150: A Century and a Half of Locomotive Trials. 1980.

17060 —— Two Miles a Minute: The Story behind the Conception and Operation of Britain's High Speed and Advanced Passenger Trains. Camb. 1980. Repr. 1983.

17061 FORD (ROGER) *and* PERREN (BRIAN). HSTs at Work. 1988.

17062 ALLEN (CECIL JOHN). Locomotive Practice and Performance in the 20th Century. Camb. 1949.

17063 BLOOM (ALAN) *and* WILLIAMS (DAVID CHRISTOPHER). Locomotives of British Railways. Norwich. 1980.

17064 BARNES (ROBIN). Locomotives that Never Were: Some 20th Century British Projects. 1985.

17065 LOWE (JAMES W.). Building Britain's Locomotives. Ashbourne. 1979.

17066 TATLOW (PETER). A History of Highland Locomotives. Oxf. 1979.

17067 COURT (JOHN HUBERT). North British Steam Locomotives Built 1857–1956 for Railways Overseas. 1978.

17068 —— North British Steam Locomotives Built 1833–1948 for Railways in Britain. Truro. 1979.

17069 CAMPBELL (ROY HUTCHESON). 'The North British Locomotive Company between the Wars'. *Business Hist.* 20 (1978), 201–34.

17070 DAY-LEWIS (SEAN). Bulleid: Last Giant of Steam. Lond./NY. 1964. 2nd rev. edn 1977.

17071 HARESNAPE (BRIAN) *comp.* Bulleid Locomotives. 1977. Rev. edn 1985.

17072 ROGERS (HUGH CUTHBERT BASSET). Bulleid Pacifics at Work. 1980.

17073 BULLEID (HENRY ANTHONY VAUGHAN). Master Builders of Steam. 1963. 2nd edn 1983.

17074 ELLIS (CUTHBERT HAMILTON). Twenty Locomotive Men. 1958.

17075 NOCK (OSWALD STEVENS). The Locomotives of Sir Nigel Gresley. 1945.

17076 —— The Locomotives of R.E.L. Maunsell, 1911–1937. Bristol. 1954.

17077 WARREN (JAMES G. H.). A Century of Locomotive Building by Robert Stephenson & Co. 1823–1923. Newcastle upon Tyne. 1931.

17078 ROLT (LIONEL THOMAS CASWELL). A Hunslet Hundred: One Hundred Years of Locomotive Building by the Hunslet Engine Company. Dawlish. 1964.

17079 CHARLES ROBERTS & COMPANY. Charles Roberts & Company Limited 1836–1951. Wakefield. 1956.

17080 WILSON (ROBERT BURDETT). Sir Daniel Gooch: Memoirs and Diary. Newton Abbot. 1972.

17081 HARESNAPE (BRIAN). Railway Design since 1830. [In 2 vols. the second of which covers 1914–1969.]. 1969.

17082 ALLEN (CECIL JOHN). Modern Railways: Their Engineering, Equipment and Operation. 1959.

17083 JOHNSON (JOHN) *and* LONG (ROBERT A.). British Railways Engineering, 1948–1980. 1981.

17084 LARKIN (EDGAR J.) *and* LARKIN (JOHN G.). The Railway Workshops of Britain, 1823–1985. 1986.

17085 COOK (PAULINE LESLEY). Railway Workings: The Problem of Contraction. Camb. 1964.

17086 WEBB (BRIAN). The British Internal Combustion Locomotive 1894–1940. Newton Abbot. 1973.

17087 CLARK (RONALD H.). The Development of the English Traction Engine. Norwich. 1960.

17088 KIDNER (ROGER WAKELY). A Short History of Mechanical Traction and Travel. [In 6 parts, pts. 5 and 6 concern the 20th century.]. 1946, 1947.

17089 WILKES (PETER). An Illustrated History of Traction Engines. Bourne End. 1979.

17090 MILLER (DENIS NEVILLE). A Source Book for Traction Engines. 1983.

17091 BENNETT (HAROLD). Traction Engines. Aylesbury. 1985. 2nd edn 1988.

17092 MORLAND (ANDREW). Traction Engines. 1988.

17093 HAINING (PETER). The Traction Engine Companion. 1983.

17094 WHITEHEAD (PETER ARTHUR). Wallis and Steevens. Farnham. 1983.

17095 NOCK (OSWALD STEVENS). British Railway Signalling: A Survey of Fifty Years' Progress. 1969.

17096 ESSERY (R. J.), ROWLAND (D. P.), *and* STEEL (W. D.). British Goods Wagons from 1887 to the Present Day. Newton Abbot. 1970.

17097 LARKIN (EDGAR J.) *and* LARKIN (JOHN G.). The Railway Workshops of Britain, 1823–1986. 1988.

5. ROADS AND ROAD VEHICLES

(a) Roads

17098 HINDLEY (GEORGE). A History of Roads. 1971.

17099 GREGORY (JOHN WALTER). The Story of the Road from the Beginning to the Present Day. 1931. 2nd rev. edn 1938, by C. J. Gregory.

17100 HARTMANN (CYRIL HUGHES). The Story of the Roads. 1927.

17101 MAYBURY (*Sir* HENRY P.). '[Roads]: A Review and a Forecast'. *Motor Traction* (26 Apr. 1920), 413–14.

17102 JENISON (MADGE). Roads. 1949.

17103 SCHIELDROP (EDGAR BONSAK). The Highway. 1939.

17104 JEFFREYS (REES). The King's Highway. 1949.

17105 DAY (ALAN CHARLES LYNN). Roads. 1963.

17106 BIRT (DAVID). Roads. 1978.

17107 TAYLOR (CHRISTOPHER). Roads and Tracks of Britain. 1979.

17108 ADDISON (*Sir* WILLIAM). The Old Roads of England. 1980.

17109 CHARLESWORTH (GEORGE E.). A History of British Motorways. 1984.

17110 DRAKE (JAMES) *et al.* Motorways. 1969.

17111 BEESLEY (M. E.) *and* REYNOLDS (D. J.). The London-Birmingham Motorway. 1960.

17112 WILLIAMS (THOMAS EIFION HOPKINS). Motorways in Urban Areas. Newcastle upon Tyne. 1965.

17113 LLEWELYN-DAVIES & PARTNERS. Motorways in an Urban Environment. 1971.

17114 SAMUELSON (G. D.). Motorways and Industry: The West Midland Conurbation. 1968.

17115 DAVIS (JOYCE S.) *ed.* Motorways in Britain: Today and Tomorrow. 1971.

17116 TYME (JOHN). Motorways Versus Democracy: Public Inquiries into Road Proposals and their Political Significance. 1978.

17117 INSTITUTION OF CIVIL ENGINEERS. Landscaping of Motorways. 1962.

17118 —— Twenty Years of British Motorways: Proceedings of a Conference. 1980.

17119 BRITISH ROAD FEDERATION. The Motorways. [Progress Reports Series.]. 1966.

17120 —— Finance and Roads. 1963.

17121 ELLIOTT (DEREK WILLIAM) *and* STREET (HARRY). Road Accidents. 1968.

17122 AUSTIN (MICHAEL). Accident Blackspot: A Critical Study of Road Safety Policy and Practice. Harmondsworth. 1966.

17123 WILLETT (TERENCE CHARLES). The Motoring Offender: A Study of Serious Motoring Offenders and Offences in an English Police District. 1962.

17124 WILLIAMS (THOMAS EIFION HOPKINS) *ed.* Urban Survival and Traffic: The Proceedings of a Symposium. 1962.

17125 RITTER (PAUL). Planning for Man and Motor. 1964.

17126 BRITISH ROAD FEDERATION AND TOWN PLANNING INSTITUTE. People and Cities: Report of the 1963 London Conference. 1964.

17127 TETLOW (THOMAS) *and* GOSS (ANTHONY). Homes, Towns and Traffic. 1965.

17128 REYNOLDS (D. J.). Economics, Town Planning and Traffic. 1966.

17129 WILLIAMS (J. T.) *ed.* The Urban Road in Relation to the Conservation and Renewal of the Environment. [Report by a Professional Institutions Council for Conservation Working Party.]. 1974.

17130 U.K. URBAN MOTORWAYS COMMITTEE. New Roads in Towns: Report of the Urban Motorways Committee to the Secretary of State for the Environment. 1972.

17131 PRESCOTT-CLARKE (PATRICIA). Public Consultation and Participation in Road Planning. 1975.

17132 HART (DOUGLAS ALLEN). Strategic Planning in London: The Rise and Fall of the Primary Road Network. Oxf. 1976.

17133 SCOTTISH ASSOCIATION FOR PUBLIC TRANSPORT. A Better Glasgow: A Statement. Glasgow. 1974.

17134 WATKINS (L. H.). Environmental Impact of Roads and Traffic. 1981.

17135 ASSOCIATION OF COUNTY COUNCILS. Highway Maintenance: A Code of Good Practice. 1989.

17136 U.K. MINISTRY OF TRANSPORT. Roads in Urban Areas. 1966.

17137 —— Better Use of Town Roads: The Report. 1967.

17138 —— Road Pricing: The Economic and Technical Possibilities of a Panel. 1964.

17139 —— Highway Statistics. [Pub. annually.] 1963.

17140 —— The Transport Needs of Great Britain in the Next Twenty Years: Report of a Group under the Chairmanship of Sir Robert Hall. 1963.

17141 —— Interim Report on the 70 m.p.h. Speed Limit Trial. 1966.

17142 —— Report on the 70 m.p.h. Speed Limit Trial. 1967.

17143 STARKIE (DAVID NICHOLAS MARTIN). Traffic and Industry: A Study of Traffic Generation and Spatial Interaction. 1967.

17144 ROAD RESEARCH LABORATORY. Sample Survey of the Roads and Traffic of Great Britain. [Road Research Technical Papers.]. 1962.

17145 —— Fifty Point Traffic Census 1956/57. [Pub. annually.]. Crowthorne. 1958.

17146 —— Fifty Point Traffic Census: The First Five Years. 1962.

17147 STEWART (JOHN MURRAY WILSON). A Pricing System for Roads. Edin. 1965.

17148 ROTH (GABRIEL JOSEPH). Paying for Roads: The Economics of Traffic Congestion. Harmondsworth. 1967.

17149 —— A Self-financing Road System. 1966.

17150 SMEED (RUBEN JACOB). The Traffic Problems in Towns. Manch. 1961.

17151 STREET (ANDREW). Challenge and Opportunity: The Case for a More Realistic Level of Highway and Infrastructure and Investment. 1984.

17152 MUNT (PETER WILLIAM). Traffic Characteristics of Greater London's Roads. 1979.

17153 COXON (R. T.). Roads and Rails of Birmingham, 1900–1939. 1979.

17154 KLAPPER (CHARLES FREDERICK). Roads and Rails of London 1900–1933. 1976.

17155 GLENN (D. FEREDAY). Roads, Rails and Ferries of the Solent Area, 1919–1969. 1980.

17156 JONES (AUSTIN EDWIN). Roads and Rails of West Yorkshire, 1890–1950. 1984.

17157 JOYCE (JAMES). Roads and Rails of Manchester, 1900–1950. 1983.

17158 —— Roads, Rails and Ferries of Liverpool, 1900–1950. 1983.

17159 —— Roads and Rails of Tyne and Wear, 1900–1980. 1985.

17160 WRIGHT (GEOFFREY NORMAN). Roads and Trackways of the Yorkshire Dales. Ashbourne. 1985.

17161 CRUMP (W. B.). Huddersfield Highways Down the Ages. Huddersfield. 1988.

17162 WATT (ARCHIBALD). Highways and Byways around Stonehaven. Aberdeen. 1976. 3rd edn 1978.

(b) Bicycles

17163 HARRISON (A. E.). 'The Competitiveness of the British Cycle Industry'. *Econ. Hist. Rev.* 2nd ser. 22 (1969), 287–303.

17164 WOODFORDE (JOHN). The Story of the Bicycle. 1970.

17165 McGURN (JAMES). On Your Bicycle: An Illustrated History of Cycling. 1987.

17166 CLAYTON (NICK). Early Bicycles. Princes Risborough. 1986.

17167 CAUNTER (CYRIL FRANCIS). The History and Development of Cycles. 1955.

17168 CROWLEY (TERENCE ELDON). Discovering Old Bicycles. 1973. 2nd edn 1978.

17169 JONES (IAN K.). The Safety Bicycle. Princes Risborough. 1986.

17170 WATSON (RODERICK) *and* GRAY (MARTIN). The Penguin Book of the Bicycle. Harmondsworth. 1978.

17171 HILLMAN (ELLIS M.). Bicycles: Boon or Menace? 1978.

17172 MATHEW (DON). The Bike is Back: A Bicycle Policy for Britain. 1980. [Friends of the Earth.].

17173 SMITH (COLIN). Back to the Good Old Bike. Hornchurch. 1982.

17174 CHAMP (ROBERT GORDON). The Illustrated History of Sunbeam Bicycles and Motorcycles. Haynes. 1989.

(c) Motorcycles

17175 MILLER (DENIS NEVILLE) *comp.* A Source Book of Motorcycles. 1977.

17176 CAUNTER (CYRIL FRANCIS). The History and Development of Motorcycles. 1955. 2nd edn 1970.

17177 TRAGATSCH (ERWIN) *ed.* The Illustrated Encyclopaedia of Motorcycles. 1977. 2nd edn 1983.

17178 AYTON (CYRIL J.) *et al.* The History of Motor Cycling. 1979.

17179 —— Guide to Pre-War British Motorcycles. Feltham. 1985.

17180 POSTHUMUS (CYRIL). The Motorcycle Story. 1979.

17181 BACON (ROY HUNT). Military Motor Cycles of World War Two: All Makes from Europe, Russia, Japan and the U.S.A., 1939 to 1945. 1985.

17182 WILSON (STEVE). British Motorcycles since 1950. Camb. 1982.

17183 WARD (IAN) *and* CADDELL (LAURIE) *eds.* Great British Bikes. 1984.

17184 SMITH (BARBARA M. D.). A History of the British Motorcycle Industry 1945–1975. Birm. 1981.

17185 HOLLIDAY (BOB). The Norton Story. 1972. 2nd edn Camb. 1976. Rev. 1981.

17186 —— The Unapproachable Norton. 1979.

17187 REYNOLDS (JIM). A Pictorial History of Norton Motor Cycles. Feltham. 1985.

17188 LOUIS (HARRY) *and* CURRIE (BOB). The Story of Triumph Motor Cycles. Camb. 1975. 3rd edn 1981.

17189 DAVIES (IVOR). A Pictorial History of Triumph Motor Cycles. Feltham. 1985.

17190 NELSON (JOHN RAYMOND). Bonnie: The Development History of the Triumph Bonneville. Yeovil. 1979.

17191 NEELD (PETER). 'Wolverhampton Motorcycles: The Growth and Decline of an Industry'. *Transport Hist.* 9 (1978), 52–9.

17192 JONES (BARRY M.). The Story of Panther Motorcycles. Camb. 1983.

17193 HARTLEY (PETER). The Story of Rudge Motorcycles. Wellingborough. 1985.

17194 CLARK (RONALD HARRY). Brough Superior: The Rolls-Royce of Motorcycles. Norwich. 1974. 3rd rev. edn Yeovil. 1984.

17195 MORLEY (DON). Classic [Post-war] British Scramblers. 1986.

17196 CURRIE (BOB). Classic Competition Motorcycles from the National Motorcycle Museum. Wellingborough. 1987.

17197 —— Great British Motorcycles of the 60s. 1981.

17198 —— Classic British Motor Cycles: The Final Years. 1984.

17199 SCOTT (CHRISTOPHER) *and* JACKSON (STUART). Accidents to Young Motorcyclists: A Statistical Investigation. 1960.

17200 WEBSTER (MICHAEL). Motor Scooters. Princes Risborough. 1986.

(d) Trams and Tramways

17201 KLAPPER (CHARLES FREDERICK). The Golden Age of Tramways. 1961. 2nd edn 1978.

17202 WILSON (FRANK). The British Tram. 1961.

17203 MCKAY (JOHN P.). Tramways and Trolleys: The Rise of Urban Mass Transport in Europe. Princeton, N.J. 1976.

17204 JOYCE (JAMES) *comp.* The British Tramways Scene. 1961.

17205 —— Tramway Heyday. 1964.

17206 —— Tramways of the World. 1965.

17207 —— Tramway Twilight: The Story of Britain's Tramways from 1945 to 1962. 1962.

17208 THOMPSON (JULIAN). British Trams in Camera. 1978.

17209 JOHNSON (PETER). British Trams and Tramways in the 1980s. Shepperton. 1985.

17210 TURNER (KEITH). Old Trams. Aylesbury. 1985.

17211 SLEEMAN (JOHN F.). 'The British Tramway Industry: The Growth and Decline of a Public Utility'. *Manch. Sch. Econ. Soc. Studs* 10 (1939), 157–74.

17212 MAGGS (COLIN G.). Bath Tramways. Lingfield. 1971.

17213 MAYOU (ARCHIE) *et al.* Birmingham Corporation Trams and Trolley Buses. Glossop. 1982.

17214 JOHNSON (PETER). Trams in Blackpool. Leicester. 1986.

17215 HIGGS (PHILIP). Blackpool's Trams: 'As Popular as the Tower'. Bolton. 1984.

17216 MAUND (THOMAS BRUCE). The Tramways of Birkenhead and Wallasey. 1987.

17217 RANSOM (W. P.). The Story of Bournemouth Corporation Transport, Part I—The Trams. Bournemouth. 1982.

17218 ELLIOTT (ALF G.). A Portrait of the Brighton Trams, 1901–1939. Portslade. 1979.

17219 PENNICK (NIGEL). Trams in Cambridgeshire. Camb. 1983.

17220 MARSDEN (BARRY MICHAEL). Chesterfield Trams and Trolleybuses. Barnsley. 1984.

17221 BADDELEY (GEOFFREY E.) *et al.* The Tramways of Croydon. 1960.

17222 BROTCHIE (ALAN WALTER) *and* GRIEVES (R. L.). Dumbarton's Trams and Buses. Dundee. 1986.

17223 STEVENSON (JAMES LAING). The Last Tram, Edinburgh. Edin. 1986.

17224 HUNTER (D. L. G.). 'The Edinburgh Cable Tramways'. *J. Transport. Hist.* 1 (1953/4), 170–84.

17225 OAKLEY (CHARLES ALLEN). The Last Tram. [Written for Glasgow Corporation Transport Department at the closing of the tramways system, 4th Sept. 1962]. Glasgow. 1962.

17226 CORMACK (IAN LESLIE). Glasgow Tramways 1872–1962: Ninety Glorious Years. 1962.

17227 —— Green Goddesses go East: A Brief History of the ex-Liverpool Trams in Glasgow 1933–1960. 1961.

17228 BROOK (ROY). The Tramways of Huddersfield: A History of Huddersfield Corporation Tramways, 1883–1940. Huddersfield. 1960.

17229 YOUNG (ANDREW DAVID). One Hundred Years of Leeds Tramways. Leeds. 1979.

17230 DICKINSON (D. G.) and LANGLEY (C. J.). 'Twopence to the Terminus?: A Study of Tram and Bus Fares in Leeds during the Inter-War Period'. *J. Transport. Hist.* 3rd ser. 7 (1986/7), 45–60.

17231 WILSON (BRIAN GEOFFREY). London United Tramways: A History, 1884–1933. 1971.

17232 DAY (JOHN ROBERT). London's Trams and Trolley Buses. 1977. 2nd edn 1979.

17233 JOYCE (JAMES). 'Operation Tramway': The End of London's Trams, 1950–1952. 1987.

17234 THOMAS (DAVID BERNARD). Trams and Buses of Newport, 1845 to 1981. Risca. 1982.

17235 DUNBAR (CHARLES S.). Tramways in Wandsworth and Battersea. 1971.

17236 JONES (AUSTIN EDWIN). Trams and Buses of West Yorkshire. 1985.

17237 SIMPSON (FRANK D.). The Wolverton and Stony Stratford Steam Trams. Bromley Common. 1982.

(e) Trolley Buses

17238 OWEN (NICHOLAS). The History of the British Trolley Bus. Newton Abbot. 1974.

17239 BILBE (GRAHAM) et al eds. 100 Years of Trolleybuses: A Pictorial Review, 1882–1982. Strood. 1982.

17240 JOYCE (JAMES). Trolleybus Trails: A Survey of British Trolleybus Systems. 1964.

17241 KAYE (DAVID). Old Trolleybuses. Princes Risborough. 1988.

17242 RANSOM (W. P.). The Story of Bournemouth Corporation Transport, Part 2—Trolleybus Era. Bournemouth. 1982.

17243 BREARLEY (HAROLD). The Bradford Trolley Bus System: Being the History of Britain's First and Last Trolley Buses. Huddersfield. 1975.

17244 UDEN (MICHAEL JOHN) and KING (J. S.). Sixty Years of Bradford Trolley Buses. Guildford. 1971.

17245 FIELDSEND (ANDREW). Fifty Years of Cleethorpes Trolley Buses 1937–1987. Cleethorpes. 1987.

17246 DEANS (BRIAN TEMPLETON). A Short History of Glasgow's Trolley Buses, 1949–1967. Glasgow. 1977.

17247 BROOK (ROY). The Trolleybuses of Huddersfield. Rochdale. 1976.

17248 DAY (JOHN ROBERT). London's Trams and Trolley Buses. 1977. New edn 1979.

17249 CANNEAUX (TOM P.) and HANSON (NOEL H.). The Trolley Buses of Newcastle upon Tyne 1935–1966. Newcastle upon Tyne. 1985.

17250 BURROWS (G.). The Trolley Buses of South Shields 1936–1964. Strood. 1977.

(f) Buses and Coaches

17251 LEE (CHARLES EDWARD). 'Sources of Bus History'. *J. Transport Hist.* 2 (1955/6), 152–7.

17252 NEWMAN (A. G.). 'Bus Services and Local History'. *Local Historian* 13 (1979), 280–295.

17253 BRUCE (JAMES GRAEME). A Source Book of Buses. 1981.

17254 JOYCE (JAMES). The Story of Passenger Transport in Britain. 1967.

17255 BOOTH (GAVIN). The British Motor Bus: An Illustrated History. 1977.

17256 —— The British Bus Today and Tomorrow. 1983.

17257 HIBBS (JOHN) ed. The Omnibus: Readings in the History of Road Passenger Transport. Newton Abbot. 1971.

17258 —— The History of British Bus Services. 1968. 2nd rev. edn 1989.

17259 —— The Country Bus. Newton Abbot. 1986.

17260 —— 'Road Passenger Transport in Ulster and its Relationship with the Railways'. *Transport Hist.* 3 (1970), 121–40.

17261 —— 'The London Independent Bus Operators 1922–1934'. *Transport Hist.* 5 (1972), 274–83.

17262 —— Regulation: An International Study of Bus and Coach Licensing. Cardiff. 1985.

17263 KLAPPER (CHARLES FREDERICK). Buses and Trams. 1949.

17264 —— The Golden Age of Buses. 1978.

17265 LEE (CHARLES EDWARD). The Early Motor Bus. 1962. [London Transport Commission.].

17266 KAYE (DAVID). The British Bus Scene in the 1930s. 1981.

17267 MILLAR (ALAN). British Buses of the 1930s. Camb. 1982.

17268 CREIGHTON (JOHN). British Buses since 1945. Poole. 1983.

17269 GILHAM (JOHN C.). Buses and Coaches 1945–1965. 1976.

17270 TOWNSIN (ALFRED ALAN). The British Bus Story, 1946–1950: A Golden Age. Glossop. 1983.

17271 —— Buses and Trams. 1984.

17272 JOYCE (JAMES). British Buses in the 1950s. 1984.

17273 ROWE (LYNDON F.). Municipal Buses of the 1960s. Truro. 1980.

17274 JAMES (ALAN). Buses and Coaches. 1971.

17275 KAYE (DAVID). Old Buses. Princes Risborough. 1982.

17276 U.K. MINISTRY OF TRANSPORT. Rural Bus Services: Report of Local Enquiries. 1965.

17277 COLLINS (JUDITH) comp. Buses in Urban Areas 1970–1976. 1976.

17278 BOOTH (GAVIN). The Classic Buses. 1980.

17279 —— Buses. Hove. 1982.

17280 THOMAS (ALAN). Buses. 1982.

17281 DODGSON (JOHN SEATON) *and* TOPHAM (T.). Bus Deregulation and Privatisation: An International Perspective. Aldershot. 1988.

See also Fleetbooks Series, ed. Alan M. Witton.

17282 WITTON (ALAN M.) *ed.* Buses of Greater Manchester. Manch. 1973. 3rd edn 1977. 6th edn 1983. [No.1 in series.].

17283 WITTON (ALAN M.) *and* DENHAM (J. R.) *eds.* Buses of South and East Yorkshire. Manch. 1974. 4th edn 1981 by D. Akrigg *et al.* Under new title, 'Buses of South Yorkshire, Humberside and Lincolnshire'. 5th edn 1984. [No. 2.].

17284 —— *Eds.* Buses of West Yorkshire. Manch. 1974. 5th edn 1984. [No. 3.].

17285 WITTON (ALAN M.) *ed.* Buses of Lancashire and Cumbria. Manch. 1975. 4th edn 1982. [No. 4.].

17286 WITTON (ALAN M.) *and* TELFER (ROBERT LACHLAN) *eds.* Buses of Mersey, North Wales and the Isle of Man. Manch. 1975. 5th edn 1984. [No. 5.].

17287 WITTON (ALAN M.) *and* HEATHCOTE (R.) *eds.* Buses of the West Midlands. Manch. 1975. 4th edn 1982. [No. 6.].

17288 WITTON (ALAN M.) *ed.* Buses of the East Midlands. Manch. 1976. 4th edn 1983. [No. 7.].

17289 —— *Ed.* Buses of North East England. Manch. 1976. 4th edn 1983. [No. 8.].

17290 —— Buses of South Wales. Manch. 1976. 3rd edn 1982. [No. 9.].

17291 —— Buses of Eastern England. Manch. 1977. 3rd edn 1982. [No. 10.].

17292 WITTON (ALAN M.) *and* TELFER (ROBERT LACHLAN) *eds.* Buses of South East England. Manch. 1977. 3rd edn 1984. [No. 11.].

17293 WITTON (ALAN M.) *ed.* Buses of South West England and the Channel Islands. Manch. 1977. 4th edn 1983. [No. 12.].

17294 MILLAR (ALAN) *ed.* Buses of Western Scotland. Manch. 1977. 2nd edn by David G. Wilson. 1980. [No. 13.].

17295 —— *Ed.* Buses of Eastern Scotland. Manch. 1977. 2nd rev. edn 1981. [No. 14.].

17296 WITTON (ALAN M.) *and* TELFER (ROBERT LACHLAN) *eds.* Buses of Inner London. Manch. 1978. 3rd edn 1982. [No. 15.].

17297 WITTON (ALAN M.) *ed.* Buses of Outer London. Manch. 1979. 3rd edn 1986. [No. 16.].

17298 —— Buses of South Central London. Manch. 1984. [No. 17.].

17299 KEELEY (MALCOLM) *et al.* Birmingham City Transport: A History of its Buses and Trolleybuses. Glossop. 1977.

17300 FERGUSSON (R. P.) *et al.* The First in the Kingdom: 1881–1981: A History of Buses and Trams in Blackburn and Darwen. Blackburn. 1981.

17301 DOUGILL (DAVID). Blackpool's Buses. Glossop. 1982.

17302 TURNER (TOM) *comp.* Fifty Years of Birkenhead Buses. Wallasey. 1978.

17303 SEAL (MARK). Cambridge Buses. Camb. 1978.

17304 GRAY (PAUL). Coventry Corporation Transport. Birm. 1978.

17305 BLACKER (KEN C.) *et al.* London's Buses. 1977.

17306 GRAY (JOHN ANTHONY) *comp.* London's Country Buses. 1980.

17307 CURTIS (COLIN HARTLEY). Buses of London: An Illustrated Review of every London Bus Type Purchased since 1908. 1977.

17308 ROBBINS (GORDON JUXON) *and* THOMAS (ALAN). Kaleidoscope of London Buses between the Wars. 1980.

17309 McCALL (ALBERT WILLIAM). London in 1947: The Fare and Ticket System of London Transport's Buses, Trams, Trolleybuses and Coaches. Luton. 1974.

17310 LONDON TRANSPORT BOARD. Reshaping London's Bus Services. 1966.

17311 BLAKE (JIM) *and* TURNER (BARRY) *comp.* At London's Service: Fifty Years of London Transport Road Services. 1983.

17312 GROVES (F. P.). Nottingham City Transport. Glossop. 1978.

17313 WARN (CHRISTOPHER ROBERT). Buses in Northumberland and Durham pt.1—1900–1930. Newcastle upon Tyne. 1978.

17314 HUNTER (DAVID LINDSAY GEORGE). Scottish Buses before 1929. Leeds. 1973. 2nd edn Sheffield. 1978.

17315 MacFARLANE-WATT (A. K.). Southampton City Transport: A History of its Motor Bus Services. Glossop. 1977.

17316 TAYLOR (CHRIS) *and* WHITTON (ALAN M.). Welsh Bus Handbook. 1987.

17317 MACK (ROBERT FREDERICK). An Album of West Yorkshire P.T.E. Buses. Sheffield. 1980.

17318 BROWN (STUART). Alexander's Buses. 1984.

17319 W. ALEXANDER & SONS LTD. W. Alexander & Sons Ltd. Part 3—1938 to 1961. 1981.

17320 STANIER (D. J.). Blue Bus Services: An Illustrated History of the well-known Derbyshire Bus Company. Ilkeston. 1979.

17321 WARREN (KENNETH). Fifty Years of the Green Line. 1980.

17322 —— The Motor Bus in London Country. 1984.

17323 McCALL (ALBERT WILLIAM). Green Line: The History of London's Country Bus Services. 1980.

17324 CLARK (RICHARD). In Shades of Green: The Story of the Country Routemasters. 1980.

17325 ALDERSON (ROY CLAUDE). A History of the Midland Red. Newton Abbot. 1984.

17326 ANDERSON *and* FRANKIS (G. G. A.). A History of the Royal Blue Express Coach Services. Newton Abbot 1970. 2nd rev. edn 1985.

17327 —— A History of the Western National. Newton Abbot. 1979.

17328 HUNTER (DAVID LINDSAY GEORGE). From S.M.T. [Scottish Motor Traction Company] to Eastern Scottish: An 80th Anniversary Story. Edin. 1987.

17329 WARWICK (ROGER M.). An Illustrated History of United Counties Omnibus Company Ltd. 2 pts. Northampton. 1978.

17330 JENKINSON (KEITH A.). Northern Rose: The History of West Yorkshire Road Car Co. Ltd. Bradford. 1987.

17331 COCKSHOTT (JOHN) *and* WALKER (M.) *comp.* The West Yorkshire Road Car Company Ltd. Part Two: 1935 to 1975. 1975.

(g) Motor Cars, the Motor Car Industry, other Road Vehicles

(i) Motor Cars

17332 HOUGHTON (GRAHAM). A History of the Motor Car. 1987.

17333 DUNCAN (HERBERT O.). The World on Wheels. Paris. 1926.

17334 SUMNER (PHILIP L.). Motor Cars up to 1930. 1969.

17335 OLIVER (GEORGE A.). Early Motor Cars: 1904–1915. 1959.

17336 —— Early Motor Cars: The Vintage Years 1919–1930. 1961.

17337 —— Early Motor Cars: 1925–1939: English Sports Cars. 1967.

17338 DU CROS (ARTHUR). Wheels of Fortune. 1938.

17339 ROLT (LIONEL THOMAS CASWELL). Horseless Carriage: The Motor Car in England. 1950.

17340 BUCHANAN (COLIN DOUGLAS). Mixed Blessings: The Motor Car in Britain. 1958.

17341 JONES (M. W.). One Hundred Years of Motoring: An R.A.C. Social History of the Car. Croydon. 1981.

17342 POSTHUMUS (CYRIL). Motor Cars. Hove. 1982.

17343 —— Classic Sports Cars. 1980.

17344 DUSSEK (IAN). Motor Cars of the 1930s. Aylesbury. 1989.

17345 —— Sports Cars 1910–1960. 1987.

17346 SPICER (SIMON J. L.). The Motor Cars We Owned: Austin, Ford, Morris, Vauxhall, 1920–1930. Hornchurch. 1981.

17347 TOWNROE (PETER MICHAEL) *ed.* The Social and Political Consequences of the Motor Car. Newton Abbot. 1974.

17348 PLOWDEN (WILLIAM). The Motor Car and Politics, 1896–1970. 1971. Harmondsworth. 1973.

17349 GEORGIANO (GEORGE NICOLAS) *ed.* The Complete Encyclopaedia of Motor Cars 1885–1965. 1969. 2nd edn 1973.

17350 —— A Source Book of Veteran Cars. 1974.

17351 —— A Source Book of Vintage and Post-Vintage Cars. 1974.

17352 —— A History of Sports Cars. 1970. 2nd edn 1974.

17353 —— *Ed.* A Source Book of Racing and Sports Cars. 1973.

17354 —— *Ed.* The Encyclopaedia of Motor Sport. 1971.

17355 HUTTON-STOTT (FRANCIS) *and* SHAPLAND (D. G.) *comps.* Guide to Veteran Cars. 1963. 2nd rev. edn 1978.

17356 WARE (MICHAEL E.). Veteran Motor Cars. Aylesbury. 1983.

17357 WOOD (JONATHAN). Classic Motor Cars. Princes Risborough. 1985.

17358 BODDY (BILL). Vintage Motor Cars. Princes Risborough. 1985.

17359 DYMOCK (ERIC). Postwar Sports Cars: The Modern Classics. 1981.

17360 HUDSON (BRUCE ANGUS). Post-War British Thoroughbreds and Specialist Cars. Yeovil. 1981.

17361 WARD (IAN). The Sports Car. Poole. 1982.

17362 CAMPBELL (COLIN). The Sports Car: Its Design and Performance. 1954. 4th edn 1978.

17363 NYE (DOUG). Sports Cars. 1980.

17364 COURT (WILLIAM). Poverty and Glory: The History of Grand Prix Motor Racing. Wellingborough. 1988.

17365 CAUNTER (CYRIL F.). The Light Car: A Technical History of Cars with Engines less than 1600 c.c. Capacity. 1970.

17366 HOUGH (RICHARD ALEXANDER) *and* FROSTICK (MICHAEL). A History of the World's High Performance Cars. 1967.

17367 MONTAGU OF BEAULIEU (EDWARD J. B.) *and* BIRD (ANTHONY). Steam Cars 1770–1970. 1971.

17368 CHURCH (ROY). 'Myths, Men and Motor Cars: A Review Article'. *J. Transport Hist.* n.s. 4 (1977), 102–12.

17369 SILBERSTON (A.). 'Hire Purchase Controls and the Demand for Cars'. *Econ. J.* 73 (1963), 32–53.

17370 TANNER (JOHN CURNON). Car Ownership Trends and Forecasts. Crowthorne. 1977.

17371 BANNISTER (DAVID). Car Availability and Usage: A Modal Split Model Based on these Concepts. Reading. 1977.

17372 MOGRIDGE (MARTIN H.) *and* ELDRIDGE (DEREK A.). Car Ownership in London. 1970.

17373 GRAY (PERCY G.). Private Motoring in England and Wales: Report [dealing] with a Quarterly Series of Surveys carried out for the Ministry of Transport from October 1961 to January 1964. 1969.

17374 BEESLEY (M. E.) *and* KAIN (J. F.). 'Urban Form, Car Ownership and Public Policy: An Appraisal of "Traffic in Towns"'. *Urban Studs* 1 (1964), 174–203.

17375 INSTITUTION OF MUNICIPAL ENGINEERS. The Problem of Car Parking: A One Day Convention. 1960.

17376 U.K. MINISTRY OF HOUSING AND LOCAL GOVERNMENT. Parking in Town Centres. 1965.

17377 U.K. MINISTRY OF TRANSPORT. Parking—The Next Stage: A New Look . . . at London's Parking Problem. 1963.

17378 ROADS CAMPAIGN COUNCIL. Parking Matters No. 1—A Community Problem. 1962.

17379 BRITISH ROAD FEDERATION. Car Parking: A National Survey, Nov. 1961. 1961.

17380 —— Car Parking: A National Survey, May 1964. 1964.

17381 —— Car Parking. 1968.

17382 THOMSON (J. MICHAEL). Some Characteristics of Motorists in Central London: Results of a Parking Survey in April 1966. 1968.

17383 U.K. LONDON G.L.C. PARKING WORKING PARTY. Car Parking Supply and Demand—Central Area. 1962.

17384 ROTH (GABRIEL JOSEPH). Parking Space for Cars: Assessing the Demand. Camb. 1965.

17385 —— Paying for Parking. 1965.

17386 BRIERLEY (JOHN). Fourth Report on Car Parking in the Central Area. 1964.

17387 —— Car Parking and the Environment. 1971. 2nd edn 1979.

17388 BIXBY (BOB). A Study of Park and Ride Use and the Influence of Parking Availability on Patronage. Oxf. 1978.

17389 BAKER (MARY) *et al.* Park Now, Pay Later?: A Study of Offensive Parking in the Heart of London. 1981.

17390 ATKINS (COLIN KEITH). People and the Motor Car: A Study of the Movement of People Related to their Residential Environment. Birm. 1964.

17391 MINISTRY OF TRANSPORT. Cars for Cities: A Study of Trends in the Design of Vehicles. 1967.

17392 BENDIXSON (TERENCE). Instead of Cars. 1974.

17393 AUTOMOBILE ASSOCIATION. The Motorist Today: Some Findings of General Interest from a Survey Commissioned by the Automobile Association. 1966.

17394 BARTY-KING (HUGH). The A.A.: A History of the First 75 Years of the Automobile Association 1905–1980. Basingstoke. 1980.

(ii) The Motor Car Industry

17395 CASTLE (HAROLD GEORGE). Britain's Motor Industry. 1950.

17396 TURNER (GRAHAM). The Car Makers. 1963.

17397 JEFFRIES (GREG). The Motor Industry. 1969.

17398 HOLME (ALAN). The Motor Vehicle Industry. 1970. Rev. edn Aylesbury, 1979, by Maureen Woodhall.

17399 RICHARDSON (KENNETH). The British Motor Industry, 1896–1939. 1977.

17400 BHASKAR (KRISH). The Future of the United Kingdom Motor Industry. 1979.

17401 DUNNET (PETER J. S.). The Decline of the British Motor Industry: The Effects of Government Policy 1945–1979. 1980.

17402 WAYMARK (PETER). The Car Industry: A Study in Economics and Geography. Bath. 1983.

17403 WILKS (STEPHEN). Industrial Policy and the Motor Industry. Manch. 1984.

17404 MARSDEN (DAVID) *et al.* The Car Industry: Labour Relations and Industrial Adjustment. 1985.

17405 MILLER (M.) *and* CHURCH (ROY ANTHONY). 'Motor Manufacturing'. Ch. in British Industry between the Wars. Neil Keith Buxton and Derek Howard Aldcroft, *eds.* 1979.

17406 THOMS (DAVID) *and* DONNELLY (TOM). The Motor Car Industry in Coventry since the 1890s. 1985.

17407 CHANNEL FOUR TELEVISION HISTORY WORKSHOP. Making Cars: A History of Car-Making in Cowley. 1985.

17408 MYERS (STEPHEN). Cars from Sheffield: The Rise and Fall of the Sheffield Motor Car Industry 1900–1930. Sheffield. 1986.

17409 GEORGE (A. D.). 'The Manchester Motor Industry 1900–1938'. *Transport Hist.* 9 (1978), 217–22.

17410 —— 'The Manchester Motor Industry 1900–1938: Further Notes'. *Transport Hist.* 10 (1979), 171–5.

17411 MACDONALD (A. CRAIG) *and* BROWNING (A. S. E.). A History of the Motor Car Industry in Scotland. 1961. [Institution of Mechanical Engineers.].

17412 RHYS (D. G.). 'Concentration in the Inter-War Motor Industry'. *J. Transport Hist.* n.s. 3 (1976), 241–64.

17413 LEWCHUK (WAYNE). 'The Return to Capital in the British Motor Vehicle Industry 1896–1939'. *Business Hist.* 27 (1985), 3–25.

17414 TURNER (H. A.) *and* BESCOBY (J.). 'Strikes, Redundancy, and the Demand Cycle in the Motor Car Industry'. *Bull. Oxf. Univ. Inst. Econ. Soc. Stat.* 23 (1961), 179–85.

17415 LYDDON (D.). 'Workplace Organisation in the British Car Industry: A Critique of Jonathan Zeitlin'. *History Workshop* 15 (1983), 61–75.

17416 COWLING (KEITH GEORGE) *and* CUBBIN (JOHN). Price Formation under Oligopoly: An Analysis of the U.K. Motor Industry. Coventry. 1971.

17417 —— 'Price, Quality and Advertising Competition: An Econometric Investigation of the United Kingdom Market'. *Economica* 37 (1971), 378–94.

17418 CUBBIN (JOHN). 'Quality Change and Pricing Behaviour in the United Kingdom Car Industry, 1956–1968'. *Economica* 42 (1975), 43–58.

17419 U.K. N.E.D.C.—ECONOMIC DEVELOPMENT COMMITTEE FOR THE MOTORING MANUFACTURING INDUSTRY. The Effect of Government Economic Planning on the Motor Industry. 1968.

17420 —— Regional Planning and the Motor Industry. 1969.

17421 —— Motor Industry Statistics: 1958/67—Data Book. 1969.

17422 CHURCH (ROY). Herbert Austin: The British Motor Car Industry to 1941. 1979.

17423 WYATT (ROBERT JOHN). The Austin 1905–1952. Newton Abbot. 1981.

17424 —— The Austin Seven: The Motor for the Million 1922–1939. 1968. 2nd edn Newton Abbot. 1972. 3rd edn 1982.

17425 HEALEY (GEOFFREY). Austin Healey: The Story of the Big Healeys. 1977.

17426 HARVEY (CHRIS). Healey: The Handsome Brute. Oxf. 1978.

17427 WILLIAMS (KAREL) *et al.* The Breakdown of Austin Rover: A Case-Study in the Failure of Business Strategies and Industrial Policy. Leamington Spa. 1987.

17428 ROBSON (GRAHAM). The Rover Story. 1977. 3rd edn Camb. 1984.

17429 TAYLOR (JAMES). The Classic Rovers, 1934–1977: A Collector's Guide. 1983.

17430 HUTCHINGS (TONY). Land Rover: The Early Years. Petersfield. 1982.

17431 OLIVER (GEORGE A.). The Rover Seven. 1971.

17432 OVERY (RICHARD JAMES). William Morris, Viscount Nuffield. 1976.

17433 ANDREWS (PHILIP WALTER SAWFORD) *and* BRUNNER (ELIZABETH). The Life of Lord Nuffield. 1959.

17434 EDWARD (HARRY). The Morris Motor Car: 1913–1983. Ashbourne. 1983.

17435 SKILLETER (PAUL). Morris Minor: The World's Supreme Small Car. 1981.

17436 LEYLAND MOTOR CORPORATION. Seventy Years of Progress. 1967.

17437 —— Proposed Amalgamation with the Rover Company Ltd. 1967.

17438 TURNER (GRAHAM). The Leyland Papers. 1971.

17439 DANIELS (JEFF). British Leyland: The Truth about the Cars. 1980.

17440 WILLMAN (PAUL) *et al.* Innovation and Management Control: Labour Relations at British Leyland Cars. Camb. 1985.

17441 GOLDING (ROB). The Mini. 1979. New edn 1984.

17442 HARVEY (CHRIS). Mighty Minis. Yeovil. 1986.

17443 NOCKOLDS (HAROLD). The Magic of a Name: A History of Rolls Royce. 1945. Rev. edn 1950.

17444 LLOYD (IAN). Rolls-Royce : The Growth of a Firm. 1978.

17445 —— Rolls-Royce: The Years of Endeavour. 1978.

17446 HARVEY-BAILEY (ALEC). Rolls-Royce: The Formative Years, 1906–1939. 1981. 2nd edn 1983.

17447 HARVEY-BAILEY (ALEC) *and* EVANS (MIKE). Rolls-Royce: The Pursuit of Excellence. 1984.

17448 EVANS (MIKE). In the Beginning: The Manchester Origins of Rolls-Royce. Derby. 1984.

17449 EVES (EDWARD). Rolls-Royce: 75 Years of Motoring Excellence. 1979.

17450 BENNETT (MARTIN). Rolls-Royce: The History of the Car. 1974. 2nd edn Yeovil. 1983.

17451 GEORGIANO (GEORGE NICOLAS). The Classic Rolls-Royce. 1985.

17452 WOOD (JONATHAN). The Rolls-Royce. Princes Risborough. 1987.

17453 SCHRADER (HALWART). Rolls Royce and Bentley from 1931. Nishen. 1989.

17454 COURTNEY (GEOFF) *and* STOWERS (ROGER). The Power behind Aston Martin. Oxf. 1978.

17455 WHITE (ANDREW). Jaguar: The History of a Great British Car. Camb. 1980. Wellingborough. 1985.

17456 BUSENKELL (RICHARD L.). Jaguar since 1945. Camb. 1983.

17457 FARRANT (JEREMY P.). The History of Scout Motors Limited of Salisbury. 1967.

(iii) Other Motor Vehicles

17458 BARKER (THEODORE CARDWELL). The Economic and Social Effects of the Spread of Motor Vehicles. 1987.

17459 —— The Transport Contractors of Rye: John Jempson and Son: A Chapter in the History of Road Haulage. 1982.

17460 DUNBAR (CHARLES S.). The Rise of Road Transport 1919–1939. 1981.

17461 GRIFFIN (JOHN BARRET). History of Past and Present Motor Vehicle Transport over 58 Years. Bognor Regis. 1980.

17462 SETH-SMITH (MICHAEL). The Long Haul: A Social History of the British Commercial Vehicle Industry. 1975.

17463 KLAPPER (CHARLES FREDERICK). British Lorries 1900–1945. 1973.

17464 STEVENS-STRATTON (SEYMOUR WALTER). British Lorries, 1945–1983. 1st pub. 1978, covering period 1945–75. 2nd edn 1983.

17465 CIVIC TRUST Heavy Lorries Nine Years On . . . 1979.

17466 WARDROPER (JOHN). Juggernaut. 1981.

17467 THOMAS (ALAN). Lorries, Vans and Trucks. Hove. 1982.

17468 WOODHAMS (JOHN). Old Lorries. Princes Risborough. 1985.

17469 BALDWIN (NICK). Lorries and Vans. 1979.

17470 —— Old Delivery Vans. Princes Risborough. 1987.

17471 —— The Illustrated History of Leyland Trucks. Sparkford. 1986.

17472 KENNET (PAT). Leyland [Commercial Vehicles]. Camb. 1983.

17473 TURNBULL (GERARD L.). Traffic and Transport: An Economic History of Pickfords. 1979.

17474 MILES (PHILIP C.). Road Transport in Hull and East Yorkshire. Hendon. 1988.

17475 GEORGIANO (GEORGE NICOLAS). The World's Commercial Vehicles 1830–1964: A Record of 134 Years of Vehicle Production. 1965.

17476 —— Trucks: An Illustrated History 1896–1920. 1979.

17477 —— A History of the London Taxi Cab. Newton Abbot. 1972.

17478 —— The London Taxi. Princes Risborough. 1985.

17479 CREIGHTON (JOHN). Fire Engines of Yesterday. Hornchurch. 1984.

17480 —— Fire Engines in the United Kingdom. 1981. 2nd edn Horn-church. 1986.

17481 WHITEHAED (TREVOR). Fire Engines. Princes Risborough. 1981.

17482 MILLER (DENIS NEVILLE). A Source Book of Fire Engines. 1983.

17483 OLIVER (GEORGE A.). Cars and Coachbuilding: 100 Years of Road Vehicle Development. 1981.

17484 HEBDEN (JULIA) *and* ROBINSON (R. V. F.). Small Firms in the Motor Vehicle Distribution and Repair Industry. 1971.

17485 HAMER (MICHAEL). Wheels within Wheels: A Study of the Road Lobby. 1974.

17486 —— Getting Nowhere Fast. 1976.

6. AVIATION

(a) Flight and Aviation—General and Early Histories

17487 SCHIELDROP (EDGAR BONSAK). The Air. Lond./Phil., Pa. 1940.

17488 HARPER (HARRY). The Evolution of the Flying Machine: Balloon, Airship, Aeroplane. 1930.

17489 STEWART (OLIVER). First Flights. 1957.

17490 TURNER (CHARLES CYRIL). The Old Flying Days. 1927.

17491 DAVY (MAURICE JOHN BERNARD) *comp*. Science Museum: Collections Illustrating Aeronautics: 1—Heavier-than-air Craft. 1929. Rev. edn 1949.

17492 —— 2–The Propulsion of Aircraft. 1930. Rev. edn 1936.

17493 —— 3–Lighter-than-air Craft. 1934. Rev. edn 1950.

17494 —— Interpretive History of Flight: A Survey of the History and Development of Aeronautics, with particular reference to contemporary influences and conditions. 1937. 2nd edn 1948.

17495 GAMBLE (WILLIAM H.). History of Aeronautics: A Selected List of References to Material in the New York Public Library. N.Y. 1938.

17496 BROWN (CECIL LEONARD MORLEY). The Conquest of the Air: An Historical Survey. 1927.

17497 BRITTAIN (*Sir* HARRY ERNEST). By Air. 1933.

17498 SETRIGHT (LEONARD JOHN KENSELL). The Power to Fly: The Development of the Piston Engine in Aviation. 1971.

17499 ANDERSON (JOHN DAVID). Introduction to Flight: Its Engineering and History. N.Y./Lond. 1978.

17500 DUKE (NEVILLE) *and* LANCHBERRY (EDWARD). Sound Barrier: The Story of High-speed Flight. 1953. 6th edn 1954.

17501 —— *Eds.* The Crowded Sky: An Anthology of Flight from its beginnings to the Age of the Guided Missile. 1959. Abgd. 1964.

17502 GIBBS SMITH (CHARLES HARVARD). The Aeroplane: A Historical Survey of its Origins and Development. 1960.

17503 —— Aviation: An Historical Survey from its Origins to the End of World War Two. 1970. [Science Museum pub.].

17504 —— A Brief History of Flying, from Myth to Space Travel. 1967. [Science Museum booklet.].

17505 —— A History of Flying. 1953. N.Y. 1954.

17506 —— The Rebirth of European Aviation. 1974.

17507 —— Flight through the Ages: A Complete Illustrated Chronology from the Dreams of Early History to the Age of Space Exploration. 1974.

17508 KING (HORACE FREDERICK). The First 50 Years of Powered Flight. 1953.

17509 —— *Comp.* From Kitty Hawk to Concorde: Jane's 100 Significant Aircraft. 1970.

17510 REAY (DAVID ANTHONY). The History of Man-powered Flight. Oxf. 1977.

17511 STINTON (DARROL). The Design of the Aeroplane. 1985.

17512 SAUNDBY (ROBERT). Early Aviation: Man Conquers the Air. 1971.

17513 PENROSE (HARALD). British Aviation: The Great War and Armistice 1915–1919. N.Y. 1969.

17514 —— British Aviation: The Adventuring Years 1920–1929. 1973.

17515 NAYLER (JOSEPH) *and* OWER (ERNEST). Aviation: Its Technical Development. 1965.

17516 —— Aviation of To-day: Its History and Development. 1930.

17517 —— Flight To-day. 1936. 4th edn 1957.

17518 MILLER (RONALD EUGENE) *and* SANDERS (DAVID). The Technical Development of Modern Aviation. 1968.

17519 MONDEY (DAVID). Women of the Air. 1981.

17520 COOKSLEY (PETER GEORGE). Flight Royal: The Queen's Flight and Royal Flying in Five Reigns. Camb. 1981.

17521 BURNS (MICHAEL) *ed*. The Queen's Flight. Poole. 1986.

17522 JONES (DAVID). The Time Shrinkers—Africa: The Development of Civil Aviation between Britain and Africa. 1977.

17523 FEARON (PETER). 'The Growth of Aviation in Britain'. *J. Contemp. Hist.* 20 (1985), 21–40.

17524 NEGUS (GEOFFREY) *and* STADDON (TOMMY). Aviation in Birmingham. Leics. 1984.

17525 JOHNSON (HOWARD). Wings over Brooklands: The Story of the Birthplace of British Aviation. Weybridge. 1981.

17526 WALKER (PERCY BROOKSBANK). Early Aviation at Farnborough: The History of the Royal Aircraft Establishment vol. 2—The First Aeroplanes. 1974.

17527 ROBINSON (BRIAN R.). Aviation in Manchester: A Short History. Stockport. 1977.

17528 GIBSON (MICHAEL L.). Aviation in Northamptonshire: An Illustrated History. Northampton. 1982.

17529 NEW (P. T.). The Solent Sky: A Local History of Aviation from 1908 to 1946, with special reference to Southampton (Eastleigh) Airport. Chandlers Ford. 1976.

17530 GILLIES (JOHN DOUGLAS) *and* WOOD (JAMES L.). Aviation in Scotland. 1966.

17531 CORLETT (JOHN). Aviation in Ulster. Belfast. 1981.

(b) Aircraft Development

17532 HIGHAM (ROBIN DAVID STEWART). The British Airship 1908–1931: A Study in Weapons Policy. 1961.

17533 MASEFIELD (*Sir* PETER GORDON). To Ride the Storm: The Story of Airship R.101. 1982.

17534 GURNEY (JOHN). The R.101. Knotting. 1980.

17535 ROBINSON (DOUGLAS H.). Giants in the Sky: A History of the Rigid Airship. Seattle. 1973.

17536 CLARKE (BASIL). The History of Airships. N.Y. 1961.

17537 BOTTING (DOUGLAS). The Giant Airships. 1981.

17538 CHAMBERLAIN (GEOFFREY). Airships—Cardington: A History of Cardington Airship Station and its Role in World Airship Development. Lavenham. 1984.

17539 ROYAL AERONAUTICAL SOCIETY. Airships and their Maritime Implications. 1981.

17540 KNELL (KENNETH ALFRED). Bring Back the Airship?: A Question together with an Historical Appraisal of the Giant Rigid Dirigible 1900–1937. Camb. 1980.

17541 FINLAY (WILFRID) *and* HANCOCK (GILLIAN). Famous Flights of Airships and Balloons. 1979.

17542 BAKER (JOHN A.). British Balloons: A Register of all Balloons and Airships Built or Registered in the British Isles since 1950. 1981.

17543 WOLTERS (RICHARD A.). The World of Silent Flight. N.Y./Lond. 1979.

17544 MRAZEK (JAMES EDWARD). Fighting Gliders of World War Two. 1977.

17545 LLOYD (ALAN). The Gliders. 1982. 2nd edn 1984.

17546 COATES (ANDREW). Jane's World Seaplanes and Motor Gliders. 1978. 2nd edn 1980.

17547 HARDY (MICHAEL JOHN). Gliders and Seaplanes of the World. 1982.

17548 RANCE (ADRIAN B.) *ed*. Seaplanes and Flying Boats of the Solent. Southampton. 1981.

17549 HENNING (G. R.) *and* TRACE (K.). 'Britain and the Motorship: A Case of the Delayed Adoption of New Technology'. *J. Econ. Hist.* 35 (1975), 353–85.

17550 MUNSON (KENNETH). Helicopters and other Rotorcraft since 1907. 1968.

17551 TAYLOR (MICHAEL JOHN HADDRICK). History of Helicopters. 1984.

17552 —— Helicopters of the World. 1976. 3rd edn 1981.

17553 POLMAR (NORMAN). Military Helicopters of the World: Military Rotor-Wing Aircraft since 1917. 1981.

17554 GARDNER (RICHARD ERIC). British Service Helicopters: A Pictorial History. 1985.

17555 EVERETT-HEATH (JOHN). British Military Helicopters. 1986.

17556 HOBBS (JACK). Bristol Helicopters: A Tribute to Raoul Hafner. Bristol. 1984.

17557 LAMBERMONT (PAUL MARCEL). Helicopters and Autogyros of the World. 1958. Rev. edn 1970.

17558 GABLEHOUSE (CHARLES). Helicopters and Autogiros: A History of Rotating-wing and V/STOL Aviation. 1967. Rev. edn Phil., Pa. 1969.

17559 WHITEHOUSE (ARTHUR). The Military Aeroplane: Its History and Development. N.Y. 1971.

17560 WHITTLE (FRANK). Jet, the Story of a Pioneer. 1953.

17561 MYLES (BRUCE). Jump Jet: The Revolutionary V/STOL Fighter. 1978.

17562 BROOKS (PETER WRIGHT). The Modern Airliner: Its Origins and Development. 1961.

17563 TAYLOR (MICHAEL JOHN). Jet Fighters. 1982.

17564 —— Modern Jet Aircraft. 1984.

17565 BOUGHTON (TERENCE). The Story of the British Light Aeroplane. 1963.

17566 SCLAIFER (ROBERT) and HERON (S. D.). The Development of Aircraft Engines and the Development of Aviation Fuels. Boston, Mass. 1950.

17567 THE TIMES. 'Concorde: A Special Report'. 4 Mar. 1969, Suppl. 1–12.

17568 COSTELLO (JOHN) and HUGHES (TERRY). The Battle for Concorde. Salisbury. 1971.

17569 WILSON (ANDREW). The Concorde Fiasco. 1973.

17570 ADAMS (JOHN G. U.). 'Concorde Wondering where to go'. Geog. Mag. 47 (1974), 6.

17571 BRITISH AIRCRAFT CORPORATION. Concorde: The Questions Answered. 1975.

17572 KNIGHT (GEOFFREY EGERTON). Concorde, the Inside Story. 1976.

17573 CALVERT (BRIAN). Flying Concorde. Shrewsbury. 1981.

17574 BRABAZON (JOHN THEODORE CUTHBERT MOORE) Baron. The Brabazon Story. 1956.

17575 —— Forty Years of Flight. Oxf. 1949.

17576 SYKES (Sir FREDERICK). From Many Angles. 1942.

17577 READER (WILLIAM J.). Architect of Air Power: The Life of the First Viscount Weir of Eastwood, 1877–1959. 1968.

(c) The British Aircraft Industry and British Airlines

17578 FEARON (PETER). 'The Formative Years of the British Aircraft Industry'. Bus. Hist. Rev. 43 (1969), 476–95.

17579 —— 'Aircraft Manufacturing'. Ch. in British Industry between the Wars. Neil Keith Buxton and Derek Howard Aldcroft, eds. 1979.

17580 FEARON (PETER). 'The British Airframe Industry and the State 1918–1935'. Econ. Hist. Rev. 2nd ser. 27 (1974), 236–51.

17581 ROBERTSON (A. J.). 'The British Airframe Industry and the State in the Inter-war Period: A Comment'. Econ. Hist. Rev. 2nd ser. 28 (1975), 648–57.

17582 FEARON (PETER). 'The British Airframe Industry and the State in the Inter-War Period: A Reply'. Econ. Hist. Rev. 2nd ser. 28 (1975), 658–62.

17583 BALCHIN (NIGEL MARLIN). The Aircraft Builders: An Account of British Aircraft Production, 1939–1945. 1947. [Prepared for the Ministry of Aircraft Production by the Central Office of Information.].

17584 MILLER (HARRY). The Predicament of the Aircraft Industry. 1966.

17585 HARTLEY (KEITH). 'The United Kingdom Military Aircraft Market'. Yorks. Bull. Econ. Soc. Res. 19 (1967), 15–36.

17586 —— 'The Export Performance of the British Aircraft Industry'. Yorks. Bull. Econ. Soc. Res. 24 (1972), 81–6.

17587 REED (ARTHUR). Britain's Aircraft Industry: What Went Right? What Went Wrong? 1973.

17588 ELLIS (KEN). British Homebuilt Aircraft since 1920. L/pool. 1975. 2nd edn 1979.

17589 ELLIS (PAUL). British Commercial Aircraft: 60 Years in Pictures. 1980.

17590 GUNSTON (BILL). The Plane Makers. 1980.

17591 PATTIE (GEOFFREY). Is there a Future for the British Aerospace Industry? 1975.

17592 SOCIETY OF BRITISH AEROSPACE COMPANIES. Keep Britain Flying: The Case for Britain's Aerospace Industry. 1965.

17593 EDWARDS (Sir GEORGE). The British Aerospace Industry: A National Asset. 1983.

17594 HAYWARD (KEITH). Government and British Civil Aerospace: A Case Study in Post-war Technology Policy. Manch. 1983.

17595 HARKER (RONALD W.). Rolls-Royce from the Wings: Military Aviation, 1925–1971. Oxf. 1976.

17596 SCOTT (JOHN DICK). Vickers: A History. 1962.

17597 EVANS (HAROLD). Vickers: Against the Odds 1956–1977. Sevenoaks. 1978.

17598 SCROPE (HUGH E.). Guide to the Vickers Archives. [In Cambridge Univ. Library.]. Camb. 1985.

17599 HEDLEY (MARTIN). Vickers VC 10. 1982.

17600 SHARP (MARTIN C.). D.H.: A History of De Havilland. Lond. 1960. Rev. edn Shrewsbury. 1982.

17601 JACKSON (AUBREY JOSEPH). De Havilland Aircraft since 1909. 1962. 2nd edn 1978.

17602 BIRTLES (PHILIP). De Havilland. 1984.

17603 RIDING (RICHARD) ed. De Havilland: The Golden Years, 1919–1939. Sutton. 1981.

17604 ARCHER (J. K.). 'De Havilland Aircraft (1908–1960)'. Transport History 9 (1978), 60–9.

17605 COWELL (J. GRAHAM). D.H. Comet: The World's First Jet Airliner. Hounslow. 1976.

17606 BIRTLES (PHILIP). De Havilland Vampire, Venom and Sea Vixen. 1986.

17607 DE HAVILLAND (Sir GEOFFREY). Sky Fever. [Autobiog.]. Shrewsbury. 1979.

17608 GARDNER (CHARLES). The British Aircraft Corporation: A History. 1981. Repr. 1985.

17609 BESWICK (FRANK) Baron. The Role of British Aerospace in the British Economy. Belf. 1979.

17610 TAPPER (OLIVER). Roots in the Sky: A History of British Aerospace Aircraft. 1980.

17611 BRAYBROOK (ROY). British Aerospace Harrier and Sea Harrier. 1984.

17612 WRIGHT (ALAN JAMES). Airbus. 1984.

17613 ROBERTSON (ALAN C.). Lion Rampant and Winged: A Commemorative History of Scottish Aviation Ltd. 1986.

17614 PARDOE (JOHN). Jetstream: A Production History. Glasgow 1977. 2nd edn 1979.

17615 PRESTON (J. M.). A Short History: A History of Short Bros. Aircraft Activities in Kent, 1908–1964. Rochester. 1978.

17616 WHITE (MOLLY O'LOUGHLIN). Belfast: The Story of Short's Big Lifter. Leics. 1984.

17617 MIDDLETON (DON H.). Airspeed: The Company and its Aeroplanes. Lavenham. 1982.

17618 FEARON (PETER). 'The Vicissitudes of a British Aircraft Company: Handley Page Ltd. between the Wars'. *Bus. Hist.* 20 (1978), 63–86.

17619 CHAPMAN (TED). Cornwall Aviation Company. Falmouth. 1979.

17620 MERTON-JONES (ANTHONY CHARLES). British Independent Airlines since 1946. Uxbridge. 1976.

17621 HUMPHRIES (B. K.). 'Nationalisation and the Independent British Airlines 1945–1951'. *J. Transport Hist.* n.s. 3 (1976), 265–81.

17622 JENKINS (CLIVE). British Airlines: A Study of Nationalised Civil Aviation. 1953. [Fabian Research Series.].

17623 HIGHAM (ROBIN DAVID STEWART). British Imperial Air Routes, 1918 to 1939: The Story of Britain's Overseas Airlines. 1960.

17624 —— 'British Airways Limited 1935–1940'. *J. Transport Hist.* 4 (1959/60), 113–32.

17625 ASHWORTH (MARK) and FORSYTH (PETER). Civil Aviation Policy and the Privatisation of British Airways. 1984.

17626 BRITISH AIRWAYS. The Story of British Airways. 1979.

17627 CAMPBELL-SMITH (DUNCAN). The British Airways Story: Struggle for Take-off. Sevenoaks. 1986.

17628 CORKE (ALISON). British Airways: The Path to Profitability. 1986.

17629 QUIN-HARKIN (A. J.). 'Imperial Airways, 1924–1940'. *J. Transport Hist.* 1 (1954), 197–215.

17630 DAVIES (RONALD EDWARD GEORGE). A History of the World's Airlines. 1964.

17631 CRAMP (B. G.). British Midland Airways. Hounslow. 1979.

17632 BANKS (HOWARD). The Rise and Fall of Freddy Laker. 1982.

17633 STADDON (TOMMY). A History of Cambrian Airways, the Welsh Airline, from 1935 to 1976. Hounslow. 1979.

17634 CLEIFE (PHILIP). Airway to the Isles. 1966.

17635 ROBERTSON (A. J.). 'The New Road to the Isles: Highland Airways and Scottish Airways'. *J. Transport Hist.* 3rd ser. 7 (1986/7), 61–6.

17636 U.K. BOARD OF TRADE. The Safety Performance of U.K. Airline Operators: Special Review. 1968.

17637 BROWN (DAVID B.). The History of the Guild of Air Pilots and Air Navigators, 1929–1964. 1967.

(d) Air Transport, Civil Aviation, and Airports

17638 THURSTON (ALBERT PETER). The Future of Aerial Transport. [Ministry of Reconstruction]. 1919.

17639 BIRKENHEAD (E.). 'The Financial Failure of British Air Transport Companies, 1919–1924'. *J. Transport Hist.* 4 (1960), 133–45.

17640 DAVIES (RONALD EDWARD GEORGE). A History of World Air Transport. Oxf. 1964.

17641 BRITISH INDEPENDENT AIR TRANSPORT ASSOCIATION. Annual Report 1962/3+.

17642 WHEATCROFT (STEPHEN). Air Transport Policy. 1964.

17643 GRUMBRIDGE (JACK LOVIS). Marketing Management in Air Transport. 1966.

17644 STRATFORD (ALAN H.). Air Transport in the Supersonic Era. 1967.

17645 HUDSON (KENNETH). Air Travel: A Social History. Bath. 1972.

17646 HUDSON (KENNETH) and PETTIFER (JULIAN). Diamonds in the Sky: A Social History of Air Travel. 1979. [BBC pub.].

17647 JACKSON (AUBREY JOSEPH). Air Travel. 1979.

17648 WALTERS (BRIAN). The Illustrated History of Air Travel. 1979.

17649 TAYLOR (LAURIE). Air Travel: How Safe is it? Oxf. 1988.

17650 FOLDES (LUCIEN). 'Domestic Air Transport Policy'. *Economica* 28 (1961), 156–75, 270–85.

17651 BROOKS (PETER WRIGHT). 'The Development of Air Transport'. *J. Transport Econ. Policy* 1 (1967), 164–83.

17652 GWILLIAM (KENNETH MASON). 'Regulation of Air Transport'. *Yorks. Bull. Econ. Soc. Res.* 18 (1966), 20–33.

17653 WORCESTER (RICHARD). Roots of British Air Policy. 1966.

17654 GARDNER (RICHARD ERIC) and WRAGG (DAVID W.). Plane Talk: A Report on British Aviation Policy. 1970.

17655 AYRSHIRE COUNTY COUNCIL. The Future of Scottish Civil Aviation: Issues in the Interests of Scotland. Ayr. 1960.

17656 U.K. CENTRAL OFFICE OF INFORMATION. British Civil Aviation. 1968. Rev. edn 1974.

17657 ENDRES (GUNTER G.). British Civil Aviation. 1985.

17658 BALDWIN (GORDON ROBERT). Regulating the Airlines: Administrative Justice and Agency Discretion. Oxf. 1985.

17659 DOGANIS (RIGAS SOTIRIS). A National Airport Plan. 1967. [Fabian Society Tract.].

17660 —— Who Travels by Air: A Survey of Air Passengers at Birmingham Airport. Birm. 1967.

17661 DOGANIS (RIGAS SOTIRIS) *and* THOMPSON (G. F.). 'Airport Profitability and Management Effectiveness'. *Manch. Sch. Econ. Soc. Stud.* 43 (1975), 331–52.

17662 MYERSCOUGH (JOHN). 'Airport Provision in the Inter-War Years'. *J. Contemp. Hist.* 20 (1985), 41–70.

17663 U.K. MINISTRY OF AVIATION. Report of the Air Freight Working Party. 1963.

17664 —— A Survey of Passenger Traffic at London's Airports. 1965.

17665 HANLON (JAMES PATRICK). Price Discrimination and Air Passenger Fares. Birm. 1978.

17666 U.K. CIVIL AVIATION AUTHORITY. Passengers at Major Airports in Scotland and Central England: Origin and Destination Survey, July–Nov., 1975. 1976.

17667 COLVIN (MICHAEL). Airport U.K.: A Policy for the U.K.'s Civil Airports. 1982.

17668 ALLEN (ROY). Major Airports of the World. 1979.

17669 STROUD (JOHN). Airports of the World. 1980.

17670 WRIGHT (ALAN JAMES). British Airports. 1980. 3rd edn 1988.

17671 CHEATER (B. J.) *ed.* Birmingham Airport: 40th Anniversary Official Handbook. Gloucs. 1979.

17672 NASH (JOANNA) *et al.* 'Croydon Aerodrome'. *Transport Hist.* 8 (1977), 254–72.

17673 CLUETT (DEREK) *et al.* Croydon Airport: The Great Days, 1928–1939. 1980.

17674 —— Croydon Airport: The Australian Connection: Flights and other Links between Croydon Airport and Australia. 1988.

17675 WORRALL (GEOFF). Exeter Airport in Peace and War: A Pictorial History. Exeter. 1988.

17676 KING (JOHN) *and* TAIT (GEOFFREY). Golden Gatwick: Fifty Years of Aviation. 1980.

17677 PARSONS (DAVID) *et al.* Gatwick Airport and the Labour Market. 1983.

17678 U.K. BRITISH AIRPORTS AUTHORITY. (London Airports Traffic Study). Gatwick Airport: 1966 Traffic Characteristics. 1967.

17679 —— Heathrow Airport: 1966 Traffic Characteristics. 1967.

17680 BUTLER (PHILIP HENRY). An Illustrated History of Liverpool Airport. L/pool. 1983.

17681 BROOKS (PETER WRIGHT). 'A Short History of London's Airports'. *J. Transp. Hist.* 3 (1957), 12–22.

17682 LONDON GREATER LONDON COUNCIL. Airport Strategy for Great Britain, pt. 1—The London Area: A Consultation Document. 1976.

17683 STARKIE (DAVID) *and* THOMPSON (DAVID). Privatising London's Airports. 1985.

17684 MCKIE (DAVID). A Sadly Mismanaged Affair: A Political History of the Third London Airport. 1973.

17685 ALAN STRATFORD AND ASSOCIATES. Studies of the Site for a Third London Airport. 1966.

17686 BRANCKER (J. W. S.). The Stansted Black Book: a Representation to the President of the Board of Trade by the North West Essex and East Hertfordshire Preservation Association. Dunmow. 1967.

17687 COOK (OLIVE). The Stansted Affair: A Case for the People. 1967.

17688 STANDING CONFERENCE ON LONDON AND SOUTH EAST REGIONAL PLANNING. The Third London Airport: Report by the Technical Panel. 1967.

17689 —— Joint Report by the Administrative and Technical Panels. 1969.

17690 U.K. MINISTRY OF HOUSING AND LOCAL GOVERNMENT. Report of the Inquiry into the Local Objections to the Proposed Development of Land at Stansted as the Third Airport for London. 1967.

17691 U.K. MINISTRY OF AVIATION. Report of the Inter-Departmental Committee on the Third London Airport to the Minister of Aviation, June 1963. 1964.

17692 TURRALL-CLARKE (ROBERT). Stansted: A Paper on Proposals for a Third London Airport at Stansted and a new Passenger Terminal at Heathrow. 1984.

17693 SCHOLEFIELD (R. A.) *and* MCDONALD (S. D.) *comps.* First and Foremost: 50 Years of Manchester's Civic Airports. Manch. 1978.

17694 KIDDAY (MIKE) *and* TIERNEY (DAVID). Britain's Northern Gateway [Manchester International Airport.]. Bradford. 1982.

17695 ALAN STRATFORD AND ASSOCIATES. An Airport Programme for Yorkshire and Humberside, 1970–1985. Maidenhead. 1967.

(e) *Rocket Technology and Air-Cushioned Vehicles*

17696 EMME (EUGENE M.) *ed.* The History of Rocket Technology. Detroit, Mitch. 1964.

17697 KERROD (ROBIN). Spacecraft. 1980. Rev. edn 1989.

17698 NICOLSON (IAN). The Road to the Stars. Newton Abbot. 1978.

17699 —— Sputnik to Space Shuttle: 25 Years of the Space Age. 1982.

17700 GATLAND (KENNETH WILLIAM). Manned Spacecraft. Lond. 1967. 2nd edn Poole. 1971. 3rd edn 1976.

17701 BAKER (DAVID). The History of Manned Space Flight. 1981.

17702 —— The Rocket: The History and Development of Rocket and Missile Technology. 1978.

17703 BROWN (MARTIN P.). Compendium of Communication and Broadcast Satellites, 1958 to 1980. N.Y. 1981.

17704 PORTER (RICHARD W.). The Versatile Satellite. Oxf. 1977.

17705 HAYWARD (LESLIE H.). A History of Air Cushion Vehicles. 1963.

17706 JOHNSON (PETER STEWART). The Economics of Invention and Innovation, with a Case Study of the Development of the Hovercraft. 1975.

17707 McLEAVY (ROY) *ed*. Hovercraft and Hydrofoils. 1980.

17708 WATTS (ANTHONY JOHN) *comp*. A Source Book of Hydrofoils and Hovercraft. 1978.

17709 BRITISH ASSOCIATION FOR THE ADVANCEMENT OF SCIENCE. On a Cushion of Air: A Conference. 1985.

17710 FILBY (PETER). T.V.R.: Success against the Odds. 1976.

17711 KING (HORACE FREDERICK). Aeromarine Engines: The Beginnings of Marine Aircraft, Winged Hulls, Air Cushion and Air Lubricated Craft, Planing Boats and Hydrofoils. 1966.

9

URBAN AND RURAL LIFE, STANDARD OF LIVING, HOUSING, AND THE ENVIRONMENT

It may be apparent that the categories drawn together in this section could have been shuffled in alternative directions or, indeed, been presented as entirely discrete sections in their own right. There are obvious links with literature on social and health issues considered in other full sections. The reader should therefore also consult sub-sections elsewhere where kindred matters are collected. Nevertheless, while these links should be pointed out, the items brought together in this section do cohere in important respects.

The literature on towns reflects the attention which this topic has attracted—whether those concerned would describe themselves as urban geographers, urban historians, or urban sociologists. Naturally the approaches and perspectives offered by these disciplines vary but together they have ensured that the literature on urban development in Britain is now sophisticated and mature. After an initial sub-section, the material is divided into 'large' and 'small' towns—a boundary which is inevitably somewhat arbitrary but which may meet the needs of different users. Separate sub-sections deal with towns in Scotland, Wales, and Northern Ireland. The phenomenon of the 'new town' attracted considerable literature and receives a separate sub-section, as does 'suburbia'. As has been noted, work by urban geographers and sociologists will have featured in these categories but an attempt has also been made to identify specifically work in these disciplines. The reader should also consult 'geography' and 'sociology' elsewhere.

'Housing' has no obvious home. However, given that it is often, if misleadingly, thought to be largely an urban problem it has been sandwiched in a separate section between 'towns' and 'town and country planning'. It was at least part of the aspiration of 'planning' that it would help to solve 'bad housing' by looking at the built environment in a comprehensive way. 'New towns', although already identified as such in a category within 'towns', were so much a part of this movement that they also have a separate category under 'town and country planning'. Indeed, while these three sub-sections have their own logic, interested readers should regard them as closely linked and consult them as a group.

The two subsequent sub-sections deal comparably with 'rural life' generously interpreted. The sub-section on villages and rural communities is the counterpart of the urban sub-sections which have just been alluded to. There is a wealth of work on local communities in Britain and it cannot all be included. It is rare to find a village without some kind of local history, often the outcome of collective research by local history groups. Some villages have received the attention of professional historians or sociologists, but much local study is undertaken by enthusiastic 'amateurs'. The result, overall, is a wide and somewhat unpredictable range of studies reflecting the diversity of bodies and individuals involved in the study of localities in the countries of Britain.

Whilst agriculture, fishing, and forestry might have been formed into a sub-section of 'industry', these industries have been grouped in close proximity to the rural life with which they are intimately associated. Separate categories identify literature which provides information on general problems affecting these industries but also identify the distinct picture in different parts of England and in Scotland, Wales, and Northern Ireland. While 'gardening' can be perceived as a leisure pursuit or, indeed, as an aesthetic activity, it has been grouped in a sub-section to follow commercially orientated 'market gardening'.

Two final sub-sections deal with 'the environment' and 'food and living standards'. Both clearly have links elsewhere—with politics, economics, industry, and health in particular—but they also contain material which has a strong bearing on urban and rural life, housing, and food and drink. 'Food and living standards' forms a natural bridge into the subsequent section.

A. TOWNS

1. GENERAL

17712 CLINE (RICHARD), LEVINE (BARRY MICHAEL), *and* BARRICK (JOHN) *comps*. Planning in the United States and the United Kingdom, 1970–1983.

17713 PEARSE (INNES HOPE) *and* WILLIAMSON (GEORGE SCOTT). The Case for Action: A Survey of Everyday Life Under Modern Industrial Conditions, with Special Reference to the Question of Health. 1931.

17714 PEARSE (INNES HOPE) *and* CROCKER (LUCY H.). The Peckham Experiment: A Study in the Living Structure of Society. 1943.

17715 WILLIAMSON (GEORGE SCOTT) *and* PEARSE (INNES HOPE). Science, Synthesis and Sanity: An Inquiry into the Nature of Living. 1965.

17716 NORTH WEST ECONOMIC PLANNING COUNCIL. Education, Arts and Amenities Group. The Social Planning of Urban Renewal: A Report on the Social Planning of Urban Renewal, with Particular Reference to the North West . . . Prepared by a Working Party of the . . . Group. [Chairman: J. Goldberg].

17717 WHITE (BRENDA). The Literature and Study of Urban and Regional Planning. 1974.

17718 UNIVERSITY COLLEGE, LONDON. DEPARTMENT OF TOWN PLANNING. SOCIAL RESEARCH UNIT. A Preliminary Bibliography of Recent Social Studies and Related Literature Relevant to Town and Country Planning in Great Britain. 1956.

17719 UNIVERSITY COLLEGE, LONDON. CENTRE FOR URBAN STUDIES. Land Use Planning and the Social Sciences: A Selected Bibliography: Literature on Town and Country Planning and Related Social Studies in Great Britain, 1930–1963. 1964.

17720 SUTCLIFFE (ANTHONY) *comp*. A History of Modern Town Planning: A Bibliographical Guide. Birm. 1977.

17721 COCKBURN (CYNTHIA). The Structure of Urban and Regional Planning Research in Britain. 1968. [Information Papers, Centre for Environmental Studies, 3.].

17722 —— A Bibliography on Planning Education. 1970. [Information Papers, Centre for Environmental Studies, 13.).

17723 BLOXSIDGE (R.). 'Local Authority Contribution: A Bibliographic Note'. *Town Planning Rev.* 46 (1975), 466–80.

17724 YEARBOOKS. 1964/5–1967/8. (Nos 31–4).

17725 JOURNAL OF THE ROYAL TOWN PLANNING INSTITUTE.

17726 URBAN HISTORY YEARBOOK. Leicester. 1974.

17727 MILLWARD (STANLEY) *ed*. Urban Renewal. Salford. 1966.

17728 CHERRY (GORDON EMANUEL). The Evolution of British Town Planning: A History of Town Planning in the United Kingdom During the 20th Century and of the Royal Town Planning Institute, 1914–74. Leighton Buzzard. 1974.

17729 —— Urban Change and Planning: A History of Urban Development in Britain Since 1750. Henley-on-Thames. 1972.

17730 —— Town Planning in its Social Context. 1970.

17731 —— *Ed*. Urban Planning Problems. 1974.

17732 —— *Ed*. Rural Planning Problems. 1976.

17733 —— National Parks and Recreation in the Countryside. 1975.

17734 BURTON (THOMAS LEONARD) *and* CHERRY (GORDON EMANUEL). Social Research Techniques for Planners. 1970.

17735 ASHWORTH (WILLIAM). The Genesis of Modern British Town Planning: A Study in Economic and Social History of the Nineteenth and Twentieth Centuries. 1954.

17736 BELL (COLIN) *and* BELL (ROSE). City Fathers: The Early History of Town Planning in Britain. 1969.

17737 ALDRIDGE (HENRY R.). The Case for Town Planning: A Practical Manual for the Use of Councillors, Officers, and Others Engaged in the Preparation of Town Planning Schemes. Appendix by Frank Elgood and Edmund Abbott. National Housing and Town Planning Council. 1916.

17738 —— The Administration of the Town Planning Duties of Local Authorities. A Supplement to 'the Case for . . .'. National Housing and Town Planning Council. 1922.

17739 JAST (L. STANLEY). 'Municipalities and Industrial Development'. *Ways and Means* (4 Sept. 1920), 238–40.

17740 SHEPARD (ODELL). 'Little Town'. *Unpartizan Rev.* (Mar. 1920), 373–87.

17741 GROVES (ERNEST R.). 'The Urban Complex'. *Sociol. Rev.* (Aut. 1920), 73–81. [Psychological Aspects of the Movement of People from the Country Districts to Town and City].

17742 ROBINSON (G. W. S.). 'British Conurbations in 1951: Some Corrections'. *Sociol. Rev.* 4(1) (1956), 91–8.

17743 FREEMAN (THOMAS WALTER). The Conurbations of Great Britain. Manch. 1959. Rev. edn 1966. See chapter by Catherine Snodgrass, 'Scottish Conurbations'. 1959.

17744 OUR TOWNS: A CLOSE-UP. A Study Made in 1939–42 with Certain Recommendations by the Hygiene Committee of the Women's Group on Public Welfare (in Association with the N.C.S.S.), with a Preface by the Rt. Hon. Margaret Bondfield. 1943.

17745 NATIONAL COUNCIL OF SOCIAL SERVICE. The Size and Social Structure of a Town: A Report. 1943.

17746 MARCHANT (*Sir* JAMES) ed. Post War Britain. 1945. [Includes chapter by E. D. Simon 'Building the Homes of the Future'.].

17747 COLE (GEORGE DOUGLAS HOWARD). Building and Planning. 1945.

17748 U.K. 1950. MINISTRY OF TOWN AND COUNTRY PLANNING. Report of the Committee on the Qualifications of Planners (The Schuster Report). Cmnd 8059. 1950.

17749 BROWN (ALFRED JOHN) *and* SHERRARD (HOWARD MACOUN). Town and Country Planning. 1951.

17750 SAVAGE (*Sir* WILLIAM GEORGE). The Making of Our Towns. 1952.

17751 —— Rural Housing. 1919.

17752 McALLISTER (GILBERT) *and* McALLISTER (ELIZABETH GLEN) eds. Homes, Towns and Countryside: A Practical Plan for Britain. 1945. [Includes chapter by L. Friedman 'The Culture of Living'.]. 1945.

17753 —— Town and Country Planning. A Study of Physical Environment: The Prelude to Post-War Reconstruction. 1976.

17754 OSBORN (*Sir* FREDERIC JAMES). Green-Belt Cities: The British Contribution. 1946.

17755 OSBORN (*Sir* FREDERIC JAMES) *and* WHITTICK (ARNOLD). The New Towns: The Answer to Megalopolis. 1963.

17756 —— Town and Country Planning. 1947. [National Book League. Reader's Guide.].

17757 —— *Ed.* With Preface. Garden Cities of Tomorrow, By Sir Ebenezer Howard. Introductory Essay By Lewis Mumford. Repr. 1960.

17758 CONWAY (FREDA). 'The Industrial Structure of Towns'. *Manch. Sch. Econ. Soc. Res.* (1953), 154–64.

17759 HARMER (D. J.). The Administrative Machinery of Planning at Local and Regional Levels. 1956.

17760 INTERNATIONAL SEMINAR ON URBAN RENEWAL. 1st Seminar. The Hague. 1958. Urban Renewal. Amsterdam. 1958.

17761 SELF (PETER JOHN OTTER). Cities in Flood. 1957. New edn 1961.

17762 —— The Planning of Industrial Location. 1953.

17763 —— Town Planning in Greater London. 1962.

17764 SELF (PETER JOHN OTTER) *and* STORING (HERBERT J.). The State and the Farmer. 1962.

17765 LONG (JOYCE R.) ed. The Wythall Inquiry: A Planning Test Case with an Introduction by P. J. O. Self. 1961.

17766 SHANKLAND (G.). 'The Crisis in Town Planning'. *Univ. Left R.* 1(1) (1957), 37–42.

17767 WILSON (A. G.). 'Models in Urban Planning: A Synoptic Review of Recent Literature'. *Urban Studs* 5(3) (1968), 249–76.

17768 HALL (*Sir* ROBERT). Planning. Camb. 1962. [Rede Lectures.].

17769 GLASS (RUTH). 'The Evaluation of Planning: Some Sociological Considerations'. *Inl Soc. Sci. J.* xi(3) (1959), 393–409.

17770 —— 'Centre for Urban Studies'. *Town Planning Rev.* 34(3) (1963–4), 169–85.

17771 BLUNDELL (LIONEL ALLEYNE) *and* DOBRY (GEORGE). Town and Country Planning. 1963.

[Republished, revised by original authors with J. H. Shaw as 'An Introduction to Town and Country Planning'.]. Sydney/Lond. 1969.

17772 KEEBLE (LEWIS). Principles and Practice of Town and Country Planning. 3rd edn 1964.

17773 JACKSON (JOHN NICHOLAS). Surveys for Town and Country Planning. 1963.

17774 ASH (MAURICE ANTHONY). The Human Cloud: A Reconsideration of Civic Planning. 1962. [TCPA].

17775 BURNS (WILFRED). New Towns for Old: The Technique of Urban Renewal. 1963.

17776 —— Newcastle: A Study in Replanning at Newcastle Upon Tyne. 1967.

17777 —— British Shopping Centres: New Trends in Layout and Distribution. 1959.

17778 STONE (P. A.). 'Urban Standards and National Resources'. *Town Planning Rev.* 36(3) (1965), 181–96.

17779 —— 'Urban Development and National Resources'. *Urban Studs* 1(2) (1964), 113–27.

17780 GANS (H. J.). 'The Failure of Urban Renewal: A Critique and Some Proposals'. *Commentary* xxxix (1963), 29–37.

17781 GOSS (ANTHONY). The Architect and Town Planning: A Report Presented to the Council of the RIBA. 1965.

17782 —— British Industry and Town Planning. 1962.

17783 TETLOW (JOHN) *and* GOSS (ANTHONY). Homes, Towns and Traffic. 1965.

17784 PINNICK (ALFRED WILLIAM). Country Planners in Action. Sidcup. 1964.

17785 MILLWARD (STANLEY) *ed.* Urban Renewal: Extracts From Papers Presented at a Symposium Held at the Royal College of Advanced Technology, Salford, 1965. Salford. 1965.

17786 GRUEN (VICTOR). The Heart of Our Cities: The Urban Crisis: Diagnosis and Cure. 1965.

17787 LLEWELYN-DAVIES (R.). 'Town Design'. *Town Planning Rev.* 37(3) (1966), 157–72.

17788 JOHNSON-MARSHALL (PERCY EDWIN ALAN). Rebuilding Cities. Edin. 1966.

17789 CREESE (WALTER LITTLEFIELD). The Search for Environment: The Garden City: Before and after. New Haven, Conn. 1966.

17790 SENIOR (DEREK) *ed.* The Regional City: An Anglo-American Discussion of Metropolitan Planning. 1966.

17791 MANDELKER (DANIEL ROBERT). Green Belts and Urban Growth: English Town and Country Planning in Action. Madison, Wis. 1962.

17792 BELLAN (R. C.). 'The Future Growth of Britain's Cities'. *Town Planning Rev.* 37(3) (1966), 173–88.

17793 KING (E. J.). 'Urbanization and Education in Britain'. *Inl Rev. Educ.* 13(4) (1967), 431–50.

17794 URBAN PLANNING SYMPOSIUM, 1965. Proceedings . . . Organised by the Building Research Station at the Bartlett School of Architecture. Garston. 1965.

17795 MOINDROT (CLAUDE). Villes et Campagnes Britanniques. Paris. 1967.

17796 MITCHELL (ELIZABETH BUCHANAN). The Plan that Pleased. 1967. TCPA.

17797 SEELEY (IVOR HUGH). Planned Expansion of Country Towns. 1968.

17798 YOUNG (MICHAEL DUNLOP). Forecasting and the Social Sciences. 1968. [See chapters by D. Grove 'Physical Planning and Social Change' and Peter Hall 'The Spread of Towns into the Country'.]. 1968.

17799 KNIGHT (B.). 'Town and Country Planning. A Quinquennial Review'. *Curr. Legal Probl.* 21 (1968), 195–214.

17800 NEEDLEMAN (L.). 'The Comparative Economics of Improvement and New Building'. *Urban Studs* 6(2) (1969), 196–209.

17801 MEDHURST (FRANKLIN) *and* LEWIS (JOHN PARRY). Urban Decay: An Analysis and A Policy. 1969. [Chapter by Elizabeth Gittus.].

17802 ASH (MAURICE ANTHONY). Regions of Tomorrow: Towards the Open City. 1969.

17803 U.K. CENTRAL OFFICE OF INFORMATION. Ref. Pamphlets 9. Town and Country Planning in Britain. 1968.

17804 U.K. M.H.L.G. Town Centres: Approach to Renewal. 1962.

17805 BENJAMIN (BERNARD). 'Statistics in Town Planning'. *J. Roy. Stat. Soc.* 132(1) (1969), 1–28.

17806 STONE (PETER ALBERT). Urban Development in Britain: Standards, Costs and Resources, 1964–2004. Vol. 1. Population Trends and Housing. Camb. 1970.

17807 —— The Structure, Size and Costs of Urban Settlements. 1973.

17808 —— Housing, Town Development, Land and Costs. 1963.

17809 —— Building Economy, Design, Production and Organisation: A Synoptic View. Oxf. 1966.

17810 LAQUEUR (WALTER) *et al. eds.* Urbanism: The City in History. 1969.

17811 TOYNBEE (ARNOLD JOSEPH). Cities on the Move. 1970.

17812 —— *Ed.* Cities of Destiny. 1967.

17813 TIMMS (DUNCAN). The Urban Mosaic: Towards a Theory of Residential Differentiation. Camb. 1971.

17814 JOHNSTON (RONALD JOHN). Urban Residential Patterns: An Introductory Review. Lond./N.Y. 1972.

17815 CLAVAL (P.). 'Les Villes Britanniques'. *Norvis* 17(67) (1970), 347–70.

17816 PAHL (RAYMOND EDWARD). Whose City?: And Other Essays on Urban Society. 2nd Edn Harmondsworth. 1975.

17817 —— London: What Next? The Case for A Joint Inner London Rehabilitation Organisation (a Lecture). 1973.

17818 —— Whose City?: And other Essays on Sociology and Planning. 1970.

17819 —— Urban Sociology and Planning: Urban Social Theory and Research. 1969.

17820 —— *Ed.* Readings in Urban Sociology. Oxf. 1968.

17821 —— 'Poverty and the Urban System'. In M. Chisholm and G. Mariner. Spatial Policy Problems of the British Economy. Camb. 1971.

17822 —— Patterns of Urban Life. 1970.

17823 —— Urbs in Rure: The Metropolitan Fringe in Hertfordshire. 1965.

17824 RIEMER (S.). 'The Nucleated City'. *Brit. J. Sociol.* 22(3) (1971), 231–9.

17825 ROYAL TOWN PLANNING INSTITUTE. Town Planners and their Future. 1971.

17826 —— Research Committee. Planning Research: A Register of Research for all those Concerned with Town and Country Planning: (Recording work commenced or completed during the period 1964–7). 3rd edn 1968.

17827 ANDREWS (H. F.). 'A Cluster Analysis of British Towns'. *Urban Studs* 8(3) (1971), 271–84.

17828 BELL (GWEN) *and* TYRWHITT (JACQUELINE) *Eds.* Human Identity in the Urban Environment. Harmondsworth. 1972.

17829 EVERSLEY (DAVID EDWARD CHARLES). 'Old Cities, Falling Populations and Rising Costs'. *GLC Intelligence Unit. Q. Bull.* No. 18 (March 1972).

17830 —— 'Urban Planning in Britain Today'. *GLC Intelligence Unit. Q. Bull.* No. 19 (June 1972).

17831 MARTIN (*Sir* LESLIE) *and* MARCH (LIONEL) *eds.* Urban Space and Structures. Camb. 1972. [Cambridge Urban and Architectural Studies. 1.].

17832 MILES (PHYLLIS MARY) *and* MILES (HAYDN BRADDOCK). Town Ecology. 1967.

17833 MARTIN (GEOFFREY HAWARD). The Town. 1961. [A visual history of modern Britain.].

17834 ELKS (J.). 'Urban Renewal'. *Architect and Surveyor* xvii (1972), 9–12.

17835 CAMERON (GORDON CAMPBELL) *and* WINGO (LOWDON) *eds.* Cities, Regions and Public Policy. Edin. 1973.

17836 STEWART (MURRAY) *ed.* the City: Problems of Planning: Selected Readings. Harmondsworth. 1972.

17837 DIAMOND (DEREK ROBIN) *and* MACLOUGHLIN (JOHN BRIAN) *eds.* Education for Planning: The Development of Knowledge and Capability for Urban Governance: Progress in Planning. Oxf. 1973.

17838 MacLOUGHLIN (JOHN BRIAN). Control and Urban Planning. 1973.

17839 —— Urban and Regional Planning: A Systems Approach. 1969.

17840 CLAWSON (MARION) *and* HALL (PETER). Planning and Urban Growth: An Anglo-American Comparison. Baltimore. 1973.

17841 BERRY (BRIAN JOE LOBLEY) *and* KASARDA (JOHN D.). Contemporary Urban Ecology. N.Y./Lond. 1977.

17842 BERRY (BRIAN JOE LOBLEY) *and* HORTON (FRANK E.). Geographic Perspectives on Urban Systems, with Integrated Readings. Englewood Cliffs, N.J. 1970.

17843 BERRY (BRIAN JOE LOBLEY). The Human Consequences of Urbanisation: Divergent Paths in the Urban Experience of the Twentieth Century. 1973.

17844 —— *Ed.* City Classification Handbook: Methods and Applications. 1972.

17845 HERBERT (D. T.). Urban Geography, a Social Perspective. Newton Abbot. 1972.

17846 COWAN (PETER) *ed.* The Future of Planning: A Study Sponsored by the Centre for Environmental Studies. 1973. Repr. 1974.

17847 CENTRE FOR ENVIRONMENTAL STUDIES: Working Papers.

17848 3. WILSON (ALAN GEOFFREY). Urban and Regional Models in Geography and Planning. 1974.

17849 5 and 6. U.K. SOCIAL SCIENCE RESEARCH COUNCIL and CENTRE FOR ENVIRONMENTAL STUDIES Joint Conference, Glasgow, 1968. The Future of the City; The Future of the Region. 2 vols 1968.

17850 —— 7. GRACEY (H.). Urban Sociology and Planning: Sociology of Planning and Urban Growth. 1969.

17851 —— 20. WILSON (ALAN GEOFFREY). Research for Regional Planning. 1968.

17852 WILLIAMS (RAYMOND). The Country and the City. 1973.

17853 HOLMAN (ROBERT) *and* HAMILTON (LYNDA). 'The British Urban Programme'. *Policy and Politics* ii(2) (1973), 97–112.

17854 THORNLEY (JENNIFER) *and* MCLOUGHLIN (JOHN BRIAN). Aspects of Urban Management. Paris. 1974.

17855 LEES (L. H.). 'Study of Cities and the Study of Social Processes: Two Directions in Recent Urban History; Essay Review'. *J. Soc. Hist.* 7 (1974), 330–9.

17856 BARNES (W.). 'The Financial and Social Costs of Urban Renewal'. *Housing Rev.* xxii (1974), 35–40.

17857 BEST (ROBIN HEWITSON) *et al.* 'Density Size-Rule'. (With Comment by J. Forbes). *Urban Studs* 11 (1974), 201–10.

17858 ENTWISTLE (E. W.). 'Going to Town in a Changed Country'. *Geog. Mag.* 46 (1974), 487–91.

17859 JAMES (J. R.). 'Lessons From the Past'. *Town & Country Planning* 43 (1975), 162–7.

17860 JOWELL (JEFFREY). 'Development Control'. *Pol. Q.* 46 (1975), 340–4.

17861 BLOWERS (ANDREW). 'Structure Plans'. *Town & Country Planning* 43 (1975), 400–2.

17862 LOCK (D.). 'Structure Plans: Beware False Promises'. *Town & Country Planning* 43 (1975), 340–2.

17863 McCALLUM (D.). 'Comparative Study in Planning: A Review Article'. *Town Planning Rev.* 46 (1975), 157–64.

17864 SELF (PETER JOHN OTTER). 'When the Minister Decides'. *Town & Country Planning* 43 (1975), 343–5.

17865 —— 'Town Planning in Retreat'. *Pol. Q.* 27(2) (1956), 209–15.

17866 NEWTON (KENNETH). 'Big Books about Small Mercies: Urban Planning in Britain and the United States'. [Review article.]. *Urban Aff. Q.* 11 (1975), 144–52.

17867 TRAVIS (A. S.). 'Containment of Urban England'. [Review article.]. *Town Plan. Rev.* 46 (1975), 157–64.

17868 HALL (D.). 'Local Community Recognition'. *Town & Country Planning* 43 (1975), 309–10.

17869 HALL (PETER). 'Containment of Urban England'. [Review article with Discussion.]. *Geog. J.* 40 (1974), 386–417.

17870 HANCOCK (TOM). 'Cause for Hope'. *Town & Country Planning* 43 (1975), 4–7.

17871 —— 'Trojan Mule'. *Town & Country Planning* 43 (1975), 199–201.

17872 HATHWAY (A.). 'Effects of Town Expansion on Central Areas in Britain'. *Ekistics* 37 (1974), 110–13.

17873 FYSON (ANTHONY). 'Confusion is Good for You'. *Town & Country Planning* 43 (1975), 323–4.

17874 TAYLOR (NICHOLAS). The Village in the City. 1973.

17875 SPENCER (JOHN CARRINGTON) *et al.* Stress and Release in an Urban Estate: A Study in Action Research. 1964.

17876 SMITHSON (ALISON M.) *and* SMITHSON (PETER). Urban Structuring. Lond./N.Y. 1967.

17877 —— Ordinances and Light: Urban Theories 1952–1960 and their Applications in a Building Project, 1963–1970. 1970.

17878 SMITH (PETER FREDERICK). The Syntax of Cities. 1977. [Hutchinson's 'Built Environment' Series.].

17879 —— The Dynamics of Urbanism. 1974. [Hutchinson's 'Built Environment' Series.].

17880 SHANKLAND-COX AND ASSOCIATES PARTNERSHIP *and* INSTITUTE OF COMMUNITY STUDIES. Inner Area Study: Lambeth.

17881 —— Multi-service Project Report. 1976.

17882 —— Second Report on Multiple Deprivation. 1977.

17883 —— Poverty and Multiple Deprivation. 1975.

17884 —— Inner London: Policies for Dispersal and Balance: Final Report of the Lambeth Inner Area Study, 1977 by Graham Shankland, Peter Willmott and David Jordan.

17885 —— Multi-Space Project: Report. 1977.

17886 —— People, Housing and District. 1974.

17887 —— Housing and Population Projections. 1975.

17888 —— Housing Stress. 1975.

17889 —— London's Inner Area: Problems and Possibilities: Discussion Paper. 1976.

17890 —— The Complications of Social Ownership. 1976.

17891 —— Interim Report on Local Services. 1974.

17892 —— Study of Intending Migrants: Report. 1978.

17893 —— Labour Market Study. 1974.

17894 —— Local Employers' Study. 1977.

17895 —— Policies and Structure: Report . . . 1975.

17896 BATLEY (RICHARD). 'An Explanation of Non-Participation in Planning'. *Policy and Politics* i(2) (1971), 95–114.

17897 COMMUNITY ACTION. 'Action Report: Compulsory Purchase'. *Community Action* (ix) (July–Aug. 1973); (x) (Sept.–Oct. 1973); (xi) (Nov.–Dec. 1973).

17898 DIAMOND (D. R.). 'Planning the Urban Environment'. *Geog.* 60 (1975), 189–93.

17899 DONNISON (DAVID VERNON). 'Age of Innocence is Past: Some Ideas about Urban Research and Planning'. *Urban Studs* 12 (1975), 263–72.

17900 GLADSTONE (FRANCIS). The Politics of Planning. 1976.

17901 ROSE (RICHARD) *ed.* The Management of Urban Change in Britain and Germany. 1974.

17902 ROBSON (WILLIAM ALEXANDER). Great Cities of the World: Their Government, Politics and Planning. 1954. Rev. edn with D. E. Regan. 1972.

17903 LASKI (HAROLD J.), JENNINGS (W. IVOR), *and* ROBSON (WILLIAM ALEXANDER) *eds.* Century of Municipal Progress: The Last Hundred Years. 1936.

17904 PRED (ALLAN RICHARD). City Systems in Advanced Economies: Past Growth, Present Processes and Future Development Options. 1977.

17905 BATTY (MICHAEL). Urban Modelling: Algorithms, Calibrations, Predictions. Camb. 1976.

17906 PILCH (I. L.). An Analysis of the Problems and Practices of Urban Development in the United States and Britain. Ann Arbor, Mich. 1954. [Microfilm.].

17907 LONDON SCHOOL OF ECONOMICS AND POLITICAL SCIENCE. DEPARTMENT OF GEOGRAPHY. British Cities: Urban Population and Employment Trends, 1951–71. 1976.

17908 LEWIS (DAVID NEVILLE) *ed.* Urban Structure. 1968.

17909 KIRBY (ANDREW). The Inner Cities: Causes and Effects. Corbridge. 1978.

17910 JACKSON (JOHN NICHOLAS). The Urban Future: A Choice Between Alternatives. 1972.

17911 HIORNS (FREDERICK ROBERT). Town Building in History. 1956. An outline review of conditions, influences, ideas and methods affecting 'planned' towns through five thousand years.

17912 BLOWERS (ANDREW), HAMNETT (CHRIS), *and* SARRE (PHILIP). The Future of Cities. 1974. [Open U. set book.].

17913 SMITH (DAVID LAWRENCE). Amenity and Urban Planning. 1974.

17914 HOUGHTON-EVANS (WILLIAM). Planning Cities: Legacy and Portent. 1975.

17915 HANCOCK (TOM) *ed*. Growth and Change in the Future City Region. 1976. [Contains papers given to an international symposium organised by the British Council.].

17916 EVERSLEY (DAVID EDWARD CHARLES) *and* MOODY (MARY), *assisted by* BARRITT (ADRIAN). The Growth of Planning Research Since the Early 1960s. 1976. [SSRC].

17917 EVERSLEY (DAVID EDWARD CHARLES) *et al*. Population Growth and Planning Policy: An Analysis of Social and Economic Factors Affecting Housing and Employment Location in the West Midlands. 1965.

17918 EVERSLEY (DAVID EDWARD CHARLES). The Planner in Society: The Changing Role of a Profession. 1973.

17919 —— Cutting Down Our Cities to Size: A Balance Sheet for Planners and Treasurers. 1971.

17920 HARVEY (DAVID). Social Justice and the City. 1973. Harmondsworth. 1975.

17921 HARLOE (MICHAEL) *ed*. 1st Conference on Urban Change and Conflict. 1975. Proceedings. 1976.

17922 —— 2nd Conference on Urban Change and Conflict. 1977. Proceedings. 1978.

17923 CHERRY (GORDON EMANUEL). Urban and Regional Planning: Promise and Potential in the West Midlands. Birmingham. 1976. [Inaugural lecture.].

17924 HARRISON (GEORGE ANTHONY) *and* GIBSON (JOHN B.) *eds*. Man in Urban Environments. Oxf. 1976.

17925 BOR (WALTER G.). The Making of Cities. 1972.

17926 BRAND (JANET) *and* COX (MARGARET) *eds*. The Urban Crisis: Social Problems and Planning. 1975. [Strathclyde Seminar Report.].

17927 GLASS (DAVID VICTOR). The Town and Changing Civilisation. 1935.

17928 EYRE (REGINALD E.). Hope for Our Towns and Cities: The Right Approach to Urban Affairs. 1977.

17929 DYOS (HAROLD JAMES) *ed*. The Study of Urban History; The Proceedings of an International Round-Table Conference of the Urban History Group. 1968.

17930 —— Urbanity and Suburbanity. Leicester. 1973. [Inaugural lecture.].

17931 DAVIES (ROSS) *and* HALL (PETER) *eds*. Issues in Urban Society. Harmondsworth. 1978.

17932 CURL (JAMES STEVENS). European Cities and Society: A Study of the Influence of Political Climate on Town Design. 1970.

17933 COWAN (PETER). The Office: A Facet of Urban Growth. 1969.

17934 —— *Ed*. Developing Patterns of Urbanization. Edin. 1970. [Centre for Environmental Studies. Study Group on Developing Patterns of Urbanization.].

17935 AMBROSE (P.). 'Gentlemen Prefer Offices'. *Geog. Mag.* 47 (1974), 3–5.

17936 COX (KEVIN) *ed*. Urbanization and Conflict in Market Societies. 1978.

17937 COX (WILLIAM HARVEY). Cities, the Public Dimension. Harmondsworth. 1976.

17938 COCKBURN (CYNTHIA). The Local State: Management of Cities and People. 1977. Repr. 1978.

17939 CENTRE FOR URBAN STUDIES. Quinquennial Report. 1958/1962.

17940 BLAIR (THOMAS LUCIEN). The International Urban Crisis. 1974.

17941 MOSER (CLAUS ADOLF) *and* SCOTT (WOLF). British Towns: A Statistical Study of their Social and Economic Differences. 1961.

17942 ABRAMS (PHILIP) *and* WRIGLEY (EDWARD ANTHONY). Towns in Societies: Essays in Economic History and Historical Sociology. Camb. 1978.

17943 ANDERSON (NELS). Our Industrial Urban Civilization. 1964.

17944 —— The Urban Community: A World Perspective. 1960.

17945 —— *Ed*. Urbanism and Urbanization. Leiden. 1964.

17946 CULLINGWORTH (JOHN BARRY). Environmental Planning 1939–1969. Vol. 1: Reconstruction and Land Use Planning 1939–1947. 1975.

17947 —— Restraining Urban Growth: The Problem of Overspill. 1960. (Fabian Society).

17948 —— New Towns for Old: The Problem of Urban Renewal. 1962. [Fabian Research Series: 229.].

17949 —— Problems of an Urban Society. 3 vols. The Social Framework of Planning. 1972; The Social Content of Planning. 1972/3; Planning for Change. 1973.

17950 —— Town and Country Planning in Britain. 4th edn. 1972. 6th edn. 1976. 10th edn. 1988.

17951 —— Town and Country Planning in England and Wales: An Introduction. 1964. 2nd edn revised 1967. The Changing Scene. Compl. rev. 3rd edn 1970.

17952 CURRIE (LAUCHLIN BERNARD). Taming the Megalopolis: A Design for Urban Growth. Oxf. 1976.

17953 LOMAS (GRAHAM). 'Out for the Count'. *Town & Country Planning* 43 (1975), 292–4. [Census.].

17954 BOURNE (LARRY STUART). Urban Systems: Strategies for Regulation: A Comparison of Policies in Britain, Sweden, Australia and Canada. Oxf. 1975.

17955 LICHFIELD (NATHANIEL), KETTLE (PETER), *and* WHITBREAD (MICHAEL). Evaluation in the Planning Process. Oxf. 1975.

17956 LASSIERE (A.). The Environmental Evaluation of Transport Plans. 1976.

17957 LEVIN (PETER HIRSCH). Government and the Planning Process: An Analysis and Appraisal of Government Decision-Making Processes with Special Reference to the Launching of New Towns and Town Development Schemes. 1976.

17958 ROBERTS (JOHN TREVOR). General Improvement Areas. Farnborough. 1976.

17959 MacEWEN (MALCOLM) *ed.* Future Landscapes. 1976.

17960 LAMBERT (CLAIRE MARIE). Structure and Local Plan Documents. 2nd edn 1977.

17961 —— Structure Plans: List A: Structure Plan Documents. 1976.

17962 JOHNSTONE (PAMELA) *and* LAMBERT (CLAIRE MARIE). Structure Plans: List B: The Literature and Debate on Structure Plans and Structure Planning. 1976.

17963 McIVER (GLENYS) *comp. and* LAMBERT (CLAIRE MARIE) *ed.* Planning: List A: Basic List for the General Library; List B: Extended List of Publications; List C: For Local Authority Planning Departments. 1976.

17964 LAMBERT (CLAIRE MARIE) *comp.* The Department of the Environment: Organisation and Functions. Rev. edn 1976.

17965 BROADBENT (THOMAS ANDREW). Planning and Profit in the Urban Economy. 1977.

17966 HALL (PETER GEOFFREY) *et al.* The Containment of Urban England. 2 Vols. 1973. vol. 1: Urban and Metropolitan Growth Processes; Vol. 2: The Planning System: Objective, Operations and Impacts.

17967 CLAWSON (MARION) *and* HALL (PETER GEOFFREY). Planning and Urban Growth: An Anglo-American Comparison. Baltimore, Md./Lond. 1973.

17968 HALL (PETER GEOFFREY). The Theory and Practice of Regional Planning. 1970.

17969 —— Urban and Regional Planning. 1975.

17970 —— *Ed.* Labour's New Frontiers. 1964. [Contains his Chapter, 'Regional and Urban Planning'.].

17971 —— Great Planning Disasters. 1980.

17972 NATIONAL ECONOMIC DEVELOPMENT OFFICE. New Homes in the Cities.

17973 SELF (PETER JOHN OTTER). The Planning of Industrial Location. 1953.

17974 ROSENAU (H.). The Ideal City in its Architectural Evolution. 1959.

17975 CIVIC TRUST. The Local Amenity Movement. [Includes chapters by Anthony Barker.]. 1976.

17976 BUCHANAN (RONALD HULL), JONES (E.), *and* McCOURT (D.) *eds.* Man and his Habitat. Lond./N.Y. 1971. [Essays presented to Emyr Estyn Evans.].

17977 DOXIADIS (C. A.). Between Dystopia and Utopia. 1968.

17978 —— Ekistics: An Introduction to the Science of Human Settlements. 1968.

17979 ABERCROMBIE (*Sir* LESLIE PATRICK). Town and Country Planning. 3rd edn 1959.

17980 MACINTYRE (D.). 'Compensation and Remedies: The Justice Report: A Review'. *Town Planning Rev.* 45 (1974), 147–56. [Land.].

2. TOWNS: LARGE

17981 MARTIN (E. W. L.). Where London Ends: English Provincial Life After 1750. 1958.

17982 ROSING (KENNETH EARL) *and* WOOD (PETER A.). Character of a Conurbation: A Computer Atlas of Birmingham and the Black Country. 1971.

17983 LLEWELYN-DAVIES, WEEKS, FORESTIER-WALKER, *and* BOR. Unequal City. 1977. [Inner area study (Final Report): Birmingham. Report prepared for Dept of Environment.].

17984 LLEWELYN-DAVIES, WEEKS (AND PARTNERS). Inner Area Study: Birmingham (part of Small Heath). [All published by the Dept. of the Environment in London.].

17985 —— 1. Project Report. 1974.

17986 —— 2. Progress Report. 1974.

17987 —— 3. Second Progress Report. 1974.

17988 —— 4. Interim Review. 1975.

17989 —— 5. MORTON-WILLIAMS (JEAN) *and* STOWELL (RICHARD). Small Heath, Birmingham: a Social Survey. 2 vols 1975.

17990 —— 6. Third Progress Report. 1975.

17991 —— 7. Little Green: A Case Study in Urban Renewals. 1975.

17992 —— 8. Fourth Progress Report. 1975.

17993 —— 9. Industrial Employment and Property Availability. 1976.

17994 —— 9–10. Housing Policies for the Inner City. 1976.

17995 —— 10. The Management of Urban Renewal. 1976.

17996 —— 12. Circumstances of Families. 1977.

17997 —— 13. & 15. Educational Action Projects. 1977. [2 vols in 1.].

17998 —— 14. You and Me: Here We Are. 1977. Artist Placement Group Project.

See also B. M. D. Smith for employment.

17999 —— 16. Family Service Unit: 435. Neighbourhood Centre. 1977.

18000 —— 18.–19. Environmental Action Projects. 1977–8. [2 vols in 1.].

18001 —— 20. Small Heath Community Federation: A Study in Local Influence. 1978.

18002 —— 22. Small Heath Informations and Advice Centre. 1978.

18003 —— 25. Shape Housing and Community Project. 1978.

18004 BRIGGS (ASA) *Baron*. Borough and City, 1865–1938. 1952. [History of Birmingham, vol. 2.].

18005 SUTCLIFFE (ANTHONY) *and* SMITH (ROGER). Birmingham, 1939–1970. 1974. [History of Birmingham, vol. 3.].

18006 CORBETT (JOHN). The Birmingham Trades Council, 1866–1966. 1966.

18007 BIRMINGHAM PUBLIC LIBRARIES: REFERENCE DEPT. Birmingham: Domesday to 1948. 1948.

18008 BIRMINGHAM INFORMATION DEPT. Publication No. 131: Birmingham. 1960.

18009 —— Publication No. 141: Birmingham. 1965.

18010 MORETON (C. G. N.) *and* TATE (J.). 'Vacancy Reserve'. *Town Planning Rev.* 46 (1975), 5–30. [Birmingham.].

18011 SMITH (R.). 'Post-War Birmingham: Planning and Development'. *Town Planning Rev.* 45 (1974), 189–206.

18012 SMITH (BARBARA MARY DIMOND). The Inner City Economic Problem: A Framework for Analysis and Local Authority Policy. Birm. 1977.

18013 RUDDY (SHEILA) *and* BLACK (JIM). Industrial Relocation in Birmingham: The 'Short' Questionnaire Enquiry. Birm. 1974.

18014 ZUCKERMAN (JOAN *Lady*) *and* ELEY (GEOFFREY). The Birmingham Heritage. 1979.

18015 RICHARDSON (CLEMENT). A Geography of Bradford. Bradford. 1976.

18016 MACINNES (C. M.) *and* WHITTARD (W. F.) *eds*. Bristol and its Adjoining Counties. Bristol. 1975.

18017 LITTLE (BRYAN DESMOND GREENWAY). The City and County of Bristol: A Study in Atlantic Civilization. 1954.

18018 —— Cheltenham. 1952.

18019 —— Exeter. 1953.

18020 —— The Three Choirs Cities. 1952.

18021 RICHARDSON (KENNETH) *asstd by* HARRIS (ELIZABETH). Twentieth Century Coventry. 1972.

18022 DAVIES (R. L.). 'Nucleated and Ribbon Components of the Urban Retail System in Britain'. *Town Planning Rev.* 45 (1974), 91–111. [Coventry.].

18023 LICHFIELD (N.) *and* CHAPMAN (H.). 'Cost–Benefit Analysis in Urban Expansion: A Case Study. Ipswich'. *Urban Studs* 7(2) (1970), 153–88.

18024 WILKINSON (HENRY ROBERT) *et al*. Kingston-upon-Hull and Haltemprice: Social Area Analysis. 1966.

18025 GILLETT (EDWARD). A History of Hull. Oxf. 1980.

18026 SYMES (DAVID) *ed*. Humberside in the Eighties: A Spatial View of the Economy. Hull. 1987.

18027 FRASER (DEREK) *ed*. A History of Modern Leeds. Manch. 1980.

18028 BERESFORD (MAURICE W.) *and* JONES (GLANVILLE R. J.) *eds*. Leeds and its Region. 1967.

18029 PYE (N.) *ed*. Leicester and Its Region. Leics. 1982.

18030 WILKINSON (R.) *and* SIGSWORTH (E. M.). 'A Survey of Slum Clearance Areas in Leeds'. *Yorks. Bull. Econ. Soc. Res.* 15(1) (1963), 25–31.

18031 SCHUMAN (S.). 'La Planification Urbaine en Évolution: Le Cas de Liverpool'. *Aménag. Ternt Dévelop. Région* 4 (1971), 73–125.

18032 WILSON (HUGH) *and* WOMERSLEY (LEWIS). Inner Area Study: Liverpool. Published by DOE. 1900.

18033 —— Work Programme. 1975.

18034 —— Third Study Review. 1975.

18035 —— Vacant Land. 1976.

18036 —— Fourth Study Review. 1976.

18037 —— Social Area Analysis. 1977.

18038 —— Environmental Care Project. 1977.

18039 —— Change or Decay (final report). 1977.

18040 —— Getting a Job. 1977.

18041 —— Economic Development of the Inner Area. 1977.

18042 —— Inner Area Play (report of action projects on adventure playgrounds and play on wheels). 1977.

18043 —— Community Care of the Elderly. 1977.

18044 —— Single Parent Families. 1977.

18045 CASTLE (I. M.) *and* GITTUS (ELIZABETH). 'The Distribution of Social Defects in Liverpool'. *Sociol. Rev.* n.s. v(1) (1957), 43–64.

18046 HART (J. F.). Some Statistics of Social Contrast in Liverpool from the 1971 Census. L/pool. 1977. [Liverpool Council for Voluntary Service.].

18047 WALLER (P.). Democracy and Sectarianism: A Political and Social History of Liverpool 1868–1939. L/pool. 1981.

18048 SMITH (JOHN FREDERICK), HEMM (GORDON), *and* SHENNAN (A. ERNEST). Liverpool: Past–Present–Future. L/pool. 1948. [Foreword by Lord Woolton.].

18049 MAYS (JOHN BARRON). 'Cultural Conformity in Urban Areas: An Introduction to the Crown Street Study in Liverpool'. *Sociol. Rev.* 6(1) (1958), 95–108.

18050 KERR (MADELINE). The People of Ship Street. 1958. [A study of Toxteth.].

18051 CORNELIUS (JOHN). Liverpool 8. 1982.

18052 GOULD (WILLIAM T. S.) *and* HODGKISS (ALAN G.) *eds*. The Resources of Merseyside. L/pool. 1982.

18053 LAWTON (R.) *and* CUNNINGHAM (C. M.) *eds*. Merseyside: Social and Economic Studies. 1970.

18054 ANDERSON (B. L.) *and* STONEY (P. J. M.) *eds*. Commerce, Industry and Transport: Studies in Economic Change on Merseyside. L/pool. 1983.

18055 MARRINER (SHEILA). The Economic and Social Development of Merseyside, 1750–1960. 1982.

18056 MANCHESTER UNIVERSITY SETTLEMENT. Survey Committee. Ancoats: A Study of a Clearance Area. Manch. 1945.

18057 FRANGOPULO (NICHOLAS JOSEPH) ed. Rich Inheritance: A Guide to the History of Manchester. Manch. 1963.

18058 SHERCLIFF (WILLIAM HENRY). Manchester: A Short History of its Development. Manch. 1961. 2nd edn 1965.

18059 WHITE (H. P.) ed. The Continuing Conurbation: Change and Development in Greater Manchester. Aldershot. 1980.

18060 CARTER (CHARLES F.) ed. Manchester and Its Region. Manch. 1962.

18061 WILLIAMS (GWYNDAF). Metropolitan Manchester: A Social Atlas. Manch. 1975.

18062 PECORA (A.). 'La Struttura Urbana di Manchester'. Boll. Soc. Geog. Ital. 8(9–10) (1956), 428–43.

18063 MCCORD (NORMAN). North East England: An Economic and Social History. 1979.

18064 CHAPMAN (RICHARD A.) ed. Public Policy Studies: The North East of England. Edin. 1985.

18065 GRAY (DUNCAN). Nottingham through 500 Years: A History of Town Government. Nottingham. 2nd edn. 1960.

18066 EDWARDS (K. C.) ed. Nottingham and Its Region. Nottingham. 1966.

18067 MARTIN (A. F.) and STEEL (R. W.) eds. The Oxford Region: A Scientific and Historical Survey. Oxf. 1954.

18068 SMITH (C. G.) and SCARGILL (D. I.) eds. Oxford and Its Region. Oxf. 1975.

18069 ROWLEY (TREVOR) ed. The Oxford Region. Oxf. 1980.

18070 COLLISON (PETER) and MOGEY (J.). 'Residence and Social Class in Oxford'. Amer. J. Sociol. 64(6) (1959), 599–605.

18071 HAWSON (HERBERT KEEBLE). Sheffield: The Growth of a City, 1893–1926. Sheffield. 1968.

18072 BEATTIE (GEOFFREY). Survivors of Steel City: A Portrait of Sheffield. 1986.

18073 LINTON (DAVID L.) ed. Sheffield and Its Region: A Scientific and Historical Survey. 1956.

18074 DARKE (R.) and DARKE (J.). 'Sheffield Revisited'. Built Environment 1 (1972), 557–61.

18075 FORD (PERCY) ed. Southampton: A Civic Survey. 1931.

18076 —— Work and Wealth in a Modern Port: An Economic Survey of Southampton. 1934.

18077 FORD (PERCY), THOMAS (CLIFFORD JOHN), and ASHTON (E. T.). The Southampton Survey.

18078 —— 1 A Survey of the Industrial Prospects of the Southampton Region. Interim Report. 1950.

18079 —— 2 Shops and Planning, etc. 1953.

18080 —— 3 Housing Targets, etc. 1953.

18081 —— 4 Problem Families. 1955.

18082 MONKHOUSE (F. J.). A Survey of Southampton and Its Region. Southampton. 1964.

18083 MASON (C. M.) and WITHERICK (M. E.) eds. Dimensions of Change in a Growth Area: Southampton since 1960. Aldershot. 1981.

18084 PATTERSON (A. TEMPLE). Southampton: A Biography. 1970.

18085 WARRILLOW (ERNEST JAMES DALZELL). A Sociological History of the City of Stoke-on-Trent. Stoke-on-Trent. 1960.

18086 BRENNAN (TOM). Midland City: Wolverhampton Social and Industrial Survey. 1948.

18087 —— Reshaping a City. Glas. 1959.

3. TOWNS: SMALL

18088 CONLEN (MICHAEL ROBERT GUNTER). Alnwick, Northumberland: A Study in Town-Plan Analysis. 1960. [Institute of British Geographers Publication No. 27.].

18089 INSTITUTE OF BRITISH GEOGRAPHERS—Publications—No. 27. Alnwick, Northumberland: A Study in Town-Plan Analysis. 1960.

18090 HOLDGATE (M. W.). A History of Appleby, County Town of Westmorland. Appleby. 1956.

18091 DUNNING (JOHN HARRY). Economic Planning and Town Expansion: A Case Study of Basingstoke. Southampton. 1963.

18092 HAIGH (M. H.). The History of Batley, 1800–1974. 1985.

18093 SEABROOK (JEREMY). City Close-up. 1971. [Blackburn.].

18094 GILBERT (EDMUND WILLIAM). Brighton, Old Ocean's Bauble. 1954.

18095 —— University Towns. 1962. [A lecture: University of Sussex, OP 1.].

18096 —— The University Town in England and West Germany: Marburg, Göttingen, Heidelberg and Tübingen, Viewed Comparatively with Oxford and Cambridge. Chicago, Ill. 1961.

18097 HALLIDAY (A. J.). The Development of Burton-on-Trent. 1956.

18098 STEERS (J. A.) ed. The Cambridge Region. Camb. 1965.

18099 HART (GWEN MURIEL). A History of Cheltenham. Leics. 1965.

18100 BARBER (ROSS). Iron Ore and After: Boom Time, Depression and Survival in a West Cumbrian Town, Cleator Moor, 1840–1960. York. 1976.

18101 CHALONER (WILLIAM HENRY). The Social and Economic Development of Crewe, 1780–1923. Manch. 1950.

18102 WILMOT (P.). The Evolution of a Community: A Study of Dagenham after Forty Years. 1963.

18103 BULMER (MARTIN) *ed.* Mining and Social Change: Durham County in the Twentieth Century. 1988.

18104 POCOCK (DOUGLAS CHARLES DAVID). Durham: Images of a Cathedral City. Durham. 1975. [Durham University, Dept. of Geography. Occasional publications No. 6.].

18105 BARLOW (FRANK) *ed.* Exeter and its Region. Exeter. 1969.

18106 LEWES (FREDERICK MARTIN MEREDITH) *and* KIRKNESS (ANNE). Exeter—University and City: A Study of the Economic and Social Interactions Caused by University Growth. 1973.

18107 PATMORE (JOHN ALLAN). An Atlas of Harrogate. Harrogate. 1963.

18108 LOCK (C. M.). The Hartlepools. 1948. [Civic improvement.].

18109 W. E. A. (Hatfield Branch). A Short Picture History of Hatfield and its People. 1966.

18110 WILKINSON (ELLEN). The Town that was Murdered: The Life-Story of Jarrow. 1939.

18111 DAVIES (CLARICE STELLA) *ed.* A History of Macclesfield. Manchester. 1961.

18112 RUNCIE (ROBERT) *ed.* Cathedral and City: St Albans Ancient and Modern. 1977.

18113 ROWSE (ALFRED LESLIE). St Austell: Church, Town, Parish. St Austell. 1960.

18114 SHORTT (HUGH DE SAUSMAREZ) *ed.* City of Salisbury. 1957.

18115 ROBSON (BRIAN TURNBULL). Urban Analysis: A Study of City Structure with Special Reference to Sunderland. Camb. 1969.

18116 —— Urban Growth: An Approach. 1973.

18117 —— Urban Social Areas. 1975. 1978 repr.

18118 HUDSON (KENNETH). An Awkward Size for a Town: A Study of Swindon at the 100,000 Mark. Newton Abbot. 1967.

18119 HARLOE (MICHAEL). Swindon: A Town in Transition: A Study in Urban Development and Overspill Policy. 1975.

18120 GLAISTER (JANET) *and* BRENNAN (TOM). County Town: A Civic Survey for the Planning of Worcester. Worcester. 1946.

18121 FEINSTEIN (CHARLES H.) *ed.* York 1831–1981: 150 Years of Scientific Endeavour and Social Change. York. 1981.

18122 WILLMOT (G. F.), BIGGINS (J. M.), *and* TILLOTT (P. M.) *eds.* York: A Survey, 1959—Prepared for the British Association. 1959.

4. TOWNS: SCOTLAND

18123 WHYTE (I. D.) *and* WHYTE (K. A.). Sources for Scottish Historical Geography: An Introductory Guide. Norwich. 1981.

18124 ADAMS (IAN HUGH). The Making of Urban Scotland. 1978.

18125 GORDON (GEORGE) *and* DICKS (BRIAN) *eds.* Scottish Urban History. Aberd. 1983.

18126 GORDON (GEORGE) *ed.* Perspectives on the Scottish City. Aberd. 1985.

18127 GRIEVE (ROBERT) *and* ROBERTSON (DONALD JAMES). The City and the Region. Edin. 1964.

18128 CHAPMAN (DENNIS). The Location of Dwellings in Scottish Towns: An Inquiry into some of the Factors Relevant to the Planning of New Urban Communities, Made for the Department of Health for Scotland. 1943. [Wartime social survey, n.s. no. 34.].

18129 JONES (S. J.) *ed.* Dundee and District. Dundee. 1968.

18130 DUNDEE: An Evocation of Town Life before the War: From Memories Collected from Local Inhabitants. Blairgowrie. 1978.

18131 WALKER (W. M.). Juteopolis: Dundee and its Textile Workers, 1885–1923. Edin. 1979.

18132 PEACOCK (HELEN) *ed.* The Unmaking of Edinburgh: The Decay, Depopulation and Destruction of Central Edinburgh: An Argument for City Centre Living and a Call for Action. Edin. 1976.

18133 BARCLAY (J. B.) *ed.* Looking at Lothian: Monographs on the Economy, Industry, Government, Culture and Services in Edinburgh and Lothian. Edin. 1979.

18134 OAKLEY (CHARLES ALLEN). The Second City. 2nd edn 1967.

18135 DAICHES (DAVID). Glasgow. 1977.

18136 MILLER (RONALD) *and* TIVY (JOY) *eds.* The Glasgow Region: A General Survey. Glas. 1958.

18137 CHECKLAND (SYDNEY GEORGE). The Upas Tree: Glasgow 1875—1975: A Study in Growth and Contraction. Glas. 1976. 2nd edn 1981.

18138 KEATING (MICHAEL). The City that Refused to Die: Glasgow: The Politics of Urban Regeneration. Aberd. 1988.

18139 BRENNAN (T.). 'Gorbals: A Study in Redevelopment'. *Scot. J. Pol. Econ.* 4(2) (1957), 114–26.

18140 SOPPELSA (J.). 'L'Expansion Urbaine Récente de Glasgow'. *A. Géog.* 76(417) (1967), 528–51.

18141 ORR (S. C.). 'Urban Renewal in Glasgow'. *Scot. J. Pol. Econ.* 6(2) (1959), 139–44.

18142 HENDERSON (R. A.). 'Industrial Overspill from Glasgow: 1958–1968'. *Urban Studs* 11 (1974), 61–79.

18143 RIDDELL (J. F.). Clyde Navigation: A History of the Development and Deepening of the River Clyde. Edin. 1979.

18144 PORTEOUS (ROBERT). Grangemouth's Modern History, 1768–1968. Grangemouth. 1970.

18145 MOORE (JOHN). Doune Valley Diary: The Critical Decade, 1963–72. Cumnock. 1980.

18146 HOUSE (JACK). Dunoon, 1868–1968. Dunoon. 1968.

18147 MILNE (COLIN). The Story of Gourock, 1858–1958. Gourock. 1958.

18148 McLELLAN (JACK). Larkhall: Its Historical Development. Larkhall. 1979.

18149 SMITH (R. D. P.). 'The Changing Urban Hierarchy in Scotland'. *Regional Studs* 12 (1978), 331–51.

18150 DONNISON (DAVID) *and* MIDDLETON (ALAN) *eds.* Rejuvenating the Inner City: The Scottish Experience. 1987.

18151 —— The North-East of Scotland: A Survey Prepared for the Aberdeen Meeting of the British Association for the Advancement of Science. Aberd. 1963.

18152 OGILVIE (ALAN G.) *et al. eds.* Scientific Survey of South and East Scotland. Edin. 1951.

18153 TIMMS (DUNCAN) *ed.* The Stirling Region. Stirling. 1974.

18154 BUTT (JOHN) *and* GORDON (GEORGE) *eds.* Strathclyde: Changing Horizons. Edin. 1985.

5. TOWNS: WALES

18155 CARTER (HAROLD). The Growth of the Welsh City System. Cardiff. 1969. [Inaugural lecture.].

18156 CARTER (HAROLD) *and* DAVIES (WAYNE K. D.). Urban Essays: Studies in the Geography of Wales. 1970.

18157 DAVIES (EDWARD JOHN). The Blaenavon Story. 2nd edn Pontypool. 1975. [Sometime chairman, Blaenavon UDC.].

18158 GRAY-JONES (ARTHUR). A History of Ebbw Vale. Risca. 1970. Repr. 1971.

18159 —— The Cardiff Region: A Survey Prepared for the Meeting of the British Association held in Cardiff, 31st August to 7th September 1960. Cardiff. 1960.

18160 REES (WILLIAM). Cardiff: A History of the City. Cardiff. 1962.

18161 JONES (S. LLOYD) *ed.* Cardiff, 1889–1974: The Story of the County Borough. Cardiff. 1974.

18162 REES (*Sir* JAMES FREDERICK). 'Cities of Men' in The Problem of Wales and other Essays. Cardiff. 1963.

18163 STACEY (M.). 'Urban Redevelopment: The Case of the Lower Swansea Valley'. *Urban Studs* 3(1) (1966), 22–34.

18164 GORDON (GEORGE) *ed.* Regional Cities in the U.K., 1890–1980. 1986. [Includes Cardiff.].

6. TOWNS: IRELAND

18165 PARKE (J. M. C.). Belfast: Areas of Special Social Need: Report by Project Team. 1976.

18166 BECKETT (JAMES CAMLIN) *and* GLASSCOCK (ROBIN EDGAR) *eds.* Belfast: The Origin and Growth of an Industrial City. 1967.

18167 EVANS (E. ESTYN) *et al. eds.* Belfast in Its Regional Setting: A Scientific Study. 1952.

18168 HAMILTON (PAUL). Up the Shankill. Belf. 1979.

18169 BARTON (BRIAN). Belfast in the Blitz. Belf. 1989.

18170 HARKNESS (DAVID) *and* O'DOWD (MARY). The Town in Ireland. Belf. 1981.

18171 JONES (EMRYS). A Social Geography of Belfast. 1960.

18172 DAWSON (G. M.). 'Defensive Planning in Belfast'. *Irish Geographer* 17 (1984), 27–41.

18173 McGURNAGHAN (M.). 'Integrated Operations and Urban Renewal: The Belfast Experience, 1981–1985'. *Administration (Dublin)* 34 (1986), 505–26.

7. NEW TOWNS

18174 CHAMPION (A. G.), CLEGG (K.), *and* DAVIES (R. L.). Facts About the New Towns: A Socio-economic Digest. 1983.

18175 VEAL (ANTHONY JAMES). New Communities in the United Kingdom: A Classified Bibliography. Birmingham. 1973. Supplement. 1975.

18176 VEAL (ANTHONY JAMES) *and* DUESBERY (W. K.) *comps.* A First List of U.K. Student Theses and Dissertations in Planning and Urban and Regional Studies. Birmingham. 1976.

18177 New Town Development Corporations. Annual Reports. 1948/9+.

18178 McGOVERN (P. D.). 'The Scottish New Towns'. *Town & Country Planning* 35(6) (1967), 287–92.

18179 CLARK (B. D.). 'Les Nouvelles Villes d'Écosse'. *C. Sociol. Econ.* 11 (1964), 353–86.

18180 CARTER (CHRISTOPHER J.). The Scottish New Towns: Their Contribution to Post-War Growth and Development in Central Scotland. Dundee. 1984.

18181 —— Innovation in Planning Thought and Practice at Cumbernauld New Town, 1956–1962. Dundee. 1983.

18182 KEATING (MICHAEL) *and* CARTER (CHRISTOPHER J.). 'Policy-Making and the Scottish Office: The Designation of Cumbernauld New Town'. *Public Admin* 65 (1987), 391–407.

18183 CUMBERNAULD DEVELOPMENT CORPORATION. Investigating Cumbernauld New Town: A Factual Guide for Every Organisation Faced with Development Problems. Cumbernauld. 1965.

18184 ZWEIG (FERDYNAND). The Cumbernauld Study. 1970.

18185 COLEMAN (SOLOMON DAVID). Mental Health and Social Adjustment in a New Town: An Exploratory Study in East Kilbride. Glasgow. 1965.

18186 SMITH (ROGER). East Kilbride: The Biography of a Scottish New Town, 1947–1973. 1979.

18187 FERGUSON (K.). Glenrothes: The First Twenty Five Years. 1974.

18188 SCOTTISH DEVELOPMENT DEPARTMENT. Irvine New Town: Final Report on Planning Proposals. A Report to the Secretary of State for Scotland by Henry Wilson and Lewis Womersley . . . 1966. Edin. 1967.

18189 LUCAS (PETER). A Reporter's Look at the Development of One of Britain's Biggest New Towns. 1985. [Basildon.].

18190 PARRIS (H.) *and* PARRIS (J.). Bracknell: The Making of Our New Town. Bracknell. 1981.

18191 OGILVY (AUDREY). Bracknell and Its Migrants: Twenty-One Years of New Town Growth. 1975.

18192 HUSSEY (C.). The Hampstead Garden Suburb: Its Achievements and Significance. 1937.

18193 GREEN (BRIGID GRAFTON). Hampstead Garden Suburb, 1907–1977. 1977.

18194 SLACK (KATHLEEN M.). Henrietta's Dream: A Chronicle of the Hampstead Garden Suburb, 1905–1982. 1982.

18195 GIBBERD (FREDERICK), HARVEY (BEN HYDE) WHITE (LEN), *et al.* Harlow: A Story of a New Town. 1980.

18196 PURDOM (CHARLES BENJAMIN). The Garden City after the War: A Discussion of the Position of the Garden City at Letchworth, and a Proposal for a National Housing Policy. Letchworth. 1917.

18197 —— The Letchworth Achievement. 1963.

18198 WALKER (DEREK). The Architecture and Planning of Milton Keynes. 1982.

18199 ANSTIS (GORDON). Redditch: Success in the Heart of England: The History of Redditch New Town, 1964–85. 1985.

18200 LING (ARTHUR). Runcorn New Town: Master Plan, Prepared for the Runcorn Development Corporation. Runcorn. 1967.

18201 BALCHIN (JACK). First New Town: An Autobiography of the Stevenage Development Corporation, 1946–1980. Stevenage. 1980.

18202 ORLANS (HAROLD). Stevenage: A Sociological Study of a New Town. 1952.

18203 GREATER LONDON COUNCIL. Thamesmead Annual Report. 1973–4.

18204 —— Thamesmead: Housing a Balanced Community. 1974.

18205 SKINNER (I.). Thamesmead. 1976.

18206 HOLLEY (STEPHEN). Washington: Quicker by Quango: The History of Washington New Town, 1964–1983. 1983.

18207 WELWYN ASSOCIATON. Welwyn Garden City: Its Meaning and Methods. Welwyn. 1929.

18208 FILLER (R.). A History of Welwyn Garden City. Chichester. 1986.

18209 U.K. MINISTRY OF HOUSING AND LOCAL GOVERNMENT. Central Lancashire: Study for a City. 1967.

18210 Central Lancashire New Town Proposal: Impact on North-East Lancashire. 1968.

18211 HUDSON (R.) *with* JOHNSON (M. R. D.) *et al.* New Towns in North East England. Durham. 1976.

18212 LINDSAY (WALTON) *with* CHEESMAN (ROBERT), *and* DE PORZECANSKI (MARTHA). New Towns: A Comparative Atlas. Camb. 1972.

18213 DE PORZECANSKI (MARTHA) *with* CHEESMAN (ROBERT), *and* LINDSAY (WALTON). New Towns: The Evolution of Planning Criteria. Camb. 1972.

18214 LLOYD (T. ALWYN). 'The "New Town" Proposals'. *Town Planning Rev.* viii (1920), 197–9.

18215 OSBORN (*Sir* FREDERIC JAMES). Green-Belt Cities. 1946. 2nd edn 1969.

18216 —— New Towns: Their Origins, Achievements and Progress. 3rd edn 1977.

18217 OSBORN (*Sir* FREDERIC JAMES) *and* WHITTICK (ARNOLD). The New Towns: The Answer to Megalopolis. Rev. edn 1969.

18218 ALDRIDGE (MERYL). The British New Towns: A Programme Without a Policy. 1979.

18219 CULLINGWORTH (J. B.). Environmental Planning, 1939–1969: vol.3. New Towns Policy. 1980.

18220 U.K. MINISTRY OF TOWN AND COUNTRY PLANNING. New Towns Committee: Final Report. Cmnd. 6876 (Reith Committee). 1946.

18221 BEVERIDGE (WILLIAM HENRY) *Baron.* New Towns and the Case for Them. 1952.

18222 MACKENZIE (NORMAN I.). The New Towns: The Success of Social Planning. 1955.

18223 RODWIN (LLOYD). The British New Towns Policy: Problems and Implications. Camb., Mass. 1956.

18224 HART (W. O.). 'British New Towns Today'. *Land. Econ.* 32 (1956), 57–68.

18225 SYKES (J.). 'La Politique de Localisation des Industries en Grande-Bretagne: les Villes Nouvelles'. *R. Sci. Financ.* (1) (1958), 43–64.

18226 DUFF (ALAN COLQUHOUN). Britain's New Towns: An Experiment in Living. 1961.

18227 CULLINGWORTH (JOHN BARRY) *and* KARN (VALERIE ANN). The Ownership and Management of Housing in the New Towns: Report. 1968.

18228 GRIMSHAW (P. N.). 'Britain's Second Generation New Towns'. *Progress* 53(298) (1968–9), 49–54.

18229 TRINTIGNAC (A.). 'La Planification en Grande-Bretagne: Le Développement des Villes Nouvelles'. *Docum. Rech. Econ. Soc.* 8(3) (1960), 5–125.

18230 DUNNING (J.). 'Manufacturing Industry in the New Towns'. *Manch. Sch. Soc. Studs* xxviii(2) (1970).

18231 ROSNER (R.). Neue Städte in England. Munich. 1962.

18232 WILLMOTT (PETER). 'Some Social Characteristics of a Scottish and an English New Town'. *Town Planning Rev.* 34(4) (1963-4), 309-17.

18233 STEELE (D. B.). 'New Towns for Depressed Areas'. *Town Planning Rev.* 34(3) (1963-4), 199-213.

18234 RANKIN (N. H.). 'Social Adjustment in a North-West New Town'. *Sociol. Rev.* 11(3) (1963), 289-302.

18235 CAGE (E. E. H.). 'Industrial and Social Developments in English New Towns'. *Administration (Dublin)* 12(3) (1964), 181-9.

18236 MOSSE (R.). 'Les Nouvelles Villes en Grande-Bretagne'. *Rev. Sociol.* 197(1966), 311-16.

18237 CORDEN (CAROL). Planned Cities: New Towns in Britain and America. Beverley Hills, Ca. 1977.

18238 KIRK (C. W. G. T.). 'New Towns in Great Britain'. *Publ. Management* 48(3) (1966), 70-80.

18239 MERLIN (P.). 'Les Villes Nouvelles en Grande-Bretagne'. *A. Géog.* 87(421) (1968), 278-95.

18240 HERAUD (B. J.).'Social Class and the New Towns'. *Urban Studs* 5(1) (1968), 33-58.

18241 —— 'The New Towns and London's Housing Problem'. *Urban Studs* 3(1) (1966), 8-21.

18242 OGILVY (A. A.). 'The Self-Contained New Town: Employment and Population'. *Town Planning Rev.* 39(1) (1968), 38-54.

18243 THOMAS (RAY). Aycliffe to Cumbernauld: A Study of Seven New Towns in their Regions. PEP broadsheets. No. 516. 1969.

18244 —— *Ed.* Perspectives on New Town Development. Milton Keynes. 1976.

18245 —— Commuting Flows and the Growth of London's New Towns, 1951-1971. Milton Keynes. 1977.

18246 —— London's New Towns: A Study of Self-Contained and Balanced Communities. PEP. 1969.

18247 McDOUGALL (R. S.). 'The Administrative Problems of Building a New Town in the United Kingdom'. *J. Admin Oversees* 8(1) (1964), 17-25.

18248 SCHAFFER (FRANK). The New Town Story. 1970. 2nd edn 1972.

18249 HURLEY (C. W.). 'The New Towns of Northumberland'. *Stud. Comp. Loc. Gvt* 5(1) (1971), 51-6.

18250 CHALINE (C.). 'La Nouvelle Génération des "New Towns" Britanniques'. *A. Géog.* 80(442) (1971), 666-86.

18251 TOWN AND COUNTRY PLANNING ASSOCIATION. New Towns: The British Experience. 1972.

18252 EVANS (HAZEL MEYRICK) *ed.* New Towns: The British Experience. 1972.

18253 U.K. CENTRAL OFFICE OF INFORMATION. The New Towns of Britain. 5th edn 1974.

18254 HUTTMAN (J.) *and* HUTTMAN (E. D.). 'Dutch and British Towns: Self-Containment and Socioeconomic Balance'. *Growth & Change* 4(1) (1973), 30-7.

18255 BLAKE (P.) comp. 'Britain's New Towns: Facts and Figures'. *Town & Country Planning* 43 (1975), 81-97.

18256 CHAMPION (A. G.). 'Population Characteristics of the British New Towns'. *Town & County Planning* 43 (1975), 63-9.

18257 TRANCIK (R.). 'Studlands Park, England: A Sociophysical Evaluation of a New Community'. *Ekistics* 39 (1975), 417-22.

18258 LEVIN (P. H.). Government and the Planning Process: An Analysis and Appraisal of Government Decision-Making Processes with Special Reference to the Launching of the New Towns and Town Development Schemes. 1976.

18259 FIELDS (A. MIRYAM) *and* CROFTS (C.). Some Aspects of Planned Migration to New and Expanding Towns. 1977. [GLC research memorandum 527.].

18260 HAGGERTY (M.). The New Towns. 1981.

18261 FOTHERGILL (S.) *et al.* 'The Impact of the New and Expanded Town Programme on Industrial Location in Britain, 1960-1978'. *Regional Studs* 17 (1983), 251-60.

18262 DUPREE (HENRY). Urban Transportation: The New Town Solution. Aldershot. 1987.

18263 POCOCK (D. C. D.). 'Some Features of the Population of Corby New Town'. *Sociol. Rev.* 8(2) (1960), 209-21.

18264 ANTRIM NEW TOWN: Outline Plan: Report of the Steering Committee. Belf. 1965.

18265 WELSH OFFICE. A New Town in Mid-Wales: Consultants' Proposals. A Report to the Secretary of State for Wales by Economic Associates Ltd. 1966.

18266 RIDEN (PHILIP). Rebuilding a Valley: A History of Cwmbran Development Corporation. Cwmbran. 1988.

8. URBAN GEOGRAPHY

18267 FREEMAN (THOMAS WALTER). Geography and Planning. 1958.

18268 BALE (J. R.). 'Towards a Definition of the Industrial Estate: A Note on a Neglected Aspect of Urban Geography'. *Geography* 59 (1974), 31-4.

18269 BECKINSALE (ROBERT PERCY) *and* HOUSTON (JAMES MAC-INTOSH). Urbanization and its Problems. Essays in Honour of Edmund W. Gilbert. 1968.

18270 CARTER (HAROLD). The Study of Urban Geography. 1972. 2nd edn 1975.

18271 HERBERT (DAVID T.). Urban Geography: A Social Perspective. Newton Abbot. 1972.

18272 THORPE (DAVID). The Geographer and Urban Studies. Durham. 1966.

18273 JONES (EMRYS). Towns and Cities. 1966. Repr. 1969.

18274 —— The City in Geography: An Inaugural Lecture . . . at L.S.E. 1962.

18275 JOHNSON (JAMES HENRY). Urban Geography: An Introductory Analysis. 2nd edn 1972. Repr. 1976.

9. URBAN SOCIOLOGY

18276 KUPER (LEO) ed. Living in Towns: Selected Research Papers in Urban Sociology of the Faculty of Commerce and Social Science, University of Birmingham. 1963.

18277 MANN (PETER HENRY). An Approach to Urban Sociology. 1965.

18278 —— An Approach to Methods of Sociological Enquiry. Oxf. 1968.

18279 NOTTRIDGE (HAROLD EDGAR). The Sociology of Urban Living. Lond./Boston, Mass. 1972.

18280 MOSER (*Sir* CLAUS ADOLF) *and* SCOTT (WOLF). British Towns: A Statistical Study of Their Social and Economic Differences. 1961.

18281 MORRIS (RAYMOND NEVILLE). Urban Sociology. 1968.

18282 PEACH (GUTHLAC CERI KLAUS) ed. Urban Social Segregation. 1975.

18283 PICKVANCE (C. G.) ed. and trans. Urban Sociology: Critical Essays. 1976.

18284 SPECIAL PUBLICATION. INSTITUTE OF BRITISH GEOGRAPHERS, No.5. Social Patterns in Cities. 1973.

18285 NEWTON (K.). 'City Politics in Britain and the United States'. *Pol. Studs* 17(2) (1969), 208–18.

18286 MORGAN (B. S.). 'Segregation of Socioeconomic Groups in Urban Areas: A Comparative Analysis'. *Urban Studs* 12 (1975), 47–60.

18287 GLASS (RUTH). 'Urban Sociology in Great Britain'. *Current Sociology* iv(4) (1955), 5–76. Reprinted in part in Readings in Urban Sociology. R. E. Pahl ed. Oxf. 1968.

18288 —— 'Urban Sociology' in A. T. Welford *et al.* ed. Society: Problems and Methods of Study. 1962.

18289 GOIST (PARK DIXON). 'Patrick Geddes and the City'. *Amer. Inst. Plan. J.* 40 (1974), 31–7.

18290 HATT (PAUL KITCHENER) *and* REISS (ALBERT JOHN) eds. Cities and Society. 2nd edn. repr. 1961.

18291 RAYNOR (JOHN) *and* HARDEN (JANE) eds. Readings in Urban Education. Vol. 1. Cities, Communities and the Young. Vol 2. Equality and City Schools. Milton Keynes. 1973.

18292 WARD (COLIN). Vandalism. 1973.

18293 —— The Child in the City. 1978.

10. SUBURBIA

18294 THORNS (DAVID CHRISTOPHER). Suburbia. 1972.

18295 HALL (PETER) 'The Urban Culture and the Suburban Culture' in R. Wells and C. Walton, *eds.* Man in the City of the Future. 1968. 99–145.

18296 JOHNSON (JAMES HENRY) *ed.* Suburban Growth: Geographical Processes at the Edge of the Western City. 1974.

18297 THOMPSON (F. M. L.) *ed.* The Rise of Suburbia. Leicester. 1982.

18298 BULL (P. J.). 'The Spatial Components of Intra-Urban Manufacturing Change: Suburbanisation in Clydeside, 1958–1968'. *Trans. Inst. Brit. Geog.* 3 (1978), 91–100.

18299 HAMNETT (CHRIS). 'The Post-War Restructuring of the British Housing and Labour Markets'. *Environment and Planning* A 16 (1984), 147–61.

18300 —— 'The Changing Socioeconomic Structure of London and the South East, 1961–1981'. *Regional Studs* 20 (1986), 391–406.

18301 WILLIAMS (GUY R.). London in the Country: The Growth of Suburbia. 1975.

18302 EDWARDS (ARTHUR M.). The Design of Suburbia: A Critical Study in Environmental History. 1981.

18303 BARRETT (HELENA) *and* PHILLIPS (JOHN). Suburban Style: The British House, 1840–1960. 1987.

11. LONDON

18304 THOMAS (D.). 'London's Green Belt: The Evolution of an Idea'. *Geog. J.* 129(1) (1963), 14–24.

18305 FRIEDLANDER (DOV). 'London's Urban Transition, 1851–1951'. *Urban Studs* 11, (1974), 127–41.

18306 —— 'The Spread of Urbanization in England and Wales, 1851–1951'. *Pop. Studs* 24(3) (1970), 423–43.

18307 SHARPE (L. J.). 'New Plan for London?'. *Nat. Civic. Rev.* 49(10) (1960), 543–8.

18308 DALEY (A.) *and* BENJAMIN (B.). 'London as a Case Study'. *Pop. Studs* 17(3) (1964), 249–62.

18309 LEE (R. K.). 'Planning and Social Change in East London'. *East London Papers* xiv(1), (1972).

18310 RYAN (M.) *and* ISAACSON (P.). 'Structure Planning in Dockland'. *Pol. Q.* 45 (1974), 323–32.

18311 CRAVEN (E.). 'Private Residential Expansion in Kent 1956–1964: A Study of Pattern and Process in Urban Growth'. *Urban Studs* 6(1) (1969), 1–16.

18312 THOMPSON (ERIC J.). 'Analyses of Census Data for London'. Greater London Council Bulletins 4 and 8.

18313 WHITEHEAD (J. W. R.). 'The Settlement Morphology of London's Cocktail Belt'. *Tijd Econ. Soc. Geog.* 58(1) (1967), 20–7.

18314 KIRWAN (DANIEL JOSEPH). Palace and Hovel; or, Phases of London life. Being Personal Observations of an American in London by Day and Night. *Ed.* by A. Allan. 1963.

18315 ASH (MAURICE ANTHONY). 'What Mr Crosland Should do About London'. *Town & Country Planning* 43 (1975), 148–51.

18316 —— 'End of Dispersal'. *Town & Country Planning* 43 (1975), 55–7.

18317 —— 'End of the Affair [Community Land Bill]'. *Town & Country Planning* 43 (1975), 244–5.

18318 —— 'Planning Reprieved'. *Town & Country Planning* 43 (1975), 420–3.

18319 CHRISTIE (I.). 'Covent Garden: Approaches to Urban Renewal'. *Town Planning Rev.* 45 (1974), 30–62.

18320 —— 'Act Two'. *Economist* 254 (1975), 100.

18321 —— 'Vegetarians' Subsidy'. *Economist* 256 (1975), 73.

18322 DROVER (G.). 'London and New York: Residential Density Planning Policies and Development'. *Town Planning Rev.* 46 (1975), 165–84.

18323 TOWN AND COUNTRY PLANNING ASSOCIATION. The Paper Metropolis: The Report of a Study of the Growth of Office Employment in London and a Survey of Decentralised Offices, etc. 1962.

18324 ECONOMIST INTELLIGENCE UNIT. A Survey of Factors Governing the Location of Offices in the London Area; . . . Prepared for the Location of Offices Bureau. 1964.

18325 LOCATION OF OFFICES BUREAU. A Wise Move. 1965.

18326 RHODES (GERALD) *ed.* The New Government of London: The First Five Years. 1972.

18327 RUCK (S. K.) and RHODES (GERALD). The Government of Greater London. 1970.

18328 RHODES (GERALD). The Government of London: The Struggle for Reform. 1970.

18329 —— Town Government in South-East England: A Comparative Study of Six Local Authorities. . . . 1967.

18330 SMALLWOOD (FRANK). Greater London: The Politics of Metropolitan Reform. Indianapolis, Ind. 1965.

18331 WILLMOTT (PETER). Whatever's Happening to London?: An Analysis of Changes in Population Structure and their Effects on Community Life. 1975.

18332 —— 'Some Social Trends'. *Urban Studs* vi(3) (1969). Reprinted in Problems of an Urban Society. Vol. 3. Planning for Change. *Ed.* by J. B. Cullingworth. 1973.

18333 WILCOX (DAVID) and RICHARDS (DAVID). London: The Heartless City. 1977.

18334 CHESTERTON (ADA ELIZABETH). In Darkest London. 1926.

18335 WEBBER (RICHARD). Social Area Analysis of Greater London. 1974.

18336 —— The Social Structure of Haringey. 1977.

18337 WEBBER (RICHARD) *and* CRAIG (JOHN). Socioeconomic Classification of Local Authority Areas. 1978.

18338 SHEPHERD (JOHN), WESTAWAY (JOHN), *and* LEE (TREVOR). A Social Atlas of London. Oxf. 1974.

18339 SKINNER (FRANK W.) *ed.* People Without Roots: A Study Undertaken in the Borough of Tower Hamlets 1966–67, and an Appraisal of Services Provided by the Voluntary and Statutory Agencies. 1967.

18340 SMITH (*Sir* HUBERT LLEWELLYN) *Director.* The New Survey of London Life and Labour. 9 vols. 1930–5. Vols 3 and 6. Survey of Social Conditions. 1932–4.

18341 ROBINSON (ARTHUR J.) *and* CHESSHYRE (D. H. B.). The Green: A History of the Heart of Bethnal Green and the Legend of the Blind Beggar. 1978.

18342 RASMUSSEN (STEEN EILER). London: The Unique City. Rev. edn 1937. Rev. edn 1982.

18343 GREATER LONDON COUNCIL. London: Facts and Figures.

18344 MITCHELL (ROSAMOND JOSCELYNE) *and* LEYS (MARY DOROTHY ROSE). A History of London Life. 1958.

18345 —— A History of the English People. 1951.

18346 THOROGOOD (H.). East of Aldgate.

18347 WILLIS (F.). London General. 1953.

18348 SMITH (A.). The East Enders. 1961.

18349 LEFF (VERA) *and* BLUNDEN (GEOFFREY HALSTEAD). The Willesden Story: History . . . Commissioned by the Willesden Council to Record the Work and Achievements of the Borough of Willesden and to Tell the Story of its People. 1965.

18350 JONES (EMRYS) *and* SINCLAIR (D. J.) *eds.* Atlas of London and the London Region. Oxf. 1969.

18351 MARTIN (JOHN EDWARD). Greater London: An Industrial Geography. 1966.

18352 JACKSON (THOMAS ALFRED). The History and Working Class Associations and Traditions of Clerkenwell Green; Written on the Occasion of the Opening of the Bookshop of Marx House. 1933.

18353 JACKSON (ALAN ARTHUR). Semi-Detached London: Suburban Development, Life and Transport 1900–39. 1973.

18354 HALL (PETER GEOFFREY). The Industries of London Since 1861. 1963.

18355 CHALINE (C.). 'Les 'Expanded Towns' de la Région de Londres'. *A. Géog.* 78(430) (1969), 636–53.

18356 —— 'Nouveaux Aspects de la Cité de Londres'. *A. Géog.* 70(379) (1961), 273–86.

18357 GLASS (RUTH) *et al.* London: Aspects of Change. 1964. [Centre for Urban Studies.].

18358 —— Urban Sociology in Great Britain. 1955.

18359 DONNISON (DAVID VERNON) *and* EVERSLEY (DAVID EDWARD CHARLES) *eds.* London Urban Patterns, Problems, and Policies: A Study Sponsored by the

Centre for Environmental Studies. 1973. [See chapter by B. J. Parker 'Some Sociological Implications of Slum Clearance Programmes'.].

18360 COPPOCK (JOHN TERENCE) *and* PRINCE (HUGH COUNSELL) *eds*. Greater London. 1964.

18361 TRENT (CHRISTOPHER). Greater London: Its Growth and Development Through Two Thousand Years. 1965.

18362 LONDON GLC. Survey of London. Vols. 33–4 : The Parish of St Anne, Soho. 1966.

18363 CLAYTON (ROBERT) *ed*. The Geography of Greater London: A Source Book. 1964.

18364 ASH (MAURICE ANTHONY). A Guide to the Structure of London. Bath. 1972.

18365 ASH (BERNARD). The Golden City: London Between the Fires, 1666–1941. 1964.

18366 CARTER (EDWARD JULIAN). The Future of London. Harmondsworth. 1962.

18367 BOAST (MARY). The Story of Bermondsey. 1978.

18368 LEFF (VERA) *and* BLUNDEN (GEOFFREY HALSTEAD). Riverside Story : The Story of Bermondsey and its People, 1900–1965. 1965.

18369 POULSEN (CHARLES). Victoria Park: A Study in the History of East London. 1976.

18370 STUART (DOROTHY MARGARET). London Through the Ages: The Story of a City and its Citizens, 54 BC—AD 1944. 1956.

B. HOUSING

18371 MAHON (DAVID). No Place in the Country: A Report on Second Homes in England and Wales. *Ed.* Moura Constable.   1973.

18372 CAERNARVONSHIRE COUNTY PLANNING DEPARTMENT. Second Homes. Caernarvon. 1973.

18373 DE VANE (RICHARD). Second Home Ownership: A Case Study. Cardiff. 1975.

18374 BIELCKUS (C. L.), ROGERS (A. W.), *and* WIBBERLEY (G. P.). Second Homes in England and Wales: A Study of the Distribution and Use of Rural Properties Taken Over as Second Homes. Ashford. 1972.

18375 MARTIN (IAN). Second Homes in Denbighshire. Denbighshire Planning Dept. Ruthin. 1972.

18376 SHUCKSMITH (MARK). No Homes For Locals? Farnborough. 1981. [Lake District.].

18377 PARIS (CHRIS) *and* POPPLESTONE (GERRY). Squatting: A Bibliography. 1978.

18378 —— 'Squatting and the Criminal Law Act: Problem Or Solution?'. *Cent. Environ. Studs Rev.* 2 (1977), 38–45.

18379 KINGHAN (MIKE). Squatters in London. 1977.

18380 HINTON (JAMES). 'Self-Help and Socialism: The Squatters Movement of 1946'. *Hist. Workshop* 25 (1988), 100–26.

18381 FRANKLIN (A.). Squatting in England, 1969–79: A Case Study of Social Conflict in Advanced Industrial Capitalism. Bristol. 1984.

18382 FAWKES (S.) *and* HARGREAVES (J.) *comps*. Squatting. 1976.

18383 BAILEY (RON). The Story of the Illegal Eviction of Squatters in Redbridge. 1969.

18384 —— The Squatters. Harmondsworth. 1973.

18385 TOWNROE (BERNARD STEPHEN). The Slum Problem. 1928.

18386 —— Britain Rebuilding: The Slum and Overcrowding Campaigns. 1936.

18387 SIMON (ERNEST DARWIN) *Baron*. How to Abolish the Slums. 1929.

18388 —— Houses For All. 1924.

18389 —— The Anti-Slum Campaign. 1933.

18390 QUIGLEY (HUGH) *and* GOLDIE (ISMAY). Housing and Slum Clearance in London. 1934.

18391 CURRIE (G. W.). The Housing Problem in London. 1928.

18392 MARTIN (CHARLES ROBERT ARTHUR). Slums and Slummers: A Sociological Treatise on the Housing Problem. 1935.

18393 MARSHALL (HOWARD P.) *and* TREVELYAN (AVICE). Slum. 1933.

18394 —— CENTRAL HOUSING ADVISORY COMMITTEE. Moving From the Slums: Seventh Report of the Housing Management Sub-Committee [Chairman, James Macalister Mackintosh.]. 1956.

18395 BARNES (HARRY). Housing: The Facts and the Future. 1923.

18396 —— The Slum: Its Story and Solution. 1931. 2nd edn 1934.

18397 JENKINSON (CHARLES). Sentimentality? Or Common-sense? Leeds. 1931.

18398 —— Our Housing Objective. 1943.

18399 HAMMERTON (HOWARD J.). This Turbulent Priest: The Story of C. Jenkinson, Parish Priest and Housing Reformer. 1952.

18400 CONQUEST (JOAN). The Naked Truth: Shocking Revelations About the Slums by an Ex-nursing Sister. 1933.

18401 MARTIN (JOHN). Corner of England. 1932.

18402 ROBERTS (ROBERT). The Classic Slum: Salford Life in the First Quarter of the Century. Manchester. 1971.

18403 HARRISON (PAUL). Inside the Inner City. Harmondsworth. 1983.

18404 BUXTON (RICHARD JOSEPH). Local Government. 2nd edn Harmondsworth. 1973. [Ch. 2 on 'Slum Clearance'.].

18405 COVENTRY COMMUNITY WORKSHOP AND SHELTER. Council Houses: The New Slums. Coventry. 1973.

18406 JENNINGS (HILDA). Societies in the Making: A Study of Development and Redevelopment within a County Borough. 1962.

18407 FLETT (HAZEL) and PEAFORD (MARGARET). The Effect of Slum Clearance on Multi-occupation. Bristol. 1977.

18408 KIRBY (D. A.). Slum Housing and Residential Renewal: The Case in Urban Britain. 1979.

18409 PARIS (CHRIS) and BLACKABY (BOB). Not Much Improvement: Urban Renewal Policy in Birmingham. 1979.

18410 ENGLISH (JOHN), MADIGAN (RUTH), and NORMAN (PETER). Slum Clearance: The Social and Administrative Context in England and Wales. 1976.

18411 ENGLISH (JOHN) and NORMAN (PETER). An Appraisal of Slum Clearance Procedures in England and Wales. Glasgow. 1974.

18412 ENGLISH (JOHN). One Hundred Years of Slum Clearance in England and Wales: Policies and Programmes, 1868–1970. Glasgow. 1974.

18413 DENNIS (NORMAN). People and Planning: The Sociology of Housing in Sunderland. 1970.

18414 WILKINSON (R.). 'A Statistical Analysis of Attitudes to Moving'. *Urban Studs* 2 (1965), 1–14.

18415 SCHORR (ALVIN LOUIS). Slums and Social Insecurity. 1964.

18416 SAMUEL (RAPHAEL) et al. 'The Long Pursuit: Studies in the Government's Slum Clearance Programme'. *New Left Rev.* 13–14 (1962), 38–100.

18417 FIELD-FISHER (THOMAS GILBERT) and IBBOTSON (STANLEY). The Protection From Eviction Act (1964). 1965.

18418 —— Rent Act (1965). 1965.

18419 —— et al. Rent Regulation and Control. 1967.

18420 MCGARRY (ROBERT EDGAR). The Rent Acts. 10th edn 2 vols. 1967.

18421 BARNETT (MALCOLM JOEL) Lord. The Politics of Legislation: The Rent Act. 1957. 1969.

18422 NOTTING HILL HOUSING SERVICE. The Rent Act and the Housing Market in North Kensington. 1970.

18423 HAYEK (FRIEDRICH AUGUST) et al. Verdict on Rent Control. 1972.

18424 WICKS (MALCOLM). Rented Housing and Social Ownership. 1973.

18425 SUTCLIFFE (ANTHONY) ed. Multi-storey Living: The British Working Class Experience. 1974.

18426 PARKER (ROY ALFRED). The Rents of Council Houses. 1967.

18427 HARLOE (MICHAEL), ISSACHAROFF (RUTH), and MINNS (RICHARD). The Organization of Housing: Public and Private Enterprise in London. 1974.

18428 GRAY (HAMISH). The Cost of Council Housing. 1968.

18429 ENGLISH (JOHN) and JONES (COLIN) eds. The Sale of Council Houses. Glasgow. 1977.

18430 BARR (ALBERT WILLIAM CLEEVE). Public Authority Housing. 1958.

18431 BARNSBY (GEORGE). A History of Housing in Wolverhampton 1750–1975. Wolverhampton. 1976.

18432 HOATH (DAVID CHARLES). Council Housing. 1978.

18433 MURIE (ALAN SHAW). The Sale of Council Houses: A Study in Social Policy. Birmingham. 1975.

18434 MURIE (ALAN SHAW) et al. Housing Policy and the Housing System. 1976.

18435 FORREST (RAY) and MURIE (ALAN SHAW). Selling the Welfare State: The Privatisation of Council Housing. 1987.

18436 CROOK (A. D. H.). 'Privatisation of Housing and the Impact of the Conservative Government's Initiatives on Low Cost Home Ownership and Private Renting Between 1979 and 1984 in England and Wales: The Privatisation Policies'. *Environment Planning* 18 (1986), 639–59, 827–36.

18437 SZELENYI (IVAN) ed. Cities in Recession: Critical Responses to the Urban Policies of the New Right. 1984.

18438 HOGGART (K.). 'Political Party Control and the Sale of Local Authority Dwellings'. *Environment Planning* 3 (1985), 463–74.

18439 DUNN (RICHARD), FORREST (RAY), and MURIE (ALAN SHAW). 'The Geography of Council House Sales in England, 1979–1985'. *Urban Studs* 24 (1987), 47–9.

18440 BEIRRE (P.). Fair Rent and Legal Fiction: Housing Rent Legislation in a Capitalist Society. 1977.

18441 GRAY (F.). 'Selection and Allocation in Council Housing'. *Trans Inst. Brit. Geog.* n.s. 1 (1976), 34–46.

18442 MARRINER (SHEILA). 'Sir Alfred Mond's Octopus: A Nationalised House-Building Business'. *Business Hist.* xxi (1979), 23–44.

18443 ATTENBURROW (J. J.). Some Impressions of the Private Sector of the Housing Market. 1968.

18444 —— Society of Labour Lawyers. Housing Group. The End of the Private Landlord. 1973.

18445 PENNANCE (FREDERICK GEORGE) and GRAY (HAMISH). Choice in Housing. 1958.

18446 PENNANCE (FREDERICK GEORGE) AND WEST (WILLIAM ALEXANDER). Housing Market Analyses and Policy. 1969.

18447 BASSETT (KEITH) and SHORT (J. R.). Housing and Residential Structures: Atlantic Approaches. 1980.

18448 BOLEAT (MARK). National Housing Finance Systems. 1985.

18449 FUERST (J. S.) *ed.* Public Housing in Europe and America. 1974.

18450 MUSIL (JIRI). Housing Needs and Policy in Great Britain and Czechoslovakia. Edin./Lond. 1966.

18451 UNGERSON (CLARE) *and* KARN (VALERIE ANN). The Consumer Experience of Housing: Cross-National Perspectives. Farnborough. 1980.

18452 SCOFFHAM (ERNEST R.). The Shape of British Housing. 1984.

18453 MALPASS (PETER) *and* MURIE (ALAN SHAW). Housing Policy and Practice. 1982.

18454 MERRETT (STEPHEN) *with* GRAY (FRED). Owner-Occupation in Britain. 1982.

18455 BUTT (JOHN). 'Working Class Housing in Scottish Cities, 1900–1950'. In 'Scottish Urban History'. *Ed.* by George Gordon and Brian Dicks. Aberd. 1983. 233–68.

18456 WATSON (C. J.). 'Vacancy Chains, Filtering and the Public Sector (West Central Region of Scotland)'. *Amer. Inst. Plan. J.* 40 (1974), 346–52.

18457 MENZIES (WILLIAM C.). 'On What Principle Should the Rents of Houses to be Erected by Local Authorities be Based and Tenants Selected?'. *Trans. Inc. San. Assn. Scot.* (1919), 173–82.

18458 WORSDALL (FRANK). The Tenement: A Way of Life: A Social, Historical and Architectural Study of Housing in Glasgow. Edin. 1979.

18459 WHITE (I. E.). Tenement Town. 1946.

18460 WHYTE (*Sir* WILLIAM EDWARD) *and* GORDON (WILLIAM). The Law of Housing in Scotland. 1934.

18461 COCHRANE (R. G. A.). The Law of Housing in Scotland. 1977.

18462 —— SCOTTISH HOUSING ADVISORY COMMITTEE. Choosing Council Tenants. Report. Edin. 1950.

18463 —— SCOTLAND-DEPARTMENT OF HEALTH. Scottish Housing Handbook. Edin. 1952.

18464 WHYTE (*Sir* WILLIAM EDWARD). Scotland's Housing and Planning Problems. 1942.

18465 —— Planning For Scotland. 1938.

18466 McDONALD (JOHN ROBERT HARRISON). Modern Housing: A Review of Present Housing Requirements in Scotland: A Resumé of Postwar Housing At Home and Abroad and some Practical Suggestions for Future Housing. Glas. 1931.

18467 ENGLISH (JOHN). Housing Allocation in Paisley and Ferguslie Park. Glas. 1975.

18468 —— Housing Allocations and Social Segregation. Paisley. 1978.

18469 DUNCAN (THOMAS LINDSAY CAMERON), COWAN (ROBERT HAMISH), *and* McCABE (MARY GARDEN MORROW). Housing Improvement Policies in Scotland: A Survey of Local Authorities. Glas. 1974.

18470 DUNCAN (THOMAS LINDSAY CAMERON) *and* COWAN (ROBERT HAMISH). Improvement Grants in Scotland, 1967–73. Glas. 1974.

18471 CRAMOND (RONALD DUNCAN). Housing Policy in Scotland, 1919–1964: A Study in State Assistance. Edin./Lond. 1966.

18472 —— Allocation of Council Houses: A Report of a Survey of Methods of Allocation of Tenancies by Local Authorities in Scotland. Edin. 1964.

18473 CULLINGWORTH (JOHN BARRY). A Profile of Glasgow Housing. Edin. 1968.

18474 CULLINGWORTH (JOHN BARRY) *and* WATSON (C. J.). Housing on Clydeside, 1970: Reports. Edin. 1971.

18475 KEMP (P.). The Changing Ownership Structure of the Privately Rented Sector: A Case Study of Partick East, 1964–1978. Glas. 1980.

18476 KARN (VALERIE A.). East Kilbride Housing Survey: A Study of Housing in a New Town. Birm. 1970.

18477 MUNROE (MOIRA) *and* MACLENNAN (DUNCAN). 'Intra-Urban Changes in Housing Prices: Glasgow 1972–83'. *Housing Studs* 2 (1987), 65–81.

18478 JACOBS (SIDNEY). The Right to a Decent House. 1976. [Focus on Glasgow].

18479 CHRISTIAN ACTION. The Gorbals 1965: A Report of an Investigation into the Housing and Social Conditions of the Gorbals and Adjacent Slum Areas of Glasgow. 1965.

18480 BALLANTINE (WILLIAM MACDONALD). Rebuilding A Nation: A Descriptive Account of Housing in Modern Scotland. Edin. 1944.

18481 CAIRNCROSS (*Sir* ALEXANDER KIRKLAND) *ed.* The Scottish Economy. Camb. 1954. [Chapter by Robert Baird 'Housing'.].

18482 JEPHCOTT (A. PEARL) *and* ROBINSON (HILARY). Homes in High Flats: Some of the Human Problems Involved in Multi-storey Housing. Edin. 1971.

18483 McLARTY (MALCOLM RONALD), PATON (G.), *and* CAMPBELL (H.) *eds.* A Source Book and History of Administrative Law in Scotland. 1956.

18484 NIVEN (DOUGLAS). The Development of Housing in Scotland. 1979.

18485 BEGG (TOM). Fifty Special Years: A Study in Scottish Housing. 1988.

18486 AL-QADDO (HUSAIN) *and* RODGER (RICHARD). 'The Implementation of Housing Policy: The Scottish Special Housing Association'. *Public. Admin* 65 (1987), 313–29.

18487 DAMER (SEAN). 'Wine Alley: The Sociology of a Dreadful Enclosure'. *Sociol. Rev.* n.s. 22 (1974), 221–48.

18488 —— Northern Ireland Housing Statistics. 1979+. Annual. [Previously published with slightly modified titles.].

18489 U.K. Planning and Housing Act (N.I.), 1931. Belf. 1931.

18490 HADDEN (TOM B.) *and* TRIMBLE (W. DAVID). Housing Law in Northern Ireland. 1984.

18491 NORTHERN IRELAND. Report of Enquiry Into the Housing Schemes of the Belfast Corporation Held by R. D. Megaw. 2 vols. 1926.

18492 U.K MINISTRY OF HEALTH AND LOCAL GOVERNMENT. Housing Return for Northern Ireland. Belf. 1953+.

18493 —— Inspector's Report on Belfast Corporation's Housing Inquiry. Belf. 1954.

18494 FIELD (D. E.) *and* NEILL (D. G.). A Survey of New Housing in Belfast. 1957.

18495 MATTHEW (ROBERT HOGG). Belfast Regional Survey and Plan: Interim Report on Housing Sites in the Belfast Area. Belf. 1961.

18496 U.K. Proposals For Dealing with Unfit Houses. Belf. 1959.

18497 BIRRELL (WILLIAM DEREK), HILLYARD (P. A. R.), MURIE (ALAN SHAW), *and* ROCHE (D. S. D.). Housing in Northern Ireland. 1971.

18498 RUSSELL (J. L.). Housing Amidst Civil Unrest. 1980.

18499 FLEMING (M. C.). 'Housebuilding Productivity in Northern Ireland'. *Urban Studs* 4(2) (1967), 122–36.

18500 FLEMING (M. C.) *and* NELLIS (J. G.). 'The Inflation of House Prices in Northern Ireland in the 1970s'. *Econ. & Soc. Rev.* 13 (1981), 1–19.

18501 ROSE (LIONEL) 'Rogues and Vagabonds': The Vagrant Underworld in Britain, 1815–1985. 1988.

18502 SANDFORD (JEREMY). Down and Out in Britain. 1971.

18503 —— Cathy Come Home. 1967.

18504 STEWART (JOHN M.). Of No Fixed Abode: Vagrancy and the Welfare State. Manch. 1975.

18505 LIVERPOOL PERSONAL SERVICE SOCIETY. Rehabilitation of Homeless Families : A Report of an Experiment in the Rehousing of Selected Families in Rehabilitation Houses, Under Casework Supervision. L/pool. 1961.

18506 BROWN (MURIEL). Problems of Homelessness: An Experiment in Co-operation, Manchester, 1954–1963. Manchester. 1964.

18507 BRANDON (DAVID). Homeless. 1974.

18508 BAILEY (RON). The Homeless and the Empty Houses. Harmondsworth. 1977.

18509 GREVE (JOHN). London's Homeless. 1964.

18510 GREVE (JOHN), PAGE (DILYS), *and* GREVE (STELLA). Homelessness in London. Edin./Lond. 1971.

18511 MINNS (R.). 'Homeless Families and Some Organizational Determinants of Deviancy'. *Policy and Politics* 1(i) (1972).

18512 GLASTONBURY (BRYAN). Homeless Near A Thousand Homes: A Study of Families Without Homes in South Wales and the West of England. 1971.

18513 DRAKE (MADELINE), O'BRIEN (MAUREEN), *and* BIEBOLEK (TONY). Single and Homeless. 1981.

18514 WOODWARD (PATRICIA J.) *and* DAVIDGE (ELIZABETH M.). 'Homelessness Four Years On'. *J. Planning & Environment Law* (1982), 158–67.

18515 SMITH (P. F.). 'The Housing (Homeless Persons) Act 1977—Four Years On'. *J. Planning & Environment Law* (1982). 143–57.

18516 HOLMANS (A. E.). Housing Policy in Britain: A History. 1987.

18517 MURIE (ALAN SHAW), NINER (PAT), *and* WALTON (CHRISTOPHER). Housing Policy and the Housing System. 1976.

18518 BALCHIN (P. N.). Housing Policy and Housing Needs. 1981.

18519 DONNISON (DAVID VERNON) *and* UNGERSON (CLARE). Housing Policy. Harmondsworth. 1982. [This is a rewrite of Donnison's 'The Government of Housing'. Harmondsworth. 1967].

18520 DONNISON (DAVID VERNON). Housing Policy since the War. Welwyn. 1960.

18521 DUCLAUD-WILLIAMS (ROGER HUGH). The Politics of Housing in Britain and France. 1978.

18522 ENGLANDER (DAVID). Landlord and Tenant in Urban Britain 1838–1918. Oxf. 1983.

18523 CASE (F. E.). 'Code Enforcement in Urban Renewal'. *Urban Studs* 5(3), (1968), 277–89.

18524 CAVE (P. W.). 'Occupancy Duration and the Analysis of Residential Change'. *Urban Studs* 6(1) (1969), 58–69.

18525 MCKIE (R.). 'Cellular Renewal: A Policy For the Older Housing Areas'. *Town Planning Rev.* 45 (1974), 274–90.

18526 GAY (OONAGH). 'Prefabs: A Study in Policy Making'. *Public Admin.* 65 (1987), 407–22.

18527 SIGSWORTH (ERIC M.) *and* WILKINSON (R. K.). 'Rebuilding or Renovation?'. *Urban Studs* 4 (1967), 109–21.

18528 —— 'The Finance of Improvements: A Study of Low Quality Housing in Three Yorkshire Towns'. *Yorks. Bull. Econ. Soc. Res.* 23 (1971), 113–28.

18529 SPENCER (K. M.). 'Older Urban Areas and Housing Improvement Policies'. *Town Planning Rev.* 41(3) (1970), 250–62.

18530 ADAMSON (S.). 'The Politics of Improvement Grants'. *Town Planning Rev.* 46 (1975), 375–86.

18531 BROOKES (J. A) *and* HUGHES (K.). 'Housing Redevelopment and Rehabilitation: A Case Study in Comparative Economics'. *Town Planning Rev.* xlvi(2) (1975), 215–25.

18532 WILKINSON (R. K.). 'Determinants of Relative House Prices: A Case of Academic Astigmatism?'. With a Reply by M. Ball. *Urban Studs* 11 (1974), 227–33.

18533 NEEDLEMAN (LIONEL). The Economics of Housing. 1965.

18534 —— 'The Comparative Economics of Improvement and New Building'. *Urban Studs* 6(2) (1969).

18535 NEVITT (ADELA ADAM). Housing, Taxation and Subsidies: A Study of Housing in the United Kingdom. 1966.

18536 MORRIS (MICHAEL WOLFGANG LAURENCE). The Disaster of Direct Labour: An Examination of Council Building Departments. 1978

18537 DIRECT LABOUR COLLECTIVE. Building With Direct Labour: Local Authority Building and the Crisis in the Construction Industry. 1978.

18538 HADJIMATHEOU (GEORGE G.). Housing and Mortgage Markets: The UK Experience. Farnborough. 1976.

18539 BETHAM (E.) *ed.* House-Building 1934–1936: A Complete Key to Available House-Building Finance From All Sources. 1936?

18540 BALLMAN (*Sir* H.). Capital, Confidence and the Community. 1938.

18541 HEALES (H. C.) *and* KIRBY (C. H.). Housing Finance in Great Britain. 1938.

18542 BALL (MICHAEL) *and* KIRWAN (RICHARD M.). The Economics of an Urban Housing Market: Bristol Area Study. 1975.

18543 AUGHTON (H.). Housing Finance: Myth, Reality and Reform. 1971.

18544 GOUDIE (JAMES). Councils and the Housing Finance Act. 1972.

18545 JARMAIN (J. R.). Housing Subsidies and Rents. 1948.

18546 KARN (VALERIE ANN). Housing Standards and Costs: A Comparison of British Standards and Costs with those in the U.S.A., Canada and Europe. Birm. 1973.

18547 —— Priorities For Local Authority Mortgage Lending: A Case Study of Birmingham. 1976.

18548 MCKENZIE-HALL (JOHN EDWARDES). Low Cost Homes to Rent or Buy: An Introduction to the Function, Formation and Operation of Housing Associations and Societies. 1971.

18549 MERRETT (ANTHONY JOHN WATKIN) *and* SYKES (ALLEN). Housing Finance and Development: An Analysis and A Programme For Reform. 1965.

18550 RICHARDSON (H. W.). 'Determinants of Urban House Prices'. *Urban Studs* II (1974), 189–99.

18551 PRITCHARD (ROGER MARTIN). Housing and the Spatial Structure of the City: Residential Mobility and the Housing Market in an English City since the Industrial Revolution. Camb. 1976. [Leicester.].

18552 JOHNSON (JAMES H.), SALT (JOHN) *and* WOOD (PETER A.). Housing and Migration of Labour in England and Wales. 1974.

18553 BALCHIN (PAUL N.). Housing Improvement and Social Inequality: Case Study of an Inner City. Farnborough. 1979.

18554 PICK (JOYCE). No Caravan: No Home. 1977.

18555 U.K. SOCIAL SURVEY. A Survey of Residential Caravan Life by Gray (P. G.) *and* Parr (Elizabeth A.). An Inquiry. 1959.

18556 BIRD (BARBARA) *and* O'DELL (ALAN). Mobile Homes in England and Wales, 1975: Report of Surveys. Watford. 1977.

18557 DEVONSHIRE PLANNING DEPARTMENT. A Survey of Residential Caravanners in Devon, 1959. Exeter. 1959.

18558 MCKIE (ROBERT). Housing and the Whitehall Bulldozer: A Study of the Maintenance of Demand and a Proposal for the Cellular Renewal of Twilight Zones. 1971.

18559 COLCLOUGH (JOHN RICHARD). The Construction Industry of Great Britain. 1965.

18560 U.K. 1964 NATIONAL ECONOMIC DEVELOPMENT COUNCIL. The Construction Industry. 1964.

18561 POWELL (CHRISTOPHER). 'Fifty Years of Progress'. *Built Environment* iii (1974), 532–5.

18562 ROCHE (F.). 'A Place to Live—Political or Technical'. *Housing & Planning Rev.* xxxi(I) (1975).

18563 SHARP (D.). 'Integrated Housing in Haringey?: Roman Halter and Associates, Architects'. *Ekistics*, 37 (1974), 297–300.

18564 FENTER (FRANCES MARGARET). Copec Adventure: The Story of Birmingham Copec House Improvement Society. Birmingham. 1960.

18565 NATIONAL FEDERATION OF HOUSING SOCIETIES: A Guide to Housing Associations and Housing Societies. 1971.

18566 U.K. DoE Housing Associations. 1971.

18567 U.K. DoE Housing Finance Act 1972: Memorandum on Housing Associations. 1972.

18568 WEST (WILLIAM ALEXANDER). The Concise Law of Housing. 1965.

18569 —— The Law of Housing: 3rd edn by Keith Davies 1974.

18570 ROSENBERG (NATHAN). Economic Planning in the British Building Industry 1945–9. Philadelphia, Pa. 1960.

18571 BACON (EDMUND N.). Design of Cities. 1967.

18572 CHALINE (CLAUDE). La Métropole Londonienne: Croissance et Planification Urbaine. Paris. 1973.

18573 —— L'Urbanisme en Grande-Bretagne. Paris. 1972.

18574 THOMPSON (MEG) *comp.* Housing: A Select List. 1975.

18575 SMITH (E. J.). Housing: The Present Opportunity. 1918.

18576 SAVAGE (WILLIAM GEORGE). Rural Housing. 1915.

18577 ORBACH (LAURENCE F.). Homes For Heroes: A Study of the Evolution of British Public Housing, 1913–1921. 1978.

18578 ROBERTSON (J.). Housing and the Public Health. 1919.

18579 SAYLE (A.) *and* ROSEVEAR (JOHN A.). The Houses of the Workers. 1924.

18580 REISS (RICHARD LEOPOLD). Reconstruction, With Particular Reference to Housing. 1918.

18581 —— The Home I Want. 1919.

18582 —— The New Housing Handbook. 1924.

18583 NATIONAL HOUSING AND TOWN PLANNING COUNCIL. Housing and Town Planning after the War: Memorandum. 1917.

18584 —— Future Housing Policy: Report of A Deputation from the . . . Council to Government. 1922.

18585 HUTTON (J. E.). Welfare and Housing: A Practical Record of War-Time Management. 1918.

18586 CLARKE (JOHN JOSEPH). The Housing Problem: Its History, Growth, Legislation and Procedure. 1920.

18587 —— Some Factors Relating to the Re-housing of Slum Dwellers—A Paper. 1923.

18588 —— Housing in Relation to Public Health and Social Welfare. 1925.

18589 CHALMERS (ARCHIBALD KERR) *and* MANN (*Sir* JOHN). Can the 'Undesirable Tenant' be Trained in Citizenship? Glas. 1933.

18590 ADDISON (CHRISTOPHER) *Baron*. The Betrayal of the Slums. 1922.

18591 ALDRIDGE (HENRY R.). The National Housing Manual. 1923.

18592 —— The Extent and Character of the National Housing Needs. Manchester. 1925.

18593 —— If You Are Blitzed: How to Claim Compensation. 1944.

18594 MARTIN (JOHN G.). The Truth about the Present Housing Situation. 1928.

18595 SHELTON (A. W.). 'Housing': Facts and Factors For Trade Unionists and Workers. 1918.

18596 HOPE (EDWARD WILLIAM). 'General Principles of Housing and Town Planning in Relation to Health'. *J. State Medicine* (Nov. 1919), 321–6.

18597 ABERCROMBIE (*Sir* L. PATRICK). 'The Influence of Town Planning Upon Tuberculosis'. *J. State Medicine* (Jan. 1920), 1–11.

18598 MANCHESTER UNIVERSITY SETTLEMENT. Some Social Aspects of Pre-War Tenements and Post-War Flats. Manch. 1932.

18599 Manchester. A Review of the Manchester Housing Schemes Built Under the Various Housing and Planning Acts in Operation During 1919–1933. Manch. 1934.

18600 LONDON COUNTY COUNCIL. Housing: Being One of A Series of Popular Handbooks on the London County Council and What It Does For London. 1924.

18601 —— Housing: With Particular Reference to Post-War Housing Schemes. 1928.

18602 —— Housing 1928–30. 1931.

18603 —— Housing and Public Health Committee. Working Class Housing on the Continent and the Application of Continental Ideas to the Housing Problem in the County of London: Report by Chmn of the Cttee Lewis Silkin. 1936.

18604 —— London Housing. 1937.

18605 —— Housing: A Survey of the Postwar Housing Work of the London County Council 1945–1949. 1949.

18606 ENGLAND (KATHLEEN M.). Housing: A Citizen's Guide to the Problem. 1931.

18607 INMAN (JOHN). Poverty and Housing Conditions in a Manchester Ward. Manchester. 1934.

18608 SIMON (ERNEST D.) *Baron and* INMAN (JOHN). The Rebuilding of Manchester. 1935.

18609 FREMANTLE (*Sir* FRANCIS EDWARD). The Housing Problem: A Concise Survey. 1934.

18610 —— The Housing of the Nation. 1927.

18611 Council For Research on Housing Construction. Housing Standards and Statistics. 1935.

18612 —— Slum Clearance and Rehousing: The First Report. 1934.

18613 —— Housing Finance: Report on Subsidies For Rehousing in Urban Areas. 1935.

18614 CHAPMAN (DENNIS). Heating in Dwellings Inquiry. 1946.

18615 —— Lighting in Dwellings Inquiry. 1943.

18616 —— Sound in Dwellings . . . An Inquiry. 1945.

18617 —— A Survey of Noise in British Homes. 1948.

18618 ROWNTREE (BENJAMIN SEEBOHM) *and* PIGOU (A. C.). Lectures on Housing: The Warburton Lectures for 1914. Manchester. 1914.

18619 —— Portrait of a City's Housing. 1943. 1945 edn. *Ed. and introd.* by R. L. Reiss.

18620 BOWLEY (MARIAN ELLEN ALBERTA). Housing and the State. 1919–1944. 1945.

18621 —— Housing Statistics. In M. G. Kendall *ed.* The Sources and Nature of the Statistics of the U.K. 1952.

18622 —— Britain's Housing Shortage. 1944.

18623 —— Innovations in Building Materials: An Economic Study. 1960.

18624 —— The British Building Industry: Four Studies in Response and Resistance to Change. Camb. 1966.

18625 SHEPPARD (RICHARD HERBERT). Building For the People. 1948.

18626 —— Cast Iron in Building. 1945.

18627 —— Prefabrication in Building. 1946.

18628 SHEPPARD (RICHARD HERBERT) *and* WRIGHT (HILTON). Building for Daylight . . . with an Introductory Historical Note on English Window Design by John Gloag. 1948/49.

18629 SABATINO (RICHARD A.). Housing in Great Britain, 1945–49. Dallas, Tex. 1956.

18630 ELSAS (MORITZ JOHN). Housing before the War and after. 1942. 2nd edn 1945.

18631 —— Housing and the Family. 1947.

18632 MADGE (JOHN). Human Factors in Housing. 1948.

18633 —— The Rehousing of Britain. 1945.

18634 —— *Ed.* Tomorrow's Houses and Building Methods, Structures and Materials. 1946.

18635 JEVONS (ROSAMOND) *and* MADGE (JOHN). Housing Estates: A Study of Bristol Corporation Policy and Practice Between the Wars. Bristol. 1946.

18636 U.K. 1950. Ministry of Works. An Inquiry into Domestic Hotwater Supply in Great Britain. Part 1. 1950.

18637 MUMFORD (LEWIS). 'The High-Rise Fashion'. *Town & Country Planning* (1953), 312–18.

18638 MANN (JEAN). 'Warehousing the People: Deprecating the Present Tendency to Build Tenement Flats'. *Town & Country Planning* (1953), 361–4.

18639 CHAPMAN (DENNIS). The Home and Social Status. 1955.

18640 TURVEY (RALPH). The Economics of Real Property: An Analysis of Property Values and Patterns of Use. 1957.

18641 CULLINGWORTH (JOHN BARRY). 'The Measurement of Housing Need'. *Brit. J. Sociol.* 9(4) (1958), 341–58.

18642 —— 'Postwar Housing Policy and Administration in England and Wales'. *Ind. J. Public Admin.* 2(2) (1956), 101–10.

18643 MUNBY (DENYS L.). Home Ownership. 1957.

18644 MILLWARD (STANLEY). An Appraisal of the Housing Situation and Future Trends. 1966.

18645 —— *Ed.* Urban Renewal. Salford. [Annual, 1965+].

18646 JENSEN (ROLF). High Density Living. 1966.

18647 DARKE (J.) *and* DARKE (ROY). Health and Environment: High Flats. 1970.

18648 MORRIS (RAYMOND NEVILLE) *and* MOGEY (JOHN MCFARLANE). The Sociology of Housing: Studies at Berinsfield. 1965.

18649 MORRIS (RAYMOND NEVILLE). Urban Sociology. 1968.

18650 COCKBURN (C.). 'Housing Policy'. *Soc. Wk* 14(3) (1957), 336–42.

18651 ASHWORTH (HERBERT). Housing: Demand and Supply. 1946.

18652 —— Housing: Housing Standards. 1947.

18653 —— Housing in Great Britain. 1957.

18654 KELLY (BURNHAM) *in association with* DAY (CASTLE N.). Design and the Production of Houses. 1959.

18655 BURNETT (F. T.) *and* SCOTT (S. F.). 'A Survey of Housing Conditions in the Urban Areas of England and Wales, 1960'. *Sociol. Rev.* X (1962), 35–79.

18656 NEWMAN (D. K.). 'Housing in Britain and America'. *Monthly Lab. Rev.* 83 (1960), 449–59; 561–8.

18657 ANON. 'Long-Term View of Housing'. *Nat. Inst. Econ. Res. Rev.* 18 (1961), 19–37.

18658 SHEFFIELD HOUSING DEVELOPMENT COMMITTEE. Ten Years of Housing in Sheffield, 1953–1963. 1963.

18659 SHEFFIELD SOCIAL SURVEY. A Report on the Housing Problem in Sheffield. 1931.

18660 LONDON COUNTY COUNCIL. Housing Londoners (1945–1960): The Part Played by the London County Council. 1961.

18661 —— 200,000 Homes. 1962.

18662 —— East End Housing: A Review of the Council's Post War Housing Achievements in Bethnal Green, Poplar and Stepney. 1964.

18663 YOUNG (KEN) *and* KRAMER (JOHN). Strategy and Conflict in Metropolitan Housing: Suburbia Versus the Greater London Council 1965–1975. 1978.

18664 WENDT (PAUL FRANCIS). Housing Policy—the Search For Solutions: A Comparison of the United Kingdom, Sweden, West Germany and the United States since World War II. Berkeley, Calif. 1962.

18665 ALDERSON (STANLEY). Housing. Harmondsworth. 1962.

18666 BARTON (DEREK). A Hope for Housing? 1963.

18667 BARLEY (MAURICE WILLMORE). The House and Home. 1963.

18668 —— The English Farmhouse and Cottage. 1961.

18669 HARDY (DENNIS) *and* WARD (COLIN). Arcadia for all: The Legacy of a Makeshift Landscape. 1984.

18670 CARMICHAEL (JOHN DAVID). Vacant Possession: A Study of Britain's 50 Year-Old Housing Problem. 1964.

18671 ABRAMS (CHARLES). Housing in the Modern World. 1964.

18672 GLASS (RUTH) *and* WESTERGAARD (JOHN HARALD). London's Housing Needs: Statements of Evidence to the Committee on Housing in Greater London. 1965.

18673 GLASS (RUTH) *and* DAVIDSON (F. G.). 'Housing Structure and Household Needs'. *Pop. Studs* IV(4) (1951), 395–420.

18674 GREATER LONDON COUNCIL. Housing Department. [Annual Report 1965/6.].

18675 —— Department of Planning and Transportation. [Annual Reports.].

18676 CHAPMAN (J. S.) *and* WHEELER (B.). The Characteristics of London's Households. 1970.

18677 CHAPMAN (J. S.) *and* BRACEWELL (I. B.). The Condition of London's Housing: A Survey. 1970.

18678 MCDONAGH (THERESA). Local Authority Housing Supply and Allocations in Greater London, 1966–1971. 1972.

18679 RODDIS (ROLAND JOSEPH). The Housing Act 1964. 1965.

18680 WOOLF (MYRA). Government Social Survey. The Housing Survey in England and Wales, 1964. 1967.

18681 TUCKER (JAMES). Honourable Estates. 1966.

18682 TURNER (MERFYN LLOYD). Safe Lodging: The Road to Norman House. 1961.

18683 —— Norman House: The First Five Years. 1961.

18684 —— A Pretty Sort of Prison. 1964.

18685 REES (BRONWEN). No Fixed Abode. 1965.

18686 HEMMING (M. F. W.). 'The Price of Accommodation'. *Nat. Inst. Econ. Soc. Res. Rev.* (Aug. 1964).

18687 HOWES (E. G.). 'Housing in Britain, France and Western Germany'. *Planning* 3l(490) (1965), 219–66.

18688 EVERSLEY (DAVID EDWARD CHARLES). 'Life, Leisure and Houses'. *Architects J.* (1967), 1337–9.

18689 MARRIOTT (OLIVER). The Property Boom. 1967.

18690 GREVE (J.). 'Housing Policies and Prospects'. *Pol. Q.* 40(1) (1969), 23–34.

18691 SHARP (EVELYN) *Baroness*. Housing in Britain: Successes, Failures and the Future. 1970.

18692 ROSE (HILARY). The Housing Problem. 1963.

18693 GRIFFITHS (HUGH) *et al.* Report of the Inquiry into the Collapse of Flats at Ronan Point, Canning Town: Presented to the Ministry of Housing and Local Government. 1968.

18694 NEVITT (ADELA ADAM). 'Conflicts in British Housing Policy'. *Pol. Q.* 39(4) (1968), 439–50.

18695 ALLAUN (FRANK). Heartbreak Housing. 1968.

18696 —— No Place Like Home: Britain's Housing Tragedy (From the Victim's View) and how to Overcome it. 1972.

18697 HOLMANS (A. E.). 'A Forecast of Effective Demand for Housing in Great Britain in the 1970s'. *Social Trends* 1 (1970). (No page nos.).

18698 WILSON (DES). I Know it was the Place's Fault. 1970.

18699 —— Minority Report: A Diary of Protest 1970–73. 1973.

18700 SEYD (P.). 'Shelter: The National Campaign for the Homeless'. *Pol. Q.* 46 (1975), 418–31.

18701 NEVITT (ADELA ADAM). 'A "Fair" Deal For Housing'. *Pol. Q.* 42 (Oct.–Dec. 1971), 428–33.

18702 SHELTER. Shelter 1976: Ten Years On: A Progress Report. 1976.

18703 CLARK (COLIN GRANT) *and* Jones (G. T.). The Demand for Housing. 1971.

18704 DUKE (CHRISTOPHER). Colour and Rehousing: A Study of Redevelopment in Leeds. 1971.

18705 KARNALIJNSLYPER (N.) *and* WARD (R.). The Housing Position and Residential Distribution of Ethnic Minorities in Britain: A Bibliography. Birm. 1982.

18706 HENDERSON (J.) *and* KARN (VALERIE A.). Race, Class and State Housing: Inequality and the Allocation of Public Housing in Britain. Aldershot. 1987.

18707 SMITH (SUSAN J.). The Politics of 'Race': Citizenship, Segregation and White Supremacy in Britain. Camb. 1988.

18708 LEE (T. R.). Race and Residence: The Concentration and Dispersal of Immigrants in London. Oxf. 1977.

18709 PEACH (CERI) *and* SHAH (S.). 'The Contribution of Council House Allocation to West Indian Desegregation in London 1961–1971'. *Urban Studs* 17 (1980), 333–41.

18710 PEPPER (SIMON). Housing Improvement: Goals and Strategy. 1971.

18711 HOLE (WINIFRED VERE) *and* POUNTNEY (MELVILLE TREVOR). Trends in Population, Housing and Occupancy Rates, 1861–1961. 1971.

18712 HOLE (WINIFRED VERE) *and* ATTENBURROW (J. J.). Houses and People: A Review of User Studies at the Building Research Station. 1966.

18713 —— 'Housing Standards and Social Trends'. *Urban Studs.* ii (1965), 137–46.

18714 CROSLAND (CHARLES ANTHONY RAVEN). Towards a Labour Housing Policy. 1971.

18715 KARN (VALERIE ANN). Aycliffe Housing Survey: A Study of Housing in a New Town. Birmingham. 1970.

18716 —— East Kilbride Housing Survey.

18717 —— Crawley Housing Survey.

18718 —— Stevenage Housing Survey.

18719 STONE (PETER ALBERT). Housing, Town Development, Land and Costs. 1963.

18720 —— Urban Development in Britain: Standards, Cost and Resources, 1964–2004. Vol. 1. Population Trends and Housing. Camb. 1970.

18721 —— Building Economy, Design, Production and Organisation: A Synoptic View. Oxf. 1966.

18722 CHAPMAN (STANLEY DAVID) *ed.* The History of Working-Class Housing: A Symposium. Newton Abbot. 1971.

18723 COCKBURN (CHRISTINE) *and* CORLETT (T.). Housing since the Rent Act: An Interim Report from the Rowntree Trust Housing Study. Welwyn. 1961.

18724 —— *Et al.* Essays on Housing. Welwyn. 1964.

18725 GLASS (RUTH). 'Housing in Cambden [*sic*]'. *Town Planning Rev.* 41(1) (1970), 15–40.

18726 MITCHELL (AUSTIN). 'Clay Cross'. *Pol. Q.* 45 (1974), 165–78.

18727 DEPARTMENT OF HEALTH AND SOCIAL SECURITY. The Census of Residential Accommodation. Vol. 1. 1970.

18728 DONNISON (DAVID VERNON) *and* EVERSLEY (DAVID EDWARD CHARLES) *eds.* London Urban Patterns, Problems and Policies. 1973.

18729 KILROY (B.). 'Housing: The Rehabilitation v. Redevelopment Cost See-Saw: The Effect of High Land Prices'. *Local Government Finance* lxxvii(4), (1973).

18730 KIRSCHENBAUM (A.). 'Spatial Clustering, Segregation and Urban Planning: A Methodological Approach'. *Urban Studs* 11 (1974), 323–7.

18731 LAMBERT (J.) *et al.* 'Neighbourhood Politics and Housing Opportunities'. *Comm. Dvlpt J.* x(2) (1975).

18732 PERRY (JANE). The Fair Housing Experiment: Community Relations Councils and the Housing of Minority Groups. PEP. 1973.

18733 DAVIDSON (B. R.). 'Effects of Land Speculation on the Supply of Housing in England and Wales'. *Urban Studs* 12 (1975), 91–9.

18734 COUPER (M.) *and* BRINDLEY (T.). 'Housing Classes and Housing Values'. *Sociol. Rev.* n.s. 23 (1975). 563–76.

18735 COWAN (P.) 'Depreciation, Obsolescence and Ageing'. *Architects J.* (1965), 395–401.

18736 BERRY (FRED). Housing: The Great British Failure. 1974.

18737 —— 'Retreat From Parker Morris'. *Municipal Rev.* xlvii (1976), 68–70.

18738 MCDONALD (G.). 'Metropolitan Housing Policy and the Stress Area'. *Urban Studs* 11 (1974), 27–37.

18739 NUTT (BEV) *et al.* Obsolescence in Housing: Theory and Applications. Farnborough. 1976.

18740 GITTUS (ELIZABETH). Flats, Families and the Under-Fives. 1976.

18741 BURNETT (JOHN). A Social History of Housing, 1815–1970. Newton Abbot. 1978.

18742 HARRISON (MOLLY). People and Furniture: Social Background to the English Home. Lond./Totowa, NJ. 1971.

18743 —— The Kitchen in History. 1972.

18744 LOMAS (GRAHAM MAURICE). The Inner City: A Preliminary Investigation of the Dynamics of Current Labour and Housing Markets with Special Reference to Minority Groups in Inner London. 1974.

18745 HOUSING RESEARCH FOUNDATION. Home Ownership in England and Wales. 1970.

18746 —— Home Ownership For Lower Income Families. 1974.

18747 GAULDIE (ENID). Cruel Habitations: A History of Working Class Housing, 1780–1918. 1974.

18748 MILLER (CHRISTINE) *comp.* Housing in London. 2nd edn 1975.

18749 SMITH (DAVID JOHN) *and* WHALLEY (ANNE). Racial Minorities and Public Housing. PEP Broadsheet No. 556. 1975.

18750 PUGH (HILARY ANGELA) *comp.* Housing Co-operatives and Co-ownership Schemes. 1976.

18751 ANDREWS (C. LESLEY). Where we Live. DoE. 1976.

18752 MACKAY (DAVID). Multiple Family Housing: From Aggregation to Integration. 1977.

18753 PITT (JAMES). Gentrification in Islington: The Return of the Middle Classes to an Inner London Borough and the Subsequent Effects on Housing. 1977.

18754 KELLY (FRANCES) *and* WINTOUR (JIM). The Housing Crisis Nationwide. 1977.

18755 STAFFORD (DAVID CHRISTOPHER). The Economics of Housing Policy. 1977.

18756 LANSLEY (P. STEWART). Housing and Public Policy. 1979.

18757 RAWSON (MARILYN) *and* ROGERS (ALAN). Rural Housing and Structure Plans: A Review of Plans Submitted by July 1976. Ashford. 1976.

18758 SIMPSON (MICHAEL ANTHONY) *and* LLOYD (TERENCE HENRY) *eds.* Middle Class Housing in Britain. Newton Abbot. 1977.

18759 CULLINGWORTH (JOHN BARRY). Housing and Local Government in England and Wales. 1966.

18760 —— Essays on Housing Policy: The British Scene. 1979.

18761 LAMBERT (JOHN) *et al.* Housing Policy and the State: Allocation, Access and Control. 1978.

18762 KING (A. D.) *ed.* Buildings and Society: Essays on the Social Development of the Built Environment. 1980.

18763 CHECKLAND (OLIVE) *and* CHECKLAND (SYDNEY). 'Housing Policy: The Formative Years: A Review Article'. *Town Planning Rev.* 46 (1975), 315–22.

18764 DUNLEAVY (PATRICK). The Politics of Mass Housing in Britain, 1945–75. Oxf. 1981.

18765 WOLMAN (HAROLD L.). Housing and Housing Policy in the U.S. and the U.K. Lexington, Mass. 1975.

18766 WARD (COLIN). Housing: An Anarchist Approach. 1976.

18767 WATES (NICHOLAS HERON). The Battle For Tolmers Square. 1976.

18768 GILL (OWEN). Luke Street: Housing Policy, Conflict and the Creation of the Delinquent Area. 1977.

C. TOWN AND COUNTRY PLANNING

1. GENERAL STUDIES

18769 SUTCLIFFE (ANTHONY). British Town Planning: The Formative Years. Leicester. 1981.

18770 GIBBERD (FREDERICK). The Evolution of British Town Planning. 1974.

18771 TAYLOR (R.) *et al.* Britain's Planning Heritage. 1975.

18772 LAW (CHRISTOPHER M.). British Regional Development since World War One. Newton Abbot. 1980. Lond. 1981.

18773 HOLFORD (WILLIAM GRAHAM) *Baron.* Civic Design: An Inquiry into the Scope and Nature of Town Planning. 1949.

18774 —— Design in City Centres. 1953. [M. H. L. G.].

18775 LLOYD (DAVID W.) *ed.* The Making of English Towns. 1984.

18776 ABERCROMBIE (*Sir* [LESLIE] PATRICK). Town and Country Planning. 1933. 3rd edn. 1959.

18777 —— Country Planning and Landscape Design. 1934.

18778 —— Planning in Town and Country: Difficulties and Possibilities. 1937.

18779 HEALEY (PATSY). 'The Professionalisation of Planning in Britain: Its Form and Consequences'. *Town Planning Rev.* 57 (1986), 492–507.

18780 —— *Et al.* The Implementation of Planning Policies and the Role of Development Plans: Final Report to the Department of the Environment. Oxf. 1985.

18781 CHERRY (GORDON E.) *ed.* Pioneers in British Town Planning. 1981.

18782 —— Planning and the Environment in the Modern World. 3 vols. 1984.

18783 —— The Politics of Town Planning. 1982.

18784 —— Town Planning in its Social Context. 1970.

18785 —— Urban and Regional Planning. Birm. 1976.

18786 —— Urban Change and Planning: A History of Urban Development since 1750. Henley-on-Thames. 1972.

18787 —— Urban Planning Problems. 1974.

18788 BURTON (THOMAS LEONARD) *and* CHERRY (GORDON EMANUEL). Social Research Techniques for Planners. Birm. 1970.

18789 WRIGHT (MYLES). Lord Leverhulme's Unknown Venture: The Lever Chair and the Beginnings of Town and Regional Planning 1908–1940. 1982.

18790 CULLINGWORTH (JOHN BARRY). Town and Country Planning in Britain. 1964. 9th edn. 1985.

18791 —— Environmental Planning 1939–1969: Vol. 1—Reconstruction and Land Use Planning 1939–1947. 1975. [HMSO Ser.—Peacetime Series].

18792 —— Environmental Planning 1939–1969. Vol. 3—New Towns Policy. 1980.

18793 —— Environmental Planning 1939–1969. Vol. 4—Land Values, Compensation and Betterment. 1980.

18794 CHERRY (GORDON EMANUEL). Environmental Planning 1939–1969: Vol. 2—National Parks and Recreation in the Countryside. 1975.

18795 RATCLIFFE (JOHN). An Introduction to Town and Country Planning. 1974. 2nd edn 1981.

18796 SIMON (ERNEST DARWIN) *Baron.* Rebuilding Britain: A Twenty Year Plan. 1945.

18797 WRIGHT (HENRY MYLES). 'The First Ten Years: Post War Planning and Development in England'. *Town Planning Rev.* 26 (1955), 73–92.

18798 MURPHY (LAWRENCE R.). 'Rebuilding Britain: The Government's Role in Housing and Town Planning, 1945–1957'. *Historian* 32 (1970), 410–27.

18799 BRENNAN (TOM). Reshaping a City. 1959.

18800 LICHFIELD (NATHANIEL). Cost–Benefit Analysis in Town Planning. Camb. 1968.

18801 HEAP (*Sir* DESMOND). Town and Country Planning, or, how to Control Land Development. Chichester. 1973. 2nd edn. 1981.

18802 WILLIS (KENNETH GEORGE). The Economics of Town and Country Planning. 1980.

18803 —— Contemporary Issues in Town Planning. Aldershot. 1986.

18804 THORNLEY (ANDREW). Thatcherism and Town Planning. 1981.

18805 AMBROSE (PETER). Whatever Happened to Planning? 1986.

18806 GLASSON (JOHN). An Introduction to Regional Planning: Concepts, Theory and Practice. 1974. 2nd edn 1978.

18807 HALL (PETER). Urban and Regional Planning. Harmondsworth 1974. 2nd edn 1982.

18808 CHAPMAN (SYDNEY). Town and Countryside: Future Planning Policies for Britain. 1978. [Conservative Political Centre.].

18809 GAULT (IAN). Greenbelt Policies in Development Plans. Oxf. 1981.

18810 SLEE (BILL). Country Parks: A Review of Policy and Management Issues. Gloucs. 1982.

18811 ELSON (MARTIN J.). Country Estate Management. Oxf. 1980.

18812 COPPOCK (JOHN TERENCE) *and* GEBBET (LEONARD FRANK). Land Use and Town and Country Planning. Oxf. 1985. [Reviews of U.K. Statistical Sources, vol. 8.].

18813 JESS (P. M.) *ed.* Planning and Development in Rural Areas: Report of a Conference. Belf. 1984.

18814 GILG (ANDREW W.). Countryside Planning: The First Three Decades, 1945–76. 1979.

18815 BLACKSELL (MARK) *and* GILG (ANDREW W.). The Countryside: Planning and Change. 1981.

18816 BLACKSELL (MARK) *and* BOWLER (IAN). Contemporary Issues in Rural Planning. Exeter. 1984.

18817 BLUNDEN (JOHN) *and* CURRY (NIGEL). A Future for our Countryside. Oxf. 1988.

18818 SELMAN (PAUL E.). Ecology and Planning: An Introductory Study. 1981.

18819 TOWN AND COUNTRY PLANNING ASSOCIATION. Planning and Plutonium: Evidence of the Town and Country Planning Association to the Public Inquiry into an Oxide Reprocessing Plant at Windscale. 1978.

18820 STOTT (MARTIN) *and* TAYLOR (PETER). The Nuclear Controversy: A Guide to the Issues of the Windscale Inquiry. 1980.

18821 PUNTER (JOHN). 'A History of Aesthetic Control: Pt. 1— 1909–1953: The Control of the External Appearance of Development in England and Wales'. *Town Planning Rev.* 57 (1986), 351–81.

18822 —— 'A History of Aesthetic Control: Pt. 2—1953–1985: The Control of the External Appearance of Development in England and Wales'. *Town Planning Rev.* 58 (1987), 29–62.

18823 BOARDMAN (PHILIP). The World of Patrick Geddes: Biologist, Town Planner, Re-educator, Peace-Warrior. 1978.

18824 SIMPSON (MICHAEL). Thomas Adams and the Modern Town Planning Movement in Britain, Canada and the United States, 1900–1940. 1985.

18825 JACKSON (FRANK). Sir Raymond Unwin: Architect, Planner and Visionary. 1985.

18826 WALLACE (D. B.). 'Rural Policy: A Review Article'. *Town Planning Rev.* 52 (1981), 215–22.

18827 CLOKE (PAUL J.). Implementing Rural Planning. 1987.

18828 CLOKE (PAUL J.) *and* LITTLE (JO). 'The Implementation of Rural Policies: A Survey of Country Planning Authorities'. *Town Planning Rev.* 57 (1986), 265–84.

18829 BRUCE (GEORGE). Some Practical Good: The Cockburn Association, 1875–1975: A Hundred Years' Participation in Planning in Edinburgh. Edin. 1975.

18830 BASSETT (PHILIPPA) *comp.* A List of the Historical Records of the Town and Country Planning Institute. Birm. 1980.

18831 CLARKE (CHRIS). Planning in the North. Newcastle upon Tyne. 1981.

See also the journals:

18832 TOWN PLANNING REVIEW. 1910+.

18833 TOWN AND COUNTRY PLANNING. 1936+.

18834 THE PLANNER. 1914+.

2. TOWN AND COUNTRY PLANNING BY AREA (EXCLUDING LONDON)

18835 HALL (ANTHONY). The Changing Face of Alloa. Alloa. 1984.

18836 KENT COUNTY COUNCIL. Expansion at Ashford: An Appraisal of its Impact on East Kent. Maidstone. 1967.

18837 U.K. MINISTRY OF HOUSING AND LOCAL GOVERNMENT. Ashford Study: Consultants' Proposals for Designation: A Report. 1967.

18838 BALLYMENA AREA PLAN. Report of the Steering Committee. Belf. 1966.

18839 DEVONSHIRE PLANNING DEPARTMENT. Barnstaple Feasibility Study. Exeter. 1966.

18840 ABERCROMBIE (*Sir* [LESLIE] PATRICK), OWENS (JOHN), *and* MEALAND (HENRY ANTHONY). A Plan for Bath: A Report . . . 1945.

18841 STEEL (ROBERT). Basingstoke Town Development: A Review of the First Six Years. Winchester. 1967.

18842 BEDFORDSHIRE COUNTY PLANNING OFFICE. County Development Plan: Town Map No. 3—Biggleswade . . . Bedford. 1963.

18843 BELFAST DESIGN PARTNERSHIP. Belfast Urban Area Plan. 2 vols. Belfast. 1970.

18844 SOUTHERN (CHRISTINE). The Changing Face of Bolton. Hendon. 1975.

18845 BRECONSHIRE COUNTY PLANNING DEPARTMENT. Brecon Borough Town Expansion: A Feasibility Study. Brecon. 1967.

18846 BRISTOL PLANNING GROUP. Bristol: The Central Area and its Waterways. Bristol. 1968.

18847 ABERCROMBIE (*Sir* [LESLIE] PATRICK) *and* BRUETON (BERTRAND F.). Bristol and Bath Regional Planning Scheme. Bath. 1930.

18848 CAMBRIDGE DEPARTMENT OF ARCHITECTURE AND PLANNING. The Future Shape of Cambridge: Report of the City Architect and Planning Officer. Camb. 1966.

18849 —— Industry and Employment: A Report on Cambridge and the Surrounding Area. Camb. 1969.

18850 CAMBRIDGE AND ISLE OF ELY PLANNING DEPARTMENT. Cambridge Study Area: A Progress Report. 2 pts. Camb. 1970.

18851 HOLFORD (WILLIAM GRAHAM) *Baron, and* WRIGHT (HENRY MYLES). Cambridge Planning Proposals. Camb. 1950.

18852 SENIOR (DEREK). A Guide to the Cambridgeshire Plan. Camb. 1957.

18853 GREENWOOD (CHARLES). A Plan for Redevelopment [. . . of the City of Chester]. Chester. 1946.

18854 TASKER (SIDNEY). 'Chester: The Challenge and the Change'. *Town Planning Rev.* 37 (1966/7), 189–206.

18855 ABERCROMBIE (*Sir* [LESLIE] PATRICK) *and* MATTHEW (*Sir* ROBERT HOGG). The Clyde Valley Regional Plan, 1946: A Report . . . Edin. 1949.

18856 COVENTRY CITY COUNCIL. City of Coventry: 1966 Review of the Development Plan, Analysis and Statement. Coventry. 1967.

18857 RICHARDSON (KENNETH) *and* HARRIS (ELIZABETH). Twentieth Century Coventry. 1972.

18858 UNIVERSITY OF SUSSEX (School of Social Studies). Crawley Expansion Study: The Report and Recommendations. Chichester. 1969.

18859 DEVON COUNTY COUNCIL. The Changing Face of Devon. Taunton. 1979.

18860 DIDCOT AND DISTRICT ARCHAEOLOGICAL AND HISTORICAL SOCIETY. The Changing Face of Didcot. Didcot. 1977.

18861 ABERCROMBIE (*Sir* [LESLIE] PATRICK) *and* JOHNSON (THOMAS H.). Doncaster Regional Planning Scheme. Doncaster. 1922.

18862 MOSELEY (MALCOLM J.) *ed.* Power, Planning and People in Rural East Anglia. Norwich. 1982.

18863 ABERCROMBIE (*Sir* [LESLIE] PATRICK). East Kent Regional Planning Scheme: Preliminary Survey. 1925.

18864 —— East Kent Regional Planning Scheme: Final Report. 1928.

18865 TWYMAN (PAUL HADLEIGH). Industrial Location in East Kent, with Special Reference to Factory Relocation and Branch Plant Establishment. 1967.

18866 ABERCROMBIE (*Sir* [LESLIE] PATRICK) *and* PLUMSTEAD (DEREK). A Civic Survey and Plan for the City and Royal Burgh of Edinburgh. Edin. 1949.

18867 MACEWEN (ANNE). 'Edinburgh: An Experiment in Positive Conservation'. *Town Planning Rev.* 46 (1975), 395–406.

18868 LYNCH (LAURENCE GERRARD). The Changing Face of Ellesmere Port. Ellesmere Port. 1976.

18869 WILSON (HUGH) *and* WOMERSLEY (LEWIS). Exeter Town Centre Interim Report No. 1. Exeter. 1966.

18870 —— Second Interim Report: Accommodation to be Provided in the Guildhall Area. Exeter. 1966.

18871 EAST SUFFOLK COUNTY COUNCIL. Felixstowe Town Map, 1963: Report of Survey and Analysis (County Development Plan, Second Quinquennial Review, Amendment No. 3). Ipswich. 1963.

18872 GLASGOW CORPORATION TOWN PLANNING EXHIBITION, 1946. Your Glasgow: Its Future: An Exhibition Illustrating the Proposals Contained in the First and Second Planning Reports Submitted by the City Engineer to the Highways and Planning Committee. Glasg. 1946.

18873 GLASGOW CORPORATION PLANNING DEPARTMENT. The Springburn Study: Urban Renewal in a Regional Context. Glasg. 1967.

18874 —— Central Area. Glasg. 1975.

18875 —— Open Space and Recreation. Glasg. 1975.

18876 —— Social and Community Facilities. Glasg. 1975.

18877 —— Transportation. Glasg. 1975.

18878 HART (THOMAS). The Comprehensive Development Area: A Study of the Legal and Administrative Problems of Comprehensive Land Development with Special Reference to Glasgow. Edin. 1968.

18879 PAYNE (GORDON EDGAR). A Physical, Social and Economic Survey and Plan [of Gloucestershire]. Gloucester. 1946.

18880 U.K. BRITISH TRANSPORT DOCKS BOARD. Grimsby: A Plan for Industry to Expand. 1968.

18881 LUTYENS (*Sir* EDWIN LANDSEER) *and* ABERCROMBIE (*Sir* [LESLIE] PATRICK). A Plan for the City of Kingston upon Hull. Hull. 1945.

18882 U.K. MINISTRY OF HOUSING AND LOCAL GOVERNMENT. The County Borough of Ipswich: A Planning Study for Town Development: A Report. 1964.

18883 SHANKLAND COX & ASSOCIATES. Expansion of Ipswich . . . a Report to the Minister of Housing and Local Government. 1966.

18884 —— Comparative Costs: A Supplementary Report. 1966.

18885 LANCASHIRE COUNTY COUNCIL. Preliminary Plan for Lancashire. Lancs. 1951.

18886 SIMMONS (JACK). Leicester Past and Present. Vol. 2: Modern City, 1860–1974. 1974.

18887 VEREKER (CHARLES) *and* MAYS (JOHN BARRON). Urban Redevelopment and Social Change: A Study of Social Conditions in Central Liverpool, 1955–56. 1961.

18888 MUCHNICK (DAVID MARTIN). Urban Renewal in Liverpool: A Study of the Politics of Redevelopment. 1970.

18889 BRADBURY (RONALD). Liverpool Builds 1945–1965. L/pool. 1967.

18890 SIMON (ERNEST DARWIN) *Baron and* INMAN (JOHN). The Rebuilding of Manchester. 1935.

18891 HOLFORD (WILLIAM GRAHAM) *Baron, and* EDEN (WILLIAM ARTHUR). The Future of Merseyside: Town and Country Planning Schemes. L/pool. 1937.

18892 CHAPMAN (DENNIS). A Social Survey of Middlesbrough . . . an Inquiry into some of the Factors Relevant to the Planning of Urban Communities Made for the Ministry of Town and Country Planning. 3 Pts. 1946–8.

18893 WOODS (KATHERINE SEYMOUR). Development of Country Towns in the South-West Midlands during the 1960s. Oxf. 1968.

18894 MATTHEW (ROBERT). New Life in Old Towns: Report . . . on Two Pilot Studies on Urban Renewal in Nelson and Rawtenstall Municipal Boroughs. 1971.

18895 DAVIES (JON GOWER). The Evangelistic Bureaucrat: A Study of a Planning Exercise in Newcastle-upon-Tyne. 1974.

18896 U.K. MINISTRY OF HOUSING AND LOCAL GOVERNMENT. Expansion of Northampton: Consultant's Proposals for Designation: A Report to the Ministry . . . 1968. [By Hugh Wilson and Lewis Womersley et al.].

18897 NORWICH PLANNING DEPARTMENT. REPORTS No. 1— Central Area Appraisal. Norwich. 1966.

18898 NORWICH PLANNING DEPARTMENT. REPORTS No. 2— Revitalisation Appraisal. Norwich. 1966.

18899 BOURKE (WALTER L.) Earl of Mayo, and ABERCROMBIE (Sir [LESLIE] PATRICK). Regional Planning Report on Oxfordshire. 1931.

18900 HOPKINS (STEVE). Planning in Oxford: An Historical Survey and Bibliography. Oxf. 1978.

18901 U.K. MINISTRY OF HOUSING AND LOCAL GOVERNMENT. Peterborough, 1965. 1964. [By Henry Wells.].

18902 WATSON (JAMES PATON) and ABERCROMBIE (Sir [LESLIE] PATRICK). A Plan for Plymouth: Report. 1943.

18903 THOMAS (Sir PERCY). Expansion of Rhayader: A Pilot Study: A Report to the Mid Wales Industrial Development Association. 1967.

18904 McWILLIAM (COLIN). Scottish Townscape. 1975.

18905 HAWSON (H. KEEBLE). Sheffield: The Growth of a City, 1893–1926. Sheffield. 1968.

18906 ABERCROMBIE (Sir [LESLIE] PATRICK). Sheffield: A Civic Survey and Suggestions Towards a Development Plan. Sheffield. 1924.

18907 —— Et al. Sheffield and District Regional Planning Scheme. Sheffield. 1931.

18908 'SHREWSBURY CHRONICLE' and THE SHROPSHIRE COUNTY LIBRARY. The Changing Face of Shrewsbury. Shrewsbury. 1977.

18909 'SHREWSBURY CHRONICLE'. The Changing Face of Shrewsbury: Second Series . . . Shrewsbury. 1981.

18910 URBAN STRUCTURE RESEARCH PROJECT. A Study Area in Southend-on-Sea. Colchester. 1973.

18911 THOMAS (TREVOR M.). 'Derelict Land in South Wales'. Town Planning Rev. 37 (1966/7), 125–41.

18912 ABERCROMBIE (Sir [LESLIE] PATRICK) and ABERCROMBIE (LASCELLES). Stratford-upon-Avon: Report on Future Development. Stratford-upon-Avon. 1923.

18913 HILTON (K. J.) ed. The Lower Swansea Valley Project. 1967.

18914 —— 'The Lower Swansea Valley Project'. Geog. 48 (1963), 296–9.

18915 SCOTT (COLIN) ed. The Expansion of Swindon, Wiltshire: A Bibliography. 1981.

18916 PAYNE (GORDON EDGAR). The Tay Valley Plan. Dundee. 1950.

18917 CAMBLIN (GILBERT). The Town in Ulster. Belf. 1951.

18918 ABERCROMBIE (Sir [LESLIE] PATRICK) and NICKSON (RICHARD SCHOLEFIELD). Warwick: Its Preservation and Redevelopment. Warwick. 1949.

18919 U.K. MINISTRY OF HOUSING AND LOCAL GOVERNMENT. Expansion of Warrington: Consultant's Proposals. 1966.

18920 —— Worcester Expansion Study: Report for the Ministry . . . 2 vols. 1964.

18921 BROOKEFIELD (H. C.). 'Worthing: A Study of a Modern Coastal Town'. Town Planning Rev. 23 (1952/3), 145–62.

3. LONDON PLANNING

18922 ASSOCIATION OF BUILDING TECHNICIANS. Your London has a Plan. 1943.

18923 CARTER (EDWARD JULIAN). The Future of London. Harmondsworth 1962.

18924 YOUNG (KEN) and GARSIDE (PATRICIA). Metropolitan London: Politics and Urban Change, 1837–1981. N.Y. 1982.

18925 THOMAS (DAVID). London's Green Belt. 1970.

18926 MUNTON (RICHARD). London's Green Belt: Containment in Practice. 1983.

18927 FIELD (BRIAN). Local Planning in London: A Survey. 1979.

18928 —— The Evolution of London's Planning System and the Changing Role of the Boroughs. 1982.

18929 TOWN PLANNING INSTITUTE. Planned London: The Town Planning Institute Conference Handbook, London 14–16 June, 1969. 1969.

18930 FOLEY (DONALD LESLIE). Controlling London's Growth: Planning the Great Wen 1940–1960. Berkeley, Calif./ Camb. 1963.

18931 —— Governing the London Region: Reorganisation and Planning in the 1960s. Berkeley, Calif./Camb. 1972.

18932 HOLFORD (WILLIAM GRAHAM) Baron. Ch. in Ruth Glass et al. London: Aspects of Change. 1964.

18933 —— The City of London: Destruction and Survival. 1951.

18934 HALL (PETER GEOFFREY). London 2000. 1963. Rev. edn 1970.

18935 ADAMS (THOMAS). 'Town Planning in Greater London'. *Town Planning Rev.* 5 (1914), 91–106.

18936 ABERCROMBIE (*Sir* [LESLIE] PATRICK). The Greater London Plan 1944. 1945.

18937 FORSHAW (JOHN H.) *and* ABERCROMBIE (*Sir* [LESLIE] PATRICK) The County of London Plan. 1943. [Prepared for London County Council.].

18938 ROBSON (WILLIAM ALEXANDER). The Heart of Greater London: Proposals for a Policy. 1965.

18939 COOPER (R. A. H.). The Greater London Problem: Report of the Chairman of the Planning Committee . . . 2 Pts. Bedford. 1964.

18940 SELF (PETER JOHN OTTER). Town Planning in Greater London. 1962.

18941 —— Metropolitan Planning: The Planning System of Greater London. 1971.

18942 U.K. DEPARTMENT OF THE ENVIRONMENT. Greater London Development Plan: Report of the Panel of Enquiry. 1973. [The Layfield Report.].

18943 BRENT DEPARTMENT OF PLANNING AND RESEARCH. Background to Brent: A Report. Brent. 1967.

18944 BYRNE (STEPHEN). The Changing Face of Lewisham. 1965.

18945 DUNCAN (LELAND LEWIS). History of the Borough of Lewisham; . . . 1963.

4. CONSERVATION AND PRESERVATION OF VILLAGES, TOWNS, AND CITIES (GENERAL AND SPECIFIC WORKS)

18946 ABERCROMBIE (*Sir* [LESLIE] PATRICK). 'The Preservation of Rural England'. *Town Planning Rev.* 12 (1926), 5–56.

18947 BANKS (FRANCIS RICHARD). Old English Towns. 1964.

18948 —— English Villages. 1963.

18949 DENNIER (D. ANNE). 'The English Village Revisited'. *Town Planning Rev.* 53 (1982), 273–91.

18950 BETJEMAN (*Sir* JOHN). The English Town in the Last Hundred Years. Camb. 1956.

18951 DOBBY (ALAN). Conservation and Planning. 1978.

18952 REYNOLDS (JOSEPHINE) *ed.* Conservation Planning in Town and Country. L/pool. 1976.

18953 SHEAIL (JOHN). Rural Conservation in Inter-war Britain. Oxf. 1981.

18954 CLIFFORD (J.) *et al.* A Political Analysis of British Rural Conservation Issues and Policies . . . 1979.

18955 GORST (J. M.). The Future of the Village. 1971.

18956 LEWIS (JOHN PARRY). Building Cycles and Britain's Growth (Incorporating Materials of the Late Bernard Weber). 1965.

18957 RIGHTER (ROSEMARY). Save our Cities: [A Report on the Save our Cities Conference . . .]. 1977.

18958 ROWLEY (RICHARD TREVOR) *and* BREAKELL (MIKE) *eds.* Planning and the Historic Environment. 1975.

18959 SCOTTISH GEORGIAN SOCIETY. Building Preservation Trusts: A Challenge for Scotland. Edin. 1984.

18960 SMITH (JOHN FRANCIS) *comp.* A Critical Bibliography of Building Conservation: Historic Towns, Buildings, their Furnishings and Fittings. 1978.

18961 THORNCROFT (MICHAEL ERIC TREVOR). The Economics of Conservation. 1975.

18962 WARD (PAMELA) *ed.* Conservation and Development in Historic Towns and Cities. Newcastle upon Tyne. 1968.

18963 WORSKETT (ROY). The Character of Towns: An Approach to Conservation. 1969.

18964 CIVIC TRUST. Financing the Preservation of Old Buildings: A Report. 1971.

18965 —— Index of Conservation Areas, 1967–1970. (With Supplement). 1971.

18966 U.K. DEPARTMENT OF THE ENVIRONMENT. New Life for Old Buildings. 1971.

18967 DEVELOPMENT CONTROL POLICY NOTES. No. 7— Preservation of Historic Buildings and Areas. 1969. Rev. edn 1976.

18968 U.K. MINISTRY OF HOUSING AND LOCAL GOVERNMENT. Protecting our Historic Buildings: A Guide to the Legislation. 1969.

18969 PRESERVATION POLICY GROUP. Report to the Ministry of Housing and Local Government. 1970. [Chairman, Lord Kennet.].

18970 COLIN BUCHANAN *and* PARTNERS. Bath: A Study in Conservation: Report to the Ministry of Housing and Local Government and Bath City Council. 1968.

18971 BATH CONSERVATION STUDY TEAM. City of Bath Conservation Study: First Stage Report. Bath. 1976.

18972 DENNIER (D. ANNE). 'Chester: Conservation in Practice'. *Town Planning Rev.* 46 (1975), 383–94.

18973 DONALD W. INSALL *and* ASSOCIATES. Chester: A Study in Conservation. 1968.

18974 BURROWS (G. S.). Chichester: A Study in Conservation. 1960.

18975 MATTHEW (*Sir* ROBERT HOGG), REID (JOHN), *and* LINDSAY (MAURICE). The Conservation of Georgian Edinburgh: The Proceedings and Outcome of a Conference. Edin. 1972.

18976 SWAINE (ANTHONY). Faversham: Its History, its Present Role and the Pattern of its Future. Faversham. 1969.

18977 GUERNSEY SOCIETY. The Guernsey Farmhouse: A Survey. Guernsey. 1963.

18978 [LONDON] DOCKLANDS JOINT COMMITTEE. (Docklands Development Team). Conservation and the Role of the River. 1975.

18979 DIX (GERALD). 'Norwich: A Fine Old City'. *Town Planning Rev.* 46 (1975), 417–34.

18980 DUMBLETON (BOB). The Second Blitz: The Demolition and Rebuilding of Town Centres in South Wales. Cardiff. 1977.

18981 BRETT (LIONEL GORDON BALIOL) *Viscount Esher.* York: A Study in Conservation: Report. 1968.

18982 SCARGILL (D. I.). 'Conservation and the Oxford Green Belt'. In ROWLEY (TREVOR) *ed.* The Oxford Region. Oxf. 1980.

18983 HAYTHORNTHWAITE (GERALD). The Sheffield Green Belt. Sheffield. 1984.

5. NEW TOWNS AND VILLAGES

18984 VIET (JEAN) *comp.* New Towns: A Selected Bibliography. 1960. [HMSO.].

18985 WHITE (LEONARD EDWARD). New Towns: Their Challenge and Opportunity. 1951. [NCSS.].

18986 BEVERIDGE (WILLIAM HENRY) *Baron.* New Towns: The Case for them. 1952.

18987 MACKENZIE (NORMAN). The New Towns: The Success of Social Planning. 1955. [Fabian Soc. pub.].

18988 U.K. CENTRAL OFFICE OF INFORMATION. The New Towns of Britain. 1961. 5th edn 1974.

18989 SHARP (EVELYN) *Dame.* 'Britain's Fifteen New Towns'. *Town and Country Planning* 29 (1961), 4–10.

18990 RODWIN (LLOYD). The British New Towns: Policy, Problems and Implications. Camb., MA/Oxf. 1956.

18991 OSBORN (*Sir* FREDERICK JAMES) *and* WHITTICK (ARNOLD). The New Towns: The Answer to Megalopolis. 1963.

18992 —— New Towns: Their Origins, Achievements and Progress. 1969. 3rd edn 1977.

18993 BURNS (WILFRED). New Towns for Old. 1963.

18994 STEELE (D. B.). 'New Towns for Depressed Areas'. *Town Planning Rev.* 34 (1963/4), 199–212.

18995 WILLIAMS (MICHAEL). New Towns. 1969. 3rd edn 1981.

18996 U.K. MINISTRY OF HOUSING AND LOCAL GOVERNMENT. The New Towns. 1969.

18997 SCHAFFER (FRANK). The New Town Story. 1970. 2nd edn 1972.

18998 LINDSAY (WALTON). New Towns: A Comparative Atlas. Camb. 1972.

18999 CRESSWELL (PETER). Justifying New Towns: And, Criteria for Evaluating New Towns. Milton Keynes. 1975. 2nd edn 1978.

19000 CORDEN (CAROL). Planned Cities: New Towns in Britain and America. Lond./Beverley Hills. 1977.

19001 CHAMPION (ANTHONY GERARD) *et al.* Facts about the New Towns: A Socio-economic Digest. Corbridge. 1977.

19002 EVANS (HAZEL) *ed.* New Towns: The British Experience. 1973.

19003 KIDD (SUSAN) *comp.* New Towns in the United Kingdom. 1977. [Dept. of Environment.].

19004 ALDRIDGE (MERYL). The British New Towns: A Programme without a Policy. 1979.

19005 CHECKLAND (SYDNEY G.). 'The British New Towns as Politics: A Review Article'. *Town Planning Rev.* 52 (1981), 223–7.

19006 LICHFIELD (NATHANIEL) *and* WENDT (PAUL F.). 'Six English New Towns: A Financial Analysis'. *Town Planning Rev.* 40 (1969), 283–314.

19007 POTTER (STEPHEN). The Alternative New Towns: The Record of the Town Development Programme 1952–1984. Milton Keynes. 1984.

19008 —— Transport and New Towns. Milton Keynes. 1976.

19009 HOLFORD (WILLIAM GRAHAM) *Baron.* Corby New Town. Corby. 1952.

19010 GRAY (FRED) *ed.* Crawley, Old Town, New Town. Brighton. 1983.

19011 CUMBERNAULD DEVELOPMENT CORPORATION. The Financing of Cumbernauld New Town. Cumbernauld. 1977.

19012 OPHER (PHILIP) *and* BIRD (CLINTON). Cumbernauld, Irvine, East Kilbride: An Illustrated Guide. Oxf. 1980.

19013 MILLAR (HUGO BELSHES). The History of Cumbernauld and Kilsyth from Earliest Times. Cumbernauld. 1962. Extd edn 1980.

19014 CARTER (CHRISTOPHER J.). Innovations in Planning Thought and Practice at Cumbernauld New Town, 1956–1962. Milton Keynes. 1983.

19015 WILLMOTT (PETER). 'East Kilbride and Stevenage: Some Social Characteristics of a Scottish and an English New Town'. *Town Planning Rev.* 36 (1963/4), 307–16.

19016 ADAMS (W. ERIC). The New Town of Harlow. Harlow. 1954.

19017 STRAWHORN (JOHN). The History of Irvine: Royal Burgh and New Town. Edin. 1985.

19018 HIGGS (LESLIE). New Town: Social Involvement in Livingston: An Account of the Formative Years. Glasg. 1977.

19019 RODERICK (W. P.). 'The London New Towns: Origin of Migrants from Greater London up to December 1968'. *Town Planning Rev.* 42 (1971), 323–42.

19020 THOMAS (RAY). Commuting Flows and the Growth of London's New Towns 1951–1971. Milton Keynes. 1977.

19021 OPHER (PHILIP) *and* BIRD (CLINTON). Milton Keynes: An Illustrated Guide. Oxf. 1981.

19022 WALKER (DEREK). The Architecture and Planning of Milton Keynes. 1982.

19023 ANSTIS (GORDON). Redditch: Success in the Heart of England: The History of Redditch New Town 1964–1985. Stevenage. 1985.

19024 OPHER (PHILIP) and BIRD (CLINTON). Runcorn, Warrington: An Illustrated Guide. Oxf. 1980.

19025 STEVENAGE DEVELOPMENT CORPORATION. The New Town of Stevenage. Stevenage. 1949.

19026 MULLAN (BOB). Stevenage Ltd: Aspects of the Planning and Politics of Stevenage New Town, 1945–1978. 1980.

19027 BALCHIN (JACK). First New Town: An Autobiography of the Stevenage Development Corporation 1946–1980. Stevenage. 1980.

19028 ASHBY (MARGARET). The Book of Stevenage. Buckingham. 1982.

19029 BRAY (CARL). New Villages: Case Studies No. 1—New Ash Green [Kent]. Oxf. 1981.

19030 —— New Villages: Case Studies No. 2—South Woodham Ferrers [Essex]. Oxf. 1981.

D. RURAL LIFE

1. GENERAL STUDIES

19031 Countryside Planning Yearbook. Norwich. 1980+. [Annual.].

19032 PHILLIPS (DAVID) and WILLIAMS (ALLAN). Rural Britain: A Social Geography. Oxf. 1984.

19033 JONES (GWYN EVANS). Rural Life: Patterns and Processes. 1973.

19034 FRANKLIN (SAMUEL HARVEY). Rural Societies. 1971.

19035 BRACEY (HOWARD EDWIN). English Rural Life: Village Activities, Organisations and Institutions. 1959.

19036 —— 'Rural Settlement in Great Britain'. Sociol. Rur. 3 (1963), 69–78.

19037 —— 'A Note on Rural Depopulation and Social Provision'. Sociol. Rev. 6 (1958), 67–74.

19038 —— 'Some Aspects of Rural Depopulation in the U.K.'. Sociol. Rev. 23 (1958), 385–91.

19039 —— Village Survey. 1953. 2nd edn 1957.

19040 —— Country Town Survey. 1954. 2nd edn 1961.

19041 —— People and the Countryside. 1970.

19042 —— Et al. Industry and the Countryside: The Impact of Industry on Amenities in the Countryside; Report of a Preliminary Enquiry for the Royal Society of the Arts. 1963.

19043 BRACEY (HOWARD EDWIN) and BRUSH (JOHN E.). 'Rural Service Centers in South Western Wisconsin and Southern England'. Geog. Rev. 45 (1955), 559–69.

19044 NEWBY (HOWARD). Social Change in Rural England. Madison, Wisconsin. 1979.

19045 NEWBY (HOWARD) et al. Property, Paternalism and Power: Class and Control in Rural England. 1978.

19046 —— Green and Pleasant Land? Social Change in Rural England. 1979. Harmondsworth. 1980.

19047 HORN (PAMELA). Rural Life in England in the First World War. Dublin. 1984.

19048 TAYLOR (CHRISTOPHER). Village and Farmstead: A History of Rural Settlement in England. 1983.

19049 PROTHERO (ROWLAND EDMUND) Lord Ernle. The Land and its People: Chapters in Rural Life and History. 1925.

19050 —— Whippingham to Westminster. 1938. [Reminiscences.].

19051 SAVAGE (Sir WILLIAM GEORGE). Rural Housing. 1915. New enlgd edn 1919.

19052 —— 'Housing Problems and Rural Districts'. J. of State Medicine (Nov. 1919), 327–35.

19053 MARTIN (E. M.). The Happy Fields: A Country Record. Stratford. 1917. 3rd edn Lond./NY. 1923.

19054 MACKLEY (TOM). Towards the Dawn: The Revolution in Rural England. 1919. [ILP pamphlet.].

19055 PEASE (C. A.). Socialism in the Village. 1920. [ILP pamphlet.].

19056 GREEN (Sir JOHN LITTLE). Political Pills for Farming Ills: An Exposure of the Lloyd George Rural Land Plan. Peterborough. 1926.

19057 BENSUSAN (SAMUEL LEVY). Latter-Day Rural England 1927. 1928.

19058 —— Comment from the Countryside. 1928.

19059 —— The Town versus the Countryside: A Plea for Better Understanding. 1923.

19060 MARTIN (ERNEST WALTER). Where London Ends: English Provincial Life after 1750: Being an Account of the English Country Town and the Lives, Work and Development of Provincial People through a Period of Two Hundred Years. 1958.

19061 LEWIS (GARETH J.). Rural Communities. Newton Abbot. 1979.

19062 WOODRUFFE (BRIAN J.). Rural Settlement Policies and Plans. 1976.

19063 SNELSON (HENRY STANBRIDGE EGERTON). The Story of Rural Community Councils. 1963.

19064 SAVILLE (JOHN). Rural Depopulation in England and Wales 1851–1951. 1957.

19065 U.K. CENTRAL OFFICE OF INFORMATION. Rural Depopulation: Report of an Inter-departmental Group. 1976.

19066 HANRAHAN (PATRICK J.) *and* CLOKE (PAUL J.). 'Towards a Critical Appraisal of Rural Settlement Planning in England and Wales'. *Sociol. Rur.* 23 (1983), 109–29.

19067 CLOKE (PAUL J.). 'Counter-Urbanisation: A Rural Perspective'. *Geog.* 70 (1985), 113–22.

19068 MARTIN VOORHEES ASSOCIATES. Review of Rural Settlement Policies, 1945–1980. 1981.

19069 VINCE (S. W.). Reflections on the Structure and Distribution of Rural Population in England and Wales, 1921–1931. 1952. [Institute of British Geographers Transactions and Papers, No. 18.].

19070 MITCHELL (G. DUNCAN). 'Depopulation and the Rural Social Structure'. *Sociol. Rev.* 62 (1950), 69–85.

19071 —— 'Social Disintegration in a Rural Community'. *Human Relations* 3 (1950), 279–306.

19072 UNITED NATIONS STUDY GROUP ON RURAL DEVELOPMENT. People in the Countryside: Studies in Rural Social Development: A Report. 1966.

19073 CHAMPION (A. G.). 'Population Trends in Rural Britain'. *Population Trends* 26 (1981), 20–3.

19074 GLYN-JONES (ANNE). Rural Recovery: Has it Begun? A Study of a Parish in North-West Devon, 1964–1978. Exeter. 1979.

19075 SHAW (J. MARTIN) *ed.* Rural Deprivation and Planning. Norwich. 1979.

19076 STANDING CONFERENCE OF RURAL COMMUNITY COUNCILS. The Decline of Rural Services. 1978.

19077 MOSELEY (MALCOLM J.). Social Issues in Rural Norfolk. Norwich. 1978.

19078 PACKMAN (JOHN) *and* TERRY (M. H. C.). Services in Rural Norfolk, 1950–1980: A Survey of the Changing Patterns of Service in Rural Norfolk over the last Thirty Years. Norwich. 1981.

19079 HODGE (IAN) *and* WHITBY (MARTIN). Rural Employment: Trends, Opinions and Choices. 1981.

19080 ASSOCIATION OF COUNTY COUNCILS. Rural Deprivation. 1979.

19081 KINSEY (BILL H.). Creating Rural Employment. 1987.

19082 WALKER (ALAN) *ed.* Rural Poverty: Poverty, Deprivation and Planning in Rural Areas. 1978.

19083 NEATE (SIMON). Rural Deprivation: An Annotated Bibliography of Economic and Social Problems in Rural Britain. Norwich. 1981.

19084 SALSBURY (JOHN). 'And is There Honey Still—?': A Look at Rural Deprivation. 1985. [United Reformed Church pub.].

19085 OPENSHAW (KEITH). The Remoter Rural Areas. 1966.

19086 ASHTON (J.) *and* LANG (W. H.) *eds.* The Remoter Areas of Britain. Edin. 1972.

19087 U.K. MINISTRY OF TRANSPORT. Rural Transport Surveys: Report of the Preliminary Results. 1963.

19088 —— Rural Bus Services: Report of Local Enquiries. 1965.

19089 THOMAS (DAVID ST JOHN). The Rural Transport Problem. 1963.

19090 WIBBERLEY (GERALD PERCY). The Changing Rural Economy of Britain. Ashford. 1964.

19091 —— 'Some Aspects of Problem Rural Areas in Britain'. *Geog. J.* 120 (1954), 43–61.

19092 THOMPSON (DENYS). Change and Tradition in Rural England: An Anthology of Writings on Country Life. Camb. 1980.

19093 KIGHTLEY (CHARLES). Country Voices: Life and Lore in Farm and Village. 1984.

19094 WILLIAMS (WILLIAM MORGAN). The Country Craftsman: A Study of some Rural Crafts and the Rural Industries Organisation in England. 1958.

19095 JONES (JOHN LLOYD). Rural Crafts in England. Newport. 1979.

19096 HARMAN (RICHARD) *comp.* Countryside Mood. 1943.

19097 —— Countryside Character. 1946.

19098 —— Countryside Company. 1949.

19099 SEYMOUR (JOHN). The Countryside Explained. 1977.

19100 RUSSELL (ANTHONY). The Country Parish. 1986.

19101 WARD (SUE). War in the Countryside, 1939–1945. 1988.

19102 GILG (ANDREW WINTON). Countryside Planning: The First Three Decades: 1945–1976. Newton Abbot. 1978.

19103 BLACKSELL (M.) *and* GILG (ANDREW WINTON). The Countryside: Planning and Change. 1981.

19104 CLARK (GORDON). Housing and Planning in the Countryside. 1982.

19105 CHAPMAN (CHRIS). The Right Side of the Hedge: Country Life Today. Newton Abbot. 1977.

19106 SHOARD (MARION). The Theft of the Countryside. 1980.

19107 MAPES (ROY E. A.). 'The Development of Certain Social Variables in an English Rural Context'. *Rural Sociol.* 27 (1962), 208–12.

19108 THORNS (DAVID C.). 'The Changing System of Rural Stratification'. *Sociol. Rur.* 8 (1968), 161–74.

19109 BRANDON (P. F.). 'A 20th Century Squire in his Landscape'. *Southern Hist.* 4 (1982), 191–220.

19110 CHENEVIX TRENCH (CHARLES POCKLINGTON). The Poacher and the Squire: A History of Poaching and Game Preservation in England. 1967.

19111 INGRAM (ARTHUR). Trapping and Poaching. Aylesbury. 1978.

19112 WALSH (EDWARD GEOFFREY). The Poacher's Companion. 1982.

19113 PLUMMER (DAVID BRIAN). Rogues and Running Dogs. Lichfield. 1978. Revd edn Woodbridge. 1980.

19114 BEDSON ('GRANDAD'). The Notorious Poacher: Memoirs of an Old Poacher. Hindhead. 1981. Revd. edn Liss. 1986.

19115 WINDER (GEORGE). Modern Rural Rides: An Account of a Ride Through the Counties of Sussex, Hampshire and Wiltshire, with some Reference to the Agricultural Act of 1947 and to other Farming and Historical Matters. 1964.

19116 MUSEUM OF ENGLISH RURAL LIFE. Guide to the Museum of English Rural Life. Reading. 1983.

19117 BASSETT (PHILLIPA) *comp.* A List of Historical Records of the Council for the Preservation of Rural England. Birm. 1980.

2. VILLAGES

19118 FINBERG (JOSCELYNE). Exploring Villages. 1958.

19119 DARLEY (GILLIAN). Villages of Vision. 1975.

19120 SAMUEL (RAPHAEL) *ed.* Village Life and Labour. 1975.

19121 MUIR (RICHARD). The Lost Villages of Britain. 1982.

19122 SUTTON (HARRY THOMAS) *comp.* Villages. 1978. [National Trust pub.].

19123 MATLESS (DAVID). 'Doing the English Village 1945–90: An Essay in Imaginative Geography' in Paul Cloke, Marcus Dorl, David Matless, Martin Phillips, and Nigel Thrift, Writing the Rural: Five Cultural Geographies, 1994.

19124 DOUGLAS (PETER). Village Life. Woodbridge. 1981.

19125 CLARK (COLIN). 'Stability of Village Populations'. *Urban Studs* 12 (1975), 109–11.

19126 NATIONAL COUNCIL OF SOCIAL SERVICE. Village Halls: Their Construction and Management. 1928. 4th edn 1938.

19127 —— Village Halls and Social Centres in the Countryside: A Handbook of Information. 5th edn of above, 1945.

19128 —— The Village Hall: The Site and the Building. 1953.

19129 —— The Village Hall: The Interior. 1954.

19130 —— The Village Hall: Design and Construction. 1959.

19131 —— The Village Hall: Maintenance. 1970.

19132 CAWKWELL (TIMOTHY) *and* OGDEN (ELIZABETH). Long Live the Village Hall!: A Survey of the Use of Village Halls. Northampton. 1982.

19133 BEST (ROBIN HEWITSON) *and* ROGERS (ALAN WILLIAM). The Urban Countryside: The Land-Use Structure of Small Towns and Villages in England and Wales. 1973.

See also the VILLAGE SERIES, pub. by Dent & Co. Ltd. London:

19134 RAWE (DONALD R.). Cornish Villages. 1978.

19135 LEWIS (JUNE R.). Cotswold Villages. 1974.

19136 SMITH (KENNETH). Cumbrian Villages. 1973.

19137 BIGNELL (ALAN). Kent Villages. 1975.

19138 LOFTHOUSE (JESSICA). Lancashire Villages. 1973.

19139 LINDSAY (MAURICE). Lowland Scottish Villages. 1980.

19140 KENNETT (DAVID H.). Norfolk Villages. 1980.

19141 WATSON (GEOFFREY). Northumberland Villages. 1976.

19142 HAINES (GEORGE HENRY). Shropshire and Herefordshire Villages. 1974.

19143 NEWMAN (PAUL). Somerset Villages. 1986.

19144 JOBSON (ALLAN). Suffolk Villages. 1971.

19145 PITT (DEREK) *and* SHAW (MICHAEL). Surrey Villages. 1971.

19146 BAKER (MICHAEL H. C.). Sussex Villages. 1977.

19147 CAVE (LYNDON F.). Warwickshire Villages. 1976.

19148 WOODRUFFE (BRIAN J.). Wiltshire Villages. 1982.

19149 WOOD (GEOFFREY BERNARD). Yorkshire Villages. 1971. 2nd edn 1980.

3. ENGLISH VILLAGES AND RURAL COMMUNITIES

19150 BAKER (W. P.). The English Village. Oxf. 1953.

19151 ROBERTS (BRIAN K.). The Making of the English Village: A Study in Historical Geography. Harlow. 1987.

19152 PEAKE (HAROLD JOHN EDWARD). The English Village: The Origin and Decay of its Community. 1922.

19153 BROWN (JONATHAN) *and* WARD (SADIE B.). Village Life in England 1860–1940: A Photographic Record. 1985.

19154 KENDALL (DIANA). 'Portrait of a Disappearing English Village'. *Sociol. Rur.* 3 (1963), 157–65.

19155 CROSSLAND (PHYLLIS). Years of Grace: A Biographical Story of Life in a Rural Area of England, 1850–1973. Penistone. 1985.

19156 EDWARDS (J. ARWELL). 'The Viability of Lower Size Order Settlements in Rural Areas: The Case of North East England'. *Sociol. Rur.* 11 (1971), 247–76.

19157 PYE-SMITH (CHARLES) *and* NORTH (RICHARD) Working the Land. 1984.

19158 NALSON (JOHN SPENCER). Mobility of Farm Families: A Study of Occupational and Residential Mobility in an Upland Area of England. Manch. 1968.

19159 PORTER (ENID). Cambridgeshire Customs and Folklore. 1969.

19160 MARTIN (ERNEST WALTER). The Shearers and the Shorn: A Study of Life in a Devon Community. 1965.

19161 GLYN-JONES (ANNE). Village into Town: A Study of Transition in South Devon. Exeter. 1977.

19162 INNES (KATHLEEN ELIZABETH). Life in a Hampshire Village. 1944.

19163 PAHL (RAYMOND EDWARD). Urbs in Rure: The Metropolitan Fringe in Hertfordshire. 1965.

19164 —— 'Class and Community in an English Commuter Village'. *Sociol. Rur.* 5 (1965), 5–23.

19165 MARSHALL (JOHN DUNCAN) *and* WALTON (JOHN K.). The Lake Counties from 1830 to the Mid-20th Century: A Study in Regional Change. Manch. 1981.

19166 HOSKINS (WILLIAM GEORGE). The Midland Peasant: The Economics and Social History of a Leicester Village. Lond./N.Y. 1957.

19167 PACKMAN (JOHN). Services in Rural Norfolk: 1950–1980. Norwich. 1981.

19168 CORDEAUX (E. H.) *and* MERRY (D. H.). A Bibliography of Printed Works Relating to Oxfordshire (excluding the University and the City). Oxf. 1955. 3rd edn 1981.

19169 DEW (GEORGE JAMES). Oxfordshire Village Life: The Diaries of George James Dew (1846–1928) Relieving Officer. Abingdon. 1983. [*Ed.* by Pamela Horn].

19170 CONNELL (JOHN). The End of Country Life in Central Surrey. 1978.

19171 BRACEY (HOWARD EDWIN). Social Provision in Rural Wiltshire. 1952.

19172 RADFORD (ELIZABETH). The New Villagers: Urban Pressure on Rural Areas in Worcestershire. 1970.

19173 BLAKEBOROUGH (JOHN FREEMAN FAIRFAX). Yorkshire Village Life, Humour and Characteristics. 1955.

19174 O'KELLY (TERENCE) *comp*. The Villages of Abinger Common and Wotton, Surrey: Snippets of History. Horsham. 1988.

19175 BLYTHE (RONALD). Akenfield: Portrait of an English Village. 1969.

19176 DAVIS (JEAN) *comp*. Aldbury People 1885–1945. Aldbury. 1988.

19177 HAVINDEN (MICHAEL ASHLEY). Estate Villages: A Study of the Berkshire Villages of Ardington and Lockinge. 1966.

19178 WILLIAMS (WILLIAM MORGAN). A West Country Village, Ashworthy: Family, Kinship and Land. 1963.

19179 STACEY (MARGARET). Tradition and Change: A Study of Banbury. 1960.

19180 —— *Et al.* Power, Persistence and Change: A Second Study of Banbury. 1975.

19181 KILBY (JOHN) *et al.* Bygone Birstall: A Century of Change. Birstall. 1988.

19182 HORSLEY (JOHN E.). A Short History of Brixham. Devon. 1988.

19183 BOOTH (JOHN). The Day War Broke out: Stories of Life in a Village at War [Cawood, Yorkshire]. Westbury. 1982.

19184 CHELLASTON HISTORY GROUP. A History of Chellaston. Chellaston. 1988.

19185 GREEN (KENNETH R.). Old Cottingham Remembered. Beverley. 1988.

19186 ROBIN (JEAN). Elmdon: Continuity and Change in a North-West Essex Village, 1861–1964. Camb. 1980.

19187 HOLLAND (ALEC JOHN). Our Exbury: Life in an English Village in the 1920s and Early 30s. Southampton. 1982.

19188 BROWN (JAMES). Gamlingay: 600 Years of Life in an English Village. Lond. 1989.

19189 WILLIAMS (WILLIAM MORGAN). The Sociology of an English Village: Gosforth. 1954.

19190 LEE (BARBARA). Groombridge Old and New: Memoirs of Village Life in the First Half of the 20th Century. Camb. 1978.

19191 HANHAM LOCAL HISTORY SOCIETY. Hanham our Home (1920–1940). Hanham. 1988.

19192 GILLETT (JOHN W.). Once upon a Hard Times: Life in the Village of Higher Cloughfield. Rawtenstall. 1981.

19193 PEAKE (HENRY JOHN EDWARD) *and* SUMMERS (WILLIAM H.) *eds*. The Story of Hungerford in Berkshire. 1926.

19194 WILLMOTT (PHYLLIS). Growing up in a London Village [Lee, Kent]: Family Life between the Wars. 1979.

19195 DEVENISH (DOROTHY). A Wiltshire Home: A Study of Little Durnford. 1948.

19196 MORTIMER LOCAL HISTORY GROUP. Mortimer between the Wars. 1984.

19197 COOK (JEAN) *and* TAYLOR (LESLIE). A Village within the City: The Story of Old Headington, Oxford. Oxf. 1987.

19198 SEND AND RIPLEY HISTORICAL SOCIETY. Ripley and Send, then and now: The Changing Scene of Surrey Village Life. Ripley. 1984.

19199 DRUCE (FRED). The Light of Other Days: Country Life around Ross, 1870–1940. Ross-on-Wye. 1984.

19200 ST BERNARD HISTORY GROUP. A Short History of St Bernard. St Bernard. 1988.

19201 BURDETT (HARRY). Life in Sapcote, Leicestershire, 1914–1924. Sapcote. 1984.

19202 LYONS (NICK) *ed*. Scotton: Aspects of Village Life. Scotton. 1980.

19203 MASON (CAROLYN). Snowshill: A Gloucestershire Village. Cheltenham. 1987.

19204 CRICHTON (RUTH MORLEY). Commuters' Village: A Study of Commuting and Commuters in the Berkshire Village of Stratfield Mortimer. Dawlish. 1964.

19205 PRESTRIDGE (COLIN). A History of Stubbington. Southampton. 1988.

19206 AMBROSE (PETER). The Quiet Revolution: Social Change in a Sussex Village, 1871–1971. 1974.

19207 GILL (CRISPIN). The Isles of Scilly. Newton Abbot. 1975.

19208 CROSBY (ALAN). A History of Thetford. Chichester. 1986.

19209 JEANS (RICHARD). Upwell: History of a Fenland Village. Upwell. 1988.

19210 LITTLEJOHN (J.). Westrigg: The Sociology of a Cheviot Parish. 1963.

19211 BRAGG (MELVYN). Speak for England: An Oral History of England, 1900–1975: Based on Interviews with Inhabitants of Wigton, Cumberland. 1976.

19212 BURTON (MARY). Wingerworth through the Ages. Ilkeston. 1988.

19213 USMAR (JOHN) *et al.* Old Witheridge: Byegone Days in a Devon Village. Exeter. 1988.

19214 SMITH (NICOLA) *ed.* Woodstreet: The Growth of a Village. Wood Street. 1988.

19215 RICE (OUIDA). Village Memories: Glimpses of Village Life During the First Fifty Years of this Century as Seen through the Eyes of the Villagers of Woughton-on-the-Green, Milton Keynes. Milton Keynes. 1982.

19216 WILLIAMSON (BILL). Class, Culture and Community: A Biographical Study of Social Change in Mining. 1982. [Throckley, Northumberland.].

4. SCOTTISH VILLAGES AND RURAL COMMUNITIES

19217 THE THIRD STATISTICAL ACCOUNT OF SCOTLAND.

19218 STRAWHORN (JOHN) *and* BOYD (WILLIAM). Ayrshire. Edin. 1951.

19219 SMITH (ALEXANDER). The County of Fife. Edin. 1952.

19220 SNODGRASS (CATHERINE P.). The County of East Lothian. Edin. 1953.

19221 HAMILTON (HENRY) *ed.* The County of Aberdeen. Glasg. 1960.

19222 MacDONALD (COLIN M.) *ed.* The County of Argyll. Glasg. 1961.

19223 HAMILTON (HENRY) *ed.* The County of Banff. Glasg. 1961.

19224 MOISLEY (H. A.) *and* THAIN (A. G.) *eds.* The County of Renfrew and the County of Bute. Glasg. 1962.

19225 HOUSTON (GEORGE) *ed.* The County of Dumfries. Glasg. 1962.

19226 MATHER (ALEXANDER S.). The County of Ross and Cromarty. Edin. 1987.

19227 LAIRD (JOHN) *and* RAMSAY (D. G.) *eds.* The Stewartry of Kirkcudbright and the County of Wigtown. Glasg. 1965.

19228 HAMILTON (HENRY) *ed.* The Counties of Moray and Nairn. Glasg. 1965.

19229 RENNIE R. C. *and* GORDON (T. C.) *eds.* The County of Stirling, The County of Clackmannan. Glasg. 1966.

19230 SMITH (JOHN S.) *ed.* The County of Caithness. Edin. 1988.

19231 —— *Ed.* The County of Sutherland. Edin. 1988.

19232 BULLOCH (J. P. B.) *and* URQUHART (J. M.) *eds.* The County of Peebles and the County of Selkirk. Glasg. 1974.

19233 ILLSLEY (WILLIAM ALLEN) *ed.* The County of Angus. Arbroath. 1977.

19234 TAYLOR (DAVID B.) *ed.* The Counties of Perth and Kinross. Coupar Angus. 1979.

19235 SMITH (DENNIS) *ed.* The County of Kincardine. Edin. 1988.

19236 COULL (JAMES R.) *ed.* The County of Shetland. Edin. 1985.

19237 MILLER (RONALD) *ed.* The County of Orkney. Edin. 1985.

19238 BARRON (HUGH) *ed.* The County of Inverness. 1985.

19239 JONES (D. T.) *et al.* Rural Scotland during the War. 1926.

19240 WHYTE (IAN D.). The Historical Geography of Rural Settlement in Scotland: A Review. Edin. 1982.

19241 HUTCHINSON (BERTRAM). 'Depopulation and Rural Life in Scotland'. *Nature* 171 (1953), 643–4. [Prepared for Dept. of Health, Scotland.].

19242 CAIRD (J. B.). 'The Making of the Scottish Rural Landscape'. *Scot. Geog. Mag.* 80 (1964), 72–80.

19243 FENTON (ALEXANDER). Scottish Country Life. Edin. 1976.

19244 SHUCKSMITH (MARK) *and* ARDEN (R. J.). Scotland's Rural Housing: A Forgotten Problem. Edin. 1984.

19245 MATHER (ALEXANDER SMITH). An Annotated Bibliography of Rural Land Use in the Highlands and Islands of Scotland. Aberd. 1981.

19246 BIRD (S. ELIZABETH). 'The Impact of Private Estate Ownership on Social Development in a Scottish Rural Community'. *Sociol. Rur.* 22 (1982), 43–56.

19247 GRANT (JAMES SHAW). Highland Villages. 1977.

19248 BECKER (A.). 'Field Work among Scottish Shepherds and German Peasants: 'Whohs' and their Handicaps'. *Social Forces* 35 (1956), 10–15.

19249 GREEN (P.). 'Drymen, Village Growth and Community Problems'. *Sociol. Rur.* 4 (1964), 52–62.

19250 BROADY (MAURICE). 'Drumbie Enquiry: David and Goliath in Scottish Rural Development'. *Comm. Dvlpt J.* 9 (1974), 187–90.

19251 EASTWOOD DISTRICT LIBRARIES. A Planned Village: A History of Eaglesham. Giffnock. 1988.

19252 PAGE (W.). Holbrook: The Story of a Village 1900–1983. Edin. 1983.

19253 Committee of Inquiry into the Functions and Powers of the Islands' Councils of Scotland. Cmnd 9216. Parliamentary Papers, 1983–4.

19254 CHALMERS (CHICK). Islanders. 1975.

19255 THOMSON (DERICK S.) *and* GRIMBLE (IAN) *eds*. The Future of the Highlands. 1968.

19256 ALEXANDER (*Sir* KENNETH). Rural Renewal: Experience in the Highlands and Islands. Camb. 1984.

19257 ABERCROMBIE (KEITH). Rural Development in Lewis and Harris: The Western Isles of Scotland. 1981.

19258 MacDONALD (DONALD). Lewis: A History of the Island. Edin. 1978.

19259 ENNEW (JUDITH). The Western Isles Today. Camb. 1980.

19260 BANKS (NOEL). Six Inner Hebrides: Eigg, Rum, Canna, Muck, Coll, Tiree. Newton Abbot. 1977.

19261 WYLIE (GUS). The Hebrides. Glasg. 1978.

19262 JAATINEN (STIG TYRGIL HJALMARSON). The Human Geography of the Outer Hebrides with Special Reference to the Latest Trends in Land Use. Helsinki. 1957/8.

19263 MACDHOMNAILL (DOMNALL IAIN). Uibhist a Deas: Beagun mu Eachdraidh is mu Bheul-aithris an Eilein. Stornoway. 1981. [South Uist history.].

19264 MacLEAN (CHARLES). Island on the Edge of the World: The Story of St Kilda. Edin. 1977.

19265 STEEL (TOM). The Life and Death of St Kilda: The Moving Story of a Vanished Island Community. Rev. edn 1988.

19266 DOWNIE (ROBERT ANGUS). The Islands of the Clyde. Perth. 1982.

19267 PHILIP (KATHLEEN). The Story of Gigha: The Flourishing Island. 1979.

19268 SHARPE (RICHARD). Raasey: A Study in Island History: Documents and Sources, People and Places. 1978.

See also from the Islands Series pub. by David & Charles, Newton Abbot

19269 McLELLAN (ROBERT). The Isle of Arran. Newton Abbot. 1970. 3rd edn 1985.

19270 MUNRO (IAN S.). The Island of Bute. Newton Abbot. 1973.

19271 THOMPSON (FRANCIS). Harris and Lewis, Outer Hebrides. Newton Abbot. 1973. 3rd edn 1987.

19272 CARMICHAEL (ALISDAIR). Kintyre: Best of all the Isles. Newton Abbot. 1974.

19273 MacNAB (P. A.). The Isle of Mull. Newton Abbot. 1973.

19274 BAILEY (PATRICK). Orkney. Newton Abbot. 1971.

19275 NICOLSON (JAMES ROBERT). Shetland. Newton Abbot. 1972. 3rd rev. edn 1979.

19276 DONALDSON (GORDON). Isles of Home: Sixty Years of Shetland. 1983.

19277 SILLAR (FREDERICK CAMERON) *and* MEYLER (RUTH M.). Skye. Newton Abbot. 1973.

19278 BECKWITH (LILLIAN). The Hills is Lonely. 1959. 2nd edn 1979. Rev. edn 1986. [Hebridean social life and customs.].

19279 —— The Sea for Breakfast. 1961. Rev. edn 1986.

19280 —— Bruach Blend. 1978. Rev. edn 1980.

19281 —— A Rope-in Case. 1968. Rev. edn 1987.

19282 CAIRD (J. B.) *and* MOISLEY (HENRY ALAN). 'Leadership and Innovation in the Crofting Communities of the Outer Hebrides'. *Sociol. Rev.* 9 (1961), 85–102.

19283 MacLENNAN (ANGUS). The Furrow Behind Me: The Autobiography of a Hebridean Crofter. 1962. [Transl. by John Lorne Campbell.].

19284 STEWART (KATHARINE). Crofts and Crofting. Edin. 1980.

19285 GOLD (JOHN ROBERT) *and* GOLD (MARGARET M.). The Crofting System: A Select Bibliography. Oxf. 1979.

19286 HUNTER (JAMES). The Making of the Crofting Community. Edin. 1976.

19287 MacLEAN (ALISDAIR). Night Falls on Ardnamurchan: The Twilight of a Crofting Family. 1984.

19288 CAMERON (DAVID KERR). Willie Gavin, Crofter Man: Portrait of a Vanished Lifestyle. 1980.

5 · VILLAGE AND RURAL COMMUNITIES IN WALES AND NORTHERN IRELAND

19289 DAVIES (ELWYN) *and* REES (ALWYN) *eds*. Welsh Rural Communities. Card. 1960.

19290 THOMASON (GEORGE FREDERICK). Rural Depopulation in Wales. 1974.

19291 LEWIS (GARETH J.). 'A Welsh Rural Community in Transition: A Case Study in Mid-Wales'. *Sociol. Rur.* 10 (1970), 143–61.

19292 —— 'Commuting and the Village in Mid-Wales'. *Geog.* 52 (1967), 294–304.

19293 LEWIS (GARETH J.) *and* MAUND (D. J.). 'Intra-community Segregation: A Case Study in Rural Herefordshire'. *Sociol. Rur.* 19 (1979), 135–47.

19294 TROPP (E. H.). 'Dispersed Settlement and the Rural Community [in Wales]'. *Rural Sociol.* 18 (1953), 338–44.

19295 WILLIAMS (HOWARD). 'Three Types of Rural Welsh Community'. *Sociol. Rur.* 16 (1976), 279–90.

19296 WILIAM (EURWYN). Home-Made Homes: Dwellings of the Rural Poor in Wales. Card. 1988.

19297 BOLLON (CHRIS). Attitudes to Second Homes in Rural Wales. Card. 1978.

19298 U.K. MINISTRY OF EDUCATON. Education in Rural Wales. 1949.

19299 BOWEN (E. G.). 'Rural Settlements in South West Wales'. *Geographical Teacher* 13 (1925/6), 317–24.

19300 EMMETT (ISABEL). A North Wales Village: A Social Anthropological Study. 1964.

19301 FRANKENBERG (RONALD). Village on the Border: A Social Study of Religion, Politics, and Football in a North Wales Community. 1957.

19302 O'CONNOR (PHILIP). Living in Croesor. 1962.

19303 REES (ALWYN DAVID). Life in a Welsh Countryside: A Social Study of Llanfihangel yng Ngwynfa. Card. 1951.

19304 JENKINS (DAVID). An Agricultural Community in South West Wales. Card. 1971.

19305 JONES (J.). 'Village Life: Redbrook on Wye, 1914–1931'. *Presenting Monmouthshire* 40 (1975), 32–5.

19306 DAVIES (C.). 'Montgomeryshire: The Life of a Rural Community'. *Contemp. Rev.* 199 (1961), 124–8.

19307 MOGEY (JOHN MACFARLANE). Rural Life in Northern Ireland: Five Regional Studies. 1947.

19308 —— 'Characteristics of the Rural Community in Northern Ireland'. *Rural Sociol.* 18 (1953), 243–8.

19309 O'NEILL (TIMOTHY P.). Life and Tradition in Rural Ireland. 1977.

19310 HANNAN (DAMIAN). Rural Exodus: A Study of the Forces Influencing the Larger-Scale Migration of Irish Rural Youth. 1970.

19311 GEARY (ROBERT CHARLES) *and* HUGHES (J. G.). Internal Migration in Ireland. [With appendix by C. J. Gillman 'Country Migration : An Alternative Approach'.]. Dublin. 1970.

19312 GAILEY (ALAN). Rural Houses in the North of Ireland. Edin. 1984.

19313 LIVINGSTONE (PEADAR). The Fermanagh Story. Fermanagh. 1969.

6. PARISHES IN ENGLAND

19314 NATIONAL ASSOCIATION OF LOCAL COUNCILS. The Future of English Local Government from the Viewpoint of the Parishes. 1981.

19315 EDWARDS (FREDERICK LAWRENCE). The Parish Councillor's Guide: The Law and Practice of Parish, Town and Community Councils in England and Wales. 1922. 8th edn 1950. 15th edn 1986. *Ed.* by John Prophet.

19316 CLOKE (PAUL J.) *and* LITTLE (JO). Social Profiles of Ten Case Study Parishes. Lampeter, Dyfed. 1984.

19317 CLOSE (ROY K.). A Village of Parts: A History of Amberley Parish. Stroud. 1986.

19318 HARBORD (REGINALD ENGLEDOW). The Parish of Ardeley: A Short History. Spring Grange. 1950.

19319 ASTON LOCAL HISTORY GROUP. Some Aspects of the History of Aston cum Aughton. Aston. 1977.

19320 JONES (JOHN MORRIS). Manors of Aston Parish: An Introduction to the Historical Geography of Aston Manor. Birm. 1978.

19321 BARSBY (PERCY JOSEPH). Bygone Days in the Parish of Attenborough. Attenborough, Notts. 1986.

19322 ICELY (HENRY EDWARD MCLAUGHLIN). Blockley through Twelve Centuries: Annals of a Cotswold Parish. Kineton. 1974. New edn Bungay. 1984.

19323 FORTESCUE (S. E. D.). People and Places, Great and Little Brokham. Great Brokham. 1978.

19324 CHATWIN (A. H.). Bushbury—Parish and People, 1550–1950. Rotherham. 1983.

19325 NEWMAN (ROGER). Chatterton, A Hampshire Parish: Bramshot and Liphook. Petersfield. 1976.

19326 LEE (JOHN MICHAEL). Social Leaders and Public Persons: A Study of County Government in Cheshire since 1888. Oxf. 1963.

19327 BIRTILL (GEORGE). 'Changing Years': Chorley and District between two Wars. Chorley. 1976.

19328 STEEL (DAVID IAN ANTHONY). A Lincolnshire Village: The Parish of Corby Glen in its Historical Context. 1979.

19329 BALL (JEAN) *et al.* Under the Oaks: The Historical Record of the Parish of Ebrington. Ebrington. 1978.

19330 SPUFFORD (PETER) *and* SPUFFORD (MARGARET). Eccleshall: The Story of a Staffordshire Market Town and its Dependent Villages. Keele. 1964.

19331 BAILEY (GEOFFREY). The Parish of Farlington. Farlington. 1975.

19332 HARRIS (WILLIAM LESLIE). Filton, Gloucestershire: Some Account of the Village and Parish. Bristol. 1981.

19333 DEACON (MARJORIE). Great Chesterfield: A Common Field Parish in Essex. Saffron Walden. 1983.

19334 WILSHERE (JOHN). Great Stretton: History, Parish Registers, Probate Inventories. Leicester. 1984.

19335 SMALLEY (KEITH AUBREY). Greenford, the Historical Geography of a North West London Parish. 1963.

19336 MITCHELL (MARCIA) *and* MURDOCH (IAN). High Halden, The Parish and the People. Ashford. 1981.

19337 BEVANS (EDNA) *and* GILLETT (MILDRED). Kinson 1894–1931: A Social Survey as Recorded in the Minutes of the Kinson Parish Council. 2 Pts. Bournemouth. 1982.

19338 SHEAIL (PHILIP). A Downland Village: Portrait of a Hampshire Parish. Winchester. 1979.

19339 PRESTON (JOHN HAROLD). The Story of Hampstead. 1948.

19340 COOPER (WILLIAM). Henley-in-Arden. Birm. 1946.

19341 BOWRA (EDWARD). Ightham: Notes on Local History. Ightham. 1978.

19342 WEATE (MARY). The Parish of Lapley-with-Weaton Aston. Lapley, Staffs. 1982.

19343 HOWSE (VIOLET MARY). Lyford: A Parish History. Faringdon. 1981.

19344 HOPKINS (PETER). Lymplesham: A Dip into the History of a Somerset Parish. Lympsham [*sic*]. 1983.

19345 HUDLESTON (NIGEL ANDREW). History of Malton and Norton. Scarborough. 1962.

19346 SMITH (BRIAN STANLEY). A History of Malvern. Leicester. 1964.

19347 CHAMBERS (V. H.). Old Meppershall: A Parish History. Meppershall, Beds. 1979.

19348 PLAYNE (ARTHUR TWISDEN). A History of the Parishes of Minchinhampton and Avening. 1915. Repr. Dursley. 1978.

19349 MORLEY VILLAGE HISTORY COMMITTEE. A History of the Parish of Morley, Derbyshire. Ilkeston. 1977.

19350 TWIST (SYDNEY JAMES). Murston Village and Parish: A History. Sittingbourne. 1981.

19351 BENTLEY (E. W.). Oakford: The History of a Devon Parish. Oakford, Devon. 1982.

19352 BRAY (MARJORIE). Oxhey: The History of a Parish. Oxhey, Hertfordshire. 1979.

19353 ROBERTS (ARTHUR STARKEY). Prescot Parish Memories. L/pool. 1982.

19354 CURTIS (GERALD). The Story of the Sampfords: The Parishes of Great and Little Sampford, Essex, from the Earliest Times to the Conclusion of the Second World War. Great Sampford. 1981.

19355 LUCEY (BERYL). Twenty Centuries in Sedlecombe: An East Sussex Parish. 1978.

19356 SAVILLE (GEORGE EDWARD). The Parish of Spernhall: A History. Spernhall, Warwickshire. 1984.

19357 SCOTT-TUCKER (J. H.) *ed.* The Parish of Stoke Fleming, Devon: Elizabeth I and before, to Elizabeth II Coronation, 2nd June 1953. 1953.

19358 CANNER (A. C.). The Parish of Tintagel: Some Historical Notes. Camelford. 1982.

19359 DALBY (MARK). Tottenham Parish Church and Parish: A Brief History and Guide. 1979. 2nd rev. edn 1980.

19360 ALLISON (J. E.). Sidelights on Tranmere. Birkenhead. 1976.

19361 HAMER (JOHN). By Wapple Way: Warnham: The Story of a Sussex Parish. Warnham. 1980.

19362 MILLIKEN (HAROLD TURNER). Changing Scene: Two Hundred Years of Church and Parish Life in Worsley. Worsley. 1976. 2nd rev. edn 1978.

19363 WROUGHTON HISTORY GROUP. Studies in the History of Wroughton Parish. Wroughton, Wiltshire. 1982.

7. PARISHES IN SCOTLAND AND WALES

19364 NEILL (JOHN). Records and Reminiscences of Bonhill Parish. Dumbarton. 1979. 1st pub. 1912.

19365 RANKIN (ERIC). Cockburnspath: A Documentary Social History of a Border Parish. Edin. 1981.

19366 SIMPSON (ERIC). Dalgety: The Story of a Parish. Dalgety Bay. 1980.

19367 SEATH (J. W.) *and* SEATH (R. E.). Dunbarney: A Parish with a Past. Coupar Angus. 1985.

19368 NEVILLE (THOMAS ERIC). East Kilbride: The History of Parish and Village. Glasg. 1965.

19369 MacKAY (MORAY SUTHERLAND). Notes on the Parish of Kilmadock and Borough of Doune. Doune. 1955. New edn Stirling. 1984.

19370 EASTWOOD DISTRICT LIBRARIES. 'Fairest Parish': A History of Mearns. Giffnock. 1988.

19371 FRASER (DUNCAN). Portrait of a Parish [St.Cyrus]. Montrose. 1970. 2nd edn 1979.

19372 WAUGH (JAMES). Slamannan Parish through the Changing Years. Falkirk. 1979.

19373 MUNRO (HENRIETTA). Pictures of Old Thurso and District: Studies of the Past. Thurso. 1978.

19374 MOISLEY (HENRY ALAN). Uig: A Hebridean Parish. Nottingham. 1961.

19375 LITTLEJOHN (JAMES). Westrigg: The Sociology of a Cheviot Parish. 1963.

19376 REES (EDWIN HENRY VERDUN). The Parish of Betws Penpont, Brecon. Brecon. 1969.

19377 JONES (GLYN MEREDITH). Sully: A Village and Parish in the Vale of Glamorgan. Sully. 1986.

E. AGRICULTURE, FISHING, FORESTRY, AND GARDENING

1. FARMING AND AGRICULTURE: BIBLIOGRAPHICAL AND SURVEY WORKS

19378 Guide to the Institute of Agricultural History and Museum of English Rural Life. Reading. 1982.

19379 —— Agricultural Land Commission Report. 1948–63.

19380 LILLEY (G. P.). Information Sources in Agriculture and Food Sciences. 1981.

19381 STRATTON (JOHN M.). Agricultural Records, A.D. 220–1968. 1969. 2nd edn 1977, covering period up to 1977.

19382 U.K. MINISTRY OF AGRICULTURE, FISHERIES AND FOOD. A Century of Agricultural Statistics: Great Britain, 1866–1966. 1968.

19383 —— Agricultural and Food Statistics: A Guide to Official Sources. 1969.

19384 —— Agricultural Statistics, United Kingdom. 1867+. [Annual.].

19385 COPPOCK (JOHN TERENCE). An Agricultural Atlas of England and Wales. 1964.

19386 FUSSELL (GEORGE EDWIN). 'The Collection of Agricultural Statistics in Great Britain: Its Origin and Evaluation'. *Agric. Hist.* 18 (1944), 161–86.

19387 BESTERMAN (THEODORE). Agriculture: A Bibliography of Bibliographies. Totowa, N.J. 1971.

19388 MORGAN (RAINE). Dissertations on British Agrarian History: A Selected List of Theses Awarded Higher Degrees in British and Foreign Universities between 1876 and 1978. Reading. 1981.

19389 BEALES (HUGH LANCELOT) *and* CHAMBERS (JONATHAN DAVID). A Select Bibliography of Rural Economic History. Edin. 1933.

19390 DENMAN (DONALD ROBERT) *et al.* Bibliography of Rural Land Economy and Land Ownership, 1900–1957. Camb. 1958.

19391 —— Agricultural History Review. 1953+.

19392 BEECHAM (HELEN AUDREY). 'List of Books and Articles on Agrarian History Issued since September 1965'. *Agric. Hist. Rev.* 15 (1967), 46–53.

19393 SHEAIL (JOHN). 'List of Books and Articles on Agrarian History Issued since June 1968'. *Agric. Hist. Rev.* 18 (1970), 64–71.

19394 WHETHAM (EDITH HOLT) *et al.* A Record of Agricultural Policy 1947–1952; 1952–1954; 1954–1956; 1956–1958; 1958–1960. Camb. 1952–60.

19395 BURRELL (ALISON MARGARET) *et al.* A Statistical Handbook of United Kingdom Agriculture. 1984.

19396 MARKS (HILARY F.). 100 Years of British Food and Farming: A Statistical Survey. 1989.

19397 BASSETT (PHILIPPA) *comp.* A List of the Historical Records of the National Farmers' Union of Scotland. Reading. 1980.

19398 HIRSCH (GUENTER PAUL HERMANN). 'Static Structure with a Changed Content: The Agrarian Situation in Great Britain since 1835'. In Transactions of the 3rd World Congress of Sociology, vol. 2. 1956.

19399 —— Young Farmers' Clubs: Report on a Survey in England and Wales on Their History, Organisation and Activities . . . 1952.

19400 ROYAL AGRICULTURAL SOCIETY OF ENGLAND. A Survey of Agricultural Libraries in England and Scotland. 1957.

19401 FREAM (WILLIAM). Elements of Agriculture. 1892. 9th edn 1914, *ed.* by J. R. Ainsworth-Davis. 14th edn 1962, *ed.* by Douglas Hepworth Robinson. 16th edn 1983, *ed.* by Colin Raymond William Spedding, under new title, Fream's Agriculture: A Textbook Prepared Under the Authority of the Royal Agricultural Society of England.

19402 PROTHERO (ROWLAND EDMUND) *Baron Ernle.* English Farming Past and Present. 1912. 2nd edn 1917. New 6th edn 1961, with an Introduction by George Edwin Fussell and Oliver R. McGregor.

19403 CHRISTIE (MABEL ELIZABETH). The Evolution of the English Farm. 1927. 2nd edn 1952.

19404 ROBINSON (DOUGLAS HEPWORTH). The New Farming. 1938. New edn 1951.

19405 FRANKLIN (THOMAS BEDFORD). A History of Agriculture. 1948.

19406 ORWIN (CHARLES STEWART). A History of English Farming. 1949.

19407 WHITLOCK (RALPH). A Short History of Farming in Britain. 1965.

19408 —— Royal Farmers. 1980.

19409 —— Farming in History. Hove. 1983.

19410 HUGGETT (FRANK EDWARD). A Short History of Farming. 1970.

19411 COLLINS (EDWARD JOHN T.). The Economics of Upland Britain 1750–1950: An Illustrated Review. Reading. 1978.

19412 WHETHAM (EDITH HOLT). The Agrarian History of England and Wales, vol. 8—1914–1939. Camb. 1978. [Series General Editor, Joan M. Thirsk.].

19413 WILKES (PETER). An Illustrated History of Farming. Bourne End. 1978.

19414 KIRK (JOHN HENRY). The Development of Agriculture in Germany and the United Kingdom, 2: U.K Agricultural Policy 1870–1970. Ashford. 1979.

19415 HARVEY (CHARLES NIGEL). The Industrial Archaeology of Farming in England and Wales. 1980.

19416 BROWN (JONATHAN). Agriculture in England, 1870–1947. Manch. 1987.

19417 HOLDERNESS (B. A.). British Agriculture since 1945. Manch. 1985.

19418 SEDDON (QUENTIN). The Quiet Revolution: Farming and the Countryside in the 21st Century. 1989.

19419 GRIGG (DAVID). English Agriculture: An Historical Perspective. Oxf. 1989.

19420 BENYON (V. H.). Agriculture and Economics. Exeter. 1979.

19421 BOWERS (JOHN K.). 'British Agricultural Policy since the Second World War'. *Agric. Hist. Rev.* 33 (1985), 66–76.

19422 WELLS (RAYMOND J. G.). 'British Agriculture—A Rare Success Story'. *Round Table*, 289 (1984), 86–92.

19423 TRACY (M. E.). 'Fifty Years of Agricultural Policy'. *J. Agric. Econ.* 27 (1976), 331–49.

19424 CLAIRE (JOHN D.). Agricultural Change since 1750. Basing. 1988.

19425 ROBINSON (GUY MARTIN). Agricultural Change: Geographical Studies of British Agriculture. Edin. 1988.

2. FARMING AND AGRICULTURE: CHRONOLOGICAL STUDIES

19426 HALL (*Sir* ALFRED DANIEL). Agriculture after the War. 1916.

19427 ASHBY (ARTHUR WILFRED). Allotments and Small Holdings in Oxfordshire. 1917.

19428 —— Some Principles of Organisation and Operation in Agricultural Co-operative Societies. Oxf. 1952.

19429 SHEAIL (JOHN). 'Land Improvement and Reclamation: The Experiences of the First World War in England and Wales'. *Agric. Hist. Rev.* 24 (1976), 110–25.

19430 HIBBARD (BENJAMIN HORACE). Effects of the Great War upon Agriculture in the United States and Great Britain. N.Y. 1919.

19431 DEWEY (PETER E.). British Agriculture in the First World War. 1989.

19432 COOPER (ANDREW FENTON). British Agricultural Policy, 1912–1936: A Study in Conservative Politics. Manch. 1989.

19433 CREASY (JOHN). The Countryside between the Wars 1918–1940: A Photographic Record. 1984.

19434 WHETHAM (EDITH HOLT). 'The Agriculture Act 1920 and its Repeal: The "Great Betrayal"'. *Agric. Hist. Rev.* 22 (1974), 36–49.

19435 ORWIN (CHARLES STEWART). 'Commodity Prices and Farming Policy'. *J. Roy. Agric. Soc. Eng.* 83 (1922), 3–14.

19436 ENFIELD (*Sir* RALPH ROSCOE). The Agricultural Crisis, 1920–1923. 1924.

19437 WATSON (*Sir* JAMES ANDERSON SCOTT) *and* MORE (JAMES ANTHONY). Agriculture: The Science and Practice of British Farming. 1924. 10th edn 1956.

19438 —— The Farming Year. 1938. New edn 1963.

19439 —— *Ed.* Agriculture in the British Economy. 1957.

19440 —— The Pace of Farming Progress. Belf. 1952.

19441 —— Rural Britain Today and Tomorrow. Edin./Lond. 1934.

19442 —— Special Article on Farming after the War. Bath. 1941. [Bath and West and Southern Counties Society pamphlet.].

19443 —— The History of the Royal Agricultural Society of England, 1839–1939. 1939.

19444 WATSON (*Sir* JAMES ANDERSON SCOTT) *and* HOBBS (MARY ELLIOT). Great Farmers. 1937. Rev. edn 1951.

19445 GREEN (*Sir* JOHN LITTLE). Political Pills and Farming Ills: An Exposure of the Lloyd George Rural Land Plan. Peterborough. 1926.

19446 MESSER (MALCOLM). The Agricultural Depression of 1931: Its Nature and Incidence. 1932.

19447 FORDHAM (MONTAGUE). Britain's Trade and Agriculture: Their Recent Evolution and Future Development. 1932.

19448 VENN (JOHN ARCHIBALD). The Foundations of Agricultural Economics, with an Economic History of British Agriculture during and after the Great War. 1933.

19449 PERCIVAL (JOHN). Wheat in Great Britain. 1934. 2nd edn 1948.

19450 JEFFCOCK (WILLIAM PHILIP). Agricultural Politics, 1915–1935. Ipswich. 1937.

19451 ASTOR (WALDORF *Viscount*) *and* ROWNTREE (BENJAMIN SEEBOHM). British Agriculture: The Principles of Future Policy. 1939.

19452 —— The Agricultural Dilemma. 1935.

19453 —— Food Production in Western Europe: An Economic Survey of Agriculture in Six Countries. 1940.

19454 —— Mixed Farming and Muddled Thinking: An Analysis of Current Agricultural Policy. 1946.

19455 ADDISON (CHRISTOPHER) *Baron*. A Policy for British Agriculture. 1939.

19456 FITZGERALD (BRIAN VESEY). Programme for Agriculture: By Lord Addison and Others. 1941.

19457 HARKNESS (*Sir* DOUGLAS ALEXANDER EARSMAN). War and British Agriculture. 1941.

19458 HALL (*Sir* ALFRED DANIEL). Reconstruction and the Land: An Approach to Farming in the National Interest. 1941.

19459 OXFORD UNIVERSITY AGRICULTURAL ECONOMICS RESEARCH UNIT. Country Planning: A Study of Rural Problems. Oxf. 1944.

19460 KIRK (JOHN HENRY). 'The Output of British Agriculture during the War'. *J. Procs. Agric. Econ. Soc.* 7 (1946), 30–45.

19461 MARSHALL (FRANCIS HUGH ADAM) *and* HAMMOND (JOHN). The Science of Animal Breeding in Britain: A Short History. Lond./N.Y. 1946.

19462 CRIPPS (ANTHONY). The Agriculture Act, 1947. 1948.

19463 BORCHERT (JOHN R.). 'The Agriculture of England and Wales, 1939–1946'. *Agric. Hist.* 22 (1948), 56–62.

19464 DIGBY (MARGARET). Agricultural Co-operation in Britain. 1949. Rev. edn 1957 by Digby *and* Sheila Gorst.

19465 —— Co-operative Land Use: The Challenge to Traditional Co-operation. Oxf. 1963.

19466 SARGENT (MALCOLM). Agricultural Co-operation. 1982.

19467 SMITH (ROBERT TROW). English Husbandry from the Earliest Times to the Present Day. 1951.

19468 —— Life from the Land. Lond./N.Y. 1969.

19469 HURD (ANTHONY RICHARD). A Farmer in Whitehall: Britain's Farming Revolution, 1939–1950. 1951.

19470 WHETHAM (EDITH HOLT). British Farming 1939–1949. 1952.

19471 —— Beef Cattle and Sheep, 1910–1940: A Description of the Production and Marketing of Beef Cattle and Sheep in Great Britain from the Early 20th Century to the Second World War. 1976.

19472 —— The Economic Background to Agriculture Policy. 1960.

19473 SYKES (FRIEND). Food, Farming and the Future. 1951.

19474 OJALA (ERIC MERVYN). Agriculture and Economic Progress. 1952.

19475 ROBINSON (DOUGLAS HEPWORTH) *and* HAY (WILLIAM DAVID). Self Sufficiency on the Farm. Bath. 1952. [Bath and West and Southern Counties Society pamphlet.].

19476 MARTELLI (GEORGE). The Elveden Enterprise: A Story of the Second Agricultural Revolution. 1952.

19477 HILTON (NORMAN). 'The Land's End Peninsula—The Influence of History on Agriculture'. *Geog. J.* 119 (1953), 57–72.

19478 —— 'Technology, Economy and Society in a Long-Settled Area [Land's End]'. *Rural Sociol.* 26 (1961), 381–94.

19479 WYE COLLEGE DEPARTMENT OF AGRICULTURAL ECONOMICS. Researches in Farm Management 1923–1950. Ashford. 1953.

See also many other works on British Agriculture published by Wye College (various departments).

19480 AGRICULTURAL RESEARCH COUNCIL. The Agricultural Research Service. 1953. 3rd edn 1969.

19481 ORWIN (CHARLES STEWART). 'Rural Revolution'. *Agriculture* 61 (1954), 264–8.

19482 HAINSWORTH (PETER HUGH). Agriculture: A New Approach. 1954.

19483 ROYAL AGRICULTURAL SOCIETY OF ENGLAND. County Agricultural Surveys

19484 —— 1—A Survey of the Agriculture of Kent. [By George Henry Garrard.]. 1954.

19485 —— 2—A Survey of the Agriculture of Sussex. [By Richard Henry Bishop Jesse.]. 1960.

19486 —— 3—A Survey of the Agriculture of Northumberland. [By Henry Cecil Pawson.]. 1961.

19487 —— 4—A Survey of the Agriculture of Cheshire. [By Wilfred Bernard Mercer.]. 1963.

19488 —— 5—A Survey of the Agriculture of Hertfordshire. [By Harold William Gardner.]. 1967.

19489 —— 6—A Survey of the Agriculture of Yorkshire. [By William Harwood Long.]. 1969.

19490 —— 7—A Survey of the Agriculture of Suffolk. [By P. J. O. Trist.] 1971.

19491 HARVEY (CHARLES NIGEL). The Farming Kingdom. 1955.

19492 STURMEY (STANLEY GEORGE). 'Owner Farming in England and Wales, 1900 to 1950'. *Manch. Sch. Econ. Soc. Studs* 23 (1955), 245–68.

19493 MURRAY (*Sir* KEITH ANDERSON). Agriculture. 1956.

19494 HUNT (KENNETH EDWARD) *and* CLARK (KENNETH ROY). The State of British Agriculture, 1955–1956. Oxf. 1956.

19495 HOOPER (SHADRACH GEORGE). The Finance of Farming in Great Britain. 1956.

19496 CHEW (HILARY C.). 'Changes in Land Use and Stock over England and Wales, 1939–1951'. *Geog. J.* 122 (1956), 466–70.

19497 THOMAS (W. J.). 'Postwar Agricultural Policy in the United Kingdom'. *Trans. Man. Stat. Soc.* (1958/60), 10 Dec. 1958. 1–24.

19498 DALE (HAROLD E.). Daniel Hall, Pioneer in Scientific Agriculture. 1956.

19499 HALLETT (GRAHAM). 'The Economic Position of British Agriculture'. *Econ. J.* 69 (1959), 522–40.

19500 COPPOCK (JOHN TERENCE). 'The Changing Arable in England and Wales 1870–1956'. *Tijd. Econ. Soc. Geog.* 50 (1959), 121–30.

19501 ALLEN (GEORGE ROLLASON). Agricultural Marketing Policies. Oxf. 1959.

19502 WIBBERLEY (GERALD PERCY). Agriculture and Urban Growth: A Study of the Competition for Rural Land. 1959.

19503 WILLIAMS (HUGH TREVOR) *ed.* Principles for British Agricultural Policy. 1960.

19504 U.K. MINISTRY OF AGRICULTURE, FISHERIES AND FOOD. A Survey among Grassland Farmers: Comprehensive Report . . . 1960.

19505 MORGAN (WILLIAM). A Survey of Capital and Credit in Agricultural Co-operative Societies in Great Britain. Oxf. 1960.

19506 BRITTON (DENIS KING). The Economic Arithmetic of Agriculture. Nottingham. 1961.

19507 —— The Changing Structure of British Agriculture. Newton Abbot. 1968.

19508 —— Cereals in the United Kingdom: Production, Marketing and Utilisation. Oxf. 1969.

19509 SMITH (LOUIS PATRICK FREDERICK). The Evolution of Agricultural Co-operation. Oxf. 1961.

19510 MINOPRIO (P.). 'Assistance for Small Farmers in the United Kingdom'. *Q. Rev. Agric. Econ.* 14 (1961), 31–46.

19511 ATTWOOD (EDWIN ARTHUR) and EVANS (HOWELL GRIFFITHS). The Economics of Hill Farming. Card. 1961.

19512 —— 'The Origins of State Support for British Agriculture'. *Manch. Sch. Econ. Soc. Studs* 31 (1963), 129–48.

19513 CHISHOLM (MICHAEL DONALD INGLIS). 'Agricultural Production, Location and Rent'. *Oxf. Econ. Papers* 13 (1961), 342–59.

19514 BRAMLEY (MARGARET). The Small Farmer: Present Situation and Future Prospects. 1961.

19515 —— Farming and Food Supplies: The Case for the Expansion of British Agriculture. 1965.

19516 SELF (PETER JOHN OTTER) and STORING (HERBERT JAMES). The State and the Farmer: British Agricultural Policies and Politics. 1962.

19517 —— 'The Farmers and the State'. *Pol. Q.* 29 (1958), 17–27.

19518 U.K. MINISTRY OF AGRICULTURE, FISHERIES AND FOOD. Classification of Agricultural Land in Britain: A Survey of the Physical and Economic Factors which used to be Taken into Account. 1962.

19519 BEST (ROBIN HEWITSON) and COPPOCK (JOHN TERENCE). The Changing use of Land in Britain. 1962.

19520 McCRONE (ROBERT GAVIN LOUDON). The Economics of Subsidising Agriculture: A Study of British Policy. Glasg. 1962.

19521 BENYON (VICTOR HOWELL) and HARRISON (J. E.). The Political Significance of the British Agricultural Vote. 1962.

19522 PENNOCK (JAMES ROLAND). ' "Responsible Government", Separate Powers and Special Interests: Agricultural subsidies in Britain and America'. *Amer Pol. Sci. Rev.* 56 (1962), 621–33.

19523 DIXON (P. J.). 'The United Kingdom Agricultural Review'. *Q. Rev. Agric. Econ.* 15 (1962), 142–8.

19524 HALLETT (GRAHAM) and JAMES (PHILIP GWYN). Farming for Consumers. 1963.

19525 FRANKEL (HENRYK). Economic Changes in British Agriculture, 1959–1964. Oxf. 1964.

19526 JAWETZ (MICHAEL BOGDAN). Agriculture in the British Economy, 1953–1963. Aberystwyth. 1964.

19527 JONES (ERIC LIONEL). Seasons and Prices: The Role of the Weather in English Agricultural History. 1964.

19528 STURROCK (FORD GIBSON). The Optimum Size of a Family Farm. 1965.

19529 STURROCK (FORD GIBSON) and CATHIE (JOHN). Farm Modernisation and the Countryside. Camb. 1980.

19530 PATVARDHAN (V. S.). British Agricultural Marketing. Poona/Lond. 1965.

19531 NASH (ERIC FRANCIS). Agricultural Policy in England. Card. 1965.

19532 LEVY (HERMANN JOACHIM). Large and Small Holdings: A Study of English Agricultural Economics. 1966.

19533 GASSON (RUTH). 'Part-Time Farmers in South East England'. *J. Agric. Econ.* 9 (1966), 135–9.

19534 HUNT (K. E.) and CLARKE (K. R.). The State of British Agriculture. Oxf. 1966.

19535 FUSSELL (GEORGE EDWIN). Farming Techniques from Prehistoric to Modern Times. Oxf. 1966.

19536 —— The Story of Farming. 1969.

19537 —— Farms, Farmers and Society: Systems of Food Production and Population Numbers. Lawrence. 1978

19538 —— 'Farming Systems and Society: A Historical Survey'. *Trans. Newcomen Soc.* 39 (1966/7), 47–64.

19539 THOMAS (HAROLD A.). 'Aspects of the Economics of Land Ownership'. *J. Agric. Econ.* 18 (1967), 197–219.

19540 WELLER (JOHN BRIAN). Modern Agriculture and Rural Planning. 1967.

19541 GAVIN (*Sir* WILLIAM). Ninety Years of Family Farming: The Study of Lord Rayleigh's and Strutt & Parker's Farms. 1967.

19542 ROGERS (SIDNEY JOHN). Economic Change and Agriculture. Newcastle upon Tyne. 1967.

19543 SUTHERLAND (DOUGLAS). The Landowners. 1968.

19544 NELSON (J. S.). The Mobility of Farm Families. 1968.

19545 WELLER (JOHN). Modern Agriculture and Rural Planning. 1968.

19546 DONALDSON (JOHN GEORGE STUART) et al. Farming in Britain Today. 1969.

19547 METCALF (DAVID). The Economics of Agriculture. Harmondsworth. 1969.

19548 COWLING (KEITH) et al. The Resource Structure of Agriculture: An Economic Analysis. Oxf. 1970.

19549 HOWARTH (RICHARD W.). 'The Political Strength of British Agriculture'. *Pol. Studs* 17 (1969), 458–69.

19550 DONALDSON (JOHN GEORGE STUART) *Baron, et al.* Farming in Britain Today. 1969. Rev. edn Harmondsworth. 1972.

19551 ELTRINGHAM (DENHAM). Agriculture. 1970.

19552 ROOKE (PATRICK JOHN). Agriculture and Industry. 1970.

19553 U.K. CENTRAL OFFICE OF INFORMATION. Agriculture in Britain. 1970. 7th edn 1977.

19554 PHILLIPS (TRUMAN) *and* RITSON (CHRISTOPHER). 'Agricultural Expansion and the U.K. Balance of Payments'. *Nat. West. Bank Q. Rev.* (Feb. 1970), 50–8.

19555 JOSLING (TIMOTHY EDWARD). Agriculture and Britain's Trade Policy Dilemma. 1970.

19556 GARNER (FRANK HAROLD). Modern British Farming Systems: An Introduction. 1972.

19557 BAKER (ALAN R.) *and* BUTLIN (ROBIN A.) eds. Studies of Field Systems in the British Isles. 1972.

19558 GILES (ANTHONY KENT) ed. University of Reading, Agricultural Economics 1923–1973. Reading. 1973. [50th anniversary of the dept.].

19559 EDWARDS (ANGELA) *and* ROGERS (ALAN) eds. Agricultural Resources: An Introduction to the Farming Industry of the United Kingdom. 1974.

19560 WESTMACOTT (RICHARD) *and* WORTHINGTON (TOM). New Agricultural Landscapes: Report of a Study undertaken on Behalf of the Countryside Commission during 1972. 1974.

19561 BELL (COLIN) *and* NEWBY (HOWARD). 'Capitalist Farmers in the British Class Structure'. *Sociol. Rur.* 14 (1974), 86–107.

19562 BERESFORD (TRISTRAM). We Plough the Fields: Agriculture in Britain Today. Harmondsworth. 1975.

19563 TAYLOR (CHRISTOPHER). Fields in the English Landscape. 1975.

19564 —— Village and Farmstead: A History of Rural Settlement in England. 1984.

19565 LITTLECHILD (S. C.) *and* REVELL (B. J.). 'Setting Guaranteed Prices in the United Kingdom Cereals Market 1967–1972'. *Econ. J.* 85 (1975), 562–77.

19566 BAINER (ROY). 'Science and Technology in Western Agriculture'. *Agric. Hist.* 49 (1975), 56–72.

19567 HARRISON (ALAN). Farmers and Farm Businesses in England. Reading. 1975.

19568 PRIEBE (HERMANN). The Changing Role of Agriculture 1920–1970. 1976.

19569 DAVIES (ELVET TALFRYN). The Dartmoor and Exmoor National Parks: Changes in Farming Structure, 1952–1972. Exeter. 1976.

19570 DAVEY (BRIAN), JOSLING (TIMOTHY EDWARD), *and* McFARQUHAR (ALISTER) eds. Agriculture and the State: British Policy in a World Context. 1976.

19571 DAVIDSON (JOAN) *and* LLOYD (RICHARD) eds. Conservation and Agriculture. Chich. 1977.

19572 MINISTRY OF AGRICULTURE, FISHERIES AND FOOD. The Changing Structure of Agriculture, 1968–1975. 1977.

19573 WILSON (GRAHAM K.). Special Interests and Policy Making: Agricultural Policies and Politics in Britain and the United States of America, 1956–1970. 1977.

19574 BOWLER (IAN ROBERT). Government and Agriculture: A Spatial Perspective. 1979.

19575 NEWBY (HOWARD). Green and Pleasant Land? 1979.

19576 BELL (ROBERT WILLIAM). The History of the Jersey Cattle Society of the United Kingdom, 1878–1978. Reading. 1979.

19577 BATEMAN (D. I.). 'A. W. Ashby: An Assessment'. *J. Agric. Econ.* 31 (1980), 1–14.

19578 WHETHAM (EDITH HOLT). Agricultural Economists in Britain 1900–1940. Oxf. 1981.

19579 UNIVERSITY OF READING, CENTRE FOR AGRICULTURAL STRATEGY. The Efficiency of British Agriculture. Reading. 1980.

19580 McGREGOR (I. M.). Hillfarms: Profitability and Prospects. Ayr. 1981.

19581 NAYLOR (E. L.). 'Farm Structure Policy in North East England'. *Scot. J. Pol. Econ.* 28 (1981), 266–72.

19582 HUTCHINSON (*Sir* JOSEPH) *and* OWERS (A. C.). Change and Innovation in Norfolk Farming: 70 Years of Experiment and Advice at the Norfolk Agricultural Station, Michaelmas **1908** to Michaelmas 1978. Chichester. 1980.

19583 CLARK (KEN R.). The State of British Agriculture, 1981. Oxf. 1981.

19584 NEWBY (HOWARD). 'Rural Sociology and its Relevance to the Agricultural Economist: A Review'. *J. Agric. Econ.* 33 (1982), 125–65.

19585 BODY (RICHARD). Agriculture: The Triumph and the Shame. 1982.

19586 HOWARTH (RICHARD W.). Farming for Farmers? A Critique of Agricultural Support Policy. 1985.

19587 BUCKWELL (A. E.), HARVEY (D. R.), THOMSON (K. J.), *and* PARTON (K. A.). The Costs of the Common Agricultural Policy. 1982.

19588 BOWERS (JOHN KENNETH) *and* CHESHIRE (PAUL). Agriculture, the Countryside and Land Use: An Economic Critique. 1983.

19589 ARCHER (FRED). Fred Archer, Farmer's Son: A Cotswold Childhood in the 1920s. 1984.

19590 REFFOLD (HENRY). Pie for Breakfast: Reminiscences of a Farmhand. Beverley. 1984.

19591 KEITH (JAMES). Fifty Years of Farming. 1954.

19592 CRAMP (HAROLD ST.GEORGE). A Yeoman Farmer's Son: A Leicestershire Childhood. Oxf. 1986.

19593 NEWMAN (NOEL). Recollections of 70 Years' Farming in Bottisham [East Cambridgeshire]. Staine. 1986.

19594 SYMES (DAVID G.) *and* MARSDEN (TERRY K.). 'Complementary Roles and Asymmetrical Lives: Farmer's Wives in a Large Farm Environment'. *Sociol. Rur.* 23 (1983), 229–41.

19595 GASSON (RUTH). 'The Roles of Farm Women in England'. *Sociol. Rur.* 20 (1980), 165–80.

19596 —— The Role of Women in British Agriculture. 1980.

19597 —— Farm Families with other Gainful Activities. 1986.

19598 —— 'Part-Time Farming: Strategy for Survival?'. *Sociol. Rur.* 26 (1986), 364–76.

19599 THEAR (KATIE). Part-time Farming. 1982.

19600 TRANTER (R. B.) *ed.* Strategies for Family-Worked Farms in the United Kingdom: Proceedings of a Symposium . . . Reading. 1983.

19601 LONG (NORMAN) *ed.* Family and Work in Rural Societies: Perspectives on Non-Wage Labour. 1984.

19602 ERRINGTON (ANDREW) *ed.* The Farm as a Family Business: An Annotated Bibliography. Reading. 1986.

19603 VENABLES (ROBERT). Preserving the Family Farm. 1987. [Inheritance and Transfer Tax.].

19604 HEAD (VICTOR). A Triumph of Hope: The Story of the National Farmers Union Mutual Insurance Society Limited. Stratford upon Avon. 1985.

19605 AGRICULTURE AND FOOD RESEARCH COUNCIL. Science and Change in Agriculture. 1988.

19606 PETERS (G. H.). Agriculture. 1988. [Royal Historical Society Publication.].

19607 McLEAVY (TONY). Agricultural Change. Edin. 1989.

19608 DARLEY (G.). The National Trust Book of the Farm. 1981.

19609 JONES (R. B.). The Pattern of Farming in the East Midlands. Nottingham. 1954.

19610 HALL (VANCE). A History of the Yorkshire Agricultural Society, 1837–1987. 1987.

19611 PAWSON (HENRY CECIL). A Survey of the Agriculture of England. 1961.

19612 BECKETT (JOHN V.). Laxton: England's Last Open Field System. Oxf. 1989.

3. FARMING IN SCOTLAND, WALES, AND NORTHERN IRELAND/AGRICULTURAL TRADE WITH OVERSEAS COUNTRIES

19613 Agriculture in Scotland. 1912+. [Annual.].

19614 COPPOCK (JOHN T.). An Agricultural Atlas of Scotland. Edin. 1976.

19615 FRANKLIN (THOMAS BEDFORD). A History of Scottish Farming. 1952.

19616 U.K. DEPT OF AGRICULTURE FOR SCOTLAND. Types of Farming in Scotland. Edin. 1952.

19617 SYMON (JAMES ALEXANDER). Scottish Farming: Past and Present. Edin. 1959.

19618 COWLING (KEITH GEORGE) *and* METCALF (DAVID). 'Determinants of Wage Inflation in Scottish Agriculture, 1948–1963'. *Manch. Sch. Econ. Soc. Studs* 32 (1966), 189–96.

19619 MACKENZIE (DAVID). Farming in the Western Isles. 1954.

19620 GOLD (JOHN) *and* GOLD (MARGARET R.). The Crofting System: A Selected Bibliography. Oxf. 1979.

19621 BRYDEN (JOHN M.) *and* HOUSTON (GEORGE FREDERICK BARCLAY). Agrarian Change in the Scottish Highlands: The Role of the Highlands and Islands Development Board in the Agricultural Economy of the Crofting Counties. Glasg. 1976.

19622 SENIOR (W. H.) *and* SWAN (W. B.). Survey of Agriculture in Caithness, Orkney and Shetland. Inverness. 1972.

19623 DUNN (J. M.). 'Some Features of Small Full-time and Part-time Farms in Scotland'. *Scot. Agric. Econ.* 19 (1969), 205–20.

19624 FAIRWEATHER (BARBARA). Old Highland Farming. Glencoe. 1978.

19625 ANDERSON (JOHN L.). Profitability of Farming in South East Scotland, 1980/1, 1981/2, 1982/3. Edin. 1982. 1983. 1984.

19626 TWEDDLE (JOHN M.). Profitability of Farms in the West of Scotland 1986/1987. Ayr. 1988.

19627 URQUHART (R.). History of the Scottish Milk Marketing Board. Edin. 1979.

19628 Welsh Agricultural Statistics. 1979+. [Annual.].

19629 EVANS (BRIAN M.). 'Sources for the Study of the History of Welsh Agriculture'. *Amateur Historian* 7 (1967), 154–60.

19630 EVANS (HYWEL E.). 'Seventy Five Years of Welsh Agriculture: Progress and the Future'. *Agriculture* 76 (1969), 449–53.

19631 STAPLEDON (*Sir* REGINALD GEORGE) *ed.* A Survey of the Agriculture and Waste Lands of Wales. 1936.

19632 ATTWOOD (EDWIN ARTHUR). 'The Economic Structure of Welsh Farming'. *Agriculture* 64 (1957), 112–16.

19633 ATTWOOD (EDWIN ARTHUR) *and* EVANS (H. G.). The Economics of Hill Farming. Card. 1961.

19634 ASHBY (ARTHUR WILFRED). Economic Conditions in Welsh Agriculture. Aberystwyth. 1928.

19635 —— Some Characteristics of Welsh Farming. 1933.

19636 ASHBY (ARTHUR WILFRED) *and* EVANS (IVOR LESLIE). The Agriculture of Wales and Monmouthshire. Card. 1944.

19637 U.K. MINISTRY OF AGRICULTURE, FISHERIES AND FOOD. Welsh Agricultural Land Sub-Commission: The Mid-Wales Investigation Report. 1955.

19638 HOWELLS (ROSCOE). Farming in Wales. 1965.

19639 AITCHISON (J.). 'The Agricultural Landscape of Wales'. *Cambria* 7 (1980), 43–68.

19640 COLYER (RICHARD J.). Man's Proper Study: A History of Agricultural Education in Aberystwyth, 1878–1978. Llandysul. 1982.

19641 JENKINS (J. GERAINT). 'Technological Improvement and Social Change in South Cardiganshire'. *Agric. Hist. Rev.* 13 (1965), pp. 94–105.

19642 JONES (WILLIAM DYFRI) *AND* GREEN (DAVID ALFRED GEORGE). Rough Grazings in the Hills and Uplands of Wales: Productivity and Potential. 1987.

19643 GREEN (DAVID ALFRED GEORGE). Resource Productivity in Hill and Upland Farming Systems in Wales. Aberystwyth. 1987.

19644 REES (DEREK). Rings and Rosettes: The History of the Pembrokeshire Agricultural Society, 1784–1977. 1977.

19645 General Report of Northern Ireland Agriculture. 1942+. [Annual.].

19646 Statistical Review of Northern Ireland Agriculture. 1966+. [Annual.].

19647 SHEEHY (SEAMUS JOSEPH) *et al.* Agriculture in Northern Ireland and the Republic of Ireland. Dublin/Belf. 1981.

19648 SYMONS (LESLIE) *ed.* Land Use in Northern Ireland: The General Report of the Survey. 1964.

19649 MOSS (JOAN E.). Part-Time Farming in Northern Ireland: A Study of Small Scale Beef and Sheep Farms. Belf. 1980.

19650 Growth Possibilities for Small Scale Beef Cattle and Sheep Farms. Belf. 1983. [Dept. of Agric., N. Ireland.].

19651 BUTTERWICK (MICHAEL WILLOUGHBY). 'British Agricultural Policy and the E.E.C.'. *Int. J. Agrarian Affs* 4 (1964), 99–113.

19652 BUTTERWICK (MICHAEL WILLOUGHBY) *and* ROLFE (EDMUND NEVILLE). Food, Farming and the Common Market. 1968.

19653 RYAN (M. C.). 'A Pressure Group prepares for Europe: The Country Landowners Association, 1961–72'. *Parl. Affs* 26 (1973), 307–17.

19654 ROGERS (SIDNEY JOHN) *and* DAVEY (BRIAN HUMPHREY) *eds.* The Common Agricultural Policy and Britain. 1973.

19655 ROYAL AGRICULTURAL SOCIETY OF ENGLAND. E.E.C. Policy and British Agriculture in the 1980s: Conference Papers, 12 March 1980. Tunbridge Wells. 1980.

19656 BEATTIE (IAN). The European Community and its Common Agricultural Policy. Edin. 1984.

19657 BOWLER (IAN ROBERT). Agriculture under the Common Agricultural Policy: A Geography. Manch. 1985.

19658 OPPENHEIM (PHILIP) *and* DERRICK (JOHN). Biting the Hand that Feeds You: A Study into the Effects on Agriculture and the Economy as a Whole, of the Common Agricultural Policy and Agricultural Support. 1985.

19659 NASH (ERIC FRANCIS) *and* ATTWOOD (EDWIN ARTHUR). The Agricultural Policies of Britain and Denmark: A Study in Reciprocal Trade. 1961.

4. FARM WORKERS, MACHINERY, TECHNIQUES

19660 GREEN (FREDERICK ERNEST). A History of the English Agricultural Labourer, 1870–1920. 1920.

19661 DEWEY (PETER E.). 'Agricultural Labour Supply in England and Wales during the First World War'. *Econ. Hist. Rev.* 2nd ser. 28 (1975), 100–12.

19662 HOWKINS (ALUN). Poor Labouring Men: Rural Radicalism in Norfolk 1872–1923. 1985.

19663 GROVES (REG). Sharpen the Sickle!: The History of the Farmworkers' Union. 1949.

19664 GILES (ANTHONY KENT) *and* COWIE (WILLIAM JOHN GAVIN). The Farm Worker: His Training, Pay and Status. 1964.

19665 MEJER (EUGENIUSZ). Agricultural Labour in England and Wales: Pt. 1—1900–1920, Pt. 2—Farm Workers' Earnings, 1917–1951. Sutton Bonington. 1949. 1951.

19666 NEWBY (HOWARD). The Deferential Worker: A Study of Farm Workers in East Anglia. 1977. Harmondsworth. 1979.

19667 FOX (ALAN W.). 'Agricultural Wages in England and Wales in the Last Half Century'. Ch. in Walter Edward Minchinton *ed.* Essays in Agrarian History, vol. 2. Newton Abbot. 1968.

19668 U.K. MINISTRY OF AGRICULTURE, FISHERIES AND FOOD. The Changing Structure of the Agricultural Labour Force in England and Wales: Numbers of Workers, Hours and Earnings 1944–1965. 1967.

19669 TYLER (GODFREY J.). 'Factors Affecting the Size of the Labour Force and the Level of Earnings in U.K. Agriculture 1948–1965'. *Oxf. Agrarian Studs* 1 (1972), 20–45.

19670 HUGHES (J. D.). 'A Note on the Decline in Numbers of Farm Workers in Great Britain'. *Farm Economist* 8 (1957), 34–9.

19671 GILES (A. K.) *and* COWIE (W. J. G.). The Farm Worker: His Training, Pay and Status. 1964.

19672 ALLEN (GEORGE). 'The National Farmers' Union as a Pressure Group'. *Contemp. Rev.* 195 (1959), 257–68 and 321–34.

19673 HILES (M.). The Young Farmers' Club Movement. 1956.

19674 NEWBY (HOWARD). 'The Low Earnings of Agricultural Workers: A Sociological Approach'. *J. Agric. Econ* 23 (1972), 15–24.

19675 —— 'Agricultural Workers in the Class Structure'. *Sociol. Rev.* 20 (1972), 413–39.

19676 WINYARD (STEVE). 'Cold Comfort Farm': A Study of Farm Workers and Low Pay. 1982. [Low Pay Unit.].

19677 COLLINS (EDWARD JOHN THOMAS). Sickle to Combine: A Review of Harvest Techniques from 1800 to the Present Day. Reading. 1969.

19678 WEST (LESLEY A.). 'An Agricultural Machinery Museum'. *Agric. Hist.* 41 (1967), 267–73.

19679 KEMP (PETER KEMP). The Bentall Story: Commemorating 150 Years' Service, 1805–1955. 1955.

19680 SHERWEN (THEO). The Bomford Story: A Century of Service to Agriculture. 1978.

19681 KENNET (PAT). The Foden Story: From Farm Machinery to Diesel Trucks. Camb. 1978.

19682 NIALL (IAN). To Speed the Plough: Mechanisation comes to the Farm. 1977.

19683 LEE (RICHARD). A Source Book of Tractors and Farm Machinery. 1979.

19684 BELL (BRIAN). Farm Machinery. Ipswich. 1979. 3rd edn 1989.

19685 MILLER (JANE). Farm Machinery. 1987.

19686 PARTRIDGE (MICHAEL). Farm Tools through the Ages. Reading. 1973.

19687 WHETHAM (EDITH HOLT). 'The Mechanisation of British Farming, 1910–1945'. *J. Agric. Econ.* 31 (1960), 317–30.

19688 LONG (W. HARWOOD). 'The Development of Mechanisation in English Farming'. *Agric. Hist. Rev.* 11 (1963), 15–16.

19689 TYLER (COLIN) *and* HAINING (JOHN). Ploughing by Steam: A History of Steam Cultivation over the Years. Hemel Hempstead. 1970.

19690 HAINING (PETER). The Scarecrow: Fact and Fable. 1988.

19691 JONES (G. E.). 'The Nature and Consequences of Technical Change in Farming'. *Folk Life* 31 (1960), 317–30.

19692 STURROCK (FORD GIBSON). Economies of Scale in Farm Mechanisation: A Study of Costs on Large and Small Scale Farms. Camb. 1978.

19693 LEE (NORMAN EDWARD). Harvests and Harvesting through the Ages. 1960.

19694 ASHTON (J.) *and* LORD (R. F.) *eds.* Research, Education and Extension in Agriculture. Edin. 1969.

19695 RUSSELL (*Sir* EDWARD JOHN). A History of Agricultural Science in Great Britain, 1620–1954. 1966.

19696 WALLACE (D. B.). 'The Crop Scientist and the Farmer in England 1940–1960'. *J. Agric. Econ.* 26 (1975), 21–36.

19697 SANDERS (HAROLD GEORGE). An Outline of British Crop Husbandry. 1939. 3rd edn 1958.

19698 LOCKHART (JAMES ARTHUR RENWICK) *AND* WISEMAN (ANTHONY JOHN LEY). Introduction to Crop Husbandry. Oxf. 1966. 4th edn 1978.

19699 COOKE (G. W.) *ed.* Agricultural Research 1931–1981: A History of the Agricultural Research Council and a Review of Developments in Agricultural Science During the Last 50 Years. 1981.

19700 HILL FARM RESEARCH ORGANISATION. Science and Hill Farming: 25 years of Work at the Hill Farming Research Organisation, 1954–1979. Penicuick. 1979.

19701 PAWSON (HENRY CECIL). Cockle Park Farm: An Account of the Cockle Park Farm Experimental Station from 1896 to 1956. 1960.

19702 HARRISON (RUTH). Animal Machines: The New Factory Farming Industry. 1964.

19703 BELLERBY (JOHN ROTHERFORD) *ed.* Factory Farming. 1970.

19704 GOLD (MARK). Assault and Battery: What Factory Farming Means for Humans. 1983.

19705 CARNELL (PAUL). Alternatives to Factory Farming. 1983.

19706 WELLER (JOHN BRIAN). Farm Buildings. 2 vols 1965, 1972.

19707 HARVEY (CHARLES NIGEL). A History of Farm Building in England and Wales. Newton Abbot. 1979. New edn 1984.

19708 PETERS (JOHN EDWARD COLCLOUGH). Discovering Traditional Farm Buildings. Princes Risborough. 1981.

19709 WILIAM (EURWYN). The Historical Farm Buildings of Wales. Edin. 1986.

19710 WALKER (BRUCE). Farm Buildings in the Grampian Region: An Historical Exploration: A Report. Aberd. 1979.

5. FORESTRY

19711 JAMES (NOEL DAVID GLANES). A History of English Forestry. Oxf. 1981.

19712 —— The Forester's Companion. Oxf. 1955. 3rd edn 1982.

19713 —— A Forestry Centenary: The Forestry Society of England, Wales and Northern Ireland. Oxf. 1982.

19714 BERESFORD-PIERSE (*Sir* HENRY). 'A Century of Forestry: Forestry in the UK over the Last Century'. *Nature* 169 (1952), 130–4.

19715 —— Forest, Food and People. 1968.

19716 HORNBY (JOHN WILKINSON). Forestry in Britain. 1957.

19717 DRINKELE (GEOFF). Forestry, Fishing, Mining and Power. 1976.

19718 HINDE (THOMAS). Forests of Britain. 1985. Repr. 1987.

19719 HAVINS (PETER J. NEVILLE). The Forests of England. 1976.

19720 WHITLOCK (RALPH). Historic Forests of England. Bradford-on-Avon. 1979.

19721 ANDERSON (MARK LOUDEN). A History of Scottish Forestry, vol. 2: From the Industrial Revolution to Modern Times. 1967.

19722 DAVIES (JOHN). The Scottish Forester. Edin. 1979.

19723 LOCKE (GEORGE MICHAEL LOCHHEAD). The Place of Forestry in Scotland: A Basis for Local Authority Planning. Edin. 1976.

19724 EDLIN (HERBERT L.). 'The Forestry Commission in Scotland, 1919–69'. *Scot. Geog. Mag.* 85 (1969), 84–95.

19725 RYLE (C. B. E.). 'Forestry in the Economic Development of Wales'. *Q. J. Forestry* 55 (1961), 197–205.

19726 LINNARD (WILLIAM). Welsh Woods and Forests: History and Utilization. Card. 1982.

19727 YOUTH HOSTEL ASSOCIATION (ENGLAND and WALES). Landscape and Forestry in Mid-Wales: A Land Use Survey. 1974.

19728 O'CARROLL (NIAL) *ed.* The Forests of Ireland: History, Distribution and Silviculture. Dublin. 1984.

19729 EDLIN (HERBERT LEESON). England's Forests Old and New: A Survey of the Woodlands Old and New in the English and Welsh Counties. 1958.

19730 —— The Living Forest: A History of Trees and Timbers. 1958.

19731 —— National Forest Parks. 1961.

19732 —— *Ed.* The New Forest. 1961.

19733 —— *Ed.* North Yorkshire Forests. 1963. 3rd edn 1972.

19734 —— *Ed.* The Forests of North East Scotland. Edin. 1963.

19735 —— *Ed.* The Forests of Central and Southern Scotland. Edin. 1969.

19736 —— *Ed.* Glamorgan Forests. 1961.

19737 PASSMORE (ANTHONY). Verderers of the New Forest: A History of the New Forest, 1877–1977. 1977.

19738 STAGG (DAVID J.). Woodmen of the New Forest. Brocklehurst. 1986.

19739 HART (CYRIL EDWIN). Royal Forest: A History of Dean's Woods as Producers of Timber. Oxf. 1966.

19740 WILLIAMS (GUY RICHARD). The Royal Parks of London. 1978.

19741 BARRINGTON (C. A.). Forestry in the Weald: Kent, Surrey, Sussex and East Hampshire. 1968.

19742 WARD (BERNARD). Trees in Epping Forest. 1980.

19743 RYLE (GEORGE). Forest Service: The First Forty Five Years of the Forestry Commission of Great Britain. Newton Abbot. 1969.

19744 WOOD (ROBERT FRANCIS). Fifty Years of Forestry Research: A Review of Work Conducted and Supported by the Forestry Commission 1920–1970. 1974. [HMSO.].

19745 WOOD (ROBERT FRANCIS) *and* ANDERSON (I. A.) *comps.* Forestry in the British Scene. 1968. [Forestry Commission pub.].

19746 BAKER (RICHARD ST. BARBE). My Life, my Trees. Forres. 1970. 2nd edn 1985. [Autobiography of a forester.].

19747 NUDDS (ANGUS). The Woods Belong to me: A Gamekeeper's Life. Poole. 1985.

19748 JOHNSTON (DAVID ROBERT), GRAYSON (ARNOLD JOHN), *and* BRADLEY (ROGER THUBRON). Forest Planning. 1967.

19749 U.K. NATURAL RESOURCES (TECHNICAL) COMMITTEE. Forestry, Agriculture and Marginal Land. 1957.

19750 U.K. DEPARTMENT OF EDUCATION AND SCIENCE. Report of the Land Use Study Group: Forestry, Agriculture and Multiple use of Rural Land. 1966.

19751 CARROLL (M. R.). Multiple Use of Woodlands. Camb. 1978.

19752 BROOKS (ALAN) *comp.* Woodlands. Reading. 1980.

19753 RACKHAM (OLIVER). Trees and Woodland in the British Landscape. 1976. Repr. 1981.

19754 WATKINS (C.) *and* WHEELER (PHILIP THEODORE). The Study and Use of British Woodlands: Conference Proceedings, University of Nottingham. Nottingham. 1981.

19755 MILES (ROGER OLIVER). Forestry in the English Landscape: A Study of the Cultivation of Trees and their Relationship to Natural Amenity and Plantation Design. 1967.

19756 BANCROFT (COLIN). Forestry for the Quality of Life: Evaluation and Analysis of the Impact of Forestry on Recreation. Edin. 1978.

19757 MILLER (ROBERT). State Forestry for the Axe: A Study of the Forestry Commission and Denationalisation by the Market. 1981.

19758 GROVE (RICHARD). The Future of Forestry: The Urgent Need for a New Policy. 1983. [British Association of Nature Conservationists.].

19759 LOWE (PHILIP) *et al.* Countryside Conflicts: The Politics of Farming, Forestry and Conservation. 1986.

19760 TOMPKINS (STEVE). Forestry in Crisis. 1989.

19761 HADFIELD (MILES). Discovering England's Trees. Aylesbury. 1970. 2nd edn 1979.

19762 ROYAL FORESTRY SOCIETY OF ENGLAND, NORTHERN IRELAND AND WALES. A Book of Trees: An Anthology of Trees and Woodlands. Tring. 1973.

19763 PHILLIPS (ROGER). Trees in Britain, Europe and North America. 1978. Repr. 1983.

19764 MITCHELL (ALAN). The Trees of Britain and Northern Europe. 1982.

19765 MARTIN (ELIZABETH ANN). Trees of Britain and Europe. 1978.

19766 HOWARD (ALEXANDER L.). 'The Ash Tree'. *Nature* 154 (1944), 27–9.

19767 —— 'The Beech Tree'. *Nature* 154 (1944), 492–4.

19768 —— 'The Cedar Tree'. *Nature* 153 (1944), 595–8.

19769 —— 'Deciduous Cypress'. *Nature* 154 (1944), 775–6.

19770 —— 'The Elm Tree'. *Nature* 152 (1943), 636–8.

19771 —— 'The Oak Tree'. *Nature* 153 (1944), 438–41.

19772 —— 'The Plane Tree'. *Nature* 152 (1943), 421–2.

19773 —— 'The Scots Pine'. *Nature* 154 (1944), 679–80.

19774 —— 'The Sycamore Tree'. *Nature* 153 (1944), 348–9.

19775 —— 'The Willow Tree'. *Nature* 154 (1944), 835–7.

19776 —— 'The Yew Tree'. *Nature* 154 (1944), 215–16.

19777 GIBBS (JOHN NEWTON) *and* HOWELL (R. S.). Dutch Elm Disease Survey, 1971, 1972–1973. 1972, 1975. [HMSO.].

19778 EAST SUSSEX COUNTY PLANNING DEPARTMENT. A Report of the East Sussex County Council Campaign to Control Dutch Elm Disease. Lewes. 1977.

19779 SUFFOLK COUNTY COUNCIL. Dutch Elm Disease in Suffolk: Report of a 1978 Survey. Ipswich. 1979.

19780 U.K. FORESTRY COMMISSION. Census of Woodlands 1947–1949, Woods of Five Acres and Over. 1952, 1953. [In various vols, *comp.* by J. S. Chard.].

19781 —— Census of Woodlands, 1965–1967: A Report on Britain's Forest Resources. 1970. [By George Michael Lochhead Locke.].

19782 —— Census of Woodland and Trees 1979–1982. Edin. 1984. [In various vols.].

19783 —— Forestry Commission Conservancy: South West England: Census of Woodlands and Trees, 1979–1982. Edin. 1983.

19784 —— Forestry in Great Britain: A Review of Progress to 1964. 1964.

19785 —— The Forestry Commission in Scotland. 1953. Rev. edn 1957.

19786 —— Forestry in Scotland. 1967.

19787 —— Forestry in England. 1958.

19788 —— Forestry in Northern Ireland. Belf. 1970.

19789 —— Forestry in Wales. 1950. New edn 1960.

19790 U.K. H.M. TREASURY. Forestry in Great Britain: An Inter-departmental Cost/Benefit Study. 1972.

19791 U.K. MINISTRY OF AGRICULTURE, FISHERIES AND FOOD. Forestry Policy. 1972.

19792 HOUSE (FRANK HOLMAN). Timber at War: An Account of the Organisation and Activities of the Timber Control, 1939–1945. 1965.

19793 EDLIN (HERBERT LEESON). Timber! Your Growing Investment. 1969.

19794 SCOTTISH COUNCIL RESEARCH INSTITUTE. The Structure of the Scottish Timber Industry. Edin. 1978.

19795 LEIGH (JACK HAROLD). The Timber Trade: An Introduction to Commercial Aspects. Oxf. 1971. 2nd edn 1980.

19796 ADAM WILSON & SONS. Adam Wilson & Sons: The History of a Firm of Timber Merchants: Founded 1956. Ayr. 1980.

19797 BEAVER (PATRICK). The Alsford Tradition: A Century of Quality Timber 1882–1982. 1982.

19798 BRUNSKILL (RONALD WILLIAM). Timber Building in Britain. 1985.

6. THE FISHING INDUSTRY

19799 Sea Fisheries: Statistical Tables. 1948+. [Annual.].

19800 GIBBS (WILLIAM EDWARD). The Fishing Industry. 1922.

19801 ALWARD (GEORGE LOWE). The Sea Fisheries of Great Britain and Ireland: A Record of the Development of the Fishing Industry and its Worldwide Ramifications. Grimsby. 1932.

19802 GRAHAM (GODFREY MICHAEL). The Fish Gate. 1943.

19803 WILLSON (FRANCIS MICHAEL GLENN). Governmental Services to the Sea-fish Industry of Great Britain. Rome. 1957.

19804 TAYLOR (RAYMOND ARCHBOLD). The Economics of White Fish Distribution in Great Britain. 1960.

19805 DAY (E. E. D.). 'The British Sea Fishing Industry'. *Geog.* 54 (1969), 165–80.

19806 CUSHING (DAVID). Fisheries Resources of the Sea and their Management. Oxf. 1975.

19807 DYSON (JOHN). Business in Great Waters: The Story of British Fishermen. 1977.

19808 TOPHAM (TONY). Decasualisation of Employment in the Fishing Industry. Hull. 1979.

19809 CUNNINGHAM (STEPHEN). Fisheries Economics: An Introduction. 1985.

19810 MASON (JAMES). Scallop and Queen Fisheries in the British Isles. Farnham. 1983.

19811 MATHESON (COLIN). Wales and the Sea Fisheries. 1929.

19812 HUGHES (P. A.). The Sea Fishing Industry of Northern Ireland: An Economic Study. Belf. 1970.

19813 DICKINSON (MICHAEL G.) *ed.* A Living from the Sea: Devon's Fishing Industry and its Fishermen. Exeter. 1987.

19814 PEARSON (GORDON). Hull and East Coast Fishing. Kingston-upon-Hull. 1976.

19815 COULL (JAMES REID) *et al.* The Fisheries in the Shetland Area: A Study in Conservation and Development. Aberdeen. 1979.

19816 EKBERG (CHARLES). Grimsby Fish: The Story of the Port and the Decline and Fall of the Deep Water Industry. Buckingham. 1984.

19817 SUTHERLAND (IAN). The Rise of the Fishing Industry in Humberside. 1987.

19818 TAYLOR (R. A.). The Economics of White Fish Distribution in Great Britain. 1960.

19819 TUNSTALL (JEREMY). The Fishermen. 1962.

19820 FESTING (SALLY). Fishermen. Newton Abbot. 1977.

19821 BUTCHER (DAVID). The Trawlermen. Reading. 1980.

19822 FRANK (P.). 'Women's Work in the Yorkshire Inshore Fishing Industry'. *Oral Hist.* 4 (1976), 57–72.

19823 BOCHEL (MARGARET). The Story of the Nairn Fisher Girls at the Gutting. Nairn. 1979.

19824 U.K. MINISTRY OF AGRICULTURE, FISHERIES AND FOOD. Sea Fisheries Statistical Tables, 1947–. [Pub. annually.].

19825 U.K. DEPARTMENT OF AGRICULTURE AND FISHERIES FOR SCOTLAND. Fisheries of Scotland: Report, 1967–. Edin. 1968–

19826 —— Scottish Sea Fisheries Statistical Tables. An annual publication under various titles. Edin.

19827 U.K. CENTRAL OFFICE OF INFORMATION. Report of the Committee of Inquiry into the Fishing Industry. 1961.

19828 HOOD (C. C.). 'British Fishing and the Iceland Saga'. *Pol. Q.* 44 (1973), 349–52.

19829 U.K. MINISTRY OF AGRICULTURE, FISHERIES AND FOOD. The Sea Fisheries Dispute between the United Kingdom and Iceland, 14 July 1971 to 19 May 1973. 1973.

19830 GILCHRIST (*Sir* ANDREW). Cod Wars and How to Lose Them. Edin. 1978.

19831 JONSSON (H.). Friends in Conflict: The Anglo-Icelandic Cod War and the Law of the Sea. 1982.

19832 GREEN (LESLIE S.). 'The Territorial Sea and the Anglo-Icelandic Dispute'. *J. Pub. Law* 9 (1960), 53–72.

19833 WISE (MARK). The Common Fisheries Policy of the European Community. 1984.

19834 FARNELL (JOHN). In Search of a Common Fisheries Policy. Aldershot. 1984.

7. MARKET GARDENING

19835 WEBBER (RONALD). Market Gardening: The History of Commercial Flower, Fruit and Vegetable Growing. Newton Abbot. 1972.

19836 —— The Early Horticulturalists. Newton Abbot. 1968.

19837 NEWSHAM (JOHN CLARK). The Horticultural Notebook: A Manual for the Use of Horticultural Advisers, Gardeners, Nurserymen, Students and all Horticulturalists. 1906. 3rd rev. edn 1914. 4th rev. edn 1950 by W. E. Shewell-Cooper.

19838 —— Fruit Growing for Profit. 1922.

19839 BAKER (JOHN OVEREND). Market Gardening. 1944.

19840 ROBINSON (R. A.) *et al.* Market Gardening. 1951.

19841 URWIN (ALAN CHARLES BELL). Commercial Nurseries and Market Gardens. 1982.

19842 WALLS (IAN GASCOINE). Growing Vegetables, Fruit and Flowers for Profit. Newton Abbot. 1986.

19843 U.K. CENTRAL OFFICE OF INFORMATION. Horticulture in Britain, pt. 1—Vegetables. 1967.

19844 —— Horticulture in Britain, pt. 2—Fruit and Flowers. 1970.

19845 RIGG (T.). 'The Market Garden District of Biggleswade, Bedfordshire'. *J. Board Agric.* 24 (1917), 834–5.

19846 BEAVINGTON (FRANK). 'The Development of Market Gardening in Bedfordshire 1799–1939'. *Agric. Hist. Rev.* 23 (1973), 23–47.

19847 —— 'Early Market Gardening in Bedfordshire'. *Trans. Inst. Br. Geog.* 37 (1965), 91–100.

19848 BENNETT (LEWIS GODFREY). The Marketing of Horticultural Produce Grown in Bedfordshire, West Cornwall, Wisbech and the Lea Valley. 1957. [University of Reading, Dept. of Agricultural Economics occasional paper.].

19849 —— The Horticultural Industry of Middlesex. 1952. [As above.].

19850 UNIVERSITY OF READING DEPARTMENT OF AGRICULTURAL ECONOMICS. Market Gardening in the Melbourne Area of Derbyshire. 1952.

19851 FOLLEY (ROGER ROWLAND WESTWELL). Commercial Horticulture in Britain: Its Character and Competitive Strength. 1957.

19852 —— Market Gardening in East Kent: Results for 1950, 1951, and 1952 Crops. 1954. [Wye College pub.].

19853 —— East Kent Horticulture. 1957.

19854 FOLLEY (ROGER ROWLAND WESTWELL) *and* HUNT (A. R.). Ten Years of Market Gardening: A Business Study of some Small-Scale Market Gardens Covering the Period 1950–1960. Ashford. 1963.

19855 FLETCHER (HAROLD ROY). The Story of the Royal Horticultural Society, 1804–1968. 1969.

8. GARDENS AND GARDENING

19856 HADFIELD (MILES). A History of British Gardening. 1969. 3rd rev. edn 1989. 1st pub. 1960, under title, Gardening in Britain.

19857 —— The Gardener's Companion. 1950.

19858 —— Pioneers in Gardening. 1955.

19859 —— The English Landscape Garden. Aylesbury. 1977. 2nd edn 1988.

19860 —— *Et al.* British Gardeners: A Biographical Dictionary. 1980.

19861 COX (EVAN HILLHOUSE METHUEN). The Modern English Garden. 1927.

19862 —— A History of Gardening in Scotland. 1935.

19863 ROHDE (ELEANOUR SINCLAIR). The Story of the Garden. Boston, MA/Lond. 1932. Repr. 1989.

19864 WETHERED (HERBERT NEWTON). A Short History of Gardens. 1933.

19865 HYAMS (EDWARD SOLOMON). The English Garden. 1966.

19866 —— A History of Gardens and Gardening. N.Y. 1971.

19867 —— Great Historical Gardens of the World. 1969.

19868 COATS (PETER). Great Gardens of the Western World. 1963.

19869 —— Great Gardens of Britain. 1967.

19870 BERRALL (JULIA S.). The Garden: An Illustrated History from Ancient Egypt to the Present Day. 1966. Harmondsworth. 1978.

19871 —— A History of Flower Arrangement. 1953.

19872 HUXLEY (ANTHONY). An Illustrated History of Gardening. 1978. Repr. 1983. [For the Royal Horticultural Society.].

19873 HARRIS (JOHN) *ed.* The Garden: A Celebration of 1000 Years of British Gardening. 1979.

19874 KING (RONALD). The Quest for Paradise: A History of the World's Gardens. Weybridge. 1979.

19875 PACKER (BILL). The Making of the English Garden. 1988.

19876 THACKER (CHRISTOPHER). The History of Gardens. 1979.

19877 —— England's Historic Gardens. 1989.

19878 STEARN (WILLIAM THOMAS). 'The Garden History Society's Tenth Anniversary and some Historians of Garden History'. *Garden Hist.* 11 (1977), 42–52.

19879 GARDEN HISTORY. Vol. 1, 1972–. [The Journal of the Garden History Society.].

19880 SEAGER (ELIZABETH) *comp.* Gardens and Gardeners. Oxf. 1984.

19881 VERNEY (PETER). The Gardens of Scotland. Batsford. 1976.

See also the Gardens of Britain Series, Batsford 1977–:

19882 SYNGE (PETER M.). 1—Devon and Cornwall. 1977.

19883 PATERSON (ALLEN). 2—Dorset, Hampshire and the Isle of Wight. 1978.

19884 BISGROVE (RICHARD). 3—Berkshire, Oxfordshire, Buckinghamshire, Bedfordshire and Hertfordshire. 1978.

19885 WRIGHT (TOM). 4—Kent, East and West Sussex and Surrey. 1978.

19886 LEMMON (KENNETH). 5—Yorkshire and Humberside. 1978.

19887 ANTHONY (JOHN). 6—The East Midlands: Derbyshire, Leicestershire, Lincolnshire. 1979.

19888 MACLEOD (DAWN). The Gardener's London: Four Centuries of Gardening, Gardeners and Garden Usage. 1972.

19889 —— Oasis of the North: A Highland Garden. 1958. 2nd edn 1963.

19890 KING (RONALD). Royal Kew. 1985.

19891 COATS (PETER). The Gardens of Buckingham Palace. 1978.

19892 BALLARD (PHILLADA). An Oasis of Delight: The History of the Birmingham Botanical Gardens. 1983.

19893 HUNKIN (J. W.). 'The Garden at Tresco [Isle of Wight]'. *Endeavour* 8 (1949), 125–9.

19894 OSBORN (T. G. B.). 'The Oxford Botanic Garden'. *Endeavour* 10 (1951), 70–7.

19895 BATEY (MAVIS). The Historic Gardens of Oxford and Cambridge. 1989.

19896 HELLYER (ARTHUR GEORGE LEE). Gardens to Visit in Britain. Feltham. 1970.

19897 —— Wartime Gardening for Home Needs. 1939.

19898 GORER (RICHARD). The Development of Garden Flowers. 1970.

19899 BEALES (PETER). 20th Century Roses. 1988.

19900 CLIFFORD (DEREK). A History of Garden Design. 1962. New edn 1966.

19901 CROWE (SYLVIA). Garden Design. 1958. Repr. Chichester. 1981.

19902 MIDGLEY (KENNETH). Garden Design: Prepared in Conjunction and Collaboration with the Royal Horticultural Society. Harmondsworth. 1966. Lond. 1977. Revd. and expanded edn 1984.

19903 BROOKES (JOHN), DOUGLAS (WILLIAM LAKE) *et al.* Garden Design: History, Principles, Elements, Practice. 1984.

19904 TURNER (TOM). English Garden Design: History and Styles since 1650. Woodbridge. 1986.

19905 COWELL (FRANK RICHARD). The Garden as Fine Art: From Antiquity to Modern Times. 1978.

F. THE ENVIRONMENT

1. GENERAL

19906 GRESSWELL (PETER). The Environment: An Alphabetical Handbook. 1971.

19907 ALDOUS (TONY). Battle for the Environment. Glasg. 1972.

19908 —— Goodbye, Britain? 1975.

19909 CALDER (NIGEL). The Environmental Game. 1967.

19910 —— The Human Conspiracy. 1976. [BBC pub.].

19911 —— *Ed.* Nature in the Round: A Guide to Environmental Science. 1973.

19912 —— Technopolis: Social Control of the Uses of Science. 1969.

19913 ARVILL (ROBERT) *pseud.* Man and Environment: Crisis and the Strategy of Choice. Harmondsworth. 1967.

19914 GOLDSMITH (EDWARD) *ed.* Can Britain Survive? 1971.

19915 LLEWELYN-DAVIES (RICHARD) *Baron.* The Future of Environmental Studies. Edin. 1967.

19916 SEARS (PAUL BIGELOW). The Biology of the Living Landscape: An Introduction to Ecology. 1964.

19917 HUTCHINSON (GEORGE EVELYN). The Ecological Theater and the Evolutionary Play. New Haven, Conn. 1965.

19918 GOODMAN (GORDON T.) *ed.* Ecology and the Industrial Society: A Symposium of the British Ecological Society. N.Y. 1965.

19919 FRASER DARLING (*Sir* FRANK) *ed.* West Highland Survey: An Essay in Human Ecology. 1955.

19920 —— Impacts of Man on the Biosphere. 1969.

19921 —— Wilderness and Plenty: The Reith Lectures 1969. 1970.

19922 NICHOLSON (MAX). The Environmental Revolution: A Guide for the New Masters of the World. 1970.

19923 —— The System: The Misgovernment of Modern Britain. 1967.

19924 U.K. DEPARTMENT OF THE ENVIRONMENT. Improving the Environment. 1971.

19925 —— Environmental Standards: A Description of United Kingdom Practice: The Report of an Inter-departmental Working Party. 1977.

19926 —— Environmental Protection: Problems, Progress, Practice, Principles and Prospects. 1984.

19927 —— Digest of Environmental Statistics: Environmental Protection and Conservation. [Pub. annually 1976–.].

19928 —— Bottle Banks: The Expansion of the Bottle Bank Scheme in London and the Surrounding Area. 1982.

19929 U.K. CENTRAL OFFICE OF INFORMATION. Environmental Planning in Britain. 1979.

19930 CHRISTIE (IAN) *et al.* 'Needed: A National Environmental Planning Policy'. *Town Planning Rev.* 45 (1974), 1–4.

19931 MORGAN (R. P. C.). 'Nature Provides, Man Erodes'. *Geog. Mag.* 46 (1974), 528–35.

19932 MILTON (J. P.). 'Communities that Seek Peace with Nature'. *Futurist* 8 (1974), 264–6.

19933 DAY (MICHAEL). 'Environmental Improvement in Glasgow'. *Town and Country Planning* 43 (1975), 317–20.

19934 BECKERMAN (WILFRED). 'Economists, Scientists and Environmental Catastrophe'. *Oxf. Econ. Papers* 24 (1972), 327–34.

19935 —— Pricing for Pollution: An Analysis of Market Pricing and Governmental Regulation in Environment Consumption and Policy. 1975.

19936 U.K. COUNTRYSIDE COMMISSION. Coastal Preservation and Development: A Study of the Coastline of England and Wales . . . 1969.

19937 U.K. ENVIRONMENTAL BOARD. Sub-Group on New Development: Interim Report. 1976. [Chairman, *Sir* Hugh Wilson.].

19938 U.K. ENVIRONMENTAL BOARD. Sub-Group on Older Areas: Interim Report. 1976. [Chairman, A. A. Wood.].

19939 NATIONAL COUNCIL OF SOCIAL SERVICE. People and their Settlements: Aspects of History, Transport and Strategic Planning in the U.K.: Papers for a Conference . . . 1976.

19940 CONSERVATIVE POLITICAL CENTRE. Clean and Pleasant Land: Studies on the Environment . . . 1970.

19941 LABOUR PARTY RESEARCH DEPARTMENT. Pollution and our Environment: A Report . . . 1970.

19942 HILTON-YOUNG (WAYLAND) *Baron Kennet.* Controlling our Environment. 1970.

19943 ROUTLEDGE (ROBERTA A.). 'Statutory Control of Land Use on Environmental Grounds in England 1485–1945'. *Journal of Legal History* I (1982), 77–89.

19944 BENNETT (ROBERT JOHN) *and* CHORLEY (RICHARD JOHN). Environmental Systems: Philosophy, Analysis and Control. 1978.

19945 CHAPMAN (GRAHAM PETER). Human and Environmental Systems: A Geographical Appraisal. 1977.

19946 KNEESE (ALLEN VICTOR). Economics and the Environment. Harmondsworth. 1977.

19947 BOHM (PETER) *and* KNEESE (ALLEN VICTOR) *eds.* The Economics of Environment: Papers from Four Nations. 1971.

19948 FREEMAN (ALBERT MYRICK), HAVEMAN (ROBERT H.), *and* KNEESE (ALLEN VICTOR). The Economics of Environment Policy. N.Y./Lond. 1973.

19949 PEARCE (DAVID WILLIAM). Environmental Economics. 1976.

19950 PEARCE (DAVID WILLIAM) *and* PETTMEN (B. O.). Research in Environmental Economics in the U.K. 1973. Hull. 1974.

19951 —— Research in Environmental Economics in the U.K. 1974. Hull. 1975.

19952 HARVEY (BRIAN W.) *and* HALLET (JOHN D.). Environment and Society: An Introductory Analysis. 1977.

19953 U.K. WELSH DEVELOPMENT AGENCY. The Changing Face of Wales. Pontypridd. 1976.

19954 ARMSTRONG (PATRICK). Changing Landscape: The History and Ecology of Man's Impact on the Face of East Anglia. 1976.

19955 EYLES (JOHN). Environmental Satisfaction and London's Docklands: Problems and Policies in the Isle of Dogs. 1976.

19956 BARKER (ANTHONY) *et al*. The Local Amenity Movement. 1976.

19957 —— 'Studying Amenity Societies'. *Town and Country-Planning* 43 (1975), 302–4.

19958 WOODFORD (GEORGE P.) *et al*. The Value of Standards for the External Residential Environment. 1976. Repr. 1977.

19959 MARSH (ALAN). 'Silent Revolution, Value Priorities and the Quality of Life in Britain'. *Amer. Pol Sci. Rev.* 69 (1975), 21–30.

19960 BROOKES (S. K.) and RICHARDSON (JEREMY JOHN). 'The Environmental Lobby in Britain'. *Parl. Affs* 28 (1975), 312–28.

19961 GIGGS (J. A.) *and* MATHER (P. M.). 'Factional Ecology and Factor Invariance: An Investigation'. *Econ. Geog.* 51 (1975), 366–82.

19962 STRETTON (HUGH). Capitalism, Socialism and the Environment. Camb. 1976.

19963 KIMBER (RICHARD) *and* RICHARDSON (JEREMY JOHN) eds. Campaigning for the Environment. 1974.

19964 COPPOCK (JOHN TERENCE) *and* WILSON (C. B.) eds. Environmental Quality. Edin. 1984.

19965 BROOKS (PETER FRED). Problems of the Environment: An Introduction. 1974.

19966 —— The Work of the Environmental Health Committee. Chichester. 1973.

19967 HOUSE (JOHN WILLIAM) *ed*. The U.K Space: Resources, Environment, and the Future. 1973.

19968 HEY (RICHARD DAVID) *and* DAVIES (TREVOR P.) eds. Science, Technology and Environmental Management: Based on a symposium of 'Applied Environmental Science' Held at the 1973 Annual Conference of the Institute of British Geographers. Farnb. 1975.

19969 JONES (JOHN OWEN) *and* JONES (ELIZABETH A.). Index of Human Ecology. 1974.

19970 JOHNSON (STANLEY). The Politics of the Environment, The British Experience. 1973.

19971 —— The Green Revolution. 1972.

19972 POLE (W.) *ed*. Environmental Institutions. Camb. 1972.

19973 BURCH (WILLIAM R.), CHEEK (NEIL H.), *and* TAYLOR (LEE). Social Behaviour, Natural Resources and the Environment. 1972.

19974 ROSE (JOHN) *ed*. Technological Injury: The Effect of Technological Advances on the Environment, Life and Society. 1973.

19975 DAWSON (JOHN A.) *and* DOORNKAMP (JOHN C.). Evaluating the Human Environment: Essays in Applied Geography. 1973.

19976 PEPPER (DAVID). The Roots of Modern Environmentalism. 1984.

19977 EAGLES (PAUL J. F.). The Planning and Management of Environmentally Sensitive Areas. 1984.

See also series entitled Environment and Man. Glasgow 1975–. John Lenihan and William Fletcher. (*Gen. eds*).

Vol. 1 Energy Resources and the Environment. 1975.

2 Food, Agriculture and the Environment. 1975.

3 Health and the Environment. 1976.

4 Reclamation. 1976.

5 The Marine Environment. 1977.

6 The Chemical Environment. 1977.

7 Measuring and Monitoring the Environment. 1978.

8 The Built Environment. 1978.

9 The Biological Environment. 1979.

10 Economics of the Environment. 1979.

2. POLLUTION

(a) General Studies

19978 LAMBERT (CLAIRE M.) *comp*. Environmental Pollution: Sources of Information on Environmental Pollution in the United Kingdom. 1983. [For Dept. of Environment.].

19979 HENDERSON (KAY) *ed*. Pollution: Sources of Information. 1972.

19980 SHERLOCH (ROBERT LIONEL). Man as a Geological Agent: An Account of his Actions on Inanimate Nature. 1922.

19981 GREGORY (PETER). Our Polluted Homes. 1965.

19982 BARR (JOHN). The Assaults on our Senses. 1970.

19983 BUGLER (J.). Polluting Britain. Harmondsworth. 1972.

19984 RICHARDSON (G.). Policing Pollution: A Study of Regulation and Enforcement. Oxf. 1982.

19985 COX (PETER) *and* PEEL (JOHN). Population and Pollution: Proceedings of the Eighth Annual Symposium of the Eugenic Society. 1971.

19986 HODGES (LAURENT). Environmental Pollution. N.Y./Lond. 1972. 2nd edn 1977.

19987 GOULDEN (P. D.). Environmental Pollution Analysis. 1978.

19988 HOLDGATE (MARTIN WYATT). A Perspective on Environmental Pollution. Camb. 1979.

19989 HOLDGATE (MARTIN WYATT) *and* WHITE (GILBERT F.) eds. Environmental Issues. 1977.

19990 DIX (H. M.). Environmental Pollution: Atmosphere, Land, Water, and Noise. Chichester. 1981.

19991 VICTOR (PETER ALLEN). The Economics of Pollution. 1972.

19992 —— Pollution: Economy and Environment. 1972.

19993 JACOBY (NEIL) *and* PENNANCE (FREDERICK GEORGE). The Polluters: Industry or Government? 1972.

19994 CLAYTON (KEITH MARTIN) *and* CHILVER (RICHARD CLEMENTSON) *eds*. Pollution Abatement. Newton Abbot. 1973.

19995 FREEMAN (ALBERT MYRICK). The Benefits of Environmental Improvement: Theory and Practice. Baltimore, Md./Lond. 1979.

19996 —— Air and Water Pollution Control: A Benefit-Cost Assessment. N.Y./Chichester. 1982.

19997 DIAMANT (RUDOLPH MAXIMILIAN EUGEN). The Prevention of Pollution. 1974.

19998 McKNIGHT (ALLAN DOUGLAS) *et al*. Environmental Pollution Control: Technical, Economic and Legal Aspects. 1974.

19999 FISHER (ANTHONY CLINTON). Resource and Environmental Economics. Camb. 1981.

20000 HIGGINS (IRVING JOHN) *and* BURNS (R. G.). The Chemistry and Microbiology of Pollution. 1975.

20001 McLOUGHLIN (JAMES). Law and Practice Relating to Pollution Control in the United Kingdom. 1977.

20002 —— The Law Relating to Pollution: An Introduction. Manch. 1972.

20003 HALL (IRENE M.). Community Action Versus Pollution: A Study of a Residents Group in a Welsh Urban Area. Card. 1976.

20004 MILLER (CHRISTOPHER) *and* WOOD (CHRISTOPHER). Planning and Pollution: An Examination of the Role of Land Use Planning in the Protection of Environmental Quality. Oxf. 1983.

20005 CHICKEN (JOHN CHARLES). Hazard Control Policy in Britain. Oxf. 1975.

20006 WOOD (CHRISTOPHER MAXWELL) *et al*. The Geography of Pollution: A Study of Greater Manchester. Manch. 1974.

20007 BLENKINSOP (ARTHUR). 'Control of Pollution'. *Town & Country Plan*. 43 (1975), 226–7.

20008 LOWE (P. D.). 'The Royal Commission on Environmental Pollution'. *Pol. Q*. 46 (1975), 87–94.

20009 ROLPH (C. H.). 'Dirtiest Village'. *New Statesman* 90 (1975), 406.

20010 —— 'Dustmanship'. *New Statesman* 89 (1975), 274–5.

20011 Digest of Environmental Pollution Statistics. 1978+.

20012 U.K. ROYAL COMMISSION ON ENVIRONMENTAL POLLUTION. First Report. 1971. Repr. 1976. [Chairman, *Baron* Eric Ashby.].

20013 —— Second Report: Three Issues in Industrial Pollution. 1972. Repr. 1978.

20014 —— Third Report: Pollution in some British Estuaries and Coastal Waters. 1972.

20015 —— Fourth Report: Pollution Control: Progress and Problems. 1974. [Chairman after 1973, *Sir* Bryan Hilton Flowers.].

20016 —— Fifth Report: Air Pollution Control: An Integrated Approach. 1976.

20017 —— Sixth Report: Nuclear Power and the Environment. 1976.

20018 —— Seventh Report: Agriculture and Pollution. 1979–80.

20019 —— Eighth Report: Oil Pollution of the Sea. 1980–1.

20020 —— Ninth Report: Lead in the Environment. 1982–3.

20021 —— Tenth Report: Tackling Pollution—Experience and Prospects. 1983–4.

20022 —— Eleventh Report: Managing Waste: The Duty of Care. 1985–6.

20023 —— Twelfth Report: Best Practicable Environmental Option. 1987–8.

20024 U.K. CENTRAL UNIT ON ENVIRONMENTAL POLLUTION. Controlling Pollution: A Review of Government Action Related to Recommendations by the Royal Commission on Environmental Pollution. 1975.

20025 U.K. WELSH OFFICE. Pollution: The Challenge to Wales. Card. 1972.

20026 SCORER (RICHARD SEGAR). A Radical Approach to Pollution, Population and Resources. 1973.

20027 ASHBY (ERIC) *Baron*. Pollution, Nuisance or Nemesis?: A Report on the Control of Pollution. 1972. [Report for the Dept. of Environment.].

20028 —— Pollution and the Public Conscience. Newcastle upon Tyne. 1972. [Earl Grey Memorial Lecture.].

20029 —— Reconciling Man with the Environment. 1978.

20030 SCARROW (HOWARD A.). 'The Impact of British Domestic Air Pollution Legislation'. *Brit. J. Pol. Sci*. 2 (1972), 261–82.

(b) Specific Studies

(i) Air Pollution

20031 ALEXANDER (BASIL A.). Acid Rain and the Environment: Sources of Information. 1985.

20032 HARRIS (FREDERICK WILLIAM). Atmospheric Pollution: Its Sources, Extent and Measurement. Glasg. 1934.

20033 SHAW (*Sir* WILLIAM NAPIER) *and* OWENS (JOHN SWITZER). The Smoke Problem of Great Cities. 1925.

20034 NATIONAL SMOKE ABATEMENT SOCIETY. Annual Report. 1930–50.

20035 —— Yearbook. 1951–6.

20036 —— Clean Air Yearbook. 1957+.

20037 MINISTRY OF HEALTH. Mortality and Morbidity during the London Fog of December 1952. 1954.

20038 WILKINS (E. T.). 'Air Pollution Aspects of the London Fog of December 1952'. *Q. J. Roy. Meteorological Soc*. 80 (1954), 267–78.

20039 COMMITTEE ON AIR POLLUTION. Interim Report. Cmnd 9011. Parliamentary Papers, VIII (1954): Report. Cmnd 9322. Parliamentary Papers, VIII (1953–4).

20040 CARR (DONALD EATON). The Breath of Life. 1965.

20041 SCORER (RICHARD SEGAR). Pollution in the Air: Problems, Policies and Priorities. 1973.

20042 —— Air Pollution. 1968.

20043 ASHBY (ERIC) *Baron, and* ANDERSON (MARY). The Politics of Clean Air. Oxf. 1981.

20044 U.K. HEALTH AND SAFETY EXECUTIVE. Industrial Air Pollution. 1975.

20045 THOMPSON (RUSSELL). Atmospheric Contamination: A Review of the Air Pollution Problem. Reading. 1978.

20046 MEETHAM (ALFRED ROGER). Atmospheric Pollution: Its History, Origins and Prevention. 1952. 4th rev. edn Oxf. 1981.

20047 ELSON (DEREK M.). Atmospheric Pollution: Causes, Effects and Control Policies. Oxf. 1987.

20048 CENTRAL ELECTRICITY GENERATING BOARD. Towards a Clean Air Policy. 1966.

20049 LAWTHER (PATRICK JOSEPH). Air Pollution and Public Health: A Personal Appraisal. 1975.

20050 CRESSWELL (COLIN RANDALL). Notes on Air Pollution Control. 1974.

20051 FRANKER (MAURICE). The Control of Industrial Air Pollution. 1974. [For the Alkali Inspectorate.].

20052 U.K. DEPARTMENT OF THE ENVIRONMENT. Clean Air Today. 1974.

20053 —— Air Pollution Information: Your Rights and Obligations. 1977.

20054 —— Information about Industrial Emissions to the Atmosphere. 1973.

20055 —— Towards Cleaner Air: A Review of Britain's Achievements. 1973.

20056 U.K. HEALTH AND SAFETY EXECUTIVE. Industrial Air Pollution. 1975.

20057 BRIMBLECOMBE (PETER). The Big Smoke: A History of Air Pollution in London since Medieval Times. 1987.

20058 SCHWAR (M. J. R.) *and* BELL (D. J.). Thirty Years On: A Review of Air Pollution in London. 1983.

20059 WOOD (C. M.) *et al.* The Geography of Pollution: A Study of Greater Manchester. Manch. 1974.

20060 MANCHESTER AREA COUNCIL FOR CLEAN AIR AND NOISE CONTROL. 25 Year Review: A Review of some Aspects of Air Pollution and Noise Control in the Area of the Council 25 Years after the Clean Air Act, 1956. Manch. 1981.

20061 BUCK (STEPHEN FRANK) *and* BROWN (D. A.). Mortality from Lung Cancer and Bronchitis in Relation to Smoke and Sulphur Dioxide Concentration, Population Density, and Social Index. 1964. [Tobacco Research Council.].

20062 WICKEN (ALAN JOHN) *and* BUCK (STEPHEN FRANK). Report on a Study of Environmental Factors Associated with Lung Cancer and Bronchitis Mortality on Areas of North East England. 1964. [Tobacco Research Council.].

20063 ROYAL COLLEGE OF PHYSICIANS OF LONDON. Air Pollution and Health: Summary and Report on Air Pollution. 1970.

20064 SHERWOOD (P. T.) *and* BOWERS (I. H.). Air Pollution from Road Traffic: A Review of the Present Position. Crowthorne. 1970.

20065 CULLEY (E. W.) *et al.* Air Pollution Statistics for London: Sulphur Dioxide and Smoke: April 1981–March 1983. 1984.

20066 ALLEN (G. O.). 'Sixteen Years: A Saga of Smoke Control'. *Clean Air* 3 (1973), 12–15. [Scunthorpe.].

20067 WALL (GEOFFREY). 'Public Response to Air Pollution in South Yorkshire, England'. *Environt & Behavior* 5 (1973), 219–48.

20068 BLOWERS (ANDREW). Something in the Air: Corporate Power and the Environment. 1984. [The London Brick Co., 1978–83, and Environmentalists.].

(ii) Water Pollution.

20069 Water Statistics, 1964+.

20070 The Torrey Canyon: Report of the Committee of Scientists on the Scientific and Technological Aspects of the Torrey Canyon Disaster. 1968.

20071 PETROW (RICHARD). The Black Tide: In the Wake of the Torrey Canyon. 1968.

20072 GILL (CRISPIN), BOOKER (FRANK), *and* SOPER (TONY). The Wreck of the Torrey Canyon. Newton Abbot. 1967.

20073 U.K. DEPARTMENT OF TRADE. (Marine Division). The Battle against Oil Pollution at Sea. 1976.

20074 —— Accidental Oil Pollution of the Sea: A Report by Officials on Oil Spills and Clean-up Measures. 1976. [Chairman, G. D. Crane.].

20075 U.K. DEPARTMENT OF THE ENVIRONMENT. Report of the Coastal Pollution Research Committee of the Water Pollution Research Laboratory. 1975. [Chairman, J. T. Calvert.].

20076 —— Cleaning up the Mersey: A Consultation Paper on Tackling Water Pollution in the Rivers and Canals of the Mersey . . . 1982.

20077 —— Report of the River Pollution Survey of England and Wales. 1970.

20078 —— Oil Pollution on the Coastline: A Study . . . 1981.

20079 DEVON COUNTY COUNCIL. A Scheme for Coastal Pollution Counter Measures. Exeter. 1985.

20080 WARDLEY-SMITH (J.) *ed.* The Control of Oil Pollution on the Sea and Inland Waters: The Effects of Oil Spills on the Marine Environment and Methods of Dealing with Them. 1976. Rev. edn 1983.

20081 —— The Prevention of Oil Pollution. 1979.

20082 CLARK (ROBERT BERNARD) *ed.* The Long-Term Effects of Oil Pollution on Marine Populations, Communities and Ecosystems. 1982.

20083 ABECASSIS (DAVID WILLIAM). The Law and Practice Relating to Oil Pollution from Ships. 1978.

20084 BRITISH PETROLEUM ENVIRONMENTAL CONTROL CENTRE. The Christos Bitas Incident: Success out of a Disaster: A Report on the Oil Spill Clean-up. [Irish Sea.]. 1979.

20085 HAWKINS (K.). Environment and Enforcement: Regulation and the Social Definition of Pollution. Oxf. 1984.

20086 PRITCHARD (SONIA ZAIDE). Oil Pollution Control. 1987.

20087 INSTITUTE OF WATER CONTROL. Health and Safety in the Water Industry: Symposium, Reading University, 5–6 April 1983. Maidstone. 1983.

20088 BRITTAN (YVONNE). The Impact of Water Pollution Control on Industry: A Case Study of 50 Dischargers. Oxf. 1984.

20089 WELSH WATER AUTHORITY. (Dee Working Party). Report of the Dee Working Party on Actions Required and Taken Following the Pollution Incident Affecting the River Dee and Water Supplies, January 1984. Brecon. 1985.

20090 HOWARTH (WILLIAM). Water Pollution Law. 1988.

20091 STANBRIDGE (H. H.). A History of Sewage Treatment in Britain. Maidstone. 1976. [In several parts.].

20092 WISDOM (ALLEN SIDNEY). Sewerage and Sewage Disposal. Chichester. 1979.

20093 BARTLETT (RONALD ERNEST). Developments in Sewerage. 1979.

20094 BOOTH (ADRIAN JOHN). Sheffield's Sewage Works Railways. Yatton. 1987.

20095 DOXAT (J.). The Living Thames: The Restoration of a Great River. 1977.

20096 WHEELER (A. C.). The Tidal Thames: The History of the River and its Fishes. 1979.

20097 FUNNELL (E. B.) *and* HEY (R. D.) *eds.* The Management of Water Resources in England and Wales. 1974.

20098 PARKER (D. J.) *and* PENNING-ROWSELL (E. C.). Water Planning in Britain. Harmondsworth. 1979.

20099 SMITH (K.). Water in Britain. 1972.

20100 KIRBY (C.). Water in Britain. Harmondsworth. 1979.

20101 JORDAN (A. G.), RICHARDSON (J. J.), *and* KIMBER (R. H.). 'The Origins of the Water Act of 1973'. *Pub. Admin.* 55 (1977), 317–34.

20102 PORTER (ELIZABETH). Water Management in England and Wales. Camb. 1978.

20103 BRAND (JACK). 'The Politics of Fluoridisation: A Community Conflict'. *Pol. Studs* 19 (1971), 430–9.

20104 DOORNKAMP (J. C.), GREGORY (K. J.), *and* BURN (A. S.). Atlas of Drought in Britain, 1975–76. 1980.

20105 MARSH (TERRY). The 1984 Drought. Wallingford. 1985.

20106 —— London's Water Supply, 1903–53: A Review of the Work of the Metropolitan Water Board. 1953.

20107 RYDZ (DAVID L.). 'The Formation of the Great Ouse Water Authority'. *Pub. Admin.* 49 (1971), 163–84, 245–68.

(iii) *Pesticides and Chemicals*

20108 SHEAIL (JOHN). Pesticides and Nature Conservation: The British Experience 1950–1975. Oxf. 1985.

20109 GREEN (MAURICE BERKELEY). Pesticides: Boon or Bane? 1976.

20110 IRWIN (ALAN) *and* LUCAS (KENNETH). 'The Control of Chemical Carcinogens in Britain'. *Policy & Politics* 11 (1983), 439–60.

20111 EDWARDS (CLIVE ARTHUR). Environmental Pollution by Pesticides. 1973.

20112 IRVINE (DAVID EDWARD GUTHRIE) *and* KNIGHT (BRIAN) *eds.* Pollution and the Use of Chemicals in Agriculture. 1974.

20113 FLETCHER (WILLIAM WHIGHAM). The Pest War. Oxf. 1974.

20114 WALKER (COLIN). Environmental Pollution by Chemicals. 1971. 2nd rev. edn 1975.

20115 MELLANBY (KENNETH). Pesticides and Pollution. 1967.

20116 —— The Biology of Pollution. 1972.

20117 PERRING (FRANKLYN H.) *and* MELLANBY (KENNETH) *eds.* The Ecological Effects of Pesticides. 1977.

20118 BROWN (ANTHONY WILLIAM ALDRIDGE). The Ecology of Pesticides. NY/Chichester. 1978.

20119 U.K. DEPARTMENT OF EDUCATION AND SCIENCE. Review of the Present Safety Arrangements for the use of Toxic Chemicals in Agriculture and Food Storage: Report of the Advisory Committee on Pesticides and other Toxic Chemicals. 1967. [Chairman, *Sir* JAMES COOK.].

20120 WILLIAMS (DAVID IVOR) *and* ANGLESEA (DOUGLAS). Experiments on Land Pollution. Hove. 1978.

20121 CAIRNEY (THOMAS) *ed.* Reclaiming Contaminated Land. Glasg. 1987.

20122 IMPERIAL CHEMICAL INDUSTRIES. (Plant Protection Division). Jealott's Hill: 50 Years of Agricultural Research 1928–1978. Bracknell. 1978. [*Ed.* by F. C. PEACOCK.].

(iv) *Nuclear Radiation and Waste*

20123 HADDOW (ALEXANDER) *ed.* The Biological Hazards of Atomic Energy: Being the Papers Presented at the Conference Convened by the Institute of Biology and the Atomic Scientists Association in 1950. 1952.

20124 MEDICAL RESEARCH COUNCIL. The Hazards of Nuclear and Allied Radiations. 1956.

20125 HIMSWORTH (*Sir* HAROLD PERCIVAL). The Hazards to Man of Nuclear and Allied Radiations: A Second Report to the Medical Research Council. 1960.

20126 MEDICAL RESEARCH COUNCIL. Introductory Manual on the Control of Health Hazards from Radio-Active Material. 1961.

20127 —— The Exposure of the Population to Radiation from Fall-Out: A Report to the Medical Research Council by their Committee on Protection against Ionizing Radiations. 1964.

20128 ELECTRICAL POWER ENGINEERS ASSOCIATION. (Nuclear Waste Working Party). Some Implication of Radioactive Waste from Nuclear Power Generation in the U.K. up to the year 2000. 2 vols .Chertsey. 1978.

20129 BRITISH NUCLEAR ENERGY SOCIETY. Radioactive Waste Management Conference, 1984. 1984.

20130 TAYLOR (PETER JOHN) *comp*. The Impact of Nuclear Waste Disposals to the Marine Environment. Oxf. 1982.

20131 LAU (FOO-SUN). A Dictionary of Nuclear Power and Waste Management. Letchworth. 1987.

20132 COUGHTREY (P. J.) *ed*. Ecological Aspects of Radionuclide Release. Oxf. 1983. [British Ecological Society pub.].

20133 POLITICAL ECOLOGY RESEARCH GROUP. An Investigation into the Hazards Associated with the Maritime Transport of Spent Nuclear Reactor Fuel to the British Isles. Oxf. 1980.

20134 —— Safety Aspects of the Advanced Gas-Cooled Reactor: A Report Commissioned by Torness Community Concern. Oxf. 1980.

20135 —— An Investigation into the Incidence of Cancer in the Areas Affected by Discharges from the Nuclear Fuels Reprocessing Plant at Windscale, Cumbria. Oxf. 1980.

20136 U.K. DEPARTMENT OF THE ENVIRONMENT. The Windscale Enquiry: Report. 2 vols. 1978. [Chairman Mr Justice PARKER.].

20137 FERGUSON (J. M.). 'Managing Clinical Waste'. *Waste Management* 77 (1987), 144–55.

(v) Noise Pollution

20138 CUNIFF (PATRICK F.). Environmental Noise Pollution. NY/Lond. 1977.

20139 NOISE ABATEMENT LEAGUE. Quiet: A Magazine Devoted to the Prevention of Avoidable Noise. Vol. 1, No. 1—vol. 5, No. 23, Mar. 1936–winter 1948.

20140 PEARCE (DAVID WILLIAM) *comp*. The Economics of Noise Nuisance: A Bibliography. S/hampton. 1973.

20141 TAYLOR (RUPERT). Noise. 1970. 2nd edn Harmondsworth. 1975. 3rd edn 1978.

20142 BUGLIARELLO (GEORGE) *et al*. The Impact of Noise Pollution: A Socio-Technological Introduction. 1976.

20143 HARRIS (ANTHONY H.). Is Quiet a Luxury Good?: A Survey Approach. Aberd. 1978.

20144 MILNE (ANTONY). Noise Pollution: Impact and Counter-Measures. Newton Abbot. 1979.

20145 PENN (CHRISTOPHER N.). Noise Control. 1979.

20146 LARA SAENZ (A.) *and* STEPHENS (RAYMOND WILLIAM BAR-ROW) *eds*. Noise Pollution: Effects and Control. Chichester. 1986.

20147 WEBB (JOHN DAVID) *ed*. Noise Control in Industry. Sudbury. 1976. 2nd edn 1978.

20148 MIDDLETON (A. H.). Machinery Noise. Oxf. 1977.

20149 GREATER LONDON COUNCIL. Traffic Noise. 1966.

20150 MORGAN (NOEL). A Select Bibliography of Aircraft Noise. 1984.

20151 POOLE (JOHN BRIAN) *and* ANDREWS (E. KAY). The Evolution of British Policy on Aircraft Noise. 1971.

20152 GOMERSALL (ALAN) *comp*. Aircraft Noise. 1975. [G.L.C. pamphlet.].

20153 —— Community Noise. 1975. [G.L.C.].

20154 GLC ENVIRONMENTAL SCIENCE GROUP. Concorde Noise and its Effect on London. 1975.

20155 U.K. CENTRAL OFFICE OF INFORMATION. Aircraft Noise Annoyance around London (Heathrow) Airport: A Survey made in 1961 for the Wilson Committee on the Problem of Noise. 2 pts. 1963.

20156 NOISE ABATEMENT SOCIETY. The Third London Airport: Foulness. 1968.

20157 —— The Law on Noise. 1969.

20158 U.K. DEPARTMENT OF THE ENVIRONMENT. Noise in the Next Ten Years: A Report . . . 1974.

20159 —— Aircraft Engine Noise Research: Report. 1974.

(vi) Lead Pollution

20160 U.K. DEPARTMENT OF THE ENVIRONMENT. Lead in the Environment and its Significance to Man . . . 1974.

20161 BRUNEKREEF (B.). Childhood Exposure to Environmental Lead: A Technical Report. 1986.

20162 CONSERVATION SOCIETY. (Pollution Working Party). The Health Effects of Lead on Children: A Review of Literature Published since 1976. Chertsey. 1978.

20163 U.K. CENTRAL OFFICE OF INFORMATION. Lead in Drinking Water: A Survey in Great Britain, 1975–1976: Report of an Inter-departmental Working Group. 1977. [HMSO.].

20164 HARRISON (ROY M.). Lead Pollution: Causes and Control. 1981. Repr. 1984.

20165 RATCLIFFE (JENNIFER M.). Lead in Man and the Environment. Chichester. 1981.

20166 PRICE (BRIAN). Lead in Petrol: An Energy Analysis. 1982. [Friends of the Earth pub.].

20167 KOLLERSTON (NICK). Lead on the Brain: A Plain Guide to Britain's Number One Pollutant. 1982.

20168 HEALEY (MICHAEL A.). Lead, the Environment and Health: A Report. Nottingham. 1982.

20169 WILSON (DES). The Lead Scandal: The Fight to Save Children from Damage by Lead in Petrol. 1983.

20170 RUTTER (MICHAEL). Lead Versus Health: Sources and Effects of Low Level Lead Exposure. Chichester. 1983.

20171 ROGERS (RICK). Lead Poison. 1978.

20172 KING (P. S. D.). Lead in Water: A Review of Environmental Factors Affecting the Use of Lead in Building. 1984.

20173 LANSDOWN (RICHARD) *and* YULE (WILLIAM) *eds*. The Lead Debate: The Environment, Toxicology and Child Health. 1986.

(vii) Food Pollution

20174 LUCAS (JACK). Our Polluted Food: A Survey of the Risks. 1975.

20175 FARM AND FOOD SOCIETY. Agriculture and Pollution. 1980.

20176 MANSFIELD (PETER) *and* MUNRO (JEAN). Chemical Children: How to Protect your Family from Harmful Pollutants. 1987.

20177 MILLSTONE (ERIK). Food Additives. Harmondsworth. 1986.

20178 JONES (NORMAN RICHARD). Food Additives: Descriptions, Functions and U.K. Legislation. Leatherhead. 1976.

20179 HANSSEN (MAURICE) *and* MARSDEN (JILL). E for Additives: The Complete "E" Numbers Guide. Wellingb. 1984.

20180 ERLICHMAN (JAMES). Gluttons for Punishment. Harmondsworth. 1986.

(viii) Floods

20181 BARKER (DUDLEY). The Official Story of the Great Floods of 1947 and their Sequel. 1948.

20182 STEERS (J. A.). 'The East Coast Floods, January 31st to February 1st, 1953'. *Geog. Jnl* 119 (1953), 280–95.

20183 ROSSITER (J. R.). 'The North Sea Storm Surge of 31st January and 1st February 1953'. *Phil. Trans. Roy. Soc. London* Series A, 246 (1954), 371–99.

20184 SUMMERS (D.). The East Coast Floods. Newton Abbot. 1978.

20185 STEERS (J. A.) *et al.* 'The Storm Surge of 11th January 1978 on the East Coast of England'. *Geog. J.* 145 (1979), 195–205.

20186 NEWSON (M. D.). Flooding and the Flood Hazard in the United Kingdom. Oxf. 1975.

3. CONSERVATION OF NATURAL RESOURCES

20187 SHEAIL (JOHN). Nature in Trust: The History of Nature Conservation in Britain. Glasg. 1976.

20188 —— Rural Conservation in Inter-war Britain. Oxf. 1981.

20189 COUNCIL FOR THE PRESERVATION OF RURAL ENGLAND. The Case for National Parks in Great Britain. 1938.

20190 TANSLEY (*Sir* ARTHUR GEORGE). Our Heritage of Wild Nature: A Plea for Organised Nature Conservation. 1945.

20191 HUXLEY (*Sir* JULIAN SORREL) Conservation of Nature in England and Wales. 1947. Cmnd 7122.

20192 RAMSAY (*Sir* JAMES DOUGLAS). National Parks: A Scottish Survey. 1947. Cmnd 7235.

20193 CONSERVATION SOCIETY. (Resources/Environment Committee-Economics Working Party). The Economics of Conservation: An Outline Plan for the United Kingdom. Chertsey. 1973.

20194 KAIN (ROGER). Planning and the Environment in the Modern World. Vol. 3: Planning for Conservation. 1980.

20195 HOOKE (J. M.) *and* KAIN (ROGER J. P.). Historical Change in the Physical Environment: A Guide to Sources and Techniques. 1982.

20196 RACKHAM (O.). 'Documentary Evidence for the Historical Ecologist'. *Landscape Hist.* 1 (1979), 29–33.

20197 CAMPBELL (BERNARD GRANT). Human Ecology: The Story of our Place in Nature from Prehistory to the Present. 1983.

20198 GILG (ANDREW W.). Countryside Planning: The First Three Decades, 1945–1976. 1979.

20199 OWEN (OLIVER SYLVANOUS). Natural Resource Conservation: An Ecological Approach. NY/Lond. 1971. 4th edn 1985.

20200 JOHNSON (BRIAN). The Conservation and Development Programme for the United Kingdom. 1983.

20201 LOWENTHAL (DAVID) *and* BINNEY (MARCUS) *eds*. Our Past before us: Why do we Save it? 1981.

20202 GALLAGHER (JANETTE) *and* GOODCHILD (PETER) *comps*. Conservation Reading List: A Select Reading List on the Conservation of Historic Parks and Gardens, with special reference to Great Britain. York. 1984.

20203 DAVIDSON (JOAN) *and* LLOYD (RICHARD) *eds*. Conservation and Agriculture. Chichester. 1977.

20204 MABEY (RICHARD). The Common Ground: A Place for Nature in Britain's Future? 1981.

20205 GREEN (BRYN). Countryside Conservation: The Protection and Management of Amenity Ecosystems. 1981. 2nd edn 1985.

20206 NORTON-TAYLOR (RICHARD). Whose Land is it Anyway?: Agriculture, Planning and Land Use in the British Countryside. Welling. 1982.

20207 JOHNSON (STANLEY P.). The Politics of Environment: The British Experience. 1973.

20208 PYE-SMITH (CHARLIE) *and* ROSE (CHRIS). Crisis and Conservation: Conflict in the British Countryside. Harmondsworth. 1984.

20209 SLESSER (MALCOLM). The Politics of Environment. 1972.

20210 CARLISLE (KENNETH). Conserving the Countryside: A Tory View. 1984. [Conservative Political Centre pub.].

20211 DRABBLE (PHIL). What Price the Countryside? 1985.

20212 HELLIWELL (DENIS RODNEY). Planning for Nature Conservation. Chichester. 1985.

20213 TYLDESLEY (DAVID). Gaining Momentum: An Analysis of the Role and Performance of Local Authorities in Nature Conservation. Oxf. 1986.

20214 EMERY (MALCOLM). Promoting Nature in Cities and Towns: A Practical Guide. 1986.

20215 GUBBAY (SUSAN). A Coastal Directory for Marine Nature Conservation. Ross-on-Wye. 1988.

20216 SMITH (DUNCAN). What Kind of Growth: People or Profits? 1984. [Conservation Society pub.].

20217 PEARCE (DEREK WILLIAM) *ed.* The Economics of Natural Resource Depletion. 1975.

20218 INTERNATIONAL UNION FOR CONSERVATION OF NATIVE AND NATURAL RESOURCES, U.K. COMMITTEE. Earth's Survival: A Conservation and Development Programme for the U.K. 1981.

20219 PEARCE (DEREK WILLIAM) *and* WALTER (INGO) *eds.* Resource Conservation: The Social and Economic Dimensions of Recycling. 1978.

20220 RATCLIFFE (DEREK) *ed.* A Nature Conservation Review: The Selection of Biological Sites of National Importance to Nature Conservation in Britain. 2 vols 1977.

20221 STAMP (*Sir* LAURENCE DUDLEY). Nature Conservation in Britain [with a List of Conservation Areas in England, Wales and Scotland Compiled by the late James Fisher]. 1970. 2nd edn 1974.

20222 BASSETT (PHILIPPA) *comp.* A List of the Historical Records of the British Ecological Society. Birm. 1980.

20223 —— A List of the Historical Records Retained by the Friends of the Lake District. Birm. 1980.

20224 BERRY (GEOFFREY) *and* BEARD (GEOFFREY). The Lake District, A Century of Conservation. Edin. 1980.

20225 STEWART (JENNIFER D.). Environmental Record Centres: A Decade of Progress? Duxford. 1980.

20226 GREGORY (ROY). The Price of Amenity: Five Studies in Conservation and Government. 1971.

20227 HAW (RICHARD CLAUDE). The Conservation of Natural Resources. 1959.

20228 CONSERVATION OF THE NEW FOREST: A Report for Consultation Prepared by Officers Drawn from the Forestry Commission . . . [and others]. Winchester. 1970.

20229 GREATER LONDON COUNCIL. (Department of Transportation and Development). Ecology and Nature Conservation in London. 1984.

20230 CLENET (DEIRDRE). Nature Conservation in Croydon: A Nature Conservation Strategy for London. 1988.

20231 O'RIORDAN (TIMOTHY). Perspectives on Resource Management. 1971.

20232 —— Environmentalism. 1976.

20233 O'RIORDAN (TIMOTHY) *and* HEY (RICHARD DAVID) *eds.* Environmental Impact Assessment. Farnb. 1976.

20234 UNITED KINGDOM NATURE CONSERVANCY. Second Conference, 1965. Reports. 1965/6.

20235 NEW UNIVERSITY OF ULSTER INSTITUTE OF CONTINUING EDUCATION. Nature Conservation and Agriculture: A Conference . . . Londonderry. 1980.

20236 LOWE (PHILIP) *et al.* Countryside Conflicts: The Politics of Farming, Forestry and Conservation. Aldershot. 1986.

20237 ALLEN (ROBERT). How to Save the World: Strategy for World Conservation. 1980. Repr. 1982.

20238 AYENSU (EDWARD SOLOMON). Our Green and Living World: The Wisdom to Save it. Camb. 1984.

20239 LAURIE (IAN C.). Nature in Cities: The Natural Environment in the Design and Development of Urban Green Spaces. Chichester. 1979.

20240 GOUDIE (ANDREW). The Nature of the Environment: An Advanced Physical Geography. Oxf. 1984.

20241 SCOTT (PETER). The Eye of the Wind. Rev. edn 1977.

20242 —— Sir Peter Scott at 80: A Retrospective. Gloucester. 1989.

4. ENVIRONMENTALISM

20243 BASSET (PHILLIPPA) *comp.* Lists of Historical Records of Environmental Organisations. Birm./Reading. 1980.

20244 BARBER (MICHAEL J. C.). Directory for the Environmental Organisations in Britain and Ireland 1986–7. 1986.

20245 LOWE (PHILIP) *and* GOYDER (JANE). Environmental Groups in Politics. 1983.

20246 KIMBER (R. H.) *and* RICHARDSON (J. J.) *eds.* Campaigning for the Environment. 1974.

20247 BROOKES (S. K.) *and* RICHARDSON (J. J.). 'The Environmental Lobby in Britain'. *Parl. Affs* 28 (1975), 312–28.

20248 BROOKES (S. K.), JORDAN (A. G.), KIMBER (R. H.), *and* RICHARDSON (J. J.). 'The Growth of the Environment as a Political Issue in Britain'. *Brit. J. Pol. Sci.* 6 (1976), 245–55.

20249 LOWE (PHILIP). 'Amenity and Equality: A Review of Local Environmental Pressure Groups in Britain'. *Environment and Planning A.* 9 (1977), 35–58.

20250 BROWN (MICHAEL) *and* MAY (JOHN). The Greenpeace Story. 1989.

5. LAND USE

20251 JONES (JOHN OWEN) *ed.* Land Use Planning: The Methodology of Choice: A Compilation of Review Articles and Annotated Bibliography. Slough. 1972.

20252 LONDON UNIVERSITY (UNIVERSITY COLLEGE). CENTRE FOR URBAN STUDIES. Land Use Planning and the Social Sciences: A Selected Bibliography. Literature on Town and Country Planning and Related Social Studies in Great Britain, 1930–63. 1964. Supplement. 1970.

20253 DENMAN (D. R.) *et al.* Bibliography of Rural Land Economy and Land Ownership, 1900–1957: A Full List of Works Relating to the British Isles and Selected Works from the United States and Western Europe. Camb. 1958.

20254 BEST (ROBIN HEWITSON). The Major Land uses of Great Britain: An Evaluation of the Conflicting Records and Estimates of Land Utilization since 1900. Ashford. 1959.

20255 BEST (ROBIN HEWITSON) *and* COPPOCK (JOHN TERENCE). The Changing use of Land in Britain. 1962.

20256 —— Land for New Towns: A Study of Land Use, Densities, and Agricultural Displacement. 1964. [TCPA.].

20257 BEST (ROBIN HEWITSON) *and* CHAMPION (A. G.). Regional Conversions of Agricultural Land to Urban Use in England and Wales, 1945–1967. 1969.

Mentions book with Rogers under 'Rural Life'.

20258 DAY (HENRY ALBERT). The Land Question Solved! 1919.

20259 STAPLEDON (*Sir* REGINALD GEORGE) *ed.* A Survey of the Agricultural and Waste Lands of Wales. 1936. [For the Cahn Hill Improvement Scheme.].

20260 STAMP (*Sir* LAURENCE DUDLEY). The Land of Britain: Its use and misuse. 3rd enlgd edn 1962.

20261 INSTITUTE OF BRITISH GEOGRAPHERS. Land Use and Resources: Studies in Applied Geography: A Memorial Volume to Sir Dudley Stamp. 1968.

20262 HALL (PETER GEOFFREY) *ed.* Land Values: The Report of the Proceedings of a Colloquium Held in London on March 13 and 14, 1965 under the Auspices of the Acton Society Trust. 1965.

20263 COX (ANDREW). Adversary Politics and Land: The Conflict over Land and Property Policy in Post-War Britain. Camb. 1984.

20264 LEAN (WILLIAM) *and* GOODALL (BRIAN). Aspects of Land Economics. 1966.

20265 LEAN (WILLIAM). Economics of Land Use Planning—Urban and Regional. 1969.

20266 DENMAN (DONALD ROBERT). Land in the Market: A Fresh Look at Property, Land and Prices. 1964. [IEA.].

20267 DENMAN (DONALD ROBERT), ROBERTS (ROBERT ALUN), *and* SMITH (H. J. F.). Commons and Village Greens: A Study in Land Use, Conservation and Management Based on a National Survey of Commons in England and Wales, 1961–1966. 1967. [Financed by the Nuffield Foundation.].

20268 LAND USE: Pamphlet: U.K. 1958 M. of Ag., F. & F. Warwickshire: A Study of the Loss of Agricultural Land for Urban Development. 1958.

20269 PANORAMA [published by the Isle of Thanet Geographical Association], vol. 10. [The first twenty-four published land use maps.]. 1964.

20270 HEALEY (P.). Local Plans in British Land Use Planning. Oxf. 1983.

20271 COLEMAN (ALICE M.). Land Use Survey Handbook: An Explanation of the Second Land Use Survey of Britain. . . 4th edn 1965.

20272 SCOTLAND. 1962. Development plans. 1962.

20273 —— (a) Areas of Great Landscape Value.

20274 —— (b) Tourist Development Proposals. Edin. 1962.

20275 READ (COLIN). Changes in the Settlement Pattern and Land Use in the Solihull District of Warwickshire since 1945. 1967.

20276 STABLER (MICHAEL). Agricultural Economics and Land Use. 1973.

20277 McCULLOCH (F. J.) *et al.* Land Use in an Urban Environment: A General View of Town and Country Planning. L/pool. 1961.

20278 LOVEJOY (DEREK) *ed.* Land Use and Landscape Planning. Aylesbury. 1973.

20279 INSTITUTE OF TERRESTRIAL ECOLOGY, NATIONAL ENVIRONMENT RESEARCH COUNCIL. Upland Land Use in England and Wales. 1978.

20280 STAMP (L. DUDLEY) *ed.* The Land of Britain. The Report of the Land Utilisation Survey of Britain. 1937.

20281 DOUGLAS (ROY IAN). Land, People and Politics: A History of the Land Question in the United Kingdom 1878–1952. 1976.

20282 COPPOCK (JOHN TERENCE). The Geographer and the Use of Land. Edin. 1966. [Inaugural lecture.].

20283 —— Review of United Kingdom Statistical Sources. Vol. viii: John Coppock. Land Use: L. F. Gebbett, Town and Country Planning. Oxf. 1978.

20284 COPPOCK (JOHN TERENCE) *and* SEWELL (W. R. DERRICK) *eds.* Spatial Dimensions of Public Policy. Oxf. 1976.

20285 CLARK (COLIN GRANT). Population Growth and Land Use. 1967. 2nd edn 1977.

20286 —— The Value of Agricultural Land. Oxf. 1973.

20287 LINDSEY COUNTY COUNCIL. Disused Railways in Lindsey: Policy for After-Use. Lincoln. 1971.

20288 HOWAT (BILL). Policy Planning and the First Regional Reports in Scotland. 1979.

20289 WILKINSON (MIKE). Regional Reports and Structure Plans in Scotland. 1979.

20290 BALCHIN (PAUL N.) and KIEVE (JEFFREY LAWRENCE). Urban Land Economics. 1977.

20291 HARRISON (ANTHONY J.). Economics and Land Use Planning. 1977.

20292 CRUICKSHANK (J. G.). 'Value of Land'. *Geog. Mag.* xlvi (1974), 684–91.

20293 NICHOLLS (D. C.). 'Towards a Rational Land Policy'. *Town & Country Plan.* 43 (1975), 168–70.

20294 THORPE (H.). 'Homely Allotment: From Rural Dole to Urban Amenity: A Neglected Aspect of Urban Land Use'. *Geog.* 60 (1975), 169–83.

20295 TIVY (JOY). 'Britain's One-Third of Waste Land'. *Geog. Mag.* 47 (1975), 314–19.

20296 TOWN AND COUNTRY PLANNING ASSOCIATION. 'To Mr John Silkin: Statement on the White Paper on Land'. *Town & Country Plan.* 43 (1975), 230–4.

20297 FORDHAM (RICHARD CHARLES). Measurement of Urban Land Use. Camb. 1974.

20298 —— 'Urban Land Use Change in the United Kingdom During the Second Half of the Twentieth Century'. *Urb. Studs* 12 (1975), 71–84.

20299 WESTERGAARD (JOHN HARALD). 'Land Use Planning since 1951: The Legislative and Administrative Framework in England and Wales'. *Town Planning Rev.* xxxv(3) (1964), 219–37.

20300 OXENHAM (JOHN RUDOLPH). Reclaiming Derelict Land. 1966.

20301 U.K. 1963. MHLG. New Life for Dead Lands: Derelict Acres Reclaimed. 1963.

20302 BARR (J.). Derelict Britain. Harmondsworth. 1969.

20303 WALLWORK (K.). Derelict Land. Newton Abbot. 1974.

20304 SYMONS (L. T.). Land Use in Northern Ireland. 1969.

6. LANDSCAPE

20305 GOULD (J. D.). 'Landscape and the Machine: A Comment'. *Econ. Hist. Rev.* S2 27 (1974), 455–60.

20306 ASTON (MICHAEL) and BOND (JAMES). The Landscape of Towns. 1976.

20307 CULLEN (GORDON). Townscape. 1961.

20308 JOHNS (EWART). British Townscapes. 1965.

20309 POCOCK (DOUGLAS CHARLES DAVID) and HUDSON (RAY). Images of the Urban Environment. 1978.

20310 TANDY (CLIFF). Landscape of Industry . . . with a section on Hydrology by Peter Nelson. 1975.

20311 —— *Cons. ed.* Handbook of Urban Landscape. 1972.

20312 Y.H.A. (England and Wales). Landscape and Forestry in Mid-Wales: A Land Use Survey. 1974.

20313 MACEWEN (MALCOLM) ed. Future Landscapes. 1976.

20314 CONZEN (M. R. G.). The Urban Landscape: Historical Development and Management. *Ed.* by J. W. R. Whiteland. 1981.

20315 JELLICOE (GEOFFREY ALAN). Motopia: A Study in the Evolution of Urban Landscapes. 1961.

20316 —— Studies in Landscape Design. 1960.

20317 CHADWICK (GEORGE F.). The Park and the Town: Public Landscape in the 19th and 20th Centuries. NY 1966.

20318 TURNOR (CHRISTOPHER REGINALD). The Smaller English House, 1500–1939. 1952.

20319 COLVIN (HOWARD MONTAGU) and HARRIS (J.) eds. The Country-Seat: Studies in the History of the British Country House. 1970.

20320 WILLIAMS (S.). 'Arts of a New Town'. *Contemp. Rev.* ccvii (1965), 99–104.

20321 NAIRN (IAN). Britain's Changing Towns. 1967.

20322 CROWE (SYLVIA). Garden Design. 1958.

20323 HARVEY (S.) and RETTIG (S.) eds. Fifty Years of Landscape Design, 1934–1984. 1985.

20324 BROWN (JANE) ed. The Art and Architecture of English Gardens: Designs for the Garden from the Collection of the Royal Institute of British Architects, 1609 to the Present Day. 1989.

7. PLANNING AND THE LAW

20325 CLARKE (JOHN JOSEPH). Outlines of the Law of Housing and Planning, Including Public Health, Highways and the Acquisition of Land. 1933. 2nd edn 1934. [Retitled 'The Law of Housing and Planning'. 3rd edn 1936. 4th edn 1937; retitled 'Law of Housing and Planning, and allied subjects'. 5th edn 1949.].

20326 —— An Introduction to Planning, with Reference to the Town and Country Planning Act, 1947. 1948.

20327 —— A Synopsis of the Town and Country Planning Act, 1947. 1949.

20328 —— [An Introduction to Planning.]. Planning Land. An Introduction Including the Acts of 1953 and 1954. 2nd edn 1955.

20329 FRANK (D. G. H.) and SEWARD (G. W.). The Enforcement of Planning Control under the Town and Country Planning Act. 1947.

20330 HARGREAVES (ANTHONY DALZELL). An Introduction to the Principles of Land Law: . . . 4th edn by George Grove and J. F. Garner. 1963.

20331 REISS (RICHARD LEOPOLD). The Town-Planning Handbook—Including Full Text of the Town-Planning–Consolidating Act, 1925. 1926.

20332 KELSALL (ROGER KEITH). Citizens' Guide to the New Town and Country Planning. Oxf. 1949.

20333 HEAP (DESMOND). On the Town and Country Planning Act. 1954.

20334 —— An Outline of the New Planning Law. Being an Analysis of the Town and Country Planning Act 1947 . . . Together with the New Towns Act, 1946, and the Licensing Planning (Temporary Provisions) Acts, 1945 and 1946. 1949.

20335 —— Encyclopaedia of the Law of Planning. 1949.

20336 —— Encyclopedia of the Law of Town and Country Planning. 1959+.

20337 —— An Outline of the New Planning Law. 6th edn 1973.

20338 —— An Outline of Planning Law. 3rd edn 1960. 4th edn 1963. 5th edn 1969.

20339 CLARKE (JOHN JOSEPH). The Gist of Planning Law: A Guide to the Town and Country Planning Acts, 1962 and 1963 and Cognate Legislation, with Comparative Index. 1964.

20340 —— Town and Country Planning Act. 1932.

20341 HEAP (DESMOND) ed. Introducing the Land Commission Act, 1967: The Book of Lectures. 1967.

20342 HARRIS (BRYAN) and NUTLEY (W. G.). Betterment Levy and the Land Commission. 1967.

20343 HILL (HAROLD ARTHUR). Town and Country Planning Acts. 5th edn by Charles Fay and Michael Rich, assisted by Francis Daly and John Grove. 1967.

20344 LAMB (PERCY CHARLES) et al. The Law and Practice of Town and Country Planning. 1951.

20345 JUSTICE. COMMITTEE ON ADMINISTRATIVE LAW. Compensation for Compulsory Acquisition and Remedies for Planning Restrictions: A Report of a Sub-Committee of the Committee on Administrative Law. 1969.

20346 KERRIGAN (D. P.) and JAMES (J. D.). The Town and Country Planning Act, 1954, with a General Introduction and Annotations. 1955.

20347 GARNER (JOHN FRANCIS). Slum Clearance and Compensation. 1960. 2nd edn 1965.

20348 —— An Englishman's Home is his Castle? Nottingham. 1966. [Inaugural lecture.].

20349 —— The Public Control of Land. 1956.

20350 DAVIES (MAURICE ROBERT RUSSELL). Principles and Practice of Planning, Compulsory Purchase and Rating Law. 1956.

20351 —— The Law of Burial, Cremation and Exhumation. 1956.

20352 —— The Law of Road Traffic. 2nd edn 1957. 3rd edn 1961.

20353 LAWRANCE (DAVID MALCOLM). Compulsory Purchase and Compensation: An Outline of the Law Governing the Compulsory Acquisition of Land for Public Purposes . . . 4th edn 1967.

20354 BOYNTON (JOHN KEYWORTH). Compulsory Purchase and Compensation: A Practical Guide to the Law. 1964.

20355 SCOTLAND. 1963. Land Compensation (Scotland) Act, 1963. Table of comparison showing how earlier enactments are dealt with in the Act. Edin. 1963.

20356 POOLEY (BEVERLEY J.). The Evolution of British Planning Legislation. Ann Arbor, Mich. 1960.

20357 TELLING (ARTHUR EDWARD). Planning Law and Procedure. 5th edn 1977. With R. M. C. Duxbury. 7th edn 1986.

20358 RATCLIFFE (JOHN). An Introduction to Town and Country Planning. 1974. Repr. 1975.

20359 McLARTY (MALCOLM RONALD) ed. A Source Book and History of Administrative Law in Scotland by Various Authors. 1956. [Ch. by W. Gordon, Housing and Town Planning.].

20360 BLUNDELL (LIONEL ALLEYNE) and DOBRY (GEORGE). Planning Appeals and Inquiries. 2nd edn by Paul Rose and Michael Barnes. 1970. Earlier edn 1963.

20361 BLUNDELL (LIONEL ALLEYNE), DOBRY (GEORGE), and CAWS (K. B.). Town and Country Planning. 1963.

20362 BURTON (ANTHONY W.) and JOHNSON (ROBINA). Public Participation in Planning: A Review of Experience in Scotland. Glasg. 1976.

20363 U.K. 1942: MINISTRY OF WORKS AND PLANNING. Final Report of the Expert Committee on Compensation and Betterment. Cmnd 6386. 1942. [Uthwatt Report.].

20364 LONG (JOYCE R.) ed. The Wythall Inquiry: A Planning Test Case, with an Introduction by P. J. O. Self. 1961.

20365 U.K. People and Planning. Report of the Committee on Public Participation in Planning. 1969. [Skeffington Report.]

20366 U.K. MINISTRY OF HOUSING AND LOCAL GOVERNMENT. Betterment Levy: An Explanatory Memorandum on Part 3 of the Land Commission Act. 1967.

20367 —— Land Commission Act, 1967: A Guide for Builders and Developers on Betterment Levy. 1967.

20368 —— Land Commission Act, 1967: A Guide for Estate Agents and Surveyors on Betterment Levy. 1967.

20369 —— The Land Commission and You. 1967.

20370 U.K. DEPARTMENT OF THE ENVIRONMENT. Community Land Act, 1975. 1976.

20371 —— The Community Land Scheme. Booklet 1: An Introduction. 1976; Booklet 2: Planning Applications and Permissions for Relevant Development. 1976.

20372 U.K. WELSH OFFICE. 1973. Community Ownership of Development Land in Wales: Summary Consultation Document. Cardiff. 1975.

20373 FERRIS (JOHN). Participation in Urban Planning: The Barnsbury Case: A Study of Environmental Improvement in London. 1972.

20374 HAAR (CHARLES MONROE) ed. Law and Land: Anglo-American Planning Practice. Cambridge, Mass. 1964.

20375 —— Land Planning Law in a Free Society: A Study of the British Town and Country Planning Act. Cambridge, Mass. 1951.

20376 BRYAN (*Sir* ANDREW MEIKLE). Planning Permission and the Place of the Public Enquiry in the Development of Mineral Resources in Britain: Problems of Potash Extraction in Yorkshire. 1971. [Reprinted from Transactions of the Inst. of Mining and Metallurgy.].

8. THEORISTS

20377 DAY (M.) *and* GARSTANG (K.). 'Socialist Theories and Sir Raymond Unwin'. *Town & Country Plan.* 43 (1975), 346–9.

20378 LESSER (W.). 'Patrick Geddes: The Practical Visionary'. *Town Plan. Rev.* 45 (1974), 311–27.

20379 UNWIN (*Sir* RAYMOND). The Legacy of Raymond Unwin: A Human Pattern for Planning. *Ed. and introd.* by Walter Creese. Camb., Mass. 1967.

20380 —— Town Planning in Practice: An Introduction to the Art of Designing Cities and Suburbs. 2nd edn 1932.

20381 GEDDES (*Sir* PATRICK). Cities in Evolution: An Introduction to the Town Planning Movement and to the Study of Civics: With a New Introduction by Percy Johnson-Marshall. 1968.

20382 ABERCROMBIE (*Sir* L. PATRICK). 'A Civic Society: An Outline of its Scope, Formation and Functions'. *Town Plan. Rev.* viii (Apr. 1920), 79–92.

20383 MELLER (HELEN ELIZABETH). Patrick Geddes: Social Evolutionist and City Planner. 1990.

9. CONSERVATION

20384 LANCASTER (OSBERT). 'The Future of the Past: Some Thoughts on Preservation'. *J. Roy. Inst. Brit. Arch.* 60 3rd ser. (1953), 175–9.

20385 MILLER (M. K.). 'Letchworth Conservation Area'. *Town & Country Plan.* 43 (1975), 253–5.

20386 MILLWAY (B.). 'The Town is a Museum: King's Lynn, Norfolk'. *Can. Geog. J.* 91 (1975), 49–55.

20387 —— 'European Architectural Heritage Year 1975—a Symposium'. *Town Plan. Rev.* (a special issue) 46 (1975), 355–480.

20388 FRICKER (L. J.). 'Historic Gardens and Landscapes: The Conservation of a National Asset'. *Town Plan. Rev.* 46 (1975), 407–14.

20389 TASKER (G. H.). 'Chester—The Challenge of Change'. *Town Plan. Rev.* 37(3) (1966), 189–206.

20390 TARN (J. N.). 'Derbyshire Heritage: The Conservation of Ordinariness'. *Town Plan. Rev.* 46 (1975), 451–65.

20391 WHITLOCK (R.). 'Conservation by Design: An Exercise in Rural Co-operation'. *Town & Country Plan.* 43 (1975), 260–3.

20392 SKINNER (DAVID N.). A Situation Report on Green Belts in Scotland. Edin. 1976.

20393 HENDRY (JOHN). 'Conservation in Northern Ireland'. *Town Plan. Rev.* 48 (1977), 373–88.

10. ECONOMICS OF URBAN AREAS

20394 GOODALL (BRIAN). The Economics of Urban Areas. 1972.

20395 BUTTON (KENNETH JOHN). Urban Economics: Theory and Policy. 1976.

20396 —— The Economics of Urban Transport. Farn. 1977. Repr. 1978.

20397 HARLOE (MICHAEL) ed. Captive Cities: Studies in the Political Economy of Cities and Regions. 1977.

20398 JACOBS (JANE). The Economy of Cities. Lond. 1970. Harmondsworth. 1972.

20399 RICHARDSON (HARRY WARD). The Economics of Urban Size. Farn. 1973. Repr. 1975.

20400 —— The New Urban Economics and Alternatives. 1977.

20401 RICHARDSON (HARRY WARD), VIPOND (JOAN), *and* FURBEY (ROBERT). Housing and Urban Spatial Structure: A Case Study. Farn. 1975.

20402 LICHFIELD (NATHANIEL). Economics of Planned Development. 1956.

20403 —— Cost-benefit Analysis in Urban Redevelopment. 1962.

20404 —— Cost-benefit Analysis in Town Planning: A Case Study of Cambridge. Camb. 1966.

20405 PARKER (HERBERT RONALD). Paying for Urban Development. 1959. [Fabian pamphlet.].

20406 KIRWAN (RICHARD MARTIN) *and* MARTIN (D. B.). The Economics of Urban Residential Renewal and Improvement. 1972. [CES Working Paper 77.].

II. Geography

20407 FREEMAN (THOMAS WALTER). Geography and Planning. 1958.

20408 BALE (J. R.). 'Towards a Definition of the Industrial Estate: A Note on a Neglected Aspect of Urban Geography'. *Geog.* 59 (1974), 31–4.

20409 BECKINSALE (ROBERT PERCY) *and* HOUSTON (JAMES MACINTOSH). Urbanization and its Problems. Essays in Honour of Edmund W. Gilbert. 1968.

20410 CARTER (HAROLD). The Study of Urban Geography. 1972. 2nd edn 1975.

20411 HERBERT (DAVID T.). Urban Geography: A Social Perspective. Newton Abbot. 1972.

20412 THORPE (DAVID). The Geographer and Urban Studies. Durham. 1966.

20413 JONES (EMRYS). Towns and Cities. 1966. Repr. 1969.

20414 —— The City in Geography: An Inaugural Lecture . . . at L.S.E. 1962.

20415 JOHNSON (JAMES HENRY). Urban Geography: An Introductory Analysis. 2nd edn 1972. Repr. 1976.

G. FOOD AND LIVING STANDARDS

I. General Consumerism

20416 BURNETT (JOHN). A History of the Cost of Living. Harmondsworth. 1969.

20417 U.K. COUNCIL FOR ART AND INDUSTRY. The Working Class Home: Its Furnishing and Equipment. 1937.

20418 U.K. MINISTRY OF LABOUR. Enquiry into Working-Class Expenditure. 1937.

20419 LIVERPOOL UNIVERSITY SOCIAL SCIENCE DEPARTMENT. (Statistics Division). New Merseyside Series 12—The Cost of Living of Representative Working Class Families. L/pool. 1941.

20420 JOHNSON (PAUL). Saving and Spending: The Working Class Economy in Britain 1870–1939. Oxf. 1985.

20421 BANKS (JOSEPH AMBROSE). The English Middle-Class Concept of the Standard of Living and its Relation to Marriage and Family Size. 1952.

20422 JONES (DAVID CARADOG). The Cost of Living of a Sample of Middle-Class Families. 1928.

20423 LAMBERT (P.). Prix, Salaires et Coût de la Vie en Grande Bretagne. Liège. 1947.

20424 CLARK (COLIN GRANT). The Cost of Living. 1957.

20425 U.K. CENTRAL OFFICE OF INFORMATION. (Reference Division). The Standard of Living in Britain. 1965.

20426 U.K. MINISTRY OF SOCIAL SECURITY. Circumstances of Families: Report on an Enquiry by the Ministry of Pensions and National Insurance, with the Co-operation of the National Assistance Board, Subsequently Combined to form the Ministry of Social Security. 1967.

20427 GODFREY (H. R.). My Family Budget. 1941.

20428 MADGE (CHARLES HENRY). The War-Time Pattern of Saving and Spending. Camb. 1943.

20429 SCHULTZ (T.). 'Income, Family Structure and Food Expenditure before and after the War'. *Bull. Oxf. Inst. Stats* 24 (1962), 447–68.

20430 U.K. SOCIAL SURVEY. The British Household. 1948.

20431 U.K. MINISTRY OF LABOUR. Report of an Enquiry into Household Expenditure in 1953–1954. 1957.

20432 HOWE (JAMES RONALD). Two Parent Families: A Study of their Resources and Needs in 1968, 1969, 1970: An Analysis based on Family Expenditure Data. 1971.

20433 U.K. DEPARTMENT OF EMPLOYMENT. Family Expenditure Survey. [Pub. annually 1970–9.]. 1971–1980.

20434 U.K. CENTRAL STATISTICAL OFFICE. Estimates of household expenditure in the United Kingdom at current prices, 1970–1975: Comparison between the Family Expenditure Survey and National Accounts. 1977.

20435 ATKINSON (ANTHONY BARNES) *et al.* Parents and Children: Incomes in Two Generations. 1983.

20436 SEN (AMARTYA) *et al.* The Standard of Living: The Tanner Lectures. Camb. 1987.

20437 PREST (ALAN RICHMOND) *and* ADAMS (ARTHUR AVERY). Consumers' Expenditures in the United Kingdom, 1900–1919. Camb. 1954.

20438 CARR-SAUNDERS (ALEXANDER MORRIS) *et al.* Consumer's Co-operation in Great Britain: An Examination of the British Co-operative Movement. 1938.

20439 STONE (*Sir* JOHN RICHARD NICHOLAS) *et al.* The Measurement of Consumers' Expenditure and Behaviour in the United Kingdom, 1920–1938. 2 vols. Camb. 1954–66.

20440 —— 'The Changing Patterns of Consumption'. Ch. in Problems of Economic Dynamics and Planning: Essays in Honour of Michal Kalecki. Oxf. 1966.

20441 —— Consumers' Wants and Expenditures: A Survey of British Studies since 1945. Camb. 1961.

20442 DAMERON (KENNETH) *ed.* Consumer Problems in Wartime. 1944.

20443 KEMSLEY (WILLIAM FREDERICK FENN). Consumers' Expenditure Surveys: Reports of Four Enquiries Carried out 1956–1958. 1960. [Social Survey.].

20444 GRASSAM (PETER BATES). The Voice of the Consumer: Some Aspects of the Relations between Electricity Boards and their Consumers. 1961.

20445 FULOP (CHRISTINA). Consumers in the Market: A Study of Choice, Competition and Sovereignty. 1967.

20446 —— Retailing and the Consumer. 1968. 2nd edn 1970.

20447 —— Revolution in Retailing. 1961.

20448 —— The Consumer Movement and the Consumer. 1977.

20449 —— Advertising, Competition and Consumer Behaviour: Public Policy and the Market. 1981.

20450 LIPPITT (VERNON G.). Determinants of Consumer Demand for House Furnishings and Equipment. 1959.

20451 BALL (R. J.) and DRAKE (PAMELA S.). 'The Impact of Credit Control on Consumer Durable Spending in the United Kingdom, 1957–1961'. *Rev. of Econ. Studs* 30 (1963), 181–94.

20452 DEATON (ANGUS S.). 'Analysis of Consumer Demand in the United Kingdom, 1900–1970'. *Econometrica* 43 (1974), 341–67.

20453 —— Models and Projections of Demand in Post-War Britain. 1975.

20454 —— *ed.* Essays in the Theory and Measurement of Consumer Behaviour in Honour of Sir Richard Stone. Camb. 1981.

20455 SAMUEL (SUSAN) *comp.* Consumer Bibliography. 1976.

20456 HIRST (I. R. C.) and REEKIE (W. DUNCAN) *eds.* The Consumer Society. 1977.

20457 BORRIE (GORDON JOHNSON) and DIAMOND (AUBREY LIONEL). The Consumer, Society and the Law. Harmondsworth. 1964. 3rd edn 1973.

20458 PYATT (FRANK GRAHAM). Priority Patterns and the Demand for Household Durable Goods. Camb. 1964.

20459 ALLEN (DAVID ELLISTON). British Tastes: An Enquiry into the Likes and Dislikes of the Regional Consumer. 1968.

20460 CONSUMER COUNCIL. Annual Report 1963/4–1970. 1964–71.

20461 —— Consumer Consultative Machinery in the Nationalised Industries: A Consumer Council Study. 1968.

20462 ABRAMS (MARK). The Teenage Consumer. 1959.

20463 —— The Elderly Consumer. 1982.

20464 ROBERTS (EIRLYS RHIWEN CADWALADR). Consumers. 1966.

20465 WRAITH (RONALD EDWARD). The Consumer Cause: A Short Account of its Organisation, Power and Importance. 1976.

20466 MARTIN (JOHN) and SMITH (GEORGE WILLIAM). The Consumer Interest. 1968.

20467 EHRENBERG (ANDREW SAMUEL CHRISTOPHER) and PYATT (FRANK GRAHAM) *eds.* Consumer Behaviour: Selected Readings. Harmondsworth. 1971.

20468 HUDSON (KENNETH). Food, Clothes and Shelter: 20th Century Industrial Archaeology. 1978.

20469 —— The Archaeology of the Consumer Society: The Second Industrial Revolution in Britain. 1983.

20470 PICKERING (JOHN FREDERICK) *et al.* The Acquisition of Consumer Durables: A Cross-Sectional Investigation. 1977.

20471 ADLER (MAX K.). Marketing and Market Research. 1967.

20472 —— *ed.* Leading Cases in Market Research. 1971.

20473 CORLEY (T. A. B.). 'Consumer Marketing in Britain, 1914–60'. *Bus. Hist.* 29 (1987), 65–83.

20474 MITCHELL (JEREMY) *ed.* Marketing and the Consumer Movement. 1978.

20475 DAVENPORT-HINES (RICHARD PETER) *ed.* Markets and Bagmen: Studies in the History of Marketing and British Industrial Performance 1830–1939. Aldershot. 1986.

20476 ROBERTSON (ANDREW). Strategic Marketing: A Response to Consumerism. 1978.

20477 MAYNARD (HAROLD H.) and DAMERON (KENNETH). Retail Marketing and Merchandising. 1938.

20478 LEVY (HERMANN). Retail Trade Associations: A New Form of Monopolist Organisation in Britain: A Report to the Fabian Society. 1942.

20479 —— The Shops of Britain: A Study of Retail Distribution. 1948.

20480 DAVIS (DOROTHY). A History of Shopping. 1966.

20481 MILLAR (ROBERT). The Affluent Sheep. 1963.

20482 ROBERTSON (SHEILA). Shopping in History. Hove. 1984.

20483 MACKEITH (MARGARET). The History and Conservation of Shopping Arcades. 1986.

20484 CROSSLEY (ALEC). Shopping in Oxford: A Brief History. Oxf. 1983.

20485 DAVIES (ROSS L.) and REYNOLDS (JONATHAN). The Development of Teleshopping and Teleservices. 1983.

20486 Glasgow: Report on Aspects of Future Shopping Provision. Glasgow. 1971.

20487 GUNDRY (ELIZABETH). A Foot in the Door: An Exposé of High Pressure Sales Methods. 1965.

20488 TURNER (HARRY). The Gentle Art of Salesmanship. 1985.

20489 STEVENSON (ALAN LESLIE). The Shops Acts, 1912–1936, and the Factories Act, 1937. 1938.

20490 —— The Shops Act, 1950, and the Factories Act, 1937, as amended by the Factories Act, 1948, so far as it relates to the powers and duties of local authorities. 1952.

20491 REGAN (PAUL). 'The 1986 Shops Bill'. *Parl. Affs* 41 (1988), 218–35.

20492 GOODE (ROYSTON MILES). Hire-Purchase Law and Practice. 1962.

20493 BROWN (HAROLD JOHN). The Practitioner's Guide to Hire-Purchase Cases. 1965.

20494 HOGAN (THOMAS BRIAN). The Hire-Purchase Act of 1965 with annotations. 1965.

20495 DIAMOND (AUBREY LIONEL). Introduction to Hire Purchase Law. 1967.

2. NUTRITION AND DIET

20496 McCARRISON (Sir ROBERT). Nutrition and Health . . . 1944. 3rd rev. edn 1961.

20497 —— Studies in Deficiency Disease. 1921.

20498 M'GONIGLE (GEORGE CUTHBERT MURA). Nutrition: The Position in England Today. 1936.

20499 ORR (JOHN BOYD) Baron Boyd-Orr. Feast and Famine: The Wonderful World of Food. 1959.

20500 —— Food and the People. 1943.

20501 —— Food, Health and Income: Report of a Survey of Adequacy of Diet in Relation to Income. 1936. 2nd edn 1937.

20502 —— Food: The Foundation of World Unity. 1948.

20503 —— The Nation's Food. 1944. [Labour's Nutrition Policy.].

20504 —— The National Food Supply and its Influence on Public Health. 1934.

20505 —— Not Enough Food for Fitness. 1937.

20506 —— Nutrition in War. 1940.

20507 ORR (JOHN BOYD) Baron Boyd-Orr, and LUBBOCK (DAVID). Feeding the People in War-Time. 1940.

20508 McCOLLUM (ELMER VERNER). A History of Nutrition: The Sequence of Ideas in Nutrition Investigations. Boston, Mass. 1957.

20509 LAMBERT (ROYSTON). Nutrition in Britain, 1950–1960: A Critical Discussion of the Standards and Findings of the National Food Survey. Welwyn. 1964.

20510 BURNETT (JOHN). Plenty and Want: A Social History of Diet in England from 1815 to the Present Day. 1966. 3rd edn 1989.

20511 ROLLESTON (Sir HUMPHRY DAVY) and MONCRIEFF (ALAN AIRD) eds. Diet in Health and Disease. 1939.

20512 BRITISH MEDICAL ASSOCIATION. Nutrition and the Public Health: Medicine, Agriculture, Industry, Education. 1939.

20513 U.K. MINISTRY OF FOOD. Food and Nutrition. Vols. 1–7. 1947–1952.

20514 —— Food Consumption Levels in the United Kingdom, 1947, 1949. 1947, 1949.

20515 —— Wartime Diet for Growing Children. 1942.

20516 —— Wise Eating in Wartime. 1942.

20517 —— Your Baby's Food in Wartime. 1942.

20518 —— The World Food Shortage. 1946.

20519 —— (Scientific Advisor's Division). Manual of Nutrition. 1945. 3rd edn 1953. [By Magnus Pike.].

20520 U.K. MINISTRY OF HEALTH. (Advisory Committee on Nutrition). Report to the Minister of Health on Diets in Poor Law Children's Homes. 1934.

20521 CHILDREN'S NUTRITIONAL COUNCIL. (Aberdeen Branch). A Budgetary and Dietary Survey of Low Income Families: Aberdeen, August 1942. Aberd. 1943.

20522 BULKLEY (MILDRED EMILY). The Feeding of School-children. 1914.

20523 WILLIAMS (EDDIE). The Nutrition of Children. Card. 1939.

20524 —— School Milk and Meals. 1944.

20525 —— School Dinners for all the World's Children. 1945.

20526 GREEN (MARJORIE HELEN). Malnutrition among Schoolchildren. 1938.

20527 —— Nutrition and Local Government: What your Local Authority Can Do. 1938.

20528 CLARK (FREDERICK LE GROS). A Social History of the School Meals Service. 1948.

20529 BISSET (LIZ) and COUSSINS (JEAN). Badge of Poverty: A New Look at the Stigma attached to Free School Meals. 1982. [Child Poverty Action Group pub.].

20530 LANG (TIM). Now You See Them, Now You Don't: A Report on the Fate of School Meals and the Loss of 300,000 Jobs. Accrington. 1981.

20531 CLARK (FREDERICK LE GROS) and PIRIE (NORMAN WINGATE). Four Thousand Million Mouths: Scientific Humanism and the Shadow of World Hunger. 1951.

20532 SOUTAR (MARY STEWART) et al. Nutrition and the Size of the Family: Report on a New Housing Estate, 1939. Birm. 1942.

20533 ROWETT RESEARCH INSTITUTE. Family Diet and Health in Pre-war Britain: A Dietary and Clinical Survey: Report to the Carnegie United Kingdom Trust. Dunfermline. 1955.

20534 STEVEN (MAISIE). The Good Scots Diet: What Happened to it? Aberd. 1985.

20535 MEDICAL RESEARCH COUNCIL. (Special Report Series No. 289). Studies on Expenditure of Energy and Consumption of Food by Miners and Clerks, Fife 1952. 1955.

20536 U.K. MINISTRY OF FOOD. (National Food Survey Committee). The Urban Working Class Household Diet, 1940–1949. 1951.

20537 —— (National Food Survey Committee). Domestic Food Consumption and Expenditure. Annual reports 1950–5.

20538 U.K. MINISTRY OF AGRICULTURE, FISHERIES AND FOOD. Agricultural and Food Statistics: A Guide to Official Sources. 1969.

20539 —— Food Standards Committee: Report on Claims and Misleading Descriptions. 1966.

20540 VAN DEN BERGHS LIMITED. Getting the Most Out of Food: A Series of Studies on the Modern Approach to Feeding and Nutrition. 1965.

20541 YUDKIN (JOHN). This Nutrition Business. 1976.

20542 —— Nutrition. 1977.

20543 —— *Ed.* The Diet of Man: Needs and Wants: International Symposium . . . 1978.

20544 —— Pure, White and Deadly: The Problem of Sugar. 1972.

20545 —— Our Changing Fare. 1966.

20546 —— Changing Food Habits. 1964.

20547 YUDKIN (JOHN) *et al. eds.* Sugar: Chemical, Biological and Nutritional Aspects of Sucrose. 1971.

20548 DAVIDSON (*Sir* LEYBOURNE STANLEY PATRICK). Human Nutrition and Dietetics. 1959.

20549 OFFICE OF HEALTH ECONOMICS. Malnutrition in the 1960s? 1967.

20550 PANEL OF NUTRITION OF THE ELDERLY. A Nutrition Survey of the Elderly: Report . . . 1972.

20551 HOLLINGSWORTH (DOROTHY FRANCES). 'Nutritional Policies in Great Britain, 1939–46'. *Jnl Amer. Dietetic Assoc.* 23 (1947), 96–100.

20552 GREAVES (J. P.) *and* HOLLINGSWORTH (DOROTHY FRANCES). 'Trends in Food Consumption in the United Kingdom'. *World Rev. Nutrition & Diatetics* 6 (1966), 34–89.

20553 HOLLINGSWORTH (DOROTHY FRANCES) *and* RUSSELL (MARGARET) *eds.* Nutritional Problems in a Changing World. Barking. 1973.

20554 HOLMES (FREDERICK L.). 'The Transformation of the Science of Nutrition'. *J. Hist. Biol.* 7 (1975), 135–44.

20555 ODDY (DEREK) *and* MILLER (DEREK) *eds.* The Making of the Modern British Diet. 1976.

20556 —— Diet and Health in Modern Britain. 1985.

20557 MOUNT (JAMES LAMBERT). The Food and Health of Western Man. 1975.

20558 McLAREN (DONALD STEWART) *ed.* Nutrition in the Community. 1976.

20559 —— Nutrition and its Disorders. Edin. 1972.

20560 BENDER (ARNOLD ERIC). Food Processing and Nutrition. 1978.

20561 —— A Dictionary of Nutrition and Food Technology. 1960. 5th edn 1982.

20562 WALKER (CAROLINE) *and* CANNON (GEOFFREY). The Food Scandal: What's Wrong with the British Diet and how to Put it Right. 1984. Rev. edn 1985.

20563 HARRIS (LESLIE JUNIUS). Vitamins in Theory and Practice. Camb./N.Y. 1935.

20564 —— Vitamins: A Digest of Current Knowledge . . . 1959.

20565 HUNTER (CAROL). Vitamins: What They Are and Why We Need Them. Wellingb. 1978.

20566 MERVYN (LEONARD) *comp.* The Dictionary of Vitamins: The Complete Guide to Vitamins and Vitamin Therapy. Wellingb. 1984.

20567 GREER (RITA). The Good Nutrients Guide: The Complete Handbook of Vitamins, Minerals and other Nutrients. 1985.

3. FOOD-GENERAL HISTORY

20568 SUTTON (DAVID CHRISTOPHER) *comp.* The History of Food: A Preliminary Bibliography of Printed Sources. Coventry. 1982.

20569 ROBERTSON (SHEILA). Food in History. Hove. 1983.

20570 WILSON (CONSTANCE ANNE). Food and Drink in Britain from the Stone Age to Recent Times. 1973. Harmondsworth. 1984.

20571 JOHNSON (JAMES P.). A Hundred Years Eating: Food, Drink, and Daily Diet in Britain since the Late 19th Century. Dublin. 1977.

20572 BARKER (THEODORE CARDWELL) *et al. eds.* Our Changing Fare: 200 Years of British Food Habits. 1966.

20573 DRUMMOND (*Sir* JACK CECIL) *and* WILBRAHAM (ANNE). The Englishman's Food: A History of Five Centuries of English Diet. 1939. Rev. with a new ch. by Dorothy Frances Hollingsworth. 1958.

20574 CHALMERS (ARCHIBALD KERR). Economy in Food during War. Glasg. 1915.

20575 LONDON COUNTY COUNCIL. (Education Officers Department). Economy in the Consumption of Food: Practical Hints on Catering for a Small Household in Wartime. 1917.

20576 HOPKINS (*Sir* FREDERICK GOWLAND). 'On the Choice of Food in War Time'. *J. State Medicine* July 1917, 193–202.

20577 CLYNES (J. R.). 'Food Control in War and Peace'. *Econ. J.* 30 (1920), 147–55.

20578 PROTHERO (ROWLAND EDMUND) *Lord Ernle.* 'The Food Campaign of 1916–1918'. *J. Roy. Agric. Soc. Eng.* 82 (1922), 1–48.

20579 BARNETT (L. MARGARET). British Food Policy in the First World War. Boston, Mass./Lond. 1985.

20580 MIDDLETON (*Sir* THOMAS HUDSON). Food Production in War. Oxf. 1923.

20581 BEVERIDGE (WILLIAM HENRY) *Baron.* British Food Control. 1928.

20582 ADDISON (CHRISTOPHER) *Viscount*. The Nation and its Food. 1929.

20583 JONES (*Sir* THOMAS GEORGE). The Unbroken Front: The British Ministry of Food, 1916–1944. 1944.

20584 HAMMOND (RICHARD JAMES). 'British Food Supplies, 1914–1939'. *Econ. Hist. Rev.* 16 (1946), 1–14.

20585 OLSON (MANCUR) *Jnr*. The Economics of Wartime Shortage: A History of British Food Supplies in the Napoleonic Wars and in World Wars One and Two. Durham, NC. 1963.

20586 CRAWFORD (*Sir* WILLIAM SMITH) *and* BROADLEY (*Sir* HERBERT). The People's Food. 1938.

20587 TITMUSS (RICHARD MORRIS) *and* CLARK (FREDERICK LE GROS). Our Food Problem: A Study of National Security. Harmondsworth. 1939.

20588 WALWORTH (GEORGE). Feeding the People in Peace and War. 1940.

20589 VERULAM (FRANK). Production for the People. 1940.

20590 DRIVER (CHRISTOPHER). The British at Table, 1940–1980. 1983.

20591 KITCHIN (ARTHUR HENDERSON) *and* PASSMORE (REGINALD). The Scotsman's Food. 1949.

20592 CURTIS-BENNETT (NOEL). The Food of the People. 1949.

20593 ARTER (WALLACE). 'Food from Airfields'. *Town and Country Planning* 21 (1953), 527–30.

20594 FENELON (KEVIN GERARD). Britain's Food Supplies. 1952.

20595 HAMMOND (RICHARD JAMES). Food. 2 vols. 1951–6.

20596 HARTLEY (DOROTHY). Food in England. 1954. 2nd edn 1979. Repr. 1985.

20597 WARDLE (CHRIS). Changing Food Habits in the United Kingdom. 1977.

20598 BARTY-KING (HUGH). Food for Man and Beast: The Story of the London Corn Trade Association, the London Cattle Food Association, and the Grain and Feed Trade Association, 1878–1978. 1978.

20599 TAYLOR (DEREK). Fortune, Fame and Folly: British Hotels and Catering from 1878 to 1978. 1977.

20600 ECONOMIC DEVELOPMENT COMMITTEE FOR FOOD MANUFACTURING. Food Statistics: A Guide to the Major Official and Unofficial U.K. Sources. 1968.

20601 FOOD QUALITY AND SAFETY. A Century of Progress: Proceedings of the symposium celebrating the centenary of the Sale of Food and Drugs Act, 1875, London, October 1975. 1976. [Chairman, Lord Zuckerman.].

20602 OVINGTON (JOHN DERRICK) *ed*. The Better Use of the World's Fauna for Food. 1963.

20603 REDMAYNE (PAUL). Britain's Food. 1963.

20604 HUXLEY (ELSPETH). Brave New Victuals: An Inquiry into Modern Food Production. 1965.

20605 COOPER (DEREK). The Bad Food Guide. 1967.

20606 McCULLOUGH (WINIFRED). The Shape of Food to Come. 1964.

20607 ALLEN (DAVID ELLISTON). British Tastes: An Enquiry into the Likes and Dislikes of the Regional Consumer. 1968.

20608 PIRIE (NORMAN WINGATE). Food Resources, Conventional and Novel. Harmondsworth. 1969.

20609 BRITISH MARKET RESEARCH BUREAU. Food: Facts and Fallacies. 1969.

20610 MELLANBY (KENNETH). Can Britain Feed Itself? 1975.

20611 GREEN (DANIEL). The Politics of Food. 1975.

20612 BENNETT (JON). The Hunger Machine: The Politics of Food. Camb. 1987. [Ch. 4 t.v. pub.].

20613 McLAUGHLIN (TERENCE). A Diet of Tripe: The Chequered History of Food Reform. Newton Abbot. 1978.

20614 CENTRE FOR AGRICULTURAL STRATEGY, UNIVERSITY OF READING. National Food Supply in the United Kingdom. Reading. 1979.

20615 CRITCHLEY (RON A.). United Kingdom Food Trends over the Last Decade. Rustington. 1977.

20616 FOOD AND FOODWAYS: EXPLORATIONS IN THE HISTORY AND CULTURE OF HUMAN NOURISHMENT. Vol. I– 1985–.

20617 MABEY (DAVID). In Search of Food: Traditional Eating and Drinking in Britain. 1978.

20618 MENNELL (STEPHEN). All Manners of Food: Eating and Taste in England and France from the Middle Ages to the Present. Oxf. 1985.

20619 RITSON (CHRISTOPHER) *et al*. *eds*. The Food Consumer. 1986.

20620 ACUMEN MARKETING GROUP. A Report on the Take Away Food Market in Britain. 1978.

20621 JUKES (DAVID J.). Food Legislation of the United Kingdom: A Concise Guide. 1984. 2nd edn 1987.

20622 CURRY (DAVID). The Food War, the European Community and the Battle for World Food Markets. 1982.

20623 MATHIAS (PETER). Retailing Revolution: A History of Multiple Retailing in the Food Trades Based upon the Allied Suppliers Group of Companies. 1967.

20624 HARDMAN (ROGER J.). The British Food Processing Industry. 1981.

20625 ASHBY (ANDREW W.). 'Britain's Food Manufacturing Industry and its Economic Development'. *J. Agric. Econ.* 29 (1978), 213–21.

20626 THOMPSON (JOHN K.). The Structure of Scottish Agriculture and Food Industries. Edin. 1978.

20627 BURNS (JIM) *et al*. *eds*. The Food Industry: Economics and Policies. 1983.

20628 PAINE (FRANK ALBERT) *ed*. Modern Processing, Packaging and Distribution Systems for Food. Glasg. 1987.

20629 SHEARD (PETER R.) *and* WINWOOD (ROBERT J.). A Guide to the British Food Manufacturing Industry. Bristol. 1986. 2nd edn 1988.

20630 SAVAGE (*Sir* WILLIAM GEORGE). The Bacteriological Examination of Food and Water. Camb. 1914. 2nd edn 1916.

20631 —— Food and Public Health. 1919.

20632 —— *et al.* The Bacteriology of Canned Meat and Fish. 1922.

20633 —— Canned Foods in Relation to Health. Camb. 1923.

20634 —— Food Poisoning and Food Infections. Camb. 1920.

20635 —— Report on the Methods Used for the Inspection of Canned Foods and their Reliability for this Purpose. 2 Pts., 1920, 1922.

20636 COOPER (ROBERT MONTAGUE HUNTE). The Danger of Food Contamination by Aluminium. 1931.

20637 FILBY (FREDERICK ARTHUR). A History of Food Adulteration and Analysis. 1934.

20638 ASHFORD (ETHEL BRIGHT) *and* SAVAGE (*Sir* WILLIAM GEORGE). The Food and Drugs Act, 1938. 1938.

20639 FRANCIS (CLARENCE). A History of Food and its Preservation: A Contribution to Civilisation. Princeton, NJ. 1937.

20640 BAUMGARTNER (JOHN GEORGE). Canned Foods: An Introduction to their Microbiology. 1943. 4th edn 1956, by Baumgartner and Albert Charles Hersom. 7th edn. Edin. 1980 by Hersom, under title, Canned Foods: Thermal Processing and Microbiology.

20641 MacINTOSH (R. W. D.). Frozen Foods: The Growth of an Industry. 1962.

20642 READER (W. J.). Birdseye: The Early Years. 1963.

20643 U.K. MINISTRY OF FOOD. Dehydration: U.K. Progress Reports, Scientific, Technical and Economic. 1943.

20644 SPICER (ARNOLD). Advances in Preconcentration and Dehydration of Foods. 1975.

20645 THORNE (STUART). The History of Food Preservation. 1986.

20646 PAULUS (INGEBORG). The Search for Pure Food: A Sociology of Legislation in Britain. 1974.

20647 WEBB (TONY). Food Irradiation in Britain? 1985.

20648 WEBB (TONY) *and* HENDERSON (ANGELA). Food Irradiation: Who Wants it? 1986.

4. FOODSTUFFS

(a) Milk

20649 CRICHTON-BROWNE (*Sir* JAMES). 'Milk and Health'. *Jnl State Medicine* (May 1918), 140–80.

20650 WHETHAM (EDITH HOLT). The London Milk Trade, 1900–1930. Reading. 1970.

20651 HARVEY (WILLIAM CLUNIE) *and* HILL (HARRY). Milk: Production and Control. 1936. 4th edn 1967.

20652 ENOCK (ARTHUR GUY). This Milk Business: A Study from 1895–1943. 1943.

20653 BARNES (F. A.). 'The Evolution of the Salient Patterns of Milk Production in England and Wales'. *Trans. Inst. Brit. Geog.* 25 (1958), 167–95.

20654 U.K. MINISTRY OF AGRICULTURE, FISHERIES AND FOOD. Machine Milking. 1959.

20655 —— The Milk Marketing Scheme, 1933 as Amended to June 27 1955. 1955.

20656 BAKER (STANLEY). Milk to Market: Forty Years of Milk Marketing. 1973.

20657 MANNING (PHYLLIS). A History of the National Investigation into the Economics of Milk Production, 1934–1951. Oxf. 1960.

20658 ROSCOE (BETTY JOAN). Economic Aspects of Milk Production in South West England, 1968–1969. 1970.

20659 WHETSTONE (LINDA). The Marketing of Milk: An Empirical Study of the Origins, Performance and Future of the Milk Marketing Board. 1970.

20660 FOOT (A. S.). 'Changes in Milk Production, 1930–70'. *Roy. Agric. Soc. J.* 131 (1970), 30–42.

20661 URQUHART (ROBERT). A History of the Scottish Milk Marketing Board. Paisley. 1979.

20662 WINTER (MICHAEL). 'Corporatism and Agriculture in the U.K.: The Case for the Milk Marketing Board'. *Sociologus Ruralis* 24 (1984), 106–19.

20663 GROVES (CHARLES RICHARD). The Marketing of Milk and Milk Products in the U.K.: A Review and Assessment. Ayr. 1982.

20664 GRAFTON GREEN (BRIGID). Milk for the Millions. 1983. [History of the Express Dairy Service.].

20665 SOPER (MICHAEL HENRY RAY). Dairy Farming and Milk Production. 1983.

20666 ROBINSON (KENNETH RICHARD) *ed.* Modern Dairy Technology. Vol. 1: Advances in Milk Processing. 1986.

20667 BELL (ROBERT WILLIAM). The History of the Jersey Cattle Society of the United Kingdom, 1878–1978. 1979.

(b) Meat

20668 FORSHAW (ALEC) *and* BERGSTROM (THEO). Smithfield: Past and Present. 1980.

20669 CAPIE (FORREST). The Demand for Meat in England and Wales 1920–1938. Coventry. 1974.

20670 —— 'Consumer Preference: Meat in England and Wales'. *Bull. Econ. Res.* 28 (1976), 85–94.

20671 HARRISON (GODFREY PERCIVAL). Borthwicks: A Century in the Meat Trade, 1863–1963. 1963.

20672 THOMAS (WYNFORD VAUGHAN). Dalgety: The Romance of a Business. 1984.

20673 U.K. MINISTRY OF AGRICULTURE, FISHERIES AND FOOD. Beef Production. 1959.

20674 WOOD (DOUGLAS). Economic Aspects of Pigmeat Marketing. Oxf. 1965.

20675 MATHESON (MARY J.) *and* PHILLPOT (BRYAN PASSMORE). The Regional Pattern of the Demand for Meat in the United Kingdom. Christchurch, N.Z. 1967.

20676 WOODWARD (JUDITH). Regulating the Meat Product Industry. Bradford. 1986.

20677 WALSH (JAN). The Meat Machine: The Inside Story of the Meat Business. 1986.

20678 WALTHAM FOREST ORAL HISTORY GROUP. Pig's Head and Pease Pudding: Memories of the Butchery Trade and the Use of Meat before the Second World War. 1985.

20679 WHITE (R. L.) *and* WATTS (H. D.). 'The Spatial Evolution of an Industry: The Example of Broiler Production'. *Trans. Inst. Brit. Geog.* n.s. 2 (1977), 175–91.

20680 WAINWRIGHT (DAVID). Brooke Bond: A Hundred Years. 1970.

20681 VINCHEZI (PENNY). Taking Stock. 1985.

20682 KNIGHTLEY (PHILLIP). The Vestey Affair. 1981.

(c) Sugar and Confectionery

20683 DEERR (NOEL). The History of Sugar. 2 vols 1949. 1950.

20684 LEWIS (FRANK). Essex and Sugar: Historic and other Connections. 1976.

20685 CHALMIN (P.). Tate and Lyle: Sugar Giant. 1987.

20686 —— 'The Strategy of a Multi-national in the World Sugar Economy: The Case of Tate and Lyle, 1870–1980'. In Alice Teichova, Maurice Lévy Leboyer, and Helga Nussbaum *eds*. Multinational Enterprises in Historical Perspective. Camb. 1986.

20687 HUGILL (ANTONY). Sugar and all that: A History of Tate & Lyle. 1978.

20688 WATTS (H. D.). 'Conflict and Collusion in the British Sugar Industry: 1924–1928'. *J. Hist. Geog.* 6 (1980), 291–314.

20689 MINTZ (SIDNEY WILFRED). Sweetness and Power: The Place of Sugar in Modern History. NY/Harmondsworth. 1986.

20690 POLITICAL AND ECONOMIC PLANNING. A Survey of the Chocolate and Sugar Confectionary Industry. 1967. [A joint survey for the Economic Development Committee for the Chocolate and Sugar Confectionary Industry.].

20691 POTTER (TIM). The British Confectionary Industry (Chocolate and Sugar). 1980. [Jordan & Sons (Surveys) Ltd.].

20692 HUGHES (M. L.) *et al*. The Chocolate Confectionary Industry. Manch. 1981.

20693 —— Industrial Challenge: The Experience of Cadburys of Bourneville in the Post-War Years. 1964.

20694 BOYNTON (SANDRA). Chocolate: The Consuming Passion. 1982.

20695 BECKETT (S. T.) *ed*. Industrial Chocolate Manufacture and Use. Glasg. 1988.

20696 WAGNER (GILLIAN). The Chocolate Conscience. 1987. [Philanthropic endeavours of the Fry, Rowntree, and Cadbury Families.].

20697 MACKINTOSH (HAROLD VINCENT). By Faith and Works: The Autobiography of the Rt. Hon. the First Viscount Mackintosh, D. L., LL. D. 1966.

20698 VERNON (ANNE). A Quaker Businessman: The Life of Joseph Rowntree 1836–1929. 1958. York. 1982.

20699 CROSFIELD (JOHN FOTHERGILL). A History of the Cadbury Family. 2 vols. 1985.

(d) Other Foodstuffs

20700 HORDER (THOMAS JEEVES) *Baron*, DODDS (*Sir* EDWARD CHARLES), *and* MORAN (THOMAS). Bread: The Chemistry and Nutrition of Flour and Bread, with an Introduction to their Chemistry and Technology. 1954.

20701 SPICER (ARNOLD). Bread: Social, Nutritional and Agricultural Aspects of Wheaten Bread. 1975.

20702 MCCANCE (ROBERT ALEXANDER) *and* WIDDOWSON (ELSIE AMY). Breads, White and Brown: Their Place in Thought and Social History. 1956.

20703 EMERSON (JOHN) *et al*. The United Kingdom Market for Bread. Manch. 1982.

20704 BIBBY (J. B.) *and* BIBBY (C. L.). A Miller's Tale: A History of J. Bibby & Sons Ltd., L/pool. 1978.

20705 CORLEY (T. A. B.). Quaker Enterprise in Biscuits: Huntley & Palmers of Reading, 1822–1972. 1972.

20706 SMYTH (ROBERT LESLIE). The Distribution of Fruit and Vegetables. 1959.

20707 YAMAGUCHI (MAS). World Vegetables: Principles, Production and Nutritive Values. Chichester. 1983.

20708 BEAVER (PATRICK). Yes! We Have Some: The Story of Fyffes. 1976.

20709 MULTHAUF (ROBERT PHILIP). Neptune's Gift: A History of Common Salt. Balt., Md./Lond. 1978.

20710 TOMLIN (DAVID M.). The Salt Industry of the River Tees. Eindhoven. 1982.

20711 FORREST (DENYS). Tea for the British: The Social and Economic History of a Famous Trade. 1973.

20712 TURNER (JOHN). The Tea Trade. 1979.

20713 INTERNATIONAL TEA COMMITTEE. The First Fifty Years: 1933–1983. 1984.

20714 VAN STUYVENBERG (JOHANNES HERMANUS). Margarine: An Economic, Social and Scientific History, 1869–1969. L/pool. 1969.

20715 SCHWITZER (MATEJ KAREL). Margarine and other Food Fats: Their History, Production and Use. 1956.

20716 U.K. MINISTRY OF AGRICULTURE AND FISHERIES. Eggs and Poultry: Report of Reorganising Committee for Great Britain. 1935. [Chairman: F. N. Blundell.].

20717 U.K. MINISTRY OF AGRICULTURE, FISHERIES AND FOOD. The Egg Trade and the E.E.C. 1972.

20718 U.K. MINISTRY OF FOOD. The Testing of Eggs for Quality. 1949.

20719 FORD (E.). The Nation's Sea-Fish Supply. 1937.

20720 SHAW (SUSAN) *and* MUIR (JAMES F.). Salmon: Economics and Marketing. 1987.

20721 U.K. MINISTRY OF AGRICULTURE, FISHERIES AND FOOD. Oyster Cultivation in Britain. 1956.

20722 CRANE (EDITH EVA) *ed.* Honey. NY 1975.

20723 —— The Archaeology of Beekeeping. 1983.

20724 BELL (HERBERT TAIT). A Short History of British Bee-Keeping . . . Ilford. 1967.

(e) Alcoholic Beverages and Public Houses

20725 LOCKHART (*Sir* ROBERT HAMILTON BRUCE). Scotch: The Whisky of Scotland in Fact and Story. 1951. 5th edn 1974. New edn 1981.

20726 McDOWALL (R. J. S.). The Whiskies of Scotland. 2nd edn 1971.

20727 GUNN (NEIL MILLER). Whisky and Scotland: A Practical and Spiritual Survey. 1935. Repr. 1977.

20728 DAICHES (DAVID). Scotch Whisky: Its Past and Present. 1976. 3rd rev. edn 1978.

20729 MOSS (MICHAEL STANLEY) *and* HUME (JOHN ROBERT). The Making of Scotch Whisky: A History of the Scotch Whisky Distilling Industry. Edin. 1981.

20730 THOMPSON (JOHN K.). Ownership and Control of the Scotch Whisky Industry. Glasg. 1980.

20731 SPILLER (BRIAN). The Chameleon's Eye: James Buchanan & Co. Ltd., 1884–1984. 1984.

20732 MONCKTON (HERBERT ANTHONY). A History of English Ale and Beer. 1966.

20733 YOUNG (JIMMY). A Short History of Ale. Newton Abbot. 1979.

20734 WYKES (ALAN). Ale and Hearty: Gleanings from the History of Brews and Brewing. 1979.

20735 VAIZEY (JOHN). The Brewing Industry 1886–1951. 1960.

20736 HAWKINS (KEVIN) *and* PASS (C. L.). The Brewing Industry: A Study in Industrial Organisation and Public Policy. 1979.

20737 LOVETT (MAURICE). Brewing and Breweries. Princes Risborough. 1981.

20738 DONNACHIE (IAN). A History of the Brewing Industry in Scotland. Edin. 1979.

20739 MITCHELL (COLIN). The British Brewing Industry: Market Overview. 1980. [Jordan & Son (Surveys) Ltd.].

20740 SMITH (MICHAEL ALFRED). Brewing Industry Policy, the Public House and Alcohol Consumption Patterns in the United Kingdom. Salford. 1980.

20741 WATTS (H. D.). 'Market Areas and Spatial Rationalization: The British Brewing Industry after 1945'. *Tijd. Econ. Soc. Geog.* 68 (1977), 224–40.

20742 JANES (HURFORD). Hall & Woodhouse, 1777–1977: Independent Family Brewers. 1977.

20743 PARRY (DAVID) *and* PARRY (DONALD). Bygone Breweries of South Yorkshire. Swinton. 1983.

20744 LUCKETT (FRED) *et al. eds.* A History of Brewing in Warwickshire. Coventry. 1983.

20745 WILSON (RICHARD G.). Greene King: A Business and Family History. 1983.

20746 GOURVISH (TERENCE RICHARD). Norfolk Beers from English Barley: A History of Steward and Patteson, 1793–1963. Norwich. 1987.

20747 TILTSCHER (ROBERT). The British Beers, Wines and Spirits Industry. 1982. [Jordan & Son (Surveys) Ltd.].

20748 QUINION (MICHAEL BRIAN). A Drink for its Time: Farm Cider Making in the Western Counties. Hereford. 1979.

20749 WILLIAMS-DAVIES (JOHN). Cider Making in Wales. Card. 1984.

20750 WILKINSON (LANCELOT PATRICK). Bulmers of Hereford: A Century of Cider-Making. Newton Abbot. 1987.

20751 O'CONNOR (JOHN). Britain's Wine Industry: Industry Commentary. 1986.

20752 BRIGGS (ASA). Wine for Sale: Victoria Wine and the Liquor Trade 1860–1984. Batsford. 1985.

20753 WILLIAMS (ERNEST EDWIN). The New Public House. 1924. [Temperance Assoc. pub.].

20754 ELWALL (ROBERT). Bricks and Beer: English Pub Architecture 1830–1939. 1983.

20755 OLIVER (BASIL). The Renaissance of the English Public House. 1947.

20756 DUGDALE (HARRY). The Management of a Public House. 1946.

20757 MASS-OBSERVATION. The Pub and the People. 1943.

20758 MARPLAN LIMITED. The British Pub. 1978.

20759 —— Pub Opening Hours. 1978.

10
MEDICINE AND HEALTH

The sub-sections into which this section has been divided include areas which are relatively discrete: nursing, mental and physical handicap, and medical education, for example. However, even in these instances, the literature cannot avoid straying into the vast territory represented by 'hospitals' and, even more, by the 'National Health Service'. Hence it is again necessary to look at these sub-sections as a totality. Naturally enough, the literature does not obediently restrict itself to the sub-sections that have been identified. Nevertheless, it is believed that they are sufficiently self-contained to make the division helpful to the user. The sub-sections which conclude this section and the earlier section on 'man and medicine' are more severely 'scientific' and pose distinct problems. 'Alcoholism' and 'drugs' have obvious links with 'food and drink' on the one hand, and with social behaviour on the other. Relevant material can therefore be found appropriately elsewhere. The items grouped in this section in general tackle the specifically medical issues involved. There is, however, clearly a limit beyond which any attempt to cover the medical issues involved would not be appropriate in this bibliography. The same point holds for the other concluding sub-sections which do not purport to provide a guide to the copious literatures of these medically related scientific disciplines. In any event, given the international nature of much scientific research, there is a certain artificiality in speaking of, for example, 'British genetics'.

1. MEDICAL EDUCATION, PROFESSIONAL BODIES, GREAT MEDICAL MEN, INSTITUTES

20760 The Hospitals and Health Services Year Book. 1889+.

20761 MEDICAL RESEARCH COUNCIL: MINISTRY OF HEALTH. Clinical Research in Relation to the National Health Service. 1953.

20762 U.K. MINISTRY OF HEALTH. Report of the Committee to Consider the Future Numbers of Medical Practitioners and the Appropriate Intake of Medical Students. [Chairman: *Sir* Henry Willink.]. 1957.

20763 PARKHOUSE (JAMES). Medical Manpower in Britain. Edin. 1979.

20764 U.K. 1964 CENTRAL OFFICE OF INFORMATION. Medical Research in Britain. 1964.

20765 WOODFORD (F. PETER). The Ciba Foundation: An Analytic History, 1949–1974. Amsterdam/Oxf. 1974.

20766 Medical Research Council Annual Report. 1920+.

20767 THOMSON (A. LANDSBOROUGH). Half a Century of Medical Research: Vol. 1 Origins and Policy of the Medical Research Council (UK) Vol. 2 The Programme of the Medical Research Council. 1973–5.

20768 JARAMILLO-ARANGO (J.). The British Contribution to Medicine. Edin. 1953.

20769 U.K. MINISTRY OF HEALTH. Postgraduate Medical Education and the Specialities, With Special Reference to the Problem in London. [Chairman: *Sir* George Pickering.]. 1962.

20770 U.K. D.H.S.S. Royal Commission on Medical Education, 1965–1968. Report. Cmnd. 3569. Parliamentary Papers, xxv (1968).

20771 WARTMAN (WILLIAM BECHMANN). Medical Teaching in Western Civilisation. Chicago, Ill. 1961.

20772 HALL (A. RUPERT) *and* BAMBRIDGE (B. A.). Physic and Philanthropy: A History of the Wellcome Trust, 1936–1986. Camb. 1986.

20773 WELLCOME INSTITUTE OF THE HISTORY OF MEDICINE. Portraits of Doctors and Scientists in the Wellcome Institute of the History of Medicine. A catalogue by Renate Burgess. Lond. 1973.

20774 WICKSTEAD (J. H.). The Growth of a Profession: The Chartered Society of Psychotherapy, 1894–1945. 1948.

20775 WIDDESS (JOHN DAVID HENRY). A History of the Royal College of Physicians of Ireland, 1654–1963. Edin. 1963.

20776 —— The Royal College of Surgeons in Ireland and its Medical School, 1784–1966. 2nd edn Edin. 1967.

20777 WALLIS (THOMAS EDWARD). History of the School of Pharmacy, University of London. 1964.

20778 TURNER (GEORGE GREY). The Newcastle upon Tyne School of Medicine, 1834–1934. Newcastle upon Tyne. 1934.

20779 THOMSON (H. CAMPBELL). The Story of the Middlesex Hospital Medical School. Written at the Request of the Council of the School on the Occasion of the Centenary. 1935.

20780 RITCHIE (JOHN). History of the Laboratory of the Royal College of Physicians of Edinburgh. Edin. 1953.

20781 RODDIE (IAN CAMPBELL). An Excellent Medical School. An Inaugural Lecture Delivered Before the Queen's University of Belfast. Belf. 1965.

20782 PORTER (WILLIAM SMITH). The Medical School in Sheffield, 1828–1928. Sheffield. 1928.

20783 ROLLESTON (*Sir* HUMPHRY DAVY). The Cambridge Medical School: A Biographical History. Camb. 1932.

20784 ROOK (ARTHUR) *ed.* Cambridge and its Contribution to Medicine. 1971.

20785 ROYAL COLLEGE OF SURGEONS OF ENGLAND. A Record of the Years from 1901–1950. 1951.

20786 SHADRAKE (A. M.). British Medical Periodicals, 1938–1961. Chicago, Ill. 1963.

20787 SHAW (*Sir* WILLIAM FLETCHER). Twenty-Five Years: The Story of the Royal College of Obstetricians and Gynaecologists 1929–1954. 1954.

20788 LITTLE (ERNEST MUIRHEAD) *comp.* History of the British Medical Association, 1832–1932. 1932.

20789 SMITH (S. WATSON). The Chronicle of the First World Tour of the British Medical Association. 1936.

20790 VAUGHAN (PAUL). Doctor's Commons: A Short History of the British Medical Association. 1959.

20791 LYLE (H. WILLOUGHBY). King's and Some King's Men: Being a Record of the Medical Department of King's College London from 1830–1909 and of King's College Hospital Medical School from 1909 to 1934. 1935.

20792 —— An Addendum. 1950.

20793 HUNT (THOMAS) *ed.* The Medical Society of London, 1773–1973. 1972.

20794 GRAY (JAMES). History of the Royal Medical Society, 1737–1937. Edin. 1952.

20795 DOBSON (JESSIE) *and* WALKER (R. MILNES). Barbers and Barber—Surgeons of London. Oxf. 1979.

20796 FORBES (ROBERT M.). Sixty Years of Medical Defence. 1968.

20797 DAVIDSON (M.). The Royal Society of Medicine, the Realization of an Ideal (1805–1955). 1955.

20798 DEWHURST (KENNETH) *ed.* Oxford Medicine: Essays on the Evolution of the Oxford Clinical School to Commemorate the Bicentenary of the Radcliffe Infirmary 1770–1970. Oxf. 1970.

20799 DAUKES (SIDNEY HERBERT). The Medical Museum: Modern Developments, Organization and Technical Methods Based on a New System of Visual Teaching: An Amplification of a Thesis. 1929.

20800 COPEMAN (WILLIAM SIDNEY CHARLES). The Worshipful Society of Apothecaries of London: A History, 1617–1967. Oxf./NY. 1967.

20801 O'MALLEY (C. D.) *ed.* The History of Medical Education. Berkeley, Calif. Lond. 1970. [Separate sections on England and Scotland.].

20802 GIBSON (THOMAS). The Royal College of Physicians and Surgeons of Glasgow. Edin. 1983.

20803 CRAIG (WILLIAM STUART). History of the Royal College of Physicians of Edinburgh. Oxf. 1976.

20804 COPE (*Sir* ZACHARY). The Royal College of Surgeons of England: A History. 1959.

20805 —— The History of St Mary's Hospital Medical School. 1954.

20806 COOKE (A. M.). A History of the Royal College of Physicians. Vol. 3. Oxf. 1972.

20807 CAMERON (HECTOR CHARLES). The British Paediatric Association 1928–1952. Vol. 1. 1955.

20808 NEALE (ALBERT VICTOR). The British Paediatric Association 1952-1968. Vol. 2. 1970.

20809 BROCKBANK (EDWARD MANSFIELD). A Centenary History of the Manchester Medical Society. Manch. 1934.

20810 ECKSTEIN (HARRY HORACE). Pressure Group Politics: The Case of the British Medical Association. 1960.

20811 JEFFERYS (MARGOT) *and* ELLIOTT (PATRICIA MARY). Women in Medicine: The Results of an Inquiry Conducted by the Medical Practitioners' Union in 1962–1963. 1966.

20812 ABEL-SMITH (BRIAN) *and* GALES (KATHLEEN) *with the assistance of* MACFARLANE (GILLIAN). British Doctors at Home and Abroad. Welwyn. 1964.

20813 SINCLAIR (DAVID). Basic Medical Education. 1972.

20814 BRITISH MEDICAL ASSOCIATION. Recruitment to the Medical Profession: The Report of a Special Committee, May 1962. 1962.

20815 HUWS-JONES (R.). The Doctor and the Social Services. 1971.

20816 HARVEY (GORDON) *and* ILIFFE (STEVE). Pickets in White: The Junior Doctors Dispute of 1975: A Study of the Medical Profession in Transition. 1977.

20817 BERLANT (JEFFREY LIONEL). Profession and Monopoly: A Study of Medicine in the United States and Great Britain. Berkeley, Calif. 1973.

20818 U.K. HOUSE OF COMMONS Select Committee on Public Expenditure. 1972. Private Practice. 1972.

20819 U.K. ROYAL COMMISSION ON DOCTORS' AND DENTISTS' REMUNERATION, 1957–1960. Report. Cmnd. 939. 1960.

20820 U.K. ROYAL COMMISSION ON MEDICAL EDUCATION. 1965–1968. Cmnd. 3569. 1968.

20821 ROYAL COLLEGE OF PHYSICIANS OF LONDON. Portraits Catalogue II. By Gordon Wolstenholme and John F. Kerslake. Amsterdam/Oxf. 1977.

20822 PICKERING (*Sir* GEORGE). Quest for Excellence in Medical Education: A Personal Survey. Oxf. 1978.

20823 POYNTER (FREDERICK NOEL LAWRENCE) *ed.* The Evolution of Medical Practice in Britain. 1961.

20824 —— The Evolution of Medical Education in Britain. 1966.

20825 PARRY (NOEL) *and* PARRY (JOSÉ). The Rise of the Medical Profession: A Study of Collective Social Mobility. 1976.

20826 BRACKENBURY (*Sir* HENRY BRITTEN). Patient and Doctor. 1935.

20827 HODSON (MARK). Doctors and Patients: A Relationship Examined. 1967.

20828 OFFICE OF HEALTH ECONOMICS. The Finance of Medical Research. 1964.

20829 PAPPWORTH (MAURICE HENRY). Human Guinea Pigs: Experimenta-tion on Man. 1967.

20830 PLATT (ROBERT) *Baron*. Doctor and Patient: Ethics, Morals, Government. Oxf. 1963.

20831 ROYAL COLLEGE OF PHYSICIANS OF LONDON, President, Sir R. Platt. Smoking and Health, a Report.

20832 STEVENS (ROSEMARY). Medical Practice in Modern England: The Impact of Specialization and State Medicine. New Haven, Conn. 1966.

20833 McLACHLAN (GORDON) *ed.* Patient, Doctor, Society: A Symposium of Introspection. 1972.

20834 —— *ed.* Portfolio for Health 2. The Developing Programme of the D.H.S.S. in Health Services Research. 1973.

20835 MALLESON (ANDREW). Need your Doctor be so Useless? 1973.

20836 KLEIN (RUDOLF) *with* HOWLETT (ANN). Complaints Against Doctors: A Study of Professional Accountability. 1973.

20837 KEITH (ARTHUR). Menders of the Maimed. Philadelphia, Pa. 1952.

20838 COX (ALFRED). Among the Doctors. 1950.

20839 TURNER (ERNEST SACKVILLE). Call the Doctor: A Social History of Medical Men. Lond./NY. 1958.

20840 COMFORT (ALEXANDER). The Anxiety Makers: Some Curious Preoccupations of the Medical Profession. 1967.

20841 MUNK (WILLIAM). Lives of the Fellows of the Royal College of Physicians of London. Vol. 5: Continued to 1965. 1968.

20842 POWER (*Sir* D'ARCY) *and* LE FANU (WILLIAM R.). The Lives of the Fellows of the Royal College of Surgeons of England. Vol. 3: 1930–1951. 1953.

20843 ROBINSON (RONALD H. O. B.) *and* LE FANU (WILLIAM R.). The Lives of the Fellows of the Royal College of Surgeons of England. Vol. 4: 1952–1964. Edin. 1970.

20844 ROSS (*Sir* JAMES PATERSON) *and* LE FANU (WILLIAM R.). The Lives of the Fellows of the Royal College of Surgeons of England. Vol. 5: 1965–1973. 1981.

20845 GIBSON (JOHN). Great Doctors and Medical Scientists. Lond./NY. 1967.

20846 McLACHLAN (GORDON) *ed.* Medical Education: A Scottish–American Symposium. Oxf. 1977.

20847 POWER (*Sir* D'ARCY). British Masters of Medicine. Lond. 1936.

20848 PEEL (*Sir* JOHN) *comp.* The Lives of the Fellows of the Royal College of Obstetricians and Gynaecologists 1929–1969. 1976.

20849 BRAIN (WALTER RUSSELL) *Baron*. Doctors Past and Present. Springfield, Ill. 1964.

20850 —— The Doctor's Place in Society. 1963.

20851 MATTHEWS (LESLIE G.). The Royal Apothecaries. 1962.

20852 GRIFFITH (EDWARD F.). Doctors by Themselves. An Anthology with a Foreword by the Rt. Hon. the Lord Horder. 1951.

20853 CROWTHER (JAMES GERALD). Six Great Doctors. 1957.

20854 FERRIS (PAUL FREDERICK). The Doctors. 1965. Rev. edn 1967.

20855 CANTLIE (*Sir* NEIL). A History of the Army Medical Department. Vol. 2. Edin./Lond. 1974.

20856 DREW (ROBERT H.). Medical Officers in the British Army. 1660–1960. Vol. 2. 1898–1960. 1968.

20857 ABRAHAM (JAMES JOHNSTON). Surgeon's Journey: The Autobiography of J. Johnston Abraham. 1957.

20858 McLEAVE (HUGH). A Time to Heal: The Life of Ian Aird, the Surgeon. 1964.

20859 HUMPHRIES (S. V.). The Life of Hamilton Bailey, Surgeon, Author and Teacher of Surgery. Beckenham. 1973.

20860 BERGER (JOHN) *and* MOHR (JEAN). A Fortunate Man: The Story of a Country Doctor. 1967.

20861 BOURNE (GEOFFREY HOWARD). We Met at Bart's: The Autobiog-raphy of a Physician. 1963.

20862 DOBSON (JESSIE) *and* WAKELEY (*Sir* CECIL). George Buckston Browne. Edin./Lond. 1957.

20863 NOBLE (W. C.). Coli—Great Healer of Men: The Biography of Dr Leonard Colebrook. 1974.

20864 CRICHTON-BROWNE (*Sir* JAMES). From the Doctor's Notebook. 1937.

20865 —— The Doctor Remembers. 1938.

20866 THOMAS (ALFRED NOYES). Doctor Courageous: The Story of Grantley Dick-Read. 1957.

20867 GRENFELL (*Sir* WILFRED). A Labrador Doctor. 1920.

20868 HOLLAND (*Sir* HENRY). Frontier Doctor: An Autobiography. 1958.

20869 HUNT (RICHARD). The Shadowless Lamp: Memoirs of an R.A.M.C. Surgeon. 1971.

20870 MAIR (ALEX). Sir James Mackenzie, M.D. 1853–1925: General Practitioner. Edin./Lond. 1973.

20871 MARTINDALE (LOUISA). A Woman Surgeon. 1951.

20872 HORDER (T. M.). The Little Genius: A Memoir of the First Lord Horder. 1966.

20873 FRY (JOHN), HUNT (OF FAWLEY), *Baron* and PINSENT (R. J. F. H.) *eds.* A History of the Royal College of General Practitioners: The First 25 Years. Lancaster/Boston, Mass. 1983.

20874 CUSHING (HARVEY). The Life of Sir William Osler. 2 vols Lond./NY/Toronto. 1925.

20875 BETT (WALTER R.). Osler: The Man and the Legend. 1951.

20876 FRANKLIN (A. W.) *ed.* A Way of Life and Other Selected Writings of William Osler. NY. 1958.

20877 WATSON (FRANCIS LESLIE). Dawson of Penn. 1950.

20878 ATKINS (HEDLEY). The Surgeon's Craft. Manch./Lond. 1965.

20879 CARTWRIGHT (FREDERICK F.). The Development of Modern Surgery. 1967.

20880 SARGENT (WILLIAM). The Unquiet Mind: The Autobiography of a Physician in Psychological Medicine. 1967.

20881 JAMESON (ERIC). The Natural History of Quackery. 1961.

20882 INGLIS (BRIAN). Fringe Medicine. 1964.

20883 —— A History of Medicine. 1965.

20884 —— Drugs, Doctors and Disease. 1965.

20885 GREENWOOD (MAJOR). Some British Pioneers of Social Medicine. [Heath Clark Lectures 1946, delivered at the London School of Hygiene and Tropical Medicine]. Lond./NY. 1948.

20886 —— Authority in Medicine: Old and New. The Linacre Lecture. 1943. Cambridge. 1943.

20887 —— Epidemics and Crowd Diseases: An Introduction to the Study of Epidemiology. 1935.

20888 —— *Et al.* Experimental Epidemiology. MRC. 1936.

20889 GREAT TEACHERS of Surgery in the Past: A Collection of Articles which have Appeared in the *British Journal of Surgery* over the Period January, 1964 to January, 1968. Bristol/Baltimore, Md. 1969.

20890 GIBSON (WILLIAM CARLETON). Creative Minds in Medicine: Scientific, Humanistic, and Cultural Contributions by Physicians. Springfield, Ill. 1963.

20891 —— *ed.* British Contributions to Medical Science. [The Woodward–Wellcome Symposium, University of British Columbia 1970.]. 1971.

20892 COPE (*Sir* ZACHARY). Almroth Wright, Founder of Modern Vaccine-Therapy. 1966.

20893 BAILEY (HENRY H.) *and* BISHOP (W. J.). Notable Names in Medicine and Surgery. 1944.

20894 THORNTON (JOHN L.). A Select Bibliography of Medical Biography. With an Introductory Essay on Medical Biography. 2nd edn 1970.

20895 SOURKES (THEODORE L.). Nobel Prize Winners in Medicine and Physiology, 1901–1965. Lond./NY/ Toronto. 1967. [Revision of earlier work by Lloyd G. Stevenson.].

20896 ROYAL COLLEGE OF PHYSICIANS OF LONDON. The Roll of the Royal College of Physicians of London. By William Munk. 2nd edn rev. and enl. Vol. 4 Lives of the Fellows of the Royal College of Physicians. 1826–1925. Compiled by G. H. Brown. Lond. 1955. Vol. 5 compiled by Richard R. Trail. 1954–1965. 1968.

20897 PEEL (*Sir* JOHN) *comp.* The Lives of the Fellows of the Royal College of Obstetricians and Gynaecologists. 1929–1969. 1976.

20898 SHAW (*Sir* WILLIAM F.). Twenty-Five Years: The Story of the Royal College of Obstetricians and Gynaecologists, 1929–1954. Edin. 1954.

20899 ROYAL COLLEGE OF SURGEONS OF ENGLAND. Lives of the Fellows of the Royal College of Surgeons of England. Revised by *Sir* d'Arcy Power with the assistance of W. C. Spencer and G. E. Gask. Bristol. 1930.

20900 —— Guide to the Surgical Instruments and Objects in the Historical Series, with their History and Development. By C. J. S. Thompson with a Foreword by the conservator, *Sir* Arthur Keith. 1930.

20901 ROBINSON (RONALD H. O. B.) *and* LE FANU (WILLIAM R.). Lives of the Fellows of the Royal College of Surgeons of England. 1952. With a Foreword by *Sir* Cecil Wakeley. Edin. 1970.

20902 CHICK (HARIETTE), HUME (MARGARET), *and* MACFARLANE (MARJORIE). War on Disease: A History of the Lister Institute. 1971.

20903 CLARK (CATHERINE MARGARET) *and* MACKINTOSH (JAMES MACALISTER). The School and the Site: A Historical Memoir to Celebrate the Twenty-Fifth Anniversary of the [London] School [of Hygiene and Tropical Medicine.]. 1954.

20904 WILSON (ROBERT MACNAIR). The Beloved Physician Sir James MacKenzie: A Biography. 1926.

20905 SPENCE (JAMES CALVERT) *Sir*. The Purpose and Practice of Medicine: Selections from the Writings of Sir James Spence. With a Memoir by Sir J. Charles. 1960.

20906 WAUCHOPE (GLADYS MARY). The Story of a Woman Physician: An Autobiography. Bristol. 1963.

20907 TURNER (HELEN). Henry Wellcome: The Man, his Collection and his Legacy. 1980.

20908 WILLCOX (PHILIP H. A.). The Detective–Physician: The Life and Work of Sir William Willcox. 1970.

20909 HISTORY of the Birmingham Medical School. 1823–1925. Birm. 1925.

2. MEDICINE

20910 ALLAN (FRANK N.). 'Diabetes before and after Insulin'. *Med. Hist.* 16 (1972), 266–73.

20911 AMULREE (BASIL W. S. H.) *Baron*. 'James MacKenzie and the Future of Medicine'. *J. Roy. Coll. Gen. Practitioners* 17 (1969), 3–11.

20912 BETT (WALTER R.). 'The Medical Press and Circular, 1839–1939'. *Bull. Hist. Med.* 7 (1939), 1004–7.

20913 BISHOP (W. J.). 'The Autobiographies of British Medical Men'. *Proc. Roy. Soc. Med.* 26 (1933), 16–22.

20914 —— 'Transport and the Doctor in Great Britain'. *Bull. Hist. Med.* 22 (1948), 427–40.

20915 BOOTH (JEREMY). 'A Short History of Blood Pressure Measurement'. *Proc. Roy. Soc. Med.* 70 (1977), 793–9.

20916 FARR (A. D.). 'Some Problems in the History of Haemoglobinometry, 1878–1931'. *Med. Hist.* 22 (1978), 151–60.

20917 BORELL (MERRILEY). 'Organotherapy, British Physiology and Discovery of the Internal Secretions'. *J. Hist. Biol.* 9 (1976), 235–68.

20918 BRACEGIRDLE (BRIAN). 'The History of Histology: A Brief Survey of Sources'. *Hist. Sci.* 15 (1977), 77–101.

20919 BROWN (W. LANGDON). 'The History of the Introduction of Biochemistry into Medicine'. *Proc. Roy. Soc. Med.* 25 (1932), 1046–54.

20920 BRUCE (*Sir* DAVID). 'Prevention of Disease: Inaugural Address Delivered to the British Association at Toronto on August 6'. *Nature* 114 (1924), 213–27.

20921 BULL (J. W. D.). 'The History of Neuroradiology'. *Proc. Roy. Soc. Med.* 63 (1970), 637–43.

20922 BURNET (*Sir* FRANK MACFARLANE). 'Immunology as a Scholarly Discipline'. *Perspect. Biol. Med.* 16 (1972), 1–10.

20923 CARTER (K. CODELL). 'The Germ Theory, Beri Beri, and the Deficiency Theory of Disease'. *Med. Hist.* 21 (1977), 119–36.

20924 CARTWRIGHT (FREDERICK F.). 'The Place of Medical History in Undergraduate Education'. *Proc. Roy. Soc. Med.* 42 (1969), 1053–60.

20925 CHICK (HARRIETTE). 'The Lister Institute of Preventive Medicine'. *Endeavour* 8 (1949), 106–11.

20926 CLARK (*Sir* WILFRID LE GROS). 'The Humanity of Man'. *Nature* 191 (1961), 970–82.

20927 CLARK (GEORGE). 'The History of the Medical Profession: Aims and Methods'. *Med. Hist.* 10 (1966), 213–20.

20928 CLARKE (EDWIN S.). 'Practical Medical History'. *Proc. Roy. Soc. Med.* 61 (1968), 316.

20929 —— 'The History of the Neurological Sciences'. *Proc. Roy. Soc. Med.* 63 (1970), 21–3.

20930 POYNTER (NOEL). 'Lord Cohen of Birkenhead'. *Med. Hist.* 22 (1978), 90–1.

20931 COHEN (HENRY) *Baron*. 'The Liverpool Medical School and its Physicians (1642–1934)'. *Med. Hist.* 16 (1972), 310–20.

20932 CUMMINGS (MARTIN M.). 'Books, Computers and Medicine'. *Med. Hist.* 10 (1966), 130–7.

20933 DENNY (LIONEL). 'The Royal Hospitals of the City of London'. *Ann. Roy. Coll. Surg.* 52 (1973), 86–101.

20934 DENT (C. E.). 'Rickets (and Osteomalacia) Nutritional and Metabolic (1919–1969)'. *Proc. Roy. Soc. Med.* 63 (1970), 401–8.

20935 DODDS (CHARLES). 'The Rise of Clinical Chemistry'. *J. Roy. Coll. Phys.* 1 (1967), 143–7.

20936 DORMAN (CLAUDE E.). 'Reflections on Sir Alexander Fleming'. *Chemistry* 51 (7) (1978), 6–10.

20937 DOTT (NORMAN). 'The History of Surgical Neurology in the 20th Century'. *Proc. Roy. Soc. Med.* 64 (1971), 1051–5.

20938 ECCLES (*Sir* JOHN CAREW). 'Alexander Forbes and his Achievement in Electro-physiology'. *Perspect. Biol. Med.* 13 (1970), 388–404.

20939 —— 'From Electrical to Chemical Transmission in the Central Nervous System'. *Notes Rec. Roy. Soc. Lond.* 30 (1976), 219–30.

20940 —— 'The Discipline of Science with Special Reference to the Neurosciences'. *Daedalus* 102(2) (1973), 85–99.

20941 FELL (HONOR B.). 'Fiftieth Anniversary of the Strangeways Research Laboratory, Cambridge'. *Nature* 196 (1962), 316–18.

20942 FISHER (DONALD). 'The Rockefeller Foundation and the Development of Scientific Medicine in Great Britain'. *Minerva* 16 (1978), 20–41.

20943 —— 'Rockefeller Philanthropy and the British Empire: The Creation of the London School of Hygiene and Tropical Medicine'. *Hist. Educ.* 7 (1978), 129–43.

20944 FLOREY (HOWARD WALTER) *Baron, and* ABRAHAM (E. P.). 'The Work on Penicillin at Oxford'. *J. Hist. Med.* 6 (1951), 302–16.

20945 —— 'L'Introduction de la Pénicilline dans la Médicine'. (Conférence du Palais de la Découverte, 10 Jan. 1946) Alençon. 1949–50.

20946 FLORKIN (MARCEL). 'The Nature and Therapy of Pernicious Anaemia: A Trail of Biomedical Research'. *Clio Medica* 8 (1973), 223–7.

20947 FRANKLIN (KENNETH J.). 'The History of Research upon the Renal Circulation'. *Proc. Roy. Soc. Med.* 42 (1949), 721–30.

20948 —— 'A Short History of the International Congresses of Physiologists'. *Ann. Sci.* 3 (1938), 241–335.

20949 FRANKLIN (R. H.). 'Grey Turner and the Evolution of Oesophageal Surgery'. *Ann. Roy. Coll. Surg.* xlix (1971), 165–77.

20950 GIBSON (WILLIAM CARLETON). 'Medical Pioneers in Aviation'. *J. Hist. Med.* 17 (1962), 83–93.

20951 GORDON (LINDA). 'The Politics of Birth Control, 1920–1940: The Impact of the Professionals'. *Inl. J. Health Serv.* 5(2) (1975), 253–77.

20952 GOULD (STEPHEN JAY). 'D'Arcy Thompson and the Science of Form'. *New Lit. Hist.* 2 (1971), 229–58.

20953 GRAHAM (GEORGE). 'The Formation of the Medical and Surgical Professional Units in the London Teaching Hospitals'. *Ann. Sci.* 26 (1970), 1–22.

20954 GRAY (PHILIP HOWARD). 'Historical Notes on the Aerial Predator Reaction and the Tinbergen Hypothesis'. *J. Hist. Behav. Sci.* 2 (1960), 330–4.

20955 GRANT (R. P.). 'National Biomedical Research Agencies: A Comparative Study of Fifteen Countries'. *Minerva* 4 (1966), 466–88.

20956 GRAY (T. CECIL). 'History of Anaesthesia in Liverpool'. *Med. Hist.* 16 (1972), 375–82.

20957 HADDOW (ALEXANDER). 'Sir Ernest Laurence Kennaway, F.R.S., 1881–1958: Chemical Causation of Cancer Then and Today'. *Perspect. Biol. Med.* 17 (1974), 543–91.

20958 HALL (DIANA LONG). 'The Critic and the Advocate: Contrasting British Views on the State of Endocrinology in the Early 1920s'. *J. Hist. Biol.* 9 (1976), 269–85.

20959 HANDLEY (R. S.). 'Gordon-Taylor, Breast Cancer and the Middlesex Hospital'. *Ann. Roy. Coll. Surg.* 49 (1971), 151–64.

20960 HARTSTON (WILLIAM). 'Care of the Sick Poor in England, 1572–1948'. *Proc. Roy. Soc. Med.* 59 (1966), 577–82.

20961 HIGHHAM (A. R. C.). 'The History of St Paul's Hospital, London'. *Proc. Roy. Soc. Lond.* 50 (1957), 164–6.

20962 HILL (AUSTIN BRADFORD) *and* HILL (BRIAN). 'The Life of Sir Leonard Erskine Hill, F.R.S., (1866–1952)'. *Proc. Roy. Soc. Med.* 61 (1968), 307–16.

20963 HOFF (HEBBEL E.) *and* GEDDES (L. A.). 'The Technological Background of Physiological Discovery: Ballistics and the Graphic Method'. *J. Hist. Med.* 15 (1960), 345–63. [See also 133–46.].

20964 HOLTON (GERALD) *ed.* 'The Making of Modern Science: Biographical Studies'. *Daedalus* (Boston), 99 (1970), 723–1120.

20965 HUBBLE (*Sir* DOUGLAS). 'William Osler and Medical Education'. *J. Roy. Coll. Phys.* 9 (1975), 269–78.

20966 HUGHES (ARTHUR F. W.). 'A History of Endocrinology'. *J. Hist. Med.* 32 (1977), 292–313.

20967 HUNT (JOHN H.). 'The Foundation of a College: The Conception, Birth and Early Days of the College of General Practitioners'. *J. Roy. Coll. Gen. Practitioners* 23 (1973), 5–20.

20968 HUNTER (RICHARD). 'Psychiatry and Neurology: Psychosyndrome or Brain Damage?'. *Proc. Roy. Soc. Med.* 66 (1973), 359–64.

20969 KEITH (ARTHUR). 'The Nature of Man's Structural Imperfections'. *Nature* 116 (1925), 821–3, 867–9.

20970 KELLY (MICHAEL). 'Sir James Mackenzie and Cellular Pathology'. *Med. Hist.* 4 (1960), 170–85.

20971 LEFANU (W. R.). 'British Periodicals of Medicine: A Chronological List'. *Bull. Inst. Hist. Med.* 5 (1937), 735–61, 827–46. 6 (1938), 614–48.

20972 —— 'The Royal College of Surgeons of England and Medical History'. *Bull. Hist. Med.* 38 (1964), 184–6.

20973 PARASCANDOLA (JOHN) *and* IHDE (AARON J.). 'Edward Mellanby and the Antirachitic Factor'. *Bull. Hist. Med.* 51 (1977), 507–15.

20974 STILES (WALTER STANLEY). 'Colour Vision—A Retrospect'. *Endeavour*, 11 (1952), 33–40.

20975 STOLKIND (E.). 'The History of Bronchial Asthma and Allergy'. *Proc. Roy. Soc. Med.* 26 (1933), 36–42.

20976 LLOYD (C. C.). 'The Conquest of Scurvy'. *Brit. J. Hist. Sci.* (1963), 357–63.

20977 LYON (ROBERT A.). 'The Development of International Health Organizations'. *Ann. Med. Hist.* 1 (1939), 519–24.

20978 McCONAGHEY (R. M. S.). 'Ernest Ward and Collective Investigations'. *J. Roy. Coll. Gen. Practitioners* 24 (1974), 568–71.

20979 MacGREGOR (ALASDAIR B.). 'The Search for a Chemical Cure for Cancer'. *Med. Hist.* 10 (1966), 374–85.

20980 MacKENZIE (DONALD). 'Eugenics in Britain'. *Soc. Stud. Sci.* vi (1976), 499–532.

20981 HUXLEY (JULIAN S.). 'Eugenics and Society'. *Eugenics Rev.* xxviii (1936), 11–31.

20982 MACNALTY (*Sir* ARTHUR SALUSBURY). 'Some Pioneers of the Past in Neurology'. *Med. Hist.* 9 (1965), 249–59.

20983 MACMAHON (H. EDWARD). 'Malignant Nephro-sclerosis—50 Years Later'. *J. Hist. Med.* 21 (1966), 125–46.

20984 McMICHAEL (*Sir* JOHN). 'The Contributions of Clinical Medicine to Physiology'. *Advan. Sci.* 20 (1963), 254–8.

20985 MACNALTY (*Sir* ARTHUR SALUSBURY). 'The Prevention of Smallpox: From Edward Jenner to Monckton Copeman'. *Med. Hist.* 12 (1968), 1–18.

20986 MAEGRAITH (B. G.). 'History of the Liverpool School of Tropical Medicine'. *Med. Hist.* 16 (1972), 354–68.

20987 MANTON (IRENE). 'Recollections in the History of Electron Microscopy'. *Proc. Roy. Microsc. Soc.* 13. (1978), 45–57.

20988 MARTIN (J. PURDON). 'British Neurology in the Last 50 Years: Some Personal Experiences'. *Proc. Roy. Soc. Med.* 14 (1971), 1055–9.

20989 MEACHEN (GEORGE NORMAN). A Short History of Tuberculosis. 1936.

20990 MEDAWAR (PETER). 'Scientific Method and Medicine'. *Perspect. Biol. Med.* 19 (1975), 345–50.

20991 MERRILL (E. D.). 'Microfilm Records of the Linnean Society of London'. *Science* 96 (1942), 352.

20992 MILLER (EDWIN C.). 'Forty Years of Plant Physiology: Some General Impressions'. *Science* 97 (1943), 315–19.

20993 NITZBERG (WILLIAM D.). 'The Malaria Parasite: Discovery of its Development and Transmission'. *Synthesis* (Cambridge) 2(2) (1974), 28–41.

20994 YOELI (M.). 'Sir Ronald Ross and the Evolution of Malarial Research'. *Bull. NY Acad. Med.* 49 (1973), 722–35.

20995 NORMAN (HUBERT J.). 'Some Factors in the Reform in the Treatment of the Insane'. *Proc. Roy. Soc. Med.* 24 (1931), 1068–74.

20996 O'BANNION (KATHLEEN). 'A Comparative History of Modern Psychic Research'. *Synthesis* (Cambridge) 4(1) (1977), 33–48.

20997 OLBY (ROBERT C.). 'The Macromolecular Concept and the Origins of Molecular Biology'. *J. Chem. Educ.* 47 (1970), 168–74.

20998 —— 'The Origins of Molecular Genetics'. *J. Hist. Biol.* 7 (1974), 93–100.

20999 PATON (WILLIAM DRUMMOND MACDONALD). 'Sir Henry Dale (1875–1968): Some Letters and Papers'. *Rev. Roy. Soc. Lond.* 30 (1976), 231–48.

21000 PAYNE (L. M.). 'In Pursuit of Medical History'. *Proc. Roy. Soc. Med.* 66 (1973), 867–70.

21001 PRATT (JOSEPH HYDE). 'A Reappraisal of Researches Leading to the Discovery of Insulin'. *J. Hist. Med.* 9 (1954), 281–9.

21002 RIEPPEL (F. W.). 'Die Medizinschule von Edinburgh'. *Ciba. Rev.* 2 10 (1948), 4162–96.

21003 HOBSON (W.) *ed.* The Theory and Practice of Public Health. 1961. 5th edn 1979.

21004 HOLLAND (WALTER W.), DETELS (ROGER), *and* KNOX (GEORGE). Oxford Textbook of Public Health. 2 vols 1984.

21005 ROLLESTON (*Sir* HUMPHRY DAVY). 'The Progress and Pioneers of Preventive Medicine'. *Ann. Med. Hist.* 6 (1934), 94–109.

21006 ROLLIS (RICHARD H.). 'Cellular Pathology and the Development of the Deficiency Disease Concept'. *Bull. Hist. Med.* 34 (1960), 291–317.

21007 SACHS (A.). 'The Centenary of British Military Pathology'. *J. Roy. Army Med. Corps.* 150 (1955), 100–21.

21008 SCHERF (DAVID). 'A Cardiologist Remembers'. *Perspect. Biol. Med.* 40/41 (1968), 615–30.

21009 SHELLEY (HARRY S.). 'The Enlarged Prostate: A Brief History of its Treatment'. *J. Hist. Med.* 24 (1969), 452–73.

21010 SHROCK (RICHARD H.). 'Library Collections in Social Medicine'. *Bull. Amer. Lib. Assoc.* (1936), 351–62.

21011 McKEOWN (THOMAS) *and* LOWE (C. R.). An Introduction to Social Medicine. 1966.

21012 SINCLAIR (R. G.). 'High Blood Pressure—Ancient, Modern and Natural'. *J. Roy. Coll. Gen. Practitioners* 18 (1969), 201–13.

21013 STUCK (WALTER G.). 'Historic Backgrounds of Orthopaedic Surgery'. *Ann. Med. Hist.* 7 (1935), 36–48.

21014 TELEKY (LUDWIG). 'Certifying Surgeons—Examining Surgeons, a Century of Activity (Great Britain 1844–1944)'. *Bull. Hist. Med.* 16 (1944), 382–8.

21015 TOWERS (BERNARD). 'Medical Scientists and the View that History is Bunk'. *Perspect. Biol. Med.* 10 (1966), 44–55.

21016 UNDERWOOD (EDGAR ASHWORTH). 'The History of Cholera in Great Britain'. *Proc. Roy. Soc. Med.* 41 (1948), 165–73.

21017 —— 'The Centenary of British Public Health'. *Brit. Med. J.* 1 (1948), 1–9.

21018 —— 'The Quest for Child Health—The Historical Beginnings'. *Rep. Ann. Conf. Nat. Ass. Matern. Child Welfare* (London 1951), 3–10. 1951.

21019 —— 'Guy's Hospital'. *Nature* 176 (1955), 893–4.

21020 URDANG (GEORGE). 'The First Century of the Pharmaceutical Society of Great Britain'. *J. Amer. Pharm. Ass.* 3 (1942), 420–6.

21021 COWEN (DAVID L.). 'The Edinburgh Pharmacoepia: 1 Historical Development and Significance, 2 Bibliography'. *Med. Hist.* 1 (1957), 123–39, 340–51.

21022 ANNING (S. T.). 'The Apothecaries of the General Infirmary at Leeds'. *Med. Hist.* 5 (1961), 221–38.

21023 WADDINGTON (IVAN). 'The Development of Medical Ethics: A Sociological Analysis'. *Med. Hist.* 19 (1975), 36–51.

21024 WALLACE (A. T.). 'Sir Robert Philip: A Pioneer in the Campaign Against Tuberculosis'. *Med. Hist.* 5 (1961).

21025 WILLIAMS (HARLEY). 'The Morphology of State Medicine in Great Britain'. *Proc. Roy. Soc. Med.* 25 (1932), 1745–52.

21026 WILSON (LEONARD G.). 'The Clinical Definition of Scurvy and the Discovery of Vitamin C'. *J. Hist. Med.* 30 (1975), 40–60.

21027 WOOD (H. C. S.). 'The Birth of a Vitamin'. *Chemy Br.* 2 (1966), 536–41.

21028 WOOD (A.). 'History of the Cavendish Laboratory, Cambridge'. *Endeavour* 4 (1945), 131–5.

21029 COPE (*Sir* ZACHARY). A History of the Acute Abdomen. 1965.

21030 RAPER (H. R.). Man against Pain: The Epic of Anesthesia. NY. 1945.

21031 KEYS (THOMAS EDWARD). The History of Surgical Anaesthesia. NY. 1945. Repr. NY. 1963.

21032 THOMAS (K. BRYN). The Development of Anaesthetic Apparatus: A History Based on the Charles King Collection of the Association of Anaesthetists of Great Britain and Ireland. Oxf. 1975.

21033 SYKES (WILLIAM STANLEY). Essays on the First Hundred Years of Anaesthesia. 2 vols. Edin. 1960–1.

21034 ARMSTRONG DAVISON (M. H.). The Evolution of Anaesthesia. Baltimore, Md. 1965.

21035 KEELE (KENNETH DAVID). Anatomies of Pain. Oxf. 1957.

21036 —— 'James MacKenzie and Pain'. *J. Hist. Med.* 17 (1962), 116–28.

21037 FULTON (JOHN FARQUHAR) *and* STANTON (MADELINE E.). The Centennial of Surgical Anesthesia. An Annotated Catalogue. NY. 1946.

21038 UNDERWOOD (E. ASHWORTH). Before and After Morton. A Historical Survey of Anesthesia *et seq.* for the Centenary Exhibition at the Wellcome Historical Medical Museum. 1946. Repr. from *British Medical Journal*, 2 (1946), 525.

21039 FAULCONER (A.) *and* KEYS (T. E.). Foundations of Anesthesiology. 2 vols. Springfield, Ill. 1965.

21040 CHOULANT (JOHANN LUDWIG). History and Bibliography of Anatomic Illustration. *Transl. and annotated* by Frank Mortimer. NY. 1962.

21041 DOBSON (JESSIE). Anatomical Eponyms. Being a Biographical Dictionary of those Anatomists whose Names have Become Incorporated into Anatomical Nomenclature. First published 1946. 2nd edn Edin./Lond. 1962.

21042 BRAY (GEORGE W.). Recent Advances in Allergy (Asthma, Hay Fever, Eczema, Migraine etc.). Foreword by A. F. Hurst. Lond./ Philadelphia, Pa. 1931. [Practically a complete history of the field.].

21043 U.K. D.H.S.S. and OFFICE OF POPULATION CENSUSES AND SURVEYS. Report on hospital in-patient enquiry for the year 1972. Preliminary tables. 1973.

21044 WHITTAM (RONALD). General Physiology and the Biological Sciences; An Inaugural Lecture. Leics. 1967.

21045 BRITISH MEDICAL BULLETIN. Vol. 20, no. 1. Experimental Psychology. 1964.

21046 GARRISON (FIELDING HUDSON). A Medical Bibliography: A Check-list of Texts Illustrating the History of the Medical Sciences. Originally compiled by F. H. G. and now revised, with additions and annotations, by Leslie T. Morton. Lond. 1943. 2nd edn 1954. 3rd edn 1970.

21047 COLE (JOHN) *ed.* Wales and Medicine: An Historical Survey from Papers Given at the 9th British Congress on the History of Medicine at Swansea and Cardiff, 4–8 Sept. 1973. 1975.

21048 COMRIE (JOHN DIXON). History of Scottish Medicine Vol. II. 18th century to *ca.* 1930. 1932.

21049 ROBINSON (DOUGLAS H.). The Dangerous Sky: A History of Aviation Medicine. Henley-on-Thames/Seattle, Wash. 1973.

21050 ANDERSON (HENRY GRAEME). The Medical and Surgical Aspects of Aviation. With chapters on Applied Physiology of Aviation by Martin Flack and The Aeroneuroses of War Pilots by Oliver H. Gotch. 1919.

21051 FULTON (JOHN FARQUHAR). Aviation Medicine in its Preventive Aspects: An Historical Survey. 1948.

21052 HOFF (EBBE CURTIS) *and* FULTON (JOHN FARQUHAR). A Bibliography of Aviation Medicine. Springfield, Ill. 1942.

21053 ELLIS (HAROLD). A History of Bladder Stone. Oxf. 1969.

21054 SMITHERS (DAVID WALDRON). Possibilities in Cancer Prevention. Glasg. 1965.

21055 CAIRNS (JOHN). Cancer, Science and Society. 1978.

21056 OFFICE OF HEALTH ECONOMICS. 'The Common Illness of our Time': A Study of the Problem of Ischaemic Heart Disease. 1966.

21057 ROLLESTON (*Sir* HUMPHRY DAVY). Cardio-vascular Diseases since Harvey's Discovery. The Harveian Oration, 1928. 1928.

21058 —— 'History of Aortic Regurgitation'. *Ann. Med. Hist.* 2 (1940), 271–9.

21059 —— 'History of Haematology'. *Proc. Roy. Soc. Med.* (1933–4).

21060 EAST (CHARLES FREDERICK TERENCE). The Story of Heart Disease. [The Fitzpatrick lectures for 1956 and 1957, given before The Royal College of Physicians of London.] 1957.

21061 LEIBOWITZ (JOSHUA O.). The History of Coronary Heart Disease. [Publications of the Wellcome Institute of the History of Medicine.] Lond./Berkeley, Calif. 1970.

21062 NOONAN (J. T.). Contraception: The History of its Treatment by the Catholic Theologians and Canonists. Harvard, Mass. 1965.

21063 HIMES (NORMAN E.). Medical History of Contraception. NY. 1963.

21064 STOPES (MARIE CARMICHAEL). Contraception (Birth Control): Its Theory, History and Practice: A Manual for the Medical and Legal Professions. 1923.

21065 WOOD (CLIVE) *and* SUITTERS (BERYL). The Fight for Acceptance: A History of Contraception. Aylesbury. 1970.

21066 BONE (MARGARET). Family Planning Services in England and Wales. An Enquiry Carried out on Behalf of the Department of Health and Social Security [by] the Office of Population Censuses and Surveys. 1973.

21067 —— The Family Planning Services: Changes and Effects: A Survey Carried out on Behalf of the D.H.S.S. Office of Population Censuses and Surveys. 1978.

21068 FINCH (B. E.) *and* GREEN (HUGH). Contraception through the Ages. Springfield, Ill. 1963.

21069 GREEN (SHIRLEY). The Curious History of Contraception. 1971.

21070 PUSEY (W. A.). The History of Dermatology. Springfield, Ill. 1933.

21071 STRIKER (C.). Famous Faces in Diabetes. Boston, Mass. 1961.

21072 PAPASPYROS (N. S.). The History of Diabetes Mellitus. 1952. New edn Stuttgart. 1964.

21073 LASSEK (A. M.). Human Dissection: Its Drama and Struggle. Springfield, Ill. 1958.

21074 KEVORKIAN (J.). The Story of Dissection. NY. 1959.

21075 COLWELL (HECTOR A.). An Essay on the History of Electrotherapy and Diagnosis. 1922.

21076 ROLLESTON (*Sir* HUMPHRY DAVY). The Endocrine Organs in Health and Disease. With a Historical Review. 1936.

21077 CHRISTOPHERS (SAMUEL RICKARD). 'Symposium to Commemorate the "Birth of Medical Entomology" Dedicated to Sir Rickard Christophers on his 100th birthday'. *Trans. Roy. Soc. Trop. Med. Hyg.* 67 (1973), 728–54.

21078 —— A Tribute to Sir Rickard Christophers on his 100th Birthday. *Trans. Roy. Ent. Soc. Lond.* 125 (1974), 253–6.

21079 U.K. CENTRAL HEALTH SERVICES COUNCIL. Joint Sub-Committee of the Standing Medical Advisory Committee and the Advisory Committee on the Health and Welfare of Handicapped Persons. 1969. People with epilepsy report. [J. J. A. Reid, Chairman.].

21080 SCOTLAND. SCOTTISH HEALTH SERVICES COUNCIL. Standing Medical Advisory Committee. 1968. The medical care of epilepsy in Scotland report. Edin. 1968.

21081 OFFICE OF HEALTH ECONOMICS. Studies in Current Health Problems. No. 38 Epilepsy in Society. 1971.

21082 BAGLEY (CHRISTOPHER). The Social Psychology of the Child with Epilepsy. 1971.

21083 GRMEK (M. D.). On Ageing and Old Age: Basic Problems and Historic Aspects of Gerontology and Geriatrics. (Monographiae biologicae. Vol. V No. 2). The Hague. 1958.

21084 ROLLESTON (*Sir* HUMPHRY DAVY). Medical Aspects of Old Age. Being a revised and enlarged edition of the Linacre lecture, 1922. 1932.

21085 GLASGOW POSTGRADUATE MEDICAL BOARD. Current Achievements in Geriatrics. 1964.

21086 COPEMAN (WILLIAM SIDNEY CHARLES). A Short History of the Gout and the Rheumatic Diseases. Berkeley, Calif./Los Angeles, Calif. 1964.

21087 TIMSON (J.). 'Social Factors in the Incidence of Spina Bifida and Anencephaly'. *J. Biosoc. Sci.* 2(1) (1970), 81–4.

21088 BOON (R. A.) *and* ROBERTS (D. F.). 'The Social Impact of Haemophilia'. *J. Biosoc. Sci.* 2(3) (1970), 237–364.

21089 YOUNG (J. H.). Caesarian Section: The History and Development of the Operation from Earliest Times. 1944.

21090 JAMESON (E. M.). Gynaecology and Obstetrics. (Clio Medica, No. 17). NY. 1962.

21091 GRAHAM ([FLACK] HARVEY [ISAAC HARVEY]). Eternal Eve. The History of Gynecology and Obstetrics. Lond./Garden City. 1951.

21092 PARISH (HENRY JAMES). A History of Immunization. Edin./Lond. 1965.

21093 —— Bacterial and Virus Diseases: Antisera, Toxoids, Vaccines and Tuberculins in Prophylaxis and Treatment. Edin. 1948.

21094 —— Victory with Vaccines: The Story of Immunization. Edinburgh. 1968. [A popular version of A History of Immunization.].

21095 FISHBEIN (MORRIS) *ed.* A Bibliography of Infantile Paralysis. With selected abstracts and annotations compiled by L. Hektoen and E. M. Salmonsen. 1789–1949. 2nd edn Philadelphia, Pa. 1951.

21096 COLLIER (RICHARD). The Plague of the Spanish Lady: The Influenza Pandemic of 1918–1919. 1974.

21097 BEVERIDGE (WILLIAM IAN BEARDMORE). Influenza, the Last Great Plague: An Unfinished Story of Discovery. 1977.

21098 CUTTER (I. S.) *and* VIETS (H. R.). A Short History of Midwifery. Philadelphia, Pa. 1964.

21099 BAIRD (*Sir* DUGALD). The Interplay of Changes in Society, Reproductive Habits and Obstetric Practice in Scotland between 1922 and 1972. 1975. [Offprint from *British Journal of Preventive and Social Medicine*.].

21100 KERR (JOHN MARTIN MUNRO), JOHNSTONE (R. W.), *and* PHILLIPS (MILES H.). Historical Review of British Obstetrics and Gynaecology, 1800–1950. Edin./Lond. 1954.

21101 CIANFRANI (T.). A Short History of Obstetrics and Gynaecology. Springfield, Ill./Oxf. 1960.

21102 SNYDER (CHARLES). A Bibliography of the History of Ophthalmology for 1952–1954. *Arch. Ophthalmol.* 55 (1956), 397–407 and continuing.

21103 ARRINGTON (G. E.). A History of Ophthalmology. (MD monographs on Medical History, Vol. 3). NY. 1959.

21104 CHANCE (B.). Ophthalmology. (Clio Medica, No. 20). NY. 1962.

21105 BICK (EDGAR M.). Source Book of Orthopaedics. 2nd edn Baltimore, Md. 1948. [A facsimile reprint of the 1948 edn with more than 600 additional references was published in New York in 1968.].

21106 STEVENSON (R. S.) *and* GUTHRIE (DUNCAN). A History of Oto-laryngology. Edin./Baltimore, Md. 1949.

21107 FOSTER (WILLIAM DEREK). A History of Parasitology. Edin./Lond. 1965.

21108 LONG (E. R.). A History of Pathology. 2nd edn Lond./NY. 1965.

21109 —— *Ed.* Selected Readings in Pathology. 2nd edn. Springfield, Ill. 1961.

21110 FOSTER (WILLIAM DEREK). A Short History of Clinical Pathology. With a chapter on the organisation of clinical pathology to the present day, by S. C. Dyke. Edin./Lond. 1961.

21111 KRUMBHAAR (EDWARD BELL). Pathology. (Clio Medica, No. 19). NY. 1962.

21112 COURT (SEYMOUR DONALD MAYNEORD) *ed.* The Medical Care of Children. 1963.

21113 —— Fit for the Future: Report of the Committee on Child Health Services. 2 vols. 1976.

21114 BRITISH PAEDIATRIC ASSOCIATION. Paediatrics in the seventies: developing the child health services. *Ed.* by Donald Court and Anthony Jackson. 1972.

21115 PARSONS (*Sir* LEONARD GREGORY) *ed.* Modern Trends in Paediatrics. 1951.

21116 PARSONS (*Sir* LEONARD GREGORY) and BARLING (SEYMOUR GILBERT) *eds.* Diseases of Infancy and Childhood. 1st edn 2 vols. 1933. 2nd edn 2 vols. 1954.

21117 —— 'Child Health and the Universities'. In Modern Trends in Public Health by Sir A. Massey, *ed.* 1949.

21118 ABT (I. A.) *ed.* Abt-Garrison History of Pediatrics. Reprinted from Pediatrics by various authors (with new chapters on the history of pediatrics in recent times by A. I. Abt). Philadelphia, Pa. 1965.

21119 COULTER (J. S.). Physical Therapy. NY. 1932.

21120 OFFICE OF HEALTH ECONOMICS. Pneumonia in Decline. 1963.

21121 —— The Price of Poliomyelitis. 1963.

21122 —— The Residue of Poliomyelitis [by Michael Lee]. 1965.

21123 FISHER (P. J.). The Polio Story. 1967.

21124 BERG (L. H.). Polio and its Problems. Philadelphia, Pa. 1948.

21125 GLASSER (OTTO) *et al.* Physical Foundations of Radiology. 3rd edn 1961.

21126 DEWING (S.). Modern Radiology in Historical Perspective. Springfield, Ill. 1962.

21127 BRITISH LEAGUE AGAINST RHEUMATISM. Rheumatism: The Price We Pay. The impact of the rheumatic diseases on the individual and the country. 1977.

21128 OFFICE OF HEALTH ECONOMICS. Rheumatism and Arthritis in Britain. 1973.

21129 LAWRENCE (J. S.). Rheumatism in Populations. 1977.

21130 FRIEDMAN (R.) The Story of Scabies. Vol. I. The Prevalence (Civil and Military), Prevention and Treatment of Scabies, and the Biology of Acarus Scabiei, from the Earliest Times to the Beginning of World War II. NY. 1947.

21131 HESS (A. F.). Scurvy: Past and Present. Philadelphia, Pa. 1920.

21132 MILLER (G.). The Adoption of Inoculation for Smallpox in England and France. Philadelphia, Pa. 1957.

21133 ELDRIDGE (MARGARET). A History of the Treatment of Speech Disorders. Edin./Melbourne. 1968.

21134 HURWITZ (A.) *and* DEGENSHEIM (G. A.). Milestones in Modern Surgery. 1958.

21135 ZIMMERMAN (LEO M.) *and* VEITH (ILZA). Great Ideas in the History of Surgery. 1961.

21136 WATSON-JONES (REGINALD). Surgery is Destined to the Practice of Medicine. Edin. 1961.

21137 GILLIES (*Sir* HAROLD DELF). Plastic Surgery of the Face. Based on selected cases of war injuries of the face, including burns. 1920.

21138 —— The Development and Scope of Plastic Surgery. [Northwestern University Medical School. The Charles H. Mayo Lecture in Surgery. 4.]. Chicago, Ill. 1935.

21139 GILLIES (*Sir* HAROLD DELF) *with* MILLARD (DAVID RALPH) *Jnr*. The Principles and Art of Plastic Surgery. 1957.

21140 GIBSON (JOHN). The Development of Surgery. 1967.

21141 NISSEN (R.) *and* WILSON (R. H. L.). Pages in the History of Chest Surgery. Springfield, Ill. 1960.

21142 ROSS (JAMES A.). The Edinburgh School of Surgery after Lister. Edin. 1978.

21143 POWER (*Sir* D'ARCY). A Short History of Surgery. 1933.

21144 —— A Mirror for Surgeons: Selected Readings in Surgery. Boston, Mass. 1939.

21145 MEADE (RICHARD H.). An Introduction to the History of General Surgery. Philadelphia, Pa. 1968.

21146 —— A History of Thoracic Surgery. Oxf. 1961.

21147 LEONARDO (R. A.). History of Surgery. NY. 1943.

21148 RICHARDSON (ROBERT G.). The Surgeon's Heart: A History of Cardiac Surgery. 1969.

21149 LEARMONTH (*Sir* JAMES RÖGNVALD). The Contribution of Surgery to Preventive Medicine. (Heath Clark Lectures, 1949, delivered at the London School of Hygiene and Tropical Medicine). Lond./NY. 1951.

21150 GRAHAM ([ISAAC HARVEY FLACK] HARVEY). Surgeons All. 1939. Amer. edn: The Story of Surgery. NY. 1939.

21151 BISHOP (W. J.). A History of Surgical Dressing. Chesterfield. 1959.

21152 ELLIOTT (ISABELLE M.) *and* ELLIOTT (JAMES RAWLINGS). A Short History of Surgical Dressing. 1964.

21153 CARTWRIGHT (FREDERICK F.). The Development of Modern Surgery from 1830. 1967.

21154 MACNALTY (*Sir* ARTHUR SALUSBURY). A Report on Tuberculosis. 1932.

21155 MYERS (J. ARTHUR). Captain of all these Men of Death. Tuberculosis Historical Highlights. Foreword by Richard M. Burke. Intro. by Gaylord W. Anderson. St Louis, Mo. 1977.

21156 WAKSMAN (SELMAN A.). The Conquest of Tuberculosis. Berkeley, Calif. 1964.

21157 —— The Antibiotic Era: A History. 1975.

21158 FLICK (L. F.). Development of our Knowledge of Tuberculosis. Philadelphia, Pa. 1925.

21159 DUBOS (RENÉ JEAN) *and* DUBOS (J.). The White Plague: Tuberculosis, Man and Society. Boston, Mass. 1952.

21160 HEAF (FREDERICK ROLAND GEORGE) *and* RUSBY (NORMAN LLOYD). Recent Advances in Respiratory Tuberculosis. 4th edn 1948.

21161 —— *Ed*. Symposium of Tuberculosis. 1957.

21162 CUMMINS (S. LYLE). Tuberculosis in History, From the 17th Century to our own Times. With an introduction by Sir Arthur Salusbury MacNalty. Baltimore, Md. 1949.

21163 BANKOFF (G.). The Conquest of Tuberculosis. 1946.

21164 BURKE (R. M.). An Historical Chronology of Tuberculosis. 2nd edn Springfield, Ill. 1955.

21165 IMMEROUT (M. A.) *ed*. Classical Articles in Urology. Springfield, Ill. 1967.

21166 BALLENGER (E. G.). History of Urology. 2 vols Baltimore, Md. 1933.

21167 BLENKINSOP (LAYTON JOHN) *and* RAINEY (JOHN WAKE-FIELD) *eds*. Veterinary Services. [History of the Great War based on official documents.]. 1925.

21168 GRUBBÉ (E. H.). X-ray Treatment: Its Origin, Birth and Early History. St Paul and Minneapolis, Minn. 1949.

3. GENERAL ON MAN AND MEDICINE

21169 OSLER (*Sir* WILLIAM). The Evolution of Modern Medicine. New Haven, Conn. 1921.

21170 LIBBY (W.). History of Medicine in its Salient Features. Boston, Mass. 1922.

21171 PHILIP (*Sir* ROBERT). The Strategic Front of Medicine Today. Being the Presidential Address at the Meeting of the British Medical Association held in Edinburgh, July 1927. Edin. 1927.

21172 CRUIKSHANK (ERNEST WILLIAM HENDERSON). The Value of Scientific Thought in the Advance of Modern Medicine. 1928.

21173 ROLLESTON (*Sir* HUMPHRY DAVY). Aspects of Age, Life and Disease. 1928.

21174 COLLIE (*Sir* ROBERT JOHN) *ed*. Recent Progress in Medicine and Surgery, 1919–1933. 1933.

21175 RITCHIE-CALDER (PETER). *Baron of Balmashannar*. The Conquest of Suffering. 1934.

21176 GALDSTON (IAGO). Progress in Medicine: A Critical Review of the Last Hundred Years. NY. 1940.

21177 ROBINSON (VICTOR). The Story of Medicine. New edn NY. 1943.

21178 HUXLEY (J. S.) *et al*. Reshaping Man's Heritage. 1944. [Ch. by James MacAllister Mackintosh on Preventive Medicine.].

21179 LEONARDO (R. A.). History of Medical Thought. NY. 1946.

21180 PEARSON (SIDNEY VERE). Men, Medicine and Myself. 1946.

21181 —— The State Provision of Sanatoriums. 1913.

21182 SHROCK (RICHARD HARRISON). The Development of Modern Medicine, an Interpretation of the Social and Scientific Factors Involved. New edn NY. 1947.

21183 METTLER (C. C.). History of Medicine: A Correlative Text Arranged According to Subjects. Philadelphia, Pa. 1947.

21184 PODOLSKY (E.). Doctors, Drugs and Steel: The Story of Medicine's Battle Against Death. Lond./NY. 1947.

21185 MAJOR (RALPH H.). A History of Medicine. 2 vols. Springfield, Ill./Oxf. 1954–5. [Second volume has chapter on 20th century.].

21186 —— 'Note on the History of Asthma'. In Science, Medicine and History. *Ed.* Edgar Ashworth Underwood.

21187 MIDDLETON (WILLIAM). Intellectual Crossroads. An Appreciation of Ralph H. Major. *Perspect. Biol. Med.* 14 (1971), 651–8.

21188 HORDER (THOMAS JEEVES). *Baron.* Fifty Years of Medicine, Being the Harben Lectures for 1952: Delivered at the Royal Institute of Public Health and Hygiene, December 9, 10 and 11, 1952, with Sir A. MacNalty in the chair. 1953.

21189 —— Health and a Day. 1937.

21190 WALKER (KENNETH MACFARLANE). The Story of Medicine. 1954.

21191 ACKERKNECHT (ERWIN H.). A Short History of Medicine. NY. 1955.

21192 —— Therapeutics from the Primitives to the 20th Century. With an appendix: History of Dietetics. NY. 1974.

21193 —— *Ed.* Metabolism and Respiration, from Erasistratus to Lavoisier. Metabolism from Liebig to the Present. The History of Metabolic Diseases. *Ciba Symp.* 6 (1944), 1815–44.

21194 BETT (WALTER R.). The History and Conquest of Some Common Diseases. Norman, Okla. 1954.

21195 ATKINSON (D. T.). Magic, Myth and Medicine. Cleveland, Ohio. 1956.

21196 GUTHRIE (DOUGLAS JAMES). A History of Medicine. Lond./Edin. 1958. [Deals with earlier period but some remarks on 20th century figures in history of science, and a nice brief sketch of Sir William Osler.].

21197 CALDER (RITCHIE). Medicine and the Man: The Story of the Art and Science of Healing. NY. 1958.

21198 —— The Life Savers. [1962]. [A popular account of contributions of research chemists to the development of life-saving drugs.].

21199 GARRISON (FIELDING HUDSON). An Introduction to the History of Medicine, with Medical Chronology, Suggestions for Study and Bibliographic Data. 4th edn Philadelphia, Pa./Lond. 1961.

21200 POYNTER (FREDERICK NOEL LAWRENCE) *and* KEELE (K. D.). A Short History of Medicine. (Science in Society, No. 2). 1961.

21201 POYNTER (FREDERICK NOEL LAWRENCE). Compilation of Printed Books in the Wellcome Historical Medical Library. 1962.

21202 BONNAR (ALPHONSUS). Medicine and Men. 1962. Repr. 1964.

21203 SINGER (CHARLES) *and* UNDERWOOD (EDGAR ASHWORTH). A Short History of Medicine. 2nd edn Oxf. 1962. [Good section on modern medicine. Extensive bibliography.].

21204 ROGERS (F. B.). A Syllabus of Medical History. Boston, Mass. 1962.

21205 KING (LESTER S.). The Growth of Medical Thought. Chicago, Ill. 1963. [Low on details of achievements, high on concepts and ideas.].

21206 —— ed. A History of Medicine: Selected Readings. Harmondsworth. 1971.

21207 —— ed. Mainstreams of Medicine: Essays on the Social and Intellectual Context of Medical Practice. Austin, Tex. 1971.

21208 KEELE (KENNETH DAVID). The Evolution of Clinical Methods in Medicine. Lond./NY. 1969. (Being the Fitzpatrick Lectures delivered at the Royal College of Physicians 1960–1.).

21209 MCMANUS (J. I. F. A.). The Fundamental Ideas of Medicine: A Brief History of Medicine. Springfield, Ill. 1963.

21210 HARMAN (J. B.). Perspectives of Medicine. 1964.

21211 LAPAGE (GEOFFREY). Man Against Disease. NY./Lond. 1964.

21212 STAROBINSKI (J.). A History of Medicine. NY. 1964.

21213 WIGHTMAN (WILLIAM PERSEHOUSE DELISLE). The Emergence of Scientific Medicine. Edin. 1971.

21214 GREEN (J. R.). Medical History for Students. Springfield, Ill. 1968.

21215 LLOYD (WYNDHAM E. B.). A Hundred Years of Medicine. 2nd edn Lond./NY. 1968. [First publ. 1936.].

21216 STEVENSON (L.) *and* MULTHAUF (R.). *eds.* Medicine, Science and Culture. Baltimore, Md. 1968.

21217 BUTTERFIELD (WILLIAM JOHN HUGHES). Priorities in Medicine. 1968.

21218 POYNTER (FREDERICK NOEL LAWRENCE) ed. Medicine and Culture: Proceedings of an Historical Symposium Organized Jointly by the Wellcome Institute of the History of Medicine, London, and the Wenner-Gren Foundation for Anthropological Research. NY. 1969.

21219 BALDRY (PETER EDWARD). The Battle Against Heart Disease; A Physician Traces the History of Man's Achievements in this Field for the General Reader. 1971.

21220 CLARKE (EDWIN) ed. Modern Methods in the History of Medicine. 1971.

21221 —— 'The History and Sociology of the Medical Sciences'. *Actes xiie Cong. Inl. Hist. Sci.* 8 (1968), 21–4.

21222 —— Modern Methods in the History of Medicine. 1971.

21223 POYNTER (FREDERICK NOEL LAWRENCE). Medicine and Man. 1971.

21224 BEVERIDGE (WILLIAM IAN BEARDMORE). Frontiers in Comparative Medicine. 1972.

21225 MORLEY (PETER). Marginal Medicine. 1976.

21226 ROBSON (JAMES SCOTT). Medicine Yesterday and Today. Edinburgh. 1978. [Inaugural lecture.].

21227 ENGLAND (J. M.). Medical Research. A Statistical and Epidemiological Approach. Edin. 1975.

21228 McLACHLAN (GORDON) *and* SHEGOG (RICHARD A.) *eds.* Computers in the Service of Medicine: Essays on Current Research and Applications. 1968. [Publ. for NPHT.].

21229 LEACH (GERALD). The Biocrats: Implications of Medical Progress. Revised edn Harmondsworth. 1972.

21230 GODBER (*Sir* GEORGE). Change in Medicine. 1976. [NPHT.].

21231 CARTWRIGHT (FREDERICK F). A Social History of Medicine. 1977.

21232 BAILEY (NORMAN THOMAS JOHN). Mathematics, Statistics, and Systems for Health. Chichester. 1977.

21233 REISER (STANLEY JOEL). Medicine and the Reign of Technology. Camb. 1978.

21234 SNYDER (LAURENCE HASBROUCK). Blood Grouping in Relation to Clinical and Legal Medicine. 1929. [Includes a history of blood transfusion.].

21235 LANGDON-BROWN (WALTER). Some Chapters in Cambridge Medical History. Camb. 1946.

21236 GILBERT (J. B.). Disease and Destiny: A Bibliography of Medical References to the Famous. 1962.

21237 UNDERWOOD (EDGAR ASHWORTH) ed. Science, Medicine and History. Essays in honour of Charles Singer. 1953. Includes George E. Gask and John Todd, 'The Origin of Hospitals' and Douglas James Guthrie, 'The Evolution of Cardiology'.

21238 WOGLOM (W. H.). Discoverers for Medicine. 1949.

21239 FLEETWOOD (J.). History of Medicine in Ireland. Dublin. 1951.

21240 JARAMILLO-ARANGO (J.). The British Contribution to Medicine. Edin./Lond. 1953.

21241 BROWNING (ETHEL). Health and Fitness. 1937.

21242 —— Health in Middle Life. 1938.

21243 —— Modern Drugs in General Practice. 1940. 2nd edn 1947.

21244 —— Toxic Solvents. 1953. [Earlier work 1937 and later 1959 and 1965.].

21245 —— The Vitamins + Bibliography. 1931.

21246 —— Harmful Effects of Ionising Radiations. Amsterdam. 1959.

21247 —— Toxicity of Industrial Metals. 1961.

4. MEDICINE-THE WORLD

21248 BESTERMAN (THEODORE). Medicine: A Bibliography of Bibliographies. Totowa, N.J. 1971.

21249 ROLLESTON (*Sir* HUMPHRY) *gen. ed.* The British Encyclopaedia of Medical Practice. 13 vols (1936–41).

21250 —— *gen. ed.* Cumulative Supplement. 1939–52.

21251 HORDER *Lord, gen. ed.* The British Encyclopaedia of Medical Practice. 13 vols. 2nd edn 1950–53.

21252 —— Cumulative Supplement, Including Index of New Subjects. (1967). 1931.

21253 —— *ed. in chief.* Medical Progress. 1968.

21254 BLAKE (JOHN) *and* ROOS (CHARLES). Medical Reference Works. (1679–1966). A selected bibliography. Chicago, Ill. 1967.

21255 CLARK (MARY VIRGINIA) *comp.* Supplement 1. (1967–1968). Chicago, Ill. 1970.

21256 KELLY (EMERSON CROSBY). Encyclopedia of Medical Sources. Baltimore, Md. 1948.

21257 JOINT COMMITTEE OF THE GENERAL COUNCIL OF THE BAR OF ENGLAND AND WALES, THE LAW SOCIETY AND THE BRITISH MEDICAL ASSOCIATION. Medical Evidence in Courts of Law: The Report. 1965.

21258 WOODRUFF (*Sir* MICHAEL FRANCIS ADDISON). The One and the Many: 'Patient Care in the World of Today' and 'The Cost of Progress', Two Lectures on Ethical Considerations Relating to the Practice of Medicine. 1970.

21259 —— And Ghosts Shall Drive You On. Glasg. 1976. [The MacEwen Memorial Lecture. 17.].

21260 —— On Science and Surgery. Edin. 1977.

5. MISCELLANEOUS

21261 HURD-MEAD (K. C.). History of Women in Medicine. 1938.

21262 LEESON (JOYCE) *and* GRAY (JUDITH). Women and Medicine. 1978.

21263 ALLDAY (RICHARD KIME). On Medicine in Britain and the National Health Service. With a foreword by A. H. Douthwaite. Bristol. 1962.

21264 COOPER (MICHAEL HYMIE) *and* CULYER (ANTHONY JOHN). The Price of Blood. I.E.A. 1968.

21265 LEFF (SAMUEL) *and* LEFF (VERA). The School Health Service. 1959.

21266 LEFF (SAMUEL). Social Medicine. 1953.

21267 GOODMAN (NEVILLE MARRIOTT). Wilson Jameson: Architect of National Health. (With a Foreword by Sir George Godber). 1970.

21268 McCLEARY (GEORGE FREDERICK). National Health Insurance. 1932.

21269 LEVY (HERMANN). National Health Insurance—A Critical Study. Camb. 1944.

21270 LICHT (S.) *ed.* Occupational Therapy Source Book. Baltimore, Md. 1948.

21271 RADCLIFFE (WALTER). Milestones in Midwifery. Bristol. 1967.

21272 RODDIS (L. H.). A Short History of Nautical Medicine. NY. 1941.

21273 HOFFMAN (FREDERICK L.). 'The Mortality from Respiratory Diseases in the Glass Industry'. *J. Ind. Hygiene* (May 1920), 1–5.

21274 SHEPARD (NORMAN A.) *and* KRALL (STANLEY). 'Poisons in the Rubber Industry. The Rash Produced by Hexamethylene-tetramine and a Means of Prevention'. *J. Ind. Hygiene* (May 1920), 33–8.

21275 HALDANE (JOHN SCOTT). 'Stone Dust and Mine Explosion'. *Times Eng. Suppt* 14 (Jan. 1916).

21276 —— 'The Effects of Dust Inhalation [on Miners]'. *Trans. Mining Engineers* 55(4) (1918), 264–93.

21277 DAVIES (H. W.). 'Dust Inhalation and Miners' Phthisis'. *Sci. Prog.* (Oct. 1919), 329–30.

21278 —— 'A Scheme for Mining Centres'. *J. Inl Welfare* (May 1920), 115–19.

21279 OLIVER (*Sir* THOMAS). 'Phthisis and Occupation'. *J. Ind. Hygiene* (July 1920), 115–19.

21280 COSSONS (W. E.). 'The Case for Pithead Baths in Great Britain'. *J. Ind. Hygiene* (Nov. 1920), 241–6.

21281 ROGAN (JOHN M.) *ed.* Medicine in the Mining Industries. 1972.

21282 BRYAN (*Sir* ANDREW). The Evolution of Health and Safety in Mines. 1975.

21283 ROLLESTON (*Sir* HUMPHRY). 'The Aims and Methods of Graduate Study'. *Brit. Med. J.* (17 Jan. 1920), 77–9.

21284 ELLIOT SMITH (G.). 'Medical Research'. *Nature* (8 July 1920), 573–5. (15 July 1920), 605–7.

21285 —— 'The Profession of Medicine'. (Educational number). *Brit. Med. J.* (4 Sept. 1920), 339–79.

21286 PORTER (CHARLES). 'Citizenship and Health—Questions in War-Time'. *J. State Medicine* (Sept. 1917), 276–82. (Oct. 1917), 300–6.

21287 HOPE (E. W.). 'Civil Sanitation and the War'. *J. State Medicine* (Jan. 1918), 18–26.

21288 WHYTE (W. E.). (a): 'The Coming of the New Public Health Era'. (b): 'The National Aspect of Public Health'. (Presidential address). *Trans. Inc. San. Assn Scot.* 1919. (1920), 1–14.

21289 COLLIS (EDGAR L.). 'Aims of the Welsh National Medical School, with Special Reference to Preventive Medicine'. *Lancet* (3 Jan. 1920), 6–11.

21290 HARRIS (HENRY J.). 'The British National Health Insurance System, 1911–19'. *Mthly Labor. R.* (January 1920), 45–59.

21291 BASKETT (BERTRAM G. M.). 'Public Health *Versus* the State'. (Insurance act *not* in interests of public health and followed by an increase in deaths from tuberculosis.). *Brit. Med. J.* (10 Jan. 1920). [Corresp. 17–31 Jan., 14 and 28 Feb., 6–20 Mar., and 10 Apr. 1920.].

21292 —— 'Arbitration on Rate of Medical Remuneration'. *Brit. Med. J.Suppt* (28 Feb. 1920), 46–54.

21293 HARE (E. H.) *and* SHAW (G. K.). 'A Study in Family Health. i. Health in Relation to Family Size. ii. A Comparison of the Health of Fathers, Mothers and Children'. *Brit. J. Psychiatry*, 3(475) (1965), 461–71.

6. HEALTH CARE

21294 GILL (D. G.) *and* HOROBIN (G. W.). 'Doctors, Patients and the State: Relationships and Decision-making'. *Sociol. Rev.* 20(4) (1972), 505–20.

21295 PEACOCK (ALAN) *and* SHANNON (R.). 'The New Doctor's Dilemma'. *Lloyds Bank Rev.* 87 (1968), 26–38.

21296 MCKINLAY (J. B.). 'Who is Really Ignorant—Physician or Patient?'. *J. Health Soc. Behav.* 16 (1975), 3–11.

21297 MADDOX (H.). 'The Work and Status of Mental Nurses'. *Sociol. R.* 2(2) (1954), 195–208.

21298 JONES (*Sir* ROBERT). 'The Orthopaedic Outlook in Military Surgery'. *Brit. Med. J.* 41–5 (12 Jan. 1917).

21299 —— 'Military Orthopaedic Treatment [in the U.K.]'. *Lancet* (27 July 1918) 115–19.

21300 MALLET (*Sir* BERNARD). 'The Effects of the War as Shown in Vital Statistics'. *J. State Medicine* (Aug. 1918), 225–47.

21301 GEORGE (W. L.). 'High Birth Rates and Low Lives'. *Forth Rev.* (Mar. 1920), 453–60.

21302 TURNER (J. G.). 'What Steps can be Taken to Improve the Teeth of the Nation?'. *J. State Medicine* (Sept. 1918), 269–82.

21303 DUNN (SAMUEL). 'The Care of Young Children's Teeth'. *Trans. Inc. San. Assn Scot.*, 1919, (1920) 157–72.

21304 BURNET (JAMES). 'Teeth and the Worker'. *J. Ind. Hyg.* (Mar. 1920), 546–9.

21305 ELLIOTT (RALPH W.). 'The Industrial Dental Clinic from the Standpoint of the Industrial Surgeon'. *J. Ind. Hyg.* (Apr. 1920), 575–81.

21306 CANTLIE (*Sir* JAMES). 'Organizing the Civil Medical Profession on Army Lines'. *J. Trop. Medicine* (Mar. 1919), 40–3.

21307 DINGLE (REGINALD JAMES). 'Doctors and the Public: Do we Suffer from Medical Priestcraft?'. *Rev. of Revs* (June 1920), 404–7.

21308 MACDONALD (PETER). 'The Discussion at Cambridge on the Future of Medical Practice'. *Brit. Med. J.* (18 Sept. 1920), 450–1.

21309 HARRIS (D. FRASER). 'The Medical and Allied Professions as a State Service'. *Sci. Mthly* (Sept. 1920), 235–45.

21310 ASTOR (WALDORF). 'Health Problems and a State Ministry of Health'. *J. State Med.* (1918), 170–7.

21311 HOPE (EDWARD WILLIAM). 'Some Constructive Suggestions in Regard to the Proposed Ministry of Health'. *J. State Med.* (Aug. 1918), 248–56.

21312 —— 'The Influence of a Ministry of Health on Local Organization and Administration'. *J. State Med.* (Nov. 1918), 338–44.

21313 SMITH (Sir WILLIAM). 'The Work of the Ministry of Health'. *J. State Med.* (Sept. 1919), 262–7.

21314 FREMANTLE (FRANCIS E.). 'Local Administration of the Work of the Ministry of Health'. *J. State Med.* (Sept. 1919), 268–70.

21315 KEITH (ARTHUR). 'Anthropometry and National Health'. *J. State Med.* (Feb. 1919), 33–42.

21316 HALL (G. ROME). 'A Study of Certain Effects of Occupation and Race on the Health of Recruits'. *Lancet* (5 June 1920), 1218–20.

21317 SCHARLIEB (MARY). 'A Terrible Census'. *19th Cent.* (July 1920), 128–35.

21318 GALLOWAY (*Sir* JAMES). 'The War Physical Census'. *Brit. Med. J.* (11 Sept. 1920), 381–4.

21319 ZOLA (I. K.). 'Medicine as an Institution of Social Control'. *Sociol. Rev.* n.s. 20(4) (1972), 487–504.

21320 WATKIN (BRIAN). 'Management in the Reorganised Health Service: The Framework'. *Nursing Mirror* 140 No. 3 (1975).

21321 —— 'Moneymatters'. *Nursing Mirror* No. 7.

21322 —— 'Best Laid Plans'. *Nursing Mirror* No. 8.

21323 —— 'Personnel Priorities'. *Nursing Mirror* No. 9.

21324 —— 'Changing Times'. *Nursing Mirror* No. 10.

21325 WILLCOCKS (A. J.). 'A Survey of Social Research into the National Health Service'. *Soc. Econ. Admin* (Autumn 1969).

21326 SOMERS (H. M.) *and* SOMERS (A. R.). 'The Health Service: Diagnosis and Prognosis'. *Pol. Q.* 27(4) (1956), 410–22.

21327 REISSMAN (C. K.). 'The Use of Health Services by the Poor'. *Social Policy* (May–June 1974).

21328 MARTIN (F. M.) *and* REHIN (G. F.). 'Towards Community Care. Problems and Policies in the Mental Health Service'. *PEP Broadsheet* 508 (1969), 197–275.

[N.B. This entry was originally cited as *Planning*, but the name was changed at the end of 1968].

21329 MCKEOWN (T.). 'The Next Forty Years in Public Health'. *Pop. Studs* 17(3) (1964), 269–92.

21330 LOWE (C. R.) *and* MCKEOWN (T.). 'Incidence of Infectious Disease in the First Three Years of Life, Related to Social Circumstances'. *Brit. J. Prev. Soc. Med.* 8(1) (1954), 24–8.

21331 BENJAMIN (BERNARD). 'The Urban Background to Public Health Changes in England and Wales, 1900–1950'. *Pop. Studs* 17(3) (1964), 225–48.

21332 ROSSDALE (M.). 'A Socialist Health Service'. *New Left Rev.* (Mar./Apr. 1966).

21333 RYAN (M.). 'Health Centre Policy in England and Wales'. *Brit. J. Sociol.* 19(1) (1968), 34–46.

21334 SHEPHERD (M.). 'General Practice, Mental Illness and the British National Health Service'. *Amer. J. Pub. Health* 62 (1974), 230–2.

21335 MILES (A. W.). 'The Health Services—What Structural Changes are Possible?'. *Pol. Q.* 39(2) (1968), 195–204.

21336 MILBANK MEMORIAL FUND QUARTERLY. 'International Comparisons of Medical Care'. ii (3) (1972).

21337 MANGOLD (G.). 'Social Aspects of the British National Health Service'. *Sociol. Soc. Res.* 42(2) (1957), 92–8.

21338 LAWRENCE (R. J.). 'The Health Services in Northern Ireland'. *Public Admin.* (London) 34(3) (1956), 289–306.

21339 LEES (D. S.). 'The Logic of the British National Health Service'. *J. Law Econ.* (5) (1962), 111–18.

21340 LEWIS (P.). 'Médecine Privée et Médecine Publique en Grande-Bretagne'. *Projet* 75 (1973), 593–8.

21341 LAST (J. M.). 'Le Personnel Médical en Grande-Bretagne'. *C. Sociol. Démogr. Médic.* 9(1) (1969), 26–31.

21342 KLEIN (RUDOLF). 'Profession of Medicine'. *Pol. Q.* 46 (1975), 338–40.

21343 —— 'Policy Making in the National Health Service'. *Pol. Studs* 22 (1974), 1–14.

21344 —— 'National Health Service after Reorganization'. *Pol. Q.* 44(3) (1973), 316–28.

21345 —— 'Toothless Watchdogs or N.H.S. Scourge?'. *Update Rev.* (Feb. 1975).

21346 GREEN (STEPHEN). 'Professional/Bureaucratic Conflict: The Case of the Medical Profession in the National Health Service'. *Sociol. Rev.* n.s. 2 (1975), 121–41. [Scotland.].

21347 DONALD (B. L.). 'Planning and Health Care: The Approach in a Reorganised N.H.S.'. *Longrange planning* vii no. 6 (1974).

21348 ASHFORD (J. R.) *and* PEARSON (N. G.). 'Who uses the Health Services and Why?'. *J. Roy. Stat. Soc.* Series A (General), cxxxiii(3), (1970).

21349 BUTLER (J. R.). 'Illness and the Sick Role: An Evaluation in Three Communities'. *Brit. J. Sociol.* 21(3) (1970), 241–61.

7. HOSPITALS

21350 ROBERTSON (JAMES). Young Children in Hospital. 1958. 2nd edn with a postscript 1970.

21351 —— Hospitals and Children. 1962.

21352 U.K. CENTRAL HEALTH SERVICES COUNCIL. Committee on the Welfare of Children in Hospital. 1959.

21353 STACEY (MARGARET) *ed.* Hospitals, Children and Their Families: The Report of a Pilot Study. 1970.

21354 U.K. Census of Children and Adolescents in Hospitals, 1960–1965. 1967.

21355 WIELAND (GEORGE FRED) *and* LEIGH (HILARY) *eds.* Changing Hospitals: A Report on the Hospital Internal Communications Project. 1971.

21356 —— Standards for Morale: Cause and Effect in Hospitals. 1964.

21357 REVANS (REGINALD WILLIAM) *ed.* Hospitals: Communication, Choice and Change. 1974.

21358 U.K. 1969 D.H.S.S. Report of the Committee of Inquiry into Allegations of Ill-Treatment of Patients and other Irregularities at the Ely Hospital. Cardiff. Cmnd. 3975. 1969.

21359 U.K. 1971 D.H.S.S. Report of the Farleigh Hospital Committee of Inquiry. Cmnd. 4557. 1971.

21360 U.K. 1972 D.H.S.S. Report of the Committee of Inquiry into Whittingham Hospital. Cmnd 4861. 1972.

21361 U.K. 1973 D.H.S.S. Report on Hospital Complaints Procedure (The Davies Report). 1973.

21362 U.K. 1963 MINISTRY OF HEALTH. Communication between Doctors, Nurses and Patients: An Aspect of Human Relations in the Hospital Service. 1963.

21363 U.K. 1966 MINISTRY OF HEALTH. The Hospital Building Programme. A Revision of the Hospital Plan for England and Wales. 1966.

21364 U.K. 1961 MINISTRY OF HEALTH. Report of the Joint Working Party on the Medical Staffing Structure in the Hospital Service. 1961.

21365 U.K. 1962 MINISTRY OF HEALTH. A Hospital Plan for England and Wales. Cmnd 1604. 1962.

21366 U.K. 1964 WESSEX REGIONAL HOSPITAL BOARD. What do They Really Want? A Report on a Questionnaire addressed to General Practitioners in the Wessex region. Winchester. 1964.

21367 U.K. MINISTRY OF HEALTH. Hospital Survey—Various Areas in Separate Volumes. 1945.

21368 U.K. SCOTLAND: DEPARTMENT OF HEALTH. Scottish Hospitals Survey. 1946.

21369 WATERHOUSE (R. E.). Children in Hospital: A Hundred Years of Children in Birmingham. 1962.

21370 U.K. 1969 D.H.S.S. The Functions of the District General Hospital. Report of the Committee.

21371 REVANS (REGINALD WILLIAM). Standards for Morale: Cause and Effect in Hospitals. 1966.

21372 U.K. 1966 MINISTRY OF HEALTH. Report of the Committee on Senior Nursing Staff Structure. [Chairman: Brian Salmon.]. 1966.

21373 SCOTLAND 1964. Medical Staffing Structure in Scottish Hospitals: Report of the Committee. 1964.

21374 U.K. 1964 WELSH HOSPITAL BOARD. Disappointed Expectations? Report on a Survey of Professional and Technical Staff in the Hospital Service in Wales, 1963, by Anne Crichton and Marion P. Crawford. 1964.

21375 PINKER (ROBERT). English Hospital Statistics, 1861–1938. 1966.

21376 OFFICE OF HEALTH ECONOMICS. Hospital Costs in Perspective. 1963.

21377 —— Efficiency in the Hospital Service. 1967.

21378 NUFFIELD PROVINCIAL HOSPITALS TRUST. A Balanced Teaching Hospital: A Symposium at Birmingham. 1965.

21379 —— Studies in the Functions and Design of Hospitals. 1955.

21380 NURTON (DOREEN). Hospitals of the Long-stay Patient: A Study of Their Practical Nursing Problems and Solutions. Oxf. 1967.

21381 LUCK (GEORGE MICHAEL), LUCKMAN (JOAN), SMITH (B. W.), *and* STRINGER (J.). Patients, Hospitals and Operational Research. 1974.

21382 INSTITUTE OF HOSPITAL ADMINISTRATORS. Hospital Waiting Lists—A Report of the Study and Research Committee of the IHA. 1973.

21383 HILL (DOUGLAS WILLIAM). The Burden on the Community. 1962.

21384 GAMMON (MAX). U.K. N.H.S. Hospital Service: Manpower and Numbers of Beds Occupied Daily, 1965–1973: Preliminary Communication. 1975.

21385 FORSYTH (GORDON) *and* LOGAN (ROBERT F. L.). The Demand for Medical Care: A Study of the Case Load in the Barrow in Furness Group of Hospitals. 1960.

21386 FAXON (N. W.) *ed.* The Hospitals in Contemporary Life. 1949.

21387 FERGUSON (THOMAS) *and* MacPHAIL (ANGUS NORMAN). Hospital and Community. 1954.

21388 COHEN (GERDA LESLEY). What's Wrong with the Hospitals? Harmondsworth. 1964.

21389 CARTWRIGHT (ANN). Human Relations and Hospital Care. Lond./NY. 1964.

21390 HART (F.) *and* WALDEGRAVE (A. J.). A Study of Hospital Administration. 1948.

21391 SIDEBOTHAM (R.). 'An Experiment in Comparative Costing in the Hospitals Service'. *Manch. Sch. Econ. Soc. Studs* 28(2) (1960), 127–35.

21392 GRIFFITH (JOHN R.) *and* REES (E. T.). Hinges of Administration: A Survey of the Characteristics of Hospital Administrative and Clerical Staff. Lond./NY. 1963.

21393 ROWBOTHAM (RALPH). Hospital Organization. 1973.

21394 ROBINSON (GEOFFREY A.). Hospital Administration. 1962. 2nd edn 1966.

21395 MONTACUTE (C.). Costing and Efficiency in Hospitals: A Critical Survey of Costing as an Aid to the Management of Hospitals, 1962. 1962.

21396 DAVIES (JULIA). A Study of Hospital Management Training in its Organisation Context: An Evaluation of First-Line Management Training Courses for Ward Sisters in the Manchester Region. Manch. 1972.

21397 HUNTER (BEATRICE). The Administration of Hospital Wards: Factors Influencing Length of Stay in a Hospital. Manch. 1972.

21398 GRANT (COLIN). Hospital Management. Edin. 1973.

21399 MARTIN (JOHN). Hospitals in Trouble. 1984.

21400 DOMBERGER (SIMON), MEADOWCROFT (SHIRLEY), *and* THOMPSON (DAVID). 'The Impact of Competitive Tendering on the Costs of Hospital Domestic Services'. *Fiscal Studs* 8 (1987), 39–54.

21401 —— The Institute of Hospital Administrators: The First Fifty Years, 1902–1952. *Hospital* 48 (1952), 285–321.

21402 KNOWLES (JOHN HILTON) *ed.* The Teaching Hospital: Evolution and Contemporary Issues. 1967.

21403 —— Hospitals, Doctors and the Public Interest. 1966.

21404 FORSYTH (GORDON) *and* LOGAN (ROBERT F. L.). Gateway or Dividing Line?: A Study of Hospital Out-Patients in the 1960's. 1968.

21405 SOUTHWICK (A. F.) *Jnr.* The Doctor, the Hospital and the Patient in England: Rights and Responsibilities under the National Health Service. Ann Arbor, Mich. 1967.

21406 DUNCUM (BARBARA MARY) *ed.* Children in Hospital: Studies in Planning: A Report of Studies Made by the Division for Architectural Studies of the Nuffield Foundation. 1963.

21407 COPE (DAVID E.). Organisation, Development and Active Research in Hospitals. Aldershot. 1981.

21408 RISLEY (M.). The House of Healing: The Story of the Hospital. 1962.

21409 LABOUR PARTY. The Hospital Problem. 1924.

21410 HOBSON (JOHN MORRISON). Some Early and Later Houses of Pity. 1926.

21411 BRITISH HOSPITALS ASSOCIATION. Report of the Voluntary Hospitals Commission, April 1937. 1937.

21412 BRITISH HOSPITALS CONTRIBUTORY SCHEMES ASSOCIATION (1948). Conference 1950–1961. National Health and Hospital Contributory Schemes: Conference Addresses, 1950–1961. Bristol. 1963.

21413 BELL (T.) *et al.* Reform of the Hospital Service. 1967.

21414 DAINTON (COURTNEY). The Story of England's Hospitals. Lond. 1961. Springfield, Ill. 1962.

21415 ABEL-SMITH (BRIAN) *and* PINKER (ROBERT). The Hospitals, 1800–1948: A Study in Social Administration in England and Wales. Camb., Mass./Lond. 1964.

21416 —— Register of Approved Private Hospitals and Nursing Homes. 3rd edn Exeter. 1977.

21417 IVES (A. G. L.). British Hospitals. 1948.

21418 POYNTER (FREDERICK NOEL LAWRENCE) *ed.* The Evolution of Hospitals in Britain. 1964.

21419 BURROUGH (E. J. R.). Unity in Diversity: The Short Life of the United Oxford Hospitals. Abingdon. 1978.

21420 KERSLEY (GEORGE DURANT) *and* COSH (JOHN A.). The History of the Royal National Hospital for Rheumatic Diseases. Bath. 1965.

21421 COHEN (R. A.). The History of the Birmingham Dental Hospital and Dental School, 1858–1958. Birm. 1958.

21422 U.K. 1966 BIRMINGHAM REGIONAL HOSPITAL BOARD. B.R.H.B. 1947–1966: A Chronicle of the Activities of the B.R.H.B. Since Their Inception in 1947, Indicating the Principal Trends in Society and Medicine which Have Influenced their Policies. Birm. 1966.

21423 BRISTOL HOSPITALS FUND. A Record of 25 Years Service, 1939–1964. 1964.

21424 PERRY (C. BRUCE). The Bristol Royal Infirmary 1904–1974. Bristol. 1981.

21425 ROBERTS (NESTA). Cheadle Royal Hospital: A Bicentenary History. Altrincham. 1967.

21426 STANDING JOINT ADVISORY COMMITTEE OF THE UNIVERSITY OF LEEDS, THE BOARD OF GOVERNORS OF THE UNITED LEEDS HOSPITALS AND THE LEEDS REGIONAL HOSPITAL BOARD. Working Party Appointed to Review the Hospital Services in Leeds. Report. Harrogate. 1960.

21427 ANNING (STEPHEN TOWERS). The General Infirmary at Leeds. Vol. 2. The Second Hundred Years, 1869–1965. Edin./Lond. 1966.

21428 FRIZELLE (ERNEST R.) *and* MARTIN (JANET D.). The Leicester Royal Infirmary, 1771–1971. 1971.

21429 MacWILLIAM (HENRY HERBERT). Memories of Walton Hospital, Liverpool. 1965.

21430 LONDON COUNTY COUNCIL. The L.C.C. Hospitals: A Retrospect. 1949.

21431 SINCLAIR (R.). The London Hospital. 1956.

21432 CLARK-KENNEDY (A. E.). The London: A Study in the Voluntary Hospital System. Vol. 2 1840–1948. 1963.

21433 RIVETT (G.). The Development of the London Hospital System, 1823–1982. 1982.

21434 COWAN (PETER). 'Some Observations Concerning the Increase of Hospital Provision in London Between 1850 and 1960'. *Med. Hist.* 14 (1970), 42–52.

21435 BUTRYM (ZOFIA). Medical Social Work in Action: A Study of Medical Social Work at Hammersmith Hospital. 1968.

21436 WOODALL (SAMUEL JAMES). The Manor House Hospital: A Personal Record. 1966.

21437 WRIGHT (A. D.). St Mary's Hospital and Paddington. 1958/9.

21438 POWER (*Sir* D'ARCY). A Short History of St. Bartholomew's Hospital, 1123–1923: Past and Present. 1923.

21439 MEDVEI (VICTOR CORNELIUS) *and* THORNTON (JOHN L.) *eds.* The Royal Hospital of Saint Bartholomew 1123–1973. 1974.

21440 BOW GROUP HOSPITAL MANAGEMENT COMMITTEE. Poplar Hospital, London E14, 1855–1955. 1955.

21441 AYERS (GWENDOLINE MARGERY). England's First State Hospitals and the Metropolitan Asylums Board, 1867–1930. 1971.

21442 GUY'S HOSPITAL GAZETTE. Special Number in Commemoration of the Bicentenary of the Hospital and the Centenary of the Medical School, 1725–1925. *Ed.* by George Housden and Gordon Gould Cameron. 1925.

21443 NEWELL (PHILIP). Greenwich Hospital: A Royal Foundation. 1984.

21444 CAMERON (HECTOR CHARLES). Mr Guy's Hospital, 1726–1948. 1954.

21445 HUMBLE (JOSEPH GRAEME) *and* HANSELL (PETER). Westminster Hospital 1716–1966. 1966.

21446 RHODES (PHILIP). Doctor John Leake's Hospital; A History of the General Lying-in Hospital, York Road, Lambeth 1765–1971: The Birth, Life and Death of a Maternity Hospital. 1977.

21447 COWELL (BETTY) *and* WAINWRIGHT (DAVID). The History of the Royal College of Midwives 1881–1981. 1981.

21448 SORSBY (ARNOLD). The Royal Eye Hospital, 1857–1957. 1957.

21449 PRIESTLEY (H. E.). The Evelina: The Story of a London Children's Hospital. 1869–1969.

21450 MINNEY (RUBEIGH JAMES). The Two Pillars of Charing Cross: The Story of a Famous Hospital. 1967.

21451 MCINNES (EILIDH MARGARET). St Thomas's Hospital. 1963.

21452 U.K. 1975 D.H.S.S. Rationalisation of Services: A Revised Hospital Plan for Inner London. 1975.

21453 PEARCE (S. B. P.). An Ideal in the Working: The Story of the Magdalen Hospital 1758–1958. 1958.

21454 HOLMES (*Sir* GEORGE MORGAN). The National Hospital, Queen Square, 1860–1948. 1954.

21455 JEWESBURY (ERIC C. O.). The Royal Northern Hospital, 1856–1956. The Story of a Hundred Years' Work in North London. 1956.

21456 MORSON (CLIFFORD) *ed.* St Peter's Hospital for Stone, 1860–1960. Edin./Lond./Baltimore, Md. 1960.

21457 GRAY (JAMES DOUGLAS ALLAN). The Central Middlesex Hospital. 1963.

21458 COLLINS (EDWARD TREACHER). History and Traditions of the Moorfields Eye Hospital. 1929.

21459 DICKS (HENRY VICTOR). Fifty Years of the Tavistock Clinic. 1970.

21460 EDWARDS (GEORGE). The Victoria Hospital for Children, Tite Street, Chelsea, London S.W.3: A Short Commemorative History, 1866–1964. 1964.

21461 HIGGINS (T. T.). 'Great Ormond Street', 1852-1952. 1952.

21462 STANCLIFFE (F. S.). The Manchester Royal Eye Hospital, 1814–1964: A Short History. Manch. 1964.

21463 BROCKBANK (WILLIAM). Portrait of a Hospital, 1752-1948. To Commemorate the Bicentenary of the Royal Infirmary, Manchester. 1952.

21464 YOUNG (JOHN HARLEY). St Mary's Hospital, Manchester, 1790–1963. Edin./Lond. 1964.

21465 ROBB-SMITH (A. H. T.). A Short History of the Radcliffe Infirmary. Oxf. 1970.

21466 GIBSON (ALEXANDER GEORGE). The Radcliffe Infirmary. 1926.

21467 SALISBURY GENERAL HOSPITAL. Salisbury 200: The Bicentenary of Salisbury Infirmary 1766–1966. Salisb. 1967.

21468 PARSONS (*Sir* LEONARD GREGORY) *et al.* The Hospital Services of the Sheffield and East Midlands Area. 1945.

21469 MORRIS (STEPHEN BERNARD). A Short History of Whitchurch Hospital, 1908–1959. Birm. 1965.

21470 MCMENEMY (WILLIAM HENRY). A History of the Worcester Royal Infirmary. 1947.

21471 ILLINGWORTH (*Sir* CHARLES F. W.), MACKINTOSH (JAMES MACALISTER), *and* PETERS (R. J.). Report for Scottish

Department of Health: Scottish Hospitals Survey. 1946.

21472 Scottish Hospital In-patient Statistics. 1961+. [Annual.]

21473 GUTHRIE (DOUGLAS JAMES) *et al.* The Royal Edinburgh Hospital for Sick Children 1860–1960. Edin./ Baltimore, Md. 1960.

21474 TURNER (A. LOGAN). Story of a Great Hospital. The Royal Infirmary of Edinburgh, 1729–1929. 1938.

21475 RUSSELL (BRIAN FITZGERALD) *ed.* St John's Hospital for Diseases of the Skin, 1863–1963. Edin. 1963.

21476 ROBERTSON (EDNA). The Yorkhill Story: The History of the Royal Hospital for Sick Children, Glasgow. Glasg. 1972.

21477 THOMSON (ARCHIBALD McCLENNAN WRIGHT). The History of the Glasgow Eye Infirmary, 1824–1962. Glasg. 1963.

21478 WATSON (WILLIAM NAIRN BOOG). A Short History of Chalmers Hospital. Edin. 1964.

21479 FERRIER (JOHN). The Greenock Infirmary 1806–1960. Greenock. 1968.

21480 FARNDALE (JAMES). The Day Hospital Movement in Great Britain. Oxf. 1961.

21481 IRVING (GORDON). Dumfries and Galloway Royal Infirmary: The First Two Hundred Years, 1776–1975. Dumfries. 1975.

21482 HENDERSON (BROWN). The History of the Glasgow Dental Hospital and School 1879–1959. Glasg. 1960.

21483 GIBSON (HENRY J. C.). Dundee Royal Infirmary 1798 to 1948. Dundee. 1948.

21484 WILSON (L. M.), BUTTAR (CHARLES), *and* MORRIS (E. W.). 'The Future of the Poor-law Infirmary'. *Lancet* (25 Dec. 1920), 1287–94, 1307–8.

21485 BURNETT (*Sir* E. NAPIER). 'Voluntary Hospitals: Results of a Preliminary Survey'. *Brit. Med. J.* (22 May 1920), 710–12; *World's Work* (Dec.), 62-5.

21486 GRIFFITH (J.). 'Administrative Structure of the Hospital Service'. *Public Admin. (Lond.)* 36(1) (1958), 71–81.

21487 FRASER (B.). 'Long-term Planning in the Hospital Service'. *Public Admin. (Lond.)* 42, (1964) 101–12.

21488 FELDSTEIN (M. S.). 'Hospital Planning and the Demand for Care'. 13. *Oxf. Univ. Inst. Stat.* 26(4) (1964), 361–8.

21489 —— 'Hospital Bed Scarcity: An Analysis of the Effects of Inter-regional Differences'. *Economica* 45(128) (1965), 393–409.

21490 DAVIES (C.). 'Professionals in Organisations: Some Preliminary Observations on Hospital Consultants'. *Sociol. Rev.* 20(4) (1972), 553–67.

21491 CULYER (ANTHONY JOHN) *and* CULLIS (J. G.). 'Hospital Waiting Lists and the Supply and Demand of In-patient Care'. *Soc. Econ. Admin.* 9(1) (1975), 13–25.

21492 BUTTAR (CHARLES). 'The Municipalization of Hospitals. The Bradford Experiment'. *Brit. Med. J.* (2 Oct. 1920), 527; (9 Oct. 1920), 552–3, (13 Nov. 1920), 753–4.

21493 MARTIN (DENIS VINCENT). Adventure in Psychiatry: Social Change in a Mental Hospital. 1962.

21494 FREEMAN (HUGH LIONEL) *ed.* Psychiatric Hospital Care: A Symposium. 1965.

21495 ULLMANN (LEONARD P.). Institution and Outcome: A Comparative Study of Psychiatric Hospitals. Oxf. 1967.

21496 FINZI (JEAN), KING (CHRYSTAL), *and* BOORER (DAVID) *eds.* Volunteers in Hospitals—A Guide for Organisers. 1971.

21497 PICKSTONE (JOHN). Medicine and Industrial Society: A History of Hospital Development in Manchester and its Region, 1752–1946. 1985.

21498 DU BOULAY (SHIRLEY). Cecily Saunders: Founder of the Modern Hospice Movement. 1984.

8. GENERAL PRACTICE

21499 —— The Medical Directory. 1845+.

21500 HOGARTH (JAMES). The Payment of the General Practitioner: Some European Comparisons. NY./Oxf. 1963.

21501 FRY (JOHN), Hunt of Fawley [*Baron*], *and* PINSENT (R. J. F. H.) *eds.* A History of the Royal College of General Practitioners: The First 25 Years. 1983.

21502 FORBES (ROBERT). Sixty Years of Medical Defence. 1948. [On the work of the Medical Defence Union, 1883–1943.].

21503 THE GENERAL PRACTITIONER AND THE HOSPITAL SERVICE. Report by a Joint Sub-Committee of the Medical Hospital and Specialist Services, and the General Practitioners Services: Standing Advisory Committees. Edin. 1952.

21504 BISHOP (WILLIAM JOHN). The Evolution of the General Practitioner in England in Science, Medicine and History: Essays in Honour of Charles Singer. 1953.

21505 TAYLOR (STEPHEN JAMES LAKE). *Baron Taylor.* Good General Practice: A Report of a Survey [initiated by the] Nuffield Provincial Hospitals Trust. 1954.

21506 CLYNE (M. G.). Night Calls: A Study in General Practice. 1961.

21507 KELLNER (ROBERT). Family Ill-health: An Investigation in General Practice. 1963.

21508 COPE (*Sir* ZACHARY). The Worshipful Society of Apothecaries of London and the Evolution of the Family Doctor. 1963.

21509 GENERAL PRACTITIONERS' ASSOCIATION. Abuse and Misuse: A Critical Problem in the Family Doctor Service: The Report of a G.P.A. Study Group. 1965.

21510 COLLINS (J.). Social Casework in General Medical Practice. 1965.

21511 CARGILL (DAVID). The G.P.: What's Wrong? 1965.

21512 LOCK (STEPHEN PENFORD). Health Centres and Group Practices: Articles Collected from the British Medical Journal. 1966.

21513 DILLANE (JOHN BEVAN). General Practice in the New Towns of Britain. 1966.

21514 CARTWRIGHT (ANN). Patients and Their Doctors: A Study of General Practice. 1967. [Reports of the Institute of Community Studies.].

21515 BUTRYM (ZOFIA). Social Work in Medical Care. 1967.

21516 FORMAN (JAMES ADAM SHOLTO) *and* FAIRBAIRN (E). Social Case Work in General Practice: A Report on an Experiment Carried out in General Practice. 1968. [NPHT.].

21517 GISH (OSCAR). Doctor Migration and World Health: The Impact of the International Demand for Doctors on Health Services in Developing Countries. 1971.

21518 —— A Reappraisal of the Brain Drain. 1976.

21519 —— *ed.* Health Manpower and the Medical Auxiliary: Some Notes and an Annotated Bibliography. 1971.

21520 DOPSON (LAURENCE). The Changing Scene in General Practice. 1971.

21521 GOLDBERG (ELSA MATHILDE) *and* NEILL (JUNE E.). Social Work in General Practice. 1972.

21522 BUTLER (JOHN RICHARD) *et al.* Family Doctors and Public Policy: A Study of Manpower Distribution. 1973.

21523 HALE (GEOFFREY) *and* ROBERTS (NESTA). A Doctor in Practice. 1974.

21524 GATHORNE-HARDY (JONATHAN). Doctors: The Lives and Work of G.P's. 1984.

21525 HEANEY (CHARLES THOMAS). The Payment of General Practitioners in Great Britain 1834–1974. 1975. [London Ph.D. thesis.].

21526 STIMSON (GERRY V.) *and* WEBB (BARBARA). Going to See the Doctor: The Consultation Process in General Practice. 1975.

21527 OWEN (H.). Administration in General Practice. 1975.

21528 MARSH (GEOFFREY) *and* KAIM-CAUDLE (P. R.). Team Care in General Practice. 1976.

21529 RESEARCH INSTITUTE FOR CONSUMER AFFAIRS. Essays and Enquiries. 2. General Practice: A Consumer Commentary Prepared by Enid Hutchinson. 1963.

21530 U.K. M.O.H. The Field of Work of the Family Doctor: Report by Annis Gillie, Chmn. 1963, repr. 1964.

21531 MANAGEMENT CONSULTANTS' ASSOCIATION. The G.P. A Report Prepared for the General Practitioners' Association. 1964.

21532 MEDICAL PRACTITIONERS' UNION. Our Blueprint for the Future. 1964.

21533 ACKERS (JAMES) *et al.* What's Wrong with General Practice: A Memo. 1965.

21534 COLLEGE OF GENERAL PRACTITIONERS. Council: Reports from General Practice, (2) Report of Present State and Future Needs of General Practice. 1965. (3) Additional Payment for Wide Experience and Notable Service in General Practice: An Outline Scheme. 1965.

21535 MEDICAL PRACTITIONERS' UNION. Newsletter special: H.M. Government's offer to G.P.s: the M.P.U. comments. Medical World Conference Programme. 1965.

21536 SEARLE (J. R.). Chapter on 'Medical Emigration, a Study in the Inadequacy of Official Statistics'. In Duncan Burn *et al.* Lessons from Central Forecasting. 1965.

21537 YOUNG FABIAN GROUP. Young Fabian Pamphlets. 9. General Practice. 1965.

21538 BALINT (MICHAEL) *et al.* A Study of Doctors: Mutual Selection and the Evaluation of Results in a Training Programme for Family Doctors. 1966.

21539 FRY (J.). 'The Family Doctor'. *Twentieth Cent.* 164 (977) (1968), 51–61.

21540 MECHANIC (D.). 'Correlates of Frustration among British General Practitioners'. *J. Health Soc. Behav.* 11(2) (1970), 87–103.

21541 MARMOR (THEODORE R.) *and* THOMAS (DAVID). 'Doctors, Politics and Pay Disputes: "Pressure Group Politics" Revisited'. *Brit. J. Pol. Sci.* 2 (1972), 421–42.

21542 SEARLE (J. R.). 'Medical Emigration from Britain, 1930–1961'. *Brit. Med. J.* (17 Mar. 1962), 782–6.

21543 GISH (OSCAR). 'British Doctor Migration, 1962-67'. *Brit. J. Med. Educ.* 4 (1970), 279–88.

9. NATIONAL HEALTH SERVICE

21544 MATHERS (NANCY M.). National Health Service: A Bibliography. 1978.

21545 —— Digest of Health Statistics for England and Wales. 1969.

21546 BEST (K. W.). A Select Bibliography on the National Health Service. 1980.

21547 ROYAL INSTITUTE OF PUBLIC ADMINISTRATION. Health Services in Britain. A Select Bibliography. 3rd edn. 1975.

21548 ROSS (*Sir* JAMES STIRLING). The National Health Service in Great Britain: An Historical and Descriptive Study. Oxf. 1952.

21549 JEWKES (JOHN) *and* JEWKES (SYLVIA). The Genesis of the British National Health Service. Oxf. 1961.

21550 HONIGSBAUM (FRANK). Health, Happiness and Security. 1989.

21551 BRITISH MEDICAL ASSOCIATION. The British Medical Association's Proposals for a General Medical Service for the Nation. 1930.

21552 MACNALTY (*Sir* ARTHUR SALUSBURY). The History of State Medicine in England. Being the Fitzpatrick Lectures of the Royal College of Physicians of London for 1936 and 1937. 1948.

21553 MACKINTOSH (JAMES M.). Trends of Opinion about the Public Health, 1901–1951. Oxf. 1953.

21554 BRITISH MEDICAL ASSOCIATION. The White Paper—An Analysis. 1944.

21555 MURRAY (DAVID STARK). Why a National Health Service? The Part Played by the Socialist Medical Association. 1972.

21556 WATKINS (STEVE). Medicine and Labour: The Politics of a Profession. 1987.

21557 COMMUNIST PARTY OF GREAT BRITAIN. Good Health for All: An Examination of the Government's Proposals for a National Health Service. 1944.

21558 LEFF (VERA). Going our Way?: A Short Novel. 1945.

21559 VIEL (BENJAMIN). La Medicina Socializada y su Aplicación en Gran Bretaña, Unión Soviética y Chile. Santiago. 1961.

21560 MIDDLESEX COUNTY COUNCIL. Plan for the Development of the Health and Welfare Services over the Next Ten Years, 1962–1972 (approved on 31st October, 1962). 1962.

21561 OFFICE OF HEALTH ECONOMICS. The Personal Health Services: A Perspective of the General Medical and the Pharmaceutical Services. 1963.

21562 —— Report of the Committee of Enquiry into the Cost of the National Health Service. Cmnd 9663. Parliamentary Papers, xx (1955–6).

21563 ABEL-SMITH (BRIAN) *and* TITMUSS (RICHARD MORRIS). The Cost of the National Health Service in England and Wales. Camb. 1956.

21564 ECKSTEIN (HARRY). The English Health Service: Its Origin, Structure, and Achievements. Camb., Mass. 1958.

21565 GEMMILL (PAUL FLEMING). Britain's Search for Health: The First Decade of the National Health Service. Philadelphia, Pa. 1960.

21566 LEES (DENNIS SAMUEL). Health Through Choice: An Economic Study of the British National Health Service. 1961. [IEA Hobart paper IL.].

21567 —— 'Health Through Choice'. In Dennis Samuel Lees *et al.* Freedom or free-for-all? Essays in Welfare, Trade and Choice. 1965.

21568 DUBOIS (A.). 'Le Service National de Santé en Angleterre'. *R. Social.* 139 (1961), 57–87.

21569 MIRFIN (DERICK) *ed.* Buying Better Health: An Abstract of Discussions at a Colloquium on the Finance of National Health, Sponsored by the Acton Society Trust. 1961. 1962.

21570 LINDSEY (ALMONT). Socialized Medicine in England and Wales—The National Health Service, 1948–1961. Chapel Hill, NC. 1962.

21571 JOHNSON (DONALD McINTOSH). The British National Health Service. 1962.

21572 FORSYTH (GORDON). Doctors and State Medicine: A Study of the British Health Service. 1966. 2nd edn 1973.

21573 EVANG (KARL), MURRAY (DAVID STARK), *and* LEAR (WALTER JAY). Medical Care and Family Security: Norway, England, and the U.S.A. Englewood Cliffs, NJ. 1963.

21574 PAGE (A. T.). Pennies for Health: The Story of the British Hospitals Contributory Schemes Association. Bristol. 1949.

21575 PAVITT (LAURENCE A.). The Health of the Nation. The Second Stage of the National Health Service. 1964. [Fabian Soc.].

21576 FARNDALE (WILLIAM ARTHUR JAMES) *ed.* Trends in the National Health Service. Oxf. 1964.

21577 FRY (JOHN) *and* FARNDALE (WILLIAM ARTHUR JAMES) *eds.* International Medical Care: A Comparison and Evaluation of Medical Care Services Throughout the World. Oxf. 1972.

21578 BUCHANAN (JAMES MCGILL). The Inconsistencies of the National Health Service: A Study in the Conflict Between Individual Demand and Collective Supply. IEA. 1965.

21579 WADSWORTH (MICHAEL EDWIN JOHN). The Consumer and the Health Service. 1968.

21580 WADSWORTH (MICHAEL EDWIN JOHN) *and* ROBINSON (DAVID) *eds.* Studies in Everyday Medical Life. 1976.

21581 POWELL (JOHN ENOCH). Medicine and Politics: 1975 and After. Tunbridge Wells. 1976.

21582 —— A New Look at Medicine and Politics. 1966.

21583 PAVITT (LAURENCE A.). The Health of the Nation: The Second Stage of the N.H.S. 1963. [Fabian Society Research Series, No. 236.].

21584 CONSERVATIVE CENTRAL OFFICE. Design for a Nation's Health. 1963.

21585 GUASPARRI (GIANCARLO). Per un Servizio Sanitario Nazionale: Il 'National Health Service'. Milan. 1964.

21586 MANAGEMENT CONSULTANTS' ASSOCIATION. The G.P.A. Report Prepared for the General Practitioners' Association. 2 vols. 1964.

21587 TAYLOR (CYRIL). Is your General Practitioner Really Necessary? 1964.

21588 U.K. 1964. MINISTRY OF HEALTH. Recent N.H.S. Prescribing Trends: Mainly Based on Prescribing During 1961 and 1962. 1964.

21589 —— National Health Service Prescribing. 1963.

21590 BUCHANAN (JAMES MCGILL). The Inconsistencies of the National Health Service. 1965.

21591 ASSOCIATION OF PUBLIC HEALTH INSPECTORS. Environmental Health. 1964.

21592 DAVIES (WYNDHAM) *ed.* Collectivism or Individualism in Medicine? 1965.

21593 —— Reforming the National Health Service. 1966. [C.P.C.].

21594 OFFICE OF HEALTH ECONOMICS. The Local Health Services. 1965.

21595 SEATON (COLIN ROBERT). Aspects of the National Health Service Acts. Oxf. 1966.

21596 BRAIN (WALTER RUSSELL) *Baron Brain.* Medicine and Government. 1967.

21597 FELDSTEIN (MARTIN STUART). Economic Analysis for Health Service Efficiency: Econometric Studies of the British National Health Service. Amsterdam. 1967.

21598 WISEMAN (J.). 'Cost–Benefit Analysis and Health Service Policy'. In Alan Peacock and Donald Robertson *eds.* Public Expenditure Appraisal and Control. Edin. 1963.

21599 NASEEM (MUHAMMAD). The Dilemma of the Welfare State. 1966.

21600 DRUITT (BASIL). The Growth of the Welfare State. 1966.

21601 COOTES (RICHARD JOHN). The Making of the Welfare State. 1966.

21602 WILLCOCKS (ARTHUR JOHN). The Creation of the National Health Service: A Study of Pressure Groups and a Major Policy Decision. 1967.

21603 WEBSTER (CHARLES). The Health Services since the War: Vol. 1: Problems of Health Care: The National Health Service before 1957. 1988.

21604 DRAPER (PETER) *et al.* The N.H.S.: Three Views. 1970. [Fabian Soc.].

21605 BRITISH MEDICAL ASSOCIATION. Primary Medical Care. 1970.

21606 —— Health Services Financing: A Report Commissioned in 1967 by the British Medical Association and Carried out by an Advisory Panel under the Chairmanship of Dr Ivor M. Jones. 1970. [A similar publication published also in 1968.].

21607 LEE (MICHAEL). Opting out of the N.H.S. PEP. 1971.

21608 CHAPLIN (K. W.) *ed.* Health Care in the United Kingdom—Its Organisation and Management. 1982.

21609 NAVARRO (VINCENTE). Class Struggle: The State and Medicine: An Historical and Contemporary Analysis of the Medical Sector in Great Britain. 1978.

21610 FOX (DANIEL M.). Health Policies, Health Politics: The British and American Experience, 1911–1965. Princeton, NJ. 1986.

21611 HOLLINGSWORTH (J. ROGER). A Political Economy of Medicine: Great Britain and the United States. Baltimore, Md. 1986.

21612 FERRER (HAROLD PETER) *ed.* The Health Services: Administration, Research and Management. 1972.

21613 DAVIES (WYNDHAM). Health or Health Service? Reform of the British National Health Service. 1972.

21614 —— The Pharmaceutical Industry, a Personal Study: A Medical, Economic and Political Survey of the Worldwide Pharmaceutical Industry. Oxf. 1967.

21615 ANDERSON (ODIN WALDEMAR). Health Care: Can There be Equity? The United States, Sweden and England. NY./Lond. 1972.

21616 BODENHAM (KENNETH EDWARD) *and* WELLMAN (F.). Foundations for Health Service Management: A Scicon Report for the Scottish Home and Health Department on the Requirements for a Health Service Information System. Nuffield Provincial Hospital Trust. 1972.

21617 EDWARDS (BRIAN) *and* WALKER (P.). *Si vis pacem*: Preparations for Change in the National Health Service. 1973.

21618 BURNS (EVELINE MABEL). Health Services for Tomorrow: Trends and Issues. NY./Lond. 1973.

21619 BROWN (RONALD GORDON SCLATER). The Changing National Health Service. 1973. 2nd edn 1978.

21620 —— Reorganising the National Health Service: A Case Study in Administrative Change. Oxf. 1979.

21621 BROWN (RONALD GORDON SCLATER) *with* GRIFFIN (S.) *and* HAYWOOD (STUART COLLINGWOOD). A series of progress reports from the research team studying the reorganization of the National Health Service on Humberside, 1972–5, entitled:

(1) Preparations for Change. Hull. 1973.

(2) Waiting for Guidance. Hull. 1973.

(3) The Shadow and Substance. Hull. 1974.

(4) New Bottles: Old Wine? Hull. 1975.

21622 HAYWOOD (STUART COLLINGWOOD) *and* ALASZIEWSKI (A.). Crisis in the Health Service: The Politics of Management. 1980.

21623 HAYWOOD (STUART COLLINGWOOD). Managing the Health Service. 1974.

21624 —— The Curate's Egg: Good in Parts: Senior Officers' Reflections on the N.H.S. Hull. 1979.

21625 —— 'The Politics of Management in Health Care: A British Perspective'. *J. Health Politics Policy & Law* 8 (1983), 424–43.

21626 COCHRANE (ARCHIBALD LEMAN). Effectiveness and Efficiency: Random Reflections on Health Services. Nuffield Provincial Hospital Trust. 1972.

21627 DOUGLAS-WILSON (I.) *and* MCLACHLAN (GORDON). Health Service Prospects: An International Survey. 1973. [Published on *The Lancet's* 150th anniversary.].

21628 FRASER (DEREK). The Evolution of the British Welfare State: A History of Social Policy since the Industrial Revolution. 1973.

21629 CUMING (MAURICE H. W.). Personnel Management in the National Health Service. 1978.

21630 DIMMOCK (STUART J.). 'Incomes Policy and Health Services in the United Kingdom'. In Industrial Relations and Health Services. Amarjit Sethi and Stuart Dimmock, eds. 1982.

21631 CULYER (ANTHONY JOHN). The National Health Service: An Economic Perspective. 1975.

21632 CULYER (ANTHONY JOHN) *and* WRIGHT (K. G.). Economic Aspects of Health Services. 1978.

21633 —— Need and the N.H.S.: Economics and Social Choice. 1976.

21634 CULYER (ANTHONY JOHN), WISEMAN (JACK), *and* WALKER (ARTHUR). An Annotated Bibliography of Health Economics. 1977.

21635 JONES (TOM) *and* PROWLE (MALCOLM). Health Service Finance: An Introduction. 1984.

21636 GATHERER (ALEXANDER) *and* WARREN (M. D.) *eds.* Management and the Health Service. Oxf./NY.1971.

21637 MCLACHLAN (GORDON) *ed.* In Low Gear?: An Examination of 'Cogwheels'. Essays by Gordon Forsyth *et al.* Publ. for NPHT. 1971.

21638 —— Measuring for Management: Quantitative Methods in Health Service Management. Essays by J. R. Ashford *et al.* Publ. for NPHT. 1975.

21639 —— Medical Education and Medical Care: A Scottish– American Symposium. Publ. for NPHT. 1977.

21640 MCLACHLAN (GORDON) *and* CAWLEY (ROBERT) *eds.* Policy for Action: A Symposium on the Planning of a Comprehensive District Psychiatric Service. Publ. for NPHT. 1973.

21641 —— *ed.* Positions, Movements, and Directions in Health Services Research: The Papers and Proceedings of a Meeting. Publ. for NPHT. 1976.

21642 —— Probes for Health: Essays from the Health Services Research Centre, University of Birmingham. Publ. for NPHT. 1975.

21643 [WORKING GROUP FOR THE EVALUATION OF THE QUALITY OF CARE.]. A Question of Quality? Roads to Assurance in Medical Care: [a report by the W.G.E.Q.C.], Contributors Sir George Godber *et al.* Publ. for NPHT. 1976.

21644 —— The Way Ahead in Postgraduate Medical Education: Papers by Stanley Clayton *et al.* Publ. for NPHT. 1974.

21645 —— *ed.* Bridging in Health: Reports of Studies on Health Services for Children, by F. S. W. Brimblecombe *et al.* Publ. for NPHT. 1975.

21646 —— The British National Health Service: Policy Trends and Their Implication for Education. 1975.

21647 —— *ed.* By Guess or by What? Information without Design in the N.H.S.: Papers by Peter D. Fox and Others. Publ. for NPHT. 1978.

21648 —— *ed.* Challenges for Change: Essays on the Next Decade in the National Health Service. Publ. for NPHT. 1971.

21649 —— *ed.* Five Years After: A Review of Health Care Research Management After Rothschild: Including an Essay by Thomas P. Whitehead. Oxf. 1978.

21650 U.K. D.H.S.S. Report of the Working Party on Medical Administrators (Hunter report). 1972.

21651 —— National Health Service: The Administrative Structure of the Medical and Related Services in England and Wales. (Green Paper). 1968.

21652 —— The Future of the National Health Service. (Green Paper II). 1970.

21653 —— National Health Service Reorganisation. 1971. [Consultative document.].

21654 —— National Health Service Reorganisation: England. Cmnd 5055. 1972.

21655 —— Management Arrangements for the Reorganised National Health Service. 1972.

21656 —— Democracy in the National Health Service. Membership of Health Authorities. 1974.

21657 LONG (A. F.) *and* MERCER (G.) *eds.* Manpower Planning in the National Health Service. Aldershot. 1981.

21658 GODBER (*Sir* GEORGE EDWARD). The Health Service: Past, Present and Future. 1975.

21659 —— Change in Medicine. 1975.

21660 —— Attainable Goals in Health. 1976.

21661 GAMMON (MAX). Public and Private Provision for Medical Care in Great Britain. 1975.

21662 —— Health and Security: A Report on the Public Provision for Medical Care in Great Britain. 1977.

21663 LEVITT (RUTH). The Reorganised National Health Service. 1976. 3rd edn with Andrew Wall. 1984.

21664 ELCOCK (HOWARD). 'Regional Government in Action: The Members of Two Regional Health Authorities'. *Public Admin.* 56 (1978), 379–97.

21665 CIBA FOUNDATION. Health Care in a Changing Setting. The U.K. Experience. (Symposium 43, n.s.). 1976.

21666 DONALDSON (R. J.). The New Health Service in Britain: Its Organization Outlined. 1977.

21667 —— Royal Commission on the National Health Service: Report. Cmnd 7615. Parliamentary Papers (1979–80). [Chairman: Sir Alec Merrison.].

21668 FARRELL (C.). 'The Royal Commission on the National Health Service'. *Policy & Politics* 8 (1980), 189–202.

21669 OFFICE OF HEALTH ECONOMICS. The Reorganised N.H.S. 1977.

21670 BUXTON (MARTIN J.). Health and Inequality. 1976.

21671 BUXTON (MARTIN J.) *and* KLEIN (RUDOLF E.). Allocating Health Resources: A Commentary on the Report of the Working Party on Resource Allocation. 1978.

21672 KLEIN (RUDOLF E.). The Politics of the National Health Service. 2nd edn 1989.

21673 INGLE (STEPHEN) *and* TETHER (PHILIP). Parliament and Health Policy: The Role of M.P.s 1970–1975. Aldershot. 1981.

21674 BARNARD (KEITH) *and* LEE (KENNETH) *eds*. Conflicts in the National Health Service. 1977.

21675 HAM (CHRISTOPHER). Health Policy in Britain: The Organisation and Politics of the N.H.S. 2nd edn 1985.

21676 VAISEY (JOHN). National Health. 1984.

21677 HELLER (TOM D.). Restructuring the Health Service. 1977.

21678 SKEET (MURIEL HILDA). Health Needs Help: Results of a Study into the Role and Preparation of Volunteers Working Within the Reorganised National Health Service. 1977.

21679 SKEET (MURIEL HILDA) *and* ELLIOTT (KATHERINE) *eds*. Health Auxiliaries and the Health Team. 1978.

21680 WATKIN (BRIAN). The National Health Service: The First Phase: 1948–1974 and After. 1978.

21681 —— Inequalities in Health: Report of a Research Working Group. 1980. [Chairman: Sir Douglas Black.].

21682 TOWNSEND (PETER) *and* DAVIDSON (NICK) *eds*. Inequality in Health: The Black Report. Harmondsworth. 1982.

21683 DAVIDSON (NICK). A Question of Care: The Changing Face of the National Health Service. 1987.

21684 SMALL (NEIL). Politics and Planning in the N.H.S. Milton Keynes. 1989.

21685 HAM (CHRISTOPHER). Policy Making in the National Health Service: A Case Study of the Leeds Regional Hospital Board. 1981.

21686 WOODS (KEVIN J.). 'The National Health Service in London: A Review of the Impact of N.H.S. Policy Since 1976'. *London J.* 9 (1983), 165–83.

21687 ABEL-SMITH (BRIAN). National Health Service: The First Thirty Years. 1978.

21688 —— Value for Money in Health Services: A Comparative Study. 1978.

21689 —— An International Study of Health Expenditure and its Relevance for Health Planning. Geneva. 1967.

21690 ALSOP (JUDITH). Health Policy and the National Health Service. 1984.

21691 SCOTTISH CONSERVATIVE WOMEN'S ORGANISATION. 1977/78. How Well is the Health Service? A Report of the Findings of a Survey. Edin. 1979.

21692 RYAN (T. M.). Day Nursery Provision Under the Health Service. England and Wales, 1948–1963. 1964.

21693 U.K. MINISTRY OF HEALTH AND DEPARTMENT OF HEALTH FOR SCOTLAND. A National Health Service. Cmnd. 6502. 1944.

21694 CARPENTER (MICK). Working for Health: The History of COHSE. 1988.

21695 —— Health Services in Scotland, 1953–1980. Succeeded by: Health in Scotland, 1981.

21696 MCLACHLAN (GORDON) *ed*. Improving the Common Weal: Aspects of Scottish Health Services, 1900–1984. Edin. 1987.

21697 LAWRENCE (R. J.). 'The Health Service in Northern Ireland'. *Public Admin.* 34 (1956), 289–308.

21698 STOWE (Sir KENNETH). On Caring for the National Health. 1988.

10. NURSING

21699 THOMPSON (ALICE M. C.) *ed*. A Bibliography of Nursing Literature, 1859–1960, With a Historical Introduction. 1968.

21700 —— *ed*. A Bibliography of Nursing Literature, 1961–1970. 1974.

21701 WALSH (FRANCES) *ed*. A Bibliography of Nursing Literature, 1971–1975. 1985.

21702 SEYMER (LUCY RIDGELY). A General History of Nursing. 2nd edn 1949.

21703 PAVEY (AGNES E.). The Story of the Growth of Nursing as an Art, a Vocation and a Profession. 1938. 3rd edn 1951.

21704 BEITH (J. HAY). One Hundred Years of Army Nursing: The Story of the British Army Services from the Time of Florence Nightingale to the Present Day. 1952.

21705 N.P.H.T. Report on a Study of the Work of Public Health Nurses. 1953.

21706 CHARLEY (IRENE H.). The Birth of Industrial Nursing: Its History and Development in Great Britain. 1954.

21707 BENDALL (EVE R. D.) *and* RAYBOULD (ELIZABETH). A History of the General Nursing Council for England and Wales, 1919–1969. 1969.

21708 BOWMAN (G.). The Lamp and the Book: The Story of the Royal College of Nursing, 1916–1966. 1967.

21709 COLWELL (B.) *and* WAINWRIGHT (D.). Behind the Blue Door: The History of the Royal College of Midwives, 1881–1981. 1981.

21710 BALY (MONICA E.). A History of the Queen's Nursing Institute: 100 years, 1887–1987. 1987.

21711 SHROCK (RICHARD HARRISON). The History of Nursing: An Interpretation of the Social and Medical Factors Involved. Philadelphia, Pa./Lond. 1959.

21712 STOCKS (MARY DANVERS). A Hundred Years of District Nursing. 1960.

21713 ABEL-SMITH (BRIAN). A History of the Nursing Profession. 1960.

21714 DIETZ (LENA DIXON). History of Modern Nursing. Philadelphia, Pa./ Lond. 1963.

21715 MARSH (DAVID CHARLES) *and* WILCOCKS (ARTHUR JOHN). Focus on Nurse Recruitment: A Snapshot from the Provinces. 1965.

21716 RAMSDEN (GERTRUDE A.) *and* SKEET (MURIEL H.). Marriage and Nursing: A Survey. 1967.

21717 HOCKEY (LISBETH). Feeling the Pulse: A Study of District Nursing in Six Areas. 1966.

21718 COMMITTEE ON NURSING. (Chairman, Asa Briggs). Report Presented to Parliament by the Secretary of State for Social Services, the Secretary of State for Scotland, and the Secretary of State for Wales. Cmnd 5113. [1972].

21719 HOCKEY (LISBETH). Use or Abuse? A Study of the State Enrolled Nurse in the Local Authority Nursing Service. 1972.

21720 BROWN (RONALD GEORGE SCLATER) *and* STONES (R. W. H.). The Male Nurse. 1973.

21721 LANCASTER (ARNOLD). Nursing and Midwifery Sourcebook. 1979.

21722 THOMPSON (IAN E.), MELIA (KATH M.), *and* BOYD (KENNETH M.). Nursing Ethics. Edin. 1981.

21723 WHITE (ROSEMARY). Social Change and the Development of the Nursing Profession: A Study of the Poor Law Nursing Service, 1848–1948. 1978.

21724 MACLEAN (UNA). Nursing in Contemporary Society. 1974.

21725 NATIONAL BOARD FOR PRICES AND INCOMES. Pay of Nurses and Midwives in the National Health Service. Report No. 60. Cmnd. 3585. 1968.

21726 WHINCUP (MICHAEL HYNES). Legal Rights and Duties in Medical and Nursing Service. Beckenham. 1976.

21727 BRIDGES (DAISY CAROLINE). A History of the International Council of Nurses, 1899–1964: The First Sixty Five Years. 1967.

21728 DAVIES (CELIA) *ed.* Rewriting Nursing History. 1980.

21729 COWELL (BETTY) *and* WAINWRIGHT (D.). Behind the Blue Door: The History of the Royal College of Midwives, 1881–1981. 1981.

21730 QUINN (SHEILA) *ed.* Nursing in the European Community. 1980.

21731 WALLACE (ELAINE). A History of the Council for the Education and Training of Health Visitors: An Account of its Establishment and Field of Activities, 1962–1975. 1979.

21732 YOUNG (PATRICIA). 'A Short History of the Chartered Society of Physiotherapy'. *Physiotherapy* 55 (1969), 271–8.

21733 AKESTER (JOYCE M.) *and* MACPHAIL (ANGUS N.). Health Visiting in the Sixties. 1963.

21734 CLARK (J.). What do Health Visitors do? A Review of the Research, 1960–1980. 1981.

21735 WILKIE (ELAINE). A History of the Council for the Education and Training of Health Visitors: An Account of its Establishment and Field of Activities, 1962–1975. 1979.

11. MENTAL AND PHYSICAL HANDICAP

21736 UNSWORTH (CLIVE). The Politics of Mental Health Legislation. Oxf. 1987.

21737 JONES (KATHLEEN). A History of the Mental Health Services. 1972.

21738 JONES (GRETA). Social Hygiene in Twentieth Century Britain. 1986.

21739 —— Better Services for the Mentally Handicapped. Cmnd. 4683. Parliamentary Papers, 20 (1970–1).

21740 MIDDLEMISS (J. R.). 'An Analysis of 200 Cases of Mental Defect'. *J. Mental Sci.* (July 1920), 254–74.

21741 WHITE (E. BARTON). Abstract of a Report on the Mental Division of the Welsh Metropolitan War Hospital, Whitchurch, Cardiff, Sept. 1917–Sept. 1919. *J. Mental Sci.* (Oct. 1920), 438–49.

21742 U.K. 1963 GENERAL REGISTER OFFICE. A Cohort Study of Patients First Admitted to Mental Hospitals in 1950 and 1955, by Eileen Brooks. 1963.

21743 U.K. LEEDS REGIONAL HOSPITAL BOARD. Census of Psychiatric Patients in the Board Area, by Brian Ward *et al.* Leeds. 1964.

21744 U.K. 1967 MINISTRY OF HEALTH. A Census of Patients in Psychiatric Beds, 1963, by Eileen Brooks. 1967.

21745 SEGAL (STANLEY SOLOMON). Mental Handicap: A Select Annotated Bibliography. Slough. 1972.

21746 MARTIN (FREDERICK M.). Between the Acts: Community Mental Health Services, 1959–1983. 1984.

21747 BUTLER (THOMAS). Mental Health, Social Policy and the Law. 1985.

21748 —— Royal Commission on the Law Relating to Mental Illness and Mental Deficiency, 1954–1957. Cmnd 169. Parliamentary Papers, 16 (1956–7).

21749 NATIONAL ASSOCIATION FOR MENTAL HEALTH (Subsequently MIND). Mental Breakdown: A Guide for Families. 1958.

21750 —— Report: In-service Training for Social Work with the Mentally Ill. 1976.

21751 —— Report: The Next Step: Community Care for Former Psychiatric Patients in Six Towns. 1977.

21752 LAWSON (ANNETTE RUTH LE VAY). The Recognition of Mental Illness in London. 1966.

21753 ASHDOWN (MARGARET) and BROWN (SIBYL CLEMENT). Social Service and Mental Health: An Essay on Psychiatric Social Workers. 1953.

21754 SCOTT (P. M.). 'Mental Health and Family Welfare: Need for an Integrated Policy'. *Public Admin.* 33(2) (1955), 163–75.

21755 ROSE (A. M.) ed. Mental Health and Mental Disorder: A Sociological Approach. 1956.

21756 O'CONNOR (NEIL) and TIZARD (JACK). The Social Problem of Mental Deficiency. Lond./NY. 1956.

21757 O'CONNOR (NEIL). 'The Social Effectiveness of the Mentally Handicapped'. *Advan. Sci.* 13(53) (1957), 373–7.

21758 TREDGOLD (ROGER FRANCIS) ed. Bridging the Gap: From Fear to Understanding in Mental Illness. 1958.

21759 NORRIS (VERA). Mental Illness in London. 1959.

21760 FREEMAN (HUGH LIONEL). 'Mental Health Services in an English County Borough before 1974'. *Med. Hist.* 28 (1984), 111–28.

21761 RAPOPORT (ROBERT NORMAN) with RAPOPORT (RHONA). Community as Doctor: New Perspective on a Therapeutic Community. 1960.

21762 —— The Therapeutic Community Revisited. 1968.

21763 BROOKS (EILEEN M.). 'Mental Health and the Population'. *Eugenics Rev.* 51(4) (1960), 209–15.

21764 PEAR (T. H.). The Moulding of Modern Man: A Psychologist's View of Information, Persuasion and Mental Persuasion Today. 1961.

21765 CAPLAN (GERALD). An Approach to Community Mental Health. 1961.

21766 —— Principles of Preventive Psychiatry. 1964.

21767 JEPSEN (S.). 'Rehabilitation of Mental Patients—A New Group Work Approach'. *Soc. Work* 18(2) (1961), 13–17.

21768 NATIONAL ASSOCIATION FOR MENTAL HEALTH. Violence and the Mental Health Services: Proceedings of a Conference. 1962.

21769 FREEMAN (HUGH LIONEL) and FARNDALE (WILLIAM ARTHUR JAMES) eds. Trends in Mental Health Services: A Symposium of Original and Reprinted Papers. Oxf. 1963.

21770 —— New Aspects of Mental Health Services. Oxf. 1967.

21771 LAING (RONALD DAVID) and ESTERSON (A.). Sanity, Madness and the Family: The Families of Schizophrenics. 1964. 2nd edn 1970.

21772 HARE (EDWARD HENRY) and SHAW (G. K.). Mental Health on a New Housing Estate: A Comparative Study of Health in Two Districts of Croydon. 1965.

21773 HARGROVE (APHRA LOCKE). Serving the Mentally Handicapped: A Record of the Work of the Central Association for Mental Welfare. 1965.

21774 POND (D. A.) and RYLE (A.). 'Marriage and Neurosis in a Working Class Population'. *Brit. J. Psychiatry* 109(462) (1963), 592–8.

21775 FORREST (A. D.), FRASER (R. H.), and PRIEST (R. G.). 'Environmental Factors in Depressive Illness'. *Brit. J. Psychiatry* 3(472) (1965), 243–53.

21776 FRASER (B.). 'The Mental Health Services'. *Public Admin.* 46(1) (1962), 29–42.

21777 EARLY (D. F.) and MAGNUS (R. V.). 'Population Trends in a Mental Hospital'. *Brit. J. Psychiatry* 112, (1966), 395–602.

21778 POLITICAL AND ECONOMIC PLANNING. Mental Subnormality in London: A Survey of Community Care. 1966.

21779 DALE (SHEILA). The Handicapped Person in the Community: Using the Literature. Milton Keynes. 1975. [An annotated bibliography.].

21780 LANE (DAVID), NOBLE (SHEILA), TIDBALL (MICHAEL), and TWIGG (SAM). The Quiet Revolution: The Planning, Development and Provision of Community Services for the Mentally Handicapped. 1983.

21781 MAYNARD (ALAN) and TINGLE (RACHEL). 'The Objectives and Performance of the Mental Health Services in England and Wales'. *J. Soc. Pol.* 4 (1975), 151–68.

21782 DONGES (G. S.). Policymaking for the Mentally Handicapped. Aldershot. 1982.

21783 MALIN (NIGEL) ed. Reassessing Community Care (with particular reference to provision for people with mental handicap and for people with mental illness). 1987.

21784 MILLS (ENID). Living with Mental Illness: A Study in East London. 1962.

21785 KERSHAW (JOHN DUNKERLEY). Handicapped Children. Harmonds-worth. 2nd edn 1966.

21786 HEIMLER (EUGENE). Mental Illness and Social Work. 1967/8.

21787 MALIN (NIGEL), RACE (DAVID), and JONES (GLENYS). Services for the Mentally Handicapped in Britain. 1980.

21788 GATHERER (ALEXANDER) and REID (JOHN JAMES ANDREW). Public Attitudes and Mental Health Education. Northampton. 1967.

21789 THOMPS (D.). The Experience of Handicap. 1982.

21790 CRAFT (MICHAEL JOHN) and MILES (LEWIS). Patterns of Care for the Subnormal. Oxf. 1967.

21791 GUNZBURG (HERBERT CHARLES). Social Competence and Mental Handicap: An Introduction to Social Education. 1968.

21792 —— ed. Experiments in the Rehabilitation of the Mentally Handicapped. 1974.

21793 MARTIN (FREDERICK MORRIS) and REHIN (GEORGE FÄNDERICH). Towards Community Care. P.E.P. 1969.

21794 REHIN (GEORGE FÄNDERICH) AND MARTIN (FREDERICK MORRIS). Problems of Performance in Community Care: A Report of a Community Mental Health Services Study. 1968.

21795 MITTLER (PETER). The Mental Health Services in the Community. 1968. [Fabian occasional paper.].

21796 JONES (MAXWELL). Social Psychiatry in Practice: The Idea of the Therapeutic Community. Harmondsworth. 1968.

21797 —— Beyond the Therapeutic Community: Social Learning and Social Psychiatry. New Haven, Conn./Lond. 1968.

21798 —— et al. Small Group Psychotherapy. Harmondsworth. 1971.

21799 MORRIS (PAULINE). Put Away: A Sociological Study of Institutions for the Mentally Retarded. 1969.

21800 HOENIG (JULIUS) and HAMILTON (MARIAN WATLING). The Desegregation of the Mentally Ill. 1969.

21801 POTTER (R. S. J.). 'Administrative and Social Work Problems of Services for the Handicapped'. Social Work (July 1966).

21802 VAIL (D. J.). The British Mental Hospital System. Springfield, Ill. 1965.

21803 IRVINE (ELIZABETH ERNESTINE) ed. Casework and Mental Illness. 1967.

21804 ASSOCIATION OF PSYCHIATRIC SOCIAL WORKERS. Casework and Mental Illness. 1967.

21805 SMITH (ALWYN) and CARSTAIRS (VERA). Patients under Psychiatric Care in Hospital in Scotland, 1963. Edin. 1966.

21806 TIMMS (NOEL). Psychiatric Social Work in Great Britain, 1939–1962. 1964.

21807 TAYLOR (STEPHEN JAMES LAKE) Baron, and CHAVE (SIDNEY). Mental Health and Environment. 1964.

21808 SPENCER (JOHN CARRINGTON) et al. Stress and Release in an Urban Estate: A Study in Action Research. 1964.

21809 TODD (FRANCES JOAN). Social Work with the Mentally Subnormal. 1967.

21810 ROBERTS (NESTA). Mental Health and Mental Illness. 1967.

21811 MUNRO (ALISTAIR). 'Parental Deprivation in Depressive Patients'. Brit. J. Psychiatry 112(486) (1966), 443–58.

21812 —— 'Some Familial and Social Factors in Depressive Illness'. Brit. J. Psychiatry 112(486) (1966), 429–42.

21813 PILONSKY (I.) and STIRLAND (J. D.). 'A Study of Long-term Patients Attending a General Hospital Psychiatric Department'. Brit. J. Psychiatry 112(486) (1966), 833–8.

21814 LUCAS (C. J.), KELVIN (R. P.), and OJHA (A. B.). 'Mental Health and Student Wastage'. Brit. J. Psychiatry 112(486) (1966), 277–84.

21815 LITTLE (A.). An 'Expectancy' Estimate of Hospitalization Rates for Mental Illness in England and Wales'. Brit. J. Sociol. 16(3) (1965), 221–31.

21816 SODDY (KENNETH) and AHRENFELDT (ROBERT H.) eds. Mental Health in the Service of the Community. 1967.

21817 MYERS (JEROME KEELEY), BEAN (LEE L.), and PEPPER (MAX P.). A Decade Later: A Follow-up Study of Social Class and Mental Illness. 1968.

21818 BROWN (GEORGE W.), N BHROLCHAIN (M.), and HARRIS (TIRRIL). 'Social Class and Psychiatric Disturbance among Women in an Urban Population'. Sociol. 9 (1975), 225–34.

21819 APTE (ROBERT Z.). Halfway House: A New Dilemma in Institutional Care. 1968.

21820 GREENLAND (C.). Mental Illness and Civil Liberty: A Study of Mental Health Review Tribunals in England and Wales. 1970.

21821 RAMON (SHULAMIT). Psychiatry in Britain: Meaning and Policy. 1985.

21822 CLARK (D. H.). 'Administrative Psychiatry, 1942-1962'. Brit. J. Psychiatry 109 (1963), 178–201.

21823 HENDERSON (D. K.). The Evolution of Psychiatry in Scotland. Edin. 1964.

21824 EVANS (RICHARD I.). R. D. Laing: The Man and his Ideas. 1976.

21825 LAING (R. D.). Wisdom, Madness and Folly: The Making of a Psychiatrist. 1985.

21826 COOPER (J.). Psychiatry and Anti-psychiatry. 1970.

21827 —— et al. Psychiatric Diagnosis in New York and London: A Comparative Study of Mental Hospital Admissions. 1972.

21828 LYNN (RICHARD). Personality and National Character. Oxf. 1971.

21829 —— National Differences in Anxiety. Dublin. 1971.

21830 BAGLEY (CHRISTOPHER). 'Mental Illness in Immigrant Minorities in London'. J. Biosoc. Sci. 3(4) (1971), 449–59.

21831 STEPHEN (ELSPETH) ed. Residential Care for the Mentally Retarded. Oxf. 1970.

21832 TIZARD (JACK). Community Services for the Mentally Handicapped. 1964.

21833 HASSALL (C.), SPENCER (A. M.), and CROSS (K. W.). 'Some Changes in the Composition of a Mental Hospital Population'. Brit. J. Psychiatry 3(474) (1965), 420–8.

21834 GOLDBERG (E. M.). 'Hospital Work and Family: A Four-Year Study of Young Mental Hospital Patients'. *Brit. J. Psychiatry* 112(483) (1966), 177–98.

21835 GOLDBERG (E. M.) *and* MORRISON (S. L.). 'Schizophrenia and Social Class'. *Brit. J. Psychiatry* 109(463) (1963), 785–808.

21836 TIZARD (JACK). The Integration of the Handicapped in Society. Exeter. 1973.

21837 —— Mental Retardation: Concepts of Education and Research. 1974.

21838 TIZARD (JACK) *and* GRAD (J.). The Mentally Handicapped and Their Families: A Social Survey. 1961.

21839 TREDGOLD (ALFRED FRANK). Tredgold's Mental Retardation. 11th edn *ed.* by R. Tredgold and Kenneth Soddy, 1970. 12th edn *ed.* by Michael Craft, 1979. First ten editions under title 'A Textbook of Mental Deficiency'.

21840 TRIPARTITE COMMITTEE OF B.M.A., R.C.P. AND S.M.O.H. The Mental Health Services after Reunification. 1972.

21841 SUTHERLAND (J. F.) *ed.* Towards Community Mental Health. 1971.

21842 BALDWIN (JOHN ALEXANDER). The Mental Hospital in the Psychiatric Service: A Case-Register Study. 1971.

21843 McLACHLAN (GORDON) *ed.* Approaches to Action: A Symposium on Services for the Mentally Ill and Handicapped. 1972.

21844 McLACHLAN (GORDON) *and* CAWLEY (ROBERT) *eds.* Policy for Action: A Symposium on the Planning of a Comprehensive District Psychiatric Service. 1973.

21845 FREEMAN (A. E.). 'Traditional and Social Perspectives on Mental Illness'. *Brit. J. Psychiatry Community Health* 4(3) (1970–1), 192–201.

21846 BASTIDE (ROGER). The Sociology of Mental Disorder. 1972.

21847 WING (JOHN KENNETH). 'Rehabilitation of Psychiatric Patients'. *Brit. J. Psychiatry* 109(462) (1963), 635–41.

21848 SYKES (P.). 'The Future of the Large Hospital in Services to the Mentally Handicapped'. *Mental Handicap. Bull.* (Mar. 1973).

21849 ADAMS (MARGARET) *and* LOVEJOY (HOWARD) *eds.* The Mentally Subnormal: Social Work Approaches. 2nd edn 1972.

21850 ADAMS (MARGARET). Mental Retardation and its Social Dimensions. NY/Lond. 1971.

21851 U.K. D.H.S.S. Better Services for the Mentally Handicapped. Cmnd. 4683. 1971.

21852 BONE (MARGARET), SPAIN (BERNIE), *and* MARTIN (FREDERICK MORRIS). Plans and Provisions for the Mentally Handicapped. 1972.

21853 McMASTER (JOHN MCGREGOR). Towards an Educational Theory for the Mentally Handicapped. 1973.

21854 BOEHRINGER (GILL MACE) *and* McCABE (SARAH). The Hospital Order in London Magistrates' Courts. Oxf. 1973.

21855 BAYLEY (MICHAEL). Mental Handicap and Community Care: A Study of Mentally Handicapped People in Sheffield. 1973.

21856 WING (JOHN KENNETH), COOPER (JOHN EDWARD), *AND* SARTORIUS (N.). Measurement and Classification of Psychiatric Symptoms. 1974.

21857 WING (JOHN KENNETH) *and* BRANSBY (E. R.) *eds.* Psychiatric Case Registers. 1970.

21858 CLARK (DAVID HAZELL). Social Therapy in Psychiatry. Harmondsworth. 1974.

21859 DUNHAM (H. WARREN). 'Social Class and Mental Disorder'. *Brit. J. Soc. Psychiatry Community Health* 4(2) (1970–71), 176–83.

21860 DURKIN (ELIZABETH). Hostels for the Mentally Disordered. 1971. [Fabian pamphlet.].

21861 MILLER (K. S.) *et al.* 'Compulsory Mental Hospitalization in England and Wales'. *J. Health Soc. Behaviour* 15 (1974), 151–6.

21862 HUNTER (RICHARD ALFRED) *and* MacALPINE (IDA). Psychiatry for the Poor: 1881 Colney Hatch Asylum-Friern Hospital 1973: A Medical and Social History. Folkestone. 1974.

21863 HEWITT (CECIL ROLPH). Believe What You Like: What Happened between the Scientologists and the National Association for Mental Health. 1973.

21864 FORREST (ALISTAIR DOUGLAS) *et al.* New Perspectives in Mental Handicap. Edin./Lond. 1973.

21865 ENNALS (DAVID). Out of Mind. 1973.

21866 JONES (KATHLEEN) *and* BROWN (JOHN) *et al.* Opening the Door: A Study of New Policies for the Mentally Handicapped. 1975.

21867 HANNAM (CHARLES). Parents and Mentally Handicapped Children. Harmondsworth. 1975.

21868 KIRMAN (BRIAN HERBERT). Mental Handicap: A Brief Guide. 1975.

21869 ARMISTEAD (NIGEL). Community Services for the Mentally Ill. 1976.

21870 U.K. D.H.S.S. 1976. The Facilities and Services of Mental Illness and Mental Handicap Hospitals in England, 1974. 1976.

21871 —— 1977. In-patient Statistics from the Mental Health Enquiry for England, 1974. 1977.

21872 THOMPSON (RICHARD). Residential and Day Care Services for the Mentally Handicapped and Mentally Ill in the London Boroughs, 1966–1974. 1976.

21873 WING (JOHN KENNETH). Reasoning about Madness. Oxf. 1978.

21874 WING (JOHN KENNETH) *and* HAILEY (ANTHEA) *eds.* Evaluating a Community Psychiatric Service: The Camberwell Register, 1964–1971. 1972.

21875 DOERNER (KLAUS). Madmen and the Bourgeoisie: A Social History of Insanity and Psychiatry. Oxf. 1981.

21876 LADER (MALCOLM HAROLD). Psychiatry on Trial. Harmondsworth. 1977.

21877 —— U.K. Report of the Royal Commission on the Law Relating to Mental Illness and Mental Deficiency. Cmnd 169. 1957.

21878 ROLPH (C. H.) *pseud.* Mental Disorder: A Brief Examination of the Report of the Royal Commission on the Law Relating to Mental Illness and Mental Deficiency, 1954–1957. 1958.

21879 FLEMING (ALAN CHALMERS) *and* PATERSON (HEW FERGUS). Mental Disorder and the Law. Edin. 1966.

21880 GOSTIN (LARRY O.). A Human Condition: The Mental Health Act from 1959–1975: Observations, Analysis and Proposals for Reform. Vol. 1 1975.[MIND].

21881 WING (JOHN KENNETH) *ed.* Early Childhood Autism: Clinical, Educational and Social Aspects. Oxf. 1966. 2nd edn 1976 *ed.* by Lorna Wing.

21882 SHABERMAN (RAPHAEL B.). Autistic Children: The Nature and Treatment of Childhood Autism. 1971.

21883 COLLIE (*Sir* ROBERT JOHN). 'The Care of Pensioners and Disabled Combatants in Relation to National Health and Wealth'. *J. State Medicine* (Feb. 1919), 43–53.

21884 SAINSBURY (PETER). Suicide in London—An Ecological Study. 1955.

21885 SHEARER (ANN). Handicapped Children in Residential Care: A Study of Policy Failure. 1980.

21886 SHERIDAN (MARY DOROTHY). The Handicapped Child and his Home. 1965.

21887 LORING (JAMES) *and* MASON (ANITA) *eds.* The Spastic Schoolchild and the Outside World. 1966.

21888 PRITCHARD (DAVID G.). Education and the Handicapped, 1760–1960. 1963.

21889 TOWNSEND (PETER BRERETON). The Disabled in Society. [Lecture.]. 1967.

21890 U.K. OFFICE OF POPULATION, CENSUSES AND SURVEYS (Social Survey Division). Amelia Isabella Harris *with* Elizabeth Cox *and* Christopher R. Smith. Handicapped and Impaired in Great Britain. 2 vols. 1971.

21891 —— Part 2 by BUCKLE (JUDITH R.). Work and Housing of Impaired Persons in Great Britain. 1971.

21892 U.K. ECONOMIC INTELLIGENCE UNIT. Care with Dignity: An Analysis of Costs of Care for the Disabled. Horsham. 1973.

21893 THOMAS (JESSIE ELLEN). Hope for the Handicapped. 1967.

21894 SAINSBURY (SALLY). Registered as Disabled. 1970.

21895 —— Measuring Disability. 1974.

21896 YOUNGHUSBAND (*Dame* EILEEN L.) *et al.* Living with Handicap. 1972.

21897 ONES (KATHLEEN). Eileen Younghusband: A Biography. 1984.

21898 RUSSELL (PHILIPPA). The Wheelchair Child. 1978.

21899 WOODS (GRACE E.). The Handicapped Child: Assessment and Management. Oxf. 1975.

21900 ROUAULT (GEORGES Y.). The Handicapped and Their Employment: A Statistical Study of the Situation in the Member States of the European Communities. 1978.

21901 NICHOLSON (JOHN HENRY). Help for the Handicapped: An Enquiry into the Opportunities of the Voluntary Services. 1958.

21902 KERSHAW (JOHN DUNKERLEY). Handicapped Children. 1961. 3rd edn 1973.

21903 MILLER (ERIC JOHN) *and* GWYNNE (G. V.). A Life Apart: A Pilot Study of Residential Institutions for the Physically Handicapped and the Young Chronic Sick. Lond./Philadelphia, Pa. 1972.

21904 MACMORLAND (B.). An ABC of Services and General Information for Disabled People. 1974.

21905 CHAMBERLAIN (ROMA). The Prevalence of Illness in Children. Tunbridge Wells. 1979.

21906 BURTON (LINDY). The Family Life of Sick Children. 1975.

21907 LANSDOWN (RICHARD). More than Sympathy: The Everyday Needs of Sick and Handicapped Children and Their Families. 1980.

21908 MCMICHAEL (JOAN CATHERINE). Handicap: A Study of Physically Handicapped Children and Their Families. 1971.

21909 LEES (DENNIS) *and* SHAW (STELLA). Impairment, Disability and Handicap: A Multi-disciplinary View. 1974.

21910 LANCASTER-GAYE (DEREK) *ed.* Personal Relationships, the Handicapped and the Community: Some European Thoughts and Solutions. 1972.

21911 KING (ROY DAVID), RAYNES (NORMA V.), *and* TIZARD (JACK). Patterns of Residential Care: Sociological Studies in Institutions for Handicapped Children. 1971.

21912 HEWETT (SHEILA) *et al.* The Family and the Handicapped Child: A Study of Cerebral Palsied Children in Their Own Homes. 1970.

21913 GREAVES (MARY). Work and Disability: Some Aspects of the Employment of Disabled Persons in Great Britain. 1969.

21914 GLASER (W. A.). Sheltered Employment of the Disabled—An International Survey. Geneva. 1967.

21915 FERGUSON (THOMAS) *and* KERR (AGNES W.). Handicapped Youth: A Report on the Employment Problems of Handicapped Young People in Glasgow. 1960.

21916 DISABLEMENT INCOME GROUP. Social Security and Disability: A Study of the Financial Provisions for Disabled People in Seven West European Countries. Godalming. 1971.

21917 DINNAGE (ROSEMARY) *comp.* The Handicapped Child: Research Review. Vols 1 and 2. Vol. 3 by Doria Pilling. 1970–3.

21918 COLLIS (EDGAR LEIGH). A Way of Life for the Handicapped Child: A New Approach to Cerebral Palsy. 1947.

21919 CLARKE (JOAN SIMEON). Disabled Citizens. 1951.

21920 BRYANT (PETER), MITTLER (PETER), *and* O'CONNOR (NEIL). The Handicapped Child: Recent Research Findings. 1971.

21921 BOSWELL (DAVID MARK) *and* WINGROVE (JANET MADGE) *eds.* The Handicapped Person in the Community. Milton Keynes. 1974.

21922 TOPLISS (EDA). Provision for the Disabled. Oxf./Lond. 1975. 2nd edn 1979.

21923 TOPLISS (EDA) *and* GOULD (G.). A Charter for the Disabled: The Chronically Sick and Disabled Persons Act, 1970. Oxf. 1981.

21924 TAYLOR (W. W.) *and* TAYLOR (I. W.). Services for Handicapped Youth in England and Wales. NY. 1967.

21925 MALIN (NIGEL), RACE (DAVID), *and* JONES (GLENYS). Services for the Mentally Handicapped in Britain. 1980.

21926 CLARK (FREDERICK LE GROS). Blinded in War: A Model for the Welfare of all Handicapped People. Royston. 1969.

21927 ROSE (JUNE). Changing Focus: The Development of Blind Welfare in Britain. 1970.

21928 PEARSON (*Sir* CYRIL ARTHUR). The Conquest of Blindness. 1921.

21929 DARK (SIDNEY). The Life of Sir Arthur Pearson, Bt. 1922.

21930 SORSBY (A.). Blindness in England, 1951–1954. 1956.

21931 ADVANI (L.). Blind Welfare in the United Kingdom. New Delhi. 1955.

21932 THOMAS (MARY G.). The Royal National Institute for the Blind, 1868–1956. 1957.

21933 WOLL (B.), KYLE (J.), *and* DEUCHAR (M.). Perspectives on British Sign Language and Deafness. 1981.

21934 MEACHER (MICHAEL). Taken for a Ride: Special Residential Homes for Old People: A Study of Separation in Social Policy. 1972.

21935 HAZELL (KENNETH) *ed.* Social and Medical Problems of the Elderly. 1960. 4th edn 1976.

21936 CRAFT (MICHAEL JOHN) *ed.* Psychopathic Disorders and Their Assessment. Oxf. 1966.

21937 —— Ten Studies in Psychopathic Personality: A Report to the Home Office and the Mental Health Research Fund. Bristol. 1965.

21938 —— Concluding chapter in Born to Trouble: Portrait of a Psychopath. *ed.* Ronald Lloyd and S. Williamson. 1968.

21939 LAING (R. D.). Wisdom, Madness and Folly: The Making of a Psychiatrist, 1927–1957. 1985.

21940 JONES (*Sir* ROBERT). 'The Problem of the Disabled'. *J. State Medicine* (Mar. 1918), 77–86; (Apr. 1918), 120–8. [Orthopaedic hospitals: treatment, care, and training after operation.].

21941 GREGORY (PETER). Deafness and Public Responsibility: The Provision of Hearing Aids. Welwyn. 1964.

21942 REES (JOHN TUDOR) *and* USILL (HARLEY VERNEAU) *eds.* They Stand Apart: A Critical Survey of the Problems of Homosexuality. 1955.

12. SOCIAL MEDICINE/PUBLIC HEALTH

21943 LEWIS (JANE). What Price Community Medicine? The Philosophy, Practice and Politics of Public Health since 1919. Brighton. 1986.

21944 HONIGSBAUM (FRANK). The Division in British Medicine: A History of the Separation of General Practice from Hospital Care, 1911–1968. 1979.

21945 STEVENSON (ALAN CARRUTH). Recent Advances in Social Medicine. 1950.

21946 CHEESEMAN (ERIC ARTHUR). Epidemics in Schools. An Analysis of the Data Collected during the Years 1935 to 1939. 1950.

21947 —— Sociological Review. Monographs No. 5. Sociology and Medicine: Studies within the Framework of the British National Health Service. Keele. 1962.

21948 SMITH (ALWYN). The Science of Social Medicine. 1968.

21949 ROBINSON (DAVID). Patients, Practitioners and Medical Care: Aspects of Medical Sociology. 1973. 2nd edn 1978.

21950 —— The Process of Becoming Ill. 1971.

21951 ROBINSON (DAVID) *and* HENRY (STUART). Self-Help and Health: Mutual Aid for Modern Problems. 1977.

21952 WADSWORTH (MICHAEL) and ROBINSON (DAVID) *eds.* Studies in Everyday Medical Life. 1976.

21953 HALMOS (PAUL) *ed.* Sociology and Medicine. Keele. 1962.

21954 BUTRYM (ZOFIA TERESA). Medical Social Work in Action: A Report of a Study of Medical Social Work at Hammersmith Hospital. 1968.

21955 —— British Sociological Association, Medical Sociology Group ed. Medical Sociology in Great Britain, 1969–1970: A Selective Review of the Research and Teaching Activities of some British Medical Sociologists. 1970.

21956 JOHNSON (MALCOLM L.) ed. and comp. Medical Sociology in Britain: A Register of Research and Teaching. 1974.

21957 McKEOWN (THOMAS). Medicine in Modern Society: Medical Planning Based on Evaluation of Medical Achievement. 1965.

21958 GARRAD (JESSIE) and ROSENHEIM (Sir MAX). Social Aspects of Clinical Medicine. 1970.

21959 MCKEOWN (THOMAS) and LOWE (CHARLES RONALD). An Introduction to Social Medicine. Oxf. 1966. 2nd edn. 1974.

21960 COX (CAROLINE) and MEAD (ADRIENNE) eds. A Sociology of Medical Practice. 1975.

21961 BREARLEY (C. PAUL) et al. The Social Context of Health Care. 1978.

21962 TUCKETT (DAVID) ed. An Introduction to Medical Sociology. 1976.

21963 FIELD (DAVID) and CLARKE (BRIAN A.). Medical Sociology in Britain: A Register of Teaching and Research. 4th edn 1982.

21964 CHECKLAND (OLIVE) and LAMB (MARGARET) eds. Health Care as Social History. Aberdeen. 1982.

21965 MAUDE (ANGUS EDMUND UPTON). The Consuming Society. 1967.

21966 MACGREGOR (IAN MURRAY). The 2 Year Mass Radiography Campaign in Scotland, 1957–1958. Edin. 1961.

21967 WICKEN (A. J.). Environmental and Personal Factors in Lung Cancer and Bronchitis Mortality in Northern Ireland, 1960–1962. 1966.

21968 ALLISON (RICHARD SYDNEY). Sea Diseases: The Story of A Great Natural Experiment in Preventive Medicine in the Royal Navy. 1943.

21969 DAVIES (TREVOR ARTHUR LLOYD). Respiratory Disease in Foundry Men: Report of A Survey. 1971.

21970 ROYDEN (A. MAUDE). 'Report of the Royal Commission on Venereal Diseases'. Inl. J. Ethics (Jan. 1917), 171–88.

21971 EDWARDS (GRIFFITH) et al. 'Alcoholics Admitted to Four Hospitals in England'. Q. J. Stud. Alcohol 35 (No. 2a), 499–522; (No. 3a), 841–55 (1974).

21972 CAMPBELL (JANET MARY) Dame. Maternity Services. 1935.

21973 McKENNELL (AUBREY CECIL). Adults' and Adolescents' Smoking Habits and Attitudes: A Report on a Survey Carried Out for the Ministry of Health. 1967.

21974 INTERNATIONAL LABOUR ORGANIZATION. Monographs on the Organization of Medical Care within the Framework of Social Security. United Kingdom National Health Service. Geneva. 1968.

21975 FARNDALE (WILLIAM ARTHUR JAMES) and Larman (Edward Cyril). Legal Liability for Claims Arising from Hospital Treatment. Beckenham. 1973.

21976 FARNDALE (WILLIAM ARTHUR JAMES). Medical Negligence. Rev. edn. Beckenham. 1976.

21977 BECK (ANN). A History of the British Medical Administration of East Africa, 1900–1950. Camb., Mass. 1970.

21978 —— Medicine, Tradition and Development in Kenya and Tanzania, 1920–1970. Waltham, Mass. 1981.

21979 WATKIN (BRIAN) ed. Documents on Health and Social Services, 1834 to the Present Day. 1975.

21980 WADSWORTH (MICHAEL EDWIN JOHN), BUTTERFIELD (WILLIAM JOHN HUGHES) and BLANEY (ROGER). Health and Sickness: The Choice of Treatment: Perception of Illness and Use of Services in an Urban Community. 1973.

21981 WALKER (JOSEPH VICCARS). Health and the Citizen: A Study in Design for Living. 1951.

21982 WALKER (M. E. M.). Pioneers of Public Health: The Story of Some Benefactors of the Human Race. Edin. 1930.

21983 —— U.K. SOCIAL SURVEY. Reports N.S. No. 21. Diphtheria Immunisation Enquiry; A Survey of 2,026 Parents Made in July–August 1942 for the Ministry of Health. 1942.

21984 —— N.S. No. 69. Diphtheria Immunisation. 1945.

21985 U.K. MINISTRY OF HEALTH. Health Education: Report of A Joint Committee. 1964.

21986 U.K. 1966 DES. Health in Education. 1966.

21987 U.K. MINISTRY OF HEALTH. The Incidence and Causes of Blindness in England and Wales, 1948–1962, by Arnold Sorsby, 1966. [For earlier report see 1956.].

21988 U.K. MATERNITY AND CHILD WELFARE: Report on the Provisions Made by Public Health Authorities and Voluntary Agencies. 1917.

21989 U.K. MINISTRY OF HEALTH. HEALTH AND WELFARE: The Development of Community Care: Revision to 1973–1974 of Plans for the Health and Welfare Services of the Local Authorities in England and Wales. 1964.

21990 U.K. 1963 MINISTRY OF HEALTH. Health and Welfare: The Development of Community Care. Cmnd 1973. 1963.

21991 —— Health and Personal Social Services Statistics for England. 1976.

21992 —— Health and Personal Social Services Statistics for Wales. 1976.

21993 U.K. HEALTH SERVICE COMMISSIONER. First Report. Session 1974. Annual Report for 1973–1974. 1974. HMSO.

21994 U.K. HEALTH AND SAFETY EXECUTIVE. Health and Safety Statistics. 1975.

21995 CENTRAL OFFICE OF INFORMATION. Health Services in Britain. 9th edn. 1977.

21996 STOCKS (PERCY). Sickness in the Population of England and Wales in 1944–1947. [Studies in Medical and Population Subjects. 2]. 1949.

21997 —— Regional and Local Differences in Cancer Death Rates. [Smps. 1]. 1947.

21998 —— Cancer Registration in England and Wales: An Enquiry into Treatment and its Results. (Smps. 3).

21999 SUSSER (MERVYN WILFRID) *and* WATSON (WILLIAM). Sociology in Medicine. 1962. 2nd edn. 1971. [Not confined to the U.K.].

22000 SOCIALIST MEDICAL ASSOCIATION OF GREAT BRITAIN. Medicine Tomorrow: A Précis of Articles on the Present Medical System and of Plans for the Future of Medicine which have appeared in *Medicine Today and Tomorrow*: with A Summary of a Scheme for an Immediate Socialized Medical Service.

22001 SPENCE (*Sir* JAMES CALVERT) *et al.* A Thousand Families in Newcastle Upon Tyne: An Approach to the Study of Health and Illness in Children. 1954.

22002 STEVENS (ROSEMARY). The Impact of Specialized and State Medicine: Medical Practice in Modern England. New Haven, Conn. 1966.

22003 SIGERIST (HENRY ERNST). Medicine and Human Welfare. New Haven, Conn. 1941.

22004 —— Landmarks in the History of Hygiene. Lond./ NY. 1956.

22005 —— Civilisation and Disease. Ithaca, NY. 1943.

22006 RHODES (PHILIP). The Value of Medicine. 1976.

22007 PEARSE (JAMES). The Co-Ordination of the Public Health Services in the Counties of Essex, Hampshire, Gloucester and West Sussex. 1928.

22008 PLATT (ROBERT) *Baron, and* PARKES (*Sir* ALAN STERLING). Social and Genetic influences on Life and Death. Edin. 1968.

22009 MEADE (J. E.) *and* PARKES (*Sir* ALAN STERLING) *eds.* Biological Aspects of Social Problems. 1965.

22010 NUFFIELD PROVINCIAL HOSPITALS TRUST. Towards a Measure of Medical Care: Operational Research in the Health Services: a Symposium. 1962.

22011 NORTON (ALAN). The New Dimensions of Medicine. 1964. Revised as: Drugs, Science and Society: The New Dimensions of Medicine. 1973.

22012 MOSS (JOHN). Health and Welfare Services Handbook. Being A General Guide To the Health and Welfare Services Administered By Local Authorities, Together with National Insurance and National Assistance. 2nd edn 1955; 3rd edn 1962. [First published in 1948 under the title: Haddin's Health and Welfare Services Handbook.].

22013 ACHESON (ROY M.) *and* HAGARD (SPENCER) Health, Society and Medicine. 3rd edn. 1984.

22014 ROSEN (GEORGE). A History of Public Health. NY. 1958.

22015 —— From Medical Police To Social Medicine: Essays on the History of Health Care. NY. 1974.

22016 MILLER (HENRY GEORGE). Medicine and Society. 1973.

22017 McLACHLAN (GORDON) *ed.* Problems and Progress in Medical Care. Series 1, 1964; Series 2, 1966.

22018 —— *ed.* Medical Education and Medical Care: A Scottish-American Symposium Arranged By the Nuffield Provincial Hospitals Trust and the Josiah Macy Jr Foundation. 1976. Oxford. 1977.

22019 LEFF (SAMUEL) *and* LEFF (VERA). From Witchcraft to World Health. 1956.

22020 —— Health and Humanity. 1960.

22021 COMMUNITY HEALTH: Including Community Medicine, Public Health, and Social Service: A Select List of Books, Periodicals and Non-Book Materials. 1977.

22022 NEWMAN (*Sir* GEORGE). The Rise of Preventive Medicine. 1932.

22023 HONIGSBAUM (FRANK). The Struggle for the Ministry of Health, 1914–1919. 1971.

22024 NEWSHOLME (*Sir* ARTHUR). Fifty Years in Public Health. 1935.

22025 —— The Ministry of Health. 1925.

22026 —— Medicine and the State: The Relation between the Private and Official Practice of Medicine, With Special Reference to Public Health. 1932.

22027 —— The Last Thirty Years in Public Health. 1936.

22028 —— The Evolution of Preventive Medicine. Lond./Baltimore, Md. 1927.

22029 —— The Story of Modern Preventive Medicine. Lond./Baltimore, Md. 1929.

22030 MURRAY (DAVID STARK). Health for All. 1942.

22031 —— Why a National Health Service? The Part Played by the Socialist Medical Association. 1971.

22032 MORRIS (*Sir* MALCOLM ALEXANDER). The Story of English Public Health. 1919.

22033 McLACHLAN (GORDON) *ed.* A Question of Quality? Roads to Assurance in Medical Care. 1976.

22034 GLASGOW CORPORATION PUBLIC HEALTH DEPARTMENT. Report of the Medical Officer of Health: City of Glasgow. 1898–1972.

22035 —— Labour Party. Health Care: Report of a Working Party. 1973.

22036 LAIDLER (P. W.). Locations: Health and Sanitation. Being an Extract from the Annual Report of the Medical Officer of Health, East London, 1st July 1934–30th June 1935. East London. 1936.

22037 ADDISON (CHRISTOPHER). The Health of the People and How It May Be Improved. 1914.

22038 CARNEGIE UNITED KINGDOM TRUST. Report on the Physical Welfare of Mothers and Children. Dunfermline. 1917.

22039 —— Vols. I and II: England and Wales, by E. W. Hope and Dame Janet Mary Campbell.

22040 —— Vol. III: Scotland, by W. Leslie Mackenzie.

22041 —— Vol. IV: Ireland, by Edward Coey Bigger.

22042 BALFOUR (*Sir* ANDREW) *and* Scott (*Sir* HENRY HOLLAND). Health Problems of the Empire, Past, Present and Future. 1924.

22043 HOPE (EDWARD WILLIAM) *and* STALLYBRASS (CLARE OSWALD). Textbook of Public Health. 9th edn, Edin. 1926; 13th edn *rev.* by W. M. Frazer. Edin. 1953.

22044 HOPE (EDWARD WILLIAM). Health at the Gateway: Problems and International Obligations of a Seaport City. Camb. 1931.

22045 FREMANTLE (*Sir* FRANCIS EDWARD). The Health of the Nation. 1927.

22046 LONDON COUNTY COUNCIL. EDUCATION COMMITTEE SPECIAL SERVICES SUB-COMMITTEE. Report by the School Medical Officer on the Average Heights and Weights of Elementary School Children in the County of London in 1938. 1940.

22047 MASSEY (*Sir* ARTHUR) *ed.* Modern Trends in Public Health. 1949.

22048 —— Epidemiology in Relation to Air Travel. 1933.

22049 MacCLEARY (GEORGE FREDERICK). The Maternity and Child Welfare Movement. 1935.

22050 —— The Early History of the Infant Welfare Movement. 1933.

22051 —— The Development of British Maternity and Child Welfare Services. 1945.

22052 M'GONIGLE (GEORGE CUTHBERT MURA) *and* KIRBY (J.). Poverty and Public Health. 1936.

22053 JAMESON (*Sir* WILLIAM WILSON) *and* PARKINSON (GEORGE SINGLETON). A Synopsis of Health. 9th edn 1947.

22054 CATTELL (RAYMOND BERNARD) *et al.* Human Affairs. 1937.

22055 CLARK (FREDERICK LE GROS) *ed.* National Fitness: A Brief Essay on Contemporary Britain. 1938.

22056 CAMPBELL (*Dame* JANET MARY) , *and* VERNON (HORACE MIDDLETON). National Health Services and Preventive Methods for Improving National Health. 1943.

22057 MACKINTOSH (JAMES MACALISTER). The Health of Scotland. Edin. 1943.

22058 —— The Nation's Health. 1944.

22059 —— The War and Mental Health in England. NY. 1944.

22060 —— Trends of Opinion About the Public Health, 1901–51. 1953.

22061 —— Topics in Public Health. Edin. 1965.

22062 MacGREGOR (*Sir* ALEXANDER STUART MURRAY). Public Health in Glasgow, 1905–1946. Edin. 1967.

22063 CHALMERS (ARCHIBALD KERR). The Health of Glasgow, 1818–1925: An Outline. Glasg. 1930.

22064 CRAIG (WILLIAM STUART McRAE). Child and Adolescent Life in Health and Disease: A Study in Social Paediatrics. Edin. 1946.

22065 ELLIS (RICHARD WHITE BERNARD) *ed.* Child Health and Development. 1947.

22066 —— Disease in Infancy and Childhood. 1951.

22067 CREW (FRANCIS ALBERT ELEY). Measurement of the Public Health : Essays on Social Medicine. Edin. 1948.

22068 GEFFEN (DENNIS HERBERT) *and* BROWN (LESLIE FARRER). Public Health and Social Services. 1940. 3rd edn 1949.

22069 FRAZER (WILLIAM MOWLL). A History of English Public Health, 1834–1939. 1950.

22070 —— The Public Health Department of the City of Liverpool. 1934.

22071 CLARKE (JOHN JOSEPH). Introduction to Public Health Law. 1949.

22072 GRUNDY (FRED). The New Public Health: An Introduction to Personal Health and the Welfare Services for Health Visitors, Social Workers and Midwives. 1908. 4th edn 1957.

22073 BROTHERSTON (JOHN HOWIE FLINT). Observations on the Early Public Health Movement in Scotland. 1952.

22074 CHARLES (*Sir* JOHN ALEXANDER). Research and Public Health. 1961.

22075 REHIN (GEORGE FAENDERICH) *and* MARTIN (F. M.). Patterns of Performance in Community Care: A Report of a Community Mental Health Services Study. 1968.

22076 ROYAL SOCIETY OF HEALTH *and* COLLEGE OF GENERAL PRACTITIONERS. The G.P. and Preventive Medicine: Report of the Joint Meeting on the Role of the General Practitioner in Preventive Medicine. 1964.

22077 TEELING-SMITH (GEORGE) *ed.* Surveillance and Early Diagnosis in General Practice: Proceedings of Colloquium. Oxf. 1965.

22078 FERGUSON (THOMAS) *et al.* Public Health and Urban Growth. 1964.

22079 NEILSON (MARY GEORGINA CUMMING) *and* CROFTON (EILEEN). The Social Effects of Chronic Bronchitis: A Scottish Study. Edin. 1965.

22080 MORRIS (JEREMY NOAH). Uses of Epidemiology. 1957. 3rd edn Edin. 1957.

22081 OWEN (DAVID). In Sickness and in Health: The Politics of Medicine. 1976.

22082 —— A Unified Health Service. Oxf. 1968.

22083 PAIGE (DEBORAH) *and* JONES (KIT). Health and Welfare Services in Britain in 1975. Camb. 1966.

22084 PARKER (WILLIAM SHEPHERD). Public and Community Health. 1964.

22085 RYAN (M.). 'Health Centre Policy in England and Wales.' *Brit. J. Sociol*, 19 (1968), 34–46.

22086 MONCRIEFF (ALAN AIRD). Child Health and the State. 1953.

22087 MILLER (FREDERICK JOHN WILLIAM) *et al.* Growing Up in Newcastle-Upon-Tyne: A Continuing Study of Health and Illness in Young Children with their Families. 1960.

22088 MEDICAL SERVICES REVIEW COMMITTEE. A Review of the Medical Services in Great Britain. 1962.

22089 BROCKINGTON (COLIN FRASER). A Short History of Public Health. 2nd edn 1966.

22090 FLINN (MICHAEL WALTER). Public Health Reform in Britain. 1968.

22091 HOLLAND (WALTER W.), DETELS (ROGER), *and* KNOX (GEORGE). Oxford Textbook of Public Health. Vols. 1 and 2. Oxf. 1984.

22092 DAVIES (JAMES BRIAN MEREDITH). Community Care and Social Services. 3rd edn. 1977.

22093 CARTWRIGHT (ANN), HOCKEY (LISBETH), *and* ANDERSON (JOHN L.). Life before Death. 1973.

22094 DALZELL-WARD (ARTHUR JAMES). A Textbook of Health Education. 1974.

22095 HICKS (DONALD). Primary Health Care: A Review. 1976.

22096 DINGWALL (ROBERT) *et al. eds.* Health Care and Health Knowledge. 1977.

22097 OLIVER (BERYL). The British Red Cross in Action. 1966.

22098 ROBERTSON (WILLIAM). Meat and Food Inspection. 2nd edn 1920.

22099 ROYAL COLLEGE OF PHYSICIANS AND OTHERS. A Review of the Medical Services in Great Britain: Report of a Committee. 1962. [Chairman: *Sir* Arthur Porritt.].

22100 SHRIGLEY (SHEILA M.). Selected References on Health and Social Services for Ethnic Minorities in Britain, 1965–1977. 1982.

22101 STEWART (ALEXANDER PATRICK) *and* JENKINS (J. EDWARD). The Medical and Legal Aspects of Sanitary Reform. 1969.

22102 U.K. D.H.S.S. CARE OF THE DYING: Proceedings of a National Symposium held on 29 November 1972. 1973.

22103 U.K. D.H.S.S. CENTRAL HEALTH SERVICES COUNCIL. REHABILITATION: Report of a Sub-Committee of the Standing Medical Advisory Committee. 1972.

22104 WILCOCKS (CHARLES). Medical Advance, Public Health and Social Evolution. Oxf. 1965.

22105 WILLIAMS (HUBERT CECIL MAURICE). Public Health in a Seaport Town. Southampton. 1961.

22106 WILLIAMS (JOHN HARGREAVES HARLEY). A Century of Public Health in Britain, 1832–1929. 1932.

22107 WILSON (MICHAEL). Health is for People. 1975.

22108 WYNN (MARGARET) *and* WYNN (ARTHUR). The Protection of Maternity and Infancy: A Study of the Services for Pregnant Women and Young Children in Finland with Some Comparisons with Britain. 1974.

22109 HALLAS (JACK). Community Health Councils in Action: A Review. 1976.

22110 LEWIS (JANE) *ed.* Community Health Councils: Four Case Studies. 1976.

22111 LEVITT (RUTH). The People's Voice in the N.H.S.: Community Health Councils after Five Years. 1980.

22112 KLEIN (RUDOLPH) *and* LEWIS (JANE). The Politics of Consumer Representation: A Study of Community Health Councils. 1976.

22113 HONIGSBAUM (FRANK). 'Unity in British Public Health Administration: The Failure of Reform, 1926–1929'. *Med. Hist*, 12 (1968), 109–22.

13. MEDICAL SERVICES: ARMED FORCES

22114 GARRISON (FIELDING HUDSON). Notes on the History of Military Medicine. Washington, DC. 1922.

22115 CREW (FRANCIS ALBERT ELEY) *ed.* The Army Medical Services: Administration. 2 vols 1953–1955. Campaigns, 5 vols 1956–1966. [History of the Second World War, United Kingdom Medical Series.].

22116 COLE (HOWARD NORMAN). On Wings of Healing: The Story of the Airborne Medical Services, 1940–1960. Edin. 1963.

22117 MACNALTY (*Sir* ARTHUR SALUSBURY) *gen. ed.* History of the Second World War. United Kingdom Medical Series, to which he contributed the following volumes:

22118 —— *ed.* The Civilian Health and Medical Services. Vol. I, 1953. Vol. II, 1954.

22119 MACNALTY (Sir ARTHUR SALUSBURY) *and* MELLOR (W. FRANKLIN) *eds.* Medical Services in War: The Principal Medical Lessons of the Second World War. 1968.

22120 —— 'Health and the Family'. in Sir J. Marchant, *ed.* Rebuilding family life in the post-War world. 1945.

14. ALCOHOLISM

22121 Offences of Drunkenness, England and Wales. 1950+.

22122 MOODY (SUSAN). Drunken Offenders in Scotland: A Review of the Relevant Literature. 1979.

22123 Report of the Department Committee on Scottish Licensing Law. Cmnd 5354. Parliamentary Papers, 15 (1972–3).

22124 TRENCH (SALLY). Bury Me in my Boots. 1968.

22125 REA (F. B.). Alcoholism: Its Psychology and Cure. 1956.

22126 OFFICE OF HEALTH ECONOMICS. Studies in Current Health Problems. No. 34. Alcohol Abuse. 1970.

22127 MOSS (MILTON CEDRIC) and DAVIES (EDWARD BERESFORD). A Survey of Alcoholism in an English County: A Study of the Prevalence, Distribution and Effects of Alcoholism in Cambridgeshire. Altrincham. 1967.

22128 Scotland 1965. Alcoholics: Health Services for their Treatment and Rehabilitation. [Report.]. Edin. 1965.

22129 KESSEL (WILLIAM IVOR NEIL) and WALTON (HENRY J.). Alcoholism. Harmondsworth. 1965.

22130 CAHN (SIDNEY). The Treatment of Alcoholics: An Evaluative Study. NY. 1970.

22131 JONES (HOWARD). Alcoholic Addiction: A Psycho-Social Approach to Abnormal Drinking. 1963.

22132 RITSON (B.) and HASSALL (C.). The Management of Alcoholism. Edin. 1970.

22133 NELSON (JAMES) pseud. No More Walls. 1978.

22134 SWINSON (RICHARD P.) and EAVES (DEREK). Alcoholism and Addiction. Plymouth. 1978.

22135 O'CONNOR (JOYCE). The Young Drinkers: A Cross-National Study of Social and Cultural Influences. 1978. [Anglo-Irish.].

22136 U.K. ADVISORY COMMITTEE ON ALCOHOLISM. The Pattern and Range of Services for Problem Drinkers: Report. 1978. [Chairman, W. I. N. Kessel.].

22137 CHRISTIAN ECONOMIC AND SOCIAL RESEARCH FOUNDATION. The Differences between Scottish Drunkenness and Drunkenness in England and Wales. 1977.

22138 ROBINSON (DAVID). From Drinking to Alcoholism: A Sociological Commentary. 1976.

22139 BRAKE (GEORGE THOMPSON). Alcohol: Its Consumption and Control: Objective Facts about a Widespread Habit: The Personal and Social Problems Involved with its Abuse: And Efforts to Control it by Legislation in England and Wales and in Other European Countries. 1976.

22140 WILLIAMS (GWYLMOR PRYS) and BRAKE (GEORGE THOMPSON). Drink in Great Britain, 1900 to 1979. 1980.

22141 —— Drink: Ups and Downs of Methodist Attitudes to Temperance. 1974.

22142 WILSON (GEORGE B.). Alcohol and the Nation. 1940. [1800–1935.].

22143 SHADWELL (ARTHUR). Drink in 1914–1922: A Lesson in Control. 1900.

22144 WILLIAMS (GWYLMOR PRYS). Chronic Alcoholics: A Report on the Incidence Apparent to Health Visitors and Probation Officers, with a Discussion of the Probable Order of Magnitude of the Incidence in England And Wales. 1964.

22145 —— Social Effects of Ending Resale Price Maintenance of Alcoholic Beverages, 1966 and 1967, England and Wales. 1968.

22146 WINTERTON (WILFRED). Breath-Taking History. 1968.

22147 WILLIAMS (LINCOLN). Alcoholism Explained. 1967.

22148 DAVIES (JOHN) and STACEY (BARRY). Teenagers and Alcohol: A Developmental Study in Glasgow. 1973. [Vol. 2 of an Enquiry conducted Under Contract to the Social Survey by the Dept. of Psychology, University of Strathclyde.].

22149 JAHODA (GUSTAV) Children and Alcohol. Vol. 1 of the above.

22150 COOK (TIMOTHY). Vagrant Alcoholics. 1975.

22151 WILLIAMS (GWYLMOR PRYS). Supermarket Off-Licences and the Growth of Drunkenness among Young Women and Young Persons since 1966. 1975.

22152 HAWKER (A.). Adolescence and Alcohol: Report of an Enquiry into Adolescent Drinking Patterns Carried out from October 1975 to June 1976. 1978.

22153 SHAW (STAN J.), CARTWRIGHT (ALAN K. J.), SPRATLEY (TERRY A.), and HARWIN (JUDITH). Responding to Drinking Problems. 1978.

22154 EDWARDS (GRIFFITH). The Treatment of Drinking Problems. 1982.

22155 ARCHARD (PETER). Vagrancy, Alcoholism and Social Control. 1979.

22156 EDWARDS (GRIFFITH) and GRANT (MARCUS) eds. Alcoholism: New Knowledge and New Responses. 1977.

22157 MASS-OBSERVATION. The Pub and the People. 1943.

22158 DORN (NICHOLAS). Alcohol, Youth and the State : Drinking Practice Controls and Health Education. 1983.

22159 HUDSON (CELIA A.) and JEREMY (DAVID J.). A Survey of Alcohol Education in the United Kingdom. 1985.

22160 VERNON (HORACE MIDDLETON). The Alcohol Problem. 1928.

22161 MAUDESLEY ALCOHOL PILOT PROJECT. Designing a Comprehensive Community Response to Problems of Alcohol Abuse: Report to the D.H.S.S. by the M.A.P.P. By A. K. J. Cartwright, S. J. Shaw, and T. A. Spratley. 1975.

22162 HORE (BRIAN D.). Alcohol Dependence. 1976.

22163 VALLANCE (M.). 'Alcoholism: A Two-Year Follow-Up Study of Patients Admitted to the Psychiatric Department of a General Hospital'. *Brit. J. Psychiatry* 3(473) (1965), 348–56.

22164 D'ABERNON (VINCENT LEONARD) Lord. 'Public Health and the Control of the Liquor Traffic'. *J. State Medicine* (Nov. 1917), 321–32.

22165 —— Preface to Vernon (Horace Middleton). The Alcohol Problem. 1928.

22166 RAWNSLEY (HARDWICKE DRUMMOND). 'Liquor Control and the Carlisle Experiment'. *Hibbert J.* (Apr. 1920), 557–71.

22167 CHANCE (*Sir* FREDERICK WILLIAM) 'Public House Reform At Carlisle'. [*19th century and after.*]. 1072–82 (Dec. 1920). [Published as a pamphlet in 1922.].

22168 DELL (ANTHONY). 'The Problem of the Liquor Trade'. *Fort. Rev.* (May 1920), 781–92.

22169 MARTIN (ANNA). 'The Future of the Public-House from the Working Woman's Point of View'. *Englishwoman* (June 1920), 169–76.

22170 PICTON-TURBERVILL (BEATRICE). 'The Case for State Purchase and Control of the Liquor Traffic: A Question for Women'. *Fort. Rev.* (June 1920), 947–54.

22171 PLATT (T. COMYN). 'Is Prohibition Coming?'. *Nat. Rev.* (Sept. 1920), 55–62.

22172 MAURICE (ARTHUR BARTLETT). 'Dora' [No Crying Liquor Problem Today.]. *Unpartizan Rev.* (Oct. 1920), 288–96.

22173 MACKAY (LYDIA M.). 'Curious Misunderstanding with Regard to the Temperance (Scotland) Act. 1913'.

22174 —— 'Scotland—Prohibition and Public Opinion'. *Ways and Means* (30 Oct. 1920).

22175 SHERWELL (ARTHUR). 'The Scottish Liquor Polls'. *Nation* (20 Nov. 1920), 268–9.

22176 OWENS (JOHN). 'The Drink Problem'. *Welsh Outlook* (June 1917), 205–7.

22177 REES (THOMAS). 'The Moral Responsibility for the Liquor Trade'. *Welsh Outlook* (May 1918), 161–3.

22178 RHYS (J. T.). 'The Prime Minister's Temperance Proposals: A Plea for Support'. *Welsh Outlook* (Oct. 1917), 364–5.

22179 GEORGE (W.). 'A Practical Temperance Policy'. *Welsh Outlook* (Nov. 1917), 387–8.

22180 THOMAS (D. LLEUFER). 'A Plea for Regional Treatment in Wales'. *Welsh Outlook* (June 1918), 189–91.

15. DRUGS

22181 PHILLIPSON (RICHARD V.). 'The Implementation of the Second Report of the Interdepartmental Committee on Drug Addiction'. In Richard V. Phillipson, *ed.*, Modern Trends in Drug Dependence and Alcoholism. 1970. 75–98.

22182 SMART (CAROL). 'Social Policy in Drug Addiction: A Critical Study of Policy Development'. *Brit. J. Addiction* 79 (1984), 31–9.

22183 EDWARDS (GRIFFITH). 'British Policies on Opiate Addiction: Ten Years Working of the Revised Response and Option for the Future'. *Brit. J. Psychiatry* 134 (1979), 1–13.

22184 STIMSON (G. V.). 'British Drug Policies in the 1980s: A Preliminary Analysis and Suggestions for Research'. *Brit. J. Addiction* 82 (1987), 477–88.

22185 JOHNSON (DONALD MCINTOSH). Indian Hemp: A Social Menace. 1952.

22186 SCHUR (EDWIN MICHAEL). Narcotic Addiction in Britain and America: The Impact of Public Policy. Bloomington, Ind. 1962. 1963.

22187 O'CALLAGHAN (SEAN). Drug Addiction in Britain. 1970.

22188 —— The Drug Traffic. 1969.

22189 ZACUNE (J.) *and* HENSMAN (C.). Drugs, Alcohol and Tobacco in Britain. 1971.

22190 GLATT (M. M.) *et al.* The Drug Scene in Great Britain. 1987.

22191 CLARIDGE (GORDON SYDNEY). Drugs and Human Behaviour. 1970.

22192 SCHOFIELD (MICHAEL). The Strange Case of Pot. Harmondsworth. 1971.

22193 COCKETT (R.). Drug Abuse and Personality in Young Offenders. Lond./NY. 1971.

22194 IMLAH (NORMAN). Drugs in Modern Society. 1970.

22195 YOUNG (JOCK). The Drugtakers: The Social Meaning of Drug Use. 1971.

22196 ROSENBAUM (MAX). Drug Abuse and Drug Addiction. 1974.

22197 D.H.S.S. Treatment and rehabilitation: Report of the Advisory Council on the Misuse of Drugs. 1982.

22198 HOME OFFICE. The Rehabilitation of Drug Addicts: Report of the Advisory Committee on Drug Dependence. 1968.

22199 JUDSON (HORACE FREELAND). Heroin Addiction in Britain. NY. 1974.

22200 PICARDIE (J.) *and* WADE (G.). Heroin, Chasing the Dragon. Harmondsworth. 1985.

22201 STIMSON (G. V.) *and* OPPENHEIMER (E.). Heroin Addiction: Treatment and Control in Britain. 1982.

22202 SPEAR (H. B.). 'The Growth of Heroin Addiction in the United Kingdom'. *Brit. J. Addiction* 64 (1969), 245–55.

22203 DORN (NICHOLAS) *and* SOUTH (NIGEL) *eds.* A Land Fit for Heroin? Drug Policies, Prevention and Practice in Britain in the 1980s. 1987.

22204 BEAN (PHILIP). The Social Control of Drugs. 1974.

22205 BERRIDGE (VIRGINIA) and EDWARDS (GRIFFITH). Opium and the People: Opiate Use in Nineteenth-century England. 1981. [Has a final part on the past in relation to the present.].

22206 EDWARDS (GRIFFITH) and BUSCH (CAROL) eds. Drug Problems in Britain: A Review of Ten Years. 1981.

22207 BERRIDGE (VIRGINIA). 'Drugs and Social Policy: The Establishment of Drug Control in Britain, 1900–1980'. Brit. J. Addiction 79 (1984), 17–29.

22208 LAW (RICHARD). Controlled Drugs: Law and Practice. 1984.

22209 PARSSINEN (TERRY M.). Secret Passions, Secret Remedies. Narcotic Drugs in British Society, 1820–1930. Manch. 1983.

22210 LAURIE (PETER). Drugs: Medical, Psychological and Social Facts. Harmondsworth. 1967.

22211 MARTIN (J.). Some Aspects of Prescribing. 1957.

22212 CENTRAL OFFICE OF INFORMATION. The Prevention and Treatment of Drug Dependence in Britain. 1973.

22213 HAPPOLD (F. H.). Medicine at Risk: The High Price of Cheap Drugs. 1967.

22214 INGLIS (BRIAN). The Forbidden Game: A Social History of Drugs. 1975.

22215 LEWIN (L.). Phantastica: Narcotic and Stimulating Drugs, their Use and Abuse. [Transl. from the 2nd German edn.]. NY. 1931.

22216 LARSON (P. S.), HAAG (H. B.), and SILVETTE (H.). Tobacco: Experimental and Clinical Studies. A Comprehensive Study of the World's Literature. Baltimore, Md. 1961.

22217 WEBSTER (CHARLES). 'Tobacco Smoking Addiction: A Challenge to the National Health Service'. Brit. J. Addiction, 79 (1984), 7–16.

22218 EWING (J. A.), ROUSE (B. A.), KEELER (M. H.), and BAKEWELL (W. E.) Jnr. 'Why Students "Turn on": Marijuana and Other Drug Use in an Undergraduate Male Population'. Brit. J. Soc. Psychiatry Community Health 4(4) (1970–1), 255–65.

22219 MCKENNELL (A. C.). 'Smoking Motivation Factors'. Brit. J. Soc. Clin. Psychol. 9 (1) (1970), 8–22.

22220 BEAN (PHILIP). 'Social Aspects of Drug Abuse: A Study of London Drug Offenders'. J. Crim. Law Criminal Pol. Sci. 62(1) (1971), 80–6.

22221 JOHNSON (B. D.). 'Understanding British Addiction Statistics'. Bull. Narcotics 22 (1975), 49–66.

22222 LEE (J. M.). 'The Political Significance of Licensing Legislation'. Parl. Affs 14(2) (1961), 211–28.

22223 MORTIMER (M.). 'The Drug Traffic'. Quart. Rev. 298(623), (1960), 25–31.

22224 NOBLE (P.) and BARNES (G.). 'Drug Taking in Adolescent Girls: Factors Associated with the Progression to Narcotic Use'. Brit. Med. J. 5762 (1971), 620–3.

22225 PLANT (MARTIN A.). 'Drug Takers in an English Town: Factors Associated with the Use of Injected Drugs'. Brit. J. Criminol. 15 (1975), 181–6.

22226 GOLDSMITH (MARGARET). The Trail of Opium, the Eleventh Plague. 1939.

22227 WATSON (JOYCE M.). Solvent Abuse: The Adolescent Epidemic? 1986.

16. DISEASE DISTRIBUTION

22228 ACKERKNECHT (ERWIN H.). History and Geography of the Most Important Diseases. NY. 1965.

22229 HOWE (GEORGE MELVYN). National Atlas of Disease Mortality in the United Kingdom. 1963. Rev. and enl. edn 1970.

22230 —— Man, Environment and Disease in Britain: a Medical Geography in Britain Through the Ages. Harmondsworth. 1976. [Earlier publ. NY/Newton Abbot, 1972.].

22231 —— ed. A World Geography of Human Diseases. 1977.

22232 HOWE (GEORGE MELVYN) and LORAINE (JOHN A.) eds. Environmental Medicine. 1973.

22233 GARDNER (M. J.), WINTER (PAUL D.), and BARKER (D. J. P.). Atlas of Mortality from Selected Diseases in England and Wales, 1968–1978. 1984.

22234 LOGAN (W. P. D.) and BROOKE (EILEEN M.). The Survey of Sickness, 1943–1952. 1958.

22235 LOGAN (W. P. D.). Cancer Mortality by Occupation and Social Class, 1851–1971. 1982.

22236 CASE (R. A. M.). 'Cohort Analysis of Cancer Mortality in England and Wales, 1911–1954 by Site and Sex'. Brit. J. Preventative & Social Medicine 10 (1956), 172–99.

22237 Investigation of a Possible Increased Incidence of Cancer in West Cumbria: Report of the Independent Advisory Group, 1984. [Chairman: Sir Douglas Black.].

22238 COOK-MOZAFFARI (P. J.) et al. Cancer Incidence in Mortality in the Vicinity of Nuclear Power Installations in England and Wales, 1959–1980. 1987.

22239 TOMS (JANE R.) ed. Trends in Cancer Survival in Great Britain: Cases Registered between 1960 and 1974. 1982.

22240 BRYDER (LINDA). Below the Magic Mountain: A Social History of Tuberculosis in Twentieth Century Britain. Oxf. 1988.

22241 LOGAN (W. P. D.) and BENJAMIN (B.). Tuberculosis Statistics for England and Wales, 1938–1955: An

Analysis of Trends and Geographical Distribution. 1957.

22242 BELL (K. P.) *and* PURCELL (H.). 'Recent Trends in Coronary Mortality and their Implications for the U.K.: Are we Winning or Losing?' *Postgrad. Medic. J.* 60 (1984), 1–46.

22243 RODGERS (S. C.) *and* WEATHERALL (J. A. C.). Anencephalus, Spina-Bifida and Congenital Hydrocephalus: England and Wales, 1964–1972. 1976.

17. GENETICS

22244 BABLOCK (E. B.). 'The Development of Fundamental Concepts in the Science of Genetics'. *Portugaliae Acta Biologica* Ser. A (1949), 1–45.

22245 BACSICH (PAUL). 'Transplantation'. *Philosophical J.* vii (1970), 1–28.

22246 GREAT BRITAIN HEALTH AND SAFETY COMMISSION. Genetic Manipulation: Regulations and Guidance Notes. 1978.

22247 TRIMMER (ERIC J.). Rejuvenation: The History of an Idea. 1967.

22248 MCKUSICK (VICTOR A.) *et al.* Medical Genetics 1961–1963. An annotated review. Oxf. 1966.

22249 Report of the Committee of Enquiry into Human Fertilization and Embryology. Cmnd 9314. 1984.

18. PHARMACY, ETC.

22250 LAWALL (C. H.). Four Thousand Years of Pharmacy: An Outline History of Pharmacy and Allied Sciences. Philadelphia, Pa. 1927.

22251 URDANG (GEORGE). Pharmacy's Part in Society. Madison, Wis. 1946.

22252 KREMERS (EDWARD) *and* URDANG (GEORGE). Kremers and Urdang's History of Pharmacy. 4th ed. Philadelphia, Pa. 1976.

22253 MATTHEWS (LESLIE G.). History of Pharmacy in Britain. Edin./Lond. 1962.

22254 TREASE (G. E.). Pharmacy in History. 1964.

22255 POYNTER (FREDERICK NOËL LAWRENCE) *ed.* The Evolution of Pharmacy in Britain. Lond./Springfield, Ill. 1965.

22256 DOYLE (PAUL A.) *ed.* Readings in Pharmacy. NY/Lond. 1962.

22257 WALL (CECIL) *et al.* A History of the Worshipful Society of Apothecaries of London. 1963.

22258 U.K. DEPARTMENT OF TRADE AND INDUSTRY. Business Monitor: Production Series P97. 1970+.

22259 DUNLOP (*Sir* DERRICK MELVILLE). The Problem of Modern Medicines and their Control. Glas. 1971.

22260 OFFICE OF HEALTH ECONOMICS. The Pharmacist in Society. 1964.

22261 BELL (*Sir* WILLIAM JAMES) *and* O'KEEFE (JOHN ALFRED). Sale of Food and Drugs. 14th edn 1968.

22262 U.K. CENTRAL OFFICE OF INFORMATION. Reference Division. The British Pharmaceutical Industry. 1965.

22263 ASSOCIATION OF THE BRITISH PHARMACEUTICAL INDUSTRY. Attitude to the Pharmaceutical Industry by Family Doctors and the Public, 1962, 1964 and 1965. 1966.

22264 —— The Pharmaceutical Industry and the Nation's Health. 3rd edn 1967, 4th edn 1969.

22265 BERMAN (A.) *ed.* Pharmaceutical Historiography. Madison, Wis. 1967.

22266 U.K. OFFICE OF HEALTH ECONOMICS. Pharmaceutical Research: The Case for Growth in Britain. 1967.

22267 HATCHER (JOHN). Founders of Medical Laboratory Science. *Ed.* and introduced by A. D. Farr. 1978.

22268 REDWOOD (HEINZ). The Pharmaceutical Industry: Trends, Problems and Achievements. 1988.

22269 COOPER (M. H.). Prices and Profits in the Pharmaceutical Industry. Oxf. 1966.

22270 REEKIE (W. DUNCAN) *and* WEBER (MICHAEL H.). Profits, Politics and Drugs. 1979.

22271 LANG (RONALD W.). The Politics of Drugs: The British and Canadian Pharmaceutical Industries and Governments. Farnb. 1974.

22272 SUNDAY TIMES INSIGHT TEAM. Suffer the Children: The Story of Thalidomide. 1979.

22273 JEPHCOTT (*Sir* HARRY). The First Fifty Years. 1969. [Glaxo.].

22274 SLINN (JUDY). A History of May and Baker. 1984.

22275 IMPERIAL CHEMICAL INDUSTRIES. Pharmaceuticals Division. Pharmaceutical Research in I.C.I. 1936–1957. Alderley. 1957.

22276 BENDER (GEORGE A.). Great Moments in Pharmacy. Detroit, Mich. 1966.

22277 CHAPMAN-HUSTON (DESMOND) *and* CRIPPS (ERNEST C.). Through a City Archway: The Story of Allen and Hanburys, 1715–1954. 1954.

22278 CRIPPS (ERNEST C.). Plough Court: The Story of a Notable Pharmacy 1715–1927. 1927.

22279 BELLAMY (JOYCE M.). A Hundred Years of Pharmacy in Hull: In Commemoration of the Centenary of the Hull Chemists' Association, 1868–1968. Hull. 1968.

22280 MAUROIS (ANDRÉ). The Life of Sir Alexander Fleming: Discoverer of Penicillin. Lond./NY. 1959.

22281 LUDOVICI (L. J.). Fleming: Discoverer of Penicillin. Bloomington, Ind. 1955.

22282 MACFARLANE (GWYN). Alexander Fleming: The Man and the Myth. 1984.

22283 —— Howard Florey: The Making of a Great Scientist. Oxf. 1979.

22284 WILLIAMS (TREVOR I.). Howard Florey: Penicillin and After. Oxf. 1984.

22285 BICKEL (LENNARD). Rise up to Life: A Biography of Howard Florey who Made Penicillin and Gave it to the World. 1972.

22286 HARRIS (S.). Banting's Miracle: The Story of the Discoverer of Insulin. Philadelphia, Pa. 1946.

22287 GALDSTON (IAGO). Behind the Sulfa Drugs: A Short History of Chemotherapy. NY. 1943.

22288 GOLDSMITH (MARGARET). The Road to Penicillin: A History of Chemotherapy. 1946.

22289 FLEMING (ALEXANDER). Chemotherapy: Yesterday, Today and Tomorrow. Camb. 1946.

22290 —— ed. Penicillin. Its Practical Application. 1st edn 1946. 2nd edn 1950.

22291 RATCLIFF (JOHN DRURY). Yellow Magic: The Story of Penicillin. 1945.

22292 MASTERS (DAVID). Miracle Drugs: The Inner History of Penicillin. 1946.

22293 SOKOLOFF (B.). The Miracle Drugs. NY/Chicago, Ill. 1949.

22294 HARE (RONALD). The Birth of Penicillin and the Disarming of Microbes. 1970.

22295 BRADSHAW (SAMUEL). The Drugs You Take: (A Plain Man's Guide to Patent Medicines). 1966.

22296 DUNLOP (Sir DERRICK MELVILLE). Medicines in Our Time. 1973. [N.P.H.T.].

22297 KREIG (MARGARET B.). Green Medicine: The Search for Plants that Heal. Lond./Chicago, Ill. 1965.

22298 THOMAS (K. BRYN). Curare: Its History and Usage. Philadelphia, Pa. 1963.

22299 SHUSTER (LOUIS) ed. Readings in Pharmacology. Boston, Mass. 1962.

22300 HOLMSTEDT (B. O.) and LILJESTRAND (GÖRAN). Readings in Pharmacology. Oxf./NY. 1963.

22301 POYNTER (FREDERICK NOËL LAWRENCE) ed. Chemistry in the Service of Medicine. Lond./Philadelphia, Pa. 1963. [Papers read at the Second British Congress on the History of Medicine and Pharmacy. London 27–9 September 1961. Preface.]. (1963).

22302 PATON (WILLIAM DRUMMOND MACDONALD). The Growth of Pharmacology with Special Reference to its Dependence on the Advance in Chemical Knowledge. Proc. 10th Int. Congr. Hist. Sci. (Ithaca, 1962). Paris. 1964.

19. PHYSIOLOGY

22303 HALDANE (JOHN SCOTT). The New Physiology and Other Addresses. 1919.

22304 —— Respiration. New Haven, Conn. 1922.

22305 BARCLAY (ALFRED E.), FRANKLIN (KENNETH J.), and PRICHARD (MARJORIE M. L.). The Foetal Circulation and Cardiovascular System, and the Changes that they Undergo at Birth. Oxf. 1944.

22306 BARCROFT (Sir JOSEPH). The Respiratory Function of the Blood. Camb. 1914.

22307 CAIRNS (JOHN), STENT (GUNNAR S.), and WATSON (JAMES D.) eds. Phage and the Origins of Molecular Biology. Cold Spring Harbor, NY. 1966.

22308 DALE (Sir HENRY HALLETT). Adventures in Physiology, with Excursions into Autopharmacology: A Selection from the Scientific Papers of Sir Henry Hallett Dale. With an introduction and recent comments by the author. 1953.

22309 FISHMAN (ALFRED P.) and RICHARDS (DICKINSON W.) eds. Circulation of the Blood: Men and Ideas. NY. 1964.

22310 FRANKLIN (KENNETH J.). 'History and the Physiologist'. In Edgar Ashworth Underwood, ed., Science, Medicine and History. 1953.

22311 —— A Short History of Physiology. 1933. 2nd edn. 1949.

22312 —— 'Fifty Years of Physiology'. Proc. Roy. Soc. Med. xliii (1950), 789–96.

22313 —— Joseph Barcroft, 1872-1947. Oxf. 1953.

22314 FULTON (JOHN FARQUHAR). Physiology. (Clio Medica No. 5). NY. 1931.

22315 —— ed. Selected Readings in the History of Physiology. Completed by WILSON (LEONARD G.). 2nd edn Springfield, Ill. 1966.

22316 WILSON (LEONARD G.). Physiology of the Nervous System. 1938. 2nd edn 1943.

22317 —— 'Reflections on the History of Reflex Action'. Arch. Iberoamer. Hist. Med. 8 (1956), 27–32.

22318 —— 'Somatic Functions of the Central Nervous System'. Ann. Rev. Physiol. 15 (1953), 305–28.

22319 GOODFIELD (GWYNETH JUNE). The Growth of Scientific Physiology: Physiological Method and the Mechanist—Vitalist Controversy, Illustrated by the Problems of Respiration and Animal Heat. 1960.

22320 HILL (Sir ARCHIBALD VIVIAN). Trails and Trials in Physiology: A Bibliography, 1909–1964: With Reviews of Certain Topics and Methods and a Reconnaissance for Further Research. 1965.

22321 HUGHES (A.). A History of Cytology. NY. 1959.

22322 KEILIN (DAVID) ed. The History of Cell Respiration and Cytochrome. Camb. 1966.

22323 LIDDELL (EDWARD GEORGE TANDY). The Discovery of Reflexes. 1960.

22324 MAISEL (A. Q.). The Hormone Quest. NY. 1965.

22325 MEITES (JOSEPH), DONOVAN (BERNARD T.), *and* MCCANN (SAMUEL M.) *eds.* Pioneers in Neuroendocrinology. NY. 1975.

22326 MENDELSOHN (EVERETT). Heat and Life: The Development of the Theory of Animal Heat. Camb., Mass./Lond. 1964.

22327 GRAUBARD (MARK). Circulation and Respiration: The Evolution of an Idea. NY. 1964.

22328 PIRENNE (M. H.). Vision and the Eye. 1948.

22329 HODGKIN (*Sir* ALAN LLOYD). *et al.* The Pursuit of Nature: Informal Essays on the History of Physiotherapy. 1977.

22330 SHERBET (G. V.). The Biophysical Characterization of the Cell Surface. 1978.

22331 SHERRINGTON (*Sir* CHARLES SCOTT). The Integrative Action of the Nervous System. 1906. 1947 edn with a new foreword by the author and a bibliography of his writings.

22332 SWAZEY (JUDITH P.). Reflexes and Motor Integration: Sherrington's Concept of Integrative Action. Camb., Mass. 1969.

22333 STARLING (ERNEST HENRY). A Century of Physiology: Being the First of a Series of Centenary Addresses. 1927. [University College Centenary Celebrations.].

22334 STILES (WALTER STANLEY). Mechanisms of Colour Vision: Selected Papers of W. S. Stiles. With a new introductory essay. 1978.

22335 WALKER (KENNETH MACFARLANE). The Story of Blood. 1958. NY. 1963.

22336 WIGHTMAN (WILLIAM PERSEHOUSE DELISLE). The Emergence of General Physiology. Belf. 1956.

22337 WILLIUS (FREDERICK A.) *and* DRY (THOMAS J.). A History of the Heart and the Circulation. Philadelphia, Pa./Lond. 1948.

22338 WILLIUS (FREDERICK A.) *and* KEYES (THOMAS E.). Classics of Cardiology: A Collection of Classic Works on the Heart and Circulation. With comprehensive biographic accounts of the authors. 2 vols. NY. 1961.

22339 ANNUAL REVIEW OF PHYSIOLOGY. Vol. 1. Stanford, Calif. 1939.

22340 JOURNAL OF PHYSIOLOGY.

Author Index to Vol. 1–60. Issued by the Physiological Society and published as a supplement to the *Journal of Physiology*. June 1928. London. Camb. 1928.

Further indexes published for vols. 61–100, 101–15, 116–34, 135–54, 155–75.

20. VIROLOGY, ETC.

22341 WATERSON (ANTHONY PETER) *and* WILKINSON (LISE). An Introduction to the History of Virology. Camb. 1978.

22342 WILKINSON (LISE). 'The Development of the Virus Concept as Reflected in Corpora of Studies on Individual Pathogens'. *Med. Hist.* 18 (1974), 211–21.

22343 BEDSON (*Sir* SAMUEL PHILLIPS), DOWNIE (ALLEN WATT), MACCALLUM (FREDERICK OGDEN), *and* HARRIS (CHARLES HERBERT STUART). Virus and Rickettsial Diseases. 2nd edn 1955. 4th edn 1967.

22344 BIGGER (J. W.). Man against Microbe. NY. 1939.

22345 WEBSTER (CHARLES). Biology, Medicine and Society, 1840–1940. Camb. 1981.

22346 GRAINGER (T. H.) *ed.* A Guide to the History of Bacteriology. NY. 1958.

22347 BULLOCH (W.). The History of Bacteriology. 1960.

22348 FOSTER (WILLIAM DEREK). A History of Medical Bacteriology and Immunology. 1970.

22349 BALDRY (PETER EDWARD). The Battle against Bacteria: A History of the Development of Antibacterial Drugs. For the General Reader. Camb. 1965.

22350 —— The Battle Against Bacteria: A Fresh Look. A History of Man's Fight against Bacterial Disease with Special Reference to the Development of Antibacterial Drugs. Camb. 1976.

22351 CARTWRIGHT (FREDERICK F.) *and* BIDDISS (MICHAEL D.). Disease and History. 1972.

22352 CREIGHTON (CHARLES). A History of Epidemics in Britain; with Additional Material by EVERSLEY (D. E. C.), UNDERWOOD (EDGAR ASHWORTH), *and* OVENALL (LYNDA). 2 vols. 2nd edn 1965.

22353 ROBERTS (R. S.). 'Epidemics and Social History: An Essay Review'. *Med. Hist.* 12 (1968), 305–16.

22354 HAMER (WILLIAM). Epidemiology Old and New. 1929.

22355 GILL (CLIFFORD ALLCHIN). The Genesis of Epidemics and the Natural History of Disease: An Introduction to the Science of Epidemiology based upon the Study of Epidemics of Malaria, Influenza and Plague. 1928.

22356 MURRAY (D. STARK). Science Fights Death. 1936.

22357 WINSLOW (C. E. A.). The Conquest of Epidemic Disease. 1943.

22358 —— Man and Epidemics. Princeton, N.J. 1952.

22359 HARE (RONALD). Pomp and Pestilence: Infectious Disease: Its Origins and Conquest. Lond./NY. 1954.

22360 BUSVINE (J. R.). Insects, Hygiene and History. 1976.

22361 BURNET (*Sir* FRANK MACFARLANE). Biological Aspects of Infectious Disease. 3rd edn entitled Natural History of Infectious Diseases. NY/Lond. 1952.

22362 —— Changing Patterns: An Atypical Autobiography. Melbourne/Lond. 1968.

22363 HENSCHEN (FOLKE). The History of Diseases. 1966.

22364 WEYMOUTH (A.). Through the Leper Squint: A Study of Leprosy from Pre-Christian Times to the Present Day. 1938.

22365 RUSSELL (PAUL F.). Man's Mastery of Malaria. Lond./NY/Toronto. 1955. [University of London, Heath Clark Lectures, 1953, delivered at the London School of Hygiene and Tropical Medicine.].

22366 ROSS (*Sir* RONALD). Memoirs. 1923. [With a full account of the malaria problem and its solution.].

22367 WARSHAW (L. J.). Malaria: The Biography of a Killer. NY. 1955.

22368 WAIN (H.). The Unconquered Plague: A Popular Story of Gonorrhea. NY. 1947.

22369 EDWARDS (FREDERICK WALLACE). Mosquitoes and their Relation to Disease: Their Life-History, Habits and Control. 1916. 3rd edn 1923. [B.M. Nat. Hist. Economic Series 4.].

22370 —— British Mosquitoes and their Control. 1925. 2nd edn 1934. [B. M. Nat. Hist. Economic Series 4A.].

22371 —— British Blood Sucking Flies. 1929. [B.M. Nat. Hist.].

22372 EBERSON (FREDERICK). The Microbe's Challenge. Lancaster, Pa. 1941.

22373 —— Microbes Militant: A Challenge to Man: The Story of Modern Preventive Medicine and Control of Infectious Diseases. NY. 1948.

22374 SIEGFRIED (ANDRÉ). Germs and Ideas. Edin./Lond. 1965.

22375 SHERWOOD TAYLOR (FRANK). The Conquest of Bacteria. From Salvarsan to Sulphapyridine. NY. 1942.

22376 ZINSSER (HANS). Rats, Lice and History. Being a Study in Biography which, after Twelve Preliminary Chapters Indispensable for the Preparation of the Lay Reader, Deals with the Life History of Typhus Fever. Lond./Boston, Mass. 1935.

22377 SCOTT (*Sir* HENRY HAROLD). Some Notable Epidemics: With Preface by W. W. Jameson. 1934.

22378 —— A History of Tropical Medicine: Based on the Fitzpatrick Lectures Delivered before the Royal College of Physicians of London, 1937–1938. 2 vols 1939. 2nd imp. 1942.

22379 ROGERS (LEONARD). 'Happy Toil: Fifty-Five Years of Tropical Medicine'. 1950.

22380 —— Recent Advances in Tropical Medicine. 1929. 2nd edn 1930.

22381 PRINZING (F.). Epidemics Resulting from Wars. Oxf. 1916.

22382 PAUL (HUGH). The Control of Diseases, Social and Communicable. With a foreword by Sir Graham S. Wilson. 1st edn London, 1952. 2nd edn Edin., 1964.

22383 ORDISH (GEORGE). The Constant Pest: A Short History of Pests and their Control. Lond./NY. 1976.

22384 OLIVER (W. W.). Stalkers of Pestilence: The Story of Man's Ideas of Infection. NY. 1930.

22385 MANSON-BAHR (PHILIP). Patrick Manson: The Father of Tropical Medicine. Lond./Edinburgh. 1962.

22386 —— 'The Malaria Story'. *Proc. Roy. Soc. Med.* 54 (1961), 91–100.

22387 McNEILL (WILLIAM HARDY). Plagues and People. Oxf. 1977.

22388 LONGMATE (NORMAN). King Cholera. 1966.

22389 FIENNES (RICHARD). Man, Nature and Disease. Lond./NY. 1964.

22390 CRITCHLEY (MACDONALD). The Black Hole and Other Essays. 1964.

22391 —— 'The Origins of Aphasiology'. *Scot. Med. J.* 9 (1964), 231–42.

21. DENTISTRY

22392 FORBES (ERIC G.). 'The Professionalisation of Dentistry: The United Kingdom'. *Med. Hist.* 29 (1985), 169–81.

22393 SLACK (GEOFFREY LAYTON) *and* BURT (BRIAN A.) *eds.* Dental Public Health: An Introduction to Community Dentistry. Bristol. 1974.

22394 McNEILL (DONALD R.). The Fight to Fluoridation. NY. 1957.

22395 BRITISH DENTAL ASSOCIATION. Fluoridation of Domestic Water Supplies. 1965.

22396 NATIONAL PURE WATER ASSOCIATION. Fluoride: Facts and Fancy. Manch. 1964.

22397 ROYAL COLLEGE OF PHYSICIANS OF LONDON. Fluoride, Teeth and Health: A Report. 1976.

22398 SYMPOSIUM ON FLUORIDATION OF WATER SUPPLIES. Fluoride and Health. Glasg. 1978.

22399 MOSER (*Sir* CLAUS ADOLF), GALES (KATHLEEN), *and* MORPURGO (P. W. K.). Dental Health and the Dental Services: An Assessment of Available Data. A Report Prepared for the N.P.H.T. 1962.

22400 GRAY (P. G.), TODD (J. E.), SLACK (G. L.), *and* BULMAN (G. L.). Adult Dental Health in England and Wales in 1968. 1970.

22401 LUFKIN (A. W.). A History of Dentistry. 2nd edn Philadelphia, Pa. 1948.

22402 SMITH (MAURICE). A Short History of Dentistry. 1958.

22403 BRITISH DENTAL ASSOCIATION. The Advance of the Dental Profession: A Centenary History, 1880–1980. 1979.

22404 LINDSAY (LILIAN). A Short History of Dentistry. 1933.

22405 PROSKAUER (C.) *and* WITT (F. H.). Pictorial History of Dentistry. Cologne. 1962.

22406 SAMSON (EDWARD). Men, Manners and Molars. Foreword by John Menzies Campbell. 1963.

22407 DENTAL BRANCH LIBRARY. The Thoughts of a Dental Chair Man. 1976.

22408 —— The Dentist and the State. 1973.

22409 COPE (V. ZACHARY). 'The Making of the Dental Profession in Britain'. *Proc. Roy. Soc. Med.* 57 (1984), 919–26.

22410 CAMPBELL (JOHN MENZIES). 'What About Dental History?' *Edin. Dent. Hosp. Gaz.* 4 (1963), 11–15.

22411 DOUBLEDAY (F. N.). 'The Contributions of King's College, London, to the Science of Dentistry'. *Proc. Roy. Soc. Med.* 42 (1949), 783–90.

22. PSYCHOLOGY, PSYCHOTHERAPY, PSYCHIATRY

22412 SHEPHERD (MICHAEL) *and* DAVIES (DAVID LEWIS). Studies in Psychiatry: A Survey of Work Carried Out in the Department of Psychiatry of the Institute of Psychiatry, under the Chairmanship of Sir Aubrey Lewis, 1945–66. 1968.

22413 HENDERSON (*Sir* DAVID KENNEDY). The Evolution of Psychiatry in Scotland. With a foreword by Sir James Learmonth. Edin. 1964.

22414 CARSTAIRS (GEORGE MORRISON). Research in Social Psychiatry. Edin. 1961. [Inaugural Lecture.].

22415 STAFFORD-CLARK (DAVID). Psychiatry To-day. 2nd edn Harmondsworth. 1963.

22416 HAYS (PETER). New Horizons in Psychiatry. Harmondsworth. 1964.

22417 BURT (*Sir* CYRIL LUDOWIC) *ed.* How the Mind Works. 2nd edn 1948.

22418 HEARNSHAW (LESLIE SPENCER). A Short History of British Psychology, 1840–1940. 1964.

22419 WOODWORTH (ROBERT SESSIONS) *and* SHEEHAN (MARY R.). Contemporary Schools of Psychology. 9th edn 1965.

22420 FOSS (BRIAN M.) *ed.* New Horizons in Psychology. Harmondsworth. 1966.

22421 KING (E. M. C.). 'The Organisation of Voluntary Service in a Psychiatric Hospital'. *Brit. J. Soc. Psychiatry Community Health* 5(1) (1971), 16–20.

22422 WALKER (NIGEL). A Short History of Psychotherapy in Theory and Practice. 1957.

11

EDUCATION

The divisions which can be made in this field do not cause undue difficulties. 'History of Education' is a long-established area and the initial sub-sections reflect this fact. The sub-sections that immediately follow take 'education' into more contentious territory. Items that have been listed in these categories include both contemporary contributions to the vigorous debates that have taken place and some initial attempts to assess their longer-term significance. Inevitably, the sub-sections which specifically identify 'education and . . .' 'society', 'religion', and 'politics' have correlates in the appropriate sections of the bibliography.

The subsequent sub-sections are organized by type of school. The literature is varied and is itself a reflection of educational realities. Many grammar and public schools have long been accustomed to commissioning histories—in some cases a generosity of spirit which extends to headmasters. These works are in general informative and helpful but, as in the case of other social institutions or companies where commissioned histories predominate, there is always the danger that they reflect a certain internal perspective on the schools concerned. The same point holds true for the histories of teacher-training institutions and universities. The issues raised by university growth are covered in one sub-section while another provides details of these histories of individual universities. By contrast, it should be noted that while 'comprehensivization' has been extensively discussed, there are comparatively few histories of comprehensive schools.

Further sub-sections identify literature on the educational needs of particular social groups and the diversity of the educational position in Scotland, Wales, and Northern Ireland is recognized by separate sub-divisions.

1. EDUCATION IN GENERAL

22423 COMBER (NORMAN MEDERSON). Agricultural Education in Great Britain. 1948.

22424 COOK (THOMAS GOLDIE) ed. Education and the Professions. 1973.

22425 TURNER (JOHN DERFEL) and RUSHTON (JAMES) eds. Education for the Professions. Manch. 1976.

22426 KNOWLES (JOHN HILTON) comp. The Teaching Hospital: Evolution and Contemporary Issues. 1966.

22427 POYNTER (FREDERICK NOEL LAWRENCE) ed. The Evolution of Medical Education in Britain. 1967.

22428 GULBENKIAN. Educational Discussion 1965: 'Higher Education for the Professions'. *Univ. Q.* 20 (1966), 147–208.

22429 WHEATCROFT (GEORGE SHORROCK ASHCOMBE). The Education and Training of the Modern Lawyer: An Inaugural Lecture. 1962.

22430 WILLIAMS (GRANVILLE LLEWELLYN). Learning the Law. 1945. 5th edn 1954.

22431 HANBURY (HAROLD GREVILLE). The Vinerian Chair and Legal Education. Oxf. 1958.

22432 GRAVESON (RONALD HARRY). 'The Aims and Methods of Legal Education'. *Medico-Legal J.* 15 (1947), 79–89.

22433 BRODETSKY (PAUL). 'Law as a Liberal Study'. *Adult Educ.* 32 (1959), 53–61.

22434 KAHN-FREUND (*Sir* OTTO). 'Reflections on Legal Education'. *Modern Law Rev.* 29 (1966), 121–36.

22435 GREEN (ANDREW WILSON). Bibliography on British Legal Education. 1973.

22436 COULSON (SIDNEY JOHN) *ed.* Theology and the University: An Ecumenical Investigation. 1964.

22437 HARDY (GODFREY HAROLD). Bertrand Russell and Trinity. Camb. 1970.

22438 HILKEN (THOMAS JOHN NORMAN). Engineering at Cambridge University: 1783–1965. Camb. 1967.

22439 ROTHBLATT (SHELDON). Tradition and Change in English Liberal Education: An Essay in History and Culture. 1976.

22440 SMITH (MARJORIE JEAN). Professional Education for Social Work in Britain: An Historical Account. 1965.

22441 WALKER (ROBERT MILNES). Medical Education in Britain. 1965.

22442 LEAVIS (FRANK RAYMOND). Education and the University. 1943. New edn 1948.

22443 TILLYARD (EUSTACE MANDEVILLE WETENHALL). The Muse Unchained: An Intimate Account of the Revolution in English Studies at Cambridge. 1958.

22444 SUTHERLAND (GILLIAN RAY). 'The Study of the History of Education'. *Hist.* 54 (1969), 49–59.

22445 SWIFT (D. F.) *and* ACLAND (H.). 'The Sociology of Education in Britain, 1960–1968: A Bibliographical Review'. *Soc. Sci. Info.* 8 (1969), 31–64. Paris.

22446 LEWIS (E. W.). 'The Development of Geography in the Polytechnics of England and Wales'. *Geog. J.* 139 (1973), 509–15.

22447 BUTT (JOHN). 'English at the Universities, 1901–1951'. *Univ. Q.* 5 (1950–1), 218–24.

22448 CLARK (GEORGE S. R. KITSON). 'A Hundred Years of the Teaching of History at Cambridge, 1873–1973'. *Hist. J.* 16 (1973), 535–53.

22449 HARRISON (BRIAN HOWARD). 'History at the Universities, 1968: A Commentary'. *Hist.* 53 (1968), 357–80.

22450 ELLIOTT (BRIAN J.). 'The League of Nations Union and History Teaching in England: A Study in Benevolent Bias'. *Hist. Educ.* 6 (1977), 131–41.

22451 SZERETER (R.). 'History and the Sociological Perspective in Educational Studies'. *Univ. Birm. Hist. J.* 12 (1969–70), 1–19.

22452 HARTE (NEGLEY B.). One Hundred and Fifty Years of History Teaching at University College London. 1982.

22453 JENKINS (E. W.). 'The Development of School Biology 1918–1945'. *Hist. Educ.* 8 (1979), 58–73.

22454 —— From Armstrong to Nuffield: Studies in Twentieth-Century Science Education in England and Wales. 1979.

22455 RAYNER (JOSEPHINE). 'A la Recherche de la Sensibilité Perdue: Notes on the State of University Music at the Present Time'. *Musical Opinion* 91 (1967).

22456 PARKES (DAVID). 'Keble College: Its Organs and Organ Scholars, 1896–1964'. *Organ* 44 (1964), 75–83.

22457 MOULD (ALAN). 'Choir Schools in a Changing Educational System'. *English Church Music* (1973), 10–17.

22458 GOTTESMAN (H. H.). 'Students and the Art Schools'. *Contemp. Rev.* 213 (1968), 257–63.

22459 LEVY (MERVYN). 'The Royal College of Art'. *Studio* 165 (1963), 186–95.

22460 BEDNARCZYK (B.). 'The First University School of Architecture in England, 1841–1960'. In British Universities Annual 1964, 123–31.

22461 ALLEN (W. A.). 'The Education of Architects: The Robbins Committee and After'. *J. Roy. Inst. Brit. Arch.* 71 (1964), 210–19.

22462 BELL (QUENTIN). The Schools of Design. 1963.

22463 BLACHFORD (GEORGE). A History of Handicraft Teaching. 1961.

22464 SINCLAIR (DAVID CECIL). Medical Students and Medical Sciences: Some Problems of Education in Britain and the United States. 1955.

22465 NEWMAN (CHARLES E.). 'The Aims and Methods of Medical Education'. *Medico-Legal J.* 15 (1947), 74–9.

22466 GRAHAM (GEORGE). 'The Formation of the Medical and Surgical Professional Units in the London Teaching Hospitals'. *Ann. Sci.* 26 (1970), 1–22.

22467 FRANKLIN (K. J.). 'A Short Sketch of the History of the Oxford Medical School'. *Ann. Sci.* 1 (1936), 431–46.

22468 EVANS (LESTER J.). 'Medical Education in Perspective'. *Lancet* (20 Dec. 1958), 1323–5.

22469 ELLIS (JOHN). 'Preparation for the Profession: The Present and the Future'. *Lancet* (12 Nov. 1960), 1041–5.

22470 BUTLER (J. R.). 'Sociology and Medical Education'. *Sociol. Rev.* 17 (1969), 87–96.

22471 BERZON (DEREK). 'Medical Students and General Practice'. *Lancet* (30 Aug. 1958), 441–2.

22472 ARNOTT (W. MELVILLE). 'The Climate of Medical Education'. *Lancet* (3 Jan. 1959), 1–7.

22473 WHITTERIDGE (GWENETH). The Royal Hospital of St Bartholomew: A Short History. 1952.

22474 RIPMAN (HUJOHN ARMSTRONG) *ed.* Guy's Hospital, 1725–1948. 1951.

22475 MANSON-BAHR (*Sir* PHILIP HEINRICH). A History of the School of Tropical Medicine in London, 1899–1949. 1956.

22476 COPE (*Sir* VINCENT ZACHARY). History of St Mary's Hospital Medical School: One Hundred Years of Medical Education. 1954.

22477 HALL (*Sir* ARTHUR JOHN). The Sheffield School of Medicine. 1944.

22478 COPE (*Sir* VINCENT ZACHARY). The Royal College of Surgeons of England. 1959.

22479 WALLIS (THOMAS EDWARD). History of the School of Pharmacy, University of London. 1964.

22480 STAFFORD (HELEN MURIEL). Queenswood: The First Sixty Years, 1894–1954. Hatfield. 1954.

22481 SEYMER (LUCY RIDGELY). Florence Nightingale's Nurses: The Nightingale Training School, 1860–1960. 1960.

22482 ELTON (GODFREY) *Baron ed.* The First Fifty Years of the Rhodes Trust and the Rhodes Scholarship, 1903–1953. 1955.

22483 CLARK (RONALD WILLIAM). A Biography of the Nuffield Foundation. 1972.

22484 PEDDIE (JOHN RONALD). The Carnegie Trust for the Universities of Scotland, 1901–1951: The First Fifty Years. Edin. 1951.

22485 DONALD (LOUISE). 'The British Federation of University Women, 1907–1957'. *Aberd. Univ. Rev.* 37 (1957), 149–55.

22486 TYLECOTE (MABEL). The Education of Women at Manchester University, 1883 to 1933. Manch. 1941.

22487 ANDERSON (KITTY) *Dame.* Women and the Universities: A Changing Pattern. Bedford College. 1965.

22488 SUTHERLAND (MARGARET B.). Sex Bias in Education. 1981.

22489 HOLLINGS (F.). 'Women in Further Education'. In P. Venables. Technical Education. 1956.

22490 PAGE (WILLIAM ROBERTS). Introducing the Younger Woman: The Story of an Experiment in Further Education for Younger Women out at Work. 1965.

22491 TUCKER (D. G.). 'Broader Education in a Technological Department'. *Univ. Q.* 13 (Feb. 1959), 157–63.

22492 VENABLES (*Sir* PETER PERCY FREDERICK RONALD). 'Emergence of Colleges of Advanced Technology in Britain'. In Year Book of Education (1959), 224–36.

22493 PALMER (W. B.). 'The Colleges of Advanced Technology and the Universities'. *Univ. Rev.* (Oct. 1959), 14–20.

22494 WALTERS (GERALD). 'The Colleges of Advanced Technology and the University Tradition'. *Univ. Rev.* 34 (1962), 66–71.

22495 COLE (PAUL). 'The Future of the C.A.T.'s'. *Twentieth Cent.* clxxii (1963), 26–34.

22496 WYATT (H. V.). 'CATs and Robbins'. *Univ. Q.* 19 (1964), 23–32.

22497 VENABLES (*Sir* PETER PERCY FREDERICK RONALD). 'Dualism in Higher Education'. *Univ. Q.* 20 (1965), 16–29.

22498 BUCHANAN (R. A.). 'The Technological Universities'. *Univ. Q.* 21 (1966), 71–90.

22499 VENABLES (*Sir* PETER PERCY FREDERICK RONALD). Higher Education Developments: The Technological Universities, 1956–1976. 1978.

22500 'The Technological Universities and Education for the Professions'. *J. Roy. Inst. Brit. Architects* 74 (1967), 239–43.

22501 CLUNIES-ROSS (EDWARD). 'Educational Technology in Adult and Community Education'. *Community Dvlpt J.* 9 (1974), 206–11.

22502 COALES (J. F.). 'Education for Automation: Technical Education and Training in an Age of Rapid Technological Advance'. *Brit. J. Educ. Studs* (May 1958), 99–118.

22503 BUTLER (KEITH). 'A Role for the Tech.'. *Adult Educ.* 37 (1965), 257–63.

22504 BOSWORTH (G. S.). 'Towards Creative Activity in Engineering'. *Univ. Q.* 17 (1963), 286–97.

22505 ARMYTAGE (WALTER HARRY GREEN). 'Some Sources for the History of Technical Education in England'. *Brit. J. Educ. Studs* 6 (1957), 64–73.

22506 DAVIES (LAURENCE). Liberal Studies and Higher Technology. Cardiff. 1965.

22507 ADAMS (MOLLIE). 'Liberal Studies in Technological Education'. *Univ. Q.* 17 (1963), 274–85.

22508 WARNER (F. E.). 'Education in Science and Technology'. *Pol. Q.* 38 (1967), 41–50.

22509 TAYLOR (P. W.). 'The Development of Higher Technological Education in Britain, 1945–1951'. *J. Educ. Admin Hist.* 8 (1975), 20–30.

22510 SINCLAIR (J. F.) *et al.* 'Educating Management'. *Twentieth Cent.* 175 (1966), 49–58.

22511 ROBINSON (F.) *and* WINDER (R.). 'Vacation Training of Undergraduate Engineers'. *Engineer* (Dec. 1959), 743–4.

22512 RICHARDSON (*Sir* ERIC). 'Education in a Technologically Based Society'. *J. Roy. Soc. Arts* 117 (1969), 454–69.

22513 PIPPARD (A. J. S.). 'Engineering Studies in British Universities'. *Univ. Q.* 2 (1947–8), 166–73.

22514 PETERS (A. J.). 'The Changing Idea of a Technical Education'. *Brit. J. Educ. Studs* 11 (1963), 142–66.

22515 PETCH (J. A.). 'Whither Education?'. *Manch. Lit. Phil. Soc. Memoirs and Procs* 108 (1965–6), 58–70.

22516 MONKHOUSE (PATRICK) *ed.* 'The Education and Training of the Technologist'. *Univ. Q.* 16 (1961–2), 143–55.

22517 de MALHERBE (M. C.) *and* OPPENHEIM (A. K.). 'Changing Structure of Engineering Education'. *Engineer* 212 (1961), 1025–8.

22518 LITTLER (KEITH T.). 'Work Experience and the British School Pupil'. *Community Dvlpt J.* 8 (1973), 99–103.

22519 KEMENY (P. J.). 'Dualism in Secondary Technical Education'. *Brit. J. Sociol.* 21 (1970), 86–94.

22520 JENKINS (E. W.). 'The Scientific Education of Girls since 1902'. *Durham Res. Rev.* 6 (1974), 873–86.

22521 JACKSON (*Sir* WILLIS). 'Some Aspects of Engineering Education'. *Engineer* 211 (1961), 980–1.

22522 HANSON (C.). 'Education and the Interaction of Technologies'. In The Integration of Technologies. *Ed.* Leslie Holliday. 1966.

22523 DIAMOND (J.). 'University Engineering Education, 1960–1980'. *Advan. Sci.* 27 (1970), 164–70.

22524 DANCY (J. C.). 'Technology in a Liberal Education'. *Advan. Sci.* 22 (1965), 379–87.

22525 COOMBE (R. A.). 'A Technological Education'. In The Integration of Technologies. *Ed.* Leslie Holliday. 1966.

22526 WOOD (ETHEL MARY). A History of the Polytechnic. 1965.

22527 ROBINSON (ERIC EMBLETON). The New Polytechnics. 1968.

22528 DONALDSON (LEX). Policy and the Polytechnics: Pluralistic Drift in Higher Education. Farnb. 1975.

22529 LANE (MICHAEL). Design for Degrees: New Degree Courses and the CNAA, 1964–1974. 1975.

22530 BROOKS (COLLIN). An Educational Adventure: A History of the Woolwich Polytechnic. 1955.

22531 LOCKE (MICHAEL). Traditions and Controls in the Making of a Polytechnic: Woolwich Polytechnic, 1890–1970. 1978.

22532 PRATT (JOHN) *and* BURGESS (TYRRELL). Polytechnics: A Report. 1974.

22533 COLLISON (PETER). 'Research Note: Career Contingencies of English University Teachers'. *Brit. J. Sociol.* 13 (1962), 286–93.

22534 MONTEFIORE (ALAN). Neutrality and Commitment: The University and Political Commitment. Camb. 1975.

22535 HOPSON (BARRIE). 'Modernising University Teaching'. *New Society* (1 Dec. 1966), 827–30.

22536 NIBLETT (WILLIAM ROY). 'Graduate Schools in British Universities'. *Nature* 187 (1960), 560–1.

22537 HALSEY (ALBERT HENRY). 'British Universities and Intellectual Life'. *Univ. Q.* 12, 2 (Feb. 1958), 141–52.

22538 HARRISON (MARTIN JOHN) *and* WEIGHTMAN (K.). 'Academic Freedom and Higher Education in England'. *Brit. J. Sociol.* 25 (1974), 32–46.

22539 COLLIER (K. G.). 'An Experiment in University Teaching'. *Univ. Q.* 20 (1966), 336–48.

22540 HALSEY (ALBERT HENRY) *and* TROW (MARTIN AARON). The British Academics. 1971.

22541 LAYTON (DAVID) *ed.* University Teaching in Transition. 1968.

22542 ADAMS (*Sir* WALTER). 'Refugee Scholars of the 1930s'. *Pol. Q.* 39 (1968), 7–14.

22543 BENTWICH (NORMAN). The Rescue and Achievement of Refugee Scholars: The Story of Displaced Scholars and Scientists, 1933–1952. The Hague. 1953.

22544 PERKIN (HAROLD JAMES). Key Profession: The History of the Association of University Teachers. 1969.

22545 WILLIAMS (GARETH), BLACKSTONE (TESSA), *and* METCALF (DAVID). The Academic Labour Market: Economic and Social Aspects of a Profession. Amsterdam/NY/Lond. 1974.

22546 NEWBOULD (GERALD D.). Academic Salaries: A Personal Application of Managerial Economics. Bradford. 1975.

22547 MCWILLIAMS-TULLBERG (RITA). Women at Cambridge: A Man's University—though of a Mixed Type. 1975.

22548 JOBLING (R. G.). 'Some Sociological Aspects of University Development in England'. *Sociol. Rev.* 17 (1969), 11–26.

22549 JONES (K.). 'The Twenty-Four Steps: An Analysis of Institutional Admission Procedures'. *Sociol.* 6 (1972), 405–15.

22550 FURNEAUX (WALTER DESMOND CHARLES). The Chosen Few: An Examination of Some Aspects of University Selection in Britain. 1961.

22551 PEDDIE (JOHN RONALD). The Trevelyan Scholarships: A Report on an Experiment in University Selection. Kineton. 1975.

22552 BLOCK (GEOFFREY D. M.). 'Jewish Students at the Universities of Great Britain and Ireland, Excluding London, 1936–1939'. *Sociol. Rev.* 35 (1942), 183–97.

22553 KLINGENDER (F. D.). 'Changing Patterns of Student Recruitment in England'. *Univ. Q.* 9 (1954–5), 168–76.

22554 ALLEN (ROY GEORGE DOUGLAS). 'Population of British Universities in the 1960s: The Age-Group Bulge'. *Nature* 177 (1956), 115–16.

22555 TAYLOR (WALLIS). 'Population of British Universities in the 1960s'. *Nature* 178 (1956), 135–6.

22556 ZWEIG (FERDYNAND). The Student in the Age of Anxiety: A Survey of Oxford and Manchester Students. 1963.

22557 HARMAN (CHRIS) *et al.* Education, Capitalism and the Student Revolt. 1968.

22558 BLACKSTONE (TESSA) *et al.* Students in Conflict: L.S.E. in 1967. 1970.

22559 FISK (T.). 'Nature and Causes of Student Unrest'. *Pol. Q.* 40 (1969), 419–25.

22560 ROOKE (M. A.). Anarchy and Apathy: Student Unrest, 1968–1970. 1971.

22561 MARTIN (DAVID). Anarchy and Culture: The Problem of the Contemporary University. 1969.

22562 COOPER (B.) *and* FOX (J. M.). 'Students' Study Habits, Attitudes and Academic Attainment'. *Univ. Q.* 23 (1969), 203–12.

22563 WILSON (BRYAN RONALD). The Youth Culture and the Universities. 1970.

22564 CROUCH (COLIN). The Student Revolt. 1970.

22565 ASHBY (*Sir* ERIC) *and* ANDERSON (MARY). The Rise of the Student Estate in Britain. 1970.

22566 HUTCHISON (D.) *and* MCPHERSON (A.). 'Competing Inequalities: The Sex and Social Class Structure of the First Year Scottish Student Population, 1962–1972'. *Sociol.* 10 (1976), 111–16.

22567 MANN (PETER HENRY). Students and Books. 1974.

22568 JACKS (DIGBY). Student Politics and Higher Education. 1975.

22569 HAJNAL (JOHN). The Student Trap: A Critique of University and Sixth Form Curricula. Harmondsworth. 1972.

22570 BELOFF (MAX). 'October for the Rebels'. *Encounter* 31 (1968), 48–56.

22571 RUDD (ERNEST) *and* SIMPSON (RENATE). The Highest Education: A Study of Graduate Education in Britain. 1975.

22572 ENTWISTLE (NOEL JAMES) *and* WILSON (JOHN D.). Degrees of Excellence: The Academic Achievement Game. 1977.

22573 WILLIAMS (PETER) ed. The Overseas Student Question: Studies for a Policy. 1981.

22574 KELSALL (ROGER KEITH) *et al.* Graduates: The Sociology of an Elite. 1972.

22575 NEAVE (GUY RICHARD). How they Fared: The Impact of the Comprehensive School upon the University. 1975.

22576 ADAMSON (JOHN WILLIAM). The Illiterate Anglo-Saxon. Camb. 1946.

22577 WHITELEY (WINIFRED MARY). The Uneducated English. 1969.

22578 HARTOG (MABEL HELENE). Lady P. J. Hartog: A Memoir. 1949.

22579 GULLIVER (DORIS). Dame Agnes Weston. Chichester. 1971.

22580 MAUD (JOHN R.). '1851–1951: A Century of British Education'. *J. Roy. Soc. Arts* (June 1951).

22581 ADULT EDUCATION.

22582 ANNUAL SURVEY, U.G.C. ACADEMIC YEAR 1963–4. [Practice began in 1960 when the Committee's statistical returns for the year 1958–9 (Cmnd 1166) were prefaced by a general statement.].

22583 BRITISH EDUCATIONAL RESEARCH JOURNAL.

22584 BRITISH JOURNAL OF EDUCATIONAL PSYCHOLOGY I. 1931.

22585 BRITISH JOURNAL OF EDUCATIONAL STUDIES I. 1952–1953.

22586 BRITISH JOURNAL OF SOCIOLOGY OF EDUCATION I. 1980.

22587 DURHAM RESEARCH REVIEW from 8 No. 40 spring 1978+. Newcastle.

22588 EDUCATION.

22589 EDUCATION COMMITTEES YEAR BOOK.

22590 EDUCATION AND SCIENCE.

22591 EDUCATION (SCOTLAND) REPORTS, ETC.

22592 EDUCATION YEARBOOK.

22593 EDUCATIONAL ADMINISTRATION.

22594 EDUCATIONAL MANAGEMENT AND ADMINISTRATION.

22595 EDUCATIONAL RESEARCH.

22596 EDUCATIONAL REVIEW.

22597 HISTORY OF EDUCATION.

22598 JOURNAL OF ADULT EDUCATION.

22599 JOURNAL OF CURRICULUM STUDIES I. 1968–9.

22600 JOURNAL OF EDUCATION FOR TEACHING.

22601 JOURNAL OF EDUCATIONAL ADMINISTRATION AND HISTORY.

22602 JOURNAL OF PHILOSOPHY OF EDUCATION.

22603 OXFORD REVIEW OF EDUCATION I. 1975.

2. EDUCATIONAL DOCUMENTS, ETC.

22604 MACLURE (JOHN STUART) *comp.* Educational Documents: England and Wales, 1816–1963. 1965. 2nd edn 1968.

22605 LELLO (JOHN). The Official View on Education: A Summary of the Major Educational Reports since 1944. Oxf. 1964.

22606 PATTISON (BRUCE). 'The Crowther Report'. *Contemp. Rev.* (Apr. 1960), 221–4.

22607 HUTCHINSON (E. M.). 'Crowther—A Personal Comment'. *Adult Educ.* 33 (1960), 27–30.

22608 OLLERENSHAW (KATHLEEN MARY) *Dame*. 'Newsom and Tomorrow'. *Contemp. Rev.* 206 (1965), 31–6.

22609 WATKINS (KENNETH W.). 'Plowden—is it Enough?'. *Pol. Q.* 38 (1967), 177–83.

22610 BLACKSTONE (TESSA). 'The Plowden Report'. *Brit. J. Sociol.* 18 (1967), 291–302.

22611 JAMES (T.). 'Commissions of Little Consequence'. *Round Table* 58 (1968), 409–16.

22612 ALEXANDER (*Sir* WILLIAM PICKEN). The Burnham Primary and Secondary Schools Report, 1954: A Commentary by Dr W. P. Alexander. 1955.

22613 GORDON (PETER). Curriculum Change in the Nineteenth and Twentieth Centuries. 1978.

22614 HURT (JOHN). Elementary Schooling and the Working Classes 1860–1918. 1979.

22615 DEAN (D. W.). 'H. A. L. Fisher, Reconstruction and the Development of the 1918 Education Act'. *Brit. J. Educ. Studs* 18 (1970), 259–76.

22616 ANDREWS (LAWRENCE). The Education Act 1918. 1976.

22617 DEAN (D. W.). 'Conservatism and the National Education System 1922–1940'. *J. Contemp. Hist.* 6 (1971), 150–65.

22618 JENKINS (E. W.). 'The Thomson Committee and the Board of Education 1916–1922'. *Brit. J. Educ. Studs* 21 (1973), 76–87.

22619 AKENSON (D. H.). 'Patterns of English Educational Change: The Fisher and the Butler Acts'. *Hist. Educ. Q.* 11 (1971), 143–56.

22620 DOHERTY (BERNARD). 'The Hadow Report, 1926'. *Durham Res. Rev.* 4 (1964), 117–27.

22621 DEAN (D. W.). 'The Difficulties of a Labour Educational Policy: The Failure of the Trevelyan Bill, 1929–1931'. *Brit. J. Educ. Studs* 17 (1969), 286–300.

22622 COCKIN (FREDERIC ARTHUR). 'The Education Act Comes of Age'. *Theology* 48 (1965), 315–22.

22623 DREWETT (A. J.). 'Education and the State: A Christian Critique of the 1944 Education Act'. *Churchman* (June 1947), 53–62.

22624 MIDDLETON (NIGEL). 'Lord Butler and the Education Act of 1944'. *Brit. J. Educ. Studs* 20 (1972), 178–91.

22625 WELLS (MURIEL MAUDE) *and* TAYLOR (PERCY STRAWSON). The New Law of Education. 1949. 4th edn 1954.

22626 BEATTIE (DAVID JOY) *and* TAYLOR (PERCY STRAWSON). The New Law of Education. 1944.

22627 IKIN (ALFRED EDWARD). The Education Act 1944, with Explanatory Notes. 1944.

22628 BARRELL (GEOFFREY RICHARD). Teachers and the Law. 1958. 2nd edn 1963.

22629 TAYLOR (GEORGE) *and* SAUNDERS (JOHN BEECROFT). The Law of Education. 1965. 8th edn 1976.

22630 PRING (BERYL). Education, Capitalist and Socialist. 1937.

22631 DENT (HAROLD COLLETT). A New Order in English Education. 1942.

22632 SHEPHERD (THOMAS BOSWELL). Living Education; Some Views on Education between the Wars and its Prospects for the Future. 1944.

22633 DENT (HAROLD COLLETT). Education in Transition. 1944.

22634 MOORE (RALPH WESTWOOD) *ed.* Education: Today and Tomorrow. 1945.

22635 SHARP (JOHN). Educating One Nation. 1959.

22636 CORBETT (ANNE). Much to do about Education: A Critical Survey of the Fate of the Major Educational Reports. 1969. 4th edn 1978.

22637 CROSLAND (CHARLES ANTHONY RAVEN). 'Some Thoughts on English Education'. *Encounter* 94 (1961), 49–58.

22638 BLOND (ANTHONY). 'An Old Etonian Looks at State Education'. *Time and Tide* 43 (1962), 6–11.

22639 WALL (W. D.). 'Vogues in British Educational Theory'. *Twentieth Cent.* 172 (1963), 91–108.

22640 SMITH (ROBERT IRVINE). 'Curriculum Reform'. *New Society* (12 May 1966), 12–15.

22641 JAMES (T.). 'Permissive Politics in Retreat'. *Round Table* lix (1969), 161–9.

22642 ROBINSON (ERIC EMBLETON). 'Education as a Social Service'. *Pol. Q.* 40 (1969), 56–65.

22643 BLISHEN (EDWARD) *ed.* Education Today: The Existing Opportunities. 1963.

22644 ELVIN (HERBERT LIONEL). Education and Contemporary Society. 1965.

22645 COX (CHARLES BRIAN) *and* DYSON (ANTHONY EDWARD) *eds.* Black Paper Three: Goodbye Mr Short. 1970.

22646 SHIPMAN (MARTEN DORRINGTON). Education and Modernization. 1971.

22647 SHORT (EDWARD). Education in a Changing World. 1971.

22648 COX (CHARLES BRIAN) *and* DYSON (ANTHONY EDWARD). The Black Papers on Education. 1971.

22649 BOYSON (RHODES). The Crisis in Education. 1975.

22650 —— *ed.* Education: Threatened Standards: Essays on the Reasons for the Present Decline in Educational Achievement and Suggestions for its Improvement. Enfield. 1972.

22651 VAIZEY (JOHN ERNEST) *Baron.* Education: The State of the Debate in America, Britain and Canada. 1976.

3. HISTORY OF EDUCATION

22652 ARMYTAGE (WALTER HARRY GREEN). Four Hundred Years of English Education. Camb. 1964. 2nd edn 1970.

22653 CURTIS (STANLEY JAMES). History of Education in Great Britain. 1948.

22654 —— An Introductory History of English Education since 1800. 1960.

22655 —— Education in Britain since 1900. 1952.

22656 CURTIS (STANLEY JAMES) *and* BOULTWOOD (MYRTLE EMMA A.). A Short History of Educational Ideas. 1953.

22657 BARNARD (HOWARD CLIVE). A Short History of English Education from 1760. 1947.

22658 EAGLESHAM (ERIC JOHN ROSS). The Foundations of Twentieth-Century Education in England. 1967.

22659 LOWNDES (GEORGE ALFRED NORMAN). The Silent Social Revolution: An Account of the Expansion of Public Education in England and Wales, 1895–1935. 1937.

22660 MUSGRAVE (PETER WILLIAM). Society and Education in England since 1800. 1968.

22661 WEST (EDWIN GEORGE). Education and the State: A Study in Political Economy. 1965.

22662 WARD (HERBERT). The Educational System of England and Wales and its Recent History. Camb. 1935.

22663 —— Notes for the Study of English Education from 1900 to 1930. 1931.

22664 PETERSON (ALEXANDER DUNCAN CAMPBELL). A Hundred Years of Education. 1952.

22665 WARDLE (DAVID). English Popular Education, 1780–1970. Camb. 1970.

22666 —— The Rise of the Schooled Society: The History of Formal Schooling in England. 1974.

22667 PEERS (ROBERT). Fact and Possibility in English Education. 1963.

22668 PARRY (JOHN PENRHYN). The Provision of Education in England and Wales: An Introduction. 1971.

22669 PALMER (RICHARD). Starting School: A Study in Policies. 1971.

22670 NORWOOD (*Sir* CYRIL). The English Educational System. 1928.

22671 MOORE (RALPH WESTWOOD) *ed.* Education: Today and Tomorrow. 1945.

22672 MORRIS (BEN). Objectives and Perspectives in Education: Studies in Educational Theory, 1955–1970. 1972.

22673 MORRISH (IVOR). Education since 1800. 1970.

22674 MIDDLETON (NIGEL GORDON) *and* WEITZMAN (SOPHIA). A Place for Everyone: A History of State Education from the End of the 18th Century to the 1970s. 1976.

22675 MARVIN (FRANCIS SYDNEY). The Nation at School. 1933.

22676 LOWNDES (GEORGE ALFRED NORMAN). The English Educational System. 1955.

22677 LITTLE (KENNETH). The Development of State Education. 1973.

22678 LAWSON (JOHN) *and* SILVER (HAROLD). A Social History of Education in England. 1973.

22679 KANDEL (ISAAC LEON). The New Era in Education: A Comparative Study. 1955.

22680 JARMAN (THOMAS LECKIE). Landmarks in the History of Education: English Education as Part of the European Tradition. 1951. 2nd edn 1963.

22681 JACKS (MAURICE LEONARD). Modern Trends in Education. 1950.

22682 HUTCHINSON (MICHAEL EDWARD). Education in Britain. 1966.

22683 GRAVES (JOHN TIARKS RANKE). Policy and Progress in Secondary Education, 1902–1942. 1943.

22684 GOSDEN (PETER HENRY JOHN HEATHER) *ed.* How they were Taught: An Anthology of Contemporary Accounts of Learning and Teaching in England, 1800–1950. Oxf. 1969.

22685 FIELD (FRANK) *ed.* Twentieth Century State Education. 1971.

22686 EVANS (KEITH). The Development and Structure of the English Educational System. 1975.

22687 DENT (HAROLD COLLETT). British Education. 1946.

22688 —— Change in English Education. 1952.

22689 —— The Educational System of England and Wales. 1961.

22690 —— 1870–1970: A Century of Growth in English Education. 1970.

22691 —— Growth in English Education, 1946–1952. 1954.

22692 —— Secondary Education for all. 1949.

22693 EVERETT (SAMUEL). Growing up in English Secondary Schools: Significance for American Practice. 1959.

22694 VAN DER EYKEN (WILLEM). Education, the Child and Society: A Documentary History, 1900–1973. Harmondsworth. 1973.

22695 SCOTT-JAMES (ROLFE ARNOLD) *ed.* Education in Britain. 1944.

22696 RICHMOND (WILLIAM KENNETH). Education in England. Harmondsworth. 1945.

22697 —— The Education Industry. 1969.

22698 —— Education in Britain since 1944: A Personal Retrospect. 1978.

22699 SEABORNE (MALCOLM VIVIAN JOHN). Education. 1966.

22700 ROSE (BRIAN). Modern Trends in Education. 1971.

22701 MARSHALL (SYBIL MARY). An Experiment in Education. Camb. 1963.

22702 BRUBACHER (JOHN SEILER). A History of the Problems of Education. 1947.

22703 BROGAN (COLM). The Educational Revolution. 1955.

22704 CARMICHAEL (JAMES). Educational Revolution. 1969.

22705 BIRCHENOUGH (CHARLES). History of Elementary Education in England and Wales from 1800 to the Present Day. 1938.

4. TEACHERS

22706 THOMPSON (DONNA FAY). Professional Solidarity among the Teachers of England. N.Y. 1927.

22707 TROPP (ASHER). The School Teachers: The Growth of the Teaching Profession in England and Wales, from 1800 to the Present Day. 1957.

22708 ROY (WALTER). The Teachers' Union: Aspects of Policy and Organisation in the National Union of Teachers, 1950–1966. 1968.

22709 MORTON (BERNARD) *ed.* Action, 1919–1969: A Record of the Growth of the National Association of Schoolmasters. 1969.

22710 MANZER (RONALD ALEXANDER). Teachers and Politics: The Role of the National Union of Teachers in the Making of National Education Policy in England and Wales since 1944. Manch. 1970.

22711 BOURNE (RICHARD). The Struggle for Education, 1870–1970: A Pictorial History of Popular Education and the National Union of Teachers. 1970.

22712 COATES (ROBERT DAVID). Teaching Unions and Interest Group Politics: A Study in the Behaviour of Organised Teachers in England and Wales. 1972.

22713 GOSDEN (PETER HENRY JOHN HEATHER). The Evolution of a Profession: A Study of the Contribution of Teachers' Associations to the Development of School Teaching as a Professional Occupation. Oxf. 1972.

22714 BROWNE (J. D.). Teachers of Teachers: A History of the Association of Teachers in Colleges and Departments of Education. 1979.

22715 FREEMAN (JOHN). Team Teaching in Britain. 1969.

22716 TEMPEST (N. R.) *comp.* 'Some Sources for the History of Teacher Training in England and Wales'. *Brit. J. Educ. Studs* 9 (1960), 57–66.

22717 BROWNE (J. D.). 'Bachelors of Education'. *Higher Ed. J.* 14 (1964), 12–16.

22718 TURNER (JOHN D.). 'New Directions in Teacher Education'. *Manch. Lit. Phil. Soc. Memoirs and Procs* 115 (1973), 32–56.

22719 PETERSON (A. D. C.). 'The Higher Education of Teachers'. *Hibbert J.* 59 (1961), 146–53.

22720 HILLIARD (F. H.). 'Divinity Studies in Colleges for the Education and Training of Teachers'. *Theology* 67 (1964), 438–42.

22721 FLOUD (JEAN ESTHER). 'Teaching in the Affluent Society'. *Brit. J. Sociol.* 13 (1962), 299–308.

22722 EVANS (A. A.). 'Where will we Teach the Teachers?'. *Twentieth Cent.* 172 (1963), 40–50.

22723 BARNETT (J. V.). 'Teacher Training: University Control and Supply of Teachers'. *Higher Ed. J.* 14 (1964), 17–21.

22724 WISEMAN (STEPHEN). 'Higher Degrees in Education in British Universities'. *Brit. J. Educ. Studs* 2 (1953), 54–66.

22725 CONWAY (FREDA). 'School-Teachers' Salaries, 1945–1959'. *Manch. Sch. Econ. Soc. Studs* 30 (1962), 153–79.

22726 HILL (ALFRED TUXBURY). The Emergency Training Scheme for Teachers in England and Wales. Ann Arbor, Mich. 1950.

22727 MINISTRY OF EDUCATION. Challenge and Response: An Account of the Emergency Scheme for the Training of Teachers. 1950.

22728 RICHARDSON (CYRIL ALBERT) *et al.* The Education of Teachers in England, France and the U.S.A. Paris. 1953.

22729 JEFFREYS (MONTAGU VAUGHAN CASTELMAN). Revolution in Teacher Training. 1961.

22730 TAYLOR (WILLIAM). Society and the Education of Teachers. 1969.

22731 KAYE (BARRINGTON). Participation in Learning: A Progress Report on Some Experiments in the Training of Teachers. 1970.

22732 WILLEY (FREDERICK THOMAS) *Baron, and* MADDISON (R. E.). An Enquiry into Teacher Training. 1971.

22733 PARRY (JOHN PENRHYN). The Lord James Tricycle: Some Notes on Teacher Education and Training. 1972.

22734 TYSON (JOHN COLIN) *and* TUCK (JOHN PHILIP). The Origins and Development of the Training of Teachers in the University of Newcastle upon Tyne. Newcastle. 1971.

22735 LOMAX (DONALD ERNEST) *ed.* The Education of Teachers in Britain. 1973.

22736 PARTINGTON (GEOFFREY). Women Teachers in the Twentieth Century in England and Wales. Windsor. 1976.

22737 TAYLOR (WILLIAM). Society and the Education of Teachers. 1969.

22738 —— *ed.* Towards a Policy for the Education of Teachers. 1969.

22739 HILLIARD (F.) *ed.* Teaching the Teachers. 1971.

22740 WRAGG (EDWARD CONRAD). Teaching Teaching. 1974.

22741 NIBLETT (WILLIAM ROY), HUMPHREYS (DARLOW W.), *and* FAIRHURST (JOHN R.). The University Connection. Windsor. 1975. [Good historical survey.].

22742 DENT (HAROLD COLLETT). The Training of Teachers in England and Wales 1800–1975. 1977.

22743 LYNCH (JAMES). The Reform of Teacher Education in the United Kingdom. Guildford. 1979.

5. TEACHER-TRAINING INSTITUTIONS

22744 BERRY (MICHAEL). Teacher Training Institutions in England and Wales: A Bibliographical Guide to their History. 1973.

22745 BIBBY (CYRIL). The First Fifty Years: A Brief History of Kingston upon Hull Training College, 1913–1963. Hull. 1964.

22746 BRADBURY (JOHN LEWIS). Chester College and the Training of Teachers, 1839–1975. Chester. 1975.

22747 CITY OF LEEDS TRAINING COLLEGE. A Short History of the City of Leeds Training College, 1907–1957. 1957.

22748 DYMOND (DOROTHY) *ed.* The Forge: The History of Goldsmiths' College, 1905–1955. 1955.

22749 MILLINGTON (ROY). A History of the City of Sheffield Training College. 1955.

22750 PRITCHARD (FRANK CYRIL). The Story of Westminster College, 1851–1951. 1951.

22751 SMART (R.). Bedford Training College, 1882–1982: A History of a Froebel College and its Schools. Bedford. 1982.

22752 ZEBEDEE (DONALD HENRY JOHN). Lincoln Diocesan Training College, 1862–1962. Lincoln. 1962.

22753 SIMMS (T. H.). Homerton College, 1695–1978: From Dissenting Academy to Approved Society in the University of Cambridge. Camb. 1979.

22754 MCGREGOR (G. P.). Bishop Otter College: And Policy for Teacher Education, 1839–1980. 1981.

22755 BARTLE (G. F.). A History of Borough Road College. 1976.

22756 KENDALL (GUY). A Headmaster Reflects. 1937.

22757 SEARBY (PETER). The Training of Teachers in Cambridge University: The First Sixty Years, 1879–1939. Camb. 1982.

22758 BOYD (MICHAEL V.). The Church of England Colleges, 1890–1944: An Administrative Study. Leeds. 1984.

6. ASPECTS OF INSTRUCTION

22759 TURNER (JOHN DERFEL). Language Laboratories in Great Britain. 1962.

22760 LEFF (SAMUEL) *and* LEFF (VERA). The School Health Service. 1959.

22761 SUTTON (GORDON). Artisan or Artist?: A History of the Teaching of Arts and Crafts in English Schools. Oxf. 1967.

22762 CHALL (JEANNE STERNLIGHT). Learning to Read: The Great Debate: An Inquiry into the Science, Art and Ideology of Old and New Methods of Teaching Children to Read, 1910–1965. 1970.

22763 HARRISON (MORRIS). Instant Reading: The Story of the Initial Teaching Alphabet. 1964.

22764 RICHMOND (WILLIAM KENNETH). Teachers and Machines: An Introduction to the Theory and Practice of Programmed Learning. 1965.

22765 GARNETT (EMMELINE). Area Resource Centres: An Experiment. 1972.

22766 ALLAWAY (ALBERT JOHN). The Educational Centres Movement: A Comprehensive Survey. 1961.

22767 BOARD (BERYL) *ed.* The Effects of Technological Progress on Education: A Classified Bibliography from British Sources, 1945–1957. 1959.

22768 CALLENDER (PATRICIA). Programmed Learning: Its Development and Structure. 1969.

22769 CORBETT (ANNE). Innovation in Education, England. Paris. 1971.

22770 SAETTLER (PAUL). A History of Instructional Technology. 1968.

22771 COPPEN (HELEN ELIZABETH). Survey of British Research in Audio-visual Aids, 1945–1971. 1972.

22772 VERNEY (R. E.). 'The History of Student Health Services in Great Britain'. *Univ. Q.* 9 (1954–5), 23–31.

22773 PEEL (E. A.). 'Programmed Learning'. *J. Roy. Soc. Arts* 115 (1967), 711–25.

22774 EYSENCK (HANS JURGEN). 'The Teaching Machine, and the Revolution in Education'. *Encounter* 26 (1966), 7–13.

22775 BRAMWELL (R. D.). 'The Impact of New Media on the Teacher's Work, with Special Reference to Britain'. *Year Book of Education* (1960), 138–55.

22776 ANNETT (JOHN). Computer-Assisted Learning, 1969–1975: A Report Prepared for SSRC. 1976.

22777 APTER (MICHAEL JOHN). The New Technology of Education. 1968.

22778 TUCKER (NICHOLAS). Understanding the Mass Media: A Practical Approach for Teaching. Camb. 1966.

7. PLANNING AND ADMINISTRATION

22779 H.M. INSPECTOR OF SCHOOLS. Aspects of Secondary Education in England. 1979.

22780 GORDON (PETER). Selection for Secondary Education. 1980.

22781 SARAN (RENE). Policy Making in Secondary Education: A Case Study. 1973.

22782 BYRNE (EILEEN MAIRE). Planning and Educational Inequality: A Study of the Rationale of Resource-allocation. Windsor. 1974.

22783 MACFARLANE (ERIC). Sixth-Form Colleges: The 16–19 Comprehensives. 1978.

22784 BRIAULT (ERIC) *and* SMITH (FRANCES). Falling Rolls in Secondary Schools. 2 vols. Windsor. 1980.

22785 SIMON (BRIAN). Intelligence, Psychology and Education: A Marxist Critique. 1971.

22786 GIPPS (CAROLINE), STEADMAN (STEPHEN), BLACKSTONE (TESSA), *and* STIERER (BARRY). Testing Children: Standardized Testing in Local Education Authorities and Schools. 1983.

22787 GIPPS (CAROLINE) *and* GOLDSTEIN (HARVEY). Monitoring Children: An Evaluation of the Assessment of Performance Unit. 1983.

22788 GOSDEN (PETER HENRY JOHN HEATHER). The Development of Educational Administration in England and Wales. Oxf. 1966.

22789 BRAND (J. A.). 'Ministry Control and Local Autonomy in Education'. *Pol. Q.* 36 (1965), 154–63.

22790 PILE (*Sir* WILLIAM). 'Corporate Planning for Education in the Department of Education and Science'. *Public Admin.* 52 (1974), 13–25.

22791 SMITH (WILLIAM OWEN LESTER). To whom do Schools Belong? An Introduction to the Study of School Government. Oxf. 1942. 2nd edn 1945.

22792 BISHOP (ANTHONY SAVELL). The Rise of a Central Authority for English Education. 1971.

22793 FOWLER (GERALD TEASDALE) et al. Decision Making in British Education. 1973.

22794 KAZAMIAS (ANDREAS MICHAEL). Politics, Society and Secondary Education in England. Philadelphia, Pa. 1966.

22795 MALE (GEORGE A.). The Struggle for Power: Who Controls the Schools in England and the United States? 1974.

22796 LAWRENCE (BERNARD). The Administration of Education in Britain. 1972.

22797 KOGAN (MAURICE). Educational Policy-Making: A Study of Interest Groups and Parliament. 1975.

22798 VAIZEY (JOHN ERNEST) Baron. The Control of Education. 1963.

22799 SELBY-BIGGE (Sir LEWIS AMHERST). The Board of Education. 1927. 2nd edn 1934.

22800 MAUD (JOHN REDCLIFFE) Baron. 'The Twentieth Century Administrator'. In Pioneers of English Education. A. V. Judges ed. 1952.

22801 BRADSHAW (D. C. A.) ed. Studies in the Government and Control of Education since 1860. 1970.

22802 SUNGAKA (H.). 'The History of Education and the Study of Educational Administration'. J. Educ. Admin Hist. 14 (1982), 62–5.

8. EDUCATION AND SOCIETY

22803 HALSEY (ALBERT HENRY) et al. Education, Economy and Society. 1961.

22804 MUSGRAVE (PETER WILLIAM). The Sociology of Education. 1965. 3rd edn 1979.

22805 PRINGLE (MIA LILLY KELLMER). Deprivation and Education. 1965.

22806 KING (EDMUND JAMES). Education and Social Change. 1966.

22807 COSIN (BEN RUPERT) ed. Education: Structure and Society; Selected Readings. Harmondsworth. 1972.

22808 BYRNE (DAVID). The Poverty of Education: A Study in the Politics of Opportunity. 1975.

22809 LAWTON (DENIS). Education and Social Justice. 1977.

22810 MUSGROVE (FRANK). School and the Social Order. Chichester. 1979.

22811 JACKSON (BRIAN). Streaming: An Education System in Miniature. 1964.

22812 BIRLEY (DEREK) and DUFTON (ANNE). An Equal Chance: Equalities and Inequalities of Educational Opportunity. 1971.

22813 WINDSOR (JOHN). 'Education and the Class Barrier'. Twentieth Cent. 172 (1965), 105–13.

22814 MARTIN (BERNICE). 'Progressive Education Versus the Working Classes'. Critical Q. 13 (1971), 297–320.

22815 LITTLE (ALAN NEVILE) and WESTERGAARD (JOHN HARALD). 'The Trend of Class Differentials in Educational Opportunity in England and Wales'. Brit. J. Sociol. 15 (1964), 301–16.

22816 EVETTS (J.). 'Equality of Educational Opportunity: The Recent History of a Concept'. Brit. J. Sociol. 21 (1970), 425–30.

22817 BANKS (OLIVE). 'The Sociology of Education, 1952–1982'. Brit. J. Educ. Studs 30 (1982), 32–42.

22818 DURES (ALAN). Schools. 1971.

22819 DOBINSON (CHARLES HENRY). Schooling 1963–70. 1973.

22820 DEMPSTER (JACK JAMES BAMPFYLDE). Selection for Secondary Education. 1954.

22821 CARTER (MICHAEL PERCY). Home, School and Work: A Study of the Education and Employment of Young People in Britain. Oxf. 1963.

22822 RICHARDSON (ELIZABETH). Authority and Organisation in the Secondary School. 1975.

22823 SIMPSON (JAMES HERBERT). Schoolmaster's Harvest: Some Findings of Fifty Years, 1894–1944. 1954.

22824 BALLARD (CHARLES MARTIN). The Story of Teaching. Harmondsworth. 1969.

22825 BURKE (VINCENT). Teachers in Turmoil. Harmondsworth. 1971.

22826 HERRIOTT (ROBERT EUGENE) and ST JOHN (NANCY HOYT). Social Class and the Urban School: The Impact of Pupil Background on Teachers and Principals. 1966.

22827 TUCKER (NICHOLAS). Understanding the Mass Media: A Practical Approach for Teaching. Camb. 1966.

22828 MUSGROVE (FRANK). The Family, Education and Society. 1966.

22829 HOWSON (GEOFFREY). A History of Mathematics Teaching in England. Camb. 1982.

22830 COOPER (BARRY). Renegotiating Secondary School Mathematics: A Study of Curriculum Change and Stability. Lond./Philadelphia, Pa. 1985.

22831 MIDWINTER (ERIC CLARE). Schools in Society: The Evolution of English Education. 1980.

22832 RAY (JOHN). The Growth of Schools: 1750 to the Present Day. 1972.

22833 FLOUD (JEAN E.) ed. Social Class and Educational Opportunity. 1956.

22834 SARAN (RENE). Policy-Making in Secondary Education: A Case Study. Oxf. 1973.

22835 AINSWORTH (MARJORIE E.) and BATTEN (ERIC J.). The Effects of Environmental Factors on Secondary

Educational Attainment in Manchester: A Plowden Follow-up. 1974.

22836 MAYS (JOHN BARRON). Education and the Urban Child. Liverpool. 1982.

22837 —— Half a Future. 1963.

22838 —— Education and Schooling. 1975.

22839 RICHMOND (W. KENNETH). The Education Industry. 1969.

9. REFERENCE

22840 BARON (GEORGE). Society, Schools and Progress in England. 1965.

22841 RUTTER (MICHAEL), TIZARD (JACK), and WHITMORE (KINGSLEY). Education, Health and Behaviour. 1970.

22842 COHEN (LOUIS), THOMAS (JOHN), and MANION (LAWRENCE) eds. Educational Research and Development in Britain 1970–1980. Windsor. 1982.

22843 GORDON (PETER) ed. The Study of Education: A Collection of Inaugural Lectures. 2 vols. 1980.

22844 SMITH (JAMES V.). The Meritocratic Intellect: Studies in the History of Educational Research. Aberd. 1980.

22845 GOSDEN (P. H. J. H.). How they were Taught: An Anthology of Contemporary Accounts of Learning and Teaching in England 1800–1950. Oxf. 1969.

22846 BUTCHER (H. J.) ed. Educational Research in Britain. 1968.

22847 BUTCHER (H. J.) and PONT (H. B.). Educational Research in Britain, 3. 1973.

22848 TAYLOR (WILLIAM) ed. Research Perspectives in Education. 1973.

22849 PETERS (R. S.). Education and the Education of Teachers. 1977.

22850 WILSON (JOHN). Philosophy and Practical Education. 1977.

22851 BRENT (ALLEN). Philosophical Foundations for the Curriculum. 1978.

22852 —— Philosophy and Educational Foundations. 1981.

22853 COOPER (DAVID E.). Illusions of Equality. 1980.

22854 BAILLY (CHARLES) and BUDGES (DAVID). Mixed Ability Grouping: A Philosophical Perspective. 1983.

22855 BANTOCK (G. HERMAN). Studies in the History of Educational Theory. Vol. 2 The Minds and the Masses 1760–1980. 1984.

22856 CHAZAN (MAURICE), MOORE (TERENCE), WILLIAMS (PHILIP), and WRIGHT (JACK). The Practice of Educational Psychology. 1974.

22857 BARON (GEORGE). A Bibliographical Guide to the English Educational System. 1951. 3rd edn 1965.

22858 BELL (ROBERT ELLIOTT) ed. Education in Great Britain and Ireland: A Source Book. 1973.

22859 RICHMOND (WILLIAM KENNETH). The Literature of Education: A Critical Bibliography, 1945–1970. 1972.

22860 YEAR BOOK OF EDUCATION. 1932—Annual.

22861 BRITISH EDUCATION INDEX. 1954—3 times a year, cumulates annually.

22862 BARNARD (HOWARD CLIVE) and LAUWERYS (JOSEPH ALBERT) comps. A Hand Book of British Educational Terms, Including an Outline of the British Educational System. 1963.

22863 LIVERPOOL UNIVERSITY (INSTITUTE OF EDUCATION). British Government Publications Concerning Education: An Introductory Guide. 1966.

22864 MAY (JONATHAN). A Student's Guide to the Development of Education in England and Wales. 1968. 2nd edn 1970.

22865 BOYD (WILLIAM) and RAWSON (WYATT TREVELYAN). The Story of the New Education. 1965.

22866 BELL (ROBERT ELLIOTT) and GRANT (NIGEL DUNCAN CAMERON). Patterns of Education in the British Isles. 1977.

22867 SMITH (WILLIAM OWEN LESTER). Compulsory Education in England. Paris. 1951.

22868 —— Education in Great Britain. 1949.

22869 RAY (JOHN). The Growth of School: 1750 to the Present Day. 1972.

22870 MINISTRY OF EDUCATION. Education, 1900–1950: The Report of the Ministry of Education. 1951.

22871 MINISTRY OF EDUCATION. Education in 1963. 1964.

22872 WATERHOUSE (RACHEL ELIZABETH). The Birmingham and Midland Institute, 1854–1954. Birm. 1954.

10. EDUCATION AND RELIGION

22873 MURPHY (JAMES). The Religious Problem in English Education: The Crucial Experiment. Liverpool. 1959.

22874 —— Church, State and Schools in Britain, 1800–1970. 1971.

22875 CRUICKSHANK (MARJORIE). Church and State in English Education, 1870 to the Present Day. 1963.

22876 HULME (ANTHONY). School in Church and State. 1960.

22877 NIBLETT (WILLIAM ROY). Christian Education in a Secular Society. 1960.

22878 —— ed. Moral Education in a Changing Society. 1963.

22879 BROWN (CHARLES KENNETH FRANCIS). The Church's Part in Education, 1833–1941. With special reference to the work of the National Society. 1942.

22880 BELL (ENID HESTER CHATAWAY MOBERLY). A History of the Church Schools Company, 1883–1958. 1958.

22881 BARNES (ARTHUR STAPYLTON). The Catholic Schools of England. 1926.

22882 EVENNETT (HENRY OUTRAM). The Catholic Schools of England and Wales. Camb. 1944.

22883 CHADWICK (HUBERT). St Omers to Stonyhurst: A History of Two Centuries. 1962.

22884 McCANN (PHILIP JUSTIN) *and* CARY-ELWES (COLUMBA) *eds.* Ampleforth and its Origins: Essays. 1952.

22885 LEVI (PETER). Beaumont 1861–1961. 1961.

22886 BATTERSBY (WILLIAM JOHN). The De La Salle Brothers in Great Britain: The Story of a Century of Effort and Achievement in the Domain of English Education. 1954.

22887 LEETHAM (C. R.). 'Purpose of the Catholic Public School'. *Wiseman Rev.* 491 (1962), 88–95.

22888 CLARKE (WILLIAM KEMP LOWTHER). A History of the S.P.C.K. 1959.

22889 BROTHERS (JOAN). Church and School: A Study of the Impact of Education on Religion. L/pool. 1964.

22890 SPERRY (WILLIAM LEAROYD). Religion and Education. 1971.

22891 BATTERSBY (W. J.). 'Educational Work of the Religious Orders of Women, 1850–1950'.

22892 —— 'Secondary Education for Boys'. Both in The English Catholics, 1850–1950, by George Andrew Beck. 1950.

22893 WHEELER (GORDON). 'Catholics and the Universities'. *New Blackfriars* 46 (1964), 78–81.

22894 BOYLE (J. D.). 'Education: The Catholic Contribution'. *Month* 30 (1963), 281–91.

22895 CARRIGAN (DELIA). The Catholic Teachers' Colleges in the United Kingdom, 1850–1960. Washington, D.C. 1961.

22896 PRITCHARD (FRANK CYRIL). Methodist Secondary Education: A History of the Contribution of Methodism to Secondary Education in the United Kingdom. 1949.

22897 —— The Story of Woodhouse Grove School. Bradford. 1978.

22898 BAKER (D.). Partnership in Excellence: A Late-Victorian Educational Venture—The Leys School, Cambridge 1873–1975. Camb. 1975.

22899 STEWART (WILLIAM ALEXANDER CAMPBELL). Quakers and Education, As Seen in their Schools in England. 1953.

22900 STROUD (L. JOHN). 'Friends and Some Aspects of Education'. *Friends Q.* 20 (1978), 379–86.

22901 STEINBERG (B.). 'Jewish Education in Great Britain during World War II'. *Jew. Soc. Studs* 29 (1967), 27–63.

22902 IQBAL (M.). 'Ethnicity and Ethnic Groups: Education and Islam in Britain, a Muslim View'. *New Community* 5 (1977), 397–404.

22903 CANNON (CHARMIAN). 'The Influence of Religion on Educational Policy, 1902–1944'. *Brit. J. Educ. Studs* 12 (1964), 143–60.

22904 DAVIS (ROBERT) *ed.* Woodbrooke, 1903–1953: A Brief History of a Quaker Experiment in Religious Education. 1953.

22905 SUTHERLAND (GEORGE ARTHUR). Dalton Hall: A Quaker Venture. 1963.

22906 RANDLES (RALPH H. S.). History of the Friends' School, Lancaster. Lancaster. 1982.

22907 BROWN (SIDNEY WILLIAM). Leighton Park: A History of the School. 1952.

11. EXAMINATIONS

22908 JENKINS (E. W.). 'Public Examinations and Science Teaching Methods in Grammar Schools since 1918'. *Durham Res. Rev.* 6 (1971), 548–56.

22909 WATKINS (K. W.). 'The Politics of Examinations (with particular reference to the C.S.E.)'. *Pol. Q.* 36 (1965), 59–66.

22910 NUTTALL (DESMOND LEWES). The 1968 CSE Monitoring Experiment. 1971.

22911 SUTHERLAND (GILLIAN RAY). 'Measuring Intelligence: English Local Education Authorities and Mental Testing, 1919–1939'. In Biology, Medicine and Society 1840–1940. C. Webster *ed.* 315–35. Camb. 1981.

22912 —— 'The Magic of Measurement: Mental Testing and English Education, 1900–1940'. *Trans. Roy. Hist. Soc.* 5th ser. 27 (1977), 155–72.

22913 ROACH (JOHN PETER CHARLES). 'Examinations and the Secondary Schools 1900–1945'. *Hist. Educ.* 8 (1979), 45–58.

22914 FISHER (P.). External Examinations in Secondary Schools in England and Wales 1944–1964. Leeds. 1982.

22915 MONTGOMERY (ROBERT JOHN). Examinations: An Account of their Evolution as Administrative Devices in England. 1965.

22916 WISEMAN (STEPHEN) *ed.* Examinations and English Education. Manchester. 1961.

22917 PETCH (JAMES ALEXANDER). Fifty Years of Examining: The Joint Matriculation Board, 1903–1953. 1953.

22918 RADFORD (H. GORDON). 'The Certificate of Secondary Education'. *Higher Ed. J.* 14 (1963), 6–9.

12. EDUCATION: POLITICS

22919 PARKINSON (MICHAEL). The Labour Party and the Organisation of Secondary Education, 1918–1965. 1970.

22920 BARKER (RODNEY STEVEN). Education and Politics, 1900–1951: A Study of the Labour Party. Oxf. 1972.

22921 GRIGGS (CLIVE). The Trades Union Congress and the Struggle for Education 1868–1925. 1983.

22922 KOGAN (MAURICE). The Politics of Educational Change. Manch. 1978.

22923 GARDNER (D. E. M.). Susan Isaacs. 1969.

13. SECONDARY MODERN, COMPREHENSIVE, GRAMMAR SCHOOLS

22924 TAWNEY (R. H.) *ed.* Secondary Education for All: A Policy for Labour. 1922.

22925 HUGHES (BILLY) *and* RUBINSTEIN (DAVID). 'Labour Governments and Comprehensive Schooling, 1945–51'. *Hist. Workshop* 7 (1979), 156–69.

22926 BENN (CAROLINE). 'Comprehensive School Reform and the 1945 Labour Government'. *Hist. Workshop* 10 (1980), 197–204.

22927 GRIER (LYNDA). 'The Evolution of Secondary Education in England'. *Advancement of Science* 4 (1947), 255–64.

22928 DENT (HAROLD COLLETT). 'English Secondary Education: Retrospect and Prospect'. *J. Roy. Soc. Arts* 112 (1964), 728–43.

22929 JUDGE (HARRY). A Generation of Schooling: English Secondary Schools since 1944. Oxf. 1984.

22930 GRAY (JOHN), MCPHERSON (ANDREW F.), *and* RAFFE (DAVID J.). Reconstructions of Secondary Education: Theory, Myth and Practice since the War. 1983.

22931 BANTOCK (G. H.). 'The Reorganisation of Secondary Education'. *Advan. Sci.* 17 (1960), 133–9.

22932 KNEEBONE (RICHARD MELVIN TAYLOR). I Work in a Secondary Modern School. 1957.

22933 TAYLOR (WILLIAM). The Secondary Modern School. 1963.

22934 LOUKES (HAROLD). Secondary Modern. 1956.

22935 CHAPMAN (J. VINCENT). Your Secondary Modern Schools: An Account of their Work in the Late 1950s. 1959.

22936 BANKS (OLIVE). Parity and Prestige in English Secondary Education. 1955.

22937 MANDER (JOHN). Old Bottles and New Wine: A Talk about Secondary Modern Schools. 1948.

22938 BANKS (OLIVE) *and* FINLAYSON (DOUGLAS). Success and Failure in the Secondary School. 1973.

22939 HOLLY (DOUGLAS). Society, Schools and Humanity: The Changing World of Secondary Education. 1971.

22940 ACKSON (BRIAN) *and* MARSDEN (DENNIS). Education and the Working Class. 1962.

22941 BERNBAUM (GERALD). Social Change and the Schools, 1918–1944. 1967.

22942 FORD (JULIENNE). Social Class and the Comprehensive School. 1969.

22943 DOUGLAS (J. W. B.), ROSS (J. M.), *and* SIMPSON (H. R.). All our Future: A Longitudinal Study of Secondary Education. 1968.

22944 BUNTON (WILLIAM JAMES). Comprehensive Education: A Select, Annotated Bibliography. Windsor. 1971.

22945 SIMON (BRIAN). The Common Secondary School. 1955.

22946 PEDLEY (ROBIN) *ed.* Comprehensive Schools Today: An Interim Survey. 1955.

22947 —— Comprehensive Education: A New Approach. 1956.

22948 —— The Comprehensive School. Harmondsworth. 1967. 3rd edn 1979.

22949 VERNON (PHILIP EWART) *ed.* Secondary School Selection. 1957.

22950 COLE (ROGER). Comprehensive Schools in Action. 1964.

22951 GROSS (RICHARD EDMUND) *ed.* British Secondary Education: Overview and Appraisal. 1965.

22952 BERG (LEILA). Risinghill: Death of a Comprehensive School. Harmondsworth. 1968.

22953 MONKS (THOMAS GORDON). Comprehensive Education in England and Wales: A Survey of Schools and their Organisation. 1968.

22954 RUBINSTEIN (DAVID) *and* SIMON (BRIAN). The Evolution of the Comprehensive School, 1926–1966. 1969. 2nd edn 1973 [to 1972.].

22955 ELTON (E. A.). Secondary Education in the East Riding of Yorkshire, 1944–1974. 1974.

22956 ECCLES (P. R.). 'Secondary Reorganisation in Tynemouth, 1962–69'. *J. Educ. Admin. Hist.* 6 (1974), 35–44.

22957 BRYANT (MARGARET E.). The London Experience of Secondary Education. 1986.

22958 BOURNE (RICHARD). 'Going Comprehensive in Greater London'. *London J.* 2 (1976), 85–96.

22959 BENN (CAROLINE) *and* SIMON (BRIAN). Half Way There—Report on the British Comprehensive School Reform. 1970. 2nd edn 1972.

22960 BATLEY (RICHARD) *et al.* Going Comprehensive: Educational Policy-Making in Two County Boroughs. 1970.

22961 HEWITSON (JOHN). The Grammar School Tradition in a Comprehensive World. 1961.

22962 HALSALL (ELIZABETH) *ed.* Becoming Comprehensive: Case Histories. Oxf. 1970.

22963 GRIFFITHS (ALUN). Secondary School Reorganisation in England and Wales. 1970.

22964 BROWN (R. J.) *and* RIBBINS (P. M.). 'Policy Making in English Local Government: The Case of Secondary School Reorganisation'. *Public Admin.* 57 (1979), 182–202.

22965 BATLEY (RICHARD), O'BRIEN (OSWALD), *and* PARRIS (HENRY). Going Comprehensive: Educational Policy-Making in Two County Boroughs. 1972. [A comparison of Gateshead with Darlington.].

22966 MARSDEN (DENNIS). Politicians, Equality and Comprehensives. 1971.

22967 BALDWIN (RAYMOND WHITTIER). The Great Comprehensive Gamble: Statistics of Secondary Education Examinations, 1966–1973. 1975.

22968 WOODS (R.). 'Margaret Thatcher and Secondary Reorganisation'. *J. Educ. Admin Hist.* 13 (1981), 33–42.

22969 FENWICK (IAN GRAHAM KEITH). The Comprehensive School, 1944–1970: The Politics of Secondary School Reorganization. 1976.

22970 BURGESS (ROBERT G.). Experiencing Comprehensive Education: A Study of Bishop McGregor School. 1983.

22971 TAYLOR (W.). 'The Changing Social Function of the English Secondary Modern School'. *Inl J. Comp. Sociol.* 2 (1961), 176–87.

22972 DAVIES (HUNTER). The Creighton Report: A Year in the Life of a Comprehensive School. 1976.

22973 DAWSON (PETER). Making a Comprehensive Work. Oxf. 1981.

22974 PISSARIDES (C. A.). 'Staying on at School in England and Wales'. *Economica* 48 (1981), 345–63.

22975 LELLO (JOHN). 'The Comprehensive Schools: A Summary of Opinions'. *Contemp. Rev.* 201 (1962), 72–8.

22976 BILSKI (RAPHAELLA). 'Ideology and the Comprehensive Schools'. *Pol. Q.* 44 (1973), 197–211.

22977 O'CONNELL (P. J.). 'Comprehensive Schools and the Catholic Community'. *Blackfriars* 45 (1964), 76–80.

22978 DAVIES (HAROLD). The Boys' Grammar School Today and Tomorrow. 1945.

22979 CAMPBELL (FLANN CANMER). Eleven Plus and All That: The Grammar School in a Changing Society. 1956.

22980 YATES (ALFRED) *and* PIDGEON (D. A.). Admission to Grammar Schools. 1957.

22981 STEVENS (FRANCES M.). The Living Tradition: The Social and Educational Assumptions of the Grammar School. 1960.

22982 DAVIES (HAROLD). Culture and the Grammar School. 1965.

22983 DALE (REGINALD ROWLAND) *and* GRIFFITH (STEPHEN). Down Stream: Failure in the Grammar School. 1965.

22984 WHITFIELD (GEORGE). 'The Grammar Schools through Half a Century'. *Brit. J. Educ. Studs* 5 (1957), 101–18.

22985 DAVIS (ROBIN). The Grammar School. Harmondsworth. 1967.

22986 GALLIE (WALTER BRYCE). An English School. 1949.

22987 JONES (ARTHUR EDWARD). A Small School in the Great War: The Story of Sutton County School and its Old Boys in World War One. Carshalton. 1975.

22988 KING (RONALD). Values and Involvement in a Grammar School. 1969.

22989 STEVENS (FRANCES M.). The New Inheritors: Some Questions about the Education of Intelligent 'First Generation' Children. 1970.

22990 NISBET (JOHN D.) *and* ENTWISTLE (NOEL JAMES). Age of Transfer to Secondary Education. 1966.

22991 —— The Transition to Secondary Education. 1969. [Scotland.].

22992 WALLIS (PETER JOHN). Histories of Old Schools: A Revised List for England and Wales. Newcastle. 1966.

22993 RUMSBY (THOMAS WALTER). The English Grammar School. 1938.

22994 BRISTOL. Charles Peter Hill, The History of Bristol Grammar School. 1951.

22995 HAMPTON. Bernard Garside, A Brief History of Hampton School, 1557–1957. 1957.

22996 HULL. John Lawson, A Town Grammar School through Six Centuries: A History of Hull Grammar School against its Local Background. 1963.

22997 LOUGHBOROUGH. Bernard Elliott, The History of Loughborough College School. Loughb. 1971.

22998 MANCHESTER. James Anson Graham and Brian Arthur Phythian *eds.* The Manchester Grammar School, 1515–1965. Manch. 1965.

22999 NOTTINGHAM. Adam Waugh Thomas, A History of Nottingham High School, 1513–1953. Nottingham. 1957.

23000 RUTHERFORD. William Maw, The Story of Rutherford Grammar School, Newcastle upon Tyne. 1964.

23001 WORCESTER. Frederick Vernon Follett, A History of the Worcester Royal Grammar School. Worcester. 1951.

14. PREPARATORY SCHOOLS

23002 MASTERS (PHILIP LESLIE). Preparatory Schools Today. 1966.

23003 KENWARD (JAMES). Preparatory School. 1958.

23004 LEINSTER-MACKAY (DONALD). The Rise of the English Preparatory School. 1984.

15. PUBLIC SCHOOLS

23005 The Public and Preparatory Schools Year Book: The Official Book of Reference for the Headmasters' Conference and of the Incorporated Association of Preparatory Schools. 1891+ [Now titled 'Independent Schools Year Book'.].

23006 WILKINS (HAROLD TOM). Great English Schools. 1925.

23007 DARWIN (BERNARD RICHARD MEIRION). The English Public School. 1929.

23008 RODGERS (JOHN CHARLES). The Old Public Schools of England. 1938.

23009 MACK (EDWARD CLARENCE). Public Schools and British Opinion since 1860. 1942. New edn NY. 1971.

23010 PARTRIDGE (EDWARD HINCKS). Freedom in Education: The Function of the Public Boarding School. 1943.

23011 FLEMING REPORT. The Public Schools and the General Educational System. 1944.

23012 LEESON (SPENCER SPOTTISBURY GWATKIN) *Bishop of Peterborough*. The Public School Question. 1948.

23013 GILKES (ANTHONY NEWCOMBE). Independent Education: In Defence of Public Schools. 1957.

23014 OGILVIE (VIVIAN). The English Public School. 1957.

23015 SNOW (GEORGE D'OYLY). The Public School in the New Age. 1959.

23016 DANCY (JOHN CHRISTOPHER). The Public Schools and the Future. 1963.

23017 CHILD (H. A. T.) *ed*. The Independent Progressive School. 1962.

23018 NEWSOM REPORT. The Public Schools Commission First Report. 1966.

23019 KALTON (GRAHAM). The Public Schools: A Factual Survey of the Headmasters' Conference Schools in England and Wales. 1966.

23020 WEINBERG (IAN). The English Public Schools: The Sociology of an Elite Education. NY. 1967.

23021 LAMBERT (ROYSTON). The Hothouse Society: An Exploration of Boarding School Life through the Boys' and Girls' own Writings. 1968.

23022 FRASER (WILLIAM RAE). Residential Education. Oxf. 1968.

23023 BAMFORD (THOMAS WILLIAM). Rise of the Public Schools: A Study of Boys' Public Boarding Schools in England and Wales from 1837 to the Present Day. 1967.

23024 —— Public School Data: A Compilation of Data on Public and Related Schools (Boys) Mainly from 1866. Hull. 1974.

23025 HOWARTH (THOMAS EDWARD BRODIE). Culture, Anarchy and the Public Schools. 1969.

23026 GLENNERSTER (HOWARD). Paying for Private Schools. 1970.

23027 DONNISON REPORT. The Public Schools Commission Second Report. 3 vols. 1970.

23028 GARDNER (ROBERT BRIAN). The Public Schools: An Historical Survey. 1973.

23029 GATHORNE-HARDY (JONATHAN). The Public School Phenomenon, 1597–1977. 1977.

23030 WALFORD (GEOFFREY) *ed*. British Public Schools: Policy and Practice. 1984.

23031 NEWSOME (DAVID HAY). 'Public Schools and Christian Ideals'. *Theology* 64 (1961), 486–92.

23032 EDE (J. CHUTER). 'The Place of the Public Schools in our Educational System'. *Hibbert J.* 60 (1962), 91–109.

23033 LUNT (R. G.). 'The Public Schools Question'. *Hibbert J.* 40 (1962), 110–15.

23034 WILKINSON (RUPERT HUGH). 'The Future of the Public Schools: A Reply'. *Encounter* 23 (1964), 90–1.

23035 WATT (DAVID). 'The Fate of the Public Schools'. *Encounter* 22 (1964), 61–5.

23036 WARD (DAVID). 'The Public Schools and Industry in Britain after 1870'. *J. Contemp. Hist.* 2 (1967), 37–52.

23037 SZERETER (R.). 'A Note on the Staffing of the Public Schools, 1939–1964'. *Brit. J. Sociol.* 18 (1967), 187–90.

23038 OTLEY (C. B.). 'Militarism and Militarization in the Public Schools, 1900–1972'. *Brit. J. Sociol.* 29 (1978), 321–39.

23039 WILKINSON (RUPERT HUGH). The Prefects: British Leadership and the Public School Tradition: A Comparative Study in the Making of Rulers. 1964.

23040 BOYD (DAVID). Elites and their Education. Windsor. 1973.

23041 WAKEFORD (JOHN). The Cloistered Elite: A Sociological Analysis of the English Public Boarding School. 1969.

23042 RAE (JOHN). The Public School Revolution: Britain's Independent Schools, 1964–1979. 1981.

23043 ARDINGLY. Reginald Perry, Ardingly, 1858–1946: A History of the School. 1951.

23044 BRADFIELD. J. Blackie, Bradfield, 1850–1975. Bradfield. 1976.

23045 BRENTWOOD. R. R. Lewis, The History of Brentwood School. Brentwood. 1981.

23046 BROMSGROVE. Henry Edward McLaughlan Icely, Bromsgrove School through the Centuries. Oxf. 1953.

23047 BRYANSTON. M. C. Morgan, Bryanston, 1929–1978. Blandford. 1978.

23048 CHARTERHOUSE. Edward Mellor Jameson, Charterhouse. 1937.

23049 —— William Foster Veale, From a New Angle: Reminiscences of Charterhouse, 1880–1945. Winchester. 1957.

23050 CHELTENHAM. M. C. Morgan, Cheltenham College: The First Hundred Years. 1968.

23051 CHRIST'S HOSPITAL. George A. T. Allan, Christ's Hospital. 1927.

23052 —— The Christ's Hospital Book. 1953.

23053 CITY OF LONDON. Aubrey Edward Douglas-Smith, The City of London School. Oxf. 1937. 2nd edn 1965.

23054 CLIFTON. Nicholas Geoffrey Lemprière Hammond, *ed*. Centenary Essays on Clifton College. Bristol. 1962.

23055 —— Octavius Francis, A History of Clifton College, 1860–1934. 1935.

23056 DULWICH. Sheila Hodges, God's Gift: A Living History of Dulwich College. 1981.

23057 ELTHAM. C. Witting, *ed.* A History of Eltham College for the Sons of Missionaries. 1952.

23058 ETON. Maurice Christopher Hollis, Eton: A History. 1960.

23059 —— Richard Ollard, An English Education: A Perspective of Eton. 1982.

23060 FELSTED. Michael Rommily Craze, The History of Felsted School, 1564–1947. Ipswich. 1955.

23061 HAILEYBURY. Robert Leslie Ashcroft, Haileybury, 1908–1961. Haileybury. 1961.

23062 HARROW. Edward Dalrymple Laborde, Harrow School: Yesterday and Today. 1948.

23063 KING EDWARD'S, BIRMINGHAM. Thomas Winter Hutton, King Edward's School, Birmingham, 1552–1952. Oxf. 1952.

23064 LANCING. Basil Walter Thomas Handford, Lancing: A History of S.S. Mary and Nicolas College, Lancing, 1848–1930. Oxf. 1933.

23065 MALVERN. Ralph Klaus Blumenau, A History of Malvern College, 1865 to 1965. 1965.

23066 MARLBOROUGH. H. C. Brentnall *and* E. G. H. Kempson, *eds.* Marlborough College, 1843–1943. Camb. 1943.

23067 MERCHANT TAYLORS'. Frederick William Marsden Draper, Four Centuries of Merchant Taylors' School, 1561–1961. 1962.

23068 MILL HILL. John Clyde Goodfellow Binfield, 'Et Virtutem et Musas: Mill Hill School and the Great War'. Studies in Church History, 20 (1983), 351–82.

23069 OUNDLE. William George Walker, A History of the Oundle Schools. 1956.

23070 POCKLINGTON. Percy Cooper Sands *and* Christopher Matthew Haworth, A History of Pocklington School, East Yorkshire, 1514–1950. 1951.

23071 RADLEY. Alfred Kenneth Boyd, The History of Radley College, 1847–1947. Oxf. 1948.

23072 ROSSALL. William Furness, *ed.* The Centenary History of Rossall School. Aldershot. 1945.

23073 RUGBY. John Barclay Hope Simpson, Rugby since Arnold: A History of Rugby School from 1842. 1967.

23074 —— Claude Ronald Evers, Rugby. 1939.

23075 SEDBERGH. Henry Lowther Clarke, History of Sedbergh School, 1525–1925. Sedburgh. 1925.

23076 SHERBORNE. Arthur Bellyse Gourlay, A History of Sherborne School. Winchester. 1951.

23077 SHREWSBURY. James Basil Oldham, A History of Shrewsbury School 1552–1952. Oxf. 1952.

23078 TAUNTON. S. P. Record, Proud Century: The First Hundred Years of Taunton School. Taunton. 1948.

23079 TONBRIDGE. David Churchill Somervell, A History of Tonbridge School. 1947.

23080 U.C.S. LONDON. H. J. K. Usher *et al.* An Angel without Wings: The History of University College School, 1830–1980. 1981.

23081 VICTORIA. D. J. Cotterill. Victoria College, Jersey, 1852–1972. Chichester. 1977.

23082 WELLINGTON. David Hay Newsome, A History of Wellington College, 1859–1959. 1959.

23083 WESTMINSTER. John Dudley Carleton, Westminster. 1938. Rev. edn 1965.

23084 —— Lawrence Edward Tanner, Westminster School. 1934. 2nd edn 1951.

23085 WINCHESTER. John D'Ewes Evelyn Firth, Winchester College. 1949.

23086 —— Thomas James Henderson Bishop *and* Rupert Hugh Wilkinson, Winchester and the Public School Elite: A Statistical Analysis. 1967.

23087 —— Roger Custance, Winchester College: Sixth-Centenary Essays. Oxf. 1982.

23088 GARDINER (DOROTHY). English Girlhood at School. 1929.

23089 KAMM (JOSEPHINE). Hope Deferred: Girls' Education in English History. 1965.

23090 TURNER (BARRY). Equality for Some: The Story of Girls' Education. 1974.

23091 KAMM (JOSEPHINE). Indicative Past: A Hundred Years of the Girls' Public Day School Trust. 1971.

23092 OLLERENSHAW (*Dame* KATHLEEN). The Girls' Schools. 1967.

23093 GLENDAY (NONITA) *and* PRICE (MARY). Reluctant Revolutionaries: A Century of Head Mistresses, 1874–1974. 1974.

23094 NEWSON (SIR JOHN HUBERT). The Education of Girls. 1948.

23095 MARLAND (MICHAEL) *ed.* Sex Differentiation and Schooling. 1983.

23096 STEWART (WILLIAM ALEXANDER CAMPBELL) *and* MCCANN (WILLIAM PHILIP). The Educational Innovators. Vol. II Progressive Schools, 1881–1967. 1968.

23097 —— Progressives and Radicals in English Education, 1750–1950. 1 vol. 1972.

23098 SKIDELSKY (ROBERT JACOB ALEXANDER). English Progressive Schools. Harmondsworth. 1969.

23099 ABBOTSHOLME. Bernard Mordaunt Ward, Reddie of Abbotsholme. 1934.

23100 BEDALES. Geoffrey Crump, Bedales since the War. 1936.

23101 —— John Haden Badley, Memories and Reflections. 1955.

23102 —— James L. Henderson, Irregularly Bold: A Study of Bedales School. 1978.

23103 DARTINGTON HALL. Victor Bonham-Carter, Dartington Hall: The History of an Experiment. 1958.

23104 —— Anthony Emery, Dartington Hall. Oxf. 1970.

23105 —— M. Young, The Elmhirsts of Dartington: The Creation of a Utopian Community. 1982.

23106 SUMMERHILL. Alexander Sutherland Neill, That Dreadful School. 1937.

23107 —— Summerhill: A Radical Approach to Education. 1962.

16. SCHOOLS FOR GIRLS

23108 CLARKE (AMY KEY). A History of the Cheltenham Ladies' College, 1853–1953. 1953.

23109 CANDLER (W. I.) *et al.* King Edward VI High School for Girls, Birmingham, pt. I, 1883–1925. 1928. Pt. 2, 1926–1970. 1971.

23110 SCRIMGEOUR (RUBY MARGARET) *ed.* North London Collegiate School, 1850–1950. 1950.

23111 DE ZOUCHE (DOROTHY EVA). Roedean School, 1885–1955. Brighton. 1955.

23112 LAUREL BANK SCHOOL, 1903–1953. Glasgow. 1953.

23113 KAMM (JOSEPHINE). Indicative Past: A Hundred Years of the Girls' Public Day School Trust. 1971.

23114 OLLERENSHAW (*Dame* KATHLEEN MARY). The Girls' Schools. 1967.

23115 RIDLER (ANNE) Olive Willis and Downe Honse. 1967.

17. EDUCATION: HANDICAPS

23116 AXFORD (WENDY ANNE) *comp.* Handicapped Children in Britain: Their Problems and Education; Books and Articles Published in Great Britain from the 1944 Education Act to 1958. 1959.

23117 PRITCHARD (DAVID GWYN). Education and the Handicapped, 1760–1960. 1963.

23118 JACKSON (STEPHEN). Special Education in England and Wales. 1966.

23119 BELL (DONALD) *ed.* An Experiment in Education: The History of Worcester College for the Blind, 1866–1966. 1967.

23120 DAYNES (EDWARD). The Growth of Special Education in London. 1970.

23121 PALFREY (COLIN). 'Remedial Education and the Adult Offender'. *Howard J.* 14 (1974), 78–85.

23122 BRIDGES (SYDNEY ALEXANDER). Gifted Children and the Brentwood Experiment. 1969.

23123 MIDWINTER (ERIC CLARE). Projections: An Educational Priority Area at Work. 1972.

23124 —— Priority Education: An Account of the Liverpool Project. Harmondsworth. 1972.

23125 BROOKS (ROBERT). Bright Delinquents: The Story of a Unique School (A Longitudinal Study of the Outcome of the Work of Kneesworth Hall School, 1953–1970). Slough. 1972.

23126 HOGAN (JAMES MARTIN). Impelled into Experiences: The Story of the Outward Bound Schools. 1968.

23127 HEAD (DAVID) *ed.* Free Way to Learning: Educational Alternatives in Action. Harmondsworth. 1974.

18. EDUCATION: YOUNG CHILDREN

23128 WHITBREAD (NANETTE). The Evolution of the Nursery-infant School: A History of Infant and Nursery Education in Great Britain, 1800–1970. 1972.

23129 TIZARD (BARBARA). Pre-school Education in Great Britain: A Research Review. 1975.

23130 TIZARD (JACK) *et al.* All our Children: Pre-school Services in a Changing Society. 1976.

23131 SHARP (RACHEL) *et al.* Education and Social Control: A Study in Progressive Primary Education. 1975.

23132 SELLECK (RICHARD JOSEPH WHEELER). English Primary Education and the Progressives, 1914–1939. 1972.

23133 BRANDIS (WALTER) *and* BERNSTEIN (BASIL). Selection and Control: Teachers' Ratings of Children in the Infant School. 1974.

23134 YARDLEY (ALICE). The Infant School. 1973.

23135 RUSK (ROBERT ROBERTSON). A History of Infant Education. 1933.

23136 ROSS (ALEXANDER MICHAEL). The Education of Childhood: The Primary School of Today, its Growth and Work. 1960.

23137 RAYMONT (THOMAS). A History of the Education of Young Children. 1937.

23138 PLOWDEN REPORT. Children and their Primary Schools: A Report of the Central Advisory Council for Education (England). 2 vols 1967.

23139 CRAFT (MAURICE), RAYNOR (JOHN), *and* COHEN (LOUIS) *eds.* Linking Home with School. 1967. 3rd edn 1980.

23140 RAZZEL (ARTHUR GEORGE). Juniors: A Postscript to Plowden. Harmondsworth. 1968.

23141 NEWSON (JOHN), NEWSON (ELIZABETH), *with* BARNES (PETER). Perspectives on School at Seven Years Old. 1977.

23142 KENT (JILL) *and* KENT (PENDARELL). Nursery Schools for All. 1970.

23143 HOWE (ELSPETH). Under 5: A Report on Nursery Education. 1966.

23144 LUNN (JOAN C. BARKER). Streaming in the Primary School. 1970.

23145 RICHARDS (COLIN) *comp.* The Study of Primary Education: A Source Book. Vol. 1 1984.

23146 HIGGINSON (JAMES HENRY). Changing Thought in Primary and Secondary Education. 1969.

23147 CROWE (BRENDA). The Playgroup Movement: A Report. 1971.

23148 H.M. INSPECTORS OF SCHOOLS. Primary Education in England. 1978.

23149 CLEGG (Sir ALEC) ed. The Changing Primary School: Its Problems and Priorities: A Statement by Teachers. 1972.

23150 CHAZAN (MAURICE) ed. Aspects of Primary Education. Cardiff. 1972.

23151 BRAMWELL (RUPERT DENIS). Elementary School Work 1900–1925. Durham. 1961.

23152 BRADBURN (ELIZABETH). Margaret McMillan: Framework and Expansion of Nursery Education. Redhill. 1976.

23153 BOARD OF EDUCATION. Consultative Committee on the Primary School. 1931.

23154 BLYTH (WILLIAM ALAN LANDSELL). English Primary Education: A Sociological Description. 2 vols. 1965.

23155 BLACKSTONE (TESSA ANN VOSPER). A Fair Start: The Provision of Pre-school Education. 1971.

23156 BLACKIE (JOHN ERNEST HALDANE). Transforming the Primary School. 1974.

23157 —— Inside the Primary School. 1967.

23158 AULD (ROBIN). The William Tyndale Junior and Infants Schools: A Report of the Public Inquiry. 1976.

23159 SCHOOLS COUNCIL/FORD FOUNDATION. British Primary Schools Today. 3 vols. 1972.

23160 ANON. Rising Standards in Scottish Primary Schools 1953–63. 1968.

23161 GRETTON (JOHN) and JACKSON (MARK). William Tyndale: Collapse of a School or a System. 1976.

23162 ELLIS (TERRY), HADDOW (BRIAN), MCWHIRTER (JACKIE), and MCCOLGAN (DOROTHY). William Tyndale—the Teachers' Story. 1976.

23163 EYKEN (WILLEM VAN DER). The Pre-school Years. Harmondsworth. 1967.

23164 BRUNER (JEROME SEYMOUR). Under Five in Britain. 1980.

23165 CROWE (BRENDA). The Playgroup Movement. 1973.

23166 JACKSON (BRIAN) and JACKSON (SONIA). Childminder: A Study in Action Research. 1979.

23167 CLARK (MARGARET M.) and CHEYNE (WILLIAM M.). Studies in Pre-school Education: Empirical Studies in Pre-school Units in Scotland and their Implications for Educational Practice. Edin. 1979.

23168 HAYSTEAD (J.), HOWARTH (V.), and STRACHAN (A.). Pre-school Education and Care. Edin. 1980.

23169 DALE (REGINALD ROWLAND). Mixed or Single-sex Schools? 3 vols .1974.

19. EDUCATION: IMMIGRANTS

23170 SILBERMAN (LEO) and SPICE (B.). Colour and Class in Six Liverpool Schools. Lpool. 1950.

23171 LONDON. London Head Teachers Association. Memorandum on Immigrant Children in London Schools. 1965.

23172 INNER LONDON EDUCATION AUTHORITY. The Education of Immigrant Pupils. [ILEA 959.]. 1967.

23173 HAWKES (NICOLAS). Immigrant Children in British Schools. 1966.

23174 MILLER (H.). 'Race Relations and the Schools in Great Britain'. Phylon 27(3) (1966), 247–67.

23175 BURGIN (TREVOR) and EDSON (PATRICIA). Spring Grove: The Education of Immigrant Children. 1967.

23176 LONDON. London Council of Social Service. Commonwealth Children in Britain. 1967.

23177 POWER (JOHN). Immigrants in School: A Survey of Administrative Policies. 1967.

23178 OAKLEY (ROBIN). New Backgrounds: The Immigrant Child at Home and at School. 1968.

23179 BOWKER (GORDON). The Education of Coloured Immigrants. 1968.

23180 BHATNAGAR (JOTI). Immigrants at School. 1970.

23181 COARD (BERNARD). How the West Indian Child is Made Educationally Sub-Normal in the British School System. 1971. [Caribbean Education and Community Workers Association.].

23182 EYSENCK (HANS JURGEN). Race, Intelligence and Education. 1971. Repr. 1973.

23183 TOWNSEND (G.) and BRITTAIN (E.). Organisation in Multi-racial Schools. N.F.E.R. Windsor. 1972.

23184 U.K. Select Committee on Race Relations and Immigration (House of Commons Session 1972–73) Education. Report. Vol. 1 1973.

23185 BAGLEY (CHRISTOPHER). 'Immigrant Children: A Review of Problems and Policy in Education'. J. Social Pol. 2 (1973), 114.

23186 —— 'Race Relations and Theories of Status Consistency'. Race 11(3) (1970), 267–88.

23187 MABEY (CHRISTINE). Social and Ethnic Mix in Schools and the Relationship with Attainments of Children Aged 8 and 11. C.E.S. Res. Paper 9. 1974.

23188 TAYLOR (FRANCINE). Race, School and Community: A Survey of Research and Literature on Education in Multi-racial Britain. N.F.E.R. Windsor. 1974.

23189 MILNER (DAVID). Children and Race. Harmondsworth. 1975.

23190 NATIONAL CATHOLIC COMMISSION FOR RACIAL JUSTICE. When Creed and Colour Matter: A Survey on Black Children and Catholic Schools. 1975.

23191 VERMA (GAJENDRA K.) *and* BAGLEY (CHRISTOPHER). Race and Education across Cultures. 1975.

23192 GILES (RAYMOND H.). The West Indian Experience in British Schools: Multi-racial Education and Social Disadvantage in London. 1977.

23193 CRAFT (MAURICE) *ed.* Teaching in a Multicultural Society. Nottingham. 1981.

23194 ROBERTS (C. D.). 'Education in a Multi-cultural Society'. *New Community* 2 (1973), 230–6.

23195 ROGERS (MARGARET). 'Education in a Multi-ethnic Britain: A Teacher's Eye View'. *New Community* 2 (1973), 221–9.

23196 LEE (ROSEMARY). 'The Education of Immigrant Children in England'. *Race* 7 (1965), 131–45.

20. COST OF EDUCATION

23197 HALSEY (A. H.), FLOUD (J. E.), *and* ANDERSON (C. A.). Education, Economy and Society. N.Y. 1961.

See chapter, FLOUD (J. E.) *and* SCOTT (W.). 'Recruitment to Teaching in England and Wales'. 1956.

23198 BARON (G.) *and* TROPP (A.). Teachers in England and America. 1961.

23199 VAIZEY (JOHN ERNEST) *Baron.* The Costs of Education. 1958.

23200 VAIZEY (JOHN ERNEST) *and* SHEEHAN (JOHN). Resources for Education: An Economic Study of Education in the United Kingdom, 1920–1965. 1968.

23201 PEACOCK (ALAN TURNER) *and* WISEMAN (JACK). Education for Democrats: A Study of the Financing of Education in a Free Society. 1964.

23202 PEACOCK (ALAN TURNER). Educational Finance: Its Sources and Uses in the United Kingdom. Edin. 1968.

23203 WEST (EDWIN GEORGE). Economics, Education and the Politician. 1968.

23204 CUMMING (CHRISTOPHER EDWARD). Studies in Educational Costs. Edin. 1971.

23205 WOODHALL (MAUREEN). Economic Aspects of Education: A Review of Research in Britain. Slough. 1972.

23206 BAGLEY (JOHN JOSEPH) *and* BAGLEY (ALEXANDER JOHN). The State and Education in England and Wales, 1833–1968. 1969.

23207 OULTON (NICHOLAS). 'The Distribution of Education and the Distribution of Income'. *Economica* 41 (1974), 387–402.

23208 O'KEEFE (DENNIS J.). 'Some Economic Aspects of Raising the School Leaving Age in England and Wales in 1947'. *Econ. Hist. Rev.* 28 (1975), 500–16.

23209 ZIDERMAN (A.). 'Rates of Return on Investment in Education: Recent Results for Britain'. *J. Human Resources* 8 (1973), 85–97.

23210 VAIZEY (JOHN ERNEST) *Baron.* 'Block Grants and Control of Education'. *Pol. Q.* (Apr. 1958), 155–65.

23211 ROWLEY (C. K.). 'The Political Economy of British Education'. *Scot. J. Pol. Econ.* 16 (1969), 152–76.

23212 DOWLING (H. M.). 'Education and the Economy'. *Q. Rev.* 302 (1964), 142–8.

23213 ADNETT (N. J.). 'The Eclipse of British Classical Political Economy: The Case of Education'. *Bull. Econ. Res.* 22 (29) (1977), 22–36.

21. HEADMASTERS

23214 RÉE (HARRY). Educator Extraordinary: The Life and Achievements of Henry Morris 1889–1961. 1973.

23215 NEILL (A. S.). 'Neill, Neill! Orange Peel!' A Personal View of Ninety Years. 1973.

23216 CROALL (JONATHAN). Neill of Summerhill: The Permanent Rebel. 1983.

23217 DELL (JOHN ALEXANDER). Arthur Rowntree: Headmaster, Bootham School, York, 1899–1927. York. 1958.

23218 EDWARDS (DAVID LAWRENCE). F. J. Shirley: An Extraordinary Headmaster. 1969.

22. SCOTTISH SCHOOLS

23219 HIGHET (JOHN). A School of One's Choice: A Sociological Study of the Fee-Paying Schools of Scotland. 1969.

23220 MAGNUSSON (MAGNUS). The Clacken and the Slate: The Story of the Edinburgh Academy, 1824–1974. 1974.

23221 The Glasgow Academy: The First Hundred Years, 1846–1946. Glasg. 1946.

23222 RAE (JOSEPH A.) *ed.* The History of Allan Glen's School, 1853–1953. Glasg. 1953.

23223 ASHMALL (HARRY A.). The High School of Glasgow. Glasg. 1976.

23224 THOMPSON (J.). A History of Daniel Stewart's College, 1855–1955. Edin. 1955.

23225 MACKAY (COLIN H.). Kelvinside Academy 1878–1978. Glasg. 1978.

23226 WILLIAMSON (JOHN). A History of Morrison's Academy, Crieff. Crieff. 1980.

23. MISCELLANEOUS

23227 McCLOY (R. J.). 'Community Colleges: Their First Fifty Years and the Corporate Ideal'. *Local Gvt Studs* 8 (1974), 47–56 and 9 (1974), 35–46.

23228 WESTERN (S. C.). 'Community College and School'. *Adult Educ.* 38 (1965), 191–7.

23229 SILVER (PAMELA) *and* SILVER (HAROLD). The Education of the Poor: The History of a National School, 1824–1974. 1974.

23230 MACLURE (JOHN STUART). One Hundred Years of London Education, 1870–1970. 1970.

23231 LONDON COUNTY COUNCIL. Education Library Catalogue 1935. Suppl. 1935–1945. 1948.

23232 SIMON (BRIAN) *ed.* Education in Leicestershire, 1540–1940. Leics. 1968.

23233 FAIRBAIRN (A. N.) *ed.* The Leicestershire Plan. 1980.

23234 GOSDEN (PETER HENRY JOHN HEATHER) *and* SHARP (P. R.). The Development of an Education Service: The West Riding 1889–1974. Oxf. 1978.

23235 WRIGHT (MARGARET SCOTT) *and* JOHN (AUDREY L.). Student Nurses in Scotland: Characteristics of Success and Failure. Edin. 1968.

23236 POMERANZ (RUTH). The Lady Apprentices: A Study of Transition in Nurse Training. 1973.

23237 ROYAL SCHOOL OF MINES. Centenary of the Royal School of Mines, 1851–1951: Some Notes on the History of the School. 1951.

23238 IMON (BRIAN) *ed.* The Radical Tradition in Education in Britain. 1972.

23239 —— Studies in the History of Education: vol. 3 The Politics of Educational Reform, 1920–1940. 1974.

23240 JUDGES (A. V.). 'The Educational Influence of the Webbs'. *Brit. J. Educ. Studs* 10 (1961), 33–48.

23241 GORDON (PETER) *and* WHITE (JOHN). Philosophers as Educational Reformers: The Influence of Idealism on British Educational Thought and Practice. 1979.

23242 YATES (ALFRED). The First Twenty Five Years: A Review of the N.F.E.R. 1946–1971. 1971.

23243 EDWARDS (REESE). The Middle School Experiment. 1972.

23244 EDWARDS (ANTHONY DAVIES). The Changing Sixth Form in the Twentieth Century. 1970.

23245 KING (RUPERT WEARING). The English Sixth Form College: An Educational Concept. Oxf. 1968.

23246 TYERMAN (MAURICE JOSEPH). Truancy. 1968.

23247 EDMUNDS (EDWARD LESLIE). The School Inspector. 1962.

23248 BLACKIE (JOHN ERNEST HALDANE). Inspecting and the Inspectorate. 1970.

23249 SPENCER (FREDERICK HERBERT). An Inspector's Testament. 1938.

23250 SMART (NICHOLAS). Crisis in the Classroom: An Enquiry into State Education Policy. 1968.

23251 TIBBLE (JOHN WILLIAM) *ed.* The Extra Year: The Raising of the School-Leaving Age. 1970.

23252 BIRLEY (DEREK). The Education Officer and his World. 1970.

24. FURTHER EDUCATION

23253 BRATCHELL (DENNIS FRANK). The Aims and Organisation of Further Education. Oxf. 1968.

23254 CANTOR (LEONARD MARTIN) *and* ROBERTS (IOLO FRANCIS). Further Education in England and Wales. 1969. 2nd edn 1972.

23255 —— Further Education Today. 1979.

23256 BRISTOW (ADRIAN). Inside the Colleges of Further Education. 1970.

23257 EDWARDS (HERBERT JAMES). The Evening Institute: Its Place in the Education System of England and Wales. 1961.

23258 PETERS (A. JOHN). British Further Education: A Critical Textbook. Oxf. 1967.

23259 SMITH (CHRISTOPHER SELBY). The Costs of Further Education: A British Analysis. Oxf. 1970.

23260 MATTERSON (ALAN). Polytechnics and Colleges. 1981.

23261 EVANS (B. J.). 'Further Education Pressure Groups: The Campaign for Continued and Technical Education in 1944'. *Hist. Educ.* 11 (1982), 45–55.

23262 MILLIS (CHARLES THOMAS). Education for Trades and Industries: A Historical Survey. 1932.

23263 ABBOTT (ALBERT). Education for Industry and Commerce in England. 1933.

23264 JONES (TUDOR JENKYN). Future Education and Training for British Industry. 1943.

23265 THOMSON (DAVID CLEGHORN) *ed.* Training Worker Citizens. 1949.

23266 SILBERSTON (DOROTHY MARION). Youth in a Technical Age: A Study of Day Release. 1959.

23267 WELLENS (JOHN). The Training Revolution: From Shop-Floor to Board-Room. 1963.

23268 —— Technical Education: Its Aims, Organisation and Future Development. 1955.

23269 VENABLES (*Sir* PETER PERCY FREDERICK RONALD). British Technical Education. 1959.

23270 VENABLES (*Sir* PETER PERCY FREDERICK RONALD) *and* WILLIAMS (W. J.). The Smaller Firm and Technical Education. 1961.

23271 —— The Changing Pattern of Technical and Higher Education. 1970.

23272 VENABLES (ETHEL). The Young Worker at College: A Study of a Local Tech. 1967.

23273 TIPTON (BERYL FRANCES A.). Conflict and Change in a Technical College. 1973.

23274 REESE-EDWARDS (KENNETH HARRY). The Secondary Technical School. 1960.

23275 PAYNE (GEORGE LOUIS). Britain's Scientific and Technical Manpower. Stanford, Calif. 1960.

23276 JAHODA (MARIE). The Education of Technologists: An Exploratory Case-Study at Brunel College. 1963.

23277 PAGE (GRAHAM TERRY). Engineering among the Schools. 1965.

23278 MOORE (BRYAN MCASKIE). Block or Day Release?: A Comparative Study of Engineering Apprentices. Slough. 1969.

23279 ARGLES (OWEN MICHAEL VENABLES). South Kensington to Robbins: An Account of English Technical and Scientific Education since 1851. 1964.

23280 PINION (FRANCIS BERTRAM). Educational Values in an Age of Technology. Oxf. 1964.

23281 PAGE (GRAHAM TERRY). The Industrial Training Act and After. 1967.

23282 BEVERSTOCK (ALBERT GEORGE). Industrial Training Practices. 1969.

23283 COTGROVE (STEPHEN FREDERICK). Technical Education and Social Change. 1958.

23284 BANTOCK (GEOFFREY HERMAN). Education in an Industrial Society. 1963.

23285 RODERICK (GORDON WYNNE). The Emergence of a Scientific Society. 1967.

23286 HASLEGRAVE (HERBERT LESLIE). Fifty Years of Progress, 1894–1944: An Historical Survey of the Work of the Association of Technical Institutions. 1947.

23287 ARROWSMITH (HAROLD). Pioneering in Education for the Technologies: The Story of Battersea College of Technology, 1891–1962. 1966.

23288 THOMS (D. W.). The History of Technical Education in London, 1904–1940. 1976.

23289 MINISTRY OF EDUCATION. Technical Education in Wales. 1961.

23290 CHARLTON (DAVID) *et al.* The Administration of Technical Colleges. Manch. 1971.

23291 BURGESS (TYRRELL) *and* PRATT (JOHN). Policy and Practice: The Colleges of Advanced Technology. 1970.

25. UNIVERSITIES: GENERAL

23292 SILVER (HAROLD) *and* TEAGUE (S. JOHN) *comps.* The History of British Universities, 1800–1969 excluding Oxford and Cambridge: A Bibliography. 1970.

23293 HEYCK (THOMAS WILLIAM). 'The Idea of a University in Britain, 1870–1970'. *Hist. Eur. Ideas* 8 (1987), 205–19.

23294 WATTS (ANTHONY GORDON). Diversity and Choice in Higher Education. 1972.

23295 MINOGUE (KENNETH R.). The Concept of a University. 1973.

23296 STEWART (W. A. C.). Higher Education in Postwar Britain. 1988.

23297 CHRISTOPHERSON (*Sir* DERMAN). The University at Work. 1973.

23298 NIBLETT (WILLIAM ROY). Universities between Two Worlds. 1974.

23299 —— *et al.* The University Connection. Windsor. 1975.

23300 THOMAS (DAVID JOHN). Universities. 1973.

23301 SILBER (JOHN R.). 'Poisoning the Wells of Academe'. *Encounter* 43 (1974), 30–43.

23302 ROWSE (ALFRED LESLIE). 'Mushroom Universities'. *Encounter* 43 (1974), 89–92.

23303 MOODIE (GRAEME C.) *and* EUSTACE (ROWLAND). Power and Authority in British Universities. 1974.

23304 ABERCROMBIE (NICHOLAS), CULLEN (IAN), GODSON (VIDA), MAJOR (SANDRA), *and* TIMSON (LESLEY). The University in an Urban Environment. 1974.

23305 CERYCH (L.). 'An International View of British Higher Education'. *Higher Ed.* 3 (1974), 253–63.

23306 SEABURY (PAUL). Universities in the Western World. 1975.

23307 SPURWAY (NEIL). Authority in Higher Education. 1968.

23308 NORRIS (GRAEME). The Effective University: A Management by Objectives Approach. 1978.

23309 REEVES (MARJORIE ETHEL) *ed.* Eighteen Plus: Unity and Diversity in Higher Education. 1965.

23310 COLLIER (KENNETH GERALD). New Dimensions in Higher Education. 1968.

23311 BROWNRIGG (M.). 'The Economic Impact of a New University'. *Scot. J. Pol. Econ.* 20 (1973), 123–39.

23312 WOODHALL (MAUREEN) *and* BLAUG (MARK). Productivity trends in British University Education, 1938–1962'. *Minerva* iii (1965).

23313 ALEXANDER (WILLIAM M.). 'The Universities and the State'. *Aberd. Univ. Rev.* 48 (1936), 102–14.

23314 VERRY (DONALD) *and* DAVIES (BLEDDYN). University Costs and Outputs. Amsterdam. 1976.

23315 WOODHALL (MAUREEN). Economic Aspects of Education: A Review of Research in Britain. 1972.

23316 PREST (ALAN RICHMOND). Financing University Education. 1966.

23317 PICKFORD (MICHAEL). University Expansion and Finance. 1975.

23318 PHILLIPSON (NICHOLAS A.). Universities, Society and the Future. Edin. 1983.

23319 SIMPSON (RENATE). How the Ph.D. Came to Britain: A Century of Struggle for Postgraduate Education. 1983.

23320 SCOTT (PETER). The Crisis of the University. 1984.

23321 MAYNELL (I. C. M.). Universities in Partnership: The Inter-University Council and the Growth of Higher Education in Developing Countries, 1946–70. Edin. 1980.

23322 ASHBY (ERIC) *Baron, with* ANDERSON (MARY). Universities: British, Indian, African: A Study in the Ecology of Higher Education. 1966.

23323 ASHBY (ERIC) *Baron*. Adapting Universities to a Technological Society. San Francisco, Calif. 1974.

23324 FRY (MARGERY). 'The University Grants Committee: An Experiment in Administration'. *Univ. Q.* 2 (1948), 221–30.

23325 MOODIE (GRAEME C.). 'Buffer, Coupling and Broker: Reflections on Sixty Years of the U.G.C.'. *Higher Ed.* 12 (1983), 331–47.

23326 SHATTOCK (MICHAEL) *and* BERDAHL (ROBERT O.). 'The British University Grants Committee, 1919–83: Changing Relationships with Government and the Universities'. *Higher Ed.* 13 (1984), 471–500.

23327 SHINN (CHRISTINE HELEN). Paying the Piper: The Development of the U.G.C. 1910–1946. Falmer. 1986.

23328 DODDS (HAROLD WILLIS) *et al.* Government Assistance to Universities in Great Britain. NY. 1952.

23329 WISEMAN (H. VICTOR). 'Parliament and the University Grants Committee'. *Public Admin.* 34 (1956), 75–91.

23330 BERDAHL (ROBERT O.). British Universities and the State. Camb. 1959.

23331 CAINE (*Sir* SYDNEY). 'Universities and the State'. *Pol. Q.* 37 (1966), 237–54.

23332 HALLETT (GRAHAM). 'Universities and the State: A Lecturer's View'. *Pol. Q.* 40 (1969), 163–72.

23333 WALKLAND (S. A.). 'The Public Accounts Committee, the UGC, and the Universities'. *Parl. Affs* 22 (1969), 349–60.

23334 Review of the University Grants Committee. Cmnd 81. Parliamentary Papers (1986–7).

23335 Higher Education: Meeting the Challenge. Cmnd 114. Parliamentary Papers (1986–7).

23336 DAALDER (HANS) *and* SHILS (EDWARD) eds. Universities, Politicians and Bureaucrats: Europe and the United States. Camb. 1982.

23337 BEVERIDGE (WILLIAM HENRY) *Baron Beveridge*. Power and Influence. 1953.

23338 BROWN (BEATRICE CURTIS) *ed*. Isabel Fry, 1869–1959: Portrait of a Great Teacher. 1960.

23339 ILLINGWORTH (*Sir* CHARLES). University Statesman: The Story of Sir Hector Hetherington. Glasg. 1971.

23340 IRVINE (MABEL). The Avenue of Years: The Life of Sir James Irvine. Edin. 1970.

23341 SCOTT (*Lady* DRUSILLA). A. D. Lindsay: A Biography. Oxf. 1971.

23342 FIRTH (CATHERINE BEATRICE). Constance Louisa Maynard: Mistress of Westfield College. 1949.

23343 GRIER (LYNDA). The Life of Winifred Mercier. 1937.

23344 —— Achievement in Education: The Work of Michael Ernest Sadler, 1885–1935. 1952.

23345 COLLISON (PETER). 'University Chancellors, Vice-Chancellors and College Principals: A Social Profile'. *Sociology* 3 (1 Jan. 1969).

23346 AIKEN (*Sir* ROBERT). Administration of a University. 1966.

23347 ASHBY (ERIC) *Baron*. Masters and Scholars. 1970.

23348 BLACKETT (PATRICK M. S.). Universities and the Nation's Crisis. Manch. 1963.

23349 KAY (RONALD). UCCA: Its Origins and Development 1950–1985. Cheltenham. 1985.

23350 LOGAN (*Sir* DOUGLAS). The Birth of a Pension Scheme: A History of the Universities' Superannuation Scheme. Lpool. 1985.

23351 DUNSHEATH (PERCY). The Graduate in Industry. 1947.

23352 ASHBY (ERIC) *Baron*. Technology and the Academics: An Essay on Universities and the Scientific Revolution. 1958.

23353 SANDERSON (J. MICHAEL). 'The Universities and Industry in England, 1919–1939'. *Yorks. Bull. Econ. Soc. Res.* 21 (1969), 39–65.

23354 —— 'The University of London and Industrial Progress'. *J. Contemp. Hist.* 7 (1972), 243–62.

23355 —— The Universities and British Industry, 1850–1970. 1972.

23356 PSACHAROPOULOS (G.). 'On some Positive Aspects of the Economics of the Brain Drain'. *Minerva* 9 (1971), 231–42.

23357 REPORT OF A COMMITTEE APPOINTED BY THE CAMBRIDGE UNIVERSITY APPOINTMENTS BOARD, University Education and Business. Camb. 1945.

23358 FINNISTON (*Sir* HAROLD MONTAGUE). 'University Science and Industry'. *Pol. Q.* 38 (1967).

23359 WILSON (CHARLES HENRY) *and* LAING (*Sir* MAURICE). Conference on Industry and the Universities—Aspects of Interdependence. Report of Proceedings. 1965.

23360 REDCLIFFE-MAUD *Lord*. National Progress and the University. Cape Town. 1972.

23361 ARMYTAGE (WALTER HARRY GREEN). Civic Universities: Aspects of a British Tradition. 1955.

23362 —— 'Community Service Stations: The Transformation of the Civic Universities, 1898–1930'. *Univ. Rev.* 25 (1953), 76–90.

23363 —— 'Flexner to Truscot: The Stocktaking Phase of Civic University Development, 1930–1944'. *Univ. Rev.* 26 (1953), 4–11.

23364 —— 'The Civic Universities and Social Readjustment, 1944–1954'. *Univ. Rev.* 26 (1954), 52–7.

23365 —— 'The Rise of Civic Universities in England' in Year Book of Education, 1959: Higher Education, 69–80.

23366 FLEXNER (ABRAHAM). Universities: American, English, German. 1930.

23367 BARKER (*Sir* ERNEST). Universities in Great Britain: Their Position and their Problems. 1931.

23368 ROBERTSON (*Sir* CHARLES GRANT). The British Universities. 1930. 2nd edn 1944.

23369 IRVINE (*Sir* JAMES). The Academic Burden in a Changing World. Aberd. 1942.

23370 TRUSCOT (BRUCE) *pseud.* Red Brick University. 1943.

23371 —— Redbrick and these Vital Days. 1945.

23372 ROBERTS (*Sir* SYDNEY CASTLE). British Universities. 1947.

23373 MOBERLEY (*Sir* WALTER HAMILTON). Universities and the State. Camb. 1948.

23374 —— The Crisis in the University. 1949.

23375 NIBLETT (WILLIAM ROY). 'The Development of British Universities since 1945'. In The Yearbook of Education, 1952, 165–78.

23376 HUMBERSTONE (THOMAS LLOYD). University Controversies. 1953.

23377 HETHERINGTON (*Sir* HECTOR JAMES WRIGHT). The British University System, 1914–1954. Edin. 1955.

23378 KNELLER (GEORGE FREDERICK). Higher Learning in Britain. 1955.

23379 SIMMONS (JACK). 'The Last Forty Years'. *Twentieth Cent.* 159 (1956), 112–22.

23380 NOBLE (PETER S.). 'The Redbrick Universities'. *Twentieth Cent.* 159 (1956), 99–111.

23381 ZUCKERMAN (SOLLY) *Baron.* 'Growth of Higher Education'. *Univ. Q.* 12 (1957–8), 241–9.

23382 MORRIS (*Sir* CHARLES R.). 'Where are we Going in English Education?'. *Univ. Q.* (1958), 153–61.

23383 DUFF (*Sir* JAMES FITZJAMES). Universities in Britain. 1959.

23384 HOBMAN (D. L.). 'University Expansion'. *Q. Rev.* (Oct. 1960), 396–401.

23385 BOWDEN (B. V.). 'Too Few Academic Eggs'. *Univ. Q.* 14 (1960), 7–23.

23386 ROWE (A. P.). If the Gown Fits. Melbourne. 1960.

23387 —— 'Redbrick and Whitewash'. *Univ. Q.* 14 (1960), 247–64.

23388 VAIZEY (JOHN ERNEST) *Baron.* 'The Reform of Higher Education'. *Univ. Rev.* 33 (1961), 59–65.

23389 NICHOLL (DONALD). 'Universities in Transition: Oxbridge and Redbrick'. *Wiseman Rev.* 488 (1961), 141–5.

23390 MADGWICK (PETER J.). 'Gentlemen Versus Players'. *Adult Educ.* 33 (1961), 260–6.

23391 FULTON (JOHN SCOTT) *Baron.* 'The Future Pattern of University Education in the United Kingdom'. *J. Roy. Soc. Arts* 109 (1961), 840–56.

23392 DENT (HAROLD COLLETT). Universities in Transition. 1961.

23393 BUTTERFIELD (*Sir* HERBERT). The Universities and Education Today. 1962.

23394 NIBLETT (WILLIAM ROY) *ed.* The Expanding University. 1962.

23395 KING (ALEXANDER). 'Higher Education, Professional Manpower and the State'. *Minerva* 1 (1963), 182–90.

23396 FLOUD (JEAN) *and* ROSSELLI (JOHN). 'Studying Higher Education in Britain and America'. *Univ. Q.* 17 (1963), 126–48.

23397 LOGAN (*Sir* DOUGLAS WILLIAM). Universities: The Years of Challenge. 1963.

23398 UNIVERSITY GRANTS COMMITTEE. University Development 1957–1962. 1964.

23399 Report of the Committee Appointed by the Prime Minister under the Chairmanship of Lord Robbins, 1961–63. Cmnd 2154. Parliamentary Papers (1962–3).

23400 CARSWELL (JOHN). Government and the Universities in Britain: Programme and Performance, 1960–1980. Camb. 1985.

23401 EAGLESHAM (ERIC JOHN ROSS). 'The Changing Idea of a University'. *Dur. Univ. J.* 57 (1964), 3–9.

23402 ANNAN (NOEL GILROY) *Baron.* 'The Universities'. *Encounter* 20 (1963), 3–14.

23403 —— 'The Reform of Higher Education in 1986'. *Hist. of Education* 16 (1987), 217–26.

23404 CUNNINGHAM (R. F.). 'The Robbins Report: The Future of Higher Education'. *Wiseman Rev.* (Spring 1964), 8–22.

23405 GOMME (ANDOR). 'Publicity or Promise? The New Universities'. *Delta* (1964), 2–19.

23406 HALSEY (ALBERT HENRY). 'Second Thoughts on Robbins: the Academic Hierarchy-Appendix Three'. *Univ. Q.* 18 (1964), 129–35.

23407 TROW (MARTIN). 'Second Thoughts on Robbins: A Question of Size and Shape'. *Univ. Q.* 18 (1964), 136–52.

23408 GRIMOND (JOSEPH) *Baron.* 'Beyond Robbins'. *Contemp. Rev.* 205 (1964), 223–7.

23409 ALLEN (HARRY CRANBROOK). 'Democracy and the Robbins Report'. *Contemp. Rev.* 205 (1964), 57–62.

23410 MORRIS (*Sir* CHARLES). 'The Robbins Report'. *Brit. J. Educ. Studs* 43 (1964), 5–15.

23411 —— 'Second Thoughts on Robbins: University Commentary'. *Univ. Q.* xviii (1964), 119–28.

23412 LITTLE (ALAN N.). 'Will More Mean Worse? An Inquiry into the Effects of University Expansion'. *Brit. J. Sociol.* 12 (1961), 351–62.

23413 MACLURE (J. STUART) *et al.* 'Who Killed Cock Robbins?'. *Twentieth Century* 174 (1966), 40–53.

23414 ROBBINS (LIONEL CHARLES) *Baron, and* FORD (BORIS). 'Report on Robbins'. *Univ. Q.* xx (1965), 5–15.

23415 ROBBINS (LIONEL CHARLES) *Baron*. Higher Education. 1963.

23416 ARMYTAGE (WALTER HARRY GREEN). 'From Formula to Policy in Education'. *Pol. Q.* 35 (1964), 182–92.

23417 FULTON (JOHN SCOTT) *Baron*. Experiment in Higher Education. 1964.

23418 NIBLETT (WILLIAM ROY). 'The Changing Image of the University: A British View'. *Educ. Forum* 30 (1965), 23–31.

23419 REYNOLDS (PHILIP ALAN). 'The University in the 1960s: An Anachronism'. *Higher Educ.* 6 (1977), 403–15.

23420 BROOK (GEORGE LESLIE). The Modern University. 1965.

23421 AULT (W. O.). 'British Crisis in Higher Education'. *Midwest Q.* 6 (1965), 175–90.

23422 ROBBINS (LIONEL CHARLES) *Baron*. The University in the Modern World and other Papers in Higher Education. 1966.

23423 ROSS (MURRAY G.). New Universities in the Modern World. 1966.

23424 MOUNTFORD (*Sir* JAMES FREDERICK). British Universities. 1966.

23425 ARMYTAGE (WALTER HARRY GREEN). 'New Pluralism in British Higher Education'. *J. World Hist.* 10 (1967), 818–31.

23426 ANNAN (NOEL GILROY) *Baron*. 'The Reform of Higher Education'. *Pol. Q.* 38 (1967), 234–52.

23427 McQUAIL (D.). 'Elite Education and Political Values'. *Pol. Studs* 16 (1968), 257–66.

23428 LONG (JOYCE RUTH). Universities and the General Public. Birm. 1968.

23429 BELOFF (MICHAEL). 'The Plateglass Universities'. *Encounter* 30 (1968), 14–23.

23430 —— The Plateglass Universities. 1968.

23431 BUTLER (RICHARD AUSTEN) *Baron*. The Responsibilities of Education: The Professions, Industry, the Universities and Government. 1968.

23432 LAWLOR (JOHN) ed. The New University. 1968.

23433 CAINE (*Sir* SYDNEY). British Universities: Purpose and Prospect. 1969.

23434 LASKY (MELVYN J.). 'Revolution Diary'. *Encounter* 31 (1968), 81–92.

23435 CLARK (COLIN). 'An Unorthodox Proposal: University Education in the Welfare State'. *Encounter* 30 (1968), 24–9.

23436 CUNLIFFE (MARCUS). 'Campus Universities and the others'. *Encounter* 32 (1969), 65–70.

23437 CAMPBELL (F.). 'Latin and the Elite Tradition in Education'. *Brit. J. Sociol.* 19 (1968), 308–25.

23438 MOOS (MALCOLM). 'Darkness over the Ivory Tower'. *Contemp. Rev.* 215 (1969), 22–9.

23439 LAYARD (PETER RICHARD GRENVILLE) *et al.* The Impact of Robbins. 1969.

23440 GREEN (VIVIAN HUBERT HOWARD). The Universities. Harmondsworth. 1969.

23441 BOWDEN (BERTRAM VIVIAN) *Baron*. 'English Universities: Problems and Prospects'. *Rev. Pol.* 32 (1970), 3–31.

23442 RICE (A. K.). The Modern University: A Model Organization. 1970.

23443 KOGAN (MAURICE) *with* KOGAN (DAVID). The Attack on Higher Education. 1983.

23444 ASHWORTH (J. M.). 'Reshaping Higher Education in Britain'. *J. Roy. Soc. Arts* 130 (1982), 713–29.

23445 DRIVER (CHRISTOPHER). The Exploding University. 1971.

23446 BIRKS (TONY). Building the New Universities. 1972.

23447 LAWLOR (JOHN JAMES). Higher Education: Patterns of Change in the 1970s. 1972.

26. PARTICULAR UNIVERSITIES

23448 POWELL (JOHN PERCIVAL). Universities and University Education: A Select Bibliography. Slough. 1966.

23449 CORDEAUX (E. H.) *and* MERRY (D. H.). A Bibliography of Printed Works Relating to the University of Oxford. Oxford. 1968.

Aberdeen

23450 SIMPSON (WILLIAM DOUGLAS), ed. The Fusion of 1860: A Record of the Centenary Celebrations and a History of the United University of Aberdeen, 1860–1960. Edin. 1963.

23451 ANDERSON (ROBERT D). The Student Community at Aberdeen, 1860–1939. Aberd. 1988.

23452 HARGREAVES (JOHN D.) *with* FORBES (ANGELA). Aberdeen University, 1945–1981: Regional Roles and National Needs. Aberd. 1989.

Aberystwyth

23453 ELLIS (EDWARD LEWIS). The University College of Wales, Aberystwyth, 1872–1972. Cardiff. 1972.

Aston

23454 WALFORD (GEOFFREY). Restructuring Universities: Politics and Power in the Management of Change. 1987. [A study which focuses upon Aston.].

Bath

23455 WALTERS (GERALD), ed. A Technological University: An Experiment in Bath. Bristol. 1966.

23456 MOORE (G. H. The University of Bath: The Formative Years 1949–1969: A Short History of the Circumstances which Led to the Foundation of the University of Bath. Bath. 1982.

Belfast

23457 MOODY (THEODORE WILLIAM) *and* BECKETT (JAMES CAM-LIN). Queen's, Belfast, 1845–1949: The History of a University. 2 vols. 1959.

23458 MALCOLM (THOMAS). Civil Engineering in Queen's, 1845–1963. Belfast. 1964.

Birmingham

23459 VINCENT (ERIC W). *and* HINTON (PERCIVAL). The University of Birmingham: Its History and Significance. Birm. 1947.

23460 VINCENT (ERIC W., *ed*. The Medical School of the University of Birmingham. 1939.

23461 STEPHENSON (*Sir* ROBERT), Administration of a University: An Account of the Management of Academic Affairs in the University of Birmingham. 1966.

Bristol

23462 COTTLE (BASIL) *and* SHERBORNE (JAMES WILSON). The Life of a University. Bristol. 1951. New edn 1959.

23463 BUTCHER (EMILY ELIZABETH). Clifton Hill House, the First Phase, 1909–1959. Bristol. 1961.

Brunel

23464 TOPPING (J.). The Beginnings of Brunel University: From Technical College to University. Oxf. 1981.

Cambridge

23465 DEACON (RICHARD). The Cambridge Apostles: A History of Cambridge University's Elite Intellectual Secret Society. 1985.

23466 WARMINGTON (E. 'Society and Education in Cambridge 1902–1922'. *The New Universities Q*. 30 (1975), 28–35.

23467 JOHNSON (HARRY G.). 'How Good was Keynes' Cambridge?'. *Encounter* 47 (1976), 82–91.

23468 ZIMAN (JOHN). 'The College System at Oxford and Cambridge'. *Minerva* 1 (1963), 191–208.

23469 CRADOCK (PERCY), *ed*. Recollections of the Cambridge Union, 1815–1939. Camb. 1953.

23470 McWILLIAMS-TULLBERY (RITA) . Women at Cambridge. 1975.

23471 CRAWLEY (CHARLES W). Trinity Hall: The History of a Cambridge College. Camb. 1976.

23472 HOWARTH (THOMAS EDWARD BRODIE). Cambridge between Two Wars. 1978.

23473 PETER (CARPENTER). 'Churchill and his "Technological" College'. *J. Educ. Admin. & Hist*. 17 (1985), 69–75.

23474 GODWIN (*Sir* HARRY), Cambridge and Clare. Camb. 1985.

23475 GREVE (W. W). Fitzwilliam College, Cambridge 1869–1969: Its History as the Non-Collegiate Institution of the University and its Beginnings as an Independent College. Camb. 1983.

23476 STEPHEN (BARBARA). Girton College, 1869–1932. Camb. 1933.

23477 ELSIE (MEGSON BARBARA *and* LINDSAY (JEAN OLIVIA. Girton College, 1869–1959: An Informal History. Camb. 1961.

23478 BRADBROOK (MURIEL CLARA). 'That Infidel Place': A Short History of Girton College, 1869–1969. 1969.

23479 BRITTAIN (FREDERICK). A Short History of Jesus College, Cambridge. 1940.

23480 WILKINSON (PATRICK LANCELOT). A Century of King's, 1873–1972. Camb. 1980.

23481 —— Kingsmen of a Century: 1873–1972. Camb. 1980.

23482 MURRAY (ROSALIND). New Hall, 1954–1972: The Making of a College. Camb. 1980.

23483 TWIGG (JOHN). A History of Queens' College, Cambridge, 1448–1986. 1986.

23484 RICH (EDWIN ERNEST). St Catharine's College, Cambridge: Quincentenary Essays. Camb. 1973.

23485 CROOK (A. C.). Penrose to Cripps: A Century of Building at the College of St John the Evangelist. Camb. 1978.

Cardiff

23486 JONES (GWYN) *and* QUINN (MICHAEL). Fountains of Praise: University College, Cardiff, 1883–1983. Cardiff. 1983.

City

23487 TEAGUE (SIDNEY JOHN). The City University: A History. 1980.

23488 TROW (C. W.). 'From College to University: A Review of Progress at City University since 1966'. *Quest* 3 (1969), 8–11.

Dundee

23489 SHAFE (M. MICHAEL), *comp*. University Education in Dundee, 1881–1981. Dundee. 1982.

23490 SOUTHGATE (DONALD). University Education in Dundee: A Centenary History. Edin. 1982.

Durham

23491 WHITING (EDWIN CHARLES). The University of Durham, 1832–1932. 1933.

23492 WHITWORTH (THOMAS ANTHONY). Yellow Sandstone and Mellow Brick: An Account of Hatfield College, Durham, 1846–1971. Durham. 1971.

Edinburgh

23493 TURNER (A. LOGAN). History of the University of Edinburgh, 1883–1933. Edin. 1933.

23494 TOMASZEWSKI (WIKTOR), *ed*. The University of Edinburgh and Poland. Edin. 1968.

23495 DONALDSON (GORDON), *ed*. Four Centuries: Edinburgh University Life 1583–1983. Edin. 1983.

Essex

23496 EDWARD (SLOMAN ALBERT). A University in the Making. 1964.

Exeter

23497 HETHERINGTON (HECTOR JAMES WRIGHT), *Sir*. The University College at Exeter. Exeter. 1963.

23498 WILLIAM (CLAPP BRIAN). The University of Exeter: A History. 1982.

Glasgow

23499 MACKIE (JOHN DUNCAN). The University of Glasgow, 1451–1951: A Short History. Glasgow. 1954.

23500 MACKENNA (R. OGILVIE). Glasgow University Athletic Club. The Story of the First Hundred Years. Glasg. 1981.

Hull

23501 BAMFORD (T. W.). The University of Hull: The First Fifty Years. Oxf. 1978.

23502 HAYWARD (JOHN). 'Responses to Contraction: The University of Hull, 1979–1984'. *Minerva* 24 (1986), 74–97.

Keele

23503 GALLIE (WALTER BRYCE). A New University: A.D. Lindsay and the Keele Experiment. 1960.

23504 MOUNTFORD (*Sir* JAMES FREDERICK), Keele: An Historical Critique. 1972.

Lampeter

23505 ARCHDALL (HENRY KINGSLEY). St David's College, Lampeter: Its Past, Present and Future. Lampeter. 1952.

23506 THOMAS (J. R. L.). Moth or Phoenix? St David's College and the University of Wales and the University Grants Committee. Llandysul. 1980.

23507 PRICE (D. T. WILLIAM). History of St David's University College, Lampeter. Vol. 2 1889–1971. Cardiff, 1990.

Lancaster

23508 McCLINTOCK (MARION E.). University of Lancaster, Quest for Innovation: A History of the First Ten Years, 1964–1974. Lancaster. 1974.

Leeds

23509 SHIMMIN (ARNOLD NIXON). The University of Leeds: The First Half Century. 1954.

23510 HEPPENSTALL (RAYNER). 'Leeds, 1929–1934'. *Twentieth Cent.* 159 (1956), 169–77.

23511 GOSDEN (PETER HENRY JOHN HEATHER) *and* TAYLOR (ARTHUR JOHN), *eds*. Studies in the History of a University, 1874–1974, to Commemorate the Centenary of the University of Leeds. Leeds. 1975.

23512 ANNING (S. T.). A History of the Leeds School of Medicine: One and a Half Centuries, 1831–1981. Leeds. 1982.

Leicester

23513 SIMMONS (JACK). New University. Leics. 1958.

Liverpool

23514 DUMBELL (STANLEY). The University of Liverpool, 1903–1953. 1953.

23515 KELLY (THOMAS). For Advancement of Learning: University College and the University of Liverpool, 1881–1981. Liverpool. 1981.

London

23516 LOGAN (*Sir* DOUGLAS WILLIAM). The University of London: An Introduction. 1956. 2nd edn 1962.

23517 DUNSHEATH (PERCY) *and* MILLER (MARGARET). Convocation in the University of London: The First Hundred Years. 1958.

23518 HARTE (NEGLEY). The University of London, 1836–1986. 1986.

23519 TUKE (MARGARET JANSON). A History of Bedford College for Women, 1849–1937. 1939.

23520 WARMINGTON (ERIC HERBERT). The History of Birkbeck College, University of London, during the Second World War, 1939–1945. 1954.

23521 DYMOND (DOROTHY), *ed*. The Forge: The History of Goldsmith's College 1905–1955. 1955.

23522 LINSTEAD (*Sir* REGINALD PATRICK), Imperial College of Science and Technology: A Decade of Expansion. 1963.

23523 LONDON UNIVERSITY, IMPERIAL COLLEGE OF SCIENCE AND TECHNOLOGY. Report on a Decade of Expansion, 1953–1963. 1963.

23524 HALL (A. RUPERT). Science for Industry: A Short History of the Imperial College of Science and Technology and Its Antecedents. 1982.

23525 HUELIN (GORDON). King's College, London, 1828–1978. 1978.

23526 BEVERIDGE (WILLIAM HENRY), *Baron Beveridge*. The London School of Economics and its Problems, 1919–1937. 1960.

23527 HAYEK (F. A.). 'The London School of Economics, 1895–1945'. *Economica* 13 (1946), 1–31.

23528 KIDD (HARRY). The Trouble at L.S.E. 1966–1967. 1969.

23529 MOSS (G. P.) *and* SAVILLE. (M. V.). From Palace to College: An Illustrated Account of Queen Mary College (University of London). 1985.

23530 KAYE (ELAINE). A History of Queen's College, London, 1848–1972. 1972.

23531 GRYLLS (ROSALIE GLYNN). Queen's College, 1848–1948. 1948.

23532 BINGHAM (CAROLINE). The History of Royal Holloway College, 1886–1986. 1987.

23533 MOORE (MORETON), *ed*. Royal Holloway and Bedford New College: Centenary Lectures, 1886–1986. 1988.

23534 SONDHEIMER (JANET). Castle Adamant in Hampstead: A History of Westfield College, 1882–1982. 1983.

23535 DIXON (C. W.). The Institute: A Personal Account of the History of the University of London Institute of Education, 1932–1972. 1986.

23536 WALLIS (THOMAS EDWARD). History of the school of pharmacy, university of london. 1964.

Loughborough

23537 CANTOR (LEONARD MARTIN) *and* MATTHEWS (GEOFFREY F.). Loughborough from College to University: A History of Higher Education at Loughborough, 1909–1966. Loughborough. 1977.

23538 MATTHEWS (GEOFFREY F.). 'The College of Advanced Technology Experiment: An Historical Review of Loughborough's Experience 1957–1966'. *Hist. Educ.* 10 (1981), 133–46.

Manchester

23539 CHARLTON (HENRY BUCKLEY). Portrait of a University 1851–1951. Manch. 1951.

23540 CARDWELL (DONALD STEPHEN LOWELL), *ed.* Artisan to Graduate. Manch. 1974.

23541 GREGORY (IAN GABRIEL), *ed.* In Memory of Burlington Street: An Appreciation of the Manchester University Unions, 1861–1957. Manch. 1958.

23542 LAWRENSON (THOMAS EDWARD). Hall of Residence: St Anselm Hall in the University of Manchester, 1907–1957. Manch. 1957.

Newcastle

23543 BETTENSON (E. M.). The University of Newcastle upon Tyne 1834–1971. Newcastle. 1971.

Nottingham

23544 WOOD (ALFRED CECIL). History of University College, Nottingham, 1881–1948. Oxf. 1953.

Open

23545 A University of the Air. Cmnd 2922. Parliamentary Papers (1965–6).

23546 HEWBRIDGE (D. G.). The Open University: A Select Bibliography. Milton Keynes. 1975.

23547 PETERSON (ALEXANDER DUNCAN CAMPBELL). 'A University of the Air?'. *Univ. Q.* 18 (1964), 180–6.

23548 STONE (BRIAN). 'The Place of the Open University in Higher Education Today'. *Contemp. Rev.* 217 (1970), 65–71.

23549 PERRY (WALTER LAING MACDONALD), *Baron.* 'The Open University'. *Roy. Inst. Great Brit. Procs* 44 (1971), 95–112.

23550 FERGUSON (JOHN). 'The Open University in Britain'. *World Year Bk of Educ. 1972–1973* (1972), 373–85.

23551 TUNSTALL (JEREMY), *ed.* The Open University Opens. 1974.

23552 FERGUSON (JOHN). The Open University from within. 1975.

23553 SCHEIBLE (KONRAD). Die Offene Universität in Grossbritannien. Tübingen. 1975.

Oxford

23554 LINDSAY (KENNETH). 'Post-War Oxford, 1918–1922'. *Contemp. Rev.* 221 (1972), 29–31.

23555 CLARK (COLIN). 'Oxford Reformed: Notes during a Controversy'. *Encounter* 24 (1965), 44–52.

23556 EGGLESTON (JOHN). 'Secondary Schools and Oxbridge Blues'. *Brit. J. Sociol.* 16 (1965), 232–42.

23557 BELOFF (MAX). 'What's Wrong with Oxford?'. *Encounter* 27 (1966), 16–22.

23558 Oxford University, Report of Commission of Inquiry. 2 vols. 1966.

23559 HALSEY (ALBERT HENRY). 'Oxford after Franks'. *Univ. Q.* 20 (1966), 259–66.

23560 CARTER (*Sir* CHARLES FREDERICK), 'The Franks Report: From the Outside'. *Univ. Q.* 20 (1966), 381–8.

23561 CAUTE (DAVID). 'Crisis in All Souls: A Case History in Reform'. *Encounter* 26 (1966), 3–15.

23562 BROGAN (*Sir* DENIS WILLIAM), 'The Price of Oxbridge'. *Virginia Q. Rev.* 45 (1969), 29–45.

23563 HOLLIS (MAURICE CHRISTOPHER). The Oxford Union. 1965.

23564 WALTER (DAVID). The Oxford Union: Playground of Power. 1985.

23565 LAWSON (F. H.). The Oxford Law School, 1850–1965. Oxf. 1968.

23566 JONES (JOHN). Balliol College: A History, 1263–1939. Oxf. 1988.

23567 BAKER (JOHN NORMAN LEONARD). Jesus College, Oxford, 1571–1971. 1972.

23568 GREEN (VIVIAN H. H.). The Commonwealth of Lincoln College, 1427–1977. Oxf. 1979.

23569 BUXTON (JOHN) *and* WILLIAMS (PENRY HERBERT). New College, Oxford, 1379–1979. Oxf. 1979.

23570 HALSEY (A. H.). 'Norman Chester and Nuffield College'. In David Butler and A. H. Halsey *eds*, Policy and Politics: Essays in Honour of Norman Chester. 1978. 1–12.

23571 REEVES (MARJORIE ETHEL). St Anne's College: An Informal History. 1979.

23572 FOOTMAN (DAVID). Antonin Besse of Aden: The Founder of St Antony's College, Oxford. London. 1985.

23573 GRIFFIN (PENNY), *ed.* St Hugh's: One Hundred Years of Women's Education in Oxford. 1986.

23574 JESSUP (FRANK WILLIAM). Wolfson College, Oxford: The Early Years. 1979.

Reading

23575 CHILDS (WILLIAM MacBRIDE). Making of a University. 1933.

23576 HOLT (JAMES CLARKE). The University of Reading: The First Fifty Years. Reading. 1977.

St Andrews

23577 CANT (RONALD GORDON). The University of St Andrews: A Short History. Edin. 1946.

Salford

23578 GORDON (COLIN). The Foundation of the University of Salford. 1975.

Sheffield

23579 CHAPMAN (ARTHUR WILLIAM). The Story of a Modern University: A History of the University of Sheffield. 1955.

23580 MANN (PETER HENRY). Growth at Redbrick: A Case Study of Sheffield University. Oxf. 1966.

Southampton

23581 PATTERSON (ALFRED TEMPLE). The University of Southampton: A Centenary History of the Evolution and Development of the University of Southampton, 1862–1962. Shampton. 1962.

Sussex

23582 DAICHES (DAVID), *ed.* The Idea of a New University, an Experiment in Sussex. 1964.

23583 BLIN-STOYLE (ROGER) *and* IVEY (GEOFF), *eds.* The Sussex Opportunity: A New University and the Future. Brighton. 1986.

Wales

23584 EVANS (*Sir* EMRYS). The University of Wales: An Historical Sketch. Cardiff. 1953.

23585 Wales University Commission, Final Reports. Cardiff. 1964.

Warwick

23586 THOMPSON (EDWARD PALMER), *ed.* Warwick University Ltd: Industry, Management and the Universities. Harmondsworth. 1970.

York

23587 LORD JAMES OF RUSHOLME. 'The Start of a New University'. *Trans. Manch. Stat. Soc.* (1965–6), 1–26.

27. EDUCATION IN SCOTLAND

23588 MacMEEKEN (A. M.). The Intelligence of a Representative Group of Scottish Children. 1939.

23589 —— The Intelligence of Scottish Children: A National Survey of an Age-Group. 1933.

23590 —— The Trend of Scottish Intelligence: A Comparison of the 1947 and 1932 Surveys of the Intelligence of 11-Year-Old Pupils. 1949.

23591 —— Social Implications of the 1947 Scottish Mental Survey. 1953.

23592 —— Educational and other Aspects of the 1947 Scottish Mental Survey. 1958.

23593 SCOTTISH EDUCATION DEPARTMENT. Education in Scotland in 1963. Edin. 1964.

23594 —— Primary Education in Scotland. Edin. 1965.

23595 MACPHERSON (JOHN S.). Eleven-Year-Olds Grow Up: A Seven Year Follow Up of a Representative Sample from the 1947 Scottish Mental Survey. 1958.

23596 MAXWELL (JAMES). The Level and Trend of National Intelligence: The Contribution of the Scottish Mental Surveys. 1961.

23597 THE SCOTTISH SCHOLASTIC SURVEY. 1953. 1963.

23598 HOLMES (EILEEN M.). Education in Scotland. 1942.

23599 KNOX (HENRY MACDONALD). Two Hundred and Fifty Years of Scottish Education 1696–1946. Edin. 1953.

23600 MACKINTOSH (MARY). Education in Scotland Yesterday and Today. Glasg. 1962.

23601 HUNTER (SANDY LESLIE). The Scottish Educational System. 1968.

23602 BONE (THOMAS RENFREW). Studies in the History of Scottish Education, 1872–1939. 1967.

23603 —— School Inspection in Scotland, 1840–1966. 1968.

23604 SCOTLAND (JAMES). 'Scottish Education, 1952–1982'. *Brit. J. Educ. Studs* 30 (1982), 122–35.

23605 OSBORNE (GERALD STANLEY). Scottish and English Schools: A Comparative Survey of the Past Fifty Years. 1966.

23606 —— Change in Scottish Education. 1968.

23607 BOYD (WILLIAM). Evacuation in Scotland: A Record of Events and Experiments. Bickley. 1944.

23608 MAXWELL (JAMES). Sixteen Years On: A Follow-Up of the 1947 Scottish Survey. 1969.

23609 SCOTLAND (JAMES). The History of Scottish Education: Vol. 2: From 1872 to the Present Day. 1969.

23610 FINDLAY (IAN RUSSELL). Education in Scotland. Newton Abbot. 1973.

23611 MacMEEKEN (A. M.). Gaelic-Speaking Children in Highland Schools. 1961.

23612 TREBLE (J. H.). 'The Working of the 1918 Education Act in Glasgow Archdiocese'. *Innes Rev.* 31 (1980), 27–44.

23613 CRUICKSHANK (MARJORIE). A History of the Training of Teachers in Scotland. 1970.

23614 WALKER (N. T.). 'Proposed New School Examination Structure in Scotland'. *Brit. J. Educ. Studs* 9 (1960), 67–8.

23615 PILLEY (JOHN). 'Teacher Training in Scotland'. *Univ. Q.* (May 1958), 283–7.

23616 CAMPBELL (C. A. C.). 'The Scottish Universities and Adult Education'. *Adult Educ.* (Dec. 1947), 66–70.

23617 McPHERSON (ANDREW) *and* NEAVE (GUY R.). The Scottish Sixth: A Sociological Evaluation of Sixth Year Studies and the Changing Relationship Between School and University in Scotland. Windsor. 1976.

23618 MACKINNON (KENNETH). Language, Education and Social Processes in a Gaelic Community. 1977.

23619 RYRIE (ALEXANDER C.). Routes and Results: A Study of the Later Years of Schooling. SCRE. Edin. 1981.

23620 RAFFE (DAVID). Fourteen to Eighteen: The Changing Pattern of Schooling in Scotland. Aberd. 1984.

28. EDUCATION: WALES

23621 LEWIS (E. GLYN). Bilingualism and Bilingual Education. Oxf. 1981.

23622 —— 'Bilingualism in Education in Wales'. In Sage Studies in Bilingual Education. Bernard Spolsky and Robert L. Cooper *eds*. Rowley, Mass. 1978.

23623 MINISTRY OF EDUCATION. The Future of Secondary Education in Wales. 1949.

23624 ELLIS (THOMAS IORWERTH). The Development of Higher Education in Wales. Wrexham. 1935.

23625 JONES (WILLIAM RICHARD). Bilingualism in Welsh Education. Cardiff. 1966.

23626 EVANS (GWILYM JOHN). The Entrance Scholarship Examination in Caernarvonshire, 1897–1961: With a Monograph in Welsh Showing the Relation of the Examination to the Development of the Country's Bilingual Policy, 1900–1965. Caernarvon. 1966.

23627 JONES (WILLIAM RICHARD). A Survey of Educational Attainment in Wales: A Report on the 1960 National Survey. Cowbridge. 1969.

23628 DAVIES (JAMES ARTHUR). Education in a Welsh Rural County, 1870–1973. 1973.

23629 GEEN (A. C.). 'Educational Policy-Making in Cardiff, 1944–1970'. *Public Admin.* 59 (1981), 313–29.

23630 EVANS (LESLIE WYNNE). Studies in Welsh Education: Welsh Educational Structure and Administration, 1880–1925. Cardiff. 1974.

23631 JENKINS (T. R.). 'Teacher Training in Welsh Colleges of Education, 1960–1970'. *J. Educ. Admin. Hist.* 8 (1975).

23632 DEPT. OF EDUCATION AND SCIENCE. Central Advisory Council for Education (Wales). 1967.

23633 Primary Education in Wales.

23634 GITTINS (CHARLES). 'Primary Education in Wales'. *Trans. Hon. Soc. Cymmr.* n.s. 1 (1969), 35–42.

23635 ELLIS (THOMAS IORWERTH). 'The Development of Modern Welsh Secondary Education'. *Trans. Hon. Soc. Cymmr.* 34 (1933), 1–39.

23636 GLOVER (ERNEST PERCIVAL). The First Sixty Years, 1896–1956: The Newport High School for Boys. Newport. 1957.

29. EDUCATION: NORTHERN IRELAND

23637 AKENSON (DONALD HARMAN). Education and Enmity: The Control of Schooling in Northern Ireland, 1920–1950. Newton Abbot. 1973.

23638 McNEILLY (NORMAN). Exactly Fifty Years: The Belfast Education Authority and its Work, 1923–1973. Belf. 1974.

23639 JAMIESON (JOHN). The History of the Royal Belfast Academical Institution 1810–1960. Belf. 1960.

23640 SUTHERLAND (M. B.). 'Progress and Problems in Education in Northern Ireland, 1952–1982'. *Brit. J. Educ. Studs* 136–49. (No date or vol. no.).

30. ADULT EDUCATION

23641 Adult Education in 1961+.

23642 THOMAS (J. E.) *and* DAVIES (J.H.) *eds*. A Select Bibliography of Adult Continuing Education in Great Britain. 1984.

23643 STYLER (W. E.). A Bibliographical Guide to Adult Education in Rural Areas, 1918–1978. Hull. 1973.

23644 KELLY (THOMAS) *ed*. A Select Bibliography of Adult Education in Great Britain, Including Works Published to the End of the Year 1950. 1952. 3rd edn 1974.

23645 —— A History of Adult Education in Great Britain. 2nd edn Liverpool. 1970.

23646 —— Outside the Walls: 60 Years of University Extension at Manchester, 1886–1946. Manch. 1950.

23647 —— Adult Education in Liverpool: A Narrative of Two Hundred Years. L/pool. 1960.

23648 BAYLISS (F. J.). 'The Response to Adult Education in Industry'. *Adult Educ.* 37 (1964), 55–67.

23649 STYLER (WILLIAM EDWARD). 'Adult Education and the Affluent Society'. *Adult Educ.* 34 (1961), 18–22.

23650 WILTSHIRE (H. C.). 'The Great Tradition in University Adult Education'. *Adult Educ.* 29 (1956–7), 88–97.

23651 PEERS (ROBERT). 'The Extra-Mural Work of Universities under War Conditions'. *Adult Educ.* 12 (1939), 85–7.

23652 WISEMAN (H. VICTOR). 'University Extension Work since 1945'. *Adult Educ.* 24 (1957), 180–92.

23653 BLYTH (J. A.). English University Adult Education 1908–1958: The Unique Tradition. Manch. 1983.

23654 EDWARDS (HERBERT JAMES). The Evening Institute: Its Place in the Education System of England and Wales. 1961.

23655 DENT (HAROLD COLLETT). Part Time Education in Great Britain: An Historical Outline. 1949.

23656 SMITHERS (ALAN GEORGE). Sandwich Courses: An Integrated Education? Windsor. 1976.

23657 FROW (EDMUND). A Survey of the Half-Time System in Education. Manch. 1970.

23658 CHERRINGTON (PAUL). 'Management Education in Britain'. *Adult Educ.* 38 (1965), 21–6.

23659 MANN (D. J.). 'Education for Management'. *J. Roy. Soc. Arts* 113 (1965), 970–87.

23660 LEE (D. J.). 'Industrial Training and Social Class'. *Sociol. Rev.* 14 (1966), 269–86.

23661 STUTTARD (GEOFFREY). 'Potentialities of the Industrial Training Act'. *Adult Educ.* 38 (1966), 254–8.

23662 WOODHALL (MAUREEN). 'Investment in Industrial Training: Effects of the Industrial Training Act on the Volume and Costs of Training'. *Brit. J. Indust. Relns* 12 (1974), 71–90.

23663 ALLAWAY (ALBERT JOHN). Adult Education in England: A Brief History. Leics. 1957.

23664 HARRISON (JOHN FLETCHER CLEWS). Learning and Living, 1790–1960: A Study in the History of the English Adult Education Movement. 1961.

23665 HUDSON (JAMES WILLIAM). The History of Adult Education. 1969.

23666 HARRISON (JOHN FLETCHER CLEWS). History of the Working Men's College, 1854–1954. 1954.

23667 HAWKINS (THORNTON HORACE) *and* BRAMBLE (LIONEL JOHN FARNHAM). Adult Education: The Record of the British Army. 1947.

23668 HUNTER (GUY). Residential Colleges: Some New Developments in British Adult Education. Pasadena, Calif. 1952.

23669 FLEMING (HORACE). Beechcroft: The Story of the Birkenhead Settlement, 1914–1924, An Experiment in Adult Education. 1938.

23670 CRAIK (WILLIAM WHITE). The Central Labour College, 1909–1929: A Chapter in the History of Adult Working Class Education. 1964.

23671 BUCHANAN (DEREK). Emergent Patterns in L.E.A. Adult Education. 1969.

23672 ALLAWAY (ALBERT JOHN). Challenge and Response: W.E.A. East Midland District 1919–1969. Nottingham. 1969.

23673 —— The First Fifty years of the W.E.A.s in Leicester. Leics. 1959.

23674 RAYBOULD (SIDNEY GRIFFITHS). The Workers Educational Association: The Next Phase. 1949.

23675 —— Fifty Years of Adult Study: University of London Goldsmiths' College School of Adult and Social Studies Golden Jubilee, 1931–1981. 1981.

23676 PRICE (THOMAS WILLIAM). The Story of the Workers' Educational Association, 1903–1924, 1924.

23677 STOCKS (MARY DANVERS) *Baroness*. The W.E.A.: The First Fifty Years. 1953.

23678 POLLINS (HAROLD). A History of Ruskin College. Oxf. 1984.

23679 MANSBRIDGE (ALBERT). Fellow Men: A Gallery of England, 1876–1946. 1948.

23680 RAYBOULD (SIDNEY GRIFFITHS) *ed.* Trends in English Adult Education. 1959.

23681 PEERS (ROBERT). Adult Education: A Comparative Study. 1958.

23682 —— *ed.* Adult Education in Practice. 1934.

23683 MARTIN (G. CURRIE). The Adult School Movement. 1924.

23684 LOVETT (TOM). Adult Education, Community Development and the Working Class. 1975.

23685 LOWE (JOHN). Adult Education in England and Wales: A Critical Survey. 1970.

23686 REES (DAVID BEN). Preparation for Crisis: Adult Education, 1945–80. 1982.

23687 DEVEREUX (WILLIAM A.). Adult Education in Inner London 1870–1980. 1982.

23688 STYLER (WILLIAM EDWARD). Adult Education in East Yorkshire, 1875–1960. Hull. 1965.

23689 WHITE (A. C. T.). The Story of Army Education 1643–1963. 1963.

23690 FIELDHOUSE (ROGER). Adult Education and the Cold War. Liberal Values Under Siege, 1946–1951. Leeds. 1985.

23691 WELCH (EDWIN). The Peripatetic University: The Cambridge Local Lectures, 1873–1973. 1973.

23692 PASHLEY (BARRY WILLIAM). University Extension Reconsidered. Leics. 1968.

23693 RAYBOULD (SIDNEY GRIFFITHS). The English Universities and Adult Education. 1952.

23694 —— University Extramural Education in England, 1945–1962: A Study in Finance and Policy. 1964.

23695 BEET (E. A.). 'New Universities and Adult Education'. *Adult Educ.* 33 (1960), 124–8.

23696 LAWSON (K. H.). 'Universities and Workers' Education in Britain'. *Inl. Lab. Rev.* 101 (1970), 1–14.

23697 WOOLFORD (A. J.). 'New Universities and Adult Education'. *Adult Educ.* 33 (1961), 266–7.

23698 BRUCE (MAURICE). The University of Sheffield, Department of Extramural Studies, 1947–1968: A Personal Survey. Sheffield. 1968.

23699 FEUCHTWANGER (E. J.). The Department of Adult Education; University of Southampton, 1928–1978: An Appreciation. Shampton. 1978.

23700 THORNTON (A. H.) *and* STEPHENS (M. D.) *eds.* The University and its Region: The Extra-Mural Contribution. Nottingham. 1977.

23701 MARRIOTT (STUART). Extramural Empires: Service and Self-Interest in English University Adult Education, 1873–1983. 1984.

23702 BLYTH (JOHN A.). English University Adult Education, 1908–1958. The Unique Tradition. Manch. 1983.

23703 TAYLOR (R.) *et al.* University Adult Education in Britain and the United States. 1985.

23704 STEAD (PETER). Coleg Harlech: The First Fifty Years. Cardiff. 1977.

23705 UNIVERSITY OF WALES. Survey of Adult Education in Wales. Cardiff. 1940.

23706 HOPKINS (P. G. H.). 'Labour Education in Britain'. *Adult Educ.* 38 (1965), 15–20.

23707 ELLIS (EDWARD L.). 'Dr Thomas Jones, C. H. and Education'. *Trans. Hon. Soc. Cymmr.* (1982), 86–109.

23708 HUTCHINSON (EDWARD MOSS) *ed.* Aims and Action in Adult Education, 1921–1971. 1971.

23709 DUKE (CHRISTOPHER). Paper Awards in Liberal Adult Education. 1973.

23710 EDWARDS (H. J.). The Evening Institute: Its Place in the Education System of England and Wales. 1961.

23711 HALL (W. ARNOLD). The Adult School Movement in the Twentieth Century. Nottingham. 1985.

23712 DAVIS (R.) *ed.* Woodbrooke College, 1903–1953: A Brief History of a Quaker Experiment in Religious Education. 1953.

23713 BARLOW (F. RALPH). Woodbrooke, 1953–1978: A Documentary Account of Woodbrooke's Third 25 Years. York. 1978.

23714 HAY (WENDY) *comp.* Adult Literacy in Britain: An Annotated Bibliography. 1978.

23715 HARGREAVES (D.). On the Move: The BBC's Contribution to the Adult Literacy Campaign in the United Kingdom between 1972 and 1976. 1977.

23716 ROBINSON (J.). Learning Over the Air: 60 Years of Partnership in Adult Learning. 1982.

31. WORLD WAR TWO

23717 GOSDEN (PETER HENRY JOHN HEATHER). Education in the Second World War: A Study in Policy and Administration. 1976.

23718 LLOYD (CYRIL). British Services Education. 1950.

23719 WILSON (NORMAN SCARLYN). Education in the Forces, 1939–1946: The Civilian Contribution. 1949.

23720 HARGREAVES (REGINALD). 'Education: The Army's Contribution'. *Quart. Rev.* 300 (1962), 291–302.

23721 SUMMERFIELD (P.). 'Education and Politics in the British Armed Forces in the Second World War'. *Inl. Rev. Soc. Hist.* 26 (1981), 133–58.

12

CULTURE, RECREATION, LEISURE, AND SPORT

The material assembled in this section covers a wide range of subjects but their individual identification is not too difficult. Contributions to the meaning of 'culture' in general in British society, and the languages used in Britain, are identified in the initial sub-section. Individual arts are then grouped. It is recognized that while it is reasonable to include early sub-sections which deal with architecture, art (painting), design and fashion, and sculpture, individuals executed work in more than one of these categories. Likewise scholars have not infrequently grouped them together in certain critical or historical studies. The user must therefore see these particular sub-sections as a totality. The same point also applies particularly to the following sub-sections: music and ballet; film, photography, radio; the press, books and publishing, literature; theatre and comedy. In all of these cases, there is inevitably some overlap of title and subject-matter. Nevertheless, the activity is sufficiently discrete for separate sub-sections to be useful. Perhaps not surprisingly, they are notably full since those whose business is primarily with communication clearly like writing about each other. Even so, many of these items represent the raw material of history rather than history itself. Within the sub-sections concerned, particular genres, tendencies, and types have been identified, so far as possible, but no cultural discrimination has been exercised between them—that is to say a 'great composer' has to live alongside a 'pop star'. The literary range is wide but it would not be appropriate to provide the amplitude to which a bibliography exclusively devoted to literature might aspire. As in the case of music, the attempt has been made, within this restriction, to be comprehensive in approach and not to presuppose the existence of a canon of British writers who should alone be considered. The emphasis has been primarily upon providing access to the writers and studies of their works rather than upon providing a full list of the works themselves. That distinction, however, cannot be invariably maintained.

The group of sub-sections that follows relates to particular academic disciplines. For reasons that will readily be apparent, some disciplines are much more self-aware than others—historians not least among them. It is perhaps natural that the 'humanities' should be particularly articulate about themselves. These sub-sections therefore attempt to give the user access both to information on leading scholars and also on the main trends within particular disciplines. In this process, natural science and natural scientists may be short-changed but it may be argued that the 'cultural' content of arts disciplines has a greater specifically British significance than the content of scientific disciplines.

A further group of sub-sections provides items relating in manifold aspects to leisure, tourism, national parks, and gardens. Linkages with rural life and the environment need to be primarily noted, but the topic also has obvious broad social, economic, and political implications. Again, although separately identified, this set of sub-sections should be seen as a totality.

Sport has then been treated in a separate group of sub-sections. The initial one covers the topic in general and it is followed by literature on particular sports. Attention naturally is concentrated on those sports with major followings. The literature does have problems. As in so many other areas, a sub-discipline has emerged in recent decades which has identified a specific area of 'sports history' and where penetrating scholarly work has been produced. On the other hand, to take two examples, biographies of sporting heroes or of football clubs in particular, do not in general reach a level which can be called scholarly. To have included every such item would perhaps have satisfied their respective fans but would have overloaded the bibliography with material which has temporary value and meets the needs only of a particular constituency. The compromise which has been adopted gives some idea of the range of material without claiming to be fully comprehensive.

1. CULTURE IN GENERAL

23722 FORD (BORIS) *ed.* The Cambridge Guide to the Arts in Britain. Vol. 8. The Edwardian Age and the Inter-War Years. 1989. Vol. 9: Since the Second World War. Camb. 1988.

23723 WILLIAMS (RAYMOND HENRY). Keywords: A Vocabulary of Culture and Society. Glasg. 1976.

23724 —— Culture and Society, 1780–1950. 1958.

23725 —— The Long Revolution. 1961.

23726 EAGLETON (TERRY) *ed.* Raymond Williams: Critical Debates. 1988.

23727 BERGONZI (BERNARD) *ed.* The Twentieth Century. 1970.

23728 COX (CHARLES BRIAN) *and* DYSON (ANTHONY EDWARD) *eds.* The 20th Century Mind: History, Ideas and Literature in Britain. Vol. 1. 1900–1918. 1972.

23729 HALLIDAY (FRANK ERNEST). An Illustrated Cultural History of England. 1967.

23730 CLARKE (JOHN), CRITCHER (CHARLES), *and* JOHNSON (RICHARD). Working Class Culture. 1979.

23731 BIDDISS (MICHAEL DENIS). The Age of the Masses: Ideas and Society in Europe since 1870. Harmondsworth. 1977.

23732 LEMAHIEU (D. L.). A Culture for Democracy: Mass Communication and the Cultivated Mind in Britain between the Wars. Oxf. 1988.

23733 FILMER (P.). 'The Literary Imagination and the Explanation of Socio-Cultural Change in Modern Britain'. *Archiv. Eur. Sociol.* 10 (1969), 271–91.

23734 DAICHES (DAVID) *ed.* A Companion to Scottish Culture. 1981.

23735 THOMSON (DERICK SMITH). A Companion to Gaelic Culture. 1983.

23736 CHAPMAN (MALCOLM). The Gaelic Vision in Scottish Culture. 1978.

23737 LONGLEY (MICHAEL) *ed.* Causeway: The Arts in Ulster. Belf. 1971.

23738 BELL (SAM HANNA) *et al.* The Arts in Ulster: A Symposium. 1951.

23739 BROWN (TERENCE). Ireland: A Social and Cultural History, 1922–1979. 1981.

23740 HAWCROFT (FRANCIS WILSON). The Arts. 1967.

23741 CARPENTER (MAURICE). A Rebel in the Thirties. Colchester. 1976.

23742 WAIN (JOHN BARRINGTON). 'My Nineteen Thirties'. *Evergreen Rev.* 14 (1960), 71–87.

23743 SPENDER (*Sir* [HAROLD] STEPHEN). 'The Modern as Vision of a Whole Situation'. *Partisan Rev.* 29 (1962), 350–65.

23744 AMIS (*Sir* KINGSLEY WILLIAM). 'Lone Voices: Views of the Fifties'. *Encounter* 15 (1960), 6–11.

23745 ALLSOP (KENNETH). The Angry Decade: A Survey of the Cultural Revolt of the Nineteen-Fifties. 1958.

23746 DEWS (PETER). 'National and Provincial'. *Critical Q.* 11 (1960), 355–9.

23747 KITCHIN (LAURENCE TYSON). 'Backwards and Forwards'. *Twentieth Cent.* 169 (1961), 165–71.

23748 OSBORNE (HAROLD). 'The New Sensibility of the 1960s'. *Brit. J. Aesthetics* 16 (1976), 99–107.

23749 CORNELIUS (DAVID KRAUSE) *and* ST VINCENT (ERWIN) *eds.* Cultures in Conflict: Perspectives on the Snow-Leavis Controversy. Chicago, Ill. 1964.

23750 SNOW (CHARLES PERCY) *Baron*. The Two Cultures and the Scientific Revolution. 1961.

23751 —— The Two Cultures and a Second Look. Camb. 1964.

23752 LEAVIS (FRANK RAYMOND). Two Cultures?: The Significance of C. P. Snow. 1962.

23753 JOHNSON (LESLEY). The Cultural Critics: From Matthew Arnold to Raymond Williams. 1979.

23754 HASSALL (CHRISTOPHER VERNON). Edward Marsh, Patron of the Arts: A Biography. 1959.

23755 MARSH (*Sir* EDWARD HOWARD). A Number of People: A Book of Reminiscences. 1939.

23756 ARTS COUNCIL OF GREAT BRITAIN: ANNUAL REPORT AND ACCOUNTS. 1946+.

23757 MINIHAN (JANET). The Nationalization of Culture: The Development of State Subsidies to the Arts in Great Britain. 1977.

23758 WILLATT (*Sir* ROBERT HUGH). The Arts Council of Great Britain: The First Twenty-Five Years. 1972.

23759 HARRIS (JOHN S.). Government Patronage of the Arts in Great Britain. Chicago, Ill. 1970.

23760 PEARSON (N.). The State and the Visual Arts. Milton Keynes. 1982.

23761 BALDRAY (H.). The Case for the Arts. 1981.

23762 WHITE (ERIC WALTER). The Arts Council in Great Britain. 1975.

23763 HUTCHINSON (ROBERT). The Politics of the Arts Council. 1982.

23764 SHAW (*Sir* ROY). The Arts and the People. 1987.

23765 OSBORNE (CHARLES). Giving it Away: The Memoirs of an Uncivil Servant. 1986.

23766 MYERSCOUGH (JOHN). The Economic Importance of the Arts in Britain. 1988. [Myerscough has also published three studies of particular regions: Merseyside, Glasgow, and Ipswich, all in 1988.].

23767 ROSENBAUM (STANFORD PATRICK) *ed*. The Bloomsbury Group: A Collection of Memoirs, Commentary and Criticism. 1975.

23768 JOHNSTONE (JOHN KEITH). The Bloomsbury Group: A Study of E. M. Forster, Lytton Strachey, Virginia Woolf and their Circle. 1954.

23769 GREEN (MARTIN). Children of the Sun: A Narrative of 'Decadence' in England after 1918. 1977.

23770 BLUNT (ANTHONY FREDERICK). 'From Bloomsbury to Marxism'. *Studio Inl.* 186 (1973), 164–8.

23771 DAVID (HUGH). The Fitzrovians: A Portrait of Bohemian London 1900–1950. 1988.

23772 HYNES (SAMUEL LYNN). The Auden Generation: Literature and Politics in England in the 1930s. 1976.

23773 MUSTE (JOHN MARTIN). Say that we saw Spain Die: Literary Consequences of the Spanish Civil War. 1966.

23774 STANSKY (PETER) *and* ABRAHAMS (WILLIAM). Journey to the Frontier: Julian Bell and John Cornford: Their Lives and the 1930s. 1966.

23775 WEINTRAUB (STANLEY). The Last Great Cause: The Intellectuals and the Spanish Civil War. 1968.

23776 HOSKINS (KATHARINE BAIL). Today the Struggle: Literature and Politics in England during the Spanish War. 1969.

23777 MUIR (EDWIN). The Present Age, from 1914. 1939.

23778 SMITH (ELTON EDWARD). The Angry Young Man of the Thirties. 1975.

23779 DAY-LEWIS (CECIL). The Mind in Chains: Socialism and the Cultural Revolution. 1937.

23780 SPENDER (*Sir* HAROLD STEPHEN). The Struggle of the Modern. 1963.

23781 HEWISON (ROBERT). Under Siege: Literary Life in London 1939–45. Rev. edn 1988.

23782 —— In Anger: Culture in the Cold War 1945–60. 1981.

23783 YVARD (P.). 'Literature and Society in the Fifties in Great Britain'. *J. Eur. Studs* 3 (1973), 36–44.

23784 BAKER (DENYS VAL). Britain Discovers herself. 1950.

23785 HEWISON (ROBERT). Too Much: Art and Society in the Sixties 1960–75. 1986.

23786 CRAIG (DAVID). 'The New Poetry of Socialism'. *New Left Rev.* 17 (1962), 73–84.

23787 SINFIELD (ALAN). Literature, Politics and Culture in Post-war Britain. Oxf. 1989.

23788 APPLEYARD (BRYAN). The Pleasures of Peace: Art and Imagination in Post-War Britain. 1989.

2. BRITISH LANGUAGES

23789 PARTRIDGE (ERIC) *and* CLARK (JOHN W.). British and American English since 1900. 1951.

23790 MCCRUM (ROBERT). The Story of English. 1986.

23791 ORTON (HAROLD) *et al*. Survey of English Dialects: The Basic Material. Leeds. 1962–71.

23792 —— The Linguistic Atlas of England. 1978.

23793 UPTON (CLIVE), SANDERSON (STEWART), *and* WIDDOWSON (JOHN). Wordmaps: A Dialect Atlas of England. 1987.

23794 KIRK (JOHN M.), SANDERSON (STEWART), *and* WIDDOWSON (JOHN). Studies in Linguistic Geography: The Dialects of English in Britain and Ireland. 1985.

23795 BURKE (PETER) *and* PORTER (ROY). The Social History of Language. Camb. 1990.

23796 TRUDGILL (PETER). International English: A Guide to Varieties of Standard English. 1982.

23797 —— *ed*. Language in the British Isles. Camb. 1984.

23798 —— On Dialect: Social and Geographical Perspectives. Oxf. 1983.

23799 —— Sociolinguistics: An Introduction. 1974.

23800 —— *ed.* Sociolinguistic Patterns in British English. 1978.

23801 —— Accent, Dialect and the School. 1975.

23802 —— Dialects of English: Studies in Grammatical Variation. 1990.

23803 —— The Dialects of England. Oxf. 1990.

23804 TRUDGILL (PETER) *and* HUGHES (ARTHUR). English Accents and Dialects: An Introduction to Social and Regional Varieties of British English. 1979.

23805 PRICE (GLANVILLE). The Languages of Britain. 1984.

23806 BURCHFIELD (ROBERT). The English Language. 1985.

23807 DEAR (I. C. B.). Oxford English: A Guide to the Language. Oxf. 1986.

23808 WAKELIN (MARTIN F.). English Dialects: An Introduction. 1972. Rev. edn 1977.

23809 LOCKWOOD (W. B.). Languages of the British Isles, Past and Present. 1975.

23810 HONEY (JOHN). Does Accent Matter: The Pygmalion Factor. 1989.

23811 GREENBAUM (SIDNEY) *ed.* The English Language Today. 1984.

23812 BARBER (CHARLES LAURENCE). Linguistic Change in Present-Day English. Edin. 1964.

23813 TRUDGILL (PETER). The Social Differentiation of English in Norwich. Camb. 1974.

23814 KHAN (VERITY SAIFULLAH). Bilingualism and Linguistic Minorities in Britain: Developments, Perspectives. 1977.

23815 WRIGHT (PETER). The Language of British Industry. 1974.

23816 —— Cockney Dialect and Slang. 1981.

23817 LASKER (GABRIEL WARD). Surnames and Genetic Structure. Camb. 1985.

23818 DURKACZ (V. E.). The Decline of the Celtic Languages. Edinburgh. 1983.

23819 DODSON (CHARLES JOSEPH) *ed.* Bilingual Education: Evaluation, Assessment and Methodology. Cardiff. 1985.

23820 Bilingualism and British Education: The Dimensions of Diversity: Papers from a Conference convened in January 1976. 1976.

23821 DERRICK (JUNE). Language Needs of Minority Group Children: Learners of English as a Second Language. Slough. 1977.

23822 HARRIS (JOHN). Phonological Variation and Change Studies in Hiberno-English. Camb. 1985.

23823 JONES (W. R.). Bilingualism in Welsh Education. Card. 1966.

23824 BETTS (CLIVE). Culture in Crisis: The Future of the Welsh Language. Upton. Wirral. 1976.

23825 AITCHISON (J. W.) *and* CARTER (H.). The Welsh Language 1961–1981: An Interpretative Atlas. Card. 1985.

23826 PRYCE (W. T. R.). 'Welsh and English in Wales 1750–1971: A Spatial Analysis Based on the Linguistic Affiliation of Parochial Communities'. *Bull. Bd Celtic Studs* 28, 1–36.

23827 THOMAS (NED). The Welsh Extremist: A Culture in Crisis. 1971.

23828 WILLIAMS (COLIN H.). 'Language Contact and Language Change in Wales, 1901–1971: A Study in Historical Geolinguistics'. *Welsh Hist. Rev.* 10 (1980), 207–38.

23829 —— 'Non-Violence and the Development of the Welsh Language Society. 1962–c.1974'. *Welsh Hist. Rev.* (1977), 426–55.

23830 —— 'Public Gain and Private Grief: The Rate of Language Loss Among Welsh Speakers Between 1921 and 1981'. *Trans. Hon. Soc. Cymmr.* (1985), 27–48.

23831 BOWEN (E. G.) *and* (CARTER H.). 'Distribution of the Welsh Language in 1971: An Analysis'. *Geog.* 60 (1975), 1–15.

23832 Council for Wales and Monmouthshire Report on the Welsh Language Today. Cmmd 2198, Parliamentary Papers xx (1963–4).

23833 Legal Status of the Welsh Language. Cmmd 2785 Parliamentary Papers xxiii (1964–5) [Sir David Hughes Parry.].

23834 PARRY (*Sir* DAVID HUGHES). 'The Status of the Welsh Language in English Law' in Robert H. C. Holland and Georg Schwarzenberger, *eds.* Law, Justice and Equity: Essays in tribute to G. W. Keeton. 1967.

23835 COUPLAND (NIKOLAS). Dialect in Use: Sociolinguistic Variations in Cardiff English. Card. 1988.

23836 BALL (MARTIN J.) *and* JONES (GLYN E.) *eds.* Welsh Phonology: Selected Readings. Card. 1984.

23837 JONES (RICHARD GERALLT). A Bid for Unity: The Story of Undeb Cymru Fydd 1946–1966. Aberystwyth. 1971.

23838 DAVIES (GWENNANT). The Story of the Urdd: The Welsh League of Youth 1922–1972. Aberystwyth. 1973. [A condensed version of R. E. Griffith, Urdd Gobaith Cymru. 3 vols. Aberystwyth. 1971–3.].

23839 DONN (THOMAS MACKENZIE). 'The Debate about the Gaelic Language of Scotland since 1832'. *Trans. Gaelic Soc. Inverness* 49 (1974), 26–52.

23840 MACKINNON (KENNETH M.). 'The School in Gaelic Scotland'. *Trans. Gaelic Soc. Inverness* 47 (1971–2), 374–89.

23841 —— Gaelic in Scotland 1971: Some Sociological and Demographic Considerations of the Census Report for Gaelic. Hatfield. 1978.

23842 —— Language, Education and Social Processes in a Gaelic Community. 1977.

23843 —— 1981 Census on Gaelic in the Highland Region. Inverness. 1984.

23844 —— The Lion's Tongue: The Story of the Original and Continuing Language of the Scottish People. Inverness. 1984.

23845 —— Scottish Opinion on Gaelic: a Report on A National Attitude Survey. Hatfield. 1981.

23846 DORIAN (NANCY C.). Language Death: The Life Cycle of a Scottish Gaelic Dialect. Philadelphia, Pa. 1971.

23847 AITKEN (A. J.) *and* MCARTHUR (TOM) *eds.* Languages of Scotland. Edin. 1979.

23848 AITKEN (A. J.) *ed.* Lowland Scots. Edin. 1973.

23849 MCCLURE (J. DERRICK), AITKEN (A. J.), *and* LAW (JOHN THOMAS). The Scots Language: Planning for Modern Usage. Edin. 1980.

23850 STEVENSON (JAMES A. C.). Scoor-Oot: A Dictionary of Scots Words and Phrases in Current Use. 1989.

23851 MACAULAY (RONALD K. S.). Language, Social Class and Education: A Glasgow Study. Edin. 1977.

23852 ROBINSON (MAIRI) *ed.-in-chief.* The Concise Scots Dictionary. Aberd. 1985.

23853 ULSTER FOLK AND TRANSPORT MUSEUM. The English Dialects of Ulster: An Anthology of Articles on Ulster Speech by G. B. Adams. Belf. 1986.

23854 MILROY (JAMES). Regional Accents of English: Belfast. Belf. 1981.

23855 ULSTER FOLK MUSEUM. Ulster Dialects: An Introductory Symposium. Belf. 1964.

23856 SUTCLIFFE (D.). British Black English. Oxf. 1982.

3. ARCHITECTURE

23857 Architects' Yearbook. 1945–74.

23858 Architecture Journal. 1894–.

23859 Architectural Periodicals Index. Royal Institute of British Architects 1972–.

23860 WATERS (G. M.). Dictionary of British Architects Working 1900–1950. 2 vols. Eastbourne. 1975–6.

23861 WODEHOUSE (L.) *ed.* British Architects 1840–1975: A Guide to Information Sources. Detroit, Mich. 1978.

23862 KAMEN (RUTH H.). British and Irish Architectural History: Bibliography and Guide to Sources of Information. 1981.

23863 WARE (DORA). A Short Dictionary of British Architects. 1967.

23864 WATKIN (DAVID). The Rise of Architectural History. 1980.

23865 SUMMERSON (*Sir* JOHN NEWENHAM). The Architectural Association, 1847–1947. 1947.

23866 MACE (ANGELA). The Royal Institute of British Architects: a Guide to its Archive and History. 1985.

23867 GOTCH (JOHN ALFRED). The Growth and Work of the Royal Institute of British Architects, 1834–1934. 1934.

23868 REILLY (*Sir* CHARLES HERBERT). Representative British Architects of the Present Day. 1931.

23869 KAYE (BARRINGTON LAURENCE BURNETT). The Development of the Architectural Profession in Britain: A Sociological Study. 1960.

23870 JENKINS (FRANK). Architect and Patron: A Survey of Professional Relations and Practice in England from the Sixteenth Century to the Present Day. 1961.

23871 LIPMAN (ALAN). 'Architectural Education and the Social Commitment of Contemporary British Architecture'. *Sociol. Rev.* 18 (1970), 5–27.

23872 BLOMFIELD (*Sir* REGINALD THEODORE). Memoirs of an Architect. 1932.

23873 HUSSEY (CHRISTOPHER EDWARD CLIVE). The Life of Sir Edwin Lutyens. 1950.

23874 BUTLER (ARTHUR STANLEY GEORGE) *et al.* The Architecture of Sir Edwin Lutyens. 3 vols. 1950.

23875 WILLIAMS-ELLIS (*Sir* BERTRAM CLOUGH). Architect Errant. 1971.

23876 SUDJIC (DEYAN). Norman Foster, Richard Rogers, James Stirling: New Directions in British Architecture. 1986.

23877 CHERRY (GORDON E.) *and* PENNY (LEITH). Holford: A Study in Architecture, Planning and Civic Design. 1986.

23878 HOUFE (S.). Sir Albert Richardson: The Professor. 1980.

23879 BRETT (LIONEL). Our Selves Unknown: An Autobiography. 1985.

23880 KNOBEL (LANCE). The Faber Guide to Twentieth-Century Architecture: Britain and Northern Europe. 1985.

23881 HITCHCOCK (HENRY-RUSSELL). Architecture: Nineteenth and Twentieth Centuries. 1958.

23882 MORGAN (HAROLD ANTHONY) *and* PRICE (ARNOLD THOMAS). Architecture of the Twentieth Century. Sydney. 1961.

23883 BANHAM ((PETER) RAYNER). Guide to Modern Architecture. 1962.

23884 —— The New Brutalism: Ethic or Aesthetic? 1966.

23885 —— Age of the Masters: A Personal View of Modern Architecture. 1975.

23886 —— The Architecture of the Well-Tempered Environment. 1969.

23887 —— Megastructure: Urban Features of the Recent Past. 1976.

23888 BRAUN (HUGH STANLEY). The Story of English Architecture. 1950.

23889 SUMMERSON (*Sir* JOHN NEWENHAM). Architecture in England. 1947. Rev. edn 1948.

23890 SHARP (DENNIS). Sources of Modern Architecture. 1967.

23891 RICHARDS (*Sir* JAMES MAUDE). An Introduction to Modern Architecture. 2nd edn 1956.

23892 DANNATT (TREVOR). Modern Architecture in Britain: Selected Examples of Recent Buildings. 1959.

23893 SCULLY (VINCENT JOSEPH). Modern Architecture: The Architecture of Democracy. 1968.

23894 PEVSNER (*Sir* NIKOLAUS BERNHARD LEON). Pioneers of Modern Design from William Morris to Walter Gropius. 1960.

23895 PETER (JOHN). Masters of Modern Architecture. 1959.

23896 NELLIST (JOHN BOWMAN). British Architecture and its Background. 1967.

23897 WEBB (MICHAEL). Architecture in Britain Today. 1969.

23898 JACOBUS (JOHN M.). Twentieth-Century Architecture: The Middle Years, 1940–1965. 1966.

23899 SUMMERSON (*Sir* JOHN NEWENHAM) *ed.* Ten Years of British Architecture 1945–55. 1956.

23900 MILLS (EDWARD DAVID). The New Architecture in Great Britain, 1946–1953. 1953.

23901 JACKSON (ANTHONY). The Politics of Architecture: A History of Modern Architecture in Britain. 1970.

23902 SAINT (ANDREW). A Change of Heart: English Architecture since the War—A Policy for Protection. 1992.

23903 MAXWELL (ROBERT MILLER). New British Architecture. 1972.

23904 MacEWEN (MALCOLM). Crisis in Architecture. 1974.

23905 JACKSON (ANTHONY). The Politics of Architecture: A History of Modern Architecture in Britain. 1970.

23906 LYALL (SUTHERLAND). The State of British Architecture. 1980.

23907 MURRAY (PETER) *and* TROMBLEY (STEPHEN) *eds.* Modern British Architecture since 1945. 1984.

23908 THE PRINCE OF WALES. A Vision of Britain. 1989.

23909 HUTCHINSON (MAXWELL). The Prince of Wales: Right and Wrong. 1989.

23910 RICHARDS (*Sir* JAMES MAUDE). 'The Hollow Victory: 1932–1972'. *J. Roy. Inst. Brit. Architects* 80 (1972), 192–7.

23911 LYONS (ERIC) *et al.* '25 years of British Architecture, 1952–1977'. *J. Roy. Inst. Brit. Architects* 84 (1977), 171–226.

23912 COLQUHOUN (ALAN). 'The Modern Movement in Architecture'. *Brit. J. Aesthetics* 2 (1962), 59–65.

23913 SMITHSON (PETER DENHAM). 'The Idea of Architecture in the Fifties'. *Architects J.* (21 Jan. 1960), 119–26.

23914 ALLSOPP (BRUCE). Towards a Humane Architecture. 1974.

23915 PEVSNER (*Sir* NIKOLAUS BERNHARD LEON). The Buildings of England. 46 vols. 1951–74.

23916 LAMBERT (SAM). New Architecture in London. 1963.

23917 McCALLUM (IAN ROBERT MORE). A Pocket Guide to Modern Buildings in London. 1951.

23918 McKEAN (CHARLES) *and* JENKINS (TOM) *eds.* Modern Buildings in London: A Guide. 1976.

23919 GERRARD (JOHN). 'Architecture in Glasgow since World War One'. *Scot. Art Rev.* 14 (1975), 13–15.

23920 ALLSOPP (BRUCE) *ed.* Modern Architecture of Northern England. 1969.

23921 McKEAN (CHARLES). Architectural Guide to Cambridge and East Anglia since 1920. 1982.

23922 MacKEITH (MARGARET). Shopping Arcades: A Gazeteer of Extant British Arcades 1817–1939. 1985.

23923 —— The History and Conservation of Shopping Arcades. 1985.

23924 MARTIN (BRUCE). School Buildings, 1945–51. 1952.

23925 MILLS (EDWARD DAVID). The Modern Factory. 1951.

23926 DUFFY (F.). 'Office Landscaping, 1958–1978'. *Architectural Rev.* 165 (1979), 54–9.

23927 ELWALL (R.). Bricks and Beer: English Pub Architecture 1830–1939. 1983.

23928 SPENCE (*Sir* BASIL URWIN). Phoenix at Coventry: The Building of a New Cathedral. 1962.

23929 SPRING (M.). 'The Natwest Tower'. *Building* (23 Jan. 1981), 38–51.

23930 ANSCOMBE (ISABELLE). Omega and After: Bloomsbury and the Decorative Arts. 1981.

23931 BARON (WENDY). Miss Ethel Sands and her Circle. 1977.

4. ART

23932 JOHNSON (J.) *and* GREUTZNER (A.). The Dictionary of British Artists 1880–1940. 1966.

23933 LUCAS (EDNA LOUISE) *comp.* Art books: A Basic Bibliography of the Fine Arts. Greenwich, Conn. 1968.

23934 COURTAULD INSTITUTE OF ART. Annual Bibliography of the History of British Art.

23935 THE YEAR'S ART 1880–1947. 1970+.

23936 CHAMBERLAIN (MARY WALLS) *comp.* Guide to Art Reference Books. Chicago, Ill. 1959.

23937 PARRY-CROOKE (CHARLOTTE). Contemporary British Artists. 1979.

23938 WATERS (GRANT). Dictionary of British Artists Working 1900–1950. 2 vols. Eastbourne. 1975.

23939 ABSE (JOAN). The Art Galleries of Britain and Ireland: A Guide to their Collections. 1976.

23940 HILL (MAUREEN) *ed.* National Portrait Gallery: Concise Catalogue, 1856–1969. 1970.

23941 HENDY (*Sir* PHILIP). The National Portrait Gallery. 1960.

23942 SAVAGE (LEONARD GEORGE GRIMSON). The Market in Art. 1969.

23943 REITLINGER (GERALD ROBERTS). The Economics of Taste. 3 vols. 1961–70.

23944 HERRMANN (FRANK). Sotheby's: Portrait of an Auction House. 1980.

23945 —— *ed.* The English as Collectors: A Documentary Chrestomathy. 1972.

23946 AGNEW (JULIAN). A Dealer's Record: Agnew's 1967–1981. 1981.

23947 FORD (JOHN). Ackermann 1783–1983: The Business of Art. 1983.

23948 SUTTON (DENYS). Christies since the War, 1945–1958. 1958.

23949 MARKS (RICHARD). Burrell: A Portrait of a Collector: Sir William Burrell 1861–1958. Glasg. 1983.

23950 HUDSON (DEREK ROMMEL) *and* LUCKHURST (KENNETH WILLIAM). The Royal Society of Arts, 1754–1954. 1954.

23951 HUTCHISON (SYDNEY CHARLES). The History of the Royal Academy, 1768–1968. 1968.

23952 CLARK (KENNETH MACKENZIE). Another Part of the Wood: A Self-Portrait. 1974.

23953 —— The Other Half: A Self Portrait. 1977.

23954 SECREST (MERYLE). Kenneth Clark : A Biography. 1985.

23955 PICK (JOHN). Arts Administration. 1980.

23956 —— The State and the Arts. Eastbourne. 1980.

23957 JENKINS (HUGH). *Baron.* The Culture Gap: An Experience of Government and the Arts. 1979.

23958 PEARSON (NICHOLAS). The State and the Visual Arts: A Discussion of State Intervention in the Visual Arts in Britain, 1760–1981. Milton Keynes. 1982.

23959 LAMBERT (RICHARD STANTON). Art in England. Harmondsworth. 1938.

23960 HUBBARD (ERIC HESKETH). A Hundred Years of British Painting, 1851–1951. 1951.

23961 SUNDERLAND (JOHN). Painting in Britain, 1525–1975. Oxf. 1976.

23962 SHORT (ERNEST HENRY). A History of British Painting. 1953.

23963 SHONE (RICHARD). British Painting 1910–1945. 1967.

23964 —— The Century of Change: British Painting since 1900. 1977.

23965 MORPHET (RICHARD). British Painting 1910–1945. 1967.

23966 BOWNESS (ALAN). Recent British Painting. 1967.

23967 ROTHENSTEIN (*Sir* JOHN KNEWSTUB MAURICE). British Art Since 1900. 1962.

23968 —— Modern English Painters: Sickert to Smith. 1952.

23969 —— Modern English Painters: Lewis to Moore. 1956.

23970 —— Modern English Painters: Wood to Hockney. 1974.

23971 —— Autobiography. Summer's Lease 1901–1938. 1965. Brave Day, Hideous Night 1939–1965. 1967. Time's Thievish Progress. 1970.

23972 WOODS (GERALD). Art Without Boundaries, 1950–1970. 1972.

23973 ROSENTHAL (ERWIN ISAAK JAKOB). Contemporary Art in the Light of History. 1971.

23974 READ (*Sir* HERBERT EDWARD). Contemporary British Art. Harmondsworth. 1951.

23975 —— A Concise History of Modern Painting. 1959.

23976 OSBOURNE (HAROLD) *ed.* The Oxford Companion to Art. Oxf. 1970.

23977 PIPER (DAVID). The Genius of British Painting. 1975.

23978 GAUNT (WILLIAM). British Painting from Hogarth's Day to ours. 1945.

23979 —— A Concise History of English Painting. 1964.

23980 BAKER (CHARLES HENRY COLLINS) *and* JAMES (MONTAGUE). British Painting. 1934.

23981 BLAKE (CHRISTOPHER). Modern English Art. 1937.

23982 RAY (PAUL CHARLES). The Surrealist Movement in England. 1971.

23983 BERTRAM (CYRIL ANTHONY GEORGE). A Century of British Painting, 1851–1951. 1951.

23984 BURY (ADRIAN) *comp.* Two Centuries of British Water-Colours and Drawings. 1950.

23985 FORD (BRINSLEY). Three Centuries of British Water-Colours and Drawings. 1951.

23986 HARRISON (CHARLES). English Art and Modernism 1900–1939. 1981.

23987 FRY (ROGER ELLIOT). Reflections on British Painting. 1934.

23988 GRIGSON (GEOFFREY EDWARD HARVEY). English Drawing from Samuel Cooper to Gwen John. 1955.

23989 DREW (JOANNA) *ed.* Landscape in Britain 1850–1950. 1983.

23990 FINCH (CHRISTOPHER). Image as Language: Aspects of British Art, 1950–1968. 1969.

23991 NAYLOR (GILLIAN). The Arts and Crafts Movement: A Study of its Sources, Ideals, and Influence on Design Theory. 1971.

23992 WADDINGTON (CONRAD HAL). Behind Appearance: A Study of the Relations between Painting and Natural Sciences in this Century. Edin. 1969.

23993 THOMPSON (DAVID). 'Recent British Painting: The Stuyvesant Collection'. *Studio* 174 (1967), 153–261.

23994 ROBERTSON (BRYAN CHARLES FRANCIS). '1893–1963: British Painting'. *Studio* 165 (1963), 136–47.

23995 MATTHEWS (J. H.). 'Surrealism and England'. *Comp. Lit. Studs* 1 (1964), 55–72.

23996 CANDY (JOHN EDWIN). Mainstream of Modern Art. 1959.

23997 LUCIE-SMITH (JOHN MCKENZIE) EDWARD). Movements in Art since 1945. 1969.

23998 —— Art in Britain, 1969–1970. 1970.

23999 BARRETT (DENIS CYRIL). Pop Art. 1970.

24000 MELLY ([ALAN HEYWOOD] GEORGE). Revolt into Style: The Pop Arts in Britain. 1970.

24001 BARNES (KEN). Twenty Years of Pop. 1973.

24002 CASH (TONY) *ed.* Anatomy of Pop. 1970.

24003 LIPPARD (LUCY ROWLAND). Pop Art. 1967.

24004 LESLIE (PETER). Fab: The Anatomy of a Phenomenon. 1965.

24005 BARBER ([JOHN LYSBERG] NOEL). Conversations with Painters. 1964.

24006 CANNON-BROOKES (PETER). Michael Ayrton: An Illustrated Commentary. Birmingham. 1978.

24007 LEIRIS (MICHEL). Francis Bacon: Full Face and in Profile. 1983.

24008 SYLVESTER ([ANTHONY BERNARD] DAVID). Interviews with Francis Bacon. 1975.

24009 VAIZEY (MARINA). Peter Blake. 1985.

24010 LIPKE (WILLIAM). David Bomberg: A Critical Study of his Life and Work. 1967.

24011 DE BELLEROCHE (WILLIAM). Brangwyn Talks. 1944.

24012 BRANGWYN (RODNEY). Brangwyn. 1978.

24013 FINCH (CHRISTOPHER). Patrick Caulfield. Harmondsworth. 1971.

24014 LEWIS (R.). Sir William Russell Flint 1880–1968. Edin. 1980.

24015 GILL (EVAN ROBERTSON). Bibliography of Eric Gill. 1953.

24016 GILL (ARTHUR ERIC HOWTON). Autobiography. 1940.

24017 SPEAIGHT (ROBERT WILLIAM). The Life of Eric Gill. 1966.

24018 YORKE (MALCOLM). Eric Gill: A Man of Flesh and Spirit. 1981.

24019 MacCARTHY (FIONA). Eric Gill. 1989.

24020 HERMAN (JOSEF). Related Twilights: Notes from an Artist's Diary. 1975.

24021 HERON (PATRICK). Ivon Hitchens. Harmondsworth. 1955.

24022 JOHN (AUGUSTUS EDWIN). Autobiography. 1975.

24023 BARP (THOMAS WADE). Augustus John. 1934.

24024 ROTHENSTEIN (*Sir* JOHN KNEWSTUB MAURICE). Augustus John. 1944.

24025 EASTON (MALCOLM) *and* HOLROYD (MICHAEL [de COURCY]). The Art of Augustus John. 1974.

24026 HOLROYD (MICHAEL [de COURCY]). Augustus John. 2 vols. 1974–5.

24027 CHITTY (*Lady* SUSAN ELSPETH RUSSEL). Gwen John 1876–1936. 1981.

24028 LANGDALE (C.) *and* JENKINS (D. F.). Gwen John: An Interior Life. Oxf. 1985.

24029 JOHNSTONE (WILLIAM). Points in Time. 1980.

24030 HUDSON (DEREK ROMMEL). For Love of Painting: The Life of Sir David Kelly. 1975.

24031 KNIGHT (*Dame* LAURA). Painting an Adventure. 1935.

24032 LAVERY (*Sir* JOHN). The Life of a Painter. 1940.

24033 MICHEL (WALTER). Wyndham Lewis: Paintings and Drawings. Berkeley, Calif. 1971.

24034 FARRINGTON (JANE). Wyndham Lewis. 1980.

24035 ANDREWS (ALLEN). The Life of L. S. Lowry, 1887–1976. 1977.

24036 LEVY (MERVYN MONTAGUE). The Paintings of L. S. Lowry. 1975.

24037 —— The Drawings of L. S. Lowry, Public and Private. 1976.

24038 ROHDE (SHELLEY). A Private View of L. S. Lowry. 1976.

24039 DIXON (E.). Charles Rennie Mackintosh: A Selective Bibliography. 1981.

24040 HOWARTH (THOMAS). Charles Rennie Mackintosh and the Modern Movement. 1952. 2nd edn 1977.

24041 BILLCLIFFE (ROGER). Mackintosh Watercolours. NY. 1978.

24042 WILKINSON (ALAN G.). The Drawings of Henry Moore. 1977.

24043 BOOTH (STANLEY). Sir Alfred Munnings 1878–1959. 1978.

24044 NASH (PAUL). Outline: An Autobiography. 1949.

24045 EASTES (MARGOT). Paul Nash: The Master of the Image, 1889–1946. 1973.

24046 CAUSEY (ANDREW). Paul Nash. Oxf. 1980.

24047 NASH (STEVEN). Ben Nicholson: Fifty Years of his Art. Buffalo, NY. 1978.

24048 BROWSE (LILIAN GERTRUDE). William Nicholson. 1943.

24049 ARNOLD (BRUCE). Orpen: An Autobiography. 1949.

24050 BOWNESS (ALAN) *and* LAMBERTINI (LUIGI). Victor Pasmore, with a Catalogue Raisonné of the Paintings, Constructs and Graphics 1926–1979. 1980.

24051 WATNEY (JOHN). Mervyn Peake. 1976.

24052 WEST (ANTONY). John Piper. 1979.

24053 INGRAMS (RICHARD REID) *and* PIPER (JOHN EGERTON CHRISTMAS). Piper's Places: John Piper in England and Wales. 1983.

24054 HUDSON (DEREK ROMMEL). James Pryde, 1886–1941. 1949.

24055 HUDSON (DEREK ROMMEL). Arthur Rackham: His Life and Work. 1960.

24056 CONSTABLE (FRIEDA). The England of Eric Ravilious. 1982.

24057 BINYON (HELEN). Eric Ravilious: Memoir of an Artist. 1983.

24058 HOUFE (S.). Sir Albert Richardson: The Professor. Luton. 1980.

24059 KUDLIEKA (ROBERT). Bridget Riley. 1978.

24060 SPEAIGHT (ROBERT WILLIAM). William Rothenstein: The Portrait of an Artist in his Time. 1962.

24061 BROWSE (LILLIAN GERTRUDE). Sickert. 1960.

24062 EMMONS (ROBERT). The Life and Opinions of Walter Richard Sickert. 1941.

24063 BARON (WENDY). Sickert. 1973.

24064 LILLY (MARJORIE). Sickert: The Painter and his Circle. 1971.

24065 SUTTON (DENYS). Walter Sickert: A Biography. 1976.

24066 HALLIDAY (FRANCIS) *and* RUSSELL (JOHN). Matthew Smith. 1962.

24067 LEVY (MERVYN MONTAGUE). Ruskin Spear. 1985.

24068 ROTHENSTEIN (*Sir* JOHN KNEWSTUB MAURICE). Stanley Spencer, the Man: Correspondence and Reminiscences. 1979.

24069 ROTHENSTEIN (ELIZABETH). Stanley Spencer. 1945.

24070 CARLINE (RICHARD). Stanley Spencer at War. 1978.

24071 LEDER (CAROLYN). Stanley Spencer: The Astor Collection. 1976.

24072 ROBINSON (DUNCAN). Stanley Spencer: Views from a Berkshire Village. Oxf. 1979.

24073 MacCOLL (DUGALD SUTHERLAND). Life, Work and Setting of Philip Wilson Steer. 1945.

24074 LAUGHTON (BRUCE). Philip Wilson Steer, 1860–1942. Oxf. 1971.

24075 COOPER (DOUGLAS). The Work of Graham Sutherland. 1961.

24076 ALLEY (RONALD). Graham Sutherland. 1982.

24077 BERTHOUD (ROGER). Graham Sutherland: A Biography. 1982.

24078 HAYES (JOHN). The Art of Graham Sutherland. Oxf. 1980.

24079 TASSI (ROBERTO). *trans. ed. and* by Julian Andrews Sutherland: The Wartime Drawings. 1979.

24080 TOWNSEND (WILLIAM). The Townsend Journals: An Artist's Record of his Times, 1928–1951. 1976.

24081 LETHABY (WILLIAM RICHARD). Philip Webb and his Work. 1935.

24082 WHISTLER (LAURENCE) *and* FULLER (RONALD). The Work of Rex Whistler. 1960.

24083 WHISTLER (LAURENCE). The Laughter and the Urn: A Biography of Rex Whistler. 1985.

24084 WILLIAMS (JOHN KYFFIN). Across the Straits: An Autobiography. 1973.

24085 GORDON (E.). The Royal Scottish Academy of Painting, Sculpture and Architecture 1826–1976. Edin. 1976.

24086 FERGUSSON (JOHN DUNCAN). Modern Scottish Painting. Glasg. 1943.

24087 FIRTH (JACK). Scottish Watercolour Painting. Edin. 1979.

24088 FINLAY (IAN). Art in Scotland. 1948.

24089 GODFREY (RICHARD). Printmaking in Britain: A General History from its Beginnings to the Present Day. Oxf. 1978.

24090 HUNNISETT (B.). A Dictionary of British Steel Engravers. Leigh-on-Sea. 1980.

24091 GARRETT (ALBERT). A History of British Wood Engraving. Tunbridge Wells. 1978.

24092 —— British Wood Engraving of the Twentieth Century. 1980.

24093 RICHARDS (*Sir* JAMES MAUDE) *comp.* The Wood Engravings of Eric Ravilious. 1972.

24094 CRAMER (GERALD), GRANT (ALISTAIR), *and* MITCHISON (DAVID). Henry Moore: Catalogue of Graphic Work. 1931–1979. 3 vols. Geneva. 1980.

24095 TASSI (ROBERTO). Graham Sutherland: Complete Graphic Work. 1978.

24096 GRANT (MAURICE HAROLD). A Dictionary of British Etchers. 1952.

24097 GUICHARD (K. M.). British Etchers, 1850–1940. 1977. 2nd edn 1981.

24098 BALSTON (THOMAS). English Wood-Engraving, 1900–1950. 1951.

24099 NEWBOLT (*Sir* FRANCIS GEORGE). History of the Royal Society of Painter-Etchers and Engravers, 1880–1930. 1931.

24100 DARTON (FREDERICK JOSEPH HARVEY). Modern Book Illustration in Great Britain and America. 1931.

24101 LAMBERT (MARGARET) *and* MARX (ENID). English Popular Art. 1951.

24102 LOW (*Sir* DAVID [ALEXANDER CECIL]). British Cartoonists, Caricaturists and Comic Artists. 1942.

24103 —— Ye Madde Designer. 1935.

24104 —— Low's Autobiography. 1956.

24105 SEYMOUR-URE (COLIN KNOWLTON) *and* SCHOFF (J.). David Low. 1985.

24106 FEAVER (WILLIAM) *and* GOULD (A.). Masters of Caricature: From Hogarth and Gillray to Scarfe and Levine. 1981.

24107 CECIL (EDWARD CHRISTIAN DAVID GASCOYNE). *Lord.* Max: A Biography. 1964.

5. DESIGN AND FASHION

24108 EHRESMANN (DONALD L.). Applied and Decorative Arts: A Bibliographic Guide to Basic Reference Works, Histories and Handbooks. Littleton, Colo. 1977.

24109 COULSON (ANTHONY J.). A Bibliography of Design in Britain 1851–1970. 1979.

24110 BETJEMAN (*Sir* JOHN). Ghastly Good Taste. 1933.

24111 GLOAG (JOHN EDWARDS). The English Tradition in Design. 1947. Rev. edn 1960.

24112 BATTERSBY (MARTIN). The Decorative Twenties. 1969.

24113 —— The Decorative Thirties. 1971.

24114 CARRINGTON (NOEL). Design and Decoration in the Home. 1952.

24115 MacCARTHY (FIONA). British Design since 1880: A Visual History. 1982.

24116 HUYGEN (FREDERIQUE). British Design: Images and Reality. 1989.

24117 MCDERMOTT (CATHERINE). Street Style: British Design in the 1980s. 1987.

24118 OSBORNE (JUNE). Stained Glass in England. 1981.

24119 RICKARDS (MAURICE). The Rise and Fall of the Poster. Newton Abbot. 1971.

24120 DARRACOTT (JOSEPH) *and* DARRACOTT (BELINDA). First World War Posters: Second World War Posters. 1972.

24121 CARLINE (RICHARD COTTON). Pictures in the Post: The Story of the Picture Postcard. Bedford. 1959.

24122 TOLLER (JANE). British Samplers: A Concise History. Chichester. 1980.

24123 ANSON (PETER FREDERICK). Fashions in Church Furnishings, 1840–1940. 1960.

24124 HINKS (PETER). Twentieth Century British Jewellery 1900–1980. 1983.

24125 DOUGLAS (RONALD WALTER) *and* FRANK (SUSAN). A History of Glassmaking. Henley-on-Thames. 1972.

24126 ELVILLE (E. M.). English and Irish Cut-Glass, 1750–1950. 1953.

24127 WHISTLER (LAURENCE). The Image on the Glass. 1975.

24128 BRENTNALL (MARGARET). John Hutton: Artist and Glass Engraver, a Biography. 1985.

24129 BUNT (CYRIL GEORGE EDWARD) *and* ROSE (ERNEST ARTHUR). Two Centuries of English Chintz, 1750–1950. Leigh-on-Sea. 1957.

24130 EYLES (DESMOND). Royal Doulton 1815–1965. 1965.

24131 GODDEN (GEOFFREY ARTHUR). British Porcelain: An Illustrated Guide. 1974.

24132 RIDE (PAUL) *and* GOWING (CHRISTOPHER). British Studio Ceramics in the 20th Century. 1989.

24133 COYSH (ARTHUR WILFRED). British Art Pottery, 1870–1940. 1976.

24134 DIGBY (GEORGE FREDERICK WINGFIELD). The Work of the Modern Potter in England. 1952.

24135 CAMERON (ELIZABETH) *and* LEWIS (PHILIPPA). Potters on Pottery. 1976.

24136 HOGBEN (CAROL) *ed.* The Art of Bernard Leach. 1978.

24137 ROSE (MURIEL). Artist Potters in England. 1955. 2nd edn 1970.

24138 CLARK (GARTH). Michael Cardew: A Portrait. 1978.

24139 TURNER (WALTER JAMES) *ed.* British Craftsmanship. 1948.

24140 MacCARTHY (FIONA). All Things Bright and Beautiful: Design in Britain, 1830 to Today. 1972. New edn A History of British Design 1830–1970. 1979.

24141 LISTER (RAYMOND GEORGE). Decorative Cast Ironwork in Great Britain. 1960.

24142 KORNWOLF (JAMES DAVID). M. H. Baillie Scott and the Arts and Crafts Movement: Pioneers of Modern Design. 1972.

24143 GILLIAT (MARY). English Style in Interior Decoration. 1967.

24144 DICKSON (ELIZABETH). Colefax and Fowler: The Best in English Interior Design. 1989.

24145 JOEL (DAVID). The Adventure of British Furniture, 1851–1951. 1953. New edn. Furniture Design Set Free: The British Furniture Revolution from 1851 to the Present Day. 1969.

24146 AGIUS (P.). British Furniture, 1880–1925. Woodbridge. 1978.

24147 RUSSELL (GORDON). Designer's Trade: An Autobiography of Gordon Russell. 1968.

24148 BAYNES (KENNETH) *and* BAYNES (KATE). Gordon Russell. 1980.

24149 FARR (MICHAEL AUSTIN LINES). Design in British Industry: A Mid-Century Survey. Camb. 1955.

24150 BAYLEY (S.). In Good Shape: Style in Industrial Products 1900–1960. 1979.

24151 SPARKE (PENNY) *ed.* Did Britain Make It? British Design in Context 1946–1986. 1986.

24152 CARRINGTON (NOEL). Industrial Design in Britain. 1976.

24153 BLAKE (JOHN E.) *and* BLAKE (AVRIL). The Practical Idealists: Twenty Five Years of Designing for Industry. 1969.

24154 MacCARTHY (FIONA). Eye for Industry: Royal Designers for Industry 1936–1986. 1986.

24155 McDOWELL (COLIN) *and* NUTTGENS (Patrick). McDowell's Directory of Twentieth Century Fashion. 1984.

24156 HOWELL (GEORGINA) *ed.* In Vogue: Six Decades of Fashion. 1975.

24157 BELL (QUENTIN [CLAUDIAN STEPHEN]). On Human Finery. 1947. Rev. edn 1976.

24158 MANSFIELD (ALAN) *and* CUNNINGTON (PHILLIS). Handbook of English Costume in the Twentieth Century 1900–1950. 1973.

24159 CUNNINGTON (C. W.) *and* CUNNINGTON (PHILLIS). English Women's Clothing in the Present Century. 1952.

24160 BROOKE (IRIS). English Costume 1900–50. 1951.

24161 GLYNN (PRUDENCE LOVEDAY). In Fashion. 1978.

24162 WAUGH (NORAH). The Cut of Women's Clothes 1600–1930. 1968.

24163 BARWICK (SANDRA). A Century of Style. 1984.

24164 DE COURTAIS (GEORGINE). Women's Hairdress and Hairstyles in England from AD 600 to the Present Day. 1973.

24165 ROBINSON (JULIAN). Fashion in the Forties and Fifties. 1976.

24166 DORNER (JANE). Fashion in the Forties and Fifties. 1975.

24167 BERNARD (BARBARA). Fashion in the '60s. 1978.

24168 AMIES (HARDY). Just So Far. 1954.

24169 —— Still Here: An Autobiography. 1984.

24170 KENNETT (FRANCES) *et al.* Norman Hartnell. 1985.

24171 QUANT (MARY). Quant by Quant. 1966.

24172 BENNETT-ENGLAND (RODNEY). Dress Optional: The Revolution in Menswear. 1967.

24173 GUPPY (A.). Children's Clothes 1939–1970: The Advent of Fashion. 1978.

24174 DAWNEY (JEAN). How I Became a Fashion Model. 1960.

24175 SHRIMPTON (JEAN). The Truth about Modelling. 1964.

6. SCULPTURE

24176 HAMMACHER (ABRAHAM MARIE). Modern English Sculpture. 1967.

24177 GRANT (MAURICE HAROLD). A Dictionary of British Sculpture from the XIIIth to the XXth century. 1953.

24178 LICHT (FRED STEPHEN). Sculpture: Nineteenth and Twentieth Centuries. 1967.

24179 MULLINS (EDWARD). 'The Open-Air Vision: A Survey of Sculpture in London since 1945, with Check List'. *Apollo* 76 (1962), 455–63.

24180 SPENCER (CHARLES). 'The Phenomenon of British Sculpture'. *Studio* 169 (1965), 98–105.

24181 SEUPHOR (MICHEL). The Sculpture of this Century. 1960.

24182 NAIRNE (SANDY) *and* SEROTA (NICHOLAS) *eds.* British Sculpture in the Twentieth Century. 1981. [Exhibition Catalogue: Whitechapel Gallery.].

24183 NEFF (TERRY ANN) *ed.* A Quiet Revolution: British Sculpture since 1945. 1987.

24184 BOWNESS (ALAN). Lynn Chadwick. 1962.

24185 EPSTEIN (*Sir* JACOB). Let there be Sculpture: An Autobiography. 1940. New edn 1955. Rev. edn 1963.

24186 BUCKLE (CHRISTOPHER RICHARD SANDFORD). Jacob Epstein: Sculptor. 1963.

24187 HEPWORTH (BARBARA). A Pictorial Autobiography. Bath. 1970.

24188 HODIN (JOSEPH PAUL). Barbara Hepworth. 1963.

24189 BOWNESS (ALAN) *ed.* Barbara Hepworth 1960–69. 1971.

24190 HAMMACHER (ABRAHAM). Barbara Hepworth. Rev. edn 1981.

24191 TEAGUE (EDWARD H.). Henry Moore: Bibliography and Reproduction Index. 1981.

24192 READ (*Sir* HERBERT EDWARD). Henry Moore. 2 vols. 1949–55.

24193 HALL (DONALD ANDREW). Henry Moore: The Life and Work of a Great Sculptor. 1966.

24194 RUSSELL (JOHN). Henry Moore. Harmondsworth. 1968.

24195 FINN (DAVID). Henry Moore. 1987.

24196 PACKER (WILLIAM). Henry Moore: An Illustrated Biography. 1985.

24197 BERTHOUD (ROGER). The Life of Henry Moore. 1987.

24198 MOORE (HENRY) *et al.* Sculpture and Environment. 1977.

24199 SPENDER (*Sir* HAROLD STEPHEN). Henry Moore: Sculptures in Landscape. 1978.

24200 MELVILLE (ROBERT). Henry Moore: Sculpture and Drawings 1921–1969. 1970.

24201 JAMES (PHILIP BRUTTON) *ed.* Henry Moore on Sculpture: A Collection of the Sculptor's Writings and Spoken Words. 1966. Rev. edn 1971.

24202 SCHNEEDE (UWE). Eduardo Paolozzi. 1971.

24203 KIRKPATRICK (DIANE). Eduardo Paolozzi. 1970.

24204 WHITFORD (FRANK) *et al.* Eduardo Paolozzi. 1976.

7. BALLET

24205 FORRESTER (FELICITÉE SHEILA). Ballet in England: A Bibliography and Survey *c.*1700–June 1966. 1968.

24206 GUMMER (DOROTHY). 'Ballet and the Dance: British Publications, 1955–1968'. *Brit. Book News* (Apr. 1969), 247–51.

24207 WHITE (JOAN W.) *ed.* Twentieth-Century Dance in Britain: A History of Major Dance Companies in Britain. 1985.

24208 NOBLE (PETER). British Ballet. 1950.

24209 BARNES (CLIVE). Ballet in Britain since the War. 1953.

24210 —— *Et al.* Ballet Here and Now. 1963.

24211 BLAND (ALEXANDER). Observer of the Dance 1958–1982: In Memory. 1985.

24212 BRINSON (PETER). The Ballet in Britain. 1962.

24213 GUEST (IVOR). 'The Post-War Contribution to the History of British Ballet'. *Theatre Notebook* 21 (1966), 42–6.

24214 HASKELL (ARNOLD LIONEL DAVID). 'The Birth of the English Ballet'. *J. Roy. Soc. Arts* lxxxvi (1939), 784–802.

24215 —— The National Ballet: A History and a Manifesto. 1943.

24216 —— Ballet 1945–1950. 1952.

24217 HALL (FERNAU). Modern English Ballet: An Interpretation. 1950.

24218 LESTER (SUSAN) *ed.* Ballet Here and Now. 1961.

24219 MONEY (KEITH). The Royal Ballet Today. 1968.

24220 BLAND (ALEXANDER). The Royal Ballet: The First Fifty years. 1981.

24221 HODGSON (M.). 'London Festival Ballet: Looking at its First Quarter Century, 1950–1975'. *Dance Mag.* 50 (1976), 51–61.

24222 WILLIAMSON (AUDREY MAY). Ballet of Three Decades. 1958.

24223 VAUGHAN (D.). 'Frederick Ashton'. *Dance Mag.* 48 (1974), 43–58.

24224 DOMINIC (ZOE) *and* GILBERT (JOHN SELWYN). Frederick Ashton: A Choreographer and his Ballets. 1971.

24225 DE VALOIS (*Dame* NINETTE). Come Dance with Me: A Memoir 1898–1956. 1957.

24226 —— Step by Step: The Formation of an Establishment. 1977.

24227 DOLIN (*Sir* ANTON). Last Words: A Final Autobiography. 1985.

24228 WHEATCROFT (ANDREW) *comp.* Dolin: Friends and Memories. 1982.

24229 CHAPPELL (WILLIAM). Fonteyn: Impressions of a Ballerina. 1951.

24230 FRANK (ELIZABETH). Margot Fonteyn. 1958.

24231 MONEY (KEITH). Fonteyn: The Making of a Legend. 1973.

24232 —— The Art of Margot Fonteyn. 1975.

24233 FONTEYN (*Dame* MARGOT). An Autobiography. 1975.

24234 GILLARD (DAVID). Beryl Grey: A Biography. 1977.

24235 HASKELL (ARNOLD). Balletomane at Large: An Autobiography. 1972.

24236 SALTER (ELIZABETH). Helpmann: The Authorized Biography of Sir Robert Helpmann CBE. Sydney. 1978.

24237 THORPE (EDWARD). Kenneth Macmillan: The Man and his Ballets. 1985.

24238 RAMBERT (*Dame* MARIE). Quicksilver: The Autobiography of Marie Rambert. 1972.

24239 GORE (WALTER). Ballet Rambert, 1926–1946. 1946.

24240 BRADLEY (LIONEL J. H.). Sixteen Years of Ballet Rambert. 1946.

24241 CLARKE (MARY). Dancers of Mercury: The Story of Ballet Rambert. 1962.

24242 CRISP (CLEMENT), SAINSBURY (ANYA), *and* WILLIAMS (PETER) *eds.* Ballet Rambert: 50 Years and On. 1981.

24243 WOOD (MICHAEL). The Sadler's Wells Ballet, 1931–1956: A Record of Twenty Five Years. 1956.

24244 CLARKE (MARY). The Sadler's Wells Ballet: A History and an Appreciation. 1955.

24245 SEXTON (CHRISTOPHER). Peggy Van Praagh: A Life of Dance. 1985.

24246 MANCHESTER (PHYLLIS WINIFRED). Vic–Wells: A Ballet Progress. 1942.

24247 PERCIVAL (JOHN). Experimental Dance. 1971.

24248 —— Theatre in my Blood: A Biography of John Cranko. 1983.

24249 AUSTIN (RICHARD). Lynn Seymour: An Authorised Biography. Sydney. 1980.

24250 SEYMOUR (LYNN) *with* GARDNER (PAUL). Lynn: The Autobiography of Lynn Seymour. 1984.

8. MUSIC

24251 British Music Yearbook. 1972–.

24252 MACKERNESS (ERIC DAVID). A Social History of English Music. 1964.

24253 EHRLICH (CYRIL). The Music Profession in Britain since the Eighteenth Century: A Social History. Oxf. 1985.

24254 MELLERS (WILFRID). Music and Society: England and the European Tradition. 1946.

24255 GROVE (*Sir* GEORGE) *comp.* Grove's Dictionary of Music and Musicians. 3rd edn by Henry Copes Colles 5 vols 1927. 4th edn + suppl. vols by Colles. 1940.

24256 Baker's Biographical Dictionary of Musicians. 7th edn.

24257 SADIE (STANLEY) *ed.* The New Grove Dictionary of Music and Musicians. 20 vols 1980.

24258 EWEN (DAVID). The Complete Book of Twentieth Century Music. 1952.

24259 DUCKLES (VINCENT). Music Reference and Research Materials. 1964. 3rd edn 1974.

24260 SCHOLES (PERCY ALFRED). Oxford Companion to Music. 1938. 10th edn John Owen Ward. 1970.

24261 ARNOLD (DENIS). The New Oxford Companion to Music. 2 vols. Oxf. 1983.

24262 WESTRUP (*Sir* JACK) *and* HARRISON (F. LL.). Collins Encyclopaedia of Music. 1959. Rev. edn by Conrad Wilson. 1976.

24263 BLOM (ERIC WALTER). Music in England. Harmondsworth. 1942. Rev. edn 1947.

24264 BACHARACH (A. L.) *ed.* British Music in our Time. Harmondsworth. 1946. New edn 1951.

24265 BRAY (TREVOR). Twentieth Century Music, 1900–1945. Milton Keynes. 1974.

24266 PALMER (RUSSELL). British Music. 1948.

24267 TREND (MICHAEL). The Music Makers: Heirs and Rebels of the English Musical Renaissance, Edward Elgar to Benjamin Britten. 1985.

24268 PIRIE (PETER). The English Musical Renaissance: Twentieth Century British Composers and their Works. 1979.

24269 MANNING (ROSEMARY). From Holst to Britten. 1949.

24270 HOWES (FRANK STEWART). Music 1945–1950. 1951.

24271 —— The English Musical Renaissance. 1966.

24272 FRANK (ALAN). Modern British Composers. 1953.

24273 HILL (RALPH). Music. 1950.

24274 DEMUTH (NORMAN FRANK). Musical Trends in the Twentieth Century. 1952.

24275 CULSHAW (JOHN). A Century of Music. 1952.

24276 STRADLING (ROBERT) *and* HUGHES (MEIRION). The English Musical Renaissance 1860–1940: Construction and Deconstruction. 1993.

24277 GIBBIN (LEONARD DOUGLAS). The Music Trader's Guide to Works by Twentieth Century British Composers. 1955.

24278 FLUCK (ALAN). The Sour Sweet Music: A Beginner's Guide to Contemporary Music. 1957.

24279 HARTOG (HOWARD) *ed.* European Music in the Twentieth Century. 1957. Rev. edn 1961.

24280 HUTCHINGS (ARTHUR). 'Music in Britain, 1918–1960'. In The New Oxford History of Music: The Modern Age 1890–1960. Martin Cooper, *ed.* 1974.

24281 KENNEDY (GEORGE MICHAEL SINCLAIR) *ed.* The Oxford Dictionary of Music. New edn 1985.

24282 YOUNG (PERCY MARSHALL). A History of British Music. 1967.

24283 MYERS (ROLLO HUGH). Twentieth Century Music. 1960. 2nd edn 1968.

24284 ROUTH (FRANCIS). Contemporary British Music: The Twenty Five Years from 1945 to 1970. 1972.

24285 GRAVES (CHARLES LARCOM). Post-Victorian Music. NY. 1970.

24286 SEARLE (HUMPHREY) *and* LAYTON (ROBERT). Twentieth Century Composers. Vol. 3: Britain, Scandinavia and the Netherlands. 1972.

24287 THOMPSON (KENNETH). A Dictionary of Twentieth Century Composers, 1911–1971. 1973.

24288 FOREMAN (LEWIS) *ed.* British Music Now: A Guide to the Work of Younger Composers. 1975.

24289 SCHAFER (MURRAY). British Composers in Interview. 1963.

24290 RAYNOR (HENRY). Music in England. 1980.

24291 McIVEAGH (DIANE) *et al.* Twentieth Century English Masters: Elgar, Delius, Vaughan Williams, Holst, Walton, Tippett. 1984.

24292 GRIFFITHS (PAUL). New Sounds: New Personalities: British Composers of the 1980s. 1985.

24293 PEACOCK (*Sir* ALAN) *and* WEIR (RONALD). The Composer in the Market Place. 1975.

24294 BANTOCK (MYRRHA). Granville Bantock: A Personal Portrait. 1972.

24295 BAX (*Sir* ARNOLD). Farewell my Youth. 1943.

24296 SUTHERLAND (COLIN SCOTT). Arnold Bax (1973); FOREMAN (LEWIS). Bax: A Composer and his Times. 1983. 2nd edn 1988.

24297 HALL (MICHAEL). Harrison Birtwhistle. 1984.

24298 BLISS (*Sir* ARTHUR). As I Remember.

24299 THOMPSON (KENNETH L.). The Works of Arthur Bliss. Rev. edn 1971.

24300 PALMER (CHRISTOPHER) Bliss. 1976.

24301 HURD (MICHAEL). Immortal Hour: The Life and Period of Rutland Boughton. 1962.

24302 NETTEL (REGINALD). Havergal Brian and his Music. 1976.

24303 EASTHAUGH (KENNETH). Havergal Brian: The Making of a Composer. 1976.

24304 PIRIE (PETER J.). Frank Bridge. 1971.

24305 PAYNE (ANTHONY), FOREMAN (LEWIS), *and* BISHOP (JOHN). The Music of Frank Bridge. 1976.

24306 WILSON (PAUL), EVANS (JOHN), *and* REED (PHILIP). A Britten Source Book. 1987.

24307 MITCHELL (DONALD CHARLES) *and* KELLER (HANS) *eds.* Benjamin Britten: A Commentary on his Works. 1952.

24308 KENDALL (ALAN). Benjamin Britten. 1973.

24309 WHITE (ERIC WALTER). Benjamin Britten: His Life and Operas. New edn 1983.

24310 DUNCAN (RONALD). Working with Britten: A Personal Memoir. Bideford. 1981.

24311 MITCHELL (DONALD CHARLES) and EVANS (JOHN). Pictures from a Life. 1978.

24312 —— Britten and Auden in the Thirties: The Year 1936. 1981.

24313 WHITTALL (ARNOLD). The Music of Britten and Tippett: Studies in Theme and Technique. Camb. 1982.

24314 HOLST (IMOGEN). Britten. 1966. 3rd edn 1980.

24315 HOWARD (PATRICIA). The Operas of Benjamin Britten. 1969.

24316 EVANS (PETER). The Music of Benjamin Britten. 1979.

24317 BLYTH (ALAN) ed. Remembering Britten. 1981.

24318 KENNEDY (GEORGE MICHAEL SINCLAIR). Britten. 1981.

24319 PALMER (CHRISTOPHER) ed. The Britten Companion. 1984.

24320 HEADINGTON (CHRISTOPHER). Britten. NY. 1982.

24321 BUSH (ALAN). In My Eighth Decade and other Essays. 1980.

24322 GRIFFITHS (PAUL). Peter Maxwell Davies. 2nd edn 1982.

24323 COLLES (HENRY COPE). Walford Davies: A Biography. 1942.

24324 HESELTINE (PHILIP). Delius. 1923. Rev. edn under the name Peter Warlock. 1952.

24325 HUTCHINGS (ARTHUR JAMES BRAMWELL). Delius. 1948.

24326 BEECHAM (Sir THOMAS). Delius. 1959.

24327 JEFFERSON (ALAN). Delius. 1972.

24328 PALMER (CHRISTOPHER). Delius: Portrait of a Cosmopolitan. 1976.

24329 REDWOOD (CHRISTOPHER) ed. A Delius Companion. 1976. 2nd edn 1980.

24330 POWELL (DORA M.). Edward Elgar: Memories of a Variation. 1937. 2nd edn 1947.

24331 KENNEDY (GEORGE MICHAEL SINCLAIR). Portrait of Elgar. 1968.

24332 MAINE (BASIL STEPHEN). Elgar, his Life and Works. 1933. Bath. 1973.

24333 FOSS (HUBERT). 'Elgar and his Age'. Music and Letters 16 (1935), 5–12.

24334 REED (WILLIAM HENRY). Elgar as I Knew him. 1936. 2nd edn 1973.

24335 YOUNG (PERCY MARSHALL). Letters of Edward Elgar and other Writings. 1956.

24336 PARROTT (HORACE IAN). Elgar. 1971.

24337 MCVEAGH (DIANE M.). Edward Elgar: His Life and Music. 1955.

24338 YOUNG (PERCY MARSHALL). Elgar O.M. A Study of his Music. 1955. Rev. edn 1973.

24339 —— ed. Letters of Edward Elgar and other Writings. 1956.

24340 —— ed. A Future for English Music and other Lectures. 1968.

24341 —— Alice Elgar: Enigma of a Victorian Lady. 1978.

24342 REDWOOD (CHRISTOPHER) ed. An Elgar Companion. Birm., Al. 1982.

24343 MOORE (JERROLD NORTHOP). Edward Elgar: A Creative Life. Oxf. 1984.

24344 —— ed. Elgar and his Publishers: Letters of a Creative Life. 2 vols Oxf. 1987.

24345 —— Comp. Elgar: A Life in Photographs. Oxf. 1972.

24346 NORTHCOTT (BAYAN) ed. The Music of Alexander Goehr. 1980.

24347 GOOSSENS (EUGENE). Overture and Beginners. A Musical Autobiography. 1951.

24348 PALMER (CHRISTOPHER). 'Patrick Hadley: The Man and his Music'. Music and Letters 45 (1974), 151–66.

24349 DEANE (BASIL). Alun Hoddinott. Cardiff. 1977.

24350 HOLST (IMOGEN). Gustav Holst: A Biography. 1938. 2nd edn 1969.

24351 The Music of Gustav Holst. 1951. 3rd edn 1974. With additional material as: Holst's Music Remembered. 1985.

24352 SHORT (MICHAEL) ed. Gustav Holst: Letters to W. G. Whittaker. Glasg. 1974.

24353 —— Gustav Holst: A Centenary Documentation. 1974.

24354 PALMER (CHRISTOPHER). Herbert Howells: A Study. 1978.

24355 LANGMIRE (JOHN). John Ireland: Portrait of a Friend. 1969.

24356 SCOTT-SUTHERLAND (COLIN). John Ireland. 1980.

24357 SEARLE (MURIEL). John Ireland: The Man and his Music. Tunbridge Wells. 1979.

24358 SHEAD (RICHARD). Constant Lambert. 1973.

24359 MOTION (ANDREW). The Lamberts: George, Constant and Kit. 1986.

24360 LUTYENS (ELIZABETH). A Goldfish Bowl. 1972.

24361 HARRIES (MEIRION) and HARRIES (SUSIE). A Pilgrim Soul. 1989.

24362 OTTAWAY (HUGH). Edmund Rubbra: An Appreciation. 1981.

24363 FOREMAN (LEWIS) ed. Edmund Rubbra. Rickmansworth. 1977.

24364 SHAW (MARTIN). Up to Now. 1929.

24365 ST JOHN (CHRISTOPHER). Ethel Smyth: A Biography. 1959.

24366 COLLIS (LOUISE). Impetuous Heart. The Story of Ethel Smyth. 1984.

24367 The Memoirs of Dame Ethel Smyth. Harmondsworth. 1987. Originally published as As Time Went on . . . 1936, and What Happened Next. 1940.

24368 KEMP (IAN). Tippett, the Composer and his Music. 1984.

24369 BOWEN (MEIRION). Michael Tippett. 1982.

24370 MATTHEWS (DAVID). Michael Tippett: An Introductory Study. 1980.

24371 HURD (MICHAEL). Tippett. 1978.

24372 WHITE (ERIC WALTER). Tippett and his Operas. 1979.

24373 LEWIS (GERAINT) ed. Michael Tippett: A Celebration. Tunbridge Wells. 1985.

24374 YOUNG (PERCY MARSHALL). Vaughan Williams. 1953.

24375 FOSS (HUBERT JAMES). Ralph Vaughan Williams: A Study. 1950.

24376 HOWES (FRANK STEWART). The Music of Ralph Vaughan Williams. 1954.

24377 DICKINSON (ALAN EDGAR FREDERIC). Vaughan Williams. 1963.

24378 OTTAWAY (HUGH). Vaughan Williams: Symphonies. 1972.

24379 KENNEDY (GEORGE MICHAEL SINCLAIR). The Works of Ralph Vaughan Williams. 1964. New edn 1980.

24380 MELLERS (WILFRID). Vaughan Williams and the Vision of Albion. 1989.

24381 VAUGHAN WILLIAMS (URSULA). R. V. W.: A Biography of Ralph Vaughan Williams. 1964.

24382 VAUGHAN WILLIAMS (RALPH). National Music and other Essays. Oxf. 1963.

24383 VAUGHAN WILLIAMS (RALPH) and HOLST (GUSTAV). ed. by Ursula Vaughan Williams and Imogen Holst. Heirs and Rebels: Letters Written to Each Other and Occasional Writings on Music.

24384 DOUGLAS (ROY). Working with R. V. W. Oxf. 1972.

24385 HOWES (FRANK STEWART). The Music of William Walton. 1942.

24386 TURNEY (NEIL). William Walton: His Life and Music. 1984.

24387 WALTON (Lady SUSANA). William Walton, Behind the Façade. Oxf. 1988.

24388 KENNEDY (MICHAEL). Portrait of Walton. Oxf. 1989.

24389 GRAY (CECIL). Peter Warlock: A Memoir of Philip Heseltine. 1934.

24390 COPLEY (I. A.). The Music of Peter Warlock: A Critical Survey. 1979.

24391 SUMNER (WILLIAM LESLIE). The Organ: Its Evolution, Principles of Construction and Use. 1952. 4th edn 1973.

24392 WILLIAMS (PETER). A New History of the Organ from the Greeks to the Present Day. 1980.

24393 CLUTTON (CECIL) and NILAND (AUSTIN). The British Organ. 1963. 2nd edn 1982.

24394 ROWNTREE (JOHN PICKERING) and BRENNAN (JOHN FREDERICK). The Classical Organ in Britain, 1955–1974. Oxf. 1975.

24395 EHRLICH (CYRIL). The Piano: A History. 1976.

24396 SETON (Sir BRUCE) and GRANT (JOHN). The Pipes of War: A Record of the Achievements of Pipers of Scottish and Overseas Regiments during the War 1914–18. Glasg. 1920.

24397 YOUNG (PERCY MARSHALL). The Choral Tradition: An Historical and Analytical Survey from the Sixteenth Century to the Present Day. 1962.

24398 EDWARDS (R. A.). And the Glory: The Huddersfield Choral Society 1836–1986. Leeds. 1986.

24399 TERTIS (LIONEL). My Viola and I. 1974.

24400 BLADES (JAMES). Drum Roll: A Professional Adventure from the Circus to the Concert Hall. 1977.

24401 COHEN (HARRIET). A Bundle of Time: The Memoirs of Harriet Cohen. 1969.

24402 OGDON (BRENDA LUCAS) and KERR (MICHAEL). Virtuoso: The Story of John Ogdon. 1981.

24403 LASSIMONE (DENISE). Myra Hess. 1966.

24404 MOORE (GERALD). Am I too Loud? Memoirs of an Accompanist. 1962.

24405 —— Farewell Recital: Further Memoirs. 1978.

24406 NEWTON (IVOR). At the Piano—Ivor Newton: The World of an Accompanist. 1966.

24407 MENUHIN (Sir YEHUDI). Unfinished Journey. 1977.

24408 DOLMETSCH (MABEL). Personal Recollections of Arnold Dolmetsch. 1957.

24409 EASTON (CAROL). Jacqueline du Pré: A Biography. 1989.

24410 BAKER (Dame JANET). Full Circle: An Autobiographical Journal. 1982.

24411 HARDWICK (MICHAEL) and HARDWICK (MOLLIE). Alfred Deller: A Singularity of Voice. 1968.

24412 EVANS (Sir GERAINT) with GOODWIN (NOEL). Sir Geraint Evans: A Knight at the Opera. 1984.

24413 CARDUS (Sir NEVILLE) ed. Kathleen Ferrier 1912–1953. 1954.

24414 FERRIER (WINIFRED). The Life of Kathleen Ferrier, by her Sister. 1955.

24415 RINGBY (CHARLES). Kathleen Ferrier: A Biography. 1955.

24416 LETHBRIDGE (PETER). Kathleen Ferrier. 1959.

24417 LEONARD (MAURICE). Kathleen: The Life of Kathleen Ferrier 1912–1953. 1988.

24418 FRANKLIN (DAVID). Basso Cantate: An Autobiography. 1969.

24419 HAMMOND (JOAN). A Voice, a Life: An Autobiography. 1970.

24420 MUTAFIAN (CLAUDE). Gwyneth Jones. Paris. 1980.

24421 THORPE (MARION) ed. Peter Pears: A Tribute on his 75th Birthday. 1985.

24422 STEWART (MARGARET). [Lady Wilson], English Singer: The Life of Stewart Wilson. 1970.

24423 KENNEDY (GEORGE MICHAEL SINCLAIR). History of the Royal Manchester College of Music, 1893–1972. Manch. 1971.

24424 COLLES (HENRY COPE). The Royal College of Music: A Jubilee Record. 1933.

24425 COLLES (HENRY COPE) and CRUFT (JOHN). The Royal College of Music: A Centenary Record. 1982.

24426 BAILEY (CECIL). Hugh Percy Allen. 1948.

24427 REID (CHARLES). John Barbirolli. 1971.

24428 KENNEDY (GEORGE MICHAEL SINCLAIR). Barbirolli. 1971.

24429 REID (CHARLES). Thomas Beecham: An Independent Biography. 1961.

24430 CARDUS (NEVILLE). Sir Thomas Beecham. 1961.

24431 PROCTOR-GREGG (HUMPHREY). Beecham Remembered. 1976.

24432 JEFFERSON (ALAN). Sir Thomas Beecham: A Centenary Tribute. 1979.

24433 BOULT (Sir ADRIAN CEDRIC). My own Trumpet. 1973.

24434 KENNEDY (MICHAEL). Adrian Boult. 1987.

24435 FREER (DAVID) ed. Hamilton Harty. Belf. 1979.

24436 KENYON (NICHOLAS). Simon Rattle. 1987.

24437 RONALD (Sir LANDON). Myself and Others, Written, Lest I Forget. 1931.

24438 MATHEWMAN (PHYLLIS). Sir Malcolm Sargent. 1959.

24439 REID (CHARLES). Malcolm Sargent: A Biography. 1968.

24440 ROBINSON (PAUL). Solti. 1979.

24441 WOOD (Sir HENRY). My Life of Music. 1938.

24442 COX (DAVID). The Henry Wood Proms. 1980.

24443 ORGA (ATES). The Proms. Newton Abbot. 1974.

24444 AYRE (LESLIE). The Proms. 1968.

24445 HALL (BARRIE). The Proms and the Man who Made them. 1981.

24446 KING (ALEXANDER HYATT). Some British Collectors of Music, c.1600–1960. Camb. 1963.

24447 FOX-STRANGWAYS (A. H.). Cecil Sharp. 1933.

24448 KARPELES (MAUD). Cecil Sharp: His Life and Work. 1967.

24449 NETTEL (REGINALD). A Social History of Traditional Song. 1969.

24450 DEAN-SMITH (MARGARET). A Guide to English Folk-Song Collections, 1822–1952, with an Index to their Contents, Historical Annotations and an Introduction. L/pool. 1954.

24451 GODBOLT (JIM). A History of Jazz in Britain, 1919–50. 1984.

24452 MORGAN (ALUN) and HORRICKS (RAYMOND). Modern Jazz: A Survey of Developments since 1939. 1956.

24453 HARRIS (REX). Jazz. Harmondsworth. 1952.

24454 BOULTON (DAVID). Jazz in Britain. 1958.

24455 CARR (IAN). Music Outside: Contemporary Jazz in Britain. 1973.

24456 MELLY (GEORGE). Owning up. 1965.

24457 —— Rum, Bum and Concertina. 1977.

24458 COLLIER (GRAHAM). Cleo and John: A Biography of the Dankworths. 1976.

24459 GOLDBLOT (JIM). All This and 10%. 1976.

24460 LYTTELTON (HUMPHREY). I Play as I Please: The Memoirs of an Old Etonian Trumpeter. 1954.

24461 —— Second Chorus. 1958.

24462 —— Take it from the Top: An Autobiographical Scrapbook. 1975.

24463 SCOTT (RONNIE). Some of My Best Friends are Blues. 1979.

24464 HEATH (TED). Listen to my Music: An Autobiography. 1957.

24465 TAYLOR (PAUL). Popular Music since 1955: A Critical Guide to the Literature. 1985.

24466 LEE (EDWARD). Music of the People: A Study of Popular Music in Great Britain. 1970.

24467 CABLE (MICHAEL). The Pop Music Inside Out. 1977.

24468 GAMMOND (PETER) and CLAYTON (PETER). A Guide to Popular Music. 1960.

24469 PEARSALL (RONALD). Popular Music of the Twenties. 1976.

24470 BRAYBROOKE (PATRICK). The Amazing Mr Noel Coward. 1933.

24471 HENSON (BRIAN) and MORGAN (COLIN). The first Hits: The Definitive Guide to the Hits of the 1940s and 1950s. 1988.

24472 COTTRELL (JOHN). Julie Andrews: The Story of a Star. 1969.

24473 WINDELER (ROBERT). Julie Andrews: A Biography. 1970. Rev. edn 1982.

24474 KON (ANDREA). This is my Song: Biography of Petula Clark. 1984.

24475 DAWSON (PETER). Fifty Years of Song. 1951.

24476 FIELDS (GRACIE). Sing As We Go: The Autobiography. 1960.

24477 BURGESS (MURIEL) with KEEN (TOM). Gracie Fields. 1980.

24478 MOULES (JOAN). Our Gracie: The Life of Dame Gracie Fields. 1983.

24479 BLACK (PETER). The Biggest Aspidistra in the World. 1972.

24480 WALLACE (IAN). Promise Me You'll Sing Mud!. 1975. Nothing Quite Like It. 1982.

24481 PARKER (DEREK) *and* PARKER (JULIA). The Story and the Song: A Survey of English Musical Plays 1916–78. 1979.

24482 GUNZL (KURT). British Musical Theatre. Vol. 2: 1945–84. 1986.

24483 WILSON (SANDY). Ivor. 1975.

24484 ELLIS (VIVIAN). I'm on a See-Saw. 1953.

24485 MASCHWITZ (ERIC). No Chip on my Shoulder. 1957.

24486 HEADINGTON (CHRISTOPHER). The Performing World of the Musician, with a Profile of Andrew Lloyd Webber. 1981.

24487 MCKNIGHT (GERALD). Andrew Lloyd Webber. 1984.

24488 WALSH (MICHAEL). Andrew Lloyd Webber: His Life and Works. 1989.

24489 WILSON (SANDY). I Could Be Happy: An Autobiography. 1975.

24490 COHN (NICK). Pop from the Beginning. 1969.

24491 FRITH (SIMON). Sound Effects: Youth, Leisure and the Politics of Rock. 1983. Rev. edn of Sociology of Rock. 1978.

24492 —— Music for Pleasure. Camb. 1988.

24493 LESLIE (PETER). FAB: The Anatomy of a Phenomenon. 1965.

24494 MABEY (RICHARD). The Pop Process. 1969.

24495 RODGERS (DAVE). Rock 'n 'Roll. 1982.

24496 BIRD (ARCHIBALD BRIAN). Skiffle: The Story of Folk-Song with a Jazz Beat. 1958.

24497 TERRY (CAROL D.). Here, There and Everywhere: The First International Beatles Bibliography 1962–1982. Ann Arbor, Mich. 1985.

24498 DAVIES (HUNTER). The Beatles. 1968. 2nd edn 1985.

24499 MELLERS (WILFRID). Twilight of the Gods: The Beatles in Retrospect. 1973.

24500 NORMAN (PHILIP). Shout! The True Story of the Beatles. 1982.

24501 STOKES (GEOFFREY). The Beatles. 1988.

24502 THOMSON (ELIZABETH) *and* GUTMAN (DAVID). The Lennon Companion: Twenty-Five Years of Comment. 1987.

24503 BROWN (PETER). The Love you Make: An Inside Story of the Beatles. 1983.

24504 BLAKES (JOHN). All you Needed was Love: The Beatles after the Beatles. 1981.

24505 COLEMAN (RAY). Brian Epstein: The Man who Made the Beatles. 1989.

24506 —— John Winston Lennon. 2 vols. 1984.

24507 GOODMAN (ALBERT). The Lives of John Lennon. 1988.

24508 FLIPPO (CHET). McCartney: The Biography. 1988.

24509 SALEWICZ (CHRIS). McCartney: The Definitive Biography. 1986.

24510 BLACK (CILLA). Step Inside. 1985.

24511 GILLAMAN (PETER) *and* GILLMAN (LENI). Alias David Bowie. 1986.

24512 JUBY (KERRY). Kate Bush—The Whole Story. 1988.

24513 COLEMAN (RAY). Survivor: The Authorised Biography of Eric Clapton. 1985.

24514 OLDFIELD (MIKE). Dire Straits. 1983.

24515 BRIGHT (SPENCER). Peter Gabriel: An Authorised Biography. 1988.

24516 GALLO (ARMONADO). Genesis: Evolution of a Rock Band. 1978.

24517 TOBERMAN (BARRY). Elton John: A Biography. 1988.

24518 DAVIS (STEPHEN). Hammer of the Gods: The Led Zeppelin Saga. NY. 1985.

24519 LULU. Lulu: Her Autobiography. 1985.

24520 RICHARD (CLIFF). Which One's Cliff? The Autobiography. 1981.

24521 DONCASTER (PATRICK) *and* JASPER (TONY). Cliff. 1981.

24522 JASPER (TONY). Survivor: A Tribute to Cliff. 1989.

24523 DIMMICK (MARY LAVERNE). The Rolling Stones: An Annotated Bibliography. Pittsburgh, Pa. 1979.

24524 NORMAN (PHILIP). The Life and Good Times of the Rolling Stones. 1989.

24525 SCHOFIELD (CAREY). Jagger. 1983.

24526 READ (MIKE) *ed.* The Story of the Shadows: An Autobiography. 1983.

24527 O'BRIEN (LUCY). Dusty. 1989. [Dusty Springfield.].

24528 KENNEDY (JOHN). Tommy Steele. 1958.

24529 STOLL (DENIS GRAY). Music Festivals of the World. Oxf. 1963.

24530 BRUCE (GEORGE). Festival in the North. Edin. 1975.

24531 SCHOLES (PERCY ALFRED). The Mirror of Music, 1844–1944: A Century of Musical Life in Britain as Reflected in the Pages of the *Musical Times*. 2 vols. 1947.

24532 CARDUS (*Sir* NEVILLE). The Delights of Music: A Critic's Choice. 1966.

24533 —— Autobiography. New edn 1975.

24534 CAREY (HUGH). Duet for Two Voices: An Informal Biography of Edward Dent Compiled from his Letters to Clive Carey. Camb. 1979.

24535 MAINE (BASIL). The Best of Me: A Study in Autobiography. 1937.

24536 ROSENTHAL (HAROLD). My Mad World of Opera. 1982.

24537 GRIERSON (MARY). Donald Francis Tovey: A Biography Based on Letters. 1952.

24538 YOUNG ((CHARLES) KENNETH). Music's Great Days in the Spas and Watering Places. 1968.

24539 SMITH (WILLIAM JAMES). Five Centuries of Cambridge Musicians, 1464–1964. Camb. 1964.

24540 RUSSELL (THOMAS). Philharmonic Project. 1952.

24541 PETTIT (STEPHEN). The Philarmonia Orchestra. 1985.

24542 KENYON (NICHOLAS). The BBC Symphony Orchestra: The First Fifty Years, 1930–1980. 1981.

24543 FOSS (HUBERT JAMES) and GOODWIN (NOEL). London Symphony: Portrait of an Orchestra, 1904–1954. 1954.

24544 PEARTON (MAURICE). The LSO at 70: A History of the Orchestra. 1974.

24545 KENNEDY (GEORGE MICHAEL SINCLAIR). The Hallé 1858–1983: A History of the Orchestra. Manch. 1982.

24546 REES (CLIFFORD BURWIN). One Hundred Years of the Hallé. 1957.

24547 KALLAWAY (WILLIAM). London Philharmonic: Music Makers since 1932. 1972.

24548 RUSSELL (THOMAS). Philharmonic Decade. 1945.

24549 —— Philharmonic Project. 1952.

24550 NETTEL (REGINALD). The Orchestra in England: A Social History. 1946. New edn 1956.

24551 SCOTTISH NATIONAL ORCHESTRA. SNO: An Anniversary Study of the Scottish National Orchestra (1950–1971), the Scottish Orchestra (1891–1950) and their Antecedents. Glasg. 1971.

24552 REID (CHARLES). Fifty Years of Robert Mayer Concerts, 1923–1972. 1972.

24553 WHITE (ERIC WALTER). A History of English Opera. 1983.

24554 —— The Rise of English Opera. 1951.

24555 —— 'A Decade of English Opera, 1951–60'. Theatre Notebook 15 (1961), 110–15.

24556 —— 'A Further Decade of English Opera, 1961–70'. Theatre Notebook 25 (1971), 146–51.

24557 WALLACE (IAN). 'From the Cambridge Theatre to Glyndebourne'. Opera 26 (1975), 931–40.

24558 TUCKER (NORMAN). 'The Place of Opera in the artistic Life of the Country'. J. Roy. Soc. Arts 110 (1962), 752–63.

24559 MILNES (R.). '50 Years of Opera at Oxford'. Opera 26 (1975), 940–6.

24560 NORTHOUSE (CAMERON). Twentieth Century Opera in England and the United States. Boston, Mass./Lond. 1976.

24561 ARUNDEL (DENNIS). The Story of Sadler's Wells, 1683–1964. 1965.

24562 ROSENTHAL (HAROLD DAVID). Opera at Covent Garden: A Short History. 1967.

24563 —— Two Centuries of Opera at Covent Garden. 1958.

24564 HALTRECHT (MONTAGUE). The Quiet Showman: Sir David Webster and the Royal Opera House. 1975.

24565 BING (Sir RUDOLF). 5,000 Nights at the Opera. 1972.

24566 LASCELLES (GEORGE) Earl of Harewood. The Tongs and the Bones: Memoirs. 1981.

24567 WILSON (CONRAD). Scottish Opera—The First Ten Years. 1972.

24568 LOVELAND (KENNETH). 'Welsh National Opera after Thirty Years'. Opera 27 (1976), 325–31.

24569 JEFFERSON (ALAN). The Operas of Richard Strauss in Britain, 1910–1963. 1963.

24570 HUGHES (SPIKE). Glyndebourne: A History of the Festival Opera Founded in 1934 by Audrey and John Christie. 1965. Rev. edn 1981.

24571 HIGGINS (JOHN). Glyndebourne: A Celebration. 1984.

24572 BLUNT (WILFRID JASPER WALTER). John Christie of Glyndebourne. 1968.

24573 READ (OLIVER). The Recording and Reproduction of Sound. Indianapolis, Ind. 1949.

24574 GELATT (ROLAND). The Fabulous Phonograph: The Story of the Gramaphone from Tin Foil to High Fidelity. 1956.

24575 SIMPSON (ROBERT WILFRED LEVICK) and PRENN (OLIVER) eds. Guide to Modern Music on Records. 1958.

24576 GAMMOND (PETER) and HORRICKS (RAYMOND) eds. The Music goes Round and Round: A Cool Look at the Record Industry. 1980.

24577 MILLER (R.). The Incredible Music Machine. 1982.

24578 BROWN (MICK). Richard Branson: The Inside Story. 1988.

24579 CULSHAW (JOHN). Putting the Record Straight. 1981.

24580 SOUTHALL (BRIAN). Abbey Road: The Story of the World's Most Famous Recording Studio. 1982.

24581 MARTIN (GEORGE) with HORNSBY (JEREMY). All you Need is Ears. 1979.

9. FILM

24582 BRITISH UNIVERSITIES FILM AND VIDEO COUNCIL. Researcher's Guide to British Film and Television Collections. 1981. Rev. edn 1985.

24583 WELCH (JEFFREY EGAN). Literature and Film: An Annotated Bibliography, 1909–1977. NY./Lond. 1981.

24584 ENSER (ALFRED GEORGE SIDNEY). Filmed Books and Plays: A List of Books and Plays from which Films have been Made, 1918–1974. 1968. Rev. edn 1975.

24585 NATIONAL FILM ARCHIVE. Catalogue. 3 vols. 1951–66.

24586 DYMENT (ALAN). The Literature of the Cinema: A Bibliographical Guide to the Film as Art and Entertainment, 1936–1970. 1972.

24587 GIFFORD (DENIS). The British Film Catalogue, 1895–1970: A Guide to Entertainment Films. 2 vols. 1973. Rev. edn to 1985. Newton Abbot. 1986.

24588 THE YEAR'S WORK IN FILM. Annual 1949–.

24589 MACCANN (RICHARD DYER) *and* PERRY (EDWARD S.). The New Film Index: A Bibliography of Magazine Articles in English, 1930–1970. N.Y. 1975.

24590 BRITISH NATIONAL FILM CATALOGUE. 1963–.

24591 JONES (KAREN) *ed.* International Index to Film Periodicals. 1972–.

24592 THOMSON (DAVID). A Biographical Dictionary of the Cinema. 1975. Rev. edn 1980.

24593 JACKSON-WRIGLEY (MAURICE) *and* LEYLAND (ERIC). The Cinema: Historical, Technical and Bibliographical: A Survey for Librarians and Students. 1939.

24594 THORPE (F.) *and* PRONAY (NICHOLAS). British Official Films in the Second World War: A Descriptive Catalogue. 1980.

24595 ALDGATE (ANTHONY) *and* RICHARDS (JEFFREY). Britain Can Take It: The British Cinema in the Second World War. 1986.

24596 TAYLOR (PHILIP M.). Britain and the Cinema in the Second World War. 1988.

24597 DICKINSON (MARGARET) *and* STREET (SARAH). Cinema and State: The Film Industry and the Government 1927–84. 1985.

24598 LOW (RACHAEL). The History of the British Film, 1914–1918. 1951. The History of the British Film, 1918–1929. 1971. The History of the British Film, 1929–1939: Documentary and Educational Films of the 1930s. 1979. The History of the British Film, 1929–1939: Films of Comment and Persuasion of the 1930s. 1979.

24599 LOW (RACHAEL) *and* MANVELL (ROGER ARNOLD). The History of the British Film. 3 vols 1948–9.

24600 SPENCER (DOUGLAS ARTHUR) *and* WALEY (HUBERT DAVID). The Cinema Today. 1939. 2nd edn 1956.

24601 SMITH (MALCOLM) *and* MILES (PETER). Cinema, Literature and Society: Elite and Mass Culture in Inter-war Britain. 1987.

24602 FIELD (MARY). Children and Films: A Study of Boys and Girls in the Cinema. Dunfermline. 1954.

24603 MANVELL (ROGER ARNOLD). Film. 1947.

24604 —— The Film and the Public. Harmondsworth. 1955.

24605 THOMSON (MICHAEL). Silver Screen in the Silver City: A History of Cinemas in Aberdeen, 1896–1987. 1988.

24606 CLARK (M. J.) *ed.* Politics and the Media: Film and Television for the Political Scientist and Historian. Oxf. 1979.

24607 RICHARDS (JEFFREY). Visions of Yesterday. 1973.

24608 ATWELL (DAVID). Cathedrals of the Movies: A History of British Cinemas and their Audiences. 1980.

24609 ALDGATE (ANTHONY). Cinema and History: British Newsreels and the Spanish Civil War. 1979.

24610 ALDGATE (ANTHONY). '1930 Newsreels: Censorship and Controversy'. *Sight and Sound* 46 (1977), 154–7.

24611 WARD (KENNETH). 'British Documentaries of the 1930s'. *Hist.* 62 (1977), 426–31.

24612 SWANN (PAUL). The British Film Documentary Movement 1926–1946. Camb. 1989.

24613 PRONAY (NICHOLAS). 'British Newsreels in the 1930s: 1. Audience and Producers'. *Hist.* 56 (1971), 411–18. 2. Their Policies and Impact. *Hist.* 57 (1972), 63–72.

24614 PRONAY (NICHOLAS) *and* SPRING (D. W.). Propaganda, Politics and Film, 1918–45. 1982.

24615 ROTHA (PAUL). Documentary Diary: An Informal History of the British Documentary Film, 1928–1939. 1973.

24616 SUSSEX (ELIZABETH). The Rise and Fall of the British Documentary. Berkeley, Calif./Lond. 1975.

24617 RICHARDS (JEFFREY) *and* ALDGATE (ANTHONY). Best of British: Cinema and Society 1930–1970. Oxf. 1983.

24618 McPHERSON (DON) *ed.* Traditions of Independence: British Cinema in the Thirties. 1980.

24619 SHORT (K. R. M.) *ed.* Feature films as History. 1981.

24620 ARMES (ROY). Patterns of Realism. 1971.

24621 —— Film and Reality: An Historical Survey. 1974.

24622 —— A Critical History of British Cinema. 1978.

24623 CURRAN (JAMES) *and* PORTER (VINCENT) *eds.* British Cinema History. 1983.

24624 BARNES (JOHN). The Beginnings of the Cinema in England. Newton Abbot. 1976.

24625 VERMILYE (JERRY). The Great British Films. 1978.

24626 BETTS (ERNEST). The Film Business: A History of British Cinema, 1896–1972. 1973.

24627 —— Inside Pictures, with some Reflections from the Outside. 1960.

24628 BIRD (JOHN). Cinema Parade: Fifty Years of Film Shows. Birm. 1947.

24629 WOOD (LESLIE). The Miracle of the Movies. 1947.

24630 BOX (KATHLEEN LOIS). The Cinema and the Public: An Enquiry into Cinema-going Habits and Expenditure Made in 1946. 1948.

24631 RICHARDS (JEFFREY) *and* SHERIDAN (D.) *eds.* Mass-Observation at the Movies. 1987.

24632 SPRAOS (JOHN). The Decline of the Cinema: An Economist's Report. 1962.

24633 BUTLER (IVAN). Cinema in Britain: An Illustrated Survey. 1973.

24634 —— 'To Encourage the Art of the Film': The Story of the British Film Institute. 1971.

24635 COWIE (PETER). Seventy Years of Cinema. 1969.

24636 GIFFORD (DENIS). British Cinema: An Illustrated Guide. 1968.

24637 OAKLEY (CHARLES ALLEN). Where We Came in: Seventy Years of the British Film Industry. 1964.

24638 DURGNAT (R.). A Mirror for England: British Movies from Austerity to Affluence. 1970.

24639 PERRY (GEORGE). The Great British Picture Show. 1974.

24640 WALKER (ALEXANDER). Hollywood, England: The British Film Industry in the Sixties. 1974.

24641 WALKER (JOHN). The Once and Future Film: British Cinema in the Seventies and Eighties. 1985.

24642 DICKINSON (MARGARET) *and* STREET (SARAH). Cinema and State: The Film Industry and the Government, 1927–84. 1985.

24643 WILSON (DAVID) *ed.* Sight and Sound: A Fiftieth Anniversary Collection. 1982.

24644 HOGENKAMP (B.). 'Film and the Workers' Movement in Britain, 1929–1939'. *Sight and Sound* 45 (1976), 69–76.

24645 CROW (DUNCAN). 'The First Golden Age'. *Sight and Sound* 23 (1954), 148–51.

24646 BALCON (*Sir* MICHAEL ELIAS). 'The British Film during the War'. *Penguin Film. Rev.* 1 (1946), 66–73.

24647 YOUNG (HOWARD IRVING). 'British Studios in Wartime'. *Screen Writer* 50 (1946), 11–17.

24648 ANSTEY (EDGAR). 'Wildlife Films in the Post-war British Cinema'. *J. Soc. for Film and Television Arts* 32 (1968), 3–6.

24649 HUNTLEY (JOHN). British Technicolor Films. 1949.

24650 FORMAN (*Sir* DENIS). Films, 1945–1950. 1952.

24651 AUSTEN (D.). 'The Fifties: Let's Go to the Pictures'. *Films and Filming* 20 (1974), 20–5.

24652 JOHNSTON (CLAIRE) *and* DAWSON (JAN). 'Declarations of Independence'. *Sight and Sound* 29 (1970), 28–32.

24653 JOHNSON (IAN). 'We're all Right Jack'. *Films and Filming* 8 (1962), 44–8.

24654 CHANAN (MICHAEL). 'Commitment and Disillusion: British Cinema, 1956–1969'. *Art Inl* 13 (1969), 61–4.

24655 CURTIS (DAVID). 'English Avant-garde Film: An Early Chronology'. *Studio Inl* 190 (1975), 176–82.

24656 HOUSTON (PENELOPE). The Contemporary Cinema. Harmondsworth. 1963.

24657 PIRIE (DAVID). A Heritage of Horror: The English Gothic Cinema 1946–72. 1973.

24658 MANVELL (ROGER ARNOLD). New Cinema in Britain. 1969.

24659 WOOD (ALAN). Mr Rank: A Study of J. Arthur Rank and British Films. 1952.

24660 NOBLE (PETER) *comp.* Anthony Asquith. [n.d.].

24661 MINNEY (RUBEIGH JAMES). 'Puffin' Asquith. 1973.

24662 MONTAGU (IVOR GOLDSMID SAMUEL) *et al.* 'Michael Balcon, 1896–1977'. *Sight and Sound* 47 (1978), 9–11.

24663 BALCON (*Sir* MICHAEL ELIAS). Michael Balcon Presents . . . a Lifetime of Films. 1969.

24664 —— *et al.* Twenty Years of British Film, 1925–1945. 1947.

24665 BRUNEL (ADRIAN). Nice Work: An Autobiography of 30 Years of British Films. 1949.

24666 POWELL (MICHAEL). A Life in Movies. 1986.

24667 BROWN (GEOFF). 'Ealing, your Ealing'. *Sight and Sound* 46 (1977), 164–7.

24668 BARR (CHARLES). Ealing Studios. 1977.

24669 FORBES (BRYAN). Notes for a Life. 1974.

24670 HARDY (FORSYTH). John Grierson: A Documentary Biography. Lond./Boston, Mass. 1979.

24671 EVANS (GARY). John Grierson and the National Film Board: The Politics of Wartime Propaganda, 1939–1945. Toronto. 1984.

24672 BEVERIDGE (JAMES). John Grierson: Film Master. Lond./NY. 1978.

24673 MANVELL (ARNOLD ROGER) *et al.* 'John Grierson'. *J. Soc. Film and Television Arts* 2 (1972), 1–9.

24674 LAVALLEY (ALBERT JOSEPH). Focus on Hitchcock. 1972.

24675 TABORI (PAUL). Alexander Korda. 1959.

24676 KULIK (KAROL). Alexander Korda: The Man who Could Work Miracles. 1975.

24677 PRATLEY (GERALD). The Cinema of David Lean. 1974.

24678 CASTELLI (LOUIS). David Lean: A Guide to References and Resources. Boston, Mass. 1980.

24679 BROWN (GEOFF). 'Richard Massingham: The Five-Inch Film Maker'. *Sight and Sound* 45 (1976), 156–9.

24680 PEARSON (GEORGE WILLIAM). Flashback: The Autobiography of a British Film-Maker. 1957.

24681 PERRY (GEORGE). Movies from the Mansion: A History of Pinewood Studios. 1976.

24682 MOSS (ROBERT). The Films of Carol Reed. 1987.

24683 BAXTER (JOHN). An Appalling Talent: Ken Russell. 1973.

24684 ROSENFELDT (DIANE). Ken Russell: A Guide to References and Resources. Boston, Mass. 1978.

24685 HANKE (KEN). Ken Russell's Films. Metuchen, NJ/Lond. 1984.

24686 SILVIVIA (DALE). Laurence Olivier and the Art of Film Making. Toronto/Lond. 1985.

24687 NOBLE (PETER). British Screen Stars. 1946.

24688 MORLEY (SHERIDAN). The Other Side of the Moon: The Life of David Niven. 1985.

24689 HINXMAN (MARGARET) *and* D'ARCY (SUSAN). The Films of Dirk Bogarde. 1974.

24690 WILCOX (HERBERT). 'British Films, Past and Future'. *Roy. Soc. Arts J.* 112 (1964), 514–22.

24691 FRENCH (PHILIP). 'The Alphaville of Admass, Or how we Learned to Stop Worrying and Love the Boom'. *Sight and Sound* 35 (1966), 107–11.

24692 BILLINGTON (KEVIN) *et al.* 'The Crisis we Deserve'. *Sight and Sound* 39 (1970), 172–8.

24693 GORDON (D.). 'Ten Points about the Crisis in the British Film Industry'. *Sight and Sound* 43 (1974), 66–72.

24694 BROWN (GEOFF). 'Which Way to the Way Ahead? Britain's Years of Reconstruction'. *Sight and Sound* 47 (1978), 242–7.

10. PHOTOGRAPHY

24695 GAISFORD (JOHN) *ed.* Time Gone By: A Photographic Record of Great Britain from 1856 to 1956. 1977.

24696 JAY (BILL). Victorian Candid Camera: Paul Martin, 1864–1944. 1973.

24697 JEFFREY (IAN) *and* MELLOR (DAVID). 'Style and Ideology in British Art and Photography, 1900–1940'. *Studio Inl* 190 (1975), 27–34.

24698 FONVIELLE (L.). 'New Standpoints: Photography 1940–1955'. *Aperture* 81 (1978), 60–76.

24699 ELLIS (A.). 'Playback: British Photography 1955–1965'. *Brit. J. Photography* 130 (1983), 420–5.

24700 BEATON (*Sir* CECIL [WALTER HARDY]). Photobiography. 1951.

24701 —— The Happy Years: Diaries, 1944–1948. 1972.

24702 —— The Strenuous Years: Diaries, 1948–1955. 1973.

24703 —— The Restless Years: Diaries, 1955–1963. 1976.

24704 —— The Parting Years: Diaries, 1963–1974. 1978.

24705 —— *with* BUCKLAND (GAIL). The Magic Image: The Genius of Photography from 1839 to the Present Day. 1975.

24706 BUCKLE (RICHARD) *ed.* Self-Portrait with Friends: The Selected Diaries of Cecil Beaton, 1926–1974. 1979.

24707 VICKERS (HUGO). Cecil Beaton: The Authorized Biography. 1985.

24708 NUNN (GEORGE WALTER ARTHUR). British Sources of Photographs and Pictures. 1952.

24709 ARMSTRONG-JONES (ANTONY CHARLES ROBERT) *Earl of Snowdon.* A Photographic Autobiography. 1979.

24710 SINCLAIR (DAVID). Snowdon: A Man of our Times. 1982.

24711 LICHFIELD (PATRICK) *Earl of Lichfield.* Not the Whole Truth: An Autobiography. 1986.

24712 PARKINSON (NORMAN). Lifework. 1983.

24713 WILLIAMS (VAL). Women Photographers: The Other Observers. 1900 to the Present Day. 1986.

24714 SPALDING (FRANCES). Vanessa Bell. 1983.

11. RADIO

24715 BRITISH BROADCASTING CORPORATION, HIGGENS (GAVIN) *ed.* British Broadcasting. 1922–82: A Select Bibliography. 1983.

24716 COLLISON (ROBERT L.). Broadcasting in Britain: A Bibliography. Camb. 1961.

24717 MACDONALD (BARRIE). Broadcasting in the United Kingdom: A Guide to Information Sources. 1988.

24718 BRIGGS (ASA) *Baron.* The History of Broadcasting in the United Kingdom. 1. The Birth of Broadcasting. 1961: 2. The Golden Age of Wireless. 1965: 3. The War of Words. 1970.

24719 —— The BBC: The First Fifty Years. Oxf. 1985.

24720 BLACK (PETER). The Biggest Aspidistra in the World: A Personal Celebration of Fifty Years of the BBC. 1972.

24721 WOOD (ROBERT). A World in your Ear: The Broadcasting of an Era, 1923–64. 1979.

24722 PEGG (M.). Broadcasting and Society 1918–39. 1983.

24723 GRISEWOOD (FREDDIE). My Story of the BBC. 1959.

24724 CLAYRE (ALASDAIR). The Impact of Broadcasting or Mrs Buckle's Wall is Singing. 1973.

24725 MARQUIS (A. G.). 'Written on the Wind: The Impact of Radio during the 1930s'. *J. Contemp. Hist.* 19 (1984), 385–415.

24726 BBC ANNUAL REPORT AND HANDBOOK. Annually from 1928. Since 1980 it has been entitled the BBC HAND-BOOK.

24727 GEDDES (KEITH). Broadcasting in Britain, 1922–1972. 1972.

24728 PAWLEY (EDWARD). BBC Engineering 1922–1972.

24729 REID (COLIN). Action Stations: A History of Broadcasting House. 1986.

24730 BBC 'Radio Times' 50th Anniversary Souvenir 1923–1973. 1973.

24731 REITH (JOHN CHARLES WALSHAM) *Baron.* Broadcast over Britain. 1924.

24732 BURROWS (ARTHUR). The Story of Broadcasting. 1924.

24733 MOSELEY (SIDNEY ALEXANDER). Broadcasting in my Time. 1935.

24734 ALLIGAHN (GARRY). Sir John Reith. 1938.

24735 BOYLE (ANDREW PHILIP MORE). Only the Wind will Listen. 1972.

24736 STUART (CHARLES HARBORNE) *ed.* The Reith Diaries. 1975.

24737 STUART (DOUGLAS). A Very Sheltered Life. 1970.

24738 ANDREWS (EAMONN). This is my Life. 1963.

24739 DAY (Sir ROBIN). Grand Inquisitor: Memoirs. 1989.

24740 DIMBLEBY (JONATHAN). Richard Dimbleby: A Biography. 1975.

24741 MIALL (ROWLAND LEONARD). Richard Dimbleby, Broadcaster: By his Colleagues. 1966.

24742 PLOMLEY (FRANCIS ROY). Days Seemed Longer: Early Years of a Broadcaster. 1980.

24743 SNAGGE (JOHN DERRICK MORDAUNT). Those Vintage Years of Radio. 1972.

24744 BRIGGS (SUSAN ANNE). Those Radio Times. 1981.

24745 SAERCHINGER (CESAR). The Voice of Europe. 1938.

24746 LEAN (EDWARD TANGYE). Voices in the Darkness: The Story of the European Radio War. 1943.

24747 ROLO (CHARLES JACK). Radio Goes to War.

24748 KRABBE (HENNING) ed. Voices from Britain: Broadcast History, 1939–1945. 1947.

24749 PEDERICK (G.). Battledress Broadcasters: A History of the British Forces Broadcasting Services. 1964.

24750 TAYLOR (DOREEN). A Microphone and a Frequency: Forty Years of Forces Broadcasting. 1983.

24751 GIELGUD (VAL). British Radio Drama 1922–1956. 1957.

24752 —— Years in a Mirror. 1964.

24753 DRAKAKIS (JOHN) ed. British Radio Drama. Camb. 1981.

24754 PRIESSNITZ (HORST P.). Das englische 'radio play' seit 1945. Berlin. 1980.

24755 PALMER (RICHARD). School Broadcasting in Britain. 1947.

24756 HEPPENSTALL (RAYNER). Portrait of the Artist as a Professional Man. 1969.

24757 COASE (RONALD HARRY). British Broadcasting: A Study in Monopoly. 1950.

24758 SIMON (Sir ERNEST DARWIN). The BBC from within. 1953.

24759 PAULU (BURTON). British Broadcasting: Radio and Television in the United Kingdom. Minneapolis, Minn. 1956. London. 1957.

24760 —— British Broadcasting in Transition. 1961.

24761 —— Television and Radio in the United Kingdom. 1981.

24762 CROZIER (MARY). Broadcasting: Sound and Television. 1958.

24763 STURMEY (STANLEY GEORGE). The Economic Development of Radio. 1958.

24764 U.K. CENTRAL OFFICE OF INFORMATION. Sound and Television Broadcasting in Britain. 1964. 2nd edn 1966.

24765 —— Broadcasting in Britain. 2nd edn 1975.

24766 BBC Pamphlets. The European Service of the BBC: Two Decades of Broadcasting to Europe 1938–1959. 1959.

24767 CLARK (J. BERESFORD). 'The BBC's External Services'. Inl Affs 35 (1939), 170–80.

24768 SHORT (K. R. M.) ed. Western Broadcasting over the Iron Curtain. 1986.

24769 BROOK (NORMAN CRAVEN) Baron Normanbrook. The Functions of the BBC's Governors. 1965.

24770 BRIGGS (ASA) Baron. Governing the BBC. 1979.

24771 GRISEWOOD (HARMAN). One Thing at a Time: An Autobiography. 1968.

24772 EDWARDS (DONALD). Political Broadcasting. 1965.

24773 SMITH (JUSTIN DAVIS). 'The Struggle for Control of the Air Waves: The Attlee Governments, the BBC and Industrial Unrest 1945–51'. In Tony Gorst, Lewis Johnman, and Scott Lucas eds. Post-War Britain 1945–64: Themes and Perspectives. 1989.

24774 NEWBY (PERCY HOWARD). The Third Programme. 1965.

24775 WHITEHEAD (KATE). The Third Programme. Oxf. 1989.

24776 WHITLEY (OLIVER JOHN). Broadcasting and the National Culture. 1965.

24777 STEPHENSON (DONALD). The BBC's Foreign Relations. 1967.

24778 CURRAN (Sir CHARLES JOHN). Broadcasting from West of Suez. 1968.

24779 —— Money, Management and Programmes. 1969.

24780 THORNE (BARRIE). The BBC's Finances and Cost Control. 1970.

24781 LAMB (KENNETH HENRY LOWRY). The BBC and its Public. 1970.

24782 REID (COLIN). Action Stations: A History of Broadcasting House. 1987.

24783 SILVEY (ROBERT). Who's Listening? The Story of BBC Audience Research. 1974.

24784 MADGE (TIM). Beyond the BBC. 1988.

24785 GREENE (Sir HUGH CARLETON). What Price Culture? An Examination of Broadcasting Finance . . . 1966.

24786 SCUPHAM (J.). Broadcasting and the Community. 1967.

24787 WEDELL (EBERHARD GEORGE). Broadcasting and Public Policy. 1968.

24788 EMMETT (B. P.). 'New Role for Research in Broadcasting'. Pub. Op. Q. 32 (1968), 654–65.

24789 SMITH (TREVOR A.). 'The Debate on Broadcasting's Future'. Contemp. Rev. 221 (1972), 169–73.

24790 SMITH (ANTHONY) comp. and ed. British Broadcasting. Newton Abbot. 1974.

24791 SMITH (ANTHONY). The Shadow in the Cave: A Study of the Relationship between the Broadcaster, his Audience and the State. 1973. Rev. edn 1976.

24792 ALLEN (R.). 'Waiting for Annan'. *Sight and Sound* 44 (1975), 250–3.

24793 NEWBY (PERCY HOWARD). Broadcasting: A Professional View. 1977.

24794 —— The Uses of Broadcasting. 1978.

24795 BURNS (TOM). The BBC: Public Institution and Private World. 1977.

24796 HILL (CHARLES). Behind the Screen: The Broadcasting Memoirs of Lord Hill of Luton. 1974.

24797 CURRAN (*Sir* CHARLES). A Seamless Robe: Broadcasting Philosophy and Practice. 1979.

24798 TRETHOWAN (*Sir* IAN). Split Screen. 1984.

24799 MILNE (ALISDAIR). 'DG': The Memoirs of a Broadcaster. 1988.

24800 BRITISH BROADCASTING CORPORATION. Serving Neighbourhood and Nation. 1977.

24801 HALE (JULIAN). Radio Power: Propaganda and International Broadcasting. 1975.

24802 VENMORE-ROWLAND (JOHN). Radio Caroline: The Story of the First British Off-Shore Radio Station. 1967.

24803 HARRIS (PAUL). When Pirates ruled the Waves. 1968. Rev. edn as Broadcasting from the High Seas: The History of Offshore Radio in Europe 1958–1976. 1977.

24804 LAING (DAVID). The Sound of our Time. 1969.

24805 BARON (M.). Independent Radio: The Story of Independent Radio in the U.K. 1975.

24806 RADCLIFFE (P.). The Piccadilly Story: Profile of a Radio Station. 1979.

24807 SEYMOUR-URE (COLIN KNOWLTON). 'Parliamentary Privilege and Broadcasting'. *Parl. Affs* 16 (1963), 411–18.

24808 ROWE (E. A.). 'Broadcasting and the 1929 General Election'. *Ren. Mod. Studs* 12 (1968), 108–19.

24809 USHERWOOD (STEPHEN). 'The BBC and the General Strike'. *Hist. Today* 22 (1972), 858–65.

24810 MACKENZIE (F. R.). 'Eden, Suez and the BBC—A Reassessment'. *Listener* 82 (1969), 841–3.

24811 FRANCIS (RICHARD). Broadcasting to a Community in Conflict: The Experience in Northern Ireland. 1977.

24812 BURNETT (GEORGE) *ed.* Scotland on the Air. Edin. 1938.

24813 BRIGGS (ASA) *Baron.* 'Local and Regional in Northern Sound Broadcasting'. *Northern Hist.* 10 (1975), 165–87.

24814 MANSELL (GERARD EVELYN HERBERT). Broadcasting to the World: Forty Years of BBC External Services. 1973.

24815 —— Let Truth be Told: 50 Years of BBC External Broadcasting. 1982.

24816 WALKER (ANDREW). Voice from the World: 50 Years of Broadcasting to the World 1932–1982. 1982.

24817 FIELDEN (LIONEL). The Natural Bent. 1960.

24818 GORHAM (MAURICE). Sound and Fury. 1948.

24819 GRISEWOOD (HARMAN JOSEPH GERARD). One Thing at a Time. 1968.

24820 NOBBS (GEORGE). The Wireless Stars. Norwich. 1972.

24821 BRIDSON (DOUGLAS GEOFFREY). Prospero and Ariel: The Rise and Fall of Radio: A Personal Recollection. 1971.

24822 PARKER (DEREK). Radio: The Great Years. 1977.

24823 GREENE (*Sir* HUGH CARLETON). The Third Floor Front: A View of Broadcasting in the Sixties. 1969.

24824 TRACEY (MICHAEL). A Variety of Lives: A Biography of Sir Hugh Carleton Greene. 1983.

12. TELEVISION

24825 INDEPENDENT BROADCASTING AUTHORITY. Annual Reports and Accounts. 1954/5–1971/2.

24826 Television and Radio: IBA Guide to Independent Broadcasting. 1976+.

24827 ABRAMS (MARK). 'Child Audiences for Television in Great Britain'. *Journalism Q.* 33 (1956), 35–41.

24828 HIMMELWEIT (HILDE THERESE), OPPENHEIM (A. N.), *and* VINCE (PAMELA). Television and the Child. Oxf. 1958.

24829 DUNN (GWEN). The Box in the Corner: Television and the Under-Fives: A Study. 1977.

24830 EMMETT (B. P.). 'The Television Audience in the United Kingdom'. *J. Roy. Stat. Soc.* 119 (1956), 284–311.

24831 ROBINSON (JOHN) *ed.* Educational Television and Radio in Britain. 1966.

24832 MACLEAN (RODERICK). Television in Education. 1968.

24833 PARSONS (CHRISTOPHER). True to Nature: Twenty-Five Years of Wildlife Filming with the BBC Natural History Film Unit. 1982.

24834 HALLORAN (JAMES DERMOT), BROWN (R. L.), *and* CHANEY (D. C.). Television and Delinquency. Leics. 1970.

24835 BAIN (ANDREW DAVID). The Growth of Television Ownership in the United Kingdom. Camb. 1964.

24836 PIEPE (ANTHONY), EMERSON (MILES), *and* LANNON (JUDY). Television and the Working Class. Farnb. 1975.

24837 WHITEHOUSE (MARY). Cleaning-up T.V.: From Protest to Participation. 1967.

24838 —— Who does She Think She is? 1971.

24839 COLLINS (MARTIN ALAN). The Television Audience: Patterns of Viewing. 1975.

24840 BELSON (WILLIAM ALBERT). 'Effects of Television on the Interests and Initiative of Adult Viewers in Greater London'. *Brit. J. Psychol.* 50 (1959), 145–58.

24841 SHAW (*Sir* ROY). 'Television: Freedom and Responsibility'. *Blackfriars* 47 (1966), 453–65.

24842 BLACK (PETER). The Mirror in the Corner: People's Television. 1972.

24843 SWIFT (JOHN). Adventure in Vision: The First Twenty-Five Years of Television. 1950.

24844 GORHAM (MAURICE ANTHONY CONEYS). Broadcasting and Television since 1900. 1952.

24845 TOMICHE (F. J.). 'Aperçu sur quelques Effets de la Télévision en Grande Bretagne'. *Temps. Mod.* 15 (1959), 1080–97.

24846 ROSS (GORDON). Television Jubilee: The Story of 25 Years of B.B.C. Television. 1961.

24847 BBC. BBC Television: A British Engineering Achievement. 1961.

24848 PAWLEY (EDWARD). 'BBC Television 1939–60: A Review of Progress'. *Proc. Inst. Elec. Eng.* (1961), 375–97.

24849 LEWIS (P. M.). Community Television and Cable in Britain. 1978.

24850 BEADLE (*Sir* GERALD). Television: A Critical Review. 1963.

24851 BLUMLER (JAY GEORGE). 'British Television—The Outlines of a Research Strategy'. *Brit. J. Sociol.* 15 (1964), 223–33.

24852 HOOD (STUART). A Survey of Television. 1967.

24853 McLEAN (*Sir* FRANCIS CHARLES). Colour Television. 1967.

24854 BELSON (WILLIAM ALBERT). The Impact of Television: Methods and Findings in Program Research. 1967.

24855 BLUEM (ALBERT WILLIAM) *and* MANVELL (ROGER) *comps.* The Progress of Television: An Anglo-American Survey. 1967.

24856 SHULMAN (MILTON). The Least Worst Television in the World. 1973.

24857 WORSLEY (T. C.). Television: The Ephemeral Art. 1970.

24858 SUTTON (SHAWN). The Largest Theatre in the World. 1982.

24859 COOKE (ALISTAIR). Masterpieces: A Decade of Classics in British Television. 1982.

24860 BRANDT (GEORGE W.). British Television Drama. Camb. 1981.

24861 TAYLOR (JOHN RUSSELL). Anatomy of a Television Play. 1962.

24862 McARTHUR (COLIN). Television and History. 1978.

24863 SENDALL (BERNARD). The History of Independent Television in Britain. 1. Origins and Foundation, 1946–62. 1982. 2. Expansion and Change, 1958–68. 1983. Recognition and Responsibility, 1968–80. 1985. The Companies and their Programmes. 1989.

24864 HARRIS (J. S.). 'Television as a Political Issue in Britain'. *Can. J. Econ. Pol. Sci.* 21 (1955), 328–38.

24865 WILSON (HARPER HUBERT). Pressure Group: The Campaign for Commercial Television. 1961.

24866 TAPLIN (WALTER). The Origin of Television Advertising in the United Kingdom. 1961.

24867 FRASER (R.). 'Independent Television in Britain'. *Public Admin.* 36 (1958), 115–24.

24868 ALTMAN (WILFRID), THOMAS (DENIS), *and* SAWERS (DAVID). From Monopoly to Competition. 1962.

24869 SUCHY (J. T.). 'How Does Commercial Television Affect British Viewing?'. *Journalism Q.* 35 (1958), 65–71.

24870 JENKINS (DAVID CLIVE). Power behind the Screen: Ownership, Control and Motivation in British Commercial Television. 1961.

24871 ALTMAN (WILFRID) *et al.* T.V: From Monopoly to Competition and Back? 1962.

24872 TAPLIN (WALTER). The Origins of Television Advertising in the United Kingdom. 1961.

24873 GABLE (J.). The Tuppeny Punch and Judy Show: 25 Years of T.V. Commercials. 1980.

24874 HENRY (BRIAN). British Television Advertising: The First 30 Years. 1986.

24875 THOMAS (HOWARD). With an Independent Air: Encounters during a Lifetime of Broadcasting. 1977.

24876 TINKER (J.). The Television Barons. 1980.

24877 HENNESSY (DAVID JAMES GEORGE) *Baron Windlesham.* Broadcasting in a Free Society. Oxf. 1980.

24878 BRIGGS (ASA) *and* SPICER (JOANNE). The Franchise Affair: Creating Fortune and Failure in Independent Television. 1986.

24879 LEAPMAN (MICHAEL). Treachery? The Power Struggle at TV-AM. 1984.

24880 LAMBERT (STEPHEN). Channel Four: Television with a Difference. 1982.

24881 BLANCHARD (SIMON) *and* MORLEY (DAVID). What's this Channel Fo(u)r? 1982.

24882 ISAACS (JEREMY). Storm over 4. 1989.

24883 MOORFOOT (REX). Television in the Eighties: The Total Equation. 1982.

24884 KUHN (RAYMOND). The Politics of Broadcasting. 1985.

24885 LEAPMAN (MICHAEL). The Last Days of the Beeb. 1987.

24886 GOLDIE (GRACE WYNDHAM). Facing the Nation: Television and Politics 1936–1976. 1977.

24887 TRENAMAN (JOSEPH) *and* McQUAIL (DENIS). Television and the Political Image: A Study of the Impact of Television on the 1959 General Election. 1961.

24888 PICKLES (WILLIAM). 'Political Attitudes in the Television Age'. *Pol. Q.* 30 (1959), 54–66.

24889 DAY (*Sir* ROBIN). The Case for Televising Parliament. 1965.

24890 BLUMLER (JAY GEORGE) *and* MADGE (JOHN). Citizenship and Television. 1965.

24891 BLUMLER (JAY GEORGE) *and* McQUAIL (DENIS). Television in Politics: Its Uses and Influence. 1968.

24892 WHALE (JOHN HILARY). The Half-Shut Eye: Television and Politics in Britain and America. 1969.

24893 MORLEY (PETER) *et al.* 'Television and the 1970 Election'. *J. Soc. Film & Television Arts* 40 (1970), 1–20.

24894 SMITH (ANTHONY) *ed.* Television and Political Life: Studies in Six European Countries. 1979.

24895 BLUMLER (JAY GEORGE) *et al.* The Challenge of Election Broadcasting. Leeds. 1978.

24896 PATEMAN (TREVOR). Television and the February 1974 General Election. 1974.

24897 HOWARD (ANTHONY MITCHELL). 'The Parties, Elections and Television'. *Sight and Sound* 47 (1978), 206–9.

24898 TRACEY (MICHAEL). The Production of Political Television in Britain. 1978.

24899 TUMBER (HOWARD). Television and the Riots. 1982.

24900 ADAMS (V.). The Media and the Falklands Campaign. 1986.

24901 GUNTER (BARRIE), SVENNING (MICHAEL), *and* WOBER (MALLORY). Television Coverage of the 1983 General Election: Audiences, Appreciation and Public Opinion. Aldershot. 1986.

24902 SVENNING (MICHAEL) *and* GUNTER (BARRIE). 'Television Coverage of the 1984 European Parliamentary Election'. *Parl. Affs* 39 (1984), 165–78.

24903 MAGEE (BRYAN). The Television Interviewer. 1966.

24904 DAY (*Sir* ROBIN). Television: A Personal Report. 1961.

24905 BAKEWELL (JOAN DAWSON) *and* GARNHAM (NICHOLAS). The New Priesthood: British Television Today. 1970.

24906 BARRETT (MICHAEL). Michael Barrett. 1973.

24907 BOSANQUET (REGINALD). Let's Get through Wednesday: My Twenty Five Years with ITN. 1980.

24908 DOUGALL (ROBERT). In and Out of the Box. 1973.

24909 FRISCHAUER (WILLI). David Frost. 1972.

24910 HARDING (GILBERT CHARLES). Along my Line. 1953.

24911 —— Master of None. 1958.

24912 KENNEDY (LUDOVIC). On my Way to the Club. 1989.

24913 MITCHELL (LESLIE). Leslie Mitchell Reporting. 1981.

24914 COCKERELL (MICHAEL). Live from Number 10: The Inside Story of Prime Ministers and Television. 1988.

24915 JACOBS (DAVID). Jacob's Ladder. 1963.

24916 SAVILE (JIMMY). As it Happens: Jimmy Savile OBE: His Autobiography. 1974.

24917 WOGAN (TERRY). Wogan on Wogan. Harmondsworth. 1987.

24918 KUMAR (KRISHAN). 'Holding the Middle Ground: The BBC, the Public and the Professional Broadcaster'. *Sociol.* 9 (1975).

24919 TYRRELL (ROBERT). The Work of the Television Journalist. 1972. 2nd edn 1981.

24920 TEDDER (EDDIE) *ed.* Who's Who in Television. 3rd edn 1985.

24921 DAVIS (ANTHONY). Television: Here is the News. 1976.

24922 GLASGOW MEDIA GROUP. Bad News. 1976.

24923 COX (*Sir* GEOFFREY). See it Happen: The Making of ITN. 1983.

24924 MITCHELL (AUSTIN VERNON). 'The Decline of Current Affairs Television'. *Pol. Q.* 44 (1973), 127–36.

24925 TRACEY (MICHAEL). In the Culture of an Eye—Ten Years of Weekend World. 1983.

24926 HETHERINGTON (ALASTAIR). News, Newspapers and Television. 1985.

13. BOOKS AND PUBLISHING

24927 MYERS (ROBIN). The British Book Trade from Caxton to the Present Day: A Bibliographical Guide. 1973.

24928 FEATHER (JOHN). A History of British Publishing. 1988.

24929 GROSS (GERALD) *ed.* Publishers on Publishing. 1961.

24930 KINGSFORD (REGINALD JOHN LETHBRIDGE). The Publishers Association 1896–1946. Camb. 1970.

24931 ROLPH (CECIL H.). Books in the Dock. 1969.

24932 NORRIE (IAN). Sixty Precarious Years: A Short History of the National Book League. 1985.

24933 BARNES (JAMES JOHN). Free Trade in Books: A Study of the London Book Trade since 1800. 1964.

24934 LANE (MICHAEL) *and* BOOTH (JEREMY). Books and Publishers: Commerce against Culture in Post-War Britain. Lexington, Mass. 1980.

24935 ARNOLD (RALPH CHRISTIAN MARSHALL). Orange Street and Brickhole Lane. 1963.

24936 MUMBY (FRANK) *and* NORRIS (IAN). Bookselling and Book Publishing: A History from the Earliest Times to the Present Day. 1930. 5th edn 1974.

24937 PLANT (MARJORIE). The English Booktrade: An Economic History of the Making and Sale of Books. 1939. 3rd edn 1974.

24938 DEANE (MARJORIE). 'United Kingdom Publishing Statistics'. *J. Roy. Stat. Soc.* (1951). 468–89.

24939 WEYBRIGHT (VICTOR). The Making of a Publisher: A Life in the 20th Century Book Revolution. 1968.

24940 CURWEN (PETER J.). The U.K. Publishing Industry. Oxf. 1981.

24941 GARDINER (LESLIE). Bartholomew: 150 Years. 1976.

24942 BOLITHO (HECTOR) *ed.* A Batsford Century . . . 1843–1943. 1943.

24943 ADAM AND CHARLES BLACK, 1807–1957. Some Chapters in the History of a Publishing House. 1957.

24944 CLARK (ALAN M.). Catalogue: Exhibition; 150 Years of Publishing, Blackie & Son, 1809–1959. 1959.

24945 TREDREY (FRANK). The House of Blackwood 1804–1954. Edin./Lond. 1954.

24946 LAMBERT (JACK) *and* RATCLIFFE (MICHAEL). The History of the Bodley Head 1887–1987. 1987.

24947 JONES (H. KAY). Butterworths: History of a Publishing House. 1980.

24948 BLACK (MICHAEL H.). Cambridge University Press, 1584–1984. Camb. 1984.

24949 ROBERTS (S. C.). Adventures with Authors. Camb. 1966. [Cambridge University Press.].

24950 HOWARD (MICHAEL SPENCER). Jonathan Cape: Publisher. 1971.

24951 NOWELL-SMITH (SIMON). The House of Cassell 1848–1958. 1958.

24952 FLOWER (*Sir* NEWMAN). Just as it Happened. 1954. [Chairman of Cassell.].

24953 WAUGH (ARTHUR). A Hundred Years of Publishing, being the Story of Chapman and Hall Ltd. 1930.

24954 MAIR (CARLENE). The Chappell Story 1811–1961. 1961.

24955 WARNER (OLIVER). Chatto and Windus: A Brief Account of the Firm's Origins, History and Development. 1973.

24956 KEIR (DAVID EDWIN). The House of Collins: The Story. 1952.

24957 STOKES (ROY). Michael Sadleir 1888–1957. 1980. [Constable].

24958 SIMON (HERBERT). Songs and Words: A History of the Curwen Press. 1973.

24959 —— Good Books Come from Devon: The David and Charles Twenty-First Birthday Book. Newton Abbot. 1981.

24960 ATHILL (DIANA). Instead of a Letter. 1976. [Partner in André Deutsch.].

24961 HODGES (SHEILA). Gollancz: The Story of a Publishing House 1928–1978. 1978.

24962 GOLLANCZ (*Sir* VICTOR). My Dear Timothy: An Autobiographical Letter to his Grandson. 1952; More for Timothy: Being the Second Instalment of an Autobiographical Letter to his Grandson. 1953; Reminiscences of Affection. 1968.

24963 EDWARDS (RUTH DUDLEY). Victor Gollancz: A Biography. 1987.

24964 SAMUELS (STUART). 'The Left Book Club'. *J. Contemp. Hist.* 1 (1966), 65–86.

24965 LEWIS (JOHN). The Left Book Club: An Historical Record. 1970.

24966 HART-DAVIS (RUPERT). The Arms of Time: A Memoir. 1979. [Hart-Davis.].

24967 HILL (ALAN). In Pursuit of Publishing. 1988. [Heinemann.].

24968 Jamie: An 80th Birthday Tribute from his Friends. 1980. [The publisher Hamish Hamilton.].

24969 BARTY-KING (HUGH). HMSO: The Story of the First 200 Years 1786–1986. 1986.

24970 ATTENBOROUGH (JOHN). A Living Memory: Hodder and Stoughton, Publishers 1868–1975. 1975.

24971 ENGLAND (EDWARD). An Unfading Vision: The Adventure of Books. 1982. [Hodder and Stoughton.].

24972 JOSEPH (RICHARD). Michael Joseph: Master of Words. 1986. (Chairman of Michael Joseph.).

24973 DROOP (JOHN PERCIVAL). The University Press of Liverpool: A Record of Progress 1899–1946. 1947.

24974 E. & S. LIVINGSTONE Ltd., Footprints in the Sands of Time, 1863–1963: The Story of the House of Livingstone: Medical, Scientific, Nursing and Dental Publishers. Edin. 1963.

24975 BRIGGS (ASA) *Lord, ed.* Essays in the History of Publishing in Celebration of the 250th Anniversary of the House of Longman, 1724–1974. 1974.

24976 MORGAN (CHARLES LANGBRIDGE). The House of Macmillan 1843–1943. 1943.

24977 NOWELL-SMITH (SIMON) *ed.* Letters to Macmillan. 1967.

24978 DICKSON (LOVAT). The House of Words. 2 vols. 1963. [Jonathan Cape and Macmillan.].

24979 DUFFY (MAUREEN). A Thousand Capricious Chances: A History of the Methuen List 1889–1989. 1989.

24980 CUMBERS (FRANK). The Book Room: The Story of the Methodist Publishing House and Epworth Press. 1956.

24981 DREYFUS (JOHN), McKITTERICK (DAVID), *and* RENDELL (SIMON). A History of the Nonesuch Press. 1981.

24982 MEYNELL (*Sir* FRANCIS). My Lives. [Nonesuch and Bodley Head.].

24983 BARKER (NICOLAS). The Oxford University Press and the Spread of Learning 1478–1978: An Illustrated History. Oxf. 1978.

24984 SUTCLIFFE (PETER). The Oxford University Press: An Informal History. Oxf. 1978.

24985 PENGUIN BOOKS. Penguin Progress 1935–1960. Published on the Occasion of the Silver Jubilee of Penguin Books. Harmondsworth. 1960.

24986 MORPURGO (JACK ERIC). Allen Lane: King Penguin, a Biography. 1979.

24987 WILLIAMS (*Sir* WILLIAM EMRYS). Allen Lane: A Personal Portrait. 1973.

24988 MUMBY (FRANK A.). The House of Routledge 1834–1934. 1934.

24989 MacLEOD (ROBERT DUNCAN). The Scottish Publishing Houses. Glasg. 1953.

24990 THOMSON (GEORGE MALCOLM). Martin Secker and Warburg: The First Fifty Years: A Memoir. 1986.

24991 BROCK (WILLIAM H.) *and* MEADOWS (A. JACK). The Lamp of Learning: Taylor and Francis and the Development of Science Publishing. 1984.

24992 CRAKER (TREVOR). Opening Accounts and Closing Memories: Thirty Years with Thames and Hudson. 1985.

24993 WARBURG (FREDERIC JOHN). An Occupation for Gentlemen. 1959; All Authors are Equal: The Publishing Life of Frederic Warburg 1936–71. 1971.

24994 FYVEL (T. R.). 'Remembering Fred Warburg: A London Publisher and his Time'. *Encounter* 59 (1982), 32–6.

24995 LIVEING (EDWARD). Adventure in Publishing: The House of Ward Lock 1854–1954. 1954.

24996 KING (ARTHUR) *and* STUART (ALBERT FREDERICK). The House of Warne: One Hundred Years of Publishing. 1965.

24997 UNWIN (PHILIP). The Publishing Unwins. 1972.

24998 UNWIN (*Sir* STANLEY). The Truth about Publishing. 8th edn revised and partly rewritten by Philip Unwin. 1976.

24999 CAVENDISH (JEAN MAVIS). A Handbook of British Publishing Practice. 1974.

25000 LUSTY (*Sir* ROBERT FRITH). Bound to be Read. 1975. [Michael Joseph and Hutchinson.].

25001 BELLAMY (B. E.). Private Presses and Publishing in England since 1945. 1980.

25002 CAVE (RODERICK GEORGE JAMES MUNRO). The Private Press. 1971. Rev. edn 1983.

25003 McCLEERY (ALISTAIR). 'The Porpoise Press, 1930–1939'. *Publishing Hist.* 21 (1987), 69–92.

25004 HARROP (D.). A History of the Gregynog Press. Pinner. 1980.

25005 THOMAS (JOY). The Bookselling Business. 1974.

25006 W. and G. FOYLE Ltd. Foyles Sixty Years, 1904–1964. 1964.

25007 NORRINGTON (*Sir* ARTHUR LIONEL PUGH). Blackwells, 1879–1979: The History of a Family Firm. Oxf. 1983.

25008 WILSON (*Sir* CHARLES H.). First with the News: The Story of W. H. Smith since 1792. 1985.

25009 HEPBURN (JAMES). The Author's Empty Purse and the Rise of the Literary Agent. Oxf. 1968.

25010 WATSON (GRAHAM). Book Society. 1980.

25011 CARTER (JOHN). Books and Book Collectors. 1956.

25012 PETERS (JEAN) *ed.* Book Collecting: A Modern Guide. 1977.

25013 BROOK (GEORGE LESLIE). Books and Book-Collecting. 1980.

25014 LEWIS (JOHN). The Twentieth Century Book: Design and Illustration. 1967.

25015 WILLIAMSON (HUGH). Methods of Book Design: The Practice of an Industrial Craft. Oxf. 1956. 2nd edn 1966.

25016 CLAIR (COLIN). A History of Printing in Britain. 1965.

25017 TWYMAN (MICHAEL). Printing 1770–1970: An Illustrated History of its Development and Uses in England. 1970.

25018 BLAGDEN (CYPRIAN). The Stationers' Company: A History 1403–1959. 1960.

25019 HANDOVER (PHYLLIS MARGARET). Printing in London from 1476 to Modern Times. 1960.

25020 SESSIONS (WILLIAM K.) *and* SESSIONS (MARGARET). Printing in York from the 1480s to the Present Day. York. 1976.

25021 CLOWES (WILLIAM BEAUFOY). Family Business 1803–1953. 1953.

25022 MORAN (JAMES). Clays of Bungay. Bungay. 1978.

25023 UNWIN (PHILIP). The Printing Unwins: A Short History of Unwin Brothers, the Gresham Press 1826–1976. 1976.

25024 MORISON (STANLEY) *and* DAY (KENNETH). The Typographic Book 1450–1935. 1963.

25025 MORAN (JAMES). Stanley Morison: His Typographic Achievement. 1971.

25026 BARKER (NICOLAS). Stanley Morison. 1972.

25027 JONES (HERBERT). Stanley Morison Displayed: An Examination of his Early Typographic Work. 1976.

25028 MORAN (JAMES). Printing Presses: History and Development from the Fifteenth Century to Modern Times. 1973.

25029 McKITTERICK (DAVID) *ed.* Stanley Morison and D. B. Updike: Selected Correspondence. 1980.

25030 BROPHY (BRIGID ANTONIA). A Guide to Public Lending Right. Aldershot. 1983.

25031 BONHAM-CARTER (VICTOR). The Fight for Public Lending Rights 1951–1979. 1988.

14. THE PRESS

25032 U.K. CENTRAL OFFICE OF INFORMATION. The British Press. 1958. 3rd edn 1976.

25033 HANDOVER (PHYLLIS MARGARET). A History of the London Gazette, 1665–1965. 1965.

25034 TREWIN (JOHN COURTENAY) *and* KING (EVELYN M.). Printer to the House: The Story of Hansard. 1952.

25035 LINTON (DAVID) *and* BOSTON (RAY) *eds.* The Newspaper Press in Britain; An Annotated Bibliography. 1987.

25036 ATKINSON (FRANK). The English Newspaper since 1900. 1960.

25037 CRANFIELD (GEOFFREY ALAN). The Press and Society from Caxton to Northcliffe. 1978.

25038 KOSS (STEPHEN EDWARD). The Rise and Fall of the Political Press in Britain. Vol. 2. The Twentieth Century. 1984.

25039 ANDREWS (Sir WILLIAM LINTON) *and* TAYLOR (HENRY ARCHIBALD). Lords and Labourers of the Press. 1972.

25040 GERALD (JAMES) EDWARD). The British Press under Government Economic Controls. Minneapolis, Minn. 1956.

25041 SINCLAIR (ROBERT GEORGE). The British Press. 1949.

25042 INNIS (HAROLD ADAMS). The Press: A Neglected Factor in the Economic History of the Twentieth Century. 1949.

25043 MADGE (CHARLES) *and* HARRISSON (TOM). Mass Observation: The Press and its Readers. 1949.

25044 HERD (HAROLD). The March of Journalism: The Story of the British Press from 1622 to the Present Day. 1952.

25045 HORNBY (ROBERT). The Press in Modern Society. 1965.

25046 ROBBINS (ALAN PITT). Newspapers Today. 1956.

25047 WILLIAMS (FRANCIS) *Baron Francis-Williams*. Dangerous Estate: The Anatomy of Newspapers. 1957. New edn with introd. by Michael Foot. 1987.

25048 WILLIAMS (RAYMOND HENRY). 'The Press the People want'. *Univ. Left Rev.* 5 (1958), 42–7.

25049 TAYLOR (HENRY ARCHIBALD). The British Press: A Critical Survey. 1961.

25050 BELSON (WILLIAM ALBERT). Studies in Readership. 1962.

25051 ABRAMS (MARK ALEXANDER). Education, Social Class and Newspaper Reading. 1963.

25052 —— The Newspaper Reading Public of Tomorrow. 1964.

25053 PAPAS (WILLIAM). The Press. 1964.

25054 CHRISTOPH (JAMES B.). 'The Press and Politics in Britain and America'. *Pol. Q.* 34 (1963), 137–50.

25055 SEYMOUR-URE (COLIN KNOWLTON). The Press, Politics and the Public: An Essay on the Role of the National Press in the British Political System. 1968.

25056 ELY (JOHN HART). 'Trial by Newspaper and its Cures'. *Encounter* 38 (1967), 80–92.

25057 KING (CECIL HARMSWORTH). The Future of the Press. 1967.

25058 HUGGETT (FRANK EDWARD). The Newspapers. 1968.

25059 THOMAS (HARFORD). Newspaper Crisis: A Study of Developments in the National Press of Britain, 1966–67. Zurich. 1967.

25060 WILLIAMS (FRANCIS) *Baron Francis-Williams*. The Right to Know. 1969.

25061 BOSTON (RICHARD) ed. The Press we Deserve. 1970.

25062 MORRIS (CLAUD). I Bought a Newspaper. 1963.

25063 WARD (KENNETH). Mass Communications and the Modern World. 1989.

25064 BARNETSON (WILLIAM DENHOLM) *Baron*. The Economics of Newspapers and News Agencies. Edin. 1973.

25065 HARRISON (STANLEY). Poor Men's Guardians: A Record of the Struggles for a Democratic Newspaper Press, 1763–1973. 1974.

25066 SMITH (ANTHONY CHARLES) *et al*. Paper Voices: The Popular Press and Social Change 1935–1965. 1975.

25067 ANGLO (MICHAEL). Service Newspapers of the Second World War. 1977.

25068 KIMBLE (P.). Newspaper Reading: The Third Year of the War. 1942.

25069 SMITH (ANTHONY DAVID) *ed*. The British Press since the War. Newton Abbot. 1974.

25070 HIRSCH (FRED) *and* GORDON (DAVID). Newspaper Money: Fleet Street and the Search for the Affluent Reader. 1975.

25071 KALDOR (NICHOLAS) *Baron, and* SILVERMAN (RODNEY). A Statistical Analysis of Advertising Expenditure and of the Revenue of the Press. Camb. 1948.

25072 BOYCE (GEORGE), CURRAN (JAMES), *and* WINGATE (PAULINE). Newspaper History from the Seventeenth Century to the Present Day. 1978.

25073 CLARK (PETER A.). Sixteen Million Readers: Evening Newspapers in the U.K. Eastbourne. 1981.

25074 CURRAN (JAMES) *ed*. The British Press: A Manifesto. 1978.

25075 JENKINS (SIMON). Newspapers: The Power and the Money. 1979.

25076 CURRAN (JAMES) *and* SEATON (JEAN). Power without Responsibility: The Press and Broadcasting in Britain. 1981.

25077 COGLAN (W. N.). The Readership of Newspapers and Periodicals in Great Britain, 1936: A Report on Circulations. 1937.

25078 MADGE (CHARLES) *and* HARRISSON (TOM) *eds*. The Press and its Readers. 1949.

25079 HOBSON (J. W.) *and* HENRY (HARRY) *eds*. Hulton Readership Survey. [Annual.]. 1947–55.

25080 HENRY (HARRY). The Dynamics of the British Press 1961–1984: Patterns of Circulation and Cover Prices. 1986.

25081 HEREN (LOUIS [PHILIP]). The Power of the Press? 1985.

25082 HOLLINGSWORTH (MARK). The Press and Political Dissent: A Question of Censorship. 1986.

25083 BRENDON (PIERS). The Life and Death of the Press Barons. 1982.

25084 HAMBRO (CARL JOACHIM). Newspaper Lords in British Politics. 1958.

25085 CUDLIPP (HUGH) *Baron*. The Prerogative of the Harlot: Press Barons and Power. 1980.

25086 JENKINS (SIMON). Market for Glory: Fleet Street Ownership in the Twentieth Century. 1986.

25087 KING (CECIL HARMSWORTH). Strictly Personal: Some Memories. 1969.

25088 —— With Malice Toward None: A War Diary. 1970.

25089 —— Without Fear or Favour. 1971.

25090 —— The Cecil King Diary, 1965–1970. 1972.

25091 —— The Cecil King Diary, 1970–1974. 1975.

25092 HUBBACK (DAVID F.). No Ordinary Press Baron: A Life of Walter Layton. 1985.

25093 CLARKE (TOM M.). My Northcliffe Diary. 1931.

25094 OWEN (LOUISE). Northcliffe: The Facts. 1931.

25095 RYAN (ALFRED PATRICK). Lord Northcliffe. 1953.

25096 GREENWALL (HARRY JAMES). Northcliffe: Napoleon of Fleet Street. 1957.

25097 POUND (REGINALD) *and* HARMSWORTH (ARTHUR GEOFFREY ANNESLEY). Northcliffe. 1959.

25098 FERRIS (PAUL FREDERICK). The House of Northcliffe: A Biography of an Empire. 1972.

25099 MINNEY (RUBEIGH JAMES). Viscount Southwood. 1954.

25100 BRADDON (RUSSELL READING). Roy Thomson of Fleet Street. 1965.

25101 THOMSON (ROY) *Baron*. After I was Sixty: A Chapter of Autobiography. 1975.

25102 GOLDENBERG (SUSAN). The Thomson Empire. 1984.

25103 REGAN (SIMON). Rupert Murdoch: A Business Biography. 1976.

25104 LEAPMAN (MICHAEL). Barefaced Cheek: The Apotheosis of Rupert Murdoch. 1983. [Arrogant Aussie: The Rupert Murdoch Story.] Secaucus, NJ.

25105 MUNSTER (GEORGE). A Paper Prince. Ringwood, Australia. 1985.

25106 GOODHART (DAVID) *and* WINTOUR (PATRICK). Eddie Shah and the Newspaper Revolution. 1986.

25107 MACARTHUR (BRIAN). Eddie Shah, Today and the Newspaper Revolution. Newton Abbot. 1988.

25108 DROGHEDA ((CHARLES) GARRETT (PONSONBY) MOORE) *Earl of*. Double Harness: Memoirs. 1978.

25109 MACDONAGH (MICHAEL). In London during the Great War: The Diary of a Journalist. 1935.

25110 COOK (Sir EDWARD TYAS) *ed*. The Press in Wartime, with some Account of the Official Press Bureau. 1920.

25111 RAPPOPORT (ARMIN). The British Press and Wilsonian neutrality. Lond./Stanford, Calif.. 1951.

25112 BOSWORTH (RICHARD J. B.). 'The British Press, the Conservatives and Mussolini, 1920–1934'. *J. Contemp. Hist.* 5 (1970), 163–82.

25113 KESERICH (CHARLES). 'The British Labour Press and Italian Fascism, 1922–1925'. *J. Contemp. Hist.* 10 (1975), 579–90.

25114 GREENE (T. R.). 'The English Catholic Press and the Second Spanish Republic, 1931–36'. *Church Hist.* 45 (1976), 70–84.

25115 GANNON (FRANKLIN REID). The British Press and Germany, 1936–1939. Oxf. 1971.

25116 SHARF (ANDREW). The British Press and the Jews under Nazi Rule. 1964.

25117 GRANZOW (BRIGITTE). A Mirror of Nazism. British Opinion and the Emergence of Hitler, 1929–33. 1964.

25118 KIESER (ROLF). Englands Appeasementpolitik und der Aufstieg des Dritten Reichs im Spiegel der britischen Presse 1933–1939: ein Beitrag zur Vorgeschichte des zweiten Weltkrieges. Winterthur. 1964.

25119 HOOD (PETER). Ourselves and the Press: A Social Study of News Advertising and Propaganda. 1939.

25120 GOODHART (ARTHUR LEHMAN). 'The Mysteries of the Kennedy Assassination and the English Press'. *Law Q. Rev.* 83 (1967), 22–63.

25121 McLACHLAN (DONALD HARVEY). 'The Press and Public Opinion'. *Brit. J. Sociol.* 6 (1955), 159–68.

25122 BIRCH (ANTHONY HAROLD), CAMPBELL (PETER WALTER), and LUCAS (P. G.). 'The Popular Press in the British General Election of 1955'. *Pol. Studs* 4 (1956), 297–306.

25123 MUSSON (ALBERT EDWARD). 'Parliament and the Press: An Historical Survey'. *Parl. Affs* 9 (1958), 151–9, 277–88, 404–17.

25124 BEAVAN (JOHN COWBURN) *Baron Ardwick*. 'Editorial Policy-Making and the Royal Commission on the Press'. *Govt. Opp.* 10 (1975), 12–23.

25125 BOYD-BARRETT (OLIVER), SEYMOUR-URE (COLIN KNOWLTON), *and* TUNSTALL (JEREMY). Studies on the Press: Working Paper, Royal Commission on the Press, 3. 1977.

25126 JONES (NICHOLAS). Strikes and the Media. 1986.

25127 HUTCHINSON (DAVID) *ed*. Headlines—The Media in Scotland. Edin. 1978.

25128 WHATES (HAROLD RICHARD GRANT). The Birmingham Post, 1857–1957. Birmingham. 1957.

25129 AVERIS (ERNEST) *ed*. Hold the Front Page. Bristol. 1984.

25130 CHESTER (LEWIS) *and* FENBY (JONATHAN). The Fall of the House of Beaverbrook. 1979.

25131 PHILLIPS (ALASTAIR). Glasgow's Herald: Two Hundred Years of a Newspaper, 1783–1983. Glasg. 1983.

25132 DUTT (RAJANI PALME). The Rise and Fall of the Daily Herald. 1964.

25133 FIENBURGH (WILFRED). Twenty-five Momentous Years: A 25th Anniversary in the History of the Daily Herald. 1955.

25134 EDELMAN (MAURICE). The Mirror: A Political History. 1966.

25135 CUDLIPP (HUGH) *Baron*. Publish and be Damned. 1953.

25136 ALLEN (ROBERT) *and* FROST (JOHN). Daily Mirror. Camb. 1981.

25137 LAWSON (EDWARD FREDERICK) *Lord Burnham*. Peterborough Court: The Story of the Daily Telegraph. 1955.

25138 RUST (WILLIAM). The Story of the Daily Worker. *Ed. and completed* by Allen Hutt. 1949.

25139 KYNASTON (DAVID). The Financial Times: A Centenary History. 1988.

25140 THE GUARDIAN. The Story of the Guardian. 1964.

25141 AYERST (DAVID GEORGE OGILVY). Guardian: Biography of a Newspaper. 1971.

25142 AYERST (DAVID GEORGE OGILVY) *ed.* The Guardian Omnibus, 1821–1971. 1973.

25143 FRAENKEL (JOSEF). Exhibition of the Jewish Press in Great Britain: 1823–1963. 1963.

25144 JENKINS (TUDOR). The Londoner. 1962.

25145 HINDLE (WILFRID HOPE). The Morning Post, 1772–1937: Portrait of a Newspaper. 1937.

25146 WILSON (KEITH M.). A Study in the History and Politics of the 'Morning Post'. Lampeter. 1991.

25147 GLENTON (GEORGE) *and* PATTINSON (WILLIAM). The Last Chronicle of Bouverie Street. 1963.

25148 McEWEN (JOHN M.). 'Lloyd George's Acquisition of the Daily Chronicle in 1918'. *J. Brit. Studs* 22 (fall 1982).

25149 MARTELL (EDWARD) *and* BUTLER (EWAN). The Murder of the News Chronicle and the Star. 1960.

25150 HOPKINSON (*Sir* [HENRY] TOM) *ed.* Picture Post 1938–50. 1970. New fwd 1984.

25151 The Glorious Privilege: The History of The Scotsman. Edin. 1967.

25152 McKAY (RON) *and* BARR (BRIAN). The Story of the Scottish Daily News. Edin. 1976.

25153 SEWELL (GORDON). Echoes of a Century (1864–1964): The Centenary History of Southern Newspapers limited. Shampton. 1964.

25154 SUNDAY TIMES. The Sunday Times: A Pictorial Biography of One of the World's Great Newspapers. 1961.

25155 HOBSON (*Sir* HAROLD), KNIGHTLEY (PHILLIP), *and* RUSSELL (LEONARD). The Pearl of Days: An Intimate Memoir of the Sunday Times 1822–1972. 1972.

25156 JACOBS (ERIC). Stop Press: The Inside Story of The Times Dispute. 1980.

25157 HOGGART (RICHARD) *ed.* Your Sunday Paper. 1967.

25158 History of The Times vol. IV The 150th Anniversary and Beyond: 1. 1912–1920 2. 1921–1948. 1952. Vol. V Struggles in War and Peace, 1939–1966 by Iverach McDonald. 1984.

25159 HOWARD (PHILIP (NICHOLAS CHARLES])). We Thundered out. 1985.

25160 HILL (DOUGLAS) *ed.* Tribune 40: The First Forty Years of a Socialist Newspaper. 1977.

25161 SCHOFIELD ((EDWARD) GUY). The Men that Carry the News: A History of the United Newspapers Limited. 1976.

25162 DUNCUM (PHILIP) *ed.* The Westminster Press Provincial Papers. 1952.

25163 GIBB (MILDRED ANN) *and* BECKWITH (FRANK). The Yorkshire Post: Two Centuries. Leeds. 1954.

25164 ROTH (CECIL) *comp.* The Jewish Chronicle 1841–1941. 1949.

25165 SCOTT (J. W. ROBERTSON). The Life and Death of a Newspaper. 1952.

25166 FERGUSON (JOAN PRIMROSE SCOTT). Directory of Scottish Newspapers. Edin. 1984.

25167 A county-by-county listing of newspapers is in progress, of which the following have so far appeared.

25168 BLUHM (ROBIN K.). Wiltshire County. 1975.

25169 BERGESS (WINIFRID F.). Kent County. 1982.

25170 MANDERS (FRANK W. D.). Durham and Northumberland County. 1982.

25171 MELLORS (ANNE) *and* RADFORD (JAN). Derbyshire County. 1986.

25172 BROOK (MICHAEL). Nottinghamshire County. 1986.

25173 HARRISON (ROYDEN) Warwick Guide to British Labour Periodicals 1790–1970. 1976.

25174 ARNOT (ROBERT PAGE). Forging the Weapon: The Struggle of the Labour Monthly 1921–1941. 1941.

25175 MARTIN (WALLACE). The 'New Age' under Orage: Chapters in English Cultural History. Manch. 1967.

25176 SELVER (PAUL). A. R. Orage and the New Age Circle. 1959.

25177 HYAMS (EDWARD SOLOMON). The New Statesman: The History of the First Fifty Years: 1913–1963. 1963.

25178 —— *Ed.* New Statesmanship: An Anthology. 1963.

25179 HOPKINSON (Sir TOM) *ed.* Picture Post 1938–50. Harmondsworth. 1970.

25180 KEE (ROBERT) *ed.* The Picture Post Album. 1989.

25181 INGRAMS (RICHARD) *ed.* The Life and Times of Private Eye, 1961–1971. Harmondsworth. 1971.

25182 MARNHAM (PATRICK). The Private Eye Story: The First Twenty-one Years. 1982.

25183 PRICE (R. G. G.). A History of Punch. 1957.

25184 THE QUEEN. A Profile of The Queen. 1958.

25185 CREWE (QUENTIN) *ed.* The Frontiers of Privilege—A Century of Social Conflict as Reflected in The Queen. 1961.

25186 THOMAS (Sir WILLIAM BEACH). The Story of The Spectator 1828–1928. 1928.

25187 POUND (REGINALD). The Strand Magazine, 1891–1950. 1966.

25188 COCKBURN (PATRICIA). The Years of The Week. 1968.

25189 JENKINS (GWYN). 'The Welsh Outlook 1914–33'. *Nat. Lib. Wales J.* 24 (1986) 463–92.

25190 DOUGHAN (DAVID) *and* SANCHEZ (DENISE). Feminist Periodicals 1855–1984: An Annotated Critical Bibliography of British, Irish, Commonwealth and International Titles. Brighton. 1988.

25191 WHITE (CYNTHIA LESLIE). Women's Magazines, 1693–1968. 1970.

25192 —— The Women's Periodical Press in Britain, 1946–1976. 1977.

25193 DANCYGER (IRENE). A World of Women: An Illustrated History of Women's Magazines. Dublin. 1978.

25194 WINSHIP (JANICE). Femininity and Women's Magazines: A Case Study of Woman's Own: 'First in Britain for Women'. Milton Keynes. 1983.

25195 —— Inside Women's Magazines. 1987.

25196 ANDERSON (CONNIE). Magazines Teenagers Read: With Special Reference to Trend, Jackie and Valentine. Oxf. 1968.

25197 POMPHREY (GEORGE). What Children Think of their Comics: With an Analysis of Current Comics and a Brief Assessment of Current Trends. 1964.

25198 ORWELL (GEORGE). 'Boys' Weeklies' in Selected Essays. 1957.

25199 HOGGART (RICHARD). The Uses of Literacy: Aspects of Working-Class Life, with Special Reference to Publications and Entertainments. 1957.

25200 NOYCE (JOHN LEONARD) *ed.* The Directory of British Alternative Periodicals 1965–1974. Hassocks. 4th edn 1979.

25201 SANDYS (RUTH) *and* HARRIS (BRENDA). The Underground and Alternative Press in Britain during 1974: A Bibliographical Guide. Hassocks. 1976.

25202 FOUNTAIN (NIGEL). Underground: The London Alternative Press 1966–74. 1988.

25203 GREEN (JONATHAN). Days in My Life: Voices from the English Underground 1961–1971. 1988.

25204 ANDREWS (Sir WILLIAM LINTON). Problems of an Editor: A Study in Newspaper Trends. 1962.

25205 —— The Autobiography of a Journalist. 1964.

25206 ANDREWS (Sir WILLIAM LINTON) *and* TAYLOR (HENRY ARCHIBALD). Lords and Laborers of the Press: Men who Fashioned the Modern British Newspaper. Carbondale, Ill. 1970.

25207 BARBER (NOEL). The Natives were Friendly: An Autobiography. 2nd edn 1985.

25208 McLACHLAN (DONALD HARVEY). In the Chair: Barrington-Ward of The Times 1927–1948. 1971.

25209 BARTLETT (VERNON). I Know what I Liked. 1974.

25210 BAXTER (Sir [ARTHUR] BEVERLEY). Strange Street: An Autobiography. 1935.

25211 BLATCHFORD (ROBERT). As I Lay A-Thinking: Some Memories and Reflections of an Ancient and Quiet Watchman. 1926.

25212 LEVENTHAL (FRED MARC). The Last Dissenter: H. N. Brailsford and his World. Oxf. 1985.

25213 BURROWES (JOHN). Frontline Report: A Journalist's Notebook. Edin. 1984.

25214 CAMERON ((MARK] JAMES (WALTER]). Point of Departure. 1967.

25215 BROOKES (CHRISTOPHER). His own Man: The Life of Neville Cardus. 1985.

25216 COUGH (ROBERT). A Public Eye. 1981.

25217 CONNOR (ROBERT). Cassandra: Reflections in a Mirror. 1969.

25218 THOMSON (GEORGE MALCOLM). Lord Castlerosse: His Life and Times. 1973.

25219 MOSLEY (LEONARD OSWALD). Castlerosse. 1956.

25220 CHRISTIANSEN (ARTHUR). Headlines all my Life. 1961.

25221 CLARK (WILLIAM DONALDSON). From Three Worlds: Memoirs. 1986.

25222 COCKBURN (CLAUD FRANCIS). In Time of Trouble. 1956. Crossing the line. 1958. Claud: Autobiography. Rev. edn Harmondsworth. 1967. Cockburn Sums Up: An Autobiography. 1981.

25223 COOTE (Sir COLIN REITH). Editorial: The Memoirs of Colin R. Coote. 1965.

25224 TAYLOR (ALAN JOHN PERCIVALE) *ed.* Off the Record: W. P. Crozier's Political Interviews, 1933–43. 1972.

25225 CUDLIPP (HUGH). At Your Peril. 1962.

25226 —— Walking on the Water. 1976.

25227 DAVENPORT (NICHOLAS). Memoirs of a City Radical. 1974.

25228 WRENCH (Sir JOHN EVELYN LESLIE). Geoffrey Dawson and our Times. 1955.

25229 KENNEDY (AUBREY LEO). 'Geoffrey Dawson'. *Quart. Rev.* 294 (1956), 155–68.

25230 DELMER ([DENIS] SEFTON). Trail Sinister. 1961. Black Boomerang. 1962.

25231 TAYLOR (HENRY ARCHIBALD). Robert Donald: Being the Authorized Biography of Sir Robert Donald, G.B.E., LL.D., Journalist and Friend of Statesmen. 1934.

25232 DUNNETT (ALASTAIR). Among Friends: An Autobiography. 1984.

25233 EDWARDS (ROBERT). Goodbye Fleet Street. 1988.

25234 EINZIG (PAUL). In the Centre of Things: The Autobiography of Paul Einzig. 1960.

25235 EVANS (HAROLD MATTHEW). Good Times, Bad Times. 1983. NY. 1984.

25236 FYFE (HENRY HAMILTON). Sixty Years of Fleet Street. 1949.

25237 HART-DAVIS (DUFF). Peter Fleming: A Biography. 1974.

25238 KOSS (STEPHEN EDWARD). Fleet Street Radical: A. G. Gardiner and the Daily News. 1973.

25239 GARVIN (KATHARINE). J. L. Garvin: A Memoir. 1948.

25240 AYERST (DAVID GEORGE OGILVY). Garvin of The Observer. 1985.

25241 GILES (FRANK THOMAS ROBERTSON). Sundry Times. 1986.

25242 GOULDON (MARK). Mark my Words! The Memoirs of a Journalist/Publisher. 1978.

25243 GRIEVE (MARY). Millions Made my Story. 1964.

25244 HAMILTON (DENNIS). Editor in Chief: Fleet Street Memoirs. 1989.

25245 HARRIS (H. WILSON). Life so Far. 1954.

25246 HEREN (LOUIS [PHILIP]). Growing up on The Times. 1978.

25247 HETHERINGTON ([HECTOR) ALASTAIR). Guardian Years. 1981.

25248 HOPKINSON (Sir [HENRY] TOM). Of This Our Time: A Journalist's Story 1905–1950. 1982.

25249 —— Under the Tropic. 1984.

25250 HOUSE (JACK). Pavement in the Sun. 1967.

25251 HUDSON (DEREK). Writing Between the Lines: An Autobiography. 1965.

25252 HULTON (E. G. W.). Conflicts. 1966.

25253 INGLIS (BRIAN). Downstart. 1989.

25254 JAMESON (DEREK). Touched by Angels. 1989.

25255 JOHNSON (FRANK). Out of Order. 1982.

25256 JOHNSON (PAUL BEDE). The Pick of Paul Johnson. 1985.

25257 LAMB (*Sir* LARRY). Sunrise. 1989.

25258 LEITCH (DAVID). Deadline: Collected Journalism. 1984.

25259 LEVIN (BERNARD). Enthusiasms. 1983.

25260 MacCOLL (RENÉ). Deadline and Dateline. 1955.

25261 MCDONALD (IVERACH). A Man of The Times: Talks and Travels in a Disrupted World. 1976.

25262 HAVIGHURST (ALFRED F.). Radical Journalist: H. W. Massingham (1860–1924). 1974.

25263 MASSINGHAM (HAROLD J.) *ed.* H. W. M.: A Selection from the Writings of H.W. Massingham. 1925.

25264 MARTIN (BASIL KINGSLEY). Father Figures: 1897–1931. 1966. Editor: 1931–1945. 1968.

25265 ROLPH (CECIL HEWITT). Kingsley: The Life, Letters and Diaries of Kingsley Martin. 1973.

25266 JONES (MERVYN) *ed.* Kingsley Martin: Portrait and Self Portrait. 1969.

25267 MONKS (NOEL). Eyewitness. 1956.

25268 MOORHEAD (ALAN). A Late Education: Episodes in a Life. 1970.

25269 FYFE (HENRY HAMILTON). T. P. O'Connor. 1934.

25270 PILGER (JOHN). Heroes. 1986.

25271 PRICE (GEORGE WARD). Extra-Special Correspondent. 1957.

25272 PRIESTLAND (GERALD). Journalism as I See it. Guildford. 1979.

25273 PRINGLE (JOHN). Have Pen Will Travel. 1973.

25274 PROCTOR (HENRY). The Street of Disillusion. 1958.

25275 PRYCE-JONES (ALAN). The Bonus of Laughter. 1987.

25276 REAKES (GEORGE LEONARD). Man of the Mersey. 1956.

25277 REDWOOD ([WILLIAM ARTHUR] HUGH). Bristol Fashion. 1948.

25278 CLARK (WILLIAM). Hugh Redwood: With God in Fleet Street. 1976.

25279 ROLPH (CECIL HEWITT). Living Twice: An Autobiography. 1974.

25280 HAMMOND (JOHN LAURENCE LE BRETON). C. P. Scott of the Manchester Guardian. 1934.

25281 WILSON (TREVOR GORDON). The Political Diaries of C.P. Scott, 1911–1918. 1970.

25282 NICHOLS (H. D.) *et al.* C. P. Scott, 1846–1932: The Making of the Manchester Guardian. 1946.

25283 SCOTT (J. W. ROBERTSON). 'We' and Me: Memories of Four Eminent Editors I Worked with. 1956.

25284 SHERIDAN (CLAIRE). To the Four Winds. 1957.

25285 HARRIS (HENRY WILSON). J. A. Spender. 1946.

25286 SCHUSTER (PETER). Henry Wickham Steed und die Habsburgermonarchie. Graz. 1970.

25287 STOTT (MARY). Forgetting's no Excuse: The Autobiography of Mary Stott, Journalist, Campaigner and Feminist. 1973.

25288 —— Before I Go: Reflections on my Life and Times. 1985.

25289 STRACHEY (AMY). St Loe Strachey: His Life and his Paper. 1930.

25290 STROUD (JEAN). Special Correspondent. 1969.

25291 STUART (Sir CAMPBELL). Opportunity Knocks Once. 1952.

25292 DRIBERG (THOMAS EDWARD NEIL). 'Swaff': The Life and Times of Hannen Swaffer. 1974.

25293 TAYLOR (ALLAN). From a Glasgow Slum to Fleet Street. 1949.

25294 LANE (MARGARET). Edgar Wallace: The Biography of a Phenomenon. 1938. Rev. edn 1964.

25295 WATERFIELD (LINA). Castle in Italy. 1961.

25296 WEBSTER (JACK). A Grain of Truth: A Scottish Journalist Remembers. Edin. 1981.

25297 WILLIAMS (FRANCIS) *Baron Francis-Williams*. Nothing so Strange. 1970.

25298 TYRHOVA-WILLIAMS (ARIADNA). Cheerful Giver: The Life of Harold Williams. 1935.

25299 WINTOUR (CHARLES VERE). Pressures on the Press: An Editor Looks at Fleet Street. 1972.

25300 BAYNES (KEN) *ed.* Scoop, Scandal and Strife: A Study of Photography in Newspapers. 1971.

25301 DEAN (EDWARD J.). Lucky Dean: Reminiscences of a Press Photographer. 1944.

25302 GRANT (BERNARD). To the Four Corners: The Memoirs of a News Photographer. 1933.

25303 DEVON (STANLEY). 'Glorious': The Life Story of Stanley Devon. 1957.

25304 FENBY (JONATHAN). The International News Services. 1986.

25305 BOYD-BARRETT (OLIVER). The International News Agencies. 1980.

25306 JONES (*Sir* RODERICK). A Life in Reuters. 1951.

25307 STOREY (GRAHAM). Reuter's Century, 1851–1951. 1951.

25308 LAWRENSON (JOHN RALPH) *and* BARBER (LIONEL). The Price of Truth: The Story of the Reuters Millions. Edin. 1985. Lond. 1986.

25309 MILLS (JOHN SAXON). The Press and Communications of the Empire. 1924.

25310 SCOTT (JAMES MAURICE). Extel 100: Centenary History of the Exchange Telegraph. 1972.

25311 BAINBRIDGE (CYRIL) *ed.* One Hundred Years of Journalism: Social Aspects of the Press. 1984.

25312 BELOFF (NORA). Freedom under Foot: The Battle over the Closed Shop in British Journalism. 1976.

25313 BUNDOCK (CLEMENT J.). The National Union of Journalists: A Jubilee History. 1957.

25314 MANSFIELD (FREDERICK J.). 'Gentlemen, the Press!': Chronicles of a Crusade. 1943.

25315 BOORMAN (HENRY ROY PRATT) *comp.* The Newspaper Society: 125 Years of Progress. Maidstone. 1961.

25316 TUNSTALL (JEREMY). Journalists at Work: Specialist Correspondents, the News Organizations, News Sources, and Competitor-Colleagues. 1971.

25317 —— The Westminster Lobby Correspondents: A Sociological Study of National Political Journalism. 1970.

25318 —— *Ed.* Media Sociology: A Reader. 1970.

25319 HALMOS (PAUL) *ed.* The Sociology of Mass-Media Communicators. Keele. 1969.

25320 COHEN (STANLEY) *and* YOUNG (JOCK). The Manufacture of News: Social Problems, Deviance and the Mass Media. 1973. 2nd edn 1981.

25321 CHIBNALL (STEVE). Law-and-Order News: An Analysis of Crime Reporting in the British Press. 1977.

25322 KNIGHTLEY (PHILLIP). The First Casualty. 1975.

25323 SCOTT (GEORGE EDWIN). Reporter Anonymous: The Story of the Press Association. 1968.

25324 MASON (A.). 'The Local Press and the General Strike: An Example from the North-East'. *Dur. Univ. J.* 61 (1969), 147–51.

25325 JACKSON (IAN). The Provincial Press and the Community. Manchester. 1971.

25326 COX (WILLIAM HARVEY) *and* MORGAN (DAVID). City Politics and the Press: Journalists and the Government of Merseyside. Camb. 1973.

25327 MURPHY (DAVID). The Silent Watchdog: The Press in Local Politics. 1976.

25328 HARTLEY (NICHOLAS). Concentration of Ownership in the Provincial Press. 1977.

25329 THE PRESS COUNCIL. The Press and the People. [Annual Report.]. 1954–.

25330 LEVY (HERMAN PHILLIP). The Press Council: History, Procedure and Cases. 1967.

25331 MURRAY (GEORGE McINTOSH). The Press and the Public: The Story of the British Press Council. 1972.

25332 ROBERTSON (GEOFFREY). The People against the Press: An Inquiry into the Press Council. 1983.

25333 PAUL (NOEL STRANGE) *ed.* Principles for the Press: A Digest of Press Council Decisions 1953–84. 1985.

25334 HEDLEY (PETER) *and* AYNSLEY (CYRIL). The D-Notice Affair. 1967.

25335 HARRIS (BRYAN). The Courts, the Press and the Public. Chichester. 1976.

25336 COCKERELL (MICHAEL), HENNESSY (PETER), *and* WALKER (DAVID). Sources Close to the Prime Minister: Inside the Hidden World of the News Manipulators. 1984. Rev. edn 1985.

25337 CLEVERLEY (GRAHAM). The Fleet Street Disaster: British National Newspapers as a Case Study in Mismanagement. 1976.

25338 SISSON (KEITH). Industrial Relations in Fleet Street: A Study in Pay Structure. Oxf. 1975.

25339 HENRY (HARRY) *ed.* Behind the Headline: The Business of the British Press. 1978.

25340 MARTIN (RODERICK). New Technology and Industrial Relations in Fleet Street. Oxf./NY. 1981.

25341 MELVERN (LINDA). The End of the Street. 1986.

25342 SIMPSON (D. H.). Commercialisation of the Regional Press. Aldershot. 1981.

25343 MORISON (STANLEY). The English Newspaper, 1632–1932. Camb. 1932.

25344 HUTT (ALLEN). Newspaper Design. 1960. 2nd edn 1967.

25345 —— The Changing Newspaper: Typographical Trends in Britain and America, 1622–1972. 1973.

25346 MARDH (INGRID). Headlinese: On the Grammar of English Front Page Headlines. Lund. 1980.

15. WRITERS AND LITERATURE

25347 ABSE (DANNIE). A Poet in the Family. 1974.

25348 —— A Strong Dose of Myself. 1983.

25349 CURTIS (TONY). Dannie Abse. Cardiff. 1985.

25350 ACTON (HAROLD). Memoirs of an Aesthete. 1948.

25351 —— More Memoirs of an Aesthete. 1970.

25352 GOHN (JACK). Kingsley Amis: A Checklist. Kent, Ohio. 1976.

25353 SALWAK (DALE). Kingsley Amis: A Reference Guide. Boston, Mass. 1978.

25354 GARDNER (PAUL). Kingsley Amis. 1981.

25355 BLOOMFIELD (B. C.) and MENDELSON (EDWARD). W. H. Auden: A Bibliography 1924–1969. Charlottesville, Va. 2nd edn 1972.

25356 BLAIR (JOHN G.). The Poetic Art of W. H. Auden. Princeton, NJ. 1965.

25357 CALLAN (EDWARD). Auden: A Carnival of Intellect. NY./Oxf. 1983.

25358 FARNAM (DOROTHY). Auden in Love. 1984.

25359 FULLER (JOHN). A Reader's Guide to W. H. Auden. 1970.

25360 CARPENTER (HUMPHREY). W. H. Auden: A Biography. 1981.

25361 HAFFENDEN (JOHN) ed. W. H. Auden: The Critical Heritage. 1983.

25362 HOGGART (RICHARD). W. H. Auden. 1957. Rev. edns 1961, 1966.

25363 OSBORNE (CHARLES). Auden: The Life of a Poet.

25364 JOHNSON (RICHARD). Man's Place: An Essay on Auden. Ithaca, NY/Lond. 1973.

25365 MENDELSON (EDWARD). Early Auden. 1981.

25366 ROWSE (ALFRED LESLIE). The Poet Auden: A Personal Memoir. 1987.

25367 GOODARD (JAMES) and PRINGLE (DAVID). J. G. Ballard: The First Twenty Years. Hayes. 1976.

25368 FODASTI (MARTHA). George Barker. Boston, Mass. 1969.

25369 BATES (HERBERT ERNEST). Autobiography. 1. The Vanished World. 2. The Blossoming World. 1971. 3. The World in Ripeness. 1972.

25370 RIEWALD (J. G.). Sir Max Beerbohm: Man and Writer. The Hague. 1953.

25371 CECIL (DAVID) Lord. Max: A Biography. 1964.

25372 HART-DAVIS (RUPERT) ed. Letters of Max Beerbohm 1892–1956. 1988.

25373 BELL (NEIL). My Writing Life. 1955.

25374 SPEAIGHT (ROBERT WILLIAM) ed. Letters from Hilaire Belloc. 1958.

25375 SPEAIGHT (ROBERT WILLIAM). Hilaire Belloc. 1957.

25376 HAYNES (RENÉE). Hilaire Belloc. 1953.

25377 MORTON (J. B.). Hilaire Belloc: A Memoir. 1955.

25378 WILSON (ANDREW N.). Hilaire Belloc. 1984.

25379 EMERY (NORMAN). Arnold Bennett, 1867–1931: A Bibliography. Hanley. 1967.

25380 HEPBURN (JAMES) ed. Letters of Arnold Bennett. 3 vols 1966–1970.

25381 —— The Art of Arnold Bennett. Bloomington, Ind. 1963.

25382 —— Arnold Bennett: Sketches for Autobiography. 1979.

25383 —— Arnold Bennett: The Critical Heritage. 1981.

25384 SWINNERTON (FRANK) pref. Arnold Bennett's Letters to his Nephew. 1936.

25385 LUCAS (JOHN). Arnold Bennett: A Study of his Fiction. 1974.

25386 ALLEN (WALTER). Arnold Bennett. 1948.

25387 BARKER (DUDLEY). Writer by Trade: A View of Arnold Bennett. 1966.

25388 SWINNERTON (FRANK). Arnold Bennett. 1950. Rev. edn 1961.

25389 POUND (REGINALD). Arnold Bennett: A Biography. 1952.

25390 YOUNG (KENNETH). Arnold Bennett. 1975.

25391 DRABBLE (MARGARET). Arnold Bennett: A Biography. 1974.

25392 BENTLEY (PHYLLIS ELEANOR). 'O Dream, O Destinations': An Autobiography. 1962.

25393 STAPLETON (MARGARET) with an essay by Ralph J. Mills. Sir John Betjeman: A Bibliography of Writings by and about him. Metuchen, NJ. 1974.

25394 BETJEMAN (Sir JOHN). Summoned by Bells. 1960.

25395 STANFORD (DEREK). John Betjeman: A Study. 1961.

25396 HILLIER (BEVIS). John Betjeman: A Life in Pictures. 1984.

25397 TAYLOR-MARTIN (PATRICK). John Betjeman: His Life and Work. 1983.

25398 KIRKPATRICK (B. J.). A Bibliography of Edmund Blunden with a Personal Introduction by Rupert Hart-Davis. Oxf. 1979.

25399 MALLON (THOMAS). Edmund Blunden. Boston, Mass. 1983.

25400 STOREY (BARBARA). Enid Blyton: A Biography. 1974.

25401 RAY (SHEILA G.). The Blyton Phenomenon: The Controversy Surrounding the World's Most Successful Children's Writer. 1982.

25402 ABBOTT (CLAUDE COLLEER) and BERTRAM (ANTHONY). Poet and Painter: Being Correspondence Between Gordon Bottomley and Paul Nash, 1910–1946. 1955.

25403 SELLERY (J'NAN M.). Elizabeth Bowen: A Descriptive Bibliography. c.1981.

25404 BOWEN (ELIZABETH). Afterthought. 1962.

25405 GLENDINNING (VICTORIA). Elizabeth Bowen: Portrait of a Writer. 1977.

25406 BROOKE (JOCELYN). Elizabeth Bowen. 1952.

25407 KENNEY (EDWIN). Elizabeth Bowen. Lewisburg, Pa. 1974.

25408 BOWRA (*Sir* CECIL MAURICE). Memories, 1898–1939. 1966.

25409 SALWAK (DALE). John Braine and John Wain: A Reference Guide. Boston, Mass. 1980.

25410 LEE (JAMES W.). John Braine. Boston, Mass. 1968.

25411 BRENAN (GERALD). Personal Record, 1920–1972. 1974.

25412 GUERARD (ALBERT JOSEPH). Robert Bridges. 1942.

25413 THOMPSON (EDWARD JOHN). Robert Bridges, 1844–1930. 1945.

25414 BRITTAIN (VERA MARY) ed. and HADLEY-TAYLOR (GEOFFREY). Selected letters (1920–1935) Winifred Holtby and Vera Brittain. Hull. 1960.

25415 BRITTAIN (VERA MARY). Testament of Youth: An Autobiographical Study of the Years 1900–1925. 1933.

25416 —— Testament of Experience: An Autobiographical Study of the Years 1925–50. 1957.

25417 BISHOP (ALAN) ed. Chronicle of Friendship: Diary of the Thirties 1932–1939. 1985.

25418 BAILEY (AGATHA). Vera Brittain. Harmondsworth. 1987.

25419 KEYNES (*Sir* GEOFFREY LANGDON). The Letters of Rupert Brooke. Lond. 1968.

25420 —— A Bibliography of Rupert Brooke. 1954. 2nd edn 1959.

25421 HASSALL (CHRISTOPHER). Rupert Brooke: A Biography. 1964.

25422 HASTINGS (MICHAEL). The Handsomest Young Man in England. 1967.

25423 LEHMANN (JOHN). Rupert Brooke: His Life and his Legend. 1980.

25424 BOLD (ALAN). George Mackay Brown. Edin. 1978.

25425 HANNA (ARCHIBALD). John Buchan 1875–1940. A Bibliography. Hamden, Conn. 1953.

25426 SMITH (JANET ADAM). John Buchan and his World. 1979.

25427 DANIELL (DAVID). The Interpreter's House: A Critical Assessment of John Buchan. 1975.

25428 TURNER (ARTHUR). Mr. Buchan, Writer. 1944.

25429 TERRELL (CARROLL F.) Ed. Basil Bunting: Man and Poet. Orone, Maine. 1981.

25430 BOYTINCK (PAUL). Anthony Burgess: An Enumerative Bibliography. Norwood, Pa. 1974.

25431 BURGESS (ANTHONY). Little Wilson and Big God. 1987.

25432 DE VITIS (A. A.). Anthony Burgess. Boston, Mass. 1972.

25433 COALE (SAMUEL). Anthony Burgess. NY. 1981.

25434 ALEXANDER (PETER). Roy Campbell: A Critical Biography. Oxf. 1982.

25435 CAMPBELL (ROY). Light on a Dark Horse. 1951.

25436 SMITH (ROWLAND). Lyric and Polemic: The Literary Personality of Roy Campbell. Montreal/Lond. 1972.

25437 ALLEN (WALTER). Joyce Cary. 1953. Rev. edn 1963.

25438 BLOOM (ROBERT). The Indeterminate World: A Study of the Novels of Joyce Cary. Philadelphia, Pa. 1962.

25439 ECHERAU (MICHAEL). Joyce Cary and the Dimensions of Order. 1979.

25440 FISHER (BARBARA). Joyce Cary: The Writer and his Theme. Gerrard's Cross. 1980.

25441 LARSEN (GOLDEN). The Dark Descent: Social Change and Moral Responsibility in the Novels of Joyce Cary. 1965.

25442 WRIGHT (ANDREW). Joyce Cary: A Preface to his Novels. 1958.

25443 HALL (DENNIS). Joyce Cary: A Reappraisal. 1983.

25444 NOBLE (R. W.). Joyce Cary. Edin. 1973.

25445 BISHOP (ALAN). Gentleman Rider: A Biography of Joyce Cary. 1989.

25446 FOSTER (MALCOLM). Joyce Cary: A Biography. 1968.

25447 SISSON (CHARLES JASPER). Raymond Wilson Chambers, 1874–1942. 1946.

25448 CHRISTIE (AGATHA). An Autobiography. 1977.

25449 MORGAN (JANET). Agatha Christie: A Biography. 1984.

25450 OSBORNE (CHARLES). The Life and Crimes of Agatha Christie. 1982.

25451 WAGONER (MARY S.). Agatha Christie. Boston, Mass. 1986.

25452 CHURCH (RICHARD THOMAS). Autobiography. Over the Bridge: An Essay in Autobiography. 1955. The Golden Sovereign. 1957. The Voyage Home. 1964.

25453 CLARKE (ARTHUR C.). Astounding Days: A Science Fictional Autobiography. 1989.

25454 LIDDELL (ROBERT). The Novels of Ivy Compton-Burnett. 1955.

25455 BURKHART (CHARLES). I. Compton-Burnett. 1965.

25456 SPURLING (HILARY). Ivy when Young: The Early Life of Ivy Compton-Burnett 1884–1919. 1974. Secrets of a Woman's Heart: The Later Life of Ivy Compton-Burnett 1920–1969. 1984.

25457 SPRIGGE (ELIZABETH). The Life of Ivy Compton-Burnett. 1973.

25458 DICK (KAY). Ivy and Stevie: Ivy Compon-Burnett and Stevie Smith: Conversations and Reflections. 1971.

25459 SPENDER (*Sir* STEPHEN). Cyril Connolly: A Memoir. 1978.

25460 SHELDEN (MICHAEL). Friends of Promise: Cyril Connolly and the World of Horizon. 1989.

25461 CONNOLLY (CYRIL). Enemies of Promise. 1948. 1973 edn.

25462 BLAKISTON (NOEL) *ed.* A Romantic Friendship: The Letters of Cyril Connolly to Noel Blakiston. 1975.

25463 COX (CHARLES BRIAN). Joseph Conrad: The Modern Imagination. 1974.

25464 NAJDER (ZDZISLAW). Joseph Conrad: A Chronicle. Camb. 1983.

25465 SHERRY (NORMAN) *ed.* Conrad: The Critical Heritage. 1973.

25466 CADOGAN (MARY). Richmal Crompton: The Woman behind William. 1986.

25467 DAHL (ROALD). Boy: Tales of Childhood. 1984.

25468 DAVIE (DONALD). These the Companions: Recollections. 1982.

25469 —— Trying to Explain. Manchester. 1980.

25470 DEKKER (GEORGE) *ed.* Donald Davie and the Responsibilities of Literature. Manch. 1983.

25471 STONESIFER (RICHARD). W. H. Davies: A Critical Biography. 1963.

25472 DAY-LEWIS (SEAN). C. Day-Lewis: An English Literary Life. 1980.

25473 DAY-LEWIS (CECIL). The Buried Day. 1960.

25474 RIDDELL (JOSEPH N.). C. Day-Lewis. Boston, Mass. 1971.

25475 ROSS (DORIS). Walter de la Mare. Boston, Mass. 1966.

25476 DICKINSON (PATRIC). The Good Minute: An Autobiographical Study. 1965.

25477 GRAHAM (DESMOND FRANCIS). Keith Douglas, 1920–1944: A Biography. 1974.

25478 WOOLF (CECIL). A Bibliography of Norman Douglas. 1954.

25479 HOLLOWAY (MARK). Norman Douglas: A Biography. 1976.

25480 ROSE (ELLEN CRONAN). The Novels of Margaret Drabble: Equivocal Figures. 1980.

25481 CREIGHTON (JOANNE). Margaret Drabble. 1985.

25482 SADLER (LYNN VEACH). Margaret Drabble. Boston, Mass. 1986.

25483 KELLY (RICHARD). Daphne du Maurier. Boston, Mass. 1987.

25484 MOORE (HENRY) *ed.* The World of Lawrence Durrell. Carbondale, Ill. 1962.

25485 FRASER (G. S.). Lawrence Durrell: A Critical Study. 1968.

25486 WICKES (GEORGE) *ed.* Lawrence Durrell and Henry Miller: A Private Correspondence. 1963.

25487 MARTIN (MILDRED). A Half-Century of Eliot Criticism: An Annotated Bibliography of Books and Articles in English, 1916–1965. Lewisburg, Pa. 1972.

25488 BEHR (CAROLINE). T. S. Eliot: A Chronology of his Life and Works. 1983.

25489 ACKROYD (PETER). T. S. Eliot. 1984.

25490 GORDON (LYNDALL). Eliot's New Life. Oxf. 1988.

25491 BANTOCK (GEOFFREY HERMAN). T. S. Eliot on Education. 1970.

25492 BERGONZI (BERNARD). T. S. Eliot. 1972.

25493 BRAYBROOKE (NEVILLE) *ed.* T. S. Eliot: A Symposium for his 70th Birthday. 1958.

25494 BROWNE (E. MARTIN). The Making of T. S. Eliot's Plays. Camb. 1969.

25495 BUSH (RONALD). T. S. Eliot: A Study in Character and Style. NY./Oxf. 1984.

25496 GARDNER (*Dame* HELEN). The Art of T. S. Eliot.

25497 —— The Composition of the *Four Quartets.* 1978.

25498 MARTIN (GRAHAM) *ed.* T. S. Eliot in Perspective. 1970.

25499 MATTHEWS (THOMAS STANLEY). Great Tom: Notes Towards the Definition of T. S. Eliot. 1974.

25500 SENCOURT (ROBERT). T. S. Eliot: A Memoir. 1971.

25501 TATE (JOHN ORLEY ALLEN). T. S. Eliot: The Man and his Work. 1967.

25502 PINION (F. B.). A T. S. Eliot Companion: His Life and Works. 1985.

25503 KOJECKY (ROGER). T. S. Eliot's Social Criticism. 1971.

25504 GARDNER (PHILIP) *and* GARDNER (AVRIL). The God Approached: A Commentary on the Poems of William Empson. 1978.

25505 GILL (ROMA) *ed.* William Empson: The Man and his Work. 1974.

25506 WALSH (WILLIAM). D. J. Enright: Poet of Humanism. Camb. 1974.

25507 BENKOVITZ (MIRIAM). A Bibliography of Ronald Firbank. 1963. 2nd edn Oxf. 1982.

25508 PEARSON (JOHN GEORGE). The Life of Ian Fleming. 1966.

25509 HARVEY (DAVID DOW). Ford Madox Ford 1873–1939: A Bibliography of Works and Criticism. Princeton, NJ. 1962.

25510 LUDWIG (RICHARD) ed. Letters of Ford Madox Ford. Princeton, NJ. 1965.

25511 CASSELL (RICHARD). Ford Madox Ford: A Study of his Novels. Baltimore, Md. 1961.

25512 LID (M. W.). Ford Madox Ford: The Essence of his Art. Berkeley, Calif. 1964.

25513 GOLDRING (DOUGLAS). The Last Pre-Raphaelite: A Record of the Life and Writings of Ford Madox Ford. 1948.

25514 McSHANE (FRANK). The Life and Work of Ford Madox Ford. 1965.

25515 —— ed. Ford Madox Ford: The Critical Heritage. 1972.

25516 MOSER (THOMAS). The Life and Fiction of Ford Madox Ford. Princeton, NJ. 1980.

25517 STERNLICHT (SANFORD). C. S. Forester. Boston, Mass. 1981.

25518 KIRKPATRICK (B. J.). A Bibliography of E. M. Forster. 1965.

25519 FURBANK (P. N.). E. M. Forster, a Life: vol. 1. The Growth of the Novelist 1874–1914. 1977. Vol. 2. Polycrates' Ring 1914–1970. 1978.

25520 IAGO (MARY) and FURBANK (P. N.) eds. Selected Letters of E. M. Forster vol. 2. Camb., Mass. 1985.

25521 ADVARSI (RUKUN). E. M. Forster as Critic. 1984.

25522 BRANDER (LAURENCE). E. M. Forster: A Critical Study. 1968.

25523 KING (FRANCIS). E. M. Forster. 1978.

25524 CAVALIERO (GLEN). A Reading of E. M. Forster, 1979.

25525 GRANSDEN (KARL WATTS). E. M. Forster. 1962.

25526 MYERS (KAREN). 'John Fowles: An Annotated Bibliography 1963–76'. Bull. Biblio. 33 4 (1976).

25527 PALMER (WILLIAM). The Fiction of John Fowles: Tradition, Art and the Loneliness of Selfhood. Columbia, NY. 1974.

25528 HUFFAKER (ROBERT). John Fowles. Boston, Mass. 1980.

25529 AUSTIN (ALLAN). Roy Fuller. Boston, Mass. 1979.

25530 MARROT (H. V.). A Bibliography of The Works of John Galsworthy. Lond./NY. 1978.

25531 GARRETT (EDWARD) ed. Letters from John Galsworthy 1900–1932. 1934.

25532 FRECHET (ALEC). John Galsworthy: A Reassessment. 1982.

25533 BARKER (DUDLEY). The Man of Principle. 1963.

25534 MOTTRAM (R. H.). For Some We Loved: An Intimate Portrait of Ada and John Galsworthy. 1956.

25535 MOTTRAM (R. H.). John Galsworthy. 1953. New edn 1963.

25536 CAMPBELL (IAN). Lewis Grassic Gibbon. Edin. 1985.

25537 MALCOLM (WILLIAM R.). A Blasphemer and Reformer: A Study of James Leslie Mitchell/Lewis Grassic Gibbon. Aberd. 1984.

25538 MUNRO (IAN S.). Leslie Mitchell–Lewis Grassic Gibbon. Edin./Lond. 1966.

25539 HYNES (SAMUEL LYNN). William Golding. NY. 1964.

25540 MEDCALF (STEPHEN ELLIS). William Golding. 1975.

25541 JOHNSTON (ARNOLD). Of Earth and Darkness: The Novels of William Golding. Columbia, NY. 1980.

25542 CAREY (JOHN) ed. William Golding: The Man and his Books: A Tribute on his 75th Birthday. 1986.

25543 WATTS (CEDRIC) and DAVIES (LAURENCE). Cunninghame Graham: A Critical Biography. Camb. 1979.

25544 GRAHAM (STEPHEN). Part of the Wonderful Scene: Autobiography. 1964.

25545 GREEN (PETER MORRIS). Kenneth Grahame, 1859–1932: A Study of his Life, Work and Times. 1959.

25546 HIGGINSON (FRED HALL). A Bibliography of the Works of Robert Graves. 1966. Rev. edn 1987 as Robert Graves: A Bibliography.

25547 O'PREY (PAUL) ed. In Broken Images: Selected Letters of Robert Graves 1914–1946. 1982.

25548 —— Between Moon and Moon: Selected Letters of Robert Graves 1946–1972. 1984.

25549 CASSARY (ROBERT). Robert Graves. Boston, Mass. 1980.

25550 COHEN (J. M.). Robert Graves. Edin./Lond. 1960.

25551 DAY (DOUGLAS). Swifter than Reason: The Poetry and Criticism of Robert Graves. Lond./Chapel Hill, NC. 1963.

25552 KIRKHAM (MICHAEL). The Poetry of Robert Graves. 1969.

25553 SEYMOUR-SMITH (MARTIN). Robert Graves. 1956. Rev. edn 1965.

25554 —— Robert Graves: His Life and Work. 1982.

25555 RUSSELL (JOHN). Henry Green: Nine Novels and an Unpacked Bag. New Brunswick, NJ. 1960.

25556 WEATHERHEAD (KINGSLEY). A Reading of Henry Green. Seattle, Wash. 1961.

25557 ODOM (KEITH). Henry Green. Boston, Mass. 1978.

25558 VANN (J. D.). Graham Greene: A Checklist of Criticism.

25559 MILLER (ROBERT). Graham Greene: A Descriptive Catalog. Lexington, Ky. 1978.

25560 WOBBE (R. A.). Graham Greene: A Bibliography and Guide to Research. NY. 1979.

25561 WYNDHAM (FRANCIS). Graham Greene. 1955.

25562 ALLOTT (KENNETH) *and* ALLOTT (MIRIAM). The Art of Graham Greene. 1951. New edn 1963.

25563 LODGE (DAVID JOHN). Graham Greene. NY. 1966.

25564 HYNES (SAMUEL LYNN) *ed*. Graham Greene: A Collection of Critical Essays. Englewood Cliffs, NJ. 1973.

25565 GREENE (GRAHAM). A Sort of Life: An Autobiography. 1971.

25566 —— Ways of Escape. 1980.

25567 SCOTT (ALEXANDER) *and* GIFFORD (DOUGLAS) *eds*. Neil M.Gunn: The Man and the Writer. Edin. 1973.

25568 PICK (J. B.) *ed*. Neil M. Gunn: Selected Letters. 1987.

25569 GUNN (NEIL M.). The Atom of Delight. 1956.

25570 HART (FRANCIS RUSSELL) *and* PICK (J. B.). Neil M. Gunn: A Highland Life. 1981.

25571 HURD (MICHAEL). The Ordeal of Ivor Gurney. Oxf. 1978.

25572 ELLIS (PETER BERRESFORD). H. Rider Haggard: A Voice from the Infinite. 1978.

25573 BLOOMFIELD (PAUL). L. P. Hartley. 1962. Rev. edn 1970.

25574 JONES (EDWARD T.). L. P. Hartley. Boston, Mass. 1978.

25575 MULKEEN (ANNE). Wild Thyme, Winter Lightning: The Symbolic Novels of L. P. Hartley. 1974.

25576 CARTER (JOHN) *and* SPARROW (JOHN). A. E. Housman: A Bibliography. 1952. Rev. edn by William White. 1982.

25577 RICHARDS (FRANKLIN THOMAS GRANT). Housman, 1897–1936. 1941.

25578 SAGAR (KEITH) *and* TABOR (STEPHEN). Ted Hughes: A Bibliography 1946–80. 1983.

25579 SAGAR (KEITH). The Art of Ted Hughes. Camb. 1975.

25580 —— The Achievement of Ted Hughes. Manch. 1983.

25581 GIFFORD (TERRY) *and* ROBERTS (NEIL). Ted Hughes: A Critical Study. 1981.

25582 WEST (THOMAS). Ted Hughes. 1985.

25583 WILLIAMS (IOAN). Emyr Humphreys. Cardiff. 1980.

25584 GREEN (ROBERT). R. C. Hutchinson: The Man and His Books. 1985.

25585 CORYTON (RAY). Hutchinson: Two Men of Letters: Correspondence between R. C. Hutchinson, Novelist, and Martyn Skinner, Poet, 1957–1974. 1979.

25586 BASS (ELVEN E.). Aldous Huxley: An Annotated Bibliography of Criticism. 1981.

25587 BEDFORD (SYBILLE). Aldous Huxley: A Biography. 2 vols. 1973–4.

25588 SMITH (GROVER) *ed*. Letters of Aldous Huxley. 1969.

25589 ATKINS (JOHN). Aldous Huxley: A Literary Study. 1956. 2nd edn 1967.

25590 HUXLEY (JULIAN) *ed*. Aldous Huxley 1894–1963: A Memorial Volume. 1965.

25591 GHOSE (SISIRKUMAR). Aldous Huxley: Cynical Salvationist. 1962.

25592 WESTBY (SELMER) *and* BROWN (CLAYTON). Christopher Isherwood: A Bibliography 1923–1967. Los Angeles, Calif. 1968.

25593 ISHERWOOD (CHRISTOPHER). Christopher and his Kind, 1929–1939. NY. 1976.

25594 —— My Guru and Other Disciples. 1980.

25595 FRYER (JONATHAN). Isherwood: A Biography of Christopher Isherwood. 1977.

25596 KING (FRANCIS). Christopher Isherwood. 1976.

25597 PIAZZA (PAUL). Christopher Isherwood: Myth and Anti-myth. NY. 1978.

25598 FINNEY (BRIAN). Christopher Isherwood: A Critical Biography. 1979.

25599 LEHMANN (JOHN). Christopher Isherwood: A Personal Memoir. 1987.

25600 JAMES. MACBRYDE (GWENDOLYN) *ed*. Montague Rhodes James: Letters to a Friend. 1956.

25601 PFAFF (RICHARD WILLIAM). Montague Rhodes James. 1980.

25602 JAMESON (MARGARET STORM). Journey from the North. 2 vols. 1969–70.

25603 QUIGLEY (ISABEL). Pamela Hansford Johnson. 1968.

25604 HAGUE (RENÉ) *ed*. Dai Greatcoat: A Self-Portrait of David Jones in his letters. 1980.

25605 PRYOR (RUTH) *ed*. David Jones: Letters to Vernon Watkins. Card. 1976.

25606 BLAMIRES (DAVID). David Jones: Artist and Writer. Manch. 1971.

25607 BLISSETT (WILLIAM). The Long Conversation: A Memoir of David Jones. Oxf. 1981.

25608 WARD (ELIZABETH). David Jones: Mythmaker. Manch. 1983.

25609 PRICE (CECIL). Gwyn Jones. 1976.

25610 ROYLE (TREVOR). James and Jim: A Biography of James Kennaway. Edin. 1983.

25611 KENNAWAY (SUSAN). The Kennaways. 1981.

25612 HOLROYD (MICHAEL). Hugh Kingsmill: A Critical Biography. 1964.

25613 KIRKUP (JAMES). I Of All People: An Autobiography of Youth. 1988.

25614 PEARSON (SIDNEY A.). Arthur Koestler. Boston, 1978.

25615 SPERBER (MURRAY) *ed*. Arthur Koestler: A Collection of Critical Essays. Englewood Cliffs, NJ 1977.

25616 ATKINS (JOHN). Arthur Koestler. 1956.

25617 CALDER (JENNI). Chronicles of Conscience: A Study of George Orwell and Arthur Koestler. 1968. Pittsburgh, Pa. 1969.

25618 HAMILTON (IAIN). Koestler: A Biography. 1982.

25619 KOPS (BERNARD). The World is a Wedding. 1963.

25620 BLOOMFIELD (BARRY CAMBRAY). Philip Larkin: A Bibliography 1933–1976. 1980.

25621 BROWNJOHN (ALAN). Philip Larkin. 1975.

25622 MOTION (ANDREW). Philip Larkin. 1982.

25623 PETCH (SIMON). The Art of Philip Larkin. Sydney. 1981.

25624 TIMMS (DAVID). Philip Larkin. Edin. 1973.

25625 MARTIN (BRUCE). Philip Larkin. Boston, Mass. 1978.

25626 SALWAK (DALE) ed. Philip Larkin: The Man and His Work. 1988.

25627 ROBERTS (WARREN). A Bibliography of D. H. Lawrence. 1963.

25628 MOORE (HARRY THORNTON) ed. D. H. Lawrence: Collected Letters. 2 vols. 1962.

25629 SECKER (MARTIN). Letters from D. H. Lawrence 1911–30. 1970.

25630 ZYTARUK (GEORGE J.) and BOULTON (JAMES THOMPSON) eds. The Letters of D. H. Lawrence. 2. 1913–1916. Camb. 1981. 3. 1916–1921. Camb. 1984.

25631 LEAVIS (FRANK RAYMOND). D. H. Lawrence: Novelist. 1964.

25632 GORDON (DAVID JAMES). D. H. Lawrence as a Literary Critic. 1966.

25633 CAVITCH (DAVID). D. H. Lawrence and the New World. 1969.

25634 ARNOLD (ARMIN). D. H. Lawrence and America. 1958.

25635 BURNS (AIDAN). Nature and Culture in D. H. Lawrence. 1980.

25636 MURFIN (ROSS). The Poetry of D. H. Lawrence: Texts and Contexts. Lincoln, Neb./Lond. 1983.

25637 DELAVENAY (EMILE). D. H. Lawrence: The Man and his Work: The Formative Years 1885–1919. 1972.

25638 ALLDRITT (KEITH). The Visual Imagination of D. H. Lawrence. 1971.

25639 DELANEY (PAUL). D. H. Lawrence's Nightmare: The Writer and his Circle in the Years of the Great War. Hassocks. 1979.

25640 DRAPER (RONALD PHILIP) ed. D. H. Lawrence: The Critical Heritage. 1970.

25641 NIVEN (ALASTAIR). D. H. Lawrence: The Writer and his Work. 1980.

25642 MOORE (HARRY THORNTON). The Life and Works of D. H. Lawrence. 1951. 2nd edn 1963. Rev. edn as The Priest of Love. 1974.

25643 NEHLS (EDWARD) ed. D. H. Lawrence: A Complete Biography. 3 vols. Madison, Wis. 1957–9.

25644 SAGAR (KEITH MILSOM). The Art of D. H. Lawrence. Camb. 1966.

25645 —— D. H. Lawrence: A Calendar of his Works. Manch. 1979.

25646 —— The Life of D. H. Lawrence: An Illustrated Biography. 1980.

25647 ALDINGTON (RICHARD). The Life of D. H. Lawrence 1885 to 1930: Portrait of a Genius, But. . . . 1951.

25648 ZYTARUK (GEORGE). The Quest for Rananim: D. H. Lawrence's Letters to S.S. Koteliansky, 1914–1930. Montreal. 1970.

25649 HOUGH (GRAHAM). The Dark Sun: A Study of D. H. Lawrence. 1957.

25650 MOORE (HARRY THORNTON) and MONTAGUE (DALE) eds. Frieda Lawrence and her Circle. Letters from, to and about Frieda Lawrence. 1981.

25651 LUCAS (ROBERT). Frieda Lawrence. 1973.

25652 LEHMANN (JOHN). Autobiography. The Whispering Gallery. 1955. I am my Brother. 1960. The Ample Proposition. 1966.

25653 LE STOURGEON (DIANA). Rosamond Lehmann. NY. 1965.

25654 TINDALL (GILLIAN). Rosamond Lehmann. 1985.

25655 SINGLETON (MARY ANN). The Fiction of Doris Lessing. Lewisburg, Pa. 1976.

25656 DRAINE (BETSY). Substance under Pressure: Artistic Coherence and Evolving Form in the Works of Doris Lessing. Madison, Wis. 1983.

25657 SELIGMAN (DEE). Doris Lessing: An Annotated Bibliography of Criticism. Westport, Conn. 1981.

25658 HAMILTON (IAN). Alun Lewis: Selected Poetry and Prose: With a Biographical Introduction. 1966.

25659 LEWIS (ALUN). Letters from India, Introd. Alfred Leslie Rowse. Card. n.d.

25660 CHRISTOPHER (JOE R.) and OSTLIN (JOAN). C. S. Lewis: An Annotated Checklist of Writings about him and his Works. Kent, Ohio. 1975.

25661 LEWIS (WARREN HAMILTON) and HOOPER (WALTER) eds. Letters of C. S. Lewis. 1966.

25662 GREEN (ROGER LANCELYN) and HOOPER (WALTER). C. S. Lewis: A Biography. 1974.

25663 SAYER (GEORGE). Jack: C. S. Lewis and his Times. 1988.

25664 KILBY (CLYDE S.) and MEAD (MARJORIE LAMP) eds. Brothers and Friends: The Diaries of Major Warren Hamilton Lewis. San Francisco, Calif. 1982.

25665 SIBLEY (BRIAN). Shadowlands: The Story of C. S. Lewis and Joy Davidman. 1985.

25666 CHRISTOPHER (JOE E.). C. S. Lewis. Boston, Mass. 1987.

25667 CARPENTER (HUMPHREY). The Inklings: C. S. Lewis, J. R. R. Tolkien, Charles Williams and Their Friends. 1979.

25668 WILSON (ANDREW N.). C. S. Lewis: A Biography. 1990.

25669 MORROW (BRADFORD) and LA FOURCADE (BERNARD). A Bibliography of the Writings of Wyndham Lewis. Santa Barbara, Calif. 1978.

25670 ROSE (W. K.) ed. The Letters of Wyndham Lewis. 1963.

25671 GRIGSON (GEOFFREY). A Master of our Time: A Study of Wyndham Lewis. 1951.

25672 JAMESON (FREDERIC). Fables of Aggression: Wyndham Lewis, the Modernist as Fascist. Berkeley, Calif. 1979.

25673 MEYERS (JEFFREY). The Enemy: A Biography of Wyndham Lewis. 1980.

25674 TOMLIN (ERIC WALTER FREDERICK). Wyndham Lewis. 1955.

25675 WAGNER (GEOFFREY). Wyndham Lewis: A Portrait of the Artist as the Enemy. 1957.

25676 LINDSAY (MAURICE). Thank You for Having Me: A Personal Memoir. 1983.

25677 —— ed. As I Remember: Ten Scottish Authors Recall how Writing Began for Them. 1979.

25678 LUCAS (AUDREY). E. V. Lucas. 1939.

25679 SMITH (CONSTANCE BABINGTON). Rose Macaulay: Letters to a Sister. 1964.

25680 BOLD (ALAN). MacDiarmid, Christopher Murray Grieve: A Critical Biography. 1988.

25681 BUTHLEY (KENNETH). Hugh MacDiarmid. Edin. 1964.

25682 GLEN (DUNCAN) ed. Hugh MacDiarmid: A Critical Survey. Edin. 1972.

25683 GISH (NANCY K.). Hugh MacDiarmid: The Man and his Work. 1984.

25684 BOLD (ALAN) ed. The Letters of Hugh MacDiarmid. 1984.

25685 SCOTT (P. H.) and DAVIES (A. C.). The Age of MacDiarmid: Essays on Hugh MacDiarmid and his Influence on Contemporary Scotland. Edin. 1980.

25686 GOULD (TONY). Insider Outsider: The Life and Times of Colin MacInnes. 1983.

25687 THOMAS (DAVID A.) and THOMAS (JOYCE). Compton Mackenzie: A Bibliography. 1986.

25688 LINKLATER (ANDRO). Compton Mackenzie: A Life. 1987.

25689 MACKENZIE (Sir COMPTON). My Life and Times. 10 vols. 1963–71.

25690 ARMITAGE (C. M.). A Bibliography of the Works of Louis MacNeice. 1973.

25691 SMITH (ELTON EDWARD). Louis MacNeice. Boston, Mass. 1970.

25692 COULTON (BARBARA). MacNeice in the BBC. 1980.

25693 MANNIN (ETHEL). Brief Voice. 1959.

25694 HANDLEY-TAYLOR (GEOFFREY) comp. John Masefield O.M. A Bibliography and Eighty-First Birthday Tribute. 1966.

25695 LAMONT (CORLISS). Remembering John Masefield. 1972.

25696 LAMONT (CORLISS) and LAMONT (LANSING) eds. Letters of John Masefield to Florence Lamont. 1979.

25697 BUCHAN (WILLIAM) ed. John Masefield, Letters to Reyna. 1983.

25698 VANSITTART (PETER) ed. John Masefield's Letters from the Front 1915–1917. 1984.

25699 STERNLICHT (SANFORD). John Masefield. Boston, Mass. 1977.

25700 SPARK (MURIEL). John Masefield. 1953.

25701 STRANG (LEONARD ALFRED GEORGE). John Masefield. 1952.

25702 SMITH (CONSTANCE BABINGTON). John Masefield: A Life. 1978.

25703 STOTT (RAYMOND TOOLE). A Bibliography of the Works of Somerset Maugham. 1973.

25704 SANDERS (CHARLES) ed. W. Somerset Maugham: An Annotated Bibliography of Writings about him. DeKalb, Ill. 1970.

25705 MAUGHAM (ROBERT CECIL ROMER) Viscount. Somerset and all the Maughams. 1966.

25706 —— Conversations with Willie: Recollections of W. Somerset Maugham. 1978.

25707 CALDER (ROBERT LAURIN). W. Somerset Maugham and the Quest for Freedom. 1972.

25708 —— Willie: The Life of Somerset Maugham. 1989.

25709 CURTIS (ANTHONY). The Pattern of Maugham. 1974.

25710 —— Somerset Maugham. 1977.

25711 RAPHAEL (FREDERIC MICHAEL). Somerset Maugham and his World. 1977.

25712 MORGAN (TED). Somerset Maugham. 1980.

25713 MILNE (ALAN ALEXANDER). It's Too Late Now: The Autobiography of a Writer. 1939.

25714 HASTINGS (SELINA). Nancy Mitford: A Biography. 1985.

25715 ACTON (HAROLD). Nancy Mitford: A Memoir. 1975.

25716 LEWIS (ELUNED) ed. Selected Letters of Charles Morgan. 1967.

25717 DUFFIN (HENRY CHARLES). The Novels and Plays of Charles Morgan. 1959.

25718 MORTIMER (JOHN). Clinging to the Wreckage: Part of a Life. 1982.

25719 MELLOWN (ELGIN). A Bibliography of the Writings of Edwin Muir. Birm., Ala. 1964. Rev. edn 1966.

25720 MUIR (EDWIN). An Autobiography. 1954.

25721 BUTTER (PETER HERBERT). Edwin Muir: Man and Poet. Edin. 1966.

25722 —— ed. Selected Letters of Edwin Muir. 1974.

25723 MELLOWN (ELGIN). Edwin Muir. Boston, Mass. 1979.

25724 KNIGHT (ROGER). Edwin Muir: An Introduction to his Work. 1980.

25725 WISEMAN (CHRISTOPHER). Beyond the Labyrinth: A Study of Edwin Muir's Poetry. Victoria, BC. 1978.

25726 MUIR (WILLA). Belonging. 1968.

25727 NOBLE (ANDREW) ed. Edwin Muir: Uncollected Scottish Criticism. 1982.

25728 BALDANZA (FRANK). Iris Murdoch. NY. 1974.

25729 BYATT (ANTONIA SUSAN). Degrees of Freedom: The Novels of Iris Murdoch. 1965.

25730 DIPPLE (ELIZABETH). Iris Murdoch: Work for the Spirit. 1982.

25731 TODD (RICHARD). Iris Murdoch. 1984.

25732 MURRY. LILLEY (GEORGE). A Bibliography of John Middleton Murry 1899–1957. 1974.

25733 LEA (FRANK ALFRED). John Middleton Murry. 1959.

25734 MAIRET (PHILIP [PE] AUGUST). John Middleton Murry. 1958.

25735 HANKIN (C. A.) ed. The Letters of John Middleton Murry to Katherine Mansfield. 1983.

25736 MURRY (KATHERINE MIDDLETON). Beloved Quixote: The Unknown John Middleton Murry. 1989.

25737 BUFKIN (E. C.). P. H. Newby. Boston, Mass. 1975.

25738 MEYERS (JEFFREY) and MEYERS (VALERIE). Orwell: An Annotated Bibliography of Criticism. NY. 1977.

25739 CRICK (BERNARD ROWLAND). George Orwell: A Life. 1980.

25740 —— George Orwell: Nineteen Eighty Four. Oxf. 1984.

25741 MEYERS (JEFFREY) ed. George Orwell: The Critical Heritage. 1975.

25742 WOODCOCK (GEORGE). The Crystal Spirit: A Critical Study of George Orwell. 1967.

25743 ZWERDLING (ALEX). Orwell and the Left. New Haven, Conn./Lond. 1974.

25744 HUNTER (LYNETTE). George Orwell: The Search for a Voice. Milton Keynes. 1984.

25745 HOLLIS (MAURICE CHRISTOPHER). A Study of George Orwell. 1956.

25746 REES (Sir RICHARD LODOWICK EDWARD MONTAGU). George Orwell: Fugitive from the Camp of Victory. 1961.

25747 GROSS (MIRIAM) ed. The World of George Orwell. 1971.

25748 STANSKY (PETER DAVID LYMAN) and ABRAHAMS (WILLIAM MILLER). The Unknown Orwell. 1972. Orwell: The Transformation. 1979.

25749 FYVEL (T. R.). George Orwell: A Personal Memoir. 1982.

25750 BOLTON (W. F.). The Language of 1984: Orwell's English and Ours. 1984.

25751 WADHAMS (STEPHEN) ed. Remembering Orwell. Harmondsworth. 1984.

25752 COPPARD (AUDREY) and CRICK (BERNARD) eds. Orwell Remembered. 1984.

25753 BUITENHUIS (PETER) and NADEL (IRA BRUCE) eds. George Orwell: A Reassessment. 1988.

25754 NORRIS (CHRISTOPHER) ed. Inside the Myth: Orwell: Views from the Left. 1984.

25755 STALLWORTHY (JON HOWIE). Wilfred Owen. 1974.

25756 LANE (ARTHUR). An Adequate Response: The War Poetry of Wilfred Owen and Siegfried Sassoon. Detroit, Mich. 1972.

25757 OWEN (HAROLD). Journey from Obscurity: Wilfred Owen 1893–1918. 3 vols. 1963–5.

25758 GILMORE (MAEVE). A World Away: A Memoir of Mervyn Peake. 1970.

25759 WATNEY (JOHN). Mervyn Peake. 1976.

25760 ALEXANDER (PETER). William Plomer: A Biography. Oxf. 1989.

25761 LINDER (LESLIE) ed. Beatrix Potter, 1866–1943: Centenary Catalogue. 1966.

25762 QUINBY (JANE). Beatrix Potter: A Bibliographical Checklist. NY. 1954.

25763 LANE (MARGARET). The Tale of Beatrix Potter: A Biography. 1946. Rev. edn 1968.

25764 SPURLING (HILARY). Handbook to Anthony Powell's Music of Time. 1977.

25765 TUCKER (JAMES). The Novels of Anthony Powell. 1976.

25766 MORRIS (ROBERT). The Novels of Anthony Powell. Pittsburgh, Pa. 1968.

25767 POWELL (ANTHONY). To Keep the Ball Rolling. 4 vols 1976–82.

25768 HOOKER (JEREMY). John Cowper Powys. Card. 1973.

25769 HUMFREY (BELINDA) ed. Essays on John Cowper Powys. Card. 1972.

25770 CAVALIERO (GLEN). John Cowper Powys: Novelist. Oxf. 1973.

25771 COLLINS (H. P.). John Cowper Powys. 1966.

25772 HOPKINS (KENNETH). The Powys Brothers: A Biographical Appreciation. 1967.

25773 BRAINE (JOHN GERARD). J. B. Priestley. 1978. N.Y. 1979.

25774 PRIESTLEY (J. B.) Autobiography and Reminiscence. Midnight in the Desert. 1937. Rain upon Godshill. 1939. Margin Released. 1962. Instead of the Trees. 1977.

25775 DAY (ALAN EDWIN). J. B. Priestley: An Annotated Bibliography. NY. 1980.

25776 COOPER (SUSAN). J. B. Priestley: Portrait of an Author. 1970.

25777 BROME (VINCENT). J. B. Priestley. 1988.

25778 PRITCHETT (*Sir* VICTOR SAWDON). A Cab at the Door. 1968. Midnight Oil. 1971. NY. 1972. The Turn of the Years. 1981.

25779 ROSSEN (JANICE). The World of Barbara Pym. 1987.

25780 SALWAK (DALE) *ed.* The Life and Work of Barbara Pym. 1987.

25781 HOLT (HAZEL) *and* PYM (HILARY) *eds.* A Very Private Eye: The Diaries, Letters and Notebooks of Barbara Pym. 1984.

25782 BROGAN (HUGH). The Life of Arthur Ransome. 1984.

25783 BERRY (FRANCIS). Herbert Read. 1981.

25784 SKELTON (ROBIN) *ed.* Herbert Read: A Memorial. 1971.

25785 LIDDIARD (JEAN). Isaac Rosenberg: The Half-Used Life. 1975.

25786 COHEN (JOSEPH). Journey into the Trenches: The Life of Isaac Rosenberg 1890–1918. 1975.

25787 PARSONS (IAN) *ed.* The Collected Works of Isaac Rosenberg. 1979.

25788 NICOLSON (NIGEL). Portrait of a Marriage. 1973. [Vita Sackville-West and Harold Nicolson.].

25789 DE SALBO (LOUISE) *and* LEASHA (MITCHELL). The Letters of Vita Sackville-West to Virginia Woolf. 1984.

25790 GLENDINNING (VICTORIA). Vita: The Life of Vita Sackville-West. 1983.

25791 STEVENS (MICHAEL). V. Sackville-West: A Critical Biography. 1973.

25792 KEYNES (*Sir* GEOFFREY LANGDON). A Bibliography of Siegfried Sassoon. 1962.

25793 CORRIGAN (D. FELICITAS). Siegfried Sassoon: Poet's Pilgrimage. 1973.

25794 BRABAZON (JAMES). Dorothy L. Sayers: The Life of a Courageous Woman. 1981.

25795 HITCHMAN (JANET). Such a Strange Lady: An Introduction to Dorothy L.Sayers 1893–1957. 1975.

25796 BRUNSDALE (MITZI). Dorothy L. Sayers. 1990.

25797 SWINDEN (PATRICK). Paul Scott: Images of India. 1980.

25798 GERARD (DAVID E.). Alan Sillitoe: A Bibliography. 1988.

25799 ATHERTON (STANLEY S.). Alan Sillitoe: A Critical Assessment. 1979.

25800 SISSON (C. H.). On The Look Out. Manch. 1989.

25801 FIFOOT (RICHARD). A Bibliography of Edith, Osbert and Sacheverell Sitwell. 1963. Rev. edn 1971.

25802 SITWELL (*Sir* OSBERT). Laughter in the Next Room.

25803 LEHMANN (JOHN). A Nest of Tigers: Edith, Osbert and Sacheverell Sitwell in their Times. 1968.

25804 GLENDINNING (VICTORIA). Edith Sitwell: A Unicorn among Lions. Oxf. 1983.

25805 SITWELL (EDITH). Taken Care Of: An Autobiography. 1965.

25806 LEHMANN (JOHN) *and* PARKER (DEREK) *eds.* Edith Sitwell: Selected Letters. 1970.

25807 PEARSON (JOHN). Façades: Edith, Osbert and Sacheverell Sitwell. 1980.

25808 McBRIAN (WILLIAM) *and* BARBARA (JACK). Stevie: A Biography of Stevie Smith. 1985.

25809 SPALDING (FRANCES). Stevie Smith: A Critical Biography. 1988.

25810 SNOW (PHILIP ARTHUR). Stranger and Brother: A Portrait of C. P. Snow. 1982.

25811 HALPERIN (JOHN). C. P. Snow: An Oral Biography: Together with a Conversation with Lady Snow (Pamela Hansford Johnson). Brighton. 1983.

25812 BOYTINCK (PAUL). C. P. Snow: A Reference Guide. Boston, Mass., 1980.

25813 RAMANATHAN (SUGUNA). The Novels of C. P. Snow: A Critical Introduction. 1978.

25814 TOMMAGA (THOMAS) *and* SCHNEIDERMAYER (WILMA). Iris Murdoch and Muriel Spark: A Bibliography. Metuchen, NJ. 1976.

25815 KEMP (PETER). Muriel Spark. 1974. NY. 1975.

25816 STUBBS (PATRICIA). Muriel Spark. 1973.

25817 MASSIE (ALLAN). Muriel Spark. 1979.

25818 KULKARNI (H. B.). Stephen Spender: Works and Criticism: An Annotated Bibliography. NY. 1976.

25819 SPENDER (*Sir* STEPHEN HAROLD). World within World: Autobiography. 1953.

25820 —— The Thirties and After: Poetry, Politics and People (1933–75). 1978.

25821 GOLDSMITH (JOHN) *ed.* Stephen Spender Journals 1939–1983. 1985.

25822 STANFORD (DEREK). Inside the Forties: Literary Memoirs 1937–1957. 1977.

25823 BULL (ANGELA). Noel Streatfeild. 1984.

25824 SWINNERTON (FRANK ARTHUR). An Autobiography. 1937.

25825 —— Figures in the Foreground: Literary Reminiscences, 1917–1940. 1963.

25826 THOMAS (D. M.). Memories and Hallucinations. 1988.

25827 ROLPH (J. ALEXANDER). Dylan Thomas: A Bibliography. 1956.

25828 MAUD (RALPH) *and* GLOVER (A.). Dylan Thomas in Print: A Bibliographical History. 1970.

25829 FERRIS (PAUL FREDERICK). Dylan Thomas. 1977.

25830 —— The Collected Letters of Dylan Thomas. 1985.

25831 FITZGIBBON (CONSTANTINE). The Life of Dylan Thomas. 1965.

25832 —— *ed.* Selected Letters. 1966.

25833 HOLBROOK (DAVID KENNETH). Llareggub Revisited: Dylan Thomas and the State of Modern Poetry. Bath. 1974.

25834 SINCLAIR (ANDREW ANNANDALE). Dylan Thomas: The Poet of his People. 1975.

25835 COX (CHARLES BRIAN). Dylan Thomas: A Collection of Critical Essays. Englewood Cliffs, NJ. 1966.

25836 BRINNAN (JOHN MALCOLM). Dylan Thomas in America. 1956.

25837 JONES (DANIEL). My Friend Dylan Thomas. 1977.

25838 TREMLETT (GEORGE). Caitlin: Life with Dylan Thomas. 1986.

25839 TINDALL (WILLIAM YORK). A Reader's Guide to Dylan Thomas. 1962.

25840 CARPENTER (HUMPHREY). J. R. R. Tolkien: A Biography. 1977.

25841 —— *ed.* Letters of J. R. R. Tolkien: A Selection. 1981.

25842 ROGERS (DEBORAH WEBSTER) *and* ROGERS (IVOR). J. R. R. Tolkien. Boston, Mass. 1980.

25843 KOCHER (PAUL HAROLD). Master of Middle Earth: The Achievement of J. R. R. Tolkien. 1972.

25844 MITFORD (JESSICA). Faces of Philip: A Memoir of Philip Toynbee. 1984.

25845 JUDD (DENIS). Alison Uttley: The Life of a Country Child (1884–1976): The Authorised Biography. 1986.

25846 WAIN (JOHN). Sprightly Running: Part of an Autobiography. 1962.

25847 SALWAK (DALE). John Wain. Boston, Mass. 1981.

25848 BLACKETT (MONICA). The Mask of the Maker: A Portrait of Helen Waddell. 1973.

25849 HART-DAVIS (*Sir* RUPERT CHARLES). Hugh Walpole: A Portrait of a Man, an Epoch and a Society. 1952.

25850 HARMAN (CLAIRE). Sylvia Townsend Warner. 1989.

25851 MAXWELL (WILLIAM) *ed.* The Letters of Sylvia Townsend Warner. 1982.

25852 ACKLAND (VALENTINE). For Sylvia: An Honest Account. 1985.

25853 MULFORD (WENDY) *ed.* This Narrow Place: Sylvia Townsend Warner and Valentine Ackland: Life, Letters and Politics 1930–1951. 1988.

25854 POLK (DORA). Vernon Watkins and the Spring of Vision. Swansea. 1977.

25855 NORRIS (LESLIE) *ed.* Vernon Watkins 1906–1967. 1970.

25856 DAVIS (ROBERT MURRAY) *et al.* Bibliography of Evelyn Waugh. NY. 1986.

25857 WAUGH (EVELYN). A Little Learning: The First Volume of Autobiography. 1964.

25858 DAVIE (MICHAEL) *ed.* The Diaries of Evelyn Waugh. 1976.

25859 AMORY (MARK) *ed.* The Letters of Evelyn Waugh. 1980.

25860 DONALDSON (FRANCES). Evelyn Waugh: Portrait of a Country Neighbour. 1967.

25861 GALLAGHER (DONAT) *ed.* The Essays, Articles and Reviews of Evelyn Waugh. 1983.

25862 SYKES (CHRISTOPHER). Evelyn Waugh: A Biography. 1975.

25863 STANNARD (MARTIN) *ed.* Evelyn Waugh: The Critical Heritage. 1984.

25864 HEATH (JEFFREY). Evelyn Waugh and his Writing. 1982.

25865 BRADBURY (MALCOLM STANLEY). Evelyn Waugh. 1964.

25866 CREW (DUDLEY). A Fragment of Friendship: A Memory of Evelyn Waugh when Young. 1974.

25867 BROOKE (JOYCELYN) *ed.* Denton Welch: Extracts from his Published Works. 1963.

25868 WELLS (GEOFFREY H.). The Works of H. G. Wells, 1887–1925. A Bibliography, Dictionary and Subject-Index. 1926.

25869 WELLS (HERBERT GEORGE). Experiment in Autobiography. 2 vols. 1934.

25870 DICKSON (LOVAT). H. G. Wells: His Turbulent Life and Times. 1969.

25871 MACKENZIE (NORMAN) *and* MACKENZIE (JEANNE). The Time Traveller: The Life of H. G. Wells. 1973.

25872 PARRINDER (PATRICK) *ed.* H. G. Wells: The Critical Heritage. 1972.

25873 HAYNES (ROSLYNN). H. G. Wells: Discoverer of the Future: The Influence of Science on his Thought. 1980.

25874 BLOOM (ROBERT). Anatomies of Egotism: A Reading of the Last Novels of H. G. Wells. Lincoln, Neb/Lond. 1977.

25875 GLENDINNING (VICTORIA). Rebecca West: A Life. 1987.

25876 HADFIELD (ALICE MARY). Charles Williams: An Explanation of his Life and Work. Oxf./NY. 1983.

25877 GLENN (LOUIS). Charles W. S. Williams: A Checklist. Kent, Ohio. 1975.

25878 CARPENTER (HUMPHREY WILLIAM BOUVERIE). The Inklings: C. S. Lewis, J. R. R. Tolkien, Charles Williams and their Friends. 1978.

25879 WILLIAMS (EMLYN). George. 1961. Emlyn. 1973.

25880 STAPE (JOHN HENRY). Angus Wilson: A Bibliography 1947–1987. 1988.

25881 GRANSDEN (KARL WATTS). Angus Wilson. 1969.

25882 FAULKNER (PETER). Angus Wilson: Mimic and Moralist. 1980.

25883 JASEN (DAVID A.). A Bibliography and Reader's Guide to the First Editions of P. G. Wodehouse. 1971.

25884 DONALDSON (FRANCES). P. G. Wodehouse: A Literary Biography. 1981.

25885 WODEHOUSE (P. G.). Wodehouse on Wodehouse. 1980.

25886 CONNOLLY (JOSEPH). P. G. Wodehouse: An Illustrated Biography. 1979.

25887 KIRKPATRICK (BROWNLEE JEAN). A Bibliography of Virginia Woolf. 1957. 3rd edn Oxf. 1980.

25888 BELL (ANNE OLIVIER). The Diary of Virginia Woolf. 1915–1941. 5 vols. 1971–84.

25889 NICOLSON (NIGEL) ed. The Letters of Virginia Woolf. 1912–1941. Vols. 2–6. 1976–80.

25890 BELL (QUENTIN). Virginia Woolf: Mrs Woolf 1912–1941. 1972.

25891 GUIGET (JEAN). Virginia Woolf and her Works. 1965.

25892 KELLEY (ALICE VAN BUREN). The Novels of Virginia Woolf. 1977.

25893 McLAURIN (ALLEN). Virginia Woolf: The Echoes Enslaved. Camb. 1973.

25894 MOODY (A. DALE). Virginia Woolf. Edin./Lond. 1963.

25895 MAJUMDAR (ROBIN) and McLAURIN (ALLEN). Virginia Woolf: The Critical Heritage. 1975.

25896 POOLE (ROGER). The Unknown Virginia Woolf. Camb. 1978.

25897 ROSE (PHYLLIS). Woman of Letters: A Life of Virginia Woolf. 1978.

16. THEATRE

25898 CAVANAGH (JOHN). British Theatre: A Bibliography 1901–1985. Mottisfont. 1989.

25899 MIKHAIL (EDWARD HALIM). English Drama, 1900–1950: A Guide to Information Sources. 1977.

25900 —— Contemporary British Drama, 1950–1976: An Annotated Critical Bibliography. 1976.

25901 HOWARD (D.) comp. Directory of Theatre Research and Information Sources in the U.K. 1980.

25902 —— Stage Yearbook. 1948–69.

25903 —— British Theatre Directory. 1972+.

25904 HARTNOLL (PHYLLIS MAY) ed. The Oxford Companion to the Theatre. 1951. 3rd edn 1967.

25905 HUDSON (LYNTON ALFRED). The English Stage, 1850–1950. 1951.

25906 MAY (ROBIN). A Companion to the Theatre: The Anglo-American Stage from 1920. Guildford. 1973.

25907 HUNT (HUGH) ed. et al. The Revels History of Drama in English vol. 7: 1880 to the Present Day. 1978.

25908 DIETRICH (RICHARD F.). British Drama 1890 to 1950. 1989.

25909 RUSINKO (SUSAN). British Drama 1950 to the Present: A Critical History. 1989.

25910 AGATE (JAMES EVERSHED). Ego: The Autobiography of James Agate. 9 vols. 1935–48.

25911 —— The Selective 'Ego': The Diaries of James Agate. Newly edited by Tim Beaumont. 1976.

25912 —— A Short View of the English Stage. 1900–1926. 1926.

25913 —— First Nights. 1934.

25914 —— More First Nights. 1937.

25915 —— The Amazing Theatre. 1939.

25916 —— Immoment Toys: A Survey of Light Entertainment on the London Stage, 1920–1943. 1945.

25917 ARTHUR (Sir GEORGE COMPTON ARCHIBALD). From Phelps to Gielgud: Reminiscences of the Stage through Sixty-Five Years. 1936.

25918 BROWN (IVOR). The Way of my World. 1954.

25919 —— Old and Young. 1971.

25920 —— 'Forty Years back'. Drama 3 (1959), 25–7.

25921 DARLINGTON (WILLIAM AUBREY CECIL). Six Thousand and one Nights: Forty Years a Critic. 1960.

25922 HOBSON (Sir HAROLD). Verdict at Midnight: Sixty Years of Dramatic Criticism. 1952.

25923 —— The Theatre Now. 1953.

25924 —— Indirect Journey. 1978.

25925 MACQUEEN-POPE (WALTER JAMES). The Footlights Flickered. 1959.

25926 MAROWITZ (CHARLES). Confessions of a Counterfeit Critic: A London Theatre Notebook, 1958–1971. 1973.

25927 SHORT (ERNEST HENRY). Sixty Years of Theatre. 1951.

25928 WORSLEY (THOMAS CUTHBERT). The Fugitive Art: Dramatic Commentaries, 1947–1951. 1952.

25929 ELSOM (JOHN). Post-War British Theatre Criticism. 1981.

25930 WEINTRAUB (S.) ed. Modern British Dramatists 1900–1945. 2 vols Detroit, Mich. 1982.

25931 —— British Dramatists since World War Two. 2 vols. Detroit, Mich. 1982.

25932 KIRKPATRICK (D. L.) ed. Contemporary Dramatists. 4th edn 1988.

25933 KING (KIMBALL). Twenty Modern British Playwrights: A Bibliography 1956 to 1976. 1977.

25934 HAYMAN (RONALD). Arden. 1968.

25935 HUNT (ALBERT). Arden: A Study of his Plays. 1974.

25936 GRAY (FRANCES). John Arden. 1982.

25937 PAGE (MALCOLM). John Arden. Boston, Mass. 1984.

25938 BILLINGTON (MICHAEL). Alan Ayckbourn. 1983.

25939 WATSON (IAN). Conversations with Ayckbourn. 1981.

25940 SEBBA (ANNA). Enid Bagnold: The Authorized Biography. 1986.

25941 MORGAN (MARGERY). A Drama of Political Man: A Study in the Plays of Granville Barker. 1961.

25942 KENNEDY (DENNIS). Granville Barker and the Dream of Theatre. Camb. 1985.

25943 McELDERRY (BRUCE R.). Max Beerbohm. NY. 1972.

25944 HAYMAN (RONALD). Robert Bolt. 1969.

25945 HAY (MALCOLM) *and* ROBERTS (PHILIP). Edward Bond: A Companion to the Plays. 1978.

25946 TRUSSLER (SIMON). Bond. 1976.

25947 SCHARINE (RICHARD). The Plays of Bond. 1977.

25948 COULT (TONY). The Plays of Bond. 1978.

25949 HIRST (DAVID L.). Edward Bond. 1985.

25950 FARMER (A. J.). 'Bottomley'. *Etudes Anglaises* 9 (1956).

25951 BRIDIE (JAMES). One Way of Living. 1939.

25952 TOBIN (TERENCE). James Bridie (Osborne Henry Mavor). Boston, Mass. 1980.

25953 BANNISTER (WINIFRED). James Bridie and his Theatre. 1955.

25954 MORLEY (SHERIDAN ROBERT). A Talent to Amuse: A Biography of Coward. 1969.

25955 CASTLE (CHARLES). Noel. 1972.

25956 GRAY (FRANCES). Noel Coward. 1987.

25957 LESLEY (COLE), PAYN (GRAHAM), *and* MORLEY (SHERIDAN). Noel Coward and His Friends. 1979.

25958 PAYN (GRAHAM) *and* MORLEY (SHERIDAN) eds. The Noel Coward Diaries. 1982.

25959 DOUGLAS-HOME (WILLIAM). Autobiography. Half-Term Report. 1954. Mr Home Pronounced Hume: An Autobiography. 1979.

25960 DUNCAN (RONALD). Autobiography. All Men are Islands. 1964. How to Make Enemies. 1968. Obsessed. 1977.

25961 STANFORD (DEREK). Christopher Fry: An Appreciation. 1951.

25962 THOMAS (GWYN) ed. John Gwilym Jones: Cyfrol Deyrnged. Llandybie. 1974.

25963 JARMAN (FRANCIS) ed. The Quality of Mercer: Bibliography of Writings by and about the Playwright Mercer. 1974.

25964 LAHR (JOHN). Prick up your Ears: The Biography of Orton. 1978.

25965 —— ed. Joe Orton's Diaries. 1986.

25966 CHARNEY (MAURICE). Joe Orton. 1984.

25967 NORTHOUSE (CAMERON) *and* WALSH (THOMAS P.). John Osborne: A Reference Guide. Boston, Mass. 1974.

25968 HAYMAN (RONALD). John Osborne. 2nd edn 1970.

25969 OSBORNE (JOHN). A Better Class of Person: An Autobiography 1929–1956. 1981.

25970 CARTER (ALAN). John Osborne. 1969. 2nd edn Edin. 1973.

25971 BURKMAN (KATHERINE H.) The Dramatic World of Harold Pinter. Columbus, Ohio.1971.

25972 HAYMAN (RONALD). Pinter. 1968. 4th edn 1980.

25973 SCHROLL (HERMAN). Harold Pinter: A Study of his Reputation, 1958–1969. NY. 1971.

25974 DUKORE (BERNARD FRANK). Harold Pinter. 1982.

25975 QUIGLEY (AUSTIN E.). The Pinter Problem. 1975.

25976 BAKER (WILLIAM) *and* ELY (STEPHEN). Harold Pinter. Edin. 1973.

25977 ESSLIN (MARTIN JULIUS). Pinter: A Study of his Plays. 1973.

25978 THOMSON (PETER). 'Harold Pinter: A Retrospect'. *Crit. Q.* 20 (1978), 21–31.

25979 GALE (STEVEN). Harold Pinter: An Annotated Bibliography. Lond./Boston, Mass. 1978.

25980 PLATER (ALAN). 'Twenty Five Years Hard: A Playwright's Personal Retrospective'. *Theatre Q.* 7 (1977), 34–42.

25981 DARLOW (MICHAEL) *and* HODSON (GILLIAN). Rattigan: The Man and his Work. 1978.

25982 TAYLOR (JOHN RUSSELL). Shaffer. 1974.

25983 GIANAKARIS (C. J.). Peter Shaffer. 1987.

25984 SHERRIFF (R. C.). No Leading Lady: An Autobiography. 1968.

25985 BIGSBY (CHRISTOPHER WILLIAM EDGAR). Stoppard. 1976.

25986 HAYMAN (RONALD). Stoppard. 1977. 3rd edn 1979.

25987 WHITAKER (THOMAS R.). Tom Stoppard. 1985.

25988 BRASSELL (TIM). Tom Stoppard, an Assessment. 1988.

25989 BILLINGTON (MICHAEL). Stoppard the Playwright. 1986.

25990 RUSINKO (SUSAN). Tom Stoppard. Boston, Mass. 1986.

25991 TAYLOR (JOHN R.). David Storey. 1974.

25992 LEEMING (GLENDA) *and* TRUSSLER (SIMON). The Plays of Wesker. 1971.

25993 LEEMING (GLENDA). Arnold Wesker. 1983.

25994 WHITING. HAYMAN (RONALD). John Whiting. 1969.

25995 SALMON (ERIC). The Dark Journey: John Whiting as Dramatist. 1979.

25996 BROWN (JOHN RUSSELL). Theatre Language. 1972.

25997 BULL (JOHN). New British Political Dramatists: Howard Brenton, David Hare, Trevor Griffiths and David Edgar. 1984.

25998 —— Who was Who in the Theatre, 1912–1976. 4 vols. 1976.

25999 FINDLATER (RICHARD). The Unholy Trade. 1952.

26000 —— The Player Kings. 1971.

26001 —— These Are Our Actors: A Celebration of the Theatre Acting of Peggy Ashcroft, John Gielgud, Laurence Olivier and Ralph Richardson. 1983.

26002 BILLINGTON (MICHAEL). The Modern Actor. 1973.

26003 SANDERSON (MICHAEL). From Irving to Olivier: A Social History of the Acting Profession in England 1880–1983. 1984.

26004 RICHARDS (SANDRA L.). The Rise of the English Actress. 1988.

26005 COCHRAN. COCHRAN (CHARLES B.). The Secrets of a Showman. 1925.

26006 —— I had almost Forgotten. 1932.

26007 —— Cock-a-Doodle-do. 1941.

26008 —— Showman Looks On. 1945.

26009 GRAVES (CHARLES). The Cochran Story: A Biography of Sir Charles Blake Cochran, Kt. 1951.

26010 ACKLAND (JOSS). I Must Be In There Somewhere. 1989.

26011 BILLINGTON (MICHAEL). Peggy Ashcroft. 1988.

26012 BARKWORTH (PETER). First Houses. 1983.

26013 BLOOM (CLAIRE). Limelight and After: The Education of an Actress. 1982.

26014 BOGARDE (DIRK). Dirk Bogarde: The Complete Autobiography. 1988. [Four vols originally published 1977/86.].

26015 BRANAGH (KENNETH). Beginnings. 1989.

26016 COTTRELL (JOHN). Richard Burton: A Biography. 1971. Rev. edn 1974.

26017 JUNOR (PENNY). Burton: The Man behind the Myth. 1985.

26018 BRAGG (MELVYN). Rich: The Life of Richard Burton. 1988.

26019 JENKINS (GRAHAM) *with* TURNER (BARRY). Richard Burton My Brother. 1988.

26020 CALLOW (SIMON). Being an Actor. 1984.

26021 CAMPBELL (*Mrs* PATRICK). My Life and some Letters. 1922.

26022 DENT (ALAN). Mrs Patrick Campbell. 1961.

26023 COLLINS (JOAN). Past Imperfect: An Autobiography. Rev. edn 1985.

26024 COOPER (*Lady* DIANA). The Light of Common Day. 1959.

26025 ZIEGLER (PHILIP). Diana Cooper. 1981.

26026 COOPER (GLADYS). An Autobiography. 1931.

26027 MORLEY (SHERIDAN). Gladys Cooper: A Biography. 1979.

26028 CRAIG (EDWARD A.). Gordon Craig: The Story of his Life. 1968.

26029 FLETCHER (IFAN KYRLE) *and* ROOD (ARNOLD). Edward Gordon Craig: A Bibliography. 1967.

26030 INNES (CHRISTOPHER). Edward Gordon Craig. Camb. 1983.

26031 CUSHING (PETER). Past Forgetting: Memoirs of the Hammer Years. 1988.

26032 JACOBS (GERALD). Judi Dench. A Great Deal of Laughter. An Authorized Biography. 1985.

26033 DENISON (MICHAEL). Overture and Beginners. 1973.

26034 —— Double Act. 1985.

26035 TREWIN (JOHN COURTENAY). Robert Donat: A Biography. 1968.

26036 DORS (DIANA). Behind Closed Dors. 1979.

26037 DU MAURIER (DAPHNE). Gerald, A Portrait. 1934.

26038 TREWIN (JOHN COURTENAY). Edith Evans. 1954.

26039 BATTERS (JEAN). Edith Evans: A Personal Memoir. 1977.

26040 FORBES (BRYAN). Ned's Girl: The Authorised Biography of Dame Edith Evans. 1977.

26041 FAULKNER (TRADER). Peter Finch: A Biography. 1979.

26042 DUNDY (ELAINE). Finch, Bloody Finch. A Biography of Peter Finch. 1980.

26043 FORBES (BRYAN). Notes for a Life. 1974.

26044 HAYMAN (RONALD). John Gielgud. 1971.

26045 BRANDRETH (GYLES). John Gielgud: A Celebration. 1984.

26046 HARWOOD (RONALD) *ed.* The Ages of Gielgud: An Actor at Eighty. 1984.

26047 GIELGUD (*Sir* JOHN). Early Stages. 1939. Distinguished Company. 1972. An Actor and his Time. 1979. 1981.

26048 GRENFELL (JOYCE). Joyce Grenfell Requests the Pleasure. 1976.

26049 GRENFELL (JOYCE) *and* MOORE (KATHARINE). An Invisible Friendship. An Exchange of Letters 1957–1979. New edn. 1991.

26050 GUINNESS (*Sir* ALEC). Blessings in Disguise: An Autobiography. 1985.

26051 TAYLOR (JOHN RUSSELL). Alec Guinness: A Celebration. 1984.

26052 HARRISON (REX). Rex, An Autobiography. 1974.

26053 MOSELEY (ROY) *et al.* Rex Harrison: The First Biography. 1987.

26054 HARRISON (ELIZABETH). Love, Honour and Dismay. 1976.

26055 HICKEY (DES) *and* SMITH (GUS). The Prince, Being the Public and Private Life of Larushka Mischa Skikne, a Jewish Lithuanian Vagabond Player, otherwise known as Laurence Harvey. 1975.

26056 HAWKINS (JACK). Anything for a Quiet Life. 1983.

26057 WOODWARD (IAN). Glenda Jackson: A Study in Fire and Ice. 1986.

26058 SINGER (KURT). The Charles Laughton Story. 1954.

26059 HYAM (CHARLES). Charles Laughton: An Intimate Biography. N.Y. 1976.

26060 CALLOW (SIMON). A Difficult Actor. 1987.

26061 DENT (ALAN). Vivien Leigh: A Bouquet. 1969.

26062 EDWARDS (ANNE). Vivien Leigh: A Biography. 1977.

26063 TAYLOR (JOHN RUSSELL). Vivien Leigh. 1984.

26064 VICKERS (HUGO). Vivien Leigh. 1988.

26065 WALKER (ALEXANDER). Vivien: The Life of Vivien Leigh. 1988.

26066 MASON (JAMES). Before I Forget. 1981.

26067 MORLEY (SHERIDAN). James Mason: Odd Man Out. 1989.

26068 DE ROSSO (DIANA). James Mason. 1989.

26069 MILLS (*Sir* JOHN). Up in the Clouds, Gentlemen Please. 1980.

26070 MORE (KENNETH). Happy Go Lucky: My Life. 1959.

26071 NEAGLE (ANNA). Anna Neagle says 'There's Always Tomorrow'. 1974.

26072 TREWIN (JOHN COURTENAY). John Neville. 1961.

26073 NIVEN (DAVID). The Moon's a Balloon. 1971.

26074 —— Bring on the Empty Horses. 1975.

26075 MORLEY (SHERIDAN). The Other Side of the Moon: The Life of David Niven. 1985.

26076 MACQUEEN-POPE (W.). Ivor: The Story of an Achievement. A Biography of Ivor Novello. 1951.

26077 NOBLE (PETER). Ivor Novello: Man of the Theatre. 1951.

26078 WILSON (SANDY). Ivor. 1975.

26079 COTTRELL (JOHN). Laurence Olivier. 1977.

26080 BRAGG (MELVYN). Laurence Olivier. 1984.

26081 HOLDEN (ANTHONY). Olivier. 1988.

26082 TANITCH (ROBERT). Olivier: The Complete Career. 1985.

26083 OLIVIER (LAURENCE). Confessions of an Actor. 1982.

26084 —— On Acting. 1976.

26085 WAPSHOTT (NICHOLAS). Peter O'Toole: A Biography. 1983.

26086 FINDLATER (RICHARD). Michael Redgrave: Actor. 1956.

26087 REDGRAVE (*Sir* MICHAEL). In My Mind's Eye: An Autobiography. 1983.

26088 RIX (*Sir* BRIAN). My Farce from my Elbow. An Autobiography. 1975.

26089 —— Farce about Face. 1989.

26090 TANITCH (ROBERT). Ralph Richardson: A Tribute. 1982.

26091 O'CONNOR (GARRY). Ralph Richardson: An Actor's Life. 1982. 2nd edn 1986.

26092 WALKER (ALEXANDER). No Bells on Sunday: The Journals of Rachel Roberts: Edited with a Documentary Biography. 1984.

26093 BARROW (KENNETH). Flora: An Appreciation of the Life and Work of Dame Flora Robson. 1981.

26094 DUNBAR (JANET). Flora Robson. 1960.

26095 TANITCH (ROBERT). Leonard Rossiter. 1985.

26096 RUTHERFORD (*Dame* MARGARET). An Autobiography. 1972.

26097 SIMMONS (DAWN LANGLEY). Margaret Rutherford: A Blithe Spirit. 1985.

26098 TREWIN (JOHN COURTENAY). Paul Scofield. 1956.

26099 SINDEN (NORMAN). A Touch of the Memoirs. 1982.

26100 —— Laughter in the Second Act. 1985.

26101 STAMP (TERENCE). Stamp Album. 1987.

26102 —— Coming Attraction. 1988.

26103 TAYLOR (ELIZABETH). Elizabeth Takes Off: An Autobiography. 1988.

26104 MORLEY (SHERIDAN). Elizabeth Taylor: A Celebration. 1977.

26105 SPRIGGE (ELIZABETH). Sybil Thorndike Casson. 1971.

26106 MORLEY (SHERIDAN ROBERT). Sybil Thorndike: A Life in the Theatre. 1977.

26107 CASSON (JOHN). Lewis & Sybil: A Memoir. 1972.

26108 USTINOV (PETER). Dear Me. 1977.

26109 HARWOOD (RONALD). Sir Donald Wolfit. 1971.

26110 WINTOUR (CHARLES). Celebration: Twenty-Five Years of British Theatre. 1981.

26111 THORNDIKE (SYBIL *and* RUSSELL). Lilian Baylis. 1938.

26112 FINDLATER (RICHARD). Lilian Baylis: The Lady of the Old Vic. 1975.

26113 WILLIAMS (HARCOURT) *ed.* Vic–Wells: The Work of Lilian Baylis. 1938.

26114 DAVIES (HUNTER). The Grades: The First Family of British Entertainment. 1981.

26115 BLACK (KITTY). Upper Circle: A Theatrical Chronicle. 1984.

26116 HUGGETT (RICHARD). Binkie Beaumont: Eminence Grise of the West End Theatre 1933–73. 1989.

26117 GUTHRIE (*Sir* TYRONE). A Life in the Theatre. 1966.

26118 FORSYTH (JAMES). Tyrone Guthrie. 1976.

26119 TREWIN (JOHN COURTENAY). Peter Brook: A Biography. 1971.

26120 BROOK (PETER). The Shifting Point: Forty Years of Theatrical Exploration 1946–1987. 1988.

26121 JONES (EDWARD T.). Following Directions: A Study of Peter Brook. NY. 1985.

26122 WILLIAMS (DAVID) *comp.* Peter Brook: A Theatrical Casebook. 1988.

26123 WEBSTER (MARGARET). The Same, Only Different: Five Generations of a Great Theatre Family. 1969.

26124 COLE (REX VICAT). The Art and Life of Byam Shaw. 1932.

26125 PEARSON (HESKETH). The Last Actor-Managers. 1974.

26126 PURDOM (CHARLES BENJAMIN). Harley Granville Barker: Man of the Theatre, Dramatist and Scholar. 1955.

26127 SALMON (ERIC). Granville Barker: A Secret Life. 1983.

26128 BRAHMS (CARYL) *and* SHERRIN (NED). Too Dirty for the Windmill: A Memoir of Caryl Brahms. 1986.

26129 ISAAC (WINIFRED). Ben Greet and the Old Vic: A Biography of Sir Philip Ben Greet. 1964.

26130 ROBERTS (PETER). The Old Vic Story: A Nation's Theatre, 1818–1976. 1976.

26131 BROWNE (E. MARTIN) *with* BROWNE (HENZIE). Two in One. Camb. 1981.

26132 DOBBS (BRIAN). Drury Lane: Three Centuries of the Theatre Royal 1663–1971. 1972.

26133 MacDERMOTT (NORMAN). Everymania: The History of the Everyman Theatre, Hampstead, 1920–1926. 1975.

26134 GRANVILLE-BARKER (HARLEY). A National Theatre. 1930.

26135 WHITWORTH (GEOFFREY ARUNDEL). The Making of a National Theatre. 1951.

26136 TREWIN (JOHN COURTENAY). 'The National Theatre'. *Contemp. Rev.* 218 (1971), 28–33.

26137 EMMET (ALFRED). 'The Long Prehistory of the National Theatre'. *Theatre Q.* 6 (1976), 55–62.

26138 BARRY (MICHAEL) *and* TYNAN (KENNETH). 'The National Theatre'. *Author* 88 (1967), 159–63.

26139 COOK (JUDITH) *ed.* The National Theatre. 1976.

26140 DUNCAN (BARRY) *and* TOMALIN (NICHOLAS). The History of the National Theatre. 1978.

26141 GOODWIN (TIM). Britain's National Theatre: The First Twenty Five Years. 1987.

26142 DENT (EDWARD JOSEPH). A Theatre for Everybody: The Story of the Old Vic and Sadler's Wells. 1945.

26143 MARSHALL (NORMAN). The Other Theatre. 1947.

26144 WILLIAMSON (AUDREY MAY). Old Vic Drama: A Twelve Years' Study of Plays and Players. 1953.

26145 —— Old Vic Drama 2. 1947–1957. 1957.

26146 BARRY (DUNCAN). The St James's Theatre: Its Strange and Complete History, 1835–1957. 1964.

26147 BEAUMAN (SALLY). The Royal Shakespeare Company: A History of Ten Decades. Oxf. 1982.

26148 GOODWIN (JOHN LONNEN) *comp.* Royal Shakespeare Theatre Company, 1960–1963. 1964.

26149 —— *ed.* Peter Hall's Diaries: The Story of a Dramatic Battle. 1983.

26150 ADDENBROOKE (DAVID). The Royal Shakespeare Company: The Peter Hall Years. 1974.

26151 HAYMAN (RONALD). 'The Royal Court, 1956–1972'. *Drama* 105 (1972), 45–53.

26152 FINDLATER (RICHARD) *ed.* At the Royal Court: 25 Years of the English Stage Company. 1981.

26153 TSCHUDIN (MARCUS). A Writer's Theatre: George Devine and the English Stage Company at the Royal Court, 1956–1965. Berne. 1972.

26154 WARDLE (IRVING). The Theatre of George Devine. 1978.

26155 BROWNE (TERRY). Playwrights' Theatre: The English Stage Company at the Royal Court Theatre. 1975.

26156 ROBERTS (PHILIP). The Royal Court Theatre 1965–1972. 1986.

26157 ROOSE-EVANS (JAMES). London Theatre, from the Globe to the National. Oxf. 1977.

26158 ELSOM (JOHN). Theatre outside London. 1971.

26159 ROWELL (G.) *and* JACKSON (A.). The Repertory Movement: A History of Regional Theatre in Britain. Camb. 1984.

26160 KEMP (THOMAS CHARLES) *and* TREWIN (JOHN COURTENAY). The Stratford Festival: A History of the Shakespeare Memorial Theatre. Birm. 1953.

26161 TREWIN (JOHN COURTENAY). The Birmingham Repertory Theatre, 1913–1963. 1963.

26162 BARKER (KATHLEEN). The Theatre Royal, Bristol, 1766–1966: Two Centuries of Stage History. 1974.

26163 VEITCH (NORMAN). The People's: Being a History of the People's Theatre, Newcastle upon Tyne, 1911–1939. Gateshead on Tyne. 1950.

26164 CARPENTER (HUMPHREY). OUDS: A Centenary of the Oxford University Dramatic Society 1885–1985. Oxf. 1985.

26165 PICKERING (KENNETH W.). Drama in the Cathedral: The Canterbury Festival Plays 1928–1948. Worthing. 1985.

26166 HAYMAN (RONALD). The First Thrust: The Chichester Festival Theatre. 1975.

26167 WILKINSON (RONALD). The Grand Theatre and Opera House Leeds, 1878–1978: First Hundred Years. Leeds. 1978.

26168 OXFORD PLAYHOUSE 1938–64. Oxford University Theatre 1961–4. Oxf. 1964.

26169 O'MALLEY (MARY) *and* BOYD (JOHN) *eds.* A Needle's Eye. Belf. 1979.

26170 McDONALD (JAN). What is a Citizens' Theatre? Dundee. 1984.

26171 BRUCE (GEORGE). Pitlochry Festival Theatre. 21, a Record of Achievement, 1951 to 1972. Scotland's Theatre in the Hills. Pitlochry. 1972.

26172 HUTCHINSON (DAVID). The Modern Scottish Theatre. 1977.

26173 WORTH (KATHARINE JOYCE). Revolutions in Modern English Drama. 1973.

26174 WILLIAMS (RAYMOND HENRY). Modern Tragedy. 1966.

26175 WHITING (JOHN). On Theatre. 1966.

26176 AXTON (MARIE) *and* WILLIAMS (RAYMOND HENRY). English Drama: Forms and Development: Essays in Honour of Muriel Clara Bradbrook. Camb. 1977.

26177 TREWIN (JOHN COURTENAY). The Theatre since 1900. 1951.

26178 ROY (EMIL). British Drama since Shaw. 1972.

26179 REYNOLDS (ERNEST RANDOLPH). Modern English Drama: A Survey on the Theatre from 1900. 1949. Rev. edn 1950.

26180 NICOLL (ALLARDYCE). English Drama, 1900–1930: The Beginnings of the Modern Period. Camb. 1973.

26181 —— British Drama: An Historical Survey from the Beginning to the Present Time. 1925. 4th edn 1947.

26182 GASCOIGNE ((ARTHUR) BAMBER). Twentieth Century Drama. 1962.

26183 PELLIZZI (CAMILLO). English Drama: The Last Great Phase. 1935.

26184 LANDSTONE (CHARLES). Off-Stage: A Personal Record of the First Twelve Years of State Sponsored Drama in Great Britain. 1953.

26185 CLUNES (ALEC SHERIFF DE MORO). British Theatre History. Camb. 1955.

26186 —— The British Theatre. 1964.

26187 TREWIN (JOHN COURTENAY). The Gay Twenties: A Decade of the Theatre. 1958.

26188 —— The Turbulent Thirties: A Further Decade of the Theatre. 1960.

26189 JURAK (M.). 'Commitment and Character Portrayal in the British Politico-Poetic Drama of the 1930's'. *Educ. Theatre J.* 26 (1974), 342–51.

26190 CLURMAN (HAROLD). The Fervent Years: The Story of the Group Theatre and the Thirties. 1946.

26191 SIDNEIL (MICHAEL J.). Dances of Death: The Group Theatre of London in the Thirties. 1984.

26192 TREWIN (JOHN COURTENAY). 'Theatre between the Wars—Classical Stage'. *Plays and Players* 16 (1969), 60–5.

26193 CHISHOLM (CECIL). Repertory: An Outline of the Modern Theatre Movement. 1934.

26194 NORGATE (M.). '40 Years back—London Plays of Autumn 1938'. *Drama* 130 (1978), 35–42.

26195 DEAN (BASIL). The Theatre at War. 1956.

26196 —— Seven Ages. An Autobiography 1888–1927. 1970.

26197 —— Mind's Eye. An Autobiography 1927–1972. 1973.

26198 HUDSON (LYNTON ALFRED). The Twentieth Century Drama. 1946.

26199 WILSON (SHEILA). The Theatre in the Fifties. 1963.

26200 TYNAN (KENNETH PEACOCK). A View of the English Stage, 1944–1963. 1975.

26201 TYNAN (KATHLEEN). The Life of Kenneth Tynan. 1988.

26202 TREWIN (JOHN COURTENAY). Drama, 1945–1950. 1951.

26203 —— A Play Tonight. 1952.

26204 WILLIAMSON (AUDREY MAY). Theatre of Two Decades. 1951.

26205 —— Contemporary Theatre, 1953–1956. 1956.

26206 ESSLIN (MARTIN). 'Must Contemporary Drama be Sordid?'. *Drama* 72 (1964).

26207 FINDLATER (RICHARD). 'The System'. *World Theatre* 13 (1964), 9–22.

26208 KITCHIN (LAURENCE). 'Realism in the English Mid-Century Drama'. *World Theatre* 14 (1965), 17–26.

26209 —— Mid-Century Drama. 1960. Rev. edn 1962.

26210 —— Drama in the Sixties: Form and Interpretation. 1966.

26211 TREWIN (JOHN COURTENAY). Drama in Britain, 1951–1964. 1965.

26212 ALVAREZ (AL). 'The Anti-Establishment Drama'. *Partisan Rev.* 26 (1959), 606–11.

26213 ARMSTRONG (WILLIAM). 'Tradition and Innovation in the London Theatre, 1960–1961'. *Modern Drama* 4 (1961), 184–95.

26214 ASHMORE (JEROME). 'Interdisciplinary Roots of the Theatre of the Absurd'. *Modern Drama* 14 (1971), 72–83.

26215 KNIGHT (GEORGE WILSON). The Golden Labyrinth: A Study of British Drama. 1962.

26216 ATKINS (THOMAS). 'The London Theatre: A Devaluation'. *Kenyon Rev.* 31 (1969), 348–66.

26217 LANDSTONE (CHARLES). 'From John Osborne to Shelagh Delaney'. *World Theatre* 8 (1959), 203–16.

26218 TARN (ADAM). 'Major Dramatic Trends: 1948–1968'. *World Theatre* 17 (1969), 9–33.

26219 TYNAN (KENNETH PEACOCK) *et al.* 'British Playwriting'. *Encore* (June 1957), 13–35.

26220 TAYLOR (JOHN RUSSELL). 'British Drama of the Fifties'. *World Theatre* 11 (1962), 241–54.

26221 DOWNER (ALAN SEYMOUR). British Drama: A Handbook and Brief Chronicle. NY. 1950.

26222 WILLIAMS (RAYMOND HENRY). 'New English Drama'. *Twentieth Cent.* 170 (1961), 169–80.

26223 BROWN (JOHN RUSSELL) *and* HARRIS (BERNARD ALOYSIUS) *eds.* Contemporary Theatre. 1962.

26224 TAYLOR (JOHN RUSSELL). Anger and after: A Guide to the New British Drama. 1962. 2nd edn 1977.

26225 POPKIN (HENRY) *ed.* The New British Drama. NY. 1964.

26226 BENTLEY (ERIC RUSSELL). The Theatre of Commitment, and other Essays on Drama in our Society. 1967.

26227 MAROWITZ (CHARLES) *and* TRUSSLER (SIMON) *eds.* Theatre at Work: Playwrights and Productions in the Modern British Theatre. 1967.

26228 ARMSTRONG (WILLIAM ARTHUR) *ed.* Experimental Drama. 1963.

26229 STOLL (KARL-HEINZ). The New British Drama: A Bibliography with Particular Reference to Arden,

Bond, Osborne, Pinter, Wesker. Frankfurt am Main. 1975.

26230 HINCHCLIFFE (ARNOLD P.). British Theatre 1950–70. Oxf. 1974.

26231 TAYLOR (JOHN RUSSELL). The Second Wave: British Drama for the Seventies. 1971. 2nd edn 1978.

26232 DAVIDSON (PETER). Contemporary Drama: The Popular Dramatic Tradition in England. 1982.

26233 DAVIES (ANDREW). Other Theatres: The Development of Alternative and Experimental Theatre in Britain. 1987.

26234 ANSORGE (PETER). Disrupting the Spectacle: Five Years of Experimental and Fringe Theatre in Britain. 1975.

26235 BARKER (CLIVE). British Alternative Theatre. 1985.

26236 RABEY (DAVID IAN). British and Irish Political Drama in the Twentieth Century: Implicating the Audience. 1986.

26237 GOORNEY (HOWARD) and MacCOLL (EWAN) eds. Agit-Prop to Theatre Workshop: Political Playscripts 1930–1950. Manch. 1986.

26238 CHAMBERS (COLIN). A History of Unity Theatre. 1986.

26239 WANDOR (MICHELENE). Carry on Understudies: Theatre and Sexual Politics. 1986.

26240 VINSON (JAMES) ed. Contemporary Dramatists. 1973.

26241 MacCOLL (EWAN). 'Grass Roots of Theatre Workshop'. Theatre Q. 3 (1973), 58–68.

26242 COPPIETERS (FRANK). 'Arnold Wesker's Centre 42: A Cultural Revolution Betrayed'. Theatre Q. 5 (1975), 37–54.

26243 EDGAR (DAVID). 'Ten Years of Political Theatre, 1968–1978'. Theatre Q. 8 (1979), 25–33.

26244 LAMBERT (JACK WALTER). Drama in Britain, 1964–1973. 1974.

26245 COLBY (DOUGLAS). As the Curtain Rises: On Contemporary British Drama, 1966–1976. 1978.

26246 HAYMAN (RONALD). The Set-Up: An Anatomy of the English Theatre Today. 1974.

26247 —— British Theatre since 1945: A Reassessment. Oxf. 1979.

26248 HOBSON (Sir HAROLD). Theatre in Britain: A Personal View. Oxf. 1984.

26249 GOORNEY (HOWARD). The Theatre Workshop Story. 1981.

26250 CROSSE (GORDON). Shakespearean Playgoing 1890–1952. 1953.

26251 TREWIN (JOHN COURTENAY). Shakespeare on the English Stage 1900–1964: A Survey of Productions. 1964.

26252 HARBEN (NILOUFER). Twentieth Century English History Plays: From Shaw to Bond. 1987.

26253 LAVER (JAMES). 'Costume Research in the Last Twenty One Years'. Theatre Notebook 21 (1966), 21–3.

26254 GOODWIN (JOHN) ed. British Theatre Design. 1989.

26255 MAY (FREDERICK). 'Drama in the Universities'. Univ. Q. (Feb. 1951), 155–61.

26256 WICKHAM (GLYNNE). 'The Study of Drama in the British Universities, 1945–1966'. Theatre Notebook 21 (1966), 15–21.

26257 MORLEY (SHERIDAN ROBERT). Review Copies: Plays and Players in London, 1970–1974. 1975.

26258 HART (OLIVE ELY). The Drama in Modern Wales: A Brief History of Welsh Playwriting from 1900 to the Present Day. Philadelphia, Pa. 1928.

26259 OWEN (MYRA). 'Theatre in Wales, 1946–1961'. Drama 61 (1961), 26–9.

26260 FINDLATER (RICHARD). Emlyn Williams. 1956.

26261 WILLIAMS (EMLYN). George: An Early Autobiography, 1905–1927. 1961.

26262 —— Emlyn: An Early Autobiography, 1927–1935. 1973.

26263 DALE-JONES (DON). Emlyn Williams. Card. 1979.

26264 SHERRIFFS (RONALD). 'Governmental Support to the Theatre in Great Britain'. Theatre Survey 6 (1965), 91–115.

26265 PICK (JOHN). The West End: Management and Snobbery. Eastbourne. 1983.

26266 MAROWITZ (CHARLES) and TRUSSLER (SIMON) eds. Theatre at Work: Playwrights and Productions in the Modern British Theatre. 1967.

17. COMEDY

26267 MAYER (DAVID). Annotated Bibliography of Pantomime and Guide to Study Sources. 1975.

26268 WILMUT (ROGER). Kindly Leave the Stage! The Story of Variety, 1919–1960. 1985.

26269 —— From Fringe to Flying Circus: Celebrating a Unique Generation of Comedy 1960–1980. 1980.

26270 WILMETH (DON B.). American and English Popular Entertainment. A Guide to Information Sources. Detroit, Mich. 1980.

26271 WILSON (ALBERT EDWARD). Christmas Pantomime: The Story of an English Institution. 1934.

26272 FROW (GERALD). "Oh, Yes it is!": A History of Pantomime. 1985.

26273 SHORT (ERNEST). Fifty Years of Vaudeville. 1946.

26274 BREWER (CHARLES). The Spice of Variety. 1948.

26275 MACQUEEN-POPE (W.). The Melodies Linger on: The Story of Music Hall. 1950.

26276 ROSE (CLARKSON). Beside the Seaside. 1960.

26277 MANDER (RAYMOND) and MITCHENSON (JOE). British Music Hall: A Story in Pictures. 1965.

26278 MACINNES (COLIN). Sweet Saturday Night. 1967.

26279 VAN DAMM (SHEILA). We Never Closed: The Windmill Story. 1967.

26280 MELLOR (G. J.). The Northern Music Hall. Newcastle upon Tyne. 1970.

26281 NATHAN (DAVID). The Laughtermakers: A Quest for Comedy. 1971.

26282 TOOK (BARRY). Laughter in the Air: An Informal History of British Radio Comedy. 2nd edn 1981.

26283 NOBBS (GEORGE). The Wireless Stars. Norwich. 1972.

26284 FISHER (JOHN). Funny Way to be a Hero. 1973.

26285 LOCKHART (HOWARD). On My Wavelength. Aberd. 1973.

26286 MACKIE (ALBERT D.). The Scotch Comedians from the Music Hall to Television. Edin. 1973.

26287 BUSBY (ROY). British Music Hall: An Illustrated Who's Who from 1850 to the Present Day. 1976.

26288 ACKROYD (PETER). Dressing up: Transvestism and Drag: The History of an Obsession. 1979.

26289 MIDWINTER (ERIC). Make 'em Laugh: Famous Comedians and their Worlds. 1979.

26290 CHESTER (CHARLIE). The Grand Order of Water Rats: A Legend of Laughter. 1984.

26291 HEWISON (ROBERT). Footlights: A Hundred Years Of Cambridge Comedy. 1983.

26292 —— Monty Python: The Case Against. 1981.

26293 PERRY (GEORGE). Life of Python. 1986.

26294 ASKEY (ARTHUR). Before Your Very Eyes. 1975.

26295 BARKER (ERIC). Steady, Barker! The Autobiography. 1956.

26296 BARKER (RONNIE). It's Hello from Him. 1988.

26297 BENTINE (MICHAEL). The Long Banana Skin. 1975.

26298 BOYCE (MAX). Max Boyce: His Songs and Poems. St Albans. 1976.

26299 BYGRAVES (MAX). 'I Wanna Tell You a Story!'. 1976.

26300 GEHRING (WES D.). Charlie Chaplin: A Bio-bibliography. Westport, Conn. 1983.

26301 LYONS (TIMOTHY J.). Charlie Chaplin: A Guide to References and Resources. 1979.

26302 HUFF (THEODORE). Charlie Chaplin. 1952.

26303 CHAPLIN (CHARLES). My Autobiography. 1964.

26304 ROBINSON (DAVID). Chaplin: His Life and Art. 1985.

26305 CHESTER (CHARLIE). The World is Full of Charlies: Recollections of a Lifetime in Show Business. 1974.

26306 CAMPBELL (DUNCAN) ed. Billy Connolly: The Authorised Version, Compiled and with an Introduction by Duncan Campbell. 1976.

26307 BILLINGTON (MICHAEL). How Tickled I am. A Celebration of Ken Dodd. 1977.

26308 EDWARDS (JIMMY). Take it from Me. 1953.

26309 FISHER (JOHN). What a Performance: The Life of Sid Field. 1975.

26310 FLANAGAN (BUD). My Crazy Life: The Autobiography. 1961.

26311 OWEN (MAUREEN). The Crazy Gang: A Personal Reminiscence. 1986.

26312 FLETCHER (CYRIL). Nice One Cyril: Being the Odd Odyssey and Anecdotage of a Comedian. 1978.

26313 RANDALL (ALAN) and SEATON (RAY). George Formby: A Biography. 1974.

26314 GREEN (HUGHIE). Opportunity Knocked. 1965.

26315 HANCOCK (Mrs FREDDIE) and NATHAN (DAVID). Hancock. 1969. Rev. edn 1986.

26316 WILMUT (ROGER). Tony Hancock: 'Artiste'. 1978.

26317 HANDLEY (TOMMY). Handley's Pages. 1938.

26318 KAVANAGH (TED). Tommy Handley. 1949.

26319 THE ITMA YEARS. 1974.

26320 WORSLEY (FRANCIS). 'ITMA' 1938–1948. 1948.

26321 SMITH (JOHN). The Benny Hill Story. 1988.

26322 HACKFORTH (NORMAN). Solo for Horne: The Biography of Kenneth Horne. 1976.

26323 HOUSTON (RENÉE). Don't Fence me in. 1974.

26324 HOWERD (FRANKIE). On the Way I Lost it. 1976.

26325 JEWEL (JIMMY). Three Times Lucky. 1982.

26326 UNDERWOOD (PETER). Life's A Drag! Danny La Rue & the Drag Scene. 1974.

26327 LAUDER (HARRY). Roamin' in the Gloamin'. 1928.

26328 IRVING (GORDON). Great Scot: The Life Story of Sir Harry Lauder, Legendary Laird of the Music Hall. 1968.

26329 EAST (JOHN M.). Max Miller: The Cheeky Chappie. 1977.

26330 SCUDAMORE (PAULINE). Spike Milligan: A Biography. 1985.

26331 BEHAN (DOMINIC). Milligan: The Life and Times of Spike Milligan. 1988.

26332 DONOVAN (PAUL). Dudley. 1988. [Moore.].

26333 MORECAMBE (GARY). Funny Man, Eric Morecambe. 1982.

26334 MORECAMBE (ERIC) and WISE (ERNIE). There's No Answer to that: An Autobiography with Help from Michael Freedland. 1981.

26335 OLIVER (VIC). Mr. Showbusiness: The Autobiography. 1954.

26336 PICKLES (WILFRID). Between You and Me. The Autobiography. 1949.

26337 —— Sometime . . . Never. 1951.

26338 RAY (TED). Raising the Laughs. 1952.

26339 WILSON (A. E.). Prime Minister of Mirth. The Biography of Sir George Robey. 1956.

26340 COTES (PETER). George Robey: 'The Darling of the Halls'. 1972.

26341 ROBEY (EDWARD). The Jester and the Court: Reminiscences. 1976.

26342 SECOMBE (*Sir* HARRY). Goon Abroad. 1982.

26343 —— Arias and Raspberrries. 1989.

26344 WALKER (ALEXANDER). Peter Sellers: The Authorised Biography. 1981.

26345 EVANS (PETER). Peter Sellers: The Mask behind the Mask. 1981.

26346 SHERRIN (NED). A Small Thing—Like an Earthquake— Memoirs. 1983.

26347 TRAIN (JACK). Up and Down the Line: The Autobiography. 1956.

26348 WALL (MAX) *and* FORD (PETER). The Fool on the Hill. 1975.

26349 WARNER (JACK). Jack of all Trades: An Autobiography. 1975.

26350 FREEDLAND (MICHAEL). Kenneth Williams: A Biography. 1989.

26351 CHIPPERFIELD (JIMMY). My Wild Life. 1975.

18. ANTHROPOLOGY

26352 KUPER (ADAM). Anthropology and Anthropologists: The Modern British School. 2nd edn 1983.

26353 ACKERMAN (ROBERT). J. G. Frazer: His Life and his Work. Camb. 1987.

26354 EVANS-PRITCHARD (E. E.). A Bibliography of the Writings of E. E. Evans-Pritchard. 1974.

26355 DOUGLAS (MARY). Edward Evans-Pritchard. 1980.

19. ARCHAEOLOGY

26356 HUDSON (KENNETH A.). A Social History of Archaeology: The British Experience. 1981.

26357 LONGWORTH (IAN) *and* CHERRY (JOHN). Archaeology in Britain since 1945. 1986.

26358 CRAWFORD (OSBERT GUY STANHOPE). Said and Done: The Autobiography of an Archaeologist. 1955.

26359 DANIEL (GLYN). Some Small Harvest. 1946.

26360 LEAKEY (LOUIS SEYMOUR BAZETT). By the Evidence: Memoirs 1932–1951. NY. 1974.

26361 COLE (SONIA). Leakey's Luck: The Life of Louis Seymour Bazett Leakey 1903–1972. 1975.

26362 WHITE (MULVEY MINA). Digging Up Adam: The Story of L.S.B. Leakey. NY. 1965.

26363 LEAKEY (MARY D.). Disclosing the Past. 1984.

26364 LEAKEY (RICHARD). One Life: An Autobiography. 1978.

26365 DROWER (M. S.). Flinders Petrie: A Life in Archaeology. 1985.

26366 HAWKES (JACQUETTA). Adventurer in Archaeology: The Biography of Sir Mortimer Wheeler. 1982.

26367 MILLER (RONALD). The Piltdown Man. 1972.

20. ASTRONOMY AND ASTRONOMERS

26368 HAINING (PETER). Eyewitness to the Galaxy: Britain's Contribution to Research in Space. 1985.

26369 HALE (GEORGE) ELLERY. The New Heavens. Lond./NY. 1922.

26370 MacPHERSON (HECTOR). Modern Astronomy: Its Rise and Progress. 1926.

26371 JEANS (*Sir* JAMES HOPWOOD). Problems of Cosmogony and Stellar Dynamics. Camb. 1919.

26372 —— Eos: Or the Wider Aspects of Cosmogony. 1928.

26373 —— The Mysterious Universe. Camb. 1930.

26374 —— The Stars in their Course. Camb. 1931.

26375 —— The Universe Around Us. Camb. 1944.

26376 —— The Growth of Physical Science. Camb. 1947.

26377 EDDINGTON (*Sir* ARTHUR STANLEY). The Internal Constitution of the Stars. Camb. 1926.

26378 —— The Expanding Universe. Camb. 1933.

26379 CHANDRASEKHAR (S.). Eddington: The Most Distinguished Astrophysicist of his Time. Camb. 1983.

26380 DOIG (PETER). A Concise History of Astronomy. 1951.

26381 PFEIFFER (JOHN). The Changing Universe: The Story of the New Astronomy. 1956.

26382 KING (HENRY CHARLES). The Background of Astronomy. 1957.

26383 HOYLE (*Sir* FRED). The Small World of Fred Hoyle: An Autobiography. 1986.

26384 —— The Nature of the Universe. Oxf. 1950.

26385 —— Astronomy. Garden City, NY. 1962.

26386 —— Of Men and Galaxies. Seattle, Wash. 1964.

26387 —— From Stonehenge to Modern Cosmology. San Francisco, Calif. 1972.

26388 HOYLE (*Sir* FRED) *and* WICKRAMSINGHE (CHANDRA). Lifecloud: The Origin of Life in the Universe. 1978.

26389 BLACKWELL (D. E.). The Future of Optical Astronomy. Oxf. 1962.

26390 TOULMIN (STEPHEN) *and* GOODFIELD (JUNE). The Fabric of the Heavens: The Development of Astronomy and Dynamics. 1961.

26391 PANNEKOEK (ANTONIE). A History of Astronomy. 1961.

26392 ARMITAGE (ANGUS). A Century of Astronomy. Lond./NY. 1950.

26393 RONAN (COLIN A.). Changing Views of the Universe. 1961.

26394 —— Their Majesties' Astronomers: A Survey of Astronomy in Britain between the Two Elizabeths. 1967.

26395 —— Astronomy: Illustrated Sources in History. Newton Abbot. 1973.

26396 MOORE (PATRICK). The Picture History of Astronomy. NY. 1961.

26397 —— Watchers of the Stars: The Scientific Revolution. NY. 1974.

26398 —— Man the Astronomer. 1973.

26399 —— The Development of Astronomical Thought. Edin. 1969.

26400 LOVELL (Sir ALFRED CHARLES BERNARD) and LOVELL (JOYCE). Discovering the Universe. 1963.

26401 LOVELL (Sir ALFRED CHARLES BERNARD), LOVELL (JOYCE), and MARGERISON (TOM) eds. The Explosion of Science: The Physical Universe. 1967.

26402 LOVELL (Sir ALFRED CHARLES BERNARD). Meteor Astronomy. 1954.

26403 —— The Exploration of Outer Space. 1961.

26404 —— Our Present Knowledge of the Universe. Manch. 1967.

26405 —— ed. Astronomy. Barking. 1970.

26406 —— The Origins and International Economics of Space Exploration. NY. 1973.

26407 —— Man's Relation to the Universe. San Francisco, Calif.. 1975.

26408 —— In the Centre of Immensities. 1978.

26409 BRINTON (HENRY). Measuring the Universe. 1962.

26410 KING (HENRY CHARLES). Exploration of the Universe: The Story of Astronomy. 1964.

26411 NORTH (JOHN D.). The Measure of the Universe: A History of Modern Cosmology. 1965.

26412 BEET (ERNEST A.). Astronomy Old and New. 1967.

26413 CALDER (NIGEL). Violent Universe: An Eye-Witness Account of the Commotion in Astronomy, 1968–9.

26414 KING (HENRY CHARLES). The History of the Telescope. 1955.

26415 ASPDEN (HAROLD). Modern Aether Science. Shampton. 1972.

26416 LOVELL (Sir ALFRED CHARLES BERNARD) and CLEGG (J. A.). Radio Astronomy. 1952.

26417 LOVELL (Sir ALFRED CHARLES BERNARD), CLEGG (J. A.), and HANBURY BROWN (R.). The Exploration of Space by Radio. 1957.

26418 BOK (BART J.). 'New Science of Radio Astronomy'. *Sci. Mthly* 80 (1955), 333–45.

26419 TAYLOR (GORDON RATTRAY). 'The Men with Long Eyes: Astronomical Revolution'. *Encounter* 39 (1967), 40–50.

26420 SOUTHWORTH (GEORGE C.). 'Early History of Radio-Astronomy'. *Sci. Mthly* 82 (1956), 55–66.

26421 JENNINGS (R. E.). 'The History of British Infrared Astronomy'. *Q. Jnl Roy. Astronom. Soc.* 27 (1986), 454–61.

26422 SAWARD (DUDLEY). Bernard Lovell: A Biography. 1984.

26423 LOVELL (Sir ALFRED CHARLES BERNARD). 'The Effects of Defence Science on the Advance of Astronomy'. *J. Hist. Astron. Soc.* 8 (1977), 151–73.

26424 —— 'The Early History of the Anglo-Australian 150 inch Telescope (AAT)'. *Q. J. Roy. Astronom. Soc.* 26 (1985), 393–495.

26425 —— 'The Emergence of Radio Astronomy in the UK after World War II'. *Q. J. Roy. Astronom. Soc.* 28 (1987), 1–9.

26426 —— The Story of Jodrell Bank. Lond./NY. 1968.

26427 —— Out of the Zenith: Jodrell Bank, 1957–70. 1973.

26428 —— The Jodrell Bank Telescopes. Oxf. 1985.

26429 HEY (J. S.). The Evolution of Radio Astronomy. 1973.

26430 EDGE (DAVID OWEN) and MULKAY (MICHAEL JOSEPH). Astronomy Transformed: The Emergence of Radio Astronomy in Britain. Lond./NY. 1976.

26431 WORVILLE (ROY). The Radio Universe: An Introduction to Radio Astronomy and Outer Space. 1977.

26432 NATIONAL MARITIME MUSEUM, GREENWICH. Man is not Lost: A Record of Two Hundred Years of Astronomical Navigation with the Nautical Almanac, 1767–1967. 1968.

26433 COTTER (CHARLES H.). A History of Nautical Astronomy. Lond./NY. 1968.

26434 —— 'Nautical Astronomy: Past, Present and Future'. *J. Navigation* 29 (1976), 334–40.

26435 MacPHERSON (HECTOR). Modern Cosmologies: A Historical Sketch of Researches and Theories Concerning the Structure of the Universe. 1929.

26436 McCREA (WILLIAM HUNTER). 'Cosmology—A Brief Review'. *Q. J. Roy. Astron. Soc.* 4 (1963), 185–202.

26437 NERLICH (GRAHAM). The Shape of Space. Camb. 1976.

26438 SINGH (JAGJIT). Modern Cosmology. Rev. edn Harmondsworth. 1970. First edn published as Great Ideas and Theories of Modern Cosmology. 1961.

26439 COWLING (T. G.). 'Mathematicians, Astrology and Cosmogony'. *Q. J. Roy. Astron. Soc.* 18 (1977), 199–212.

26440 EDGE (DAVID). 'The Sociology of Innovation in Modern Astronomy'. *Q. J. Roy. Astron. Soc.* 18 (1977), 326–39.

26441 WHITROW (GERALD JAMES). The Structure of the Universe: An Introduction to Cosmology. 1949.

26442 —— The Structure and Evolution of the Universe. Lond./NY. 1959.

26443 —— What is Time? 1972.

26444 —— Time, Gravitation and the Universe: The Evolution of Relativistic Theories. 1973.

26445 WHITTAKER (*Sir* EDMUND TAYLOR). The Beginning and End of the World. Durham. 1942.

26446 McCREA (WILLIAM HUNTER). 'The Royal Greenwich Observatory, 1675–1975: Some of its External Relations'. *Q. J. Roy. Astron. Soc.* 17 (1976), 4–24.

26447 —— Royal Greenwich Observatory: An Historical Review Issued on the Occasion of its Tercentenary. 1975.

26448 —— 'Three Hundred Years of Greenwich'. *Nature* 255 (1975), 581–606.

26449 TAYLOR (R. J.) *ed.* History of the Royal Astronomical Society vol. 2: 1920–1980. Oxf. 1987.

26450 KNOX-SHAW (H.). 'The Radcliffe Observatory'. *Vistas Astron.* 1 (1955), 144–9.

26451 KING (HENRY CHARLES). 'The Planetarium'. *Endeavour* 18 (1959), 35–44.

26452 BAROCAS (V.). 'The Preston Observatory'. *Physics Educ.* 8 (1973), 471–4.

26453 BEET (E. A.). 'The King's Observatory at Richmond'. *J. Brit. Astron. Ass.* (1977), 260–3.

21. BIOCHEMISTRY

26454 NEEDHAM (JOSEPH). A Chart to Illustrate the History of Biochemistry and Physiology. Camb. 1929.

26455 NEEDHAM (JOSEPH) *and* GREEN (D. E.) *eds.* Perspectives in Biochemistry: Thirty One Essays Presented to Sir F. G. Hopkins. Camb. 1937.

26456 BALDWIN (ERNEST HUBERT FRANCIS). The Nature of Biochemistry. 1962.

26457 BROOKS (C. M.) *and* CRANEFIELD (P. F.) *eds.* The Historical Development of Physiological Thought: A Symposium. NY. 1959.

26458 CLARK (BRIAN FREDERICK CARL). The Genetic Code. Lond. 1977.

26459 COHEN (*Baron*). Sherrington: Physiologist, Philosopher and Poet. Liverpool. 1958.

26460 GRANIT (RAGNAR). Charles Scott Sherrington: An Appraisal. Garden City, NY. 1967.

26461 CLARK (RONALD W.). The Life of Ernst Chain. 1985.

26462 KREBS (*Sir* HANS) *and* MARTIN (ANNE). Reminiscences and Reflections. Oxf. 1981.

26463 KREBS (*Sir* HANS). 'Some Facts of Life: Biology and Politics'. *Roy. Inst. Great Brit. Procs* 44 (1971), 169–84.

26464 NEEDHAM (JOSEPH) *and* BALDWIN (ERNEST HUBERT FRANCIS) *eds.* Hopkins and Biochemistry 1861–1947: Papers

Concerning Sir Frederick Gowland Hopkins, with a Foreword by A. C. Chibnall . . . a Commemoration Volume. 1949.

26465 FLORKIN (MARCEL). A History of Biochemistry. 1977.

26466 LEICESTER (HENRY M.). Development of Biochemical Concepts from Ancient to Modern Times. Camb., Mass. 1974.

26467 FRUTON (J. S.). Molecules and Life: Historical Essays on the Interplay of Chemistry and Biology. Lond./NY. 1972.

26468 —— Selected Bibliography of Biographical Data for the History of Biochemistry since 1800. Philadelphia, Pa. 1974.

26469 —— 'The Emergence of Biochemistry'. *Science* 192 (1976), 327–34.

26470 YOUNG (*Sir* FRANK GEORGE). 'Biochemistry in Retrospect and Prospect'. *J. Roy. Soc. Arts* 120 (1972), 298–307.

26471 TEICH (MIKULAS). 'The History of Modern Biochemistry: The Second Phase c.1920–1940/45'. *Actes XIIe Cong. Int. Hist. Sci.* 8 (1968–pub. 1971), 199–203.

26472 MORTON (RICHARD ALAN). 'Biochemistry at Liverpool 1902–1971'. *Medic. Hist.* 16 (1972), 321–53.

26473 GLASS (JUSTINE). The Earth Heals Everything: The Story of Biochemistry. 1964.

26474 GOODWIN (TREVOR W.) *ed.* British Biochemistry Past and Present: Biochemical Society Symposium No. 30, Held in London, December 1969. 1970.

26475 —— History of the Biochemistry Society 1911–1986. 1987.

26476 NEEDHAM (JOSEPH) *ed.* The Chemistry of Life: Eight Lectures on the History of Biochemistry. Camb. 1970.

26477 OLBY (ROBERT). The Path to the Double Helix. Foreword by Francis Crick. 1974.

26478 SMELLIE (ROBERT MARTIN STUART). A Matter of Life— DNA. Edin. 1969.

26479 WATSON (JAMES DEWEY). The Double Helix: A Personal Account of the Discovery of the Structure of DNA. Lond./NY. 1968. New edn 1981.

26480 HOAGLAND (MAHLON). Discovery: The Search for DNA's Secrets. Boston, Mass. 1981.

26481 WATSON (JAMES D.) *and* TOOZE (JOHN). The DNA Story: A Documentary History of Gene Cloning. San Francisco, Calif. 1981.

26482 KOHLER (ROBERT E.). From Medical Chemistry to Biochemistry: The Making of a Biomedical Discipline. Camb. 1982.

26483 —— 'Walter Fletcher, F. G. Hopkins and the Dunn Institute of Biochemistry: A Case Study in the Patronage of Science'. *Isis* 69 (1978), 318–53.

26484 —— 'The Enzyme Theory and the Origin of Biochemistry'. *Isis* 64 (1973), 181–96.

22. BIOLOGY AND BIOLOGISTS

26485 BESTERMAN (THEODORE). Biological Sciences: A Bibliography of Bibliographies. Totowa, NJ 1972.

26486 BOWLER (PETER J.). Theories of Human Evolution: A Century of Debate, 1844–1944. Oxf. 1986.

26487 THOMSON (*Sir* JOHN ARTHUR). The Control of Life. 1921.

26488 —— What is Man? 1923.

26489 —— The Gospel of Evolution. 1925.

26490 DRONAMRAJU (KRISHNA R.) *ed.* Haldane and Modern Biology. Baltimore, Md./Lond. 1968.

26491 —— Haldane: The Life and Work of J. B. S. Haldane with Special Reference to India. Aberd. 1985.

26492 HALDANE (JOHN BURDON SANDERSON). Adventures of a Biologist. NY. 1940.

26493 CLARK (RONALD W.) J. B. S.: The Life and Work of J. B. S. Haldane. 1968.

26494 JONES (GRETA). Science, Politics and the Cold War. 1988.

26495 —— 'British Scientists, Lysenko and the Cold War'. *Econ. and Soc.* 8 (1979), 26–58.

26496 PAUL (DIANE B.). 'A War on Two Fronts: J. B. S. Haldane and the Response to Lysenkoism in Britain'. *J. Hist. Biol.* 16 (1986), 1–37.

26497 MITCHISON (NAOMI). 'The Haldanes: Personal Notes and Historical Lessons'. *Roy. Inst. Great Brit. Procs* 47 (1974), 1–21.

26498 HALDANE (JOHN SCOTT). The Philosophical Basis of Biology. 1931.

26499 —— The Philosophy of a Biologist. 1933.

26500 HUXLEY (*Sir* JULIAN SORELL). Essays of a Humanist. 1964.

26501 CLARK (RONALD W.). The Huxleys. 1967.

26502 HUXLEY (*Sir* JULIAN SORELL). Memories vol. 1 1970. Vol. 2 1973.

26503 BAKER (J. R.). Julian Huxley: Scientist and World Citizen: A Biographical Memoir. Paris. 1978.

26504 WERSKEY (PAUL GARY). 'Haldane and Huxley: First Appraisals'. *J. Hist. Biol.* 4 (1971), 171–83.

26505 WHITE (M. J. D.). 'The Infinite Variety of Haldane'. *Science* 164 (1969), 678–80.

26506 MEDAWAR (*Sir* PETER). Memoir of a Thinking Radish. Oxf. 1986.

26507 ROTHSCHILD (MIRIAM). Dear Lord Rothschild: Birds, Butterflies and History. 1983.

26508 KOESTLER (ARTHUR) *and* SMYTHIES (JOHN R.) *eds.* The Alpbach Symposium, 1968: Beyond Reductionism: New Perspectives in the Life Sciences. 1969.

26509 KORNBERG (*Sir* HANS LEO). The Unity of Life. Leics. 1962.

26510 GUNTHER (ALBERT E.). William Carmichael McIntosh MD, FRS of St Andrews, 1838–1931: A Pioneer of Marine Biology. Edin. 1977.

26511 THOMPSON (D'ARCY R.). D'Arcy Wentworth Thompson: The Scholar-Naturalist 1860–1948. 1958.

26512 FRANK (ROBERT G.) *Jnr.* 'The A. V. Hill Papers at Churchill College, Cambridge'. *J. Hist. Biol.* 9 (1978), 211–14.

26513 DAWES (B.). A Hundred Years of Biology. 1952.

26514 BODENHEIMER (F. S.). The History of Biology: An Introduction. 1958.

26515 ZUCKERMAN (SOLLY) *Baron, ed.* Classics in Biology: A Course of Selected Readings by Authorities: With an Introductory Reading Guide. NY. 1960.

26516 CROW (WILLIAM BERNARD). A Synopsis of Biology. Bristol. 1960.

26517 TAYLOR (GORDON RATTRAY). The Science of Life: A Picture History of Biology. 1963.

26518 HANDLER (PHILIP) *ed.* Biology and the Future of Man. 1970.

26519 FULLER (WATSON) *ed.* The Social Impact of Modern Biology. 1971.

26520 RUSE (MICHAEL). The Philosophy of Biology. 1973.

26521 BUTLER (JOHN ALFRED VALENTINE). Science and Human Life: Successes and Limitation. 1957.

26522 —— Modern Biology and its Human Implications. 1976.

26523 ALLEN (GARLAND E.). Life Science in the Twentieth Century. NY. 1975. Camb. 1978.

26524 MAGNER (LOIS N.). A History of the Life Sciences. NY. 1979.

26525 GARDINER (J. S.) *and* TANSLEY (A. G.). The Natural History of Wicken Fen. Camb. 1923–32.

26526 FITTER (R. S. R.). London's Natural History. 1945.

26527 BEEBE (W.). The Book of Naturalists: An Anthology of the best Natural History. NY. 1944.

26528 ALLEN (DAVID ELLISTON). The Naturalist in Britain: A Social History. 1976. Harmondsworth. 1978.

26529 —— 'Natural History and Social History'. *J. Soc. Bibliogr. Nat. Hist.* 7 (1976), 509–16.

26530 WILLIAMS (E. G.). The Chester Society of Natural Science. Chester. 1977.

26531 SHERBORN (CHARLES DAVIES) *comp.* Where is the—Collection? An Account of the Various Natural History Collections which Have Come under the Notice of the Compiler. Camb. 1940.

26532 PERRY (RICHARD). A Naturalist on Lindisfarne. 1946.

26533 HUTCHINSON (A. LESLIE). Botany, Birds, Bugs and Barrows on the Isle of Wight: The Jubilee History of the Isle of Wight Natural History and Archaeological Society, 1919–69. Newport. 1970.

26534 GODDARD (T. RUSSELL). History of the Natural History Society of Northumberland, Durham and Newcastle upon Tyne, 1829–1929. Newcastle. 1929.

23. BOTANY

26535 TURRILL (W. B.) *ed.* Vistas in Botany: A Volume in Honour of the Bicentenary of the Royal Botanic Gardens, Kew. Lond./NY. 1959.

26536 DANIELS (GILBERT S.). Artists from the Royal Botanic Gardens, Kew. Pittsburgh, Pa. 1974.

26537 FLETCHER (HAROLD R.) *and* BROWN (WILLIAM H.). The Royal Botanic Garden, Edinburgh, 1670–1970. Edin. 1970.

26538 RATTER (J. A.). 'Three Hundred Years of Botany in Edinburgh'. *Nature* 226 (1970), 904–7.

26539 GAGER (C. STUART). 'Botanic Gardens of the World: Materials for a History'. 2nd edn *Brooklyn Bot. Gard. Rec.* 27 (1938), 151–406.

26540 DARLINGTON (C. D.). 'The Oxford Botanic Gardens: 1621–1971'. *Nature* 233 (1971), 455–6.

26541 BALLARD (PHILLADA). An Oasis of Delight: The History of Birmingham Botanical Gardens. 1983.

26542 GAGE (A. T.). A History of the Linnean Society of London. 1938. It has been added to by W. T. Stearn as A Bicentenary History of the Linnean Society of London. 1988.

26543 ALLEN (DAVID ELLISTON). The Botanists: A History of the Botanical Society of the British Isles through One Hundred and Fifty Years. 1986.

26544 FLETCHER (HAROLD R.). The Story of the Royal Horticultural Society, 1804–1968. 1969.

26545 International Address Book of Botanists: Being a Dictionary of Individuals and Scientific Institutions, Universities, Societies etc. in all Parts of the World Interested in the Study of Botany. Camb. 1931.

26546 BRITTEN (JAMES), BOULGER (GEORGE S.), *and* RENDLE (A. B.). A Bibliographical Index of Deceased British and Irish Botanists. 1931.

26547 BOWER (FREDERICK ORPEN). Sixty Years of Botany in Britain (1875–1935): Impressions of an Eye Witness. Lond./NY. 1938.

26548 GILMOUR (JOHN). British Botanists. 1944.

26549 DESMOND (RAY). Dictionary of British and Irish Botanists and Horticulturalists, Including Plant Collectors and Botanical Artists, with Historical Introduction by William T. Stearn. 1977.

26550 BOR (ELEANOR). Adventures of a Botanist's Wife. 1952.

26551 JAMES (WILLIAM OWEN). Botany—Here and Now. 1959.

26552 STEER (WILLIAM CAMPBELL) *ed.* Fifty Years of Botany. NY. 1958.

26553 COATS (ALICE M.). The Quest for Plants: A History of the Horticultural Explorers. 1969.

26554 CLOKIE (H. N.). An Account of the Herbaria of the Department of Botany in the University of Oxford. 1964.

26555 WALTERS (S. M.). The Shaping of Cambridge Botany: A Short History of Whole-Plant Botany in Cambridge from the Time of Ray into the Present Century. Camb. 1981.

26556 GODWIN (*Sir* HARRY). Cambridge and Clare. Camb. 1985.

26557 MILLER (EDWIN C.). 'Forty Years of Plant Physiology: Some General Impressions'. *Science* 97 (1943), 315–19.

26558 BLUNT (WILFRID) *with the assistance of W. T. Stearn*. The Art of Botanical Illustration. 1950. 4th edn 1967.

26559 GILBERT-CARTER (H.). Glossary of the British Flora. Camb. 1950.

26560 SALMON (CHARLES EDGAR). Flora of Surrey. 1931.

26561 HORWOOD (ARTHUR REGINALD) *and* GAINSBOROUGH (CHARLES WILLIAM FRANCIS NOEL) *Earl of*. The Flora of Leicestershire and Rutland: A Topographical, Ecological and Historical Account, with Biographies of Former Botanists (1620–1933). 1933.

26562 MILNE-REDHEAD (E.) *ed.* The Conservation of British Flora. 1963.

26563 TURRILL (W. B.). British Plant Life. 1948. 3rd edn 1962.

26564 GRIGSON (GEOFFREY). A Dictionary of English Plant Names. 1974.

26565 COWAN (MAY). Inverewe: A Garden in the North West Highlands. 1964.

24. CLASSICAL SCHOLARSHIP

26566 WOOD (HERBERT GEORGE). Terrot Reaveley Glover: A Biography. Camb. 1953.

26567 MURRAY (GEORGE GILBERT AIMÉ). An Unfinished Autobiography, with Contributions by his Friends. *ed.* by Jean Smith and Arnold Toynbee. 1960.

26568 LLOYD JONES ([PETER] HUGH [JEFFERD]). 'Gilbert Murray'. *American Scholar* 51 (1981–2), 55–72.

26569 WEST (FRANCIS). Gilbert Murray: A Life. 1984.

26570 WILSON (*Sir* DUNCAN). Gilbert Murray OM 1855–1957. Oxf. 1987.

26571 LLOYD JONES (HUGH). Blood for Ghosts: Classical Influence in the Nineteenth and Twentieth Centuries. 1982.

26572 LLOYD JONES (HUGH) *ed.* Maurice Bowra: A Celebration. 1974.

25. ECONOMICS AND ECONOMISTS

26573 STURGES (PAUL) *and* STURGES (CLAIRE) *eds.* Who's Who in British Economics: A Dictionary of Economists in Higher Education, Business and Government. Aldershot. 1990.

26574 STURGES (R. P.). Economists' Papers 1750–1950: A Guide to Archives and other Manuscript Sources for the History of British and Irish Economic Thought. 1975.

26575 O'BRIEN (DENIS PATRICK) *and* PRESLEY (JOHN R.) *eds.* Pioneers of Modern Economics. 1981.

26576 COATS (A. W.) *and* COATS (S. E.). 'The Changing Social Composition of the Royal Economic Society, 1890–1960 and the Professionalization of British Economics'. *Brit. J. Sociol.* 24 (1973), 165–87.

26577 BOOTH (A. E.) *and* COATS (A. W.). 'The Market for Economists in Britain 1944–1975'. *Econ. J.* 88 (1978), 436–54.

26578 SHACKLE (GEORGE LENNOX SHARMAN). The Years of High Theory: Invention and Tradition in Economic Thought, 1926–1939. Camb. 1967.

26579 GILBERT (CHRISTOPHER L.). The Development of British Econometrics 1945–85. Oxf. 1986.

26580 CAIRNCROSS (*Sir* ALEXANDER KIRKLAND) *ed.* The Robert Hall Diaries. Vol. 1. 1947–53. Vol. 2 1954–61. 1989–90.

26581 —— *ed. and* WATTS (NINA). The Economic Section 1939–61: A Study in Economic Advising. 1989.

26582 POLLITT (BRIAN) *and* McFARLANE (BRUCE) *eds.* Selected Papers of Maurice Dobb. 2 vols. 1986.

26583 BUTLER (EAMONN). Hayek: His Contribution to the Political and Economic Thought of our Time. 1983.

26584 MACHLUP (FRITZ) *ed.* Essays on Hayek. 1977.

26585 HOBSON (JOHN ATKINSON) *et al.* Some Aspects of Recent British Economics. 1923.

26586 BRAILSFORD (HENRY NOEL). The Life-Work of J. A. Hobson. 1948.

26587 MITCHELL (HARVEY). 'Hobson Revisited'. *J. Hist. Ideas* 26 (1965), 397–416.

26588 HOBSON (JOHN ATKINSON). Confessions of an Economic Heretic. 1938. Reissued Brighton. 1976.

26589 ALLETT (JOHN). The New Liberalism: The Political Economy of J. A. Hobson. Toronto/Lond. 1981.

26590 MOGGRIDGE (DONALD EDWARD) *and* ROBINSON (EDWARD AUSTIN GOSSAGE) *eds.* The Collected Writings of John Maynard Keynes. 30 vols. 1971–88.

26591 SKIDELSKY (ROBERT JACOB ALEXANDER). John Maynard Keynes: Hopes Betrayed, 1883–1920. 1983.

26592 HARROD (*Sir* ROY). The Life of John Maynard Keynes. 1951.

26593 HESSION (CHARLES H.). John Maynard Keynes. 1984.

26594 MANTOUX (ÉTIENNE). The Carthaginian Peace: Or the Economic Consequences of Mr. Keynes. 1946.

26595 LEKACHMAN (ROBERT). The Age of Keynes. 1969.

26596 HARRIS (SEYMOUR EDWIN). John Maynard Keynes: Economist and Policy Maker. 1955.

26597 MURAD (ANATOL). What Keynes Means: A Critical Clarification of the Economic Theories of John Maynard Keynes. NY. 1962.

26598 MOGGRIDGE (DONALD EDWARD). Keynes. 1976. 2nd edn 1980.

26599 KEYNES (MILO) *ed.* Essays on John Maynard Keynes. 1951.

26600 WARNER (M.). 'The Webbs, Keynes and the Economic Problem in the Inter-War Years'. *Pol. Studs* 14 (1966), 81–6.

26601 CLARKE (PETER F.). The Keynesian Revolution in the Making, 1924–36. Oxf. 1988.

26602 STEWART (MICHAEL JAMES). Keynes and After. 1967.

26603 ROBINSON (EDWARD AUSTIN GOSSAGE). 'John Maynard Keynes: Economist, Author, Statesman'. *Econ. J.* 82 (1972), 531–46.

26604 HICKS (*Sir* JOHN RICHARD). The Crisis in Keynesian Economics. Oxf. 1974.

26605 WORSWICK (GEORGE DAVID NORMAN) *and* TREVITHICK (JAMES) *eds.* Keynes and the Modern World. Camb. 1983.

26606 JOHNSON (ELIZABETH) *and* JOHNSON (HARRY G.). The Shadow of Keynes: Understanding Keynes, Cambridge and Keynesian Economics. Oxf. 1978.

26607 SKIDELSKY (ROBERT JACOB ALEXANDER) *ed.* The End of the Keynesian Era. 1977.

26608 HARCOURT (G. C.) *ed.* Keynes and his Contemporaries. 1985.

26609 THIRLWALL (ANTHONY PHILIP) *ed.* Keynes as a Policy Adviser. 1982.

26610 PATINKIN (DON). Keynes's Monetary Thought. Durham, NC. 1976.

26611 PATINKIN (DON) *and* LEITH (J. CLARK) *eds.* Keynes, Cambridge and the *General Theory*. 1977.

26612 MOGGRIDGE (DONALD EDWARD) *and* HOWSON (SUSAN). 'Keynes on Monetary Policy, 1910–1946'. *Oxf. Econ. Papers* 26 (1974), 226–47.

26613 KAHN (RICHARD F.). 'On Re-reading Keynes'. *Procs Brit. Acad.* (1975), 361–91.

26614 KAHN (RICHARD F.). The Making of Keynes's General Theory. Camb. 1984.

26615 GILLMAN (JOSEPH MOSES). 'An Evaluation of John Maynard Keynes'. *Science and Society* xix (1955), 107–33.

26616 BLEANEY (M.). The Rise and Fall of Keynesian Economics. 1985.

26617 MacDOUGALL (*Sir* DONALD). Don & Mandarin: Memoirs of an Economist. 1987.

26618 ROBBINS (LIONEL CHARLES) *Baron*. Autobiography of an Economist. 1971. Against Inflation: Speeches in the Second Chamber 1965–1977. 1979.

26619 O'BRIEN (DENNIS PATRICK). Lionel Robbins. 1982.

26620 GRAM (HARVEY) *and* WALSH (VIVIAN). 'Joan Robinson's Economics in Retrospect'. *J. Econ. Lit.* 21 (1983), 518–50.

26621 JONES (JAMES HARRY). Josiah Stamp: Public Servant. 1964.

26. GEOGRAPHY

26622 BREWER (J. GORDON) *ed.* The Literature of Geography: A Guide to its Organisation and Use. 1973. 2nd edn 1978.

26623 GODDARD (STEPHEN) *ed.* A Guide to Information Sources in the Geographical Sciences. 1983.

26624 MILL (HUGH ROBERT). Record of the Royal Geographical Society, 1830–1930. 1930.

26625 BRIGHAM (ALBERT PERRY). 'The Centenary of the Royal Geographical Society'. *Geog. Rev.* (1931), 142–5.

26626 CLOSE (CHARLES). 'Addresses on the History of the Royal Geographical Society at the Centenary Meeting, Oct 21st'. *Geog. J.* 76 (1930), 455–76.

26627 CRONE (GERALD ROE). The Royal Geographical Society: A Record, 1931–1955. 1955.

26628 CAMERON (IAN). To the Farthest Ends of the Earth: The History of the Royal Geographical Society, 1830–1980. 1980.

26629 STEEL (ROBERT WALTER). The Institute of British Geographers: The First Fifty Years. 1984.

26630 FREEMAN (THOMAS WALTER). A History of Modern British Geography. 1980.

26631 —— One Hundred Years of Geography. 1961.

26632 —— The Geographer's Craft. Manch./NY. 1967.

26633 BAKER (JOHN NORMAN LEONARD). The History of Geography. Oxf. 1963.

26634 CLARKE (JOHN INNES). Population Geography. Oxf. 1963.

26635 CRONE (GERALD ROE). Background to Geography. 1964.

26636 —— Background to Political Geography. 1967.

26637 HOUSE (JOHN WILLIAM). The Frontiers of Geography. Newcastle upon Tyne. 1965.

26638 MINSHULL (ROGER). Regional Geography: Theory and Practice. 1967.

26639 HARVEY (DAVID). Explanation in Geography. 1969.

26640 COOKE (RONALD URWICK) *and* JOHNSON (JAMES HENRY) *eds.* Trends in Geography: An Introductory Survey. Oxf. 1969.

26641 MINSHULL (ROGER). The Changing Nature of Geography. 1970.

26642 BAKER (ALAN REGINALD HAROLD) *ed.* Progress in Historical Geography. Newton Abbot. 1972.

26643 BROWN (ERIC HERBERT) *ed.* Geography Yesterday and Tomorrow. Oxf. 1980.

26644 STEEL (ROBERT WALTER) *ed.* British Geography, 1918–1945. Camb. 1987.

26645 CRONE (GERALD ROE). 'British Geography in the Twentieth Century'. *Geog. J.* 125 (1964), 197–220.

26646 FITZGERALD (WALTER). 'Progress in Geographical Method'. *Nature* 153 (1944), 481–3.

26647 KELTIE (JOHN SCOTT). 'A Half Century of Geographical Progress'. *Scot. Geog. Mag.* 31 (1915), 617–36.

26648 MACKINDER (*Sir* HALFORD JOHN). 'Progress of Geography in the Field and in the Study during the Reign of His Majesty King George the Fifth'. *Geog. J.* 86 (1935), 1–12.

26649 STAMP (*Sir* LAURENCE DUDLEY) *and* WOOLDRIGE (SIDNEY WILLIAM) *eds.* London Essays in Geography. 1951.

26650 TAYLOR (GRIFFITH) *ed.* Geography in the Twentieth Century: A Study of Growth, Fields, Techniques, Aims and Trends. A Symposium by Twenty-two Authors from Canada, the United States, England, Czechoslovakia and Poland. 2nd edn NY./Lond. 1953.

26651 JOHNSTON (RONALD JOHN) *and* CLAVAL (P.). Geography since the Second World War. 1984.

26652 JOHNSTON (RONALD JOHN). Geography and Geographers: Anglo-American Human Geography since 1945. 3rd edn 1987.

26653 GRAVES (NORMAN JOHN) *ed.* New Movements in the Study and teaching of Geography. 1972.

26654 DICKINSON (ROBERT ERIC) *and* HOWARTH (OSBERT JOHN RADCLIFFE). The Making of Geography. Oxf. 1933.

26655 DICKINSON (ROBERT ERIC). The Makers of Modern Geography. 1969.

26656 —— The Regional Concept: The Anglo-American Leaders. 1976.

26657 CRONE (GERALD ROE). Modern Geographers: An Outline of Progress in Geography since AD 1800. Rev. edn 1970.

26658 GILBERT (EDMUND WILLIAM). British Pioneers in Geography. Newton Abbot. 1972.

26659 —— Sir Halford Mackinder, 1861–1947: An Appreciation of his Life and Work. 1961.

26660 PARKER (WILLIAM HENRY). Mackinder: Geography as an Aid to Statecraft. Oxf. 1982.

26661 WISE (MICHAEL JOHN) *and* RAWSTRON (ERIC MITCHELL) *eds.* R. O. Buchanan and Economic Geography. 1973.

26662 GOUDIE (ANDREW SHAW). 'Vaughan Cornish: Geographer: with a Bibliography of his Published Works'. *Trans. Inst. Brit. Geog.* 55 (1972), 1–16.

26663 EDWARDS (KENNETH CHARLES). 'Sixty Years after Herbertson: The Advance of Geography as a Spatial Science'. *Geog.* 59 (1974), 1–9.

26664 WHITTOW (JOHN BYRON) *and* WOOD (PETER DENIS) *eds.* Essays in Geography for Austin Miller. Reading. 1965.

26665 MILLER (RONALD) *and* WATSON (JAMES WREFORD) *eds.* Geographical Essays in Memory of Alan G. Ogilvie. 1959.

26666 REEVES (EDWARD AYEARST). The Recollections of a Geographer. 1935.

26667 INSTITUTE OF BRITISH GEOGRAPHERS: Special Publications No. 1. Land Use and Resources: Studies in Applied Geography; a Memorial Volume to Sir Dudley Stamp. 1968.

26668 BOWEN (EMRYS GEORGE). Geography, Culture and Habitat: Selected Essays (1925–1975) of E. G. Bowen, Selected and Introduced by Harold Carter and Wayne Davies. Llandyssul. 1976.

26669 ROBINSON (G.) *and* PATTEN (JOHN). 'Edmund W. Gilbert and the Development of Historical Geography with a Bibliography of his Work'. *J. Hist. Geog.* 6 (1980), 409–19.

26670 HODGSON (H. B.). 'Notes on the History of the Teaching of Geography'. *Geog.* 22 (1937), 44–8.

26671 CLARK (ROSE B.). 'Geography in the Schools of Europe'. In Isaiah Bowman. Geography in Relation to the Social Sciences. NY. 1934.

26672 STAMP (*Sir* JOSIAH). 'Geography and Economic Theory'. *Geog.* 22 (1937), 1–14.

26673 FREEMAN (THOMAS WALTER). Geography and Planning. 1958.

26674 BOWEN (EMRYS GEORGE). Geography at Aberystwyth: Essays Written on the Occasion of the Departmental Jubilee 1917–18—1967–68. Card. 1968.

26675 STEEL (ROBERT WALTER) *and* LAWTON (RICHARD) *eds.* Liverpool Essays in Geography: A Jubilee Collection. 1967.

26676 LEWIS (E. W.). 'Development of Geography in the Polytechnics of England and Wales'. *Geog. J.* 139 (1973), 509–15.

26677 MILLER (RONALD) *and* TIVY (JOY) *eds.* The Glasgow Region: A General Survey. Prepared for . . . the British Association. Glasg. 1958.

26678 RICHARDSON (C.). A Geography of Bradford. 1976.

26679 BELSHAW (DERYKE GERALD ROSTEN). The Changing Economic Geography of the Merthyr Valley. Merthyr Tydfil. 1956.

26680 SMITH (WILFRED). Economic Geography of Great Britain. 1949. 2nd edn 1953.

26681 GREEN (FRANK HENRY WINN). 'Recent Changes in Land Use and Treatment'. *Geog. J.* 142 (1976), 12–26.

26682 MONKHOUSE (FRANCIS JOHN). The Material Resources of Britain: An Economic Geography of the United Kingdom. 1971.

26683 STAMP (*Sir* LAURENCE DUDLEY). The Land of Britain. 1948.

26684 STAMP (*Sir* LAURENCE DUDLEY) *and* BEAVER (STANLEY HENRY). The British Isles: A Geographic and Economic Survey. 6th edn 1971.

26685 CHISHOLM (MICHAEL). Human Geography: Evolution or Revolution? Harmondsworth. 1975.

26686 CHISHOLM (MICHAEL) *and* RODGERS (BRIAN) *eds.* Studies in Human Geography. 1973.

26687 WATSON (JAMES WREFORD) *and* SISSONS (JOHN BRIAN) *eds.* The British Isles: A Systematic Geography. 1964.

26688 JONES (EMRYS) *and* EYLES (JOHN). An Introduction to Social Geography. Oxf. 1977.

26689 EYRE (SAMUEL ROBERT) *and* JONES (GLANVILLE REES JEFFREYS) *eds.* Geography as Human Ecology: Methodology by Example. 1966.

Cartography

26690 FORDHAM (HERBERT GEORGE). Hand-List of Catalogues and Works of Reference Relating to Carto-Bibliography and Kindred Subjects for Great Britain and Ireland, 1720–1927. Camb. 1928.

26691 —— The Evolution of the Maps of the British Isles. Address Delivered in the Whitworth Hall of the University of Manch., January 26 1923. Manch. 1923.

26692 —— Maps: Their History, Characteristics and Uses: A Handbook for Teachers. Camb. 1923.

26693 SHEPPARD (T.). 'The Evolution of (British) Topographical and Geological Maps'. British Association. 1920. 391–405.

26694 SOMERVILLE (HENRY BOYLE TOWNSHEND). The Chart Makers. 1928.

26695 EDWARDS (FRANCIS). Ancient Geography: A Catalogue of Atlases and Maps of all Parts of the World from the xv Century to the Present Day. 1929.

26696 HINKS (ARTHUR ROBERT). Maps and Survey. Camb. 1933.

26697 COWAN (WILLIAM). The Maps of Edinburgh 1544–1929. Second rev. edn with Census of Copies in Edinburgh Libraries by Charles B. Boog Watson. 1932.

26698 CLOSE (CHARLES FREDERICK). The Map of England, or about England, with an Ordnance Map. 1932.

26699 PHILIP (GEORGE). The Story of the Last Hundred Years: A Geographical Record, 1834–1934. 1934.

26700 JERVIS (WALTER WILLSON). The World in Maps: A Study in Map Evolution. 1936.

26701 LYNAM (EDWARD WILLIAM O'FLAHERTY). British Maps and Mapmakers. 1945.

26702 BROWN (LLOYD A.). The Story of Maps. 1949.

26703 CRONE (GERALD ROE). Maps and Their Makers: An Introduction to the History of Cartography. 1953.

26704 BERESFORD (MAURICE WARWICK). History on the Ground: Six Studies in Maps and Landscapes. 1957.

26705 DEBENHAM (FRANK). The World is Round: The Story of Man and Maps. 1959.

26706 ROYAL SOCIETY OF LONDON: British National Committee for Geography: Cartographic Activity in Great Britain. Report Two. Prepared by the Cartography Subcommittee of the British National Committee for Geography. 1964.

26707 GREAT BRITAIN, ORDNANCE SURVEY. The History of Triangulation of Great Britain, 1935–1962. Written and Compiled by the Officers of the Department under the Authority of the Director-General of the Ordnance Survey. 1967.

26708 HOWSE (DEREK) *and* SANDERSON (MICHAEL). The Sea Chart: An Historical Survey Based on the Collections in the National Maritime Museum, with an Introduction by G.S. Ritchie. Newton Abbot/NY. 1973.

26709 GARDINER (LESLIE). Bartholomew: 150 Years. Edin. 1976.

26710 —— One Hundred Years of Map-Making: The Story of W. & A. K Johnston. Edin. 1925.

26711 HARDY (GEORGE ALFRED). 'Ordnance Survey 1: 50000 Map Series'. *Geog. J.* 140 (1974), 275–83.

26712 HARLEY (J. B.). Ordnance Survey Maps: A Descriptive Manual. 1975.

26713 BLACKSELL (MARK). 'Reformed England and Wales'. *Geog. Mag.* 46 (1974), 235–6.

26714 BRICKER (CHARLES). Landmarks of Mapmaking: An Illustrated Survey of Maps and Mapmakers. Oxf. 1976.

26715 MacLEOD (M. N.). 'The Evolution of British Cartography'. *Endeavour* 3 (1944), 62–7.

26716 TOOLEY (RONALD VERE). Maps and Mapmakers. 1949.

26717 LYNAM (EDWARD WILLIAM O'FLAHERTY). The Mapmaker's Art: Essays on the History of Maps. Lond./NY. 1953.

26718 BALDOCK (E. D.). 'Milestones of Mapping'. *Cartographer* 3 (1966), 89–102.

26719 ROBINSON (ADRIAN H. W.) *and* WALLWORK (KENNETH L.). Map Studies, with Related Field Excursions. 1970.

26720 DICKINSON (GORDON CAWOOD). Maps and Air Photographs. 1969. 2nd edn. 1979.

27. HISTORIANS AND THE DISCIPLINE OF HISTORY

26721 WATSON (CHARLES A.). The Writing of History in Britain: A Bibliography of Post-1945 Writings about British Historians and Biographers. NY. 1982.

26722 RICHARDSON (R. C.). The Study of History: A Bibliographical Guide. Manch. 1988.

26723 GOLDSTEIN (DORA S.). 'The Organizational Development of the British Historical Profession, 1884–1921'. *Bull. Inst. Hist. Res.* 55 (1982), 180–93.

26724 HARCUP (SARA E.). Historical, Archaeological and Kindred Societies in the British Isles: A List. 1965.

26725 STIEG (MARGARET F.). The Origin and Development of Scholarly Historical Periodicals. Birm., Ala. 1986.

26726 KENYON (JOHN PHILIPPS). The History Men: The Historical Profession in England since the Renaissance. 1983.

26727 HALE (*Sir* JOHN RIGBY) *ed.* The Evolution of British Historiography from Bacon to Namier. 1967.

26728 STERN (FRITZ) *ed.* The Varieties of History from Voltaire to the Present. 1956. 2nd edn 1970.

26729 ELTON (*Sir* GEOFFREY RUDOLPH) *comp.* Modern Historians on British History 1485–1945: A Critical Bibliography, 1945–1969. 1970.

26730 CANNON (JOHN ASHTON) *ed.* The Historian at Work. 1980.

26731 CANNON (JOHN ASHTON), DAVIS (RALPH HENRY CARLESS), DOYLE (WILLIAM), *and* GREENE (JACK P.). The Blackwell Dictionary of Historians. Oxf. 1988.

26732 KAYE (HARVEY J.). The British Marxist Historians. Oxf. 1984.

26733 NEALE (R. S.). Writing Marxist History: British Society, Economy and Culture since 1700. Oxf. 1985.

26734 CORNFORTH (MAURICE) *ed.* Rebels and their Causes: Essays in Honour of A. L. Morton. 1978.

26735 SAMUEL (RAPHAEL). 'British Marxist Historians 1880–1980'. *New Left Rev.* 120 (1980), 21–96.

26736 DENLEY (PETER) *and* HOPKIN (DEIAN) *eds.* History and Computing. Manchester. 1987. [Proceedings of the initial meeting of the Association for History and Computing: further volumes will emerge from subsequent meetings.].

26737 CANNADINE (DAVID). 'British History: Past, Present and Future?'. *Past and Present* 116 (1987), 169–91.

26738 CALHOUN (CRAIG). 'History and Sociology in Britain: A Review Article'. *Comp. Studs Soc. Hist.* 29 (1987), 626–39.

26739 SMITH (PAUL) *ed.* The Historian and Film. Camb. 1976.

26740 THOMPSON (PAUL). The Voice of the Past: Oral History. Oxf. 1978. Rev. edn 1988.

26741 The Local Historian. 1952+.

26742 General Introduction to the Victoria County History of England. 1970. [Lists the 150 volumes published by that date and includes indexes of the articles and authors involved.].

26743 ELRINGTON (CHRISTOPHER R.) ed. Supplement to the General Introduction to the Victoria County History. 1989. [Lists and indexes the further 50 volumes that have been published, together with a general account of the progress of the Victoria County History project.].

26744 STEPHENS (W. B.). Sources for English Local History. Camb. 1981.

26745 OLIVER (GEORGE). Using Old Photographs: A Guide for the Local Historian. 1988.

26746 RIDEN (PHILIP). Local History: A Practical Handbook for Beginners. 1983.

26747 —— Record Sources for Local History. 1987.

26748 LEWIS (CHRISTOPHER). Particular Places: An Introduction to English Local History. 1989.

26749 SMITH (DAVID). Maps and Plans for the Local Historian and Collector. 1988.

26750 EVANS (GEORGE EWART). The Strength of the Hills: An Autobiography. 1983.

26751 —— Where Beards Wag All: The Relevance of the Oral Tradition. 1977.

26752 WILLIAMS (GARETH). George Ewart Evans. Card. 1991.

26753 HENIGE (DAVID). Oral Historiography. 1982.

26754 Oral History. 1972+.

26755 MOODY (DAVID). Scottish Local History: An Introductory Guide. 1986.

26756 —— Scottish Family History. 1988.

26757 ARMSTRONG (NORMA). Local Collections in Scotland. Glasg. 1973.

26758 LIBRARY. British Humanities Index: Regional Lists. 1954–68.

26759 County Magazine Index: An Index to Magazines Covering the Rural and Country Life of the Counties of England. 1979+ Qly.

26760 SELDON (ANTHONY) ed. Contemporary History: Practice and Method. Oxf. 1988.

26761 PERKIN (HAROLD). 'Social History in Britain'. *J. Soc. Hist.* 10 (1976), 129–43.

26762 BEALES (DEREK EDWARD DAWSON). History and Biography: An Inaugural Lecture. Camb. 1982.

26763 COLEMAN (DONALD C.). History and the Economic Past: An Account of the Rise and Decline of Economic History in Britain. Oxf. 1987.

26764 KADISH (ALON). Historians, Economists and Economic history. 1989. [Detailed account of the emergence of economic History as an academic discipline in England.].

26765 SCOTT (CHRISTINA). A Historian and his World: A Life of Christopher Dawson 1889–1970. 1984.

26766 MANDELBAUM (SEYMOUR J.). 'H. J. Dyos and British Urban History'. *Econ. Hist. Rev.* 2nd ser. 38 (1985), 437–47; Francis Michael L. Thompson. 'Dyos and the Urban Past'. *Lond. J.* 9 (1983), 67–70; B. M. Stave. 'A Conversation with H. J. Dyos: Urban History in Great Britain'. *J. Urban Hist.* 5 1979 469–500; David Cannadine and David Reader, *eds.* Exploring the Urban Past: Essays in Urban History by H. J. Dyos. Camb. 1982.

26767 ELTON (*Sir* GEOFFREY RUDOLPH). The History of England. Camb. 1984.

26768 —— 'The Historian's Social Function'. *Trans. Roy. Hist. Soc.* 5th ser. 27 (1977), 197–211.

26769 The Historical Association, 1906–1956. 1957.

26770 ROBBINS (KEITH GILBERT). '*History*, the Historical Association and the "National Past"'. *Hist.* (1981), 413–25; 'National Identity and History: Past, Present and Future'. *Hist.* (1990), 369–87; Insular Outsider? 'British History' and European Integration. Reading. 1990.

26771 HUMPHREYS (ROBERT ARTHUR). The Royal Historical Society, 1868–1968. 1969.

26772 DONALDSON (GORDON). 'A Lang Pedigree: An Essay to Mark the Centenary of the Scottish History Society 1886–1986'. *Scot. Hist. Rev.* 65 (1986), 1–16.

26773 TAYLOR (ARTHUR JOHN). 'History at Leeds, 1877–1974: The Evolution of a Discipline'. *Northern Hist.* 10 (1975), 141–64; George S. R. Kitson Clark. 'A Hundred Years of the Teaching of History at Cambridge 1873–1973'. *Hist. J.* 16 (1973), 535–53.

26774 BARLOW (G.) *and* HARRISON (BRIAN HOWARD). History at the Universities. 1966.

26775 HARRISON (BRIAN HOWARD). 'History at the Universities, 1968: A Commentary'. *Hist.* (1968), 357–80.

26776 BOURNE (JOHN M.). History at the Universities. 1985.

26777 —— 'History at the Universities [1966–1986]'. *Hist.* 71 (1986), 54–60.

26778 STREET (PAMELA). Arthur Bryant: Portrait of a Historian. 1979.

26779 ELLIOTT (JOHN H.) *and* KOENIGSBERGER (H. G.) *eds.* The Diversity of History: Essays in Honour of Sir Herbert Butterfield. 1970.

26780 McINTIRE (C. T.) ed. Herbert Butterfield: Writings on Christianity and History. NY. 1979.

26781 HOBART (MICHAEL). 'History and Religion in the Thought of Herbert Butterfield'. *J. Hist. Ideas.* 32 (1971), 543–54.

26782 TURNER (J. MUNSEY). 'The Christian and the Study of History: Sir Herbert Butterfield (1900–79)'. *Procs Wes. Hist. Soc.* 46 (1987), 1–12.

26783 CHADWICK (WILLIAM OWEN). 'Acton and Butterfield'. *J. Eccl. Hist.* 38 (1987), 386–405.

26784 ELTON (GEOFFREY RUDOLPH). 'Herbert Butterfield and the Study of History'. *Hist. J.* 27 (1984), 729–43.

26785 THOMPSON (KENNETH W.) *ed.* Herbert Butterfield: The Ethics of History and Politics. Lanham. 1980.

26786 COLL (ALBERTO R.). The Wisdom of Statecraft: Sir Herbert Butterfield and the Philosophy of International Politics. Durham, NC. 1986.

26787 BEALES (DEREK EDWARD DAWSON) *and* BEST (GEOFFREY FRANCIS ARTHUR) *eds.* History, Society and the Churches: Essays in Honour of Owen Chadwick. Camb. 1985.

26788 GREEN (SALLY). Prehistorian: A Biography of V. Gordon Childe. Bradford-on-Avon. 1981.

26789 ASHLEY (MAURICE PERCY). Churchill as Historian. 1968.

26790 HAY (DENYS). 'Sir George Clark (1890–1979)'. *Eng. Hist. Rev.* 95 (1980), 1–27.

26791 COBB (RICHARD CHARLES). Still Life: Sketches from a Tunbridge Wells Childhood. 1983; Something to Hold Onto: Autobiographical Sketches. 1988.

26792 COLLINGWOOD (ROBIN GEORGE). An Autobiography. 1938.

26793 VAN DER DUSEN (W. J.). History as a Science: The Philosophy of R. G. Collingwood. The Hague. 1981.

26794 SCHURMAN (DONALD M.). Julian S. Corbett, 1854–1922, Historian of British Maritime Policy. 1981.

26795 COULTON (G. C.). Fourscore Years: An Autobiography. 1944.

26796 FISHER (HERBERT ALBERT LAURENS). Unfinished Autobiography. Herbert Fisher, 1865–1940: A Short Biography. By David Ogg.

26797 EYCK (FRANK). G. P. Gooch: A Study in History and Politics. 1982.

26798 GOOCH (GEORGE PEABODY). Under Six Reigns. 1958.

26799 HANCOCK (WILLIAM KEITH). Country and Calling. 1954; Professing History. Sydney. 1976.

26800 LANGHORNE (RICHARD). Diplomacy and Intelligence during the Second World War: Essays in Honour of F. H. Hinsley. Camb. 1985.

26801 THANE (PAT), CROSSICK (GEOFFREY), *and* FLOUD (RODERICK) *eds.* The Power of the Past: Essays for Eric Hobsbawm. Camb. 1984.

26802 HUIZINGA (J. H.). Confessions of a European in England. 1958.

26803 WINTER (J. M.) *ed.* War and Economic Development: Essays in Memory of David Joslin. Camb. 1975.

26804 MOREY (ADRIAN). David Knowles: A Memoir. 1979.

26805 BROOKE (CHRISTOPHER N. L.). David Knowles. Oxf. 1975.

26806 HODGSON (S.). Ramsay Muir: An Autobiography and Some Essays. 1943.

26807 NAMIER (JULIA). Lewis Namier: A Biography. 1971; Lewis Namier. By Linda Colley. 1988.

26808 PETRIE (*Sir* CHARLES ALEXANDER). A Historian Looks at his World. By Sir Charles Alexander Petrie. 1972.

26809 PLUMB (J. H.). The Making of an Historian: The Collected Papers of J. H. Plumb. Vol. 1 1988.

26810 BOSSY (JOHN ANTONY) *and* JUPP (PETER J.) *eds.* Essays Presented to Michael Roberts. Belf. 1976.

26811 ROTH (IRENE). Cecil Roth: Historian without Tears. 1983.

26812 ROWSE (ALFRED LESLIE). A Man of the Thirties. 1979.

26813 BROOKS (PETER NEWMAN) *ed.* Christian Spirituality: Essays in Honour of Gordon Rupp. 1975.

26814 TAYLOR (ALAN JOHN PERCIVALE). Politicians, Socialism and Historians. 1980; A Personal History. 1983; An Old Man's Diary. 1984.

26815 TAYLOR (EVA H.). A Life with Alan: The Diary of A. J. P. Taylor's Wife, Eva from 1978 to 1985. 1987.

26816 WRIGLEY (CHRIS J.) *comp.* A. J. P. Taylor: A Complete Annotated Bibliography and Guide to his Historical and other Writings. Brighton. 1980.

26817 KAYE (HARVEY J.) *and* McCLELLAND (KEITH) *eds.* E. P. Thompson: Critical Debates. Oxf. 1988.

26818 MORTON (S. FIONA). A Bibliography of Arnold J. Toynbee. Oxf. 1980.

26819 McNEILL (WILLIAM H.). Arnold J. Toynbee: A Life. Oxf. 1989.

26820 TOYNBEE (ARNOLD JOSEPH). Acquaintances. 1967; Experiences. 1969.

26821 PEPER (CHRISTIAN D.) *comp.* An Historian's Conscience. A Correspondence between Arnold J. Toynbee and Columba Cary-Elwes. Oxf. 1987.

26822 CLOGG (RICHARD). Politics and the Academy: Arnold Toynbee and the Koraes Chair. 1986.

26823 McDOUGALL (W. A.). '"Mais ce n'est pas l'histoire": Some Thoughts on Toynbee, McNeill and the Rest of us'. *J. Mod. Hist.* 58 (1986), 19–42.

26824 THOMPSON (KENNETH W.). Toynbee's Philosophy of World History and Politics. Baton Rouge, La. 1985.

26825 TREVELYAN. George Macaulay Trevelyan: A Memoir by his Daughter [Mary Caroline Moorman]. 1980.

26826 HERNON (JOSEPH M.). 'The Last Whig Historian and Consensus History: George Macaulay Trevelyan, 1876–1962'. *Amer. Hist. Rev.* 81 (1976), 66–97.

26827 WHEELER-BENNETT (*Sir* JOHN WHEELER). Knaves, Fools, and Heroes in Europe between the Wars. 1974; Friends, Enemies and Sovereigns. 1976.

26828 COLEMAN (DONALD C.) *and* MATHIAS (PETER) *eds.* Enterprise and History: Essays in Honour of Charles Wilson. Camb. 1984.

26829 WOODWARD (*Sir* ERNEST LLEWELLYN). Short Journey. 1943.

28. PHILOSOPHY AND PHILOSOPHERS

26830 AYER (*Sir* ALFRED JULES). Philosophy in the Twentieth Century. 1982.

26831 EDWARDS (P.) *ed.* The Encyclopaedia of Philosophy. 1967.

26832 MUIRHEAD (J. H.) *ed.* Contemporary British Philosophy: Personal Statements. 1st ser. 1924. 2nd ser. 1925.

26833 LEWIS (HYWEL DAVID) *ed.* Contemporary British Philosophy. 3rd ser. 1956. 4th ser. 1976.

26834 MACE (CECIL ALEC) *ed.* British Philosophy in the Mid-century: A Cambridge Symposium. 1957. 2nd edn 1966.

26835 PASSMORE (JOHN ARTHUR). A Hundred Years of Philosophy. 1957. 2nd edn 1966.

26836 PAUL (LESLIE ALLEN). The English Philosophers. 1953.

26837 WARNOCK (*Dame* [HELEN] MARY). Ethics since 1900. 1960. 2nd edn 1966.

26838 WARNOCK (*Sir* GEOFFREY). English Philosophy since 1900. 1958. Oxf. 2nd edn 1969.

26839 MAGEE (BRYAN) *ed.* Modern British Philosophy. 1971.

26840 —— Modern British Philosophy. Oxf. 1986.

26841 MEHTA (VED). Fly and the Fly Bottle. 1963.

26842 SHANKER (S. G.) *ed.* Philosophy in Britain Today. 1986.

26843 HUDSON (W. DONALD). Modern Moral Philosophy. 1983.

26844 GRAHAM (KEITH). John Austin: A Critique of Ordinary Language Philosophy. Hassocks. 1977.

26845 FANN (K. T.). Symposium on J. L. Austin. 1969.

26846 AYER (*Sir* ALFRED JULES). Part of my Life. 1977; More of My Life. 1984.

26847 FOSTER (JOHN). Ayer. 1985.

26848 COLLINGWOOD (ROBIN GEORGE). The Idea of Nature. Oxf. 1945.

26849 —— The Later Philosophy of R. G. Collingwood. Oxf. 1962.

26850 KRAUSZ (MICHAEL) *ed.* Critical Essays on the Philosophy of R.G. Collingwood. Oxf. 1972.

26851 JOAD (CYRIL EDWIN MITCHINSON). Under the Fifth Rib: A Belligerent Autobiography. 1932.

26852 WORALL (JOHN) *and* CURRIE (GREGORY) *eds.* Philosophical Papers of Imre Lakatos. Camb. 1978.

26853 MACE (MARJORIE) *ed.* C. A. Mace: Selected Papers. 1973.

26854 GELWICK (RICHARD). The Way of Discovery: An Introduction to the Thought of Michael Polanyi. NY. 1977.

26855 POPPER (*Sir* KARL RAIMUND). The Open Society and Its Enemies. 2 vols. 1945.

26856 MAGEE (BRYAN). Popper. 1973.

26857 O'HEAR (ANTHONY). Karl Popper. 1980.

26858 POPPER (*Sir* KARL). Unended Quest: An Intellectual Autobiography. Glasg. 1976.

26859 MILLER (DAVID) *ed.* A Pocket Popper. 1983.

26860 BURKE (T. E.). The Philosophy of Karl Popper. Manch. 1983.

26861 MARTIN (WERNER). Bertrand Russell: A Bibliography of his Writings 1895–1976. Hamden, Conn. 1981.

26862 RUSSELL (BERTRAND ARTHUR WILLIAM). Autobiography. 3 vols. 1967–9.

26863 BELL (ROBERT H.). 'Confession and Concealment in the Autobiography of Bertrand Russell'. *Biography* 8 (1985), 318–35.

26864 RUSSELL (BERTRAND ARTHUR WILLIAM). My Philosophical Development. 1959.

26865 CLARK (RONALD W.). The Life of Bertrand Russell. 1975.

26866 TAIT (KATHERINE). My Father, Bertrand Russell. 1975.

26867 CRAWSHAY-WILLIAMS (RUPERT). Russell Remembered. 1970.

26868 WOOD (ALAN). Bertrand Russell: The Passionate Sceptic. 1957.

26869 PEARS (DAVID FRANCIS). Bertrand Russell and the British Tradition in Philosophy. 1967.

26870 PEARS (DAVID FRANCIS) *ed.* Bertrand Russell: A Collection of Critical Essays. 1972.

26871 RYAN (ALAN). Bertrand Russell: A Political Life. 1988.

26872 SCHOENMAN (RALPH) *ed.* Bertrand Russell: Philosopher of the Century. 1967.

26873 SCHILPP (PAUL ARTHUR). The Philosophy of Bertrand Russell. Evanston, Ill. 1944. 3rd edn NY. 1951.

26874 AYER (*Sir* ALFRED JULES). Russell. 1972.

26875 SAINSBURY (R. M.). Russell. 1979.

26876 ROBERTS (GEORGE W.) *ed.* Bertrand Russell Memorial Volume. 1979.

26877 KILMISTER (C. W.). Russell. 1984.

26878 LYONS (WILLIAM). Gilbert Ryle. Brighton. 1980.

26879 FOWLER (DEAN R.). Alfred North Whitehead. *Zygon* 11 (1976), 50–69.

26880 WOODBRIDGE (BARRY). Alfred North Whitehead: A Primary–Secondary Bibliography. Bowling Green, Ohio. 1977.

26881 BAMBOROUGH (RENFORD). Wisdom: Twelve Essays. Oxf. 1974.

26882 WITTGENSTEIN (LUDWIG). Letters to C. K. Ogden. Oxf. 1973.

26883 PEARS (DAVID FRANCIS). Wittgenstein. 1970.

26884 ANSCOMBE (GERTRUDE ELIZABETH M.). Introduction to Wittgenstein's 'Tractatus'. 1951.

26885 KENNY (ANTHONY J. P.). Wittgenstein. 1973.

26886 BLACK (MAX). A Companion to Wittgenstein's 'Tractatus'. Oxf. 1964.

26887 MALCOLM (NORMAN). Ludwig Wittgenstein: A Memoir. Oxf. 1958.

29. POLITICAL SCIENCE

26888 LOVENDUSKI (JONI). The Profession of Political Science in Britain. Glasg. 1981.

26889 CHESTER (D. NORMAN). 'Political Studies in Britain: Recollections and Comments'. *Pol. Studs* 23 (1975), 29–42.

26890 HARRISON (WILFRID). 'The Early Years of Political Studies'. *Pol. Studs* 23 (1975), 43–60.

26891 CHESTER (*Sir* D. NORMAN). Economics, Politics and Social Studies at Oxford, 1900–85. 1986.

26892 PINDER (JOHN) ed. Fifty Years of Political and Economic Planning (PEP): Looking Forward 1931–1981. Aldershot. 1981.

30. CENSORSHIP

26893 RADCLIFFE (CYRIL JOHN) *Baron*. Censors. 1961.

26894 —— Freedom of Information: A Human Right. Glasg. 1953.

26895 LLOYD (PETER). Not for Publication. 1968.

26896 THOMAS (DONALD). A Long Time Burning: The History of Literary Censorship in England. 1969.

26897 THOMPSON (ANTHONY HUGH). Censorship in Public Libraries in the United Kingdom during the Twentieth Century. Epping. 1975.

26898 O'HIGGINS (PAUL). Censorship in Britain. 1972.

26899 KNOWLES (DOROTHY). The Censor, the Drama and the Film, 1900–1934. 1934.

26900 FINDLATER (RICHARD). Banned! A Review of Theatrical Censorship in Britain. 1967.

26901 HOPKIN (DEIAN). 'Domestic Censorship in the First World War'. *J. Contemp. Hist.* 5 (1970), 151–69

26902 CONNOLLY (L. W.). 'The Abolition of Theatre Censorship in Great Britain: The Theatres Act of 1968'. *Queen's Q.* 75 (1968), 569–83.

26903 BRODY (STEPHEN). Screen Violence and Film Censorship: A Review of Research: A Home Office Research Unit Report. 1977.

26904 DAVIES (CHRISTIE). Permissive Britain: Social Change in the Sixties and Seventies. 1975.

26905 DHAVAN (RAJEEV) *and* DAVIES (CHRISTIE) eds. Censorship and Obscenity. 1978.

26906 PHELPS (GUY). Film Censorship. 1975.

26907 —— 'Censorship and the Press'. *Sight and Sound* 43 (1973), 138–40.

26908 TREVELYAN (JOHN). What the Censor Saw. 1973.

26909 RICHARDS (JEFFREY). 'The British Board of Film Censors and Content Control in the 1930s: Images of Britain and Foreign Affairs'. *Hist. J. Film, Radio, Television* 1 (1981), 95–116; 2 (1982), 39–48.

26910 ROBERTSON (JAMES C.). The British Board of Film Censors: Film Censorship in Britain, 1896–1950. 1985.

26911 —— The Hidden Cinema: British Film Censorship in Action 1913–1972. 1989.

26912 —— 'British Film Censorship Goes to War'. *Hist. J. Film, Radio, Television* 2 (1982), 49–64.

26913 HUNNINGS (NEVILLE MARCH). Film Censors and the Law. 1967.

31. LEISURE

26914 DEPARTMENT OF THE ENVIRONMENT. Leisure and the Quality of Life: Report of a Central Steering Group of Officials on Four Local Experiments (Chairman: W. M. Fox.). 2 vols. 1977.

26915 ROWNTREE (BENJAMIN SEEBOHM) *and* LAVERS (GEORGE RUSSELL). English Life and Leisure: A Social Study. 1951.

26916 WALVIN (JAMES). Leisure and Society 1830–1950. 1978.

26917 WALTON (JOHN K.) *and* WALVIN (JAMES) eds. Leisure in Britain 1780–1939. Manch. 1983.

26918 JONES (STEPHEN G.). Workers at Play: A Social and Economic History of Leisure, 1918–1939. 1986.

26919 HOWKINS (ALUN) *and* LOWERSON (JOHN). Trends in Leisure, 1919–1939. 1979.

26920 ANDERSON (NELS). Work and Leisure. 1961.

26921 BROMHEAD (PETER ALEXANDER). 'State and Leisure'. *Pol. Q.* 35 (1964), 87–98.

26922 CULLINGWORTH (JOHN BARRY). 'Planning for Leisure'. *Urban Studs* 1 (1964), 1–25.

26923 ROBERTS (KENNETH). Leisure. 1970.

26924 GLASSER (RALPH). Leisure: Penalty or Prize? 1970.

26925 ASHTON (ELWYN THOMAS). People and Leisure. 1971.

26926 LEIGH (JOHN). Young People and Leisure. 1971.

26927 SMITH (MICHAEL ALFRED), PARKER (STANLEY ROBERT), *and* SMITH (CYRIL S.) eds. Leisure and Society in Britain. 1973.

26928 PARKER (STANLEY ROBERT). The Future of Work and Leisure. 1971.

26929 —— The Sociology of Leisure. 1976.

26930 —— *ed.* Annotated Bibliography on Leisure: Great Britain (1962–1972). 1972.

26931 CLAYRE (ALASDAIR). Work and Play: Ideas and Experience of Work and Leisure. 1974.

26932 RAPOPORT (RHONA) *and* RAPOPORT (ROBERT) *with* STRELITZ (ZIONA). Leisure and the Family Life Cycle. 1975.

26933 LEWES (FREDERICK MARTIN MEREDITH), PARKER (STANLEY ROBERT), *and* LICKORISH (LEONARD JOHN). Leisure and Tourism. 1975.

26934 LEWES (FREDERICK MARTIN MEREDITH) *and* MENNELL (STEPHEN). Leisure, Culture and Local Government: A Study of Policies and Provision in Exeter. Exeter. 1976.

26935 HARRIS (BRYAN) *and* RYAN (GERARD). An Outline of the Law relating to Common Land and Public Access to the Countryside. 1967.

26936 HAWORTH (JOHN TREVOR) *and* VEAL (ANTHONY JAMES) *eds.* Leisure and the Community: Conference Proceedings: Papers from a Conference Held by the Leisure Studies Association at Birmingham in 1976. Birm. 1976.

26937 CLARKE (JOHN) *and* CRITCHER (CHAS). The Devil Makes Work: Leisure in Capitalist Britain. 1985.

32. TOURISM

26938 BRITISH TOURIST AUTHORITY. Annual Reports. 1971+.

26939 —— Patterns in British Holidaymaking, 1951–1968; A Summary of Statistical Information about British Holidaymakers in the United Kingdom and Abroad, with Special Reference to Holiday Patterns in the Major Regions. 1969.

26940 —— A Survey of the Tourist Trade in Scotland. 1956.

26941 —— Investing in Tourism: Aid to Tourist Projects in England's Development Areas, 1971–76. 1977.

26942 BROWNRIGG (MARK) *and* GREIG (MICHAEL). Tourism and Regional Development. Glasg. 1976.

26943 —— The Economic Impact of Tourist Spending in Skye. Inverness. 1974.

26944 HUNT (AUDREY). A Survey of Scottish Tourism: A Survey Carried out by the Social Survey for the Scottish Development Department in 1964. 1966.

26945 ARCHER (BRIAN). The Impact of Domestic Tourism. Card. 1973.

26946 NICHOLLS (DEREK CLIFFORD) *and* YOUNG (A.). Recreation and Tourism in the Loch Lomond Area: A Report to the County Council of Dumbarton. Glasg. 1968.

26947 LICKORISH (LEONARD JOHN) *and* KERSHAW (ANDREW GABRIEL). The Travel Trade. 1958.

26948 HOLLOWAY (J. CHRISTOPHER). The Business of Tourism. 1983.

26949 LEWES (FREDERICK MARTIN MEREDITH), CULYER (A. J.), *and* BRADY (GILLIAN A.). The Holiday Industry in Devon and Cornwall. 1970.

26950 RUBINSTEIN (DAVID) *and* SPEAKMAN (COLIN). Leisure, Transport and the Countryside. 1969.

33. RECREATION AND NATIONAL PARKS

26951 BURTON (THOMAS LEONARD) *ed.* Recreation Research and Planning: A Symposium. 1970.

26952 BURTON (THOMAS LEONARD) *and* WIBBERLEY (GERALD PERCY). Outdoor Recreation in the British Countryside. Ashford. 1965.

26953 MUTCH (WILLIAM EDWARD SCOTT). Public Recreation in National Forests: A Factual Survey. 1968.

26954 PATMORE (JOHN ALLAN). Land and Leisure in England and Wales. Newton Abbot. 1970.

26955 CHERRY (GORDON EMANUEL). Environmental Planning 1939–1969 Volume II: National Parks and Recreation in the Countryside. 1975.

26956 GREAVES (JOAN). National Parks and Access to the Countryside and Coast: Trends in Research, 1964–1968. 3rd edn 1968.

26957 GOODALL (BRIAN). National Forests and Recreational Opportunities. Reading. 1975.

26958 COPPOCK (JOHN TERENCE) *and* DUFFIELD (BRIAN). Recreation in the Countryside: A Spatial Analysis. 1975.

26959 COPPOCK (JOHN TERENCE) *ed.* Second Homes: Curse or Blessing? Oxf. 1977.

26960 BELL (M.) *ed.* Britain's National Parks. Newton Abbot. 1975.

26961 COPPOCK (JOHN TERENCE). 'Ideals for National Parks'. *Geog. Mag.* 46 (1974), 627–33.

26962 SHEAIL (JOHN). 'The Concept of National Parks in Great Britain 1900–1950'. *Trans. Inst. Brit. Geog.* 66 (1975), 41–56.

26963 RODGERS (HARRY BRIAN) *et al.* 'Recreation and Resources'. *Geog. J.* (1973), 467–97.

26964 GITTINS (J. W.). 'Conservation and Capacity: A Case Study of the Snowdonia National Park'. *Geog. J.* (1976), 482–6.

26965 MacEWEN (ANNE) *and* MacEWEN (MALCOLM). National Parks: Conservation or Cosmetics. 1982.

26966 —— Greenprints for the Countryside: The Story of Britain's National Parks. 1987.

26967 ADDISON (W.). Portrait of Epping Forest. 1977.

26968 CROWE (A.). The Parks and Woodlands of London. 1987.

26969 STEPHENSON (TOM). Forbidden Land. Manch. 1989.

26970 JAMES (D.) *ed.* Outward Bound. 1957.

26971 WAINWRIGHT (D.). Youth in Action: The Duke of Edinburgh's Award Scheme 1956–1966. 1966.

26972 SHEAIL (JOHN). Nature in Trust: The History of Nature Conservation in Britain. Glasg. 1976.

26973 RACKHAM (OLIVER). Ancient Woodland: Its History, Vegetation and Uses in England. 1980.

26974 FAWCETT (JANE). The Future of the Past: Attitudes to Conservation, 1174–1974. 1976.

34. GARDENS

26975 HADFIELD (MILES), HARLING (ROBERT), *and* HIGHTON (L.). British Gardeners: A Biographical Dictionary. 1980.

26976 HADFIELD (MILES). A History of British Gardening. 1979.

26977 MILLIKEN (HAROLD TURNER). The Road to Bodnant: The Story behind the Foundation of the Famous North Wales Garden. Manch. 1975.

26978 ALLEN (MARJORY) *Lady Allen of Hurtwood.* Memoirs of an Uneducated Lady. 1975.

26979 HYAMS (EDWARD). The English Garden. NY. 1966.

26980 —— A History of Gardens and Gardening. 1971.

26981 CONSTANTINE (STEPHEN). 'Amateur Gardening and Popular Recreation in the 19th and 20th Centuries'. *J. Soc. Hist.* 14 (1980–1), 387–406.

35. HOLIDAYS

26982 PIMLOTT (JOHN ALFRED RALPH). The Englishman's Holiday. 1947.

26983 BRUNNER (E.). Holiday Making and the Holiday Trends. 1945.

26984 HAMILTON (RONALD). Now I Remember: A Holiday History of Britain. 1983.

26985 WALTON (JOHN K.). The Blackpool Landlady: A Social History. 1978.

26986 WALVIN (JAMES). Beside the Seaside: A Social History of the Popular Seaside Holiday. 1978.

26987 BUTLIN (*Sir* BILLY) *with* DACRE (PETER). The Butlin Story: 'A Showman to the End'. 1982.

26988 WARD (COLIN). 'Goodnight Campers!' The History of the British Holiday Camp. 1986.

26989 FARRANT (S.). 'London by the Sea: Resort Development on the South Coast of England, 1880–1939'. *J. Contemp. Hist.* 22 (1987), 137–62.

26990 WILLIAMS (FRANCIS) *Baron.* Journey into Adventure: The Story of the Workers Travel Association. 1960.

26991 ADAMSON (S. H.). Seaside Piers. 1977.

26992 JONES (STEPHEN G.). 'State Intervention in Sport and Leisure in Britain between the Wars'. *J. Contemp. Hist.* 22 (1987), 163–82.

26993 —— 'Trade-Union Policy between the Wars: The Case of Holidays with Pay in Britain'. *Inl Rev. Soc. Hist.* 31 (1986), 40–67.

26994 OWEN (CHARLES). Britons Abroad: A Report on the Package Tour. 1968.

26995 JACKSON (STANLEY). The Savoy: The Romance of a Great Hotel. 1964.

26996 TAYLOR (DEREK) *and* BUSH (DAVID). The Golden Age of British Hotels. 1974.

26997 MONTGOMERY-MASSINGBERD (HUGH) *and* WATKIN (D.). The London Ritz: A Social and Architectural History. 1981.

26998 FORTE (CHARLES) *Baron.* Forte: The Autobiography of Charles Forte. 1986.

26999 RONAY (EGON). The Unforgettable Dishes of my Life. 1989.

27000 TAYLOR (DEREK). Fortune, Fame and Folly: British Hotels and Catering 1878–1978. 1977.

27001 SWINGLEHURST (EDMOND). Cook's Tours: The Story of Popular Travel. 1982.

27002 STUDDARD (R. M.). Town and Country: The Amenity Question. 1959.

27003 WHITAKER (BENJAMIN CHARLES GEORGE) *and* BROWNE (KENNETH). Parks for People. 1971.

27004 ROODIS (ROLAND JOSEPH). The Law of Parks and Recreation Grounds. 3rd edn 1970.

27005 VEAL (ANTHONY JAMES) *comp.* Environmental Protection and Recreation: A Review and Annotated Bibliography. Birm. 1974.

27006 ALLEN (MARJORY) *Lady Allen of Hurtwood.* New Playgrounds. 1964.

27007 CHADWICK (GEORGE FLETCHER). The Park and the Town: Public Landscape in the 19th and 20th Centuries. 1966.

27008 CARRINGTON (RONALD). Alexandra Park and Palace: A History. 1975.

27009 OPIE (IONA) *and* OPIE (PETER). Children's Games in Street and Playground. Oxf. 1969.

27010 HOLME (ANTHEA) *and* MASSIE (PETER). Children's Play: A Study of Needs and Opportunities: A Study for the Council for Children's Welfare. 1970.

27011 BENJAMIN (JOSEPH). In Search of Adventure: A Study of the Junk Playground. 1961.

27012 RUCK (S. KENNETH). Municipal Entertainment and the Arts in Greater London. 1965.

27013 SANDFORD (JEREMY) *and* LAW (ROGER). Synthetic Fun: A Short Soft Glance. Harmondsworth. 1967.

27014 SEELEY (IVOR HUGH). Outdoor Recreation and the Urban Environment. 1973.

27015 SHEPPARD (D.). Play Spaces for Children on Estates. 1973.

27016 DEPARTMENT OF THE ENVIRONMENT. 1977. Recreation and Deprivation in Inner Urban Areas. 1977.

27017 SNELL (HENRY) *Lord*. The Case for Sunday Games: Against Sabbatarian Prejudice. 1923.

27018 SOCIETY FOR PROMOTING DUE OBSERVANCE OF THE LORD'S DAY. Sunday Opening of Theatres and Music Halls: Manifesto to the Christian People of England. 1926.

36. SPORT

27019 British Journal of Sports History 1984–6 but now The International Journal of the History of Sport. 1987+.

27020 COX (RICHARD W.). Sport—A Guide to Historical Sources in the U.K. 1983.

27021 'A Survey of Literature on the History of Sport in Britain'. *Brit. J. Sports Hist.* 1 (1984), 41–59. [Cox has continued to produce an Annual Bibliography in the International Journal.].

27022 DUFFIELD (BRIAN) *et al.* A Digest of Sports Statistics. 1983.

27023 MASON (TONY) *ed.* Sport in Britain: A Social History. Camb. 1989.

27024 HARGREAVES (JOHN). Sport, Power and Culture: A Social and Historical Analysis of Popular Sports in Britain. Camb. 1986.

27025 DUNNING (ERIC). The Sociology of Sport: A Selection of Readings. 1971.

27026 MANGAN (J. ANTHONY) *ed.* Physical Education and Sport: Sociological and Cultural Perspectives. Oxf. 1973.

27027 BIRLEY (DEREK). 'Sportsmen and the Deadly Game'. *Brit. J. Sports Hist.* 3 (1986), 288–310.

27028 CASHMORE (ERNEST). Black Sportsmen. 1982.

27029 ALLISON (LINCOLN) *ed.* The Politics of Sport. Manch. 1986.

27030 BALE (JOHN). Sport and Place: A Geography of Sport in England, Scotland and Wales. 1982.

27031 —— 'Sport and National Identity: A Geographical View'. *Brit. J. Sports Hist.* 3 (1986), 18–41.

37. RUGBY

27032 DUNNING (ERIC) *and* SHEARD (KENNETH). Barbarians, Gentlemen and Players: A Sociological Study of the Development of Rugby Football. Oxf. 1979.

27033 REYBURN (WALLACE REYBURN). The Lions. 1967.

27034 SALMON (THOMAS). The First Hundred Years: The Story of Rugby Football in Cornwall. Illogan. 1983.

27035 GRIFFITHS (JOHN). The Book of English International Rugby 1871–1982. 1982.

27036 OWEN (OWEN LLEWELLYN). The History of the Rugby Football Union. 1955.

27037 SMITH (J. V.). 'Good Morning President': Rugby from the Top. 1985.

27038 TETLEY (UEL A.) *and* MCWHIRTER (ALAN ROSS). Centenary History of the Rugby Football Union. 1970.

27039 REYBURN (WALLACE MACDONALD). The Men in White: The Story of English Rugby. 1975.

27040 BOWKER (BARRY MORRISON). England Rugby: A History of the National Side, 1871–1976. 1976.

27041 STARMER-SMITH (NIGEL). The Barbarians: The Official History of the Barbarians Football Club. 1977.

27042 DIFFLEY (SEAN). The Men in Green: The Story of Irish Rugby. 1973.

27043 ORR (DAVID) *ed.* City of Derry Rugby Football Club: A Centenary 1881–1981. Londonderry. 1981.

27044 VAN ESBECK (EDMUND). One Hundred Years of Irish Rugby: The Official History of the Irish Rugby Football Union. Dublin. 1974.

27045 SMITH (DAVID) *and* WILLIAMS (GARETH). Fields of Praise: The Official History of the Welsh Rugby Union, 1881–1981. Card. 1981.

27046 RICHARDS (ALUN). A Touch of Glory: 100 Years of Welsh Rugby. 1980.

27047 TAYLOR (JOHN). Decade of the Dragon. 1980.

27048 EDWARDS (GARETH OWEN). Gareth—An Autobiography. 1978.

27049 JOHN (BARRY). The Barry John Story. 1974.

27050 THORBURN (SANDY). The History of Scottish Rugby. 1980.

27051 MASSIE (ALLAN). A Portrait of Scottish Rugby. 1984.

27052 GATE (ROBERT). Rugby League: An Illustrated History. 1989.

27053 MACKLIN (KEITH). The Story of Rugby League. 1984.

38. FOOTBALL

27054 WALVIN (JAMES). The People's Game: A Social History of English Football. 1975.

27055 MASON (TONY). Association Football and English Society 1863–1915. Brighton. 1980.

27056 FISHWICK (NICHOLAS). English Football and Society 1910–1950. Manch. 1989.

27057 MOORHOUSE (HERBERT F.). 'Professional Football and Working Class Culture: English Theories and Scottish Evidence'. *Sociol. Rev.* 32 (1984), 285–315.

27058 VEITCH (C.). ' "Play Up! Play Up! and Win the War!" Football, the Nation, and the First World War 1914–15'. *J. Contemp. Hist.* 20 (1985), 363–78.

27059 YOUNG (PERCY MARSHALL). A History of British Football. 1968.

27060 GREEN (GEOFFREY). History of the Football Association. 1953.

27061 KEETON (GEORGE W.). The Football Revolution: A Study of the Changing Pattern of Association Football. Newton Abbot. 1972.

27062 DOUGLAS (PETER). The Football Industry. 1974.

27063 INGLIS (SIMON). Soccer in the Dock: A History of British Football Scandals 1900–1965. 1985.

27064 MORRIS (DESMOND). The Soccer Tribe. 1985.

27065 FOOTBALL ASSOCIATION AND FOOTBALL LEAGUE. The Financing and Taxation of Football Clubs. 1982.

27066 DEPARTMENT OF EDUCATION AND SCIENCE. Report of the Committee on Football. 1968.

27067 INGHAM (ROGER) ET AL. 'Football Hooliganism': The Wider Context. 1978.

27068 SPORTS COUNCIL. Public Disorder and Sporting Events: A Report by a Joint Panel of the Sports Council and the SSRC (Chairman: Cyril Smith.). 1978.

27069 WAGG (STEPHEN). The Football World: A Contemporary Social History. Brighton. 1984.

27070 FARRER (MORLEY) *and* LAMMING (DOUGLAS). A Century of English International Football 1872–1972. 1972.

27071 PAWSON (TONY). 100 Years of the FA Cup: The Official Centenary History. 1972.

27072 INGLIS (SIMON). League Football and the Men who Made it: The Official Centenary History of the Football League 1888–1988. 1988.

27073 WOOLNOUGH (BRIAN). Black Magic: The Rise of the Black Footballer. 1983.

27074 BALE (JOHN). 'Changing Regional Origins of an Occupation: The Case of Professional Footballers in 1950 and 1980'. *Geog.* 68 (1983), 140–8.

27075 BASS (H.). Glorious Wembley: The Official History of Britain's Foremost Entertainment Centre. Enfield. 1982.

27076 ROBERTS (JOHN). Everton: The Official Centenary History. 1978.

27077 JOHNSON (IAN). The Aston Villa Story. 1981.

27078 YOUNG (PERCY MARSHALL). Bolton Wanderers. 1961.

27079 —— Football in Sheffield. 1962.

27080 —— Football on Merseyside. 1963.

27081 —— Manchester United. 1960.

27082 GREEN (GEOFFREY). There's only one United: The Official Centenary History of Manchester United 1878–1978. 1978.

27083 GIBSON (JOHN). The Newcastle United Story. 1985.

27084 CREEK (FREDERICK NORMAN SMITH). A History of the Corinthian Football Club. 1933.

27085 ROUS (Sir STANLEY). Football Worlds: A Lifetime in Sport. 1978.

27086 MILLER (DAVID). Father of Football: The Story of Sir Matt Busby. 1970.

27087 CRAMPSEY (BOB). The Scottish Footballer. Edin. 1979.

27088 MURRAY (BILL). The Old Firm: Sectarianism, Sport and Society in Scotland. Edin. 1984.

27089 ARCHER (IAN). The Rangers Story. 1985.

27090 MCNEE (GERRY). The Story of Celtic: An Official History. 1978.

27091 WICKIE (JAMES). Across the Great Divide. Edin. 1984.

27092 Football Crowd Behaviour: Report by a Working Group appointed by the Secretary of State for Scotland under the Chairmanship of Frank McElhone. Edin. 1977.

27093 BRODIE (MALCOLM). 100 Years of Irish Football. Belf. 1980.

27094 PARKINSON (MICHAEL). Best: An Intimate Biography. 1975.

39. CRICKET

27095 Wisden's Cricketers' Almanack. 1864+.

27096 PADWICK (E. W.) *comp.* A Bibliography of Cricket. 1984.

27097 TRUEMAN (FRED) *and* MOSEY (DON). Cricket Statistics Year by Year 1946–1987. 1988.

27098 SWANTON (E. W.). A History of Cricket. 1962.

27099 HILL (JEFFREY). ' "First Class" Cricket and the Leagues: Some Notes on the Development of English Cricket, 1900–1940'. *Inl. J. Hist. Sport* 4 (1987), 68–81.

27100 SANDIFORD (KEITH A. P.). 'The Professionalization of Modern Cricket'. *Brit. J. Sports Hist.* 2 (1985), 270–89.

27101 LEWIS (TONY). Double Century: The Story of MCC and Cricket. 1987.

27102 FLINT (RACHEL HAYHOE) *and* RHEINBERG (NETTA). Fair Play: The Story of Women's Cricket. 1976.

27103 COWDREY (MICHAEL COLIN). MCC: The Autobiography of a Cricketer. 1977.

27104 ROGERSON (SIDNEY). Wilfred Rhodes. 1960.

27105 MIDWINTER (ERIC). The Lost Season: Cricket in Wartime, 1939–45. 1987.

27106 ARLOTT (JOHN). Fred: Portrait of a Fast Bowler. 1983.

27107 GRAVENEY (THOMAS WILLIAM). The Heart of Cricket. 1983.

27108 BLOFIELD (HENRY). The Packer Affair. 1978.

40. BOXING

27109 BUTLER (FRANK). A History of Boxing in Britain: A Survey of the Noble Art from its Origins to the Present Day. 1972.

27110 COOPER (HENRY). An Autobiography. 1974.

41. GAMBLING

27111 CORNISH (D. B.). Gambling: A Review of the Literature. 1978.

27112 HILTON (JOHN) ed. Why I Go In For the Pools. 1936.

27113 Royal Commission on Betting, Lotteries and Gaming: 1949–1951. Report. Cmnd 8190. Parliamentary Papers viii 1950–1.

27114 Royal Commission on Gambling. Cmnd 7200. Parliamentary Papers 1977–8.

27115 HALLIDAY (JON) and FULLER (PETER). The Psychology of Gambling. 1974.

27116 DOWNES (DAVID MALCOLM) et al. Gambling, Work and Leisure: A Study across Three Areas. 1976.

27117 MOODY (GORDON). The Facts about the 'Money Factories': An Independent View of Betting and Gambling in Britain Now. 1972.

27118 PERKINS (ERNEST BENSON). Gambling and English Life. 1950.

27119 McKIBBIN (ROSS IAN). 'Working-Class Gambling in Britain 1880–1939'. Past and Present 82 (1979), 147–78.

27120 —— 'Work and Hobbies in Britain 1880–1950'. In The Working Class in Modern British History: Essays in Honour of Henry Pelling. Jay Murray Winter, ed. Camb. 1983. 127–46.

42. HORSE RACING, SHOW-JUMPING, AND FOX-HUNTING

27121 LODER (EILEEN P.). Bibliography of the History and Organisation of Horse Racing and Thoroughbred Breeding in Great Britain and Ireland: Books published in Great Britain and Ireland 1565–1973. 1978.

27122 VAMPLEW (WRAY). The Turf: A Social and Economic History of Horse Racing. 1976.

27123 LONGRIGG (ROGER). The History of Horseracing. 1972.

27124 CARR (Sir RAYMOND). English Fox-Hunting: A History. 1976.

27125 THOMAS (RICHARD H.). The Politics of Hunting. Aldershot. 1983.

27126 HILL (CHRISTOPHER R.). Horse Power: The Politics of the Turf. Manch. 1987.

27127 MORTIMER (ROGER). The Jockey Club. 1958.

27128 —— A History of the Derby Stakes. 1984.

27129 GREEN (REG). A Race Apart: The History of the Grand National. 1988.

27130 SETH-SMITH (MICHAEL). Knight of the Turf: The Life and Times of Sir Gordon Richards. 1980.

27131 CULRING (WILLIAM). The Captain: A Biography of Captain Sir Cecil Boyd-Rochfort, Royal Trainer. 1970.

27132 WILLIAMS (DORIAN). Horse of the Year: The Story of a Unique Horseshow. Newton Abbot. 1976.

27133 ANSELL (Sir MICHAEL). Soldier On: An Autobiography. 1973.

27134 RIPPON (ANGELA). Mark Phillips: The Man and his Horses. Newton Abbot. 1982.

27135 BROOME (DAVID) with GILES (BRIAN). Twenty-Five Years in Show Jumping. 1981.

43. CYCLING AND MOTORSPORT

27136 OAKLEY (WILLIAM). Winged Wheel: The History of the First Hundred Years of the Cyclists Touring Club. Godalming. 1977.

27137 HARRIS (REG). Two Wheels to the Top. 1976.

27138 HAMILTON (MAURICE). The British Grand Prix. 1989.

27139 ROGERS (MARTIN). An Illustrated History of Speedway. 1978.

27140 CAMPBELL (GINA) with MEECH (MICHAEL). Bluebirds: The Story of the Campbell Dynasty. 1988.

27141 HUNT (JAMES). James Hunt Against all the Odds. 1978.

27142 SCOTT (MICHAEL). Barry Sheene. 1984.

44. ATHLETICS

27143 LOVESEY (PETER) and MCNAB (THOMAS). The Guide to British Track and Field Literature 1275–1968. 1969.

27144 LOVESEY (PETER). The Official Centenary History of the Amateur Athletic Association. 1979.

27145 BANNISTER (ROGER). First Four Minutes. 1955.

27146 MILLER (DAVID). Seb Coe—Coming Back. 1984.

27147 HEMERY (DAVID). Another Hurdle. 1976.

27148 PETER (MARY) with WOOLDRIDGE (IAN). Mary P: Autobiography. 1974.

27149 DAVIES (LYNN). Winner Stakes All: Lynn Davies Face to Face with Peter Williams. 1970.

45. TENNIS

27150 ROBERTSON (MAX). Wimbledon. 1981.

27151 PERRY (FRED). Fred Perry. 1984.

27152 WADE (VIRGINIA). Courting Triumph. 1978.

46. GOLF

27153 COUSINS (GEOFFREY). Golf in Britain: A Social History from the Beginnings to the Present Day. 1975.

27154 DARWIN (BERNARD) *et al.* A History of Golf in Britain. 1952.

27155 MORTIMER (CHARLES GORDON) *and* PIGNON (FRED). The Story of the Open Golf Championship 1860–1950. 1952.

27156 ALLISS (PETER). The Open: The British Golf Championship since the War. 1984.

27157 JACKLIN (TONY). Jacklin: The Champion's Own Story. 1970.

27158 WARD-THOMAS (PAT). The Royal and Ancient. Edin. 1980.

47. MISCELLANEOUS

27159 HOPKINSON (ALAN). The Mountain Men: The Early History of Rock Climbing in North Wales. 1977.

27160 HALOT (ANN). 'Hikers and Ramblers: Surviving a Thirties' Fashion'. *Inl J. Hist. Sport* 4 (1987), 56–67.

27161 SMITH (DAVID BUCHANAN). Curling: An Illustrated History. Edin. 1981.

27162 BIRD (DENNIS L.). Our Skating Heritage: A Centenary History of the National Skating Association of Great Britain, 1879–1979. 1979.

27163 PHILLIPS-BIRT (DOUGLAS). A History of Seamanship. 1971.

27164 —— When Luxury Went to Sea. Newton Abbot. 1971.

27165 WALKER (ANITA). Francis Chichester: A Biography. NY. 1975.

27166 HEATH (EDWARD). Sailing: A Course of my Life. 1975.

27167 KNOX-JOHNSTON (ROBIN). A World of my Own. 1969.

27168 EMMONS (FREDERICK). The Atlantic Liners 1925–70. Newton Abbot. 1972.

27169 RICHARDSON (PHILIP JOHN SAMPEY). A History of English Ballroom Dancing, 1910–1945. 1946.

27170 McCARTHY (ALBERT JOHN). The Dance Band Era: The Dancing Decades from Ragtime to Swing, 1910–1950. 1971.

27171 BANHAM (MARY) *and* HILLIER (BEVIS). A Tonic to the Nation: The Festival of Britain 1951. 1976.

27172 HOWARD (ALEXANDER). Endless Cavalcade: A Diary of British Festivals and Customs. 1965.

48. EXPLORATION

27173 BUCHAN (JOHN). The Last Secrets: The Final Mysteries of Exploration. 1922.

27174 DEBENHAM (FRANK). Discovery and Exploration: An Atlas-History of Man's Journeys into the Unknown. 2nd edn 1968.

27175 MITCHELL (J. LESLIE). Earth Conquerors: The Lives and Achievements of the Great Explorers. NY. 1934.

27176 OUTHWAITE (LEONARD). Unrolling the Map: The Story of Exploration. 1935.

27177 KEY (CHARLES E.). The Story of Twentieth-Century Exploration. 1937.

27178 SYKES (PERCY). A History of Exploration from the Earliest Times to the Present Day. 1934. 3rd edn 1950.

27179 WOOD (H. J.). Exploration and Discovery. 1952.

27180 SHARAF ('ABD AL-AZIZ TURAYH). A Short History of Geographical Discovery. 1967.

27181 PALMER (KATHERINE V. H.). 'An Annotated Bibliography of Scientific Oceanographic Expeditions (Voyages)'. *Amer. Phil. Soc. Yb.* (1968), 326–7.

27182 WILKINS (*Sir* GEORGE HUBERT). Flying the Arctic. 1928.

27183 —— Undiscovered Australia. 1928.

27184 —— Under the North Pole. 1931.

27185 —— Thoughts through Space. 1952.

27186 THOMAS (LOWELL). Sir Hubert Wilkins (1888–1958). His World of Adventure: An Autobiography Recounted by Lowell Thomas. 1962.

27187 SPENCER (W. BALDWIN). Spencer's Last Journey: Being the Journal of an Expedition to Tierra del Fuego by the late Sir Baldwin Spencer: With a Memoir by R. R. Marett and T. K. Penniman. With contributions by Sir James Frazer and H. Balfour. Oxf. 1931.

27188 SHARP (C. ANDREW). The Discovery of the Pacific Islands. Oxf. 1960.

27189 SCOTT (ERNEST). Australian Discovery. 1929.

27190 PETRIE (WILLIAM MATTHEW FLINDERS). Eastern Exploration, Past and Future. 1918.

27191 DROWER (M. S.). Flinders Petrie: A Life in Archaeology.

27192 GREGORY (JOHN WALTER) *and* GREGORY (C. J.). To the Alps of Chinese Tibet: An Account of a Journey of Exploration up to and among the Snow-Clad Mountains of the Tibetan Frontier. 1923.

27193 BELL (*Sir* CHARLES ALFRED). Tibet, Past and Present. Oxf. 1924.

27194 BAGNOLD (RALPH ALGER). Libyan Sands: Travel in a Dead World. 1935.

27195 AXELSON (ERIK) *ed.* South African Explorers. 1954.

27196 HOWARD (CECIL) *ed.* West African Explorers. 1951.

27197 ELDER (JOHN RAWSON). The Pioneer Explorers of New Zealand. 1929.

27198 CHEESMAN (ROBERT ERNEST). Lake Tana and the Blue Nile: An Abyssinian Quest. 1936.

27199 CARRUTHERS (DOUGLAS). Beyond the Caspian: A Naturalist in Central Asia. Edin. 1949.

27200 POUND (REGINALD). Evans of the Broke: A Biography of Admiral Lord Mountevans. 1963.

27201 MOUNTEVANS (EDWARD RATCLIFFE GARTH RUSSELL) *Baron*. Keeping the Seas. 1920.

27202 —— South with Scott. 1921.

27203 —— British Polar Explorers. 1944.

27204 —— Adventurous Life. 1946.

27205 —— The Desolate Antarctic. 1950.

27206 —— Arctic Solitudes. Lond./NY. 1953.

27207 GLEN (*Sir* ALEXANDER RICHARD). Young Men in the Arctic: The Story of the Oxford University Expedition to Spitzbergen, 1933. 1935.

27208 GLEN (*Sir* ALEXANDER RICHARD) *and* CROFT (NOEL ANDREW COTTON). Under the Pole Star: The Oxford University Arctic Expedition, 1935–36. 1937.

27209 MARKHAM (CLEMENTS R.). The Lands of Silence: A History of Arctic and Antarctic Exploration. Camb. 1921.

27210 SHACKLETON (EDWARD ARTHUR ALEXANDER) *Baron*. Arctic Journeys: The Story of the Oxford University Ellesmere Land Expedition, 1934–35. 1937.

27211 HAYES (JAMES GORDON). The Conquest of the North Pole: Recent Arctic Exploration. NY./Lond. 1934.

27212 MILL (HUGH ROBERT). The Life of Sir Ernest Shackleton. 1923.

27213 HURLEY (FRANK). Argonauts of the South: Being a Narrative of the Voyagings and Polar Seas Adventures.

27214 JOYCE (ERNEST EDWARD MILLS). The South Polar Trail: The Log of the Imperial Trans-Antarctic Expedition. 1929.

27215 HAYES (JAMES GORDON). Antarctica: A Treatise on the Southern Continent. 1928.

27216 RYMILL (JOHN). Southern Lights: The Official Account of the British Graham Land Expedition, 1934–37, with Two Chapters by A. Stephenson and an Historical Introduction by Hugh Robert Mill. 1938.

27217 CROFT (ANDREW). Polar Exploration: Epics of the Twentieth Century. 1939.

27218 HENRY (THOMAS). The White Continent: The Story of Antarctica. 1951.

27219 MILL (HUGH ROBERT). An Autobiography. 1951.

27220 CHRISTIE (E. W. HUNTER). The Antarctic Problem: An Historical and Political Study. 1951.

27221 KIRWAN (*Sir* ARCHIBALD LAURENCE PATRICK). A History of Polar Exploration. NY. 1960. Eng. edn The White Road. 1959.

27222 BRUNT (*Sir* DAVID) *ed.* Royal Society International Geophysical Year Antarctic Expeditions: Halley Bay, Coats Land, Falkland Islands Dependencies, 1955–1959. 4 vols. 1960–4.

27223 MOTT (P. G.). Wings over Ice: An Account of the Falkland Islands and Dependencies Aerial Survey Expedition 1955–57. 1986.

27224 PRIESTLEY (*Sir* RAYMOND EDWARD) *et al., eds.* Antarctic Research: A Review of British Scientific Research in Antarctica. 1964.

27225 COLEMAN-COOKE (JOHN). Discovery II in the Antarctic: The Story of British Research in the Southern Seas. 1963.

27226 HARDY (*Sir* ALISTER CLAVERING). Great Waters: A Voyage of Natural History to Study Whales, Plankton and the Waters of the Southern Ocean in the Old Royal Research Ship Discovery, with Results Brought up to Date by the Findings of the R.R.S. Discovery II. 1967.

27227 BRITISH ANTARCTIC SURVEY. Annual Report 1975+.

27228 CRANFIELD (INGRID). The Challengers: British and Common-wealth Adventure since 1945. 1976.

27229 FIENNES (RANULPH). Living Dangerously: An Autobiography. 1987.

27230 GRANT (CHRISTINA PHELPS). The Syrian Desert: Caravans, Travel and Exploration. London. 1937. NY. 1938.

27231 PHILBY (HARRY ST JOHN BRIDGER). The Heart of Arabia. 1922.

27232 —— A Pilgrim in Arabia. 1943.

27233 THOMAS (BERTRAM SIDNEY). Alarms and Excursions in Arabia. 1931.

27234 SCOTT (HUGH). In the High Yemen. 1942.

27235 NEATE (JILL). Mountaineering Literature: A Bibliography of Material Published in English. Milnthorpe. Rev. edn 1986.

27236 CLARK (RONALD WILLIAM) *and* PYATT (EDWARD CHARLES). Mountaineering in Britain: A History from the Earliest Times to the Present Day. 1957.

27237 IRVING (RONALD GRAHAM LOCK). A History of British Mountaineering. 1955.

27238 BRUCE (CHARLES GRANVILLE) *et al.* The Assault on Mount Everest, 1922. 1923.

27239 SOMERVELL (THEODORE HOWARD). After Everest: The Experiences of a Mountaineer and Medical Missionary. 1936.

27240 HUNT (HENRY CECIL JOHN) *Baron, and* HILLARY (*Sir* EDMUND). 'The Ascent of Mount Everest'. *Geog. J.* 119 (1953), 386–99.

27241 HUNT (HENRY CECIL JOHN) *Baron*. The Ascent of Everest. 1953. NY. 1954.

27242 —— Life is Meeting. 1978.

27243 HILLARY (*Sir* EDMUND) *and* HILLARY (PETER). Ascent: Two Lives Explored: The Autobiographies of Sir Edmund and Peter Hillary. NY. 1986.

27244 BONINGTON (CHRISTIAN). The Everest Years: A Climber's Life. 1986.

27245 BROWN (JOE). The Hard Years: An Autobiography. 1967.

27246 WHILLANS (DONALD) *and* ORMEROD (ALICK). Don Whillans: Portrait of a Mountaineer. Harmondsworth. 1976.

27247 BONINGTON (CHRISTIAN). I Chose to Climb. 1966. The Next Horizon: Autobiography. 1973.

27248 HUGHES (ARTHUR JOSEPH). History of Air Navigation. 1946.

27249 SMITH (ROBERT ALLAN). Radio Aids to Navigation. Camb. 1947.

27250 HEWSON (*Sir* JOSEPH BUSHBY). A History of the Practice of Navigation. Glasg. 1951.

27251 MAY (WILLIAM EDWARD). A History of Marine Navigation. [With a chapter on modern developments by Leonard Holder.]. Henley-on-Thames. 1973.

27252 WRIGHT (MONTE D.). Most Probable Position: A History of Aerial Navigation to 1941. Lawrence, Ka. 1973.

49. SCIENCE AND THEOLOGY

27253 HALDANE (J. S.). The Sciences and Philosophy. 1929.

27254 DINGLE (HERBERT). Science and Human Experience. 1931.

27255 DAVIDSON (MARTIN). The Heavens and Faith. 1936.

27256 DAMPIER (formerly WHETHAM) (WILLIAM CECIL). A History of Science and its Relations with Philosophy and Religion. Camb. 1929. 4th edn 1948. Reprinted with a postscript by I. Bernard Cohen. Camb. 1966.

27257 INGE (WILLIAM RALPH). God and the Astronomers. 1933.

27258 NEEDHAM (JOSEPH). History is on Our side: A Contribution to Political Religion and Scientific Faith. 1946.

27259 POLANYI (MICHAEL). The Study of Man. Lond./ Chicago, Ill. 1959.

27260 PASSMORE (JOHN). The Perfectibility of Man. 1970.

27261 ECCLES (*Sir* JOHN CAREW). Facing Reality: Philosophical Adventures by a Brain Scientist. 1970.

27262 —— The Human Mystery. 1979.

27263 ECCLES (*Sir* JOHN CAREW) *and* POPPER (*Sir* KARL RAIMUND). The Self and its Brain. Berlin and Lond. 1977.

27264 AUSTIN (WILLIAM H.). The Relevance of Natural Science to Theology. 1976.

INDEX

A.E.R.E. (U.K.) Energy Technology Support Unit: The Prospect for the Generation of Electricity from Wind Energy in the United Kingdom: A Report prepared for the Department of Energy, 7166

ACAS and Central Office of Information: Disciplinary Practice and Procedures in Employment, 4162

Aaron, Benjamin: Industrial Conflict: A Comparative Legal Survey, 5759

Aaronovitch, Sam: The Ruling Class: A Study of British Finance Capital, 5429, 9756; 'The Concentration of British Manufacturing', 5530 Monopoly: A Study of British Monopoly Capitalism, 9757

Abbas, Mekki: The Sudan Question: The Dispute over the Anglo-Egyptian Condominium 1884–1951, 14412

Abbot, George C.: 'Political Disintegration: The Lessons of Anguilla', 13061

Abbotsholme: Reddie of Abbotsholme, 23099

Abbott, Albert: Education for Industry and Commerce in England, 23263

Abbott, Claude Colleer: Poet and Painter: Being Correspondence between Gordon Bottomley and Paul Nash, 1910–1946, 25402

Abbott, Joan: 'The Concept of Mobility', 9590; Student Life in a Class Society, 9854; 'Students' Class in Three Northern Universities', 9855

Abbott, Pamela: Women and Social Class, 9605

Abbott, Simon: 'Race Studies in Britain', 11004; The Prevention of Racial Discrimination in Britain, 11168

Abbott, Wilbur Cortez: An Introduction to the Documents Relating to the International Status of Gibraltar, 1704–1934, 12848

Abdela, Lesley: Women with X Appeal: Women Politicians in Britain Today, 7835

Abecassis, David William: The Law and Practice Relating to Oil Pollution from Ships, 20083

Abel, Deryck Robert Endsleigh: Ernest Benn: Counsel for Liberty, 1573; A History of British Tariffs, 1923–1942, 3761

Abel-Smith, Brian: Socialism and Affluence: Four Fabian Essays, 2136; ed. Social Policy: An Introduction, 8831; 'Public Expenditure on the Social Services', 8938; The Poor and the Poorest: A New Analysis of the Ministry of Labour's Family Expenditure Surveys of 1953–54 and 1960, 9057; Child Poverty, 9058; The Hospitals, 1800–1948: A Study in Social Administration in England and Wales, 9254, 21415; British Doctors at Home and Abroad, 20812; The Cost of the National Health Service in England and Wales, 21563; National Health Service: The First Thirty Years, 21687; Value for Money in Health Services: A Comparative Study, 21688; An International Study of Health Expenditure and its Relevance for Health Planning, 21689; A History of the Nursing Profession, 21713

Abell, Paul Henry: Transport and Industry in Greater Manchester, 16331

Abercrombie, Keith: Rural Development in Lewis and Harris: The Western Isles of Scotland, 19257

Abercrombie, Lascelles: Stratford-upon-Avon: Report on Future Development, 18912

Abercrombie, Sir [Leslie] Patrick: Town and Country Planning, 17979; 'The Influence of Town Planning upon Tuberculosis', 18597; Town and Country Planning, 18776; Country Planning and Landscape Design, 18777; Planning in Town and Country: Difficulties and Possibilities, 18778; A Plan for Bath: A Report . . ., 18840; Bristol and Bath Regional Planning Scheme, 18847; The Clyde Valley Regional Plan, 1946: A Report, 18855; Doncaster Regional Planning Scheme, 18861; East Kent Regional Planning Scheme: Preliminary Survey, 18863; Final Report, 18864; A Civic Survey and Plan for the City and Royal Burgh of Edinburgh, 18866; A Plan for the City of Kingston upon Hull, 18881; Regional Planning Report on Oxfordshire, 18899; A Plan for Plymouth: Report, 18902; Sheffield: A Civic Survey and Suggestions towards a Development Plan, 18906; Sheffield and District Regional Planning Scheme, 18907; Stratford-upon-Avon: Report on Future Development, 18912; Warwick: Its Preservation and Redevelopment, 18918; The Greater London Plan 1944, 18936; The County of London Plan, 1943, 18937; 'The Preservation of Rural England', 18946; 'A Civic Society: An Outline of its Scope, Formation and Functions', 20382

Abercrombie, Nicholas: Capital, Labour and the Middle Classes, 9734; The University in an Urban Environment, 23304

Aberdeen University: (Dept. of Geography) Royal Grampian Country: A Report of the Scottish Tourist Board, 5290

Abortion Statistics 1974+ Annual, 7875

Abraham, E. P.: 'The Work on Penicillin at Oxford', 20944; 'L'Introduction de la Penicilline dans la Médicine', 20945

Abraham, James Johnston: Surgeon's Journey: The Autobiography of J. Johnston Abraham, 20857

Abraham, Joseph Hayim: Sociology, 8052; The Origins and Growth of Sociology, 8051

Abraham, Neville: Big Business and Government: The New Disorder, 4973

Abrahams, P.: Jamaica, 13049

Abrahams, William Miller: Journey to the Frontier: Julian Bell and John Cornford: Their Lives and the 1930s, 1943, 23774; Orwell: The Transformation; The Unknown Orwell, 25748

Abramovitz, Moses: The Growth of Public Employment in Great Britain 1890–1950, 775

Abrams, Charles: Housing in the Modern World, 18671

Abrams, Mark Alexander: ed. Values and Social Change in Britain, 238; 'Public Opinion Polls and the British General Election', 2268; 'Opinion Polls and the 1970 British General Election', 2271; Must Labour Lose?, 2316; ed. Britain and her Export Trade, 4801; The Condition of the British People, 1911–1945: A Study Prepared for the Fabian Society, 7574; Social Surveys and Social Action, 8773; Education, Social Class and Reading of Newspapers and Magazines, 9473; 'Social Class and British Politics', 9474; 'British Elite Attitudes and the European Common Market', 14154; The Teenage Consumer, 20462; The Elderly Consumer, 20463; 'Child Audiences for Television in Great Britain', 24827; Education, Social Class and Newspaper Reading, 25051; The Newspaper Reading Public of Tomorrow, 25052

Abrams, Philip: ed. Work, Urbanism and Inequality: U.K. Society Today, 3858; Communes, Sociology and Society, 8053; 'The Young Voter in British Politics', 8419; 'The Young Activist in British Politics', 8420; Towns in Societies: Essays in Economic History and Historical Sociology, 17942

Abramson, Paul R.: 'Generational Change and Continuity and British Partisan Choice, 2227; 'Social Class and Political Change in Western Europe: A Cross-national Longitudinal Analysis', 9437; 'Il Nuovo Ruolo delle Classi in Europa', 9438; 'Social Mobility and Political Attitudes: A Study of Intergenerational Mobility among Young British Men', 9439

Abromeit, Heidrun: British Steel: An Industry between the State and Private Sector, 6579

Abse, Dannie: A Poet in the Family, 25347; A Strong Dose of Myself, 25348

Abse, Joan: The Art Galleries of Britain and Ireland: A Guide to their Collections, 23939

Abse, Leo: Private Member, 1338

Abshagen, Karl Heinz: King, Lords and Gentlemen: Influence and Power of the English Upper Classes, 681

Abt, I. A.: ed. Abt-Garrison History of Pediatrics, 21118

Acheson, Roy M.: Health, Society and Medicine, 22013

Ackerknecht, Erwin H.: A Short History of Medicine, 21191; Therapeutics from the

Primitives to the 20th Century, 21192; *ed.* Metabolism and Respiration, from Erasistratus to Lavoiser, Metabolism from Liebig to the Present, 21193; History and Geography of the most Important Diseases, 22228

Ackerman, Robert: J.G. Frazer: His Life and His Work, 26353

Ackers, James: What's Wrong with General Practice: A Memo, 21533

Ackland, Joss: I Must Be in There Somewhere, 26010

Ackland, Valentine: For Sylvia: An Honest Account, 25852

Ackroyd, Carol: The Technology of Police Control, 10733

Ackroyd, Peter: T. S. Eliot, 25489; Dressing up: Transvestism and Drag: The History of an Obsession, 26288

Ackworth, Bernard: The Navies of Today and Tomorrow, 15334

Ackworth, Evelyn: The New Matriarchy, 7694

Acland, Eric: The House of Windsor, George V to George VI, 470

Acland, H.: 'The Sociology of Education in Britain, 1960–1968: A Bibliographical Review', 22445

Acland, Sir Francis Dyke: Japan Must be Stopped, 13576

Acland, Sir Richard: The Forward March, 1905; What it Will Be like in the New Britain, 1906; How it Can Be Done, 1907

Acompline, 56

Acton Society Trust: The Acton Society Trust: Its Aims, Work and Publications, 7974

Acton, Harold: Memoirs of an Aesthete, 25350; More Memoirs of an Aesthete, 25351; Nancy Mitford: A Memoir, 25715

Acton, Thomas Alan: *ed.* Current Changes amongst British Gypsies and their Place in International Patterns of Development, 11345; Gypsy Politics and Social Change: The Development of Ethnic Ideology and Pressure Politics among British Gypsies from Victorian Reformism to Romany Nationalism, 11346

Acumen Marketing Group: A Report on the Take Away Food Market in Britain, 20620

Adam Wilson & Sons: Adam Wilson & Sons: The History of a Firm of Timber Merchants: Founded 1956, 19796

Adam and Charles Black, 1807–1957: Some Chapters in the History of a Publishing House, 24943

Adam, Colin Forbes: Life of Lord [George Ambrose] Lloyd, 1454

Adam, Ruth: A Woman's Place, 1910–75, 7842; Beatrice Webb: A Life, 1858–1943, 2149

Adamec, Ludwig: Afghanistan's Foreign Affairs to the Mid-Twentieth Century: Relations with the USSR, Germany and Britain, 13848

Adams, Arthur Avery: Consumers' Expenditures in the United Kingdom, 1900–1919, 20437

Adams, Barbara: Gypsies and Government Policy in England: A Study of the Travellers' Way of Life in Relation to the Policies and Practices of Central and Local Government, 11347

Adams, Brian Warren: London's North Western Electric: A Jubilee History, 16962

Adams, David Philip: The Evolution of Modern Britain, 3498

Adams, Ian Hugh: The Making of Urban Scotland, 2453, 18124

Adams, Jack: The South Wales Borderers, 15753

Adams, John G. U.: Transport Planning: Vision and Practice, 16259; 'Concorde Wondering Where to Go', 17570

Adams, M. E.: Voluntary Service Overseas— The Story of the First Ten Years, 9159

Adams, Margaret: *ed.* The Mentally Subnormal: Social Work Approaches, 21849; Mental Retardation and its Social Dimensions, 21850

Adams, Michael: Suez and After: Year of Crisis, 14369

Adams, Mollie: 'Liberal Studies in Technological Education', 22507

Adams, Paul: Children's Rights: Towards the Liberation of the Child, 7513

Adams, R. H.: Club Life and the Approved School Boy, 10522

Adams, R. J. Q.: Arms and the Wizard: Lloyd George and the Ministry of Munitions, 1915–1916, 1022

Adams, Rex: The Employers' Challenge: A Study of the National Shipbuilding and Engineering Disputes of 1957, 5618; Trade Union Officers: A Study of Full-time Officers, Branch Secretaries and Shop Stewards in British Trade-Unions, 6716

Adams, Thomas: 'Town Planning in Greater London', 18935

Adams, Tony: 'The Formation of the Co-operative Party Re-Considered', 1898

Adams, Valerie: 'Logistics Support for the Falklands Campaign', 16094; The Media and the Falklands Campaign, 16121, 24900

Adams, W. Eric: The New Town of Harlow, 19016

Adams, W. S.: 'Lloyd George and the Labour Movement', 1025

Adams, Sir Walter: 'Foreigners in Britain', 10967; 'Refugee Scholars of the 1930s', 22542

Adamson, G.: 'Should Foster Mums be Paid?', 8096; The Care Takers, 8097

Adamson, John William: The Illiterate Anglo-Saxon, 22576

Adamson, S. H.: Seaside Piers, 26991

Adamson, S.: 'The Politics of Improvement Grants', 18530

Adamthwaite, Anthony: 'The British Government and the Media, 1937–1938', 15218

Adcock, Cyril J.: 'Social Class and the Ranking of Occupations', 9468

Addenbrooke, David: The Royal Shakespeare Company: The Peter Hall Years, 26150

Addison, Christopher, Viscount: Politics from Within, 1911–1918, 1064; Four and a Half Years: A Personal Diary from June 1914 to January 1919, 1065; The Betrayal of the Slums, 18590; A Policy for British Agriculture, 19455; The Nation and its Food, 20582; The Health of the People and how it May be Improved, 22037

Addison, Paul: 'The Political Beliefs of Winston Churchill, 988; Now the War is Over: A Social History of Britain from 1945 to 1951, 7536

Addison, Sir William: The Old Roads of England, 17108; Portrait of Epping Forest, 26967

Addleshaw, George William Outram: The Architectural Setting of Anglican Worship: An Inquiry into the Arrangements for Public Worship in the Church of England from the Reformation to the Present Day, 11607

Adelman, Paul: The Decline of the Liberal Party, 1910–1931, 1820

Adeney, Martin: Community Action: Four Examples, 9262

Adinarayan, Samuel Pundipeddi: The Case for Colour: An Analysis of the Causes, Manifestations and Effects of Colour Prejudices. A Survey of Remedial Measures and some Suggestions for a Cure, 11154

Adler, Bill: *ed.* The Churchill Wit, 988

Adler, Max K.: Marketing and Market Research, 20471; *ed.* Leading Cases in Market Research, 20472

Adler, Michael H.: The Writing Machine, 7054

Adley, Robert: Covering My Tracks: Recollections of the Last Years of Steam, 17049

Admiralty: East of Malta, West of Suez: The Admiralty Account of the Naval War in the Eastern Mediterranean, September 1939 to March 1941, 14885; The Mediterranean Fleet, Greece to Tripoli: The Admiralty Account of Naval Operations, April 1941 to January 1943, 14886; Fleet Air Arm, 14984; Merchantmen at War: The Official Story of the Merchant Navy, 1939–1944, 15125; The Royal Marines: The Admiralty Account of their Achievement, 1939–1943, 15410

Adnett, N. J.: 'The Eclipse of British Classical Political Economy: The Case of Education', 23213

Adult Education in 1961+, 23641

Adult Education, 22581

Advani, L.: Blind Welfare in the United Kingdom, 21931

Advarsi, Rukun: E. M. Forster as Critic, 25521

Advertising Association: Advertising Expenditure 1948, 4321; Advertising Expenditure 1960–1974, 4322

Advertising: An Annotated Bibliography, 1972, 4318

Advisory, Conciliation and Arbitration Service [ACAS]: Industrial Relations Handbook, 4157; First Annual Report, 4158; The Contract Cleaning Industry: A Report, 4159; The Laundry Wages Council, 4160; Workplace Communications, 4161

Ady, Peter Honorine: The British Economy 1945–1950, 3616; British Economy in the 1950s, 3617

Agar, Augustus: Baltic Episode: A Classic of Secret Service in Russian Waters, 15126; Footprints in the Sea, 15304; Showing the Flag, 15305

Agate, James Evershed: Ego: The Autobiography of James Agate, 25910; The Selective 'Ego': The Diaries of James Agate, 25911; A Short View of the English Stage, 25912; First Nights, 25913; More First Nights, 25914; The Amazing Theatre, 25915; Immoment Toys: A Survey of Light Entertainment on the London Stage, 1920–1943, 25916

Agate, John: The Care of the Aged, 8596; atrics for Nurses and Social Workers, 8597; ed. Medicine in Old Age, 8598

Agee-Hosenball Defence Committee: Scrap the Act: Empire and Immigration: A Historical Background to the 1971 Immigration Act, 11125

Agius, P.: British Furniture, 1880–1925, 24146

Agnew, John A.: 'Political Regionalism and Scottish Nationalism in Gaelic Scotland', 2494

Agnew, Julian: A Dealer's Record: Agnew's 1967–1981, 23946

Agricultural History Review: 1953+, 19391

Agricultural Land Commission Report: 1948–63, 19379

Agricultural Research Council: The Agricultural Research Service, 19480

Agricultural Statistics, United Kingdom: 1867+, 19384

Agriculture and Food Research Council: Science and Change in Agriculture, 19605

Agriculture in Scotland: 1912+, 19613

Aguolu, C. C.: Nigeria: A Comprehensive Bibliography in the Humanities and Social Sciences 1900–1971, 12753

Ahern, Geoffrey: Inner City God: The Nature of Belief in the Inner City, 11846

Ahern, Tom: The Railways and the People: An Appeal to Passengers and Workers, 16770

Ahmad, Ishtiar: Anglo-Iranian Relations 1905–1919, 13852

Ahmed, Mesbahuddin: The British Labour Party and the Indian Independence Movement 1917–1939, 13134

Ahmed, N.: 'Race Relations in Britain', 11226

Ahrenfeldt, Robert Henry: ed. Cultural Factors in Delinquency, 10573; Medical Records in the Criminal Court, 10574; ed. Mental Health in the Service of the Community, 21816

Ahrons, Ernest L.: The British Steam Railway Locomotive 1825–1925, 17026

Aickman, Robert: The River Runs Uphill: A Story of Success and Failure, 16449

Aiken, Alex: Courage Past: A Duty Done, 15454

Aiken, Sir Robert: Administration of a University, 23346

Ainslie, J. R.: ed. English Catholic Worship: Liturgical Renewal in England since 1900, 11976

Ainsworth, John Francis: The Royal Sussex Regiment, 1701–1966, 15731

Ainsworth, Marjorie E.: The Effects of Environmental Factors on Secondary Educational Attainment in Manchester: A Plowden Follow-up, 22835

Ainsworth, Peter: Police Work, 10784

Air Force List: 1949+, 15780

Air Ministry: R.A.F. Middle East: The Official Story of Air Operations in the Middle East from February 1942 to January 1943, 15939; The Origins and Development of Operational Research in the Royal Air Force, 15952

Air Training Corps: Twenty-First Birthday 1941–62, 15921

Aitchison, J. W.: 'The Agricultural Landscape of Wales', 19639; The Welsh Language 1961–1981: An Interpretative Atlas, 23825

Aitken, A. J.: ed. Languages of Scotland, 23847; ed. Lowland Scots, 23848; The Scots Language: Planning for Modern Usage, 23849

Aitken, Alexander Craig: Gallipoli to the Somme, 14466

Aitken, H. H.: Northumberland Village Halls, 9258

Aitken, Jonathan: Officially Secret, 767

Aitken, William Maxwell, Baron Beaverbrook: The Decline and Fall of Lloyd George: And Great was the Fall Thereof, 1018

Aitken-Swan, Jean: Fertility Control and the Medical Profession, 7520

Ajayi, J. F. A.: ed. History of West Africa, 12727

Akenson, Donald Harman: 'The Irish Civil War and the Drafting of the Free-State Constitution', 2684; Small Differences: Irish Catholics and Irish Protestants, 1815–1922: An International Perspective, 2717; Education and Enmity: The Control of Schooling in Northern Ireland 1920–1950, 2863, 12171, 23637; 'Patterns of English Educational Change: The Fisher and the Butler Acts', 22619

Akester, Joyce M.: Health Visiting in the Sixties, 21733

Akinsanya, J.: A Bibliography of Race and Race Relations, 10889

Akker, J.: Trade Unions in a Changing Society, 6778

Akrigg, D.: Buses of South Yorkshire, Humberside and Lincolnshire, 17283

Al-Qaddo, Husain: 'The Implementation of Housing Policy: The Scottish Special Housing Association', 18486

Al-Rahman, Muddathir 'Abd: Imperialism and Nationalism in the Sudan: A Study in Constitutional and Political Development, 14415

Alareon, Jose: 'Depression and Attempted Suicide: A Study of 91 Cases Seen in a Casualty Department', 10816

Alasziewski, A.: Crisis in the Health Service: The Politics of Management, 21622

Albery, Paul: The Story of the Bahamas, 13019

Albion, Robert Greenhalgh: Naval and Maritime History: An Annotated Bibliography, 15227; Maritime and Naval History, 16452

Albjerg, Victor L.: 'British Finance, 1914–1939', 4554

Albrecht-Carrié, René: Britain and France: Adaptations to a Changing Context of Power, 14237

Albrow, Martin C.: 'The Influence of Accommodation upon 64 Reading University Students', 9858

Aldcroft, Derek H.: ed. British Economic Fluctuations, 1790–1939, 3405; ed. Growth in 20th Century Britain, 3406; The British Economy, 1870–1939, 3407; British Railways in Transition: The Economic Problems of Britain's Railways since 1914, 3408, 16725; British Transport since 1914: An Economic History, 3409, 16181; The British Economy, 3523; 'Economic Progress in Britain in the 1920's: A Reappraisal', 3561; 'Economic Progress in Britain in the 1920's: A Rejoinder', 3563; 'Economic Growth in Britain in the Inter-War Years: A Reassessment', 3589; The Inter-War Economy: Britain 1918–1939, 3590; The British Economy between the Wars, 3591; ed. British Industry between the Wars: Instability and Industrial Development, 1919–1939, 5001; The East Midlands Economy: An Economic and Business Review of the East Midlands Region, 5157; Business, Banking and Urban History: Essays in Honour of S. G. Checkland, 5251; 'The Effectiveness of Direct Controls in the British Economy, 1946–1950', 6110; 'The Development of the Managed Economy before 1939', 6140; 'The Diminishing Scope of Government Trading, 1946–1954', 6141; Building in the British Economy Between the Wars, 6174; Studies in British Transport History, 1870–1970, 16182; 'A New Chapter in 20th Century History: The Transport Revolution', 16183; British Transport: An Economic Survey from the 17th Century to the 20th Century, 16184; Rail Transport and Sea Transport, 16185; 'The Eclipse of English Coastal Shipping, 1913–1921', 16469; 'The Decontrol of British Shipping and Railways after the First World War', 16470; British Industry between the Wars, 16610; 'The Railways and Economic Growth: A Review Article', 16726; The Atlas of British Railway History, 16727; ed. British Industry between the Wars, 17579

Alden, Jeremy: Regional Development Policies for Rural Wales: Mid-Wales, 5359; Rural Schleswig-Holstein and Mid Wales: A Comparative Study of Regional Development, 5360

Alderman, Geoffrey: Modern Britain 1700–1983: A Domestic History, 302; Pressure Groups and Government in Great Britain, 2061; 'Symposium: Pressure Groups', 2074; The Jewish Vote in Great Britain since 1945, 2232, 11324; British Elections: Myth and Reality, 2361; 'The Railway Companies and the Growth of Trade Unionism in the Late Nineteenth and Early Twentieth Centuries', 6813; The Jewish Community in British Politics, 11323; London Jewry and London Politics, 1889–1986, 11325; 'Anglo-Jewry: The Politics of an Image', 11326

Alderman, R. Keith: 'Problems of Ministerial Turnover in Two Labour Cabinets', 732; The Tactics of Resignation: A Study in British Cabinet Government, 744; 'The Timing of Cabinet Reshuffles', 745; 'Rejuvenating the Cabinet: The Records of Post-War British Prime Ministers

Compared', 746; 'The Prime Minister and the Appointment of Ministers: An Exercise in Political Bargaining', 957; 'Discipline in the Parliamentary Labour Party, 1945–1951', 1725; 'Parliamentary Party Discipline in Opposition: The Parliamentary Labour Party, 1951–1964', 1728

Alderman, Ralph: A Bibliography of British Honduras 1900–1970, 13022

Alderson, John Cottingham: 'The Role of the Police in Society', 10731; The Police We Deserve, 10732

Alderson, Roy Claude: A History of the Midland Red, 17325

Alderson, Stanley: Yea or Nay? Referenda in the United Kingdom, 2386; 'The Referendum Under the British Constitution', 2387; Housing, 18665

Aldgate, Anthony: Britain Can Take It: The British Cinema in the Second World War, 24595; Cinema and History: British Newsreels and the Spanish Civil War, 24609; '1930 Newsreels: Censorship and Controversy', 24610; Best of British: Cinema and Society 1930–1970, 24617

Aldington, Richard: Lawrence of Arabia: A Biographical Enquiry, 13818; Lawrence of Arabia, 14515; The Life of D. H. Lawrence 1885 to 1930, 25647

Aldous, Joan: International Bibliography of Research in Marriage and the Family, 1900–1964, 9922

Aldous, Tony: Battle for the Environment, 19907; Goodbye, Britain?, 19908

Aldred, Chris: Women at Work, 7857

Aldrich, Richard: ed. British Intelligence, Strategy and the Cold War, 1945–1951, 16007

Aldridge, Alan: 'In the Absence of a Minister: Structures of Subordination in the Role of the Deaconess in the Church of England', 11672

Aldridge, Henry R.: The Case for Town Planning: A Practical Manual for the Use of Councillors, Officers, and Others engaged in the Preparation of Town Planning Schemes, 17737; The Administration of the Town Planning Duties of Local Authorities, 17738; The National Housing Manual, 18591; The Extent and Character of the National Housing Needs, 18592; If you are Blitzed: How to Claim Compensation, 18593

Aldridge, Meryl: The British New Towns: A Programme without a Policy, 18218, 19004

Alexander, Alan: The Politics of Local Government in the United Kingdom, 3127; 'Symposium: Local Government', 3128; Local Government since Reorganisation, 3187; Borough Government and Politics: Reading 1835–1985, 3339

Alexander, Andrew,'British Politics and the Royal Prerogative of Appointment since 1945', 462; The Making of the Prime Minister, 1970, 966

Alexander, B.: British Volunteers for Liberty: Spain 1936–1939, 13990

Alexander, Basil A.: Acid Rain and the Environment: Sources of Information, 20031

Alexander, Jeffrey C.: Sociological Theory since 1945, 8095

Alexander, Sir Kenneth John Wilson: 'Political Economy of Change', 6793; 'Membership Participation in a Printing Trade Union', 6794; A Study of Industrial Change, 16631; Rural Renewal: Experience in the Highlands and Islands, 19256

Alexander, Michael: Privileged Nightmare, 15041

Alexander Peter: Roy Campbell: A Critical Biography, 25434; William Plomer: A Biography, 25760

Alexander, Roy: The Cruise of the Raider 'Wolf', 14681

Alexander, Sally: ed. Women's Fabian Tracts, 7765

Alexander, W. & Sons Ltd: W. Alexander & Sons Ltd, Part 3: 1938–1961, 17319

Alexander, William M.: 'The Universities and the State', 23313

Alexander, Sir William Picken: The Burnham Primary and Secondary Schools Report, 1954: A Commentary by Dr W. P. Alexander, 22612

Alford, Bernard William Ernest: Depression and Recovery? British Economic Growth, 1918–1939, 3565; British Economic Performance, 1945–1975, 3626; A History of the Carpenters Company, 6189; W. D. & H. O. Wills and the Development of the U.K. Tobacco Industry,1786–1965, 6535

Alford, R. R.: Party and Society, 2231

Algie, Jimmy: A Management Game for Social Services, 9248

Ali, Tariq: The Coming British Revolution, 1985; 'The Critical Condition of British Socialism': ed. 1968 and After: Inside the Revolution, 2005; Street Fighting Years: An Autobiography of the Sixties, 2006; 'Why Labour Lost', 2350

Allan, Charles M.: 'Fiscal Marksmanship, 1951–1963', 4603; The Theory of Taxation, 4851

Allan, Frank N.: 'Diabetes before and after Insulin', 20910

Allan, George A. T.: Christ's Hospital, 23051; The Christ's Hospital Book, 23052

Allaun, Frank: Heartbreak Housing, 18695; No Place Like Home: Britain's Housing Tragedy (From the Victim's View) and how to Overcome it, 18696.

Allaway, Albert John: The Educational Centres Movement: A Comprehensive Survey, 22766; Adult Education in England: a Brief History, 23663; Challenge and Response: W.E.A. East Midland District 1919–1969, 23672; The First Fifty Years of the W.E.A.in Leicester, 23673

Allday, Richard Kime: On Medicine in Britain and the National Health Service, 21263

Alldritt, Keith: The Visual Imagination of D. H. Lawrence, 25638

Allen, A. J.: The English Voter, 2219

Allen, Arthur Bruce: Twentieth Century Britain, 338

Allen, Barbara K.: Financial Help in Social Work: A Study of Preventative Work with Families under the Children and Young Persons Act, 1963, 10093

Allen, Cecil John: A Century of Scientific Instrument Making, 1853–1953, 7103; Railways of Britain, 16768; The Great Eastern Railway, 16842; The Great Northern, 16846; The Great Western, 16856; Salute to the Great Western, 16857; Salute to the London Midland and Scottish, 16874; The London and North Eastern Railway, 16889; The North Eastern Railway, 16905; Salute to the Southern, 16912; Locomotive Practice and Performance in the 20th Century, 17062; Modern Railways: Their Engineering, Equipment and Operation, 17082

Allen, Charles: ed. Tales from the Dark Continent: Images of British Colonial Africa in the Twentieth Century, 12685; The Savage Wars of Peace, 16178

Allen, Christopher: Unions and Economic Crisis: Britain, West Germany and Sweden, 6827

Allen, David Elliston: British Tastes: An Enquiry into the Likes and Dislikes of the Regional Consumer, 20459, 20607; The Naturalist in Britain: A Social History, 26528; 'Natural History and Social History', 26529; The Botanists: A History of the Botanical Society of the British Isles through One Hundred and Fifty Years, 26543

Allen, G. O.: 'Sixteen Years: A Saga of Smoke Control', 20066

Allen, Garland E.: Life Science in the Twentieth Century, 26523

Allen, Geoffrey Freeman: Railways of the Twentieth Century, 16730; The Illustrated History of Britain's Railways, 16731; British Rail after Beeching, 16780; The Southern since 1948, 16916

Allen, George Cyril: The Structure of Industry in Britain: A Study in Economic Change, 3427, 4959; 'Advice from Economists Forty Five Years Ago', 3571; British Industries and their Organisation, 4958; Monopoly and Restrictive Practices, 4990

Allen, George Henry: The Great War, 14450

Allen, George Rollason: Agricultural Marketing Policies, 19501; 'The National Farmers' Union as a Pressure Group', 19672

Allen, Harry Cranbrook: Great Britain and the United States: A History of Anglo-American Relations (1783–1952), 13998; ed. Contrast and Connection: Bicentennial Essays in American History, 13999; The Anglo-American Predicament: The British Commonwealth, the United States and European Unity, 14071; 'The Anglo-American Relationship in the Sixties', 14072; 'Democracy and the Robbins Report', 23409

Allen, Hubert Raymond: Battle of Britain. The Recollections of H. R. 'Dizzy' Allen, D.F.C., 14800; The Legacy of Lord Trenchard, 15967

Allen, Isobel: Women in Top Jobs: Four Studies in Achievement, 7714

Allen, J. de V.: ed. A Collection of Treaties and other Documents Affecting the States of Malaysia 1761–1963, 12899

Allen, James Albert: Studies in Innovation in the Steel and Chemical Industries, 6569

Allen, John Ernest: British War Budgets, 4911

Allen, Louis: 'Transfer of Power in Burma', 13206; Singapore 1941–42, 15070

Allen, M. J.: Women in Top Jobs: Four Studies in Achievement, 7714

Allen, Marjory: Memoirs of an Uneducated Lady, 26978; New Playgrounds, 27006

Allen, Sir Peter: Transport Pioneers of the Twentieth Century, 16208

Allen, R.: 'Waiting for Annan', 24792

Allen, Sir Richard: Malaysia: Prospect and Retrospect: The Impact and Aftermath of Colonial Rule, 12940

Allen, Robert: Daily Mirror, 25136

Allen, Robert: How to Save the World: Strategy for World Conservation, 20237

Allen, Robert: The Presbyterian College, Belfast, 1853–1953, 12176

Allen, Roy George Douglas: 'Movements in Retail Prices since 1953', 3812 'The Economic Effects of the British Value-Added Tax', 4847; 'Mutual Aid between the U.S. and the British Empire, 1941–1945, 14061; 'Population of British Universities in the 1960s: The Age-group Bulge', 22554

Allen, Roy: Major Airports of the World, 17668

Allen, Sandra: ed. Conditions of Illusion: Papers from the Women's Movement, 7769

Allen, Sheila: Homeworking: Myths and Realities, 7644; ed. Sexual Divisions and Society: Process and Change, 7793; ed. Dependence and Exploitation in Work and Marriage, 7794; Sociology in a Technological University, 8054; 'Class, Culture and Generation', 9450; New Minorities, Old Conflicts: Asian and West Indian Migrants in Great Britain, 11270; Work, Race and Immigration, 11424; Unions and Immigrant Workers: How They See Each Other, 11425

Allen, Victor Leonard: The Sociology of Industrial Relations: Studies in Method, 5744; 'The Centenary of the British Trades Union Congress, 1868–1968, 6705; 'The Reorganisation of the Trades Union Congress, 1918–1927', 6707; Power in Trade Unions, 6710; Trade Union Leadership, 6711; Militant Trade Unionism: A Re-analysis of Industrial Action in an Inflationary Situation, 6712, 6822; Trade Unions and the Government, 6869; 'The Growth of Trade Unionism in Banking, 1914–1927', 6890; The Militancy of British Miners, 6900

Allen, W. A.: 'The Education of Architects: The Robbins Committee and After', 22461

Allen, W. Gore: The Reluctant Politician: Derick Heathcote Amory, 1067; We The Undersigned: A History of the Royal London Insurance Society Ltd. and its Times, 1861–1961, 4216

Allen, Walter: Arnold Bennett, 25386; Joyce Cary, 25437

Alleridge, Patricia: 'Criminal Insanity: Bethlem to Broadmoor', 10262

Allett, John: The New Liberalism: The Political Economy of J. A. Hobson, 26589

Alley, Ronald: Graham Sutherland, 24076

Alligahn, Garry: Sir John Reith, 24734

Allingham, Margery: The Oaken Heart, 15184

Allison, J. E.: Sidelights on Tranmere, 19360

Allison, Lincoln: ed. The Politics of Sport, 27029

Allison, Richard Sydney: Sea Diseases: The Story of a Great Natural Experiment in Preventive Medicine in the Royal Navy, 21968

Allison, Ronald: The Queen: The Life and Work of Elizabeth II, 512

Alliss, Peter: The Open: The British Golf Championship since the War, 27156

Allott, Kenneth and Allott, Miriam: The Art of Graham Greene, 25562

Allsop, Kathleen: A New Deal for Young Workers, 3923

Allsop, Kenneth: The Angry Decade: A Survey of the Cultural Revolt of the Nineteen-Fifties, 23745

Allsopp, Bruce: Towards a Humane Architecture, 23914; ed. Modern Architecture of Northern England, 23920

Allward, Maurice: Gloster Javelin, 15877; Buccaneer, 15881

Allyn, Emily: Lords versus Commons: a Century of Conflict and Compromise, 1830–1930, 679

Alpert, M.: 'Humanitarianism and Politics in the British Response to the Spanish Civil War, 1936–9', 13994

Alport, Cuthbert J. M., Baron: The Sudden Assignment: Central Africa 1961–1963, 12786

Alsop, Judith: Health Policy and the National Health Service, 21690

Alt, James E.: Cabinet Studies: A Reader, 718; 'Partisanship and Policy Choice: Issue Preference in the British Electorate, February 1974', 2332; 'Angels in Plastic: The Liberal Surge in 1974', 2333

Altermatt, U.: et al. Innen—und Aussenpolitik: Primat oder Independenz?, 13920

Altham, Edward: Jellicoe, 15264

Altman, Wilfred: T.V: From Monopoly to Competition and Back?, 24871; From Monopoly to Competition, 24868

Alvarez, Al: The Savage God: A Study of Suicide, 10813. 'The Anti-Establishment Drama', 26212

Alward, George Lowe: The Sea Fisheries of Great Britain and Ireland: A Record of the Development of the Fishing Industry and its Worldwide Ramifications, 19801

Alyson-Smith, K.: 'A Study of Immigrant Group Relations in North London', 11447

Ambrose, David: Lesotho, 12711

Ambrose, G. P.: Monmouthshire County Council 1888–1974, 3385

Ambrose, P.: 'Gentlemen Prefer Offices', 17935

Ambrose, Peter John: Whatever Happened to Planning?, 18805; The Quiet Revolution: Social Change in a Sussex Village, 1871–1971, 19206

American Doctoral Dissertations: 1934–, 88

Amery, Julian: Approach March: A Venture in Autobiography, 1341; Reply to Strachey, 10900

Amery, Leopold Charles Maurice Stennett: Thoughts on the Constitution, 577; My Political Life, 1066; A Balanced Economy, 3614; The Washington Loans Agreement, 3725

Amies, Hardy: Just so far, 24168; Still here: An Autobiography, 24169

Amis, Sir Kingsley William: Harold's Years: Impressions from the New Statesman and the Spectator, 7605; 'Lone Voices: Views of the Fifties', 23744

Amory, Mark: ed. The Letters of Evelyn Waugh, 25859

Amos, Charles William Hale: ed. Call to Action in Defence of Church and State in England, 1933–35, 11625

Amos, Sir Maurice Sheldon: The English Constitution, 578

Amos, Valerie: 'Black Women in Britain: A Bibliographical Essay', 7624

Amphlett, Edgar Montague: 'Employers' Wage Policy', 3889

Amulree, Basil W. S. H., Baron: 'James MacKenzie and the Future of Medicine', 20911

Anderson, Dame Adelaide Mary: Women in the Factory, 1893 to 1921, 7665

Anderson, Alan: 'The Labour Laws and the Cabinet Legislative Committee of 1926–1927', 6861

Anderson, Bruce Louis: ed. Commerce, Industry and Transport: Studies in Economic Change on Merseyside, 5186, 16692, 18054

Anderson, Charles Arnold: ed. Education, Economy and Society: A Reader in the Sociology of Education, 9521, 23197

Anderson, Connie: Magazines Teenagers Read: With Special Reference to Trend, Jackie and Valentine, 25196

Anderson, Edgar: 'British Policy toward the Baltic States, 1918–1920', 13876

Anderson, Gregory: ed. The White Blouse Revolution: Female Office Workers since 1870, 7768

Anderson, Henry Graeme: The Medical and Surgical Aspects of Aviation, 21050

Anderson, I. A.: Forestry in the British Scene, 19745

Anderson, John David: Introduction to Flight: Its Engineering and History, 17499

Anderson, John L.: Life before Death, 22093; Profitability of Farming in South East Scotland, 1980/81, 1981/82, 1982/83, 19625

Anderson, John Richard Lane: East of Suez: A Study of Britain's Greatest Trading Enterprise, 4800, 6521

Anderson, Dame Kitty: Women and the Universities: A Changing Pattern, 22487

Anderson, Mark Louden: A History of Scottish Forestry, vol. 2: From the Industrial Revolution to Modern Times, 19721

Anderson, Mary: 'Studies in the Politics of Environmental Protection: The Historical Roots of the British Clean Air Act, 1956', 7033; The Rise of the Student Estate in Britain, 9862, 22565; The Politics of Clean Air, 20043; Universities: British, Indian, African: a Study in the Ecology of Higher Education, 23322

Anderson, Matthew Smith: The Eastern Question, 1774–1923: A Study in International Relations, 13799

Anderson, Michael: *ed.* The Sociology of the Family: Selected Readings, 10094

Anderson, Mosa: Noel Buxton: A Life, 1387

Anderson, Nancy: *ed.* Australian Trade Policy 1942–1966, 12638

Anderson, Nels: Our Industrial Urban Civilization, 17943; The Urban Community: A World Perspective, 17944; *ed.* Urbanism and Urbanization, 17945; Work and Leisure, 26920

Anderson, Odin Waldemar: Health Care: Can There be Equity?, 21615

Anderson, Perry: 'The Left in the Fifties', 1735; *ed.* Towards Socialism, 2134, 2155; Arguments within English Marxism, 2159

Anderson, R. C.: A History of the Royal Blue Express Coach Services, 17326; A History of the Western National, 17327

Anderson, Robert Charles Beckett: History of the Argyll and Sutherland Highlanders, 1st Battalion, 1909–1939, 15568

Anderson, Robert D.: The Student Community at Aberdeen, 1860–1939, 23451

Anderson, Robert: Efficiency in the Social Services, 8950

Anderson, Terry H.: The United States, Great Britain and the Cold War 1944–1947, 14108

Anderson, Verity: The Last of the Eccentrics: A Life of Rosslyn Bruce, 11774

Anderton, David A.: Jet Fighters and Bombers, 15873

Andreades, Andreas Michael: Philip Snowden: The Man and his Financial Policy, 1319

Andrew, Christopher M.: 'The British Secret Service and Anglo-Soviet Relations: Part 1: From the Trade Negotiations to the Zinoviev Letter', 13932; 'British Intelligence and the Breach with Russia in 1927', 13933; 'More on the Zinoviev Letter', 13939; *ed.* Intelligence and International Relations 1900–1945, 15996; 'The Missing Dimension': Governments and the Intelligence Communities in the Twentieth Century, 15997; Secret Service: The Making of the British Intelligence Community, 15998; 'Whitehall, Washington and the Intelligence Services', 16009; 'F. H. Hinsley and the Cambridge Moles: Two Patterns of Intelligence Recruitment', 16022

Andrews, Allen: The Prosecutor: The Life of M. P. Pugh, Prosecuting Solicitor and Agent for the Director of Public Prosecutions, 10765; The Life of L. S. Lowry, 1887–1976, 24035

Andrews, C. Lesley: Where We Live, 18751

Andrews, E. Kay: The Evolution of British Policy on Aircraft Noise, 20151

Andrews, Eamonn: This is my Life, 24738

Andrews, H. F.: 'A Cluster Analysis of British Towns', 17827

Andrews, Irene Osgood: Economic Effects of the War upon Women and Children in Great Britain, 3745

Andrews, Lawrence: The Education Act 1918, 22616

Andrews, Leonard Martin: Canon's Folly, 11772

Andrews, Philip Walter Sawford: Capital Development in Steel: A Study of the United Steel Companies Ltd., 6600; The Life of Lord Nuffield, 17433

Andrews, Sir William Linton: Lords and Laborers of the Press: Men who Fashioned the Modern British Newspaper, 25039, 25206; Problems of an Editor: A Study in Newspaper Trends, 25204; The Autobiography of a Journalist, 25205

Andrews, William G.: 'Social Change and Electoral Politics in Britain: A Case Study of Basingstoke, 1964 and 1974', 9454

Andry, Robert George: The Short-term Prisoner: A Study in Forensic Psychology, 10389; Delinquency and Parental Pathology: A Study in Forensic and Clinical Psychology, 10390

Angell, Sir Norman: After All: The Autobiography of Norman Angell, 13465

Anglesea, Douglas: Experiments on Land Pollution, 20120

Anglo, Michael: Service Newspapers of the Second World War, 25067

Animashawun, G. K.: 'African Students in Britain', 11508

Annan, Noel Gilroy, Baron: The Disintegration of an Old Culture, 7582; 'The Universities', 23402; 'The Reform of Higher Education in 1986', 23403; 'The Reform of Higher Education', 23426

Annett, John: Computer-assisted Learning, 1969–1975: A Report Prepared for SSRC, 22776

Anning, Stephen Towers: 'The Apothecaries of the General Infirmary at Leeds', 21022; The General Infirmary at Leeds, 21427; A History of the Leeds School of Medicine: One and a Half Centuries, 1831–1981, 23512

Annual Catalogue 1985+, 181

Annual Register, 1758+, 305.

Annual Register: A Record of World Events: 1974+, 263

Annual Report of the Chief Registrar of Friendly Societies: 1894–1974, continued as: Annual Report of the Certification Officer, 9116

Annual Review of Physiology: Vol. 1, 22339

Annual Supplements 1974–1981, 157

Annual Survey, U.G.C. Academic Year 1963–64, 22582

Anon: 'Long-Term View of Housing', 18657

Anon: Rising Standards in Scottish Primary Schools 1953–63, 23160

Anscombe, Gertrude Elizabeth M.: Introduction to Wittgenstein's 'Tractatus', 26884

Anscombe, Isabelle: Omega and after: Bloomsbury and the Decorative Arts, 23930

Ansell, Sir Michael: Soldier On: An Autobiography, 27133

Anson, Harold: T. B. Strong: Bishop, Musician, Dean, Vice-Chancellor, 11758

Anson, Peter Frederick: The Call of the Cloister: Religious Communities and Kindred Bodies in the Anglican Communion, 11667; The Religious Orders and Congregations of Great Britain and

Ireland, 11960; The Catholic Church in Modern Scotland, 1560–1937, 12271; Fashions in Church Furnishings, 1840–1940, 24123

Anson, Sir William Reynell: The Law and Custom of the Constitution, 597

Ansorge, Peter: Disrupting the Spectacle: Five Years of Experimental and Fringe Theatre in Britain, 26234

Anstey, Edgar: 'Wildlife Films in the Post-War British Cinema', 24648

Anstis, Gordon: Redditch: Success in the Heart of England: The History of Redditch New Town 1964–1985, 18199, 19023

Anthony, John: The Gardens of Britain 6— The East Midlands: Derbyshire, Leicestershire, Lincolnshire, 19887

Anthony, L. J.: Sources of Information on Atomic Energy, 6658

Anthony, Peter D.: Industrial Relations and the Personnel Specialists, 5705, 9781; The Conduct of Industrial Relations, 5706; The Ideology of Work, 5707

Anthony, Vivian Stanley: Britain's Overseas Trade: The Recent History of British Trade, 1868–1968, 4799

Antrim New Town: Outline Plan: Report of the Steering Committee, 18264

Anwar, Muhammad: 'Asian Participation in the October 1974 General Election', 2239; Votes and Policies: Ethnic Minorities and the General Election 1979, 2240; Ethnic Minorities and the 1983 General Election: A Research Report, 2241; Race and Politics: Ethnic Minorities in the British Political System, 2242

Appadorai, A.: *ed.* Speeches and Documents on the Indian Constitution 1925–1947, 13116

Apple, Raymond: The Hampstead Synagogue, 1892–1967, 12429

Appleby, Robert: Profitability and Productivity in the United Kingdom, 1954–1964, 5984

Appleyard, Bryan: The Pleasures of Peace: Art and Imagination in Post-war Britain, 23788

Appleyard, John Rollo: Workers' Participation in Western Europe, 6016; The History of the Institution of Electrical Engineers, 1871–1931, 7102

Appleyard, Reginald Thomas: British Emigration to Australia, 7320; 'The Return Movement of U.K. Migrants from Australia, 7321

Apps, Michael: The Four 'Ark Royals', 15025

Apte, Robert Z.: Halfway House: A New Dilemma in Institutional Care, 21819

Apter, David E.: Ghana in Transition, 12738

Apter, Michael John: The New Technology of Education, 22777

Archard, Peter: Vagrancy, Alcoholism and Social Control, 22155

Archbishop of Canterbury's Group on The Divorce Law: Putting Asunder . . . [Mortimer Report.], 10008

Archbishop's Commission on the Christian Doctrine of Marriage: Marriage, Divorce and the Church: The Report of a Commission Appointed by the Archbishop of Canterbury to Prepare a Statement on the Christian Doctrine of Marriage, 9921

Archdall, Henry Kingsley: St. David's College, Lampeter: Its Past, Present and Future, 23505

Archer, Anthony: 'The Passing of the "Simple Faithful"', 11957; The Two Catholic Churches: A Study in Oppression, 11975

Archer, Brian: Regional Income Multipliers: The Anglesey Study, 5347; The Impact of Domestic Tourism, 26945

Archer, Fred: Fred Archer, Farmer's Son: A Cotswold Childhood in the 1920s, 19589

Archer, Ian: The Rangers Story, 27089

Archer, J. K.: 'De Havilland Aircraft (1908–1960)', 17604

Archer, Peter Kingsley: ed. Social Welfare and the Citizen, 8775; The Queen's Courts, 10283

Archer, T. C.: 'Britain and Scandinavia: Their Relations within EFTA, 1960–1968', 13887

Archibald, Edward Hunter Holmes: The Metal Fighting Ship in the Royal Navy, 1860–1970, 15344

Architects' Yearbook: 1945–74, 23857

Architectural Periodicals Index: Royal Institute of British Architects 1972–, 23859

Architecture Journal: 1894–, 23858

Archives: 1948–, 74

Arden, R. J.: Scotland's Rural Housing: A Forgotten Problem, 19244

Arden-Clarke, Sir Charles: 'Gold Coast into Ghana: Some Problems of Transition', 12743

Ardener, Shirley: ed. The Incorporated Wife, 9945

Ardingly: Ardingly, 1858–1946: A History of the School, 23043

Arends, Andrew: Mr Attlee's Engine Room: Cabinet Committee Structure and the Labour Governments 1945–51, 729

Argles, Owen Michael Venables: South Kensington to Robbins: An Account of English Technical and Scientific Education since 1851, 23279

Argy, Victor: Inflation and Unemployment, 4019

Argyle, Michael: 'The Measurement of Supervisory Methods', 5866; Religious Behaviour, 12381

Aris, Stephen: The Jews in Business, 11291, 12412

Arkle, E. W.: 'The London and North Eastern Railway [1922–1948]', 16886

Arkley, Joyce: The Over-Sixties. A Survey of Social Problems and Unmet Needs among a Sample of Men and Women Aged about Sixty or Over, 8581

Arlott, John: Fred: Portrait of a Fast Bowler, 27106

Armes, Roy: Patterns of Realism, 24620; Film and Reality: An Historical Survey, 24621; A Critical History of British Cinema, 24622

Armistead, Nigel: Data for 1975 Report on Children's Day Care Facilities in London, 8098; Community Services for the Mentally Ill, 21869

Armitage, Angus: A Century of Astronomy, 26392

Armitage, C. M.: A Bibliography of the Works of Louis MacNeice, 25690

Armitage, Frank: The British Paint Industry, 6619

Armitage, Susan: The Politics of Decontrol of Industry: Britain and the United States, 6125

Armour, Charles: 'The BBC and the Development of Broadcasting in British Colonial Africa 1946–1956', 12698

Armstrong Davison, M. H.: The Evolution of Anaesthesia, 21034

Armstrong, Eric George Abbot: Improving Industrial Relations: The Advisory Role of A.C.A.S, 4155, 5825; 'The Conciliatory Negotiation of Change: A Case Study of the Norwich Footwear Arbitration Board, 1909–1980', 5824

Armstrong, Noel: Let's Make Britain Great Again, 374

Armstrong, Norma: Local Collections in Scotland, 26757

Armstrong, Patrick: Changing Landscape: The History and Ecology of Man's Impact on the Face of East Anglia, 19954

Armstrong, Peter J.: Safety or Profit: Industrial Accidents and the Conventional Wisdom, 4138; Ideology and Shopfloor Industrial Relations, 5815; White Collar Workers, Trade Unions and Class, 9673

Armstrong, R.: 'Educational Elements in Community Work in Britain', 9407

Armstrong, Roger: Joint Consultation Revisited, 6048

Armstrong, Walter Alan: 'Size of Plant, Size of Enterprise and Concentration in British Manufacturing Industry 1935–1958', 5056 An Introduction to Historical Demography, 7370; Farmworkers: A Social and Economic History 1770–1980, 9709

Armstrong, William Arthur: 'Tradition and Innovation in the London Theatre, 1960–1961', 26213; ed. Experimental Drama, 26228

Armstrong-Jones, Antony Charles Robert, Earl of Snowdon: A Photographic Autobiography, 24709

Army League: The British Army in the Nuclear Age, 15438

Armytage, Walter Harry Green: 'Some Sources for the History of Technical Education in England', 22505; Four Hundred Years of English Education, 22652; Civic Universities: Aspects of a British Tradition, 23361; 'Community Service Stations: the Transformation of the Civic Universities, 1898–1930', 23362; 'Flexner to Truscot: the Stocktaking Phase of Civic University Development, 1930–1944', 23363; 'The Civic Universities and Social Readjustment, 1944–1954', 23364; 'The Rise of Civic Universities in England', 23365; 'From Formula to Policy in Education', 23416; 'New Pluralism in British Higher Education', 23425

Arndt, Heinz Wolfgang: The Economic Lessons of the 1930's, 3587

Arnold, Armin: D. H. Lawrence and America, 25634

Arnold, Bruce: Margaret Thatcher: A Study in Power, 1048; What Kind of Country? Modern Irish Politics, 2988; Orpen: An Autobiography, 24049

Arnold, Denis: The New Oxford Companion to Music, 24261

Arnold, Lorna: A Very Special Relationship, 12621

Arnold, Ralph Christian Marshall: Orange Street and Brickhole Lane, 24935

Arnold, Robert McCulloch: The Golden Years of the Great Northern Railway [Ireland], Part One, 16850; Part Two—Newry, Armagh, Clones, 16851

Arnot, Robert Page: The Miners: Years of Struggle. A History of the Miners' Federation of Great Britain, 6816; The Miners: In Crisis and War: A History of the Miners' Federation of Great Britain (from 1930 onwards), 6817; A History of the Scottish Miners from the Earliest Times, 6818; The Miners: One Union, One Industry: A History of the National Union of Mineworkers, 1939–1946, 6905; The General Strike, May 1926: Its Origins and History, 6943; A History of the Scottish Miners from the Earliest Times, 9650; The Impact of the Russian Revolution in Britain, 13914; Forging the Weapon: The Struggle of the Labour Monthly 1921–1941, 25174

Arnott, Alison June Elphinstone: The Scottish Criminal, 10181

Arnott, M. C.: ed. The County of Wigtown, 10115

Arnott, W. Melville: 'The Climate of Medical Education', 22472

Arnstein, Walter Leonard: Britain, Yesterday and Today: 1830 to the Present, 286; 'The Liberals and the General Election of 1945: A Skeptical Note', 2291

Aronson, Lawrence: The Origins of the Cold War: A Comparative Perspective: American, British and Canadian Relations with the Soviet Union 1941–1948, 14103

Arregger, Constance E.: ed. Graduate Women at Work: A Study by a Working Party of the British Federation of University Women, 7711

Arrington, G. E.: A History of Opthalmology, 21103

Arrowsmith, Harold: Pioneering in Education for the Technologies: The Story of Battersea College of Technology, 1891–1962, 23287

Arslanian, Artin H.: 'British Wartime Pledges, 1917–1918: The Armenian Case', 13846

Artell, Robert: The London and South Western Railway, 16892

Arter, Wallace: 'Food from Airfields', 20593

Arthur, Sir George Compton Archibald: From Phelps to Gielgud: Reminiscences of the Stage through Sixty Five Years, 25917

Arthur, Max: Northern Ireland—Soldiers Talking, 2899

Arthur, Paul: Northern Ireland since 1968, 2784; 'Devolution as Administrative Convenience: A Case Study of Northern Ireland', 2804; The Government and Politics of Northern Ireland, 2805

Arthurs, Alan: 'Industrial Relations in the Civil Service: Beyond GCHQ', 5848

Artis, Michael John: 'Monetary Policy and Financial Intermediaries: The Hire Purchase Financial Houses', 4611; Foundations of British Monetary Policy, 4612; 'Effects of the Devaluation of 1967 on the Current Balance of Payments', 4711

Arts Council of Great Britain: Annual Report and Accounts: 1946+, 23756

Arundel, Dennis: The Story of Sadler's Wells, 1683–1964, 24561

Arvill, Robert *pseud*.: Man and Environment: Crisis and the Strategy of Choice, 19913

Ascoli, David: The Queen's Peace. The Origins and Development of the Metropolitan Police, 10785

Ash, Bernard: The Lost Dictator. A Biography of Field-Marshal Sir Henry Wilson, 14521; Norway, 1940, 14913; Someone had Blundered: The Story of the 'Repulse' and the 'Prince of Wales', 15030; The Golden City: London between the Fires, 1666–1941, 18365

Ash, John Colin Keith: Forecasting the United Kingdom Economy, 3521

Ash, Maurice Anthony: The Human Cloud: A Reconsideration of Civic Planning, 17774; Regions of Tomorrow: Towards the Open City, 17802; 'What Mr Crosland should do about London', 18315; 'End of Dispersal', 18316; 'End of the Affair [Community Land Bill]', 18317; 'Planning Reprieved', 18318; A Guide to the Structure of London, 18364

Ashby, Andrew W.: 'Britain's Food Manufacturing Industry and its Economic Development', 20625

Ashby, Arthur Wilfred: 'The Social Origins of Farmers in Wales', 9584; Allotments and Small Holdings in Oxfordshire, 19427; Some Principles of Organisation and Operation in Agricultural Co-operative Societies, 19428; Economic Conditions in Welsh Agriculture, 19634; Some Characteristics of Welsh Farming, 19635; The Agriculture of Wales and Monmouthshire, 19636

Ashby, Eric W. [Baron]: 'Studies in the Politics of Environmental Protection: The Historical Roots of the British Clean Air Act, 1956', 7033; The Rise of the Student Estate in Britain, 9862, 22565; Pollution, Nuisance or Nemesis?: A Report on the Control of Pollution, 20027; Pollution and the Public Conscience, 20028; Reconciling Man with the Environment, 20029; The Politics of Clean Air, 20043; British, Indian, African: A Study in the Ecology of Higher Education, 23322; Adapting Universities to a Technological Society, 23323; Masters and Scholars, 23347; Technology and the Academics: an Essay on Universities and the Scientific Revolution, 23352

Ashby, Margaret: The Book of Stevenage, 19028

Ashcroft, M. Y.: *ed.* A History of the North Riding of Yorkshire County Council 1889–1974, 3372

Ashcroft, Robert Leslie: Haileybury, 1908–1961, 23061

Ashdown, Margaret: Social Service and Mental Health: An Essay on Psychiatric Social Workers, 8711, 21753

Ashford, Douglas E.: British Dogmatism and French Pragmatism: Central-Local Policymaking in the Welfare State, 3210; 'The Effects of Central Finance on the British Local Government System', 3273; The Emergence of the Welfare State, 8992

Ashford, Ethel Bright: The Food and Drugs Act, 1938, 20638

Ashford, J. R.: 'Who Uses the Health Services and Why?', 21348

Ashley, A. M. D.: Joyful Servant: The Ministry of Percy Harthill, 11785

Ashley, B.: 'A Sociological Analysis of Students' Reasons for Becoming Teachers', 9871

Ashley, Jack: Journey into Silence, 1343

Ashley, Maurice Percy: Churchill as Historian, 988, 26789; The People of England: A Short Social and Economic History, 3509, 7620

Ashley, Peter: Social Security after Beveridge, 9044

Ashley, Sir William James: The Economic Organisation of England: An Outline History, 3439

Ashmall, Harry A.: The High School of Glasgow, 23223

Ashmore, Edward Bailey: Air Defence, 14644

Ashmore, Jerome: 'Interdisciplinary Roots of the Theatre of the Absurd', 26214

Ashmore, Owen: The Development of Power in Britain, 6406

Ashton, D. N.: Young Workers, 8458

Ashton, Elwyn Thomas: 'Problem Families and their Household Budgets', 3800; Social Work and the Social Sciences, 8783; The Southampton Survey, 18077; 1. A Survey of the Industrial Prospects of the Southampton Region, 18078; 2. Shops and Planning etc, 18079; 3. Housing Targets etc, 18080; 4. Problem Families, 18081; People and Leisure, 26925

Ashton, J.: The Remoter Areas of Britain, 19086; *ed.* Research, Education and Extension in Agriculture, 19694

Ashton, Raymond K.: The United Kingdom Financial Accounting Standard: A Descriptive and Financial Approach, 4195

Ashton, Stephen R.: British Policy towards the Indian States, 1905–1939, 13158

Ashton, Thomas Southcliffe: *ed.* Papers in English Monetary History, 4548

Ashton-Gwatkin, Frank Trelawny Arthur: The British Foreign Service: A Discussion of the Development and Function of the British Foreign Service, 13329

Ashworth, Andrew: The English Sentencing System, 10310; Sentencing and Penal Policy, 10311; Sentencing in the Crown Court, 10312

Ashworth, Herbert: The Building Society Story, 4386; Housing: Demand and Supply, 18651; Housing: Housing Standards, 18652; Housing in Great Britain, 18653

Ashworth, J. M.: 'Reshaping Higher Education in Britain', 23444

Ashworth, Mark: Public Finances in Perspective, 4660; Civil Aviation Policy and the Privatisation of British Airways, 17625

Ashworth, William: An Economic History of England, 1870–1939, 3410; Contracts and Finance, 3442; Fifty Years: The Story of the Association of Certified and Corporate Accountants, 1904–1954, 4181; The History of the British Coal Industry. Vol.5: 1946–1982, 6247; The Genesis of Modern British Town Planning: A Study in Economic and Social History of the Nineteenth and Twentieth Centuries, 17735

Askey, Arthur: Before Your Very Eyes, 26294

Aspden, Harold: Modern Aether Science, 26415

Aspden, J. C.: A Municipal History of Eastbourne 1938–1974, 3327

Aspinall-Oglander, Cecil Faber: Roger Keyes: Being the Biography of Admiral of the Fleet Lord Keyes of Zeebrugge and Dover, 15267

Aspinwall, Bernard: 'Broadfield Revisited: Some Scottish Catholic Responses to Wealth 1918–40', 12276; 'Popery in Scotland: Image and Reality, 1820–1920', 12277

Asprey, Robert Brown: The First Battle of the Marne, 14575

Asquith, Lady Cynthia Mary Evelyn: The Duchess of York, 507

Asquith, Cyril [Baron Asquith of Bishopstone]: Life of Herbert Henry Asquith, Lord Oxford and Asquith, 971

Asquith, Herbert Henry [Earl of Oxford and Asquith]: Fifty Years of Parliament, 971; Memories and Reflections, 1852–1957, 971; Studies and Sketches, 971; The Genesis of the War, 971; Moments of Memory: Recollections and Impressions, 971

Asquith, Margot [Emma Alice Margaret, Countess of Oxford and Asquith]: Autobiography, 971; More or Less about Myself, 971; More Memories, 971; Places and Persons, 971

Associated British Ports: Guide to the Nineteen Ports, 16670

Associated Industrial Consultants Ltd.: The Economic and Industrial Development of the South West, 5218

Association of British Chemical Manufacturers: Report on the Chemical Industry, 6213

Association of Building Technicians: Your London has a Plan, 18922

Association of County Councils: Highway Maintenance: A Code of Good Practice, 17135; Rural Deprivation, 19080

Association of Multi-Racial Playgroups: Occasional Papers, No. 1: Action in the Priority Areas: A Note on the Aims and Workings of the Association of Multi-Racial Playgroups, 11051; No. 2. Work in the Midlands, 11052

Association of Psychiatric Social Workers: Casework and Mental Illness, 21804

Association of Public Health Inspectors: Environmental Health, 21591

Association of Social Workers of Great Britain (Education Sub-Committee): New Thinking about Administration, 9243

Association of the British Pharmaceutical Industry: Attitudes to the Pharmaceutical Industry by Family Doctors and the Public, 1962, 1964 and 1965, 22263; The Pharmaceutical Industry and the Nation's Health, 22264

Aster, Sidney: 1939: The Making of the Second World War, 13769; Anthony Eden, 1007

Aston Local History Group: Some Aspects of the History of Aston cum Aughton, 19319

Aston, Michael: The Landscape of Towns, 20306

Astor, David: 'Why the Revolt against Hitler was Ignored: On the British Reluctance to Deal with German Anti-Nazis', 13685

Astor, William Waldorf [Viscount]: Temperance and Politics, 1349; Our Imperial Future, 1352; British Agriculture: The Principles of Future Policy, 19451; The Agricultural Dilemma, 19452; Food Production in Western Europe: An Economic Survey of Agriculture in Six Countries, 19453; Mixed Farming and Muddled Thinking: An Analysis of Current Agricultural Policy, 19454; 'Health Problems and a State Ministry of Health', 21310

Atherton, Stanley S.: Alan Sillitoe: A Critical Assessment, 25799

Athill, Diana: Instead of a Letter, 24960

Atholl, Justin: Prison on the Moor: The Story of Dartmoor Prison, 10397

Atkin, John: 'Official Regulation of British Overseas Investment 1914–1931', 3551, 4775

Atkin, Ronald: Dieppe 1942. The Jubilee Disaster, 14823

Atkins, Colin Keith: People and the Motor Car: A Study of the Movement of People Related to their Residential Environment, 17390

Atkins, H. W.: The Royal Armoured Corps, 15599

Atkins, Hedley: The Surgeon's Craft, 20878

Atkins, John: Aldous Huxley: A Literary Study, 25589; Arthur Koestler, 25616

Atkins, R. T.: ed. Guide to Government Departments and other Libraries, 97

Atkins, Thomas: 'The London Theatre: A Devaluation', 26216

Atkinson, Anthony Barnes: Unequal Shares: Wealth in Britain, 3791; ed. Wealth, Income and Inequality: Selected Readings, 3792; Parents and Children: The Economics of Inequality, 3793; The Distribution of Personal Wealth in Britain, 3794; The Tax Credit Scheme and the Redistribution of Income, 3835; ed. Personal Distribution of Incomes, 3836; Poverty in Britain and the Reform of Social Security, 4083, 9065; Incomes in two Generations, 20435

Atkinson, Christopher Thomas: The Devonshire Regiment, 1914–1918, 15613; The Dorsetshire Regiment, 15615; History of the Royal Dragoons, 1661–1934, 15617; The Royal Hampshire Regiment. Vol.2 1914–1918, 15647; The Queen's Own Royal West Kent Regiment, 1914–1919, 15672; The History of the South Wales Borderers 1914–1918, 15750; The South Wales Borderers, 24th Foot, 1689–1937, 15751

Atkinson, D. T.: Magic, Myth and Medicine, 21195

Atkinson, Francis Gaston Bryant: London's North Western Electric: A Jubilee History, 16962

Atkinson, Frank: The English Newspaper since 1900, 25036

Atkinson, Fred: Oil and the British Economy, 6512

Atkinson, R.: The Development of the Rate Support Grant (R.S.G.) System, 3275

Attali, Jacques: A Man of Influence: Sir Siegmund Warburg, 1902–82, 4477

Attenborough, John: A Living Memory: Hodder and Stoughton, Publishers 1868–1975, 24970

Attenburrow, J. J.: Some Impressions of the Private Sector of the Housing Market, 18443; Houses and People: A Review of User Studies at the Building Research Station, 18712; 'Housing Standards and Social Trends', 18713

Atterbury, Paul: A Golden Adventure: The First Fifty Years of Ultramar, 6523

Attfield, John W.: ed. 1939: The Communist Party of Great Britain and the War, 1931

Attiwill, Kenneth: The Singapore Story, 15071; The Rising Sunset, 15188

Attlee, Clement Richard [Earl Attlee]: As it Happened, 975; 'Eight Decades of Change', 976; Purpose and Policy: Selected Speeches, 976; The Labour Party Perspective, 976; The Social Worker, 976; War Comes to Britain. Speeches . . . 976

Attridge, John: Rotherham Transport History, 16352

Attwater, Donald: The Catholic Church in Modern Wales: A Record of the Past Century, 12301

Attwood, Edwin Arthur: The Economics of Hill Farming, 19511, 19633; 'The Origins of State Support for British Agriculture', 19512; 'The Economic Structure of Welsh Farming', 19632; The Agricultural Policies of Britain and Denmark: A Study in Reciprocal Trade, 19659

Attwood, Margaret: Introduction to Personnel Management, 5476

Atwell, David: Cathedrals of the Movies: A History of British Cinemas and their Audiences, 24608

Auckland, R. G.: Catalogue of British 'Black' Propaganda to Germany, 1941–45, 15106

Auer, Michel: The Illustrated History of the Camera from 1839 to the Present, 7060

Aughey, Arthur: Conservatives and Conservatism, 1626; 'Law Before Violence? The Protestant Paramilitaries in Ulster Politics', 2960; Ulster Unionism and the Anglo-Irish Agreement, 3004

Aughton, H.: Housing Finance: Myth, Reality and Reform, 18543

Augustino, D. K.: ed. Alcohol and the Family: A Comprehensive Bibliography, 10096

Aulach, Harindar: 'Britain and the Sudeten Issue, 1938: The Evolution of a Policy', 13734; 'The British View of the Czechs in the Era before the Munich Crisis', 13735

Auld, Robin: The William Tyndale Junior and Infants Schools: A Report of the Public Inquiry, 23158

Ault, W. O.: 'British Crisis in Higher Education', 23421

Aunger, E. A.: 'Religion and Occupational Class in Northern Ireland', 2896

Aurora, Gurdip Singh: The New Frontiersmen: A Sociological Study of Indian Immigrants in the United Kingdom, 11213; 'Process of Social Adjustment of Indian Immigrants in Britain', 11214

Austen, D.: 'The Fifties: Let's Go to the Pictures', 24651

Austin, Allan: Roy Fuller, 25529

Austin, Claire: Board of Visitor Adjudications, 10459

Austin, Dennis: Britain and South Africa, 12715; West Africa and the Commonwealth, 12732; Politics in Ghana 1946–1960, 12747; ed. From Rhodesia to Zimbabwe: Behind and beyond Lancaster House, 12810; 'Sanctions and Rhodesia', 12813; Malta and the End of Empire, 12860

Austin, Michael: Accident Blackspot: A Critical Study of Road Safety Policy and Practice, 17122

Austin, Richard: Lynn Seymour: An Authorised Biography, 24249

Austin, William H.: The Relevance of Natural Science to Theology, 27264

Automobile Association: The Motorist Today: Some Findings of General Interest from a Survey Commissioned by the Automobile Association, 17393

Auty, Phyllis: British Policy in South-East Europe in the Second World War, 14936; British Policy towards Wartime Resistance in Yugoslavia and Greece, 14937

Aveling, John C. H.: Rome and the Anglicans, 12334

Averis, Ernest: ed. Hold the Front Page, 25129

Aves, Geraldine Maitland: The Voluntary Worker in the Social Services, 9205

Avison, E.: 'Immigrants in a Small Borough', 11474

Avison, Neville Howard: Crime in England and Wales, 10180

Awdrey, Wilbert: ed. A Guide to the Steam Railways of Britain, 17028

Axelson, Erik: ed. South African Explorers, 27195

Axford, Wendy Anne: Handicapped Children in Britain: Their Problems and Education; Books and Articles Published in Great Britain from the 1944 Education Act to 1958, 23116

Axton, Marie: English Drama: Forms and Development: Essays in Honour of Muriel Clara Bradbrook, 26176

Ayany, S. G.: A History of Zanzibar, 12845

Ayearst, Morley: The British West Indies: The Search for Self-Government, 13008

Ayensu, Edward Solomon: Our Green and Living World: The Wisdom to Save it, 20238

Ayer, Sir Alfred Jules: Philosophy in the Twentieth Century, 26830; Part of my Life, 26846; Russell, 26874

Ayers, Gwendoline Margery: England's First State Hospitals and the Metropolitan Asylums Board, 1867–1930, 21441

Ayerst, David George Ogilvy: Guardian: Biography of a Newspaper, 25141; ed. The Guardian Omnibus, 1821–1971, 25142; Garvin of The Observer, 25240

Ayles, Jonathan: 'Privatisation of the British Steel Corporation', 6580

Aynsley, Cyril: The D-Notice Affair, 25334

Ayodele, J.: Pan-Africanism and Nationalism in West Africa, 1900–1945, 12731

Ayr and Troon: Official Ports Handbook, 16673

Ayre, Leslie: The Proms, 24444

Ayres, Eugene: Energy Sources—Wealth of the World, 7211

Ayres, N.: Born and Bred Unequal, 9508

Ayrshire County Council: The Future of Scottish Civil Aviation: Issues in the Interests of Scotland, 17655

Ayton, Cyril J.: Guide to Pre-war British Motorcycles, 17179; The History of Motor Cycling, 17178

Azikwe, Nnamdi: My Odyssey: An Autobiography, 12767

Azimi, Fakhreddin: Iran: The Crisis of Democracy 1941–1953, 13859

Aziz, K. K.: Britain and Muslim India, 13159; The Making of Pakistan, 13192; Britain and Pakistan: A Study of British Attitudes Towards the East Pakistan Crisis of 1971, 13193

BBC: Sound Archives Library: Broadcasting House, 227; Sound Archives Library: Catalogue of Records Talks and Speeches, 228; [Audience Research Department] Statistics of what People are doing Half-hour by Half-hour from Six-thirty am until Midnight, 9914; British Broadcasting, 24715; Annual Report and Handbook: Annually from 1928, 24726; 'Radio Times' 50th Anniversary Souvenir 1923–1973, 24730; Pamphlets: The European Service of the BBC: Two Decades of Broadcasting to Europe 1938–1959, 24766; Serving Neighbourhood and Nation; BBC Television: A British Engineering Achievement, 24847

Baber, Colin: ed. Modern South Wales: Essays in Economic History, 5380

Babington, Anthony: The Power to Silence: A History of Punishment in Britain, 10331; Military Intervention in Britain: From the Gordon Riots to the Gibraltar Incident, 15447

Babington Smith, Constance: Iulia de Beausobre: A Russian Christian in the West, 12351; Evidence in Camera: The Story of Photographic Intelligence in World War II, 15200

Bablock, E. B.: 'The Development of Fundamental Concepts in the Science of Genetics', 22244

Bacharach, A. L.: ed. British Music in our Time, 24264

Bachmann, Hans: Die Britische Sterling und Devisenkontrolle, 4703

Backus, J. H.: 'Archbishop Temple and the Orthodox: A Note on the Preparations for the Joint Doctrinal Commission of 1931', 12311

Bacon, Edmund N.: Design of Cities, 18571

Bacon, Sir Reginald Hugh Spencer: The Jutland Scandal, 14650; The Dover Patrol, 1915–1917, 14679; The Life of Lord Fisher of Kilverstone, 15252; The Life of John Rushworth, Earl Jellicoe, 15263; From 1900 Onward, 15306; Modern Naval Strategy, 15339

Bacon, Robert William: Britain's Economic Problem: Too Few Producers, 3680

Bacon, Roy Hunt: Military Motor Cycles of World War Two: All Makes from Europe, Russia, Japan and the U.S.A., 1939 to 1945, 17181

Bacon, W. F.: 'The Growth of Pension Rights and their Impact on the National Economy', 4054

Bacsich, Paul: 'Transplantation', 22245

Baddeley, Geoffrey E.: The Tramways of Croydon, 17221

Baden-Powell, Dorothy: Operation Jupiter. S.O.E.'s Secret War in Norway, 15082, 15192

Bader, Sir Douglas Robert Steuart: Fight for the Sky: The Story of the Spitfire and the Hurricane, 15849

Badger, Alfred Bowen: Man in Employment: The Fundamental Principles of Industrial Relations, 5643

Badham, Paul: ed. Religion, State and Society in Modern Britain, 11561

Badley, John Haden: Memories and Reflections, 23101

Baghot, John Henry: Juvenile Delinquency: A Comparative Study of the Position in Liverpool and in England and Wales, 10547; Punitive Detention: An Inquiry into the Results of Treatment (Under Section 54 of the Children and Young Persons Act 1939) of Juvenile Delinquents in Liverpool during the Years 1940, 1941, and 1942, 10548

Bagis, A. I.: ed. Four Centuries of Turco-British Relations: Studies in Diplomatic, Economic and Cultural Affairs, 13843

Bagley, Alexander John: The State and Education in England and Wales, 1833–1968, 23206

Bagley, Christopher: The Cost of a Child: Problems in the Relief and Measurement of Poverty, 9066; Dealing with Delinquents, 10598; '"Black Suicide": A Report of 25 English Cases and Controls', 10807; 'Race Relations and the Press: An Empirical Analysis', 11039; Social Structure and Prejudice in Five English Boroughs, 11171; 'Status Consistency, Relative Deprivation and Attitudes to Immigrants', 11414; Racial Prejudice, 11198; The Social Psychology of the Child with Epilepsy, 21082; 'Mental Illness in Immigrant Minorities in London', 21830; 'Immigrant Children: A Review of Problems and Policy in Education', 23185; 'Race Relations and Theories of Status Consistency', 23186; Race and Education Across Cultures, 23191

Bagley, John Joseph: The Earls of Derby 1485–1985, 1184; The State and Education in England and Wales, 1833–1968, 23206

Bagnold, Ralph Alger: Libyan Sands. Travel in a Dead World, 27194

Bagwell, Philip Sidney: Britain and America 1850–1939: A Study of Economic Change, 3708, 14005; Industrial Relations, 5768; The Railwaymen: History of the National Union of Railwaymen, 6820, 6845, 16733; Vol.2. The Beeching Era and After, 6846; The Transport Revolution from 1770, 16192; End of the Line?: The Fate of Public Transport under Thatcher, 16193; The Railway Clearing House and the British Economy 1842–1922, 16734

Baher, Edwina: At Risk: An Account of the Battered Child Research Department, NSPCC, 9958

Bailey, Agatha: Vera Brittain, 25418

Bailey, Anthony: Acts of Union: Reports on Ireland, 1973–1979, 2883

Bailey, Cecil: Hugh Percy Allen, 24426

Bailey, Frederick Marshman: Mission to Tashkent, 13250

Bailey, Geoffrey: The Parish of Farlington, 19331

Bailey, Henry H.: Notable Names in Medicine and Surgery, 20893

Bailey, Sir Jack: The British Co-operative Movement, 1890

Bailey, M. B.: 'Community Orientations Towards Social Casework', 8681

Bailey, Martin Neil: 'Wages and Employment under Uncertain Demand', 5903

Bailey, Maurice Howard: Britain and World Affairs in the Twentieth Century, 13235

Bailey, Norman Thomas John: Mathematics, Statistics, and Systems for Health, 21232

Bailey, Oliver F.: 'The Kensingtons': 13th London Regiment, 15694

Bailey, Patrick: Orkney, 19274

Bailey, R. J.: 'The Local Ombudsman', 3255

Bailey, Richard: Managing the British Economy: A Guide to Economic Planning in Britain since 1962, 6123; 'Coal in Britain and Europe: Problems and Solutions', 6304; Energy: The Rude Awakening, 7218

Bailey, Ron: The Story of the Illegal Eviction of Squatters in Redbridge, 18383; The Squatters, 18384; The Homeless and the Empty Houses, 18508

Bailey, Roy: ed. Radical Social Work and Practice, 8755; ed. Contemporary Social Problems in Britain, 8841

Bailey, S.: 'High Spending Cities: An Historical Perspective', 3268

Bailey, S. D.: 'This Colossal Engine of Finance', 814

Bailey, Stephen: Cross on Local Government Law, 3105

Bailey, Sydney Dawson: ed. The Future of the House of Lords, 677

Bailey, Thomas Andrew: The Marshall Plan Summer, 14126; The Lusitania Disaster: An Episode in Modern Warfare and Diplomacy, 14662

Bailie, W. D.: ed. A History of Congregations in the Presbyterian Church in Ireland 1610–1982, 12175

Baillie, Albert Victor: My First Eighty Years, 11773

Baillie-Grohman, Harold Tom: Greek Tragedy, 14854

Baillie-Stewart, Norman: The Officer in the Tower, [as told to John Murdoch], 15183

Bailly, Charles: Mixed Ability Grouping: A Philosophical Perspective, 22854

Baily, Leslie William Alfred: Craftsman and Quaker: the Story of James T. Baily, 1876–1957, 12140

Bain, Andrew David: The Control of the Money Supply, 4575; The Growth of Television Ownership in the United Kingdom, 24835

Bain, George Sayers: A Bibliography of British

Industrial Relations, 5568; A Bibliography of British Industrial Relations, 1971–1979, 5569; *ed.* Industrial Relations in Britain, 5826; Social Stratification and Trade Unionism: A Critique, 6722, 9607; 'Union Growth Revisited: 1948–1974 in Perspective', 6767; 'The Growth of White-collar Unionism in Great Britain', 6784; Profiles of Union Growth: A Comparative Statistical Portrait of Eight Countries, 6802; The Growth of White-collar Unionism, 6853

Bain, Kenneth: Treason at 10: Fiji at the Crossroads, 12883

Bainbridge, Cyril: *ed.* One Hundred Years of Journalism: Social Aspects of the Press, 25311

Bainer, Roy: 'Science and Technology in Western Agriculture', 19566

Bains, J. S.: *ed.* Studies in Political Science, 6074

Baird, Sir Dugald: The Interplay of Changes in Society, Reproductive Habits and Obstetric Practice in Scotland between 1922 and 1972, 21099

Baj, J.: 'Twentieth Century Cohort Marriage and Divorce in England and Wales', 9940

Bakalar, James B.: Drug Control in a Free Society, 10831

Baker's Biographical Dictionary of Musicians, 24256

Baker, Alan Reginald Harold: *ed.* Studies of Field Systems in the British Isles, 19557; *ed.* Progress in Historical Geography, 26642

Baker, Arthur: The House is Sitting, 635

Baker, Blake: 'The Communist Party', 1956; The Far Left: An Exposé of the Extreme Left in Britain, 2009

Baker, Charles Henry Collins: British Painting, 23980

Baker, Charles Whiting: Government Control and Operation of Industry in Great Britain and the United States During the World War, 6107

Baker, D.: Partnership in Excellence: A Late-Victorian Educational Venture: The Leys School, Cambridge, 1873–1975, 22898

Baker, David: The History of Manned Spaceflight, 17701; The Rocket: The History and Development of Rocket and Missile Technology, 17702

Baker, Denys Val: Britain Discovers Herself, 23784

Baker, Derek: *ed.* Religious Motivation: Biographical and Sociological Problems for the Church Historian, 12380

Baker, Edgar Charles Richard: The Fighter Aces of the R.A.F., 1939–1945, 15891; Pattle—Supreme Fighter in the Air, 15892

Baker, Edward Cecil: A Guide to Records in the Windward Islands, 13073

Baker, Edward Ronald: Road Traffic Law Summary, 16239

Baker, Frank: Industrial Organisations and Health, 4130

Baker, J. R.: Julian Huxley: Scientist and World Citizen: A Biographical Memoir, 26503

Baker, Dame Janet: Full Circle: An Autobiographical Journal, 24410

Baker, John: The Neighbourhood Advice Centre: A Community Project in Camden, 9412

Baker, John A.: British Balloons: A Register of all Balloons and Airships Built or Registered in the British Isles since 1950, 17542

Baker, John Norman Leonard: Jesus College, Oxford, 1571–1971, 23567; The History of Geography, 26633

Baker, John Overend: Market Gardening, 19839

Baker, M. H.: Sabah: The First Ten Years as a Colony 1946–1956, 12953

Baker, Margaret: Social Worker, 8656

Baker, Mary: Park Now, Pay Later?: A Study of Offensive Parking in the Heart of London, 17389

Baker, Michael: The Changing London Midland Scene 1948–1983, 16871; London to Brighton: 150 Years of Britain's Premier Holiday Line, 16967; The Waterloo to Weymouth Line, 16980; Sussex Villages, 19146

Baker, Paul: Yeoman, Yeoman: The Warwickshire Yeomanry, 1920–1956, 15738

Baker, Peter: Attitudes to Coloured People in Glasgow, 11486

Baker, Richard St. Barbe: My Life, my Trees, 19746

Baker, Stanley: Milk to Market: Forty Years of Milk Marketing, 20656

Baker, W. J.: A History of the Marconi Company, 6679

Baker, W. P.: The English Village, 19150

Baker, William Avery: From Paddle Steamer to Nuclear Ship: A History of the Engine-Powered Vessel, 16602

Baker, William: Harold Pinter, 25976

Bakewell, Joan Dawson: The New Priesthood: British Television Today, 24905

Bakewell, W. E. Jnr.: 'Why Students "Turn on": Marijuana and other Drugs in an Undergraduate Male Population, 22218

Bakke, Edward Wright: Insurance or Dole? The Adjustments of Unemployment Insurance to Economic and Social Facts in Britain, 4026

Balchin, Jack: First New Town: An Autobiography of the Stevenage Development Corporation 1946–1980, 18201, 19027

Balchin, Nigel Marlin: Income and Outcome: A Study of Personal Finance, 3797; The Aircraft Builders: An Account of British Aircraft Production, 1939–1945, 17583

Balchin, Paul N.: Regional and Urban Economics, 5126; Housing Policy and Housing Needs, 18518; Housing Improvement and Social Inequality: Case Study of an Inner City, 18553; Urban Land Economics, 20290

Balcon, Sir Michael Elias: 'The British Film during the War', 24646; Michael Balcon Presents . . . a Lifetime of Films, 24663; Twenty Years of British Film, 1925–1945, 24664

Baldamus, Wilhelm: Efficiency and Effort: An Analysis of Industrial Administration, 4956; 'The Problem Family: A Sociological Approach', 10026

Baldanza, Frank: Iris Murdoch, 25728

Baldock, E. D.: 'Milestones of Mapping', 26718

Baldock, Peter: Community Work and Social Work, 8757

Baldray, H.: The Case for the Arts, 23761

Baldry, Peter Edward: The Battle against Heart Disease; A Physician traces the History of Man's Achievements in this Field for the General Reader, 21219; The Battle against Bacteria: A History of the Development of Antibacterial Drugs, 22349; The Battle against Bacteria: A Fresh Look, 22350

Baldwin, Arthur Windham [Earl Baldwin]: My Father: The True Story, 977

Baldwin, Ernest Hubert Francis: The Nature of Biochemistry, 26456; *ed.* Hopkins and Biochemistry 1861–1947, 26464

Baldwin, George Benedict: Beyond Nationalisation: the Labor Problems of British Coal, 6292, 7253; 'Structural Reform in the British Miners' Union', 6904

Baldwin, Gordon Robert: Regulating the Airlines: Administrative Justice and Agency Discretion, 17658

Baldwin, John Alexander: The Urban Criminal: A Study in Sheffield, 10188; *ed.* Criminal Justice: Selected Readings, 10189; 'The Role of Interrogation in Crime Discovery and Conviction', 10243; Courts, Prosecution and Conviction, 10305; Confessions in Crown Court Trials, 10306; Jury Trials, 10307; Negotiated Justice: Pressures to Plead Guilty, 10308 'Juries, Foremen and Verdicts', 10309; 'Delinquent Schools in Tower Hamlets: A Critique', 10593; 'Police Powers and the Citizen', 10774; The Mental Hospital in the Psychiatric Service: A Case—Register Study, 21842

Baldwin, Mark: Canal Books: A Guide to the Literature of the Waterways, 16379; *ed.* British Freight Waterways Today and Tomorrow, 16442. *ed.* Canals: A New Look: Essays in Honour of Charles Hadfield, 16378

Baldwin, Nicholas [Nick]: 'Research in Transport History: The International Transport Workers' Federation Archive', 16209; Lorries and Vans, 17469; Old Delivery Vans, 17470; The Illustrated History of Leyland Trucks, 17471

Baldwin, Raymond Whittier: The Great Comprehensive Gamble: Statistics of Secondary Education Examinations, 1966–1973, 22967

Baldwin, Robert: Police Powers and Politics, 10721

Baldwin, Stanley [Earl Baldwin]: On England, and Other Addresses, 978; Our Inheritance: Speeches and Addresses, 978; Service of our Lives: Last Speeches as Prime Minister, 978; This Torch of Freedom: Speeches and Addresses, 978

Bale, John R.: 'Towards a Definition of the Industrial Estate: A Note on a Neglected Aspect of Urban Geography', 18268, 20408; Sport and Place: A Geography of Sport in England, Scotland and Wales, 27030; 'Sport and National Identity: A Geographical View', 27031;'Changing Regional Origins of an Occupation: The Case of Professional Footballers in 1950 and 1980', 27074

Balfour, Sir Andrew: Health Problems of the Empire, Past, Present and Future, 22042

Balfour, Campbell: Incomes Policy and the Public Sector, 3850; Industrial Relations in the Common Market, 5758

Balfour, Harold [Baron Balfour of Inchrye]: Wings over Westminster, 1070

Balfour, Sir John: Not Too Correct an Aureole: The Recollections of a Diplomat, 13251

Balfour, John Patrick Douglas [Lord Kinross]: The Windsor Years: The Life of Edward, as Prince of Wales, King and Duke of Windsor, 491

Balfour, Michael Leonard Graham: Four Power Control in Germany and Austria 1945–1946, 14190; Propaganda in War, 1939–1945: Organizations, Policies and Publics in Britain and Germany, 15101, 15220

Balint, Michael: A Study of Doctors: Mutual Selection and the Evaluation of Results in a Training Programme for Family Doctors, 21538

Ball, Alan R.: British Political Parties: the Emergence of a Modern Party System, 1582

Ball, Colin: What the Neighbours Say: A Report on a Study of Neighbours, 9436

Ball, D. B.: Crime in our Time, 10187

Ball, Desmond: The Ties that Bind: Intelligence Co-operation in UK/USA Countries- The United Kingdom, The United States of America, Canada, Australia and New Zealand, 16008

Ball, Frank Norman: Unemployment Insurance in Great Britain, 1911–1948, 4030

Ball, George W. : Britain and the United States: Four Views to Mark the Silver Jubilee, 14011

Ball, Ian M.: Pitcairn: Children of the Bounty, 12892

Ball, Jean: Under the Oaks: The Historical Record of the Parish of Ebrington, 19329

Ball, Joan: Cops and Robbers: An Investigation into Armed Bank Robbery, 4442, 10236

Ball, Martin J.: ed. Welsh Phonology: Selected Readings, 23836

Ball, Mia: The Worshipful Company of Brewers: A Short History, 6152

Ball, Michael: The Transformation of Britain, 3707; The Economics of an Urban Housing Market: Bristol Area Study, 18542

Ball, R. J.: ed. Inflation, 3999; 'Inflationary Mechanism in the U.K. Economy', 4016; 'Some Econometric Analyses of the Long-Term Rate of Interest in the United Kingdom, 1921–1961', 4557; 'The Impact of Credit Control on Consumer Durable Spending in the United Kingdom, 1957–1961', 20451

Ballantine, William Macdonald: Rebuilding A Nation: A Descriptive Account of Housing in Modern Scotland, 18480

Ballantyne, James: ed. Researcher's Guide to British Newsreels, 220

Ballard, Charles Martin: The Story of Teaching, 22824

Ballard, Phillada: An Oasis of Delight: The History of the Birmingham Botanical Gardens, 19892, 26541

Balleine, George Reginald: A History of the Evangelical Party in the Church of England, 11654

Ballenger, E. G.: History of Urology, 21166

Ballhatchet, K.: Race, Sex and Class under the Raj: Imperial Attitudes and Policies and their Critics 1793–1905, 13118

Ballman, Sir H.: Capital, Confidence and the Community, 18540

Ballymena Area Plan: Report of the Steering Committee, 18838

Balogh, Thomas [Baron]: Labour and Inflation, 4000; The Economics of Poverty: Essays, 9059; 'Post-War Britain and the Common Market', 14161

Balopolous, Elias T.: Fiscal Policy Models of the British Economy, 4662

Balsom, Denis: 'The Scottish and Welsh Devolution Referenda of 1979', 2411; A Political and Electoral Handbook for Wales, 2583; 'Plaid Cymru: The Welsh National Party', 2610; The Nature and Distribution of Support for Plaid Cymru, 2611

Balston, Thomas: English Wood-Engraving, 1900–1950, 24098

Baly, Monica E.: A History of the Queen's Nursing Institute: 100 Years, 1887–1987, 21710

Bamber, Greg: 'Microchips and Industrial Relations', 5812

Bamborough, Renford: Wisdom: Twelve Essays, 26881

Bambridge, B. A.: Physic and Philanthropy: A History of the Wellcome Trust, 1936–1986, 20772

Bamford, James: The Puzzle Palace: America's National Security Agency and its Special Relationship with Britain's GCHQ, 16019

Bamford, Thomas William: Rise of the Public Schools: A Study of Boys' Public Boarding Schools in England and Wales from 1837 to the Present Day, 23023; Public School Data: A Compilation of Data on Public and Related Schools (Boys) Mainly from 1866, 23024; The University of Hull: the First Fifty Years, 23501

Bancroft, Colin: Forestry for the Quality of Life: Evaluation and Analysis of the Impact of Forestry on Recreation, 19756

Band, Edward: Working His Purpose Out: The History of the English Presbyterian Mission, 1847–1947, 12362

Banerji, Arun Kumar: India and Britain 1947–68: The Evolution of Post-Colonial Relations, 13191

Bangura, Y.: Britain and Commonwealth Africa: The Politics of Economic Relationships, 12707

Banham, Martin: 'The Nigerian Student in Britain', 11507

Banham, Mary: A Tonic to the Nation: The Festival of Britain 1951, 27171

Banham, [Peter] Rayner: Guide to Modern Architecture, 23883; The New Brutalism: Ethic or Aesthetic?, 23884; Age of the

Masters: A Personal View of Modern Architecture, 23885; The Architecture of the Well-Tempered Environment, 23886; Megastructure: Urban Features of the Recent Past, 23887

Banister, David: Travel and Energy Use in Great Britain 1969 to 1979: Trends and Options, 16234; Car Availability and Usage: A Modal Split Model Based on these Concepts, 17371

Bank Education Service: The City of London and its Markets, 4282; A History of Banking, 4437; The Clearing System, 4438; The Role of the Banks, 4439; Banks and Overseas Trade, 4440

Bank of England: The UK Recovery in the 1930s, 3595; Report for the Year Ended 28th February, 1950, 4486

Bankers Almanac and Yearbook, 4441

Banking Insurance Finance Union: Beyond 1984: A Perspective of the Impact of New Technology and Working Procedure in the National Westminster Bank, 4505

Bankoff, G.: The Conquest of Tuberculosis, 21163

Banks, C.: 'Public Attitudes to Crime and the Penal System', 10346

Banks, Francis Richard: Old English Towns, 18947; English Villages, 18948

Banks, Howard: The Rise and Fall of Freddy Laker, 17632

Banks, Joseph Ambrose: Industrial Participation: Theory and Practice: A Case Study, 6001; Trade Unionism, 6749; 'Sociological Aspects of Technical Change in a Steel Plant', 7925; ed. Studies in British Society, 7996; Sociology as a Vocation, 8064; The Sociology of Social Movements, 8065; Community Action: Arguments, 9261; The English Middle-Class Concept of the Standard of Living and its Relation to Marriage and Family Size, 20421

Banks, Mary MacLeod: British Calendar Customs, 9910

Banks, Michael: 'Professionalism in the Conduct of Foreign Policy', 13354

Banks, Noel: Six Inner Hebrides: Eigg, Rum, Canna, Muck, Coll, Tiree, 19260

Banks, Olive: The Attitudes of Steelworkers to Technical Change, 7252; Faces of Feminism: A Study of Feminism as a Social Movement, 7795; 'The Sociology of Education, 1952–1982', 22817; Parity and Prestige in English Secondary Education, 22936; Success and Failure in the Secondary School, 22938

Banks, R. F.: 'The Reform of British Industrial Relations: The Donovan Report and the Labour Government's Policy Proposals', 5721; 'British Collective Bargaining: The Challenge of the 1970s', 5722

Banks, Robert: Britain's Home Defence Gamble, 15140

Bannister, David: Transport Mobility and Deprivation in Inter-urban Areas, 16273

Bannister, Roger: First Four Minutes, 27145

Bannister, Winifred: James Bridie and his Theatre, 25953

Bannock, Graham Bertram: The Juggernauts: The Age of the Big Corporation, 5524

Banting, K. G.: *ed.* The Politics of Constitutional Change in Industrial Nations, 582

Bantock, Geoffrey Herman: Studies in the History of Educational Theory, 22855; 'The Reorganisation of Secondary Education', 22931; Education in an Industrial Society, 23284; T. S. Eliot on Education, 25491

Bantock, Myrrha: Granville Bantock: A Personal Portrait, 24294

Banton, Michael Parker: The Coloured Quarter: Negro Immigrants in an English City, 10913; White and Coloured: The Behaviour of British People Towards Coloured Immigrants, 10914; Race Relations, 10915; The Idea of Race, 10916; Rational Choice: A Theory of Racial and Ethnic Relations, 10917; The Race Concept, 10918; Racial Minorities, 10919; 'Sociology and Race Relations', 10920; Racial and Ethnic Competition, 10921; 'Optimism and Pessimism about Racial Relations', 10922; 'The Beginning and the End of the Racial Issue in British Politics', 11087; Promoting Racial Harmony, 11141

Baptist Union Directory: 1862+, 12017

Barbara, Jack: Stevie: A Biography of Stevie Smith, 25808

Barber, B. J.: The West Riding County Council 1889–1974: Historical Studies, 3373

Barber, Charles Laurence: Linguistic Change in Present-Day English, 23812

Barber, Dolan: One-Parent Families, 9943

Barber, Edward *and* Barber, Elinor Gellert: *eds.* European Social Class: Stability and Change, 9531

Barber, James: The Uneasy Relationship: Britain and South Africa, 12722

Barber, [John Lysberg] Noel: The Fall of Shanghai: The Communist Takeover in 1949, 13635; Sinister Twilight. The Fall and Rise again of Singapore, 15072; The War of the Running Dogs: How Malaya Defeated the Communist Guerrillas 1948–60, 16154; Conversations with Painters, 24005; The Natives were Friendly: An Autobiography, 25207

Barber, Lionel: The Price of Truth: The Story of the Reuters Millions, 25308

Barber, Michael J. C.: Directory for the Environmental Organisations in Britain and Ireland 1986–7, 20244

Barber, Ross: Iron Ore and After: Boom Time, Depression and Survival in a West Cumbrian Town, Cleator Moor, 1840–1960, 18100

Barbour, George Freeland: Church and Nation in Scotland Today, 12209

Barbour, Nevill: 'England and the Arabs', 13826

Barbour, Robert F.: 'The Young Offenders', 10679

Barclay, Alfred E.: The Foetal Circulation and Cardiovascular System, and the Changes that they Undergo, 22305

Barclay, Christopher: Competition and the Regulation of Banks, 4445

Barclay, Cyril Nelson: Armistice 1918, 14597; On their Shoulders. British Generalship in the Lean Years, 1939–1942, 14743; Against

Great Odds—including Extracts from the Personal Account of . . . General Sir Richard N. O'Connor, 14776; History of the Cameronians (Scottish Rifles), 15581; History of the Duke of Wellington's Regiment, 1919–1952, 15623; History of the 16th/5th: The Queen's Royal Lancers, 1925–61, 15688; *ed.* The London Scottish in the Second World War, 1939–1945, 15696; The History of the Royal Northumberland Fusiliers in the Second World War, 15704; The History of the Sherwood Foresters (Nottinghamshire and Derbyshire Regiment), 1919–1957, 15717; The History of the 53rd (Welsh) Division in the Second World War, 15757; The First Commonwealth Division: The Story of the British Commonwealth Land Forces in Korea 1950–1953, 16128

Barclay, Glen St John: 'Background to EFTA: An Episode in Anglo-Scandinavian Relations', 13886; Their Finest Hour, 14801

Barclay, H. M.: Parliamentary Dictionary, 649

Barclay, J. B.: *ed.* Looking at Lothian: Monographs on the Economy, Industry, Government, Culture and Services in Edinburgh and Lothian, 18133

Barclay, Oliver R.: Whatever Happened to the Jesus Lane Lot?, 11663

Barclay, Peter M.: Social Workers: Their Role and Tasks: The Report of a Working Party, 8843

Barclays Bank D.C.O.: A Banking Centenary: Barclays Bank (Dominion, Colonial and Overseas) 1836–1936, 4493

Barclays Bank: UK Economic Survey, 3692

Barcroft, Sir Joseph: The Respiratory Function of the Blood, 22306

Bardanne, Jean: Perfide Albion: An Examination of British Foreign Policy in Relation to France and Germany after the European War, 14256

Bardens, Denis C.: Churchill in Parliament, 988

Bareau, Paul: The Future of the Sterling System, 4704

Baring, Maurice: R.F.C.H.Q., 15798

Barkas, Geoffrey: The Camouflage Story (from Aintree to Alamein), 15097

Barke, Michael [Mike]: Social Change in Benwell, Written in . . . Conjunction with Benwell Community Project, 9410; Transport and Trade, 16256

Barker, Anthony: *ed.* Quangos in Britain, 2080; 'The Planning and Control of Public Expenditure', 4762; The Local Amenity Movement, 19956; Studying Amenity Societies', 19957

Barker, Arthur James: Suez: The Seven Day War, 14371; The Neglected War: Mesopotamia, 1914–1918, 14558; Dunkirk: The Great Escape, 14845; Eritrea 1941, 14888; British and American Infantry Weapons of World War II, 15483; The East Yorkshire Regiment, 15748; Fortune Favours the Brave: The Hook, Korea, 1953, 16127

Barker, Bernard: *ed.* Ramsay MacDonald's Political Writings, 1033; 'Anatomy of Reformism: The Social and Political Ideas

of the Labour Leadership in Yorkshire', 1699

Barker, Brian: When the Queen was Crowned, 513

Barker, Clive: British Alternative Theatre, 26235

Barker, D. J. P.: Atlas of Mortality from Selected Diseases in England and Wales, 22233

Barker, Dennis: Ruling the Waves: An Unofficial Portrait of the Royal Navy, 15284

Barker, Diana Leonard: *ed.* Sexual Divisions and Society: Process and Change, 7793; *ed.* Dependence and Exploitation in Work and Marriage, 7794; 'Young People and their Homes: Spoiling and "Keeping Close" in a South Wales Town', 8418

Barker, Dudley: British Aid to Developing Nations, 9175; The Official Story of the Great Floods of 1947 and their Sequel, 20181; Writer by Trade: A View of Arnold Bennett, 25387; The Man of Principle, 25533

Barker, Elisabeth: Churchill and Eden at War, 1011

Barker, Eric: Steady, Barker! The Autobiography, 26295

Barker, Sir Ernest: The Character of England, 321, 7564; Britain and the British People, 7563; British Constitutional Monarchy, 462; Ireland in the Last Fifty Years (1866–1916), 2673; National Character and the Factors in its Formation, 7565; The Development of Public Services in Western Europe, 1660–1930, 8976; Reflections on Family Life, 10018; Mothers and Sons in War-time and other Pieces, 10019; The Ideas and Ideals of the British Empire, 12554; Universities in Great Britain: Their Position and Their Problems, 23367

Barker, Kathleen: The Theatre Royal, Bristol, 1766–1966: Two Centuries of Stage History, 26162

Barker, Nicolas: The Oxford University Press and the Spread of Learning 1478–1978: An Illustrated History, 24983; Stanley Morison, 25026

Barker, Paul: The Social Sciences Today, 8055

Barker, Rachel: Conscience, Government and War: Conscientious Objection in Great Britain 1939–1945, 13520

Barker, Ralph Hammond: The Children of the Benares, 15093; Down in the Drink: The Hurricats, 15830; True Stories of the Goldfish Club, 15902; The Ship-busters: The Story of R.A.F. Torpedo Bombers, 15968; Strike Hard, Strike Sure: Epics of the Bombers, 15969; The Thousand Plan, 15970; The Blockade Busters, 15971

Barker, Rodney Steven: 'Political Myth: Ramsay MacDonald and the Labour Party', 1032; Political Ideas in Modern Britain, 2084; Education and Politics, 1900–1951: A Study of the Labour Party, 2102, 22920; 'The Labour Party and Education for Socialism', 2103; 'Guild Socialism Revisited?', 2121

Barker, Ronnie: It's Hello from Him, 26296

Barker, Terence S.: 'Devaluation and the Rise in U.K. Prices, 4712; 'The Import Content of Final Expenditures for the United Kingdom, 1954–1972', 4792

Barker, Theodore Cardwell: A History of the Carpenters Company, 6189; Pilkington Brothers and the Glass Industry, 6482; The Glassmakers Pilkington: The Rise of An International Company, 1826–1976, 6483; *ed.* Population and Society, 1850–1980, 7425; *ed.* The Long March of the Common Man, 1750–1960, 7531; An Economic History of Transport in Britain, 16201; A History of London Transport: Passenger Travel and the Development of the Metropolis, 16316; The Economic and Social Effects of the Spread of Motor Vehicles, 17458; The Transport Contractors of Rye: John Jempson and Son: A Chapter in the History of Road Haulage, 17459; *ed.* Our Changing Fare: 200 Years of British Food Habits, 20572

Barker, William: Local Government Statistics: A Guide to Statistics on Local Government Finance and Service in the United Kingdom at August 1964, 3101, 4882

Barker, William Alan: *ed.* Documents of English History 1832–1950, 280; A General History of England, 1832–1960, 331

Barkley, John Monteith: The Presbyterian Orphan Society, 1866–1966, 8099; *ed.* Handbook to Church Hymnary, 11930; A Short History of the Presbyterian Church in Ireland, 12173; 'The Presbyterian Church in Ireland and the Government of Ireland Act 1920', 12174; 'Presbyterian-Roman Catholic Relations in Ireland (1780–1975)', 12178

Barkworth, Peter: First Houses, 26012

Barley, Maurice Willmore: The House and Home, 18667; The English Farmhouse and Cottage, 18668

Barling, Seymour Gilbert: *ed.* Diseases of Infancy and Childhood, 21116; *ed.* 'Child Health and the Universities', 21117

Barlow, F. Ralph: Woodbrooke, 1953–1978: A Documentary Account of Woodbrooke's Third 25 Years, 23713

Barlow, Frank: *ed.* Exeter and its Region, 18105

Barlow, G.: History at the Universities, 26774

Barlow, Graham: 'Some Latent Influences in a Pay-claim: An Examination of a White-collar Dispute', 5720

Barltrop, Robert: The Monument: The Story of the Socialist Party of Great Britain, 1968

Barman, Christian: The Man who Built London Transport: A Biography of Frank Pick, 16317

Barman, S.: The English Borstal System, 10518

Barman, Thomas: 'Britain and France, 1967', 14226; 'Britain, France and West Germany', 14227

Barmann, Lawrence F.: Baron Friedrich von Hügel and the Modernist Crisis in England, 11981

Barna, Tibor: The Redistribution of Incomes through Public Finance in 1937, 3829; Investment and Growth Policies in British Industrial Firms, 4964

Barnaby, Kenneth Cloves: The Institution of Naval Architects 1860–1960, 16503; Some Ship Disasters and their Causes, 16515; 100 Years of Specialised Shipbuilding and Engineering: John I. Thorneycroft Centenary, 16635

Barnard, Howard Clive: A Short History of English Education from 1760, 22657; A Hand Book of British Educational Terms, including an Outline of the British Educational System, 22862

Barnard, Keith: *ed.* Conflicts in the National Health Service, 21674

Barnes, Alfred: The Political Aspect of Co-operation, 1884

Barnes, [Anthony] John [Lane]: Baldwin, a Biography, 977; *ed.* The Leo Amery Diaries, 1068

Barnes, Arthur Stapylton: The Catholic Schools of England, 22881

Barnes, Clive: Ballet in Britain since the War, 24209; Ballet here and now, 24210

Barnes, Sir [Ernest] John [Ward]: Ahead of his Age: Bishop Barnes of Birmingham, 11717

Barnes, F. A.: 'The Evolution of the Salient Patterns of Milk Production in England and Wales', 20653

Barnes, G. M.: *ed.* Alcohol and the Family: A Comprehensive Bibliography, 10096

Barnes, G.: 'Drug Taking in adolescent Girls: Factors Associated with the Progression to Narcotic Use', 22224

Barnes, George Nicoll: From Workshop to War Cabinet, 1071

Barnes, Harry Elmer: An Introduction to the History of Sociology, 7892; Society in Transition: Problems of a Changing Age, 7893; *ed.* The History and Prospects of the Social Sciences, 7894; Housing: The Facts and the Future, 18395; The Slum: Its Story and Solution, 18396

Barnes, James John: Hitler's Mein Kampf in Britain & America: A Publishing History, 13679; Free Trade in Books: A Study of the London Book Trade since 1800, 24933

Barnes, John: The Beginnings of the Cinema in England, 24624

Barnes, Ken: Twenty Years of Pop, 24001

Barnes, Michael: Britain on Borrowed Time, 3656

Barnes, Patricia P.: Hitler's Mein Kampf in Britain & America: A Publishing History, 13679

Barnes, Paul: Building Societies: The Myth of Mutuality, 4369

Barnes, Peter: Perspectives on School at Seven Years Old, 23141

Barnes, Robert Money: A History of the Regiments and Uniforms of the British Army, 15544; Military Uniforms of Britain and the Empire, 1742 to the Present Time, 15545

Barnes, Robin: Locomotives that Never Were: Some 20th Century British Projects, 17064

Barnes, Trevor: Terry Waite: Man with a Mission, 11817

Barnes, W.: 'The Financial and Social Costs of Urban Renewal', 17856

Barnet, A.S.: 'Some Factors Underlying Racial Discrimination in Housing', 11188

Barnetson, William Denholm, Baron: The Economics of Newspapers and News Agencies, 25064

Barnett, Arthur: The Western Synagogue through Two Centuries (1761–1961), 11290, 12427

Barnett, Correlli Douglas: The Collapse of British Power, 330; The Collapse of British Power, 13236; The Desert Generals, 14745; Britain and Her Army, 1509–1970: A Political and Social Survey, 15429

Barnett, J. V.: 'Teacher Training: University Control and Supply of Teachers', 22723

Barnett, L. Margaret: British Food Policy in the First World War, 20579

Barnett, [Malcolm] Joel [Lord]: Inside the Treasury, 816; The Politics of Legislation: The Rent Act, 18421

Barnsby, George: A History of Housing in Wolverhampton 1750–1975, 18431

Barocas, V.: 'The Preston Observatory', 26452

Baron, Christina: Fair Shares in Parliament: Or, How to Elect More Women MPs, 7829

Baron, George: 'The Teachers' Registration Movement', 9844; Society, Schools and Progress in England, 22840; A Bibliographical Guide to the English Educational System, 22857; Teachers in England and America, 23198

Baron, M.: Independent Radio: The Story of Independent Radio in the U.K, 24805

Baron, Wendy: Miss Ethel Sands and her Circle, 23931; Sickert, 24063

Barooah, D. P.: Indo-British Relations 1950–1960, 13189

Barp, Thomas Wade: Augustus John, 24023

Barr, Albert William Cleeve: Public Authority Housing, 18430

Barr, Brian: The Story of the Scottish Daily News, 25152

Barr, Charles: Ealing Studios, 24668

Barr, Hugh: Volunteers in Prison After-care: The Report of the Teamwork Associates, 10480; Probation Research: A Study of Group Work in the Probation Service, 10481; Trends and Regional Comparisons in Probation, 10482

Barr, J.: Derelict Britain, 20302

Barr, James: The Scottish Church Question, 12250; The United Free Church of Scotland, 12251

Barr, John: The Assaults on our Senses, 19982

Barr, N. A.: 'Real Rates of Return to Financial Assets since the War', 4571; Public Finance in Theory and Practice, 4590

Barraclough, Geoffrey: An Introduction to Contemporary History, 318

Barraclough, K. C.: Sheffield Steel, 6603

Barratt, Sir C.: 'The Town Clerk in British Local Government', 3246

Barratt, Rex: The Hey-Day of the Great Atlantic Liners, 16579

Barrell, Geoffrey Richard: Teachers and the Law, 22628

Barresi, C. M.: 'The Urban Community: Attitudes towards Neighbourhood and Urban Renewal', 9416

Barrett, [Denis] Cyril: Pop Art, 23999

Barrett, Helena: Suburban Style: The British House, 1840–1960, 18303

Barrett, John Oliver: Rawdon College

(Northern Baptist Education Society) 1804–1954: A Short History, 12041

Barrett, Michael: Michael Barrett, 24906

Barrick, John: Planning in the United States and the United Kingdom, 1970–1983, 17712

Barrie, Derek Stiven: South Wales, 16820

Barrington, C. A.: Forestry in the Weald: Kent, Surrey, Sussex and East Hampshire, 19741

Barritt, Adrian: The Growth of Planning Research since the Early 1960s, 17916

Barritt, Denis Phillips: The Northern Ireland Problem: A Study in Group

Relations, 2826, 12161; Orange and Green: A Quaker Study of Community Relations in Northern Ireland, 12160

Barron, Andrew: Gossip: A History of High Society from 1920 to 1970, 9747

Barron, Hugh: ed. The County of Inverness, 19238

Barros, James: Office without Power: Secretary-General Sir Eric Drummond, 1919–1933, 13478; Britain, Greece and the Politics of Sanctions: Ethiopia, 1935–36, 13783

Barrow, Kenneth: Flora: An Appreciation of the Life and Work of Dame Flora Robson, 26093

Barry, Brian: Sociologists, Economists and Democracy, 7911

Barry, Duncan: The St James's Theatre: Its Strange and Complete History, 1835–1957, 26146

Barry, E. Eldon: Nationalisation in British Politics: The Historical Background, 6077

Barry, Frank Russell: Period of My Life, 11718; Mervyn Haigh, 11736

Barry, Michael: 'The National Theatre', 26138

Barry, Norman P.: Hayek's Road to Serfdom Revisited: Essays by Economists, Philosophers and Political Scientists on 'The Road to Serfdom' after Forty Years, 2096; Hayek's Social and Economic Philosophy, 2097

Barry, Thomas B.: Guerilla Days in Ireland: A First Hand Account of the Black and Tan War, 1919–1921, 2750

Barry, William Sydney: The Fundamentals of Management, 5430; Managing a Transport Business, 5431

Barrymaine, Norman: The Story of Peter Townsend, 544

Barsby, Percy Joseph: Bygone Days in the Parish of Attenborough, 19321

Bartholomew, David John: ed. Manpower Planning: Selected Readings, 5946

Bartholomew: Road Atlas Britain, 132

Barthop, Michael: The Armies of Britain, 1485–1980, 15431; Crater to the Creggan: A History of the Royal Anglian Regiment, 1964–1974, 15597; The Northamptonshire Regiment, 15703

Bartle, G. F.: A History of Borough Road College, 22755

Bartlett, A. F.: Industrial Relations: A Study in Conflict, 5778

Bartlett, Charles P.: Bomber Pilot, 1916–1918, 14641

Bartlett, Christopher J.: A History of Post-war Britain, 1945–1974, 300

British Foreign Policy in the Twentieth Century, 13247

Bartlett, Ellis Ashmead: Some of My Experiences in the Great War, 14467; Ashmead Bartlett's Despatches from the Dardanelles, 14537; The Uncensored Dardanelles, 14538

Bartlett, Ernest Henry: The House of Windsor, George V to George VI, 470

Bartlett, J. Neville: Carpeting the Millions: The Growth of Britain's Carpet Industry, 6429

Bartlett, Percy: Barrow Cadbury: A Memoir, 12144

Bartlett, Ronald Ernest: Developments in Sewerage, 20093

Bartlett, Vernon Oldfield: The Colour of Their Skin, 10974; I Know what I Liked, 25209

Bartley, Jeff: 'London at the Polls: A Review of the 1981 GLC Election and Analysis', 3300

Barton, Brian: Belfast in the Blitz, 18169; Brookeborough: The Making of a Prime Minister, 3072

Barton, D. B.: A Historical Survey of the Mines and Mineral Railways of East Cornwall and West Devon, 6356; Essays in Cornish Mining History, 6357

Barton, Derek: A Hope For Housing?, 18666

Barton, R. M.: A History of the China-Clay Industry, 6630

Bartram, Peter: David Steel: His Life and Politics, 1526

Barty-King, Hugh: The Baltic Exchange, 4252; Light Up the World: The Story of the Success of the Dale Electric Group, 1935–1985, 6682; The A.A.: A History of the First 75 Years of the Automobile Association 1905–1980, 17394; Food for Man and Beast: The Story of the London Corn Trade Association, the London Cattle Food Association, and the Grain and Feed Trade Association, 1878–1978, 20598; HMSO: The Story of the first 200 years 1786–1986, 24969

Barwick, Sandra: A Century of Style, 24163

Barzilay, David: The British Army in Ulster, 2898

Baskerville, Doris Renwick: Behavioural Patterns of Families in a London

Borough: A Study of Marital and Parental Roles, 10069

Baskett, Bertram G. M.: 'Public Health versus the State', 21291; 'Arbitration on Rate of Medical Remuneration', 21292

Basnett, David: The Future of Collective Bargaining, 5821

Bass, Elven E.: Aldous Huxley: An Annotated Bibliography of Criticism, 25586

Bass, H.: Glorious Wembley: The Official History of Britain's Foremost Entertainment Centre, 27075

Basset, Bernard: The English Jesuits from Campion to Martindale, 11963

Bassett, Keith: Housing and Residential Structures: Atlantic Approaches, 18447

Bassett, Philip: Strike Free: New Industrial Relations in Britain, 5850

Bassett, Philippa: A List of the Historical Records of the County Councils

Association, 3108; A List of the Historical Records of the Town and Country Planning Institute, 18830; A List of Historical Records of the Council for the Preservation of Rural England, 19117; A List of the Historical Records of the National Farmers' Union of Scotland, 19397; A List of the Historical Records of the British Ecological Society, 20222; A List of the Historical Records Retained by the Friends of the Lake District, 20223; Lists of Historical Records of Environmental Organisations, 20243

Bassett, Reginald: 'Telling the Truth to the People: The Myth of the Baldwin "Confession"', 977; Democracy and Foreign Policy: A Case History, the Sino-Japanese Dispute, 1931–1933, 13595

Bassett, Thomas Myrfyn: The Welsh Baptists, 12298

Bastide, Roger: The Sociology of Mental Disorder, 21846

Bastin, John Sturgus: Malaysia: Selected Historical Readings, 12900

Batchelor, John H.: Artillery, 15492; Fighter. A History of Fighter Aircraft, 15826

Bateman, D. I.: 'A. W. Ashby: An Assessment', 19577

Baterry, Roy: Women in Khaki: The Story of the British Woman Soldier, 15459

Bates, Herbert Ernest: Autobiography, 25369

Bates, James: 'Company Finance in the United Kingdom', 4259

Bates, Leonard Maurice: The Thames on Fire: The Battle of London River 1939–1945, 16698

Batey, Mavis: The Historic Gardens of Oxford and Cambridge, 19895

Bath Conservation Study Team: City of Bath Conservation Study: First Stage Report, 18971

Bather, Leslie: The British Constitution, 613

Batley, Richard: The Neighbourhood Scheme: Cases of Central Government Intervention in Local Deprivation, 9379; Evaluation of Two Neighbourhood Schemes in Liverpool and Teesside, 9380; 'An Explanation of Non-Participation in Planning', 17896; Going Comprehensive: Educational Policy-Making in Two County Boroughs, 22960, 22965

Batstone, Eric: Shop Stewards in Action, 5789

Batta, I.D.: 'Study of Juvenile Delinquency amongst Asians and Half-Asians: A Comparative Study in a Northern Town, based on Official Statistics', 10632

Batten, Edgar: National Economics for Britain's Day of Need, 3556

Batten, Eric J.: The Effects of Environmental Factors on Secondary Educational Attainment in Manchester: A Plowden Follow-up, 22835

Batten, Madge: The Human Factor in Casework, 8652

Batten, Mollie: 'Theological Education', 11903

Batten, Thomas Reginald: The Human Factor in Casework, 8652; The Non-Directive Approach in Group and Community Work, 9397; Training for Community Development: A Critical Study of Method,

9398; The Human Factor in Community Work, 9399

Batters, Jean: Edith Evans: A Personal Memoir, 26039

Battersby, Martin: The Decorative Twenties, 24112; The Decorative Thirties, 24113

Battersby, William John: The De La Salle Brothers in Great Britain: The Story of a Century of Effort and Achievement in the Domain of English Education, 22886; 'Educational Work of the Religious Orders of Women, 1850–1950', 22891; 'Secondary Education for Boys', 22892

Battersea United Charities: The Battersea United Charities, 1641–1966, 9132

Battiscombe, Georgina: Queen Alexandra, 471

Batty, Michael: Urban Modelling: Algorithms, Calibrations, Predictions, 17905

Baugh, G. C.: Shropshire and its Rulers: A Thousand Years, 3367

Baugh, William Ellis: Introduction to the Social Services, 8874

Baughan, Peter E.: North and Mid Wales, 16819

Bauman, Zygmunt: Between Class and Elite: The Evolution of the Labour Movement, A Sociological Study, 9577

Baumgartner, John George: Canned Foods: An Introduction to their Microbiology, 20640

Baumhogger, Goswin: The Struggle for Independence: Documents on the Recent Development of Zimbabwe 1975–1980, 12791

Bax, Anthony: ed. The Macmillan Guide to the UK 1978–1979, 279

Bax, Sir Arnold: Farewell My Youth, 24295

Baxendale, Arthur Salisbury: Britain's Coming Great Crash, 3554

Baxter, Sir [Arthur] Beverley: Strange Street: An Autobiography, 25210

Baxter, David: Two Years To Do, 16067

Baxter, J. L.: 'Long-term Unemployment in Great Britain, 1953–1971', 6980

Baxter, John: An Appalling Talent: Ken Russell, 24683

Baxter, Paul: ed. Race and Social Difference, 11019

Baxter, R.: 'The Working Class and Labour Politics', 1797, 9628

Baxter, Raymond Eric: Ports and Inland Waterways/Civil Aviation, 16449

Baxter, Ron: Ports and Inland Waterways and Civil Aviation, 16186

Bayer, J. A.: 'British Policy towards the Russian-Finnish Winter War 1939–1940', 13881

Bayldon, Joan: Cyril Bardsley, Evangelist, 11715

Bayley, J. C. R.: 'The Administration and Evaluation of Research Units and Projects', 8789

Bayley, Michael: Mental Handicap and Community Care: A Study of Mentally Handicapped People in Sheffield, 21855

Bayley, S.: In Good Shape: Style in Industrial Products 1900–1960, 24150

Bayliss, F. J.: 'The Independent Members of British Wages Councils and Boards', 5639;

'West Indians at Work in Nottingham', 11236; 'The Response to Adult Education in Industry', 23648

Bayliss, G. M.: Bibliographic Guide to the Two World Wars: An Annotated Survey of English-Language Reference Materials, 14432

Bayne, Stephen Fielding: An Anglican Turning Point: Documents and Interpretations, 11597

Baynes, John: History of the Cameronians (Scottish Rifles): Vol. 4, The Close of Empire, 1948–1968, 15582

Baynes, Kate and Baynes, Kenneth: Gordon Russell, 24148

Baynes, Ken: ed. Scoop, Scandal and Strife: A Study of Photography in Newspapers, 25300

Bazalgette, John: Freedom, Authority and the Young Adult: A Report to the Department of Education and Science on the Young Adult Project: In Particular Examining how the Resources of Adults are Used by Young People as they take up full Adult Roles in Society, 8453

Beacham, Arthur: Industries in Welsh Country Towns, 5310; 'The Ulster Linen Industry', 5397

Beadle, Sir Gerald: Television: A Critical Review, 24850

Beadon, Roger Hammet: Some Memories of the Peace Conference, 13425; The Royal Army Service Corps, 15770

Beaglehole, T. H.: 'From Rulers to Servants: The I.C.S. and the British Demission of Power in India', 13124

Beales, Derek Edward Dawson: History, Society and the Churches: Essays in Honour of Owen Chadwick, 11866, 26787; History and Biography: An Inaugural Lecture, 26762

Beales, Hugh Lancelot: The Making of Social Policy, 8861; ed. Memoirs of the Unemployed, 9622; A Select Bibliography of Rural Economic History, 19389

Beales, Peter: 20th Century Roses, 19899

Bealey, Frank William: 'Size of Place and the Labour Vote in Britain, 1918–66', 1722; ed. The Social and Political Thought of the British Labour Party, 2099; Constituency Politics: a Study of Newcastle-under-Lyme, 3334; The Politics of Independence A Study of a Scottish Town, 3378; Unions in Prosperity, 6729.

Bean, Charles Edward Woodrow: ed. Photographic Record of the War: Reproductions of Pictures Taken by the Australian Official Photographers, 14616

Bean, J. M. W., ed. The Political Culture of Modern Britain: Studies in Memory of Stephen Koss, 2297

Bean, Lee L.: A Decade Later: A Follow-up Study of Social Class and Mental Illness, 21817

Bean, Philip: Punishment: A Philosophical and Criminological Inquiry, 10382; Rehabilitation and Deviance, 10381; The Social Control of Drugs, 10828, 22204; 'Social Aspects of Drug Abuse: A Study of London Drug Offenders', 22220

Bean, Ron: 'Militancy, Policy Formation and Membership Opposition in the Electrical Trade Union, 1945–1961', 6892; 'Liverpool Shipping Employers and the Anti-Communist Activities of J. M. Hughes, 1920–1925', 16566; 'The Port of Liverpool: Employers and Industrial Relations, 1919–1939', 16692

Beard, Geoffrey: The Lake District, A Century of Conservation, 20224

Beasant, John: The Santo Rebellion: An Imperial Reckoning, 12889

Beaton, Sir Cecil [Walter Hardy]: Photobiography, 24700; The Happy Years: Diaries, 1944–1948, 24701; The Strenuous Years: Diaries, 1948–1955, 24702; The Restless Years: Diaries, 1955–1963, 24703; The Parting Years: Diaries, 1963–74, 24704; The Magic Image: The Genius of Photography from 1839 to the Present Day, 24705

Beattie, Alan J.: 'Recent Developments in the British Constitution', 615; ed. English Party Politics, 1577

Beattie, David Joy: The New Law of Education, 22626

Beattie, Geoffrey: Survivors of Steel City: A Portrait of Sheffield, 18072

Beattie, Ian: The European Community and its Common Agricultural Policy, 19656

Beauman, Katharine Bentley: Partners in Blue: The Story of Women's Service with the Royal Air Force, 14988; Wings on her Shoulders, 14989

Beauman, Sally: The Royal Shakespeare Company: A History of Ten Decades, 26147

Beaumont, Bill: Probation Work: Critical Theory and Socialist Practice, 10463

Beaumont, Joan: Comrades in Arms: British Aid to Russia, 1941–1945, 13964; 'Trade, Strategy and Foreign Policy in Conflict: The Rolls Royce Affair 1946–1947', 13970

Beaumont, Philip B.: Government as Employer—Setting an Example?, 882

Beavan, John Cowburn, Baron Ardwick: 'Editorial Policy-Making and the Royal Commission on the Press', 25124

Beaver, Patrick: The Alsford Tradition: A Century of Quality Timber 1882–1982, 19797; Yes! We Have Some: The Story of Fyffes, 20708

Beaver, Stanley Henry: The British Isles: A Geographic and Economic Survey, 5036, 26684

Beaverbrook, William Maxwell Aitken, Lord: My Early Life, 1077

Beavington, Frank: 'The Development of Market Gardening in Bedfordshire 1799–1939', 19846; 'Early Market Gardening in Bedfordshire', 19847

Bebbington, David William: Evangelicalism in Modern Britain. A History from the 1730s to the 1980s, 11660; ed. The Baptists in Scotland: A History, 12258; 'The Oxford Group Movement between the Wars', 12398

Bechhofer, Frank: ed. Population Growth and the Brain Drain, 7383

Bechhofer-Roberts, Carl Eric: Sir John Simon:

Being an Account of the Life and Career . . ., 1315; Philip Snowden: An Impartial Portrait, 1320

Bechmann, Arnold: 'The Conservative Research Department: The Care and Feeding of Future British Political Elites', 1647

Beck, Ann: 'Colonial Policy and Education in British East Africa', 12819; A History of the British Medical Administration of East Africa, 1900–1950, 21977; Medicine, Tradition and Development in Kenya and Tanzania, 1920–1970, 21978

Beck, George Andrew: The English Catholics, 1850–1950: Essays to Commemorate the Centenary of the Restoration of the Hierarchy of England and Wales, 11939, 22891, 22892

Beck, Keith M.: The Greatness of the Great Western, 16863

Beck, Peter J.: 'From the Geneva Protocol to the Greco-Bulgarian Dispute: The Development of the Baldwin Government's Policy towards the Peace-Keeping Role of the League of Nations, 1924–1925', 13484; 'The Anglo-Persian Oil Dispute, 1932–1933', 13856; 'The Anglo-Argentine Dispute over the Title to the Falkland Islands: Changing British Perceptions on Sovereignty since 1910', 16084

Becker, A.: 'Field Work among Scottish Shepherds and German Peasants: 'Whohs' and their Handicaps', 19248

Becker, Howard: ed. Modern Sociological Theory in Continuity and Change, 7950

Beckerman, Wilfred: ed. The Labour Government's Economic Record, 1964–1970, 1749; 'The National Plan: A Discussion before the Royal Statistical Society, November 24 1965', 3650; ed. Labour's Economic Record, 1964–1970, 3665; The British Economy in 1975, 3674; 'What Stopped the Inflation? Unemployment or Commodity Prices?, 4020; An Introduction to National Income Analysis, 3808, 4885; Poverty and Social Security in Britain since 1961, 9111; 'Economists, Scientists and Environmental Catastrophe', 19934; Pricing for Pollution: An Analysis of Market Pricing and Governmental Regulation in Environment Consumption and Policy, 19935

Beckett, Ian: A Nation at Arms: A Social Study of the British Army in the First World War, 14447

Beckett, James Camlin: The Making of Modern Ireland, 1603–1923, 2642; 'Northern Ireland', 2838; ed. Ulster since 1800: A Political and Economic Survey, 2904; The Anglo-Irish Tradition, 2974; ed. Belfast: The Origin and Growth of an Industrial City, 18166; Queen's Belfast, 1845–1949: The History of a University, 23457

Beckett, John V.: Laxton: England's Last Open Field System, 19612

Beckett, S. T.: ed. Industrial Chocolate Manufacture and Use, 20695

Beckett, Wendy: Contemporary Women Artists, 7739

Beckinsale, Robert Percy: Urbanization and its Problems. Essays in Honour of Edmund W. Gilbert, 18629, 20409

Beckwith, Frank: The Yorkshire Post: Two Centuries, 25163

Beckwith, Lillian: The Hills is Lonely, 19278; The Sea for Breakfast, 19279; Bruach Blend, 19280; A Rope-in Case, 19281

Bedales: Bedales since the War, 23100; Memories and Reflections, 23101; Irregularly Bold: A Study of Bedales School, 23102

Bédarida, François: A Social History of England, 1851–1975, 7558; 'France, Britain and the Nordic Countries', 13880; Britain and France: Ten Centuries, 14243; La Stratégie Secrète de la Drôle de Guerre: Le Conseil Supreme Interallié, Septembre 1939–Avril 1940, 14272

Beddington, William Richard: A History of the Queen's Bays (The 2nd Dragoon Guards): 1929–1945, 15618

Bedeman, Trevor: 'The February Election (1974)', 2334

Bedford, Alan: 'Women and Parole', 10434

Bedford, Sybille: Aldous Huxley: A Biography, 25587

Bedfordshire County Council: A Hundred Years at your Service 1889–1989, 3347

Bedfordshire County Planning Officer: County Development Plan: Town Map No. 3: Biggleswade, 18842

Bednarczyk, B.: 'The First University School of Architecture in England, 1841–1960', 22460

Bedoyère, Michael de la: The Life of Baron von Hügel, 11982

Bedson,'Grandad': The Notorious Poacher: Memoirs of an Old Poacher, 19114

Bedson, Sir Samuel Phillips: Virus and Rickettsial Diseases, 22343

Beebe, W.: The Book of Naturalists: An Anthology of the Best Natural History, 26527

Beeby-Thompson, A.: Oil Pioneer: Selected Experiences and Incidents Associated with Sixty Years of World-wide Petroleum Exploration and Oil Field Development, 7180

Beecham, Helen Audrey: 'List of Books and Articles on Agrarian History Issued since September 1965', 19392

Beecham, Sir Thomas: Delius 24326

Beeching, Wilfred A.: Century of the Typewriter, 7055

Beedle, James: 43 Squadron Royal Flying Corps, Royal Air Force: The History of the Fighting Cocks, 1916–1966, 15924

Beer, Edwin John: The Beginning of Rayon, 6421

Beer, Max: 'The Independent Labour Party', 1867; 'The Reorganisation of the Socialist Parties', 1967

Beer, Samuel Hutchison: Treasury Control: The Co-ordination of Financial and Economic Policy, 809; Modern British Politics: A Study of Parties and Pressure Groups, 1585

Beerman, René: 'Juvenile Delinquency in Great Britain and the USSR', 10613;

Delinquency: Its Roots, Causes and Prospects, 10614

Beesley, Michael Edwin: Urban Transport: Studies in Economic Policy, 16304; The London-Birmingham Motorway, 17111; 'Urban Form, Car Ownership and Public Policy: An Appraisal of "Traffic in Towns"', 17374

Beesley, Patrick: Very Special Intelligence: The Story of the Admiralty's Operational Intelligence Centre, 1939–1945, 15425

Beeson, Trevor Randall: Britain Today and Tomorrow, 7607; The Church of England in Crisis, 11600

Beet, E. H.: 'New Universities and Adult Education', 23695

Beet, Ernest A.: Astronomy Old and New, 26412; 'The King's Observatory at Richmond', 26453

Beetham, David: Immigrant School Leavers and the Youth Employment Service in Birmingham, 11458; Transport and Turbans: A Comparative Study in Local Politics, 11459

Beevor, Anthony: The Spanish Civil War, 13984

Beevor, J. G.: S.O.E. Recollections and Reflections, 1940–1945, 15083

Begg, Hugh M.: 'Expenditure on Regional Assistance to Industry: 1960/61–1973/74', 4768, 5103

Begg, Tom: Fifty Special Years: A Study in Scottish Housing, 18485

Behan, Dominic: Milligan: The Life and Times of Spike Milligan, 26331

Beharrell, Peter: ed. Trade unions and the Media, 6834

Behr, Caroline: T. S. Eliot: A Chronology of his Life and Works, 25488

Behrend, Hilde: A National Survey of Attitudes to Inflation and Incomes Policy, 3830; 'A Fair Day's Work', 3880

Behrens, Catherine Betty Abigail: Merchant Shipping and the Demands of War, 16488

Behrens, Robert: The Conservative Party from Heath to Thatcher: Policies and Politics 1974–1979, 1624; '"Blinkers for the Cart-Horse": The Conservative Party and the Trade Unions 1974–8', 1653

Beirre, P.: Fair Rent and Legal Fiction: Housing Rent Legislation in a Capitalist Society, 18440

Beith, Alan: The Case for the Liberal Party and the Alliance, 2180

Beith, J. Hay: One Hundred Years of Army Nursing: The Story of the British Army Services from the Time of Florence Nightingale to the Present Day, 21704

Belbin, Eunice: 'The Problems of Industrial Training', 5625; Training in the Clothing Industry: A Study of Recruitment Training and Education, 5958

Belchem, David: Victory in Normandy, 14944

Belfast Design Partnership: Belfast Urban Area Plan, 18843

Belfield, Eversley: Corps Commander, 14957

Bell, Andrew: 'Fascist Parties in Post-War Britain', 2011

Bell, Anne Olivier: The Diary of Virginia Woolf, 25888

Bell, Archibald Colquhoun: A History of the Blockade of Germany and of the Countries Associated with her in the Great War: Austria-Hungary, Bulgaria and Turkey, 1914–1918, 14604; Sea Power and the Next War, 15337; History of the Manchester Regiment: Vol. 3, 1st and 2nd Battalions, 1922–1948, 15697

Bell, Brian: Farm Machinery, 19684

Bell, Sir Charles Alfred: Tibet, Past and Present, 27193

Bell, Christopher Richard Vincent: A History of East Sussex Council 1889–1974, 3354

Bell, Colin: Inside the Whale: The Personal Accounts of Social Research, 8034; Community Studies: An Introduction to the Sociology of the Local Community, 9365; ed. Sociology of Community: A Selection of Readings, 9366; 'The Sources of Variation in Agricultural Workers' Images of Society', 9706; Middle Class Families: Social and Geographical Mobility, 9723; 'Mobility and the Middle Class Extended Family', 9724; City Fathers: The Early History of Town Planning in Britain, 17736; 'Capitalist Farmers in the British Class Structure', 19561

Bell, Coral: The Debatable Alliance: An Essay in Anglo-American Relations, 14079

Bell, D. J.: Thirty Years On: A Review of Air Pollution in London, 20058

Bell, D. Wallace: Industrial Participation, 6034

Bell, Desmond: 'Acts of Union: Youth Sub-Culture and Ethnic Identity amongst Protestants in Northern Ireland', 8526

Bell, Donald: ed. An Experiment in Education: The History of Worcester College for the Blind, 1866–1966, 23119

Bell, Douglas Herbert: A Soldier's Diary of the Great War, 14468

Bell, Enid Hester Chataway Moberly: A History of the Church Schools Company, 1883–1958, 22880

Bell, G.: Sudan Political Service, 1899–1956, 14426

Bell, Geoffrey: The Protestants of Ulster, 2946; The British in Ireland, 2947

Bell, Geoffrey L.: 'Incomes Policy: The British Experience', 3815; 'Changes in the Money Supply in the United Kingdom, 1954–1964', 4615

Bell, George Kennedy Allen: Randall Davidson, Archbishop of Canterbury, 11690; ed. Documents on Christian Unity, 12315

Bell, Gwen: ed. Human Identity in the Urban Environment, 17828

Bell, Sir Harold Idris: 'Welsh Nationalism Today', 2595

Bell, Herbert Tait: A Short History of British Bee-keeping . . ., 20724

Bell, Sir Hugh: High Wages: Their Cause and Effect, 3863

Bell, J. Bowyer: The Secret Army: The IRA 1916–1979, 2763; 'The Escalation of Insurgency: The Provisional Irish Republican Army's Experience, 1969–1971', 2764; 'The Chroniclers of Violence in Northern Ireland: The First Wave Interpreted', 2880; 'The Chroniclers Revisited: The Analysis of Tragedy', 2881; On Revolt: Strategies of National Liberation, 16173

Bell, J. D. M.: 'Stability of Membership in Trade Unions', 6763; 'The Development of Industrial Relations in Nationalized Industries in Post-war Britain', 5775

Bell, J. Graham: The Business of Transport, 16229

Bell, James H.: The Sewermen at Work: Report of the Investigation into the Health and Conditions of Work of Glasgow Sewermen, 9667

Bell, Julian: ed. We Did Not Fight: 1914–1918, 13449

Bell, K. P.: 'Recent Trends in Coronary Mortality and their Implications for the U.K.: Are we Winning or Losing?', 22242

Bell, Kathleen M.: 'The Development of Community Care', 8716

Bell, M.: ed. Britain's National Parks, 26960

Bell, Neil: My Writing Life, 25373

Bell, Philip Michael Hett: Disestablishment in Ireland and Wales, 12279; A Certain Eventuality: Britain and the Fall of France, 14264

Bell, Philip Wilkes: The Sterling Area in the Post-War World: Internal Mechanism and Cohesion, 1946–1952, 4697

Bell, Quentin [Claudian Stephen]: The Schools of Design, 22462; On Human Finery, 24157; Virginia Woolf: Mrs Woolf 1912–1941, 25890

Bell, R.: 'Smethwick', 11475

Bell, Robert Elliott: ed. Education in Great Britain and Ireland: A Source Book, 22858; Patterns of Education in the British Isles, 22866

Bell, Robert H.: 'Confession and Conceal-ment in the Autobiography of Bertrand Russell', 26863

Bell, Robert William: The History of the Jersey Cattle Society of the United Kingdom, 1878–1978, 19576, 20667

Bell, Robert: A History of the British Railways during the War, 1939–1945, 16753; 'The London and North Eastern Railway [1922–1948]', 16886

Bell, Rose: City Fathers: The Early History of Town Planning in Britain, 17736

Bell, Sam Hanna: The Arts in Ulster: A Symposium, 23738

Bell, T.: Reform of the Hospital Service, 21413

Bell, Tom: The Communist Party: A Short History, 1922

Bell, Wendell: ed. The Democratic Revolution in the West Indies, 13013

Bell, Sir William James: Sale of Food and Drugs, 22261

Bellamy, B. E.: Private Presses and Publishing in England since 1945, 25001

Bellamy, Joyce M.: ed. Dictionary of Labour Biography, 45, 1661; 'Cotton Manufacture in Kingston-upon-Hull', 6469; A Hundred Years of Pharmacy in Hull, 22279

Bellan, R. C.: 'The Future Growth of Britain's Cities', 17792

Bellerby, John Rotherford: Economic Recon-struction, 3736. ed. Factory Farming, 19703

Bello, Sir Ahmadu: My Life, 12766

Bellows, Thomas J.: The People's Action Party of Singapore: Emergence of a Dominant Party System, 12962

Beloff, Max [Baron]: Wars and Welfare: Britain 1914–1945, 292; 'The Whitehall Factor: The Role of the Higher Civil Service 1919–1939', 785; 'Reflections on the British General Election 1966', 2327; Imperial Sunset: Britain's Liberal Empire, 1897–1921, 12525; The Future of British Foreign Policy, 13233; 'The Projection of Britain Abroad', 13353; 'The Special Relationship: An Anglo-American Myth', 14085; 'October for the Rebels', 22570; 'What's Wrong with Oxford?', 23557

Beloff, Michael: 'The Plateglass Universities', 23429; The Plateglass Universities, 23430

Beloff, Nora: Freedom under Foot: The Battle over the Closed Shop in British Journalism, 6887, 25312; Transit of Britain: A Report on Britain's Changing Role in the Post-War World, 13238; The General Says No: Britain's Exclusion from Europe, 14157

Belshaw, Cyril S.: Island Administration in the South West Pacific, 12878

Belshaw, Deryke Gerald Rosten: The Changing Economic Geography of the Merthyr Valley, 26679

Belson, William Albert: Bibliography of Methods of Social and Business Research, 7922; The Impact of Television: Methods and Findings in Program Research, 8100, 24854; Television Violence and Adolescent Boys, 8430; Juvenile Theft: Its Causal Factors, 10200, 10633; 'The Extent of Stealing by London Boys', 10594; The Public and the Police, 10729; 'Effects of Television on the Interests and Initiative of Adult Viewers in Greater London', 24840; Studies in Readership, 25050

Belzung, L. D.: 'Consequences of Voluntary Early Retirement: A Case Study of a New Labour Force Phenomenon', 5883

Ben-David, Joseph: 'Professions in the Class System of Present Day Societies', 9831

Ben-Tovin, Gideon: 'The Politics of Race in Britain, 1962–1970: A Review of the Major Trends and of the Recent Literature', 10891

Bendall, Eve R. D.: A History of the General Nursing Council for England and Wales, 1919–1969, 21707

Bender, Arnold Eric: Food Processing and Nutrition, 20560; A Dictionary of Nutrition and Food Technology, 20561

Bender, George A.: Great Moments in Pharmacy, 22276

Bender, Michael Philip: Community Psychology, 8679

Bendixson, Terence: Instead of Cars, 17392

Benemy, Frank William Georgeson: The Queen Reigns, She Does not Rule, 443; The Elected Monarch: The Development of the Power of the Prime Minister, 956; Whitehall—Town Hall: A Brief Account of Central and Local Government, 3156; Industry, Income and Investment: The Common Sense of Economics, 3644, 4901

Benewick, Robert J.: The Fascist Movement

in Britain, 2026; 'The Floating Voter and the Liberal View of Representation, 2225

Benham, Frederick Charles: Great Britain under Protection, 3764; British Monetary Policy, 4561

Benjamin, Bernard: Pensions: The Problems of Today and Tomorrow, 4053; General Insurance, 4231; The Population Census, 7386; Demographic Analysis, 7387; Social and Economic Factors Affecting Mortality, 7388; Health and Vital Statistics, 7389; ed. Medical Records, 7390; An Analysis of Trends and Geographical Distribution, 7464, 22241; 'Inter-generation Differences in Occupation: A Sample Comparison in England and Wales of Census and Birth Registration Records', 9587; Tuberculosis Statistics for England and Wales, 1938–1955: 'Statistics in Town Planning', 17805; 'London as a Case Study', 18308; 'The Urban Background to Public Health Changes in England and Wales, 1900–1950', 21331

Benjamin, Joseph: In Search of Adventure: A Study of the Junk Playground, 27011

Benjamin, Roger W.: 'Local Government in Post-Industrial Britain; Studies of the Royal Commission on Local Government', 3174

Benkovitz, Miriam: A Bibliography of Ronald Firbank, 25507

Benn's Media Directory, 147

Benn, Anthony Neil Wedgwood [Tony]: The Regeneration of Britain, 1080; Out of the Wilderness: Diaries 1963–1967, 1081; Office without Power: Diaries 1968–1972, 1082; Against the Tide: Diaries 1973–1976, 1083; Conflicts of Interest: Diaries 1977–1980, 1084; Speeches by Tony Benn, 1085; Arguments for Socialism, 1086; Arguments for Democracy, 1087; Parliament, People and Power: Agenda for a Free Society, 1088; Fighting Back: Speaking out for Socialism in the Eighties, 1089; The Crisis and the Future of the Left: The Debate of the Decade, 2007; The Social and Political Implications of Automation, 7250

Benn, Caroline: 'Comprehensive School Reform and the 1945 Labour Government', 22926; Half Way There—Report on the British Comprehensive School Reform, 22959

Benn, Sir Ernest John Pickstone: 'Recollections of the Ministry of Reconstruction', 838; Happier Days: Recollections and Reflections, 1572. The Return to Laissez-Faire, 2169; Modern Government as a Busybody in Other Men's Matters, 2170; State the Enemy, 2171; Honest Doubt: Being a Collection of Papers on the Price of Modern Politics, 3573; Unemployment and Work, 7004

Bennet, D.: Margot, 971

Bennet, Harold: Traction Engines, 17091

Bennett, A.: 'Training and Selection of Nurses from Commonwealth Countries', 10955

Bennett, Gareth Vaughan: ed. Essays in Modern English Church History, in Memory of Norman Sykes, 11565

Bennett, Geoffrey Martin: Battle of the River Plate, 1503; The Battle of Jutland, 14654;

Coronel and the Falklands, 14667; Naval Battles of the First World War, 14675; Cowan's War: The Story of British Naval Operations in the Baltic, 1918–1920, 14676; The Loss of the 'Prince of Wales' and 'Repulse', 15031; Charlie B: A Biography of Admiral Lord Beresford of Metemmeh and Curraghmore, G.C.B., G.C.V.O., LL.D., D.C.L., 15258

Bennett, George: Kenya: A Political History: The Colonial Period, 12822; The Kenyatta Election: Kenya 1960–1961, 12829

Bennett, Jeremy: British Broadcasting and the Danish Resistance Movement, 1940–1945, 15107

Bennett, John D.: A Bibliography of British Industrial Relations 1971–1979, 5569; 'A Bibliography of Industrial Relations, 1980', 5570; 'A Bibliography of Industrial Relations, 1981', 5571; 'Industrial Relations Material in Warwick University Library', 5572

Bennett, Jon: The Hunger Machine: The Politics of Food, 20612

Bennett, Lewis Godfrey: The Marketing of Horticultural Produce grown in Bedfordshire, West Cornwall, Wisbech and the Lea Valley, 19848; The Horticultural Industry of Middlesex, 19849

Bennett, Martin: Rolls-Royce: The History of the Car, 17450

Bennett, Richard Lawrence: A Picture of the Twenties, 299; The Black and Tans, 2751, 14696

Bennett, Robert John: Environmental Systems: Philosophy, Analysis and Control, 19944

Bennett, Stuart: A History of Control Engineering 1800–1930, 6377

Bennett, Tom: Welsh Shipwrecks, 16509

Bennett-England, Rodney: Dress Optional: The Revolution in Menswear, 24172.

Benney, Mark: How People Vote: A Study of Electoral Behaviour in Greenwich, 2302; Over to Bombers, 5592; Low Company: Describing the Evolution of a Burglar, 10274

Bennison, D. J.: The Impact of Town Centre Shopping Schemes in Britain: Their Impact on Traditional Environments, 6647

Benson, C.: 'Report of the Commissioner of Prisons, 1953', 10345

Benson, James: "The Admiralty Regrets . . . .": The Story of His Majesty's Submarines 'Thetis' and 'Thunderbolt', 15380; Above us the Waves: The Story of Midget Submarines and Human Torpedoes, 15381

Benson, John: Bibliography of the British Coal Industry, 6244; Studies in the Yorkshire Coal Industry, 6330; 'A Bibliography of the Coal Industry in Wales', 6336

Bensusan, Samuel Levy: Latter-day Rural England 1927, 19057; Comment from the Countryside, 19058; The Town versus the Countryside: A Plea for Better Understanding, 19059

Benthal, Rowan: My Store of Memories, 6651

Bentine, Michael: The Long Banana Skin, 26297

Bentley, E. W.: Oakford: The History of a Devon Parish, 19351

Bentley, Eric Russell: The Theatre of Commitment, and Other Essays on Drama in our Society, 26226

Bentley, James: 'British and German High Churchmen in the Struggle against Hitler', 11863

Bentley, Michael J.: ed. High and Low Politics in Modern Britain, 1690. 'Liberal Politics and the Grey Conspiracy of 1921', 1818; The Climax of Liberal Politics: The Liberal Mind, 1914–1929, 2165; British Liberalism in Theory and Practice 1868–1918, 2166

Bentley, Phyllis Eleanor: 'O Dream, O Destinations': An Autobiography, 25392

Bentwich, Helen: Mandate Memories 1918–1948, 14308

Bentwich, Norman De Mattos: The Rescue and Achievement of Refugee Scholars: The Story of Displaced Scholars and Scientists 1933–1952, 9811, 22543'; The Social Transformation of Anglo-Jewry 1883–1960', 11298; England in Palestine, 14306; My 77 Years: An Account of My Life and Times 1883–1960, 14307; Mandate Memories 1918–1948, 14308

Benwell Ideas Group: Four Big Years: The History of Benwell's Independent Funding Organisation 1973–1977, 9411

Benyon, Victor Howell: Agriculture and Economics [in Britain, 1920–1977], 3539, 19420; The Political Significance of the British Agricultural Vote, 19521

Benz, Wolfgang: ed. Sommer 1939: Die Grossmächte und der Europäische Krieg, 13762

Berber, Fritz J.: ed. Locarno: A Collection of Documents, 13656

Berdahl, Robert O.: 'The British University Grants Committee, 1919–83: Changing Relationships with Government and the Universities', 23326; British Universities and the State, 23330

Berent, Jerzy: 'Fertility and Social Mobility', 7483, 9586

Beresford, David: Ten Men Dead: The Story of the 1981 Irish Hunger Strikes, 2892

Beresford, Maurice Warwick: The West Riding County Council 1889–1974: Historical Studies, 3373; ed. Leeds and its Region, 18028; History on the Ground: Six Studies in Maps and Landscapes, 26704

Beresford, Paul: Good Council Guide: Wandsworth 1978–1987, 3318; 'Struggles in the Welfare State: Wandsworth—The Cuts and the Fightback', 3319

Beresford, Tristram: We Plough the Fields: Agriculture in Britain Today, 19562

Beresford-Pierse, Sir Henry: 'A Century of Forestry: Forestry in the UK over the Last Century', 19714; Forest, Food and People, 19715

Berg, L. H.: Polio and its Problems, 21124

Berg, Leila: Look at Kids, 8101; Risinghill: Death of a Comprehensive School, 22952

Berger, Brigitte: Sociology: A Biographical Approach, 8026

Berger, John: A Fortunate Man: The Story of a Country Doctor, 20860

Berger, Peter Ludwig: Sociology: A Biographical Approach, 8026; Invitation to Sociology: A Humanistic Perspective, 8027

Bergess, Winifrid F.: Kent County, 25169

Berghahn, Marion: German-Jewish Refugees in England: The Ambiguities of Assimilation, 11322

Bergonzi, Bernard: ed. The Twentieth Century, 23727; T. S. Eliot, 25492

Bergstrom, Theo: Smithfield: Past and Present, 20668

Berkeley, Humphrey John: The Power of the Prime Minister, 955; Crossing the Floor, The Odyssey of Enoch: A Political Memoir, 1295; 'Catholics in English Politics', 11979

Berkeley, Reginald Cheyne: The History of the Rifle Brigade in the War of 1914–1918, 15712

Berkova, Zdenka: Direct Investment in the United Kingdom by Smaller European Firms, 4750

Berkovitch, Israel: Coal on the Switchback: The Coal Industry since Nationalisation, 6314

Berlant, Jeffrey Lionel: Profession and Monopoly: A Study of Medicine in the United States and Great Britain, 20817

Berlin, Sir Isaiah: Mr. Churchill in 1940, 988; Personal Impressions, 14043

Berman, A.: ed. Pharmaceutical Historiography, 22265

Berman, Lawrence S.: 'Changes in the Money Supply in the United Kingdom, 1954–1964', 4615

Bermant, Chaim: The Cousin-hood: The Anglo-Jewish Gentry, 11288; Troubled Eden: An Anatomy of British Jewry, 11289

Bernard, Barbara: Fashion in the '60s, 24167

Bernard, T. L.: 'Implications of Social Class Factors in Contemporary English Secondary Education', 9497

Bernbaum, Gerald: Social Change and the Schools, 1918–1944, 22941

Bernhard, Richard C.: 'English Law and American Law on Monopolies and Restraints of Trade', 5512

Bernstein, Barton J.: 'Uneasy Alliance: Roosevelt, Churchill and the Atomic Bomb, 1940–1945', 14060

Bernstein, Basil: 'Social Class, Speech Systems and Psychotherapy', 9480; 'Some Sociological Determinants of Perception', 9481; 'Language and Social Class', 9482; 'Social Class Difference: The Relevance of Language to Socialization', 9483; 'Social Class Differences in Conceptions of the Uses of Toys', 9484; Selection and Control: Teachers' Ratings of Children in the Infant School, 23133

Bernstein, Jeremy: The Analytical Engine: Computers—Past, Present and Future, 7088

Berrall, Julia S.: The Garden: An Illustrated History from Ancient Egypt to the Present Day, 19870; A History of Flower Arrangement, 19871

Berreman, Gerald D.: 'Race, Caste and other Invidious Distinctions in Social Stratification', 11184

Berridge, Geoffrey: Economic Power in Anglo-South African Diplomacy: Simonstown, Sharpeville and After, 12716

Berridge, Virginia: Opium and the People: Opiate Use in Nineteenth-Century England, 22205; 'Drugs and Social Policy: The Establishment of Drug Control in Britain, 1900–1980', 22207

Berrington, Hugh Bayard: Backbench Opinion in the House of Commons, 1945–1955, 699. 'The Conservative Party: Revolts and Pressures, 1955–1961', 1637; 'The General Election of 1964', 2320; 'The February Election (1974)', 2334

Berry, Brian Joe Lobley: Contemporary Urban Ecology, 17841; Geographic Perspectives on Urban Systems, with Integrated Readings, 17842; The Human Consequences of Urbanisation: Divergent Paths in the Urban Experience of the Twentieth Century, 17843; ed. City Classification Handbook: Methods and Applications, 17844

Berry, C. L.: 'The Coronation Oath and the Church of England', 462

Berry, David: The Sociology of Grass Roots Politics: A Study of Party Membership, 1795, 3330

Berry, Francis: Herbert Read, 25783

Berry, Frank: Bench, Saw and Plane: A Cotswold Apprenticeship, 5966

Berry, Fred: Housing: The Great British Failure, 18736; 'Retreat From Parker Morris', 18737

Berry, Geoffrey: The Lake District: A Century of Conservation, 20224

Berry, Juliet: Social Work with Children, 8102

Berry, Michael: Teacher Training Institutions in England and Wales: A Bibliographical Guide to their History, 22744

Berry, Paul: Daughters of Cain: The Story of Eight Women Executed since Edith Thompson in 1923, 10795

Berthoud, Richard: The Disadvantages of Inequality: A Study of Social Deprivation: A PEP Report, 9088; The Examination of Social Security, 9089; Family Income Support, 9090; Poverty and the Development of Anti-Poverty Policy in the United Kingdom, 9091; Unemployed Professionals and Executives, 9776

Berthoud, Roger: Graham Sutherland: A Biography, 24077; The Life of Henry Moore, 24197

Berton, Pierre: The Royal Family: The Story of the British Monarchy from Victoria to Elizabeth, 469

Bertram, [Cyril] Anthony [George]: A Century of British Painting, 1851–1951, 23983; Poet and Painter: Being Correspondence between Gordon Bottomley and Paul Nash, 1910–1946, 25402

Bertram, George Colin Lawder: West Indian Immigration, 11243

Berzon, Derek: 'Medical Students and General Practice', 22471

Bescoby, John: 'An Analysis of Post-war Labour Disputes in the British Car Manufacturing Firms', 5650; 'Strikes, Redundancy, and the Demand Cycle in the Motor Car Industry', 17414

Beshir, Mohammed Omer: The Southern Sudan: Background to Conflict, 14428; Educational Development in the Sudan 1898–1956, 14429; Revolution and Nationalism in the Sudan, 14430

Bessell, Peter: Cover-Up: The Jeremy Thorpe Affair, 1534

Bessell, Robert: Introduction to Social Work, 8650

Bessey, G. S.: The Training of Part-time Youth Leaders and Assistants, 8498

Best, Geoffrey Francis Arthur ed.: War, Economy and the Military Mind, 14699; History, Society and the Churches: Essays in Honour of Owen Chadwick, 11866, 26787

Best, K. W.: A Select Bibliography on the National Health Service, 21546

Best, Richard A.: 'Co-operation with Like-Minded People': British Influence on American Security Policy 1945–1949, 14075

Best, Robin Hewitson: 'Recent Changes and Future Prospects of Land Use in England and Wales', 5055; 'Density Size-Rule', 17857; The Urban Countryside: The Land-Use Structure of Small Towns and Villages in England and Wales, 19133; The Changing Use of Land in Britain, 19519, 20255; The Major Land Uses of Great Britain: An Evaluation of the Conflicting Records and Estimates of Land Utilization since 1900, 20254; Land for New Towns: A Study of Land Use, Densities, and Agricultural Displacement, 20256; Regional Conversions of Agricultural Land to Urban Use in England and Wales, 1945–1967, 20257

Besterman, Theodore: A World Bibliography of Bibliographies and of Bibliographical Catalogues, Calendars, Abstracts, Digests, Indexes and the Like, 9; Agriculture: A Bibliography of Bibliographies, 19387; Biological Sciences: A Bibliography of Bibliographies, 26485

Beswick, Frank [Baron]: The Role of British Aerospace in the British Economy, 17609

Beth, Ronald: The Specials: History of the Special Constabulary in England, Wales and Scotland, 10760

Betham, E.: ed. House-Building 1934–1936: A Complete Key to Available House-Building Finance from all Sources, 18539

Bethell, Nicholas [Baron]: The Last Secret: Forcible Repatriation to Russia, 1944–1947, 13967; The Great Betrayal: The Untold Story of Kim Philby's Biggest Coup, 13975; The Palestine Triangle: The Struggle between the British, the Jews and the Arabs, 14298

Betjeman, Sir John: London's Historic Railway Stations, 16990; The English Town in the Last Hundred Years, 18950; Ghastly Good Taste, 24110; Summoned by Bells, 25394

Bett, Walter R.: Osler: The Man and the Legend, 20875; 'The Medical Press and Circular, 1839–1939', 20912; The History and Conquest of some Common Diseases, 21194

Bettenson, E. M.: The University of Newcastle Upon Tyne 1834–1971, 23543

Better Services for the Mentally Handicapped, 21739

Bettey, Joseph Harold: *ed.* English Historical Documents 1906–1939, 281

Betts, Clive: Culture in Crisis: The Future of the Welsh Language, 23824

Betts, Ernest: The Film Business: A History of British Cinema, 1896–1972, 24626; Inside Pictures, with some Reflections from the Outside, 24627

Betts, Raymond F.: Uncertain Dimensions: Western Overseas Empires in the Twentieth Century, 12476

Beuret, Geoff: Decision Making for Energy Futures: A Case Study of the Windscale Inquiry, 6670

Bevan, A.: 'The U.K. Potato Crisp Industry, 1960–1972: A Study of New Entry Competition, 6624

Bevan, Aneurin: In Place of Fear, 1095

Bevan, Hugh: Source Book of Family Law, 10014

Bevan, Vaughan: The Development of British Immigration Law, 11093

Bevans, Edna: Kinson 1894–1931: A Social Survey as Recorded in the Minutes of the Kinson Parish Council, 19337

Beveridge, Andrew: Apprenticeship Now: Notes on the Training of Young Entrants to Industry, 5955

Beveridge, James: John Grierson: Film Master, 24672

Beveridge, Janet: Beveridge and his Plan, 9038

Beveridge, John: 'The British Universities' Industrial Relations Association: The First 35 Years', 5859

Beveridge, William Henry [Baron]: Why I am a Liberal, 1356; Social Insurance and Allied Services: Report, 9025; The Beveridge Report in Brief: Social Insurance and Allied Services, 9026; Pillars of Security, 9027; Full Employment in a Free Society, 9028; Beveridge on Beveridge. Recent Speeches, 9029; New Towns and the Case for them, 18221, 18986; British Food Control, 20581; Power and Influence, 23337; The London School of Economics and its Problems, 1919–1937, 23526

Beveridge, William Ian Beardmore: Influenza, the Last Great Plague: An Unfinished Story of Discovery, 21097; Frontiers in Comparative Medicine, 21224

Beverstock, Albert George: Industrial Training Practices, 23282

Bevins, Reginald: The Greasy Pole: A Personal Account of the Realities of British Politics, 1105

Bew, Paul: 'The Problem of Irish Unionism', 2729; The State in Northern Ireland, 1921–1971: Political Forces and Social Causes, 2787

Beynon, Huw: Perceptions of Work: Variations within a Factory, 5469; Living with Capitalism: Class Relations and the Modern Factory, 5788; Digging Deeper: Issues in the Miners' Strike, 6920

Bhasin, V. K.: Superpower Rivalry in the Indian Ocean, 13196

Bhaskar, Krish: The Future of the United Kingdom Motor Industry, 17400

Bhatnagar, Joti: Immigrants at School, 23180

Bhatt, S.: 'Ethnic Identity and Preferences among Asian Immigrant Children in Glasgow: A Replicated Study', 11224

Bhide, M. Y.: 'Vocational Guidance in the United Kingdom', 5867

Bialer, Uri: The Shadow of the Bomb: The Fear of Air Attack and British Politics, 1932–1939, 13516; 'Humanization of Air Warfare in British Foreign Policy on the Eve of the Second World War', 13517

Bianchi, William J.: Belize: The Controversy between Guatemala and Great Britain over the Territory of British Honduras in Central America, 13026

Bibby, C. L. *and* Bibby, J. B.: A Miller's Tale: A History of J. Bibby & Sons Ltd., Liverpool, 6396, 20704

Bibby, Harold Cyril: Race, Prejudice and Education, 11151; The First Fifty Years: A Brief History of Kingston upon Hull Training College, 1913–1963, 22745

Bibliographical Index: A Cumulative Bibliography of Bibliographies, 11

Bibliography of the English-Speaking Caribbean, 1979+, 12996

Bibliography on Women Workers, 1861–1965: Geneva, 7710

Bick, Edgar M.: Source Book of Orthopaedics, 21105

Bickel, Lennard: Rise up to Life: A Biography of Howard Florey who Made Penicillin and Gave it to the World, 22285

Bickerstaffe, Rodney: Privatisation and Low Pay: The Impact of Government Policies, 3959

Bickmore, D. P.: The Atlas of Britain and Northern Ireland, 123

Biddiss, Michael Denis: Disease and History, 22351; The Age of the Masses: Ideas and Society in Europe since 1870, 23731

Biddle, Gordon: Lancashire Waterways, 16443; Great Railway Stations of Britain: Their Architecture, Growth and Development, 16988; Railway Stations in the North West, 16993

Biddle, John: The Canals of North West England, 16405

Bidman, Geoffrey: Race and Law, 11126

Bidwell, [Reginald George] Shelford: The Chindit War: The Campaign in Burma 1944, 15065; The Women's Royal Army Corps, 15460; Fire-Power: British Army Weapons and Theories of War, 1904–1945, 15482; Gunners at War: A Tactical Study of the Royal Artillery in the Twentieth Century, 15603; The Royal Horse Artillery, 15651

Bidwell, Robin: The Two Yemens, 13864

Bidwell, Sidney: Red, White and Black: Race Relations in Britain, 11056

Biebolek, Tony: Single and Homeless, 18513

Bielckus, C. L.: Second Homes in England and Wales: A Study of the Distribution of Rural Properties taken over as Second Homes, 18374

Bienefeld, M. A.: Working Hours in British Industry: An Economic History, 3884; Wages, Relative Prices and the Export of Capital, 3885

Bigger, J. W.: Man against Microbe, 22344

Biggins, J. M.: *ed.* York: A Survey, Prepared for the British Association, 18122

Biggs-Davison, Sir John: The Hand is Red, 2951; The Cross of Saint Patrick: The Catholic Unionist Tradition in Ireland, 2952; The Uncertain Ally, 14067

Bigland, Eileen: The Riddle of the Kremlin, 15187; The Story of the W.R.N.S, 15329

Bignell, Alan: Kent Villages, 19137

Bigsby, Christopher William Edgar: Stoppard, 25985

Bigwood, George: The Lancashire Fighting Territorials, 15679

Bilainkin, George: 'France Despairs for British Ally', 14234

Bilbe, Graham: *et al., ed.* 100 Years of Trolleybuses: A Pictorial Review, 1882–1982, 17239

Bilboul, Roger R.: *ed.* Retrospective Index to Theses of Great Britain and Ireland, 1716–1950: Vol. 1, Social Sciences and Humanities and addenda to 1971, 7919

Bild, Ian: The Jews in Britain, 11331

Bilingualism and British Education: The Dimensions of Diversity: Papers from a Conference Convened in January 1976, 23820

Bill, James A.: *ed.* Mussaddiq, Iranian Nationalism and Oil, 13861

Billcliffe, Roger: Mackintosh Watercolours, 24041

Billig, Michael: 'Fascist Parties in Post-War Britain', 2011; Fascists: A Psychological View of the National Front, 2044; 'Patterns of Racism: Interviews with National Front Members', 11197

Billington, Kevin: 'The Crisis we Deserve', 24692

Billington, Michael: Alan Ayckbourn, 25938; Stoppard the Playwright, 25989; The Modern Actor, 26002; Peggy Ashcroft, 26011; How tickled I Am, 26307

Bilski, Raphaella: 'Ideology and the Comprehensive Schools', 22976

Bilton, Michael: Speaking Out: Untold Stories from the Falklands War, 16119

Binder, B. J. A.: 'Relations between Central and Local Government since 1975: Are the Associations Failing?', 3195

Binfield, John Clyde Goodfellow: So Down to Prayers: Studies in English Nonconformity, 1780–1920, 12013; Pastors and People: The Biography of a Baptist Church: Queen's Road, Coventry, 12037; 'Et Virtutem et Musas: Mill Hill School and the Great War', 23068

Bing, Geoffrey H. C.: Reap the Whirlwind: An Account of Kwame Nkrumah's Ghana from 1950 to 1966, 12751

Bing, Sir Rudolf: 5,000 Nights at the Opera, 24565

Bingham, Barry: Falklands. Jutland and the Bight, 14663

Bingham, Caroline: The History of Royal Holloway College, 1886–1986, 23532

Bingham, T. H.: Report on the Supply of Petroleum and Petroleum Products to Rhodesia, 12811

Binney, Marcus: *ed.* Change and Decay: The

Future of Our Churches, 11845; *ed.* Our Past before us: Why Do we Save it?, 20201

Binns, Denis: A Gypsy Bibliography, 11353

Binyon, Gilbert Clive: The Christian Socialist Movement in England, 1997

Binyon, Helen: Eric Ravilious: Memoir of an Artist, 24057

Birch, Anthony Harold: Representative and Responsible Government: An Essay on the British Constitution, 569; 'The Popular Press in the British General Election of 1955', 2314, 25122; Small Town Politics: A Study of Political Life in Glossop, 3328

Birch, Jack Ernest Lionel: *ed.* The History of the T.U.C., 1868–1968, 6704

Birch, Jack William: The Isle of Man: A Study in Economic Geography, 2625, 5163

Birch, Reginald Charles: The Shaping of the Welfare State, 9002

Birch, Stephanie: Managers on the Move: A Study of British Managerial Mobility, 7277

Birchall, Ian: The Smallest Mass Party in the World: Building the Socialist Workers' Party 1951–1979, 1975

Birchenough, Charles: History of Elementary Education in England and Wales from 1800 to the Present Day, 22705

Bird, Anthony: Steam Cars 1770–1970, 17367

Bird, Archibald Brian: Skiffle: The Story of Folk-Song with a Jazz Beat, 24496

Bird, Barbara: Mobile Homes in England and Wales, 1975: Report of Surveys, 18556

Bird, Clinton: Cumbernauld, Irvine, East Kilbride: An Illustrated Guide, 19012; Milton Keynes: An Illustrated Guide, 19021; Runcorn, Warrington: An Illustrated Guide, 19024

Bird, Dennis L.: Our Skating Heritage: A Centenary History of the National Skating Association of Great Britain, 1879–1979, 27162

Bird, James Harold: The Major Seaports of the United Kingdom, 16647

Bird, John: Cinema Parade: Fifty years of Film Shows, 24628

Bird, S. Elizabeth: 'The Impact of Private Estate Ownership on Social Development in a Scottish Rural Community', 19246

Birdseye, P.: 'Why the Rate Burden is Cause for Concern', 3266

Birdwood, Christopher Bromhead [Baron]: The Worcestershire Regiment, 1922–1950, 15741

Birkenhead, E.: 'The Financial Failure of British Air Transport Companies, 1919–1924', 17639

Birks, Tony: Building the New Universities, 23446

Birley, Derek: An Equal Chance: Equalities and Inequalities of Educational Opportunity, 22812; The Education Officer and his World, 23252; 'Sportsmen and the Deadly Game', 27027

Birmingham Community Club: Community Club Birmingham, 1916–1955: A Short Account of an Effort in Friendliness, 9306

Birmingham Community Development Project: (Final Reports No. 1—The Transport Industry). Driven on Wheels, 9301; (Final Reports No. 2—Employment).

The Scrapheap, 9302; (Final Reports No. 3—Immigration and the State). People in Paper Chains, 9303; (Final Reports No. 4—Young Workers). Youth on the Dole, 9304; (Final Reports No. 5—Housing). Leasehold Loophole, 9305

Birmingham Information Dept: Publication No. 131: Birmingham, 18008; Publication No. 141: Birmingham, 18009

Birmingham Planet: Smethwick Survey. Issues of 3–17 June 1965, 11454

Birmingham Public Libraries: Reference Dept: Birmingham: Domesday to 1948, 18007

Birmingham University Centre for Contemporary Cultural Studies: Report, 373; (Women's Studies Group). Women Take Issue: Aspects of Women's Subordination, 7810; First Report, 10112

Birmingham, Stephen: Duchess: The Story of Wallis Warfield Simpson, 480

Birn, Donald S.: The League of Nations Union, 13494; 'The League of Nations Union and Collective Security', 13495

Birnie, Arthur: An Economic History of the British Isles, 3606

Birrell, [William] Derek: Policy and Government in Northern Ireland: Lessons of Devolution, 2806;'The Stormont-Westminster Relationship', 2807; 'The Northern Ireland Civil Service from Devolution to Direct Rule', 2815; Voluntary Organisations in the United Kingdom and their Role in Combatting Poverty, 9218; *ed.* Social Administration: Readings in Applied Social Science, 9245;'A Socio-Political Opinion Profile of Clergymen in Northern Ireland', 12165; Housing in Northern Ireland, 18497

Birt, David: Roads, 17106

Birt, William Raymond: XXII Dragoons, 1760–1945: The Story of a Regiment, 15619

Birtchnell, John: 'Depression and Attempted Suicide: A Study of 91 Cases Seen in a Casualty Department', 10816

Birtill, George: 'Changing Years': Chorley and District between Two Wars, 19327

Birtles, Philip: De Haviland Vampire, Venom and Sea Vixen, 15878, 17606; De Havilland, 17602

Bisceglia, Louis R.: 'Norman Angell and the "Pacifist Muddle"', 13466; 'The Politics of a Peace Prize', 13467

Bisgrove, Richard: The Gardens of Britain 3—Berkshire, Oxfordshire, Buckinghamshire, Bedfordshire and Hertfordshire, 19884

Bish, Francis: *ed.* Comparing Urban Delivery Systems: Structure and Performance, 3174

Bishku, M. B.: 'The British Press and the Future of Egypt, 1919–1922', 14403

Bishop, Alan: *ed.* Chronicle of Friendship: Diary of the Thirties 1932–1939, 25417; Gentleman Rider: A Biography of Joyce Cary, 25445

Bishop, Anthony Savell: The Rise of a Central Authority for English Education, 22792

Bishop, Donald Gordon: The Administration of Britain's Foreign Relations, 13355

Bishop, Edward Barry: The Battle of Britain, 14802; The Wooden Wonder: The Story of

the De Havilland Mosquito, 15829; The Debt We Owe: The Royal Air Force Benevolent Fund, 1919–1969, 15907

Bishop, Gertrude Muriel Fennell: They All Come out, 10388

Bishop, J. W.: 'Law in the Control of Terrorism and Insurrection: The British Laboratory Experience', 2867

Bishop, John: The Music of Frank Bridge, 24305

Bishop, Patrick: The Provisional IRA, 2766; The Winter War: The Falklands, 16105

Bishop, W. J.: Notable Names in Medicine and Surgery, 20893; 'The Autobiographies of British Medical Men', 20913; 'Transport and the Doctor in Great Britain', 20914; A History of Surgical Dressing, 21151; The Evolution of the General Practitioner in England in Science, Medicine and History, 21504

Biss, Peter: Social Policy and the Young Delinquent, 10609

Bissanti, Andrea Antonio: 'Considerazioni Geografica sulla Distribuzione della Populazione in Eta Pensionabile in Gran Bretagna', 4055

Bisset, Liz: Badge of Poverty: A New Look at the Stigma Attached to Free School Meals, 20529

Bitting, A. W.: Appetizing or the Art of Canning: Its History and Development, 6199

Bixby, Bob: A Study of Park and Ride Use and the Influence of Parking Availability on Patronage, 17388

Blachford, George: A History of Handicraft Teaching, 22463

Black, Boyd: 'Industrial Relations in Northern Ireland: A Survey', 5842

Black, Charles Stewart: The Scottish Church: A Short Study in Ecclesiastical History, 12208

Black, Cilla: Step Inside, 24510

Black, Clinton V.: History of Jamaica, 13050

Black, Duncan: The Incidence of Income Taxes, 4854

Black, H. J.: History of the Corporation of Birmingham: Vol. 6, 1936–1950, 3320

Black, J. B.: Organising the Propaganda Instrument: The British Experience, 15219

Black, Jim: Industrial Relocation in Birmingham, 18013

Black, John: The Economics of Modern Britain: An Introduction to Macroeconomics, 3681

Black, Kitty: Upper Circle: A Theatrical Chronicle, 26115

Black, Max: A Companion to Wittgenstein's 'Tractatus', 26886

Black, Michael H.: Cambridge University Press, 1584–1984, 24948

Black, Peter: The Biggest Aspidistra in the World: A Personal Celebration of Fifty Years of the BBC, 24479, 24720; The Mirror in the Corner: People's Television, 24842

Black, Robert Wilson: Robert Wilson Black, 12028

Black, William George: The Parochial Ecclesiastical Law of Scotland as Modified by the Church of Scotland Acts, 1921 and 1925, 12212

Blackaby, Bob: Not Much Improvement: Urban Renewal Policy in Birmingham, 18409

Blackaby, Frank T.: British Economic Policy, 1960–1974, 3647; An Incomes Policy for Britain: Policy Proposals and Research Needs, 3849

Blackburn, Fred: George Tomlinson, 1328

Blackburn, J. A.: 'The British Cotton Industry in the Common Market', 6456

Blackburn, Raymond: I am an Alcoholic, 1360

Blackburn, Robert Martin: Perceptions of Work: Variations within a Factory, 5469; 'White Collar Unionization: A Conceptual Framework', 6785; Union Character and Social Class: A Study of White-collar Unionism, 6856, 9596; Social Stratification and Occupations, 9595

Blackburn, Robin M.: ed. Towards Socialism, 2134; ed. The Incompatibles: Trade Union Militancy and Consensus, 6911; ed. Student Problems, Diagnosis, Action, 9859

Blackburne, Kenneth: 'Changing Patterns of Caribbean International Relations: Britain and the "British" Caribbean', 13017

Blacker, Carlos Paton: 'Sir Alexander Carr-Saunders, 14th January 1886–6th October 1966', 7262; 'Family Planning and Eugenic Movements in the Mid-Twentieth Century', 7501

Blacker, Ken C.: London's Buses, 17305

Blackett, Monica: The Mask of the Maker: A Portrait of Helen Waddell, 25848

Blackett, Patrick Maynard Stewart: Technology, Industry and Economic Growth, 5987; Universities and the Nation's Crisis, 23348

Blackham, Harold John: Living as a Humanist, 11893; Religion in a Modern Society, 11894

Blackham, R. J.: The Unemployment Insurance Acts, 1920–1927, 4023

Blackie, J.: Bradfield, 1850–1975, 23044

Blackie, John Ernest Haldane: Transforming the Primary School, 23156; Inside the Primary School, 23157; Inspecting and the Inspectorate, 23248

Blackledge, William James: The Legion of Marching Madmen, 14559

Blackler, Rosamunde: Fifteen Plus: School Leavers and the Outside World, 8452

Blacklock, Michael: The Royal Scots Greys (The 2nd Dragoons), 15595

Blackman, Raymond Victor Bernard: Ships of the Royal Navy, 15357

Blackmore, John: 'Relationship Between Self-reported Delinquency and Official Convictions among Adolescent Boys', 10628

Blackmore, Ruth Matteson: ed. Cumulative Subject Index to the Public Affairs Information Service Bulletin 1915–74, 83; Cumulative Index to the Annual Catalogues of Her Majesty's Stationery Office 1922–1972, 183

Blacksell, Mark: The Countryside: Planning and Change, 18815, 19103; Contemporary Issues in Rural Planning, 18816; 'Reformed England and Wales', 26713

Blackstone, Tessa Ann Vosper [Baroness]: Social Policy and Administration: A Bibliography, 9236; Economic and Social Aspects of a Profession, 9837, 22545; Students in Conflict: L.S.E. in 1967, 22558; 'The Plowden Report', 22610; Testing Children: Standardized Testing in Local Education Authorities and Schools, 22786; A Fair Start: The Provision of Pre-school Education, 23155

Blackwell, D. E.: The Future of Optical Astronomy, 26389

Blackwell, Trevor: The Politics of Hope: Britain at the End of the Twentieth Century, 1688

Blackwood, Alan: Transport in History, 16194

Blades, James: Drum Roll: A Professional Adventure from the Circus to the Concert Hall, 24400

Blagden, Cyprian: The Stationers' Company: A History 1403–1959, 25018

Blain, Alexander Nicholas John: 'Industrial Relations Theory: A Critical Review', 5732; Pilots and Management: Industrial Relations in the United Kingdom Airlines, 5757

Blair, Ian: Investigating Rape: A New Approach for Police, 10870

Blair, John G.: The Poetic Art of W.H. Auden, 25356

Blair, L.: 'The Civil Servant: Political Reality and Legal Myth', 904

Blair, May: Once Upon the Lagan: The Story of the Lagan Canal, 16426

Blair, Thomas Lucien: The International Urban Crisis, 17940

Blake, Avril: The Practical Idealists: Twenty Five Years of Designing for Industry, 24153

Blake, Christopher: Modern English Art, 23981

Blake, George: Lloyds' Register of Shipping, 1760–1960, 16522; Gellatly's 1862–1962: A Short History of the Firm, 16554; The Ben Line: The History of Wm. Thompson & Co. of Leith and Edinburgh and of the Ships Owned and Managed by them, 1825–1955, 16555; British Ships and Shipbuilders, 16605

Blake, Jim: At London's Service: Fifty Years of London Transport Road Services, 17311

Blake, John: 'The Planner and Immigration', 11421

Blake, John: Medical Reference Works, 21254

Blake, John E.: The Practical Idealists: Twenty Five Years of Designing for Industry, 24153

Blake, John William: Northern Ireland in the Second World War, 2820, 15150

Blake, P.: 'Britain's New Towns: Facts and Figures', 18255

Blake, Pamela: The Plight of One-Parent Families, 9949

Blake, Robert Norman William [Baron]: ed. The Dictionary of National Biography 9th Supplement [1971–1980.], 20; The Dictionary of National Biography 10th Supplement [1981–1985], 21; The Decline of Power, 1915–1964, 295; The Conservative Party from Peel to Thatcher, 1612; Stalinism in Britain, 1944; A History of Rhodesia, 12793; ed. The Private Papers of Douglas Haig, 1914–1919, 14505

Blakeborough, John Freeman Fairfax: Yorkshire Village Life, Humour and Characteristics, 19173

Blakes, John: All you Needed was Love: The Beatles after the Beatles, 24504

Blakey, Michael: The Story of Bedfordshire Railways, 16921

Blakiston, Noel: ed. A Romantic Friendship: The Letters of Cyril Connolly to Noel Blakiston, 25462

Blamires, David: David Jones: Artist and Writer, 25606

Blanchard, Simon: What's this Channel Fo(u)r?, 24881

Blanchflower, D. G.: Profit-sharing: Can it Work?, 6050

Bland, Alexander: Observer of the Dance 1958–1982: In Memory, 24211; The Royal Ballet: The first Fifty years, 24220

Bland, David: History of Book Illustration, 7071; The Illustration of Books, 7072

Blandford, John: The D.C.O. Story: A History of Banking in Many Countries, 1925–1971, 4494

Blandy, R.: 'Brain Drains in an Integrating Europe', 7330

Blaney, Roger: Health and Sickness: The Choice of Treatment: Perception of Illness and Use of Services in an Urban Community, 21980

Blank, Maurice Victor: Take-overs and Mergers, 5545

Blank, Stephen: Industry and Government in Britain: The Federation of British Industries in Politics, 1945–1965, 5487, 6126

Blatchford, Robert: As I lay a-Thinking: Some Memories and Reflections of an Ancient and Quiet Watchman, 25211

Blaug, Mark: Productivity Trends in British University Education, 1938–1962', 23312

Blaxall, Arthur: Suspended Sentence, 10340

Blaxland, William Gregory: J. H. Thomas: A Life for Unity, 1327; Amiens: 1918, 14579; Destination Dunkirk: The Story of Gort's Army, 14844; The Plain Cook and the Great Showman: The First and Eighth Armies in North Africa, 14889; The Regiments Depart: A History of the British Army, 1945–1970, 15446; The Farewell Years: The Final Historical Records of the Buffs, Royal East Kent Regiment, 1948–1967, 15669; The Buffs: Royal East Kent Regiment, the 3rd Regiment of Foot, 15670; The Queen's Own Buffs, the Royal East Kent Regiment, 3rd, 50th and 97th Foot, 15671; The Middlesex Regiment, 15699

Bleakley, David: Crisis in Ireland, 2861; Peace in Ulster, 2927; Faulkner: Conflict and Consent in Irish Politics, 3085

Bleaney, M.: The Rise and Fall of Keynesian Economics, 26616

Blenkinsop, Arthur: 'Control of Pollution', 20007

Blenkinsop, Layton John: ed. Veterinary Services (History of the Great War based on official documents), 21167

Blight, Gordon: The History of the Royal

Berkshire Regiment (Princess Charlotte of Wales), 1920–1947, 15604

Blin-Stoyle, Roger: ed. The Sussex Opportunity: A New University and the Future, 23583

Blishen, Edward: A Cack-Handed War, 13523; ed. Education Today: The Existing Opportunities, 22643

Bliss, Sir Arthur: As I Remember, 24298

Blissett, William: The Long Conversation: A Memoir of David Jones, 25607

Bloch, J.: British Intelligence and Covert Action: Africa, Middle East and Europe since 1945, 16006

Bloch, Michael: ed. Wallis and Edward: Letters 1931–1937: The Intimate Correspondence of the Duke and Duchess of Windsor, 493; ed. Duke of Windsor's War, 494; ed. Operation Widi: the Plot to Kidnap the Duke of Windsor, July 1940, 495; ed. Secret File of the Duke of Windsor, 496

Block, F.: 'Expanding Capitalism: The British and American Cases', 5518

Block, Geoffrey D. M.: A Source Book of Conservatism, 1610; Transport in Wales, 16340; 'Jewish Students at the Universities of Great Britain and Ireland, Excluding London, 1936–1939', 22552

Blofield, Henry: The Packer Affair, 27108

Blom, Eric Walter: Music in England, 24263

Blom-Cooper, Louis Jacques: Final Appeal: A Study of the House of Lords in its Judicial Capacity, 10294; ed. Law and Morality, 10295; ed. Progress in Penal Reform, 10392; A Calender of Murder: Criminal Homicide in England since 1957, 10791; 'Prostitution: A Socio-legal Comment on the Case of Dr Ward', 10842

Blomfield, J. M.: Children under Five: The Results of a National Survey, 8165

Blomfield, Sir Reginald Theodore: Memoirs of an Architect, 23872

Blond, Anthony: 'An Old Etonian Looks at State Education', 22638

Blond, Georges: Ordeal below Zero: The Heroic Story of the Arctic Convoys in World War II, 15123

Blondel, Jean: Voters, Parties and Leaders: The Social Fabric of British Politics, 2253; Constituency Politics: A Study of Newcastle-under-Lyme, 3334

Bloom, Alan: Steam Engines at Bessingham: The Story of a Live Steam Museum, 17050; Locomotives of British Railways, 17063

Bloom, Claire: Limelight and After: The Education of an Actress, 26013

Bloom, Leonard: The Social Psychology of Race Relations, 11016

Bloom, Robert: Anatomies of Egotism: A Reading of the Last Novels of H. G. Wells, 25874

Bloom, Robert: The Indeterminate World: A Study of the Novels of Joyce Cary, 25438

Bloom, Ursula: The Duke of Windsor, 490; The Great Queen Consort, 521

Bloomfield, Barry Cambray: W.H. Auden: A Bibliography 1924–1969, 25355; Philip Larkin: A Bibliography 1933–1976, 25620

Bloomfield, Paul: Uncommon People: A Study of England's Elite, 9759; L. P. Hartley, 25573

Blouet, Brian W.: Sir Halford Mackinder 1861–1947: Some New Perspectives, 1461

Blowers, Andrew: 'Structure Plans', 17861; The Future of Cities, 17912; Something in the Air: Corporate Power and the Environment, 20068

Bloxsidge, R.: 'Local Authority Contribution: A Bibliographic Note', 17723; Yearbooks 1964/5–1967/8, 17724

Bluem, Albert William: comps. The Progress of Television: An Anglo-American Survey, 24855

Bluhm, Robin K.: Wiltshire County, 25168

Blum, Fred Herman: Work and Community: The Scott Barder Commonwealth and the Quest for a New Social Order, 6216; Ethics of Industrial Man: An Empirical Study of Religious Awareness and the Experience of Society, 11895

Blumberg, Paul: Industrial Democracy: The Sociology of Participation, 5704

Blume, S. S.: 'Professional Civil Servants: A Study in the Sociology of Public Administration, 916

Blumenau, Ralph Klaus: A History of Malvern College, 1865 to 1965, 23065

Blumenson, Martin: Anzio: The Gamble that Failed, 14860; Kasserine Pass, 14890; Liberation, 14942

Blumler, Jay George: 'Trade Unionists, the Mass Media and Unofficial Strikes', 6961; 'British Television—The Outlines of a Research Strategy', 24851; Citizenship and Television, 24890; Television in Politics: Its Uses and Influence, 24891; The Challenge of Election Broadcasting, 24895

Blundell, Lionel Alleyne: Town and Country Planning, 17771, 20361; Planning Appeals and Inquiries, 20360

Blundell, Walter Derek George: Royal Navy Battleships, 1895–1946, 15349; Royal Navy Warships 1939–1945, 15355; British Aircraft Carriers, 15392

Blunden, Edmund Charles: Undertones of War, 14469; War Poets 1914–1918, 14470

Blunden, Geoffrey Halstead: The Willesden Story: History . . . Commissioned by the Willesden Council to Record the Work and Achievements of the Borough of Willesden and to Tell the Story of its People, 18349; Riverside Story: The Story of Bermondsey and its People, 1900–1965, 18368

Blunden, John Russell: The Mineral Resources of Britain: A Study in Exploitation and Planning, 6313; A Future for our Countryside, 18817

Blunden, Ronald M.: A Survey of Adoption in Great Britain, 8201

Blunden, William Ross: The Land Use/Transport System, 16245

Blunkett, David: Democracy in Crisis: The Town Halls Respond, 3342

Blunt, Anthony Frederick: 'From Bloomsbury to Marxism', 23770

Blunt, Wilfrid Jasper Walter: John Christie of Glyndebourne, 24572; The Art of Botanical Illustration, 26558

Blyth, Alan: ed. Remembering Britten, 24317

Blyth, H. E.: Through the Eye of a Needle: The Story of the English Sewing Cotton Company, 6432

Blyth, John A.: English University Adult Education 1908–1958: The Unique Tradition, 23653, 23702

Blyth, William Alan Landsell: English Primary Education: A Sociological Description, 23154

Blythe, Ronald: The Age of Illusion: England in the Twenties and Thirties, 1919–1940, 299, 7554; Akenfield: Portrait of an English Village, 19175

Blyton, William Joseph: Anglo-German Future, 13758

Boaden, Noel T.: 'Innovation and Change in English Local Government', 3237

Boadle, Donald Graeme: 'The Formation of the Foreign Office Economic Relations Section, 1930–1937', 13341

Board of Education: Consultative Committee on the Primary School, 23153

Board, Beryl: ed. The Effects of Technological Progress on Education: A Classified Bibliography from British Sources, 1945–1957, 22767

Boardman, Philip: Patrick Geddes: Maker of the Future, 8070; The World of Patrick Geddes: Biologist, Town Planner, Re-Educator, Peace-Warrior, 8071, 18823

Boardman, Robert: ed. The Management of Britain's External Relations, 13360; Britain and the People's Republic of China, 1949–1974, 13637

Boas, George: The Cult of Childhood, 8103

Boast, Mary: The Story of Bermondsey, 18367

Bocca, Geoffrey: She Might Have Been Queen, 488; Elizabeth and Philip, 510

Bochel, Dorothy: Probation and After-care: Its Development in England and Wales, 10479

Bochel, John M.: 'Candidate Selection in the Labour Party: What the Selectors Seek', 1788; The Referendum Experience: Scotland 1979, 2474; 'The Decline of the Scottish National Party—An Alternative View', 2502; The Scottish Local Elections 1974: Results and Statistics, 3203

Bochel, Margaret: The Story of the Nairn Fisher Girls at the Gutting, 19823

Bocock, Robert: 'British Sociologists and Freud: A Sociological Analysis of the Absence of a Relationship', 8081; Ritual in Industrial Society: A Sociological Analysis of Ritualism in Modern England, 9915

Boddy, Bill: Vintage Motor Cars, 17358

Boddy, Martin: The Building Societies, 4362

Bodelsen, Carl Adolf Gotlieb: The Government and Institutions of England, 703

Bodenham, Kenneth Edward: Foundations for Health Service Management: A Scicon Report for the Scottish Home and Health Department on the Requirements for a Health Service Information System, 21616

Bodenheimer, F. S.: The History of Biology: An Introduction, 26514

Bodensieck, H.: Preussen, Deutschland und der Westen, 13689

Bodington, Clive Eaton: The Baldwin-Bruce Economic Policy: Its Scientific Basis, 3553

Bodington, Stephen: Developing the Socially Useful Economy, 3694

Body, Alfred Harris: Old Road: A Lancashire Childhood, 1912–1926, 8231; Canals and Waterways, 16384

Body, Geoffrey: Railways of the Southern Region, 16915

Body, Richard: Agriculture: The Triumph and the Shame, 19585

Boehm, Eric H.: ed. Historical Periodicals Directory, 162

Boehm, Klaus: British Parliamentary Election Results, 1950–1964, 2217; The British Patent System. 1. Administration, 5016

Boehringer, Gill Mace: The Hospital Order in London Magistrates' Courts, 21854

Bogarde, Dirk: Dirk Bogarde: The Complete Autobiography, 26014

Bogdanor, Vernon: ed. The Age of Affluence 1951–1964, 300, 10169; The People and the Party System: The Referendum and Electoral Reform in British Politics, 2392; The Constitution and Political Consequence of Devolution, 2408; Devolution, 2409

Bohm, Peter: Social Efficiency: A Concise Introduction to Welfare Economics, 8947; ed. The Economics of Environment: Papers from Four Nations, 19947

Böhmler, Rudolf: Monte Cassino, 14861

Bohning, Wolf-Rudiger: The Migration of Workers in the United Kingdom and the European Community, 7331

Bok, Bart J.: 'New Science of Radio Astronomy', 26418

Bolam, Charles Gordon: The English Presbyterians: From Elizabethan Puritanism to Modern Unitarianism, 12116

Bold, Alan: George Mackay Brown, 25424; MacDiarmid, Christopher Murray Grieve: A Critical Biography, 25680; ed. The Letters of Hugh MacDiarmid, 25684

Boldt, Joseph R.: The Winning of Nickel: Its Geology, Mining and Extractive Metallurgy, 7201

Boldy, Duncan: The Elderly in Grouped Dwellings: A Profile, 8607

Boleat, Mark: The Building Societies Association, 4377; Building Societies: A Descriptive Study, 4378; The Building Society Industry, 4379; National Housing Finance Systems, 18448

Bolitho, [Henry] Hector: A Century of British Monarchy, 448; King Edward VIII, 476; George VI, 504; Alfred Mond, First Lord Melchett, 1479; Task for Coastal Command: The Story of the Battle of the South West Approaches, 14982; Command Performance: The Authentic Story of the Last Battle of Coastal Command, R.A.F., 14983; The Galloping Third: The Story of the 3rd King's Own Hussars, 15657; ed. A Batsford Century . . . 1843–1943, 24942

Bollon, Chris: Attitudes to Second Homes in Rural Wales, 19297

Bolsover, Philip: ed. The CND Story: The First 25 Years of CND in the Words of the People Involved, 13531

Bolsterli, Margaret Jones: The Early Community at Bedford Park: 'Corporate Happiness' in the First Garden Suburb, 9389

Bolton, Sir George Lewis French: A Banker's World: The Revival of the City, 1957–1970, 4418

Bolton, W. F.: The Language of 1984: Orwell's English and Ours, 25750

Bonavia, Michael Robert: The Economics of Transport, 16204; The Nationalisation of Britain's Transport: The Early History of the British Transport Commission, 1948–1953, 16205; The Channel Tunnel Story, 16364; Railway Policy between the Wars, 16750; British Rail: The First 25 Years, 16790; The Four Great Railways, 16839; A History of the L.N.E.R, 16885

Bond, Brian James: ed. War and Society: A Yearbook of Military History, 14700; Liddell Hart: A Study of his Military Thought, 14739; Chief of Staff: The Diaries of Lieutenant General Sir Henry Pownall, 1. 1933–1940, 14777; 'Educational Changes at R.M.A. Sandhurst 1966–1983', 15774

Bond, James: The Landscape of Towns, 20306

Bond, Maurice Francis: Guide to the Records of Parliament, 556; 'Materials for Transport History amongst Records of Parliament', 16210

Bond, Reginald Copleston: History of the King's Own Yorkshire Light Infantry in the Great War, 1914–1918, 15744

Bondfield, Margaret: A Life Work, 1114

Bondy, Louis T.: Racketeers of Hatred, 2019

Bone, Sir David William: Landfall at Sunset: The Life of a Contented Sailor, 15307; Merchantmen-at-Arms, 15407; Merchantmen Rearmed, 15408

Bone, Edith: Seven Years Solitary, 10441

Bone, Margaret: Family Planning in Scotland in 1982: A Survey Carried out on Behalf of the Scottish Home and Health Department, 7523; Family Planning Services in England and Wales, 21066; The Family Planning Services: Changes and Effects: A Survey Carried out on Behalf of the D.H.S.S, 21067; Plans and Provisions for the Mentally Handicapped, 21852

Bone, Thomas Renfrew: Studies in the History of Scottish Education, 1872–1939, 23602; School Inspection in Scotland, 1840–1966, 23603

Bonfield, Arthur Earl: 'The Role of Legislation in Eliminating Racial Discrimination', 11101

Bonham, Dennis Geoffrey: Perinatal Mortality: The First Report of the 1958 Perinatal Mortality Survey, Under the Auspices of the National Birthday Trust Fund, 7454

Bonham, John: The Middle Class Vote, 2255, 9719; 'Two Studies in the Middle Class Vote', 9720

Bonham-Carter, Mark: 'Legislation and the Race Relations Board', 11117

Bonham-Carter, Victor: Authors by Profession: Vol. 2, 9801; Soldier True: The Life and Times of Field-Marshal Sir William Robertson, 1860–1933, 14518; Dartington Hall: The History of an Experiment, 23103; The Fight for Public Lending Rights 1951–1979, 25031

Bonham-Carter, Violet [Baroness] Asquith: Winston Churchill as I Knew him, 988; The Impact of Personality in Politics, 1567

Bonhomme, Samuel: Enoch Powell and West Indian Immigrants, 11264

Bonington, Christian: The Everest Years: A Climber's Life, 27244; I Chose to Climb; The Next Horizon: Autobiography, 27247

Bonnar, Alphonsus: Medicine and Men, 21202

Bonner, Arnold: British Co-operation: The History, Principles and Organisation of the British Co-operative Movement, 1894; Economic Planning and the Co-operative Movement, 3532

Bonnet, Kevin: Thatcherism: A Tale of Two Nations, 1054

Bonnor, Jean: 'The Four Labour Cabinets', 1729

Bonsall, Peter: ed. Urban Transportation Planning: Current Themes and Future Prospects, 16307

Bonsor, Noel Reginald Pixelle: North Atlantic Story, 16578

Bontecou, Eleanor: 'The English Policy as to Communists and Fascists in the Civil Service', 901

Booer, T. G.: 'Can Britain's Exports Grow?', 4780

Booker, Frank: The Great Western Railway, a New History, 16858; The Wreck of the Torrey Canyon, 20072

Bookmann, H.: ed. Geschichte und Gegenwart, 14222

Books in English: 1971–, 6

Boon, R. A.: 'The Social Impact of Haemophilia', 21088

Boorer, David: Volunteers in Hospitals—A Guide for Organisers, 21496

Boorman, Henry Roy Pratt: The Newspaper Society: 125 years of Progress, 25315

Booth, Alan E.: 'Some Wartime Observations on the Role of the Economist in Government', 797; Employment, Capital and Economic Policy: Great Britain 1918–1939, 3564; 'Unemployment in the Inter-war Period: A Multiple Problem', 6997; 'The Market for Economists in Britain 1944–1975', 26577

Booth, Adrian John: Sheffield's Sewage Works Railways, 20094

Booth, Arthur Harold: British Hustings, 1924–1950, 2273; Orange and Green: A Quaker Study of Community Relations in Northern Ireland, 12160

Booth, Gavin: The British Motor Bus: An Illustrated History, 17255; The British Bus Today and Tomorrow, 17256; The Classic Buses, 17278; Buses, 17279

Booth, Jeremy: 'A Short History of Blood Pressure Measurement', 20915; Books and Publishers: Commerce against Culture in Post-war Britain, 24934

Booth, John: The Day War Broke Out: Stories of Life in a Village at War [Cawood, Yorkshire], 19183

Booth, Stanley: Sir Alfred Munnings 1878–1959, 24043

Booth, Timothy A.: Home Truths: Old People's Homes and the Outcome of Care,

8637; Planning for Welfare: Social Policy and the Expenditure Process, 9252

Booth, William: 'The Liberals and the 1923 General Election', 2283

Boothby, Robert John Graham [Baron]: I Fight to Live, 1361; My Yesterday, Your Tomorrow, 1362; Boothby: Recollections of a Rebel, 1363; Industry and the State: A Conservative View, 2186; The New Economy, 3735

Boothe, L. E.: 'A Fettered Envoy: Lord Grey's Mission to the United States 1919–1920', 13430

Boothroyd, John Basil: Philip: An Informal Biography, 517

Bor, Eleanor: Adventures of a Botanist's Wife, 26550

Bor, Walter G.: The Making of Cities, 17925

Boraston, Ian: Shop Stewards in Action, 5789; Workplace and Union: A Study of Local Relationship in Fourteen Unions, 6721

Boraston, John Herbert: ed. Sir Douglas Haig's Depatches, 14506

Borchert, John R.: 'The Agriculture of England and Wales, 1939–1946', 19463

Borell, Merriley: 'Organotherapy, British Physiology and Discovery of the Internal Secretions', 20917

Borissow, Michael: Angels without Wings: The Dramatic Inside Stories of the R.A.F. Search and Rescue Squadrons, 15913

Borley, H. V.: The History of the Great Northern Railway 1843 -1922, 16845

Borna, Shaheen: 'Free Enterprise Goes to Prison', 10460

Bornstein, Sam: Two Steps Back: Communists and the Wider Labour Movement, 1939–1945: A Study in Relations between 'Vanguard' and Class, 1953; Against the Stream: A History of the Trotskyist Movement in Britain 1924–1938, 1982; The War and the International: A History of the Trotskyist Movement in Britain 1937–1949, 1983

Bornstein, Stephen: Unions and Economic Crisis: Britain, West Germany and Sweden, 6827

Borrell, Clive: Crime in Britain Today, 10139

Borrie, Gordon Johnson: The Consumer, Society and the Law, 20457

Bosanquet, Nicholas: ed. Labour and Inequality, 3782. 'Government and Unemployment, 1966–1970: A Study of Policy and Evidence', 6981; New Deal for the Elderly, 8636; Labour and Equality: A Study in Social Policy, 1964–1970, 8914; Race and Employment in Britain: A Report, 11034

Bosanquet, Reginald: Let's Get through Wednesday: My Twenty Five Years with ITN, 24907

Boshier, Roger: 'Does Conviction Affect Employment Opportunities?', 5904

Boskoff, Alvin: ed. Modern Sociological Theory in Continuity and Change, 7950

Bosl, Karl: ed. Die demokratisch-parlamentarische Struktur der ersten Tschechoslowakischen Republik, 13730

Boss, Peter: Exploration into Childcare, 8104

Bossom, Alfred Charles [Baron]: Our House, 675

Bossy, John Antony: ed. Essays Presented to Michael Roberts, 26810

Boston, Ray: ed. The Newspaper Press in Britain: An Annotated Bibliography, 25035

Boston, Richard: ed. The Press We Deserve, 25061

Boston, Sarah: Women Workers and the Trade Union Movement, 7751, 7859

Boswell, David Mark: ed. The Handicapped Person in the Community, 21921

Boswell, Jonathan S.: Business Policies in the Making: Three Steel Companies Compared, 6605

Bosworth, G. S.: 'Towards Creative Activity in Engineering', 22504

Bosworth, Richard J. B.: 'The British Press, the Conservatives and Mussolini, 1920–1934', 13774, 25112

Bothwell, Robert: Canada since 1945: Power, Politics and Provincialism, 12641

Bott, Edward Hugh: British Industry: Its Changing Structure in Peace and War, 4971

Bott, Elizabeth J.: Family and Social Network, 9923; Family and Social Network: Roles, Norms and External Relationships in Ordinary Urban Families, 10038

Bottcher, Winifried: ed. Britische Europaideen 1940–1970: Eine Bibliographie, 14119

Botting, Douglas S.: The Second Front, 14943; The Giant Airships, 17537

Botting, Joseph Henry Alfred: 'Studenti Africani a Londra', 11511

Bottomley, Allan Keith: ed. Criminal Justice: Selected Readings, 10189; Criminal Justice: Selected Readings, 10239; Criminology in Focus: Past Trends and Future Prospects, 10240; Understanding Crime Rates, 10241; Decisions in the Penal Process, 10313, 10395; 'Bail Procedures in Magistrates' Courts', 10317; Prison Before Trial: A Study of Remand Decisions in Magistrates' Courts, 10330

Bottomley, Arthur: The Use and Abuse of Trade Unions, 6730; Control of Commonwealth Immigration: An Analysis of the Evidence Taken by the Select Committee on Race Relations and Immigration 1969–1970 by Arthur Bottomley and George Sinclair, 11006

Bottomore, Thomas Burton: Sociology: A Guide to Problems and Literature, 7970; 'La Sociologie Anglaise Contemporaine', 7971; Classes in Modern Society, 9540; Elites and Society, 9760

Bottoms, Anthony Edward: The Urban Criminal: A Study in Sheffield, 10188; Criminals Coming of Age: A Study of Institutional Adaptation on the Treatment of Adolescent Offenders, 10625; 'Delinquency among Immigrants', 10631

Botwell, Harold D.: Over Shap to Carlisle: The Lancaster and Carlisle Railway in the 20th Century, 16953

Boucher, David: The Movement for Women's Liberation in Britain and the USA, 7636

Boughton, Terence: The Story of the British Light Aeroplane, 17565

Boulger, George S.: A Bibliographical Index of Deceased British and Irish Botanists, 26546

Boult, Sir Adrian Cedric: My own Trumpet, 24433

Boulton, David K.: Migration and Social Adjustment: Kirkby and Maghall, 7282

Boulton, David: The U.V.F. 1966–1973: An Anatomy of Loyalist Rebellion, 2958; Objection Overruled, 13455; Jazz in Britain, 24454

Boulton, James Thompson: ed. The Letters of D. H. Lawrence, 25630

Boultwood, Myrtle Emma A.: A Short History of Educational Ideas, 22656

Bound, John Alexander: Coastwise Shipping and the Small Ports, 16649

Bourdillon, Anne Frances Claudine: ed. A Survey of the Social Services in the Oxford District, 8871; Voluntary Social Services: Their Place in the Modern State, 9136

Bourke, Sean: The Springing of George Blake, 16027

Bourke, Walter L. [Earl of Mayo]: Regional Planning Report on Oxfordshire, 18899

Bourne, Geoffrey Howard: We Met at Bart's: The Autobiography of a Physician, 20861

Bourne, J.: 'Powell, the Minorities and the 1970 Election', 2237

Bourne, John M.: History at the Universities, 26776; 'History at the Universities [1966–1986]', 26777

Bourne, Larry Stuart: Urban Systems: Strategies for Regulation: A Comparison of Policies in Britain, Sweden, Australia and Canada, 17954

Bourne, Richard: The Struggle for Education, 1870–1970: A Pictorial History of Popular Education and the National Union of Teachers, 22711; 'Going Comprehensive in Greater London', 22958

Bourner, Tom: 'Initial Employment Experience of Sociology Graduates in the United Kingdom, 1976–1978', 5973

Bourret, Florence Mabel: Ghana: The Road to Independence 1919–1957, 12740

Bouvard, Marguerite: Labor Movements in the Common Market Countries: The Growth of a European Pressure Group, 6877

Bovill, D. I. N.: Peak Hour and Directional Factors, 16238

Bow Group Hospital Management Committee: Poplar Hospital, London E14, 1855–1955, 21440

Bow Group: Employee Participation in British Companies: An Examination of all Levels of Employee Participation in Industry, 6019

Bowden, Bertram Vivian [Baron]: 'Too Few Academic Eggs', 23385; 'English Universities: Problems and Prospects', 23441

Bowden, Tom: The Breakdown of Public Security: The Case of Ireland 1916–1921 and Palestine 1936–1939, 2697, 14319; 'The I.R.A. and the Changing Tactics of Terrorism', 2772; 'Bloody Sunday: A Reappraisal', 2839

Bowen, E. G.: 'Distribution of the Welsh Language in 1971: An Analysis', 23831

Bowen, Elizabeth: Afterthought, 25404

Bowen, Emrys George: 'Rural Settlements in South West Wales', 19299; Geography,

Culture and Habitat: Selected Essays (1925–1975) of E.G. Bowen, 26668; Geography at Aberystwyth: Essays written on the Occasion of the Departmental Jubilee 1917–18–1967–68, 26674

Bowen, Ian: Acceptable Inequalities: An Essay on the Distribution of Income, 3831; Economics and Demography, 7371

Bowen, Meirion: Michael Tippett, 24369

Bowen, Peter: Social Control in Industrial Organisations: Industrial Relations and Industrial Sociology: A Strategic and Occupational Study of British Steelmaking, 5781

Bower, Sir Frank: 'Some Reflections on the Budget', 4910

Bower, Frederick Orpen: Sixty years of Botany in Britain (1875–1935): Impressions of an Eye Witness, 26547

Bower, Tom: The Red Web: MI6 and the KGB Master Group, 16011

Bower, Sir William Guy Nott: ed. National Coal Board: The First Ten Years, 6293

Bowers, D.: 'The Degree of Unionization, 1948–1968', 6746; 'The Degree of Unionization, 1948–1968: A Reply', 6748

Bowers, I. H.: Air Pollution from Road Traffic: A Review of the Present Position, 20064

Bowers, John Kenneth: ed. Inflation, Development and Integration; Essays in honour of A. J. Brown, 4012; 'British Agricultural Policy since the Second World War', 19421; Agriculture, the Countryside and Land Use: An Economic Critique, 19588

Bowes, Stuart: The Police and Civil Liberties, 10734

Bowey, Angela: Payment Systems and Productivity, 3954; Job and Pay Comparisons: How to identify Similar Jobs in Different Companies and compare their Rates of Pay, 5899

Bowie, R. R.: Suez 1956, 14366

Bowker Publications: Irregular Series and Annuals: An International Directory, 150; Ulrich's International Periodicals Directory, 149; Ulrich's Update: A Quarterly Update, 151

Bowker, Barry Morrison: England Rugby: A History of the National Side, 1871–1976, 27040

Bowker, Gordon: The Education of Coloured Immigrants, 23179

Bowlby, Edward John Mostyn: Childcare and the Growth of Love, 8105; Attachment and Loss, 8106; Forty-four Juvenile Thieves: Their Characters and Home Life, 10550

Bowle, John Edward: Viscount Samuel: A Biography, 1308; The Imperial Achievement: The Rise and Transformation of the British Empire, 12591

Bowler, Ian Robert: Contemporary Issues in Rural Planning, 18816; Government and Agriculture: A Spatial Perspective, 19574; Agriculture under the Common Agricultural Policy: A Geography, 19657

Bowler, Peter J.: Theories of Human Evolution: A Century of Debate, 1844–1944, 26486

Bowley, Agatha Hilliam: A Study of the Factors Influencing the General Development of the Child during the Pre-school Years by Means of Record Forms, 8107; Psychological Aspects of Child Care, 8108; Child Care, 8109; ed. Psychological Care of the Child in Hospital, 8110; ed. The Spiritual Development of the Child, 8111; The Problems of Family Life: An Environmental Study, 10020

Bowley, Sir Arthur Lyon: Some Economic Consequences of the Great War, 3747; Wages, Earnings and Hours of Work in the United Kingdom, 1914–1947, 3881; Wages and Income in the United Kingdom since 1860, 3882; Prices and Wages in the United Kingdom, 1914–1920, 3883; The National Income 1924: A Comparative Study of the Income of the U.K., 1911, and 1924, 4886; Studies in National Income 1924–1938, 4887;Livelihood and Poverty: A Study in the Economic Conditions of Working Class Households in Northampton, Warrington, Stanley and Reading, 9020; Has Poverty Diminished? A Sequel to 'Livelihood and Poverty', 9021

Bowley, Marian Ellen Alberta: Housing and the State, 18620; Housing Statistics, 18621; Britain's Housing Shortage, 18622; Innovations in Building Materials: An Economic Study, 18623; The British Building Industry: Four Studies in Response and Resistance to Change, 6194, 18624

Bowman, A. Ian: Swifts and Queens: Passenger Transport on the Forth and Clyde Canal, 16424; Kirkintilloch Shipbuilding, 16625

Bowman, Cliff: Strategic Management: Corporate Strategy and Business Policy, 5456

Bowman, G.: The Lamp and the Book: The Story of the Royal College of Nursing, 1916–1966, 21708

Bowman, Isaiah: Geography in Relation to the Social Sciences, 26671

Bowman, John: De Valera and the Ulster Question, 1917–1973, 3047

Bown, Ian: Britain's Industrial Survival, 4965

Bowness, Alan: Recent British Painting, 23966; Victor Pasmore, with a Catalogue Raisonné of the Paintings, Constructs and Graphics 1926–1979, 24050; Lynn Chadwick, 24184; ed. Barbara Hepworth, 24189

Bowra, Sir Cecil Maurice: Memories, 1898–1939, 25408

Bowra, Edward: Ightham: Notes on Local History, 19341

Bowyer, Chaz: ed. Bomber Pilot, 1916–1918, 14641; The History of the RAF, 15785; ed. Hurricane at War, 15833; ed. Mosquito at War, 15834; Guns in the Sky: The Air Gunners of World War II, 15893; Path Finders at War, 14994; Bombing Colours: R.A.F. Bombers, Their Marking and Operations, 1937–1973, 15862; Fighter Command 1936–1963, 15909; The Flying Elephants: A History of No.27 Squadron, Royal Flying Corps, Royal Air Force 1915–1969, 15923

Bowyer, Michael John Frederick, Mosquito, 15835, 15853; Fighting Colours: R.A.F. Fighting Camouflage and Markings, 1937–1969, 15863; Action Stations: Military Airfields of East Anglia, 15936; Wartime Military Airfields of East Anglia, 1939–1945, 15953

Box, Charles Edward: Liverpool Overhead Railway 1893–1956, 16957

Box, Kathleen Lois: The Cinema and the Public: An Enquiry into Cinema-going Habits and Expenditure Made in 1946, 24630

Box, Muriel: Rebel Advocate: A Biography of Gerald Gardiner, 1419

Box, Steven: Science, Industry and Society: Studies in the Sociology of Science, 7946; 'Scientific Identity, Occupational Selection and Role Strain', 9832; 'New Criminology: For a Social Theory of Deviance', 10165; 'The Facts Don't Fit: On the Relationship between Social Class and Criminal Behaviour', 10166; Deviance, Reality and Society, 10186; 'Politics of Accountability: Disarming Complaints against the Police', 10722

Boyce, Anthony John: ed. Population Structure and Human Variation, 7391; ed. The Structure of Human Populations, 9442

Boyce, David George: Nationalism in Ireland, 2722; ed. Revolution in Ireland 1879–1923, 2723; The Irish Question and British Politics, 1868–1986, 2724; '"Normal Policing": Public Order in Ireland since Partition', 2800; 'British Conservative Opinion, the Ulster Question and the Partition of Ireland 1912–1921', 2980; Englishmen and Irish Troubles: British Public Opinion and the Making of Irish Policy, 1918–1922, 2981; 'From War to Neutrality: Anglo-Irish Relations, 1921–1950', 2982; Newspaper History from the Seventeenth Century to the Present Day, 25072

Boyce, Max: Max Boyce: His Songs and Poems, 26298

Boyce, Robert W.: 'Insects and International Relations: Canada, France, and British Agricultural Sanitary Import Restrictions between the Wars', 12651; 'Britain's First "No" to Europe: Britain and the Briand Plan, 1929–1930, 14257

Boyd, A.: 'The Social Importance of Trade Unions', 6777

Boyd, Alfred Kenneth: The History of Radley College, 1847–1947, 23071

Boyd, Andrew: The Rise of the Irish Trade Unions 1729–1970, 2669; Holy War in Belfast, 2840, 12157; Brian Faulkner and the Crisis of Ulster Unionism, 3086

Boyd, D.: Royal Engineers, 15628

Boyd, David: Elites and their Education, 23040

Boyd, Francis: Richard Austen Butler, 1123

Boyd, James I. C.: The Isle of Man Railway . . . 1962, 2636

Boyd, John: ed. A Needle's Eye, 26169

Boyd, Kenneth M.: Nursing Ethics, 21722

Boyd, Michael V.: The Church of England Colleges, 1890–1944: An Administrative Study, 22758

Boyd, William: Ayrshire, 19218; Evacuation in Scotland: A Record of Events and Experiments, 23607

Boyd, William: The Story of the New Education, 22865

Boyd-Barrett, Oliver: Studies on the Press: Working Paper, Royal Commission on the Press, 25125; The International News Agencies, 25305

Boyd-Carpenter, John: Memoirs, 1115

Boyes, John: The Canals of East England, 16406

Boyfield, R.: 'T.U.C. Machinery for Disputes between Unions, 6760

Boylan, Henry: A Dictionary of Irish Biography, 51, 2659

Boyle, Andrew Philip More: 'Poor Dear Bracken': The Quest for Brendan Bracken, 1368; Montagu Norman, A Biography, 4423; The Climate of Treason: Five who Spied for Russia, 15080, 16029; No Passing Glory. The Full and Authentic Biography of Group Captain Cheshire, 15894; Trenchard, 15966; Only the Wind Will Listen, 24735

Boyle [Baron] Edward: Current Issues in Community Work: A Study by the Community Work Group, 8672

Boyle, J. D.: 'Education: The Catholic Contribution', 22894

Boyle, Kevin: 'The Tallents Report on the Craig-Collins Pact of 30 March 1922', 2683; Justice in Northern Ireland: A Study in Social Confidence, 2854; Law and the State: The Case of Northern Ireland, 2855; Ten Years On: The Legal Control of Political Violence, 2856; The Anglo-Irish Agreement: Commentary, Text and Official Review, 2999

Boyle, Sir Lawrence: Equalisation and the Future of Local Government Finance, 4863

Boyle, Peter G.: 'The British Foreign Office View of Soviet-American Relations 1945-1946', 13971; 'Britain, America and the Transition from Economic to Military Assistance, 1948-1951', 14076; 'The British Foreign Office and America's Foreign Policy 1947-1948', 14077

Boyns, T.: 'Occupation in Wales, 1851-1971', 5344

Boynton, Sir John Keyworth: Job at the Top: The Chief Executive in Local Government, 3244; Compulsory Purchase and Compensation: A Practical Guide to the Law, 20354

Boynton, Sandra: Chocolate: The Consuming Passion, 20694

Boyson, Rhodes: ed. Down with the Poor, 9071; The Crisis in Education, 22649; ed. Education: Threatened Standards: Essays on the Reasons for the Present Decline in Educational Achievement and Suggestions for its Improvement, 22650

Boytinck, Paul: Anthony Burgess: An Enumerative Bibliography, 25430; C. P. Snow: A Reference Guide, 25812

Bozorth, Richard M.: 'Magnetism', 7137

Braae, G. P.: 'Investment and Housing in the United Kingdom, 1924-1938', 6192

Brabant, Frank Herbert: Neville Stuart Talbot, 1879-1943: A Memoir, 11760

Brabazon, James: Dorothy L. Sayers, 25794

Brabazon, John Theodore Cuthbert Moore [Baron]: The Brabazon Story, 17574; Forty Years of Flight, 17575

Brace, Harold W.: History of Seed-crushing in Great Britain, 6198

Bracegirdle, Brian: Engineering in Chester: 200 Years of Progress, 6376; 'The History of Histology: A Brief Survey of Sources', 20918

Bracewell, I. B.: The Condition of London's Housing: A Survey, 18677

Bracey, Howard Edwin: In Retirement: Pensioners in Great Britain and the United States, 8589; Neighbours: On New Estates and Subdivisions in England and the USA, 9349; Social Provision in Rural Wiltshire, 9395, 19171; English Rural Life: Village Activities, Organisations and Institutions, 19035; 'Rural Settlement in Great Britain', 19036; 'A Note on Rural Depopulation and Social Provision', 19037; 'Some Aspects of Rural Depopulation in the U.K.', 19038; Village Survey, 19039; Country Town Survey, 19040; People and the Countryside, 19041 Industry and the Countryside: The Impact of Industry on Amenities in the Countryside; Report of a Preliminary Enquiry for the Royal Society of Arts, 19042; 'Rural Service Centers in South Western Wisconsin and Southern England', 19043

Brackenbury, Sir Henry Britten: Patient and Doctor, 20826

Brackman, Arnold C.: The other Nuremberg: The Untold Story of the Tokyo War Crimes Trials, 13620

Bradbrook, Muriel Clara: 'That Infidel Place': A Short History of Girton College, 23478

Bradburn, Elizabeth: Margaret McMillan: Framework and Expansion of Nursery Education, 23152

Bradbury, John Lewis: Chester College and the Training of Teachers, 1839-1975, 22746

Bradbury, Malcolm Stanley: Evelyn Waugh, 25865

Bradbury, Ronald: Liverpool Builds 1945-1965, 18889

Bradbury, Savile: The Microscope Past and Present, 7106

Braddock, David Wilson: The Campaigns in Egypt and Libya, 1940-1942, 14891

Braddock, John and Braddock, Margaret Elizabeth: The Braddocks, 1371

Braddon, Russell Reading: Suez: Splitting of a Nation, 14379; All the Queen's Men: The Household Cavalry and the Brigade of Guards, 15655; Roy Thomson of Fleet Street, 25100

Braden, Charles Samuel: Christian Science Today: Power, Policy, Practice, 12454

Bradfield: Bradfield, 1850-1975, 23044

Bradford, Ernle Dusgate Selby: The Mighty 'Hood', 15026

Bradford, J. Selby: The Story of Dunkirk, 14843

Bradley, Harriet: Men's Work, Women's Work: A History of the Sex-Typing of Jobs in Britain, 7800

Bradley, Ian: Breaking the Mould? The Birth and Prospects of the Social Democratic Party, 1830; The English Middle Classes are Alive and Kicking, 9728

Bradley, John Francis Nejez: Allied Intervention in Russia, 1917-1920, 13924, 14568

Bradley, Keith: Worker Capitalism: The New Industrial Relations, 5829; Profit Sharing in the Retail Sector: The Relative Performance of the John Lewis Partnership, 6052

Bradley, Sir Kenneth Granville: The Diary of a District Officer, 12495; The Colonial Service as a Career, 12496; Once a District Officer, 12497; The Living Commonwealth, 12583; Britain's Purpose in Africa, 12680

Bradley, Lionel J. H.: Sixteen Years of Ballet Rambert, 24240

Bradley, R. L.: 'The English Borstal System', 10540

Bradley, Roger Thubron: Forest Planning, 19748

Bradshaw, D. C. A.: ed. Studies in the Government and Control of Education since 1860, 22801

Bradshaw, David N.: World Photography Sources, 212

Bradshaw, Jonathan: Welfare Rights and Social Action: The York Experiment, 8749

Bradshaw, Paul Frederick: The Anglican Ordinal: Its History and Development from the Reformation to the Present Day, 11609

Bradshaw, Samuel: The Drugs You Take: (A Plain Man's Guide to Patent Medicines), 22295

Brady, Gillian A.: The Holiday Industry in Devon and Cornwall, 26949

Brady, L. W.: T. P. O'Connor and the Liverpool Irish, 1498

Bragg, Melvyn: Speak for England: An Oral History of England, 1900-1975: Based on Interviews with Inhabitants of Wigton, Cumberland, 19211; Rich: The Life of Richard Burton, 26018; Laurence Olivier, 26080

Braham, John: Practical Manpower Planning, 5945

Braham, Peter: 'Discrimination and Disadvantage in Employment: The Experience of Black Workers', 11319

Brahms, Caryl: Too Dirty for the Windmill: A Memoir of Caryl Brahms, 26128

Brailey, Mary J.: Women's Access to Council Housing, 7846

Brailsford, Henry Noel: The Life-work of J. A. Hobson, 26586

Brain, Walter Russell [Baron]: Doctors Past and Present, 20849; The Doctor's Place in Society, 20850; Medicine and Government, 21596

Braine, John Gerard: J. B. Priestley, 25773; Autobiography and Reminiscence. Midnight in the Desert; Instead of the Trees; Margin Released; Rain Upon Godshill, 25774

Braithwaite, Eustace Edward Ricardo: Paid Servant, 11245; To Sir, with Love, 11246

Braithwaite, John: Crime, Shame and Re-integration, 10280

Braithwaite, Lewis: Canals in Towns, 16385

Brake, George Thompson: Inside the Free Churches, 12010; Policy and Politics in

British Methodism, 1932–1982, 12083; Alcohol: Its Consumption and Control: Objective Facts about a Widespread Habit, 22139; Drink in Great Britain, 1900 to 1979, 22140; Drink: Ups and Downs of Methodist Attitudes to Temperance, 22141

Brake, Mike: The Sociology of Youth Culture and Sub-cultures, 8539; ed. Radical Social Work and Practice, 8755

Braley, E.F.: ed. Letters of Herbert Hensley Henson, 11742; ed. More Letters of Herbert Hensley Henson, 11743

Bramall, Margaret: Adoption and Fostering: Papers, 8112

Bramble, Lionel John Farnham: Adult Education: The Record of the British Army, 23667

Bramley, Margaret: The Small Farmer: Present Situation and Future Prospects, 19514; Farming and Food Supplies: The Case for the Expansion of British Agriculture, 19515

Brammall, Ronald: The Tenth: A Record of Service of the 10th Battalion, The Parachute Regiment, 1942–1945 and the 10th Battalion, The Parachute Regiment (T. A.). 1947–1965, 15708

Bramsen, Bo: The Hambros 1779–1979, 4470

Bramsted, Ernest K.: 'Apostles of Collective Security: The L.N.U. and its Functions', 13496

Bramwell, Rupert Denis: 'The Impact of New Media on the Teacher's Work, with Special Reference to Britain', 22775; Elementary School Work 1900–1925, 23151

Branagh, Kenneth: Beginnings, 26015

Branch, Alan Edward: Elements of Shipping, 16460; Dictionary of Shipping/International Trade Terms and Abbreviations, 16461

Branch, Margaret: Gifted Children: Recognising and Developing Exceptional Ability, 8113

Branckner, J. W. S.: The Stansted Blackbook: a Representation to the President of the Board of Trade by the North West Essex and East Hertfordshire Preservation Association, 17686

Brand, Alexander: A Century's Progress in Jute Manufacture, 1833–1933, 6427

Brand, Carl Fremont: The British Labour Party: A Short History, 1677; 'The British General Election of 1950', 2304; 'The British General Election of 1951', 2307; 'The British General Election of 1955', 2313; 'The British General Election of 1959', 2317; 'The British General Election of 1964', 2321; 'The British General Election of 1966', 2326; 'The British General Election of 1970', 2330; 'British Labour and the International during the Great War', 13373

Brand, Jack A.: The Labour Party in Scotland in 1979: Advance or Retreat?, 2372, 2523; The National Movement in Scotland, 2496; Local Government Reform in England 1888–1974, 3131; Political Stratification and Democracy, 3375; 'The Politics of Fluoridisation: A Community Conflict', 20103; 'Ministry Control and Local Autonomy in Education', 22789

Brand, Janet: ed. The Urban Crisis: Social Problems and Planning, 17926

Brand, Mary Vivian: The Social Catholic Movement in England, 1920–1955, 11835

Brand, Robert Henry: War and National Finance, 3743

Brandell, Ulf: 'Sweden versus Great Britain and the Soviet Union during the Second World War', 13885

Brander, A. Michael: The Emigrant Scots, 2466, 7336; The Royal Scots (The Royal Regiment), 15592

Brander, Laurence: E. M. Forster: A Critical Study, 25522

Brandis, Walter: Social Class, Language and Communication, 9544; Selection and Control: Teachers' Ratings of Children in the Infant School, 23133

Brandon, David: Homeless, 18507

Brandon, Henry: In the Red: The Struggle for Sterling, 1964–1966, 4708

Brandon, Leonard George: A Short Economic and Social History of England, 3485

Brandon, P. F.: 'A 20th Century Squire in his Landscape', 19109

Brandon, Ruth: Wrongful Imprisonment: Mistaken Convictions and their Consequences, 10394; The Burning Question: The Anti-Nuclear Movement since 1945, 13532

Brandreth, Gyles: John Gielgud: A Celebration, 26045

Brandt, George W.: British Television Drama, 24860

Brangwyn, Rodney: Brangwyn, 24012

Brannen, Julia: Give and Take in Families: Studies in Resource Distribution, 10053

Brannen, Peter: 'Social Relations and Social Perspectives among Shipbuilding Workers: A Preliminary Statement', 9662; 'The Contours of Solidarity: Social Stratification and Industrial Relations in Shipbuilding', 9663

Bransby, E. R.: ed. Psychiatric Case Registers, 21857

Branson, Noreen: Britain in the Nineteen Twenties, 299; Britain in the Nineteen Thirties, 299; Poplarism 1919–25: George Lansbury and the Councillors' Revolt, 1702; A History of the Communist Party of Great Britain, 1927–1981, 1918

Branston, Ursula: Some Reflections on British Foreign Policy, 13220

Branton, Noel: The Economic Organisation of Modern Britain, 3440

Brash, William Bardsley: Methodism, 12068; The Story of Our Colleges, 1835–1935: A Centenary Record of Ministerial Training in the Methodist Church, 12107

Brasher, Norman Henry: Britain in the Twentieth Century, 1900–1964, 334; Studies in British Government, 778

Brasnett, Margaret: Voluntary Social Action: A History of the National Council of Social Service, 1919–1969, 9206

Brassell, Tim: Tom Stoppard, an Assessment, 25988

Brassey's Naval Annual 1886, 16455

Bratchell, Dennis Frank: The Aims and Organisation of Further Education, 23253

Braun, Hugh Stanley: The Story of English Architecture, 23888

Bray, Carl: New Villages: Case Studies, No. 1. New Ash Green [Kent], 19029; No. 2. South Woodham Ferrers [Essex], 19030

Bray, George W.: Recent Advances in Allergy (Asthma, Hay Fever, Eczema, Migraine etc.), 21042

Bray, Jeremy: Decision in Government, 779

Bray, Marjorie: Oxhey: The History of a Parish, 19352

Bray, Trevor: Twentieth Century Music, 1900–1945, 24265

Braybon, Gail: Women Workers in the First World War, 7705

Braybrook, Roy: The Battle for the Falklands: Air Forces, 16091; British Aerospace Harrier and Sea Harrier, 17611

Braybrooke, Neville: ed. T. S. Eliot: A Symposium for his 70th Birthday, 25493

Braybrooke, Patrick: The Amazing Mr. Noel Coward, 24470

Brazier, S.: 'Inter-Authority Planning', 5109

Breach, Robert Walter: A History of Our Own Times: Britain 1900–1964, 332; ed. British Economy and Society, 1870–1970: Documents, Descriptions, Statistics, 3444, 7619

Breakell, Mike: ed. Planning and the Historic Environment, 18958

Breakwell, Glynis Marie: Young Women in 'Gender-Atypical' Jobs: The Case of Trainee Technicians in the Engineering Industry, 7847

Brearley, Alan: The Woollen Industry, 6417

Brearley, Christopher Paul: Social Work, Ageing and Society, 8615; Risk and Social Work, 8768; The Social Context of Health Care, 21961

Brearley, Harold: The Bradford Trolley Bus System: Being the History of Britain's First and Last Trolley Buses, 17243

Brearley, Harry: Steel-makers, 6542

Breathnach, S.: The Irish Police: From Earliest Times to the Present Day, 2938

Brebner, John Bartlet: North American Triangle: The Interplay of Canada, the United States and Great Britain, 14003

Brech, Michael: Inward Investment: Policy Options for the United Kingdom, 4749

Breconshire County Planning Department: Brecon Borough Town Expansion: A Feasibility Study, 18845

Breed, Bryan: White Collar Bird, 10215

Breen, D. H.: 'Anglo-American Rivalry and the Evolution of Canadian Petroleum Policy to 1930', 12655

Breen, Henry H.: St Lucia: Historical, Statistical and Descriptive, 13089

Bremme, G.: Freiheit und sozialer Sicherheit. Motive und Prinzipien sozialer Sicherung dargestellt in England und Frankreich, 8777

Bremner, Marjorie K.: Dependency and the Family: A Psychological Study in Preferences between Family and Official Decision Making, 10083

Bren, Mary Winifred Josephine Macalister: Youth and Youth Groups, 8423

Brenan, Gerald: Personal Record, 1920–1972, 25411

Brendon, Piers: Our Own Dear Queen, 447; Winston Churchill, 988; The Life and Death of the Press Barons, 25083

Brennan, John: Employment of Graduates from Ethnic Minorities: A Research Report, 9885

Brennan, John Frederick: The Classical Organ in Britain, 1955–1974, 24394

Brennan, Thomas [Tom]:'Party Politics and Local Government in Western South Wales', 3382; Social Change in South-West Wales, 5381, 9653; The Social Pattern: A Handbook of Social Statistics of South-West Wales, 5382; 'Cheerful Delinquents and Grey Scrabblers: An Hypothesis on Problem Behaviour', 10565; Midland City: Wolverhampton Social and Industrial Survey, 18086; Reshaping a City, 18087, 18799; County Town: A Civic Survey for the Planning of Worcester, 18120; 'Gorbals: A Study in Redevelopment', 18139

Brennan, Wilfrid Kayan: Money, Banks and Banking, 4417

Brenner, M. F.: 'Public Pricing of Natural Resources', 6303

Brent Department of Planning and Research: Background to Brent: A Report, 18943

Brent, Allen: Philosophical Foundations for the Curriculum, 22851; Philosophy and Educational Foundations, 22852

Brent, Peter: T. E. Lawrence, 13820

Brentnall, H. C.: ed. Marlborough College, 1843–1943, 23066

Brentnall, Margaret: The Cinque Ports and Romney Marsh, 16679; John Hutton: Artist and Glass Engraver, a Biography, 24128

Brenton, Maria: Yearbook of Social Policy in Britain, 1987–88, 8809; The Voluntary Sector in British Social Services, 9217

Brentwood: The History of Brentwood School, 23045

Brereton, Bridget: ed. 'East Indians in the Caribbean: Colonialism and the Struggle for Identity', 13010

Brereton, John Maurice: The 7th Queen's Hussars, 15661

Bretherton, Russell Frederick: Public Investment and the Trade Cycle in Great Britain, 4731

Brett, C. E. B.: 'The Lessons of Devolution in Northern Ireland', 2808

Brett, George Albert: History of the South Wales Borderers and the Monmouthshire Regiment, 1937–1952, 15752

Brett, Lionel Gordon Baliol, Viscount Esher: York: A Study in Conservation: Report, 18981; Our Selves Unknown: An Autobiography, 23879

Brett, Maurice V.: Journals and Letters of Reginald, Viscount Esher, 1190

Brett, Oliver Sylvain Baliol: Journals and Letters of Reginald, Viscount Esher, 1190

Brett, Sidney Reed: British History, 1901–1961, 351

Brewer, Charles: The Spice of Variety, 26274

Brewer, J. Gordon: ed. The Literature of Geography: A Guide to its Organisation and Use, 26622

Brewer, John D.: 'The British Union of Fascists and Anti-Semitism in Birming-

ham', 2023, 11340; Mosley's Men: The British Union of Fascists in the West Midlands, 2024

Brewis, T. N.: 'Selective Credit and Investment Controls in the United Kingdom', 4743

Brewster, Chris: Understanding Industrial Relations, 5841

Briant, Keith Rutherford: Marie Stopes: A Biography, 7516

Briault, Eric: Falling Rolls in Secondary Schools, 22784

Brice, Martin Hubert: The Royal Navy and the Sino-Japanese Incident 1937–41, 14685

Bricker, Charles: Landmarks of Mapmaking: An Illustrated Survey of Maps and Mapmakers, 26714

Brickhill, Paul: The Dambusters, 15889; Reach for the Sky. The Story of Douglas Bader, 15890

Briden, Timothy: Moore's Introduction to English Canon Law, 11589

Bridge, Ann: see O'Malley, Lady

Bridge, Brian: Employment Service for the Disadvantaged: A Report to the Personal Social Services Council on Current Needs and Provision, Including a Study of Supported Employment, 5981

Bridge, Carl: Holding India to the Empire: The British Conservative Party and the 1935 Constitution, 13152; 'Conservatism and Indian Reform (1929–1939): Towards a Prerequisites Model in Imperial Constitution-making', 13153

Bridgeman, Harriet: ed. Society Scandals, 9746

Bridger, Peter A.: A Hindu Family in Great Britain, 12468

Bridges, Antony: Scapa Ferry, 15300

Bridges, B.: 'Britain and Japanese Espionage in Pre-War Malaya: The Shinozaki Case', 12925

Bridges, Daisy Caroline: A History of the International Council of Nurses, 1899–1964: The First Sixty Five Years, 21727

Bridges, Edward Ettingdene [Baron]: The Treasury, 804; Portrait of a Profession: The Civil Service, 924

Bridges, Lee: 'Race Relations Research: From Colonialism to Neo-Colonialism? Some Random Thoughts', 11038; 'Victims, the "Urban Jungle" and the New Racism', 11204

Bridges, Sydney Alexander: Gifted Children and the Brentwood Experiment, 23122

Bridgford, Jeff: 'British and French Shipbuilding: The Industrial Relations of Decline', 5849

Bridgman, Leonard: The Clouds Remember: The Aeroplanes of World War I, 14639

Bridie, James: One Way of Living, 25951

Bridson, Douglas Geoffrey: Prospero and Ariel: The Rise and Fall of Radio: A Personal Recollection, 24821

Brierley, John: Fourth Report on Car Parking in the Central Area, 17386; Car Parking and the Environment, 17387

Brierley, Peter: U.K. Christian Handbook-1983+, 11547; ed. Prospects for Scotland:

Report of the 1984 Census of the Churches, 12244; ed. Prospects for Wales: Report of the 1982 Census of the Churches, 12295

Briggs, Asa [Baron]: 'They Saw It Happen', 282, 7591; ed. Essays in Labour History in Memory of G. D. H. Cole, 1666, 1032, 1893; ed. Vol. 2, 1667, 6824, 13678; ed. Vol. 3, 1668, 6824; Wine for Sale: Victoria Wine and the Liquor Trade, 1860–1984, 6170, 20752; 'Social History 1900–1945', 7592; Social Thought and Social Action: A Study of the Work of Seebohm Rowntree, 1871–1954, 8075, 9019; 'The Welfare State in Historical Perspective', 8974; Toynbee Hall: The First Hundred Years, 9135; A History of Birmingham, vol.2: Borough and City 1865–1938, 5141, 18004; A Social History of England, 7593; The History of Broadcasting in the United Kingdom, 24718; The BBC: The First Fifty Years, 24719; Governing the BBC, 24770; 'Local and Regional in Northern Sound Broadcasting', 24813; The Franchise Affair: Creating Fortune and Failure in Independent Television, 24878; ed: Essays in the History of Publishing in Celebration of the 250th Anniversary of the House of Longman, 1724–1974, 24975

Briggs, Dennis: Dealing with Delinquents, 10597

Briggs, John H. Y.: 'She-Preachers, Widows and Other Women: The Feminine Dimension in Baptist Life since 1600', 12039

Briggs, Milton: An Economic History of England, 3486

Briggs, Susan Anne: The Home Front: War Years in Britain, 1939–1945, 15174; Those Radio Times, 24744

Brigham, Albert Perry: 'The Centenary of the Royal Geographical Society', 26625

Bright, Arthur A., Jnr: The Electric-Lamp Industry: Technological Change and Economic Development from 1800–1947, 6676

Bright, David: 'The Industrial Relations of Recession', 5834

Bright, Joan: ed. The Ninth Queen's Royal Lancers, 1936–1945: The Story of an Armoured Regiment in Battle, 15686; History of the Northumberland Hussars Yeomanry, 1924–1949, 15705

Bright, Laurence: ed. The Committed Church, 11956

Bright, Spencer: Peter Gabriel: An Authorised Biography, 24515

Brignall, T. J.: Accounting for British Steel: A Financial Analysis of the Failure of the British Steel Corporation 1967–80, and Who Was to Blame, 6606

Brill, Kenneth: Children in Homes, 8114; ed. John Groser: East End Priest, 11783

Brimblecombe, Peter: The Big Smoke: A History of Air Pollution in London since Medieval Times, 20057

Brindley, T.: 'Housing Classes and Housing Values', 18734

Brinnan, John Malcolm: Dylan Thomas in America, 25836

Brinson, Peter: The Ballet in Britain, 24212

Brinton, Henry: Measuring the Universe, 26409

Brinton, Howard Haines: Friends for 300 Years, 12137

Briscoe, Catherine: *ed.* Community Work: Learning and Supervision, 9378

Briscoe, Lynden: The Textile and Clothing Industries of the United Kingdom, 6458

Bristol Development Department: The Story of Social Welfare in Bristol, 1696–1948, 8870

Bristol Hospitals Fund: A Record of 25 Years Service, 1939–1964, 21423

Bristol Planning Group: Bristol: The Central Area and its Waterways, 18846

Bristol: The History of Bristol Grammar School, 22994

Briston, Richard J.: The Growth and Impact of Institutional Investors: A Report, 4270

Bristow, Adrian: Inside the Colleges of Further Education, 23256

Bristow, S. E.: 'Women Councillors: An Explanation of the Under-representation of Women in Local Government', 7832

Bristow, Stephen L.: 'Partisanship, Participation and Legitimacy in Britain's E.E.C. Referendum, 2393

Britain: An Official Handbook: 1954+, 270

British Aircraft Corporation: Concorde: The Questions Answered, 17571

British Airways: The Story of British Airways, 17626

British Aluminium Company: The History of the British Aluminium Company Limited, 1894–1955, 6149

British Antarctic Survey: Annual Report 1975+, 27227

British Association for the Advancement of Science and the Association of

British Chambers of Commerce: Decimal Coinage and the Metric System: Should Britain Change?, 4723

British Association for the Advancement of Science: Birmingham and its Regional Setting: A Scientific Survey, 5143; A Scientific Survey of Blackpool and District, 5145; Bristol and its Adjoining Counties, 5147; A Scientific Survey of Cambridge District, 5148; The Cambridge Region, 5149; Durham County and City, with Teesside, 5152; Handbook to Hull and the East Riding of Yorkshire, 5160, 5162; Leeds and its Region, 5167; A Scientific Survey of Leicester and District, 5168; Leicester and its Region, 5169; Handbook to Liverpool and District, 5170; Manchester and its Region: A Survey, 5176; A Scientific Survey of Merseyside, 5181; Official Handbook to Newcastle and District, 5187; Handbook to Newcastle upon Tyne, 5188; A Scientific Survey of North-Eastern England, 5202; A Scientific Survey of Nottingham and District, 5208; A Survey of Southampton and its Region, 5220; The Oxford Region: A Scientific and Historical Survey, 5213; Handbook to York, 5235; Scientific Survey of Aberdeen and District, 5281; A Scientific Survey of Dundee and District, 5283, 5284; Glasgow: Sketches by Various authors, 5289; The North East of Scotland, 5300; A

Scientific Survey of South Eastern Scotland, 5301; The Stirling Region, 5302; The Cardiff Region: A Survey, 5351; Swansea and its Region, 5383; Belfast in its Regional Setting, 5395; Research and Social Work, 8888 On a Cushion of Air: A Conference, 17709

British Code of Advertising Practice Committee: (Economists Advisory Group) The Economics of Advertising, 4311; The British Code of Advertising Practice, 4312

British Council for Overseas Students in Britain: A Handbook for All who Are Interested in the Welfare of Overseas Students, 11506

British Council of Churches and the Conference of British Missionary Societies: World Poverty and British Responsibility, 9183

British Dental Association: Fluoridation of Domestic Water Supplies, 22395; The Advance of the Dental Profession: A Centenary History, 1880–1980, 22403

British Dependencies in the Caribbean and North Atlantic 1939–1952, 12999

British Education Index, 22861

British Educational Research Journal, 22583

British Honduras: Report of an Inquiry Held by Sir Reginald Sharpe QC into Allegations of Contacts between the People's United Party and Guatemala, 13025

British Hospitals Association: Report of the Voluntary Hospitals Commission, April 1937, 21411

British Hospitals Contributory Schemes Association, 1948: Conference 1950–1961: National Health and Hospital Contributory Schemes, 21412

British Humanities Index: 1962–, 80

British Independent Air Transport Association: Annual Report 1962/3+, 17641

British Institute of Management: (Occasional Papers). Industrial Democracy: Some Implications for Management: An Exploratory Study, 6011

British Institute of Management: Women Managers: The Future, 5455

British Institute of Recorded Sound, became National Sound Archive in 1983, as part of the British Library, 226

British Iron and Steel Federation: The Welsh Steel Industry, 6571

British Journal of Educational Psychology 1, 22584

British Journal of Educational Studies 1, 22585

British Journal of Sociology of Education 1, 22586

British Journal of Sports History 1984–6, but now: *The International Journal of the History of Sport*, 27019

British League against Rheumatism: Rheumatism: The Price We Pay: The Impact of the Rheumatic Diseases on the Individual and the Country, 21127

British Library General Catalogue of Printed Books to 1975, 100.

British Library General Subject Catalogue 1975–1985, 106.

British Library Lending Division: British Reports, Translations and Theses, 424

British Library: Inventory of Bibliographic Databases produced in the UK, 53

British Maritime League: British Merchant Shipping: An Examination of the Causes of Decline in the British Merchant Fleet since 1975, 16490

British Market Research Bureau: Food: Facts and Fallacies, 20609

British Media Publications: Willing's Press Guide, 148

British Medical Association: All our Tomorrows: Growing Old in Britain, 8648; Nutrition and the Public Health: Medicine, Agriculture, Industry, Education, 20512; Recruitment to the Medical Profession: The Report of a Special Committee, May 1962, 20814; Vol. 20, no. 1. Experimental Psychology, 21045; The British Medical Association's Proposals for a General Medical Service for the Nation, 21551; The White Paper—An Analysis, 21554; Primary Medical Care, 21605; Health Services Financing, 21606;

British Museum Publications: Catalogue of the Newspaper Library at Colindale, 145

British Music Yearbook: 1972–, 24251

British National Bibliography, 5

British National Conference on Social Work: Children and Young People: A Guide to Studies for the British National Conference on Social Work at the University of Edinburgh, 8115

British National Conference on Social Welfare 1964: Communities and Social Change: Implications for Social Welfare: A Guide to Studies for the Conference, 8858, 9342; Report of the Fifth Conference, 8859

British National Film Catalogue: 1963–, 24590

British Nuclear Energy Society: Radioactive Waste Management Conference, 1984, 20129

British Paediatric Association: Paediatrics in the Seventies: Developing the Child Health Services, 21114

British Petroleum Environmental Control Centre: The Christos Bitas Incident: Success out of a Disaster: A Report on the Oil Spill Clean-up, 20084

British Phonograph Committee: The British Record: The Gramophone Record Industry's Services to the Nation from 1898 to the Present Day, 6486

British Political Yearbook: 1947, 275

British Ports Association: Annual Report 1980–1984, 16668; Annual Statistical Abstract of the United Kingdom Ports Industry 1982, 16669

British Road Federation and Town Planning Institute: The Motorways, 17119; Finance and Roads, 17120; People and Cities: Report of the 1963 London Conference, 17126; Car Parking: A National Survey, Nov. 1961, 17379; Car Parking: A National Survey, May 1964, 17380; Car Parking, 17381

British Shipping Review 1978+, 16521

British Social Attitudes: 1984+, 237

British Sociological Association, Medical Sociology Group ed: Medical Sociology in Great Britain, 1969–1970: A Selective

Review of the Research and Teaching Activities of Some British Medical Sociologists, 21955

British Theatre Directory: 1972+, 25903

British Tourist Authority: The Channel Tunnel: An Opportunity and a Challenge for British Tourism, 16366; Annual Reports, 26938; Patterns in British Holidaymaking, 1951–1968, 26939; A Survey of the Tourist Trade in Scotland, 26940; Investing in Tourism: Aid to Tourist Projects in England's Development Areas, 1971–76, 26941

British Transport Commission: Passenger Transport in Glasgow and District, 16337

British Transport Docks Board: Annual Report and Accounts 1963–81, 16644; The Ports of Grimsby and Immingham 1981, 16688; Hull: Official Guide 1982, 16691

British Universities Film and Video Council/Institute of Contemporary British History: Post-War British History: A Select List of Videos and Films available in the U.K., 221; Researcher's Guide to British Film and Television Collections, 24582

British Waterways Board: Annual Report and Accounts, 16372

British and Commonwealth Shipping Company Ltd.: Annual Report 1977–1978, 16563

Brittain, E.: Organisation in Multi-racial Schools, 23183

Brittain, Frederick: A Short History of Jesus College, Cambridge, 23479

Brittain, Sir Harry Ernest: By Air, 17497

Brittain, Sir Herbert: The British Budgetary System, 4913; 'The Treasury's Responsibilities', 6120

Brittain, John Michael: ed. Inventory of Information Resumés in the Social Sciences, 7921

Brittain, Vera Mary: Pethick-Lawrence: A Portrait, 1288; The Women at Oxford: A Fragment of History, 7680; Lady into Woman: A History of Women from Victoria to Elizabeth II, 7681; ed. Selected Letters (1920–1935) Winifred Holtby and Vera Brittain, 25414; Testament of Youth: An Autobiographical Study of the Years 1900–1925, 25415; Testament of Experience: An Autobiographical Study of the Years 1925–50, 25416

Brittan, Samuel: The Price of Economic Freedom, 4934; The Treasury under the Tories, 1951–1964, 5004, 6099; Steering the Economy, 6122

Brittan, Yvonne: The Impact of Water Pollution Control on Industry: A Case Study of 50 Dischargers, 20088

Britten, James: A Bibliographical Index of Deceased British and Irish Botanists, 26546

Brittenden, Frederick Henry: A Guide to the Selective Employment Tax, 5879

Britton, Clare: Child Care and Social Work: A Collection of Papers Written between 1954 and 1963, 8116

Britton, Denis King: The Economic Arithmetic of Agriculture, 19506; The Changing Structure of British Agriculture, 19507; Cereals in the United Kingdom: Production, Marketing and Utilisation, 19508

Britton, John Nigel Haskings: Regional Analysis and Economic Geography: A Case Study of Manufacturing in the Bristol Region, 5146

Broad, [Charles] Lewis: The Abdication Twenty-five Years after; A Re-appraisal, 476; The Path to Power: The Rise to the Premiership from Rosebery to Wilson, 962; Mr. Churchill, 988; Sir Anthony Eden: The Chronicles of a Career, 1007

Broad, D. W.: Centennial History of the Liverpool Section, Society of Chemical Industry, 1881–1981, 6203

Broad, Geoffrey: 'Shop Steward Leadership and the Dynamics of Workplace Industrial Relations', 5835

Broadbent, Sir Ewen: The Military and Government: From Macmillan to Heseltine, 827

Broadbent, Thomas Andrew: Planning and Profit in the Urban Economy, 17965

Broadberry, S. N.: The British Economy Between the Wars: A Macroeconomic Survey, 3593; 'Fiscal Policy in Britain in the 1930s', 4645

Broadley, Sir Herbert: The People's Food, 20586

Broadway, Frank Edward: ed. Case Studies in Human Relations, Productivity and Organization, 5481; State Intervention in British Industry, 1964–1968, 6112; Upper Clyde Shipbuilders: A Study of Government Intervention in Industry, 16621

Broady, Maurice: ed. Marginal Regions: Essays on Social Planning, 9327; Planning for People: Essays on the Social Context of Planning, 9328; 'The Sociological Adjustment of Chinese Immigrants in Liverpool', 11378; 'The Chinese in Great Britain', 11379; 'Drumbie Enquiry: David and Goliath in Scottish Rural Development', 19250

Brock, Eleanor and Brock, Michael: ed. H. H. Asquith: Letters to Venetia Stanley, 971

Brock, George: Thatcher, 1048

Brock, Jenny: 'Prelates in Parliament', 11632

Brock, William H.: The Lamp of Learning: Taylor and Francis and the Development of Science Publishing, 24991

Brock, William Ranulf: Britain and the Dominions, 12540

Brockbank, Edward Mansfield: A Centenary History of the Manchester Medical Society, 20809

Brockbank, William: Portrait of a Hospital, 1752–1948, 21463

Brockington, Colin Fraser: The Social Needs of the Over-80's: The Stockport Survey, 8582; A Short History of Public Health, 22089

Brockway, Archibald Fenner [Baron]: Inside the Left: Thirty Years of Platform, Press, Prison and Parliament, 1372; German Diary, 1373; Outside the Right, 1374; Towards Tomorrow: The Autobiography of Fenner Brockway, 1375; 98 Not Out, 1376; Socialism over Sixty Years: The Life of Jowett of Bradford, 1864–1944, 1439;

English Prisons to-day: Being the Report of the Prison System Enquiry Committee, 10337; This Shrinking Explosive World: A Study of Race Relations, 10957; Immigration: What is the Answer? Two Opposing Views, 11406; African Journeys, 12694

Brodetsky, Paul: 'Law as a Liberal Study', 22433

Brodie, Charles Gordon: Forlorn Hope, 1915: The Submarine Passage of the Dardanelles, 14539

Brodie, Malcolm: 100 Years of Irish Football, 27093

Brodie, Mary: Traffic Generation, 16242

Brodrick, Alan Houghton: Near to Greatness: A Life of the Sixth Earl Winterton, 1548

Brodrick, William St. John Fremantle [Earl of Midleton]: Records and Reactions, 1856–1939, 1377

Brodsky, Samuel L.: 'Understanding and Treating Sexual Offenders', 10857

Brody, Stephen: Screen Violence and Film Censorship: A Review of Research: A Home Office Research Unit Report, 26903

Brogan, Colm: Fifty Years on: British Socialism, 1900–1950, 1675; The Educational Revolution, 22703

Brogan, Sir Denis William,: The English People: Impressions and Observations, 320; 'Anglo-American Relations, Retrospect and Prospect', 14073; 'The Price of Oxbridge', 23562

Brogan, Hugh: The Life of Arthur Ransome, 25782

Brogden, Michael: The Police: Autonomy and Consent, 10711; 'The Emergence of the Police: The Colonial Dimension', 10776

Brolchain, M.: 'Social Class and Psychiatric Disturbance among Women in an Urban Population', 21818

Bromage, Mary Cogan: De Valera and the March of a Nation, 3050

Brome, [Herbert] Vincent: Aneurin Bevan: A Biography, 1096; J. B. Priestley, 25777

Bromhead, Evelyn: Fair Shares in Parliament: Or, How to Elect More Women MPs, 7829

Bromhead, Peter Alexander: Britain's Developing Constitution, 621; 'The British Constitution in 1974', 622; 'The British Constitution in 1975', 623; The House of Lords and Contemporary Politics, 1911–1957, 670; 'Mr Wedgwood Benn, the Peerage and the Constitution', 672; Private Members' Bills in the British Parliament, 693; 'The General Election of 1966', 2328; Life in Modern Britain, 7595; 'State and Leisure', 26921

Bromley, Peter Mann: Family Law, 10016

Bromley, Simon: Thatcherism: A Tale of Two Nations, 1054

Brommage, Mary Cogan: Churchill and Ireland, 988

Bromsgrove: Bromsgrove School through the Centuries, 23046

Brook, George Leslie: The Modern University, 23420; Books and Book-collecting, 25013

Brook, Michael: Nottinghamshire County, 25172

Brook, Norman Craven [Baron Norman-brook]: The Functions of the BBC's Governors, 24769

Brook, Peter: The Shifting Point: Forty Years of Theatrical Exploration 1946–1987, 26120

Brook, Roy: The Tramways of Huddersfield: A History of Huddersfield Corporation Tramways, 1883–1940, 17228; The Trolleybuses of Huddersfield, 17247

Brook, Stephen: The Club: The Jews of Modern Britain, 12417

Brooke, Christopher N. L.: David Knowles, 26805

Brooke, Eileen M.: The Survey of Sickness, 1943–1952, 22234

Brooke, Iris: English Costume 1900–50, 24160

Brooke, Jocelyn: Elizabeth Bowen, 25406; ed. Denton Welch: Extracts from his Published Works, 25867

Brooke, Peter: Ulster Presbyterianism. The Historical Perspective 1610–1970, 12172

Brookefield, H. C.: 'Worthing: A Study of a Modern Coastal Town', 18921

Brookes, Andrew, Bomber Squadron at War, 15973

Brookes, Barbara: Abortion in Britain, 1900–1967, 7880

Brookes, Christopher: His Own Man: The Life of Neville Cardus, 25215

Brookes, Ewart Stanley: Prologue to a War: The Navy's Part in the Narvik Campaign, 14914; The Gates of Hell, 15127; Destroyer, 15386; Glory Passed them by, 15397

Brookes, J. A.: 'Housing Redevelopment and Rehabilitation: A Case Study in Comparative Economics', 18531

Brookes, John: Garden Design: History, Principles, Elements, Practice, 19903

Brookes, Kenneth: Battle Thunder: The Story of Britain's Artillery, 15503

Brookes, S. K.: 'The Environmental Lobby in Britain', 20247; 'The Growth of the Environment as a Political Issue in Britain', 19960, 20248

Brookfield, H. C.: Colonialism, Development and Independence—The Case of the Melanesian Islands in the South Pacific, 12877

Brooks, Alan: Woodlands, 19752

Brooks, C. M.: ed. The Historical Development of Physiological Thought: A Symposium, 26457

Brooks, Collin: Devil's Decade: Portraits of the Nineteen Thirties, 299; Can Chamberlain Save Britain?: The Lesson of Munich, 13749; An Educational Adventure: A History of the Woolwich Polytechnic, 22530

Brooks, David: 'Lloyd George—For and Against', 1023

Brooks, Dennis: Black Employment in the Black Country: A Study of Walsall, 11483; Race and Labour in London Transport, 11452, 16329

Brooks, Edwin: This Crowded Kingdom: An Essay on Population Pressure in Great Britain, 7405

Brooks, Eileen M.: 'Mental Health and the Population', 21763

Brooks, Peter Fred: Problems of the

Environment: An Introduction, 19965; The Work of the Environmental Health Committee, 19966

Brooks, Peter Newman: ed. Christian Spirituality: Essays in Honour of Gordon Rupp, 26813

Brooks, Peter Wright: The Modern Airliner: Its Origins and Development, 17562; 'The Development of Air Transport', 17651; A Short History of London's Airports, 17681

Brooks, Robert: Bright Delinquents: The Story of a Unique School (A Longitudinal Study of the Outcome of the Work of Kneesworth Hall School, 1953–1970), 23125

Brookshire, J. H.: 'Clement Attlee and Cabinet Reform 1930–1945', 728

Broom, John: John Maclean, 2528

Broom, L.: 'Bridging Occupations', 5872

Broome, David: Twenty Five Years in Show Jumping, 27135

Brophy, Brigid Antonia: A Guide to Public Lending Right, 25030

Brophy, John: The Five Years: A Conspectus of the Great War, 14456; Songs and Slang of the British Soldier: 1914–1918, 14471; The Long Trail, 14472; Britain's Home Guard, 15147; Advanced Training for the Home Guard, 15148

Brosnan, Peter: Cheap Labour: Britain's False Economy, 3960

Brotchie, Alan Walter: Dumbarton's Trams and Buses, 17222

Brothers, Joan: ed. The Uses of Sociology, 7979; Church and School: A Study of the Impact of Education on Religion, 22889

Brotherston, John Howie Flint: Observations on the Early Public Health Movement in Scotland, 22073

Brotherton, Christopher M.: ed. Industrial Relations: A Social Psychological Approach, 5801

Brothwell, J. F.: 'Budget Adjustments with a Consumption Tax', 4904

Brotz, Howard: 'The Position of the Jews in English Society', 11299

Brough, Ian: Social Values and Industrial Relations: A Study of Fairness and Equality, 5764

Brown, Alan: Profits, Wages and Wealth, 3927; 'Initial Employment Experience of Sociology Graduates in the United Kingdom, 1976–1978', 5973

Brown, Alfred John: Town and Country Planning, 17749

Brown, Alfred Victor: A History of Britain, 1939–1968, 333

Brown, Anthony Cave: The Secret Servant: The Life of Sir Stewart Menzies. Churchill's Spymaster, 16010

Brown, Anthony William Aldridge: The Ecology of Pesticides, 20118

Brown, Antony: Hazard Unlimited: The Story of Lloyd's of London, 4241; 300 Years of Lloyds, 4262; Red for Remembrance: The British Legion 1921–1971, 15469

Brown, Arthur Joseph: 'Inflation and the British Economy', 3985; The Great Inflation, 1939–1951, 4619, 5003; Regional Economic Problems: Comparative Experiences of Some Market Economies,

5091; 'Surveys of Applied Economics: Regional Economics, with Special Reference to the United Kingdom', 5092; 'Regional Problems and Regional Policy', 5093; The Framework of Regional Economies in the United Kingdom, 5094

Brown, Beatrice Curtis: ed. Isabel Fry, 1869–1959: Portrait of a Great Teacher, 23338

Brown, Callum G.: The Social History of Religion in Scotland since 1730, 12187

Brown, Cecil Leonard Morley: The Conquest of the Air: An Historical Survey, 17496

Brown, Charles Kenneth Francis: The Church's Part in Education, 1833–1941, 22879

Brown, Charles Victor: Public Sector Economics, 4661

Brown, Clayton: Christopher Isherwood: A Bibliography 1923–1967, 25592

Brown, D. A.: Mortality from Lung Cancer and Bronchitis in Relation to Smoke and Sulphur Dioxide Concentration, Population Density, and Social Index, 20061

Brown, David: A Sociology of Industrialisation: An Introduction, 5017; 'Women, Shiftworking and the Sexual Division of Labour', 5921

Brown, David: A New Threshold: Guidelines for the Churches in their Relations with Muslim Communities, 12458

Brown, David B.: 'Mountbatten as First Sea Lord', 15273; Carrier Air Groups, 15914; The Royal Navy and the Falklands War, 16089; The History of the Guild of Air Pilots and Air Navigators, 1929–1964, 17637

Brown, Eric Herbert: ed. Geography Yesterday and Tomorrow, 26643

Brown, Sir [Ernest] Henry Phelps: 'The Brookings Study of the Poor Performance of the British Economy', 3661; A Century of Pay: The Course of Pay and Production in France, Germany, Sweden, the United Kingdom and the United States of America, 1860–1960, 3907; Earnings in Industries of the United Kingdom, 1948–1959', 3908; 'Equal Pay for Equal Work', 3909; The Inequality of Pay, 3910; Pay and Profits, 3911; A Perspective of Wages and Prices, 3912; 'Accumulation, Productivity and Distribution in the British Economy, 1870–1938', 4744; The Origins of Trade Union Power, 6739; 'The Sizes of Trade-unions: A Study in the Laws of Aggregation', 6756

Brown, G.: The Iron and Steel Industry, 6546

Brown, Geoff: 'Ealing, your Ealing', 24667; 'Richard Massingham: The Five-inch Film Maker', 24679; 'Which Way to the Way Ahead?', 24694

Brown, George [Lord George-Brown]: In My Way: The Political Memoirs of Lord George Brown, 1118

Brown, George: 'Social Class and Psychiatric Disturbance among Women in an Urban Population', 21818

Brown, Gordon: Maxton: A Biography, 1471, 2534

Brown, H. P.: 'The National Economic Development Organisation', 6090

Brown, Harold John: The Practitioner's Guide to Hire-purchase Cases, 20493

Brown, Ian M.: Personnel Management in Five Public Services: Its Development and Future, 5475

Brown, Ivor: The Way of my World, 25918; Old and Young, 25919; 'Forty Years back', 25920

Brown, J. D.: Carrier Operations in World War II, 15040

Brown, J. W.: 'The Fertility of the English Middle Classes: A Statistical Study', 7475

Brown, James Alexander Campbell: The Social Psychology of Industry: Human Relations in the Factory, 5480

Brown, James: Gamlingay: 600 Years of Life in an English Village, 19188

Brown, Jane: ed. The Art and Architecture of English Gardens: Designs for the Garden from the Collection of the Royal Institute of British Architects, 1609 to the Present Day, 20324

Brown, Joan C.: Low Pay and Poverty in the United Kingdom, 3963; Family Income Support Part One: Family Income Supplement, 4093; Part Twelve: The Future of Family Income Support, 4094; Poverty and the Development of Anti-Poverty Policy in the United Kingdom, 9091

Brown, Joe: The Hard Years: An Autobiography, 27245

Brown, John Falcon: Guinness and Hops, 6159

Brown, John Russell: Theatre Language, 25996; ed. Contemporary Theatre, 26223

Brown, John: Community versus Crime, 10170; Policing by Multi-racial Consent: The Handsworth Experiment, 10713; The Police and the Community, 10723; The Unmelting Pot: An English Town and its Immigrants, 11489; Opening the Door: A Study of New Policies for the Mentally Handicapped, 21866

Brown, Jonathan: Village Life in England 1860–1940: A Photographic Record, 19153; Agriculture in England, 1870–1947, 19416

Brown, Judith Margaret: Modern India: The Origins of an Asian Democracy, 13109; Gandhi's Rise to Power: Indian Politics 1915–1922, 13136; Gandhi and Civil Disobedience: The Mahatma in Indian Politics 1928–1934, 13137; Gandhi, 13138; 'Imperial Façade: Some Constraints upon and Contradictions in the British Position in India, 1919–1935', 13149

Brown, Kenneth D.: John Burns, 1121; ed. Essays in Anti-Labour History: Responses to the Rise of Labour in Britain, 1627; The English Labour Movement 1700–1951, 6695; A Social History of the Nonconformist Ministry in England and Wales 1800–1930, 11906; 'Patterns of Baptist Ministry in the Twentieth Century', 12019

Brown, L. B.: 'English Migrants to New Zealand: The Decision to Move', 7313; 'Social Class and the Ranking of Occupations', 9468

Brown, Leslie Farrer: Public Health and Social Services, 22068

Brown, Leslie Wilfred: 'Anglican-Methodist Unity—a Symposium', 12309

Brown, Lloyd A.: The Story of Maps, 26702

Brown, M. J.: Online Bibliographical Databases: A Directory and Sourcebook, 52

Brown, Malcolm: Scapa Flow, 15302

Brown, Martin James: ed. Social Issues and the Social Services, 8821

Brown, Martin P.: Compendium of Communication and Broadcast Satellites, 1958 to 1980, 17703

Brown, Michael Barratt: 'Determinants of the Structure and Level of Wages in the Coal Mining Industry since 1956', 6298; 'The Trade Union Question', 6783

Brown, Michael: The Greenpeace Story, 20250

Brown, Michele: Queen Elizabeth II: The Silver Jubilee Book, 1952–1977, 514

Brown, Mick: Richard Branson: The Inside Story, 24578

Brown, Muriel: Introduction to Social Administration in Britain, 9244; Problems of Homelessness: An Experiment in Co-operation, Manchester, 1954–1963, 18506

Brown, Pat: The Other Side of Growing Older, 8643

Brown, Peter: The Love you Make: An Inside Story of the Beatles, 24503

Brown, R. G. S.: The Administrative Process in Britain, 912

Brown, R. J.: 'Policy Making in English Local Government: The Case of Secondary School Reorganisation', 22964

Brown, R. L.: 'Pop Music in an English Secondary School System', 8421; Television and Delinquency, 24834

Brown, Richard K.: 'Participation, Conflict and Change in Industry', 5681; 'Research and Consultancy in Industrial Enterprises: A Review of the Contribution of the Tavistock Institute of Human Relations to the Development of Industrial Sociology', 5682; 'Social Relations and Social Perspectives among Shipbuilding Workers: A Preliminary Statement', 9662; 'The Contours of Solidarity: Social Stratification and Industrial Relations in Shipbuilding', 9663

Brown, Roger V.: Banking in Britain, 4443

Brown, Ronald George Sclater: The Management of Welfare: A Study of British Social Service Administration, 9246; The Administrative Process in Britain, 9247; The Changing National Health Service, 21619; Reorganising the National Health Service: A Case Study in Administrative Change, 21620; A Series of Progress Reports from the Research Team Studying the Reorganisation of the National Health Service on Humberside, 1972–75, 21621; The Male Nurse, 21720

Brown, Sibil Clement: The Field Training of Social Workers: A Survey, 8710; Social Services and Mental Health: An Essay in Psychiatric Social Workers, 8711, 21753

Brown, Sidney William: Leighton Park: A History of the School, 22907

Brown, Stuart: Alexander's Buses, 17318

Brown, Susannah: 'A Comparison of the Size of Families of Roman Catholics and Non-Catholics in Great Britain', 7490

Brown, Terence: Ireland: A Social and Cultural History, 1922–1979, 23739

Brown, W. Langdon: 'The History of the Introduction of Biochemistry into Medicine', 20919

Brown, Wilfrid [Baron]: Some Problems of a Factory: An Analysis of Industrial Institutions, 5603; Bismarck to Bullock: Conversations about Institutions in Politics and Industry in Britain and Germany between Wilfrid Brown and Wolfgang Hirsch-Weber, 5604; The Earnings Conflict, 5900

Brown, William Adams: England and the New Gold Standard, 1919–1926, 4670

Brown, William H.: The Royal Botanic Garden, Edinburgh, 1670–1970, 26537

Brown, William: Factors Shaping Shop Steward Organisation in Britain, 5796; ed. Changing Contours of British Industrial Relations, 5800; 'Industrial Relations: The Next Decade', 5833

Browne, Douglas Gordon: The Rise of Scotland Yard: A History of the Metropolitan Police, 10752; The Floating Bulwark: The Story of the Fighting Ship: 1514–1942, 15350; Private Thomas Atkins; A History of the British Soldier from 1840 to 1940, 15449; The Tank in Action, 15516

Browne, E. Martin: The Making of T. S. Eliot's Plays, 25494; Two in One, 26131

Browne, J. D.: Teachers of Teachers: A History of the Association of Teachers in Colleges and Departments of Education, 22714; 'Bachelors of Education', 22717

Browne, Kenneth: Parks for People, 27003

Browne, Margaret H.: A Century of Pay: The Course of Pay and Production in France, Germany, Sweden, the United Kingdom and the United States of America, 1860–1960, 3907; 'Earnings in Industries of the United Kingdom, 1948–1959', 3908

Browne, Noel: Against the Tide, 3010

Browne, Terry: Playwrights' Theatre: The English Stage Company at the Royal Court Theatre, 26155

Browning, A. S. E.: A History of the Motor Car Industry in Scotland, 17411

Browning, Ethel: Health and Fitness, 21241; Health in Middle Life, 21242; Modern Drugs in General Practice, 21243; Toxic Solvents, 21244; The Vitamins + Bibliography, 21245; Harmful Effects of Ionising Radiations, 21246; Toxicity of Industrial Metals, 21247

Browning, Peter: The Treasury and Economic Policy 1964–1985, 806

Brownjohn, Alan: Philip Larkin, 25621

Brownlie, Alistair R.: ed. Crime Investigation: Art or Science?, 10717

Brownrigg, Mark: 'The Economic Impact of a New University', 23311; Tourism and Regional Development, 26942; The Economic Impact of Tourist Spending in Skye, 26943

Browse, Lilian Gertrude: Sickert, 24061; William Nicholson, 24048

Brubacher, John Seiler: A History of the Problems of Education, 22702

Bruce, Charles Granville: The Assault on Mount Everest, 1922, 27238

Bruce, Sir David: 'Prevention of Disease: Inaugural Address Delivered to the British Association at Toronto on August 6', 20920

Bruce, Frederick Fyvie: The English Bible: A History of Translations, 11916

Bruce, George: A Wine Day's Work: The London House of Deinhard, 1835–1985, 6171; Some Practical Good: The Cockburn Association, 1875–1975: A Hundred Years' Participation in Planning in Edinburgh, 18829; Festival in the North, 24530; Pitlochry Festival Theatre. 21, a Record of Achievement, 1951–1972. Scotland's Theatre in the Hills, 26171

Bruce, James Graeme: A Source Book of Buses, 17253

Bruce, John McIntosh: British Aeroplanes, 1914–1918, 14640

Bruce, Martin Hubert: The Tribals: Biography of a Destroyer Class, 15385

Bruce, Maurice: The Rise of the Welfare State: English Social Policy, 1601–1971, 8977; The Coming of the Welfare State, 8978; British Foreign Policy: Isolation or Intervention?, 13748; The University of Sheffield, Department of Extramural Studies, 1947–1968: A Personal Survey, 23698

Bruce, Steve: God Save Ulster: The Religion and Politics of Paisleyism, 3076; No Pope of Rome: Anti-Catholicism in Modern Scotland, 12246; 'Ideology and Isolation: A Failed Scots Protestant Movement', 12259

Bruce-Gardyne, Jock [Baron]: Ministers and Mandarins, 736; Mrs. Thatcher's First Administration: Confounding the Prophets, 1048; Ministers and Mandarins: Inside the Whitehall Village, 1378

Bruegel, Johann Wolfgang: Czechoslovakia before Munich; The German Minority Problem and British Appeasement Policy, 13731; Tschechen und Deutsche 1918–1938, 13732; 'Der Runciman Bericht', 13733

Brueton, Bertrand F.: Bristol and Bath Regional Planning Scheme, 18847

Brunekreef, B.: Childhood Exposure to Environmental Lead: A Technical Report, 20161

Brunel Institute of Organization and Social Studies: Organising Some Social Service Departments, 9235

Brunel, Adrian: Nice Work: An Autobiography of 30 years of British Films, 24665

Bruner, Jerome Seymour: Under Five in Britain, 23164

Brunner, Elizabeth: Capital Development in Steel: A Study of the United Steel Companies Ltd., 6600; The Life of Lord Nuffield, 17433; Holiday Making and the Holiday Trends, 26983

Brunsdale, Mitzi: Dorothy L. Sayers, 25796

Brunskill, Ronald William: Timber Building in Britain, 19798

Brunt, Barry Maynard: The Contemporary Economic Problems of Merthyr Tydfil, 5355

Brunt, Sir David: ed. Royal Society International Geophysical Year Antarctic Expeditions: Halley Bay, Coats Land, Falkland Islands Dependencies, 1955–1959, 27222

Bruton, Michael J.: Local Planning in South Wales, 5378

Brush, John E.: 'Rural Service Centers in South Western Wisconsin and Southern England', 19043

Brutton, E. D.: British Steam, 1948–1955, 17043

Bryan, Sir Andrew Meikle: The Evolution of Health and Safety in Mines, 4140; Planning Permission and the Place of the Public Enquiry in the Development of Mineral Resources in Britain: Problems of Potash Extraction in Yorkshire, 20376; The Evolution of Health and Safety in Mines, 21282

Bryan, Beverley: The Heart of the Race: Black Women's Lives in Britain, 7726

Bryan, Gordon: Scottish Nationalism and Cultural Identity in the Twentieth Century: An Annotated Bibliography of Secondary Sources, 2509

Bryanston: Bryanston, 1929–1978, 23047

Bryant, Peter: The Handicapped Child: Recent Research Findings, 21920

Bryant, Sir Arthur Wynne Morgan: George V, 473; ed. In Search of Peace (Speeches of Neville Chamberlain), 987; The Spirit of Conservatism, 2187; The Turn of the Tide 1939–1943: A Study Based on the Diaries and Autobiographical Notes of Field Marshal the Viscount Alanbrooke, 14749; Triumph in the West, 1943–1946: A Study Based on the Diaries and Autobiographical Notes of Field Marshal the Viscount Alanbrooke, 14750; Jackets of Green: A Study of the History, Philosophy and Character of the Rifle Brigade, 15713

Bryant, Christopher Gordon Alistair: Sociology in Action: A Critique of Selected Conceptions of the Social Role of the Sociologist, 8028

Bryant, David: 'Social Contacts on the Hyde Park Estate, Sheffield', 9417

Bryant, Margaret E.: The London Experience of Secondary Education, 22957

Bryant, Richard: 'Professionals in the Firing Line', 8747; Change and Conflict: A Study of Community Work in Glasgow, 8748; Welfare Rights and Social Action: The York Experiment, 8749

Bryce, James [Viscount Bryce of Dechmont]: Essays and Addresses in Wartime, 1379

Bryden, John M.: Agrarian Change in the Scottish Highlands: The Role of the Highlands and Islands Development Board in the Agricultural Economy of the Crofting Counties, 19621

Bryden, Ronald: 'Generation in Exodus', 8417

Bryder, Linda: Below the Magic Mountain: A Social History of Tuberculosis in Twentieth Century Britain, 22240

Bryer, R. A.: Accounting for British Steel: A Financial Analysis of the Failure of the British Steel Corporation 1967–80, and who Was to Blame, 6606

Bryman, A.: Clergy, Ministers and Priests, 11588

Buchan, Alastair: 'Mothers and Daughters (or Greeks and Romans)', 14082

Buchan, John [Baron Tweedsmuir]: The King's Grace 1910–1935, 473; The Last Secrets: The Final Mysteries of Exploration, 27173

Buchan, Susan C. [Baroness Tweedsmuir]: John Buchan, 1385

Buchan, William: John Buchan: A Memoir, 1384; ed. John Masefield, Letters to Reyna, 25697

Buchanan, Angus: Three Years of War in East Africa, 14522

Buchanan, Colin Douglas: The State of Britain, 7608; Transport and the Community, 16221; Mixed Blessings: The Motor Car in Britain, 17340

Buchanan, D. S.: Merchant Shipping: A Guide to Government Publications, 16519

Buchanan, Derek: Emergent Patterns in L.E.A. Adult Education, 23671

Buchanan, Sir George William: My Mission to Russia and other Diplomatic Memories, 13252

Buchanan, James Mcgill: The Inconsistencies of the National Health Service: A Study in the Conflict between Individual Demand and Collective Supply, 21578, 21590

Buchanan, Robert Angus: 'The Contribution of Industrial Archaeology to the History of Technology', 7146; Industrial Archaeology: Retrospect and Prospect, 7147; 'The Technological Universities', 22498

Buchanan, Ronald Hull: Man and his Habitat, 17976

Buchman, Frank Nathan Daniel: Remaking the World, 12405

Buck, Philip Wallenstein: Amateurs and Professionals in British Politics, 1918–1959, 1555; 'First Time Winners in the British House of Commons since 1918', 1556; ed. How Conservatives Think, 2184

Buck, Stephen Frank: Mortality from Lung Cancer and Bronchitis in relation to Smoke and Sulphur Dioxide Concentration, Population Density, and Social Index, 20061; Report on a Study of Environmental Factors associated with Lung Cancer and Bronchitis Mortality on Areas of North East England, 20062

Buckingham, Graeme L.: Productivity Agreements and Wage Systems, 5994

Buckland, Gail: The Magic Image: The Genius of Photography from 1839 to the Present Day, 24705

Buckland, Patrick: A History of Northern Ireland, 2782; The Factory of Grievances: Devolved Government in Northern Ireland 1921–1939, 2783; Irish Unionism, 2948; 'The Unity of Ulster Unionism, 1886–1939', 2949; Irish Unionism, 1885–1923: A Documentary History, 2950; James Craig, 3073

Buckle, Christopher Richard Sandford: Jacob Epstein: Sculptor, 24186

Buckle, Richard: ed. Self-Portrait with Friends: The Selected Diaries of Cecil Beaton, 1926–1974, 24706

Buckley, Christopher: Greece and Crete, 1941, 14852; Road to Rome, 14862; Norway. The Commandos' Dieppe, 14920

Buckley, Peter J.: Direct Investment in the United Kingdom by Smaller European

Firms, 4750; The Future of the Multinational Enterprise, 5561; The Industrial Relations Position of Foreign-owned Firms in Britain, 5845

Buckley, Roger: 'Britain and the Emperor: The Foreign Office and Constitutional Reform in Japan, 1945–1946', 13614; Occupation Diplomacy: Britain, the United States and Japan, 1945–1952, 13615. 'Joining the Club: The Japanese Question and Anglo-American Peace Diplomacy 1950–1951', 13616

Buckley, Walter: ed. Power and Control: Social Structures and their Transformation, 9457

Buckmaster, Owen Stanley, Viscount: Roundabout: The Autobiography of Viscount Buckmaster, 5502

Buckwell, A. E.: The Costs of the Common Agricultural Policy, 19587

Budd, A.: The Politics of Economic Planning, 6137

Budd, Susan: Varieties of Unbelief: Atheists and Agnostics in English Society 1850–1960, 11890

Budge, Ian: 'Strategic Issues and Votes: British General Elections 1950–1979', 2362; Scottish Political Behaviour, 2475; Belfast: Approach to Crisis: A Study of Belfast Politics, 1613–1970, 2908; Political Stratification and Democracy, 3375; Electors' Attitudes Towards Local Government. A Survey of a Glasgow Constituency', 3376

Budgen, Nicholas: Immigration, Race and Politics: A Birmingham View, 11455

Budges, David: Mixed Ability Grouping: A Philosophical Perspective, 22854

Bufkin, E. C.: P. H. Newby, 25737

Bufwack, Mary S.: Village without Violence: An Examination of a Northern Irish Community, 2895

Bugge, Gunther: 'Some Problems Relating to the History of Science and Technology', 7148

Bugler, J.: Polluting Britain, 19983

Bugliarello, George: The Impact of Noise Pollution: A Socio-Technological Intro-duction, 20142

Building Societies Association: Facts about Building Societies, 4371; Studies in Building Society Activity 1974–1979, 4372; Future Constitution and Power of Building Societies, 4373; Building Societies and the Savings Market, 4374; Understanding Building Societies, 4375; New Legislation for Building Societies, 4376

Building Societies Institute Research Group: Insurance in Building Society Practice, 4365; Building Society Branches:Their Development and Organisation, 4380; [International School 1964]. The Influence of Building Societies on the Present and Future Patterns of Society, 4381

Building Societies Yearbook, 4355

Buitenhuis, Peter: The Great War of Words: Literature as Propaganda 1914–18 and After, 15215; ed. George Orwell: A Reassessment, 25753

Bulbring, Maud: 'Post-War Refugees in Great Britain', 11395

Bulkley, Mildred Emily: A Bibliographical Survey of Contemporary Sources for the Economic and Social History of the War, 3741; The Feeding of Schoolchildren, 20522

Bull, Angela: Noel Streatfeild, 25823

Bull, David: ed. Family Poverty: Programmes for the Seventies, 9070

Bull, George Antony: Industrial Relations: The Boardroom Viewpoint, 5760

Bull, Gregory H.: Regional and Urban Economics, 5126

Bull, Hedley: ed. The Special Relationship: Anglo-American Relations since 1945, 14084

Bull, J. W. D.: 'The History of Neuroradiology', 20921

Bull, John: New British Political Dramatists: Howard Brenton, David Hare, Trevor Griffiths and David Edgar, 25997

Bull, P. J.: 'The Spatial Components of Intra-Urban Manufacturing Change: Suburbanisation in Clydeside, 1958–1968', 18298

Bull, Peter Cecil: To Sea in a Sieve, 15308

Bullard, Sir Reader William: The Camels Must Go, 13253; Britain and the Middle East from Earliest Times, 13800

Bulleid, Henry Anthony Vaughan: Master Builders of Steam, 17073

Bullen, Roger: ed. The Foreign Office 1782–1982, 13336

Bullmore, Francis Tresillian King: The Dark Haven, 14992

Bulloch, J. P. B.: ed. The County of Peebles and the County of Selkirk, 19232

Bulloch, John: MI5: The Origin and History of the British Counter-Espionage Service, 16013; Akin to Treason, 16033; Spy Ring: The Full Story of the Naval Secrets Case, 16046

Bulloch, W.: The History of Bacteriology, 22347

Bullock, Alan Louis Charles [Baron]: The Life and Times of Ernest Bevin, 1101; ed. The Liberal Tradition from Fox to Keynes, 2163; Report of the Committee of Inquiry on Industrial Democracy, 6023; Great Britain in the World of the Twentieth Century, 13216

Bullock, Frederick William Bagshawe: A History of Training for the Ministry of the Church of England in England and Wales from 1875 to 1974, 11908; The History of Ridley Hall, Cambridge, 11909

Bullock, M.: Accessibility to Employment in the Northern Region Report, 16290

Bullock, Roger: After Grace—Teeth: A Comparative Study of the Residential Experiment of Boys and Approved Schools, 10509

Bulman, G. L.: Adult Dental Health in England and Wales in 1968, 22400

Bulman, Inga: ed. Youth Service and Inter-professional Studies, 8451

Bulmer, Martin I. A.: ed. Mining and Social Change: Durham County in the Twentieth Century, 5151; Essays on the History of British Sociological Research, 8086; ed. Social Policy Research, 8819; Social Science and Social Policy, 8820; 'Sociological

Models of the Mining Community', 9646; Studies in Working Class Imagery, 9647; Working Class Images of Society, 9648; ed. Mining and Social Change: Durham County in the Twentieth Century, 18103

Bulmer-Thomas, Ivor: The Growth of the British Party System, 1575

Bulpitt, James Graham: Party Politics in English Local Government, 3142

Bundock, Clement James: The Story of the National Union of Printing, Bookbinding and Paper Workers, 6884; The National Union of Journalists: A Jubilee History, 1907–1957, 6897, 25313

Bunker, Gordon: ed. Race and Ethnic Relations: Sociological Readings, 11055

Bunselmayer, Robert E.: The Cost of the War, 1914–1919: British Economic War Aims and the Origins of Reparations, 13416

Bunt, Cyril George Edward: Two Centuries of English Chintz, 1750–1950, 24129

Bunt, Sidney: Jewish Youth in Britain: Past, Present and Future, 8514

Bunting, Sir John: R. G. Menzies: A Portrait, 12624

Bunton, William James: Comprehensive Education: A Select, Annotated Bibliography, 22944

Bunyan, Tony: The History and Practice of the Political Police in Britain, 10735

Burch, David: Overseas Aid and the Transfer of Technology, 9186

Burch, Martin: 'The British Cabinet: A Residual Executive', 734; A Political and Electoral Handbook for Wales, 2583

Burch, William R.: Social Behaviour, Natural Resources and the Environment, 19973

Burchard, Joseph Randall: The British Labour Movement in European Politics, 1933–1939, 13560

Burchell, R. W.: The Affluent Suburb, 18295

Burchett, Wilfred Graham: Wingate's Phantom Army, 14790

Burchfield, Robert: The English Language, 23806

Burden, Rodney: Falklands: The Air War, 16093

Burdett, Harry: Life in Sapcote, Leicester-shire, 1914–1924, 19201

Bureau International du Travail: La Situation Syndicale au Royaume-Uni, 6728

Burge, Cyril Gordon: The Annals of 100 Squadron, 15915

Burgess, Alfred Robert Paul: The True Book about the British Army, 15440

Burgess, Anthony: Little Wilson and Big God, 25431

Burgess, J.: A History of Cumbrian Methodism, 12110

Burgess, Keith: The Origins of British Industrial Relations, 5574

Burgess, Muriel: Gracie Fields, 24477

Burgess, Renate: Portraits of Doctors and Scientists in the Wellcome Institute of the History of Medicine, 20773

Burgess, Robert G.: Experiencing Comprehensive Education: A Study of Bishop McGregor School, 22970

Burgess, Tyrrell: Ten Billion Pounds: Whitehall's Takeover of the Town Halls,

3267, 4867; Polytechnics: A Report, 22532; Policy and Practice: The Colleges of Advanced Technology, 23291

Burghart, Richard: ed. Hinduism in Great Britain: The Perpetuation of Religion in an Alien Cultural Milieu, 12467

Burgin, Trevor: Spring Grove: The Education of Immigrant Children, 23175

Burk, Kathleen: ed. War and the State: The Transformation of British Government 1914–1919, 793, 14439; Morgan Grenfell 1838–1988: The Biography of a Merchant Bank, 4471; The First Privatisation: The Politicians, the City and the Denationalisation of Steel, 6576; 'Great Britain, America, and the Sinews of War, 1914–1918, 13403; Britain in the United States, 1917–1918: The Turning Point', 13404; 'The Diplomacy of Finance: British Financial Missions to the United States 1914–1918', 13405; 'The Mobilization of Anglo-American Finance During World War I', 13406; 'Britain and the Marshall Plan', 14129

Burke's Peerage and Baronetage 1826+, 34

Burke, M.: Signalman, 16805

Burke, Peter: Sociology and History, 8092; The Social History of Language, 23795

Burke, R. M.: An Historical Chronology of Tuberculosis, 21164

Burke, T. E.: The Philosophy of Karl Popper, 26860

Burke, Vincent: Teachers in Turmoil, 22825

Burke-Gaffney, John Joseph: The Story of the King's Regiment, 1914–1948, 15678

Burkett, Jack: Library and Information Networks in the United Kingdom, 94; Library and Information Networks in Western Europe, 95

Burkhart, Charles: I. Compton-Burnett 25455

Burkitt, Brian: Trade Unions and Wages, 3942; 'The Degree of Unionization, 1948–1968', 6746; 'The Degree of Unionization, 1948–1968: A Reply', 6748

Burkman, Katherine H.: The Dramatic World of Harold Pinter, 25970

Burleigh, John Henderson Seaforth: A Church History of Scotland, 12195

Burley, Kevin: British Shipping and Australia, 1920–1939, 16465

Burlingham, Dorothy: Infants without Families: The Case for and against Residential Nurseries, 8121; Staffing of Local Authority Children's Departments: A Report by the Scottish Advisory Council on Child Care, 8122

Burman, P.: ed. Change and Decay: The Future of Our Churches, 11845

Burman, R.: 'The Jewish Woman as Breadwinner: The Changing Value of Women's Work in a Manchester Immigrant Community', 11330

Burn, A. S.: Atlas of Drought in Britain, 1975–76, 20104

Burn, Duncan Lyall: ed. The Structure of British Industry: A Symposium, 4970; 'Recent Trends in the History of the Steel Industry', 6548; The Economic History of Steelmaking, 1867–1939: A Study in Competition, 6560; The Steel Industry,

1939–1959, 6565; Nuclear Power and the Energy Crisis, 6663; Lessons from Central Forecasting, 21536

Burne, Alfred Higgins: Mesopotamia, the Last Phase, 14560; Strategy as Exemplified in the Second World War, 14702; The Woolwich Mess, 15457

Burnet, Sir Frank MacFarlane: 'Immunology as a Scholarly Discipline', 20922; Biological Aspects of Infectious Disease, 22361; Natural History of Infectious Disease, 22361; Changing Patterns. An Atypical Autobiography, 22362

Burnet, George Bain: The Holy Communion in the Reformed Church in Scotland, 1560–1960, 12199; The Story of Quakerism in Scotland, 1650–1850, 12261

Burnet, James: 'Teeth and the Worker', 21304

Burnett, David: Dorset Shipwrecks, 16508

Burnett, F. T.: 'A Survey of Housing Conditions in the Urban Areas of England and Wales, 1960', 18655

Burnett, George: ed. Scotland on the Air, 24812

Burnett, Gordon B.: 'The Habitual Drunkenness Offender', 10881

Burnett, John: 'Autobiographies of Childhood: The Experience of Education', 8119; Destiny Obscure: Autobiographies of Childhood Education and Family from the 1820's to the 1920's, 8120; A Social History of Housing, 1815–1970, 18741; A History of the Cost of Living, 20416; Plenty and Want: A Social History of Diet in England from 1815 to the Present Day, 20510

Burnett, Sir E. Napier: 'Voluntary Hospitals: Results of a Preliminary Survey', 21485

Burney, Elizabeth: Black in a White World, 10950; Housing on Trial: A Study of Immigrants and Local Government, 11491

Burnham, Thomas Hall: Iron and Steel in Britain, 1870–1930, 6545

Burns, Aidan: Nature and culture in D. H. Lawrence, 25635

Burns, Sir Alan Cuthbert: Colonial Civil Servant, 12508; Fiji, 12881; The History of the British West Indies, 13001

Burns, Charles C.: Maladjusted Children, 10652

Burns, Donald George: Travelling Scholars: An Enquiry into the Adjustment and Attitudes of Overseas Students Holding Commonwealth Bursaries in England and Wales, 11504

Burns, Emile: The General Strike, May 1926: Trades Councils in Action, 6942

Burns, Eveline Mabel: Wages and the State: A Comparative Study of the Problems of State Wage Regulation, 3886; British Unemployment Programs, 1920–1938, 7008; Health Services for Tomorrow: Trends and Issues, 21618

Burns, James H.: 'The Scottish Committees of the House of Commons, 1948–1959', 2478

Burns, Jim: ed. The Food Industry: Economics and Policies, 20627

Burns, Jimmy: The Land that Lost its Heroes: The Falklands, the Postwar and Alfonsin, 16111

Burns, Michael: ed. The Queen's Flight, 17521

Burns, R. G.: The Chemistry and Microbiology of Pollution, 20000

Burns, Russell W.: The History of Radar Development to 1945, 15114

Burns, Terry: 'Inflationary Mechanism in the U.K. Economy', 4016

Burns, Tom R.: The Management of Innovation, 5427; ed. Industrial Man: Selected Readings, 5709; Sociological Explanation, 7980; ed. Social Theory and Economic Change, 7981; The Child Care Service at Work, 8118; ed. Power and Control: Social Structures and their Transformation, 9457 The BBC: Public Institution and Private World, 24795

Burns, Wilfred: New Towns for Old: The Technique of Urban Renewal, 17775, 18993; Newcastle: A Study in Replanning at Newcastle upon Tyne, 17776; British Shopping Centres: New Trends in Layout and Distribution, 17777

Burpitt, Harry Reginald: 'The Provision of Occupations for Children out of School Hours.', 8123

Burrage, Michael: 'Culture and Britain's Economic Growth', 3438; 'The Group Ties of Occupations in Britain and the United States', 5898

Burrell, Alison Margaret: A Statistical Handbook of United Kingdom Agriculture, 19395

Burrell, Brian: Combat Weapons: Hand Guns and Shoulder-arms of World War II, 15499

Burridge, Trevor David: Attlee: A Political Biography, 975; 'A Postscript to Potsdam: The Churchill-Laski Electoral Clash', 2294; British Labour and Hitler's War, 13565; 'Barnacles and Trouble Makers: Labour's Left Wing and British Foreign Policy 1939–1945', 13570

Burrington, Gillian A.: How to Find out about the Social Sciences, 7920

Burrough, E. J. R.: Unity in Diversity: The Short Life of the United Oxford Hospitals, 21419

Burroughes, H. R.: 'Political and Administrative Problems of Development Planning: The Case of the C.E.G.B. and the Supergrid', 6389

Burrowes, John: Frontline Report: A Journalist's Notebook, 25213

Burrowes, Reynold A.: The Wild Coast: An Account of Politics in Guyana, 13046

Burrows, Arthur: The Story of Broadcasting, 24732

Burrows, E. Michael: Regional Economic Problems: Comparative Experiences of some Market Economies, 5091

Burrows, G.: The Trolley Buses of South Shields 1936–1964, 17250; Chichester: A Study in Conservation, 18974

Burrows, John: 'The Investigation of Crime in England and Wales', 10276

Burrows, Paul: The Economics of Unemployment Insurance, 4033

Burt, Brian A.: ed. Dental Public Health: An Introduction to Community Dentistry, 22393

Burt, Sir Cyril Ludovic: 'The Delinquent Child', 10546; ed. How the Mind Works, 22417

Burton, Alfred Joseph: Electronic Computers and their Business Applications, 7087

Burton, Anthony: *ed.* Canals: A New Look: Essays in Honour of Charles Hadfield, 16378; The Waterways of Britain: A Guide to the Canals and Rivers of England, Scotland and Wales, 16427

Burton, Anthony W.: Public Participation in Planning: A Review of Experience in Scotland, 20362

Burton, F. N.: 'The Role of Invisible Trade in the United Kingdom Balance of Payments, 1952–1966', 4921

Burton, Frank Patrick: The Politics of Legitimacy: Struggles in a Belfast Community, 9392

Burton, Harry: Investment and Unit Trusts in Britain and America, 4265

Burton, Hyde Clarke: The Great Betrayal: An Indictment of the Conservative Governments' Departure from Conservative Principles, 1951–1963, 1636

Burton, Lindy: The Family Life of Sick Children: A Study of Families coping with Chronic Childhood Disease, 8124, 21906; Care for the Child Facing Death, 8125; Vulnerable Children: Three Studies of Children in Conflict, 8126

Burton, Mary: Wingerworth through the Ages, 19212

Burton, Thomas Leonard: Social Research Techniques for Planners, 17734, 18788; *ed.* Recreation Research and Planning: A Symposium, 26951; Outdoor Recreation in the British Countryside, 26952

Bury, Adrian: Two Centuries of British Water-Colours and Drawings, 23984

Busby, Roy: British Music Hall: An Illustrated Who's Who from 1850 to the Present Day, 26287

Busch, Briton Cooper: Britain, India and the Arabs, 1914–1921, 13828

Busch, Carol: *ed.* Drug Problems in Britain. A Review of Ten Years, 10833, 22206

Busenkell, Richard L.: Jaguar since 1945, 17456

Busfield, Joan: Thinking about Children: Sociology and Fertility in Post-war England, 7496

Bush, Alan: In My Eighth Decade and other Essays, 24321

Bush, David: The Golden Age of British Hotels, 26996

Bush, Eric Wheeler: Gallipoli, 14540

Bush, J.: Behind the Lines: East London Labour, 1914–1919, 1780

Bush, Martha: Immigrant Housing, 11493

Bush, Michael Laccohee: The English Aristocracy, 9745

Bush, Peter: Undergraduate Income and Expenditure, 9883

Bush, Ronald: T. S. Eliot: A Study in Character and Style, 25495

Bushby, John: Air Defence of Great Britain, 15992

Bushell, Thomas Alexander: 'Royal Mail': A Centenary History of the Royal Mail Line 1839–1939, 16535; Eight Bells: The Royal Mail Lines War Story, 1939–1945, 16536

Business Atlas of Great Britain, 130

Busk, Sir Douglas Laird: The Craft of Diplomacy, 13254

Bussey, Ellen M.: 'Coloured Minorities and Present British Policies', 10954

Bussey, Gertrude: Women's International League for Peace and Freedom 1915–1965, 13439

Bussey, Sarah: 'The Labour Victory in Winchester in 1945', 2299

Bustani, Emile: 'The Arab World and Britain', 13824

Busvine, J. R.: Insects, Hygiene and History, 22360

Butcher, David: Official Publications in Britain, 176; The Trawlermen, 19821

Butcher, Emily Elizabeth: Clifton Hill House, the First Phase, 1909–1959, 23463

Butcher, H. J.: Educational Research in Britain, 3, 22847; *ed.* Educational Research in Britain, 22846

Butcher, Hugh: Pensioned Off: A Study of Elderly People in Cleator Moor, 8617; Information and Action Services for Rural Areas: A Study in West Cumbria, 9414

Butcher, Tony: The Civil Service Today, 874

Buthley, Kenneth: Hugh MacDiarmid, 25681

Butler, Arthur Stanley George: The Architecture of Sir Edward Lutyens, 23874

Butler, David Edgeworth: British Political Facts 1900–1985, 64; 'The Benn Archive', 1093; *ed.* Policy and Politics: Essays in Honour of Norman Chester, 1592, 23570; The Electoral System in Britain Since 1918, 2222; 'The Redistribution of Seats', 2223; Political Change in Britain: Forces Shaping Electoral Choice, 2224; The British General Election of 1951, 2305; The British General Election of 1955, 2311; The British General Election of 1959, 2315; The British General Election of 1964, 2319; The British General Election of 1966, 2325; The British General Election of 1970, 2329; The British General Election of February 1974, 2331; The British General Election of 1979, 2339; The British General Election of 1983, 2343; British General Elections since 1945, 2364; European Elections and British Politics, 2380; Party Strategies in Britain: A Study of the 1984 European Elections, 2382; The British General Election of October 1974, 2338; The 1975 Referendum, 2389; 'On the Analytical Division of Social Class', 9489

Butler, E. C. L.: The Building Societies Institute 1934–1978: An Historical Account, 4382

Butler, Eamonn: Economy and Local Government, 4881; Hayek: His Contribution to the Political and Economic Thought of our Time, 26583

Butler, Ewan: The Story of Dunkirk, 14843; The Murder of the News Chronicle and the Star, 25149

Butler, Frank: A History of Boxing in Britain: A Survey of the Noble Art from its Origins to the Present Day, 27109

Butler, Gareth: British Political Facts 1900–1985, 64

Butler, Sir Harold Beresford: Confident Morning, 13255

Butler, Ivan: Cinema in Britain; An Illustrated Survey, 24633; 'To Encourage the Art of the Film': The Story of the British Film Institute, 24634

Butler, J. R.: 'Illness and the Sick Role: An Evaluation in Three Communities', 21349; 'Sociology and Medical Education', 22470

Butler, Sir James Ramsay Montague: A History of England, 1815–1939, 297; Lord Lothian 1882–1940, 1457; September 1939–June 1941, 14720; June 1941–August 1942, 14721

Butler, John Alfred Valentine: Science and Human Life: Successes and Limitation, 26521; Modern Biology and its Human Implications, 26522

Butler, John Richard: Family Doctors and Public Policy: A Study of Manpower Distribution, 21522

Butler, Keith: 'A Role for the Tech.', 22503

Butler, Mollie: August and Rab: A Memoir, 1130

Butler, Neville Roy: Perinatal Mortality: The First Report of the 1958 Perinatal Mortality Survey, Under the Auspices of the National Birthday Trust Fund, 7454

Butler, Phillip Henry: An Illustrated History of Liverpool Airport, 17680

Butler, Richard Austen [Baron]: The Art of the Possible: The Memoirs of Lord Butler, K.G. C.H., 1125; The Art of Memory: Friends in Perspective, 1126; The 1944 Act in Perspective, 1127; The Conservatives, 1619; The Responsibilities of Education: The Professions, Industry, the Universities and Government, 23431

Butler, Thomas: Mental Health, Social Policy and the Law, 21747

Butlin, Sir Billy: The Butlin Story: 'A Showman to the End', 26997

Butlin, Robin A.: *ed.* Studies of Field Systems in the British Isles, 19557

Butrym, Zofia Teresa: The Nature of Social Work, 8759; Medical Social Work in Action: A Study of Medical Social Work at Hammersmith Hospital, 21435; Social Work in Medical Care, 21515; Medical Social Work in Action: A Report of a Study of Medical Social Work at Hammersmith Hospital, 21954

Butt Philip, Alan: The Welsh Question: Nationalism in Welsh Politics, 1945–1970, 2601

Butt, John: An Economic History of Scotland 1100–1939, 5270; 'Achievement and Prospect: Transport History in the 1970s and 1980s', 16212; *ed.* Strathclyde: Changing Horizons, 18154; 'Working Class Housing in Scottish Cities, 1900–1950', 18455

Butt, John: 'English at the Universities, 1901–1951', 22447

Butt, Ronald: The Power of Parliament, 592; 'The Common Market and Conservative Party Politics 1961–1962', 14159

Buttar, Charles: 'The Future of the Poor-Law Infirmary', 21484; 'The Municipalization of Hospitals. The Bradford Experiment', 21492

Butter, Peter Herbert: Edwin Muir: Man and Poet, 25721; *ed.* Selected Letters of Edwin Muir, 25722

Butterfield, Sir Herbert: The Universities and Education Today, 23393

Butterfield, Peter: 'Grouping, Pooling, and Competition: The Passenger Policy of the London and North Eastern Railway 1929–1939', 16887

Butterfield, William John Hughes: Priorities in Medicine, 21217; Health and Sickness: The Choice of Treatment: Perception of Illness and Use of Services in an Urban Community, 21980

Butteriss, Margaret: Job Enrichment and Employee Participation: A Study, 6015

Butterwick, Michael Willoughby: 'British Agricultural Policy and the E.E.C.', 19651; Food, Farming and the Common Market, 19652

Butterworth, Eric: ed. The Sociology of Modern Britain: An Introductory Reader, 7600; ed. Social Problems of Modern Britain, 7601, 8818; Social Welfare in Modern Britain, 7602; Immigrants in West Yorkshire: Social Conditions and the Lives of Pakistanis, Indians and West Indians, 11223; A Muslim Community in Britain, 12459

Butterworth, R.: 'Islington Borough Council: Some Characteristics of Single-Party Rule', 3312

Button, Kenneth John: Case Studies in Regional Economies, 5100; Urban Economics: Theory and Policy, 5399, 20395; The Economics of Urban Transport, 5400, 16301, 20396; ed. The Shetland Way of Oil: Reactions of a Small Community to Big Business, 6533, 9385

Buxton, John: New College, Oxford, 1379–1979, 23569

Buxton, Martin J.: Social Policy and Public Expenditure: Constraints and Choices, 8952; ed. The Uncertain Future: Demographic Change and Social Policy, 8953; Health and Inequality, 21670; Allocating Health Resources: A Commentary on the Report of the Working Party on Resource Allocation, 21671

Buxton, Neil Keith: The Economic Development of the British Coal Industry: From Industrial Revolution to the Present Day, 3421, 6271; 'Economic Progress in Britain in the 1920's: A Reappraisal', 3562; 'Economic Growth in Scotland between the Wars: The Role of Production Structure and Rationalization', 3586; ed. British Industry Between the Wars: Instability and Industrial Development, 1919–1939, 5001, 16610, 17405, 17579; British Employment Statistics: A Guide to Sources and Methods, 5911; 'Entrepreneurial Efficiency in the British Coal Industry Between the Wars', 6268; 'Entrepreneurial Efficiency in the British Coal Industry Between the Wars: Reconfirmed', 6269; 'Avoiding the Pitfalls: Entrepreneurial Efficiency in the Coal Industry again', 6270; 'Efficiency and Organization in Scotland's Iron and Steel Industry during the Interwar Period', 6544; 'The Role of the "New" Industries in Britain During the 1930s: A Reinterpretation', 7235; 'The Scottish Shipbuilding Industry between the Wars: A Comparative Study', 16617

Buxton, Noel: The Question of the Bosphorus and the Dardanelles, 14553

Buxton, Richard Joseph: Local Government, 18404

Byatt, Antonia Susan: Degrees of Freedom: The Novels of Iris Murdoch, 25729

Bygraves, Max: "I Wanna Tell you a Story!", 26299

Bynner, John Morgan: The Young Smoker: A Study of Smoking among Schoolboys Carried Out for the Ministry of Health, 8117

Byre, Angela: Human Rights at the Workplace: A Handbook for Industrial Relations Practitioners, 4167

Byrne, David: 'The 1930 "Arab Riot" in South Shields: A Race Riot that Never Was', 11484

Byrne, David: The Poverty of Education: A Study in the Politics of Opportunity, 22808

Byrne, Dominic: Making Ends Meet: Working for Low Wages in the Civil Service, 3964

Byrne, Eileen Maire: Planning and Educational Inequality: A Study of the Rationale of Resource-allocation, 22782

Byrne, F. J.: ed. The Scholar Revolutionary: Eoin MacNeill 1867–1945, 3062

Byrne, Paul: The Campaign for Nuclear Disarmament, 13530

Byrne, Stephen: The Changing Face of Lewisham, 18944

Byrne, Tony: Local Government in Britain: Everyone's Guide to how it all Works, 3138

Bytheway, Bill: 'The Social Differentiation of Ability', 9494

Bywater, Hector Charles: Navies and Nations: A Review of Naval Developments since the Great War, 15331; Cruisers in Battle, 15390

C. Hoare & Co. Ltd: Hoare's Bank: A Record 1672–1955, 4512

C.N.R.S.: Les Relations Franco-Britanniques de 1935 à 1939, 14242; Les Relations Franco-Allemandes, 1933–1939, 14261; Français et Britanniques dans le Drôle de Guerre, 14271

Cable, John: Advertising and Economic Behaviour, 4307

Cable, Michael: The Pop Music Inside Out, 24467

Cadbury, Laurence John: This Question of Population: Europe in 1970, 7358

Caddell, Laurie: ed. Great British Bikes, 17183

Cadogan, Sir Alexander: The Diaries of Sir Alexander Cadogan, 1938–1945, 13256

Cadogan, Mary: You're a Brick Angela!: A New Look at Girls Fiction from 1839 to 1975, 8127; Richmal Crompton: The Woman behind William, 25466

Caernarvonshire County Council: Hydro-electric Power in North Wales, 5362

Caernarvonshire County Planning Department: Second Homes, 18372

Cagan, Philip: The Effect of Pension Plans on Aggregate Savings: Evidence from a Sample Survey, 3970; 'Inflation and Market Structure, 1967–1973', 3995

Cage, E. E. H.: 'Industrial and Social Developments in English New Towns', 18235

Cage, R. A.: The Scots Abroad, 2468

Cahn, Sidney: The Treatment of Alcoholics: An Evaluative Study, 22130

Cain, Edward R.: 'Conscientious Objection in France, Britain and the United States', 13457

Cain, Maureen Elizabeth: Society and the Policeman's Role, 10728

Caine, Sir Sydney: 'Universities and the State', 23331; British Universities: Purpose and Prospect, 23433

Caird, James Brown: 'Migrating Scots', 7338; 'The Making of the Scottish Rural Landscape', 19242; 'Leadership and Innovation in the Crofting Communities of the Outer Hebrides', 19282

Cairncross, Sir Alexander Kirkland: ed. The Scottish Economy: A Statistical Account of Scottish Life, 3471, 5246, 18481; An Introduction to Economics, 3499; Changing Perceptions of Economic Policy: Essays in Honour of the Seventieth Birthday of Sir Alec Cairncross, 3500; Years of Recovery: British Economic Policy, 1945–1951, 3624; ed. Britain's Economic Prospects Reconsidered, 3667; Sterling in Decline: The Devaluations of 1931, 1949, and 1967, 4693; The Price of War. British Policy on German Reparations 1941–1949, 14195; A Country to Play with: Level-of-Industry Negotiations in Berlin, 1945–1946, 14196; ed. The Robert Hall Diaries, 26580; ed. The Economic Section 1939–1961: A Study in Economic Advising, 26581

Cairncross, Frances: Capital City: London as a Financial Centre, 4245

Cairney, Thomas: ed. Reclaiming Contaminated Land, 20121

Cairns, A. C. H.: The Chemical Industry: Its Position in the U.K. Economy, 6204

Cairns, John C.: 'A Nation of Shopkeepers in Search of a Suitable France: 1919–1940', 14241; 'Great Britain and the Fall of France: A Study in Allied Disunity', 14267

Cairns, John: Cancer, Science and Society, 21055; Phage and the Origins of Molecular Biology, 22307

Cairns, William J.: Onshore Impacts of Offshore Oil, 6524

Caiyer, Stephen L.: British Honduras: Past and Present, 13024

Calder, Angus: ed. Speak for Yourself: A Mass-Observation Anthology, 1937–1949, 229, 7532; 'Never Again: December 1942 to August 1945', 1904; The People's War: Britain, 1939–1945, 7533

Calder, Jenni: Chronicles of Conscience: A Study of George Orwell and Arthur Koestler, 25617

Calder, Kenneth J.: Britain and the Origins of the New Europe, 1914–1918, 13390

Calder, Nigel: The Environmental Game, 19909; The Human Conspiracy, 19910; ed. Nature in the Round: A Guide to Environmental Science, 19911; Technopolis: Social Control of the Uses of Science, 19912; Violent Universe: An Eye-witness Account of the Commotion in Astronomy, 26413

Calder, Ritchie [Baron Ritchie-Calder of

Balmashannar]: The Conquest of Suffering, 21175; Medicine and the Man: The Story of the Art and Science of Healing, 21197; The Life Savers, 21198

Calder, Robert Laurin: W. Somerset Maugham and the Quest for Freedom, 25707; Willie: The Life of Somerset Maugham, 25708

Calhoun, Craig: 'History and Sociology in Britain: A Review Article', 26738

Calhoun, Daniel Fairchild: The United Front: The TUC and the Russians, 1923–1928, 13940

Callaghan, James: Time and Chance, 982; A House Divided: The Dilemma of Northern Ireland, 2836

Callaghan, John: British Trotskyism: Theory and Practice, 1986; The Far Left in British Politics, 2001

Callahan, Raymond: Burma, 1942–1945, 15058; The Worst Disaster: The Fall of Singapore, 15073

Callan, Edward: Auden: A Carnival of Intellect, 25357

Callan, Hilary: ed. The Incorporated Wife, 9945; Ethnology and Society: Towards an Anthropological View, 10998

Callard, P.: 'Punishment by the State, Its Motives and Form', 10332

Callaway, Helen: Gender, Culture and Empire: European Woman in Colonial Nigeria, 7749, 12764

Callcott, M.: 'The Nature and Extent of Political Change in the Inter-war Years: The Example of County Durham', 1785

Callcott, W. R.: 'The Last War Aim: British Opinion and the Decision for Czechoslovak Independence. 1914–1919', 13395

Callender, Sir Geoffrey Arthur Romaine: The Naval Side of British History, 1485–1945, 15231

Callender, Jean A.: 'The Road to Independence: Antigua and Barbuda—A Select Bibliography', 13058

Callender, Patricia: Programmed Learning: Its Development and Structure, 22768

Calley, Malcolm J. C.: God's People: West Indian Pentecostal Sects in England, 11256, 12449

Callies, G.: 'Les Comités d'entreprise en Grande-Bretagne', 5626

Callow, Clive: Power from the Sea: The Search for North Sea Oil and Gas, 6407

Callow, Simon: Being an Actor, 26020; A Difficult Actor, 26060

Callwell, Sir Charles Edward: Field Marshal Sir Henry Wilson: His Life and Diaries, 14520; The Dardanelles, 14541

Calvert, Brian: Flying Concorde, 17573

Calvert, Harry Greenall: The Northern Ireland Problem, 2827; Constitutional Law in Northern Ireland: A Study in Regional Government, 2853

Calvert, J.: The Shipping Industry: Statistical Sources, 16520

Calvert, Michael: Chindits: Long Range Penetration, 14930; Prisoners of Hope, 14931

Calvert, Peter: The Concept of Class, 9582; Guatemala, 13034; The Falklands Crisis, 16101

Calvert, Roger: Inland Waterways of Britain, 16437; The Future of Britain's Railways, 16779

Calvocoressi, Peter: The British Experience, 1940–1975, 300; 'Foreigners in Britain', 10967; 'The Lure of the Horizon: Aspects of British Foreign Policy with particular Reference to Africa and Asia', 12837; Middle East Crisis, 14368; Total War: Causes and Courses of the Second World War, 14703

Camblin, Gilbert: The Town in Ulster, 18917

Cambon, Pierre Paul: Correspondence, 1870–1924, 14255

Cambridge Department of Architecture and Planning: The Future Shape of Cambridge: Report of the City Architect and Planning Officer, 18848; Industry and Employment: A Report on Cambridge and the Surrounding Area, 18849

Cambridge Department of Criminal Science: The Results of Probation, 10478; Sexual Offences: A Report, 10840

Cambridge History of the British Empire: Vol. III: The Empire–Commonwealth, 1870–1919, 12469.

Cambridge Institute of Criminology: Bibliographical Series, 10128

Cambridge and Isle of Ely Planning Department: Cambridge Study Area: A Progress Report, 18850

Cameron, David Kerr: Willie Gavin, Crofter Man: Portrait of a Vanished Lifestyle, 19288

Cameron, Elizabeth: Potters on Pottery, 24135

Cameron, George G.: The Scots Kirk in London, 12232

Cameron, Gordon C.: Industrial Movement and the Regional Problem, 5062; ed. Cities, Regions and Public Policy, 5063, 17835; The Relevance to the U.S. of British and French Regional Population Strategies, 5064; ed. Scottish Economic Planning and the Attraction of Industry, 5260; 'Post-War Strikes in the North-East Shipbuilding and Ship-Repairing Industry, 1946–1961', 16638

Cameron, Hector Charles: Diet and Disease in Infancy, 8129; Diseases of Children, 8130; The Nervous Child, 8131; The Nervous Child and School, 8132; 'Maternity and Child Welfare Work.' Lancet (24 Apr 1920), 8133; The British Paediatric Association 1928–1952, 20807; Mr Guy's Hospital, 1726–1948, 21444

Cameron, Ian: Wings of Morning: The Story of the Fleet Air Arm in the Second World War, 14987; Red Duster, White Ensign: The Story of the Malta Convoys, 15124; To the Farthest Ends of the Earth: The History of the Royal Geographical Society, 1830–1980, 26628

Cameron, J. M.: 'The Thirties in Britain: The Marxist Mood', 1941

Cameron, John S.: Solvent Abuse: A Guide for the Carer, 8543

Cameron, Lewis Legertwood Legg: The Challenge of Need: A History of Social Service by the Church of Scotland, 1869–1969, 12218; A Badge to be Proud of: A History of the Church of Scotland Huts and Canteens, 12219

Cameron, Neil [Baron]: In the Midst of Things: The Autobiography of Lord Cameron of Dalhousie: Marshal of the Royal Air Force, 15954

Cameron, [Mark] James [Walter]: Point of Departure, 25214

Camp, John: One Hundred Years of Medical Murder, 10799

Camp, William Newton Alexander: The Glittering Prizes: A Biographical Study of F. E. Smith, First Earl of Birkenhead, 1112

Campaign for the Care of the Deprived Child: Justice for Children: The Scottish System and its Application to Ireland, 8134

Campbell, A. D.: 'Changes in Scottish Incomes, 1924–1949', 3799

Campbell, Alan: The Industrial Relations Act: An Introduction, 5738

Campbell, Anne: Girl Delinquents, 10659

Campbell, Arthur Fraser: Jungle Green, 14933; The Siege: A Story from Kohima, 14934

Campbell, Beatrix: The Iron Ladies: Why do Women Vote Tory?, 2266, 7851; Sweet Freedom, 7797; Unofficial Secrets: Child Sex Abuse: The Cleveland Case, 8128; Wigan Pier Revisited: Poverty and Politics in the 80's, 9110

Campbell, Bernard Grant: Human Ecology: The Story of our Place in Nature from Prehistory to the Present, 20197

Campbell, C. A. C.: 'The Scottish Universities and Adult Education', 23616

Campbell, Colin: The Sports Car: Its Design and Performance, 17362

Campbell, Dorothy Adams: Eyes in Industry: A Complete Book on Eyesight Written for Industrial Workers, 4120

Campbell, Duncan: War Plan U.K., 15143; ed. Billy Connolly: The Authorised Version, Compiled and with an Introduction by Duncan Campbell, 26306

Campbell, F.: 'Latin and the Elite Tradition in Education', 23437

Campbell, Flann Canmer: Eleven Plus and All That: The Grammar School in a Changing Society, 22979

Campbell, George Archibald: The Civil Service in Britain, 848

Campbell, Sir Gerald: Of True Experience, 13257

Campbell, Gina: Bluebirds: The Story of the Campbell Dynasty, 16369, 27140

Campbell, H.: ed. A Source Book and History of Administrative Law in Scotland, 18483

Campbell, Hilary: 'Students and University Teachers: A Case Study of Informal Pressures', 9868

Campbell, Horace: 'Rastafari: Culture of Resistance', 11272

Campbell, Ian: Lewis Grassic Gibbon, 25536

Campbell, Sir Ian: The Kola Run: A Record of Arctic Convoys, 1941–1945, 15128

Campbell, J. D.: The Savings Bank of Glasgow, 4344

Campbell, J.: Changes in Mortality Trends: England and Wales 1931–1961: A Study of Trends in the Death Rates in England and Wales Analysed by Sex, Age and Cause of Death, as Part of a Survey of Trends in the United States and other Countries, 7455

Campbell, Dame Janet Mary: Maternal Mortality, 7443; Infant Mortality: International Inquiry of the Health Organisation of the League of Nations, English Section, 7444; High Maternal Mortality in Certain Areas, 7445; Maternity Services, 21972; National Health Services and Preventative Methods for improving National Health, 22056

Campbell, John: Lloyd George: The Goat in the Wilderness, 1922–1931, 1018; Nye Bevan and the Mirage of British Socialism, 1100; F. E. Smith, First Earl of Birkenhead, 1113; Roy Jenkins: A Biography, 1244

Campbell, John Menzies: 'What About Dental History?', 22410

Campbell, John Ross: Forty Fighting Years, the Communist Record, 1920–1960: Some Highlights in the Life of the Communist Party of Great Britain, 1930; 'The Development of Incomes Policy in Britain', 3813

Campbell, Judith: Elizabeth and Philip, 511

Campbell, Mrs. Patrick: My Life and some Letters, 26021

Campbell, Peter Walker: 'The Popular Press in the British General Election of 1955', 2314, 25122

Campbell, Roy Hutcheson: Scotland since 1707: The Rise of an Industrial Society, 2435, 5259; ed. Scottish Industrial History: A Miscellany, 2464; 'The Scottish Office and the Special Areas in the 1930's', 2482; 'Scottish Economic History', 3472; ed. Entrepreneurship in Britain, 1750–1939, 5415; A Source Book of Scottish Economic and Social History, 7528; 'The Church and Social Reform', 11843; 'The North British Locomotive Company between the Wars', 17069

Campbell, Roy: Light on a Dark Horse, 25435

Campbell, William Alec: A Century of Chemistry on Tyneside, 1868–1968, 6200; The Chemical Industry, 6201

Campbell-Johnson, Alan: Sir Anthony Eden: A Biography, 1007; Eden: the Making of a Statesman, 1010; Viscount Halifax: A Biography, 1220; Mission with Mountbatten, 13180; 'Reflections on the Transfer of Power', 13181

Campbell-Platt, K.: Ethnic Minorities in Society: A Reference Guide, 11519

Campbell-Smith, Duncan: The British Airways Story: Struggle for Take-off, 17627

Campion, Gilbert Francis Montriou [Baron] Campion: Parliament: A Survey, 550; An Introduction to the Procedure of the House of Commons, 650; British Government since 1918, 705

Campion, Harry: Public and Private Property in Great Britain, 3774; 'Changes in Salaries in Great Britain, 1924–1939', 3869

Camps, Miriam: 'Britain and the European Crisis', 14153; Britain and the European Community, 1955–1963, 14152

Canada in London: An Unofficial Glimpse of Canada's Sixteen High Commissioners 1880–1980, 12646

Candler, W. I.: King Edward VI High School for Girls, Birmingham, pt 1, 1883–1925, pt 2, 1926–1970, 23109

Candy, John Edwin: Mainstream of Modern Art, 23996

Cannadine, David: 'The Context, Performance and Meaning of Ritual: The British Monarchy and "The Invention of Tradition" c. 1820–1977', 451; 'British History: Past, Present and Future?', 26737; Exploring the Urban Past: Essays in Urban History by H. J. Dyos, 26766

Canneaux, Tom P.: The Trolley Buses of Newcastle upon Tyne 1935–1966, 17249

Canner, A. C.: The Parish of Tintagel: Some Historical Notes, 19358

Canning, Bernard J.: Padraig H. Pearse and Scotland: Cuimhneachan an Phiarsaigh, 1879–1979, 3068

Canning, John: ed. Living History: 1914, 389

Canning, Paul: British Policy towards Ireland 1921–1941, 2967

Cannon, Charmian: 'The Influence of Religion on Educational Policy, 1902–1944', 22903

Cannon, Geoffrey: The Food Scandal: What's Wrong with the British Diet and how to Put it Right, 20562

Cannon, Isidore Cyril: 'Ideology and Occupational Community: A Study of Compositors', 5884, 9711

Cannon, James P.: The Socialist Workers' Party in World War Two: Writings and Speeches, 1940–1943, 1974

Cannon, John Ashton: The Oxford Illustrated History of the British Monarchy, 427; 'The Survival of the British Monarchy', 452; ed. The Historian at Work, 26730; ed. The Blackwell Dictionary of Historians, 26731

Cannon, Tom: Advertising: The Economic Implications, 4319

Cannon-Brookes, Peter: Michael Ayrton: An Illustrated Commentary, 24006

Cant, Ronald Gordon: The University of St. Andrews: a Short History, 23577

Cantlie, Sir James: 'Organizing the Civil Medical Profession on Army Lines', 21306

Cantlie, Sir Neil: A History of the Army Medical Department, 20855

Cantor, Leonard Martin: Further Education in England and Wales, 23254; Further Education Today, 23255; Loughborough from College to University: a History of Higher Education at Loughborough, 1909–1966, 23537

Cantor, Milton: ed. Class, Sex and the Woman Worker, 7802

Capes, Mary: Stress in Youth: A Five Year Study of the Psychiatric Treatment, Schooling and Care of 150 Adolescents, 8454

Capie, Forrest: Depression and Protectionism: Britain between the Wars, 3584; The Inter-War British Economy: A Statistical Abstract, 3592; 'The British Tariff and Industrial Protection in the 1930's', 3758; Bank Deposits and the Quantity of Money in the United Kingdom 1870–1921, 4434; Profits and Profitability in British Banking 1870–1939, 4435; Was the War Loan Conversion a Success?, 4436; A Monetary History of the United Kingdom, 1870–1982, 4544; The Demand for Meat in England and Wales 1920–1938, 20669; 'Consumer Preference: Meat in England and Wales', 20670

Caplan, Gerald: An Approach to Community Mental Health, 21765; Principles of Preventive Psychiatry, 21766

Caplan, Neil: Futile Diplomacy Vol.1 Early Arab-Zionist Negotiation Attempts 1913–1931. Vol.2 Arab-Zionist Negotiations and the End of the Mandate, 14278; 'Britain, Zionism and the Arabs, 1917–1925', 14291

Capon, John: And Then There Was Light . . . The Story of the Nationwide Festival of Light, 11657

Caraman, Philip: C.C. Martindale: A Biography, 11995

Carberry, Thomas F.: Consumers in Politics: A History and General Review of the Co-operative Party, 1895

Carden, Robert W.: 'Before Bizonia: Britain's Economic Dilemma in Germany, 1945–1946', 14193

Carden, W. M.: ed. Public Assistance to Industry: Protection and Subsidies in Britain and Germany, 6460

Cardiff Region: A Survey Prepared for the Meeting of the British Association Held in Cardiff, 31st August to 7th September 1960, 18159

Cardozo, David Abraham Jessurun: Think and Thank: The Montefiore Synagogue and College, Ramsgate, 1833–1933, 12435

Cardus, Sir Neville: ed. Kathleen Ferrier 1912–1953, 24413; Sir Thomas Beecham, 24430; The Delights of Music: A Critic's Choice, 24532; Autobiography, 24533

Cardwell, Donald Stephen Lowell: 'Dyes and Dyeing', 7049; 'The History of Technology: Now and in the Future', 7144; 'The Academic Study of the History of Technology', 7145; ed. Artisan to Graduate, 23540

Carew, Anthony: The Lower Deck of the Royal Navy 1900–39: The Invergordon Mutiny in Perspective, 15294

Carew, Karl G.: 'Great Britain and the Greco-Turkish War, 1921–1922', 13838

Carew, Tim: Wipers, 14580; The Vanished Army, 14928; The Longest Retreat: The Burma Campaign, 1942, 14929; The Glorious Glosters: A Short History of the Gloucestershire Regiment 1945–1970, 15637; The Royal Norfolk Regiment, 15701; The Korean War, 16140

Carey, Alexander Timothy: Colonial Students: A Study of the Social Adaptation of Colonial Students in London, 11497

Carey, Hugh: Duet for Two Voices: An informal Biography of Edward Dent Compiled from his Letters to Clive Carey, 24534

Carey, John: ed. William Golding: The Man and His Books: A Tribute on his 75th Birthday, 25542

Carey, Lynette: The Sociology of Planning: A Study of Social Activity on New Housing Estates, 9367

Cargill, David: The G.P.: What's Wrong?, 21511

Cargill, Gavin: Blockade '75: The Story of the Fishermen's Blockade of the Ports, 16656

Cargill, Kenneth: Scotland 2000: Eight Views on the State of a Nation, 2459

Caribbean Commission: Current Caribbean Bibliography, 1951+, 12995

Carl, Ernst: One against England: The Death of Lord Kitchener and the Plot against the British Fleet, 14501

Carland, John M.: 'Shadow and Substance: Mackenzie King's Perceptions of British Intentions at the 1923 Imperial Conference', 12649

Carlebach, Julius: Caring for Children in Trouble, 8135

Carlen, Pat: Women's Imprisonment: A Study in Social Control, 10436

Carleton, John Dudley: Westminster, 23083

Carlile, John Charles: My Life's Little Day, 12027

Carline, Richard Cotton: Stanley Spencer at War, 24070; Pictures in the Post: The Story of the Picture Postcard, 24121

Carlisle, Kenneth: Conserving the Countryside: A Tory View, 20210

Carlsson, Gosta: 'The Decline of Fertility: Innovation or Adjustment Process?', 7489

Carlton, Charles: Bigotry and Blood: Documents on the Ulster Troubles, 2922

Carlton, David: MacDonald versus Henderson: The Foreign Policy of the Second Labour Government, 1231, 13552. 'Great Britain and the League Council Crisis of 1926', 13485;'Disarmament with Guarantees: Lord Cecil 1922–1927', 13486; 'Great Britain and the Coolidge Naval Disarmament Conference of 1927', 13489; 'The Anglo-French Compromise on Arms Limitation, 1928', 13490; 'The Problem of Civil Aviation in British Disarmament Policy, 1919–1934', 13491; 'The Dominions and British Policy in the Abyssinian Crisis', 13787; 'Eden, Blum and the Origins of Non-Intervention', 13981; Anthony Eden: A Biography, 1006; Britain and the Suez Crisis, 14388

Carlton, J.: 'Restructuring the Electricity Supply Industry', 6390

Carmichael, Alisdair: Kintyre: Best of all the Isles, 19272

Carmichael, James: Educational Revolution, 22704

Carmichael, Jane: First World War Photographers, 14617

Carmichael, John David: William Temple's Political Legacy: A Critical Assessment, 11713; Vacant Possession: A Study of Britain's 50 Year-old Housing Problem, 18670

Carne, Daphne: The Eyes of the Few, 15008

Carnegie Endowment for International Peace: Economic and Social History of the World War, 14433

Carnegie United Kingdom Trust: The Carnegie Bursary Scheme for the Training of Young Leaders, 8456; Report on the Physical Welfare of Mothers and Children, 22038; Vols. I and II: England and Wales, 22039; Vol. II: Scotland, 22040; Vol. IV Ireland, 22041

Carnell, Paul: Alternatives to Factory Farming, 19705

Carney, James Joseph: Institutional Change and the Level of Employment: A Study of British Unemployment, 1918–29, 7007

Carpenter, Alfred Francis Blakeney: The Blocking of Zeebrugge, 14658

Carpenter, Edward Frederick: Cantuar: The Archbishops in their Office, 11688; ed. The Archbishop Speaks, 11695

Carpenter, Humphrey William Bouverie: W. H. Auden: A Biography, 25360; J. R. R. Tolkien: A Biography, 25667, 25840; ed. Letters of J. R. R. Tolkien: A Selection, 25841; The Inklings: C. S. Lewis, J. R. R. Tolkien, Charles Williams and their Friends, 25878; OUDS: A Centenary of the Oxford University Dramatic Society 1885–1985, 26164

Carpenter, James Anderson: Gore: A Study in Liberal Catholic Thought, 11733

Carpenter, L. P.: G. D. H. Cole: An Intellectual Portrait, 2119; 'Corporatism in Britain 1930–1945', 2120

Carpenter, Maurice: A Rebel in the Thirties, 23741

Carpenter, Mick: Working for Health: The History of COHSE, 21694

Carpenter, N.: Programs for Older People in Great Britain, 8567

Carpenter, Peter: 'Churchill and his "Technological" College', 23473

Carpenter, Spencer Cecil: Winnington-Ingram: A Biography of Arthur Foley Winnington-Ingram. Bishop of London, 1901–1939, 11766; Duncan-Jones of Chichester, 11780

Carr, Donald Eaton: Energy and the Earth Machine, 7163; The Breath of Life, 20040

Carr, Edward Hallett: 'The Zinoviev Letter', 13938

Carr, Gordon: The Angry Brigade: The Cause and the Case, 2008

Carr, Griselda: Contraception and Family Design: A Study of Birth Planning in Contemporary Society, 7507

Carr, Ian: Music outside: Contemporary Jazz in Britain, 24455

Carr, James Cecil: History of the British Steel Industry, 6550

Carr, Sir Raymond: English Fox-hunting: A History, 27124

Carr, William Guy: By Guess and by God: The Story of the British Submarines in the War, 15366

Carr-Hill, Roy: Crime: The Police and Criminal Statistics, 10237

Carr-Saunders, Sir Alexander Morris: Consumer's Co-operation in Great Britain: An Examination of the British Co-operative Movement, 1885, 20438; Memorandum on the Present Position and Needs of the Social Sciences with Particular Reference to Population Problems, 7261; The Professions, 9766; Young Offenders: An Enquiry into Juvenile Delinquency, 10549

Carrier, John Wolfe: 'Social Policy and Social Change—Explanations of the Development of Social Policy', 8889; ed. Race and Ethnic Relations: Sociological Readings, 11055

Carrier, Norman Henry: External Migration: A Study of the Available Statistics

1850–1950, 7311; 'An Examination of Generation Fertility in England and Wales', 7372; 'The Resort to Divorce in England and Wales, 1858–1957', 9987

Carrigan, Delia: The Catholic Teachers' Colleges in the United Kingdom, 1850–1960, 22895

Carrington, Athol Sprott: Accounting: Concepts, Systems, Applications, 4191

Carrington, Charles Edmund: The Life and Reign of King George V, 472; The British Overseas: Exploits of a Nation of Shopkeepers, 12564; Soldiers from the Wars Returning, 14473

Carrington, Noel: Design and Decoration in the Home, 24114; Industrial Design in Britain, 24152

Carrington, Peter Alexander Rupert, Lord: Reflect on Things Past: The Memoirs of Lord Carrington, 1133

Carrington, Ronald: Alexandra Park and Palace: A History, 27008

Carroll, F. M.: American Opinion and the Irish Question, 1910–1923: A Study in Opinion and Policy, 2677

Carroll, Joseph Thomas: Ireland in the War Years, 2704

Carroll, M. R.: Multiple Use of Woodlands, 19751

Carruthers, Douglas: Beyond the Caspian: A Naturalist in Central Asia, 27199

Carse, Stephen: The Financing Procedures of British Foreign Trade, 4808

Carson, R. L.: 'Multiplication Tables: The Progress of Catholicism in England and Wales, 1702–1949', 11958

Carson, Wesley George: 'Some Sociological Aspects of Strict Liability and the Enforcement of Factory Legislation', 5734; The Development of Factory Legislation: The Sociology of a Law and its Enforcement, 5770; ed. Delinquency in Britain: Sociological Readings, 10266; Crime and Delinquency in Britain: Sociological Readings, 10622; Later edition with the Title 'The Sociology of Crime and Delinquency in Britain', 10623

Carson, William Arthur: Ulster and the Irish Republic, 2943

Carstairs, Andrew McLaren: The Tayside Industrial Population: The Changing Character and Distribution of the Industrial Population in the Tayside Area, 1911–1951, 5303

Carstairs, George Morrison: This Island Now: The Surge of Social Change in the Twentieth Century, 7596; Research in Social Psychiatry, 22414

Carstairs, Vera: Patients under Psychiatric Care in Hospital in Scotland, 1963, 21805

Carsten, Francis L.: War Against War: British and German Radical Movements in the First World War, 13445; Britain and the Weimar Republic: The British Documents, 13646

Carswell, John Patrick: The Civil Servant and his World, 930; Government and the Universities in Britain: Programme and Performance, 1960–1980, 23400

Carter, A. H.: 'The Lesser Evil: Some Aspects

of Income Tax Administration in the U.S.A. and the U.K., 4837

Carter, Alan: John Osborne, 25970

Carter, April: The Politics of Women's Rights, 7864

Carter, Bob: 'The 1951-1955 Conservative Government and the Racialisation of Black Immigration', 11099

Carter, Byrum E.: The Office of Prime Minister, 954

Carter, Carolle J.: The Shamrock and the Swastika: German Espionage in Ireland in World War Two, 2712

Carter, Sir Charles Frederick: ed. Manchester and its Region, 1806; The Northern Ireland Problem: A Study in Group Relations, 2826, 12161; 'Government Scientific Policy and the Growth of the British Economy', 3640; ed. Industrial Policy and Innovation, 4974; 'The Franks Report: from the Outside', 23560

Carter, Christopher J.: The Scottish New Towns: Their Contribution to Post-War Growth and Development in Central Scotland, 18180; Innovation in Planning Thought and Practice at Cumbernauld New Town, 1956-1962, 18181, 19014; 'Policy-Making and the Scottish Office: The Designation of Cumbernauld New Town', 18182

Carter, Clive: Cornish Shipwrecks, 16506

Carter, E. F. Cato: The Real Business: A Narrative of the Vital Role developed by Loss Adjusters, 4213

Carter, Edward Julian: The Future of London, 18366, 18923

Carter, Ernest Frank: Britain's Railway Liveries: Colours, Crests and Linings, 1825-1948, 16796; An Historical Geography of the Railways of the British Isles, 16835

Carter, Gwendolen Margaret: The British Commonwealth and International Security: The Role of the Dominions, 1919-1939, 12517

Carter, Harold: National Atlas of Wales, 137; The Growth of the Welsh City System, 18155; Urban Essays: Studies in the Geography of Wales, 18156; The Study of Urban Geography, 18270, 20410; The Welsh Language 1961-1981: An Interpretative Atlas, 23825; 'Distribution of the Welsh Language in 1971: An Analysis', 23831

Carter, Henry: The Methodist Heritage, 12070

Carter, John: Books and Book Collectors, 25011; A.E. Housman: A Bibliography, 25576

Carter, K. Codell: 'The Germ Theory, Beri Beri, and the Deficiency Theory of Disease', 20923

Carter, Lady Mary: A Living Soul in Holloway, 10387

Carter, Michael Percy: 'Report on a Survey of Sociological Research in Britain', 7985; Home, School and Work: A Study of the Education and Employment of Young People in Britain, 8436, 22821; Education, Employment and Leisure: A Study of Ordinary Young People, 8437; Into Work, 8438; The Social Background of Delinquency, 10554

Carter, Paul: ed. Forth and Clyde Canal Guidebook, 16423

Carter, Robert: Probation and Parole: Selected Readings, 10494

Carter, William Horsfall: Speaking European: The Anglo-Continental Cleavage, 14173

Cartland, Barbara: Ronald Cartland, 1388

Cartter, Alan Murray: The Redistribution of Income in Post-War Britain: A Study of the Effects of the Central Government Fiscal Program in 1948-1949, 3807

Cartwright, Alan K. J.: Responding to Drinking Problems, 22153

Cartwright, Ann: Patients and their Doctors: A Study of General Practice, 21514; Human Relations and Hospital Care, 21389; Life before Death, 22093

Cartwright, Frederick F.: The Development of Modern Surgery, 20879; 'The Place of Medical History in Undergraduate Education', 20924; The Development of Modern Surgery from 1830, 21153; A Social History of Medicine, 21231; Disease and History, 22351

Cartwright, John F.: Politics in Sierra Leone 1947-67, 12770

Cartwright, Mary: How Many Children?, 9925; Parents and Family Planning Services, 9926; Recent Trends in Family Planning and Contraception, 9927; Changes in Family Building Plans: A Follow-up Study to 'How Many Children?', 9928

Cartwright, T. J.: Royal Commissions and Departmental Committees in Britain: a Case Study in Institutional Adaptiveness and Public Participation in Government, 686

Carus-Wilson, Eleanora Mary: ed. Essays in Economic History, 3487

Carvel, John Lees: Fifty Years of Machine Mining Progress, 1899-1949, 6283

Carvell, John: Citizen Ken, 1453

Carver, Richard Michael Power [Baron]: The War Lords: Military Commanders of the Twentieth Century, 14742; Out of Step: The Memoirs of Field Marshal Lord Carver, 14757; Harding of Petherton: Field Marshal, 14762; El Alamein, 14892; Second to None: The Royal Scots Greys, 1919-1945, 15594

Carver, Vida: An Ageing Population, 8635

Cary, Arthur Joyce Lunel: Britain and West Africa, 12728

Cary-Elwes, Columba: ed. Ampleforth and its Origins: Essays, 22884

Casburn, Maggie: Receiving Juvenile Justice, 10644

Case, F. E.: 'Code Enforcement in Urban Renewal', 18523

Case, Robert Alfred Martin: The Chester Beatty Research Institute. Serial Bridged Life Tables; England and Wales, 1841-1960, 7378; 'Cohort Analysis of Cancer Mortality in England and Wales, 1911-1954 by Site and Sex', 22236

Casey, Richard Gardiner [Baron]: The Future of the Commonwealth, 12578; Personal Experience, 1939-1946, 12629; Friends and Neighbours: Australia and the World, 12630

Cash, Aubrey: Gifted Children: Recognising and Developing Exceptional Ability, 8113

Cash, Tony: ed. Anatomy of Pop, 24002

Cashinella, Brian: Crime in Britain Today, 10139

Cashmore, Ernest: No Future: Youth and Society, 8527; Dictionary of Race and Ethnic Relations, 11524; Rastaman: The Rastafarian Movement in England, 12446; Black Sportsmen, 27028

Cassar, George H.: Kitchener, Architect of Victory, 14510

Cassary, Robert: Robert Graves, 25549

Cassel, Karl Gustav: The Downfall of the Gold Standard, 4695

Cassell, Michael: Inside Nationwide: One Hundred Years of Co-operation, 4389

Cassell, Richard: Ford Madox Ford: A Study of his Novels, 25511

Cassels, Alan: 'Repairing the Entente Cordiale and the New Diplomacy', 13652, 14249

Cassen, Robert H.: 'Social Priorities and Economic Policy', 9054; Does Aid Work? Report to an Intergovernmental Task Force, 9189

Casserley, Henry Cecil: Welsh Railways in the Heyday of Steam, 17046

Casson, John: Using Words: Verbal Communications in Industry, 5703; Lewis & Sybil. A Memoir, 26107

Casson, Mark: The Future of the Multinational Enterprise, 5561; Alternatives to Multinational Enterprise, 5562; The Firm and the Market: Studies on Multinational Enterprise and the Scope of the Firm, 5563

Castelli, Louis: David Lean: A Guide to References and Resources, 24678

Castle, Barbara: The Castle Diaries, 1974-1976, 1139; The Castle Diaries, 1964-1970, 1140

Castle, Charles: Noel, 25955

Castle, Colin M.: Better by Yards, 16620

Castle, Harold George: Britain's Motor Industry, 17395

Castle, I. M.: 'The Distribution of Social Defects in Liverpool', 18045

Castle, Tony: Basil Hulme: A Portrait, 11993

Castles, Stephen: Immigrant Workers and Class Structure in Western Europe, 11422

Cathcart, Helen: Princess Margaret, 526; Prince Charles: the Biography, 532; Anne, The Princess Royal: A Princess for our Times, 534

Cathcart, Rex: The Most Contrary Region: The B.B.C. in Northern Ireland, 2886

Cathie, John: Farm Modernisation and the Countryside, 19529

Catholic Archives, 11933

Catholic Directory of England and Wales: 1839+, 11932

Catlin, Sir George E. C.: For God's Sake, Go! An Autobiography, 2112

Cato, Conrad: The Navy in Mesopotamia, 1914-1917, 14561

Cattell, Raymond Bernard: Human Affairs, 22054

Catterall, Peter: 'The State of the Literature on Post-War British History', 425; British

History 1945–1987: An Annotated Bibliography, 426

Caulcott, T. H.: 'The Control of Public Expenditure', 4736

Caulfield, Max: The Easter Rebellion, 2736

Caunter, Cyril F.: The History and Development of Cycles, 7057, 17167; The History and Development of Motorcycles, 17176; The Light Car: A Technical History of Cars with Engines less than 1600 c.c. Capacity, 17365

Causey, Andrew: Paul Nash, 24046

Caute, David: Under the Skin: The Death of White Rhodesia, 12802; 'Crisis in All Souls: a Case History in Reform', 23561

Cavaliero, Glen: A Reading of E. M. Forster, 25524; John Cowper Powys: Novelist, 25770

Cavanagh, John: British Theatre: A Bibliography 1901–1985, 25898

Cave, Lyndon F.: Warwickshire Villages, 19147

Cave, P. W.: 'Occupancy Duration and the Analysis of Residential Change', 18524

Cave, Roderick George James Munro: The Private Press, 25002

Cavenagh, Winifred Elizabeth: Four Decades of Students in Social Work, 8662; The Child and the Court, 10650; The Problem Family, 10651

Cavendish, Anthony: Inside Intelligence, 16017

Cavendish, Jean Mavis: A Handbook of British Publishing Practice, 24999

Caves, Richard Earl: Britain's Economic Prospects, 3657

Cavitch, David: D.H. Lawrence and the New World, 25633

Cawkwell, Timothy: Long Live the Village Hall!: A Survey of the Use of Village Halls, 19132

Cawley, Robert: ed. Policy for Action: A Symposium on the Planning of a Comprehensive District Psychiatric Service, 21640; ed. Movements, and Directions in Health Services Research: The Papers and Proceedings of a Meeting, 21641; ed. Probes for Health: Essays from the Health Services Research Centre, University of Birmingham, 21642; ed. [Working Group for the Evaluation of The Quality of Care.]. A Question of Quality? Roads to Assurance in Medical Care: [a report by the W.G.E.Q.C.], 21643; ed. The Way Ahead in Postgraduate Medical Education, 21644; ed. Bridging in Health: Reports of Studies on Health Services for Children, by F. W. S. Brimblecombe et al., 21645; ed. The British National Health Service: Policy Trends and their Implication for Education, 21646; ed. By Guess or by What? Information without Design in the N.H.S., 21647. ed. Challenges for Change: Essays on the Next Decade in the National Health Service, 21648; ed. Five Years After: A Review of Health Care Research Management after Rothschild, 21649; ed. Policy for Action: A Symposium on the Planning of a Comprehensive District Psychiatric Service, 21844

Caws, K. B.: Town and Country Planning, 20361

Ceadel, Martin: 'The First British Referendum: The Peace Ballot, 1934–5', 13506; 'The "King and Country" Debate, 1933: Student Politics, Pacifism and the Dictators', 13509; Pacifism in Britain 1914–1945: The Defining of a Faith, 13515

Cecil, Edward Christian David Gasgoyne [Lord]: Max: A Biography, 24107, 25371

Cecil, Hugh Richard Heathcote [Baron] Quickswood: Anglo-Catholicism Today, 11650

Cecil, Robert: A Divided Life: A Biography of Donald Maclean, 16038

Cell, John W.: 'On the Eve of Decolonisation: The Colonial Office's Plans for the Transfer of Power in Africa',12695

Celtic League Annual, 1969–1972:-, 2427

Cemach, Harry Paul: Work Study in the Office, 5419

Census Research Unit, University of Durham: People in Britain: A Census Atlas, 142

Center for Naval Analyses: Naval Abstracts, 15228

Central Board of Finance of the Church of England: Church Statistics: Some Facts and Figures about the Church of England, 11548

Central Electricity Authority: Report and Statement of Accounts, 6383

Central Electricity Generating Board: Annual Report and Accounts, 6384; Towards a Clean Air Policy, 20048

Central Housing Advisory Committee: Moving from the Slums: Seventh Report of the Housing Management Sub-Committee, 18394

Central Office of Information: Technical and Specialised Periodicals published in Britain: A Selected List, 161; The Treatment of Offenders in Britain, 10206; Paiforce: The Official History of the Persia and Iraq Command 1941–1946, 13857; Health Services in Britain, 21995; The Prevention and Treatment of Drug Dependence in Britain, 22212

Central Policy Review Staff: Relations between Central Government and Local Authorities, 3222

Central Statistical Office, 57; United Kingdom Balance of Payments, 1963–1973, 4928

Centre for Agricultural Strategy, University of Reading: National Food Supply in the United Kingdom, 20614

Centre for Contemporary Cultural Studies: The Empire Strikes Back: Race and Racism in 70s Britain, 11089

Centre for Environmental Studies: Working Papers, 17847

Centre for Studies in Social Policy: Social Policy and Public Expenditure, 8943

Centre for Urban Studies: Quinquennial Report, 17939

Cerych, L.: 'An International View of British Higher Education', 23305

Cesarani, David: ed. The Making of Modern Anglo-Jewry, 11285

Ch'en, Wei-kiung: The Doctrine of Civil Service Neutrality in Party Conflicts in the United States and Great Britain, 894

Chadwick-Jones, J. K.: 'Italian Workers in a British Factory: A Study of Informal Selection and Training', 11385

Chadwick, George Fletcher: The Park and the Town: Public Landscape in the 19th and 20th centuries, 20317, 27007

Chadwick, Hubert: St Omers to Stonyhurst: A History of Two Centuries, 22883

Chadwick, Lynn: Lynn Chadwick, 24184

Chadwick, William Owen: The History of the Church: A Select Bibliography, 11527; Michael Ramsey: A Life, 11700; Hensley Henson, 11739; The Founding of Cuddesdon, 11910; ed. From Uniformity to Unity, 1662–1962, 12001; Britain and the Vatican during the Second World War, 14116; 'Acton and Butterfield', 26783

Chadwick-Jones, John K.: 'Shift-working: Physiological Effects and Social Behaviour', 5885; Automation and Behaviour: A Social Psychological Study, 7251

Chafetz, Janet Saltzman: 'Room at the Top: Social Recognition of British and American Females over Time', 7815

Chalfont, Alun Gwynne Jones [Baron]: Montgomery of Alamein, 14772

Chaline, Claude: 'La Nouvelle Génération des "New Towns" Britanniques', 18250; 'Les 'Expanded Towns' de la Région de Londres', 18355; 'Nouveaux Aspects de la Cité de Londres', 18356; La Métropole Londonienne: Croissance et Planification Urbaine, 18572; L'Urbanisme en Grande-Bretagne, 18573

Chall, Jeanne Sternlight: Learning to Read: The Great Debate: An Inquiry into the Science, Art and Ideology of Old and New Methods of Teaching Children to Read, 1910–1965, 22762

Challinor, Raymond: The Origins of British Bolshevism, 1926; The Lancashire and Cheshire Miners, 9651

Chalmers, Archibald Kerr: Can the 'Undesirable Tenant' be Trained in Citizenship?, 18589; Economy in Food during War, 20574; The Health of Glasgow, 1818–1925: An Outline, 22063

Chalmers, Chick: Islanders, 19254

Chalmers, Eric Brownlie: ed. Monetary Policy in the Sixties: The U.K., the U.S.A. and West Germany, 4608; ed. United Kingdom Monetary Policy, 4609; The Money World: A Guide to Money and Banking in the Age of Inflation, 4637

Chalmers, William Scott: Max Horton and the Western Approaches, 14981; The Life and Letters of David, Earl Beatty, 15248

Chalmin, P.: Tate and Lyle: Sugar Giant, 20685; 'The Strategy of a Multi-National in the World Sugar Economy: The Case of Tate and Lyle, 1870–1980', 20686

Chaloner, William Henry: Bibliography of British Economic and Social History, 395, 3387, 7527; Trade and Transport: Essays in Economic History in Honour of T. S. Willan, 3413, 16213, 16618; 'The British Miners and the Coal Industry between the Wars', 6277; 'The British Miners and the Coal Industry between the Wars', 9632; The Social and Economic Development of Crewe, 1780–1923, 18101

Chamberlain, Christopher W.: 'The Growth of Support for the Labour Party in Britain', 1755; 'Lower Class Attitudes to Property: Aspects of the Counter Ideology', 9451; 'Lower Class Attitudes towards the British Political System', 9691

Chamberlain, Geoffrey: Airships—Cardington: A History of Cardington Airship Station and its Role in World Airship Development, 17538

Chamberlain, Sir [Joseph] Austen: Peace in our Time: Addresses on Europe and the Empire, 1144; Down the Years: A Volume of Essays on Men and Affairs, 1145; Seen in Passing . . . (1937), 1146

Chamberlain, Mary Walls: Guide to Art Reference Books, 23936

Chamberlain, Muriel Evelyn: Decolonization: The Fall of the European Empires, 12594; Britain and India, 13107

Chamberlain, Peter: Modern British Tanks and Fighting Equipment, 15517; British and American Tanks of World War II, 15518; The Churchill Tank: The Story of Britain's Most Famous Tank, 1939–1965, 15519; Tanks of World War I: British and German, 15520

Chamberlain, Roma: The Prevalence of Illness in Children, 21905

Chamberlin, E. R.: Life in Wartime Britain, 15172

Chambers, Colin: A History of Unity Theatre, 26238

Chambers, Frances: Guyana, 13035; Trinidad and Tobago, 13063

Chambers, Gerry: ed. The British Crime Survey: Scotland, 10269

Chambers, Joanna: Abortion Politics, 7879

Chambers, Jonathan David: A Select Bibliography of Rural Economic History, 19389

Chambers, Peter: Called Up: The Personal Experience of Sixteen National Servicemen, 16066

Chambers, Ralph Frederick: The Strict Baptist Chapels of England, 12032

Chambers, Rosalind: Social Science and Social Pathology, 7929, 10173

Chambers, V. H.: Old Meppershall: A Parish History, 19347

Chamier, John Adrian: The Birth of the Royal Air Force: The Early History and Experiences of the Flying Services, 14619

Champ, Robert Gordon: The Illustrated History of Sunbeam Bicycles and Motorcycles, 17174

Champernowne, David Gawen: 'Comparisons of Measures of Inequality of Income Distribution', 3844; The Distribution of Incomes between Persons, 3845; 'A Model of Income Distribution', 3846; 'The Determinants of Wage Inflation: United Kingdom, 1946–1956: A Discussion', 3990

Champion, Anthony Gerard: The Urban and Regional Transformation of Britain, 5122; Changing Places: Britain's Demographic, Economic and Social Complexion, 7439; Facts about the New Towns: A Socio-economic Digest, 18174; 'Population Characteristics of the British New Towns', 18256; Facts about the New Towns: A Socio-economic Digest, 19001; 'Population Trends in Rural Britain', 19073; Regional Conversions of Agricultural Land to Urban Use in England and Wales, 1945–1967, 20257

Champion, Leonard George: 'Reflections upon the Present Curriculum of Theological Colleges', 11902

Chan, K. C.: 'Britain's Reaction to Chiang Kai-Shek's Visit to India, February 1942', 13163

Chanan, Michael: 'Commitment and Disillusion: British Cinema, 1956–1969', 24654

Chance, B.: Ophthalmology, 21104

Chance, Sir Frederick William: 'Public House Reform at Carlisle', 22167

Chance, Michael: Our Princesses and their Dogs, 509

Chandler, Dean: The Rise of the Gas Industry in Britain, 6398

Chandler, George: Four Centuries of Banking, 4400; Liverpool Shipping: A Short History, 16474

Chandler, M. J.: A Guide to Records in Barbados, 13074

Chandrasekhar, B. K.: 'Trade Union Government: Regulation by Registration—A Comparative Study', 6791

Chandrasekhar, P.: 'The Rhodesian Crisis and the Use of Force', 12814

Chandrasekhar, S.: Eddington: The Most Distinguished Astrophysicist of his time, 26379

Chaney, D. C.: Television and Delinquency, 24834

Chang, Joseph Y. S.: ed. Hong Kong in the 1980s, 12977; ed. Hong Kong in Transition, 12978; ed. 'A Draft Agreement between the Government of the United Kingdom of Great Britain and Northern Ireland and the Government of the People's Republic of China on the Future of Hong Kong', 12979

Chang, Tse Chun: 'The British Balance of Payments, 1924–1933', 4919

Channel Four Television History Workshop: Making Cars: A History of Car-making in Cowley, 17407

Channon, Derek French: British Banking Strategy and the International Challenge, 4444

Channon, Geoffrey: 'The Great Western Railway under the British Railways Act of 1921', 16866

Chant, Chris: The Illustrated History of the Air Forces of World War I and World War II, 15799

Chantler, P.: The British Gas Industry: An Economic Study, 6411

Chaplin, Charles: My Autobiography, 26303

Chaplin, Howard Douglas: The Queen's Own Royal West Kent Regiment, 1951–1961, 15674

Chaplin, K. W.: ed. Health Care in the United Kingdom—Its Organisation and Management, 21608

Chapman, Agatha Louisa: Wages and Salaries in the United Kingdom, 1920–1938, 3887

Chapman, Arthur William: The Story of a Modern University: A History of the University of Sheffield, 23579

Chapman, Brian: The Profession of Government, 710

Chapman, Chris: The Right Side of the Hedge: Country Life Today, 19105

Chapman, Dennis: People and their Homes, 9515; The Home and Social Status, 9516, 18639; Sociology and the Stereotype of the Criminal, 10214, 10259; The Location of Dwellings in Scottish Towns: An Inquiry into some of the Factors Relevant to the Planning of New Urban Communities, made for the Department of Health for Scotland, 18128; Heating in Dwellings Inquiry, 18614; Lighting in Dwellings Inquiry, 18615; Sound in Dwellings . . . An Inquiry, 18616; A Survey of Noise in British Homes, 18617; A Social Survey of Middlesbrough . . . an Inquiry into some of the Factors Relevant to the Planning of Urban Communities made for the Ministry of Town and Country Planning, 18892

Chapman, Graham Peter: Human and Environmental Systems: A Geographical Appraisal, 19945

Chapman, H.: 'Cost Benefit Analysis in Urban Expansion: A Case Study, 18023

Chapman, J. S.: The Characteristics of London's Households, 18676; The Condition of London's Housing: A Survey, 18677

Chapman, J. Vincent: Your Secondary Modern Schools: An Account of their Work in the Late 1950s, 22935

Chapman, Jennifer: The Last Bastion, 11670

Chapman, Keith: North Sea Oil and Gas: A Geographical Perspective, 6492

Chapman, Malcolm: The Gaelic Vision in Scottish Culture, 23736

Chapman, Paul G.: The Youth Training Scheme in the U.K., 8546

Chapman, Peter: Fuel's Paradise: Energy Options for Britain, 7215

Chapman, Richard Arnold: ed. The Role of Commissions in Policy Making, 685; ed. Open Government, 771; The Dynamics of Administrative Reform, 782; 'The Fulton Report: A Summary', 857; 'The Civil Service after Fulton', 862; The Higher Civil Service in Britain, 868; Leadership in the British Civil Service: A Study of Sir Percival Waterfield and the Creation of the Civil Service Selection Board, 914; 'Administrative Culture and Personnel Management: The British Civil Service in the 1980s', 920; Ethics in the British Civil Service, 925; 'The Bank Rate Decision of 19 September 1957: A Case Study in Joint Decision Making', 4572; Decision Making: A Case Study of the Decision to Raise the Bank Rate in December 1957, 4639; ed. Public Policy Studies: The North East of England, 18064

Chapman, Stanley David: The Rise of Merchant Banking, 4463

Chapman, Sydney David: ed. The History of Working-Class Housing: A Symposium, 18722; Town and Countryside: Future Planning Policies for Britain, 18808

Chapman, Ted: Cornwall Aviation Company, 17619

Chapman-Huston, Desmond: Through a City Archway. The Story of Allen and Hanburys, 1715–1954, 22277

Chappell, D.: 'No Questions Asked: A Consideration of the Criminal Crime of Receiving', 10213

Chappell, Edgar Leyshon: Wake up Wales!: A Survey of Welsh Home Rule Activities, 2592

Chappell, William: Fonteyn: Impressions of a Ballerina, 24229

Chaput, Rolland A.: Disarmament in British Foreign Policy, 13487

Charities Digest: 1882+, 9114

Charles, Sir John Alexander: Research and Public Health, 22074

Charles Roberts & Company: Charles Roberts & Company Limited 1836–1951, 17079

Charles, Enid: The Effects of Present Trends in Fertility and Mortality upon the Future Population of England and Wales and upon its Age Composition, 7476; The Practice of Birth Control: An Analysis of Birth-control Experiences of Nine Hundred Women, 7477; The Twilight of Parenthood: A Biological Study of the Decline of the Population Growth, 7478; The Menace of Underpopulation, 7479

Charles, Rodger: The Development of Industrial Relations in Britain, 1911–1939: Studies in the Evolution of Collective Bargaining at National and Industrial Level, 5578, 6127

Charlesworth, George E.: A History of the Transport and Road Research Laboratory 1933–1983, 16225; A History of British Motorways, 17109

Charlesworth, Harold Karr: The Economics of Repressed Inflation, 3984

Charley, Irene H.: The Birth of Industrial Nursing: Its History and Development in Great Britain, 21706

Charlot, Monica: 'La Reforme des Relations du Travail en Grande-Bretagne', 5750; Le Syndicalisme en Grande Bretagne, 6735; ed. Naissance d'un Problème Racial: Minorités de Couleur en Grande Bretagne, 11172; Britain and Europe since 1945, 14188

Charlton, David: The Administration of Technical Colleges, 23290

Charlton, Henry Buckley: Portrait of a University 1851–1951, 23539

Charlton, Lionel Evelyn Oswald: Britain at War: The Royal Air Force and U.S.A.A.F, 14976

Charlton, Michael: The Little Platoon: Diplomacy and the Falklands Dispute, 16096

Charmley, John: Duff Cooper: The Authorized Biography, 1151; Lord Lloyd and the Decline of the British Empire, 1455

Charney, Maurice: Joe Orton, 25966

Chartered Institute of Bankers: Bank Strategies for the 1990's, 4455

Chartered Institute of Transport: Consumers in Transport, 16258

Charterhouse: Charterhouse, 23048; From a New Angle: Reminiscences of Charterhouse, 1880–1945, 23049

Charteris, John: At G.H.Q., 15480

Charters, David A.: 'Intelligence and Psychological Warfare Operations in Northern Ireland', 2901

Chater, Anthony: Race Relations in Britain, 10949

Chaterton, Michael: 'Assessing Police Effectiveness—Future Prospects', 10777

Chatfield, Michael: A History of Accounting Thought, 4170; An Introduction to Financial Accounting, 4171

Chatham House Study Group: Britain in Western Europe: WEU and the Atlantic Alliance, 14146

Chatterton, Edward Keble: Dardanelles Dilemma: The Story of Naval Operations, 14542; The Big Blockade, 14605; Q-Ships and their Story, 14683; The Sea Raiders, 14684; Britain at War: The Royal Navy and Allies, 14690; Fighting the U-Boats, 14794; Beating the U-boats, 14795

Chatterton, George James Stewart: The Wings of Pegasus, 15007

Chatwin, A. H.: Bushbury—Parish and People, 1550–1950, 19324

Chave, Sidney: Mental Health and Environment, 21807

Chayen, Edna: Persistent Criminals: A Study of all Criminals Liable to Preventative Detention in 1956, 10202

Chazan, Maurice: The Practice of Educational Psychology, 22856; ed. Aspects of Primary Education, 23150

Cheater, B. J.: ed. Birmingham Airport: 40th Anniversary Official Handbook, 17671

Checkland, Olive: 'Housing Policy: The Formative Years: A Review Article', 18763; ed. Health Care as Social History, 21964

Checkland, Sydney G.: Scottish Banking: A History, 1695–1973, 4404; 'Scottish Economic History: Recent Work', 5250; ed. Dictionary of Scottish Business Biography, 1860–1960, 9786; The Upas Tree: Glasgow 1875–1975: A Study in Growth and Contraction, 18137; 'Housing Policy: The Formative Years: A Review Article', 18763; 'The British New Towns as Politics: A Review Article', 19005

Chee, Chan Heng: A Sensation of Independence: A Political Biography of David Marshall, 12963

Cheek, Neil H.: Social Behaviour, Natural Resources and the Environment, 19973

Cheeseman, Eric Arthur: Epidemics in Schools, 21946

Cheeseman, H. R.: Bibliography of Malaya: Being a Classified List of Books wholly or partly in English Relating to the Federation of Malaya and Singapore, 12898

Cheesman, David: Neighbourhood Care and Old People: A Community Development Project, 8606

Cheesman, Robert Ernest: Lake Tana and the Blue Nile: An Abyssinian Quest, 27198

Cheesman, Robert: New Towns: A Comparative Atlas, 18212; The Evolution of Planning Criteria, 18213

Cheetham, Juliet: Social Work with Immigrants, 8762; Social Work Services for Ethnic Minorities in Britain and the USA,

8763; Social and Community Work in a Multicultural Society, 8764; Unwanted Pregnancy and Counselling, 9944

Chellaston History Group: A History of Chellaston, 19184

Cheltenham: Cheltenham College. The First Hundred Years, 23050

Chenevix Trench, Charles Pocklington: The Poacher and the Squire: A History of Poaching and Game Preservation in England, 19110

Chennels, E.: 'Professional Civil Servants: A Study in the Sociology of Public Administration, 916

Cherns, Albert Bernard: ed. Social Science Research and Industry, 5745; 'The Problems Facing the Social Science Research Council during its First Year of Existence', 7937; 'Organised Social Science Research in Great Britain', 7938; Research in Universities, Independent Institutes and Government Departments: Eleven Contributions to a Discussion', 7939; ed. Social Science and Government: Policies and Problems, 8817

Cherrett, Paul: After Grace—Teeth: A Comparative Study of the Residential Experiment of Boys and Approved Schools, 10509

Cherrington, Paul: 'Management Education in Britain', 23658

Cherry, Gordon E.: Employment Problems in a County Town: A Study of Bridgnorth, Shropshire, 7015; The Evolution of British Town Planning: A History of Town Planning in the United Kingdom during the 20th Century and of the Royal Town Planning Institute, 1914–74, 17728; ed. Urban Change and Planning: A History of Urban Development since 1750, 17729, 18786; ed. Town Planning in its Social Context, 17730, 18784; ed. Urban Planning Problems, 17731, 18787; ed. Rural Planning Problems, 17732; National Parks and Recreation in the Countryside, 17733; Social Research Techniques for Planners, 17734, 18788; ed. Urban and Regional Planning, 17923, 18785; ed. Pioneers in British Town Planning, 18781; ed. Planning and the Environment in the Modern World, 18782; ed. The Politics of Town Planning, 18783; Environmental Planning 1939–1969 Volume II: National Parks and Recreation in the Countryside, 18794, 26955; Holford: A Study in Architecture, Planning and Civic Design, 23877

Cherry, John: Archaeology in Britain since 1945, 26357

Cheshire, Paul: Agriculture, the Countryside and Land Use: An Economic Critique, 19588

Chesser, Eustace: Cruelty to Children, 8137; Challenge of the Middle Years, 8552; Living with Suicide, 10819; Live and Let Live: The Moral of the Wolfenden Report, 10860

Chesshyre, D. H. B.: The Green: A History of the Heart of Bethnal Green and the Legend of the Blind Beggar, 18341

Chester, Charlie: The Grand Order of Water

Rats: A Legend of Laughter, 26290; The World is Full of Charlies. Recollections of a Lifetime in Showbusiness, 26305

Chester, Sir [Daniel] Norman: The Organisation of British Central Government, 1914–1956, 711; Central and Local Government: Financial and Administrative Relations, 3120, 3221; Lessons of the British War Economy, 3734; The Nationalised Industries: An Analysis of the Statutory Provisions, 6060; The Nationalisation of British Industry, 1945–1951, 6061; 'The Treasury, 1962', 6097; 'The British Treasury and Economic Planning', 6098; 'Political Studies in Britain: Recollections and Comments', 26889; Economics, Politics and Social Studies at Oxford, 1900–85, 26891

Chester, Lewis: Cops and Robbers: Jeremy Thorpe: A Secret Life, 1533; An Investigation into Armed Bank Robbery, 10236; et al. The Zinoviev Letter, 13935; The Fall of the House of Beaverbrook, 25130

Chester, Robert: 'Contemporary Trends in the Stability of English Marriage', 9978; ed. Equalities and Inequalities of Family Life, 10012

Chester, T. E.: 'The Nationalised Industries in Great Britain', 6124; 'The Distribution of Power in Nationalised Industries', 6134

Chesterton, A. K.: Mosley: Portrait of a Leader, 1487

Chesterton, Ada Elizabeth: In Darkest London, 18334

Cheung, Steven N. S.: The Myth of Social Cost: A Critique of Welfare Economics and their Implications for Public Policy, 8955

Chew, Hilary C.: 'Changes in Land Use and Stock over England and Wales, 1939–1951', 19496

Cheyne, Alexander C.: The Transforming of the Kirk: Victorian Scotland's Religious Revolution, 12213

Cheyne, William M.: Studies in Pre-school Education: Empirical Studies in Pre-school Units in Scotland and their Implications for Educational Practice, 23167

Chiari, Joseph: Britain and France, the Unruly Twins, 14238

Chibnall, Steve: Law-and-order News: An Analysis of Crime Reporting in the British Press, 25321

Chick, Harriette: War on Disease: A History of the Lister Institute, 20902; 'The Lister Institute of Preventive Medicine', 20925

Chicken, John Charles: Hazard Control Policy in Britain, 20005

Child, H. A. T.: ed. The Independent Progressive School, 23017

Child, John: 'Quaker Employers and Industrial Relations', 5669; Industrial Relations in the British Printing Industry: The Quest for Security, 5670; The Society of London Bookbinders, 1780–1951, 6840

Children and Society: Special Issue 'Lessons of Cleveland', 8138

Childrens Nutritional Council, Aberdeen Branch: A Budgetary and Dietary Survey of Low Income Families: Aberdeen, August 1942, 20521

Childs, William MacBride: Making of a University, 23575

Chilver, Richard Clementson: ed. Pollution Abatement, 19994

Chin, K. W.: The Defence of Malaysia and Singapore: The Transformation of a Security System, 1957–1971, 12941

Chingford Community Association: Chingford Community Association, 1940–1965, 9352

Chinkin, C. M.: 'The Local Ombudsman', 3255

Chinn, George Morgan: The Machine Gun, 15501

Chinoy, Ely: 'Social Stratification: Theory and Synthesis', 9505

Chiplin, Brian: Sex Discrimination in the Labour Market, 7788; 'Sexual Discrimination in the Labour Market', 7789

Chipperfield, Jimmy: My Wild Life, 26351

Chisholm, Cecil: Repertory: An Outline of the Modern Theatre Movement, 26193

Chisholm, Michael Donald Inglis: Geography and Economics, 5074; 'Regional Policies for the 1970s', 5075; The Changing Pattern of Employment: Regional Specialisation and Industrial Localisation in Britain, 5076; ed. Spatial Policy Problems of the British Economy, 5077, 17821; Regional Forecasting: Proceedings of the Twenty Second Symposium of the Colston Research Society, 5078; 'Agricultural Production, Location and Rent', 19513; Human Geography: Evolution or Revolution?, 26685; ed. Studies in Human Geography, 26686

Chisolm, Cecil: The £.s.d. of Retirement, 8610; Retire and Enjoy It, 8611; Retire into the Sun: A Survey of Some Possibilities in Nine Paradises, 8612

Chitty, Lady Susan Elspeth Russel: Gwen John 1876–1936, 24027

Chlords, Alexander George: ed. A Bibliographical Guide to the Law of the United Kingdom, the Channel Islands and the Isle of Man, 10286

Choen, Henry [Baron]: 'The Liverpool Medical School and its Physicians (1642–1934)', 20931

Chorley, Richard John: Environmental Systems: Philosophy, Analysis and Control, 19944

Chou, Ru-chi: 'A Comparison of the Size of Families of Roman Catholics and Non-Catholics in Great Britain', 7490

Choulant, Johann Ludwig: History and Bibliography of Anatomic Illustration, 21040

Chowdharay-Best, George: The Cross of Saint Patrick: The Catholic Unionist Tradition in Ireland, 2952

Chown, J. F.: 'Merchant Banks in Britain and the New Europe', 4464

Chown, Sheila M.: Ageing and Semi-skilled: A Survey in Manufacturing Industry on Merseyside, 8571; The Home Help Service in England and Wales, 8591

Chrimes, Mike: ed. Thames Tunnel to Channel Tunnel: 150 Years of Civil Engineering, 16365

Chrimes, Stanley Bertram: English Constitutional History, 575; English Constitutional History: A Select Bibliography, 629; ed. The General Election in Glasgow, February 1950, 2301

Christ's Hospital: Christ's Hospital, 23051; The Christ's Hospital Book, 23052

Christensen, Eric: Automation and the Workers, 7247

Christian Action: The Gorbals 1965: A Report of An Investigation into the Housing and Social Conditions of the Gorbals and Adjacent Slum Areas of Glasgow, 18479

Christian Economic and Social Research Foundation: The Differences between Scottish Drunkenness and Drunkenness in England and Wales, 22137

Christian, Roy: The 'Country Life' Book of Old English Customs, 9907; Old English Customs, 9908

Christiansen, Arthur: Headlines all my Life, 25220

Christiansen, Clara E.: Scholar's Guide to Intelligence Literature, 15994

Christiansen, Rex: The West Midlands, 16815; Thames and Severn, 16821

Christie, Agatha: An Autobiography, 25448

Christie, E. W. Hunter: The Antarctic Problem: An Historical and Political Study, 27220

Christie, Ian: 'Covent Garden: Approaches to Urban Renewal', 18319; 'Act Two', 18320; 'Vegetarians' Subsidy', 18321; 'Needed: A National Environmental Planning Policy', 19930

Christie, Mabel Elizabeth: The Evolution of the English Farm, 19403

Christoph, James B.: 'Political Rights and Administrative Impartiality in the British Civil Service', 899; 'The Press and Politics in Britain and America', 25054

Christopher, Anthony: Policy for Poverty, 9067

Christopher, Joe E.: C. S. Lewis: An Annotated Checklist of Writings about him and his Works, 25660; C. S. Lewis, 25666

Christophers, Samuel Rickard: 'Symposium to Commemorate the "Birth of Medical Entomology" Dedicated to Sir Rickard Christophers on his 100th birthday', 21077; A Tribute to Sir Rickard Christophers on his 100th Birthday, 21078

Christopherson, Sir Derman: The University at Work, 23297

Chronological Table of the Statutes: Northern Ireland, 2778

Church Commissioners for England: Annual Report: 1949+, 11534

Church History: 1932+, 11539

Church of England: (Church Information Office): Homes for Old People: A Church of England Guide to Helping with Accommodation and other Practical Problems, 8574

Church of England: Facts and Figures about the Church of England, 11535

Church of England: Faith in the City: A Call for Action by Church and Nation, 11844

Church of England Committee for Diocesan Moral and Social Welfare Councils: A

Directory of Social and Moral Welfare Work, 9203

Church of England Committee of Social Services: Directory of Church of England Social Services, 9204

Church of England Council for Social Work: Annual Report, 9201

Church of England Moral Welfare Council: Sexual Offenders and Social Punishment, 10841

Church of England: National Assembly Board for Social Responsibility. Fatherless by Law? The Law and Welfare of Children Designated Illegitimate, 8139

Church of England Official Yearbook: 1885+, 11532

Church of Scotland Yearbook: 1930+, 12188

Church, Richard Thomas: Autobiography, 25452

Church, Roy Anthony: 'Myths, Men and Motor Cars: A Review Article', 17368; 'Motor Manufacturing', 17405; Herbert Austin: The British Motor Car Industry to 1941, 17422

Churchill Machine Tool Company: The Story of the Churchill Machine Tool Co. Ltd.: A History of Precision Grinding: Golden Jubilee, 1906–1956, 6378

Churchill, Randolph Spencer: Churchill, 988; Churchill: His Life in Photographs, 988; The Rise and Fall of Sir Anthony Eden, 1007; Lord Derby . . . : The Official Life of Edward, Lord Derby, 17th Earl of Derby 1865–1948, 1183; The Fight for the Tory Leadership: A Contemporary Chronicle, 1639

Churchill, Sir Winston Leonard Spencer: Great Contemporaries, 319, 988; The World Crisis, 988; A History of the English Speaking Peoples, 988; The Second World War, 988, 14704; Arms and the Covenant, 989; Step by Step, 1936–1939, 990; Into Battle, 991; The Unrelenting Struggle, 992; Onwards to Victory, 993; The End of the Beginning, 994; The Dawn of Liberation, 995; Victory, 996; The Sinews of Peace, 997; Europe Unite, 998; In the Balance, 999; Stemming the Tide, 1000; Secret Session Speeches, 1003; Unwritten Alliance: Speeches, 1953–1959, 1003; War speeches 1940–1945, 1003

Cianfrani, T.: A Short History of Obstetrics and Gynecology, 21101

Ciba Foundation: Health Care in a Changing Setting: The UK Experience, 21665

Cienciala, Anna M.: Poland and the Western Powers, 1938–1939: A Study in the Interdependence of Eastern and Western Europe, 13893

Cioffi, Frank: 'The Measurement of Supervisory Methods', 5866

City of Leeds Training College: A Short History of the City of Leeds Training College, 1907–1957, 22747

City of London: The City of London School, 23053

City of Westminster Chamber of Commerce: Travelling to Work: Report of a Working Party, 16279

Civic Trust: Heavy Lorries Nine Years On

. . ., 17465; The Local Amenity Movement, 17975; Financing the Preservation of Old Buildings: A Report, 18964

Civil Service Commission: Annual Report 1855+, 875

Clabby, John: The History of the Royal Army Veterinary Corps, 1919–1961, 15771

Clack, Garfield: Industrial Relations in a British Car Factory, 5693; Labour Relations in the Motor Industry: A Study of Industrial Unrest and an International Comparison, 7242

Clair, Colin: A History of Printing in Britain, 6634, 25016

Claire, John D.: Agricultural Change since 1750, 19424

Clammer, Richard: Passenger Ships of the River Dart and Kingsbridge Estuary, 16594

Clancy, Roger: Ships, Ports and Pilots: A History of the Piloting Profession, 16496

Clapham, Sir John Harold: An Economic History of Modern Britain, 3457; The Bank of England, 4483; Monetary Policy, 4649

Clapp, Brian William: The University at Exeter: a History, 23498

Clare, Albert: The City Temple, 1640–1940, 12054

Claridge, Gordon Sydney: Drugs and Human Behaviour, 22191

Clark, Alan M.: Catalogue: Exhibition; 150 Years of Publishing, Blackie & Son, 1809–1959, 24944

Clark, Alan: The Donkeys, 14475; The Fall of Crete, 14853

Clark, Alan: ed. Anglican/Roman Catholic Dialogue, 12333

Clark, Brian Drummond: Industrial Movement and the Regional Problem, 5062; 'Les Nouvelles Villes d'Ecosse', 18179

Clark, Brian Frederick Carl: The Genetic Code, 26458

Clark, Catherine Margaret: The School and the Site: A Historical Memoir to Celebrate the Twenty-Fifth Anniversary of the [London] School [of Hygiene and Tropical Medicine.], 20903

Clark, Colin Grant: England's Fight against Communism and its Relation to the Industrial Crisis, 3558; The Economic Position of Great Britain, 3602; The Conditions of Economic Progress, 3603; The Economics of 1960, 3604; National Income, 1924–1931, 4893; National Income and Outlay, 4894; Poverty before Politics: A Proposal for Reverse Income Tax, 9014; The Demand for Housing, 18703; 'Stability of Village Populations', 19125; Population Growth and Land Use, 20285; The Cost of Living, 20424; The Value of Agricultural Land, 20286; 'An Unorthodox Proposal: University Education in the Welfare State', 23435; 'Oxford Reformed: Notes During a Controversy', 23555

Clark, D. H.: 'Administrative Psychiatry, 1942–1962', 21822

Clark, David Bernard: A Survey of Anglicans and Methodists in Four Towns, 12307

Clark, David George: The Industrial Manager: His Background and Career Pattern, 9804

Clark, David Hazell: Social Therapy in Psychiatry, 21858

Clark, David: Battle for the Counties: A Guide to the County Council Elections, 3201

Clark, David: De-industrialisation and Employment Decline in the West Midlands and Coventry, 5227

Clark, Frederick Le Gros: Ageing in Industry: An Inquiry based on Figures derived from Census Reports into the Problems of Ageing under the Conditions of Modern Industry, 5862; Age and the Working Lives of Men: An Attempt to reduce the Statistical Evidence to its Practical Shape, 5863; Women, Work and Age: To Study the Employment of Working Women Throughout their Middle Lives, 7684; The Economic Rights of Women, 7689; Work, Age and Leisure: Causes and Consequences of the Shortened Working Life, 8588; A Social History of the School Meals Service, 20528; Four Thousand Million Mouths: Scientific Humanism and the Shadow of World Hunger, 20531; Our Food Problem: A Study of National Security, 20587; Blinded in War: A Model for the Welfare of all Handicapped People, 21926; ed. National Fitness: A Brief Essay on Contemporary Britain, 22055

Clark, Garth: Michael Cardew: A Portrait, 24138

Clark, George: Whatever Happened to the Welfare State? A Working Note on Social Problems and Poverty in Great Britain in the Early 1970's, 9085; 'The History of the Medical Profession: Aims and Methods', 20927

Clark, George S. R. Kitson: The English Inheritance: An Historical Essay, 11569; 'A Hundred Years of the Teaching of History at Cambridge, 1873–1973', 22448, 26773

Clark, Gordon: Housing and Planning in the Countryside, 19104

Clark, Gregory: 'Doc': 100 Year History of the Sick Berth Branch, 15327

Clark, Ivo MacNaughton: A History of Church Discipline in Scotland, 12203

Clark, J. Beresford: 'The BBC's External Services', 24767

Clark, J.: What do Health Visitors do? A Review of the Research, 1960–1980, 21734

Clark, John W.: British and American English since 1900, 23789

Clark, Ken R.: The State of British Agriculture, 1981, 19583

Clark, Kenneth Mackenzie: Another Part of the Wood: A Self-Portrait, 23952; The Other Half: A Self Portrait, 23953

Clark, Kenneth Roy: The State of British Agriculture, 1955–1956, 19494

Clark, M. J.: ed. Politics and the Media: Film and Television for the Political Scientist and Historian, 24606

Clark, Margaret M.: Studies in Pre-school Education: Empirical Studies in Pre-school Units in Scotland and their Implications for Educational Practice, 23167

Clark, Mary Virginia: Supplement 1 (1967–1968), 21255

Clark, Peter A.: Sixteen Million Readers: Evening Newspapers in the U.K, 25073

Clark, Richard: In Shades of Green: The Story of the Country Routemasters, 17324

Clark, Robert Bernard: ed. The Long-term Effects of Oil Pollution on Marine Populations, Communities and Ecosystems, 20082

Clark, Rodney: Venture Capital in Britain, America and Japan, 4478

Clark, Ronald Harry: A Short History of the Midland and Great Northern Joint Railway, 16900; The Development of the English Traction Engine, 17087; Brough Superior: The Rolls-Royce of Motorcycles, 17194

Clark, Ronald W.: The Scientific Breakthrough: The Impact of Modern Invention, 7143; A Biography of the Nuffield Foundation, 9154, 22483; Battle for Britain: Sixteen Weeks that Changed the Course of History, 14803; The Birth of the Bomb: The Untold Story of Britain's Part in the Weapon that Changed the World, 15207; The Rise of the Boffins, 15208; The Life of Ernst Chain, 26461; J.B.S.: The Life and Work of J. B. S. Haldane, 26493; The Huxleys, 26501; The Life of Bertrand Russell, 26865; Mountaineering in Britain: A History from the Earliest Times to the Present Day, 27236

Clark, Rose B.: 'Geography in the Schools of Europe', 26671

Clark, Walter Houston: The Oxford Group: Its History and Significance, 12403

Clark, Sir Wilfrid Le Gros: 'The Humanity of Man', 20926

Clark, William Donaldson: Less than Kin: A Study of Anglo-American Relations, 14000; From Three Worlds: Memoirs, 25221

Clark, William: Hugh Redwood: With God in Fleet Street, 25278

Clark-Kennedy, Archibald Edmund: The London: A Study in the Voluntary Hospital System, 9214, 21432; London Pride: The Story of a Voluntary Hospital, 9215; Edith Cavell: Pioneer and Patriot, 14608

Clarke, Amy Key: A History of the Cheltenham Ladies' College, 1853–1953, 23108

Clarke, Arthur C.: Astounding Days: A Science Fictional Autobiography, 25453

Clarke, Basil: The History of Airships, 17536

Clarke, Brian A.: Medical Sociology in Britain: A Register of Teaching and Research, 21963

Clarke, C. F. O.: ed. Police/Community Relations: Report of a Conference, 10725

Clarke, Chris: Planning in the North, 18831

Clarke, Dudley Wrangel: The Eleventh at War: Being the Story of the XIth Hussars through the Years, 1934–1945, 15664

Clarke, Edward Brian Stanley: From Kent to Kohima: Being the History of the 4th Battalion, the Queen's Own Royal West Kent Regiment, 1939–1947, 15673

Clarke, Edwin S.: 'Practical Medical History', 20928; 'The History of the Neurological Sciences', 20929; ed. Modern Methods in the History of Medicine, 21220, 21222; ed. 'The History and Sociology of the Medical Sciences', 21221

Clarke, Henry Lowther: History of Sedbergh School, 1525–1925, 23075

Clarke, Joan Simeon: The Assistance Board, 4086; Social Security, 4087 ed. Beveridge on Beveridge. Recent Speeches, 9029 Disabled Citizens, 21919

Clarke, John Finbar: Power on Land and Sea: 160 Years of Industrial Enterprise on Tyneside: A History of R. & W. Hawthorn Leslie & Co. Ltd, Engineers and Shipbuilders, 16639

Clarke, John Innes: 'Rural and Urban Sex Ratios in England and Wales', 7369; Population Geography, 26634

Clarke, John Joseph: A History of Local Government of the United Kingdom, 3157; The Local Government of the United Kingdom, 3158; Public Assistance: Being the Relevant Sections from 'Social Administration, Including the Poor Laws', 4085; Social Welfare, 8875; Social Administration, including the Poor Laws, 9239; The Housing Problem: Its History, Growth, Legislation and Procedure, 18586; Some Factors relating to the Re-Housing of Slum Dwellers—A Paper, 18587; Housing in relation to Public Health and Social Welfare, 18588; Outlines of the Law of Housing and Planning, including Public Health, Highways and the Acquisition of Land, 20325; An Introduction to Planning, with Reference to the Town and Country Planning Act, 1947, 20326; A Synopsis of the Town and Country Planning Act, 1947, 20327; [An Introduction to Planning.] Planning Land. An Introduction Including the Acts of 1953 and 1954, 20328; The Gist of Planning Law: A Guide to the Town and Country Planning Acts, 1962 and 1963 and Cognate Legislation, with Comparative Index, 20339; Town and Country Planning Act, 20340; Introduction to Public Health Law, 22071

Clarke, John: Working Class Culture, 23730; The Devil makes Work: Leisure in Capitalist Britain, 26937

Clarke, K. R.: The State of British Agriculture, 19534

Clarke, Kenneth: Immigration, Race and Politics: A Birmingham View, 11455

Clarke, L.: Broadening the Battlefield: The H-Blocks and the Rise of Sinn Fein, 2891

Clarke, Mary: Dancers of Mercury: The Story of Ballet Rambert, 24241; The Sadler's Wells Ballet: A History and an Appreciation, 24244

Clarke, Michael: Regulating the City: Competition, Scandal and Reform, 4287; Industrial Relations, 5684

Clarke, Oliver Fielding: Unfinished Conflict: An Autobiography, 11776

Clarke, P.: Black Paradise: The Rastafarian Movement, 12445

Clarke, Peter Frederick: 'Liberals, Labour and the Franchise', 2282; The Keynesian Revolution in the Making, 1924–36, 26601

Clarke, Peter: Geoffrey Howe: A Quiet Revolutionary, 1240

Clarke, R. V. G.: Tackling Vandalism, 10661

Clarke, Raymond Thurston: ed. Working with

Communities: A Study of Community Work in Great Britain, Based upon a Conference Sponsored by the Society of Neighbourhood Workers, 9396

Clarke, Robin: The Science of War and Peace, 15209

Clarke, Roger: Concentration in British Industry 1935–1975: A Study of the Growth, Causes and Effects of Concentration in British Manufacturing Industries, 5527

Clarke, Ronald Oliver: Workers' Participation in Management in Britain, 5459, 6018, 6128; Workers' Participation and Industrial Democracy, 6017

Clarke, Sir Richard William Barnes: New Trends in Government, 786; Anglo-American Collaboration in War and Peace 1942–1949, 3727, 14054; The Management of the Public Sector of the National Economy, 6117

Clarke, Stephen V. O.: Central Bank Co-operation, 1924–1931, 4560

Clarke, Tom M.: Trade Unions under Capitalism, 6913; My Northcliffe Diary, 25093

Clarke, William Kemp Lowther: A Hundred Years of Hymns Ancient and Modern, 11926; A History of the S.P.C.K, 12358, 22888

Clarke, William Malpas: Inside the City: A Guide to London as a Financial Centre, 4283; How the City of London Works: An Introduction to its Financial Markets, 4284; Britain's Invisible Earnings: The Report of the Committee on Invisible Exports, 4782

Clarkson, Leslie Albert: ed. Irish Population, Economy and Society: Essays in Honour of the late K.H. Connell, 2649, 2795

Classified Index to the Library of Aerial Photographs, 210

Clausen, Rosemary: Government Social Survey. Labour Mobility in Great Britain, 1953–1963: An Enquiry undertaken for the Ministry of Labour and National Service in 1963, 7273; Social Welfare for the Elderly: A Study in Thirteen Local Authority Areas in England, Wales and Scotland: Vols 1. and 2, 8593

Claval, P.: 'Les Villes Britanniques', 17815; Geography since the Second World War, 26651

Clawson, Marion: Planning and Urban Growth: An Anglo-American Comparison, 17840, 17967

Clay, Charles John Jervis: Clay and Wheble's Modern Merchant Banking: A Guide to the Workings of the Accepting Houses of the City of London, 4467

Clay, Sir Henry: Lord Norman, 4426

Clay, John F.: ed. Essays in Steam: An Anthology of Articles from the Journal of the Stephenson Locomotive Society, 17025

Clay, Reginald S.: The History of the Microscope, 7105

Claypon, Janet Elizabeth Lane: The Child Welfare Movement, 8140; Hygiene of Women and Children, 8141; Maternity and Child Welfare. Pt.1: A Memorandum on Health Visiting, 8142; Pt. 2: An Extract from the Third Report on Infant Mortality by the Medical Officer of the Board, Sir A. Newsholme, 8142; Milk and its Hygienic Relations, 8143

Clayre, Alasdair: The Impact of Broadcasting or Mrs Buckle's Wall is Singing, 24724; Work and Play: Ideas and Experience of Work and Leisure, 26931

Clayton, Anthony: Khaki and Blue: The Military Police in British Colonial Africa, 12678, 12706; Government and Labour in Kenya 1895–1963, 12836

Clayton, Cheryl Anne: The Coal Industry and the Iron and Steel Industry of Great Britain under Nationalization, 1945–1958: An Analytical Study, 6299

Clayton, David: Capital Taxation and Land Ownership in England and Wales: A Preliminary Assessment, 3773

Clayton, George: Insurance Company Investment: Principles and Policy, 4227; British Insurance, 4228; 'British Financial Intermediaries in Theory and Practice', 4610

Clayton, Gerold Fancourt: The Wall is Strong, 10386

Clayton, Keith Martin: ed. Pollution Abatement, 19994

Clayton, Nick: Early Bicycles, 17166

Clayton, Peter: A Guide to Popular Music, 24468

Clayton, Richard: Civil Action Against the Police, 10780

Clayton, Robert: ed. The Geography of Greater London: A Source Book, 18363

Clayton, Thomas [Tom]: Men in Prison, 10260; The Protectors: The Inside Story of Britain's Private Security Forces, 10882

Cleary, A. J.: 'The Placings Service of the Ministry of Labour', 5865

Cleary, Esmond John: 'Liberal Voting at the General Election of 1951', 2310; The Building Society Movement, 4358; The Economic Consequences of the Severn Bridge and its Associated Motorways, 5365

Cleary, John Martin: Catholic Social Action in Britain, 1909–1959: A History of the Catholic Social Guild, 9138, 11836

Cleaves, R. W.: Congregationalism 1960–1976: The Story of the Federation, 12051

Clegg, Sir Alexander [Alec] Bradshaw: Children in Distress. 8144; ed. The Changing Primary School: Its Problems and Priorities: A Statement by Teachers, 23149

Clegg, Hugh Armstrong: How to run an Incomes Policy: And why We Made such a Mess of the Last One, 3848; ed. The System of Industrial Relations in Great Britain: Its History, Law and Institutions, 5614; The System of Industrial Relations in Great Britain, 5615; The Changing System of Industrial Relations in Great Britain, 5616; Industrial Courts Act 1919: Report of a Court of Inquiry into a Dispute concerning the Operation of Fork Lift Trucks at the Albert Edward Dock, North Shields, 5617; The Employers' Challenge: A Study of the National Shipbuilding and Engineering Disputes of 1957, 5618; History of British Trade Unions since 1889: vol. II, 1911–1933,

6693; Trade Union Officers: A Study of Full-time Officers, Branch Secretaries and Shop Stewards in British Trade-unions, 6716; Workplace and Union: A Study of Local Relationship in Fourteen Unions, 6721; 'Some Consequences of the Great Strike', 6821; General Union in a Changing Society: A Short History of the National Union of General and Municipal Workers, 1889–1964, 6896; 'Strikes', 6929

Clegg, J. A.: Radio Astronomy, 26416; The Exploration of Space by Radio, 26417

Clegg, K.: Facts about the New Towns: A Socio-Economic Digest, 18174

Clegg, Stewart: Power, Rule and Domination: A Critical and Empirical Understanding of Power in Sociological Theory and Organization Life, 9764

Clegg, William Paul: Docks and Ports—2—London, 16699

Cleife, Philip: Airway to the Isles, 17634

Clemens, Cyril: The Man from Limehouse: Clement Richard Attlee, Earl Attlee, 975

Clement, Henry Anthony: British history, 1865–1965, 350

Clements, E. M. B.: 'Bodyweight of Men Related to Structure, Age and Social Status'. and, 'Chest Girth of Men Related to Structure, Age, Bodyweight and Social Status', 9504

Clements, J. A.: 'Royal Navy Ship-Based Air Defence 1939 -1984', 15393

Clements, Keith Winston: 'Baptists and the Outbreak of the First World War', 11855; Lovers of Discord: Twentieth-Century Theological Controversies in England, 11871; ed. Baptists in the Twentieth Century, 12018

Clements, Lawrie: Trade Unions under Capitalism, 6913

Clements, Richard: Glory without Power: A Study of Trade Unionism in our Present Society, 6726

Clements, Roger Victor: Local Notables and the City Council, 3325; Managers: A Study of their Careers in Industry, 5421

Clements, Simon: ed. The Committed Church, 11956; The McCabe Affair: Evidence and Comment, 11971

Clenet, Deirdre: Nature Conservation in Croydon: A Nature Conservation Strategy for London, 20230

Cleverley, Graham: The Fleet Street Disaster: British National Newspapers as a Case Study in Mismanagement, 25337

Clew, Kenneth R.: The Kennet and Avon Canal, 16413

Cliff, P. B.: The Rise and Development of the Sunday School Movement in England, 1780 to 1980, 11907

Cliff, Sheila: 'I Dread to Think About Christmas': A Study of Poor Families in 1976, 9087

Clifford, Derek: A History of Garden Design, 19900

Clifford, Hon. Sir Bede Edmund Hugh: Proconsul, 12498

Clifford, J.: A Political Analysis of British Rural Conservation Issues and Policies . . ., 19954

Clifford, James: Aspects of Economic Development, 1760–1960, 3488

Clifford, Juliet Mary: International Aid: A Discussion of the Flow of Public Resources from Rich to Poor Countries, with Particular Reference to British Policy, 9185

Clifford, Nicholas Rowland: Retreat from China, 13627

Clifton, Michael: Amigo: Friend of the Poor. Bishop of Southwark, 1904–1949, 11989

Clifton: Centenary Essays on Clifton College, 23054; A History of Clifton College, 1860–1934, 23055

Cline, Catherine Ann: E. D. Morel, 1873–1924: The Strategies of Protest, 1481; Recruits to Labour: The British Labour Party 1914–1931, 1695

Cline, Marjorie W.: Scholar's Guide to Intelligence Literature, 15994

Cline, Peter K.: 'Re-opening the Case of the Lloyd George Coalition and the Post-war Economic Transition 1918–1919', 6105

Cline, Richard: Planning in the United States and the United Kingdom, 17712

Clinker, Charles Ralph: Railway History: A Handlist of the Principal Sources of Original Material, with Notes and Guidance on its use, 16715; ed. A Regional History of the Railways of Great Britain, 16808; The Railways of Cornwall, 1809–1963, 16926

Clinton, Alan: The Trade Union Rank and File: Trades Councils in Britain, 1900–1940, 6718; The Post Office Workers: A Trade Union and Social History, 6859; 'Trade Councils during the First World War', 6907

Clipsham, Ernest F.: 'The Baptist Historical Society: Sixty Years Achievement', 12020

Clive, Lewis: The People's Army, 15433

Cloake, J.: Templer, Tiger of Malaya: The Life of Field Marshal Sir Gerald Templer, 12930, 16161

Clogg, Richard: British Policy in South-East Europe in the Second World War, 14936; British Policy towards Wartime Resistance in Yugoslavia and Greece, 14937; Politics and the Academy: Arnold Toynbee and the Koraes Chair, 26822

Cloke, Paul J.: Implementing Rural Planning, 18827; 'The Implementation of Rural Policies: A Survey of Country Planning Authorities', 18828; 'Towards a Critical Appraisal of Rural Settlement Planning in England and Wales', 19066; 'Counter-Urbanisation: A Rural Perspective', 19067; Writing the Rural: Five Cultural Geographies, 19123; Social Profiles of Ten Case Study Parishes, 19316

Clokie, H. N.: An Account of the Herbaria of the Department of Botany in the University of Oxford, 26554

Close, Charles Frederick: Addresses on the History of the Royal Geographical Society at the Centenary Meeting, Oct 21st', 26626; The Map of England, or about England, with an Ordnance Map, 26698; '

Close, David H.: 'Conservatives and Coalition after the First World War', 1628; 'The Collapse of Resistance to Democracy: Conservatism, Adult Suffrage and Second Chamber Reform, 1911–1928', 2276

Close, Roy K.: A Village of Parts: A History of Amberley Parish, 19317

Clough, Monica: The Field of Thistles: Scotland's Past and Scotland's People, 2458

Clowes, William Beaufoy: Family Business 1803–1953, 25021

Cluett, Derek: Croydon Airport: The Great Days, 1928–1939, 17673; Croydon Airport: The Australian Connection: Flights and other Links between Croydon Airport and Australia, 17674

Clunes, Alec Sheriff De Moro: British Theatre History, 26185; The British Theatre, 26186

Clunies-Ross, Edward: 'Educational Technology in Adult and Community Education', 22500

Clurman, Harold: The Fervent Years: The Story of the Group Theatre and the Thirties, 26190

Clutterbuck, Richard: Industrial Conflict and Democracy: The Last Chance, 6046; Riot and Revolution in Singapore and Malaya, 1945–1963, 12929; The Long, Long War: The Emergency in Malaya 1948–1960, 16155; Guerrillas and Terrorists, 16174

Clutton, Cecil: The British Organ, 7074, 24393

Clyne, M. G.: Night Calls: A Study in General Practice, 21506

Clynes, John Robert: Memoirs, 1148; 'Food Control in War and Peace', 20577

Cmnd 2922. A University of the Air. Parliamentary Papers (1965–6), 23545

Co-operative Party: The People's Industry: A Statement on Social Ownership, 1899; Discussion Pamphlets: Co-operation and Modern Socialism, 1900; The Challenge of Monopoly, 1901

Co-operative Women's Guild: Maternity: Letters from Working-Women, 7650

Coad, Ray: Laing: The Biography of Sir John W. Laing, CBE, 1879–1978, 6185

Coakley, Jerry: The City of Capital: London's Role as a Financial Centre, 4244

Coale, Ansley J.: 'Age Patterns of Marriage', 9976

Coale, Samuel: Anthony Burgess, 25433

Coales, J. F.: 'Education for Automation: Technical Education and Training in an Age of Rapid Technological Advance', 22502

Coard, Bernard: How the West Indian Child is Made Educationally Sub-normal in the British School System, 23181

Coase, Ronald Harry: British Broadcasting: A Study in Monopoly, 24757

Coates, A.: Western Pacific Islands, 12875

Coates, Andrew: Jane's World Seaplanes and Motor Gliders, 17546

Coates, Bryan Ellis: Regional Variations in Britain: Studies in Economic and Social Geography, 5080; Geography and Inequality, 5081; 'South Yorkshire County is Born and Analysed' 5233

Coates, David: The Labour Party and the Struggle for Socialism, 1757; Labour in Power?, 1758; The Economic Decline of Modern Britain: The Debate Between Left and Right, 3699; The Economic Revival of Modern Britain: The Debate Between Left and Right, 3700; Social Stratification and Trade Unionism: A Critique, 6722, 9607

Coates, J. A. C.: Workers' Participation in Western Europe, 6016

Coates, J. B.: 'West Indians at Work in Nottingham', 11236

Coates, Kenneth [Ken] Sidney: The Crisis of British Socialism: Essays on the Rise of Harold Wilson and the Fall of the Labour Party, 1752; ed. What Went Wrong?, 1763; ed. Industrial Democracy in Great Britain: A Book of Readings and Witnesses for Workers' Control, 5698, 6007; Democracy in the Mines, 5700; The Shop Steward's Guide to the Bullock Report, 5699; Can the Workers Run Industry?, 6003; ed. The New Worker Co-operatives, with Contributions by Tony Benn and Others, 6004; Beyond Wage Slavery, 6005; The Right to Useful Work: Planning by the People, 6006; ed. The New Unionism: The Case for Workers' Control, 6008; Work-ins, Sit-ins and Industrial Democracy, 6938; Poverty: The Forgotten Englishman, 9068; Poverty, Deprivation and Morale in a Nottingham Community: St. Ann's: A Report of the Preliminary Findings of the St. Ann's Study Group, 9069

Coates, Robert David: Teaching Unions and Interest Group Politics: A Study in the Behaviour of Organised Teachers in England and Wales, 22712

Coates, William Peyton and Coates, Zelda Kahan: A History of Anglo-Soviet Relations, 13909; Armed Intervention in Russia 1918–1922, 13919, 14567

Coats, A. W.: 'Some Wartime Observations on the Role of the Economist in Government', 797; 'Britain: The Rise of Specialists', 798; and Coats, S. E. 'The Changing Social Composition of the Royal Economic Society 1890–1960 and the Professionalisation of British Economics', 9833, 26576; 'The Market for Economists in Britain 1944–1975', 26577

Coats, Alice M.: The Quest for Plants: A History of the Horticultural Explorers, 26553

Coats, Peter: Great Gardens of the Western World, 19868; Great Gardens of Britain, 19869; The Gardens of Buckingham Palace, 19891

Cobb, Richard Charles: Something to Hold onto: Autobiographical Sketches, 26791; Still Life: Sketches from a Tunbridge Wells Childhood, 26791

Cochran, Charles B.: The Secrets of a Showman, 26005. I had almost Forgotten, 26006; Cock-a-Doodle-do, 26007; Showman Looks on, 26008

Cochrane, Archibald Leman: Effectiveness and Efficiency: Random Reflections on Health Services, 21626

Cochrane, D. G.: 'Britannic Irish and Hibernian Irish in Ulster's Racial Conflict', 2928

Cochrane, R. G. A.: The Law of Housing in Scotland, 18461

Cockburn, Alexander: ed. The Incompatibles: Trade Union Militancy and Consensus, 6911; ed. Student Problems, Diagnosis, Action, 985

Cockburn, Christine: 'Housing Policy', 18650; Housing Since the Rent Act: An Interim Report from the Rowntree Trust Housing Study, 18723; Essays on Housing, 18724

Cockburn, Claud Francis: Claud: Union Power: The Growth and Challenge in Perspective, 6715; Autobiography; Cockburn Sums Up: An Autobiography; Crossing the Line; In Time of Trouble, 25222

Cockburn, Cynthia: The Structure of Urban and Regional Planning Research in Britain, 17721; A Bibliography on Planning Education, 17722; The Local State: Management of Cities and People, 17938

Cockburn, Patricia: The Years of The Week, 25188

Cocker, M.: Destroyers of the Royal Navy 1893–1981, 15388

Cockerell, Hugh Anthony Lewis: The British Insurance Business, 1547–1970: An Introduction and Guide to Historical Records in the United Kingdom, 4205; Sixty Years of the Chartered Insurance Institute, 1897–1957, 4207; Friends for Life: Friends' Provident Life Office, 1832–1982, 4236; Lloyd's of London: A Portrait, 4243

Cockerell, Michael: Live from Number 10: The Inside Story of Prime Ministers and Television, 24914

Cockerill, A. W.: Sir Percy Sillitoe, 16016

Cockett, I. E. N.: Research Projects of Employment within the London Boroughs 1966–Nov. 1976, 7017

Cockett, R.: 'Borstal Training: A Follow-up Study', 10539; Drug Abuse and Personality in Young Offenders, 10669, 22193

Cockin, Frederic Arthur: 'The Education Act Comes of Age', 22622

Cockman, Frederick George: The Story of Bedfordshire Railways, 16921; The Railways of Hertfordshire, 16943

Cocks, Edward John: The Tincal Trail: A History of Borax, 6222; A History of the Zinc Smelting Industry in Britain, 6617

Cocks, Frederick Seymour: E. D. Morel: The Man and His Work, 1480

Cocks, Michael: Labour and the Benn Factor, 1094, 1774

Cockshott, John: The West Yorkshire Road Car Company Ltd. Part Two: 1935 to 1975, 17331

Codlin, Ellen M.: Aslib Directory of Information Sources in the United Kingdom, 93

Coe, W. E.: The Engineering Industry of the North of Ireland, 6379

Coffey, Thomas M.: Agony at Easter: The 1916 Uprising, 2738

Cogan, David: The Attack on Higher Education, 23443

Coggan, Frederick Donald: ed. Christ and the Colleges: A History of the Inter-Varsity Fellowship, 11664; Cuthbert Bardsley, Bishop, Evangelist, Pastor, 11716

Coggan, Philip: The Money Machine: How the City Works, 4285

Coghlan, F.: Armaments, Economic Policy and Appeasement: Background to British Foreign Policy 1931–1937, 14710

Coglan, W. N.: The Readership of Newspapers and Periodicals in Great Britain, 1936: A Report on Circulations, 25077

Cohen, Albert Kircidel: Delinquent Boys: The Culture of the Gang, 10559

Cohen, Sir Andrew Benjamin: New Work and Ideas in the Field of Technical Co-operation: . . . the Henry Morley Lecture to the Royal Society of Arts, 9172; British Policy in Changing Africa, 12679

Cohen [Baron]: Sherrington: Physiologist, Philosopher and Poet, 26459

Cohen, Brian: 'The Employment of Immigrants: A Case Study within the Wool Industry', 10966; Colour, Citizenship and British Society, 10993; 'Economic Effects of Immigration', 11410

Cohen, Charles Desmond: British Economic Policy, 1960–1969, 3646; The Common Market Ten Years After: An Economic Review of Britain's Membership of the E.E.C. 1973–1983, 4821

Cohen, Dorothy: Advertising, 4333

Cohen, Emmeline Waley: The Growth of the British Civil Service, 1780–1939, 843; Autonomy and Delegation in County Government, 3197

Cohen, Gavriel: Churchill and Palestine, 1939–1942, 14333; The British Cabinet and the Question of Palestine, April–July 1943, 14334

Cohen, Gerda Lesley: What's Wrong with the Hospitals?, 21388

Cohen, Harriet: A Bundle of Time: The Memoirs of Harriet Cohen, 24401

Cohen, Israel: A Jewish Pilgrimage: The Autobiography of Israel Cohen, 12433

Cohen, J. M.: Robert Graves, 25550

Cohen, Joseph: Journey into the Trenches: The Life of Isaac Rosenberg 1890–1918, 25786

Cohen, Louis: ed. Educational Research and Development in Britain 1970–1980, 22842; ed. Linking Home with School, 23139

Cohen, Michael J.: 'Sir Arthur Wauchope, the Army and the Rebellion in Palestine, 1936', 14312; 'British Strategy and the Palestine Question, 1936–1939', 14313; Palestine, Retreat from the Mandate: The Making of British Policy, 1936–1945, 14323; Churchill and the Jews, 14324; Origins and Evolution of the Arab-Zionist Conflict, 14325; 'Appeasement in the Middle East: The British White Paper on Palestine, May 1939', 14326; 'The British White Paper on Palestine, May 1939: Part II, the Testing of a Policy, 1942–1945', 14327; 'Why Britain Left: The End of the Mandate', 14328; 'American Influence on British Policy in the Middle East during World War Two: First Attempts at Co-ordinating Allied Policy on Palestine', 14329; 'The Genesis of the Anglo-American Committee on Palestine, November 1945: A Case Study on the Assertion of American Hegemony', 14330; Palestine and the Great Powers 1945–1948, 14341

Cohen, Percy: Unemployment Insurance and Assistance in Britain, 4027

Cohen, Philip: Knuckle Sandwich: Growing Up in the Working Class City, 8324, 10667

Cohen, R. A.: One Hundred Years: A History of the University of Birmingham Dental Students' Society [1886–1986.], 9887; The History of the Birmingham Dental Hospital and Dental School, 1858–1958, 21421

Cohen, Robin: 'The Interaction between Race and Colonialism: A Case Study of the Liverpool Race Riots of 1919', 11464

Cohen, S. A.: English Zionists and British Jews: The Communal Politics of Anglo-Jewry, 1895–1920, 12416

Cohen, Stanley: Psychological Survival: The Experience of Long-term Imprisonment, 10385; 'The Teddy Boys', 10619; The Manufacture of News: Social Problems, Deviance and the Mass Media, 10626, 25320; Folk Devils and Moral Panics: The Creation of the Mods and Rockers, 10630; 'Mods, Rockers and the Rest', 10681

Cohen, Yoel: Media Diplomacy: The Foreign Office in the Mass Communications Age, 13363

Cohn, Nick: Pop from the Beginning, 24490

Colby, Douglas: As the Curtain Rises: On Contemporary British Drama, 1966–1976, 26245

Colclough, John Richard: The Construction Industry of Great Britain, 6193, 18559

Cole, C. R.: 'The Conflict Within: Sir Stephen Tallents and Planning Propaganda Overseas before the Second World War', 15217

Cole, Christopher: ed. Royal Flying Corps, 1915–1916, 14623; ed. Royal Air Force, 1918, 14624; ed. McCudden, V.C, 14625

Cole, Dorothy: The Economic Circumstances of Old People, 8575

Cole, George Douglas Howard: Great Britain in the Post-war World, 357; John Burns, 1119; A Short History of the British Working Class Movement 1789–1947, 1673, 9619; A History of the Labour Party from 1914, 1680; 'The Independent Labour Party', 1868; A Century of Co-operation, 1886; The British Co-operative Movement in a Socialist Society, 1887; A History of Socialist Thought, 2098; 'Why Britain Went Socialist', 2289; Introduction to Economic History, 1750–1950, 3467; Economic Planning, 3535; The Post-War Condition of Britain, 3615; The Payment of Wages, 3862; British Trade and Industry, Past and Future, 4966; The Case for Industrial Partnership, 5637; Labour in the Coal Mining Industry, 1914–1921, 6254; The Common People, 1746–1938, 7529; 'Sociology and Social Policy', 8791; The Next Ten Years in British Social and Economic Policy, 8792; British Social Services, 8793; Beveridge Explained: What the Beveridge Report on Social Security Means, 9032; Studies in Class Structure, 9517; Building and Planning, 17747

Cole, Howard Norman: The Story of Catterick Camp 1915–1972, 15456; On Wings of Healing: The Story of the Airborne Medical Services, 1940–1960, 15906, 22116

Cole, John: The Thatcher Years: A Decade of Revolution in British Politics, 1052

Cole, John: ed. Wales and Medicine: An Historical Survey from Papers given at the 9th British Congress on the History of Medicine at Swansea and Cardiff, 4–8 Sept. 1973, 21047

Cole, Lesley: Noel Coward and His Friends, 25957

Cole, Luella Winifred: Psychology of Adolescence, 8459

Cole, Dame Margaret Isabel: ed. The Story of Fabian Socialism, 2108; The Life of G.D.H.Cole, 2122; Growing up into Revolution, 2123; Beatrice Webb, 2147; 'The Woman's Vote: What has it Achieved?' 7816; Marriage Past and Present, 9967

Cole, Paul: The Future of the C.A.T'.s', 22495

Cole, Rex Vicat: The Art and Life of Byam Shaw, 26124

Cole, Richard Lee: One Methodist Church, 1860–1960: Vol. 4 of the History of Methodism in Ireland, 12184

Cole, Roger: Comprehensive Schools in Action, 22950

Cole, Sonia: Leakey's Luck: The Life of Louis Seymour Bazett Leakey 1903–1972, 26361

Cole, William Alan: British Economic Growth, 1688–1959: Trends and Structure, 5006

Coleman, Alice M.: Land Use Survey Handbook: An Explanation of the Second Land Use Survey of Britain . . ., 20271

Coleman, C.: Understanding Crime Rates, 10241

Coleman, David A.: Demography of Immigrants and Minority Groups in the United Kingdom, 2718, 2862, 7397; 'Recent Trends in Marriage and Divorce in Britain and Europe', 9939

Coleman, Donald Cuthbert: History and the Economic Past: An Account of the Rise and Decline of Economic History in Britain, 3545, 26763; Courtaulds: An Economic and Social History, 6419; ed. Enterprise and History: Essays in Honour of Charles Wilson, 26828

Coleman, P. G.: 'Social Gerontology in England, Scotland and Wales: A Review of Recent and Current Research', 8622

Coleman, Peter W.: Catholics and the Welfare State, 9003

Coleman, Ray: Brian Epstein: The Man who made the Beatles, 24505; John Winston Lennon, 24506; Survivor: The Authorised Biography of Eric Clapton, 24513

Coleman, Solomon David: Mental Health and Social Adjustment in a New Town: An Exploratory Study in East Kilbride, 18185

Coleman, Terry: The Liners: A History of the North Atlantic Crossing, 16577

Coleman-Cooke, John: Discovery II in the Antarctic: The Story of British Research in the Southern Seas, 27225

Colfax, John David: ed. Radical Sociology, 8040

Colin Buchanan and Partners: The Conurbations: A Study, 16310. Bath: A Study in Conservation: Report to the Ministry of Housing and Local Government and Bath City Council, 18970

Coll, Alberto R.: The Wisdom of Statecraft: Sir Herbert Butterfield and the Philosophy of International Politics, 26786

Collard, D.: Economic Issues in Immigration—An Exploration of the Liberal Approach to Public Policy on Immigration, 11435

Collard, Jean: Who Divorces?, 9990

Collard, John A.: A Maritime History of Rye, 16478

Colledge, James Joseph: Ships of the Royal Navy: An Historical Index, 15342; Warships of World War Two, 15354

College of General Practitioners: Council: Reports from General Practice, 21534; The G.P. and Preventative Medicine: Report of the Joint Meeting on the Role of the General Practitioner in Preventative Medicine, 22076

Colles, Henry Cope: Walford Davies:, A Biography, 24323; The Royal College of Music: A Jubilee Record, 24424; The Royal College of Music: A Centenary Record, 24425

Collett, R. J.: Northern Ireland Statistics: A Guide to Principal Sources, 2780

Collie, Sir Robert John: Workmen's Compensation: Its Medical Aspect, 4114; ed. Recent Progress in Medicine and Surgery, 1919–1933, 21174; 'The Care of Pensioners and Disabled Combatants in Relation to National Health and Wealth', 21883

Collier, Basil: Barren Victories: Versailles to Suez (1918–1956), 14007; The Lion and the Eagle: British and American Strategy, 1900–1950, 14008; A Short History of the Second World War, 14705; The Defence of the United Kingdom, 14725; The Battle of Britain, 14804; A History of Air Power, 14979; Leader of the Few: The Authorised Biography of Air Chief Marshal the Lord Dowding of Bentley Priory, 15956

Collier, Graham: Cleo and John: A Biography of the Dankworths, 24458

Collier, John: Just the Other Day: an Informal History of Great Britain since the War, 353

Collier, Kenneth Gerald: 'An Experiment in University Teaching', 22539; New Dimensions in Higher Education, 23310

Collier, Sir Laurence: Flight from Conflict, 13258

Collier, Richard Hugheson: The Sands of Dunkirk, 14842; The City that Wouldn't Die, 15166; The Plague of the Spanish Lady: The Influenza Pandemic of 1918–1919, 21096

Collier, Simon: 'The First Falklands War: Argentine Attitudes', 16108

Collingwood, Robin George: An Autobiography, 26792; The Idea of Nature, 26848; The Later Philosophy of R. G. Collingwood, 26849

Collins, Anthea: Non-specialist Graduates in Industry, 5967; The Arts Graduate in Industry, 5968

Collins, Sir Charles Henry: Public Administration in Hong Kong, 12970; Public Administration in Ceylon, 12985

Collins, E. A.: 'The Price of Financial Control', 4605

Collins, Edward John Thomas: The Economics of Upland Britain 1750–1950: An Illustrated Review, 19411; Sickle to Combine: A Review of Harvest Techniques from 1800 to the Present Day, 19677

Collins, Edward Treacher: History and Traditions of the Moorfields Eye Hospital, 21458

Collins, H. P.: John Cowper Powys, 25771

Collins, J.: Social Casework in General Medical Practice, 21510

Collins, Joan: Past Imperfect: An Autobiography, 26023

Collins, Judith: Buses in Urban Areas 1970–1976, 17277

Collins, Larry: Mountbatten and Independent India 16 August 1947–18 June 1948, 13184

Collins, Lewis John: Faith under Fire, 11777

Collins, M.: Women Graduates and the Teaching Profession, 9841

Collins, Martin Alan: The Television Audience: Patterns of Viewing, 24839

Collins, Michael Frank: Transport Organisation in a Great City: The Case of London, 16324

Collins, Michael: The Inter-War British Economy: A Statistical Abstract, 3592; Money and Banking in the U.K.: A History, 4456

Collins, Robert John: Lord Wavell, 1883–1941: A Military Biography, 14784

Collins, Robert O.: ed. The British in the Sudan 1898–1956, 14417; Shadows in the Grass: Britain in the Southern Sudan, 1918–1956, 14427

Collins, Sydney F.: Coloured Minorities in Britain: Studies in British Race Relations, Based on African, West Indian, and Asiatic Immigrants, 10901; 'The British-born Coloured', 10902; 'The Moslem Family in Britain', 10903

Collins, Wallace Barrymore: Jamaican Migrant, 11255

Collins, Wendy: Women, 7803

Collis, Arthur T.: These our Children: An Account of the Home Life and Social Environment of Children in an Industrial Slum District, 8145; 'Social Work. A Current Assessment of Training and Related Topics', 8691; 'Casework in a Statutory and Voluntary Setting', 8723

Collis, Edgar Leigh: Industrial Pneumoconiosis, with Special Reference to Dust-Pthisis, 4108; The Health of Industrial Workers, 4109; ed. The Industrial Clinic: A Handbook dealing with Health in Work, 4110; 'Aims of the Welsh National Medical School, with Special Reference to Preventive Medicine', 21289; A Way of Life for the Handicapped Child: A New Approach to Cerebral Palsy, 21918

Collis, Henry: B-P's Scouts: An Official History of the Boy Scouts Association, 8515

Collis, Louise: Impetuous Heart. The Story of Ethel Smyth. 24366; The Memoirs of Dame Ethel Smyth, 24367

Collis, Maurice Stewart: Nancy Astor, 1344; Last and First in Burma, 1941–1948, 13204, 15057

Collis, Pat: Neighbourhood Information and

Advice Centres: Oldham Community Development Project, 9300

Collison, Frances: 'Young Offenders, Gambling and Video Game Playing', 10532

Collison, Peter Cheeseborough: The Cutteslowe Walls: A Study in Social Class, 9537; 'University Chancellors, Vice-Chancellors and College Principals: A Social Profile', 9834, 23345; 'Immigrants and Residence', 11436; 'Residence and Social Class in Oxford', 18070; 'Research Note: Career Contingencies of English University Teachers', 22533

Collison, Robert L.: Published Library Catalogues: An Introduction to their Contents and Use, 99; Kenya, 12821; Broadcasting in Britain: A Bibliography, 24716

Collotti, Enzo: L'Internazionale Operaia e Socialista tra le due Guerre, 13554

Colls, Robert M.: The Colliers Rant: Song and Culture in the Industrial Village, 9697

Collyer, David G.: Battle of Britain Diary: July-September 1940, 14805

Colman, Andrew M.: 'Scientific Racism and the Evidence on Race and Intelligence', 11174

Colmer, John: Coleridge to Catch 22: Images of Society, 7606

Colquhoun, Alan: 'The Modern Movement in Architecture', 23912

Colquhoun, Maureen: A Woman in the House, 1396

Colton, Mary: Fair and Equal, 7766

Colville, Sir John Rupert: The Churchillians, 988; Man of Valour: The . . . of Field Marshal the Viscount Gort, 14760

Colvin, Howard Montagu: ed. The Countryseat: Studies in the History of the British Country House, 20319

Colvin, Ian Duncan: The Life of Edward Carson, 1136; The Chamberlain Cabinet: How the Meetings in 10 Downing Street, 1937–1939, Led to the Second World War, 13701

Colvin, Michael: British Shipping: The Right Course, 16463; Airport U.K.: A Policy for the U.K.'s Civil Airports, 17667

Colwell, B.: Behind the Blue Door: The History of the Royal College of Midwives, 1881–1981, 21709

Colwell, Hector A.: An Essay on the History of Electrotherapy and Diagnosis, 21075

Colyer, Richard J.: Man's Proper Study: A History of Agricultural Education in Aberystwyth, 1878–1978, 19640

Colyer, William Thomas: The Workers Passport: A Study of the Legal Restrictions on Migrant Workers: Prepared by the Labour Defence Council, 11097

Coman, Peter: Catholics and the Welfare State, 11841

Comber, Norman Mederson: Agricultural Education in Great Britain, 22423

Comeau, Marcel Gerard: Operation Mercury: An Airman in the Battle of Crete, 15896

Comfort, A. F.: Guide to Government Data: A Survey of Unpublished Social Science Material in Libraries of Government Departments in London, 247

Comfort, Alexander: The Anxiety Makers: Some Curious Preoccupations of the Medical Profession, 20840

Comfort, George O.: Professional Politicians: A Study of British Party Agents, 1608

Comitas, Lambros: The Complete Caribbeana 1900–1975: A Topical Bibliography, 12997

Commercial Bank of Scotland Ltd: Our Bank: The Story of the Commercial Bank of Scotland Ltd. 1810–1941, 4520

Commission for Racial Equality: A Guide to the New Race Relations Act 1976: Employment, 11127; Employment, 11128; Immigrant Control Procedures: Report of a Formal Investigation, 11441; Your Rights to Equal Treatment under the New Race Relations Act 1976

Commissiong, Barbara: The English-Speaking Caribbean: A Bibliography of Bibliographies, 12994

Committee on Air Pollution: Interim Report, 20039

Committee of Enquiry into Certain Matters concerning the Port Transport Industry, 16658

Committee of Enquiry into Shipping: Report: Cmnd 4337, Parliamentary Papers, XXVII 1969–70, 16523

Committee of Inquiry into Local Government in Scotland: Report, 3170

Committee of Inquiry into the Functions and Powers of the Islands Councils in Scotland, 3171

Committee of Inquiry on Decimal Currency: Minutes and Papers Presented to the Committee, 4727

Committee of London Clearing Banks: The London Clearing Banks, 4461; Banks and Industry: Some Recent Developments, 4462

Committee on Nursing, 21718

Common Wealth Information Bulletin: 1943–1946, 1908

Common Wealth News Letter: 1950–1954, 1910; We Hold These Truths: A Manifesto for Libertarians, 1912

Common Wealth Party: A New Kind of Politics: A Party in the Making, 1911

Common Wealth Review, 1944–1949, 1909

Commonwealth Survey: 1953–1967, 271

Communist Party of Britain, Marxist/Leninist: Congress '76, 1963; Counter Attack, 1964; The Protracted Struggle of the Working Class, 1965

Communist Party of Great Britain: The British Road to Socialism, 1957; Forging the Weapon: A Handbook for Members of the Communist Party, 1958; A Policy for Britain: General Election Programme of the Communist Party, 1959; Communist Policy for Great Britain: The General Election, 1960; Speeches and Documents of the 6th (Manchester) Conference of the Communist Party of Great Britain . . . 1924, 1961; (Historians Group) Labour-Communist Relations, 1920–1939, 1962; Communist Railway Workers: How to End Muddle on the Railways, 16751; Good Health for all: An Examination of the

Government's Proposals for a National Health Service, 21557

Community Action: 'Action Report: Compulsory Purchase', 17897

Community Development Programme, Political Economy Collective, Newcastle Upon-Tyne: Back-Street Factory, 9286; From Rags to Ruins: Batley, Woollen Textiles and Industrial Change, 9287; Housing Action?: The Myth of Area Improvement, 9288

Community Development Working Group: 'The British National Community Development Project', 9297.Community Health: Including Community Medicine, Public Health, and Social Service: A Select List of Books, Periodicals and Non-Book Materials, 22021

Community Relations Commission: Unemployment and Homelessness, 11040; 'Some of my Best Friends . . . ': A Report on Race Relations Attitudes, 11041; Housing in Multi-racial Areas: Prepared by a Working Party of Housing Directors, 11042; Black Employees: Job Levels and Discrimination, 11043; Caring for the Under-Fives in a Multi-Racial Society, 11053; Evidence to the Royal Commission on the National Health Service, 11060; The Multi-Racial Community: A Guide for Local Councillors, 11061; Urban Deprivation, Racial Inequality and Social Policy, 11062; The Views of Social Workers in Multi-Racial Areas, 11064; Meeting their Needs: An Account of Language Tuition Schemes for Ethnic Minority Women, 11063; (Youth and Community Section.) Seen but Not Served: Black Youth and the Youth Service, 11065; Race Relations in Britain: A Select Bibliography with Emphasis on Commonwealth Immigrants, 11521

Community Work Group: Current Issues in Community Work, 9415

Community: Journal of the UK Community Relations Commission Jan, 1970–Apr. 1971. Ceased Publication. New Community published from 1972 onwards, 10999

Comprehensive Dissertation Index 1861–1972: Volume 28: History, 91

Compton, Maurice: British Industry: Its Changing Structure in Peace and War, 4971

Compton, Paul Alwyn: Northern Ireland: A Census Atlas, 141; 'Fertility, Nationality and Religion in Northern Ireland', 2862; 'Aspects of Intercommunity Population Balance in Northern Ireland', 7298; 'Estimates of the Religious Composition of Northern Ireland Local Government Districts in 1981 and Change in the Geographical Pattern of Religious Composition between 1971 and 1981', 12156

Comrie, John Dixon: History of Scottish Medicine Vol. II. 18th Century to ca.1930, 21048

Comyns-Carr, Sir Arthur Strettell: 'Our Economy and Our Nationalised Industries', 6070; Recent Mining Legislation, Including the Coal Mines Act, 1930, 6258

Conan, A. R.: 'Postscript on the Balance of

Payments', 4922; 'The Balance of Payments Policy in Operation', 4923

Conant, James Bryant: Anglo-American Relations in the Atomic Age, 14065

Concannon, H.: 'The Growth of Arbitration Work in A.C.A.S.', 4154

Condell, Diana: Working for Victory? Images of Women in the First World War, 1914–18, 7704

Confederation of British Industry: The Future of Regional Policy, 5121; Britain Means Business: The Full Proceedings of the C.B.I. First National Conference, 5492; Twenty Five Years of 'Ups' and 'Downs', 5493

Congdon, Tim: Monetary Control in Britain, 4640

Congregational Year Book: 1846+, 12044

Conkling, Edgar C.: A Geographical Analysis of Diversification in South Wales, 5372

Conlen, Michael Robert Gunter: Alnwick, Northumberland: A Study in Town-plan Analysis, 18088

Conlin, James: Local and Central Government: Police Administration, 10738

Connell, Charles: Monte Cassino: The Historic Battle, 14863

Connell, John Henry Robertson: The 'Office': A Study of British Foreign Policy and its Makers, 1919–1951, 13331; Auchinleck, 14754; Wavell, Soldier and Scholar to June 1941, 14783

Connell, John: The End of Country Life in Central Surrey, 19170

Connell, Jon: Fraud: The Amazing Case of Doctor Savundra, 10273

Conniford, Michael Peter: British Light Military Trucks, 1939–1945, 15484; A Summary of the Transport used by the British Army 1939–1945, 15500

Connolly, Cyril: The Missing Diplomats, 16034; Enemies of Promise, 25461

Connolly, D. J.: 'Social Repercussions of New Cargo Handling Methods in the Port of London', 16702

Connolly, Joseph: P.G.Wodehouse: An Illustrated Biography, 25886

Connolly, L. W.: 'Politics and Royalty: Welsh Nationalism and the Investiture of the Prince of Wales, 1969', 2599; 'The Abolition of Theatre Censorship in Great Britain: The Theatres Act of 1968', 26902

Connolly, Michael: ed. 'Local Government in Northern Ireland', 3386

Connor, Robert: Cassandra: Reflections in a Mirror, 25217

Connor, Tom: Irish Youth in London Survey, 11370

Connor, Sir William Neil: George Brown: A Profile and Pictorial Biography, 1117

Conquest, Joan: The Naked Truth: Shocking Revelations about the Slums by an Ex-Nursing Sister, 18400

Conservation Society: (Pollution Working Party) The Health Effects of Lead on Children: A Review of Literature published since 1976, 20162; (Resources/Environment Committee-Economics Working Party). The Economics of Conservation: An Outline Plan for the United Kingdom, 20193

Conservation of The New Forest: A Report for Consultation Prepared by Officers Drawn from the Forestry Commission . . . [and others]. Winchester, 20228

Conservative Central Office: Design for a Nation's Health, 21584

Conservative Party Annual Conference Reports: 1948+, 1611

Conservative Political Centre: Service Overseas: The Young Idea, 9171; Clean and Pleasant Land: Studies on the Environment . . . , 19940

Conservative and Unionist Party: The Conservative Manifesto for Scotland, 1983, 2542; (Scottish Constitutional Committee) Scotland's Government: A Report . . . , 2543

Constable, Frieda: The England of Eric Ravilious, 24056

Constantine, Sir Leary Nicholas: Colour Bar, 11238

Constantine, Stephen: 'Amateur Gardening and Popular Recreation in the 19th and 20th centuries', 26981

Constitutional Development of the West Indies 1922–1968: A Selection from Major Documents, 12992

Construction Industry Advisory Committee: Managing Health and Safety in Construction, 4148

Consumer Council: Annual Report 1963/64–1970, 20460; Consumer Consultative Machinery in the Nationalised Industries: A Consumer Council Study, 20461

Control of Immigration Statistics: United Kingdom 1980+ Annual, 11092

Conversations Between the Church of England and the Methodist Church: A Report to the Archbishop of Cantebury and York and the Conference of the Methodist Church, 12306

Conway, Freda: 'The Industrial Structure of Towns', 17758; 'School-teachers' Salaries, 1945–1959', 22725

Conway, John S.: 'The Vatican, Great Britain and Relations with Germany, 1938–1940', 14114

Conway, Leonard Thomson: The International Position of the London Money Market, 1931–1937, 4413

Conway-Jones, Hugh: Gloucester Docks: An Illustrated History, 16687

Conzen, M. R. G.: The Urban Landscape: Historical Development and Management, 20314

Coogan, Tim Pat: Ireland, A Personal View, 2658; The IRA, 2767; On the Blanket: The H-Block Story, 2889

Cook, Alice Hanson: The Working Mother: A Survey of Problems and Programmes in Nine Countries, 7770

Cook, Chris P.: The Longman Handbook of Modern British History 1714–1987, 65; Sources in British Political History 1900–1951, 78; Post-war Britain: A Political History, 300; ed. The Politics of Reappraisal, 1918–1939, 785, 13144; ed. The Labour Party: An Introduction to its History, Structure and Politics, 1683; A

Short History of the Liberal Party 1900–1976, 1819; The Age of Alignment: Electoral Politics 1922–1929, 2280; ed. By-Elections in British Politics, 2356; The First European Elections: A Handbook and Guide, 2381; Trends in British Politics since 1945, 3501; The Slump: Society and Politics during the Depression, 3588, 7568; Longman Atlas of Modern British History: A Visual Guide to British Society and Politics, 1700–1970, 7569; Commonwealth Political Facts, 12470; ed. A Guide to the Steam Railways of Britain, 17028

Cook, E. Thomas: ed. The Empire and the World, 12547

Cook, Sir Edward Tyas: ed. The Press in Wartime, with some Account of the Official Press Bureau, 25110

Cook, Hugh: The North Staffordshire Regiment, 15726

Cook, Jean: A Village within the City: The Story of Old Headington, Oxford, 19197

Cook, Judith: ed. The National Theatre, 26139

Cook, Nancy Gwendolyn: Attempted Suicide: Its Social Significance and Effects, 10802

Cook, Olive: The Stanstead Affair: A Case for the People, 17687

Cook, P.: Ombudsman: An Autobiography, 3256

Cook, Pauline Lesley: Energy Policy: Strategies for Uncertainty, 7220; Railway Workings: The Problem of Contraction, 17085

Cook, Thomas Goldie: ed. Education and the Professions, 22424

Cook, Timothy: Vagrant Alcoholics, 22150

Cook-Mozaffairi, P. J.: Cancer incidence in Mortality in the Vicinity of Nuclear Power installations in England and Wales, 1959–1980, 22238

Cooke, A. M.: A History of the Royal College of Physicians, 20806

Cooke, Alistair: Masterpieces: A Decade of Classics in British Television, 24859

Cooke, Colin Arthur: The Life of Richard Stafford Cripps, 1156

Cooke, Douglas: ed. Youth Organisations of Great Britain: With a Foreword by the Countess of Albemarle, 8460

Cooke, G. W.: ed. Agricultural Research 1931–1981: A History of the Agricultural Research Council and a Review of Developments in Agricultural Science during the Last 50 Years, 19699

Cooke, Ronald Urwick: ed. Trends in Geography: An Introductory Survey, 26640

Cooke, Sidney Russell: The Oil Trusts and Anglo-American Relations, 14019

Cooke, Terence E.: Mergers and Acquisitions, 5549

Cooke, W. F.: 'The Pattern of Opposition in British and American Unions', 6780

Cookridge, E. H.: Inside S.O.E. The Story of Special Operations in Western Europe, 1940–45, 15193; George Blake: Double Agent, 16025; The Third Man. The Truth about 'Kim' Philby, Double Agent, 16047

Cooksley, Peter George: Flight Royal: The Queen's Flight and Royal Flying in Five Reigns, 17520

Coombe, R. A.: 'A Technological Education', 22525

Coombes, David L.: Westminster to Brussels: the Significance for Parliament of Accession to the European Community, 565; The Member of Parliament and the Administration: the Case of the Select Committee on Nationalised Industries, 656; Representative Government and Economic Power, 4975

Cooney, E. W.: 'Party Politics and Local Government in Western South Wales', 3382; Social Change in South-West Wales, 5381; The Social Pattern: A Handbook of Social Statistics of South-West Wales, 5382

Cooper, Alan: Research Libraries and Collections in the United Kingdom, 96

Cooper, Alfred Duff, Viscount Norwich: Old Men Forget, 1149; Haig, 14507

Cooper, Andrew Fenton: British Agricultural Policy, 1912–1936: A Study in Conservative Politics, 1630, 19432

Cooper, Artemis: ed. A Durable Fire: The Letters of Duff and Diana Cooper, 1913–1950, 1150

Cooper, Barry: 'Students' Study Habits, Attitudes and Academic Attainment', 22562; Renegotiating Secondary School Mathematics: A Study of Curriculum Change and Stability, 22830

Cooper, Barry: Transport Planning and Practice, A Review, 16260

Cooper, Basil Knowlan: Electric Trains in Britain, 17051

Cooper, Bruce M.: Industrial Relations: A Study in Conflict, 5778

Cooper, Bryan: Fighter. The Adventure of North Sea Oil, 7173; The Battle of the Torpedo Boats, 15400; Tank Battles of World War I, 15522; A History of Fighter Aircraft, 15826

Cooper, Christine: The Illegitimate Child, 8146

Cooper, David E.: Illusions of Equality, 22853

Cooper, David Graham: The Death of the Family, 10097

Cooper, Derek: The Bad Food Guide, 20605

Cooper, Lady Diana: The Light of Common Day, 26024

Cooper, Douglas: The Work of Graham Sutherland, 24075

Cooper, Gladys: An Autobiography, 26026

Cooper, Henry: An Autobiography, 27110

Cooper, J. M., Jnr: 'The Command of Gold Reversed: American Loans to Britain, 1915–1917', 13399; 'The British Response to the House-Grey Memorandum: New Evidence and New Questions', 13400

Cooper, Joan D.: Patterns of Family Placement: Current Issues in Fostering and Adoption, 8147; The Creation of the British Personal Social Services 1962–1974, 8844

Cooper, John Edward: Psychiatry and Anti-psychiatry, 21826; et al Psychiatric Diagnosis in New York and London: A Comparative Study of Mental Hospital Admissions, 21827; Measurement and Classification of Psychiatric Symptoms, 21856

Cooper, John St.John: Invasion! The D-Day Story, June 6, 1944, 14940

Cooper, M. H.: Prices and Profits in the Pharmaceutical Industry, 22269

Cooper, Malcolm: The Birth of Independent Air Power: British Air Policy in the First World War, 14618

Cooper, Michael Hymie: The Price of Blood, 21264

Cooper, Paul: 'Competing Explanations of the Merseyside Riots', 10873

Cooper, R. A. H.: The Greater London Problem: Report of the Chairman of the Planning Committee . . ., 18939

Cooper, R.: 'Trends in Medical Social Work in the United Kingdom and the United States', 8724

Cooper, R.A.: Export Performance and the Pressure of Demand, 4818

Cooper, Robert L.: ed. Sage Studies in Bilingual Education, 23622

Cooper, Robert Montague Hunte: The Danger of Food Contamination by Aluminium, 20636

Cooper, Steven: F.I.S. Part Five: Health Benefits, 4096; Poverty and the Development of Anti-Poverty Policy in the United Kingdom, 9091; Rural Poverty in the United Kingdom, 9107

Cooper, Susan: J. B.Priestley: Portrait of an Author, 25776

Cooper, W. B.: Methodism in Portsmouth, 1750–1932, 12109

Cooper, William: Henley-in-Arden, 19340

Coote, Anna: Sweet Freedom, 7797; Battered Women and the Law, 9951

Coote, Sir Colin Reith: A Companion of Honour: The Story of Walter Elliot, 1187; Editorial: The Memoirs of Colin R. Coote, 25223

Cootes, Richard John: The Making of the Welfare State, 21601

Cope, David E.: Organisation, Development and Active Research in Hospitals, 21407

Cope, Sir Vincent Zachary: The Royal College of Surgeons of England: A History, 20804; History of St Mary's Hospital Medical School: One Hundred Years of Medical Education, 20805, 22476; Almroth Wright, Founder of Modern Vaccine-therapy, 20892; A History of the Acute Abdomen, 21029; The Worshipful Society of Apothecaries of London and the Evolution of the Family Doctor, 21508; 'The Making of the Dental Profession in Britain, 22409; The Royal College of Surgeons of England, 22478

Copeman, Frederick: Reason in Revolt, 1945

Copeman, George H.: Leaders of British Industry: A Study of the Careers of more than a Thousand Public Company Directors, 4987, 9796; The Challenge of Employee Shareholding: How to Close the Gap between Capital and Labour, 6000

Copeman, William Sidney Charles: The Worshipful Society of Apothecaries of London: A History, 1617–1967, 20800; A Short History of the Gout and the Rheumatic Diseases, 21086

Copley, A. R. H.: Gandhi against the Tide, 13139

Copley, I. A.: The Music of Peter Warlock: A Critical Survey, 24390

Coppard, Audrey: ed. Orwell Remembered, 25752

Coppen, Helen Elizabeth: Survey of British Research in Audio-visual Aids, 1945–1971, 22771

Copperthwaite, Nigel: Local Government in the Community, 3143

Coppieters, Emmanuel: English Bank Note Circulation, 1694–1954, 4416

Coppieters, Frank: 'Arnold Wesker's Centre 42: A Cultural Revolution Betrayed', 26242

Copping, George: A Fascinating Story: The History of OCCA, 1918–1968, 6221

Coppock, John Terence: ed. Greater London, 18360; Land Use and Town and Country Planning, 18812; An Agricultural Atlas of England and Wales, 19385; 'The Changing Arable in England and Wales 1870–1956', 19500; An Agricultural Atlas of Scotland, 19614; ed. Environmental Quality, 19964; The Changing Use of Land in Britain, 19519, 20255; Land for New Towns: A Study of Land Use, Densities, and Agricultural Displacement, 20256; The Geographer and the Use of Land, 20282; ed. Spatial Dimensions of Public Policy, 20284; Recreation in the Countryside: A Spatial Analysis, 26958; ed. Second Homes: Curse or Blessing?, 26959;'Ideals for National Parks', 26961

Copps, J. A.: 'The Union in British Socialist Thought', 6786

Corbally, Marcus Joseph Patrick Matthew: The Royal Ulster Rifles, 1793–1957, 15562

Corbett, Anne: Much to do about Education: A Critical Survey of the Fate of the Major Educational Reports, 22636; Innovation in Education, England, 22769

Corbett, John: The Birmingham Trades Council, 1866–1966, 6838, 6909, 18006

Corbett, Sir Julian Stafford: History of the Great War: Naval Operations, 14674

Corbin, Marie: ed. The Couple, 10107

Cordeaux, E. H.: A Bibliography of Printed Works Relating to Oxfordshire (excluding the University and the City), 19168; A Bibliography of Printed Works Relating to the University of Oxford, 23449

Corden, Carol: Planned Cities: New Towns in Britain and America, 18237, 19000

Corina, Maurice: Trust in Tobacco: The Anglo-American Struggle for Power, 6536; Pile It High, Sell It Cheap: The Authorised Biography of Sir John Cohen, 6648; From Silks and Oak Counters: Debenhams 1878–1978, 6652

Corish, Patrick J.: The Irish Catholic Experience: A Historical Survey, 2719

Cork, Sir Kenneth: Cork on Cork: Sir Kenneth Cork takes Stock, 4204

Corke, Alison: British Airways: The Path to Profitability, 17628

Corlett, John: Aviation in Ulster, 17531

Corlett, T.: Housing Since the Rent Act: An Interim Report from the Rowntree Trust Housing Study, 18723; Essays on Housing, 18724

Corley, Thomas Anthony Bertram: Domestic Electrical Appliances, 6677; 'Consumer Marketing in Britain, 1914–60', 20473;

Quaker Enterprise in Biscuits: Huntley & Palmers of Reading, 1822–1972, 20705

Cormack, Ian Leslie: Glasgow Tramways 1872–1962: Ninety Glorious Years, 17226; Green Goddesses go East: A Brief History of the ex-Liverpool Trams in Glasgow 1933–1960, 17227

Cormack, Patrick: Westminster Palace and Parliament, 547

Cornelius, David Krause: ed. Cultures in Conflict: Perspectives on the Snow-Leavis Controversy, 23749

Cornelius, John: Liverpool 8, 18051

Corner, D. C.: Investment and Unit Trusts in Britain and America, 4265; 'Exports and the British Trade Cycle: 1929', 4777

Cornes, Paul: Open Prisons, 10368

Cornford, James Peters: British Elites 1870–1950, 9755

Cornforth, Maurice: ed. Rebels and their Causes: Essays in Honour of A. L. Morton, 26734

Cornish, D. B.: Gambling: A Review of the Literature, 27111

Cornish, Graham Peter: Archival Collections of Non-Book Material, 207

Cornish, Margaret: Troubled Waters: Memoirs of a Canal Boatwoman, 16389

Cornwall County and Diocesan Record Office: Handlist of Records: Turnpike Roads, Canals, Ferries, 16420

Cornwallis-Jones, Arthur Thomas: Education for Leadership: The International Administrative Staff Colleges, 1948–1984, 5486

Corran, Henry Stanley: The Isle of Man, 2615; A History of Brewing, 6167

Corrigan, D. Felicitas: Siegfried Sassoon: Poet's Pilgrimage, 25793

Coryton, Ray: Hutchinson: Two Men of Letters: Correspondence between R.C. Hutchinson, Novelist, and Martyn Skinner, Poet, 25585

Cosgrave, Patrick: Margaret Thatcher: A Tory and Her Party, 1048; Thatcher: The First Term, 1048; R.A. Butler: An English Life, 1129; Carrington: A Life and a Policy, 1132; The Lives of Enoch Powell, 1300

Cosh, John A.: The History of the Royal National Hospital for Rheumatic Diseases, 21420

Cosin, Ben Rupert: ed. Education: Structure and Society: Selected Readings, 22807

Cosmo, Graham: The Role of A.C.A.S.: Conciliation in Equal Pay and Sex Discrimination Cases, 4166

Cossons, W. E.: 'The Case for Pithead Baths in Great Britain', 21280

Costello, John: Jutland, 1916, 14657; The Battle of the Atlantic, 14796; Mask of Treachery, 16031; The Battle for Concorde, 17568

Costelloe, Rachel/Ray: Careers and Openings for Women:A Survey of Women's Employment and a Guide for those Seeking Work, 7668; 'The Cause': A Short History of the Women's Movement in Great Britain, 7669; ed, Our Freedom and its Results, 7670; Women's Suffrage and Women's Service: The History of the London and National Society for Women's Service, 7671

Coster, Ian: The Sharpest Edge in the World: The Story of the Rise of a Great Industry, 6541

Costigliola, Frank C.: 'Anglo-American Financial Rivalry in the 1920's', 3709

Cotes, Peter: George Robey: 'The Darling of the Halls', 26340

Cotgrove, Stephen Frederick: The Science of Society: An Introduction to Sociology, 7944; The Sociology of Science and Technology, 7945; Science, Industry and Society: Studies in the Sociology of Science, 7946; 'Scientific Identity, Occupational Selection and Role Strain', 9832; Technical Education and Social Change, 23283

Cotter, Charles H.: A History of Nautical Astronomy, 26433; 'Nautical Astronomy: Past, Present and Future', 26434

Cotterill, D. J.: Victoria College, Jersey, 1852–1972, 23081

Cottis, S. P.: 'Restrictive Practices Legislation: An Industrial View', 6109

Cottle, Basil: The Life of a University, 23462

Cotton, James: ed. The Korean War in History, 16144

Cottrell, John: Julie Andrews: The Story of a Star, 24472; Richard Burton: A Biography, 26016; Laurence Olivier, 26079

Cottrell, P. L.: ed. Money and Power: Essays in Honour of L. S. Pressnell, 4648

Cough, Robert: A Public Eye, 25216

Coughlan, A.: Fooled Again? The Anglo-Irish Agreement and After, 3005

Coughtrey, P. J.: ed. Ecological Aspects of Radionuclide Release, 20132

Couldery, Frederick Alan James: Accounting Standards Study Book, 4194

Coull, James Reid: ed. The County of Shetland, 19236; The Fisheries in the Shetland Area: A Study in Conservation and Development, 19815

Coulshed, Veronica: Social Work Practice: An Introduction, 8903

Coulson, Anthony J.: A Bibliography of Design in Britain 1851–1970, 24109

Coulson, Sidney John: ed. Theology and the University: An Ecumenical Investigation, 22436

Coult, Tony: The Plays of Bond, 25948

Coulter, John Stanley: Physical Therapy, 21119

Coulter, Jack Leonard Sagar: ed. The Royal Naval Medical Services, 15326

Coulton, Barbara: MacNeice in the BBC, 25692

Coulton, G.C.: Fourscore Years: An Autobiography, 26795

Council for Children's Welfare: A Family Service and a Family Court, 8718

Council for Research on Housing Construction: Housing Standards and Statistics, 18611; Slum Clearance and Rehousing: The First Report, 18612; Housing Finance: Report on Subsidies For Rehousing in Urban Areas, 18613

Council for Wales and Monmouthshire: Report on the Welsh Holiday Industry, 5346; Report on the Welsh Language Today: Cmnd 2198, Parliamentary Papers xx, (1963–64), 23832

Council for the Preservation of Rural England: The Case for National Parks in Great Britain, 20189

Council of Christians and Jews: Annual Report 1960, 11309; The Corner of the Earth: Souvenir of an Anglo-Jewish Exhibition in the Undercroft of Westminster Abbey in the 900th Anniversary Year, 11310

Counihan, David: Royal Progress: Britain's Changing Monarchy, 431

Counter Information Services: The Wealthy, 3788

Countryside Planning Yearbook: Norwich, 1980+, 19031

County Magazine Index: An Index to Magazines covering the Rural and Country Life of the Counties of England: 1979+ , 26759

Couper, M.: 'Housing Classes and Housing Values', 18734

Coupland, Nikolas: Dialect in Use: Sociolinguistic Variations in Cardiff English, 23835

Coupland, Sir Reginald: Welsh and Scottish Nationalism: A Study, 2418

Courage, G.: The History of 15/19 the King's Royal Hussars 1939–1945, 15668

Course, Edwin Alfred: London Railways, 16960

Course, Alfred George: The Merchant Navy: A Social History, 16485

Court, John Hubert: North British Steam Locomotives Built 1857–1956 for Railways Overseas, 17067; North British Steam Locomotives Built 1833–1948 for Railways in Britain, 17068

Court, Seymour Donald Mayneord: ed. The Medical Care of Children, 21112; ed. Fit for the Future: Report of the Committee on Child Health Services, 21113

Court, Thomas H.: The History of the Microscope, 7105

Court, William Henry Bassano: A Concise Economic History of Britain from 1750 to Recent Times, 3476; Scarcity and Choice in History, 3496; 'Problems of the British Coal Industry between the Wars', 6276; Coal, 6289

Court, William: Poverty and Glory: The History of Grand Prix Motor Racing, 17364

Courtauld Institute of Art: Annual Bibliography of the History of British Art, 23934

Courtney, Anthony: Sailor in a Russian Frame, 1397

Courtney, Geoff: The Power behind Aston Martin, 17454

Courtney, Nicholas: Princess Anne: A Biography, 535

Cousins, Frank: 'Race Relations in Employment in the United Kingdom', 10994

Cousins, Geoffrey: The Story of Scapa Flow, 15301; Golf in Britain: A Social History from the Beginnings to the Present Day, 27153

Cousins, James M.: 'The Contours of Solidarity: Social Stratification and Industrial Relations in Shipbuilding', 9663

Cousins, Paul: 'London Votes 1983: The General Election', 2375; 'The GLC Election 1981', 3299; '1982: The Battle for the Boroughs', 3307

Coussins, Jean: The Equality Report: One Year of the Equal Pay Act, the Sex Discrimination Act, the Equal Opportunities Commission, 7779; Badge of Poverty: A New Look at the Stigma attached to Free School Meals, 20529

Coutts, John: The Salvationists, 12128

Coventry City Council: City of Coventry: 1966 Review of the Development Plan, Analysis and Statement, 18856

Coventry Community Development Project (Inter-Project Editorial Team): CDP Final Report: Part One: Coventry and Hillfields, 9282; CDP Final Report: Part Two: Background Working Papers, 9283; School Life and Working Life: A Report Carried out for the Home Office CDP in Coventry, 1971–1975, 9284; Gilding the Ghetto: The State and the Poverty Experiments, 9285

Coventry Community Workshop and Shelter: Council Houses: The New Slums, 18405

Coventry, John Seton: 'Ecumenism in England since the Council', 12332; Reconciling, 12349

Cowan, Arthur Robert: The Sterling Area, 4699; The Problem of Sterling, 4700

Cowan, Ian Borthwick: The Scottish Episcopal Church: The Ecclesiastical History and Polity, 12264

Cowan, May: Inverewe: A Garden in the North West Highlands, 26565

Cowan, Peter: The Office: A Facet of Urban Growth, 17933; ed. Developing Patterns of Urbanization, 17934; ed. The Future of Planning: A Study Sponsored by the Centre for Environmental Studies, 17846; Depreciation, Obsolescence and Ageing', 18735; 'Some Observations Concerning the Increase of Hospital Provision in London Between 1850 and 1960', 21434

Cowan, Robert Hamish: Housing Improvement Policies in Scotland: A Survey of Local Authorities, 18469; Improvement Grants in Scotland, 1967–73, 18470

Cowan, William: The Maps of Edinburgh 1544–1929, 26697

Coward, John: 'Recent Characteristics of Roman Catholic Fertility in Northern and Southern Ireland', 7524

Cowden, James E.: The Price of Peace: Elder Dempster, 1939–1945, 15133

Cowdrey, Michael Colin: MCC: The Autobiography of a Cricketer, 27103

Cowell, Betty: Behind the Blue Door: The History of the Royal College of Midwives, 1881–1981, 21447, 21729

Cowell, Frank A.: Measuring Inequality, 3857

Cowell, Frank Richard: The Garden as Fine Art: From Antiquity to Modern Times, 19905

Cowell, J. Graham: D.H. Comet: The World's First Jet Airliner, 17605

Cowen, David L.: 'The Edinburgh Pharmacoepia: 1 Historical Development and Significance, 2 Bibliography', 21021

Cowen, Sir Zelman: The British Commonwealth of Nations in a Changing World, 12579

Cowie, H. T.: 'American Investment in British Industry', 3724

Cowie, John Stewart: Mines, Minelayers and Minelaying, 15395

Cowie, John: Delinquency in Girls, 10621

Cowie, Leonard Wallace: The Industrial Revolution 1750 to the Present Day, 3497

Cowie, Peter: Seventy years of Cinema, 24635

Cowie, Valerie: Delinquency in Girls, 10621

Cowie, William John Gavin: The Farm Worker: His Training, Pay and Status, 19664, 19671

Cowles, E.: Sand-hills and Mountains: Memoirs of a Civil Servant, 931

Cowles, Virginia: Winston Churchill: The Era and the Man, 988; The Phantom Major: The Story of David Stirling and the S.A.S. Regiment, 15724

Cowley, Brian Lee: The Self, the Individual and the Community: Liberalism in the Political Thought of F.A. Hayek and Sidney and Beatrice Webb, 2093

Cowley, John: Community or Class Struggle, 9394

Cowley, Ruth: What About Women? Information Sources for Women's Studies, 7625

Cowling, Keith George: Advertising and Economic Behaviour, 4307; Optimality in Firms' Advertising Policies: An Empirical Analysis, 4308; Mergers and Economic Performance, 4992; Monopolies and Mergers Policy: A View on the Green Paper, 5535; Monopoly Capitalism, 5536; Price Formation under Oligopoly: An Analysis of the U.K. Motor Industry, 17416; 'Price, Quality and Advertising Competition: An Econometric Investigation of the United Kingdom Market', 17417; The Resource Structure of Agriculture: An Economic Analysis, 19548; 'Determinants of Wage Inflation in Scottish Agriculture, 1948–1963', 19618

Cowling, Maurice John: The Impact of Labour, 1920–1924: The Beginning of Modern British Politics, 1701; ed. Conservative Essays, 2199; Religion and Public Doctrine in Modern England, 11564; The Impact of Hitler, 13696

Cowling, T. G.: 'Mathematicians, Astrology and Cosmogony', 26439

Cox, Alfred: Among the Doctors, 20838

Cox, Andrew: Adversary Politics and Land: The Conflict over Land and Property Policy in Post-War Britain, 20263

Cox, Barry: The Fall of Scotland Yard, 10757

Cox, Bernard: Paddle Steamers, 16588

Cox, Caroline: Rape of Reason: The Corruption of the Polytechnic of North London, 9866; ed. A Sociology of Medical Practice, 21960

Cox, Charles Brian: ed. Black Paper Three: Goodbye Mr Short, 22645; The Black Papers on Education, 22648; ed. The 20th Century Mind: History, Ideas and Literature in Britain, 23728; Joseph Conrad: The Modern Imagination, 25463; Dylan Thomas: A Collection of Critical Essays, 25835

Cox, David: 'The Labour Party in Leicester: A Study in Branch Development', 1778

Cox, David: The Henry Wood Proms, 24442

Cox, Derek Maurice: The Community Approach to Youth Work in East London, 8461

Cox, Evan Hillhouse Methuen: The Modern English Garden, 19861; A History of Gardening in Scotland, 19862

Cox, Sir Geoffrey: The Road to Trieste, 14864; The Race for Trieste, 14865; See it Happen: The Making of ITN, 24923

Cox, Idris: The Fight for Socialism in South Wales, 1848–1948, 2567; Forward to a New Life for South Wales, 2568; Drive the Spectre from Wales, 2569

Cox, James T.: Practice and Procedure in the Church of Scotland, 12190

Cox, Jeffrey: The English Churches in a Secular Society: Lambeth 1870–1930, 11587

Cox, Kevin: Geography, Social Contexts and Welsh Voting Behaviour 1861–1951, 2584; ed. Urbanization and Conflict in Market Societies, 17936

Cox, Margaret: ed. The Urban Crisis: Social Problems and Planning, 17926

Cox, Peter R.: 'The Demographic Characteristics of Britain Today, and their Implications', 7379; 'Demographic Development in Great Britain since the Royal Commisssion on Population', 7380; Demography, 7487; Population and Pollution: Proceedings of the Eighth Annual Symposium of the Eugenic Society, 19985

Cox, Richard W.: Sport—A Guide to Historical Sources in the U.K, 27020; 'A Survey of Literature on the History of Sport in Britain', 27021

Cox, William Harvey: 'The 1983 General Election in Northern Ireland: Anatomy and Consequences', 2374; Cities, the Public Dimension, 17937; City Politics and the Press: Journalists and the Government of Merseyside, 25326

Coxall, W. N.: Political Realities: Parties and Pressure Groups, 2062

Coxhead, Elizabeth: Women in the Professions, 7811

Coxon, Anthony Peter Macmillan: The Images of Occupational Prestige, 5917, 9551; The Fate of the Anglican Clergy: A Sociological Study, 11677

Coxon, R. T.: Roads and Rails of Birmingham, 1900–1939, 17153

Coyle, G.: 'Some Principles and Methods in Social Work Education', 8725

Coyne, John: Management Buy-outs, 5548

Coysh, Arthur Wilfred: British Art Pottery, 1870–1940, 24133

Crabtree, Cyril: The Industrial Relations Act: A Comprehensive Guide, 5741

Cracknell, Douglas George: Constitutional Law and the English Legal System, 609

Cradock, Percy: ed. Recollections of the Cambridge Union, 1815–1939, 23469

Craft Skills, A Report on: in the Building Industry: by a Working Group, Chairman Donald Ensom, 6175

Craft, Maurice: ed. Youth Service and Interprofessional Studies, 8451; ed. Family, Class and Education: A Reader, 9543, 10092; ed. Linking Home with School, 23139; ed. Teaching in a Multicultural Society, 23193

Craft, Michael John: 'The Treatment of Adolescents with Personality Disorders', 10682; Patterns of Care for the Subnormal, 21790; ed. Psychopathic Disorders and their Assessment, 21936; ed. Ten Studies in Psychopathic Personality: A Report to the Home Office and the Mental Health Research Fund, 21937; ed. Concluding Chapter in Born to Trouble: Portrait of a Psychopath, 21938

Cragg, Rowland: Anvil and Loom: A Survey of British Industries, 6461

Craig, Christine: The Employment of Cambridge Graduates, 9877

Craig, David: 'The New Poetry of Socialism', 23786

Craig, Edward A.: Gordon Craig: The Story of his Life, 26028

Craig, Frederick Walter Scott: British Parliamentary Election Results, 1885–1918, 2204; British Parliamentary Election Results, 1918–1949, 2205; British Parliamentary Election Results, 1950–1970, 2206; British Parliamentary Election Results, 1974–1983, 2207; British Parliamentary Election Statistics, 1918–1970, 2208; British Parliamentary Election Results 1983–1987, 2209; British Electoral Facts 1832–1987, 2210; Boundaries of Parliamentary Constituencies, 1885–1972, 2211; Britain Votes Four: British General Election Manifestos, 1900–1974, 2212; Minor Parties at British Parliamentary Elections, 1885–1974, 2213; Chronology of British Parliamentary By-Election Results, 1833–1987, 2214; ed. Europe Votes I, 2377; ed. Europe Votes II, 2378; ed. City and Royal Burgh of Glasgow: Municipal Election Results 1948–73, 3204; Greater London Votes 1: The Greater London Council 1964–1970, 3297

Craig, Gary: ed. Jobs And Commnunity Action, 9374

Craig, Gordon Alexander: ed. The Diplomats, 1919–1939, 13330

Craig, H.: The Legislative Council of Trinidad and Tobago, 13064

Craig, John: 'Humberside: Employment, Unemployment and Migration: The Evolution of Industrial Structure 1951–1966', 7020; Population Density and Concentration in Great Britain 1931, 1951 and 1961, 7406; Socioeconomic Classification of Local Authority Areas, 7407, 18337

Craig, Sir John Herbert McCutcheon: A History of Red Tape, 849; The Mint: A History of the London Mint from AD 287 to 1948, 4721

Craig, Mary: Longford: A Biographical Portrait, 1263

Craig, Rachel: The Youth Training Scheme: A Study of Non-Participants and Early Leavers, 8549

Craig, Robert S.: Social Concern in the Thought of William Temple, 11712

Craig, Robin: Steam Tramps and Cargo Liners 1850–1950, 16596

Craig, Walter Lennox: Sterling Decimal Coinage: A Colonial Plea for Modernising our Money, 4722

Craig, William Stuart McCrae: History of the Royal College of Physicians of Edinburgh, 20803; Child and Adolescent Life in Health and Disease: A Study in Social Paediatrics, 22064

Craigie, Sir Robert Leslie: Behind the Japanese Mask, 13259

Craik, William White: Bryn Roberts and the National Union of Public Employees, 6842; The Central Labour College, 1909–1929: a Chapter in the History of Adult Working Class Education, 23670

Craker, Trevor: Opening Accounts and Closing Memories; Thirty Years with Thames and Hudson, 24992

Cramer, Gerald: Henry Moore: Catalogue of Graphic Work 1931–1979, 24094

Crammond, Edgar: The Economic Position of Great Britain, 3555

Cramond, Ronald Duncan: 'Housing and Mobility', 7339; Housing Policy in Scotland, 1919–1964: A Study in State Assistance, 18471; Allocation of Council Houses: A Report of a Survey of Methods of Allocation of Tenancies by Local Authorities in Scotland, 18472

Cramp, B. G.: British Midland Airways, 17631

Cramp, Harold St.George: A Yeoman Farmer's Son: A Leicestershire Childhood, 19592

Crampsey, Bob: The Scottish Footballer, 27087

Cramshaw, Nancy: The Cyprus Revolt: An Account of the Struggle for Union with Greece, 12866

Crane, Edith Eva: ed. Honey, 20722; ed. The Archaeology of Beekeeping, 20723

Crane, Paul: Gays and the Law, 10851

Cranefield, P. F.: ed. The Historical Development of Physiological Thought: A Symposium, 26457

Cranfield, Geoffrey Alan: The Press and Society from Caxton to Northcliffe, 25037

Cranfield, Ingrid: The Challengers: British and Commonwealth Adventure since 1945, 27228

Cranforth, John: Working in the Community, 9403

Crankshaw, William P.: Report on a Survey of the Welsh Textile Industry, 6462

Craster, Sir Herbert Henry Edmund: ed. Speeches on Foreign Policy by Viscount Halifax, 1218

Craven, Edward: Regional Devolution and Social Policy, 2410, 8954; ed. The Uncertain Future: Demographic Change and Social Policy, 8953; 'Private Residential Expansion in Kent 1956–1964: A Study of Pattern and Process in Urban Growth', 18311

Crawford, Anne: ed. The Europa Biographical Dictionary of British Women, 7622

Crawford, C.: The Free Two Pence: Section 137 of Local Government Act 1972 and Section 83 of the Local Government (Scotland) Act 1973, 3263

Crawford, Iain: The Profumo Affair, 9904

Crawford, John G.: ed. Australian Trade Policy 1942–1966, 12638; 'Britain, Australia and the Common Market', 14167

Crawford, M.: 'The 1965 Reforms in the British Tax System', 4843

Crawford, M. P.: 'Retirement and Role Playing', 8623

Crawford, Oliver: The Door Marked Malaya, 16167

Crawford, Osbert Guy Stanhope: Said and Done: The Autobiography of an Archaeologist, 26358

Crawford, Robert George: Loyal to King Billy: A Profile of the Ulster Protestants, 2945

Crawford, Sir William Smith: The People's Food, 20586

Crawfurd, Horace Evelyn: That's the Way the Money Goes: A Study of the Relations between British Industry and Taxation, 6062

Crawley, Aidan: Leap Before You Look: A Memoir, 1398

Crawley, Charles W.: Trinity Hall: The History of a Cambridge College, 23471

Crawshay-Williams, Rupert: Russell Remembered, 26867

Craze, Michael Rommily: The History of Felsted School, 1564–1947, 23060

Creasy, John: The Countryside between the Wars 1918–1940: A Photographic Record, 19433

Creaton, Heather J.: ed. Institute of Historical Research 1958–1959, 408; ed. Institute of Historical Research 1960–1961, 409; ed. Institute of Historical Research 1962–1964, 410; ed. Institute of Historical Research 1965–1966, 411; ed. Institute of Historical Research 1967–1968, 412; ed. Institute of Historical Research 1969–1970, 413; ed. Institute of Historical Research 1971–1972, 414; ed. Institute of Historical Research 1973–1974, 415

Credland, Geoffrey Denis: Scotland: The Vital Market, 5254; Scotland: A New Look, 5255

Creech-Jones, Violet: 'Select Committee on Estimates: Report on Child Care.' Howard J, 8148

Creedy, John: State Pensions in Britain, 8640

Creek, Frederick Norman Smith: A History of the Corinthian Football Club, 27084

Creese, Walter Littlefield: The Search for Environment: The Garden City: Before and After, 17789

Creigh, S. W.: ed. Industrial Conflict in Britain, 6959

Creighton, Charles: A History of Epidemics in Britain, 22352

Creighton, Donald: The Forked Road: Canada 1939–1957, 12642

Creighton, Joanne: Margaret Drabble, 25481

Creighton, John: British Buses since 1945, 17268; Fire Engines of Yesterday, 17479; Fire Engines in the United Kingdom, 17480

Creighton, Louise: 'Women Police', 7661

Creighton, W. B.: Working Women and the Law, 7780

Crellin, Eileen: Born Illegitimate: Social and Educational Implications, 8149

Cressey, Donald Ray: Criminal Organization: Its Elementary Forms, 10185, 10264

Cressey, Peter: Employee Participation in Scottish Industry and Commerce: A Survey of Attitudes and Practices, 6040; Participation in the Electronics Sector: The Comco Case Study, 6041

Cresswell, Colin Randall: Notes on Air Pollution Control, 20050

Cresswell, Peter: 'Interpretations of "Suicide"', 10817

Cresswell, Peter: Justifying New Towns: And, Criteria for Evaluating New Towns, 18999

Cresswell, Roy: ed. Passenger Transport and the Environment, 16233

Cressy, Edward: Discoveries and Inventions of the Twentieth Century, 7139

Creswell, John: Naval Warfare: An Introductory Study, 15338; Generals and Admirals: The Story of Amphibious Command, 15477

Crew, Albert: The Unemployment Insurance Acts, 1920–1927, 4023; The Profession of an Accountant, 9797; The Profession of a Secretary, 9798; London Prisons of Today and Yesterday: Plain Facts and Coloured Impressions, 10380

Crew, Dudley: A Fragment of Friendship: A Memory of Evelyn Waugh when Young, 25866

Crew, Francis Albert Eley: Measurement of the Public Health : Essays on Social Medicine, 22067; ed. The Army Medical Services: Administration, 22115

Crewe, Ivor: Thatcherism: Its Origins, Electoral Impact and Implications for Downs's Theory of Party Strategy, 1056; British Parliamentary Constituencies: A Statistical Compendium, 2221; 'Partisanship and Policy Choice: Issue Preference in the British Electorate, February 1974', 2332; 'Angels in Plastic: The Liberal Surge in 1974', 2333; ed. Political Communications: The General Election Campaign of 1987, 2355

Crewe, Quentin: ed. The Frontiers of Privilege—A Century of Social Conflict as Reflected in The Queen, 25185

Crichton, Anne: Industrial Relations and the Personnel Specialists, 5705, 9781

Crichton, J. D.: ed. English Catholic Worship: Liturgical Renewal in England since 1900, 11976

Crichton, Richard: The Coldstream Guards, 1946–1970, 15611

Crichton, Ruth Morley: Commuter's Village: A Study of Community and Commuters in the Berkshire Village of Stratfield Mortimer, 9350, 19204

Crichton-Browne, Sir James: 'Milk and Health', 20649; From the Doctor's Notebook, 20864; The Doctor Remembers, 20865

Crick, Bernard Rowland: The Crisis of British Government in the Nineteen Sixties, 552; ed. On Reform: a Centenary Tribute, 553; The Reform of Parliament, 564; 'The Prospects for Parliamentary Reform', 588; ed. The Commons in Transition, 633; ed. Protest and Discontent, 2137; 'Socialist Literature in the 1950s', 2161; ed. The Future of the Social Services, 8823; George

Orwell: A Life, 25739; George Orwell: Nineteen Eighty Four, 25740; *ed.* Orwell Remembered, 25752

Crick, Michael: The March of Militant, 1794, 1991

Crick, Wilfrid Frank: A Hundred Years of Joint Stock Banking, 4409; Thirty Years of Monetary Change, 1914–1945, 4568

Cripps, Anthony: The Agriculture Act, 1947, 19462

Cripps, Ernest C.: Through a City Archway. The Story of Allen and Hanburys, 1715–1954, 22277; Plough Court. The Story of a Notable Pharmacy 1715–1927, 22278

Cripps, Francis: Local Government Finance and its Reform: A Critique of the Layfield Committee's Report, 4875

Cripps, John: Accommodation for Gypsies: A Report on the Working of the Caravan Sites Act, 1968, Presented to the Secretary of State for the Environment, December 1976, 11354

Cripps, T. F.: 'Analysis of the Duration of Male Unemployment in Great Britain, 1932–1973', 7009

Crisp, Clement: Ballet Rambert: 50 Years and On, 24242

Crisp, Dorothy: The Dominance of England, 13222

Crisp, Robert: Brazen Chariots: An Account of Tank Warfare in the Western Desert, November-December 1941, 15523

Crispin, A.: 'Local Government Finance: Assessing the Central Government's Contribution', 3274

Critcher, Charles: Working Class Culture, 23730; The Devil Makes Work: Leisure in Capitalist Britain, 26937

Critchley, Julian: Heseltine: The Unauthorised Biography, 1234; Westminster Blues, 1399

Critchley, MacDonald: The Black Hole and Other Essays, 22390; 'The Origins of Aphasiology', 22391

Critchley, Ron A.: United Kingdom Food Trends over the Last Decade, 20615

Critchley, Thomas Alan: The Civil Service Today, 846; A History of Police in England and Wales, 1900–1966, 10697; The Conquest of Violence: Order and Liberty in Britain, 10698

Croall, Jonathan: Neill of Summerhill: The Permanent Rebel, 23216

Crocker, Lucy H.: The Peckham Experiment: A Study in the Living Structure of Society, 9308, 17714

Crockett, Anthony John Sinclair: Green Beret, Red Star: The Story of Two Years' Struggle Against the Maylayan[sic] Terrorist, 16164

Crockett, Geoffrey: British Managers: A Study of their Education, Training, Mobility and Earnings, 5452

Crockford's Clerical Directory:1858+, 11533

Croft, Andrew: Polar Exploration: Epics of the Twentieth Century, 27217

Croft, Noel Andrew Cotton: Under the Pole Star: The Oxford University Arctic Expedition, 1935–36, 27208

Crofton, Eileen: The Social Effects of Chronic Bronchitis: A Scottish Study, 22079

Crofts, C.: Some Aspects of Planned Migration to New and Expanding Towns, 18259

Crombie, A. D.: A Sociology of Organisations, 5676

Crompton, Mary: Workers' Attitudes and Technology, 5897

Crompton, Rosemary: Economy and Class Structure, 9550; White-collar Proletariat: Deskilling and Gender in Clerical Work, 9670

Crompton, W. G.: '"Efficient and Economical Policy?": The Performance of the Railway Companies 1922–1933', 16836

Cromwell, Valerie: 'The Foreign and Commonwealth Office' in 'The Times Survey of Foreign Ministries of the World', 13334

Cromwell, William C.: 'The Marshall Plan, Britain and the Cold War', 14131

Crone, Gerald Roe: The Royal Geographical Society: A Record, 1931–1955, 26627; Background to Geography, 26635; Background to Political Geography, 26636; 'British Geography in the Twentieth century', 26645; Modern Geographers: An Outline of Progress in Geography since AD 1800, 26657; Maps and their Makers: An Introduction to the History of Cartography, 26703

Cronin, James E.: Industrial Conflict in Modern Britain, 5802, 6915; Labour and Society in Britain 1918–1979, 7621; *ed.* Social Conflict and the Political Order in Modern Britain, 13573

Cronin, Sean: Irish Nationalism: A History of its Roots and Ideology, 2726

Crook, A.C.: Penrose to Cripps: A Century of Building at the College of St. John the Evangelist, 23485

Crook, A. D. H.: 'Privatisation of Housing and the Impact of the Conservative Government's Initiatives on Low Cost Home Ownership and Private Renting between 1979 and 1984 in England and Wales: The Privatisation Policies', 18436

Crook, Richard C.: 'Decolonisation, the Colonial State and Chieftaincy in the Gold Coast', 12746

Crookenden, N.: Dropzone Normandy: The Story of the American and British Airborne Assault on D-Day 1944, 14947

Crookes, T. G.: 'Burgess "H" Score in Psychiatric Patients', 10537

Croome, David Robin: Money in Britain, 1959–1969, 4627

Croome, Desmond Felix: Rails through the Clay: A History of London's Tube Railways, 17000

Croome, Honoria Renée Minturn: The Economy of Britain: A History, 3463

Cropley, A. J.: 'Intelligence, Family Size and Socio-economic Status.', 10098

Cros, Janet Teissier du: Divided Loyalties, 15181

Crosbie, A. J.: 'Brunei in Transition', 12952

Crosbie, David: Pensioned Off: A Study of Elderly People in Cleator Moor, 8617

Crosby, Alan: A History of Thetford, 19208

Crosby, Andrew C.: Creativity and Performance in Industrial Organization, 4944

Crosby, Gerda Richards: Disarmament and Peace in British Politics, 1914–1919, 13443

Crosby, Sir Josiah: Siam: The Crossroads, 13260

Crosby, Travis L.: The Impact of Civilian Evacuation in the Second World War, 8150

Crosfield, John Fothergill: A History of the Cadbury Family, 20699

Crosland, Charles Anthony Raven: The Future of Socialism, 1158; The Politics of Education, 1159; Socialism Now, and other Essays, 1160; Britain's Economic Problem, 3613; Towards a Labour Housing Policy, 18714. 'Some Thoughts on English Education', 22637

Crosland, Margaret: Beyond the Lighthouse: English Women Novelists in the Twentieth Century, 7740

Crosland, Susan: Tony Crosland, 1162

Crosley, A. S.: 'Early Development of the Railless Electric Trolleybus, in particular its Application in Great Britain and elsewhere up to 1924', 7045

Cross, Alfred Rupert Neale: Punishment, Prison and the Public: An Assessment of Penal Reform in 20th Century England by an Armchair Penologist, 10383

Cross, Charles: Cross on Local Government Law, 3105; Local Government and Politics, 3146

Cross, Colin: *ed.* Life with Lloyd George: The Diary of A. J. Sylvester, 1931–1945, 1018; The Fascists in Britain, 2021; Philip Snowden, 1318; The British Empire, 12478; The Fall of the British Empire, 1918–1968, 12586

Cross, Crispin: Ethnic Minorities in the Inner City: The Ethnic Dimension in Urban Deprivation in England, 11066

Cross, Frank Leslie: *ed.* The Oxford Dictionary of the Christian Church, 11529; Darwell Stone, 11813

Cross, John Arthur: 'Problems of Ministerial Turnover in Two Labour Cabinets', 732; The Tactics of Resignation: A Study in British Cabinet Government, 744; Timing of Cabinet Reshuffles', 745; 'Rejuvenating the Cabinet: The Records of Post-War British Prime Ministers Compared', 746; 'Ministerial Responsibility and the British Civil Service', 906; Lord Swinton, 1170; Sir Samuel Hoare: A Political Biography, 1236; 'Withdrawal of the Conservative Party Whip', 1643; 'The Regional Decentralisation of British Government Departments', 2401; Whitehall and the Commonwealth: British Departmental Organisation for Commonwealth Relations, 1900–1966, 12506

Cross, K. W.: 'Some Changes in the Composition of a Mental Hospital', 21833

Cross, Rod: Economic Theory and Policy in the U.K.: An Outline and Assessment of the Controversies, 3684

Crosse, Gordon: Shakespearean Playgoing 1890–1952, 26250

Crossland, Phyllis: Years of Grace: A Biographical Story of Life in a Rural Area of England, 1850–1973, 19155

Crossley, Alec: Shopping in Oxford: A Brief History, 20484

Crossley, B.: 'Community Care: A Study of the Psychiatric Morbidity of a Salvation Army Hospital', 9123

Crossley, David W.: The Wealth of England 1085–1966, 3777

Crossley, John Rodney: The "Guardian" Wages Index: A Series of Indexes of Wages Rates in British Industry since 1948, 3925

Crossley, Sir Julian: The D.C.O. Story: A History of Banking in Many Countries, 1925–1971, 4494

Crossman, Richard Howard Stafford: The Diaries of a Cabinet Minister, 1164; The Backbench Diaries of Richard Crossman, 1165; Inside View: Three Lectures on Prime Ministerial Government, 1166; Paying for the Social Services, 8912; 'The Rift in Anglo-American Relations', 14068; Palestine Mission: A Personal Record, 14345; A Nation Reborn: The Israel of Weizmann, Bevin and Ben-Gurion, 14360; ed. Oxford and the Groups, 12406

Crouch, Colin: Class Conflict and the Industrial Relations Crisis: Compromise and Corporatism in the Policies of the British State, 5785; The Politics of Industrial Relations, 5786; ed. The Resurgence of Class Conflict in Western Europe Since 1968, 9561; The Student Revolt, 9865, 22564

Crouch, W. W.: 'Local Government under the British Labour Government', 3163

Crouzet, François: Britain and France: Ten Centuries, 14243

Crow, Duncan: British A.F.V.s. [Armoured Fighting Vehicles] 1919–1940, 15495; British and Commonwealth A.F.V.s. 1940–1946, 15496; 'The First Golden Age', 24645

Crow, William Bernard: A Synopsis of Biology, 26516

Crowder, Michael: ed. The Cambridge History of Africa, 12675; ed. History of West Africa, 12727; West Africa under Colonial Rule, 12729; The Story of Nigeria, 12754

Crowe, A.: The Parks and Woodlands of London, 26968

Crowe, Brenda: The Playgroup Movement: A Report, 23147; The Playgroup Movement, 23165

Crowe, Sybil Eyre: 'Sir Eyre Crowe and the Locarno Pact', 13658; 'The Zinoviev Letter: A Reappraisal', 13937

Crowe, Sylvia: Garden Design, 19901, 20322

Crowley, Terence Eldon: Discovering Old Bicycles, 17168

Crowther, James Gerald: Six Great Doctors, 20853

Crowther, M. Anne: British Social Policy, 1914–1939, 8849; The Workhouse System 1834–1929: The History of an English Social Institution, 8850

Crowther-Hunt, Norman, Lord: The Civil Servants: An Inquiry into Britain's Ruling Class, 871

Crozier, Andrew Joseph: Appeasement and Germany's Last Bid for Colonies, 13721; 'Prelude to Munich: British Foreign Policy and Germany, 1935–1938', 13736

Crozier, Brian: ed. The Grenada Documents, 13086

Crozier, Frank Percy: A Word to Gandhi: The Lesson of Ireland, 2688; A Brass Hat in No Man's Land, 14476

Crozier, Mary: An Old Silk Family, 1745–1945: The Brocklehursts of Brocklehurst—Whiston Amalgamated Limited, 6424

Crozier, Mary: Broadcasting: Sound and Television, 24762

Crozier, Stephen Forster: The History of the Corps of Royal Military Police, 15762

Cruft, John: The Royal College of Music: A Centenary Record, 24425

Cruickshank, Charles Greig: S.O.E. in the Far East: Special Operations Executive, 15084; Deception in World War II, 15095; The Fourth Arm: Psychological Warfare 1938–1945, 15099, 15221

Cruickshank, J. G.: 'Value of Land', 20292

Cruickshank, Marjorie: Children and Industry, 8151; A History of the Training of Teachers in Scotland, 9850, 23613; Church and State in English Education, 1870 to the Present Day, 22875

Cruikshank, Ernest William Henderson: The Value of Scientific Thought in the Advance of Modern Medicine, 21172

Crump, Geoffrey: Bedales since the War, 23100

Crump, Norman Easedale: By Rail to Victory, 16755

Crump, W. B.: Huddersfield Highways Down the Ages, 17161

Cruttwell, Charles Robert Mowbray Fraser: A History of the Great War, 1914–1918, 14451

Cubbin, John: Mergers and Economic Performance, 4992; Price Formation under Oligopoly: An Analysis of the U.K. Motor Industry, 17416; 'Price, Quality and Advertising Competition: An Econometric Investigation of the United Kingdom Market', 17417; 'Quality Change and Pricing Behaviour in the United Kingdom Car Industry, 1956–1968', 17418

Cudlipp, Hugh [Baron]: The Prerogative of the Harlot: Press Barons and Power, 25085; Publish and be Damned, 25135; At your Peril, 25225; Walking on the Water, 25226

Cudlipp, R.: 'One Man's Thoughts on Anglo-Japanese Relations', 13618

Cullen, Gordon: Townscape, 20307

Cullen, Ian: The University in an Urban Environment, 23304

Cullen, S.: 'The Development of the Ideals and Policy of the British Union of Fascists, 1932–40', 2203

Culley, E. W.: Air Pollution Statistics for London: Sulphur Dioxide and Smoke: April 1981–Mar 1983, 20065

Cullingworth, John Barry: Regional and Urban Studies: A Social Science Approach, 5065; The Politics of Research, 7959; The Needs of New Communities, 9357; 'The Swindon Social Survey: A Second Report on the Social Implications of Overspill', 9358; Vol. 1—Reconstruction and Land Use Planning 1939–1947, 17946, 18791; Housing on Clydeside, 1970: Restraining Urban Growth: The Problem of Overspill, 17947; New Towns for Old: The Problem of Urban Renewal, 17948; Problems of an Urban Society, 17949; Town and Country Planning in Britain, 17950, 18790; Town and Country Planning in England and Wales: An Introduction, 17951; Vol.3. New Town Policy, 18219, 18792; Environmental Planning, 1939–1969: The Ownership and Management of Housing in the New Towns: Report, 18227; A Profile of Glasgow Housing, 18473; Reports, 18474; 'The Measurement of Housing Need', 18641; 'Postwar Housing Policy and Administration in England and Wales', 18642; Housing and Local Government in England and Wales, 18759; Essays on Housing Policy: The British Scene, 18760; Vol. 4—Land Values, Compensation and Betterment, 18793; 'Planning for Leisure', 26922

Culliss, J. G.: 'Hospital Waiting Lists and the Supply and Demand of In-patient Care', 21491

Culring, William: The Captain: A Biography of Captain Sir Cecil Boyd-Rochfort, Royal Trainer, 27131

Culshaw, John: A Century of Music, 24275; Putting the Record Straight, 24579

Culyer, Anthony John: The Economics of Social Policy, 8833, 8949; The Political Economy of Social Policy, 8834; ed. Economic Policies and Social Goals: Aspects of Public Choice, 8948; Keynes, Beveridge and Beyond, 9048; 'Social Indicators: Health', 9466; The Price of Blood, 21264; 'Hospital Waiting Lists and the Supply and Demand of In-patient Care', 21491; The National Health Service: An Economic Perspective, 21631; Economic Aspects of Health Services, 21632; Need and the N.H.S.: Economics and Social Choice, 21633; An Annotated Bibliography of Health and Economics, 21634; The Holiday Industry in Devon and Cornwall, 26949

Cumbernauld Development Corporation: Investigating Cumbernauld New Town: A Factual Guide for every Organisation Faced with Development Problems, 18183; The Financing of Cumbernauld New Town, 19011

Cumbers, Frank Henry: The Book Room: The Story of the Methodist Publishing House and Epworth Press, 12106, 24980

Cumbria County Council: A Century of Service 1889–1989, 3352

Cuming, Geoffrey John: A History of Anglican Liturgy, 11606

Cuming, Maurice H. W.: Personnel Management in the National Health Service, 21629

Cumings, Bruce: Korea: The Origins of the Korean War, 16138; The Unknown War, 16143

Cumming, Christopher Edward: Studies in Educational Costs, 23204

Cumming, Henry Harford: Franco-British Rivalry in the Post-War Near East, 13831

Cumming, Sir John Guest: A Contribution towards a Bibliography Dealing with Crime and Cognate Subjects, 10287

Cumming, Michael: The Powerless Ones: Gliding in Peace and War, 15886

Cummings, Gordon: Investor's Guide to the Stock Market, 4294

Cummings, John Morrison: Railway Motor Buses and Bus Services in the British Isles, vol.2, 1902–1933, 16737

Cummings, Martin M.: 'Books, Computers and Medicine', 20932

Cummins, J. David: The Investment Activities of Life Insurance Companies, 4234

Cummins, S. Lyle: Tuberculosis in History, From the 17th Century to our own Times, 21162

Cumpston, Ina Mary: The Growth of the British Commonwealth, 1880–1932, 12486

Cuneo, John Robert: The Air Weapon, 1914–1916, 14620

Cuniff, Patrick F.: Environmental Noise Pollution, 20138

Cunliffe, M. A.: 'The Use of Supervision in Casework Practice', 8689

Cunliffe, Marcus Falkner: History of the Royal Warwickshire Regiment, 1919–1955, 15737; The Royal Irish Fusiliers, 1793–1950, 15556; 'Campus Universities and the Others', 23436

Cunliffe-Lister, Philip, Earl Swinton: Sixty Years of Power: Some Memories of the Men who Wielded it, 1169

Cunningham of Hyndhope [Lord]: A Sailor's Odyssey, 15250

Cunningham, Sir Alan: 'Palestine: The Last Days of the Mandate', 14348

Cunningham, Catherine M.: ed. Merseyside Social and Economic Studies, 5184, 10113, 18053

Cunningham, George: ed. Britain and the World in the Seventies: A Collection of Fabian Essays, 7603

Cunningham, R. F.: 'The Robbins Report: the Future of Higher Education', 23404

Cunningham, Stephen: Fisheries Economics: An Introduction, 19809

Cunningham, W. B.: ed. Canada, the Commonwealth and the Common Market, 12652

Cunningham-Boothe, Ashley: ed. British Forces in the Korean War, 16133

Cunnington, Phillis: Handbook of English Costume in the Twentieth Century 1900–1950, 24158; and Cunnington, C. W.: English Women's Clothing in the Present Century, 24159

Cunnison, James: In their Early Twenties: A Study of Glasgow Youth, 8412; The Young Wage Earner: A Study of Glasgow Boys, 8413; 'The Impact of National Service', 8414

Cunnison, Sheila: Wages and Work Allocation: A Study of Social Relations in a Garment Workshop, 5878

Curl, James Stevens: European Cities and Society: A Study of the Influence of Political Climate on Town Design, 17932

Curran, Sir Charles John: Broadcasting from West of Suez, 24778; Money, Management and Programmes, 24779; A Seamless Robe: Broadcasting Philosophy and Practice, 24797

Curran, James: ed. British Cinema History, 24623; Newspaper History from the Seventeenth Century to the Present Day, 25072; ed. The British Press: A Manifesto, 25074; Power without Responsibility: The Press and Broadcasting in Britain, 25076

Curran, John: Energy and Human Needs, 7208

Curran, Joseph M.: The Birth of the Irish Free State 1921–1923, 2686

Curran, Sir Samuel C.: Energy and Human Needs, 7208

Currell, Melville: Political Women, 2259; 'British Inter-industrial Earnings Differentials, 1924–1955', 7231

Current Biography: 1940+, 43

Current Law Statutes Annotated: 1948+, 262

Currie, Bob: The Story of Triumph Motor Cycles, 17188; Classic Competition Motorcycles from the National Motorcycle Museum, 17196; Great British Motorcycles of the 60s, 17197; Classic British Motor Cycles: The Final Years, 17198

Currie, Edwina: Life Lines, 1400

Currie, G. W.: The Housing Problem in London, 18391

Currie, Gregory: ed. Philosophical Papers of Imre Lakatos, 26852

Currie, Lauchlin Bernard: Taming the Megalopolis: A Design for Urban Growth, 17952

Currie, Robert: Churches and Churchgoers: Patterns of Church Growth in the British Isles since 1700, 11546; Methodism Divided: A Study in the Sociology of Ecumenicalism, 12075

Curry, David: The Food War, the European Community and the Battle for World Food Markets, 20622

Curry, Nigel: Working Conditions in Universities: A Pilot Study, 4146; A Future for our Countryside, 18817

Curtice, John: 'Electoral Choice and the Production of Government: The Changing Operation of the Electoral System in the United Kingdom since 1955', 2363

Curtis, Anthony: The Pattern of Maugham, 25709; Somerset Maugham, 25710

Curtis, Colin Hartley: Buses of London: An Illustrated Review of Every London Bus Type purchased since 1908, 17307

Curtis, David: 'English Avant-garde Film: An Early Chronology', 24655

Curtis, Edmund: A History of Ireland, 313

Curtis, Gerald: The Story of the Sampfords: The Parishes of Great and Little Sampford, Essex, from the Earliest Times to the Conclusion of the Second World War, 19354

Curtis, Helene: Part-time Social Work: A Study of Opportunities for the Employment of Trained Social Workers, 8705

Curtis, Lettice: The Forgotten Pilots: A Story of the Air Transport Auxiliary, 1939–1945, 15901

Curtis, Liz: Ireland and the Propaganda War: The Media and the Battle for 'Hearts and Minds', 2884; Nothing but the Same Old Story: The Roots of Anti-Irish Racism, 11365

Curtis, Philip: A Hawk among Sparrows: A Biography of Austin Farrer, 11781

Curtis, Stanley James: History of Education in Great Britain, 22653; An Introductory History of English Education since 1800, 22654; Education in Britain since 1900, 22655; A Short History of Educational Ideas, 22656

Curtis, Tony: Dannie Abse, 25349

Curtis-Bennett, Noel: The Food of the People, 20592

Curwen, Peter J.: Inflation, 4009; The U.K Publishing Industry, 24940

Curzon, George Nathaniel [Baron] Scarsdale: Selections of the Day: Being a Selection of Speeches and Writings, 1171; Leaves from a Viceroy's Note-Book and other Papers, 1172

Cushing, David: Fisheries Resources of the Sea and their Management, 19806

Cushing, Harvey: The Life of Sir William Osler, 20874

Cushing, Peter: Past Forgetting: Memoirs of the Hammer Years, 26031

Custance, Roger: Winchester College: Sixth-centenary Essays, 23087

Cuthbert, Norman H.: An Economic Survey of Northern Ireland, 5385; ed. Company Industrial Relations Policies: The Management of Industrial Relations in the 1970's, 5766; The Lace Makers' Society: A Study of Trade Unionism in the British Lace Industry 1760–1960, 6882

Cutler, Horace: The Cutler Files, 3291

Cutter, I. S.: A Short History of Midwifery, 21098

Cyprus: The Dispute and the Settlement: R.I.I.A, 12871

Cyr, Anthony: British Foreign Policy and the Atlantic Area: The Techniques of Accommodation, 14093

Cyr, Arthur: Liberal Party Politics in Britain, 1826

Cyriax, George: The Bargainers: A Survey of Modern Trade Unionism, 6727; 'How to Make Trade Unions more Responsible', 6776

D'Abernon, Edgar Vincent, Viscount: Diary of an Ambassador, 13261; 'Public Health and the Control of the Liquor Traffic', 22164; Preface to Vernon, Horace Middleton: The Alcohol Problem, 22165

D'Abernon, Viscountess: Red Cross and Berlin Embassy, 1915–1926, 13262

D'Arcy, Susan: The Films of Dirk Bogarde, 24689

D.H.S.S.: Social Service Teams: The Practitioner's View, 8722; The Census of Residential Accommodation, 18727; Treatment and Rehabilitation: A Report of the Advisory Council on the Misuse of Drugs, 22197

D.S.I.R.: Automation: Man, Steel and Technical Change, 7245; A Report on Technical Trends and their Impact on Management and Labour, 7246

Daalder, Hans: Cabinet Reform in Britain, 1914–1963, 717; ed. Universities, Politicians and Bureaucrats: Europe and the United States, 23336

Dada, L.: A Bibliography of Race and Race Relations, 10889

Dadzie, Stella: The Heart of the Race: Black Women's Lives in Britain, 7726

Dahl, Roald: Boy: Tales of Childhood, 25467

Dahrendorf, Ralf: Class and Conflict in an Industrial Society, 9524; Inequality, Hope and Progress, 9525; 'La Situation de la Classe Ouvrière en Angleterre', 9675

Dahya, Badr: 'Pakistanis in Britain: Transients or Settlers?', 11209; 'Yemenis in Britain: An Arab Migrant Community', 11210

Daiches, David: Glasgow, 18135; Scotch Whisky: Its Past and Present, 20728; ed. The Idea of a New University, an Experiment in Sussex, 23582; ed. A Companion to Scottish Culture, 23734

Dainton, Courtney: The Story of England's Hospitals, 21414

Dalby, G. R.: Social Enterprise: A Study of the Activities of Voluntary Societies and Voluntary Workers in an Industrial Town, 9145

Dalby, Mark: Tottenham Parish Church and Parish: A Brief History and Guide, 19359

Dale, Harold Edward: The Higher Civil Service of Great Britain, 844; Daniel Hall, Pioneer in Scientific Agriculture, 19498

Dale, Sir Henry Hallett: Adventures in Physiology, with Excursions into Autopharmacology: A Selection from the Scientific Papers of Sir Henry Hallett Dale, 22308

Dale, Jennifer: Feminists and State Welfare, 7865; Social Theory and Social Welfare, 8886

Dale, John Rodney: The Clerk in Industry: A Survey of the Occupational Experience, Status, Education and Vocational Training of a Group of Male Clerks Employed by Industrial Companies, 9671, 9799

Dale, Peter: Guide to Libraries and Information Units, 97

Dale, Reginald Rowland: Down Stream: Failure in the Grammar School, 22983; Mixed or Single-sex Schools?, 23169

Dale, Sheila: The Handicapped Person in the Community: Using the Literature, 21779

Dale-Jones, Don: Emlyn Williams, 26263

Daley, A.: 'London as a Case Study', 18308

Dalton, C. P.: 'The Place of the Petroleum Industry in the U.K.', 6511

Dalton, Hugh Neale, Baron: Call Back Yesterday: Memoirs, 1887–1931, 1176; The Fateful Years: Memoirs, 1931–1945, 1177. High Tide and After: Memoirs, 1945–1960, 1178; 'The Measurement of the Inequality of Incomes', 3796

Daly, M. W.: ed. Modernization in the Sudan: Essays in Honor of Richard Hill, 14411

Daly, Mary E.: Social and Economic History of Ireland since 1800, 2646

Dalyell, Tam: Devolution: Thatcher's Torpedo, 1051; Dick Crossman, 1163; The End of Britain, 2407; One Man's Falklands, 16077

Dalzell-Ward, Arthur James: A Textbook of Health Education, 22094

Damer, Sean: 'Wine Alley: The Sociology of a Dreadful Enclosure', 18487

Dameron, Kenneth: ed. Consumer Problems in War-time, 20442; Retail Marketing and Merchandising, 20477

Damesick, Peter J.: Regional Problems, Problem Regions and Public Policy in the United Kingdom, 5127

Dampier, (formerly Whetham), William Cecil: A History of Science and its Relations with Philosophy and Religion, 27256

Dancy, John Christopher: 'Technology in a Liberal Education', 22524; The Public Schools and the Future, 23016

Dancyger, Irene: A World of Women: An Illustrated History of Women's Magazines, 25193

Dane, Edmund: British Campaigns in Africa and the Pacific, 1914–1918, 14523; British Campaigns in the Nearer East, 1914–1918, 14562

Dane, R. A.: The Railways of Peterborough, 16971

Dangerfield, Christabel: Insight into Industry: An Introduction to the Growth of Present Day Conditions of British Industry, 5713

Daniel, Glyn: Some Small Harvest, 26359

Daniel, John Edward: Welsh Nationalism, What it Stands for, 2594

Daniel, John: 'Welsh Opinion: Ecumenical Developments', 12302

Daniel, Susie: ed. The Painthouse: Words from an East End Gang, 8462

Daniel, William Wentworth: The Next Stage of Incomes Policy, 3853; 'Industrial Behaviour and Orientation to Work: A Critique', 5714; Workplace Industrial Relations and Technical Change, 5715; The Right to Manage?: A Study of Leadership and Reform in Employee Relations, 5716; The Impact of Employment Protection Laws, 6989; Where Are They Now? A Follow Up Study of the Unemployed, 9698; Racial Discrimination in England: Based on the PEP Report, 11164

Daniell, David: The Interpreter's House: A Critical Assessment of John Buchan, 25427

Daniell, David Scott: Cap of Honour: The Story of the Gloucestershire Regiment (The 28th/61st Foot). 1694–1975, 15636; Regimental History: The Royal Hampshire Regiment: Vol.3 1918–54, 15648; 4th Hussars: The Story of the 4th Queen's Own Hussars, 1685–1958, 15669; History of the East Surrey Regiment, 1920–1952, 15729

Daniels, Gerald: comp. Passengers No More, 1952–1962: Closures of Stations and Branch Lines, 16774

Daniels, Gilbert S.: Artists from the Royal Botanic Gardens, Kew, 26536

Daniels, Jeff: British Leyland: The Truth about the Cars, 17439

Daniels, Peter Walters: Office Location and the Journey to Work: A Comparative Study of Five Urban Areas, 16278

Daniélou, J.: The Pelican Guide to Modern Theology, 11549

Dankelmann, O.: 'Zur Geschichte und Funktion Britischer Sozial-Reformistischen Völkerbundskonzeptionen 1916 bis 1919', 13473

Dann, Graham M. S.: Barbados, 13075

Dannatt, Trevor: Modern Architecture in Britain: Selected Examples of Recent Buildings, 23892

Darby, John: Conflict in Northern Ireland: The Development of a Polarised Community, 2824; ed. Violence and the Social Services in Northern Ireland, 2825, 8885

Dare, R.: 'Instinct and Organization: Intellectuals and British Labour after 1931', 1714

Dark, Sidney: Archbishop Davidson and the English Church, 11692; Wilson Carlile, the Laughing Cavalier of Christ, 11775; The Life of Sir Arthur Pearson, Bt, 21929

Darke, Bob: The Communist Technique in Britain, 1954

Darke, J. and Darke, R.: 'Sheffield Revisited', 18074; Health and Environment: High Flats, 18647

Darley, Gillian: The National Trust Book of the Farm, 19608; Villages of Vision, 19119

Darling, J. T.: 'Presbyterian Church of England Records', 12122

Darlington, C. D.: 'The Oxford Botanic Gardens: 1621–1971', 26540

Darlington, William Aubrey Cecil: Six Thousand and one Nights: Forty Years a Critic, 25921

Darlow, Michael: Rattigan: The Man and his Work, 25981

Darnell, Regna: 'History of Anthropology in Historical Perspective', 10123

Darracott, Belinda and Darracott, Joseph: First World War Posters: Second World War Posters, 24120

Darragh, James: The Catholic Hierarchy of Scotland. A Biographical List, 1653–1985, 12270

Darter, Pat: The Women's Movement, 7623

Dartington Hall: The History of an Experiment, 23103; Dartington Hall, 23104; Dartington Hall: The Elmhirsts of Dartington: The Creation of a Utopian Community, 23105

Darton, Frederick Joseph Harvey: Modern Book Illustration in Great Britain and America, 24100

Darvill, Giles: Preparing for Community Social Work, 8839

Darwin, Andrew: Canals and Rivers of Britain, 16383

Darwin, Bernard Richard Meirion: War on the Line, 16754; The English Public School, 23007; A History of Golf in Britain, 27154

Darwin, John G.: 'Imperialism in Decline: Tendencies in British Imperial Policy between the Wars', 12543; Britain and Decolonisation 1945–65, 12592; Britain, Egypt and the Middle East: Imperial Policy in the Aftermath of War, 1918–1922, 13830; 'The Chanak Crisis and the British Cabinet', 13837

Dash, Jack: Good Morning Brothers!, 9665

Daugherty, Marion Roberts: The Currency-Banking Controversy, 4415

Daukes, Sidney Herbert: The Medical Museum: Modern Developments, Organization and Technical Methods based on a New System of Visual Teaching: An Amplification of a Thesis, 20799

Daunton-Fear, Mary: 'Social Inquiry Reports: Comprehensive and Reliable?', 10485

Davenport, Nicholas Ernest Harold: The Split Society, 3643, 9528; The Oil Trusts and Anglo-American Relations, 14019; Memoirs of a City Radical, 25227

Davenport-Hines, Richard Peter Treadwell: Dudley Docker: The Life and Times of a Trade Warrior, 5504; ed. Markets and Bagmen: Studies in the History of Marketing and British Industrial Performance 1830–1939, 20475

Davey, Brian Humphrey: ed. Agriculture and the State: British Policy in a World Context, 19570; ed. The Common Agricultural Policy and Britain, 19654

Davey, Colin: ed. Anglican/Roman Catholic Dialogue, 12333

Davey, Cyril James: The March of Methodism, 12071; The Methodist Story, 12072

Davey, Richard, My Life on the Footplate, 16736

David, Edward: 'The Liberal Party Divided, 1916–1918', 1812

David, Hugh: The Fitzrovians: A Portrait of Bohemian London 1900–1950, 23771

David, Wilfrid L.: ed. Public Finance, Planning and Economic Development: Essays in Honour of Lady Hicks, 4582

Davidge, Elizabeth M.: 'Homelessness Four Years On', 18514

Davidoff, Leonore: ed. Our Work, Our Lives, Our Words, 7646; The Best Circles: Society, Etiquette and the Season, 9753

Davidow, Jeffrey: A Peace in Southern Africa. The Lancaster House Conference on Rhodesia, 1979, 12808

Davidson, Andrew Rutherford: The History of the Faculty of Actuaries in Scotland 1856–1956, 4225

Davidson, Audrey: Phantasy in Childhood, 8152

Davidson, B. R.: 'Effects of Land Speculation on the Supply of Housing in England and Wales', 18733

Davidson, Basil: Special Operations Europe: Scenes from the Anti-Nazi War, 15085

Davidson, F. G.: 'Household Structure and Housing Needs', 10025, 18673

Davidson, J. W.: Samoa Mo Samoa: The Emergence of the Independent State of Western Samoa, 12894

Davidson, Joan: ed. Conservation and Agriculture, 19571, 20203

Davidson, John Colin Campbell, Viscount: Memoirs of a Conservative: J. C. C. Davidson's Memoirs and Papers, 1910–1937, 1182

Davidson, Sir John: Haig, Master of the Field, 14503

Davidson, Sir Leybourne Stanley Patrick: Human Nutrition and Dietetics, 20548

Davidson, M.: The Royal Society of Medicine, the Realization of an Ideal (1805–1955), 20797

Davidson, Martin: The Heavens and Faith, 27255

Davidson, Nick: ed. Inequality in Health: The Black Report, 21682; A Question of Care:

The Changing Face of the National Health Service, 21683

Davidson, Peter: Contemporary Drama: The Popular Dramatic Tradition in England, 26232

Davidson, Scott: Grenada: A Study in Politics and the Limits of International Law, 13087

Davie, Donald [Alfred]: A Gathered Church: The Literature of the English Dissenting Interest, 1700–1930, 11997; These the Companions: Recollections, 25468; Trying to Explain, 25469

Davie, Grace: Inner City God: The Nature of Belief in the Inner City, 11846

Davie, Michael: ed. The Diaries of Evelyn Waugh, 25858

Davie, Ronald Butler Neville: Children and Families with Special Needs, 8153; From Birth to Seven: The Second Report of the NCDS—1958 Cohort, 8285

Davies, A. C.: The Age of MacDiarmid: Essays on Hugh MacDiarmid and his influence on Contemporary Scotland, 25685

Davies, A. L.: ed. Cornwall County Council 1889–1989: A History of 100 Years of County Government, 3351

Davies, Andrew: Other Theatres: The Development of Alternative and Experimental Theatre in Britain, 26233

Davies, Anne H.: One Hundred Years: A History of the University of Birmingham Dental Students' Society [1886–1986.], 9887

Davies, Bernard David: The Social Education of the Adolescent, 8463; The Use of Groups in Social Work Practice, 8658

Davies, Bleddyn Price: Variations in Services for the Aged: A Causal Analysis, 8603; University Costs and Outputs, 23314

Davies, C. T.: 'Educational Elements in Community Work in Britain', 9407

Davies, C.: 'Montgomeryshire: The Life of a Rural Community', 19306

Davies, C.: 'Professionals in Organisations: Some Preliminary Observations on Hospital Consultants', 21490

Davies, Celia: ed. Rewriting Nursing History, 21728

Davies, Charles Norman: The Effects of Abnormal Physical Conditions at Work, 4127; ed. Health Conditions in the Ceramic Industry, 4128

Davies, Christie: Wrongful Imprisonment: Mistaken Convictions and their Consequences, 10394; Permissive Britain: Social Change in the Sixties and Seventies, 26904; ed. Censorship and Obscenity, 26905

Davies, Clarice Stella: North Country Bred: A Working Class Family Chronicle, 10063; ed. A History of Macclesfield, 18111

Davies, Clive: 'Pre-Trial Imprisonment: A Liverpool Study', 10318

Davies, D. Hywel: The Welsh Nationalist Party, 1925–1945: A Call to Nationhood, 2606

Davies, [Daniel] Horton [Marlais]: Worship and Theology in England, 11920; Varieties of English Preaching, 1900–1960, 11921; The English Free Churches, 12005

Davies, David Lewis: Studies in Psychiatry: A Survey of Work carried out in the Department of Psychiatry of the Institute of Psychiatry, under the Chairmanship of Sir Aubrey Lewis, 1945–66, 22412

Davies, David Richard: In Search of Myself, 11778

Davies, E. R.: A History of the First Berkshire County Council, 3348

Davies, Edmund Frank: Illyrian Adventure: The Story of the British Military Mission to Enemy-Occupied Albania, 1943–44, 14938

Davies, Ednyfed Hudson: 'Welsh Nationalism', 2598

Davies, Edward Beresford: A Survey of Alcoholism in an English County: A Study of the Prevalence, Distribution and Effects of Alcoholism in Cambridgeshire, 22127

Davies, Edward John: The Blaenavon Story, 18157

Davies, Elvet Talfryn: The Dartmoor and Exmoor National Parks: Changes in Farming Structure, 1952–1972, 19569

Davies, Elwyn: Celtic Studies in Wales: A Survey Prepared for the Second International Congress of Celtic Studies, 2432; ed. Welsh Rural Communities, 19289

Davies, Ernest Albert John: 'National' Capitalism: The Government's Record as Protector of Private Monopoly, 3598; National Enterprise: The Development of the Public Corporation, 6145

Davies, G. A.: The Channel Tunnel, 16357

Davies, George Colliss Boardman: Men for the Ministry: The History of the London College of Divinity, 11912

Davies, Glyn: Building Societies and their Branches: A Regional Economic Survey, 4363; National Giro: Modern Money Transfer, 4533

Davies, Gwennant: The Story of the Urdd: The Welsh League of Youth 1922–1972, 23838

Davies, H. W. E.: 'Recent Industrial Changes in South Wales', 5371; 'Dust Inhalation and Miners' Phthisis', 21277; 'A Scheme for Mining Centres', 21278

Davies, Harold: The Boys' Grammar School Today and Tomorrow, 22978; Culture and the Grammar School, 22982

Davies, Hunter: The Creighton Report: A Year in the Life of a Comprehensive School, 22972; The Beatles, 24498; The Grades: The First Family of British Entertainment, 26115

Davies, Ioan: Social Mobility and Political Change, 9542

Davies, Ivor Norman Richard: 'Sir Maurice Hankey and the Inter—Allied Mission to Poland, July-August 1920', 13888; 'Lloyd George and Poland, 1919 to 1920', 13889

Davies, Ivor: A Pictorial History of Triumph Motor Cycles, 17189

Davies, J. H.: ed. A Select Bibliography of Adult Continuing Education in Great Britain, 23642

Davies, James Arthur: Education in a Welsh Rural County, 1870–1973, 23628

Davies, James Brian Meredith: Community Care and Social Services, 22092

Davies, Jean: A National Survey of Attitudes to Inflation and Incomes Policy, 3830

Davies, Jean: Girl Offenders Aged 17 to 20 Years, 7729, 10624

Davies, Jeffrey Rowe: Investment in the British Economy, 4753

Davies, John: Teenagers and Alcohol: A Developmental Study in Glasgow, 22148, 22149

Davies, John: The Scottish Forester, 19722

Davies, Jon Gower: The Evangelistic Bureaucrat: A Study of a Planning Exercise in Newcastle-upon-Tyne, 18895

Davies, Julia: A Study of Hospital Management Training in its Organisation Context: An Evaluation of First-Line Management Training Courses for Ward Sisters in the Manchester Region, 21396

Davies, Keith: Local Government Law, 3106

Davies, Kenneth: The Clyde Passenger Steamers, 16591

Davies, Laurence: Cunninghame Graham: A Critical Biography, 25543

Davies, Laurence: Liberal Studies and Higher Technology, 22506

Davies, Lynn: Winner Stakes All: Lynn Davies Face to Face with Peter Williams, 27149

Davies, Martin J.: Building Societies and their Branches: A Regional Economic Survey, 4363; Every Man his own Landlord: A History of Coventry Building Society, 4392

Davies, Martin: The Essential Social Worker, 8904; Prisoners of Society: Attitudes and After-care, 10409; Probationers in their Social Environment: A Study of Male Probationers Aged 17-20, together with an Analysis of those Reconvicted within Twelve Months, 10476; Financial Penalties and Probation, 10477

Davies, Maurice Robert Russell: Principles and Practice of Planning, Compulsory Purchase and Rating Law, 20350; The Law of Burial, Cremation and Exhumation, 20351; The Law of Road Traffic, 20352

Davies, Peter Neville: Trading in West Africa 1840-1920, 4813; The Trade Makers: Elder Dempster in West Africa, 1852-1972, 16556; Henry Tyrer: A Liverpool Shipping Agent and his Enterprise 1879-1979, 16567; Sir Alfred Jones: Shipping Entrepreneur par Excellence, 16568

Davies, P. R.: The Effects of Abnormal Physical Conditions at Work, 4127

Davies, P.: 'The Social Patterns of Immigrant Areas', 11002

Davies, R. L.: 'Nucleated and Ribbon Components of the Urban Retail System in Britain', 18022; Facts about the New Towns: A Socio-Economic Digest, 18174

Davies, R. R.: ed. Welsh Society and Nationhood: Historical Essays Presented to Glanmor Williams, 2556

Davies, R. V.: ed. Watchdog's Tales: The District Audit Service: The First 138 Years, 3249

Davies, Rhys John: Widowed Mothers Pensions, 4046

Davies, Ronald Edward George: A History of the World's Airlines, 17630; A History of World Air Transport, 17640

Davies, Ross L.: Urban Change in Britain and the Retail Response, 6643; The Impact of Town Centre Shopping Schemes in Britain: Their Impact on Traditional Environments, 6647; Women at Work, 7776; ed. Issues in Urban Society, 17931; The Development of Teleshopping and Teleservices, 20485

Davies, Rupert Eric: The Church in Our Times: An Ecumenical History from a British Perspective, 11581, 12322; ed. The Testing of the Churches 1932-1982, 11582; Religious Authority in an Age of Doubt, 11877; A History of the Methodist Church in Great Britain, 12066; Methodism, 12073; ed. John Scott Lidgett: A Symposium, 12087

Davies, S. C.: 'Trade Union Rivalry and the Bridlington Agreement', 6757

Davies, S. D.: 'The History of the Avro Vulcan', 15880

Davies, Sidney Herbert: 'The Health Factor in Education', 8154; 'On Offspring: By A Parent', 8155

Davies, Trevor Arthur Lloyd: Respiratory Diseases in Foundry Men, 21969

Davies, Trevor P.: ed. Science, Technology and Environmental Management: Based on a symposium of 'Applied Environmental Science' held at the 1973 Annual Conference of the Institute of British Geographers, 19968

Davies, Trevor: Bolton, May 1926: A Review of the General Strike as it Affected Bolton and District, 6927

Davies, Wayne K. D.: Urban Essays: Studies in the Geography of Wales, 18156

Davies, William James Keith: Light Railways of the First World War: A History of Tactical Rail Communications on the British Fronts 1914-18, 14645; Light Railways: Their Rise and Decline, 16777

Davies, Wyndham: ed. Collectivism or Individualism in Medicine?, 21592; ed. Reforming the National Health Service, 21593; Health or Health Service? Reform of the British National Health Service, 21613; The Pharmaceutical Industry, a Personal Study: A Medical, Economic and Political Survey of the Worldwide Pharmaceutical Industry, 21614

Davis, Alan: The Management of Deprivation: Final Report of Southwark Community Development Project, 9281

Davis, Anthony: Television: Here is the News, 24921

Davis, Charles: A Question of Conscience, 11972

Davis, Dorothy: A History of Shopping, 20480

Davis, E. W.: The London Clearing Banks, 4458

Davis, Henry William Carless: ed. The Dictionary of National Biography 3rd Supplement [1912-1921], 14

Davis, J.: 'ATFERO: The Atlantic Ferry Organisation', 12657

Davis, Jean: Aldbury People 1885-1945, 19176

Davis, Joyce S.: ed. Motorways in Britain: Today and Tomorrow, 17115

Davis, Kingsley: 'The Theory of Change and Response in Modern Demographic History', 7374; World Population in Transition, 7375

Davis, P. A.: A Sledgehammer to Crack a Nut: An Examination of the Race Relations Bill, 11102

Davis, R.: 'Ulster Protestants and the Sinn Fein Press', 2956

Davis, Ralph Henry Carless: The Blackwell Dictionary of Historians, 26731

Davis, Ralph: Twenty One and a Half Bishop Lane: A History of J.H. Fenners & Co. Ltd., 1861-1961, 6365

Davis, Reginald: Elizabeth our Queen, 509

Davis, Richard P.: Arthur Griffith, 3056; Arthur Griffith and Non-Violent Sinn Fein, 3057

Davis, Robert: ed. Woodbrooke 1903-1953: A Brief History of a Quaker Experiment in Religious Education, 12152, 22904, 23712

Davis, Robert Murray: Bibliography of Evelyn Waugh, 25856

Davis, Robin: The Grammar School, 22985

Davis, Stephen: Hammer of the Gods: The Led Zeppelin Saga, 24518

Davis, Tenney L.: The Chemistry of Powder and Explosives, 7058

Davis, William: Three Years Hard Labour: The Road to Devaluation, 4718

Davison, Evelyn Hope: 'The Southampton Generic Course', 8692; Social Casework: A Basic Textbook for Students of Casework and for Administrators in the Social Services, 8706

Davison, Robert Barry: West Indian Migrants: Social and Economic Facts of Migration from the West Indies, 11251; Commonwealth Immigrants, 11252; Black British: Immigrants to England, 11253

Davison, Sir Ronald Conway: British Unemployment: The Modern Phase since 1930, 7006

Davy, George Mark Oswald: The Seventh and Three Enemies, 15662

Davy, Maurice John Bernard: Science Museum: Collections Illustrating Aeronautics: 1—Heavier-than-air Craft, 17491; 2—The Propulsion of Aircraft, 17492; 3—Lighter-than-air Craft, 17493; Interpretive History of Flight: A Survey of the History and Development of Aeronautics, 17494

Dawe, Donovan Arthur: Skilbecks: Drysalters, 1650-1950, 6475

Dawes, B.: A Hundred Years of Biology, 26513

Dawes, Frank: A Cry from the Streets: The Boys' Club Movement in Britain from the 1850's to the Present Day, 8523

Dawney, Jean: How I Became a Fashion Model, 24174

Dawson, Andrew H.: 'The Idea of the Region: The Reorganisation of Scottish Local Government', 3181

Dawson, G. M.: 'Defensive Planning in Belfast', 18172

Dawson, Jan: 'Declarations of Independence', 24652

Dawson, Jenny: Crime and Society: Readings in History and Theory, 10263

Dawson, John A.: Evaluating the Human Environment: Essays in Applied Geography, 19975

Dawson, John Lewis: *ed.* Disappointed Ghosts: Essays by African, Asian and West Indian Students, 11500

Dawson, Peter: Fifty Years of Song, 24475

Dawson, Peter: Making a Comprehensive Work, 22973

Dawson, Raymond: 'Theory and Reality in the Anglo-American Alliance', 14078

Day, Alan Charles Lynn: 'The Bank of England in the Modern State', 4487; The Future of Sterling, 4701; Roads, 17105

Day, Alan Edwin: J. B. Priestley: An Annotated Bibliography, 25775

Day, Castle N.: Design and the Production of Houses, 18654

Day, D.: Menzies and Churchill at War, 12628

Day, Douglas: Swifter than Reason: The Poetry and Criticism of Robert Graves, 25551

Day, E. E. D.: 'The British Sea Fishing Industry', 19804

Day, John Robert: The Story of the London Underground, 17001; London's Trams and Trolley Buses, 17232, 17248

Day, John: Bristol Brass: A History of the Industry, 6608

Day, Kenneth: The Typographic Book 1450–1935, 25024

Day, M.: 'Socialist Theories and Sir Raymond Unwin', 20377

Day, Michael: 'Environmental Improvement in Glasgow', 19933

Day, Peter Russell: Communication in Social Work, 8720

Day, Sir Robin: Grand Inquisitor: Memoirs, 24739; The Case for televising Parliament, 24889; Television: A Personal Report, 24904

Day, Henry Albert: The Land Question Solved!, 20258

Day-Lewis, Cecil: The Mind in Chains: Socialism and the Cultural Revolution, 23779; The Buried Day, 25473

Day-Lewis, Sean: Bulleid: Last Giant of Steam, 17070; C. Day-Lewis: An English Literary Life, 25472

Dayer, Roberta Albert: 'The British War Debts to the United States and the Anglo-Japanese Alliance, 1920–1923', 14016

Daynes, Edward: The Growth of Special Education in London, 23120

De Breffny, Brian: *ed.* The Irish World, 2655

De Belleroche, William: Brangwyn Talks, 24011

De Bunsen, Victoria Alexandrina: Charles Roden Buxton: A Memoir, 1386

De Courcy, John: The History of the Welsh Regiment, 1919–1951, 15756

De Courtais, Georgine: Women's Hairdress and Hairstyles in England from AD 600 to the Present day, 24164

De Crespigny, Anthony: *ed.* Contemporary Political Philosophers, 2086

De Golyer, Everett L. Jnr: 'The Steam Locomotive: A Selective Bibliography', 17024

De Guingand, Sir Francis Wilfred: From Brass Hat to Bowler Hat, 5505; Operation Victory, 14759

De Havilland, Sir Geoffrey: Sky Fever, 17607

De Jong, Gordon F.: 'Population Redistribution Policies: Alternatives from the Netherlands, Great Britain and Israel', 7340

De Jouvenel, Bertrand: Problems of Socialist England, 3609

De Kadt, Emanuel J.: 'Research Note: Sociology Graduate Students at the L.S.E.', 7976

De Kerbrech, Richard P.: Damned by Destiny: A Complete Account of all the World's Projects for Passenger Liners which never Entered Service, 16585

De Malherbe, M. C.: 'Changing Structure of Engineering Education', 22517

De Maré, Eric Samuel: The Canals of England, 16393

De Novo, John A.: 'The Culberston Economic Mission and Anglo-American Tensions in the Middle East, 1944–1945', 3723

De Paor, Liam: The Peoples of Ireland: From Pre-history to Modern Times, 2650; Divided Ulster, 2917

De Porzecanski, Martha: New Towns: A Comparative Atlas, 18212; New Towns: The Evolution of Planning Criteria, 18213

De Rosso, Diana: James Mason, 26068

De Salbo, Louise: The Letters of Vita Sackville-West to Virginia Woolf, 25789

De Schweinitz, Karl: England's Road to Social Security: From 'The Statute of Laborers' to the 'Beveridge Report' of 1942, 9047

De Silva, K. M.: *ed.* History of Ceylon vol.iii: From the Beginning of the Nineteenth Century to 1948, 12982

De Valois, Dame Ninette: Come Dance with Me: A Memoir 1898–1956, 24225; Step by Step: The Formation of an Establishment, 24226

De Vane, Richard: Second Home Ownership: A Case Study, 18373

De Vitis, A. A.: Anthony Burgess, 25432

De Watteville, Herman Gaston: The British Soldier: His Daily Life from Tudor to Modern Times, 15435

De Witt, John J.: Indian Workers' Associations in Britain, 11218

De Zayas, Alfred M.: Nemesis at Potsdam: the Anglo-Americans and the Expulsion of the Germans: Background, Execution, Consequences, 14204

De Zouche, Dorothy Eva: Roedean School, 1885–1955, 23111

De'Ath, Wilfred: Barbara Castle: A Portrait from Life, 1141; *ed.* Just Me and Nobody Else, 10475

De-La-Noy, Michael: Young Once Only: A Study of Boys on Probation, 10474

DeLancey, Mark: Cameroon, 12773

Deacon, Alan: In Search of the Scrounger: The Administration of Unemployment Insurance in Britain, 1920–1931, 4035; 'Labour and the Unemployed: The Administration of Insurance in the Twenties', 6998

Deacon, Marjorie: Great Chesterfield: A Common Field Parish in Essex, 19333

Deacon, Richard: The Silent War: A History of Western Naval Intelligence, 15426; A History of the British Secret Services, 15999; 'C': A Biography of Sir Maurice

Oldfield, Head of MI6, 16012; The Cambridge Apostles: A History of Cambridge University's Elite Intellectual Secret Society, 23465

Deakin, Brian Measures: Effects of the Temporary Employment Subsidy, 4953; Productivity in Transport: A Study of Employment, Capital, Output, Productivity, and Technical Change, 16226

Deakin, Frederick William Dampier: The Embattled Mountain, 14939

Deakin, Nicholas: 'Colour and the 1966 General Election', 2234; 'Housing and Race Relations', 11005; *ed.* Colour and the British Electorate: Six Case Studies, 2233, 10941; 'Powell, the Minorities and the 1970 Election', 2237; 'Research and the Policy-Making Process in Local Government', 3257; Leaving London: Planned Mobility and the Inner-city, 7280; 'Harold Macmillan and the Control of Commonwealth Immigration', 10940; 'Foreigners in Britain', 10967; Colour, Citizenship and British Society, 10993; 'Survey of Race Relations in Britain', 11007; 'Racial Integration and Whitehall: A Plan for Reorganisation', 11008

Dean, Basil: Mind's Eye: An Autobiography, 26197; Seven Ages.: An Autobiography, 26196; The Theatre at War, 26195

Dean, Britten: 'British Informal Empire: The Case of China', 13623

Dean, Charles Graham Troughton: The Loyal Regiment: North Lancashire, 1919–1953, 15682

Dean, D. W.: 'Coping with Coloured Immigration: The Cold War and Colonial Policy, The Labour Government and Black Communities in Great Britain, 1945–51', 11098; 'H.A.L. Fisher, Reconstruction and the Development of the 1918 Education Act', 22615; 'Conservatism and the National Education System 1922–1940', 22617; 'The Difficulties of a Labour Educational Policy: The Failure of the Trevelyan Bill, 1929–1931', 22621

Dean, Edward J.: Lucky Dean: Reminiscences of a Press Photographer, 25301

Dean, Sir Maurice: The Royal Air Force and Two World Wars, 15795

Dean, Ralph Stanley: William Temple, 1882–1944, 11705

Dean-Smith, Margaret: A Guide to English Folk-song Collections, 1822–1952, With an Index to their Contents, Historical Annotations and an Introduction, 24450

Deane, Basil: Alun Hoddinott, 24349

Deane, Charles: The Isle of Man T.T, 2637

Deane, Herbert Andrew: The Political Ideas of Harold Laski, 2114

Deane, Marjorie: 'United Kingdom Publishing Statistics', 24938

Deane, Phyllis Mary: British Economic Growth, 1688–1959: Trends and Structure, 5006

Deans, Brian Templeton: A Short History of Glasgow's Trolley Buses, 1949–1967, 17246

Dear, I. C. B.: Oxford English: A Guide to the Language, 23807

Dearden, John: Iron and Steel Today, 6564

Dearle, Norman Burrell: The Labour Costs of the World War to Great Britain 1914–1922, 3744

Dearlove, John: The Reorganisation of British Local Government: Old Orthodoxies and Political Perspectives, 3188; The Politics of Policy in Local Government: The Making and Maintenance of Public Policy in the Royal Borough of Kensington and Chelsea, 3313

Dearmer, Nancy: The Life of Percy Dearmer, 11779

Dearmer, Percy: Songs of Praise Discussed, 11931

Deaton, Angus S.: 'Analysis of Consumer Demand in the United Kingdom, 1900–1970', 20452; Models and Projections of Demand in Post-war Britain, 20453; Essays in the Theory and Measurement of Consumer Behaviour in Honour of Sir Richard Stone, 20454

Debenham, Frank: The World is Round: The Story of Man and Maps, 26705; Discovery and Exploration: An Atlas-History of Man's Journeys into the Unknown, 27174

Debo, Richard K.: 'Lloyd George and the Copenhagen Conference of 1919–20: The Initiation of Anglo-Soviet Negotiations', 13929

Debrett's Peerage and Baronetage 1769+, 35.

Decline in the UK Registered Merchant Fleet: HC Paper 94, Parliamentary Papers, 1986–87, 16524

Dee, B. D.: Sudan Political Service, 1899–1956, 14426

Deem, Rosemary: Women and Schooling, 7736; ed. Schooling for Women's Work, 7737

Deep, Samuel David: Human Relations in Management, 5484

Deere, Alan C.: Nine Lives, 15900

Deerr, Noel: The History of Sugar, 20683

Deeson, Arthur F. L.: Great Swindlers, 1367

Degen, Gunther R.: Shop Stewards: Ihre Zentrale Bedeutung für die Gewerkschaftsbewegung in Grossbritannien, 5779

Degensheim, G. A.: Milestones in Modern Surgery, 21134

Degras, Henry Ernest see Benney, Mark

Deighton, Anne: ed. Britain and the Cold War, 14104

Deighton, Herbert Stanley: 'History and the Study of Race Relations', 10923

Deighton, Len: Battle of Britain, 14806; Fighter: The True Story of the Battle of Britain, 14807

Dekker, George: ed. Donald Davie and the Responsibilities of Literature, 25470

Delafons, J.: 'Working in Whitehall: Changes in Public Administration, 1952–1982', 889

Delage, Edmond: The Tragedy of the Dardanelles, 14543

Delaney, Paul: D. H. Lawrence's Nightmare: The Writer and his Circle in the Years of the Great War, 25639

Delavenay, Emile: D.H. Lawrence: The Man and his Work: The Formative Years 1885–1919, 25637

Deli, P.: 'The Image of the Russian Purges in the Daily Herald and the New Statesman', 13948

Dell, Anthony: 'The Problem of the Liquor Trade', 22168

Dell, John Alexander: Arthur Rowntree: Headmaster, Bootham School, York, 1899–1927, 23217

Dell, Susanne: 'Bail Procedures in Magistrates' Courts', 10317; Murder into Manslaughter. The Diminished Responsibility Defence in Practice, 10800

Delmer, [Denis] Sefton: Trail Sinister, 25230

Dempsey, Mike: ed. Bubbles: Early Advertising Art from A. & F. Pears Ltd., 4300; ed. Pipe Dreams: Early Advertising Art from the Imperial Tobacco Company, 4301

Dempsey, William S.: The Story of the Catholic Church in the Isle of Man, 12451

Dempster, Derek David: The Narrow Margin: The Battle of Britain and the Rise of Air Power, 1930–1940, 14816

Dempster, Jack James Bampfylde: Selection for Secondary Education, 22820

Demuth, Clare: Immigration: A Brief Guide to the Numbers Game, 11427

Demuth, Norman Frank: Musical Trends in the Twentieth Century, 24274

Dench, G.: Maltese in London: A Case Study in the Erosion of Ethnic Consciousness, 11390

Dench, Leslie Alan: comp. Passengers No More, 1952–1962: Closures of Stations and Branch Lines, 16774

Dendy Marshall, Chapman Frederick: Centenary History of the Liverpool and Manchester Railway, 16955

Deng, Francis M.: ed. The British in the Sudan 1898–1956, 14417

Denham, J. R.: ed. Buses of South and East Yorkshire, 17283; ed. Buses of West Yorkshire, 17284

Denison, Michael: Overture and Beginners, 26033; Double Act, 26034

Denley, Peter: ed. History and Computing, 26736

Denman, Donald Robert: Bibliography of Rural Land Economy and Land Ownership, 1900–1957: A Full List of Works Relating to the British Isles and Selected Works from the United States and Western Europe, 19390, 20253; Land in the Market: A Fresh Look at Property, Land and Prices, 20266; Commons and Village Greens: A Study in Land Use, Conservation and Management based on a National Survey of Commons in England and Wales, 1961–1966, 20267

Denmark, J. C.: 'Community Care: A Study of the Psychiatric Morbidity of a Salvation Army Hospital', 9123

Denney, Anthony: Children in Need, 8156

Dennier, D. Anne: 'The English Village Revisited', 18949; 'Chester: Conservation in Practice', 18972

Denning, Lord: Cmnd 2152.Parliamentary Papers, xxiv (1962–63) [The Profumo Affair], 9896

Dennis, Norman: English Ethical Socialism: Thomas More to R.H. Tawney, 2105; 'Research and Social Work', 8680; 'The Popularity of the Neighbourhood Community Idea', 9418; Coal is Our Life: An Analysis of a Yorkshire Mining Community, 9637; People and Planning: The Sociology of Housing in Sunderland, 18413

Dennis, Peter: Troubled Days of Peace: Mountbatten and the South-East Asia Command, 1941–1946, 13165; Decision by Default: Peacetime Conscription and British Defence, 1919–1939, 14716

Dennison, Stanley Raymond: The Location of Industry and the Depressed Areas, 5038; 'The British Restrictive Trade Practices Act of 1956', 6108

Denny, Barbara: King's Bishop: The Lords Spiritual of London, 11617

Denny, Lionel: 'The Royal Hospitals of the City of London', 20933

Denny, Lowell: America Conquers Britain: A Record of Economic War, 3713

Denny, William: William Denny and Brothers Ltd., Leven Shipyard, Dumbarton, 1844–1932, 16640

Dent, Alan: Mrs Patrick Campbell, 26022; Vivien Leigh: A Bouquet, 26061

Dent, C. E.: 'Rickets (and Osteomalacia) Nutritional and Metabolic (1919–1969)', 20934

Dent, Edward Joseph: A Theatre for Everybody: The Story of the Old Vic and Sadler's Wells, 26142

Dent, Harold Collett: The Training of Teachers in England and Wales, 1800–1975, 9848; A New Order in English Education, 22631; Education in Transition, 22633; British Education, 22687; Change in English Education, 22688; The Educational System of England and Wales, 22689; 1870–1970: A Century of Growth in English Education, 22690; Growth in English Education, 1946–1952, 22691; Secondary Education for all, 22692; The Training of Teachers in England and Wales 1800–1975, 22742; 'English Secondary Education: Retrospect and Prospect', 22928; Universities in Transition, 23392; Part Time Education in Great Britain: An Historical Outline, 23655

Dent, Philip: 'The d'Abernon Papers: Origins of "Appeasement"', 13661

Dental Branch Library: The Thoughts of a Dental Chair Man, 22407; The Dentist and the State, 22408

Denton, Geoffrey: Economic Planning in Britain, France, and Germany, 3437; Beyond Bullock: The Economic Implications of Worker Participation in Control and Ownership of Industry, 6024

Denver, David T.: 'Candidate Selection in the Labour Party: What the Selectors Seek', 1788; 'Political Communication: Scottish Local Newspapers and the General Election of February 1974', 2369; 'The Decline of the Scottish National Party—An Alternative View', 2502; The Scottish Local Elections 1974: Results and Statistics, 3203

Deosaran, Ramesh: Eric Williams: The Man, His Ideas and His Politics, 13071

Deosaran, Winston: ed. 'East Indians in the Caribbean: Colonialism and the Struggle for Identity', 13010

Department of Education and Science: Central Advisory Council for Education (Wales), 23632; Primary Education in Wales, 23633

Department of the Environment: Planning Maps of England and Wales, 134; Atlas of the Environment: England and Wales 1976+, 135; Leisure and the Quality of Life: Report of a Central Steering Group of Officials on Four Local Experiments, 26914; Report of the Committee on Football, 27066

Derber, Milton: 'Labor Relations in British Metalworking', 5620; Labor-management Relations at Plant Level under Industry-wide Bargaining: A Study of the Engineering (Metalworking) Industry in Birmingham (England), 5621; 'Adjustment Problems of a Long Established Industrial Relations System: An Appraisal of British Engineering 1954–1961', 5622; 'Collective Bargaining in Great Britain and the United States', 5623

Derrick, Deborah: Selected and Annotated Bibliography of Youth, Youth Work, and the Provision for Youth, 8410

Derrick, John: Biting the Hand that Feeds you: A Study into the Effects on Agriculture and the Economy as a Whole, of the Common Agricultural Policy and Agricultural Support, 19658

Derrick, June: Language Needs of Minority Group Children: Learners of English as a Second Language, 23821

Derrick, P.: 'Wages and Dividends', 3934

Derry, Thomas Kingston: British History from 1782 to 1933, 349; Outlines of English Economic History, 3399; The Campaign in Norway, 14915

Desai, Rashmi: Indian Immigrants in Britain, 11219

Descloitres, Robert: Les Travailleurs Étrangers, leur Adaptation au Travail Industriel et à la Vie Urbaine, 10960

Desmarais, Ralph H.: 'Lloyd George and the Development of the British Government's Strikebreaking Organisation', 1030, 6971; 'The British Government's Strike Breaking Organisation and Black Friday', 6862

Desmond, Ray: Dictionary of British and Irish Botanists and Horticulturalists, including Plant Collectors and Botanical Artists, with Historical Introduction by William T. Stearn, 26549

Detels, Roger: Oxford Textbook of Public Health, 21004, 22091

Deuchar, M.: Perspectives on British Sign Language and Deafness, 21933

Deutsch, Richard R.: Northern Ireland, 1921–1974: A Select Bibliography, 2776; Northern Ireland, 1968–1974: A Chronology of Events, 2819; Mairead Corrigan, Betty Williams: Two Women Who Ignored Danger in Campaigning for Peace in Northern Ireland, 7746

Development Control Policy Notes: No. 7—Preservation of Historic Buildings and Areas, 18967

Developments towards Self-Government in the Caribbean: A Symposium Held under the Auspices of the Netherlands Universities Foundation for International Co-operation at The Hague, September 1954, 13000

Devenish, Dorothy: A Wiltshire Home: A Study of Little Durnford, 19195

Deverell, Cyril Spencer: Business Administration and Management, 5436; Office Personnel: Organisation and Management, 5437; Management Planning and Control, 5438

Devereux, William A.: Adult Education in Inner London 1870–1980, 23687

Devlin, Bernadette: The Price of My Soul, 3087

Devlin, P.: Yes, We Have No Bananas: Outdoor Relief in Belfast 1920–1939, 2792

Devlin, Patrick, Baron: Trial by Jury, 10298; Law and Morals, 10299; Samples of Lawmaking, 10300; The Enforcement of Morals 10301; What's Wrong with the Law, 10302; The Judge, 10303

Devon County Council: The Changing Face of Devon, 18859; A Scheme for Coastal Pollution Counter Measures, 20079

Devon, Stanley: 'Glorious': The Life Story of Stanley Devon, 25303

Devons, Ely: An Introduction to British Economic Statistics, 3432; The "Guardian" Wages Index: A Series of Indexes of Wages Rates in British Industry since 1948, 3925; 'Wage Rates by Industry, 1948–1965', 3926; Planning in Practice, 6119

Devonshire Planning Department: A Survey of Residential Caravanners in Devon, 1959, 18557; Barnstaple Feasibility Study, 18839

Dew, George James: Oxfordshire Village Life: The Diaries of George James Dew (1846–1928) Relieving Officer, 19169

Dewar, G. D. H.: V.A.T. 73: An Accountant's Guide to V.A.T., 4860

Dewar, Hugo: Communist Politics in Britain: The CPGB from its Origins to the Second World War, 1929

Dewar, Kenneth Gilbert Balmain: The Navy from Within, 15309

Dewar, M.: Brush Fire Wars: Minor Campaigns of the British Army since 1945, 16175

Dewey, Peter E.: 'Agricultural Labour Supply in England and Wales during the First World War', 9702, 19661; British Agriculture in the First World War, 19431

Dewhurst, Kenneth: ed. Oxford Medicine: Essays on the Evolution of the Oxford Clinical School to commemorate the Bicentenary of the Radcliffe Infirmary 1770–1970, 20798

Dewing, Richard Henry: The Army, 15434

Dewing, S.: Modern Radiology in Historical Perspective, 21126

Dewis, Malcolm: The Law on Health and Safety at Work, 4142; ed. Tolley's Health and Safety at Work Handbook, 4143

Dewitt, David B.: Canada as a Principal Power: A Study in Foreign Policy and International Relations, 12643

Dews, Peter: 'National and Provincial', 23746

Dex, Shirley: Women's Occupational Mobility: A Lifetime Perspective, 5925

Dhavan, Rajeev: ed. Censorship and Obscenity, 26905

Di Roma, Edward: A Numerical Finding List of British Command Papers Published 1832–1961/2, 203

Diack, William: 'The Scottish Mines', 6345

Diamant, Rudolph Maximilian Eugen: The Prevention of Pollution, 19997

Diamond, Aubrey Lionel: The Consumer, Society and the Law, 20457; Introduction to Hire Purchase Law, 20495

Diamond, Derek Robin: Business in Britain: A Philip Management Planning Atlas, 131; ed. Education for Planning: The Development of Knowledge and Capability for Urban Governance: Progress in Planning, 17837; 'Planning the Urban Environment', 17898

Diamond, J.: 'University Engineering Education, 1960–1980', 22523

Dichfield, John: Board of Visitor Adjudications, 10459

Dick, Kay: Ivy and Stevie: Ivy Compton-Burnett and Stevie Smith: Conversations and Reflections, 25458

Dickens, Linda: 'Resolving Industrial Disputes: The Role of A.C.A.S. Conciliation, 4164

Dickens, Peter: Narvik: Battles in the Fjords, 14916

Dickie, John Purcell: The Coal Problem—A Survey: 1910–1936, 6267

Dickie, John: The Uncommon Commoner: A Study of Sir Alec Douglas-Home, 1004

Dickie, M. A. M.: 'Community Development in Scotland', 9419

Dickinson, Alan Edgar Frederic: Vaughan Williams, 24377

Dickinson, D. G.: 'Twopence to the Terminus?': A Study of Tram and Bus Fares in Leeds during the Inter-war Period', 17230

Dickinson, Gordon Cawood: Maps and Air Photographs, 26720

Dickinson, Henry W.: A Short History of the Steam Engine, 7080

Dickinson, Leslie: The Immigrant School Leaver: A Study of Pakistani Pupils in Glasgow, 11225

Dickinson, Margaret: Cinema and State: The Film Industry and the Government 1927–84, 24597, 24642

Dickinson, Patric: The Good Minute: An Autobiographical Study, 25476

Dickinson, Robert Eric: City Region and Regionalism: A Geographical Contribution to Human Ecology, 5040; City and Region: A Geographical Interpretation, 5041; Regional Ecology: The Study of Man's Environment, 5042; Regional Concept: The Anglo-American Leaders, 5043, 26656; The Making of Geography, 26654; The Makers of Modern Geography, 26655

Dickman, H. J.: Haverfordwest Rural District Council: A History of the Council 1894–1974, 3380

Dicks, Brian: ed. Scottish Urban History, 2452, 18125, 18455

Dicks, Henry Victor: Fifty Years of the Tavistock Clinic, 21459

Dicks-Mireaux, L. A.: 'The Determinants of Wage Inflation: United Kingdom, 1946–1956', 3989; 'The Inter-Relationship between Cost and Price Changes,

1946–1959: A Study in Inflation in Post-War Britain', 3991

Dickson, Diane: World Catalogue of Theses on the Pacific Islands, 12872

Dickson, Elizabeth: Colefax and Fowler: The Best in English Interior Design, 24144

Dickson, Lovat: Richard Hillary, 15897; The House of Words, 24978; H. G. Wells: His Turbulent Life and Times, 25870

Dickson, Michael G.: ed. A Living from the Sea: Devon's Fishing Industry and its Fishermen, 19813

Dickson, Nora: A World Elsewhere: Voluntary Service Overseas, 9160

Dickson, Peter George Muir: The Sun Insurance Office 1710–1960, 4209

Dickson, Tony: ed. Scottish Capitalism: Class, State and Nation from before the Union to the Present, 2489; ed. Capital and Class in Scotland, 2490

Dictionary of National Biography: The Concise Dictionary, 22

Didcot and District Archaeological and Historical Society: The Changing Face of Didcot, 18860

Diebold, William: The Schuman Plan: A Study in Economic Co-operation 1950–1959, 14143; 'Britain, the Six and the World Economy', 14160

Diefenbaker, John: One Canada: Memoirs of the Right Honourable John Diefenbaker Vol.I: The Crusading Years 1895–1956, 12664; Vol.II: The Years of Achievement 1957–1962, 12665; Vol.III: The Tumultuous Years, 12666

Dietrich, Richard F.: British Drama 1890 to 1950, 25908

Dietz, Frederick Charles: An Economic History of England, 3404

Dietz, Lena Dixon: History of Modern Nursing, 21714

Dietz, Peter: ed. Garrison: The British Military Towns, 15442

Diffley, Sean: The Men in Green: The Story of Irish Rugby, 27042

Digby, Anne: Pauper Palaces, 4070; British Welfare Policy: Workhouse to Workforce, 8798

Digby, George Frederick Wingfield: The Work of the Modern Potter in England, 24134

Digby, Margaret: Agricultural Co-operation in Britain, 19464; Co-operative Land Use: The Challenge to Traditional Co-operation, 19465

Digest of Environmental Pollution Statistics: 1978+, 20011

Digest of Health Statistics for England and Wales, 21545

Dignan, D. K.: 'Australia and British Relations with Japan, 1914–1921', 12611

Dilks, David N.: Neville Chamberlain: vol. 1: Pioneering and Reform, 1869–1929, 983; 'New Perspectives on Chamberlain', 983; Sir Winston Churchill, 988; Three Visitors to Canada: Stanley Baldwin, Neville Chamberlain and Winston Churchill, 12659; 'The Great Dominion: Churchill's Farewell Visits to Canada 1952 and 1954', 12660; ed. Retreat from Power: Studies in

Britain's Foreign Policy of the Twentieth Century, 13243; ed. The Diaries of Sir Alexander Cadogan, 1938–1945, 13256; 'Appeasement Revisited', 13717; '"We Must Hope for the Best and Prepare for the Worst": The Prime Minister, the Cabinet and Hitler's Germany, 1937–1939', 13718; 'Great Powers and Scandinavia in the "Phoney War"', 13883; 'The Twilight War and the Fall of France: Chamberlain and Churchill in 1940', 14270; 'The Missing Dimension': Governments and Intelligence Communities in the Twentieth Century, 15997

Dillane, John Bevan: General Practice in the New Towns of Britain, 21513

Dillistone, Frederick William: Charles Raven, 11805; Into all the World: A Biography of Max Warren, 11818; C. H. Dodd: Interpreter of the New Testament, 12058

Dillon, G. Martin: Political Murder in Northern Ireland, 2846; The Falklands, Politics and War, 16076

Dilmot, George: Scotland Yard: Its History and Organisation, 1829–1929, 10749

Dimbleby, David: An Ocean Apart, 14012

Dimbleby, Jonathan: Richard Dimbleby: A Biography, 24740

Dimmick, Mary Laverne: The Rolling Stones: An Annotated Bibliography, 24523

Dimmock, Stuart J.: 'Incomes Policy and Health Services in the United Kingdom', 21630

Dimock, Marshall Edward: British Public Utilities and National Development, 6408

Dingle, Herbert: 'Particle and Field Theories of Gravitation', 7136; Science and Human Experience, 27254

Dingle, Reginald James: 'Doctors and the Public: Do We Suffer from Medical Priestcraft?', 21307

Dingley, Cyril S.: The Story of B.I.P. 1894–1962, 6234

Dingwall, Robert: The Sociology of the Professions: Lawyers, Doctors and Others, 9817; ed. Health Care and Health Knowledge 22096

Dinnage, Rosemary: Foster Home Care: Facts and Fallacies: A Review of Research in the United States, Western Europe, Israel and Great Britain between 1948 and 1966, 8157; Residential Home Care: A Review of Research in the United States, Western Europe, Israel and Great Britain between 1948 and 1966, 8158; The Handicapped Child: Research Review, 21917

Dinnerstein, L.: 'America, Britain and Palestine: The Anglo-American Committee of Enquiry', 14331

Dinwiddy, Robert: The Effects of Certain Social and Demographic Changes on Income Distribution, 3856

Dipple, Elizabeth: Iris Murdoch: Work for the Spirit, 25730

Direct Labour Collective: Building with Direct Labour: Local Authority Building and the Crisis in the Construction Industry, 18537

Disablement Income Group: Social Security and Disability: A Study of the Financial

Provisions for Disabled People in Seven West European Countries, 21916

Discussion Papers in Social Research, University of Glasgow: No. 17. Poverty in Scotland: An Analysis of Official Statistics, 9100

Diskin, Michael: The Development of Party Competition among Unionists in Ulster 1966–1982, 2955

Disney, Alfred N.: ed. Origin and Development of the Microscope, 7104

Dissertation Abstracts International: 1938–, 87

Distinguished People of Today: 1988+, 39

Ditchfield, John: Grievance Procedures in Prisons: A Study of Prisoners' Applications and Petitions, 10370

Dittmar, Frederick James: British Warships, 1914–1919, 15353

Ditz, Gerhard William: Joint Consultation in the British Coal Industry, 5999; British Coal Nationalized, 6284

Divine, David: The Nine Days of Dunkirk, 14841; Mutiny at Invergordon, 15297

Divine, Robert A.: Blowing in the Wind: The Nuclear Test Ban Debate 1954–1960, 13541

Dix, Carol: Say I'm Sorry to Mother: Growing Up in the Sixties, 7692

Dix, Frank L.: Royal River Highway: A History of Passenger Boats and Services on the River Thames, 16593

Dix, Gerald: 'Norwich: A Fine Old City', 18979

Dix, H. M.: Environmental Pollution: Atmosphere, Land, Water, and Noise, 19990

Dixey, R.: 'It's a Great Feeling When You Win: Women and Bingo', 7727

Dixon, C. W.: The Institute: a Personal Account of the History of the University of London Institute of Education, 1932–1972, 23535

Dixon, Daniel: Can You Retire? Some Thoughts about the Individual, Administrative and Economic Aspects of Retirement, 3971

Dixon, Donald F.: 'The Development of the Solus System of Petrol Distribution in the United Kingdom, 1950–1960', 6508; 'Petrol Distribution in the United Kingdom, 1900–1950', 6509

Dixon, E.: Charles Rennie Mackintosh: A Selective Bibliography, 24039

Dixon, Julia: Portrait of Social Work: A Study of Social Services in a Northern Town, 8732

Dixon, P. J.: 'The United Kingdom Agricultural Review', 19523

Dixon, Piers: Double Diploma: The Life of Sir Pierson Dixon, Don and Diplomat, 13263

Dixon, William Hepworth: The Match Industry: Its Origin and Development, 6613

Dixson, Anne: Solving Local Government Problems: Practical Applications of Operations Research in Cities and Regions, 3243

Dobb, Maurice Herbert: Wages, 3865; 'Inflation and all That', 3997; Studies in the Development of Capitalism, 4967; Trade Union Experience and Policy, 1914–1918, 6699

Dobbie, S.: Faith and Fortitude: The Life and Work of General Sir William Dobbie, 12857, 14793

Dobbins, E. Lloyd: South Wales as the Chief Industrial Centre of the United Kingdom, 5366

Dobbins, Richard: The Growth and Impact of Institutional Investors: A Report, 4270

Dobbs, Brian: Drury Lane: Three Centuries of the Theatre Royal 1663–1971, 26132

Dobby, Alan: Conservation and Planning, 18951

Dobie, Edith: Malta's Road to Independence, 12859

Dobie, William Jardine: Law and Practice of the Sheriff Courts in Scotland, 10322

Dobinson, Charles Henry: Schooling 1963–70, 22819

Dobry, George: Planning Appeals and Inquiries, 20360; Town and Country Planning, 17771, 20361

Dobson, Alan P.: The Politics of the Anglo-American Economic Special Relationship, 1940–1987, 3716; U.S. Wartime Aid to Britain, 1940–1946, 3728

Dobson, Jessie: Barbers and Barber-Surgeons of London, 20795; George Buckston Browne, 20862; Anatomical Eponyms. Being a Biographical Dictionary of those Anatomists whose Names have become Incorporated into Anatomical Nomenclature, 21041

Dobson, N.: A History of Belize, 13029

Docherty, Kathryn: U.S. Investment in Scotland, 5267

Dockar-Drysdale, Barbara: Therapy in Children: Collected Papers, 8159

Docklands [London] Joint Committee: (Docklands Development Team). Conservation and the Role of the River, 18978

Dockrill, Michael L.: 'The Foreign Office Reforms, 1919–1921', 13340; Peace without Promise: Britain and the Peace Conferences, 1919–1923, 13420; The Cold War 1945–1963, 14102.'The Foreign Office, Anglo-American Relations and the Korean War June 1950–June 1951', 16145

Dodd, Kenneth N.: Computers, 7082

Dodds, Charles: 'The Rise of Clinical Chemistry', 20935

Dodds, Sir Edward: Bread: The Chemistry and Nutrition of Flour and Bread, with an Introduction to their Chemistry and Technology, 20700

Dodds, Harold Willis: Government Assistance to Universities in Great Britain, 23328

Dodds, James Colin: The Investment Behaviour of British Life Insurance Companies, 4220

Dodds, Norman Noel: Gypsies, Didikois and other Travellers, 11342

Dodds-Parker, Sir Douglas: Political Eunuch, 1402; Setting Europe Ablaze, 15086

Dodge, David Lawrence: Social Stress and Chronic Illness: Mortality Patterns in Industrial Society, 7453

Dodge, Frederick Brian: Road Traffic Law Summary, 16239

Dodgson, John Seaton: The Rail Problem, 16784; Bus Deregulation and Privatisation: An International Perspective, 17281

Dodson, Charles Joseph: ed. Bilingual Education: Evaluation, Assessment and Methodology, 23819

Doerner, Klaus: Madmen and the Bourgeoisie: A Social History of Insanity and Psychiatry, 21875

Doganis, Rigas Sotiris: A National Airport Plan, 17659; Who Travels by Air: A Survey of Air Passengers, 17660; 'Airport Profitability and Management Effectiveness', 17661

Doherty, Bernard: 'The Hadow Report, 1926', 22620

Doherty, Frank: The Stalker Affair, 2937

Dohrmann, Bernd: Die Englische Europapolitik in der Wirtschaftskrise 1921–1923, 13654

Doig, Peter: A Concise History of Astronomy, 26380

Dolby, George W.: 'The Changing Face of Methodism: 2. The Methodist Church Act, 1976', 12079

Dolby, James: The Steel Navy: A History in Silhouette, 1860–1962, 15351

Dolin, Sir Anton: Last Words: A Final Autobiography, 24227

Doll, Richard: Effects on Health of Exposure to Asbestos, 4137

Dolmetsch, Mabel: Personal Recollections of Arnold Dolmetsch, 24408

Domberger, Simon: 'The Impact of Competitive Tendering on the Costs of Hospital Domestic Services', 21400

Dominian, Jack: Marriage in Britain, 1945–1980, 9970

Dominic, Zoe: Frederick Ashton: A Choreographer and his Ballets, 24224

Donald, B. L.: 'Planning and Health Care: The Approach in a Reorganised N.H.S.', 21347

Donald W.Insall and Associates: Chester: A Study in Conservation, 18973

Donald, Louise: 'The British Federation of University Women, 1907–1957', 22485

Donaldson, Lady Frances: Edward VIII, 486; King George VI and Queen Elizabeth, 507; Evelyn Waugh: Portrait of a Country Neighbour, 25860; P.G.Wodehouse: A Literary Biography, 25884

Donaldson, Gordon Ian: The Scots Overseas, 2467, 7335; The Eastern Counties, 6813; Scotland, Church and Nation through Six Centuries, 12210; Northwards by Sea, 16480; Isles of Home: Sixty Years of Shetland, 19276; ed. Four Centuries: Edinburgh University Life 1583–1983, 23495; 'A Lang Pedigree: An Essay to Mark the Centenary of the Scottish History Society 1886–1986', 26772

Donaldson, John George Stuart [Baron]: Farming in Britain Today, 19456, 19550

Donaldson, Lex: Policy and the Polytechnics: Pluralistic Drift in Higher Education, 22528

Donaldson, Peter: A Guide to the British Economy, 3524, 5005

Donaldson, R. J.: The New Health Service in Britain, 21666

Doncaster, Patrick: Cliff, 24521

Donges, G. S.: Policymaking for the Mentally Handicapped, 21782

Donn, Thomas Mackenzie: 'The Debate about the Gaelic Language of Scotland since 1832', 23839

Donnachie, Ian Lowe: ed. Forward! Labour Politics in Scotland 1888–1988, 2513; The Industrial Archaeology of Galloway, 5287; Industrial History in Pictures: Scotland, 5265; Old Galloway, 5288; A History of the Brewing Industry in Scotland, 6166, 20738; Poverty and Social Policy 1885–1950, 8969

Donnelly, Desmond: Gaderene '68: The Crimes, Follies and Misfortunes of the Wilson Government, 1403; David Brown's: The Story of a Family Business, 1860–1960, 6363

Donnelly, Eugene Lawrence: Manpower Training and Development, 5938

Donnelly, Tom: The Motor Car Industry in Coventry since the 1890s, 17406

Donner, Sir Patrick: Crusade: A Life against the Calamitous Twentieth Century, 1404

Donnison Report: The Public Schools Commission Second Report, 23027

Donnison, David Vernon: 'Economics and Politics of the Regions', 5110; 'The Movements of Households in England', 7341; The Child and the Social Services, 8160, 8812; The Neglected Child and the Social Services: A Study of the Work done in Manchester and Salford by Social Services of all Kinds for 118 Families whose Children came into Public Care, 8161; Pattern of Disadvantage: ed. A Commentary on 'From Birth to Seven.', 8162; Health, Welfare and Democracy in Greater London, 8813; Social Policy and Administration: Studies in the Development of Social Service at the Local Level, 8814; An Approach to Social Policy, 8815; ed. Policy and Administration Revisited: Studies in the Development of Social Service at the Local Level, 8816; The Politics of Poverty, 9109; The Ingelby Report: Three Critical Essays, 10059; 'Age of Innocence is Past: Some Ideas about Urban Research and Planning', 17899; ed. Rejuvenating the Inner City: The Scottish Experience, 18150; ed. London Urban Patterns, Problems, and Policies: A Study sponsored by the Centre for Environmental Studies, 18359, 18728; Housing Policy, 18519; Housing Policy since the War, 18520

Donnison, F. S. V.: Burma, 13202

Donoughue, Bernard [Baron]: Herbert Morrison: Portrait of a Politician, 1283; The People in Parliament: An Illustrated History of the Labour Party, 1670; Trade Unions in a Changing Society, 6778

Donovan, Bernard T.: Pioneers in Neuroendocrinology, 22325

Donovan, Paul: Dudley, 26332

Dony, John George: A History of the Straw Hat Industry, 6236

Dookhan, Isaac: A History of the British Virgin Islands 1672–1970, 13062

Dooley, Pat: The Irish in Britain, 11358

Doornkamp, John C.: Evaluating the Human Environment: Essays in Applied Geography, 19975; Atlas of Drought in Britain, 1975–76, 20104

Dopson, Laurence: The Changing Scene in General Practice, 21520

Doran, A.: 'Evidence Concerning the Relationship between Health and Retirement', 8626

Dorfman, Gerald Allen: Wage Politics in Britain, 1945–1967, 5767, 6875; British Trade Unionism Against the Trades Union Congress, 6906

Dorian, Nancy C.: Language Death: The Life Cycle of a Scottish Gaelic Dialect, 23846

Dorl, Marcus: Writing the Rural: Five Cultural Geographies, 19123

Dorling, Henry Taprell: Western Mediterranean 1942–1945, 14866; Swept Channels: Being an Account of the Work of the Minesweepers in the Great War, 15394

Dorman, Claude E.: 'Reflections on Sir Alexander Fleming', 20936

Dorn, Nicholas: Alcohol, Youth and the State : Drinking Practice Controls and Health Education, 22158; ed. A Land Fit for Heroin?, 22203

Dorner, Jane: Fashion in the Forties and Fifties, 24166

Dorrington, J. G.: 'A Structural Approach to Estimating the Built-In Flexibility of United Kingdom Taxes on Personal Income', 3825

Dors, Diana: Behind Closed Dors, 26036

Dosser, Douglas: British Taxation and the Common Market, 4846

Dossor, Carol: World Catalogue of Theses on the Pacific Islands, 12872

Dott, Norman: 'The History of Surgical Neurology in the 20th Century', 20937

Doubleday, F. N.: 'The Contributions of King's College, London to the Science of Dentistry', 22411

Dougall, Robert: In and Out of the Box, 24908

Dougan, David: The Shipwrights: The History of the Shipconstructors' and Shipwrights' Association, 1882–1963, 6831; The History of North East Shipbuilding, 16626

Doughan, David: Feminist Periodicals 1855–1984: An Annotated Critical Bibliography of British, Irish, Commonwealth and International Titles, 25190

Doughty, Martin: Merchant Shipping and War: A Study of Defence Planning in 20th Century Britain, 16487

Dougill, David: Blackpool's Buses, 17301

Douglas, David: Pit Life in County Durham: Rank and File Movements and Workers Control, 9641

Douglas, Hugh: The Underground Story, 17002

Douglas, James William Bruce: The Home and the School: A Study of Ability and Attainment in the Primary School, 8163; 'Broken Families and Child Behaviour.', 8164; Children Under Five: The Results of a National Survey, 8165; 'Delinquency and Social Class', 10599, 10635; All our Future: A Longitudinal Study of Secondary Education, 22943

Douglas, Mary: Edward Evans-Pritchard, 26355

Douglas, Peter: Village Life, 19124; The Football Industry, 27062

Douglas, R. P. A.: An Outline of the Law Relating to Harbours in Great Britain Managed under Statutory Powers, 16664

Douglas, Ronald Walter: A History of Glassmaking, 6484, 24125

Douglas, Roy: Working with R.V.W, 24384

Douglas, Roy Ian: 'Chamberlain and Eden, 1937–38', 983; The History of the Liberal Party, 1895–1970, 1809; 'The National Democratic Party and the British Worker's League', 2013; 'The Background to the "Coupon" Election Arrangements', 2279; In the Year of Munich, 13756; The Advent of War, 1939–1940, 13767; ed. 1939: A Retrospect Forty Years After, 13768; From War to Cold War 1942–1948, 14099; Land, People and Politics: A History of the Land Question in the United Kingdom 1878–1952, 20281

Douglas, Torin: The Complete Guide to Advertising, 4331

Douglas, William Lake: Garden Design: History, Principles, Elements, Practice, 19903

Douglas, William Sholto [Baron]: Years of Command, 15955

Douglas-Home, Charles: Evelyn Baring: The Last Proconsul, 12831

Douglas-Home, Sir Alec [Baron Home of the Hirsel]: The Way the Wind Blows: An Autobiography, 1004; Peaceful Change: A Selection of Speeches, 1005

Douglas-Home, William: Autobiography. Half Term Report, 25959; Mr. Home Pronounced Hume: An Autobiography, 25959

Douglas-Smith, Aubrey Edward: The City of London School, 23053

Douglas-Wilson, I.: Health Service Prospects: An International Survey, 21627

Douty, H. M.: 'Union Impact on Wage Structures', 3870

Dover, Victor: 'Marine Insurance through Two Wars', 4214

Dow, J. B. A.: A Source Book of Scottish Economic and Social History, 7528

Dow, John Christopher Roderick: The Management of the British Economy 1945–1960, 3625, 5010; 'The Determinants of Wage Inflation: United Kingdom, 1946–1956', 3989

Dow, Leslie: Merchant's Marks, 4542

Dowell, Susan: Dispossessed Daughters of Eve, 11671

Dowie, J. A.: '1919–1920 is in Need of Attention', 3546; 'Growth in the Inter-War Period: Some More Arithmetic', 3547

Dowling, H. M.: 'Education and the Economy', 23212

Dowling, M. J.: Employee Participation in Manufacturing Industry: Themes and Implications, 6042; Employee Participation in Manufacturing Industry: Trade Union Attitudes, 6043; Employee Participation in Manufacturing Industry: Management Attitudes, 6044

Down, C. G.: The History of the Somerset Coalfield, 6323

Downer, Alan Seymour: British Drama: A Handbook and Brief Chronicle, 26221

Downes, Cathy: Special Trust and Confidence: The Making of an Officer, 15465

Downes, David Malcolm: Signs of Trouble: Aspects of Delinquency, 10151; 'Social Reaction to Deviance and its Effects on Crime and Criminal Careers', 10194; Deviant Interpretations, 10604; The Delinquent Solution: A Study in Subcultural Theory, 10605, 10647; Delinquent Subcultures in East London, 10646; Gambling, Work and Leisure: A Study across Three Areas, 27116

Downey, James E.: Us and Them: Britain, Ireland and the Northern Ireland Question, 1962–1982, 2987

Downie, Allen Watt: Virus and Rickettsial Diseases, 22343

Downie, Robert Angus: The Islands of the Clyde, 19266

Downs, Norton: ed. Essays in Honor of Conyers Read, 13681

Downs, Robert B.: British and Irish Library Resources: A Bibliographical Guide, 72

Dowse, Robert E.: 'Party Discipline in the House of Commons', 1602; 'The Left-wing Opposition During the First Two Labour Governments', 1709; 'The Parliamentary Labour Party in Opposition', 1743; 'The Entry of Liberals into the Labour Party, 1910–1920', 1817; Left in the Centre: The Independent Labour Party, 1893–1940, 1870; 'The ILP 1914–1932: A Bibliographical Study', 1871; 'The Politics of Birth Control', 7510; 'The Independent Labour Party and Foreign Politics, 1918–1923', 13544

Doxat, John: Shinwell Talking: A Conversational Biography to Celebrate his 100th Birthday, 1312; The Living Thames: The Restoration of a Great River, 20095

Doxey, G. V.: The High Commission Territories and South Africa, 12712

Doxiadis, C. A.: Between Dystopia and Utopia, 17977; Ekistics: An Introduction to the Science of Human Settlements, 17978

Doyle, Sir Arthur Conan: The British Campaign in Europe, 1914–1918, 14461

Doyle, Paul A.: ed. Readings in Pharmacy, 22256

Doyle, Peter: ed. Inflation, 3999

Doyle, William: The Blackwell Dictionary of Historians, 26731

Drabble, Margaret: Arnold Bennett: A Biography, 25391

Drabble, Phil: What Price the Countryside?, 20211

Draine, Betsy: Substance under Pressure: Artistic Coherence and Evolving Form in the Works of Doris Lessing, 25656

Drakakis, John: ed. British Radio Drama, 24753

Drakatos, C.: 'Short Term Fluctuations in the Velocity of Circulation of Money in the U.K., 1954–1961', 4607

Drake, Barbara: Women in Trade Unions, 7754

Drake, James: Motorways, 17110

Drake, Keith: Britain's Exports and the Balance of Payments, 5009

Drake, Madeline: Single and Homeless, 18513

Drake, Michael: *ed.* Population in Industrialisation, 7384; *ed.* The Population Explosion: An Interdisciplinary Approach, 7385; *ed.* Population and Society, 1850–1980, 7425

Drake, Pamela S.: 'The Impact of Credit Control on Consumer Durable Spending in the United Kingdom, 1957–1961', 20451

Drake, St. Clair: 'The "Colour Problem" in Britain: A Study of Social Definitions', 11149

Draper, Elizabeth: Birth Control in the Modern World: The Role of the Individual in Population Control, 7514

Draper, Frederick William Marsden: Four Centuries of Merchant Taylors' School, 1561–1961, 23067

Draper, Hilary: Private Police, 10770

Draper, Michael: Falklands: The Air War, 16093

Draper, Peter: The N.H.S.: Three Views, 21604

Draper, Ronald Philip: *ed.* D.H. Lawrence: The Critical Heritage, 25640

Draper, Theodore: The Six Weeks War: France, May 10–June 25, 1940, 14840

Dreikurs, R.: 'The War between the Generations.', 8166

Dreiziger, F.: *ed.* Mobilization for Total War: The Canadian, American and British Experience, 1914–1918, 1939–1945, 13406

Drennan, James: British Union of Fascists: Oswald Mosley and British Fascism, 2015

Drew, Joanna: *ed.* Landscape in Britain 1850–1950, 23989

Drew, Robert H.: Medical Officers in the British Army.1660–1960, 20856

Drewe, Paul: Migration Policy in Europe: A Comparative Study, 11423

Drewett, A. J.: 'Education and the State: A Christian Critique of the 1944 Education Act', 22623

Drewry, Gavin: 'The Outsider and House of Commons Reform: Some Evidence from the Crossman Diaries', 651; The Civil Service Today, 874; Final Appeal: A Study of the House of Lords in its Judicial Capacity, 10294; *ed.* Law and Morality, 10295; 'Prelates in Parliament', 11632

Dreyer, Sir Charles: The Sea Heritage: A Study of Maritime Warfare, 15235

Dreyfus, John: A History of the Nonesuch Press, 24981

Driberg, Thomas Edward Neil: The Best of Both Worlds: A Personal Diary, 1405; Ruling Passions, 1406; The Mystery of Moral Rearmament: A Study of Frank Buchman and His Movement, 12402; Guy Burgess: A Portrait with Background, 16036; 'Swaff': The Life and Times of Hannen Swaffer, 25292

Drinkele, Geoff: Forestry, Fishing, Mining and Power, 19717

Driver, Christopher: A Future for the Free Churches?, 12008; The Disarmers: A Study in Protest, 13526; The British at Table, 1940–1980, 20590; The Exploding University, 23445

Driver, Philip: Harwich: A Nautical History, 16689

Drogheda, [Charles] Garrett [Ponsonby] Moore [Earl of]: Double Harness: Memoirs, 25108

Dromey, Jack: Grunwick: The Workers' Story, 6751

Dronamraju, Krishna R.: *ed.* Haldane and Modern Biology, 26490; *ed.* Haldane: The Life and Work of J. B. S. Haldane with Special Reference to India, 26491

Droop, John Percival: The University Press of Liverpool: A Record of Progress 1899–1946, 24973

Drover, G.: 'London and New York: Residential Density Planning Policies and Development', 18322

Drower, G. M. F.: Neil Kinnock: The Path to Leadership, 1443

Drower, M. S.: Flinders Petrie: A Life in Archaeology, 26365, 27191

Druce, Fred: The Light of Other Days: Country Life around Ross, 1870–1940, 19199

Drucker, Henry M.: 'Leadership Selection in the Labour Party', 1691; 'Changes in the Labour Party Leadership', 1692; 'Intra-Party Democracy in Action: The Election of the Leader and Deputy Leader by the Labour Party in 1983', 1693; *ed.* Multi-Party Britain, 2003, 2043, 2503; Doctrine and Ethos in the Labour Party, 2158; Breakaway: The Politics of Nationalism and Devolution, 2416; The Scottish Labour Party, 2522

Drucker, Peter Ferdinand: Managing for Results, 5443; The Age of Discontinuity: Guidelines to our Changing Society, 5444; The Effective Executive, 5445; Technology, Management and Society, 5446

Drudy, P. J.: *ed.* Ireland and Britain since 1922, 2973, 11362; 'Migration between Ireland and Britain since Independence', 11368

Druitt, Basil: The Growth of the Welfare State, 21600

Drummond, G. Gordon: The Invergordon Smelter: A Case Study in Management, 6150

Drummond, Ian Macdonald.: British Economic Policy and the Empire, 1919–1939, 3594, 12536; The Floating Pound and the Sterling Area 1931–1939, 4690; 'Empire Trade and Russian Trade: Economic Diplomacy in the 1930s', 4788; The Floating Pound and the Sterling Area, 1931–1939, 5002; British Economic Policy and the Empire, 1919–1939, 5007; Imperial Economic Policy, 1917–1939: Studies in Expansion and Protection, 5008; Canada since 1945: Power, Politics and Provincialism, 12641

Drummond, Sir Jack Cecil: The Englishman's Food: A History of Five Centuries of English Diet, 20573

Drummond, John Dorman: Blue for a Girl: The Story of the W.R.N.S, 15317; H.M. U-boat, 15368

Drummond, Joseph Margach: The Finance of Local Government: England and Wales, 3261, 4871

Drury, Elizabeth: *ed.* Society Scandals, 9746

Dry, Thomas J.: A History of the Heart and the Circulation, 22337

Du Boulay, Shirley: Cecily Saunders: Founder of the Modern Hospice Movement, 21498

Du Cane, Peter: An Engineer of Sorts, 16636

Du Maurier, Daphne: Gerald, A Portrait, 26037

Du-Cros, Arthur: Wheels of Fortune, 17338

Dubin, Martin David: 'Toward the Concept of Collective Security: The Bryce Group's "Proposals for the Avoidance of War", 1914–1917', 13475

Dubois, A.: 'Le Service National de Santé en Angleterre', 21568

Dubos, J. *and* R.J.: The White Plague: Tuberculosis, Man and Society, 21559

Dubs, Alf: Lobbying: An Insider's Guide to the Parliamentary Process, 2072

Duckham, Baron Frederick *and* Duckham, Helen: Great Pit Disasters: Great Britain to the Present Day, 6317; A History of the Scottish Coal Industry, 6321

Duckles, Vincent: Music Reference and Research Materials, 24259

Duclaud-Williams, Roger Hugh: The Politics of Housing in Britain and France, 18521

Ducrocq, P.: Youth in Contemporary Britain, 8464

Dudley, James: The Life of Edward Grubb, 1854–1939: A Spiritual Pilgrimage, 12143

Dudley, Norman Alfred: Work Measurement: Some Research Studies, 5887

Duesbery, W. K.: *comp.* A First List of U.K Student Theses and Dissertations in Planning and Urban and Regional Studies, 18176

Duff, Alan Colquhoun: Britain's New Towns: An Experiment in Living, 18226

Duff, Charles St. Lawrence: Six Days to Shake an Empire: Events and Factors behind the Irish Rebellion of 1916, 2737

Duff, David Skene: Elizabeth of Glamis, 507; Queen Mary, 475

Duff, Sir James Fitzjames: Universities in Britain, 23383

Duffield, Brian: Recreation in the Countryside: A Spatial Analysis, 26958; A Digest of Sports Statistics, 27022

Duffin, Henry Charles: The Novels and Plays of Charles Morgan, 25717

Duffy, F.: 'Office Landscaping, 1958–1978', 23926

Duffy, Maureen: A Thousand Capricious Chances: A History of the Methuen List 1889–1989, 24979

Duffy, Norman Francis: 'Occupational Status, Job Satisfaction and Levels of Aspiration', 5869; *ed.* The Sociology of the Blue Collar Worker, 9659

Dufton, Anne: An Equal Chance: Equalities and Inequalities of Educational Opportunity, 22812

Dugdale, Blanche Elizabeth Campbell: Arthur James Balfour, First Earl of Balfour, 980; *ed.* Opinions and Argument from Speeches and Addresses of the Earl of Balfour . . . 1910–1927, 981

Dugdale, Harry: The Management of a Public House, 20756

Dugdale, John: *ed.* War Comes to Britain. Speeches . . . 976

Duggan, John P.: Neutral Ireland and the Third Reich, 2711

Duggan, Margaret: Runcie: The Making of an Archbishop, 11701; *ed.* Padre in Colditz: The Diary of J. Ellison Platt MBE, 15043

Duignan, Peter: *ed.* Colonialism in Africa 1870–1960, 12676; *ed.* African Proconsuls: European Governors in Africa, 12705

Duke, Christopher: Colour and Rehousing: A Study of Redevelopment in Leeds, 11492, 18704; Paper Awards in Liberal Adult Education, 23709

Duke, Neville: Sound Barrier: The Story of High-speed Flight, 17500; *ed.* The Crowded Sky: An Anthology of Flight from its Beginnings to the Age of the Guided Missile, 17501

Dukes, Ethel: Children of Today and Tomorrow, 8167

Dukore, Bernard Frank: Harold Pinter, 25974

Dulffer, Jost: 'Das Deutsch-Englische Flottenabkommen vom 18 Juni 1935', 13667

Dulwich: God's Gift: A Living History of Dulwich College, 23056

Dumbell, Stanley: The University of Liverpool, 1903–1953, 23514

Dumbleton, Bob: The Second Blitz: The Demolition and Rebuilding of Town Centres in South Wales, 18980

Dummett, Ann: Citizenship and Nationality, 11070; A Portrait of English Racism, 11175

Dumsday, William Henry: The Relieving Officers' Handbook: Being a Complete and Practical Guide to the Law Relating to the Powers, Duties and Liabilities of Relieving Officers, 4068

Dunbabin, John P. D.: British Rearmament in the 1930s: A Chronology and a Review, 14711

Dunbar, Charles S.: Tramways in Wandsworth and Battersea, 17235; The Rise of Road Transport 1919–1939, 17460

Dunbar, David Stuart: Planning and Pricing for Decimalisation, 4729

Dunbar, Janet: Flora Robson, 26094

Duncan, Andrew: The Reality of Monarchy, 430

Duncan, Barry: Invergordon '31: How the Men of the RN Struck and Won, 15295; The History of the National Theatre, 26140

Duncan, George Sang: Bibliography of Glass, From the Earliest Records to 1940, 6485

Duncan, Herbert O.: The World on Wheels, 17333

Duncan, J. S. R.: The Sudan: A Record of Achievement, 14423; Sudan's Path to Independence, 14424

Duncan, Judith Anne: The Scottish Criminal, 10181; The State of Crime in Scotland, 10183

Duncan, Leland Lewis: History of the Borough of Lewisham, 18945

Duncan, Otis Dudley: Social Characteristics of Urban and Rural Communities, 9333

Duncan, Robert: The Warwick Guide to British Labour Periodicals 1790–1970: A Checklist, 1662

Duncan, Ronald: Working with Britten: A Personal Memoir, 24310; Autobiography. All Men are Islands; How to Make Enemies; Obsessed, 25960

Duncan, S. S.: Housing Disadvantage and Residential Mobility: Immigrants and Institutions in a Northern Town, 11490

Duncan, Thomas Lindsay Cameron: The Kings Heath Study: Report of an Exploratory Survey of Attitudes to House and Neighbourhood Improvement in an Older Part of Birmingham, 9383; Housing Improvement Policies in Scotland: A Survey of Local Authorities, 18469; Improvement Grants in Scotland, 1967–73, 18470

Duncum, Barbara Mary: *ed.* Children in Hospital: Studies in Planning: A Report of Studies Made by the Division for Architectural Studies of the Nuffield Foundation, 21406

Duncum, Philip: *ed.* The Westminster Press Provincial Papers, 25162

Dundee: An Evocation of Town Life before the War: From Memories Collected from Local Inhabitants, 18130

Dundy, Elaine: Finch, Bloody Finch. A Biography of Peter Finch, 26042

Dunham, H. Warren: 'Social Class and Mental Disorder', 21859

Dunhill, Mary: Our Family Business, 6538

Dunkerley, David: Occupations and Society, 5906

Dunleavy, Patrick: The Politics of Mass Housing in Britain, 1945–75, 18764

Dunlop, Sir Derrick Melville: The Problem of Modern Medicines and their Control, 22259; Medicines in Our Time, 22296

Dunlop, Anne B.: Young Men in Detention Centres, 10517; Young Women in Detention Centres, 10592

Dunlop, J. T.: 'Cyclical Variations on the Wage Structure', 3867

Dunn, Gwen: The Box in the Corner: Television and the Under-fives: A Study, 24829

Dunn, J. M.: 'Some Features of Small Full-time and Part-time Farms in Scotland', 19623

Dunn, Laurence: British Warships, 15346

Dunn, Richard: 'The Geography of Council House Sales in England, 1979–1985', 18439

Dunn, S. Watson: Advertising: Its Role in Modern Marketing, 4315

Dunn, Samuel: 'The Care of Young Children's Teeth', 21303

Dunn, Stephen: The Closed Shop in British Industry, 5836

Dunn, Walter Scott: Second Front Now 1943, 14922

Dunne, Agnes Clarissa: Ageing in Industry: An Inquiry Based on Figures derived from Census Reports into the Problems of Ageing under the Conditions of Modern Industry, 5862

Dunnet, Peter J. S.: The Decline of the British Motor Industry: The Effects of Government Policy 1945–1979, 17401

Dunnett, Alastair: Among Friends: An Autobiography, 25232

Dunnett, Andrew: Understanding the British Economy, 3525

Dunnett, Sir James: 'The Civil Service: Seven Years after Fulton', 861

Dunnill, Frank: The Civil Service: Some Human Aspects, 929

Dunning, Eric: Barbarians, The Sociology of Sport: A Selection of Readings, 27025; Gentlemen and Players: A Sociological Study of the Development of Rugby Football, 27032

Dunning, John H.: Insurance in the Economy, 4218; An Economic Study of the City of London, 4254; American Investment in British Manufacturing Industry, 4754, 4999; British Industry: Change and Development in the Twentieth Century, 4941; The Role of American Investment in the British Economy, 5000; 'Employment for Women in the Development Areas 1939–1951', 7817; Economic Planning and Town Expansion: A Case Study of Basingstoke, 18091; 'Manufacturing Industry in the New Towns', 18230

Dunphy, Elaine M.: Oil: A Bibliography, 6488

Dunsch, Jürgen: Die 'Europapolitik' der Britischen Labour Party 1970–1975, 14186

Dunsheath, Percy: The Graduate in Industry, 23351; Convocation in the University of London: the First Hundred Years, 23517

Dunsire, Andrew: 'So You Think You Know what Government Departments are . . . ?', 819; Cutback Management in Public Bureaucracies: Popular Theories and Observed Outcomes in Whitehall, 897; The Making of an Administrator, 911

Dupree, Henry: Urban Transportation: The New Town Solution, 18262

Dupree, Marguerite: *ed.* Lancashire and Whitehall: The Diary of Sir Raymond Streat, 6446

Dupuy, Trevor Nevitt: Land Battles: North Africa, Sicily and Italy, 14893

Durand, Algernon Thomas Marion: The London Rifle Brigade, 1919–1950, 15695

Durand, Sir Henry Mortimer: The 13th Hussars in the Great War, 15665

Durant, Ruth: Watling: A Survey of Social Life on a New Housing Estate, 9325

Durbin, Elizabeth: New Jerusalem: The Labour Party and the Economics of Democratic Socialism, 3695

Durcan, J. W.: Strikes in Post-War Britain: A Study of Stoppages of Work due to Industrial Disputes, 1948–1973, 6916; 'The State Subsidy Theory of Strikes: An Examination of Statistical Data for the Period 1956–7', 6932

Dures, Alan: Schools, 22818

Durgnat, R.: A Mirror for England: British Movies from Austerity to Affluence, 24638

Durham County Council: Durham City: An Interim Traffic Management Study, 16348

Durham Research Review from VIII No.40 Spring 1978+, 22587

Durham, M.: 'British Revolutionaries and the Suppression of the Left in Lenin's Russia, 1918–1924', 13930

Durkacz, V. E.: The Decline of the Celtic Languages, 23818

Durkin, Elizabeth: Hostels for the Mentally Disordered, 21860

Dury, George Harry: The British Isles: A Systematic and Regional Geography, 5050; The East Midlands and the Peak, 5131

Dussek, Ian: Motor Cars of the 1930s, 17344; Sports Cars 1910–1960, 17345

Dutt, Rajani Palme: The Rise and Fall of the Daily Herald, 25132; Britain's Crisis of Empire, 12565; The Crisis of Britain and the British Empire, 12566

Dutter, L. E.: 'The Structure of Vote Preferences: The 1921, 1925, 1973 and 1975 Northern Irish Parliamentary Elections', 2798

Dutton, David J.: Austen Chamberlain: Gentleman in Politics, 1147; 'The Deposition of King Constantine of Greece, June 1917: An Episode in Anglo-French Diplomacy', 13387; 'The Calais Conference of December 1915', 13407

Dutton, Patricia A.: A Case Study of the G.E.C./A.E.I./English Electrical Mergers, 5543

Dwyer, Denis John: A History of the Royal Naval Barracks, Portsmouth, 15299

Dwyer, T. Ryle: Strained Relations: Ireland at Peace and the USA at War, 1941–1945, 2708; Michael Collins and the Treaty: His Differences with De Valera, 3029; Irish Neutrality and the U.S.A. 1939–1947, 2709; De Valera's Darkest Hour: In Search of National Independence 1919–1932, 3045; De Valera's Finest Hour: In Search of National Independence 1932–1959, 3046

Dyer, B. R.: Kent Railways, 16946

Dyer, Malcolm: A History of British Railways Diesel and Electric Locomotive Liveries, 16795

Dyer, Michael: 'Size of Place and the Labour Vote in Britain, 1918–66', 1722

Dyhouse, Carol: Feminism and the Family in England, 1880–1930, 7641

Dyment, Alan: The Literature of the Cinema: A Bibliographical Guide to the Film as Art and Entertainment, 1936–1970, 24586

Dymock, Eric: Postwar Sports Cars: The Modern Classics, 17359

Dymond, Dorothy: ed. The Forge: The History of Goldsmiths' College, 1905–1955, 22748, 23521

Dyos, Harold James: British Transport: An Economic Survey from the 17th Century to the 20th Century, 16184; 'Transport History in University Theses', 16211; ed. The Study of Urban History; The Proceedings of an International Round-Table Conference of the Urban History Group, 17929; ed. Urbanity and Suburbanity, 17930

Dyson, Anthony Edward: ed. Black Paper Three: Goodbye Mr Short, 22645; The Black Papers on Education, 22648; ed. The 20th Century Mind: History, Ideas and Literature in Britain. Vol. 1. 1900–1918, 23728

Dyson, Anthony Oakley: 'The Church's Educational Institutions: Some Theological Institutions', 11901

Dyson, John: Business in Great Waters: The Story of British Fishermen, 19807

Döring, H.: 'Krisenbewusstsein im Establishment? Stimmen zur Verfassungsverein seit 1974, 586

E. & S. Livingstone Ltd.: Footprints in the Sands of Time, 1863–1963: The Story of the House of Livingstone: Medical, Scientific, Nursing and Dental Publishers, 24974

E.S.R.C., 55

Eade, Charles: ed. Churchill by his Contemporaries, 988

Eager, Alan: Guide to Irish Bibliographical Material: A Bibliography of Irish Bibliographies and Sources of Information, 2638

Eagger, Arthur Austin: Venture in Industry: The Slough Industrial Health Service, 1947–1963, 4123

Eagles, Paul J. F.: The Planning and Management of Environmentally Sensitive Areas, 19977

Eaglesham, Eric John Ross: The Foundations of Twentieth-century Education in England, 22658; 'The Changing Idea of a University', 23401

Eagleton, Terry: ed. Raymond Williams: Critical Debates, 23726

Eames, Aled: Ships and Seamen of Anglesey, 1558–1918: Studies in Maritime and Local History, 16482

Eames, E.: 'Not Welcome: The Punjabi Visitor and British Officialdom', 11208

Earl, Lawrence: Yangtse Incident: The Story of H.M.S. Amethyst, April 20, 1949 to July 31, 1949., 14693

Earle, J. B. E.: A Century of Road Materials: The History of the Roadstone Division of Tarmac Ltd., 6180; Blacktop: A History of the British Flexible Roads Industry, 6181

Early, D. F.: 'Population Trends in a Mental Hospital', 21777

Early, Richard Elliott: The Blanket Makers, 1669–1969: A History of Charles Early and Marriott (Witney) Ltd., 6440

East Suffolk County Council: Felixstowe Town Map, 1963: Report of Survey and Analysis, 18871

East Sussex County Planning Department: A Report of the East Sussex County Council Campaign to control Dutch Elm Disease, 19778

East, Charles Frederick Terence: The Story of Heart Disease, 21060

East, John M.: Max Miller: The Cheeky Chappie, 26329

Eastes, Margot: Paul Nash: The Master of the Image, 1889–1946, 24045

Easthaugh, Kenneth: Havergal Brian: The Making of a Composer, 24303

Easthope, Gary: A History of Social Research Methods, 8091, 8899; 'Religious War in Northern Ireland', 12167

Easton, Alan: 50 North: An Atlantic Battleground, 15136

Easton, Carol: Jacqueline du Pré: A Biography, 24409

Easton, Malcolm: The Art of Augustus John, 24025

Eastwood District Libraries: A Planned Village: A History of Eaglesham, 19251; 'Fairest Parish': A History of Mearns, 19370

Eastwood, Gerry G.: George Isaacs: Printer, Trade Union Leader, Cabinet Minister, 1242; Harold Laski, 2116; Skilled Labour Shortages in the United Kingdom with Particular Reference to the Engineering Industry, 5907

Eaton, George E.: Alexander Bustamente and Modern Jamaica, 13052

Eaton, Jack: 'Workers' Participation in Management: A Survey of Post-war Organised Opinion', 5458; Industrial Relations in the Chemical Industry, 5797, 6202

Eaton, John: Economics of Peace and War: An Analysis of Britain's Economic Problems, 3740; Whatever Happened to Britain? The Economics of Decline, 3685

Eatwell, Roger: 'Labour and the Lessons of 1931', 1713

Eaves, Derek: Alcoholism and Addiction, 22134

Eaves, John: Emergency Powers and the Parliamentary Watchdog: Parliament and the Executive in Great Britain, 1939–1951, 722

Eayrs, George: British Methodism: A Handbook and Short History, 12067

Eayrs, James George: ed. The Commonwealth and Suez: A Documentary Survey, 14372

Eberson, Frederick: The Microbe's Challenge, 22372; Microbes Militant: A Challenge to Man: The Story of Modern Preventive Medicine and Control of Infectious Diseases, 22373

Ebsco Publishing: The Serials Directory: An International Reference Book, 152

Ebsworth, Robert: Factors Shaping Shop Steward Organisation in Britain, 5796

Eccles, David McAdam [Viscount Eccles]: Life and Politics: A Moral Diagnosis, 1185; By Safe Hand: The Wartime Letters of Sybil and David Eccles, 1939–1942, 1186

Eccles, Sir John Carew: 'Alexander Forbes and his Achievement in Electro-physiology', 20938; 'From Electrical to Chemical Transmission in the Central Nervous System', 20939; 'The Discipline of Science with Special Reference to the Neurosciences', 20940; Facing Reality: Philosophical Adventures by a Brain Scientist, 27261; The Human Mystery, 27262; The Self and its Brain, 27263

Eccles, P. R.: 'Secondary Reorganisation in Tynemouth, 1962–69', 22956

Eccleshall, Robert: British Liberalism: Liberal Thought from the 1640s to the 1980s, 2164

Echerau, Michael: Joyce Cary and the Dimensions of Order, 25439

Eckstein, Harry Horace: Pressure Group Politics: The Case of the British Medical Association, 20810; The English Health Service: Its Origin, Structure, and Achievements, 21564

Eco, U.: A Pictorial History of Inventions, 7141

Ecology Party: Working for the Future, 1859; How to Survive the Nuclear Age: What the Government Will Not Tell You, 1860; Nuclear Disarmament and Beyond, 1861; Politics for Life, 1862; Towards a Green Europe, 1863

Economic Development Committee for Food Manufacturing: Food Statistics: A Guide to the Major Official and Unofficial U.K. Sources, 20600

Economic History Review 'List of Publications on the Economic History of Great Britain and Ireland', 3391

Economist Intelligence Unit: Britain and Europe: A Study of the Effects on British Manufacturing Industry of a Free Trade Area and the Common Market, 4822; A Survey of Factors governing the Location of Offices in the London Area, prepared for the Location of Offices Bureau, 5175; A Survey of Factors Governing the Location of Offices in the London Area; . . . Prepared for the Location of Offices Bureau, 18324

Economists Advisory Group: The British and German Banking System: A Comparative Study, 4446

Eddington, Sir Arthur Stanley: The Internal Constitution of the Stars, 26377; The Expanding Universe, 26378

Ede, J. Chuter: 'The Place of the Public Schools in our Educational System', 23032

Edelman, Maurice: The Mirror: A Political History, 25134

Edelstein, J. D.: 'The Pattern of Opposition in British and American Unions', 6780; 'Countervailing Powers and the Political Process in the British Mineworkers Union', 6781; 'Democracy in a National Union: The British AEU', 6782

Edelstein, J. M.: *ed*. A Garland for Jake Zeitlin, 17024

Eden, Guy: Portrait of Churchill, 988

Eden, Robert Anthony [Earl of Avon]: Facing the Dictators, 1008; Full Circle, 1008; The Reckoning, 1008; Foreign Affairs, 1015; Freedom and Order: Selected Speeches, 1939–1946, 1015; Days for Decision, 1015

Eden, William Arthur: The Future of Merseyside: Town and Country Planning Schemes, 18891

Eder, Norman R.: National Health Insurance and the Medical Profession in Britain, 1913–1939, 4111

Edgar, David: 'Racism, Fascism and the Politics of the National Front', 2045, 11196; 'Ten Years of Political Theatre, 1968–1978', 26243

Edgar, J.: 'The Big Rush: Britons Emigrate', 7312

Edge, David Owen: Astronomy Transformed: The Emergence of Radio Astronomy in Britain, 26430; 'The Sociology of Innovation in Modern Astronomy', 26440

Edgell, Stephen: 'Marriage and the Concept of Companionship', 9979

Edinburgh, H.R.H. the Prince Philip, Duke of: Selected Speeches 1948–1955, 522

Edinburgh Royal College of Physicians: (Publications—No.22). The Care of the Elderly in Scotland, 8583

Edlin, Herbert Leeson: 'The Forestry Commission in Scotland, 1919–69', 19724; England's Forests Old and New: A Survey of the Woodlands Old and New in the English and Welsh Counties, 19729; The Living Forest: A History of Trees and Timbers, 19730; National Forest Parks, 19731; *ed*. The New Forest, 19732; *ed*. North Yorkshire Forests, 19733; *ed*. The Forests of North East Scotland, 19734; *ed*. The Forests of Central and Southern Scotland, 19735; *ed*. Glamorgan Forests, 19736; Timber! Your Growing Investment, 19793

Edmonds, Charles: A Subaltern's War: Being a Memoir of the Great War from the Point of View of a Romantic Young Man, 14474

Edmonds, Sir James Edward: A Short History of World War I, 14458; Italy, 1915–1919, 14556; France and Belgium, 14581

Edmonds, Robin: Setting the Mould: The United States and Britain 1945–1950, 14074

Edmunds, Edward Leslie: The School Inspector, 23247

Edmunds, Vincent: 'Child Development, Mental Deficiency and Child Delinquency', 8168; *ed*. Medical Ethics: A Christian View, 8168

Edson, Patricia: Spring Grove: The Education of Immigrant Children, 23175

Education (Scotland) Reports Etc., 22591

Education Committees Year Book, 22589

Education Yearbook, 22592

Education and Science, 22590

Education, 22588

Educational Administration, 22593

Educational Management and Administration, 22594

Educational Research, 22595

Educational Review, 22596

Edward VIII: A King's Story: the Memoirs of H.R.H The Duke of Windsor, 476

Edward VIII: The Crown and the People, 1902–1953, 485

Edward, A. T.: British Bluejacket, 1915–1940, 15290

Edward, Harry: The Morris Motor Car: 1913–1983, 17434

Edwardes, Michael: The Myth of the Mahatma: Gandhi, the British and the Raj, 13140; The Last Years of British India, 13170

Edwardes, Sir Michael: Back from the Brink, 5506

Edwards, A. M.: The Design of Suburbia: A Critical Study of Environmental History, 9391

Edwards, Alfred George, Archbishop of Wales: Memories, 12281

Edwards, Angela: *ed*. Agricultural Resources: An Introduction to the Farming Industry of the United Kingdom, 19559

Edwards, Anne: 'Inmate Adaptations and Socialization in the Prison', 10339

Edwards, Anne: Vivien Leigh: A Biography, 26062

Edwards, Anthony Davies: The Changing Sixth Form in the Twentieth Century, 23244

Edwards, Arthur M.: The Design of Suburbia: A Critical Study in Environmental History, 18302

Edwards, Arthur Trystan: Merthyr, Rhondda and the Valleys, 5356

Edwards, Barry K.: Derby City Transport Route History, 1840–1982, 16351

Edwards, Bob: Multinational Companies and the Trade Unions, 5557

Edwards, Brian: Si vis pacem: Preparations for Change in the National Health Service, 21617

Edwards, Clive Arthur: Environmental Pollution by Pesticides, 20111

Edwards, David Lawrence: '101 years of the Lambeth Conference', 11640; Leaders of the Church of England, 1828–1944, 11676; Ian Ramsey, Bishop of Durham: A Memoir, 11754; *ed*. The Honest to God Debate, 11873; Religion and Change, 11887; The British Churches turn to the Future, 12347; F. J. Shirley: An Extraordinary Headmaster, 23218

Edwards, Donald: Political Broadcasting, 24772

Edwards, Francis: Ancient Geography: A Catalogue of Atlases and Maps of all Parts of the World from the XV Century to the Present Day, 26695

Edwards, Frederick Lawrence: The Parish Councillor's Guide: The Law and Practice of Parish, Town and Community Councils in England and Wales, 19315

Edwards, Frederick Wallace: Mosquitoes and their Relation to Disease: Their Life-History, Habits and Control, 22369; British Mosquitoes and their Control, 22370; British Blood Sucking Flies, 22371

Edwards, G. E.: 'The Scottish Grand Committee, 1958 to 1970', 2479

Edwards, Gareth Owen: Gareth—An Autobiography, 27048

Edwards, George: The Victoria Hospital for Children, Tite Street, Chelsea, London S.W.3: A Short Commemorative History, 1866–1964, 21460

Edwards, Sir George: The British Aerospace Industry: A National Asset, 17593

Edwards, Griffith: *ed*. Drug Problems in Britain: A Review of Ten Years, 10833, 22206; 'Alcoholics Admitted to Four Hospitals in England', 21971; The Treatment of Drinking Problems, 22154; *ed*. Alcoholism: New Knowledge and New Responses, 22156; 'British Policies on Opiate Addiction: Ten Years Working of the Revised Response and Option for the Future', 22183; Opium and the People: Opiate Use in Nineteenth-century England, 22205

Edwards, H. W. J.: 'The Course of Welsh Nationalism Today', 2596

Edwards, Harold Raymond: Competition and Monopoly in the British Soap Industry, 6395

Edwards, Herbert James: The Evening Institute: Its Place in the Educational System of England and Wales, 23257, 23654, 23710

Edwards, J. Arwell: 'The Viability of Lower Size Order Settlements in Rural Areas: The Case of North East England', 19156

Edwards, J. G.: Sir John Cecil Power, Bart. 1870–1950, 1507

Edwards, Jill: The British Government and the Spanish Civil War 1936–1939, 13983

Edwards, Jimmy: Take It from Me, 26308

Edwards, John Llewelyn Jones: 'A New Doctrine in Criminal Punishment', 10333

Edwards, John R.: Social Patterns in Birmingham, 1966: A Reference Manual, 9382

Edwards, John Richard: Company Legislation and Changing Patterns of Disclosure in British Company Accounts, 1900–1940, 4184

Edwards, Kathleen Louise: The Story of the Civil Service Union, 6879

Edwards, Kenneth: Britain at War: The Royal Navy and Allies, 14690; The Mutiny at Invergordon, 15296

Edwards, Kenneth Charles: ed. Nottingham and its Region, 5209, 18066; 'Sixty years after Herbertson: The Advance of Geography as a Spatial Science', 26663

Edwards, Kenneth Harry Reese: Chronology of the Development of the Iron and Steel Industries of Teesside, 6562

Edwards, Lewis Arthur: Inland Waterways of Great Britain, 16371, 16441

Edwards, Lynne: Decision Making for Energy Futures: A Case Study of the Windscale Inquiry, 6670

Edwards, Maldwyn Lloyd: Methodism and England: A Study of Methodism in its Social and Political Aspects, 1850–1932, 12100

Edwards, Ness: History of the South Wales Miners' Federation, 6899

Edwards, Owen Dudley: Celtic Nationalism, 2419; ed. 1916: The Easter Rising, 2739; The Sins of the Fathers: Roots of Conflict in Northern Ireland, 2841, 12159; Eamon de Valera, 3053

Edwards, P.: ed. The Encyclopaedia of Philosophy, 26831

Edwards, Paul K.: Managing the Factory: A Survey of General Managers, 5457; 'Britain's Changing Strike Problem', 6958

Edwards, Peter G.: 'The Foreign Office and Fascism, 1914–1929', 13775; 'The Austen Chamberlain-Mussolini Meetings', 13776; 'Britain, Fascist Italy and Ethiopia, 1925–1928', 13777; 'Britain, Mussolini and the "Locarno-Geneva" System', 13778

Edwards, R. A.: And the Glory: The Huddersfield Choral Society 1836–1986, 24398

Edwards, Reese: The Middle School Experiment, 23243

Edwards, Robert: Industrial Democracy, 6045; Goodbye Fleet Street, 25233; Edwards, Roger: Business in Britain: A Philip Management Planning Atlas, 131

Edwards, Sir Ronald Stanley: Status, Productivity and Pay—A Major Experiment: A Study of the Electricity Supply Industry's Agreements and their Outcome, 1961–1971, 3914, 5692; Business Enterprise: Its Growth and Organisation, 4945; ed. Studies in Business Organisation, 4946; ed. Business Growth, 4947; An Experiment in Industrial Relations: The Electricity Supply Industry's Status Agreement for Staff, 5691

Edwards, Rowland Alexander: Church and Chapel: A Study of the Problem of Reunion in the Light of History, 12325

Edwards, Ruth Dudley: Harold Macmillan: A Life in Pictures, 1046; An Atlas of Irish History, 2664; James Connolly, 3031; Patrick Pearse: The Triumph of Failure, 3069; Victor Gollancz: A Biography, 24963

Edwards, Susan M.: Women on Trial, 10877

Edwards, Thomas Joseph: Military Customs, 15548; A Short History of the 4th Queen's Own Hussars, 15658

Edwards, William: British Foreign Policy from 1815 to 1933, 13210

Eebelo, H. S.: Reaction to Colonialism: A Prelude to the Politics of Independence in Northern Zambia, 1893–1939, 12779

Eekelaar, John M.: ed. Family Violence: An International and Interdisciplinary Study, 9954; Family Law and Social Policy, 9955; Family Security and Family Breakdown, 9956; Custody after Divorce: The Disposition of Custody in Divorce Cases in Great Britain, 9957

Egerton, Frank N.: 'A Bibliographical Guide to the History of General Ecology and Popular Ecology', 10121

Egerton, George W.: 'Britain and the "Great Betrayal": Anglo-American Relations and the Struggle for United States Ratification of the Treaty of Versailles', 13429; Great Britain and the Creation of the League of Nations: Strategy, Politics and International Organization, 13470; 'The Lloyd George Government and the Creation of the League of Nations', 13471

Egerton, Hugh Edward: British Colonial Policy in the Twentieth Century, 12538

Eggleston, John: 'Secondary Schools and Oxbridge Blues', 23556

Eggleston, John Francis: Mr. Selwyn Lloyd: The Balance of Payments and the Dollar Reserve, 4924

Ehrenberg, Andrew Samuel Christopher: ed. Consumer Behaviour: Selected Readings, 20467

Ehrenstrom, Nils: ed. Institutionalism and Church Unity, 12077

Ehresmann, Donald L.: Applied and Decorative Arts: A Bibliographic Guide to Basic Reference Works, Histories and Handbooks, 24108

Ehrlich, Cyril: The Music Profession in Britain since the Eighteenth Century: A Social History, 9802, 24253; The Piano: A History, 24395

Ehrlich, Ludwik: The War and the English Constitution, 574

Ehrman, John Patrick William: Cabinet Government and War, 1890–1940, 724; 'Lloyd George and Churchill as War Ministers', 1026; August 1943–August 1945, 14722

Eichengreen, Barry: Sterling in Decline: The Devaluations of 1931, 1949, and 1967, 4693; ed. The Gold Standard in Theory and History, 4694

Einzig, Paul: The Control of the Purse: Progress and Decline of Parliament's Financial Control, 663; Inflation, 3983; Montagu Norman: A Study in Financial Statesmanship, 4425; The Tragedy of the Pound, 4672; The Comedy of the Pound, 4673; Appeasement before, during and after the War, 13705; In the Centre of Things: The Autobiography of Paul Einzig, 25234

Eisen, Janet: Anglo-Dutch Relations and European Unity, 1940–1948, 14132

Eisenberg, Dennis: The Re-Emergence of Fascism, 2031

Eisenberg, J.: Leonard Woolf: A Political Biography, 2130

Eisermann, G.: ed. Die Gegenwärtige Situation der Soziologie, 7983

Ekberg, Charles: Grimsby Fish: The Story of the Port and the Decline and Fall of the Deep Water Industry, 19816

Elbaum, Bernard: The Decline of the British Economy, 3697

Elcock, Howard J.: Local Government: Politicians, Professionals and the Public in Local Authorities, 3135; 'English Local Government Reformed: The Politics of Humberside', 3358; Budgeting in Local Government: Managing the Margins, 4876; 'Politicians, Organisations and the Public—The Provision of Gypsy Sites', 11356; Portrait of a Decision: The Council of Four and the Treaty of Versailles, 13419; 'Britain and the Russo-Polish Frontier, 1919–1921', 13890; 'Regional Government in Action: The Members of Two Regional Health Authorities', 21664

Elder, John Rawson: The Pioneer Explorers of New Zealand, 27197

Eldersveld, S. J.: 'British Polls and the 1950 General Election', 2269

Eldridge, Derek A.: Car Ownership in London, 17372

Eldridge, John Eric Thomas: 'Plant Bargaining in Steel: North East Case Studies', 5672; The Demarcation Dispute in the British Shipbuilding Industry: A Study in the Sociology of Conflict, 5673; Industrial Disputes: Essays in the Sociology of Industrial Relations, 5674; Sociology and Industrial Life, 5675; A Sociology of Organisations, 5676; Recent British Sociology, 8084

Eldridge, Margaret: A History of the Treatment of Speech Disorders, 21133

Electrical Power Engineers Association: (Nuclear Waste Working Party) Some Implication of Radioactive Waste from Nuclear Power Generation in the U.K. up to the year 2000, 20128

Electrical Trades Union: The Story of the E.T.U. The Official History of the Electrical Trades Union, 6893

Electricity Council: Electricity Supply in Great Britain: A Chronology from the Beginnings of the Industry, 6385

Eley, Geoffrey: The Birmingham Heritage, 18014

Elias, Norbert: The Established and the Outsiders: A Sociological Enquiry into Community Problems, 9351, 11155; 'Studies in the Genesis of the Naval Profession', 9838

Elias, Peter: British Managers: A Study of their Education, Training, Mobility and Earnings, 5452

Eliasberg, Vera F.: The Growth of Public

Employment in Great Britain 1890–1950, 775

Elkin, Stephen L.: 'Structural Effects and Individual Attitudes: Racial Prejudice in English Cities', 11182

Elks, J.: 'Urban Renewal', 17834

Ellacott, Samuel Ernest: Ships under the Sea, 15369

Ellenberger, George Fothergill: History of the King's Own Yorkshire Light Infantry, 1939–1948, 15746

Ellinwood, Dewitt C.: ed. India and World War I, 13126

Elliot Smith, G.: 'Medical Research', 21284; 'The Profession of Medicine', 21285

Elliot, Bernard: The History of Loughborough College School, 22997

Elliot, Sir John: On and Off the Rails, 16827

Elliot, John H. ed.: The Diversity of History: Essays in Honour of Sir Herbert Butterfield, 26779

Elliot, Kenneth: Albany: Birth of a Prison— End of an Era, 10407

Elliot, R. S. P.: Ulster: A Case Study in Conflict Theory, 2918

Elliott, Alf G.: A Portrait of the Brighton Trams, 1901–1939, 17218

Elliott, Blanche B.: A History of English Advertising, 4298

Elliott, Brian J.: 'Bourgeois Social Movements in Britain: Repertoires and Responses', 2079; 'Austerity and the Politics of Resistance', 3212; 'Property and Political Power: Edinburgh 1875–1975, 3374; 'The League of Nations Union and History Teaching in England: A Study in Benevolent Bias', 22450

Elliott, Dave: The Politics of Nuclear Power, 6668

Elliott, Derek William: Road Accidents, 17121

Elliott, Doreen: Residential Care: A Reader in Current Theory and Practice, 8878

Elliott, Isabelle M. and Elliott, James Rawlings: A Short History of Surgical Dressing, 21152

Elliott, James Gordon: The Frontier, 1839–1947, 14611

Elliott, John: Conflict or Co-operation? The Growth of Industrial Democracy, 6029

Elliott, Katherine: ed. Health Auxiliaries and the Health Team, 21679

Elliott, Michael J.: The Role of Law in Central-Local Relations, 3223

Elliott, Osborn: Men at the Top, 5422

Elliott, Patricia Mary: Women in Medicine: The Results of an Inquiry Conducted by the Medical Practitioners' Union in 1962–1963, 20811

Elliott, Peter: Allied Escort Ships of World War II: A Complete Survey, 15122

Elliott, Philip: The Sociology of the Professions, 9773

Elliott, Ralph W.: 'The Industrial Dental Clinic from the Standpoint of the Industrial Surgeon', 21305

Elliott, Robert F.: ed. Incomes Policies, Inflation and Relative Pay, 3946; Pay in the Public Sector, 3947; Pay Differentials in Perspective: A Study of Manual and Non-Manual Worker's Pay over the Period

1951–1975, 3948; Salary Changes and Salary Structure: A Study of Clerical Workers Pay, 3949

Elliott, Sydney: Northern Ireland Parliamentary Election Results, 1921–1972, 2797

Elliott, William Yandell: The New British Empire, 12541; ed. The British Commonwealth at War, 12552

Ellis, A.: 'Playback: British Photography 1955–1965', 24699

Ellis, Aytoun: Heir of Adventure: The Story of Brown, Shipley and Co. Merchant Bankers 1810–1960, 4468; Yorkshire Magnet: The Story of John Smith's Tadcaster Brewery, 6160

Ellis, Brian: The West Midlands, 5230

Ellis, Charles Howard: The Transcaspian Episode, 14557

Ellis, Cuthbert Hamilton: British Railway History vol. 2: 1877–1947, 16719; The Flying Scotsman 1862–1962: Portrait of a Train, 16798; Royal Journey: A Retrospect of Royal Trains in the British Isles, 16799; Four Main Lines, 16838; The History of the Great Northern Railway, 16845; London Midland and Scottish: A Railway in Retrospect, 16873; The Midland Railway, 16895; The North British Railway, 16903; The South Western Railway, its Mechanical History and Background, 1838–1932, 16919; The London, Brighton and South Coast Railway, 16965; Twenty Locomotive Men, 17074

Ellis, Edward Lewis: The University College of Wales, Aberystwyth, 1872– 1972, 23453; 'Dr Thomas Jones, C.H. and Education, 23707

Ellis, Harold: A History of Bladder Stone, 21053

Ellis, Herbert: Hippocrates RN, 15328

Ellis, John: Members from the Unions, 1557; 'Preparation for the Profession: The Present and the Future', 22469

Ellis, Ken: British Homebuilt Aircraft since 1920, 17588

Ellis, Lionel Frederic: France and Flanders, 1939–1940, 14726; Victory in the West, 14727; Welsh Guards at War, 15760

Ellis, Paul: British Commercial Aircraft: 60 Years in Pictures, 17589

Ellis, Peter Berresford: Celtic Inheritance, 2424; Wales, A Nation Again: The Nationalist Struggle for Freedom, 2613; A History of the Irish Working Class, 2668; ed. James Connolly: Selected Writings, 3040; H.Rider Haggard: A Voice from the Infinite, 25572

Ellis, Peter: The 150th Anniversary of the Opening of the Canterbury and Whitstable Railway: A Pioneer Line and the Area it Served, 16923

Ellis, Richard White Bernard: ed. Child Health and Development, 22065; ed. Disease in Infancy and Childhood, 22066

Ellis, Terry: William Tyndale: The Teachers' Story, 23162

Ellis, Thomas Iorwerth: The Development of Higher Education in Wales, 23624; 'The Development of Modern Welsh Secondary Education', 23635

Ellis, Valerie: Social Stratification and Trade Unionism: A Critique, 6722, 9607; Change in Trade Unions: the Development of U.K. Unions since the 1960's, 6741

Ellis, Vivian: I'm on a See-Saw, 24484

Ellison, Mary: The Deprived Child and Adoption, 8169

Elman, Peter: The Jewish Marriage, 11287

Elmhirst, Edward Mars: Merchant's Marks, 4542

Elmslie, William Alexander Leslie: Westminster College, Cambridge: An Account of its History, 1899–1949, 11905

Elrington, Christopher R.: ed. Supplement to the General Introduction to the Victoria County History, 26743

Elsas, Moritz John: Housing before the War and after, 18630; Housing and the Family, 18631

Else, P. K.: 'The Unplanning of Public Expenditure: Recent Problems in Expenditure Planning and the Consequences of Cash Limits', 4769

Else, R.: 'Corporate Planning and Community Work in Britain', 9406

Elsom, John: Post-War British Theatre Criticism, 25929; Theatre outside London, 26158

Elson, Derek M.: Atmospheric Pollution: Causes, Effects and Control Policies, 0047

Elson, Martin J.: Country Estate Management, 18811

Elson, Peter: Tyneside Shipbuilding 1920–1960: A Personal Selection of Photographs, 16628

Eltham: A History of Eltham College for the Sons of Missionaries, 23057

Eltis, Walter A.: ed. The Money Supply and the Exchange Rate, 4651

Elton, Arthur: 'The Rise of the Gas Industry in England and France', 6399

Elton, Sir Arthur: 'The Film as Source Material for History', 219

Elton, E. A.: Secondary Education in the East Riding of Yorkshire, 1944–1974, 22955

Elton, Sir Geoffrey Rudolph: Modern Historians on British History 1485–1945: A Critical Bibliography, 1945–1969, 26729; The History of England, 26767; 'The Historian's Social Function', 26768; 'Herbert Butterfield and the Study of History', 26784

Elton, Godfrey, [Baron]: The Life of James Ramsay MacDonald, 1032; The Unarmed Invasion: A Survey of Afro-Asian Immigration, 11398; Imperial Commonwealth, 12555; ed: The First Fifty Years of the Rhodes Trust and the Rhodes Scholarship, 1903–1953, 22482

Eltringham, Denham: Agriculture, 19551

Elville, E. M.: English and Irish Cut-glass, 1750–1950, 24126

Elvin, Herbert Lionel: Education and Contemporary Society, 22644

Elwall, Robert: Bricks and Beer: English Pub Architecture 1830–1939, 20754, 23927

Elwell-Sutton, L. P.: Persian Oil: A Study in Power Politics, 13858

Elwyn-Jones, Frederick, Baron: In My Time: An Autobiography, 1188

Ely, John Hart: 'Trial by Newspaper and its Cures', 25056

Ely, Peter: Social Work in a Multi-Racial Society, 8766

Ely, Stephen: Harold Pinter, 25976

Emden, Cecil Stuart: The Civil Servant in the Law and the Constitution, 892

Emden, Paul Herman: Jews of Britain: A Series of Biographies, 12432

Emerson, A. R.: 'The Age Distribution of an Industrial Group [Scottish Railwaymen]', 9657

Emerson, John: The United Kingdom Market for Bread, 20703

Emerson, Miles: Television and the Working Class, 24836

Emery, Anthony: Dartington Hall, 23104

Emery, Frederick Edmund: Freedom and Justice within Walls: The Bristol Prison Experiment, 10377

Emery, Malcolm: Promoting Nature in Cities and Towns: A Practical Guide, 20214

Emery, Norman: Arnold Bennett, 1867–1931: A Bibliography, 25379

Emmanuel, Patrick: Crown Colony Politics in Grenada 1917–1951, 13085

Emme, Eugene M.: The History of Rocket Technology, 17696

Emmerson, James Thomas: The Rhineland Crisis, 7 March 1936: A Study in Multilateral Diplomacy, 13671

Emmet, Alfred: 'The Long Prehistory of the National Theatre', 26137

Emmet, Dorothy Mary: Rules, Roles and Relations, 9490

Emmett, B. P.: 'New Role for Research in Broadcasting', 24788; 'The Television Audience in the United Kingdom', 24830

Emmett, Isabel: Youth and Leisure in an Urban Sprawl, 8465; A North Wales Village: A Social Anthropological Study, 19300

Emmons, Frederick: The Atlantic Liners 1925–1970, 16569, 27168

Emmons, Robert: The Life and Opinions of Walter Richard Sickert, 24062

Endacott, George Beer: A Collection of Documents Illustrating the History of Hong Kong, 12966; A History of Hong Kong, 12967; An Eastern Entrepôt: Government and People in Hong Kong, 1841–1962: A Constitutional History, 12968

Enderville, Peter: The Industrial Relations Position of Foreign-owned Firms in Britain, 5845

Endicott, Stephen Lyon: Diplomacy and Enterprise: British China Policy, 1933–1937, 13629

Endres, Gunter G.: British Civil Aviation, 17657

Enfield, Sir Ralph Roscoe: The Agricultural Crisis, 1920–1923, 19436

Engel, Solomon: Inside the Whale: The Personal Accounts of Social Research, 8034

England, Edward: ed. David Watson: A Portrait by his Friends, 11821; An Unfading Vision: The Adventure of Books, 24971

England, J. M.: Medical Research. A Statistical and Epidemiological Approach, 21227

England, J.: 'The Basis for National Front Support', 2051

England, Kathleen M.: Housing: A Citizen's Guide to the Problem, 18606

Englander, David: Landlord and Tenant in Urban Britain 1838–1918; War and Politics: The Experiences of the Serviceman in the Two World Wars, 15448

Engleman, Stephen Robert: The Industrial Relations Act: A Review and Analysis, 5773

English Historical Review, 418

English, A.: The Battle for the Falklands: Naval Forces, 16088

English, John: ed. Social Services in Scotland, 8884; Ferguslie Park: Profile of a Deprived Community, 9278; A Profile of Ferguslie Park, 9279; Slum Clearance: The Social and Administrative Context in England and Wales, 18410; An Appraisal of Slum Clearance Procedures in England and Wales, 18411; One Hundred Years of Slum Clearance in England and Wales: Policies and Programmes, 1868–1970, 18412; ed. The Sale of Council Houses, 18429; Housing Allocation in Paisley and Ferguslie Park, 18467; Housing Allocations and Social Segregation, 18468

English, John: Canada since 1945: Power, Politics and Provincialism, 12641

Ennals, David: Out of Mind, 21865

Ennew, Judith: The Western Isles Today, 19259

Enock, Arthur Guy: This Milk Business: A Study from 1895–1943, 20652

Enser, Alfred Guy Sidney: A Subject Bibliography of the First World War: Books in English 1914–1978, 14431; Filmed Books and Plays: A List of Books and Plays from which Films Have Been Made, 1918–1974, 24584

Ensign, Marie S.: ed. Historical Periodicals Directory, 162

Entwistle, E. W.: 'Going to Town in a Changed Country', 17858

Entwistle, Howard: Class, Culture and Education, 9560

Entwistle, Noel James: Degrees of Excellence: The Academic Achievement Game, 9884; Degrees of Exellence: The Academic Achievement Game, 22572; Age of Transfer to Secondary Education, 22990; The Transition to Secondary Education, 22991

Eppel, Emanuel Montague *and* Eppel, May 'A Pioneer Investigation of the Needs, Interests, and Attitudes of 380 Young Workers Attending a County College', 8416; Adolescents and Morality: A Study of Some Moral Values and Dilemmas of Working Adolescents in the Context of a Changing Climate of Opinion, 8466; 'Connotations of Morality: The Views of Some Adults on the Standards and Behaviour of Adolescents', 8467

Epstein, Sir Jacob: Let there be Sculpture: An Autobiography, 24185; Jacob Epstein: Sculptor, 24186

Epstein, Leon David: 'Political Sterilization of Civil Servants: The United States and Great Britain', 900; 'New MPs and the Politics of the PLP', 1746; British Class Consciousness and the Labour Party', 1798; 'The Nuclear Deterrent and the British General Election of 1964', 2323; 'British Class Consciousness and the Labour Party', 9501; Britain—Uneasy Ally, 14066; British Politics in the Suez Crisis, 14370

Ereira, Alan: The Invergordon Mutiny, 15293

Erickson, Charlotte: British Industrialists: Steel and Hosiery, 1850–1950, 6568

Erickson, Eric Homburger: Childhood and Society, 8170

Erlichman, James: Gluttons for Punishment, 20180

Ermisch, J. F.: 'Economic Opportunities, Marriage Squeezes, and the Propensity to Marry: An Economic Analysis of Period Marriage Rates in England and Wales', 7436

Ernle, Lord: 'Women's Land Army', 7662

Errington, Andrew: ed. The Farm as a Family Business: An Annotated Bibliography, 19602

Erskine, David Hervey: The Scots Guards, 1919–1955, 15589

Ervin, Spencer: The Scottish Episcopal Church: The Ecclesiastical History and Polity, 12264

Ervine, St. John Greer: Craigavon: Ulsterman, 3074

Esco Foundation for Palestine: Inc. Palestine: A Study of Jewish, Arab and British Policies, 14294

Escott, Harry: A History of Scottish Congregationalism, 12255

Esh, Saul: ed. Jewish Life in Modern Britain . . ., 11305, 12423

Eshag, Eprime: The Present System of Trade and Payments versus Full Employment and Welfare State, 3645; From Marshall to Keynes: An Essay on the Monetary Theory of the Cambridge School, 4573

Essame, H.: Corps Commander, 14957

Essery, Robert J.: An Illustrated History of L.M.S. Coaches, 1923–1957, 16882; An Illustrated History of L.M.S. Locomotives, 16883; An Illustrated History of Midland Wagons, 16897; British Goods Wagons from 1887 to the Present Day, 17096

Essex County Council: 100 Not Out: A Centenary of Service: Essex County Council 1889–1989, 3355; Land Use/Transportation Study: Brentwood, 16243; Land Use/Transportation Study: Colchester, 16244

Essex Welfare Committee: Welfare Services in Essex, 1957–1965: A Report Submitted to the Welfare Committee of the County Council of Essex by the County Welfare Officer, W. E. Boyce, 8863

Esslin, Martin Julius: Pinter: A Study of his Plays, 25977; 'Must Contemporary Drama be Sordid?', 26206

Esterson, A.: Sanity, Madness and the Family: The Families of Schizophrenics, 21771

Estey, Martin S.: 'Trends in Concentration of Union Membership, 1897–1962', 6765

Estorick, Eric: Stafford Cripps, 1155

Estrin, Saul: Profit Sharing in the Retail Sector: The Relative Performance of the John Lewis Partnership, 6052

Etchells, Frederick: The Architectural Setting

of Anglican Worship: An Inquiry into the Arrangements for Public Worship in the Church of England from the Reformation to the Present Day, 11607

Ethell, Jeffrey: Air War South Atlantic, 16092

Etholiad Cyffredinol 1987 yng Nghymru: The 1987 General Election in Wales, 2376

Eton: An English Education: A Perspective of Eton, 23059

Eton: Eton: A History, 23058

Eubank, Weaver Keith: Munich, 13740

European Journal of Sociology: Special Issue on 'Welfare State', 8864

Eustace, Rowland: Power and authority in British universities, 23303

Evang, Karl: Medical Care and Family Security: Norway, England and the U.S.A., 21573

Evans, A. A.: 'Where will we Teach the Teachers?', 22722

Evans, Alfred Dudley: The History and Economics of Transport, 16189

Evans, Alistair: A Guide to Manpower Information, 5950

Evans, Arthur F.: The History of the Oil Engine. A Review in Detail of the Development of the Oil Engine from the Year 1680 to the Beginning of the Year 1930, 7056

Evans, B. J.: 'Further Education Pressure Groups: The Campaign for Continued and Technical Education in 1944', 23261

Evans, Brian M.: 'Sources for the Study of the History of Welsh Agriculture', 19629

Evans, David John: Geographical Perspectives on Juvenile Delinquency, 10684

Evans, Dorothy Elizabeth: Women and the Civil Service: A History of the Development of the Employment of Women in the Civil Service, 946

Evans, Douglas: ed. Destiny or Delusion: Britain and the Common Market, 14177; While Britain slept: The Selling of the Common Market, 14182

Evans, E. Estyn: ed. Belfast in Its Regional Setting: A Scientific Study, 18167

Evans, Sir Emrys: The University of Wales: an Historical Sketch, 23584

Evans, Eric Wyn: 'British Labour and the Common Market', 1742; 'Work Stoppages in the United Kingdom, 1951–1964: A Quantitative Study', 6956; 'Work Stoppages in the United Kingdom 1965–1970: A Quantitative Study', 6957; ed. Industrial Conflict in Britain, 6959; Employment and Unemployment in the Hull Region, 1951–1968, 7012; The Miners of South Wales, 9652

Evans, Gary: John Grierson and the National Film Board: The Politics of Wartime Propaganda, 1939–1945, 24671

Evans, Sir Geoffrey: Slim as Military Commander, 14782

Evans, George Ewart: The Strength of the Hills: An Autobiography, 26750; Where Beards Wag All: The Relevance of the Oral Tradition, 26751

Evans, Sir Geraint: Sir Geraint Evans: A Knight at the Opera, 24412

Evans, Gwilym John: The Entrance

Scholarship Examination in Caernarvonshire,1897–1961: with a Monograph in Welsh Showing the Relation of the Examination to the Development of the County's Bilingual Policy, 1900–1965, 23626

Evans, Harold Matthew: Good Times, Bad Times, 25235

Evans, Harold: Vickers against the Odds, 1956–1977, 6369, 17597

Evans, Hazel Meyrick: ed. New Towns: The British Experience, 18252, 19002

Evans, Hilary and Evans, Mary: Picture Researchers Handbook: An International Guide to Picture Sources and how to use them, 211

Evans, Howell Griffiths: The Economics of Hill Farming, 19511, 19633 'The Origins of State Support for British Agriculture', 19512

Evans, Hywel E.: 'Seventy Five Years of Welsh Agriculture: Progress and the Future', 19630

Evans, Ivor Leslie: The Agriculture of Wales and Monmouthshire, 19636

Evans, John: A Britten Source Book, 24306; Pictures from a Life, 24311; Britten and Auden in the Thirties: The Year 1936, 24312

Evans, Keith: The Development and Structure of the English Educational System, 22686

Evans, Les: ed. The Socialist Workers' Party in World War Two: Writings and Speeches, 1940–1943, 1974

Evans, Leslie Wynne: Studies in Welsh Education: Welsh Educational Structure and Administration, 1880–1925, 23630

Evans, Lester J.: 'Medical Education in Perspective', 22468

Evans, Mike: Rolls-Royce: The Pursuit of Excellence, 17447; In the Beginning: The Manchester Origins of Rolls-Royce, 17448

Evans, Neil: 'The South Wales Race Riots of 1919', 11469; 'The South Wales Race Riots of 1919: A Documentary Postscript', 11470; 'Regulating the Reserve Army: Arabs, Blacks and the Local State in Cardiff, 1919–1945', 11471

Evans, Nigel: Nuclear Power: Features, Cash and Benefits, 6664

Evans, P. A.: A Hard Day's Night: The Problem of the Residential Child Care Worker, 8171

Evans, Peter C. C.: Prison Crisis, 10379; The Police Revolution, 10701

Evans, Peter: Peter Sellers: The Mask behind the Mask, 26345

Evans, Peter: The Music of Benjamin Britten, 24316

Evans, Richard I.: R. D. Laing: The Man and his Ideas, 21824

Evans, Roger: The Story of the Fifth Royal Inniskilling Dragoon Guards, 15554; The Years Between: The Story of the 7th Queen's Own Hussars, 1911–1937, 15660

Evans, Simon Caradoc: ed. Energy Options in the United Kingdom, 7209

Evans, Stanley George: The Church in the Backstreets, 9199

Evans, Stephen F.: The Slow Rapprochement:

Britain and Turkey in the Age of Kemal Ataturk, 1919–1938, 13841

Evans, Stephen: 'The Use of Injunctions in Industrial Disputes, May 1984–April 1987', 5857

Evans, Thomas John: Sir Rhys Hopkin Morris: . . . the Man and his Character, 2580

Evans, Trefor Ellis: ed. The Killearn Diaries 1934–1946: The Diplomatic and Personal Record of Lord Killearn, Sir Miles Lampson, High Commissioner and Ambassador to Egypt, 13285, 14401; ed. Mission to Egypt 1934–1946: Lord Killearn, High Commissioner and Ambassador, 14402

Evans, Sir Trevor: Bevin, 1102; Pathway to Tomorrow: The Impact of Automation on People: A Survey of the International Conference on Automation, Full Employment and a Balanced Economy at Rome in June 1967, 7249

Evans, William: My Mountbatten Years: In the Service of Lord Louis, 15277

Evans, William Arthur: Advertising Today and Tomorrow, 4326

Evans, Winifred May: Young People in Society, 8468

Evans-Pritchard, E. E.: A Bibliography of the Writings of E. E. Evans-Pritchard, 26354

Evatt, Herbert Vere: The King and His Dominion Governors: A Study of the Reserve Powers of the Crown in Great Britain and the Dominions, 461

Eve, John: Accounting: An Insight, 4193

Evelegh, R.: Peacekeeping in a Democratic Society: The Lessons of Northern Ireland, 2850

Evely, Richard: Concentration in British Industry: An Empirical Study of the Structure of Industrial Production, 1935–1951, 4979; Steel is Power: The Case for Nationalisation, 6549; 'Some Aspects of the Structure of British Industry, 1935–1951', 7227

Evennett, Henry Outram: The Catholic Schools of England and Wales, 22882

Everard, Stirling: History of the Gas, Light and Coke Company, 1812–1949, 6409

Everest, J. H.: The First Battle of the Tanks, Cambrai, November 20th 1917, 15524

Everett, Helen: The British Coal Dilemma, 6257

Everett, Samuel: Growing up in English Secondary Schools: Significance for American Practice, 22693

Everett-Heath, John: British Military Helicopters, 15885, 17555

Everitt, Alistair: The Left in Britain: A Checklist and Guide, 1996

Everitt, Don: The K Boats: A Dramatic First Report on the Navy's Most Calamitous Submarines, 15379

Evers, Claude Ronald: Rugby, 23074

Eversley, David Edward Charles: Religion and Employment in Northern Ireland, 2864; 'Employment Planning and Income Maintenance', 3839; The Overspill Problem in the West Midlands, 5224; Population Growth and Planning Policy: An Analysis of Social and Economic Factors Affecting

Housing and Employment Location in the West Midlands, 5225, 7416, 17917; An Introduction to Historical Demography, 7370; *ed.* Population in History: Essays in Historical Demography, 7399; Social Theories of Fertilty and the Malthusian Debate, 7485; The Dependants of the Coloured Commonwealth Population of England and Wales, 10984; A Question of Numbers?, 11428; 'Old Cities, Falling Populations and Rising Costs', 17829; 'Urban Planning in Britain Today', 17830; The Growth of Planning Research since the Early 1960s, 17916; The Planner in Society: The Changing Role of a Profession, 17918; Cutting down our Cities to Size: A Balance Sheet for Planners and Treasurers, 17919; *ed.* London Urban Patterns, Problems and Policies, 18359, 18728; 'Life, Leisure and Houses', 18688

Every, George: *ed.* Herbert Kelly: No Pious Person, 11797

Eves, Edward: Rolls-Royce: 75 Years of Motoring Excellence, 17449

Evetts, J.: 'Equality of Educational Opportunity: The Recent History of a Concept', 22816

Evriade, Marios L.: Cyprus, 12861

Ewart-Biggs, Jane [Baroness]: Lady in the Lords, 1407; Pay, Pack and Follow: Memoirs, 13264

Ewbank, A. J.: 'Trade Unionists, the Mass Media and Unofficial Strikes', 6961

Ewen, David: The Complete Book of Twentieth Century Music, 24258

Ewing, A. F.: 'Monopoly and Competition in the British Textile Industry', 6466

Ewing, J. A.: 'Why Students "Turn On": Marijuana and other Drugs in an Undergraduate Male Population, 22218

Ewing, John: The Royal Scots 1914–1919, 15590

Ewing, Keith: The Funding of Political Parties in Britain, 1598

Exley, C. H.: The Guide to Poor Relief, 4069

Eyck, Frank: G. P. Gooch: A Study in History and Politics, 26797

Eyden, Joan Lily Mary: Social Policy in Action, 8887

Eyken, Willem Van Der: The Pre-school Years, 23163

Eyles, David R.: Road Traffic and Environment, 16236; Road Traffic and Urban Environment in Inner London, 16237

Eyles, Desmond: Royal Doulton, 1815–1965, 6628, 24130

Eyles, John: Environmental Satisfaction and London's Docklands: Problems and Policies in the Isle of Dogs, 19955; An introduction to Social Geography, 26688

Eyre, Frank: English Rivers and Canals, 16391

Eyre, Reginald E.: Hope for Our Towns and Cities: The Right Approach to Urban Affairs, 17928

Eyre, Samuel Robert: *ed.* Geography as Human Ecology: Methodology by example, 26689

Eysenck, Hans Jurgen: Crime and Personality, 10184; 'Personality and Recidivism in Borstal Boys', 10536; 'The Teaching Machine, and the Revolution in Education', 22774; Race, Intelligence and Education, 23182

Eysenck, Sybil B. G.: 'Personality and Recidivism in Borstal Boys', 10536

Ezra, Sir Derek Joseph: Coal and Energy: The Need to Exploit the World's Most Abundant Fossil Fuel, 6346

Fabian Society: Labour and Inequality, 9566; Politics for Racial Equality, 10962

Fabian, A. P.: 'The Contribution of Psychoanalysis to Child Guidance in Art', 8210

Fabian, Robert: The Anatomy of Crime, 10227

Fabunmi, L. A.: The Sudan in Anglo-Egyptian Relations: A Case Study in Power Politics 1800–1956, 14413

Fair, John D.: 'Walter Bagehot, Royal Mediation, and the Modern British Constitution, 1869–1931', 462; British Interparty Conferences: A Study of the Procedure of Conciliation in British Politics, 1867–1921, 1599; 'British Conservatism in the Twentieth Century: An Emerging Ideological Tradition', 2185

Fairbairn, A. N.: *ed.* The Leicestershire Plan, 23233

Fairbairn, Nicholas: A Life is too Short, 1408

Fairburn, James A.: *ed.* Mergers and Merger Policy, 5553

Fairclough, Tony: Great Western Steam through the Years, 16864

Fairfield, Cecily I.: The Vassall Affair, 16056

Fairfield, S.: *ed.* The Macmillan Guide to the UK 1978–1979, 279

Fairhead, Suzan: Persistent Petty Offenders, 10169

Fairhurst, John R.: The University Connection, 22741

Fairlamb, David: Savings and Co-operative Banking, 4341

Fairley, Peter: British Inventions in the 20th Century, 7142

Fairlie, Henry: Suicide of a Nation? An Inquiry into the State of Britain Today, 381; 'Aneurin Bevan and the Art of Politics', 1099

Fairweather, Barbara: Old Highland Farming, 19624

Fairweather, E.: Only the Rivers Run Free: Northern Ireland: The Women's War, 7743

Fairweather, George William: Experimental Methods for Social Policy Research, 8872

Falconer, Ronald: The Kilt beneath My Cassock, 12230

Faligot, Roger: La Résistance Irlandaise, 1916–1976, 2769; Nous avons tué Mountbatten: L'I.R.A. Parle, 2770; James Connolly et le Mouvement Revolutionnaire Irlandais, 3035

Falk, Nicholas: Planning the Social Services, 8840

Falk, Stanley Lawrence: Seventy Days to Singapore: The Malayan Campaign 1941–1942, 15067

Falklands Campaign: A Digest of Debates in the House of Commons 2 April to 15 June 1982, 16974

Falklands War: The Official History, 16085

Falkus, Malcolm: *ed.* Historical Atlas of Britain, 139; Always under Pressure: A History of North Thames Gas since 1949, 6402

Fallick, Leslie J.: *ed.* Incomes Policies, Inflation and Relative Pay, 3946; Pay in the Public Sector, 3947; Differentials in Perspective: A Study of Manual and Non-Manual Worker's Pay over the Period 1951–1975, 3948; Changes and Salary Structure: A Study of Clerical Workers Pay, 3949

Fallin, J. F.: 'The Irish Civil War and the Drafting of the Free-State Constitution', 2684

Fallon, Ivan: Takeovers, 5551

Fallon, Thomas: The River Police: The Story of Scotland Yard's Little Ships, 10751

Falls, Cyril Bentham: The First World War, 14452; A Hundred Years of War, 14459; Egypt and Palestine, 14493; Macedonia, 14533; Armageddon, 1918, 14598

Family Planning Association: (Working Party). Family Planning in the Sixties: A Report, 9924; The West Indian Comes to England, 11244

Fann, K. T.: Symposium on J. L. Austin, 26845

Fanning, J. Ronan: 'The Response of the London and Belfast Governments to the Declaration of the Republic of Ireland, 1948–1949', 2976

Fannon, D. G.: Community Centres: Some Service Experiences, 9257

Fanshel, D.: Foster-parenthood: A Role Analysis, 8172

Farber, Ruth: 'Informal View of British Social Work Agencies', 8750

Farid, S. M.: 'On The Pattern of Cohort Fertility', 7494

Farm and Food Society: Agriculture and Pollution, 20175

Farman, Christopher: The General Strike: May 1926, 6944

Farmer, A. J.: 'Bottomley', 25950

Farmer, Bernard James: Bibliography of the Works of Sir Winston S. Churchill, 1001

Farmer, Henry George: History of the Royal Artillery Band, 1762–1953, 15491

Farmer, Mary E.: 'The Positivist Movement and the Development of English Sociology', 7984; The Family, 10091

Farnam, Dorothy: Auden in Love, 25358

Farndale, James: The Day Hospital Movement in Great Britain, 21480

Farndale, William Arthur James: *ed.* Trends in the Services for Youth, 8478; *ed.* Trends in Social Welfare, 8865; *ed.* Trends in the National Health Service, 21576; *ed.* International Medical Care: A Comparison and Evaluation of Medical Care Services throughout the World, 21577; *ed.* Trends in Mental Health Services: A Symposium of Original and Reprinted Papers, 21769; *ed.* New Aspects of Mental Health Services, 21770; Legal Liability for Claims Arising from Hospital Treatment, 21975; Medical Negligence, 21976

Farnell, John: In Search of a Common Fisheries Policy, 19834

Farnie, Douglas Anthony: East and West of Suez: The Suez Canal in History, 1854–1958, 14361; The Manchester Ship Canal and the Rise of the Port of Manchester, 1894–1975, 16409

Farquharson, Dorothea: 'Dissolution of the Institute of Sociology', 7949

Farquharson, John: The Western Allies and the Politics of Food: Agrarian Management in Post-War Germany, 14191; 'Land Reform in the British Zone 1945–1947', 14192; '"Emotional but Influential": Victor Gollancz, Richard Stokes and the British Zone in Germany: 1945–1949', 14200

Farr, A. D.: 'Some Problems in the History of Haemoglobinometry, 1878–1931', 20916; ed. Founders of Medical Laboratory Science, 22267

Farr, Diana: Five at 10: Prime Ministers' Consorts since 1957, 970

Farr, Michael Austin: Lines: Design in British Industry: A Mid-Century Survey, 24149

Farrant, Jeremy P.: The History of Scout Motors Limited of Salisbury, 17457

Farrant, S.: 'London by the Sea: Resort Development on the South Coast of England, 1880–1939', 26989

Farrar, L. L.: Divide and Conquer: German Efforts to Conclude a Separate Peace, 1914–1918, 13377; 'Opening to the West: German Efforts to Conclude a Separate Peace with England, July 1917–March 1918', 13378

Farrar, Peter N.: ed. British Forces in the Korean War, 16133; 'Britain's Proposal for a Buffer Zone South of the Yalu in November 1950: Was it a Neglected Opportunity to End the Fighting in Korea?', 16148

Farrar-Hockley, Anthony Heritage: The Somme, 14582; Death of an Army, 14603; The War in the Desert, 14894; Airborne Carpet: Operation Market Garden, 14950; The Edge of the Sword, 16131

Farrell, Christine: Across the Generations: Old People and Young Volunteers, 8471; 'The Royal Commission on the National Health Service', 21668

Farrell, M. J.: 'The Structure of the British Coal Mining Industry in 1955', 6301

Farrell, Michael: Northern Ireland: The Orange State, 312, 2790; The Poor Law and the Workhouse in Belfast 1838–1948, 2788; The Struggle in the North, 2789; ed. Twenty Years On, 2791; Arming the Protestants: The Formation of the Ulster Special Constabulary and the Royal Ulster Constabulary 1920–1927, 2931

Farrer, David: G—For God Almighty. A Personal Memoir of Lord Beaverbrook, 1073

Farrer, Morley: A Century of English International Football 1872–1972, 27070

Farrier, Richard: The Suicide Syndrome, 10823

Farrington, David Philip: 'Unemployment, School Leaving and Crime', 10530; 'The Persistence of Labelling Effects', 10590; Who Becomes Delinquent?: Second Report of the Cambridge Study in Delinquent Development, 10611; The Delinquent Way of Life: Third Report of the Cambridge Study in Delinquent Development, 10612

Farrington, Jane: Wyndham Lewis, 24034

Farson, N.: Bomber's Moon: London in the Blitzkrieg, 15158

Fatchett, Derek John: Workers' Participation and Industrial Democracy, 6017; Workers' Participation in Management in Britain, 5459, 6018; Worker Participation, 6020

Faulconer, A.: Foundations of Anesthesiology, 21039

Faulk, Henry: The Re-education of German Prisoners of War in Britain 1945–1948, 15052

Faulkner, Alan Henderson: The Warwick Canals, 16421

Faulkner, Brian, [Baron]: Memoirs of a Statesman, 3084

Faulkner, Peter: Angus Wilson: Mimic and Moralist, 25882

Faulkner, Trader: Peter Finch: A Biography, 26041

Fausten, Dietrich K.: The Consistency of British Balance of Payments Policies, 4929

Fawcett, Charles Bungay: Provinces of England: A Study of some Geographical Aspects of Devolution, 2403

Fawcett, Harold William: The Fighting at Jutland, 14649

Fawcett, J. E. S.: 'Gibraltar: The Legal Issues', 12851

Fawcett, Jane: The Future of the Past: Attitudes to Conservation, 1174–1974, 26974

Fawcett, Dame Millicent Garrett: The Women's Victory—and After: Personal Reminiscences, 1911–1918, 2258, 7660; What I Remember, 7659

Fawkes, Richard: Fighting for a Laugh. Entertaining British and American Armed Forces, 15151

Fawkes, S.: Squatting, 18382

Faxon, N. W.: ed. The Hospitals in Contemporary Life, 21386

Fay, Charles Rule: Great Britain from Adam Smith to the Present Day, 3468

Fay, Judith: Phantasy in Childhood, 8152

Fay, Sir Samuel: The War Office at War, 829

Fay, Stephen: Portrait of an Old Lady: Turmoil at the Bank of England, 4490

Fayle, Charles Edwin: The War and the Shipping Industry, 16471

Fearon, Peter: ed. British Economic Fluctuations, 1790–1939, 3405; ed. Growth in 20th Century Britain, 3406; 'The Growth of Aviation in Britain', 17523; 'The Formative Years of the British Aircraft Industry', 17578; 'Aircraft Manufacturing', 17579; 'The British Airframe Industry and the State 1918–1935', 17580; 'The British Airframe Industry and the State in the Interwar Period: A Reply', 17582; 'The Vicissitudes of a British Aircraft Company: Handley Page Ltd. between the Wars, 17618

Feather, John: A History of British Publishing, 24928

Feaver, William: Masters of Caricature: From Hogarth and Gillray to Scarfe and Levine, 24106

Feaveryear, Sir Albert Edgar: The Pound Sterling: A History of English Money, 4671

Federation of British Industry: Fuel and Energy Policy, 7191

Feehan, John M.: Bobby Sands and the Tragedy of Ireland, 2894

Feeney, V. E.: 'The Civil Rights Movement in Northern Ireland', 2851

Feiling, Sir Keith Grahame: Study of the Modern History of Great Britain, 1862–1946, 337; The Life of Neville Chamberlain, 983

Feinstein, Charles Hilliard: ed. The Managed Economy: Essays in British Economic Policy and Performance since 1929, 3478, 4016, 4644; British Economic Growth, 1856–1973, 3514; Domestic Capital Formation in the United Kingdom, 1920–1938, 4732; Studies in Capital Formation in the United Kingdom 1750–1950, 4733; National Income, Expenditure and Output of the United Kingdom, 1855–1965, 4892; ed. York 1831–1981: 150 Years of Scientific Endeavour and Social Change, 18121

Fekete, Liz: 'Victims, the "Urban Jungle" and the New Racism', 11204

Feldman, David: Metropolis: London Histories and Representations since 1800, 3282

Feldman, Maurice Philip: Psychology in the Industrial Environment, 5746

Feldstein, Martin Stuart: 'Hospital Planning and the Demand for Care', 21488; 'Hospital Bed Scarcity: An Analysis of the Effects of Inter-regional Differences', 21489; Economic Analysis for Health Service Efficiency: Econometric Studies of the British National Health Service, 21597

Fell, Honor B.: 'Fiftieth Anniversary of the Strangeways Research Laboratory, Cambridge', 20941

Fellman, James D.: International List of Geographical Serials, 166

Fels, Allan: The British Prices and Incomes Board, 3816

Fels, Gerhard: ed. Public Assistance to Industry: Protection and Subsidies in Britain and Germany, 6460

Felstead, Sidney T.: Horatio Bottomley, 1366

Felsted: The History of Felsted School, 1564–1947, 23060

Fenby, Jonathan: The Fall of the House of Beaverbrook, 25130; The International News Services, 25304

Fenelon, Kevin Gerard: Britain's Food Supplies, 20594

Fensham, Peter James: The Dynamics of a Changing Technology: A Case Study in Textile Manufacturing, 6444

Fenter, Frances Margaret: Copec Adventure: The Story of Birmingham Copec House Improvement Society, 18564

Fenton, Alexander: Scottish Country Life, 19243

Fenton, Steve: Ageing Minorities: Black People as they Grow Old in Britain, 8633

Fenwick, Ian Graham Keith: The Comprehensive School, 1944–1970: The Politics of Secondary School Reorganization, 22969

Ferguson, Edward: Desperate Siege: The Battle of Hong Kong, 15066

Ferguson, J. M.: 'Managing Clinical Waste', 20137

Ferguson, Joan Primrose Scott: Directory of Scottish Newspapers, 25166

Ferguson, John: 'The Open University in Britain', 23550; The Open University from Within, 23552

Ferguson, K.: Glenrothes: The First Twenty Five Years, 18187

Ferguson, Marjorie: Forever Feminine: Women's Magazines and the Cult of Femininity, 7866

Ferguson, N. A.: 'Women's Work: Employment Opportunities and Economic Roles, 1918–1939', 3567

Ferguson, Rob: Television on History: Representations of Ireland, 2885

Ferguson, Ron: Chasing the Wild Goose, 12224

Ferguson, Sheila: Children in Care and After, 8173; In their Early Twenties: A Study of Glasgow Youth, 8412; The Young Wage Earner: A Study of Glasgow Boys, 8413; 'The Impact of National Service', 8414; Studies in the Social Services, 8857; The Young Delinquent in his Social Setting: A Glasgow Case study, 10553; Hospital and Community, 21387; Handicapped Youth: A Report on the Employment Problems of Handicapped Young People in Glasgow, 21915; Public Health and Urban Growth, 22078

Ferguson, William: Scotland 1689 to the Present, 316, 2433

Fergusson, Sir Bernard Edward: The Trumpet in the Hall 1930–1958, 14758; Wavell: Portrait of a Soldier, 14785; Beyond the Chindwin, 15062; The Watery Maze: The Story of Combined Operations, 15478

Fergusson, John Duncan: Modern Scottish Painting, 24086

Fergusson, R. P.: The First in the Kingdom: 1881–1981: A History of Buses and Trams in Blackburn and Darwen, 17300

Fergusson, Sir James: The Sixteen Peers of Scotland: An Account of the Elections of the Representative Peers of Scotland, 1707–1959, 2477; The Curragh Incident, 2734

Ferns, J. L.: 'Electricity Supply and Industrial Archaeology', 6388

Ferrer, Harold Peter: ed. The Health Services: Administration, Research and Management, 21612

Ferri, Elsa: Growing up in a One-Parent Family: A Long-term Study of Child Development, 8277, 9947; Disadvantaged Families and Playgroups, 8278; Coping Alone, 8279

Ferrier, John: The Greenock Infirmary 1806–1960, 21479

Ferrier, R. W.: The History of the British Petroleum Company: Vol. 1: The Developing Years, 1901–1932, 6520

Ferrier, Winifred: The Life of Kathleen Ferrier, By her Sister, 24414

Ferris, John: Participation in Urban Planning: The Barnsbury Case: A Study of Environmental Improvement in London, 20373

Ferris, Paul Frederick: Gentlemen of Fortune: The World's Merchant and Investment Bankers, 4466; The Nameless: Abortion in Britain Today, 7878; The Doctors, 20854; The House of Northcliffe: A Biography of an Empire, 25098; Dylan Thomas, 25829; The Collected Letters of Dylan Thomas, 25830

Fest, Wilfried B.: 'British War Aims and German Peace Feelers during the First World War (December 1916–November 1918)', 13379

Festing, Sally: Fishermen, 19820

Fetter, Frank Whitson: Monetary and Financial Policy, 4665

Feuchtwanger, E. J.: The Department of Adult Education; University of Southampton, 1928–1978: An Appreciation, 23699

Fey, Harold Edward: ed. Ecumenical Advance: A History of the Ecumenical Movement, 1948–1968, 12317

Ffoulkes, Charles: The Gun-founders of England, 6611

Ffrench-Blake, Richard Lifford Valentine: A History of the 17th/21st Lancers, 1922–59, 15689

Fiegehen, Guy C.: Poverty and Progress in Britain, 1953–1973: A Statistical Study of Low Income Households, their Numbers, Types and Expenditure Patterns, 9093

Field, Brian: Local Planning in London: A Survey, 18927; The Evolution of London's Planning System and the Changing Role of the Boroughs, 18928

Field, Clive D.: 'The Social Structure of English Methodism: Eighteenth–Twentieth Centuries', 12098; 'A Sociological Profile of English Methodism, 1900–1932', 12099

Field, D. E.: A Survey of New Housing in Belfast, 18494

Field, David: Young Workers, 8458; Medical Sociology in Britain: A Register of Teaching and Research, 21963

Field, Eric: Advertising: The Forgotten Years, 4313

Field, Frank: ed. The Wealth Report, 3790; F.I.S. Part Six: What Price a Child? A Historical Review of the Relative Cost of Dependants, 4097; To Him who Hath: A Study of Poverty and Taxation, 4855, 9094; The Conscript Army: A Study of Britain's Unemployed, 6988, 9699; 'I Dread to Think About Christmas': A Study of Poor Families in 1976, 9087; Poverty: The Facts, 9095; Inequality in Britain: Freedom, Welfare and the State, 9096; Poverty and Politics: The Inside Story of the Child Poverty Action Groups' Campaigns in the 1970's, 9097; Family Income Support, 9098; ed. Twentieth Century State Education, 22685

Field, G. C.: Pacifism and Conscientious Objection, 13525

Field, Mary: Children and Films: A Study of Boys and Girls in the Cinema, 24602

Field, S.: Ethnic Minorities in Britain: A Study of Trends in their Position since 1961, 11074

Field, Veronica: On the Strength: The Story of the British Army Wife, 15461

Field, Xenia: Under Lock and Key: A Study of Women in Prison, 7733, 10376

Field-Fisher, Thomas Gilbert: The Protection from Eviction Act (1964), 18417; Rent Act (1965), 18418; Rent Regulation and Control, 18419

Fielden, Lionel: The Natural Bent, 24817

Fieldhouse, David Kenneth: Unilever Overseas: The Anatomy of a Multinational, 1895–1965, 5558, 6220; Colonialism 1870–1945: An Introduction, 12481; Oxford and the Idea of the Commonwealth: Essays presented to Sir Edgar Williams, 12489

Fieldhouse, Roger: Adult Education and the Cold War. Liberal Values under Siege, 1946–1951, 23690

Fielding, Nigel: The National Front, 2047

Fields, A. Miryam: Some Aspects of Planned Migration to New and Expanding Towns, 18259

Fields, Gracie: Sing as We Go: The Autobiography, 24476

Fields, Rona M.: A Society on the Run: A Psychology of Northern Ireland, 2849

Fieldsend, Andrew: Fifty Years of Cleethorpes Trolley Buses 1937–1987, 17245

Fienburgh, Wilfred: Steel is Power: The Case for Nationalisation, 6549; Twenty-five Momentous years: A 25th Anniversary in the History of the Daily Herald, 25133

Fiennes, Gerald: I Tried to Run a Railway, 16828

Fiennes, Ranulph: Living Dangerously: An Autobiography, 27229

Fiennes, Richard: Man, Nature and Disease, 22389

Fifoot, Richard: A Bibliography of Edith, Osbert and Sacheverell Sitwell, 25801

Fifty Years of Adult Study: University of London Goldsmiths' College School of Adult and Social Studies Golden Jubilee, 1931–1981, 23675

Figes, Eva: Little Eden: A Child at War, 15090

Fijalkowski-Bereday, G. Z.: 'The Equalising Effects of the Death Duties', 4829

Filby, Frederick Arthur: A History of Food Adulteration and Analysis, 20637

Filby, Peter: T.V.R.: Success against the Odds, 17710

Filler, R.: A History of Welwyn Garden City, 18208

Filmer, P.: 'The Literary Imagination and the Explanation of Socio-Cultural Change in Modern Britain', 23733

Financial Times Business Information: Monthly Index to the Financial Times, 170

Finberg, Joscelyne: Exploring Villages, 19118

Finch, B. E.: Contraception through the Ages, 21068

Finch, Christopher: Image as Language: Aspects of British Art, 1950–1968, 23990; Patrick Caulfield, 24013

Finch, Harold: Memoirs of a Bedwellty M.P., 1409

Finch, J.: Labour of Love: Women, Work and Caring, 9150

Finch, Janet: Married to the Job: Wives' Incorporation in Men's Work, 10090

Finch, Roger: A Cross in the Topsail: An

Account of the Shipping Interests of R. & W. Paul Ltd., Ipswich, 16558

Findlater, Richard: What are Writers Worth?, 9800; The Unholy Trade, 25999 The Player Kings, 26000; These Are Our Actors: A Celebration of the Theatre Acting of Peggy Ashcroft, John Gielgud, Laurence Olivier and Ralph Richardson, 26001; Michael Redgrave: Actor, 26086; Lilian Baylis: The Lady of the Old Vic, 26112; ed. At the Royal Court: 25 Years of the English Stage Company, 26152; 'The System', 26207; Emlyn Williams, 26260; Banned! A Review of Theatrical Censorship in Britain, 26900

Findlay, Ian Russell: Education in Scotland, 23610

Fine, Ben: The Peculiarities of the British Economy, 3526; ed. Policing the Miners' Strike, 6922, 10768; 1,000,000 Delinquents, 10558

Finefrock, Michael M.: 'Ataturk, Lloyd George, and the Megali Idea: Cause and Consequence of the Greek Plan to Seize Constantinople from the Allies, June–August 1922', 13840

Fineman, Stephen: Social Work Stress and Intervention, 8962

Finer, Herman: 'The British Cabinet, the House of Commons and the War', 726; The British Civil Service: An Introductory Essay, 841; English Local Government, 3159; Local Government in England and Wales, 3161

Finer, Samuel E.: 'The Individual Responsibility of Ministers', 747; The Changing British Party System 1945–79, 1588; Anonymous Empire: A Study of the Lobby in Great Britain, 2064

Fink, Carole: The Genoa Conference: European Diplomacy 1921–1922, 13650

Finlay, Ian: Art in Scotland, 24088

Finlay, Wilfrid: Famous Flights of Airships and Balloons, 17541

Finlayson, A.: The Motivation and Characteristics of Internal Migrants: A Socio-medical Study of Young Migrants in Scotland, 7343

Finlayson, Angela: 'Married Women who Work in Early Motherhood', 7826

Finlayson, D. A.: 'Scottish Members of Parliament: Problems of Devolution', 2472

Finlayson, Douglas: Success and Failure in the Secondary School, 22938

Finlayson, Iain: The Scots, 2437

Finn, Dan: Training without Jobs: New Deals and Broken Promises: From Raising the School Leaving Age to the Youth Training Scheme, 8550

Finn, David: Henry Moore, 24195

Finn, J. E.: 'Public Support for Emergency/Anti-Terrorist Legislation in Northern Ireland: A Preliminary Analysis', 2868

Finn, Walter Henry: ed. Family Therapy in Social Work: A Collection of Papers, 10041

Finnegan, Frances: Poverty and Social Policy: An Historical Study of Batley, 9104; Poverty and Prostitution, 9105

Finnegan, John: Industrial Training Management, 5892; The Right People in the Right Jobs, 5893

Finney, Brian: Christopher Isherwood: A Critical Biography, 25598

Finnie, Hazel: Checklist of British Official Serial Publications, 191

Finniston, Sir Harold Montague: 'University Science and Industry', 23358

Finzi, Jean: Volunteers in Hospitals—A Guide for Organisers, 21496

Firmin, Stanley: Murderers in Our Midst, 10797

Firn, John: The Erosion of a Relationship: India and Britain since 1960, 13190

First, Ruth: The South African Connection: Western Investment in Apartheid, 12717

Firth, Catherine Beatrice: Constance Louisa Maynard: Mistress of Westfield College, 23342

Firth, Jack: Scottish Watercolour Painting, 24087

Firth, John D'Ewes Evelyn: Winchester College, 23085

Firth, Sir Raymond William: ed. Two Studies on Kinship in London, 10022, 11388; 'Family and Kin Ties in Britain and their Social Implications: Introduction', 10023; Families and their Relatives: Kinship in a Middle-Class Sector of London: An Anthropological Study, 10024

Fisch, Harold: The Dual Image: The Study of the Figure of the Jew in English Literature, 11286

Fischer, C. J.: 'Juvenile Delinquency and Police Discretion in an Inner-city Area', 10671

Fischer, David W.: North Sea Oil: An Environment Interface, 7176

Fischer, Louis: 'British Labour and the Soviets', 13918

Fischler, Guido: Der Britische Energiemarkt und die Atomkraftnutzung, 7196

Fish, M. S.: 'After Stalin's Death: The Anglo-American Debate over a New Cold War', 14110

Fishbein, Morris: ed. A Bibliography of Infantile Paralysis, 21095

Fishbein, Warren H.: Wage Restraint by Consensus, Britain's Search for an Incomes Policy Agreement, 1965–1979, 3921

Fisher, Alan George Bernard: Economic Progress and Financial Aspects of Social Security: An International Survey, 4098

Fisher, Anthony Clinton: Resource and Environmental Economics, 19999

Fisher, Barbara: Joyce Cary: The Writer and his Theme, 25440

Fisher, Donald: 'The Rockefeller Foundation and the Development of Scientific Medicine in Great Britain', 20942; Rockefeller Philanthropy and the British Empire: The Creation of the London School of Hygiene and Tropical Medicine', 20943

Fisher, Elsie Maude: Self-Portrait of Youth: Or, the Urban Adolescent, 8475

Fisher, Graham: The Queen's Life and Her Twenty-Five years of Monarchy, 509; Prince Andrew: Boy, Man and Prince, 533

Fisher, Herbert Albert Laurens: An Unfinished Autobiography, 1411, 26796; James Bryce, Viscount Bryce of Dechmont, O.M., 1380

Fisher, John: Burgess and Maclean: A New Look at the Foreign Office Spies, 16040

Fisher, John: Funny Way to be a Hero, 26284; What a Performance: The Life of Sid Field, 26309

Fisher, Sir Nigel: The Tory Leaders: Their Struggle for Power, 965 Harold Macmillan: A Biography, 1034; Iain Macleod, 1268

Fisher, P. J.: The Polio Story, 21123

Fisher, P.: External Examinations in Secondary Schools in England and Wales 1944–1964, 22914

Fisher, Robert: The Assessment of the Effects on English Borstal Boys of Different Correctional Training and Treatment Programmes, 10521

Fisher, Samuel [Baron Fisher of Camden]: Brodetsky: Leader of the Anglo-Jewish Community, 11300

Fisher, Stephen, British Shipping and Seamen, 1630–1960: Some Studies, 16457; ed. West Country Maritime and Social History: Some Essays, 16479

Fisher, Victor: 'Labour Evolution and Social Revolution', 6810

Fishman, Alfred P.: ed. Circulation of the Blood: Men and Ideas, 22309

Fishwick, Nicholas: English Football and Society 1910–1950, 27056

Fisk, Robert: In Time of War: Ireland, Ulster and the Price of Neutrality 1939–1945, 2707; The Point of No Return: The Strike which Broke the British in Ulster, 2921

Fisk, T.: 'Nature and Causes of Student Unrest', 22559

Fitter, R. S. R.: London's Natural History, 26526

Fitzgerald, Brian Vesey: Gypsies of Britain: An Introduction to their History, 11341; Programme for Agriculture: By Lord Addison and Others, 19456

Fitzgerald, Desmond J. L.: History of the Irish Guards in the Second World War, 15559

Fitzgerald, Fergus: ed. Memoirs of Desmond Fitzgerald, 1913–1916, 3054

Fitzgerald, Garret Ernest: Towards a New Ireland, 2654

Fitzgerald, Hilde: Studies in the Social Services, 8857

Fitzgerald, M.: Ethnic Minorities and the 1983 General Election, 2243; ed. Welfare in Action, 8909; Crime and Society: Readings in History and Theory, 10238, 10263; Prisoners in Revolt, 10366; Stranger on the Line: The Secret History of Phone Tapping, 10781; British Prisons, 10367

Fitzgerald, Patrick: British Intelligence and Covert Action: Africa, Middle East and Europe since 1945, 16006; Strangers on the Line: The Secret History of Phone-Tapping, 16065

Fitzgerald, Walter: 'Progress in Geographical Method', 26646

Fitzgibbon, Constantine: The Life and Times of Eamon de Valera, 3052; Red Hand: The Ulster Colony, 2909; The Life of Dylan Thomas, 25831; ed. Letters of Dylan Thomas, 25832

Fitzhardinge, L. F.: 'Australia, Japan and

Great Britain, 1914–1918: A Study in Triangular Diplomacy', 12612

Fitzherbert, Katrin: West Indian Children in London, 11261

Fitzpatrick, David: ed. Ireland and the First World War, 2675; Irish Emigration 1801–1921, 2702; Politics and Irish Life 1913–1921, 2703

Fitzroy, Olivia: Men of Valour: The History of the VII King's Royal Irish Hussars, 15452, 15561

Fitzsimons, Matthew Anthony: 'British Foreign Policy and Southern and Far Eastern Asia', 13619; 'The Masque of Uncertainty: Britain and Munich', 13751; Empire by Treaty: Britain and the Middle East in the Twentieth Century, 13801

Flack, Jeremy: Today's Royal Air Force in Colour, 15789

Flackes, W. D.: Northern Ireland: A Political Directory, 1968–1979, 2821; 1968–1983, 2822

Flagg, Amy C.: Notes on the History of Shipbuilding in South Shields 1746–1946, 16627

Flanagan, Bud: My Crazy Life: The Autobiography, 26310

Flanagan, Desmond: 1869–1969: A Centenary Story of the Co-operative Union of Great Britain and Ireland, 6800

Flanders, Allan David: The Fawley Productivity Agreements: A Case Study of Management and Collective Bargaining, 5608; Industrial Relations: What is wrong with the System? An Essay on its Theory and Failure, 5609; The Future of Voluntarism in Industrial Relations, 5610; Collective Bargaining: Prescription for Change, 5611; ed. Collective Bargaining: Selected Readings, 5612; Management and Unions: The Theory and Reform of Industrial Relations, 5613, 5729; ed. The System of Industrial Relations in Great Britain: Its History, Law and Institutions, 5614; 'The Reform of Collective Bargaining—From Donovan to Durkheim', 5690; Experiment in Industrial Democracy: A Study of the John Lewis Partnership, 6002

Flanders, M. June: 'The Effects of Devaluation on Exports', 4787

Flayhart, William H.: The Q.E.2, 16583

Fleay, C.: 'The Labour Spain Committee: Labour Party Policy and the Spanish Civil War', 13991

Fleetwood Port: Handbook 1984, 16685

Fleetwood, J.: History of Medicine in Ireland, 21239

Flegmann, Vilma: Public Expenditure and the Select Committees of the House of Commons, 4773

Fleming Report: The Public Schools and the General Educational System, 23011

Fleming, Alan Chalmers: Mental Disorder and the Law, 21879

Fleming, Alexander: Chemotherapy: Yesterday, Today and Tomorrow, 22289; ed. Penicillin. Its Practical Application, 22290

Fleming, Charlotte Mary: Adolescence, its

Social Psychology: With an Introduction to Recent Findings from the Fields of Anthropology, Physiology, Medicine, Psychometrics and Sociometry, 8431

Fleming, D. P.: The Cold War and Its Origins 1917–1960, 14095

Fleming, Horace: Beechcroft: the Story of the Birkenhead Settlement, 1914–1924, an Experiment in Adult Education, 23669

Fleming, Sir John Ambrose: Fifty Years of Electricity: The Memories of an Electrical Engineer, 7097; Memories of a Scientific Life, 7098

Fleming, John Robert: A History of the Church in Scotland, 1843–1929, 12196

Fleming, M. C.: 'Housebuilding Productivity in Northern Ireland', 18499 'The Inflation of House Prices in Northern Ireland in the 1970s', 18500

Fleming, Nicholas: August 1939: The Last Days of Peace, 13766

Fleming, Tom: Voices out of the Air: The Royal Christmas Broadcasts, 1932–1981, 463

Flemming, John Stanton: Inflation, 4007

Fletcher, A.: 'Workers' Participation in Management: A Survey of Post-war Organised Opinion', 5458

Fletcher, Cyril: Nice One Cyril: Being the Odd Odyssey and Anecdotage of a Comedian, 26312

Fletcher, Eric George Molyneaux, [Baron]: Random Reminiscences, 1412; 'Trade Union Reaction to Industrial Change', 6774

Fletcher, G. A.: The Discount Houses in London: Principles, Operations and Change, 4511

Fletcher, Geoffrey Scowland: Down among the Meths Men, 10218

Fletcher, Harold R.: The Story of the Royal Horticultural Society, 1804–1968, 19855, 26544; The Royal Botanic Garden, Edinburgh, 1670–1970, 26537

Fletcher, Ifan Kyrle: Edward Gordon Craig: A Bibliography, 26029

Fletcher, John William: A Measure to Society, 10217

Fletcher, John: 'Industrial Relations Material in Warwick University Library', 5572

Fletcher, Joseph Francis: William Temple: Twentieth Century Christian, 11707

Fletcher, M. H.: The WRNS: A History of the Women's Royal Naval Service, 15319

Fletcher, Max E.: 'From Coal to Oil in British Shipping', 16603

Fletcher, Ronald: 'The British Sociological Association Conference 1957', 7961; ed. The Making of Sociology: A Study of Social Theory, Vol. 1: Beginnings and Foundations, 8004; ed. The Making of Sociology: A Study of Social Theory: Vol. 2: Developments, 8004; ed. The Science of Society and the Unity of Mankind, 8005; 'Social Changes in Britain', 9476; Human Needs and Social Order, 9477; Britain in the Sixties: The Family and Marriage, an Analysis and Moral Assessment, 9478, 10047; The Shaking of the Foundations: Family and Society, 10048

Fletcher, Sheila: Women First: The Female

Tradition in English Physical Education, 1880–1980, 7738; Maude Royden, 11808

Fletcher, William Whigham: The Pest War, 20113

Flett, Hazel: The Effect of Slum Clearance on Multi-Occupation, 18407

Flexner, Abraham: Universities: American, English, German, 23366

Flick, L. F.: Development of our Knowledge of Tuberculosis, 21158

Flindall, Roy Philip: The Church of England, 1815–1948: A Documentary History, 11604

Flinn, Michael Walter: An Economic and Social History of Britain since 1700, 3479, 7615; 'Exports and the Scottish Economy in the Depresssion of the 1930's', 3585; Scottish Population History from the 17th Century to the 1930s, 7430; ed. Essays in Social History, 7616; Public Health Reform in Britain, 22090

Flint, Betty M.: The Child and the Institution: A Study of Deprivation and Recovery, 8174

Flint, James: '"Must God Go Fascist?": English Catholic Opinion and the Spanish Civil War', 13987

Flint, John E.: 'Scandal at the Bristol Hotel: Some Thoughts on Racial Discrimination in Britain and West Africa and its Relationship to the Planning of Decolonisation 1939–1947', 11201, 12735; 'The Failure of Planned Decolonisation in British Africa', 12692

Flint, Rachel Hayhoe: Fair Play: The Story of Women's Cricket, 27102

Flippo, Chet: McCartney: The Biography, 24508

Flood, R. Anthony: 'Suicide in Bristol', 10818

Florence, Philip Sargant: The Logic of British and American Industry: A Realistic Analysis of Economic Structure and Government, 4998; Ownership, Control and Success of Large Companies: An Analysis of English Industrial Structure and Policy, 1939–1951, 5011; Post-war Investment, Location and Size of Plant, 5012; Industry and the State, 6064

Florey, Howard Walter, [Baron]: 'The Work on Penicillin at Oxford', 20944; 'L'introduction de la Penicilline dans la Médicine', 20945

Florkin, Marcel: 'The Nature and Therapy of Pernicious Anaemia: A Trail of Biomedical Research', 20946; A History of Biochemistry, 26465

Flory, Harriette: 'The Arcos Raid and the Rupture of Anglo-Soviet Relations, 1927', 13942

Floud, Jean Esther: ed. Social Class and Educational Opportunity, 9520, 22833; ed. Education, Economy and Society: A Reader in the Sociology of Education, 9521;'Teaching in the Affluent Society', 22721; Education, Economy and Society, 23197; 'Studying Higher Education in Britain and America', 23396

Floud, Roderick: ed. The Economic History of Britain since 1700, 3513; 'The Economic History of Britain since 1700', 7592

Flower, Raymond: Lloyds of London: An Illustrated History, 4261

Flower, Sir Newman: Just as it Happened, 24952

Flowers, Arthur W.: Forty Years of Steam, 1926–1966, 7061

Fluck, Alan: The Sour Sweet Music: A Beginner's Guide to Contemporary Music, 24278

Flynn, M. *and* Flynn, P.: 'Social Malaise Research: A Study in Liverpool', 9420

Fodasti, Martha: George Barker, 25368

Fogarty, Michael Patrick: Contrasting Values in Western Europe: Unity, Diversity and Change, 239; Prospects of the Industrial Areas of Great Britain, 3425, 5039; Further Studies in Industrial Organisation, 3426; The Just Wage, 3933; Pensions Where Next?, 4048; Under-Governed and Over-Governed, 4049; *ed.* Further Studies in Industrial Organisation, 5595; Personality and Group Relations in Industry, 5630; The Rules of Work, 5631; Women and Top Jobs: An Interim Report, 7713; Women in Top Jobs: Four Studies in Achievement, 7714; Sex, Career and Family: Including an International Review of Women's Roles, 7715; Women in Top Jobs 1968–1979, 7716; Retirement Age and Retirement Costs, 8645; Retirement Policy: The Next Fifty Years, 8646; 'Tendences Nouvelles du "Welfare State"', 8975; 'Britain and Europe since 1945', 14147

Fogelman, Kenneth: Growing Up in Great Britain: Papers from the National Child Development Study, 8280; Britain's Sixteen-Year-Olds: Preliminary Findings from the Third Follow-Up of the NCDS—1958 Cohort, 8286

Foldes, Lucien P.: 'Estimates of Marginal Tax Rates for Dividends and Bond Interest in the United Kingdom, 1919–1970', 4555; 'Domestic Air Transport Policy', 17650

Foley, Cedric John: The Boilerplate War, 15347; ABC of British Army Vehicles, Armoured Cars, Tanks and Guns, 15507

Foley, Charles: *ed.* The Memoirs of General Grivas, 12868

Foley, Donald Leslie: Governing the London Region: Reorganisation and Planning in the Sixties, 3289, 18931; Controlling London's Growth: Planning the Great Wen 1940–1960, 18930

Foley, Gerald: The Energy Question, 7219

Follet, Frederick Vernon: A History of the Worcester Royal Grammar School, 23001

Folley, Roger Rowland Westwell: Commercial Horticulture in Britain: Its Character and Competitive Strength, 19851; Market Gardening in East Kent: Results for 1950, 1951, and 1952 Crops, 19852; East Kent Horticulture, 19853; Ten Years of Market Gardening: A Business Study of Some Small-scale Market Gardens covering the Period 1950–1960, 19854

Fontaine, Judith M.: Scholar's Guide to Intelligence Literature, 15994

Fonteyn, Dame Margot: An Autobiography, 24233

Fonvielle, L.: 'New Standpoints: Photography 1940–1955', 24698

Food Quality and Safety: A Century of Progress: Proceedings of the Symposium Celebrating the Centenary of the Sale of Food and Drugs Act, 1875, London, October 1975, 20601

Food and Foodways: Explorations in The History and Culture of Human Nourishment: Vol. 1, 20616

Foot, A. S.: 'Changes in Milk Production, 1930–70', 20660

Foot, Hugh Mackintosh [Baron Caradon]: A Start in Freedom, 12504

Foot, Michael Mackintosh: Aneurin Bevan, 1098; Another Heart and other Pulses: The Alternative to the Thatcher Society, 1193

Foot, Michael Richard Daniell: British Foreign Policy since 1898, 13218; Men in Uniform: Military Manpower in Modern Industrial Societies, 15444

Foot, Paul Mackintosh: The Politics of Harold Wilson, 1060; Why you should be a Socialist: The Case for a New Socialist Party, 1973; The Rise of Enoch Powell, 1292, 11186; Immigration and Race in British Politics, 11404

Foot, R. J.: 'Anglo-American Relations in the Korean Crisis: The British Effort to avert an Expanded War, December 1950–January 1951', 16149

Foot, Sir Dingle: British Political Crises, 1563

Foot, Sylvia: Emergency Exit, 12869

Football Association and Football League: The Financing and Taxation of Football Clubs, 27065

Football Crowd Behaviour: Report by a Working Group Appointed by the Secretary of State for Scotland under the Chairmanship of Frank McElhone: Edin, 27092

Foote, Bernard L.: The Caribbean Commission: Background of Co-operation in the West Indies, 13094

Foote, Geoffrey: A Chronology of Post-War British Politics, 66; The Labour Party's Political Thought: A History, 2101

Footman, David: Antonin Besse of Aden: the Founder of St. Antony's College, Oxford, 23572

Foran, W. R.: The Kenya Police 1887–1960, 12835

Forbes, Angela: Aberdeen University, 1945–1981: Regional Roles and National Needs, 23452

Forbes, Bryan: Ned's Girl: Notes for a Life, 24669, 26043; The Authorised Biography of Dame Edith Evans, 26040

Forbes, Eric G.: 'The Professionalisation of Dentistry: The United Kingdom', 22392

Forbes, Neil: 'London Banks, the German Standstill Agreements, and "Economic Appeasement" in the 1930s', 13688

Forbes, Patrick: The Grenadier Guards in the War of 1939–1945, 15643; 6th Guards Tank Brigade, 15734

Forbes, R. N.: The History of the Institute of Bankers in Scotland, 1875–1975, 4513

Forbes, Robert M.: Sixty Years of Medical Defence, 20796, 21502

Ford, A. W.: The Anglo-Iranian Oil Dispute of 1951–1952: A Study of the Rule of Law in the Relations of States, 13862

Ford, Boris: 'Report on Robbins', 23414; *ed.* The Cambridge Guide to the Arts in Britain. Vol. 8. The Edwardian Age and the Inter-war Years. Vol. 9: Since the Second World War, 23722

Ford, Brian John: Allied Secret Weapons: The War of Science, 15116

Ford, Brinsley: Three Centuries of British Water-Colours and Drawings, 23985

Ford, Donald: The Deprived Child and the Community, 8175, 10561; The Delinquent Child and the Community, 10560

Ford, E.: The Nation's Sea-fish Supply, 20719

Ford, Grace *and* Ford, Percy: A Guide to Parliamentary Papers, 192; Breviate of Parliamentary Papers 1900–1916, 193; Breviate of Parliamentary Papers 1917–1939, 194; Breviate of Parliamentary Papers 1940–1954: War and Reconstruction, 195; Select List of British Parliamentary Papers, 1955–1964, 196

Ford, J. R.: 'An Estimate of the Future Population of England and Wales', 7365

Ford, Jack: In the Steps of John Wesley: The Church of the Nazarene in Britain, 12117

Ford, Janet: 'The Role of the Building Society Manager in the Urban Stratification System: Autonomy Versus Constraint', 4383

Ford, John: Ackermann 1783–1983: The Business of Art, 23947

Ford, Julienne: Social Class and the Comprehensive School, 9541, 22942; 'The Facts Don't Fit: On the Relationship between Social Class and Criminal Behaviour', 10166

Ford, Percy: Incomes, Means Tests and Personal Responsibility, 3798; Social Theory and Social Practice: An Exploration of Experience, 8779; Coastwise Shipping and the Small Ports, 16649; The Southampton Survey, 18077; 1. A Survey of the Industrial Prospects of the Southampton Region, 18078; 2. Shops and Planning etc, 18079; 3. Housing Targets etc, 18080; 4. Problem Families, 18081; *ed.* Southampton: A Civic Survey, 18075; *ed.* Work and Wealth in a Modern Port: An Economic Survey of Southampton, 18076

Ford, Peter: The Fool on the Hill, 26348

Ford, Roger: HSTs at Work, 17061

Forder, Anthony: Concepts in Social Administration: A Framework for Analysis, 8735, 9232; Theories of Welfare, 8736; 'Recent Developments in Social Work', 8737; Penelope Hall's Social Services of England and Wales, 8740; Social Casework and Administration, 9231

Fordham, Herbert George: Hand-list of Catalogues and Works of Reference Relating to Carto-Bibliography and Kindred Subjects for Great Britain and Ireland, 1720–1927, 26690; The Evolution of the Maps of the British Isles, 26691; Maps: Their History, Characteristics and Uses: A Handbook for Teachers, 26692

Fordham, Montague: Britain's Trade and Agriculture: Their Recent Evolution and Future Development, 19447

Fordham, Peta: Inside the Underworld, 10216

Fordham, Richard Charles: Measurement of Urban Land Use, 20297; 'Urban Land Use Change in the United Kingdom during the Second Half of the Twentieth Century', 20298

Fordham, Wilfred Gurney: Recent Mining Legislation, including the Coal Mines Act, 1930, 6258

Foreign Office List: Annual, 13326

Foreman, Lewis: ed. British Music Now: A Guide to the Work of Younger Composers, 24288; Bax: A Composer and his Times, 24296; The Music of Frank Bridge, 24305; ed. Edmund Rubbra, 24363

Foreman, Nell: Archive Sound Collections: An Interim Directory of Institutional Collections of Sound Recordings in Great Britain Holding Material other than that Currently Commercially Available, 223

Forester, Margery: Michael Collins: The Lost Leader, 3025

Forester, Tom: The Labour Party and the Working Class, 1799

Forman, James Adam Sholto: Social Case Work in General Practice: A Report on an Experiment carried out in General Practice, 21516

Forman, Sir Denis: Films, 1945–1950, 24650

Forrest, Alistair Douglas: 'Environmental Factors in Depressive Illness', 21775; New Perspectives in Mental Handicap, 21864

Forrest, Denys: Tea for the British: The Social and Economic History of a Famous Trade, 20711

Forrest, Ray: Selling the Welfare State: The Privatisation of Council Housing, 18435; 'The Geography of Council House Sales in England, 1979–1985', 18439

Forrester, A.: Beyond our Ken: A Guide to the Battle for London, 3296

Forrester, Duncan B.: Christianity and the Future of Welfare, 11850; ed. Studies in the History of Worship in Scotland, 12200

Forrester, Felicitée Sheila: Ballet in England: A Bibliography and Survey c.1700–June 1966, 24205

Forshaw, Alec: Smithfield: Past and Present, 20668

Forshaw, John H.: The County of London Plan. 1943, 18937

Forster, Charles Ian Kennerley: The Changing Balance of Fuel and Power, 6300

Forsyth, David James Cameron: U.S. Investment in Scotland, 4755, 5267; Studies in the British Coal Industry, 6307

Forsyth, Gordon: The Demand for Medical Care: A Study of the Case Load in the Barrow in Furness Group of Hospitals, 21385; Gateway or Dividing Line?: A Study of Hospital Out-Patients in the 1960's, 21404; Doctors and State Medicine: A Study of the British Health Service, 21572

Forsyth, James: Tyrone Guthrie, 26118

Forsyth, Peter: Civil Aviation Policy and the Privatisation of British Airways, 17625

Forte, Charles, Baron: Forte: The Autobiography of Charles Forte, 27998

Forte, F.: ed. Public Expenditure and Government Growth, 6148

Fortes, Meyer: Kinship and Social Order: The Legacy of Lewis Henry Morgan, 8067, 10124

Fortescue, S. E. D.: People and Places, Great and Little Brokham, 19323

Forth, Geoffrey N.: Accounting: An Insight, 4193

Forty, A.: 'Lorenzo of the Underground [Frank Pick]', 16318

Forty, George: Desert Rats at War, 14895; Called Up: A National Service Scrapbook, 16070

Foschepoth, Josef: 'British Interest in the Division of Germany after the Second World War', 14199; ed. Die britische Deutschland—und Besatzungspolitik 1945–1949, 14213

Fosh, Patricia: ed. Industrial Relations and the Law in the 1980's: Issues and Future Trends, 5843; The Active Trade Unionist: A Study of Motivation and Participation at Branch Level, 6719

Foss, Brian M.: ed. New Horizons in Psychology, 22420

Foss, Hubert James: 'Elgar and his Age', 24333; Ralph Vaughan Williams: A Study, 24375; London Symphony: Portrait of an Orchestra, 1904–1954, 24543

Foss, Michael: The Royal Fusiliers, 15634

Fossey, John Cobb: Prelude to 1937: Being a Sketch of the Critical Years 1931–1936, 299

Foster, Christopher David: Local Government Finance in a Unitary State, 3262, 4872; The Transport Problem, 16224

Foster, D. F.: The Mackenzie King Record, 12661

Foster, J.: 'The Redistributive Effect of Inflation on Building Society Shares and Deposits 1961–1974', 4010, 4367

Foster, Janet: British Archives, 71

Foster, John: Ayer, 26847

Foster, John: The Politics of the U.C.S. Work-in, 16623

Foster, Malcolm: Joyce Cary: A Biography, 25446

Foster, Peggy: Access to Welfare: An Introduction to Welfare Rationing, 8967

Foster, R. C. G.: History of the Queen's Royal Regiment Vol. 8 1924–48, 15711

Foster, Roy F.: Modern Ireland 1600–1972, 2645

Foster, William Derek: A History of Parasitology, 21107; A Short History of Clinical Pathology, 21110; A History of Medical Bacteriology and Immunology, 22348

Fothergill, Stephen: The State of the Nation, 125; The Economics of Nuclear Power, 6669; 'The Impact of the New and Expanded Town Programme on Industrial Location in Britain, 1960–1978', 18261

Foulkes, David: The Welsh Veto: The Wales Act 1978 and the Referendum, 2577; 'The Work of the Local Commissioner for Wales', 3381

Fountain, Nigel: Underground: The London Alternative Press 1966–74, 25202

Fowler, Alan: Effective Negotiation, 5853

Fowler, Dean R.: Alfred North Whitehead, 26879

Fowler, Gerald Teasdale: Decision Making in British Education, 22793

Fowler, John Henry: The Life and Letters of Edward Lee Hicks, Bishop of Lincoln, 1910–1919, 11738

Fowler, Sir [Peter] Norman: Police in the Seventies, 10700; After the Riots: The Police in Europe, 10724

Fowler, W.: The Battle for the Falklands: Land Forces, 16087

Fowler, Wilton B.: British-American Relations, 1917–1918: The Role of Sir William Wiseman, 13397

Fowles, D.: et al. 100 Not Out: A Look Back at 100 Years of Staffordshire County Council, 3368

Fox, Adam: Dean Inge, 11787

Fox, Alan W.: 'Agricultural Wages in England and Wales in the Last Half Century', 19667

Fox, Alan: Industrial Sociology and Industrial Relations: An Assessment of the Contribution which Industrial Sociology can Make towards Understanding and Resolving some of the Problems now Being Considered by the Royal Commission [Donovan Commission], 5685; 'Management Ideology and Labour Relations', 5686; A Sociology of Work in Industry, 5687; Socialism and Shop Floor Power, 5688; History and Heritage: The Social Origins of the British Industrial Relations System, 5689; 'The Reform of Collective Bargaining—From Donovan to Durk-heim', 5690; A History of the National Union of Boot and Shoe Operatives, 1874–1957, 6878; The Milton Plan: An Exercise in Manpower Planning and the Transfer of Production, 7351

Fox, Anthony: British Parliamentary Constituencies: A Statistical Compendium, 2221

Fox, Daniel M.: Health Policies, Health Politics: The British and American Experience, 1911–1965, 21610

Fox, Sir Frank: The Royal Inniskilling Fusiliers in the World War, 15555; The History of the Royal Gloucestershire Hussars Yeomanry, 1898–1922, 15638

Fox, Hubert: ed. Marion Fox, Quaker: A Selection of her Letters, 12142

Fox, J. M.: 'Students' Study Habits, Attitudes and Academic Attainment', 22562

Fox, John P.: 'Britain and the Inter-Allied Military Commission of Control', 13653

Fox, Joseph Tylor: 'The Care of the Epileptic Child', 8176

Fox, Judith: Families and their Needs, with Particular Reference to One-Parent Families, 9941

Fox, Sir Lionel Wreay: The English Prison Systems: An Account of the Prison and Borstal System in England and Wales after the Criminal Justice Act 1948, with an Historical Introduction and an Examination of the Principles of Imprisonment as Legal Punishment, 10403, 10516; The Modern English Prison, 10404

Fox, Richard Michael: The History of the Irish Citizen Army, 2757; James Connolly: The Forerunner, 3041

Fox, Robert: 'I Counted Them All Out and I Counted Them All Back': The Battle for the

Falklands, 16106; Eyewitness Falklands: A Personal Account of the Falklands Campaign, 16107

Fox, Robin: Kinship and Marriage: An Anthropological Perspective, 10077

Fox, William Thornton Rickert: Anglo-American Relations in the Post-War World, 14059

Fox-Strangways, A. H.: Cecil Sharp, 24447

Foyle, W. & G. Ltd: Foyles Sixty Years 1904–1964, 25006

Fraenkel, Josef: Exhibition of the Jewish Press in Great Britain: 1823–1963, 25143

Francis-Williams, [Lord]: Ernest Bevin: Portrait of a Great Englishman, 1103; Ernest Bevin: An Illustrated Life, 1881–1951, 1104

Francis, Clarence: A History of Food and its Preservation: A Contribution to Civilisation, 20639

Francis, Constance: The Welfare of the Needy, 8890

Francis, E. V.: London and Lancashire History: The History of the London and Lancashire Insurance Co. Ltd, 4215

Francis, Hywel: The Fed: A History of the South Wales Miners in the Twentieth Century, 6320, 6901; 'No Surrender in the Valleys: The 1984–1985 Miners' Strike in South Wales', 6335; 'The Politics of Coal in South Wales, 1945–48', 6337; Miners against Fascism: Wales and the Spanish Civil War, 13988; 'Welsh Miners and the Spanish Civil War', 13989

Francis, Mary: The First European Elections: A Handbook and Guide, 2381

Francis, Octavius: A History of Clifton College, 1860–1934, 23055

Francis, Richard: Broadcasting to a Community in Conflict: The Experience in Northern Ireland, 24811

Franco, Paul: The Political Philosophy of Michael Oakeshott, 2091

Frangopulo, Nicholas Joseph: Tradition in Action: The Historical Evolution of the Greater Manchester County, 3363; ed. Rich Inheritance: A Guide to the History of Manchester, 18057

Frank, Alan: Modern British Composers, 24272

Frank, D. G. H.: The Enforcement of Planning Control under the Town and Country Planning Act, 20329

Frank, Elizabeth: Margot Fonteyn, 24230

Frank, P.: 'Women's Work in the Yorkshire Inshore Fishing Industry', 19822

Frank, Robert G., Jnr: 'The A. V. Hill Papers at Churchill College, Cambridge', 26512

Frank, Susan: A History of Glassmaking, 6484, 24125

Frank, William Francis: The New Industrial Law, 5596; 'The State and Industrial Arbitration in the United Kingdom', 5597; An Introduction to Industrial Administration, 5598

Franke, Reiner: 'Die Tschechoslowakei in der politischen Meinung Englands, 1918–1938', 13730

Frankel, Henryk: Economic Changes in British Agriculture, 1959–1964, 19525

Frankel, Joseph: British Foreign Policy 1945–1973, 13241

Frankel, M.: 'Joint Industrial Planning in Great Britain', 5640

Frankel, P. H.: 'Oil Supplies during the Suez Crisis: On Meeting a Political Emergency', 6507

Frankenberg, Ronald: Communities in Britain: Social Life in Town and Country, 9356; Village on the Border: A Social Study of Religion, Politics, and Football in a North Wales Community, 19301

Franker, Maurice: The Control of Industrial Air Pollution, 20051

Frankis, G. G. A.: A History of the Royal Blue Express Coach Services, 17326; A History of the Western National, 17327

Frankland, Noble: Prince Henry, Duke of Gloucester, 538; The Bombing Offensive against Germany: Outlines and Perspectives, 15972; The Strategic Air Offensive, 15981

Franklin, A. W.: ed. A Way of Life and other Selected Writings of William Osler, 20876

Franklin, A.: Squatting in England, 1969–79: A Case Study of Social Conflict in Advanced Industrial Capitalism, 18381

Franklin, David: Basso Cantate: An Autobiography, 24418

Franklin, Harry: Unholy Wedlock: The Failure of the Central African Federation, 12787

Franklin, Kenneth J.: 'The History of Research upon the Renal Circulation', 20947; 'A Short History of the International Congresses of Physiologists', 20948; 'History and the Physiologist', 22310; A Short History of Physiology, 22311; 'Fifty Years of Physiology', 22312; 'A Short Sketch of the History of the Oxford Medical School', 22467; Joseph Barcroft, 1872–1947, 22313; The Foetal Circulation and Cardiovascular System, and the Changes that they Undergo, 22305

Franklin, Marjorie E.: ed. Camp: An Epitome of Experiences at Hawkspur Camp 1936–1940, 10543

Franklin, Peter J.: The U.K. Life Assurance Industry: A Study in Applied Economics, 4224

Franklin, R. H.: 'Grey Turner and the Evolution of Oesophageal Surgery', 20949

Franklin, Samuel Harvey: Rural Societies, 19034

Franklin, Thomas Bedford: A History of Agriculture, 19405; A History of Scottish Farming, 19615

Franks, Norman L. R.: The Greatest Air Battle. Dieppe 19th August 1942, 14824

Franks, Oliver Shewell [Baron]: Central Planning and Control in War and Peace, 801; Britain and the Tide of World Affairs, 13217

Fransman, L.: British Nationality Law and the 1981 Act, 11135

Fraser Darling, Sir Frank: 'The Ecological Approach to the Social Sciences', 7916; ed. West Highland Survey: An Essay in Human Ecology, 19919; ed. Impacts of Man on the Biosphere, 19920; ed. Wilderness and Plenty: The Reith Lectures 1969, 19921

Fraser, B.: 'Long-term Planning in the Hospital Service', 21487; 'The Mental Health Services', 21776

Fraser, Brian: Sure and Stedfast: A History of the Boys' Brigade, 1883–1983, 8510

Fraser, Sir David: Alanbrooke, 14748

Fraser, Derek: The Evolution of the British Welfare State: A History of Social Policy since the Industrial Revolution, 8987, 21628; ed. A History of Modern Leeds, 18027

Fraser, Duncan: Portrait of a Parish [St. Cyrus]. Montrose, 19371

Fraser, G. S.: Lawrence Durrell: A Critical Study, 25485

Fraser, Grace Lovat: Textiles by Britain, 6463

Fraser, Herbert Freeman: Great Britain and the Gold Standard, 4691

Fraser, J. M.: The Place of Women in the Church, 12217

Fraser, John Munro: Human Relations in a Fully Employed Democracy, 5477; Principles and Practice of Supervisory Management, 5478; Introduction to Personnel Management, 5479

Fraser, K. C.: A Bibliography of the Scottish National Movement 1844–1973, 2498

Fraser, Morris: Children in Conflict, 2860

Fraser, Peter: 'Cabinet Secrecy and War Memoirs', 762; Lord Esher: A Political Biography, 1189

Fraser, R. H.: 'Environmental Factors in Depressive Illness', 21775

Fraser, R.: 'Independent Television in Britain', 24867

Fraser, Ronald: ed. Work: Twenty Personal Accounts . . . With a Concluding Essay by Raymond Williams, 5886

Fraser, Ruth F.: Religion and Politics: A Bibliography Selected from the Atlas Religious Database, 11530

Fraser, Thomas G.: 'India in Anglo-Japanese Relations during the First World War', 13127; Partition in Ireland, India and Palestine: Theory and Practice, 13174; ed. The Middle East 1914–1979, 13797

Fraser, W. Hamish: Workers and Employers. Documents on Trade Unions and Industrial Relations in Britain since the Eighteenth Century, 5566, 6801

Fraser, William Rae: Residential Education, 23022

Frasure, Carl Maynard: British Policy on War Debts and Reparations, 3752

Frasure, Robert C.: 'Constituency Agents and British Politics', 1609; 'Backbench Opinion Revisited: The Case of the Conservatives', 1644

Frazer, Patrick: The Clearing Banks: Their Role and Activities, 4460

Frazer, William Mowll: A History of English Public Health, 1834–1939, 22069; The Public Health Department of the City of Liverpool, 22070

Fream, William: Elements of Agriculture, 19401

Frechet, Alec: John Galsworthy: A Reassessment, 25532

Free Presbyterian Church of Scotland: A History of the Free Presbyterian Church of Scotland, 12254

Freeden, Michael: *ed.* Reappraising J. A. Hobson: Humanism and Welfare, 2113; Liberalism Divided: A Study in British Political Thought 1914–1939, 2181

Freedland, M. R.: The Contract of Employment, 7223

Freedland, Michael: Kenneth Williams: A Biography, 26350

Freedman, Lawrence: Signals of War: The Falklands Conflict of 1982, 16079; 'Bridgehead Revisited: The Literature of the Falklands', 16080; Britain and the Falklands War, 16081; 'Intelligence Operations in the Falklands', 16095

Freedman, Maurice: *ed.* Social Organisation: Essays Presented to Raymond Firth, 9536; 'The Relations of Race: A Review of New Writing', 10924; *ed.* A Minority in Britain: Social Studies of the Anglo-Jewish Community, 11284, 12413

Freeman, A. E.: 'Traditional and Social Perspectives on Mental Illness', 21845

Freeman, Alan: The Benn Heresy, 1091

Freeman, Albert Myrick: The Economics of Environment Policy, 19948; The Benefits of Environmental Improvement: Theory and Practice, 19995; Air and Water Pollution Control: A Benefit-Cost Assessment, 19996

Freeman, Gary P.: Immigrant Labour and Racial Conflict in Industrial Societies: The French and the British Experience 1945–1975, 11199

Freeman, Hugh Lionel: *ed.* Psychiatric Hospital Care: A Symposium, 21494; 'Mental Health Services in an English County Borough before 1974', 21760; *ed.* Trends in Mental Health Services: A Symposium of Original and Reprinted Papers, 21769; *ed.* New Aspects of Mental Health Services, 21770

Freeman, J. P. G.: Britain's Nuclear Arms Control Policy in the Context of Anglo-American Relations 1957–1968, 13540

Freeman, John: Prisons Past and Future, 10449

Freeman, John: Team Teaching in Britain, 22715

Freeman, Kathleen: If Any Man Build: The History of the Save the Children Fund, 8178, 9196

Freeman, Michael David Alan: The Rights and Wrongs of Children, 8177

Freeman, Michael: The Atlas of British Railway History, 16727

Freeman, Ruth: Quakers and Peace, 12147

Freeman, Simon: Conspiracy of Silence: The Secret Life of Anthony Blunt, 16630

Freeman, Thomas Walter: Ireland: Its Physical, Historical, Social and Economic Geography, 2663; Geography and Regional Administration: England and Wales 1830–1968, 3133; Lancashire, Cheshire and the Isle of Man, 5132; Ireland's General and Regional Geography, 5384; The Conurbations of Great Britain, 17743; Geography and Planning, 18267, 20407, 26673; A History of Modern British Geography, 26630; One Hundred Years of Geography, 26631; The Geographer's Craft, 26632

Freeman-Grenville, G. S. P.: Atlas of British History, 144

Freer, David: *ed.* Hamilton Harty, 24435

Fremantle, Sir Francis Edward: The Housing Problem: A Concise Survey, 18609; The Housing of the Nation, 18610; 'Local Administration of the Work of the Ministry of Health', 21314; The Health of the Nation, 22045

Fremantle, Sir Sydney Robert: My Naval Career, 1880–1928, 15311

French, David: British Strategy and War Aims 1914–16, 13369, 14441; British Economic and Strategic Planning 1905–15, 14440

French, Edward Gerald: The Life of Field Marshal Sir John French, First Earl of Ypres, 14502; Goodbye to Boot and Saddle, or, the Tragic Passing of British Cavalry, 15436

French, John Oliver: Plumbers in Unity: History of the Plumbing Trades Union, 1865–1965, 6843

French, Philip N.: *ed.* the Age of Austerity, 1945–1951, 300, 7576; 'The Alphaville of Admass, or How We Learned to Stop Worrying and Love the Boom', 24691

Frenkel, Stephen: Shop Stewards in Action, 5789

Freud, Anna: Infants without Families: The Case for and against Residential Nurseries, 8121; Staffing of Local Authority Children's Departments: A Report by the Scottish Advisory Council on Child Care, 8122; Infants without Families and Reports on the Hampstead Nurseries, 8179

Frey, Cynthia W.: 'Meaning Business: The British Application to Join the Common Market, November 1966–October 1967', 14171

Frey, Linda and Frey, Marrsha: *eds.* Women in Western European History: A Select Chronological and Topical Bibliography: The Nineteenth and Twentieth Centuries, 7627

Freymond, Jean F.: Political Integration in the Commonwealth Caribbean: A Survey of Recent Attempts with Special Reference to the Associated States (1967–1974), 13016

Freyre, Gilberto De Mello: The Racial Factor in Contemporary Politics, 10952

Fricker, L. J.: 'Historic Gardens and Landscapes: The Conservation of a National Asset', 20388

Fried, M. H.: *ed.* Colloquium on Overseas Chinese, 11379

Friedlander, Cecil Paul: The Police: Servants or Masters?, 10730

Friedlander, Dov: Internal Migration in England and Wales 1851–1951, 7275; 'London's Urban Transition, 1851–1951, 18305; 'The Spread of Urbanization in England and Wales, 1851–1951', 18306

Friedman, Ellen: Women, 7803

Friedman, Irvine Sigmund: British Relations with China: 1931–1939, 13628

Friedman, Isaiah: The Question of Palestine, 1918: British-Jewish-Arab Relations, 14284

Friedman, R.: The Story of Scabies, 21130

Friend, John Francis: The Long Trek, 15063

Friesel, Evytar: The British, Zionism and Palestine: Perceptions and Policies during the Mandate Period, 14322

Frisby, J. H.: The Northampton Gas Undertaking 1823–1949, 7164

Frischauer, Willi: David Frost, 24909

Frith, Simon: Sound Effects: Youth, Leisure and the Politics of Rock, 24491; Music for Pleasure, 24492

Fritz, Stephen E.: 'La Politique de la Ruhr and Lloyd George's Conference Diplomacy: The Tragedy of Anglo-French Relations 1919–1923', 14246

Frizelle, Ernest R.: The Leicester Royal Infirmary, 1771–1971, 21428

Frost, Brian: *ed.* The Tactics of Pressure: A Critical Review of Six British Pressure Groups, 2076

Frost, John: Daily Mirror, 25136

Frost, John: A Drop too Many, 14954

Frost, Richard: Race against Time: Human Relations and Politics in Kenya before Independence, 12825

Frost, Richard: The British Commonwealth and the World, 12556; *ed.* The British Commonwealth and World Society, 12562

Frost, Stanley B.: 'Selection and Training of Candidates for the Ministry: Postgraduate Theological Training', 11900

Frost, W.: *ed.* Zwischen Ruhrkontrolle und Mitbestimmung, 14209

Frostick, Michael: A History of the World's High Performance Cars, 17366

Frothingham, Thomas Goddard: A True Account of the Battle of Jutland, May 31, 1916, 14648; The Naval History of the World War, 14673

Frow, Edmund: Engineering Struggles: Episodes in the Story of the Shop Stewards' Movement, 5819; 'The History of British Trade Unions: A Select Bibliography', 6689; A Survey of the Half-Time System in Education, 23657

Frow, Gerald: "Oh, Yes It Is!" A History of Pantomime, 26272

Frow, Ruth: Engineering Struggles: Episodes in the Story of the Shop Stewards' Movement, 5819; 'The History of British Trade Unions: A Select Bibliography', 6689; 'Strikes': A Documentary History, 6970

Fruin, David John: Social Workers and their Workloads in Northern Ireland Welfare Departments, 8746

Fruton, J. S.: Molecules and Life: Historical Essays on the Interplay of Chemistry and Biology, 26467; Selected Bibliography of Biographical Data for the History of Biochemistry since 1800, 26468; 'The Emergence of Biochemistry', 26469

Fry, Anne: Media Matters: Social Work, the Press and Broadcasting, 8908

Fry, Geoffrey Kingdon: The Growth of Government: the Development of Ideas about the Role of the State and the Machinery and Functions of Government in Britain since 1780, 709; 'Thoughts on the Present State of the Convention of Ministerial Responsibility', 748; 'Some Weaknesses in the Fulton Report on the British Home Civil Service', 858; 'Some

Developments in the British Home Civil Service Since the Fulton Report', 859; 'Policy Planning Units—Ten Years On', 863; Statesmen in Disguise: The Changing Role of the Administrative Class of the British Home Civil Service, 1853–1966, 867

Fry, Gerald W.: Pacific Basin and Oceania, 12874

Fry, J.: 'The Family Doctor', 21539

Fry, Joan Mary: Friends Lend a Hand in Alleviating Unemployment: The Story of a Social Experiment Extending over 20 Years, 1926–1946, 12149

Fry, John, Lord Hunt of Fawley: ed. A History of the General Practitioner: Some European Comparisons, 21501

Fry, John, Lord Hunt of Fawley: ed. A History of the Royal College of General Practitioners: The First 25 Years, 20873; ed. International Medical Care: A Comparison and Evaluation of Medical Care Services throughout the World, 21577

Fry, Sir Leslie: As Luck Would Have It, 13265

Fry, Michael Graham: 'Britain, the Allies and the Problem of Russia, 1918–1919', 13928; 'The North Atlantic Triangle and the Abrogation of the Anglo-Japanese Alliance',14014; Illusions of Security: North Atlantic Diplomacy, 1918–1922, 14015

Fry, Michael: Patronage and Principle: A Political History of Modern Scotland, 2446

Fry, Richard: Bankers in West Africa: The Story of the Bank of British West Africa Ltd., 4531

Fry, Roger Elliot: Reflections on British Painting, 23987

Fry, [Sara] Margery: The Single Woman, 7675; The Ancestral Child, 8182; Children as Citizens, 8183; Old Age Looks at Itself, 8557; The Future Treatment of the Adult Offender, 10405; 'The University Grants Committee: an Experiment in Administration', 23324

Fry, V. C.: The Taxation of Occupational Pension Schemes in the United Kingdom, 3981

Fryde, E. B.: ed. Handbook of British Chronology, 69

Fryer, J. A.: Travel to Work in Greater London: Selected Results from the 1971 Census, 16280

Fryer, Jonathan: Isherwood: A Biography of Christopher Isherwood, 25595

Fryer, Peter: The Birth Controllers, 7515; Mrs Grundy: Studies in English Prudery, 9894; Private Case—Public Scandal, 9895; Staying Power: The History of Black People in Britain, 11078; Black People in the British Empire: An Introduction, 11079

Fuchser, L. W.: Neville Chamberlain and Appeasement: A Study in the Politics of History, 983

Fuerst, J. S.: ed. Public Housing in Europe and America, 18449

Fulbrook, Julian: Administrative Justice and the Unemployed, 4039

Fulcher, James: 'Industrial Conflict in Britain and Sweden', 5776

Fulford, Sir Roger Thomas Baldwin: The Pictorial Life Story of King George VI, 503;

The Liberal Case, 2174; Votes for Women: The Story of a Struggle, 2256; Glyn's 1753–1953: Six Generations in Lombard Street, 4491

Fuller, Edward: The Right of the Child: A Chapter in Social History, 8180, 9197; Child Welfare in England, with Special Reference to the Family, 8181

Fuller, Jean Overton: The German Penetration of S.O.E.: France 1941–1944, 15087

Fuller, John Frederic Charles: Empire Unity and Defence, 12542; India in Revolt, 13145; The Second World War, 1939–1945: A Strategical and Tactical History, 14706; On Future Warfare, 14731; Memoirs of an Unconventional Soldier, 14732; Towards Armageddon: The Defence Problem and its Solution, 14733; Tanks in the Great War, 1914–1918, 15525

Fuller, John: A Reader's Guide to W.H. Auden, 25359

Fuller, Margaret Dorothy: West Country Friendly Societies': An Account of Village Benefit Clubs and their Brass Pole Heads, 4073, 9131

Fuller, Peter: The Psychology of Gambling, 27115

Fuller, Ronald: The Work of Rex Whistler, 24082

Fuller, Roy Broadbent: The Building Societies Acts, 1874–1960, 4370

Fuller, Watson: ed. The Social Impact of Modern Biology, 26519

Fullerton, Brian: Accessibility to Employment in the Northern Region Report, 16290

Fullick, Roy: Suez: The Double War, 14383

Fulop, Christina: Consumers in the Market: A Study of Choice, Competition and Sovereignty, 20445; Retailing and the Consumer, 20446; Revolution in Retailing, 20447; The Consumer Movement and the Consumer, 20448; Advertising, Competition and Consumer Behaviour: Public Policy and the Market, 20449

Fulton, H. W.: 'The GLC's Parliamentary Business', 3303

Fulton, John Farquhar: The Centennial of Surgical Anesthesia. An Annotated Catalogue, 21037; Aviation Medicine in its Preventive Aspects: An Historical Survey, 21051; A Bibliography of Aviation Medicine, 21052; Physiology, 22314; ed. Selected Readings in the History of Physiology, 22315

Fulton, John Scott [Baron]: 'The Future Pattern of University Education in the United Kingdom', 23391; Experiment in Higher Education, 23417

Funk, Arthur Layton: 'Negotiating the "Deal with Darlan"', 14274

Funnell, E. B.: ed. The Management of Water Resources in England and Wales, 20097

Furbank, P. N.: E. M. Forster, a Life, 25519; ed. Selected Letters of E. M. Forster, 25520

Furber, Elizabeth Chaplin: Changing Views on British History: Essays on Historical Writing since 1939, 372, 5256

Furbey, Robert: Housing and Urban Spatial Structure: A Case Study, 5405, 20401

Furneaux, Walter Desmond Charles: The Chosen Few: An Examination of Some Aspects of University Selection in Britain, 22550

Furness, Eric Longfellow: British Monetary and Fiscal Policy in Relation to the Operation of the Gold Standard, 1925–1931, 4684

Furness, William: ed. The Centenary History of Rossall School, 23072

Furnia, Arthur Homer: The Diplomacy of Appeasement: Anglo-French Relations and the Prelude to World War II, 1931–1938, 13707

Furse, Sir Ralph Dolignon: Aucuparius: Recollections of a Recruiting Officer, 12509

Furth, Charles: Life since 1900, 354, 7614

Fussell, George Edwin: 'The Collection of Agricultural Statistics in Great Britain: Its Origin and Evaluation', 19386; Farming Techniques from Prehistoric to Modern Times, 19535; The Story of Farming, 19536; Farms, Farmers and Society: Systems of Food Production and Population Numbers, 19537; 'Farming Systems and Society: A Historical Survey', 19538

Fussell, Paul: The Great War and Modern Memory, 14477

Fyfe, Christopher: A History of Sierra Leone, 12769

Fyfe, George: From Box-Kites to Bombers, 14637; Sopwith Camel: King of Combat, 14638

Fyfe, Henry Hamilton: T. P. O'Connor, 1496, 25269; Sixty Years of Fleet Street, 25236

Fyle, Nigel: Black Settlers in Britain 1555–1958, 11075

Fyrth, J.: ed. Britain, Fascism and the Popular Front, 13563; The Signal Was Spain: The Aid Spain Movement in Britain, 1936–39, 13993

Fyson, Anthony: 'Confusion is Good for You', 17873

Fyvel, Raphael Joseph: ed. The Future of Sociology, 7947

Fyvel, Toscoe Raphael: ed. The Future of Sociology, 7947; 'Remembering Fred Warburg: A London Publisher and his Time', 24994; George Orwell: A Personal Memoir, 25749; Troublemakers: Rebellious Youth in an Affluent Society, 10568; The Insecure Offenders: Rebellious Youth in the Welfare State, 10569

GLC Environmental Science Group: Concorde Noise and its Effect on London, 20154

Gabarino, Joseph W.: 'Managing Conflict in Industrial Relations: U.S. Experience and Current Issues in Britain, 5717; 'British Experiments with Industrial Relations Reform', 5718

Gabiné, Bernard Luthard: A Finding List of British Royal Commission Reports, 1860–1935, 684

Gable, J.: The Tuppenny Punch and Judy Show; 25 Years of T.V, 24873

Gablehouse, Charles: Helicopters and Autogiros: A History of Rotating-wing and V/STOL Aviation, 17558

Gabor, Andre: 'The Economics of the Welfare State in Britain', 8972

Gabor, Dennis: 'Holography, 1948–1971', 7160

Gabriel, John: 'The Politics of Race in Britain, 1962–1970: A Review of the Major Trends and of the Recent Literature', 10891

Gaddis, John Lewis: The United States and the Origins of the Cold War 1941–1947, 14097; 'The Emerging Post-Revisionist Synthesis and the Origins of the Cold War', 14098

Gaffikin, Prudence: 'A Scheme for the Study of Nature and Nutrition in Relation to Child Welfare', 8184

Gage, A. T.: A History of the Linnean Society of London, 26542

Gager, C. Stuart: 'Botanic Gardens of the World: Materials for a History', 26539

Gailey, Alan: Rural Houses in the North of Ireland, 19312

Gailey, H. A.: Clifford: Imperial Consul, 12499; A History of the Gambia, 12772

Gainsborough, Charles William Francis Noel [Earl of]: The Flora of Leicestershire and Rutland: A Topographical, Ecological and Historical Account, with Biographies of Former Botanists (1620–1933), 26561

Gaisford, John: ed. Time Gone By: A Photographic Record of Great Britain from 1856 to 1956, 24695

Gajda, Patricia A.: Postscript to Victory: British Policy and the German–Polish Borderland, 1919–1925, 13892

Galambos, P.: 'The Role of Invisible Trade in the United Kingdom Balance of Payments, 1952–1966', 4921; 'Work Stoppages in the United Kingdom, 1951–1964: A Quantitative Study', 6956; 'Work Stoppages in the United Kingdom 1965–1970: A Quantitative Study', 6957; 'On the Growth of the Employment of Non-manual Workers in the British Manufacturing Industries, 1948–1962', 7019

Galbraith, John S.: 'British War Aims in World War I: A Commentary on "Statesmanship"', 13370

Galdston, Iago: Progress in Medicine: A Critical Review of the Last Hundred Years, 21176; Behind the Sulfa Drugs: A Short History of Chemotherapy, 22287

Gale, Sir Richard Nelson: Call to Arms, 14761

Gale, Steven H.: Harold Pinter: An Annotated Bibliography, 25971

Gale, Walter Keith Vernon: Iron and Steel, 6584; The British Iron and Steel Industry: A Technical History, 6591; The Black Country Iron Industry: A Technical History, 6592

Gales, Kathleen: 'Twentieth Century Trends in the Work of Women in England and Wales', 7774; A Survey of Manpower Demand Forecasts for the Social Services, 8942; British Doctors at Home and Abroad, 20812; Dental Health and the Dental Services: An Assessment of Available Data, 22399

Gallacher, William: Revolt on the Clyde, 1413; The Chosen Few: A Sketch of Men and Events in Parliament, 1936–1940, 1414; The Rolling of the Thunder, 1415; Rise Like Lions, 1416; The Tyrant's Might is Passing, 1417; The Last Memoirs of William Gallacher, 1418; 'Shapurji Saklatvala 1874–1936', 1516

Gallagher, Donat: ed. The Essays, Articles and Reviews of Evelyn Waugh, 25861

Gallagher, Eric: Christians in Ulster 1968–1980, 2925, 12170; 'The Irish Churches 1968–1983', 12169

Gallagher, Frank: The Indivisible Island: The History of the Partition of Ireland, 2701; The Anglo-Irish Treaty, 2969

Gallagher, Janette: Conservation Reading List: A Select Reading List on the Conservation of Historic Parks and Gardens, with Special Reference to Great Britain, 20202

Gallagher, John: ed. The Decline, Revival and Fall of the British Empire, 12591

Gallagher, Margaret: Unequal Opportunities: The Case of Women and the Media, 7848

Gallagher, Nancy E.: 'Anglo-American Rivalry and the Establishment of a Medical Research Institute in Egypt, 1942–1948', 14404

Gallagher, Thomas: ed. Contemporary Irish Studies, 2660; 'Religion, Reaction and Revolt in Northern Ireland: The Impact of Paisleyism in Ulster', 12177; 'Protestant Extremism in Urban Scotland 1930–1939: Its Growth and Contraction', 12247; Glasgow: The Uneasy Peace: Religious Tension in Modern Scotland, 12248; Edinburgh Divided: John Cormack and No Popery in the 1930s, 12249

Galletly, Guy: The Big Bang: The Financial Revolution in the City of London and What it Means to You after the Crash, 4295

Gallico, Paul William: The Hurricane Story, 15850

Gallie, Duncan: In Search of the New Working Class: Automation and Social Integration within the Capitalist Enterprise, 9700

Gallie, Walter Bryce: An English School, 22986; A New University: A. D. Lindsay and the Keele Experiment, 23503

Gallo, Armonado: Genesis: Evolution of a Rock Band, 24516

Galloway, Allan Douglas: Faith in a Changing Culture, 11885

Galloway, Sir James: 'The War Physical Census', 21318

Gallup Political Index: 1960+, 233

Gallup, George H.: ed. The Gallup International Public Opinion Polls: Great Britain 1937–1975, 230

Gamba-Stonehouse, Virginia: Signals of War: The Falklands Conflict of 1982, 16079; The Falklands/Malvinas War: A Model for North-South Crisis Prevention, 16082

Gamble, Andrew: The Conservative Nation, 1622; Britain in Decline: Economic Policy, Political Strategy and the British State, 3415

Gamble, David P.: The Gambia, 12771

Gamble, William H.: History of Aeronautics: A Selected List of References to Material in the New York Public Library, 17495

Game, Chris: The Changing Politics of Local Government, 3145

Gammell, Christopher John: The Branch Line Age: The Minor Railways of the British Isles in Memoriam and Retrospect, 16786; L.M.S. Branch Lines, 16880

Gammie, Alexander: William Quarrier and the Story of the Orphan Homes of Scotland, 8185; In Glasgow's Underworld: The Social Work of the Salvation Army, 9122

Gammon, Max: Public and Private Provision for Medical Care in Great Britain, 21661; Health and Security: A Report on the Public Provision for Medical Care in Great Britain, 21662; U.K. N.H.S. Hospital Service: Manpower and Numbers of Beds Occupied Daily, 1965–1973: Preliminary Communication, 21834

Gammond, Peter: A Guide to Popular Music, 24468; ed. The Music goes Round and Round: A Cool Look at the Record Industry, 24576

Gamser, H. G.: 'Interunion Disputes in Great Britain and the United States', 6953

Gann, Lewis Henry: ed. Colonialism in Africa 1870–1960, 12676; ed. African Proconsuls: European Governors in Africa, 12705; A History of Northern Rhodesia: Early Days to 1953, 12775; A History of Southern Rhodesia to 1953, 12792

Gannon, Franklin Reid: The British Press and Germany, 1936–1939, 13675, 25115

Gannon, Jack: Catholic Political Culture and the Constitution of Ireland, 12168

Gans, H. J.: 'The Failure of Urban Renewal: A Critique and Some Proposals', 17780

Ganz, Gabriele: Government and Industry, 4976

Garbett, Cyril Forster: Church and State in England, 11626; Cyril Forster Garbett: Archbishop of York, 11696; In an Age of Revolution, 11697

Garbett, Mike: The Lancaster at War, 15842

Garbutt, Paul Elford: Naval Challenge: The Story of Britain's Post-War Fleet, 15236; London Transport and the Politicians, 16328; A Survey of Railway Development and Practice, 16749; How the Underground Works, 17003

Gard, Elizabeth: British Trade Unions, 6734

Garden History: Vol. 1, 1972–, 19879

Gardener, Edward P. M.: U.K. Banking Supervision: Evolution, Practice and Issues, 4453

Gardiner, Dorothy: English Girlhood at School, 23088

Gardiner, George: Margaret Thatcher: From Childhood to Leadership, 1048

Gardiner, Gerald: 'The Purpose of Criminal Punishment', 10334; (Foreword) The Homicide Act, 10790

Gardiner, J. S.: The Natural History of Wicken Fen, 26525

Gardiner, Leslie: The 'Royal Oak' Courts Martial, 15038, 15310; Bartholomew: 150 Years, 24941; One Hundred Years of Map-Making: The Story of W & A. K Johnston, 26710

Gardiner, Robert: A World of Peoples, 10945

Gardner, Avril: The God Approached: A Commentary on the Poems of William Empson, 25504

Gardner, Charles: The British Aircraft Corporation: A History, 17608

Gardner, D. E. M.: Susan Isaacs, 22923

Gardner, Geoffrey: 'The Measurement of Supervisory Methods', 5866

Gardner, George Lawrence Harter: English Catholicism in the Present Day, 11935

Gardner, Dame Helen: The Art of T .S. Eliot, 25496; The Composition of the Four Quartets, 25497

Gardner, Leslie: The Royal Oak Courts Martial, 15038

Gardner, M. J.: Atlas of Mortality from Selected Diseases in England and Wales, 22233

Gardner, Paul: Kingsley Amis, 25354

Gardner, Philip: The God Approached: A Commentary on the Poems of William Empson, 25504

Gardner, Richard Eric: The Flying Navy, 15419; British Service Helicopters: A Pictorial History, 17554; Plane Talk: A Report on British Aviation Policy, 17654

Gardner, Richard Newton: Sterling-Dollar Diplomacy, 4620, 14090; Sterling-Dollar Diplomacy in Current Perspective, 14091

Gardner, [Robert] Brian: Churchill in his Times: A Study in a Reputation, 1939–1945, 988; Allenby, 14500; The Big Push: A Portrait of the Battle of the Somme, 14583; The Public Schools: An Historical Survey, 23028

Gardner, Ward: Health at Work, 4141

Garigue, P.: 'Kinship and Organisation of Italians in London', 11388

Garland, David: Punishment and Welfare: A History of Penal Strategies, 10335, 10444; The Power to Punish, 10396

Garlick, Kenneth Benjamin: Garlick's Methodist Registry, 12064

Garner, Frank Harold: Modern British Farming Systems: An Introduction, 19556

Garner, John Francis: 'Racial Restrictive Covenants in England and the United States', 11173; Slum Clearance and Compensation, 20347; An Englishman's Home is his Castle?, 20348; The Public Control of Land, 20349

Garner, Lloyd P.: 'A Quarter Century of Anglo-Jewish Historiography', 12408

Garnett, David: War in the Air, September 1939 to May 1941, 15947

Garnett, Emmeline: Area Resource Centres: An Experiment, 22765

Garnett, John C.: 'BAOR and NATO', 16180

Garnett, Ronald George: A Century of Co-operative Insurance: The Co-operative Insurance Society, 1867–1967: A Business History, 4217

Garnham, Nicholas: The New Priesthood: British Television Today, 24905

Garrad, Jessie: Social Aspects of Clinical Medicine, 21958

Garran, Peter: 'Britain and Europe: Past, Present and Future', 14175

Garrard, John Adrian: ed. The Middle Class in Politics, 2078, 3374, 9735; 'Parallels of Protest: English Reactions to Jewish and Commonwealth Immigration', 11297

Garratt, Colin: The Last Days of British Steam Railways, 17030

Garratt, Geoffrey Theodore: Gibraltar and the Mediterranean, 12849

Garrett, Albert: A History of British Wood Engraving, 24091; British Wood Engraving of the Twentieth Century, 24092

Garrett, Alexander Adnett: History of the Society of Incorporated Accountants, 1885–1957, 4182

Garrett, Edward: ed. Letters from John Galsworthy 1900–1932, 25531

Garrett, John: The Management of Government, 787; Managing the Civil Service, 913

Garrett, Richard: The British Sailor, 15292

Garrison, Fielding Hudson: A Medical Bibliography: A Check-list of Texts Illustrating the History of the Medical Sciences, 21046; An Introduction to the History of Medicine, with Medical Chronology, Suggestions for Study and Bibliographic Data, 21199; Notes on the History of Military Medicine, 22114

Garside, Bernard: A Brief History of Hampton School, 1557–1957, 22995

Garside, Patricia L.: Metropolitan London: Politics and Urban Change 1837–1981, 3280, 18924

Garside, R. F.: 'Old Age Mental Disorders in Newcastle-upon-Tyne: A Factorial Study of Medical Psychiatric and Social Characteristics', 8624

Garside, William Redvers: 'The North-eastern Coalfield and the Export Trade, 1919–1939', 6338; The Durham Miners, 1919–1960, 6819; 'Juvenile Unemployment and Public Policy Between the Wars', 7001; The Measurement of Unemployment: Methods and Sources in Great Britain 1850–1979, 7023

Garstang, K.: 'Socialist Theories and Sir Raymond Unwin', 20377

Garvey, Jude: A Guide to the Transport Museums of Britain, 16370

Garvie, Alfred Ernest: Memories and Meanings of My Life, 12061

Garvin, Katharine: J.L. Garvin: A Memoir, 25239

Garvin, Tom: Nationalist Revolutionaries in Ireland 1858–1928, 2725

Gas Council: Annual Report and Accounts, 6397

Gascoigne, J.: New Periodical Titles, 1969–1973, 156

Gascoigne, [Arthur] Bamber: Twentieth Century Drama, 26182

Gascoyne-Cecil, [Edgar Algernon] Robert [Viscount Cecil]: All the Way, 1391; A Great Experiment, 1392

Gaselee, Stephen: The Foreign Office, 13327

Gaskell, T. F.: The Adventure of North Sea Oil, 7173

Gaskin, Maxwell: The Scottish Banks: A Modern Survey, 4405; The Economic Impact of North Sea Oil on Scotland, 6526

Gasson, Ruth: 'Occupations Chosen by the Sons of Farmers', 5891; 'Part-time Farmers in South East England', 19533; 'The Roles of Farm Women in England', 19595; The Role of Women in British Agriculture, 19596; Farm Families with other Gainful Activities, 19597; 'Part-time Farming: Strategy for Survival?', 19598

Gaston, P.: Thirty-Eighth Parallel: The British in Korea, 16132

Gate, Robert: Rugby League: An Illustrated History, 27052

Gater, Anthony: Thrusters and Sleepers: A Study in Industrial Management, 5439, 9790

Gates, Eleanor M.: End of the Affair: The Collapse of the Anglo-French Alliance, 1939–1940, 14265

Gates, John D.: The Astor Family, 1350

Gates, Lionel Chasemore: The History of the Tenth Foot, 1919–1950, 15693

Gateshill, Bernard: The Commission for Local Administration: A Preliminary Appraisal, 3253

Gath, Dennis: Child Guidance and Delinquency in a London Borough, 10627

Gatherer, Alexander: Management and the Health Services, 9249; ed. Management and the Health Service, 21636; Public Attitudes and Mental Health Education, 21788

Gathorne-Hardy, Jonathan: The Rise and Fall of the British Nanny, 8186; Doctors: The Lives and Work of G.P.'s, 21524; The Public School Phenomenon, 1597–1977, 23029

Gatland, Kenneth William: Manned Spacecraft, 17700

Gaudart, D. J.: Social Situation of Women in Europe: The Effects of the Opportunities of General and Vocational Training on the Social Position of Women, 7720

Gauldie, Enid: Cruel Habitations: A History of Working Class Housing, 1780–1918, 18747

Gault, Ian: Greenbelt Policies in Development Plans, 18809

Gaunt, William: British Painting from Hogarth's Day to Ours, 23978; A Concise History of English Painting, 23979

Gauvain, [Catherine Joan] Suzette: ed. Occupational Health: A Guide to Sources of Information, 4139

Gavin, Catherine Irvine: Britain and France: A Study of 20th Century Relations, 14236

Gavin, R. J.: Aden under British Rule 1839–1967, 13873

Gavin, Sir William: Ninety Years of Family Farming: The Study of Lord Rayleigh's and Strutt & Parkers Farms, 19541

Gavron, Hannah: The Captive Wife: Conflicts of Housebound Mothers, 7709

Gavston, Arthur: The Sinking of the Belgrano, 16113

Gay, John Dennis: The Geography of Religion in England, 11545

Gay, Oonagh: 'Prefabs: A Study in Policy Making', 18526

Gay, Philip William: The British Pottery Industry, 6626

Gayler, Joshua Leonard: A Sketch Map Economic History of Britain, 3519

Gazit, Mordecai: 'American and British Diplomacy and the Bernadotte Mission', 14357

Geach, Bob: The Rights of Children, 8187

Geach, Hugh: Justice for Children, 10634

Geary, Robert Charles: Religion and

Demographic Behaviour . . . 12155; Internal Migration in Ireland, 19311

Geary, Roger: Policing Industrial Disputes: 1893 to 1985, 10769

Gebbet, Leonard Frank: Land Use and Town and Country Planning, 18812

Geddes, Sir Eric Campbell: Mass Production: The Revolution which Changes Everything, 5861

Geddes, Keith: Broadcasting in Britain, 1922–1972, 24727

Geddes, L. A.: 'The Technological Background of Physiological Discovery: Ballistics and the Graphic Method', 20963

Geddes, Sir Patrick: Cities in Evolution: An Introduction to the Town Planning Movement and to the Study of Civics: With a New Introduction by Percy Johnson-Marshall, 20381

Geddes, Philip: Inside the Bank of England, 4489

Geen, A. C.: 'Educational Policy-Making in Cardiff, 1944–1970', 23629

Geertz, H.: 'Old Age in London and San Francisco: Some Families Compared', 8630

Geffen, Dennis Herbert: Public Health and Social Services, 22068

Gehring, Wes D.: Charlie Chaplin: A Bio-bibliography, 26300

Geiss, Immanuel: The Pan-African Movement, 11046

Gelatt, Roland: The Fabulous Phonograph: The Story of the Gramophone from Tin Foil to High Fidelity, 24574

Gelb, Alan: Worker Capitalism: The New Industrial Relations, 5829

Gelber, Harry Gregor: Australia, Britain and the EEC 1961 to 1963, 12637

Gelber, Lionel Morris: America in Britain's Place, 14006; The Alliance of Necessity: Britain's Crisis, the New Europe and American Interests, 14174

Gelfand, M. David: ed. Half a Century of Municipal Decline 1935–1985, 3130

Gelwick, Richard: The Way of Discovery: An Introduction to the Thought of Michael Polanyi, 26854

Gemmill, Paul Fleming: Britain's Search for Health: The First Decade of the National Health Service, 21565

General Council of British Shipping: Annual Report, 16468

General Introduction to the Victoria County History of England: 1970, 26742

General Practitioner and the Hospital Service: Report by a Joint Sub-committee of the Medical Hospital and Specialist Services, and the General Practitioners Services: Standing Advisory Committees, 21503

General Practitioners' Association: Abuse and Misuse: A Critical Problem in the Family Doctor Service: The Report of a G.P.A. Study Group, 21509

General Register Office Scotland: Occupational Mortality, 1969–1973, 7470

General Report of Northern Ireland Agriculture: 1942+, 19645

Geneste, M. E.: 'Britain, France and the Defence of Europe', 14235

Gennard, John: The Closed Shop in British Industry, 5836; 'Industrial Relations Theory: A Critical Review'; Financing Strikers, 6931

Gentleman, Hugh: Scotland's Travelling People: Problems and Solutions: A Report of the Study of a Minority Group within Scotland's Population, with Recommendations as to the Possible Solutions to these Problems, 11344

George, A. D.: 'The Manchester Motor Industry 1900–1938', 17409; 'The Manchester Motor Industry 1900–1938: Further Notes', 17410

George, A. Raymond: A History of the Methodist Church in Great Britain, 12066. 'The Changing Face of Methodism: 1. The Methodist Service Book', 12078

George, Cyril Oswald: British Budgets, 4902

George, Frank H.: Computers, Science and Society, 7096

George, J. T. A.: 'An Examination of the Work of Local Authority Child Welfare Clinics', 8188

George, Kenneth Desmond: The Welsh Economy, 2587; ed. The Welsh Economy, 3475; Industrial Organisation: Competition, Growth and Structural Change in Britain, 5749; 'Changes in British Industrial Concentration 1951–1958', 7233; 'The Changing Structure of Competitive Industry', 7234

George, Margaret: The Hollow Men: An Examination of British Foreign Policy between the Years 1933 and 1939, 13704

George, Mike: Developing the Socially Useful Economy, 3694

George, Vic[tor]: Social Security and Society, 4082, 8799, 9050; 'Stereotypes of Male and Female Roles and their Influence on People's attitudes to One Parent Families', 7871; Foster Care: Theory and Practice, 8189; Ideology and Social Welfare, 8797; Social Security: Beveridge and After, 9049; Motherless Families, 9942; 'The Assimilation of Cypriot Immigrants in London', 11389

George, W. L.: 'High Birth Rates and Low Lives', 21301

George, W.: 'A Practical Temperance Policy', 22179

George, William: My Brother and I, 1018

Georghallides, G. S.: 'The Management of Public Records under the British Colonial Administration in Cyprus', 12863

Georgiano, George Nicolas: ed. A History of Transport, 16190; ed. The Complete Encyclopaedia of Motor Cars 1885–1965, 17349; ed. A Source Book of Veteran Cars, 17350; ed. A Source Book of Vintage and Post-vintage Cars, 17351; ed. A History of Sports Cars, 17352; ed. A Source Book of Racing and Sports Cars, 17353; ed. The Encyclopaedia of Motor Sport, 17354; The Classic Rolls-Royce, 17451; The World's Commercial Vehicles 1830–1964: A Record of 134 Years of Vehicle Production, 17475; Trucks: An Illustrated History 1896–1920, 17476; A History of the London Taxi Cab, 17477; The London Taxi, 17478

Geraghty, Tony: Who Dares Wins: The Story of the Special Air Service, 1950–1980, 15723

Gerald, [James] Edward: The British Press under Government Economic Controls, 25040

Gerard, David E.: Alan Sillitoe: A Bibliography, 25798

Gerard, David: ed. Values and Social Change in Britain, 238; Charity and Change: Norms, Beliefs and Effectiveness—A Profile of the Voluntary Sector, 9225; Charities in Britain: Conservatism or Change?, 9226

Geraud, André, 'Rise and Fall of the Anglo-French Entente', 14224

Gerbert, P.: ed. 'La Candidature de la Grande Bretagne aux Communautés Européennes 1967–1968: Les Données de la Problème', 14172

Gernsheim, Helmut: Churchill: His Life in Photographs, 988

Gerrard, John: 'Architecture in Glasgow since World War One', 23919

Gershon, Karen: We Came as Children: A Collective Autobiography, 11306

Gervasi, Sean D.: 'Social Priorities and Economic Policy', 9054

Geyser, Otto: Watershed for South Africa: London, 1961, 12718

Ghana: Survey of the Gold Coast on the Eve of Independence, 12742

Ghose, Sisirkumar: Aldous Huxley: Cynical Salvationist, 25591

Ghosh, S. C.: 'Pressure and Privilege: The Manchester Chamber of Commerce and the Indian Problem, 1930–1934', 13146; 'Decision-Making and Power in the British Conservative Party: A Case Study of the Indian Problem, 1929–34', 13154

Gianakaris, C. J.: Peter Shaffer, 25983

Gibb, Mildred Ann: The Yorkshire Post: Two Centuries, 25163

Gibbens, Trevor Charles Noel: Shoplifting, 10226; Psychiatric Studies of Borstal Lads, 10529, 10572; ed. Cultural Factors in Delinquency, 10573; Medical Remands in the Criminal Court, 10574; 'Borstal Boys after 25 Years', 10673; 'The Misuse of Drugs', 10837; 'Prostitution', 10854

Gibberd, Frederick: Harlow: A Story of a New Town, 18195; The Evolution of British Town Planning, 18770

Gibbin, Leonard Douglas: The Music Trader's Guide to Works by Twentieth Century British Composers, 24277

Gibbon, Frederick P.: William A. Smith of the Boys' Brigade, 8511

Gibbon, Peter: The State in Northern Ireland, 1921–1971: Political Forces and Social Causes, 2787

Gibbons, Chester H.: Materials Testing Machines, 7075

Gibbs Smith, Charles Harvard: The Aeroplane: A Historical Survey of its Origins and Development, 17502; Aviation: An Historical Survey from its Origins to the End of World War Two, 17503; A Brief History of Flying, from Myth to Space Travel, 17504; A History of Flying, 17505; The Rebirth of European Aviation, 17506; Flight through the Ages: A Complete Illustrated Chronology from the Dreams of

Early History to the Age of Space Exploration, 17507

Gibbs, Charles Robert Vernon: British Passenger Liners of the Five Oceans: A Record of the British Passenger Lines and their Liners from 1838 to the Present Day, 16580

Gibbs, D. N.: 'The National Serviceman and Military Delinquency', 10167

Gibbs, Jack P.: 'Conceptions of Deviant Behaviour: The Old and the New', 10575; 'Crime, Unemployment and Status Integration', 10576

Gibbs, John Morel: Morel's of Cardiff: The History of a Family Shipping Firm, 16559

Gibbs, John Newton: Dutch Elm Disease Survey, 1971, 1972–1973, 19777

Gibbs, Mary Ann: The Years of the Nannies, 8190

Gibbs, Norman Henry: Grand Strategy, 14717

Gibbs, William Edward: The Fishing Industry, 19800

Gibson, A. H.: British Finance, 1914–1921, 4545

Gibson, Alan: The Social Education of the Adolescent, 8463

Gibson, Alexander George: The Radcliffe Infirmary, 21466

Gibson, Colin: 'Association Between Divorce and Social Class in England and Wales', 9453, 9975

Gibson, Evelyn: Robbery in London: An Enquiry, 10179; Murder, 1957 to 1968: A Home Office Statistical Division Report on Murder in England and Wales (with an annex by the Scottish Home and Health Department on Murder in Scotland), 10796

Gibson, Henry J. C.: Dundee Royal Infirmary 1798 to 1948, 21483

Gibson, I. F.: The Economic History of the Scottish Iron and Steel Industry, 6563

Gibson, John: 'In Search of an Explanation of Social Mobility', 9589; 'Biological Aspects of a High Socio-economic Group', 9593; 'Biological Aspects of a High Socio-economic Group II: IQ Components and Social Mobility', 9594; Great Doctors and Medical Scientists, 20845; The Development of Surgery, 21140

Gibson, John: The Newcastle United Story, 27083

Gibson, John B.: ed. Man in Urban Environments, 17924

Gibson, John Sibbald: The Thistle and the Crown: A History of the Scottish Office, 2481

Gibson, Langhorne: The Riddle of Jutland, 14651

Gibson, Mary Barnet: Unemployment Insurance in Great Britain, 4024

Gibson, Michael L.: Aviation in Northamptonshire: An Illustrated History, 17528

Gibson, N.: 'Economic Conditions and Policy in Northern Ireland', 5390

Gibson, R.: The Family Doctor: His Life and History, 9820

Gibson, Thomas: The Royal College of Physicians and Surgeons of Glasgow, 20802

Gibson, William Carleton: Creative Minds in Medicine: Scientific, Humanistic, and Cultural Contributions by Physicians, 20890; ed. British Contributions to Medical Science. (The Woodwood-Wellcome Symposium), 20891; 'Medical Pioneers in Aviation', 20950

Gibson-Jarvie, Robert: The City of London: A Financial and Commercial History, 4246; The London Metal Exchange: A Commodity Market, 4247

Giddens, Anthony: The Class Structure of the Advanced Societies, 9547; ed. Social Class and the Division of Labour: Essays in Honour of Ilya Neustadt, 9548; 'Elites in the British Class Structure', 9765; ed. The Sociology of Suicide: A Selection of Readings, 10809; ed. Elites and Power in British Society, 11686

Gielgud, Sir John: An Actor and his Time, 26047; Distinguished Company, 26047; Early Stages, 26047

Gielgud, Val: British Radio Drama 1922–1956, 24751; Years in a Mirror, 24752

Gifford, Denis: The British Film Catalogue, 1895–1970: A Guide to Entertainment Films, 24587; British Cinema: An Illustrated Guide, 24636

Gifford, Douglas: ed. Neil M. Gunn: The Man and the Writer, 25567

Gifford, John Liddle King: The Devaluation of the Pound, 4685

Gifford, Prosser: ed. The Transfer of Power in Africa: Decolonization 1940–1960, 12697

Gifford, Terry: Ted Hughes: A Critical Study, 25581

Gifford, Tony: Supergrasses: The Use of Accomplice Evidence in Northern Ireland: A Report, 2870

Giggs, J. A.: 'Factional Ecology and Factor Invariance: An Investigation', 19961

Gilbert, Alan D.: Churches and Churchgoers: Patterns of Church Growth in the British Isles since 1700, 11546; Religion and Society in Industrial England, 11562; The Making of Post-Christian Britain, 11563

Gilbert, Bentley Brinkerhoff: Britain since 1918, 286; 'Third Parties and Voters' Decisions: The Liberals and the General Election of 1945', 2290; 'The Liberals and the General Election of 1945: A Modest Rejoinder', 2292; The Evolution of National Insurance in Great Britain: The Origins of the Welfare State, 4038, 8988; British Social Policy 1914–1939, 8856

Gilbert, Christopher L.: The Development of British Econometrics 1945–85, 26579

Gilbert, Edmund William: Sir Halford Mackinder, 1861–1947: An Appreciation of his Life and Work, 1460, 26659; Brighton, Old Ocean's Bauble, 18094; University Towns, 18095; The University Town in England and West Germany: Marburg, Göttingen, Heidelberg and Tübingen, Viewed Comparatively with Oxford and Cambridge, 18096; British Pioneers in Geography, 26658

Gilbert, Felix: ed. The Diplomats, 1919–1939, 13330

Gilbert, Heather: As a Tale is Told: A Church of Scotland Parish 1913–54, 12233

Gilbert, J. B.: Disease and Destiny: A Bibliography of Medical References to the Famous, 21236

Gilbert, J. C.: 'British Investment and Unit Trusts since 1960', 4746

Gilbert, John Selwyn: Frederick Ashton: A Choreographer and his Ballets, 24224

Gilbert, Martin John: ed. A Century of Conflict, 1850–1950, 306, 14085; Winston Churchill: The Wilderness Years, 988; Churchill's Political Philosophy, 988; Churchill, 988; Churchill: A Photographic Portrait, 988; Lloyd George, 1018; ed. Plough My Own Furrow: The Story of Lord Allen of Hurtwood as told through his Writings and Correspondence, 1340; Britain and Germany between the Wars, 13700; The Appeasers, 13709; The Roots of Appeasement, 13712; Auschwitz and the Allies, 14701

Gilbert, Victor F.: Labour and Social History Theses: American, British and Irish University Theses and Dissertations in the Field of British and Irish Labour History, Presented between 1900 and 1978, 1660; Theses and Dissertations in Economic and Social History in Yorkshire Universities, 1920–1974, 3394; Women's Studies: A Bibliography of Dissertations 1870–1982, 7628; Immigrants, Minorities and Race Relations: A Bibliography of Theses and Dissertations Presented at British and Irish Universities, 1900–1981, 10887; 'Race and Labour in Britain: A Bibliography', 11525

Gilbert-Carter, H.: Glossary of the British Flora, 26559

Gilchrist, Sir Andrew: Bangkok: Top Secret, 14927; Cod Wars and How to Lose Them, 19830

Gilder, Lesley: Research Libraries and Collections in the United Kingdom, 96

Giles, Anthony Kent: ed. University of Reading, Agricultural Economics 1923–1973, 19558; The Farm Worker: His Training, Pay and Status, 19664, 19671

Giles, Frank Thomas Robertson: Sundry Times, 25241

Giles, Howard: Speech Style and Social Evaluation, 9549

Giles, John: The Ypres Salient, 14584; The Somme: Then and Now, 14585

Giles, Raymond H.: The West Indian Experience in British Schools: Multi-racial Education and Social Disadvantage in London, 23192

Giles-Sims, Jean: Wife Battering: A Systems Theory Approach, 9953

Gilg, Andrew W.: Countryside Planning: The First Three Decades, 1945–1976, 18814, 19102, 20198; The Countryside: Planning and Change, 18815, 19103

Gilham, John C.: Buses and Coaches 1945–1965, 17269

Gilkes, Anthony Newcombe: Independent Education: In Defence of Public Schools, 23013

Gill, Alec: Lost Trawlers of Hull: 900 Losses between 1835 and 1987, 16599

Gill, Arthur Eric Howton: Autobiography, 24016

Gill, Clifford Allchin: The Genesis of Epidemics and the Natural History of Disease: An Introduction to the Science of Epidemiology based upon the Study of Epidemics of Malaria, Influenza and Plague, 22355

Gill, Colin: Industrial Relations in the Chemical Industry, 5797, 6202

Gill, Conrad: A History of Birmingham, vol.2: Borough and City 1865–1938, 5141

Gill, Crispin: The Isles of Scilly, 19207; The Wreck of the Torrey Canyon, 20072

Gill, D. G.: 'Doctors, Patients and the State: Relationships and Decision-making', 21294

Gill, Deirdre Rockingham: Job Evaluation in Practice: A Survey of 213 Organisations in the U.K., 5780

Gill, Derek: Illegitimacy, Sexuality and the Status of Women, 7801

Gill, Evan Robertson: Bibliography of Eric Gill, 24015

Gill, John: 'One Approach to the Teaching of Industrial Relations', 5719

Gill, Owen: Whitegate: An Approved School in Transition, 10514; 'Residential Treatment for Young Offenders: The Boys' Perspectives', 10515; Luke Street: Housing Policy, Conflict and the Creation of the Delinquent Area, 18768

Gill, Robin: Theology and Social Structure, 11832

Gill, Roma: ed. William Empson: The Man and his Work, 25505

Gillard, David: Beryl Grey: A Biography, 24234

Gillard, Michael: Nothing to Declare: The Political Corruptions of John Poulson, 3186

Giller, Elizabeth: Justice for Children, 10634

Giller, Henry: Juvenile Delinquency: Trends and Perspectives, 10603; Justice for Children, 10634

Gillespie, Sarah C.: A Hundred Years of Progress: The Record of the Scottish Typographical Association, 1853–1952, 6885

Gillett, Arthur: One Million Volunteers: The Story of the Volunteer Youth Service, 8522

Gillett, Edward: A History of Hull, 18025

Gillett, John W.: Once upon a Hard Times: Life in the Village of Higher Cloughfield, 19192

Gillett, Mildrid: Kinson 1894–1931: A Social Survey as Recorded in the Minutes of the Kinson Parish Council, 19337

Gilliat, Mary: English Style in Interior Decoration, 24143

Gillies, Sir Harold Delf: Plastic Surgery of the Face, 21137; The Development and Scope of Plastic Surgery, 21138; The Principles and Art of Plastic Surgery, 21139

Gillies, Hunter: 'Murder in the West of Scotland', 10789

Gillies, John Douglas: Aviation in Scotland, 17530

Gilling-Smith, Gordon Dryden: The Complete Guide to Pensions and Superannuation, 4042

Gillingham, John: ed. Historical Atlas of Britain, 139

Gillingwater, David: Regional Planning and Social Change: A Responsive Approach, 5098; ed. The Regional Planning Process, 5099; Case Studies in Regional Economies, 5100

Gillion, Frederick Arthur: 'An Attempt towards Church Unity: Anglicans and Methodists in England Propose a First Step', 12308

Gillis, John R.: For Better, for Worse: British Marriages, 1600 to the Present, 9971

Gillman, Joseph Moses: 'An Evaluation of John Maynard Keynes', 26615

Gillman, Leni and Gillman, Peter: 'Collar the Lot': How Britain Interned and Expelled its Wartime Refugees, 15049; Alias David Bowie, 24511

Gillman, R. J. H.: Barclays Bank, 1926–1969: Some Recollections, 4492

Gillon, Stair A.: The K.O.S.B. in the Great War, 15577

Gilmore, Maeve: A World Away: A Memoir of Mervyn Peake, 25758

Gilmore, William C.: The Grenada Intervention: Analysis and Documentation, 13082

Gilmour, Andrew: An Eastern Cadet's Anecdotage, 12921

Gilmour, Sir Ian Hedworth John: The Body Politic, 618; Inside Right: A Study of Conservatism, 2196; Britain Can Work, 4638

Gilmour, John: British Botanists, 26548

Gilroy, Paul: 'Managing the "Under-Class": A Further Note on the Sociology of Race Relations in Britain', 11072

Giner, Salvador: Sociology, 8008; ed. Contemporary Europe: Class, Status and Power, 9546

Ginnings, Arthur T.: Arbitration: A Practical Guide, 4156, 5839

Ginns, Michael: Transport in Jersey: An Historical Survey of Public Transport Facilities by Rail and Road in the Island of Jersey 1788–1961, 16344

Ginsberg, Morris: On Justice in Society, 8786; 'Social Change', 9506; 'Enforcement of Morals', 10864

Ginsburg, Alan L.: 'The Determination of the Factors Affecting American and British Exports in the Inter-War and Post-War Periods', 3717

Gipps, Caroline: Testing Children: Standardized Testing in Local Education Authorities and Schools, 22786; Monitoring Children: An Evaluation of the Assessment of Performance Unit, 22787

Girdlestone, Gathorne Robert: 'The Care of Crippled Children', 8191; A Description of the National Scheme for the Welfare of Crippled Children, 8192; The Care and Cure of Crippled Children: The Scheme of the Central Committee for the Care of Cripples, 8193

Girouard, Mark: The Return to Camelot: Chivalry and the English Gentleman, 9916, 14444

Girtin, Thomas: The Mark of the Sword: A Narrative History of the Cutler's Company, 1189–1975, 6599

Girvin, Brian: ed. Politics and Society in Contemporary Ireland, 2996

Gish, Nancy K.: Hugh MacDiarmid: The Man and His Work, 25683

Gish, Oscar: 'Color and Skill: British Immigration 1955–1968', 11437; Doctor Migration and World Health: The Impact of the International Demand for Doctors on Health Services in Developing Countries, 21517; A Reappraisal of the Brain Drain, 21518; ed. Health Manpower and the Medical Auxiliary: Some Notes and an Annotated Bibliography, 21519; 'British Doctor Migration, 1962–67', 21543

Gittins, Charles: 'Primary Education in Wales', 23634

Gittins, Diana: Fair Sex: Family Size and Structure 1900–1939, 10051; The Family in Question, 10052

Gittins, J. W.: 'Conservation and Capacity: A Case Study of the Snowdonia National Park', 26964

Gittler, Joseph Bertram: ed. Review of Sociology, 10905; ed. Minority Groups, 10906

Gittus, Elizabeth: 'The Distribution of Social Defects in Liverpool', 18045; Flats, Families and the Under-Fives, 18740

Giuseppi, John: The Bank of England: A History from its Foundation in 1694, 4482

Gladden, Edgar Norman: Civil Service or Bureaucracy?, 885; British Public Service Administration, 886; A History of Public Administration, 887; 'An Old Hand Remembers: A Personal Account, 1932–1947', 932

Gladstone, Alan: ed. Employers' Associations and Industrial Relations: A Comparative Study, 5837

Gladstone, Erskine William: The Royal Navy, 15234; The Army, 15439; The Shropshire Yeomanry, 1795–1945: The Story of a Volunteer Cavalry Regiment, 15718

Gladstone, Francis J.: Charity, Law and Social Justice, 9227; The Politics of Planning, 17900

Gladwin, David Daniel Francis: The Canals of Britain, 16382; English Canals, 16392; The Canals of the Welsh Valleys and their Tramroads, 16396; British Waterways: An Ilustrated History, 16428

Gladwyn, Hubert Miles Gladwyn Jebb [Baron]: Memoirs, 13266

Glaister, Janet: County Town: A Civic Survey for the Planning of Worcester, 18120

Glamorgan—Glyncorrwg Community Development Project: Transport and the Younger Unemployed, 9293; State of the Community Report: Community Health and Welfare, 9294; Job Getting and Holding Capacities, 9295

Glaser, Barney Galland: Status Passage, 9545

Glaser, W. A.: Sheltered Employmentof the Disabled—An International Survey, 21914

Glasgow Academy: The First Hundred Years, 1846–1946. 23221

Glasgow Corporation Planning Department: The Springburn Study: Urban Renewal in a Regional Context, 18873; Central Area, 18874; Open Space and Recreation, 18875; Social and Community Facilities, 18876; Transportation, 18877

Glasgow Corporation Public Health Department: Report of the Medical Officer of Health: City of Glasgow, 22034

Glasgow Corporation Town Planning Exhibition, 1946: Your Glasgow: Its Future: An Exhibition Illustrating the Proposals contained in the First and Second Planning Reports Submitted by the City Engineer to the Highways and Planning Committee, 18872

Glasgow Corporation: Greater Glasgow Transportation Studies, 16336

Glasgow Postgraduate Medical Board: Current Achievements in Geriatrics, 21085

Glasgow University Media Group: War and Peace News, 16122; Bad News, 24922

Glasgow Women's Group: Uncharted Lives: Extracts from Scottish Women's Experiences, 1850 1982, 7742

Glasgow, George: MacDonald as Diplomatist: The Foreign Policy of the First Labour Government in Great Britain, 13550

Glasgow: Report on Aspects of Future Shopping Provision, 20486

Glass, Archibald: A History of the Greenock Provident Savings Bank, 1815–1976, 4346

Glass, David Victor: Population: Policies and Movements in Europe, 7359; The Trend and Pattern of Fertility in Great Britain: A Report on the Family Census of 1946, 7360; Population and Emigration, 7398; ed. Population in History: Essays in Historical Demography, 7399; ed. Population and Social Change, 7400; The Development of Population Statistics: A Collective Reprint of Materials Concerning the History of Census Taking and Vital Registration in England and Wales, 7401; 'Some Indications of Differences between Urban and Rural Mortality in England and Wales and Scotland', 7458; 'Family Planning Programmes and Action in Western Europe', 7505; 'The Application of Social Research', 7960; ed. Social Mobility in Britain, 9585; The Town and Changing Civilisation, 17927

Glass, Justine: The Earth Heals Everything: The Story of Biochemistry, 26473

Glass, Ruth: ed. The Social Background of a Plan: A Study of Middlesbrough, 9326; 'Household Structure and Housing Needs', 10025, 18673; Insider-outsiders: The Position of Minorities, 10938; Newcomers: The West Indians in London, 11248; 'London: Aspects of Change', 11359; London: Aspects of Change, 11444, 16326, 18357, 18932; 'The Evaluation of Planning: Some Sociological Considerations', 17769; 'Centre for Urban Studies', 17770; 'Urban Sociology in Great Britain', 18287, 18358; 'Urban Sociology', 18288; London's Housing Needs: Statements of Evidence to the Committee on Housing in Greater London, 18672; 'Housing in Cambden (sic)', 18725

Glassberg, Andrew D.: Representation and the Urban Community, 3305

Glasscock, Robin Edgar: ed. Belfast: The Origin and Growth of an Industrial City, 18166

Glasser, Otto: Physical Foundations of Radiology, 21125

Glasser, Ralph: The Net and the Quest: Patterns of Community and Housing: How they can Survive Progress, 9388; Leisure: Penalty or Prize?, 26924

Glassner, Martin Ira: 'The Foreign Relations of Jamaica and Trinidad and Tobago 1960–1965', 13051

Glasson, John: An Introduction to Regional Planning: Concepts, Theory and Practice, 5097, 18806

Glastonbury, Bryan: Managing People in the Personal Social Services, 8961; 'Community Perceptions and Personal Social Services', 9402; Homeless near a Thousand Homes: A Study of Families without Homes in South Wales and the West of England, 18512

Glatt, Max Meier: 'Alcoholism, Crime and Juvenile Delinquency', 10636; The Drug Scene in Great Britain, 10825, 22190; ed. Dependence: Current Problems and Issues, 10826; A Guide to Addiction and its Treatment, 10827; The Alcoholic and the Help he needs, 10878

Glazer, Nathan: ed. Ethnic Pluralism and Public Policy: Achieving Equality in the United States and Britain, 11082

Glees, Anthony: Exile Politics during the Second World War: The German Social Democrats in Britain, 15053; The Secrets of the Service: British Intelligence and Communist Subversion 1939–51, 16002

Gleeson, J.: They Feared No Evil: The Women Agents of Britain's Secret Armies 1939–1945, 15201

Glen, Sir Alexander Richard: Young Men in the Arctic: The Story of the Oxford University Expedition to Spitzbergen, 1933, 27207; Under the Pole Star: The Oxford University Arctic Expedition, 1935–36, 27208

Glen, Duncan: ed. Hugh MacDiarmid: A Critical Survey, 25682

Glenday, Nonita: Reluctant Revolutionaries: A Century of Head Mistresses, 1874–1974, 23093

Glendinning, Caroline: ed. Women and Poverty in Britain, 7723

Glendinning, Victoria: Elizabeth Bowen: Portrait of a Writer, 25405; Vita: The Life of Vita Sackville-West, 25790; Edith Sitwell: A Unicorn among Lions, 25804; Rebecca West: A Life, 25875

Glenn, D. Fereday: Roads, Rails and Ferries of the Solent Area, 1919–1969, 16334, 17155

Glenn, Louis: Charles W. S. Williams: A Checklist, 25877

Glennerster, Howard: National Assistance: Service or Charity?, 4080; Social Science Budgets and Social Policy: British and American Experience, 8951; Paying for Private Schools, 23026

Glenny, M. V.: 'The Anglo-Soviet Trade Agreement, March 1921', 4790

Glenton, George: The Last Chronicle of Bouverie Street, 25147

Glickman, David L.: 'The British Imperial Preference System', 3763

Glickman, Harvey: 'The Toryism of English Conservatism', 2193; The Problem of Internal Security in Great Britain 1948–1953, 10884

Glickman, M. J. A.: From Crime to Rehabilitation, 10246

Glorious Privilege: The History of The Scotsman, 25151

Gloag, John Edwards: The English Tradition in Design, 24111

Glover, A.: Dylan Thomas in Print: A Bibliographical History, 25828

Glover, Edward: The Roots of Crime, 10182

Glover, Edwin Maurice: The 70 Days: The Story of the Japanese Campaign in British Malaya, 15069

Glover, Elizabeth Reaveley: Probation and Re-education, 10473

Glover, Ernest Percival: The First Sixty Years, 1896–1956: The Newport High School for Boys, 23636

Glover, Frederick J.: 'Government Contracting, Competition and Growth in the Heavy Woollen Industry', 6467

Glover, Graham: British Locomotive Design, 1825–1960, 17053

Glover, Janet Reaveley: The Story of Scotland, 2438

Glubb, Sir John Bagot: Britain and the Arabs: A Study of Fifty Years, 1908–1958, 13809

Gluckmann, Herman May: Closed Systems and Open Minds: The Limits of Naivety in Social Anthropology, 10125

Glyn, Andrew: The British Economic Disaster, 3682; 'The Stock Market Valuation of British Companies and the Cost of Capital, 1955–1969', 4735

Glyn-Jones, Anne: Rural Recovery: Has it Begun? A Study of a Parish in North-West Devon, 1964–1978, 19074; Village into Town: A Study of Transition in South Devon, 19161

Glynn, John: Public Sector Financial Control and Accounting, 4771

Glynn, Prudence Loveday: In Fashion, 24161

Glynn, Sean: Inter-War Britain: A Social and Economic History, 3566, 7559; 'Unemployment in the Inter-war Period: A Multiple Problem', 6997

Godber, Sir George Edward: Change in Medicine, 21230, 21659; The Health Service: Past, Present and Future, 21658; Attainable Goals in Health, 21660

Godbolt, Jim: A History of Jazz in Britain, 1919–50, 24451

Goddard, John Burgess: ed. The Urban and Regional Transformation of Britain, 5122

Goddard, Stephen: ed. A Guide to Information Sources in the Geographical Sciences, 26623

Goddard, T. Russell: History of the Natural History Society of Northumberland, Durham and Newcastle-upon-Tyne, 1829–1929, 26534

Goddard, Ted: Pembrokeshire Shipwrecks, 16513

Goddard, Sir Victor: Skies to Dunkirk: A Personal Memoir, 15958

Godden, Geoffrey Arthur: English China, 6627; British Porcelain: An Illustrated Guide, 24131

Godfrey, H. R.: My Family Budget, 20427

Godfrey, J.: West Sussex County Council: The First Hundred Years, 3370

Godfrey, Richard: Printmaking in Britain: A General History from its Beginnings to the Present Day, 24089

Godley, Wynne: Local Government Finance and its Reform: A Critique of the Layfield Committee's Report, 4875

Godson, Vida: The University in an Urban Environment, 23304

Godwin's Concise Guide to Local Authorities in England and Wales: 1974, 3091

Godwin, George: Crime and Social Action, 10176

Godwin, Sir Harry: Cambridge and Clare, 23474, 26556

Goetschius, George W.: Working with Unattached Youth, 8469; Working with Community Groups: Using Community Development as a Method of Social Work, 9400

Goffee, Robert E.: 'The Butty System and the Kent Coalfield', 6339; The Entrepreneurial Middle Class, 9727

Gohn, Jack: Kingsley Amis: A Checklist, 25352

Goist, Park Dixon: 'Patrick Geddes and the City', 18289

Golant, W.: 'C. R. Attlee in the First and Second Labour Governments', 975; 'Mr. Attlee', 975; 'The Early Political Thought of C. R. Attlee', 975; 'The Emergence of C. R. Attlee as Leader of the Parliamentary Labour party in 1935', 975

Golby, John: The Monarchy and the British People 1760 to the Present, 439

Gold, John Robert and Gold, Margaret M.: The Crofting System: A Select Bibliography, 19285, 19620

Gold, Mark: Assault and Battery: What Factory Farming Means for Humans, 19704

Goldberg, Elsa[Else] Matilda[Mathilde]: 'Rising Eighteen in a London Suburb: Some Aspects of the Life and Health of Young Men', 8445; Helping the Aged: A Field Experiment in Social Work, 8600; Welfare in the Community: Talks on Social Work to Welfare Officers, 8717; Social Workers and their Workloads in Northern Ireland Welfare Departments, 8746; Social Work in General Practice, 21521; 'Hospital Work and Family: A Four-year Study of Young Mental Hospital Patients', 21834; 'Schizophrenia and Social Class', 21835

Goldberg, Mary: 'Confrontation Groups in a Girls' Approved School', 10500

Goldberg, Percy Selvin: The Manchester Congregation of British Jews 1857–1957, 11317, 12439

Goldberg, Walter H.: Mergers: Motives, Modes, Methods, 5547

Goldblot, Jim: All this and 10%, 24459

Goldenberg, Susan: The Thomson Empire: The First Fifty Years, 5507, 25102

Goldfarb, Amira: Workers' Participation in Management: Expectations and Experience, 6014

Goldie, Frederick: A Short History of the Episcopal Church in Scotland from the Reformation to the Present Time, 12265

Goldie, Grace Wyndham: Facing the Nation: Television and Politics 1936–1976, 24886

Goldie, Ismay: Housing and Slum Clearance in London, 18390

Goldie, M.: 'The Social Characteristics of Militant and Anti-militant Students', 9869

Golding, E. W.: Power Supplies, 7192

Golding, Lewis: Dictionary of Local Government in England and Wales, 3092

Golding, Peter: Images of Welfare: Press and Public Attitudes to Poverty, 9009

Golding, Rob: The Mini, 17441

Goldman, Aaron L.: 'Stephen King-Hall and the German Newsletter Controversy of 1939', 13676; 'Sir Robert Vansittart's Search for Italian Co-operation against Hitler, 1933–1936', 13785; 'Defence Regulation 18B: Emergency Internment of Aliens, and Political Dissenters in Great Britain during World War II', 15051

Goldman, Ronald: Angry Adolescents, 8470

Goldrick, Michael Kevin D'Arcy: The Administration of Transportation in Greater London, 16323

Goldring, Douglas: The Last Pre-Raphaelite: A Record of the Life and Writings of Ford Madox Ford, 25513

Goldring, Patrick: The Friend of the Family: The Work of Family Service Units, 10099

Goldsmith, A. O.: 'Challenges of Delinquency Casework Treatment', 10639

Goldsmith, Edward: ed. Can Britain Survive?, 19914

Goldsmith, John: ed. Stephen Spender Journals 1939–1983, 25821

Goldsmith, Margaret: The Trail of Opium, the Eleventh Plague, 22226; The Road to Penicillin: A History of Chemotherapy, 22288

Goldsmith, Michael: ed. New Research in Central-Local Relations, 3218; ed. The Middle Class in Politics, 9735

Goldstein, Dora S.: 'The Organizational Development of the British Historical Profession, 1884–1921', 26723

Goldstein, Harvey: Britain's Sixteen-Year-Olds: Preliminary Findings from the Third Follow-Up of the NCDS—1958 Cohort, 8286; Monitoring Children: An Evaluation of the Assessment of Performance Unit, 22787

Goldstein, Joseph: The Government of a British Trade Union, 6708

Goldstrom, J. M.: ed. Irish Population, Economy and Society: Essays in Honour of the Late K. H. Connell, 2649, 2795

Goldsworthy, David J.: Colonial Issues in British Politics, 1945–1961: From 'Colonial Development' to 'Wind of Change', 11015, 12568

Goldthorpe, John Ernest: An Introduction to Sociology, 7986

Goldthorpe, John Harry: 'Industrial Relations in Great Britain: A Critique of Reformism', 5769; 'Class, Status and Party in Modern Britain', 9445; 'Affluence and the British Class Structure', 9446; The Social Grading of Occupations: A New Approach and Scale, 9552; The Affluent Worker: Political Attitudes and Behaviour, 9627; 'The Affluent Worker and the Thesis of "Embourgoisement": Some Preliminary Research Findings', 9680

Gollancz, Sir Victor: ed. Betrayal of the Left, 1721; ed. The Making of Women: Oxford Essays, 7658; Our Threatened Values, 14201; In Darkest Germany, 14202; My Dear Timothy: An Autobiographical Letter to his Grandson, 24962

Gollin, Alfred Manuel: Proconsul in Politics: A Study of Lord Milner in Opposition and in Power, 1273

Gomersall, Alan: Aircraft Noise, 20152; Community Noise, 20153

Gomme, Andor: 'Publicity or Promise? The New Universities', 23405

Gonvertch, Peter: Unions and Economic Crisis: Britain, West Germany and Sweden, 6827

Gonzalez Arnao, Mariano: 'El Batallon Britanico en la Guerra Civil Espanola', 13992

Gooch, George Peabody: Under Six Reigns, 26798

Gooch, John: 'The Maurice Debate, 1918', 1813

Good, James: The Church of England and the Ecumenical Movement, 12344

Good, Robert: UDI: The International Politics of the Rhodesian Rebellion, 12805

Goodacre, Iris: Adoption Policy and Practice: A Study, 8194

Goodair, Christine M.: Current British Periodicals: A Bibliographical Guide, 159

Goodall, Brian: The Economics of Urban Areas, 5398, 20394; Aspects of Land Economics, 20264; National Forests and Recreational Opportunities, 26957

Goodall, Norman: 'Nathaniel Micklem', 12060; The Ecumenical Movement: What it is and What it Does, 12318; Ecumenical Progress: A Decade of Change in the Ecumenical Movement, 1961–1971, 12319; Second Fiddle: Recollections and Reflections, 12320; A History of the London Missionary Society, 1895–1945, 12360

Goodchild, Barry: 'Class Differences in Environmental Perception: An Exploratory Study', 9452

Goodchild, Peter: Conservation Reading List: A Select Reading List on the Conservation of Historic Parks and Gardens, with Special Reference to Great Britain, 20202

Goode, Charles Tony: The Railways of East Yorkshire, 16932

Goode, Royston Miles: Hire-purchase Law and Practice, 20492

Gooden, R. Y.: 'Modern English Silver-smithing', 7159

Goodenough, S.: Jam and Jerusalem: A History of the Women's Institution, 7654

Goodey, Charles: The First Hundred Years: The Story of Richards Shipbuilders, 16641

Goodfield, [Gwyneth] June: The Growth of Scientific Physiology: Physiological Method and the Mechanist-Vitalist Controversy, Illustrated by the Problems of Respiration and Animal Heat, 22319; The Fabric of the Heavens: The Development of Astronomy and Dynamics, 26390

Goodhart, Arthur Lehman: 'The Mysteries of the Kennedy Assassination and the English Press', 25120

Goodhart, C. B.: 'On the Incidence of Illegal Abortion', 7885

Goodhart, David: Eddie Shah and the Newspaper Revolution, 25106

Goodhart, Philip Carter: The 1922: The Story of the Conservative Backbenchers Parliamentary Committee, 1631; The Referendum, 2385; Full Hearted Consent: The Story of the Referendum Campaign and the Campaign for the Referendum, 2391; A Nation of Consumers, 5034; Fifty Ships that Saved the World: The Foundations of the Anglo-American Alliance, 14052

Goodin, Robert E.: Not Only the Poor: The Middle Classes and the Welfare State, 8993

Goodland, N. L.: 'Farm Workers—Past and Present', 9704

Goodman, Albert: The Lives of John Lennon, 24507

Goodman, Derick: Crime of Passion, 10225

Goodman, Gordon T.: ed. Ecology and the Industrial Society: A Symposium of the British Ecological Society, 19918

Goodman, John Francis Bradshaw: Shop Stewards in British Industry, 5711; Rule Making and Industrial Peace: Industrial Relations in the Footwear Industry, 5712; 'The British Universities' Industrial Relations Association: The First 35 Years', 5859; The Mond Legacy: A Family Saga, 6205; 'Les Grèves au Royaume-Uni: Statistiques et Tendances Récentes', 6962

Goodman, Nancy: Girl Offenders Aged Seventeen to Twenty Years, 7729; Studies of Women Offenders, 10875

Goodman, Neville Marriott: Wilson Jameson: Architect of National Health, 21267

Goodman, W. L.: The History of Wood-working Tools, 6187; Woodwork, 6188

Goodwin, Crauford David Wycliffe: A Decade of the Commonwealth, 1955–1964, 12584

Goodwin, Geoffrey Lawrence: Britain and the United Nations, 13538

Goodwin, Harold Sidney: William Temple's Political Legacy: A Critical Assessment, 11713

Goodwin, John Lonnen: Royal Shakespeare Theatre Company, 1960–1963, 26148; ed. Hall's Diaries: The Story of a Dramatic Battle, 26149; ed. British Theatre Design, 26254

Goodwin, Noel: Sir Geraint Evans: A Knight at the Opera, 24412; London Symphony: Portrait of an Orchestra, 1904–1954, 24543

Goodwin, R. M.: 'The Supply of Bank Money in England and Wales 1920–1938', 4653

Goodwin, Tim: Britain's National Theatre: The First Twenty Five Years, 26141

Goodwin, Trevor W.: ed. British Biochemistry Past and Present: Biochemical Society Symposium no.30, Held in London, December 1969, 26474; ed. History of the Biochemistry Society 1911–1986, 26475

Goody, John Rankine: Production and Reproduction: A Comparative Study of the Domestic Domain, 7421

Goold, J. Douglas: Peace without Promise: Britain and the Peace Conferences, 1919–1923, 13420; 'Lord Hardinge as Ambassador to France, and the Anglo-French Dilemma over Germany and the Near East, 1920–1922', 14244

Goorney, Howard: ed. Agit-Prop to Theatre Workshop: Political Playscripts 1930–1950, 26237; The Theatre Workshop Story, 26249

Goossens, Eugene; Overture and Beginners: A Musical Autobiography, 24347

Gopal, Sarvepalli: The Viceroyalty of Lord Irwin 1926–1931, 13141

Gordin, Ian R.: The Retirement Industry in the South West: A Survey of its Size, Distribution and Economic Aspects, 8614

Gordon, Andrew: Handley Page Victor, 15883

Gordon, Andrew Macdonald: Scottish Catholics and the Reformation, 1500–1956, 12275

Gordon, Anne Wolrige: Peter Howard: Life and Letters, 12400

Gordon, B.: One Hundred Years of Electricity, 1881–1981, 6392

Gordon, Cecil: 'The Age Distribution of an Industrial Group [Scottish Railwaymen]', 9657

Gordon, Colin: The Foundations of the University of Salford, 23578

Gordon, D.: 'Ten Points about the Crisis in the British Film Industry', 24693

Gordon, David: Newspaper Money: Fleet Street and the Search for the Affluent Reader, 25070

Gordon, David James: D. H. Lawrence as a Literary Critic, 25632

Gordon, Donald Craigie: The Moment of Power: Britain's Imperial Epoch, 12484

Gordon, E.: The Royal Scottish Academy of Painting, Sculpture and Architecture 1826–1976, 24085

Gordon, E. Olga M. Huntly: The Minister's Wife, 12229

Gordon, George Stuart: Mons and the Retreat: The Operations of the British Army in the Present War, 14586

Gordon, George: ed. Scottish Urban History, 2452, 18125, 18455; ed. Perspectives on the Scottish City, 18126; ed. Strathclyde: Changing Horizons, 18154; ed. Regional Cities in the U.K., 1890–1980, 18164

Gordon, Hampden Charles: The War Office, 828

Gordon, I. E.: 'Maternal Attitudes to Child Socialization: Some Social and National Differences', 8249

Gordon, Ian: 'Social Class and Political Attitudes: The Case of Labour Councillors', 1802; 'London at the Polls: A Review of the 1981 GLC Election and Analysis', 3300

Gordon, Keith V.: The King in Peace and War, 503

Gordon, Laurence Lee: Military Origins, 15549

Gordon, Lincoln: The Public Corporation in Great Britain, 4989

Gordon, Linda: 'The Politics of Birth Control, 1920–1940: The Impact of the Professionals', 20951

Gordon, Lyndall: Eliot's New Life, 25490

Gordon, Michael R.: 'Civil Servants, Politicians and Parties: Shortcomings in the British Policy Process', 905; Conflict and Consensus in Labour's Foreign Policy, 1914–1965, 13568

Gordon, Paul: Policing Scotland, 10772; Policing Immigration: Britain's Internal Controls, 11106; British Immigration Control: A Brief Guide, 11442; Racism and Discrimination in Britain: A Select Bibliography 1970–1983, 11523

Gordon, Peter: Curriculum Change in the Nineteenth and Twentieth Centuries, 22613; Selection for Secondary Education, 22780; ed. The Study of Education: A Collection of Inaugural Lectures, 22843; Philosophers as Educational Reformers: The Influence of Idealism on British Educational Thought and Practice, 23241

Gordon, Strathearn: Our Parliament, 566

Gordon, T. C.: The County of Stirling, The County of Clackmannan, 19229

Gordon, William: The Law of Housing in Scotland, 18460

Gordon-Walker, Patrick Chrestien, [Baron Gordon-Walker]: The Cabinet: Political Authority in Britain, 720

Gore, Elizabeth: The Better Fight: The Story of Dame Lilian Barker, 10528

Gore, John Francis: King George V: A Personal Memoir, 473

Gore, Walter: Ballet Rambert, 1926–1946, 24239

Gore-Booth, [Lord]: With Great Truth and Respect, 13267

Gorer, Geoffrey: The Danger of Equality and Other Essays, 2135; Death, Grief and Mourning in Contemporary Britain, 10110; Sex and Marriage in England Today: A Study of the Views and Experience of the Under 45's, 10101

Gorer, Richard: The Development of Garden Flowers, 19898

Gorham, Maurice Anthony Coneys: Sound and Fury, 24818; Broadcasting and Television Since 1900, 24844

Gorny, Joseph: The British Labour Movement and Zionism 1917–1948, 13561, 14283

Gorodetsky, Gabriel: The Precarious Truce: Anglo-Soviet Relations, 1924–1927, 13934; Stafford Cripps' Mission to Moscow 1940–1942, 1157, 13959; 'The Hess Affair and Anglo-Soviet Relations on the Eve of Barbarossa', 13960; 'Churchill's Warning to Stalin: A Reappraisal', 13961

Gorst, Anthony [Tony]: ed. Post-war Britain 1945–64: Themes and Perspectives, 425, 14392, 24773; 'Suez 1956: A Consumer's Guide to Papers at the Public Record Office', 14387; 'Suez 1956: Strategy and the Diplomatic Process', 14389

Gorst, J. M.: The Future of the Village, 18955

Gortner, Harold F.: Administration in the Public Sector, 9253

Gosden, Peter Henry John Heather: The Evolution of a Profession: A Study of the Contribution of Teachers' Associations to the Development of School Teaching as a Professional Occupation, 9847, 22713; ed. How they were Taught: An Anthology of

Contemporary Accounts of Learning and Teaching in England, 1800–1950, 22684, 22845; The Development of Educational Administration in England and Wales, 22788; The Development of an Education Service: The West Riding 1889–1974, 23234; ed. Studies in the History of a University, 1874–1974, to Commemorate the Centenary of the University of Leeds, 23511; Education in the Second World War: A Study in Policy and Administration, 23717

Gosling, John: The Shame of a City: An Inquiry into the Vice of London, 10846

Gospel, Howard F.: 'The Mond-Turner Talks 1927–1933: A Study in Industrial Co-operation', 5590

Goss, Anthony: British Industry and Town Planning, 5051, 17782; Homes, Towns and Traffic, 17127, 17783; The Architect and Town Planning: A Report Presented to the Council of the RIBA, 17781

Goss, Sue: Councils in Conflict: The Rise and Fall of the Municipal Left, 3230; Local Labour and Local Government: A Study of Interests, Politics and Policy in Southwark 1919 to 1982, 3315

Gossage, Sir Ernest Leslie: The Royal Air Force, 15793

Gostin, Larry O.: A Human Condition: The Mental Health Act from 1959–1975: Observations, Analysis and Proposals for Reform, 21880

Gotch, John Alfred: The Growth and Work of the Royal Institute of British Architects, 1834–1934, 23867

Gothard, W. P.: 'The Brightest and the Best': A Study of Graduates and their Occupational Choices in the 1970s, 5974

Goto, S.: 'Daiichiji Taisen to Igirisu Kaigun Gyofuteiki Sengyokai no Shihon Chikuseki o Chusin ni', 16473

Gott, Richard Willoughby: The Appeasers, 13709

Gottesman, H. H.: 'Students and the Art Schools', 22458

Gotthold, D. W. and Gotthold, J. J.: Indian Ocean, 13195

Gottlieb, David: Adolescent Behaviour in Urban Areas: A Bibliographic Review and Discussion of the Literature, 8409; The Emergence of Youth Societies: A Cross Cultural Approach, 8432

Gottlieb, Wolfram Wilhelm: Studies in Secret Diplomacy during the First World War, 13391

Gotts, G. L.: Party Politics in Local Government in South Wales, with Special Reference to Cardiff, Glamorgan and Pontypridd, 2570

Gottschalk, Andrew William: British Industrial Relations: An Annotated Bibliography, 5567; Productivity Bargaining: A Case Study and Simulation Exercise, 5708; 'Proposals for Change in the British System of Industrial Relations—An Evaluation', 5733

Goudie, Andrew Shaw: The Nature of the Environment: An Advanced Physical Geography, 20240.; Vaughan Cornish:

Geographer: With a Bibliography of his Published Works', 26662

Goudie, James: Councils and the Housing Finance Act, 18544

Gough, Sir Hubert de la Poer: The Fifth Army, 14601; The March Retreat, 14602

Gough, T. J.: The Economics of Building Societies, 4385

Gough, Terry: The Southern in Kent and Sussex, 16918

Gould, A.: Masters of Caricature: From Hogarth and Gillray to Scarfe and Levine, 24106

Gould, Sir Alfred Pearce: Sir Alfred Pearce Gould, 12031

Gould, David: The London and Birmingham Railway Fifty Years On, 16968

Gould, Donald: The Black and White Medical Show: How Doctors Serve and Fail their Customers, 9821

Gould, G.: A Charter for the Disabled: The Chronically Sick and Disabled Persons Act, 1970, 21923

Gould, J. D.: 'Landscape and the Machine: A Comment', 20305

Gould, Robert: Canals in Derbyshire: A Bibliography, 16422

Gould, [Samuel] Julius: ed. Penguin Survey of the Social Sciences, 7933; ed. Penguin Social Sciences Survey, 1968, 7934; Dictionary of the Social Sciences, 7935; Leeds Jewry: Its Historical and Social Structure . . . With an Introduction by Julius Gould, 11315; ed. Jewish Life in Modern Britain: Papers and Proceedings of a Conference . . . Held on . . . 2nd April 1962, 11305, 12423

Gould, Stephen Jay: 'D'Arcy Thompson and the Science of Form', 20952

Gould, Tony: Stories from the Dole Queue, 9690; Insider Outsider: The Life and Times of Colin MacInnes, 25686

Gould, William T. S.: ed. The Resources of Merseyside, 18052

Goulden, P. D.: Environmental Pollution Analysis, 19987

Goulding, James: R.A.F. Bomber Command and its Aircraft 1936–1940, 15009 Camouflage and Markings: R.A.F. Fighter Command, Northern Europe, 1936–1945, 15815

Gouldon, Mark: Mark my Words! The Memoirs of a Journalist/Publisher, 25242

Gourlay, Arthur Bellyse: A History of Sherborne School, 23076

Gourlay, Logan: The Beaverbrook Years, 1078; ed. Beaverbrook I Knew, 1079

Gourvish, Terence Richard: Norfolk Beers from English Barley: A History of Steward and Patteson, 1793–1963, 6163, 20746; British Railways, 1948–1973: A Business History, 16788

Govan Area Resource Centre: Resources for Community Action: Final Report of Govan Area Resource Centre, 9431

Government Publications 1954–1985, 180

Government Publications: Monthly and Consolidated Lists: 1936–1954, 179

Gowen, Robert Joseph: 'Great Britain and the Twenty One Demands of 1915: Co-operation Versus Effacement', 13624

Gower, L. C. B.: 'The Profession and Practice of Law in England and America', 9815

Gowing, Christopher: British Studio Ceramics in the 20th Century, 24132

Gowing, Margaret M.: The British War Economy, 3754; 'The Organisation of Manpower in Britain during the Second World War', 5929; Civil Industry and Trade, 7257

Goyder, Jane: Environmental Groups in Politics, 20245

Grace, D. R.: Ransomes of Ipswich: A History of the Firm and Guide to its Records, 6373

Gracey, H.: Urban Sociology and Planning: Sociology of Planning and Urban Growth, 17850

Grad, J.: The Mentally Handicapped and Their Families: A Social Survey, 21838

Grady, F. J.: 'The Exclusion of Catholics from the Lord Chancellorship, 1673–1954', 11945

Grady, Henry F.: British War Finance, 1914–1919, 3751

Grady, John: British Banking 1960–1985, 4449

Grafftey-Smith, Sir Laurence Baton: Bright Levant, 13268

Grafton Green, Brigid: Milk for the Millions, 20664

Grafton, Peter: Men of the Great Western, 16862

Graham, Allan Barnes: Social Problems: Are our Disabled Sailors and Soldiers to be Properly Provided for by the State?, 6993

Graham, Desmond Francis: Keith Douglas, 1920–1944: A Biography, 25477

Graham, Dominick: Fire-Power: British Army Weapons and Theories of War, 1904–1945, 15482

Graham, George: 'The Formation of the Medical and Surgical Professional Units in the London Teaching Hospitals', 20953, 22466

Graham, Gerald Sandford: Tides of Empire, 12591; Britain and Canada, 12647

Graham, Godfrey Michael: The Fish Gate, 19802

Graham, Harvey: Eternal Eve, 21091; Surgeons All, 21150

Graham, James Anson: ed. The Manchester Grammar School, 1515–1965, 22998

Graham, John Geoffrey: British History, 1914 to the Present Day, 340

Graham, John W.: Conscription and Conscience: A History 1916–1919, 13456

Graham, John W.: Seventeen Stations to Dingle: The Liverpool Overhead Railway Remembered, 16958; The Line beneath the Liners: 100 Years of Mersey Railway Sights and Sounds, 17023

Graham, Keith: John Austin: A Critique of Ordinary Language Philosophy, 26844

Graham, R. J.: ed. Acts of the Convocations of Canterbury and York, 1921–1970, 11687

Graham, Robert A.: 'Vatican Radio between London and Berlin, 1940–41', 14113

Graham, Stephen: Part of the Wonderful Scene: Autobiography, 25544

Graham-Dixon, Sue: Never Darken My Door: Working for Single Parents and their Children 1918–1978: National Council for One Parent Families, 8195, 9155

Grainger, T. H.: *ed.* A Guide to the History of Bacteriology, 22346

Gram, Harvey: 'Joan Robinson's Economics in Retrospect', 26620

Graml, Hermann: *ed.* Sommer 1939: Die Grossmächte und der Europäische Krieg, 13762

Grangemouth/Falkirk Regional Survey and Plan: 2 vols, 5292

Granit, Ragnar: Charles Scott Sherrington: An Appraisal, 26460

Gransden, Karl Watts: E. M. Forster, 25525; Angus Wilson, 25881

Grant, Alexander Thomas Kingdom: A Study of the Capital Market in Britain from 1919 to 1936, 4255, 4647; The Machinery of Finance and the Management of Sterling, 4710

Grant, Alistair: Henry Moore: Catalogue of Graphic Work 1931–1979, 24094

Grant, Sir Allen John: Steel and Ships: The History of John Brown's, 16630

Grant, Bernard: To the Four Corners: The Memoirs of a News Photographer, 25302

Grant, Bruce: The Crisis of Loyalty: A Study of Australian Foreign Policy, 12618

Grant, Cedric H.: The Making of Modern Belize: Politics, Society and British Colonialism in Central America, 13030

Grant, Charles: The Black Watch, 15571; The Coldstream Guards, 15607

Grant, Christina Phelps: The Syrian Desert: Caravans, Travel and Exploration, 27230

Grant, Colin: Hospital Management, 21398

Grant, Douglas: The Thin Blue Line: A History of the City of Glasgow Police, 10763

Grant, G. L.: The Standard Catalogue of Provincial Banks and Banknotes, 4408

Grant, Hubert Brian: Marriage, Separation and Divorce, 10004

Grant, I.: National Council of Women of Great Britain: The First Sixty Years, 1895–1955, 7651

Grant, Ian: The City at War, 15164

Grant, Isabel Frances: The Economic History of Scotland, 5239

Grant, James Shaw: Highland Villages, 19247

Grant, Jeanne Valerie: Personnel Administration and Industrial Relations, 5710

Grant, John Webster: Free Churchmanship in England, 1870–1940, with Special Reference to Congregationalism, 12003

Grant, John: The Pipes of War: A Record of the Achievements of Pipers of Scottish and Overseas Regiments during the War 1914–18, 24396

Grant, John: The Politics of Urban Transport Planning, 16305

Grant, Marcus: *ed.* Alcoholism: New Knowledge and New Responses, 22156

Grant, Maurice Harold: A Dictionary of British Etchers, 24096; A Dictionary of British Sculpture from the XIIIth to the XXth century, 24177

Grant, Neil: The Easter Rising, Dublin 1916: The Irish Rebel against British Rule, 2742

Grant, Nigel Duncan Cameron: Patterns of Education in the British Isles, 22866

Grant, R. P.: 'National Biomedical Research Agencies: A Comparative Study of Fifteen Countries', 20955

Grant, Roderick: The Great Canal, 16412

Grant, Ronald Melville: Industrial Relations, 5731

Grant, William Russell: Principles of Rehabilitation, 10435

Grant, Wyn P.: 'Business Interests and the British Conservative Party', 1655; Pressure Groups: Politics and Democracy in Britain, 2075; 'Welsh and Scottish Nationalism', 2422; 'The Politics of the Green Pound, 1974–1979', 4719; 'The Confederation of British Industries', 5488; 'The Politics of the C.B.I.: 1974 and After', 5489; The Confederation of British Industries, 5490; Government and the Chemical Industry: A Comparative Study of Britain and West Germany, 6227; 'Representation of Retail Interests in Britain', 6637

Grantham, J. T.: 'Hugh Dalton and the International Post-War Settlement: Labour Party Foreign Policy Formulation, 1943–1944', 13569; 'British Labour and the Hague "Congress of Europe": National Sovereignty Defended', 14133

Granville, Wilfred: Inshore Heroes: The Story of H.M. Motor Launches in Two World Wars, 15401

Granville-Barker, Harley: A National Theatre, 26134

Granzow, Brigitte: A Mirror of Nazism: British Opinion and the Emergence of Hitler, 1929–1933, 13674, 25117

Grassam, Peter Bates: The Voice of the Consumer: Some Aspects of the Relations between Electricity Boards and their Consumers, 20444

Grattan, Hartley C.: The South-West Pacific: A Modern History, 12876

Graubard, Mark: Circulation and Respiration: The Evolution of an Idea, 22327

Graubard, Stephen Richards: British Labour and the Russian Revolution, 1917–1924, 13917

Graveney, Thomas William: The Heart of Cricket, 27107

Graves, Charles Larcom: Post-Victorian Music, 24285; The Cochran Story. A Biography of Sir Charles Blake Cochran, Kt, 26009

Graves, Charles: The Home Guard of Britain, 15146

Graves, John: The Red Dragon: The Story of the Welsh Fusiliers, 1919–1945, 15755

Graves, John Tiarks Ranke: Policy and Progress in Secondary Education, 1902–1942, 22683

Graves, Norman John: *ed.* New Movements in the Study and Teaching of Geography, 26653

Graves, Robert: The Long Week-end: A Social History of Great Britain, 1918–1939, 7557; Goodbye to All That, 14478

Graveson, Ronald Harry: 'The Aims and Methods of Legal Education', 22432

Gray, Adrian: The London to Brighton Line 1841–1977, 16966

Gray, Cecil: Peter Warlock: A Memoir of Philip Heseltine, 24389

Gray, Daniel Hale: Manpower Planning: An Approach to the Problem, 5934

Gray, Donald: Earth and Altar. The Evolution of the Parish Communion in the Church of England to 1945, 11620

Gray, Duncan: The Youth Training Scheme: The First Three Years, 8548; Nottingham through 500 Years: A History of Town Government, 18065

Gray, Edwyn: The Devil's Device: The Story of Robert Whitehead, Inventor of the Torpedo, 7077; A Damned un-English Weapon: The Story of British Submarine Warfare 1914–1918, 15370

Gray, F.: 'Selection and Allocation in Council Housing', 18441

Gray, Frances: John Arden, 25936; Noel Coward, 25956

Gray, Fred: Owner-Occupation in Britain, 18454; *ed.* Crawley, Old Town, New Town, 19010

Gray, Hamish: Universal or Selective Social Benefits?, 8934; The Cost of Council Housing, 18428; Choice in Housing, 18445

Gray, Howard Levy: War-Time Control of Industry: The Experience of England, 3742

Gray, James Douglas Allan: History of the Royal Medical Society, 1737–1937, 20794; The Central Middlesex Hospital, 21457

Gray, James: *ed.* W.R., The Man and His Work: A Brief Account of the Life and Work of William Robinson, M.A., B.Sc., D.D., 1888–1963, 12120

Gray, John: Reconstructions of Secondary Education: Theory, Myth and Practice since the War, 22930

Gray, John Anthony: London's Country Buses, 17306

Gray, Judith: Women and Medicine, 21262

Gray, Martin: The Penguin Book of the Bicycle, 17170

Gray, P. G. C.: Children in Care and the Recruitment of Foster Parents, 8196; U.K. Social Survey: A Survey of Residential Caravan Life: An Enquiry, 18555; Adult Dental Health in England and Wales in 1968, 22400

Gray, Paul: Coventry Corporation Transport, 17304

Gray, Percy G.: Private Motoring in England and Wales: Report [dealing] with a Quarterly Series of Surveys carried out for the Ministry of Transport from October 1961 to January 1964, 17373

Gray, Philip Howard: 'Historical Notes on the Aerial Predator Reaction and the Tinbergen Hypothesis', 20954

Gray, Richard A.: Serial Bibliographies in the Humanities and Social Sciences, 13

Gray, Robert: Edward VIII: The Man we Lost: A Pictorial Study, 484

Gray, S. M.: Report on the Supply of Petroleum and Petroleum Products to Rhodesia, 12811

Gray, T. Cecil: 'History of Anaesthesia in Liverpool', 20956

Gray, Tony: The Orange Order, 2940

Gray-Jones, Arthur: A History of Ebbw Vale, 18158

Grayling, Christopher: Just Another Star?

Anglo-American Relations since 1945, 14088

Grayshon, Matthew Clifford: Initial Bibliography of Immigration and Race, 11520

Grayson, Arnold John: Forest Planning, 19748

Great Britain Health and Safety Commission: Genetic Manipulation: Regulations and Guidance Notes, 22246

Great Britain, Ordnance Survey: The History of Triangulation of Great Britain, 1935–1962, 26707

Great Teachers of Surgery in the Past: A Collection of Articles which have appeared in the British Journal of Surgery over the Period January, 1964 to January, 1968, 20889

Greater London Council: Greater London Transportation Survey, 16321; Greater London Transport: A Plan for Action 1976/77, 16322; Thamesmead Annual Report, 18203; Thamesmead: Housing a Balanced Community, 18204; London: Facts and Figures, 18343; Housing Department, 18674; Department of Planning and Transportation, 18675; Traffic Noise, 20149; (Department of Transportation and Development) Ecology and Nature Conservation in London, 20229

Greaves, Charles Desmond: The Easter Rising in Song and Ballad, 2745; The Irish Crisis, 2845; The Life and Times of James Connolly, 3030

Greaves, Harold Richard Goring: The British Constitution, 571; 'The Last Revolution and the Next, 1930–1970', 589; 'British Central Government, 1914–1956', 784; The Civil Service in the Changing State, 845

Greaves, J. P.: 'Trends in Food Consumption in the United Kingdom', 20552

Greaves, Joan: National Parks and Access to the Countryside and Coast: Trends in Research, 1964–1968, 26956

Greaves, Mary: Work and Disability: Some Aspects of the Employment of Disabled Persons in Great Britain, 21913

Greaves, Robert William: 'Church and Chapel: The Historical Background of Home Reunion, 1559–1952', 12304

Grebenik, E.: The Trend and Pattern of Fertility in Great Britain: A Report on the Family Census of 1946, 7360

Green Party: Green Politics, 1864; Will They Thank Us for This?, 1865; General Election Manifesto, 1866

Green, Andrew Wilson: Bibliography on British Legal Education, 22435

Green, Arthur John: Devolution and Public Finance: Stormont from 1921 to 1972, 2813

Green, Brigid Grafton: Hampstead Garden Suburb, 1907–1977, 18193

Green, Bryan Sidney Richard: An Introduction to Sociology, 7978; 'Youth and Work: Problems and Perspectives', 8440

Green, Bryn: Countryside Conservation: The Protection and Management of Amenity Ecosystems, 20205

Green, Charles Alfred Howell: The Setting of the Constitution of the Church in Wales, 12286

Green, D. E.: ed. Perspectives in Biochemistry: Thirty one Essays presented to Sir F. G. Hopkins, 26455

Green, D. G.: Power and Party in an English City: An Account of Single Party Rule, 3335

Green, Daniel: The Politics of Food, 20611

Green, David Alfred George: Rough Grazings in the Hills and Uplands of Wales: Productivity and Potential, 19642; Resource Productivity in Hill and Upland Farming Systems in Wales, 19643

Green, Dennis William: Flying Boats, 15424; Famous Fighters of the Second World War, 15867; Famous Bombers of the Second World War, 15868; Aircraft of the Battle of Britain, 15869

Green, Edwin: The British Insurance Business, 1547–1970: An Introduction and Guide to Historical Records in the United Kingdom, 4205; Banking: An Illustrated History, 4401; Debtors to their Profession: A History of the Institute of Banking, 4402; The Making of a Modern Banking Group: A History of the Midland Banking Group since 1900, 4496; Midland: 150 Years of Banking Business, 4497; A Business of National Importance: The Royal Mail Shipping Group, 1902–1937, 16537; From Cape to Cape: The History of the Lyle Shipping Company, 16552

Green, Francis: The Restructuring of the United Kingdom Economy, 3706

Green, Frank Henry Winn: 'Recent Changes in Land Use and Treatment', 26681

Green, Frederick Ernest: A History of the English Agricultural Labourer, 1870–1920, 19660

Green, Geoffrey: History of the Football Association, 27060; There's only one United: The Official Centenary History of Manchester United 1878–1978, 27082

Green, Howard: The British Army in the First World War, 14462

Green, Hugh: Contraception through the Ages, 21068

Green, Hughie: Opportunity Knocked, 26314

Green, Ivan: The Book of the Cinque Ports: Their Origin, Development and Decline, 16680

Green, J. R.: Medical History for Students, 21214

Green, Jeffry P.: '"Beef Pie with a Suet Crust": A Black Childhood in Wigan, 1906–1920', 11482

Green, Sir John Little: Political Pills and Farming Ills: An Exposure of the Lloyd George Rural Land Plan, 19056, 19445

Green, Jonathan: Days in My Life: Voices from the English Underground 1961–1971, 25203

Green, Kenneth R.: Old Cottingham Remembered, 19185

Green, Leslie S.: 'The Territorial Sea and the Anglo-Icelandic Dispute', 19832

Green, Marjorie Helen: Malnutrition among Schoolchildren, 20526; Nutrition and Local Government: What your Local Authority can do, 20527

Green, Martin: Children of the Sun: A

Narrative of 'Decadence' in England after 1918, 23769

Green, Maurice Berkeley: Pesticides: Boon or Bane?, 20109

Green, Oliver: The London Underground: An Illustrated History, 17006

Green, P.: 'Drymen, Village Growth and Community Problems', 19249

Green, Peter Morris: Kenneth Grahame, 1859–1932: A Study of His Life, Work and Times, 25545

Green, Reg: A Race Apart: The History of the Grand National, 27129

Green, Robert: R. Hutchinson: The Man and His Books, 25584

Green, Roger Lancelyn: C. S. Lewis: A Biography, 25662

Green, Sally: Prehistorian: A Biography of V. Gordon Childe, 26788

Green, Shirley: The Curious History of Contraception, 21069

Green, Stephen: 'Professional/Bureaucratic Conflict: The Case of the Medical Profession in the National Health Service', 21346

Green, Steven: '"Black Suicide": A Report of 25 English Cases and Controls', 10807

Green, Vivian Hubert Howard: The Universities, 23440; The Commonwealth of Lincoln College, 1427–1977, 23568

Green, William: Aircraft of the Battle of Britain, 14808

Greenaway, D.: ed. Public Choice, Public Finance and Public Policy, 6147

Greenaway, J. R.: The Dynamics of Administrative Reform, 782

Greenbaum, Sidney: ed. The English Language Today, 23811

Greenberg, Bradley S.: 'British Children and Television Violence', 8197

Greenberger, Allen Jay: The British Image of India: A Study in the Literature of Imperialism, 1880–1960, 13117

Greene, Graham: A Sort of Life: An Autobiography, 25565; Ways of Escape, 25566

Greene, Gwendolen Maud: ed. Letters from Baron Friedrich von Hügel to a Niece, 11985

Greene, Sir Hugh Carleton: What Price Culture? An Examination of Broadcasting Finance, 24785; The Third Floor Front: A View of Broadcasting in the Sixties, 24823

Greene, Jack P.: The Blackwell Dictionary of Historians, 26731

Greene, Owen: London after the Bomb: What a Nuclear Attack Really Means, 15142

Greene, T. R.: 'The English Catholic Press and the Second Spanish Republic, 1931–36', 25114

Greengrass, H. W.: The Discount Market in London: Its Organisation and Recent Development, 4260

Greenhalgh, Christine A.: Occupational Status and Mobility of Men and Women, 5923

Greenhill, Basil Jack: The Merchant Schooners 1870–1940, 16597

Greenhill, Richard: Employee Remuneration and Profit Sharing, 6039

Greenland, C.: Mental Illness and Civil Liberty: A Study of Mental Health Review Tribunals in England and Wales, 21820

Greenleaf, Horace: Britain's Big Four: The Story of the London, Midland and Scottish, London and North Eastern, Great Western, and Southern Railways, 16837

Greenleaf, W. H.: 'The Character of Modern British Politics', 1590; Oakeshott's Philosophical Politics, 2090; The British Political Tradition, 2081; 'Laski and British Socialism', 2117; 'The Character of Modern British Conservatism', 2197

Greenwall, Harry James: Northcliffe: Napoleon of Fleet Street, 25096

Greenway, Ambrose: A Century of North Sea Passenger Steamers, 16592

Greenway, D. E.: ed. Handbook of British Chronology, 69

Greenwood, Charles: A Plan for Redevelopment [. . . of the City of Chester], 18853

Greenwood, George Arthur: England To-day: A Social Study, 7553; 'The Era of the Child: "A New Mind and a New Earth in a Single Generation"', 8198

Greenwood, J. R.: 'Promoting Working Class Candidatures in the Conservative Party: The Limits of Central Office Power', 1650

Greenwood, John A., and Seear, Nancy, Baroness: Some Problems in the Implementation of an Equal Pay Policy, 7814

Greenwood, Major: An Inquiry into the Prevalence and Aetiology of Tuberculosis among Industrial Workers, 4105; The Incidence of Industrial Accidents upon Individuals with Special Reference to Multiple Accidents, 4106; Sickness Absence and Labour Wastage, 4107; Industrial Pneumoconiosis, with Special Reference to Dust-Pthisis, 4108; The Health of Industrial Workers, 4109; 'The Fertility of the English Middle Classes: A Statistical Study', 7475; 'Deaths by Violence, 1837–1937', 10291; Some British Pioneers of Social Medicine (Heath Clark Lectures 1946), 20885; Authority in Medicine: Old and New, the Linacre Lecture 1943, 20886; Epidemics and Crowd Diseases: An Introduction to the Study of Epidemiology, 20887; et al. Experimental Epidemiology, 20888

Greenwood, Royston: Patterns of Management in Local Government, 3238; In Pursuit of Corporate Rationality: Organisational Developments in the Post-Reorganisation Period, 3239; Corporate Planning in English Local Government: An Analysis with Readings 1967–72, 3241; 'Changing Patterns of Budgeting in English Local Government', 3277

Greenwood, Sean: 'Bevin, the Ruhr and the Division of Germany: August 1945/December 1946', 14198

Greenwood, Victoria: Abortion on Demand, 7884

Greer, Germaine: The Female Eunuch, 7860; Sex and Destiny: The Politics of Human Fertility, 7861

Greer, Hardy: U.K. Report on Confidential Enquiries into Maternal Deaths in Northern Ireland 1960–1963, 7452

Greer, J. I. 'A Socio-Political Opinion Profile of Clergymen in Northern Ireland', 12165

Greer, P. Eugene: Road versus Rail: Documents on the History of Public Transport in Northern Ireland 1921–1948, 16343

Greer, Rita: Building Societies, 4366; The Good Nutrients Guide: The Complete Handbook of Vitamins, Minerals and other Nutrients, 20567

Greer, Rupert: Building Societies, 4366

Greeves, Ivan S.: London Docks 1800–1980: A Civil Engineering History, 16697

Greg, A. R.: British Honduras, 13028

Gregg, Pauline: A Social and Economic History of Britain 1760–1972, 329, 3504, 8997

Gregory, Alison M.: 'Some Factors Affecting the Career Choice and Career Perceptions of Sixth Form School Leavers', 5896

Gregory, Barry: British Airborne Troops, 1940–1945, 15010

Gregory, C. J.: To the Alps of Chinese Tibet: An Account of a Journey of Exploration up to and among the Snow-Clad Mountains of the Tibetan Frontier, 27192

Gregory, Denis: ed. Work Organization: Swedish Experience and British Context, 5792

Gregory, Derek: Monetary and Financial Policy, 4665

Gregory, Frank: Crisis in Procurement: A Case Study of the TSR-2, 15888

Gregory, Ian Gabriel: ed. In Memory of Burlington Street: an Appreciation of the Manchester University Unions, 1861–1957, 23541

Gregory, J.: 'Social Justice', 8761

Gregory, J. E.: The Westminster Bank through a Century, 4504

Gregory, John Duncan: On the Edge of Diplomacy: Rambles and Reflections, 1902–1928, 13269

Gregory, John Walter: The Story of the Road from the Beginning to the Present Day, 17099; To the Alps of Chinese Tibet: An Account of a Journey of Exploration up to and among the Snow-Clad Mountains of the Tibetan Frontier, 27192

Gregory, K. J.: Atlas of Drought in Britain, 1975–76, 20104

Gregory, Peter: Deafness and Public Responsibility: The Provision of Hearing Aids, 21941

Gregory, Peter: Telephones for the Elderly, 8608; Lifeline Telephone Service for the Elderly: An Account of a Pilot Project in Hull, 8609; Our Polluted Homes, 19981

Gregory, Roy: The Price of Amenity: Five Studies in Conservation and Government, 20226

Gregory, Theodore Emmanuel Guggenheim: ed. Select Statutes, Documents and Reports Relating to British Banking, 1832–1928, 4397

Greig, James William: 'On the Guardianship, Maintenance and Education of Infants', 8199; 'Training of the Schoolgirl in Infant Care', 8200

Greig, Michael: Tourism and Regional Development, 26942; The Economic Impact of Tourist Spending in Skye, 26943

Grenatstein, J. L.: Canada since 1867: A Bibliographical Guide, 12640

Grenfell, David Rhys: Coal, 6282

Grenfell, Joyce: Joyce Grenfell Requests the Pleasure, 26048; An Invisible Friendship. An Exchange of Letters, 26049

Grenfell, Russell: The Bismarck Episode, 15035; Main Fleet to Singapore, 15068; The Men who Defend us, 15289

Grenfell, Sir Wilfred: A Labrador Doctor, 20867

Grenville, Wilfred: The RNVR, 15323

Gresswell, Peter: The Environment: An Alphabetical Handbook, 19906

Gretton, John: Transport U.K, 16269

Gretton, John: William Tyndale: Collapse of a School or a System, 23161

Gretton, Sir Peter: Former Naval Person: Winston Churchill and the Royal Navy, 988; 'The Nyon Conference: The Naval Aspect', 13795

Gretton, Richard Henry: A Modern History of the English People, 1910–1922, 352

Greutzner, A.: The Dictionary of British Artists 1880–1940, 23932

Greve, John: 'Housing Policies and Prospects', 18690; Comparative Social Administration, 9234; London's Homeless, 18509; and Greve, Stella: Homelessness in London, 18510

Greve, W. W.:Fitzwilliam College, Cambridge 1869–1969: Its History as the Non-Collegiate Institution of the University and its Beginnings as an Independent College, 23475

Grew, Benjamin Dixon: Prisoner Governor, 10378

Grey, Alexander: Urban Fares Policy, 16306

Grey, C. G.: Sea-flyers, 15857

Grey, Charles Grey: A History of the Air Ministry, 830

Grey, Edward, Viscount Grey of Fallodon: Thoughts on Public Life, 1205; Twenty Five Years 1892–1916, 1206

Grey, Eleanor: A Survey of Adoption in Great Britain, 8201

Grey, Jeffrey: The Commonwealth Armies and the Korean War: An Alliance Study, 16134

Greystoke, A. L.: Take-overs and Mergers, 5545

Grieb, Kenneth J.: ed. Research Guide to Central America and the Caribbean, 12990

Grier, Lynda: 'The Evolution of Secondary Education in England', 22927; The Life of Winifred Mercier, 23343; Achievement in Education: the Work of Michael Ernest Sadler, 1885–1935, 23344

Grierson, Flora: The Story of Woodstock Gloves, 6415

Grierson, Mary: Donald Francis Tovey: A Biography Based on Letters, 24537

Grieve, Mary: Millions made my Story, 25243

Grieve, Robert: [Edinburgh] The City and the Region, 5285, 18127

Grieve, W. Grant: Tunnellers: The Story of the Tunnelling Companies, Royal Engineers during the World War, 15629

Grieves, Keith: The Politics of Manpower 1914–1918, 5928

Grieves, R. L.: Dumbarton's Trams and Buses, 17222

Griff, Catherine: Directors of Industry: The British Corporate Network 1904–1976, 5454, 9787

Griffin, A.: A Brief Guide to the Sources for the Study of Burma in the India Office Records, 13200

Griffin, Alan Ramsay: Coal Mining, 6310; The British Coalmining Industry: Retrospect and Prospect, 6315; 'On the Writing of Miners' Trade Union History' 6319; Mining in the East Midlands, 1550–1947, 6328; The Miners of Nottinghamshire, 1914–1944: A History of the Nottinghamshire Miners' Unions, 6898

Griffin, John Barret: History of Past and Present Motor Vehicle Transport over 58 Years, 17461

Griffin, K. B.: 'A Note on Wages, Prices and Unemployment', 6996

Griffin, Penny: ed. St. Hugh's: One Hundred Years of Women's Education in Oxford, 23573

Griffin, S.: A Series of Progress Reports from the Research Team Studying the Reorganisation of the National Health Service on Humberside, 1972–75, 21621

Griffith, Arthur: The Resurrection of Hungary: A Parallel for Ireland, with Appendices on Pitt's Policy and Sinn Fein, 3058

Griffith, Edward F.: Doctors by Themselves: An Anthology, 20852

Griffith, Hubert Freeling: R.A.F. in Russia, 15946

Griffith, John Aneurin Grey: Parliamentary Scrutiny of Government Bills, 648; Central Departments and Local Authorities, 3225; Coloured Immigrants in Britain, 11396; 'Administrative Structure of the Hospital Service', 21486

Griffith, John R.: Hinges of Administration: A Survey of the Characteristics of Hospital Administrative and Clerical Staff, 21392

Griffith, [Llewelyn] Wyn: The British Civil Service, 1854–1954, 847; ed. A Celt Looks at the World, 12284

Griffith, M.: 'A Geographical Study of Mortality in an Urban Area', 7459

Griffith, Stephen: Down Stream: Failure in the Grammar School, 22983

Griffiths, Alun: Secondary School Reorganisation in England and Wales, 22963

Griffiths, Brian: Inflation: The Price of Prosperity, 4008; 'Resource Efficiency, Monetary Policy and the Reform of the U.K. Banking System, 4633; 'The Development of Restrictive Practices in the U.K. Monetary System, 4634; 'Two Monetary Enquiries in Great Britain: The Macmillan Report of 1931 and the Radcliffe Committee of 1959', 4635; Monetarism in the United Kingdom, 4636

Griffiths, Ernest S.: The Modern Development of City Government in the United Kingdom and the United States, 3113

Griffiths, Hugh: Report of the Inquiry into the Collapse of Flats at Ronan Point, Canning Town: Presented to the Ministry of Housing and Local Government, 18693

Griffiths, I. L.: 'The New Welsh Anthracite Industry', 6340

Griffiths, James: Pages from Memory, 1207

Griffiths, John: The Book of English International Rugby 1871–1982, 27035

Griffiths, Paul: New Sounds: New Personalities: British Composers of the 1980s, 24292

Griffiths, Paul: Peter Maxwell Davies, 24322

Griffiths, Sir Percival Joseph: Empire into Commonwealth, 12482; The British in India, 13119; The British Impact on India, 13120

Griffiths, Peter: A Question of Colour, 10953

Griffiths, Ralph A.: The Oxford Illustrated History of the British Monarchy, 427; ed. Welsh Society and Nationhood: Historical Essays Presented to Glanmor Williams, 2556

Griffiths, Richard: Fellow Travellers of the Right: British Enthusiasts for Nazi Germany 1933–1939, 2027

Griffiths, Robert: S. O. Davies: A Socialist Faith, 1401

Grigg, David: English Agriculture: An Historical Perspective, 19419

Grigg, Edward, Lord Altrincham: Kenya's Opportunity: Memories, Hopes and Ideas, 12824

Grigg, John: Lloyd George: From Peace to War, 1912–1916, 1018; 'Aftermath of Empire: Britain and India since Independence', 13186; 1943: The Victory that Never Was, 14923

Grigg, Mary: The White Question, 10959

Grigg, Sir Percy James: Prejudice and Judgement, 1420

Griggs, Clive: The Trades Union Congress and the Struggle for Education 1868–1925, 22921

Grigson, Geoffrey Edward Harvey: English Drawing from Samuel Cooper to Gwen John, 3988; A Master of our Time: A Study of Wyndham Lewis, 25671; A Dictionary of English Plant Names, 26564

Grimble, Ian: ed. The Future of the Highlands, 5297, 19255

Grime, Eric Keith: Recent Developments in the Transport Network and the Growth of Population in South East Buckinghamshire, 16349

Grimond, Jo, [Lord]: Memoirs, 1421; A Personal Manifesto, 1422; The Referendum, 2388; The Common Welfare, 8806; 'Beyond Robbins', 23408

Grimshaw, P. N.: 'Britain's Second Generation New Towns', 18228

Grinling, Charles Herbert: The History of the Great Northern Railway 1843–1922, 16845

Grinnell-Milne, Duncan William: Wind in the Wires, 14995

Gripaios, Hector: Tramp Shipping, 16494

Grisewood, Freddie: My Story of the BBC, 24723

Grisewood, Harman Joseph Gerard: One Thing at a Time: An Autobiography, 24771, 24819

Grizzard, Nigel: Jews in an Inner London Borough: A Study of the Jewish Population of Hackney Based on the 1971 Census, 11320

Grmek, M. D.: On Ageing and Old Age: Basic Problems and Historic Aspects of Gerontology and Geriatrics, 21083

Groom, Arthur John Richard: ed. The Commonwealth in the 1980s, 12526; ed. The Management of Britain's External Relations, 13360

Gross, Gerald: ed. Publishers on Publishing, 24929

Gross, Miriam: ed. The World of George Orwell, 25747

Gross, Richard Edmund: ed. British Secondary Education: Overview and Appraisal, 22951

Grossman, Herschel I.: 'The Cyclical Pattern of Unemployment Wage Inflation', 3899; 'Macroeconomic Effects of Productive Public Expenditure', 4765

Group RAF: A Complete History, 1936–1945, 15938

Grove, Sir George: Grove's Dictionary of Music and Musicians, 24255

Grove, Jack William: Central Administration in Britain, 712; Government and Industry in Great Britain, 6071

Grove, Richard: The Future of Forestry: The Urgent Need for a New Policy, 19758

Grover, George Walter Montague: A Short History of the Royal Marines, 15411

Grover, H. W.: 'Reflections on Early X-ray Engineering', 7161

Grover, R. F.: New Zealand, 12668

Groves, Charles Pelham: The Planting of Christianity in Africa, 12370

Groves, Charles Richard: The Marketing of Milk and Milk Products in the U.K.: A Review and Assessment, 20663

Groves, D.: Labour of Love: Women, Work and Caring, 9150

Groves, Ernest R.: 'The Urban Complex', 17741

Groves, F. P.: Nottingham City Transport, 17312

Groves, R.: Economic and Social Change in the West Midlands, 5228

Groves, Reg[inald]: The Balham Group: How British Trotskyism began, 1984; Conrad Noel and the Thaxted Movement: An Adventure in Christian Socialism, 11834; Sharpen the Sickle!: The History of the Farmworkers' Union, 19663

Grubb, Sir Kenneth: Crypts of Power: An Autobiography, 11784

Grubbé, E. H.: X-ray Treatment: Its Origin, Birth and Early History, 21168

Grubel, Herbert G.: 'The Reduction of the Brain Drain: Problems and Policies', 7309

Gruen, Victor: The Heart of Our Cities: The Urban Crisis: Diagnosis and Cure, 17786

Grumbridge, Jack Lovis: Marketing Management in Air Transport, 17643

Grunbaum, Werner F.: 'The British Security Program 1948–1958', 16003

Grundy, Fred: The New Public Health: An Introduction to Personal Health and the

Welfare Services for Health Visitors, Social Workers and Midwives, 22072

Gruner, W. D.: 'Friedenssicherung und Politisch-soziales System: Grossbritannien auf der Pariser Friedenskonferenzen 1919', 13421

Grunewald, Donald: 'The Anglo-Guatemalan Dispute over the Colony of Belize (British Honduras)', 13023

Grunfeld, Judith: Shefford: The Story of a Jewish School Community in Evacuation, 1939–1945, 11327, 15161

Grunhut, Max: 'Progress in Criminal Statistics: Comments on Criminal Statistics, England and Wales, 1953', 10195; Penal Reform, 10555; Juvenile Offenders Before the Courts, 10556

Grusky, Oscar: 'Career Patterns and Characteristics of British Naval Officers', 15287

Grygier, Tadeusz: ed. Criminology in Transition: Essays in Honour of Hermann Mannheim, 10175

Grylls, Rosalie Glynn: Queen's College, 1848–1948, 23531

Guardian, The: 1986+, 171; The Story of the Guardian, 25140

Guasparri, Giancarlo: Per un Servizio Sanitario Nazionale: Il 'National Health Service', 21585

Gubbay, Jon: Economy and Class Structure, 9550

Gubbay, Susan: A Coastal Directory for Marine Nature Conservation, 20215

Gudgin, Graham: Industrial Location Processes and Regional Employment Growth, 5096

Guedalla, Philip: Mr. Churchill: A Portrait, 988; ed. Slings and Arrows: Sayings Chosen from the Speeches of the Rt. Hon. D. Lloyd George, 1031; Middle East, 1940–1942: A Study in Air Power, 15945

Guerard, Albert Joseph: Robert Bridges, 25412

Guernsey Society: The Guernsey Farmhouse: A Survey, 18977

Guest, David E.: Worker Participation, 6020

Guest, Ivor: 'The Post-War Contribution to the History of British Ballet', 24213

Guichard, K. M.: British Etchers, 1850–1940, 24097

Guichard, Louis: The Naval Blockade, 1914–1918, 14606

Guide to Government and other Libraries and Research Bureaux, 248

Guide to Records in the Leeward Islands, 13057

Guide to the Institute of Agricultural History and Museum of English Rural Life, 19378

Guiget, Jean: Virginia Woolf and her Works, 25891

Guildford, Ronald: The Education of Slow Learning Children, 8379

Guinn, Paul: British Strategy and Politics, 1914–1918, 13364

Guinness, Sir Alec: Blessings in Disguise: An Autobiography, 26050

Gulbenkian: Educational Discussion 1965: 'Higher Education for the Professions', 22428

Gull, Edward Manico: British Economic Interests in the Far East, 4809, 13578

Gullet, Sir Henry Somer: ed. Photographic Record of the War: Reproductions of Pictures taken by the Australian Official Photographers, 14616

Gullick, J. M.: Malaya, 12906

Gulliver, Doris: Dame Agnes Weston, 22579

Gulvin, G.: The Scottish Hosiery and Knitwear Industry 1680–1980, 6243

Gulvin, K. R.: Kent Home Guard: A History, 15149

Gumbel, Walter: The Iron and Steel Act, 1949, With General Introduction and Annotations, 6551

Gumbley, Walter: 'The English Dominicans from 1555 to 1950', 11961; Obituary Notices of the English Dominicans, 1555–1952, 11980

Gummer, Dorothy: 'Ballet and the Dance: British Publications, 1955–1968', 24206

Gummer, John Selwyn: When the Coloured People Come, 11480; The Chavasse Twins, 11729

Gundry, Dudley William: 'The Church, the Universities and Theological Studies', 11898; 'University Theology in a Technological Age', 11899

Gundry, Elizabeth: A Foot in the Door: An Exposé of High Pressure Sales Methods, 20487

Gungwu, Wang: ed. Malaysia: A Survey, 12908

Gunn, L. A.: 'Politicians and Officials: Who is Answerable?', 907

Gunn, Neil Miller: Whisky and Scotland: A Practical and Spiritual Survey, 20727; The Atom of Delight, 25569

Gunning, Hugh: Borderers in Battle, 15575

Gunston, Bill: Early Supersonic Fighters of the West, 15870; Bombers of the West, 15871; The Plane Makers, 17590

Gunstone, John: Pentecostal Anglicans, 12134

Gunter, Barrie: Television Coverage of the 1983 General Election: Audiences, Appreciation and Public Opinion, 24901; 'Television Coverage of the 1984 European Parliamentary Election', 24902

Gunther, Albert E.: William Carmichael McIntosh MD, FRS of St Andrews, 1838–1931: A Pioneer of Marine Biology, 26510

Gunzburg, Herbert Charles: Social Competence and Mental Handicap: An Introduction to Social Education, 21791; ed. Experiments in the Rehabilitation of the Mentally Handicapped, 21792

Günzl, Kurt: British Musical Theatre, 24482

Guppy, A.: Children's Clothes 1939–1970: The Advent of Fashion, 24173

Gupta, R. L.: Conflict and Harmony: Indo-British Relations: A New Perspective, 13188

Gupta, S.: 'Input and Output Trends in British Manufacturing Industry, 1948–1954', 7232

Gurney, Christabel: The South African Connection: Western Investment in Apartheid, 12717

Gurney, John: The R.101, 17534

Gusfield, Joseph R.: ed. Protest, Reform and

Revolt: A Reader in Social Movements, 7597; Community: A Critical Response, 9381

Guthrie, Douglas James: A History of Oto-laryngology, 21106; A History of Medicine, 21196; The Royal Edinburgh Hospital for Sick Children 1860–1960, 21473

Guthrie, John: A History of Marine Engineering, 16502

Guthrie, Sir Tyrone: A Life in the Theatre, 26117

Gutman, David: The Lennon Companion: Twenty-Five Years of Comment, 24502

Guttery, David Reginald: The Queen's Own Worcestershire Hussars, 1922–1956, 15742

Guttsman, Wilhelm Leo: The English Ruling Class, 9750; The British Political Elite, 9751; 'Social Stratification and Political Elite', 9752

Guy's Hospital Gazette: Special Number in Commemoration of the Bicentenary of the Hospital and the Centenary of the Medical School, 1725–1925, 21442

Guy, Clifford M.: Retail Location and Retail Planning in Britain, 6655

Gwenault, Paul Herbert: The Control of Monopoly in the United Kingdom, 4968

Gwilliam, Kenneth Mason: Transport and Public Policy, 16219; Economics and Transport Policy, 16220; A Pilot Study of the Haven Ports of Harwich, Felixstowe and Ipswich, 16684; 'Regulation of Air Transport', 17652

Gwyer, J. M. A.: June 1941–August 1942, 14721

Gwyn, William B.: British Progress and Decline, 3502

Gwynn, Denis Rolleston: The Life of John Redmond, 1512, 3014; The Irish Free State, 1922–1927, 2680; The History of Partition, 1912–1925, 2681; The Life and Death of Roger Casement, 3018; A Hundred Years of Catholic Emancipation, 1829–1929, 11936

Gwynn, J. B.: 'Some Economic Aspects of Immigration', 11401

Gwynn, Stephen Lucius: Redmond's Last Years, 1513, 3015; ed. The Letters and Friendships of Sir Cecil Spring Rice: A Record, 13309

Gwynne, G. V.: A Life Apart: A Pilot Study of Residential Institutions for the Physically Handicapped and the Young Chronic Sick, 21903

Gwynne-Jones, Alun, [Lord Chalfont]: et al. Disarmament: Nuclear Swords or Unilateral Ploughshares, 13543

Gyford, John: National Parties and Local Politics, 3144; The Changing Politics of Local Government, 3145; Local Politics in Britain, 3152; 'The Development of Party Politics in the Local Authority Associations', 3194

H.M. Inspector of Schools: Aspects of Secondary Education in England, 22779; Primary Education in England, 23148

H.M.S.O.: Index to Chairmen of Committees: 1982+, 190; General Index to Parliamentary Papers, 1900–1949, 199; General Alphabetical Index: 1950 to 1958–9, 200; 1959 to 1969, 201; Public General Acts and

Measures: 1945+, 249; Statutes in Force: 1972+, 250; Index to the Statutes Covering the Legislation in Force on 31 December 1985, 251; Chronological Table of the Statutes, 252; The Statutory Rules and Orders and Statutory Instruments Revised to December 31 1948, 253; Table of Government Orders Covering the General Instruments to 31 December 1986, 255; Statutory Rules and Orders 1945-, 254; List of Statutory Instruments: 1900+, 256; Index to Government Orders in Force on 31 December 1985, 257; Index to Local and Personal Acts and Special Orders and Special Procedure Orders, 1801-1947, 258; Supplementary Index to Local and Personal Acts, 1948-1966, 259; Local and Personal Acts 1800+, 260; Royal Commission on the Constitution, 1969-1973, 688

Haag, H. B.: Tobacco: Experimental and Clinical Studies. A Comprehensive Study of the World's Literature, 22216

Haar, Charles Monroe: ed. Law and Land: Anglo-American Planning Practice, 20374; ed. Land Planning Law in a Free Society: A Study of the British Town and Country Planning Act, 20375

Habakkuk, Sir Hrothgar John: Production Growth and Economic Development Since 1750, 7419

Haber, Ludwig Fritz: The Chemical Industry, 1900-1930: International Growth and Technological Change, 6231; 'Government Intervention at the Frontiers of Science: British Dyestuffs and Synthetic Organic Chemicals, 1914-39', 7158

Habgood, John: Church and Nation in a Secular Age, 11577

Hachey, Thomas E.: The Problem of Partition: Peril to World Peace, 2690; Britain and Irish Separatism: From the Fenians to the Free State, 1867-1922, 2691; 'The Neutrality Issue in Anglo-Irish Relations during World War Two', 2971; 'The Archbishop of Canterbury's Visit to Palestine: An Issue in Anglo-Vatican Relations in 1931', 12303; ed. Anglo-Vatican Relations 1914-1919, 13415; ed. Confidential Dispatches: Analyses of America by the British Ambassador, 1939-1945, 14041; 'British War Propaganda and American Catholics, 1918', 15212

Hacker, Barton C.: 'Resistance to Innovation: The British Army and the Case against Mechanization, 1919-1939', 7044; The Military and the Machine, 15508

Hackforth, Norman: Solo for Horne: The Biography of Kenneth Horne, 26322

Hackman, Maria: Workplace Industrial Relations in the Engineering Industry in the United Kingdom and the Federal Republic of Germany, 5662

Hadden, Tom B.: Justice in Northern Ireland: A Study in Social Confidence, 2854; Law and the State: The Case of Northern Ireland, 2855; Ten Years On: The Legal Control of Political Violence, 2856; The Anglo-Irish Agreement: Commentary, Text and Official Review, 2999; Housing Law in Northern Ireland, 18490

Haddow, Alexander: ed. The Biological Hazards of Atomic Energy: Being the Papers presented at the Conference Convened by the Institute of Biology and the Atomic Scientists Association, 20123; 'Sir Ernest Laurence Kennaway, F.R.S., 1881-1958: Chemical Causation of Cancer Then and Today', 20957

Haddow, Alfred Cort: We Europeans: A Survey of Racial Problems, 11146

Haddow, Brian: William Tyndale: The Teachers' Story, 23162

Haddy, Pamela: 'British Inter-industrial Earnings Differentials, 1924-1955', 7231

Hadfield, Alice Mary: Charles Williams: An Explanation of his Life and Work, 25876

Hadfield, Miles: Discovering England's Trees, 19761; A History of British Gardening, 19856, 26976; The Gardener's Companion, 19857; Pioneers in Gardening, 19858; The English Landscape Garden, 19859; British Gardeners: A Biographical Dictionary, 19860, 26975

Hadfield, [Ellis] Charles [Raymond]: British Canals: An Illustrated History, 16373; 'Sources for the History of British Canals', 16374; Introducing Canals: A Guide to British Waterways Today, 16375; Canals and Waterways, 16376; World Canals: Inland Navigation Past and Present, 16377; English Rivers and Canals, 16391; The Canals of Southern England, 16398; The Canals of South West England, 16399; The Canals of South and Southeast England, 16400; The Canals of the East Midlands, 16401; The Canals of the West Midlands, 16402; The Canals of South Wales and the Border, 16403; The Canals of Yorkshire and North East England, 16404; The Canals of North West England, 16405; Introducing Inland Waterways, 16433; Waterways to Stratford, 16434

Hadjimatheou, George G.: Housing and Mortgage Markets: The U.K Experience, 18538

Hadley, Guy: Citizens and Founders: A History of the Worshipful Company of Founders, London 1365-1975, 6540

Hadley, Roger: Across the Generations: Old People and Young Volunteers, 8471

Hadley, William Waite: Munich: Before and After, 13737

Hadley-Taylor, Geoffrey: ed. Selected Letters (1920-1935) Winifred Holtby and Vera Brittain, 25414

Haffenden, John: ed. W. H. Auden: The Critical Heritage, 25361

Hafford, E. R. and Hafford, J. H. P.: Employer and Employed: Ford Ayrton & Co. Ltd.: Silk Spinners with Worker Participation, Leeds and Low Bentham, 1870-1970, 6425

Hagard, Spenser: Health, Society and Medicine, 22013

Haggard, Sir Rider: The After-War Settlement and Employment of Ex-Service Men in the Overseas Dominions, 15466

Hagger, Alfred James: Inflation: A Theoretical Survey and Synthesis, 4015

Hagger, D. F.: 'Recent Industrial Changes in South Wales', 5371

Haggerty, M.: The New Towns, 18260

Haggie, Paul: Britannia at Bay: The Defence of the British Empire against Japan 1931-1941, 13602, 14686

Haglund, David G.: 'George C.Marshall and the Question of Military Aid to England, May-June 1940', 14037

Hagmann, H. M.: Report on the Demographic and Social Pattern of Migrants in Europe, Especially with Regard to International Migrations, 11420

Hague, Douglas Chambers: Public Policy and Private Interests: the Institutions of Compromise, 791; The IRC—An Experiment in Industrial Intervention, 4977; The Economics of Man-made Fibres, 6426

Hague, Graham and Hague, Judy: The Unitarian Heritage: An Architectural Survey of Chapels and Churches in the Unitarian Tradition in the British Isles, 12115

Hague, René: ed. Dai Greatcoat: A Self-Portrait of David Jones in his Letters, 25604

Hahn, Catherine: World Photography Sources, 212

Hahn, Frank H.: 'The Theory of Economic Growth: A Survey', 7230

Hahn, Peter L.: 'The Anglo-Egyptian Negotiations 1950-1952', 14405; 'Containment and Egyptian Nationalism: The Unsuccessful Effort to establish the Middle East Command 1950-1953', 14406

Haigh, Alan: Yorkshire Railways: Including Cleveland and Humberside, 16987

Haigh, Austin Anthony Francis: Congress of Vienna to Common Market: An Outline of British Foreign Policy, 1815-1972, 13223

Haigh, Christopher: ed. The Cambridge Historical Encyclopaedia of Great Britain and Ireland, 301

Haigh, M. H.: The History of Batley, 1800-1974, 18092

Hailey, Anthea: ed. Evaluating a Community Psychiatric Service: The Camberwell Register, 1964-1971, 21874

Haileybury: Haileybury, 1908-1961, 23061

Haim, André: Adolescent Suicide, 10820

Hain, Peter: Crisis and the Future of the Left: The Debate of the Decade, 2007; Radical Liberalism and Youth Politics, 2179; ed. Policing the Police, 10710

Haines, George Henry: Shropshire and Herefordshire Villages, 19142

Haining, John: Ploughing by Steam: A History of Steam Cultivation over the Years, 19689

Haining, Peter: Eurotunnel: An Illustrated History of the Channel Tunnel Scheme, 16362; The Traction Engine Companion, 17093; The Scarecrow: Fact and Fable, 19690; Eyewitness to the Galaxy: Britain's Contribution to Research in Space, 26368

Hainsworth, P.: The Baha'i Faith, 12461

Hainsworth, Peter Hugh: Agriculture: A New Approach, 19482

Hair, P. E. H.: 'Deaths from Violence in Britain: A Tentative Secular Survey', 7460

Hajnal, John: 'Age at Marriage and Proportions Marrying', 9963; The Student Trap: A Critique of University and Sixth Form Curricula, 22569

Hakim, Catherine: Secondary Analysis in Social Research: A Guide to Data Sources with Examples, 177

Halasz, D.: Metropolis, 3098

Halcrow, Morrison: Keith Joseph: A Single Mind, 1251

Haldane Committee Report: Report of the Machinery of Government Committee, 713

Haldane, John Burdon Sanderson: Adventures of a Biologist, 26492

Haldane, John Scott: 'Stone Dust and Mine Explosion', 21275; 'The Effects of Dust Inhalation [on Miners]', 21276; The New Physiology and Other Addresses, 22303; Respiration, 22304; The Philosophical Basis of Biology, 26498; The Philosophy of a Biologist, 26499; The Sciences and Philosophy, 27253

Haldane, Richard Burdon, Viscount Haldane: Viscount Grey of Fallodon, 1201; An Autobiography, 1212; 'The Future of the Boys' Brigade Organisation and the Cadet Movement', 8513

Haldane, Thomas Graeme Nelson: The Socialization of the Electrical Supply Industry, 6410

Hale, Barbara M.: The Subject Bibliography of the Social Sciences and Humanities, 7918

Hale, Geoffrey: A Doctor in Practice, 21523

Hale, George, Ellery: The New Heavens, 26369

Hale, Sir John Rigby: ed. The Evolution of British Historiography from Bacon to Namier, 26727

Hale, Julian: Radio Power: Propaganda and International Broadcasting, 24801

Hale, Susan: The Idle Hill: A Prospect for Young Workers in a Rural Area, 8472

Hale, Thomas F.: 'The Labour Party and the Monarchy', 449

Hale, W.: ed. Four Centuries of Turco-British Relations: Studies in Diplomatic, Economic and Cultural Affairs, 13843

Hall, A. Rupert: 'The History of Time', 7157; Physic and Philanthropy: A History of the Wellcome Trust 1936–1986, 9228, 20772; Science for Industry: A Short History of the Imperial College of Science and Technology and its Antecedents, 23524

Hall, Sir Alfred Daniel: Agriculture after the War, 19426; Reconstruction and the Land: An Approach to Farming in the National Interest, 19458

Hall, Anthony: The Changing Face of Alloa, 18835

Hall, Anthony Stewart: The Point of Entry: A Study of Client Reception in the Social Services, 8877; A Management Game for Social Services, 9248

Hall, Sir Arthur John: The Sheffield School of Medicine, 22477

Hall, Barrie: The Proms and the Man who Made Them, 24445

Hall, C. B.: 'Socio-Economic Patterns of England and Wales', 9496

Hall, C. C.: Sheffield Transport, 16345

Hall, D. J.: Industrial Relations Problems and the Industrial Relations Act, 5761

Hall, D.: 'Local Community Recognition', 17868

Hall, Daniel George Edward: A Brief Survey of English Constitutional History, 601

Hall, Dennis: Joyce Cary: A Reappraisal, 25443

Hall, Diana Long: 'The Critic and the Advocate: Contrasting British Views on the State of Endocrinology in the Early 1920s', 20958

Hall, Donald Andrew: Henry Moore: The Life and Work of a Great Sculptor, 24193

Hall, Dorothy V.: Making Things Happen: History of the National Federation of Business and Professional Women's Clubs of Great Britain and Northern Ireland, 7652

Hall, Fernau: Modern English Ballet: An Interpretation, 24217

Hall, Frederick George: A History of the Bank of Ireland, 4527

Hall, G. Rome: 'A Study of Certain Effects of Occupation and Race on the Health of Recruits', 21316

Hall, Gladys Mary: Prostitution: A Survey and a Challenge, 10845

Hall, Henry L.: The Colonial Office: A History, 12501; Australia and England: A Study in Imperial Relations, 12610

Hall, Hessel Duncan: Commonwealth: A History of the British Commonwealth of Nations, 12477; The British Commonwealth of Nations: A Study of its Past and Future Development, 12531; Mandates, Dependencies and Trusteeship, 12532, 12561; 'The Genesis of the Balfour Declaration of 1926', 12534; The British Commonwealth of Nations, 12537; ed. The British Commonwealth at War, 12552

Hall, Hines H.: 'The Foreign Policy-Making Process in Britain, 1934–1935 and the Origins of the Anglo-German Naval Agreement', 13668; 'Lloyd George, Briand and the Failure of the Anglo-French Entente', 14247

Hall, Irene M.: Community Action versus Pollution: A Study of a Residents Group in a Welsh Urban Area, 20003

Hall, Irma Nelson: Psychology of Adolescence, 8459

Hall, James Logan: Online Bibliographical Databases: A Directory and Sourcebook, 52

Hall, Jean Graham: 'The Prostitute and the Law', 10848

Hall, John Challice: Sources of Family Law, 10017

Hall, John Martin: London: Metropolis and Region, 5174

Hall, Lady Laura Margaret: A Bibliography in Economics, 3389

Hall, M. Penelope: The Church in Social Work: A Study of Moral Welfare Work undertaken by the Church of England, 8738; The Social Services of Modern England, 8739; Penelope Hall's Social Services of England and Wales, 8740; The Church in Social Work: A Study of Moral Welfare Work Undertaken by the Church of England, 11833

Hall, Maximilian: The City Revolution: Causes and Consequences, 4290

Hall, Michael: Harrison Birtwhistle, 24297

Hall, Noel E.: 'Colonial Development and Welfare: The Emergence of a New British Policy', 12559

Hall, Peter Geoffrey: 'The Location of the Clothing Trades in London, 1861–1951', 6242; ed. Labour's New Frontiers, 9179; Planning and Urban Growth: An Anglo-American Comparison, 17840, 17967; 'Containment of Urban England', 17869; ed. Issues in Urban Society, 17931; The Containment of Urban England, 17966; The Theory and Practice of Regional Planning, 17968; Urban and Regional Planning, 17969, 18807; ed. Labour's New Frontiers, 17970; Great Planning Disasters, 17971; The Industries of London since 1861, 18354; London 2000, 18934; 'The Urban Culture and the Suburban Culture', 18295; ed. Land Values: The Report of the Proceedings of a Colloquium Held in London on March 13 and 14 1965 under the Auspices of the Acton Society Trust, 20262

Hall, Phoebe: Change, Choice and Conflict in Social Policy, 8854; Reforming the Welfare: The Politics of Change in the Personal Social Services, 8855; Caring for Quality in the Caring Services, 8946

Hall, R.: 'Changes in the Industrial Structure of Britain', 7229

Hall, Ray: 'Recent Changes in the Birthrate of England and Wales', 7495

Hall, Sir Robert: Planning, 17768

Hall, Ruth E.: Marie Stopes: A Biography, 7517; Ask Any Woman: A London Inquiry into Rape and Sexual Assault, 10868

Hall, Sir Stephen King: Our Own Times, 1913–1934, 299

Hall, Stephen: Oil and the British Economy, 6512

Hall, Stuart McPhail: Resistance through Rituals: Youth Sub-cultures in Post-war Britain, 8528, 10534; Policing the Crisis: Mugging, the State and Law and Order, 10270;

Hall, Tony: Nuclear Politics: The History of Nuclear Power in Britain, 6666

Hall, Unity: Philip: The Man Behind the Monarchy, 520

Hall, Vance: A History of the Yorkshire Agricultural Society, 1837–1987, 19610

Hall, W. Arnold: The Adult School Movement in the Twentieth Century, 23711

Hall-Williams, John Eryle: The English Penal System in Transition, 10400; Changing Prisons, 10401

Hallas, Jack: Community Health Councils in Action: A Review, 22109

Halle, Kay: Impossible Churchill: A Treasury of Winston Churchill's Wit, 988; Randolph Churchill: The Young Unpretender: Essays by His Friends, 1394

Hallet, Christine: The Personal Social Services in Local Government, 9251

Hallet, John D.: Environment and Society: An Introductory Analysis, 19952

Hallett, Graham: Maritime Industry and Port Development in South Wales, 16710; 'The Economic Position of British Agriculture', 19499; Farming for Consumers, 19524; 'Universities and the State: a Lecturer's View', 23332

Halley, James J.: Famous Maritime Squadrons of the R.A.F., 15812; Famous Fighter Squadrons of the R.A.F. 15813; Royal Air Force Unit Histories, 15918

Halliday, A. J.: The Development of Burton-on-Trent, 18097

Halliday, Ernest Milton: The Ignorant Armies: The Anglo-American Archangel Expedition, 1918–1919, 14569

Halliday, Francis: Matthew Smith, 24066

Halliday, Frank Ernest: An Illustrated Cultural History of England, 23729

Halliday, John: Korea: The Unknown War, 16143

Halliday, Jon: The Psychology of Gambling, 27115

Halliday, Richard John:'The Sociological Movement, the Sociological Society and the Genesis of Academic Sociology in Britain', 7992

Halloran, James Dermot: ed. The Uses of Sociology, 7979; The Effects of Mass Communication with Special Reference to Television: A Survey, 8202; ed. Effects of Television, 8203; Television and Delinquency, 24834

Halmos, A. M.: Change in Trade Unions: the Development of U.K. Unions since the 1960's, 6741

Halmos, Paul: ed. The Teaching of Sociology to Students of Education and Social Work, 8011; Sociology and Medicine, 8012, 21953; ed. Moral Issues in the Training of Teachers and Social Workers, 8013, 8690; Sociological Studies in Economics and Administration, 8014; Sociology of Sociology, 8015; The Sociology of Mass-Media Communicators, 8016, 25319; The Personal Service Society, 8017, 8805; ed. The Sociology of Science, 8018; ed. Professionalism and Social Change, 8019; The Personal and Political: Social Work and Political Action, 8020, 8804; Introduction to Welfare: Concepts and History, 8021; ed. The Development of Industrial Societies, 9535; The Faith of the Counsellors, 9966; ed. Sociological Studies in the British Penal System, 10329

Halot, Ann: 'Hikers and Ramblers: Surviving a Thirties' Fashion', 27160

Halpenny, Bruce Barrymore: Action Stations: Military Airfields of Greater London, 15937

Halperin, John: C. P. Snow: An Oral Biography: Together with a Conversation with Lady Snow (Pamela Hansford Johnson), 25811

Halpern, Louis: British War Finance, 1939–1944, 3753

Halpern, Paul G.: 'The Anglo-French-Italian Naval Convention of 1915', 13371; The Keyes Papers: Selections from the Private and Official Correspondence of Admiral of the Fleet Baron Keyes of Zeebrugge, 15268

Halsall, Elizabeth: ed. Becoming Comprehensive: Case Histories, 22962

Halsey, Albert Henry: ed. Policy and Politics: Essays in Honour of Norman Chester, 1592, 23570; Power in Co-operatives: A Study of the Internal Politics of British Retail Societies, 1897; English Ethical Socialism:

Thomas More to R. H.Tawney, 2105; Trends in British Society since 1900: A Guide to the Changing Social Structure of Britain, 7584, 9555; Change in British Society, 7585, 9554; 'Sociological Aspects of Technical Change in a Steel Plant', 7925; ed. Traditions of Social Policy: Essays in Honour of Violet Butler, 8069; 'The Views of Adolescents on Some Aspects of Social Class Structure', 9503; ed. Education, Economy and Society, 9521, 22803, 23197; 'Social Mobility in Britain: A Review', 9556; The British Academics, 9835, 22540; 'British Academics and the Professorship', 9836; 'Second Thoughts on Robbins: the Academic Hierarchy-Appendix Three', 23406; 'British Universities and Intellectual Life', 22537; 'Oxford after Franks', 23559; 'Norman Chester and Nuffield College', 23570

Haltrecht, Montague: The Quiet Showman: Sir David Webster and the Royal Opera House, 24564

Ham, Christopher: Health Policy in Britain: The Organisation and Politics of the N.H.S, 21675; Policy Making in the National Health Service: A Case Study of the Leeds Regional Hospital Board, 21685

Hambro, Carl Joachim: Newspaper Lords in British Politics, 25084

Hamer, David Allan: John Morley: Liberal Intellectual, 1281

Hamer, John: By Wapple Way: Warnham: The Story of a Sussex Parish, 19361

Hamer, Michael: Wheels within Wheels: A Study of the Road Lobby, 17485; Getting Nowhere Fast, 16232, 17486

Hamer, William: Epidemiology Old and New, 22354

Hamill, Desmond: Pig in the Middle: The Army in Northern Ireland, 1969–1984, 2897

Hamill, James: Foreign Multinationals and the British Economy: Impact and Policy, 5565

Hamilton Jenkin, A. K.: Mines and Miners of Cornwall, 6358

Hamilton, Adrian: North Sea Impact: Offshore and the British Economy, 6493

Hamilton, Alan: The Real Charles, 531

Hamilton, C. M.: 'Attempted Suicide in Glasgow', 10814

Hamilton, Dennis: Editor in Chief: Fleet Street Memoirs, 25244

Hamilton, Ernest William, Lord: The First Seven Divisions: Being a Detailed Account of the Fighting from Mons to Ypres, 14587

Hamilton, Frederick Edwin Ian: Regional Economic Analysis in Britain and the Commonwealth: A Bibliographical Guide, 3388

Hamilton, Sir H. P.: 'Sir Warren Fisher and the Public Service', 934

Hamilton, Henry: The County of Aberdeen, 19221; ed. The County of Banff, 19223; ed. The Counties of Moray and Nairn, 19228

Hamilton, Iain: Koestler: A Biography, 25618

Hamilton, Ian: Alun Lewis: Selected Poetry and Prose: With a Biographical Introduction, 25658

Hamilton, Sir Ian: Gallipoli Diary, 14544

Hamilton, James Alan Bousfield: Britain's

Railways in World War One, 16738; Railway Accidents of the 20th Century, 16741

Hamilton, Lynda: 'The British Urban Programme', 17853

Hamilton, M. B.: ed, Britain's Crisis in Sociological Perspective, 7604

Hamilton, Marian Watling: The Desegregation of the Mentally Ill, 21800

Hamilton, Mary Agnes: J. Ramsay MacDonald: 1032; Arthur Henderson: A Biography, 1230; Our Freedom and its Results, 7670; Women at Work: A Brief Introduction to Trade Unionism for Women, 7858

Hamilton, Maurice: The British Grand Prix, 27138

Hamilton, Nigel: Monty: The Making of a General, 1887–1942, 14769; Monty: Master of the Battlefield, 1942–1944, 14770; Monty: The Field Marshal, 1944–1976, 14771

Hamilton, Paul: Up the Shankill, 18168

Hamilton, Roberta: The Liberation of Women: A Study of Patriarchy and Capitalism, 7804

Hamilton, Ronald: Now I Remember: A Holiday History of Britain, 26984

Hamilton, William Baskerville: A Decade of the Commonwealth, 1955–1964, 12584

Hamilton, William: My Queen and I, 545

Hammacher, Abraham Marie: Modern English Sculpture, 24176; Barbara Hepworth, 24190

Hammerton, Howard J.: This Turbulent Priest: The Story of C. Jenkinson, Parish Priest and Housing Reformer, 18399

Hammond, Joan: A Voice, a Life: An Autobiography, 24419

Hammond, John Laurence Le Breton: C. P. Scott of The Manchester Guardian, 25280

Hammond, John: The Science of Animal Breeding in Britain: A Short History, 19461

Hammond, Nicholas Geoffrey Lemprière: Venture into Greece: With the Guerillas, 1943–44, 14848; ed. Centenary Essays on Clifton College, 23054

Hammond, Reginald Charles Holt: Railways Tomorrow: A Story of Railway Transport Problems, 16772; Railways in the New Air Age, 16773

Hammond, Richard James: The Economy of Britain: A History, 3463; 'British Food Supplies, 1914–1939', 20584; Food, 20595

Hammond, William Hobson: Persistent Criminals: A Study of All Criminals Liable to Preventative Detention in 1956, 10202

Hamnett, Chris: The Future of Cities, 17912; 'The Post-War Restructuring of the British Housing and Labour Markets', 18299; 'The Changing Socioeconomic Structure of London and the South East, 1961–1981', 18300

Hampshire, Arthur Cecil: The Royal Navy: Its Transition to the Nuclear Age, 15240; Lilliput Fleet: The Story of the Royal Naval Patrol Service, 15402

Hampton, William A.: 'Parliament and the Civil Service', 590; Local Government and Local Politics, 3140; Democracy and Community: A Study of Politics in

Sheffield, 3340, 9359; Forty Years of Labour Rule In Sheffield, 3341

Hampton: A Brief History of Hampton School, 1557–1957, 22995

Hamway, John: Industrial Relations: The Boardroom Viewpoint, 5760

Hamzah, B. A.: 'Oil and Independence in Brunei: A Perspective', 12951

Hanak, Harry: Great Britain and Austria-Hungary during the First World War: A Study in the Formation of Public Opinion, 13392; 'The Government, the Foreign Office and Austria-Hungary, 1914–1918', 13393; 'Stafford Cripps as British Ambassador in Moscow, May 1940 to June 1941', 13958

Hanbury Brown, R. : The Exploration of Space by Radio, 26417

Hanbury, Harold Greville: The English Courts of Law, 10284; The Vinerian Chair and Legal Education, 22431

Hancock, Alan: Advertising, 4316; ed. The Social Workers, 8715

Hancock, Clive: Hewlett Johnson, Priest, Prophet and Man of Action, 11795

Hancock, Gillian: Famous Flights of Airships and Balloons, 17541

Hancock, I.: White Liberals, Moderates and Radicals in Rhodesia 1953–1980, 12803

Hancock, Keith J.: 'Unemployment and the Economists in the 1920s', 6994; 'The Reduction of Unemployment as a Problem of Public Policy 1920–1929', 6995

Hancock, Mrs Freddie: Hancock, 26315

Hancock, Philip D.: A Bibliography of Works on Scotland 1916–1950, 2444

Hancock, Thomas: 'Crisis and Community Structure', 9421;'Cause for Hope', 17870; 'Trojan Mule', 17871; ed. Growth and Change in the Future City Region, 17915

Hancock, Sir [William] Keith: The British War Economy, 3754; Survey of British Commonwealth Affairs, 12574; Smuts: The Fields of Force, 1919–1950, 12723; Selections from the Smuts Papers, 12724; Country and Calling, 26799

Handbook of the United Free Presbyterian Church of Scotland: 1931+, 12252

Handford, Basil Walter Thomas: Lancing: A History of S.S. Mary and Nicolas College, Lancing, 1848–1930, 23064

Handler, Joel F.: 'The Coercive Children's Officers', 8204

Handler, Philip: ed. Biology and the Future of Man, 26518

Handley, R. S.: 'Gordon-Taylor, Breast Cancer and the Middlesex Hospital', 20959

Handley, Tommy: Handley's Pages, 26317

Handley-Taylor, Geoffrey: John Masefield O.M.: A Bibliography and Eighty-First Birthday Tribute, 25694

Handover, Phyllis Margaret: Printing in London from 1476 to Modern Times, 6635, 25019; A History of the London Gazette, 1665–1965, 25033

Handsaker, Marjorie L. and Handsaker, Morrison: 'Arbitration in Great Britain', 5651

Handy, Charles B.: Understanding Voluntary Organisations, 9219

Hanham Local History Society: Hanham our Home (1920–1940), 19191

Hanham, Harold John: Scottish Nationalism, 2493

Hanke, Ken: Ken Russell's Films, 24685

Hankey, Maurice Pascal Alers [Baron Hankey]: The Development of the Higher Control of the Machinery of Government, 714; Diplomacy by Conference: Studies in Public Affairs 1926–1946, 1223; The Supreme Control at the Paris Peace Conference, 1919: A Commentary, 13427; The Supreme Command, 1914–1918, 15472

Hankin, C. A.: ed. The Letters of John Middleton Murry to Katherine Mansfield, 25735

Hanlon, James Patrick: Road Traffic, 16298; Price Discrimination and Air Passenger Fares, 17665

Hann, Danny: Government and North Sea Oil, 6494; The Economics of North Sea Oil Taxation, 6495

Hanna, Archibald: John Buchan 1875–1940, 25425

Hanna, W. A.: The Formation of Malaysia, 12938

Hanna, William: Industrial Hygiene and Medicine, 4113

Hannaford, R. G. Magnus: Commercial Apprenticeships, 5954

Hannah, Leslie: The Rise of the Corporate Economy, 3431, 6088; Concentration in Industry: Theory, Measurement and the U.K. Experience, 4993; 'Management Innovation and the Rise of the Large-scale Company in Inter-war Britain', 5495; Engineers, Managers and Politicians: The First Fifteen Years of Nationalised Electricity Supply in Britain, 5496, 6387; Electricity before Nationalisation: A Study in the Development of the Electricity Supply Industry in Britain to 1948, 6386

Hannah, W. H.: Bobs: Kipling's General: Life of Field Marshal Earl Roberts of Kandahar, V.C, 14517

Hannam, Charles: Parents and Mentally Handicapped Children, 21867

Hannan, Damian: Rural Exodus: A Study of the Forces Influencing the Larger-scale Migration of Irish Rural Youth, 19310

Hannington, Walter: The Problem of Distressed Areas, 5037. Never on our Knees, 1566, 6805; Unemployed Struggles, 1919–1936: My Life and Struggles amongst the Unemployed, 7025

Hanrahan, Brian: 'I Counted Them All Out and I Counted Them All Back': The Battle for the Falklands, 16106

Hanrahan, Patrick J.: 'Towards a Critical Appraisal of Rural Settlement Planning in England and Wales', 19066

Hansard Society: Parliamentary Reform, 1933–1960: A Survey of Suggested Reforms, 549

Hansell, Peter: Westminster Hospital 1716–1966, 21445

Hanson, Albert Henry: ed. The Commons in Transition, 633; Parliament at Work: A Case-Book of Parliamentary Procedure, 647; Parliament and Public Ownership, 664

Hanson, Charles: The Closed Shop: A Comparative Study in Public Policy and Trade Union Security in Britain, the USA and West Germany, 5817; 'Education and the Interaction of Technologies', 22522

Hanson, D. G.: Service Banking: The Arrival of the All-Purpose Bank, 4535

Hanson, Noel H.: The Trolley Buses of Newcastle upon Tyne 1935–1966, 17249

Hanssen, Maurice: E for Additives: The Complete 'E' Numbers Guide, 20179

Happold, F. H.: Medicine at Risk: The High Price of Cheap Drugs, 22213

Haralambos, Michael: Sociology: Themes and Perspectives, 8093

Haraszti, Eva H.: Treaty-Breakers or 'Realpolitiker': The Anglo-German Naval Agreement of June 1935, 13666; The Invaders: Hitler occupies the Rhineland, 13672; 'Three Documents Concerning Great Britain's Policy in East-Central Europe in the Period After the Munich Agreement', 13754

Harben, Niloufer: Twentieth Century English History Plays: From Shaw to Bond, 26252

Harbey, B.: The Rifle Brigade, 15715

Harbhajan, Singh Janjua: Sikh Temples in the U.K. and the People behind their Management, 12466

Harbinson, John Fitzsimons: The Ulster Unionist Party, 1882–1973: Its Development and Organisation, 2953

Harbord, Reginald Engledow: The Parish of Ardeley: A Short History, 19318

Harbottle, Michael: The Impartial Soldier, 12870

Harbury, Colin Desmond: An Introduction to the United Kingdom Economy, 3537; 'Inheritance and the Economic Distribution of Personal Wealth in Great Britain', 3768; 'Wealth, Women and Inheritance', 3769

Harbutt, Fraser J.: 'Churchill, Hopkins, and the "Other" Americans: An Alternative Perspective on Anglo-American Relations, 1941–1945', 14048; The Iron Curtain: Churchill, America and the Origins of the Cold War, 14105

Harcourt, G. C.: ed. Keynes and his Contemporaries, 26608

Harcup, Sara E.: Historical, Archaeological and Kindred Societies in the British Isles: A List, 26724

Hard, Arnold Henry: The Story of Rayon and Other Synthetic Textiles, 6422; Berisfords, the Ribbon People: Jubilee, 1858–1958, 6423

Harden, Jane: ed. Readings in Urban Education, 18291

Harden, Maximilian Felix Ernst: Germany, France and England, 14254

Hardie, David William Ferguson: A History of the Modern British Chemical Industry, 6226; 'The Chemical Industry of Merseyside', 6228; A History of the Chemical Industry in Widnes, 6229

Hardie, Frank Martin: The Political Influence of the British Monarchy, 1868–1952, 428; 'The King and the Constitutional Crisis', 464; The Abyssinian Crisis, 13782; Britain and Zion: The Fateful Entanglement, 14287

Harding, D. W.: 'Political Scepticism in Britain', 2132

Harding, Gilbert Charles: Along my Line, 24910; Master of None, 24911

Harding, Stephen D.: Contrasting Values in Western Europe: Unity, Diversity and Change, 239

Hardinge, Charles, Lord: My Indian Years 1910–1916, 13125; Old Diplomacy, 13270

Hardinge, Helen Mary [Lady]: Loyal to Three Kings, 543

Hardingham, Roger: Celebrating 150 Years of the London and South Western Railway, 16893

Hardman, Roger J.: The British Food Processing Industry, 20624

Hardwick, Michael and Hardwick, Mollie: Alfred Deller: A Singularity of Voice, 24411

Hardwick, P. J. W.: Tax Expenditures in the United Kingdom, 4858

Hardy, Alfred Cecil: Everyman's History of the Sea War, 14691

Hardy, Sir Alister Clavering: Great Waters: A Voyage of Natural History to Study Whales, Plankton and the Waters of the Southern Ocean in the old Royal Research Ship Discovery, with Results brought up to date by the Findings of the R.R.S. Discovery II, 27226

Hardy, Dennis: Arcadia for All: The Legacy of a Makeshift Landscape, 18669

Hardy, Forsyth: John Grierson: A Documentary Biography, 24670

Hardy, George Alfred: 'Ordnance Survey 1: 50000 Map Series', 26711

Hardy, Godfrey Harold: Bertrand Russell and Trinity, 22437

Hardy, H.: The Minesweepers' Victory, 15398

Hardy, Henry: ed. Personal Impressions, 14043

Hardy, L. J.: 'Absenteeism and Attendance in the British Coal-Mining Industry: An Examination of Post-war Trends', 6308

Hardy, Michael John: Mosquito Victory, 15853; Gliders and Seaplanes of the World, 17547

Hardy, Richard Harry Norman: Beeching: Champion of the Railway?, 16826

Hardy, Sydney James: History of the Royal Scots Greys (The Second Dragoons). August 1914–March 1919, 15596

Hardyman, J. T.: Two Minutes from Sloane Square: A Brief History of the Conference of Missionary Societies in Great Britain and Ireland, 1912–1977, 12371

Hare, Anthony Edward Christian: The First Principles of Industrial Relations, 5641

Hare, Edward Henry: Mental Health on a New Housing Estate: A Comparative Study of Health in Two Districts of Croydon, 21772; 'A Study in Family Health, I: Health in Relation to Family Size; II: A Comparison of the Health of Fathers, Mothers and Children', 21293

Hare, P. G.: An Introduction to British Economic Policy, 3529; Planning the British Economy, 3530

Hare, Ronald: The Birth of Penicillin and the Disarming of Microbes, 22294; Pomp and Pestilence: Infectious Disease: Its Origins

and Conquest, 22359

Haresnape, Brian: British Rail 1948–1983: A Journey by Design , 16791; The London Midland and Scottish Railway, 16872; Bulleid Locomotives, 17071; Railway Design since 1830, 17081

Harewood, Jack: 'Changes in the Use of Birth Control Methods', 7512

Harford, Barbara: ed. Greenham Common; Women at the Wire, 13440

Harford, John Battersby: Handley Carr Glyn Moule, Bishop of Durham, 1901–20: A Biography, 11751

Hargave, John Gordon: Professor Skinner, Alias Montagu Norman, 4424

Hargreaves, Anthony Dalzell: 'Modern Real Property', 3765; An Introduction to the Principles of Land Law: . . ., 20330

Hargreaves, D.: On the Move: The BBC's Contribution to the Adult Literacy Campaign in the United Kingdom between 1972 and 1976, 23715

Hargreaves, Eric Lyde: The National Debt, 4579; Civil Industry and Trade, 7257

Hargreaves, J.: Squatting, 18382

Hargreaves, John D.: The End of Colonial Rule in West Africa: Essays in Contemporary History, 12734; 'The Anglo-Japanese Alliance, 1902–1952', 13584; Aberdeen University, 1945–1981: Regional Roles and National Needs, 23452

Hargreaves, John: Computers and the Changing World: A Theme for the Automation Age, 7083

Hargreaves, John: Sport, Power and Culture: A Social and Historical Analysis of Popular Sports in Britain, 27024

Hargreaves, Reginald: 'Education: The Army's Contribution', 23720

Hargrove, Aphra Locke: Serving the Mentally Handicapped: A Record of the Work of the Central Association for Mental Welfare, 21773

Harker, Ronald W.: Rolls-Royce from the Wings: Military Aviation, 1925–1971, 15825, 17595

Harkness, David W.: The Restless Dominion, 2714; 'The Constitution of Ireland and the Development of National Identity', 2715; Northern Ireland since 1920, 2786; 'Aspects of Government and Society in Northern Ireland 1920–1968', 2811; 'Reforms in Northern Ireland', 2812; 'The Difficulties of Devolution: The Post-War Debate at Stormont', 2831; 'Mr De Valera's Dominion: Irish Relations with Britain and the Commonwealth, 1932–1938', 2989; 'Patrick McGilligan, Man of Commonwealth', 3063; The Town in Ireland, 18170

Harkness, Sir Douglas Alexander Earsman: War and British Agriculture, 19457

Harle, R.: 'The Role of Trade Unions in Increasing Productivity', 6773

Harley, J. B.: Ordnance Survey Maps: A Descriptive Manual, 128, 26712

Harling, Robert: British Gardeners: A Biographical Dictionary, 26975

Harloe, Michael: ed. Captive Cities: Studies in the Political Economy of Cities and Regions, 5401, 20397; ed. 1st Conference on

Urban Change and Conflict, 17921; ed. 2nd Conference on Urban Change and Conflict, 17922; Swindon: A Town in Transition: A Study in Urban Development and Overspill Policy, 18119; The Organisation of Housing: Public and Private Enterprise in London, 18427

Harlow, P. A.: A Decade of Quantity Surveying: Review of the Literature, 1970–1979, 6195

Harman, Chris: Education, Capitalism and the Student Revolt, 22557

Harman, Claire: Sylvia Townsend Warner, 25850

Harman, J. B.: Perspectives of Medicine, 21210

Harman, Nicholas: Dunkirk. The Necessary Myth, 14839

Harman, Reginald Gordon: The Conway Valley Railway—Branch Line Handbooks, 16925; The Hayling Island Railway, 16939; Railways in the Isle of Sheppey, 16944

Harman, Richard: Countryside Mood, 19096; Countryside Character, 19097; Countryside Company, 19098

Harmer, D. J.: The Administrative Machinery of Planning at Local and Regional Levels, 17759

Harmsworth, Arthur Geoffrey Annesley: Northcliffe, 25097

Haron, M. J.: Palestine and the Anglo-American Connection, 1945–1950, 14335; 'Note: United States-British Collaboration on Illegal Immigration to Palestine, 1945–1947', 14336

Harper, Harry: The Evolution of the Flying Machine: Balloon, Airship, Aeroplane, 17488

Harper, John Ernest Troyte: The Riddle of Jutland, 14651

Harper, Marjory: Emigration from North-East Scotland, 2469

Harper, Ross: The Glasgow Rape Case, 10869

Harries, Meirion and Harries, Susie: A Pilgrim Soul, 24361

Harrington, J. F.: 'The Third Polish Uprising in Upper Silesia, 1921: A Case Study in Anglo-French Relations', 13891

Harrington, Michael: The Conservative Party, 1918–1970, 1614

Harrington, V. P.: Population in Ireland: A Census Atlas, 140

Harrington, William: The 1945 Revolution, 2295

Harris, Charles Herbert Stuart: Virus and Rickettsial Diseases, 22343

Harris, Amelia Isabella: Government Social Survey: Labour Mobility in Great Britain, 1953–1963: An Enquiry Undertaken for the Ministry of Labour and National Service in 1963, 7273; Social Welfare for the Elderly: A Study in Thirteen Local Authority Areas in England, Wales and Scotland: Vols 1. and 2, 8593

Harris, Anthony H.: Is Quiet a Luxury Good?: A Survey Approach, 20143

Harris, Sir Arthur: Bomber Offensive, 15974

Harris, Bernard Aloysius: ed. Contemporary Theatre, 26223

Harris, Brenda: The Underground and

Alternative Press in Britain during 1974: A Bibliographical Guide, 25201

Harris, Bryan: Betterment Levy and the Land Commission, 20342; The Courts, the Press and the Public, 25335; An Outline of the Law Relating to Common Land and Public Access to the Countryside, 26935

Harris, Chauncey D.: International List of Geographical Serials, 166; Annotated World List of Selected Current Geographical Serials, 167

Harris, Christopher C.: 'Relationships through Marriage in a Welsh Urban Area', 10044; The Family and Social Change: A Study of Family and Kinship in a South Wales Town, 10045; ed. Readings in Kinship in Urban Society, 10088; The Family: An Introduction, 10089; 'Church, Chapels and the Welsh', 12294

Harris, Clive: 'The 1951–1955 Conservative Government and the Racialisation of Black Immigration', 11099

Harris, D. Fraser: 'The Medical and Allied Professions as a State Service', 21309

Harris, Donald Bertram: Eric Milner-White, 1884–1963, 11801

Harris, Donald: Capital Accumulation and Income Distribution, 3859

Harris, Edward: Swansea: Its Port and Trade and their Development, 16711

Harris, Elizabeth: Twentieth Century Coventry, 18021, 18857

Harris, Evelyn Marjorie: Married Women in Industry, 7677

Harris, Frederick William: Atmospheric Pollution: Its Sources, Extent and Measurement, 20032

Harris, George Herbert: Vernon Faithfull Storr: A Memoir, 11814

Harris, George Montagu: Local Government in Many Lands: A Comparative Study, 3117; Municipal Self-Government in Britain: A Study of the Practice of Local Government in Ten of the Larger British Cities, 3118; Comparative Local Government, 3119

Harris, Henry: The Irish Regiments in the First World War, 15553; The Royal Irish Fusiliers, 15557

Harris, Henry J.: 'The British National Health Insurance System, 1911–19', 21290

Harris, Henry Wilson: Life So Far, 25245; J. A. Spender, 25285

Harris, J.: ed. The Country-seat: Studies in the History of the British Country House, 20319

Harris, John Raymond: ed. Liverpool and Merseyside: Essays in the Economic and Social History of the Port and its Hinterland, 5172

Harris, John Sharp: British Government Inspection: the Local Services and the Central Departments, 789; Government Patronage of the Arts in Great Britain, 23759; 'Television as a Political Issue in Britain', 24864

Harris, John: Corporate Management and Financial Planning: The British Rail Experience, 16789

Harris, John: Dunkirk. The Storms of War, 14838

Harris, John: Phonological Variation and Change Studies in Hiberno-English, 23822

Harris, John: The Big Slump, 3653

Harris, John: ed. The Garden: A Celebration of 1000 Years of British Gardening, 19873

Harris, José: William Beveridge: A Biography, 1359, 9042; Unemployment and Politics: A Study of English Social Policy 1886–1914, 6991; 'The Social Thought of William Beveridge', 9041

Harris, Kenneth: Attlee, 975; David Owen: Personally Speaking, 1285

Harris, Laurence: The Peculiarities of the British Economy, 3526; The City of Capital: London's Role as a Financial Centre, 4244

Harris, Leonard Mortimer: Long to Reign Over Us? The Status of the Royal Family in the Sixties, 444

Harris, Leslie Junius: Vitamins in Theory and Practice, 20563; Vitamins: A Digest of Current Knowledge . . . , 20564

Harris, Michael Louis John: Great Western Coaches from 1890, 16865

Harris, Nigel: Competition and the Corporate Society: British Conservatives, the State and Industry, 1945–1964, 6116

Harris, P. J.: Local Government in Southern Nigeria, 12759

Harris, Paul: When Pirates ruled the Waves, 24803

Harris, Peter: Estate Planning and Life Assurance, 4232

Harris, Peter: Hong Kong: A Study in Bureaucratic Politics, 12975; 'Hong Kong Confronts 1997: An Assessment of the Sino-British Agreement', 12976

Harris, R. J. P.: 'Inter-Authority Planning', 5109; 'Inter-regional Movement of Manufacturing Industry: A Comparative Evaluation of the Findings in the Nottinghamshire-Derbyshire Sub-region', 5212

Harris, Ralph: Politics without Prejudice: A Political Appreciation of the Rt. Hon Richard Austen Butler, 1122; ed. Radical Reaction: Essays in Competition and Affluence, 3634; British Economic Policy 1970–1974, 3670; Advertising and the Public, 4309; Advertising in a Free Society, 4310; Pricing or Taxing?, 4874

Harris, Reg: Two Wheels to the Top, 27137

Harris, Rex: Jazz, 24453

Harris, Richard William: Not So Humdrum: The Autobiography of a Civil Servant, 933

Harris, Robert: The Making of Neil Kinnock, 1442; Gotcha: The Media, the Government and the Falklands Crisis, 16123

Harris, Rosemary: Prejudice and Tolerance in Ulster, 2926

Harris, S.: Banting's Miracle: The Story of the Discoverer of Insulin, 22286

Harris, Sarah: Women in Twentieth Century Britain, 7867

Harris, Seymour Edwin: John Maynard Keynes: Economist and Policy Maker, 26596

Harris, Sydney: 'The Identity of Jews in an English City', 11313

Harris, Tirrel: 'Social Class and Psychiatric Disturbance among Women in an Urban Population', 21818

Harris, William Leslie: Filton, Gloucestershire: Some Account of the Village and Parish, 19332

Harrison, A. E.: 'The Competitiveness of the British Cycle Industry', 17163

Harrison, Alan: Farmers and Farm Businesses in England, 19567

Harrison, Anthony J.: The Distribution of Personal Wealth in Britain, 3794; The Framework of Economic Activity: The International Economy and the Rise of the State in the Twentieth Century, 6101; Transport U.K, 16269; Economics and Land Use Planning, 20291

Harrison, B.: The RAF: A Pictorial History, 15788

Harrison, Brian Howard: 'History at the Universities, 1968: A Commentary', 22449, 26775; History at the Universities, 26774

Harrison, Charles: English Art and Modernism 1900–1939, 23986

Harrison, D. E. W.: Worship in the Church of England, 11605

Harrison, Derek: Salute to Snow Hill: The Rise and Fall of Birmingham's Snow Hill Railway Station, 1852–1977, 16997

Harrison, Derrick Inskip: These Men are Dangerous: The Special Air Service at War, 15004

Harrison, Elizabeth: Love, Honour and Dismay, 26054

Harrison, F. Ll.: Collins Encyclopaedia of Music, 24262

Harrison, Frederick: The Bible in Britain, 11917

Harrison, Geoffrey Ainsworth: ed. Population Structure and Human Variation, 7391, 9441; 'Social Class and Marriage Patterns in some Oxfordshire Populations', 9440; ed. The Structure of Human Populations, 9442

Harrison, George Anthony: ed. Man in Urban Environments, 17924

Harrison, Godfrey Percival: Borthwicks: A Century in the Meat Trade, 1863–1963, 20671

Harrison, J. E.: The Political Significance of the British Agricultural Vote, 19521

Harrison, John Fletcher Clews: Learning and Living, 1790–1960: A Study in the History of the English Adult Education Movement, 23664; History of the Working Men's College, 1854–1954, 23666

Harrison, John: The District Officer in India 1930–1947, 13121

Harrison, Martin John: 'Political Finance in Britain', 1594; Trade Unions and the Labour Party since 1945, 6870; 'Academic Freedom and Higher Education in England', 22538

Harrison, Mary M. M.: Local Government Administration in England and Wales, 3125

Harrison, Michael J.: A Sociology of Industrialisation: An Introduction, 5017

Harrison, Michael: Mulberry: The Return In Triumph, 14949

Harrison, Molly: People and Furniture: Social Background to the English Home, 18742; The Kitchen in History, 18743

Harrison, Morris: Instant Reading: The Story of the Initial Teaching Alphabet, 22763

Harrison, Paul: 'The Children Act under Attack', 8205; Inside the Inner City, 18403

Harrison, R. M.: Men out of Work: A Study of Unemployment in Three English Towns, 7016

Harrison, Rex: Rex, An Autobiography, 26052

Harrison, Roy M.: Lead Pollution: Causes and Control, 20164

Harrison, Royden: The Warwick Guide to British Labour Periodicals 1790–1970: A Check List, 1662; 'Labour Government: Then and Now', 1753

Harrison, Ruth: Animal Machines: The New Factory Farming Industry, 19702

Harrison, Stanley: Poor Men's Guardians: A Record of the Struggles for a Democratic Newspaper Press, 1763–1973, 25065

Harrison, Wilfrid: 'The Early Years of Political Studies', 26890

Harrisson, Tom: Mass Observation: The Press and its Readers, 25043; ed. The Press and its Readers, 25078

Harrod, Sir [Henry] Roy [Forbes]: The British Economy, 3520, 3639; Policy against Inflation, 3619; The Life of John Maynard Keynes, 26592

Harrod, Jeffrey: Trade Union Policy: A Study of British and American Trade Union Activities in Jamaica, 6826

Harrop, D.: A History of the Gregynog Press, 25004

Harrop, Martin: 'The Basis for National Front Support', 2051; ed. Political Communications: The General Election Campaign of 1987, 2355

Harrow: Harrow School: Yesterday and Today, 23062

Hart, Basil Henry Liddell: 'T. E. Lawrence': In Arabia and After, 13816; History of the Second World War, 14708; The Real War, 1914–1918, 14454; A History of the World War 1914–1918, 14455; Reputations. 14736; Deterrence and Defence, 14737; The Tanks: The History of the Royal Tank Regiment and its Predecessors, 15735

Hart, Cyril Edwin: Royal Forest: A History of Dean's Woods as Producers of Timber, 19739

Hart, David W.: A Review of Community Councils in Scotland, 1983–1984, 9433

Hart, Douglas Allen: ed. The Regional Planning Process, 5099; Strategic Planning in London: The Rise and Fall of the Primary Road Network, 16320, 17132

Hart, F.: A Study of Hospital Administration, 21390

Hart, Francis Russell: Neil M. Gunn: A Highland Life, 25570

Hart, Gwen Muriel: A History of Cheltenham, 18099

Hart, J. F.: Some Statistics of Social Contrast in Liverpool from the 1971 Census, 18046

Hart, Jennifer Margaret Murray: The British Police, 10688

Hart, Nicky: When Marriage Ends: A Study in Status Passage, 9998

Hart, Olive Ely: The Drama in Modern Wales: A Brief History of Welsh Playwriting from 1900 to the Present Day, 26258

Hart, Peter Edward: 'The Dynamics of Earnings, 1963–1973', 3873; Mergers and Concentration in British Industry, 4988, 5526; Concentration in British Industry 1935–1975: A Study of the Growth, Causes and Effects of Concentration in British Manufacturing Industries, 5527; Studies in Profit, Business Saving and Investment in the United Kingdom, 1920–1962, 5983; 'The Sizes of Trade-unions: A Study in the Laws of Aggregation', 6756; 'Profits in Non-manufacturing Industries in the United Kingdom, 1920–1938', 7228

Hart, R. A.: 'Wage Inflation and the Phillips Relationship', 3897; 'Engineering Earnings in Britain, 1914–1968', 6382

Hart, Sydney: Discharged Dead: A True Story of Britain's Submarines at War, 15374

Hart, Thomas: The Comprehensive Development Area: A Study of the Legal and Administrative Problems of Comprehensive Land Development with Special Reference to Glasgow, 18878

Hart, Sir William: 'The Conurbations and the Regions', 5057; 'British New Towns Today', 18224

Hart-Davis, Duff: ed. End of an Era: Letters and Journals of Sir Alan Lascelles 1887–1920, 465; Peter Fleming: A Biography, 25237

Hart-Davis, Sir Rupert Charles: The Arms of Time: A Memoir, 24966; ed. Letters of Max Beerbohm 1892–1956, 25372; Hugh Walpole: A Portrait of a Man, an Epoch and a Society, 25849

Hartcup, Guy: Code Name Mulberry. The Planning, Building and Operation of the Mulberry Harbours, 14956; The Challenge of War: Scientific and Engineering Contributions to World War Two, 15117

Harte, Negley B.: 'Trends in Publications on the Economic and Social History of Great Britain and Ireland, 1925–1974', 3392; ed. Study of Economic History, 3393; ed. Textile History and Economic History: Essays in Honour of Miss Julia de Lacy Mann, 6413; One Hundred and Fifty Years of History Teaching at University College London, 22452; The University of London, 1836–1986, 23518

Hartigan, Maureen: The History of the Irish in Britain: A Bibliography, 11367

Hartley, Arthur Bamford: Unexploded Bomb: A History of Bomb Disposal, 15511

Hartley, Dorothy: Food in England, 20596

Hartley, Sir Harold: The Contribution of Engineering to the British Economy, 6360

Hartley, Jean: Steel Strike: A Case Study in Industrial Relations, 6939

Hartley, Keith: Export Performance and the Pressure of Demand, 4818; Employment and Unemployment in the Hull Region, 1951–1968, 7012; 'The United Kingdom Military Aircraft Market', 17585; 'The Export Performance of the British Aircraft Industry', 17586

Hartley, Marie: Life and Tradition in West Yorkshire, 5234

Hartley, Nicholas: Concentration of Ownership in the Provincial Press, 25328

Hartley, Peter: The Story of Rudge Motorcycles, 17193

Hartley, Stephen: The Irish Question as a Problem in British Foreign Policy 1914–1918, 2964, 13408

Hartley, Trevor Clayton: Government and Law: an Introduction to the Working of the Constitution in Britain, 625

Hartley, W. Freda: 'The Farewell Rally of the Women's Land Army and a Retrospect', 7663

Hartman, Paul: 'Industrial Relations in the News Media', 5783

Hartmann, Cyril Hughes: The Story of the Roads, 17100

Hartmann, Paul: 'A British Scale for Measuring White Attitudes to Coloured People', 11018; Racism and the Mass Media: A Study of the Mass Media in the Formation of White Beliefs and Attitudes in Britain, 11176

Hartnoll, Phyllis May: ed. The Oxford Companion to the Theatre, 25904

Hartog, Howard: ed. European Music in the Twentieth Century, 24279

Hartog, Mabel Helene: Lady P. J. Hartog: A Memoir, 22578

Hartston, William: 'Care of the Sick Poor in England, 1572–1948', 20960

Hartwell, [Ronald] Max: ed. British Economy and Society, 1870–1970: Documents, Descriptions, Statistics, 3444, 7619

Hartwell-Jones, Griffith: A Celt Looks at the World, 12284

Harvard Theological Review, 11544

Harvey, Ben Hyde: Harlow: A Story of a New Town, 18195

Harvey, Brian W.: Environment and Society: An Introductory Analysis, 19952

Harvey, C. R. M.: Export Performance and the Pressure of Demand, 4818

Harvey, Charles E.: 'Old Traditions, New Departures: The Later History of the Bristol and West Building Society', 4393; ed. Studies in the Business History of Bristol, 4393; The Rio Tinto Company: An Economic History of a Leading International Mining Concern, 1873–1951, 6351

Harvey, Charles Nigel: The Industrial Archaeology of Farming in England and Wales, 19415; The Farming Kingdom, 19491; A History of Farm Building in England and Wales, 19707

Harvey, Chris: Healey: The Handsome Brute, 17426; Mighty Minis, 17442

Harvey, D. R.: The Costs of the Common Agricultural Policy, 19587

Harvey, David Dow: Ford Madox Ford 1873–1939: A Bibliography of Works and Criticism, 25509

Harvey, David: Social Justice and the City, 17920; Explanation in Geography, 26639

Harvey, Denis: The Gypsies: Waggon-Time and After, 11357

Harvey, George Leonard Hunton: The Church and the Twentieth Century, 11575

Harvey, Gordon: Pickets in White: The Junior Doctors Dispute of 1975: A Study of the Medical Profession in Transition, 20816

Harvey, Ian: To Fall Like Lucifer, 1429

Harvey, Jack: The British Constitution, 613

Harvey, James T.: 'Problems of Inflation', 3998

Harvey, Joan M.: ed. Walford's Guide to Current British Periodicals in the Humanities and Social Sciences, 160

Harvey, John: ed. Diplomatic Diaries of Oliver Harvey, 1937–1940, 13271; ed. War Diaries of Oliver Harvey, 1941–1945, 13272

Harvey, Richard Jon: Industrial Relations (including the 1971 Industrial Relations Act), 5739

Harvey, S.: ed. Fifty Years of Landscape Design, 1934–1984, 20323

Harvey, Stephen: The Northern Ireland Economy: With Special Reference to Industrial Development, 5392

Harvey, William Clunie: Milk: Production and Control, 20651

Harvey, William Frederick James: 'Pi' in the Sky: A History of No.22 Squadron, Royal Flying Corps and R.A.F. in the War of 1914–1918, 15917

Harvey-Bailey, Alec: Rolls-Royce: The Formative Years, 1906–1939, 17446; Rolls-Royce: The Pursuit of Excellence, 17447

Harvie, Christopher: 'Labour in Scotland during the Second World War', 2366, 2514; No Gods and Precious Few Heroes: Scotland 1914–1980, 2442; Scotland and Nationalism: Scottish Society and Politics 1701–1977, 2443; ed. Forward! Labour Politics in Scotland 1888–1988, 2513

Harvie-Watt, G. S.: Most of My Life, 1430

Harwin, Judith: Alcohol and the Family, 10095

Harwood, Ronald: ed. The Ages of Gielgud: An Actor at Eighty, 26046; Sir Donald Wolfit, 26109

Harzfeld, Lois A.: Periodical Indexes in the Social Sciences and Humanities: A Subject Guide, 243

Haseler, Stephen: The Gaitskellites: Revisionism in the British Labour Party 1951–1964, 1198, 1736; The Tragedy of Labour, 1764

Haskell, Arnold Lionel David: 'The Birth of the English Ballet', 24214; The National Ballet: A History and a Manifesto, 24215; Ballet 1945–1950, 24216; Balletomane at Large: An Autobiography, 24235

Haslegrave, Herbert Leslie: Fifty Years of Progress, 1894–1944: An Historical Survey of the Work of the Association of Technical Institutions, 23286

Haslem, E. B.: The History of the Royal Air Force, Cranwell, 15779

Haslett, E.: The Anglo-Irish Agreement: Northern Ireland Perspectives, 3006

Hasluck, Eugene Lewis: Local Government in England, 3116; The Second World War, 14707

Hasluck, Sir Paul: Sir Robert Menzies, 12623; Mucking About, 12634

Hassal, C.: 'Some Changes in the Composition of a Mental Hospital', 21833; The Management of Alcoholism, 22132

Hassall, Christopher Vernon: Edward Marsh, Patron of the Arts: A Biography, 937, 23754; Rupert Brooke: A Biography, 25421

Hasson, J. A.: 'Development in the British Coal Industry', 6302

Haste, Cate: Keep the Home Fires Burning: Propaganda in the First World War, 15214

Hastings, Adrian: A History of English Christianity 1920–1985, 11557; Robert Runcie, 11702; ed. Bishops and Writers: Aspects of the Evolution of Modern English Catholicism, 11944; Church and Mission in Modern Africa, 12369

Hastings, Anthony: 'Role Relations and Value Adaptation: A Study of the Professional Accountant in Industry', 9828

Hastings, Max: The Fight for Civil Rights in Northern Ireland, 2914; Bomber Command, 15983; The Battle for the Falklands, 16102; The Korean War, 16142; Ulster '69

Hastings, Michael: The Handsomest Young Man in England, 25422

Hastings, R. F.: 'The Birmingham Labour Movement 1918–1945', 1783

Hastings, Robert Hood William Stewart: The London Rifle Brigade, 1919–1950, 15695

Hastings, Selina: Nancy Mitford: A Biography, 25714

Hastings, Somerville: The Family and the Social Services, 10076

Hastings, Stephen: Murder of the TSR-2, 15887

Haswell, Jock: The British Army: A Concise History, 15430

Hatch, Stephen: Graduate Study and After, 5970, 9872

Hatcher, John: Founders of Medical Laboratory Science, 22267

Hatfield, H. Stafford: The Inventor and his World, 7076

Hatfield, Michael: The House the Left Built: Inside Labour Policy Making 1970–1975, 1761

Hathaway, R. M.: Ambiguous Partnership: Britain and America, 1944–1947, 14062

Hathway, A.: 'Effects of Town Expansion on Central Areas in Britain', 17872

Hatt, Paul Kitchener: ed. Cities and Society, 18290

Hattersley, Roy: Goodbye to Yorkshire, 1224; A Yorkshire Boyhood, 1225; Choose Freedom: The Future for Democratic Socialism, 1226

Hauser, Mark M.: The Economics of Unemployment Insurance, 4033

Hauser, Oswald: England und das Dritte Reich: Eine Dokumentierte Geschichte der Englisch-deutschen Beziehungen von 1933 bis 1939 auf Grund Unveröffentlicher Akten aus dem britischen Staatsarchiv, 13697; 'The year 1937: The Decisive Turning-Point in British-German Relations', 13723

Hauser, Philip Morris: ed. Population and World Politics, 10910

Haut, F. J. G.: The History of the Electric Locomotive, 17052

Haveman, Robert H.: The Economics of Environment Policy, 19948

Havighurst, Alfred Freeman: Britain in Transition: The Twentieth Century, 286; Modern England 1901–1970, 392; Radical Journalist: H.W. Massingham, 25262

Havinden, Michael Ashley: Estate Villages: A Study of the Berkshire Villages of Ardington and Lockinge, 19177

Havins, Peter J. Neville: The Forests of England, 19719

Haw, Richard Claude: The Conservation of Natural Resources, 20227

Hawcroft, Francis Wilson: The Arts, 23740

Hawke, Gary Richard: Economics for Historians, 3453

Hawker, A.: Adolescence and Alcohol: Report of an Enquiry into Adolescent Drinking Patterns Carried out from October 1975 to June 1976, 22152

Hawkes, Jacquetta: Adventurer in Archaeology: The Biography of Sir Mortimer Wheeler, 26366

Hawkes, Nicolas: Immigrant Children in British Schools, 23173

Hawkes, Nigel: The Computer Revolution, 7095

Hawkins, Bill: Whatever Happened at Fairfields?, 16633

Hawkins, Chris: The British Economy: What Will our Children Think?, 3683

Hawkins, D. C.: 'Britain and Malaysia—Another View: Was the Decision to Withdraw Entirely Voluntary or Was Britain Pushed a Little?', 12914

Hawkins, Jack: Anything for a Quiet Life, 26056

Hawkins, Keith: comp. Deprivation of Liberty for Young Offenders: A Select Bibliography on Approved Schools, Attendance Centres, Borstals, Detention Centres and Remand Homes, 1940–1965, 10499

Hawkins, Kevin H.: Business and Society: Tradition and Change, 5449; British Industrial Relations, 1945–1975, 5580, 6129; 'Productivity Bargaining: A Reassessment', 5751; The Management of Industrial Relations, 5752; Case Studies in Industrial Relations, 5753; ed. Company Industrial Relations Policies: The Management of Industrial Relations in the 1970's, 5766; The Brewing Industry: A Study in Industrial Organisation and Public Policy, 6153, 20736; A History of Bass Charrington, 6156; Environment and Enforcement: Regulation and the Social Definition of Pollution, 20085

Hawkins, Thornton Horace: Adult Education: The Record of the British Army, 23667

Hawksworth, J. M.: 'Some Developments in Local Government 1944–1948', 3164

Haworth, Christopher Matthew: A History of Pocklington School, East Yorkshire, 1514–1950, 23070

Haworth, John Trevor: ed. Leisure and the Community: Conference Proceedings: Papers from a Conference held by the Leisure Studies Association at Birmingham in 1976, 26936

Hawson, Herbert Keeble: Sheffield: The Growth of a City, 1893–1926, 18071, 18905

Hawthorn, Geoffrey: Population Policy: A Modern Delusion, 7403; The Sociology of Fertility, 7521; Enlightenment and Despair: A History of Sociology, 8029

Hawtrey, Sir Ralph George: Incomes and Money, 3826; An Incomes Policy, 3827;

Cross Purposes in Wage Policy, 3905; A Century of Bank Rate, 4427; Towards the Rescue of Sterling, 4668; The Pound at Home and Abroad, 4669

Hawtrey, S. C.: Parliamentary Dictionary, 649

Haxby, David: *ed.* Frontiers of Criminology: Summary of the Proceedings, 10253; Probation: A Changing Service, 10472

Hay, Alan M.: 'South Yorkshire County is Born and Analysed', 5233

Hay, Denys: 'Sir George Clark (1890–1979)', 26790

Hay, Doddy: War under the Red Ensign: The Merchant Navy, 1939–45, 15134

Hay, Ian: Arms and the Men, 14479; The British Infantrymen: An Informal History, 15450

Hay, James Roy: *ed.* The Development of the British Welfare State 1880–1975, 9006

Hay, Malcolm: Edward Bond: A Companion to the Plays, 25945

Hay, Margaret: Children of Today and Tomorrow, 8167

Hay, Peter: Pre-Grouping Trains on British Railways: The L.N.E.R. Companies, 16888

Hay, Wendy: Adult Literacy in Britain: An Annotated Bibliography, 23714

Hay, William David: Self Sufficiency on the Farm, 19475

Hayburn, R.: 'The National Unemployed Workers' Movement 1921–1936: A Re-Appraisal', 1937

Hayden, A. J.: *ed.* British Hymn Writers and Composers: A Check List Giving their Dates and Places of Birth and Death, 11923

Hayek, Friedrich August, von: The Road to Serfdom, 2094; Law, Legislation and Liberty, 2095; Verdict on Rent Control, 18423; 'The London School of Economics, 1895–1945', 23527

Hayes, Denis: Conscription Conflict: The Conflict of Ideas in the Struggle for and against Military Conscription in Britain between 1901 and 1939, 13459; Challenge of Conscience: The Story of the Conscientious Objectors of 1939–45, 13518

Hayes, Frank: 'South Africa's Departure from the Commonwealth 1960–1961', 12720

Hayes, James Gordon: The Conquest of the North Pole: Recent Arctic Exploration, 27211; Antarctica: A Treatise on the Southern Continent, 27215

Hayes, John: The Art of Graham Sutherland, 24078

Hayes, Paul Martin: Modern British Foreign Policy: the Twentieth Century, 1880–1939, 13224

Hayman, Bernard: Harbour Seamanship, 16665

Hayman, Ronald: Arden, 25934; Robert Bolt, 25944; John Osborne, 25968; Pinter, 25972; Stoppard, 25986; John Whiting, 25994; John Gielgud, 26044; 'The Royal Court, 1956–1972', 26151; The First Thrust: The Chichester Festival Theatre, 26166; The Set-up: An Anatomy of the English Theatre Today, 26246; British Theatre since 1945: A Reassessment, 26247

Hayman, Roy: The Institute of Fuel: The First 50 Years, 6516

Haynes, Charles Edward: The Essentials of the British Constitution, 616

Haynes, Sir George E.: 'Social Work in the Sixties', 8726

Haynes, K. J.: The Living Pattern of Some Old People, 8578

Haynes, Renée: Hilaire Belloc, 25376

Haynes, Roslynn: H. G. Wells: Discoverer of the Future: The Influence of Science on his Thought, 25873

Haynes, William Warren: Nationalization in Practice: The British Coal Industry, 6291

Hays, Peter: New Horizons in Psychiatry, 22416

Hays, Samuel Frimmer: National Income and Expenditure in Britain and O.E.C.D. Countries, 4586; 'Productivity Bargaining before the War and Now', 5989; The Engineering Industries, 6380

Haystead, J.: Pre-school Education and Care, 23168

Hayter, Diane: The Labour Party: Crisis and Prospects, 1800

Hayter, Sir William: The Kremlin and the Embassy, 13273; A Double Life: The Memoirs of Sir William Hayter, 13274

Haythornthwaite, Gerald: The Sheffield Green Belt, 18983

Hayward, John: 'Responses to Contraction: the University of Hull, 1979–1984'. 23502

Hayward, Keith: Government and British Civil Aerospace: A Case Study in Post-war Technology Policy, 17594

Hayward, Leslie H: A History of Air Cushion Vehicles, 17705

Haywood, Harold: A Role for Voluntary Youth Work, 8521

Haywood, Stuart Collingwood: A Series of Progress Reports from the Research Team Studying the Reorganisation of the National Health Service on Humberside, 1972–75, 21621; Crisis in the Health Service: The Politics of Management, 21622; Managing the Health Service, 21623; The Curate's Egg: Good in Parts: Senior Officers' Reflections on the N.H.S., 21624; 'The Politics of Management in Health Care: A British Perspective', 21625

Hazell, Kenneth: Social and Medical Problems of the Elderly, 8616; *ed.* Social and Medical Problems of the Elderly, 21935

Hazlehurst, Cameron: A Guide to the Papers of British Cabinet Ministers 1900–1951, 79, 963; 'Asquith as Prime Minister, 1908–1916', 971; 'The Baldwinite Conspiracy', 977; Menzies Observed, 12622

Hazlewood, Rex: B-P's Scouts: An Official History of the Boy Scouts Association, 8515

Head, David: *ed.* Free way to Learning: Educational Alternatives in Action, 23127

Head, Victor: A Triumph of Hope: The Story of the National Farmers Union Mutual Insurance Society Limited, 19604

Headey, Bruce Wyndham: British Cabinet Ministers: the Role of Politicians in Executive Office, 723

Headington, Christopher: Britten, 24320; The Performing World of the Musician, with a Profile of Andrew Lloyd Webber, 24486

Headlam, Arthur Cayley: The Church of England, 11590

Headrick, T. E.: The Town Clerk in English Local Government, 3245

Heady, J. A.: Social and Biological Factors in Infant Mortality, 7456

Heaf, Frederick Roland George: Recent Advances in Respiratory Tuberculosis, 21160; *ed.* Symposium of Tuberculosis, 21161

Heal, David Walter: The Steel Industry in Post-war Britain, 6590; Iron and Steel; Shipbuilding, 16612

Heal, G. M.: Public Policy and the Tax System, 4853

Heal, Kevin: Non-Accidental Injury to Children under the Age of Seventeen, 9961; 'The Police, the Public and the Prevention of Crime', 10773

Heald, D.: 'Restructuring the Electricity Supply Industry', 6390

Heald, David: Making Devolution Work, 2417; 'The Impact of the Devolution Commitment on the Scottish Body Politic', 2470

Heald, Gordon: The Gallup Survey of Britain, 231

Heales, H. C.: Housing Finance in Great Britain, 18541

Healey, Denis Winston: The Time of my Life, 1228

Healey, Francis George: Rooted in Faith: Three Centuries of Nonconformity, 1662–1962, 12000

Healey, Geoffrey: Austin Healey: The Story of the Big Healeys, 17425

Healey, Michael A.: De-industrialisation and Employment Decline in the West Midlands and Coventry, 5227; Lead, the Environment and Health: A Report, 20168

Healey, P.: Local Plans in British Land Use Planning, 20270

Healey, Patsy: 'The Professionalisation of Planning in Britain: Its Form and Consequences', 18779; The Implementation of Planning Policies and the Role of Development Plans: Final Report to the Department of the Environment, 18780

Health Services in Scotland, 1953–1980, 21695

Health Visitor: 'Child Health and Education in the Seventies: A National Study in England, Scotland and Wales of all Children Born 5–11th April 1970', 8206

Health and Personal Social Services Statistics for England, 21991

Health and Personal Social Services for Wales, 21992

Healy, Timothy Michael: Letters and Leaders of My Day, 3012

Heaney, Charles Thomas: The Payment of General Practitioners in Great Britain 1834–1974, 21525

Heanor and District Historical Society: Two Centuries of Transport in the Heanor [Derbyshire] Area, 16354

Heap, Sir Desmond: Town and Country Planning, or, How to Control Land Development, 18801: On the Town and Country Planning Act, 20333; An Outline of the New Planning Law, 20334, 20337; Encyclopaedia of the Law of Planning, 20335, 20336; An Outline of Planning Law, 20338; *ed.* Introducing the Land Commission Act, 1967: The Book of Lectures, 20341

Heard, Gerald: These Hurrying Years: an Historical Outline, 1900–1933, 355

Hearder, Harry: *ed.* British Government and Administration: Studies Presented to S. B. Chrimes 708

Hearl, Derek: 'The United Kingdom', 2383

Hearn, Cyril Victor: A Duty to the Public: A Frank Assessment of Today's Police Force, 10695

Hearnshaw, Leslie Spencer: A Short History of British Psychology, 1840–1940, 22418

Heasman, D. J.: 'The Monarch, the Prime Minister and the Dissolution of Parliament', 462; 'The Ministerial Hierarchy', 742; 'Parliamentary Paths to High Office', 743; '"My Station and its Duties": The Attlee Version', 975

Heasman, Kathleen: Christians and Social Work, 9200

Heasman, Michael Anthony: Social and Biological Factors in Infant Mortality, 7456

Heater, Derek Benjamin: Britain and the Outside World, 13242

Heath, Anthony: Social Mobility, 9604

Heath, Sir Edward Richard George: Old World, New Horizons: Britain, the Common Market, and the Atlantic Alliance, 1017; Sailing: A Course of my Life, 27166

Heath, Graham: The Illusory Freedom: The Intellectual Origins and Social Consequences of the Sexual 'Revolution', 7808

Heath, Jeffrey: Evelyn Waugh and his Writing, 25864

Heath, Ted: Listen to my Music: An Autobiography, 24464

Heathcote, K. A.: 'The Ports of Great Britain', 16651

Heathcote, R.: *ed.* Buses of the West Midlands, 17287

Heaton, Paul Michael: The Abbey Line: History of a Cardiff Shipping Venture, 16560; The Reardon Smith Line: History of a South Wales Shipping Venture, 16561

Heavyside, G. Tom: Steam Renaissance: The Decline and Rise of Steam, 17045

Hebden, Donald C.: The Trustee Savings Bank of Yorkshire and Lincoln: The Story of its Formation and of the Six Savings Banks from which it was Constituted, 4353

Hebden, John E.: 'Men and Women's Pay in Britain, 1968–1975', 3943; Management Structure and Computerization, 5447; Pathways to Participation, 6025

Hebden, Julia: Small Firms in the Motor Vehicle Distribution and Repair Industry, 17484

Hebdidge, Dick: Subculture: The Meaning of Style, 8540

Hecht, Robert A.: 'Great Britain and the Stimson Note of January 7 1932', 13599

Hechter, Michael: 'Regional Inequality and National Integration: The Case of the British Isles', 2395; 'The Persistence of Regionalism in the British Isles', 2396, 5084; Internal Colonialism: The Celtic Fringe in British National Development 1536–1966, 2420, 5083.'Industrialization and National Development in the British Isles', 5082; 'Political Economy of Ethnic Change', 11048

Heckstall-Smith, Anthony: Greek Tragedy, 14854; Tobruk, 14896

Heclo, Hugh: The Private Government of Public Money, 808, 5528; From Relief to Income Maintenance: Modern Social Policy-Making in Britain and Sweden, 4084

Heddle, A.: Forty Five Years: A History of the Woolwich and District Invalid Children's Aid Association, 1892–1937, 8207

Hedley, Martin: Vickers VC 10, 17599

Hedley, Peter: The D-Notice Affair, 25334

Heenan, John Carmel: Cardinal Hinsley, 11990; Not the Whole Truth, 11991; A Crown of Thorns: An Autobiography, 1951–1963, 11992

Heeney, Brian: The Women's Movement in the Church of England 1850–1930, 11669

Heffer, Eric Samuel: The Class Struggle in Parliament: A Socialist View of Industrial Relations, 5765

Heginbotham, Herbert: The Youth Employment Service, 8473; 'Young Immigrants and Work', 10964

Heidenheimer, A. J.: 'Trade Unions, Benefit Systems and Party Mobilization Styles: Horizontal Influences on the British Labour and German Social Democratic Parties', 6792; The Politics of Public Education, Health and Welfare in the USA and Western Europe: How Growth and Reform Potentials have differed', 8940

Heidensohn, Frances: The Deviance of Women: A Critique and an Inquiry', 10196; 'The Able Criminal', 10197; Crime and Society, 10281; 'Prisons for Women', 10453; Women and Crime, 10874

Heiman, Marcel: *ed.* Psychoanalysis and Social Work, 8210

Heimler, Eugene: Mental Illness and Social Work, 21786

Heineman, Benjamin Walter: The Politics of the Powerless: A Study of the Campaign against Racial Discrimination, 11170

Heinemann, Margot: Britain in the Nineteen Thirties, 299; '1956 and the Communist Party', 1932; Wages Front, 3877; Britain's Coal: A Study of the Mining Crisis, 6281

Heiser, Francis Bernhard: The Story of St Aidan's College, Birkenhead, 1847–1947, 11911

Heller, Frank: What Do the British Want from Participation and Industrial Democracy?, 6038

Heller, Joseph: British Policy Towards the Ottoman Empire, 1908–1914, 13821; 'Failure of a Mission: Count Bernadotte and Palestine 1948', 14356

Heller, Richard: 'East Fulham Revisited', 2285

Heller, Tom D.: Restructuring the Health Service, 21677

Hellier, Paul: Payment Systems and Productivity, 3954

Helliwell, Denis Rodney: Planning for Nature Conservation, 20212

Hellyer, Arthur George Lee: Gardens to Visit in Britain, 19896; Wartime Gardening for Home Needs, 19897

Helm, Robert M.: The Gloomy Dean: The Thought of William Ralph Inge, 11790

Helmick, Raymond C.: 'Church Structure and Violence in Northern Ireland', 12164

Helmore, Leonard Mervyn: The District Auditor, 3250

Helweg, Arthur Wesley: Sikhs in England: The Development of a Migrant Community, 12465

Hemery, David: Another Hurdle, 27147

Hemm, Gordon: Liverpool: Past—Present—Future, 18048

Hemming, James: Problems of Adolescent Girls, 8427

Hemming, M. F. W.: 'A Statistical Summary of the Extent of Import Control in the United Kingdom since the War', 4804; Studies in Capital Formation in the United Kingdom 1750–1950, 4805; 'The Regional Problem', 5058; 'The Price of Accommodation', 18686

Hemming, Richard: Poverty and Incentives: The Economics of Social Security, 9112

Henderson, Angela: Food Irradiation: Who Wants it?, 20648

Henderson, Arthur: Labour and Foreign Affairs, 13549

Henderson, Brown: The History of the Glasgow Dental Hospital and School 1879–1959, 21482

Henderson, C. A. P.: *ed.* Current British Directories, 59

Henderson, Sir David Kennedy: Society and Criminal Conduct, 10248; The Evolution of Psychiatry in Scotland, 21823, 22413

Henderson, Dorothy: 'Social Class Difference: The Relevance of Language to Socialization', 9483; Social Class, Language and Communication, 9544

Henderson, G. P.: Directory of British Associations and Associations in Ireland, 63

Henderson, George David: The Claims of the Church of Scotland, 12191; The Scottish Ruling Elder, 12192; Presbyterianism, 12197; Church and Ministry: A Study in Scottish Experience, 12198

Henderson, Hubert Douglas: The Inter-War Years and other Papers, 3578

Henderson, Ian: 'White Populism in Southern Rhodesia', 12798

Henderson, Ian: Power Without Glory: A Study of Ecumenical Politics, 12207

Henderson, J. L.: 'The Evolution of Child Care', 8211

Henderson, J.: Race, Class and State Housing: Inequality and the Allocation of Public Housing in Britain, 18706

Henderson, James L.: Irregularly Bold: A Study of Bedales School, 23102

Henderson, Joan: The Industrial Relations Act at Work, 5742; The Industrial Relations Act in the Courts, 5743; Effective Joint Consultation, 6009

Henderson, K. D. D.: Sudan Republic, 14418; Set Under Authority, 14419

Henderson, Kay: *ed.* Pollution: Sources of Information, 19979

Henderson, Sir Nevile Meyrick: Failure of a Mission: Berlin 1937–1939, 13275; Water under the Bridges, 13276

Henderson, Sir Nicholas: The Private Office: A Personal View of Five Foreign Secretaries and of Government from the Inside, 13277; 'America and the Falklands: Case Study in the Behaviour of an Ally', 16098; Channels and Tunnels: Reflections on Britain and Abroad, 16363

Henderson, Patrick David: *ed.* Economic Growth in Britain, 3652

Henderson, Paul: Community Work and the Local Authority: A Case Study of the Batley Community Development Project, 9299

Henderson, R. A.: 'Industrial Overspill from Glasgow: 1958–1968', 18142

Henderson, S. P. A.: Directory of British Associations and Associations in Ireland, 63

Henderson, Thomas: The Savings Bank of Glasgow: A Short History, 4342; The Savings Bank of Glasgow: One Hundred Years of Thrift, 4343

Hendin, Herbert: Black Suicide, 10821

Hendry, John: 'Conservation in Northern Ireland', 20393

Hendy, Sir Philip: The National Portrait Gallery, 23941

Henige, David: Oral Historiography, 26753

Henke, Josef: England in Hitlers politischem Kalkül, 1935–1939, 13695

Hennessy, R. A. S.: The Electric Revolution, 6681

Hennessy, B.: Trade Unions and the British Labour Party', 6772

Hennessy, David James George, Baron Windlesham: Politics in Practice, 1547; Broadcasting in a Free Society, 24877

Hennessy, J. M.: Trustee Savings Bank Legislation and Management, 4340

Hennessy, James: Britain and Europe since 1945: A Bibliographical Guide, 14118

Hennessy, Peter: Cabinet, 721; Mr Attlee's Engine Room: Cabinet Committee Structure and the Labour Governments 1945–51, 729; 'Fulton: 20 Years On', 864; Whitehall, 873; Routine Punctuated by Orgies: The Central Policy Review Staff, 910; 'Britain's Cold War Security Purge: The Origins of Positive Vetting', 16005; 'The Documentary Spoor of Burgess and Maclean', 16039

Henniker, Alan Major: Transportation on the Western Front, 1914–1918, 14646

Henning, G. R.: 'Britain and the Motorship: A Case of the Delayed Adoption of New Technology', 17549

Henrey, Robert: Mrs Bloomsbury Fair, 9911

Henriques, Sir Basil Lucas Quixano: The Homemenders: The Prevention of Unhappiness in Children, 8212; The Indiscretions of a Magistrate: Thoughts on the Work of the Juvenile Court, 8213

Henriques, Louis Fernando: Coal is Our Life: An Analysis of a Yorkshire Mining Community, 9637; Prostitution and Society, 10863

Henry, B. C.: 'Helping Women Addicts at the Coke Hill, England', 10829

Henry, Brian: *ed.* British Television Advertising: The First Thirty Years, 4302, 24874

Henry, Harry: *ed.* Hulton Readership Survey, 25079; The Dynamics of the British Press 1961–1984: Patterns of Circulation and Cover Prices, 25080; *ed.* Behind the Headline: The Business of the British Press, 25339

Henry, J. A.: *ed.* The First Hundred Years of the Standard Bank, 4507

Henry, Joan: Who Lie in Gaol, 7734

Henry, S. D.: 'Scottish Baptists and the First World War', 11856

Henry, S. G. B.: 'Incomes Policy and Wage Inflation: Empirical Evidence for the U.K., 1976–1977', 3854

Henry, Stuart: The Hidden Economy: The Context and Control of Borderline Crime, 10275; Self-Help and Health: Mutual Aid for Modern Problems, 21951

Henry, Thomas: The White Continent: The Story of Antarctica, 27218

Henschen, Folke: The History of Diseases, 22363

Hensher, David A.: *ed.* Urban Transport Economics, 16300

Hensman, C.: Drugs, Alcohol and Tobacco in Britain, 22189

Henson, Brian *and* Morgan, Colin, The First Hits: The Definitive Guide to the Hits of the 1940s and 1950s. 1988

Henson, Herbert Hensley: Herbert Hensley Henson, Retrospect of an Unimportant Life, 11740; More Letters of Herbert Hensley Henson, 11743; The Oxford Groups, 12399

Henwood, Melanie: Inside the Family: The Changing Roles of Men and Women, 10054

Hepburn, A. C.: The Conflict of Nationality in Modern Ireland, 2731

Hepburn, James: The Author's Empty Purse and the Rise of the Literary Agent, 25009; *ed.* Letters of Arnold Bennett, 25380; The Art of Arnold Bennett, 25381; *ed.* Arnold Bennett: Sketches for Autobiography, 25382; *ed.* Arnold Bennett: The Critical Heritage, 25383

Heppenstall, Rayner: 'Leeds, 1929–1934', 23510; Portrait of the Artist as a Professional Man, 24756

Hepple, Alexander: Race, Jobs and the Law in Britain, 10971; Business and Employment,. 1. Race Relations, 10972; The Position of Coloured Workers in British Industry, 10973

Hepple, B. A.: Public Employee Trade Unionism in the United Kingdom: The Legal Framework, 6858; Equal Pay and the Industrial Tribunals, 7782

Hepple, Peter: *ed.* The Joint Problems of the Oil and Water Industries, 6517; *ed.* The Petroleum Industry in the United Kingdom, 6518

Hepworth, Barbara: A Pictorial Autobiography, 24187

Hepworth, Mike: Blackmail: Publicity and Secrecy in Everyday Life, 10272

Hepworth, Noel Peers: The Finance of Local Government, 3260, 4866

Hepworth, R.: 'The Effects of Technological Change in the Yorkshire Coalfield, 1960–1965', 6342

Heraud, Brian Jeremy: Sociology and Social Work: Perspectives and Problems, 8788; 'Social Class and the New Towns', 18240; 'The New Towns and London's Housing Problem', 18241

Herbert, Alan Patrick: Independent Member, 1431

Herbert, Charles: Twenty Five Years as Archbishop of Canterbury: A Biography of Archbishop Davidson, 11691; Twenty Five Years as Bishop of London: A Biography of Bishop Winnington-Ingram, 11768

Herbert, David T.: Urban Geography: A Social Perspective, 17845, 18271, 20411

Herbert, G. W.: Parents and Children in the Inner City, 10108

Herbert, Jesse Basil: *ed.* Occasional Addresses, 1893–1916 by the Earl of Oxford and Asquith 974; *ed.* Speeches by the Earl of Oxford and Asquith, 974; *ed.* The Justice of Our Case . . . Four Speeches, 974; *ed.* The Paisley Policy,1920, 974; *ed.* The War: Its Causes and its Messages: Speeches . . . August-October 1914, 974

Herbert, Mike: Accounting, 4202

Herd, Harold: Panorama, 1900–1942, 356; The March of Journalism: The Story of the British Press from 1622 to the Present Day, 25044

Heren, Louis [Philip]: The Power of the Press?, 25081; Growing up on The Times, 25246

Heriot Watt University: The Esk Valley: A Sub-regional Study of Eastern Midlothian: A Study Carried out for Midlothian County Council, 5286

Herman, Josef: Related Twilights: Notes from an Artist's Diary, 24020

Herman, Valentine: 'Adjournment Debates in the House of Commons', 647; *ed.* The Backbencher and Parliament: A Reader, 698; Cabinet Studies: A Reader, 718

Hermann, P. W.: Die Communist Party of Great Britain: Untersuchungen zur geschichtlichen Entwicklung, Organisation, Ideologie und Politik der C.P.G.B. von 1920–1970, 1923

Hermans, F. A.: 'Electoral System and Political Systems: Recent Developments in Britain, 2226

Hermon, Celia: Commuters Pastimes, 16288

Herne, Leslie William: A Guide to British History, 1868–1959, 298

Hernon, Joseph M.: 'The Last Whig Historian and Consensus History: George Macaulay Trevelyan, 1876–1962', 26826

Hernton, Calvin C.: Sex and Racism, 10975

Heron, Alistair: Ageing and Semi-skilled: A Survey in Manufacturing Industry on Merseyside, 8571; The Home Help Service in England and Wales, 8591

Heron, Liz: *ed.* Truth, Dare or Promise: Girls Growing Up in the Fifties, 7691; Changes of Heart: Reflections on Women's Independence, 7796

Heron, Patrick: Ivon Hitchens, 24021

Heron, S. D.: The Development of Aircraft Engines and the Development of Aviation Fuels, 17566

Herrick, J.: Vision and Realism: A Hundred Years of "The Freethinker", 11896

Herriott, Robert Eugene: Social Class and the Urban School: The Impact of Pupil Background on Teachers and Principals, 22826

Herrman, I.: Britain and Zion: The Fateful Entanglement, 14287

Herrmann, Frank: Sotheby's: Portrait of an Auction House, 23944; ed. English as Collectors: A Documentary Chrestomathy, 23945

Herron, Andrew: Kirk by Divine Right: Church and State: Peaceful Co-Existence, 12223

Herson, Zoe: Women at the Top: Achievement and Family Life, 7806

Hersov, Lionel: ed. Child Psychiatry: Modern Approaches, 8342

Heseltine, Michael: Where there's a Will, 1233

Heseltine, Philip: Delius, 24324

Heskin, Ken: Northern Ireland: A Psychological Analysis, 2887

Heslinga, Marcus Willem: The Irish Border as a Cultural Divide: A Contribution to the Study of Regionalism in the British Isles, 2665

Hess, A. F.: Scurvy: Past and Present, 21131

Hess, Alan Charles: Some British Industries: Their Expansion and Achievements, 1936–1956, 7205

Hession, Charles H.: John Maynard Keynes, 26593

Hetherington, Alastair: News, Newspapers and Television, 24926; Guardian Years, 25247

Hetherington, Sir Hector James Wright: The British University System, 1914–1954, 23377; The University College at Exeter, 23497

Hetherington, John: Air-Borne Invasion, 14951

Hetherington, P.: British Paternalism and Africa, 1920–1940, 12687

Hetherington, S. J.: Katharine Atholl, 1353

Heubel, E. J.: 'Church and State in England: The Price of Establishment', 11628

Heuser, Beatrice: Western Containment Policies in the Cold War: The Yugoslav Case 1948–1953, 13974

Heussler, Robert V.: Yesterday's Rulers: The Making of the British Colonial Service, 12510; The British in Northern Nigeria, 12758; ed. British Malaya: A Bibliographical and Biographical Compendium, 12897; British Rule in Malaya: The Malayan Civil Service and its Predecessors, 1867–1942, 12919; Completing a Stewardship: The Malayan Civil Service 1942–1957, 12920

Hewat, Elizabeth Glendinning Kirkwood: Vision and Achievement, 1796–1956: A History of the Foreign Missions of the Churches United in the Church of Scotland, 12236

Hewbridge, D. G.: The Open University: A Select Bibliography, 23546

Hewett, Sheila: The Family and the Handicapped Child: A Study of Cerebral Palsied Children in Their Own Homes, 21912

Hewins, Angela: ed. Mary, after the Queen: Memories of a Working Girl, 7635

Hewins, William Albert Samuel: The Apologia of an Imperialist: Forty Years of Empire Policy, 1433

Hewison, Robert: Under Siege: Literary Life in London 1939–45, 23781; In Anger: Culture in the Cold War 1945–60, 23782; Too Much: Art and Society in the Sixties 1960–75, 23785; Footlights: A Hundred Years of Cambridge Comedy, 26291; Monty Python: The Case Against, 26292

Hewitson, John: The Grammar School Tradition in a Comprehensive World, 22961

Hewitt, Cecil Rolph: Believe What You Like: What Happened between the Scientologists and the National Association for Mental Health, 21863

Hewitt, Christopher: 'Catholic Grievances, Catholic Nationalism and Violence in Northern Ireland during the Civil Rights Period: A Reconsideration', 2852

Hewitt, George Henry Gordon: ed. Strategist for the Spirit: Leslie Hunter, Bishop of Sheffield, 11747; The Problems of Success: A History of the Church Missionary Society, 1910–42, 12359

Hewitt, James: The Irish Question, 2843

Hewitt, Margaret: Children in English Society: Vol. 2. From the 18th Century to the Children's Act 1948, 8306

Hewitt, Patricia: ed. Danger! Women at Work. [Report of a Conference Organised by the National Council for Civil Liberties on 11th February 1974.], 7767

Hewitt, William H.: A Bibliography of Police Administration, Public Safety and Criminology, to July 1 1965, 10288; British Police Administration, 10737

Hewlett, Sir William Meyrick: Forty Years in China, 13278

Hewlings, David: 'The Treatment of Murderers', 10801

Hewson, Sir Joseph Bushby: A History of the Practice of Navigation, 27250

Hey, J. S.: The Evolution of Radio Astronomy, 26429

Hey, Richard David: ed. Science, Technology and Environmental Management: Based on a symposium of 'Applied Environmental Science' Held at the 1973 Annual Conference of the Institute of British Geographers, 19968; ed. The Management of Water Resources in England and Wales, 20097; ed. Environmental Impact Assessment, 20233

Heyck, Thomas William: 'The Idea of a University in Britain, 1870–1970', 23293

Heyer, Fritz: Das Britische Finanzsystem, 4659

Heyes, Alan: London Midland Steam: The Closing Years, 16870

Heywood, Jean Schofield: Children in Care: The Development of the Service for the Deprived Child, 8214; An Introduction to Teaching Casework Skills, 8215; Casework

and Pastoral Care, 8216, 9202; 'Recent Developments in the Structure and Practice of Child Care', 8217; Financial Help in Social Work: A Study of Preventative Work with Families under the Children and Young Persons Act, 1963, 10093

Heywood, Robert W.: 'London, Bonn, the Königswinter Conferences and the Problem of European Integration', 14221

Hezlet, Sir Arthur Richard: The 'B' Specials: A History of the Ulster Special Constabulary, 2932, 10762; The Submarine and Sea Power, 15376

Hibbard, Benjamin Horace: Effects of the Great War upon Agriculture in the United States and Great Britain, 19430

Hibbert Journal, 11542

Hibbert, Christopher: Edward, the Uncrowned King, 483; The Roots of Evil: A Social History of Crime and Punishment, 10174; The Battle of Arnhem, 14953

Hibbs, John Alfred Blyth: Transport for Passengers: A Study in Enterprise without Licence, 16222; Transport Studies: An Introduction, 16223; ed. The Omnibus: Readings in the History of Road Passenger Transport, 17257; ed. The History of British Bus Services, 17258; ed. The Country Bus, 17259; ed. 'Road Passenger Transport in Ulster and its Relationship with the Railways', 17260; ed. 'The London Independent Bus Operators 1922–1934', 17261; ed. Regulation: An International Study of Bus and Coach Licensing, 17262

Hickey, Des: The Prince, Being the Public and Private life of Larushka Mischa Skikne, a Jewish Lithuanian Vagabond Player, otherwise Known as Laurence Harvey, 26055

Hickey, John Vincent: Urban Catholics: Urban Catholicism in England and Wales from 1829 to the Present Day, 11948; Religion and the Northern Ireland Problem, 12154

Hickie, John: Ulster: A Case Study in Conflict Theory, 2918

Hickinbotham, Sir Tom: Aden, 13869

Hickman, Mary: The History of the Irish in Britain: A Bibliography, 11367

Hicks, Donald: Primary Health Care: A Review, 22095

Hicks, Sir John Richard: The Social Framework: An Introduction to Economics, 3435; After the Boom: Thoughts on the 1966 Economic Crisis, 3654; Crisis '75, 3675; The Theory of Wages, 3866; The Problem of Valuation for Rating, 4864; The Incidence of Local Rates in Great Britain, 4865; The Problem of Budgetary Reform, 4917; The Crisis in Keynesian Economics, 26604

Hicks, Lady Ursula Kathleen: British Public Finances: Their Structure and Development, 1880–1952, 662, 4581; The Finance of British Government, 1920–1936, 4580, 6130; Public Finance, 4581; The Problem of Valuation for Rating, 4864; The Incidence of Local Rates in Great Britain, 4865

Hickson, D. J.: 'Professionalisation in Britain: A Preliminary Measure', 9769

Higenbotham, S.: Amalgamated Society of Woodworkers: Our Society's History, 6851

Higgens, Gavin L.: Printed Reference Material, 241; ed. British Broadcasting, 24715

Higgin, G. W.: The Relationship of Social Status and Rank in the R.A.F, 14980

Higgins, Irving John: The Chemistry and Microbiology of Pollution, 20000

Higgins, Joan: The Poverty Business: Britain and America, 9103

Higgins, John: Glyndebourne: A Celebration, 24571

Higgins, Sydney: The Benn Inheritance: The Story of a Radical Family, 1090

Higgins, Sydney Herbert: A History of Bleaching, 6474

Higgins, T. T.: 'Great Ormond Street', 1852–1952, 21461

Higginson, Fred Hall: A Bibliography of the Works of Robert Graves, 25546

Higginson, James Henry: Changing Thought in Primary and Secondary Education, 23146

Higgs, Leslie: New Town: Social Involvement in Livingston: An Account of the Formative Years, 19018

Higgs, Philip: Blackpool's Trams: 'As Popular as the Tower', 17215

Higham, Charles: Wallis: Secret Lives of the Duchess of Windsor, 497

Higham, Robin David Stewart: The British Rigid Airship, 1908–1931: A Study in Weapons Policy, 14643; The Military Intellectuals in Britain 1918–1939, 14729; The British Airship 1908–1931: A Study in Weapons Policy, 17532; British Imperial Air Routes, 1918 to 1939: The Story of Britain's Overseas Airlines, 17623; 'British Airways Limited 1935–1940, 17624

Higher Education: Meeting the Challenge: Cmnd 114, 23335

Highet, Campbell: The Glasgow and South-Western Railway, 16934

Highet, John: The Churches in Scotland Today: A Survey of their Principles, Strength, Work and Statements, 12241; The Scottish Churches: A Review of their State 400 Years after the Reformation, 12242; 'Churchgoing in Scotland', 12243; A School of One's Choice: A Sociological Study of the Fee-paying Schools of Scotland, 23219

Highfield, John Somerville: 'The Supply of Electricity', 7168

Highham, A. R. C.: 'The History of St Paul's Hospital, London', 20961

Highton, L.: British Gardeners: A Biographical Dictionary, 26975

Hignett, Norman Howarth: Portrait in Grey, Being a Full Length Portrait of Prison Conditions and Administration, and of the Philosophy which Supports Them, 10365

Hikins, Harold R.: ed. Building the Union: Studies on the Growth of the Workers' Movement: Merseyside, 1756–1967, 6889

Hiles, M.: The Young Farmers' Club Movement, 19673

Hilken, Thomas John Norman: Engineering at Cambridge University: 1783–1965, 22438

Hill Farm Research Organisation: Science and Hill Farming: 25 Years of Work at the Hill Farming Research Organisation, 1954–1979, 19700

Hill, Alan: In Pursuit of Publishing, 24967

Hill, Alfred Bostock: Internal Migration—And its Effects upon Death Rates, 7266

Hill, Alfred Tuxbury: The Emergency Training Scheme for Teachers in England and Wales, 22726

Hill, Sir Archibald Vivian: Trails and Trials in Physiology: A Bibliography, 1909–1964: With Reviews of Certain Topics and Methods and a Reconnaissance for Further Research, 22320

Hill, Arthur Cheney Clifton: The British Attack on Unemployment, 7003

Hill, Austin Bradford and Hill, Brian: 'The Life of Sir Leonard Erskine Hill, F.R.S., (1866–1952)', 20962

Hill, C. J.: 'Great Britain and the Saar Plebiscite of 13 January 1935', 13669

Hill, Charles Peter: British Economic and Social History, 1700–1975, 3506; The History of Bristol Grammar School, 22994

Hill, Charles: Behind the Screen: The Broadcasting Memoirs of Lord Hill of Luton, 24796

Hill, Christopher R.: Horse Power: The Politics of the Turf, 27126

Hill, Clifford Stanley Horace: ed. Race: A Christian Symposium, 10951; How Colour Prejudiced is Britain?, 11159; Immigration and Integration: A Study of the Settlement of Coloured Minorities in Britain, 11160; West Indian Migrants and the London Churches, 11250, 12444; Black Churches: West Indian and African Sects in Britain, 12447; 'From Church to Sect: West Indian Religious Sect Development in Britain', 12448

Hill, Cyril F.: ed. Origin and Development of the Microscope, 7104

Hill, David: ed. The Burden on the Community, 8931; 'The Attitudes of West Indian and English Adolescents in Britain', 10995

Hill, Dilys M.: Participating in Local Affairs, 9362

Hill, Douglas William: The Burden on the Community, 21383

Hill, Douglas: ed. Tribune 40: The First Forty Years of a Socialist Newspaper, 25160

Hill, Harold Arthur: The Local Government Act 1929 (Annotated), 3114; Town and Country Planning Acts, 20343

Hill, Harry: Milk: Production and Control, 20651

Hill, J. R.: British Sea Power in the 1980s, 15409

Hill, Jeffrey: '"First Class" Cricket and the Leagues: Some Notes on the Development of English Cricket, 1900–1940', 27099

Hill, John Michael Meath: The Seafaring Career: A Study, 9688

Hill, Margaret Neville: An Approach to Old Age and its Problems, 8572

Hill, Maureen: ed. National Portrait Gallery: Concise Catalogue, 1856–1969, 23940

Hill, Michael James: The Sociology of Public Administration, 817, 9256; Men Out of Work: A Study of Unemployment in Three English Towns, 7016, 9694; The State, Administration and the Individual, 818; Analysing Social Policy, 8835; Community Action and Race Relations: A Study of Community Relations Committees in Britain, 11011; ed. A Sociological Yearbook of Religion in Britain, 12231, 12390; A Sociology of Religion, 12388

Hill, Sir Norman: War and Insurance, 4221

Hill, Prudence: To Know the Sky: The Life of Air Chief Marshal Sir Roderic Hill, 15959

Hill, R.: Destroyer Captain, 15312

Hill, Ralph: Music, 24273

Hill, Reuben: International Bibliography of Research in Marriage and the Family, 1900–1964, 9922

Hill, Richard Leslie: A Bibliography of the Anglo-Egyptian Sudan, From the Earliest Times to 1937, 14409; A Biographical Dictionary of the Sudan, 14410

Hill, Robert: The Great Coup, 15113

Hill, Stephen: The Dockers: Class and Tradition in London, 16662

Hill, T. P.: 'Wages and Labour Turnover', 3937

Hillary, Sir Edmund: 'The Ascent of Mount Everest'. 27240; and Hillary, Peter: Ascent: Two Lives Explored: The Autobiographies of Sir Edmund and Peter Hillary, 27243

Hillebrandt, Patricia M.: Analysis of the British Construction Industry, 6178

Hiller, Peter: 'Social Reality and Social Stratification', 9449

Hilliard, David: God's Gentlemen: A History of the Melanesian Mission, 1849–1942, 12363

Hilliard, Frank H.: A Short History of Education in British West Africa, 12730; 'Divinity Studies in Colleges for the Education and Training of Teachers', 22720; ed. Teaching the Teachers, 22739

Hillier, Bevis: John Betjeman: A Life in Pictures, 25396; A Tonic to the Nation: The Festival of Britain 1951, 27171

Hillier, Caroline: The Bulwark Shore: Thanet and the Cinque Ports, 16678

Hilling, D.: 'The Restructuring of the Severn Estuary Ports', 16654; ed. Seaport Systems and Spatial Change: Technology, Industry and Development Strategies, 16654

Hillman, Ellis M.: Bicycles: Boon or Menace?, 17171

Hillman, James: Suicide and the Soul, 10812

Hillman, Judy: Geoffrey Howe: A Quiet Revolutionary, 1240

Hillmer, Norman: 'Defining the First British Commonwealth: The Hankey Memorandum and the 1926 Imperial Conference', 12535

Hills, George: Rock of Contention: A History of Gibraltar, 12853

Hills, J.: 'Candidates: The Impact of Gender', 2264; 'Women Local Councillors: A Reply to Bristow', 7833

Hills, John: Public Finances in Perspective, 4660

Hills, R. I.: The General Strike in York, 1926, 6952

Hills, Reginald John Taylor: Phantom Was There, 15481; The Royal Dragoons, 15620; The Life Guards, 15692

Hillson, Norman: I Speak of Germany: A Plea for Anglo-German Friendship, 13692; Alexander of Tunis: A Biographical Portrait, 14751

Hillyard, Paddy A. R.: Justice in Northern Ireland: A Study in Social Confidence, 2854; Law and the State: The Case of Northern Ireland, 2855; Ten Years On: The Legal Control of Political Violence, 2856; Housing in Northern Ireland, 18497

Hilmore, Peter: Live Aid, 9192

Hilton Young, E., Lord Kennet: The System of National Finance, 4664

Hilton Young, Wayland, Baron Kennet: The Profumo Affair 9898, Controlling our Environment, 19942

Hilton, George Woodman: The Truck System, including A History of the British Truck Acts, 1465–1960, 7221; The Illustrated History of Paddle Steamers, 16587

Hilton, James: The Duke of Edinburgh, 515

Hilton, John: Rich Man, Poor Man, 3775, 9030; ed. Why I go in for the Pools, 27112

Hilton, K. J.: The Lower Swansea Valley Project, 18913; ed. 'The Lower Swansea Valley Project', 18914

Hilton, Norman: 'The Land's End Peninsula—The Influence of History on Agriculture', 19477; 'Technology, Economy and Society in a Long-settled Area [Land's End]', 19478

Himbury, D. Mervyn: British Baptists: A Short History, 12025; The South Wales Baptist College, 1807–1957, 12042, 12299

Himes, Norman E.: Medical History of Contraception, 21063

Himmelfarb, Gertrude: 'The Intellectual in Politics: The Case of the Webbs', 2152

Himmelweit, Hilde Therese: How Voters Decide: A Longitudinal Study of Political Attitudes and Voting Extended over Fifteen Years, 2254; Television and the Child, 8218, 24828; 'The Views of Adolescents on Some Aspects of Social Class Structure', 9503

Himsworth, Sir Harold Percival: The Hazards to Man of Nuclear and Allied Radiations: A Second Report to the Medical Research Council, 20125

Hinchcliffe, Arnold P.: British Theatre 1950–70, 26230

Hinchliff, Peter Bingham: The One-sided Reciprocity: A Study in the Modification of the Establishment, 11629

Hinde, Richard Standish Elphinstone: The British Penal System 1773–1950, 10328, 10399

Hinde, Thomas: Forests of Britain, 19718

Hindell, Keith: 'Scarborough and Blackpool: An Analysis of some Votes at the Labour Party Conferences of 1960 and 1961', 1737; Abortion Law Reformed, 7876; Abortion and Contraception: A Study of Patient's Attitudes, 7877; 'The Genesis of the Race Relations Bill', 11100

Hinden, Rita: ed. R. H. Tawney: the Radical Tradition, 2146; Empire and After: A Study of British Imperial Attitudes, 12567

Hindess, Barry: The Decline of Working Class Politics, 1796, 9687; The Use of Official Statistics in Sociology: A Critique of Positivism and Ethnomethodology, 8022; Philosophy and Methodology in the Social Sciences, 8023

Hindle, Wilfrid Hope: The Morning Post, 1772–1937: Portrait of a Newspaper, 25145

Hindley, George: A History of Roads, 17098

Hinds, Donald: Journey to an Illusion: The West Indians in Britain, 11257

Hines, Albert Gregorio: 'Trade Unions and Wage Inflation in the United Kingdom 1893–1961', 3992; 'Wage Inflation in the United Kingdom, 1948–1962: A Disaggregated Study', 3993

Hines, N.: Lost Girls, 10844

Hines, Tony: Accounting and Finance, 4203

Hingston, W.: Never Give Up: The History of the King's Own Yorkshire Light Infantry, 1919–1942, 15745

Hinings, B.: Clergy, Ministers and Priests, 11588

Hinks, Arthur Robert: Maps and survey, 26696

Hinks, Peter: Twentieth Century British Jewellery 1900–1980, 24124

Hinnings, C. R.: 'Role Relations and Value Adaptation: A Study of the Professional Accountant in Industry', 9828

Hinsley, Sir Francis Harry: ed. British Foreign Policy under Sir Edward Grey, 1204; The Naval Side of British History, 1485–1945, 15231; Command of the Sea: The Naval Side of British History from 1918 to the End of the Second World War, 15232; Hinton, Christopher, Baron: Heavy Current Electricity in the United Kingdom: History and Development, 6393

Hinton, James: Labour and Socialism: A History of the British Labour Movement 1867–1974, 1684; Trade Unions and Revolution: The Industrial Politics of the early British Communist Party, 1934; The First Shop Stewards' Movement, 6698; Protests and Visions: Peace Politics in Twentieth Century Britain, 13437; 'Self-Help and Socialism: The Squatters Movement of 1946', 18380

Hinton, Percival: The University of Birmingham: its History and Significance, 23459

Hinxman, Margaret: The Films of Dirk Bogarde, 24689

Hiorns, Frederick Robert: Town Building in History, 17911

Hiorns, R. W.: Demographic Patterns in Developed Societies, 7435, 9939

Hiro, Dilip: Black British, White British, 11012; The Indian Family in Britain, 11013; 'Three Generations of Tiger Bay', 11014

Hirsch, Fred: 'Britain's Debts and World Liquidity', 4613; The Pound Sterling: A Polemic, 4707; Newspaper Money: Fleet Street and the Search for the Affluent Reader, 25070

Hirsch, Guenter Paul Hermann: 'Static Structure with a Changed Content: The Agrarian Situation in Great Britain since 1835', 19398; Young Farmers' Clubs: Report on a Survey in England and Wales on their History, Organisation and Activities . . . , 19399

Hirsch, Steven: The Suicide Syndrome, 10823

Hirshfield, Claire: 'In Search of Mrs Ryder: British Women in Serbia during the Great War', 13388

Hirst, David L.: Edward Bond, 25949

Hirst, Francis Wrigley: The History of Local Government in England, 3112; The Consequences of the War to Great Britain, 3748; British War Budgets, 4911

Hirst, I. R. C.: ed. The Consumer Society, 20456

Hirst, Lloyd: Coronel and After, 14665

Hirst, Margaret E.: The Quakers in Peace and War, 12148

Historical Association: Annual Bibliography of Historical Literature, 417; The Historical Association, 1906–1956, 26769

Historical Magazine of the Protestant Episcopalian Church: 1966+, 11536

Historical Manuscripts Commission: Accessions to Repositories and Reports Added to the National Register of Archives, 73; Record Repositories in Great Britain: A Geographical Directory, 76

Historical Records of the Queen's Own Cameron Highlanders: vol. 7 1949–61, 15583

Historical abstracts, 1

History Today Special Issue on 'The History of Blacks in Britain', 11076

History of Education, 22597

History of The Times: Vol. IV: The 150th Anniversary and Beyond, 25158

History of the Birmingham Medical School: 1823–1925, 20909

Hitchcock, Francis Clere: 'Stand To': A Diary of the Trenches, 1915–1918, 14480

Hitchcock, Henry-Russell: Architecture: Nineteenth and Twentieth Centuries, 23881

Hitchins, D. M. W. N.: 'Wealth, Women and Inheritance', 3769

Hitchman, Harry G.: Harwich: A Nautical History, 16689

Hitchman, Janet: They Carried the Sword, 8219; Such a Strange Lady: An Introduction to Dorothy L. Sayers 1893–1957, 25795

Hitt, W. H.: Economic Issues in Immigration—An Exploration of the Liberal Approach to Public Policy on Immigration, 11435

Hoagland, Mahlon: Discovery: The Search for DNA's Secrets, 26480

Hoar, Geoffrey: The Missing Macleans, 16037

Hoare, John: Tumult in the Clouds: A Story of the Fleet Air Arm, 15421

Hoare, Michael: Sure and Stedfast: A History of the Boys' Brigade, 1883–1983, 8510

Hoare, Samuel John Gurney, Baron Templewood: Nine Troubled Years, 1235; Ambassador on Special Mission, 13279; The Fourth Seal: The End of a Russian Chapter, 13916

Hoath, David Charles: Council Housing, 18432

Hobart, Frank William Arthur: Pictorial History of the Machine Gun, 15510

Hobart, Michael: 'History and Religion in the Thought of Herbert Butterfield', 26781

Hobbs, Arthur O.: A Guide to the Representation of the People Act of 1918, 2274

Hobbs, Jack: Bristol Helicopters: A Tribute to Raoul Hafner, 17556

Hobbs, Mary Elliot: Great Farmers, 19444

Hobbs, William H.: 'The British Arctic Air Route Expedition', 7042

Hobday, Peter: Industrial Relations: The Boardroom Viewpoint, 5760

Hobhouse, Leonard Trelawney: Sociology and Philosophy: A Centenary Collection of Essays and Articles, 8037

Hobhouse, Stephen: English Prisons To-day: Being the Report of the Prison System Enquiry Committee, 10337

Hobkirk, E. I. W.: The Training of Girls in the Scottish Borstal System, 10545

Hobley, Leonard Frank: Living and Working: A Social and Economic History of England, 1760–1960, 3477

Hobman, D. L.: 'University Expansion', 23384

Hobman, David: The Social Challenge of Ageing, 8586

Hobsbawm, Eric John Ernest: ed. The Invention of Tradition. 451; 'Twentieth Century British Politics', 1589; ed. The Forward March of Labour Halted?, 1767; Politics for a Rational Left: Political Writing 1977–1988, 1769; 'The British Communist Party', 1938; Industry and Empire: An Economic History of Britain since 1750, 3493; 'Trade Union Historiography', 6688; 'From Social History to the History of Society', 7907; Labouring Men: Studies in the History of Labour, 9686

Hobson, Bulmer: A Short History of the Irish Volunteers, 2756; Ireland Yesterday and Tomorrow, 3059

Hobson, Sir Harold: The Pearl of Days: An Intimate Memoir of the Sunday Times 1822–1972, 25155; Verdict at Midnight: Sixty Years of Dramatic Criticism, 25922; The Theatre now, 25923; Indirect Journey, 25924; Theatre in Britain: A Personal View, 26248

Hobson, J. W.: ed. Hulton Readership Survey, 25079

Hobson, John Atkinson: Free-thought in the Social Sciences, 7891; Some Aspects of Recent British Economics, 26585; Confessions of an Economic Heretic, 26588

Hobson, John Morrison: Some Early and Later Houses of Pity, 21410

Hobson, Sir Oscar Rudolf: A Hundred Years of the Halifax: The History of the Halifax Building Society, 1853–1953, 4388

Hobson, W.: ed. The Theory and Practice of Public Health, 21003

Hoch, P. K.: 'Immigration into Britain: No Utopia: Refugee Scholars in Britain', 11440

Hocken, Peter: Streams of Renewal: The Origins and Early Development of the Charismatic Movement in Great Britain, 12131

Hockey, John: Squaddies: Portrait of a Subculture, 15455

Hockey, Lisbeth: Feeling the Pulse: A Study of District Nursing in Six Areas, 21717; Use or Abuse? A Study of the State Enrolled Nurse in the Local Authority Nursing Service, 21719; Life before Death, 22093

Hockley, Graham C.: Public Finance: An Introduction, 4657

Hodder-Williams, Richard: Public Opinion Polls and British Politics, 2267; White Farmers in Rhodesia, 1890–1965, 12796

Hodge, Alan: The Long Week-end: A Social History of Great Britain, 1918–1939, 7557

Hodge, Ian: Rural Employment: Trends, Opinions and Choices, 19079

Hodges, Frank: The Nationalisation of the Coal Industry, 6252

Hodges, Laurent: Environmental Pollution, 19986

Hodges, Michael: Multinational Corporations and National Government: A Case Study of the United Kingdom's Experience, 1964–1970, 5556

Hodges, Peter: British Military Markings 1939–1945, 15509

Hodges, Sheila: God's Gift. A Living History of Dulwich College, 23056; Gollancz: The Story of a Publishing House 1928–1978, 24961

Hodgetts, John Edwin: Organisation, Staffing and Control of the British Civil Service, 909

Hodgkin, Sir Alan Lloyd: et al. The Pursuit of Nature: Informal Essays on the History of Physiotherapy, 22329

Hodgkiss, Alan Geoffrey: ed. Merseyside in Maps, 5183; ed. The Resources of Merseyside, 18052

Hodgman, Donald R.: 'British Techniques of Monetary Policy: A Critical Review', 4629

Hodgson, Godfrey: Lloyd's of London: A Reputation at Risk, 4242

Hodgson, H. B.: 'Notes on the History of the Teaching of Geography', 26670

Hodgson, Leonard Grundy: Building Societies: Their Origin, Methods and Principles, 4356

Hodgson, M.: 'London Festival Ballet: Looking at its First Quarter Century, 1950–1975', 24221

Hodgson, Robin: Britain's Home Defence Gamble, 15140

Hodgson, S.: Ramsay Muir: An Autobiography and Some Essays, 26806

Hodgson, Stuart: Lord Halifax: An Appreciation, 1219; The Liberal Policy for Industry, 7206

Hodgson, Vera: Few Eggs and No Oranges: A Diary Showing how People in London and Birmingham Lived through the War Years, 1940–45, 15175

Hodin, Joseph Paul: Barbara Hepworth, 24188

Hodjera, Zoran: 'Short Term Capital Movements of the United Kingdom, 1963–1967', 4614

Hodson, Gillian: Rattigan: The Man and his Work, 25981

Hodson, Henry Vincent: Slump and Recovery, 1929–1937: A Survey of World Economic Affairs, 3582; ed. The British Commonwealth and the Future, 12548; The British Empire, 12549; Twentieth Century Empire, 12563; The Great Divide: Britain, India, Pakistan, 13173

Hodson, Mark: Doctors and Patients: A Relationship Examined, 20827

Hodson, Patricia M.: The Manchester Ship Canal: A Guide to Historical Sources, 16411

Hoe, Susanna: The Man who Gave his Company Away: A Biography of Ernest Barder, Founder of the Scott Barder Commonwealth, 6217

Hoenig, Julius: The Desegregation of the Mentally Ill, 21800

Hoff, Ebbe Curtis: A Bibliography of Aviation Medicine, 21052

Hoff, Hebbel E.: 'The Technological Background of Physiological Discovery: Ballistics and the Graphic Method', 20963

Hoffman, Frederick Ludwig: National Health Insurance and the Friendly Societies, 4103; 'The Mortality from Respiratory Diseases in the Glass Industry', 21273

Hoffman, John David: The Conservative Party in Opposition, 1945–1951, 1634

Hoffman, W.: 'The Growth of Industrial Production in Great Britain: A Quantitative Study', 4996

Hoffmann, Alther Gustav: British Industry, 1700–1950, 4955

Hofstetter, P.: 'Le Problème Noir en Grande Bretagne', 11148

Hogan, James Martin: Impelled into Experiences: The Story of the Outward Bound Schools, 23126

Hogan, Michael J.: Informal Entente: The Private Structure of Cooperation in Anglo-American Economic Diplomacy, 1918–1928, 14020; 'Informal Entente: Public Policy and Private Management in Anglo-American Petroleum Affairs, 1918–1924', 14021; The Marshall Plan: America, Britain and the Reconstruction of Western Europe, 1947–1952, 14127; Palestine and the Anglo-American Connection, 1945–1950, 14335; 'Note: United States-British Collaboration on Illegal Immigrants to Palestine, 1945–1947', 14336

Hogan, Thomas Brian: The Hire-purchase Act of 1965 with Annotations, 20494

Hogarth, James: The Payment of the General Practitioner: Some European Comparisons, 21500

Hogben, Carol: ed. The Art of Bernard Leach, 24136

Hogben, Lancelot: ed. Political Arithmetic: A Symposium of Population Studies, 7354

Hogenkamp, B.: 'Film and the Workers' Movement in Britain, 1929–1939', 24644

Hogg, Alexander: ed. Scotland and Oil, 6529, 7172

Hogg, Ian Vernon: A History of Artillery, 7078, 15487; Military Smallarms of the Twentieth Century, 15485; Military Pistols and Revolvers: The Handguns of the Two World Wars, 15486; British Artillery Weapons and Ammunition, 1914–1918, 15488

Hogg, Margaret H.: Has Poverty Diminished? A Sequel to 'Livelihood and Poverty', 9021

Hogg, Oliver Frederick Gillian: The Royal Arsenal: Its Background, Origin and Subsequent History, 6612, 15490; Artillery: Its Origins, Heyday and Decline, 7079

Hogg, Quintin McGarel, Lord Hailsham:

New Charter: Some Proposals for Constitutional Reform, 617; The Door Wherein I Went, 1209; A Sparrow's Flight: Memoirs, 1210; The Purpose of Parliament, 1211; The Case for Conservatism, 2189

Hogg, William Richey: Ecumenical Foundations: A History of the International Missionary Council and its Nineteenth-Century Background, 12354

Hoggart, Keith: 'Property Tax Resources and Political Party Control in England 1974–1984', 3269; 'Responses to Local Fiscal Stress: Local Government Expenditures in England 1976–85', 3272; Politics, Geography and Social Stratification, 9609; 'Political Party Control and the Sale of Local Authority Dwellings', 18438

Hoggart, Richard: The Uses of Literacy: Aspects of Working Class Life, with Special Reference to Publications and Entertainments, 9674, 25199; ed. Your Sunday Paper, 25157; W. H. Auden, 25362

Hoggart, Simon David: Michael Foot: A Portrait, 1192

Hogwood, Brian W.: ed. Regional Government in England, 2404; The Tartan Fringe: Quangos and other Associated Animals in Scotland, 2491; Government and Shipbuilding: The Politics of Industrial Change, 16613

Hohler, Sir Thomas Beaumont: Diplomatic Petrel, 13280

Hohman, Helen Fisher: The Development of Social Insurance and Minimum Wage Legislation in Great Britain, 4025, 8918

Hoinville, Gerald: ed. Britain into Europe: Public Opinion and the E.E.C. 1961–1975, 14183

Holbrook, David Kenneth: Llareggub Revisited: Dylan Thomas and the State of Modern Poetry, 25833

Holdaway, Simon: ed. The British Police, 10705; ed. Inside the British Police: A Force at Work, 10706

Holden, Alan S.: Children in Care, 8220

Holden, Anthony: The Queen Mother: A Birthday Tribute, 507; Charles, Prince of Wales, 528; Olivier, 26081

Holden, K.: The Economics of Wage Controls, 3955

Holden, Matthew: The Desert Rats, 14897; The British Soldier, 15451

Holden, Pat: Women Administrative Officers in Colonial Africa, 1944–1960, 7748

Holderness, B. A.: British Agriculture since 1945, 19417

Holdgate, Martin Wyatt: A History of Appleby, County Town of Westmorland, 18090; A Perspective on Environmental Pollution, 19988; ed. Environmental Issues, 19989

Holdich, Patrick G. H.: 'A Policy of Percentages? British Policy and the Balkans after the Moscow Conference of October 1944', 13965

Hole, Winifred Vere: Trends in Population, Housing and Occupancy Rates 1861–1961, 7420, 18711; 'Social Effects of Planned Rehousing', 9422; Houses and People: A Review of User Studies at the Building Research Station, 18712; 'Housing Standards and Social Trends', 18713

Holford, John: Reshaping Labour: Organisation, Work and Politics: Edinburgh in the Great War and After, 2524

Holford, William Graham, [Baron]: Civic Design: An Inquiry into the Scope and Nature of Town Planning, 18773; Design in City Centres, 18774; Cambridge Planning Proposals, 18851; The Future of Merseyside: Town and Country Planning Schemes, 18891; The City of London: Destruction and Survival, 18933; Corby New Town, 19009

Holgate, Eileen: ed. Communicating with Children: Collected Papers, 8221

Holland, Alec John: The Age of Industrial Expansion: British Economic and Social History since 1700, 3483; Our Exbury: Life in an English Village in the 1920s and Early 30s, 19187

Holland, Bernard: ed. Baron Friedrich von Hügel: Selected Letters, 1896–1924, 11984

Holland, Sir Henry: Frontier Doctor: An Autobiography, 20868

Holland, Jack: Too Long a Sacrifice: Life and Death in Ireland since 1969, 2888

Holland, Robert F.: European Decolonization 1918–81, 12593; 'The End of an Imperial Economy: Anglo-Canadian Disengagement in the 1930s', 12656

Holland, Robert H. C.: ed. Law, Justice and Equity: Essays in Tribute to G. W. Keeton, 23833

Holland, Stuart: The Socialist Challenge, 2157

Holland, Walter W.: Oxford Textbook of Public Health, 21004, 22091

Hollenweger, Walter: The Pentecostals, 12130

Holles, Robert Owen: Now Thrive The Armourers: A Story of Action with the Gloucesters in Korea, 16130

Hollet, Dave: From Cumberland to Cape Horn: The Complete History of the Sailing Fleet of Thomas and John Brocklebank of Whitehaven and Liverpool, 16562

Holley, Stephen: Washington: Quicker by Quango: The History of Washington New Town, 1964–1983, 18206

Holliday, Bob: The Norton Story, 17185; The Unapproachable Norton, 17186

Holliday, Leslie: ed. The Integration of Technologies, 22522, 22525

Hollier, Harold M.: 'The Kensingtons' 13th London Regiment, 15694

Hollingdale, Stuart Havelock: Electronic Computers, 7089

Hollings, F.: 'Women in Further Education', 22489

Hollingsworth, Dorothy Frances: 'Nutritional Policies in Great Britain, 1939–46', 20551; 'Trends in Food Consumption in the United Kingdom', 20552; ed. Nutritional Problems in a Changing World, 20553

Hollingsworth, J. Roger: A Political Economy of Medicine: Great Britain and the United States, 21611

Hollingsworth, John Brian: The Illustrated Encyclopaedia of the World's Steam Passenger Locomotives from the 1820s to the Present Day, 17029

Hollingsworth, Mark: The Press and Political Dissent: A Question of Censorship, 25082

Hollingsworth, Thomas Henry: Migration: A Study Based on Scottish Experience between 1939 and 1964, 7276; 'The Demography of the British Peerage', 7367; The Demography of the English Peerage, 7368

Hollis, Sir Leslie Chasemore: The Captain General: A Life of H.R.H Prince Philip, 516

Hollis, [Maurice] Christopher: Parliament and its Sovereignty, 628; Along the Road to Frome, 1237; 'The Conservative Party in History', 1641; The Two Nations: A Financial Study of English History, 3400; The Homicide Act: With a Foreword by Gerald Gardiner, 10790; Social Evolution in Modern English Catholicism, 11946; Eton: A History, 23058; The Oxford Union, 23563; A Study of George Orwell, 25745

Holloway, J. Christopher: The Business of Tourism, 26948

Holloway, Mark: Norman Douglas: A Biography, 25479

Holloway, Roger: The Queen's Own Royal West Kent Regiment: The Dirty Half-Hundred, 15675

Holloway, Vernon: 'Institutional Treatment of Young Offenders', 10683

Hollowell, Peter Gilbert: The Lorry Driver, 7238, 9666

Holly, Douglas: Society, Schools and Humanity: The Changing World of Secondary Education, 22939

Holman, Dennis: Lady Louis. Life of the Countess Mountbatten of Burma, 540

Holman, Robert: ed. Social Welfare in Modern Britain, 7602, 8818; Trading in Children: A Study of Private Fostering, 8222; 'The Place of Fostering in Social Work', 8223; Poverty: Explanations of Social Deprivation, 9079; ed. Deprived Families in Britain, 9080; 'The British Urban Programme', 17853

Holmans, A. E.: 'The Growth of Public Expenditure in the United Kingdom since 1950', 4763; 'Current Population Trends in Britain', 7366; Housing Policy in Britain: A History, 18516; 'A Forecast of Effective Demand for Housing in Great Britain in the 1970s', 18697

Holme, Alan: The Motor Vehicle Industry, 17398

Holme, Anthea: Working Mothers and their Children: A Study for the Council for Children's Welfare, 7688; Social Workers and Volunteers, 9212; Children's Play: A Study of Needs and Opportunities: A Study for the Council for Children's Welfare, 27010

Holme, Bryan: Advertising: Reflections of a Century, 4296

Holmes, A. R.: Midland: 150 Years of Banking Business, 4497

Holmes, Colin: Theses and Dissertations in Economic and Social History in Yorkshire Universities, 1920–1974, 3394; 'Violence and Race Relations in Britain, 1953–1968', 11181; ed. Anti-Semitism in British Society, 1876–1939, 11338; ed. Immigrants and Minorities in British Society, 11431;

'Immigration into Britain: The Myth of Fairness: Racial Violence in Britain', 11432; John Bull's Island: Immigration and British Society 1871–1971, 11433

Holmes, Eileen M.: Education in Scotland, 23598

Holmes, Frederick L.: 'The Transformation of the Science of Nutrition', 20554

Holmes, G. V.: The Likes of Us, 8224

Holmes, Sir George Morgan: The National Hospital, Queen Square, 1860–1948, 21454

Holmes, Graeme: Britain and America: A Comparative Economic History, 1850–1939, 3711

Holmes, J. Derek: 'English Catholicism from Hinsley to Heenan', 11947

Holmes, John W.: The Better Part of Valor: Essays on Canadian Diplomacy, 12653

Holmes, Martin: Political Pressure and Economic Policy: The British Government 1970–1974, 3673; The Labour Government 1974–1979, 3676; The First Thatcher Government, 1979–1983: Contemporary Conservatism and Economic Change, 3689

Holmes, Richard: The Bitter End, 15074

Holmstedt, B. O.: Readings in Pharmacology, 22300

Holmyard, E. J.: 'Priests of Pomona', 7041

Holroyd, Michael [De Courcy]: The Art of Augustus John, 24025; Augustus John, 24026; Hugh Kingsmill: A Critical Biography, 25612

Holst, Gustav and Vaughan Williams, Ralph: Heirs and Rebels: Letters Written to each other and Occasional Writings on Music, 24383

Holst, Imogen: Britten, 24314; Gustav Holst: A Biography, 24350; The Music of Gustav Holst, 24351

Holt, A. T.: Political Parties in Action: The Battle of Barons Court, 2324

Holt, Arthur: Transport: A Report by a Committee under the Chairmanship of Mr. Arthur Holt. M.P., 16246

Holt, Edgar Crawshaw: Protest in Arms: The Irish Troubles, 1916–1923, 2746, 14697

Holt, Geoffrey Ogden: The North West, 16818; A Short History of the Liverpool and Manchester Railway, 16956

Holt, Hazel: ed. A Very Private Eye: The Diaries, Letters and Notebooks of Barbara Pym, 25781

Holt, James Clarke: The University of Reading: the First Fifty Years, 23576

Holt, Peter Malcolm: Egypt and the Fertile Crescent, 1516–1922: A Political History, 14396; A Modern History of the Sudan from the Funf Sultanate to the Present Day, 14414

Holt, Raymond Vincent: The Unitarian Contribution to Social Progress in England, 12114

Holtby, Robert Tinsley: Eric Graham, 1888–1964, 12266

Holton, Gerald: ed. 'The Making of Modern Science: Biographical Studies', 20964

Holton, J. E.: 'The Status of the Coloured in Britain', 10936

Homa, Bernard: Orthodoxy in Anglo-Jewry, 1880–1940, 12424

Home Office Research Unit: Report No 11: Studies of Female Offenders, 10203

Home Office: The Rehabilitation of Drug Addicts: Report of the Advisory Committee on Drug Dependence, 22198

Homosexual Law Reform Society: Memorandum, 10866; Homosexuality: The Law into Action, 10867

Hondelink, Engelbert Rutgerus: Review of Dr. Beeching's Report, 1776; Suburban Passenger Services: A Paper on 'Commuter Traffic', 16286; Stopping Tracks, 16775

Honderich, Ted: ed. Social Ends and Political Means, 8796

Honey, John: Does Accent Matter: The Pygmalion Factor, 23810

Honigsbaum, Frank: Health, Happiness and Security, 21550; The Division in British Medicine: A History of the Separation of General Practice from Hospital Care, 1911–1968, 21944; The Struggle for the Ministry of Health, 1914–1919, 22023; 'Unity in British Public Health Administration: The Failure of Reform, 1926–1929', 22113

Honoré, Deborah Duncan: Trevor Huddleston: Essays on his Life and Work, 11745

Hood, C. C.: 'British Fishing and the Iceland Saga', 19828

Hood, Catriona: Children of West Indian Immigrants: A Study of One-year-olds in Paddington, 11263

Hood, Christopher: 'So You Think You Know what Government Departments Are . . . ?', 819; Cutback Management in Public Bureaucracies: Popular Theories and Observed Outcomes in Whitehall, 897; Big Government in Hard Times, 3677

Hood, Dina Wells: Working for the Windsors, 487

Hood, Katherine: Room at the Bottom: National Insurance in the Welfare State, 4032

Hood, Neil: ed. Industry, Policy and the Scottish Economy, 5277; Foreign Multinationals and the British Economy: Impact and Policy, 5565

Hood, Peter: Ourselves and the Press: A Social Study of News Advertising and Propaganda, 25119

Hood, Roger Grahame: ed. Crime, Criminology and Public Policy: Essays in Honour of Sir Leon Radzinowicz, 10129; Key Issues in Criminology, 10130; Criminology and the Administration of Criminal Justice: A Bibliography, 10292; 'Social Work in Prison', 10338; Borstal Re-assessed, 10525; Homeless Borstal Boys: A Study of their After-care and After-conduct, 10526; The Research Potential of the Case Records of Approved School Boys: A Detailed Study of the Information Available in the Records of Boys at an Approved School Classifying Centre, 10527; ed. Community Homes and the Approved School System, 10654; ed. Residential Treatment of Disturbed and Delinquent Boys, 10655

Hood, Stuart: A Survey of Television, 24852

Hood, W.: 'Inter-Industry Wage Levels in United Kingdom Manufacturing', 3916

Hoogvelt, Ankie M.: 'Ethnocentrism, Authoritarianism and Powellism', 11187

Hooke, J. M.: Historical Change in the Physical Environment: A Guide to Sources and Techniques, 20195

Hooker, Ian: 'Industrial Relations Law Commentary: Proposed Changes in the Law', 5809

Hooker, James R.: Black Revolutionary: George Padmore's Path from Communism to Pan-Africanism, 12689

Hooker, Jeremy: John Cowper Powys, 25768

Hoole, Kenneth: North East England, 16812; North Eastern Branch Lines since 1925, 16907; North Eastern Railway Buses, Lorries and Autocars, 16908; The East Coast Main Line since 1925, 16930; Railway Stations in the North East, 16992

Hooper, David: Official Secrets: The Use and Abuse of the Act, 766

Hooper, Douglas: The Dynamics of a Changing Technology: A Case Study in Textile Manufacturing, 6444

Hooper, Geoffrey William Winsmore: The Fighting at Jutland, 14649

Hooper, Richard: ed. Colour in Britain . . . Based on a BBC Radio Series, 10942

Hooper, Shadrach George: The Finance of Farming in Great Britain, 19495

Hooper, Walter: ed. Letters of C. S. Lewis, 25661; C. S. Lewis: A Biography, 25662

Hope, Chris: Nuclear Power: Features, Cash and Benefits, 6664

Hope, Edward William: Industrial Hygiene and Medicine, 4113; 'General Principles of Housing and Town Planning in Relation to Health', 18596; 'Civil Sanitation and the War', 21287; 'Some Constructive Suggestions in Regard to the Proposed Ministry of Health', 21311; 'The Influence of a Ministry of Health on Local Organization and Administration', 21312; Textbook of Public Health, 22043; Health at the Gateway: Problems and International Obligations of a Seaport City, 22044

Hope, Ian: The Campbells of Kilmun: Shipowners 1853–1980, 16557

Hope, Keith: The Social Grading of Occupations: A New Approach and Scale, 9552; ed. The Analysis of Social Mobility: Methods and Approaches, 9553

Hope, Ronald: The Merchant Navy, 16486

Hopewell, Sydney: One Hundred and Fifty Years of Modern Britain, 1815 to the Present Day, 345

Hopkin, Deian: ed. History and Computing, 26736; 'Domestic Censorship in the First World War', 26901

Hopkins, A. G.: An Economic History of West Africa, 12733

Hopkins, Eric: A Social History of the English Working Classes 1815–1945, 7613

Hopkins, Sir Frederick Gowland: 'On the Choice of Food in War Time', 20576

Hopkins, Harry: The New Look: A Social History of the Forties and Fifties in Britain, 7575

Hopkins, Kenneth: The Powys Brothers: A Biographical Appreciation, 25772

Hopkins, Leon: The Hundredth Year [of the Institute of Chartered Accountants], 4198

Hopkins, P. G. H.: 'Labour Education in Britain', 23706

Hopkins, Peter: Lymplesham: A Dip into the History of a Somerset Parish, 19344

Hopkins, Sarah: *ed.* Greenham Common; Women at the Wire, 13440

Hopkins, Sheila: A Perspective of Wages and Prices, 3912

Hopkins, Steve: Planning in Oxford: An Historical Survey and Bibliography, 18900

Hopkinson, Alan: The Mountain Men: The Early History of Rock Climbing in North Wales, 27159

Hopkinson, Sir Alfred: 'Adoption', 8225; 'Wife Desertion and Adoption of Children', 8226

Hopkinson, Angela: Single Mothers: The First Year: A Scottish Study of Mothers bringing up Children on their Own, 7873

Hopkinson, Sir [Henry] Tom: *ed.* Picture Post 1938–50, 25150, 25179; Of This Our Time: A Journalist's Story 1905–1950, 25248; Under the Tropic, 25249

Hoppen, Karl Theodore: Ireland since 1800: Conflict and Conformity, 2647

Hopson, Barrie: 'Modernising University Teaching', 22535

Horden, Anthony: Legal Abortion: The English Experience, 7881

Horder, Thomas Jeeves [Baron]: Bread: The Chemistry and Nutrition of Flour and Bread, with an Introduction to their Chemistry and Technology, 20700; Fifty Years of Medicine, being the Harben Lectures for 1952, 21188; Health and a Day, 21189; *gen. ed.* The British Encyclopaedia of Medical Practice, 21251; *gen. ed.* Cumulative Supplement, Including Index of New Subjects, 21252; *gen. ed.* Medical Progress, 21253

Horder, T. M.: The Little Genius: A Memoir of the First Lord Horder, 20872

Hordern, Charles: East Africa, 14524

Hore, Brian D.: Alcohol Dependence, 22162

Horn, Joyce M.: History Theses 1971–1980: Historical Research for Higher Degrees in the Universities of the United Kingdom, 90

Horn, Pamela: Rural Life in England in the First World War, 19047

Hornby, John Wilkinson: Forestry in Britain, 19716

Hornby, Robert: 'Parties in Parliament, 1959–1963: The Labour Party', 1744; The Press in Modern Society, 25045

Hornby, William: Factories and Plant, 5047

Horne, Alistair: Macmillan, 1894–1956, 1037; Macmillan, 1957–1986, 1038; Death of a Generation: From Neuve Chapelle to Verdun and the Somme, 14588

Horne, H. Oliver: A History of Savings Banks, 4335; Savings Banks at Kintore and Inverurie: A Short History, 4347; Insch and Upper Garioch Savings Bank, 4348; Forres Savings Bank 1839–1939, 4349; Ellon Savings Bank 1839–1939, 4350; Stonehouse Savings Bank, 1838–1938, 4351

Horne, M. A. C.: The Central Line, 17017; The Northern Line: A Short History, 17018; The Victoria Line: A Short History, 17019

Horner, A. A.: Population in Ireland: A Census Atlas, 140

Horner, Lady Frances: Time Remembered, 971

Horner, Simon A.: The Isle of Man and the Channel Islands: A Study of their Status in Constitutional, International and European Law, 2623

Hornsby, Jeremy: All you Need is Ears, 24581

Hornsby-Smith, Michael P.: Roman Catholics in England: Studies in Social Structure since the Second World War, 11950

Hornsey College of Art: The Hornsey Affair, 9867

Horobin, Gordon W.: *ed.* Experience with Abortion: A Case Study of North-East Scotland, 7882; 'Community and Occupation in the Hull Fishing Industry', 9423; 'The Social Differentiation of Ability', 9494; 'Adjustment and Assimilation: The Displaced Person', 10907; 'Doctors, Patients and the State: Relationships and Decision-making', 21294

Horowitz, Dan: 'The British Conservatives and the Racial Issue in the Debate on Decolonization', 10992, 12597; 'Attitudes of British Conservatives towards Decolonisation in Africa', 12702

Horricks, Raymond: Modern Jazz: A Survey of Developments since 1939, 24452; *ed.* The Music goes Round and Round: A Cool Look at the Record Industry, 24576

Horrocks, Sir Brian: Corps Commander, 14957

Horrocks, Meryl: Social Development in the New Communities, 9401

Horrocks, Sidney: The State as Publisher: A Librarian's Guide to the Publications of His Majesty's Stationery Office, 172; Lancashire Business Histories, 3422

Horsfall, John: The Iron Masters of Penns, 1720–1970, 6604

Horsley, John E.: A Short History of Brixham, 19182

Horsley, Lee: Churches and Churchgoers: Patterns of Church Growth in the British Isles since 1700, 11546

Horsman, George: Inflation in the 20th Century, 4021

Horton, A. V. M.: The British Residency in Brunei 1906–1959, 12950

Horton, Frank E.: Geographic Perspectives on Urban Systems, with Integrated Readings, 17842

Horwood, Arthur Reginald: The Flora of Leicestershire and Rutland: A Topographical, Ecological and Historical Account, with Biographies of Former Botanists (1620–1933), 26561

Hosking, Gordon Albert: Pension Schemes and Retirement Benefits, 3968, 8577

Hoskins, George Owen: Iron and Steel in Britain, 1870–1930, 6545

Hoskins, Katharine Bail: Today the Struggle: Literature and Politics in England during the Spanish War, 23776

Hoskins, William George : Provincial England: Essays in Social and Economic History, 3517; The Midland Peasant: The Economics and Social History of a Leicester Village, 19166

Hoskyns, Sir John: 'Whitehall and Westminster: An Outsider's View', 738

Hospitals and Health Services Year Book, 1889+, 20760

Houfe, S.: Sir Albert Richardson: The Professor, 23878, 24058

Hough, Graham: The Dark Sun: A Study of D. H. Lawrence, 25649

Hough, John Aspey: The Co-operative Movement in Britain, 1888

Hough, Richard Alexander: The Battle of Jutland, 14653; The Hunting of Force Z: The Brief, Controversial Life of the Modern Battleship, and its Tragic Close with the Destruction of 'Prince of Wales' and 'Repulse', 15032; First Sea Lord: An Authorised Biography of Admiral Lord Fisher, 15255; Mountbatten: Hero of our Time, 15275; Dreadnought: A History of the Modern Battleship, 15348; A History of the World's High Performance Cars, 17366

Houghton, Douglas [Baron]: 'The Labour Backbencher', 1747; Paying for the Social Services, 8936

Houghton, Graham: A History of the Motor Car, 17332

Houghton, R. W.: *ed.* Public Finance, 4658

Houghton, Vincent Paul: Initial Bibliography of Immigration and Race, 11520

Houghton-Evans, William: Planning Cities: Legacy and Portent, 17914

Houlihan, Michael: World War I Trench Warfare, 14481

Hourani, Albert H.: Britain and the Arab World, 13807

House, Frank Holman: Timber at War: An Account of the Organisation and Activities of the Timber Control, 1939–1945, 19792

House, Jack: Dunoon, 1868–1968, 18146; Pavement in the Sun, 25250

House, John William: The North East, 5135; *ed.* Northern Geographical Essays: In Honour of G. H. J. Daysh, 5194; *ed.* North Eastern England, 5195; *ed.* Rural North-East England 1951–1961: Report to the Development Commissioners, 5196; *ed.* People on the Move: The South Tyne in the Sixties: Report to the Minister of Labour, 5197; Migrants of North-East England 1951–1961: Character, Age and Sex, 5198; Northumbrian Tweedside: The Rural Problem, 5207; Northern Region and Nation: A Short Migration Atlas 1960–1961. Papers on Migration and Mobility in Northern England, No. 4, 7270; Mobility of the Northern Business Manager. Report of the Ministry of Labour. P.M.N.E. No. 8, 7271; Where Did the School Leavers Go? Report of the Ministry of Labour. P.M.N.E. No. 7, 7272; Pit Closure and the Community: Report to the Minister of Labour, Newcastle-upon-Tyne, 9643; Northern Graduates of '64: Braindrain or Brainbank?, 9876; *ed.* The U.K. Space Resources, Environment, and the Future, 19967; The Frontiers of Geography, 26637

Household, Humphrey: Gloucestershire Railways in the 20th Century, 16935

Housing Research Foundation: Home Ownership in England and Wales, 18745;

Home Ownership for Lower Income Families, 18746

Houston, George Frederick Barclay: *ed.* The County of Dumfries, 19225; Agrarian Change in the Scottish Highlands: The Role of the Highlands and Islands Development Board in the Agricultural Economy of the Crofting Counties, 19621

Houston, James Dobbie: The Fairfields Project, 16632

Houston, James Macintosh: Urbanization and its Problems. Essays in Honour of Edmund W. Gilbert, 18269, 20409

Houston, Penelope: The Contemporary Cinema, 24656

Houston, Renée: Don't Fence Me in, 26323

Hovi, O.: The Baltic Area in British Policy, 1918–1921, vol. I: From the Compiègne Armistice to the Implementation of the Versailles Treaty, 11, 13877

Howard League for Penal Reform: The Howard Journal of Penology and Crime Prevention 1921–1975, 10261

Howard, Alexander L.: 'The Ash Tree', 19766;'The Beech Tree', 19767; 'The Cedar Tree', 19768; 'Deciduous Cypress', 19769; 'The Elm Tree', 19770; 'The Oak Tree', 19771; 'The Plane Tree', 19772; 'The Scots Pine', 19773; 'The Sycamore Tree', 19774; 'The Willow Tree', 19775; 'The Yew Tree', 19776

Howard, Alexander: Endless Cavalcade: A Diary of British Festivals and Customs, 27172

Howard, Anthony Mitchell: The Making of the Prime Minister, 964; Rab: The Life of R. A. Butler, 1131; *ed.* The Crossman Diaries: Selections from the Diaries of a Cabinet Minister, 1964–1970, 1167; 'The Parties, Elections and Television', 24897

Howard, Cecil: *ed.* West African Explorers, 27196

Howard, D.: Directory of Theatre Research and Information Sources in the U.K, 25901

Howard, Derek Lionel: The English Prisons: Their Past and Future, 10362; The Education of Offenders: A Select Bibliography, 10363

Howard, Esmé William, Baron Howard of Penrith: Theatre of Life, 13281

Howard, George: Guardians of the Queen's Peace: The Development and Work of Britain's Police, 10689

Howard, Sir Michael Eliot: Central Organisation for Defence, 825, 15475; The Mediterranean Strategy in the Second World War, 14718; August 1942–August 1943, 14719; The Coldstream Guards, 1920–1946, 15610

Howard, Michael Spencer: Jonathan Cape: Publisher, 24950

Howard, Patricia: The Operas of Benjamin Britten, 24315

Howard, Peter: Britain and the Beast, 12397

Howard, Philip [Nicholas Charles]: The British Monarchy in the Twentieth Century, 432; The Royal Palaces, 457; We Thundered out, 25159

Howard, Robert Sugden: The Movement of Manufacturing Industry in the United Kingdom 1945–1965, 5046

Howard-White, Frank Buller: Nickel: An Historical Review, 7202

Howard-Williams, Jeremy N.: Night Intruder: A Personal Account of the Radar War between the RAF and Luftwaffe Night-fighter Forces, 15115

Howarth, David: Sovereign of the Seas: The Story of British Sea Power, 14677; Dawn of D-Day, 14952; The Story of P & O: The Peninsular and Orient Steamship Navigation Company, 16532

Howarth, Ken: Dark Days: Memoirs and Reminiscences of the Lancashire and Cheshire Coalmining Industry up to Nationalisation, 9645

Howarth, Osbert John Radcliffe: The Making of Geography, 26654

Howarth, Patrick: George VI: A Biography, 506; Under Cover: The Men and Women of the Special Operations Executive, 15081

Howarth, Richard W.: 'The Political Strength of British Agriculture', 19549; Farming for Farmers? A Critique of Agricultural Support Policy, 19586

Howarth, Thomas Edward Brodie: Prospect and Reality: Great Britain 1945–1955, 300; Culture, Anarchy and the Public Schools, 23025; Cambridge between Two Wars, 23472

Howarth, Thomas: Charles Rennie Mackintosh and the Modern Movement, 24040

Howarth, V.: Pre-school Education and Care, 23168

Howarth, William: Water Pollution Law, 20090

Howarth-Williams, Martin: R. D. Laing: His Work and its Relevance to Sociology, 8033

Howat, Bill: Policy Planning and the First Regional Reports in Scotland, 20288

Howat, Gerald Malcolm David: From Chatham to Churchill: British History, 1760–1965, 346

Howe, David: An Introduction to Social Work: Theory Making Sense in Practice, 8905

Howe, Ellis: The British Federation of Master Printers, 1900–1950, 6835; The Society of London Bookbinders, 1780–1951, 6840; The Black Game: British Subversive Operations against Germany during the Second World War, 15102

Howe, Elspeth: Under 5: A Report on Nursery Education, 23143

Howe, George Melvyn: National Atlas of Disease Mortality in the United Kingdom: Prepared on Behalf of the Royal Geographical Society, 7457, 22229; Man, Environment and Disease in Britain: A Medical Geography of Britain through the Ages, 22230; *ed.* A World Geography of Human Diseases, 22231; *ed.* Environmental Medicine, 22232

Howe, James Ronald: Two Parent Families: A Study of their Resources and Needs in 1968, 1969, 1970: An Analysis based on Family Expenditure Data, 20432

Howe, M.: 'The Iron and Steel Board and Steel Pricing, 1953–1967', 6570

Howe, Sir Ronald Martin: The Story of

Scotland Yard: A History of the C.I.D from the earliest Times to the Present Day, 10755

Howe, W. Stewart: Competition in British Industry: Restrictive Practices Legislation in Theory and Practice, 4935

Howell, Catherine: Part-time Social Work: A Study of Opportunities for the Employment of Trained Social Workers, 8705

Howell, David: A Lost Left: Three Studies in Socialism and Nationalism, 1330, 1706, 2526; British Social Democracy: A Study in Development and Decay, 1760

Howell, Georgina: *ed.* In Vogue: Six Decades of Fashion, 24156

Howell, R. S.: Dutch Elm Disease Survey, 1971, 1972–1973, 19777

Howell, Trevor H.: 'Origins of British Geriatrics', 7040

Howell-Thomas, Dorothy: Socialism in West Sussex: A History of the Chichester Constituency Labour Party, 1786; Mutual Understanding: The Social Services and Christian Belief, 11842

Howells, John Gwilym: Family Psychiatry, 10072

Howells, Kim: 'The Politics of Coal in South Wales, 1945–48', 6337

Howells, Roscoe: Farming in Wales, 19638

Howerd, Frankie: On the Way I Lost it, 26324

Howes, E. G.: 'Housing in Britain, France and Western Germany', 18687

Howes, Frank Stewart: Music 1945–1950, 24270; The English Musical Renaissance, 24271; The Music of Ralph Vaughan Williams, 24376; The Music of William Walton, 24385

Howes, Graham: The Police and the Community, 10723

Howes, Ismene V.: The Church in Social Work: A Study of Moral Welfare Work Undertaken by the Church of England, 11833

Howes, Keith: Spotlight on Sources of Information about Children, 8272

Howie, Will: *ed.* Thames Tunnel to Channel Tunnel: 150 Years of Civil Engineering, 16365

Howitt, Frederick Oliver: Bibliography of the Technical Literature on Silk, 6443

Howitt, Sir Harold: History of the Institute of Chartered Accountants in England and Wales 1870–1965, 4199

Howkins, Alun: Poor Labouring Men: Rural Radicalism in Norfolk 1872–1923, 9708, 19662; Trends in Leisure, 1919–1939, 26919

Howlett, Ann: Complaints Against Doctors: A Study of Professional Accountability, 20836

Howse, Derek: The Sea Chart: An Historical Survey based on the Collections in the National Maritime Museum, with an Introduction by G. S. Ritchie, 26708

Howse, Violet Mary: Lyford: A Parish History, 19343

Howson, Geoffrey: A History of Mathematics Teaching in England, 22829

Howson, Henry F.: London's Underground, 17004

Howson, Susan: Domestic Monetary Management in Britain, 1919–1938, 4578; 'The Managed Floating Pound, 1932–1939',

4687; 'The Management of Sterling, 1932–1939', 4688; 'Sterling's Managed Float: The Operation of the Exchange Equalisation Account, 1932–1939', 4689; The Economic Advisory Council, 1930–1939, 6139; 'Keynes on Monetary Policy, 1910–1946', 26612

Hoyle, B. S.: ed. Seaport Systems and Spatial Change: Technology, Industry and Development Strategies, 16654

Hoyle, Bernard: ed. British Economic Performance, 1880–1980, 3511

Hoyle, Sir Fred: The Small World of Fred Hoyle: An Autobiography, 26383; The Nature of the Universe, 26384; Astronomy, 26385; Of Men and Galaxies, 26386; From Stonehenge to Modern Cosmology, 26387; Lifecloud: The Origin of Life in the Universe, 26388

Hoyles, James Arthur: The Church and the Criminal, 10221

Hoyos, F. A.: Barbados: A History from the Amerindians to Independence, 13078

Hoyt, Edwin Palmer: Disaster at the Dardanelles, 1915, 14545; The Life and Death of H.M.S. Hood, 15027

Htin Aung, Maung: The Stricken Peacock: Anglo-Burmese Relations 1752–1948, 13201

Huang, Su-shu: 'Jeans' Criterion of Gravitational Instability', 7135

Hubback, David F.: No Ordinary Press Baron: A Life of Walter Layton, 25092

Hubback, Eva Marian: The Population of Britain, 7361; Population Facts and Policies, 7362

Hubback, Judith: Wives who Went to College, 7678; 'The Fertility of Graduate Women', 7679

Hubbard, Eric Hesketh: A Hundred Years of British Painting, 1851–1951, 23960

Hubbard, Gilbert E.: British Far Eastern Policy, 13580

Hubble, Sir Douglas: 'William Osler and Medical Education', 20965

Hubert, Jane: 'Kinship and Geographical Mobility in a Sample from a London Middle-Class Area', 10065

Huby, Meg: Cutback Management in Public Bureaucracies: Popular Theories and Observed Outcomes in Whitehall, 897

Huddleston, J.: 'Trade Unions in a Technological Society', 6775

Hudgins, Michael W.: Jnr. 'The Floating Pound Sterling of the Nineteen Thirties', 4686

Hudleston, Nigel Andrew: History of Malton and Norton, 19345

Hudson, Bruce Angus: Post-war British Thoroughbreds and Specialist Cars, 17360

Hudson, Celia A.: A Survey of Alcohol Education in the United Kingdom, 22159

Hudson, Derek Rommel: The Royal Society of Arts, 1754–1954, 23950; For the Love of Painting: The Life of Sir David Kelly, 24030; James Pryde, 1886–1941, 24054; Arthur Rackham: His Life and Work, 24055; Writing Between the Lines: An Autobiography, 25251

Hudson, Graham S.: The Aberford Railway and the History of the Garforth Collieries, 16920

Hudson, James William: The History of Adult Education, 23665

Hudson, Kenneth A.: Pawnbroking, An Aspect of British Social History, 4538; The History of English China Clays: Fifty Years of Pioneering and Growth, 6349; Behind the High Street, 6645; A Dictionary of the Teenage Revolution and its Aftermath, 8529; The Jargon of the Professionals, 9775; Air Travel: A Social History, 17645; Diamonds in the Sky: A Social History of Air Travel, 17646; An Awkward Size for a Town: A Study of Swindon at the 100,000 Mark, 18118; Food, Clothes and Shelter: 20th Century Industrial Archaeology, 20468; The Archaeology of the Consumer Society: The Second Industrial Revolution in Britain, 20469; A Social History of Archaeology: The British Experience, 26356

Hudson, Lynton Alfred: The English Stage, 1850–1950, 25905; The Twentieth Century Drama, 26198

Hudson, Miles: Triumph or Tragedy?: Rhodesia to Zimbabwe, 12801

Hudson, Ray: New Towns in North East England, 18211; Images of the Urban Environment, 20309

Hudson, W. Donald: Modern Moral Philosophy, 26843

Hudson, W. J.: Casey, 12632

Huelin, Gordon: Old Catholics and Anglicans 1931–1981, 12337; King's College, London, 1828–1978, 23525

Huff, Graham: 'Young Offenders, Gambling and Video Game Playing', 10532

Huff, Theodore: Charlie Chaplin, 26302

Huffaker, Robert: John Fowles, 25528

Huggett, Frank Edward: A Dictionary of British History 1815–1973, 68; Life below Stairs: Domestic Servants in England from Victorian Times, 9701; Goodnight Sweetheart: Songs and Memories of the Second World War, 15152; A Short History of Farming, 19410; The Newspapers, 25058

Huggett, Renée: Daughters of Cain: The Story of Eight Women Executed since Edith Thompson in 1923, 10795

Huggett, Richard: Binkie Beaumont: Eminence Grise of the West End Theatre 1933–73, 26116

Hughes, A.: A History of Cytology, 22321

Hughes, Anselm: The Rivers of the Flood: A Personal Account of the Catholic Revival in England in the Twentieth Century, 11987

Hughes, Arthur: English Accents and Dialects: An Introduction to Social and Regional Varieties of British English, 23804

Hughes, Arthur F. W.: 'A History of Endocrinology', 20966

Hughes, Arthur Joseph: History of Air Navigation, 27248

Hughes, Billy: 'Labour Governments and Comprehensive Schooling, 1945–51', 22925

Hughes, Cledwyn, Baron Cledwyn of Penrhos: The Referendum: The End of an Era: A Lecture . . . , 2578

Hughes, Colin A.: Race and Politics in the Bahamas, 13020; 'Experiment towards Closer Union in the British West Indies', 13099

Hughes, David Lloyd: Holyhead: The Story of a Port, 16690

Hughes, Edward: ed. The Criminal Justice Act 1948, 10296

Hughes, Emmot J.: ed. The Historian as Diplomat: Charles Kingsley Webster and the United Nations, 1939–1946, 13536; 'Winston Churchill and the Formation of the United Nations Organisation', 13537

Hughes, Emrys: The Prince, the Crown and the Cash, 454; Sir Alec Douglas-Home, 1004; Macmillan: Portrait of a Politician, 1036; Keir Hardie, 1424; Sydney Silverman: Rebel in Parliament, 1520

Hughes, Ernest William: Human Relations in Management, 5483

Hughes, Gordon Alexander: Public Policy and the Tax System, 4853

Hughes, Goronwy Alun: ed. Men of No Property: Historical Studies of Welsh Trade Unions, 6848

Hughes, J. G.: Religion and Demographic Behaviour . . . 12155; Internal Migration in Ireland, 19311

Hughes, J. R. T.: 'Measuring British Economic Growth', 3648

Hughes, John Dennis: Industrial Restructuring: Some Manpower Problems, 5782; ed. Trade Unions in Great Britain, 6737, 6832; 'A Note on the Decline in Numbers of Farm Workers in Great Britain', 19670

Hughes, John G.: The Greasepaint War: Show Business, 1939–45, 15153

Hughes, K.: 'Housing Redevelopment and Rehabilitation: A Case Study in Comparative Economics', 18531

Hughes, M. L.: The Chocolate Confectionary Industry, 20692

Hughes, Michael: The Anatomy of Scottish Capital: Scottish Companies and Scottish Capital, 1900–1979, 5273

Hughes, P. A.: The Sea Fishing Industry of Northern Ireland: An Economic Study, 19812

Hughes, P.: 'Decentralisation in Tower Hamlets', 3317

Hughes, Richard: The Administration of War Production, 795

Hughes, Robert: The Red Dean: The Life and Riddle of Dr. Hewlett Johnson, Born 1874, Died 1966, Dean of Canterbury 1931 to 1963, 11796

Hughes, Roger: Oceania: A Basic Annotated Bibliography, 12873

Hughes, S.: Investment in the British Economy, 4753

Hughes, Spike: Glyndebourne: A History of the Festival Opera Founded in 1934 by Audrey and John Christie, 24570

Hughes, Terry: Jutland, 1916, 14657; The Battle of the Atlantic, 14796; The Battle for Concorde, 17568

Hughes, William Ravenscroft: Indomitable Friend: The Life of Corder Catchpool, 1883–1952, 12141

Hugill, Antony: Sugar and all that: A History of Tate & Lyle, 20687

Hugo, Grant: Britain in Tomorrow's World: Principles of Foreign Policy, 13232

Huguet, Victor Jacques Marie: Britain and the War: A French Indictment, 14463

Huizinga, J. H.: Confessions of a European in England, 26802

Hull Development Committee: The City and County of Kingston upon Hull, 5165

Hull, Daniel R.: Casting of Brass and Bronze, 6609

Hull, Roger Harold: The Irish Triangle: Conflict in Northern Ireland, 2878

Hull: A Town Grammar School through Six Centuries: A History of Hull Grammar School against its Local Background, 22996

Hulme, Anthony: School in Church and State, 22876

Hulton, E. G. W.: Conflicts, 25252

Human Resources Abstracts: 1965+, 3

Humberstone, Thomas Lloyd: University Controversies, 23376

Humble, Joseph Graeme: Westminster Hospital 1716–1966, 21445

Humble, Richard: The Rise and Fall of the British Navy, 15244; Fraser of North Cape: The Life of Admiral of the Fleet Lord Fraser (1881–1981), 15257

Humblett, J. E.: 'A Comparative Study of Management in Three European Countries: Preliminary Findings', 5428

Hume, John Robert: Beardmore: The History of a Scottish Industrial Giant, 6375, 16643; A Bed of Sails: The History of P. MacCallum and Sons Ltd. 1781–1981: A Study in Survival, 16550; Workshop of the Empire: Engineering and Shipbuilding in the West of Scotland, 16615; Clyde Shipbuilding from Old Photographs, 16616; Shipbuilders to the World: 125 Years of Harland & Wolff, Belfast, 1861–1986, 16634; Glasgow Stations, 16989; The Making of Scotch Whisky: A History of the Scotch Whisky Distilling Industry, 20729

Hume, Margaret: War on Disease: A History of the Lister Institute, 20902

Humes, James C.: Churchill: Speaker of the Century, 988,

Humes, Walter M.: ed. Scottish Culture and Scottish Education 1800–1980, 2454

Humfrey, Belinda: ed. Essays on John Cowper Powys, 25769

Humphrey, Michael: The Hostage Seekers: A Study of Childless and Adopting Couples, 8228

Humphreys, Betty Vance: Clerical Unions in the Civil Service, 6852

Humphreys, Darlow W.: The University Connection, 22741

Humphreys, Graham: South Wales, 5138

Humphreys, John H.: The General Election 1935 and Constitutional Reform, 2287

Humphreys, Patrick: How Voters Decide: A Longitudinal Study of Political Attitudes and Voting Extended over Fifteen Years, 2254

Humphreys, Robert Arthur: The Royal Historical Society, 1868–1968, 26771

Humphreys, [Travers] Christmas: The Development of Buddhism in England, 12463; Sixty Years of Buddhism in England (1907–1967): A History and Survey, 12464

Humphries, B. K.: 'Nationalisation and the Independent British Airlines 1945–1951', 17621

Humphries, S. V.: The Life of Hamilton Bailey, Surgeon, Author and Teacher of Surgery, 20859

Humphries, Stephen: Hooligans or Rebels? An Oral History of Working Class Children and Youth, 8227, 10664

Humphry, Derek: Police Power and Black People, 11017; Passports and Politics, 11045; Because They're Black, 11169

Humphrys, Graham: 'No Welcome in the Hillsides', 7342

Hunkin, J. W.: 'The Garden at Tresco [Isle of Wight]', 19893

Hunnings, Neville March: Film Censors and the Law, 26913

Hunnisett, B.: A Dictionary of British Steel Engravers, 24090

Hunt, A. R.: Ten Years of Market Gardening: A Business Study of some Small-scale Market Gardens Covering the Period 1950–1960, 19854

Hunt, Alan: 'Class Structure in Britain Today', 9499; Class and Class Structure, 9500

Hunt, Albert: Arden: A Study of his Plays, 25935

Hunt, Audrey: ed. Women and Paid Work: Issues of Equality, 7787; The Elderly at Home: A Survey carried out on Behalf of the Department of Health and Social Security, 8592; Families and their Needs, with Particular Reference to One-Parent Families, 9941; A Survey of Scottish Tourism: A Survey carried out by the Social Survey for the Scottish Development Department in 1964, 26944

Hunt, B. D.: ed. War Aims and Strategic Policy in the Great War, 1914–1918, 13368; Sailor-Scholar: Admiral Sir Herbert Richmond 1871–1946, 15279

Hunt, D.: 'The Channel Tunnel Enters the First Phase', 16360

Hunt, Sir David Wathen Stather: On the Spot: An Ambassador Remembers, 13282; A Don at War, 15079

Hunt, Deirdre: The Engineering Industry in the Grampian Region: A Study for the North East Scotland Development Authority, 5291

Hunt, Dennis D.: Common Sense Industrial Relations, 5791

Hunt, Felicity: Lessons for Life: The Schooling of Girls and Women, 1850–1950, 7693

Hunt, [Henry Cecil] John, [Baron]: 'The Ascent of Mount Everest'. 27240; The Ascent of Everest, 27241; Life is Meeting, 27242

Hunt, Hugh: ed. The Revels History of Drama in English, 25907

Hunt, J. Leslie: Twenty-One Squadrons: History of the Royal Auxiliary Air Force 1925–1957, 15920

Hunt, J.: 'Race Relations in Britain', 11162

Hunt, James: James Hunt against all the Odds, 27141

Hunt, John H.: 'The Foundation of a College: The Conception, Birth and Early Days of the College of General Practitioners', 20967

Hunt, John: Managing People at Work: A Manager's Guide to Behaviour in Organisations, 5473

Hunt, Kenneth Edward: The State of British Agriculture, 1955–1956, 19494; The State of British Agriculture, 19534

Hunt, L. B.: 'The Worshipful Company of Goldsmiths', 7039

Hunt, M.: ed. Open Government, 771

Hunt, Morton Magill: The World of the Formerly Married, 10001

Hunt, P.: 'The Case Study Method in Management Training', 5417

Hunt, Richard: The Shadowless Lamp: Memoirs of an R.A.M.C. Surgeon, 20869

Hunt, Roland: The District Officer in India 1930–1947, 13121

Hunt, Thomas: ed. The Medical Society of London, 1773–1973, 20793

Hunter, Anthony: Dardanelles Patrol, 14554

Hunter, Beatrice: The Administration of Hospital Wards: Factors Influencing Length of Stay in a Hospital, 21397

Hunter, Carol: Vitamins: What They Are and Why We Need Them, 20565

Hunter, David Lindsay George: 'The Edinburgh Cable Tramways', 17224; Scottish Buses before 1929, 17314; From S.M.T. [Scottish Motorway Traction Company] to Eastern Scottish: An 80th Anniversary Story, 17328

Hunter, Donald: The Diseases of Occupations, 4121

Hunter, Guy: ed. Industrialisation and Race Relations: A Symposium, 10943; Residential Colleges: Some New Developments in British Adult Education, 23668

Hunter, James: The Making of the Crofting Community, 19286

Hunter, John: Direct Participation in Action: The New Bureaucracy, 6028

Hunter, Kathleen: History of Pakistanis in Britain, 11212

Hunter, Laurence Colvin: Pay, Productivity and Collective Bargaining, 3940; ed. The British Balance of Payments, 4932; 'Unemployment and Industrial Relations', 5860; Labour Problems of Technological Change, 6208; 'The State Subsidy Theory of Strikes—A Reconsideration', 6933; Migration in Scotland 1958–1973, 7284; The Nationalised Transport Industries, 16191

Hunter, Leslie: Oil, 7179; The Needle is Threaded: 'The History of an Industry', 6438

Hunter, Leslie Stannard: ed. The English Church: A New Look, 11599

Hunter, Leslie David Stevenson: The Road to Brighton Pier, 1740

Hunter, Lynette: George Orwell: The Search for a Voice, 25744

Hunter, Richard Alfred: 'Psychiatry and Neurology: Psychosyndrome or Brain Damage?', 20968; Psychiatry for the Poor: 1881 Colney Hatch Asylum-Friern Hospital 1973: A Medical and Social History, 21862

Hunter, Sandy Leslie: The Scottish Educational System, 23601

Hunter, Thomas: Officers of the Black Watch, 1725–1937, 15573

Huntley, John: British Technicolor Films, 24649

Hurcombe, Linda: Dispossessed Daughters of Eve, 11671

Hurd, Anthony Richard: A Farmer in Whitehall: Britain's Farming Revolution, 1939–1950, 19469

Hurd, Sir Archibald Spicer: The British Fleet in the Great War, 14672; The Eclipse of British Sea Power: An Increasing Peril, 15335

Hurd, Douglas: An End to Promises: Sketch of a Government, 1970–1974, 1241

Hurd, Michael: Immortal Hour: The Life and Period of Rutland Boughton, 24301; Michael Tippett, 24371; The Ordeal of Ivor Gurney, 25571

Hurd-Mead, K. C.: History of Women in Medicine, 21261

Hurewitz, Jacob Coleman: Diplomacy in the Near and Middle East: A Documentary Record, 1535–1956, 13796

Hurley, C. W.: 'The New Towns of Northumberland', 18249

Hurley, Frank: Argonauts of the South: Being a Narrative of the Voyagings and Polar Seas Adventures, 27213

Hurley, Michael: ed. Irish Anglicanism, 1869–1969: Essays on the Role of Anglicanism in Irish Life presented to the Church of Ireland on the Occasion of the Centenary of its Disestablishment, 12181

Hurll, Fred: B-P's Scouts: An Official History of the Boy Scouts Association, 8515

Hurn, David Abner: Archbishop Roberts, S.J.: His Life and Writings, 11994

Hurren, Bernard John: Perchance: A Short History of British Naval Aviation, 15417; The Swordfish Saga: Story of the Fairey Swordfish Torpedo Bomber, 15841

Hurst, Alexander Robert Burnett: Livelihood and Poverty: A Study in the Economic Conditions of Working Class Households in Northampton, Warrington, Stanley and Reading, 9020

Hurstfield, Joel: 'The Control of British Raw Material Supplies, 1919–1939', 7254; Control of Raw Materials, 7255

Hurt, John: Elementary Schooling and the Working Classes 1860–1918, 22614

Hurwitz, A.: Milestones in Modern Surgery, 21134

Hurwitz, Samuel Justin: State Intervention in Great Britain: A Study of Economic Control and Social Response, 1914–1919, 6102

Husbands, Christopher Temple: Racial Exclusionism and the City: The Urban Support of the National Front, 2050; 'The Basis for National Front Support', 2051; 'The London Borough Council Elections of 6 May 1982: Results and Analysis', 3306; 'The London Borough Council Elections of 8 May 1986: Results and Analysis', 3308; 'A British Scale for Measuring White Attitudes to Coloured People', 11018; 'Race' in Britain: Continuity and Change, 11073; Racism and the Mass Media: A Study of the Mass Media in the Formation of White Beliefs and Attitudes in Britain, 11176

Husler, Angelo: Contribution à l'étude de l'élaboration de la politique étrangère Britannique, 1945–1956, 14121

Hussey, Christopher Edward Clive: The Hampstead Garden Suburb: Its Achievements and Significance, 18192; The Life of Sir Edwin Lutyens, 23873

Hustwit, Jane: Information in Social Welfare: A Study of Resources, 8879

Hutber, Patrick: The Decline and Fall of the Middle Class: And How it Can Fight Back, 9732

Hutcheson, Alexander Macgregor: ed. Scotland and Oil, 6529, 7172

Hutcheson, B. R.: 'A Prognostic (predictive) Classification of Juvenile Court First Offenders Based on a Follow Up Study', 10586

Hutcheson, John A.: 'British Conservatism in the Twentieth Century: An Emerging Ideological Tradition', 2185

Hutchings, Arthur James Bramwell: 'Music in Britain, 1918–1960', 24280; Delius, 24325

Hutchings, David F.: The Q.E.2: A Ship for all Seasons, 16582

Hutchings, Tony: Land Rover: The Early Years, 17430

Hutchins, John Greenwood Brown: Transportation and the Environment, 16231

Hutchins, Kenneth Richard: Urban Transport: Public or Private?, 16303

Hutchinson, A. Leslie: Botany, Birds, Bugs and Barrows on the Isle of Wight: The Jubilee History of the Isle of Wight Natural History and Archaeological Society, 1919–69, 26533

Hutchinson, Bertram: 'Depopulation and Rural Life in Scotland', 19241

Hutchinson, David: ed. Headlines—The Media in Scotland, 25127; The Modern Scottish Theatre, 26172

Hutchinson, Edward Moss: 'Crowther—A Personal Comment', 22607; ed. Aims and Action in Adult Education, 1921–1971, 23708

Hutchinson, George: Edward Heath: A Personal and Political Biography, 1016

Hutchinson, George Evelyn: The Ecological Theater and the Evolutionary Play, 19917

Hutchinson, Sir Herbert John: Tariff-Making and Industrial Reconstruction: An Account of the Work of the Import Duties Advisory Committee, 1932–1939, 3760

Hutchinson, Sir Joseph: Change and Innovation in Norfolk Farming: 70 Years of Experiment and Advice at the Norfolk Agricultural Station, Michaelmas 1908 to Michaelmas 1978, 19582

Hutchinson, Maxwell: The Prince of Wales: Right and Wrong, 23909

Hutchinson, Michael Edward: Education in Britain, 22682

Hutchinson, Robert: The Politics of the Arts Council, 23763

Hutchinson, Walter Victor: ed. Hutchinson's Pictorial History of the War, 14615

Hutchison, D.: 'Competing Inequalities: The Sex and Social Class Structure of the First Year Scottish Student Population, 1962–1972', 22566

Hutchison, Graham Seton: Machine Guns: Their History and Tactical Employment, 15504

Hutchison, Keith: The Decline and Fall of British Capitalism, 3610

Hutchison, Kenneth: 'Searching for Gas and Oil Under the North Sea', 6403; High Speed Gas: An Autobiography, 6404

Hutchison, Sydney Charles: The History of the Royal Academy, 1768–1968, 23951

Hutchison, Terence Wilmot: Economics and Economic Policy in Britain 1946–1966: Some Aspects of their Interrelations, 3608

Hutt, Clive: 'The Reporting of Industrial Relations on Breakfast Television', 5858

Hutt, [George] Allen: The Final Crisis, 3597; British Trade Unionism: A Short History, 6691; The Condition of the Working Class in Great Britain, 9620; The Post War History of the British Working Class, 9621; Newspaper Design, 25344; The Changing Newspaper: Typographical Trends in Britain and America, 1622–1972, 25345

Hutt, Rosemary: 'Trade Unions as Friendly Societies, 1912–1952', 6745

Hutter, Bridget: ed. Controlling Women: The Normal and the Deviant, 7844

Huttman, E. D. and Huttman, J.: 'Dutch and British Towns: Self-Containment and Socioeconomic Balance', 18254

Hutton, Bernard J.: Frogman Spy: The Incredible Case of Commander Crabb, 16041

Hutton, Geoffrey: New Ways in Management Training: A Technical College Develops its Service to Industry, 5418

Hutton, Graham: Whatever Happened to Productivity?, 5995

Hutton, J. E.: Welfare and Housing: A Practical Record of War-Time Management, 18585

Hutton, John P.: 'Model of Short Term Capital Movements, the Foreign Exchange Market and Official Intervention in the U.K. 1963–1970, 4734

Hutton, Thomas Winter: King Edward's School, Birmingham, 1552–1952, 23063

Hutton-Stott, Francis: comps. Guide to Veteran Cars, 17355

Huws-Jones, R.: The Doctor and the Social Services, 20815

Huxley, Anthony: An Illustrated History of Gardening, 19872

Huxley, Elspeth: Back Street New Worlds: A Look at Immigrants in Britain, 11397; The Sorcerer's Apprentice: A Journey Through East Africa, 12818; Brave New Victuals: An Inquiry into Modern Food Production, 20604

Huxley, George: The Plight of the Railways, 16781

Huxley, Sir Julian Sorell: We Europeans: A Survey of Racial Problems, 11146; 'Race' in Europe, 11147; Conservation of Nature in England and Wales, 20191; 'Eugenics and Society', 20981; Reshaping Man's Heritage, 21178; ed. Aldous Huxley 1894–1963: A Memorial Volume, 25590; Essays of a Humanist, 26500; Memories vol.1 1970, 26502

Huygen, Frederique: British Design: Images and Reality, 24116

Hyam, Charles: Charles Laughton: An Intimate Biography, 26059

Hyam, Ronald: 'Africa and the Labour Government 1945-1951', 12693; 'The Politics of Partition in Southern Africa, 1908-1961', 12708; 'The Political Consequences of Seretse Khama: Britain, the Bangwato and South Africa 1948-1952', 12713; 'The Geopolitical Origins of the Central African Federation: Britain, Rhodesia and South Africa, 1948-1953', 12782

Hyams, Edward Solomon: The English Garden, 19865, 26979; A History of Gardens and Gardening, 19866, 26980; Great Historical Gardens of the World, 19867; The New Statesman: The History of the First Fifty Years: 1913-1963, 25177; ed. New Statesmanship: An Anthology, 25178

Hyamson, Albert Montefiore: The Sephardim of England: A History of the Spanish and Portuguese Jewish Community, 1492-1951, 12425; Jews' College, London, 1855-1955, 12436; Palestine under the Mandate 1920-1948, 14296

Hyde, Francis Edwin: Liverpool and the Mersey: An Economic History of a Port 1700-1970, 5171, 16694; Cunard and the North Atlantic, 1840-1973: A History of Shipping and Financial Management, 16526; Shipping Enterprise and Management, 1830-1939: Harrisons of Liverpool, 16547

Hyde, Harford Montgomery: Baldwin: The Unexpected Prime Minister, 977; Neville Chamberlain, 983; Carson: The Life of Sir Edward Carson, Lord Carson of Duncairn, 1134; Lord Reading: The Life of Rufus Isaacs, First Marquess of Reading, 1304; ed. The Trial of Sir Roger Casement, 3019; Solitary in the Ranks: Lawrence of Arabia as Airman and Private Soldier, 14512; The Quiet Canadian. The Secret Service Story of Sir William Stephenson, 15194; British Air Policy between the Wars, 1918-1939, 15989; George Blake Superspy, 16026; The Atom Bomb Spies, 16042

Hyman, Alan: The Rise and Fall of Horatio Bottomley: The Biography of a Swindler, 1365

Hyman, Richard: Trade Unions and Revolution: The Industrial Politics of the early British Communist Party, 1934; Disputes Procedure in Action: A Study of the Engineering Industry Disputes Procedure in Coventry, 5762; Industrial Relations: A Marxist Introduction, 5763; Social Values and Industrial Relations: A Study of Fairness and Equality, 5764; The Workers' Union, 6833; Strikes, 6972

Hyndman, A.: 'The Welfare of Coloured People in London', 11445

Hynes, Samuel Lynn: The Auden Generation: Literature and Politics in England in the 1930s, 23772; William Golding, 25539; ed. Graham Greene: A Collection of Critical Essays, 25564

Iago, Mary: ed. Selected Letters of E. M. Forster, 25520

Ianni, Francis A.: A Family Business: Kinship and Social Control in Organised Crime, 10220

Ibbotson, Stanley: The Protection from Eviction Act (1964), 18417; Rent Act (1965), 18418

Icely, Henry Edward McLaughlin: Blockley through Twelve Centuries: Annals of a Cotswold Parish, 19322; Bromsgrove School through the Centuries, 23046

Ignotus, Paul: 'Foreigners in Britain', 10967

Ihde, Aaron J.: 'Edward Mellanby and the Antirachitic Factor', 20973

Ikin, Alfred Edward: The Education Act 1944, with Explanatory Notes, 22627

Ilbert, Sir Courtenay Peregrine: Parliament: its History, Constitution and Practice, 563

Ilersic, Alfred Roman: Government Finance and Fiscal Policy in Post-War Britain, 4570; The Taxation of Capital Gains, 4856

Iliffe, John: A Modern History of Tanganyika, 12842

Iliffe, Steve: Pickets in White: The Junior Doctors Dispute of 1975: A Study of the Medical Profession in Transition, 20816

Illingworth, Sir Charles F. W.: Report for Scottish Department of Health: Scottish Hospitals Survey, 21471; University Statesman: the Story of Sir Hector Hetherington, 23339

Illsley, Raymond: 'Measuring the Status of Occupations', 5880; The Motivation and Characteristics of Internal Migrants: A Socio-medical Study of Young Migrants in Scottland (sic), 7343; 'Women from Broken Homes', 7682

Illsley, William Allen: ed. The County of Angus, 10116, 19233

Imlah, Norman: Drugs in Modern Society, 22194

Immerout, M. A.: ed. Classical Articles in Urology, 21165

Immigration Appeals: Report of the Committee. Cmnd 3387, 11105

Imperial Chemical Industries: (Plant Protection Division) Jealott's Hill: 50 Years of Agricultural Research 1928-1978, 20122; Pharmaceuticals Division. Pharmaceutical Research in I.C.I. 1936-1957, 22275

Imperial Metal Industries (Kynoch): Under Five Flags: The Story of Kynoch Works, Witton, Birmingham, 1862-1962, 7198

Ince, Basil A.: Decolonization and Conflict in the United Nations: Guyana's Struggle for Independence, Camb, 13044; 'The Diplomacy of New States: The Commonwealth Caribbean and the Case of Anguilla', 13060

Inchbald, G.: Camels and Others: The Imperial Camel Corps in World War I, 14612

Independent Advisory Group: Investigation of a Possible Increased Incidence of Cancer in West Cumbria, 22237

Independent Broadcasting Authority: Annual Reports and Accounts, 24825

Independent Labour Party: Annual Conference Report, 1877

Index of Conservation Areas, 1967-1970: (With Supplement), 18965

Index to Theses accepted for the Higher Degrees in the Universities of Great Britain and Ireland: 1953-, 86

Industrial Challenge: The Experience of Cadburys of Bourneville in the Post-War Years, 20693

Industrial Injuries Advisory Council: Bronchitis and Emphysema, 4149

Industrial Participation Association: Industrial Democracy—An Acceptable Solution: A Submission to the Government, 6027

Industrial Society: Productivity Agreements: The Process of Negotiating and Communicating, 5992

Ineichen, Bernard: 'Home Ownership and Manual Workers' Lifestyles', 9712

Inequalities in Health: Report of a Research Working Group: 1980, 21681

Inge, William Ralph: Diary of a Dean: St Paul's, 1911-1934, 11788; Outspoken Essays, 11789; God and the Astronomers, 27257

Ingham, Geoffrey K.: Capitalism Divided?: The City and Industry in British Social Development, 4281; 'Organizational Size, Orientation to Work and Industrial Behaviour', 5696

Ingham, Keith P. D.: Understanding the Scottish Economy, 5276

Ingham, Kenneth: Jan Christian Smuts: The Conscience of a South African, 12725

Ingham, Mike: 'Industrial Relations in British Local Government', 5847

Ingham, Roger: 'Football Hooliganism': The Wider Context, 27067

Ingilby, Joan: Life and Tradition in West Yorkshire, 5234

Ingle, Stephen J.: The British Party System, 1587; 'The Recent Revival of the British Liberal Party: Some Geographical, Social and Political Aspects', 1825; Parliament and Health Policy: The Role of M.P.s 1970-1975, 21673

Inglis, Brian: Abdication, 476; Roger Casement, 3020; The Forbidden Game. A Social History of Drugs, 10834, 22214; Private Conscience—Public Morality, 12391; Fringe Medicine, 20882; A History of Medicine, 20883; Drugs, Doctors and Disease, 20884; Downstart, 25253

Inglis, Fred: Radical Earnestness: English Social Theory 1880-1980, 2087, 8087

Inglis, Ruth: The Children's War: Evacuation 1939-1945, 15094

Inglis, Simon: Soccer in the Dock: A History of British Football Scandals 1900-1965, 27063; League Football and the Men who Made It: The Official Centenary History of the Football League 1888-1988, 27072

Ingram, Archibald Kenneth: Fifty Years of the National Peace Council: A Short History, 13434

Ingram, Arthur: Trapping and Poaching, 19111

Ingram, C. A.: Four Score and Four: The Story of the Insurance and Actuarial Society of Glasgow, 4239

Ingram, Derek: Commonwealth for a Colour-blind World, 10944, 12581; 'Ten Turbulent Years: The Commonwealth Secretariat at Work', 12521

Ingram, Kenneth E.: Basil Jellicoe, 11791; Jamaica, 13048

Ingrams, Doreen: Palestine Papers, 1917–1922: Seeds of Conflict, 14292

Ingrams, Harold: Hong Kong, 12969

Ingrams, Richard Reid: Piper's Places: John Piper in England and Wales, 24053; *ed.* The Life and Times of Private Eye, 1961–1971, 25181

Inland Waterways Association: (Development Committee). New Waterways: Interim Report, 16447; Annual Report 1979–1980, 16448

Inman, John: Poverty and Housing Conditions in a Manchester Ward, 18607; The Rebuilding of Manchester, 18608; The Rebuilding of Manchester, 18890

Inman, Peggy: Labour in the Munitions Industries, 6610

Inner London Education Authority: The Education of Immigrant Pupils, 23172

Innes, Christopher: Edward Gordon Craig, 26030

Innes, Kathleen Elizabeth: Life in a Hampshire Village, 19162

Innis, Harold Adams: The Press: A Neglected Factor in the Economic History of the Twentieth Century, 25042

Institute of Actuaries and Faculty of Actuaries: The Ivanhoe Guide to Actuaries, 4226

Institute of Bankers: Banks and Society, 4433

Institute of British Geographers— Publications: (Transport Geography Study Group), 16264; Rural Geography Study Group: Rural Accessibility and Mobility, 16314; No. 27: Alnwick, Northumberland: A Study in Town-plan Analysis, 18089; Land Use and Resources: Studies in Applied Geography: A Memorial Volume to Sir Dudley Stamp, 20261; Special Publications No: 1. Land Use and Resources: Studies in Applied Geography, 26667

Institute of Chartered Accountants of England and Wales: Setting Accounting Standards, 4196; The Making of Accounting Standards, 4197; The History of the Institute . . . 1880–1965

Institute of Chartered Accountants of Scotland: A History of the Chartered Accountants of Scotland, from the Earliest Times to 1954, 417, 9827

Institute of Community Studies: Inner Area Study: Lambeth, 17880; Multi-Service Project Report, 17881; Second Report on Multiple Deprivation, 17882; Poverty and Multiple Deprivation, 17883; Multi-Space Project: Report, 17885; People, Housing and District, 17886; Inner London: Policies for Dispersal and Balance: Final Report of the Lambeth Inner Area Study, 1977 by Graham Shankland, Peter Willmott and David Jordan, 17884; Housing and Population Projections, 17887; Housing Stress, 17888; London's Inner Area: Problems and Possibilities: Discussion Paper, 17889; The Complications of Social

Ownership, 17890; Interim Report on Local Services, 17891; Study of Intending Migrants: Report, 17892; Labour Market Study, 17893; Local Employers' Study, 17894; Policies and Structure: Report . . ., 17895

Institute of Economic Affairs: Trade Unions: Public Goods or Public 'Bads'?, 6740

Institute of Historical Research: Bibliography of Historical Works Issued in the United Kingdom, 396; Writings on British History, 401

Institute of Hospital Administrators: Hospital Waiting Lists: A Report of the Study and Research Committee of the IHA, 21382; The First Fifty Years, 1902–1952, 21401

Institute of Municipal Treasurers and Accountants: Capital Finance of Local and Public Authorities, 4879; Local Expenditure and Exchequer Grants, 4880

Institute of Personnel Management: Personnel Management: A Bibliography, 5462; Personnel Management 1913–1963: The Growth of Personnel Management and the Development of the Institute, 5463

Institute of Practitioners in Advertising: Advertising: A General Introduction, 4314; Poster Audience Survey: An Investigation into Poster Campaign Audiences based on Surveys in Ipswich and the West Midlands Conurbation, 5018

Institute of Race Relations: Coloured Immigrants in Britain, 11396

Institute of Terrestrial Ecology, National Environment Research Council: Upland Land Use in England and Wales, 20279

Institute of Water Control: Health and Safety in the Water Industry: Symposium, Reading University, 5–6 April, 1983, 20087

Institution of Civil Engineers: Landscaping of Motorways, 17117; Twenty Years of British Motorways: Proceedings of a Conference, 17118

Institution of Mechanical Engineers, Environmental Engineering Group: The King's Cross Underground Fire, 17020; The Problem of Car Parking: A One Day Convention, 17375

Insurance Annual Report, 4206

International Address Book of Botanists: Being a Dictionary of Individuals and Scientific Institutions, Universities, Societies etc: in All Parts of the World Interested in the Study of Botany, 26545

International Bibliography of Historical Sciences: 1935+, 419

International Bibliography of the History of Religions: For the Year 1952+, 11526

International Labour Organization: Monographs on the Organization of Medical Care within the Framework of Social Security, 21974

International Political Science Association: International Political Science Abstracts, 2

International Review of Missions: 1911–1969, 12352

International Seminar on Urban Renewal: 1st Seminar, 17760

International Tea Committee: The First Fifty Years: 1933– 1983, 20713

International Union for Conservation of Native and Natural Resources, U.K. Committee: Earth's Survival: A Conservation and Development Programme for the U.K., 20218

Ions, Edmund: James Bryce and American Democracy, 1870–1922, 1381; A Call to Arms: Interlude with the Military, 16068

Ipswich Permanent Building Society: One Hundred Years of Service, 1850–1950: A Brief History, 4391

Iqbal, M.: 'Ethnicity and Ethnic Groups: Education and Islam in Britain, a Muslim View', 22902

Ireland, Jenny: Savings and Co-operative Banking, 4341

Iremonger, Frederic Athelwold: William Temple, 11703

Iremonger, Valentina: *transl.* An Irish Navvy: The Diary of an Exile, 11364

Irish Church Directory and Yearbook: 1862+, 12179

Irish Social and Economic History 1974–, 2662

Irish Historical Studies: 1938–, 2661

Irish National Committee for Geography: Atlas of Ireland, 138

Ironside, D. J.: An Accessions Tax, 4828

Ironside, Edmund Oslac [Baron]: *ed.* High Road to Command: The Diaries of Major General Sir Edmund Ironside, 1920–1922, 14509

Ironside, W. Edmund [Baron]: Archangel, 1918–1919, 14570

Irvine, David Edward Guthrie: *ed.* Pollution and the Use of Chemicals in Agriculture, 20112

Irvine, Elizabeth Ernestine: *ed.* Casework and Mental Illness, 21803

Irvine, Sir James: The Academic Burden in a Changing World, 23369

Irvine, Mabel: The Avenue of Years: The Life of Sir James Irvine, 23340

Irvine, Sandy: A Green Manifesto: Policies for a Green Future, 1856

Irving, Clive: Scandal '63: A Study of the Profumo Affair, 9897

Irving, David: The War between the Generals, 14744; The Destruction of Convoy PQ.17, 15129; The Virus House, 15203; The Destruction of Dresden, 15975

Irving, Gordon: Dumfries and Galloway Royal Infirmary: The First Two Hundred Years, 1776–1975, 21481; Great Scot: The Life Story of Sir Harry Lauder, Legendary Laird of the Music Hall, 26328

Irving, Joe: The City at Work: A Guide to the Institutions that Make up the City of London and their Roles, 4280

Irving, John: The Smoke Screen of Jutland, 14655

Irving, Ronald Graham Lock: A History of British Mountaineering, 27237

Irwin, Alan: 'The Control of Chemical Carcinogens in Britain', 20110

Isaac, Winifred: Ben Greet and the Old Vic: A Biography of Sir Philip Ben Greet, 26129

Isaac-Henry, Kester: 'Taking Stock of the Local Authority Associations', 3193

Isaacs, Bernard: Survival of the Unfittest: A Study of Geriatric Patients in Glasgow, 8605

Isaacs, Gerald Rufus, 2nd Marquess of Reading: Rufus Isaacs, First Marquess of Reading, 1860–1935, 1303

Isaacs, Jeremy: Storm over 4, 24882

Isaacs, Julius: British Post-war Migration, 7394

Isaacson, P.: 'Structure Planning in Dockland', 18310

Isard, Walter: Atomic Power: An Economic and Social Analysis: A Study in Industrial Location and Regional Economic Development, 6662

Isherwood, Christopher: Christopher and his Kind, 1929–1939, 25593; My Guru and Other Disciples, 25594

Isherwood, Henry Burton: Racial Integration: The Rising Tide of Colour, 10947; Racial Contours: The Factor of Race in Human Survival, 10948

Isle of Man Official Yearbook 1983–: Ramsay, 2626

Isle of Man Register-General: Annual Report and Statistical Review of Births, Marriages and Deaths in the Isle of Man, 1951–, 2632; Census 1951. Report on Isle of Man, 2633; Census 1961: Report on Isle of Man, 2634

Isle of Man Summerland Fire Commission: Report . . . , 2635

Isles, Keith Sydney: An Economic Survey of Northern Ireland, 5385

Ismay, Hastings Lionel [Baron]: The Memoirs of General Lord Ismay, 14764

Israel, William H.: Colour and Community: A Study of Coloured Immigrants and Race Relations in an Industrial Town, 11479

Issacharoff, Ruth Miryam: Community Action and Race Relations: A Study of Community Relations Committees in Britain, 11011; The Organisation of Housing: Public and Private Enterprise in London, 18427

ITMA Years, the, 26319

Ivens, Michael W.: ed. Case Studies in Human Relations, Productivity and Organization, 5481

Ives, A. G. L.: British Hospitals, 21417

Ivey, Geoff: ed. The Sussex Opportunity: A New University and the Future, 23583

Jaatinen, Stig Tyrgil Hjalmarson: The Human Geography of the Outer Hebrides with Special Reference to the Latest Trends in Land Use, 19262

Jack, A. B.: 'Inter-regional Migration in Great Britain: Some Cross-sectional Evidence', 7344

Jacka, Alan A.: Adoption in Brief: Research and Other Literature in the United States, Canada and Great Britain, 1966–1972, An Annotated Bibliography, 8229

Jacklin, Tony: Jacklin: The Champion's Own Story, 27157

Jackman, William T.: The Development of Transport in Modern England, 16202; Economic Principles of Transportation, 16203

Jacks, Digby: Student Politics and Higher Education, 9879, 22568

Jacks, Keith: Rape of Reason: The Corruption of the Polytechnic of North London, 9866

Jacks, Maurice Leonard: Modern Trends in Education, 22681

Jackson, A.: The Repertory Movement: A History of Regional Theatre in Britain, 26159

Jackson, Alan Arthur: London's Local Railways, 16959; Rails through the Clay: A History of London's Tube Railways, 17000; Semi-Detached London: Suburban Development, Life and Transport 1900–39, 18353

Jackson, Anthony: The Politics of Architecture: A History of Modern Architecture in Britain, 23901, 23905

Jackson, Aubrey Joseph: De Havilland Aircraft since 1909, 17601; Air Travel, 17647

Jackson, Brian: Working Class Community: Some General Notions Raised by a Series of Studies in Northern England, 9658; Streaming: An Education System in Miniature, 22811; Childminder: A Study in Action Research, 23166; Education and the Working Class, 22940

Jackson, Christine: Bail or Custody, 10321

Jackson, Dudley: Do Trade Unions Cause Inflation?, 4001; Poverty, 9075

Jackson, Eleanor M.: Red Tape and the Gospel: A Study of the Significance of the Ecumenical Missionary Struggle of William Paton (1886–1943), 12375

Jackson, Frank: Sir Raymond Unwin: Architect, Planner and Visionary, 18825

Jackson, Sir Geoffrey Jackson: Concorde Diplomacy: The Ambassador's Role in the World Today, 13283

Jackson, Gordon: The History and Archaeology of Ports, 16655

Jackson, H. C.: Behind the Modern Sudan, 14425

Jackson, Hilary: Unlocking Community Resources: Four Experimental Government Small Grant Schemes, 9428

Jackson, Ian: The Provincial Press and the Community, 25325

Jackson, J. M.: ed. The City of Dundee, 10117

Jackson, James Charles: Planters and Speculators: Chinese and European Agricultural Enterprises in Malaya, 1786–1921, 12915

Jackson, John Archer: ed. Migration, 7333; ed. Social Stratification, 9510; ed. Professions and Professionalization, 9770; 'The Irish', 11359; The Irish in Britain, 11360; 'The Irish in Britain', 11361; 'The Irish in Britain', 11362

Jackson, John Hampden: England since the Industrial Revolution, 1815–1948, 3465

Jackson, John Nicholas: Surveys for Town and Country Planning, 17773; The Urban Future: A Choice between Alternatives, 17910

Jackson, Joseph Michael: The Control of Monopoly in the United Kingdom, 4968; Family Income, 10070

Jackson, Keith: Democracy in Crisis: The Town Halls Respond, 3342

Jackson, Mark: William Tyndale: Collapse of a School or a System, 23161

Jackson, Michael P.: Industrial Relations: A Textbook, 5575; Trade Unions, 6912

Jackson, Michael: The Price of Coal, 6312

Jackson, P. M.: 'Urban Fiscal Decay in U.K. Cities', 3271; Public Sector Economics, 4661

Jackson, P. W.: Local Government, 3155

Jackson, R. A.: Local Government Finance in a Unitary State, 3262, 4872

Jackson, Richard Meredith: The Machinery of Local Government, 3153

Jackson, Sir Richard: Occupied with Crime, 10716

Jackson, Robert J.: Rebels and Whips: An Analysis of Dissension, Discipline and Cohesion in British Political Parties, 1601

Jackson, Robert Louis: Occupied with Crime, 10160; ed. Twentieth Century Interpretations of Crime and Punishment: A Collection of Critical Essays, 10161

Jackson, Robert: The Prisoners 1914–18, 14448; Dunkirk: The British Evacuation 1940, 14837; Air War over Korea, 16135; Avro Vulcan, 15879; The V-Bombers, 15882; The Air War over France: May-June 1940, 15941; Storm from the Skies: The Strategic Bombing Offensive, 1943–1945, 15976; Before the Storm: The Story of Royal Air Force Bomber Command, 1939–1942, 15977

Jackson, Sheila: The Closed Shop: A Comparative Study in Public Policy and Trade Union Security in Britain, the USA and West Germany, 5817

Jackson, Sonia: Childminder: A Study in Action Research, 23166

Jackson, Stanley: The Savoy: The Romance of a Great Hotel, 26995

Jackson, Stephen: Special Education in England and Wales, 23118

Jackson, Stuart: Accidents to Young Motor-cyclists: A Statistical Investigation, 17199

Jackson, Thomas Alfred: The History and Working Class Associations and Traditions of Clerkenwell Green: Written on the Occasion of the Opening of the Bookshop of Marx House, 18352

Jackson, Valerie Jean: Population in the Countryside: Growth and Stagnation in the Cotswolds, 7413; Population Growth and Planning Policy: An Analysis of Social and Economic Factors Affecting Housing and Employment Location in the West Midlands, 7416

Jackson, William Eric: The Structure of Local Government in England and Wales, 3154; Achievement: A Short History of the London County Council, 3283

Jackson, Sir William Godfrey Fothergill: The Rock of Gibraltar, 12854; Alexander of Tunis: As Military Commander, 14753; The North African Campaign, 1940–1943, 14901; Overlord, Normandy 1944, 14946

Jackson, Sir Willis: Scientific, Technological and Technical Manpower, 5027; 'Some Aspects of Engineering Education', 22521

Jackson-Wrigley, Maurice: The Cinema: Historical, Technical and Bibliographical: A Survey for Librarians and Students, 24593

Jacob, Lucy M.: Sri Lanka: From Dominion to Republic: A Study of the Changing Relations with the United Kingdom, 12989

Jacobs, Brian D.: 'Labour against the Centre: The Clay Cross Syndrome', 3227; Racism in Britain, 11081; Black Politics and Urban Crisis in Britain, 11088

Jacobs, David: Jacob's Ladder, 24915

Jacobs, Eric: Stop Press: The Inside Story of The Times Dispute, 25156

Jacobs, Gerald: Judi Dench, 26032

Jacobs, Jane: The Economy of Cities, 5402, 20398

Jacobs, Julius: ed. London Trades Council, 1860–1950, 6908

Jacobs, P. M.: History Theses 1901–1970: Historical Research for Higher Degrees in the Universities of the United Kingdom, 89; ed. Institute of Historical Research 1955–1957, 407

Jacobs, Sidney: The Right to a Decent House, 18478

Jacobson, Jon: Locarno Diplomacy: Germany and the West 1925–1929, 13655

Jacobus, John M.: Twentieth-Century Architecture: The Middle Years, 1940–1965, 23898

Jacoby, Neil: The Polluters: Industry or Government?, 19993

Jaensch, Dean: 'The Scottish Vote 1974: A Realigning Party System', 2368

Jaffe, Lorna S.: The Decision to Disarm Germany: British Policy towards Post-War German Disarmament, 1914–1919, 13381

Jagan, Cheddi: The West on Trial: My Fight for Guyana's Freedom, 13042

Jagger, Peter John: Christian Initiation, 1552–1969: Rites of Baptism and Confirmation since the Reformation Period, 11608; A History of the Parish and People Movement, 11618; Bishop Henry de Candole: His Life and Times, 1895–1971, 11730

Jahoda, Gustav: 'Ethnic Identity and Preferences among Asian Immigrant Children in Glasgow: A Replicated Study', 11224

Jahoda, Marie: The Education of Technologists: An Exploratory Case-study at Brunel College, 23276

Jain, Jagdish Prasad: China in World Politics: A Study of Sino-British Relations, 1949–1975, 13639

Jakobovits, Immanuel: Journal of a Rabbi, 11304; If only my People . . . Zionism in My Life, 12431

James, A. E. T.: The Royal Air Force: The Past 30 Years, 15811

James, Alan: Buses and Coaches, 17274

James, Alan G.: Sikh Children in Britain, 11217

James, Arnold J.: Wales at Westminster: A History of Parliamentary Representation of Wales 1801–1979, 2582

James, C. R. L.: At the Rendezvous of History, 13068

James, D.: ed. Philip Snowden, 1317; ed. Outward Bound, 26970

James, D. E.: 'University Involvement in Community Development', 9409

James, Edward: 'Women at Work in Twentieth Century Britain: The Changing Structure of Female Employment', 7775, 7818

James, Edwin Oliver: A History of Christianity in England, 11566

James, Eric [Baron]: 'The Start of a New University', 23587

James, Eric A.: A Life of Bishop John A. T. Robinson: Scholar, Pastor, Prophet, 11756; ed. God's Truth: Essays to Commemorate the Twenty Fifth Anniversary of the Publication of Honest to God, 11874

James, Frank Cyril: England Today: A Survey of the Economic Situation, 3575

James, Harold Douglas: A Pride of Gurkhas: The 2nd King Edward VII's Own Goorkhas (The Sirmoor Rifles). 1948–1971, 15646

James, J. D.: The Town and Country Planning Act, 1954, with a General Introduction and Annotations, 20346

James, J. R.: 'Lessons from the Past', 17859

James, John Williams: A Church History of Wales, 12280

James, Larry: Power in a Trade Union: The Role of the District Committee of the A.U.E.W., 6829

James, Lawrence: Imperial Rearguard: Wars of Empire, 1918–1985, 16177

James, Margaret: ed. The Emancipation of Women in Great Britain, 7764

James, Mari: 'The Development of Party Politics in the Local Authority Associations', 3194

James, Montague: British Painting, 23980

James, Noel David Glanes: A History of English Forestry, 19711; The Forester's Companion, 19712; A Forestry Centenary: The Forestry Society of England, Wales and Northern Ireland, 19713

James, Philip Brutton: ed. Henry Moore on Sculpture: A Collection of the Sculptor's Writings and Spoken Words, 24201

James, Philip Gwyn: Farming for Consumers, 19524

James, Robert Rhodes: Churchill: A Study in Failure, 1900–1939, 988; ed. The Complete Speeches of Sir Winston Churchill, 1897–1963, 1002; Anthony Eden, 1013; Victor Cazalet: A Portrait, 1389; ed. "Chips": The Diaries of Sir Henry Channon, 1393; The British Revolution: British Politics, 1880–1939, 1578; Ambitions and Realities: British Politics 1964–70, 1579; 'Anthony Eden and the Suez Crisis', 14385; Gallipoli, 14546

James, Simon: The Economics of Taxation, 4850

James, T.: 'Commissions of Little Consequence', 22611; 'Permissive Politics in Retreat', 22641

James, William H.: 'The Incidence of Illegal Abortion', 7886; 'Social Class and Season of Birth', 9443

James, Sir William Milbourne: The British Navies in the Second World War, 15011; The Portsmouth Letters, 15259; Blue Water and Green Fields, 15313

James, William Owen: Botany—Here and Now, 26551

Jameson, Derek: Touched by Angels, 25254

Jameson, E. M.: Gynaecology and Obstetrics, 21090

Jameson, Edward Mellor: Charterhouse, 23048

Jameson, Eric: The Natural History of Quackery, 20881

Jameson, Frederic: Fables of Aggression: Wyndham Lewis, the Modernist as Fascist, 25672

Jameson, Margaret Storm: Journey from the North, 25602

Jameson, Sir William Scarlett: Ark Royal, 1939–1941, 15024

Jameson, Sir William Wilson: A Synopsis of Health, 22053

Jamie [Hamish Hamilton]: An 80th Birthday Tribute from his Friends: 1980, 24968

Jamieson, John: The History of the Royal Belfast Academical Institution 1810–1960, 23639

Jane's Merchant Shipping Review 1983, 16492

Janes, Henry Hurford: Albion Brewery, 1808–1958: The Story of Mann, Crossman and Paulin Ltd. 1959, 6161; The Red Barrel: A History of Watney Mann, 6162; Sons of the Forge: The Story of B. & S. Massey Limited, 1861–1961, 6371; Hall & Woodhouse, 1777–1977: Independent Family Brewers, 20742

Janke, Peter: Ulster: Consensus and Coercion, 2920

Janosik, Edward Gabriel: Constituency Labour Parties in Britain, 1777

Jansen, Clifford John: Social Aspects of Internal Migration: Research Report, 7268; ed. Readings in the Sociology of Migration, 7269

Jansen, Jürgen: ed. Britische Europaideen 1940–1970: Eine Bibliographie, 14119; Britische Konservative und Europa. Debattennaussagen im Unterhaus zur Westeuropäischen Integration 1945–1972, 14187

Jaques, Elliot: Measurement of Responsibility: A Study of Work, Payment and Individual Progress, 3902; Equitable Payment: A General Theory of Work, Differential Payment and Individual Progress, 3903; Time-Span Handbook: The Use of Time-Span Discretion to Measure the Level of Work in Employment Roles and to arrange an Equitable Payment Structure, 3904; The Changing Culture of a Factory, 7237; 'The Science of Society', 8803

Jaramillo-Arango, J.: The British Contribution to Medicine, 20768, 21240

Jarmain, J. R.: Housing Subsidies and Rents, 18545

Jarman, Betty: The Lively-Minded Women: The First Twenty Years of the National Housewives Register, 7653

Jarman, Francis: ed. The Quality of Mercer: Bibliography of Writings by and about the Playwright Mercer, 25963

Jarman, Thomas Leckie: Democracy and World Conflict, 1868–1970, 297; Socialism in Britain, 1681; Landmarks in the History of Education: English Education as Part of the European Tradition, 22680

Jarrett-Kerr, Martin: Patterns of Christian Acceptance: Individual Response to the Missionary Impact 1550–1950, 12377

Jarry, David: 'The Philosophical Critique of a Scientific Sociology: Some Remarks on Bryant's Defence', 8001; ed. The Middle Class in Politics, 9735

Jarvis, Frederick Victor: Advise, Assist and Befriend: A History of the Probation and After-care Service, 10462

Jarvis, Rupert C.: 'Sources for the History of Ports', 16650; 'Sources for the History of Ships and Shipping', 16451

Jasen, David A.: A Bibliography and Reader's Guide to the First Editions of P. G. Wodehouse, 25883

Jasper, Ronald Claud Dudley: Arthur Cayley Headlam: Life and Letters of a Bishop, 11737; George Bell, Bishop of Chichester, 11720

Jasper, Tony: Cliff, 24521; Survivor: A Tribute to Cliff, 24522

Jast, L. Stanley: 'Municipalities and Industrial Development', 17739

Jawetz, Michael Bogdan: Agriculture in the British Economy, 1953–1963, 19526

Jay, Bill: Victorian Candid Camera: Paul Martin, 1864–1944, 24696

Jay, Douglas Patrick Thomas, [Baron]: Change and Fortune, 1243

Jay, Peggy: The Family and the Social Services, 10076

Jeager, Marianne: How Voters Decide: A Longitudinal Study of Political Attitudes and Voting Extended over Fifteen Years, 2254

Jeans, Sir James Hopwood: Problems of Cosmogony and Stellar Dynamics, 26371; Eos: Or the Wider Aspects of Cosmogony, 26372; The Mysterious Universe, 26373; The Stars in their Course, 26374; The Universe Around Us, 26375; The Growth of Physical Science, 26376

Jeans, Richard: Upwell: History of a Fenland Village, 19209

Jebb, Richard: His Britannic Majesty: A Political View of the Crown in the Jubilee Year 1935, 473

Jebson, David: A Voice in the City: Liverpool City Mission, 12129

Jedrzejewicz, Waclaw: ed. Poland in the British Parliament 1939–1945, 13904

Jeffcock, William Philip: Agricultural Politics, 1915–1935, 19450

Jefferies, Sir Charles Joseph: The Colonial Empire and its Civil Service, 12500; Whitehall and the Colonial Service: An Administrative Memoir, 1939–1956, 12502; Ceylon—The Path to Independence, 12986; 'O.E.G.': A Biography of Sir Oliver Ernest Goanetilleke, 12987

Jefferies, Roger: Tackling the Town Hall: A Local Authority Handbook, 3096

Jeffers, W.: 'The South Wales Ports', 16709

Jefferson, Alan: Delius, 24327; Sir Thomas Beecham: A Centenary Tribute, 24432; The Operas of Richard Strauss in Britain, 1910–1963, 24569

Jefferson, Philip Clarke: ed. The Church in the 60s, 11583

Jeffery, Frederick: Irish Methodism: An Historical Account of its Traditions, Theology and Influence, 12183

Jeffery, Keith: Northern Ireland since 1968, 2784

Jefferys, James Bavington: 'National Income and Expenditure of the United Kingdom, 1870–1952', 4891; Retail Trading in Britain, 1850–1950, 6640; Trade Unions in a Labour Britain, 6723; The Story of the Engineers, 1800–1945, 6880

Jefferys, Margot: Women in Medicine: The Results of an Inquiry Conducted by the Medical Practitioners' Union in 1962–1963, 20811

Jeffrey, Ian: 'Style and Ideology in British Art and Photography, 1900–1940', 24697

Jeffrey, James R.: External Migration: A Study of the Available Statistics 1850–1950, 7311

Jeffrey, Patricia: Migrants and Refugees: Muslim and Christian Pakistani Families in Bristol, 11222

Jeffreys, Montagu Vaughan Castelman: Revolution in Teacher Training, 22729

Jeffreys, Rees: The King's Highway, 17104

Jeffreys-Jones, Rhodri: 'Review Article: The Inestimable Advantage of Not Being English: Lord Lothian's American Ambassadorship, 1939–1940', 14032

Jeffries, Greg: The Motor Industry, 17397

Jefkins, Frank: Advertising Today, 4323; Advertising Made Simple, 4324; A Dictionary of Advertising, 4325

Jeger, Lena May: Illegitimate Children and their Parents, 7508; 'The Politics of Family Planning', 7509

Jehu, Derek: Behaviour Modification and Social Work, 8721

Jellicoe, Geoffrey Alan: Motopia: A Study in the Evolution of Urban Landscapes, 20315; Studies in Landscape Design, 20316

Jellicoe, John Rushworth [Earl]: The Grand Fleet 1914–1916, 15260; The Crisis of the Naval War, 15261; The Submarine Peril: The Admiralty Policy of 1917, 15262

Jencks, C. E.: 'Social Status of Coal Miners in Britain Since Nationalisation', 6309, 9642

Jenison, Madge: Roads, 17102

Jenkin, Michael: British Industry and the North Sea: State Intervention in a Developing Industrial Sector, 6502

Jenkin, T. P.: 'The British General Election of 1951', 2308

Jenkins, Alan: The Thirties, 299; The Forties, 300; The Stock Exchange Story, 4275; Built on Teamwork, 6182

Jenkins, C. L.: Fairfields: A Study of Industrial Change, 16631

Jenkins, Clare: White-collar Unionism: The Rebellious Salariat, 6830

Jenkins, Clive: Power at the Top: A Critical Survey of the Nationalized Industries, 5423; Power Behind the Screen: Ownership and Motivation in British Commercial Television, 5424, 24870; Collective Bargaining: What You Always Wanted to Know About Trade Unions and Never Dared to Ask, 6795; The Kind of Laws the Unions Ought to Want, 6796; British Trade Unions Today, 6797; British Airlines: A Study of Nationalised Civil Aviation, 17622

Jenkins, D. F.: Gwen John: An Interior Life, 24028

Jenkins, Daniel Thomas: The British: Their Identity and their Religion, 11578

Jenkins, David: An Agricultural Community in South West Wales, 19304

Jenkins, E. W.: 'The Development of School Biology 1918–1945', 22453; From Armstrong to Nuffield: Studies in Twentieth-century Science Education in England and Wales, 22454; 'The Scientific Education of Girls since 1902', 22520; 'The Thomson Committee and the Board of Education 1916–1922', 22618; 'Public Examinations and Science Teaching Methods in Grammar Schools since 1918', 22908

Jenkins, Edwin Alfred: From Foundry to Foreign Office: The Romantic Life Story of the Rt. Hon. Arthur Henderson M.P., 1229

Jenkins, Frank: Architect and Patron: A Survey of Professional Relations and Practice in England from the Sixteenth Century to the Present Day, 23870

Jenkins, G. D.: The Price of Liberty: Personality and Politics in Colonial Nigeria, 12762

Jenkins, Geraint H.: Politics and Society in Wales, 1840–1922: Essays in Honour of Ieuan Gwynedd Jones, 2557

Jenkins, Graham: Richard Burton my Brother, 26019

Jenkins, Gwyn: 'The Welsh Outlook 1914–33', 25189

Jenkins, Hugh [Baron]: The Culture Gap: An Experience of Government and the Arts, 1434, 23957; Rank and File, 1775

Jenkins, John Geraint: The Welsh Woollen Industry, 5341; From Fleece to Fabric: The Technological History of the Welsh Woollen Industry, 5342; 'Technological Improvement and Social Change in South Cardiganshire', 5352; 'Rural Industry in Cardiganshire', 5353; ed. The Wool Textile Industry in Great Britain, 6416; Traditional Country Craftsmen, 6657; 'Technological Improvement and Social Change in South Cardiganshire', 7038, 19641; Maritime Heritage: The Ships and Seamen of Ceredigion, 16484

Jenkins, Mark: Bevanism—Labour's High Tide: The Cold War and the Democratic Mass Movement, 1731

Jenkins, R. T.: 'The Development of Nationalism in Wales', 2593; Y Bywgraffiadur Cymreig 1941–1950, 50; ed. The Dictionary of Welsh Biography down to 1940, 49

Jenkins, Rachel: Adoption and Fostering: Papers, 8112

Jenkins, Richard: ed. Racism and Equal Opportunity Policies in the 1980s, 11142

Jenkins, Roy Harries [Baron]: Asquith, 971; Mr. Attlee: An Interim Biography, 975; Baldwin, 977; 'Hugh Gaitskell: A Political Memoir', 1196; European Diary, 1977–1981, 1245. Jenkins, Roy: ed. Britain and the E.E.C. [Proceedings of the Economic Section of the British Assoc. for the Advancement of Science], 4820

Jenkins, Simon: Here to Live: A Study of English Race Relations in an English Town, 11003; With Respect, Ambassador: An Inquiry into the Foreign Office, 13335; The Battle for the Falklands, 16102; Newspapers: The Power and the Money,

25075; Market for Glory: Fleet Street Ownership in the Twentieth century, 25086

Jenkins, T. R.: 'Teacher Training in Welsh Colleges of Education, 1960–1970', 23631

Jenkins, Tom: ed. Modern Buildings in London: A Guide, 23918

Jenkins, Tudor: The Londoner, 25144

Jenkins, W.: ed. Social Science and Government: Policies and Problems, 8817

Jenkinson, Charles: This Turbulent Priest: The Story of Charles Jenkinson, Parish Priest and Housing Reformer, 11792; Sentimentality? or Commonsense?, 18397; Our Housing Objective, 18398

Jenkinson, David: An Illustrated History of L.M.S. Coaches, 1923–1957, 16882; An Illustrated History of L.M.S. Locomotives, 16883

Jenkinson, Jacqueline: 'The Glasgow Race Disturbances of 1919', 11487; 'The Black Community of Salford and Hull 1919–1921', 11488

Jenkinson, Keith A.: Northern Rose: The History of West Yorkshire Road Car Co. Ltd., 17330

Jenkinson, T.: 'What Stopped the Inflation? Unemployment or Commodity Prices?, 4020

Jenner, Peter J.: 'The Employment of Immigrants: A Case Study within the Wool Industry', 10966; 'Economic Effects of Immigration', 11410

Jennings, Bernard: A History of Lead Mining in the Pennines, 6359

Jennings, Frank: Men of the Lanes: The Autobiography of the Tramps' Parson, 11793

Jennings, Hilda: Bryn Mawr: A Study of a Distressed Area, 5348; Societies in the Making: A Study of Development and Redevelopment within a County Borough, 7572, 9346, 18406

Jennings, Humphry: ed. May the Twelfth. [Mass Observation Day Surveys 1937.], 7570

Jennings, R. E.: 'The Changing Representational Role of the Local Councillor in England', 3192

Jennings, R. E.: 'The History of British Infrared Astronomy', 26421

Jennings, Tony: Transport and the Environment, 16230

Jennings, Sir [William] Ivor: 'The Abdication of King Edward VIII', 499; 'Notes on Constitutional Developments, 1 January–August 1937', 500; Parliament, 546; Law and the Constitution, 600; The British Constitution, 610; The Queen's Government, 706; Cabinet Government, 716; Party Politics, 1574; Nationalism and Political Development in Ceylon, 12984; ed. Century of Municipal Progress: The Last Hundred Years, 17903

Jensen, Rolf: High Density Living, 18646

Jenson, Alec G.: Birmingham Transport vol.1, 16330

Jenson, J. Vernon: 'Clement R. Attlee and Twentieth Century Parliamentary Speaking', 975

Jephcott, Agnes Pearl: Married Women Working, 7683; 'Going out to Work: A Note on the Adolescent Girl in Britain', 8424; Girls Growing Up, 8425; Rising Twenty, 8426; A Troubled Area: Notes on Notting Hill, 9348, 11446; The Social Background of Delinquency, 10554; Homes in High Flats: Some of the Human Problems involved in Multi-Storey Housing, 18482

Jephcott, Sir Harry: The First Fifty Years, 22273

Jepsen, S.: 'Rehabilitation of Mental Patients—a New Group Work Approach', 21767

Jeremy, David J.: ed. Dictionary of Business Biography: A Biographical Dictionary of Business Leaders Active in the Period 1860–1950, 9785; 'Anatomy of the British Business Elite, 1860–1980', 9788; ed. Business and Religion in Britain, 11840; A Survey of Alcohol Education in the United Kingdom, 22159

Jerrold, Douglas: The Royal Naval Division, 15414

Jervis, Frank Robert Joseph: The Evolution of Modern Industry, 4980; Bosses in British Business: Management from the Industrial Revolution to the Present Day, 5412, 9795; An Introduction to Industrial Administration, 5598

Jervis, Walter Willson: The World in Maps: A Study in Map Evolution, 26700

Jervois, W. J.: The History of the Northamptonshire Regiment: 1934–1948, 15702

Jess, P. M.: ed. Planning and Development in Rural Areas: Report of a Conference, 18813

Jesse, Richard L.: 'Great Britain and Abdullah's Plan to Partition Palestine: A Natural Sorting Out', 14354; 'Britain and the Anglo-Israeli War of 1948', 14355

Jessop, Bob: Thatcherism: A Tale of Two Nations, 1054; Traditionalism, Conservatism and British Political Culture, 1623; Social Order, Reform and Revolution: A Power, Exchange and Institutionalisation Perspective, 9448

Jessup, Frank William: The History of Kent: A Select Bibliography, 5164; Wolfson College, Oxford: the Early Years, 23574

Jevons, Herbert Stanley: The British Coal Trade, 6251

Jevons, Rosamond: Housing Estates: A Study of Bristol Corporation Policy and Practice between the Wars, 18635

Jewel, Jimmy: Three Times Lucky, 26325

Jewell, Richard Edward Coxhead: The British Constitution, 619

Jewesbury, Eric C. O.: The Royal Northern Hospital, 1856–1956, 21455

Jewish Chronicle: Special Supplements to celebrate the Tercentenary of the Resettlement of the Jews in the British Isles 1656–1956, 11283

Jewish Yearbook: 1896+, 12407

Jewkes, John: Public and Private Enterprise, 4978; The New Ordeal by Planning: The Experience of the Forties and the Sixties, 6080; 'The Localisation of the Cotton Industry', 6470; The Sources of Intervention, 7140; and Jewkes, Sylvia: The

Genesis of the British National Health Service, 21549

Jingoes, Jason: A Chief is a Chief by the People, 11514

Joad, Cyril Edwin Mitchinson: Under the Fifth Rib: A Belligerent Autobiography, 26851

Jobling, Megan: Helping the Handicapped Child, 8230; Spotlight on Sources of Information about Children, 8272

Jobling, R. G.: 'Some Sociological Aspects of University Development in England', 22548

Jobson, Allan: Suffolk Villages, 19144

Joby, R. S.: The Railwaymen, 16735

Jody, Daniele: Muslims in Britain: An Annotated Bibliography, 1960–1984, 12455

Joel, David: The Adventure of British Furniture, 1851–1951, 24145

John, Angela V.: Unequal Opportunities: Women's Employment in England, 1800–1918, 7645

John, Arthur H.: ed. Glamorgan County History 5: Industrial Glamorgan from 1700 to 1970, 3384; A Liverpool Merchant House: Being a History of Alfred Booth and Company, 1863–1958, 16525

John, Audrey L.: Student Nurses in Scotland: Characteristics of Success and Failure, 23235

John, Augustus Edwin: Autobiography, 24022

John, Barry: The Barry John Story, 27049

John, Gus: (Commentary) Police Power and Black People, 11017; Because They're Black, 11169

Johnman, Lewis: ed. Postwar Britain 1945–1964: Themes and Perspectives, 425, 14392, 24773; 'Defending the Pound: The Economics of the Suez Crisis 1956', 14392

Johns, Edward Alistair: The Social Structure of Modern Britain, 7586; An Introduction to Sociology, 7978

Johns, Ewart: British Townscapes, 20308

Johnson, A.: 'Some Guides to Understanding the British Social Services', 8881

Johnson, Albert F.: A Bibliography of Ghana 1930–1961, 12736

Johnson, B. D.: 'Understanding British Addiction statistics', 22221

Johnson, B. S.: ed. The Evacuees, 15089, 15160; ed. All Bull: The National Servicemen, 16069

Johnson, Brian: The Conservation and Development Programme for the United Kingdom, 20200

Johnson, Christopher: Anatomy of U.K. Finance, 1970–1975, 4601

Johnson, Dale A.: Women in English Religion 1700–1925, 11674

Johnson, David S.: 'The Economic History of Ireland between the Wars', 2672; 'The Belfast Boycott 1920–1922', 2795; 'Northern Ireland as a Problem in the Economic War, 1932–1938', 2799

Johnson, David: The City Ablaze. The Second Great Fire of London, 29 December 1940, 15162

Johnson, Derek: 'Does Conviction Affect Employment Opportunities?', 5904

Johnson, Derek E.: Exodus of Children, 15092; East Anglia at War, 1939–1945, 15176

Johnson, Donald McIntosh: A Cassandra at Westminster, 1435; Indian Hemp: A Social Menace, 22185; On Being an Independent M.P, 1436; A Doctor in Parliament, 1437; A Doctor Reflects: Miracles and Mirages, 1438; The British National Health Service, 21571

Johnson, Douglas: Contending for the Faith: A History of the Evangelical Movement in the Universities and Colleges, 11662

Johnson, Douglas W. J.: 'Austen Chamberlain and the Locarno Agreements', 13657; Britain and France: Ten Centuries, 14243; 'Britain and France in 1940', 14268

Johnson, Edgar Augustus Jerome: An Economic History of Modern England, 3464

Johnson, Edward Lea: Family Law, 10015

Johnson, Elizabeth: The Shadow of Keynes: Understanding Keynes, Cambridge and Keynesian Economics, 26606

Johnson, Francis: The ILP in War and Peace: A Short Account of the Party from its Foundation to the Present Day, 1869

Johnson, Frank: Out of Order, 25255

Johnson, Franklyn Arthur: Defence by Committee: The British Committee of Imperial Defence, 1885–1959, 822, 15474; Defence by Ministry: The British Ministry of Defence 1944–74, 823

Johnson, G. Griffith: The Treasury and Monetary Policy, 1933–1938, 4583

Johnson, H.: 'Oil, Imperial Policy and the Trinidad Disturbances', 6506

Johnson, Harry Gordon: Inflation and the Monetarist Controversy, 4004; Readings in British Monetary Economics, 4592; 'Financial and Monetary Problems of the United Kingdom: Their Relation to British Entry into the Common Market', 4595; Money in Britain, 1959–1969, 4627; 'How Good was Keynes' Cambridge?', 23467; The Shadow of Keynes: Understanding Keynes, Cambridge and Keynesian Economics, 26606

Johnson, Hewlett: Searching for Light: An Autobiography, 11794

Johnson, Howard: The Cunard Story, 16529; Wings over Brooklands: The Story of the Birthplace of British Aviation, 17525

Johnson, Humphrey John Thewlis: Anglicanism in Transition, 11591; 'Tendencies in the Church of England: Some Recent Views', 11592; 'Anglicanism in the 20th Century: 4. The Church of England and Other Denominations', 11593

Johnson, Ian: 'We're all Right Jack', 24653; The Aston Villa Story, 27077

Johnson, J.: The Dictionary of British Artists 1880–1940, 23932

Johnson, James Edgar: Full Circle: The Story of Air Fighting, 15800

Johnson, James Henry: Housing and the Migration of Labour in England and Wales, 7283, 18552; Urban Geography: An Introductory Analysis, 18275, 20415; ed. Suburban Growth: Geographical Processes at the Edge of the Western City, 18296; ed. Trends in Geography: An Introductory survey, 26640

Johnson, James P.: A Hundred Years Eating: Food, Drink, and Daily Diet in Britain since the Late 19th Century, 20571

Johnson, John: British Railways Engineering, 1948–1980, 17083

Johnson, Leonard George: The Social Evolution of Industrial Britain: A Study in the Growth of our Industrial Society, 5644

Johnson, Lesley: The Cultural Critics: From Matthew Arnold to Raymond Williams, 23753

Johnson, Luke: Shell Expro: A History, 6497

Johnson, M. R. D.: New Towns in North East England, 18211

Johnson, Malcolm L.: ed. and comp. Medical Sociology in Britain: A Register of Research and Teaching, 21956

Johnson, Marjorie Scott: The Peace Ballot: The Official History, 13502

Johnson, Nevil: In Search of the Constitution: Reflections on State and Society in Britain, 626; Parliament and Administration: the Estimates Committee 1945–1965, 653; 'The Royal Commission on the Constitution', 687; 'Servicemen and Parliamentary Elections', 2228

Johnson, Pamela Hansford: On Iniquity: Some Personal Reflections Arising out of the Moors Murder Trial, 10794

Johnson, Paul: Gold Fields: A Centenary Portrait, 6350

Johnson, Paul: Saving and Spending: The Working Class Economy in Britain 1870–1939, 9629, 20420

Johnson, Paul Barton: Land Fit for Heroes: The Planning of British Reconstruction, 1916–1919, 6106, 8979

Johnson, Paul Bede: The Suez War, 14367; The Pick of Paul Johnson, 25256

Johnson, Peter: British Trams and Tramways in the 1980s, 17209; Trams in Blackpool, 17214

Johnson, Peter David: Money and Economic Activity in the Open Economy: The United Kingdom, 1880–1970, 4600

Johnson, Peter Stewart: The Economics of Invention, with a Case Study of the Development of the Hovercraft, 17706

Johnson, Phyllis: The Struggle for Zimbabwe: The Chimurenga War, 12806

Johnson, R. F.: Regimental Fire: The Honourable Artillery Company in World War 2, 15650

Johnson, Raymond: Mines and Quarries in Britain, 6327

Johnson, Richard: Man's Place: An Essay on Auden, 25364

Johnson, Richard: Working Class Culture, 23730

Johnson, Richard William: Members from the Unions, 1557; 'The Nationalisation of English Rural Politics: Norfolk South-West 1945–1970', 3366

Johnson, Robina: Public Participation in Planning: A Review of Experience in Scotland, 20362

Johnson, Ruth: Old Road: A Lancashire Childhood, 1912–1926, 8231

Johnson, S.: Agents Extraordinary, 15195

Johnson, Stanley P.: ed. The Population Problem, 7395; The Politics of Environment: The British Experience, 19970, 20207; The Green Revolution, 19971

Johnson, Terence James: Professionals and Power, 9772

Johnson, Thomas H.: Doncaster Regional Planning Scheme, 18861

Johnson, W. C.: Encounter in London: The Story of the London Baptist Association, 1865–1965, 12038

Johnson, W.: 'Entrepreneurial Efficiency in the British Coal Industry between the Wars: A Second Comment', 6275

Johnson, Walford: A Short Economic and Social History of 20th Century Britain, 386, 3492

Johnson-Marshall, Percy Edwin Alan: Rebuilding Cities, 17788

Johnston, A.: 'Britain, Ireland and Ulster', 2995

Johnston, Sir Alexander: The City Take-over Code, 5546

Johnston, Arnold: Of Earth and Darkness: The Novels of William Golding, 25541

Johnston, Brian: The Secret War, 15196

Johnston, Charles Hepburn: The View from Steamer Point: Being an Account of Three Years in Aden, 13871

Johnston, Claire: 'Declarations of Independence', 24652

Johnston, Colin: Glasgow Stations, 16989

Johnston, David Robert: Forest Planning, 19748

Johnston, John: The Growth of Life Assurance in the United Kingdom since 1880, 4210; 'The Growth of Life Actuaries in the United Kingdom since 1880', 4211

Johnston, L. C.: 'Historical Records of the British Transport Commission', 16206; 'British Transport Commission Archives: Work since 1953', 16207

Johnston, Luke: The Key to Making Money in the New Stock Market, 4292

Johnston, P. H. W.: British Emigration to Durban, South Africa: A Sociological Examination of Richardson's Conceptual Framework, 7327

Johnston, Ronald John.: 'A Further Look at British Political Finance', 1597; 'Campaign Expenditure and the Efficiency of Advertising at the 1974 Elections in England', 2335; The Geography of English Politics: The 1983 General Election, 2347; 'Places, Campaigns and Votes', 2348 'The Electoral Geography of an Election Campaign: Scotland in October 1974', 2371; Geography and Inequality, 5081; Urban Residential Patterns: An Introductory Review, 17814; Geography since the Second World War, 26651; Geography and Geographers: Anglo-American Human Geography since 1945, 26652

Johnston, Rosie: Inside Out, 7735

Johnston, Thomas Lothian: 'Pay Policy after the Pause', 3935; Structure and Growth of the Scottish Economy, 5266; An Introduction to Industrial Relations, 5816

Johnston, Thomas: Memories, 1248; The

History of the Working Classes in Scotland, 1249, 2520

Johnstone, John Keith: The Bloomsbury Group: A Study of E. M. Forster, Lytton Strachey, Virginia Woolf and their Circle, 23768

Johnstone, Monty: 'The Communist Party in the 1920's', 1939

Johnstone, Pamela: Structure Plans: List B: The Literature and Debate on Structure Plans and Structure Planning, 17962

Johnstone, R. W.: Historical Review of British Obstetrics and Gynaecology, 1800–1950, 21100

Johnstone, William: Points in Time, 24029

Joint Committee On Labour Problems After The War: The Problem of Demobilisation: A Statement and Some Suggestions Including Proposals for the Reform of Employment Exchanges, 6992

Joint Committee of the General Council of the Bar of England and Wales, The Law Society and the British Medical Association: Medical Evidence in Courts of Law: The Report, 21257

Joint Council for the Welfare of Immigrants: The Numbers Game . . . Evidence to the Select Committee on Race Relations and Immigration, 11429

Joint Liberal Party/ SDP Alliance Commission on Electoral Reform: Electoral Reform: Fairer Voting in Natural Communities: First Report . . . , 1850

Joint University Council for Social and Public Administration: Bibliography of Social Work and Administration: A Classified List of Articles from Selected Periodicals: 1930–1952, 9237

Joll, Caroline: Industrial Organisation: Competition, Growth and Structural Change in Britain, 5749

Jolly, A. R.: 'The Structure of the British Coal Mining Industry in 1955', 6301

Jolly, Alan: Blue Flash: The Story of an Armoured Regiment, 15602

Jolly, Rick: The Red and Green Life Machine: Diary of the Falklands Field Hospital, 16116

Jones, A. E.: Roads and Rails of West Yorkshire, 1890–1950, 16333

Jones, Anna M.: The Rural Industries of England and Wales, 6656

Jones, Anthony: Welsh Chapels, 12290

Jones, Arthur Edward: A Small School in the Great War: The Story of Sutton County School and its Old Boys in World War One, 22987

Jones, Aubrey: The Pendulum of Politics, 2188; Britain's Economy: The Roots of Stagnation, 3701; The New Inflation: The Politics of Prices and Incomes, 4005

Jones, Austin Edwin: Roads and Rails of West Yorkshire, 1890–1950, 17156; Trams and Buses of West Yorkshire, 17236

Jones, B.: ed. The Channel Tunnel and Beyond, 16361

Jones, Barry: Labour and the British State, 1686

Jones, Barry M.: The Story of Panther Motorcycles, 17192

Jones, Beti: Etholiadau Seneddol yng Nghymru 1900–1975, 2365

Jones, C. D.: 'The Performance of British Railways, 1962–1968', 16783

Jones, C. Gareth: 'The British Government and the Oil Companies, 1912–1924: The Search for an Oil Policy', 6498

Jones, Catherine Joy: Patterns of Social Policy: An Introduction to Comparative Analysis, 8810; Immigration and Social Policy in Britain, 11426

Jones, Charles L.: The Images of Occupational Prestige, 5917, 9551

Jones, Charles Mark Jenkin: The North Eastern Railway: A Centenary Story, 16904

Jones, Charles: 'Inter-Party Competition in Britain, 1950–1959', 1604

Jones, Colin: ed. The Sale of Council Houses, 18429

Jones, D. T.: Rural Scotland during the War, 19239

Jones, Daniel: My Friend Dylan Thomas, 25837

Jones, David Caradog: The Social Survey of Merseyside, 5177; Handbook of Social Statistics Relating to Merseyside, 5178; New Handbook of Social Statistics, 5179; Merseyside: The Relief of the Poor, 9023; Post-war Poverty and Unemployment Can Be Prevented, 9024; The Cost of Living of a Sample of Middle-Class Families, 20422

Jones, David: The Time Shrinkers—Africa: The Development of Civil Aviation between Britain and Africa, 17522

Jones, David: ed. Community, 9372; Community Work, 9373

Jones, Douglas: 'The Chinese in Britain: Origins and Development of a Community', 11381; 'Chinese Schools in Britain: A Minority Response to its own Needs', 11382

Jones, E. D.: Y Bywgraffiadur Cymreig 1941–1950, 50

Jones, E. R.: Northern Labour History: A Bibliography, 1776

Jones, E.: Man and his Habitat, 17976

Jones, Edgar: Accounting and the British Economy 1880–1980: The Evolution of Ernst & Whinney, 4174; A History of G.K.N. Vol.1: Innovation and Enterprise, 1759–1918, 6366; The Penguin Guide to the Railways of Great Britain, 16729

Jones, Sir Edgar R.: Toilers of the Hills: An Historical Record of those who Worked through more than a Century on Iron, Steel, and Tin Plate among the Welsh Hills and Valleys, 9631

Jones, Edward T.: L. P. Hartley, 25574; Following Directions, 26121

Jones, Elizabeth A.: Index of Human Ecology, 19969

Jones, Emrys: A Social Geography of Belfast, 18171; Towns and Cities, 18273, 20413; The City in Geography: An Inaugural Lecture . . . at L.S.E, 18274, 20414; ed. Atlas of London and the London Region, 18350; An Introduction to Social Geography, 26688

Jones, Emyr: Canrif y Chwarelwyr, 5350

Jones, Enid Huws: Margery Fry: The Essential Amateur, 10364

Jones, Eric Lionel: Seasons and Prices: The Role of the Weather in English Agricultural History, 19527

Jones, Francis Avery: 'The Norwich Schools of Surgery: The Evolution of Surgery in an English City', 7043

Jones, Frank E.: 'Some Situational Influences on Attitudes toward Immigrants', 11438

Jones, G. E.: 'The Nature and Consequences of Technical Change in Farming', 19691

Jones, G. T.: The Demand for Housing, 18703

Jones, Gareth Elwyn: People, Protest and Politics in the Twentieth Century: Case Studies in Twentieth Century Wales, 2550; Modern Wales: A Concise History 1585–1979, 2551

Jones, Gareth Stedman: Metropolis: London Histories and Representations since 1800, 3282; 'From Historical Sociology to Theoretical History', 8076; Languages of Class: Studies in English Working Class History, 1832–1932, 9669; White-collar Proletariat: Deskilling and Gender in Clerical Work, 9670

Jones, Geoffrey: 'Lombard Street on the Riviera: The British Clearing Banks and Europe 1900–1960', 4421; 'British Overseas Banks in the Middle East, 1920–70: A Study in Multinational Middle Age', 4457; Banking and Oil: The History of the British Bank of the Middle East, 4529; ed. British Multinationals: Origins, Management and Performance, 5564; The State and the Emergence of the British Oil Industry, 6489

Jones, Geoffrey Patrick: Raider: The Halifax and its Flyers, 15858

Jones, George William: 'Prime Ministers' Advisers', 959; Herbert Morrison: Portrait of a Politician, 1283; 'Mr Crossman and the Reform of Local Government, 1964–1966', 3173; Central-Local Relations in Britain, 3213; ed. Between Centre and Locality: The Politics of Public Policy, 3217; ed. New Approaches to the Study of Central-Local Government Relations, 3220; Borough Politics: A Study of the Wolverhampton Town Council 1888–1964, 3343 Jones, Glanville Rees Jeffreys: ed. Leeds and its Region, 18028; ed. Geography as Human Ecology: Methodology by Example, 26689

Jones, Glenys: Services for the Mentally Handicapped in Britain, 21787, 21925

Jones, Glyn: Britain on Borrowed Time, 3656

Jones, Glyn E.: ed. Welsh Phonology: Selected Readings, 23836

Jones, Glyn Meredith: Sully: A Village and Parish in the Vale of Glamorgan, 19377

Jones, Greta: Social Darwinism and English Thought: The Interaction between Biological and Social Theory, 8085; 'Eugenics and Social Policy between the Wars', 8846; 'The Mushroomed-Shaped Cloud: British Scientists' Opposition to Nuclear Weapons Policy 1945–1957', 13535; Social Hygiene in Twentieth Century Britain, 21738; Science, Politics and the Cold War, 26494; 'British Scientists, Lysenko and the Cold War', 26495

Jones, Gwilym Peredur: A Hundred Years of Economic Development in Great Britain, 3443; The Genesis of Freemasonry, 12394

Jones, Gwyn: Fountains of Praise: University College, Cardiff, 1883–1983, 23486

Jones, Gwyn Evans: Rural Life: Patterns and Processes, 19033

Jones, H. A.: The War in the Air, 15791

Jones, H. Kay: Butterworths: History of a Publishing House, 24947

Jones, Herbert: Stanley Morison Displayed: An Examination of his Early Typographic Work, 25027

Jones, Howard: ed. Towards a New Social Work, 8713; ed. The Residential Community: A Setting for Social Work, 8714, 10258; Crime in a Changing Society, 10254; Prison Reform Now, 10255; Reluctant Rebels: Re-education and Group Process in a Residential Community, 10256; Crime and the Penal System. A Textbook of Criminology, 10257; ed. Society against Crime: Penal Practice in Modern Britain, 10361; Open Prisons, 10368; 'The Prisons in 1960', 10402; 'Prison Officers as Therapists', 10452; Alcoholic Addiction: A Psycho-Social Approach to Abnormal Drinking, 22131

Jones, Huw A.: Recent Migration in Northern Scotland: Pattern, Process, Impact, 7332

Jones, Ian K.: The Safety Bicycle, 17169

Jones, Ian Shore: Urban Transport Appraisal, 16302

Jones, Idris Deane: Modern Welsh History ..., 2554

Jones, Ieuan Gwynedd: ed. Welsh Society and Nationhood: Historical Essays Presented to Glanmor Williams, 2556

Jones, Ivor Wynne: Shipwrecks of North Wales, 16510

Jones, J.: 'Village Life: Redbrook on Wye, 1914–1931', 19305

Jones, J. Barry: A Research Register of Territorial Politics in the United Kingdom, 1560; The Welsh Veto: The Politics of the Devolution Campaign in Wales, 2576; The Wales Act 1978 and the Referendum, 2577

Jones, J. E. Owen: 'A Brief Review of Industry in Caernarvonshire', 5349

Jones, J. Graham: 'Wales and the New Liberalism, 1926–1929', 2562; 'Wales and "War Socialism", 1926–1929', 2563; 'Forming Plaid Cymru: Laying the Foundations, 1926–1936', 2607; 'Forming Plaid Cymru: Searching for a Policy, 1926–1930', 2608

Jones, James Harry: Josiah Stamp, Public Servant: The Life of the First Baron Stamp of Shortlands, 926, 26621

Jones, James Ira Thomas: Tiger Squadron: The Story of 74 Squadron, R.A.F in Two World Wars, 15925

Jones, James Owain: The History of the Caernarvonshire Constabulary 1856–1950, 10759

Jones, John: Balliol College: A History, 1263–1939, 23566

Jones, John Charles: John Bangor, The People's Bishop: The Life and Work of John Charles Jones, Bishop of Bangor, 1949–56, 12283

Jones, John Edward: 1925–1955: Cylchwyn Plaid Cymru, 2609

Jones, John Harry: The Coal Mining Industry, 6280; Social Reconstruction: A Proposal, 8928; Social Economics, 8929

Jones, John Lloyd: Rural Crafts in England, 19095

Jones, John Morris: Manors of Aston Parish: An Introduction to the Historical Geography of Aston Manor, 19320

Jones, John Owen: Index of Human Ecology, 19969; ed. Land Use Planning: The Methodology of Choice: A Compilation of Review Articles and Annotated Bibliography, 20251

Jones, Karen: ed. International Index to Film Periodicals, 24591

Jones, Kathleen: Eileen Younghusband: A Biography, 8676, 21897; Health and Social Services Merry Go-Round, 8677; Mental Health and Social Policy, 8678; Issues in Social Policy, 8807; ed. Yearbook of Social Policy in Britain—1971, 8808; A History of the Mental Health Services, 21737; Opening the Door: A Study of New Policies for the Mentally Handicapped, 21866; 'The Twenty-four Steps: An Analysis of Institutional Admission Procedures', 22549

Jones, Kevin P.: Steam Locomotive Development: An Analytical Guide to the Literature on British Steam Locomotive Development, 1923–1962, 17044

Jones, Kit: 'Immigrants and the Social Services', 10965; The Economic Impact of Commonwealth Immigration, 11417; Health and Welfare Services in Britain in 1975, 22083

Jones, L. H.: 'Industrial Location and Unemployment', 5054

Jones, Leslie: Shipbuilding in Britain, mainly between the Two World Wars, 16606

Jones, M. E. F.: 'The Regional Impact of an Overvalued Pound in the 1920s', 4675

Jones, M. W.: One Hundred Years of Motoring: An R.A.C. Social History of the Car, 17341

Jones, Martin: Failure in Palestine: Britain and United States Policy after the Second World War, 14349

Jones, Maxwell: Social Psychiatry in Practice: The Idea of the Therapeutic Community, 21796; Beyond the Therapeutic Community: Social Learning and Social Psychiatry, 21797; et al. Small Group Psychotherapy, 21798

Jones, Mervyn: Life on the Dole, 6982, 9689; Two Ears of Corn: Oxfam in Action, 9193; ed. Kingsley Martin: Portrait and Self Portrait, 25266

Jones, Michael: 'Resolving Industrial Disputes: The Role of A.C.A.S. Conciliation, 4164

Jones, Michael Wynn: Lloyds of London: An Illustrated History, 4261

Jones, Neville: The Origins of Strategic Bombing: A Study of the Development of British Air Strategic Thought and Practice up to 1918, 15978

Jones, Nicholas: Strikes and the Media, 25126

Jones, Norman Richard: Food Additives: Descriptions, Functions and U.K. Legislation, 20178

Jones, P. N.: Colliery Settlement in the South Wales Coalfield, 1850–1926, 6316

Jones, P. R.: Vietnamese Refugees: A Study of Their Reception and Resettlement in the United Kingdom, 11391

Jones, Peter Lloyd: The Economics of Nuclear Power Programmes in the United Kingdom, 6665

Jones, Philip Nicholas: The Humberside Region, 5137; The Segregation of Immigrant Communities in the City of Birmingham, 1961, 11456; 'Workmen's Trains in the South Wales Coalfield 1870–1926', 16975

Jones, Philip: Britain and Palestine, 1914–1948: Archival Sources for the History of the British Mandate, 14277

Jones, R. B.: The Pattern of Farming in the East Midlands, 19609

Jones, R. Merfyn: The North Wales Quarrymen 1874–1922, 5363

Jones, Raymond A.: Arthur Ponsonby, 1505

Jones, Reginald V.: The Wizard War: British Scientific Intelligence, 1939–1945, 15108; Most Secret War, 15197

Jones, Richard Benjamin: The Economic and Social History of England, 1770–1977, 3494

Jones, Richard Gerallt: A Bid for Unity: The Story of Undeb Cymru Fydd 1946–1966, 23837

Jones, Robert Tudur: Congregationalism in England, 1662–1962, 12048

Jones, Robert: Anatomy of a Merger: A History of G.E.C., A.E.I. and English Electric, 4994, 6678

Jones, Sir Robert: 'The Orthopaedic Outlook in Military Surgery', 21298; 'Military Orthopaedic Treatment [in the U.K.]', 21299; 'The Problem of the Disabled', 21940

Jones, Sir Roderick: A Life in Reuters, 25306

Jones, Rowan: Public Sector Accounting, 4770

Jones, Roy Elliott: The Changing Structure of British Foreign Policy, 13240

Jones, Russell: Wages and Employment Policy, 1936–1985, 3966

Jones, S. J.: ed. Dundee and District, 18129

Jones, S. Lloyd: ed. Cardiff, 1889–1974: The Story of the County Borough, 18161

Jones, S.: Employment and Unemployment in North West Wales, 7014

Jones, Simon: Black Culture, White Youth and the Reggae Tradition from JA. to U.K., 8530

Jones, Sir Thomas George: The Unbroken Front: The British Ministry of Food, 1916–1944: Personalities and Problems, 839, 20583

Jones, Stephen G.: The British Labour Movement and Film, 1918–1939, 2104; Workers at Play: A Social and Economic History of Leisure, 1918–1939, 26918; 'State Intervention in Sport and Leisure in Britain between the Wars', 26992; 'Trade-union Policy between the Wars: The Case of Holidays with Pay in Britain', 26993

Jones, T. M.: Watchdogs of the Deep: Life in a Submarine during the Great War, 15367

Jones, Thomas: A Diary with Letters, 1930–1950, 757; Whitehall Diary, 758; Lloyd George, 1018; Whitehall Diary No.3: Ireland, 1918–1925, 2993

Jones, Tom: Health Service Finance: An Introduction, 21635

Jones, Trevor W.: 'Occupational Transition in Advanced Industrial Societies: A Reply', 5913

Jones, Tudor Jenkyn: Future Education and Training for British Industry, 23264

Jones, Vivian: ed. The Church in a Mobile Society: A Survey of the Zone of Industrial South West Wales, 12293

Jones, William Dyfri: Rough Grazings in the Hills and Uplands of Wales: Productivity and Potential, 19642

Jones, William Henry: History of the Port of Swansea, 16712

Jones, William Richard: Bilingualism in Welsh Education, 23625, 23823; A Survey of Educational Attainment in Wales: a Report on the 1960 National Survey, 23627

Jonson, P. D.: 'Money and Economic Activity in the Open Economy: The United Kingdom, 1880–1970', 4628

Jonsson, H.: Friends in Conflict: The Anglo-Icelandic Cod War and the Law of the Sea, 19831

Jordan, A. G.: Government and Pressure Groups in Britain, 2060; 'The Origins of the Water Act of 1973', 20101; 'The Growth of the Environment as a Political Issue in Britain', 20248

Jordan, Alma: The English-Speaking Caribbean: A Bibliography of Bibliographies, 12994

Jordan, Edward Kenneth Henry: Free Church Unity: A History of the Free Church Council Movement, 1896–1941, 11999

Jordan, George William: Self-Portrait of Youth: Or, the Urban Adolescent, 8475

Jordan, Henry D.: 'Foreign Government and Politics: The British Cabinet and the Ministry of Defence', 730; 'The British Cabinet and the Ministry of Defence', 826

Jordan, Percy: An Economic History of England, 3486

Jordan, William: Rethinking Welfare, 8965; Paupers: Poor Parents: Social Policy and the Cycle of Deprivation, 9083; The Making of the New Claiming Class, 9084; The Social Worker in Family Situations, 10100

Jordan, William Mark: Great Britain, France and the German Problem, 1918–1939, 14259

Jorgensen, J. J.: Uganda: A Modern History, 12840

Journal of Religious History: 1960–1+, 11538

Joseph, G.: Women at Work: The British Experience, 7772

Joseph, Joyce: 'Research Note: Attitudes of 600 Adolescent Girls to Work and Marriage', 8428

Joseph, Richard: Michael Joseph: Master of Words, 24972

Joseph, Keith Sinjohn [Baron]: Reversing the Trend, 2195; A New Strategy for Social Security, 4100

Josephs, Jeremy: Inside the Alliance: An Inside Account of the Development and Prospects of the Liberal-SDP Alliance, 1841

Josephson, Harold: ed. et al. Biographical Dictionary of Modern Peace Leaders, 13433

Josey, Alex: Lee Kuan Yew and the Commonwealth, 12965

Joshi, Heather: Female Labour Supply in Post-War Britain: A Cohort Approach, 7773

Joshi, Shirley: 'The 1951–1955 Conservative Government and the Racialisation of Black Immigration', 11099

Joshua, Harris: To Ride the Storm: The 1980 Bristol 'Riots' and the State, 10872, 11077

Josling, Timothy Edward: Agriculture and Britain's Trade Policy Dilemma, 19555; ed. Agriculture and the State: British Policy in a World Context, 19570

Josset, Christopher Robert: Money in Great Britain and Ireland, 4631

Joubert de la Ferté, Sir Philip Bennet: Birds and Fishes: The Story of Coastal Command, 14977, 15911; Rocket, 14996; The Forgotten Ones: The Story of the Ground Crews, 14998; The Third Service, the Story behind the Royal Air Force, 15801

Journal of Adult Education: 22598

Journal of Curriculum Studies: 22599

Journal of Ecclesiastical History: 1950+, 11537

Journal of Education for Teaching: 22600

Journal of Educational Administration and History: 22601

Journal of Philosophy of Education: 22602

Journal of Philosophy: 22340

Journal of Theological Studies: 1899+, 11540

Journal of Transport Economics and Policy: 1967+: 16218

Journal of Transport History: 1953/4: 16215

Journal of the Royal Town Planning Institute: 17725

Journal of the Society of Archivists:

Jowell, Jeffrey: ed. The Changing Constitution, 583, 749; 'Development Control', 17860

Jowell, Roger: 'Racial Discrimination and White Collar Workers in Britain', 11167; ed. Britain into Europe: Public Opinion and the E.E.C. 1961–1975, 14183

Jowett, Paul: Party Strategies in Britain: A Study of the 1984 European Elections, 2382

Joy, David: South and West Yorkshire: The Industrial West Riding, 16816; The Lake Counties, 16822; Railways in Lancashire, 16949; Yorkshire Railways: Including Cleveland and Humberside, 16987

Joy, Stewart: The Train that Ran Away: A Business History of Britain's Railways, 1948–1968, 16787

Joyce, Cyril Alfred: By Courtesy of the Criminal: The Human Approach to the Treatment of Crime, 10510; Fair Play, 10511; Education and Delinquency, 10512

Joyce, Ernest Edward Mills: The South Polar Trail: The Log of the Imperial Trans-Antarctic Expedition, 27214

Joyce, James: Roads, Rails and Ferries of Liverpool, 1900–1950, 16332; Roads and Rails of Manchester, 1900–1950, 17157; 17158; Roads and Rails of Tyne and Wear, 1900–1980, 17159; The British Tramways Scene, 17204; Tramway Heyday, 17205; Tramways of the World, 17206; Tramway Twilight: The Story of Britain's Tramways from 1945 to 1962, 17207; 'Operation Tramway': The End of London's Trams, 1950–1952, 17233; Trolleybus Trails: A Survey of British Trolleybus Systems, 17240; The Story of Passenger Transport in

Britain, 17254; British Buses in the 1950s, 17272

Joye, Gill: ed. Southampton's Ships: An Index to Periodical References, 16477

Joynson-Hicks, W., Viscount Brentford: The Command of the Air, 14633

Juby, Kerry: Kate Bush—The Whole Story, 24512

Judd, Denis O.: The House of Windsor, 467; The Life and Times of George V, 473; George VI: 1895–1952, 505; Prince Philip: A Biography, 519; Lord Reading, 1305; The Evolution of the Modern Commonwealth, 1902–80, 12479; Alison Uttley: The Life of a Country Child (1884–1976): The Authorised Biography, 25845

Judge, Anthony: A Source Book of Police, 10687; The Night the Police Went on Strike, 10708; A Man Apart: The British Policeman and his Job, 10718; The First Fifty Years, 10719

Judge, David: 'Backbench Specialisation: A Study in Parliamentary Questions', 700; 'Scottish Members of Parliament: Problems of Devolution', 2472

Judge, Harry: A Generation of Schooling: English Secondary Schools since 1944, 22929

Judge, Ken: Rationing Social Services: A Study of Resource Allocation and the Personal Social Services, 8958

Judges, A. V.: Pioneers of English Education, 22800; 'The Educational Influence of the Webbs', 23240

Judson, Horace Freeland: Heroin Addiction in Britain, 22199

Jukes, David J.: Food Legislation of the United Kingdom: A Concise Guide, 20621

Julienne, L.: Charles Wootton: The 1919 Race Riots in Liverpool, 11465

Junankar, P. N.: 'The Relationship between Investment and Spare Capacity in the United Kingdom, 1957–1966', 4747

Junor, Penny: Charles, 530; Diana: Princess of Wales: A Biography, 536; Margaret Thatcher: Woman, Mother, Prime Minister, 1048; Burton: The Man behind the Myth, 26017

Jupp, James: The Radical Left in Britain, 1931–1941, 1716; 'The British Social Democrats and Crisis in the British Labour Party', 1832; 'The Discontents of Youth', 8439; 'Immigrants Involvement in British and Australian Politics', 11415

Jupp, Peter J.: ed. Essays Presented to Michael Roberts, 26810

Jurak, M.: 'Commitment and Character Portrayal in the British Politico-Poetic Drama of the 1930's', 26189

Just, Marion R.: 'Causal Models of Voter Rationality, Great Britain 1959 and 1963', 2250

Justice: Committee on Administrative Law, Compensation for Compulsory Acquisition and Remedies for Planning Restrictions: A Report of a Sub-committee of the Committee on Administrative Law, 20345

Jwaideh, Alice Reid: The Policy of the United Kingdom towards Spain from the End of World War II until the British Elections of 1951, 13996

Jürgensen, Kurt: 'British Occupation Policy after 1945 and the Problems of "Re-Educating Germany"', 14205

Kaarsted, T.: Great Britain and Denmark 1914–1920, 13414

Kacewicz, George V.: Great Britain, the Soviet Union and the Polish Government in Exile (1939–1945), 13903

Kadish, Alon: Historians, Economists and Economic History, 26764

Kaelble, Hartmut: Historical Research on Social Mobility: Western Europe and the USA in the 19th and 20th Centuries, 9583

Kahan, Barbara: Growing up in Care, 8232

Kahan, Michael: 'On the Analytical Division of Social Class', 9489

Kahler, Miles: Decolonization in Britain and France: the Domestic Consequences of International Relations, 12595

Kahn, Alfred Edward: Great Britain in the World Economy, 3428; 'The British Balance of Payments and Problems of Domestic Policy', 4918

Kahn, Hilde Renate: Salaries in the Public Sector in England and Wales, 3874; Repercussions of Redundancy: A Local Survey, 6973

Kahn, Jack: The Group Process as a Helping Technique, 8653

Kahn, Peggy: Picketing: Industrial Disputes, Tactics and the Law, 6940

Kahn, Richard F.: 'On Re-reading Keynes', 26613; The Making of Keynes's General Theory, 26614

Kahn-Freund, Sir Otto: 'Industrial Relations and the Law: Retrospect and Prospect', 5723; 'Trade Unions, the Law and Society', 5724; 'Reflections on Legal Education', 22434

Kaim-Caudle, P. R.: Team Care in General Practice, 21528

Kain, J. F.: 'Urban Form, Car Ownership and Public Policy: An Appraisal of "Traffic in Towns"', 17374

Kain, Roger J. P.: Planning and the Environment in the Modern World, 20194; Historical Change in the Physical Environment: A Guide to Sources and Techniques, 20195

Kaiser, Karl: ed. Britain and West Germany: Changing Societies and the Future of Foreign Policy, 14215

Kaldor, Nicholas [Baron]: Essays on Economic Policy, 3516; A Statistical Analysis of Advertising Expenditure and of the Revenue of the Press, 4306, 25071

Kalla-Bishop, Peter Michael: Locomotives at War: Army Railway Reminiscences of the Second World War, 16756

Kallaway, William: London Philharmonic: Music Makers since 1932, 24547

Kallen, Kevin A.: Nationalised Industries, 4962

Kalton, Graham: The Public Schools: A Factual Survey of the Headmasters' Conference Schools in England and Wales, 23019

Kamen, Ruth H.: British and Irish Architectural History: Bibliography and Guide to Sources of Information, 23862

Kamm, Josephine: Rapiers and Battleaxes: The Women's Movement and its Aftermath, 7708; Hope Deferred: Girls' Education in English History, 23089; Indicative Past: A Hundred Years of the Girls' Public Day School Trust, 23091, 23113 Kammerer, Gladys Marie: British and American Child Welfare Services: A Comparative Study in Administration, 8233

Kandel, Isaac Leon: The New Era in Education: A Comparative Study, 22679

Kaniki, M. H. Y.: Tanzania under Colonial Rule, 12843

Kapur, B. K.: ed. Singapore Studies: Critical Surveys of the Humanities and Social Sciences, 12958

Karn, Valerie Ann: Retiring to the Seaside, 8618; 'Property Values amongst Indians and Pakistanis in a Yorkshire Town', 11207; The Ownership and Management of Housing in the New Towns: Report, 18227; The Consumer Experience of Housing: Cross-National Perspectives, 18451; East Kilbride Housing Survey: A Study of Housing in a New Town, 18476, 18716; Race, Class and State Housing: Inequality and the Allocation of Public Housing in Britain, 18706; Aycliffe Housing Survey: A Study of Housing in a New Town, 18715; Crawley Housing Survey, 18717; Stevenage Housing Survey, 18718; Housing Standards and Costs: A Comparison of British Standards and Costs with those in the U.S.A., Canada and Europe, 18546; Priorities for Local Authority Mortgage Lending: A Case Study of Birmingham, 18547

Karnalijnslyper, N.: The Housing Position and Residential Distribution of Ethnic Minorities in Britain: A Bibliography, 18705

Karpeles, Maud: Cecil Sharp: His Life and Work, 24448

Karran, T. J.: The Politics of Local Expenditure, 3259

Kasarda, John D.: Contemporary Urban Ecology, 17841

Kassenbaum, Gene: Women's Prisons: Sex and Social Structure, 10433

Kastell, Jean: Casework in Childcare, 8234

Katanka, Michael: 'The History of British Trade Unions: A Select Bibliography', 6689; 'Strikes': A Documentary History, 6970

Katz, Sanford M.: ed. Family Violence: An International and Interdisciplinary Study, 9954

Katzburg, Nathaniel: From Partition to White Paper: British Policy in Palestine, 1936–1940, 14321

Katznelson, Ira: Black Men and White Cities: Race Politics and Migration in the United States 1900–1930, and Britain 1948–1968, 11037; 'The Policy of Racial Buffering in Nottingham, 1954–1968', 11477

Kauffmann, Morris: The First Century of Plastics: Celluloid and its Sequel, 6224; The History of P.V.C.: The Chemical and Industrial Production of Polyvinylchloride, 6225

Kaufman, Gerald: ed. The Left: A Symposium, 1745

Kavanagh, Dennis: 'Monarchy in Contemporary Political Culture', 450; Thatcherism and British Politics: The End of Consensus?, 1055; ed. The Politics of the Labour Party, 1682; The British General Election of February 1974, 2331; The British General Election of October 1974, 2338; The British General Election of 1979, 2339; The British General Election of 1983, 2343

Kavanagh, Ted: Tommy Handley, 26318

Kavuma, P.: Crisis in Buganda 1953–1955: The Story of the Exile and Return of the Kabaka Mutesa II, 12839

Kawwa, Tasir: 'Three Sociometric Studies of Ethnic Relations in London Schools', 11448

Kay, Billy: Odyssey: Voices from Scotland's Recent Past, 2461

Kay, D. W.: 'Old Age Mental Disorders in Newcastle-upon-Tyne: A Factorial Study of Medical Psychiatric and Social Characteristics', 8624

Kay, Ernest: Pragmatic Premier: An Intimate Portrait of Harold Wilson, 1060; The Wit of Harold Wilson, 1061

Kay, G. B.: ed. The Political Economy of Colonialism in Ghana: A Collection of Documents and Statistics 1900–1960, 12737

Kay, John Alexander: The British Tax System, 4824

Kay, John Anderson: Concentration in Industry: Theory, Measurement and the U.K. Experience, 4993; ed. Mergers and Merger Policy, 5553

Kay, Maurice: Arbitration, 5807

Kay, Ronald: UCCA: its Origins and Development 1950–1985, 23349

Kay, Sheila: 'Recent Developments in Social Work', 8737

Kaye, Barrington Laurence Burnett: Participation in Learning: A Progress Report on Some Experiments in the Training of Teachers, 22731; The Development of the Architectural Profession in Britain: A Sociological Study, 23869

Kaye, David: Old Trolleybuses, 17241; The British Bus Scene in the 1930s, 17266; Old Buses, 17275

Kaye, Elaine: The History of the King's Weigh House, 12053; C. J. Cadoux: Theologian, Scholar and Pacifist, 12062; A History of Queen's College, London, 1848–1972, 23530

Kaye, Harvey J.: The British Marxist Historians, 26732; ed. E. P. Thompson: Critical Debates, 26817

Kazamias, Andreas Michael: Politics, Society and Secondary Education in England, 22794

Keane, J. P.: 'The British Steel Industry and the European Coal and Steel Community', 6587

Keane, Richard: Germany—What Next? An Examination of the German Menace in so far as it Affects Great Britain, 13760

Kearsey, Alexander Horace Cyril: Notes and Comments on the Dardanelles Campaign, 14547; A Study of the Strategy and Tactics of the Mesopotamian Campaign, 1914–1917, 14563; The Battle of Amiens

1918, and Operations 8th Aug.-3rd Sept, 14589

Keating, Michael J.: Labour and the British State, 1686; *ed.* Regional Government in England, 2404; 'The Impact of the Devolution Commitment on the Scottish Body Politic', 2470; 'Administrative Devolution in Practice: The Secretary of State for Scotland and the Scottish Office', 2471; The City—Power and Policy: A Comparative Study of the United States, Britain and France, 3211; The City that Refused to Die: Glasgow: The Politics of Urban Regeneration, 3377, 18138; 'Policy-Making and the Scottish Office: The Designation of Cumbernauld New Town', 18182

Keatley, Patrick: The Politics of Partnership, 12788

Kedourie, Elie: England and the Middle East: The Destruction of the Ottoman Empire, 1914–1921, 13822; In the Anglo-Arab Labyrinth: The McMahon-Husayn Correspondence and its Interpretations, 1914–1939, 14285; 'Sir Herbert Samuel and the Government of Palestine', 14300

Kee, Robert: The Green Flag: A History of Irish Nationalism, 2727; *ed.* The Picture Post Album, 25180

Keeble, Lewis: Principles and Practice of Town and Country Planning, 17772

Keegan, John: The Face of Battle, 14464; Six Armies in Normandy, 14945

Keegan, William: Who Runs the Economy?: Control and Influence in British Economic Policy, 3678; Mrs Thatcher's Economic Experiment, 3691

Keele, E. Teresa: 'Youth and Work: Problems and Perspectives', 8440

Keele, Kenneth David: Anatomies of Pain, 21035; 'James MacKenzie and Pain', 21036; The Evolution of Clinical Methods in Medicine, 21208; A Short History of Medicine, 21200

Keeler, Christine: Scandal!, 9900

Keeler, M. H.: 'Why Students "Turn on": Marijuana and other Drugs in an undergraduate Male Population, 22218

Keeley, Malcolm: Birmingham City Transport: A History of its Buses and Trolleybuses, 17299

Keeley, Raymond: Memoirs of L.M.S. Steam, 16881

Keeling, Bernard Sydney: The Development of the Modern British Steel Industry, 6573

Keeling, Desmond: 'The Development of Central Training in the Civil Service, 1963–1970', 919

Keen, Tom: Gracie Fields, 24477

Keene, David: The Adult Criminal, 10210

Keenleyside, M.: 'Development in Casework Method', 8688

Keep, Ewart: Designing the Stable Door: A Study of how the Youth Training Scheme was Planned, 8547

Keesings Contemporary Archives: 1931+, 269

Keeton, George W.: The United Kingdom: The Development of its Laws and Constitutions: England and Wales, Northern Ireland, the Isle of Man, 2624;

The Football Revolution: A Study of the Changing Pattern of Association Football, 27061

Keilin, David: *ed.* The History of Cell Respiration and Cytochrome, 22322

Keir, David Edwin: The Bowring Story, 16553; The House of Collins: The Story, 24956

Keir, Sir David Lindsay: The Constitutional History of Modern Britain, 576; *ed.* Cases in Constitutional Law, 607

Keith, Arthur: Menders of the Maimed, 20837; 'The Nature of Man's Structural Imperfections', 20969; 'Anthropometry and National Health', 21315

Keith, Sir Arthur Berriedale: The King and the Imperial Crown: the Powers and Duties of His Majesty, 440; The Privileges and Rights of the Crown, 441; The King, the Constitution, the Empire and Foreign Affairs, 1936–1937, 442; The Constitution of England from Queen Victoria to George VI, 568; The Constitution under Strain: Its Working from the Crisis of 1938 down to the Present Time, 573; The British Cabinet System 1830–1938, 715

Keith, Claude Hilton: I Hold My Aim: The Story of how the Royal Air Force was Armed for War, 15831

Keith, James: Fifty Years of Farming, 19591

Keith, K.: 'Finance and Structural Changes in British Industry with Particular Reference to Cotton', 6455

Keith-Lucas, Bryan: A History of Local Government in the Twentieth Century, 3123; English Local Government in the Nineteenth and Twentieth Centuries, 3124; The English Local Government Franchise, 3191; 'The Government of the County in England', 3198

Keith-Shaw, Duncan: Prime Minister Neville Chamberlain, 983

Kelf-Cohen, Reuben: Nationalisation in Britain: The End of a Dogma, 6066; Twenty Years of Nationalisation: The British Experience, 6081; British Nationalisation, 19450–1973, 6085

Kellas, James Grant: Modern Scotland, the Nation since 1870, 315, 2440; 'The Politics of Constitution-Making: the Experience of the United Kingdom', 582; The Scottish Political System, 2441

Kellaway, F. W.: *ed.* Metrication, 4728

Kellaway, William: *ed.* Institute of Historical Research 1957–60, 397; *ed.* Institute of Historical Research 1961–65, 398; *ed.* Institute of Historical Research 1966–70, 399

Keller, Hans: *ed.* Benjamin Britten: A Commentary on his Works, 24307

Kelley, Alice Van Buren: The Novels of Virginia Woolf, 25892

Kelley, Joanna: 'Askham Grange—Open Prison for Women', 10344; When the Gates Shut, 10360

Kelley, Jonathan: The Decline of Class Revisited: Class and Party in England, 1964–1979, 9610

Kelley, Lillian Winifred: Some Sources of English Presbyterian History, 12124

Kelley, Robert: 'Asquith at Paisley: The Content of British Liberalism at the End of its Era', 1815

Kellner, Peter: Callaghan: The Civil Servants: an Inquiry into Britain's Ruling Class, 871; The Road to Number Ten, 982

Kellner, Robert: Family Ill-health: An Investigation in General Practice, 21507

Kelly's Handbook to the Titled, Landed and Official Classes, 38

Kelly, Aidan: The Stock Exchange, 4274; The Story of Wedgwood, 6629

Kelly, Burnham: Design and the Production of Houses, 18654

Kelly, Sir David Victor: The Ruling Few, 13284

Kelly, Denis: *ed.* The Ironside Diaries 1937–1940, 14763

Kelly, Emerson Crosby: Encyclopedia of Medical Sources, 21256

Kelly, Frances: The Housing Crisis Nationwide, 18754

Kelly, Henry: How Stormont Fell, 2835

Kelly, Ian: Hong Kong: A Political-Geographical Analysis, 12980

Kelly, John Barrett: Arabia, the Gulf and the West, 13827

Kelly, John: 'Symposium: British Workplace Industrial Relations 1980–1984', 5856; Steel Strike: A Case Study in Industrial Relations, 6939

Kelly, Michael: 'Sir James Mackenzie and Cellular Pathology', 20970

Kelly, Michael: Advertising and Economic Behaviour, 4307

Kelly, Paul J.: Glasgow Subway 1896–1977, 17022

Kelly, Richard: Daphne du Maurier, 25483

Kelly, Richard N.: Conservative Party Conferences: The Hidden System, 1649

Kelly, Robin Arthur: Inshore Heroes: The Story of H.M. Motor Launches in Two World Wars, 15401

Kelly, Thomas: For Advancement of Learning: University College and the University of Liverpool, 1881–1981, 23515; *ed.* A Select Bibliography of Adult Education in Great Britain, Including Works Published to the End of the Year 1950, 23644; *ed.* A History of Adult Education in Great Britain, 23645; *ed.* Outside the Walls: 60 Years of University Extension at Manchester, 1886–1946, 23646; *ed.* Adult Education in Liverpool: a Narrative of Two Hundred Years, 23647

Kelsall, Helen Martin: Stratification: An Essay on Class and Inequality, 9575; The School Teacher in England and the United States: The Findings of Empirical Research, 9840

Kelsall, Roger Keith: Higher Civil Servants in Britain, from 1870 to the Present Day, 850; Industrial Relations in the Modern State: An Introductory Survey, 5591; Population, 7396; 'Married Women and Employment in England and Wales', 7819; Stratification: An Essay on Class and Inequality, 9575; 'The New Middle Class in the Power Structure of Great Britain', 9721; The School Teacher in England and the United States: The Findings of Empirical Research,

9840; 'Marriage and Family-building Patterns of University Graduates', 9977; Citizens' Guide to the New Town and Country Planning, 20332; Graduates: The Sociology of an Elite, 22574

Keltie, John Scott: 'A Half Century of Geographical Progress', 26647

Kelvin, R. P.: :'Mental Health and Student Wastage', 21814

Kelway, Albert Clifton: The Story of the Catholic Revival, 1833–1933, 11649

Kemeny, Paul James: 'The Affluent Worker Project: Some Criticisms and a Derivative Study', 9681; 'Dualism in Secondary Technical Education', 22519

Kemp, Anthony: The Bitter End, 15074

Kemp, Eric Waldram: Life and Letters of Kenneth Escott Kirk, Bishop of Oxford, 1937–1954, 11748

Kemp, Ian: Tippett, The Composer and his Music, 24368

Kemp, J. C.: The History of the Royal Scots Fusiliers, 1919–1959, 15593

Kemp, Norman: The Devices of War, 15505

Kemp, P.: The Changing Ownership Structure of the Privately Rented Sector: A Case Study of Partick East, 1964–1978, 18475

Kemp, Peter: Muriel Spark, 25815

Kemp, Peter Kemp: Victory at Sea, 1939–1945, 15015; History of the Royal Navy, 15233; ed. The Papers of Admiral Sir John Fisher, 15254; H.M. Destroyers, 15382; The Middlesex Regiment (Duke of Cambridge's Own). 1919–1952, 15698; History of the Royal Norfolk Regiment, Vol.3 1919–1951, 15700; The History of the 4th Battalion, King's Shropshire Light Infantry, 1745–1945, 15719; The Red Dragon: The Story of the Welsh Fusiliers, 1919–1945, 15755; The Bentall Story: Commemorating 150 Years' Service, 1805–1955, 19679

Kemp, Ray: Sizewell B: An Anatomy of the Inquiry, 6673

Kemp, Thomas Charles: The Stratford Festival: A History of the Shakespeare Memorial Theatre, 26160

Kempe, Sir John Arrow: Reminiscences of an old Civil Servant, 1846–1927, 928

Kempner, Thomas: Business and Society: Tradition and Change, 5449

Kempson, E. G. H.: ed. Marlborough College, 1843–1943, 23066

Kemsley, William Frederick Fenn: Consumer's Expenditure Surveys: Reports of Four Enquiries Carried out 1956–1958, 20443

Kendall, Alan: Benjamin Britten, 24308

Kendall, Diana: 'Portrait of a Disappearing English Village', 19154

Kendall, Guy: A Headmaster Reflects, 22756

Kendall, Ian: 'Social Policy and Social Change—Explanations of the Development of Social Policy', 8889

Kendall, K. A.: 'New Dimensions in Casework and Group Work Practice, Implications for Professional Education', 8682

Kendall, M. G.: The Sources and Nature of the Statistics of the U.K, 18621

Kendall, Walter: The Revolutionary Movement in Britain: 1900–1921: The Origins of British Communism, 1914; The History of the Communist Party of Great Britain, 1915

Kendle, John Edward: 'The Round Table Movement and "Home Rule All Round"', 2978; 'Federalism and the Irish Problem 1918', 2979

Kenen, Peter Bain: British Monetary Policy and the Balance of Payments, 1951–1957, 4604

Kenna, Charmian: No Time for Women: Exploring Women's Health in the 1930s and Today, 7838

Kennaway, Richard: New Zealand Foreign Policy 1951–1971, 12671

Kennaway, Susan: The Kennaways, 25611

Kennedy, Aubrey Leo: 'Reorganisation of the Foreign Office', 13342; Britain Faces Germany, 13691; 'Geoffrey Dawson', 25229

Kennedy, Caroline: An Affair of State: The Profumo Case and the Framing of Stephen Ward, 9903

Kennedy, Denis: The Widening Gulf: Northern Attitudes to the Independent Irish State, 1919–1949, 3008

Kennedy, Dennis: Granville Barker and the Dream of Theatre, 25942

Kennedy, [George] Michael [Sinclair]: ed. The Oxford Dictionary of Music, 24281; Britten, 24318; Portrait of Elgar, 24331; The Works of Ralph Vaughan Williams, 24379; Portrait of Walton, 24388; History of the Royal Manchester College of Music, 1893–1972, 24423; Barbirolli, 24428; Adrian Boult, 24434; The Hallé 1858–1983: A History of the Orchestra, 24545

Kennedy, J.: The Place of Women in the Church, 12217

Kennedy, John Fitzgerald: Why England Slept, 13761

Kennedy, John: Tommy Steele, 24528

Kennedy, Joseph: British Civilians and the Japanese War in Malaya and Singapore, 1941–45, 12927

Kennedy, Liam: ed. An Economic History of Ulster, 1820–1940, 2906, 5396

Kennedy, Ludovic: The Trial of Stephen Ward, 9902; Sub-Lieutenant: A Personal Record of the War at Sea, 15314; On my Way to the Club, 24912

Kennedy, Malcolm Duncan: The Estrangement of Great Britain and Japan, 1917–1935, 13591

Kennedy, Michael Paul: Soldier 'I': SAS, 15725

Kennedy, Paul M.: The Rise and Fall of British Naval Mastery, 15241

Kennedy, Thomas C.: The Hound of Conscience: A History of the No-Conscription Fellowship, 1914–1919, 13452; 'Public Opinion and the Conscientious Objector, 1915–1919', 13453

Kennedy, W. P. M.: 'The Regency Acts, 1937–1953', 462

Kennet, H. John: British Railways and Economic Recovery: A Sociological Study of the Transport Problem, 16758

Kennet, K. C.: 'Intelligence, Family Size and Socio-economic Status', 10098

Kennet, Pat: Leyland [Commercial Vehicles], 17472; The Foden Story: From Farm Machinery to Diesel Trucks, 19681

Kennett, David H.: Norfolk Villages, 19140; Norman Hartnell, 24170

Kennett, Stephen: Differential Migration between British Labour Markets: Some Policy Implications, 5095

Kenney, John P.: Manpower Training and Development, 5938

Kenney, M. L.: 'The Role of the House of Commons in British Policy during the 1937–1938 Session', 13681

Kenny, Sir Anthony John Patrick: The Road to Hillsborough: The Shaping of the Anglo-Irish Agreement, 2998; A Path from Rome: An Autobiography, 11974; Wittgenstein, 26885

Kent County Council: Expansion at Ashford: An Appraisal of its Impact on East Kent, 18836

Kent Planning Department: The Channel Tunnel: A Discussion of Terminal Requirements of the British Side and Possible Locations of Terminal Facilities in Kent, 16359

Kent, Janet: The Solomon Islands, 12895

Kent, Jill: Nursery Schools for All, 23142

Kent, John Henry Somerset: 'The Study of Modern Ecclesiastical History since 1930', 11549; The Age of Disunity, 12076; 'The Methodist Union in England, 1932', 12077

Kent, Marian: 'Great Britain and the End of the Ottoman Empire 1900–1923', 13396; Moguls and Mandarisn: Oil, Imperialism and the Middle East in British Foreign Policy, 1900–1940, 14301

Kent, Pendarell: Nursery Schools for All, 23142

Kent, William R. G.: John Burns, Labour's Lost Leader: A Biography, 1120

Kenward, James: Preparatory School, 23003

Kenyon, James: The Fourth Arm, 15098

Kenyon, Joe: Stories from the Dole Queue, 9690

Kenyon, John Philipps: The History Men: The Historical Profession in England since the Renaissance, 26726

Kenyon, Nicholas: Simon Rattle, 24436; The BBC Symphony Orchestra: The First Fifty Years, 1930–1980, 24542

Keogh, Dermot: The Vatican, the Bishops and Irish Politics 1919–1939, 2720; Ireland and Europe, 1919–1948, 2721

Kepars, I.: Australia, 12600

Kerckhoff, Alan C.: 'Patterns of Educational Attainment in Great Britain', 9456

Kerly, Sir Duncan Mackenzie: Kerly's Law of Trade Marks and Trade Names, 4543

Kermode, D. G.: 'The Legislative-Executive Relationship in the Isle of Man', 2620; Devolution at Work: A Case Study of the Isle of Man, 2621; The Changing Pattern of Manx Devolution, 2622

Kernek, Sterling J.: 'The British Government's Reaction to President Wilson's "Peace" Note of December 1916', 13401; 'Distractions of Peace during War: The Lloyd George Government's Reactions to

President Wilson, December 1916–November 1918', 13402

Kerr, Agnes W.: Handicapped Youth: A Report on the Employment Problems of Handicapped Young People in Glasgow, 21915

Kerr, Andrew William: A History of Banking in Scotland, 4403

Kerr, D.: 'The Changing Role of the Backbencher', 694

Kerr, J. Lennox: The RNVR, 15323

Kerr, John Martin Munro: Historical Review of British Obstetrics and Gynaecology, 1800–1950, 21100

Kerr, Madeline: The People of Ship Street, 9336, 18050

Kerr, Malcolm H.: 'Coming to Terms with Nasser: Attempts and Failures', 14377

Kerr, Michael: Virtuoso: The Story of John Ogdon, 24402

Kerr, Philip Henry, Marquess of Lothian: The American Speeches of Lord Lothian, July 1939 to December 1940, 1458

Kerrigan, D. P.: The Town and Country Planning Act, 1954, with a General Introduction and Annotations, 20346

Kerrod, Robin: Spacecraft, 17697

Kersaudy, François: Churchill and de Gaulle, 14230

Kershaw, Andrew Gabriel: The Travel Trade, 26947

Kershaw, John Dunkerley: Handicapped Children, 21785, 21902

Kershaw, Roger: 'Anglo-Malaysian Relations: Old Roles versus New Rules', 12943

Kersley, George Durant: The History of the Royal National Hospital for Rheumatic Diseases, 21420

Keserich, Charles: 'The British Labour Press and Italian Fascism, 1922–1925', 13551, 25113

Kessel, William Ivor Neil: Alcoholism, 22129

Kessler, L.: The Great York Air Raid, 15159

Kessler, Sidney: ed. Conflict at Work: Reshaping Industrial Relations—A Book of Original Essays, 5737

Ketelbey, C. D. M.: Tullis Russell, 6623

Kettenacker, Lothar: ed. The Fascist Challenge and the Policy of Appeasement, 13722; 'Die Diplomatie der Ohnmacht: Die gescheiterte Friedensstrategie in der britischen Regierung vor Ausbruch des zweiten Weltkrieges', 13762; ed. Studien zur Geschichte Englands und der deutsch—britischen Beziehungen, 14212

Kettle, Martin: Uprising! The Police, the People and the Riots in Britain's Cities, 10871

Kettle, Michael: Russia and the Allies, 1917–1920, 13921

Kettle, Peter: Evaluation in the Planning Process, 17955

Kettle, Sir Russell: Deloitte and Co. 1845–1956, 4175

Kevorkian, J.: The Story of Dissection, 21074

Key, Charles E.: The Story of Twentieth-Century Exploration, 27177

Keyes, Sir Roger John Brownlow: The Naval Memoirs of Admiral of the Fleet Sir Roger Keyes: 1) The Narrow Seas to the Dardanelles, 1910–1915. 2) Scapa Flow to the Dover Straits, 1916–1918, 14548; The Fight for Gallipoli, 14549; Amphibious Warfare and Combined Operations, 15476;

Keyes, Thomas E.: Classics of Cardiology: A Collection of Classic Works on the Heart and Circulation, 22338

Keynes, Sir Geoffrey Langdon: The Letters of Rupert Brooke, 25419; A Bibliography of Rupert Brooke, 25420; A Bibliography of Siegfried Sassoon, 25792

Keynes, John Maynard [Baron]: Essays in Biography, 328; 'A Reply to Sir William Beveridge', 9040

Keynes, W. Milo: ed. Essays on John Maynard Keynes, 3756, 26599

Keys, Thomas Edward: The History of Surgical Anaesthesia, 21031; Foundations of Anesthesiology, 21039

Khalilzadeh-Shirazi, J.: 'Market Structure and Price-cost Margins in United Kingdom Manufacturing Industries', 4942

Khan, Verity Saifullah: Bilingualism and Linguistic Minorities in Britain: Developments, Perspectives, 23814

Khong, Kim Hoong: Merdeka! British Rule and the Struggle for Independence in Malaya 1945–1957, 12913

Kibblewhite, Liz: Aberdeen in the General Strike, 6926

Kidd, Harry: The Trouble at L. S. E. 1966–1967, 23528

Kidd, Howard C.: A New Era for British Railways, 16745

Kidd, Susan: New Towns in the United Kingdom, 19003

Kidday, Mike: Britain's Northern Gateway (Manchester International Airport), 17694

Kidner, Roger Wakely: The Waterloo-Southampton Line, 16979; A Short History of Mechanical Traction and Travel, 17088

Kidson, Mary C.: Men in Middle Life, 8553

Kiernan, Reginald Hugh: The First War in the Air, 15802

Kiernan, Victor Gordon: The Lords of Human Kind: European Attitudes towards the Outside World in the Imperial Age, 11165; European Empires from Conquest to Collapse, 1815–1960, 12480; 'Labour and Imperialism', 12572

Kieser, Rolf: Englands Appeasementpolitik und der Aufstieg des Dritten Reichs im Spiegel der britischen Presse 1933–1939: ein Beitrag zur Vorgeschichte des zweiten Weltkrieges, 25118

Kiev, Ari: 'Beliefs and Delusions of West Indian Immigrants to London', 11254

Kieve, Jeffrey Lawrence: The Electric Telegraph: A Social and Economic History, 6394; Urban Land Economics, 20290

Kiffer, Mary E.: Current Biography: Cumulated Index 1940–1985, 44

Kightly, Charles: Country Voices: Life and Lore in Farm and Village, 19093

Kilby, Clyde S.: ed. Brothers and Friends: The Diaries of Major Warren Hamilton Lewis, 25664

Kilby, John: Bygone Birstall: A Century of Change, 19181

Killearn: The Killearn Diaries, 1934–1946, 13285

Killen, John: A History of Marine Aviation, 1911–1968, 14985

Killick, A. J.: Trade Union Officers: A Study of Full-time Officers, Branch Secretaries and Shop Stewards in British Trade-unions, 6716

Killingray, David: Africa and the Second World War, 12699; Khaki and Blue: The Military Police in British Colonial Africa, 12706

Killip, Christopher: The Isle of Man: A Book about the Manx, 2618

Kilmister, C. W.: Russell, 26877

Kilmuir, David Maxwell-Fyfe [Earl]: Political Adventure: The Memoirs of the Earl of Kilmuir, 1252

Kilroy, B.: 'Housing: The Rehabilitation v. Redevelopment Cost See-Saw: The Effect of High Land Prices', 18729

Kilroy-Silk, Robert: Hard Labour: The Political Diary of Robert Kilroy-Silk, 1440; 'The Problem of Industrial Relations', 5725

Kimball, Warren F.: 'Beggar My Neighbour: America and the British Interim Finance Crisis, 1940–1941', 3718, 14050; 'Naked versus Right: Roosevelt, Churchill and Eastern Europe from Tolstoy to Yalta—and a Little Beyond', 13963; ed. Churchill and Roosevelt: The Complete Correspondence, 14039; The Most Unsordid Act: Lend-Lease, 1939–1941, 14049; 'The Temptation of British Opulence, 1937–1942', 14051

Kimber, Richard H.: 'Parliamentary Questions and the Allocation of Departmental Responsibilities', 647; 'The Role of All-Party Committees in the House of Commons', 660; Political Parties in Modern Britain: An Organisational and Functional Guide, 1586; ed. Pressure Groups in Britain: A Reader, 2073; ed. Campaigning for the Environment, 19963, 20246; 'The Origins of the Water Act of 1973', 20101; 'The Growth of the Environment as a Political Issue in Britain', 20248

Kimble, David: A Political History of Ghana: The Rise of Gold Coast Nationalism, 1850–1928, 12748

Kimble, P.: Newspaper Reading: The Third Year of the War, 25068

Kimche, David and Kimche, Jon: The Secret Roads: The 'Illegal' Migration of a People 1938–1948, 14337; Both Sides of the Hill: Britain and the Palestine War, 14351

Kimmins, Charles William: The Child in the Changing Home, 8235; ed. Mental and Physical Welfare of the Child, 8236; The Child's Attitude to Life: A Study of Children's Stories, 8237; Children's Dreams, 8238; Children's Dreams: An Unexplored Land, 8239; The Triumph of the Dalton Plan, 8240

Kimmins, Mrs Charles William: 'Orthopedic Hospital Schools', 8241

Kincaid, James Collins: Poverty and Equality in Britain: A Study of Social Security and Taxation, 4081

Kindleberger, Charles Poor: Economic Growth in France and Britain, 1851–1950, 3429; Manias, Panics and Crashes: A

History of Financial Crises, 4263; Financial Crises: Theory, History and Policy, 4264; 'Foreign Trade and Growth: Lessons from British Experiences since 1913', 4779

King Edward's, Birmingham: King Edward's School, Birmingham, 1552–1952, 23063

King George VI: King George VI to His Peoples, 1936–1951: Selected Broadcasts and Speeches, 503

King, A. D.: ed. Buildings and Society: Essays on the Social Development of the Built Environment, 18762

King, Alexander: 'Higher Education, Professional Manpower and the State', 23395

King, Alexander Hyatt: Some British Collectors of Music, c.1600–1960, 24446

King, Alison: Golden Wings: The Story of some of the Women Ferry Pilots of the Air Transport Auxiliary, 14999

King, Anthony: Britain Says Yes, 2390; The British General Election of 1964, 2319; The British General Election of 1966, 2325

King, Arthur: The House of Warne: One Hundred Years of Publishing, 24996

King, Cecil Harmsworth: The Future of the Press, 25057; Strictly Personal: Some Memories, 25087; With Malice toward None: A War Diary, 25088; Without Fear or Favour, 25089; The Cecil King Diary, 1965–1970, 25090; The Cecil King Diary, 1970–1974, 25091

King, Chrystal: Volunteers in Hospitals—A Guide for Organisers, 21496

King, David Neden: Rates or Prices?: A Study of the Economics of Local Government and its Replacement by the Market, 4878; An Introduction to National Income Accounting, 4899; Financial and Economic Aspects of Regionalism and Separatism, 5086; Training within the Organization: A Study of Company Policy and Procedures for the Systematic Training of Operators and Supervisors, 5959

King, E. J.: 'Urbanization and Education in Britain', 17793

King, E. M. C.: 'The Organisation of Voluntary Service in a Psychiatric Hospital', 22421

King, Edmund James: Education and Social Change, 22806

King, Evelyn Mansfield: Closest Correspondence: The Inside Story of an M.P., 1441; Printer to the House: The Story of Hansard, 25034

King, Francis: E. M. Forster, 25523; Christopher Isherwood, 25596

King, Gillian: Imperial Outpost—Aden: Its Place in British Strategic Policy, 13870

King, Henry Charles: The Background of Astronomy, 26382; Exploration of the Universe: The Story of Astronomy, 26410; The History of the Telescope, 26414; 'The Planetarium', 26451

King, Horace Frederick: Armament of British Aircraft, 1909–1939, 14642; The First 50 Years of Powered Flight, 17508; comp. From Kitty Hawk to Concorde: Jane's 100 Significant Aircraft, 17509; Aeromarine Engines: The Beginnings of Marine Aircraft, Winged Hulls, Air Cushion and Air Lubricated Craft, Planning Boats and Hydrofoils, 17711

King, J. S.: Sixty Years of Bradford Trolley Buses, 17244

King, James Clifford: The Orange and the Green, 2730

King, Joan Faye Sendall: New Thinking for Changing Needs, 8811; The Growth of Crime: The International Experience, 10131; ed. The Probation and After-care Service 1970, 10471

King, John: Golden Gatwick: Fifty Years of Aviation, 17676

King, John: Relative Income Shares, 3855; Inflation, 4018

King, John Charles: ed. Evangelicals Today: 13 Stock-Taking Essays, 11658

King, Kimball: Twenty Modern British Playwrights: A Bibliography 1956 to 1976, 25933

King, Lester S.: The Growth of Medical Thought, 21205; ed. A History of Medicine: Selected Readings, 21206; ed. Mainstreams of Medicine: Essays on the Social and Intellectual Context of Medical Practice, 21207

King, Mervyn A.: The British Tax System, 4824

King, Michael: Bail or Custody, 10321

King, P. S. D.: Lead in Water: A Review of Environmental Factors Affecting the Use of Lead in Building, 20172

King, R.: 'Italian Migration to Great Britain', 11387

King, Roger: ed. The British Right: Conservative and Right-wing Politics in Britain, 1621, 2056; Respectable Rebels: Middle Class Campaigns in Britain in the 1970s, 2077, 9730

King, Ronald: The Quest for Paradise: A History of the World's Gardens, 19874; Royal Kew, 19890; Values and Involvement in a Grammar School, 22988

King, Roy David: Patterns of Residential Care: Sociological Studies in Institutions for Handicapped Children, 2842, 21911; The Future of the Prison System, 10406; Albany: Birth of a Prison—End of an Era, 10407; A Taste of Prison: Custodial Conditions for Trial and Remand Prisoners, 10408; 'Industrial Relations in the Prison Service', 10455; 'The Prison System: Prospects for Change', 10456

King, Rupert Wearing: The English Sixth Form College: An Educational Concept, 23245

King, Sally: The Pocket Guide to Advertising, 4334

King, Suzanne: The Youth Training Scheme: The First Three Years, 8548

King, W. T. C.: 'The Bank of England', 4485

King-Hall, Magdalen: The Story of the Nursery, 8243

King-Hall, Stephen: History of the War, 14453

Kinghan, Mike: Squatters in London, 18379

Kinghan, Nancy: United We Stood: The Official History of the Ulster Women's Unionist Council, 1911–1974, 2954

Kingsford, P. W.: Builders and Building Workers, 6177

Kingsford, Reginald John Lethbridge: The Publishers Association 1896–1946, 24930

Kingston-McCloughry, E. J.: Winged Warfare: Air Problems of Peace and War, 15988

Kinnear, Michael: The Fall of Lloyd George: The Political Crisis of 1922, 1018; The British Voter: An Atlas and Survey Since 1885, 2218

Kinross, John: Fifty Years in the City: Financing Small Business, 4476

Kinsey, Bill H.: Creating Rural Employment, 19081

Kinsey, Gordon: Martlesham Heath: The Story of the Royal Air Force Station 1917–1973, 15935

Kinsey, Richard: Losing the Fight against Crime, 10277; Police Powers and Politics, 10721

Kinvig, Robert Henry: The Isle of Man: A Social, Cultural and Political History, 2616

Kipling, Rudyard: ed. The Irish Guards in the Great War, 15558

Kirby, Andrew: Education, Health and Housing: An Empirical Investigation of Resource Accessibility, 8959; The Inner Cities: Causes and Effects, 17909

Kirby, C. H.: Housing Finance in Great Britain, 18541

Kirby, C.: Water in Britain, 20100

Kirby, D. A.: Slum Housing and Residential Renewal: The Case in Urban Britain, 18408

Kirby, David: 'International Socialism and the Question of Peace: The Stockholm Conference of 1917', 13374

Kirby, J.: Poverty and Public Health, 22052

Kirby, John Lavan: A Guide to Historical Periodicals in the English Language, 163

Kirby, Maurice W.: 'The Politics of State Coercion in Inter-War Britain: The Mines Department of the Board of Trade, 1920–1942', 837; The Decline of British Economic Power since 1870, 3512; Men of Business and Politics: The Rise and Fall of the Quaker Pease Dynasty of North-East England 1700–1943, 5501; The British Coalmining Industry, 1870–1946, 6245; 'The Control of Competition in the British Coal-mining Industry in the Thirties', 6272; 'Entrepreneurial Efficiency in the British Coal Industry between the Wars: A Comment', 6273; 'Government Intervention in Industrial Organisation: Coal Mining in the Nineteen Thirties', 6274

Kirby, Stanley Woodburn: The War against Japan, 15059

Kirk, C. W. G. T.: 'New Towns in Great Britain', 18238

Kirk, Gordon: Teacher Education and Professional Development, 9851

Kirk, John Henry: The Development of Agriculture in Germany and the United Kingdom, 2: U.K. Agricultural Policy 1870–1970, 19414; 'The Output of British Agriculture during the War', 19460

Kirk, John M.: Studies in Linguistic Geography: The Dialects of English in Britain and Ireland, 23794

Kirk-Greene, Anthony H. M.: 'The Progress of Pro-consuls: Advancement and

Migration among the Colonial Governors of British African Territories, 1900–1965', 12513; 'The Governors-General of Canada 1867–1952: A Collective Profile', 12645; 'Taking Canada into Partnership in the "White Man's Burden": The British Colonial Service and the Dominions Selection Scheme of 1923', 12650; A Biographical Dictionary of the British Colonial Governor Vol.1: Africa, 12703; ed. Africa in the Colonial Period III: The Transfer of Power: The Colonial Administrator in the Age of Decolonisation, 12704; ed. The Principles of Native Administration in Nigeria: Select Documents 1900– 1947, 12756

Kirkaldy, Adam Willis: ed. British Finance During and After the War, 1914–1921, 4546; British Shipping: Its History, Organisation and Importance, 16456

Kirkbride, Sir Alec Seath: A Crackle of Thorns: Experiences in the Middle East, 13286

Kirkham, Michael: The Poetry of Robert Graves, 25552

Kirkham, Pat: Furnishing the World: The East London Furniture Trade, 1830–1980, 6480

Kirkman, Patrick: Electronic Funds Transfer Systems: The Revolution in Cashless Banking and Payment Methods, 4534

Kirkman, William Patrick: Unscrambling an Empire: A Critique of British Colonial Policy, 1956–1966, 12585

Kirkness, Anne: Exeter—University and City: A Study of the Economic and Social Interactions Caused by University Growth, 18106

Kirkpatrick, Brownlee Jean: A Bibliography of Edmund Blunden with a Personal Introduction by Rupert Hart-Davis, 25398; A Bibliography of E. M. Forster, 25518; A Bibliography of Virginia Woolf, 25887

Kirkpatrick, D. G.: 'How Close is American to British Community Development?: Some Impressions', 9405

Kirkpatrick, D. L.: ed. Contemporary Dramatists, 25932

Kirkpatrick, Diane: Eduardo Paolozzi, 24203

Kirkpatrick, Sir Ivone: The Inner Circle, 13287

Kirkup, James: I of all People: An Autobiography of Youth, 25613

Kirkwood, David, Baron: My Life of Revolt, 1445

Kirkwood, Kenneth: Britain and Africa, 12674

Kirman, Brian Herbert: Mental Handicap: A Brief Guide, 21868

Kirschenbaum, A.: 'Spatial Clustering, Segregation and Urban Planning: A Methodological Approach', 18730

Kirton, John J.: Canada as a Principal Power: A Study in Foreign Policy and International Relations, 12643

Kirwan, Sir Archibald Laurence Patrick: A History of Polar Exploration, 27221

Kirwan, Daniel Joseph: Palace and Hovel or, Phases of London Life: Being Personal Observations of an American in London by Day and Night, 18314

Kirwan, Richard Martin: The Economics of Urban Residential Renewal and Improvement, 5410, 20406; The Economics of an Urban Housing Market: Bristol Area Study, 18542

Kirwin, F. X.: 'Migrant Employment and the Recession—The Case of the Irish in Britain', 11369

Kissack, Reginald: Church or No Church? A Study of the Development of the Concept of Church in British Methodism, 12074

Kitchen, Jack: Accounting Thought and Education: Six English Pioneers, 4180; Accounting: A Century of Development, 4183

Kitchen, Martin: British Policy towards the Soviet Union during the Second World War, 13954; 'Winston Churchill and the Soviet Union during the Second World War', 13955; The Origins of the Cold War: A Comparative Perspective: American, British and Canadian Relations with the Soviet Union 1941–1948, 14103

Kitchen, Paddy: A Most Unsettling Person: An Introduction to the Ideas and Life of Patrick Geddes, 8074

Kitchin, Arthur Henderson: The Scotsman's Food, 20591

Kitchin, Laurence Tyson: 'Backwards and Forwards', 23747; 'Realism in the English Mid-Century Drama', 26208; Mid-Century Drama, 26209; Drama in the Sixties: Form and Interpretation, 26210

Kitching, Christopher J.: The Central Records of the Church of England: A Report and Survey, 11552

Kitromilides, Pashalis: Cyprus, 12861

Kitson, Frank: Low Intensity Operations: Subversion, Insurgency, Peace-keeping, 2900, 16172; Gangs and Counter-Gangs, 16170; Bunch of Five, 16171

Kittridge, Alan: Passenger Ships of the River Dart and Kingsbridge Estuary, 16594; Passenger Steamers of the River Tamar, 16595

Kitts, Albert: Steel: The Commanding Height of the Economy, 6574

Kitzinger, Uwe Webster: The 1975 Referendum, 2389; 'Britain and the Common Market: The State of the Debate', 14158; Diplomacy and Persuasion: How Britain joined the Common Market, 14180

Klaasen, Leo Hendrik: Migration Policy in Europe: A Comparative Study, 11423

Klapper, Charles Frederick: Sir Herbert Walker's Southern Railway, 16914; Roads and Rails of London 1900–1933, 16961, 17154; The Golden Age of Tramways, 17201; Buses and Trams, 17263; The Golden Age of Buses, 17264; British Lorries 1900–1945, 17463

Klare, Hugh John: ed. Changing Concepts of Crime and its Treatment, 10249; Delinquency, Social Support and Control Systems, 10250; Anatomy of Prison, 10251; People in Prison, 10252; ed. Frontiers of Criminology: Summary of the Proceedings, 10253; 'Prison Reform—Retrospect and Prospect', 10343

Klein, Daryl: Coal Cavalcade, 6287

Klein, Ira D.: 'British Imperialism in Decline: Tibet 1914–1921', 13143; 'Whitehall, Washington and the Anglo-Japanese Alliance, 1919–1921', 13588, 14013

Klein, Josephine: Samples from English Cultures, 7588

Klein, L. R.: 'Savings and Finances of the Upper Income Classes', 3766

Klein, Rudolf E.: Social Policy and Public Expenditure: An Interpretative Essay, 8944; Constraints and Choices, A Commentary on the Public Expenditure White Paper, 8945; Caring for Quality in the Caring Services, 8946; Complaints against Doctors: A Study of Professional Accountablity, 20836; 'Profession of Medicine', 21342; 'Policy Making in the National Health Service', 21343; 'National Health Service after Reorganization', 21344; 'Toothless Watchdogs or N.H.S. Scourge?', 21345; Allocating Health Resources: A Commentary on the Report of the Working Party on Resource Allocation, 21671; The Politics of the National Health Service, 21672; The Politics of Consumer Representation: A Study of Community Health Councils, 22112

Klein, Sydney: Murder, 1957 to 1968: A Home Office Statistical Division Report on Murder in England and Wales (with an annex by the Scottish Home and Health Department on Murder in Scotland), 10796

Klein, Thomas M.: 'The United Kingdom Balance of Payments Accounts', 4925

Klein, Viola: Britain's Married Women Workers, 7697; Women Workers: Working Hours and Services, 7698; Employing Married Women, 7699; The Feminine Character: History of an Ideology, 7700; Working Wives: A Survey of Facts and Opinions concerning the Gainful Employment of Married Women in Britain, 7701; 'Der Gegenwärtige Situation der Soziologie in Gross Britannien', 7983

Kleine-Ahlbrandt, William Laird: The Policy of Simmering: A Study of British Policy during the Spanish Civil War, 1936–1939, 13980

Kleinman, Philip: The Saatchi and Saatchi Story, 4332

Klieman, Aaron S.: Foundations of British Policy in the Arab World: The Cairo Conference of 1921, 13829; 'The Divisiveness of Palestine: Foreign Office versus Colonial Office on the Issue of Partition, 1937', 14314

Klingender, Francis Donald: The Condition of Clerical Labour in Britain, 9778; 'Changing Patterns of University Recruitment in England', 9856; Russia—Britain's Ally, 1812–1942, 13910; 'Changing Patterns of Student Recruitment in England', 22553

Klitz, J. Kenneth: North Sea Oil: Resource Requirements for Development of the U.K. Sector, 7174

Klug, Francesca: Racism and Discrimination in Britain: A Select Bibliography 1970–1983, 11523

Klugmann, James: History of the Communist Party of Great Britain, 1917

Kluke, Paul: 'Winston Churchill und die allierte Intervention im revolutionären Russland', 13920

Knaplund, Paul: The British Empire 1815–1939, 12557

Knapp, John: 'Britain's Growth Performance: The Enigma of the 1950's', 3633

Knappen, M. M.: 'Review Article: The Abdication of Edward VIII', 501

Knatchbull-Hugessen, Sir Hugh Montgomery: Diplomat in Peace and War, 13288

Kneebone, Richard Melvin Taylor: I Work in a Secondary Modern School, 22932

Kneen, J. J.: The Place-Names of the Isle of Man, with their Origin and History, 2617

Kneese, Allen Victor: Economics and the Environment, 19946; ed. The Economics of Environment: Papers from Four Nations, 19947; The Economics of Environment Policy, 19948

Knell, Kenneth Alfred: Bring Back the Airship?: A Question Together with an Historical Appraisal of the Giant Rigid Dirigible 1900–1937, 17540

Kneller, George Frederick: Higher Learning in Britain, 23378

Knickerbocker, Frances Wentworth: Free Minds: John Morley and his Friends, 1280

Knight, Arthur: Private Enterprise and Public Intervention: The Courtaulds Experience, 6420

Knight, B.: 'Town and Country Planning. A Quinquennial Review', 17799

Knight, Brian: ed. Pollution and the Use of Chemicals in Agriculture, 20112

Knight, D.: Beyond the Pale: The Christian Political Fringe, 2058

Knight, Elizabeth Mary: Migrants of North-East England 1951–1961: Character, Age and Sex, 5198

Knight, Geoffrey Egerton: Concorde, the Inside Story, 17572

Knight, George Wilson: The Golden Labyrinth: A Study of British Drama, 26215

Knight, James: Northern Ireland: The Elections of the Twenties, 2796

Knight, K. G.: 'Strikes and Wage Inflation in British Manufacturing Industry 1950–1968', 3994, 6934

Knight, Laura: Painting an Adventure, 24031

Knight, R.: 'Unionism among Retail Clerks in Post-war Britain', 6771

Knight, Robert: 'Harold Macmillan and the Cossacks: Was there a Klagenfurt Conspiracy?', 13969

Knight, Roger: Edwin Muir: An Introduction to his Work, 25724

Knight, Rose: Wages and Salaries in the United Kingdom, 1920–1938, 3887

Knightley, Phillip: An Affair of State: The Profumo Case and the Framing of Stephen Ward, 9903, 9905; The Secret Lives of Lawrence of Arabia, 13819; Lawrence of Arabia, 14516; The Spy who betrayed a Generation, 16053; Philby: The Life and Views of the KGB Masterspy, 16054; The Vestey Affair, 20682; The Pearl of Days: An Intimate Memoir of the Sunday Times 1822–1972, 25155; The First Casualty, 25322

Knobel, Lance: The Faber Guide to Twentieth-Century Architecture: Britain and Northern Europe, 23880

Knoop, Douglas: The Genesis of Freemasonry, 12394

Knott, George H.: Trial of Sir Roger Casement, 3023

Knowles, C. C.: A History of Building Regulation in London, 1189–1972, With an Account of the District Surveyors' Association, 6197

Knowles, Dick: 'Social Contacts on the Hyde Park Estate, Sheffield', 9417

Knowles, Dorothy: The Censor, the Drama and the Film, 1900–1934, 26899

Knowles, John Hilton: ed. The Teaching Hospital: Evolution and Contemporary Issues, 21402; ed. Hospitals, Doctors and the Public Interest, 21403; The Teaching Hospital: Evolution and Contemporary Issues, 22426

Knowles, Kenneth Guy Jack Charles: 'Earnings and Engineering, 1926–1948', 3930; 'Some Notes on Engineering Earnings', 3931; 'Differences between the Wages of Skilled and Unskilled Workers, 1880–1950', 3932; Strikes: A Study in Industrial Conflict, 6928

Knox, David: 'Britain's Black Powerhouse: Michael X', 10956

Knox, Edmund Arbuthnott: Reminiscences of an Octogenarian, 1847–1934, 11749

Knox, Francis: The Growth of Central Government Manpower, 776

Knox, George: Oxford Textbook of Public Health, 21004, 22091

Knox, Henry MacDonald: Two Hundred and Fifty Years of Scottish Education 1696–1946, 23599

Knox, James: The Triumph of Thrift: The Story of the Savings Bank of Airdrie, 4345

Knox, Paul Leslie: 'Social Indicators and the Concept of Level of Living', 3840; Geography and Inequality, 5081

Knox, Wilfred Lawrence: The Catholic Movement in the Church of England, 11647

Knox, William James: Decades of the Ulster Bank, 1836–1964, 4526

Knox, William: James Maxton, 1472, 2535

Knox-Johnston, Robin: A World of my own, 27167

Knox-Shaw, H.: 'The Radcliffe Observatory', 26450

Knox: The Knox Brothers: Edmund ('Evoe') 1881–1971, Dillwyn (1883–1943), Wilfred (1886–1950), Ronald (1888–1957), 11798

Kobler, Arthur L.: The End of Hope: A Sociological-Clinical Study of Suicide, 10811

Koch, Hans-Joachim Werner: 'Das Britische Russlandbild im Spiegel der Britischen Propaganda 1914–1918', 13411

Kochan, Miriam: Prisoners of England, 15054

Kocher, Paul Harold: Master of Middle Earth: The Achievement of J. R. R. Tolkien, 25843

Koenigsberger, H. G. ed.: The Diversity of History: Essays in Honour of Sir Herbert Butterfield, 26779

Koestler, Arthur: ed. Suicide of a Nation? An Inquiry into the State of Britain Today, 381;

Promise and Fulfilment: Palestine, 1917–1949, 14282; ed. The Alpbach Symposium, 1968: Beyond Reductionism: New Perspectives in the Life Sciences, 26508

Kogan, David: The Battle for the Labour Party, 1766

Kogan, Maurice: The Battle for the Labour Party, 1766; Educational Policy-making: A Study of Interest Groups and Parliament, 22797; The Politics of Educational Change, 22922; The Attack on Higher Education, 23443

Kohan, Charles Mendel: Works and Buildings, 5048

Kohler, David F.: Ethnic Minorities in Britain: Statistical Data, 11054; Immigration and Race Relations, 11430

Kohler, K. H.: 'Parental Deprivation, Family Background and Female Delinquency', 10163

Kohler, Robert E.: From Medical Chemistry to Biochemistry: The Making of a Biomedical Discipline, 26482; 'Walter Fletcher, F. G. Hopkins and the Dunn Institute of Biochemistry: A Case Study in the Patronage of Science', 26483; 'The Enzyme Theory and the Origin of Biochemistry', 26484

Kohn, Leo: The Constitution of the Irish Free State, 2685

Kojecky, Roger: T. S. Eliot's Social Criticism, 25503

Kolb, William L.: ed. Dictionary of the Social Sciences, 7935

Kolinsky, Martin: ed. Divided Loyalties: British Regional Assertion and European Integration, 2398

Kollerston, Nick: Lead on the Brain: A Plain Guide to Britain's Number One Pollutant, 20167

Kolling, Mirjam: Führungsmacht in Westeuropa? Grossbritanniens Anspruch und Scheitern, 1944–1950, 14135; 'Grossbritanniens Westeuropapolitik 1944–1947 und die Stabilisierung der bürgerlichen Herrschaft in Frankreich', 14136

Kolz, Arno W. F.: 'British Economic Interests in Siberia during the Russian Civil War, 1918–1920', 4776

Kon, Andrea: This is my Song: Biography of Petula Clark, 24474

Koot, Gerald M.: English Historical Economy, 1870–1926: The Rise of Economic History, 3542

Kops, Bernard: The World is a Wedding, 25619

Korah, Valentine: 'Counter-Inflation Legislation: Whither Parliamentary Sovereignty?', 666

Kornberg, Allan: 'Constituency Agents and British Politics', 1609

Kornberg, Sir Hans Leo: The Unity of Life, 26509

Kornitzer, Margaret: Adoption and Family Life, 8244

Kornwolf, James David: M.H. Baillie Scott and the Arts and Crafts Movement: Pioneers of Modern Design, 24142

Kosack, Godula: Immigrant Workers and Class Structure in Western Europe, 11422

Kosmin, Barry A.: Steel City Jews: A Study of Ethnicity and Social Mobility in the Jewish Population of the City of Sheffield, South Yorkshire, 11318; 'Exclusion and Opportunity: Traditions of Work amongst British Jews', 11319; Jews in an Inner London Borough: A Study of the Jewish Population of Hackney Based on the 1971 Census, 11320; British Jewry in the Eighties: A Statistical and Geographical Study, 12419

Kosminsky, Peter: Speaking Out: Untold Stories from the Falklands War, 16119

Koss, Stephen Edward: Asquith, 971; 'Lloyd George and Nonconformity: The Last Rally', 1029; 'The Destruction of Britain's Last Liberal Government', 1811; Fleet Street Radical: Lord Haldane: A Scapegoat for Liberalism, 1215; Nonconformity in Modern British Politics, 12014; The Rise and Fall of the Political Press in Britain, 25038; A. G. Gardiner and the Daily News, 25238

Koster, C. J.: ed. New Periodical Titles, 1960–1968, 155

Kotelawala, Sir John: An Asian Prime Minister's Story, 12988

Kozlov, V. I.: 'Etnorasovye izmeneniya v sostave naseleniya Velikobritanii'. ('Ethnic and Racial Changes in the Population of Great Britain'), 7437

Krabbe, Henning: ed. Voices from Britain: Broadcast History, 1939–1945, 24748

Krall, Stanley: 'Poisons in the Rubber Industry, 21274

Kramer, John: Strategy and Conflict in Metropolitan Housing: Suburbia versus the Greater London Council 1965–1975, 18663

Krausse, Gerald H. and Krausse, Sylvia C. E.: Brunei, 12948

Krausz, A.: Sheffield Jewry: Commentary on a Community, 12440

Krausz, Ernest: Sociology in Britain: A Survey of Research, 7997; 'Factors of Social Mobility in a British Minority Group', 9601; Ethnic Minorities in Britain, 11001; 'An Anglo-Jewish Community: Leeds', 11314; Leeds Jewry: Its History and Social Structure . . . With an Introduction by Julius Gould, 11315, 12438; A Sociological Field Study of Jewish Suburban Life in Edgware 1962–63: With Special Reference to Minority Identification, 11316; 'Occupation and Social Advancement in Anglo-Jewry', 12442

Krausz, Michael: ed. Critical Essays on the Philosophy of R. G. Collingwood, 26850

Krebs, Sir Hans: Reminiscences and Reflections, 26462; 'Some Facts of Life: Biology and Politics', 26463

Kreider, Carl Jonas: The Anglo-American Trade Agreement: A Study of British and American Commercial Policies, 1934–1939, 3712

Kreig, Margaret B.: Green Medicine: The Search for Plants that Heal, 22297

Kremers, Edward: Kremers and Urdang's History of Pharmacy, 22252

Krieger, Joel: Undermining Capitalism: State Ownership and the Dialectic of Control in the British Coal Industry, 6263

Krieger, Leonard: 'The Idea of the Welfare State in Britain and the United States', 8983

Krieger, Wolfgang: Labour Party und Weimarer Republik, Ein Beitrag zur Aussenpolitik der britischen Arbeiterbewegung zwischen Programmatik und Parteitaktik (1918–1924), 13559

Krishan, Y.: 'Mountbatten and the Partition of India', 13178

Krogman, Wilton Marion: 'Fifty Years of Physical Anthropology: The Men, the Material, the Concepts, the Methods', 10122

Krug, Mark M.: Aneurin Bevan: A Cautious Rebel, 1097

Krumbhaar, Edward Bell: Pathology, 21111

Kudlieka, Robert: Bridget Riley, 24059

Kuehl, Warren F.: Dissertations in History 1970—June 1980: An Index to Dissertations Completed in History Departments of United States and Canadian Universities, 92

Kuehn, Douglas: Takeovers and the Theory of the Firm: An Empirical Analysis of the United Kingdom, 1957–1967, 4984; Gangs, Groups and Clubs Voluntary Youth Leaders, 8520; ed. Social Group Work in Great Britain, 8659; ed. Spontaneous Youth Groups, 8660; ed. Community Organisation in Great Britain, 8661, 9341

Kuhn, Annette: 'An Analysis of Graduate Job Mobility', 5901

Kuhn, Raymond: The Politics of Broadcasting, 24884

Kulik, Karol: Alexander Korda: The Man who Could Work Miracles, 24676

Kulkarni, H. B.: Stephen Spender: Works and Criticism: An Annotated Bibliography, 25818

Kumar, D.: ed. The Cambridge Economic History of India, 13112

Kumar, Krishan: 'Holding the Middle Ground: The BBC, the Public and the Professional Broadcaster', 24918

Kunz, Philip R.: 'Immigrants and Socialization: A New Look', 10969

Kuper, Adam: Anthropology and Anthropologists: The Modern British School, 26352

Kuper, Leo: ed. Living in Towns: Selected Research Papers in Urban Sociology of the Faculty of Commerce and Social Science, University of Birmingham, 18276

Kurtz, Harold: 'The Lansdowne Letter', 13384

Kushner, Tony: Traditions of Intolerance: Historical Perspectives on Fascism and Race Discourse in Britain, 11205

Kuzminov, I.: 'The Unemployment Problem in Great Britain', 7024

Kyba, P.: Covenants without the Sword: Public Opinion and British Defence Policy, 1931–1935, 13507

Kyle, J.: Perspectives on British Sign Language and Deafness, 21933

Kynaston, David: The Chancellor of the Exchequer, 803; The Financial Times: A Centenary History, 25139

La Feber, W.: 'Roosevelt, Churchill and Indo-China: 1942–1945', 14057

La Fourcade, Bernard: A Bibliography of the Writings of Wyndham Lewis, 25669

La Preslé, A. De: 'Racisme et Libertés Publiques en Angleterre', 10983

Laborde, Edward Dalrymple: Harrow School: Yesterday and Today, 23062

Labour Party: Labour Party Bibliography, 1656; Report of the Annual conference, 1657; A Pictorial History of the Labour Party, 1900–1975 to celebrate the Seventy-Fifth Anniversary of its Birth, 1669

Labour Party Campaign Handbook: Transport, 16255

Labour Party Research Department: The National Front Investigated, 2052; A State of Collapse: The UK Economy under the Tories, 3698; Shift Work and Unsocial Hours: A Negotiators' Guide, 5926; Beveridge Report: What it Means: A Brief and Clear Analysis Showing how it Affects Various Sections, what changes it proposes, its Financial Basis, etc., 9031; Twelve Wasted Years, 1748 Pollution and our Environment: A Report . . . , 19941

Labour Party Scottish Council: Labour: The Real Voice of Scotland in Europe: Labour's Campaign Document for the European Elections, 1989, 2539

Labour Party and Trades Union Congress: Fuel and Power: An Immediate Policy. Joint Statement, 7190

Labour Party in Scotland: The Better Way for Scotland: The Labour Party Manifesto for Scotland, 1979, 2537; Scotland Will Win: Manifesto of the Labour Party in Scotland, 1987, 2538

Labour Party: Scottish Election Special, 2536; Industrial Democracy: A Discussion Document, 6010; Report of a Working Party on Race Relations, 10961; The Hospital Problem, 21409; Health Care: Report of a Working Party, 22035

Lacey, A. Douglas: The Rise of the Gas Industry in Britain, 6398

Lacey, Robert: Majesty: Elizabeth II and the House of Windsor, 508

Lacey, T. A.: 'The Political Basis of Trade Unionism', 6809

Ladd, James David: The Invisible Raiders: The History of the SBS from World War Two to the Present, 15325; Assault from the Sea, 1939–1945: The Craft, the Landings, the Men, 15415

Lader, Malcolm Harold: Psychiatry on Trial, 21876

Laffan, Michael: The Partition of Ireland 1911–1925, 2682

Laffargue, Jean-Pierre: Financial Crises: Theory, History and Policy, 4264

Laffin, John: Jack Tar: The Story of the British Sailor, 15291; Tommy Atkins: The Story of the English Soldier, 15453

Laffin, M.: Professionalism and Policy: The Role of the Professions in the Central/Local Relationship, 3224; 'The Changing Role and Responsibilities of Local Authority Chief Officers', 3247

Lafitte, François: The Internment of Allies, 15050

Lahey, R. J.: 'The Origins and Approach of the Malines Conversations', 12313

Lahr, John: Prick up your Ears: The Biography of Orton, 25964; *ed.* Orton's Diaries, 25965

Laidler, David E. W.: Inflation and Labour Markets, 4006; 'The Demand for Money in the United Kingdom, 1956–1967: Preliminary Estimates', 4623

Laidler, P. W.: Locations: Health and Sanitation, 22036

Laing, David: The Sound of our Time, 24804

Laing, Margaret: Edward Heath: Prime Minister, 1016

Laing, Sir Maurice: Conference on Industry and the Universities—Aspects of Interdependence, 23359

Laing, Ronald David: Wisdom, Sanity, Madness and the Family: The Families of Schizophrenics, 21771; Madness and Folly: The Making of a Psychiatrist, 1927–1957, 21825, 21939

Laird, Dorothy: Queen Elizabeth the Queen Mother and Her Support to the Throne During Four Reigns, 507; How the Queen Reigns: An Authentic Study of the Queen's Personality and Life Work, 509

Laird, John: *ed.* (Third Statistical Account of Scotland) The Stewartry of Kirkcudbright, 10114; 19227

Laishley, Jenny: 'Skin Colour Awareness and Preference in London Nursery-school Children', 11450

Lamb, Andrew: 'International Banking in London, 1975–85', 4537

Lamb, John Alexander: *ed.* Fasti Ecclesiae Scoticanae: The Succession of Ministers in the Church of Scotland since the Reformation, 12189

Lamb, Kenneth Henry Lowry: The BBC and its Public, 24781

Lamb, Sir Larry: Sunrise, 25257

Lamb, Margaret: *ed.* Health Care as Social History, 21964

Lamb, P. G.: Electricity in Bristol 1863–1948, 7167

Lamb, Percy Charles: The Law and Practice of Town and Country Planning, 20344

Lamb, Richard: Montgomery in Europe, 1943–45, 14774

Lambermont, Paul Marcel: Helicopters and Autogyros of the World, 17557

Lambert, Angela: Unquiet Souls: The Indian Summer of the British Aristocracy 1880–1918, 9744

Lambert, Claire Marie: Transport Policy Consultation Document, 1976: Responses to the Government's Transport Policy Consultation Document: A Select List of Material, 16254; Structure and Local Plan Documents, 17960; Structure Plans: List A: Structure Plan Documents, 17961; List B: The Literature and Debate on Structure Plans and Structure Planning, 17962; *ed.* Planning: List A: Basic List for the General Library; List B: Extended List of Publications; List C: For Local Authority Planning Departments, 17963; The Department of the Environment: Organisation and Functions, 17964;

Environmental Pollution: Sources of Information on Environmental Pollution in the United Kingdom, 19978

Lambert, G.: 'Career Objectives, Group Feeling and Legislative Party Voting Cohesion: The British Conservatives, 1959–68', 1642

Lambert, J.: 'Neighbourhood Politics and Housing Opportunities', 18731

Lambert, Jack Walter: The History of the Bodley Head 1887–1987, 24946; Drama in Britain, 1964–1973, 26244

Lambert, John Richard: Crime, Police and Race Relations: A Study in Birmingham, 10159, 11460; Housing Policy and the State: Allocation, Access and Control, 18761

Lambert, Lydia: Children who Wait: A Study of Children Needing Substitute Families, 8329

Lambert, Margaret: English Popular Art, 24101

Lambert, P.: Prix, Salaires et Coût de la Vie en Grande Bretagne, 20423

Lambert, Richard Stanton: *ed.* Memoirs of the Unemployed, 9622; Art in England, 23959

Lambert, Royston: Nutrition in Britain, 1950–1960: A Critical Discussion of the Standards and Findings of the National Food Survey, 20509; The Hothouse Society: An Exploration of Boarding School Life Through the Boys' and Girls' own Writings, 23021

Lambert, Sam: New Architecture in London, 23916

Lambert, Stephen: Channel Four: Television with a Difference, 24880

Lambert, Walker E.: 'Some Situational Influences on Attitudes toward Immigrants', 11438

Lambertini, Luigi: Victor Pasmore, with a Catalogue Raisonné of the Paintings, Constructs and Graphics 1926–1979, 24050

Lamberton, William Melville: Reconnaissance and Bomber Aircraft of the 1914–1918 War, 14634

Lambeth Palace: The Lambeth Conferences 1867–1948, 11636; The Lambeth Conference, 11639

Lammers, Donald Ned: Explaining Munich: The Search for Motive in British Policy, 13741; 'From Whitehall after Munich: The Foreign Office and the future Course of British Policy', 13755; British Foreign Policy, 1919–1934: The Problem of Soviet Russia, 13943; 'The Second Labour Government and the Restoration of Relations with Soviet Russia (1929)', 13944; 'The Engineers' Trial (Moscow, 1933) and Anglo-Soviet Relations', 13945; 'Britain, Russia and the Revival of Entente Diplomacy, 1934', 13946

Lamming, Douglas: A Century of English International Football 1872–1972, 27070

Lamont, Archibald: Scotland—The Wealthy Nation: A Scientist's Survey of Scots' Resources, 5245

Lamont, Corliss *and* Lamont, Laming: Remembering John Masefield, 25695; *ed.* Letters of John Masefield to Florence Lamont, 25696

Lancashire County Council: Preliminary Plan for Lancashire, 18885

Lancaster, Arnold: Nursing and Midwifery Sourcebook, 21721

Lancaster, J. Y.: The Iron and Steel Industry of West Cumberland: An Historical Survey, 6598

Lancaster, Joan C.: *ed.* Institute of Historical Research: Bibliography of Historical Works Issued in the United Kingdom 1946–56, 396; A Guide to Lists and Catalogues of the India Office Records, 13105

Lancaster, Lorraine: 'Some Conceptual Problems in the Study of Family and Kin Ties in the British Isles', 10046

Lancaster, Osbert: 'The Future of the Past: Some Thoughts on Preservation', 20384

Lancaster, Thomas D.: 'Britain, Spain and the Gibraltar Question', 12852

Lancaster-Gaye, Derek: *ed.* Personal Relationships, the Handicapped and the Community: Some European Thoughts and Solutions, 21910

Lancelot, John Bennett: Francis James Chavasse, Bishop of Liverpool, 11728

Lanchberry, Edward: Sound Barrier: The Story of High-speed Flight, 17500; The Crowded Sky: An Anthology of Flight from its beginnings to the Age of the Guided Missile, 17501

Lancing: Lancing: A History of S.S. Mary and Nicolas College, Lancing, 1848–1930, 23064

Land Use: Pamphlet: U.K. 1958 M. of Ag., F. & F. Warwickshire: A Study of the Loss of Agricultural Land for Urban Development, 20268

Land, Hilary: Change, Choice and Conflict in Social Policy, 8854; Large Families in London: A Study of 86 Families, 10037

Landau, Simha F.: 'Juveniles and the Police', 10674

Landsberg, Stephen E.: 'Taste Change in the United Kingdom, 1900–1955', 9893

Landstone, Charles: 'From John Osborne to Shelagh Delaney', 26217; Off-Stage: A Personal Record of the First Twelve Years of State Sponsored Drama in Great Britain, 26184

Lane, Arthur: An Adequate Response: The War Poetry of Wilfred Owen and Siegfried Sassoon, 25756

Lane, David: The End of Inequality? Stratification under State Socialism, 9569

Lane, David: The Quiet Revolution: The Planning, Development and Provision of Community Services for the Mentally Handicapped, 21780

Lane, Margaret: Edgar Wallace: The Biography of a Phenomenon, 25294; The Tale of Beatrix Potter: A Biography, 25763

Lane, Michael: Design for Degrees: New Degree Courses and the CNAA, 1964–1974, 22529; Books and Publishers: Commerce against Culture in Post-war Britain, 24934

Lane, Peter: Documents on British Economic and Social Policy, 3396; Banks, 4432

Lane, Peter: Prince Charles: A Study in Development, 529

Lane, Peter: The Conservative Party, 1613; The Liberal Party, 1821

Lane, Tony: Strike at Pilkingtons, 6937; Grey Dawn Breaking: British Merchant Seafarers in the Late Twentieth Century, 16458

Lane-Claypon, Janet Elizabeth: 'The Privileges of Organisation and Administration in Child Welfare Work', 8245

Lang, Iain: Just the Other Day: an Informal History of Great Britain since the War, 353

Lang, Ronald W.: The Politics of Drugs: The British and Canadian Pharmaceutical Industries and Governments, 22271

Lang, Tim: Now You See Them, Now You Don't: A Report on the Fate of School Meals and the Loss of 300,000 Jobs, 20530

Lang, W. H.: ed. The Remoter Areas of Britain, 19086

Langdale, C.: Gwen John: An Interior Life, 24028

Langdon, Christopher: Just Another Star? Anglo-American Relations since 1945, 14088

Langdon-Brown, Walter: Some Chapters in Cambridge Medical History, 21235

Langer, J. D.: 'The Harriman-Beaverbrook Mission and the Debate over Unconditional Aid for the Soviet Union, 1942', 13962

Langford, C. M.: Birth Control Practice and Marital Fertility in Great Britain: A Report on a Survey Carried out in 1967–1968, 7503

Langford, Richard Victor: British Foreign Policy: Its Formulation in Recent Years, 13345

Langhorne, Elizabeth: Nancy Astor and her Friends, 1346

Langhorne, Richard: ed. Diplomacy and Intelligence during the Second World War: Essays in Honour of F. H. Hinsley, 14332, 16022, 26800

Langley, C. J.: 'Twopence to the Terminus?: A Study of Tram and Bus Fares in Leeds during the Inter-war Period', 17230

Langley, H. M.: 'The Woolton Papers', 1337

Langley, Martin: Merchant Shipping at Plymouth, 16493; Milbay Docks, 16706

Langley, Michael: The East Surrey Regiment (The 31st and 70th Regiments of Foot), 15730

Langmaid, Rowland John Robb: 'The Med': The Royal Navy in the Mediterranean, 1939–1945, 14887

Langmire, John: John Ireland: Portrait of a Friend, 24355

Lannon, Judy: Television and the Working Class, 24836

Lansbury, George: My Life, 1447; What I Saw in Russia, 1448; My Quest for Peace, 13512

Lansbury, Russell: 'Careers, Work and Leisure among the New Professionals', 9774

Lansdown, Richard: ed. The Lead Debate: The Environment, Toxicology and Child Health, 20173; More than Sympathy: The Everyday Needs of Sick and Handicapped Children and their Families, 21907

Lansing, John B.: 'A Comparison of the Distribution of Personal Income and Wealth in the United States and Great Britain', 3804

Lansley, John: Voluntary Organisations Facing Change: The Report of a Project to Help Councils for Voluntary Service Respond to Local Government Re-organisation, 9209

Lansley, P. Stewart: Councils in Conflict: The Rise and Fall of the Municipal Left, 3230; Beyond our Ken: A Guide to the Battle for London, 3296; Poverty and Progress in Britain, 1953–1973: A Statistical Study of Low Income Households, their Numbers, Types and Expenditure Patterns, 9093; Poor Britain, 9108; Housing and Public Policy, 18756

Lanton, Richard: Merseyside Social and Economic Studies, 10113

Lapage, Geoffrey: Man against Disease, 21211

Lapierre, Dominique: Mountbatten and Independent India 16 August 1947–18 June 1948, 13184

Lapping, Brian: End of Empire, 12590

Laqueur, Walter: ed. 'Generations in Conflict', 8442; The Terrible Secret. An Investigation into the Suppression of Information about Hitler's 'Final Solution', 15180; ed. The Second World War. Essays in Military and Political History, 15189; ed. Urbanism: The City in History, 17810

Lara Saenz, A.: ed. Noise Pollution: Effects and Control, 20146

Larkin, Edgar J. and Larkin, John G.: The Railway Workshops of Britain, 1823–1985, 17084, 17097

Larkin, Emmet: James Larkin, Irish Labour Leader, 1876–1947, 3060; 'Church, State and Nation in Modern Ireland', 12163

Larman, Edward Cyril: Legal Liability for Claims Arising from Hospital Treatment, 21975

Larn, Richard: Shipwrecks of Great Britain and Ireland, 16504; Devon Shipwrecks, 16505; Cornish Shipwrecks, 16506

Larner, Christina J.: 'The Amalgamation of the Diplomatic Service with the Foreign Office', 13337

Larsen, Golden: The Dark Descent: Social Change and Moral Responsibility in the Novels of Joyce Cary, 25441

Larson, P. S.: Tobacco: Experimental and Clinical Studies. A Comprehensive study of the World's Literature, 22216

Lascelles, George [Earl of Harewood]: The Tongs and the Bones: Memoirs, 24566

Lascelles, Thomas Spooner: The City and South London Railway, 16964

Lash, Joseph P.: Roosevelt and Churchill, 1939–1941: The Partnership that Saved the West, 14038

Lash, Nicholas Langrishe Alleyne: 'English Catholic Theology: Ten Years on', 11973

Lask, M.: 'Racial Attitudes in General Practice', 11157

Lasker, Gabriel Ward: Surnames and Genetic Structure, 23817

Laski, Harold Joseph: Parliamentary Government in England: A Commentary, 570; The Crisis of the Constitution: 1931 and After, 572; Programme for Victory: A Collection of Essays Prepared for the Fabian Society, 2118; The Decline of Liberalism, 2172; ed. Century of Municipal Progress: The Last Hundred Years, 17903

Lasky, Melvyn J.: 'Revolution Diary', 23434

Laslett, Peter: An Introduction to Historical Demography, 7370; The World We Have Lost, 7587; ed. Philosophy, Politics and Society, 7926, 8778

Laslin, Terry: Current Controversies in Economics, 3703

Lassek, A. M.: Human Dissection: Its Drama and Struggle, 21073

Lassiere, A.: The Environmental Evaluation of Transport Plans, 17956

Lassimone, Denise: Myra Hess, 24403

Last, J. M.: 'Le Personnel Médical en Grande-Bretagne', 21341

Latourette, Kenneth Scott: Christianity in a Revolutionary Age: A History of Christianity in the Nineteenth and Twentieth Centuries, 11554; A History of the Expansion of Christianity, 12365

Latukefu, Sione: The Tongan Constitution: A Brief History to Celebrate its Centenary, 12896

Lau, Foo-sun: A Dictionary of Nuclear Power and Waste Management, 20131

Lauder, Harry: Roamin' in the Gloamin', 26327

Laudreth, Amy: Called Up: The Personal Experience of Sixteen National Servicemen, 16066

Laughrey, Patrick: The People of Ireland, 2656

Laughton, Bruce: Philip Wilson Steer, 1860–1942, 24074

Laundy, Philip Alan Charles: An Encyclopedia of Parliament, 555; The Office of Speaker, 631; 'Parliament and the Church', 11627

Laurel Bank School, 1903–1953, 23112

Laurie, Bruce: ed. Class, Sex and the Woman Worker, 7802

Laurie, Ian C.: Nature in Cities: The Natural Environment in the Design and Development of Urban Green Spaces, 20239

Laurie, Peter: The Teenage Revolution, 8476; Scotland Yard: A Personal Inquiry, 10756; Drugs: Medical, Psychological and Social Facts, 22210

Lauterbach, Albert T.: 'Economic Demobilisation in Great Britain after the First World War', 3749, 6104

Lauterpacht, E.: ed. The Suez Canal Settlement: A Selection of Documents Relating to the Clearance of the Suez Canal and the Settlement of Disputes between the United Kingdom, France and the United Arab Republic, October 1956–March 1959, 14365

Lauwerys, Joseph Albert: A Hand Book of British Educational Terms, Including an Outline of the British Educational System, 22862

Laux, James Michael: War, Crises and Transformation: The British Economy in the 20th Century, 3730

Lavalley, Albert Joseph: Focus on Hitchcock, 24674

Lavelle, Patricia: James O'Mara: A Staunch Sinn Feiner 1873–1948, 1500, 3066

Laver, James: 'Costume Research in the Last Twenty One Years', 26253

Laver, Michael: 'Party Policy, Polarisation and the Breaking of Moulds: The 1983 British Party Manifestos in Context', 2354

Lavers, George Russell: English Life and Leisure: A Social Study, 26915

Lavery, Sir John: The Life of a Painter, 24032

Lavington, Frederick: The English Capital Market, 4650

Lavington, Simon H.: A History of Manchester Computers, 7062

Law Commission, the, and the Scottish Law Commission: Chronological Table of Local Legislation Part II: Local and Personal Acts 1909–1973, Private Acts 1539–1973, 261

Law Reform Commission: Putting Asunder: A Divorce Law for Contemporary Society, 10009

Law, Christopher M.: British Regional Development Since World War One, 2402, 5119, 18772

Law, Ian: A History of Race and Racism in Liverpool, 11466

Law, John Thomas: The Scots Language: Planning for Modern Usage, 23849

Law, Richard: Controlled Drugs: Law and Practice, 22208

Law, Richard Kidston: Return from Utopia, 2190

Law, Roger: Synthetic Fun: A Short Soft Glance, 27013

Law, T. S.: Homage to John Maclean, 2530

Law, William: Our Hansard: or, The True Mirror of Parliament: a Full Account of the Official Reporting of the Debates in the House of Commons, 642

Lawall, C. H.: Four Thousand Years of Pharmacy: An Outline History of Pharmacy and Allied Sciences, 22250

Lawford, Valentine George: Bound for Diplomacy, 13289; 'Inside the Foreign Office: Halifax, Eden, Bevin', 13348

Lawlor, John James: ed. The New University, 23432; Higher Education: Patterns of Change in the 1970's, 23447

Lawlor, Monica: The McCabe Affair: Evidence and Comment, 11971

Lawlor, Sheila M.: 'Ireland from Truce to Treaty: War or Peace? July to October 1921', 2679; Britain and Ireland, 1914–1923, 2965

Lawrence, Bernard: The Administration of Education in Britain, 22796

Lawrence, Daniel: Black Migrants and White Natives: A Study of Race Relations in Nottingham, 11478

Lawrence, David Malcolm: Compulsory Purchase and Compensation: An Outline of the Law Governing the Compulsory Acquisition of Land for Public Purposes . . ., 20353

Lawrence, Derek W.: 'The Enemy Unseen: The Origins of Submarine Design', 7037

Lawrence, J. S.: Rheumatism in Populations, 21129

Lawrence, John Raymond: ed. Operational Research and the Social Sciences, 7982

Lawrence, John and Lawrence, Robert: When the Fighting is over: A Personal Story of the Battle for Tumbledown Mountain and its Aftermath, 16115

Lawrence, Reginald James: The Government of Northern Ireland: Public Finance and Public Services, 1921–1964, 2802; 'Politics and Public Administration in Northern Ireland', 2803; 'Northern Ireland at Westminster', 2809; 'The Health Services in Northern Ireland', 21338, 21697

Lawrence, Reginald Frederick: Inheritance Tax, 3795

Lawrence, Thomas Edward: Revolt in the Desert, 14490; Seven Pillars of Wisdom: A Triumph, 13815; 14491

Lawrence, W. J.: No.5 Bomber Group R.A.F., 1939–1945, 15000

Lawrenson, John Ralph: The Price of Truth: The Story of the Reuters Millions, 25308

Lawrenson, Thomas Edward: Hall of Residence: St Anselm Hall in the University of Manchester, 1907–1957, 23542

Lawrie, Leslie Gordon: A Bibliography of Dyeing and Textile Printing: Comprising a List of Books from the Sixteenth Century to the Present Time, 6478

Lawson, Annette Ruth Le Vay: The Recognition of Mental Illness in London, 21752

Lawson, Cecil C. P.: A History of the Uniforms of the British Army, 15546

Lawson, Edward Frederick, Lord Burnham: Peterborough Court: The Story of the Daily Telegraph, 25137

Lawson, Frederick Henry: ed. Cases in Constitutional Law, 607; The Oxford Law School, 1850–1965, 23565

Lawson, Joan: Children in Jeopardy: The Life of a Child Care Officer, 8246

Lawson, John: A Social History of Education in England, 22678; A Town Grammar School through Six Centuries: A History of Hull Grammar School against its Local Background, 22996

Lawson, K. H.: 'Universities and Workers' Education in Britain', 23696

Lawson, Richard Grenville: Advertising Law, 4328

Lawson, William Ramage: British War Finance 1914–1915, 4655; Europe after the World War: A Financial and Economic Survey: vol. 1, 4549

Lawson, William: Family Handbook, 10068

Lawther, Patrick Joseph: Air Pollution and Public Health: A Personal Appraisal, 20049

Lawton, Charles: A Guide to the Law of Trustee Savings Banks, 4337

Lawton, Denis: Class, Structure and the Curriculum, 9557; Social Change, Educational Theory and Curriculum Planning, 9558; Education and Social Justice, 9559, 22809

Lawton, Richard: ed. Liverpool Essays in Geography: A Jubilee Collection, 5184, 26675; 'The Daily Journey to Work in England and Wales', 16276; ed. Merseyside: Social and Economic Studies, 18053

Layard, [Peter] Richard [Grenville]: Female Labour Supply in Post-War Britain: A Cohort Approach, 7773; The Causes of Poverty, 9102; The Impact of Robbins, 23439

Laybourn, Keith ed.: Philip Snowden, 1317;

The Rise of Labour: The British Labour Party 1890–1979: Problems and Perspectives of Interpretation, 1685

Laycock, Arthur Leslie: Adolescence and Social Work, 8477

Laycock, Gloria: 'Behaviour Modifications in Prisons', 10448; 'Police Force Cautioning: Policy and Practice', 10775

Layton, David: ed. University Teaching in Transition, 22541

Layton, Robert: Twentieth Century Composers, 24286

Layton-Henry, Zig: ed. Conservative Party Politics, 1625; 'The Young Conservatives 1945–1970', 1640; 'Labour's Lost Youth', 1759; 'The Electoral Participation of Black and Asian Britons: Integration or Alienation?', 2248; 'Labour's Militant Youth', 8422; Race and Politics in Britain: A Select Bibliography, 10890; The Politics of Race in Britain, 11137; Race, Government and Politics in Britain, 11143; 'Immigration into Britain: The New Commonwealth Migrants, 1945–1962', 11439

Lazare, Bernard: Antisemitism: Its History and Causes, 11336

Lazarus, David: Freeing London's Gluepot, 16325

Lazell, H. G.: From Pills to Penicillin: The Beecham Story, 6235

Lazonick, William: The Decline of the British Economy, 3697; 'Industrial Organisation and Technological Change: The Decline of the British Cotton Industry', 6448

Le Fanu, W. R.: The Lives of the Fellows of the Royal College of Surgeons of England, Vol. 3: 1930–1951, 20842; Vol. 4: 1952–1964, 20843; Vol. 5 1965–1973, 20844; Lives of the Fellows of the Royal College of Surgeons of England. 1952, 20901; 'British Periodicals of Medicine: A Chronological List', 20971; 'The Royal College of Surgeons of England and Medical History', 20972

Le Grand, Julien: ed. Privatisation and the Welfare State, 9010

Le Lohe, M. J.: 'Voter Discrimination against Asian and Black Candidates in the 1983 General Election', 2244; Ethnic Minority Participation in Local Elections, 2245

Le Mire, E. D.: 'The Socialist League Leaflets and Manifestoes: An Annotated Checklist', 1998

Le Ruez, Jacques: Economic Planning and Politics in Britain, 3451

Le Stourgeon, Diana: Rosamond Lehmann, 25653

LeMahieu, D. L.: A Culture for Democracy: Mass Communication and the Cultivated Mind in Britain between the Wars, 23732

LeMay, Godfrey Hugh Lancelot: British Government, 1914–1953: Select Documents, 596

Lea, Frank Alfred: John Middleton Murry, 25733

Lea, Sir Frederick Measham: Science and Building: A History of the Building Research Station, 6176

Leach, Bridget: 'Postal Screening for a

Minority Group: Young West Indians in Leeds', 11271

Leach, Gerald: The Biocrats: Implications of Medical Progress. Revised edn, 21229

Leach, S. N.: 'County/District Relations in Shire and Metropolitan Counties in the Field of Town and Country Planning: A Comparison', 3229

Leach, Steve: The Changing Politics of Local Government, 3145; 'The Politics and Management of Hung Authorities', 3149

Lead, Peter: The Trent and Mersey Canal, 16415

Leakey, Louis Seymour Bazett: By the Evidence: Memoirs 1932–1951, 26360

Leakey, Mary D.: Disclosing the Past, 26363

Leakey, Richard: One Life: An Autobiography, 26364

Lean, Edward Tangye: Voices in the Darkness: The Story of the European Radio War, 24746

Lean, Garth: Frank Buchman: A Life, 12404

Lean, William: Aspects of Land Economics, 20264; Economics of Land Use Planning—Urban and Regional, 20265

Leapman, Michael: Kinnock, 1444; Treachery? The Power Struggle at TV-AM, 24879; The Last Days of the Beeb, 24885; Barefaced Cheek: The Apotheosis of Rupert Murdoch, 25104

Lear, Walter Jay: Medical Care and Family Security: Norway, England and the U.S.A., 21573

Learmonth, Sir James Rögnvald: The Contribution of Surgery to Preventive Medicine, 21149

Leasha, Mitchell: The Letters of Vita Sackville-West to Virginia Woolf, 25789

Leasor, James: Green Beach, 14825; War at the Top, 14746

Leaver, John Barker: Building Societies: Past, Present and Future, 4357

Leavis, Frank Raymond: Education and the University, 22442; Two Cultures?: The Significance of C. P.Snow, 23752; D. H. Lawrence: Novelist, 25631

Lecombert, J. R. C.: 'The Import Content of Final Expenditures for the United Kingdom, 1954–1972', 4792

Leder, Carolyn: Stanley Spencer: The Astor Collection, 24071

Ledger, David: Shifting Sands: The British in South Arabia, 13865

Lee, Bang Ha: Divorce Law Reform in England, 9994

Lee, Barbara: Groombridge Old and New: Memoirs of Village Life in the First Half of the 20th Century, 19190

Lee, Bradford A.: Britain and the Sino-Japanese War, 1937–1939, 13605

Lee, C. H.: British Regional Employment Statistics 1841–1971, 7021

Lee, Charles Edward [London Transport Board]: The Metropolitan District Railway, 16963; The Welsh Highland Railway, 16984; Sixty Years of the Bakerloo, 17008; The Bakerloo Line, 17009; Seventy Years of the Central, 17010; The Central Line, 17011; The Metropolitan Line, 17012; Sixty Years of the Northern, 17013; The Northern

Line, 17014; Sixty Years of the Piccadilly, 17015; The Piccadilly Line, 17016; 'Sources of Bus History', 17251; The Early Motor Bus, 17265

Lee, Sir David: Eastward: A History of the Royal Air Force in the Far East 1945–1972, 15949; Flight from the Middle East: A History of the Royal Air Force in the Arabian Peninsula and Adjacent Territories 1945–1972, 15950; Wings in the Sun: A History of the Royal Air Force in the Mediterranean 1945–1986, 15951

Lee, Derek J.: Control of the Economy, 4599; Monopoly, 5515; Regional Planning and Location of Industry, 5073; 'Industrial Training and Social Class', 23660

Lee, Edward: Music of the People: A Study of Popular Music in Great Britain, 24466

Lee, Edwin: 'The Historiography of Singapore', 12958

Lee, Eric: Dictionary of Arbitration Law and Practice, 5852

Lee, F. E.: 'Racial Patterns in a British City: An Institutional Approach', 10926; 'Social Controls in British Race Relations', 10927

Lee, Gloria L.: Skill Seekers: Black Youth, Apprenticeships and Disadvantage, 5964

Lee, Gordon: The Half-Forgotten Army: The British Forces in Germany, 16179

Lee, John Michael: 'Parliament and the Reorganisation of Central Government', 591; 'Select Committees and the Constitution', 654; Reviewing the Machinery of Government 1942–1952. An Essay on the Anderson Committee and its Successors, 774; The Colonial Office, War, and Redevelopment Policy, 12492; 'Forward Thinking and War: The Colonial Office during the 1940s', 12493; Social Leaders and Public Persons: A Study of County Government in Cheshire since 1888, 3349, 19326; Opting out of the N.H.S, 21607; 'The Political Significance of Licensing Legislation', 22222

Lee, James W.: John Braine, 25410

Lee, Jennie [Baroness]: Tomorrow is a New Day, 1449; This Great Journey: A Volume of Autobiography, 1904–1945, 1450; My Life with Nye, 1451

Lee, Joseph J.: ed. Irish Historiography 1970–1979, 2641; Ireland, 1912–1985: Politics and Society, 2648; ed. Ireland 1945–1970, 2716

Lee, Kenneth: ed. Conflicts in the National Health Service, 21674

Lee, M. D.: 'Scottish History Since 1940', 5256

Lee, Norman: The History of Dorman Smith, 1878–1972, 6601

Lee, Norman Edward: Harvests and Harvesting through the Ages, 19693

Lee, Phil: Welfare Theory and Social Policy: Reform or Revolution?, 8836

Lee, R. K.: 'Planning and Social Change in East London', 18309

Lee, Richard: A Source Book of Tractors and Farm Machinery, 19683

Lee, Rosemary: 'The Education of Immigrant Children in England', 23196

Lee, Thomas: ed. Transactions of the Chartered Accountants Students' Societies

of Edinburgh and Glasgow: A Selection of Writings 1886–1958, 4201

Lee, Trevor Ross: Race and Residence: The Concentration and Dispersal of Immigrants in London, 11453, 18708; A Social Atlas of London, 18338

Lee, William Alexander: Thirty Years in Coal, 1917–1947: A Review of the Coal Mining Industry under Private Enterprise, 6248, 6285

Leeming, Glenda: The Plays of Wesker, 25992; Arnold Wesker, 25993

Leeper, Sir Reginald Wildig Allen: When Greek Meets Greek, 13290

Lees, Dennis Samuel: 'Public Departments and Cheap Money, 1932–1938', 4564; Freedom or Free—for all? Essays in Welfare, Trade and Choice, 8932, 21567; Economic Consequences of the Professions, 9768; 'The Logic of the British National Health Service', 21339; Health through Choice: An Economic Study of the British National Health Service, 21566; 'Health through Choice', 21567; Impairment, Disability and Handicap: A Multi—disciplinary View, 21909

Lees, John David: Political Parties in Modern Britain: An Organisational and Functional Guide, 1586; 'Aspects of Third Party Campaigning in the 1964 General Election', 2322

Lees, L. H.: 'Study of Cities and the Study of Social Processes: Two Directions in Recent Urban History; Essay Review', 17855

Lees, Ray: Politics and Social Work, 8795

Lees-Milne, James: The Enigmatic Edwardian: The Life of Reginald, 2nd Viscount Esher, 1191

Leeson, Cecil: The Probation System, 10498

Leeson, Francis L.: A Directory of British Peerages, 37

Leeson, Joyce: Women and Medicine, 21262

Leeson, Robert Arthur: Strike: A Live History 1887–1973, 6917; United we Stand. An Illustrated Account of Trade Union Emblems, 6918

Leeson, Spencer Spottisbury Gwatkin, Bishop of Peterborough: The Public School Question, 23012

Leetham, C. R.: 'Purpose of the Catholic Public School', 22887

Lefcowitz, Myron J.: Poverty and Health: A Re-Examination, 9078

Leff, Samuel: The School Health Service, 21265, 22760; Social Medicine, 21266; From Witchcraft to World Health, 22019; Health and Humanity, 22020

Leff, Vera: The Willesden Story: History . . . Commissioned by the Willesden Council to record the Work and Achievements of the Borough of Willesden and to tell the Story of its People, 18349; Riverside Story: The Story of Bermondsey and its People, 1900–1965, 18368; The School Health Service, 21265, 22760; Going our Way?: A Short Novel, 21558; From Witchcraft to World Health, 22019; Health and Humanity, 22020

Legal Research Unit: Criminal Homicide in England and Wales, 1957–1968, 10793

Legal Status of the Welsh language: Cmnd 2785 Parliamentary Papers xxiii (1964–65), 23833,

Legg, Leopold George Wickham: *ed.* The Dictionary of National Biography 5th Supplement [1931–1940], 16; *ed.* The Dictionary of National Biography 6th Supplement [1941–1950], 17

Legge, Karen: 'Work in Prison: The Process of Inversion', 10445

Legge, Sir Thomas Morrison: Industrial Maladies, 4115

Legge-Bourke, Sir Edward Alexander Henry: The King's Guards: Horse and Foot, 15676; The Queen's Guards: Horse and Foot, 15677

Legh, Thomas Wodehouse [Baron Newton]: Retrospection, 1491

Lehane, Denis Charles: Political Murder in Northern Ireland, 2846

Lehman, Edward: 'Reactions to Women in Ministry: A Survey of English Baptist Church Members', 12040

Lehmann John: Rupert Brooke: His Life and his Legend, 25423; Christopher Isherwood: A Personal Memoir, 25599; Autobiography: The Whispering Gallery, 25652; I am my Brother, 25652; The Ample Proposition, 25652; A Nest of Tigers: Edith, Osbert and Sacheverell Sitwell in their Times, 25803; *ed.* Edith Sitwell: Selected Letters, 25806

Lehmann, Ruth Pauline: *ed.* Nova Bibliotheca Anglo-Judaica: A Bibliographical Guide to Anglo-Jewish History 1937–1960, 11277; Anglo-Jewish Bibliography, 1937–1970, 11278

Leibowitz, Joshua O.: The History of Coronary Heart Disease, 21061

Leicester City Museum and Art Gallery Public Transport in Leicester, 1874–1961, 16346

Leicester, Henry M.: Development of Biochemical Concepts from Ancient to Modern Times, 26466

Leicester, James H.: *ed.* Trends in the Services for Youth, 8478

Leifer, Michael: *ed.* Constraints and Adjustments in British Foreign Policy, 13359

Leigh, David: Michael Foot: A Portrait, 1192

Leigh, Hilary: *ed.* Changing Hospitals: A Report on the Hospital Internal Communications Project, 21355; *ed.* Standards for Morale: Cause and Effect in Hospitals, 21356

Leigh, Jack Harold: The Timber Trade: An Introduction to Commercial Aspects, 19795

Leigh, John: Young People and Leisure, 8474, 26926

Leigh, Roger: The Journey to Work in Central London, 1921–1951: A Geographical Analysis, 16283

Leighton-Boyce, John Alfred Stuart: Smith's the Bankers 1658–1958, 4506

Leinster-Mackay, Donald: The Rise of the English Preparatory School, 23004

Leiper, M. A.: Sickness Absence and Labour Wastage, 4107

Leiris, Michel: Francis Bacon: Full Face and in Profile, 24007

Leissner, Aryeh: Family Advice Services: An Exploratory Study of a Sample of Such Services Organised by Children's Departments in England, 10074; Guidance and Assistance: A Study of Seven Family Advice Centres, 10075

Leitch, David: Philby: The Spy who Betrayed a Generation, 16053; Deadline: Collected Journalism, 25258

Leitch, Michael: *ed.* Great Songs of World War II: The Home Front in Pictures, 15154

Leith, J. Clark: *ed.* Keynes, Cambridge and the General Theory, 26611

Leith-Ross, Sylvia: Stepping Stones; Memoirs of Colonial Nigeria 1907–1960, 12765

Lekachman, Robert: The Age of Keynes, 26595

Leleux, Robin: The East Midlands, 16817

Lello, John: The Official View on Education: A Summary of the Major Educational Reports since 1944, 22605; 'The Comprehensive Schools: A Summary of Opinions', 22975

Lemieux, Peter H.: 'Political Issues and Liberal Support in the February 1974 British General Election', 2337

Lemmon, Kenneth: The Gardens of Britain 5: Yorkshire and Humberside, 19886

Lemon, Anthony: Postwar Industrial Growth in East Anglian Small Towns: A Study of Migrant Firms, 1945–1970, 5153

Lempert, Susanne Martina: The Social Needs of the Over-80's: The Stockport Survey, 8582

Leng, Roger: 'Police Powers and the Citizen', 10774

Lenman, Bruce: An Economic History of Modern Scotland, 1660–1976, 3411, 5271

Lennhoff, Frederick George: Exceptional Children: Residential Treatment of Emotionally Disturbed Boys at Shotton Hall, 8247

Lentin, Anthony: Lloyd George, Woodrow Wilson and the Guilt of Germany: An Essay in the Pre-History of Appeasement, 13694

Lenton, Henry Trevor: Warships of the British and Commonwealth Navies, 15343; Warships of World War Two, 15354; British Battleships and Aircraft Carriers, 15362; British Fleet and Escort Destroyers, 15363; British Cruisers, 15364; British Submarines, 15365

Lenton, John: Immigration, Race and Politics: A Birmingham View, 11455

Leonard, A.: Britain's Economy, 3430

Leonard, Dick: The Socialist Agenda: Crosland's Legacy, 1161

Leonard, Maurice: Kathleen: The Life of Kathleen Ferrier 1912–1953, 24417

Leonard, Peter: Sociology in Social Work, 8784; 'The Application of Sociological Analysis to Social Work Training', 8785

Leonard, Richard Lawrence: *ed.* The Backbencher and Parliament: A Reader, 698

Leonardo, R. A.: History of Surgery, 21147; History of Medical Thought, 21179

Leong, Cecilia: *ed.* Commemorative History of Sabah 1881–1981, 12956

Leopold, Mark: Strangers on the Line: The Secret History of Phone-Tapping, 16065

Lerner, Shirley Wacowitz: Breakaway Unions and the Small Trade Union, 6857

Lerodiokonos, Leontios: The Cyprus Question, 12865

Lerry, George G.: The Collieries of Denbighshire: Past and Present, 6326

Leruez, Jacques: 'Actualité du Problème Ethnique en Grande Bretagne', 11044

Leser, Conrad Emanuel Victor: The Problem of Valuation for Rating, 4864; 'Scottish Industries during the Inter-war Period', 5243; Some Aspects of the Industrial Structure of Scotland, 5244; 'Fertility Changes in Scottish Cities and Countries (sic)', 7498; 'The Supply of Women for Gainful Work in Britain', 7820

Leslie, Sir [John Randolph] Shane: The Oxford Movement, 1833–1933, 11646; Mark Sykes: His Life and Letters, 13812

Leslie, Peter: FAB: The Anatomy of a Phenomenon, 24004, 24493

Leslie, Robert Henderson: Steam on the Waverley Route, 16982

Lesse, L.: 'Our Current Youth in Relation to the Basic Determinants and Trends of our Future Society', 8441

Lesser, W.: 'Patrick Geddes: The Practical Visionary', 20378

Lessing, Doris: In Pursuit of the English: A Documentary, 9891

Lester, Anthony: *ed.* Essays and Speeches by Roy Jenkins, 1246; Citizens without Status, 11094; 'Fair Employment Practices: The Government's Role', 11109; Race and Law, 11126

Lester, Joan: Beyond Band Aid: Charity is not Enough, 9191

Lester, Muriel: It Occurred to Me, 8838

Lester, Susan: *ed.* Ballet here and now, 24218

Lethaby, William Richard: Philip Webb and his Work, 24081

Lethard, Audrey: The Fight for Family Planning: The Development of Family Planning Services in Britain 1921–1974, 7519

Lethbridge, Peter: Kathleen Ferrier, 24416

Leuchtenburg, W. E.: Britain and the United States: Four Views to Mark the Silver Jubilee, 14011

Leutze, James R.: 'The Secret of the Churchill-Roosevelt Correspondence: September 1939–May 1940', 14044

Leve, H. J.: Britisch Indien-Politik 1926–1932: Motive, Methoden und Misserfolg imperialer Politik am Vorabend der Dekolonisation, 13135

Levenson, Samuel: James Connolly: A Biography, 3032

Leventhal, Fred Marc: Arthur Henderson: A Biography, 1232; 'Towards Revision and Reconciliation: H.N. Brailsford and Germany, 1914–1939, 13678; The Last Dissenter: H.N. Brailsford and his World, 25212

Lever, Jeremy Frederick: The Law of Restrictive Practices and Resale Price Maintenance, 5029

Leveson, Joseph Harry: *ed.* Electronic Business Machines, 7086

Levi, Peter: Beaumont 1861–1961, 22885

Levin, Bernard: The Pendulum Years: Britain and the Sixties, 300; Enthusiasms, 25259

Levin, Peter Hirsch.: Government and the Planning Process: An Analysis and Appraisal of Government Decision-Making Processes with Special Reference to the Launching of the New Towns and Town Development Schemes, 17957, 18258

Levin, Salmond S.: ed. A Century of Anglo-Jewish Life, 1870–1970, 12414

Levine, Aaron Lawrence: 'Economic Science and Population Theory', 7377

Levine, Barry Michael: Planning in the United States and the United Kingdom, 1970–1983, 17712

Levine, E. E.: 'Renaissance in British Casework', 8686

Levine, H. M.: An American Guide to British Social Science Abstracts, 98

Levine, Victor: The Cameroons from Mandate to Independence, 12774

Levitt, Ian: Poverty in Scotland 1890–1948, 9077

Levitt, Ruth: The Reorganised National Health Service, 21663; The People's Voice in the N.H.S.: Community Health Councils after Five Years, 22111

Levy, Abraham: History of the Sunderland Jewish Community, 11321

Levy, Catriona: Ardrossan Harbour 1805–1970: A Short History, 16672

Levy, Hermann Phillip: The Press Council: History, Procedure and Cases, 25330

Levy, Hermann Joachim: Workmen's Compensation, 4028; Industrial Assurance: A Historical and Critical Study, 4029; Burial Reform and Funeral Costs, 4044; National Health Insurance—A Critical Study, 4119, 21269; Monopolies, Cartels and Trusts in British Industry, 5508; The New Industrial System: A Study of the Origin, Forms, Finance and Prospects of Concentration in Industry, 5509; Retail Trade Associations, 6641, 20478; Shops of Britain, 6642; Large and Small Holdings: A Study of English Agricultural Economics, 19532; The Shops of Britain: A Study of Retail Distribution, 20479

Levy, Mervyn Montague: 'The Royal College of Art', 22459; The Paintings of L.S. Lowry, 24036; Ruskin Spear, 24067

Levy-Leboyer, Maurice: ed. Multinational Enterprise in Historical Perspective, 4457, 20686

Lewchuk, Wayne: 'The Return to Capital in the British Motor Vehicle Industry 1896–1939', 17413

Lewenhak, Sheila: 'Women in the Leadership of the Scottish Trades Unions, 1897–1970', 7741; Women and Trade Unions: An Outline History of Women in the British Trade Union Movement, 7752

Lewes, Frederick Martin Meredith: Statistics of the British Economy, 3433; Exeter—University and City: A Study of the Economic and Social Interactions caused by University Growth, 18106; Leisure and Tourism, 26933; Leisure, Culture and Local Government: A Study of Policies and Provision in Exeter, 26934; The Holiday Industry in Devon and Cornwall, 26949

Lewin, Julius: The Struggle for Racial Equality, 10958

Lewin, L.: Phantastica: Narcotic and Stimulating Drugs, their Use and Abuse, 22215

Lewin, Ronald: Montgomery as Military Commander, 14773; Slim, the Standardbearer: A Biography of Field-Marshal the Viscount Slim, 14780; The Chief: Field Marshal Lord Wavell, Commander-in-Chief, Viceroy, 1939–1947, 14786; Man of Armour: A Study of Lieut-General Vyvyan Pope and the Development of Armoured Warfare, 15526

Lewin, Terence: 'The Indian Ocean and Beyond: British Interests', 13199

Lewis, Alan: The Psychology of Taxation, 4849

Lewis, Alun: Letters from India, 25659

Lewis, Ben William: British Planning and Nationalization, 6131

Lewis, Charles G.: ed. Manpower Planning: A Bibliography, 5935

Lewis, Christopher: Particular Places: An Introduction to English Local History, 26748

Lewis, D. S.: Illusions of Grandeur: Mosley, Fascism and British Society 1931–1981, 2030

Lewis, David Benjamin: ed. Regular Savings Plans: The Handbook for Investment Linked Assurance, 4230

Lewis, David Neville: ed. Urban Structure, 17908

Lewis, E. Glyn: Bilingualism and Bilingual Education, 23621; 'Bilingualism in Education in Wales', 23622

Lewis, E. W.: 'Development of Geography in the Polytechnics of England and Wales', 22446, 26676

Lewis, Eluned: ed. Selected Letters of Charles Morgan, 25716

Lewis, Ernest Michael Roy: Enoch Powell: Principle in Politics, 1294

Lewis, Evan David: The Rhondda Valleys: A Study in Industrial Development, 1800 to the Present Day, 5364

Lewis, Frank: Essex and Sugar: Historic and other Connections, 20684

Lewis, G. K.: 'An Introductory Note to the Study of Race Relations in Great Britain', 11009; 'Protest among the Immigrants', 11010

Lewis, Gareth J.: Rural Communities, 19061; 'A Welsh Rural Community in Transition: A Case Study in Mid-Wales', 19291; 'Commuting and the Village in Mid-Wales', 19292; 'Intra-community Segregation: A Case Study in Rural Herefordshire', 19293

Lewis, George H.: 'The Structure of Support in Social Movements: An Analysis of Organisation and Resource Mobilisation in the Youth Contra-Culture', 8524

Lewis, Geraint: ed. Michael Tippett. A Celebration, 24373

Lewis, Gordon K.: 'The Social Legacy of British Colonialism in the Caribbean', 13011; The Growth of the Modern West Indies, 13014; 'Struggle for Freedom (A Story of Contemporary Barbados)', 13076; Grenada: The Jewel Despoiled, 13088; 'The British Caribbean Federation: The West Indian Background', 13098

Lewis, Gwilym Hugh: Wings Over the Somme, 1916–1918, 14626

Lewis, Hilda North: Deprived Children: The Mersham Experiment: A Social and Clinical Study, 8248

Lewis, Hywel David: ed. Contemporary British Philosophy, 26833

Lewis, Ioan M.: The Modern History of Somaliland: from Nation to State, 12846

Lewis, J. Parry: Building Cycles and Britain's Growth, 6179

Lewis, Jane: ed. Labour and Love: Women's Experiences of Home and Family, 1850–1940, 7637; Women in England 1870–1950: Sexual Divisions and Social Change, 7744; What Price Community Medicine? The Philosophy, Practise and Politics of Public Health since 1919, 21943; ed. Community Health Councils: Four Case Studies, 22110; The Politics of Consumer Representation: A Study of Community Health Councils, 22112

Lewis, John: Christianity and the Social Revolution, 11830; The Left Book Club: An Historical Record, 24965

Lewis, John: The Twentieth Century Book: Design and Illustration, 25014

Lewis, John Parry: Welsh Economic Statistics: A Handbook of Sources, 5312; Urban Decay: An Analysis and a Policy, 17801; Building Cycles and Britain's Growth (Incorporating Materials of the Late Bernard Weber), 18956

Lewis, June R.: Cotswold Villages, 19135

Lewis, Michael Arthur: The Navy of Britain: A Historical Portrait, 15229; The History of the British Navy, 15230; England's Sea Officers: The Story of the Naval Profession, 15286

Lewis, Norman: The Commission for Local Administration: A Preliminary Appraisal, 3253; Naples 1944, 14879

Lewis, P. M.: Community Television and Cable in Britain, 24849

Lewis, P.: 'Médecine Privée et Médecine Publique en Grande-Bretagne', 21340

Lewis, Paul: 'The Role of A.C.A.S. Conciliators in Unfair Dismissal Cases, 4163

Lewis, Peter: Squadron Histories: RFC, RNAS and RAF 1912–59, 15919; The British Fighter since 1912: Fifty Years of Design and Development, 15821; The British Bomber Since 1914: Sixty-Five Years of Change and Development, 15822

Lewis, Peter: The Humberside Region, 5137

Lewis, Peter Ronald: The Literature of the Social Sciences: An Introductory Survey and Guide, 423, 7932

Lewis, Philip: The Sociology of the Professions: Lawyers, Doctors and Others, 9817

Lewis, Philippa: Potters on Pottery, 24135

Lewis R.: Sir William Russell Flint 1880–1968, 24014

Lewis, R. R.: The History of Brentwood School, 23045

Lewis, Roy: 'Britain and Biafra: A Commonwealth Civil War', 12768

Lewis, Roy: 'The Legal Enforcibility of Collective Agreements', 5735

Lewis, Roy: The Boss: The Life and Times of the British Business Man, 5420, 9789; The English Middle Classes, 9718; Professional People, 9767

Lewis, Russell: Margaret Thatcher: A Personal and Political Biography, 1048; Tony Benn: A Critical Biography, 1092

Lewis, T. M.: North Sea Oil and Scotland's Economic Prospects, 6530, 7170

Lewis, Tony: Double Century: The Story of MCC and Cricket, 27101

Lewis, Warren Hamilton: ed. Letters of C. S.Lewis, 25661

Lewis, Sir William Arthur: An Economic Survey, 1919–1939, 3402

Lewis, William John: Lead Mining in Wales, 5340, 6354

Leyland Motor Corporation: Seventy Years of Progress, 17436; Proposed Amalgamation with the Rover Company Ltd, 17437

Leyland, Eric: The Cinema: Historical, Technical and Bibliographical: A Survey for Librarians and Students, 24593

Leyland, John: The Achievement of the British Navy in the World War, 14671

Leys, Colin: European Politics in Southern Rhodesia, 12797

Leys, Mary Dorothy Rose: A History of London Life, 18344; A History of the English People, 18345

Leys, Norman: By Kenya Possessed: The Correspondence of Norman Leys and J.H. Oldham, 12827

Leys, W. A. R.: 'The Philosophical and Ethical Aspects of Group Relations', 10906

Libby, R. T.: 'Anglo-American Diplomacy and the Rhodesian Settlement: A Loss of Impetus', 12815

Libby, W.: History of Medicine in its Salient Features, 21170

Liberal Party Transport Committee: Transport: A Report by a Committee under the Chairmanship of Mr. Arthur Holt M.P., 16246

Library: Library Association: A Union List of Statistical Serials in British Libraries, 164; British Humanities Index: Regional Lists, 26758

Library of Congress Catalog: A Cumulative List of Works Represented by Library of Congress Printed Cards: Books: Subjects 1950–1954, 114; Books: Subjects 1955–1959, 115; Books: Subjects 1960–1964, 116; Books: Subjects 1965–1969, 117; Books: Subjects 1970–1974, 118

Lichfield, Nathaniel: Economics of Planned Development, 5406, 20402; Cost-benefit Analysis in Urban Redevelopment, 5407, 20403; Cost-benefit Analysis in Town Planning: A Case Study of Cambridge, 5408, 20404; Evaluation in the Planning Process, 17955; 'Cost Benefit Analysis in Urban Expansion: A Case Study, 18023; 'Six English New Towns: A Financial Analysis', 19006; Cost Benefit Analysis in Town Planning, 18800

Lichfield, Patrick [Earl of Lichfield]: Not the Whole Truth: An Autobiography, 24711

Licht, Fred Stephen: Sculpture: Nineteenth and Twentieth Centuries, 24178

Licht, S.: ed. Occupational Therapy Source Book, 21270

Lichter, Robert: Roots of Radicalism: Jews, Christians and the New Left, 9861

Lickorish, Leonard James: Leisure and Tourism, 26933; The Travel Trade, 26947

Lid, M. W.: Ford Madox Ford: The Essence of his Art, 25512

Liddell, Edward George Tandy: The Discovery of Reflexes, 22323

Liddell, Robert: The Novels of Ivy Compton-Burnett, 25454

Liddiard, Jean: Working for Victory? Images of Women in the First World War, 1914–18, 7704; Isaac Rosenberg: The Half-used Life, 25785

Liddiard, Penny: An Ageing Population, 8635

Liddle, Peter H.: ed. Home Fires & Foreign Fields: British Social and Military Experience in the First World War, 14445; Men of Gallipoli: The Dardanelles and Gallipoli Experience, August 1914 to January 1916, 14535; ed. Gallipoli 1915: Pens, Pencils and Cameras at War, 14536

Lidgett, John Scott: My Guided Life, 12086

Lieber, Robert J.: British Politics and European Unity: Parties, Elites and Pressure Groups, 14162; 'Interest Groups and Political Integration: British Entry into Europe', 14163

Liefer, Michael: 'Anglo-American Differences over Malaysia', 12937; 'Anglo-Malaysian Alienation', 12942

Liepmann, Kate K.: Apprenticeship: An Enquiry into its Adequacy under Modern Conditions, 5953:; The Journey to Work, 16274

Life Offices Association: Life Assurance in the United Kingdom 1972–1976, 4233

Light, George: ed. Ben Tillett: Fighter and Pioneer, 1536

Lijphart, Arend: 'The Northern Ireland Problem: Cases, Theories and Solutions', 2828

Likierman, Andrew: Public Expenditure and the Public Spending Process, 4772

Liljestrand, Göran: Readings in Pharmacology, 22300

Lilley, George P.: Information Sources in Agriculture and Food Sciences, 19380; A Bibliography of John Middleton Murry 1899–1957, 25732

Lilly, Marjorie: Sickert: The Painter and His Circle, 24064

Lincoln, John A.: The Restrictive Society, 4936

Lind, Mary Ann: The Compassionate Memsahibs: Welfare Activities of British Women in India, 1900–1947, 7747

Lindau, Henry: All's Fair: The Story of the British Secret Service behind the German Lines, 14614

Lindeboom, Johannes: Austin Friars: History of the Dutch Reformed Church in London, 1550–1950, 12450

Linder, Leslie: ed. Beatrix Potter, 1866–1943: Centenary Catalogue, 25761

Lindley, Clive: ed. Partnership of Principle: Writings and Speeches on the Making of the Alliance by Roy Jenkins, 1247

Lindley, Sir Francis Oswald: A Diplomat off Duty, 13291

Lindley, Robert M.: The Demand for Apprentice Recruits by the Engineering Industry. 1951–1971, 6381; 'Inter-industry Mobility of Male Employees in Great Britain, 1959–1968', 7226

Lindquist, J. H.: 'The Urban Community: Attitudes towards Neighbourhood and Urban Renewal', 9416

Lindsay, David: Friend for Life: A Portrait of Lancelot Fleming, 11731

Lindsay, Jean: The Canals of Scotland, 16394; The Trent and Mersey Canal, 16414

Lindsay, Jean Olivia: Girton College, 1869–1959: An Informal History, 23477

Lindsay, Kenneth: 'Post-war Oxford, 1918–1922', 23554

Lindsay, Lilian: A Short History of Dentistry, 22404

Lindsay, Maurice: The Conservation of Georgian Edinburgh: The Proceedings and Outcome of a Conference, 18975; Lowland Scottish Villages, 19139; Thank You For Having Me: A Personal Memoir, 25676; ed. I Remember: Ten Scottish Authors Recall how Writing Began for Them, 25677

Lindsay, Oliver: ed. A Guard's General: The Memoirs of Sir Allan Adair, 14747

Lindsay, Thomas Fanshawe: The Conservative Party, 1918–1970, 1614

Lindsay, Thomas Martin: Sherwood Rangers, 15716

Lindsay, Walton: New Towns: The Evolution of Planning Criteria 18213; New Towns: A Comparative Atlas, 18998, 18212

Lindsell, Sir Wilfred Gordon: Military Organisation and Administration, 15479

Lindsey County Council: Disused Railways in Lindsey: Policy for After-use, 20287

Lindsey, Almont: Socialized Medicine in England and Wales: The National Health Service, 1948–1961, 21570

Ling, Arthur: Runcorn New Town: Master Plan, Prepared for the Runcorn Development Corporation, 18200

Ling, Tom: Thatcherism: A Tale of Two Nations, 1054

Linge, G. J. R.: The Functions of the Cabinet Secretariat, 753

Lini, Walter: Beyond Pandemonium: From the New Hebrides to Vanuatu, 12887

Linklater, Andro: The Black Watch: The History of the Royal Highland Regiment, 15572; Compton Mackenzie: A Life, 25688

Linklater, Eric Robert Russell: The Survival of Scotland: A Review of Scottish History from Roman Times to the Present Day, 5257; The Campaign in Italy, 14867; The Black Watch: The History of the Royal Highland Regiment, 15572; Our Men in Korea, 16125

Linklater, Magnus: Jeremy Thorpe: A Secret Life, 1533; Not with Honour: The Inside Story of the Westland Scandal, 9906

Linnard, William: Welsh Woods and Forests: History and Utilization, 19726

Linstead, Sir Reginald Patrick: Imperial College of Science and Technology: A Decade of Expansion, 23522

Linton, David L.: ed. Sheffield and its Region: A Scientific and Historical Survey, 18073

Linton, David: ed. The Newspaper Press in Britain: An Annotated Bibliography, 25035

Lipgens, Walter: A History of European Integration, 14120

Lipke, William: David Bomberg: A Critical Study of his Life and Work, 24010

Lipman, A.: 'Old People's Homes: Siting and Neighbourhood Integration', 8625; 'Architectural Education and the Social Commitment of Contemporary British Architecture', 9830, 23871

Lipman, S. L.: ed. Jewish Life in Britain, 1962–1977, 12418

Lipman, Vivian David: Local Government Areas, 1834–1945, 3109; Social History of the Jews in England, 1850–1950, 11282, 12410; ed. A Century of Social Service, 1859–1959: The Jewish Board of Guardians, 9124, 11281; ed. Three Centuries of Anglo-Jewish History: A Volume of Essays, 11280; 'Trends in Anglo-Jewish Occupations', 11296; ed. Jewish Life in Britain, 1962–1977, 12418

Lippard, Lucy Rowland: Pop Art, 24003

Lippitt, Vernon G.: Determinants of Consumer Demand for House Furnishings and Equipment, 20450

Lipscombe, Frank Woodgate: The British Submarine, 15375

Lipsey, David: The Socialist Agenda: Crosland's Legacy, 1161

Lipsey, Richard G.: An Introduction to the United Kingdom Economy, 3537

Lipson, Ephraim: Europe, 1914–1939, 358; The Growth of English Society: A Short Economic History, 3461; A Planned Economy or Free Enterprise: The Lessons of History, 4584

Lipton, Michael: Assessing Economic Performance, 4576; The Erosion of a Relationship: India and Britain since 1960, 13190

Lipworth, L.: Regional and Social Factors in Infant Mortality, 7448

Liquid History: To Commemorate Fifty Years of the Port of London Authority, 1909–1959, 16701

Lischeron, Joe: 'Attitudes towards Participation among Local Authority Employees', 5777

Lister, Raymond George: Decorative Cast Ironwork in Great Britain, 24141

Lister, Ruth: As Man and Wife: A Study of the Cohabitation Rule, 4056; Supplementary Benefit Rights, 4057, 8893; The Unequal Breadwinner: A New Perspective on Women and Social Security, 7792; National Welfare Benefits Handbook, 8892; Social Assistance: The Real Challenge, 8894; Welfare Benefits, 8895

Litman, Simon: Prices and Price Control in Great Britain and the United States during the World War, 3750

Little, A. J.: ed. Schofield's Local Government Elections, 3107; 'Penal Theory, Penal Reform and Borstal Practice', 10649

Little, Alan Nevile: 'Sociology in Britain since 1945', 7975; 'The Young Voter in British Politics', 8419; 'The Young Activist in British Politics', 8420; 'The Trend of Class Differentials in Educational Opportunity in England and Wales', 9479; 'The Prevalence of Recorded Delinquency and Recidivism in England and Wales', 10164, 10648; 'The Education of Immigrant Pupils in Inner London Primary Schools', 11449; An 'Expectancy' Estimate of Hospitalization Rates for Mental Illness in England and Wales', 21815; 'The Trend of Class Differentials in Educational Opportunity in England and Wales', 22815; 'Will More Mean Worse? An Enquiry into the Effects of University Expansion', 23412

Little, Bryan Desmond Greenway: David Jones 1862–1962: A Hundred Years of Wholesale Grocery, 6487; The City and County of Bristol: A Study in Atlantic Civilization, 18017; Cheltenham, 18018; Exeter, 18019; The Three Choirs Cities, 18020

Little, D.: Malevolent Neutrality: The United States, Great Britain, and the Origins of the Spanish Civil War, 13978

Little, Ernest Muirhead: History of the British Medical Association, 1832–1932, 20788

Little, Ian Malcolm David: Concentration in British Industry: An Empirical Study of the Structure of Industrial Production, 1935–1951, 4979; 'Some Aspects of the Structure of British Industry, 1935–1951', 7227; A Critique of Welfare Economics, 8930; International Aid: A Discussion of the Flow of Public Resources from Rich to Poor Countries, with Particular Reference to British Policy, 9185

Little, Jo: 'The Implementation of Rural Policies: A Survey of Country Planning Authorities', 18828; Social Profiles of Ten Case Study Parishes, 19316

Little, Kenneth Lindsay: 'Department of Social Anthropology, the University of Edinburgh', 10126; Social Anthropology in Modern Life, 10127; Negroes in Britain: A Study of Racial Relations in English Society, 10892; Colour and Commonsense, 10893; Race and Society, 10894; 'Loudon Square—A Community Survey I', 10895, 11467; 'Loudon Square—A Community Survey II', 10896, 11468; 'The Coloured Folk of Cardiff—A Challenge to Reconstruction', 10897; 'The Position of Coloured People in Britain', 10898; The Development of State Education, 22677

Little, Tom: South Arabia: Arena of Conflict, 13875

Little, W. R.: 'Social Class Backgrounds of Young Offenders from London', 10600

Littlechild, Stephen C.: 'Setting Guaranteed Prices in the United Kingdom Cereals Market 1967–1972', 19565

Littlejohn, James: Social Stratification: An Introduction, 9570; Westrigg: The Sociology of a Cheviot Parish, 19210, 19375

Littler, Craig R.: ed. Industrial Relations and the Law in the 1980's: Issues and Future Trends, 5843

Littler, Keith T.: 'Work Experience and the British School Pupil', 22518

Liu, W. H.: 'The Evolution of Commonwealth Citizenship and U.K. Statutory Control over Commonwealth Immigration', 11096

Liveing, Edward: Adventure in Publishing: The House of Ward Lock 1854–1954, 24995

Liverpool Council of Social Service: Social Reconstruction in Liverpool: An Introductory Memorandum, 8980

Liverpool Personal Service Society: Rehabilitation of Homeless Families: A Report of An Experiment in the Rehousing of Selected Families in Rehabilitation Houses, under Casework Supervision, 18505

Liverpool Stock Exchange: The Centenary Book of the Liverpool Stock Exchange 1836–1936, 4267

Liverpool University Social Science Department: (Statistics Division) New Merseyside Series 12—The Cost of Living of Representative Working Class Families, 20419

Liverpool University Social Science Dept.: Social Aspects of a Town Development Plan: A Study of the County Borough of Dudley, 9335; The Dock Worker, 9660

Liverpool University, Institute of Education: British Government Publications Concerning Education: An Introductory Guide, 22863

Liversidge, Douglas: Queen Elizabeth II: The British Monarchy Today, 509; Prince Philip: First Gentleman of the Realm, 518; Prince Charles: Monarch in the Making, 527; The House of Commons, 637

Livi-Bacci, Massimo: Report on the Demographic and Social Pattern of Migrants in Europe, Especially with Regard to International Migrations, 11420

Livingston, William Samuel: ed. Federalism in the Commonwealth: A Bibliographical Commentary, 12471

Livingstone, Dame Adelaide Lord: The Peace Ballot: The Official History, 13502

Livingstone, Arthur Stanley: The International Student, 11503

Livingstone, Elizabeth Anne: ed. The Oxford Dictionary of the Christian Church, 11529

Livingstone, James Mccardle: The British Economy in Theory and Practice, 3446

Livingstone, Ken: If Voting Changed Anything, They'd Abolish it, 1452; 'Why Labour Lost', 2350

Livingstone, Peadar: The Fermanagh Story, 19313

Llewellyn, David T.: The Framework of U.K. Monetary Policy, 4652

Llewellyn-Davies & Partners: Motorways in an Urban Environment, 17113

Llewellyn-Davies, Richard [Baron]: 'Town Design', 17787; The Future of Environmental Studies, 19915

Llewellyn-Davies, Weeks, Forestier-Walker and Bor: Unequal City, 179831

Llewellyn-Davies, Weeks and Partners: Inner

Area Study: Birmingham (part of Small Heath), 17984; Project Report, 17985; 2. Progress Report, 17986; 3. Second Progress Report, 17987; 4. Interim Review, 17988; 5. Small Heath, Birmingham: a Social Survey, 17989; 6. Third Progress Report, 17990; 7. Little Green: A Case Study in Urban Renewals, 17991; 8. Fourth Progress Report, 17992; 9. Industrial Employment and Property Availability, 17993; 9–10. Housing Policies for the Inner City, 17994; 10. The Management of Urban Renewal, 17995; 12. Circumstances of Families, 17996; 13.and 15. Educational Action Projects, 17997; 14. You and Me: Here we Are, 17998; 16. Family Service Unit, 17999; 18.-19. Environmental Action Projects, 18000; 20. Small Heath Community Federation: A Study in Local Influence, 18001; 22. Small Heath Information and Advice Centre, 18002; 25. Shape Housing and Community Project, 18003

Lloyd Jones, [Peter] Hugh [Jefferd]: 'Gilbert Murray', 26568; Blood for Ghosts: Classical Influence in the Nineteenth and Twentieth Centuries, 26571; ed. Maurice Bowra: A Celebration, 26572

Lloyd's Bank: Lloyd's Bank in the Community, 4501

Lloyd's Register of Shipping: Annual Report, 16467

Lloyd, Alan: The War in the Trenches, 14482; The Gliders, 17545

Lloyd, Bruce: Energy Policy, 7195

Lloyd, C. C.: 'The Conquest of Scurvy', 20976

Lloyd, Cyril: British Services Education, 23718

Lloyd, David W.: ed. The Making of English Towns, 18775

Lloyd, Ian: Rolls-Royce: The Growth of a Firm, 17444; Rolls-Royce: The Years of Endeavour, 17445

Lloyd, Sir John Edward: ed. Dictionary of Welsh Biography down to 1940, 49

Lloyd, John Phillip: R.A.F. Aircraft of World War 2, 15827

Lloyd, Lorna: British Writing on Disarmament from 1914 to 1978: A Bibliography, 13432

Lloyd, Michael: 'The United Kingdom's Trade and the European Community: 1973 and 1974', 4811

Lloyd, Peter: Not for Publication, 26895

Lloyd, Richard: ed. Conservation and Agriculture, 19571, 20203

Lloyd, Roger Bradshaigh: The Church of England, 1900–1965, 11598

Lloyd, Selwyn [Baron]: Mr. Speaker, Sir, 1254; Suez 1956: A Personal Account, 1255, 14382

Lloyd, T. Alwyn: 'The "New Town" Proposals', 18214

Lloyd, Terence Henry: ed. Middle Class Housing in Britain, 9737, 18758

Lloyd, Trevor O.: Empire to Welfare State: English History, 1906–1976, 290; 'Ramsay MacDonald: Socialist or Gentleman?', 1032

Lloyd, Wyndham E. B.: A Hundred Years of Medicine, 21215

Lloyd George, David [Earl]: War Memoirs, 1019; The Truth about Reparations and War Debts, 1020; The Truth about the Peace Treaties, 1021; Is it Peace? Articles and Addresses on the European Situation, 1031

Lloyd George, Frances Louise [Countess; Stevenson, Frances Louise]: Lloyd George: A Diary, 1018; Lloyd George: The Years that are Past, 1018

Lloyd George, Richard [Earl Lloyd-George]: Lloyd George, 1018

Lloyds Register of Shipping: Rules and Regulations for the Classification of Inland Waterways Ships, 16440

Lo Bogola: An African Savage's Own Story, 11512

Loades, David M.: Rome and the Anglicans, 12334

Local Government Annotations Service: Romford, 3099

Local Government Comparative Statistics, 3103

Local Government Financial Statistics: 1953, 3102

Local Government Trends, 1973-83, 3095

Local Historian, The, 1952+, 26741

Location of Offices Bureau [Research Papers No: 1]. White Collar Commuters: A Second Survey: An Inter-regional Comparison of the Community and Working Conditions of Office Workers, 16289; A Wise Move, 18325

Lochhead, Andrew Van Sylke: ed. A Reader in Social Administration, 9238; 'Current Issues in Community Work: A Review Article', 9404

Lock, C. B. Muriel: Modern Maps and Atlases: An Outline Guide to Twentieth Century Production, 129

Lock, C. M.: The Hartlepools, 18108

Lock, D.: 'Structure Plans: Beware False Promises', 17862

Lock, H. O.: With the British Army in the Holy Land, 14492

Lock, Joan: The British Policewoman: Her Story, 7731

Lock, Stephen Penford: Health Centres and Group Practises: Articles Collected from the British Medical Journal, 21512

Locke, Arthur: The Tigers of Trengganu, 12922

Locke, George Michael Lochhead: The Place of Forestry in Scotland: A Basis for Local Authority Planning, 19723

Locke, Michael: Traditions and Controls in the Making of a Polytechnic: Woolwich Polytechnic, 1890–1970, 22531

Locke, R. R.: The End of the Practical Man: Higher Education and the Institutionalisation of Entrepreneurial Performance in Germany, France and Great Britain 1880–1940, 5453

Lockhart, Howard: On My Wavelength, 26285

Lockhart, James Arthur Renwick: Introduction to Crop Husbandry, 19698

Lockhart, John Gilbert: Cosmo Gordon Lang, 11699

Lockhart, Sir Robert Hamilton Bruce: Friends, Foes and Foreigners, 327; The Marines were there: The Story of the Royal

Marines in the Second World War, 15322; Scotch: The Whisky of Scotland in Fact and Story, 20725

Lockwood, David: 'Arbitration and Industrial Conflict', 5624; The Black-Coated Worker: A Study in Class Consciousness, 9522; 'Sources of Variation in Working Class Images of Society', 9682

Lockwood, Ernest: Colne Valley Folk: The Romance and Enterprise of a Textile Stronghold, 6464

Lockwood, P.: 'Affluence and the British Class Structure', 9446

Lockwood, W. B.: Languages of the British Isles, Past and Present, 23809

Lockyer, Cliff J.: Industrial Relations in Britain, 5793; Industrial Relations, 5794

Lockyer, John: Industrial Arbitration in Great Britain: Everyman's Guide, 5803

Lockyer, Roger Walter: The Monarchy, 433

Loder, Eileen P.: Bibliography of the History and Organisation of Horse Racing and Thoroughbred Breeding in Great Britain and Ireland: Books Published in Great Britain and Ireland 1565–1973, 27121

Lodge, David John: Graham Greene, 25563

Lodge, Juliet: ed. Direct Elections to the European Parliament, 2283; 'Euro-Elections and the European Parliament: The Dilemma over Turnout and Powers', 2384; The European Community and New Zealand, 12673; 'New Zealand, Britain and the E.E.C. in the 1970's', 14181

Loebl, Herbert: Government Factories and the Origins of British Regional Policy 1934–1948, 5128

Loewenberg, Gerhard: 'The Transformation of the British Labour Party Policy since 1945', 1734

Loewenheim, Francis L.: et al. eds. Roosevelt and Churchill: Their Secret Wartime Correspondence, 14040

Lofthouse, Jessica: Lancashire Villages, 19138

Lofts, Dudley: 'The Civil Service after Fulton', 862

Logan, Sir Douglas William: The Birth of a Pension Scheme: A History of the Universities' Superannuation Scheme, 23350; Universities: the Years of Challenge, 23397; The University of London: An Introduction, 23516

Logan, Robert F. L.: 'Rising Eighteen in a London Suburb: Some Aspects of the Life and Health of Young Men', 8445; The Demand for Medical Care: A Study of the Case Load in the Barrow in Furness Group of Hospitals, 21385; Gateway or Dividing Line?: A Study of Hospital Out-Patients in the 1960's, 21404

Logan, William Philip Dowie: Tuberculosis Statistics for England and Wales, 1938–1955: 'Mortality in the London Fog Incident, 1952', 7461; 'Mortality in England and Wales From 1848–1947', 7462; 'Social Class Variations in Mortality', 7463; An Analysis of Trends and Geographical Distribution, 7464, 22241; The Survey of Sickness, 1943–1952, 22234; Cancer Mortality by Occupation and Social Class, 1851–1971, 22235

Lomas, Glenys Barbara Gillian: Census 1971: The Coloured Population of Great Britain: Preliminary Report, 11021; The Employment and Socio-Economic Conditions of the Coloured Population, 11049

Lomas, Graham Maurice: Employment Location in Regional Economic Planning: A Case Study of the West Midlands, 5223; Population Growth and Planning Policy: An Analysis of Social and Economic Factors Affecting Housing and Employment Location in the West Midlands, 7416; ed. Social Aspects of Urban Development: United Kingdom Report on the Social Welfare Implications of Urban Development, 9355; 'Out for the Count', 17953; The Inner City: A Preliminary Investigation of the Dynamics of Current Labour and Housing Markets with Special Reference to Minority Groups in Inner London, 18744

Lomas, Peter: ed. The Predicament of the Family: A Psycho-analytical Symposium, 10078

Lomax, Donald Ernest: ed. The Education of Teachers in Britain, 22735

Lomax, Sir John Garnett: The Diplomatic Smuggler, 13292

Lomax, Kenneth: 'Britain's Growth Performance: The Enigma of the 1950's', 3633

London Bibliography of the Social Sciences, 119

London Committee of Deputies of the British Jews: Annual Report, 11303

London Conference on Overseas Students—Standing Committee: Overseas Students in Britain: A Handbook, 11502

London County Council: Housing: Being One of a Series of Popular Handbooks on the London County Council and what it Does for London, 18600; Housing: With Particular Reference to Post-War Housing Schemes, 18601; Housing 1928-30, 18602; Housing and Public Health Committee: Working Class Housing on the Continent and the Application of Continental Ideas to the Housing Problem in the County of London, 18603; London Housing, 18604; Housing: A Survey of the Postwar Housing Work of the London County Council 1945-1949, 18605; Housing Londoners (1945-1960): The Part played by the London County Council, 18660; 200,000 Homes, 18661; East End Housing: A Review of the Council's Post War Housing Achievements in Bethnal Green, Poplar and Stepney, 18662; (Education Officers Department). Economy in the Consumption of Food: Practical Hints on Catering for a Small Household in Wartime, 20575; The L.C.C. Hospitals: A Retrospect, 21430; Education Committee Special Services Sub-Committee. Report By the School Medical Officer on the Average Heights and Weights of Elementary School Children in The County of London in 1938, 22046; Education Library Catalogue 1935, 23231

London Department of Transport: Crime on the London Underground, 10782

London GLC: Airport Strategy for Great Britain, pt.1—The London Area: A Consultation Document, 17682; Survey of London. Vol 33-4: The Parish of St. Annes, Soho, 18362

London L.C.C. and G.L.C.: London Traffic Survey, 16327

London Regional Advisory Council for Youth Employment: A Guide to Employment for Boys and Girls in Greater London, 8501; Memorandum on the Problem of Post-war Entry of Juveniles into Employment, 8502

London, Royal Society of: Emigration of Scientists from the United Kingdom: Report, 5028

London School of Economics and Political Science: Department of Geography. British Cities: Woman, Wife and Worker, 7706; Urban Population and Employment Trends, 1951-71, 17907

London Transport Board: Reshaping London's Bus Services, 17310

London Transport Executive: Comments on Transport Policy: A Consultation Document, 16319

London University, Imperial College of Science and Technology: Report on a Decade of Expansion, 1953-1963, 23523

London University, University College: Centre for Urban Studies, Land Use Planning and the Social Sciences: A Selected Bibliography, 20252

London and Cambridge Economic Service: The British Economy: Key Statistics, 1900-1970, 4577

London's Water Supply, 1903-53: A Review of the Work of the Metropolitan Water Board, 20106

London: London Council of Social Service: Commonwealth Children in Britain, 23176

London: London Head Teachers Association: Memorandum on Immigrant Children in London Schools, 23171

Loney, Martin: Community against Government: The British Community Development Project, 1968-1978: A Study of Government Impotence, 9276; Rhodesia: White Racism and Imperial Response, 12795

Long, Andrew F.: ed. Manpower Planning in the National Health Service, 5951, 21657

Long, A.: A Shipping Venture: Turnbull Scott & Company, 1872-1972, 16546

Long, E. R.: A History of Pathology, 21108; ed. Selected Readings in Pathology, 21109

Long, Geoffrey: Solar Energy: Its Potential Contribution within the United Kingdom: A Report Prepared for the Department of Energy, 7165

Long, Joyce Ruth: ed. The Wythall Inquiry: A Planning Test Case, with an Introduction by P. J. O. Self, 17765, 20364; Universities and the General Public, 23428

Long, Kenneth Roy: The Music of the English Church, 11922

Long, Norman: An Introduction to the Sociology of Rural Development, 7924; ed. Family and Work in Rural Societies: Perspectives on Non-wage Labour, 19601

Long, R.: A Shipping Venture: Turnbull Scott & Company, 1872-1972, 16546

Long, Robert A.: British Railways Engineering, 1948-1980, 17083

Long, W. Harwood: 'The Development of Mechanisation in English Farming', 19688

Long, Walter Hume [Viscount]: Memories . . . 1923, 1258

Longbottom, Charles: 'Britain and the Underdeveloped World' in 'The Conservative Opportunity: Fifteen . . . Essays on Tomorrow's Toryism'.by the Bow Group, 9182

Longdon, H. A.: 'Post-war Developments in the Coal Mining Industry', 6296

Longford, Elizabeth [Countess of Longford]

Longford, Frank [Earl of]

Longhurst, Henry Carpenter: Adventure in Oil: The Story of British Petroleum, 6519

Longland, Sir John Laurence: Education and Delinquency, 10512

Longley, Michael: ed. Causeway: The Arts in Ulster, 23737

Longmate, Norman Richard: Milestones in Working Class History, 1671; The Way We Lived Then: A History of Everyday Life during the Second World War, 7535; If Britain had Fallen, 14846; When We Won the War: The Story of Victory in Europe 1945, 14941; The Home Front: An Anthology of Personal Experiences 1938-1945, 15091; Air Raid. The Bombing of Coventry, 1940, 15156; The Doodlebugs: The Story of the Flying Bombs, 15204; The Bombers; The R.A.F. Offensive against Germany, 1939-1945, 15984; King Cholera, 22388

Longrigg, Roger: The History of Horseracing, 27123

Longworth, Ian: Archaeology in Britain since 1945, 26357

Longworth, J. E.: Oldham Master Cotton Spinners Association Ltd.: Centenary Year, 6433

Lonsdale, Gordon: Spy: Twenty Years of Secret Service, 16045

Lonsdale, John: 'Some Origins of Nationalism in East Africa', 12817

Lopez-Rey Y Arrojo, Manuel: Crime: An Analytical Appraisal, 10137

Loraine, John Alexander: Syndromes of the Seventies: Population, Sex and Social Change, 7412

Lord, Fred Townley: Achievement: A Short History of the Baptist Missionary Society, 1792-1942, 12361

Lord, R. F.: ed. Research, Education and Extension in Agriculture, 19694

Lord, Richard: Controlled Drugs: Law and Practice, 10835

Lord, Walter: The Miracle of Dunkirk, 14836

Loring, James: ed. The Spastic Schoolchild and the Outside World, 21887

Lorraine, John A.: ed. Environmental Medicine, 22232

Lort-Phillips, Patrick: 'The British Liberal Revival', 1824

Lothians Regional Survey and Plan: 2 vols, 5293

Lotz, Rainer: Under the Imperial Carpet, 11086

Louden, R. Stuart: The True Face of the Kirk: An Examination of the Ethos and Traditions of the Church of Scotland, 12193

Loudon, J. B.: 'Kinship and Crisis in South Wales', 10043

Loughborough: The History of Loughborough College School, 22997

Loughlin, Martin: ed. Half a Century of Municipal Decline 1935–1985, 3130; Local Government in the Modern State, 3216

Loughran, Mary Malachy: Catholics in England between 1918 and 1945, 11934

Louis, Harry: The Story of Triumph Motor Cycles, 17188

Louis, William Roger: 'Great Britain and the African Peace Settlement of 1919', 12515; 'The United Kingdom and the Beginning of the Mandates System, 1919–1922', 12516; Imperialism at Bay: The United States and the Decolonization of the British Empire, 12598; ed. The Transfer of Power in Africa: Decolonization 1940–1960, 12697; Great Britain and Germany's Lost Colonies, 1914–1919, 13382; British Strategy in the Far East, 1919–1939, 13582; The British Empire in the Middle East 1945–1951: Arab Nationalism, the United States and Postwar Imperialism, 13804; ed. Mussaddiq, Iranian Nationalism and Oil, 13861; ed. The Special Relationship: Anglo-American Relations since 1945, 14084; ed. The End of the Palestine Mandate, 14342; 'British Imperialism and the Partitions of India and Palestine', 14346; 'Sir Alan Cunningham and the End of British Rule in Palestine', 14347; ed. Suez 1956: The Crisis and its Consequences, 14390

Loukes, Harold: Friends and their Children: A Study in Quaker Education, 12153; Secondary Modern, 22934

Love, Brian: Would You Care to Make a Contribution?, 9213

Love, Israel Kennett: Suez: The Twice Fought War, 14378

Love, James: Understanding the Scottish Economy, 5276

Loveday, Alexander: Britain and World Trade, 4798

Lovegrove, P.: Not Least in the Crusade: A Short History of the Royal Army Medical Corps, 15761

Lovejoy, Derek: ed. Land Use and Landscape Planning, 20278

Lovejoy, Howard: ed. The Mentally Subnormal: Social Work Approaches, 21849

Loveland, Kenneth: 'Welsh National Opera after Thirty Years', 24568

Loveless, C.: Guide to Government Data: A Survey of Unpublished Social Science Material in Libraries of Government Departments in London, 247

Lovell, Sir [Alfred Charles] Bernard: World Power Resources and Social Development, 7210; Discovering the Universe, 26400; The Explosion of Science: The Physical Universe, 26401; Meteor Astronomy, 26402; The Exploration of Outer Space, 26403; Our Present Knowledge of the Universe, 26404; ed. Astronomy, 26405;

The Origins and International Economics of Space Exploration, 26406; Man's Relation to the Universe, 26407; In the Centre of Immensities, 26408; Radio Astronomy, 26416; The Exploration of Space by Radio, 26417; 'The Effects of Defence Science on the Advance of Astronomy', 26423; 'The Early History of the Anglo-Australian 150 inch Telescope (AAT)', 26424; 'The Emergence of Radio Astronomy in the UK after World War II', 26425; The Story of Jodrell Bank, 26426; Out of the Zenith: Jodrell Bank, 1957–70, 26427; The Jodrell Bank Telescopes, 26428

Lovell, Colin Rhys: English Constitutional and Legal History: A Survey, 603

Lovell, George: The Church and Community Development, 9427

Lovell, John Christopher: 'Collective Bargaining and the Emergence of National Employer-organizations in the British Ship-Building Industry', 5799; A Short History of the T.U.C., 6703; British Trade Unions, 1875–1933, 6804

Lovell, Joyce: Discovering the Universe, 26400; The Explosion of Science: The Physical Universe, 26401

Lovell, Terry: Camera in Colditz, 15046

Lovell-Knight, A. V.: The Story of the Royal Military Police, 15763

Lovenduski, Joni: The Profession of Political Science in Britain, 26888

Lovering, John: The 'Success' of Bristol and the 'Failure' of South Wales, 5379

Lovesey, Peter: The Guide to British Track and Field Literature 1275–1968, 27143; The Official Centenary History of the Amateur Athletic Association, 27144

Lovett, Maurice: Brewing and Breweries, 20737

Lovett, Tom: Adult Education, Community Development and the Working Class, 9695, 23684

Lovins, Amory Bloch: Soft Energy Paths: Towards A Durable Peace, 7162

Low's Handbook to the Charities of London: 1969–70, 9125

Low, [Donald] Anthony: The Contraction of England, 12599; ed. Congress and the Raj. Facets of the Indian Struggle, 1917–1947, 13151

Low, Sir David [Alexander Cecil]: British Cartoonists, Caricaturists and Comic Artists, 24102; Ye Madde Designer, 24103; Low's Autobiography, 24104

Low, Rachael: The History of the British Film, 1914–1918, 24598; The History of the British Film, 24599

Low, T.: 'The Select Committee in Nationalised Industries', 6072

Lowe, Alexandra Vivien: Intervention in the Mixed Economy: The Evolution of British Industrial Policy, 1964–1972, 6111

Lowe, C. R.: An Introduction to Social Medicine, 21011; 'Incidence of Infectious Disease in the First Three Years of Life, Related to Social Circumstances', 21330

Lowe, Cedric J.: 'Britain and Italian Intervention, 1914–1915', 13372; 'The Failure of British Policy in the Balkans, 1914–1916', 13386

Lowe, Charles Ronald: An Introduction to Social Medicine, 21959

Lowe, Henry John: Plan for Rural Nottinghamshire, 5211

Lowe, J. F.: 'Competition in the U.K. Retail Petrol Market, 1960–1973, 6505

Lowe, James W.: Building Britain's Locomotives, 17065

Lowe, John: Adult Education in England and Wales: A Critical Survey, 23685

Lowe, Jonquil: Choose Your Pension: An Independent Guide to Choosing the Best Pension Scheme for You, 3982

Lowe, Peter: Britain in the Far East: A Survey from 1918 to the Present, 13575; 'Great Britain, Japan and the Fall of Yuan Shih-k'ai 1915–1916', 13586; Great Britain and the Origins of the Pacific War, 13606; 'Great Britain and the Coming of the Pacific War, 1939–1941', 13607; 'The Dilemmas of an Ambassador: Sir Robert Craigie in Tokyo, 1937–1941', 13608; The Origins of the Korean War, 16137

Lowe, Philip D.: 'The Withered "Greening" of British Politics: A Study of the Ecology Party', 1855; Countryside Conflicts: The Politics of Farming, Forestry and Conservation, 19759, 20236; 'The Royal Commission on Environmental Pollution', 20008; Environmental Groups in Politics, 20245; 'Amenity and Equality: A Review of Local Environmental Pressure Groups in Britain', 20249

Lowe, Rodney: Adjusting to Democracy: The Role of the Ministry of Labour in British Politics, 1916–1939, 836; 'Sir Horace Wilson, 1900–35: The Making of a Mandarin', 935; 'The Erosion of State Intervention in Britain, 1917–1924', 6054

Lowell, Abbott Lawrence: The British Commonwealth of Nations, 12537

Lowenthal, David: West Indian Societies, 11266; ed. West Indian Federation: Perspectives on a New Nation, 13101

Lowenthal, David: ed. Our Past before us: Why do we save it?, 20201

Lowerson, John: Trends in Leisure, 1919–1939, 26919

Lowndes, George Alfred Norman: The Silent Social Revolution: An Account of the Expansion of Public Education in England and Wales, 1895–1935, 22659; The English Educational System, 22676

Lowndes, Richard: Industrial Relations: A Contemporary Survey, 5755

Lowry, Charles W.: William Temple, an Archbishop for all Seasons, 11709

Lowry, L. S.: The Drawings of L. S. Lowry, Public and Private, 24037

Lowson, David Murray: City Lads in Borstal: A Study Based on 100 Lads Discharged to Addresses in Liverpool, 10524

Loyn, Henry Royston: ed. British Government and Administration: Studies presented to S. B. Chrimes, 708

Luard, [David] Evan [Trant]: Britain and China, 13622; ed. The Cold War: A Reappraisal, 14096

Lubbock, David: Feeding the People in Wartime, 20507

Lubin, Isador: The British Coal Dilemma, 6257; The British Attack on Unemployment, 7003

Lucas, Arthur Fletcher: Industrial Reconstruction and the Control of Competition: The British Experiments, 6138

Lucas, Audrey: E. V. Lucas, 25678

Lucas, C. J.:'Mental Health and Student Wastage', 21814

Lucas, Sir Charles Prestwood: The British Empire, 12529

Lucas, Edna Louise: Art Books: A Basic Bibliography of the Fine Arts, 23933

Lucas, Jack: Our Polluted Food: A Survey of the Risks, 20174

Lucas, James: Co-operation in Scotland, 1882

Lucas, John: Arnold Bennett: A Study of his Fiction, 25385

Lucas, Kenneth: 'The Control of Chemical Carcinogens in Britain', 20110

Lucas, P. G.: 'The Popular Press in the British General Election of 1955', 2314, 25122

Lucas, Peter: A Reporter's Look at the Development of one of Britain's Biggest New Towns, 18189

Lucas, Robert: Frieda Lawrence, 25651

Lucas, Robert F.: 'Macroeconomic Effects of Productive Public Expenditure', 4765

Lucas, Rosemary E.: Improving Industrial Relations: The Advisory Role of A.C.A.S, 4155, 5825

Lucas, Rowland: The Voice of a Nation?: A Concise Account of the BBC in Wales, 1923–1973, 2559

Lucas, W. Scott: ed. Post-war Britain 1945–1964: Themes and Perspectives, 425, 14392, 24773; 'Suez 1956: Strategy and the Diplomatic Process' 14389

Lucey, Beryl: Twenty Centuries in Sedlecombe: An East Sussex Parish, 19355

Lucie-Smith, [John McKenzie] Edward: Movements in Art since 1945, 23997; Art in Britain, 1969–1970, 23998

Luck, George Michael: Patients, Hospitals and Operational Research, 21381

Luckett, Fred: ed. A History of Brewing in Warwickshire, 20744

Luckhurst, Kenneth William: The Royal Society of Arts, 1754–1954, 23950

Lucking, John Horace: The Great Western at Weymouth: A Railway and Shipping History, 16868; Dorset Railways, 16929

Luckman, Joan: Patients, Hospitals and Operational Research, 21381

Ludlow, Peter Woods: 'Britain and Northern Europe, 1940–1945', 13884; 'Papst Pius XII, die britische Regierung und die deutsche Opposition im Winter 1939–40', 14115

Ludovici, L. J.: Fleming: Discoverer of Penicillin, 22281

Ludowyck, E. F. C.: The Modern History of Ceylon, 12983

Ludwig, Richard: ed. Letters of Ford Madox Ford, 25510

Luffingham, Raymond Laurence: A New Look at Industrial Medicine, 4129

Lufkin, A. W.: A History of Dentistry, 22401

Lukowitz, David C.: 'British Pacifists and Appeasement: The Peace Pledge Union',

13510; 'George Lansbury's Peace Missions to Hitler and Mussolini in 1937', 13511

Lulu: Lulu: Her Autobiography, 24519

Lumby, E. W. R.: The Transfer of Power in India 1945–1947, 13166; ed. Papers Relating to Naval Policy and Operations in the Mediterranean 1912–1914, 14668

Lumley, L. R.: History of the Eleventh Hussars, 1908–1934, 15663

Lumley, Roger: White-collar Unionism in Britain: A Survey of the Present Position, 6855

Lund, Paul: The War of the Landing Craft, 15406; Trawlers go to War, 15405

Lunn, Joan C. Barker: Streaming in the Primary School, 23144

Lunn, Kenneth: British Fascism: Essays on the Radical Right in Inter-War Britain, 2028; Hosts, Immigrants and Minorities, 11083; ed. Race and Labour in Twentieth Century Britain, 11084; Traditions of Intolerance: Historical Perspectives on Fascism and Race Discourse in Britain, 11205; ed. 'Regulating the Reserve Army: Arabs, Blacks and the Local State in Cardiff, 1919–1945', 11471; ed. 'The Glasgow Race Disturbances of 1919, 11487; ed. 'Race and Labour in Britain: A Bibliography', 11525

Lunn, Sir Arnold: '"A Most Passionate War": Some Reflections on a Left-Wing View of the Spanish Civil War', 13985; 'British Reactions to the Spanish Civil War', 13986

Lunt, James: Glubb Pasha, 13810; The Duke of Wellington's Regiment, 15624

Lunt, R. G.: 'The Public Schools Question', 23033

Lupton, Thomas: Wages and Salaries, 3918; Management and the Social Sciences, 5440, 8063; Industrial Behaviour and Personnel Management, 5465; On the Shop Floor: Two Studies in Workshop Organisation and Output, 5656; Job and Pay Comparisons: How to identify Similar Jobs in Different Companies and Compare their Rates of Pay, 5899

Lush, Archibald James: The Young Adult, 8415

Lusty, Margaret: The Foundations of Our Society, 7583

Lusty, Sir Robert Frith: Bound to be Read, 25000

Lutolf, Franz: Die britische Sterling und Devisenkontrolle, 4703

Luttrell, William Fownes: Factory Location and Industrial Movement: A Study of Recent Experience in Great Britain, 5052

Lutyens, Sir Edwin Landseer: A Plan for the City of Kingston upon Hull, 18881

Lutyens, Elizabeth: A Goldfish Bowl, 24360

Luvaas, Jay: The Education of an Army: British Military Thought 1815–1940, 14730

Lux, William: Historical Dictionary of the British Caribbean, 12991

Lyall, Francis: Of Presbyters and Kings: Church and State in the Law of Scotland, 12215

Lyall, Sutherland: The State of British Architecture, 23906

Lydall, Harold French: British Incomes and Savings, 3801, 4898; 'The Long-Term

Trend in the Size and Distribution of Incomes', 3802; 'The Life Cycle in Income, Saving and Asset Ownership', 3803; 'A Comparison of the Distribution of Personal Income and Wealth in the United States and Great Britain', 3804; The Structure of Earnings, 3901

Lyddon, D.: 'Workplace Organisation in the British Car Industry: A Critique of Jonathan Zeitlin', 17415

Lydiate, P. W. H.: The Law Relating to the Misuse of Drugs, 10836

Lyle, H. Willoughby: King's and Some King's Men: Being a Record of the Medical Department of King's College London from 1830–1909 and of King's College Hospital Medical School from 1909 to 1934, 20791; An Addendum, 20792

Lyman, Richard Wall: 'James Ramsay MacDonald and the Leadership of the Labour Party, 1918–1922, 1032; The First Labour Government, 1704; 'The British Labour Party: The Conflict between Socialist Ideals and Practical Politics between the Wars', 1705

Lynam, Edward William O'Flaherty: British Maps and Mapmakers, 26701; The Mapmaker's Art: Essays on the History of Maps, 26717

Lynch, Angela: The History of the Irish in Britain: A Bibliography, 11367

Lynch, Harriet: A National Survey of Attitudes to Inflation and Incomes Policy, 3830

Lynch, James: The Reform of Teacher Education in the United Kingdom, 22743

Lynch, Laurence Gerrard: The Changing Face of Ellesmere Port, 18868

Lyne, R. M.: Military Railways in Kent, 16947

Lynes, Tony Alfred: National Assistance and National Prosperity, 4036

Lynn, Richard: 'Maternal Attitudes to Child Socialization: Some Social and National Differences', 8249; The Universities and the Business Community, 9875; Personality and National Character, 21828; National Difference in Anxiety, 21829

Lynskey, James J.: 'The Role of British Backbenchers in the Modification of Government Policy', 696; 'Backbench Tactics and Parliamentary Party Structure', 697

Lyon, D.: The Steeple's Shadow, 12387

Lyon, Peter: ed. Britain and Canada: Survey of a Changing Relationship since 1945, 12654

Lyon, Robert A.: 'The Development of International Health Organizations', 20977

Lyons, Eric: '25 Years of British Architecture, 1952–1977', 23911

Lyons, Francis Stewart Leland: Ireland since the Famine: 1850 to the Present, 311, 2643; John Dillon: A Biography, 3011; Culture and Anarchy in Ireland 1890–1939, 2644

Lyons, Frank: 'Class Theory and Practice', 9447

Lyons, Nick: ed. Scotton: Aspects of Village Life, 19202

Lyons, Timothy J.: Charlie Chaplin: A Guide to References and Resources, 26301

Lyons, William: Gilbert Ryle, 26878

Lysaght, Charles Edward: Brendan Bracken, 1369

Lythe, Charlotte: The Renaissance of the Scottish Economy?, 5275

Lythe, [Samuel George] Edgar: British Economic History since 1760, 3469; An Economic History of Scotland, 1100–1939, 3470, 5270

Lyttelton, Humphrey: I Play as I Please: The Memoirs of an Old Etonian Trumpeter, 24460; Second Chorus, 24461; Take it from the Top: An Autobiographical Scrapbook, 24462

Lyttelton, Oliver, Lord Chandos: The Memoirs of Lord Chandos, 1265

Lytton, Lord: 'The Problem of Manchuria', 13597; The League, the Far East and Ourselves, 13598

Lyytinen, Eino: Finland in British Politics during the First World War, 13413.

MORI: British Public Opinion, 236

Mabey, Christine: 'The Education of Immigrant Pupils in Inner London Primary Schools', 11449; Social and Ethnic Mix in Schools and the Relationship with Attainments of Children Aged 8 and 11, 23187

Mabey, Christopher: Graduates in Industry: A Survey of Changing Graduate Attitudes, 5975

Mabey, David: In Search of Food: Traditional Eating and Drinking in Britain, 20617

Mabey, Richard: ed. Class: A Symposium, 9538; The Common Ground: A Place for Nature in Britain's Future?, 20204; The Pop Process, 24494

Mabileau, Albert: Local Politics and Participation in France and Britain, 3129

McAdoo, Henry R.: Rome and the Anglicans, 12334

Macassey, Sir Lynden Livingstone: 'The Industrial Courts Act, 1919', 5587; Labour Policy—False and True: A Study in Economic History and Industrial Economics, 5588

Macaulay, Ronald K. S.: Language, Social Class and Education: A Glasgow Study, 23851

McAllister, Elizabeth Glen and McAllister, Gilbert: ed. Homes, Towns and Countryside: A Practical Plan for Britain, 17752; ed. Town and Country Planning: A Study of Physical Environment: The Prelude to Post-war Reconstruction, 17753

McAllister, Gilbert: James Maxton: The Portrait of a Rebel, 1469, 2532

McAllister, Ian: United Kingdom Facts, 67; 'Attitudes, Issues and Labour Party Decline in England, 1974–1979', 1765, 2341; Protest and Survive: Alliance Support in the 1983 British General Election, 1842; The Nationwide Competition for Votes: The 1983 British General Election, 2346; 'The Scottish and Welsh Devolution Referenda of 1979', 2411; Bi-Confessionalism in a Confessional Party System: The Northern Ireland Alliance Party, 2817

Macalpine, Ida: Psychiatry for the Poor: 1881 Colney Hatch Asylum-Friern Hospital 1973: A Medical and Social History, 21862

Macamlaigh, Donall: An Irish Navvy: The Diary of an Exile, 11364

Mac an Beatha, Proinsias: James Connolly and the Workers Republic, 3034

Macarthur, Arthur: 'The Background to the Formation of the United Reformed Church (Presbyterian and Congregational) in England and Wales in 1972', 12052, 12338

Macarthur, Brian: Eddie Shah, Today and the Newspaper Revolution, 25107

McArthur, Colin: Scotch Reels: Scotland in Cinema and Television, 2455; Television and History, 24862

MacArthur, Ian C.: The Caledonian Steam Packet Company, 16549

MacArthur, Mary: Memoir of James Keir Hardie M.P. and Tributes to his Work, 1425

McArthur, Tom: ed. Languages of Scotland, 23847

McAvinchy, Ian D.: Unemployment and Mortality: Some Aspects of the Scottish Case 1950–1978, 7469

McBeath, Gordon: Manpower Planning and Control, 5949

McBrian, William: Stevie: A Biography of Stevie Smith, 25808

MacBriar, Alan Marne: Fabian Socialism and English Politics, 1884–1918, 2106

Mcbride, Elizabeth A.: British Command Papers: A Numerical Finding List 1962/63–1976/77, 204

MacBryde, Gwendolyn: ed. Montague Rhodes James: Letters to a Friend, 25600

McCabe, Mary Garden Morrow: Housing Improvement Policies in Scotland: A Survey of Local Authorities, 18469

McCabe, Sarah: Young Men in Detention Centres, 10517; Young Women in Detention Centres, 10592; The Hospital Order in London Magistrates' Courts, 21854

McCaffrey, John Francis: 'Roman Catholics in Scotland in the 19th and 20th Centuries', 12278

McCall, Albert William: London in 1947: The Fare and Ticket System of London Transport's Buses, Trams, Trolleybuses and Coaches, 17309; Green Line: The History of London's Country Bus Services, 17323

MacCallum Frederick Ogden: Virus and Rickettsial Diseases, 22343

McCallum, B. T.: 'Wage Rate Changes and the Excess Demand for Labour: An Attractive Formulation', 3898

McCallum, D.: 'Comparative Study in Planning: A Review Article', 17863

McCallum, Ian Robert More: A Pocket Guide to Modern Buildings in London, 23917

McCallum, Ronald Buchanan: Asquith, 971; The British General Election of 1945, 2288; 'Thoughts on the General Election', 2318; England and France, 1939–1943, 14262; Public Opinion and the Last Peace, 13431

McCallum, William: 'Problems of Inflation', 3998

McCance, Robert Alexander: Breads, White and Brown: Their Place in Thought and Social History, 20702

McCann, Eamonn: War and an Irish Town, 2857

McCann, Philip Justin: ed. Ampleforth and its Origins: Essays, 22884

MacCann, Richard Dyer: The New Film Index: A Bibliography of Magazine Articles in English, 1930–1970, 24589

McCann, Samuel D.: Pioneers in Neuroendocrinology, 22325

McCann, William Philip: Constituency Politics: a Study of Newcastle-under-Lyme, 3334; The Educational Innovators, 23096; Progressives and Radicals in English Education, 1750–1950, 23097

McCardle, Dorothy: The Irish Republic: A Documented Chronicle of the Anglo-Irish Conflict and the Partitioning of Ireland, with a Detailed Account of the Period, 1916–1923, 2698

McCarran, Margaret Patricia: Fabianism in the Political Life of Britain, 1919–1931, 2107

McCarrison, Sir Robert: Nutrition and Health . . . 1944, 20496; Studies in Deficiency Disease, 20497

McCart, Neil: 20th Century Passenger Ships of the P & O, 16533; Passenger Ships of the Orient Line, 16542

Mccarthy, Albert John: The Dance Band Era: The Dancing Decades from Ragtime to Swing, 1910–1950, 27170

McCarthy, C.: Trade Unions in Ireland, 1894–1960, 2670

McCarthy, Charles: Elements in a Theory of Industrial Relations, 5838

McCarthy, D. M. P.: Colonial Bureaucracy and Creating Underdevelopment in Tanganyika 1919–1940, 12841

MacCarthy, Fiona: Work for Married Women, 7707; Eric Gill, 24019; British Design Since 1880: A Visual History, 24115; All Things Bright and Beautiful: Design in Britain, 1830 to Today, 24140; Eye for Industry: Royal Designers for Industry 1936–1986, 24154

MacCarthy, Sir Desmond: ed. H. H. A.: Letters . . . to a Friend, 1915–1927, 971

McCarthy, William Edward John [Baron]: Disputes Procedures in Britain, 5663; The Closed Shop in Britain, 5664, 6910; The Role of Shop Stewards in British Industrial Relations: A Survey of Existing Information and Research, 5665; Industrial Relations in Britain: A Guide for Management and Unions, 5666; Management by Agreement: An Alternative to the Industrial Relations Act, 5667; Change in Trade Unions: The Development of U.K. Unions since the 1960's, 6741; Strikes in Post-War Britain: A Study of Stoppages of Work Due to Industrial Disputes, 1948–1973, 6916; 'The State Subsidy Theory of Strikes: An Examination of Statistical Data for the Period 1956–7', 6932; 'The Nature of Britain's Strike Problem', 6965

Macartney, Anne: Toynbee Hall: The First Hundred Years, 9135

McCartney, Wilfrid: Walls Have Mouths: A Record of Ten Year's Penal Servitude, 10359

MacCaughey, J. D.: Christian Obedience in the University: Studies in the Life of the

Student Christian Movement of Great Britain, 1930–1950, 11666

McCauley, Martin: The Origins of the Cold War, 14094

MacCleary, George Frederick: The Menace of British Depopulation: Today's Question, 7355; Race Suicide?, 7356; The Malthusian Population Theory, 7357; National Health Insurance, 21268; The Maternity and Child Welfare Movement, 22049; The Early History of the Infant Welfare Movement, 22050; The Development of British Maternity and Child Welfare Services, 22051

McCleery, Alistair: 'The Porpoise Press, 1930–1939', 25003

McClelland, Keith: ed. E. P. Thompson: Critical Debates, 26817

McClelland, W. G.: Studies in Retailing, 6644

McClintock, Frederick Hemming: Crimes of Violence: An Enquiry by the Cambridge Institute of Criminology, 10177; Crimes against the Person, 10178; Robbery in London: An Enquiry, 10179; Crime in England and Wales, 10180; Attendance Centres, 10591; Criminals Coming of Age: A Study of Institutional Adaptation on the Treatment of Adolescent Offenders, 10625; The Security Industry in the United Kingdom, 10883

McClintock, Marion E.: ed. The History of Lancashire County Council, 1889–1974, 3361; University of Lancaster, Quest For Innovation: A History of the First Ten Years, 1964–1974, 23508

McCloskey, Donald Nansen: Economic History, 3543; ed. Essays on a Mature Economy: Britain after 1840, 3503; ed. The Economic History of Britain since 1700, 3513, 7592; 'Productivity Change in British Pig Iron, 1870–1939', 6561

McCloy, R. J.: 'Community Colleges: Their First Fifty Years and the Corporate Ideal', 23227

McClure, J. Derrick: The Scots Language: Planning for Modern Usage, 23849

McColgan, Dorothy: William Tyndale—the Teachers' Story, 23162

McColgan, John: British Policy and Irish Administration 1920–1922, 2970

MacColl, Dugald Sutherland: Life, Work and Setting of Philip Wilson Steer, 24073

MacColl, Ewan: ed. Agit-Prop to Theatre Workshop: Political Playscripts 1930–1950, 26237; 'Grass Roots of Theatre Workshop', 26241

MacColl, René: Roger Casement: A New Judgement, 3021; Deadline and Dateline, 25260

McCollum, Elmer Verner: A History of Nutrition: The Sequence of Ideas in Nutrition Investigations, 20508

Mcconaghey, R. M. S.: 'Ernest Ward and Collective Investigations', 20978

McConville, J.: The Shipping Industry: Statistical Sources, 16520

McConville, Maureen: Philby: The Long Road to Moscow, 16052

McConville, Michael: 'The Role of Interrogation in Crime Discovery and Conviction', 10243; Confessions in Crown Court Trials, 10306; Courts, Prosecution and Conviction, 10305; Jury Trials, 10307; Negotiated Justice: Pressures to Plead Guilty, 10308; 'Juries, Foremen and Verdicts', 10309

McConville, Sean: The Use of Imprisonment: Essays in the Changing State of English Penal Policy, 10358

McCord, Norman: Strikes, 6919; North East England: An Economic and Social History, 5203, 18063

MacCordock, R. Stanley: British Far Eastern Policy, 13596

MacCormack, John Macdonald: The Flag in the Wind: The Story of the National Movement in Scotland, 2507

MacCormack, Neil: The Scottish Debate: Essays on Scottish Nationalism, 2504

McCormick, Brian Joseph: Industrial Relations in the Coal Industry, 5798; 'Managerial Unionism in the Coal Industry', 5868, 6807; 'Trade Union Reaction to Technological Change in the Construction Industry', 6789

McCormick, [George] Donald [King]; The Mask of Merlin: A Critical Study of David Lloyd George, 1018; The Unseen Killer: A Study of Suicide, its History, Causes and Cures, 10808; The Mystery of Lord Kitchener's Death, 14511; A History of the British Secret Service, 16000; The British Connection: Russia's Manipulation of British Individuals and Institutions, 16023

McCormick, James: The Doctor: Father-figure or Plumber?, 9818

McCormick, Paul: Enemies of Democracy, 1789. 'Prentice and the Newham North East Constituency: The Making of Historical Myths', 1790; 'The Labour Party: Three Unnoticed Changes", 1791

McCourt, D.: Man and his Habitat, 17976

McCrea, Alexander: ed. Irish Methodism in the Twentieth Century, 12185

McCrea, William Hunter: 'Cosmology—A Brief Review', 26436; 'The Royal Greenwich Observatory, 1675–1975: Some of its External Relations', 26446; Royal Greenwich Observatory: An Historical Review Issued on the Occasion of its Tercentenary, 26447; 'Three Hundred Years of Greenwich', 26448

McCrindle, Jean: Dutiful Daughters: Women Talk about their Lives, 7809

McCrone, David: 'Austerity and the Politics of Resistance', 3212; 'Property and Political Power: Edinburgh 1875–1975, 3374

McCrone, Robert Gavin Loudon: Scotland's Future: The Economics of Nationalism, 2505, 5263; Regional Policy in Britain, 5067; Scotland's Economic Progress, 1951–1960: A Study in Regional Accounting, 5262; The Economics of Subsidising Agriculture: A Study of British Policy, 19520

McCrum, Robert: The Story of English, 23790

McCulloch, F. J.: Land Use in an Urban Environment: A General View of Town and Country Planning, 20277

McCulloch, Gary: 'Labour, the Left and the British General Election of 1945', 1723, 2296

McCulloch, Wallace: Suicidal Behaviour, 10822

McCullough, Winifred: The Shape of Food to Come, 20606

McCurragh, D. F.: 'Britain's U.S. Dollar Problems, 1939–1945, 3719

McCutcheon, John Elliott: Troubled Scenes: The Story of a Pit and its People, 9638

McCutcheon, William Alan: The Canals of the North of Ireland, 16397

MacDermot, Edward Terence: History of the Great Western Railway, 16852

McDermott, Catherine: Street Style: British Design in the 1980s, 24117

McDermott, F. E.: ed. Self-determination in Social Work: A Collection of Essays, 8754

McDermott, Sir Geoffrey Lyster: The Eden Legacy and the Decline of British Diplomacy, 1009; A Biography of Hugh Gaitskell, 1199

McDermott, J.: 'Total War and the Merchant State: Aspects of British Economic Warfare against Germany, 1914–1916', 13418

Macdermott, Norman: Everymania: The History of the Everyman Theatre, Hampstead, 1920–1926, 26133

McDermott, Philip J.: Industrial Organisation and Location, 5820

MacDhomhnaill, Domnall Iain: Uibhist a Deas: Beagun mu Eachdraidh is mu Bheul-aithris an Eilein, 19263

MacDonagh, Giles: A Good German: Adam von Trott zu Solz, 13683

MacDonagh, Michael: The English King: a Study of the Monarchy and the Royal Family, Historical, Constitutional and Social, 434; The Irish at the Front, 15551; The Irish on the Somme, 15552; In London during the Great War: The Diary of a Journalist, 25109

MacDonagh, Oliver: Ireland: The Union and its Aftermath, 2653; States of Mind: A Study of Anglo-Irish Conflict 1780–1980, 2963

Mcdonagh, Theresa: Local Authority Housing Supply and Allocations in Greater London, 1966–1971, 18678

Macdonald, A. Craig: A History of the Motor Car Industry in Scotland, 17411

Macdonald, Barrie: Cinderellas of the Empire, 12884; The Phosphaters: A History of the British Phosphate Commissioners and the Christmas Island Phosphate Commission, 12885; Broadcasting in the United Kingdom: A Guide to Information Sources, 24717

Macdonald, Callum A.: 'Economic Appeasement and the German 'Moderates' 1937–1939: An Introductory Essay', 13687; 'Britain, France and the April Crisis of 1939', 14263; Korea: The War before Vietnam, 16141

MacDonald, Charles Brown: By Air to Battle, 15948

MacDonald, Colin M.: ed. The County of Argyll, 19222

MacDonald, D. F. N.: Practice and Procedure in the Church of Scotland, 12190

MacDonald, Donald Farquhar: The Age of

Transition: Britain in the Nineteenth and Twentieth Centuries, 336; The State and the Trade Unions, 6867

MacDonald, Donald: Lewis: A History of the Island, 19258

Macdonald, Frederick Charles: Handley Carr Glyn Moule, Bishop of Durham, 1901–20: A Biography, 11751

Mcdonald, G.: 'Metropolitan Housing Policy and the Stress Area', 18738

McDonald, G. W.: 'The Mond-Turner Talks 1927–1933: A Study in Industrial Co-operation', 5590

Macdonald, Hugh: 'Britain and the Falklands War: The Lessons of Interdependence', 16099

MacDonald, Ian Alexander: Resale Price Maintenance, 5030; Race Relations and Immigration Law, 11121; The New Immigration Law, 11122; Race Relations: The New Law, 11123; Immigration Law and Practice in the United Kingdom, 11124

MacDonald, Ian S.: ed. Anglo-American Relations since the Second World War, 14083

McDonald, Iverach: A Man of The Times: Talks and Travels in a Disrupted World, 25261

McDonald, J. F.: The Lack of Political Identity in English Regions: Evidence from MPs, 2405

MacDonald, James: 'Policy Planning Units—Ten Years On', 863

MacDonald, James Ramsay: American Speeches; At Home and Abroad: Essays; Wanderings and Excursions, 1033; Memoir of James Keir Hardie M.P. and Tributes to his Work, 1425; The Foreign Policy of the Labour Party, 13553

McDonald, Jan: What is a Citizens' Theatre?, 26170

Mcdonald, John: 'An Analysis of the Significance of Revisions to Some Quarterly U.K. National Income Time Series, 4897

McDonald, John Robert Harrison: Modern Housing: A Review of Present Housing Requirements in Scotland: A Resumé of Postwar Housing At Home and Abroad and Some Practical Suggestions For Future Housing, 18466

MacDonald, John Ronald Moreton: 'The Economic Future of the Highlands', 5294

Macdonald, K. I.: The Essex Reference Index: British Journals of Politics and Sociology 1950–1973, 84

MacDonald, Malcolm: People and Places: Random Reminiscences, 1266

McDonald, Mary Lynn: Social Class and Delinquency, 10601

MacDonald, Peter: 'The Discussion at Cambridge on the Future of Medical Practice', 21308

McDonald, S. D.: First and Foremost: 50 Years of Manchester's Civic Airports, 17693

Mcdonnell, Kevin George Thomas: A Survey of English Economic History, 3460

McDonough, R.: Only the Rivers Run Free: Northern Ireland: The Women's War, 7743

McDougall, E. H. V.: Fifth Quarter Century:

Some Chapters in the History of the Chartered Accountants of Scotland, 4178

MacDougall, Sir [George] Donald [Alistair]: Don and Mandarin: Memoirs of an Economist, 941, 26617; Studies in Economic Policy, 3414; 'Inflation in the United Kingdom', 3988; 'Britain's Foreign Trade Problem', 4791; Studies in Political Economy, 4933; 'Inter-war Population Changes in Town and Country', 7350

McDougall, R. S.: 'The Administrative Problems of Building a New Town in the United Kingdom', 18247

McDougall, W. A.: '"Mais ce n'est pas l'histoire": Some Thoughts on Toynbee, McNeill and the Rest of Us', 26823

McDougall, Walter A.: The Grenada Papers, 13084

McDowall, R. J. S.: The Whiskies of Scotland, 20726

McDowell, Colin: McDowell's Directory of Twentieth Century Fashion, 24155

McDowell, Robert Brendan: 'The Anglican Episcopate, 1780–1945', 11684; The Church of Ireland, 1869–1969, 12182

Mace, Angela: The Royal Institute of British Architects: A Guide to its Archive and History, 23866

Mace, Cecil Alec: ed. British Philosophy in the Mid-century: A Cambridge Symposium, 26834

Mace, Marjorie: ed. C. A. Mace: Selected Papers, 26853

Mace, Rodney: ed. Taking Stock: A Documentary History of the Greater London Council Supplies Department: Celebrating Seventy Five Years of working for London, 3304; Furnishing the World: The East London Furniture Trade, 1830–1980, 6480

McEachern, Doug: A Class Against Itself: Power and the Nationalisation of the British Steel Industry, 6553

MacEchern, Dugald: The Sword of the North: Highland Memories of the Great War, 15565

Mcelderry, Bruce R.: Max Beerbohm, 25943

McElwee, William Lloyd: Britain's Locust Years, 1918–1940, 299

McEntee, Girard Lindsley: Military History of the World War, 14457

McEvoy, F. J.: 'Canada, Ireland and the Commonwealth: The Declaration of the Irish Republic, 1948–9', 12658

McEwan, P. J. M.: ed. Twentieth Century Africa, 12677

McEwan, Peter: Industrial Organisations and Health, 4130

MacEwen, Anne: 'Edinburgh: An Experiment in Positive Conservation', 18867

MacEwen, Anne and MacEwen, Malcolm: Greenprints for the Countryside: National Parks: Conservation or Cosmetics, 26965; The Story of Britain's National Parks, 26966

McEwen, John Helias Finnie: Gallantry: Its Public Recognition and Reward, in Peace and in War, at Home and Abroad, 9892; The Fifth Camerons, 15579

McEwen, John M.: 'The Coupon Election of

1918 and Unionist Members of Parliament', 2278; Lloyd George's Acquisition of the Daily Chronicle in 1918', 25148

MacEwen, Malcolm: ed. Future Landscapes, 17959, 20313; Crisis in Architecture, 23904

MacFadyean, Sir Andrew: Recollected in Tranquillity, 5503

McFadyean, H.: Only the Rivers Run Free: Northern Ireland: The Women's War, 7743

McFarland, Dalton Edward: ed. Personnel Management: Selected Readings, 5467

Macfarland, Keith: The Korean War: An Annotated Bibliography, 16124

Mcfarlane, Bruce: ed. Selected Papers of Maurice Dobb, 26582

Macfarlane, Eric: Sixth-Form Colleges: The 16–19 Comprehensives, 22783

Macfarlane, Gillian: British Doctors at Home and Abroad, 20812

MacFarlane, Gwyn: Alexander Fleming: The Man and the Myth, 22282; Howard Florey: The Making of a Great Scientist, 22283

MacFarlane, Leslie John: British Politics 1918–1964, 1584; The British Communist Party: Its Origin and Development until 1929, 1916; 'Justifying Rebellion: Black and White Nationalism in Rhodesia', 12800; 'Hands off Russia: British Labour and the Russo-Polish War, 1920', 13931

Macfarlane, Marjorie: War on Disease: A History of the Lister Institute, 20902

MacFarlane, Ronald: 'The Welfare of Commonwealth Students', 11509; 'Overseas Students in British Universities 1957–1958', 11510

MacFarlane-Watt, A. K.: Southampton City Transport: A History of its Motor Bus Services, 17315; Women's War, 7743

McFarquhar, Alister: ed. Agriculture and the State: British Policy in a World Context, 19570

Mcfeely, Mary Drake: Lady Inspectors: The Campaign for a Better Workplace, 1893–1921, 4126

Macfie, A. L.: 'The British Decision Regarding the Future of Constantinople (November 1918–January 1920)', 13835

McGarry, John: 'The Anglo-Irish Agreement and Unlikely Prospects for Power-Sharing in Northern Ireland', 3002

McGarry, Robert Edgar: The Rent Acts, 18420

McGeown, Patrick: Heat the Furnace Seven Times More: An Autobiography, 9633

McGill, Barry: 'Asquith's Predicament, 1914–1918', 972

McGill, J.: Crisis on the Clyde: The Story of Upper Clyde Shipbuilders, 16622

McGivering, Ian C.: Management in Britain: A General Characterization, 5425

McGoldrick, Ann: Equal Treatment in Occupational Pension Schemes: A Research Report, 3979

McGoldrick, James: 'Industrial Relations and the Division of Labour in the Shipbuilding Industry since the War', 5831, 16637

McGovern, John: Neither Fear nor Favour, 1459

McGovern, P. D.: 'The Scottish New Towns', 18178

McGowan, H.: '1851–1951: A Century of British Industry', 7035

McGrath, John: The Game's a Bogey: 7:84's John Maclean Show, 2529

McGrath, Morag: Batley East and West: A Community Development Project Survey, 9298

McGregor, Robert Murdoch: The Work of a Family Doctor, 9819

M'Gonigle, George Cuthbert Mura: Nutrition: The Position in England Today, 20498; Poverty and Public Health, 22052

Macgregor, Alasdair B.: 'The Search for a Chemical Cure for Cancer', 20979

MacGregor, Sir Alexander Stuart Murray: Public Health in Glasgow, 1905–1946, 22062

McGregor, G. P.: Bishop Otter College: And Policy for Teacher Education, 1839–1980, 22754

McGregor, I. M.: Hillfarms: Profitability and Prospects, 19580

Macgregor, Ian Murray: The 2 Year Mass Radiography Campaign in Scotland, 1957–1958, 21966

Macgregor, Malcolm Blair: Towards Scotland's Social Good: A Hundred Years of Temperance Work in the Church of Scotland, 12220

MacGregor, Murray: A Short History of the Scottish Coal Mining Industry, 6322

McGregor, Oliver Ross, Baron: 'Equality, Sexual Values and Permissive Legislation: The English Experience', 7821; 'Social Facts and Social Conscience', 8776; Divorce in England: A Centenary Study, 9982; Separated Spouses: A Study of the Matrimonial Jurisdiction of Magistrates' Courts, 9983; Family Breakdown and Social Policy, 9984; 'The Stability of the Family in the Welfare State', 9985; 'Some Research Possibilities and Historical Materials for Family and Kinship Study in Britain', 9986

MacGregor, Susanne: Drugs and British Society: Responses to a Social Problem in the 1980's, 10839

MacGregor-Morris, John T.: The Inventor of the Valve: A Biography of Sir Ambrose Fleming, 7099

McGucken, W.: 'The Central Organisation of Scientific and Technical Advice in the United Kingdom during the Second World War', 796

McGuffin, John: The Guinea Pigs, 2865; Internment, 2866

McGuiness, Tony: Advertising and Economic Bahaviour, 4307

McGuire, Edward: The British Tariff System, 3759

McGuire, Maria: To Take Arms: A Year in the Provisional IRA, 2768

McGuire, P.: ed. The Painthouse: Words from an East End Gang, 8462

McGurk, Barry and McGurk, Rae: 'Personality Types among Prisoners and Prison Officers', 10447

Mcgurn, James: On Your Bicycle: An Illustrated History of Cycling, 17165

McGurnaghan, M.: 'Integrated Operations and Urban Renewal: The Belfast Experience, 1981–1985', 18173

McHardy, Jane: Ulster, 2924

McHenry, Dean Eugene: The Labour Party in Transition, 1720

Machie, T. T.: ed. Europe Votes I, 2377

Machin, Donald John: The Changing Structure of the British Pottery Industry, 1935–1968, 6625

Machin, Frank: The Yorkshire Miners: A History, 6903

Machin, [George] Ian [Thom]: Politics and the Churches in Great Britain 1869 to 1921, 11868

Machlup, Fritz: ed. Essays on Hayek, 26584

McIlheney, Colin: 'Law Before Violence? The Protestant Paramilitaries in Ulster Politics', 2960

McIlwain, Charles Howard: Constitutionalism and the Changing World, 606

McIlwee, Terry: Personnel Management in Context: The 1980s, 5474

McInnes, C. M.: The British Commonwealth and its Unsolved Problems, 12539; ed. Bristol and its Adjoining Counties, 18016

Macinnes, Colin: Sweet Saturday Night, 26278

McInnes, Eilidh Margaret: St Thomas's Hospital, 21451

MacInnes, John: Joint Consultation: Thatcherism at Work: Industrial Relations and Economic Change, 5855; A Critical Review of Post-war Experience in Britain, 6047

MacInnis, Edgar Wardwell: The Atlantic Triangle and the Cold War, 14070

Mcintire, C. T.: ed. Herbert Butterfield: Writings on Christianity and History, 26780

McIntosh, A.: et al. New Zealand in World Affairs, 12672

McIntosh, Ian Graham: The Face of Scotland, 5264

McIntosh, Mary: 'Vagrancy and Street Offences', 10849

McIntosh, Neil: The Right to Manage?: A Study of Leadership and Reform in Employee Relations, 5716

MacIntosh, R. W. D.: Frozen Foods: The Growth of an Industry, 20641

Macintyre, Alasdair Chalmers: Secularization and Moral Change, 12393

Macintyre, D.: 'Compensation and Remedies: The Justice Report: A Review', 17980

MacIntyre, Donald George Frederick Wyville: Jutland, 14652; The Battle of the Atlantic, 14797; The Battle for the Mediterranean, 14884; Narvik, 14917; The Kola Run: A Record of Arctic Convoys, 1941–1945, 15128; Fighting Ships and Seamen, 15288; Aircraft Carriers, 15391; Wings of Neptune: The Story of Naval Aviation, 15418

MacIntyre, Stuart: 'British Labour, Marxism and Working Class Apathy in the Nineteen Twenties', 1708; Little Moscows: Communism and Working Class Militancy in Inter-War Britain, 1951; 'Socialism, the Unions and the Labour Party after 1918', 6871

McIntyre, John: 'Current Theology: Scotland', 12237; 'The Structure of Theological Education', 11904

McIntyre, William David: The Rise and Fall of the Singapore Naval Base, 1919–42, 14687; Colonies into Commonwealth, 12473; The Commonwealth of Nations: Origins and Impact, 1869–1971, 12474

McIver, Glenys: ed. Planning: List A: Basic List for the General Library; List B: Extended List of Publications; List C: For Local Authority Planning Departments, 17963

MacIver, Robert Morrison: Society: An Introductory Analysis, 7530; The Elements of Social Science, 7890; Community: A Sociological Study, 9334

Mack, Edward Clarence: Public Schools and British Opinion since 1860, 23009

Mack, J. A.: 'Trade Union Leadership', 6766

Mack, J. E.: A Prince of Our Disorder: The Life of T. E. Lawrence, 14514

Mack, Joanna: Poor Britain, 9108

Mack, John Alexander: Police Warnings, 10557

Mack, John Anderson: Delinquency and the Changing Social Pattern, 10562; Family and Community: A Private Report to the Carnegie United Kingdom Trust arising out of a Review of Activities Concerned with Juvenile Delinquency, 10563

Mack, Robert Frederick: An Album of West Yorkshire P.T.E. Buses, 17317

Mackay, Alex: Social Indicators for Urban Sub-Areas: The Use of Administrative Records in the Paisley Community Development Project, 9280

Mackay, Ann: 'Stereotypes of Male and Female Roles and their Influence on People's attitudes to One Parent Families', 7871

McKay, C. G. R.: Samoana: A Personal Story of the Samoan Islands, 12893

McKay, Claude: A Long Way from Home: An Autobiography, 11515

Mackay, Colin H.: Kelvinside Academy 1878–1978, 23225

Mackay, David: Multiple Family Housing: From Aggregation to Integration, 18752

McKay, David H.: Housing and Race in Industrial Society: Civil Rights and Urban Policy in Britain and the United States, 11494

MacKay, Donald Iain: Scotland 1980: The Economics of Self-Government, 2483; Scotland: The Framework for Change, 2484; 'Wage Inflation and the Phillips Relationship', 3897; 'Exporters and Export Markets', 4794; British Employment Statistics: A Guide to Sources and Methods, 5911; 'Discussion of Public Works Programmes, 1917–1935: Some Remarks on the Labour Movement's Contribution', 6053; 'Engineering Earnings in Britain, 1914–68', 6382; The Political Economy of North Sea Oil, 6490; The Economic Impact of North Sea Oil on Scotland, 6526; Geographical Mobility and the Brain Drain: A Case Study of Aberdeen University Graduates, 1860–1960, 7337

MacKay, G. A.: The Political Economy of North Sea Oil, 6490

Mckay, G. S.: Old Age Pensions: An Historical and Critical Study, 4045

Mckay, John P.: Tramways and Trolleys: The Rise of Urban Mass Transport in Europe, 17203

MacKay, Johnston R.: 'The Impact of American Religion on Great Britain', 12453

Mackay, Lesley: The Changing Nature of Personnel Management, 9782

Mackay, Lydia M.: 'Curious Misunderstanding with regard to the Temperance (Scotland) Act, 22173; 'Scotland—Prohibition and Public Opinion', 22174

MacKay, Moray Sutherland: Notes on the Parish of Kilmadock and Borough of Doune, 19369

McKay, Ron: The Story of the Scottish Daily News, 25152

McKay, Roy: John Leonard Wilson, Confessor for the Faith, 11765

Mackay, Ruddock F.: Balfour: International Statesman, 980; Fisher of Kilverstone, 15256

McKean, Charles: ed. Modern Buildings in London: A Guide, 23918; Architectural Guide to Cambridge and East Anglia since 1920, 23921

McKechnie Brothers Limited: The McKechnie Story, 7200

McKechnie, James: A Short History of the Scottish Coal Mining Industry, 6322

McKee, Alexander: Caen: Vimy Ridge, 14590; The Friendless Sky: The Story of Air Combat in World War I, 14627; Strike from the Sky: The Story of the Battle of Britain, 14809; The Race for the Rhine Bridges, 14958; Anvil of History, 14959

McKee, Christine D.: Charitable Organisations, 9207

McKee, Lorna: The Father Figure, 10050

Mckee, Robert: Lloyds Bank, 4500

MacKeith, Margaret: The History and Conservation of Shopping Arcades, 20483; Shopping Arcades: A Gazetteer of Extant British Arcades 1817–1939, 23922; The History and Conservation of Shopping Arcades, 23923

McKelvie, Roy: The War in Burma, 14935

McKenna, Frank: The Railway Workers, 1840–1970, 16732

MacKenna, R. Ogilvie: Glasgow University Athletic Club: The Story of the First Hundred Years, 23500

McKenna, Stephen: Reginald McKenna, 1863–1943: A Memoir, 1267

McKennell, Aubrey Cecil: Adults and Adolescents' Smoking Habits and Attitudes: A Report on a Survey Carried out for the Ministry of Health, 21973; 'Smoking Motivation Factors', 22219

Mackenzie, A. D.: The Bank of England Note: A History of its Printing, 4720

McKenzie, A. W.: The Treatment of Enemy Property in the United Kingdom during and after the Second World War, 15170

MacKenzie, Alan J.: 'Communism in Britain: A Bibliography', 1913

Mackenzie, David: Farming in the Western Isles, 19619

Mackenzie, Donald: Statistics in Britain 1865–1930: The Social Construction of

Scientific Knowledge, 10109; 'Eugenics in Britain', 20980

Mackenzie, Sir Edward Montague Compton: The Windsor Tapestry, 476; Realms of Silver: One Hundred Years of Banking in the East, 4530; The House of Coalport, 1750–1950, 6288; Catholicism and Scotland, 12272; My Life and Times, 25689

Mackenzie, F. R.: 'Eden, Suez and the BBC—A Reassessment', 24810

Mackenzie, G.: 'The Class Situation of Manual Workers: The United States and Britain: A Review Article', 9679

Mackenzie, Gavin: ed. Social Class and the Division of Labour: Essays in Honour of Ilya Neustadt, 9548

MacKenzie, H. C.: Straight Fight: A Study of Voting Behaviour in the Constituency of Bristol North-East at the General Election of 1951, 2309; Marginal Seat: A Study of Voting Behaviour in the Constituency of Bristol North-East at the General Election of 1955, 2312

MacKenzie, Jeanne and MacKenzie, Norman: ed. The Diary of Beatrice Webb, 2151; ed. The Letters of Sidney and Beatrice Webb III. Pilgrimage 1912–1947, 2150

MacKenzie, Norman: ed. A Guide to the Social Sciences, 7936; The New Towns: The Success of Social Planning, 18222, 18987; The Time Traveller: The Life of H. G. Wells, 25871

Mackenzie, John M.: Propaganda and Empire: The Manipulation of British Public Opinion 1880–1960, 12527; ed. Imperialism and Popular Culture, 12528; ed. Popular Imperialism and the Military 1850–1950, 15443; The Railway Station: A Social History, 16792

Mackenzie, Julia: A Golden Adventure: The First Fifty Years of Ultramar, 6523

Mackenzie, Lady Leslie: 'The Social Care of the Child', 8254

McKenzie, Robert Threlford: British Political Parties: The Distribution of Power within the Conservative and Labour Parties, 1576; Angels in Marble: Working Class Conservatism in Urban England, 1616, 9685; ed. 'Parties, Pressure Groups and the British Political Process', 2067

Mackenzie, William James Millar: Central Administration in Britain, 712

Mackenzie, William Warrender [Baron Amulree]: Industrial Arbitration in Great Britain, 4151

Mckenzie-Hall, John Edwardes: Low Cost Homes to Rent or Buy: An Introduction to the Function, Formation and Operation of Housing Associations and Societies, 18548

McKeown, Thomas: The Modern Rise of Population, 7408; 'An Interpretation of the Decline of Mortality in England and Wales during the Twentieth Century', 7431; 'Fertility, Mortality and the Causes of Death', 7471; 'The Next Forty Years in Public Health', 21329; 'Incidence of Infectious Disease in the First Three Years of Life, Related to Social Circumstances', 21330; Medicine in Modern Society: Medical Planning Based on Evaluation of

Medical Achievement, 21957; An Introduction to Social Medicine, 21011, 21959

McKercher, Brian J. C.: Esmé Howard: A Diplomatic Biography, 13321; 'A Sane and Sensible Diplomacy: Austen Chamberlain, Japan and the Naval Balance of Power in the Pacific Ocean, 1924–1929', 13590; '"A Dose of Fascismo": Esmé Howard in Spain, 1919–1924', 13976; The Second Baldwin Government and the United States, 1924–1929: Attitudes and Diplomacy, 14022

Mackerness, Eric David: A Social History of English Music, 24252

MacKerrow, Gordon: The Economics of Nuclear Power, 6669

Mckersie, R. B.: Pay, Productivity and Collective Bargaining, 3940

McKibbin, Ross Ian: The Evolution of the Labour Party 1910–1924, 1700, 1881; 'The Economic Policy of the Second Labour Government, 1929–1931', 3569; 'Work and Hobbies in Britain 1880–1950', 27119; 'Working-class Gambling in Britain 1880–1939', 27119

Mackie, Albert D.: The Scotch Comedians from the Music Hall to Television, 26286

McKie, David: A Sadly Mismanaged Affair: A Political History of the Third London Airport, 17684

McKie, Eric: Venture in Faith: The Story of the Establishment of the Liverpool Family Service Unit and the Development of the Work with Problem Families, 10073

Mackie, John Duncan: A History of Scotland, 2439; The University of Glasgow, 1451–1951: A Short History. 23499

Mackie, Karl: 'Industrial Relations Law Commentary: Proposed Changes in the Law', 5809; 'Industrial Relations Law Commentary: The Employment Act 1980', 5810; 'Trends and Developments in Industrial Relations Law: The Employment Act 1988', 5811

Mackie, Lindsay: Women at Work, 7807

Mackie, Peter John: Economics and Transport Policy, 16220; 'The New Grants System for Local Transport—The First Five Years', 16295

McKie, Robert: 'Cellular Renewal: A Policy for the Older Housing Areas', 18525; Housing and the Whitehall Bulldozer: A Study of the Maintenance of Demand and a Proposal for the Cellular Renewal of Twilight Zones, 18558

Mackinder, Sir Halford John: 'Progress of Geography in the Field and in the Study during the Reign of His Majesty King George the Fifth', 26648

McKinlay, J. B.: 'Who is Really Ignorant—Physician or Patient?', 21296

McKinley, Donald Gilbert: Social Class and Family Life, 7690, 9534

MacKinnon, Kenneth M.: Language, Education and Social Processes in a Gaelic Community, 23618; 'The School in Gaelic Scotland', 23840; Some Sociological and Demographic Considerations of the Census Report for Gaelic, 23841; Language, Education and Social Processes in a Gaelic

Community, 23842; 1981 Census on Gaelic in the Highland Region, 23843; The Lion's Tongue: The Story of the Original and Continuing Language of the Scottish People, 23844; Gaelic in Scotland 1971: Scottish Opinion on Gaelic: A Report on a National Attitude Survey, 23845

Mackintosh, Athole Spalding: The Development of Firms: An Empirical Study with Special Reference to the Economic Effects of Taxation, 4985

Mackintosh, Harold Vincent: By Faith and Works: The Autobiography of the Rt. Hon. the First Viscount Mackintosh, D.L., LL.D., 20697

MacKintosh, James Macalister: Report for Scottish Department of Health: Scottish Hospitals Survey, 21471; The School and the Site: A Historical Memoir to Celebrate the Twenty-Fifth Anniversary of the [London] School [of Hygiene and Tropical Medicine.], 20903; Trends of Opinion about the Public Health, 1901–1951, 21553; The Health of Scotland, 22057; The Nation's Health, 22058; The War and Mental Health in England, 22059; Trends of Opinion About The Public Health, 1901–51, 22060; Topics in Public Health, 22061

Mackintosh, John Pitcairn: The Influence of the Backbencher, Now and a Hundred Years ago, 695; The British Cabinet, 719; ed. British Prime Ministers in the Twentieth Century, 967; The Devolution of Power, 2406; 'The Royal Commission on Local Government in Scotland 1966–1969', 3178; 'Britain in Europe: Historical Perspective and Contemporary Reality', 14155

Mackintosh, Mary: Education in Scotland Yesterday and Today, 23600

Mackintosh, Maureen: A Taste of Power: The Politics of Local Economics, 3294

Mackintosh, William Horatius: Disestablishment and Liberation: The Movement for the Separation of the Anglican Church from State Control, 12015

McKitterick, David: Despatches from Belfast, 3003

McKitterick, David: A History of the Nonesuch Press, 24981; ed. Stanley Morison and D. B. Updike: Selected Correspondence, 25029

McKnight, Allan Douglas: Environmental Pollution Control: Technical, Economic and Legal Aspects, 19998

McKnight, Gerald: Andrew Lloyd Webber, 24487

McKnight, Hugh: A Source Book of Canals: Locks and Canal Boats, 16380; The Shell Book of Inland Waterways, 16438; Waterways Postcards 1900–1930, 16439

McKusick, Victor A.: Medical Genetics 1961–1963, 22248

McLachlan, D. L.: 'Steel Pricing in a Recession: An Analysis of United Kingdom and ECSC Experience', 6559

McLachlan, Donald Harvey: Room 39: Naval Intelligence in Action 1939–1945, 15427; 'The Press and Public Opinion', 25121; In the Chair: Barrington-Ward of The Times 1927–1948, 25208

McLachlan, Gordon: ed. Patient, Doctor, Society: A Symposium of Introspection, 20833; ed. Portfolio for Health 2. The Developing Programme of the D.H.S.S. in Health Services Research , 20834; ed. Medical Education and Medical Care: A Scottish-American Symposium, 20846, 22018, 21639; Computers in the Service of Medicine: Essays on Current Research and Applications, 21228; ed. Policy for Action: Health Service Prospects: An International Survey, 21627; ed. In Low Gear?: An Examination of 'Cogwheels', 21637; ed. Measuring for Management: Quantitative Methods in Health Service Management, 21638; A Symposium on the Planning of a Comprehensive District Psychiatric Service, 21640, 21844; ed. Movements, and Directions in Health Services Research: The Papers and Proceedings of a Meeting, 21641; ed. Probes for Health: Essays from the Health Services Research Centre, University of Birmingham, 21642; ed. [Working Group for the Evaluation of the Quality of Care.]. A Question of Quality? Roads to Assurance in Medical Care: [a report by the W.G.E.Q.C.], 21643; ed. The Way Ahead in Postgraduate Medical Education: Papers by Stanley Clayton et al, 21644; ed. Bridging in Health: Reports of Studies on Health Services for Children, 21645; ed. The British National Health Service: Policy Trends and their Implication for Education, 21646; ed. By Guess or by What? Information without Design in the N.H.S., 21647; ed. Challenges for Change: Essays on the Next Decade in the National Health Service, 21648; ed. Five Years After: A Review of Health Care Research Management after Rothschild, 21649; ed. Improving the Common Weal: Aspects of Scottish Health Services, 1900–1984, 21696; ed. Approaches to Action: A Symposium on Services for the Mentally Ill and Handicapped, 21843; ed. Problems and Progress in Medical Care, 22017; ed. A Question of Quality? Roads to Assurance in Medical Care, 22033

McLachlan, Herbert: Essays and Addresses, 12113

McLaine, I.: Ministry of Morale: Home Front Morale and the Ministry of Information in World War II, 834

Maclaren, Archibald Allan: ed. Social Class in Scotland: Past and Present, 9533

Maclaren, Charles Benjamin Bright, Lord Aberconway: The Basic Industries of Great Britain: An Historic and Economic Survey, 4981

McLaren, Donald Stewart: ed. Nutrition in the Community, 20558; Nutrition and its Disorders, 20559

McLarty, Malcolm Ronald: ed. A Source Book and History of Administrative Law in Scotland by various Authors, 18483, 20359

Maclay, David Thomson: Treatment for Children: The Work of a Child Guidance Clinic, 8255

Maclay, Sir J. P.: Control and De-control of [British] Shipping, 16455

McLaughlin, Peter: Ragtime Soldiers: The Rhodesian Experience in the First World War, 14530

McLaughlin, Terence: A Diet of Tripe: The Chequered History of Food Reform, 20613

McLaurin, Allen: Virginia Woolf: The Echoes Enslaved, 25893; Virginia Woolf: The Critical Heritage, 25895

MacLean, Alisdair: Night Falls on Ardnamurchan: The Twilight of a Crofting Family, 19287

MacLean, Charles: Island on the Edge of the World: The Story of St. Kilda, 19264

Maclean, Donald: The Counter-Reformation in Scotland, 1560–1930, 12274

Maclean, Donald Duart: British Foreign Policy: The Years since Suez, 1956–1968, 13230

Mclean, Sir Francis Charles: Colour Television, 24853

McLean, Iain: 'The Rise and Fall of the Scottish National Party', 2499; Keir Hardie, 1427; The Legend of Red Clydeside, 2517

Maclean, J. D.: 'Decision-making in Juvenile Cases', 10585

McLean, John: The 1926 General Strike in North Lanarkshire, 6951

Maclean, Roderick: Television in Education, 24832

MacLean, Una: Nursing in Contemporary Society, 21724

Mcleave, Hugh: A Time to Heal: The Life of Ian Aird, the Surgeon, 20858

McLeavy, Roy: Hovercraft and Hydrofoils, 17707

McLeavy, Tony: Agricultural Change, 19607

McLellan, Jack: Larkhall: Its Historical Development, 18148

McLellan, R. S.: Anchor Line, 1856–1956, 16551

McLellan, Robert: The Isle of Arran, 19269

MacLennan, Angus: The Furrow Behind Me: The Autobiography of a Hebridean Crofter, 19283

MacLennan, Duncan: ed. Regional Policy: Past Experiences and New Directions, 5117; 'Intra-Urban Changes in Housing Prices: Glasgow 1972–83', 18477

MacLennan, Emma: Child Labour in London, 8256; Working Children, 8257

McLennan, Gregor: Crime and Society: Readings in History and Theory, 10263

MacLennan, J.: Scots of the Line, 15566

MacLennan, Malcolm Cameron: Inflation, Unemployment and the Market, 4017

Macleod, Alexander: 'London Magnet', 11380

Mcleod, Charles: 'All Change': Railway Industrial Relations in the Sixties, 5728, 16782

MacLeod, Dawn: The Gardener's London: Four Centuries of Gardening, Gardeners and Garden Usage, 19888; Oasis of the North: A Highland Garden, 19889

Mcleod, Hugh: Religion and the People of Western Europe, 1789–1970, 11559

Macleod, Iain Norman: Neville Chamberlain, 983

MacLeod, Innes: Old Galloway, 5288

Macleod, M. N.: 'The Evolution of British Cartography', 26715

McLeod, R. M.: Treasury Control and Social Administration, 810

Macleod, Robert Duncan: The Scottish Publishing Houses, 24989

MacLeod, Roderick: *ed.* The Ironside Diaries 1937–1940, 14763

MacLeod, Roy: *ed.* Government and Expertise: Specialists, Administrators and Professionals 1860–1919, 799

Mackley, Tom: Towards the Dawn: The Revolution in Rural England, 19054

Macklin, Keith: The Story of Rugby League, 27053

McLoughlin, James: Law and Practice Relating to Pollution Control in the United Kingdom, 20001; The Law Relating to Pollution: An Introduction, 20002

MacLoughlin, [John] Brian: *ed.* Education for Planning: The Development of Knowledge and Capability for Urban Governance: Progress in Planning, 17837; Control and Urban Planning, 17838; Urban and Regional Planning: A Systems Approach, 17839; Aspects of Urban Management, 17854

Maclure, John Stuart: Educational Documents: England and Wales, 1816–1963, 22604; One Hundred Years of London Education, 1870–1970, 23230; 'Who Killed Cock Robbins?', 23413

McMahon, Christopher William: Sterling in the Sixties, 4706

McMahon, Deirdre: Republicans and Imperialists: Anglo-Irish Relations in the 1930's, 2985; 'A Transient Apparition: British Policy towards the De Valera Government 1932–1935', 2986

MacMahon, H. Edward: 'Malignant Nephrosclerosis—50 Years Later', 20983

MacManus, Francis: *ed.* The Years of the Great Test, 2687

McManus, J. I. F. A.: The Fundamental Ideas of Medicine: A Brief History of Medicine, 21209

McMaster, John McGregor: Towards an Educational Theory for the Mentally Handicapped, 21853

MacMeeken, A. M.: The Intelligence of a Representative Group of Scottish Children, 23588; The Intelligence of Scottish Children: a National Survey of an Age Group, 23589; The Trend of Scottish Intelligence: a Comparison of the 1947 and 1932 Surveys of the Intelligence of ll-Year-Old Pupils, 23590; Social Implications of the 1947 Scottish Mental Survey, 23591; Educational and Other Aspects of the 1947 Scottish Mental Survey, 23592; Gaelic-Speaking Children in Highland Schools, 23611

McMenemy, William Henry: A History of the Worcester Royal Infirmary, 21470

MacMichael, Sir Harold: The Sudan, 14421; Sudan Political Service, 1899–1956, 14422

McMichael, Sir John: 'The Contributions of Clinical Medicine to Physiology', 20984

McMichael, Joan Catherine: Handicap: A Study of Physically Handicapped Children and Their Families, 21908

McMicking, Neil: Officers of the Black Watch, 1752–1952, 15574

Macmillan, Brenda: Managers on the Move: A Study of British Managerial Mobility, 7277

Macmillan, Harold [Earl of Stockton]: The Past Masters: Politics and Politicians, 1906–1939, 968; Memoirs, 1039; Winds of Change, 1914–1939, 1040; The Blast of War, 1939–1945, 1041; Tides of Fortune, 1945–1955, 1042; Riding the Storm, 1956–1959, 1043; Pointing the Way, 1959–1961, 1044; At the End of the Day, 1961–1963, 1045; War Diaries: The Mediterranean, 1943–45, 1046; Economic Aspects of Defence, 1047; Reconstruction: A Plea for National Policy, 1047; The Middle Way: A Study of the Problem of Economic and Social Progress in a Free and Democratic Society, 1047, 3601; The Next Five Years, 1047

MacMillan, Keith: Business and Society: Tradition and Change, 5449

MacMillan, Norman: Offensive Patrol: The Story of the RNAS, RFC and RAF in Italy, 1917–1918, 14622; The Royal Air Force in the World War, 14977; Tales of Two Air Wars, 14978

MacMillan, W. M.: The Road to Self-Rule: A Study in Colonial Evolution, 13006

MacMorland, B.: An ABC of Services and General Information for Disabled People, 21904

MacMunn, George: Egypt and Palestine, 14493

McMullan, John T.: Energy Resources and Supply, 7217

McMurtrie, Francis Edwin: Modern Naval Strategy, 15339

MacNab, P. A.: The Isle of Mull, 19273

McNab, Thomas: The Guide to British Track and Field Literature 1275–1968, 27143

McNair, Henry S.: A Survey of Children in Residential Schools for the Maladjusted in Scotland, 8258

McNair, John: James Maxton: The Beloved Rebel, 1470, 2533

McNally, Fiona: Women for Hire: A Study of the Female Office Worker, 7717

MacNalty, Sir Arthur Salusbury: Eyes in Industry: A Complete Book on Eyesight Written for Industrial Workers, 4120; 'Some Pioneers of the Past in Neurology', 20982; 'The Prevention of Smallpox: From Edward Jenner to Monckton Copeman', 20985; A Report on Tuberculosis, 21154; The History of State Medicine in England, 21552; *gen. ed.* History of the Second World War, 22117; *gen. ed.* The Civilian Health and Medical Services, 22118; *ed.* Medical Services in War: The Principal Medical Lessons of the Second World War, 22119; *ed.* 'Health and the Family', 22120

McNay, Marie: Low Pay and Family Poverty, 3965

McNeal, Julia: Colour, Citizenship and British Society, 10993

McNee, Gerry: The Story of Celtic: An Official History, 27090

McNeil, John: 'The Fife Coal Industry, 1947–1967: A Study of Changing Trends and their Implications', 6344

McNeill, Donald R.: The Fight to Fluoridation, 22394

MacNeill, Duncan: The Scottish Realm: An Approach to the Political and Constitutional History of Scotland, 2445

MacNeill, Eoin: Celtic Ireland, 2425

MacNicol, John: The Movement for Family Allowances, 1918–1945: A Study in Social Policy Development, 4091, 8845

McNeill, John Gordon Swift: What I have Seen and Heard, 1462

MacNeill, Kate: Britain Can't Afford Low Pay, 3967

McNeill, Ronald [Baron Cushendun]: Ulster's Stand for Union, 2911; The Irish Boundary Question, 2912

McNeill, William Hardy: America, Britain and Russia, their Cooperation and Conflict, 1941–1946, 14046; Plagues and People, 22387; Arnold J. Toynbee: A Life, 26819

McNeilly, Norman: Exactly Fifty Years: The Belfast Education Authority and its Work, 1923–1973, 23638

McNicoll, Iain Hugh: North Sea Oil and Scotland's Economic Prospects, 6530, 7170

McNulty, Anne: Directory of British Oral History Collections, 222

MacNutt, Frederick Brodie: Theodore, Bishop of Winchester, 11771

MacPhail, Sir Andrew: The Bible in Scotland, 11918

MacPhail, Angus Norman: Hospital and Community, 21387; Health Visiting in the Sixties, 21733

Macphee, Marshall: Kenya, 12823

McPherson, Andrew F.: 'Competing Inequalities: The Sex and Social Class Structure of the First Year Scottish Student Population, 1962–1972', 22566; Reconstructions of Secondary Education: Theory, Myth and Practice since the War, 22930; The Scottish Sixth: a Sociological Evaluation of Sixth Year Studies and the Changing Relationship Between School and University in Scotland, 23617

McPherson, Don: *ed.* Traditions of Independence: British Cinema in the Thirties, 24618

MacPherson, Fergus: Anatomy of a Conquest: The British Occupation of Zambia, 1884–1924, 12777; 'Future of East Africa 1939–1948: A Case Study of the "Official Mind of Imperialism"', 12816

MacPherson, Hector: Modern Astronomy: Its Rise and Progress, 26370; A Historical Sketch of Researches and Theories Concerning the Structure of the Universe, 26435

MacPherson, John S.: Eleven-Year-Olds Grow Up: A Seven Year Follow Up of a Representative Sample from the 1947 Scottish Mental Survey, 23595

McQuail, Denis: 'Elite Education and Political Values', 23427; Television and the Political Image: A Study of the Impact of Television on the 1959 General Election, 24887; Television in Politics: Its Uses and Influence, 24891

Macquarrie, John: Christian Unity and Christian Diversity, 12343

Macqueen-Pope, Walter James: The Footlights Flickered, 25925; Ivor: The Story of An Achievement, 26076; The Melodies Linger on: The Story of Music Hall, 26275

Macrae, Donald Gunn: 'Social Theory: Retrospect and Prospect', 7962; 'Morris Ginsberg: Five Memorial Addresses', 8006; 'Morris Ginsberg, MA, D.Litt, and F.B.A, 1889–1970', 8007; 'Social Stratification: A Trend: Report and Bibliography', 9518; Ideology and Society: Papers in Sociology and Politics, 9519

McRae, Hamish: Capital City: London as a Financial Centre, 4245

Macrae, Norman Alistair Duncan: Sunshades in October: An Analysis of the Main Mistakes in British Economic Policy since the mid-1950's, 3631

Macrae, Robert Stuart: Winston Churchill's Toyshop, 7063

McRae, Thomas Watson: North Sea Oil: Mecca or Mirage?, 7175; The Impact of Computers on Accounting, 7085

McRoberts, David: ed. Modern Scottish Catholicism, 1878–1978, 12269

Macrosty, Henry W.: 'The Overseas Trade of the United Kingdom, 1930–1939', 4789

Macksey, Kenneth: Invasion: The German Invasion of England, July 1940, 14847; Crucible of Power, 14898; Tank Force: Allied Armour in the World War, 15527; A History of the Royal Armoured Corps, 1914–1975, 15600; The Tanks: A History of the Royal Tank Regiment, 1945–1975, 15736

McShane, Frank: The Life and Work of Ford Madox Ford, 25514; ed. Madox Ford: The Critical Heritage, 25515

McShane, Harry: No Mean Fighter, 1950

MacStiofain, Sean: Memoirs of a Revolutionary, 2771

McTague, J. J.: 'Zionist-British Negotiations over the Draft Mandate for Palestine, 1920', 14293

McVeagh, Diane M.: Twentieth Century English Masters: Elgar, Delius, Vaughan Williams, Holst, Walton, Tippett, 24291; Edward Elgar: His Life and Music, 24337

McVey, Frank Lerond: The Financial History of Great Britain, 1914–1918, 4547

McWhinnie, Alexina Mary: Adopted Children: How They Grow Up: A Study of their Adjustment as Adults, 8259

McWhirter, Alan Ross: Centenary History of the Rugby Football Union, 27038

Macwhirter, Archibald: 'Unitarianism in Scotland', 12262

McWhirter, Jackie: William Tyndale—the Teachers' Story, 23162

McWilliam, Colin: Scottish Townscape, 18904

Macwilliam, Henry Herbert: Memories of Walton Hospital, Liverpool, 21429

McWilliams, William: 'The Mission Transformed: Professionalisation of Probation between the Wars', 10497

McWilliams-Tullberg, Rita: Women at Cambridge: A Men's University—Though of a Mixed Type, 9888, 23470

Madan, Raj: Coloured Minorities in Great Britain: A Comprehensive Bibliography, 11522

Madden, Albert Frederick: Essays in Imperial Government Presented to Margery Perham, 12488, 12684; Oxford and the Idea of the Commonwealth: Essays presented to Sir Edgar Williams, 12489; ed. Australia and Britain: Studies in Changing Relationships, 12608

Maddick, H.: 'Conventions of Local Authorities in the West Midlands', 3323

Maddison, R. E.: An Enquiry into Teacher Training, 22732

Maddock, Rowland Thomas: The Growth of the British Economy 1918–1968, 3458

Maddox, H.: 'The Assimilation of Negroes in a Dockland Area in Britain', 11247; 'The Work and Status of Mental Nurses', 21297

Maddox, John: Beyond the Energy Crisis, 7214

Maddox, William Percy: Foreign Relations in British Labour Politics, 1900–1924, 13555

Maddren, Nicholas: The City at War, 15164

Madge, Charles Henry: Industry after the War, 4982; ed. May the Twelfth [Mass Observation Day Surveys 1937], 7570; Society in the Mind: Elements of Social Eidos, 7910; The War-time Pattern of Saving and Spending, 20428; Mass Observation: The Press and its Readers, 25043; ed. The Press and its Readers, 25078

Madge, John Hylton: The Tools of Social Science, 7902; The Origins of Scientific Sociology, 7903; Workbook for 'People in Towns': A Course of Twenty Radio Programmes on Urban Sociology, 7904; 'Obituary John Madge (1914–1968)', 7905; Human Factors in Housing, 18632; The Rehousing of Britain, 18633; ed. Tomorrow's Houses and Building Methods, Structures and Materials, 18634; Housing Estates: A Study of Bristol Corporation Policy and Practice between the Wars, 18635; Citizenship and Television, 24890

Madge, Nic: Racial Discrimination: NCCL's Comments on the White Paper, 11183

Madge, Nicola: Cycles of Disadvantage: A Review of Research, 8344

Madge, Robin: Somerset Railways, 16973

Madge, Tim: Beyond the BBC, 24784

Madgwick, Peter Jones: Britain since 1945, 387; Government by Consultation: The Case of Wales, 2572; and Griffiths, Non: The Politics of Rural Wales: A Study of Cardiganshire, 2573; 'Gentlemen Versus Players', 23390

Madigan, Ruth: Slum Clearance: The Social and Administrative Context in England and Wales, 18410

Maegraith, B. G.: 'History of the Liverpool School of Tropical Medicine', 20986

Maehl, William H.: '"Jerusalem Deferred": Recent Writings in the History of the British Labour Movement', 1665

Magee, Bryan Edgar: Towards 2000: The World We Make, 376; One in Twenty: A Study of Homosexuality in Men and Women, 10861; The Television Interviewer, 24903; ed. Modern British Philosophy, 26839; ed. Modern British Philosophy, 26840; Popper, 26856

Magee, John: ed. Northern Ireland: Crisis and Conflict, 2877

Maggs, Colin Gordon: Railways of the Cotswolds, 16928; Bath Tramways, 17212

Magner, Lois N.: A History of the Life Sciences, 26524

Magnus, R. V.: 'Population Trends in a Mental Hospital', 21777

Magnusson, Magnus: The Clacken and the Slate: The Story of the Edinburgh Academy, 1824–1974, 23220

Magnusson, Mamie: A Length of Days: The Scottish Mutual Assurance Society 1883–1983, 4240

Magowan, Vivienne: Northern Ireland, 1968–1974: A Chronology of Events, 2819

Maguire, Eric: Dieppe, August 19, 14826

Maguire, Maria: A Bibliography of Published Works on Irish Foreign Relations, 1921–1978, 2678

Mahmoud-Harris, Mariyam: World Religions in Britain: A Series of Study Pamphlets designed to help the Ordinary Reader's Understanding of some Non-Christian Faiths Practised in Britain, 12456

Mahon, David: No Place in the Country: A Report on Second Homes in England and Wales, 18371

Mahon, John: Harry Pollitt: A Biography, 1947

Mahoney, Patrick: Battleship: The Loss of the Prince of Wales and the Repulse, 15021

Maine, Basil Stephen: Edward VIII: Duke of Windsor, 481; Our Ambassador King: King Edward VIII's Life of Devotion and Service as Prince of Wales, 482; Elgar, his Life and Works, 24332; The Best of Me: A Study in Autobiography, 24535

Mainwaring, Lynn: The Welsh Economy, 3475; ed. The Welsh Economy, 2587

Mair, Alex: Sir James MacKenzie, M.D. 1853–1925: General Practitioner, 20870

Mair, Carlene: The Chappell Story 1811–1961, 24954

Mair, John: Four Power Control in Germany and Austria 1945–1946, 14190

Mair, Lucy: Anthropology and Social Change, 10997

Mair, Peter: 'The Marxist Left', 2003; The Break-up of the United Kingdom: The Irish Experience of Regional Change 1918–1949, 2667; 'Labour and the Irish Party System Revisited: Party Competition in the 1920s', 2695

Mair, Philip Beveridge: 'Shared Enthusiasm': William Beveridge, 1357, 9043

Maire Ni Bhrolchain: 'Period Parity Progression Ratios and Birth Intervals in England and Wales 1941–1971: A Synthetic Life Table Analysis', 7525

Mairet, Philip [pe] August: Pioneer of Sociology: The Life and Letters of Patrick Geddes, 8073; John Middleton Murry, 25734

Maisel, A. Q.: The Hormone Quest, 22324

Maitland, [George Baker] Christopher: Dr Leslie Weatherhead of the City Temple, 12088

Maitron, Jean: ed. Dictionnaire Biographique du Mouvement Ouvrier International: Grande Bretagne, 46

Maizels, Joan: Social Workers and Volunteers, 9212

Majdalany, Fred: The Battle of El Alamein, 14899

Major, Henry Dewsbury Alves: English Modernism: Its Origins, Methods, Aims, 11878

Major, Ralph H.: 'Note on the History of Asthma', 21186; A History of Medicine, 21185

Major, Robin L.: 'The Competitiveness of British Exports since Devaluation', 4784; ed. Britain's Trade and Exchange Rate Policy, 4785

Major, Sandra: The University in an Urban Environment, 23304

Majumdar, Madhavi: The Renaissance of the Scottish Economy?, 5275

Majumdar, Robin: Virginia Woolf: The Critical Heritage, 25895

Makar, Ragai N.: Egypt, 14393

Makepeace, Chris: The Manchester Ship Canal: A Short History, 16410

Makin, Frank Bradshaw: The London Money Market, 4277

Malaysia: Agreement Concluded between the United Kingdom of Great Britain and Northern Ireland, the Federation of Malaya, North Borneo, Sarawak and Singapore, 12935

Malcolm, Charles Alexander: The British Linen Bank, 1746–1946, 4514; The Bank of Scotland 1695–1945, 4515

Malcolm, G. I.: Argyllshire Highlanders, 1860–1960, 15567; The Argylls in Korea, 16126

Malcolm, Norman: Ludwig Wittgenstein: A Memoir, 26887

Malcolm, Thomas: Civil Engineering in Queen's, 1845–1963, 23458

Malcolm, William R.: A Blasphemer and Reformer: A Study of James Leslie Mitchell/Lewis Grassic Gibbon, 25537

Malden, Richard Henry: The English Church and Nation, 11572

Male, George A.: The Struggle for Power: Who Controls the Schools in England and the United States?, 22795

Malet, Hugh: Coal, Cotton and Canals: Three Studies in Local Canal History, 16419

Malik, Michael Abdul: From Michael de Freitas to Michael X, 10968

Malik, Rex: What's Wrong with British Industry?, 3641

Malin, Nigel: ed. Reassessing Community Care (with particular reference to provision for people with mental handicap and for people with mental illness), 21783; Services for the Mentally Handicapped in Britain, 21787, 21925

Malin, S. R. C.: 'British World Magnetic Charts', 7134

Maliphant, Rodney: 'Delinquent Areas in the County of London: Ecological Factors', 10641

Mallaber, K. A.: 'The Sale Catalogues of British Government Publications 1836 to 1965', 182

Mallaby, Sir George: Each in his Office: Studies of Men in Power, 326; 'The Civil Service Commission: Its Place in the Machinery of Government', 877; From My Level, 938

Mallalieu, William C.: British Reconstruction and American Policy 1945–1955, 3714, 14089

Mallander, Jacqueline: Incomes In and Out of Work 1978–1982, 3861

Mallen, D.: Local Government and Politics, 3146

Malleson, Andrew: Need your Doctor be so Useless?, 20835

Mallet, Sir Bernard: British Budgets, 4902; 'The Effects of the War as Shown in Vital Statistics', 21300

Mallon, Thomas: Edmund Blunden, 25399

Mally, Gerhard: Britain and European Unity, 14164

Malmgreen, Gail: ed. Religion in the Lives of English Women, 1760–1930, 11673

Malpass, Peter: Housing Policy and Practice, 18453

Malta Round Table Conference 1955: Report, 12858

Maltby, Arthur: The Government of Northern Ireland, 1922–1972: A Catalogue and Breviate of Parliamentary Papers, 206, 2779

Maltby, D.: Transport in the United Kingdom, 16196

Malvern: A History of Malvern College, 1865 to 1965, 23065

Mamdani, Mahmood: From Citizen to Refugee: Ugandan Asians Come to Britain, 11229

Management Consultants' Association: The G.P.: A Report Prepared for the General Practitioners' Association, 21531, 21586

Manchester Area Council for Clean Air and Noise Control: 25 Year Review: A Review of some Aspects of Air Pollution and Noise Control in the Area of the Council 25 Years after the Clean Air Act, 1956, 20060

Manchester University Settlement: Survey Committee. Ancoats: A Study of a Clearance Area, 18056; Some Social Aspects of Pre-War Tenements and Post-War Flats, 18598

Manchester, Phyllis Winifred: Vic-Wells: A Ballet Progress, 24246

Manchester, William: The Last Lion: Winston Spencer Churchill: Visions of Glory, 1874–1932, 988

Manchester: A Review of the Manchester Housing Schemes Built under the Various Housing and Planning Acts in Operation during 1919–1933, 18599

Manchester: The Manchester Grammar School, 1515–1965, 22998

Mandelbaum, Seymour J.: H. J. Dyos and British Urban History, 26766

Mandelker, Daniel Robert: Green Belts and Urban Growth: English Town and Country Planning in Action, 17791

Mander, John Geoffrey Gryles: Great Britain or Little England?, 13229; Old Bottles and New Wine: A Talk about Secondary Modern Schools, 22937

Mander, Raymond: British Music Hall: A Story in Pictures, 26277

Manderson-Jones, Ronald Brandis: The Special Relationship: Anglo-American Relations and Western Unity, 1947–1956, 14069

Mandle, William Frederick: Anti-Semitism and the British Union of Fascists, 2022, 11337; 'The Leadership of the British Union of Fascists', 2033; 'Sir Oswald Mosley's Resignation from the Labour Government', 2034

Mangan, J. Anthony: ed. From 'Fair Sex' to Feminism: Sport and the Socialisation of Women in the Industrial and Post-Industrial Eras, 7648; ed. Physical Education and Sport: Sociological and Cultural Perspectives, 27026

Mangold, G.: 'Social Aspects of the British National Health Service', 21337

Manion, Lawrence: ed. Educational Research and Development in Britain 1970–1980, 22842

Manley, Douglas: The West Indian in Britain, 11242

Mann, D. J.: 'Education for Management', 23659

Mann, Jean: Woman in Parliament, 1463; 'Warehousing the People: Deprecating the Present Tendency to build Tenement Flats', 18638

Mann, Michael: Consciousness and Action among the Western Working Class, 9693

Mann, Pamela: Children in Care Revisited, 8250

Mann, Peter Henry: An Approach to Urban Sociology, 8060, 18277; An Approach to Methods of Sociological Enquiry, 18278; Students and Books, 22567; Growth at Redbrick: A Case Study of Sheffield University, 23580

Mann, Sir John: Can the 'Undesirable Tenant' be Trained in Citizenship?, 18589

Manne, Robert: 'The British Decision for Alliance with Russia, May 1939', 13949; 'The Foreign Office and the Failure of Anglo-Soviet Rapprochement', 13950; 'Some British Light on the Nazi-Soviet Pact', 13951

Manners, Elizabeth: The Vulnerable Generation, 8479

Manners, G.: Coal in Britain, 6249

Manners, Gerald: ed. Spatial Policy Problems of the British Economy, 5077; Regional Development in Britain, 5085; ed. South Wales in the Sixties: Studies in Industrial Geography, 5373; The Tinplate and Steel Industries in South West Wales', 6556

Mannheim, Hermann: Social Aspects of Crime in England between the Wars, 10134; Group Problems in Crime and Punishment and other Studies in Criminology and Criminal Law, 10135; Comparative Criminology, 10136; Young Offenders: An Enquiry into Juvenile Delinquency, 10549; Juvenile Delinquency in an English Middletown, 10551; Prediction Methods in Relation to Borstal Training, 10552

Mannheim, Karl: Man and Society in an Age of Reconstruction: Studies in Modern Social Structure. With a Bibliographical Guide to the Study of Modern Society, 7573; Systematic Sociology: An Introduction to the Study of Society, 7963

Mannin, Ethel: Brief Voice, 25693

Manning, Dame Elizabeth Leah: A Life for Education, 1464, 1465

Manning, Nick: Social Problems and Welfare Ideology, 8966

Manning, Peter Kirby: Police Work: The Social Organisation of Policing, 10707

Manning, Phyllis: A History of the National Investigation into the Economics of Milk Production, 1934–1951, 20657

Manning, Rosemary: From Holst to Britten, 24269

Manning, Thomas David: The British Destroyer, 15383

Mansbridge, Albert: Edward Stuart Talbot and Charles Gore, 11734; Fellow Men: a Gallery of England, 1876–1946, 23679

Mansel, John: The Mansel Diaries: The Diaries of Captain John Mansel, P.O.W., and Camp Forger in Germany, 1940–45, 15042

Mansell, Gerard Evelyn Herbert: Broadcasting to the World: Forty Years of BBC External Services, 24814; Let Truth be Told: 50 Years of BBC External Broadcasting, 24815

Manser, Roy: The Household Cavalry Regiment, 15654

Manser, Wiliam Arthur Peete: Britain in Balance, 3664

Mansergh, [Philip] Nicholas [Seton]: Advisory Bodies: A Study of their Uses in Relation to Central Government, 1919–1939, 690; The Prelude to Partition: Concepts and Aims in Ireland and India, 2689; The Government of Northern Ireland: A Study in Devolution, 2801; The Irish Question, 1840–1921: A Commentary on Anglo-Irish Relations . . . 1940, 2990; 'Britain and the Dominions: Consultation and Cooperation in Foreign Policy', 12518; Survey of British Commonwealth Affairs: Problems of Wartime Co-operation and Postwar Change, 1939–1952, 12575; ed. Documents and Speeches on British Commonwealth Affairs: Problems of External Policy, 1931–1939, 12576; Constitutional Relations between Britain and India: The Transfer of Power, 1942–1947, 13160

Mansfield, Alan: Ceremonial Costume: Court, Civil and Civic Costume from 1660 to the Present Day, 458; Handbook of English Costume in the Twentieth Century 1900–1950, 24158

Mansfield, Frederick J.: 'Gentlemen, the Press!': Chronicles of a Crusade, 25314

Mansfield, Norman: Failure of the Left, 1919–1939, 1711

Mansfield, Peter: Chemical Children: How to Protect your Family from Harmful Pollutants, 20176

Mansfield, Peter: The British in Egypt, 14400

Manson-Bahr, Sir Philip Heinrich: Patrick Manson: The Father of Tropical Medicine, 22385; 'The Malaria Story', 22386; A History of the School of Tropical Medicine in London, 1899–1949, 22475

Mant, Alistair: The Rise and Fall of the British Manager, 5450, 9794

Mantle, Jonathan: In for a Penny: The Unauthorised Biography of Jeffrey Archer, 1342

Manton, Irene: 'Recollections in the History of Electron Microscopy', 20987

Mantoux, Etienne: The Carthaginian Peace: Or the Economic Consequences of Mr. Keynes, 26594

Manvell, Roger Arnold: The History of the British Film, 24599; Film, 24603; The Film and the Public, 24604; New Cinema in Britain, 24658; 'John Grierson', 24673; comps. The Progress of Television: An Anglo-American Survey, 24855

Manwaring, Randle: The Heart of this People: An Outline of the Protestant Tradition in England since 1900, 11656; From Controversy to Co-Existence: Evangelicals in the Church of England 1914–1980, 11659

Manwaring-White, Sarah: The Policing Revolution: Police Technology, Democracy and Liberty, 10712

Manzer, Ronald Alexander: Teachers and Politics: The Role of the National Union of Teachers in the Making of National Education Policy in England and Wales since 1944, 9839, 22710

Map, Kurt: The British Economy and the Working Class 1946–1958: An Analysis of Post War Capitalism, 9626

Mapes, Roy E. A.: The Sociology of Planning: A Study of Social Activity on New Housing Estates, 9367; 'The Development of Certain Social Variables in an English Rural Context', 19107

March, Edgar J.: British Destroyers: A History of Development, 1892–1953, 15039, 15384

March, Lionel: ed. Urban Space and Structures, 17831

March, Norah Helena: 'Eugenic Aspects of National Baby Week', 8251; Towards Racial Health: A Handbook on the Training of Boys and Girls, 8260

Marcham, Anthony James: Foreign Policy, 13237

Marcham, Frederick George: ed. Sources of English Constitutional History, 595; A Constitutional History of Modern England, 1485 to the Present, 602

Marchant, Sir James: ed. Medical Views on Birth Control, 9929; ed. Post War Britain, 384, 17746; ed. Rebuilding Family Life in the Postwar World: An Enquiry with Recommendations, 10021

Marchington, Mick: Joint Consultation Revisited, 6048

Marcus, H. G.: Ethiopia, Great Britain and the United States 1941–1974: The Politics of Empire, 14058

Marder, Arthur Jacob: 'The Royal Navy and the Ethiopian Crisis of 1935–1936', 13792; From the Dreadnought to Scapa Flow: The Royal Navy in the Fisher Era, 1904–1919, 14669; From the Dardanelles to Oran: Studies of the Royal Navy in War and Peace, 1915–1940, 14670; Old Friends, New Enemies: The Royal Navy and the Imperial Japanese Navy, 1936–41, 14689; Operation 'Menace': The Dakar Expedition and the Dudley North Affair, 14820; ed. Fear God

and Dread Nought: The Correspondence of Admiral of the Fleet Lord Fisher of Kilverstone, 15253; Portrait of an Admiral: The Life and Papers of Sir Herbert Richmond, 15278

Mardh, Ingrid: Headlinese: On the Grammar of English Front Page Headlines, 25346

Marengo, Franco Damaso: The Code of British Trade Union Behaviour, 6717

Margerison, Tom: The Explosion of Science: The Physical Universe, 26401

Margolis, Karen: The Technology of Police Control, 10733

Margolis, Michael: Political Stratification and Democracy, 3375

Marin, U.: Italiani in Gran Bretagna, 11386

Mariner, G.: Spatial Policy Problems of the British Economy, 17821

Maritime Librarian's Association: Marine Transport: A Guide to Libraries and Sources of Information in Great Britain, 16454

Marjoribanks, Edward: The Life of Edward Carson, 1135

Mark, John: 'Change in the Brewing Industry in the Twentieth Century', 6154

Mark, Sir Robert: Policing a Perplexed Society, 10714; In the Office of Constable, 10715

Marke, Ernest: Old Man Trouble, 11513

Markham, Clements R.: The Lands of Silence: A History of Arctic and Antarctic Exploration, 27209

Markham, Richard: Location of Industry in Hertfordshire: Planning and Industry in the Post-war Period, 5159

Marks, Hilary F.: 100 Years of British Food and Farming: A Statistical Survey, 19396

Marks, John: Rape of Reason: The Corruption of the Polytechnic of North London, 9866

Marks, Jonathan: British Shipping: The Right Course, 16463

Marks, P.: 'Twentieth Century Trends in the Work of Women in England and Wales', 7774

Marks, Richard: Burrell: A Portrait of a Collector: Sir William Burrell 1861–1958, 23949

Marks, Sally: The Illusion of Peace: International Relations in Europe, 1918–1973, 13644; 'Ménage à Trois: The Negotiations for an Anglo-French-Belgian Alliance in 1922', 14248

Marks, Winifred Rose: Politics and Personnel Management: An Outline History, 1960–1976, 5470

Marland, Michael: ed. Sex Differentiation and Schooling, 23095

Marlborough: Marlborough College, 1843–1943, 23066

Marley, Felix: Unemployment Relief in Great Britain: A Study in State Socialism, 4022

Marley, Joan G.: 'Changes in Salaries in Great Britain, 1924–1939', 3869

Marlow, Barbara: Charting the British Economy, 3660

Marlowe, Derek: Nancy Astor: The Lady from Virginia, 1348

Marlowe, John: Milner: Apostle of Empire: A Life of Alfred George, the Right

Honourable Viscount Milner . . . 1854–1925, 1274; The Life of Sir Arnold Talbot Wilson, 1543; Arab Nationalism and British Imperialism: A Study in Power Politics, 13802; The Seat of Pilate: An Account of the Palestine Mandate, 14297; A History of Modern Egypt and Anglo-Egyptian Relations, 1800–1956, 14395

Marmor, Theodore R.: 'Doctors, Politics and Pay Disputes: "Pressure Group Politics" Revisited', 21541

Marmot, G.: Immigrant Mortality in England and Wales, 1970–1978: Cause of Death by Country of Birth, 7467

Marnham, Patrick: The Private Eye Story: The First Twenty-one Years, 25182

Marowitz, Charles: Confessions of a Counterfeit Critic: A London Theatre Notebook, 1958–1971, 25926; ed. Theatre at Work: Playwrights and Productions in the Modern British Theatre, 26227, 26266

Marplan Limited: Pub Opening Hours, 20759; The British Pub, 20758

Marples, Morris: Princes in the Making: A Study of Royal Education, 453

Marquand David Ian: Ramsay MacDonald, 1032; 'The Politics of Deprivation: Reconsidering the Failure of Utopianism', 2153; European Elections and British Politics, 2380

Marquand, Hilary Adair: South Wales Needs a Plan, 5369

Marquand, Judith: Wage Drift: Origins, Measurement and Behaviour, 3920

Marquis, A. G.: 'Words as Weapons: Propaganda in Britain and Germany during the First World War', 15213; 'Written on the Wind: The Impact of Radio during the 1930s', 24725

Marr, Douglas Stuart Balfour: 208 Squadron History, 15926

Marr, W. L.: 'The United Kingdom's International Migration in the Inter-war Period: Theoretical Considerations and Empirical Testing', 7438

Marreco, Constance Georgina: The Rebel Countess: The Life and Times of Constance Markievicz, 1467

Marret, Sir Robert: Latin America: British Trade and Investment, 4816

Marriage, A.: Psychiatric Studies of Borstal Lads, 10572

Marrin, Albert: The Last Crusade: The Church of England in the First World War, 11853

Marrinan, Patrick: Paisley: Man of Wrath, 3075

Marriner, Sheila: The Economic and Social Development of Merseyside, 1750–1960, 5185, 18055; 'Sir Alfred Mond's Octopus: A Nationalised House-Building Business', 18442

Marriott, Sir John Arthur Ransome: Modern England, 1885–1945, 297; The Constitution in Transition, 1910–1924, 604; This Realm of England: Monarchy, Aristocracy, Democracy, 605; Anglo-Russian Relations, 1689–1943, 13911

Marriott, Oliver: Anatomy of a Merger: A History of G.E.C., A.E.I. and English

Electric, 4994, 6678; The Property Boom, 18689

Marriott, Stuart: Extramural Empires: Service and Self-Interest in English University Adult Education, 1873–1983, 23701

Marris, Peter: Widows and their Families, 10040

Marrot, H. V.: A Bibliography of the Works of John Galsworthy, 25530

Mars, Alastair: British Submarines at War, 1939–1945, 15371

Mars, Penelope A.: 'An Economic Comparison of the Textile Industries in the U.K. and the U.S.A.', 6465

Marsden, Barry Michael: Chesterfield Trams and Trolleybuses, 17220

Marsden, Colin C.: Southern Electric Multiple Units at Work 1948–1973, 16917

Marsden, Colin J.: This is Waterloo, 16998

Marsden, David: Pay Inequalities in the European Community, 3876; The Car Industry: Labour Relations and Industrial Adjustment, 5844, 17404

Marsden, Dennis: Mothers Alone: Poverty and the Fatherless Family, 7874, 9064, 9948; Some Unemployed Men and their Families: An Exploration of the Social Contract between Society and Worker, 10104; Education and the Working Class, 22940; Politicians, Equality and Comprehensives, 22966

Marsden, Jill: E for Additives: The Complete "E" Numbers Guide, 20179

Marsden, Peter: The Historic Shipwrecks of South East England, 16507

Marsden, Philip: The Officers of the Commons, 1363–1965, 630

Marsden, Terry K.: 'Complimentary Roles and Asymmetrical Lives: Farmer's Wives in a Large Farm Environment', 19594

Marsh, Alan: Adolescent Drinking: A Survey Carried out on Behalf of the DHSS, 8537; 'Awareness of Racial Differences in West Indian and British Children', 11262; 'Silent Revolution, Value Priorities and the Quality of Life in Britain', 19959

Marsh, Arthur Ivor: Managers and Shop Stewards, 5658; Industrial Relations in Engineering, 5659; Research and Teaching in Industrial Relations: The British Experience, 5660; Industrial Relations in Engineering, 5661, 6881; Workplace Industrial Relations in the Engineering Industry in the United Kingdom and the Federal Republic of Germany, 5662; Disputes Procedures in Britain, 5663; Historical Directory of British Trade Unions, 6686; Trade Union Handbook: A Guide and Directory to the Structure, Membership, Policy and Personnel of the British Trade Unions, 6687; 'The General Federation of Trade Unions, 1945–1970', 6895

Marsh, David:'Government Popularity and the Falklands War: A Reassessment:, 2352

Marsh, David: Abortion Politics, 7879

Marsh, David: 'The Confederation of British Industries', 5488; 'The Politics of the C.B.I.: 1974 and After', 5489; The Confederation of British Industries, 5490;

'Representation of Retail Interests in Britain', 6637

Marsh, David Charles: National Insurance and Assistance in Britain, 4037; ed. The Social Sciences: An Outline for the Intending Student, 7912; ed. Changing Social Structure of England and Wales, 1871–1951, 7913; ed. Introducing Social Policy, 8913; The Future of the Welfare State, 8989; The Welfare State, 8990; ed. An Introduction to the Study of Social Administration, 9242; The Changing Social Structure of England and Wales, 1871–1951, 9467; Focus on Nurse Recruitment: A Snapshot from the Provinces, 21715

Marsh, Sir Edward Howard: A Number of People: A Book of Reminiscences, 23755

Marsh, Geoffrey: Team Care in General Practice, 21528

Marsh, John R.: The Practice of Banking, 4454

Marsh, Leonard Charles: Health and Unemployment: Some Studies of their Relationships, 7005

Marsh, Peter: Aggro: The Illusion of Violence, 10666; The Anatomy of a Strike: Unions, Employers and Punjabi Workers in a Southall Factory, 11215

Marsh, Richard William [Baron Marsh]: Off the Rails, 1269

Marsh, Terry: The 1984 Drought, 20105

Marshall, Arthur Hedley: Financial Administration in Local Government, 3122, 4869

Marshall, Chapman Frederick Dendy: A History of the Southern Railway, 16910

Marshall, Charles Blythe: The Face of Scotland, 5264

Marshall, Charles Frederick Dendy: One Hundred Years of Railways: From Liverpool and Manchester to London Midland and Scottish, 16746

Marshall, Elizabeth: Shetland's Oil Era, 6531

Marshall, Francis Hugh Adam: The Science of Animal Breeding in Britain: A Short History, 19461

Marshall, G. P.: 'The Unplanning of Public Expenditure: Recent Problems in Expenditure Planning and the Consequences of Cash Limits', 4769

Marshall, Geoffrey: Constitutional Conventions: The Rules and Forms of Political Accountability, 580; Some Problems of the Constitution, 611; 'Parliament and the Constitution', 614; Parliamentary Sovereignty and the Commonwealth, 627; ed. Ministerial Responsibility, 750; Police and Government: The Status and the Accountability of the English Constable, 10720

Marshall, Gordon: Social Class in Modern Britain, 9611

Marshall, Honor: Twilight London: A Study in Degradation, 10843

Marshall, Howard P.: Slum, 18393

Marshall, J. L.: 'Housing and Mobility', 7339

Marshall, John Duncan: ed. The History of Lancashire County Council, 1889–1974, 3361; The Lancashire and Yorkshire

Railway, 16950; The Lake Counties from 1830 to the Mid-20th Century: A Study in Regional Change, 19165

Marshall, Michael: Ocean Traders: A History of Merchant Shipping from the Portuguese Discoveries to the Present Day, 16489

Marshall, Norman: The Other Theatre, 26143

Marshall, R. K.: Virgins and Viragos: A History of Women in Scotland 1080–1980, 7745

Marshall, Roy: 'Foreigners in Britain', 10967; 'The Law and Race Relations', 11119

Marshall, Sybil Mary: An Experiment in Education, 22701

Marshall, Thomas Humphrey: 'Sociology and Social Pathology', 7964; Sociology at the Crossroads, 7965; Social Policy, 7966, 8824; Social Policy in the Twentieth Century, 7967, 8825; 'Morris Ginsberg, MA, D.Litt. and F.B.A, 1889–1970', 8007; 'The Welfare State: A Sociological Interpretation', 8973; 'The Right to Welfare', 9001; Citizenship and Social Class, and other Essays, 9511; 'General Surveys of Changes in Stratification in the Twentieth Century', 9512

Marshall, Tony: 'A Framework for the Analysis of Juvenile Delinquency Causation', 10602

Marshallsay, Diana: Select List of British Parliamentary Papers, 1955–1964, 196; ed. Ford's List of British Parliamentary Papers 1965–1974, together with Specialist Commentaries, 197; ed. Ford's List of British Parliamentary Papers 1974–1983, together with Specialist Commentaries, 198

Marsland, David: Education and Youth, 8531

Martel, Giffard Le Quesne: In the Wake of the Tank: The First Fifteen Years of Mechanisation in the British Army, 15528

Martel, Gordon: Studies in British Imperial History: Essays in honour of A. P. Thornton, 12571, 12649; ed. The Origins of the Second World War Reconsidered: The A. J. P. Taylor Debate after Twenty-Five Years, 13771

Martell, Edward: The Murder of the News Chronicle and the Star, 25149

Martelli, George: The Elveden Enterprise: A Story of the Second Agricultural Revolution, 19476

Martienssen, Anthony Kenneth: Crime and the Police, 10742

Martin Voorhees Associates: Review of Rural Settlement Policies, 1945–1980, 19068

Martin, A. F.: ed. The Oxford Region: A Scientific and Historical Survey, 18067

Martin, Andrew: Unions and Economic Crisis: Britain, West Germany and Sweden, 6827

Martin, Anna: 'The Future of the Public-House from the Working Woman's Point of View', 22169

Martin, Anne: Reminiscences and Reflections, 26462

Martin, Anne: Welsh Economic Statistics: A Handbook of Sources, 5312

Martin, [Basil] Kingsley: The Crown and the Establishment, 436; Harold Laski 1893–1950: A Biographical Memoir, 2115; Father Figures: 1897–1931, 25264

Martin, Bernice: The Development of Factory Legislation: The Sociology of a Law and its Enforcement, 5770; 'Progressive Education Versus the Working Classes', 22814

Martin, Bruce: Philip Larkin, 25625

Martin, Bruce: School Buildings, 1945–51, 23924

Martin, Charles Robert Arthur: Slums and Slummers: A Sociological Treatise on the Housing Problem, 18392

Martin, Colin: 'The Decline of Labour Party Membership', 1762

Martin, D. B.: The Economics of Urban Residential Renewal and Improvement, 5410, 20406

Martin, Daniel: A History of the Savings Bank in Carluke, 1815–1965, 4352

Martin, David Alfred: ed. Strange Gifts? A Guide to Charismatic Renewal, 12133; A General Theory of Secularization, 12384; A Sociology of English Religion, 12382; The Religious and the Secular: Studies in Secularization, 12383; ed. Sociological Yearbook of Religion in Britain, 12390; Pacifism: An Historical and Sociological Study, 13514; Anarchy and Culture: The Problem of the Contemporary University, 22561

Martin, David: The Struggle for Zimbabwe: The Chimurenga War, 12806

Martin, David: ed. The Fifth Battalion, The Cameronians (Scottish Rifles). 1914–1919, 15578

Martin, Denis Vincent: Adventure in Psychiatry: Social Change in a Mental Hospital, 21493

Martin, Derek: Thorn EMI: 50 Years of Radar: 50 Years of Company Involvement with Radar Technology, 1936–1986, 6680

Martin, Dick: 'The Decline of Labour Party Membership', 1762

Martin, E. M.: The Happy Fields: A Country Record, 19053

Martin, Edwin W.: Divided Counsel: The Anglo-American Response to Communist Victory in China, 13638

Martin, Elizabeth Ann: Trees of Britain and Europe, 19765

Martin, Ernest Walter: ed. Comparative Development in Social Welfare, 8891; Where London Ends: English Provincial Life after 1750: Being an Account of the English Country Town and the Lives, Work and Development of Provincial People through a Period of Two Hundred Years, 17981, 19060; The Shearers and the Shorn: A Study of Life in a Devon Community, 19160

Martin, Francis Xavier: Leaders and Men of the Easter Rising: Dublin 1916, 2740; ed. The Irish Volunteers, 1913–1915: Recollections and Documents, 2754; ed. Howth Gun-running and the Kilcoole Gun-running, 1914: Recollections and Documents, 2755; ed. Eoin MacNeill: Scholar and Man of Action 1867–1945, 3061; ed. The Scholar Revolutionary: Eoin MacNeill 1867–1945, 3062

Martin, Frederick Morris: ed. Social Services in Scotland, 8884; 'Two Studies in the Middle Class Vote', 9720; ed. The Scottish

Juvenile Justice System, 10645; Children out of Court, 10662; Children's Hearings, 10668; 'Towards Community Care. Problems and Policies in the Mental Health Service', 21328; Between the Acts: Community Mental Health Services, 1959–1983, 21746; Towards Community Care, 21793; Problems of Performance in Community Care: A Report of a Community Mental Health Services Study, 21794; Plans and Provisions for the Mentally Handicapped, 21852; Patterns of Performance in Community Care: A Report of a Community Mental Health Services Study, 22075

Martin, Frederick: History of the Grenadier Guards, 1656–1949, 15641

Martin, G. Currie: The Adult School Movement, 23683

Martin, Geoffrey Haward: The Town, 17833

Martin, George: All you Need is Ears, 24581

Martin, Graham: ed. T. S. Eliot in Perspective, 25498

Martin, Hugh: ed. The Baptist Hymn Book Companion, 11927

Martin, Ian: From Workhouse to Welfare: The Founding of the Welfare State, 8991; Second Homes in Denbighshire. Denbighshire Planning Dept., 18375

Martin, J.: 'Evidence Concerning the Relationship between Health and Retirement', 8626

Martin, J.: Some Aspects of Prescribing, 22211

Martin, J. A. M.: The Child with Delayed Speech, 8343

Martin, J. Purdon: 'British Neurology in the Last 50 Years: Some Personal Experiences', 20988

Martin, James: The Computerised Society: An Appraisal of the Impact of Computers on Society over the Next Fifteen Years, 7094

Martin, Janet D.: The Leicester Royal Infirmary, 1771–1971, 21428

Martin, John: Corner of England, 18401

Martin, John: Hospitals in Trouble, 21399

Martin, John: The Consumer Interest, 20466

Martin, John Edward: Greater London: An Industrial Geography, 5173, 18351

Martin, John G.: The Truth about the Present Housing Situation, 18594

Martin, John Powell: Violence and the Family, 9962; The Social Consequences of Conviction, 10190; The Police: A Study in Manpower: The Evolution of the Service in England and Wales, 10699, 10748

Martin, John Rodney: The Future of the Prison System, 10406

Martin, Laurence W.: Peace without Victory: Woodrow Wilson and the British Liberals, 13398

Martin, Sir Leslie: ed. Urban Space and Structures, 17831

Martin, Mildred: A Half-Century of Eliot Criticism: An Annotated Bibliography of Books and Articles in English, 1916–1965, 25487

Martin, Nancy: Search and Rescue: The Story of the Coastguard Service, 16518

Martin, Ralph Guy: The Woman He Loved, 478

Martin, Roderick: 'Union Democracy: An Exploratory Framework', 6779; Communism and the British Trade Unions, 1924–1933: A Study of the National Minority Movement, 1936, 6864; Working Women in Recession: Employment, Redundancy and Unemployment, 7718; *ed.* Sociology, Theology and Conflict, 7906; New Technology and Industrial Relations in Fleet Street, 25340

Martin, Ross M.: T.U.C.: The Growth of a Pressure Group, 1868–1976, 6706

Martin, T. A.: The Essex Regiment, 1929–1950, 15631

Martin, W. J.: 'Deaths by Violence, 1837–1937', 10291

Martin, Wallace: The 'New Age' under Orage: Chapters in English Cultural History, 25175

Martin, Walter T.: Social Stress and Chronic Illness: Mortality Patterns in Industrial Society, 7453

Martin, Werner: Bertrand Russell: A Bibliography of his Writings 1895–1976, 26861

Martindale, Hilda: Women Servants of the State, 1870–1938: A History of Women in the Civil Service, 947

Martindale, Louisa: A Woman Surgeon, 20871

Marvin, Francis Sydney: The Nation at School, 22675

Marvin, Will: *ed.* 'The Restless Caribbean: Changing Patterns of International Relations', 13017

Marwick, Arthur John Brereton: Britain in the Century of Total War: War, Peace and Social Change, 1900–1967, 288, 7538; Britain in our Century: Images and Controversies, 289, 7545; Clifford Allen: The Open Conspirator, 1339; 'The Independent Labour Party in the 1920s', 1873; 'Middle Opinion in the Thirties: Planning, Progress and Political Agreement', 2133; 'James Maxton: His Place in Scottish Labour History', 2531; The Deluge: British Society and the First World War, 7537; Social Change in Britain: 1920–1970, 7539; The Explosion of British Society 1914–1962, 7540; Between Two Wars, 7541; The Home Front: The British and the Second World War, 7542, 15173; War and Social Change in the Twentieth Century: A Comparative Study of Britain, France, Germany, Russia and the United States, 7543; British Society Since 1945, 7544; Women at War, 1914–1918, 7647, 14694; 'Youth in Britain, 1920–1960: Detachment and Commitment', 8442, 9853; Class: Image and Reality in Britain, France and the USA since 1930, 9461; Class in the Twentieth Century, 9462

Marwick, William Hutton: A Short History of Labour in Scotland, 2521; The Economic Development of Scotland, 5236; Scotland in Modern Times: An Outline of Economic and Social Development since the Union of 1707, 5237; 'A Bibliography of Scottish Economic History, 1951–1962', 5238

Marx, Daniel: Jnr. International Shipping: A Study of Industrial Self-Regulation by Shipping Conferences, 16565

Marx, Enid: English Popular Art, 24101

Marx, Roland: Le problème du Commonwealth dans les choix européens de la Grande-Bretagne de 1948 à 1975', 14184; Eamon de Valera, 3044

Mascall, Eric L.: 'Anglican Dogmatic Theology, 1939–1960: A Survey and a Retrospect', 11884

Maschwitz, Eric: No Chip on my Shoulder, 24485

Mascie-Taylor, C. G. Nicholas: 'Biological Aspects of a High Socio-economic Group II: IQ Components and Social Mobility', 9594

Masefield, John: The Old Front Line, 14483; The Nine Days Wonder, 14835

Masefield, Sir Peter Gordon: To Ride the Storm: The Story of Airship R.101, 17533

Mason, A.: 'The Local Press and the General Strike: An Example from the North-East', 25324

Mason, Alan: 'A Framework for the Analysis of Juvenile Delinquency Causation', 10602

Mason, Anita: *ed.* The Spastic Schoolchild and the Outside World, 21887

Mason, Carolyn: Snowshill: A Gloucestershire Village, 19203

Mason, Colin M.: Industrial Promotion by Local and Regional Authorities: The Effectiveness of Advertising Material, 5116; *ed.* Dimensions of Change in a Growth Area: Southampton since 1960, 18083

Mason, David: Raid on St. Nazaire, 14960

Mason, David Marshall: Monetary Policy, 1914–1918, 4550

Mason, Eric: The Lancashire and Yorkshire Railway in the 20th Century, 16951

Mason, Francis Kenneth: Battle over Britain, 14810; The Hawker Hurricane, 15828, 15852; Hawker Aircraft since 1920, 15851

Mason, James: Before I Forget, 26066

Mason, James: Scallop and Queen Fisheries in the British Isles, 19810

Mason, Keith: Front Seat, 6742

Mason, Oliver: Bartholomew Gazetteer of Britain, 122

Mason, Philip: The English Gentleman: The Rise and Fall of an Ideal, 9748; (Intro) Man, Race and Darwin, 10925; Christianity and Race, 10929; Common Sense about Race, 10930; Prospero's Magic: Some Thoughts on Class and Race, 10931; Race Relations: A Field Study Comes of Age, 10932; Race Relations, 10933; Patterns of Dominance, 10934; How People Differ: An Introduction to Race Relations, 10935; 'An Approach to Race Relations', 11152; 'The Colour Problem in Britain as Affects Africa and the Commonwealth', 11153

Mason, Sandra: The Flow of Funds in Britain, 4622

Mason, Timothy: Leads the Field: The History of No.12 Squadron, Royal Air Force, 15922

Mason, Tony: War and Politics: The Experiences of the Serviceman in the Two World Wars, 15448; *ed.* Sport in Britain: A Social History, 27023; Association Football and English Society 1863–1915, 27055

Mason, Ursula Stuart: The Wrens 1917–77: A History of the Women's Royal Naval Service, 15318, 15330

Mass-Observation: The Pub and the People, 20757, 22157

Massam, Bryan: Location and Space in Social Administration, 9250

Massey, Sir Arthur: *ed.* Modern Trends in Public Health, 22047; Epidemiology in Relation to Air Travel, 22048

Massey, Doreen Barbara: Spatial Divisions of Labour: Social Structures and the Geography of Production, 5124

Massey, Philip Hubert: Industrial South Wales: A Social and Political Survey, 5370

Massey, William Thomas: The Desert Campaigns, 14494; How Jerusalem Was Won, 14495; Allenby's Final Triumph, 14496

Massie, Allan: Muriel Spark, 25817; A Portrait of Scottish Rugby, 27051

Massie, Peter: Children's Play: A Study of Needs and Opportunities: A Study for the Council for Children's Welfare, 27010

Massingham, Harold J.: *ed.* H. W. M.: A Selection from the Writings of H.W. Massingham, 25263

Masterman, Charles Frederick Gurney: England after the War, 7548; After Twelve Months of War, 7549; 'The Collapse of the Middle Class', 9717

Masterman, Lucy: C. F. G. Masterman: A Biography, 1270

Masters, Anthony: Nancy Astor: A Life, 1347

Masters, David: 'So Few': The Immortal Record of the Royal Air Force, 15006; With Pennants Flying: The Immortal Deeds of the Royal Armoured Corps, 15601; Miracle Drugs: The Inner History of Penicillin, 22292

Masters, Philip Leslie: Preparatory Schools Today, 23002

Masters, Stanley H.: 'An Inter-Industry Analysis of Wages and Plant Size', 3928

Matatko, John: Key Developments in Personal Finance, 4536

Mather, Alexander Smith: The County of Ross and Cromarty, 19226; An Annotated Bibliography of Rural Land Use in the Highlands and Islands of Scotland, 19245

Mather, P. M.: 'Factional Ecology and Factor Invariance: An Investigation', 19961

Mathers, Nancy M.: National Health Service: A Bibliography, 21544

Matheson: Colin: Wales and the Sea Fisheries, 19811

Matheson, Mary J.: The Regional Pattern of the Demand for Meat in the United Kingdom, 20675

Matheson, Percy Ewing: The Life of Hastings Rashdall, 11804

Mathew, David: Catholicism in England, 11937

Mathew, Don: The Bike is Back: A Bicycle Policy for Britain, 17172

Mathew, Sir Theobald: The Office and Duties of the Director of Public Prosecutions, 10764

Mathewman, Phyllis: Sir Malcolm Sargent, 24438

Mathews, David: *ed.* Race: A Christian Symposium, 10951

Mathews, V. L.: Blue Tapestry, 15818

Mathias, Peter: Retailing Revolution: A History of Multiple Retailing in the Food Trade Based upon the Allied Suppliers Group of Companies, 6649, 20623; ed. Shipping: A Survey of Historical Records, 16450; ed. Enterprise and History: Essays in Honour of Charles Wilson, 26828

Mathiesen, Thomas: 'The Sociology of Prisons: Problems for Future Research', 10342

Matless, David: Doing the English Village 1945–90: An Essay in Imaginative Geography, 19123; Writing the Rural: Five Cultural Geographies, 19123

Matro, Robert: The Market for North Sea Crude Oil, 6496

Mattausch, John: A Commitment to Campaign: A Sociological Study of CND, 13528

Mattei-Gentili, Matteo: Le Building Society in Gran Bretagna, 4359

Matterson, Alan: Polytechnics and Colleges, 23260

Matthew, Henry Colin Gray: 'The Franchise Factor in the Rise of the Labour Party', 2281

Matthew, Sir Robert Hogg: Belfast Regional Survey and Plan: Interim Report on Housing Sites in the Belfast Area, 18495; The Clyde Valley Regional Plan, 1946: A Report, 18855; New Life in Old Towns: Report . . . on two Pilot Studies on Urban Renewal in Nelson and Rawtenstall Municipal Boroughs, 18894; The Conservation of Georgian Edinburgh: The Proceedings and Outcome of a Conference, 18975

Matthews, Charles Henry Selfe: Dick Sheppard: Man of Peace, 11811

Matthews, David G. J.: Management in Britain: A General Characterization, 5425

Matthews, David: Michael Tippett, 24370

Matthews, Geoffrey F.: Loughborough from College to University: A History of Higher Education at Loughborough, 1909–1966, 23537; 'The College of Advanced Technology Experiment: an Historical Review of Loughborough's Experience 1957–1966', 23538

Matthews, J. H.: 'Surrealism and England', 23995

Matthews, Joan Ethel: Working with Youth Groups, 8518; Youth and Youth Groups, 8423

Matthews, John: The Unity Scene, 12350

Matthews, K. G. P.: 'Was Sterling Overvalued in 1925?', 4676; 'Was Sterling Overvalued in 1925?: A Reply and Further Evidence', 4678

Matthews, Leslie G.: History of Pharmacy in Britain, 7027, 22253; The Royal Apothecaries, 20851

Matthews, Philip W.: The Bankers' Clearing House: What It Is and What it does, 4459; A History of Barclays Bank Ltd., 4495

Matthews, Robert Charles Oliver: British Economic Growth, 1856–1973, 3514; 'Why has Britain had Full Employment Since the War?', 3611; 'Some Aspects of Post-War Growth in the British Economy in Relation to Historical Experience', 3642; 'Foreign Trade and British Economic Growth', 4786; 'The Theory of Economic Growth: A Survey', 7230

Matthews, Roger: Confronting Crime, 10279

Matthews, Thomas Stanley: Great Tom: Notes towards the Definition of T. S. Eliot, 25499

Matthews, Walter Robert: William Temple: An Estimate and an Appreciation, 11704; Memoirs and Meanings, 11800

Maud, John Primatt Redcliffe [Baron]: Experiences of an Optimist, 940; Local Government in Modern England, 3160; Local Government in England and Wales, 3161; '1851–1951: A Century of British Education', 22580; 'The Twentieth Century Administrator', 22800; National Progress and the University, 23360

Maud, Ralph: Dylan Thomas in Print: A Bibliographical History, 25828

Maude, Angus Edmund Upton [Baron]: The Consuming Society, 375, 21965; The New Conservatism: An Anthology of Post-War Thought, 2191; The Common Problem, 2194; The English Middle Classes, 9718; Professional People, 9767

Maude, Sir Evelyn John: The Story of the Royal United Kingdom Beneficent Association 1863–1963, 9128

Maudesley Alcohol Pilot Project: Designing a Comprehensive Community Response to Problems of Alcohol Abuse: Report to the D.H.S.S. by the M.A.P.P., 22161

Maudling, Reginald: Memoirs, 1271

Maugham, Robert Cecil Romer [Viscount]: Somerset and all the Maughams, 25705; Conversations with Willie: Recollections of W. Somerset Maugham, 25706

Maule, Henry: Caen. Scobie, Hero of Greece: The British Campaign, 1944–45, 14849; The Brutal Battle and Break-Out for Normandy, 14961

Maund, D. J.: 'Intra-community Segregation: A Case Study in Rural Herefordshire', 19293

Maund, Thomas Bruce: The Tramways of Birkenhead and Wallasey, 17216

Maunden, A. R.: Accounting for British Steel: A Financial Analysis of the Failure of the British Steel Corporation 1967–80, and Who Was to Blame, 6606

Maunder, Pamela Ann: Modern Industry in Britain, 4983

Maunder, Peter: The British Economy in the 1970's, 3679

Maunder, W. F.: 'The New Jamaican Immigration', 11240

Maunder, W. Peter J.: Competition in British Industry: Restrictive Practices Legislation in Theory and Practice, 4935

Maurice, Arthur Bartlett: 'Dora' [No crying liquor problem today], 22172

Maurice, Sir Frederick Barton: Haldane, 1856–1928: The Life of Viscount Haldane of Cloan, 1213; Lessons of Allied Cooperation: Naval, Military and Air, 1914–1918, 15473

Maurice, Rita: ed. National Accounts Statistics: Sources and Methods, 4912

Mauricio, Rufino: Pacific Basin and Oceania, 12874

Maurois, André: The Life of Sir Alexander Fleming: Discoverer of Penicillin, 22280

Maw, William: The Story of Rutherford Grammar School, Newcastle-upon-Tyne, 23000

Mawby, Rob: 'Juvenile Delinquency and Police Discretion in an Inner-city Area', 10671

Mawhinney, Brian Stanley: Conflict and Christianity in Northern Ireland, 12158

Mawson, John: British Regional and Industrial Policy in the 1970s: A Critical Review with Special Reference to the West Midlands in the 1980s, 5226

Max, S. M.: 'Cold War on the Danube: The Belgrade Conference of 1948 and Anglo-American Effort to Reinternationalize the River', 13972; The United States, Great Britain and the Sovietization of Hungary, 1945–1948, 13973

Maxcy, George: The Multinational Motor Industry, 5559

Maxtone-Graham, John: Cunard: 150 Glorious Years, 16527

Maxwell, David Wellesley: The Principal Cause of Unemployment: A Simple Explanation of our Defective Monetary System, 4551

Maxwell, James: Social Implications of the 1947 Scottish Mental Survey, 7427; The Level and Trend of National Intelligence: the Contribution of the Scottish Mental Surveys, 23596; Sixteen Years on: A Follow-Up of the 1947 Scottish Survey, 23608

Maxwell, Leslie F.: A Bibliography of English Law from 1801 to June 1932, 10285

Maxwell, Robert Miller: New British Architecture, 23903

Maxwell, Stephen: ed. Scotland, Multinationals and the Third World, 5560

Maxwell, William Delbert: A History of Worship in the Church of Scotland, 12201

Maxwell, William: ed. The Letters of Sylvia Townsend Warner, 25851

Maxwell-Arnot, M.: 'Social Change and the Church of Scotland', 12231

Maxwell-Atkinson, J.: 'Suicide, Status Integration and Pseudo-Science', 10804; 'On the Sociology of Suicide', 10805; Discovering Suicide, 10806

May, David: Jeremy Thorpe: A Secret Life, 1533

May, Frederick: 'Drama in the Universities', 26255

May, James Lewis: The Oxford Movement: Its History and its Future, a Layman's Estimate, 11645

May, John: The Greenpeace Story, 20250

May, Jonathan: A Student's Guide to the Development of Education in England and Wales, 22864

May, Margaret: 'Delinquent and Maladjusted Girls', 10680

May, Robin: A Companion to the Theatre: The Anglo-American Stage from 1920, 25906

May, Roy: 'The Interaction between Race and Colonialism: A Case Study of the Liverpool Race Riots of 1919', 11464

May, Thomas Erskine [Baron Farnborough]:

A Treatise on the Law, Privileges, Proceedings, and Usage of Parliament, 645

May, Timothy C.: Trade Unions and Pressure Group Politics, 6714

May, Trevor: An Economic and Social History of Britain, 1760–1970, 3527

May, William Edward: A History of Marine Navigation, 27251

Maybury, Sir Henry P.: '[Roads]: A Review and a Forecast', 17101

Mayer, David: Annotated Bibliography of Pantomime and Guide to Study Sources, 26267

Mayer, John E.: The Client Speaks, 8741

Mayes, David G.: The Property Boom: The Effects of Building Society Behaviour on House Prices, 4364

Mayes, Stanley: Makarios: A Biography, 12867

Mayfield, Guy: The Church of England: Its Members and its Business, 11596

Mayhew, Christopher: Party Games, 1473; Time to Explain, 1474

Mayhew, K.: 'The Degree of Unionization, 1948–1968: A Comment', 6747

Mayhew, Pat: 'Crime in England and Wales and Scotland: A British Crime Survey Comparison', 10245

Maykovitch, Minako Kurokawa: 'Changes in Racial Stereotypes among College Students', 11145

Mayle, Peter: Thirsty Work: Ten Years of Heineken Advertising, 4305

Maynard, Alan K.: Rates or Prices?: A Study of the Economics of Local Government and its Replacement by the Market, 4878; 'The Objectives and Performance of the Mental Health Services in England and Wales', 21781

Maynard, Geoffrey: The Economy under Mrs Thatcher, 3704

Maynard, Harold H.: Retail Marketing and Merchandising, 20477

Maynard, Sir Charles Clarkson Martin: The Murmansk Venture, 14571

Maynell, I. C. M.: Universities in Partnership: The Inter-University Council and the Growth of Higher Education in Developing Countries, 1946–70, 23321

Mayo, Marjorie: et al eds. Women in the Community, 8760; Community Development and Urban Deprivation, 9371; ed. Community, 9372; ed. Community Work, 9373; ed. Jobs and Commnunity Action, 9374

Mayo, Patricia Elton: The Roots of Identity: Three National Movements in Contemporary European Politics, 2602; The Making of a Criminal: A Comparative Study of Two Delinquency Areas, 10191

Mayou, Archie: Birmingham Corporation Trams and Trolley Buses, 17213

Mays, John Barron: Growing Up in the City: A Study of Juvenile Delinquency in an Urban Neighbourhood, 8443, 10581; The Young Pretenders: A Study of Teenage Culture in Contemporary Society, 8444; Crime and the Social Structure, 10192; Crime and its Treatment, 10193; ed. Delinquency, the Family and the Social Group: A Reader, 10582; On the Threshold of Delinquency, 10583; 'Cultural Conformity in Urban Areas: An Introduction to the Crown Street Study in Liverpool', 18049; Urban Redevelopment and Social Change: A Study of Social Conditions in Central Liverpool, 1955–56, 18887; Education and the Urban Child, 22836; Half a Future, 22837; Education and Schooling, 22838

Meachen, George Norman: A Short History of Tuberculosis, 20989

Meacher, Michael: Taken for a Ride: Special Residential Homes for Confused Old People: A Study of Separatism in Social Policy, 8638, 21934; The Care of the Aged, 8596

Meacher, Molly: Rate Rebates: A Study of the Effectiveness of Means Tests, 4076; A Study of Poverty and Taxation, 4855; To Him who Hath: A Study of Poverty and Taxation, 9094

Mead, Adrienne: ed. A Sociology of Medical Practice, 21960

Mead, Marjorie Lamp: ed. Brothers and Friends: The Diaries of Major Warren Hamilton Lewis, 25664

Mead, Peter W.: Soldiers in the Air, 15001

Meade, J. E.: ed. Biological Aspects of Social Problems, 22009

Meade, James Edward: Efficiency, Equality and the Ownership of Property, 3776; Wage-Fixing Revisited, 3961; National Income and Expenditure, 4888

Meade, Richard H.: An Introduction to the History of General Surgery, 21145; A History of Thoracic Surgery, 21146

Meadowcroft, Shirley: 'The Impact of Competitive Tendering on the Costs of Hospital Domestic Services', 21400

Meadows, A. Jack: The Lamp of Learning: Taylor and Francis and the Development of Science Publishing, 24991

Meadows, Daniel: Nattering in Paradise: A Word from the Suburbs, 9390

Meadows, J.: 'High Spending Cities: An Historical Perspective', 3268; 'Urban Fiscal Decay in U.K. Cities', 3271

Mealand, Henry Anthony: A Plan for Bath: A Report . . . , 18840

Meaney, Neville: Australia and the World: A Documentary History from the 1870s to the 1970s, 12605

Means, Robin: The Development of Welfare Services for Elderly People, 8642; Social Work and the 'Undeserving Poor', 8902

Meara, Gwynne: Juvenile Unemployment in South Wales, 7000

Mearsheimer, John J.: Liddell Hart and the Weight of History, 14740

Measham, Donald Charles: Measurement and Meanings: Techniques and Methods of Studying Occupational Cognition, 5918; ed. Fourteen: Autobiography of an Age-group, 8481

Measures, J.: 'Joint Working Parties: A Case Study of the A.C.A.S. Approach to Improving Industrial Relations, 4165

Mechanic, D.: 'Correlates of Frustration among British General Practitioners', 21540

Mechie, Stewart: The Office of Lord High Commissioner, 12194; Trinity College, Glasgow, 1856–1956, 12222

Medawar, Jean: ed. Family Planning, 7506

Medawar, Sir Peter: 'Scientific Method and Medicine', 20990; Memoir of a Thinking Radish, 26506

Medcalf, Stephen Ellis: William Golding, 25540

Medhurst, Franklin: Urban Decay: An Analysis and a Policy, 17801

Medhurst, Kenneth N.: Church and Politics in a Secular Age, 11634; 'Studying a Religious Elite: The Case of the Anglican Episcopate', 11685

Medical Directory, 21499

Medical Practitioners' Union: Our Blueprint for the Future, 21532; Newsletter Special: H.M. Government's Offer to G.P.'s: The M.P.U Comments, 21535

Medical Research Council: Memorandum No. 1: Reactions of Mines Rescue Personnel to Work in Hot Environments, 4112; The Hazards of Nuclear and Allied Radiations, 20124; Introductory Manual on the Control of Health Hazards from Radio-active Material, 20126; The Exposure of the Population to Radiation from Fall-out: A Report to the Medical Research Council by their Committee on Protection against Ionizing Radiations, 20127; (Special Report Series No. 289) Studies on Expenditure of Energy and Consumption of Food by Miners and Clerks, Fife 1952, 20535; Ministry of Health: Clinical Research in Relation to the National Health Service, 20761; Annual Report, 1920+, 20766

Medical Services Review Committee: A Review of the Medical Services in Great Britain, 22088

Medlicott, William Norton: The Economic Blockade, 3605, 14723; Britain and Germany: The Search for Agreement, 1930–1937, 13703; British Foreign Policy since Versailles, 13225; Contemporary England, 1914–1964, 291

Medlik, Slavoj: Britain: Workshop or Service Centre to the World?, 7612

Medvei, Victor Cornelius: ed. The Royal Hospital of Saint Bartholomew 1123–1973, 21439

Meech, Michael: Bluebirds: The History of the Campbell Dynasty, 16369

Meech, Thomas Cox: This Generation: A History of Great Britain and Ireland from 1900 to 1926, 366

Meehan, Elizabeth: Women's Rights at Work: Campaigns and Policy in Britain and the United States, 7791

Meehan, Eugene John: The British Left Wing and Foreign Policy: A Study of the Influence of Ideology, 13567

Meehan, Patricia: Scapa Flow, 15302

Meek, E. G.: 'Social and Cultural Factors in Casework Diagnosis', 8683

Meeks, Geoffrey: 'Giant Companies in the United Kingdom, 1948–1969', 5532

Meenan, James: The Irish Economy since 1922, 2652

Meering, Agnes Brownlie: A Handbook for Nursery Nurses, 8261

Meetham, Alfred Roger: Atmospheric Pollution: Its History, Origins and Prevention, 20046

Megaw, M. Ruth: 'Australia and the Anglo-American Trade Agreement 1938', 12615; 'The Scramble for the Pacific: Anglo-United States Rivalry in the 1930s', 13612, 14024

Megginson, William James: Britain's Response to Chinese Nationalism, 1925–1927: The Foreign Office Search for a New Policy, 13625

Megson, Barbara Elsie: Girton College, 1869–1959: An Informal History, 23477; Children in Distress, 8144

Mehta, Ved: Fly and the Fly Bottle, 26841

Meirs, Richard Capel Hammer: Shoot to Kill, 16166

Meites, Joseph: Pioneers in Neuroendocrinology, 22325

Mejcher, Helmut: 'British Middle East Policy 1917–1921: The Inter-Departmental Level', 13834

Mejer, Eugeniusz: Agricultural Labour in England and Wales: Pt. 1—1900–1920, Pt. 2—Farm Workers' Earnings, 1917–1951, 19665

Mejia, Arthur: Modern British Monarchy, 438

Melia, Kath M.: Nursing Ethics, 21722

Melissen, Jan: 'Britain and Western Europe 1945–1951: Opportunities Lost', 14139

Melko, Robert L.: 'Darlan between Britain and Germany, 1940–1941', 14275

Mellanby, Kenneth: Can Britain Feed Itself?, 20610; Pesticides and Pollution, 20115; The Biology of Pollution, 20116; ed. The Ecological Effects of Pesticides, 20117

Meller, Helen Elizabeth: Patrick Geddes: Social Evolutionist and City Planner, 20383

Mellers, Wilfrid: Music and Society: England and the European Tradition, 24254; Twilight of the Gods: The Beatles in Retrospect, 24499; Vaughan Williams and the Vision of Albion, 24380

Melling, Elizabeth: History of the Kent County Council 1889–1974, 3360

Melling, Leonard: With the Eighth in Italy, 14868

Mellish, Michael: The Docks after Devlin, 16659

Mellor, David: 'Style and Ideology in British Art and Photography, 1900–1940', 24697

Mellor, G. J.: The Northern Music Hall, 26280

Mellor, Hugh: The Role of Voluntary Organisations in Social Welfare, 9117

Mellor, John: Forgotten Heroes: The Canadians at Dieppe, 14830

Mellor, John Hanson: A Century of British Fabrics, 1850–1950, 6471

Mellor, N.: 'Social Malaise Research: A Study in Liverpool', 9420

Mellor, Rosemary: 'Urban Sociology in an Urban Society', 8061

Mellor, W. Franklin: ed. Medical Services in War: The Principal Medical Lessons of the Second World War, 22119; ed. 'Health and the Family', 22120

Mellord, C. M.: 'Dyes and Dyeing', 7049

Mellors, Anne: Derbyshire County, 25171

Mellors, Colin: Local Government in the Community, 3143

Mellown, Elgin: A Bibliography of the Writings of Edwin Muir, 25719; Edwin Muir, 25723

Melly, [Alan Heywood] George: Revolt into Style: The Pop Arts in Britain, 24000; Owning up, 24456; Rum, Bum and Concertina, 24457

Melossi, Dario: The Prison and the Factory: Origins of the Penitentiary System, 10443

Melvern, Linda: The End of the Street, 25341

Melville, Robert: Henry Moore: Sculpture and Drawings 1921–1969, 24200

Melvin, Michael: Pre-trial Bail and Custody in the Scottish Sheriff Courts, 10315

Mencher, S.: 'Factors Affecting the Relationship of the Voluntary and Statutory Child-care Services in England', 8252

Mencher, Samuel: Poor Law to Poverty Program: Economic Security Policy in Britain and the United States, 4071

Mendelsohn, Everett: Heat and Life: The Development of the Theory of Animal Heat, 22326

Mendelson, Edward: Early Auden, 25365; W. H. Auden: A Bibliography 1924–1969, 25355

Mennell, Stephen: All Manners of Food: Eating and Taste in England and France from the Middle Ages to the Present, 20618; Leisure, Culture and Local Government: A Study of Policies and Provision in Exeter, 26934

Mennell, William: Takeover: The Growth of Monopoly in Britain, 1951–1961, 4991, 5513

Menon, P. K.: 'The Anglo-Guatemalan Territorial Dispute over the Colony of Belize (British Honduras)', 13031

Menon, V. P.: The Transfer of Power in India 1939–1947, 13167

Menuhin, Sir Yehudi: Unfinished Journey, 24407

Meny, Y.: ed. The Politics of Steel: Western Europe and the Steel Industry in the Crisis Years, 1974–1984, 6581

Menzies, Campbell J.: From a Trade to a Profession: Byways in Dental History, 9822

Menzies, Sir Robert Gordon: Afternoon Light: Some Memories of Men and Events, 12626; The Measure of the Years, 12627

Menzies, William C.: 'On what Principle Should the Rents of Houses to be Erected by Local Authorities be Based and Tenants Selected?', 18457

Mepham, George James: Problems of Equal Pay, 7785

Mercer, Geoffrey: ed. Manpower Planning in the National Health Service, 5951, 21657

Mercer, John: Scotland: The Devolution of Power, 2473

Merchant Taylors': Four Centuries of Merchant Taylors' School, 1561–1961, 23067

Meredith, David: 'The British Government and Colonial Economic Policy, 1919–1939', 3762, 12491

Meredith, Hugh Owen: Economic History of England: A Study in Social Development, 3466

Merlin, P.: 'Les Villes Nouvelles en Grande-Bretagne', 18239

Merger of the Foreign Office and the Commonwealth Office: H.M.S.O., 12512

Merrett, Anthony John Watkin: 'The Profitability of British and American Industry', 3722; 'Financial Control of State Industry', 6073; Housing Finance and Development: An Analysis and A Programme For Reform, 18549

Merrett, Stephen: Owner-Occupation in Britain, 18454

Merriam, Robert E.: The Battle of the Ardennes, 14962

Merrill, E. D.: 'Microfilm Records of the Linnean Society of London', 20991

Merry, D. H.: A Bibliography of Printed Works Relating to Oxfordshire (Excluding the University and the City), 19168; A Bibliography of Printed Works Relating to the University of Oxford, 23449

Merry, D. M.: 'A Statistical Analysis of Attitudes to Moving: A Survey of Slum Clearances in Leeds', 9424

Mersey Ports: Handbook 1983/84—Downham Market, 16696

Mersham Children's Reception Centre: Interim Report, 8253

Merton, Robert King: ed. Sociology Today: Problems and Prospects, 7896; ed. Social Theory and Social Structure: Toward the Codification of Theory and Research, 7897; ed. Social Theory and Social Structure, 7898

Merton-Jones, Anthony Charles: British Independent Airlines since 1946, 17620

Mervyn, Leonard: The Dictionary of Vitamins: The Complete Guide to Vitamins and Vitamin Therapy, 20566

Mesher, John: Compensation for Unemployment, 4040

Mess, Henry Adolphus: Factory Legislation and its Administration 1891–1924, 5589, 7222; Factory Legislation and its Administration, 5589; The Facts of Poverty, 9022; Voluntary Social Services since 1918, 9119; Industrial Tyneside: A Social Survey Made for the Bureau of Social Research for Tyneside, 9329

Messenger, Rosalind: The Doors of Opportunity: A Biography of Dame Caroline Haslett, D.B.E. Companion I.E.E., 7724

Messer, Malcolm: The Agricultural Depression of 1931: Its Nature and Incidence, 19446

Messina, A. M.: 'Ethnic Minority Representation and Party Competition in Britain: The Case of Ealing Borough', 3311

Metcalf, B. L.: 'Post-war Developments in the Coal Mining Industry', 6296

Metcalf, David: 'Determinants of Wage Inflation in Scottish Agriculture, 1948–1963', 19618; Low Pay, Occupational Mobility and Minimum Wage Policy in Great Britain, 3878, 5919; The Academic Labour Market: Economic and Social Aspects of a Profession, 9837, 22545; The Economics of Agriculture, 19547

Metcalfe, George Edgar: Great Britain and Ghana: Documents of Ghana History, 1807–1957, 12739

Metcalfe, John Ernest: British Mining Fields, 6325

Mettler, C. C.: History of Medicine: A Correlative Text Arranged According to Subjects, 21183

Mews, Stuart Paul: 'Religion and National Identity', 11624, 12214; 'Neo-orthodoxy, Liberalism and War: Karl Barth, P.T.Forsyth and John Oman, 1914–1918', 11857; 'Urban Problems and Rural Solutions: Drink and Disestablishment in the First World War', 11859; 'The Sword of the Spirit: A Catholic Cultural Crusade of 1940', 11865

Meyer, Frederick Victor: The Functions of Sterling, 4667; Britain, the Sterling Area and Europe, 4698; United Kingdom Trade with Europe, 4810

Meyers, Jeffrey: The Enemy: A Biography of Wyndham Lewis, 25673; Orwell: An Annotated Bibliography of Criticism, 25738; ed. George Orwell: The Critical Heritage, 25741

Meyers, Reinhard: 'Britain, Europe and the Dominions in the 1930s: Some Aspects of British, European and Commonwealth Policies', 12519; 'Sicherheit und Gleichgewicht: Das britische Kabinett und die Remilitarisierung des Rheinlandes 1936', 13673

Meyers, Valerie: Orwell: An Annotated Bibliography of Criticism, 25738

Meyler, Ruth M.: Skye, 19277

Meynell, Alix: Public Servant, Private Woman: An Autobiography, 949

Meynell, Sir Francis: My Lives, 24982

Meynell, H.: 'The Stockholm Conference of 1917', 13375

Miall, Rowland Leonard: Richard Dimbleby, Broadcaster: By his Colleagues, 24741

Miall, Stephen: History of the British Chemical Industry, 6214

Michael, James: The Politics of Secrecy, 768

Michaelson, John: Developing the Socially Useful Economy, 3694

Michel, Walter: Wyndham Lewis: Paintings and Drawings, 24033

Michie, Allan Andrew: The Crown and the People, 435; The Invasion of Europe: The Story behind D-Day, 14963

Micklem, Caryl: 'Is Britain Still Christian?', 11585

Micklem, Nathaniel: The Box and the Puppets, 12059

Micklewright, F. H. Amphlett: 'The Rise and Decline of English Neo-Malthusianism', 7373

Mid-Wales Industrial Development Association: Development in Mid-Wales: A Review of the M.W.I.D.A. 1957–1959, 5357

Middlebrook, Martin: The First Day on the Somme, 1st July 1916, 14591; Battleship: The Loss of the Prince of Wales and the Repulse, 15021; Convoy: The Battle for Convoys SC.122 and HX.229, 15130; The Battle for Hamburg: Allied Bomber Forces against a German City in 1943, 15986; Task Force: The South Atlantic 1982, 16103; The Fight for the 'Malvinas': The Argentine Forces in the Falklands War, 16110

Middlebrook, S. M.: How Malaya is Governed, 12902

Middlemas, Robert Keith: The Life and Times of George VI, 503; ed. Whitehall Diary, 758; 'Cabinet Secrecy and the Crossman Diaries', 760; Baldwin, a Biography, 977; The Clydesiders: A Leftwing Struggle for Parliamentary Power, 2516; Diplomacy of Illusion: The British Government and Germany, 1937–1939, 13702; Command the Far Seas: A Naval Campaign of the First World War, 14678

Middlemiss, J. R.: 'An Analysis of 200 Cases of Mental Defect', 21740

Middlesex County Council: Plan for the Development of the Health and Welfare Services over the Next Ten Years, 1962–1972 (Approved on 31st October, 1962), 21560

Middleton, A. H.: Machinery Noise, 20148

Middleton, Alan: ed. Rejuvenating the Inner City: The Scottish Experience, 18150

Middleton, Don H.: Test Pilots: The Story of British Test Flying 1903–1984, 15903; Airspeed: The Company and its Aeroplanes, 17617

Middleton, Drew: The British, 379; The Supreme Choice: Britain and the European Community, 14165

Middleton, Kenneth William Bruce: Britain and Russia: An Historical Essay, 13912

Middleton, Lucy: ed. Women in the Labour Movement: The British Experience, 1803, 7852

Middleton, Nigel Gordon: When Family Failed: The Treatment of Children in the Care of the Community during the First Half of the Twentieth Century, 8262; 'Lord Butler and the Education Act of 1944', 22624; A Place for Everyone: A History of State Education from the End of the 18th Century to the 1970s, 22674

Middleton, R.: 'The Problems and Consequences of Parliamentary Government: an Historical View', 639

Middleton, Roger: 'The Measurement of Fiscal Influence in Britain in the 1930s', 4646; 'The Constant Employment Budget Balance and British Budgetary Policy, 1929–1939', 4916

Middleton, Sue: Images of Welfare: Press and Public Attitudes to Poverty, 9009

Middleton, Sir Thomas Hudson: Food Production in War, 20580

Middleton, William E. Knowles: The History of the Barometer, 7064; A History of the Thermometer and its Use in Meteorology: Baltimore, 7065

Middleton, William: Intellectual Crossroads, 21187

Midgley, Kenneth: Garden Design: Prepared in Conjunction and Collaboration with the Royal Horticultural Society, 19902

Midwinter, Arthur F.: The Politics of Local Spending, 3121, 4870; Remote Bureaucracy or Administrative Efficiency? Scotland's New Local Government System, 3180; Corporate Management: The New Conventional Wisdom in British Local Government, 3240; 'Setting the Rate: Liverpool Style', 3333

Midwinter, Eric Clare: Priority Education: An Account of the Liverpool Project, 23124; Projections: An Educational Priority Area at Work, 23123; Schools in Society: The Evolution of English Education, 22831; Make 'em laugh: Famous Comedians and their Worlds, 26289; The Lost Season: Cricket in Wartime, 1939–45, 27105

Mikardo, Ian: Backbencher, 1475

Mikes, H. George: Come to Prison, 10356

Mikhail, Edward Halim: Contemporary British Drama, 1950–1976: An Annotated Critical Bibliography, 25900; English Drama, 1900–1950: A Guide to Information Sources, 25899

Milbank Memorial Fund Quarterly: 'International Comparisons of Medical Care', 21336

Milburn, Clara E.: Mrs Milburn's Diaries: An Englishwoman's day-to-day Reflections, 1939–1945, 15168

Milburn, David: A History of Ushaw College: A Study of the Origin, Foundation and Development of an English Catholic Seminary, 11964

Milburn, Josephine F.: British Business and Ghanaian Independence, 12752

Miles, A. W.: 'The Health Services—What Structural Changes are Possible?', 21335

Miles, A.: 'Workers Education: The Communist Party and the Plebs League in the 1920's', 1955

Miles, Caroline: 'Protection of the British Textile Industry', 6460; Lancashire Textiles: A Case Study of Industrial Change, 6449

Miles, Haydn Braddock: Town Ecology, 17832

Miles, Lewis: Patterns of Care for the Subnormal, 21790

Miles, Peter: Cinema, Literature and Society: Elite and Mass Culture in Inter-war Britain, 24601

Miles, Philip C.: Road Transport in Hull and East Yorkshire, 17474

Miles, Phyllis Mary: Town Ecology, 17832

Miles, Robert: Between Two Cultures?: The Case of Rastafarianism, 11269; Labour and Racism, 11191; Racism and Migrant Labour, 11192; The Relative Autonomy of Ideology: Racism and the Migration of Labour to Britain since 1945, 11193; The TUC, Black Workers and New Commonwealth Immigration, 1954–1973, 11190; White Man's Country: Racism and British Politics, 11195; ed. Racism and Political Action in Britain, 11189 'The Riots of 1958: The Ideological Construction of "Race Relations" as a Political Issue in Britain', 11194

Miles, Roger Oliver: Forestry in the English Landscape: A Study of the Cultivation of Trees and their Relationship to Natural Amenity and Plantation Design, 19755

Miles, Wilfrid: The Gordon Highlanders, 1919–1945, 15585

Miliband, Ralph: Parliamentary Socialism: A Study in the Politics of Labour, 1739; The State in Capitalist Society, 2154

Militant Liverpool Black Caucus: The Racial Politics of Militant in Liverpool . . . 1980–1986, 1995

Militant: A History of the Labour Party: Articles Reprinted from 'Militant', 1992; Pamphlet: Nuclear Time Bomb, 1994; Pamphlet: Stop the Cuts, 1993

Mill Hill: 'Et Virtutem et Musas: Mill Hill School and the Great War', 23068

Mill, Hugh Robert: An Autobiography, 27219; Record of the Royal Geographical Society, 1830–1930, 26624; The Life of Sir Ernest Shackleton, 27212

Millar, Alan: British Passenger Transport Executives—1: Strathclyde, 16338; British Buses of the 1930s, 17267; ed. Buses of Western Scotland, 17294; ed. Buses of Eastern Scotland, 17295

Millar, George: The Bruneval Raid: Flashpoint of the Radar War, 15109

Millar, Hugo Belshes: The History of Cumbernauld and Kilsyth from Earliest Times, 19013

Millar, Jane: Poverty and the One Parent Family: The Challenge to Social Policy, 4092

Millar, Robert: The Affluent Sheep, 20481; The New Classes, 9539; ed. Policing the Miners' Strike, 6922

Millar, Ronald: Death of an Army: The Siege of Kut, 1915–1916, 14564

Millar, T. B.: Australia's Foreign Policy, 12633; ed. Australian Foreign Minister: The Diaries of R. G. Casey, 1951–1960, 12631; ed. The Australian Contribution to Britain, 12609

Millard, David Ralph Jnr.: The Principles and Art of Plastic Surgery, 21139

Millard, Patricia: Trade Associations and Professional Bodies of the United Kingdom: A Directory and Classified Index, 5870

Millen, James: 'University Chancellors, Vice-Chancellors and College Principals: A Social Profile', 9834

Miller, C. H.: History of the 13th/18th Royal Hussars, Queen Mary's Own, 1922–1947, 15666

Miller, Charles: Battle for the Bundu, 14526; Lobbying Government: Understanding and Influencing the Corridors of Power, 2071

Miller, Christine: Housing in London, 18748

Miller, Christopher: Planning and Pollution: An Examination of the Role of Land Use Planning in the Protection of Environmental Quality, 20004

Miller, David: ed. A Pocket Popper, 26859; Father of Football: The Story of Sir Matt Busby, 27086; Seb Coe—Coming Back, 27146

Miller, David: ed. The Blackwell Encyclopaedia of Political Thought, 2082

Miller, David M.: The Bank of England and Treasury Notes, 1694–1970, 4488

Miller, David W.: Queen's Rebels: Ulster Loyalism in Historical Perspective, 2942; Church, State and Nation in Ireland, 1898–1921, 12162

Miller, Denis Neville: A Source Book of Motorcycles, 17175; A Source Book for Traction Engines, 17090; A Source Book of Fire Engines, 17482

Miller, Derek: The Age Between: Adolescents in a Disturbed Society, 8480; Growth to Freedom: The Psychological Treatment of the Delinquent Youth, 10584

Miller, Derek J.: ed. Diet and Health in Modern Britain, 6154, 20556; ed. The Making of the Modern British Diet, 20555

Miller, Douglas: Workplace Industrial Relations in the Engineering Industry in the United Kingdom and the Federal Republic of Germany, 5662; The Closed Shop: A Comparative Study in Public Policy and Trade Union Security in Britain, the USA and West Germany, 5817

Miller, E.: 'Divorce and the Family Structure', 9981

Miller, Edwin C.: 'Forty Years of Plant Physiology: Some General Impressions', 20992, 26557

Miller, Eric John: A Life Apart: A Pilot Study of Residential Institutions for the Physically Handicapped and the Young Chronic Sick, 21903

Miller, Eugene Willard: A Geography of Manufacturing, 5053

Miller, Frederic M.: 'National Assistance or Unemployment Assistance? The British Cabinet and Relief Policy, 1932–33, 7022; 'The Unemployment Policy of the National Government, 1931–1936', 6999

Miller, Frederick John William: Growing up in Newcastle-upon-Tyne: A Continuing Study of Health and Illness in Young Children with their Families, 22087

Miller, G.: The Adoption of Inoculation for Smallpox in England and France, 21132

Miller, Gordon Wesley: Educational Opportunity and the Home, 8263

Miller, H. Tatlock: Churchill: The Walk with Destiny, 988

Miller, H.: 'Race Relations and the Schools in Great Britain', 23174

Miller, Harry: The Way of Enterprise: A Study of the Origins, Problems and Achievements in the Growth of Post-war British Firms, 4972, 5414; The Future of North Sea Gas, 7177; Spy Ring: The Full Story of the Naval Secrets Case, 16046; Menace in Malaya, 16151; Jungle War in Malaya: The Campaign against Communism 1948–60, 16156; The Predicament of the Aircraft Industry, 17584

Miller, Henry George: Medicine and Society, 22016

Miller, Herbert Crossley: The Ageing Countryman: A Socio-Medical Report on Old Age in a Country Practice, 8579

Miller, Jane: ed. Women and Poverty in Britain, 7723; Poverty and the One-Parent Family, 9950; Farm Machinery, 19685

Miller, John Donald Bruce: Sir Winston Churchill and the Commonwealth of Nations, 988; Survey of Commonwealth Affairs: Problems of Expansion and Attrition, 1953–1969, 12577; Australian Government and Politics, 12604; ed. Australians and British: Social and Political Connections, 12607; The EEC and Australia, 12636; 'South Africa's Departure', 12719; Norman Angell and the Futility of War, 13464

Miller, John Gareth: Family Property and Financial Provision, 3787

Miller, K. S.: 'Compulsory Mental Hospitalization in England and Wales', 21861

Miller, Kenneth Eugene: Socialism and Foreign Policy: Theory and Practice in Britain to 1931, 13556

Miller, M.: 'Motor Manufacturing', 17405

Miller, M. K.: 'Letchworth Conservation Area', 20385

Miller, Margaret: Convocation in the University of London: The First Hundred Years, 23517

Miller, Paul W.: 'The Wage Effect of the Occupational Segregation of Women in Britain', 3956

Miller, R.: The Incredible Music Machine, 24577

Miller, Robert: Graham Greene: A Descriptive Catalog, 25559

Miller, Robert: State Forestry for the Axe: A Study of the Forestry Commission and Denationalisation by the Market, 19757

Miller, Ronald: The Piltdown Man, 26367

Miller, Ronald: ed. Geographical Essays in Memory of Alan G. Ogilvie 26665; ed. The County of Orkney, 19237; ed. The Glasgow Region: A General Survey, 18136; 26677

Miller, Ronald Eugene: The Technical Development of Modern Aviation, 17518

Miller, S. M.: 'The Working Class Subculture', 9676; ed. Incentives and Planning in Social Policy, 8901

Miller, Thomas Ronald: The Monkland Tradition, 6554

Miller, William Henry: The Last Atlantic Liners, 16570; Transatlantic Liners 1945–1980, 16571; Transatlantic Liners at War: The Story of the Queens, 16572; Famous Ocean Liners: The Story of Passenger Shipping from the Turn of the Century to the Present Day, 16573; British Ocean Liners: A Twilight Era, 1960–1985, 16574; Liner: 50 Years of Passenger Ship Photographs, 16575

Miller, William L.: 'Cross Voting and the Dimensionality of Party Conflict in Britain during the Period of Realignment, 1918–31', 2277; Electoral Dynamics in Britain since 1918, 2229; 'The Religious Alignment of English Elections between 1918 and 1970, 2230; 'The Religious Alignment in England at the General Elections of 1974', 2336; 'There Was No Alternative: The British General Election in 1983', 2349; The Labour Party in Scotland in 1979: Advance or Retreat?, 2372, 2523; The End of British Politics? Scots and English Political Behaviour in the Seventies, 2476; Oil and the Scottish Voter 1974–1979, 2486; Irrelevant Elections? The Quality of Local Democracy in Britain, 3141

Millerson, Geoffrey Leonard: The Qualifying Associations: A Study in Professionalization, 9771

Millet, Allan: ed. Military Effectiveness, 15470

Millet, Richard: ed. 'The Restless Caribbean: Changing Patterns of International Relations', 13017

Millham, Spencer: After Grace—Teeth: A Comparative Study of the Residential Experiment of Boys and Approved Schools, 10509

Milligan, Edward H.: The Past is Prologue: 100 Years of Quaker Overseas Work, 1868–1968, 12151

Milligan, John: The Resilient Pioneers: A History of the Elastic Rail Spike Company and its Associates, 6607

Milligan, Stephen: The New Barons: Union Power in the 1970s, 6738

Milliken, Ernest Kenneth: English Monasticism Yesterday and Today, 11959

Milliken, Harold Turner: Changing Scene: Two Hundred Years of Church and Parish Life in Worsley, 19362; The Road to Bodnant: The Story behind the Foundation of the Famous North Wales Garden, 26977

Millington, A.: The Penetration of E.C. Markets by U.K. Manufacturing Industry, 4812

Millington, Edward Geoffrey Lyall: The Unseen Eye, 15912

Millington, Roy: A History of the City of Sheffield Training College, 22749

Millis, Charles Thomas: Education for Trades and Industries: A Historical Survey, 23262

Mills, Edward David: The Modern Factory, 23925; The New Architecture in Great Britain, 1946–1953, 23900

Mills, Enid: Living with Mental Illness: A Study in East London, 21784

Mills, John: Growth and Welfare: A New Policy for Britain, 8939

Mills, Sir John: Up in the Clouds, Gentlemen Please, 26069

Mills, John Saxon: The Future of the Empire, 12530; The Press and Communications of the Empire, 25309

Mills, Lennox Algernon: Malaya: A Political and Economic Appraisal, 12903

Mills, Richard: Young Outsiders: A Study of Alternative Communities, 8482

Mills, Ronald Gerald: Electronic Computers and their Business Applications, 7087

Mills, T. C.: 'Money Substitutes and Monetary Policy in the United Kingdom, 1922–1974', 4632

Millstone, Erik: Food Additives, 20177

Millum, Trevor: Working Papers in Cultural Studies, 10168

Millward, Robert: 'Price Restraint, Anti-Inflation Policy and Public and Private Industry in the United Kingdom, 1948–1973', 3814

Millward, Stanley: ed. Urban Renewal, 17727, 17785, 18645; An Appraisal of the Housing Situation and Future Trends, 18644

Millway, B.: 'European Architectural Heritage year 1975—a Symposium', 20387; 'The Town is a Museum: King's Lynn, Norfolk', 20386

Milne, Alan Alexander: It's Too Late now: The Autobiography of a Writer, 25713

Milne, Alexander Taylor: ed. Institute of Historical Research 1901–1933, 402; ed. Institute of Historical Research 1934–1945, 403

Milne, Alisdair: 'DG': The Memoirs of a Broadcaster, 24799

Milne, Alistair Murray: The Economics of Inland Transport, 16435

Milne, Antony: Noise Pollution: Impact and Counter-measures, 20144

Milne, Colin: The Story of Gourock, 1858–1958, 18147

Milne, Edward: No Shining Armour, 1476

Milne, R. S.: 'The Experiment with "Co-ordinating Ministers" in the British Cabinet 1951–3', 731; Straight Fight: A Study of Voting Behaviour in the Constituency of Bristol North-East at the General Election of 1951, 2309; Marginal Seat: A Study of Voting Behaviour in the Constituency of Bristol North-East at the General Election of 1955, 2312

Milne-Bailey, Walter: Trade Union Documents, 6743; Trade Unions and the State, 6865

Milne-Redhead, E.: ed. The Conservation of British Flora, 26562

Milner, Chris: The Midland Mainline Today, 16898

Milner, David: Children and Race, 23189

Milner, Frederic: Economic Evolution in England, 3568

Milnes, R.: '50 Years of Opera at Oxford', 24559

Milroy, James: Regional Accents of English: Belfast, 23854

Milson, Fred[erick] William: 'Social Origins and Full-time Youth Leaders', 8446; ed. Youth Service and Inter-professional Studies, 8451; Youth in a Changing Society, 8483; Operation Integration . . . An Enquiry into the Experience of West Indians Living in Birmingham with Particular Reference to Children and Young People, 11249

Milton, J. P.: 'Communities that Seek Peace with Nature', 19932

Milton, Nan: John Maclean, 2527

Milton, Roger: A Community Project in Notting Dale, 9307

Milward, Alan Steele: The Economic Effects of the Two World Wars in Britain, 3731

Minchin, James: No Man is an Island: A Study of Singapore's Lee Kuan Yew, 12964

Minchinton, Walter Edward: The British Tinplate Industry, 6353; 'Local Social Status in England and Wales', 9475; ed. Essays in Agrarian History, 19667

Miner, John Burnham: Personnel Psychology, 5466; Personnel and Industrial Relations: A Managerial Approach, 5748

Miners, N. J.: 'Plans for Constitutional Reform in Hong Kong 1946–52', 12973; Government and Politics of Hong Kong, 12972

Mingay, Gordon Edmund: Britain and America 1850–1939: A Study of Economic Change, 3708, 14055; The Gentry: The Rise and Fall of a Ruling Class, 9739

Minihan, Janet: The Nationalization of Culture: The Development of State Subsidies to the Arts in Great Britain, 23757

Ministry of Agriculture, Fisheries and Food: The Changing Structure of Agriculture, 1968–1975, 19572

Ministry of Defence: Author and Subject Catalogues of the Royal Navy, 15226;

[Adastral Library]: Bibliography of the Royal Air Force, 15781

Ministry of Education: Challenge and Response: An Account of the Emergency Scheme for the Training of Teachers, 22727; Education, 1900–1950: The Report of the Ministry of Education, 22870; Education in 1963, 22871; Technical Education in Wales, 23289; The Future of Secondary Education in Wales, 23623

Ministry of Fuel and Power: Coal Mines Acts, 1887–1949: The Abstract and the General Regulations, 6250; South Wales Coalfields: Regional Survey Report, 6324

Ministry of Health: Mortality and Morbidity during the London Fog of December 1952, 20037

Ministry of Housing and Local Government: Planning Maps of England and Wales, 133; Committee on the Staffing of Local Government. Report of the Committee, 3235; Report of the Inspector Appointed by the Minister of Housing and Local Government to Hear Objections to the Proposals of the Local Government Commission for England for the City of York and Surrounding Areas, 3346

Ministry of Pensions: Pensions for Disablement or Death due to Service in the Forces after 2nd September 1939, 4047

Ministry of Transport: Cars for Cities: A Study of Trends in the Design of Vehicles, 17391

Minkel, Clarence: A Bibliography of British Honduras 1900–1970, 13022

Minkin, Lewis: The Labour Party Conference: A Study in the Politics of Intra-Party Democracy, 1751

Minman, John: ed. The CND Story: The First 25 Years of CND in the Words of the People Involved, 13531

Minney, Rubeigh James: Viscount Addison: Leader of the Lords, 1063; ed. The Private Papers of Hore-Belisha, 1238; The Two Pillars of Charing Cross: The Story of a Famous Hospital, 21450; 'Puffin' Asquith, 24661; Viscount Southwood, 25099

Minns, Richard: State Shareholding: The Role of the Local and Regional Authorities, 4751; Bombers and Mash: The Domestic Front 1939–45, 15171; The Organisation of Housing: Public and Private Enterprise in London, 18427; 'Homeless Families and some Organizational Determinants of Deviancy', 18511

Minogue, Kenneth R.: ed. Contemporary Political Philosophers, 2086; The Liberal Mind, 2178; The Concept of a University, 23295

Minogue, Martin: ed. Documents on Contemporary British Government, 594, 3093

Minoprio, P.: 'Assistance for Small Farmers in the United Kingdom', 19510

Minshull, Roger: Regional Geography: Theory and Practice, 26638; The Changing Nature of Geography, 26641

Minto, George Archibald: The Thin Blue Line, 10696

Mintz, Sidney Wilfred: Sweetness and Power:

The Place of Sugar in Modern History, 20689

Minutes and Proceedings of the London Yearly Meeting of the Society of Friends: 1857+, 12135

Minutes and Yearbook of the Methodist Conference: 1932+, 12063

Mirfin, Derick: *ed.* Buying Better Health: , 21569

Mishan, Ezra Joshua: 'A Survey of Welfare Economics, 1939–1951', 3627, 9053; 'Immigration: Some Economic Effects', 11408; 'Immigration: Excess Aggregate Demand and the Balance of Payments', 11409

Mishler, W.: 'Scotching Nationalism in the British Parliament: Crosscutting Cleavages among MP's', 2423

Mishra, Ramesh: Society and Social Policy: Theories and Practice of Welfare, 8963

Mitchell, Alan: The Trees of Britain and Northern Europe, 19764

Mitchell, Anne K.: Children in the Middle: Living through Divorce, 8264

Mitchell, Arthur: Labour in Irish Politics 1890–1930: The Irish Labour Movement in an Age of Revolution, 2696

Mitchell, Austin Vernon: Four Years in the Death of the Labour Party, 1768; Can Labour Win Again?, 2340; 'Clay Cross', 18726; 'The Decline of Current Affairs Television', 24924

Mitchell, Basil: Law, Morality and Religion in a Secular Society, 9913

Mitchell, Brian Redman: British Parliamentary Election Results, 1950–1964, 2217

Mitchell, Colin: The British Brewing Industry: Market Overview, 20739

Mitchell, D. J.: A History of Warwickshire County Council 1889–1989, 3369

Mitchell, Daniel J. B.: 'British Incomes Policy, the Competitive Effect and the 1967 Devaluation', 3938; 'Some Aspects of Labour Mobility and Recent Policy in Britain', 5894; 'The Constitutional Position of the Police in Scotland', 10758

Mitchell, David: 'A Ghost of a Chance: British Revolutionaries in 1919', 1940; Women on the Warpath: The Story of the Women of the First World War, 7702, 14695

Mitchell, Donald Charles: *ed.* Benjamin Britten: A Commentary on his Works, 24307; Pictures from a Life, 24311; Britten and Auden in the Thirties: The Year 1936, 24312

Mitchell, Edward: The Police: Servants or Masters?, 10730

Mitchell, Elizabeth Buchanan: The Plan that Pleased, 17796

Mitchell, Fanny Harriet: Migration in Scotland 1958–1973, 7284

Mitchell, G. E.: 'China and Britain: Their Commercial and Industrial Relations', 13636

Mitchell, Geoffrey Duncan: A Hundred Years of Sociology, 7987; *ed.* A Dictionary of Sociology, 7988; Sociology: The Study of Social Systems, 7989; Sociological Questions, 7990; Neighbourhood and Community: An Enquiry into Social Relationships on Housing Estates in Liverpool and Sheffield, 7991; Neighbourhood and Community: An Enquiry into Social Relationships on Housing Estates in Liverpool and Sheffield, 9343; Depopulation and the Rural Social Structure', 19070; 'Social Disintegration in a Rural Community', 19071

Mitchell, Hannah Maria: The Hard Way up: The Autobiography of Hannah Mitchell, Suffragette and Rebel, *ed.* Mitchell, Geoffrey, 2260

Mitchell, Sir Harold P.: In My Stride, 1477; Europe in the Caribbean: The Policies of Great Britain, France and the Netherlands towards their West Indian Territories in the Twentieth Century, 13007

Mitchell, Harvey: 'Hobson Revisited', 26587

Mitchell, J. Clyde: 'Occupational Prestige and the Social System: A Problem in Comparative Sociology', 5873; 'The Difference in an English and an American Rating of the Prestige of Occupations', 5874

Mitchell, J. Leslie: Earth Conquerors: The Lives and Achievements of the Great Explorers, 27175

Mitchell, Jeremy: *ed.* Social Science Research and Industry, 5745; *ed.* Marketing and the Consumer Movement, 20474

Mitchell, Joan Eileen: Crisis in Britain, 1951, 3612; The National Board for Prices and Incomes, 3817; 'The Functions of the National Economic Development Council', 6091

Mitchell, Juliet: Women's Estate, 7721; Women and Equality, 7722; *ed.* Essays on Women, 7799

Mitchell, Leslie: Leslie Mitchell Reporting, 24913

Mitchell, M.: 'The Effects of Unemployment on the Social Condition of Women and Children in the 1930's', 8265

Mitchell, Marcia: High Halden, The Parish and the People, 19336

Mitchell, Rosamond Joscelyne: A History of London Life, 18344; A History of the English People, 18345

Mitchell, Sheila: 'Married Women and Employment in England and Wales', 7819

Mitchell, William Harry: Sailing Ship to Supertanker: The 100 Year Story of British Esso and its Ships, 6510, 16540; The Cunard Line: A Post-war History, 1945–1974, 16528; The Cape Run: The Story of the Union Castle Service to South Africa, 16539; Tankers, 16601

Mitchenson, Joe: British Music Hall: A Story on Pictures, 26277

Mitchison, David: Henry Moore: Catalogue of Graphic Work 1931–1979, 24094

Mitchison, Naomi: 'The Haldanes: Personal Notes and Historical Lessons', 26497

Mitchison, Rosalind: A History of Scotland, 2436; Life in Scotland, 5272; British Population Change since 1860, 7410

Mitford, Jessica: Faces of Philip: A Memoir of Philip Toynbee, 25844

Mitford, Nancy: Noblesse Oblige: An Inquiry into the Identifiable Characteristics of the English Aristocracy, 9742; 'Die Englische Aristokratie', 9743

Mitra, A.: 'The British Trade Union Movement: A Statistical Analysis', 6764

Mittler, Peter: The Mental Health Services in the Community, 21795; The Handicapped Child: Recent Research Findings, 21920

Moberley, Sir Walter Hamilton: Universities and the State, 23373; The Crisis in the University, 23374

Moberly, Frederick J.: Togoland and the Cameroons, 1914–1916, 14527; Mesopotamia, 14565

Mobey, J.: 'Marriage Counselling and Family Life Education in England', 9965

Mockaitis, Thomas R.: British Counterinsurgency 1919–60, 16158

Mockler, A.: Our Enemies the French: Being an Account of the War fought between the French and the British, Syria 1941, 14882

Modern Churchman, The, 11543

Moelder, Walter: *ed.* Institutionalism and Church Unity, 12077

Moffat, Abe: My Life with the Miners, 9640

Moffat, James: Handbook to the Church Hymnary, 11929; The Presbyterian Churches, 12123

Moffat, Jonathan: Concepts in Casework Treatment, 8734

Mogey, John MacFarlane: 'Changes in Family Life Experienced by English Workers moving from Slums to Housing Estates', 10029; Family and Neighbourhood: Two Studies in Oxford, 10030; *ed.* Sociology of Marriage and Family Behaviour, 1957–1968, A Trend Report and Bibliography, 10031; 'Residence and Social Class in Oxford', 18070; The Sociology of Housing: Studies at Berinsfield, 18648; Rural Life in Northern Ireland: Five Regional Studies, 19307; 'Characteristics of the Rural Community in Northern Ireland', 19308

Moggridge, Donald Edward: 'The 1931 Financial Crisis: A New View', 3572; 'Economic Policy in the Second World War', 3756; British Monetary Policy, 1924–1931: The Norman Conquest of $4.86, 4558; 'Financial Crises and Lenders of Last Resort: Policy in the Crises of 1920 and 1929', 4559; *ed.* Money and Power: Essays in Honour of L. S. Pressnell, 4648; The Return to Gold, 1925: The Formulation of Economic Policy and and its Critics, 4680; *ed.* The Collected Writings of John Maynard Keynes, 26590; Keynes, 26598; 'Keynes on Monetary Policy, 1910–1946', 26612

Mogre, N.: 'County/District Relations in Shire and Metropolitan Counties in the Field of Town and Country Planning: A Comparison', 3229

Mogridge, Basil: 'Les Syndicats Ouvriers de la Grande-Bretagne', 6787; 'Militancy and Inter-union Rivalries in British Shipping, 1911–1929', 6814

Mogridge, Martin H.: Car Ownership in London, 17372

Mohr, Jean: A Fortunate Man: The Story of a Country Doctor, 20860

Moindrot, Claude: 'Les Mouvements de la

population dans la Région de Birmingham', 7345; 'Le Renversement du courant d'immigration Seculaire: I, 11400; 'Les Vagues d'immigration en Grande Bretagne', 11399; Villes et campagnes britanniques, 17795

Moir, Guthrie: The Suffolk Regiment, 15728

Moir, Phyllis: I was Winston Churchill's Private Secretary, 988

Moisley, Henry Alan: ed. The County of Renfrew and the County of Bute, 19224; 'Leadership and Innovation in the Crofting Communities of the Outer Hebrides', 19282; Uig: A Hebridean Parish, 19374

Moloney, Ed: Paisley, 3077

Moloney, T.: Westminster, Whitehall and the Vatican: The Role of Cardinal Hinsley, 1935–43, 14117

Mommsen, Wolfgang J.: ed. The Fascist Challenge and the Policy of Appeasement, 13722

Monck, Elizabeth Mary: The Employment and Socio-Economic Conditions of the Coloured Population, 11049

Monckton, Herbert Anthony: A History of English Ale and Beer, 20732

Moncrieff, Alan Aird: ed. Diet in Health and Disease, 20511; Child Health and the State, 22086

Moncrieff, Anthony: ed. Suez—Ten Years After, 14375

Mond, Alfred Moritz [Baron Melchett]: Industry and Politics, 1478, 6056; 1478; Liberalism and Modern Industrial Problems: Trade, Currency, Industry and Unemployment, 6055

Mondey, David: Women of the Air, 17519

Money, Ernle: Margaret Thatcher: First Lady of the House, 1048

Money, Keith: Fonteyn: The Royal Ballet Today, 24219; The Making of a Legend, 24231; The Art of Margot Fonteyn, 24232

Monger, Mark: Casework in After-care, 10469; Casework in Probation, 10470

Monk, Leonard Ashby: Britain, 1945–1970, 367

Monkhouse, Francis John: The Material Resources of Britain: An Economic Geography of the United Kingdom, 26682; A Survey of Southampton and its Region, 18082

Monkhouse, Patrick: ed. 'The Education and Training of the Technologist', 22516

Monks, Noel: Squadrons up! A First Hand History of the R.A.F, 14990; Eyewitness, 25267

Monks, Thomas Gordon: Comprehensive Education in England and Wales: A Survey of Schools and their Organisation, 22953

Monroe, Elizabeth: Britain's Moment in the Middle East, 1914–1956, 13803. 'Kuwait and Aden: A Contrast in British Policies', 13866

Monroe, W. F.: 'Evaluation of Foreign Exchange Market Intervention: The Pound Sterling, 1964–1968', 4716

Montacute, C.: Costing and Efficiency in Hospitals: A Critical Survey of Costing as an Aid to the Management of Hospitals, 1962, 21395

Montagu of Beaulieu, Edward [Baron]: Steam Cars 1770–1970, 17367

Montagu, Edwin S.: An Indian Diary, 13131

Montagu, Ivor Goldsmid Samuel: 'Michael Balcon, 1896–1977', 24662

Montague, Dale: ed. Frieda Lawrence and her Circle, 25650

Montague, Joel Benjamin, Jnr: Class and Nationality: English and American Studies, 383; Class and Nationality: English and American Studies, 9532

Montefiore, Alan: Neutrality and Commitment: The University and Political Commitment, 22534

Montefiore, Dora B.: From a Victorian to a Modern, 2257

Montefiore, Hugh: So Near and Yet So Far: Rome, Canterbury and ARCIC, 12335

Montgomery, A. E.: 'Lloyd George and the Greek Question, 1918–1922', 13839

Montgomery, B.: Shenton of Singapore: Governor and Prisoner of War, 12926

Montgomery, Bernard Law: The Memoirs of Field Marshal the Viscount Montgomery of Alamein, K.G., 14767

Montgomery, John: The Twenties, an Informal Social History, 299, 7546; The Fifties, 300, 7547

Montgomery, Robert John: Examinations: An Account of their Evolution as Administrative Devices in England, 22915

Montgomery-Massingberd, Hugh: The London Ritz: A Social and Architectural History, 27997

Moodie, Graeme Cochrane: 'The Monarch and the Selection of a Prime Minister: A Re-Examination of the Crisis of 1931', 462; Some Problems of the Constitution, 611; Opinions, Publics and Pressure Groups: An Essay on Vox Populi and Representative Government, 2360; Power and Authority in British Universities, 23303; 'Buffer, Coupling and Broker: Reflections on Sixty Years of the U.G.C.', 23325

Moody, A. Dale: Virginia Woolf, 25894

Moody, Bert: 150 Years of Southampton Docks, 16707

Moody, David: Scottish Local History: An Introductory Guide, 2460, 26755; Scottish Family History, 26756

Moody, George Thomas: Southern Electric 1909–1979: The History of the World's Largest Suburban Electrified System, 16911

Moody, Gordon: The Facts about the 'Money Factories': An Independent View of Betting and Gambling in Britain now, 27117

Moody, Mary: The Growth of Planning Research since the Early 1960s, 17916

Moody, Susan: Drunken Offenders in Scotland: A Review of the Relevant Literature, 22122

Moody, Theodore W.: ed. Irish Historiography 1936–1970, 2640; ed. Ulster since 1800: A Political and Economic Survey, 2904; The Ulster Question, 1603–1973, 2905; Queen's Belfast, 1845–1949: The History of a University, 23457

Moon, Jeremy: European Integration in British Politics 1950–1963: A Study of Issue Change, 14144

Moon, Norman Sydney: Education for

Ministry: Bristol Baptist College, 1679–1979, 12043

Moon, Sir Penderel: Wavell: The Viceroy's Journal, 13161; Divide and Quit, 13169

Moonman, Eric: Reluctant Partnership: A Critical Study of the Relationship between Government and Industry, 6083

Moorby, Ronald Leonard: A Century of Trade Marks: A Commentary on the Work and History of the Trade Mark Registry, 4541

Moore, B.: All out: The Dramatic Story of the Sheffield Demonstration against Dole Cuts on February 6th 1935, 1781

Moore, Barry Charles: 'Evaluating the Effects of British Regional Economic Policy [1950–1971]', 3632, 5102; 'Regional Policy and the Scottish Economy', 5269; Regional Policy and the Economy of Wales, 5326

Moore, Bryan McAskie: Block or Day Release?: A Comparative Study of Engineering Apprentices, 23278

Moore, Charles: The Church in Crisis: A Critical Assessment of the Current State of the Church of England, 11601

Moore, Colin: Community versus Crime, 10170

Moore, Donald: The First 150 Years of Singapore, 12918

Moore, E. Garth: Moore's Introduction to English Canon Law, 11589

Moore, Eldon: 'Social Progress and Social Decline', 7895

Moore, G. H.: The University of Bath: The Formative Years 1949–1969: A Short History of the Circumstances which Led to the Foundation of the University of Bath, 23456

Moore, Gerald: Am I too Loud?, 24404; Farewell Recital: Further Memoirs, 24405

Moore, Harry Thornton: ed. The World of Lawrence Durrell, 25484; ed. D. H. Lawrence: Collected Letters, 25628; The Life and Works of D. H. Lawrence, 25642; ed. Frieda Lawrence and her Circle, 25650

Moore, Henry: Sculpture and Environment, 24198

Moore, Jerrold Northrop: Edward Elgar: A Creative Life, 24343; Elgar and his Publishers: Letters of a Creative Life, 24344; A Life in Photographs, 24345

Moore, Joanna: The First 150 Years of Singapore, 12918

Moore, John: 'The Falklands Experience', 16112

Moore, John: Doune Valley Diary: The Critical Decade, 1963–72, 18145

Moore, John Cecil: The Fleet Air Arm: A Short Account of its History and Achievements, 14986

Moore, Katharine: An Invisible Friendship: An Exchange of Letters, 26049

Moore, Mary: Wilfred Burrows, 1858–1929: Bishop of Truro, 1912–1919, Bishop of Chichester, 1919–1929, 11727

Moore, Moreton: ed. Royal Holloway and Bedford New College: Centenary Lectures, 1886–1986, 23533

Moore, N. E. A.: 'The Civil Service College: What It Is and what It Is Not', 883; The Decimalisation of Britain's Currency, 4725

Moore, Patrick: The Picture History of Astronomy, 26396; Watchers of the Stars: The Scientific Revolution, 26397; Man the Astronomer, 26398; The Development of Astronomical Thought, 26399

Moore, Ralph Westwood: *ed.* Education: Today and Tomorrow, 22634, 22671

Moore, Robert Samuel: The Social Impact of Oil: The Case of Peterhead, 6527; Slamming the Door: The Administration of Immigration Control, 11107; Race, Community and Conflict: A Study of Sparkbrook, 11457; Racism and Black Resistance in Britain, 11180; Pitmen, Preachers and Politics: The Effects of Methodism in a Durham Mining Community, 12385

Moore, Robin James: The Crisis of Indian Unity 1917–1940, 13142; Churchill, Cripps and India, 1939–1945, 13164; Escape from Empire: The Attlee Government and the Indian Problem, 13182

Moore, Terence: The Practice of Educational Psychology, 22856

Moore, V.: The Local Ombudsman: A Review of the First Five Years, 3252; The Free Two Pence: Section 137 of Local Government Act 1972 and Section 83 of the Local Government (Scotland) Act 1973, 3263

Moore, W.: The Durham Light Infantry, 15627

Moorehead, Caroline: Troublesome People: Enemies of War, 1916–1986, 13436

Moorfoot, Rex: Television in the Eighties: The total Equation, 24883

Moorhead, Alan McCrae: Gallipoli, 14550; Montgomery, A Biography, 14768; African Trilogy, 14900; A Late Education: Episodes in a Life, 25268

Moorhouse, Geoffrey: Britain in the Sixties: The Other England, 7579; The Missionaries, 12355; The Diplomats: The Foreign Office Today, 13332

Moorhouse, Herbert F.: 'Lower Class Attitudes to Property: Aspects of the Counter Ideology', 9451; 'Lower Class Attitudes towards the British Political System', 9691; 'The Political Incorporation of the British Working Class: An Interpretation', 9692; 'Professional Football and Working Class Culture: English Theories and Scottish Evidence', 27057

Moorman, John Richard Humpidge: A History of the Church in England, 11567; 'Archbishop Davidson and the Church', 11693; Vatican Observed: An Anglican Impression of Vatican II, 12327

Moorman, Mary Caroline: George Macaulay Trevelyan: A Memoir by his Daughter, 26825

Moos, Malcolm: 'Darkness over the Ivory Tower', 23438

Moos, Siegfried: A Pioneer of Social Advance: William Henry Beveridge, 1879–1963, 1358, 9039; Aspects of Monopoly and Restrictive Practices Legislation in Relation to Small Firms, 5520

Mor-O'Brien, Anthony: 'The Merthyr Boroughs Election, November 1915', 2560; '"Conchie": Emrys Hughes and the First World War', 2581, 13454

Moran, Jack William Grace: Spearhead in Malaya, 14926

Moran, James: Natsopa Seventy-five Years: The National Society of Operative Printers and Assistants, 1889–1964, 6844; Printing Presses: History and Development from the 15th Century to Modern Times, 7066, 25028; Clays of Bungay, 25022; Stanley Morison: His Typographic Achievement, 25025

Moran, Michael: 'Monetary Policy and the Machinery of Government', 815; 'The Conservative Party and the Trade Unions since 1974', 1654; The Politics of Banking: The Strange Case of Competition and Credit Control, 4450; The Politics of Industrial Relations: The Origins, Life and Death of the 1971 Industrial Relations Act, 5790; The Union of Post Office Workers: A Study in Political Sociology, 6883

Moran, Thomas: Bread: The Chemistry and Nutrition of Flour and Bread, with an Introduction to their Chemistry and Technology, 20700

Morash, Merry: 'Gangs, Groups and Delinquency', 10672

Mordal, Jacques: Dieppe: The Dawn of Decision, 14827

Mordecai, John: The West Indies: The Federal Negotiations, 13103

More, Charles: The Industrial Age: Economy and Society in Britain 1750–1985, 3536

More, James Anthony: Agriculture: The Science and Practice of British Farming, 19437; The Farming Year, 19438; *ed.* Agriculture in the British Economy, 19439; The Pace of Farming Progress, 19440; Rural Britain Today and Tomorrow, 19441; Special Article on Farming after the War, 19442; The History of the Royal Agricultural Society of England, 1839–1939, 19443

More, Kenneth: Happy Go Lucky: My Life, 26070

Morecambe, Eric: There's No Answer to That: An Autobiography with Help from Michael Freedland, 26334

Morecambe, Gary: Funny Man, Eric Morecambe, 26333

Moreton, C. G. N.: 'Vacancy Reserve', 18010

Morey, Adrian: David Knowles: A Memoir, 26804

Morgan Jones, J.: 'The Social Origins of Farmers in Wales', 9584

Morgan, A. E.: Young Citizen, 8532

Morgan, A. Mary: *ed.* British Government Publications: An Index to Chairmen and Authors, 1941–1966, 189

Morgan, Alun: Modern Jazz: A Survey of Developments since 1939, 24452

Morgan, Austen: J. Ramsay MacDonald, 1032; James Connolly: A Political Biography, 3042

Morgan, B. S.: 'Segregation of Socioeconomic Groups in Urban Areas: a Comparative Analysis', 18286

Morgan, Charles Langbridge: The House of Macmillan 1843–1943, 24976

Morgan, D. H. J.: 'The British Association Scandal: The Effect of Publicity on a Sociological Investigation', 8036; 'The Social and Educational Background of Anglican Bishops—Continuities and Changes', 11681

Morgan, David John: The Official History of Colonial Development, 12558

Morgan, David: 'British Social Theory: Review Article', 8056

Morgan, David: City Politics and the Press: Journalists and the Government of Merseyside, 25326

Morgan, Edward Victor: The Structure of Property Ownership in Great Britain, 3767; Choice in Pensions: The Political Economy of Saving for Retirement, 3980; The Stock Exchange: Its History and Functions, 4253; An Economic Study of the City of London, 4254; Studies in British Financial Policy, 1914–1925, 4552; 'Funding Policy and the Gilt-Edged Market', 4553; 'How Serious is Welsh Unemployment?', 5313; 'Wales in Recession', 5314; 'Progress and Problems in Wales', 5315; Monopolies, Mergers and Restrictive Practices: U.K. Competition Policy 1948–1984, 5550

Morgan, Sir Gilbert Thomas: Achievements of the British Chemical Industry in the last 25 Years, 6223; British Chemistry Industry: Its Rise and Development, 6215

Morgan, Harold Anthony: Architecture of the Twentieth Century, 23882

Morgan, J. Vyrnwy: 'Industrialism in Wales', 5304

Morgan, Jane: Portrait of a Progressive: The Political Career of Christopher, Viscount Addison, 1062

Morgan, Janet P.: The House of Lords and the Labour Government, 1964–1970, 680; *ed.* The Backbench Diaries of Richard Crossman, 1165; Agatha Christie: A Biography, 25449

Morgan, John S.: 'The Break-up of the Poor Law in Britain, 1907–47: An Historical Footnote', 9052; Comparative Social Administration, 9234

Morgan, Jon: North Sea Oil in the Future: Economic Analysis and Government Policy, 7171

Morgan, Kenneth Owen: *ed.* The Age of Lloyd George, 1018; *ed.* Lloyd George Family Letters, 1885–1936, 1018; David Lloyd George, 1863–1945, 1018; Lloyd George, 1018; David Lloyd George: Welsh Radical as World Statesman, 1018; 'Lloyd George's Premiership: A Study in "Prime-Ministerial" Government', 1027; Portrait of a Progressive: The Political Career of Christopher, Viscount Addison, 1062; Keir Hardie: Radical and Socialist, 1423; Labour People: Leaders and Lieutenants Hardie to Kinnock, 1689; 'The High and Low Politics of Labour: Keir Hardie to Michael Foot', 1690; Consensus and Disunity: The Lloyd George Coalition Government 1918–22, 1814; 'Lloyd George and the Historians', 1028; Wales 1880–1980: The Rebirth of a Nation, 2546; Wales in British Politics, 1868–1922, 2547; 'Post-war Reconstruction in Wales, 1918 and 1945', 2548; 'Peace Movements in Wales 1899–1945', 2549,

13442; *ed.* Welsh Society and Nationhood: Historical Essays Presented to Glanmor Williams, 2556; 'Cardiganshire Politics: The Liberal Ascendancy, 1885–1923', 2564; 'The New Liberalism and the Challenge of Labour: The Welsh Experience, 1885–1929', 2565; 'Welsh Nationalism, the Historical Background', 2600; Freedom or Sacrilege? A History of the Campaign for Welsh Disestablishment, 12289

Morgan, M. C.: Bryanston, 1929–1978, 23047; Cheltenham College: The First Hundred Years, 23050

Morgan, Margaret: Families and their Needs, with Particular Reference to One-Parent Families, 9941

Morgan, Margery: A Drama of Political Man: A Study in the Plays of Granville Barker, 25941

Morgan, Noel: A Select Bibliography of Aircraft Noise, 20150

Morgan, Patricia: Delinquent Fantasies, 10158

Morgan, Prys Tomos Jon: *ed.* Glamorgan Society 1780–1980, 3383

Morgan, R. H.: 'The Development of an Urban Transport System: The Case of Cardiff', 16341

Morgan, R. P. C.: 'Nature Provides, Man Erodes', 19931

Morgan, Raine: Dissertations on British Agrarian History: A Selected List of Theses awarded Higher Degrees in British and Foreign Universities between 1876 and 1978, 19388

Morgan, Rodney: A Taste of Prison: The Future of the Prison System, 10406; Custodial Conditions for Trial and Remand Prisoners, 10408; 'The Prison System: Prospects for Change', 10456; 'Police Accountability: Developing the Local Infrastructure', 10778

Morgan, Roger: *ed.* Britain and West Germany: Changing Societies and the Future of Foreign Policy, 14215

Morgan, Ted: Churchill, 1874–1915, 988; Somerset Maugham, 25712

Morgan, William: A Survey of Capital and Credit in Agricultural Co-operative Societies in Great Britain, 19505

Morgan, William John: *ed.* The Welsh Dilemma: Some Essays on Nationalism in Wales, 2603

Morgan-Webb, Sir Charles: The Rise and Fall of the Gold Standard, 4681

Moriarty, Cecil Charles Hudson: Police Procedure and Administration, 10747

Morison, Stanley: The Typographic Book 1450–1935, 25024; The English Newspaper, 1632–1932, 25343

Morland, Andrew: Traction Engines, 17092

Morland, Nigel: An Outline of Sexual Criminology, 10862

Morley Village History Committee: A History of the Parish of Morley, Derbyshire, 19349

Morley, David: What's this Channel Fo(u)r?, 24881

Morley, Don: Classic [Postwar] British Scramblers, 17195

Morley, John [Viscount Morley of Blackburn]: Recollections, 1278; Memorandum on Resignation, August 1914, 1279

Morley, John: 'Can White Management Cope with Coloured Workers?', 10946

Morley, Kenneth C.: Social Activity and Social Enterprise: A Study of the Present Condition and Future Role of Voluntary Social Organisations in the Designated New Town of Redditch, 9353; 'Social Participation and Social Enterprise in Redditch (England)', 9354

Morley, Peter: 'Television and the 1970 Election', 24893

Morley, Peter: Marginal Medicine, 21225

Morley, Sheridan Robert: The Other Side of the Moon: The Life of David Niven, 24688, 26075; A Talent to Amuse: A Biography of Coward, 25954; Noel Coward and His Friends, 25957; *ed.* The Noel Coward Diaries, 25958; Gladys Cooper: A Biography, 26027; James Mason: Odd Man Out, 26067; Elizabeth Taylor: A Celebration, 26104; Sybil Thorndike: A Life in the Theatre, 26106; Review Copies: Plays and Players in London, 1970–1974, 26257

Moro, Ruben O.: The History of the South Atlantic Conflict: The War for the Malvinas, 16083

Moroney, Robert M.: The Family and the State: Considerations for Social Policy, 10106

Morphet, Janice: 'Local Authority Decentralisation—Tower Hamlets Goes all the way', 3316

Morphet, Richard: British Painting 1910–1945, 23965

Morpurgo, Jack Eric: Barnes Wallis: A Biography, 15206; Allen Lane: King Penguin, a Biography, 24986

Morpurgo, P. W. K.: Dental Health and the Dental Services: An Assessment of Available Data, 22399

Morrah, Dermot MacGregor: The Work of the Queen, 509

Morrell, James: Britain through the 80's: An Evaluation of Market and Business Prospects, 3687

Morrell. J. B.: *ed.* York: How York Governs Itself, 3344; How York is Governed by the Ministers of the Crown, 3345

Morris, A. J. Anthony: C. P. Trevelyan, 1870–1958, 1539; 'The Birmingham Post and Anglo-German Relations, 1933–1935', 13677

Morris, Alan: The Balloonatics, 14636; First of the Many: The Story of Independent Force, R.A.F, 15002

Morris, Alfred J.: *ed.* The Growth of Parliamentary Scrutiny by Committee, 661

Morris, Alison: Signs of Trouble: Aspects of Delinquency, 10151; Understanding Juvenile Justice, 10533; Justice for Children, 10634; Providing Criminal Justice for Children, 10643

Morris, Ben: Objectives and Perspectives in Education: Studies in Educational Theory, 1955–1970, 22672

Morris, Sir Charles R.: 'Where are We Going in English Education?', 23382; 'The Robbins Report', 23410; 'Second Thoughts on Robbins: University Commentary', 23411

Morris, Charles F.: Origins, Orient and 'Oriana' [History of the Orient Line.], 16541

Morris, Claud: I Bought a Newspaper, 25062

Morris, D. S.: 'The Social Composition of A City Council: Birmingham 1925–1966', 3322; 'British Interest Group Theory Re-examined: The Politics of Four Thousand Voluntary Organisations in a British City', 9210

Morris, David: The End of Marriage, 9997

Morris, Derek: *ed.* The Economic System in the United Kingdom, 3449

Morris, Desmond: The Soccer Tribe, 27064

Morris, E. W.: 'The Future of the Poor-Law Infirmary', 21484

Morris, Frank: Scottish Harbours: The Harbours of Mainland Scotland, 16667

Morris, J. Herwald: Local Government Areas, 3110

Morris, James/Jan: The Outriders: A Liberal View of Britain, 2176; The Matter of Wales, 2558; Farewell the Trumpets: An Imperial Retreat, 12589

Morris, Jeremy Noah: Uses of Epidemiology, 22080

Morris, John: The Railways of Pembrokeshire, 16970

Morris, Joseph Acton: The Growth of Industrial Britain: A Work Book and Study Guide in Social and Economic History, 3416

Morris, L. P.: 'British Secret Missions in Turkestan, 1918–1919', 13849

Morris, Sir Malcolm Alexander: The Story of English Public Health, 22032

Morris, Margaret G. N.: *ed.* Australian Trade Policy 1942–1966, 12638

Morris, Lady Mary: Social Enterprise: A Study of the Activities of Voluntary Societies and Voluntary Workers in an Industrial Town, 9145; Voluntary Work in the Welfare State, 9146; A Study of Halifax Concerned with the Recruitment, Training and Deployment of Volunteers in the Social Services, 9147

Morris, Margaret: The General Strike, 6946

Morris, Michael Wolfgang Laurence: The Disaster of Direct Labour: An Examination of Council Building Departments, 18536

Morris, Nick: Public Finances in Perspective, 4660

Morris, Pauline 'The Experience of Imprisonment', 10341; Pentonville: A Sociological Study of an English Prison, 10353; Prisoners and their Families, 10354; Put Away: A Sociological Study of Institutions for the Mentally Retarded, 10355, 21799

Morris, Sir Philip Robert: Welfare and Responsibility, 8862

Morris, Raymond Neville: Urban Sociology, 18281, 18649; The Sociology of Housing: Studies at Berinsfield, 18648

Morris, Richard: Industrial Relations in the Chemical Industry, 5797, 6202

Morris, Robert: The Novels of Anthony Powell, 25766

Morris, Ruth: Scottish Harbours: The Harbours of Mainland Scotland, 16667

Morris, Stephen Bernard: A Short History of Whitchurch Hospital, 1908–1959, 21469

Morris, Terence Patrick: The Criminal Area: A Study in Social Ecology, 10157; 'The Experience of Imprisonment', 10341; Pentonville: A Sociological Study of an English prison, 10353; A Calendar of Murder: Criminal Homicide in England Since 1957, 10791

Morris, Timothy: Innovations in Banking, 4452

Morris, William A.: Earnings and Spending, 3868

Morris-Jones, Sir Henry: Doctor in the Whip's Room, 1482

Morris-Jones, W. H.: ed. Australia and Britain: Studies in Changing Relationships, 12608; ed. From Rhodesia to Zimbabwe: Behind and beyond Lancaster House, 12810

Morrish, Ivor: Education since 1800, 22673; The Background of Immigrant Children, 11000

Morrish, Reginald: The Police and Crime Detection Today, 10156

Morrish, Robert: Towards a Caring Society: The Report of a US Study Team on its Visit to England, Scotland and Wales to Observe the Work of Local Authority Social Services, with Implications Noted for the United States, 8880

Morrison, Arthur Cecil Lockwood: ed. The Criminal Justice Act 1948, 10296

Morrison, Elizabeth: A Community Project in Notting Dale, 9307

Morrison, Frank: War on Great Cities: A Study of the Facts, 15138

Morrison, G.: The Life and Times of Eamon de Valera, 3052

Morrison, Gavin Stuart: The Big Four Remembered, 16840

Morrison, Gavin Wedderburn: The Southern Remembered, 16913

Morrison, H. S.: Modern Ulster: Its Character, Customs, Politics and Industries, 2910

Morrison, Herbert Stanley [Baron]: Government and Parliament, 561.;British Parliamentary Democracy, 562; An Autobiography, 1282; How London is Governed, 3284

Morrison, Ian: Malayan Postscript, 15061

Morrison, Lady: Memoirs of a Marriage, 1284

Morrison, S. L.: 'Schizophrenia and Social Class', 21835

Morrison, Susan: Routine Punctuated by Orgies: The Central Policy Review Staff, 910

Morrison, Sybil: I Renounce War: The Story of the Peace Pledge Union, 13513

Morriss, Richard K.: Railways of Shropshire: A Brief History, 16972

Morrow, Bradford: A Bibliography of the Writings of Wyndham Lewis, 25669

Morse, Geoffrey: Company Finance, Takeovers and Mergers, 5542; Profit-sharing: Legal Aspects of Employee Share Schemes, 6035

Morse, Sir Jeremy: How Banking has Changed, 4448

Morse, Mary: The Unattached: A Report of the Three-year Project Carried out by the National Association of Youth Clubs, 8517

Morson, Clifford: ed. St Peter's Hospital for Stone, 1860–1960, 21456

Mort, Derek: Rail Transport and Sea Transport, 16185

Morter, Peter: The Police, 10704

Mortimer Local History Group: Mortimer between the Wars, 19196

Mortimer, Charles Gordon: The Story of the Open Golf Championship 1860–1950, 27155

Mortimer, James Edward: Industrial Relations, 5697; The Kind of Laws the Unions Ought to Want, 6796; British Trade Unions Today, 6797; History of the Boilermakers' Society, 6841; Trade Unions and Technological Change, 7244

Mortimer, John: Clinging to the Wreckage: Part of a Life, 25718

Mortimer, M.: 'The Drug Traffic', 22223

Mortimer, Roger: The Jockey Club, 27127; A History of the Derby Stakes, 27128

Morton, Andrew: Duchess, 537

Morton, Bernard: ed. Action, 1919–1969: A Record of the Growth of the National Association of Schoolmasters, 22709

Morton, Frank: Report of the Inquiry into the Safety of Natural Gas as a Fuel, 7178

Morton, H. M.: 'The Trained Social Worker and After-care', 10484

Morton, Hudson T.: Anti-friction Bearings, 7067

Morton, J. B.: Hilaire Belloc: A Memoir, 25377

Morton, Jocelyn: Three Generations in a Family Textile Firm, 6442

Morton, R.: 'The Social Effects of Industrial Changes in Great Britain, the Republic of Ireland and Northern Ireland, 5671

Morton, Richard Alan: 'Biochemistry at Liverpool 1902–1971', 26472

Morton, S. Fiona: A Bibliography of Arnold J. Toynbee, 26818

Morton, Walter Albert: British Finance, 1930–1940, 4565

Moscucci, Ornella: The Science of Woman: Gynaecology and Gender in England, 1800–1929, 7840

Moseley, Malcolm J.: The Industrial Development of East Anglia, 5155; Rural Transport and Accessibility, 16312; ed. Power, Planning and People in Rural East Anglia, 18862; Social Issues in Rural Norfolk, 19077

Moseley, Roy: Rex Harrison: The First Biography, 26053

Moseley, Sidney Alexander: Broadcasting in my Time, 24733

Moser, Sir Claus Adolf: British Towns: A Statistical Study of their Social and Economic Differences, 17941, 18280; Dental Health and the Dental Services: An Assessment of Available Data, 22399

Moser, Thomas: The Life and Fiction of Ford Madox Ford, 25516

Moses, Leon N.: 'Income, Leisure and Wage Pressure', 3922

Mosey, Don: Cricket Statistics Year by Year 1946–1987, 27097

Mosley, Diana: The Duchess of Windsor, 479

Mosley, Leonard Oswald: The Glorious Fault: The Life of Lord Curzon, 1173; Backs to the Wall: London under Fire 1939–45, 7534, 15163; Battle of Britain, 14811; Castlerosse, 25219; The Last Days of the British Raj, 13168

Mosley, Nicholas: Beyond the Pale: Sir Oswald Mosley, 1933–1980, 1486; Rules of the Game: Sir Oswald and Lady Cynthia Mosley, 1896–1933, 1485

Mosley, Sir Oswald Ernald: My Life, 1483; The Greater Britain, 2035; One Hundred Questions Answered, 2036; Tomorrow We Live, 2037; My Answer, 2038; The Alternative, 2039; Mosley: Right or Wrong?, 2040; My Life, 2041

Mosley, Paul: Overseas Aid: Its Defence and Reform, 9187; The Settler Economies: Studies in the Economic History of Kenya and Southern Rhodesia, 12834

Mosley, Richard Kenneth: Westminster Workshop: A Student's Guide to the British Constitution, 560; The Story of the Cabinet Office, 598, 754

Moss, Basil Stanley: Clergy Training Today, 11913

Moss, Claude Beaufort: Anglo-Catholicism at the Crossroads, 11643; The Orthodox Revival, 1833–1933: Six Lectures on the Oxford Movement, 11644

Moss, G. P.: From Palace to College: An Illustrated Account of Queen Mary College (University of London), 23529

Moss, Joan E.: Part-time Farming in Northern Ireland: A Study of Small Scale Beef and Sheep Farms, 19649; Growth Possibilities for Small Scale Beef Cattle and Sheep Farms, 19650

Moss, John: The Relieving Officers' Handbook: Being a Complete and Practical Guide to the Law relating to the Powers, Duties and Liabililties of Relieving Officers, 4068; Health and Welfare Services Handbook, 22012

Moss, Louis: Older People and their Employment: Commentary on a Sample Survey made in Britain in the 1950's, 8562

Moss, Michael Stanley: Beardmore: The History of a Scottish Industrial Giant, 6375, 16643; A Business of National Importance: The Royal Mail Shipping Group, 1902–1937, 16537; A Bed of Sails: The History of P. MacCallum and Sons Ltd., 1781–1981: A Study in Survival, 16550; From Cape to Cape: The History of the Lyle Shipping Company, 16552; Workshop of the Empire: Engineering and Shipbuilding in the West of Scotland, 16615; Clyde Shipbuilding from Old Photographs, 16616; Shipbuilders to the World: 125 Years of Harland & Wolff, Belfast, 1861–1986, 16634; The Making of Scotch Whisky: A History of the Scotch Whisky Distilling Industry, 20729

Moss, Milton Cedric: A Survey of Alcoholism in An English County: A Study of the Prevalence, Distribution and Effects of Alcoholism in Cambridgeshire, 22127

Moss, Norman: Klaus Fuchs, the Man who stole the Atom Bomb, 16043

Moss, Peter: All our Children: Pre-School Services in a Changing Society, 8372

Moss, Robert: The Films of Carol Reed, 24682

Mosse, G.: ed. 'Generations in Conflict', 8442

Mosse, R.: 'Les Nouvelles Villes en Grande-Bretagne', 18236

Mossek, M.: Palestine Immigration Policy under Sir Herbert Samuel: British, Zionist and Arab Attitudes, 14299

Most, Eckhard: Grossbritannien und der Völkerbund: Studien zur Politik der Friedenssicherung, 1925–1934, 13482

Motion, Andrew: The Lamberts: George, Constant and Kit, 24359; Philip Larkin, 25622

Mott, J.: 'The Social Characteristics of Militant and Anti-militant Students', 9869; Adult Prisons and Prisoners in England and Wales 1970–1982, 10442

Mott, P. G.: Wings over Ice: An Account of the Falkland Islands and Dependencies Aerial Survey Expedition 1955–57, 27223

Mott-Radclyffe, Sir Charles: Foreign Body in the Eye: A Memoir of the Foreign Service, 1488, 13293

Mottram, R. H.: For some we Loved: An Intimate Portrait of Ada and John Galsworthy, 25534; John Galsworthy, 25535

Mould, Alan: 'Choir Schools in a Changing Educational System', 22457

Moule, Charles F. D.: ed. G. W. H. Lampe, 11799

Moules, Joan: Our Gracie: The Life of Dame Gracie Fields, 24478

Moulson, Thomas James: The Flying Sword: The Story of 601 Squadron, 15927

Moulton, James Louis: The Norwegian Campaign of 1940, 14918; The Royal Marines, 15412

Mounfield, P. R.: 'Early Technological Innovation in the British Footwear Industry', 7050

Mount, Ferdinand: The Subversive Family: An Alternative History of Love and Marriage, 10011

Mount, James Lambert: The Food and Health of Western Man, 20557

Mountevans, Edward Ratcliffe Garth Russell [Baron]: Keeping the Seas, 27201; South with Scott, 27202; British Polar Explorers, 27203; Adventurous Life, 27204; The Desolate Antarctic, 27205; Arctic Solitudes, 27206

Mountfield, Stuart: Western Gateway: A History of the Mersey Docks and Harbour Board, 16693

Mountford, Sir James Frederick: British Universities, 23424; Keele: an Historical Critique, 23504

Mowat, Charles Loch: Britain between the Wars, 1918–1940, 299; ed. New Cambridge Modern History, Vol. XII: The Shifting Balance of World Forces, 365; England in the Twentieth Century, 390; British History Since 1926: A Select Bibliography, 393; 'Baldwin Restored', 977; Lloyd George, 1018; 'Ramsay MacDonald and the Labour Party', 1032; 'The Fall of the Labour Government in Great Britain, August 1931', 1712

Moxon-Browne, Edward: Nation, Class and Creed in Northern Ireland, 2793

Moyes, Adrian: 'Post-war Changes in Coalmining in the West Midlands', 6329; Not by Government Alone: The Role of British Non-Government Organisations in the Development Decade, 9180; Aid in the Commonwealth, 9181

Moyes, Philip John Richard: Bomber Squadrons of the R.A.F, 15003; R.A.F. Bomber Command and its Aircraft 1936–1940, 15009; Pictorial History of the R.A.F., 15787; R.A.F. Jet Fighter Flypast, 15874; Royal Air Force Bombers of World War II, 15985

Moylan, Sir John Fitzgerald: Scotland Yard and the Metropolitan Police, 10750

Moylan, P. A.: The Form and Reform of County Government: Kent 1889–1974, 3359

Moyle, Francis Walter: Neville Gorton, Bishop of Coventry, 1943–1955, 11735

Moyle, John: The Owners of Quoted Ordinary Shares: A Survey for 1963, 3779; The Pattern of Ordinary Share Ownership 1957–1970, 3780

Moynihan, Maurice: ed. Speeches and Statements by Eamon De Valera, 1917–1973, 3048

Moynihan, Michael H.: God on Our Side: The British Padre in the First World War, 11860; ed. A Place Called Armageddon: Letters from the Great War, 14484; ed. Greater Love: Letters Home 1914–1918, 14485; People at War 1939–1945, 15177

Moyser, George H.: Local Politics and Participation in France and Britain, 3129; Church and Politics in a Secular Age, 11634; ed. Church and Politics Today, 11635; 'Studying a Religious Elite: The Case of the Anglican Episcopate', 11685; ed. Research Methods for Elite Studies, 11685

Mozley, John Kenneth: Some Tendencies in British Theology from the Publication of 'Lux Mundi' to the Present Day, 11876

Mrakovits, Andrei: Unions and Economic Crisis: Britain, West Germany and Sweden, 6827

Mrazek, James Edward: Fighting Gliders of World War Two, 17544

Mtshali, B. V.: Rhodesia: Background to Conflict, 12799

Muchnick, David Martin: Urban Renewal in Liverpool: A Study of the Politics of Redevelopment, 18888

Mudge, G. P.: 'The Menace to the English Race and to the Traditions of England in Present-day Immigration and Emigration', 11144

Muellbauer, J.: 'Prices and Inequality: The United Kingdom Experience', 3841; 'Inequality Measures, Prices and Household Composition', 3842; 'Household Composition, Engel Curves and Welfare Comparisons between Households', 3843

Muggeridge, Kitty: Beatrice Webb: A Life, 1858–1943, 2149

Muggeridge, Malcolm: The Thirties: 1930–1940 in Great Britain, 299, 7555; The Sun Never Sets: The Story of England in the Nineteen-Thirties, 7556

Mughan, Anthony: 'Attitudes, Issues and Labour Party Decline in England, 1974–1979', 1765, 2341; Party and Participation in British Elections, 2357

Muhamed, Anwar: The Myth of Return: Pakistanis in Britain, 11231

Muir, Augustus: Blythe, Greene, Jourdain & Co., 1810–1960, 4469; John White, C.H., D.D., LL.D., 12228; The First of Foot: The History of the Royal Scots, 15591

Muir, C. A.: The History of Baker Perkins, 6362

Muir, Edwin: The Present Age, from 1914, 23777; An Autobiography, 25720

Muir, James F.: Salmon: Economics and Marketing, 20720

Muir, John Ramsay Bryce: How Britain is Governed: a Critical Analysis of Modern Developments in the British System of Government, 704

Muir, Richard: The Lost Villages of Britain, 19121

Muir, Willa: Belonging, 25726

Muirhead, J. H.: ed. Contemporary British Philosophy: Personal Statements, 26832

Mukherjee, Santosh: Through No Fault of their Own: Systems for Handling Redundancy in Britain, France and Germany, 6974; Unemployment Costs, 6975

Mulford, David C.: Zambia: The Politics of Independence, 1957–1964, 12780

Mulford, Wendy: ed. This Narrow Place: Sylvia Townsend Warner and Valentine Ackland: Life, Letters and Politics 1930–1951, 25853

Mulhearn, Tony: Liverpool: A City that Dared to Fight, 3332

Mulkay, Michael Joseph: Astronomy Transformed: The Emergence of Radio Astronomy in Britain, 26430

Mulkeen, Anne: Wild Thyme, Winter Lightning: The Symbolic Novels of L. P. Hartley, 25575

Mullally, Frederic: Fascism inside Britain, 2018

Mullaly, Brian Reginald: The South Lancashire Regiment: The Prince of Wales's Volunteers, 15683

Mullan, Bob: Stevenage Ltd: Aspects of the Planning and Politics of Stevenage New Town, 1945–1978, 19026

Mullard, Chris: Black Britain, 11080

Mullen, Peter: ed. Strange Gifts? A Guide to Charismatic Renewal, 12133

Muller, William Dale: British Politics Group Research Register 1981, 1561; 'Trade Union Sponsored Members of Parliament in the Defence Dispute of 1960–1', 1738, 6866; The 'Kept Men'?: The First Century of Trade Union Representation in the British House of Commons, 1874–1975, 6860

Mullin, Chris: Error of Judgement: The Birmingham Bombings, 2773

Mullin, W. A. Roger: 'The Scottish National Party', 2503

Mulliner, H. G.: Arthur Burroughs, 11726

Mullineux, W.: U.K. Banking after Deregulation, 4451

Mullins, Edward: 'The Open-air Vision: A Survey of Sculpture in London since 1945, with Check List', 24179

Multhauf, Robert Philip: Neptune's Gift: A History of Common Salt, 20709; ed. Medicine, Science and Culture, 21216

Mumby, Frank A.: Bookselling and Book Publishing: A History from the Earliest Times to the Present Day, 24936; The House of Routledge 1834–1934, 24988

Mumford, Lewis: 'Sociology and its Prospects in Great Britain', 7958; 'The High-Rise Fashion', 18637

Munby, Denys Lawrence: Road Passenger Transport and Road Goods Transport, 16187; ed. Inland Transport Statistics, Great Britain 1900–1970: vol.1: Railways, Public Road Passenger Transport, London Transport, 16188; Home Ownership, 18643

Munch-Petersen, Thomas: 'Great Britain and the Revision of the Aland Convention, 1938–1939', 13879; The Strategy of Phoney War: Britain, Sweden and the Iron-Ore Question 1939–1940, 14919

Muncie, John: The Trouble with Kids Today, 10658

Munck, Ronnie: Industrial Sociology: An Introduction: With Northern Ireland Case Studies, 5840

Municipal Year Book and Public Services Directory: 1898–, 3094

Munk, William: Lives of the Fellows of the Royal College of Physicians of London, 20841

Munn, Charles W.: The Clydesdale Bank: The First One Hundred and Fifty Years, 4517

Munro, Alistair: 'Parental Deprivation in Depressive Patients', 21811; 'Some Familial and Social Factors in Depressive Illness', 21812

Munro, Charles Kirkpatrick: The Fountains in Trafalgar Square: Some Reflections on the Civil Service, 927

Munro, D.J.: ed. Institute of Historical Research 1946–1948, 404; ed. Institute of Historical Research 1949–1951, 405

Munro, Henrietta: Pictures of Old Thurso and District: Studies of the Past, 19373

Munro, Ian S.: Leslie Mitchell-Lewis Grassic Gibbon, 25538; The Island of Bute, 19270

Munro, Jean: Chemical Children: How to Protect your Family from Harmful Pollutants, 20176

Munro, John Stables Forbes: Britain in Tropical Africa, 1880–1960: Economic Relationships and Impact, 4807, 12686

Munro, Neil: The History of the Royal Bank of Scotland 1727–1927, 4522

Munroe, Moira: 'Intra-Urban Changes in Housing Prices: Glasgow 1972–83', 18477

Munson, James: ed. Echoes of the Great War: The Diary of the Rev. Andrew Clark 1914–1919, 14449

Munson, Kenneth George: Fighters, Attack and Training Aircraft 1914–1919, 14630; Bombers, Patrol and Reconnaissance Aircraft 1914–1919, 14631; Aircraft of World War I, 14632; Aircraft of World War Two, 15836; Bombers between the Wars, 1919–1939, 15837; Bombers in Service: Patrol and Transport Aircraft since 1960, 15872; Bombers, Patrol and Transport

Aircraft, 1939–1945, 15838; Fighters between the Wars, 1919–1939, Including Attack and Training Aircraft, 15824; Fighters, Attack and Training Aircraft 1939–1945, 15832; Helicopters and other Rotorcraft since 1907, 17550

Munster, George: A Paper Prince, 25105

Munt, Peter William: Traffic Characteristics of Greater London's Roads, 17152

Munton, Richard: London's Green Belt: Containment in Practice, 18926

Murad, Anatol: What Keynes Means: A Critical Clarification of the Economic Theories of John Maynard Keynes, 26597

Murdoch, Brian: Fighting Songs and Warring Words: Popular Lyrics of Two World Wars, 14443

Murdoch, Ian: High Halden, The Parish and the People, 19336

Murdock, Graham: 'Youth Culture and the School Revisited', 8447

Murfin, Ross: The Poetry of D. H. Lawrence: Texts and Contexts, 25636

Murie, Alan Shaw: Policy and Government in Northern Ireland: Lessons of Devolution, 2806; Regional Policy and the Attraction of Manufacturing Industry in Northern Ireland, 5391; Housing Policy and the Housing System, 18434, 18517; The Sale of Council Houses: A Study in Social Policy, 18433; Selling the Welfare State: The Privatisation of Council Housing, 18435; 'The Geography of Council House Sales in England, 1979–1985', 18439; Housing Policy and Practice, 18453; Housing in Northern Ireland, 18497;

Murland, J. R. W.: The Royal Armoured Corps, 15598

Murless, Brian J.: Bridgewater Docks and the River Parrett, 16675

Murphy, B. J.: Community Use of Community Schools at the Primary Level: Two Case Studies in Walsall, 9430

Murphy, Brian: A History of the British Economy, 1086–1970, 3490; The Computer in Society, 7084

Murphy, David: The Silent Watchdog: The Press in Local Politics, 25327

Murphy, George William: The Growth of Life Assurance in the United Kingdom since 1880, 4210. 'The Growth of Life Actuaries in the United Kingdom since 1880', 4211

Murphy, James: The Religious Problem in English Education: The Crucial Experiment, 22873; Church, State and Schools in Britain, 1800–1970, 22874

Murphy, John Augustine: Ireland in the Twentieth Century, 310, 2651; ed. De Valera and His Times, 3049

Murphy, John: Dorset at War, 15178

Murphy, John Thomas: Labour's Big Three: A Biographical Study of Clement Attlee, Herbert Morrison and Ernest Bevin, 975

Murphy, John W.: 'Making Sense of Post-modern Sociology', 8083

Murphy, Lawrence R.: 'Rebuilding Britain: The Government's Role in Housing and Town Planning, 1945–1957', 18798

Murphy, Mary Elizabeth: The British War Economy, 1939–1943, 3732

Murphy, Michael Joseph: Poverty in Cambridgeshire, 9101

Murra, Kathleen: Children's Hearings, 10668

Murray, Anne: Reforming Scotland's Prisons: A Task for the Assembly, 10369

Murray, Bill: The Old Firm: Sectarianism, Sport and Society in Scotland, 27088

Murray, David: Steel Curtain: A Biography of the British Iron and Steel Industry, 6567

Murray, David: The First Nation in Europe: A Portrait of Scotland and the Scots, 5248

Murray, David Stark: Why a National Health Service? The Part Played by the Socialist Medical Association, 21555, 22031; Medical Care and Family Security: Norway, England and the U.S.A., 21573; Health for All, 22030; Science Fights Death, 22356

Murray, Derek Boyd: The First Hundred Years: The Baptist Union of Scotland, 12257

Murray, Douglas M.: ed. Studies in the History of Worship in Scotland, 12200

Murray, George Gilbert Aimé: The League of Nations Movement: Some Recollections of the Early Days, 13469; An Unfinished Autobiography, with Contributions by his Friends, 26567

Murray, George John: Voluntary Organisations and Social Welfare: An Administrator's Impressions, 9208

Murray, George McIntosh: The Press and the Public: The Story of the British Press Council, 25331

Murray, George Thursby: Scotland: A New Look, 5255; The United Kingdom: An Economic and Marketing Study, 7258

Murray, Kathleen: ed. The Scottish Juvenile Justice System, 10645

Murray, Sir Keith Anderson: Agriculture, 19493

Murray, L.: 'Le Syndicalisme et la Planification en Grande Bretagne', 6768

Murray, Lady Mildred Octavia: The Making of a Civil Servant: Sir Oswyn Murray, G.C.B., Secretary of the Admiralty, 1917–6, 921

Murray, Marischal: Union Castle Chronicle, 1853–1953, 16538

Murray, Peter: ed. Modern British Architecture since 1945, 23907

Murray, Rosalind: New Hall, 1954–1972: the Making of a College, 23482

Murray, Williamson: 'Munich 1938: The Military Confrontation', 13744; ed. Military Effectiveness, 15470

Murray-Brown, Jeremy: ed. The Monarchy and its Future, 437

Murry, Katherine Middleton: Beloved Quixote: The Unknown John Middleton Murry, 25736

Museum of English Rural Life: Guide to the Museum of English Rural Life, 19116

Musgrave, Beatrice: Women at the Top: Achievement and Family Life, 7806

Musgrave, Peter William: The Economic Structure, 3448; Technical Change, The Labour Force and Education: A Study of the British and German Iron and Steel Industries, 1860–1964, 6572; ed. Sociology, History and Education, 7999; ed. Sociology of Education, 8000; 'How Children Use Television', 8266; Youth and the Social Order, 8434; The Family, Education and Society, 8435; Society and Education in England since 1800, 22660; The Sociology of Education, 22804

Musgrove, Frank: The Migratory Elite, 7329, 9529; School and the Social Order, 9612, 22810; Society and the Teacher's Role, 9846; 'Social Class and Levels of Aspiration in a Technological University', 9870; The Family, Education and Society, 10079, 22828

Musgrove, G.: Pathfinder Force: A History of 8 Group, 14993

Musil, Jiri: Housing Needs and Policy in Great Britain and Czechoslovakia, 18450

Musson, Albert Edward: The Growth of British Industry, 5413; Enterprise in Soap and Chemicals: Joseph Crosfield and Sons Ltd., 1815–1965, 6230; Trade Union and Social History, 6701; ed. The Typographical Association: Origins and History up to 1949, 6886; 'Parliament and the Press: An Historical Survey', 25123

Muste, John Martin: Say that We Saw Spain Die: Literary Consequences of the Spanish Civil War, 23773

Mustoe, Nelson Edwin: The Law and Organisation of the British Civil Service, 893

Mutafian, Claude: Gwyneth Jones, 24420

Mutch, William Edward Scott: Public Recreation in National Forests: A Factual Survey, 26953

Muto, Chozo: A Short History of Anglo-Japanese Relations, 13583

Myers, Charles Samuel: Present-day Applications of Psychology with Special Reference to Industry, Education and Nervous Breakdown, 5583; Mind and Work: The Psychological Factors in Industry and Commerce, 5584; Industrial Psychology in Great Britain, 5585

Myers, Frank E.: 'Social Class and Political Change in Western Industrial Systems', 9444; 'Conscription and the Politics of Military Strategy in the Attlee Government', 16071

Myers, J. Arthur: Captain of all these Men of Death: Tuberculosis Historical Highlights, 21155

Myers, Jerome Keeley: A Decade Later: A Follow-up Study of Social Class and Mental Illness, 21817

Myers, Karen: 'John Fowles: An Annotated Bibliography 1963–76', 25526

Myers, Robert A.: Dominica, 13079

Myers, Robin: The British Book Trade from Caxton to the Present Day: A Bibliographical Guide, 24927

Myers, Rollo Hugh: Twentieth Century Music, 24283

Myers, Stephen: Cars from Sheffield: The Rise and Fall of the Sheffield Motor Car Industry 1900–1930, 17408

Myerscough, John: 'Airport Provision in the Inter-war Years', 17662; The Economic Importance of the Arts in Britain, 23766

Myles, Bruce: Jump Jet: The Revolutionary V/STOL Fighter, 17561

Myrdal, Gunnar: 'How Scientific are the Social Services?', 8043; 'The Relation between Social Theory and Social Policy', 8774; Beyond the Welfare State, 9012

N.P.H.T. Report on a Study of the Work of Public Health Nurses, 21705

NOP Market Research: Political, Social, Economic Review, 235

Nabarro, Sir Gerald: Exploits of a Politician, 1490; NAB 1: Portrait of a Politician, 1489

Nachmani, Anikam: Great Power Discord in Palestine: The Anglo-American Committee of Inquiry into the Problems of European Jewry and Palestine 1945–1946, 14338. ' "It is a Matter of Getting the Mixture Right": Britain's Post-War Relations with America in the Middle East', 14339

Nadel, Ira Bruce: ed. George Orwell: A Reassessment, 25753

Nadia, A. R.: The Ethics of Feminism: A Study of the Revolt of Women, 7666

Nagle, Thomas Wheeler: A Study of British Public Opinion and the European Appeasement Policy, 1933–1939, 13706

Nairn, A. G.: 'Migrant Employment and the Recession—The Case of the Irish in Britain', 11369

Nairn, Ian: Britain's Changing Towns, 20321

Nairn, Tom: The Enchanted Glass: Britain and Its Monarchy, 446; The Break-up of Britain: Crisis and Neo-Nationalism 1965–1975, 2399; 'The English Working Class', 9677; 'The British Political Elite', 9758

Nairne, Sandy: ed. British Sculpture in the Twentieth Century, 24182

Najder, Zdzislaw: Joseph Conrad: A Chronicle, 25464

Nalson, John Spencer: Mobility of Farm Families: A Study of Occupational and Residential Mobility in an Upland Area of England, 19158

Namier, Lady Julia: Lewis Namier: A Biography, 26807

Namier, Sir Lewis Bernstein: In the Margin of History, 13699

Nandy, Dipak: 'Immigrants and the Election', 2235; 'Discrimination and the Law', 11111; 'Immigration: The Great Betrayal', 11112; The Politics of Race Relations, 11138

Napal, Doojen: Enoch Powell: A Study in Personality and Politics, 1291

Napier, Brian: 'Judicial Attitudes towards the Employment Relationship: Some Recent Developments', 10297

Naseem, Muhammad: The Dilemma of the Welfare State, 21599

Nash, Christopher Alfred: The Economics of Public Transport, 16257

Nash, Eric Francis: Agricultural Policy in England, 19531; The Agricultural Policies of Britain and Denmark: A Study in Reciprocal Trade, 19659

Nash, Joanna: Croydon Aerodrome, 17672

Nash, Paul: Outline: An Autobiography. 24044

Nash, Steven: Ben Nicholson: Fifty Years of his Art, 24047

Nasric, Abdel Rahman El: A Bibliography of the Sudan, 1938–1958, 14409

Nassibian, Akaby: Britain and the Armenian Question, 1915–1923, 13845

Nathan, David: The Laughtermakers: A Quest for Comedy, 26281; Hancock, 26315

Nathan, H. L., Baron: ed. Liberal Points of View, 2167; ed. Liberalism and Some Problems of Today, 2168

National Advisory Centre on Careers for Women: Training and Employment for the Arts Graduate: An Introduction, 5971

National Association for Mental Health, Subsequently Mind: Mental Breakdown: A Guide for Families, 21749; Report: In-service Training for Social Work with the Mentally Ill, 21750; Report: The Next Step: Community Care for Former Psychiatric Patients in Six Towns, 21751; Violence and the Mental Health Services: Proceedings of a Conference, 21768

National Association of Local Councils: The Future of English Local Government from the Viewpoint of the Parishes, 19314

National Bank of Scotland Ltd: The National Bank of Scotland Ltd., 4521

National Board for Prices and Incomes: Pay of Nurses and Midwives in the National Health Service, 21725

National Bureau for Co-operation in Child Care: Annual Report, 8267; (Proceedings of the First Annual Conference) Investment in Children: A Symposium on Positive Child Care and Constructive Education, 8268

National Catholic Commission For Racial Justice: When Creed and Colour Matter: A Survey on Black Children and Catholic Schools, 23190

National Child Development Study: 1958 Cohort. 11,000 seven-year-olds: First Report of the NCDS—1958 Cohort—Submitted to the Central Advisory Committee for Education (England), April 1966, 8284; From Birth to Seven: The Second Report of the NCDS—1958 Cohort, 8285; Britain's Sixteen-Year-Olds: Preliminary Findings from the Third Follow-Up of the NCDS—1958 Cohort, 8286

National Children's Bureau: (Information Service). Spotlight on Physical and Mental Assessment, 8269; Spotlight on Services for the Young Handicapped Child, 8270; Spotlight on Groupwork with Parents in Special Circumstances, 8271; Spotlight on Sources of Information about Children, 8272; Handicapped School-leavers: Their Further Education, Training and Employment, 8273; The Child with Cerebral Palsy, 8274; The Child with a Chronic Medical Problem, 8275; The Child with Asthma, 8276; Growing Up in a One Parent Family, 8277; Disadvantaged Families and Playgroups, 8278; Coping Alone, 8279; Growing Up in Great Britain: Papers from the National Child Development Study, 8280; Who Cares? Young People in Care Speak Out, 8281; Inequalities and Childhood: The Proceedings of a Conference Held on 26 April 1985 at Queen's Hall, Edinburgh, 8282; Warnock Seven Years On: A Scottish Perspective, 8283

National Coal Board: British Coal: The Rebirth of an Industry, Published on the Completion of the First Ten Years of Public Ownership, 6294; Scottish Division: A Short History of the Scottish Coal-mining Industry, 6331

National Council of Social Service: Public Social Services: Handbook of Information, 8866; Councils of Social Service: A Handbook, 8867; Dictionary of Social Services: Policy and Practice, 8868; Welfare State and Welfare Society: A Guide to Studies for the Sixth British National Conference on Social Welfare, April 1967, 8869; New Housing Estates and their Problems, 9310; Community Centres and Associations, 9311; Community Centres and Associations Conference, 9312; Community Organisation—An Introduction, 9313; Community Organisation: Work in Progress, 9314; The Size and Social Structure of a Town: A Report, 17745; Village Halls: Their Construction and Management, 19126; Village Halls and Social Centres in the Countryside: A Handbook of Information, 19127; The Village Hall: The Site and the Building, 19128; The Village Hall: The Interior, 19129; The Village Hall: Design and Construction, 19130; The Village Hall: Maintenance, 19131; People and their Settlements: Aspects of History, Transport and Strategic Planning in the U.K.: Papers for a Conference . . . , 19939

National Council on Inland Transport: A Future Policy for Britain's Transport, 16251

National Economic Development Office: New Homes in the Cities, 17972

National Federation of Business and Professional Women's Clubs of Great Britain and Northern Ireland: The Changing Pattern: Report on the Training of Older Women, 7687

National Federation of Community Associations: Creative Living: The Work and Purposes of Community Associations, 9309

National Federation of Housing Societies: A Guide to Housing Associations and Housing Societies, 18565

National Film Archive: Catalogue, 24585

National Front: Policy Cttee: The Case for Economic Nationalism: 2053; Policy Cttee: The Money Manufacturers: An Exposé of the Root Cause of the Financial and Economic Crisis, 2054; Education for National Survival, 2055

National Guilds League: Workers' Control on the Railways, 16742

National Housing and Town Planning Council: Housing and Town Planning after the War: Memorandum, 18583; Future Housing Policy: Report of a Deputation from the . . . Council to Government, 18584

National Industrial Conference Board: Mergers in Industry, 5510

National Industrial Development Council of Wales and Monmouthshire Ltd: Made in Wales: Where and what to Buy from Wales

and Monmouthshire, 5307; Wales and Monmouthshire: An Illustrated Review, 5308; The Second Industrial Survey of South Wales, 5368

National Institute for Social Work: Social Workers: Their Role and Tasks, 8767

National Institute of Economic Research: 'The United Kingdom Balance of Payments', 4920

National Institute of Industrial Psychology: Joint Consultation in British Industry: A Report of an Inquiry, 5998

National Maritime Museum, Greenwich: Man is not Lost: A Record of Two Hundred Years of Astronomical Navigation with the Nautical Almanac, 1767–1967, 26432

National Museum of Wales: The Maritime History of Dyfed, 16483

National Old People's Welfare Council: Age is Opportunity: A Handbook of Historical and Social Development concerning the Care of the Elderly in the United Kingdom, with Information about Practical Schemes and with some Reference to Development Overseas, 8621

National Old People's Welfare Council: Employment and Workshops for the Elderly, 8563

National Opinion Polls: NOP Political Bulletin, 234

National Portrait Gallery: 20th Century Portraits, 214; Complete Illustrated Catalogue, 215

National Pure Water Association: Fluoride: Facts and Fancy, 22396

National Smoke Abatement Society: Annual Report, 20034; Yearbook, 20035; Clean Air Yearbook, 20036

National Spiritual Assembly of the Baha'is of the British Isles: The Centenary of a World Faith: The History of the Baha'i Faith in the British Isles, 12460

National Standing Joint Council on Road and Rail Traffic Problems: The Road and Rail Crisis: Memorandum to the Prime Minister, 16834

National Union Catalog Pre-1956 Imprints: A Cumulative Author List representing Library of Congress Printed Cards and Titles reported and other American Libraries: Compiled and edited with the Co-operation of the Library of Congress and the National Union Catalog Sub-Committee of the Resources and Technical Services Division, American Library Association, 107

National Union Catalog. 1958–1962, 108; Motion Pictures and Filmstrips 1963–1967, 109; Motion Pictures and Filmstrips 1968–1972, 110; Author List 1968–1972, 111; Films 1973–1977, 112; Author List 1973–1977, 113

National Whitley Council: Fulton—The Reshaping of the Civil Service, Developments since 1970, 880

National Youth Bureau: Bibliography of Youth Social Work, 8408

Navabpour, Reza: Iran, 13850

Navarro, Vincente: Class Struggle: The State and Medicine: An Historical and

Contemporary Analysis of the Medical Sector in Great Britain, 21609

Navy List: 1814+, 15225

Nayler, Joseph L.: Aviation: Its Technical Development, 15121, 17515; Aviation of To-day: Its History and Development, 17516; Flight To-day, 17517

Naylor, E. L.: 'Farm Structure Policy in North East England', 19581

Naylor, Gillian: The Arts and Crafts Movement: A Study of its Sources, Ideals and Influence on Design Theory, 23991

Naylor, John Francis: ed. Britain, 1919–1970, 339; A Man and an Institution: Sir Maurice Hankey, the Cabinet Secretariat and the Custody of Cabinet Secrecy, 755; 'The Establishment of the Cabinet Secretariat', 756; Labour's International Policy: The Labour Party in the 1930s, 13562

Ndem, E. B.: 'The Status of Coloured People in Britain', 10909

Neagle, Anna: Anna Neagle Says 'There's Always Tomorrow', 26071

Neal, Sir Leonard F.: Industrial Relations in the 1970s, 5727

Neal, Terence Arthur: Democracy and Responsibility: British History, 1880–1965, 364

Neale, Albert Victor: The British Paediatric Association 1952–1968, 20808

Neale, R. S.: Writing Marxist History: British Society, Economy and Culture since 1700, 26733

Neale, Wilfrid Groves: The Tides of War and the Port of Bristol 1914–1918, 16676

Neame, Sir Philip: Playing with Strife: The Autobiography of a Soldier, 14775

Neary, Ian: ed. The Korean War in History, 16144

Neate, Jill: Mountaineering Literature: A Bibliography of Material Published in English, 27235

Neate, Simon: Rural Deprivation: An Annotated Bibliography of Economic and Social Problems in Rural Britain, 19083

Neave, Airey: Control by Committee: the Reform of the Committee System of the House of Commons, 657; The Flames of Calais: A Soldier's Battle, 1940, 14834

Neave, Guy Richard: How they Fared: The Impact of the Comprehensive School upon the University, 22575; The Scottish Sixth: A Sociological Evaluation of Sixth Year Studies and the Changing Relationship between School and University in Scotland, 23617

Needham, Joseph: A Chart to Illustrate the History of Biochemistry and Physiology, 26454; ed. Perspectives in Biochemistry: Thirty one Essays presented to Sir F. G. Hopkins, 26455; ed. Hopkins and Biochemistry 1861–1947, 26464; ed. The Chemistry of Life: Eight Lectures on the History of Biochemistry, 26476; History is on our Side: A Contribution to Political Religion and Scientific Faith, 27258

Needham, Robert: 'Probation Politics', 10483

Needleman, Lionel: 'Growth, Investment and Efficiency in Britain: Some Policy Suggestions', 4742; Regional Problems and

Location of Industry Policy in Britain, 5101; 'Immigration: Some Economic Effects', 11408; 'Immigration: Excess Aggregate Demand and the Balance of Payments', 11409; Reply to Criticism, 11411; 'The Comparative Economics of Improvement and New Building', 17800, 18534; The Economics of Housing, 18533

Neeld, Peter: 'Wolverhampton Motorcycles: The Growth and Decline of an Industry', 17191

Neff, Terry Ann: ed. A Quiet Revolution: British Sculpture since 1945, 24183

Negrine, R.: 'The Press and the Suez Crisis: A Myth Re-examined', 14386

Negus, Geoffrey: Aviation in Birmingham, 17524

Nehls, Edward: ed. D. H. Lawrence: A Complete Biography, 25643

Neidpath, James: The Singapore Naval Base and the Defence of Britain's Eastern Empire 1919–41, 14688

Neil, Herbert: 'History of Chromatography', 7113

Neilans, Alison: Our Freedom and its Results, 7670

Neild, P. G.: 'Financial Planning in British Industry', 4950

Neild, Robert Ralph: Pricing and Employment in the Trade Cycle: A Study of British Manufacturing Industry, 1950–1961, 3811, 5871

Neill, Alexander Sutherland: That Dreadful School, 23106; 'Neill, Neill! Orange Peel!' A Personal View of Ninety Years, 23215

Neill, D. G.: 'Housing and the Social Aspects of Town and Country Planning in Northern Ireland', 9425; A Survey of New Housing in Belfast, 18494

Neill, Desmond Gorman: The Unfinished Business of the Welfare State, 9013

Neill, J. D. H.: Elegant Flower, 12923

Neill, John: Records and Reminiscences of Bonhill Parish, 19364

Neill, June E.: Social Work in General Practice, 21521

Neill, Stephen Charles: Anglicanism, 11594; The Interpretation of the New Testament, 1861–1961, 11919; ed. A History of the Ecumenical Movement, 1517–1948, 12316; Towards Church Union, 1937–1952, 12342; ed. Concise Dictionary of the Christian World Missions, 12353; A History of Christian Missions, 12367

Neillands, Robin: By Sea and Land: The Royal Marine Commandos: A History 1942–1982, 15321

Neilson, Keith: Strategy and Supply: The Anglo-Russian Alliance, 1914–17, 13409; '"Joy Rides"? British Intelligence and Propaganda in Russia, 1914–1917', 13410

Neilson, Mary Georgina Cumming: The Social Effects of Chronic Bronchitis: A Scottish Study, 22079

Nellis, J. G.: 'The Inflation of House Prices in Northern Ireland in the 1970s', 18500

Nellist, John Bowman: British Architecture and its Background, 23896

Nelson, Geoffrey K.: 'Social Science and the British Association', 7914

Nelson, Harold I.: Land and Power: British and Allied Policy on Germany's Frontiers, 1916–1919, 13383

Nelson, J. S.: The Mobility of Farm Families, 19544

Nelson, James [pseud.]: No more Walls, 22133

Nelson, John Raymond: Bonnie: The Development History of the Triumph Bonneville, 17190

Nelson, Sara: Ulster's Uncertain Defenders: Protestant Political Paramilitary and Community Groups and the Northern Ireland Conflict, 2959

Nerlich, Graham: The Shape of Space, 26437

Nerlove, Marc: 'A Quarterly Econometric Model for the United Kingdom', 3630

Nettel, Reginald: Havergal Brian and his Music, 24302; A Social History of Traditional Song, 24449; The Orchestra in England: A Social History, 24550

Nettleford, Rex: 'Manley and the Politics of Jamaica—Towards an Analysis of Political Change in Jamaica 1938–1968', 13054; ed. Norman Washington Manley and the New Jamaica: Selected Speeches and Writings 1938–1968, 13055; ed. Jamaica in Independence: Essays on the Early Years, 13056

Neuberger, Henry: From the Dole Queue to the Sweatshop, 3962

Neuman, Andrew Martin De: The Economic Aspects of Nationalisation in Great Britain, 6063; Economic Organization of the British Coal Industry, 6260

Neusss, R. F: ed. Facts and Figures about the Church of England, 11535

Neustadt, Richard E.: Alliance Politics, 14080

Neustatter, Angela: Hyenas in Petticoats: A Look at Twenty Years of Feminism, 7798

Neustatter, W. Lindesey: The Mind of the Murderer, 10798; 'Homosexuality', 10852

Nevakivi, Jukka: Britain, France and the Arab Middle East, 1914–1920, 13832

Neve, Brian: The Referendum, 2388

Neve, Eric: The East Coast from King's Cross, 16931

Nevett, Terry R.: Advertising in Britain: A History, 4297

Neville, J. W.: Inflation and Unemployment, 4019

Neville, Robert G.: Bibliography of the British Coal Industry, 6244; Studies in the Yorkshire Coal Industry, 6330; 'A Bibliography of the Coal Industry in Wales', 6336

Neville, Thomas Eric: East Kilbride: The History of Parish and Village, 19368

Nevin, Edward Thomas: The London Clearing Banks, 4458; Mechanism of Cheap Money: A Study of British Monetary Policy, 1931–1939, 4562; 'The Origins of Cheap Money, 1931–1932', 4563; The Problem of the National Debt, 4606; 'The Cost Structure of British Manufacturing, 1948–1961', 4951; 'The Growth of the Welsh Economy', 5319; Structure of the Welsh Economy, 5320; The Social Accounts of the Welsh Economy, 1948–1952, 5321; 'The "New" Industrial Revolution in Wales', 5322

Nevinson, Henry Woodd: The Dardanelles Campaign, 14551

Nevitt, Adela Adam: Housing, Taxation and Subsidies: A Study of Housing in the United Kingdom, 18535; 'Conflicts in British Housing Policy', 18694; 'A "Fair" Deal for Housing', 18701

New Cambridge Modern History: 1957+, 365

New Fabian Research Bureau: The Road to War, being an Analysis of the National Government's Foreign Policy, 13564

New Town Development Corporations: Annual Reports, 18177

New University of Ulster Institute of Continuing Education: Nature Conservation and Agriculture: A Conference . . . , 20235

New Zealand Foreign Policy: Statements and Documents 1943–1957, 12670

New, P. T.: The Solent Sky: A Local History of Aviation from 1908 to 1946, 17529

Newall, Roy Norman: Methodist Preacher and Statesman: Eric W. Baker, 1899–1973, 12094

Newbigin, Lesslie: Unfinished Agenda: An Autobiography, 12376

Newbolt, Sir Francis George: History of the Royal Society of Painter-Etchers and Engravers, 1880–1930, 24099

Newbolt, Sir Henry: History of the Great War: Naval Operations, 14674

Newbould, Gerald David: Direct Investment in the United Kingdom by Smaller European Firms, 4750; Management and Merger Activity, 5517; Academic Salaries: A Personal Application of Managerial Economics, 22546

Newby, Eric: Love and War in the Appennines, 14869

Newby, Howard: Community Studies: An Introduction to the Sociology of the Local Community; ed. Sociology of Community: A Selection of Readings, 9366; Property, Paternalism and Power: Class and Control in Rural England, 9608, 19045; 'Agricultural Workers in the Class Structure', 9705, 19675; 'The Sources of Variation in Agricultural Workers' Images of Society', 9706; The Deferential Worker: A Study of Farmworkers in East Anglia, 9707, 19666; Green and Pleasant Land? Social Change in Rural England, 19044, 19046, 19575; 'Capitalist Farmers in the British Class Structure', 19561; 'Rural Sociology and its Relevance to the Agricultural Economist: A Review', 19584; 'The Low Earnings of Agricultural Workers: A Sociological Approach', 19674

Newby, Percy Howard: The Third Programme, 24774; Broadcasting: A Professional View, 24793; The Uses of Broadcasting, 24794

Newell, Philip: Greenwich Hospital: A Royal Foundation, 1692–1983, 9216, 21443

Newhouse, John: De Gaulle and the Anglo-Saxons, 14231

Newman, A. G.: 'Bus Services and Local History', 17252

Newman, Aubrey Norris: The Board of Deputies of British Jews, 1760–1985: A Brief

Survey, 12420; The United Synagogue, 1870–1970, 12428

Newman, Bernard: One Hundred Years of Good Company (The Story of Ruston and Hornby), Published on the Occasion of the Ruston Centenary, 1857–1957, 6370; Tunnellers: The Story of the Tunnelling Companies, Royal Engineers during the World War, 15629

Newman, Charles E.: 'The Aims and Methods of Medical Education', 22465

Newman, D. K.: 'Housing in Britain and America', 18656

Newman, E. L.: 'An American Looks at British Social Service', 8727

Newman, Sir George: The Rise of Preventive Medicine, 22022

Newman, J. R.: The N.A.O.P. Heritage: A Short Historical Review of the Growth and Development of the National Association of Operative Plasterers, 1860–1960, 6849

Newman, Jeremiah: Race: Migration and Immigration, 10970

Newman, Michael: John Strachey, 1323; British Socialists and the Question of European Unity, 1939–1945', 13571; 'Britain and the German-Austrian Customs Union Proposal of 1931', 13663; 'The Origins of Munich: British Policy in Danubian Europe, 1933–1937', 13745

Newman, Noel: Recollections of 70 Years' Farming in Bottisham [East Cambridgeshire], 19593

Newman, Paul: Somerset Villages, 19143

Newman, Roger: Chatterton, a Hampshire Parish: Bramshot and Liphook, 19325

Newman, Simon: March 1939, the British Guarantee to Poland: A Study in the Continuity of British Foreign Policy, 13900

Newman-Norton, Seraphim: The Time of Silence: A History of the Catholic Apostolic Church, 1901–1971, 12452

Newnham, Maurice: Prelude to Glory: The Story of the Creation of Britain's Parachute Army, 15706

Newport and Monmouthshire College of Technology: (Department of Business and Managerial Studies) Labour Mobility in Monmouthshire, 7278

Newsham, John Clark: The Horticultural Notebook: A Manual for the Use of Horticultural Advisers, Gardeners, Nurserymen, Students and all Horticulturalists, 19837; Fruit Growing for Profit, 19838

Newsholme, Sir Arthur: Fifty Years in Public Health, 22024; The Ministry of Health, 22025; Medicine and the State: The Relation between the Private and Official Practice of Medicine, with Special Reference to Public Health, 22026; The Last Thirty Years in Public Health, 22027; The Evolution of Preventive Medicine, 22028; The Story of Modern Preventive Medicine, 22029

Newsholme, Henry Pratt: The Population Report and the Survival of the Christian Family, 7364

Newsom Report: The Public Schools Commission First Report, 23018

Newsome, David Hay: 'Public Schools and Christian Ideals', 23031; A History of Wellington College, 1859–1959, 23082

Newson, Elizabeth and Newson, John: Four Years Old in an Urban Community, 8287; Perspectives on School at Seven Years Old, 8288, 23141; Seven Years Old in the Home Environment, 8289; Infant Care in an Urban Community, 8290; Patterns of Infant Care in an Urban Community, 8291

Newson, Sir John Hubert: The Education of Girls, 23094

Newson, M. D.: Flooding and the Flood Hazard in the United Kingdom, 20186

Newson, Marion G. C.: 'The Geographical Pattern of Population Changes in England and Wales, 1921–1951', 7299

Newton, Arthur Percival: A Hundred Years of the British Empire, 12550

Newton, C.C.Scott: 'The Sterling Crisis of 1947 and the British Response to the Marshall Plan', 4696, 14130; 'The 1949 Sterling Crisis and British Policy towards European Integration', 14140

Newton, Ivor: At the Piano—Ivor Newton, 24406

Newton, John Anthony: A Man for all Churches: Marcus Ward, 1906–1978, 12097

Newton, Kenneth: The Sociology of British Communism, 1927; The Politics of Local Expenditure, 3259; Does Politics Matter? The Determinants of Public Policy, 3148; Second City Politics: Democratic Processes and Decision Making in Birmingham, 3321; 'The Social Composition of A City Council: Birmingham 1925–1966', 3322; Balancing the Books: Financial Problems for Local Government in Western Europe, 4868; 'British Interest Group Theory Re-examined: The Politics of Four Thousand Voluntary Organisations in a British City', 9210; 'The Social Patterns of Immigrant Areas', 11002; 'Big Books about Small Mercies: Urban Planning in Britain and the United States', 17866; 'City Politics in Britain and the United States', 18285

Newton, R. F.: ed. British Hymn Writers and Composers: A Check List Giving their Dates and Places of Birth and Death, 11923

Newton, Trevor: Cost-Benefit Analysis in Administration, 813

New Scottish Local Authorities: Organisation and Management Structures, 3169

Ng, Kwee Choo: The Chinese in London, 11377

Niall, Ian: To Speed the Plough: Mechanisation comes to the Farm, 19682

Niblett, Rosalind: Disadvantaged Families and Playgroups, 8278

Niblett, William Roy: 'Graduate Schools in British Universities', 22536; The University Connection, 22741, 23299; Christian Education in a Secular Society, 22877; ed. Moral Education in a Changing Society, 22878; Universities between two worlds, 23298; 'The Development of British Universities since 1945', 23375; ed. The Expanding University, 23394; 'The Changing Image of the University: a British View', 23418

Nicholas, David J.: Money Flow in the United Kingdom Regions, 4666

Nicholas, Herbert George: The British General Election of 1950, 2300; Britain and the United States, 14001; The United States and Britain, 14002; ed. Washington Despatches: Weekly Political Reports from the British Embassy, 14042

Nicholl, Donald: 'Universities in Transition: Oxbridge and Redbrick', 23389

Nicholls, Christine S.:ed. The Dictionary of National Biography 8th Supplement [1961–1970], 19; ed. The Dictionary of National Biography 9th Supplement [1971–1980], 20; The Dictionary of National Biography 10th Supplement [1981– 1985], 21

Nicholls, D. C.: 'Towards a Rational Land Policy', 20293

Nicholls, David: Church and State in Britain since 1820, 11612

Nicholls, Derek Clifford: Recreation and Tourism in the Loch Lomond Area: A Report to the County Council of Dumbarton, 26946

Nichols, David Ian: Marriage, Divorce and the Family in Scotland, 10002

Nichols, H. D.: C. P. Scott, 1846–1932: The Making of The Manchester Guardian, 25282

Nichols, Theo: Safety or Profit: Industrial Accidents and the Conventional Wisdom, 4138; 'Living with Capitalism: Class Relations and the Modern Factory, 5788; 'Labourism and Class Consciousness: The Class Ideology of Some Northern Foremen', 9713

Nicholson, David: ed. The Leo Amery Diaries, 1068

Nicholson, David J.: Local Planning in South Wales, 5378

Nicholson, Gill: Mother and Baby Homes: A Survey of Homes for Unmarried Mothers, 7869

Nicholson, Hugh Thayer: Mergers and Associations of Professional Firms, 5534

Nicholson, John Henry: New Communities in Britain, 9339; Help for the Handicapped: An Enquiry into the Opportunities of the Voluntary Services, 21901

Nicholson, John Leonard: Distribution of Income in the United Kingdom in 1959, 1957 and 1953, 3828

Nicholson, Max: The Environmental Revolution: A Guide for the New Masters of the World, 19922; The System: The Misgovernment of Modern Britain, 19923

Nicholson, Nigel: Steel Strike: A Case Study in Industrial Relations, 6939

Nicholson, R. J.: 'Capital Stock, Employment and Output in British Industry, 1948–1964', 4741

Nicholson, Robert John: 'Distribution of Personal Incomes', 3820

Nicholson, Simon: Community Participation in City Decision Making, 9434

Nicholson, V. M.: Just the Job: The Employment and Training of Young School Leavers: A Summary Report, 5962

Nicholson, Walter Norris: The Suffolk Regiment, 1928–1946, 15727

Nickie, Charles: 'Women, Shiftworking and the Sexual Division of Labour', 5921

Nickolls, L. A.: The Crowning of Queen Elizabeth II: A Diary of the Coronation Year, 509

Nickson, Richard Scholefield: Warwick: Its Preservation and Redevelopment, 18918

Nicoll, Allardyce: English Drama, 1900–1930: The Beginnings of the Modern Period, 26180; British Drama: An Historical Survey from the Beginning to the Present Time, 26181

Nicolson, Sir Harold George: King George V: His Life and Reign, 473; The Evolution of Diplomatic Method, 13323; Peacemaking 1919: Being Reminiscences of the Paris Peace Conference, 13423; Curzon: The Last Phase, 1919–1925: A Study in Post-War Diplomacy, 13643; Friday Mornings 1941–1944, 15185

Nicolson, I. F.: The Administration of Nigeria 1900–1960: Men, Methods and Myths, 12755

Nicolson, Ian: The Road to the Stars, 17698; Sputnik to Spaceshuttle: 25 Years of the Space Age, 17699

Nicolson, James Robert: Shetland and Oil, 6528; Shetland's Fishing Vessels, 16600; Shetland, 19275

Nicolson, Nigel: People and Parliament, 559; ed. Harold Nicolson: Diaries and Letters, 1492; ed. Portrait of a Marriage, 1493, 25788; Alex: The Life of Field Marshal Earl Alexander of Tunis, 14752; The Grenadier Guards in the War of 1939–1945, 15643; ed. The Letters of Virginia Woolf 1912–1941, 25889

Nicolson, Robert: The Pitcairners, 12891

Niedhart, Gottfried: Grossbritannien und die Sowjetunion 1934–1939: Studien zur britischen Politik der Friedenssicherung zwischen den beiden Weltkriegen, 13952

Nielsen, Jorgen: Muslims in Britain: An Annotated Bibliography, 1960–1984, 12455

Niemeyer, Nannie: England: A Social and Economic History, 1830 to 1936, 363, 3462

Nightingale, Benedict: Charities, 9211

Nightingale, P. R.: A History of the East Yorkshire Regiment in the War of 1939–1945, 15747

Nightingale, Robert T.: The Personnel of the British Foreign Office and Diplomatic Service, 1851–1921, 13248

Nikolinakos, Marios: 'Notes on an Economic Theory of Racism', 11413

Niland, Austin: The British Organ, 7074, 24393

Niner, Pat: Housing Policy and the Housing System, 18517

Nisbet, James Walker: The Beveridge Plan, 9034

Nisbet, John D.: Social Change and History: Aspects of the Western Theory of Development, 8048; Age of Transfer to Secondary Education, 22990; The Transition to Secondary Education, 22991

Nisbet, Robert Alexander: The Sociological Tradition, 8044; Sociology as an Art Form, 8045; Tradition and Revolt: Historical and Sociological Essays, 8046; The Social Bond:

An Introduction to the Study of Society, 8047; The Social Philosophers: Community and Conflict in Western Thought, 8049; Twilight of Authority, 8050

Nish, Ian Hill: Alliance in Decline: A Study in Anglo-Japanese Relations, 1908–1923, 13585; ed. Anglo-Japanese Alienation, 1919–52: Papers of the Anglo-Japanese Conference on the History of the Second World War, 13592

Nissen, R.: Pages in the History of Chest Surgery, 21141

Nitzberg, William D.: 'The Malaria Parasite: Discovery of its Development and Transmission', 20993

Niven, Alastair: D. H. Lawrence: The Writer and his Work, 25641

Niven, Charles David: History of the Humane Movement, 12396

Niven, David: Bring on the Empty Horses, 26074; The Moon's a Balloon, 26073

Niven, Douglas: The Development of Housing in Scotland, 18484

Niven, Mary Margaret: Personnel Management 1913–1963: The Growth of Personnel Management and the Development of the Institute [of Personnel Management], 9779

Nkrumah, Kwame: The Autobiography of Kwame Nkrumah, 12750

Noakes, Jeremy: ed. Intelligence and International Relations 1900–1945, 15996

Nobay, A. R.: 'The Bank of England, Monetary Policy and Monetary Theory in the United Kingdom, 1951–1971', 4630

Nobbs, George: The Wireless Stars, 24820, 26283

Nobbs, Jack: Economic Problems of the 1970s, 3668

Nobes, Christopher: Comparative International Accounting, 4173; The Economics of Taxation, 4850

Noble, Andrew: ed. Edwin Muir: Uncollected Scottish Criticism, 25727

Noble, Grant: Children in Front of the Small Screen, 8292

Noble, P.: 'Drug taking in Adolescent Girls: Factors Associated with the Progression to Narcotic Use', 22224

Noble, Peter S.: 'The Redbrick Universities', 23380

Noble, Peter: Anthony Asquith, 24660, British Ballet, 24208; British Screen Stars, 24687; Ivor Novello: Man of the Theatre, 26077

Noble, R. W.: Joyce Cary, 25444

Noble, Sheila: The Quiet Revolution: The Planning, Development and Provision of Community Services for the Mentally Handicapped, 21780

Noble, Trevor: Modern Britain: Structure and Change, 7610; 'Sociology and Literature', 8062; 'Social Mobility and Class Relations in Britain', 9599; 'Intergenerational Mobility in Britain: A Criticism of the Counter-balance Theory', 9600; 'Family Breakdown and Social Networks', 10087

Noble, W. C.: Coli—Great Healer of Men: The Biography of Dr Leonard Colebrook, 20863

Nock, Oswald Stevens: 150 Years of Main

Line Railways, 16728; Railways of Britain, Past and Present, 16759; British Trains, Past and Present, 16760; Scottish Railways, 16761; British Railways in Action, 16762; Railways in the Transition from Steam, 1950–1965, 16763; Historic Railway Disasters, 16764; Railway Signalling: A Treatise on Recent Practice of British Railways, 16766; Speed Records on Britain's Railways, 16767; The Caledonian Railway, 16841; The Great Northern Railway, 16847; The Great Western Railway in the 20th Century, 16853; The Great Western Railway: An Appreciation, 16854; ed. The Great Western, 16855; British Railway Signalling: A Survey of Fifty Years Progress, A History of the L.M.S, 16875; Britain's New Railways: Electrification of the London-Midland Main Lines, 16876; The Royal Scots and the Patriots of the L.M.S, 16877; The London and North Western Railway, 16890; The London and South Western Railway, 16891; The Midland Compounds, 16894; North Western, A Saga of the Premier Line of Great Britain, 1846–1922, 16909; The Highland Railway, 16940; The Lancashire and Yorkshire Railway: A Concise History, 16952; Underground Railways of the World, 16999; O. S. Nock's Encyclopaedia of British Steam Railways and Locomotives, 17032; Steam Locomotives: The Unfinished Story of Steam Locomotives and Steam Locomotive Men on the Railways of Great Britain, 17033; British Steam Railways, 17034; Railways at the Zenith of Steam, 1920–1940, 17035; The British Steam Railway Locomotive 1925–1965, 17036; The Last Years of British Railways Steam: Reflections of Ten Years after, 17037; The Golden Age of Steam: A Critical and Nostalgic Memory of the Last 20 Years before Grouping on the Railways of Great Britain, 17038; L.M.S. Steam, 17039; L.N.E.R. Steam, 17040; Southern Steam, 17041; British Locomotives at Work, 17054; British Steam Locomotives at Work, 17055; Steam Locomotive: A Retrospect of the Work of Eight Great Locomotive Engineers, 17056; British Locomotives of the 20th Century, 17057, 16765, 17095; The Railway Engineers, 17058; Rocket 150: A Century and a Half of Locomotive Trials, 17059; Two Miles a Minute: The Story behind the Conception and Operation of Britain's High Speed and Advanced Passenger Trains, 17060; The Locomotives of Sir Nigel Gresley, 17075; The Locomotives of R. E. L. Maunsell, 1911–1937, 17076

Nockolds, Harold: The Magic of a Name: A History of Rolls Royce, 17443

Noel, Gerard Eyre: Harold Wilson and the 'New Britain', 1060; The Great Lock-out of 1926, 6945

Noel-Baker, Philip J.: The League of Nations at Work, 13481; The First World Disarmament Conference, 1932–1933 and why it failed, 13492

Noise Abatement League/Society: Quiet: A Magazine Devoted to the Prevention of

Avoidable Noise, 20139; The Third London Airport: Foulness, 20156; The Law on Noise, 20157

Nokes, Peter L.: The Professional Task in Welfare Practice, 8657

Noonan, J. T.: Contraception: The History of its Treatment by the Catholic Theologians and Canonists, 21062

Nordlie, Peter G.: Strategies for Improving Race Relations: The Anglo-American Experience, 11139

Nordlinger, Eric A.: The Working-Class Tories: Authority, Deference and Stable Democracy, 1617, 9683

Noreng, Oystein: The Oil Industry and Government Strategy in the North Sea, 6491

Norfolk County Council: 1889–1974, 3365

Norgate, M.: '40 Years back—London Plays of Autumn 1938', 26194

Norman, Adrian R. D.: The Computerised Society: An Appraisal of the Impact of Computers on Society over the Next Fifteen Years, 7094

Norman, Edward Robert: Church and Society in England, 1770–1970, 11576; Roman Catholicism in England from the Elizabethan Settlement to the Second Vatican Council, 11943

Norman, Frank: A True Story of Soho, 9337; Lock 'em Up and Count 'em: Reform of the Penal System, Stand on Me, 10357:

Norman, Hubert J.: 'Some Factors in the Reform in the Treatment of the Insane', 20995

Norman, Peter: Slum Clearance: The Social and Administrative Context in England and Wales, 18410; An Appraisal of Slum Clearance Procedures in England and Wales, 18411

Norman, Philip: Shout! The True Story of the Beatles, 24500; The Life and Good Times of the Rolling Stones, 24524

Norrie, Ian: Sixty Precarious Years: A Short History of the National Book League, 24932

Norrington, Sir Arthur Lionel Pugh: Blackwells, 1879–1979: The History of a Family Firm, 25007

Norris, Christopher: ed. Inside the Myth: Orwell: Views from the Left, 25754

Norris, Geoff: Poverty: The Facts in Scotland, 9099

Norris, Geoffrey: The Royal Flying Corps: A History, 15803

Norris, Graeme: The Effective University: A Management by Objectives Approach, 23308

Norris, Herbert William: One from Seven Hundred: A Year in the Life of Parliament, 278, 557

Norris, Ian: Bookselling and Book Publishing: A History from the Earliest Times to the Present Day, 24936

Norris, John: Waterways to Stratford, 16434

Norris, June: Human Aspects of Redevelopment, 9338

Norris, Leslie: ed. Vernon Watkins 1906–1967, 25855

Norris, Pippa: 'Conservative Attitudes in Recent British Elections: An Emerging Gender Gap', 2265; British By-Elections: The Volatile Electorate, 2358

Norris, Vera: Mental Illness in London, 21759

North East Lancashire Structure Plan: Summary Report of the Survey Plan, 5189

North-East of Scotland: A Survey Prepared for the Aberdeen Meeting of the British Association for the Advancement of Science, 18151

North Tyneside Community Devlopment Project: North Shields: Living with Industrial Change, 9289; Organisation for Change in a Working Class Area, 9290; Women's Work, 9291; Working Class Politics and Housing, 1900–1977, 9292

North West Economic Planning Council: Education, Arts and Amenities Group: The Social Planning of Urban Renewal: A Report on the Social Planning of Urban Renewal, with Particular Reference to the North-West . . . , 17716

North, Arthur John Day: Royal Naval Coastal Forces, 1939–1945, 15020

North, Dick Trevor Brooke: Productivity Agreements and Wage Systems, 5994

North, Frederick John: Coal and the Coalfields in Wales, 6332

North, John D.: The Measure of the Universe: A History of Modern Cosmology, 26411

North, John: North-West Europe, 1944–1945: The Achievement of 21st Army Group, 14964

North, Richard: Working the Land, 19157

Northcote, Hugo Stafford: Winston Churchill: Man of Destiny, 988

Northcott, Bayan: ed. The Music of Alexander Goehr, 24346

Northcott, Clarence Hunter: Personnel Management: Its Scope and Practice, 5461

Northcott, William Cecil: 'The Colour Problem in Britain', 11150; 'Decade of Change in the Churches', 11586; 'Church and State in England', 11630; 'Scotland's New Style Sabbath', 12245

Northedge, Frederick Samuel: The Troubled Giant: Britain among the Great Powers, 1916–1939, 13213; ed. The Foreign Policies of the Powers, 13231; Descent from Power: British Foreign Policy 1945–1973, 13239; '1917–1919: The Implications for Britain', 13424; Britain and Soviet Communism: The Impact of a Revolution, 13915

Northern Ireland Census 1961, 7293

Northern Ireland Community Relations Commission: Register of Completed and Ongoing Research into the Irish Conflict, 2848

Northern Ireland Economic Advisory Office: Northern Ireland, Economic Survey, 5386

Northern Ireland Housing Statistics: 1979+ Annual, 18488

Northern Ireland: Report of Enquiry into the Housing Schemes of the Belfast Corporation held by R. D. Megaw, 18941

Northern Ireland Statutes: 1922+, 2777

Northern Region Strategy Team: Movement of Manufacturing Industry: The Northern Region, 1961–1973, 5192

Northern Region Strategy Team: Rural Development in the Northern Region, 5193

Northern Universities Geographical Societies: Regional Planning in Britain: Proceedings [of a Conference], 5066

Northouse, Cameron: Twentieth Century Opera in England and the United States, 24560; John Osborne: A Reference Guide, 25967

Norton, Alan: Drugs, Science and Society: The New Dimensions of Medicine, Local Government Administration in England and Wales, 3125; The New Dimensions of Medicine, 22011

Norton, Geoffrey Gordon: The Red Devils: The Story of Britain's Airborne Forces, 15709

Norton, Michael: Community, 9387

Norton, Philip: 'The House of Commons and the Constitution: the Challenge of the 1970s', 584; ed. Parliament in the 1980s, 587; 'The Forgotten Whips: Whips in the House of Lords', 671; ed. Dissension in the House of Commons: Intra-Party Dissent in the House of Commons Division Lobbies, 1945–1974, 701; ed. 'Legislation and the Influence of the Backbench M.P.', 702; 'Party Organisation in the House of Commons', 1603; Conservatives and Conservatism, 1626; Conservative Dissidents: Dissent within the Conservative Parliamentary Party 1970–74, 1645; Law and Order and British Politics, 10152; 'Intra-Party Dissent in the House of Commons: A Case Study: The Immigration Rules, 1972', 11134

Norton, S.: 'Joint Working Parties: A Case Study of the A.C.A.S. Approach to improving Industrial Relations, 4165

Norton, W. E.: 'Debt Management and Monetary Policy in the United Kingdom', 4625

Norton-Taylor, Richard: The Ponting Affair, 765; Whose Land is it anyway?: Agriculture, Planning and Land Use in the British Countryside, 20206

Norwich Planning Department: Report No 1—Central Area Appraisal, 18897; Report No 2—Revitalisation Appraisal, 18898

Norwood, Sir Cyril: The English Educational System, 22670

Nossiter, Bernard D.: Britain: A Future that Works, 378

Notting Hill Housing Service: The Rent Act and the Housing Market in North Kensington, 18422

Nottingham: A History of Nottingham High School, 1513–1953, 22999

Nottridge, Harold Edgar: The Sociology of Urban Living, 18279

Nowell-Smith, Simon: The House of Cassell 1848–1958, 24951; ed. Letters to Macmillan, 24977

Nowlan, Kevin Barry: Ireland and the War Years and After 1939–1951, 2705; ed. Making of 1916: Studies in the History of the Rising, 2741

Noyce, John Leonard: ed. The Directory of British Alternative Periodicals 1965–1974, 25200

Noyes, A.: 'The Industrial Economy of North Staffordshire in the Second World War', 4952

Ntsekhe, V. R.: 'Social Class Backgrounds of Young Offenders from London', 10600

Nudds, Angus: The Woods belong to me: A Gamekeeper's Life, 19747

Nuffield Provincial Hospitals Trust: A Balanced Teaching Hospital: A Symposium at Birmingham, 21378; Studies in the Functions and Design of Hospitals, 21379; Towards a Measure of Medical Care: Operational Research in the Health Services: A Symposium, 22010

Nugent, Neill: ed. The British Right: Conservative and Right-wing Politics in Britain, 1621, 2056; ed. Respectable Rebels: Middle Class Campaigns in Britain in the 1970's, 2077, 9730

Nulty, Geoffrey: ed. The Historical Atlas of Cheshire Edited for the Local History Committee of the Cheshire Community Council, 5150

Nunn, George Walter Arthur: British Sources of Photographs and Pictures, 209, 24708

Nunnerley, David: President Kennedy and Britain, 14092

Nurcombe, Valerie J.: ed. Whitehall and Westminster, 184; ed. Catalogue of British Official Publications not Published by H.M.S.O., 185; ed. Directory of Specialists in Official Publications, 186; ed. British Official Publications Online: A Review of Sources, Services and Developments, 187

Nurek, M.: 'Great Britain and Poland from June 1940 to July 1941', 13906

Nurton, Doreen: Hospitals of the Long-stay Patient: A Study of their Practical Nursing Problems and Solutions, 21380

Nussbaum, Helga: ed. Multi-National Enterprises in Historical Perspective, 4457, 20686

Nutley, W. G.: Betterment Levy and the Land Commission, 20342

Nutt, Bev: Obsolescence in Housing: Theory and Applications, 18739

Nuttall, Desmond Lewes: The 1968 CSE Monitoring Experiment, 22910

Nuttall, Geoffrey Fillingham: ed. From Uniformity to Unity, 1662–1962, 12001

Nuttgens, Patrick: McDowell's Directory of Twentieth Century Fashion, 24155

Nutting, Sir [Harold] Anthony: Disarmament: An Outline of the Negotiations, 13539; Europe Will Not Wait, 14151; No End of a Lesson: The Story of Suez, 14376

Nye, Doug: Sports Cars, 17363

Oakeshott, Edward: The Blindfold Game: 'The Day' at Jutland, 14656

Oakeshott, Michael: On Human Conduct, 2089; Rationalism in Politics and Other Essays, 2088

Oakeshott, Robert: The Bargainers: A Survey of Modern Trade Unionism, 6727

Oakley, Ann: Sex, Gender and Society, 7755; The Sociology of Housework, 7756; Housewife, 7757; Becoming a Mother, 7758; Women Confined: Towards a Sociology of Childbirth, 7759; Subject Women, 7760; Taking it Like a Woman, 7761; What is Feminism?, 7762; ed. Essays on Women, 7799

Oakley, Charles Allen: Scottish Industry To-day: A Survey of Recent Developments undertaken for the Scottish Development Council, 5240; Industrial Map of Scotland, 5241; ed. Scottish Industry: An Account of what Scotland Makes and where She Makes It, 5242; 'The Social Effects of Industrial Changes in Great Britain, the Republic of Ireland and Northern Ireland, 5671; The Last Tram, 17225; The Second City, 18134; Where We Came in: Seventy Years of the British Film Industry, 24637

Oakley, Robin: The Political Year, 1970, 276; 1971, 277; New Backgrounds: The Immigrant Child at Home and at School, 23178

Oakley, William: Winged Wheel: The History of the First Hundred Years of the Cyclists Touring Club, 27136

Oakwood Library of Railway History, 16823

Oatts, Lewis Balfour: Emperor's Chambermaids: The Story of 14th/20th King's Hussars, 15667

O'Ballance, Edgar: Malaya: The Communist Insurgent War 1948–1960, 16153

O'Bannion, Kathleen: 'A Comparative History of Modern Psychic Research', 20996

O'Beirne-Ranelagh, John: 'The Irish Republican Brotherhood, 1858–1924', 2761

Obituaries from The Times, 1961–1970, 41; 1971–1975, 42

O'Brien, Conor Cruise: Neighbours, 2994; States of Ireland, 2657; ed. The Shaping of Modern Ireland, 309

O'Brien, Denis Patrick: Competition in British Industry: Restrictive Practices Legislation in Theory and Practice, 4935; ed. Pioneers of Modern Economics, 26575; Lionel Robbins, 26619

O'Brien, John: 'Ireland's Departure from the British Commonwealth', 2977

O'Brien, Lucy: Dusty, 24527

O'Brien, Margaret: The Father Figure, 10050

O'Brien, Maureen: Single and Homeless, 18513

O'Brien, Nora Connolly: James Connolly: Portrait of a Rebel Father, 3038; James Connolly Wrote for Today, 3039

O'Brien, Oswald: Going Comprehensive: Educational Policy-Making in Two County Boroughs, 22965

O'Brien, Patrick: The New Economic History of the Railways, 16724

O'Brien, Terence H.: Viscount Milner of St. James's and Cape Town, 1854–1925, 1275; Civil Defence, 14724, 15139; Milner: British Experiments in Public Ownership and Control, 6058

O'Broin, Leon: Dublin Castle and the 1916 Rising, 2743; Protestant Nationalists in Revolutionary Ireland: The Stopford Connection, 2748; Revolutionary Underground: The Story of the Irish Republican Brotherhood, 1858–1924, 2760; Michael Collins, 3028

O'Buachalla, Seamus: ed. A Significant Educationalist: The Educational Writings of P. H. Pearse, 3070

O'Callaghan, Sean: Drug Addiction in Britain, 22187; The Drug Traffic, 22188

O'Carroll, J. P.: ed. De Valera and His Times, 3049

O'Carroll, Nial: ed. The Forests of Ireland: History, Distribution and Silviculture, 19728

O'Casey, Sean: The Story of the Irish Citizen Army, 1919, 2758

Occasional Papers in Social Administration: 1961–1987, 9255

O'Cleary, Conor: 'The Effects of the European Monetary System on Anglo-Irish Relations', 3009

O'Cleireacain, Carol Chapman: 'Labour Market Trends in London and the Rest of the South-East', 5905

O'Connell, James: ed. Contemporary Irish Studies, 2660

O'Connell, P. J.: 'Comprehensive Schools and the Catholic Community', 22977

O'Connor, Denis: Glue Sniffing and Volatile Substance Abuse, 8544

O'Connor, Garry: Ralph Richardson: An Actor's Life, 26091

O'Connor, James: The Practice of Advertising, 4327

O'Connor, John: Britain's Wine Industry: Industry Commentary, 20751

O'Connor, John Joseph: Catholic Revival in England, 11938

O'Connor, Joyce: The Young Drinkers: A Cross-National Study of Social and Cultural Influences, 22135

O'Connor, Kevin: The Irish in Britain, 11363

O'Connor, Maeve: ed. Immigration: Medical and Social Aspects, 11407

O'Connor, Neil: The Social Problem of Mental Deficiency, 21756; 'The Social Effectiveness of the Mentally Handicapped', 21757; The Handicapped Child: Recent Research Findings, 21920

O'Connor, Philip: Living in Croesor, 19302

O'Connor, Thomas Power: Memoirs of an Old Parliamentarian, 1885–1929, 1497

O'Connor, Ulick: A Terrible Beauty is Born: The Irish Troubles, 1912–1922, 2752

Oddie, G.: 'Some British Attitudes towards Reform and Repression in India, 1917–1920', 13132

Oddy, Derek S.: ed. Diet and Health in Modern Britain, 6154; ed. The Making of the Modern British Diet, 20555; Diet and Health in Modern Britain, 20556

O'Dea, Desmond James: Cyclical Indicators for the Post-War British Economy, 3629

O'Dea, William T.: The Social History of Lighting, 6683

O'Dell, Alan: Mobile Homes in England and Wales, 1975: Report of Surveys, 18556

O'Dell, Andrew Charles: The Highlands and Islands of Scotland, 5130, 5298

Odell, Peter R.: Optimal Development of the North Sea's Oil Fields: A Study in Divergent Government and Company Interests and their Reconciliation, 6504

Odling-Smee, J. D.: British Economic Growth, 1856–1973, 3514

O'Doherty, Eamon: An Illustrated History of the I.R.A., 2765

O'Doherty, K.: 'The Social Effects of Industrial Changes in Great Britain, the

Republic of Ireland and Northern Ireland, 5671

Odom, Keith: Henry Green, 25557

O'Donovan, K.: Sexual Divisions in Law, 7685

O'Donovan, Patrick: 'Catholicism and Class in England', 11949

O'Donovan, William James: 'The War-time Experiences of Factory Medical Officers and the Position of Factory Medicine under Peace Conditions', 5586

O'Dowd, Mary: The Town in Ireland, 18170

O'Dwyer, Sir Maurice: ed. Speeches and Documents on the Indian Constitution 1925–1947, 13116

Oeppen, Jim: The Changing Pattern of Employment: Regional Specialisation and Industrial Localisation in Britain, 5076

O'Faolain, Sean: Constance Markievicz, 1466; De Valera, 3051

O'Farrell, Padraic: Who's Who in the Irish War of Independence 1916–1921, 2753

O'Farrell, Patrick: Ireland's English Question: Anglo-Irish Relations, 1534–1970, 2961; England and Ireland since 1800, 2962

Offences of Drunkenness, England and Wales, 22121

Office of Health Economics: Malnutrition in the 1960s?, 20549; The Finance of Medical Research, 20828; 'The Common Illness of our Time': a Study of the Problem of Ischaemic Heart Disease. The Harveian Oration 1928, 21056; Studies in Current Health Problems. No. 38 Epilepsy in Society, 21081; Pneumonia in Decline, 21120; The Price of Poliomyelitis, 21121; The Residue of Poliomyelitis, 21122; Rheumatism and Arthritis in Britain, 21128; Hospital Costs in Perspective, 21376; Efficiency in the Hospital Service, 21377; The Personal Health Services: A Perspective of the General Medical and the Pharmaceutical Services, 21561; The Local Health Services, 21594; The Reorganised N.H.S, 21669; Studies in Current Health Problems, 22126; The Pharmacist in Society, 22260

O'Flaherty, Liam: The Life of Tim Healy, 3013

Ogden, Elizabeth: Long Live the Village Hall!: A Survey of the Use of Village Halls, 19132

Ogden, F. J.: A Guide to the Representation of the People Act of 1918, 2274

Ogden, S. G.: 'Bargaining Structure and the Control of Industrial Relations', 5823

Ogdon, Brenda Lucas: Virtuoso: The Story of John Ogdon, 24402

Ogg, David: Herbert Fisher 1865–1940: A Short Biography, 1410

Ogilvie, Alan G.: ed. Scientific Survey of South and East Scotland, 18152

Ogilvie, Sir Heneage: ed. Fifty: An Approach to the Problems of Middle Age, 8554

Ogilvie, Vivian: Our Times: A Social History, 1912–1952, 7560; The English Public School, 23014

Ogilvy, Audrey A.: Bracknell and Its Migrants: Twenty-One Years of New Town Growth, 18191; 'The Self-Contained New Town: Employment and Population', 18242

Ogorkiewicz, R. M.: 'Fifty Years of British Tanks', 15538

O'Gorman, Frank: British Conservatism: Conservative Thought from Burke to Thatcher, 2183

O'Halloran, Clare: Partition and the Limits of Irish Nationalism, 3007

O'Halpin, Eunan: The Decline of the Union: British Government in Ireland 1892–1920, 2972

O'Hear, Anthony: Karl Popper, 26857

O'Higgins, Paul: Public Employee Trade Unionism in the United Kingdom: The Legal Framework, 6858; Censorship in Britain, 26898

Ohrnial, A. J. H.: 'Estimates of Marginal Tax Rates for Dividends and Bond Interest in the United Kingdom, 1919–1970', 4555

Ojala, Eric Mervyn: Agriculture and Economic Progress, 19474

Ojha, A. B.: 'Mental Health and Student Wastage', 21814

Oke, Mim Kemal: The Armenian Question, 1914–1923, 13847

O'Keefe, Dennis J.: 'Some Economic Aspects of Raising the School Leaving Age in England and Wales in 1947', 23208

O'Keefe, John Alfred: Sale of Food and Drugs, 22261

O'Kelly, Terence: The Villages of Abinger Common and Wotton, Surrey: Snippets of History, 19174

Okley, Judith: The Traveller-Gypsies, 11352

Olby, Robert C.: 'The Macromolecular Concept and the Origins of Molecular Biology', 20997; 'The Origins of Molecular Genetics', 20998; The Path to the Double Helix, 26477

Old Union Canals Society: The 'Old Union' Canals of Leicester and Northamptonshire, 16418

Oldfield, Adrian: 'The Independent Labour Party and Planning, 1920–1926', 1872; ed. The Middle Class in Politics, 9735

Oldfield, E. A. L.: History of the Army Physical Training Corps, 15768

Oldfield, Frederick E.: New Look Industrial Relations, 5683

Oldfield, J. B.: The Green Howards in Malaya (1949–1952): The Story of a Post-War Tour of Duty by a Battalion of the Line, 16165

Oldfield, Mike: Dire Straits, 24514

Oldfield, Sybil: Women against the Iron Fist: Alternatives to Militarism, 1900–1989, 7703

Oldham, James Basil: A History of Shrewsbury School 1552–1952, 23077

Oldham, Joseph Houldsworth: The Churches Survey their Task: The Report of the Conference at Oxford, July 1937, on Church, Community and State, 12323

Oldman, David: 'Measuring the Status of Occupations', 5880; 'The Social Differentiation of Ability', 9494

O'Leary, Brendan: 'The Anglo-Irish Agreement: Statecraft or Folly?', 3000; 'The Limits to Coercive Consocialisation in Northern Ireland', 3001; 'Why Was The GLC Abolished?', 3295

O'Leary, Cornelius: 'North Ireland: The Politics of Illusion', 2834; Belfast: Approach to Crisis: A Study of Belfast Politics, 1613–1970, 2908

O'Leary, E.: Trends and Regional Comparisons in Probation, 10482

O'Leary, M.: 'Pop Music in an English Secondary School System', 8421

Oliver, A. M.: The Local Government Act 1929 (Annotated), 3114

Oliver, Basil: The Renaissance of the English Public House, 20755

Oliver, Beryl: The British Red Cross in Action, 22097

Oliver, D.: ed. The Changing Constitution, 583

Oliver, David: British Combat Aircraft since 1918, 15823

Oliver, Dawn: ed. The Changing Constitution, 749

Oliver, Elizabeth: ed. Researcher's Guide to British Film and Television Collections, 216

Oliver, F. R.: 'Some Aspects of the Financial Behaviour of County Boroughs', 3276

Oliver, George: Using Old Photographs: A Guide for the Local Historian, 26745

Oliver, George A.: Early Motor Cars: 1904–1915, 17335; Early Motor Cars: The Vintage Years 1919–1930, 17336; Early Motor Cars: 1925–1939: English Sports Cars, 17337; The Rover Seven, 17431; Cars and Coachbuilding: 100 Years of Road Vehicle Development, 17483

Oliver, Ian P.: Buddhism in Britain, 12462

Oliver, John A.: Working at Stormont, 2816

Oliver, John Keith: The Church and Social Order: Social Thought in the Church of England, 1918–1939, 11831

Oliver, John Leonard: The Development and Structure of the Furniture Industry, 6481

Oliver, Robert: Fraternally Yours: A History of the Independent Order of Foresters, 4074, 9129

Oliver, Sir Thomas: Diseases of Occupation, from the Legislative, Social and Medical Points of View, 4104; Foreword to—The Health of the Child of School Age, 8293; 'Phthisis and Occupation', 21279

Oliver, Vic: Mr. Showbusiness: The Autobiography, 26335

Oliver, W. W.: Stalkers of Pestilence: The Story of Man's Ideas of Infection, 22384

Olivier, Laurence, [Baron]: Confessions of an Actor, 26083; On Acting, 26084

Olla, Paola Brundo: Le Origini Diplomatiche dell'acordo Navale Anglo-Tedesco del Giugno 1935, 13665

Ollard, Richard: An English Education: A Perspective of Eton, 23059

Ollard, Sidney Leslie: Dictionary of English Church History, 11568

Olle, James G.: An Introduction to British Government Publications, 178

Ollerenshaw, Dame Kathleen Mary: 'Newsom and Tomorrow', 22608; The Girls' Schools, 23092, 23114

Ollerenshaw, Philip: ed. An Economic History of Ulster, 1820–1940, 2906, 5396

Olson, Mancur, Jnr.: The Economics of Wartime Shortage: A History of British Food Supplies in the Napoleonic Wars and in World Wars One and Two, 3738, 20585

Olson, William Joseph: Britain's Elusive Empire in the Middle East, 1900–1921: An Annotated Bibliography, 13798; Anglo-Iranian Relations during World War I, 13853

Olsover, L.: The Jewish Communities of North-East England, 1755–1980, 12441

Olu Agbi, S.: 'The British Foreign Office and the Roosevelt-Hugessen Bid to Stabilise Asia and the Pacific in 1937', 13603; 'The Foreign Office and Yoshida's Bid for Rapprochement with Britain in 1936–1937: A Critical Reconsideration of the Anglo-Japanese Conversations', 13604

Olusanya, G. O.: The Second World War and Politics in Nigeria 1939–1953, 12761

O'Malley, C. D.: ed. The History of Medical Education, 20801

O'Malley, Ernie: The Singing Flame, 2699; On Another Man's Wound, 2700

O'Malley, Jan: The Politics of Community Action: A Decade of Struggle in Notting Hill, 9386

O'Malley, Lady: Permission to Resign, 13295

O'Malley, Mary: ed. A Needle's Eye, 26169

O'Malley, Sir Owen St. Clair: The Phantom Caravan, 13294

O'Malley, Padraig: The Uncivil Wars: Ireland Today, 2842

O'Malley, William: Glancing Back, 1499, 3065

O'Neill, Helen B.: Spatial Planning in the Small Economy: A Case Study of Ireland, 5389

O'Neill, Herbert Charles: The Royal Fusiliers in the Great War, 15632

O'Neill, John: Sociology as a Skin Trade: Essays towards a Reflective Sociology, 8035

O'Neill, Terence, Lord O'Neill of the Maine: The Autobiography of Terence O'Neill, 3081; Ulster at the Crossroads, 3082

O'Neill, Thomas Patrick: 'In Search of a Political Path: Irish Republicanism 1922–1927', 2762; Eamon De Valera, 3043

O'Neill, Timothy P.: Life and Tradition in Rural Ireland, 19309

O'Neill, William: The Woman Movement: Feminism in the United States and in England, 7854

Ongkili, James P.: Nation-Building in Malaysia 1946–1974, 12905

O'prey, Paul: ed. In Broken Images: Selected Letters of Robert Graves 1914–1946, 25547

Onslow, Richard William Alan [Earl of Onslow]: Sixty Three Years: Diplomacy, the Great War and Politics, with Notes on Travel, Sport and Other Things, 13296

Openshaw, Keith: The Remoter Rural Areas, 19085

Opher, Philip: Cumbernauld, Irvine, East Kilbride: An Illustrated Guide, 19012; Milton Keynes: An Illustrated Guide, 19021; Runcorn, Warrington: An Illustrated Guide, 19024

Opie, Iona and Opie, Peter: Children's Games in Street and Playground, 8294, 27009; The Language and Lore of Children, 8295

Opitz, Leslie: Hampshire Railways Remembered, 16938; Kent Railways Remembered, 16948

Oppenheim, A. K.: 'Changing Structure of Engineering Education', 22517

Oppenheim, A. N.: Television and the Child, 8218, 24828; 'Social Status and Clique Formation among Grammar School Boys', 8448; 'The Views of Adolescents on Some Aspects of Social Class Structure', 9503

Oppenheim, Philip: Biting the Hand that Feeds You: A Study into the Effects on Agriculture and the Economy as a Whole, of the Common Agricultural Policy and Agricultural Support, 19658

Oppenheimer, E.: Heroin Addiction: Treatment and Control in Britain, 22201

Oral History: 1972+, 26754

Oram, R. B.: The Dockers' Tragedy, 16661

Orange, Vincent: A Biography of Air Chief Marshal Sir Keith Park, 15960

Orbach, Laurence F.: Homes For Heroes: A Study of the Evolution of British Public Housing, 1913–1921, 18577

Orbell, John: From Cape to Cape: The History of the Lyle Shipping Company, 16552

Orchard, R. K.: Two Minutes from Sloane Square: A Brief History of the Conference of Missionary Societies in Great Britain and Ireland, 1912–1977, 12371

Orchard, William Edwin: From Faith to Faith: An Autobiography of Religious Development, 11996

Orde, Anne W.: Great Britain and International Security, 1920–1926, 13645; 'Grossbritannien und die Selbständigkeit Österreichs 1918–1938', 13725

Orde, Roden Powlett Graves: The Household Cavalry at War, 15653

Ordish, George: The Constant Pest: A Short History of Pests and their Control, 22383

Ordnance Survey Atlas of Great Britain, 120

Ordnance Survey Gazeteer of Great Britain, 121

Ordnance Survey Map Catalogue, 127

Orford, A. L.: The Iron and Steel Industry, 6546

Orford, Tim: Alcohol and the Family, 10095

Orga, Ates: The Proms, 24443

Organisation for Economic Co-operation and Development: Manpower Policy in the United Kingdom, 5936

Orgill, Douglas: The Gothic Line: The Autumn Campaign in Italy 1944, 14870

O'Riordan, Timothy: Sizewell B: An Anatomy of the Inquiry, 6673; Perspectives on Resource Management, 20231; Environmentalism, 20232; ed. Environmental Impact Assessment, 20233

Orlans, Harold: Stevenage: A Sociological Study of a New Town, 18202

Ormerod, A.: 'The Prospects of the British Cotton Industry', 6454

Ormerod, Alick: Don Whillans: Portrait of a Mountaineer, 27246

Ormerod, P.: 'Incomes Policy and Wage Inflation: Empirical Evidence for the U.K., 1976–1977', 3854

Ormond, Richard: ed. Dictionary of British Portraiture, 213

Oromaner, Mark Jay: 'Comparison of Influentials in Contemporary American and British Sociology: A Study in the Internationalization of Sociology', 8003

Orr, David: ed. City of Derry Rugby Football Club: A Centenary 1881–1981, 27043

Orr, John Boyd [Baron Boyd-Orr]: Feast and Famine: The Wonderful World of Food, 20499; Food and the People, 20500; Food, Health and Income: Report of a Survey of Adequacy of Diet in Relation to Income, 20501; Food: The Foundation of World Unity, 20502; The Nation's Food, 20503; The National Food Supply and its Influence on Public Health, 20504; Not Enough Food for Fitness, 20505; Nutrition in War, 20506; Feeding the People in War-time, 20507

Orr, Sarah Craig: Regional and Urban Studies: A Social Science Approach, 5065; 'Urban Renewal in Glasgow', 18141

Orton, Harold: Survey of English Dialects: The Basic Material, 23791; The Linguistic Atlas of England, 23792

Orton, Ian: An Illustrated History of Mobile Library Services in the United Kingdom, 16368

Orton, William Aylott: Labour in Transition: A Survey of British Industrial History since 1914, 6823

Orwell, George: The Road to Wigan Pier, 9624; 'Boys' Weeklies' in Selected Essays, 25198

Orwin, Charles Stewart: A History of English Farming, 19406; 'Commodity Prices and Farming Policy', 19435; 'Rural Revolution', 19481

Osanka, Franklin Mark: Modern Guerrilla Warfare, 16168

Osborn, A. F.: The Social Life of Britain's Five Year Olds: A Report of the Child Health and Education Study, 8296

Osborn, Sir Frederic James: ed. Our Crowded Planet: Essays on the Pressure of the Population, 7376; Green-Belt Cities: The British Contribution, 17754, 18215; The New Towns: The Answer to Megalopolis, 17755, 18217, 18991; Town and Country Planning, 17756; ed. Garden Cities of Tomorrow, 17757; New Towns: Their Origins, Achievements and Progress, 18216, 18992

Osborn, S.G.: 'The Persistence of Labelling Effects', 10590

Osborn, T. G. B.: 'The Oxford Botanic Garden', 19894

Osborne, Charles: Giving it Away: The Memoirs of an Uncivil Servant, 23765; Auden: The Life of a Poet, 25363; The Life and Crimes of Agatha Christie, 25450

Osborne, Eric N.: Transport in Jersey: An Historical Survey of Public Transport Facilities by Rail and Road in the Island of Jersey 1788–1961, 16344

Osborne, Gerald Stanley: Scottish and English Schools: A Comparative Survey of the Past Fifty Years, 23605; Change in Scottish Education, 23606

Osborne, Harold: 'The New Sensibility of the 1960s', 23748

Osborne, John: A Better Class of Person: An Autobiography 1929–1956, 25969

Osborne, June: Stained Glass in England, 24118

Osborne, Richard Horsley: Geographical Essays in Honour of K. C. Edwards, 5210; 'Internal Migration in England and Wales, 1951', 7346; Atlas of Population Change in the East Midland Counties 1951–1961, 7415

Osborough, Nial: 'Police Discretion not to Prosecute Juveniles', 10570

Osbourne, Harold: ed. The Oxford Companion to Art, 23976

Osgood, S. M.: 'Le Mythe de 'la Perfide Albion' en France, 1919– 1940', 14239; 'Anglophobia and other Vichy Obsessions', 14273

O'Shaughnessy, Hugh: Grenada: Revolution, Invasion and Aftermath, 13083

O'Shaughnessy, W. W.: How Botha and Smuts Conquered German South West Africa, 14528

Osler, Sir William: The Evolution of Modern Medicine, 21169

Osman, Terry: The Facts of Everyday Life, 126

Osmond, John: Creative Conflict: The Politics of Welsh Devolution, 2575; The Centralist Enemy, 2612

Ossowski, Stanislaw: Class Structure in the Social Consciousness, 9530

Ostergaard, Geoffrey Neilsen: Constitutional Relations Between the Labour and Co-operative Parties: An Historical Review, 1896; Power in Co-operatives: A Study of the Internal Politics of British Retail Societies, 1897

Osterhammel, J.: Britischer Imperialismus im Fernen Osten: Strukturen der Durchdringung und einheimischer Widerstand auf dem Chinesischen Markt, 1932–1937, 13630

Ostlin, Joan: C. S. Lewis: An Annotated Checklist of Writings about him and his Works, 25660

Ostrom, Vincent: ed. Comparing Urban Delivery Systems: Structure and Performance, 3174

O'Sullivan, Patrick: Transport Policy: Geographical, Economic and Planning Aspects, 16271

O'Sullivan, Timothy: Julian Hodge: A Biography, 4479

Osuntokua, A.: Nigeria and the First World War, 14531

Oswald, Andrew J.: Profit-sharing: Can it Work?, 6050

Otley, C. B.: 'Militarism and Militarization in the Public Schools, 1900–1972', 23038

Ottaway, Hugh: Edmund Rubbra: An Appreciation, 24362; Vaughan Williams: Symphonies, 24378

Ottaway, Kathleen: Sick Pay, 8960

Ottaway, Richard N.: ed. Humanising the Work Place: New Proposals and Perspectives, 5787

Ottey, Roy: The Strike: An Insider's Story, 6921

Ottley, George: A Bibliography of British Railway History, 3419, 16716; A Guide to the Transport History Collection in Leicester University Library, 16198; Railway History: A Guide to 61 Collections in Libraries and Archives in Great Britain, 16717

Oughton, Frederick: Fraud and White Collar Crime, 10271

Oulihan, Brian: The Politics of Local Government: Central-Local Relations, 3215

Oulton, Nicholas: 'The Distribution of Education and the Distribution of Income', 23207

Oundle: A History of the Oundle Schools, 23069

Our Towns: A Close-Up: A Study Made in 1939–42 with Certain Recommendations by the Hygiene Committee of the Women's Group on Public Welfare, 17744

Outhwaite, Leonard: Unrolling the Map: The Story of Exploration, 27176

Ovendale, Ritchie: The English-speaking Alliance: Britain, the United States, the Dominions and the Cold War, 1945–1951, 12701; 'The South African Policy of the British Labour Government 1947–1951', 12714; 'Britain, the United States and the Recognition of Communist China', 13633; Appeasement and the English-Speaking World: Britain, the United States, the Dominions and the Policy of 'Appeasement', 13720; ed. The Foreign Policies of the British Labour Governments, 1945–1951, 14124; 'The Palestine Policy of the British Labour Government 1945–1946', 14343; 'The Palestine Policy of the British Labour Government 1947: The Decision to Withdraw', 14344; Britain, the United States and the End of the Palestine Mandate 1942–1948, 14350

Ovenden, Keith: The Politics of Steel, 6577

Overseas Development Institute: British Aid 4: Technical Assistance: A Factual Survey of Britain's Aid to Overseas Development through Technical Assistance, 9174

Overy, Richard James: The Air War 1939–1945, 15796; William Morris, Viscount Nuffield, 17432

Ovington, John Derrick: ed. The Better Use of the World's Fauna for Food, 20602

Owen Jones, Evan: 'Those who Cease to Foster', 8297

Owen, Arthur Ernest Bion: comp. Handlist of the Political Papers of Stanley Baldwin in the Library of the University of Cambridge, 979

Owen, Carol: Social Stratification, 9565

Owen, Charles: No More Heroes: The Royal Navy in the Twentieth Century: Anatomy of a Legend, 15238; Britons Abroad: A Report on the Package Tour, 26994

Owen, Christine: Regional Income Multipliers: The Anglesey Study, 5347

Owen, D. B.: An American Guide to British Social Science Abstracts, 98

Owen, David Arthur Llewellyn, [Baron] : Face the Future, 1834; A Future that Will Work: Competitiveness and Compassion, 1835; Britain and the United States: Four Views to mark the Silver Jubilee, 14011; In Sickness and in Health: The Politics of Medicine, 22081; A Unified Health Service, 22082

Owen, David Edward: English Philanthropy, 1660–1960, 9151

Owen, David Elystan: Canals to Manchester, 16407; The Manchester Ship Canal, 16408

Owen, Sir David John: The Origin and Development of the Ports of the United Kingdom, 16646; A Short History of the Port of Belfast, 16674; The Port of London, Yesterday and Today, 16700

Owen, Dorothy Mary: The Records of the Established Church in England, Excluding Parochial Records, 11551

Owen, Eluned Elizabeth: The Later Life of Bishop Owen: A Son of Lleyn, 12282

Owen, Frank: Tempestuous Journey: Lloyd George, his Life and Times, 1018; The Fall of Singapore, 15075; The Royal Armoured Corps, 15599

Owen, H.: Administration in General Practice, 21527

Owen, Harold: Journey from Obscurity: Wilfred Owen 1893–1918, 25757

Owen, Henry: Steel: The Facts about Monopoly and Nationalization, 6547

Owen, John A.: The History of the Dowlais Ironworks, 1959–1970, 6597

Owen, John P.: 'Consequences of Voluntary Early Retirement: A Case Study of a New Labour Force Phenomenon', 5883

Owen, Louise: Northcliffe: The Facts, 25094

Owen, Maureen: The Crazy Gang: A Personal Reminiscence, 26311

Owen, Myra: 'Theatre in Wales, 1946–1961', 26259

Owen, Nicholas: The History of the British Trolley Bus, 17238

Owen, Oliver Sylvanus: Natural Resource Conservation: An Ecological Approach, 20199

Owen, Owen Llewellyn: The History of the Rugby Football Union, 27036

Owen, R. Fenwick: The Desert Air Force, 15819; Tedder, 15965

Owen, Roger: ed. Suez 1956: The Crisis and its Consequences, 14390

Owen, Susan: Female Labour Supply in Post-War Britain: A Cohort Approach, 7773

Owen-Jones, Stuart: Railways of Wales, 16977

Owens, Joan Llewellyn: Careers in Social Work, 8708

Owens, John: 'The Drink Problem', 22176

Owens, John: A Plan for Bath: A Report . . ., 18840

Owens, John Switzer: The Smoke Problem of Great Cities, 20033

Owens, Rosemary Cullen: Smashing Times: A History of the Irish Women's Suffrage Movement 1889–1922, 2674

Ower, Ernest: Aviation: Its Technical Development, 15121; Aviation: Its Technical Development, 17515; Aviation of To-day: Its History and Development, 17516; Flight To-day, 17517

Owers, A. C.: Change and Innovation in Norfolk Farming: 70 Years of Experiment and Advice at the Norfolk Agricultural Station, Michaelmas 1908 to Michaelmas 1978, 19582

Oxaal, Ivar: Black Intellectuals come to Power: The Rise of Creole Nationalism in Trinidad and Tobago, 13067

Oxborrow, John: Inter-War Britain: A Social and Economic History, 3566, 7559

Oxbury, Harold: Great Britons: Twentieth Century Lives, 33

Oxenham, John Rudolph: Reclaiming Derelict Land, 20300

Oxford City Council: Oxford Traffic Survey, 16350

Oxford Playhouse 1938–64: Oxford University Theatre 1961–64, 26168

Oxford Review of Education 1, 22603

Oxford University Agricultural Economics Research Institute: Changes in the Economic Pattern, 4895

Oxford University Agricultural Economics Research Unit: Country Planning: A Study of Rural Problems, 19459

Oxford University Department of Social and Administrative Studies: (New Barnett Papers, No, 1) The Family in Modern Society, 10060

Oxford University Penal Research Unit: Occasional Papers No.1 The Violent Offender: Reality or Illusion?, 10208

Oxford University, Report of Commission of Inquiry, 23558

P.E.P.: Britain and World Trade, 4814

Paasdivirta, Johani: The Victors in World War I and Finland: Finland's Relations with the British, French and United States Governments in 1918–1919, 13878

Pace, David E.: Direct Participation in Action: The New Bureaucracy, 6028, 6031

Pack, Melvyn: Employment, Capital and Economic Policy: Great Britain 1918–1939, 3564

Pack, Stanley Walter Croucher: The Battle for Crete, 14855; Operation 'Husky': The Allied Invasion of Sicily, 14871; Invasion North Africa, 1942, 14902; Britannia at Dartmouth: The Story of HMS Britannia and the Britannia Royal Naval College, 15777

Packer, Bill: The Making of the English Garden, 19875

Packer, William: Henry Moore: An Illustrated Biography, 24196

Packman, Jean: Childcare: Needs and Numbers, 8298; The Child's Generation: Child Care Policy from Curtis to Houghton, 8299; Who Needs Care? Social Work Decisions about Children, 8300, 8842

Packman, John: Services in Rural Norfolk, 1950–1980: A Survey of the Changing Patterns of Service in Rural Norfolk over the Last Thirty Years, 19078, 19167

Paddon, Michael: Thinking about Children: Sociology and Fertility in Post-war England, 7496

Padfield, Peter: Beneath the House Flag of the P & O [Peninsular and Oriental Steam Navigation Company.], 16531

Padmore, George: Africa: Britain's Third Empire, 12688

Padwick, E. W.: A Bibliography of Cricket, 27096

Pagan, A. W.: Infantry: An Account of the 1st Gloucestershire Regiment during the War, 1914–1918, 15635

Page, A. C.: 'State Intervention in the Inter-war Period: The Special Areas Acts, 1934–1937', 7225

Page, A. T.: Pennies for Health: The Story of the British Hospitals Contributory Schemes Association, 21574

Page, Bruce: Philby: The Spy who Betrayed a Generation, 16053

Page, Charles Hunt: Society: An Introductory Analysis, 7530

Page, Dilys: Homelessness in London, 18510

Page, Edward C.: Remote Bureaucracy or Administrative Efficiency? Scotland's New Local Government System, 3180; Why Should Central/Local Relations in Scotland be any different from that in England?, 3214; ed. Fiscal Stress in Cities, 3270

Page, Graham Terry: Engineering among the Schools, 23277; The Industrial Training Act and After, 23281

Page, Henry: ed. The Newer Caribbean: Decolonisation, Democracy and Development, Philadelphia, 13018

Page, I.: 'Hostels for Educationally Sub-normal Adolescents', 10566

Page, Malcolm: John Arden, 25937

Page, Robert Jeffress: New Directions in Anglican Theology: A Survey from Temple to Robinson, 11875

Page, W.: Holbrook: The Story of a Village 1900–1983, 19252

Page, William Roberts: Introducing the Younger Woman: The Story of an Experiment in Further Education for Younger Women out at Work, 22490

Paget, Elma Katie: Henry Luke Paget: Portrait and Frame, 11752

Paget, Sir Julian: Last Post: Aden 1964–1967, 13874; The Story of the Guards, 15542; Counter-Insurgency Campaigning, 16169

Paget, Stephen: ed. Henry Scott Holland . . . Memoir and Letters, 11786

Paget-Tomlinson, Edward W.: Humber Shipping: A Pictorial History, 16475

Pahl, Janice Mary: A Refuge for Battered Women: A Study of the Role of a Woman's Centre, 7841, 9952; Managers and their Wives: A Study of Career and Family Relationships in the Middle Class, 9729

Pahl, Raymond Edward: Managers and their Wives: A Study of Career and Family Relationships in the Middle Class, 9729; Whose City?: And Further Essays on Urban Society, 17816; London: What Next? The Case for a Joint Inner London Rehabilitation Organisation (a Lecture), 17817; Whose City?: And Other Essays on Sociology and Planning, 17818; Urban Sociology and Planning: Urban Social Theory and Research, 17819; Readings in Urban Sociology, 17820, 18287; 'Poverty and the Urban System', 17821; Patterns of Urban Life, 17822; Urbs in Rure: The Metropolitan Fringe in Hertfordshire, 17823, 19163; 'Class and Community in an English Commuter Village', 19164

Paige, Deborah: Health and Welfare Services in Britain in 1975, 22083

Paine, Frank Albert: ed. Modern Processing, Packaging and Distribution Systems for Food, 20628

Painter, C.: 'The Civil Service: Post-Fulton Malaise', 860

Paish, Frank Walter: How the Economy Works and other Essays, 3510; 'British Floating Debt Policy from 1919 to 1939', 3548; The Rise and Fall of Incomes Policy, 3847; 'Inflation in the United Kingdom, 1948–1957', 3986; Studies in an Inflationary Economy in the United Kingdom, 1948–1961, 3987; 'Inflation and the Balance of Payments in the U.K., 1952–1967, 4016, 4926; The Post-War Financial Problem and other Essays, 4569; 'Britain's Changing Capacity for Overseas Investment', 4740; 'Profits and Dividends: The Next Five Years', 5985; 'The Management of the British Economy', 6115

Paisley, Ian: Why I am a Protestant, 3080

Paisley, Rhonda: Ian Paisley, My Father, 3079

Pakenham, Elizabeth [Countess of Longford]: The Royal House of Windsor, 466 Elizabeth R: A Biography, 509; The Pebbled Shore: Memoirs of Elizabeth Longford, 1264

Pakenham, Francis Aungier, Earl of Longford: Born to Believe: An Autobiography, 1259; Five Lives, 1260; Eleven at No. 10: A Personal View of Prime Ministers, 1931–1984, 1262; The Grain of Wheat, 1261; Peace by Ordeal: An Account from First Hand Sources of the Negotiation and Signature of the Anglo-Irish Treaty, 1921, 2975; Ulster, 2924; Eamon De Valera, 3043 A Study of Leaders in the Church Today, 11682

Palfrey, Colin: 'Remedial Education and the Adult Offender', 23121

Palmai, G.: 'Social Class and the Young Offender', 10637

Palmer, Alan: The Gardeners of Salonika, 14532

Palmer, Christopher: ed. The Britten Companion, 24319; Bliss, 24300; Delius: Portrait of a Cosmopolitan, 24328; 'Patrick Hadley: The Man and his Music', 24348; Herbert Howells: A Study, 24354

Palmer, Ernest Barry: Mergers and Associations of Professional Firms, 5534

Palmer, Gill: 'Donovan, the Commission on Industrial Relations and Post-liberal Rationalisation', 5854

Palmer, Helen M.: ed. The Dictionary of National Biography 7th Supplement [1951–1960], 18

Palmer, Herbert John: Government and Parliament in Britain: A Bibliography, 551

Palmer, Katherine V. H.: 'An Annotated Bibliography of Scientific Oceanographic Expeditions (Voyages)', 27181

Palmer, Richard: Starting School: A Study in Policies, 22669; School Broadcasting in Britain, 24755

Palmer, Russell: British Music, 24266

Palmer, W. B.: 'The Colleges of Advanced Technology and the Universities', 22493

Palmer, William: The Fiction of John Fowles: Tradition, Art and the Loneliness of Selfhood, 25527

Pamphlets relating to Scottish Nationalism: 1844–1973, 2508

Pamuk, Elsie M.: 'Social Class Inequality in Mortality from 1921 to 1972 in England and Wales', 7472

Pandey, Bishwa Nath: *ed.* The Evolution of Modern India and Pakistan 1858 to 1947, 13113; *ed.* The Indian Nationalist Movement 1885–1947, 13114; The Break-up . . . of British India, 13172

Panel of Nutrition of the Elderly: A Nutrition Survey of the Elderly: Report . . . , 20550

Paneth, Philipp: The Guardian of the Law: The Chief Rabbi, Dr J. H. Hertz, 12437

Panic, M.: 'Gross Fixed Capital Formation and Economic Growth in the United Kingdom and West Germany, 1954–1964', 4745; 'The Profitability of British Manufacturing Industry', 5988

Panitch, Leo Victor: Social Democracy and Industrial Militancy: The Labour Party and Incomes Policy, 1945–1974, 1806

Pankrashova, M.: Why War Was Not Prevented: A Documentary Review of the Soviet-British-French Talks in Moscow, 1939, 13953

Pannekoek, Antonie: A History of Astronomy, 26391

Pannell, Norman Alfred [Baron]: Immigration: What is the Answer? Two Opposing Views, 11406

Pannick, David: Sex Discrimination Law, 7781

Panning, William H.: 'Structural Effects and Individual Attitudes: Racial Prejudice in English Cities', 11182

Panorama [published by the Isle of Thanet Geographical Association], vol: 10, 20269

Panton, Alec: A Green Manifesto: Policies for a Green Future, 1856

Papadopoulos, Andrestinos N.: Multilateral Diplomacy within the Commonwealth, 12523

Papas, William: The Press, 25053

Papaspyros, N. S.: The History of Diabetes Mellitus, 21072

Pappe, Ilan: Britain and the Arab-Israeli Conflict 1948–1951, 14358

Pappworth, Joanna: By Word of Mouth: Elite Oral History, 225

Pappworth, Maurice Henry: Human Guinea Pigs: Experimentation on Man, 20829

Parascandola, John: 'Edward Mellanby and the Antirachitic Factor', 20973

Pardoe, John: Jetstream: A Production History, 17614

Pare, Philip Norris: Eric Milner-White, 1884–1963, 11801

Parekh, Bhikhu *and* Parekh, Pramila: Cultural Conflict and the Asian Family: Report of a Conference Organised by the National Association of Indian Youth, (in Leicester in 1975), 11220

Parfit, Jesse: Spotlight on Physical and Mental Assessment, 8269; Spotlight on Services for the Young Handicapped Child, 8270; Spotlight on Groupwork with Parents in Special Circumstances, 8271; Spotlight on Sources of Information about Children, 8272; Handicapped School-leavers: Their Further Education, Training and Employment, 8273; The Community's Children: Long-term Substitute Care: A Guide for the Intelligent Layman, 8304

Paris, Chris: Squatting: A Bibliography,

18377; 'Squatting and the Criminal Law Act: Problem or Solution?', 18378; Not Much Improvement: Urban Renewal Policy in Birmingham, 18409

Parish, Henry James: A History of Immunization, 21092; Bacterial and Virus Diseases: Antisera, Toxoids, Vaccines and Tuberculins in Prophylaxis and Treatment, 21093; Victory with Vaccines: The Story of Immunization, 21094

Park, Roberta J.: *ed.* From 'Fair Sex' to Feminism: Sport and the Socialisation of Women in the Industrial and Post-Industrial Eras, 7648

Parke, J. M. C.: Belfast: Areas of Special Social Need: Report by Project Team, 18165

Parker, D. J.: Water Planning in Britain, 20098

Parker, Derek: Radio: The Great Years, 24822; *and* Parker, Julia, The Story and the Song: A Survey of English Musical Plays, 1916–78, 24481; *ed.* Edith Sitwell: Selected Letters, 25806

Parker, Ernest Walter: Into Battle, 1914–1918, 14486

Parker, Henry Michael Denne: Manpower: A Study of Wartime Policy and Administration, 800, 5931

Parker, Herbert Ronald: Paying for Urban Development, 5409, 20405

Parker, Howard John: View from the Boys: A Sociology of Down-town Adolescents, 8484; Receiving Juvenile Justice, 10644

Parker, James G.: Lord Curzon: A Biography, 1175

Parker, John: Father of the House: Fifty Years in Politics, 1501; Labour Marches on, 1726

Parker, John Edgar Sayce: 'Profitability and Growth of British Industrial Firms', 5986

Parker, Michael St.John: The British Revolution, 1750–1970: A Social and Economic History, 3491

Parker, Olive: For the Family's Sake: A History of the Mothers Union, 1876–1976, 11675

Parker, Sir Peter: For Starters: The Business of Life, 16829

Parker, R. Alistair C.: 'Dr Schacht und der Briten : Auswirkungen von Schachts Paris-Reise in August 1936', 13689; 'Great Britain, France and the Ethiopian Crisis 1935–1936', 13790; 'Britain, France and Scandinavia, 1939–1940', 13882; 'Pound Sterling, the American Treasury and British Preparations for War, 1938– 1939', 14029; 'Anglo-French Conversations, April and September 1938', 14261; Economics, Rearmament and Foreign Policy: The United Kingdom before 1939—A Preliminary Study, 14712

Parker, Robert Henry: British Accountants: A Biographical Sourcebook, 4168; Accounting in Scotland: A Historical Biography, 4172; Comparative International Accounting, 4173; Accounting Thought and Education: Six English Pioneers, 4180; The Macmillan Dictionary of Accounting, 4185; Men of Account, 4186; Management Accounting: An Historical Perspective, 4187; Readings in Accounting and Business Research,

1970–1977, 4188; The Study of Accounting History, 4189; Papers on Accounting History, 4190

Parker, Roger Jocelyn: The Windscale Inquiry, 6671

Parker, Roy Alfred: Decisions in Child Care: A Study of Prediction in Fostering, 8301; The Rents of Council Houses, 18426

Parker, Stanley Robert: A Bibliography of Industrial Sociology, including the Sociology of Occupations, 5677; The Sociology of Industry, 5678; Effects of the Redundancy Payments Act: A Survey Carried out in 1969 for the Department of Employment, 5679; Workplace Industrial Relations 1972, An Enquiry Carried out on Behalf of the Department of Employment, 5680; 'Work and Non-work in Three Occupations', 5876; Leisure and Society in Britain, 26927; The Future of Work and Leisure, 26928; The Sociology of Leisure, 26929; *ed.* Bibliography on Leisure: Great Britain (1962–1972), 26930; Leisure and Tourism, 26933

Parker, Tony: The People of Providence: A Housing Estate and some of its Inhabitants, 9435; The Plough Boy, 9703; The Unknown Citizen, 10231; Five Women, 10410; A Man of Good Abilities, 10411; The Frying Pan: A Prison and its Prisoners, 10412

Parker, William Henry: Mackinder: Geography as an Aid to Statecraft, 26660

Parker, William Shepherd: Public and Community Health, 22084

Parkes, Sir Alan Sterling: *ed.* Towards a Population Policy for the United Kingdom, 7422; *ed.* Social and Genetic Influences on Life and Death, 22008; *ed.* Biological Aspects of Social Problems, 22009

Parkes, David: 'Keble College: Its Organs and Organ Scholars, 1896–1964', 22456

Parkes, James William: A History of the Jewish People, 11311; The Conflict of the Church and the Synagogue: A Study in the Origins of Anti-Semitism, 11333; The Jewish Question, 11334; The Emergence of the Jewish Problem 1878–1939, 11335

Parkes, Oscar: British Battleships: 'Warrior' 1860 to 'Vanguard' 1950: A History of Design, Construction and Armament, 15360

Parkhouse, James: Medical Manpower in Britain, 20763

Parkin, Frank: Class, Inequality and Political Order: Social Stratification in Capitalist and Communist Societies, 9571; *ed.* Social Analysis of Class Structure, 9572; 'Working Class Conservatives: A Theory of Political Deviance', 9684; Middle Class Radicalism: The Social Bases of the British Campaign for Nuclear Disarmament, 9731, 13527

Parkin, Michael: Inflation in the United Kingdom, 4011; 'The Demand for Money in the United Kingdom, 1956–1967: Preliminary Estimates', 4623

Parkin, Sara: Green Parties: An International Guide, 1857

Parkinson, Sir Arthur Charles Cosmo: The Colonial Office from within, 1909–1945, 12507

Parkinson, C. Northcote: Always a Fusilier, 15633

Parkinson, George Anthony: The People Called Methodists: A Short Survey of the History of the Methodist Church, 12069

Parkinson, George Singleton: A Synopsis of Health, 22053

Parkinson, John Richard: 'The Progress of United Kingdom Exports', 4781; Economic Development in Northern Ireland, 5387; The Economics of Shipbuilding in the United Kingdom, 16608; 'The Financial Prospects of Shipbuilding after Geddes', 16609; 'Shipbuilding', 16610

Parkinson, Lisa: Separation, Divorce and Families, 10003

Parkinson, Michael: Best: An Intimate Biography, 27094

Parkinson, Michael: Liverpool on the Brink: One City's Struggle against Government Cuts, 3331; The Labour Party and the Organisation of Secondary Education, 1918–1965, 22919

Parkinson, Norman: Lifework, 24712

Parkinson, Roger: Peace for Our Time: Munich to Dunkirk, the Inside Story, 13773; The Auk: Auchinleck, Victor at Alamein, 14756; Dawn on our Darkness: The Summer of 1940, 14812

Parkinson, Stephen: Unions in Prosperity, 6729

Parliamentary Papers: Conduct in Local Government: Prime Minister's Committee on Local Government Rules of Conduct, 3185; Streamlining the Cities: Government Proposals for Re-organising Local Government in Greater London and the Metropolitan Counties, 3189; The Conduct of Local Authority Business, 3190; Local Government Finance: Report of the Committee of Inquiry, 3264; Royal Commission on Local Government in Greater London 1957–1960, 3285; Report of the Tribunal Appointed to Inquire into the Vassall Case, 16055; Falkland Islands Review: Report of a Committee of Privy Councillors, 16075; Third Report of the House of Commons Foreign Affairs Committee, 16078; Committee of Inquiry into the Functions and Powers of the Islands' Councils of Scotland, 19253

Parmoor, Charles Alfred Cripps [Baron]: A Retrospect: Looking back over a Life of more than Eighty Years, 1502

Parr, Elizabeth A.: Children in Care and the Recruitment of Foster Parents, 8196; U.K. Social Survey: A Survey of Residential Caravan Life: An Enquiry, 18555

Parr, H. W.: The Great Western Railway in Devon, 16867

Parr, John B.: ed. Regional Policy: Past Experiences and New Directions, 5117

Parrinder, Patrick: ed. H. G. Wells: The Critical Heritage, 25872

Parris, Henry Walter: Constitutional Bureaucracy: the Development of British Central Administration since the Eighteenth Century, 707; Staff Relations in the Civil Service: Fifty Years of Whitleyism, 878; Going Comprehensive: Educational Policy-Making in Two County Boroughs, 22965

Parris, J. and Parris, H: Bracknell: The Making of our New Town, 18190

Parris, John: Arbitration: Principles and Practice, 5830

Parrott, Sir Cecil: The Tightrope, 13297; The Serpent and the Nightingale, 13298

Parrott, [Horace] Ian: Elgar, 24336

Parry, Cyril: 'The Independent Labour Party and Gwynedd Politics, 1900–1920', 1874; The Radical Tradition in Welsh Politics: A Study of Liberal and Labour Politics in Gwynedd, 1900–1920, 2561

Parry, David and Parry, Donald: Bygone Breweries of South Yorkshire, 20743

Parry, Sir David Hughes: 'The Status of the Welsh Language in English Law', 23833

Parry, Geraint: Local Politics and Participation in France and Britain, 3129

Parry, John Penrhyn: The Provision of Education in England and Wales: An Introduction, 22668; The Lord James Tricycle: Some Notes on Teacher Education and Training, 22733

Parry, José: The Rise of the Medical Profession: A Study of Collective Social Mobility, 20825

Parry, Kenneth Lloyd: ed. Companion to Congregational Praise, 11928

Parry, Noel: The Rise of the Medical Profession: A Study of Collective Social Mobility, 20825

Parry, Richard: Scottish Political Facts, 2487

Parry-Crooke, Charlotte: Contemporary British Artists, 23937

Parry-Edwards, E. L.: 'The Next Generation—A Welsh County Record of Maternity and Child Welfare', 8302

Parsler, Ron: ed. The Social Impact of Oil in Scotland, 6532

Parsloe, Phyllida: The Work of the Probation and After-care Officer, 10468

Parsonage, M.: 'Britain and Rhodesia: The Economic Background to Sanctions', 12812

Parsons, Sir Anthony: The Pride and the Fall: Iran 1974–1979, 13299; 'The Falklands Crisis in the United Nations 31 March–14 June 1982', 16097

Parsons, Anthony Dallin: The Maroon Square: A History of the 4th Battalion, the Wiltshire Regiment in North-West Europe, 1939–1946, 15740

Parsons, Christopher: True to Nature: Twenty-Five Years of Wildlife Filming with the BBC Natural History Film Unit, 24833

Parsons, David: Gatwick Airport and the Labour Market, 17677

Parsons, Ian: ed. The Collected works of Isaac Rosenberg, 25787

Parsons, Jack: Population Fallacies, 7411

Parsons, Lady Katherine: 'Women's Work in Engineering and Shipbuilding during the War', 7664

Parsons, Kenneth A. C.: ed. St Andrew's Street Baptist Church, Cambridge: Three Historical Lectures Given on the 250th Anniversary of the Foundation of the Church, 12036

Parsons, Sir Leonard Gregory: ed. Modern Trends in Paediatrics, 21115; ed. Diseases of Infancy and Childhood, 21116; ed. 'Child Health and the Universities', 21117; The Hospital Services of the Sheffield and East Midlands Area, 21468

Parsons, R. H.: The Early Days of the Power Station Industry, 6631

Parssinen, Terry M.: Secret Passions, Secret Remedies: Narcotic Drugs on British Society, 1820–1930, 22209

Part, Sir Anthony: The Making of a Mandarin, 939

Partington, Geoffrey: Women Teachers in the Twentieth Century in England and Wales, 22736

Partington, Martin, 'Parliamentary Committees: Recent Developments', 658; comp. Welfare Rights: A Bibliography on Law and the Poor 1970–1975, 4043

Parton, K. A.: The Costs of the Common Agricultural Policy, 19587

Partridge, Edward Hincks: Freedom in Education: The Function of the Public Boarding School, 23010

Partridge, Eric Honeywood: Songs and Slang of the British Soldier: 1914–1918, 14471; The Long Trail, 14472; British and American English since 1900, 23789

Partridge, Frances: A Pacifist's War, 13521; Everything to Lose: Diaries 1945–1960, 13522

Partridge, Michael: Farm Tools through the Ages, 19686

Partridge, Ralph: Broadmoor: A History of Criminal Lunacy and its Problems, 10438

Pashley, Barry William: University Extension Reconsidered, 23692

Pasold, Eric W.: Ladybird, Ladybird: A Story of Private Enterprise, 6439

Pass, Christopher Laurence: ed. Monopoly, 5515; The Brewing Industry: A Study in Industrial Organisation and Public Policy, 6153, 20736

Passmore, Anthony: Verderers of the New Forest: A History of the New Forest, 1877–1977, 19737

Passmore, John Arthur: A Hundred Years of Philosophy, 26835; The Perfectibility of Man, 27260

Passmore, Reginald: The Scotsman's Food, 20591

Patchett, Kenneth William: 'Decision-making in Juvenile Cases', 10585

Pateman, Carole: Participation and Democratic Theory, 6013

Pateman, Trevor: Television and the February 1974 General Election, 24896

Paterson, Alan James Stuart: Classic Scottish Paddle Steamers, 16590

Paterson, Sir Alexander: Paterson on Prisons: Being the Collected Papers of Sir Alexander Paterson, 10413

Paterson, Allen: The Gardens of Britain 2: Dorset, Hampshire and the Isle of Wight, 19883

Paterson, Hew Fergus: Mental Disorder and the Law, 21879

Paterson, Thomas Thomson: Glasgow Limited: A Case-study in Industrial War and Peace, 5649

Paterson, William: Government and the Chemical Industry: A Comparative Study of Britain and West Germany, 6227

Patey, Edward H.: My Liverpool Life, 11802

Patinkin, Don: Keynes's Monetary Thought, 26610; *ed.* Keynes, Cambridge and the General Theory, 26611

Patmore, John Allan: *ed.* Merseyside in Maps, 5183; An Atlas of Harrogate, 18107; Land and Leisure in England and Wales, 26954

Paton, David MacDonald: R.O.: Reform of the Ministry: A Study in the Work of Roland Allen, 11683; The Life and Times of Bishop Ronald Hall of Hong Kong, 12364

Paton, G.: *ed.* A Source Book and History of Administrative Law in Scotland, 18483

Paton, Herbert James: The Claim of Scotland, 5258

Paton, William Drummond MacDonald: 'Sir Henry Dale (1875–1968): Some Letters and Papers', 20999; The Growth of Pharmacology with Special Reference to its Dependence on the Advance in Chemical Knowledge, 22302

Patrick, James: A Glasgow Gang Observed, 8485, 10618

Patrick, John: The Rise of Scotland, 5274

Patten, John: 'Edmund W. Gilbert and the Development of Historical Geography with a Bibliography of his Work, 26669

Patterson, Alfred Temple: A Bibliography of Sources in Regional Industrial Development, 5115; Jellicoe, 15265; The Jellicoe Papers, 15266; Tyrwhitt of the Harwich Force: The Life of Admiral of the Fleet Sir Reginald Tyrwhitt, 15280; Southampton: A Biography, 18084; The University of Southampton: a Centenary History of the Evolution and Development of Southampton, 1862–1962, 23581

Patterson, Hamish M.: *ed.* Scottish Culture and Scottish Education 1800–1980, 2454

Patterson, Henry: The State in Northern Ireland, 1921–1971: Political Forces and Social Causes, 2787; Class Conflict and Sectarianism: The Protestant Working Class and the Belfast Labour Movement, 1868–1920, 2794

Patterson, J. H.: With the Zionists in Gallipoli, 14552

Patterson, Sheila: 'Foreigners in Britain', 10967; 'Race Relations in Birmingham', 10978; Immigrants in London: Report of a Study Group Set up by the London Council of Social Service, 10979; Dark Strangers: A Sociological Study of the Absorption of a Recent West Indian Migrant Group in Brixton, South London, 10980; Immigrants in Industry, 10981; Immigration and Race Relations in Britain 1960–1967, 10982.'The Polish Exile Community in Britain', 11372

Patterson, W. J.: Social Work's Theory of Man: A New Profession's Philosophical Anthropology, 8753

Patterson, W.: Going Critical: An Unofficial History of British Nuclear Power, 6667

Patterson, William David: The Lansdowne Earnings Survey, 3917

Pattie, Geoffrey: Is there a Future for the British Aerospace Industry? 17591

Pattinson, Sir Lawrence Arthur: History of 99 Squadron Independent Force, Royal Air Force, March 1918–November 1918, 15916

Pattinson, William: The Last Chronicle of Bouverie Street, 25147

Pattison, Bruce: 'The Crowther Report', 22606

Pattison, Iain: The British Veterinary Profession, 1791–1948, 9824

Patton, Henry Edmund: Fifty Years of Disestablishment: A Sketch of the History of the Church of Ireland, 1869–1920, 12180

Patullo, Polly: Women at Work, 7807

Patvardhan, V. S.: British Agricultural Marketing, 19530

Paul, Diane B.: 'A War on Two Fronts: J. B. S. Haldane and the Response to Lysenkoism in Britain', 26496

Paul, Hugh: The Control of Diseases, Social and Communicable, 22382

Paul, J. B.: 'The Union of Democratic Control', 13463

Paul, Leslie Allen: 'The Legal Straitjacket of the Church of England', 11633; The Deployment and Payment of the Clergy, 11679; A Church by Daylight: A Reappraisement of the Church of England and its Future, 11680; The English Philosophers, 26836

Paul, Noel Strange: *ed.* Principles for the Press: A Digest of Press Council Decisions 1953–84, 25333

Paul, William James: Job Enrichment and Employee Motivation, 5730

Paul, William Pratt: The Highland Regiments: Tigers in Tartan, 15563; The Lowland Regiments: Lions Rampant, 15564

Paulden, Sydney Maurice: Whatever Happened at Fairfields?, 16633

Pauley, R.: Beyond our Ken: A Guide to the Battle for London, 3296

Paulu, Burton: Broadcasting: Radio and Television in the United Kingdom, 24759; British Broadcasting in Transition, 24760; British Television and Radio in the United Kingdom, 24761

Paulus, Ingeborg: The Search for Pure Food: A Sociology of Legislation in Britain, 20646

Pavenstedt, Eleanor: *ed.* The Drifters: Children of Disorganised Lower-Class Families, 8305

Pavey, Agnes E.: The Story of the Growth of Nursing as an Art, a Vocation and a Profession, 21703

Pavitt, Laurence A.: The Health of the Nation. The Second Stage of the National Health Service, 21575

Pawle, Shafto Gerald Strachan: The War and Colonel Warden: Based on the Recollections of Commander C. R. Thompson, Personal Assistant to the Prime Minister, 1939–1945, 988; The Secret War, 1939–1945, 15202

Pawley, Bernard Clinton and Pawley, Margaret: Rome and Canterbury through Four Centuries: The Second Vatican Council: Studies by Eight Anglican Observers, 12328; A Study of the Relations between the Church of Rome and the Anglican Churches, 1530–1973, 12329

Pawley, Edward: BBC Engineering 1922–1972, 24728; 'BBC Television 1939–60: A Review of Progress', 24848

Pawley, Margaret: Donald Coggan: Servant of Christ, 11689

Pawson, Henry Cecil: A Survey of the Agriculture of England, 19611; Cockle Park Farm: An Account of the Cockle Park Farm Experimental Station from 1896 to 1956, 19701

Pawson, Tony: 100 Years of the FA Cup: The Official Centenary History, 27071

Paxton, John: *ed.* The Statesman's Year Book Historical Companion, 266; Commonwealth Political Facts, 12470

Payley, J.: Children: Handle with Care: A Critical Analysis of the Development of Intermediate Treatment, 8303

Payn, Graham: Noel Coward and His Friends, 25957; *ed.* The Noel Coward Diaries, 25958

Payne, Anthony: Grenada: Revolution and Invasion, 13080

Payne, Anthony: The Music of Frank Bridge, 24305

Payne, Douglas: A Study of Job Satisfaction in Social Work, 8837

Payne, Ernest Alexander: The Free Church Tradition in the Life of England, 12011; Free Churchmen Unrepentant and Repentant and Other Papers, 12012; The Baptist Union: A Short History, 12024; To be a Pilgrim: A Memoir of Ernest A. Payne, 12029; James Henry Rushbrooke, 1870–1947: A Baptist Greatheart, 12030; 'Baptists and the Ecumenical Movement', 12339; Thirty Years of the British Council of Churches 1942–1972, 12346

Payne, Geoff: 'Occupational Transition in Advanced Industrial Societies', 5912; 'Understanding Occupational Transition: A Comment on Jones', 5914; 'Typologies of Middle Class Mobility', 9733

Payne, George Louis: Britain's Scientific and Technical Manpower, 23275

Payne, Gordon Edgar: A Physical, Social and Economic Survey and Plan [of Gloucestershire], 18879; The Tay Valley Plan, 18916

Payne, L. M.: 'In Pursuit of Medical History', 21000

Payne, Peter: Isle of Wight Railways Remembered, 16945

Payne, Peter Frederick: British Commercial Institutions, 6639

Payne, Peter Lester: *ed.* Studies in Scottish Business History, 5261; 'Rationality and Personality: A Study of Mergers in the Scottish Iron and Steel Industry, 1916–1936', 6543; Colvilles and the Scottish Steel Industry, 6596

Payne, Robert: The Great Man: A Portrait of Winston Churchill, 988

Payne, W. F.: Business Behaviour, 1919–1922: An Account of Post-War Inflation and Depression, 3552

Paynter, Will: My Generation, 1949; British Trade Unions and the Problem of Change, 6815, 7243

Payton-Smith, Derek Joseph: Oil, 6499

Peace, K.: 'Some Changes in the Coalmining Industry of Southern Yorkshire, 1951–1971', 6341

Peach, [Guthlac] Ceri [Klaus]: 'West Indian

Migration to Britain', 11258; West Indian Migration to Britain: A Social Geography, 11259, 11412; 'West Indian Migration to Britain: The Economic Factors', 11260; 'British Unemployment Cycles and West Indian Immigration, 1955–74', 11273; ed. Urban Social Segregation, 18282; 'The Contribution of Council House Allocation to West Indian Desegregation in London 1961–1971', 18709

Peacock, Sir Alan Turner: 'The British Economy and its Problems', 3502; 'Wage Claims and the Pace of Inflation [1948–1951]', 3888; The Economics of National Insurance, 4031; The Economic Analysis of Government, 4587; The Economic Theory of Fiscal Policy, 4588; The Growth of Public Expenditure in the United Kingdom, 4757; 'The Control and Appraisal of Public Investment in the United Kingdom since 1790', 4758; ed. Public Expenditure Appraisal and Control, 4759, 21598; ed. Public Expenditure and Government Growth, 6148; Welfare Economics: A Liberal Restatement, 9055; 'The New Doctor's Dilemma', 21295; Education for Democrats: A Study of the Financing of Education in a Free Society, 23201; Educational Finance: Its Sources and Uses in the United Kingdom, 23202; The Composer in the Market Place, 24293

Peacock, Alfred J.: 'Conscience and Politics in York 1914–18', 13451

Peacock, Bill: Waverley Route Reflections, 16983

Peacock, Helen: ed. The Unmaking of Edinburgh: The Decay, Depopulation and Destruction of Central Edinburgh: An Argument for City Centre Living and a Call for Action, 18132

Peacock, Herbert Leonard: A History of Modern Britain, 1815–1968, 344

Peacock, Roger S.: Pioneer of Boyhood: Story of Sir W. A. Smith, 8512

Peacocke, Marguerite Dorothea: Queen Mary: Her Life and Times, 475

Peaford, Margaret: The Effect of Slum Clearance on Multi-Occupation, 18407

Peake, Harold John Edward: The English Village: The Origin and Decay of its Community, 19152

Peake, Henry John Edward: ed. The Story of Hungerford in Berkshire, 19193

Peaker, Anthony: Economic Growth in Modern Britain, 3669

Pear, Thomas Hatherley: English Social Differences, 9513; Personality, Appearance and Speech, 9514; The Moulding of Modern Man: A Psychologist's View of Information, Persuasion and Mental Persuasion Today, 21764

Pearce, Brian: The Early History of the Communist Party in Great Britain, 1925

Pearce, Clifford: The Machinery of Change in Local Government 1888–1974: A Study of Central Involvement, 3132

Pearce, David William: 'Retrospect on Sterling: The Crises of 1964 and 1965', 4709; Decision Making for Energy Futures: A Case Study of the Windscale Inquiry,

6670; Environmental Economics, 19949; Research in Environmental Economics in the U.K. 1973, 19950; Research in Environmental Economics in the U.K. 1974, 19951; The Economics of Noise Nuisance: A Bibliography, 20140; ed. The Economics of Natural Resource Depletion, 20217; ed. Resource Conservation: The Social and Economic Dimensions of Recycling, 20219

Pearce, John Dalziel Wyndham: Juvenile Delinquency: A Short Text-book on the Medical Aspects of Juvenile Delinquency, 10615

Pearce, Philippa: From inside Scotland Yard, 10754

Pearce, R. D.: The Turning Point in Africa: British Colonial Policy, 1938–1948, 12690; 'The Colonial Office and Planned Decolonisation in Africa', 12691; 'The Colonial Office in 1947 and the Transfer of Power; An Addendum to John Cell', 12696; 'Government, Nationalists and Constitutions in Nigeria 1935–1951', 12763

Pearce, S. B. P.: An Ideal in the Working: The Story of the Magdalen Hospital 1758–1958, 21453

Pearl, David: 'Muslim Marriages in English Law', 11211

Pears, David Francis: Bertrand Russell and the British Tradition in Philosophy, 26869; ed. Bertrand Russell: A Collection of Critical Essays, 26870; Wittgenstein, 26883

Pears, Randolph: British Battleships, 1892–1957: The Great Days of the Fleets, 15361

Pearsall, H. W. A.: ed. Shipping: A Survey of Historical Records, 16450

Pearsall, Ronald: Popular Music of the Twenties, 24469

Pearse, Innes Hope: The Peckham Experiment: A Study in the Living Structure of Society, 9308, 17714; The Case for Action: A Survey of Everyday Life under Modern Industrial Conditions, with Special Reference to the Question of Health, 17713; Science, Synthesis and Sanity: An Inquiry into the Nature of Living, 17715

Pearse, James: The Co-ordination of The Public Health Services in the Counties of Essex, Hampshire, Gloucester and West Sussex, 22007

Pearse, Padraic H.: The Letters of Padraic H. Pearse, 3067

Pearse, Richard: The Ports and Harbours of Cornwall: An Introduction to the Study of Eight Hundred Years of Maritime Affairs, 16681

Pearson, Arthur James: The Railways and the Nation, 16778

Pearson, Sir Cyril Arthur: The Conquest of Blindness, 21928

Pearson, D.: 'The Aberdeenshire Canal: A Description and Interpretation of its Remains', 16425

Pearson, Geoffrey: Hooligan: A History of Respectable Fears, 10665

Pearson, George William: Flashback: The Autobiography of a British Film-maker, 24680

Pearson, Gordon: Hull and East Coast Fishing, 19814

Pearson, Hesketh: The Last Actor-Managers, 26125

Pearson, J. E.: 'Pilot Study of Single Women Requesting a Legal Abortion', 7887

Pearson, John George: Facades: Edith, Osbert and Sacheverell Sitwell, 25807; The Life of Ian Fleming, 25508

Pearson, Lester Bowles: Memoirs Vol.I: 1897–1948: Through Diplomacy to Politics, 12662; Memoirs Vol.II: 1948–1957: The International Years, 12663

Pearson, N. G.: 'Who Uses the Health Services and Why?', 21348

Pearson, Neville Stewart: Redundancy Payments: An Annotation and Guide to the Redundancy Payments Act, 1965, 6976

Pearson, Nicholas: The State and the Visual Arts: A Discussion of State Intervention in the Visual Arts in Britain, 1760–1981, 23760, 23958

Pearson, Richard: Education, Training and Employment, 5965; Graduate Supply and Demand into the 1990's, 9889

Pearson, Sidney A.: Arthur Koestler, 25614

Pearson, Sidney Vere: Men, Medicine and Myself, 21180; The State Provision of Sanatoriums, 21181

Pearson, Sylvia: Mothers at Work, 7812

Peart-Binns, John Stuart: Living with Paradox: John Habgood, Archbishop of York, 11698; Blunt, 11724; Cornish Bishop [J. W. Hunkin], 11746; Graham Leonard: Bishop of London, 11750; Ambrose Reeves, 11755; Eric Treacy, 11761; Wand of London, 11763; Defender of the Church of England: The Life of Bishop R. R. Williams, 11764

Pearton, Maurice: The LSO at 70: A History of the Orchestra, 24544

Pease, C. A.: Socialism in the Village, 19055

Pease, Ken: Community Service Orders, 10495

Peate, Iorwerth: Studies in Regional Consciousness and Environment, 2397

Peck, Sir John: Dublin from Downing Street, 2992, 13301

Pecora, A.: 'La Struttura Urbana di Manchester', 18062

Peddie, John Ronald: The United Steel Companies Ltd., 1918–1968, 6602; The Carnegie Trust for the Universities of Scotland, 1901–1951: The First Fifty Years, 22484; The Trevelyan Scholarships: A Report on an Experiment in University Selection, 22551

Peddie, John Taylor: The Crisis of the Pound, 4682

Peden, George C.: Warren Fisher and British Rearmament against Germany, 14713

Pederick, G.: Battledress Broadcasters: A History of the British Forces Broadcasting Services, 24749

Pedley, Robin: ed. Comprehensive Schools Today: An Interim Survey, 22946; ed. Comprehensive Education: A New Approach, 22947; ed. The Comprehensive School, 22948

Peebles, Malcolm W. H.: Evolution of the Gas Industry, 6401

Peel, Albert: The Free Churches, 1903–1926, 12004; A Brief History of English Congregationalism, 12046; These Hundred Years: A History of the Congregational Union of England and Wales, 12047

Peel, C. S. Mrs: 'Domestic Life in England To-day', 9912

Peel, D.A.: The Economics of Wage Controls, 3955

Peel, D. W.: A Garden in the Sky: The Story of Barkers of Kensington, 1870–1957, 6650

Peel, Edwin Arthur: The Nature of Adolescent Judgement, 8486; 'Programmed Learning', 22773

Peel, John: Contraception and Family Design: A Study of Birth Planning in Contemporary Society, 7507; 'The Politics of Birth Control', 7510; 'The Hull Family Survey. Pt One, The Survey Couples, 1966', 7511; Pt Two, Family Planning in the First Five Years of Marriage, 1966', 7511; ed. Equalities and Inequalities of Family Life, 10012; Population and Pollution: Proceedings of the Eighth Annual Symposium of the Eugenic Society, 19985

Peel, Sir John: The Lives of the Fellows of the Royal College of Obstetricians and Gynaecologists 1929–1969, 20848, 20897

Peele, Gillian: ed. The Politics of Reappraisal, 1918–1939, 785, 13144; British Party Politics: Competing for Power in the 1980s, 1593; 'Revolt over India', 13144

Peers, Robert: Fact and Possibility in English Education, 22667; 'The Extra-Mural Work of Universities under War Conditions', 23651; Adult Education: A Comparative Study, 23681; ed. Adult Education in Practice, 23682

Pegden, Sue: Families Five Years on, 7493

Pegg, Ian: Under the Imperial Carpet, 11086

Pegg, M.: Broadcasting and Society 1918–39, 24722

Pelling, Doria: The Child with Cerebral Palsy, 8274; The Child with a Chronic Medical Problem, 8275; The Child with Asthma, 8276

Pelling, Henry Mathison: Modern Britain, 1885–1955, 293; Churchill, 988; A Short History of the Labour Party, 1678; The British Communist Party: A Historical Profile, 1919; 'The Early History of the Communist Party of Great Britain, 1920–1929', 1920; 'The 1945 General Election Reconsidered', 2293; Britain and the Marshall Plan, 3729, 14128; A History of British Trade Unionism, 6690; America and the British Left: From Bright to Bevan, 14010

Pellizzi, Camillo: English Drama: The Last Great Phase, 26183

Pemberton, John Edward: British Official Publications, 174, 644

Pen, Jan: Income Distribution, 3832

Pencavel, John H.: 'Relative Wages and Trade Unions in the United Kingdom', 3913; 'An Investigation into Industrial Strike Activity in Britain', 6960

Pender, John: The Square Mile: A Guide to the New City of London, 4286

Pendlebury, Maurice: Public Sector Accounting, 4770

Penguin Books: Penguin Progress 1935–1960, 24985

Penhale, Francis: The Anglican Church Today: Catholics in Crisis, 11652

Penhaligon, Annette: Penhaligon, 1503

Penn, Christopher N.: Noise Control, 20145

Pennance, Frederick George: Choice in Housing, 18445; Housing Market Analyses and Policy, 18446; The Polluters: Industry or Government?, 19993

Pennick, Nigel: London's Early Tube Railways, 17007; Trams in Cambridgeshire, 17219

Penning-Rowsell, E. C.: Water Planning in Britain, 20098

Pennington, Shelley: A Hidden Workforce: Women Homeworkers in Britain, 1850–1985, 7643

Pennock, James Roland: '"Responsible Government", Separate Powers and Special Interests: Agricultural Subsidies in Britain and America', 19522

Penny, Leith: Holford: A Study in Architecture, Planning and Civic Design, 23877

Penrose, Barrie: Conspiracy of Silence: The Secret Life of Anthony Blunt, 16030

Penrose, Edith Tilton: The Theory of the Growth of a Firm, 5511

Penrose, Harald: British Aviation: The Great War and Armistice 1915–1919, 17513; British Aviation: The Adventuring Years 1920–1929, 17514

Pentney, John: 'Worms that Turned: The Inter-Party Mobility of Parliamentary Candidates since 1945', 1558

People's Autobiography of Hackney Association: The Island: The Life and Death of an East London Community 1870–1970, 9393

Peper, Christian D.: An Historian's Conscience, 26821

Pepler, Conrad: The English Religious Heritage, 11570

Peppard, Nadine: 'Migration: Some British and European Comparisons', 7328

Pepper, David: The Roots of Modern Environmentalism, 19976

Pepper, Max P.: A Decade Later: A Follow-up Study of Social Class and Mental Illness, 21817

Pepper, Simon: Housing Improvement: Goals and Strategy, 18710

Percival, A. E.: The War in Malaya, 15060

Percival, John: Experimental Dance, 24247; Theatre in my Blood: A Biography of John Cranko, 24248

Percival, John: Wheat in Great Britain, 19449

Percy, Eustace, Lord Percy of Newcastle: Some Memories, 1286

Perham, Dame Margery Freda: The Second Part of the Life of Frederick Dealtry Lugard, 12494; Colonial Sequence, 1930–1949: A Chronological Commentary upon British Colonial Policy, especially in Africa, 12681; Colonial Sequence, 1949–1969: A Chronological Commentary upon British Colonial Policy, especially in Africa, 12682; Lugard: The Years of Authority, 1898–1945: The Colonial Reckoning: The End of

Imperial Rule in Africa in the Light of British Experience, 12683

Perkin, Harold James: Intro. North Country Bred: A Working Class Family Chronicle, 10063; The Age of the Railway, 16720; Key Profession: The History of the Association of University Teachers, 22544; 'Social History in Britain', 26761

Perkins, Dudley: Husbands and Wives: A Survey of Recent Changes in the Law, 10005

Perkins, Ernest Benson: So Appointed: An Autobiography, 12084; Gambling and English Life, 27118

Perkins, James Oliver Newton: 'Europe and the Sterling Area', 4705; Britain and Australia: Economic Relationships in the 1950s, 12635

Perkins, Kevin: Menzies, the Last of the Queen's Men, 12625

Perkins, M.: The Baha'i Faith, 12461

Perlman, Morris: Local Government Finance in a Unitary State, 3262, 4872

Perman, David: Change and the Churches, 11560

Perren, Brian: HSTs at Work, 17061

Perrett, Bryan: The Matilda, 15521; Tank Tracks to Rangoon: The Story of British Armour in Burma, 15529; The Valentine in North Africa, 1942–1943, 15530; Through Mud and Blood: Infantry-Tank Operations in World War II, 15531

Perrigo, Sarah: Trouble and Strife: Women and the Labour Party, 1805

Perring, Franklyn H.: ed. The Ecological Effects of Pesticides, 20117

Perrott, Roy: The Aristocrats: A Portrait of Britain's Nobility and their Way of Life Today, 9740; Cops and Robbers: An Investigation into Armed Bank Robbery, 10236

Perry, C. Bruce: The Bristol Royal Infirmary 1904–1974, 21424

Perry, Cassandra and Perry, John: Comp. A Chief is a Chief by the People, 11514

Perry, Colin: Boy in the Blitz, 15165

Perry, Donald Gordon: A Social and Economic History Notebook, 1750–1960, 3480

Perry, Edward S.: The New Film Index: A Bibliography of Magazine Articles in English, 1930–1970, 24589

Perry, Fred: Fred Perry, 27151

Perry, George: The Great British Picture Show, 24639; Movies from the Mansion: A History of Pinewood Studios, 24681; Life of Python, 26293

Perry, Jane: All our Children: Pre-School Services in a Changing Society, 8372; The Fair Housing Experiment: Community Relations Councils and the Housing of Minority Groups, 18732

Perry, Peter John Charles: The Evolution of British Manpower Policy: From the Statute of Artificers 1563 to the Industrial Training Act 1964, 5927

Perry, Reginald: Ardingly, 1858–1964: A History of the School, 23043

Perry, Richard: A Naturalist on Lindisfarne, 26532

Perry, Walter Laing MacDonald [Baron]: 'The Open University', 23549

Petch, James Alexander: 'Whither Education?', 22515; Fifty Years of Examining: The Joint Matriculation Board, 1903–1953, 22917

Petch, Simon: The Art of Philip Larkin, 25623

Peter, John: Masters of Modern Architecture, 23895

Peter, Mary: Mary P.: Autobiography, 27148

Peters, A. John: 'The Changing Idea of a Technical Education', 22514; British Further Education: A Critical Textbook, 23258

Peters, Alan Frederick: ed. Impact of Offshore Oil Operations, 6525

Peters, Anthony R.: Anthony Eden at the Foreign Office, 1931–1938, 1012

Peters, B. G.: 'Income Inequality in Sweden and the United Kingdom: A Longitudinal Analysis', 3833

Peters, George Henry: Cost-Benefit Analysis and Public Expenditure, 4766; Agriculture, 19606

Peters, Jean: ed. Book Collecting: A Modern Guide, 25012

Peters, John Edward Colclough: Discovering Traditional Farm Buildings, 19708

Peters, R. J.: Report for Scottish Department of Health: Scottish Hospitals Survey, 21471

Peters, R. S.: Education and the Education of Teachers, 22849

Petersen, Paul D.: Religion and Politics: A Bibliography Selected from the Atlas Religious Database, 11530

Peterson, Alexander Duncan Campbell: A Hundred Years of Education, 22664; 'The Higher Education of Teachers', 22719; 'A University of the Air?', 23547

Peterson, Sir Maurice Drummond: Both Sides of the Curtain, 13300

Pethick-Lawrence, Frederick William, [Lord]: Fate Has Been Kind, 1287

Petre, Francis Loraine: The Scots Guards in the Great War, 1914–1918, 15588

Petrie, Sir Charles Alexander: The Modern British Monarchy, 429; The Chamberlain Tradition, 983, 1142; The Life and Letters of Rt. Hon. Austen Chamberlain, 1143; Walter Long and his Times, 1257; The Carlton Club, 1632; A Historian Looks at his World, 26808

Petrie, William Matthew Flinders: Eastern Exploration, Past and Future, 27190

Petrow, Richard: The Black Tide: In the Wake of the Torrey Canyon, 20071

Petter, M.: The Colonial Office, War, and Redevelopment Policy, 12492; 'Forward Thinking and War: The Colonial Office during the 1940s', 12493

Pettes, Dorothy Elizabeth: Supervision in Social Work: A Method of Student Training and Staff Development, 8719

Pettifer, Julian: Diamonds in the Sky: A Social History of Air Travel, 17646

Pettigrew, A. M.: The Awakening Giant: Continuity and Change in Imperial Chemical Industries, 6207

Pettit, Stephen: The Philarmonia Orchestra, 24541

Pettman, Barry Oliver: Industrial Democracy: A Selected Bibliography, 6037

Pettmen, B. O.: Research in Environmental Economics in the U.K. 1973, 19950; Research in Environmental Economics in the U.K. 1974, 19951

Pevsner, Sir Nikolaus Bernhard Leon: Pioneers of Modern Design from William Morris to Walter Gropius, 23894; The Buildings of England, 23915

Pfaff, Richard William: Montague Rhodes James, 25601

Pfeiffer, John: The Changing Universe: The Story of the New Astronomy, 26381

Pharoah, Timothy Martin: Transport Organisation in a Great City: The Case of London, 16324

Phelan, Keiren: Fast Attack Craft: The Evolution of Design and Tactics, 15120

Phelps, Edmund Struther: ed. Economic Justice, Selected Readings, 3434; Inflation Policy and Unemployment Theory: The Cost Benefit Approach to Monetary Planning, 4002; Microeconomic Foundations of Employment and Inflation Theory, 4003

Phelps, Guy: 'Youth Culture and the School Revisited', 8447; Film Censorship, 26906; 'Censorship and the Press', 26907

Philby, Eleanor: The Spy I Loved, 16048

Philby, Harold A. R. 'Kim': My Silent War, 16051

Philby, Harry St. John Bridger: The Heart of Arabia, 27231; A Pilgrim in Arabia, 27232

Philip, George: The Story of the Last Hundred Years: A Geographical Record, 1834–1934, 26699

Philip, Kathleen: The Story of Gigha: The Flourishing Island, 19267

Philip, P. J.: English Political Ideas from 1918 to 1939, 2083

Philip, Sir Robert: The Strategic Front of Medicine Today, 21171

Philips, Cyril H.: ed. The Evolution of Modern India and Pakistan 1858 to 1947, 13113; ed. The Partition of British India. Policies and Perspectives 1935–1947, 13156

Phillips, A. W.: 'The Relation between Unemployment and the Rate of Change in Money Wage Rates in the United Kingdom, 1861–1957', 3924

Phillips, Alastair: Glasgow's Herald: Two Hundred Years of a Newspaper, 1783–1983, 25131

Phillips, Alfred: The Lawyer and Society, 9814

Phillips, Anne: Hidden Hands: Women and Economic Policies, 7845; Feminism and Equality, 7863

Phillips, Brian M.: Building Society Finance, 4384

Phillips, Cecil Ernest Lucas: Escape of the 'Amethyst', 14692; Alamein, 14903; The Greatest Raid of all, 14924; The Raiders of Arakan, 14925; Cockleshell Heroes, 15028

Phillips, Celia M.: Ports and Inland Waterways and Civil Aviation, 16186

Phillips, Charles: The Great Eastern since 1900, 16844

Phillips, D. C.: Ransomes of Ipswich: A History of the Firm and Guide to its Records, 6373

Phillips, David: Contrasting Values in Western Europe: Unity, Diversity and Change, 239; Rural Britain: A Social Geography, 19032

Phillips, George Godfrey: Constitutional Law, 608

Phillips, Gordon Ashton: The Growth of the British Economy 1918–1968, 3458; 'The Triple Industrial Alliance in 1914', 6696; The General Strike: The Politics of Industrial Conflict, 6950; Casual Labour: The Unemployment Question in the Port Transport Industry 1880–1970, 7018, 9661

Phillips, J. B.: The Price of Success, 11803

Phillips, John: 'The Philosophical Critique of a Scientific Sociology: Some Remarks on Bryant's Defence', 8001

Phillips, John: Suburban Style: The British House, 1840–1960, 18303

Phillips, M.: The Divided House: Women at Westminster, 7831

Phillips, Margaret: Small Social Groups in England, 10120

Phillips, Marion: Women and the Miner's Lock-out: The Story of the Women's Committee for the Relief of the Miner's Wives and Children, 9127

Phillips, Martin: The Copper Industry in the Port Talbot District, 6618; Writing the Rural: Five Cultural Geographies, 19123

Phillips, Miles H.: Historical Review of British Obstetrics and Gynaecology, 1800–1950, 21100

Phillips, Owen Hood: Reform of the Constitution, 620

Phillips, Roger: Trees in Britain, Europe and North America, 19763

Phillips, Truman: 'Agricultural Expansion and the U.K. Balance of Payments', 19554

Phillips-Birt, Douglas: A History of Seamanship, 16495, 27163; When Luxury went to Sea, 16581, 27164

Phillipson, C.: The Question of the Bosphorus and the Dardanelles, 14553

Phillipson, Michael: Sociological Aspects of Crime and Delinquency, 10620

Phillipson, Nicholas A.: Universities, Society and the Future, 23318

Phillipson, Richard V.: 'The Implementation of the Second Report of the Interdepartmental Committee on Drug Addiction', Modern Trends in Drug Dependence and Alcoholism, 22181

Phillpot, Bryan Passmore: The Regional Pattern of the Demand for Meat in the United Kingdom, 20675

Philo, Greg: ed. Trade Unions and the Media, 6834

Philp, Albert Frederic: Family Failure: A Study of 129 Families with Multiple Problems, 10061; The Problem of the 'Problem Family': A Critical Review of the Literature Concerning the 'Problem Family' and its Treatment, 10062

Philpin, Charles H. E.: ed. Institute of Historical Research 1960–1961, 409

Philpott, B. P.: 'Fluctuations in Wool Prices, 1870–1953', 6430

Philpott, Bryan: Challenge in the Air, 15804

Phizacklea, Annie: ed. Racism and Political

Action in Britain, 11189; White Man's Country: Racism and British Politics, 11195

Phythian, Brian Arthur: *ed.* The Manchester Grammar School, 1515– 1965, 22998

Piachaud, D.: The Causes of Poverty, 9102

Piazza, Paul: Christopher Isherwood: Myth and Anti-Myth, 25597

Picardie, J.: Heroin, Chasing the Dragon, 22200

Pick, Frederick Walter: Contemporary History, 341

Pick, J. B.: *ed.* Neil M. Gunn: Selected Letters, 25568; Neil M. Gunn: A Highland Life, 25570

Pick, John: Arts Administration, 23955; The State and the Arts, 23956; The West End: Management and Snobbery, 26265

Pick, Joyce: No Caravan: No Home, 18554

Pickard, D. G.: 'Clerical Workers and the Trade Unions', 6770

Pickering, Sir George: Postgraduate Medical Education and the Specialities, with Special Reference to the Problem in London, 20769; Quest for Excellence in Medical Education: A Personal Survey, 20822

Pickering, John Frederick: 'Recruitment to the Administrative Class, 1960–1964', 918; Resale Price Maintenance in Practice, 5035, 6653; 'The Abandonment of Major Mergers in the United Kingdom, 1965–1975', 5537; The Causes and Consequences of Abandoned Mergers, 5538; The Implementation of British Competition Policy on Mergers, 5539; Concentration in British Manufacturing Industry into the 1970s, 5540; International Trade Performance and Concentration in British Industry, 5541; The Acquisition of Consumer Durables: A Cross-sectional Investigation, 20470

Pickering, Kenneth W.: Drama in the Cathedral: The Canterbury Festival Plays 1928–1948, 26165

Pickering, William Stuart Frederick: *ed.* A Social History of the Diocese of Newcastle, 11615; Anglo-Catholicism: A Study in Religious Ambiguity, 11653; 'Persistence of Rites of Passage: Towards an Explanation', 11889; *ed.* Anglican-Methodist Relations: Some Institutional Factors, 12305

Pickersgill, J. W.: The Mackenzie King Record, 12661

Pickett, Kathleen Gordon: Migration and Social Adjustment: Kirkby and Maghall, 7282; 'Aspects of Migration in North West England, 1959–1961', 7347; 'Bodyweight of Men Related to Structure, Age and Social Status'. and, 'Chest Girth of Men Related to Structure, Age, Bodyweight and Social Status', 9504

Pickettjohns, Edward Allister: The Social Structure of Modern Britain, 9487

Pickford, M.: The Church of Scotland: An Economic Survey, 12240

Pickford, Michael: University Expansion and Finance, 23317

Pickhaus, K.: 'Dockerstreik in Grossbritannien', 6954

Pickles, Dorothy: The Uneasy Entente: French Foreign Policy and Franco-British Misunderstandings, 14225

Pickles, Wilfrid: Between You and Me: The Autobiography, 26336; Sometime . . . Never, 26337

Pickles, William: 'Political Attitudes in the Television Age', 24888

Pickstone, John: Medicine and Industrial Society: A History of Hospital Development in Manchester and its Region, 1752–1946, 21497

Pickvance, Christopher Geoffrey: 'Life-cycle, Housing Tenure and Residential Mobility: A Path Analytical Approach', 7348; 'Some Factors Underlying Racial Discrimination in Housing', 11188; *ed.* Urban Sociology: Critical Essays, 18283

Picton-Turbervill, Beatrice: 'The Case for State Purchase and Control of the Liquor Traffic: A Question for Women', 22170

Pidgeon, D. A.: Admission to Grammar Schools, 22980

Piekalkiewicz, Janusz: Cassino: Anatomy of the Battle, 14872

Piepe, Anthony: Television and the Working Class, 24836

Pierce, Rachel M.: 'Birth Control in Britain', 7502; 'Marriage in the Fifties', 9968

Piggott, Juliet: Queen Alexandra's Royal Army Nursing Corps, 14609, 15764

Piggott, Mary: *ed.* Government Information and the Research Worker, 246

Pignon, Fred: The Story of the Open Golf Championship 1860–1950, 27155

Pigott, Stanley C.: Hollins: A Study of Industry, 1784–1949, 6457

Pigou, Arthur Cecil: Aspects of British Economic History, 1918–1925, 3557; The Economic Position of Great Britain, 3602; A Study in Public Finance, 4591; Lectures on Housing: The Warburton Lectures for 1914, 18618; Portrait of A City's Housing, 18619

Pike, David: *ed.* Family Planning, 7506

Pike, Edgar Royston: Pioneers of Social Change, 8995

Pike, Geoff: Graduate Supply and Demand into the 1990's, 9889

Pilch, I. L.: An Analysis of the Problems and Practices of Urban Development in the United States and Britain, 17906

Pilch, Michael: Pension Schemes, 3972; New Trends in Pensions, 3973; Pension Schemes Practice, 3974; Company Pension Schemes, 3975; Managing Pension Schemes: A Guide to Contemporary Pension Plans and the Social Security Act, 3976

Pile, Sir Frederick Alfred: Ack-Ack: Britain's Defence against Air Attack during the Second World War, 14818, 14819

Pile, Sir William D.: The Department of Education and Science, 833; 'Corporate Planning for Education in the Department of Education and Science', 22790

Pilger, John: Heroes, 25270

Pilkington, Edward: Beyond the Mother Country: West Indians and the Notting Hill White Riots, 10904

Pilley, John: 'Teacher Training in Scotland', 23615

Pilonsky, I.: 'A Study of Long-term Patients Attending a General Hospital Psychiatric Department', 21813

Pilpel, Robert H.: Churchill in America 1895–1961: An Affectionate Portrait, 988

Pimlott, Benjamin: Hugh Dalton, 1179; *ed.* Second World War Diary of Hugh Dalton 1940–1945, 1180; *ed.* Political Diary of Hugh Dalton, 1918–1940, 1945–1960, 1181; Labour and the Left in the 1930s, 1718; 'The Socialist League: Intellectuals and the Labour Left in the 1930s', 1719; *ed.* Fabian Essays in Socialist Thought, 2110

Pimlott, John Alfred Ralph: The Englishman's Holiday, 26982

Pinchbeck, Ivy: Children in English Society: Vol. 2: From the 18th Century to the Children's Act 1948, 8306

Pincher, Chapman: Inside Story: A Documentary of the Pursuit of Power, 16061; Their Trade is Treachery, 16062; Too Secret Too Long, 16063; The Secret Offensive: Active Measures: A Saga of Deception, Disinformation, Subversion, Terrorism, Sabotage and Assassination, 16064

Pincus, Lily: *ed.* Marriage: Studies in Emotional Conflict and Growth, 9964

Pinder, John: Britain and the Common Market, 14166; *ed.* Fifty Years of Political and Economic Planning (PEP): Looking Forward 1931–1981, 26892

Pinder, Pauline: 'Women at Work', 7822; Women at Work, 7823

Pine, Leslie Gilbert: The New Extinct Peerage 1884–1971, Containing Extinct, Abeyant, Dormant and Suspended Peerages with Genealogies and Arms, 36; Tradition and Custom in Modern Britain, 9909

Pinion, Francis Bertram: Educational Values in an Age of Technology, 23280; A T. S. Eliot Companion: His Life and Works, 25502

Pink, William: 'Youth Culture and the School: A Replication', 8455

Pinker, Robert: Social Theory and Social Policy, 8964; English Hospital Statistics, 1861–1938, 21375; The Hospitals, 1800–1948: A Study in Social Administration in England and Wales, 21415

Pinkus, Charles E.: Solving Local Government Problems: Practical Applications of Operations Research in Cities and Regions, 3243

Pinnick, Alfred William: How Malaya is Governed, 12902; Country Planners in Action, 17784

Pinon, René: L'avenir de l'entente Franco-Anglaise, 14251

Pinsent R. J. F. H.: *ed.* A History of the Royal College of General Practitioners: The First 25 Years, 20873; *ed.* A History of the General Practitioner: Some European Comparisons, 21501

Pinson, Barry: Revenue Law, Comprising Income Tax, Surtax and Profit Tax; Estate Duty; Stamp Duties; Tax and Estate Planning, 4836

Pinto-Duschinsky, Michael: British Political Finance 1830–1980, 1595; 'Trends in British Political Funding 1979–1983', 1596; 'Central Office and "Power" in the

Conservative Party', 1648; The British General Election of 1970, 2329

Piper, David: The Genius of British Painting, 23977

Piper, John Egerton Christmas: Piper's Places: John Piper in England and Wales, 24053

Piper, John Richard: 'Backbench Rebellion, Party Government and Consensus Politics: The Case of the Parliamentary Labour Party 1966–1970', 1750

Piper, L. P. S.: 'A Short History of the Camborne School of Mines', 7051

Pippard, A. J. S.: 'Engineering Studies in British Universities', 22513

Piratin, Phil: Our Flag Stays Red, 1948

Pirenne, M. H.: Vision and the Eye, 22328

Pirie, David: A Heritage of Horror: The English Gothic Cinema 1946–72, 24657

Pirie, Madsen: Economy and Local Government, 4881

Pirie, Norman Wingate: Four Thousand Million Mouths: Scientific Humanism and the Shadow of World Hunger, 20531; Food Resources, Conventional and Novel, 20608

Pirie, Peter J.: The English Musical Renaissance: Twentieth Century British Composers and their Works, 24268; Frank Bridge, 24304

Pissarides, C. A.: 'A Model of British Macro-Economic Policy, 1955–1969', 3663; 'Staying on at School in England and Wales', 22974

Piszczkowski, T.: Anglia a Polska 1914–1939: w swietle dokumentow Brytyskich, 13905

Pitcairn, Lee: 'Crisis in British Communism: An Insider's View', 1966

Pitfield, David E.: 'Regional Economic Policy and the Long-run: Innovation and Location in the Iron and Steel Industry', 6588

Pitt, Barrie William: 1918: The Last Act, 14596; Zeebrugge: St George's Day 1918, 14659; Coronel and Falkland, 14666; Churchill and the Generals, 14741; The Crucible of War: Year of Alamein, 14904

Pitt, Derek: Surrey Villages, 19145

Pitt, Douglas C.: Government Departments: An Organisational Perspective, 820

Pitt, James: Gentrification in Islington: The Return of the Middle Classes to an Inner London Borough and the Subsequent Effects on Housing, 18753

Pitt, P. H.: A History of Building Regulation in London, 1189–1972, with an Account of the District Surveyors' Association, 6197

Pitt-Rivers, J. A.: The Story of the Royal Dragoons, 1938–1945, 15621

Pitts, P. W.: Royal Wilts: The History of the Royal Wiltshire Yeomanry, 1920–1945, 15739

Pivot, Agnes: Women, 7803

Pizzurno, Alessandro: ed. The Resurgence of Class Conflict in Western Europe since 1968, 9561

Plachy, Frank: Britain's Economic Plight, 3560

Planner, the: 1914+, 18834

Planning and Transport Research Computation: Public Transport Planning and Operations, 16263

Plant, Chris: ed. New Hebrides: The Road to Independence, 12888

Plant, Marjorie: The English Booktrade: An Economic History of the Making and Sale of Books, 24937

Plant, Martin A.: Alcohol, Drugs and School-leavers, 8538; 'Drug Takers in an English Town: Factors Associated with the Use of injected Drugs', 22225

Plant, Raymond: Ideology in Modern British Politics, 1605; Social and Moral Theory in Casework, 8651

Plater, Alan: 'Twenty-five Years Hard: A Playwright's Personal Retrospective', 25980

Platt, Beryl Catherine [Baroness]: Women in Technology, 7855

Platt, D. C. M.: 'The Commercial and Industrial Interests of Ministers of the Crown', 1564

Platt, Jennifer: Realities of Social Research: An Empirical Study of British Sociologists, 8031; Social Research in Bethnal Green: An Evaluation of the Work of the Institute of Community Studies, 8032, 9363; 'Some Problems in Measuring the Jointness of Conjugal Role-relationships', 10085

Platt, John: British Coal: A Review of the Industry, its Organisation and Management, 6262, 6306

Platt, Robert [Baron]: Doctor and Patient: Ethics, Morals, Government, 20830; ed. Social and Genetic Influences on Life and Death, 22008

Platt, T. Comyn: 'Is Prohibition Coming?', 22171

Plaut, Theodor: Industrial Relations in the Modern State: An Introductory Survey, 5591

Playfair, Giles William: Crime, Punishment and Cure, 10325; The Offenders: The Case against Legal Vengeance, 10326; The Offenders: Society and the Atrocious Crime, 10327; The Punitive Obsession: An Unvarnished History of the English Prison System, 10439

Playfair, Ian Stanley Ord: The Mediterranean and Middle East, 14728

Playne, Arthur Twisden: A History of the Parishes of Minchinhampton and Avening, 19348

Playne, Caroline E.: Society at War, 1914–1916, 7551; Britain Holds On, 1917–1918, 7552

Pliatzky, Sir Leo: The Treasury under Mrs Thatcher, 807; Getting and Spending: Public Expenditure, Employment and Inflation, 811, 943

Plimmer, Charlotte and Plimmer, Denis: A Matter of Expediency: The Jettisoning of Admiral Sir Dudley North, 14822

Plomley, [Francis] Roy: Days Seemed Longer: Early Years of a Broadcaster, 24742

Plowden Report: Children and their Primary Schools: A Report of the Central Advisory Council for Education (England), 23138

Plowden, Edwin [Baron]: An Industrialist in the Treasury, 944

Plowden, Stephen: Taming Traffic, 16240; Transport Reform: Changing the Rules, 16241

Plowden, William: The Motor Car and Politics, 1896–1970, 17348

Plowman, D. E. G.: 'Local Social Status in England and Wales', 9475

Plumb, J. H.: The Making of an Historian: The Collected Papers of J. H. Plumb, 26809

Plummer, Alfred: New British Industries in the Twentieth Century, 4969; The Blanket Makers, 1669–1969: A History of Charles Early and Marriott (Witney) Ltd., 6440; The London Weavers' Company, 1600–1970, 6441

Plummer, David Brian: Rogues and Running Dogs, 19113

Plumridge, John Henry: Hospital Ships and Ambulance Trains, 14610

Plumstead, Derek: A Civic Survey and Plan for the City and Royal Burgh of Edinburgh, 18866

Pocklington: A History of Pocklington School, East Yorkshire, 1514–1950, 23070

Pockson, Jonathan R. H. H.: Accountants' Professional Negligence: Developments in Legal Liability, 9829

Pocock, Douglas Charles David: Durham: Images of a Cathedral City, 18104; 'Some Features of the Population of Corby New Town', 18263; Images of the Urban Environment, 20309

Pocock, John Grahame: The Spirit of a Regiment: Being the History of the 19th King George V's Own Lancers. 1921–1947, 15690

Pocock, Rowland Francis: Nuclear Power: Its Development in the United Kingdom, 6661

Pocock, Tom: Fighting General: The Public and Private Campaigns of General Sir Walter Walker, 16162

Podet, Allen Howard: The Success and Failure of the Anglo-American Committee of Inquiry 1945–1946: Last Chance in Palestine, 14340

Podmore, David: 'Localisation in the Hong Kong Government Service 1948–1968', 12974

Podolsky, E.: Doctors, Drugs and Steel: The Story of Medicine's Battle Against Death, 21184

Polanyi, George: Which Way Monopoly Policy?: Some Questions raised by recent Reports of the Monopolies Commission, 5525; Planning in Britain: The Experience of the 1960s, 6079; How Much Inequality? An Inquiry into the 'Evidence', 9567

Polanyi, Michael: The Study of Man, 27259

Polanyi, Richard: Policy for Poverty, 9067

Pole, W.: ed. Environmental Institutions, 19972

Polish-Catholic Mission in London 1894–1944: (Summary in English), 11375

Political Activities of Civil Servants: Report of the Committee, 891

Political Ecology Research Group: An Investigation into the Hazards Associated with the Maritime Transport of Spent Nuclear Reactor Fuel to the British Isles, 20133; Safety Aspects of the Advanced Gas-cooled Reactor: A Report Commissioned by Torness Community Concern, 20134; An Investigation into the Incidence of Cancer in the Areas affected by Discharges from the Nuclear Fuels Reprocessing Plant at Windscale, Cumbria, 20135

Political Party Yearbooks, 1885–1948, 1562
Political Quarterly 49 (1969), Special Issue on the Future of the Social Services, 8937
Political and Economic Planning Research Services Limited: Racial Discrimination, 11161
Political and Economic Planning: Growth in the British Economy: A Study of Economic Problems and Policies in Contemporary Britain, 3638; Manpower: A Series of Studies of the Composition of Britain's Labour Force, 5930; Graduate Employment: A Sample Survey, 5969; Industries Group: Report on the British Coal Industry, 6278; Report on the Gas Industry in Great Britain, 6412; Women and Top Jobs: An Interim Report, 7713; Colonial Students in Great Britain: A Report, 9880; Family Needs and the Social Services, 10042; New Commonwealth Students in Britain: With Special Reference to Students from East Africa, 11498; Anti-Discrimination Legislation, 11110; Colonial Students in Britain, 11499; A Survey of the Chocolate and Sugar Confectionary Industry, 20690; Mental Subnormality in London: A Survey of Community Care, 21778
Polk, Barbara Bovee: 'Room at the Top: Social Recognition of British and American Females over Time', 7815
Polk, Dora: Vernon Watkins and the Spring of Vision, 25854
Polk, Judd: Sterling: Its Meaning in World Finance, 4702
Polk, Kenneth: 'Youth Culture and the School: A Replication', 8455
Pollak, Andy: Paisley, 3077
Pollard, A. O.: The Royal Air Force, a Concise History, 15790
Pollard, David W.: 'The Police Act 1964', 10692
Pollard, Robert Spence Watson: Introducing the National Insurance (Industrial Injuries) Acts, 1946–1953, 4101; Beveridge in Brief, 9033; The Problem of Divorce, 9988; Family Problems and the Law, 9989
Pollard, Sidney: 'The Foundation of the Co-operative Party', 1893; The Development of the British Economy, 1914–1980, 3495; The British Economic Miracle, 3671; The Wasting of the British Economy: British Economic Policy, 1945 to the Present, 3686; The Wealth of England 1085–1966, 3777; *ed.* The Gold Standard and Employment Policies Between the Wars, 4683; The Genesis of Modern Management: A Study of the Industrial Revolution in Great Britain, 5411; A History of Labour in Sheffield, 6700
Pollins, Harold: 'Liberal Voting at the General Election of 1951', 310; 'Party Politics and Local Government in Western South Wales', 3382; An Economic History of the Jews in England, 3538, 11328; Social Change in South-West Wales, 5381; *ed.* Trade Unions in Great Britain, 6737, 6832; 'Coloured People in Post-war English Literature', 11068; 'The West Indian Comes to England', 11069; Newcomers: The West Indians in London, 11248; 'The Jews',

11329; 'Transport Lines and Social Divisions', 16326; Britain's Railways: An Industrial History, 16723; A History of Ruskin College, 23678
Pollitt, Brian: *ed.* Selected Papers of Maurice Dobb, 26582
Pollitt, Christopher: Manipulating the Machine: Changing the Pattern of Ministerial Departments 1960–83, 821; 'The Public Expenditure Survey, 1961–1972', 4764
Pollitt, Harry: Serving My Time: An Apprenticeship in Politics, 1946
Pollock, Bertram: A Twentieth-Century Bishop: Recollections and Reflections, 11753
Pollock, F. E.: 'Roosevelt, the Ogdensburg Agreement, and the British Fleet: All Done with Mirrors', 14053
Pollock, G. J.: Just the Job: The Employment and Training of Young School Leavers: A Summary Report, 5962; 'Employers and Trade Unions', 6762
Pollock, John Charles: A Cambridge Movement, 11661
Polmar, Norman: Military Helicopters of the World: Military Rotor-wing Aircraft since 1917, 17553
Polonsky, Antony B.: 'Polish Failure in Wartime London: Attempts to Forge a European Alliance, 1940–1944', 13907
Polsky, Howard W.: 'Changing Delinquent Subcultures: A Social-psychological Approach', 10638
Pomeranz, Ruth: The Lady Apprentices: A Study of Transition in Nurse Training, 23236
Pomphrey, George: What Children Think of their Comics: With an Analysis of Current Comics and a Brief Assessment of Current Trends, 25197
Pond, Chris: Low Pay-1980s Style, 3950; Low Pay: What Can Local Authorities Do?, 3951; No Return to Sweatshops! Government Economic Strategy and the Wages Councils, 3952; The Case for a National Minimum Wage, 3953; Low Pay and Family Poverty, 3965; Britain Can't Afford Low Pay, 3967; A Study of Poverty and Taxation, 4855; Taxation and Social Policy, 8916; To Him who Hath: A Study of Poverty and Taxation, 9094
Pond, D. A.: 'Marriage and Neurosis in a Working Class Population', 21774
Pond, Hugh: Salerno, 14873; Sicily, 14874
Ponsonby, Arthur Augustus William Henry [Baron]: Falsehood in Wartime, 1504, 14442; Democracy and Diplomacy: A Plea for Popular Control of Foreign Policy, 13343
Ponsonby, Sir Charles: Ponsonby Remembers, 1506
Ponsonby, Frederick Edward Grey, Lord Sysonby: Recollections of Three Reigns, 542; The Grenadier Guards in the Great War, 1914–1918, 15642
Pont, H. B.: Educational Research in Britain, 3, 22847
Ponting, Clive: The Right to Know: The Inside Story of the Belgrano Affair, 764, 908; Whitehall: Tragedy and Farce, 872

Ponting, Kenneth George: *ed.* Textile History and Economic History: Essays in Honour of Miss Julia de Lacy Mann, 6413; The Wool Trade: Past and Present, 6428
Pool, Charles George: A Hundred Years of Economic Development in Great Britain, 3443
Poole, Herbert Reginald: The Liverpool Council of Social Service 1909–1954, 9133
Poole, John Brian: The Evolution of British Policy on Aircraft Noise, 20151
Poole, K. P.: The Local Government Service in England and Wales, 3233
Poole, Michael: Managers in Focus: The British Manager in the Early 1980's, 5451; Theories of Trade Unionism: A Sociology of Industrial Relations, 5813; Industrial Relations: Origins and Patterns of National Diversity, 5814; Workers' Participation in Industry, 6021; Towards a New Industrial Democracy: Workers' Participation in Industry, 6022
Poole, Roger: The Unknown Virginia Woolf, 25896
Poole, Sydney Leonard: Cruiser: A History of the British Cruiser from 1889 to 1960, 15389
Poole, Vera E.: These our Children: An Account of the Home Life and Social Environment of Children in an Industrial Slum District, 8145
Poole-Conner, Edward Joshua: Evangelicalism in England, 11655
Pooley, Beverley J.: The Evolution of British Planning Legislation, 20356
Poolman, Kenneth: Escort Carrier, 1941–1945: An Account of British Escort Carriers in Trade Protection, 15131; Flying Boat: The Story of the 'Sunderland', 15854; The Catafighters and Merchant Aircraft Carriers, 15855
Popay, J.: Employment Trends and the Family Study, 9938
Pope, Barbara H.: *ed.* Historical Periodicals Directory, 162
Pope, David Watts: *ed.* Modern Policing, 10736
Pope, Dudley: Flag 4: The Battle of Coastal Forces in the Mediterranean, 14905; The Battle of the River Plate, 15034
Pope, Rex: *ed.* Atlas of British Social and Economic History, 143; *ed.* British Economic Performance, 1880–1980, 3511
Pope-Hennessy, James: Queen Mary, 1867–1953, 475; Lord Crewe, 1858–1945: The Likeness of a Liberal, 1152
Popham, G. T.: 'Government and Smoking: Policy Making and Pressure Groups', 6539
Popham, Hugh: FANY: The Story of the Women's Transport Services 1907–1984, 15462; The Dorset Regiment: The 39th/54th Regiment of Foot, 15616; Into Wind: A History of British Naval Flying, 15856
Popkin, Henry: *ed.* The New British Drama, 26225
Popper, Sir Karl Raimund: Unended Quest: An Intellectual Autobiography, 26858; The Open Society and Its Enemies, 26855; The Self and its Brain, 27263
Popplestone, Gerry: Squatting: A

Bibliography, 18377; 'Squatting and the Criminal Law Act: Problem or Solution?', 18378

Population Investigation Committee: London School of Economics: 'Towards a Population Policy for the United Kingdom', 7404

Porminder, Bhachu: Twice Migrants: East African Sikh Settlers in Great Britain, 11434

Porritt, Arthur: J. D. Jones of Bournemouth, 12057

Porritt, Jonathon: Seeing Green: The Politics of Ecology Explained, 1858

Porteous, J. Douglas: Canal Ports: The Urban Achievement of the Canal Age, 16387

Porteous, Robert: Grangemouth's Modern History, 1768–1968, 18144

Porter, Andrew N.: ed. British Imperial Policy and Decolonization, 1938–64, 12487; 'Iain Macleod, Decolonization in Kenya and Tradition in British Colonial Policy', 12830

Porter, Bernard: The Lion's Share: A Short History of British Imperialism, 1850–1970, 12475; Britain, Europe and the World, 1850–1982: Delusions of Grandeur, 13244; Plots and Paranoia: A History of Political Espionage in Britain, 1790–1988, 15995

Porter, Brian Ernest: Britain and the Rise of Communist China: A Study of British Attitudes, 1945–1954, 13632

Porter, Charles: 'Citizenship and Health—questions in War-time', 21286

Porter, Elizabeth: Water Management in England and Wales, 20102

Porter, Enid: Cambridgeshire Customs and Folklore, 19159

Porter, Julia: Furnishing the World: The East London Furniture Trade, 1830–1980, 6480

Porter, Kenneth I.: ed. New Periodical Titles, 1960–1968, 155

Porter, Richard W: The Versatile Satellite, 17704

Porter, Roy: The Social History of Language, 23795

Porter, Vincent: ed. British Cinema History, 24623

Porter, William Smith: The Medical School in Sheffield, 1828–1928, 20782

Portsmouth Borough Council: Borough Government in Portsmouth 1835–1974, 3338

Portwood, Derek: 'Careers and Redundancy', 5924

Posner, Michael: ed. Demand Management, 4641

Post, Gaines: 'The Machinery of British Policy in the Ethiopian Crisis', 13791

Post, K. W. J.: The Price of Liberty: Personality and Politics in Colonial Nigeria, 12762

Postan, Sir Mosei Mikhail Efimovich: British War Production, 3755; Design and Development of Weapons, 15119

Postgate, Raymond William: The Life of George Lansbury, 1446; The Common People, 1746–1938, 7529; A Pocket History of the British Working Class, 9625

Posthumus, Cyril: The Motorcycle Story, 17180; Motor Cars, 17342; Classic Sports Cars, 17343

Pott, A.: Northern Labour History: A Bibliography, 1776

Potter, Allen M.: Organised Groups in British National Politics, 2066; 'The Equal Pay Campaign Committee', 7784

Potter, David: Society and the Social Sciences: An Introduction, 8094

Potter, David C.: India's Political Administrators, 1919–1983, 13122; 'Manpower Shortage and the End of Colonialism: The Case of the Indian Civil Service', 13123

Potter, Kenneth: The Iron and Steel Act, 1949, with General Introduction and Annotations, 6551

Potter, R. S. J.: 'Administrative and Social Work Problems of Services for the Handicapped', 21801

Potter, Robert B.: Barbados, 13075

Potter, Stephen: Transport and New Towns, 16308, 19008; Transport Planning in the Urban Cities, 16309; The Alternative New Towns: The Record of the Town Development Programme 1952–1984, 19007

Potter, Tim: The British Confectionary Industry (Chocolate and Sugar), 20691

Potter, Warren: Fraternally Yours: A History of the Independent Order of Foresters, 4074, 9129

Pottinger, George: The Secretaries of State for Scotland, 1926–1976: Fifty Years of the Scottish Office, 2480

Pottle, Patrick: The Blake Escape, 16028

Poulsen, Charles: Victoria Park: A Study in the History of East London, 18369

Poulter, S. M.: English Law and Ethnic Minority Customs, 11095

Pound, Reginald: A. P. Herbert: A Biography, 1432; Selfridge: A Biography, 5500; The Lost Generation, 14434; Northcliffe, 25097; The Strand Magazine, 1891–1950, 25187; Arnold Bennett: A Biography, 25389; Evans of the Broke: A Biography of Admiral Lord Mountevans, 27200

Pountney, Melville Trevor: Trends in Population, Housing and Occupancy Rates, 1861–1961, 7420, 18711

Powell, Anthony: To Keep the Ball Rolling, 25767

Powell, Christopher G.: An Economic History of the British Building Industry, 1815–1979, 6173; 'Fifty Years of Progress', 18561

Powell, Dora M.: Edward Elgar: Memories of a Variation, 24330

Powell, Geoffrey: Suez: The Double War, 14383

Powell, John Enoch: Freedom and Reality, 1297; Still to Decide, 1298; A Nation—No Nation?, 1299; The New Conservatism: An Anthology of Post-War Thought, 2191; Medicine and Politics: 1975 and After, 21581; A New Look at Medicine and Politics, 21582

Powell, John Percival: Universities and University Education: a Select Bibliography, 23448

Powell, Leslie Hughes: The Shipping Federation: A History of the First Sixty Years, 1890–1950, 16564

Powell, Michael: A Life in Movies, 24666

Powell, W. R.: 'Nationalism in Wales', 2597

Power, Christopher: Black Settlers in Britain 1555–1958, 11075

Power, Sir D'Arcy: The Lives of the Fellows of the Royal College of Surgeons of England, Vol.3: 1930–1951, 20842; British Masters of Medicine, 20847; A Short History of Surgery, 21143; A Mirror for Surgeons: Selected Readings in Surgery, 21144; A Short History of St. Bartholomew's Hospital, 1123–1923: Past and Present, 21438

Power, Edward Raymond Roper: Population Prospects, 7353; The Social Structure of an English Country Town, 9509

Power, John: Immigrants in School: A Survey of Administrative Policies, 23177

Power, John P.: 'Estimates of the Religious Composition of Northern Ireland Local Government Districts in 1981 and Change in the Geographical Pattern of Religious Composition between 1971 and 1981', 12156

Power, Michael John: 'Neighbourhood, School and Juveniles before the Courts', 10640

Power, Paul F.: 'The Sunningdale Strategy and the Northern Majority Consent Doctrine in Anglo-Irish Relations', 2997

Powers, B. D.: Strategy without Slide Rule: British Air Strategy, 1914–1939, 15805

Powers, R. H.: 'Winston Churchill's Parliamentary Commentary on British Foreign Policy, 1935–1938', 13680

Powesland, Peter F.: Speech Style and Social Evaluation, 9549

Powlinson, Charles F.: 'Exhibit Posters on Child Welfare Work', 8307

Pownall, Henry: Chief of Staff: The Diaries of Lieutenant General Sir Henry Pownall, I. 1933–1940, 14777

Poynter, [Frederick] Noel [Lawrence]: ed. The Evolution of Medical Practice in Britain, 20823; ed. The Evolution of Medical Education in England, 20824, 22427; 'Lord Cohen of Birkenhead', 20930; A Short History of Medicine, 21200; Compilation of Printed Books in the Wellcome Historical Medical Library, 21201; ed. Medicine and Culture: Proceedings of an Historical Symposium Organised Jointly by the Wellcome Institute of the History of Medicine, London, and the Wenner-Gren Foundation for Anthropological Research, 21218; Medicine and Man, 21223; ed. The Evolution of Hospitals in Britain, 21418; ed. The Evolution of Pharmacy in Britain, 22255; ed. Chemistry in the Service of Medicine, 22301

Poynton, Thomas Llewelyn: The Institute of Municipal Treasurers and Accountants: A Short History 1885–1960, 3248

Pradhan, S. D.: ed. India and World War I, 13126

Prais, Sigbert Jon: The Evolution of Giant Firms in Britain: A Study of the Growth of Concentration in Manufacturing Industry in Britain, 1909–1970, 4939, 5533; 'New Look at the Growth of Industrial

Concentration', 4943; 'The Fertility of Jewish Families in Britain, 1971', 7497; 'Measuring Social Mobility', 9464; 'The Formal Theory of Social Mobility', 9465; 'Synagogue Marriages in Great Britain, 1966–1968', 9980; 'The Size and Structure of the Anglo-Jewish Population 1960–1965', 11295; 'Synagogue Statistics and the Jewish Population of Great Britain, 1900–1970', 12430

Prandy, Kenneth: Professional Employees: A Study of Scientists and Engineers, 5023, 9807; 'White Collar Unionization: A Conceptual Framework', 6785; Social Stratification and Occupations, 9595; White Collar Work, 9672

Pratley, Gerald: The Cinema of David Lean, 24677

Pratt, Alan Frederick Weston: Economic and Social History: A Booklist for Schools, 3390

Pratt, C.: The Critical Phase in Tanzania 1945–1968: Nyerere and the Emergence of a Socialist Strategy, 12844

Pratt, David Doig: British Chemistry Industry: Its Rise and Development, 6215

Pratt, James Davidson: A History of the Modern British Chemical Industry, 6226

Pratt, John: 'Diversion from the Juvenile Court', 10531

Pratt, John: Polytechnics: A Report, 22532; Policy and Practice: The Colleges of Advanced Technology, 23291

Pratt, Sir John T.: China and Britain, 13621

Pratt, Joseph Hyde: 'A Reappraisal of Researches Leading to the Discovery of Insulin', 21001

Pratt, Lawrence: 'The Anglo-American Naval Conversations on the Far East of January 1938', 14026

Pratt, Mark Jones: Building Societies: An Econometric Model, 4368

Pratt, Michael: Mugging as a Social Problem, 10201

Pratt, Vernon: Religion and Secularisation, 12389

Pratten, C. F.: 'Steel to Nationalise or Not to Nationalise', 6558

Pratten, Clifford F.: Effects of the Temporary Employment Subsidy, 4953; The Economies of Large Scale Production in British Industry: an Introductory Study, 4963

Prazmowska, Anita J.: Britain, Poland and the Eastern Front, 1939, 13894; 'War over Danzig? The Dilemma of Anglo-Polish Relations in the Months preceding the Outbreak of the Second World War, 13895; 'Poland's Foreign Policy: September 1938–September 1939', 13896; 'The Eastern Front and the British Guarantee to Poland of March 1939', 13897

Pred, Allan Richard: City Systems in Advanced Economies: Past Growth, Present Processes and Future Development Options, 17904

Preece, R. J. C.: 'Welsh and Scottish Nationalism', 2422

Prem, Dhani R.: The Parliamentary Lepers: A History of Colour Prejudice in Britain, 11156

Prenn, Oliver: ed. Guide to Modern Music on Records, 24575

Prentice, William R.: The Employment of Graduates, 5972

Prescott-Clarke, Patricia: 'Racial Discrimination and White Collar Workers in Britain', 11167; Public Consultation and Participation in Road Planning, 17131; Preservation Policy Group: Report to the Ministry of Housing and Local Government, 18969

Presley, John R.: ed. Pioneers of Modern Economics, 26575

Press Council: The Press and the People, 25329

Press, Jon: ed. Studies in the Business History of Bristol, 4393

Presseisen, Ernst L.: 'Foreign Policy and British Public Opinion: The Hoare-Laval Pact of 1935', 13789

Pressnell, Leslie Sedden: A Guide to the Historical Records of British Banking, 4396; '1925: The Burden of Sterling', 4674

Prest, Alan Richmond: ed. The U.K. Economy: A Manual of Applied Economics, 3445; 'The British Economy, 1945–1960', 3628; 'Some Aspects of Income Distribution in the U.K. since World War Two, 3810; Public Finance, 4589; Public Finance in Theory and Practice, 4590; 'The Sensitivity of the Yield of Personal Income Tax in the United Kingdom', 4839; The Taxation of Urban Land, 4840; The State of Taxation, 4841; Value Added Taxation: The Experience of the United Kingdom, 4842; Intergovernmental Financial Relations in the United Kingdom, 4873; Consumers' Expenditures in the United Kingdom, 1900–1919, 20437; Financing University Education, 23316

Prest, Robert: F4 Phantom: A Pilot's Story, 15904

Prestige, George Leonard: The Life of Charles Gore, A Great Englishman, 11732

Preston, Adrian: ed. War Aims and Strategic Policy in the Great War, 1914–1918, 13368

Preston, Anthony: ed. History of the Royal Navy in the 20th Century, 15245; 'V and W' Class Destroyers, 1917–1945, 15387; Sea Combat off the Falklands: The Lessons that Must Be Learned, 16090

Preston, Barbara: 'Statistics of Inequality', 3834

Preston, J. M.: A Short History: A History of Short Bros. Aircraft Activities in Kent, 1908–1964, 17615

Preston, John Harold: The Story of Hampstead, 19339

Preston, Ronald Haydn: Church and Society in the Late Twentieth Century: The Economic and Political Task, 11837

Preston, S. H.: 'An International Comparison of Excessive Adult Mortality', 7465

Prestridge, Colin: A History of Stubbington, 19205

Pribicevic, Branko: The Shop Stewards' Movement and Workers' Control, 1910–1922, 6697

Price, Alfred: Battle of Britain: The Hardest Day, 18 August 1940, 14813; Instruments of

Darkness: The History of Electronic Warfare, 15114, 15118; Aircraft versus Submarine: The Evolution of the Anti-submarine Aircraft, 1912 to 1972, 15816; Spitfire, a Documentary History, 15847; The Spifire Story, 15848; Air War South Atlantic, 16092

Price, Arnold Thomas: Architecture of the Twentieth Century, 23882

Price, Brian: Lead in Petrol: An Energy Analysis, 20166

Price, C. A.: 'The Use of Inter-marriage Statistics as an Index of Assimilation', 10937

Price, Cecil: Gwyn Jones, 25609

Price, D. L.: Ulster: Consensus and Coercion, 2920

Price, D. T. William: 'The Contribution of St. David's College, Lampeter to the Church in Wales, 1920–71', 12288; History of St. David's University College, Lampeter, 23507

Price, Denis: 'The Fall of Asquith: A Matter of Opinion', 973

Price, Emyr: Megan Lloyd George, 1456

Price, George Ward: Extra-Special Correspondent, 25271; The Story of the Salonika Army, 14534

Price, Glanville: The Languages of Britain, 23805

Price, Jean: Studies of Women Offenders, 10875

Price, Jonathan: The Best Thing on T.V.: Commercials, 4303

Price, Leolin: 'The Profession and Practice of Law in England and America', 9815

Price, Mary: Reluctant Revolutionaries: A Century of Head Mistresses, 1874–1974, 23093

Price, Morgan Philips: My Three Revolutions, 1508

Price, R. G. G.: A History of Punch, 25183

Price, Robert: Transport and Communications [in Horsforth, Yorkshire], 16356

Price, Robert J.: 'Union Growth Revisited: 1948–1974 in Perspective', 6767; Profiles of Union Growth: A Comparative Statistical Portrait of Eight Countries, 6802

Price, Seymour J.: Building Societies: Their Origin and History, 4360; From Queen to Queen: The Centenary Story of the Temperance Permanent Building Society, 1854–1954, 4394

Price, Thomas William: The Story of the Workers' Educational Association, 1903–1924, 23676

Price, Thomas: Independent African: John Chilembwe and the Origins, Setting and Significance of the Nyasaland Native Rising in 1915, 12778

Prichard, Marjorie M. L.: The Foetal Circulation and Cardiovascular System, and the Changes that they undergo, 22305

Priebe, Hermann: The Changing Role of Agriculture 1920–1970, 19568

Priessnitz, Horst P.: Das englische "radio play" seit 1945, 24754

Priest, R. G.: 'Environmental Factors in pressive Illness', 21775

Priestland, Gerald: Journalism as I See it, 25272

Priestley, Barbara: British Qualifications: A Comprehensive Guide to Educational, Technical, Professional and Academic Qualifications in Britain, 5877

Priestley, H. E.: The Evelina: The Story of a London Children's Hospital, 21449

Priestley, Philip: Justice for Juveniles: The 1969 Children and Young Persons Act: A Case for Reform?, 8308

Priestley, Sir Raymond Edward: *et al, eds.* Antarctic Research: A Review of British Scientific Research in Antarctica, 27224

Prince, Gordon Stewart: Teenagers Today, 8487

Prince, Hugh Counsell: *ed.* Greater London, 18360

Prince, Joyce: Shoplifting, 10226

Prince, Michael: God's Cop: The Biography of James Anderton, 10787

Princess Alice, Duchess of Gloucester: The Memoirs of Princess Alice, Duchess of Gloucester, 539

Princess Marie Louise: My Memories of Six Reigns, 541

Pring, Beryl: Education, Capitalist and Socialist, 22630

Pringle, David: J. G. Ballard: The First Twenty Years, 25367

Pringle, John: Have Pen Will Travel, 25273

Pringle, Mia Lilly Kellmer: Foster Home Care: Facts and Fallacies: A Review of Research in the United States, Western Europe, Israel and Great Britain between 1948 and 1966, 8157; Residential Home Care: A Review of Research in the United States, Western Europe, Israel and Great Britain between 1948 and 1966, 8158; *ed.* Investment in Children: A Symposium on Positive Child Care and Constructive Education, 8268; *ed.* Directory of Voluntary Organisations concerned with Children, 8309; *ed.* The Needs of Children: A Personal Perspective, 8310; *ed.* 'Better Adoption', 8311; *ed.* Caring for Children: A Symposium on Co-operation in Childcare, 8312; *ed.* The Emotional and Social Adjustment of Blind Children, 8313; *ed.* Investment in Children, 8314; *ed.* Putting Children First, 8315; Deprivation and Education, 22805

Pringle, Patrick: Fighting Marines, 15413

Pringle, Robert: Rajahs and Rebels: The Ibans of Sarawak under Brooke Rule, 1841–1941, 12945

Pringle, Robin: A Guide to Banking in Britain, 4407

Prins, Herschel Albert: Criminal Behaviour: An Introduction to its Study and Treatment, 10155; 'Probation and After-care', 10496

Prinzing, F.: Epidemics Resulting from Wars, 22381

Prior, Jim: A Balance of Power, 1301

Prior, Robin: Churchill's 'World Crisis' as History, 988

Pritchard, Colin: The Protest Makers: The British Nuclear Disarmament Movement of 1958–1965: Twenty Years On, 13529

Pritchard, D. D.: The Economic Conditions of the Nantlle Valley and Certain Contiguous Areas, 5361

Pritchard, David Gwyn: Education and the Handicapped, 1760–1960, 21888, 23117

Pritchard, E. P.: 'Conventions of Local Authorities in the West Midlands', 3323; 'The Responsibility of the Nationalized Industries to Parliament', 6144

Pritchard, Eric Law: The Infant, Nutrition and Management, 8316; The Physiological Feeding of Infants, 8317; The New-born Baby, 8318; The Infant: A Handbook of Modern Treatment, 8319

Pritchard, Frank Cyril: The Story of Westminster College, 1851–1951, 22750; Methodist Secondary Education: A History of the Contribution of Methodism to Secondary Education in the United Kingdom, 22896; The Story of Woodhouse Grove School, 22897

Pritchard, Jack: View from a Long Chair, 6479

Pritchard, R. John: 'The Far East as an Influence on the Chamberlain Government's Pre-War European Policies', 13610

Pritchard, Roger Martin: Housing and the Spatial Structure of the City: Residential Mobility and the Housing Market in An English City Since the Industrial Revolution, 18551

Pritchard, Sonia Zaide: Oil Pollution Control, 20086

Pritchett, Sir Victor Sawdon: A Cab at the Door, 25778

Pritt, Denis Nowell: The Autobiography of D. N. Pritt, 1509; Law, Class and Society: Book 1: Employers, Workers and Trade Unions, 6720

Probert, Belinda: Beyond Orange and Green: The Political Economy of the Northern Ireland Crisis, 2879

Probyn, Walter: Angelface: The Making of a Criminal, 10222

Proceedings of the British Academy 1903, 47

Proceedings of the Wesley Historical Society 1893+, 12065

Prochaska, Alice: History of the General Federation of Trade Unions, 1899–1980, 6894

Prochaska, Frank: The Voluntary Impulse: Philanthropy in Modern Britain, 9120

Proctor, Henry: The Street of Disillusion, 25274

Proctor, Jesse Harris: 'British West Indies Society and Government in Transition 1920–1960', 13009; 'The Development of the Idea of Federation of the British Caribbean Territories', 13095; 'Britain's Pro-Federation Policy in the Caribbean: An Inquiry into Motivation', 13096

Proctor-Gregg, Humphrey: Beecham Remembered, 24431

Pronay, Nicholas: Propaganda, Politics and Film, 1918–45, 15224, 24614; British Official Films in the Second World War: A Descriptive Catalogue, 24594; 'British Newsreels in the 1930s: 1: Audiences and Producers, 24613; 'British Newsreels in the 1930s: 2: Their Policies and Impact, 24613

Proskauer, C.: Pictorial History of Dentistry, 22405

Prosser, Hilary: Perspectives on Residential Care: An Annotated Bibliography: Research and other Literature in the United States and Great Britain 1966–1974, 8320; Born to Fail, 8398

Prothero, Rowland Edmund [Baron Ernle]: The Land and its People: Chapters in Rural Life and History, 19049; Whippingham to Westminster, 19050; English Farming Past and Present, 19402; 'The Food Campaign of 1916–1918', 20578

Proudfoot, B.: 'A Perspective on the Scottish Economy', 3474

Proudfoot, Mary: Britain and the United States in the Caribbean, 13002

Proudfoot, W. B.: 'Copying Methods Past and Present', 7155

Prowle, Malcolm: Health Service Finance: An Introduction, 21635

Pryce, Roy: 'Britain's Failure in Europe', 14150

Pryce, W. T. R.: 'Welsh and English in Wales 1750–1971: A Spatial Analysis Based on the Linguistic Affiliation of Parochial Communities', 23826

Pryce-Jones, Alan: The Bonus of Laughter, 25275

Pryce-Jones, Janet E.: Accounting in Scotland: A Historical Biography, 4172

Pryde, George Smith: A New History of Scotland, 314; Scotland from 1603 to the Present Day, 2434; 'The Development of Nationalism in Scotland', 2492

Pryke, Richard Wallis Speaight: Public Enterprise in Practice: The British Experience of Nationalization over Two Decades, 6084; The Rail Problem, 16784

Prynn, D. L.: 'Common Wealth—A British "Third Party" of the 1940s', 1902

Pryor, Ruth: *ed.* David Jones: Letters to Vernon Watkins, 25605

Prytherch, Raymond John: The Great Western Railway and other Services in the West Country and South Wales: A Bibliography of British Books Published 1950–1969, 16861

Psacharopoulos, G.: 'On Some Positive Aspects of the Economics of the Brain Drain', 23356

Public Affairs Information Service Bulletin: 1915–, 82

Public and Preparatory Schools Year Book: The Official Book of Reference for the Headmasters' Conference and of the Incorporated Association of Preparatory Schools, 23005

Pudney, John Sleigh: His Majesty King George VI: A Study, 503

Pugh, Sir Arthur: Men of Steel, by One of Them: A Chronicle of Eighty Years of Trade Unionism, 6847

Pugh, D. S.: 'The Age Distribution of an Industrial Group [Scottish Railwaymen]', 9657

Pugh, Elizabeth: Social Work in Child Care, 8321

Pugh, Hilary Angela: Housing Co-operatives and Co-ownership Schemes, 18750

Pugh, Leslie Mervyn: Matrimonial Proceedings Before Magistrates, 10007

Pugh, Martin David: Lloyd George, 1018; The

Making of Modern British Politics 1867–1939, 1583; The Tories and the People 1880–1935, 1618

Pugh, Michael: 'Pacifism and Politics in Britain, 1931–1935', 13508

Pugh, Patricia: Educate, Agitate, Organise: 100 Years of Fabian Socialism, 2109

Pugh, Ralph Bernard: The Crown Estate, 792

Pugh, Stevenson: Fighting Vehicles and Weapons of the Modern British Army, 15514

Puleston, William Dilworth: High Command in the World War, 15471

Pulling, Charles Robert Druce: Mr Punch and the Police, 10694

Pulzer, Peter George Julius: 'British General Election of 1979: Back to the Fifties or on to the Eighties?, 2342; Political Representation and Elections in Britain, 2359

Punnett, Robert Malcolm: Front Bench Opposition: the Role of the Leader of the Opposition, the Shadow Cabinet and Shadow Government in British Politics, 752; ''The Structure of the Macmillan Government 1957–1963', 953; The Prime Minister and the Dissolution of Parliament', 958

Punshon, John: Portrait in Grey: A Short History of the Quakers, 12139

Punter, John: 'A History of Aesthetic Control: Pt 1—1909–1953: The Control of the External Appearance of Development in England and Wales', 18821; 'A History of Aesthetic Control: Pt 2—1953–1985: The Control of the External Appearance of Development in England and Wales', 18822

Purcell, H.: 'Recent Trends in Coronary Mortality and their Implications for the U.K.: Are we Winning or Losing?', 22242

Purcell, Victor William Williams Saunders: The Memoirs of a Malayan Official, 12503; Malaysia, 12909; The Chinese in Malaya, 12916; Malaya:Communist or Free?, 16150

Purcell, William Ernest: British Police in a Changing Society, 10703; Fisher of Lambeth: A Portrait from Life, 11694; Portrait of Soper: A Biography of the Reverend the Lord Soper of Kingsway, 12090

Purdom, Charles Benjamin: The Garden City after the War: A Discussion of the Position of the Garden City at Letchworth, and a Proposal for a National Housing Policy, 18196; The Letchworth Achievement, 18197; Harley Granville Barker: Man of the Theatre, Dramatist and Scholar, 26126

Purdue, Michael: Sizewell B: An Anatomy of the Inquiry, 6673

Purdue, William: The Monarchy and the British People 1760 to the Present, 439

Purdy, Anthony: Burgess and Maclean, 16035

Purdy, D.: Inflation and Labour Markets, 4006

Pusey, W. A.: The History of Dermatology, 21070

Puxon, Catherine Margaret: The Family and the Law: The Laws of Marriage, Separation and Divorce, 10013

Puxon, Grattan: On the Road: . . . to Minnie Rose Smith, a Gypsy who Died of Bronchial Pneumonia, Aged Three Months, 11349

Pyatt, Edward Charles: Mountaineering in Britain: A History from the Earliest Times to the Present Day, 27236

Pyatt, Frank Graham: Priority Patterns and the Demand for Household Durable Goods, 20458; ed. Consumer Behaviour: Selected Readings, 20467

Pye Limited: The Story of Pye, 6636

Pye, Lucian W.: Guerrilla Communism in Malaya, 16152

Pye, Michael: The King over the Water: The Windsors in the Bahamas 1940–1945, 476

Pye, N.: ed. Leicester and Its Region, 18029

Pye-Smith, Charlie: Working the Land, 19157; Crisis and Conservation: Conflict in the British Countryside, 20208

Pyke, Magnus: Long Life: Expectations for Old Age, 8632

Pyke-Lees, Celia: Elderly Ethnic Minorities, 8634

Pyle, Fergus: ed. 1916: The Easter Rising, 2739

Pym, Denis: ed. Industrial Society: Social Sciences in Management, 5442

Pym, Francis: The Politics of Consent, 1302

Pym, Hilary: ed. A Very Private Eye: The Diaries, Letters and Notebooks of Barbara Pym, 25781

Pyman, Sir Harold E.: Call to Arms, 14778

Pyne, Peter: 'The Politics of Parliamentary Absenteeism: Ireland's Four Sinn Fein Parties, 1905–1926', 2692; 'The Third Sinn Fein Party, 1923–1926', 2693; 'The New Irish State and the Decline of the Republican Sinn Fein Party', 2694

Pyper, Charles Bothwell: Chamberlain and his Critics: A Statesman Vindicated, 983

Pyper, Robert: 'Sarah Tisdall, Ian Willmore and the Civil Servant's "Right to Leak"', 769

Quah, J. S. T. and Quah, Stella R.: Singapore, 12957

Quant, Mary: Quant by Quant, 24171

Quantin, Patrick: Local Politics and Participation in France and Britain, 3129

Quartararo, Rosaria: 'Imperial Defence in the Mediterranean on the Eve of the Ethiopian Crisis', 13793

Queen: A Profile of the Queen, 25184

Quesne: Charles Thomas Le: Sir Alfred Pearce Gould, 12031

Quick, Anthony: Twentieth Century Britain, 335

Quigley, Austin E.: The Pinter Problem, 25975

Quigley, Hugh: The Highlands of Scotland, 5295; A Plan for the Highlands: Proposals for a Highland Development Board, 5296; Housing and Slum Clearance in London, 18390

Quigley, Isabel: Pamela Hansford Johnson, 25603

Quill, Jeffrey: Spitfire: A Test Pilot's Story. 1983

Quilter, David C.: No Dishonourable Name: The 2nd and 3rd Battalions, Coldstream Guards, 1939–1946, 15612

Quilter, Percy Cuthbert [Baron]: ed. Discourses and Letters of Hubert Murray Burge, D.D., K.C.V.O., Bishop of Southwark, 1911–1919, Bishop of Oxford, 1919–1925, 11725

Quin-Harkin, A. J.: 'Imperial Airways, 1924–1940', 17629

Quinby, Jane: Beatrix Potter: A Bibliographical Checklist, 25762

Quinion, Michael Brian: A Drink for its Time: Farm Cider Making in the Western Counties, 20748

Quinlan, Paul D.: Clash over Romania: British and American Policies toward Romania 1938–1947, 14056

Quinn, James: 'Christian Unity in Scotland', 12341

Quinn, Michael: Fountains of Praise: University College, Cardiff, 1883–1983, 23486

Quinn, Sheila: ed. Nursing in the European Community, 21730

Quinton, Anthony, Baron : The Politics of Imperfection: The Religious and Secular Traditions of Conservative Thought in England from Hooker to Oakeshott, 2198; Britain and the United States: Four Views to Mark the Silver Jubilee, 14011; Quirk, R. N.: 'The Problem of Scientific Manuscripts in Britain', 7151

Qureshi, M. Aslam: Anglo-Pakistan Relations, 1947–1976, 13194

R.C.H.M.: Guides to Sources for British History 6: Papers of British Churchmen 1780–1940, 11531

Raab, Gillian: 'The Religious Alignment of English Elections between 1918 and 1970, 2230

Rabey, David Ian: British and Irish Political Drama in the Twentieth Century: Implicating the Audience, 26236

Rabinowicz, Oskar K.: Winston Churchill on Jewish Problems: A Half Century Survey, 988

Race Relations in Britain: Round Table 193: 29–36, 10911

Race, David: Services for the Mentally Handicapped in Britain, 21787, 21925

Rack, Henry D.: The Future of John Wesley's Methodism, 12081

Rackham, Oliver: Trees and Woodland in the British Landscape, 19753; 'Documentary Evidence for the Historical Ecologist', 20196; Ancient Woodland: Its History, Vegetation and Uses in England, 26973

Radcliffe, Cyril John [Baron]: The Dissolving Society: Oration Delivered at the London School of Economics and Political Science, 7581; Censors, 26893; Freedom of Information: A Human Right, 26894

Radcliffe, James: The Reorganisation of British Central Government, 788

Radcliffe, P.: The Piccadilly Story: Profile of a Radio Station, 24806

Radcliffe, Walter: Milestones in Midwifery, 21271

Radford, Elizabeth: The New Villagers: Urban Pressure on Rural Areas in Worcestershire, 19172

Radford, H. Gordon: 'The Certificate of Secondary Education', 22918

Radford, Jan: Derbyshire County, 25171

Radford, John Brian: Midland through the Peak: A Pictorial History of the Midland Railway Mainline Routes between Derby and Manchester, 16899

Radical Statistics Race Group: Britain: Black Population, 10888

Radice, Edward Albert: Savings in Great Britain, 1922–1935, 4336

Radice, Jonathan: Transport, 16253

Radice, Lisanne : Beatrice and Sidney Webb: Fabian Socialists, 2148

Radley: The History of Radley College, 1847–1947, 23071

Radwanski, George: Trudeau, 12667

Radzinowicz, Sir Leon: The Growth of Crime: The International Experience, 10131; Ideology and Crime: A Study of Crime in its Social and Historical Context, 10132; In Search of Criminology, 10133; 'Changing Attitudes towards Crime and Punishment', 10229; A History of English Criminal Law and its Administration, from 1750, 10290; Criminology and the Administration of Criminal Justice: A Bibliography, 10292

Rae, John: Conscience and Politics: The British Government and the Conscientious Objector to Military Service 1916–1919, 13458; The Public School Revolution: Britain's Independent Schools, 1964–1979, 23042

Rae, John B.: Harry Ferguson and Henry Ford, 5498

Rae, Joseph A.: ed. The History of Allan Glen's School, 1853–1953, 23222

Rae, Leslie: The Skills of Human Relations Training: A Guide for Managers and Practitioners, 5485

Raffe, David J.: Reconstructions of Secondary Education: Theory, Myth and Practice since the War, 22930; Fourteen to Eighteen: The Changing Pattern of Schooling in Scotland, 23620

Raffo, Peter: 'The League of Nations Philosophy of Lord Robert Cecil', 13497

Rahman, Tunku Abdul: Malaysia, The Road to Independence, 12912

Railway Conversions League: Memorandum on the Future of British Railways Being an Outline of Arguments for the Conversion into a System of Reserved Motorways, 16769

Rainey, John Wakefield: ed. Veterinary Services, 21167

Rainnie, George Fraser: ed. The Woollen and Worsted Industry: An Economic Analysis, 6418

Raison, Timothy: Why Conservative?, 2192; The Founding Fathers of Social Science, 7995

Raistrick, Arthur: A History of Lead Mining in the Pennines, 6359

Rait, Sir Robert Sangster: The History of the Union Bank of Scotland, 4518

Raleigh, Walter Alexander: The War in the Air, 15791

Rallings, Colin S.: 'Two Types of Middle-Class Labour Voter?', 9726

Ramanadham, Venkata Vemuri: Public Enterprise in Britain: Thoughts on Recent Experiences, 6067

Ramanathan, Suguna: The Novels of C. P. Snow: A Critical Introduction, 25813

Rambert, Dame Marie: Quicksilver: The Autobiography of Marie Rambert, 24238

Ramdin, Roger: The Making of the Black Working Class in Britain, 11085

Ramon, Shulamit: Psychiatry in Britain: Meaning and Policy, 21821

Ramphal, Shridath: 'The West Indies—Constitutional Background to Federation', 13100

Ramsay, Sir Alexander: Terms of Industrial Peace, 5581; The Truth about Industry, 5582

Ramsay, D. G.: ed. (Third Statistical Account of Scotland). The Stewartry of Kirkcudbright, 10114, 19227

Ramsay, Sir James Douglas: National Parks: A Scottish Survey, 20192

Ramsden, Gertrude A.: Marriage and Nursing: A Survey, 21716

Ramsden, John A.: A History of the Conservative Party: The Age of Balfour and Baldwin, 1620; '"A Party for Owners or a Party for Earners?" How far did the British Conservative Party Really Change after 1945?', 1635; The Making of Conservative Party Policy: The Conservative Research Department since 1929, 1646; Real Old Tory Politics: The Political Diaries of Sir Robert Sanders, First Lord Bayford, 1910–1935, 1354; ed. By-Elections in British Politics, 2356; Trends in British Politics since 1945, 3501

Ramsey, Arthur Michael: From Gore to Temple: The Development of Anglican Theology between 1889 and 1939, 11869

Rance, Adrian B.: ed. Seaplanes and Flying Boats of the Solent, 17548

Randall, Sir Alec Walter George: Vatican Assignment, 13302, 14111; 'British Diplomatic Representation at the Holy See', 14112

Randall, Alan: George Formby: A Biography, 26313

Randall, P. J.: 'Wales in the Structure of Central Government', 2571

Randall, Vicky: Women in Politics, 7853

Randell, Brian: The Origins of Digital Computers: A Bibliography, 7093

Randle, Michael: The Blake Escape, 16028

Randles, Ralph H. S.: History of the Friends' School, Lancaster, 22906

Ranft, B. McL.: The Beatty Papers: Selections from the Private and Official Correspondence of Admiral of the Fleet Earl Beatty, 15246; ed. Technical Change and British Naval Policy, 1860–1939, 15345; Ironclad to Trident: 100 Years of Defence Commentary: Brassey's 1886–1986: Centenary Volume of Brassey's Naval Annual, 16455

Ranger, Terence: ed. The Invention of Tradition. 451

Ranken, Michael Bruce Fernie, British Shipping in the 1990s, 16464; ed. 'The Ports of Great Britain', 16651

Rankin, Eric: Cockburnspath: A Documentary Social History of a Border Parish, 19365

Rankin, N. H.: 'Social Adjustment in a North-West New Town', 18234

Ranney, Austin: ed. Britain at the Polls 1983, 2344; ed. 'Review Article: Thirty Years of Psephology', 2345

Ransom, B.: Connolly's Marxism, 3037

Ransom, W. P.: The Story of Bournemouth Corporation Transport, Part 1—The Trams, 17217; Part 2—Trolleybus Era, 17242

Ransome-Wallace, P.: The Last Steam Locomotives of British Railways, 17031

Ransomes, Sims & Jefferies: Wherever the Sun Shines: 175 Years of Progress by Ransomes, 6372

Ranson, S.: Clergy, Ministers and Priests, 11588

Ranson, Stewart: ed. Between Centre and Locality: The Politics of Public Policy, 3217

Raper, H. R.: Man against Pain: The Epic of Anaesthesia, 21030

Raphael, Frederic Michael: Somerset Maugham and his World, 25711

Rapoport, Rhona: Recent Social Trends in Family and Work in Britain, 9937

Rapoport, Rhona and Rapoport, Robert Norman: Sex, Career and Family: Including an International Review of Women's Roles, 7715; Dual Career Families, 7719; 'Early and Later Experiences as Determinants of Adult Behaviour: Married Women's Family and Career Patterns', 7824; Fathers, Mothers and Others: Towards New Alliances, 9934; The Therapeutic Community Revisited, 21762; ed. Working Couples, 9935; Community as Doctor: New Perspective on a Therapeutic Community, 21761; Leisure and the Family Life Cycle, 26932

Rapoport, Robert Norman: Families in Britain, 9936

Rappoport, Armin: The British Press and Wilsonian Neutrality, 25111

Rasmussen, Jorgen Scott: 'Party Discipline in Wartime: The Downfall of the Chamberlain Government', 984; 'Government and Intra-party Opposition: Dissent Within the Conservative Parliamentary Party in the 1930s', 1633; The Liberal Party: A Study of Retrenchment and Revival, 1823; 'The Electoral Costs of Being a Woman in the 1979 British General Election', 2262; 'How Remarkable was 1983?', 2351; 'Women's Role in British Politics: Impediments to Parliamentary Candidature', 7834

Rasmussen, Steen Eiler: London: The Unique City, 18342

Ratcliff, John Drury: Yellow Magic: The Story of Penicillin, 22291

Ratcliffe, Barrie M.: Trade and Transport: Essays in Economic History in Honour of T. S. Willan, 3413, 16213, 16618

Ratcliffe, Derek: ed. A Nature Conservation Review: The Selection of Biological Sites of National Importance to Nature Conservation in Britain, 20220

Ratcliffe, Jennifer M.: Lead in Man and the Environment, 20165

Ratcliffe, John: An Introduction to Town and Country Planning, 18795, 20358

Ratcliffe, Michael: The History of the Bodley Head 1887–1987, 24946

Rathbone, Eleanor Florence: The Case for Family Allowances, 4088; The Disinherited Family: A Plea for the Endowment of the Family, 4089; The Ethics and Economics of Family Endowment, 4090; Our Freedom and its Results, 7670; Falsehoods and Facts about the Jews, 11274

Rathbone, Jessie: The Curious Years: History, Recent and Remote, 7562

Rathbone, Richard: ed. Africa and the Second World War, 12699; 'The Government of the Gold Coast after the Second World War', 12745

Ratter, J. A.: 'Three Hundred Years of Botany in Edinburgh', 26538

Rattray, Robert Fleming: 'The Decline and Fall of the Labour Party', 1741; 'Basic Realities of the Economic Crisis', 3607

Raven, Alan: British Battleships of World War 2: The Development and Technical History of the Royal Navy's Battleships and Battlecruisers from 1911 to 1946, 15359

Raven, C. E.: Musings and Memories, 11806

Raven, J.: The Living Pattern of Some Old People, 8578

Raverat, Gwen: Period Piece: A Cambridge Childhood, 8322

Raw, Charles: Slater Walker: An Investigation of a Financial Phenomenon, 4474, 4748

Rawcliffe, D. H.: The Struggle for Kenya, 12828

Rawe, Donald R.: Cornish Villages, 19134

Rawlings, John Dunstan Richard: Pictorial History of the Fleet Air Arm, 15420; The History of the Royal Air Force, 15786

Rawlins, Clive L.: William Barclay: The Authorised Biography, 12225

Rawlins, Randolph: 'What Really Happened in British Guiana', 13039

Rawlinson, Peter, Baron: A Price Too High, 1511

Rawnsley, Hardwicke Drummond: 'Liquor Control and the Carlisle Experiment', 22166

Rawson, Geoffrey: Beatty, 15247

Rawson, Marilyn: Rural Housing and Structure Plans: A Review of Plans submitted by July 1976, 18757

Rawson, Wyatt Trevelyan: The Story of the New Education, 22865

Rawstron, Eric Mitchell: Regional Variations in Britain: Studies in Economic and Social Geography, 5080; ed. R. O Buchanan and Economic Geography, 26661

Ray, Cyril: Regiment of the Line: The Story of the 20th Lancashire Fusiliers, 15681

Ray, John: A History of Britain, 1900–1939, 342; The Growth of School: 1750 to the Present Day, 22832, 22869

Ray, John: Lloyd George and Churchill, 1018

Ray, Paul Charles: The Surrealist Movement in England, 23982

Ray, Sheila G.: The Blyton Phenomenon: The Controversy Surrounding the World's Most Successful Children's Writer, 25401

Ray, Ted: Raising the Laughs, 26338

Raybould, Elizabeth: A History of the General Nursing Council for England and Wales, 1919–1969, 21707

Raybould, Sidney Griffiths: The Workers Educational Association: The Next Phase, 23674; ed. Trends in English Adult Education, 23680; The English Universities and Adult Education, 23693; University Extramural Education in England, 1945–1962: a Study in Finance and Policy, 23694

Rayden, William: Practice and Law of Divorce, 9996

Raymond, John: ed. The Baldwin Age, 299

Raymond, R. J.: 'American Public Opinion and Irish Neutrality, 1939–1945', 2706

Raymont, Thomas: A History of the Education of Young Children, 23137

Rayner, Josephine: 'A la Recherche de la Sensibilité Perdue: Notes on the State of University Music at the Present Time', 22455

Rayner, Robert Macey: Recent Times: A History of Britain and its Continental Background, 1868–1939, 343

Rayner, W. S.: How Botha and Smuts Conquered German South West Africa, 14528

Raynes, Harold Ernest: A History of British Insurance, 4219; Social Security in Britain: A History, 9061

Raynes, Norma V.: Patterns of Residential Care: Sociological Studies in Institutions for Handicapped Children, 2842, 21911

Raynor, Henry: Music in England, 24290

Raynor, John: The Middle Class, 9725; ed. Readings in Urban Education, 18291; ed. Linking Home with School, 23139

Raynor, Lois: 'Agency Adoptions of Non-white Children in the United Kingdom: A Quantitative Study', 10963

Razzel, Arthur George: Juniors: A Postscript to Plowden, 23140

Rea, Desmond: The Northern Ireland Economy: With Special Reference to Industrial Development, 5392

Rea, F. B.: Alcoholism: Its Psychology and Cure, 22125

Read, Colin: Changes in the Settlement Pattern and Land Use in the Solihull District of Warwickshire since 1945, 20275

Read, Donald: The English Provinces, c.1760–1960: A Study in Influence, 307

Read, Gordon: A Voice in the City: Liverpool City Mission, 12129

Read, Sir Herbert Edward: To Hell with Culture and other Essays on Art and Society, 7598; Contemporary British Art, 23974; A Concise History of Modern Painting, 23975; Henry Moore, 24192

Read, John: Explosives, 7059

Read, Mike: ed. The Story of the Shadows: An Autobiography, 24526

Read, Oliver: The Recording and Reproduction of Sound, 24573

Read, Piers Paul: The Train Robbers, 10233

Reader, David: Exploring the Urban Past: Essays in Urban History by H. J. Dyos, 26766

Reader, K. M.: The Civil Service Commission: 1855–1975, 876

Reader, Keith Stanley: The Modern British Economy in Historical Perspective, 3484

Reader, William Joseph: A House in the City: A Study of the City and the Stock Exchange based on the Records of Foster and Braithwaite 1825–1975, 4256; Grand Metropolitan: A History, 1962–1987, 6164; Fifty Years of Unilever, 1930–1980, 6218; Imperial Chemical Industries: A History. Vol. 1, The Forerunners 1870–1926, Vol. 2, The First Quarter-century 1926–1952, 6206; The Weir Group: A Centenary History, 6374; Metal Box: A History, 6614; Bowater: A History, 6621; The Middle Classes, 9736; Architect of Air Power: The Life of the First Viscount Weir of Eastwood, 1877–1959, 17577; 'At Duty's Call': A Study in Obsolete Patriotism, 14446; Birdseye: The Early Years, 20642

'Reader's Digest' Complete Atlas of the British Isles, 124

Readman, Alison: The British General Election of 1945, 2288

Reakes, George Leonard: Man of the Mersey, 25276

Reardon, A. M.: Pensions Guide, 4052

Reay, David Anthony: The History of Man-Powered Flight, 17510

Recently Published Articles: 1976–, 85

Recker, M. L.: England und der Donauraum 1919–1929, 13662

Reckitt, Maurice Benington: As it Happened: An Autobiography, 11807; Faith and Society: A Study of the Structure, Outlook and Opportunity of the Christian Social Movement in Great Britain and the U.S.A, 11825; ed. Prospect for Christianity: Essays in Catholic Social Reconstruction, 11826; Maurice to Temple: A Century of the Social Movement in the Church of England (1846–1946), 11827; P. E. T. Widdrington, A Study in Vocation and Versatility, 11828; ed. For Christ and the People: Studies of Four Socialist Priests and Prophets of the Church of England between 1870 and 1930, 11829

Record, R. G.: ' An Interpretation of the Decline of Mortality in England and Wales during the Twentieth Century', 7431

Record, S. P.: Proud Century: The First Hundred Years of Taunton School, 23078

Reddaway, John: Burdened with Cyprus: The British Connection, 12862

Reddaway, William Brian: 'Progress in British Manufacturing Industries in the Period, 1948–1954', 3622; Effects of Selective Income Tax: Final Report, 4852

Reddin, Terence: South Wales, 5374

Redford, Arthur: Labour Migration in England, 7265; Manchester Merchants and Foreign Trade, vol. 2 1850–1939, 4797

Redgrave, Sir Michael: In My Mind's Eye: An Autobiography, 26087

Redlich, Josef: The History of Local Government in England, 3112

Redman, G. P.: Strikes in Post-War Britain: A Study of Stoppages of Work Due to Industrial Disputes, 1948–1973, 6916

Redmayne, P. B.: Gold Coast to Ghana, 12741

Redmayne, Paul: Britain's Food, 20603

Redmayne, Sir Richard Augustine Studdert: British Coal—Mining Industry during the War, 6253

Redmayne, Ronald: *ed.* Ideals in Industry: Being the Story of Montague Burton Ltd., 1900–1950, 6238

Redmond, John: 'Was Sterling Overvalued in 1925?: A Comment', 4677; 'An Indicator of the Effective Exchange Rate of the Pound in the 1930s', 4692

Redwood, Christopher: *ed.* A Delius Companion, 24329; *ed.* An Elgar Companion, 24342

Redwood, Heinz: The Pharmaceutical Industry: Trends, Problems and Achievements, 22268

Redwood, [William Arthur] Hugh: Bristol Fashion, 25277

Ree, Yong-yil: 'Special Relationship at War: The Anglo-American Relationship during the Korean War', 16146

Reece, R. H. W.: The Name of Brooke: The End of White Rajah Rule in Sarawak, 12946

Reed, Arthur: Britain's Aircraft Industry: What Went Right? What Went Wrong?, 17587

Reed, Brian: 150 Years of British Steam Locomotives, 17042

Reed, Bruce: Denis Healey and the Politics of Power, 1227

Reed, Laurence: Our Export of Intelligence: A Question of National Debilitation, 7310

Reed, Malcolm Christopher: A History of James Capel and Co, 4251

Reed, Peter William: The Economics of Public Enterprise, 6087

Reed, Philip: A Britten Source Book, 24306

Reed, Richard: National Westminster Bank: A Short History, 4503

Reed, William Henry: Elgar as I Knew Him, 24334

Reekie, W. Duncan: *ed.* The Consumer Society, 20456; Profits, Politics and Drugs, 22270

Rees, A. M.: Town Councillors: A Study of Barking, 3309

Rees, Alwyn David: *ed.* Welsh Rural Communities, 19289; Life in a Welsh Countryside: A Social Study of Llanfihangel yng Ngwynfa, 19303

Rees, B.: The Personal Family and Social Circumstances of Old People: Report of an Investigation Carried Out in England in 1959 to Pilot a Future Cross-national Survey of Old Age, 8561

Rees, Bronwen: No Fixed Abode, 18685

Rees, Clifford Burwin: One Hundred Years of the Hallé, 24546

Rees, David Ben: Chapels in the Valley: A Study in the Sociology of Welsh Nonconformity, 12292; Preparation for Crisis: Adult Education, 1945–80, 23686

Rees, David Bernard: Korea: The Limited War, 16139

Rees, Derek: Rings and Rosettes: The History of the Pembrokeshire Agricultural Society, 1784–1977, 19644

Rees, E. T.: Hinges of Administration: A Survey of the Characteristics of Hospital Administrative and Clerical Staff, 21392

Rees, Edwin Henry Verdun: The Parish of Betws Penpont, Brecon, 19376

Rees, Gareth: Poverty and Social Inequality in Wales, 2588; Migration, Industrial Structuring and Class Relations: The Case of South Wales, 5377; 'No Surrender in the Valleys: The 1984–1985 Miners' Strike in South Wales', 6335

Rees, Goronwy: The Great Slump: Capitalism in Crisis 1929–1933, 3600

Rees, Graham Lloyd: Britain and the Post-War European Payments System, 4594; A Survey of the Welsh Economy, 5324; A Study of the Passenger Transport Needs of Urban Wales, 16339

Rees, Henry: British Ports and Shipping, 16648

Rees, Ioan Bowen: Government by Community, 3379

Rees, Sir James Frederick: A Survey of Economic Development, with Special Reference to Great Britain, 3398; Studies in Welsh History: Collected Papers, Lectures and Reviews, 5305; The Problem of Wales and other Essays, 5306, 18162; 'Cities of Men', 18162

Rees, John Collwyn: Equality, 9573

Rees, John Tudor: *ed.* They Stand Apart: A Critical Survey of the Problems of Homosexuality, 21942

Rees, Merlyn: 'The Social Setting', 9472

Rees, P. H.: Gower Shipwrecks, 16511

Rees, Philip: Fascism in Britain, 2010

Rees, R. D.: 'Inter-Industry Wage Levels in United Kingdom Manufacturing', 3916

Rees, Sir Richard Lodowick Edward Montagu: George Orwell: Fugitive from the Camp of Victory, 25746

Rees, Stuart: Verdicts on Social Work, 8906

Rees, Teresa L.: Migration, Industrial Structuring and Class Relations: The Case of South Wales, 5377

Rees, Thomas: 'The Moral Responsibility for the Liquor Trade', 22177

Rees, William: An Historical Atlas of Wales from Early to Modern Times, 5309; Cardiff: A History of the City, 18160

Rees-Mogg, Sir William; Sir Anthony Eden, 1007

Reese, Trevor Richard: The History of the Royal Commonwealth Society, 1868–1968, 12511; Australia in the Twentieth Century: A Short Political Guide, 12601

Reese-Edwards, Kenneth Harry: The Secondary Technical School, 23274

Reeve, Carl: James Connolly and the United States: The Road to the 1916 Irish Rebellion, 3033

Reeves, Edward Ayearst: The Recollections of a Geographer, 26666

Reeves, Jon: Adolescent Behaviour in Urban Areas: A Bibliographic Review and Discussion of the Literature, 8409; The Emergence of Youth Societies: A Cross Cultural Approach, 8432

Reeves, Marjorie Ethel: *ed.* Eighteen Plus: Unity and Diversity in Higher Education, 23309; St. Anne's College: an Informal History, 23571

Reffold, Henry: Pie for Breakfast: Reminiscences of a Farmhand, 19590

Refugees and Asylum with Special Reference to the Vietnamese, 11392

Regan, Paul: 'The 1986 Shops Bill', 20491

Regan, Philip: Relative Income Shares, 3855

Regan, Simon: Rupert Murdoch: A Business Biography, 25103

Register of Approved Private Hospitals and Nursing Homes, 21416

Rehin, George Faenderich: 'Towards Community Care: The Problems and Policies in the Mental Health Service, 21328, 21793; Patterns of Performance in Community Care: A Report of a Community Mental Health Services Study, 21794, 22075

Reid, A.: 'Glasgow Socialism', 2519

Reid, B. L.: The Lives of Roger Casement, 3022

Reid, Brian Holden: 'T. E. Lawrence and Liddell Hart', 13817; J. F. C. Fuller: Military Thinker, 14735

Reid, Charles: John Barbirolli, 24427; Thomas Beecham: An Independent Biography, 24429; Malcolm Sargent: A Biography, 24439; Fifty Years of Robert Mayer Concerts, 1923–1972, 24552

Reid, Colin: Action Stations: A History of Broadcasting House, 24729, 24782

Reid, David James: The British Revolution, 1750–1970: A Social and Economic History, 3491

Reid, Fred: Keir Hardie: The Making of a Socialist, 1428

Reid, Gordon Stanley: The Politics of Financial Control: the Role of the House of Commons, 667

Reid, Graham Livingstone: *ed.* Fringe Benefits, Labour Costs and Social Security, 3893; Nationalized Industries, 4962; Scottish Economic Planning and the Attraction of Industry, 5260; The Nationalised Fuel Industries, 6405

Reid, Ivan: *ed.* Sex Differences in Britain, 7686; Sociological Perspectives on School and Education, 8059; Social Class and Differences in Britain: A Sourcebook, 9576

Reid, James MacArthur: Scotland's Progress: The Survival of a Nation, 2447; The History of the Clydesdale Bank 1838–1938, 4516; Kirk and Nation; The Story of the Reformed Church of Scotland, 12211; James Lithgow: Master of Work 1883–1952, 16642

Reid, James[Jimmy]: Reflections of a Clyde-built Man, 9664, 16624

Reid, Janet: 'Employment of Negroes in Manchester', 11461

Reid, John: The Conservation of Georgian Edinburgh: The Proceedings and Outcome of a Conference, 18975

Reid, John James Andrew: Public Attitudes and Mental Health Education, 21788

Reid, Margaret: All Change in the City: The Revolution in Britain's Financial Sector, 4293; The Secondary Banking Crisis, 1973–75: Its Causes and Course, 4431

Reid, P. R.: The Colditz Story, 15044; The Latter Days, 15045

Reilly, Peter A.: Employee Financial Participation, 6032; Participation, Democracy and Control: Forms of Employee Involvement, 6033

Reilly, Sir Bernard: Aden and the Yemen, 13868

Reilly, Sir Charles Herbert: Representative British Architects of the Present Day, 23868

Reilly, Robin: The Sixth Floor, 15179

Reiner, Robert: The Politics of the Police, 10766

Reiser, Stanley Joel: Medicine and the Reign of Technology, 21233

Reisman, David: State and Welfare: Tawney, Galbraith and Adam Smith, 8847; Richard Titmuss: Welfare and Society, 8848

Reisman, Frank: 'The Working Class Subculture', 9676

Reiss, Albert John: Social Characteristics of Urban and Rural Communities, 9333; ed. Cities and Society, 18290

Reiss, Erna: Rights and Duties of Englishwomen: A Study in Law and Public Opinion, 7667; Our Freedom and its Results, 7670

Reiss, Richard Leopold: Reconstruction, With Particular Reference to Housing, 18580; The Home I Want, 18581; The New Housing Handbook, 18582; The Town-Planning Handbook—Including Full Text of the Town-Planning—Consolidating Act, 1925, 20331

Reissman, C. K.: 'The Use of Health Services by the Poor', 21327

Reith, Charles: A New Study of Police History, 10690

Reith, George Murray: Reminiscences of the United Free Church General Assembly, 1900–1929, 12253

Reith, John Charles Walsham, Baron: Broadcast over Britain, 24731

Reitlinger, Gerald Roberts: The Economics of Taste, 23943

Remer, Robert: The Blue-coated Worker: A Sociological Study of Police Unionism, 6828

Remillard, W. J.: 'The History of Thunder Research', 7156

Rempel, Richard A.: 'The Dilemmas of British Pacifists during World War II', 13519

Rendel, Sir George William: The Sword and the Olive: Recollections of Diplomacy and the Foreign Service, 1913–1954, 13303

Rendell, Simon: A History of the Nonesuch Press, 24981

Rendle, A. B.: A Bibliographical Index of Deceased British and Irish Botanists, 26546

Rennie, Belle: The Triumph of the Dalton Plan, 8240

Rennie, James Alan: The Scottish People, their Clans, Families and Origins, 10119

Rennie, Jane: 'The Recreational Needs of Adolescence', 8323

Rennie, R. C.: The County of Stirling, The County of Clackmannan, 19229

Renouf, Alan: Let Justice be Done: The Foreign Policy of Dr. H. V. Evatt, 12620

Renshaw, Patrick: 'Anti-Labour Politics in Britain, 1918–1927', 1707; 'Trade Unions in America and Britain', 6769; 'Black Friday, 1921', 6863; Nine Days in May, 6948; The General Strike, 6949

Rentoul, John: The Rich Get Richer: The Growth of Inequality in Britain in the 1980's, 9615

Renvoize, Jean: Children in Danger: The Causes and Prevention of Baby Battering, 9960

Report of a Committee Appointed by the Cambridge University Appointments Board: University Education and Business, 23357

Report of the Committee on the Civil Service 1966–1968 Cmnd 3638; Parliamentary Papers xviii, 1967–68: ['The Fulton Report'.], 853

Report of a Committee of Privy Councillors on Ministerial Memoirs, 759

Report of a Committee to Consider, in the Context of Civil Liberties and Human Rights, Measures to deal with Terrorism in Northern Ireland, 2873

Report of the Commission of Enquiry, North Borneo and Sarawak 1962, 12947

Report of the Commission to Consider Legal Procedures to deal with Terrorist Activities in Northern Ireland, 2872

Report of the Committee Appointed by the Prime Minister under the Chairmanship of Lord Robbins, 1961–63: Cmnd 2154, 23399

Report of the Committee of Enquiry into Human Fertilization and Embryology, 22249

Report of the Committee of Enquiry into the Cost of the National Health Service, 21562

Report of the Committee on the Political Activities of Civil Servants Cmnd 7718, Parliamentary Papers xii (1948–9), 890

Report of the Department Committee on Scottish Licensing Law, 22123

Report of the Irish Boundary Commission, 1923, 2666

Report of the Review Committee on Overseas Representation 1968–1969, 13362

Report of the Tribunal Appointed to Enquire into the Disaster at Aberfan on October 21st, 1966, 6343

Research Institute for Consumer Affairs: Essays and Enquiries: 8. Fair Trading: Protecting Consumers, 5031; Essays and Enquiries: 3. London Stations: A Users' Assessment, 16991; Essays and Enquiries, 21529

Research Services Limited: Britain Today: Her International Affiliation; Her Standing in the World, Her Daily Newspapers: A Study of the Opinions of People Listed in Who's Who, 7578; Community Survey: Scotland; Prepared for the Government Social Survey, 9360; Community Attitudes Survey: England; Prepared for the Government Social Survey, 9361

Resis, A.: 'The Churchill-Stalin Secret "Percentages" Agreement on the Balkans, Moscow, October 1944', 13966

Resler, Henrietta: Class in a Capitalist Society: A Study of Contemporary Britain, 9568

Rettig, S.: ed. Fifty Years of Landscape Design, 1934–1984, 20323

Reusch, Ulrich: Deutsches Berufsbeamtentum und britische Besatzung: Planung und Politik 1943–1947, 14203

Reuss-Ianni, Elizabeth: A Family Business: Kinship and Social Control in Organised Crime, 10220

Revans, Reginald William: ed. Hospitals: Communication, Choice and Change, 21357; Standards for Morale: Cause and Effect in Hospitals, 21371

Revell, B. J.: 'Setting Guaranteed Prices in the United Kingdom Cereals Market 1967–1972', 19565

Revell, Jack Robert Stephen: The Wealth of the Nation: The National Balance Sheet of the United Kingdom, 1957–1961, 3778, 4596; The Owners of Quoted Ordinary Shares: A Survey for 1963, 3779; Changes in British Banking: The Growth of a Secondary Banking System, 4430; Financial Structure and Government Regulation in the United Kingdom, 1952–1980, 4597; The British Financial System, 4598; Personal Wealth and Finance in Wales, 5325

Revelle, Roger: ed. Population and Social Change, 7400

Review of United Kingdom Statistical Sources: Vol. viii: John Coppock, Land Use: L. F. Gebbett, Town and Country Planning, 20283

Review of the Operation of the Prevention of Terrorism, Temporary Provisions: Acts 1974 and 1976, 2874

Review of the Operation of the Prevention of Terrorism, Temporary Provisions Act 1976, 2875

Review of the University Grants Committee: Cmnd 81, 23334

Revue d'Histoire Ecclésiastique: 1900+, 11528

Rex, John Ardenne: ed. Approaches to Sociology: An Introduction to Major Trends in British Sociology, 8024; 'Foreigners in Britain', 10967; 'The Future of Race Relations Research in Britain: Sociological Research and the Politics of Racial Justice', 11023; 'The Concept of Housing Class and the Sociology of Race Relations', 11024; 'The Future of Black Culture and Politics in Britain', 11025; Colonial Immigrants in a British City, 11026; Race, Community and Conflict: A Study of Sparkbrook, 11457

Rexford-Welch, Samuel Cuthbert: ed. The Royal Air Force Medical Services, 15905

Reyburn, Wallace MacDonald: The Lions, 27033; The Men in White: The Story of English Rugby, 27039

Reynolds, D. J.: The London-Birmingham Motorway, 17111; Economics, Town Planning and Traffic, 17128

Reynolds, David J.: An Ocean Apart, 14012; The Creation of the Anglo-American Alliance, 1937–1941: A Study in Competitive Cooperation, 14030; 'Lord Lothian and Anglo-American Relations 1939–1940', 14031; 'Roosevelt, the British Left, and the Appointment of John G. Winant as United States Ambassador to Britain in 1941', 14033; 'Competitive Co-operation: Anglo-American Relations in World War Two', 14034; 'A "Special Relationship"? America, Britain and the International Order Since World War Two', 14086; 'Re-thinking Anglo-American Relations', 14087; 'The Origins of the Cold War: The European Dimension 1944–1951',

14100; 'Britain and the New Europe: The Search for Identity since 1940', 14122

Reynolds, Ernest Edwin: Britain in the Twentieth Century, 1900–1964, 334; The Roman Catholic Church in England and Wales: A Short History, 11942

Reynolds, Ernest Randolph: Modern English Drama: A Survey on the Theatre from 1900, 26179

Reynolds, Gerald William: The Night the Police Went on Strike, 10708

Reynolds, Jim: A Pictorial History of Norton Motor Cycles, 17187

Reynolds, Jonathan: The Development of Teleshopping and Teleservices, 20485

Reynolds, Josephine: ed. Conservation Planning in Town and Country, 18952

Reynolds, Philip Alan: British Foreign Policy in the Inter-War Years, 13211; ed. The Historian as Diplomat: Charles Kingsley Webster and the United Nations, 1939–1946, 13536; 'The University in the 1960s: an anachronism', 23419

Reynolds, Quentin James: They Fought for the Sky: The Story of the First War in the Air, 14621

Reynolds, Reginald Arthur: ed. British Pamphleteers, 283

Rheinberg, Netta: Fair Play: The Story of Women's Cricket, 27102

Rheinstein, Max: Marriage Stability, Divorce and the Law, 9993

Rhodes, Albert John: Dartmoor Prison: A Record of 126 Years of Prisoner of War and Convict Life, 1806–1932, 10349

Rhodes, Benjamin D.: 'British Diplomacy and the Silent Oracle of Vermont, 1923–1929', 14023; 'The British Royal Visit of 1939 and the "Psychological Approach" to the United States', 14036

Rhodes, E.C.: Young Offenders: An Enquiry into Juvenile Delinquency, 10549

Rhodes, G. W.: Co-operative Labour Relations 1900–1962, 1889

Rhodes, Gerald: Committees of Inquiry, 683; ed. Central-Local Relations: The Experience of the Environmental Health and Trading Services, 3226; The Government of Greater London, 3279, 18327; The Government of London: The Struggle for Reform, 3287, 18328; ed. The New Government of London: The First Five Years, 3290, 18326; Public Sector Pensions, 3969, 8576; Town Government in South-East England: A Comparative Study of Six Local Authorities, 18329

Rhodes, John: 'Evaluating the Effects of British Regional Economic Policy [1950–1971]', 3632, 5102; 'Regional Policy and the Scottish Economy', 5269

Rhodes, John: The Midland and Great Northern Joint Railway, 16902

Rhodes, Philip: Doctor John Leake's Hospital; A History of the General Lying-in Hospital, York Road, Lambeth 1765–1971: The Birth, Life and Death of a Maternity Hospital, 21446; The Value of Medicine, 22006

Rhodes, R. A. W.: Beyond Westminster and Whitehall: The Sub- Central Governments of Britain, 952; 'Continuity and Change in

British Central-Local Relations: The "Conservative Threat"', 3208; 'Intergovernmental Relations in the Post-War Period', 3209; 'The Lost World of British Local Politics', 3162; The National World of Local Government, 3206; Control and Power in Central-Local Relations, 3207; Corporate Management: The New Conventional Wisdom in British Local Government, 3240

Rhodes-Wood, E. H.: A War History of the Royal Pioneer Corps, 1939–1945, 15769

Rhys, D. G.: 'Concentration in the Inter-war Motor Industry', 17412

Rhys, J. T.: 'The Prime Minister's Temperance Proposals: A Plea for Support', 22178

Rhys-Williams, Sir Brandon: Stepping Stones to Independence: National Insurance after 1990, 4041

Rhys-Williams, Lady Juliet Evangeline: A New Look at Britain's Economic Policy, 3651; Something to Look Forward to: A Suggestion for a new Social Contract, 8769; Proposals for Simplifying and Reducing Income Tax . . . 8770; Taxation and Incentive, 8771

Ribbins, P. M.: 'Policy Making in English Local Government: The Case of Secondary School Reorganisation', 22964

Rice, A. K.: The Modern University: A Model Organisation, 234442

Rice, Ouida: Village Memories: Glimpses of Village Life during the First Fifty Years of this Century as seen through the Eyes of the Villagers of Woughton-on-the-Green, Milton Keynes, 19215

Rich, Ernest Edwin: St. Catherine's College, Cambridge: Quincentenary Essays, 23484

Rich, Paul B.: Race and Empire in British Politics, 11090; Race, Government and Politics in Britain, 11091, 11143; 'Philanthropic Racism in Britain: The Liverpool Universal Settlement, the Anti-Slavery Society and the Question of "Half-caste" Children 1919–1951', 11202; 'Doctrines of Racial Segregation in Britain 1900–1944', 11203

Richard, Cliff: Which One's Cliff?, 24520

Richard, Stephen: Directory of British Official Publications: A Guide to Sources, 173; British Government Publications: An Index to Chairmen and Authors, 188

Richards, Alun: A Touch of Glory: 100 Years of Welsh Rugby, 27046

Richards, Archibald B.: Touche Ross and Co. 1899–1981: The Origins and Growth of the United Kingdom Firm, 4177

Richards, Brian: New Movement in Cities, 16293

Richards, Colin: The Study of Primary Education: A Source Book, 23145

Richards, Daniel: Honest to Self, 12300

Richards, David: London: The Heartless City, 18333

Richards, Denis George: Twentieth Century Britain, 335; The Royal Air Force 1939–1945, 15808, 15809; Portal of Hungerford: The Life of Marshal of the Royal Air Force, Viscount Portal of Hungerford, 15961

Richards, Dickinson W.: ed. Circulation of the Blood: Men and Ideas, 22309

Richards, Edith Ryley: Private View of a Public Man: The Life of Leyton Richards, 12056

Richards, Franklin Thomas Grant: Housman, 1897–1936, 25577

Richards, G. Tilghman: The History and Development of Typewriters: Based on the Collection in the Science Museum, 7053

Richards, Hamish: ed. Population. Factor Movements and Economic Development: Studies Presented to Brinley Thomas, 7424

Richards, Sir James Maude: An Introduction to Modern Architecture, 23891; 'The Hollow Victory: 1932–1972', 23910; The Wood Engravings of Eric Ravilious, 24093

Richards, Jeffrey: The Railway Station: A Social History, 16792; Britain Can Take It: The British Cinema in the Second World War, 24595; Visions of Yesterday, 24607; Best of British: Cinema and Society 1930–1970, 24617; ed. Mass-Observation at the Movies, 24631; 'The British Board of Film Censors and Content Control in the 1930s: Images of Britain and Foreign Affairs', 26909

Richards, Melville: Welsh Administrative and Territorial Units: Medieval and Modern, 3111

Richards, Pauline N.: Shift Work: A Selective Annotated Bibliography, 5916

Richards, Peter G.: Prime Ministers and Diplomats: The Making of Australian Foreign Policy 1901–1949, 12619

Richards, Peter Godfrey: ed. Ford's List of British Parliamentary Papers 1974–1983, together with Specialist Commentaries, 198; Parliament and Conscience, 558; Honourable Members: a Study of the British Backbencher, 691; The Backbenchers, 692; 'The SDP in Parliament', 1840; 'General Election (1950)', 2303; A History of Local Government in the Twentieth Century, 3123; The Local Government System, 3150; The Reformed Local Government System, 3151; The Local Government Act 1972: Problems of Implementation, 3183; Delegation in Local Government: County to District Councils, 3228; Parliament and Foreign Affairs, 13356

Richards, Richard David: Money and Banking: A Select Bibliography, 3418

Richards, Sandra L.: The Rise of the English Actress, 26004

Richardson, Al: Two Steps Back: Communists and the Wider Labour Movement, 1939–1945: A Study in Relations between 'Vanguard' and Class, 1953; Against the Stream: A History of the Trotskyist Movement in Britain 1924–1938, 1982

Richardson, Alan: 'Some Psycho-social Characteristics of Satisfied and Dissatisfied British Immigrant Skilled Manual Workers in Western Australia', 7322; British Immigrants and Australia: A Psycho-social Inquiry, 7323; 'Some Psycho-social Aspects of British Immigration to Australia', 7324; 'The Assimilation of British Immigrants in Australia', 7325

Richardson, Ann: 'Decision-Making by Non-elected Members: An Analysis of New Provisions in the 1972 Local Government Act', 3184; F.I.S. Part Four: Widow's Benefits, 4095

Richardson, Charles James: Contemporary Social Mobility, 9578

Richardson, Charles: Flashback: A Soldier's Story, 14779

Richardson, Clement: A Geography of Bradford, 1805, 26678

Richardson, Cyril Albert: The Education of Teachers in England, France and the U.S.A., 22728

Richardson, Elizabeth: Authority and Organisation in the Secondary School, 22822

Richardson, Sir Eric: 'Education in a Technologically Based Society', 22512

Richardson, Frank: Fighting Spirit: A Study of Psychological Factors in War, 15100

Richardson, G.: Policing Pollution: A Study of Regulation and Enforcement, 19984

Richardson, Harry Ward: The British Economy, 1870–1939, 3407; 'Over-Commitment in Britain before 1930', 3559; 'The Basis of Economic Recovery in the 1930's: A Review and a New Interpretation', 3579; Economic Recovery in Britain, 1932–1939, 3580; 'The Economic Significance of the Depression in Britain', 3581; 'Fiscal Policy in the 1930s', 4644; Elements of Regional Policy, 5104; Regional Economics: Location Theory, Urban Structure and Regional Change, 5105; ed. Regional Economics: A Reader, 5106; Regional Growth Theory, 5107; Regional and Urban Economics, 5108; The Economics of Urban Size, 5403, 20399; The New Urban Economics and Alternatives, 5404, 20400; Housing and Urban Spatial Structure: A Case Study, 5405, 20401; Building in the British Economy between the Wars, 6174; 'The Development of the British Dyestuffs Industry before 1939', 6477; 'The New Industries between the Wars', 7224; 'Determinants of Urban House Prices', 18550

Richardson, Helen Jane: Adolescent Girls in Approved Schools, 10508

Richardson, Ian Milne: Age and Need: A Study of Older People in North-East Scotland, 8584

Richardson, Jeremy John: 'The Role of All-Party Committees in the House of Commons', 660; Government and Pressure Groups in Britain, 2060; ed. Pressure Groups in Britain: A Reader, 2073; Steel Policy in the U.K.: The Politics of Industrial Decline, 6578; 'The Environmental Lobby in Britain', 19960, 20247; ed. Campaigning for the Environment, 19963, 20246; 'The Origins of the Water Act of 1973', 20101; 'The Growth of the Environment as a Political Issue in Britain', 20248

Richardson, John Henry: Economic and Financial Aspects of Social Security, 4099; British Economic Foreign Policy, 4778, 13346; An Introduction to the Study of Industrial Relations, 5605

Richardson, Kenneth: The British Motor Industry, 1896–1939, 17399; Twentieth Century Coventry, 18021, 18857

Richardson, Paul: Britain, Europe and the Modern World 1918–1968, 13234

Richardson, Philip John Sampey: A History of English Ballroom Dancing, 1910–1945, 27169

Richardson, Robert G.: The Surgeon's Heart: A History of Cardiac Surgery, 21148

Richardson, Roger Charles: British Economic and Social History: A Bibliographical Guide, 395, 3387, 7527; The Study of History: A Bibliographical Guide, 26722

Richardson, V. A.: 'A Measurement of Demand for Professional Engineers', 9808

Richelson, Jeffrey T.: The Ties that Bind: Intelligence Co-operation in UK/USA Countries—The United Kingdom, the United States of America, Canada, Australia and New Zealand, 16008

Richey, Paul: Fighter Pilot: A Personal Record of the Campaign in France, 1939–1940, 5899

Richmond, Anthony Henry: The Human Factor in Industry, 5594; 'Return Migration from Canada to Britain', 7319; 'Housing and Racial Attitudes in Bristol', 10986; 'The Significance of a Multi-Racial Commonwealth', 10987; 'Tendances récentes de la recherche en matière de relations raciales: Grande Bretagne', 10988; 'Sociological and Psychological Explanations of Racial Prejudice', 10989; 'Immigration as a Social Process: The Case of the Coloured Colonials in the United Kingdom', 10990; 'Teaching Race Questions in Schools', 10991; The Colour Problem: A Study of Race Relations, 11031; Readings in Race and Ethnic Relations, 11032; Colour Prejudice in Britain: A Study of West Indian Workers in Liverpool, 1941–1951, 11239, 11463; Immigration and Ethnic Conflict, 11443; Immigration and Race Relations in an English Town: A Study in Bristol, 11481

Richmond, Sir Herbert: Sea Power in the Modern World, 15336; Statesmen and Seapower, 15340

Richmond, Kenneth: 'Adolescence and Neurosis', 8411

Richmond, William Kenneth: Education in Britain since 1944: Education in England, 22696; The Education Industry, 22697; A Personal Retrospect, 22698; Teachers and Machines: An Introduction to the Theory and Practice of Programmed Learning, 22764; The Education Industry, 22839; The Literature of Education: A Critical Bibliography, 1945–1970, 22859

Richter, Irving: Political Purpose in Trade Unions, 6713

Richter, Melvin: 'Intellectual and Class Alienation: Oxford Idealist Diagnoses and Prescriptions', 9812

Rickards, Maurice: The Rise and Fall of the Poster, 24119

Ricker, John C.: The Modern Era, 362

Riddell, D. S.: 'Youth and Work: Problems and Perspectives', 8440

Riddell, George Allardice [Baron]: Lord Riddell's War Diary, 1914–1918, 1515

Riddell, John F.: The Clyde: An Illustrated History of the River and its Shipping, 16481; Clyde Navigation: A History of the Development and Deepening of the River Clyde, 18143

Riddell, Joseph N.: C. Day-Lewis, 25474

Riddell, Patrick: Fire over Ulster, 2915

Riddell, Peter: The Thatcher Government, 1050

Riddle, Ian: Shipbuilding Credit, 16614

Ride, E.: BAAG: Hong Kong Resistance 1942–1945, 12971

Ride, Paul: British Studio Ceramics in the 20th Century, 24132

Riden, Philip: Rebuilding a Valley: A History of Cwmbran Development Corporation, 18266; Local History: A Practical Handbook for Beginners, 26746; Record Sources for Local History, 26747

Rideout, R. W.: 'Strikes', 6966; 'Responsible Self-government in British Trade Unions', 6967; 'The Content of Trade Union Rules regulating Admission', 6968; The Right to Membership of a Trade Union, 6969

Ridge, John Michael: ed. Mobility in Britain Reconsidered, 9603

Ridgeway, Christopher: 'The Job Expectations of Immigrant Workers', 11419

Ridill, William John Brownlow: Eyes in Industry: A Complete Book on Eyesight Written for Industrial Workers, 4120

Riding, E. J.: Aircraft of the 1914–1918 War, 14635

Riding, Richard: ed. De Havilland: The Golden Years, 1919–1939, 17603

Ridker, Ronald G.: 'Desired Family Size and the Efficacy of Current Family Planning Programmes', 7504

Ridler, Anne: Olive Willis and Downe House, 23115

Ridley, Anthony: An Illustrated History of Transport, 16214

Ridley, F. F.: Specialists and Generalists, 865; 'The British Civil Service and Politics; Principles in Question and Traditions in Flux', 903

Ridley, Maurice Roy: Gertrude Bell, 13813

Ridley, T. M.: 'Industrial Production in the United Kingdom, 1900–1953', 4995

Riedel, H.: 'Labour Party und EWG: zum Antrag Grossbritanniens auf Mitgliedschaft in der EWG in der Zweiten Hälfte der Sechziger Jahre', 13574

Riemer, S.: 'The Nucleated City', 17824

Rieppel, F. W.: 'Die Medizinschule von Edinburgh', 21002

Riewald, J. G.: Sir Max Beerbohm: Man and Writer, 25370

Rigby, Andrew: Aberdeen in the General Strike, 6926

Rigg, T.: 'The Market Garden District of Biggleswade, Bedfordshire', 19845

Righter, Rosemary: Save our Cities: [A Report on the Save our Cities Conference . . .], 18957

Riley, Denise: 'Am I That Name?': Feminism and the Category of 'Women' in History, 7763; 'The Free Mothers: Pronatalism and

Working Women in Industry at the End of the Last War in Britain', 7843

Riley, Harold: *ed.* Acts of the Convocations of Canterbury and York, 1921–1970, 11687

Rimlinger, Gaston Victor: 'Welfare Policy and Economic Development', 8935

Rimmer, L.: Employment Trends and the Family Study, 9938

Rimmer, Malcolm: Workplace and Union: A Study of Local Relationship in Fourteen Unions, 6721; Race and Industrial Conflict: A Study in a Group of Midland Foundries, 11472

Ringby, Charles: Kathleen Ferrier: A Biography, 24415

Ripley, B. J.: Administration in Local Authorities, 3232

Ripman, Hujohn Armstrong: *ed.* Guy's Hospital, 1725–1948, 22474

Rippon, Angela: Mark Phillips: The Man and His Horses, 27134

Rippy, J. Fred: British Investment in Latin America, 1822–1949, 4752

Rise, Desmond: The Sinking of the Belgrano, 16113

Risley, M.: The House of Healing: The Story of the Hospital, 21408

Rissik, David: The D.L.I.: The History of the Durham Light Infantry, 1939–1945, 15625

Ritchie, Bernie: The Key to the Door: The Abbey National Story, 4390

Ritchie, C.: The Siren Years: Undiplomatic Diaries, 1937–1945, 15167

Ritchie, John: History of the Laboratory of the Royal College of Physicians of Edinburgh, 20780

Ritchie, L. A.: Modern British Shipbuilding: A Guide to Historical Records, 16604

Ritchie, M.: Women's Studies: A Checklist of Bibliographies, 7626

Ritchie, Margaret: Police Warnings, 10557

Ritchie, Richard: *ed.* A Nation—No Nation?, 1299

Ritchie-Noakes, Nancy: Liverpool's Historic Waterfront: Old Docks, 16657; The World's First Mercantile Dock System, 16695

Ritson, B.: The Management of Alcoholism, 22132

Ritson, Christopher: 'Agricultural Expansion and the U.K. Balance of Payments, 19554; *ed.* The Food Consumer, 20619

Ritter, Gerhard A.: 'Friedensbewegung in Grossbritannien 1914–1918/19: The Union of Democratic Control und ihr Kampf um eine gerechte Friedensordnung', 13447

Ritter, Paul: Planning for Man and Motor, 17125

Rivers, Patrick: Politics, 2069

Rivett, G.: The Development of the London Hospital System, 1823–1982, 21433

Rivett, Patrick: Integrated Planning in the Textile Industry, 6452

Rix, Sir Brian: My Farce from my Elbow, 26088; Farce about Face, 26089

Rizvi, Gowher: Linlithgow and India: A Study of British Policy and the Political Impasse in India, 1936–1943, 13157

Roach, Jack Leslie: *ed.* Radical Sociology, 8040; *and* Roach, Janet K.: Poverty, 9076

Roach, John Peter Charles: 'Examinations

and the Secondary Schools 1900–1945', 22913

Road Research Laboratory: Sample Survey of the Roads and Traffic of Great Britain, 17144; Fifty Point Traffic Census 1956/57, 17145; Fifty Point Traffic Census: The First Five Years, 17146

Road Transport Directory for the British Isles and Western Europe, 16272

Roads Campaign Council: Parking Matters No. 1—A Community Problem, 17378

Robb, James Harding: Working Class Anti-Semite: A Psychological Study in a London Borough, 11332

Robb, Peter G.: The Government of India and Reform: Policies towards Politics and the Constitution, 13128; 'The British Cabinet and Indian Reform, 1917–1919', 13129

Robb-Smith, A. H. T.: A Short History of the Radcliffe Infirmary, 21465

Robbins, Alan Pitt: Newspapers Today, 25046

Robbins, Frank: Under the Starry Plough: Recollections of the Irish Citizen Army, 2759

Robbins, Gordon Juxon: Fleet Street Blitzkrieg Diary, 15157; Kaleidescope of London Buses between the Wars, 17308

Robbins, Keith Gilbert: *ed.* The Blackwell Biographical Dictionary of British Political Life in the Twentieth Century, 48; The Eclipse of a Great Power: Modern Britain, 1870–1975, 287; The Great 20th Century Serial, 391; Sir Edward Grey: A Biography of Lord Grey of Fallodon, 1203; 'Institutions and Illusions: The Dilemma of the Modern Ecclesiastical Historian', 11550; 'Religion and Identity in Modern British History', 11580; 'Free Churchmen and the Twenty Years' Crisis: 1919–1939', 11861; 'Church and Politics: Dorothy Buxton and the German Church Struggle', 11862; 'Martin Niemöller: The German Church Struggle and English Opinion', 11864; 'Britain, 1940 and "Christian Civilization"', 11866; 'The Spiritual Pilgrimage of the Rev. R.J. Campbell', 12055; The First World War, 13366, 14465; 'British Diplomacy and Bulgaria, 1914–1915', 13385; The Abolition of War: The British 'Peace Movement', 1914–1919, 13444; 'Lord Bryce and the First World War', 13476; 'Labour Foreign Policy and International Socialism: Ramsay MacDonald and the League of Nations', 13554; 'Appeasement: New Tasks for the Historian', 13715; Appeasement, 13716; Munich 1938, 13742; 'Konrad Henlein, the Sudeten Question and British Foreign Policy', 13743; 'History, The Historical Association and the "National Past"', 26770; 'National Identity and History: Past, Present and Future', 26770; Insular Outsider? 'British History' and European Integration', 26770

Robbins, Lionel Charles [Baron]: Political Economy Past and Present: A Review of Leading Theories in Economic Policy, 3515; The Great Depression, 3577; Liberty and Equality, 9527; 'Report on Robbins', 23414; Higher Education, 23415; The University in the Modern World and Other Papers in

Higher Education, 23422; Autobiography of an Economist, 26618

Robbins, Michael: A History of London Transport: Passenger Travel and the Development of the Metropolis, vol. 2—'The 20th Century to 1970', 16316; The Railway Age, 16771

Robbins, Stephen Paul: Personnel: The Management of Human Resources, 5472

Robboy, H.: 'Not Welcome: The Punjabi Visitor and British Officialdom', 11208

Robens, Alfred [Baron]: Ten Year Stint, 6311; Engineering and Economic Progress, 6361

Roberts, Arthur Starkey: Prescot Parish Memories, 19353

Roberts, Audrey: Bibliography of Commissions of Enquiry and Other Government-Sponsored Reports on the Commonwealth Caribbean 1900–1975, 12993

Roberts, Benjamin Charles: National Wages Policy in War and Peace, 3890; Workers' Participation in Management in Britain, 5459, 6018; Trade Union Government and Administration in Great Britain, 5627; Industrial Relations: Contemporary Problems and Perspectives, 5628; 'Employers and Industrial Relations in Britain and America', 5629; Reluctant Militants: A Study of Industrial Technicians, 5756; *ed.* Manpower Policy and Employment Trends, 5933; The Trades Union Congress, 1868–1921, 6702; A Short History of the T.U.C., 6703; Trade Unions in a Free Society, 6725; 'Trade Unions in the Welfare State', 6914

Roberts, Brian K.: The Making of the English Village: A Study in Historical Geography, 19151

Roberts, Brian: Randolph: A Story of Churchill's Son, 1395

Roberts, Brynley: 'Welsh Nonconformist Archives', 12291

Roberts, C. D.: 'Education in a Multi-cultural Society', 23194

Roberts, D. A.: 'The Orange Order in Ireland: A Religious Institution?', 2941

Roberts, D. E.: The Northampton Gas Undertaking 18230–1949, 7164

Roberts, D. F.: 'The Social Impact of Haemophilia', 21088

Roberts, David M.: 'Clement Davies and the Fall of Neville Chamberlain', 985

Roberts, David William: An Outline of the Economic History of England to 1952, 3455

Roberts, Eirlys Rhiwen Cadwaladr: Consumers, 20464

Roberts, Elizabeth: A Women's Place: An Oral History of Working-Class Women 1890–1940, 7638; Women's Work 1840–1940, 7639

Roberts, Frank C.: Obituaries from The Times, 1951–1960, 40

Roberts, Geoffrey: Labour Relations in the Motor Industry: A Study of Industrial Unrest and an International Comparison, 7242

Roberts, George W.: 'Emigration from the Island of Barbados', 11241

Roberts, George W.: *ed.* Bertrand Russell Memorial Volume, 26876

Roberts, Glyn: Volunteers in Africa and Asia: A Field Study, 9161

Roberts, Henry Lithgow: Britain and the United States: Problems in Co-operation, 14064

Roberts, Iolo Francis: Further Education in England and Wales, 23254; Further Education Today, 23255

Roberts, Jim: Making the Present: A Social and Economic History of Britain, 1918–1972, 3507

Roberts, John: Everton: The Official Centenary History, 27076

Roberts, John: The Calvinistic Methodism of Wales, 12296

Roberts, John Trevor: General Improvement Areas, 17958

Roberts, Kenneth: 'The Entry into Employment: An Approach Towards a General Theory', 5888; Strike at Pilkingtons, 6937; From School to Work: A Study of the Youth Employment Service, 6987; Leisure, 26923; Youth and Leisure, 8533; The Fragmentary Class Structure, 9579

Roberts, N.: ed. Use of Social Science Literature, 12

Roberts, Neil: Ted Hughes: A Critical Study, 25581

Roberts, Nesta: Not in Perfect Mind: The Care of Mentally Frail Old People, 8570; Cheadle Royal Hospital: A Bicentenary History, 21425; A Doctor in Practice, 21523; Mental Health and Mental Illness, 21810

Roberts, Norman: ed. Use of Social Sciences Literature, 7948

Roberts, Peter: Any Colour so Long as it's Black: The First Fifty Years of Automobile Advertising, 4299; The Old Vic Story: A Nation's Theatre, 1818–1976, 26130

Roberts, Peter Geoffrey: The Coal Act, 1938, 6279

Roberts, Philip: Edward Bond: A Companion to the Plays, 25945; The Royal Court Theatre 1965–1972, 26156

Roberts, R. O.: 'The Development and Decline of the Copper and Other Non-ferrous Metal Industries in South Wales', 5343

Roberts, R. S.: 'Epidemics and Social History: An Essay Review', 22353

Roberts, Richard: A History of Schroders, 4473.

Roberts, Richard Ellis: H.R.L. Sheppard: Life and Letters, 11810

Roberts, Robert Alun: Commons and Village Greens: A Study in Land Use, Conservation and Management Based on a National Survey of Commons in England and Wales, 1961–1966, 20267

Roberts, Robert David Valpo: Status, Productivity and Pay—A Major Experiment: A Study of the Electricity Supply Industry's Agreements and their Outcome, 1961–1971, 3914, 5692; 'Joint Consultations in the Electricity Supply Industry, 1949–1959', 5645; 'Labor/Management Co-operative Committees in Britain's Electricity Supply Industry', 5646

Roberts, Robert: The Classic Slum: Salford Life in the First Quarter of the Century, 18402

Roberts, Stephen Andrew: Research Libraries and Collections in the United Kingdom, 96; ed. Inventory of Information Resumés in the Social Sciences, 7921

Roberts, Sir Sydney Castle: British Universities, 23372; Adventures with Authors, 24949

Roberts, Warren: A Bibliography of D. H. Lawrence, 25627

Robertson, A. J.: 'Clydeside Revisited: A Reconsideration of the Clyde Shipbuilding Industry, 1919–1938', 16618; 'The British Airframe Industry and the State in the Interwar Period: A Comment', 17581; 'The New Road to the Isles: Highland Airways and Scottish Airways', 17635

Robertson, Alan C.: Lion Rampant and Winged: A Commemorative History of Scottish Aviation Ltd, 17613

Robertson, Andrew: 'Technological Change, Management and Labour', 5875; The Trade Unions', 6798; Strategic Marketing: A Response to Consumerism, 20476

Robertson, Bruce: Spitfire: The Story of a Famous Fighter, 15845; British Military Aircraft Serials, 1912–1963, 15864; Bombing Colours: British Bomber Camouflage and Markings, 1914–1937, 15865; Aircraft Camouflage and Markings, 1907–1954, 15866; Robertson, Bryan Charles Francis: '1893–1963: British Painting', 23994

Robertson, Donald James: ed. Fringe Benefits, Labour Costs and Social Security, 3893; 'Earnings and Engineering, 1926–1948', 3930; Notes on Engineering Earnings', 3931; Differences between the Wages of Skilled and Unskilled Workers, 1880–1950', 3932; ed. Public Expenditure Appraisal and Control, 4759, 21598; ed. The British Balance of Payments, 4932; [Edinburgh] The City and the Region, 5285, 18127; 'Trade Unions and Wage Policy', 6761; 'The Migrating Scot', 7334

Robertson, Edna: The Yorkhill Story: The History of the Royal Hospital for Sick Children, Glasgow, 21476

Robertson, Esmonde Manning: ed. The Origins of the Second World War, 13772

Robertson, Geoffrey: Reluctant Judas: The Life and Death of the Special Branch Informer, Kenneth Lennon, 2871; The People against the Press: An Inquiry into the Press Council, 25332

Robertson, J. F.: 'Civil Service Reform in Britain', 856

Robertson, J.: Housing and the Public Health, 18578

Robertson, James C.: 'The British General Election of 1935', 2286; 'British Policy in East Africa, March 1891 to May 1935', 13779; 'The Origins of British Opposition to Mussolini over Ethiopia', 13780; 'The Hoare-Laval Plan', 13788; The British Board of Film Censors: Film Censorship in Britain, 1896–1950, 26910; The Hidden Cinema: British Film Censorship in Action 1913–1972, 26911; 'British Film Censorship goes to War', 26912

Robertson, James Hugh: Reform of British Central Government, Post-war Trends in Employment, Productivity, Output, Labour Costs and Prices by Industry in the United Kingdom, 5915; The Same Alternative: Signposts to a Self-fulfilling Future, 8068; Profit or People? The New Social Role of Money, 8956, 9459; Power, Money and Sex: Towards a New Social Balance, 8957, 9458; Hospitals and Children, 21351

Robertson, K. G.: ed. Britain's Crisis in Sociological Perspective, 7604

Robertson, Keith Barrie: Job Enrichment and Employee Motivation, 5730

Robertson, Kevin: Hampshire Railways Remembered, 16938; The Last Days of Steam around London, 17048

Robertson, Max: Wimbledon, 27150

Robertson, Norman: 'Les Relations professionelles en Grande-Bretagne: Perspectives d'un nouveau système', 5726; ed. British Trade Unionism: Select Documents, 6744

Robertson, Roland: Deviance, Crime and Socio-legal Control: Comparative Perspectives, 10150

Robertson, Sheila: Shopping in History, 20482; Food in History, 20569

Robertson, Sir Charles Grant: The British Universities, 23368

Robertson, Sir Dennis Holme: Britain in the World's Economy, 4803

Robertson, Terence: Crisis: The Inside Story of the Suez Conspiracy, 14373; Dieppe: The Shame and the Glory, 14828

Robertson, William Robert: Soldiers and Statesmen, 1914–1918, 14519

Robertson, William Stewart: Scotland Today: Economic Developments, 5268

Robertson, William: Meat and Food Inspection, 22098

Robertson, William: Welfare in Trust: A History of the Carnegie United Kingdom Trust 1913–1963, 9126

Robey, Edward: The Jester and the Court, 26341

Robin, Jean: Elmdon: Continuity and Change in a North-West Essex Village, 1861–1964, 19186

Robins, David: Knuckle Sandwich: Growing up in the Working Class City, 8234, 10667

Robins, F. W.: The Story of the Lamp (and the Candle), 7068

Robinson, Adrian H. W.: Map Studies, with Related Field Excursions, 26719

Robinson, Ann: Tax-Policy Making in the United Kingdom: A Study of Rationality, Ideology and Politics, 4825

Robinson, Arthur J.: The Green: A History of the Heart of Bethnal Green and the Legend of the Blind Beggar, 18341

Robinson, Brett Mallon: Firearms in Crime: A Home Office Statistical Division Report on Indictable Offences Involving Firearms in England and Wales, 10207

Robinson, Brian R.: Aviation in Manchester: A Short History, 17527

Robinson, Colin: North Sea Oil in the Future: Economic Analysis and Government Policy, 7171

Robinson, David: Chaplin: His Life and Art, 26304

Robinson, David: *ed.* Studies in Everyday Medical Life, 21580, 21952; Patients, Practitioners and Medical Care: Aspects of Medical Sociology, 21949; The Process of Becoming Ill, 21950; Self-Help and Health: Mutual Aid for Modern Problems, 21951; From Drinking to Alcoholism: A Sociological Commentary, 22138

Robinson, Derek: 'Wage Rates, Wage Income and Wage Policy', 3936

Robinson, Douglas H.: Giants in the Sky: A History of the Rigid Airship, 17535; The Dangerous Sky: A History of Aviation Medicine, 21049

Robinson, Douglas Hepworth: The New Farming, 19404; Self Sufficiency on the Farm, 19475

Robinson, Duncan: Stanley Spencer: Views from a Berkshire Village, 24072

Robinson, [Edward] Austin [Gossage]: Economic Planning in the United Kingdom: Some Lessons, 3534; Fifty Years of Commonwealth Economic Development, 12490; *ed.* The Collected Writings of John Maynard Keynes, 26590; 'John Maynard Keynes: Economist, Author, Statesman', 26603

Robinson, Eric Embleton: The New Polytechnics, 22527; 'Education as a Social Service', 22642

Robinson, F.: 'Vacation Training of Undergraduate Engineers', 22511

Robinson, G. W. S.: 'British Conurbations in 1951: Some Corrections', 17742

Robinson, G.: 'Edmund W. Gilbert and the Development of Historical Geography with a Bibliography of his Work, 26669

Robinson, Geoffrey A.: Hospital Administration, 21394

Robinson, Guy Martin: Agricultural Change: Geographical Studies of British Agriculture, 19425

Robinson, Sir Harry Perry: The Turning Point: The Battle of the Somme, 14599

Robinson, Henry Wheeler: Baptists in Britain, 12022

Robinson, Hilary: Coping Alone, 8279; Homes in High Flats: Some of the Human Problems involved in Multi-Storey Housing, 18482

Robinson, J.: Learning over the Air: 60 Years of Partnership in Adult Learning, 23716

Robinson, John Arthur Thomas: Honest to God, 11872; 'But That I Can't Believe!', 11886; 'The Teaching of Theology for the Ministry', 11897

Robinson, John: *ed.* Educational Television and Radio in Britain, 24831

Robinson, Julian: Fashion in the Forties and Fifties, 24165

Robinson, K.: 'Selection and the Social Background of the Administrative Class', 917

Robinson, Kenneth Ernest: *ed.* Essays in Imperial Government Presented to Margery Perham, 12488, 12684; The Dilemmas of Trusteeship; Aspects of British Colonial Policy between the Wars, 12533; A Decade of the Commonwealth, 1955–1964, 12584

Robinson, Kenneth Richard: *ed.* Modern Dairy Technology, 20666

Robinson, Leland Rex: Foreign Credit Facilities in the United Kingdom: A Sketch of Post-War Development and Present Status, 4593

Robinson, Madeline R.: 'Parliamentary Privilege and Political Morality in Britain, 1939–57', 652

Robinson, Mairi: *ed.* The Concise Scots Dictionary, 23852

Robinson, Mary: Local Authority Information Sources: A Guide to Publications, Databases and Services, 3097

Robinson, Olive: 'Part-Time Employment and Low Pay in Retail Distribution in Britain', 3941; 'White-collar Bargaining: A Case Study in the Private Sector', 5694; 'Representation of the White-collar Worker: The Bank Staff Associations in Britain', 5695; Pay and Employment in Retailing, 9668

Robinson, Paul: Solti, 24440

Robinson, R. A.: Market Gardening, 19840

Robinson, R. V. F.: Small Firms in the Motor Vehicle Distribution and Repair Industry, 17484

Robinson, Ray: *ed.* Privatisation and the Welfare State, 9010

Robinson, Ronald H. O. B.: The Lives of the Fellows of the Royal College of Surgeons of England, Vol. 4: 1956–1973, 20843; Lives of the Fellows of the Royal College of Surgeons of England. 1952, 20901

Robinson, Sidney: Seebord: The First Twenty Five Years, 6391

Robinson, Stuart: A History of Dyed Textiles: Dyes, Fibres, Painted Bark, Batik, Starch-Resist, Discharge, Tie-Dye, Further Sources for Research, 7069; A History of Printed Textiles: Block, Roller, Screen, Design, Dyes, Fibres, Discharge, Resist, Further Sources for Research, 7070

Robinson, V.: 'Correlates of Asian Immigration, 1959–74', 11234

Robinson, Victor: The Story of Medicine, 21177

Robson, Brian Turnbull: Urban Analysis: A Study of City Structure with Special Reference to Sunderland, 18115; Urban Growth: An Approach, 18116; Urban Social Areas, 18117

Robson, Graham: The Rover Story, 17428

Robson, James Scott: Medicine Yesterday and Today, 21226

Robson, Robert: The Cotton Industry in Britain, 6453

Robson, Stephen: P & O in the Falklands: A Pictorial Record, 5 April–25 September 1982, 16534

Robson, William Alexander: 'The Machinery of Government, 1939–1947', 802; The Governors and the Governed, 851; *ed.* Civil Service in Britain and France, 852; *ed.* Protest and Discontent, 2137; The Development of Local Government, 3136; Local Government in Crisis, 3137; The Government and Misgovernment of London, 3278; *ed.* Public Enterprise: Developments in Social Ownership and Control in Great Britain, 6057; Nationalised Industry and Public Ownership, 6069; 'The Political Control of Nationalised Industries in Britain', 6074; *ed.* Problems of Nationalised Industry, 6092; *ed.* Man and the Social Sciences: Twelve Lectures Delivered at the London School of Economics and Political Science, tracing the Development of the Social Sciences during the Present Century, 7942; *ed.* The Future of the Social Services, 8823; The Welfare State, 8998; Welfare State and Welfare Society: Illusion and Reality, 8999; Great Cities of the World: Their Government, Politics and Planning, 17902; *ed.* Century of Municipal Progress: The Last Hundred Years, 17903; The Heart of Greater London: Proposals for a Policy, 18938

Roche, D. J.: 'A Socio-Political Opinion Profile of Clergymen in Northern Ireland', 12165

Roche, D. S. D: Housing in Northern Ireland, 18497

Roche, F.: 'A Place to Live—Political or Technical', 18562

Rock, Paul Elliot: 'Sociology of Deviancy and Conceptions of Moral Order', 10162; 'Social Reaction to Deviance and its Effects on Crime and Criminal Careers', 10194; 'Observation on Debt Collection', 10212; Making People Pay, 10314; Deviant Interpretations, 10604; The Delinquent Solution: A Study in Subcultural Theory, 10605

Rock, William Ray: Neville Chamberlain, 983; Appeasement on Trial: British Foreign Policy and its Critics, 1938–1939, 13713; British Appeasement in the 1930s, 13714; 'British Guarantee to Poland, March 1939: A Problem in Diplomatic Decision-Making', 13899; 'Grand Alliance or Daisy Chain: British Opinion and Policy towards Russia, April–August 1939', 13947

Rocker, Rudolph: The London Years: Translated by Joseph Leftwich, 11301; Nationalism and Culture, 11302

Rodaway, Angela: A London Childhood, 8325

Rodd, James Rennell [Baron]: Social and Diplomatic Memoirs: Third Series 1902–1919, 13304

Roddie, Ian Campbell: An Excellent Medical School, 20781

Roddis, L. H.: A Short History of Nautical Medicine, 21272

Roddis, Roland Joseph: The Housing Act 1964, 18679

Roderick, Gordon Wynne: *ed.* The British Malaise: Industrial Performance, Education and Training in Britain Today, 5963; The Emergence of a Scientific Society, 23285

Roderick, W. P.: 'The London New Towns: Origin of Migrants from Greater London up to December 1968', 19019

Rodger, N. A. M.: The Admiralty, 831

Rodger, Richard: 'The Implementation of Housing Policy: The Scottish Special Housing Association', 18486

Rodgers, Barbara Noel: A Follow-up Study of Social Administration Students of Manchester University 1940–1960: Their Further Training and Subsequent Careers, with Particular Reference to the

Contribution Made by the Married Woman to Social Work, 8712; Portrait of Social Work: A Study of Social Services in a Northern Town, 8732; A New Portrait of Social Work: A Study of Social Services in a Northern Town from Younghusband to Seebohm, 8733; Comparative Social Administration, 9234

Rodgers, Dave: Rock 'n 'Roll, 24495

Rodgers, Frank: Guide to British Government Publications, 175; Serial Publications in the British Parliamentary Papers 1900–1968: A Bibliography, 202; Serial Publications in the British Parliamentary Papers, 1900–1968: A bibliography, 643

Rodgers, [Harry] Brian: 'The Changing Geography of the Lancashire Cotton Industry', 6451; 'Women and Work in New and Expanding Towns', 7825; The Battle against Poverty, 9063; ed. Studies in Human Geography, 26686; 'Recreation and Resources', 26963

Rodgers, John Charles: The Old Public Schools of England, 23008

Rodgers, S. C.: Anencephalus, Spina-Bifida and Congenital Hydrocephalus: England and Wales, 1964–1972, 22243

Rodgers, William Thomas: ed. Hugh Gaitskell, 1906–1963, 1197; The People in Parliament: An Illustrated History of the Labour Party, 1670; The Politics of Change, 1836

Rodney, Walter: The Groundings with my Brothers, 10976

Rodrigues, J.: 'Ted Knight Interviewed', 3314

Rodwin, Lloyd: The British New Towns Policy: Problems and Implications, 18223, 18990

Roe, James Moulton: A History of the British and Foreign Bible Society, 1905–1954, 11915, 12356

Roebuck, Janet: The Making of Modern English Society from 1850, 7561

Roebuck, Peter: ed. Plantation to Partition: Essays in Honour of J. L. McCracken, 2907

Roepke, Howard George: Movements of the British Iron and Steel Industry, 1720–1951, 6552

Rogan, John M.: ed. Medicine in the Mining Industries, 21281

Rogers, Alan William: Second Homes in England and Wales: A Study of the Distribution of Rural Properties taken over as Second Homes, 18374; Rural Housing and Structure Plans: A Review of Plans submitted by July 1976, 18757; The Urban Countryside: The Land-Use Structure of Small Towns and Villages in England and Wales, 19133; ed. Agricultural Resources: An Introduction to the Farming Industry of the United Kingdom, 19559

Rogers, Deborah Webster and Rogers, Ivor: J. R. R. Tolkien, 25842

Rogers, F. B.: A Syllabus of Medical History, 21204

Rogers, Hugh Cuthbert Basset: Troopships and Their History, 15399; The Mounted Troops of the British Army, 1066–1945, 15437; Weapons of the British Soldier, 15502; Bulleid Pacifics at Work, 17072

Rogers, K.: Wiltshire County Council: The First Hundred Years 1889–1989, 3371

Rogers, Leonard: 'Happy Toil: Fifty Five Years of Tropical Medicine', 22379; Recent Advances in Tropical Medicine, 22380

Rogers, Lindsay: 'The Last Tory Prime Minister', 986

Rogers, Malcolm: ed. Dictionary of British Portraiture, 213

Rogers, Margaret: 'Education in a Multi-ethnic Britain: A Teacher's Eye View', 23195

Rogers, Martin: An Illustrated History of Speedway, 27139

Rogers, Patrick: Onshore Impacts of Offshore Oil, 6524

Rogers, Patrick: St Peter's Pro-Cathedral, Belfast, 1866–1966, 12186

Rogers, Rick: Crowther to Warnock: How Fourteen Reports Tried to Change Children's Lives, 8326; Education and Social Class, 9613; Lead Poison, 20171

Rogers, Sidney John: Economic Change and Agriculture, 19542; ed. The Common Agricultural Policy and Britain, 19654

Rogers, T. G. P.: 'Recent Advances in Personnel Management', 5464

Rogerson, Sidney: The Last Off the Ebb, 14600; Wilfred Rhodes, 27104

Rogow, Arnold A.: The Labour Government and British Industry, 1945–1951, 6132; 'Labor Relations under the British Labor Governments', 6873

Rohde, Eleanour Sinclair: The Story of the Garden, 19863

Rohde, Shelley: A Private View of L. S. Lowry, 24038

Rohe, K.: ed. Krise in Grossbritannien?, 586

Rohmann, Herbert: Intonation und Lautgebung in der Sprache von Lloyd George, 1031

Rokeling, G. D.: A British Index of National Prosperity, 1920–1927, 3772

Rolf, David: 'Labour and Politics in the West Midlands Between the Wars', 1784; 'Birmingham Labour and the Background to the 1945 General Election', 2298

Rolfe, Edmund Neville: Food, Farming and the Common Market, 19652

Roll, Eric: Crowded Hours, 942; The Uses and Abuses of Economics, 3452

Rolleston, Sir Humphry Davy: ed. Diet in Health and Disease, 20511; The Cambridge Medical School: A Biographical History, 20783; 'The Progress and Pioneers of Preventive Medicine', 21005; Cardio-vascular Diseases since Harvey's Discovery, 21057; 'History of Aortic Regurgitation', 21058; 'History of Haematology', 21059; The Endocrine Organs in Health and Disease, 21076; Medical Aspects of Old Age, 21084; Aspects of Age, Life and Disease, 21173; gen. ed. 21249; gen. ed. Cumulative Supplement, 21250; 'The Aims and Methods of Graduate Study', 21283

Rollis, Richard H.: 'Cellular Pathology and the Development of the Deficiency Disease Concept', 21006

Rolls, S. C.: Steel Chariots in the Desert, 15532

Rolo, Charles Jack: Wingate's Raiders, 15064; Radio Goes to War, 24747

Rolph, Cecil Hewitt [pseud.]: 'The Police and the Public, 10726; ed. Women of the Streets: A Sociological Study of the Common Prostitute, 10847; 'Dirtiest Village', 20009; 'Dustmanship', 20010; Mental Disorder: A Brief Examination of the Report of the Royal Commission on the Law relating to Mental Illness and Mental Deficiency, 1954–1957, 21878; Books in the Dock, 24931; Kingsley: The Life, Letters and Diaries of Kingsley Martin, 25265; Living Twice: An Autobiography, 25279

Rolph, J. Alexander: Dylan Thomas: A Bibliography, 25827

Rolston, Bill: A Social Science Bibliography of Northern Ireland, 1945–1983: Material Published since 1945 Relating to Northern Ireland since 1921, 2781

Rolt, Lionel Thomas Caswell: The Dowty Story, 6364; Waterloo Ironworks: A History of Taskers of Andover, 1809–1968, 6594; The Inland Waterways of England, 16430; Inland Waterways, 16431; Navigable Waterways, 16432; A Hunslet Hundred: One Hundred Years of Locomotive Building by the Hunslet Engine Company, 17078; Horseless Carriage: The Motor Car in England, 17339

Romanyshyn, John M.: Social Welfare: Charity to Justice, 9156

Romijn, Jan: Tabu: Ugandan Asians: The Old, the Weak, the Vulnerable. A Report on . . . Work with the Elderly and Handicapped among the Ugandan Asian Evacuees in London, 11227

Romilly, Giles: Privileged Nightmare, 15041

Ronald, Sir Landon: Myself and Others, Written, Lest I Forget, 24437

Ronan, Colin A.: Changing Views of the Universe, 26393; Their Majesties' Astronomers: A Survey of Astronomy in Britain between the Two Elizabeths, 26394; Astronomy: Illustrated Sources in History, 26395

Ronay, Egon: The Unforgettable Dishes of my Life, 27999

Rood, Arnold: Edward Gordon Craig: A Bibliography, 26029

Roodis, Roland Joseph: The Law of Parks and Recreation Grounds, 27004

Rooff, Madeline: Voluntary Societies and Social Policy, 9139; A Hundred Years of Family Welfare: A Study of the Family Welfare Association [formerly Charity Organisation Society.] 1869–1969, 9140

Rook, Arthur: ed. Cambridge and its Contribution to Medicine, 20784

Rooke, M. A.: Anarchy and Apathy: Student Unrest 1968–1970, 9863, 22560

Rooke, Patrick John: The Growth of the Social Services, 8873; Agriculture and Industry, 19552

Rooney, David: Sir Charles Arden-Clarke, 12505; Kwame Nkrumah: A Political Kingdom in the Third World, 12749

Roos, Charles: Medical Reference Works, 21254

Roose-Evans, James: London Theatre, from the Globe to the National, 26157

Rooseboom, Maria: 'The History of the Microscope', 7154

Rooth, T. J. T.: 'Limits of Leverage: The Anglo-Danish Trade Agreement of 1933', 4806

Roots, Ivan Alan: English Constitutional History: A Select Bibliography, 629

Rosberg, C. G.: The Kenyatta Election: Kenya 1960–1961, 12829

Roscoe, Betty Joan: Economic Aspects of Milk Production in South West England, 1968–1969, 20658

Rose, Arnold Marshall: Union Solidarity, 6709; Theory and Method in the Social Sciences, 7930; Human Behaviour and Social Processes: An Interactionist Approach, 7931; ed. Mental Health and Mental Disorder: A Sociological Approach, 21755

Rose, Arthur Gordon: The Older Unemployed Man in Hull, 7011; The Struggle for Penal Reform, 10440; Schools for Young Offenders, 10506; 500 Borstal Boys, 10507

Rose, Brian: Modern Trends in Education, 22700

Rose, Chris: Crisis and Conservation: Conflict in the British Countryside, 20208

Rose, Clarkson: Beside the Seaside, 26276

Rose, E. James B.: Colour and Citizenship: A Report on British Race Relations, 10977; 'The Problems of Immigration and Integration', 11405

Rose, Ellen Cronan: The Novels of Margaret Drabble: Equivocal Figures, 25480

Rose, Ernest Arthur: Two Centuries of English Chintz, 1750–1950, 24129

Rose, Frank William: Personnel Management Law, 5468

Rose, Gordon Arthur: 'Trends in the Development of Criminology in Britain', 10198

Rose, Gordon: The Working Class, 9678

Rose, Hannah: 'The Immigration Act, 1970: A Case Study in the Work of Parliament', 11132; 'The Politics of Migration after the 1971 Act', 11133

Rose, Hilary: Social Welfare in the Inner City, 8910; The Housing Problem, 18692

Rose, John: ed. Technological Injury: The Effect of Technological Advances on the Environment, Life and Society, 19974

Rose, June: Changing Focus: The Development of Blind Welfare in Britain, 21927

Rose, Kenneth: Kings, Queens and Courtiers: Intimate Portraits of the Royal House of Windsor, 468; King George V, 473; The Later Cecils, 1390

Rose, Lionel: 'Rogues and Vagabonds': The Vagrant Underworld in Britain, 1815–1985, 18501

Rose, M. J.: Management Structure and Computerization, 5447

Rose, Michael Edward: The English Poor Law, 1780–1930, 4067

Rose, Muriel: Artist Potters in England, 24137

Rose, Norman Anthony: 'The Resignation of Anthony Eden', 1014. The Gentile Zionists: A Study in Anglo-Zionist Diplomacy, 1929–1939, 14295; 'Arab Rulers and Palestine, 1936: The British Reaction', 14309; ed. Baffy: The Diaries of Blanche Dugdale 1936–1947, 14310; Lewis Namier and Zionism, 14311; 'The Debate on Partition, 1937–1938: The Anglo-Zionist Aspect, 1. The Proposal, 14315; 2. The Withdrawal, 14316; 'Palestine's Role in Britain's Imperial Defence: An Aspect of Zionist Diplomacy, 1938–1939', 14317; 'The Moyne Assassination, November 1944: A Political Analysis', 14318

Rose, Peter: The Political Year, 1970, 276; 1971, 277

Rose, Phyllis: Woman of Letters: A Life of Virginia Woolf, 25897

Rose, R. Eric: The L.M.S. and the L.N.E.R. in Manchester, 16884

Rose, Richard: United Kingdom Facts, 67; 'Monarchy in Contemporary Political Culture', 450; 'The Making of Cabinet Ministers', 739; Ministers and Ministries: A Functional Analysis, 896; The Problems of Party Government, 1600; 'The Political Ideas of English Party Activists', 1606; 'The Bow Group's Role in British Politics', 1651; The Polls and the 1970 Election, 2270; Towards Normality—Public Opinion Polls in the 1979 Election, 2272; The British General Election of 1959, 2315; Must Labour Lose?, 2316; The Nationwide Competition for Votes: The 1983 British General Election, 2346; Governing without Consensus: An Irish Perspective, 2832; Northern Ireland: A Time of Choice, 2833; 'Ulster Politics: A Select Bibliography of Political Discord', 2923; ed. Fiscal Stress in Cities, 3270; British Progress and Decline, 3502; Regional Differentiation and Practical Unity in Western Nations, 5090; Public Employment in Western Nations, 6146; 'Classes sociales et partis politiques en Grande Bretagne dans une perspective historique', 9488; ed. The Management of Urban Change in Britain and Germany, 17901

Rose, Saul: 'The Labour Party and German Rearmament: A View from Transport House', 14219

Rose, W. K.: ed. The Letters of Wyndham Lewis, 25670

Rosecrance, Richard: 'Theory and Reality in the Anglo-American Alliances', 14078

Rosen, George: The History of Miners' Diseases: A Medical and Social Interpretation, 4117; A History of Public Health, 22014; From Medical Police to Social Medicine: Essays on the History of Health Care, 22015

Rosen, H.: Psychology of Union—Management Relations, 6799

Rosen, Lionel: Matrimonial Offences with Particular Reference to the Magistrates' Courts, 10006

Rosenau, H.: The Ideal City in its Architectural Evolution, 17974

Rosenbaum, Max: Drug Abuse and Drug Addiction, 22196

Rosenbaum, Naomi: 'Success in Foreign Policy: The British in Cyprus, 1878–1960', 12864

Rosenbaum, Stanford Patrick: ed. The Bloomsbury Group: A Collection of Memoirs, Commentary and Criticism, 23767

Rosenberg, Jerry M.: The Computer Prophets, 7092

Rosenberg, Joseph L.: 'The Consecration of Expediency: The Wartime Neutrality of Ireland', 2713

Rosenberg, Nathan: 'Government Economic Controls in the British Building Industry, 1945–1949', 6190; Economic Planning in the British Building Industry 1945–9, 6191, 18570

Rosenfeldt, Diane: Ken Russell: A Guide to References and Resources, 24684

Rosenhaft, Eve: 'Communism and Communists: Britain and Germany between the Wars', 1942

Rosenhead, Jonathan: The Technology of Police Control, 10733

Rosenheim, Sir Max: Social Aspects of Clinical Medicine, 21958

Rosenson, Alex: 'The Terms of the Anglo-American Financial Agreement', 3715

Rosenthal, Erwin Isaak Jakob: Contemporary Art in the Light of History, 23973

Rosenthal, Harold David: My Mad World of Opera, 24536; Opera at Covent Garden: A short History, 24562; Two Centuries of Opera at Covent Garden, 24563

Rosenthal, Joseph A.: A Numerical Finding List of British Command Papers Published 1832–1961/2, 203

Rosenzweig, L. W.: 'The Abdication of Edward VIII: A Psycho-Historical Explanation', 502

Rosevear, John A.: The Houses of the Workers, 18579

Roseveare, Henry: The Evolution of a British Institution: The Treasury, 805

Roshier, R. J.: Internal Migration in England and Wales 1851–1951, 7275

Rosie, George: The Ludwig Initiative: A Cautionary Tale of North Sea Oil, 6534

Rosing, Kenneth Earl: Optimal Development of the North Sea's Oil Fields: A Study in Divergent Government and Company Interests and their Reconciliation, 6504; Character of a Conurbation: A Computer Atlas of Birmingham and the Black Country, 17982

Roskill, Stephen Wentworth: Hankey: Man of Secrets, 1222; The Art of Leadership, 1569; The Navy at War, 1939–1945, 15016; The War at Sea, 1939–1945, 15017; H.M.S. Warspite: The Story of a Famous Battleship, 15029; A Merchant Fleet at War, 15132; Admiral of the Fleet Earl Beatty: The Last Naval Hero, 15249; Naval Policy between the Wars, 15333; The Strategy of Sea Power: Its Development and Application, 15341

Rosner, Charles: Printer's Progress: A Comparative Survey of the Craft of Printing, 1851–1951, Dedicated to 100 Years of British Printing by Balding and Mansell, Printers, 6632

Rosner, R.: Neue Städte in England, 18231

Ross of Bladensburg, Sir John: The Coldstream Guards, 1914–1918, 15609

Ross, Alan C. S.: The Forties: A Period Piece, 300

Ross, Alexander Michael: The Education of Childhood: The Primary School of Today, its Growth and Work, 23136

Ross, Arthur M.: 'Prosperity and British Industrial Relations', 5657

Ross, Charles: The Parliamentary Record, 1861–1939, 641

Ross, Donald J.: New Street Remembered: The Story of Birmingham's New Street Railway Station, 1854–1967, 16793

Ross, Doris: Walter de la Mare, 25475

Ross, George William: The Nationalization of Steel: One Step Forward, Two Steps Back?, 6575; Unions and Economic Crisis: Britain, West Germany and Sweden, 6827

Ross, Gordon: Television Jubilee: The Story of 25 Years of B.B.C. Television, 24846

Ross, J. M.: The Presbyterian Church of England: Index to the Proceedings of the General Assembly, 1921–1972, 12121; All our Future: A Longitudinal Study of Secondary Education, 22943

Ross, James A.: The Edinburgh School of Surgery after Lister, 21142

Ross, James Frederick Stanley: Parliamentary Representation, 2215; Elections and Electors, 2216; 'Women and Parliamentary Elections', 2261

Ross, Sir James Paterson: The Lives of the Fellows of the Royal College of Surgeons of England, Vol. 5: 1965–1973, 20844

Ross, Sir James Stirling: The National Health Service in Great Britain: An Historical and Descriptive Study, 21548

Ross, John: Thatcher and Friends: The Anatomy of the Tory Party, 1049

Ross, K. Graham: ed. The Foreign Office and the Kremlin: British Documents on Anglo-Soviet Relations, 1941–1945, 13956; ed.'Foreign Office Attitudes to the Soviet Union 1941–5', 13957

Ross, Murray G.: New Universities in the Modern World, 23423

Ross, Sir Ronald: Memoirs, 22366

Rossall: The Centenary History of Rossall School, 23072

Rossdale, M.: 'A Socialist Health Service', 21332

Rosselli, John: 'Studying Higher Education in Britain and America', 23396

Rossen, Janice: The World of Barbara Pym, 25779

Rosser, Colin: 'Relationships through Marriage in a Welsh Urban Area', 10044; The Family and Social Change: A Study of Family and Kinship in a South Wales Town, 10045

Rossiter, J. R.: 'The North Sea Storm Surge of 31st January and 1st February 1953', 20183

Rostas, Laszlo: The Burden of British Taxation, 1937/8 and 1941/2, 4830; Public Policy and the Tax System, 4831; Comparative Productivity in British and American Industry, 5990

Rostow, Nicholas: Anglo-French Relations, 1934–1936, 14258

Rotberg, Robert Irwin: The Rise of Nationalism in Central Africa: The Making of Malawi and Zambia, 1873–1964, 12776; 'The Federation Movement in British East and Central Africa 1889–1953', 12781

Roth, Andrew: Heath and the Heathmen, 1016; Enoch Powell: Tory Tribune, 1290

Roth, Cecil: Magna Biblioteca Anglo-Judaica: A Bibliographical Guide to Anglo-Jewish History, 11275; A History of the Jews in England, 11276, 12409; Essays and Portraits in Anglo-Jewish History, 12411; The Great Synagogue, London, 1690–1940, 12426; The Jewish Chronicle 1841–1941, 25164

Roth, G. K.: Fijian Way of Life, 12882

Roth, Gabriel Joseph: Paying for Roads: The Economics of Traffic Congestion, 17148; A Self-financing Road System, 17149; Parking Space for Cars: Assessing the Demand, 17384; Parking Space for Cars: Paying for Parking, 17385

Roth, Guenther: 'History and Sociology in the Work of Max Weber', 8077

Roth, Irene: Cecil Roth: Historian without Tears, 26811

Roth, M.: 'Old Age Mental Disorders in Newcastle-upon-Tyne: A Factorial Study of Medical Psychiatric and Social Characteristics', 8624

Rotha, Paul: Documentary Diary: An Informal History of the British Documentary Film, 1928–1939, 24615

Rothblatt, Sheldon: Tradition and Change in English Liberal Education: An Essay in History and Culture, 22439

Rothenstein, Elizabeth: Stanley Spencer, 24069

Rothenstein, Sir John Knewstub Maurice: British Art since 1900, 23967; Modern English Painters: Sickert to Smith, 23968; Modern English Painters: Lewis to Moore, 23969; Modern English Painters: Wood to Hockney, 23970; Autobiography: Summer's Lease 1901–1938, Brave Day, Hideous Night 1939–1965, Time's Thievish Progress, 23971; Augustus John, 24024; Stanley Spencer, The Man: Correspondence and Reminiscences, 24068

Rothman, Stanley: Roots of Radicalism: Jews, Christians and the New Left, 9861

Rothschild, Miriam: Dear Lord Rothschild: Birds, Butterflies and History, 26507

Rothstein, Andrew: British Foreign Policy and its Critics, 1830–1950, 13221; The Munich Conspiracy, 13739; When Britain invaded Soviet Russia: The Consul who rebelled, 13925

Rothwell, S. G.: Workers' Participation and Industrial Democracy, 6017

Rothwell, Victor Howard: British War Aims and Peace Diplomacy, 1914–1918, 13367.'The British Government and Japanese Military Assistance, 1914–1918', 13587; 'The Mission of Sir Frederick Leith-Ross to the Far East, 1935–1936', 13601

Rotner, Sheila: 'Design for a Women's Prison', 10451

Rouault, Georges Y.: The Handicapped and their Employment: A Statistical Study of the Situation in the Member States of the European Communities, 21900

Roubiczek, Paul: Across the Abyss: Diary Entries for the Year 1939–1940, 15169

Roucek, J. S.: 'Britain's Retreat from Aden and East of Suez', 13198

Rough, Douglas: Falklands: The Air War, 16093

Rous, Sir Stanley: Football Worlds: A Lifetime in Sport, 27085

Rouse, B. A.: 'Why Students "Turn on": Marijuana and other Drugs in an Undergraduate Male Population, 22218

Rouse, Ruth: ed. A History of the Ecumenical Movement, 1517–1948, 12316

Routh, Francis: Contemporary British Music: The Twenty Five Years from 1945 to 1970, 24284

Routh, Gerald Guy Cumming: Occupation and Pay in Great Britain, 1906–1960, 3891; 'The Structure of Collective Bargaining', 5636

Routh, Harold Victor: The Diffusion of English Culture outside England: A Problem for Post-war Reconstruction, 382

Routledge, Roberta A.: 'Statutory Control of Land Use on Environmental Grounds in England 1485–1945', 19943

Routley, Erik Reginald: The Music of Christian Hymnody: A Study of the Development of the Hymn Tune since the Reformation, with Special Reference to English Protestantism, 11924; The English Carol, 11925; English Religious Dissent, 12007; The Story of Congregationalism, 12049

Rowallan, Thomas Godfrey Polson Corbett [Baron]: Autobiography, 8516

Rowan, David Culloden: 'The Monetary System in the Fifties and Sixties', 4617; ed. International Handbook on Local Government Reorganization: Contemporary Developments, 3100

Rowan-Robinson, Henry: England, Italy, Abyssinia, 13781

Rowbotham, Ralph: Hospital Organization, 21393

Rowbotham, Sheila: Women's Liberation and Revolution:A Bibliography, 7629; A New World for Women: Stella Browne: Socialist Feminist, 7630; Women, Resistance and Revolution: A History of Women and Revolution in the Modern World, 7631; Women's Consciousness, Man's World, 7632; Hidden from History: 300 Years of Women's Oppression and the Fight against it, 7633; The Past before Us: Feminism in Action since the 1960s, 7634; Dutiful Daughters: Women Talk about their Lives, 7809

Rowe, A. P.: One Story of Radar, 15110; If the Gown Fits, 23386; 'Redbrick and Whitewash', 23387

Rowe, Albert W.: Making the Present: A Social and Economic History of Britain, 1918–1972, 3507

Rowe, David: Lead Manufacturing in Britain: A History, 6352

Rowe, E. A.: 'Broadcasting and the 1929 General Election', 2284, 24808

Rowe, Frederick Maurice: Two Lectures on the Development of the Chemistry of Commercial Synthetic Dyes, 1856–1938, 6476

Rowe, J. W. F.: Wages in Price and Theory, 3864

Rowe, Jane: Adoption and Fostering: Papers, 8112; Parents, Children and Adoption: A Handbook for Adoption Workers, 8327; Yours by Choice: A Guide for Adoptive Parents, 8328; Children who Wait: A Study of Children Needing Substitute Families, 8329

Rowe, Lyndon F.: Municipal Buses of the 1960s, 17273

Rowe, Thomas: ed. Gathering Moss. A Memoir of Owen Tweedy, 14438

Rowell, G.: The Repertory Movement: A History of Regional Theatre in Britain, 26159

Rowett Research Institute: Family Diet and Health in Pre-war Britain: A Dietary and Clinical Survey: Report to the Carnegie United Kingdom Trust, 20533

Rowland, Chris: The Economics of North Sea Oil Taxation, 6495

Rowland, D. P.: British Goods Wagons from 1887 to the Present Day, 17096

Rowland, Jon: Community Decay, 9369

Rowland, Keith T.: Steam at Sea: A History of Steam Navigation, 16498

Rowland, Peter: Lloyd George, 1018

Rowlands, Edward: 'The Politics of Regional Administration: The Establishment of the Welsh Office', 950

Rowlands, Marie Bernadette: The West Midlands from AD 1000, 5231

Rowles, George E.: The 'Line' is On: A Centenary Souvenir of the London Society of Compositors, 1848–1948, 6850

Rowley, Charles Kershaw: The British Monopolies Commission, 5514; Steel and Public Policy, 6586; Welfare Economics: A Liberal Restatement, 9055; 'The Political Economy of British Education', 23211

Rowley, Gwyn: 'The Greater London Council Elections of 1964 and 1967: A Study in Electoral Geography', 3298; 'Coloured Immigrants within the City: An Analysis of Housing and Travel Preferences', 11476

Rowley, J. C. R.: 'Fixed Capital Formation in the British Economy, 1956–1965', 4738

Rowley, [Richard] Trevor: ed. The Oxford Region, 18069, 18982; ed. Planning and the Historic Environment, 18958

Rowntree, Benjamin Seebohm: Poverty and Progress: A Social Survey of York, 9017; Poverty and the Welfare State: A Third Social Survey of York Dealing only with Economic Questions, 9018; British Agriculture: Lectures on Housing: The Warburton Lectures for 1914, 18618; Portrait of a City's Housing, 18619; The Principles of Future Policy, 19451; The Agricultural Dilemma, 19452; Food Production in Western Europe: An Economic Survey of Agriculture in Six Countries, 19453; Mixed Farming and Muddled Thinking: An Analysis of Current Agricultural Policy, 19454; English Life and Leisure: A Social Study, 26915

Rowntree, Griselda: 'Birth Control in Britain', 7502; 'The Resort to Divorce in England and Wales, 1858–1957', 9987; 'Some Aspects of Marriage Breakdown in Britain during the Last Thirty Years', 9991; 'Early Childhood in Broken Families', 9992

Rowntree, John A.: Internal Migration: A Study of the Frequency of Movement of Migrants, 7267

Rowntree, John Pickering: The Classical Organ in Britain, 1955–1974, 24394

Rowse, Alfred Leslie: All Souls and Appeasement, 13708; Appeasement: A Study in Political Decline, 1933–1934, 13710; Homosexuals in History. A Study of Ambivalence in Society, Literature and the Arts, 10850; St Austell: Church, Town, Parish, 18113; 'Mushroom universities', 23302; The Poet Auden: A Personal Memoir, 25366; A Man of the Thirties, 26812

Roy, Emil: British Drama since Shaw, 26178

Roy, Ian: ed. Handbook of British Chronology, 69; ed. War and Society: A Yearbook of Military History, 14700

Roy, Walter: 'Membership Participation in the National Union of Teachers', 9842; The Teachers' Union: Aspects of Policy and Organisation in the National Union of Teachers, 1950–1966, 22708

Royal Aeronautical Society: Airships and their Maritime Implications, 17539

Royal Agricultural Society of England: A Survey of Agricultural Libraries in England and Scotland, 19400; County Agricultural Surveys, 19483; 1—A Survey of the Agriculture of Kent, 19484; 2—A Survey of the Agriculture of Sussex, 19485; 3—A Survey of the Agriculture of Northumberland, 19486; 4—A Survey of the Agriculture of Cheshire, 19487; 5—A Survey of the Agriculture of Hertfordshire, 19488; 6—A Survey of the Agriculture of Yorkshire, 19489; 7—A Survey of the Agriculture of Suffolk, 19490; E.E.C. Policy and British Agriculture in the 1980s: Conference Papers, 12 March 1980, 19655

Royal Bank of Scotland: The Royal Bank of Scotland 1727–1977, 4523

Royal College of Obstetrics and Gynaecologists and Population Investigation Joint Committee: Maternity in Great Britain: A Survey of Social and Economic Aspects of Pregnancy, 7482

Royal College of Physicians and Others: A Review of the Medical Services in Great Britain: Report of a Committee, 22099

Royal College of Physicians of London: Air Pollution and Health: Summary and Report on Air Pollution, 20063; Portraits Catalogue II, 20821; Smoking and Health, a Report, 20831; The Roll of the Royal College of Physicians of London, 20896; Fluoride, Teeth and Health: A Report, 22397

Royal College of Surgeons of England: A Record of the Years from 1901–1950, 20785; Lives of the Fellows of the Royal College of Surgeons of England, 20899

Royal College of Veterinary Surgeons: A Career as a Veterinary Surgeon, 9825

Royal Commission on Betting, Lotteries and Gaming: 1949–1951: Report, 27113

Royal Commission on Equal Pay, 1944–1946: Report, 7771

Royal Commission on Gambling: Cmnd 7200, 27114

Royal Commission on Local Government in England 1966–1969, 66

Royal Commission on Local Government in Scotland 1966–1969, 3168

Royal Commission on Marriage and Divorce: 1951–55. Cmnd 9687. Parliamentary Papers, xxii (1955–56), 9920

Royal Commission on the Law Relating to Mental Illness and Mental Deficiency, 1954–1957, 21748

Royal Commission on the National Health Service: Report, 21667

Royal Forestry Society of England, Northern Ireland and Wales: A Book of Trees: An Anthology of Trees and Woodlands, 19762

Royal Historical Society: Annual Bibliography of British and Irish History, 416

Royal Institute of International Affairs: The British Caribbean: A Brief Political and Economic Survey, 13003; British Far Eastern Policy, 13577; Great Britain and Palestine, 1915–1945, 14280; Great Britain and Egypt, 1914–1951, 14398

Royal Institute of Public Administration: British Public Administration: Ripalis, 54; Policy and Practice: the Experience of Government, 772; Parliament and the Executive, 773; Select Bibliography, 840; Health Services in Britain, A Select Bibliography, 21547

Royal School of Mines: Centenary of the Royal School of Mines, 1851–1951: Some Notes on the History of the School, 23237

Royal Society of Health: The G.P. and Preventative Medicine: Report of the Joint Meeting on the Role of the General Practitioner in Preventative Medicine, 22076

Royal Society of London: Emigration of Scientists from the United Kingdom: Report of a Committee Appointed by the Council of the Royal Society, 7307; British National Committee for Geography: Cartographic Activity in Great Britain: Report Two, 26706

Royal Town Planning Institute: Town Planners and their Future, 17825; Research Committee. Planning Research: A Register of Research for all those concerned with Town and Country Planning, 17826

Royden, A. Maude: 'Report of the Royal Commission on Venereal Diseases', 21970

Roydhouse, Eric: Prices and Wages Freeze: A Narrative Guide to the Prices and Incomes Act 1966—Together with the text of the Act, 3809, 5021; Matrimonial Proceedings before Magistrates, 10007

Royle, Edward: Modern Britain, a Social History, 303

Royle, Trevor: The Best Years of their Lives: The National Service Experience 1945–63, 16072; James and Jim: A Biography of James Kennaway, 25610

Rozen, Marvin E.: 'Investment Control in Post-War Britain, 1945–1955', 4739

Rubenstein, M.: Equal Pay for Work of Equal Value, 7783

Rubin, B.: The Great Powers in the Middle

East: The Road to the Cold War, 13811

Rubin, Gerry R.: 'The Origins of Industrial Tribunals: Munitions Tribunals During the First World War', 4150; War, Law and Labour: The Munitions Acts, State Regulation and the Unions, 1915–1921, 5579

Rubinstein, David: The Labour Left and Domestic Policy 1945–1950, 1733; 'Labour Governments and Comprehensive Schooling, 1945–51', 22925; The Evolution of the Comprehensive School, 1926–1966, 22954; Leisure, Transport and the Countryside, 26950

Rubinstein, W. D.: ed. Wealth and the Wealthy in the Modern World, 3783; ed. Men of Property: The Very Wealthy in Britain since the Industrial Revolution, 3784, 9754; ed. Wealth and Inequality in Britain, 3785; 'Wealth, Elites and the Class Structure of Modern Britain', 9502

Rubner, Alexander: Fringe Benefits: The Golden Chains, 3892

Ruck, Sydney Kenneth: The Government of Greater London, 3279, 18327; 'A Policy for Old Age', 8627; London Government and the Welfare Services, 9134; Intro. Paterson on Prisons: Being the Collected Papers of Sir Alexander Paterson, 10413; Municipal Entertainment and the Arts in Greater London, 27012

Rudd, Ernest: Graduate Study and After, 5970, 9872; The Highest Education: A Study of Graduate Education in Britain, 9873, 22571; A New Look at Postgraduate Failure, 9874

Ruddy, Sheila Ann: Employment Problems in a County Town: A Study of Bridgnorth, Shropshire, 7015; Industrial Relocation in Birmingham, 18013

Rudig, Wolfgang: 'The Withered "Greening" of British Politics: A Study of the Ecology Party', 1855

Rudlin, W. A.: The Growth of Fascism in Great Britain, 2016

Rudner, Martin: 'The Organisation of the British Military Administration in Malaya 1946–1948', 12928

Rudolph, Mildred de Montjoie: Everybody's Children: The Story of the Church of England Children's Society, 1921–48, 8330

Rudzio, W.: 'Grossbritannien als Sozialistische Besatzungsmacht in Deutschland: Aspekte des deutsch-britischen Verhältnisses 1945–1948', 14212

Rugby: Rugby since Arnold: A History of Rugby School from 1842, 23073

Rugby: Rugby, 23074

Ruge, Friedrich: Scapa Flow 1919. Das Ende der deutschen Flotte, 15303

Ruine, Joan Jane: Anglo-French Diplomatic Relations, 1923–1936, 14252

Ruitenbeek, Hendrik Marinus: ed. Homosexuality: A Changing Picture, 10865

Rumbold, Sir Anthony: Watershed in India, 1914–1922, 13133

Rumpf, Erhard: Nationalism and Socialism in Twentieth Century Ireland, 2728

Rumsby, Thomas Walter: The English Grammar School, 22993

Runcie, Robert: ed. Cathedral and City: St Albans Ancient and Modern, 18112

Runciman, Sir Steven [i.e. Sir James Cochran Stevenson]: The White Rajahs: The History of Sarawak from 1841 to 1946, 12944

Runciman, Walter Garrison: ed. Philosophy, Politics and Society, 7926; Sociology in its Place, and other Essays, 7998; ed. Philosophy, Politics and Society, 8778; Relative Deprivation and Social Justice: A Study of Attitudes to Social Inequality in Twentieth Century England, 8780, 9060, 9486; Social Science and Political Theory, 8781; A Treatise on Social Theory, 8782; '"Embourgeoisement", Self-rated Class and Party Preference',9485; 'Race and Social Stratification', 11020; 'Status Consistency, Relative Deprivation and Attitudes to Immigrants', 11414

Rundle, Raymond Norman: Britain's Economic and Social Development from 1700 to the Present Day, 3441

Runnymede Trust: Briefing Papers. No. 6: Ethnic Minorities in Britain: A Select Bibliography, 11518

Rupp, [Ernest] Gordon: I Seek My Brethren: Bishop George Bell and the German Churches, 11722; A History of the Methodist Church in Great Britain, 12066

Rusama, Jaakko: Unity and Compassion: Moral Issues in the Life and Thought of George K. A. Bell, 11723

Rusby, Norman Lloyd: Recent Advances in Respiratory Tuberculosis, 21160; Symposium of Tuberculosis, 21161

Ruse, Michael: The Philosophy of Biology, 26520

Rush, Michael: Parliament and the Public, 548; The Cabinet and Policy Formation, 727

Rushbrooke, James Henry: Baptists in Britain, 12022; James Henry Rushbrooke, 1870–1947: A Baptist Greatheart, 12030

Rushton G. A.: 100 Years of Progress: Hampshire County Council 1889–1989, 3356

Rushton, James: ed. Education for the Professions, 22425

Rusinko, Susan: British Drama 1950 to the Present: A Critical History, 25909; Tom Stoppard, 25990

Rusk, Robert H.: The Training of Teachers in Scotland: A Historical Overview, 9849

Rusk, Robert Robertson: A History of Infant Education, 23135

Russell, Anthony John: The Clerical Profession, 11678; The Country Parish, 19100

Russell, B. S.: 'The British Steel Industry', 6582

Russell, Bertrand Arthur William [Earl]: Portraits from Memory and other Essays, 325; Autobiography, 26862; My Philosophical Development, 26864

Russell, Brian Fitzgerald: ed. St John's Hospital for Diseases of the Skin, 1863–1963, 21475

Russell, Sir Edward John: A History of Agricultural Science in Great Britain, 1620–1954, 19695

Russell, Gordon: Designer's Trade: An Autobiography of Gordon Russell, 24147

Russell, J. L.: Housing amidst Civil Unrest, 18498

Russell, John: Matthew Smith, 24066; Henry Moore, 24194; Henry Green: Nine Novels and an Unpacked Bag, 25555

Russell, K.: 'Politics of Accountability: Disarming Complains against the Police', 10722

Russell, Leonard: The Pearl of Days: An Intimate Memoir of the Sunday Times 1822–1972, 25155

Russell, Margaret: ed. Nutritional Problems in a Changing World, 20553

Russell, Paul F.: Man's Mastery of Malaria, 22365

Russell, Philippa: The Wheelchair Child, 21898

Russell, Robert: 'Are Maternity and Child Welfare Schemes Proceeding on Right Lines?', 8331

Russell, Ronald: The Canals of East England, 16406

Russell, Thomas: Philharmonic Project, 24540, 24549; Philharmonic Decade, 24548

Russell, W. T.: 'Deaths by Violence, 1837–1937, 10291

Russell, Wilfrid William: New Lives for Old: The Story of the Cheshire Homes, 9148; Forgotten Skies: The Story of the Air Force in India and Burma, 15944

Russell-Smith, Dame Enid: Modern Bureaucracy: The Home Civil Service, 869

Russett, Bruce Martin: Community and Contention: Britain and America in the Twentieth Century, 14009

Rust, William: The Story of the Daily Worker, 25138

Rustin, Michael: 'Different Conceptions of Party: Labour's Constitutional Debates', 1772

Rutherford, Andrew: Prison and the Reductionist Challenge, 10384

Rutherford, Dame Margaret: An Autobiography, 26096

Rutherford: The Story of Rutherford Grammar School, Newcastle-upon-Tyne, 23000

Rutter, Ernest George: Sick Pay, 8960

Rutter, Michael: Education, Health and Behaviour, 8332, 22841; Psychiatric Study, 8333; Helping Troubled Children, 8334; ed. Infant Autism: Concepts, Characteristics and Treatment, 8335; Maternal Deprivation Reassessed, 8336; et al. Neuropsychiatric Study in Childhood, 8337; Changing Youth in a Changing Society: Patterns of Adolescent Development, 8338; Fifteen Thousand Hours: Secondary Schools and their Effects on Children, 8339; Stress, Coping and Development in Children, 8340; Depression in Young People: Developmental and Clinical Perspectives, 8341; ed. Child Psychiatry: Modern Approaches, 8342; The Child with Delayed Speech, 8343; Cycles of Disadvantage: A Review of Research, 8344; Juvenile Delinquency: Trends and Perspectives, 10603; 'Children of West Indian

Immigrants: 1. Rates of Behavioural Deviance and Psychiatric Disorder', 11267; 'Children of West Indian Immigrants: 3. Home Circumstances and Family Patterns', 11268; Lead versus Health: Sources and Effects of Low Level Lead Exposure, 20170

Rutter, Owen: Red Ensign: A History of Convoy, 15135

Ryan, Alan: Property and Political Theory, 3789; The Philosophy of the Social Sciences, 8038; ed. The Philosophy of Social Explanation, 8039; Bertrand Russell: A Political Life, 26871

Ryan, Alfred Patrick: Mutiny at the Curragh, 2735; Lord Northcliffe, 25095

Ryan, Sir Andrew: The Last of the Dragomans, 13305

Ryan, Cornelius: A Bridge too Far, 14955

Ryan, Desmond: The Rising, 2744; The Invisible Army: A Story of Michael Collins, 3027; James Connolly, His Life, Work and Writings, 3036

Ryan, Gerard: An Outline of the Law relating to Common Land and Public Access to the Countryside, 26935

Ryan, Henry B.: 'Anglo-American Relations during the Polish Crisis in 1945: A Study of British Efforts to shape American Policy toward the Soviet Union', 13908; The Vision of Anglo-America: The US—UK Alliance and the emerging Cold War, 1943–1946, 14106; 'A New Look at Churchill's "Iron Curtain" Speech', 14107

Ryan, M. C.: 'A Pressure Group Prepares for Europe: The Country Landowners Association, 1961–72', 19653

Ryan, M.: 'Health Centre Policy in England and Wales', 21333, 22085

Ryan, M.: 'Structure Planning in Dockland', 18310

Ryan, Mick: The Acceptable Pressure Group: Inequality in the Penal Lobby: A Case Study of the Howard League and R.A.P, 10393

Ryan, Neil Joseph: The Making of Modern Malaysia, 12911

Ryan, Paul B.: The Lusitania Disaster: An Episode in Modern Warfare and Diplomacy, 14662

Ryan, Selwyn D.: Race and Nationalism in Trinidad and Tobago: A Study of Decolonisation in a Multiracial Society, 13070

Ryan, T. M.: Day Nursery Provision under the Health Service, 21692

Ryan, Victoria: Historical Directory of British Trade Unions, 6686

Ryan, W. J. L.: 'Wage Claims and the Pace of Inflation [1948–1951]', 3888

Ryder, Chris: The R.U.C, 2939

Ryder, Judith: Modern English Society: History and Structure, 1850–1970, 7618

Ryder, Rowland: Oliver Leese, 14766

Ryder, Sue: Child of My Love: An Autobiography, 9149

Rydz, David L.: The Parliamentary Agents: a History, 634; 'The Formation of the Great Ouse Water Authority', 20107

Ryle, Anthony: Neurosis in the Ordinary Family: A Psychiatric Survey, 10071; 'Marriage and Neurosis in a Working Class Population', 21774

Ryle, C. B. E.: 'Forestry in the Economic Development of Wales', 19725

Ryle, George: Forest Service: The First Forty Five Years of the Forestry Commission of Great Britain, 19743

Ryle, Michael: ed. The Commons in the Seventies, 636; 'Parliamentary Control of Expenditure and Taxation', 665

Rymill, John: Southern Lights: The Official Account of the British Graham Land Expedition, 1934–37, 27216

Ryott, David: John Barran's of Leeds, 1851–1951, 6240

Ryrie, Alexander C.: Getting a Trade: A Study of Apprentices' Experience of Apprenticeship, 5961; Routes and Results: a Study of the Later Years of Schooling, 23619

Rée, Harry: Educator Extraordinary: The Life and Achievements of Henry Morris 1889–1961, 23214

SDP/Liberal Alliance: Let's Get Europe Working Together: Manifesto of the SDP/Liberal Alliance for the European Elections, 1851; Britain United: The Time Has Come: The SDP/Liberal Alliance Programme for Government, 1852

Sabatino, Richard A.: Housing in Great Britain, 1945–49, 18629

Sabin, Philip A. G.: The Third World War Scare in Britain: A Critical Analysis, 13534

Sabine, Basil Ernest Vyvyan: A History of Income Tax, 4859; British Budgets in Peace and War, 1932–1945, 4903

Sabry, H. Z.: Sovereignty for Sudan, 14420

Sachs, A.: 'The Centenary of British Military Pathology', 21007

Sachs, Curt: The History of Musical Instruments, 7073

Sacks, Benjamin: J. Ramsay MacDonald in Thought and Action, 1032; 'The Independent Labour Party and World War Peace Objectives', 13545

Sadek, S. E. M.: The Balance Point between Local Autonomy and National Control, 3205

Sadie, Stanley: ed. The New Grove Dictionary of Music and Musicians, 24257

Sadler, Lynn Veach: Margaret Drabble, 25482

Sadler, Peter: Regional Income Multipliers: The Anglesey Study, 5347

Sadler, Philip: Social Research on Automation, 7248; 'Sociological Aspects of Skill', 9714

Saerchinger, Cesar: The Voice of Europe, 24745

Saettler, Paul: A History of Instructional Technology, 22770

Safavi, H. A.: Rail Commuting to Central London, 16287

Sagalyn, L. B.: The Affluent Suburb, 18295

Sagar, Keith Milsom: Ted Hughes: A Bibliography 1946–80, 25578; The Art of Ted Hughes, 25579; The Achievement of Ted Hughes, 25580; The Art of D. H. Lawrence, 25644; D. H. Lawrence: A Calendar of his Works, 25645; The Life of D. H. Lawrence: An Illustrated Biography, 25646

Sahm, Ulrich: 'Britain and Europe 1950', 14141

Sailes, George W.: At the Centre: The Story of Methodism's Central Missions, 12108

Sainsbury, Anya: Ballet Rambert: 50 Years and On, 24242

Sainsbury, Eric: Social Diagnosis in Casework, 8743; Social Work with Families, 8744; The Personal Social Services, 8745

Sainsbury, K: 'The Constitution: Some Disputed Points', 612

Sainsbury, Keith: 'British Policy and German Unity at the End of the Second World War', 14189; The North African Landings, 1942: A Strategic Decision, 14906

Sainsbury, Peter: Suicide in London—An Ecological Study, 10815, 21884

Sainsbury, R. M.: Russell, 26875

Saint, Andrew, A Change of Heart: English Architecture since the War—a Policy for Protection, 23902

Sainsbury, Sally: Registered as Disabled, 21894; Measuring Disability, 21895

St. Aubin de Teran, Lisa: Off the Rails: Memoirs of a Train Addict, 16804

St. Bernard History Group: A Short History of St. Bernard, 19200

St.John, Christopher: Ethel Smyth: A Biography, 24365

St John, Henry: 'Ecumenical Survey—Anglo Catholic Hopes', 12340

St. John, John: To the War with Waugh, 15190

St John, Nancy Hoyt: Social Class and the Urban School: The Impact of Pupil Background on Teachers and Principals, 22826

St. John-Stevas, Norman Henry Anthony: The Two Cities, 1528; The Right to Life, 10810

St. Vincent, Erwin: ed. Cultures in Conflict: Perspectives on the Snow-Leavis Controversy, 23749

Saint, Andrew: ed. Politics and the People of London: The London County Council 1889–1965, 3281

Sainthill, Loudon: Churchill: The Walk with Destiny, 988

Sainty, John Christopher: Leaders and Whips in the House of Lords, 1783–1964, 668; Officers of the House of Lords, 1485–1971, 669

Sales, H.: The Local Ombudsman: A Review of the First Five Years, 3252

Sales, Peter M.: 'W. M. Hughes and the Chanak Crisis of 1922', 12614

Salewicz, Chris: McCartney: The Definitive Biography, 24509

Salford Transport Geography Group: Implications of the 1985 Transport Bill . . . Salford, 16270

Salisbury General Hospital: Salisbury 200: The Bicentenary of Salisbury Infirmary 1766–1966, 21467

Sallis, H.: 'Joint Consultations in the Electricity Supply Industry, 1949–1959', 5645; 'Labor/Management Co-operative Committees in Britain's Electricity Supply Industry', 5646

Salmon, Charles Edgar: Flora of Surrey, 26560

Salmon, Eric: Granville Barker: A Secret Life, 26127; The Dark Journey: John Whiting as Dramatist, 25995

Salmon, Thomas: The First Hundred Years: The Story of Rugby Football in Cornwall, 27034

Salsbury, John: 'And Is There Honey Still-?': A Look at Rural Deprivation, 19084

Salt, John: Housing and Migration of Labour in England and Wales, 18552

Salter, Elizabeth: Helpmann: The Authorized Biography of Sir Robert Helpmann CBE, 24236

Salter, James Arthur, Baron: Memoirs of a Public Servant, 922; Slave of the Lamp, 923; Recovery: The Second Effort, 3576; Security: Can We Retrieve it?, 13759

Salvation Army Yearbook: 1906+, 12125

Salvidge, Stanley: Salvidge of Liverpool: Behind the Political Scenes, 1890–1928, 1571

Salwak, Dale: Kingsley Amis: A Reference Guide, 25353; John Braine and John Wain: A Reference Guide, 25409; ed. Philip Larkin: The Man and His Work, 25626; ed. The Life and Work of Barbara Pym, 25780; John Wain, 25847

Sameraweera, Vijaya: Sri Lanka, 12981

Samphier, M.: 'The Contours of Solidarity: Social Stratification and Industrial Relations in Shipbuilding', 9663

Sampson, Anthony: Macmillan: A Study in Ambiguity, 1035; The Money Lenders, 4447; The New Anatomy of Britain, 7609

Sams, Kenneth Ian: 'A Case Study of a Shipbuilding Redundancy in Northern Ireland', 5394; 'Les Relations Professionelles en Grande Bretagne: Perspectives d'un Nouveau Systeme', 5726; ed. British Trade Unionism: Select Documents, 6744

Samson, Edward: Men, Manners and Molars, 22406

Samuel, Herbert Louis, Viscount: Memoirs, 1306; The War and Liberty, 1307

Samuel, Raphael: 'The Lost World of British Communism', 1952; 'Classi e Coscienza di Classe', 9471; ed. Miners, Quarrymen and Saltworkers, 9639; 'The Long Pursuit: Studies in the Government's Slum Clearance Programme', 18416; ed. Village Life and Labour, 19120; 'British Marxist Historians 1880–1980', 26735

Samuel, Susan: Consumer Bibliography, 20455

Samuels, Harry: Redundancy Payments: An Annotation and Guide to the Redundancy Payments Act, 1965, 6976; The County Council: What It Is and what it does, 3196

Samuels, Stuart: 'The Left Book Club', 1717, 24964

Samuelson, G. D.: Motorways and Industry: The West Midland Conurbation, 17114

Sanchez, Denise: Feminist Periodicals 1855–1984: An Annotated Critical Bibliography of British, Irish, Commonwealth and International Titles, 25190

Sandall, Robert: The History of the Salvation Army, 12126

Sandberg, Lars G.: Lancashire in Decline: A Study in Entrepreneurship, Technology and International Trade, 6450

Sanders, Andrew: 'British Colonial Policy and the Role of the Amerindians in the Politics of the Nationalist Period in British Guiana', 13040

Sanders, Charles: ed. W. Somerset Maugham: An Annotated Bibliography of Writings about him, 25704

Sanders, Conrad: The Social Stigma of Occupations: The Lower Grade Worker in Service Organisations, 5920

Sanders, David: 'Government Popularity and the Falklands War: A Reassessment, 2352; The Technical Development of Modern Aviation, 17518

Sanders, Harold George: An Outline of British Crop Husbandry, 19697

Sanders, Lee: ed. Conditions of Illusion: Papers from the Women's Movement, 7769

Sanders, Michael L.: 'The Labour Spain Committee: Labour Party Policy and the Spanish Civil War', 13991; British Propaganda during the First World War, 1914–1918, 15210; 'Wellington House and British Propaganda during the First World War', 15211

Sanderson, G. N.: 'The "Swing of the Pendulum" in British General Elections 1832–1966', 2249

Sanderson, J. Michael: 'Research and the Firm in British Industry 1919–39', 7034; 'The Universities and Industry in England, 1919–1939', 23353; 'The University of London and Industrial Progress', 23354; The Universities and British Industry, 1850–1970, 23355

Sanderson, Michael: From Irving to Olivier: A Social History of the Acting Profession in England 1880–1980, 26003

Sanderson, Michael: The Sea Chart: An Historical Survey based on the Collections in the National Maritime Museum, with an Introduction by G. S. Ritchie, 26708

Sanderson, Stewart: Wordmaps: A Dialect Atlas of England, 23793; Studies in Linguistic Geography: The Dialects of English in Britain and Ireland, 23794

Sandes, Edward Warren Caulfield: The Military Engineer in India, 14613; The Royal Engineers in Egypt and the Sudan, 15630; From Pyramid to Pagoda: The Story of the West Yorkshire Regiment in the War 1939–1945 and Afterwards, 15749

Sandford, Cedric Thomas: Economic Policy, 3666; Taxing Personal Wealth: An Analysis of Capital Taxation in the United Kingdom: History, Present Structure and Future Possibilities, 3781; Economics of Public Finance: An Economic Analysis of Government Expenditure and Revenue in the United Kingdom, 4585; Tax-Policy Making in the United Kingdom: A Study of Rationality, Ideology and Politics, 4825; Taxing Inheritance and Capital Gains, 4826; Costs and Benefit of V.A.T. 1981, 4827; An Accessions Tax, 4828; Taxation and Social Policy, 8916

Sandford, Gregory: Grenada: The Untold Story, 13081

Sandford, Jeremy: Prostitutes: Portraits of People in the Sexploitation Business, 10853; Gypsies, 11350; Down and Out in Britain, 18502; Cathy Come Home, 18503; Synthetic Fun: A Short Soft Glance, 27013

Sandhu, Kernial Singh: Indians in Malaya: Some Aspects of their Immigration and Settlement (1786–1957), 12917

Sandiford, Keith A. P.: 'The Professionalization of Modern Cricket', 27100

Sandison, Francis G.: Profit Sharing and other Share Acquisition Schemes, 6036

Sands, Bobby: One Day in my Life, 2893

Sands, Percy Cooper: A History of Pocklington School, East Yorkshire, 1514–1950, 23070

Sandys, Ruth: The Underground and Alternative Press in Britain during 1974: A Bibliographical Guide, 25201

Sanger, Clyde: Stitches in Time: The Commonwealth and World Politics, 12522

Sangster, Paul: A History of the Free Churches, 12009; Dr Sangster, 12096

Sansom, Basil: ed. Race and Social Difference, 11019

Sansom, Michael C.: Worship in the Church of England, 11605

Sant, Morgan Eugene Cyril: Industrial Movement and Regional Development: The British Scene, 5087; Regional Disparities, 5088; The Industrial Development of East Anglia, 5155

Sara, E. T.: 'Progress in the United Kingdom Iron and Steel Industry', 6555

Saran, Rene: Policy Making in Secondary Education: A Case Study, 22781, 22834

Sargeant, A. V.: Men out of Work: A Study of Unemployment in Three English Towns, 7016

Sargent, John Richard: 'Recent Growth Experience in the Economy of the United Kingdom', 3659

Sargent, Malcolm: Agricultural Co-operation, 19466

Sargent, William Ewart: ed. Adolescent Problems: Their Nature and Understanding, 10578; The Unquiet Mind: The Autobiography of a Physician in Psychological Medicine, 20880

Sarkar, S.: Modern India, 1885–1947, 13111

Sarkissian, A. O.: ed. Studies in Diplomatic History and Historiography in Honour of G. P. Gooch, 13786

Sarlvik, Bo: 'Partisanship and Policy Choice: Issue Preference in the British Electorate, February 1974', 2332; 'Angels in Plastic: The Liberal Surge in 1974', 2333

Sarre, Philip: The Future of Cities, 17912

Sartorius, N.: Measurement and Classification of Psychiatric Symptoms, 21856

Sassoon, Siegfried: Memoirs of an Infantry Officer, 14487

Satow, Sir Ernest Mason: A Guide to Diplomatic Practice, 13322

Saul, Samuel Berrick: ed. Social Theory and Economic Change, 7981

Saundby, Sir Robert: Air Bombardment: The

Story of its Development, 15980; Early Aviation: Man Conquers the Air, 17512

Saundercock, Victor G.: Harbour Vessels, 16666

Saunders, Christopher: Pay Inequalities in the European Community, 3876

Saunders, Hilary Aidan St George: The Red Beret: The Story of the Parachute Regiment at War, 1940–1945, 15707; Per Ardua: The Rise of British Air Power, 1911–1939, 15797; The Royal Air Force 1939–1945, 15808, 15809

Saunders, John Beecroft: The Law of Education, 22629

Sauvy, Alfred: 'Le Renversement du Courant d'Immigration Seculaire', 11400

Savage, Christopher Ivor: An Economic History of Transport, 3423, 16200, 16201; Inland Transport, 16199, 16436

Savage, David W.: 'Ireland and British Politics, 1914–1921', 2983

Savage, Donald C.: Government and Labour in Kenya 1895–1963, 12836

Savage, Eric: Advertising, 4317

Savage, Leonard George Grimson: The Market in Art, 23942

Savage, Sir William George: The Making of Our Towns, 17750; Rural Housing, 17751, 18576, 19051; 'Housing Problems and Rural Districts', 19052; The Bacteriological Examination of Food and Water, 20630; Food and Public Health, 20631; The Bacteriology of Canned Meat and Fish, 20632; Canned Foods in Relation to Health, 20633; Food Poisoning and Food Infections, 20634; Report on the Methods Used for the Inspection of Canned Foods and their Reliability for this purpose, 20635; The Food and Drugs Act, 1938, 20638

Savile, Jimmy: As it Happens: Jimmy Savile OBE: His Autobiography, 24916

Saville, George Edward: The Parish of Spernhall: A History, 19356

Saville John: ed. Dictionary of Labour Biography, 45, 1661; ed. Essays in Labour History, 2nd series 1886–1923, 1032, 1667, 1893, 6824; ed. Essays in Labour History in Memory of G. D. H. Cole, 1666; The Labour Movement in Britain: A Commentary, 1687; ed. Essays in Labour History, 3rd series, 1918–1939, 1668, 6824, 13678; 'The XXth Congress and the British Communist Party',1933; Rural Depopulation in England and Wales 1851–1951, 19064

Saville, M. V.: From Palace to College: An Illustrated Account of Queen Mary College (University of London), 23529

Saville, Richard: ed. The Economic Development of Modern Scotland 1950–1980, 5278

Savings Bank Institute: Trustee Savings Bank Legislation and Management, 4338

Savory, Sir Douglas: 'Chamberlain, Macleod and the Facts', 983

Savory, Roger: Casement: The Flawed Hero, 3017

Saw, Reginald C. Wykeham: The Bank of England 1694–1944, and its Buildings Past and Present, 4481

Saward, Dudley: The Bomber's Eye, 15979; Bernard Lovell: A Biography, 26422

Saward, Michael: Christian Youth Groups, 8542

Sawers, David: The Sources of Intervention, 7140; From Monopoly to Competition, 24868

Sawyer, L. A.: Sailing Ship to Supertanker: The Hundred Year Story of British Esso and its Ships, 6510, 16540; The Cape Run: The Story of the Union Castle Service to South Africa, 16539; Tankers, 16601

Sawyer, Michael C.: 'The Earnings of Manual Workers: A Cross-Section Analysis', 3929; 'The Concentration of British Manufacturing', 5530; 'Concentration in British Manufacturing Industry', 5531

Saxton, Clifford Clive: The Beveridge Report Criticised, 9036

Sayer, A. P.: Army Radar, 15111

Sayer, George: Jack: C. S. Lewis and his Times, 25663

Sayers, Richard Sidney: The Vicissitudes of an Export Economy: Britain since 1880, 3481, 4815; A History of Economic Change in England, 1880–1939, 3482; 'The Springs of Technical Progress in Britain, 1919–1939', 3550; Modern Banking, 4398; Twentieth Century English Banking, 4399; The Bank of England, 1819–1944, 4480; Lloyds Bank in the History of English Banking, 4498; Gilletts in the London Money Market, 1867–1967, 4509; ed. Papers in English Monetary History, 4548; Financial Policy, 1939–1945, 4567

Sayle, A.: The Houses of the Workers, 18579

Scafe, Suzanne: The Heart of the Race: Black Women's Lives in Britain, 7726

Scammel, W. M.: 'The Treasury and Stagnation', 6121

Scammels, Brian: The Administration of Health and Welfare Services: A Study of the Provision of Care for Elderly People, 8602

Scanlon, John: Very Foreign Affairs, 13693

Scargill, D. I.: ed. Oxford and its Region, 18068; 'Conservation and the Oxford Green Belt', 18982

Scarlett, Bernard: Shipminder: The Story of H.M. Coastguard, 16517

Scarlott, Charles A.: Energy Sources—Wealth of the World, 7211

Scarman, Leslie George [Baron]: Violence and Civil Disturbances in Northern Ireland in 1969: Report of a Tribunal of Inquiry, 2847

Scarrow, Howard A.: 'The Impact of British Domestic Air Pollution Legislation', 20030

Scase, Richard: ed. Industrial Society: Class, Cleavage and Control, 9580; ed. Social Democracy in Capitalist Society: Working Class Politics in Britain and Sweden, 9581; The Entrepreneurial Middle Class, 9727

Sceats, R.: 'The Evolution of Anglo-French Relations', 14233

Schafer, Murray: British Composers in Interview, 24289

Schaffer, Evelyn B.: Child Care and the Family: A Study of Short Term Admission to Care, 8345

Schaffer, Frank: The New Town Story, 18248, 18997

Schaffer, Heinz Rudolph: Child Care and the Family: A Study of Short Term Admission to Care, 8345

Scharf, Claus: ed. Die Deutschlandspolitik Grossbritanniens und die britische Zone 1945–1949, 14214

Scharine, Richard: The Plays of Bond, 25947

Scharlieb, Dame Mary Dacomb: 'Save the Children', 3849; The Seven Ages of Women, 7655; The Welfare of the Expectant Mother, 7656; Reminiscences, 7657; Maternity and Infancy, 8346; The Hope of the Future: The Psychology of Childhood, 8347; The Management of Children in Health and Disease, 8348; 'A Terrible Census', 21317

Schatz, Arthur W.: 'The Anglo-American Trade Agreements and Cordell Hull's Search for Peace, 1936–1938', 14028

Scheible, Konrad: Die Offene Universität in Grossbritannien, 23553

Scherer, Jacqueline: Contemporary Community: Sociological Illusion or Reality?, 9370

Scherf, David: 'A Cardiologist Remembers', 21008

Schieldrop, Edgar Bonsak: The Highway, 17103; The Air, 17487

Schiller, F. C. S.: The Future of the British Empire after Ten Years, 12545

Schilling, Richard Selwyn Francis: Modern Trends in Occupational Health, 4131; Occupational Health Practice, 4132

Schilpp, Paul Arthur: The Philosophy of Bertrand Russell, 26873

Schinness, Roger: 'The Conservative Party and Anglo-Soviet Relations, 1925–1927', 13941

Schlencke, Manfred: ed. Studien zur Geschichte Englands und der deutsch-britischen Beziehungen, 14212

Schlote, Werner: British Overseas Trade from 1700 to the 1930's, 4796

Schmidt, Gustav: ed. Krise in Grossbritannien?, 586; 'Politische Tradition und Wirtschaftliche Faktoren in der Britischen Friedensstrategie 1918/19', 13422; England in der Krise, 13686

Schmidt, Heide-Irene: 'Wirtschaftliche Kriegsziele Englands und interalliierte Kooperation: Die Pariser Wirtschaftskonferenz 1916', 13417

Schmool, Marlena: 'The Fertility of Jewish Families in Britain, 1971', 7497; 'Register of Social Research on Anglo-Jewry, 1968–1971', 11294; 'The Size and Structure of the Anglo-Jewish Population 1960–1965', 11295

Schmool, Maurice: 'Synagogue Marriages in Great Britain, 1966–1968', 9980

Schneede, Uwe: Eduardo Paolozzi, 24202

Schneer, Jonathan: Ben Tillett: Portrait of a Labour Leader, 1535, 6806; Labour's Conscience: The Labour Left 1945–51, 1732; 'The Labour Left and the General Election of 1945', 2297; ed. Social Conflict and the Political Order in Modern Britain, 13573

Schneider, Fred D.: 'British Labour and Ireland, 1918–1921: The Retreat to Houndsditch', 2984; 'British Policy in West Indian Federation', 13097

Schneider, J. R. L.: 'Local Population Projections in England and Wales', 7414

Schneider, Joanna: *ed.* Women in Western European History: A Select Chronological and Topical Bibliography: The Nineteenth and Twentieth Centuries, 7627

Schneider, U.: 'Grundzüge britischer Deutschland—und Besatzungspolitik', 14206; 'Zur Deutschland—und Besatzungspolitik Grossbritanniens im Rahmen der Vier-Mächtekontrolle Deutschlands vom Kriegsende bis Herbst 1945, 14207; 'Niedersachsen unter Britischer Besatzung 1945', 14208

Schneidermayer, Wilma: Iris Murdoch and Muriel Spark: A Bibliography, 25814

Schoen, Douglas E.: Enoch Powell and the Powellites, 1293

Schoen, R.: 'Twentieth Century Cohort Marriage and Divorce in England and Wales', 9940

Schoenman, Ralph: *ed.* Bertrand Russell: Philosopher of the Century, 26872

Schoff, J.: David Low, 24105

Schofield, A. Norman: Local Government Elections, 3107

Schofield, Brian Betham: The Russian Convoys, 15137; British Sea Power: Naval Policy in the Twentieth Century, 15237; The Royal Navy Today, 15283

Schofield, Carey: Jagger, 24525

Schofield, [Edward] Guy: The Men that Carry the News: A History of the United Newspapers Limited, 25161

Schofield, Michael G.: The Sexual Behaviour of Young People, 8488; The Sexual Behaviour of Young Adults, 8489; Promiscuity, 8490; A Minority: A Report on the Life of a Male Homosexual in Great Britain, 10858; Sociological Aspects of Homosexuality: A Comparative Study of Three Types of Homosexuals, 10859; The Strange Case of Pot, 22192

Schofield, Stephen: Musketoon: Commando Raid, Glomfjord 1942, 14921

Scholefield, R. A.: First and Foremost: 50 Years of Manchester's Civic Airports, 17693

Scholes, Percy Alfred: Oxford Companion to Music, 24260; The Mirror of Music, 1844–1944: A Century of Musical Life in Britain as reflected in the Pages of the Musical Times, 24531

Schonberger, H.: 'Peacemaking in Asia: the United States, Great Britain, and the Japanese Decision to recognize Nationalist China, 1951–1952', 13617

Schonenberger, Toni: Der Britische Rückzug aus Singapore 1945–1976, 12960

Schonfield, Hugh J.: The Suez Canal in Peace and War 1868–1969, 14362

Schools Council/Ford Foundation: British Primary Schools Today, 23159

Schorr, Alvin Louis: Children and Decent People, 8351; Slums and Social Insecurity, 18415

Schottland, Charles Irwin: *ed.* The Welfare State: Selected Essays, 8996

Schrader, Halwart: Rolls Royce and Bentley from 1931, 17453

Schramm, Gottfried: 'Minderheiten gegen den Krieg. Motive und Kampfformen 1914–1918 am Beispiel Grossbritanniens und seines Empire', 13446

Schroder, Hans-Jürgen: *ed.* Die Deutschlandspolitik Grossbritanniens und die britische Zone 1945–1949, 14214

Schroder, Karsten: Parlament und Aussenpolitik in England 1911–1914, 13344

Schroeder, P. W.: 'Munich and the British Tradition', 13753

Schroeder, Peter J.: Cameroon, 12773

Schroeter, J.: Discovery of Chlorine and the Beginning of the Chlorine Industry: The Story of Chlorine down to the Present, 6211

Schroll, Herman: Harold Pinter: A Study of his Reputation, 1958–1969, 25973

Schuker, Stephen A.: The End of French Predominance in Europe: The Financial Crisis of 1924 and the Adoption of the Dawes Plan, 14253

Schultz, T.: 'Middle Class Families in France and in England', 9722; 'Income, Family Structure and Food Expenditure before and after the War', 20429

Schumacher, E. F.: 'Some Aspects of Coal Board Policy, 1947–1967', 6266

Schuman, S.: 'La Planification urbaine en évolution: le cas de Liverpool', 18031

Schumer, Leslie Arthur: Elements of Transport, 16267

Schur, Edwin Michael: Narcotic Addiction in Britain and America: The Impact of Public Policy, 22186

Schurman, Donald M. The Education of a Navy, 15285; Julian S. Corbett, 1854–1922, Historian of British Maritime Policy, 26794

Schuster, Peter: Henry Wickham Steed und die Habsburgermonarchie, 25286

Schuster, Sir George: Private Work and Public Causes: A Personal Record, 1881–1935, 9162

Schuyler, Robert Livingston: British Constitutional History since 1832, 599

Schwar, M. J. R.: Thirty Years On: A Review of Air Pollution in London, 20058

Schwartz, Anna Jacobson: 'Monetary Trends in the United States and the United Kingdom, 1878–1970: Selected Findings', 4618

Schwartz, George Leopold: Bread and Circuses, 1945–1958, 3623

Schwarz, J. E.: 'Career Objectives, Group Feeling and Legislative Party Voting Cohesion: The British Conservatives, 1959–68', 1642

Schwarzenberger, Georg: *ed.* Law, Justice and Equity: Essays in Tribute to G. W. Keeton, 23833

Schwitzer, Matej Karel: Margarine and other Food Fats: Their History, Production and Use, 20715

Schwoerer, Louis G.: 'Lord Halifax's Visit to Germany, November 1937', 13724

Science Museum, London: Books on the Chemical and Allied Industries: A Subject Catalogue of Books in the Science Library, 6212

Sclaifer, Robert: The Development of Aircraft Engines and the Development of Aviation Fuels, 17566

Sclare, A. Balfour: 'Attempted Suicide in Glasgow', 10814

Scobie, Edward: Black Britannia: A History of Blacks in Britain, 11022

Scoffham, Ernest R.: The Shape of British Housing, 18452

Scorer, Catherine:. 'The United Kingdom Prevention of Terrorism Acts 1974 and 1976', 2876

Scorer, Charles Gordon: *ed.* Medical Ethics: A Christian View, 8168

Scorer, Richard Segar: A Radical Approach to Pollution, Population and Resources, 20026; Pollution in the Air: Problems, Policies and Priorities, 20041; Air Pollution, 20042

Scotchford Archer, Margaret: *ed.* Contemporary Europe: Class, Status and Power, 9546

Scotland, Alexander: The London Cage, 16018

Scotland, James: 'Scottish Education, 1952–1982', 23604; The History of Scottish Education, 23609

Scotland: Department of Health: Depopulation and Rural Life in Scotland: A Summary Report by Bertram Hutchinson of Three Enquiries for the Department of Health for Scotland, 7426. 1963: Staffing of Local Authority Children's Departments: A Report, 8709; 1960: Custodial Sentences for Young Offenders: Report, 10541; 1966: Probation Hostels in Scotland: Final Report by the Scottish Probation Advisory and Training Council, 10487; 1962: Custodial Training for Young Offenders: Report of a Committee of the Scottish Advisory Council on the Treatment of Offenders, 10519; Department of Health: Scottish Housing Handbook, 18463; 1962: Development plans, 20272; (a) Areas of Great Landscape Value, 20273; (b) Tourist Development Proposals, 20274; 1963: Land Compensation (Scotland) Act, 1963, 20355; Scottish Health Services Council: Standing Medical Advisory Committee 1968: The Medical Care of Epilepsy in Scotland Report, 21080; 1964: Medical Staffing Structure in Scottish Hospitals: Report of the Committee, 21373; 1965: Alcoholics: Health Services for their Treatment and Rehabilitation, 22118

Scotson, John L.: The Established and the Outsiders: A Sociological Enquiry into Community Problems, 9351, 11155

Scott, Alexander: *ed.* Neil M. Gunn: The Man and the Writer, 25567

Scott, B.: Regional Problems and Location of Industry Policy in Britain, 5101

Scott, Carolyn: Dick Sheppard: A Biography, 11809

Scott, Christina: A Historian and his World: A Life of Christopher Dawson 1889–1970, 26765

Scott, Christopher: Accidents to Young Motorcyclists: A Statistical Investigation, 17199

Scott, Colin: *ed.* The Expansion of Swindon, Wiltshire: A Bibliography, 18915

Scott, Sir David: Ambassador in Black and

White: Thirty Years of Changing Africa, 13306

Scott, Lady Drusilla: A. D. Lindsay: A Biography, 23341

Scott, Ernest: Australian Discovery, 27189

Scott, George Edwin: The R.C.s: A Report on Roman Catholics in Britain Today, 11951; Reporter Anonymous: The Story of the Press Association, 25323

Scott, Sir Harold Richard: The Concise Encyclopedia of Crime and Criminals, 10289; Scotland Yard, 10753; From inside Scotland Yard, 10754

Scott, Sir Henry Harold: Health Problems of the Empire, Past, Present and Future, 22042; Some Notable Epidemics, 22377; A History of Tropical Medicine: Based on the Fitzpatrick Lectures Delivered before the Royal College of Physicians of London, 1937–1938, 22378

Scott, Hugh: In the High Yemen, 27234

Scott, J. W. Robertson: The Life and Death of a Newspaper, 25165; 'We' and Me: Memories of Four Eminent Editors I Worked With, 25283

Scott, James Maurice: Extel 100: Centenary History of the Exchange Telegraph, 25310

Scott, John: The Anatomy of Scottish Capital: Scottish Companies and Scottish Capital, 1900–1979, 5273; Directors of Industry: The British Corporate Network, 1904–76, 5454, 9787; The upper Classes: Property and Privilege, 9738

Scott, John Alexander: Problem Families in London, 10039

Scott, John Dick: Life in Britain, 388, 7594; The Administration of War Production, 795; Vickers: A History, 6368, 17596

Scott, Judith G.: 'Ecclesiological Influences in England, 1846–1963', 11610

Scott, L. P.: Growing Up in Shoreditch, 8352

Scott, Maurice Fitzgerald: A Study of United Kingdom Imports, 4793, 4817

Scott, Michael: Barry Sheene, 27142

Scott, P. M.: 'Mental Health and Family Welfare: Need for an Integrated Policy', 21754

Scott, Paul Henderson: In Bed with an Elephant, 2457; The Age of MacDiarmid: Essays on Hugh MacDiarmid and his Influence on Contemporary Scotland, 25685

Scott, Peter: 'The Development of Rural Wales', 5311

Scott, Peter: The Crisis of the University, 23320

Scott, Sir Peter: The Eye of the Wind, 20241; Sir Peter Scott at 80: A Retrospective, 20242

Scott, Peter D.: 'Gangs and Delinquent Groups in London', 10199; 'Juvenile Courts—the Juvenile's Point of View', 10571

Scott, Roger: 'The 1970 General Election in Ulster', 2367

Scott, Ronnie: Some of my Best Friends are Blues, 24463

Scott, S. F.: 'A Survey of Housing Conditions in the Urban Areas of England and Wales, 1960', 18655

Scott, W.: 'Fertility and Social Mobility among Teachers', 7484

Scott, William Henry: Management in Britain: A General Characterization, 5425; Management Structure and Computerization, 5447; Technical Change and Industrial Relations, 5632; 'The Aims of Industrial Sociology: Some Reflections', 5633; Coal and Conflict: A Study of Industrial Relations at Collieries, 5634; 'Sociological Aspects of Technical Change in a Steel Plant', 7925

Scott, Wolf: British Towns: A Statistical Study of their Social and Economic Differences, 17941, 18280

Scott-James, Rolfe Arnold: ed. Education in Britain, 22695

Scott-Moncrieff, George: The Mirror and the Cross: Scotland and the Catholic Faith, 12273

Scott-Sutherland, Colin: John Ireland, 24356

Scott-Tucker, J. H.: ed. The Parish of Stoke Fleming, Devon: Elizabeth I and before, to Elizabeth II Coronation, 2nd June 1953, 19357

Scottish Advisory Council on the Treatment and Rehabilitation of Offenders: Approved Schools, 10656

Scottish Amicable Life Assurance Society: A History of the Scottish Amicable Life Assurance Society 1826–1976, 4223

Scottish Association for Public Transport: Public Transport in Rural Scotland, 16315; A Better Glasgow: A Statement, 17133

Scottish Conservative Women's Organisation: 1977/78. A Report of the Findings of a Survey, 21691

Scottish Council Research Institute: The Structure of the Scottish Timber Industry, 19794

Scottish Council for Research in Education: Mental Survey Committee. Education and other Aspects of the 1947 Scottish Mental Survey, 7429

Scottish Council for Social Service: Party Lines: A Guide to Contacts in the Political Parties of Scotland, 2488; Third Statistical Account of Scotland—The County of Dumbarton, 5279; Community Councils, 9432; The Stewartry of Kirkcudbright, 10114; The County of Wigtown, 10115; The County of Angus, 10116; The City of Dundee, 10117; The Counties of Perth and Kinross, 10118

Scottish Council for Voluntary Organisations: Directory of National Voluntary Organisations for Scotland, 9221

Scottish Council, Development and Industry: Committee on Natural Resources in Scotland. Natural Resources in Scotland: Symposium at the Royal Society of Edinburgh, 31st October to 2nd November 1960, 7197

Scottish Development Department: Planning Maps Series, 136; Electricity in Scotland: Report of the Committee on the Generation and Distribution of Electricity in Scotland, 6684; Irvine New Town: Final Report on Planning Proposals, 18188

Scottish Education Department: Education in Scotland in 1963, 23593; Primary Education in Scotland, 23594

Scottish Episcopal Church Yearbook: 1892+, 12263

Scottish Georgian Society: Building Preservation Trusts: A Challenge for Scotland, 18959

Scottish Historical Review: 1903/4–, 2465

Scottish Home Department: Custodial Sentences for Young Offenders, 10657

Scottish Home and Health Department: A Report and Enquiry into Maternal Deaths in Scotland, 1965–1971, 7468; Prisons in Scotland. (1959 report), 10371; Prisons in Scotland (1962 report), 10372; Organisation of After-care in Scotland. Report of a Committee of the Scottish Advisory Council on the Treatment of Offenders, 10373; The Extension of Compulsory After-care to Additional Categories of Inmates and Prisoners. Report of a Committee of the Scottish Advisory Council on the Treatment of Offenders, 10374; Use of Short Sentences of Imprisonment by the Courts. Report of a Committee of the Scottish Advisory Council on the Treatment of Offenders, 10304, 10375

Scottish Hospital In-patient Statistics, 21472

Scottish Housing Advisory Committee: Choosing Council Tenants, 18462

Scottish Journal of Political Economy, Special Issue: 'Industrial Relations', 5736

Scottish Liberal Party: The Scottish Liberal Manifesto, 2544

Scottish National Orchestra: SNO: An Anniversary Study of the Scottish National Orchestra (1950–1971), The Scottish Orchestra (1891–1950) and their Antecedents, 24551

Scottish National Party: Choose Scotland: The Challenge of Independence: SNP Manifesto, 1983, 2510; Play the Scottish Card: SNP General Election Manifesto, 1987, 2511; Scotland's Future: Independence in Europe: SNP Manifesto, European Elections 15 June 1989, 2512

Scottish Office: Rate Rebates in Scotland 1969/70, 4078

Scottish Railway Development Association: Scottish Railways: The Next Five Years, 16833

Scottish Scholastic Survey: 1953, 23597

Scrimgeour, Ruby Margaret: ed. North London Collegiate School, 1850–1950, 23110

Scrope, Hugh E.: Guide to the Vickers Archives, 17598

Scruton, Roger: A Dictionary of Political Thought, 2085; The Meaning of Conservatism, 2201 'Notes on the Sociology of War', 8082

Scrutton, M.: Register of Research on Commonwealth Immigrants in Britain, 11517

Scudamore, Pauline: Spike Milligan: A Biography, 26330

Scully, Vincent Joseph: Modern Architecture: The Architecture of Democracy, 23893

Scupham, J.: Broadcasting and the Community, 24786

Scurfield, Harold: Infant and Young Child Welfare, 8350

Sea Fisheries: Statistical Tables: 1948+, 19799

Seaborne, Malcolm Vivian John: Education, 22699

Seabrook, Jeremy: The Politics of Hope: Britain at the End of the Twentieth Century, 1688; Working-class Childhood, 8353; The Unprivileged, 9495; City Close-up, 18093

Seabury, Paul: The Grenada Papers, 13084; Universities in the Western World, 23306

Seacombe, Wally: 'Sheila Rowbotham on Labour and the Greater London Council', 3292

Seager, Charles Philip: 'Suicide in Bristol', 10818

Seager, Elizabeth: Gardens and Gardeners, 19880

Seal, Anil: ed. The Decline, Revival and Fall of the British Empire, 12591

Seal, Mark: Cambridge Buses, 17303

Seal, Vera G.: Social Science and Social Pathology, 7929, 10173

Seale, Patrick: Philby: The Long Road to Moscow, 16052

Seaman, Lewis Charles Bernard: Post-Victorian Britain, 1902–1951, 298

Seaman, Robert Donald Harold: The Reform of the Lords, 678

Searby, Peter: The Training of Teachers in Cambridge University: The First Sixty Years, 1879–1939, 22757

Searight, Sarah: The British in the Middle East, 13805

Searle, Humphrey: Twentieth Century Composers, 24286

Searle, J. R.: The Campus War, 9864; Chapter on 'Medical Emigration, a Study in the Inadequacy of Official Statistics', 21536.'Medical Emigration from Britain, 1930–1961', 21542

Searle, Muriel: John Ireland: The Man and his Music, 24357

Searle-Barnes, Robert Griffiths: Pay and Productivity Bargaining: A Study of the Effects of National Wage Agreements in the Nottinghamshire Coal Fields, 3875

Sears, Paul Bigelow: The Biology of the Living Landscape: An Introduction to Ecology, 19916

Seath, J. W. and Seath, R. E.: Dunbarney: A Parish with a Past, 19367

Seaton, Colin Robert: Aspects of the National Health Service Acts, 21595

Seaton, Jean: Power without Responsibility: The Press and Broadcasting in Britain, 25076

Seaton, Ray: George Formby: A Biography, 26313

Seaward, Thelma: Productivity in Transport: A Study of Employment, Capital, Output, Productivity, and Technical Change, 16226

Sebag-Montefiore, Ruth: A Family Patchwork: Five Generations of an Anglo-Jewish Family, 12421

Sebba, Anna: Enid Bagnold: The Authorized Biography, 25940

Secker, Martin: Letters from D. H. Lawrence 1911–30, 25629

Secombe, Sir Harry: Goon Abroad, 26342; Arias and Raspberrries, 26343

Second Report from the Home Affairs Committee: Chinese Community in Britain. 3 vols HC Paper 102, Parliamentary Papers, 1984–85, 11383

Secrest, Meryle: Kenneth Clark: A Biography, 23954

Sedbergh: History of Sedbergh School, 1525–1925, 23075

Seddon, Quentin: The Quiet Revolution: Farming and the Countryside in the 21st Century, 19418

Seddon, Vicky: ed. The Cutting Edge: Women and the Pit Strike, 7750

Sedgwick, S.: London and Overseas Freighters Limited, 1949–1977: A Shore History, 16576

Seear, [Beatrice] Nancy [Baroness]: Married Women Working, 7683

A Career for Women in Industry?, 7813

Seed, Philip: The Expansion of Social Work in Britain, 8751

Seeley, Ivor H.: Local Government Explained, 3126; Planned Expansion of Country Towns, 17797; Outdoor Recreation and the Urban Environment, 27014

Seers, Dudley George: The Levelling of Incomes since 1938, 3805; Changes in the Cost-of-Living and the Distribution of Income since 1938, 3806; Inflation, 4014

Sefton, Henry R.: 'The Church of Scotland and Scottish Nationhood', 12214

Segal, Charles Solomon: Penn'orth of Chips: Backward Children in the Making, 8354; Backward Children in the Making, 8355

Segal, Stanley Solomon: From Care to Education, 8356; Mental Handicap: A Select Annotated Bibliography, 21745

Seglow, Peter: Trade Unionism in Britain, 6837

Seier, H.: ed. Studien zur Geschichte Englands und der deutsch–britischen Beziehungen, 14212

Selak, C. B.: 'The Suez Canal Base Agreement of 1954: Its Background and Implications', 14407

Selby, Sir Walford Harmood Montague: Diplomatic Twilight, 1930–1940, 13307

Selby-Bigge, Sir Lewis Amherst: The Board of Education, 22799

Seldon, Anthony: ed. Contemporary History: Practice and Method, 70, 26760; By Word of Mouth: Elite Oral History, 225

Seldon, Arthur: Advertising and the Public, 4309; Advertising in a Free Society, 4310; Pricing or Taxing?, 4874; Taxation and Welfare: A Report on Private Opinion and Public Policy, 8933; Universal or Selective Social Benefits?, 8934

Select Committee on Education and Science: Student Relations, 9852

Selected Documents Relating to Problems of Security and Co-operation in Europe 1954–1977, 14170

Selekman, Benjamin Morris and Selekman, Sylvia Kopald: British Industry Today, 4961

Self, Sir Albert Henry: Electricity Supply in Great Britain: Its Development and Organization, 6685

Self, Peter John Otter: 'The Reform of the Civil Service', 855; Regionalism: A Report to the Fabian Society, 5044; 'Regional Development Incentives', 5045; Cities in Flood, 17761; The Planning of Industrial Location, 17762, 17973; Town Planning in Greater London, 17763, 18940; The State and the Farmer, 17764, 19516; 'When the Minister Decides', 17864; 'Town Planning in Retreat', 17865; Metropolitan Planning: The Planning System of Greater London, 18941; 'The Farmers and the State', 19517

Self, Robert C.: Tories and Tariffs: The Conservative Party and the Politics of Tariff Reform 1922–1932, 1629

Seligman, Dee: Doris Lessing: An Annotated Bibliography of Criticism, 25657

Selikoff, Irving J.: Asbestos and Disease, 4136

Sell, Alan P. F.: Defending and Declaring the Faith: Some Scottish Examples 1860–1920, 12239

Sell, B. H. and Sell, K. D.: ed. Divorce in the United States, Canada and Great Britain: A Guide to Information Sources, 9919

Sell, George: ed. The Post-war Expansion of the United Kingdom Petroleum Industry, 6515

Sellar, R. J. B.: The Fife and Forfar Yeomanry, 1919–1956, 15584

Selleck, Richard Joseph Wheeler: English Primary Education and the Progressives, 1914–1939, 23132

Seller, Lindsay: Councils, Committees and Boards: A Handbook of Advisory, Consultative, Executive and Similar Bodies in British Public Life, 62

Sellers, Ian: ed. Our Heritage: The Baptists of Yorkshire, Lancashire and Cheshire, 1647–1987, 12035

Sellery, J'nan; Elizabeth Bowen: A Descriptive Bibliography, 25403

Sellman, George Raymond Stanley: A Practical Guide to Modern British Economic History, from 1700 to the Present Day, 3450

Sellman, Roger Raymond: Modern British History, 1815–1970: A Practical Guide, 298

Sellwood, A. and Sellwood, M.: Black Avalanche, 6318

Sellwood, Arthur Victor: The Saturday Night Soldiers: The Stirring Story of the Territorial Army, 15463

Selman, Paul E.: Ecology and Planning: An Introductory Study, 18818

Selsam, John Paul: The Attempts to form an Anglo-French Alliance, 1919–1924, 14250

Selver, Paul: A. R., 25176

Selwyn, Edward Gordon: Sir Edwyn Hoskyns, Bishop of Southwell, 1904–1925, 11744

Semmens, Peter: A History of the Great Western Railway, 16859

Sen, Amartya: The Standard of Living: The Tanner Lectures, 20436

Sen, Amya: Problems of Overseas Students and Nurses, 9886

Sencourt, Robert: The Reign of Edward VIII, 476; T. S. Eliot: A Memoir, 25500

Send and Ripley Historical Society: Ripley and Send, then and now: The Changing Scene of Surrey Village Life, 19198

Sendall, Bernard: The History of Independent Television in Britain, 24863

Senior, Clarence: 'Race Relations and Labour Supply in Great Britain', 10908; The West Indian in Britain, 11242

Senior, Derek: 'Organization for Regional

Planning', 5111; *ed.* The Regional City: An Anglo-American Discussion of Metropolitan Planning, 17790; A Guide to the Cambridgeshire Plan, 18852

Senior, W. H.: Survey of Agriculture in Caithness, Orkney and Shetland, 19622

Sergean, Robert: Training in the Clothing Industry: A Study of Recruitment Training and Education, 5958

Sergeant, Graham: A Textbook of Sociology, 8041; A Statistical Sourcebook for Sociologists, 8042

Sergeant, Jean-Claude: Britain and Europe since 1945, 14188

Sergeant, Winsley: Prices and Wages Freeze: A Narrative Guide to the Prices and Incomes Act 1966—Together with the Text of the Act, 3809, 5021

Serota, Nicholas: *ed.* British Sculpture in the Twentieth Century, 24182

Sessions, Margaret and William K.: Printing in York from the 1480s to the Present Day, 25020

Seth, Ronald Sydney: Lion with Blue Wings: The Story of the Glider Pilot Regiment, 1942–1945, 15933

Seth-Smith, J.: 'The New Look in Family Casework', 8687; 'Modern Trends in Social Work—the Family Casework', 8707

Seth-Smith, Michael: The Long Haul: A Social History of the British Commercial Vehicle Industry, 17462; Knight of the Turf: The Life and Times of Sir Gordon Richards, 27130

Sethi, Amarjit: Industrial Relations and Health Services, 21630

Seton, Sir Bruce: The Pipes of War: A Record of the Achievements of Pipers of Scottish and Overseas Regiments during the War 1914–18, 24396

Seton-Hutchinson, Graham: Machine Guns, 15493

Seton-Watson, Christopher and Seton-Watson, Hugh: The Making of a New Europe: R. W. Seton-Watson and the Last Years of Austria-Hungary, 13394

Seton-Watson, Robert William: Britain and the Dictators: A Survey of Post-War British Policy, 13698; After Munich, 13750

Seton-Williams, M. V.: Britain and the Arab States: A Survey of Anglo-Arab Relations, 1920–1948, 13808

Setright, Leonard John Kensell: The Power to Fly: The Development of the Piston Engine in Aviation, 17498

Setzekorn, William David: Formerly British Honduras: A Profile of the New Nation of Belize, 13032

Seuphor, Michel: The Sculpture of this Century, 24181

Seward, G. W.: The Enforcement of Planning Control under the Town and Country Planning Act, 20329

Sewel, John: The Politics of Independence: A Study of a Scottish Town, 3378; Colliery Closure and Social Change: A Study of a South Wales Mining Valley, 6334, 9644

Sewell, Gordon: Echoes of a Century (1864–1964): The Centenary History of Southern Newspapers Limited, 25153

Sewell, W. R. Derrick: *ed.* Spatial Dimensions of Public Policy, 20284

Sewill, Brendan: British Economic Policy 1970–1974, 3670

Sexsmith, Ann: The Left in Britain: A Checklist and Guide, 1996

Sexton, Christopher: Peggy Van Praagh: A Life of Dance, 24245

Seyd, Patrick: 'Factionalism within the Conservative Party: The Monday Club', 1652; The Rise and Fall of the Labour Left, 1773; 'Shelter: The National Campaign for the Homeless', 18700

Seymer, Lucy Ridgely: A General History of Nursing, 21702; Florence Nightingale's Nurses: The Nightingale Training School, 1860–1960, 22481

Seymour, John Barton: The Whitley Councils Scheme, 4152

Seymour, John: The Countryside Explained, 19099

Seymour, Lynn: Lynn: The Autobiography of Lynn Seymour, 24250

Seymour, William Walter: The History of the Rifle Brigade in the War of 1914–1918, 15712; British Special Forces, 15722

Seymour-Smith, Martin: Robert Graves, 25553; Robert Graves: His Life and Work, 25554

Seymour-Ure, Colin: 'British "War Cabinets" in Limited Wars: Korea, Suez and the Falklands', 725; 'The SDP and the Media', 1839; David Low, 24105; 'Parliamentary Privilege and Broadcasting', 24807; The Press, Politics and the Public: An Essay on the Role of the National Press in the British Political System, 25055; Studies on the Press: Working Paper, Royal Commission on the Press, 25125

Shaberman, Raphael B.: Autistic Children: The Nature and Treatment of Childhood Autism, 21882

Shacklady, Edward: The Gloster Meteor, 15876

Shackle, George Lennox Sharman: The Years of High Theory: Invention and Tradition in Economic Thought, 1926–1939, 26578

Shackleton, Edward Arthur Alexander [Baron]: Arctic Journeys: The Story of the Oxford University Ellesmere Land Expedition, 1934–35, 27210

Shackleton, Richard: *ed.* Worlds of Labour: Essays in Birmingham Labour History, 1782, 2298

Shadrake, A. M.: British Medical Periodicals, 1938–1961, 20786

Shadwell, Arthur: The Problem of Dock Labour, 7241; Drink in 1914–1922, 22143

Shafe, M. Michael: University Education in Dundee, 1881–1981, 23489

Shaftesley, John M.: *ed.* Remember the Days: Essays on Anglo-Jewish History Presented to Cecil Roth by Members of the Council of the Jewish Historical Society of England, 11279

Shah, S.: 'The Contribution of Council House Allocation to West Indian Desegregation in London 1961–1971', 18709

Shah, Samir: Immigrants and Employment in the Clothing Industry: The Rag Trade in London's East End, 11451

Shai, Aron: Origins of the War in the East: Britain, China and Japan, 1937–1939, 13609; Britain and China, 1941–1947: Imperial Momentum, 13631; 'Britain, China and the End of Empire', 13641; 'Imperialism Imprisoned: The Closure of British Firms in the People's Republic of China', 13642

Shakespeare, Sir Geoffrey: Let Candles be Brought in, 1517

Shakespeare, John Howard: The Churches at the Crossroads: A Study in Church Unity, 12006

Shallice, Tim: The Technology of Police Control, 10733

Shanas, Ethel: Old People in Three Industrial Societies, 8594

Shang, Anthony: The Chinese in Britain, 11384

Shanker, S. G.: *ed.* Philosophy in Britain Today, 26842

Shankland, G.: 'The Crisis in Town Planning', 17766

Shankland, Peter: Dardanelles Patrol, 14554; The Phantom Flotilla: The Story of the Naval Africa Expedition 1915–1916, 14682

Shankland-Cox & Associates: Inner Area Study: Lambeth, 17880; Multi-Service Project Report, 17881; Second Report on Multiple Deprivation, 17882; Poverty and Multiple Deprivation, 17883; Policies for Dispersal and Balance: Final Report of the Lambeth Inner Area Study, 1977 by Graham Shankland, Peter Willmott and David Jordan, 17884; Multi-Space Project: Report, 17885; People, Housing and District, 17886; Housing and Population Projections, 17887; Housing Stress, 17888; London's Inner Area: Problems and Possibilities: Discussion Paper, 17889; The Complications of Social Ownership, 17890; Interim Report on Local Services, 17891; Study of Intending Migrants: Report, 17892; Labour Market Study, 17893; Local Employers' Study, 17894; Policies and Structure: Report . . . , 17895; Expansion of Ipswich . . . a Report to the Minister of Housing and Local Government, 18883; Comparative Costs: A Supplementary Report, 18884

Shankland-Cox Partnership and Institute of Community Studies: Inner Area Study: Lambeth: The Groveway Project: An Experiment in Salaried Childminding, 8361

Shanks, Michael James: The Stagnant Society: A Warning, 3635; What Future for 'Neddy'?, 6089; *ed.* The Lessons of Public Enterprise, 6094; 'Politics and the Trade Unionist', 6788

Shannon, Michael Owen: *ed.* Modern Ireland: A Bibliography on Politics, Planning, Research and Development, 2639

Shannon, R.: 'The New Doctor's Dilemma', 21295

Shapiro, Dan: *ed.* The Social Impact of Oil in Scotland, 6532

Shapiro, Judith Claire: Inter-Industry Wage Determination: The Post-War U.K. Experience, 3919

Shapiro, Richard M.: Strategies for Improving Race Relations: The Anglo-American Experience, 11139

Shapiro, Stanley: 'The Great War and Reform: Liberals and Labour, 1917–1919', 1696

Shapland, D. G.: *comps.* Guide to Veteran Cars, 17355

Sharaf, 'abd Al-aziz Turayh: A Short History of Geographical Discovery, 27180

Share, Bernard: The Emergency: Neutral Ireland, 2710; *ed.* Root and Branch: Allied Irish Banks, Yesterday, Today, Tomorrow, 4528

Sharf, Andrew: The British Press and the Jews under Nazi rule, 25116

Sharma, Shiva Kumar: Der Völkerbund und die Grossmächte: ein Beitrag zur Geschichte der Völkerbundspolitik Grossbritanniens, Frankreichs und Deutschlands, 1929–1933, 13493

Sharma, Ursula: Rampal and his Family, 11216

Sharman, Dick: *ed.* Jobs and Community Action, 9374

Sharman, Mike: The Great Eastern Railway, 16843

Sharp, Alan J: 'The Foreign Office in Eclipse, 1919–1922', 13339; 'Britain and the Channel Tunnel, 1919–1920', 13649

Sharp, C. Andrew: The Discovery of the Pacific Islands, 27188

Sharp, Cecil Martin: Mosquito, 15835

Sharp, Clifford Henry: Transport Economics, 16227; The Problem of Transport, 16228; Transport and the Environment, 16230

Sharp, Dennis: 'Integrated Housing in Haringay?: Roman Halter and Associates, Architects', 18563; Sources of Modern Architecture, 23890

Sharp, Evelyn [Baroness]: Housing in Britain: Successes, Failures and the Future, 18691; 'Britain's Fifteen New Towns', 18989

Sharp, Ian Gordon: Industrial Conciliation and Arbitration in Britain, 4153, 5599, 6133

Sharp, John: Educating One Nation, 22635

Sharp, Margaret: Inward Investment: Policy Options for the United Kingdom, 4749

Sharp, Martin C.: D. H.: A History of De Havilland, 17600

Sharp, P. R.: The Development of an Education Service: The West Riding 1889–1974, 23234

Sharp, Paul: 'The Rise of the European Community in the Foreign Policy of British Governments 1961–1971', 14156

Sharp, Rachel: Education and Social Control: A Study in Progressive Primary Education, 23131

Sharpe, Eric J.: *ed.* Presbyterian Reunion in Scotland, 1907–1921: Its Background and Development, 12204

Sharpe, L. J.: Does Politics Matter? The Determinants of Public Policy, 3148; 'Elected Representatives in Local Government', 3176; 'Leadership and Representation in Local Government', 3177; 'The Failure of Local Government Modernisation in Britain: A Critique of Functionalism', 3182; *ed.* Voting in Cities: The 1964 Borough Elections, 3202; 'The Politics of Local Government in Greater London', 3286; 'New Plan for London?', 18307

Sharpe, Richard: Raasey: A Study in Island History: Documents and Sources, People and Places, 19268

Shattock, Michael: 'The British University Grants Committee, 1919–83: Changing Relationships with Government and the Universities', 23326

Shaw, Charles James Dalrymple, Lord Kilbrandon: A Background to Constitutional Reform, 689

Shaw, Duncan: *ed.* Reformation and Revolution, 12202

Shaw, E. R.: The London Money Market, 4276

Shaw, Eric: Discipline and Discord in the Labour Party: The Politics of Managerial Control in the Labour Party, 1951–86, 1727

Shaw, G. K.: 'A Study in Family Health. i. Health in Relation to Family Size; ii: A Comparison of the Health of Fathers, Mothers and Children', 21293; Mental Health on a New Housing Estate: A Comparative Study of Health in Two Districts of Croydon, 21772

Shaw, G. K.: The Economic Theory of Fiscal Policy, 4588; Fiscal Policy, 4654; *ed.* Public Choice, Public Finance and Public Policy, 6147

Shaw, Gareth: British Directories: A Bibliography and Guide to Directories Published in England and Wales (1850–1950) and Scotland (1773–1950), 58

Shaw, Graham H.: Pathways to Participation, 6025

Shaw, J. Martin: *ed.* Rural Deprivation and Planning, 19075

Shaw, Jack: On Our Conscience: The Plight of the Elderly, 8601

Shaw, James Edward: Local Government in Scotland: Past, Present and Future, 3167; Ayrshire, 1745–1950: A Social and Industrial History of the County, 5282

Shaw, John W.: Strategies for Improving Race Relations: The Anglo-American Experience, 11139

Shaw, John: The Self in Social Work, 8752

Shaw, Lulie A.: 'Impressions of Family Life in a London Suburb', 10028

Shaw, M. A.: The Atlas of Britain and Northern Ireland, 123

Shaw, Martin: Up to Now, 24364

Shaw, Michael: Surrey Villages, 19145

Shaw, Michael: Twice Vertical: The History of No. 1 (Fighter) Squadron, R.A.F., 15928

Shaw, Otto Leslie: Maladjusted Boys, 10606; Youth in Crisis: A Radical Approach to Delinquency, 10607; Prisoners of the Mind, 10608

Shaw, Richard: The Monopolies Commission and the Market Process: An Examination of the Effectiveness of Public Policy in Selected U.K. Industries, 5552

Shaw, Sir Roy: The Arts and the People, 23764; 'Television: Freedom and Responsibility', 24841

Shaw, Sir William Fletcher: Twenty-Five Years: The Story of the Royal College of Obstetricians and Gynaecologists 1929–1954, 20787, 20898

Shaw, Sir William Napier: The Smoke Problem of Great Cities, 20033

Shaw, Stan J.: Responding to Drinking Problems, 22153

Shaw, Stella: *ed.* Social Indicators and Social Policy, 8851; Impairment, Disability and Handicap: A Multi-disciplinary View, 21909

Shaw, Susan: Salmon: Economics and Marketing, 20720

Shaw, Thomas: A History of Cornish Methodism, 12111

Shay, Robert Paul: British Rearmament in the Thirties: Politics and Profits, 14709

Shea, Patrick: Voices and the Sound of Drums, 2814

Shead, Richard: Constant Lambert, 24358

Sheail, John: Rural Conservation in Inter-war Britain, 18953, 20188; 'List of Books and Articles on Agrarian History issued since June 1968', 19393; 'Land Improvement and Reclamation: The Experiences of the First World War in England and Wales', 19429; Pesticides and Nature Conservation: The British Experience 1950–1975, 20108; Nature in Trust: The History of Nature Conservation in Britain, 20187, 26792; 'The Concept of National Parks in Great Britain 1900–1950' 26962

Sheard, Kenneth: Barbarians, Gentlemen and Players: A Sociological Study of the Development of Rugby Football, 27032

Sheail, Philip: A Downland Village: Portrait of a Hampshire Parish, 19338

Sheard, Peter R.: A Guide to the British Food Manufacturing Industry, 20629

Shearer, Ann: Handicapped Children in Residential Care: A Study of Policy Failure, 21885

Shearman, Hugh Francis: Anglo-Irish Relations, 2968

Shears, Richard: The Coconut War: The Crisis on Espiritu Santo, 12890

Sheehan, John: Resources for Education: An Economic Study of Education in the United Kingdom, 1920–1965, 23200

Sheehan, Mary R.: Contemporary Schools of Psychology, 22419

Sheehy, Eugene P.: *ed.* Guide to Reference Books, 242

Sheehy, Jeanne: The Rediscovery of Ireland's Past: The Celtic Revival, 1830–1930, 2671

Sheehy, Seamus Joseph: Agriculture in Northern Ireland and the Republic of Ireland, 19647

Sheen, H.E.: Canon Peter Green: A Biography of a Great Parish Priest, 11782

Sheerman, Barrie: Collective Bargaining: What You Always Wanted to Know about Trade Unions and Never Dared to Ask, 6795; White-collar Unionism: The Rebellious Salariat, 6830

Sheffield Housing Development Committee: Ten Years of Housing in Sheffield, 1953–1963, 18658

Sheffield Social Survey: A Report on the Housing Problem in Sheffield, 18659

Sheffield, O. F.: The York and Lancaster Regiment, 1919–1953, 15743

Shegog, Richard A.: *ed.* Computers in the Service of Medicine: Essays on Current Research and Applications, 21228

Shehab, Fakhri: Progressive Taxation: A Study in the Development of the Progressive Principle in the British Income Tax, 4832

Sheils, William J.: ed. The Church and War, 11865; ed. The Church and Wealth, 12205, 12276; ed. Voluntary Religion, 12398

Shelden, Michael: Friends of Promise: Cyril Connolly and the World of Horizon, 25460

Sheldon, Alan: Industrial Organisations and Health, 4130

Sheldon, I. M.: International Trade Performance and Concentration in British Industry, 5541

Sheldrick, G.: The Hart Reguardant: Hertfordshire County Council 1889–1989, 3357

Shell, D.: 'The British Constitution in 1974', 622; 'The British Constitution in 1975', 623

Shell, F. R.: 'The British Constitution in 1980', 585

Shell, Kurt T.: 'Industrial Democracy and the British Labour Movement', 5638

Shelley, Harry S.: 'The Enlarged Prostate: A Brief History of its Treatment', 21009

Shelley, Jeffrey: ed. The General Strike, 6941

Shelter: Shelter 1976: Ten Years On: A Progress Report, 18702

Shelton, A. W.: 'Housing': Facts and Factors for Trade Unionists and Workers, 18595

Shemesh, Moshe: The Suez-Sinai Crisis: A Retrospective, 14391

Shenfield, Barbara Estelle: Social Policies for Old Age: A Review of Social Provisions for Old Age in Great Britain, 8564

Shennan, A. Ernest: Liverpool: Past—Present—Future, 18048

Shenton, Neil: Neighbourhood Information and Advice Centres: Oldham Community Development Project, 9300

Shepard, Norman A.: 'Poisons in the Rubber Industry, 21274

Shepard, Odell: 'Little Town', 17740

Shepherd, Charles: A Historical Account of the Island of St. Vincent, 13090

Shepherd, John: A Social Atlas of London, 18338

Shepherd, Michael: 'General Practice, Mental Illness and the British National Health Service', 21334; Studies in Psychiatry: A Survey of Work Carried cut in the Department of Psychiatry of the Institute of Psychiatry, under the Chairmanship of Sir Aubrey Lewis, 1945–66, 22412

Shepherd, P.: Urban Redevelopment and Changes in Retail Structure, 1961–1971, 6638

Shepherd, Thomas Boswell: Living Education; Some Views on Education between the Wars and its Prospects for the Future, 22632

Shepherd, William G.: 'Changes in British Industrial Concentration, 1951–1958', 3424; 'British Nationalized Industry: Performance and Policy', 6075; Economic Performance under Public Ownership: British Fuel and Power, 6076

Sheppard, D. K.: 'Changes in the Money Supply in the United Kingdom, 1954–1964: A Comment', 4616

Sheppard, D.: Play Spaces for Children on Estates, 27015

Sheppard, David Kent: The Growth of United Kingdom Financial Institutions 1880–1962, 4273

Sheppard, David: Built as a City, 11847; Bias to the Poor, 11848; Better Together: Christian Partnership in a Hurt City, 11849

Sheppard, Eric William: A Short History of the British Army, 15428; Britain at War: The Army, British and Allies, 15445; The Ninth Queen's Royal Lancers, 1715–1936, 15685

Sheppard, Julia: British Archives, 71

Sheppard, Mubin: Taman Budiman: Memoirs of an Unorthodox Civil Servant, 12924

Sheppard, Richard Herbert: Building for the People, 18625; Cast Iron in Building, 18626; Prefabrication in Building, 18627; Building for Daylight . . . With an Introductory Historical Note on English Window Design by John Gloag, 18628

Sheppard, T.: 'The Evolution of (British) Topographical and Geological Maps', 26693

Shepperd, G. A.: The Italian Campaign, 1943–1945: A Political and Military Re-Assessment, 14875

Shepperson, George Allcot: Independent African: John Chilembwe and the Origins, Setting and Significance of the Nyasaland Native Rising in 1915, 12778

Shepperson, Wilbur Stanley: British Emigration to North America, 7314; Emigration and Disenchantment: Portraits of Englishmen Repatriated from the United States, 7315

Sherbet, G. V.: The Biophysical Characterization of the Cell Surface, 22330

Sherborn, Charles Davies: Where is the—Collection? An Account of the Various Natural History Collections which Have Come under Notice of the Compiler, 26531

Sherborne, James Wilson: The Life of a University, 23462

Sherborne: A History of Sherborne School, 23076

Shercliff, William Henry: Manchester: A Short History of its Development, 18058

Sheridan, Claire: To the Four Winds, 25284

Sheridan, Dorothy: ed. Speak for Yourself: A Mass Observation Anthology 1937–1949, 229, 7532; 'Mass Observing the British', 7571; ed. Mass-Observation at the Movies, 24631

Sheridan, Mary Dorothy: The Handicapped Child and his Home, 21886

Sheriff, Peta: Career Patterns in the Higher Civil Service, 870

Sherloch, Robert Lionel: Man as a Geological Agent: An Account of his Actions on Inanimate Nature, 19980

Sherlock, Philip: West Indies, 13012; Norman Manley, 13053

Sherman, Alfred V.: Price Control by any Other Name: The National Board for Prices and Incomes and its Powers, 5020

Shermer, David: Blackshirts: Fascism in Britain, 2025

Sherrard, Howard Macoun: Town and Country Planning, 17749

Sherratt, Tom: Isle of Man Parliamentary Election Results 1919–1979, 2619

Sherriff, R. C.: No Leading Lady: An Autobiography, 25984

Sherriffs, Ronald: 'Governmental Support to the Theatre in Great Britain', 26264

Sherrin, Ned: Too Dirty for the Windmill: A Memoir of Caryl Brahms, 26128; A Small Thing—Like an Earthquake—Memoirs, 26346

Sherrington, Charles Ely Rose: A Hundred Years of Inland Transport, 1830–1933, 16429; The Economics of Rail Transport in Great Britain, 16744

Sherrington, Sir Charles Scott: The Integrative Action of the Nervous System, 22331

Sherry, Norman: ed. Conrad: The Critical Heritage, 25465

Sherwell, Arthur: 'The Scottish Liquor Polls', 22175

Sherwen, Theo: The Bomford Story: A Century of Service to Agriculture, 19680

Sherwood Taylor, Frank: A History of Industrial Chemistry, 6210. 'The Science Museum, London', 7149; The Conquest of Bacteria, 22375

Sherwood, K. B.: 'The Canal Boatmen's Strike of 1923', 16388

Sherwood, P. T.: Air Pollution from Road Traffic: A Review of the Present Position, 20064

Shew, Betty Spencer: Queen Elizabeth the Queen Mother, 507

Shields, Graham J.: Gibraltar, 12847

Shields, James Bowie: The Gifted Child, 8357

Shields, John Veysie Montgomery: The State of Crime in Scotland, 10183

Shils, Edward: ed. Universities, Politicians and Bureaucrats: Europe and the United States, 23336

Shimmin, Arnold Nixon: The University of Leeds: The First Half Century, 23509

Shinn, Christine Helen: Paying the Piper: The Development of the U.G.C., 23327

Shinn, R. F.: 'The King's Title, 1926: A Note on a Critical Document', 460

Shinwell, Emmanuel [Baron]: Conflict without Malice, 1309; I've Lived through it All, 1310; Lead with the Left: My First Ninety-Six Years, 1311; Shinwell Talking: A Conversational Biography to Celebrate his 100th Birthday, 1312

Shipbuilder and Marine Engine-Builder: Queen Mary, the Cunard White Star Quadruple-Screw North Atlantic Liner, 16530

Shipbuilding Enquiry Committee Report: 1965–66, 16611

Shipley, Peter: Militant Tendency: Trotskyism in the Labour Party, 1990; Revolutionaries in Modern Britain, 2002; Directory of Pressure Groups and Representative Associations, 2059; Hostile Action: The KGB and Secret Service Operations in Britain, 16001

Shipman, Marten Dorrington: Education and Modernization, 22646

Shirley, Joan: The Fall of Scotland Yard, 10757

Shirras, George Findlay: The Burden of British Taxation, 1937/8 and 1941/2, 4830; Public Policy and the Tax System, 4831

Shlaim, Avi: Britain and the Origins of European Unity 1945–1951, 14137; 'Prelude to Downfall: The British Offer to France, June 1940', 14269; Collusion across the Jordan: King Abdullah, the Zionist Movement and the Partition of Palestine, 14352

Shoard, Marion: The Theft of the Countryside, 19106

Shock, Maurice: ed. The Liberal Tradition from Fox to Keynes, 2163

Shone, Richard: British Painting 1910–1945, 23963; The Century of Change: British Painting since 1900, 23964

Shone, Sir Robert: 'The Economic Development of the United Kingdom Steel Industry', 6557

Shonfield, Sir Andrew Akiba: British Economic Policy since the War, 3620; Modern Capitalism: The Changing Balance of Public and Private Power, 3649; 'The Public Sector Versus Private Sector in Britain', 6113; 'Economic Planning in Great Britain: Pretence and Reality', 6114; ed. Social Indicators and Social Policy, 8851; The Social Sciences in the Great Debate on Science Policy, 8852

Shore, Peter: Entitled to Know, 1313

Shores, Christopher Francis: Fighter Aces, 14629; Fighters over the Desert: The Air Battles in the Western Desert, June 1940 to December 1942, 15940

Shorrick, N.: Lion in the Sky: The Story of Seletar and the Royal Air Force in Singapore, 16163

Shorrucks, A. F.: 'Age-Wealth Relationships: A Cross-Section and Cohort Analysis', 3770

Short, Anthony: The Communist Insurrection in Malaya, 1948–60, 12931, 16157

Short, Edward: Whip to Wilson, 1518; I Knew my Place, 1519; Education in a Changing World, 22647

Short, Ernest Henry: That's the Way the Money Goes: A Study of the Relations between British Industry and Taxation, 6062; A History of British Painting, 23962; Sixty Years of Theatre, 25927; Fifty Years of Vaudeville, 26273

Short, J. R.: Housing and Residential Structures: Atlantic Approaches, 18447

Short, John: Money Flow in the United Kingdom Regions, 4666

Short, K. R. M.: '"The White Cliffs of Dover": Promoting Anglo-American Alliance in World War II', 14063; ed. Film and Radio Propaganda in World War II, 15105; ed. Feature Films as History, 24619; ed. Western Broadcasting over the Iron Curtain, 24768

Short, L. B.: 'The Challenge to Scottish Calvinism', 12238

Short, Martin: The Fall of Scotland Yard, 10757

Short, Michael: ed. Gustav Holst: Letters to W. G. Whittaker, 24352; Gustav Holst: A Centenary Documentation, 24353

Short, Renée: The Case of the Long-term Prisoner, 10391

Shorter, Alfred Henry: Southwest England, 5133; Paper Making in the British Isles: A Historical and Geographical Study, 6620

Shorter, Edward: The Making of the Modern Family, 10049

Shortt, Hugh de Sausmarez: ed. City of Salisbury, 18114

Showalter, Elaine: The Female Malady: Women, Madness and English Culture, 1830–1980, 7839

Showler, Brian: The Public Employment Service, 5910, 6986

Shragge, Eric: Pensions Policy in Britain: A Socialist Analysis, 4051

Shrewsbury Chronicle: The Changing Face of Shrewsbury, 18908; The Second Series . . . Shrewsbury, 18909

Shrewsbury: A History of Shrewsbury School 1552–1952, 23077

Shrigley, Sheila M.: Selected References on Health and Social Services for Ethnic Minorities in Britain, 22100

Shrimpton, Jean: The Truth about Modelling, 24175

Shrock, Richard Harrison: 'Library Collections in Social Medicine', 21010; The Development of Modern Medicine, an Interpretation of the Social and Scientific Factors Involved, 21182; The History of Nursing: An Interpretation of the Social and Medical Factors Involved, 21711

Shropshire County Library: The Changing Face of Shrewsbury, 18908

Shuckburgh, Sir Evelyn: Descent to Suez: Diaries 1951–1956, 14384

Shucksmith, Mark: No Homes For Locals?, 18376; Scotland's Rural Housing: A Forgotten Problem, 19244

Shukla, Hari: 'Living in a Multi-Cultural Society: The Hindu Community in Britain', 12457

Shulman, Milton: The Least Worst Television in the World, 24856

Shurick, Adam Thomas: The Coal Industry, 6255

Shuster, Louis: ed. Readings in Pharmacology, 22299

Shuttleworth, Alan: Two Working Papers in Cultural Studies, 10111; Race, Community and Conflict: A Study of Sparkbrook, 11457

Shwadran, Benjamin: 'The Anglo-Iranian Oil Dispute 1948–53', 13860

Sibley, Brian: Shadowlands: The Story of C. S .Lewis and Joy Davidman, 25665

Sibley, D.: Outsiders in Urban Societies, 11355

Sicard, Gerald L.: ed. Sociology for our Times, 8058

Sicherman, Harvey: Aden and British Strategy, 1839–1968, 13867

Sidebotham, Herbert: British Policy and the Palestine Mandate, 14304; Great Britain and Palestine, 14305

Sidebotham, R.: 'An Experiment in Comparative Costing in the Hospitals Service', 21391

Sidey, Philip John: Britain in the World, 13215

Sidneil, Michael J.: Dances of Death: The Group Theatre of London in the Thirties, 26192

Siegfried, André: Germs and Ideas, 22374

Siepmann, H. A.: ed. The First Hundred Years of the Standard Bank, 4507

Sierakowski, M.: Recent Social Trends in Family and Work in Britain, 9937

Sieve, Jack E. B.: Income Distribution and the Welfare State, 3852, 9074

Sigerist, Henry Ernst: Medicine and Human Welfare, 22003; Landmarks in the History of Hygiene, 22004; Civilisation and Disease, 22005

Sigsworth, Eric Milton: Black Dyke Mills: A History with Introductory Chapters on the Development of the Worsted Industry in the Nineteenth Century, 6431; 'A Survey of Slum Clearance Areas in Leeds', 18030; 'Rebuilding or Renovation?', 18527; 'The Finance of Improvements: A Study of Low Quality Housing in Three Yorkshire Towns', 18528

Silber, John R.: 'Poisoning the Wells of Academe', 23301

Silberman, Charles Eliot: Crisis in Black and White, 11158

Silberman, Ian: Explorations in After-care: Home Office Research Studies No 9, 10467

Silberman, Leo: Analysis of Society, 7901; Colour and Class in Six Liverpool Schools, 23170

Silberston, Aubrey: The British Patent System. 1. Administration, 5016; 'Size of Plant, Size of Enterprise and Concentration in British Manufacturing Industry 1935–1958', 5056; 'Hire Purchase Controls and the Demand for Cars', 17369

Silberston, Dorothy Marion: Youth in a Technical Age: A Study of Day Release, 23266

Silburn, Richard: Poverty: The Forgotten Englishman, 9068; Poverty, Deprivation and Morale in a Nottingham Community: St.Ann's: A Report of the Preliminary Findings of the St.Ann's Study Group, 9069

Silcock, H.: 'The Comparison of Occupational Mortality Rates', 7466

Silk, Paul: How Parliament Works, 1554

Silkin, Arthur: 'The "Agreement to Differ" of 1975 and its Effects on Ministerial Responsibility', 733

Silkin, John: Changing Battlefields: The Challenge to the Labour Party, 1770

Sillar, Frederick Cameron: Skye, 19277

Sillars, Jim: Scotland: The Case for Optimism, 2485

Sillitoe, Sir Percy: Cloak without Dagger, 10761, 16015

Silver, Allan: Angels in Marble: Working Class Conservatives in Urban England, 1616, 9685

Silver, Harold: Modern English Society: History and Structure, 1850–1970, 7618; A Social History of Education in England, 22678; and Silver, Pamela: The Education of the Poor: The History of a National School, 1824–1974, 23229; The History of British Universities, 1800–1969 excluding Oxford and Cambridge: A Bibliography, 23292

Silver, Michael: 'Recent British Strike Trends: A Factual Analysis', 6936

Silver, Morris: 'Births, Marriages and Income

Fluctuations in the United Kingdom and Japan', 7488

Silverlight, John: The Victor's Dilemma: Allied Intervention in the Russian Civil War, 13922

Silverman, Herbert Albert: ed. Studies in Industrial Organisation, 4960

Silverman, Rodney: A Statistical Analysis of Advertising Expenditure and the Revenue of the Press, 4306, 25071

Silverstone, Rosalie: Careers of Professional Women, 7856

Silvester, Reginald: Official Railway Postcards of the British Isles, 16802

Silvette, H.: Tobacco: Experimental and Clinical Studies. A Comprehesive Study of the World's Literature, 22216

Silvey, Anne H.: 'Scottish Industries During the Inter-war Period', 5243

Silvey, Robert: Who's Listening?, 24783

Silvivia, Dale: Laurence Olivier and the Art of Film Making, 24686

Sim, Joe: British Prisons, 10367

Simeon, R.: ed. The Politics of Constitutional Change in Industrial Nations, 582

Simey, Margaret: Democracy Rediscovered: A Study in Police Accountability, 10779

Simey, Thomas Spensley, [Baron]: Social Science and Social Purpose, 8876; Principles of Social Administration, 9240

Simmie, James M.: The Sociology of Internal Migration: A Discussion of Theories and Analysis of a Survey in Southampton County Borough, 7281

Simmons, Charles James: Soap Box Evangelist, 1521

Simmons, Dawn Langley: Margaret Rutherford: A Blithe Spirit, 26097

Simmons, Jack: The Railways of Britain: An Historical Introduction, 16721; St. Pancras Station, 16996; 'The Pattern of Tube Railways in London', 17005; Leicester Past and Present Vol 2: Modern City, 1860–1974, 18886; 'The Last Forty Years', 23379; New University, 23513

Simms, Madeleine: Abortion Law Reformed, 7876; Abortion and Contraception: A Study of Patient's Attitudes, 7877; 'Abortion Law and Medical Freedom', 7888; 'Abortion Act after Three Years', 7889

Simms, Peter: Trouble in Guyana: An Account of People, Personalities as they were in British Guiana, 13041

Simms, T. H.: Homerton College, 1695–1978: From Dissenting Academy to Approved Society in the University of Cambridge, 22753

Simnett, William Edward: Railway Amalgamation in Great Britain, 16743

Simon, A. L.: Energy Resources, 7216

Simon, Brian: Intelligence, Psychology and Education: A Marxist Critique, 22785; The Common Secondary School, 22945; The Evolution of the Comprehensive School, 1926–1966, 22954; Half Way There—Report on the British Comprehensive School Reform, 22959; ed. Education in Leicestershire, 1540–1940, 23232; ed. The Radical Tradition in Education in Britain, 23238; ed. Studies in the History of

Education: Vol. 3, The Politics of Educational Reform, 1920–1940, 23239

Simon, Ernest Darwin [Baron]: How to Abolish the Slums, 18387; Houses for All, 18388; The Anti-Slum Campaign, 18389; The Rebuilding of Manchester, 18608, 18890; Rebuilding Britain: A Twenty Year Plan, 18796; The BBC from within, 24758

Simon, Frances Hamilton: Prediction Methods in Criminology: Including a Prediction Study of Young Men on Probation, 10465

Simon, Herbert: Songs and Words: A History of the Curwen Press, 24958; Good Books come from Devon: The David and Charles Twenty-First Birthday Book, 24959

Simon, John Allesbrook, [Viscount]: Retrospect, 1314

Simon, Julian Lincoln: 'The Effect of Income on Fertility', 7491

Simon, Rita James: 'A Comment on Sociological Research and Interest in Britain and the United States', 7993

Simonds, W. H.: 'Old People Living in Dorset: A Socio-medical Survey of Private Households', 8628

Simons, R. B.: 'The British Coal Industry—A Failure of Private Enterprise', 6286

Simper, Robert: Britain's Maritime Heritage, 16462

Simpson, Barry John: Planning and Public Transport in Great Britain, France and W. Germany, 16261

Simpson, Bill: Labour, the Unions and the Party: A Study of the Trade Unions and the British Labour Movement, 6874

Simpson, Colin: The Secret Lives of Lawrence of Arabia, 13819; Lusitania, 14661

Simpson, David Hugh: 'Investments, Employment and Government Expenditure in the Highlands, 1950–1960', 5299; Manufacturing Industry in Wales: Prospects for Employment Growth, 5345; 'An Analysis of the Size of Trade Unions', 6759; Commercialisation of the Regional Press, 25342

Simpson, Edward Smethurst: Coal and the Power Industries in Postwar Britain, 6305, 7194

Simpson, Eric: Dalgety: The Story of a Parish, 19366

Simpson, Frank D.: The Wolverton and Stony Stratford Steam Trams, 17237

Simpson, H. R.: All our Future: A Longitudinal Study of Secondary Education, 22943

Simpson, J. G.: Derby City Transport Route History, 1840–1982, 16351

Simpson, J. V.: 'A Case Study of a Shipbuilding Redundancy in Northern Ireland', 5394

Simpson, James Herbert: Schoolmaster's Harvest: Some Findings of Fifty Years, 1894–1944, 22823

Simpson, John: Crisis in Procurement: A Case Study of the TSR-2, 15888

Simpson, John Barclay Hope: Rugby since Arnold: A History of Rugby School from 1842, 23073

Simpson, Keith: A Nation at Arms: A Social

Study of the British Army in the First World War, 14447

Simpson, Michael Anthony: ed. Middle Class Housing in Britain, 9737, 18758; Thomas Adams and the Modern Town Planning Movement in Britain, Canada and the United States, 1900–1940, 18824

Simpson, Noel: The Belfast Bank, 1827–1970: 150 Years of Banking in Ireland, 4525

Simpson, Paul: The Monopolies Commission and the Market Process: An Examination of the Effectiveness of Public Policy in Selected U.K. Industries, 5552

Simpson, Renate: The Highest Education: A Study of Graduate Education in Britain, 9873, 22571; How the Ph.D. came to Britain: A Century of Struggle for Postgraduate Education, 23319

Simpson, Richard L.: 'A Note on Status, Mobility, and Anomie', 9469

Simpson, Robert Wilfred Levick: ed. Guide to Modern Music on Records, 24575

Simpson, Tony: Operation Mercury: The Battle for Crete 1941, 14856

Simpson, William Douglas: ed. The Fusion of 1860: a Record of the Centenary Celebrations and a History of the United University of Aberdeen, 1860–1960, 23450

Simpson, William John Sparrow: History of the Anglo-Catholic Revival from 1845, 11642; The Contribution of Cambridge to the Anglo-Catholic Revival, 11648

Simpson, William W.: 'Jewish-Christian Relations since the Inception of the Council of Christians and Jews', 12422

Sims, Charles: The Royal Air Force: The First Fifty Years, 15783

Sims, Edward Howell: Fighter Tactics and Strategy, 1914–1970, 15814

Sims, J.M.: ed. Institute of Historical Research 1952–1954, 406; ed. Institute of Historical Research 1955–1957, 407

Sims, John: A List and Index of Parliamentary Papers Relating to India 1908–1947, 13106

Sims, Nicholas A.: British Writing on Disarmament from 1914 to 1978: A Bibliography, 13432

Simson, Ivan: Singapore: Too Little, Too Late, 15076

Sinclair, Andrew Annandale: The Red and the Blue: Intelligence, Treason and the Universities, 16021; Dylan Thomas: The Poet of his People, 25834

Sinclair, D. J.: ed. Atlas of London and the London Region, 18350

Sinclair, David Cecil: Basic Medical Education, 20813; Medical Students and Medical Sciences: Some Problems of Education in Britain and the United States, 22464

Sinclair, David Edwin: The Glasgow Subway, 17021

Sinclair, David: Two Georges: The Making of the Modern Monarchy, 445; Dynasty: The Astors and their Times, 1351; Snowdon: A Man of Our Times, 24710

Sinclair, George: Control of Commonwealth Immigration: An Analysis of the Evidence Taken by the Select Committee on Race Relations and Immigration 1969–1970 by

Arthur Bottomley and George Sinclair, 11006

Sinclair, Ian: Hostels for Probationers, 10466

Sinclair, J. F.: 'Educating Management', 22510

Sinclair, John: Coal-Mining: Organisation and Management, 6264; Coal Mining Economics, 6295

Sinclair, Keith: A History of New Zealand, 12669

Sinclair, Peter J. N.: An Introduction to Economics, 3499; 'Economic Debates', 3501; ed. The Money Supply and the Exchange Rate, 4651

Sinclair, R. G.: 'High Blood Pressure—Ancient, Modern and Natural', 21012; The London Hospital, 21431

Sinclair, R.: ed. Social Science and Government: Policies and Problems, 8817

Sinclair, Robert George: The British Press, 25041

Sinclair, Susan: The Child Care Service at Work, 8118

Sinclair-Stevenson, Christopher: The Gordon Highlanders, 15586; The Life of a Regiment: The History of the Gordon Highlanders, vol.vi 1945–1970, 15587

Sinden, Norman: A Touch of the Memoirs, 26099; Laughter in the Second Act, 26100

Siney, Marion C.: The Allied Blockade of Germany, 1914–1916, 14607

Sinfield, Adrian: The Long-term Unemployed—Comparative Survey, 6977; Which Way for Social Work?, 8787

Sinfield, Alan: Literature, Politics and Culture in Post-war Britain, 23787

Singer, Charles: A Short History of Medicine, 21203

Singer, Hans Wolfgang: Can We Afford Beveridge?, 9037; Food Aid: The Challenge and the Opportunity, 9190

Singer, Kurt: The Charles Laughton Story, 26058

Singh, A. K. J.: Gandhi and Civil Disobedience: Documents in the India Office Records 1922–1946, 13115

Singh, Amal Kumar: Indian Students in Britain: A Survey of their Adjustment and Attitudes, 11496

Singh, Anita Inder: The Origins of the Partition of India, 1936–1947, 13175; 'Imperial Defence and the Transfer of Power in India, 1946–1947', 13176; 'Keeping India in the Commonwealth: British Political and Military Aims, 1947–1949', 13177; 'Post-Imperial British Attitudes to India: The Military Aspect 1947–1951', 13185

Singh, Avtar: Take-overs, 5519

Singh, Davinder: 'A Model of Collective Bargaining for U.K. and U.S. Manufacturing: A Comparative Study', 5804

Singh, Jagjit: Modern Cosmology, 26438

Singleton, John: 'Lancashire's Last Stand: Declining Employment in the British Cotton Industry, 1950–1970', 6447

Singleton, Mary Ann: The Fiction of Doris Lessing, 25655

Singleton-Gates, Peter: The Black Diaries: An Account of Roger Casement's Life and Times, with a Collection of his Diaries and Public Writings, 3024

Sington, Derrick: Crime, Punishment and Cure, 10325; The Offenders: The Case against Legal Vengeance, 10326; The Offenders: Society and the Atrocious Crime, 10327

Sipols, V. Y.: Why War Was Not Prevented: A Documentary Review of the Soviet-British-French Talks in Moscow, 1939, 13953

Sires, Ronald Vernon: 'Government in the British West Indies: An Historical Outline', 13004; 'British Guiana: The Suspension of the Constitution', 13036

Sisson, C. H.: The Spirit of British Administration, 888; On The Look Out, 25800

Sisson, Charles Jasper: Raymond Wilson Chambers, 1874–1942, 25447

Sisson, Keith: 'Industrial Relations: The Next Decade', 5833; ed. Personnel Management in Britain, 9780; Industrial Relations in Fleet Street: A Study in Pay Structure, 25338

Sissons, John Brian: ed. The British Isles: A Systematic Geography, 26687

Sissons, Michael: ed. The Age of Austerity, 1945–1951, 300, 7576

Sissons, P. L.: The Social Significance of Church Membership in the Burgh of Falkirk, 12216

Sitwell, Edith: Taken Care Of: An Autobiography, 25805

Sitwell, Sir Osbert: Laughter in the Next Room, 25802

Sivanandan, A.: 'Race, Class and Power: An Outline for Study', 11027; 'Race, Class and the State: The Black Experience in Britain', 11028; A Different Hunger: Writings on Black Resistance, 11029; Coloured Immigrants in Britain: A Select Bibliography Based on the Holdings of the Library of the Institute of Race Relations, 11516; Register of Research on Commonwealth Immigrants in Britain, 11517

Siviter, Roger: Waverley: Portrait of a Famous Route, 16981

Sixsmith, E. K. G.: Douglas Haig, 14504

Sizewell B Public Inquiry: Report on Application by the Central Electricity Generating Board for Consent for the Construction of a Pressurized Water Reactor and a Direction that Planning Permission be deemed granted for that Development, 6672

Sjölinder, Rolf: Presbyterian Reunion in Scotland, 1907–1921: Its Background and Development, 12204

Sked, Alan: Post-war Britain: A Political History, 300; Britain's Decline: Problems and Perspectives, 3702

Skeels, H. M.: 'A Final Follow-up Study of One Hundred Adopted Children', 8358

Skeet, Muriel Hilda: Health Needs Help: Results of a Study into the Role and Preparation of Volunteers Working within the Reorganised National Health Service, 21678; ed. Health Auxiliaries and the Health Team, 21679; Marriage and Nursing: A Survey, 21716

Skeffington, John [Baron Massereene and Ferrard]: The Lords, 676

Skelton, Robin: ed. Herbert Read: A Memorial, 25784

Skelton, Valerie: 'Property and Political Power: Edinburgh 1875–1975, 3374

Skene, Norman Henry: The British Peerage in Parliament, 674

Skentelbery, N.: Arrows to Atom Bombs: A History of the Ordnance Board, 15489

Skidelsky, Robert Jacob Alexander [Baron]: Thatcherism, 1053; Oswald Mosley, 1484; ed. The End of the Keynesian Era: Essays on the Disintegration of the Keynesian Political Economy, 6136, 26607; The Age of Affluence, 10619; English Progressive Schools, 23098; John Maynard Keynes; Hopes Betrayed, 1883–1920, 26591

Skidmore, Ian: Anglesey and Lleyn Shipwrecks, 16512

Skilleter, Paul: Morris Minor: The World's Supreme Small Car, 17435

Skinner, David N.: A Situation Report on Green Belts in Scotland, 20392

Skinner, Frank W.: ed. People without Roots: A Study undertaken in the Borough of Tower Hamlets 1966–67, and an Appraisal of Services Provided by the Voluntary and Statutory Agencies, 18339

Skinner, I.: Thamesmead, 18205

Skinner, Quentin: ed. Philosophy, Politics and Society, 8778

Sklair, Leslie: Organised Knowledge: A Sociological View of Science and Technology, 7909

Sklair, Leslie: The Sociology of Progress, 7908

Skodak, M.: 'A Final Follow-up Study of One Hundred Adopted Children', 8358

Skop, Arthur L.: 'The British Labour Party and the German Revolution, November 1918–January 1919', 13546

Skrine, Sir Clarmont Percival: World War in Iran, 13308

Skuse, Allen: Government Intervention and Industrial Policy, 6082

Slack, Geoffrey Layton: ed. Dental Public Health: An Introduction to Community Dentistry, 22393

Slack, Kathleen M.: Councils, Committees and Concern for the Old, 8568; Old People and London Government: A Study of Change, 1958–1970, 8569; Social Administration and the Citizen, 9241; Henrietta's Dream: A Chronicle of the Hampstead Garden Suburb, 1905–1982, 18194

Slack, Kenneth: The British Churches Today, 11584; George Bell, 11721

Slater, Eliot Trevor Oakeshott: Patterns of Marriage: A Study of Marriage Relationships in the Urban Working Classes, 10027; Delinquency in Girls, 10621

Slater, Gilbert: The Growth of Modern England, 3403

Slater, Jim: Return to Go: My Autobiography, 4475

Slater, Norman: A Brewer's Tale: The Story of Greenall Whitley & Co. Ltd. through Two Centuries, 6157

Slaughter, Clifford: 'The Strike of Yorkshire Mineworkers in May, 1955', 6935; Coal is Our Life: An Analysis of a Yorkshire Mining Community, 9637

Slaven, Anthony: Business, Banking and Urban History: Essays in Honour of S. G. Checkland, 5251; ed. Dictionary of Scottish Business Biography, 1860–1960, 9786; 'British Shipbuilders: Market Trends and Order Book Patterns between the Wars', 16607; Iron and Steel; Shipbuilding, 16612

Slee, Bill: Country Parks: A Review of Policy and Management Issues, 18810

Sleeman, John Frederick: The Welfare State: Its Aims, Benefits and Costs, 9011; 'The Rise and Decline of Municipal Transport', 16294; 'The British Tramway Industry: The Growth and Decline of a Public Utility', 17211

Slesser, Sir Henry Herman: A History of the Liberal Party, 1808

Slesser, Malcolm: The Politics of Environment, 20209

Slessor, Sir John Cotesworth: The Central Blue, 15962; These Remain. A Personal Anthology, Memoirs of Flying, Fighting and Field Sports, 15963; 'The Place of the Bomber in British Strategy', 15991

Slim, William: Defeat into Victory, 14781

Slinn, Judy: A History of May and Baker, 22274

Slinn, Peter: The Evolution of the Modern Commonwealth, 1902–80, 12479

Sloane, Peter J.: ed. Women and Low Pay, 3879; Women and Low Pay, 3945; Changing Patterns of Working Hours, 5909; Sex Discrimination in the Labour Market, 7788; 'Sexual Discrimination in the Labour Market', 7789

Sloman, Albert Edward: A University in the Making, 23496

Sloman, Anne: With Respect, Ambassador: An Inquiry into the Foreign Office, 13335

Smail, Robin: Breadline Wages: Low Pay in Greater Manchester, 3957; Two Nations: Poverty and Wages in the North, 3958

Smailes, Arthur Eltringham: North England, 5129

Small, Denis Sheil: A Pride of Gurkhas: The 2nd King Edward VII's Own Goorkhas (the Sirmoor Rifles). 1948–1971, 15646

Small, Edwina: Merchant Shipping at Plymouth, 16493

Small, Mabel: Growing Together: Some Aspects of the Ecumenical Movement in Scotland, 1924–1964, 12206

Small, Neil: Politics and Planning in the N.H.S, 21684

Small, Stephen: Police and People in London, 10783

Smalley, Keith Aubrey: Greenford, the Historical Geography of a North West London Parish, 19335

Smallwood, Frank: Greater London: The Politics of Metropolitan Reform, 3288, 18330

Smart, Carol Rosemary: Industrial Relations in Britain: A Guide to Sources of Information, 5573; Crime and Criminology: A Feminist Critique, 10876; 'Social Policy in Drug Addiction: A Critical Study of Policy Development', 22182

Smart, Nicholas: Crisis in the Classroom: An Enquiry into State Education Policy, 23250

Smart, R.: Bedford Training College, 1882–1982: A History of a Froebel College and its Schools, 22751

Smart, Reginald Cecil: The Economics of the Coal Industry, 6259

Smeed, Ruben Jacob: The Traffic Problems in Towns, 17150

Smellie, Kingsley Bryce Speakman: A Hundred Years of British Government, 567; A History of Local Government, 3115

Smellie, Robert Martin Stuart: A Matter of Life—DNA, 26478

Smethurst, Arthur Frederick: ed. Acts of the Convocations of Canterbury and York together with certain other Resolutions, Passed since the Reform of the Convocations in 1921, 11637

Smillie, Robert: Memoir of James Keir Hardie M.P. and Tributes to his Work, 1425; My Life for Labour, 1523

Smith John Harold: Industrial Sociology, 7969

Smith, A.: The East Enders, 18348

Smith, A. D.: 'Progress in British Manufacturing Industries in the Period, 1948–1954', 3622; The Economic Impact of Commonwealth Immigration, 11417

Smith, A. L. M.: Political Stratification and Democracy, 3375

Smith, Alexander: The County of Fife, 19219

Smith, Alwyn: Patients under Psychiatric Care in Hospital in Scotland, 1963, 21805; The Science of Social Medicine, 21948

Smith, Ann Dorothea: Women in Prisons: A Study in Penal Methods, 7732, 10437

Smith, Anne: Women Remember: An Oral History, 7640

Smith, Anthony: The Trade Unions, 6732

Smith, Anthony David: 'The Diffusion of Nationalism: Some Historical and Sociological Perspectives', 8079

Smith, Anthony David: ed. British Broadcasting, 24790; The Shadow in the Cave: A Study of the Relationship between the Broadcaster, his Audience and the State, 24791; ed. Television and Political Life: Studies in Six European Countries, 24894; Paper Voices: The Popular Press and Social Change 1935–1965, 25066l; ed. The British Press since the War, 25069

Smith, Anthony Douglas: Social Change: Social Theory and Historical Processes, 8080, 9460; Poverty and Progress in Britain, 1953–1973: A Statistical Study of Low Income Households, their Numbers, Types and Expenditure Patterns, 9093

Smith, Arnold: Stitches in Time: The Commonwealth and World Politics, 12522

Smith, Arthur: Foundations of Sociology, 8089

Smith, B. W.: Patients, Hospitals and Operational Research, 21381

Smith, Barbara Mary Dimond: Constitutional Relations between the Labour and Co-operative Parties: An Historical Review, 1896; Industrial Relocation in Birmingham: The 'Short' Questionnaire Inquiry, 5144; British Regional and Industrial Policy in the 1970s: A Critical review with special reference to the West Midlands in the 1980s, 5226; Black Country Employment, 1959–1970. An Analysis Based on Employment Exchange Data and Incorporating Comparisons between Inner and Outer Exchanges and between the Black Country and Birmingham and Great Britain, 7013; Employment Problems in a County Town: A Study of Bridgnorth, Shropshire, 7015; A History of the British Motorcycle Industry 1945–1975, 17184; The Inner City Economic Problem: A Framework for Analysis and Local Authority Policy, 18012

Smith, Brian Charles: Government Departments: An Organisational Perspective, 820; Regionalism in England, 5061

Smith, Brian Stanley: A History of Malvern, 19346

Smith, C. A.: The Place of Women in the Church, 12217

Smith, C. G.: ed. Oxford and its Region, 18068

Smith, C. J.: 'Great Britain and the 1914–1915 Straits Agreement with Russia: The British Promise of November 1914', 13412

Smith, C. T. B.: Strikes in Britain: A Research Study of Industrial Stoppages in the United Kingdom, 6930

Smith, Charles: Fifty Years with Mountbatten, 15276

Smith, Christopher Selby: The Costs of Further Education: A British Analysis, 23259

Smith, Colin: Falklands: The Air War, 16093; Back to the Good Old Bike, 17173

Smith, Constance Babington: Evidence in Camera: The Story of Photographic Intelligence in World War II, 15200; Iulia de Beausobre: A Russian Christian in the West, 12351; Rose Macaulay: Letters to a Sister, 25679; John Masefield: A Life, 25702

Smith, Cyril Stanley: Industrial Participation, 6026; 'Employment of Sociologists in Research Occupations in Britain in 1973', 8057; Adolescence: An Introduction to the Problem of Order and the Opportunities for Continuity presented by Adolescence in Britain, 8491; People in Need and other Essays: A Study of Contemporary Social Needs and of their Relation to the Welfare State, 8981; The Wincroft Youth Project, 10489; Leisure and Society in Britain, 26927

Smith, Sir Cyril: Big Cyril, 1524

Smith, David Buchanan: Curling: An Illustrated History, 27161

Smith, David Elliott: 'Relationships between the Eysenck and Personality Inventories', 10538

Smith, David John: Racial Disadvantage in Employment, 11177; The Facts of Racial Disadvantage: A National Survey, 11178; Racial Disadvantage in Britain: The PEP Report, 11179; Racial Minorities and Public Housing, 11495; Racial Minorities and Public Housing, 18749

Smith, David L.: The Railway and its Passengers: A Social History, 16794; The Little Railways of South West Scotland, 16976

Smith, David Lawrence: Amenity and Urban Planning, 17913

Smith, David M.: 'An Exploratory Study of Adults' Attitudes Towards Adolescence', 8457; 'New Movements in the Sociology of Youth: A Critique.', 8525

Smith, David Marshall: The North West, 5136; Human Geography: A Welfare Approach, 8800

Smith, David: The Fed: A History of the South Wales Miners in the Twentieth Century, 6320, 6901; 'The Struggle against Company Unionism in the South Wales Coalfield, 1926–1939', 6825; Fields of Praise: The Official History of the Welsh Rugby Union, 1881–1981, 27045

Smith, David: Life-sentence Prisoners, 10457; Reducing the Prison Population: An Exploratory Study in Hampshire, 10458; Board of Visitor Adjudications, 10459

Smith, David: Maps and Plans for the Local Historian and Collector, 26749

Smith, David: Mrs Thatcher's Economics, 3705

Smith, Dennis: 'The Royal Navy and Japan in the Aftermath of the Washington Conference, 1922–1926', 13589

Smith, Dennis: ed. The County of Kincardine, 19235

Smith, Donald John: The Horse and the Cut: The Story of the Canal Horses of Britain, 16390; 'The Gretna Train Smash', 16740; New Street Remembered: The Story of Birmingham's New Street Railway Station 1854–1967, 16995

Smith, Donald M.: ed. Families and Groups: A Unit at Work: A Description and Analysis of Work with Families, Groups and the Neighbourhood, undertaken at the East London Family Service Unit, 10103

Smith, Dudley: Harold Wilson: A Critical Biography, 1060

Smith, Duncan: What Kind of Growth: People or Profits?, 20216

Smith, E. D.: The Battles for Cassino, 14876; Counter-Insurgency Operations: Malaya and Borneo, 16160

Smith, E. J.: Housing: The Present Opportunity, 18575

Smith, E. O.: 'The Trend in Trade Union Amalgamation', 6758

Smith, Edgar C.: 'The Centenary of Steam Navigation', 16499; A Short History of Naval and Maritime Engineering, 16500; 'The Centenary of Naval Engineering', 16501

Smith, Elton Edward: The Angry Young Man of the Thirties, 23778; Louis MacNeice, 25691

Smith, Eric David: East of Kathmandu: The Story of the 7th Duke of Edinburgh's Own Gurkha Rifles, 15645

Smith, Frances: Falling Rolls in Secondary Schools, 22784

Smith, Frederick Edwin [Earl of Birkenhead]: The Last Phase, 1106; The Speeches of Lord Birkenhead, 1107; Contemporary Personalities, 1108; Law, Life and Letters, 1109; Last Essays, 1110

Smith, Frederick Winston Furneaux [Lord Birkenhead]: F. E.: The Life of F. E. Smith, First Earl of Birkenhead, 1111; Halifax 1221; Walter Monckton: The Life of Viscount Monckton of Brenchley, 1276

Smith, G. J.: Personnel Administration and Industrial Relations, 5710

Smith, G. P.: Employment and Unemployment in North West Wales, 7014

Smith, G. Rex: The Yemens, 13863

Smith, Gavin: Getting Around: Transport Today and Tomorrow, 16265

Smith, George Anthony Noel: Government against Poverty?: Liverpool Community Development Project 1970–1975, 9092, 9277

Smith, George William: Britain's Economy: Its Structure and Development, 7236; The Consumer Interest, 20466

Smith, Gerry M.: Britain in Decline?: A Select Bibliography, 3688

Smith, Gilbert: Social Work and the Sociology of Organisations, 8794

Smith, Graham: Something to Declare: 1000 Years of Customs and Excise, 4848

Smith, Graham A.: 'Jim Crow on the Home Front 1942–1945', 11200

Smith, Grover: ed. Letters of Aldous Huxley, 25588

Smith, Gus: The Prince, Being the Public and Private life of Larushka Mischa Skikne, a Jewish Lithuanian Vagabond Player, otherwise Known as Laurence Harvey, 26055

Smith, H. J. F.: Commons and Village Greens: A Study in Land Use, Conservation and Management Based on a National Survey of Commons in England and Wales, 1961–1966, 20267

Smith, H. R.: 'The Dispersal of Population from Congested Urban Centres in Scotland', 7349

Smith, Harold L.: The British Labour Movement to 1970: A Bibliography, 1659; ed. British Feminism in the Twentieth Century, 7642; 'Sex versus Class: British Feminists and the Labour Movement 1919–1929', 7672; 'The Woman-Power Problem in Britain during the Second World War', 7673

Smith, Harold Stanley Vian: The Transport Act 1953: An Explanation for the Transport User and Operator, 16299

Smith, Henry Norman: The Politics of Plenty, 3737

Smith, Henry: A Select Bibliography on the Monetary System, 3417

Smith, Sir Hubert Llewellyn: The Borderland between Public and Voluntary Action in the Social Services, 9118; The New Survey of London Life and Labour, 18340

Smith, J. A.: 'The Scottish Criminal System: Some Distinctive Features', 10247

Smith, J. H.: ed. Ford's List of British Parliamentary Papers 1965–1974, together with Specialist Commentaries, 197; 'Sociology and Management Studies', 5426; 'New Ways in Industrial Sociology', 5648; 'Bridging Occupations', 5872

Smith, J. M. A.: 'The Impact of the Motor Car on Public Transport', 16296

Smith, J. V.: 'Good Morning President': Rugby from the Top, 27037

Smith, James V.: The Meritocratic Intellect: Studies in the History of Educational Research, 22844

Smith, Janet Buchanan Adam: John Buchan, 1383; John Buchan and his World, 25426

Smith, Jenkyn Beverley: James Griffiths and his Times, 1208; Politics and Society in Wales, 1840–1922: Essays in Honour of Ieuan Gwynedd Jones, 2557

Smith, John Francis: A Critical Bibliography of Building Conservation: Historic Towns, Buildings, their Furnishings and Fittings, 18960

Smith, John Frederick: Liverpool: Past-Present-Future, 18048

Smith, John Harold: ed. Manpower Policy and Employment Trends, 5933; 'The Distribution of Power in Nationalised Industries', 6134; Married Women Working, 7683; The University Teaching of the Social Sciences: Industrial Sociology, 7968

Smith, John S.: ed. The County of Caithness, 19230; ed. The County of Sutherland, 19231

Smith, John: 74 Days: An Islander's Diary of the Falklands Occupation, 16120

Smith, John: The Benny Hill Story, 26321

Smith, Justin Davis: 'The Struggle for Control of the Air Waves: The Attlee Governments, The BBC and Industrial Unrest 1945–51', 24773

Smith, K.: Water in Britain, 20099

Smith, Kathleen Joan: A Cure for Crime: The Case of the Self-determinate Prison Sentence, 10414

Smith, Keith: The British Economic Crisis: Its Past and Future, 3693

Smith, Kenneth B.: A Geopolitical Survey of British Policy in the Arab Lands of the Middle East, 1869–1947, 13823

Smith, Kenneth: Cumbrian Villages, 19136

Smith, L. W. Merrow: Prison Screw, 10415

Smith, Lawrence: 'England's Return to the Gold Standard in 1925', 4679

Smith, Leslie: Harold Wilson: The Authentic Portrait, 1060

Smith, Lorna J. F.: 'Crime in England and Wales and Scotland: A British Crime Survey Comparison', 10245

Smith, Louis Patrick Frederick: The Evolution of Agricultural Co-operation, 19509

Smith, Malcolm S.: Rearmament and Deterrence in Britain in the 1930s, 14714; The Royal Air Force, Air Power and British Foreign Policy, 1932–1937, 14715; Cinema, Literature and Society: Elite and Mass Culture in Inter-war Britain, 24601

Smith, Marjorie Jean: Professional Education for Social Work in Britain: An Historical Account, 8731, 22440

Smith, Maurice: A Short History of Dentistry, 22402

Smith, Maurice Hamblin: The Psychology of the Criminal, 10154

Smith, May: Sickness Absence and Labour Wastage, 4107; An Introduction to Industrial Psychology, 5642

Smith, Michael A.: 'Process Technology and Powerlessness', 5889

Smith, Michael Alfred: Brewing Industry

Policy, the Public House and Alcohol Consumption Patterns in the United Kingdom, 20740; Leisure and Society in Britain, 26927

Smith, Myron J., Jnr: The Secret Wars: A Guide to Sources in English, 15993

Smith, N. A.: 'Government Versus Trade Unions in Britain', 6790

Smith, N.: The Plymouth Blitz, 15145

Smith, Neville John: Poverty in England, 1601–1932, 8968

Smith, Nicola: ed. Woodstreet: The Growth of a Village, 19214

Smith, Norman David: The Royal Air Force, 15792

Smith, P. F.: 'The Housing (Homeless Persons) Act 1977—Four Years On', 18515

Smith, Paul: ed. The Historian and Film, 26739

Smith, Peter Charles: Pedestal: The Malta Convoy of August 1942, 12856; War in the Aegean, 14907; Action: Three Studies of the Naval War in the Mediterranean Theatre during 1940, 15012; The Great Ships Pass: British Battleships at War, 1939–1945, 15019; Task Force 57: the British Pacific Fleet, 1944–1945, 15022; Fighting Flotilla: H.M.S. Laforey and her Sister Ships, 15033; Per Mare per Terram: A History of the Royal Marines, 15320; The Great Ships Pass: British Battleships at War, 1939–1945, 15356; The Story of the Torpedo Bomber, 15859

Smith, Peter Frederick: The Syntax of Cities, 17878; The Dynamics of Urbanism, 17879

Smith, Peter Gladstone: The Crime Explosion, 10153

Smith, R. A.: 'Socio-Economic Patterns of England and Wales', 9496

Smith, R. D. P.: 'The Changing Urban Hierarchy in Scotland', 18149

Smith, R. E.: British Army Vehicles and Equipment, 15506

Smith, R.: Planning Local Authority Services for the Elderly, 8595

Smith, Robert Allan: Radio Aids to Navigation, 27249

Smith, Robert Irvine: 'Curriculum Reform', 22640

Smith, Robert Trow: English Husbandry from the Earliest Times to the Present Day, 19467; Life from the Land, 19468

Smith, Roger: A History of Birmingham, vol.3: Birmingham 1939–1970, 5142, 18005; 'Postwar Birmingham: Planning and Development', 18011

Smith, Roger: East Kilbride: The Biography of a Scottish New Town, 1947–1973, 18186

Smith, Rowland: Lyric and Polemic: The Literary Personality of Roy Campbell, 25436

Smith, S. Watson: The Chronicle of the First World Tour of the British Medical Association, 20789

Smith, Selwyn Michael: The Battered Child Syndrome, 9959

Smith, Stephen: Local Taxes and Local Government, 4884

Smith, Stirling: Burying Beveridge: Conservatives and Social Security Reform, 9045

Smith, Susan J.: 'Crime in the News', 10244; The Politics of 'Race': Citizenship, Segregation and White Supremacy in Britain, 18707

Smith, T.: 'A Comparative Study of French and British Decolonization', 12596

Smith, T. Dan: 'Local Government in Newcastle: The Background to some recent Developments', 3336; An Autobiography, 3337

Smith, T. E.: The Background to Malaysia, 12936

Smith, Trevor A.: 'Party Discipline in the House of Commons', 1602; Town and County Hall: Problems of Recruitment and Training, 3236; Town Councillors: A Study of Barking, 3309; The Politics of the Corporate Economy, 6135; 'The Debate on Broadcasting's Future', 24789

Smith, Wilfred: An Economic Geography of Great Britain, 3447, 26680

Smith, Sir William: 'The Work of the Ministry of Health', 21313

Smith, William James: Five Centuries of Cambridge Musicians, 1464–1964, 24539

Smith, William Owen Lester: To Whom do Schools Belong? An Introduction to the Study of School Government, 22791; Compulsory Education in England, 22867; Education in Great Britain, 22868

Smitherman, Philip Henry: Infantry Uniforms of the British Army, 15547

Smithers, Alan George: Sandwich Courses: an Integrated Education?, 23656

Smithers, David Waldron: Possibilities in Cancer Prevention, 21054

Smithies, Edward: The Black Economy in England since 1914, 3540; Crime in Wartime Britain: A Social History of Crime in World War Two, 10268

Smithson, Alison M. and Smithson, Peter: Urban Structuring, 17876; Ordinances and Light: Urban Theories 1952–1960 and their Applications in a Building Project, 1963–1970, 17877

Smithson, Peter Denham: 'The Idea of Architecture in the Fifties', 23913

Smout, [Thomas] Christopher: A Century of the Scottish People 1830–1950, 2448; 'US Consular Reports: A Source for Scottish Economic Historians', 3473; ed. Essays in Social History, 7616; ed. The Search for Wealth and Stability: Essays in Economic and Social History Presented to M. W. Flynn, 7617; 'Scottish Marriage, Regular and Irregular, 1500–1940', 10010

Smuts, Jan Christian: Jan Christian Smuts, 12726

Smyth, Charles Hugh Egerton: The Church and the Nation: Six Studies in the Anglican Tradition, 11573; Cyril Forster Garbett: Archbishop of York, 11696

Smyth, Clifford: Ulster Assailed, 2916; Ian Paisley: Voice of Protestant Ulster, 3078

Smyth, D.: Diplomacy and Strategy of Survival: British Policy and Franco's Spain, 1940–1, 13995

Smyth, H.: Property Companies and the Construction Industry in Britain, 6186

Smyth, Hazel P.: The B & I Line: A History of the British and Irish Steam Packet Company, 16548

Smyth, Sir John George: Only Enemy, 1525; Bolo Whistler: The Life of General Sir Lashmer Whistler, 14788; Before the Dawn: A Story of Two Historic Retreats, 14833; Percival and the Tragedy of Singapore, 15077; The Will to Live: The Story of Dame Margot Turner, D.B.E., R.R.C., 15765; The History of the Royal Military Academy, Woolwich; The Royal Military College, Sandhurst, And the Royal Military Academy, Sandhurst, 1741–1961, 15772

Smyth, R.: 'Britain's African colonies and British Propaganda during the Second World War', 12700

Smyth, Robert: 'Essays in the Economics of Socialism and Capitalism', 9040

Smyth, Robert Leslie: The British Pottery Industry, 6626; The Distribution of Fruit and Vegetables, 20706

Smythe, Paul Rodney: A Bibliography of Anglican Modernism, 11553

Smythies, John R.: ed. The Alpbach Symposium, 1968: Beyond Reductionism: New Perspectives in the Life Sciences, 26508

Snagge, John Derrick Mordaunt: Those Vintage Years of Radio, 24743

Snaith, Jill: An Information Service in a Deprived Housing Estate, 9413

Snell, Henry, [Lord]: The Case for Sunday Games: Against Sabbatarian Prejudice, 27017

Snell, John Bernard: Britain's Railways under Steam, 17027

Snellgrove, Douglas Rosebery: Elderly Housebound: A Report on Elderly People who are Incapacitated, 8580

Snelling, R. C.: 'Peacemaking 1919: Australia, New Zealand and the British Empire Delegation at Versailles', 12613

Snelson, Henry Stanbridge Egerton: The Story of Rural Community Councils, 19063

Snodgrass, Catherine P.: The County of East Lothian, 19220

Snow, Charles Percy, [Baron]: The Two Cultures and the Scientific Revolution, 23750; The Two Cultures and a Second Look, 23751

Snow, George D'Oyly: The Public School in the New Age, 23015

Snow, Philip A.: A Bibliography of Fiji, Tonga and Rotuma, 12879

Snow, Philip Arthur: Stranger and Brother: A Portrait of C.P. Snow, 25810

Snowden, Ethel [Viscountess] [Mrs Philip]:British Students of Child Welfare, Tested by the 'Declaration of Geneva'. 1926, 8359

Snowden, Philip [Viscount]: An Autobiography, 1316

Snyder, Charles: A Bibliography of the History of Opthalmology for 1952–1954, 21102

Snyder, Esther M.: Israel, 14279

Snyder, G. S.: The 'Royal Oak' Disaster, 15037

Snyder, Laurence Hasbrouck: Blood Grouping in Relation to Clinical and Legal Medicine, 21234

Snyder, Rixford Kinney: The Tariff Problem in Great Britain, 1918–1923, 3757

Social Democratic Party and The Scottish Liberal Party: Working Together for Scotland: A Joint Programme for Government, 2545

Social Democratic Party: (Policy Dept.) Decentralising Government, 1843; The Politics of Prosperity and the Politics of Poverty, 1844; Attacking Poverty, 1845; Caring about People—Caring about Costs: Policy Guidelines for the Local Elections, 1846; Education Matters, 1847; Housing: A Choice for All, 1848; Policy for Women, 1849

Social Science Research Council: The Social Responsibilities of Business: A Report, 5980; Research on Poverty, 9062

Social and Economic Trends: H.M.S.O, 2774

Socialist Labour League: In Defence of Trotskyism, 1987

Socialist Medical Association of Great Britain: Medicine Tomorrow, 22000

Socialist Party of Great Britain: The Socialist Party and War, 1969; Questions of the Day, 1970; From Capitalism to Socialism, 1971; Socialism as a Practical Alternative, 1972

Socialist Workers' Party: Why Labour Fails, 1976; The Labour Party: Myth and Reality, 1977; Permanent Revolution: A Re-examination, 1978; How Marxism Works, 1979; Socialism from Below, 1980; The Future Socialist Society, 1981

Society for Promoting Due Observance of the Lord's Day: Sunday Opening of Theatres and Music Halls: Manifesto to the Christian People of England, 27018

Society of British Aerospace Companies: Keep Britain Flying: The Case for Britain's Aerospace Industry, 17592

Society for the Study of Labour History: Bulletin 1+ Sheffield, 1658

Society of Labour Lawyers: Housing Group, The End of the Private Landlord, 18444

Sociological Abstracts Inc.: Sociological Abstracts 1953, 4

Sociological Review:Special Issue: 'Aspects of the Sociology of Social Welfare', 8790; Monographs No. 5. Sociology and Medicine: Studies within the Framework of the British National Health Service, 21947

Soddy, Kenneth: Men in Middle Life, 8553; ed. Mental Health in the Service of the Community, 21816

Sofer, Anne: The London Left Takeover, 3293

Sofer, Cyril: 'Buying and Selling: A Study in the Sociology of Distribution', 4948; New Ways in Management Training: A Technical College Develops its Service to Industry, 5418; Men in Mid-Career: A Study of British Managers and Technical Specialists, 5448, 9791, 9805

Sokoloff, B.: The Miracle Drugs, 22293

Solden, Norbert C.: Women in British Trade Unions, 1874–1976, 7753, 7862

Solesbury, William: 'Ideas about Structure Plans: Past, Present and Future', 5112

Solmes, Alwyn: The English Policeman 1871–1941, 10685

Solomon, Barbara W.: The Scope of Local Initiative: A Study of Cheshire County Council 1961–1974, 3350

Solomos, John: Black Youth, Racism and the State: The Politics of Ideology and Policy, 11140; ed. Racism and Equal Opportunity Policies in the 1980s, 11142

Somers, A. R. and Somers, H. M.: 'The Health Service: Diagnosis and Prognosis', 21326

Somerset, Felicity: 'Vietnamese Refugees in Britain: Resettlement Experiences', 11393

Somervell, David Churchill: Modern Britain, 1870–1950, 296; The Reign of King George V: An English Chronicle, 473; British Politics since 1900, 1581; A History of Tonbridge School, 23079

Somervell, Theodore Howard: After Everest: The Experiences of a Mountaineer and Medical Missionary, 27239

Somerville, Henry Boyle Townshend: The Chart Makers, 26694

Sommer, Dudley: Haldane of Cloan: His Life and Times, 1856–1928, 1214

Somner, Graeme: From 70 North to 70 South: A History of the Christian Salvesen Fleet, 16545

Sondheimer, Janet: Castle Adamant in Hampstead: A History of Westfield College, 1882–1982, 23534

Sondhi, Ranjit: Divided Families: British Immigration Control in the Indian Sub-Continent, 11136

Soothill, Keith: The Prisoner's Release: A Study in the Employment of Ex-prisoners, 10464

Soper, Donald Oliver: Calling for Action: An Autobiographical Enquiry, 12092

Soper, Michael Henry Ray: Dairy Farming and Milk Production, 20665

Soper, Tony: The Wreck of the Torrey Canyon, 20072

Soppelsa, J.: 'L'expansion urbaine récente de Glasgow', 18140

Sorge, Arndt: 'The Context of Industrial Relations in Great Britain and West Germany', 5808

Sorsby, Arnold: The Royal Eye Hospital, 1857–1957, 21448; Blindness in England, 1951–1954, 21930

Sourkes, Theodore L.: Nobel Prize Winners in Medicine and Physiology, 1901–1965, 20895

Soutar, Mary Stewart: Nutrition and the Size of the Family: Report on a New Housing Estate, 1939, 20532

South Atlantic Crisis: Background, Consequences, Documentation, 16086

South, Nigel: Policing for Profit: The Private Security Sector, 10771; ed. A Land Fit for Heroin?, 22203

Southall, Brian: Abbey Road: The Story of the World's Most Famous Recording Studio, 24580

Southcott, Ernest William: The Parish Comes Alive, 11619

Southern Rhodesia: Constitutional Conference held at Lancaster House, London September-December 1979, 12807

Southern, Christine: The Changing Face of Bolton, 18844

Southgate Donald: University Education in Dundee: A Centenary History, 23490; ed. The Conservative Leadership, 1832–1932, 1615

Southgate, George Walter: England, 1867–1939, 361; English Economic History, 3459

Southwick, A. F., Jnr: The Doctor, the Hospital and the Patient in England: Rights and Responsibilities under the National Health Service, 21405

Southworth, George C.: 'Early History of Radio-Astronomy', 26420

Spackman, Ann: 'Constitutional Development in Trinidad and Tobago', 13065

Spaight, James Molony: The Beginnings of Organised Air Power: A Historical Study, 15806

Spain, Bernie: Plans and Provisions for the Mentally Handicapped, 21852

Spalding, Ethel Howard: England: a Social and Economic History, 1830–1936, 363, 3462

Spalding, Frances: Vanessa Bell, 24714; Stevie Smith: A Critical Biography, 25809

Spalding, William Frederick: The London Money Market: A Practical Guide, 4278

Spark, Muriel: John Masefield, 25700

Sparke, Penny: ed. Did Britain Make It?, 24151

Sparkes, John Richard: ed. Monopoly, 5515

Sparks, Richard Franklin: Key Issues in Criminology, 10130; Local Prisons: The Crisis in the English Penal System, 10352; ed. Community Homes and the Approved School System, 10654; ed. Residential Treatment of Disturbed and Delinquent Boys, 10655

Sparrow, Gerald: "R. A. B.": Study of a Statesman, 1124

Sparrow, John: The Coldstream Guards, 1920–1946, 15610; A. E. Housman: A Bibliography, 25576

Spate, Oskar Hermann Khristian: The Fijian People: Economic Problems and Prospects: A Report, 12880

Speaight, Robert William: The Life of Eric Gill, 24017; William Rothenstein: The Portrait of an Artist in his Time, 24060; ed. Letters from Hilaire Belloc, 25374; Hilaire Belloc, 25375

Speakman, Colin: Leisure, Transport and the Countryside, 26950

Speakman, John: Transport in Yorkshire, 16335

Spear, H. B.: 'The Growth of Heroin Addiction in the United Kingdom', 22202

Spear, Sheldon: 'Pacifist Radicalism in the Postwar British Labour Party: The Case of E. D. Morel, 1919–1924', 13500, 13547

Spearing, A.: 'George Blake versus Two Home Secretaries', 10885

Spears, Sir Edward Louis: Liaison, 1914. A Narrative of the Great Retreat, 14574; Assignment to Catastrophe, 14832

Special Publication: Institute of British Geographers, No. 5. Social Patterns in Cities, 18284

Speed, Keith: Sea Change: The Battle for the Falklands and the Future of Britain's Navy, 15243

Speed, Peter Frederick: Police and Prisons, 10745

Speers, Peter C.: 'Colonial Policy of the British Labour Party', 12573

Speirs, John: The Left in Britain: A Checklist and Guide, 1996

Speirs, M.: 'The General Federation of Trade Unions, 1945–1970', 6895

Spence, Sir Basil Urwin: Phoenix at Coventry: The Building of a New Cathedral, 23928

Spence, Sir James Calvert: The Purpose and Practice of Medicine: Selections from the Writings of Sir James Spence, 20905; A Thousand Families in Newcastle Upon Tyne: An Approach to the Study of Health and Illness in Children, 22001

Spence, John E.: 'British Policy towards the High Commission Territories', 12709; Lesotho: The Politics of Independence, 12710

Spencer Jones, Harold: 'The History of the Marine Chronometer', 7153

Spencer, A. M.: 'Some Changes in the Composition of a Mental Hospital', 21833

Spencer, Anthony Ernest Charles Winchcombe: 'Catholics in Britain and Ireland: Regional Contrasts', 2718; 'The Catholic Community as a British Melting Pot', 11953; 'Demography of Catholicism', 11954; 'The Newman Demographic Survey, 1953–1962', 11955; 'The Demography and Sociology of the Catholic Community in England and Wales', 11956

Spencer, Charles: 'The Phenomenon of British Sculpture', 24180

Spencer, Douglas Arthur: The Cinema Today, 24600

Spencer, Frederick Herbert: An Inspector's Testament, 23249

Spencer, J. H.: The Battle for Crete, 14857

Spencer, John Carrington: Stress and Release in an Urban Estate: A Study in Action Research, 17875, 21808

Spencer, Ken: Crisis in the Industrial Heartland: A Study of the West Midlands, 5229; 'Older Urban Areas and Housing Improvement Policies', 18529

Spencer, Peter D.: Financial Innovation Efficiency and Disequilibrium: Problems of Monetary Management in the U.K. 1971–1981, 4656

Spencer, W. Baldwin: Spencer's Last Journey: Being the Journal of an Expedition to Tierra del Fuego by the late Sir Baldwin Spencer, 27187

Spencer-Cooper, H. E. H.: The Battle of the Falkland Islands, 14664

Spender, John Alfred: Life of Herbert Henry Asquith, Lord Oxford and Asquith, 971; Great Britain, Empire and Commonwealth 1886–1935, 297, 12546

Spender, Sir [Harold] Stephen: 'The Character of Lloyd George', 1024; 'The Modern as Vision of a Whole Situation', 23743; The Struggle of the Modern, 23780; Henry Moore: Sculptures in Lanscape, 24199; Cyril Connolly: A Memoir, 25459; World within World: Autobiography, 25819; The Thirties and After: Poetry, Politics and People (1933–1975), 25820

Spenser, James: Limey Breaks In, 10224

Sperber, Murray: ed. Arthur Koestler: A Collection of Critical Essays, 25615

Spero, Sterling Denhard: Labor Relations in British Nationalized Industry, 5619

Sperry, William Learoyd: Religion and Education, 22890

Spice, B.: Colour and Class in Six Liverpool Schools, 23170

Spicer, Arnold: Advances in Preconcentration and Dehydration of Foods, 20644; Bread: Social, Nutritional and Agricultural Aspects of Wheaten Bread, 20701

Spicer, C. C.: Regional and Social Factors in Infant Mortality, 7448

Spicer, Joanne: The Franchise Affair: Creating Fortune and Failure in Independent Television, 24878

Spicer, Simon J. L.: The Motor Cars We Owned: Austin, Ford, Morris, Vauxhall, 1920–1930, 17346

Spiers, Edward M.: Haldane: An Army Reformer, 1216

Spiller, Brian: The Chameleon's Eye: James Buchanan & Co. Ltd., 1884–1984, 20731

Spinks, George Stephens: Religion in Britain since 1900, 11556

Spinley, Betty Martha: The Deprived and the Privileged: Personality Development in English Society, 7577, 8360

Spinner, Thomas J.: A Political and Social History of Guyana 1945–1983, 13045

Spiro, Edward: Shadow of a Spy: The Complete Dossier on George Blake, 16024; The Third Man, 16049

Spolsky, Bernard: ed. Sage Studies in Bilingual Education, 23622

Spoor, Alec: White-collar Union: Sixty Years of NALGO, 6854

Sports Council: Public Disorder and Sporting Events: A Report by a Joint Panel of the Sports Council and the SSRC, 27068

Sprake, R. F.: London and Overseas Freighters Limited, 1949–1977: A Shore History, 16576

Spraos, John: 'Linking Wages to Productivity', 3895; The Decline of the Cinema: An Economist's Report, 24632

Spratley, Terry A.: Responding to Drinking Problems, 22153

Spratt, Hereward Philip: Transatlantic Paddle Steamers, 16589

Sprigge, Elizabeth: The Life of Ivy Compton-Burnett, 25457; Sybil Thorndike Casson, 26105

Spring Rice, Sir Cecil: The Letters and Friendships of Sir Cecil Spring Rice: A Record, 13309

Spring Rice, Margery: Working-class Wives: Their Health and Conditions, 7837, 9623

Spring, D. W.: Propaganda, Politics and Film, 1918–45, 15224, 24614

Spring, David: The League of British Covenanters: A Study in English Extremism, 2057

Spring, Ernest: 'Conchie'. The Wartime Experiences of a Conscientious Objector, 13524

Spring, M.: 'The Natwest Tower', 23929

Springer, Hugh W.: 'Barbados as a Sovereign State', 13077

Springhall, John: Youth, Empire and Society: British Youth Movements, 1883–1940, 8508; Coming of Age: Adolescence in Great Britain 1860–1960, 8509; Sure and Stedfast: A History of the Boys' Brigade, 1883–1983, 8510

Springham, Betty: Problems of the British Economy, 3655

Sprinks, Neil: The Railways of Central and West Wales, 16924; ed. The Railways of South East Wales, 16974

Sproat, Iain: Wodehouse at War, 15104

Sprott, Walter John Herbert: Social Psychology, 7951; Sociology, 7952; Science and Social Action, 7953; Human Groups, 7954; Sociology and the Seven Dials, 7955; 'Principia Sociologica', 7956; Making Good Citizens—The Process of Socialization, 7957

Sproule, Anna: The Social Calender, 9749

Spufford, Margaret and Spufford, Peter: Eccleshall: The Story of a Staffordshire Market Town and its Dependent Villages, 19330

Spurling, Hilary: Ivy when Young: The Early Life of Ivy Compton-Burnett 1884–1919, 25456; Handbook to Anthony Powell's Music of Time, 25764

Spurway, Neil: Authority in Higher Education, 23307

Spyer, Geoffrey: Architect and Community: Environmental Design in an Urban Society, 9364

Squibb, G. D.: Precedence in England and Wales, 459

Squire, Duncan: Local Taxes and Local Government, 4884

Squires, Roger W.: Canals Revived: The Story of the Waterways Restoration Movement, 16386

Squires, Stuart E.: The Lost Railways of Lincolnshire, 16954

Srodes, James: Takeovers, 5551

Stabler, Michael: Agricultural Economics and Land Use, 20276

Stacey, Barry G.: 'Inter-generational Occupational Mobility in Britain', 5890; Teenagers and Alcohol: A Developmental Study in Glasgow, 22148; Vol, 22149

Stacey, C. P.: Canada and the Age of Conflict: A History of Canadian External Policies, 12644

Stacey, Francis William: Britain and Russia from the Crimean to the Second World War, 13913

Stacey, Frank Arthur: British Government, 1966–1975: Years of Reform, 777

Stacey, Margaret: Women, Power and Politics, 7849; ed. Comparability in Social Research, 7994; 'Local Social Status in England and Wales', 9475; 'Urban Redevelopment: The Case of the Lower Swansea Valley', 18163; Tradition and Change: A Study of Banbury, 19179; Power, Persistence and Change: A Second Study of Banbury, 19180; ed. Hospitals, Children and Their Families: The Report of a Pilot Study, 21353

Stacey, Nicholas Anthony Howard: English Accountancy: A Study in Social and Economic History, 1800–1954, 4169

Stacey, Nicolas David: Who Cares?, 11812

Stacey, Tom: Immigration and Enoch Powell, 11265

Stack, Frieda: 'Civil Service Associations and the Whitley Report of 1917', 881

Stack, Prunella: Movement is Life: The Autobiography of Prunella Stack, 7725

Stacpoole, Alberic: 'Anglican/Roman Catholic Relations after the Council 1965–1970', 12331; 'Ecumenism on the Eve of the Council: Anglican/Roman Catholic Relations', 12330

Stadden, Charles: Coldstream Guards—Dress and Appointments, 1658–1972, 15608

Staddon, Tommy: Aviation in Birmingham, 17524; A History of Cambrian Airways, the Welsh Airline, from 1935 to 1976, 17633

Stafford, Ann: The Age of Consent, 9973

Stafford, David: Britain and European Resistance 1940–1945: A Survey of the Special Operations Executive with Documents, 14965

Stafford, David Christopher: Key Developments in Personal Finance, 4536; The Economics of Housing Policy, 18755

Stafford, Helen Muriel: Queenswood: The First Sixty Years, 1894–1954, 22480

Stafford, Paul: 'Political Autobiography and the Art of the Possible: R.A. Butler at the Foreign Office 1938–1939', 1128; 'The Chamberlain-Halifax Visit to Rome: A Reappraisal', 13794

Stafford-Clark, David: Psychiatry To-Day, 22415

Stage Yearbook: 1948–69, 25902

Stagg, David J.: Woodmen of the New Forest, 19738

Stagner, R.: Psychology of Union—Management Relations, 6799

Stalker, John: Stalker, 2935, 10788

Stallworthy, Jon Howie: Wilfred Owen, 25755

Stallybrass, Clare Oswald: Industrial Hygiene and Medicine, 4113; Textbook of Public Health, 22043

Stammers, Michael K.: West Coast Shipping, 16476

Stamp, Gavin: The Church in Crisis: A Critical Assessment of the Current State of the Church of England, 11601

Stamp, Josiah Charles [Baron]: The Financial Aftermath of War, 3746, 4556; Taxation during the War, 4833; Wealth and Taxable Capacity, 4834; The Social Significance of Death Duties, 4835; The National Income 1924: A Comparative Study of the Income of the U.K., 1911, and 1924, 4886; 'Geography and Economic Theory', 26672

Stamp, Sir Laurence Dudley: The British Isles: A Geographic and Economic Survey, 5036, 26684; Nature Conservation in Britain [with a List of Conservation Areas in England, Wales and Scotland Compiled by the late James Fisher]. 1970, 20221; The Land of Britain: Its Use and Misuse, 20260; ed. The Land of Britain: The Report of the Land Utilisation Survey of Britain, 20280; ed. London essays in Geography, 26649; The Land of Britain, 26683

Stamp, Terence: Stamp Album, 26101; Coming Attraction, 26102

Stanbridge, H. H.: A History of Sewage Treatment in Britain, 20091

Stancliffe, F. S.: The Manchester Royal Eye Hospital, 1814–1964: A Short History, 21462

Standard Chartered Bank Ltd.: Standard Chartered Bank Ltd.: A Story Brought Up to Date, 4508

Standing Conference of Councils of Social Service: Social Work in the 1960's: Report of a Conference, 8728; Community Services for Health and Welfare Cooperation between Local Authorities and Voluntary Organisations: Report of a Conference, 8729; New Approaches to Community Work: Report, 9260

Standing Conference of Rural Community Councils: The Decline of Rural Services, 19076

Standing Conference on London and South East Regional Planning: The Third London Airport: Report by the Technical Panel, 17688; Joint Report by the Administrative and Technical Panels, 17689

Standing Joint Advisory Committee of the University of Leeds, The Board of Governors of The United Leeds Hospitals and the Leeds Regional Hospital Board: Working Party . . . , 21426

Standing, Guy: 'Government and Unemployment, 1966–1970: A Study of Policy and Evidence', 6981

Stanford, Derek: John Betjeman: A Study, 25395; Inside the Forties: Literary Memoirs 1937–1957, 25822; Christopher Fry: An Appreciation, 25961

Stanhope-Palmer, R.: Tank Trap 1940, or, No Battle in Britain, 15533

Stanier, D. J.: Blue Bus Services: An Illustrated History of the Well-known Derbyshire Bus Company, 17320

Stanier, Peter: 'The Granite Quarrying Industry in Devon and Cornwall: Part Two 1910–1985', 6348

Stannage, C. T.: 'The East Fulham By-Election: 25 October 1933', 13501

Stannard, Carol: London's Workers: Changes in the Distribution of Residence 1961–1966, 16285

Stannard, Martin: ed. Evelyn Waugh: The Critical Heritage, 25863

Stannard, Robert B.: Rail Commuting to Central London, 16287

Stansky, Peter David Lyman: ed. Churchill: A Profile, 988; Journey to the Frontier: Julian Bell and John Cornford: Their Lives and the 1930s, 1943, 23774; Orwell: The Transformation; The Unknown Orwell, 25748

Stanton, Louis Francois Honore: A Guide to the Merchant Shipping Acts, 16491

Stanton, Madeline E.: The Centennial of Surgical Anesthesia. An Annotated Catalogue, 21037

Stanwood, F.: 'Revolution and the "Old Reactionary Policy": Britain in Persia, 1917', 13854

Stanworth, P.: ed. Elites and Power in British Society, 11686

Stanyer, Jeffrey: County Government in England and Wales, 3199; 'Some Aspects of the Financial Behaviour of County Boroughs', 3276; A History of Devon County Council 1889–1989, 3353

Stape, John Henry: Angus Wilson: A Bibliography 1947–1987, 25880

Stapledon, Sir [Reginald] George: ed. A Survey of the Agriculture and Waste Lands of Wales, 19631; ed. A Survey of the Agricultural and Waste Lands of Wales, 20259

Staples, Peter: The Church of England 1961–1980, 11603

Stapleton, Margaret: with an Essay by Ralph J. Mills. Sir John Betjeman: A Bibliography of Writings by and about him, 25393

Stargardt, A. W.: Australia's Asian Policies: The History of a Debate 1839–1972, 12606

Stark, Thomas: 'Some Aspects of Income Distribution in the U.K. since World War Two, 3810; The Distribution of Personal Income in the U.K. 1949–1963, 3822

Starkie, David Nicholas Martin: Traffic and Industry: A Study of Traffic Generation and Spatial Interaction, 17143; Privatising London's Airports, 17683

Starling, Ernest Henry: A Century of Physiology: Being the First of a Series of Centenary Addresses, 21211

Starmer-Smith, Nigel: The Barbarians: The Official History of the Barbarians Football Club, 27041

Starobinski, J.: A History of Medicine, 21212

Statesman's Year Book: 1864+, 265

Statistical Abstract of the UK Ports Industry, 16645

Statistical Review of Northern Ireland Agriculture: 1966+, 19646

Stave, B. M.: A Conversation with H. J. Dyos: Urban History in Great Britain, 26766

Staveley, Ronald: ed. Government Information and the Research Worker, 246

Stead, Peter: 'Working Class Leadership in South Wales 1900–1920', 2566; Coleg Harlech: the First Fifty Years, 23704

Stead, Philip John: The Police We Deserve, 10732; The Police of Britain, 10767

Steadman, Stephen: Testing Children: Standardized Testing in Local Education Authorities and Schools, 22786

Stearn, William Thomas: 'The Garden History Society's Tenth Anniversary and some Historians of Garden History', 19878

Stebbing, John: 'Commonwealth Consultation in External Affairs: Ups and Downs over 74 Years', 12520

Steck, H. J.: 'Grassroots, Militants and Ideology: The Bevanite Revolt', 1730

Steed, Guy P. F.: 'Regional Industrial Change: Northern Ireland', 5388

Steed, Henry Wickham: 'Locarno and British Interests', 13660

Steed, Michael: 'Electoral Choice and the Production of Government: The Changing Operation of the Electoral System in the United Kingdom since 1955', 2363

Steeds, D.: Britain since 1945, 387

Steel, Sir Christopher: 'Anglo-German Relations: A British View', 14218

Steel, D. R.: The Administrative Process in Britain, 912

Steel, David Ian Anthony: A Lincolnshire Village: The Parish of Corby Glen in its Historical Context, 19328

Steel, Sir David: Against Goliath: David Steel's Story, 1527; No Entry: The Background and Implications of the Commonwealth Immigrants Act 1968, 11118

Steel, David: Sharing Profits: The Partnership Path to Economic Recovery, 6051

Steel, Robert Walter: ed. The Oxford Region: A Scientific and Historical

Survey, 18067; Basingstoke Town Development: A Review of the First Six Years, 18841; The Institute of British Geographers: The First Fifty Years, 26629; ed. British Geography, 1918–1945, 26644; ed. Liverpool Essays in Geography: A Jubilee Collection, 26675

Steel, Tom: Scotland's Story, 2456; The Life and Death of St Kilda: The Moving Story of a Vanished Island Community, 19265

Steel, W. D.: British Goods Wagons from 1887 to the Present Day, 17096

Steele, D. B.: 'New Towns for Depressed Areas', 18233, 18994

Steele, David: More Power to the Regions, 5060

Steele, Jonathan: The South African Connection: Western Investment in Apartheid, 12717

Steer, David: Police Cautions—A Study in the Exercise of Police Discretion, 10746

Steer, Herbert Philip: Caring for the Elderly, 8590

Steer, William Campbell: ed. Fifty Years of Botany, 26552

Steers, J. A.: ed. The Cambridge Region, 18098; 'The East Coast Floods, January 31st to February 1st, 1953', 20182; 'The Storm Surge of 11th January 1978 on the East Coast of England', 20185

Stein, Bruno: Work and Welfare in Britain and the U.S.A., 5979, 8900; ed. Incentives and Planning in Social Policy, 8901

Stein, Leonard: Weizmann and England . . . 1964, 11307; The Balfour Declaration, 14289

Steinberg, B.: 'Jewish Education in Great Britain during World War II', 11293, 22901

Steiner, Zara Shakow: ed. 'The Foreign and Commonwealth Office', 13334, 13340

Steiniger, Rolf: 'Grossbritannien und die Ruhr', 14209; 'Wie die Teilung Deutschlands verhindert wer den sollte: Der Robertson-Plan aus dem Jahre 1948', 14210; 'Die Rhein-Ruhr Frage im Kontext britischer Deutschlandspolitik 1945/46', 14211; ed. Die britische Deutschland—und Besatzungspolitik 1945–1949, 14213

Stengel, Erwin: Attempted Suicide: Its Social Significance and Effects, 10802; Suicide and Attempted Suicide, 10803

Stengelhofen, John: Cornwall's Railway Heritage, 16927

Stent, Gunnar S.: Phage and the Origins of Molecular Biology, 22307

Stent, Ronald: A Bespattered Page? The Internment of His Majesty's Most Loyal Enemy Aliens, 15048

Stephen, Barbara: Girton College, 1869–1932, 23476

Stephen, Elspeth: ed. Residential Care for the Mentally Retarded, 21831

Stephen, G. M.: British Warship Design since 1906, 15352

Stephen, R. D.: Steam Supreme: Recollections of Scottish Railways in the 1920s, 17047

Stephens, J.: Inventory of Abstracting and Indexing Services Produced in the United Kingdom, 245

Stephens, Michael D.: ed. The University and its Region: The Extra-Mural Contribution, 23700; ed. The British Malaise: Industrial Performance, Education and Training in Britain Today, 5963

Stephens, Raymond William Barrow: ed. Noise Pollution: Effects and Control, 20146

Stephens, W. B.: Sources for English Local History, 26744

Stephenson, Alan Malcolm George: Anglicanism and the Lambeth Conference, 11638; The Rise and Decline of English Modernism, 11879; 'Ripon Hall, 1897–1964', 11914

Stephenson, Carl: ed. Sources of English Constitutional History, 595

Stephenson, Donald: The BBC's Foreign Relations, 24777

Stephenson, Geoffrey M.: ed. Industrial Relations: A Social Psychological Approach, 5801

Stephenson, Gwendolen: Edward Stuart Talbot, 1844–1934, 11759

Stephenson, Hugh: Claret and Chips: The Rise of the SDP, 1838

Stephenson, Richard M.: 'Stratification, Education and Occupational Orientation: A Parallel Study and Overview', 9588

Stephenson, Sir Robert: Administration of a University: An Account of the Management of Academic Affairs in the University of Birmingham, 23461

Stephenson, T. E.: 'The Changing Role of Local Democracy: The Trade Union Branch and its Members', 6755

Stephenson, Tom: Forbidden Land, 26969

Stephenson, Yvonne: A Bibliography of the West Indian Federation, 13091

Stern, Fritz: ed. The Varieties of History from Voltaire to the Present, 26728

Stern, Hans Heinrich: Parent Education: An International Survey, 10066

Stern, Nicholas Herbert: Crime: The Police and Criminal Statistics, 10237

Stern, Robert M.: 'The Determination of the Factors Affecting American and British Exports in the Inter-War and Post-War Periods', 3717; 'British and American Productivity and Comparative Costs in International Trade', 3721

Stern, Walter Marcel: The Porters of London, 9656

Sternlicht, Sanford: C. S. Forester, 25517; John Masefield, 25699

Stettner, Nora: Productivity Bargaining and Industrial Change, 5993

Steven, Maisie: The Good Scots Diet: What Happened to it?, 20534

Stevenage Development Corporation: The New Town of Stevenage, 19025

Stevens, Frances M.: The Living Tradition: The Social and Educational Assumptions of the Grammar School, 22981; The New Inheritors: Some Questions about the Education of Intelligent 'First Generation' Children, 22989

Stevens, L.: Ethnic Minorities and Building Society Lending in Leeds, 4387

Stevens, Michael: V. Sackville-West: A Critical Biography, 25791

Stevens, Paul: Canada since 1867: A Bibliographical Guide, 12640

Stevens, Philip: Race, Crime and Arrests, 10265

Stevens, Robert: 'The Role of a Final Appeal Court in a Democracy: The House of Lords Today', 10293

Stevens, Rosemary: Medical Practice in Modern England: The Impact of Specialization and State Medicine, 20832; The Impact of Specialized and State Medicine: Medical Practice in Modern England, 22002

Stevens-Stratton, Seymour Walter: British Lorries, 1945–1983, 17464

Stevenson, Alan Carruth: Recent Advances in Social Medicine, 21945

Stevenson, Alan Leslie: The Shops Acts 1912–1936, and the Factories Act, 1937, 20489; The Shops Act, 1950, and the Factories Act, 1937, as Amended by the Factories Act, 1948, so far as it Relates to the Powers and Duties of Local Authorities, 20490

Stevenson, Bruce: Reader's Guide to Great Britain: A Bibliography, 422

Stevenson, David: The First World War and International Politics, 13365

Stevenson, James A. C.: Scoor-Oot: A Dictionary of Scots Words and Phrases in Current Use, 23850

Stevenson, James Laing: The Last Tram, Edinburgh, 17223

Stevenson, John: The Longman Handbook of Modern British History 1714–1987, 65; ed. High and Low Politics in Modern Britain, 1690; The Slump, 3588, 7568; Social Conditions in Britain between the Wars, 7566; British Society 1914–1945, 7567; Longman Atlas of Modern British History: A Visual Guide to British Society and Politics, 1700–1970, 7569

Stevenson, June: A New Portrait of Social Work: A Study of Social Services in a Northern Town from Younghusband to Seebohm, 8733

Stevenson, L.: ed. Medicine Science and Culture, 21216

Stevenson, Olive: Claimant or Client?: A Social Worker's View of the Supplementary Benefits Commission, 8742

Stevenson, R. S.: A History of Oto-laryngology, 21106

Stewart, A.: 'Old People Living in Dorset: A Socio-medical Survey of Private Households', 8628

Stewart, Alexander Patrick: The Medical and Legal Aspects of Sanity Reform, 22101

Stewart, Andrew: Social Stratification and Occupations, 9595

Stewart, Anthony Terence Quincey: Edward Carson, 1137; The Narrow Ground: Aspects of Ulster 1609–1969, 2902; The Ulster Crisis, 2903

Stewart, C. M.: 'An Estimate of the Future Population of England and Wales', 7365

Stewart, D.: T. E. Lawrence, 14513

Stewart, Herbert Leslie: Winged Words: Sir Winston Churchill as Writer and Speaker, 988; A Century of Anglo-Catholicism, 11641

Stewart, I. Mcd. G.: The Struggle for Crete 20 May–1 June 1941. A Story of Lost Opportunity, 14858

Stewart, J. Andrew: 'Jubilee of the National Insurance Act', 4034

Stewart, J. D.: British Pressure Groups: Their Role in Relation to the House of Commons, 2065; 'The Politics and Management of Hung Authorities', 3149; Corporate Planning in English Local Government: An Analysis with Readings 1967–72, 3241; 'Developments in Corporate Planning in British Local Government: The Bains Report and Corporate Planning', 3242

Stewart, James D.: ed. British Union Catalogue of Periodicals: A Record of the Periodicals of the World from the Seventeenth Century to the Present Day in British Libraries, 153; ed. Supplement (to 1960), 154

Stewart, Jennifer D.: Environmental Record Centres: A Decade of Progress?, 20225

Stewart, John D.: Gibraltar the Keystone, 12850

Stewart, John M.: Of No Fixed Abode: Vagrancy and the Welfare State, 18504

Stewart, John Murray Wilson: A Pricing System for Roads, 17147

Stewart, Sir K. D.: The Royal Bank in Glasgow, 1783–1983, 4524

Stewart, Katharine: Crofts and Crofting, 19284

Stewart, Margaret: Pathway to Tomorrow: The Impact of Automation on People—A Survey of the International Conference on Automation, Full Employment and a Balanced Economy at Rome in June 1967, 7249

Stewart, Margaret: Protest or Power? A Study of the Labour Party, 1756

Stewart, Margaret: The Needle is Threaded: 'The History of an Industry', 6438

Stewart, Margaret [Lady Wilson]: English Singer, 24422

Stewart, Mark B.: Collective Bargaining Arrangements, Closed Shops and Relative Pay, 5851; Occupational Status and Mobility of Men and Women, 5923

Stewart, Mary: The Child and the Social Services, 8160

Stewart, Maxwell Slutz: The Beveridge Plan, 9035

Stewart, Michael James: The Jekyll and Hyde Years: Politics and Economic Policy since 1964, 3672; 'Planning and Persuasion in a Mixed Economy', 6118; The Causes of Poverty, 9102; Keynes and after, 26602

Stewart, Michael [Baron]: Life and Labour, 1321; 'Britain, Europe and the Alliance', 14176

Stewart, Murray: ed. The City: Problems of Planning: Selected Readings, 17836

Stewart, Oliver: The Story of Air Warfare, 15794; First Flights, 17489

Stewart, P. T.: The History of the XII Royal Lancers (Prince of Wales's), 15687

Stewart, Richard Louis: Anglicans and Roman Catholics, 12336

Stewart, Rosemary: The Boss: The Life and Times of the British Businessman, 5420, 9789

Stewart, William Alexander Campbell: Quakers and Education, as seen in their Schools in England, 22899; The Educational Innovators, 23096; Progressives and Radicals in English Education, 1750–1950, 23097; Higher Education in Postwar Britain, 23296

Stewart, William Frederick Roy: Children in Flats: A Family Study, 8362

Stewart, William: James Keir Hardie: A Biography, 1426

Stieber, J.: 'Unauthorized Strikes under the American and British Industrial Relations Systems', 6963

Stieg, Margaret F.: The Origin and Development of Scholarly Historical Periodicals, 26725

Stierer, Barry: Testing Children: Standardized Testing in Local Education Authorities and Schools, 22786

Stiles, Walter Stanley: 'Colour Vision—A Retrospect', 20974; Mechanisms of Colour Vision: Selected Papers of W. S. Stiles, 22334

Stilgoe, Elizabeth: The Impact of Employment Protection Laws, 6989

Stillerman, Richard: The Sources of Intervention, 7140

Stimpson, Michael: The History of Gloucester Docks and its Associated Canals and Railways, 16686

Stimson, Gerry V.: Going to See the Doctor: The Consultation Process in General Practice, 21526; 'British Drug Policies in the 1980's: A Preliminary Analysis and Suggestions for Research', 22184; Heroin Addiction: Treatment and Control in Britain, 22201

Stinton, Darrol: The Design of the Aeroplane, 17511

Stirland, J. D.: 'A Study of Long-term Patients Attending a General Hospital Psychiatric Department', 21813

Stirling, John: 'British and French Shipbuilding: The Industrial Relations of Decline', 5849

Stobhaugh, B. P.: Women and Parliament 1918–1970, 7830

Stockdale, Sir Edmund: The Bank of England in 1934, 4484

Stockdale, Eric: 'A Short History of Prison Inspection in England', 10446

Stockdale, Frank A.: 'The Work of the Caribbean Commission', 13093

Stockford, Richard: Open Prisons, 10368

Stocks, Mary Danvers [Baroness]: Eleanor Rathbone, 1510; Ernest Simon of Manchester, 1522; A Hundred Years of District Nursing, 21712; The W.E.A.: The First Fifty Years, 23677

Stocks, Percy: Sickness in the Population of England and Wales in 1944–1947, 21996; Regional and Local Differences in Cancer Death Rates, 21997; Cancer Registration in England and Wales: An Enquiry into Treatment and its Results, 21998

Stockwell, A. J.: ed. British Imperial Policy and Decolonization, 1938–64, 12487; ed. A Collection of Treaties and other Documents affecting the States of Malaysia 1761–1963, 12899; 'The Historiography of Malaysia: Recent Writings in English on the History of the Area since 1874', 12901; British Policy and Malay Politics during the Malayan Union Experiment, 1942–48, 12932; 'British Imperial Policy and De-colonisation in Malaya 1942–1952', 12933

Stockwood, Mervyn: Chanctonbury Ring: An Autobiography, 11757

Stoff, Michael B.: 'The Anglo-American Oil Agreement and the War-time Search for Foreign Policy', 14035

Stoker, Gerry: The Politics of Local Government, 3139

Stokes, Arthur Henry: Lead and Lead Mining in Derbyshire, 6355

Stokes, Donald Elkington: Political Change in Britain: Forces Shaping Electoral Choice, 2224; 'On the Analytical Division of Social Class', 9489

Stokes, Geoffrey: The Beatles, 24501

Stokes, Roy: Michael Sadleir 1888–1957, 24957

Stokes, Sewell: Our Dear Delinquents, 10577

Stoland, Ezra: The End of Hope: A Sociological-Clinical Study of Suicide, 10811

Stolkind, E.: 'The History of Bronchial Asthma and Allergy', 20975

Stoll, Denis Gray: Music Festivals of the World, 24529

Stoll, Karl-Heinz: The New British Drama: A Bibliography with Particular Reference to Arden, Bond, Osborne, Pinter, Wesker, 26229

Stolper, Wolfgang Frederick: 'British Monetary Policy and the Housing Boom', 4566

Stone, Brian: 'The Place of the Open University in Higher Education of Today', 23548

Stone, Carol: ed. The Newer Caribbean: Decolonisation, Democracy and Development, 13018

Stone, Giovanna: National Income and Expenditure, 4889

Stone, Glyn A.: 'Britain, Non-Intervention and the Spanish Civil War', 13982; 'The Official British Attitude to the Anglo-Portuguese Alliance, 1910–1945', 13997

Stone, H. W. D.: The Principles of Urban Traffic, 16291

Stone, John: Colonist or Uitlander? A Study of the British Immigrant in South Africa, 7326

Stone, Maureen: The Education of the Black Child in Britain: The Myth of Multi-racial Education, 8363

Stone, Peter Albert: 'Urban Standards and National Resources', 17778; 'Urban Development and National Resources', 17779; Urban Development in Britain: Standards, Cost and Resources, 1964–2004, 17806, 18720; The Structure, Size and Costs of Urban Settlements, 17807; Housing, Town Development, Land and Costs, 17808, 18719; Building Economy, Design, Production and Organisation: A Synoptic View, 17809, 18721

Stone, Sir [John] Richard [Nicholas]: Inland Revenue Report on National Income, 1929, 4890; National Income and Expenditure, 4888; National Income and Expenditure, 4889; The Measurement of Consumers' Expenditure and Behaviour in the United Kingdom, 1920–1938, 20439; 'The Changing Patterns of Consumption', 20440; Consumers' Wants and Expenditures: A Survey of British Studies since 1945, 20441

Stoneman, Paul: Mergers and Economic Performance, 4992

Stones, R. W. H.: The Male Nurse, 21720

Stonesifer, Richard: W. H. Davies: A Critical Biography, 25471

Stoney, P. J. M.: ed. A Bibliography of Sources in Regional Industrial Development, 5115; Commerce, Industry and Transport: Studies in Economic Change in Merseyside, 5186, 16692, 18054; 'Unemployment Dispersion as a Determinant of Wage Inflation in the U.K., 1925–1966', 7010

Stookey, Robert W.: ed. The End of the Palestine Mandate, 14342

Stopes, Marie Carmichael: Contraception (Birth Control): Its Theory, History and Practice: A Manual for the Medical and Legal Professions, 21064

Stopford, John Morton: 'Origins of British-based Multinational Manufacturing Enterprises', 5554; Britain and the Multinationals, 5555

Storck, John: Flour for Man's Bread: A History of Milling, 6151

Storey, Barbara: Enid Blyton: A Biography, 25400

Storey, David John: ed. Small Firms in Regional Economic Development, 5125

Storey, Graham: Reuter's Century, 1851–1951, 25307

Storey, H.: 'United Kingdom Immigration Controls and the Welfare State', 11108

Storey, Richard: Consolidated Guide to the Modern Records Centre, 77

Storing, Herbert James: The State and the Farmer: British Agricultural Policies and Politics, 17764, 19516; 'The Farmers and the State', 19517

Storrs, Sir Ronald Henry Amherst: Orientations, 13310; Great Britain and the Near and Middle East, 13806

Story, Henry Harle: History of the Cameronians (Scottish Rifles), 15580

Stott, Denis Herbert: 'Delinquency and Cultural Stress', 10587; 'The Prediction of Delinquency from Non-delinquent Behaviour', 10588; 'Delinquency, Maladjustment and Unfavourable Ecology', 10589

Stott, Martin: The Nuclear Controversy: A Guide to the Issues of the Windscale Inquiry, 18820

Stott, Mary: Forgetting's no Excuse: The Autobiography of Mary Stott, Journalist, Campaigner and Feminist, 25287; Before I Go: Reflections on my Life and Times, 25288

Stott, Raymond Toole: A Bibliography of the Works of Somerset Maugham, 25703

Stout, Hiram Miller: Public Service in Great Britain, 842

Stowe, Sir Kenneth: On Caring for the National Health, 21698

Stowers, Roger: The Power behind Aston Martin, 17454

Stoye, Johannes: The British Empire: Its Structure and its Problems, 12544

Strachan, A.: Pre-school Education and Care, 23168

Strachey, Amy: St Loe Strachey: His Life and His Paper, 25289

Strachey, [Evelyn] John [St Loe]: Revolution by Reason: An Account of the Financial Proposals Submitted by Oswald Mosley at the 33rd Independent Labour Party Conference, 1876; Accept Churchill's Challenge . . . , 1878; Socialism through Peace . . . , 1879; Which Way to Worker's Control?: Towards a Socialist Policy for Industry, 1880; The Menace of Fascism, 2017; The Coming Struggle for Power, 2138; Contemporary Capitalism, 2139; 'Racial Equality (The Key to a Successful World Policy for Britain)', 10899

Strachey, Rachel/Ray: Careers and Openings for Women: A Survey of Women's Employment and a Guide for those Seeking Work, 7668; 'The Cause': A Short History of the Women's Movement in Great Britain, 7669; ed. Our Freedom and its Results, 7670; Women's Suffrage and Women's Service: The History of the London and National Society for Women's Service, 7671

Stradling, Robert and Hughes, Meirion: The English Musical Renaissance, 1860–1940, 24276

Strang, Leonard Alfred George: John Masefield, 25701

Strang, William [Baron]: Britain in World Affairs, 13212; Home and Abroad, 13311; The Diplomatic Career, 13325; The Foreign Office, 13328; 'The Formation and Control of Foreign Policy', 13347

Strange, Susan: 'Sterling and British Policy: A Political View', 4713; Sterling and British Policy: A Political Study of an International Currency in Decline, 4714; The Sterling Problem and the Six, 4715

Stranges, Anthony N.: 'From Birmingham to Billingham: High Pressure Coal Hydrogenisation in Great Britain', 6514

Stranks, Jeremy: ed. Tolley's Health and Safety at Work Handbook, 4143

Strappert, A.: Die Reorganisation der Britischen Zentralregierung seit dem Ende der 50er Jahre, in Besondere die Zentrale Lenkung, 783

Stratford, Alan H.: Air Transport in the Supersonic Era, 17644; Studies of the Site for a Third London Airport, 17685; An Airport Programme for Yorkshire and Humberside, 1970–1985, 17695

Stratta, Erica: The Education of Borstal Boys, 10523

Stratton, John M.: Agricultural Records, A.D. 220–1968, 19381

Strauss, Anselm L.: Status Passage, 9545

Strauss, Erich: Irish Nationalism and British Democracy, 2991

Strauss, Patricia: Cripps: Advocate and Rebel, 1154

Strawhorn, John: The History of Irvine: Royal Burgh and New Town, 19017; Ayrshire, 19218

Strawson, John: The Battle for North Africa, 14908; El Alamein: Desert Victory, 14909; The Battle for the Ardennes, 14966

Streat, Sir Raymond: 'Manchester and Cotton—Today', 7152

Streather, Jane: Social Insecurity: Single Mothers on Benefit, 7872

Street, Andrew: Challenge and Opportunity: The Case for a More Realistic Level of Highway and Infrastructure and Investment, 17151

Street, Eric: The History of the National Mutual Life Assurance Society 1830–1980, 4237

Street, Harry: Report on Anti-discrimination Legislation, 10985; Road Accidents, 17121

Street, Pamela: Arthur Bryant: Portrait of a Historian, 26778

Street, Sarah: Cinema and State: The Film Industry and the Government 1927–84, 24597, 24642

Stretton, Hugh: Capitalism, Socialism and the Environment, 19962

Stride, H. G.: Nickel for Coinage, 7203

Striker, C.: Famous Faces in Diabetes, 21071

Strinati, Dominic: Capitalism, the State and Industrial Relations, 5818

Stringer, J.: Patients, Hospitals and Operational Research, 21381

Stromberg, Roland N.: 'Uncertainties and Obscurities about the League of Nations', 13474

Strong, Sir Kenneth: Intelligence at the Top, 15198

Strongman, Kenneth T.: 'Stereotypical Reactions to Regional Accents', 9493

Stronnictwo, Narolowe: Centralny zjazd Delegatow, 2/1/1961, 11373

Stroud, Jean: Special Correspondent, 25290

Stroud, John: Airports of the World, 17669

Stroud, John: ed. Services for Children and their Families: Aspects of Childcare for Social Workers, 8364; An Introduction to the Child Care Service, 8365; Thirteen Penny Stamps: The Story of the Church of England Children's Society (Waifs and Strays) from 1881 to the 1970's, 8366; In the Care of the Council: Social Workers and their World, 8756

Stroud, L. John: 'Friends and Some Aspects of Education', 22900

Stuart, Albert Frederick: The House of Warne: One Hundred Years of Publishing, 24996

Stuart, Sir Campbell: Opportunity Knocks Once, 25291

Stuart, Charles Harborne: *ed.* The Reith Diaries, 24736

Stuart, Denis: County Borough: The History of Burton upon Trent 1901–74: Part 2: 1914–1974, 3326

Stuart, Dorothy Margaret: London through the Ages: The Story of a City and its Citizens, 54 BC-AD 1944, 18370

Stuart, Douglas: A Very Sheltered Life, 24737

Stuart, James Gibb: The Mind Benders: The Gradual Revolution and Scottish Independence, 2525

Stuart, James [Viscount Stuart of Findhorn]: Within the Fringe, 1324

Stubbs, J. O.: 'Lord Milner and Patriotic Labour, 1914–1918', 2012

Stubbs, Patricia: Muriel Spark, 25816

Stubbs, Peter: The History of Dorman Smith, 1878–1972, 6601

Stubbs, Peter C.: Transport Economics, 16268

Stuck, Walter G.: 'Historic Backgrounds of Orthopaedic Surgery', 21013

Studdard, R. M.: Town and Country: The Amenity Question, 27002

Studdert-Kennedy, William Gerald: Opinions, Publics and Pressure Groups: An Essay on Vox Populi and Representative Government, 2360; Dog-collar Democracy. The Industrial Christian Fellowship, 1919–1929, 11838; ' "Woodbine Willie": Religion and Politics after the Great War', 11839; Studies in Church History, 11541

Studlar, Donley T.: Protest and Survive: Alliance Support in the 1983 British General Election, 1842; 'Policy Voting in Britain: The Coloured Immigration Vote in the 1964, 1966 and 1970 General Elections', 2238; 'The Ethnic Vote: Problems of Analysis and Interpretation', 2246; 'The Impact of Race on Political Behaviour in Britain', 2247; 'The Electoral Participation of Black and Asian Britons: Integration or Alienation?', 2248; 'British Public Opinion, Colour Issues and Enoch Powell: A Longitudinal Analysis', 11185

Study Group of the Royal Institute of Public Administration: Budgeting in Public Authorities, 4877,4914

Study Group of the Institute for the Study of Conflict: The Ulster Debate, 2919

Stueck, William: 'The Limits of Influence: British Policy and American Expansion of the War in Korea', 16147

Sturges, Claire and Sturges, Rodney Paul: *ed.* Who's Who in British Economics: A Dictionary of Economists in Higher Education, Business and Government, 26573

Sturges, Rodney Paul: Economists' Papers 1750–1950: A Guide to Archives and other Manuscript Sources for the History of British and Irish Economic Thought, 3395, 26574

Sturgess, Janet: Non-Accidental Injury to Children under the Age of Seventeen, 9961

Sturivant, Ray: The History of Britain's Military Training Aircraft, 15884

Sturm, Roland: Nationalismus in Schottland und Wales 1966–1988: eine Analyse seiner Ursachen und Konsequenzen, 2421; *ed.* Politics and Society in Contemporary Ireland, 2996

Sturmey, Stanley George: 'Income Tax and Economic Stability', 4838; British Shipping and World Competition, 16459; 'Owner Farming in England and Wales, 1900 to 1950', 19492; The Economic Development of Radio, 24763

Sturrock, Ford Gibson: The Optimum Size of a Family Farm, 19528; Farm Modernisation and the Countryside, 19529; Economies of Scale in Farm Mechanisation: A Study of Costs on Large and Small Scale Farms, 19692

Stuttard, Geoffrey: 'Potentialities of the Industrial Training Act', 23661

Styler, William Edward: A Bibliographical Guide to Adult Education in Rural Areas, 1918–1978, 23643; 'Adult Education and the Affluent Society', 23649; Adult Education in East Yorkshire, 1875–1960, 23688

Subject Index of Modern Books Acquired: 1946–1950, 101; 1951–1955, 102; 1956–1960, 103; 1961–1970, 104; 1971– 1975, 105

Subject Index to Periodicals: 1918–, 81

Suchy, J. T.: 'How does Commercial Television Affect British Viewing?', 24869

Sudjic, Deyan: Norman Foster, Richard Rogers, James Stirling: New Directions in British Architecture, 23876

Sueter, Sir Murray Fraser: The Evolution of the Tank, 15534

Suffolk County Council: Dutch Elm Disease in Suffolk: Report of a 1978 Survey, 19779

Sugarman, Barry N.: 'Involvement in Youth Culture, Academic Achievement and Conformity in School: An Empirical Study of London Schoolboys', 8449; 'Social Norms in Teenage Boys' Peer Groups', 8450; 'Social Class and Values as Related to Achievement and Conduct in School', 9491

Sugden, Robert: Who Cares? An Economic and Ethical Analysis of Private Charity and the Welfare State, 9230

Suggate, Alan M.: William Temple and Christian Social Ethics Today, 11714

Suitters, Beryl: The Fight for Acceptance: A History of Contraception, 21065

Sukdeo, Fred: The Dependants of the Coloured Commonwealth Population of England and Wales, 10984

Sullivan, Anwar: *ed.* Commemorative History of Sabah 1881–1981, 12956

Sullivan, Dick: Old Ships, Boats and Maritime Museums, 16497

Sullivan, F. B: The 1944 Act in Perspective, 1127

Sullivan, K.: Girls Who Go Wrong, 7730

Sullivan, Martin Gloster: Watch How You Go: An Autobiography, 11815

Sullivan, Matthew Barry: Thresholds of Peace: Four Hundred Thousand German Prisoners and the People of Britain 1944–1948, 15055

Summer, G.: Planning Local Authority Services for the Elderly, 8595

Summerfield, Penny: Women Workers in the Second World War: Production and Patriarchy in Conflict, 7676; 'Education and Politics in the British Armed Forces in the Second World War', 23721

Summerhill: Summerhill: That Dreadful School, 23106; Summerhill: A Radical Approach to Education, 23107

Summers, Anthony: Honey Trap: The Secret World of Stephen Ward, 9901

Summers, D.: The East Coast Floods, 20184

Summers, David Lewis: HMS Ganges 1866–1966: One Hundred Years of Training Boys for the Royal Navy, 15778

Summers, J. E.: 'Strict Baptists in the 1970s', 12034

Summers, William H.: *ed.* The Story of Hungerford in Berkshire, 19193

Summerskill, Edith [Baroness]: Letters to my Daughter, 1529; A Woman's World, 1530

Summerson, Sir John Newenham: The Architectural Association, 1847–1947, 23865; Architecture in England, 23889; *ed.* Ten Years of British Architecture 1945–55, 23899

Sumner, Michael Thomas: Inflation in the United Kingdom, 4011

Sumner, Philip L.: Motor Cars up to 1930, 17334

Sumner, William Leslie: The Organ: Its Evolution, Principles of Construction and Use, 24391

Sunday Times: The Sunday Times: A Pictorial Biography of one of the World's Great Newspapers, 25154

Sunday Times Insight Team: The Falklands War: The Full Story, 16104; Suffer the Children: The Story of Thalidomide, 22272

Sunderland, John: Painting in Britain, 1525–1975, 23961

Sungaka, H.: 'The History of Education and the Study of Educational Administration', 22802

Supple, Barry Emmanuel: The Royal Exchange Assurance: A History of British Insurance, 1720–1970, 4208; *ed.* Essays in British Business History, 4937; The History of the British Coal Industry, Vol. 4: 1913–1946: The Political Economy of Decline, 6246

Surrey, A. J.: Energy Policy: Strategies for Uncertainty, 7220

Surrey, M. J. C.: 'The National Plan in Retrospect', 3662

Surtees, George: A Short History of the XXth Lancashire Fusiliers, 15680

Survey of British and Commonwealth Affairs: 1967–1970, 272

Survey of Current Affairs: 1971–1985, 273

Susser, Mervyn Wilfrid: Sociology in Medicine, 21999

Sussex, Elizabeth: The Rise and Fall of the British Documentary, 24616

Sutcliffe, Anthony: 'Political Leadership In Labour-controlled Birmingham: The Contrasting Style of Henry Watton 1959–66 and Stanley Yapp 1972–74', 3324; A History of Birmingham, vol. 3: Birmingham 1939–1970, 5142, 18005; A History of Modern Town Planning: A Bibliographical

Guide, 17720; *ed.* Multi-Storey Living: The British Working Class Experience, 18425; British Town Planning: The Formative Years, 18769

Sutcliffe, D.: British Black English, 23856

Sutcliffe, Edmund Felix: Bibliography of the English Province of the Society of Jesus, 1773–1953, 11962

Sutcliffe, Peter: The Oxford University Press: An Informal History, 24984

Sutherland, Colin Scott: Arnold Bax, 24296

Sutherland, Douglas: Fraud: The Amazing Case of Doctor Savundra, 10273; Tried and Valiant: The History of the Border Regiment, the 34th and 55th Regiments of Foot, 1702–1959, 15576; The Fourth Man, 16032; Burgess and Maclean, 16035; The Landowners, 19543

Sutherland, George Arthur: Dalton Hall: A Quaker Venture, 22905

Sutherland, Gillian Ray: 'The Study of the History of Education', 22444; 'Measuring Intelligence: English Local Education Authorities and Mental Testing, 1919–1939', 22911; 'The Magic of Measurement: Mental Testing and English Education, 1900–1940', 22912

Sutherland, Ian: The Rise of the Fishing Industry in Humberside, 19817

Sutherland, J. F.: *ed.* Towards Community Mental Health, 21841

Sutherland, Margaret B.: Sex Bias in Education, 22488; 'Progress and Problems in Education in Northern Ireland, 1952–1982', 23640

Sutten, H. M. A.: 'West Indians, Britain's New Coloured Citizens', 11235

Sutton, David Christopher: The History of Food: A Preliminary Bibliography of Printed Sources, 20568

Sutton, Denys: Christies since the War, 1945–1958, 23948; Walter Sickert: A Biography, 24065

Sutton, Gordon: Artisan or Artist?: A History of the Teaching of Arts and Crafts in English Schools, 22761

Sutton, Harold Thomas: Raiders Approach! The Fighting Tradition of the Royal Air Force Station Hornchurch, 15932

Sutton, Harry Thomas: Villages, 19122

Sutton, Paul: Grenada: Revolution and Invasion, 13080

Sutton, Shawn: The Largest Theatre in the World, 24858

Svenning, Michael: Television Coverage of the 1983 General Election: Audiences, Appreciation and Public Opinion, 24901; 'Television Coverage of the 1984 European Parliamentary Election', 24902

Swaine, Anthony: Faversham: Its History, its Present Role and the Pattern of its Future, 18976

Swan, Dennis: Competition in British Industry: Restrictive Practices Legislation in Theory and Practice, 4935

Swan, M.: British Guiana, 13037

Swan, W. B.: Survey of Agriculture in Caithness, Orkney and Shetland, 19622

Swann, Brenda Audrey Swanton: Records of Interest to Social Scientists, 1919–1939:

Employment and Unemployment, 6990, 7941

Swann, D.: 'Steel Pricing in a Recession: An Analysis of United Kingdom and ECSC Experience', 6559

Swann, Paul: The British Film Documentary Movement 1926–1946, 24612

Swanson, Edward B.: A Century of Oil and Gas in Books: A Descriptive Bibliography, 7169

Swanton, E. W.: A History of Cricket, 27098

Swanwick, Helena M.: Builders of Peace: Being Ten Years' History of the Union of Democratic Control, 13461

Swartz, Marvin: The Union of Democratic Control in British Politics during the First World War, 13462

Swazey, Judith P.: Reflexes and Motor Integration: Sherrington's Concept of Integrative Action, 22332

Sweeney, Garrett: St Edmund's House, Cambridge: The First Eighty Years, 11965

Sweeting, Robert Clifford: Modern Infantry Weapons and Training in their Use, 15515

Swift, D. F.: 'Social Class, Mobility-ideology and Eleven Plus Success', 9492; 'The Sociology of Education in Britain, 1960–1968: A Bibliographical Review', 22445

Swift, John: Adventure in Vision: The First Twenty-Five Years of Television, 24843

Swift, Susan: Scotland's Travelling People: Problems and Solutions: A Report of the Study of a Minority Group within Scotland's Population, with Recommendations as to the Possible Solutions to these Problems, 11344

Swift, Wesley Frank: Methodism in Scotland, 12260

Swift, William J.: *ed.* Great Britain and the Common Market, 1957–1969, 14168

Swinden, Patrick: Paul Scott: Images of India, 25797

Swingewood, Alan: A Short History of Sociological Thought, 8088

Swinglehurst, Edmond: Cook's Tours: The Story of Popular Travel, 27001

Swinhoe, K.: 'Lines of Division among Members of Parliament over Procedural Reform in the House of Commons', 647

Swinnerton, Frank Arthur: *pref.* Arnold Bennett's Letters to his Nephew, 25384; Arnold Bennett, 25388; An Autobiography, 25824; Figures in the Foreground: Literary Reminiscences, 1917–1940, 25825

Swinson, Richard P.: Alcoholism and Addiction, 22134

Swinton, Sir Ernest Dunlop: Eyewitness: Being Personal Reminiscences of Certain Phases of the Great War, Including the Genesis of the Tank, 15535

Sword, Keith R.: '"Their Prospects Will Not be Bright": British Responses to the Problem of the Policy "Recalcitrants", 1946–49', 11376

Sykes, A. J. M.: 'The Pattern of Industrial Relations', 5647; 'Financial Control of State Industry', 6073; 'The Approaching Crisis in the Trade Unions', 6811; 'Trade-union Workshop Organization in the Printing

Industry: The Chapel', 6812; 'The Problem of Status in Old Age', 8629; 'Navvies: Their Work Attitudes', 9715; 'Navvies: Their Social Relations', 9716; 'Some Differences in the Attitudes of Clerical and Manual Workers', 9803

Sykes, Allen: Housing Finance and Development: An Analysis and a Programme for Reform, 18549

Sykes, Christopher Hugh: Nancy: The Story of Lady Astor, 1345; Troubled Loyalty: A Biography of Adam von Trott zu Solz, 13682; Crossroads to Israel, 14281; Orde Wingate, 14791; Evelyn Waugh: A Biography, 25862

Sykes, E. I.: 'Trade Union Autonomy in Great Britain', 6752; 'Trade Unionism Today', 6753

Sykes, Sir Frederick: From Many Angles, 17576

Sykes, Friend: Food, Farming and the Future, 19473

Sykes, Joseph: British Public Expenditure, 1921–1931, 4760; A Study in English Local Authority Finance, 4862; 'La Politique de localisation des industries en Grande-Bretagne: les villes nouvelles', 18225

Sykes, Norman: The English Religious Tradition, 11571; 'Anglican-Presbyterian Relations', 12326

Sykes, P.: 'The Future of the Large Hospital in Services to the Mentally Handicapped', 21848

Sykes, Percy: A History of Exploration from the Earliest Times to the Present Day, 27178

Sykes, Stephen W.: *ed.* England and Germany: Studies in Theological Diplomacy, 11883

Sykes, William Stanley: Essays on the First Hundred Years of Anaesthesia, 21033

Sylvester, Albert James: The Real Lloyd George, 1018

Sylvester, Dorothy: *ed.* The Historical Atlas of Cheshire Edited for the Local History Committee of the Cheshire Community Council, 5150

Sylvester, [Anthony Bernard] David: Interviews with Francis Bacon, 24008

Symes, David G.: *ed.* Humberside in the Eighties: A Spatial View of the Economy, 18026; 'Complementary Roles and Asymmetrical Lives: Farmer's Wives in a Large Farm Environment', 19594

Symon, James Alexander: Scottish Farming: Past and Present, 19617

Symons, Julian: The Angry Thirties, 299; Horatio Bottomley, 1364; The General Strike, 6947

Symons, Leslie: *ed.* Land Use in Northern Ireland: The General Report of the Survey, 19648, 20304

Symposium on Fluoridation of Water Supplies: Fluoride and Health, 22398

Symposium on Race and Race Relations: Man, Race and Darwin; Papers Read at a Joint Conference of the Royal Anthropological Institute of Great Britain and Ireland, and the Institute of Race Relations, 10925

Synge, Peter M.: The Gardens of Britain 1—Devon and Cornwall, 19882

Synge, William Alfred Thackeray: The Story of the Green Howards, 1939–1945, 15640

Szacki, Jerzi: History of Sociological Thought, 8090

Szelenyi, Ivan: Cities in Recession: Critical Responses to the Urban Policies of the New Right, 3212; *ed.* Cities in Recession: Critical Responses to the Urban Policies of the New Right, 18437

Szereter, R.: 'History and the Sociological Perspective in Educational Studies', 22451; 'A Note on the Staffing of the Public Schools, 1939–1964', 23037

Taafe, Peter: Liverpool: A City that Dared to Fight, 3332

Tabb, Jai Yanai: Workers' Participation in Management: Expectations and Experience, 6014

Tabor, Stephen: Ted Hughes: A Bibliography 1946–80, 25578

Tabori, Paul: Alexander Korda, 24675

Taboulet, Georges: 'La France et l'Angleterre face au Conflit Sino-Japonais, 1937–1939', 13611

Tait, Alan A.: 'Long Term Policy and the British Budget 1962–1963', 4905; 'British Budgetary Policy, 1963–1964', 4906; 'British Budgetary Policy 1965–1966: A Sequence of Budgets and the Selective Employment Tax', 4907; 'International Constraints on Domestic Budgetary Policy: The British Budget 1967', 4908; 'Political Economy: The British Budget 1971', 4909

Tait, Geoffrey: Golden Gatwick: Fifty Years of Aviation, 17676

Tait, Katherine: My Father, Bertrand Russell, 26866

Tajfel, Henri: *ed.* Disappointed Ghosts: Essays by African, Asian and West Indian Students, 11500; 'Pregiudizi di Colore in Gran Bretagna: L'Esperienza degli Studenti d'Africa, d'Asia e delle Indie Occidentali', 11501

Takel, R. E.: Industrial Port Development: With Case Studies from South Wales and Elsewhere, 16653

Talbot, Edward: The Locomotive Names of British Railways: Their Origins and Meanings, 16797

Talbot, Godfrey: Queen Elizabeth: The Queen Mother, 507

Talbot, Ian A.: 'Mountbatten and the Partition of India: A Rejoinder', 13179

Talbot, V.: Men out of Work: A Study of Unemployment in Three English Towns, 7016

Talbot-Booth, E. C.: The British Army: Its History, Customs, Traditions and Uniforms, 15543

Tamaki, Nario: The Life Cycle of the Union Bank of Scotland 1830–1954, 4519

Tancred, Edith: Women Police, 10786

Tandy, Cliff: Landscape of Industry . . ., 20310; *ed.* Handbook of Urban Landscape, 20311

Tanfield, Jennifer: The Impact of the 1982 Budget on Individual Incomes and Real Income Movements since 1979, 3860

Tanitch, Robert: Olivier: The Complete Career, 26082; Ralph Richardson: A Tribute, 26090; Leonard Rossiter, 26095

Tann, Jennifer: The Development of the Factory, 4938; Gloucestershire Woollen Mills, 6414

Tannahill, John Allan: European Volunteer Workers in Britain, 9157

Tanner, John Curnon: Car Ownership Trends and Forecasts, 17370

Tanner, Lawrence Edward: Westminster School, 23084

Tansley, Albert Edward: The Education of Slow Learning Children, 8379

Tansley, Sir Arthur George: Our Heritage of Wild Nature: A Plea for Organised Nature Conservation, 20190; The Natural History of Wicken Fen, 26525

Tantral, Panadda: Accounting Literature in Non-Accounting Journals: An Annotated Bibliography, 4200

Taplin, Eric: The Dockers' Union: A Study of the National Union of Dock Labourers 1899–1922, 6803

Taplin, Walter: History of the British Steel Industry, 6550; The Origins of Television Advertising in the United Kingdom, 24866, 24872

Tapper, Oliver: Roots in the Sky: A History of British Aerospace Aircraft, 17610

Tapper, Ted: Young People and Society, 8534

Target, George William: Bernadette: The Story of Bernadette Devlin, 3088

Tarling, Nicholas: Britain, the Brookes and Brunei, 12949; 'Lord Mountbatten and the Return of Civil Government to Burma', 13205; The Sun Never Sets: An Historical Essay on Britain and its Place in the World, 13246

Tarling, R. J.: 'Analysis of the Duration of Male Unemployment in Great Britain, 1932–1973', 7009

Tarling, Roger: 'The Investigation of Crime in England and Wales', 10276; 'Police Force Cautioning: Policy and Practice', 10775

Tarn, Adam: 'Major Dramatic Trends: 1948–1968', 26219

Tarn, J. N.: 'Derbyshire Heritage: The Conservation of Ordinariness', 20390

Tash, Joan M.: Working with Unattached Youth, 8469

Tasker, G. H. *and* Tasker, Sidney: 'Chester—The Challenge of Change', 18854, 20389

Tassi, Roberto: Sutherland: The Wartime Drawings, 24079; Graham Sutherland, 24095

Tatchell, Peter: The Battle for Bermondsey, 1792

Tate, J.: 'Vacancy Reserve', 18010

Tate, John Orley Allen: T. S. Eliot: The Man and his Work, 25501

Tatford, Barrington: The Story of British Railways, 16752

Tatla, Darshan Singh: Women's Studies: A Bibliography of Dissertations 1870–1982, 7628; Immigrants, Minorities and Race Relations: A Bibliography of Theses and Dissertations Presented at British and Irish Universities, 1900–1981, 10887

Tatlow, Peter: A History of Highland Locomotives, 17066

Tatlow, Tissington: The Story of the Student Christian Movement, 11665

Taulbee, James L.: 'Britain, Spain and the Gibraltar Question', 12852

Taunton: Proud Century: The First Hundred Years of Taunton School, 23078

Taverne, Dick: The Future of the Left: Lincoln and After, 1829

Tavistock Institute of Human Relations: Tavistock Pamphlets No. 7. Social Research and a National Policy for Science, 7973

Tawney, Richard Henry: The Acquisitive Society, 2140; Equality, 2141; Beatrice Webb, 2142; 'The Abolition of Economic Controls, 1918–1921', 3549, 6103; *ed.* Secondary Education for all: A Policy for Labour, 22924

Taylor, A. B.: 'Urban Fiscal Decay in U.K. Cities', 3271

Taylor, A. H.: 'The Effect of Electoral Pacts on the Decline of the Liberal Party', 2251; 'The Proportional Decline Hypothesis in English Elections', 2252; 'Some Recent Parliamentary Changes and the February 1974 General Election', 2370

Taylor, Alan John Percivale: English History, 1914–1945, 285; The Struggle for Mastery in Europe, 1848–1918, 360; Essays in English History, 368; Europe: Grandeur and Decline, 369; From Napoleon to Stalin, 370; *ed.* The Abdication of King Edward VIII, 476; *ed.* Churchill: Four Faces and the Man, 988; *ed.*: Lloyd George: Twelve Essays, 1018, 13839; The Rise and Fall of Lloyd George, 1018; *ed.* My Darling Pussy: The Letters of Lloyd George and Frances Stevenson, 1913–1941, 1018; Beaverbrook, 1072; 'A Look back at British Socialism, 1922–1937', 1710; The Troublemakers: Dissent over Foreign Policy, 1792–1939, 13219; The Origins of the Second World War, 13770; The First World War: An Illustrated History, 14460; *ed.* Off the Record: W. P. Crozier's Political Interviews, 1933–43, 25224; Politicians, Socialism and Historians, 26814

Taylor, Alan R.: Prelude to Israel: An Analysis of Zionist Diplomacy 1897–1947, 14288

Taylor, Alastair M.: From Rhodesia to Zimbabwe: The Politics of Transition, 12809

Taylor, Allan: From a Glasgow Slum to Fleet Street, 25293

Taylor, Arthur John: *ed.* Studies in the History of a University, 1874–1974, to commemorate the Centenary of the University of Leeds, 23511; 'History at Leeds, 1877–1974: The Evolution of a Discipline', 26773

Taylor, Audrey M.: Gilletts: Bankers at Banbury and Oxford, 4510

Taylor, Brian: 'Coming of Age: A Study of the Evolution of the Ministry of Defence Headquarters 1974–1982', 824

Taylor, Brian: 'The Cowley Fathers and the First World War', 11854

Taylor, Chris: Welsh Bus Handbook, 17316

Taylor, Christopher: Roads and Tracks of Britain, 17107; Village and Farmstead: A History of Rural Settlement in England, 19048, 19564; Fields in the English Landscape, 19563

Taylor, Cyril: Is your General Practitioner Really Necessary? 21587

Taylor, D.: The Rhodesian: The Life of Sir Roy Welensky, 12785

Taylor, David: *ed.* The Counties of Perth and Kinross, 10118, 19234

Taylor, Derek: Fortune, Fame and Folly: British Hotels and Catering from 1878 to 1978, 20599, 27000; The Golden Age of British Hotels, 26996

Taylor, Don: Years of Challenge: The Commonwealth and the British Empire, 1945–1958, 359, 12582; 'No Cutbacks on the Horizon', 9184

Taylor, Doreen: A Microphone and a Frequency: Forty Years of Forces Broadcasting, 24750

Taylor, Elizabeth: Elizabeth Takes Off: An Autobiography, 26103

Taylor, Eric: The House of Commons at Work, 632

Taylor, Eva H.: A Life with Alan: The Diary of A.J.P. Taylor's Wife, Eva, from 1978 to 1985, 26815

Taylor, F. S.: 'Scotland: A Financial and Industrial History', 5249

Taylor, Francine: Race, School and Community: A Survey of Research and Literature on Education in Multi-racial Britain, 23188

Taylor, Frank Salmond: Banking in Scotland, 4406

Taylor, George: Born and Bred Unequal, 9508; The Law of Education, 22629

Taylor, Gordon Rattray: 'The Men with Long Eyes: Astronomical Revolution', 26419; The Science of Life: A Picture History of Biology, 26517

Taylor, Graham: Grunwick: The Workers' Story, 6751

Taylor, Griffith: *ed.* Geography in the Twentieth Century: A Study of Growth, Fields, Techniques, Aims and Trends, 26650

Taylor, H. G.: An Experiment in Co-operative Research: An Account of the First Fifty Years of the Electrical Research Association, 7101

Taylor, Harry Bernard, [Baron Taylor of Mansfield]: Uphill all the Way, 1531

Taylor, Hedley: Growing Old Together: Elderly Owner-Occupiers and their Housing, 8647

Taylor, Henry Archibald: Jix, Viscount Brentford, 1116; Communism in Great Britain: A Short History of the British Communist Party, 1921; Lords and Labourers of the Press, 25039, 25206; The British Press: A Critical Survey, 25049; Robert Donald, 25231

Taylor, Hugh A.: Northumberland History: A Brief Guide to Records and Aids in Newcastle upon Tyne, 5206

Taylor, I. W.: Services for Handicapped Youth in England and Wales, 21924

Taylor, Ian: *ed.* Critical Criminology, 10145; The New Criminology: For a Social Theory of Deviance, 10146; *ed.* Politics and Deviance, 10148

Taylor, Ian: *ed.* The Labour Party: An Introduction to its History, Structure and Politics, 1683

Taylor, J. H.: L.C.U. Story 1873–1972, 12050

Taylor, J.: The Devons: A History of the Devonshire Regiment, 1685–1945, 15614

Taylor, James Arnold: Ellermans: A Wealth of Shipping, 16543

Taylor, James: 'Cobalt, Madder and Computers—The Society's Changing Scene', 7046

Taylor, James: The Classic Rovers, 1934–1977: A Collector's Guide, 17429

Taylor, John Russell: Anatomy of a Television Play, 24861; Shaffer, 25982; David Storey, 25991; Alec Guinness: A Celebration, 26051; Vivien Leigh, 26063; 'British Drama of the Fifties', 26220; Anger and After: A Guide to the New British Drama, 26224; The Second Wave: British Drama for the Seventies, 26231

Taylor, John William Ransom: Pictorial History of the RAF, 15787; C.F.S.: Birthplace of Air Power, 15817; Modern Combat Aircraft, 15875

Taylor, John: Decade of the Dragon, 27047

Taylor, Laurie: *ed.* Politics and Deviance, 10148; Deviance and Society, 10149; Deviance, Crime and Socio-legal Control: Comparative Perspectives, 10150; Signs of Trouble: Aspects of Delinquency, 10151; Psychological Survival: The Experience of Long-term Imprisonment, 10385; Air Travel: How Safe is it?, 17649

Taylor, Lee: Social Behaviour, Natural Resources and the Environment, 19973

Taylor, Leslie: A Village within the City: The Story of Old Headington, Oxford, 19197

Taylor, Linda King: The Stock Exchange Press Guide to Investing for Income and Growth, 4291

Taylor, Lionel Roy: *ed.* The Optimum Population for Britain, 7392

Taylor, M. A.: Studies of Travel in Gloucester, Northampton and Reading, 16347

Taylor, Michael: Industrial Organisation and Location, 5820

Taylor, Michael John Haddrick: History of Helicopters, 17551; Helicopters of the World, 17552; Jet Fighters, 17563; Modern Jet Aircraft, 17564

Taylor, Nicholas: The Village in the City, 17874

Taylor, P. W.: 'The Development of Higher Technological Education in Britain, 1945–1951', 22509

Taylor, Paul: Popular Music since 1955: A Critical Guide to the Literature, 24465

Taylor, Percy Strawson: The New Law of Education, 22625; The New Law of Education, 22626

Taylor, Peter: Beating the Terrorists, 2858

Taylor, Peter: Families at War, 2859

Taylor, Peter: Health at Work, 4141

Taylor, Peter: Smoke Ring: The Politics of Tobacco, 6537

Taylor, Peter: Stalker: The Search for Truth, 2936

Taylor, Peter: The Nuclear Controversy: A Guide to the Issues of the Windscale Inquiry, 18820

Taylor, Peter J.: Information Guides: A Survey of Subject Guides to Sources of Information produced by Library and Information Services in the United Kingdom, 244

Taylor, Peter John: The Impact of Nuclear Waste Disposals on the Marine Environment, 20130

Taylor, Philip Arthur Michael: The Distant Magnet: European Emigration to the USA, 7316; Population and Emigration, 7398

Taylor, Philip Hampson: Society and the Teacher's Role, 9846

Taylor, Philip M.: British Propaganda during the First World War, 1914–1918, 15210; The Projection of Britain: British Overseas Publicity and Propaganda, 1919–1939, 15222; '"If War Should Come": Preparing the Fifth Arm for Total War, 1935–1939', 15223; Britain and the Cinema in the Second World War, 24596

Taylor, R. A.: The Economics of White Fish Distribution in Great Britain, 19818

Taylor, R. J.: *ed.* History of the Royal Astronomical Society vol.2: 1920–1980, 26449

Taylor, R.: 'The Uneasy Alliance—Labour and the Unions', 1807

Taylor, R.: Britain's Planning Heritage, 18771

Taylor, R.: University Adult Education in Britain and the United States, 23703

Taylor, Raymond Archbold: The Economics of White Fish Distribution in Great Britain, 19804

Taylor, Rex: Michael Collins, 3026

Taylor, Richard K.: *ed.* Campaigning for Peace: British Peace Movements in the Twentieth Century, 13438; The Protest Makers: The British Nuclear Disarmament Movement of 1958–1965: Twenty Years On, 13529; Against the Bomb: The British Peace Movement 1958–1965, 13533

Taylor, Robert: Labour and the Social Contract, 8911

Taylor, Rosemary: *ed.* Institute of Historical Research 1971–1975, 400

Taylor, Rupert: Noise, 20141

Taylor, Stan: The National Front in English Politics, 2049

Taylor, Stephen James Lake [Baron]: Good General Practice: A Report of a Survey [initiated by the] Nuffield Provincial Hospitals Trust, 21505; Mental Health and Environment, 21807

Taylor, Telford: Munich: The Price of Peace, 13746

Taylor, W. W.: Services for Handicapped Youth in England and Wales, 21924

Taylor, Wallis: 'Comparative Fertility in the Local Government Areas of England and Wales, 1951', 7500; 'Population of British Universities in the 1960s', 22555

Taylor, William: Society and the Education of Teachers, 22730, 22737; *ed* Towards a Policy for the Education of Teachers, 22738; *ed.* Research Perspectives in Education, 22848; The Secondary Modern School, 22933; 'The Changing Social Function of the English Secondary Modern School', 22971

Taylor-Goodby, Peter: Social Theory and Social Welfare, 8886

Taylor-Martin, Patrick: John Betjeman: His Life and Work, 25397

Teague, Edward H.: Henry Moore: Bibliography and Reproduction Index, 24191

Teague, Paul: ed. Beyond the Rhetoric: Politics, the Economy and Social Policy in Northern Ireland, 2823

Teague, Sidney John: The History of British Universities, 1800–1969 excluding Oxford and Cambridge: A Bibliography, 23292; The City University: a History, 23487

Teague, W. D.: Flour for Man's Bread: A History of Milling, 6151

Tebb, Albert Edward: An Inquiry into the Prevalence and Aetiology of Tuberculosis among Industrial Workers, 4105

Tebbit, Norman: Upwardly Mobile, 1325

Tebbutt, Melanie: Making Ends Meet: Pawnbroking and Working Class Credit, 4539

Tedder, Arthur [Baron]: With Prejudice, 15964; Air Power in War, 15990

Tedder, Eddie: ed. Who's Who in Television, 24920

Teeling, Luke William Burke: Corridors of Frustration, 1532

Teeling-Smith, George: ed. Surveillance and Early Diagnosis in General Practice: Proceedings of Colloquium, 22077

Tees and Hartlepool Ports: Handbook 1983/84—Downham Market, 16713

Teff, Harvey: Drugs, Society and the Law, 10830

Teich, Mikulas: 'The History of Modern Biochemistry: The Second Phase c.1920–1940/45', 26471

Teichova, Alice: ed. Multinational Enterprise in Historical Perspective, 4457, 20686; An Economic Background to Munich: International Business and Czechoslovakia, 1918–1938, 13747

Teleky, Ludwig: History of Factory and Mine Hygiene, 4118; 'Certifying Surgeons—Examining Surgeons, a Century of Activity (Great Britain 1844–1944)', 21014

Television and Radio: IBA Guide to Independent Broadcasting: 1976+, 24826

Telfer, Robert Lachlan: ed. Buses of Mersey, North Wales and the Isle of Man, 17286; ed. Buses of South East England, 17292; ed. Buses of Inner London, 17296

Telling, Arthur Edward: Planning Law and Procedure, 20357

Telser, Lester G.: Advertising and Competition, 4320

Temkinowa, Hanna: Gromndy Ludu Polskiego: Zarys Ideologii, 11374

Temperley, Arthur Cecil: The Whispering Gallery of Europe, 13488

Temperley, Harold Neville Vazeille: ed. History of the Peace Conference of Paris, 13426

Temperton, Paul: A Guide to Monetary Policy, 4642

Tempest, N. R.: 'Some Sources for the History of Teacher Training in England and Wales', 22716

Temple, Frederick Stephen: ed. William Temple: Some Lambeth Letters, 1942–1944, 11710

Temple, William: Christianity and Social Order, 11711

Temu, A. J.: British Protestant Missions, 12372

Ten Houton, Warren D.: The Emergence of Youth Societies: A Cross Cultural Approach, 8432

Tennant, T. Gavin: 'The Use of Remand on Bail or in Custody by the London Juvenile Courts: A Comparative Study', 10316

Teper, Susan: Patterns of Fertility in Greater London: A Comparative Study: Population Trends Project supported in the Department of Statistics, London School of Economics, by the Greater London Council (Research Intelligence Unit), 7499

Terraine, John: Douglas Haig, the Educated Soldier, 14508; The Western Front, 1914–1918, 14573; ed. General Jack's Diary 1914–1918, 14592; ed. Mons, the Retreat to Victory, 14593; ed. The Road to Passchendaele, the Flanders Offensive of 1917: A Study in Inevitability, 14594; The Life and Times of Lord Mountbatten, 15274

Terrell, Carroll F.: ed. Basil Bunting: Man and Poet, 25429

Terrell, Edward: Admiralty Brief: The Story of Inventions that Contributed to Victory in the Battle of the Atlantic, 14798

Terrell, Kermit: 'The Process of Status Attainment in the United States and Great Britain', 9455

Terrell, Thomas: On the Law of Patents, 5014

Terrill, Ross: R. H. Tawney and His Times. 2144

Terry, Carol D.: Here, There and Everywhere: The First International Beatles Bibliography 1962–1982, 24497

Terry, George Percy Warner: The Representation of the People Acts 1918 to 1928 and Amending Acts, and the Law Relating to the Registration of Jurors, 2275

Terry, M. H. C.: Services in Rural Norfolk, 1950–1980: A Survey of the Changing Patterns of Service in Rural Norfolk over the last Thirty Years, 19078

Terry, Michael: The Emergence of a Lay Elite?: Some Recent Changes in Shop Steward Organisation, 5795; Factors Shaping Shop Steward Organisation in Britain, 5796

Tertis, Lionel: My Viola and I, 24399

Tether, C. Gordon: 'Decimal Currency for Britain?', 4726

Tether, Philip: Parliament and Health Policy: The Role of M.P.s 1970–1975, 21673

Tetley, Uel A.: Centenary History of the Rugby Football Union, 27038

Tetlow, John: Homes, Towns and Traffic, 177127, 17783

Thacker, Christopher: The History of Gardens, 19876; England's Historic Gardens, 19877

Thackrah, John Richard: Malta, 12855

Thain, A. G.: ed. The County of Renfrew and the County of Bute, 19224

Thakur, Manab: Job Evaluation in Practice: A Survey of 213 Organisations in the U.K., 5780; Manpower Planning in Action, 5944; Industry as Seen by Immigrant Workers: A Summary of Research Findings from a Textile Mill, 11418

Thane, Pat: ed. The Origins of British Social Policy, 8917; The Power of the Past: Essays for Eric Hobsbawm, 26801; 'Toward Equal Opportunities? Women in Britain since 1945', 1138

Thatcher, Arthur Roger: Prices and Earnings 1951–1969, 3818

Thatcher, Carol: Diary of an Election: With Margaret Thatcher on the Campaign Trail, 2353

Third Statistical Account of Scotland, 19217

Thirlwall, Anthony Philip: 'Another Autopsy on Britain's Balance of Payments: 1958–1967', 4927; 'Changes in Industrial Composition in the U.K. and U.S. and Labour's Share of the National Income, 1948–1969, 4997; 'Types of Unemployment in the Regions of Great Britain', 5089; ed. Keynes as a Policy Adviser, 26609

Thoenes, Piet: The Elite in the Welfare State, 9763

Thomas, A. D.: Northern Graduates of '64: Braindrain or Brainbank?, 9876

Thomas, Adam Waugh: A History of Nottingham High School, 1513–1953, 22999

Thomas, Alan: Buses, 17280; Kaleidoscope of London Buses between the Wars, 17308; Vans and Trucks, 17467

Thomas, Alfred Noyes: The Queen's Sister: An Intimate Portrait of Princess Margaret, 523; Doctor Courageous: The Story of Grantley Dick-Read, 20866

Thomas, Bertram Sidney: Alarms and Excursions in Arabia, 27233

Thomas, Brinley: Migration and Economic Growth: A Study of Great Britain and the Atlantic Economy, 3710, 7317; ed. The Welsh Economy: A Study in Expansion, 5317; 'Economic and Social Planning in Wales', 5323; 'The International Circulation of Human Capital', 7308, 11403; Migration and Urban Development: A Reappraisal of British and American Long Cycles, 7318; The Economics of the Immigration White Paper, 11402

Thomas, C. J.: 'Projections of the Growth of the Coloured Immigrant Population of England and Wales', 11416

Thomas, Clifford J.: British Industry: Change and Development in the Twentieth Century, 4941; The Southampton Survey, 18077; 1. A Survey of the Industrial Prospects of the Southampton Region, 18078; 2. Shops and Planning etc, 18079; 3. Housing Targets etc, 18080; 4. Problem Families, 18081

Thomas, D.: 'London's Green Belt: The Evolution of an Idea', 18304

Thomas, D. Lleufer: 'A Plea for Regional Treatment in Wales', 22180

Thomas, D. M.: Memories and Hallucinations, 25826

Thomas, D. S.: 'International Migration', 10910

Thomas, David: 'Doctors, Politics and Pay Disputes: "Pressure Group Politics" Revisited', 21541

Thomas, David: Community in Social Policy, 9322

Thomas, David: London's Green Belt, 18925

Thomas, David: ed. Wales: A New Study, 5327

Thomas, David A.: Compton Mackenzie: A Bibliography, 25687

Thomas, David Arthur: Crete 1941: The Battle at Sea, 14859; Submarine Victory: With Ensigns Flying: The Story of H.M. Destroyers at War, 1939–1945, 15018; The Story of British Submarines in World War Two, 15372

Thomas, David Bernard: Trains and Buses of Newport, 1845 to 1981, 16342, 17234

Thomas, David John: Universities, 23300

Thomas, David N.: Organising for Social Change: A Study in the Theory and Practice of Community Work, 9375; The Making of Community Work, 9376; Community Workers in a Social Services Department: A Case Study, 9377; ed. Community Work: Learning and Supervision, 9378

Thomas, David St John: The Rural Transport Problem, 16311, 19089 The Great Days of the County Railway, 16748; ed. A Regional History of the Railways of Great Britain, 16808; The West Country, 16809; The Great Western Railway: 150 Glorious Years, 16860; L.M.S. 150: The London, Midland and Scottish Railway: A Century and a Half of Progress, 16878; The London Midland and Scottish in the West Midlands, 16879

Thomas, Denis: From Monopoly to Competition, 24868

Thomas, Donald: A Long Time Burning: The History of Literary Censorship in England, 26896

Thomas, G. H.: 'The Changing Pattern of Parliamentary Representation in Wales, 1945–1966', 2585

Thomas, George [Viscount Tonypandy]: Mr. Speaker: Memoirs of Viscount Tonypandy, 1326

Thomas, Gilbert: [John Jestin] Llewellin: A Biography, 1253, 12789

Thomas, Gwyn: ed. John Gwilym Jones: Cyfrol Deyrnged, 25962

Thomas, Harford: Newspaper Crisis: A Study of Developments in the National Press of Britain, 1966–67, 25059

Thomas, Harold A.: 'Aspects of the Economics of Land Ownership', 19539

Thomas, Howard: With an Independent Air: Encounters during a Lifetime of Broadcasting, 24875

Thomas, Hugh Swynnerton [Baron]: ed. Crisis in the Civil Service, 854; John Strachey, 1322; The Spanish Civil War, 13977; Armed Truce: The Beginnings of the Cold War 1945–1946, 14101; The Suez Affair, 14374; The Story of Sandhurst, 15773

Thomas, Ian C.: The Creation of the Welsh Office: Conflicting Purposes in Institutional Change, 951, 2579

Thomas, J. A.: 'Liturgy and Architecture, 1932–1960: Methodist Influence and Ideas', 12105

Thomas, J. R. Lloyd: Moth or Phoenix? St.

David's College and the University of Wales and the University Grants Committee, 23506

Thomas, James Edward: The English Prison Officer since 1850: A Study in Conflict, 10351; The Future of the Prison System, 10406; 'Hull '76: Observations on the Inquiries into the Prison Riot', 10454

Thomas, Jessie Ellen: Hope for the Handicapped, 21893

Thomas, Joan: A History of the Leeds Clothing Industry, 6241

Thomas, John: Gretna, Britain's Worst Railway Disaster, 16739; Scotland: The Lowlands and the Borders, 16814; The North of Scotland, 16823; The Callander and Oban Railway, 16922; The West Highland Railway, 16986

Thomas, John E.: ed. Educational Research and Development in Britain 1970–1980, 22842; ed. A Select Bibliography of Adult Continuing Education in Great Britain, 23642

Thomas, John E.: Wales at Westminster: A History of Parliamentary Representation of Wales 1801–1979, 2582

Thomas, Joy: The Bookselling Business, 25005

Thomas, Joyce: Compton Mackenzie: A Bibliography, 25687

Thomas, K. Bryn: The Development of Anaesthetic Apparatus: A History Based on the Charles King Collection of the Association of Anaesthetists of Great Britain and Ireland, 21032; Curare: Its History and Usage, 22298

Thomas, Lowell: Sir Hubert Wilkins (1888–1958), 27186

Thomas, Mark: 'Rearmament and Economic Recovery in the Late 1930's', 3583

Thomas, Mary G.: The Royal National Institute for the Blind, 1868–1956, 21932

Thomas, Maurice Walton: ed. A Survey of English Economic History, 3456; Young People in Industry, 1750–1945, 8367; 'Professionalisation in Britain: A Preliminary Measure', 9769

Thomas, Morgan D.: 'Regional Industrial Change: Northern Ireland', 5388

Thomas, Ned: The Welsh Extremist: A Culture in Crisis, 2590, 23827

Thomas, Neville Penry: A History of British Politics from the Year 1900, 1580

Thomas, Sir Percy: Expansion of Rhayader: A Pilot Study: A Report to the Mid-Wales Industrial Development Association, 18903

Thomas, R. C. W.: The War in Korea, 1950–1953, 16129

Thomas, R. E.: The Economic Consequences of the Severn Bridge and its Associated Motorways, 5365

Thomas, R. L.: 'Cross-Sectional Phillips Curve', 3896; 'Unemployment Dispersion as a Determinant of Wage Inflation in the U.K., 1925–1966', 7010

Thomas, R. T.: Britain and Vichy: The Dilemma of Anglo-French Relations, 1940–1942, 14276

Thomas, Ray: Commuting Flows and the Growth of London's New Towns

1951–1971, 16284, 18245, 19020; Aycliffe to Cumbernauld: A Study of Seven New Towns in their Regions, 18243; ed. Perspectives on New Town Development, 18244; London's New Towns: A Study of Self-contained and Balanced Communities, 18246

Thomas, Raymond Elliott: The Government of Business, 4940; Commercial Apprenticeships, 5954

Thomas, Richard H.: The Politics of Hunting, 27125

Thomas, Roger: Looking Forward to Work: A Report on the Follow-up Survey of Fifteen and Sixteen Year Old Boy School-leavers, Carried out by the Social Survey Division of the Office of Population Censuses and Surveys on Behalf of the Central Youth Employment Executive, 8492

Thomas, Roy: Industry in Rural Wales: Welsh Economic Studies, No. 3, 5318

Thomas, Ruth: Children in Homes, 8114

Thomas, Ruth: South Wales, 5375

Thomas, Samuel Evelyn: British Banks and the Finance of Industry, 4411

Thomas, Shirley: Computers: Their History, Present Applications and Future, 7091

Thomas, Terence: The British: Their Religious Beliefs and Practices 1800–1986, 11579

Thomas, Trevor Morgan: The Mineral Wealth of Wales and its Exploitation, 5316; 'Recent Trends and Developments in the British Coal Mining Industry', 6297; 'Derelict Land in South Wales', 18911

Thomas, W. J.: 'Postwar Agricultural Policy in the United Kingdom', 19497

Thomas, William Arthur: The Stock Exchange: Its History and Functions, 4253 The Finance of British Industry 1918–1976, 4257, 4756; The Provincial Stock Exchanges, 4258

Thomas, Sir William Beach: The Story of The Spectator 1828–1928, 25186

Thomason, George Frederick: 'Management Work Roles and Relationships', 5441; Rural Depopulation in Wales, 19290

Thomis, Malcolm I.: 'Conscription and Consent: British Labour and the Resignation Threat of January 1916', 1698

Thomps, D.: The Experience of Handicap, 21789

Thompson, A. Landsborough: Half a Century of Medical Research: Vol.1 Origins and Policy of the Medical Research Council (UK) Vol.2 The Programme of the Medical Research Council, 20767

Thompson, B.: The Motivation and Characteristics of Internal Migrants: A Socio-medical Study of Young Migrants in Scotland, 7343

Thompson, Alan: The Day before Yesterday: An Illustrated History of Britain from Attlee to Macmillan, 300

Thompson, Alice M. C.: ed. A Bibliography of Nursing Literature, 1859–1960, with a Historical Introduction, 21699; ed. A Bibliography of Nursing Literature, 1961–1970, 21700

Thompson, Anthony Hugh: Censorship in Public Libraries in the United Kingdom

during the Twentieth Century, 26897;
Thompson, Barbara: 'Problems of Abortion
in Britain: Aberdeen, A Case Study', 7522;
'Women from Broken Homes', 7682;
'Married Women who Work in Early
Motherhood', 7826
Thompson, C. J. S.: Royal College of
Surgeons of England: Guide to the Surgical
Instruments and Objects in the Historical
Series, with their History and Development,
20900
Thompson, Charles H.: Bibliography of the
British Coal Industry, 6244
Thompson, D'Arcy R.: D'Arcy Wentworth
Thompson: The   Scholar-Naturalist
1860–1948, 26511
Thompson, David: 'Recent British Painting:
The Stuyvesant Collection', 23993
Thompson, David: Privatising London's
Airports,   17683;   'The   Impact   of
Competitive Tendering on the Costs of
Hospital Domestic Services', 21400
Thompson, David Michael: 'The Politics of
the Enabling Act (1919)', 11621; 'War, the
Nation, and the Kingdom of God: The
Origins   of   the   National   Mission   of
Repentance and Hope, 1915–16', 11858;
'Let Sects and Parties Fall': A Short History
of the Association of the Churches of Christ
in Great Britain and Ireland, 12119;
'Theological and Sociological Approaches
to the Motivation of the Ecumenical
Movement', 12324
Thompson, Dennis Frank: The Democratic
Citizen: Social Science and Democratic
Theory in the Twentieth Century, 7940
Thompson, Denys: Change and Tradition in
Rural England: An Anthology of Writings
on Country Life, 19092
Thompson, Donna Fay: Professional
Solidarity among the Teachers of England,
22706
Thompson, Dorothy: ed. Over our Dead
Bodies: Women Against the Bomb, 13441
Thompson, Douglas Weddell: Donald Soper,
12091
Thompson, Edward John: Robert Bridges,
1844–1930, 25413
Thompson, Edward Palmer: 'On History,
Sociology and Historical Relevance', 8078;
Protest and Survive, 15141; ed. Warwick
University Ltd.: Industry, Management and
the Universities, 23586
Thompson, Eric John: Demographic Social
and Economic Trends for Wards in Greater
London, 7260; 'Analyses of Census Data for
London', 18312
Thompson, Francis G.: ed. The Significance
of Freedom, 2428; ed. The Celt in the
Seventies, 2429; ed. Celtic Unity Ten Years
On, 2430; ed. The Celtic Experience Past
and Present, 2431
Thompson, Francis: Harris and Lewis, Outer
Hebrides, 19271
Thompson, Francis Michael Longstreth:
Chartered Surveyors: The Growth of a
Profession, 9806; ed. The Rise of Suburbia,
18297; Dyos and the Urban Past, 26766
Thompson, G. F.: 'Airport Profitability and
Management Effectiveness', 17661

Thompson, Sir Geoffrey Harington: Front
Line Diplomat, 13312
Thompson, George Frederick: Community
Development in Urban Areas, 9344; The
Professional Approach to Community
Work, 9345
Thompson, Grahame: The Conservatives'
Economic Policy, 3696
Thompson, Henry Paget: Into all Lands: The
History of the Society for the Propagation of
the Gospel in Foreign Parts, 1701–1950,
12357
Thompson, Ian E.: Nursing Ethics, 21722
Thompson, J. A.: 'Lord Cecil and the Pacifists
of the League of Nations Union', 13498;
'Lord Cecil and the Historians', 13499; 'The
Peace Ballot of 1935: The Welsh
Campaign', 13503; 'The Peace Ballot and
the Public', 13504; The "Peace Ballot" and
the "Rainbow" Controversy', 13505
Thompson, J.: A History of Daniel Stewart's
College, 1855–1955, 23224
Thompson, J.L.: The Economics of Wage
Controls, 3955
Thompson, John K.: The Structure of Scottish
Agriculture and Food Industries, 20626;
Ownership and Control of the Scotch
Whisky Industry, 20730
Thompson, Joseph Allen: Modern British
Monarchy, 438; The Collapse of the British
Liberal Party: Fate or Self-Destruction?,
1822
Thompson, Julian: Ready for Anything: The
Parachute Regiment, 1940–1982, 15710; No
Picnic, 16114; British Trams in Camera,
17208
Thompson, K. J.: The Costs of the Common
Agricultural Policy, 19587
Thompson, Kenneth Alfred: 'So You Think
You Know what Government Departments
Are . . . ?', 819; Sociological Perspectives:
Selected Readings, 8002; Bureaucracy and
Church Reform: The   Organizational
Response of the Church of England to
Social Change, 1800–1965, 11611; 'The
Church of England Bishops as an Elite',
11686
Thompson, Kenneth L.: A Dictionary of
Twentieth Century Composers, 1911–1971,
24287; The Works of Arthur Bliss, 24299
Thompson, Kenneth W.: ed. Herbert
Butterfield: The Ethics of History and
Politics, 26785; Toynbee's Philosophy of
World History and Politics, 26824
Thompson, Laurence: 1940: Year of Legend,
Year of History, 371
Thompson, Meg: Housing: A Select List,
18574
Thompson, Neville: The Anti-Appeasers:
Conservative Opposition to Appeasement in
the Thirties, 13719
Thompson, Owen: 'Some Points and Practice
in the law of Infants', 8368
Thompson, Patricia G.: 'Some Factors in
Upward Social Mobility in England', 9597
Thompson, Paul: Living the Fishing, 9655;
The Voice of the Past: Oral History, 26740
Thompson, Reginald William: Churchill and
Morton, 988; The Yankee Marlborough,
988; Dieppe at Dawn: The Story of the

Dieppe Raid, 14829; The Battle for the
Rhineland, 14967; The Eighty-Five Days:
The Story of the Battle of the Scheldt,
14968; Spearhead of Invasion: D-Day,
14969; Cry Korea, 16136
Thompson, Richard: Race and Sport, 10939
Thompson, Richard: Residential and Day
Care   Services   for   the   Mentally
Handicapped and Mentally Ill in the
London Boroughs, 1966–1974, 21872
Thompson, Robert: Defeating Communist
Insurgency: Experience from Malaya and
Vietnam, 16159
Thompson, Sir Robert: The Royal Flying
Corps (per ardua ad astra), 15807
Thompson, Roger: ed.   Contrast   and
Connection: Bicentennial   Essays   in
American History, 13999
Thompson,   Russell: Atmospheric
Contamination: A Review of the Air
Pollution Problem, 20045
Thompson, Sheila: The Group Process as a
Helping Technique, 8653
Thoms, David W.: The Motor Car Industry in
Coventry since the 1890s, 17406; The
History of Technical Education in London,
1904–1940, 23288
Thomson, Andrew William John:'Collective
Bargaining under Incomes Legislation: The
Case of Britain's Buses', 5754; The
Industrial Relations Act: A Review and
Analysis, 5773; The Nationalised Transport
Industries, 16191
Thomson, Archibald McLennan Wright: The
History of the Glasgow Eye Infirmary,
1824–1962, 21477
Thomson, Sir Basil Home: The Scene
Changes, 10686
Thomson, D. P.: Eric H. Liddell: Athlete and
Missionary, 12374
Thomson, David: England in the Twentieth
Century, 294; 'General de Gaulle and the
Anglo-Saxons', 14228; 'President de Gaulle
and the Mésentente Cordiale', 14229; The
Proposal for Anglo-French Union in 1940,
14266
Thomson, David: A Biographical Dictionary
of the Cinema, 24592
Thomson, David Cleghorn: ed. Training
Worker Citizens, 23265
Thomson, David Lawrie: The Glasgow
Subway, 17021
Thomson, Derick Smith: ed. The Future of
the Highlands, 5297, 19255; A Companion
to Gaelic Culture, 23735
Thomson,   Elizabeth: The   Lennon
Companion: Twenty-Five Years of
Comment, 24502
Thomson, G.: 'Parties in Parliament,
1959–1963: The Conservatives', 1638
Thomson, G. H.: The Trend of Scottish
Intelligence, 7428
Thomson, George Malcolm: Vote of Censure,
988; Martin Secker and Warburg: The First
Fifty Years: A Memoir, 24990; Lord
Castlerosse: His Life and Times, 25218
Thomson, H. Campbell: The Story of the
Middlesex Hospital Medical School, 20779
Thomson, J. Michael: Great Cities and their
Traffic, 16292; Some Characteristics of

Motorists in Central London: Results of a Parking Survey in April 1966, 17382

Thomson, Sir John Arthur: The Control of Life, 26487; What is Man?, 26488; The Gospel of Evolution, 26489

Thomson, Malcolm: David Lloyd George: The Official Biography, 1018

Thomson, Michael: Silver Screen in the Silver City: A History of Cinemas in Aberdeen, 1896–1987, 24605

Thomson, Peter: 'Harold Pinter: A Retrospect', 25978

Thomson, Roy, Baron: After I was Sixty: A Chapter of Autobiography, 25101

Thomson, S. S.: 'Ethnic Identity and Preferences among Asian Immigrant Children in Glasgow: A Replicated Study', 11224

Thorburn, Sandy: The History of Scottish Rugby, 27050

Thornberry, Cedric: The Stranger at the Gate: A Study of the Law on Aliens and Commonwealth Citizens, 11129; 'Commitment or Withdrawal? The Place of Law in Race Relations in Britain', 11130; 'Discretion and Appeal in British Immigrant Law', 11131

Thorncroft, Michael Eric Trevor: The Economics of Conservation, 18961

Thorndike, Sybil and Thorndike, Russell: Lilian Baylis, 26111

Thorndike, Tony: 'Belizean Political Parties: The Independence Crisis and After', 13033; Grenada: Revolution and Invasion, 13080

Thorne, Barrie: The BBC's Finances and Cost Control, 24780

Thorne, Christopher Guy: The Limits of Foreign Policy: The West, the League and the Manchurian Crisis, 1931–1933, 13593; 'The Shanghai Crisis of 1932: The Basis of British Policy', 13594; 'Chatham House, Whitehall and Far Eastern Issues: 1941–1945', 13613; The Approach of War, 1938–1939, 13765; Allies of a Kind: The United States, Great Britain and the War against Japan, 1941–1945, 14045

Thorne, Stuart: The History of Food Preservation, 20645

Thornes, Barbara: Who Divorces?, 9990

Thornes, Vernon: Steel: The Commanding Height of the Economy, 6574

Thornhill, Christopher J.: Taking Tanganyika: Experiences of an Intelligence Officer, 1914–1918, 14529

Thornhill, William: ed. The Modernization of British Government, 781; ed. The Growth and Reform of English Local Government, 3134; The Nationalized Industries: An Introduction, 6093

Thornley, Andrew: Thatcherism and Town Planning, 18804

Thornley, Jennifer: State Shareholding: The Role of the Local and Regional Authorities, 4751; Aspects of Urban Management, 17854

Thorns, David Christopher: New Directions in Sociology, 8030; The Quest for Community: Social Aspects of Residential Growth, 9368; Suburbia, 18294; 'The Changing System of Rural Stratification', 19108

Thornton, A. H.: ed. The University and its Region: The Extra-Mural Contribution, 23700

Thornton, Archibald Paton: The Imperial Idea and its Enemies, 12569; For the File on the Empire, 12570; 'With Wavell on to Simla and Beyond', 13162

Thornton, John L.: A Select Bibliography of Medical Biography, 20894; ed. The Royal Hospital of Saint Bartholomew 1123–1973, 21439

Thornton, Michael: Royal Feud: The Queen Mother and the Duchess of Windsor, 489

Thorogood, H.: East of Aldgate, 18346

Thorold, Henry Karslake: Community Centres: Some Service Experiences, 9257

Thorpe, David: Urban Redevelopment and Changes in Retail Structure, 1961–1971, 6638; The Geographer and Urban Studies, 18272, 20412

Thorpe, David R.: Selwyn Lloyd, 1256

Thorpe, Don: Railways of the Manchester Ship Canal, 16969

Thorpe, Edward: Kenneth Macmillan: The Man and his Ballets, 24237

Thorpe, Frances: ed. A Directory of British Film and Television Libraries, 217; ed. International Directory of Film and TV Documentation Centres, 218; British Official Films in the Second World War: A Descriptive Catalogue, 24594

Thorpe, H.: 'Homely Allotment: From Rural Dole to Urban Amenity: A Neglected Aspect of Urban Land Use', 20294

Thorpe, Marion: ed. Peter Pears: A Tribute on his 75th Birthday, 24421

Thorpe, R.: Children: Handle with Care: A Critical Analysis of the Development of Intermediate Treatment, 8303

Thorpe, Richard: Payment Systems and Productivity, 3954

Thrift, Nigel: Class and Space: The Making of Urban Society, 9614; Writing the Rural: Five Cultural Geographies, 19123

Throup, David: Economic and Social Origins of Mau Mau 1945–1953, 12832

Thrower, W. Rayner: The Great Northern Main Line, 16849; Kings Cross in the Twenties, 16994

Thurley, Keith: Industrial Relations and Management Strategy, 5827

Thurlow, Richard C.: British Fascism: Essays on the Radical Right in Inter-War Britain, 2028; Fascism in Britain: A History, 1918–1985, 2029

Thurnley, Jean: Some Voluntary Work in the North West: A Guide, 9198

Thurston, Albert Peter: The Future of Aerial Transport, 17638

Thwaites, Alfred T.: Industrial Innovation and Regional Development: Final Report to the Department of the Environment, 5120

Thwing, Leroy: Flickering Flames: A History of Domestic Lighting through the Ages, 7081

Tibawi, Abdul Latif: Anglo-Arab Relations and the Question of Palestine, 1914–1921, 14286

Tibbatts, George: John How: A Cambridge Don, Parish Priest, Scottish Primus: A Biography, 12268

Tibble, John William: ed. The Extra Year: The Raising of the School-leaving Age, 23251

Tickell, Jerrard: Moon Squadron, 15929

Tidball, Michael: The Quiet Revolution: The Planning, Development and Provision of Community Services for the Mentally Handicapped, 21780

Tidy, Douglas: I Fear No Man: The Story of No. 74 (Fighter) Squadron, 15930

Tierney, David: Britain's Northern Gateway (Manchester International Airport) 17694

Tierney, Mark: Modern Ireland, 1850–1950, 308

Tierney, Michael: Eoin MacNeill: Scholar and Man of Action 1867–1945, 3061

Tignor, Robert L.: Egyptian Textiles and British Capital, 1930–1956, 6459; 'Decolonization and Business: The Case of Egypt', 14408

Till, Barry Dorn: The Churches Search for Unity, 12321

Tillett, Ben: Memoirs and Reflections, 1537

Tilley, J.: 'Local Government Councillors and Community Work', 9408

Tilley, Sir John Anthony Cecil: London to Tokyo, 13313; The Foreign Office, 13327

Tillman, Seth P.: Anglo-American Relations at the Paris Peace Conference of 1919, 13428

Tillot, P. M.: ed. York: A Survey, Prepared for the British Association, 18122

Tillott, Alan Theodore: From Kent to Kohima: Being the History of the 4th Battalion, the Queen's Own Royal West Kent Regiment, 1939–1947, 15673

Tillyard, Eustace Mandeville Wetenhall: The Muse Unchained: An Intimate Account of the Revolution in English Studies at Cambridge, 22443

Tillyard, Sir Frank: Unemployment Insurance in Great Britain, 1911–1948, 4030

Tilman, Robert O.: 'Malaysia: Problems of Federation', 12939; Bureaucratic Transition in Malaya, 12904

Tiltman, Hubert Hessel: James Ramsay MacDonald: Labour's Man of Destiny, 1032

Tiltscher, Robert: The British Beers, Wines and Spirits Industry, 20747

Times Guide to the European Parliament, 2379

Times Yearbook of World Affairs: 1978+, 268

Times, The: The Official Index to The Times 1906–1956, 168; The Times Index 1957+, 169; British War Production, 1939–1945: A Record, 4896

Times 'Concorde: A Special Report': 4 Mar, 17567

Timmermann, Heinrich: Friedensbewegung in den Vereinigten Staaten von Amerika und in Grossbritannien während des Ersten Weltkrieges, 13448

Timms, David: Philip Larkin, 25624

Timms, Duncan: The Urban Mosaic: Towards a Theory of Residential Differentiation, 17813; ed. The Stirling Region, 18153

Timms, Noel: ed. Values and Social Change in Britain, 238; Casework in the Child Care Service, 8369; ed. Receiving End: Consumer

Accounts of Social Help for Children, 8370; Rootless in the City, 8493; 'Knowledge, Opinion and the Social Services', 8693; 'On Wootton's Image of the Social Worker', 8694; A Sociological Approach to Social Problems, 8695; Social Casework: Principles and Practice, 8696; Recording in Social Work, 8697; Social Work: An Outline for the Intending Student, 8698; The Language of Social Casework, 8699; Social Welfare: Why and How?, 8700; Social Work Values: An Enquiry, 8701; Perspectives in Social Work, 8702; ed. Talking about Welfare: Readings in Philosophy and Social Policy, 8703; ed. Philosophy in Social Work, 8704; The Client Speaks, 8741; 'The Problem Family: A Sociological Approach', 10026; The Problem of the 'Problem Family': A Critical Review of the Literature concerning the 'Problem Family' and its Treatment, 10062; Psychiatric Social Work in Great Britain, 1939–1962, 21806

Timms, Rita: Perspectives in Social Work, 8702

Timperley, Stuart R.: 'Some Factors Affecting the Career Choice and Career Perceptions of Sixth Form School Leavers', 5896

Timpson, David John: William Timpson Ltd.: A Century of Service, 1865–1965, 6654

Tims, Margaret: Women's International League for Peace and Freedom 1915–1965, 13439

Timson, J.: 'Social Factors in the Incidence of Spina Bifida and Anencephaly', 21087

Timson, Lesley: The University in an Urban Environment, 23304

Tindall, Gillian: Rosamond Lehmann, 25654

Tindall, William York: A Reader's Guide to Dylan Thomas, 25839

Tingle, Rachel: 'The Objectives and Performance of the Mental Health Services in England and Wales', 21781

Tinker, Anthea: The Elderly in Modern Society, 8631

Tinker, David: A Message from the Falklands, 16117

Tinker, Hugh: The Banyan Tree: Overseas Immigrants from Pakistan and Bangladesh, 11221; ed. Constitutional Relations between Britain and Burma: Burma: The Struggle for Independence 1944–1948: Documents from Official and Private Sources, 13203; 'British Policy Towards the Separate Indian Identity in the Caribbean 1920–1950', 13010; Experiment with Freedom: India and Pakistan 1947, 13171; 'The Falklands after Three Years', 16100

Tinker, J.: The Television Barons, 24876

Tipper, Alison: British Directories: A Bibliography and Guide to Directories Published in England and Wales (1850–1950) and Scotland (1773–1950), 58

Tippett, Leonard Henry Caleb: A Portrait of the Lancashire Textile Industry, 6445

Tipping, David Guy: Profits in the British Economy, 1909–1938, 5982

Tipple, Graham: 'Coloured Immigrants within the City: An Analysis of Housing and Travel Preferences', 11476

Tipton, Beryl Frances A.: Conflict and Change in a Technical College, 23273

Tisdall, Patricia: Agents of Change: The Development and Practice of Management Consultancy, 9792

Titley, David Paul: Machines, Money and Men: An Economic and Social History of Great Britain from 1700 to the 1970s, 3505

Titmuss, Kathleen and Titmuss, Richard Morris: Parents' Revolt: A Study of the Declining Birthrate in Acquisitive Societies, 7481

Titmuss, Kay [Kathleen]: ed. Social Policy: An Introduction, 8831

Titmuss, Richard M.: Income Distribution and Social Change: A Study in Criticism, 3823; Professional Education for Social Work in Britain: An Historical Account, 8731; The Gift Relationship: From Human Blood to Social Policy, 8826; Problems of Social Policy, 8827; The Social Division of Welfare, 8828; Commitment to Welfare, 8829; The Irresponsible Society, 8830; ed. Social Policy: An Introduction, 8831; Poverty and Population: A Factual Study of Contemporary Social Waste, 8984; Essays on the 'Welfare State', 8985; Choice and the 'Welfare State', 8986; Our Food Problem: A Study of National Security, 20587; The Cost of the National Health Service in England and Wales, 21563

Titus, Edna Brown: ed. Union List of Serials in Libraries in the United States and Canada, 158

Tivey, Leonard James: Nationalization in British Industry, 6078; ed. The Nationalized Industries since 1960: A Book of Readings, 6086; 'The Political Consequences of Economic Planning', 6143

Tivy, Joy: ed. The Glasgow Region: A General Survey, 18136, 26677; 'Britain's One-third of Waste Land', 20295

Tizard, Barbara: Adoption: A Second Chance, 8371; Pre-school Education in Great Britain: A Research Review, 23129

Tizard, Jack: Patterns of Residential Care: Sociological Studies in Institutions for Handicapped Children, 2842, 21911; All our Children: Pre-School Services in a Changing Society, 8372, 23130; The Social Problem of Mental Deficiency, 21756; Community Services for the Mentally Handicapped, 21832; The Integration of the Handicapped in Society, 21836; Mental Retardation: Concepts of Education and Research, 21837; The Mentally Handicapped and Their Families: A Social Survey, 21838; Education, Health and Behaviour, 22841

Toberman, Barry: Elton John: A Biography, 24517

Tobias, John Jacob: 'Police and Public in the United Kingdom', 10727

Tobin, Terence: James Bridie (Osborne Henry Mavor), 25952

Tod, Robert James Niebohr: ed. Social Work in Foster Care: Collected Papers, 8373; Disturbed Children, 8374; ed. Children in Care, 8375; ed. Social Work in Adoption: Collected Papers, 8376

Todd, Frances Joan: Social Work with the Mentally Subnormal, 21809

Todd, J. E.: Adult Dental Health in England and Wales in 1968, 22400

Todd, Judith: The Conjurers: Wealth and Welfare in the Upper Income Brackets, 3824

Todd, Nigel: 'Labour Women: A Study of Women in the Bexley Branch of the British Labour Party, 1945–1950', 1804

Todd, Richard: Iris Murdoch, 25731

Toland, John: Battle: The Story of the Bulge, 14970

Toller, Jane: British Samplers: A Concise History, 24122

Tolstoy, Dimitry: The Law and Practice of Divorce and Matrimonial Causes, Including Proceedings in Magistrates' Courts, 9995

Tolstoy, Nikolai: The Minister and the Massacres, 13968

Tomalin, Nicholas: The History of the National Theatre, 26140

Tomaszewski, Wiktor: ed. The University of Edinburgh and Poland, 23494

Tombs, Jacqueline: ed. The British Crime Survey: Scotland, 10269

Tomiche, F. J.: 'Aperçu sur quelques effets de la Télévision en Grande Bretagne', 24845

Tomison, Maureen: The English Sickness: The Rise of Trade Union Political Power, 6736

Tomkins, Cyril Robert: Personal Wealth and Finance in Wales, 5325

Tomkins, Oliver Stratford: The Life of Edward Woods, 11769

Tomkinson, Martin: Nothing to Declare: The Political Corruptions of John Poulson, 3186

Tomlin, David M.: The Salt Industry of the River Tees, 20710

Tomlin, Eric Walter Frederick: Wyndham Lewis, 25674

Tomlinson, Brian R.: 'Britain and the Indian Currency Crisis, 1930–1932', 13147; The Political Economy of the Raj, 1914–1947: The Economics of Decolonisation in India, 13148; The Indian National Congress and the Raj 1929–1942, 13150; 'Indo-British Relations in the Post-Colonial Era: The Sterling Balances Negotiations, 1947–1949', 13187

Tomlinson, Jim: Problems of British Economic Policy, 1870–1945, 3412; British Macroeconomic Policy since 1940, 3522; The Unequal Struggle? British Socialism and the Capitalist Enterprise, 6095; 'Unemployment and Government Policy between the Wars: A Note', 7002

Tomlinson, John: Left-Right: The March of Political Extremism in Britain, 2004

Tomlinson, Rolfe C.: OR Comes of Age: A Review of the Work of the Operational Research Branch of the National Coal Board 1948–1969, 6265

Tomlinson, William Weaver: Tomlinson's North Eastern Railway: Its Rise and Development, 16906

Tommaga, Thomas: Iris Murdoch and Muriel Spark: A Bibliography, 25814

Tompkins, Steve: Forestry in Crisis, 19760

Tompson, Richard Stevens: The Atlantic Archipelago, 304; The Charity Commission and the Age of Reform, 9229

Toms, Jane R.: *ed.* Trends in Cancer Survival in Great Britain: Cases Registered between 1960 and 1974, 22239

Tonbridge: A History of Tonbridge School, 23079

Tonkinson, Ernest: Commercial Apprenticeships, 5954

Took, Barry: Laughter in the Air: An Informal History of British Radio Comedy, 26282

Toole, Millie: Mrs Bessie Braddock, M.P, 1370

Tooley, Ronald Vere: Maps and Mapmakers, 26716

Toomey, Alice F.: A World Bibliography of Bibliographies 1964–1974, 10

Toomey, Derek M.: 'Ambition, Occupational Values and School Organisation', 9598; 'Home Centred Working-class Parents' Attitudes towards their Sons' Education and Careers', 10084

Toon, Peter: 'English Strict Baptists', 12033

Toothill, G. C.: Electronic Computers, 7089

Tooze, John: The DNA Story: A Documentary History of Gene Cloning, 26481

Top 2000 Directories and Annuals, 60

Top 3000 Directories and Annuals, 61

Topham, Anthony [Tony]: '"Package Deals" et negociation collective en Grande-Bretagne', 5668; Industrial Democracy in Great Britain, 5698; The Shop Steward's Guide to the Bullock Report, 5699; *ed.* Industrial Democracy in Great Britain: A Book of Readings and Witnesses for Workers' Control, 6007; *ed.* The New Unionism: The Case for Workers' Control, 6008; Bus Deregulation and Privatisation: An International Perspective, 17281; Decasualisation of Employment in the Fishing Industry, 19808

Topham, Edward: The Co-operative Movement in Britain, 1888

Topliss, C. E.: Demolition, 6196

Topliss, Eda: Provision for the Disabled, 21922; A Charter for the Disabled: The Chronically Sick and Disabled Persons Act, 1970, 21923

Topping J.:The Beginnings of Brunel University: from Technical College to University, 23464

Topping, Philip R.: Government against Poverty? Liverpool Community Development Project, 1970–1975, 9092, 9277

Torrey Canyon, the: Report of the Committee of Scientists on the Scientific and Technological Aspects of the Torrey Canyon Disaster, 20069

Torrington, Derek: The Changing Nature of Personnel Management, 9782

Torstendal, Rolf: Bureaucratisation in Northwestern Europe 1880–1985: Domination and Governance, 898

Toscano, Mario: 'Eden's Mission to Rome on the Eve of the Italo-Ethiopian Conflict', 13786

Tough, Alistair: Consolidated Guide to the Modern Records Centre, 77

Toulmin, Stephen: The Fabric of the Heavens: The Development of Astronomy and Dynamics, 26390

Towers, Bernard: 'Medical Scientists and the View that History is Bunk', 21015

Towers, Brian: Productivity Bargaining: A Case Study and Simulation Exercise, 5708

Towler, Robert: The Fate of the Anglican Clergy: A Sociological Study, 11677; The Need for Certainty: A Sociological Study of Conventional Religion, 12386

Town and Country Planning Association: 'To Mr John Silkin: Statement on the White Paper on Land', 20296

Town and Country Planning: 1936+, 18833

Town Planning Institute: Planned London: The Town Planning Institute Conference Handbook, London 14–16 June, 1969, 18929

Town Planning Review: 1910+, 18832

Town and Country Planning Association: New Towns: The British Experience, 18251; The Paper Metropolis: The Report of a Study of the Growth of Office Employment in London and a Survey of Decentralised Offices, etc, 18323; Planning and Plutonium: Evidence of the Town and Country Planning Association to the Public Inquiry into an Oxide reprocessing Plant at Windscale, 18819

Town, Stephen Williams: After the Mines: Changing Employment Opportunities in a South Wales Valley, 5376, 6333

Townroe, Bernard Stephen: Britain Rebuilding: The Slum and Overcrowding Campaigns, 18386

Townroe, Bernard Stephen: The Slum Problem, 18385

Townroe, M.: *ed.* The Spiritual Development of the Child, 8111

Townroe, Peter Michael: Industrial Location and Regional Economic Policy: A Selected Bibliography, 5071, 5114; Industrial Location Decisions: A Study in Management Behaviour, 5072; 'Branch Plants and Regional Development', 5113; *ed.* The Social and Political Consequences of the Motor Car, 17347

Townsend, G.: Organisation in Multi-racial Schools, 23183

Townsend, Harry: Business Enterprise: Its Growth and Organisation, 4945; *ed.* Studies in Business Organisation, 4946; *ed.* Business Growth, 4947

Townsend, Henry: The Claims of the Free Churches, 12016; Robert Wilson Black, 12028

Townsend, K.: 'The Documentary Spoor of Burgess and Maclean', 16039

Townsend, Peter: The Last Emperor: Decline and Fall of the British Empire, 12588

Townsend, Peter Brereton: *ed.* Labour and Inequality, 3782; Sociology and Social Policy, 8025; The Family Life of Old People: An Inquiry in East London, 8558; The Development of Home and Welfare Services for Old People, 1946–1960, 8559; The Last Refuge: A Survey of Residential Institutions and Homes for the Aged in England and Wales, 8560; The Personal Family and Social Circumstances of Old People: Report of an Investigation Carried Out in England in 1959 to Pilot a Future

Cross-national Survey of Old Age, 8561; The Aged in the Welfare State: The Interim Report of a Survey of Persons aged 65 and Over in Britain, 1962 and 1963, 8585; Labour and Equality: A Study in Social Policy, 1964–1970, 8914; The Social Minority, 8915, 11030; 'The Meaning of Poverty', 9015; Poverty in the United Kingdom, 9016; The Poor and the Poorest: A New Analysis of the Ministry of Labour's Family Expenditure Surveys of 1953–54 and 1960, 9057; The Fifth Social Service: A Critical Analysis of the Seebohm Proposals, 9263; The Family of Three Generations in Britain, the United States and Denmark, 10067; *ed.* Inequality in Health: The Black Report, 21682; The Disabled in Society, 21889

Townsend, Richard: Routine Punctuated by Orgies: The Central Policy Review Staff, 910

Townsend, William: The Townsend Journals: An Artist's Record of his Times, 1928–1951, 24080

Townshend, Charles: Political Violence in Ireland: Government and Resistance since 1848, 2732; *ed.* Consensus in Ireland: Approaches and Recessions, 2785; The British Campaign in Ireland 1919–1921: The Development of Political and Military Policies, 2966, 14698; Britain's Civil Wars: Counter-Insurgency in the Twentieth Century, 16176

Townshend, Sir Charles Vere-Ferrers: My Campaign in Mesopotamia, 14566

Townshend-Rose, Henry: The British Coal Industry, 6290

Townsin, Alfred Alan: The British Bus Story, 1946–1950: A Golden Age, 17270; Buses and Trams, 17271

Toynbee, Arnold Joseph: Change and Habit: The Challenge of our Time, 9890; *ed.* The Conduct of British Empire Foreign Relations since the Peace Settlement, 12514; 'Britain and the Arabs: The Need for a New Start', 13825; Cities on the Move, 17811; *ed.* Cities of Destiny, 17812; Acquaintances, 26820

Trace, K.: 'Britain and the Motorship: A Case of the Delayed Adoption of New Technology', 17549

Tracey, Herbert: *ed.* The Book of the Labour Party: its History, Growth, Policy and Leaders, 1672, 1676; The British Trade Union Movement, 6724

Tracey, Michael: A Variety of Lives: A Biography of Sir Hugh Carleton Greene, 24824; The Production of Political Television in Britain, 24898; In the Culture of an Eye—Ten Years of Weekend World, 24925

Tracey, N.: The Origins of the Social Democratic Party, 1831

Tracy, M. E.: 'Fifty Years of Agricultural Policy', 19423

Tragatsch, Erwin: *ed.* The Illustrated Encyclopaedia of Motorcycles, 17177

Train, Jack: Up and Down the Line: The Autobiography, 26347

Trancik, R.: 'Studlands Park, England: A

Sociophysical Evaluation of a New Community', 18257

Transactions of the Newcomen Society for the Study of the History of Engineering and Technology Vol.1., 7107

Transport 1980+, 16217

Transport History 1968–1981, 16216

Tranter, Nigel L.: Population and Society 1750–1940, 7259; 'Population and Social Structure in a Bedfordshire Parish: The Cardington Listing of Inhabitants', 7418

Tranter, R. B.: *ed.* Strategies for Family-worked Farms in the United Kingdom: Proceedings of a Symposium . . . , 19600

Trask, David F.: Captains and Cabinets: Anglo-American Naval Relations, 1917–1918, 15332

Trasler, Gordon: In Place of Parents: A Study of Foster Care, 8377; The Explanation of Criminality, 10144

Travers, Tim: The Killing Ground: The British Army, the Western Front and the Emergence of Warfare, 1900–1918, 14572

Travers, Tony: The Politics of Local Government Finance, 3258, 4883; Ten Billion Pounds: Whitehall's Takeover of the Town Halls, 3267, 4867

Travis, A. S.: 'Containment of Urban England', 17867

Travis, N. J.: The Tincal Trail: A History of Borax, 6222

Trease, George Edward: Pharmacy in History, 7026, 22254

Trebilcock, R. Clive: 'A "Special Relationship": Government, Rearmament and the Cordite firms', 6142

Treble, J. H.: 'The Working of the 1918 Education Act in Glasgow Archdiocese', 23612

Tredgold, Alfred Frank: A Textbook of Mental Deficiency [Tredgold's Mental Retardation], 21839

Tredgold, Roger Francis: *ed.* Bridging the Gap: From Fear to Understanding in Mental Illness, 21758

Tredrey, Frank: The House of Blackwood 1804–1954, 24945

Tree, Ronald: When the Moon was High: Memoirs of Peace and War, 1538

Tregoning, David: Friends for Life: Friends' Provident Life Office, 1832–1982, 4236

Tregonning, Kennedy Gordon Phillip: A History of Modern Malaya, 12907; North Borneo, 12954; A History of Modern Sabah (North Borneo), 12955

Treiman, Donald J.: 'The Process of Status Attainment in the United States and Great Britain', 9455

Tremlett, George: Caitlin: Life with Dylan Thomas, 25838

Trenaman, Joseph: Out of Step: A Study of Young Delinquent Soldiers in Wartime: Their Offences, their Background, and their Treatment under an Army Experiment, 10564; Television and the Political Image: A Study of the Impact of Television on the 1959 General Election, 24887

Trench, Sally: Bury me in my Boots, 22124

Trend, Michael: The Music Makers: Heirs and Rebels of the English Musical Renaissance, Edward Elgar to Benjamin Britten, 24267

Trenowden, Ian: Operations Most Secret: S.O.E., the Malayan Theatre, 14932

Trent, Christopher: Greater London: Its Growth and Development through Two Thousand Years, 18361

Trethowan, Sir Ian: Split Screen, 24798

Trevaskis, Sir Kennedy: Shades of Amber: A South Arabian Episode, 13872

Trevelyan, Avice: Slum, 18393

Trevelyan, George Macaulay: Grey of Fallodon, 1202

Trevelyan, Humphrey, Baron: The India We Left: Charles Trevelyan, 1826–1865; Humphrey Trevelyan, 1929–1947, 13183; Worlds Apart: China 1953–1955: Soviet Union 1962–1965, 13314; Public and Private, 13315; Diplomatic Channels, 13333

Trevelyan, John: What the Censor Saw, 26908

Trevelyan, Raleigh: The Fortress: A Diary of Anzio and After, 14877; Rome '44. The Battle for the Eternal City, 14878

Trevenen, James: The Royal Air Force: The Past Thirty Years, 15784

Trevithick, James Anthony: Inflation: A Guide to the Crisis in Economics, 4013; *ed.* Keynes and the Modern World, 26605

Trevor-Roper, Hugh Redwald [Lord Dacre]: The Philby Affair: Espionage, Treason and the Secret Service 10886, 16050

Trewin, John Courtenay: Printer to the House: The Story of Hansard, 25034; Robert Donat: A Biography, 26035; Edith Evans, 26038; John Neville, 26072; Paul Scofield, 26098; Peter Brook: A Biography, 26120; 'The National Theatre', 26136; The Stratford Festival: A History of the Shakespeare Memorial Theatre, 26160; The Birmingham Repertory Theatre, 1913–1963, 26161; The Theatre since 1900, 26177; The Gay Twenties: A Decade of the Theatre, 26186; The Turbulent Thirties: A Further Decade of the Theatre, 26188; 'Theatre between the Wars—Classical Stage', 26192; Drama, 1945–1950, 26202; A Play Tonight, 26203; Drama in Britain, 1951–1964, 26211; Shakespeare on the English Stage 1900–1964: A Survey of Productions, 26251

Tribe, David: The Rise of the Mediocracy, 7611

Trimble, W. David: Housing Law in Northern Ireland, 18490

Trimmer, Eric J.: Rejuvenation: The History of an Idea, 22247

Trintignac, A.: 'La Planification en Grande-Bretagne: le développement des villes nouvelles', 18229

Tripartite Committee of B.M.A., R.C.P. and S.M.O.H.: The Mental Health Services after Reunification, 21840

Tripp, Basil Howard: The Joint Iron Council, 1945–1966, 6566

Triseliotis, John Paul: Hard to Place: The Outcome of Adoption and Residential Care, 8378; Social Work with Coloured Immigrants and their Families, 8765

Trivizas, Eugene: 'Offences and Offenders in Football Crowd Disorders', 10675; 'Sentencing the "Football Hooligan"', 10676; 'Disturbances Associated with Football Matches: Types of Incidents and Selection of Charges', 10677

Troen, Ilan: The Suez-Sinai Crisis: A Retrospective, 14391

Trombley, Stephen: *ed.* Modern British Architecture since 1945, 23907

Trompf, G. W.: 'Social Science in Historical Perspective', 7915

Troop, Hilary: Directory of British Oral History Collections, 222

Tropp, Asher: The School Teachers: The Growth of the Teaching Profession in England and Wales, from 1800 to the Present Day, 9843, 22707; Teachers in England and America, 23198

Tropp, E. H.: 'Dispersed Settlement and the Rural Community [in Wales]', 19294

Trotter, Ann: Britain and East Asia, 1933–1937, 13581; 'Tentative Steps for an Anglo-Japanese Rapprochement in 1934', 13600; 'MacDonald in Geneva in March 1933: A Study in Britain's European Policy', 13670

Trotter, Sallie Wallace Brown: No Easy Road: A Study of the Theories and Problems Involved in the Rehabilitation of the Offender, 10143

Trow, C. W.: 'From College to University: a Review of Progress at City University Since 1966', 23488

Trow, Martin Aaron: The British Academics, 9835, 22540; 'British Academics and the Professorship', 9836; 'Second Thoughts on Robbins: a Question of Size and Shape', 23407

Trower-Foyan, M.: Public Transport in Rural Areas: The Increasing Role of Central and Local Government, 16313

Trudgill, Peter: The Social Differentiation of English in Norwich, 9606; International English: A Guide to Varieties of Standard English, 23796; *ed.* Language in the British Isles, 23797; On Dialect: Social and Geographical Perspectives, 23798; Sociolinguistics: An Introduction, 23799; *ed.* Sociolinguistic Patterns in British English, 23800; Accent, Dialect and the School, 23801; Dialects of English: Studies in Grammatical Variation, 23802; The Dialects of England, 23803; English Accents and Dialects: An Introduction to Social and Regional Varieties of British English, 23804; The Social Differentiation of English in Norwich, 23813

Trueman, Fred: Cricket Statistics Year by Year 1946–1987, 27097

Truman Hanbury Buxton and Company: Trumans the Brewers (1666–1966): The Story of Truman, Hanbury, Buxton & Co. Ltd. London and Buxton, 6165

Trump, Harold James: Teignmouth: A Maritime History, 16714

Truptil, Roger Jean: British Banks and the London Money Market, 4414

Truscot, Bruce *pseud.*] Red Brick University, 23370; Redbrick and these Vital Days, 23371

Trussler, Simon: Bond, 25946; The Plays of Wesker, 25992; *ed.* Theatre at Work: Playwrights and Productions in the Modern British Theatre, 26226, 26266

Trustee Savings Bank: Report of the Inspection Committee of Trustee Savings Banks for the Year Ended 20th November—80th Annual Report 1970/71, 4339

Trythall, Anthony John: 'The Downfall of Leslie Hore-Belisha', 1239; 'Boney' Fuller: The Intellectual General 1878–1966, 14734

Tschudin, Marcus: A Writer's Theatre: George Devine and the English Stage Company at the Royal Court, 1956–1965, 26153

Tsuzuki, Chushichi: Edward Carpenter 1844–1929: Prophet of Human Fellowship, 2111

Tubbs, Douglas Burnell: The Illustrated History of the Camera from 1839 to the Present, 7060; Lancaster Bomber, 15843

Tubbs, F. R.: 'The East Malling Research Station (1913–1963)', 7108

Tuck, John Philip: The Origins and Development of the Training of Teachers in the University of Newcastle upon Tyne, 22734

Tucker, David G.: Gisbert Kapp, 1852–1922: First Professor of Electrical Engineering at the University of Birmingham, Appointed 1905, Retired 1919, 7100; 'Broader Education in a Technological Department', 22491

Tucker, James: Honourable Estates, 18681; The Novels of Anthony Powell, 25765

Tucker, Nicholas: Understanding the Mass Media: A Practical Approach for Teaching, 22778, 22827

Tucker, Norman: 'The Place of Opera in the Artistic Life of the Country', 24558

Tucker, William Rayburn: The Attitude of the British Labour Party Towards European and Collective Security Problems, 1920–1939, 13557; 'British Labor and Revision of the Peace Settlement, 1920–1925', 13558

Tuckett, Angela: The Blacksmiths' History, 6839; The Scottish Carter: The History of the Scottish Horse and Motormen's Association, 1898–1964, 6888

Tuckett, David: ed. An Introduction to Medical Sociology, 21962

Tuckey, Bob and Tuckey, Linda: Handicapped School-leavers: Their Further Education, Training and Employment, 8273

Tudope, William B.: 'Motives for the Choice of the Teaching Profession by Training College Students', 9845

Tudor, Owen Davies: On Charities, 9137

Tugwell, Maurice: Arnhem: A Case Study, 14971; Airborne to Battle: A History of Airborne Warfare, 1918–1971, 15810

Tuke, A. W.: Barclays Bank, 1926–1969: Some Recollections, 4492

Tuke, Margaret Janson: A History of Bedford College for Women, 23519

Tuker, Sir Francis Ivan Simms: Approach to Battle: A Commentary, Eighth Army, November 1941 to May 1943, 14910

Tullet, Tom: Inside Dartmoor, 10350

Tulloch, Derek: Wingate in Peace and War, 14792

Tulloch, Hugh: James Bryce's American

Commonwealth: The Anglo-American Background, 1382

Tumber, Howard: Television and the Riots, 24899

Tumelty, James: Britain Today, 380

Tunstall, Jeremy: Sociological Perspectives: Selected Readings, 8002; Old and Alone: A Sociological Study of Old People, 8587; The Fishermen, 9654, 19819; The Advertising Man in London Advertising Agencies, 9783; Studies on the Press: Working Paper, Royal Commission on the Press, 25125; Journalists at Work: Specialist Correspondents, the News Organizations, News Sources, and Competitor-Colleagues, 25316; The West-minster Lobby Correspondents: A Socio-logical Study of National Political Journalism, 25317; ed. Sociology: A Reader, 25318; ed. The Open University Opens, 23551

Turnbull, C. M.: 'British Planning for Post-War Malaya', 12934; A History of Singapore 1819–1975, 12959

Turnbull, David: Receiving Juvenile Justice, 10644

Turnbull, Gerald L.: Traffic and Transport: An Economic History of Pickfords, 16367, 17473

Turnbull, John Geoffrey: ed. A History of the Calico Printing Industry of Great Britain, 6473

Turnbull, Malcolm: The Spycatcher Trial, 16059

Turnbull, Maureen: Records of Interest to Social Scientists, 1919–1939: Employment and Unemployment, 6990; Records of Interest to Social Scientists, 1919–1939: Introduction, 7941

Turnbull, Patrick: Dunkirk: Anatomy of Disaster, 14831

Turner, A. Logan: Story of a Great Hospital: The Royal Infirmary of Edinburgh, 1729–1929, 21474; History of the University of Edinburgh, 1883–1933, 23493

Turner, Arthur Campbell: Scottish Home Rule, 2497; The Unique Partnership: Britain and the United States, 14081

Turner, Arthur: Mr Buchan, Writer, 25428

Turner, Barry: At London's Service: Fifty Years of London Transport Road Services, 17311; Equality for Some: The Story of Girls' Education, 23090

Turner, Bryan S.: Social Stratification, 9618

Turner, Charles Cyril: The Struggle in the Air, 1914–1918, 14628; Britain's Air Peril: The Danger of Neglect, together with Considerations on the Role of an Air Force, 15987; The Old Flying Days, 17490

Turner, Christopher: Family and Kinship in Modern Britain: An Introduction, 10082

Turner, Don: Kircakos: A British Partisan in Wartime Greece, 14850

Turner, Duncan Robert: The Shadow Cabinet in British Politics, 751

Turner, Ernest Sackville: Roads to Ruin: The Shocking History of Social Reform, 8994; The Phoney War on the Home Front, 15155; Gallant Gentlemen: A Portrait of the British Officer, 1660–1956, 15464; Call the Doctor: A Social History of Medical Men, 20839

Turner, George Grey: The Newcastle upon Tyne School of Medicine, 1834–1934, 20778

Turner, Graham: The North Country, 5190; The Car Makers, 17396; The Leyland Papers, 17438

Turner, Harry: The Gentle Art of Salesmanship, 20488

Turner, Helen: Henry Wellcome: The Man, his Collection and his Legacy, 20907

Turner, Henry John Mansfield: 'Is Establishment Defensible Today?', 11631

Turner, Herbert Arthur: The Progress and Poverty of Incomes Policy, 3851; 'The Donovan Report [Royal Commission Report on Trade Unions and Employers' Associations, 1965–1968]', 5497; Arbitration: A Study of Industrial Experience, 5600; Labour Relations in the Motor Industry: A Study of Industrial Unrest and an International Comparison, 5601, 7242; 'Collective Bargaining and the Eclipse of the Incomes Policy: Retrospect, Prospect and Possibilities', 5602; 'An Analysis of Post-war Labour Disputes in the British Car Manufacturing Firms', 5650; Trade Union Growth, Structure and Policy: A Comparative Study of the Cotton Unions, 6891; Is Britain really Strike Prone? A Review of the Incidence, Character and Costs of Industrial Conflict, 6964; 'Strikes, Redundancy, and the Demand Cycle in the Motor Car Industry', 17414

Turner, Ian: '"Spot of Bother"—Civil Disorder in the North-East between the Wars', 11485

Turner, Ian: 'Great Britain and the Post-War German Currency Reform', 14197

Turner, J. F.: British Aircraft of World War II, 15861

Turner, J. G.: 'What Steps Can Be Taken to Improve the Teeth of the Nation?', 21302

Turner, J. Neville: Improving the Lot of Children Born Outside Marriage: A Comparison of Three Recent Reforms: England, New Zealand and West Germany, 8380

Turner, John: The Tea Trade, 20712

Turner, John Andrew: 'The Formation of Lloyd George's "Garden Suburb": "Fabian-like Milnerite Infiltration"?', 794; 'The British Commonwealth Union and the General Election of 1918', 2014; Britain and the First World War, 14436; British Politics in the Great War: Competition and Conflict, 1915–1918, 14437

Turner, John Derfel: ed. Education for the Professions, 22425; 'New Directions in Teacher Education', 22718; Language Laboratories in Great Britain, 22759

Turner, John E.: Labour's Doorstep Politics in London, 1793; Political Parties in Action: The Battle of Barons Court, 2324

Turner, John Frayn: Invasion '44: The Full Story of D-Day, 14972; Periscope Patrol: The Saga of Malta Submarines, 15377; Service Most Silent: The Navy's Fight against Enemy Mines, 15396; V.C.'s of the Army, 1939–1951, 15550

Turner, John Munsey: Conflict and

Reconciliation: Studies in Methodism and Ecumenism in England, 1740–1982, 12082, 12310; 'Robert Featherstone Wearmouth, (1882–1963). Methodist Historian', 12103; 'The Christian and the Study of History: Sir Herbert Butterfield (1900–79)', 26782

Turner, John Raymond: Scotland's North Sea Gateway: Aberdeen Harbour AD 1136–1986, 16671

Turner, Keith: Old Trams, 17210

Turner, L. C. F.: War in the Southern Oceans, 1939–1945, 15014

Turner, Louis: Britain and the Multinationals, 5555

Turner, Merfyn Lloyd: A Pretty Sort of Prison, 10348, 18684; Dealing with Delinquents, 10597; Safe Lodging: The Road to Norman House, 18682; Norman House: The First Five Years, 18683

Turner, Phyllis Mary: Transport History: Railways, 16722

Turner, R. D.: ' An Interpretation of the Decline of Mortality in England and Wales during the Twentieth Century', 7431

Turner, Ralph H.: 'Life Situation and Subculture: A Comparison of Merited Prestige Judgements by Three Occupational Classes in Britain', 9591; 'Acceptance of Irregular Mobility in Britain and the United States', 9592

Turner, Tom: Fifty Years of Birkenhead Buses, 17302; English Garden Design: History and Styles since 1650, 19904

Turner, W. H. K.: 'Wool Textile Manufacture in Scotland: An Historical Geography', 6468

Turner, Walter James: ed. The British Commonwealth and Empire, 12551; ed. British Craftsmanship, 24139

Turney, Neil: William Walton: His Life and Music, 24386

Turnock, David: The Historical Geography of Scotland since 1707: Geographical Aspects of Modernisation, 2450; The New Scotland, 2451, 5140; The North of Scotland, 16823

Turnor, Christopher Reginald: The Smaller English House, 1500–1939, 20318

Turnour, Edward [Earl Winterton]: Orders of the Day, 1549; Fifty Tumultuous Years, 1550

Turpin, Colin: British Government and the Constitution. A Selection of Legal and non-Legal Materials with Commentary, 581; 'Ministerial Responsibility: Myth or Reality?', 749

Turrall-Clarke, Robert: Stansted: A Paper on Proposals for a Third London Airport at Stansted and a New Passenger Terminal at Heathrow, 17692

Turrill, W. B.: ed. Vistas in Botany: A Volume in Honour of the Bicentenary of the Royal Botanic Gardens, Kew, 26535; British Plant Life, 26563

Turuatzky, Louis G.: Experimental Methods for Social Policy Research, 8872

Turvey, Ralph: 'The Effect of Price Level Changes on Real Private Incomes in the United Kingdom, 1954–1960', 3786; Economic Analysis and Public Enterprise, 6096; The Economics of Real Property: An Analysis of Property Values and Patterns of Use, 18640

Tute, Warren: The Grey Top Hat: The Story of Moss Bros. of Covent Garden, 6239

Tutt, Norman: Care or Custody: Community Houses and the Treatment of Delinquency, 10319; Alternative Strategies for Coping with Crime, 10320

Tuxford, J.: 'Research and Social Work', 8680

Tweddle, John M.: Profitability of Farms in the West of Scotland 1986/1987, 19626

Twelvetrees, Alan Clyde: Community Associations and Centres: A Comparative Study, 9384

Twigg, John: A History of Queens' College, Cambridge, 1448–1986, 23483

Twigg, Sam: The Quiet Revolution: The Planning, Development and Provision of Community Services for the Mentally Handicapped, 21780

Twist, Sydney James: Murston Village and Parish: A History, 19350

Twitchett, K. J.: 'Britain and Community Europe, 1973–1979', 14185

Twyman, Michael: Printing 1770–1970: An Illustrated History of its Development and Uses in England, 25017

Twyman, Paul Hadleigh: Industrial Location in East Kent, with Special Reference to Factory Relocation and Branch Plant Establishment, 18865

Tyerman, Donald: Industry after the War, 4982

Tyerman, Maurice Joseph: Truancy, 23246

Tylecote, Andrew B.: 'The Effect of Monetary Policy on Wage Inflation', 3900

Tylecote, Mabel: The Education of Women at Manchester University, 1883 to 1933, 22486

Tyldesley, David: Gaining Momentum: An Analysis of the Role and Performance of Local Authorities in Nature Conservation, 20213

Tyler, Colin: Ploughing by Steam: A History of Steam Cultivation over the Years, 19689

Tyler, Froom: Cripps: A Portrait and a Prospect, 1153

Tyler, Godfrey J.: 'Factors Affecting the Size of the Labour Force and the Level of Earnings in U.K. Agriculture 1948–1965, 19669

Tyme, John: Motorways versus Democracy: Public Inquiries into Road Proposals and their Political Significance, 17116

Tynan, Kathleen: The Life of Kenneth Tynan, 26201

Tynan, Kenneth Peacock: 'The National Theatre', 26138; A View of the English Stage, 1944–1963, 26200; 'British Playwriting', 26219

Tyng, Sewell T.: The Campaign of the Marne, 1914, 14595

Tynwald: Report of the Proceedings of the Legislative Council 1954–, 2627; Report of the Proceedings of the House of Keys 1954–, 2628; Report of the Possible Effects on the Isle of Man of United Kingdom Entry into the Common Market, 2629; Report of the Committee of Tynwald Appointed to Examine the Representation of the People Acts, 1951 to 1961, 2630

Tyrhova-Williams, Ariadna: Cheerful Giver: The Life of Harold Williams, 25298

Tyrrell, Robert: The Work of the Television Journalist, 24919

Tyrrell, W.: A History of the Belfast Savings Bank, 4354

Tyrwhitt, Jacqueline: ed. Patrick Geddes in India, 8072; ed. Human Identity in the Urban Environment, 17828

Tyson, G. W.: 100 Years of Banking in Asia and Africa, 1863–1963, 4532

Tyson, John Colin: The Origins and Development of the Training of Teachers in the University of Newcastle upon Tyne, 22734

Tzannotos, Z.: Women and Equal Pay: The Effects of Legislation on Female Employment and Wages in Britain, 7790

U.C.S. London: An Angel without Wings: The History of University College School, 1830–1980, 23080

U.K. Admiralty. British Vessels Lost at Sea 1917–1918, 16472

U.K. Advisory Committee on Alcoholism 1978: The Pattern and Range of Services for Problem Drinkers: Report, 22136

U.K. Advisory Committee on Drug Dependence: Report on Cannabis, 10824

U.K. Advisory, Conciliation and Arbitration Service: First Annual Report, 1975, 5774

U.K. Advisory Council on the Employment of Prisoners: Work and Vocational Training in Borstals. England and Wales Report, 10542

U.K. Birmingham Regional Hospital Board [1966]: B.R.H.B. 1947–1966: A Chronicle of the Activities of the B.H.R.B. since their Inception in 1947, 21422

U.K. Board of Education Youth Advisory Council: The Youth Service after the War, 8503; The Purpose and Content of the Youth Service: A Report, 8504; The Youth Service Scheme in Scotland, 8505

U.K. Board of Inland Revenue: The Survey of Personal Incomes 1969/1970, 3837; Capital Gains Tax, 4857

U.K. Board of Trade: Accounts Relating to the Export Trade of the United Kingdom for the Years 1939, 1940 and 1941, 4819; Government Help for Your Business in the Development Areas and Northern Ireland, 5069; What the Development Areas Offer, 5070; An Industrial Survey of the Lancshire Area, 5166; An Industrial Survey of Mersyside, 5180; An Industrial History Survey of the North East Coast Area, 5199; The North East: A Programme for Regional Development and Growth, 5200; An Industrial Survey of South Wales, 5367; Mergers: A Guide to Board of Trade Practice, 5516; The Safety Performance of U.K. Airline Operators: Special Review, 17636

U.K. Boundary Commission for Wales: 1983 Review of European Assembly Constituencies, 2586

U.K. British Airports Authority: (London Airports Traffic Study) Gatwick Airport: 1966 Traffic Characteristics, 17678; Heathrow Airport: 1966 Traffic Characteristics, 17679

U.K. British Council: How to Live in Britain: A Handbook for Students from Overseas, 9881

U.K. British Family Research Committee: Families in Britain, 10055

U.K. British Railways Board: The Re-shaping of British Railways, 16830; The Development of the Major Trunk Routes, 16831; A Study of the Relative True Costs of Rail and Road Freight Transport over Trunk Routes, 16832

U.K. British Railways Southern Region: Want to Run a Railway? 16824

U.K. British Transport Commission. British Transport Commission Historical Records: Canal, Dock, Harbour, Navigation and Steamship Companies, 16453; British Railways Progress, 16825

U.K. British Transport Docks Board: Grimsby: A Plan for Industry to Expand, 18880

U.K. British Waterways Board: The Future of Waterways: Interim Report of the Board, 16445; The Facts about the Waterways, 16446

U.K. Cabinet Office: The Economic Situation: A Statement by H.M. Government, 26 October, 1964, 3637

U.K. Census of Children and Adolescents in Hospitals, 1960–1965, 21354

U.K. Central Health Services Council: Joint Sub-committee of the Standing Medical Advisory Committee and the Advisory Committee on the Health and Welfare of Handicapped Persons. People with Epilepsy Report, 21079; Committee on the Welfare of Children in Hospital, 21352

U.K. Central Office of Information: The Co-operative Movement in Britain, 1892; Social Security in Britain, 4061; [Reference Division]: Insurance in Britain, 4235; Regional Development in Britain, 5079; [Reference Division]: The English Regions—East Anglia, 5154; [Reference Division]: The English Regions—The North West, 5205; The English Regions—The South West, 5219; [Reference Division]—Scotland, 5280; [Reference Division]—Wales, 5337; [Reference Division]—Northern Ireland, 5393; Labour Relations and Conditions of Work in Britain, 5881; Manpower in Britain: The Trade Unions, 5939; Occupations and Conditions of Work, 5940; Industrial Relations, 5941; The Role of Government, 5942; Industrial Training, 5943; Regional Trends, 7589; Children in Britain, 8136; Care of the Elderly in Britain, 8619; Social Services in Britain, 8919; British Aid to Developing Nations, 9175; Britain and the Developing Countries: Overseas Aid: A Brief Survey, 9176; Financial and Technical Aid from Britain, 9177; Britain and the Developing Countries: Economic Aid: A Brief Survey, 9178; Race Relations in Britain, 11058; Immigration into Britain, 11059; British Civil Aviation, 17656; Ref. Pamphlets 9: Town and Country Planning in Britain, 17803; The New Towns of Britain, 18253, 18988; Rural Depopulation:

Report of an Inter-departmental Group, 19065; Agriculture in Britain, 19553; Report of the Committee of Inquiry into the Fishing Industry, 19827; Horticulture in Britain, pt. 1—Vegetables, 19843; Horticulture in Britain, pt. 2—Fruit and Flowers, 19844; Environmental Planning in Britain, 19929; Aircraft Noise Annoyance around London (Heathrow) Airport: A Survey made in 1961 for the Wilson Committee on the Problem of Noise, 20155; Lead in Drinking Water: A Survey in Great Britain, 1975–1976: Report of an Inter-Departmental Working Group, 20163; [1964] Medical Research in Britain, 20764; [Reference Division] The Standard of Living in Britain, 20425; The British Pharmaceutical Industry, 22262; Sound and Television Broadcasting in Britain, 24764; Broadcasting in Britain, 24765; The British Press, 25032

U.K. Central Policy Review Staff: Population and the Social Services Report, 7288, 7409; Population Panel Report, 7289; Long Term Population Distribution in Great Britain: A Study, 7290

U.K. Central Statistical Office: National Income and Expenditure, 3838; Social Trends, 7580; Estimates of Household Expenditure in the United Kingdom at current prices, 1970–1975: Comparison between the Family Expenditure Survey and National Accounts, 20434

U.K. Central Unit on Environmental Pollution: Controlling Pollution: A Review of Government Action Related to Recommendations by the Royal Commission on Environmental Pollution, 20024

U.K. Centre for Studies in Social Policy: Forty to Sixty: How We Waste the Middle Aged, 8555

U.K. Charities Aid Foundation: The Give as You Earn Directory of Charities, 9224

U.K. Charities Data Services: The Handbook of Charities 1987–1988, 9223

U.K. Civil Aviation Authority: Passengers at Major Airports in Scotland and Central England: Origin and Destination Survey, July-Nov, 1975, 17666

U.K. Civil Service Commission [1961]: The Scientific Civil Service, 5025

U.K. Colonial Office: Commonwealth Development Act, 1963, 9169

U.K. Committee on Abuse of Social Security Benefits: Report, 4063

U.K. Commonwealth Economic Committee: Sources of Energy: A Review, 7193

U.K. Council for Art and Industry: The Working Class Home: Its Furnishing and Equipment, 20417

U.K. Council for Children's Welfare: A Family Service and a Family Court, 10064

U.K. Countryside Commission: Coastal Preservation and Development: A Study of the Coastline of England and Wales, 19936

U.K. Department of Agriculture [and Fisheries] for Scotland: Types of Farming in Scotland, 19616; Fisheries of Scotland: Report, 1967–, 19825; Scottish Sea Fisheries Statistical Tables, 19826

U.K. Department of Commerce (Northern Ireland): Insurance Companies General Annual Report 1974, 4229

U.K. Department of Economic Affairs: The Development Areas: A Proposal for a Regional Employment Premium, 5068; The East Midlands Study, 5156; Humberside: A Feasibility Study, 5161; The Problems of Merseyside: An Appendix to the North West: A Regional Study, 5182; Challenge of the Changing North: A Preliminary Study, 5191; The North West: A Regional Study, 5204; A Strategy for the South East, 5216; A Region with a Future: A Draft Strategy for the South West, 5217; The West Midlands: A Regional Study, 5221; The West Midlands: Patterns of Growth: A First Report, 5222; A Review of Yorkshire and Humberside, 5232

U.K. Department of Education and Science: Survey of Earnings of Qualified Manpower in England and Wales 1966/67, 5937; A Second Report on the Training of Part-time Youth Leaders and Assistants, 8499; The Youth Service in England and Wales, 8500; Report of the Land Use Study Group: Forestry, Agriculture and Multiple Use of Rural Land, 19750; Review of the Present Safety Arrangements for the use of Toxic Chemicals in Agriculture and Food Storage: Report of the Advisory Committee on Pesticides and Other Toxic Chemicals, 20119; [1966]] Health in Education, 21986

U.K. Department of Employment: Manpower Studies Nos 1–12, 5932; Long Term Population Distribution in Great Britain—A Study, 7264; Equal Pay A Guide to the Equal Pay Act 1970, 7786; Family Expenditure Survey, 20433

U.K. Department of Employment and Central Office of Information: Industrial Relations: A Guide to the Industrial Relations Act, 5740

U.K. Department of Employment [1977], Unit for Manpower Studies: Employment in Metropolitan Areas: Project Report, 6983; British Labour Statistics Year Book, 6984; Department of Employment Gazette, 6985

U.K. Department of Employment and Productivity: A National Minimum Wage: Report of an Inter-Departmental Working Party, 3906

U.K. Department of the Environment: Children at Play, 8381; Housing Associations, 18566; Housing Finance Act 1972: Memorandum on Housing Associations, 18567; Greater London Development Plan: Report of the Panel of Enquiry, 18942; New Life for Old Buildings, 18966; Improving the Environment, 19924; Environmental Standards: A Description of United Kingdom Practice: The Report of an Inter-departmental Working Party, 19925; Environmental Protection: Problems, Progress, Practice, Principles and Prospects, 19926; Digest of Environmental Statistics: Environmental Protection and Conservation, 19927; Bottle Banks: The Expansion of the Bottle Bank Scheme in

London and the Surrounding Area, 19928; Clean Air Today, 20052; Air Pollution Information: Your Rights and Obligations, 20053; Information about Industrial Emissions to the Atmosphere, 20054; Towards Cleaner Air: A Review of Britain's Achievements, 20055; Report of the Coastal Pollution Research Committee of the Water Pollution Research Laboratory, 20075; Cleaning up the Mersey: A Consultation Paper on Tackling Water Pollution in the Rivers and Canals of the Mersey . . . , 20076; Report of the River Pollution Survey of England and Wales, 20077; Oil Pollution on the Coastline: A Study ..., 20078; The Windscale Inquiry: Report, 20136; Noise in the Next Ten Years: A Report ..., 20158; Aircraft Engine Noise Research: Report, 20159; Lead in the Environment and its Significance to Man . . . , 20160; Community Land Act, 1975, 20370; The Community Land Scheme, 20371

U.K. Department of the Environment and the Welsh Office: Rate Rebates in England and Wales 1968/69, 4077

U.K. Department of Health and Productivity: Asbestos: Health Precautions in Industry, 4133

U.K. Department of Health and Social Security [D.H.S.S.]: Strategy for Pensions: The Future Development of State and Occupational Pensions, 4050; Family Benefits and Pensions, 4064; Social Security Statistics, 4065; Youth Treatment Centres: A New Form of Provision for Severely Disturbed Children, 8388; Intermediate Treatment. A Guide for the Regional Planning of New Forms of Treatment for Children in Trouble, 8389; Report of the Committee of Inquiry into the Care and Supervision provided in Relation to Maria Colwell, 8390; Report of the Inquiry into Child Abuse in Cleveland, 1987, 8393; Adolescent Drinking: A Survey Carried out on Behalf of the DHSS, 8537; A Happier Old Age: A Discussion Document on Elderly People in Our Society, 8641; Annual Report, 8920; Annual Report on Departmental Research and Development, 8921; A Guide to Health and Personal Social Security Statistics, 8922; Studies on Community Health and Personal Social Services, 8923; Health and Personal Social Service Statistics for England, (With Summary Tables for Great Britain), 8924; Social Security Statistics, 8925; Family Planning Services in England and Wales: A Report carried out on behalf of the DHSS, 9930; The Family in Society, Preparation for Parenthood, 10102; Royal Commission on Medical Education, 1965–1968. Report, 20770; [1969] Report of the Committee of Inquiry into Allegations of Ill-Treatment of Patients and other Irregularities at the Ely Hospital, 21358; [1971] Report of the Farleigh Hospital Committee of Inquiry, 21359; [1972] Report of the Committee of Inquiry into Whittingham Hospital, 21360; [1973] Report on Hospital Complaints Procedure (The Davies Report), 21361;

[1969] The Function of the District General Hospital, 21370; [1974] Rationalisation of Services: A Revised Hospital Plan for Inner London, 21452; Report of the Working Party Medical Administrators (Hunter Report), 21650; The Administrative Structure of the Medical and Related Services in England and Wales, 21651; The Future of the National Health Service, 21652; National Health Service Reorganistion, 21653; National Health Service Reorganisation: England, 21654; Management Arrangements for the Reorganised National Health Service, 21655; Democracy in the National Health Service. Membership of Health Authorities, 21656; Better Services for the Mentally Handicapped, 21851; [1976] The Facilities and Services of Mental Illness and Mental Handicap Hospitals on England, 21870; [1977] In-Patient Statistics from the Mental Health Enquiry for England, 21871; Care of the Dying: Proceedings of a National Symposium held on 29 November 1972, 22102; Central Health Services Council, 22103

U.K. Department of Health and Social Security and Office of Population Censuses and Surveys: Report on Hospital In-Patient Enquiry for the Year 1972. Preliminary Tables, 21043

U.K. Department of Health and Social Security: Social Survey Division: (New Series), 1055: The Family Planning Services: Changes and Effects: A Survey, 9931; Family Planning Services in England and Wales, 9932; Family Planning in Scotland in 1982, 9933

U.K. Department of Health and Social Security: Supplementary Benefits Commission: Supplementary Benefits Handbook, 4058; Cohabitation: The Administration of the Relevant Provisions of the Ministry of Social Security Act 1966, 4059; Northern Ireland: Report, 4066

U.K. Department of Scientific and Industrial Research: Human Sciences Aid to Industry, 5653; Human Sciences in Industry: An Annotated Bibliography, 5654

U.K. Department of Technical Co-operation and the Central Office of Information: Department of Technical Co-operation, 9170

U.K. Department of Technical Co-operation: New Work and Ideas in the Field of Technical Co-operation: . . . the Henry Morley Lecture to the Royal Society of Arts, 9172; Report of a Committee on Training in Public Administration for Overseas Countries, 9173

U.K. Department of Trade and Industry: Business Monitor: Production Series P97, 22258

U.K. Department of Trade: (Marine Division) The Battle against Oil Pollution at Sea, 20073; Accidental Oil Pollution of the Sea: A Report by Officials on Oil Spills and Clean-up Measures, 20074

U.K. Economic Intelligence Unit: The Economic Effects of Disarmament, 3636;

Care with Dignity: An Analysis of Costs of Care for the Disabled, 21892

U.K. Economics Advisory Group: An Economic Study of the City of London, 4271

U.K. Electricity Council [1965]: The Growth of the British Distribution System: by H.L. Sheppard, 6675

U.K. Environmental Board: Sub-Group on New Development: Interim Report, 19937; Sub-Group on Older Areas: Interim Report, 19938

U.K. Equal Opportunities Commission: Women and Low Incomes: A Report Based on Evidence to the Royal Commission on Income Distribution and Wealth, 7777; Annual Report, 7778; Women and Men in Great Britain: A Research Profile, 7836

U.K. First Report of the Expenditure Committee: Probation and After-care, 10490

U.K. Forestry Commission: Census of Woodlands 1947–1949, Woods of Five Acres and Over, 19780; Census of Woodlands, 1965–1967: A Report on Britain's Forest Resources, 19781; Census of Woodland and Trees 1979–1982, 19782; Forestry Commission Conservancy: South West England: Census of Woodlands and Trees, 1979–1982, 19783; Forestry in Great Britain: A Review of Progress to 1964, 19784; The Forestry Commission in Scotland, 19785; Forestry in Scotland, 19786; Forestry in England, 19787; Forestry in Northern Ireland, 19788; Forestry in Wales, 19789

U.K. General Register Office: Census 1921: Isle of Man, 2631; The Registrar-General's Decennial Supplement, England and Wales, 7446; Decennial Supplement for 1961, 7447; Regional and Social Factors in Infant Mortality, 7448; Social and Biological Factors in Infant Mortality, 7449; [1963]: A Coherent Study of Patients First Admitted to Mental Hospitals in 1950 and 1955, 21742

U.K. Health and Safety Commission: [Advisory Committee on Asbestos] Asbestos: Final Report, 4135; Some Aspects of the Safety of Nuclear Installations in Great Britain, 4144; Lightning at Work, 4145; A Guide to the Health and Safety at Work etc. Act 1974, 4147; Industrial Air Pollution, 20044; Industrial Air Pollution, 20056; Hospital Survey, 21367; [1966] Report of the Committee on Senior Nursing Staff Structure, 21372; Health and Safety Statistics, 21994

U.K. Health Service Commissioner: First Report, Session 1974, 21993

U.K. Home Office: The Children Act, 8382; Children and Young Persons, 8384; Children in Care in England and Wales, 8386; The Children and Young Persons Act 1963, 8387; The War against Crime in England and Wales, 1959–1964, 10204; Research Bulletin—Semi-annually from Spring 1975, 10205; [1965] The Adult Offender, 10209; The Regime for Long-term Prisoners in Conditions of Maximum Security—Report of the Advisory Council on the Penal System (the Radzinowicz Report), 10416; Report of the Inquiry into Prison Escapes and Security (the Mountbatten Report), 10417; People in Prison, 10418; The Organisation of the Prison Medical Service: Report of the Working Party, 10422; Penal Practice in a Changing Society, 10423; Report on the Work of the Prison Department, 10424; Prisons and Borstals: Statements of Policy and Practice in the Administration of Prison and Borstal Institutions in England and Wales, 10425; Report of the Parole Board, 10426; People in Prison, 10427; Prisons and the Prisoner, 10428; Probation and Aftercare: Department Report, 1962–63. HMSO Report on the Work of the Probation and After-care Service, 10486; Residential Provision for Homeless Discharged Offenders, 10488; The Probation and Aftercare Service in a Changing Society, 10491; Detention Centres: Report of the Advisory Council on the Penal System, 10520; Directory of Approved Schools, Remand Homes and Special Reception Centres in England and Wales, 10544; Police Report of a Working Party on Police Cadets, 10739; Manpower, Equipment and Efficiency Reports, 10740; The Recruitment of People with Higher Educational Qualifications into the Police Service, 10741; Commonwealth Immigrants Act 1962, 11103; Admission of Commonwealth Citizens to the United Kingdom, 11104; Police/Immigrant Relations in England and Wales, 11033

U.K. Home Office: Community Development Project. (Information and Intelligence Unit): The National Community Development Project: Interim Report, 9264; Inter-Project Report, 9265; Forward Plan, 1975–76, 9266; Action-Research in Community Development, 9267; The Costs of Industrial Change, 9268; Cutting the Welfare State: Who Profits?, 9269; Limits of the Law, 9270; The Poverty of the Improvement Programme, 9271; Profits against Houses, 9272; Rates of Decline: An Unacceptable Base of Public Finance, 9273; Whatever Happened to Council Housing? A Report, 9274; Workers and the Industry Bill: Time for a Rank and File Response, 9275

U.K. House of Commons Select Committee on Public Expenditure, 1972, 20818

U.K. House of Commons Select Committee on Race Relations and Immigration: Session 1970–1971: Includes 'Housing and Race Relations' by Nicholas Deakin and Clare Ungerson in vol. 3 House of Commons Paper 508, 11005; Control of Commonwealth Immigration: An Analysis of the Evidence Taken by the Select Committee on Race Relations and Immigration 1969–1970 by Arthur Bottomley and George Sinclair, 11006; The Problems of Coloured School-leavers, 11120; (House of Commons Session 1972–73) Education Report, 23184

U.K. House of Commons Social Services Committee: Children in Care: Second

Report of the Social Service Committee, Session 1983/4, 8392

U.K. Iron and Steel Board [1963]: Research in the Iron and Steel Industry: Special Report, 7199

U.K. Leeds Regional Hospital Board: Census of Psychiatric Patients in the Board Area, 21743

U.K. London G.L.C. Parking Working Party: Car Parking Supply and Demand: Central Area, 17383

U.K. London Transport Board [1963]: London Transport Posters, with an Introduction and Notes by Harold F. Hutchison, 5019

U.K. Lord President of the Council, the Scottish Office, and the Welsh Office: Our Changing Democracy: Devolution to Scotland and Wales, 2414; Devolution to Scotland and Wales: Supplementary Statement, 2415

U.K. Mines Department: Catalogue of Publications Relating to the Mining, Quarrying and Petroleum Industries, 3420

U.K. Ministry of Agriculture, Fisheries and Food: A Century of Agricultural Statistics: Great Britain, 1866–1966, 19382; Agricultural and Food Statistics: A Guide to Official Sources, 19383; A Survey among Grassland Farmers: Comprehensive Report . . . , 19504; Classification of Agricultural Land in Britain: A Survey of the Physical and Economic Factors which used to be taken into Account, 19518, 19791; The Mid-Wales Investigation Report, 19637; The Changing Structure of the Agricultural Labour Force in England and Wales: Numbers of Workers, Hours and Earnings 1944–1965, 19668; Sea Fisheries Statistical Tables, 1947–, 19824; The Sea Fisheries Dispute between the United Kingdom and Iceland, 14 July 1971 to 19 May 1973, 19829; Agricultural and Food Statistics: A Guide to Official Sources, 20538; Food Standards Committee: Report on Claims and Misleading Descriptions, 20539; Machine Milking, 20654; The Milk Marketing Scheme, 1933 as Amended to June 27 1955, 20655; Beef Production, 20673; Eggs and Poultry: Report of Reorganising Committee for Great Britain, 20716; The Egg Trade and the E.E.C., 20717; Oyster Cultivation in Britain, 20721

U.K. Ministry of Aviation: Report of the Air Freight Working Party, 17663; A Survey of Passenger Traffic at London's Airports, 17664; Report of the Inter-Departmental committee on the Third London Airport to the Minister of Aviation, June 1963, 17691

U.K. Ministry of Education: The Training of Part-time Youth Leaders and Assistants, 8498; Education in Rural Wales, 19298

U.K. Ministry of Food: Food and Nutrition, 20513; Food Consumption Levels in the United Kingdom, 1947, 1949, 20514; Wartime Diet for Growing Children, 20515; Wise Eating in Wartime, 20516; Your Baby's Food in Wartime, 20517; The World Food Shortage, 20518; (Scientific Advisor's Division), Manual of Nutrition, 20519;

(National Food Survey Committee), The Urban Working Class Household Diet, 1940–1949, 20536; Domestic Food Consumption and Expenditure, 20537; Dehydration: U.K. Progress Reports, Scientific, Technical and Economic, 20643; The Testing of Eggs for Quality, 20718

U.K. Ministry of Health: Report on Confidential Enquiries into Maternal Deaths in England and Wales 1958–1960, 7450; Report on Confidential Enquiries into Maternal Deaths in England and Wales 1961–1963, 7451; Report on Confidential Enquiries into Maternal Deaths in Northern Ireland 1960–1963, 7452; Residential Accommodation for Elderly People, 8573; (Advisory Committee on Nutrition): Report to the Minister of Health on Diets in Poor Law Children's Homes, 20520; Report of the Committee to consider the Future Numbers of Medical Practitioners and the Appropriate Intake of Medical Students, 20762; Postgraduate Medical Education and the Specialities, with Special Reference to the Problem in London, 20769; [1963] Communication between Doctors, Nurses and Patients: An Aspect of Human Relations in the Hospital Service, 21362; [1961]: The Hospital Building Programme. [1966] A Revision of the Hospital Plan for England and Wales, 21363; Report of the Joint Working Party on the Medical Staffing Structure in the Hospital Service, 21364. [1962] A Hospital Plan for England and Wales, 21365; Hospital Survey, 21367; [1966] Report of the Committee on Senior Nursing Staff Structure, 21372; The Field of Work of the Family Doctor: Report by Annis Gillie, 21530; [1964] Recent N.H.S. Prescribing Trends, 21588; [1964] National Health Service Prescribing, 21589; [1967] A Census of Patients in Psychiatric Beds 1963, 21744; Health Education: A Report of a Joint Committee, 21985; The Incidence and Causes of Blindness in England and Wales, 1948–1962, 21987; Maternity and Child Welfare: Report of the Provisions made by Public Health Authorities and Voluntary Agencies, 21988; Health and Welfare: The Development of Community Care, 21989; Health and Welfare: The Development of Community Care 21990

U.K. Ministry of Health and Department of Health for Scotland: A National Health Service, 21693

U.K. Ministry of Housing and Local Government: Report of the Committee of Inquiry into the Impact of Rates on Households, 4075; [1967] Refuse Storage and Collection: Report of the Working Party on Refuse Collection, 5022; South Hampshire Study: Report on the Feasibility of Major Urban Growth, 5158; The South East Study, 1961–1981 [sic], 5215; Projecting Growth Patterns in Regions—Statistics for Town Planning: Series Three. Population and Households. No. 1, 7274; Depopulation in Mid-Wales, 7423; and Welsh Office: The Needs of New Communities: A Report on Social Provision in New and Expanding Communities, 9259; [Sociological Research Section]: Gypsies and Other Travellers, 11343; Parking in Town Centres, 17376; Report of the Enquiry into the Local Objections to the Proposed Development of Land at Stansted as the Third Airport for London, 17690; Report of the Committee on the Qualifications of Planners, 17748; Town Centres: Approach to Renewal, 17804; Central Lancashire New Town Proposal: Central Lancashire: Study for a City, 18209; Impact on North-East Lancashire, 18210; Housing Return for Northern Ireland, 18492; Inspector's Report on Belfast Corporation's Housing Inquiry, 18493; Ashford Study: Consultants' Proposals for Designation: A Report, 18837; The County Borough of Ipswich: A Planning Study for Town Development, A Report, 18882; Expansion of Northampton: Consultant's Proposals for Designation: A Report to the Ministry, 18896; Peterborough, 1965, 18901; Expansion of Warrington: Consultant's Proposals, 18919; Worcester Expansion Study: Report for the Ministry, 18920; Protecting our Historic Buildings: A Guide to the Legislation, 18968; The New Towns, 18996; [1963] New Life for Dead Lands: Derelict Acres Reclaimed, 20301; Betterment Levy: An Explanatory Memorandum on Part 3 of the Land Commission Act, 20366; Land Commission Act, 1967: A Guide for Builders and Developers on Betterment Levy, 20367; Land Commission Act, 1967: A Guide for Estate Agents and Surveyors on Betterment Levy, 20368; The Land Commission and You, 20369

U.K. Ministry of Labour and National Service: 'Average Earnings and Hours of Men in Manufacturing: Analysis by Establishment', 3871; Northern Ireland: Byssinosis in Flax National Insurance, 4124; The Appointed Factory Doctor Service: Report by a Sub-Committee of the Industrial Health Advisory Committee, 4125; [Factory Inspectorate]: Problems Arising from the use of Asbestos: Memorandum, 4134; Industrial Relations Handbook 1944, 5593; Occupational Changes, 1951–1961, 5882; [1964] Report of the Joint Advisory Committee for the Cutlery and Silverware Trades in Sheffield and District, 6593; The Metal Industries: A Study of Occupational Trends in the Metal Manufacturing and Metal Using Industries, 7204; Enquiry into Working-Class Expenditure, 20418; Report of an Enquiry into Household Expenditure in 1953–1954, 20431

U.K. Ministry of Overseas Development: The Young Volunteer, 9163; The Work of the Ministry of Overseas Development, 9164; Figures on Aid, 9165; Overseas Appointments, 9166; Training in Britain, 9167; Helping Universities Overseas, 9168; Training in Britain, 11505

U.K. Ministry of Propaganda: After Twelve Months of War, 7549

U.K. Ministry of Reconstruction: Welsh Advisory Council: First Interim Report, 5329

U.K. Ministry of Social Security: Circumstances of Families: Report on an Enquiry by the Ministry of Pensions and National Insurance with the Co-operation of the National Assistance Board, Subsequently Combined to form the Ministry of Social Security, 4060; Circumstances of Families: Report on an Enquiry by the Ministry of Pensions and National Insurance, with the Co-operation of the National Assistance Board, Subsequently Combined to form the Ministry of Social Security, 20426

U.K. Ministry of Town and Country Planning: New Towns Committee: Final Report, 18220

U.K. Ministry of Transport: Rural Transport Surveys: Report of Preliminary Results, 16247; The Transport Needs of Britain in the Next Twenty Years: Report, 16248; Passenger Transport in Great Britain, 16249; Highland Transport Enquiry Report, 16250; Committee of Inquiry into Shipping Services to Northern Ireland, 16466; Roads in Urban Areas, 17136; Better Use of Town Roads: The Report, 17137; Road Pricing: The Economic and Technical Possibilities of a Panel, 17138; Highway Statistics, 17139; The Transport Needs of Great Britain in the Next Twenty Years: Report of a Group under the Chairmanship of Sir Robert Hall, 17140; Interim Report on the 70 m.p.h, Speed Limit Trial, 17141; Report on the 70 m.p.h. Speed Limit Trial, 17142; Rural Bus Services: Report of Local Enquiries, 17276; Parking—The Next Stage: A New Look . . . at London's Parking Problem, 17377; Rural Transport Surveys: Report of the Preliminary Results, 19087; Rural Bus Services: Report of Local Enquiries, 19088

U.K. Ministry of Works: The Welsh Slate Industry, 5339; [1950] An Inquiry into Domestic Hotwater Supply in Great Britain, 18636

U.K. Ministry of Works and Planning: [1942] Final Report of the Expert Committee on Compensation and Betterment, 20363

U.K. National Assistance Board: Handbook for Newcomers, 4079

U.K. National Board for Prices and Incomes: Top Salaries in the Private Sector and Nationalised Industries, 3915; Productivity Agreements in the Bus Industry, 5991

U.K. National Council for Voluntary Organisations: The Voluntary Worker in the Social Services, 9121; Charitable Fund-Raising: A Report of a Working Party, 9142; Directory of Grant-making Trusts, 9143; The Voluntary Agencies Directory, 9220; Charity and Change Norms, Beliefs and Effectiveness—A Profile of the Voluntary Sector, 9225

U.K. National Economic Development Council—Economic Development Committee for the Motoring Manufacturing Industry: The Effect of Government Economic Planning on the Motor Industry, 17419; Regional Planning and the Motor Industry, 17420; Motor Industry Statistics: 1958/67—Data Book, 17421; [1964] The Construction Industry, 18560

U.K. National Economic Development Office: Value Added Tax, 4861

U.K. Natural Resources (Technical) Committee: Forestry, Agriculture and Marginal Land, 19749

U.K. Northern Ireland Office [Government of Northern Ireland]: Planning and Housing Act (N. I.), 1931, 18489; U.K. Secretary of State for Northern Ireland: The Future of Northern Ireland: A Paper for Discussion, 2829; The Government of Northern Ireland: Proposals for Further Discussion, 2830

U.K. Office of Health Economics: Pharmaceutical Research: The Case for Growth in Britain, 22266; Work Lost through Sickness, 5977

U.K. Office of Manpower Economics: Equal Pay: First Report on the Implementation of the 1970 Act, 3939

U.K. Office of Population Censuses and Surveys: 1961 Census: Great Britain: Scientific and Technological Qualifications, 5026; Classification of Occupations, 5895; Population Projections: Area Population Projection by Sex and Age for Standard Regions, Counties and Metropolitan Districts of England 1974–1991, 7285; Guide to Census Reports, Great Britain 1801–1966, 7286; Population Trends—1, 7287; U.K. Census 1961, 7292; U.K. Census 1966, 7294; General Household Survey: An Introductory Report, 7295; People in Britain: A Census Atlas, 7296; 1991 Census of Population, 7297; Census 1981, 7440; Guide to Census Reports, Great Britain 1801–1966, 7441; 1991 Census of Population: User Consultation, 7442; Young People's Employment Study: Preliminary Report, 8507; Marriage and Divorce Statistics, 1974+, 9918; U.K. Office of Population Censuses and Surveys (Social Survey Division): Families Five Years On, 10056; Family Formation 1976, 10057; Family Expenditure Survey, 10058; (Social Survey Division), 21890; Part II: Work and Housing of Impaired Persons in Great Britain, 21891

U.K. Oversea Migration Board, Annual Report, 7306

U.K. Overseas Development Administration: Overseas Development and Aid: A Guide to Sources of Information and Material, 9188

U.K. Policy Studies Institute: Westminster and Devolution, 2412

U.K. Overseas Settlement Department: 2. Life Overseas, 7302; 7. Index to Official and Voluntary Agencies in Great Britain and the Overseas Dominions, 7303; 25. Training for Women Who Wish to Settle Overseas, 7304; 30. The Empire Overseas, 7305

U.K. Parliamentary Group: Video Inquiry: Video Violence and Children: Part One — Children's Viewing Patterns in England and Wales, 8391

U.K. Patent Office: Reports of Patent, Design and Trademark Cases, 5015

U.K. Port of London Authority: The Port of London: Official Handbook of the Authority, 16703; Notes on the Port of London, 16704; The History and Development of the Port of London Authority, 16705

U.K. Proposals for Dealing with Unfit Houses, 18496

U.K. Race Relations Board: Discrimination and You, 11113; Explaining the Race Relations Act, 11114; A Guide to the Race Relations Act, 11115; Annual Reports, 11116

U.K. Register of Friendly Societies and Office of the Industrial Insurance Commissioner: Guide to the Friendly Societies' Act and the Industrial Assurance Acts, 4072, 9130

U.K. Registrar of Restrictive Trading Agreements, Office of [1964]: Guide to the Registration of Goods Under the Resale Prices Act, 1964, 5032

U.K. Report of the Wolfenden Committee: The Future of Voluntary Organisations, 9141

U.K. Report of the Committee on Invisible Exports: Britain's Invisible Earnings, 4900

U.K. Report of the Committee on the Working of the Abortion Act: (The Lane Committee), 7883

U.K. Report of the Care of Children Committee, 8383

U.K. Report of the Committee on Children and Young Persons (Scotland), 8385

U.K. Report of the Departmental Committee on Criminal Statistics (Perks Committee), 10211

U.K. Report of the Committee on Public Participation in Planning: People and Planning, 20365

U.K. Royal Commission on the Constitution 1969–1973: Devolution within the United Kingdom: Some Alternatives for Discussion, 2413

U.K. Royal Commission on the Distribution of the Industrial Population Report: Cmnd 6153, 7263

U.K. Royal Commission on Doctors' and Dentists' Remuneration, 1957–1960, 20819

U.K. Royal Commission on Environmental Pollution: First Report, 20012; Second Report: Three Issues in Industrial Pollution, 20013; Third Report: Pollution in some British Estuaries and Coastal Waters, 20014; Fourth Report: Pollution Control: Progress and Problems, 20015; Fifth Report: Air Pollution Control: An Integrated Approach, 20016; Sixth Report: Nuclear Power and the Environment, 20017; Seventh Report: Agriculture and Pollution, 20018; Eighth Report: Oil Pollution of the Sea, 20019; Ninth Report: Lead in the Environment, 20020; Tenth Report: Tackling Pollution—Experience and Prospects, 20021; Eleventh Report: Managing Waste: The Duty of Care, 20022; Twelfth Report: Best Practicable Environmental Option, 20023

U.K. Royal Commission on Marriage and Divorce: Report 1951–1955, 9999; Minutes of Evidence, Appendix and Index, 1952–1956, 10000

U.K. Royal Commission on Medical Education, 1965–1968, 20820

U.K. Royal Commission on the Law Relating to Mental Illness and Mental Deficiency, 21877

U.K. Royal Commission on the Penal System in England and Wales, 10419; Written Evidence from Government Departments, Miscellaneous Bodies and Individual Witnesses, 10420; Minutes of Evidence Taken, 10421

U.K. Royal Commission on the Police: Final Report, 10691

U.K. Royal Commission on Population: Cmnd report 7695, 7381; Papers, 7363

U.K. Scotland: Department of Health: Scottish Hospitals Survey, 21368

U.K. Scottish Education Department: The Child Care Service at Work, 8118; Social Work and the Community: Proposals for Reorganising Local Authority Services in Scotland, 8927

U.K. Scottish Home Department: Industry and Employment in Scotland, and Scottish Roads Report, 5247

U.K. Scottish Office: The Scottish Economy, 1965–1970: A Plan for Expansion, 5252; Development and Growth in Scotland, 5253

U.K. Social Science Research Council: Reviews of Current Research. 3. Research in Social Anthropology, 8066

U.K. Social Science Research Council and Centre for Environmental Studies Joint Conference: The Future of the City; The Future of the Region, 17849

U.K. Social Work Services and Scottish Education Dept.: Scottish Social Work Statistics, 8926

U.K. Social Survey Department: Workplace Industrial Relations: An Enquiry Undertaken for the Royal Commission on Trade Unions and Employers Associations [Donovan Commission] in 1966, 5701; The Adolescent in Great Britain: A Report on a Nation-wide Survey of Young Persons between 15–19 Years of Age Carried out in 1950 by the Social Survey, 8506; Older People and their Employment: Commentary on a Sample Survey made in Britain in the 1950's, 8562; The British Household, 20430; Reports N.S. No. 21: Diptheria Immunisation Enquiry, 21983; N.S. No. 69. Diptheria Immunisation, 21984

U.K. Stock Exchange (London): Stock Exchange Fact, 4268; Highest and Lowes Prices and Dividends 1940–1949, 4269

U.K. Treasury: Report of the Committee of Enquiry on Decimal Currency, 4730; The Government's Expenditure Plans 1988/89 and 1990/91, 4774; United Kingdom Balance of Payments, 1946–1949, 4930; United Kingdom Balance of Payments, 1958–1961, 4931; [1965] Report of a Committee Appointed to Review the Organisation of the Scientific Civil Service, 5024; Forestry in Great Britain: An Inter-departmental Cost/Benefit Study, 19790

U.K. Urban Motorways Committee: New Roads in Town: Report of the Urban Motorways Committee to the Secretary of State for the Environment, 17130

U.K. Water Resources Board [1966]: Morecambe Bay and Solway Barrages: Report on Desk Studies, 7028; Morecambe Bay Barrage: Desk Study: Report of Consultants, 7029; Solway Barrage: Desk Study: Report of Consultants, 7030; Water Supplies in South East England, 7031; Interim Report on Water Resources in the North, 7032

U.K. Welsh Development Agency: The Changing Face of Wales, 19953

U.K. Welsh Hospital Board [1964]: Disappointed Expectations? Report on a Survey of Professional and Technical Staff in the Hospital Services in Wales, 1963, 21374

U.K. Welsh Office (Welsh Council): Digest of Welsh Statistics, 5330; Industrial Development Policy: An Analysis of the Measures Introduced, March 1972, 5331; Location, Size, Ownership and Control Tables for Welsh Industry, 5332; Report on Water in Wales, 5333; The Steel Industry in Wales, 5334; Unemployment in Wales: A Study, 5335; Wales: Employment and Economy, a Report Submitted by the Welsh Council to the Secretary of State for Wales, 5336; Planning Services Division: Welsh Population Change 1961–1971, 7291; Pollution: The Challenge to Wales, 20025; 1973, Community Ownership of Development Land in Wales: Summary Consultation Document, 20372

U.K. 1964 Wessex Regional Hospital Board: What Do They Really Want? A Report on a Questionnaire Addressed to General Practitioners in the Wessex Region, 21366

U.K. Youth Service Development Council: Youth and Community Work in the 1970's, 8536

UNESCO: International Bibliography of Political Science, 420; International Bibliography of Sociology, 421

U.S. Educational Commission in the U.K.: Some Impressions of Social Services in Great Britain by an American Social Work Team, 8685

U.S. Library of Congress: A List of Reference on the Economic Policy of Great Britain, 1930–1940, 3599

Ubbelohde, A. R.: Man and Energy, 7212

Uden, Michael John: Sixty Years of Bradford Trolley Buses, 17244

Uhlig, R.: 'Königswinter—Symbol deutsch-britischer Verständigung nach dem Zweiten Weltkrieg', 14222

Ulah, Philip: 'Second Generation Irish Youth: Identity and Ethnicity', 11366

Ullerton, Brian: The Development of British Transport Networks, 16235

Ullman, Richard Henry: Anglo-Soviet Relations, 1917–1921, 13923

Ullmann, Leonard P.: Institution and Outcome: A Comparative Study of Psychiatric Hospitals, 21495

Ulster Folk and Transport Museum: The

English Dialects of Ulster: An Anthology of Articles on Ulster Speech, 23853; Ulster Dialects: An Introductory Symposium, 23855

Ulster Year Book: 1926–38, 1947+, 2775

Ulyatt, Michael E.: Humber Shipping: A Pictorial History, 16475

Umiastowski, Roman: Poland, Russia and Great Britain, 1941–1945, 13902

Underhill, William Ernest: ed. The Royal Leicestershire Regiment, 17th Foot: A History of the Years 1928 to 1956, 15691

Underwood, Alfred Clair: A History of the English Baptists, 12023

Underwood, Edgar Ashworth: 'The History of Cholera in Great Britain', 21016; 'The Centenary of British Public Health', 21017; 'The Quest for Child Health—The Historical Beginnings', 21018; 'Guy's Hospital', 21019; Before and after Morton: A Historical Survey of Anaesthesia for the Centenary Exhibition at the Wellcome Historical Medical Museum, 21038; ed. Science, Medicine and History, 21186, 21237, 22310; A Short History of Medicine, 21203

Underwood, Peter: Life's a Drag! Danny La Rue & the Drag Scene, 26326

Undy, R.: Change in Trade Unions: The Development of U.K. Unions since the 1960's, 6741

Unger, David Charles: The Roots of Red Clydeside: Economic and Social Relations and Working Class Politics in the West of Scotland 1900–1919, 2518

Ungerson, Clare: Moving Home: A Study of the Redevelopment Process in Two London Boroughs, 7279; Leaving London: Planned Mobility and the Inner-city, 7280; Yearbook of Social Policy in Britain, 1987–88, 8809; 'Housing and Race Relations', 11005; The Consumer Experience of Housing: Cross-National Perspectives, 18451; Housing Policy, 18519

Union Co-operative Manchester: 'Le Mouvement cooperatif britannique et la problème de la cogestion', 1891

United Kingdom Atomic Energy Authority: Annual Report, 6659; The Development of Atomic Energy, 1939–1984: Chronology of Events, 6660; Glossary of Atomic Terms, 7181; Guide to U.K.A.E.A. Documents, 7182; The Nuclear Energy Industry of the United Kingdom, 7183; The U.K.A.E.A.: Its History and Organisation, 7184; List of Publications Available to the Public, 7185; Scientific and Technical News Service, 7186; Press Releases, 7187; Annual Report, 1955, 7188; Atom, 7189

United Kingdom Nature Conservancy: Second Conference, 1965, 20234

United Nations Economic Commission for Europe: Population Structure in European Countries, 7382

United Nations Study Group on Rural Development: People in the Countryside: Studies in Rural Social Development: A Report, 19072

United Reformed Church Yearbook: 1973+, 12045

Unity Begins at Home: A Report from the First British Conference on Faith and Order, 12345

University College, London: Centre for Urban Studies: Land Use Planning and the Social Sciences: A Selected Bibliography: Literature on Town and Country Planning and Related Social Studies in Great Britain 1930–1963, 17719

University College, London: Department of Town Planning: Social Research Unit: A Preliminary Bibliography of Recent Social Studies and Related Literature Relevant to Town and Country Planning in Great Britain, 17718

University Grants Committee: University Development 1957–1962, 23398

University of Liverpool: Social Science Department: The Dock Worker: An Analysis of Conditions of Employment in the Port of Manchester, 7240; Social Research Series: The Dock Worker: An Analysis of Conditions of Employment in the Port of Manchester, 16663

University of Michigan, Program In International Business: Labor Relations and the Law in the United Kingdom and the United States, 5702

University of Reading: Department of Economics: Discussion Paper in Urban and Regional Economics, 5118; Centre for Agricultural Strategy: The Efficiency of British Agriculture, 19579; Department of Agricultural Economics: Market Gardening in the Melbourne Area of Derbyshire, 19850

University of Sussex, School of Social Studies: Crawley Expansion Study: The Report and Recommendations, 18858

University of Wales: Survey of Adult Education in Wales, 23705

Unstead, Robert John: Britain in the Twentieth Century, 347

Unsworth, Clive: The Politics of Mental Health Legislation, 21736

Unwin, Joseph Daniel: Our Economic Problems and their Solution, 3733

Unwin, Peter: Travelling by Train in the 20's and 30's, 16747

Unwin, Philip: The Publishing Unwins, 24997; The Printing Unwins: A Short History of Unwin Brothers, the Gresham Press 1826–1976, 25023

Unwin, Sir Raymond: The Legacy of Raymond Unwin: A Human Pattern for Planning, 20379; Town Planning in Practice: An Introduction to the Art of Designing Cities and Suburbs, 20380

Unwin, Sir Stanley: The Truth about Publishing, 24998

Upper Afan Community Development Project: Upper Afan CDP: Final Report to Sponsors, 9296

Upton, Clive: Wordmaps: A Dialect Atlas of England, 23793

Upton, M. A.: Mergers and Concentration in British Industry, 4988

UrbaLine, 56

Urban History Yearbook, 17726

Urban Planning Symposium, 1965: Proceedings ... Organised by the Building

Research Station at the Bartlett School of Architecture, 17794

Urban Structure Research Project: A Study Area in Southend-on-Sea, 18910

Urbanitsch, Peter: Grossbritannien und die Verträge von Locarno, 13659

Urdang, George: 'The First Century of the Pharmaceutical Society of Great Britain', 21020; Pharmacy's Part in Society, 22251; Kremers and Urdang's History of Pharmacy, 22252

Urquhart, J. M.: ed. The County of Peebles and the County of Selkirk, 19232

Urquhart, Robert Elliott: Arnhem, 14973

Urquhart, Robert: A History of the Scottish Milk Marketing Board, 19627, 20661

Urry, John: ed. Power in Britain: Sociological Readings, 7923

Urwin, Alan Charles Bell: Commercial Nurseries and Market Gardens, 19841

Urwin, Derek W.: Scottish Political Behaviour, 2475; Regional Differentiation and Practical Unity in Western Nations, 5090

Urwin, Evelyn Clifford: Henry Carter, C.B.E., 12095

Usborne, Cecil Vivian: Smoke on the Horizon: Mediterranean Fighting, 1914–1918, 14680; Blast and Counterblast: A Naval Impression of the War, 15315

Usher, Abbott Payson: A History of Mechanical Inventions, 7138; 'The Industrialization of Modern Britain', 7036

Usher, H. J. K.: An Angel without Wings: The History of University College School, 1830–1980, 23080

Usherwood, Stephen: 'The BBC and the General Strike', 24809

Usill, Harley Verneau: ed. They Stand Apart: A Critical Survey of the Problems of Homosexuality, 21942

Usmar, John: Old Witheridge: Byegone Days in a Devon Village, 19213

Ustinov, Peter: Dear Me, 26108

Utley, Thomas Edwin: Enoch Powell: The Man and His Thinking, 1289; Lessons of Ulster, 2944

Utting, J. E. G.: The Economic Circumstances of Old People, 8575

Utton, Michael Arthur: 'The Effect of Mergers on Concentrations: U.K. Manufacturing Industry, 1954–1965, 5521; 'On Measuring the Effects of Industrial Mergers', 5522

Vacher's Biographical Guide, 32

Vacher's Parliamentary Companion: A Reference Book for Parliament, National Organisations and Public Offices: 1831+, 274

Vader, John: Spitfire, 15846

Vail, D. J.: The British Mental Hospital System, 21802

Vaizey, John Ernest [Baron]: In Breach of Promise: Gaitskell, Macleod, Titmuss, Crosland, Boyle: Five Men who Shaped a Generation, 1200; The Brewing Industry, 1886–1951, 6169, 20735; The History of British Steel, 6589; National Health, 21676; Education: The State of the Debate in

America, Britain and Canada, 22651; The Control of Education, 22798; The Costs of Education, 23199; Resources for Education: An Economic Study of Education in the United Kingdom, 1920–1965, 23200; 'Block Grants and Control of Education', 23210; 'The Reform of Higher Education', 23388

Vaizey, Marina: Peter Blake, 24009

Valdin-Guillou, A.: Youth in Contemporary Britain, 8464

Vale, Lawrence J.: The Limits of Civil Defence in the USA, Switzerland, Britain and the Soviet Union: The Evolution of Policies since 1945, 15144

Vallance, Elizabeth: Women in the House: A Study of Women Members of Parliament, 1553, 7828; 'Women Candidates in the 1983 General Election', 2263; 'Equality for Women: A Note on the White Paper', 7827; Fair Shares in Parliament: Or, How to Elect More Women MPs, 7829

Vallance, Hugh Aymer: The History of the Highland Railway, 16941; The Great North of Scotland Railway, 16942

Vallance, M.: 'Alcoholism: A Two-Year Follow-up Study of Patients Admitted to the Psychiatric Department of a General Hospital', 22163

Vamplew, Wray: Salvesen of Leith, 16544; The Turf: A Social and Economic History of Horse Racing, 27122

Van Damm, Sheila: We Never Closed.: The Windmill Story, 26279

Van den Bergh, Tony: The Trade Unions—What Are They?, 6733

Van den Berghs Limited: Getting the Most out of Food: A Series of Studies on the Modern Approach to Feeding and Nutrition, 20540

Van den Haag, Ernest: 'Snobbery', 9463

Van der Dusen, W. J.: History as a Science: The Philosophy of R. G. Collingwood, 26793

Van der Eyken, Willem: Education, the Child and Society: A Documentary History, 1900–1973, 22694

Van der Poel, Jean: Selections from the Smuts Papers, 12724

Van der Stoel, M.: The British Application for Membership of the European Communities 1963–1968, 14169

Van Dorsten, Jan Adrianua: ed. Ten Studies in Anglo-Dutch Relations, 14134

Van Esbeck, Edmund: One Hundred Years of Irish Rugby: The Official History of the Irish Rugby Football Union, 27044

Van Ishoven, Armand: The Luftwaffe in the Battle of Britain, 14814

Van Stuyvenberg, Johannes Hermanus: Margarine: An Economic, Social and Scientific History, 1869–1969, 20714

Van Thal, Herbert: ed. The Prime Ministers, 969

Van Voris, Jacqueline: Constance de Markievicz: In the Cause of Ireland, 1468

Vane, Howard R.: Current Controversies in Economics, 3703

Vann, J. D.: Graham Greene: A Checklist of Criticism, 25558

Vansittart, Peter: ed. John Masefield's Letters from the Front 1915–1917, 25698

Vansittart, Robert Gilbert [Baron]: The Mist Procession, 13316; Black Record, 13317

Varah, Edward Chad: The Samaritans: To Help Those Tempted to Suicide or Despair, 9152

Varcoe, Ian: 'Scientists, Government and Organised Research in Great Britain, 1914–16: The Early History of the Department of Scientific and Industrial Research', 7110

Varga, E.: The Great Crisis and its Political Consequences: Economics and Politics, 1928–1934, 3574

Varley, D. E.: A History of the Midland Counties Lace Manufacturers Association, 1915–1958, 6472

Varma, Ved Prakash: ed. Stresses in Children, 8394

Vassall, William J. C.: Vassall: The Autobiography of a Spy, 16057

Vatikiotis, Panayiotis Jerasimof: The Modern History of Egypt, 14397

Vaughan, Adrian: Signalman's Morning, 16806; Signalman's Twilight, 16807; Signalman's Nightmare, 16808

Vaughan, D: 'Frederick Ashton', 24223

Vaughan, Paul: Doctor's Commons: A Short History of the British Medical Association, 20790

Vaughan-Thomas, Wynford: Anzio, 14880; Dalgety: The Romance of a Business, 20672

Vaughan Williams, Ralph: National Music and Other Essays, 24382; Heirs and Rebels: Letters Written to each other and Occasional Writings on Music, 24383

Vaughan Williams, Ursula: R.V.W.: A Biography of Ralph Vaughan Williams, 24381

Vaux, Nick: March to the South Atlantic, 16118

Veal, Anthony James: New Communities in the UK: A Classified Bibliography, 9429, 18175; Community Use of Community Schools at the Primary Level: Two Case Studies in Walsall, 9430; comp. A First List of U.K Student Theses and Dissertations in Planning and Urban and Regional Studies, 18176; ed. Leisure and the Community: Conference Proceedings: Papers from a Conference held by the Leisure Studies Association at Birmingham in 1976, 26936; Environmental Protection and Recreation: A Review and Annotated Bibliography, 27005

Veale, William Foster: From a New Angle: Reminiscences of Charterhouse, 1880–1945, 23049

Veerathappa, K.: The British Conservative Party and Indian Independence 1930–1947, 13155

Veitch, C.: '"Play up! Play up! and Win the War!" Football, the Nation, and the First World War 1914–15', 27058

Veitch, Norman: The People's: Being a History of the People's Theatre, Newcastle-upon-Tyne, 1911–1939, 26163

Veith, Ilza: Great Ideas in the History of Surgery, 21135

Velarde, Albert: 'Do Delinquents Really Drift?', 10670

Veliz, C.: 'Britain and the Underdeveloped World' in 'Labour's New Frontiers', 9179

Vellacott, Jo: Bertrand Russell and the Pacifists in the First World War, 13460

Venables, Ethel: The Young Worker at College: A Study of a Local Tech, 23272

Venables, Sir Peter Percy Frederick Ronald: Technical Education, 22489; 'Emergence of Colleges of Advanced Technology in Britain', 22492; 'Dualism in Higher Education', 22497; Higher Education Developments: The Technological Universities, 1956–1976, 22499; 'The Technological Universities and Education for the Professions', 22500; British Technical Education, 23269; The Smaller Firm and Technical Education, 23270; The Changing Pattern of Technical and Higher Education, 23271

Venables, Robert: Preserving the Family Farm, 19603

Veness, Thelma: School Leavers: Their Aspirations and Expectations, 8494

Venkataramani, M. S.: 'Ramsay MacDonald and Britain's Domestic Policies and Foreign Relations, 1919–1931', 1032

Venmore-Rowland, John: Radio Caroline: The Story of the First British Off-shore Radio Station, 24802

Venn, John Archibald: The Foundations of Agricultural Economics, with an Economic History of British Agriculture during and after the Great War, 19448

Verdin, Sir Richard: The Cheshire (Earl of Chester's) Yeomanry, 1898–1967: The Last Regiment to Fight on Horses, 15606

Vereker, Charles: Urban Redevelopment and Social Change: A Study of Social Conditions in Central Liverpool, 1955–1956, 9340, 18887

Vereté, Mayir: 'The Balfour Declaration and its Makers', 14290

Verma, Gajendra K.: Race and Education across Cultures, 23191

Verma, P.: 'Mergers in British Industry, 1949–1966', 5523

Vermilye, Jerry: The Great British Films, 24625

Verney, G. L.: The Desert Rats: The History of the 7th Armoured Division, 1938–1945, 14911

Verney, Peter: Anzio 1944: An Unexpected Fury, 14881; The Micks: The Story of the Irish Guards, 15560; The Gardens of Scotland, 19881

Verney, R. E.: 'The History of Student Health Services in Great Britain', 22772

Vernon, Anne: A Quaker Businessman: The Life of Joseph Rowntree, 1836–1925, 12146, 20698

Vernon, Betty D.: Ellen Wilkinson, 1891–1947, 1333; Margaret Cole, 1893–1980: A Political Biography, 1570, 2124

Vernon, Horace Middleton: Road Accidents in War-Time, 4116; National Health Services and Preventative Methods for improving National Health, 22056; The Alcohol Problem, 22160

Vernon, Philip Ewart: ed. Secondary School Selection, 22949

Vernon, Robin Anthony: Who Owns the Blue Chips? A Study of Shareholding in a Leading Company, 4266

Vernon, Roland Venables: Advisory Bodies: A Study of their Uses in Relation to Central Government, 1919–1939, 690

Verrier, Anthony: The Road to Zimbabwe 1890 to 1980, 12794; Through the Looking Glass: British Foreign Policy in the Age of Illusions, 13245; The Bomber Offensive, 15982

Verry, Donald: University Costs and Outputs, 23314

Verulam, Frank: Production for the People, 20589

Veverka, Jindrich: 'The Growth of Public Expenditure in the United Kingdom since 1950', 4761

Vian, Sir Philip: Action this Day: A War Memoir, 15281

Vickers, Hugo: Cecil Beaton: The Authorized Biography, 24707; Vivien Leigh, 26064

Vickers, Sir Geoffrey: The Art of Judgement, 5432; Industry, Human Relations and Mental Health, 5433; Towards a Sociology of Management, 5434; Making Institutions Work, 5435; 'Incentives of Labour', 5864

Victor, Peter Allen: The Economics of Pollution, 19991; Pollution: Economy and Environment, 19992

Victoria: Victoria College, Jersey, 1852–1972, 23081

Vidler, Alexander Roper: The Church in an Age of Revolution: 1789 to the Present Day, 11555; 'The Limitations of William Temple', 11708; Scenes from a Clerical Life, 11816; Twentieth Century Defenders of the Faith, 11870; The Modernist Movement in the Roman Church: Its Origins and Outcome, 11968; A Variety of Catholic Modernists, 11969; 'Abortive Renaissance: Catholic Modernists in Sussex', 11970

Vidler, John: If Freedom Fail, 10347

Viel, Benjamin: La medicina socializada y sa aplicacion en Gran Bretana, 21559

Viet, Jean: New Towns: A Selected Bibliography, 18984

Viets, H. R.: A Short History of Midwifery, 21098

Vig, Norman J.: 'Parliament, Science and Technology', 7111

Vigilante, Richard: Grenada: The Untold Story, 13081

Vince, Pamela: Television and the Child, 8218, 24828

Vince, S. W.: Reflections on the Structure and Distribution of Rural Population in England and Wales, 1921–1931, 19069

Vincent, Eric W.: The University of Birmingham: its History and Significance, 23459; ed. The Medical School of the University of Birmingham, 23460

Vincent, Jill: The State of the Nation, 125

Vincent, John Russell: 'The House of Lords', 673

Vincent, Mike: An Introduction to Industrial Relations, 5828

Vincent-Smith, John: 'Britain, Portugal and the First World War 1914–1916', 13389

Vinchezi, Penny: Taking Stock, 20681

Vine, Paul Ashley Laurence: London's Lost Route to the Sea: An Historical Account of the Inland Navigations which linked the Thames to the English Channel, 16444

Vine, Raymond Douglas: ed. A Century of Adventism in the British Isles, 12443

Vines, C. M.: A Little Nut-Brown Man: My Three Years with Lord Beaverbrook, 1074

Vinson, James: ed. Contemporary Dramatists, 26240

Violette, Eugene Morrow: ed. English Constitutional Documents since 1832, 593

Vipond, Joan:: Housing and Urban Spatial Structure: A Case Study, 5405, 20401

Vipont, Elfrida [pseud.]: The Story of Quakerism, 1652–1952, 12138

Visran, Rozina: Ayahs, Lascars and Princes: Indians in Britain 1700–1947, 11206

Vital, David: The Making of British Foreign Policy, 13357; 'The Making of British Foreign Policy', 13358

Viviani, Nancy: Nauru: Phosphate and Political Progress, 12886

Vodopivec, Katja: Maladjusted Youth: An Experiment in Rehabilitation, 10653

Vogel, Robert: A Breviate of British Diplomatic Blue Books 1919–1939, 205

Voigt, Johannes H.: Indien im Zweiten Weltkrieg, 15056

Voluntary Social Service: A Directory of National Organisations. 1928+, 9115

Von Herwath, Hans: 'Anglo-German Relations: A German View', 14217

Von Hügel, Friedrich [Baron]: Baron Friedrich von Hügel and the Modernist Crisis in England, 11981; The Life of Baron von Hügel, 11982; The Spirituality of Friedrich von Hügel, 11983; Selected Letters, 1896–1924, 11984; Letters from Baron Friedrich von Hügel to a Niece, 11985; Two Witnesses: A Personal Recollection of Hubert Parry and Friedrich von Hügel, 11986

Von Imhoff, Christoph: Zwanzig Jahre Königswinter: deutsch-englisches Gespräch 1949–1969, 14223

W.E.A. (Hatfield Branch). A Short Picture History of Hatfield and its People, 18109

Wabe, J. Stuart: Manpower Changes in the Engineering Industry, 5947; 'Labour Force Participation Rates in the London Metropolitan Region', 6012

Waddell, David Alan Gilmour: British Honduras: An Historical and Contemporary Survey, 13027

Waddilove, Lewis E.: Private Philanthropy and Public Welfare: The Joseph Rowntree Memorial Trust 1954–1979, 9153

Waddington, Conrad Hal: Behind Appearance: A Study of the Relations between Painting and Natural Sciences in this Century, 23992

Waddington, Ivan: 'The Development of Medical Ethics: A Sociological Analysis', 21023

Waddington, P. A. J.: The Training of Prison Governors, 10398

Wade, Arthur Shepers: Modern Finance and Industry: A Plain Account of the British Financial System, 4250

Wade, Aubrey: Gunner on the Western Front, 14488

Wade, Emlyn Capel Stuart: Constitutional Law, 608

Wade, G.: Heroin, Chasing the Dragon, 22200

Wade, Virginia: Courting Triumph, 27152

Wadge, D. Collett: ed. Women in Uniform, 15458

Wadhams, Stephen: ed. Remembering Orwell, 25751

Wadsworth, John Edwin: ed. The Banks and the Monetary System in the U.K., 1959–1970, 4410, 4429, 4643

Wadsworth, Michael Edwin John: The Consumer and the Health Service, 21579; ed. Studies in Everyday Medical Life, 21580; ed. Studies in Everyday Medical Life, 21952; Health and Sickness: The Choice of Treatment: Perception of Illness and Use of Services in an Urban Community, 21980

Wager, R.: Care of the Elderly: An Exercise in Cost Benefit Analysis Commissioned by Essex County Council, 8604

Wagg, Stephen: The Football World: A Contemporary Social History, 27069

Wagner, Donald O.: The Church of England and Social Reform since 1854, 11824

Wagner, Geoffrey: Wyndham Lewis: A Portrait of the Artist as the Enemy, 25675

Wagner, Gillian: Children of the Empire, 8395; The Chocolate Conscience, 20696

Wagoner, Mary S.: Agatha Christie, 25451

Wagstaffe, M.: ed. Research Methods for Elite Studies, 11685

Wah, Yeo Kim: Political Development in Singapore 1945–1955, 12961

Wain, H.: The Unconquered Plague: A Popular Story of Gonorrhea, 22368

Wain, John Barrington: 'My Nineteen Thirties', 23742; Sprightly Running: Part of an Autobiography, 25846

Wain, Kathleen: The Hambros 1779–1979, 4470

Wainwright, David: The Volunteers: The Story of Overseas Voluntary Service, 9158; Brooke Bond: A Hundred Years, 20680; Behind the Blue Door: The History of the Royal College of Midwives, 1881–1981, 21447, 21709, 21729; Youth in Action: The Duke of Edinburgh's Award Scheme 1956–1966, 26971

Wainwright, Hilary: Labour: A Tale of Two Parties, 1771; A Taste of Power: The Politics of Local Economics, 3294

Wainwright, Mary Doreen: ed. The Partition of British India Policies and Perspectives 1935–1947, 13156

Waites, Bernard A.: 'The Effect of the First World War on Class and Status in England, 1910–1920', 9616; A Class Society at War: England, 1914–1918, 9617; Popular Culture Past and Present: A Reader, 9917

Waites, Neville: ed. Troubled Neighbours: Franco-British Relations in the Twentieth Century, 14240

Wakefield, Gordon Stevens: Robert Newton Flew, 1886–1962, 12085; Methodist Devotion: The Spiritual Life in the Methodist Tradition, 1791–1945, 12104

Wakeford, Geoffrey: The Great Labour Mirage: An Indictment of Socialism in Britain, 1754

Wakeford, John: *ed.* Power in Britain: Sociological Readings, 7923; 'Fostering—A Sociological Perspective', 8396; The Cloistered Elite: A Sociological Analysis of the English Public Boarding School, 23041

Wakeley, Sir Cecil: George Buckston Browne, 20862

Wakelin, Martin F.: English Dialects: An Introduction, 23808

Waksman, Selman A.: The Conquest of Tuberculosis, 21156; The Antibiotic Era: A History, 21157

Waldegrave, A. J.: A Study of Hospital Administration, 21390

Waldegrave, William: The Binding of Leviathan: Conservatism and the Future, 2200

Walder, Alan David: The Chanak Affair, 13836

Waldron, Thomas John: The Frogmen: The Story of the Wartime Underwater Operations, 15403

Wales Council for Voluntary Action: The Wales Funding Handbook for Community and Voluntary Organisations, 9221

Wales, Prince of: A Vision of Britain, 23908

Wales University Commission, Final Reports, 23585

Wales, Peter: The British Constitution: An Introduction, 624

Waley, Daniel P.: British Public Opinion and the Abyssinian war, 1935–1936, 13784

Waley, Hubert David: The Cinema Today, 24600

Waley, Sir Sigismund David: Edwin Montagu: A Memoir and an Account of his Visits to India, 1277, 13130

Walford, A. J.: *ed.* Walford's Guide to Current British Periodicals in the Humanities and Social Sciences, 160; Guide to Reference Material, 240

Walford, Geoffrey: *ed.* British Public Schools: Policy and Practice, 23030; Restructuring Universities: Politics and Power in the Management of Change, 23454

Walkden, A. H.: 'The Estimation of Future Numbers of Private Households in England and Wales', 7417

Walker, A.: Psychiatric Studies of Borstal Lads, 10572

Walker, Alan: *ed.* Rural Poverty: Poverty, Deprivation and Planning in Rural Areas, 9106, 19082

Walker, Albert: Taxation and Social Policy, 8916

Walker, Alexander: Hollywood, England: The British Film Industry in the Sixties, 24640; Vivien: The Life of Vivien Leigh, 26065; No Bells on Sunday: The Journals of Rachel Roberts: Edited with a Documentary Biography, 26092; Peter Sellers: The Authorised Biography, 26344

Walker, Andrew: Restoring the Kingdom: The Radical Christianity of the House Church Movement, 12132

Walker, Andrew: Voice from the World: 50 Years of Broadcasting to the World 1932–1982, 24816

Walker, Anita: Francis Chichester: A Biography, 27165

Walker, Annelise: 'Delinquent and Maladjusted Girls', 10678

Walker, Sir Arnold L.: Report on Confidential Enquiries into Maternal Deaths in England and Wales 1958–1960, 7450; . . . 1961–1963, 7451

Walker, Arthur: An Annoted Bibliography of Health and Economics, 21634

Walker, B. J.: The Manpower Services Commission and Youth Training Schemes: A Critical Appraisal, 5952

Walker, Bruce: Farm Buildings in the Grampian Region: An Historical Exploration: A Report, 19710

Walker, Caroline: The Food Scandal: What's Wrong with the British Diet and how to Put it Right, 20562

Walker, Sir Charles: Thirty-Four Years in the Admiralty, 15316

Walker, Colin: Environmental Pollution by Chemicals, 20114

Walker, David Grant: 'William Temple, Archbishop of Canterbury', 11706; 'Herbert Hensley Henson, 1863–1947', 11741; *ed.* A History of the Church in Wales, 12285

Walker, David Maxwell: Scottish Courts and Tribunals, 10323

Walker, Derek: The Great Engineers: The Art of British Engineers 1837–1987, 9809; The Architecture and Planning of Milton Keynes, 18198, 19022

Walker, Eric Anderson: The British Empire, its Structure and Spirit, 12553

Walker, Frank: The Bristol Region, 5134

Walker, Fred M.: Song of the Clyde: A History of Clyde Shipbuilding, 16619

Walker, G. G.: The Honourable Artillery Company, 1537–1947, 15649

Walker, Gilbert: Economic Planning by Programme and Control in Great Britain, 3436, 6065

Walker, Graham: Thomas Johnston 1881–1965, 1250; 'The Common Wealth Labour Party in Northern Ireland 1942–1947', 1903; '"Protestantism before Party!": The Ulster Protestant League in the 1930's', 2957; The Politics of Frustration: Harry Midgley and the Failure of Labour in Northern Ireland, 3083

Walker, Hilary: Probation Work: Critical Theory and Socialist Practice, 10463

Walker, James: British Economic and Social History, 1700–1977, 3489

Walker, John: The Once and Future Film: British Cinema in the Seventies and Eighties, 24641

Walker, Joseph Viccars: Health and the Citizen: A Study in Design for Living, 21981

Walker, Kenneth F.: 'Towards Useful Theorising about Industrial Relations', 5784

Walker, Kenneth MacFarlane: The Family and Marriage in a Changing World, 9969; The Story of Medicine, 21190; The Story of Blood, 22335

Walker, M.: The West Yorkshire Road Car Company Ltd. Part Two: 1935 to 1975, 17331

Walker, M. E. M.: Pioneers of Public Health, 21982

Walker, Martin: The National Front, 2042, 2046; 'The National Front', 2043

Walker, Monica: The Urban Criminal: A Study in Sheffield, 10188; Crime, 10278; 'The Court Disposal of Young Males, by Race, in London in 1983', 10535

Walker, N. T.: 'Proposed New School Examination Structure in Scotland', 23614

Walker, Nigel David: Morale in the Civil Service: A Study of the Desk Worker, 884, 9784; 'The Habitual Criminal: An Administrative Problem', 10230; Crime and Punishment in Britain, 10324; Adolescent Maladjustment, 10595; A Short History of Psychotherapy in Theory and Practice, 22422

Walker, P.: Si vis pacem: Preparations for Change in the National Health Service, 21617

Walker, Percy Brooksbank: Early Aviation at Farnborough: The History of the Royal Aircraft Establishment vol.2—The First Aeroplanes, 17526

Walker, Peter Norman: The Courts of Law: A Guide to their History and Working, 10282

Walker, Peter R. J.: The Future of Transport in Britain, 16252

Walker, Rea: Social Workers and their Workloads in Northern Ireland Welfare Departments, 8746

Walker, Robert Milnes: Barbers and Barber—Surgeons of London, 20795; Medical Education in Britain, 22441

Walker, Tina: Biding Time: Reflections of Unemployed Young People in Kirkcaldy, 8541

Walker, Valerie: The Politics of Rural Wales: A Study of Cardiganshire, 2573

Walker, William George: A History of the Oundle Schools, 23069

Walker, William M.: 'Dundee's Disenchantment with Churchill: A Comment upon the Downfall of the Liberal Party', 1816; Juteopolis: Dundee and its Textile Workers, 1885–1923, 18131

Walker-Smith, Sir Derek: Neville Chamberlain, 983

Walkerdine, Reginald Hubert: *ed.* National Coal Board: The First Ten Years, 6293

Walkland, Stuart Alan: *ed.* The Commons in the Seventies, 636; The Legislative Process in Great Britain, 638; 'Science and Parliament: The Role of the Select Committees of the House of Commons', 655; 'Parliament, Science and Technology', 7111; 'The Public Accounts Committee, the UGC, and the Universities', 23333

Wall, Bernard: Headlong into Change: An Autobiography and a Memoir of Ideas since the Thirties, 11988

Wall, Cecil: *et al.* A History of the Worshipful Society of Apothecaries of London, 22257

Wall, Geoffrey: 'Public Response to Air Pollution in South Yorkshire, England', 20067

Wall, John: Directory of British Photographic Collections, 208

Wall, Max: The Fool on the Hill, 26348

Wall, Toby D.: 'Attitudes towards Participation among Local Authority Employees', 5777

Wall, W. D.: 'Vogues in British Educational Theory', 22639

Wallace, A. T.: 'Sir Robert Philip: A Pioneer in the Campaign against Tuberculosis', 21024

Wallace, D. B.: 'Rural Policy: A Review Article', 18826; 'The Crop Scientist and the Farmer in England 1940–1960', 19696

Wallace, Elaine: A History of the Council for the Education and Training of Health Visitors: An Account of its Establishment and Field of Activities, 1962–1975, 21731

Wallace, Elizabeth: The British Caribbean from the Decline of Colonialism to the End of Federation, 13005; 'The West Indian Federation: Decline and Fall', 13102

Wallace, G. J.: 'Felixstowe: Britain's Little Big Port', 16683

Wallace, Graham: The Guns of the Royal Air Force, 1939–1945, 15840; R.A.F. Biggin Hill, 15934

Wallace, Ian: Promise Me You'll Sing Mud!, 24480; 'From the Cambridge Theatre to Glyndebourne', 24557

Wallace, John: 'Part-Time Employment and Low Pay in Retail Distribution in Britain', 3941; Pay and Employment in Retailing, 9668

Wallace, Judith: Working Women in Recession: Employment, Redundancy and Unemployment, 7718

Wallace, L. P.: ed. Power, Public Opinion and Diplomacy: Essays in Honor of Eber Malcolm Carroll'. 13947

Wallace, Martin: Northern Ireland: Fifty Years of Self-Government, 2810; Drums and Guns: Revolution in Ulster, 2913

Wallace, Paul: The Square Mile: A Guide to the New City of London, 4286

Wallace, Tina: Slamming the Door: The Administration of Immigration Control, 11107

Wallace, William: Profit-sharing and Co-partnership, 5997; Enterprise First: The Relationship of the State to Industry, with Particular Reference to Private Enterprise, 6059

Wallace, William J. L.: The Foreign Policy Process in Britain, 13361; 'British External Relations and the European Community: The Changing Context of Foreign Policy Making', 14179

Wallace, William V.: 'The Making of the May Crisis of 1938', 13727; 'A Reply to Mr Watt', 13729

Waller Hills, John: The Finance of Government, 4663

Waller, P. J.: ed. Politics and Social Change in Modern Britain, 1591; Democracy and Sectarianism: A Political and Social History of Liverpool 1868–1939, 18047

Waller, Robert: The Almanac of British Politics, 2220; The Atlas of British Politics, 2373

Walley, Sir John: 'The United Kingdom Tax System, 1968–1970: Some Fixed Point Indicators of its Economic Impact', 4844;

Social Security: Another British Failure?, 4062, 9008; 'A General Equilibrium Assessment of the 1973 United Kingdom Tax Reform', 4845

Wallis, C. P.: 'Delinquent Areas in the County of London: Ecological Factors', 10641

Wallis, Jack Harold: The Challenge of Middle Age, 8551

Wallis, Jan: ed. Conditions of Illusion: Papers from the Women's Movement, 7769

Wallis, Jill: Valiant for Peace: A History of the Fellowship of Reconciliation 1914 to 1989, 13435

Wallis, John William: Accounting: A Modern Approach, 4192

Wallis, Peter John: Histories of Old Schools: A Revised List for England and Wales, 22992

Wallis, Thomas Edward: History of the School of Pharmacy, University of London, 20777, 22479, 23536

Wallman, Sandra: Ethnicity at Work, 11071

Walls, Ian Gascoine: Growing Vegetables, Fruit and Flowers for Profit, 19842

Wallwork, Kenneth L.: Derelict Land, 20303; Map Studies, with Related Field Excursions, 26719

Walsh, B. M.: Religion and Demographic Behaviour . . . 12155

Walsh, D. P.: Shoplifting: Controlling a Major Crime, 10223

Walsh, Dermot: The Use and Abuse of Emergency Legislation in Northern Ireland, 2869

Walsh, Edward Geoffrey: The Poacher's Companion, 19112

Walsh, Frances: ed. A Bibliography of Nursing Literature, 1971–1975, 21701

Walsh, H. G.: Current Issues in Cost-Benefit Analysis, 4767

Walsh, J.A.: Population in Ireland: A Census Atlas, 140

Walsh, Jan: The Meat Machine: The Inside Story of the Meat Business, 20677

Walsh, John Dixon: ed. Essays in Modern English Church History, in Memory of Norman Sykes, 11565

Walsh, Kieron: ed. Between Centre and Locality: The Politics of Public Policy, 3217

Walsh, M.: 'No Questions Asked: A Consideration of the Criminal Crime of Receiving', 10213

Walsh, Michael J.: 'Ecumenism in Wartime Britain: The Sword of the Spirit and Religion and Life, 1940–1945', 11977; From Sword to Ploughshare, 11978

Walsh, Michael: Andrew Lloyd Webber: His Life and Works, 24488

Walsh, Thomas P.: John Osborne: A Reference Guide, 25967

Walsh, Vivian: 'Joan Robinson's Economics in Retrospect', 26620

Walsh, William: D. J. Enright: Poet of Humanism, 25506

Walshe, Graham: Mergers and Concentration in British Industry, 4988; Recent Trends in Monopoly in Great Britain, 5529

Walter, David: The Oxford Union: Playground of Power, 23564

Walter, Ingo: ed. Resource Conservation: The Social and Economic Dimensions of Recycling, 20219

Walter, J. A.: Sent Away: A Study of Young Offenders in Court, 10580

Walters, Sir Alan A.: Britain's Economic Renaissance: Margaret Thatcher's Reforms 1979–1984, 3690; 'Money Multipliers in the United Kingdom, 1880–1962', 4602; Money in Boom and Slump: An Empirical Inquiry into British Experience since the 1880's, 4624

Walters, Bernhardt: A History of the Zinc Smelting Industry in Britain, 6617

Walters, Brian: The Illustrated History of Air Travel, 17648

Walters, David: British Railway Bridges, 16800

Walters, Dennis: Not Always with the Pack, 1540

Walters, Dorothy: 'National Income and Expenditure of the United Kingdom, 1870–1952', 4891

Walters, Gerald: 'The Colleges of Advanced Technology and the University Tradition', 22494; ed. A Technological University: An Experiment in Bath, 23455

Walters, P.: Women in Top Jobs: Four Studies in Achievement, 7714

Walters, Peter: The Scope of Local Initiative: A Study of Cheshire County Council 1961–1974, 3350

Walters, Rhoda: How Parliament Works, 1554

Walters, S. M.: The Shaping of Cambridge Botany: A Short History of Whole-Plant Botany in Cambridge from the Time of Ray into the Present Century, 26555

Waltham Forest Oral History Group: Pig's Head and Pease Pudding: Memories of the Butchery Trade and the use of Meat before the Second World War, 20678

Walton, Christopher: Housing Policy and the Housing System, 18517

Walton, D.: 'George Orwell and Antisemitism', 11339

Walton, Henry J.: Alcoholism, 22129

Walton, John K.: The Lake Counties from 1830 to the Mid-20th Century: A Study in Regional Change, 19165; ed. Leisure in Britain 1780–1939, 26917; The Blackpool Landlady: A Social History, 26985

Walton, Kenneth: The Highlands and Islands of Scotland, 5298

Walton, Mary: A History of the Diocese of Sheffield, 1914–1979, 11614

Walton, Paul: ed. Critical Criminology, 10145; The New Criminology: For a Social Theory of Deviance, 10146

Walton, Ronald Gordon: Women in Social Work, 7712, 8758; Residential Care: A Reader in Current Theory and Practice, 8878

Walton, Lady Susanna: William Walton, Behind the Facade, 24387

Walvin, James: Black and White: The Negro and English Society 1555–1945, 11035; Passage to Britain, 11036; Leisure and Society 1830–1950, 26916; ed. Leisure in Britain 1780–1939, 26917; Beside the Seaside: A Social History of the Popular Seaside Holiday, 26986; The People's Game: A Social History of English Football, 27054

Walworth, George: Feeding the People in Peace and War, 20588

Walz, Kenneth N.: Foreign Policy and Democratic Politics: The American and British Experience, 14004

Wand, John William Charles: Anglicanism in History and Today, 11595; Changeful Page: An Autobiography, 11762

Wandor, Michelene: Carry on Understudies: Theatre and Sexual Politics, 26239

Wandsworth Council for Community Relations: Ugandan Resettlement Unit. Ugandan Asians in Wandsworth: A Report Produced for Sir Charles Cunningham, Chairman of the Ugandan Resettlement Board, 11228

Wang, C.: Endphase des britischen Kolonialismus in China, 13626

Wapshott, Nicholas: Thatcher, 1048; Peter O'Toole: A Biography, 26085

Wapsiec, Jan: Sociology: An International Bibliography of Serial Literature, 1880–1980, 165

Warburg, Frederic John: All Authors are Equal: The Publishing Life of Frederic Warburg 1936–1971, 24993; An Occupation for Gentlemen, 24993

Warburg, Gabriel R.: 'The Sinai Peninsula Borders 1906–1947', 14394

Warburton, R. William: Community Workers in a Social Services Department: A Case Study, 9377

Warburton, S.: Public Transport in Rural Areas: The Increasing Role of Central and Local Government, 16313

Ward, Alan Joseph: Ireland and Anglo-American Relations, 1899–1921, 2676, 14017; ed. Northern Ireland: Living with the Crisis, 2844

Ward, Arthur Marcus: The Churches Move Together: A Brief Account of the Ecumenical Movement from the Edinburgh Conference of 1910, 12314

Ward, Audrey: Careers of Professional Women, 7856

Ward, Barbara: Faith and Freedom: A Study of Western Society, 11882

Ward, Bernard Mordaunt: Reddie of Abbotsholme, 23099

Ward, Bernard: Trees in Epping Forest, 19742

Ward, Charles Humble Dudley: History of the Welsh Guards, 15758; The Welsh Regiment of Foot Guards, 1915–1918, 15759

Ward, Colin: 'Goodnight Campers!' The History of the British Holiday Camp, 26988

Ward, Colin: Arcadia For All: The Legacy of a Makeshift Landscape, 18669

Ward, Colin: Housing: An Anarchist Approach, 18766

Ward, Colin: Vandalism, 10660, 18292; The Child in the City, 18293

Ward, Conor: 'English Catholics in Transition', 11941; 'The Catholic Family as a Minority Group', 11952

Ward, David: 'The Public Schools and Industry in Britain after 1870', 23036

Ward, David: Beyond Band Aid: Charity is not Enough, 9191

Ward, David: Women's Prisons: Sex and Social Structure, 10433

Ward, Elizabeth: David Jones: Mythmaker, 25608

Ward, George: Fort Grunwick, 6750

Ward, Herbert: The Educational System of England and Wales and its Recent History, 22662; Notes for the Study of English Education from 1900 to 1930, 22663

Ward, Hugh: 'Government Popularity and the Falklands War: A Reassessment', 2352

Ward, Ian: 'The Government and Local Accountability since Layfield', 3265

Ward, Ian: ed. Great British Bikes, 17183; The Sports Car, 17361

Ward, John Tower: The First Century: A History of Scottish Tory Organisation, 1882–1982, 2540; Workers and Employers: Documents on Trade Unions and Industrial Relations in Britain Since the 18th Century, 5566, 6801

Ward, Kenneth: 'British Documentaries of the 1930s', 24611; Mass Communications and the Modern World, 25063

Ward, Margaret: Unmanageable Revolutionaries: Women and Irish Nationalism, 2733

Ward, Michael: Passports and Politics, 11045

Ward, Pamela: ed. Conservation and Development in Historic Towns and Cities, 18962

Ward, Patrick: Social Worker, 8656

Ward, R.: The Housing Position and Residential Distribution of Ethnic Minorities in Britain: A Bibliography, 18705

Ward, Richard Heron: The Hidden Boy: The Work of C. A. Joyce as Headmaster of an Approved School, 10513

Ward, Robin Harwood: 'Some Factors Underlying Racial Discrimination in Housing', 11188

Ward, Russell: A Nation for a Continent: The History of Australia 1901–1975, 12602

Ward, Sadie B.: Village Life in England 1860–1940: A Photographic Record, 19153

Ward, Stephen George Peregrine: Faithful: The Story of the Durham Light Infantry, 15626

Ward, Stephen: Stephen Ward Speaks: Conversations with Warwick Chalton: Judge Gerald Sparrow Sums up the Profumo Affair, 9899

Ward, Sue: Pensions: What to Look for in Company Pension Schemes and how to Improve them, 3977; The Essential Guide to Pensions: A Workers' Handbook, 3978

Ward, Sue: War in the Countryside, 1939–1945, 19101

Ward, T. S.: The Distribution of Consumer Goods: Structure and Performance, 6646

Ward, W. E. F.: Fraser of Trinity and Achimota, 12373

Ward-Jackson, Cyril Henry: The 'Cellophane' Story: Origins of a British Industrial Group, 6615; Ships and Shipbuilders of a West Country Seaport: Fowey 1786–1939, 16629

Ward-Thomas, Pat: The Royal and Ancient, 27158

Warde, Alan: Consensus and Beyond: The Development of Labour Party Strategy since the Second World War, 1724

Wardle, Chris: Changing Food Habits in the United Kingdom, 20597

Wardle, D. B.: 'Sources for the History of Railways at the Public Record Office', 16718

Wardle, David: English Popular Education, 1780–1970, 22665; The Rise of the Schooled Society: The History of Formal Schooling in England, 22666

Wardle, Irving: The Theatre of George Devine, 26154

Wardley-Smith, J.: ed. The Control of Oil Pollution on the Sea and Inland Waters: The Effects of Oil Spills on the Marine Environment and Methods of Dealing with Them, 20080; ed. The Prevention of Oil Pollution, 20081

Wardrop, Keith R. H.: 'Delinquent Teenage Types', 10642

Wardroper, John: Juggernaut, 17466

Ware, Dora: A Short Dictionary of British Architects, 23863

Ware, Michael E.: Canals and Waterways, 16381; Veteran Motor Cars, 17356

Warham, Joyce: Social Policy in Context, 8896; An Introduction to Administration for Social Workers, 8897; The Organisational Context of Social Work, 8898

Warhurst, John: 'The Australia-Britain Relationship: The Future of Australia's Political Relationship to Britain', 12639

Warman, Roberta M.: 'The Erosion of Foreign Office Influence in the Making of Foreign Policy, 1916–1918', 13338

Warmington, Eric Herbert: 'Society and Education in Cambridge 1902–1922', 23466; The History of Birkbeck College, University of London, during the Second World War, 1939–1945, 23520

Warn, Christopher Robert: Buses in Northumberland and Durham, pt. 1: 1900–1930, 17313

Warner, A. W.: British Trade Unionism under a Labour Government 1945–1951, 6872

Warner, Douglas: The Shame of a City: An Inquiry into the Vice of London, 10846

Warner, F. E.: 'Education in Science and Technology', 22508

Warner, Frank: The Silk Industry of the United Kingdom: Its Origin and Development, 6437

Warner, Geoffrey: England in the Twentieth Century, 294; 'Die britische Labour-Regierung und die Einheit Westeuropas 1948–1951', 14125; '"Collusion" and the Suez Crisis of 1956', 14381; Iraq and Syria 1941, 14883

Warner, Gerald: The Scottish Tory Party: A History, 2541

Warner, Jack: Jack of all Trades: An Autobiography, 26349

Warner, Malcolm: 'The Context of Industrial Relations in Great Britain and West Germany', 5808; 'The Pattern of Opposition in British and American Unions', 6780; 'The Webbs, Keynes and the Economic Problem in the Inter-War years', 26600

Warner, Oliver Martin Wilson: Battle Honours of the Royal Navy, 14647; The British Navy: A Concise History, 15239; Cunningham of Hyndhope: Admiral of the Fleet, 15251; Admiral of the Fleet: The Life of Sir Charles Lambe, 15269; Chatto and Windus: A Brief Account of the Firm's Origins, History and Development, 24955

Warner, Philip: The Zeebrugge Raid, 14660; Auchinleck: The Lonely Soldier, 14755; Alamein, 14912; The D-Day Landings, 14948; The Special Air Service, 15005, 15721; The SBS: Special Boat Squadron, 15324; Stories of Famous Regiments, 15541

Warner, W. L.: 'The Study of Social Stratification', 10905

Warnock, Sir Geoffrey: English Philosophy since 1900, 26838

Warnock, Dame [Helen] Mary: Ethics since 1900, 26837

Warr, Sir Charles Laing: The Glimmering Landscape, an Autobiography, 12227

Warr, Peter: ed. The Psychology of Work, 5747

Warren, Charles Esmé Thornton: 'The Admiralty Regrets . . .': The Story of His Majesty's Submarines 'Thetis' and 'Thunderbolt', 15380; Above us the Waves: The Story of Midget Submarines and Human Torpedoes, 15381

Warren, Frank A.: An Alternative Vision: The Socialist Party in the 1930s, 1715

Warren, J. H.: 'The Party System in Local Government', 3147; The Local Government Service, 3231

Warren, James G. H.: A Century of Locomotive Building by Robert Stephenson & Co. 1823–1923, 17077

Warren, Kenneth: Chemical Foundations: The Alkali Industry in Britain to 1926, 6232; 'Recent Changes in the Geographical Location of the British Steel Industry', 6583; The British Iron and Steel Sheet Industry since 1840: An Economic Geography, 6585; 'Locational Problems of the Scottish Iron and Steel Industry since 1760, pt.1', 7052; Fifty Years of the Green Line, 17321; The Motor Bus in London Country, 17322

Warren, Linda: Older Women and Feminist Social Work, 8649

Warren, M. D.: ed. Management and the Health Service, 21636

Warren, Max Alexander Cunningham: Crowded Canvas: Some Experiences of a Lifetime, 11819; The Missionary Movement from Britain in Modern History, 12366

Warrillow, Ernest James Dalzell: A Sociological History of the City of Stoke-on-Trent, 18085

Warrington, A. J.: The History of the Somerset Coalfield, 6323

Warshaw, L. J.: Malaria: The Biography of a Killer, 22367

Warth, Robert D.: 'The Mystery of the Zinoviev Letter', 13936

Wartman, William Bechmann: Medical Teaching in Western Civilisation, 20771

Warwick, Christopher: Abdication, 498; Princess Margaret, 525

Warwick, Roger M.: An Illustrated History of United Counties Omnibus Company Ltd, 17329

Warwick, Ronald W.: The Q.E.2, 16583

Wass, Sir Douglas: Government and the Governed, 737

Wasserman, Gary B.: The Politics of Decolonization: Kenya Europeans and the Land Issue 1960–1965, 12833

Wasserstein, Bernard: 'Jewish Identification among Students at Oxford', 11292; Britain and the Jews of Europe 1939–1945, 11312, 15186; 'The British in Palestine: The Mandatory Government and the Arab-Jewish Conflict, 1917–1929, 14303; 'Herbert Samuel and the Palestine Problem', 14302

Water Statistics: 1964+, 20069

Waterfield, Lina: Castle in Italy, 25295

Waterfield, Percival: 'Civil Service Recruitment', 915

Waterhouse, Rachel Elizabeth: Children in Hospital: A Hundred Years of Children in Birmingham, 21369; The Birmingham and Midland Institute, 1854–1954, 22872

Waterman, Stanley: British Jewry in the Eighties: A Statistical and Geographical Study, 12419

Waters, Brian: Get our Cities Moving, 16297

Waters, Grant M.: Dictionary of British Architects Working 1900–1950, 23860; Dictionary of British Artists Working 1900–1950, 23938

Waterson, Anthony Peter: An Introduction to the History of Virology, 22341

Waterson, Mary: Gypsy Family, 11348

Wates, Nicholas Heron: The Battle for Tolmers Square, 18767

Wathen, Robert L.: 'Genesis of a Generator . . . The Early History of the Magnetron', 7112

Watkin, Brian: 'Management in the Reorganised Health Service: The Framework', 21320; 'Moneymatters', 21321; 'Best Laid Plans', 21322; 'Personnel Priorities', 21323; 'Changing Times', 21324; The National Health Service: The First Phase: 1948–1974 and After, 21680; ed. Documents on Health and Social Services, 1834 to the Present Day, 21979

Watkin, David: The Rise of Architectural History, 23864; The London Ritz: A Social and Architectural History, 27997

Watkin, Edward Ingram: Roman Catholicism in England from the Reformation to 1950, 11940

Watkins, Alan R.: The Liberal Dilemma, 2177

Watkins, C.: The Study and Use of British Woodlands: Conference Proceedings, University of Nottingham, 19754

Watkins, Ernest: The Cautious Revolution, 385

Watkins, Harold Mostyn: Coal and Men: An Economic and Social Study of the British and American Coalfields, 6261

Watkins, Kenneth William: Britain Divided: The Effect of the Spanish Civil War on British Public Opinion, 13979; 'Plowden—is it Enough?', 22609; 'The Politics of Examinations (with Particular Reference to the C.S.E.)', 22909

Watkins, L. H.: Environmental Impact of Roads and Traffic, 17134

Watkins, Steve: Medicine and Labour: The Politics of a Profession, 21556

Watkinson, Harold Arthur, Baron: Turning Points, 1329

Watney, John: Mervyn Peake, 24051, 25759

Watson, A. G.: How York Governs itself, 3344; ed. How York is Governed by the Ministers of the Crown, 3345

Watson, Anthony Heriot: Road Passenger Transport and Road Goods Transport, 16187; 'The Channel Tunnel: Investment Appraisals', 16358

Watson, Arnold R.: West Indian Workers in Britain, 11237

Watson, Bernard: A Hundred Years of War: The Salvation Army, 1865–1965, 12127

Watson, C. J.: 'Vacancy Chains, Filtering and the Public Sector (West Central Region of Scotland)', 18456; Housing on Clydeside, 1970: Reports, 18474

Watson, Charles A.: The Writing of History in Britain: A Bibliography of Post-1945 Writings about British Historians and Biographers, 26721

Watson, David: You are My God, 11820

Watson, David: ed. Talking about Welfare: Readings in Philosophy and Social Policy, 8703; ed. Philosophy in Social Work, 8704

Watson, Elizabeth M.: Electricity Supply in Great Britain: Its Development and Organization, 6685

Watson, F.: 'The Death of George V', 474

Watson, Francis Leslie: Dawson of Penn, 20877

Watson, Geoffrey: Northumberland Village, 19141

Watson, George Grimes: ed. The Unservile State: Essays in Liberty and Welfare, 2173, 8822: ed. Radical Alternative: Studies in Liberalism, 2175

Watson, Graham: Book Society, 25010

Watson, Ian: Conversations with Ayckbourn, 25939

Watson, Jack Brierley: Empire to Commonwealth, 1919 to 1970, 12483

Watson, James Dewey: Phage and the Origins of Molecular Biology, 22307; The Double Helix: A Personal Account of the Discovery of the Structure of DNA, 26479; The DNA Story: A Documentary History of Gene Cloning, 26481

Watson, James Lee: ed. Between Two Cultures: Migrants and Minorities in Britain, 11057

Watson, James Paton: A Plan for Plymouth: Report, 18902

Watson, James Wreford: ed. Geographical Essays in Memory of Alan G. Ogilvie, 26665; ed. The British Isles: A Systematic Geography, 26687

Watson, Joyce M.: Solvent Abuse: The Adolescent Epidemic?, 22227

Watson, K.: Thames and Medway Canal: A Study of Recreational Potential, 16417

Watson, Milton E.: Flagships of the Line: A Celebration of the World's Three Funnel Liners, 16584

Watson, Roderick: The Penguin Book of the Bicycle, 17170

Watson, Sir James Anderson Scott: Agriculture: The Science and Practice of British Farming, 19437; The Farming Year, 19438; ed. Agriculture in the British Economy, 19439; The Pace of Farming

Progress, 19440; Rural Britain Today and Tomorrow, 19441; Special Article on Farming after the War, 19442; The History of the Royal Agricultural Society of England, 1839–1939, 19443; Great Farmers, 19444

Watson, Tony J.: The Personnel Managers: A Study in the Sociology of Work and Employment, 5471; Sociology, Work and Industry, 5806

Watson, W. E.: ed. Origin and Development of the Microscope, 7104

Watson, William Nairn Boog: A Short History of Chalmers Hospital, 21478

Watson, William: Sociology in Medicine, 21999

Watson-Jones, Reginald: Surgery is Destined to the Practice of Medicine, 21136

Watson-Watt, Sir Robert Alexander: Three Steps to Victory: A Personal Account by Radar's Greatest Pioneer, 15112

Watt, Archibald: Highways and Byways around Stonehaven, 17162

Watt, David: 'The Politics of 1951–1971', 1559; ed. The Constitution of Northern Ireland: Problems and Prospects, 2818; 'The Fate of the Public Schools', 23035

Watt, Donald Cameron: 'Britain and North Sea Oil: Policies Past and Present', 6501; 'Britain and the Indian Ocean: Diplomacy before Defence', 13197; 'Divided Control of British Foreign Policy: Danger or Necessity?', 13349; 'Foreign Affairs, the Public Interest and the Right to Know', 13350; Personalities and Policies: Studies in the Formulation of British Foreign Policy in the Twentieth Century, 13351; 'The Home Civil Service and the New Diplomacy', 13352; 'The Anglo-German Naval Agreement of 1935: An Interim Judgement', 13664; 'Appeasement: The Rise of a Revisionist School?', 13711; 'The May Crisis of 1938: A Rejoinder to Mr Wallace', 13728; 'Anglo-German Naval Negotiations on the Eve of the Second World War', 13763; How War Came: The Immediate Origins of the Second World War 1938–1939, 13764; Succeeding John Bull: America in Britain's Place, 1900–1975, 14005; 'Grossbritannien und Europa, 1951–1959: Die Jahre konservativer Regierung', 14149; Britain Looks to Germany: British Opinion and Policy towards Germany since 1945, 14216; 'Königswinter, 1965', 14220; Britain and the Suez Canal, 14363; Documents on the Suez Crisis 26 July to 6 November 1956, 14364

Watt, Hugh: New College, Edinburgh: A Centenary History, 12221

Watt, Sir Alan: The Evolution of Australia's Foreign Policy 1938–1965, 12616; Australian Defence Policy 1951–1963: Major International Aspects, 12617

Watterson, P.A.: 'The Causes of Rapid Mortality Decline in England and Wales 1861–1921', 7473

Wattleworth, D. R.: The Iron and Steel Industry of West Cumberland: An Historical Survey, 6598

Watts, Anthony Gordon: Diversity and Choice in Higher Education, 23294

Watts, Anthony John: The U-Boat Hunters, 14799; A Source Book of Hydrofoils and Hovercraft, 17708

Watts, Cedric: Cunninghame Graham: A Critical Biography, 25543

Watts, D. G.: 'Milford Haven and its Oil Industry', 6500

Watts, David R.: Location of Industry in Hertfordshire: Planning and Industry in the Post-war Period, 5159

Watts, Eric: Fares Please: The History of Passenger Transport in Portsmouth, 16355

Watts, H. D.: 'Market Areas and Spatial Rationalization: The British Brewing Industry after 1945', 6168; 'The Spatial Evolution of an Industry: The Example of Broiler Production', 20679; 'Conflict and Collusion in the British Sugar Industry: 1924–1928', 20688; 'Market Areas and Spatial Rationalization: The British Brewing Industry after 1945', 20741

Watts, Nina: The Economic Section 1939–1961: A Study in Economic Advising, 26581

Wauchope, Arthur Grenfell: A History of the Black Watch (Royal Highlanders) in the Great War, 15569

Wauchope, Gladys Mary: The Story of a Woman Physician: An Autobiography, 20906

Waugh, Arthur: A Hundred Years of Publishing, Being the Story of Chapman and Hall Ltd, 24953

Waugh, Evelyn: A Little Learning: The First Volume of Autobiography, 25857

Waugh, James: Slamannan Parish through the Changing Years, 19372

Waugh, Norah: The Cut of Women's Clothes 1600–1930, 24162

Waughray, Vernon: Race Relations in Great Britain, 10928

Wavell, Archibald Percival [Earl]: Allenby: A Study in Greatness, 14497; Allenby in Egypt, 14498; The Palestine Campaigns, 14499

Waymark, Peter: The Car Industry: A Study in Economics and Geography, 17402

Weale, Albert: Equality and Social Policy, 8801; Political Theory and Social Policy, 8802

Weale, Martin: British Banking 1960–1985, 4449

Wearmouth, Robert Featherstone: Methodism and the Trade Unions, 12101; The Social and Political Influence of Methodism in the Twentieth Century, 12102

Weate, Mary: The Parish of Lapley-with-Weaton Aston, 19342

Weatherall, J. A. C.: Anencephalus, Spina-Bifida and Congenital Hydrocephalus: England and Wales, 1964–1972, 22243

Weatherhead, A. Kingsley: Leslie Weatherhead: A Personal Portrait, 12089; A Reading of Henry Green, 25556

Weatherhead, Alan Douglas: Firearms in Crime: A Home Office Statistical Division Report on Indictable Offences Involving Firearms in England and Wales, 10207

Weatherhead, Leslie Dixon: The Christian Agnostic, 11888

Weaver, John Reginald Homer: ed. The Dictionary of National Biography 3rd Supplement [1912–1921], 14; ed. The Dictionary of National Biography 4th Supplement [1922–1930], 15

Webb, Adrian Leonard: Income Distribution and the Welfare State, 3852, 9074; Across the Generations: Old People and Young Volunteers, 8471; Planning, Need and Scarcity: Essays on the Personal Social Services, 8832; Change, Choice and Conflict in Social Policy, 8854; Whither State Welfare?: Policy Implementation in the Personal Social Services 1979–1980, 9007; 'Social Service Administration: Principles and Practices', 9233

Webb, Barbara: 'Mobility of General Practitioners during the First Few Years in General Practice', 9602; Going to See the Doctor: The Consultation Process in General Practice, 21526

Webb, Beatrice: The Consumers Co-operative Movement, 1883; English Prisons under Local Government, 10336

Webb, Brian: The British Internal Combustion Locomotive 1894–1940, 17086

Webb, David: 'Some Factors Associated with the Employment of Sociology Graduates in the Field of Social Work', 9878

Webb, John David: ed. Noise Control in Industry, 20147

Webb, Keith: The Growth of Nationalism in Scotland, 2500

Webb, Michael: Architecture in Britain Today, 23902

Webb, Philip Richard Hylton: Source Book of Family Law, 10014

Webb, Robert Kiefer: Modern England: From the Eighteenth Century to the Present, 286

Webb, Sidney James [Baron Passfield]: 'The First Labour Government', 1703; The Consumers Co-operative Movement, 1883; English Prisons under Local Government, 10336

Webb, T.: 'Why the Rate Burden is Cause for Concern', 3266

Webb, Thomas Duncan: Deadline for Crime, 10140; Line-up for Crime, 10141; Crime is my Business, 10142

Webb, Tony: Food Irradiation in Britain?, 20647; Food Irradiation: Who Wants it?, 20648

Webb, William: Coastguard! An Official History of H.M. Coastguard, 16516

Webber, Alan: Bank Deposits and the Quantity of Money in the United Kingdom 1870–1921, 4434; Profits and Profitability in British Banking 1870–1939, 4435; A Monetary History of the United Kingdom, 1870–1982, 4544

Webber, Bernard: 'Accumulation, Productivity and Distribution in the British Economy, 1870–1938', 4744

Webber, G. C.: 'Patterns of Membership and Support for the British Union of Fascists', 2032; The Ideology of the British Right, 1918–39, 2202

Webber, Richard: Socioeconomic Classification of Local Authority Areas, 7407, 18337; Social Area Analysis of Greater

London, 18335; The Social Structure of Haringay, 18336

Webber, Ronald: Market Gardening: The History of Commercial Flower, Fruit and Vegetable Growing, 19835; The Early Horticulturalists, 19836

Webber, Rosemary: World List of National Newspapers in Libraries in the British Isles, 146

Weber, F. G.: The Evasive Neutral: Germany, Britain and the Quest for a Turkish Alliance in the Second World War, 13844

Weber, Michael H.: Profits, Politics and Drugs, 22270

Webley, Maureen: Information in Social Welfare: A Study of Resources, 8879

Webster, Charles: The Health Services since the War, 21603; 'Tobacco Smoking Addiction: A Challenge to the National Health Service', 22217; ed. Biology, Medicine and Society 1840–1940, 22345, 22911

Webster, Sir Charles Kingsley: United Kingdom Policy: Foreign, Strategic, Economic: Appreciations by Sir Charles Webster and Others, 13214; The Art and Practice of Diplomacy, 13324; The League of Nations in Theory and Practice, 13480; 'Munich Reconsidered: A Survey of British Policy', 13752; The Strategic Air Offensive, 15981

Webster, Douglas: The Social Consequences of Conviction, 10190

Webster, F. V.: Urban Passenger Transport: Some Trends and Prospects, 16281; A Theoretical Estimate of London Car Commuters Transferring to Bus Travel, 16282

Webster, Jack: A Grain of Truth: A Scottish Journalist Remembers, 25296

Webster, John B.: et al. A Bibliography on Kenya, 12820

Webster, Margaret: The Same, Only Different: Five Generations of a Great Theatre Family, 26123

Webster, Michael: Motor Scooters, 17200

Webster, Robin MacLean: Professional Ethics and Practices for Scottish Solicitors, 9816

Wedderburn, Dorothy: Workers' Attitudes and Technology, 5897; White-collar Redundancy: A Case Study, 6978; Redundancy and the Railwaymen, 6979; The Aged in the Welfare State: The Interim Report of a Survey of Persons aged 65 and Over in Britain, 1962 and 1963, 8585; 'Poverty in Britain Today: The Evidence', 9072; ed. Poverty, Inequality and Class Structure, 9073, 9574

Wedderburn, Kenneth William [Baron]: Industrial Conflict: A Comparative Legal Survey, 5759; 'The Right to Threaten Strikes', 6955

Wedell, Eberhard George: Broadcasting and Public Policy, 24787

Wedge, Peter: Born to Fail, 8398

Wedgwood, Ciceley Veronica: The Last of the Radicals: Josiah Wedgwood, M.P., 1542

Wedgwood, Josiah Clement [Baron]: Memoirs of a Fighting Life, 1541; The Economics of Inheritance, 3771

Weekes, Brian: Industrial Relations and the Limits of Law: The Industrial Effects of the Industrial Relations Act 1971, 5771; The Law and Practice of the Closed Shop, 5772; ed. Conflict at Work: Reshaping Industrial Relations—A Book of Original Essays, 5737

Weeks, Jeffry: Sex, Politics and Society: The Regulation of Sexuality since 1800, 7518

Weeks, John: Men against Tanks: A History of Anti-Tank Warfare, 15512; Infantry Weapons, 15513; Airborne Equipment: A History of its Development, 15908

Weerasinghe, Lali: Directory of Recorded Sound Resources in the United Kingdom, 224

Wehner, Gerd: Grossbritannien und Polen 1938–1939: Die britische Polen-Politik zwischen München und dem Ausbruch des Zweiten Weltkrieges, 13901

Weigall, David: Britain and the World 1815–1986: A Dictionary of International Relations, 13207

Weighell, Sidney: On the Rails, 6836, 16803

Weightman, K.: 'Academic Freedom and Higher Education in England', 22538

Weiler, Peter: British Labour and the Cold War, 13572; 'British Labour and the Cold War: The London Dock Strike of 1949', 13573

Weinberg, Aubrey: 'Class Theory and Practice', 9447

Weinberg, Gerhard L.: 'The May Crisis, 1938', 13726

Weinberg, Ian: The English Public Schools: The Sociology of an Elite Education, 23020

Weinberg, Mark Aubrey: Take-overs and Mergers, 5545

Weinberger, B.: 'Communism and the General Strike', 1935

Weinberger, J. M.: 'The British on Borah: Foreign Office and Embassy Attitudes towards Idaho's Senior Senator, 1935–1940', 14027

Weinberger, Paul Eric: Perspectives on Social Welfare: An Introductory Anthology, 8860

Weinberger, Philip: ed. Sociology for our Times, 8058

Weinder, Norman L.: ed. Modern Policing, 10736

Weiner, Herbert Elias: British Labor and Public Ownership, 6068

Weinroth, Howard: 'Peace by Negotiation and the British Anti-War Movement, 1914–1918', 13468

Weintraub, Stanley: The Last Great Cause: The Intellectuals and the Spanish Civil War, 23775; ed. British Dramatists since World War Two, 25931

Weir, Alexander Douglas: Getting a Trade: A Study of Apprentices' Experience of Apprenticeship, 5961

Weir, Angela: 'The British Women's Movement', 7805

Weir, Sir Cecil: Civilian Assignment, 936

Weir, David: ed. The Sociology of Modern Britain: An Introductory Reader, 7600; ed. Social Problems of Modern Britain, 7601; Social Welfare in Modern Britain, 7602

Weir, Lauchlan Macneill: The Tragedy of Ramsay MacDonald: A Political Biography, 1032

Weir, Mary: ed. Job Satisfaction: Challenge and Response in Modern Britain, 5908

Weir, Ronald: The Composer in the Market Place, 24293

Weir, William: 'The First One Hundred Years': A Sketch of the History of the Glasgow Pawnbrokers Association, 4540

Weitzer, Ronald: 'Policing a Divided Society: Obstacles to Normalisation in Northern Ireland', 2933; 'Accountability and Complaints against the Police in Northern Ireland', 2934

Weitzman, Martin L.: The Case for Profit-sharing, 6049

Weitzman, Sophia: A Place for Everyone: A History of State Education from the End of the 18th Century to the 1970s, 22674

Weizmann, Chaim: Trial and Error: The Autobiography of Chaim Weizmann, 12434

Welch, Colin: ed. Recollections of Three Reigns, 542

Welch, Edwin: The Peripatetic University: The Cambridge Local Lectures, 1873–1973, 23691

Welch, Jeffrey Egan: Literature and Film: An Annotated Bibliography, 1909–1977, 24583

Welch, Ruth Lillian: Migration Research and Migration in Britain: A Selected Bibliography, 7300; Migration in Britain: Data Sources and Estimation Techniques, 7301

Welch, Susan: 'The Impact of Race on Political Behaviour in Britain', 2247

Welchman, Gordon: The Hut Six Story: The Breaking of the Enigma Codes, 15199

Welensky, Sir Roy: 4000 Days: The Life and Death of the Federation of Rhodesia and Nyasaland, 12783

Welfare Cooperation between Local Authorities and Voluntary Organisations: Working in the Community: Report of a Conference . . . 1964, 8730

Welford, Alan Trafford: ed. Society: Problems and Methods of Study, 7972, 18288; Ageing and Human Skill, 8566

Welham, Philip John: Monetary Circulation in the United Kingdom: A Statistical Study, 4626

Wellcome Institute of the History of Medicine: Portraits of Doctors and Scientists in the Wellcome Institute of the History of Medicine, 20773

Wellens, John: The Training Revolution: From Shop-floor to Board-room, 5957, 23267; Technical Education: Its Aims, Organisation and Future Development, 23268

Weller, John Brian: Modern Agriculture and Rural Planning, 19540, 19545; Farm Buildings, 19706

Weller, K.: 'Don't be a Soldier!': The Radical Anti-war Movement in North London, 1914–1918, 13450

Wellesley, Sir Victor: Diplomacy in Fetters, 13318

Wellington: A History of Wellington College, 1859–1959, 23082

Wellman, F.: Foundations for Health Service Management: A Scicon Report for the Scottish Home and Health Department on the Requirements for a Health Service Information System, 21616

Wells, A.: The Battle for the Falklands: Naval Forces, 16088

Wells, Alan F.: Social Institutions, 10996

Wells, Audrey: Britain and Soviet Communism: The Impact of a Revolution, 13915

Wells, Frederick Arthur: The British Hosiery Trade: its History and Organisation, 6434; Hollins and Viyella: A Study in Business History, 6435; The British Hosiery and Knitwear Industry: Its History and Organisation, 6436

Wells, Geoffrey H.: The Works of H.G.Wells, 1887–1925: A Bibliography, Dictionary and Subject-index, 25868

Wells, Herbert George: Experiment in Autobiography, 25869

Wells, Muriel Maude: The New Law of Education, 22625

Wells, Nicholas: The Ageing Population: Burden or Challenge?, 8644

Wells, Raymond J. G.: 'British Agriculture—A Rare Success Story', 19422

Wells, Ronald: Conflict and Christianity in Northern Ireland, 12158

Wells, Sidney John: British Export Performance: A Comparative Study, 4795

Wells, Warre Bradley: Why Edward Went: Crown, Clique and Church, 477; John Redmond: A Biography, 1514, 3016

Welsby, Paul A.: A History of the Church of England 1945–1980, 11602

Welsch, Friedrich: ed. Britische Europaideen 1940–1970: Eine Bibliographie, 14119

Welsh Agricultural Statistics: 1979+, 19628

Welsh College of Advanced Technology: Occupational Survey of Manufacturing Industries in Wales Reports, 5338; Occupational Survey of Manufacturing Industries in Wales. Report 2: Survey of Chemical and Allied Industries in Wales as at April 1962, 6223

Welsh Highland Light Railway: More about the Welsh Highland Light Railway, 16985

Welsh Historical Review: 1960–, 2591

Welsh Office: A New Town in Mid-Wales: Consultants' Proposals, 18265

Welsh Water Authority: (Dee Working Party) Report of the Dee Working Party on Actions Required and Taken Following the Pollution Incident Affecting the River Dee and Water Supplies, January 1984, 20089

Welsh, Frank: Uneasy City: An Insider's View of the City of London, 4289

Welsh, L.: ed. Royal Commission on Local Government: Evidence in Brief: Summaries of Evidence to the Commission and other Material on the Subject Published in the Local Government Chronicle, 3172

Welton, Harry: The Necessary Conflict: A Commonsense View of Industrial Relations, 5655; The Trade Unions, the Employers and the State, 6868

Welwyn Associaton: Welwyn Garden City: Its Meaning and Methods, 18207

Wendt, Paul Francis: Housing Policy: The Search for Solutions: A Comparison of the United Kingdom, Sweden, West Germany and the United States since World War II, 18664; 'Six English New Towns: A Financial Analysis', 19006

Wenger, Gwynifer Clare: Mid-Wales: Deprivation or Development: A Study of Patterns of Employment in Selected Communities, 5358

Werbner, Prima: 'Avoiding the Ghetto: Pakistani Migrants and Settlement Shifts in Manchester', 11232, 11462; 'From Rags to Riches: Manchester Pakistanis in the Textile Trade', 11233

Wersey, Paul Gary: 'The Perennial Dilemma of Science Policy', 7109; 'Haldane and Huxley: First Appraisals', 26504

Wesley-Smith, Peter: Unequal Treaty, 1897–1997: China, Great Britain and Hong Kong's New Territories, 13640

West, Sir Algernon: Contemporary Portraits, 324

West, Antony: John Piper, 24052

West, Clarence J.: Bibliography of Pulp and Paper Making, 1900–1928, 6622

West, Donald James: The Habitual Prisoner, 10461; ed. The Future of Parole: Commentaries on Systems in Britain and the USA, 10492; 'The Persistence of Labelling Effects', 10590; Present Conduct and Future Delinquency: First Report of the Cambridge Study in Delinquent Development, 10610; Who Becomes Delinquent?: Second Report of the Cambridge Study in Delinquent Development, 10611; The Delinquent Way of Life: Third Report of the Cambridge Study in Delinquent Development, 10612; The Young Offender, 10616; The Habitual Offender, 10617; Murder Followed by Suicide: An Inquiry, 10792; Homosexuality, 10855; Homosexuality Re-examined, 10856

West, Edwin George: Education and the State: A Study in Political Economy, 22661; Economics, Education and the Politician, 23203

West, Francis: Gilbert Murray: A Life, 26569

West, Frank H.: F.R.B.: A Portrait of Bishop Russell Barry, 11719

West, Lesley A.: 'An Agricultural Machinery Museum', 19678

West, Nigel: MI5: British Security Operations, 1909–45, 15088; The Friends: Britain's Post-War Intelligence Operations, 16004; A Matter of Trust: MI5 1945–72, 16014; GCHQ: The Secret Wireless War 1900–1986, 16020

West, Rebecca: The Meaning of Treason, 2020

West, Richard: The Making of the Prime Minister, 964

West, Thomas: Ted Hughes, 25582

West, Trevor: Horace Plunkett: Co-operation and Politics, 3071

West, William Alexander: Housing Market Analyses and Policy, 18446; The Concise Law of Housing, 18568; The Law of Housing: 3rd edn by Keith Davies, 18569

West, William Morris Schumm: To be a Pilgrim: A Memoir of Ernest A. Payne, 12029

Westall, Oliver M.: ed. The Historian and the Business of Insurance, 4238

Westaway, John: A Social Atlas of London, 18338

Westby, Selmer: Christopher Isherwood: A Bibliography 1923–1967, 25592

Wester Wemyss, Lady Victoria: Life and Letters of Lord Wester Wemyss G.C.B., C.M.G., M.V.O. Admiral of the Fleet, 15282

Wester-Wemyss, R. E.: The Navy in the Dardanelles Campaign, 14555

Westergaard, John Harald: ed. Modern British Society: A Bibliography, 394, 7526; 'The Trend of Class Differentials in Educational Opportunity in England and Wales', 9479; Class in a Capitalist Society: A Study of Contemporary Britain, 9568; 'Journeys to Work in the London Region', 16277; London's Housing Needs: Statements of Evidence to the Committee on Housing in Greater London, 18672; 'Land Use Planning since 1951: The Legislative and Administrative Framework in England and Wales', 20299; 'The Trend of Class Differentials in Educational Opportunity in England and Wales', 22815

Western, S. C.: 'Community College and School', 23228

Westmacott, Richard: New Agricultural Landscapes: Report of a Study Undertaken on behalf of the Countryside Commission during 1972, 19560

Westminster: Westminster, 23083; Westminster School, 23084

Westoby, Adam: Social Scientists at Work, 7943

Weston, Corinne Comstock: British Constitutional History since 1832, 599

Westover, Belinda: A Hidden Workforce: Women Homeworkers in Britain, 1850–1985, 7643; ed. Our Work, Our Lives, Our Words, 7646

Westrup, Sir Jack: Collins Encyclopaedia of Music, 24262

Westwood, John: Railways at War, 16757

Wethered, Herbert Newton: A Short History of Gardens, 19864

Wetten, Desmond: The Decline of British Seapower, 15242

Weybright, Victor: The Making of a Publisher: A Life in the 20th Century Book Revolution, 24939

Weyman, Anne: ed. Modern British Society: A Bibliography, 394

Weymouth, Anthony: This Century of Change, 1853–1952, 348; Through the Leper Squint: A Study of Leprosy from Pre-Christian Times to the Present Day, 22364

Whale, Derek: The Liners of Liverpool, 16586

Whale, John Hilary: The Half-Shut Eye: Television and Politics in Britain and America, 24892

Whalley, Anne: Racial Minorities and Public Housing, 11495, 18749

Whalley-Kelly, Joseph Herbert: 'Ich dien': The Prince of Wales's Volunteers (South Lancashire) 1914–1934, 15684

Whates, Harold Richard Grant: The Birmingham Post, 1857–1957, 25128

Wheare, Sir Kenneth Clinton: Government by Committee: an Essay on the British

Constitution, 579; The Civil Service in the Constitution, 895

Wheatcroft, Andrew: War, Economy and the Military Mind, 14699; Dolin: Friends and Memories, 24228

Wheatcroft, George Shorrock Ashcombe: The Education and Training of the Modern Lawyer: An Inaugural Lecture, 22429

Wheatcroft, Mildred: The Revolution in British Management Education, 9793

Wheatcroft, Stephen: Air Transport Policy, 17642

Wheatley, David Ernest: Apprenticeships in the United Kingdom, 5960

Wheatley, Dennis: The Deception Planners, 15096

Wheeler, A. C.: The Tidal Thames: The History of the River and its Fishes, 20096

Wheeler, Allen Henry: That Nothing Failed Them: Testing Aeroplanes in War, 15839; Flying between the Wars, 15895

Wheeler, B.: The Characteristics of London's Households, 18676

Wheeler, Gerald E.: 'Isolated Japan: Anglo-American Diplomatic Cooperation, 1927–1936', 14025

Wheeler, Gordon: 'Catholics and the Universities', 22893

Wheeler, Mark C.: Britain and the War for Yugoslavia, 1940–1943, 15182

Wheeler, Philip Theodore: The Study and Use of British Woodlands: Conference Proceedings, University of Nottingham, 19754

Wheeler-Bennett, Joan: Women at the Top: Achievement and Family Life, 7806

Wheeler-Bennett, Sir John Wheeler: King George VI: His Life and Reign, 503; ed. Action this Day: Working with Churchill, 988; John Anderson, Viscount Waverley, 1069; Munich: Prologue to Tragedy, 13738; Friends, Enemies and Sovereigns 26827; Knaves, Fools, and Heroes in Europe between the Wars, 26827

Whelan, Joseph P.: The Spirituality of Friedrich von Hügel, 11983

Whelpley, James Davenport: British-American Relations, 14018

Whetham, Edith Holt: A Record of Agricultural Policy 1947–1952, 1952–1954; 1954–1956; 1956–1958; 1958–1960, 19394; The Agrarian History of England and Wales, vol. 8. 1914–1939, 19412; 'The Agriculture Act 1920 and its Repeal: The "Great Betrayal"', 19434; British Farming 1939–1949, 19470; Beef Cattle and Sheep, 1910–1940: A Description of the Production and Marketing of Beef Cattle and Sheep in Great Britain from the Early 20th Century to the Second World War, 19471; The Economic Background to Agriculture Policy, 19472; Agricultural Economists in Britain 1900–1940, 19578; 'The Mechanisation of British Farming, 1910–1945', 19687; The London Milk Trade, 1900–1930, 20650

Whetstone, Linda: The Marketing of Milk: An Empirical Study of the Origins, Performance and Future of the Milk Marketing Board, 20659

Whillans, Donald: Don Whillans: Portrait of a Mountaineer, 27246

Whincup, Michael Hynes: Legal Rights and Duties in Medical and Nursing Service, 21726

Whistler, Laurence: The Work of Rex Whistler, 24082; The Laughter and the Urn: A Biography of Rex Whistler, 24083; The Image on the Glass, 24127

Whitaker's Almanac: 1868+, 264

Whitaker's Books of the Month and Books to Come: 1970–, 8

Whitaker's Cumulative Book List: 1924–, 7

Whitaker, Benjamin Charles George: A Bridge of People: A Personal View of Oxfam's First Forty Years, 9194; The Foundations: An Anatomy of Philanthropy and Society, 9195; Crime and Society, 10138; The Police, 10693; Parks for People, 27003

Whitaker, C. S.: The Politics of Tradition: Continuity and Change in Northern Nigeria 1946–1966, 12757

Whitaker, David J.: Fighter for Peace: Philip Noel-Baker, 1889–1982, 1495

Whitaker, Graham: 'The Education of Immigrant Pupils in Inner London Primary Schools', 11449

Whitaker, John K. Jnr.: 'The Profitability of British and American Industry', 3722; 'The Floating Pound Sterling of the Nineteen Thirties', 4686

Whitaker, Thomas R.: Tom Stoppard, 25987

Whitbread and Company: Whitbread's Brewery: Incorporating the Brewer's Art, 6155

Whitbread, Michael: Evaluation in the Planning Process, 17955

Whitbread, Nanette: The Evolution of the Nursery-infant School: A History of Infant and Nursery Education in Great Britain, 1800–1970, 23128

Whitby, Martin: Rural Employment: Trends, Opinions and Choices, 19079

White, A. C. T.: The Story of Army Education 1643–1963, 23689

White, A. S.: A Bibliography of Regimental Histories of the British Army, 15539

White, Andrew: Jaguar: The History of a Great British Car, 17455

White, Archie Cecil Thomas: The Story of Army Education, 1643–1963, 15776, 23689

White, Barry: John Hume: Statesman of the Troubles, 3089

White, Brenda: The Literature and Study of Urban and Regional Planning, 17717

White, Brian Terence: British Armoured Cars, 1914–1945, 15494; British Tanks, 1915–1945, 15536

White, Cynthia Leslie: Women's Magazines, 1693–1968, 25191; The Women's Periodical Press in Britain, 1946–1976, 25192

White, E. Barton: Abstract of a Report on the Mental Division of the Welsh Metropolitan War Hospital, Whitchurch, Cardiff, Sept, 21741

White, E. W.: British Fishing Boats and Coastal Craft, 16598

White, Eric Walter: The Arts Council in Great Britain, 23762; Benjamin Britten: His Life and Operas, 24309; Tippett and his Operas, 24372; A History of English Opera, 24553; The Rise of English Opera, 24554; 'A Decade of English Opera, 1951–60', 24555; 'A Further Decade of English Opera, 1961–70', 24556

White, G. W.: A Half-Century of Cornish Methodism, 1925–1975, 12112

White, Gavin Donald: 'The Hectic Night: The Prayer Book Debate, 1927 and 1928', 11623; '"No-one is Free from Parliament": The Worship and Doctrine Measure in Parliament 1974', 11624; 'The Fall of France', 11867; 'Whose are the Tiends? The Scottish Union of 1929', 12205; 'Ideals in Urban Mission: Episcopalians in Twentieth-Century Glasgow', 12267

White, Gilbert F.: ed. Environmental Issues, 19989

White, Henry Patrick: Transport in the United Kingdom, 16196; Transport Geography, 16197; Southern England, 16810; Greater London, 16811; ed. The Continuing Conurbation: Change and Development in Greater Manchester, 18059

White, I. D.: A Historical Geography of Scotland, 2449

White, I. E.: Tenement Town, 18459

White, J. Lincoln: The Abdication of Edward VIII: A Record with all the Published Documents, 492

White, Jeremy: Central Administration in Nigeria 1914–1948: The Problem of Polarity, 12760

White, Joan W.: ed. Twentieth-Century Dance in Britain: A History of Major Dance Companies in Britain, 24207

White, John: Philosophers as Educational Reformers: The Influence of Idealism on British Educational Thought and Practice, 23241

White, Joyce Marian: English Canals, 16392

White, L. D.: Whitley Councils in the British Civil Service, 879

White, Leonard Edward: Community or Chaos: Housing Estates and their Social Problems, 9330; Small Towns: Their Social and Community Problems, 9331; New Towns: Their Challenge and Opportunity, 9332, 18985; Harlow: A Story of a New Town, 18195; New Towns: Their Challenge and Opportunity, 18985

White, Leslie William: Industrial and Social Revolution, 1750–1937, 3401

White, M. J. D.: 'The Infinite Variety of Haldane', 26505

White, Molly O'Loughlin: Belfast: The Story of Short's Big Lifter, 17616

White, Mulvey Mina: Digging up Adam: The Story of L. S. B. Leakey, 26362

White, Peter R.: Public Transport: Its Management and Operation, 16262

White, R. L.: 'The Spatial Evolution of an Industry: The Example of Broiler Production', 20679

White, Reginald James: ed. The Conservative Tradition, 2182

White, Roderick: Advertising: What It Is and How to Do It, 4330

White, Rosemary: Social Change and the Development of the Nursing Profession: A

Study of the Poor Law Nursing Service, 1848–1948, 21723

White, Stephen Leonard: The Origins of Detente: The Genoa Conference and Soviet-Western Relations, 1921–1922, 13651; Britain and the Bolshevik Revolution: A Study in the Politics of Diplomacy, 1920–1924, 13926; '"Anti-Bolshevik Control Officers" and British Foreign Policy, 1918–1920', 13927

White, Terence de Vere: Kevin O'Higgins, 3064

White, Thomas Anthony Blanco: Patents for Inventions and the Registration of Industrial Designs, 5013

White, Valerie: Wimpey: The First Hundred Years, 6183; Balfour Beattie, 1909–1984, 6184

White, William C.: 'Evolution of Electronics', 7114

Whitehead, A. P.: ed. The 1st Battalion Tyneside Scottish, The Black Watch-Royal Highland Regiment, 15570

Whitehead, Alan: The Midland in the 1930s, 16896

Whitehead, J. W. R.: 'The Settlement Morphology of London's Cocktail Belt', 18313

Whitehead, John Anthony: In the Service of Old Age: The Welfare of Psychogeriatric Patients, 8599

Whitehead, Kate: The Third Programme, 24775

Whitehead, Kenneth: History of the Somerset Light Infantry (Prince Albert's), 1946–1960, 15720

Whitehead, Peter Arthur: Wallis and Stevens, 17094

Whitehead, Trevor: Fire Engines, 17481

Whitehouse, Arthur George Joseph: Subs and Submariners, 15378; Tank: The Battles they Fought, and the Men who Drove them-from Flanders to Korea, 15537; The Military Aeroplane: Its History and Development, 17559

Whitehouse, Mary: Cleaning-up T.V.: From Protest to Participation, 24837; Who Does She Think She Is?, 24838

Whitehouse, Patrick Bruce: The Illustrated History of Britain's Railways, 16731; The Great Days of the County Railway, 16748; ed. Britain's Main Line Railways, 16785; The Great Western Railway: 150 Glorious Years, 16860; L.M.S. 150: The London, Midland and Scottish Railway: A Century and a Half of Progress, 16878; The London Midland and Scottish in the West Midlands, 16879

Whiteland, J. W. R.: ed. The Urban Landscape: Historical Development and Management, 20314

Whitelaw, William Stephen Ian [Lord]: The Whitelaw Memoirs, 1331

Whiteley, Charles Henry: The Permissive Morality, 12392

Whiteley, Denys Edward Hugh: ed. Sociology, Theology and Conflict, 7906

Whiteley, Gerald: 'The British Experience with Peacetime Conscription', 16073

Whiteley, John Stuart: The Big Four Remembered, 16840; The Southern Remembered, 16913

Whiteley, Paul: The Labour Party in Crisis, 1801; 'Social Class and Political Attitudes: The Case of Labour Councillors', 1802; Pressure for the Poor: The Poverty Lobby and Policy Making, 9113

Whiteley, Stuart: Dealing with Delinquents, 10597

Whiteley, Winifred Mary: The Permissive Morality, 12392; The Uneducated English, 22577

Whiteside, Noel: Casual Labour: The Unemployment Question in the Port Transport Industry 1880–1970, 7018

Whitestone, Nicholas: The Submarine: The Ultimate Weapon, 15373

Whitfield, George: 'The Grammar Schools through Half a Century', 22984

Whitford, Frank: Eduardo Paolozzi, 24204

Whiting, Charles: Battle of the Ruhr Pocket, 14974

Whiting, Charles Edwin: The University of Durham, 1832–1932, 23491

Whiting, Desmond Percival: Finance of Foreign Trade and Foreign Exchange, 4783; The Finance of Foreign Trade, 4823

Whiting, John: On Theatre, 26175

Whiting, R. C.: The View from Cowley: The Impact of Industrialisation upon Oxford, 1918–1939, 5214

Whitley, Henry Charles: Laughter in Heaven, 12226

Whitley, Oliver John: Broadcasting and the National Culture, 24776

Whitley, Richard D.: 'The Operation of Science Journals: Two Case Studies in British Social Science', 7132, 7900; 'Communication Nets in Science: Status and Citation Patterns in Animal Physiology', 7133; ed. Social Processes of Scientific Development, 7899

Whitley, William Thomas: A History of British Baptists, 12021; Calvinism and Evangelism in England, Especially in Baptist Circles, 12026

Whitlock, Ralph: A Short History of Farming in Britain, 19407; Royal Farmers, 19408; Farming in History, 19409; Historic Forests of England, 19720; 'Conservation by Design: An Exercise in Rural Co-operation', 20391

Whitmore, Kingsley: The Contribution of Child Guidance to the Community, 8403; Education, Health and Behaviour, 22841

Whitney, Charles E.: Discovering the Cinque Ports, 16677

Whitney, Owen: The Family and Marriage in a Changing World, 9969

Whitney, Vincent Heath: Atomic Power: An Economic and Social Analysis: A Study in Industrial Location and Regional Economic Development, 6662

Whitrow, Gerald James: 'The Limits of the Physical Universe', 7115; 'An Analysis of the Evolution of Scientific Method', 7116; 'Is the Physical Universe a Self-contained System?', 7117; The Structure of the Universe: An Introduction to Cosmology, 26441; The Structure and Evolution of the Universe, 26442; What Is Time?, 26443; Time, Gravitation and the Universe: The Evolution of Relativistic Theories, 26444

Whitson, Colin: Government and the Chemical Industry: A Comparative Study of Britain and West Germany, 6227

Whittaker, Sir Edmund Taylor: 'Chance, Freewill and Necessity in the Scientific Conception of the Universe', 7118; The Beginning and End of the World, 26445

Whittall, Arnold: The Music of Britten and Tippett: Studies in Theme and Technique, 24313

Whittam, Ronald: General Physiology and the Biological Sciences; An Inaugural Lecture, 21044

Whittard, W. F.: ed. Bristol and its Adjoining Counties, 18016

Whitteridge, Gweneth: The Royal Hospital of St Bartholomew: A Short History, 22473

Whittick, Arnold: The New Towns: The Answer to Megalopolis, 17755, 18217, 18991; Town and Country Planning, 17756; ed. Garden Cities of Tomorrow, 17757; New Towns: Their Origins, Achievements and Progress, 18992

Whittingham, Terence George: British Industrial Relations: An Annotated Bibliography, 5567; 'Proposals for Change in the British System of Industrial Relations: An Evaluation', 5733

Whittington, Geoffrey: 'Giant Companies in the United Kingdom, 1948–1969', 5532

Whittington, Graeme: A Historical Geography of Scotland, 2449

Whittle, Frank: Jet, the Story of a Pioneer, 17560

Whittle, Peter: Dark Blue for Courage: With Contributory Articles by . . . Kelwyn Cosway and others, 10709; Angels without Wings: The Dramatic Inside Stories of the R.A.F. Search and Rescue Squadrons, 15913

Whitton, Alan M.: Welsh Bus Handbook, 17316

Whitton, Frederick Ernest: The Marne Campaign, 14576

Whittow, John Byron: ed. Essays in Geography for Austin Miller, 26664

Whitworth, Geoffrey Arundel: The Making of a National Theatre, 26135

Whitworth, Reginald Henry: The Grenadier Guards, 15644

Whitworth, Thomas Anthony: Yellow Sandstone and Mellow Brick: An Account of Hatfield College, Durham, 1846–1971, 23492

Who Was Who in Theatre, 1912–1976, 25998

Who Was Who: 1897–1915, 24; 1916–1928, 25; 1929–1940, 26; 1941–1950, 27; 1951–1960, 28; 1961–1970, 29; 1971–1980, 30; A Cumulated Index, 1897–1980, 31

Who's Who in Local Government 1984/5, 3104

Who's Who: 1897, 23

Whybrow, Robert J.: The Gallup Survey of Britain, 231; Britain Speaks Out, 1937–1987: A Social History as Seen through Gallup Data, 232

Whyman, John: A Short Economic and Social History of Twentieth Century Britain, 386

Whymant, Robert: *ed.* Industry as Seen by Immigrant Workers: A Summary of Research Findings from a Textile Mill, 11418

Whyte, Ian D.: The Historical Geography of Rural Settlement in Scotland: A Review, 19240

Whyte, Ian D. *and* Whyte, K. A.: Sources for Scottish Historical Geography: An Introductory Guide, 18123

Whyte, Sir William Edward: The Law of Housing in Scotland, 18460; Scotland's Housing and Planning Problems, 18464; Planning For Scotland, 18465; (a): 'The Coming of the New Public Health Era' (b): The National Aspect of Public Health', 21288

Whyte, William Hamilton: Decasualization of Dock Labour, with Special Reference to the Port of Bristol, 7239

Wibberley, Gerald Percy: Second Homes in England and Wales: A Study of the Distribution of Rural Properties Taken Over as Second Homes, 18374; The Changing Rural Economy of Britain, 19090; 'Some Aspects of Problem Rural Areas in Britain', 19091; Agriculture and Urban Growth: A Study of the Competition for Rural Land, 19502; Outdoor Recreation in the British Countryside, 26952

Wiborg, Frank B.: Printing Ink: A History with a Treatise on Modern Methods of Manufacture and Use, 6633

Wicken, Alan John: Report on a Study of Environmental Factors associated with Lung Cancer and Bronchitis Mortality on Areas of North East England, 20062; Environmental and Personal Factors in Lung Cancer and Bronchitis Mortality in Northern Ireland, 1960–1962, 21967

Wickenden, James: Colour in Britain, 10912

Wicker, Brian: 'The New Left: Christians and Agnostics', 11891; 'Atheism and the Avant-Garde', 11892

Wickes, George: *ed.* Lawrence Durrell and Henry Miller: A Private Correspondence, 25486

Wickes, Henry Leonard: Regiments of Foot: A Historical Record of all the Foot Regiments of the British Army, 15540

Wickham, Edward Ralph: Church and People in an Industrial City, 11613

Wickham, Glynne: 'The Study of Drama in the British Universities, 1945–1966', 26256

Wickie, James: Across the Great Divide, 27091

Wickramsinghe, Chandra: Lifecloud: The Origin of Life in the Universe, 26388

Wicks, H. W.: The Prisoner Speaks, 10432

Wicks, Malcolm: Old and Cold: Hypothermia and Social Policy, 8620; Rented Housing and Social Ownership, 18424

Wickstead, A.: Lincolnshire, Lindsey: The Story of the County Council 1889–1974, 3362

Wickstead, J. H.: The Growth of a Profession: The Chartered Society of Psychotherapy, 1894–1945, 20774

Widdess, John David Henry: A History of the Royal College of Physicians of Ireland, 1654–1963, 20775; The Royal College of Surgeons in Ireland and its Medical School, 1784–1966, 20776

Widdowson, Elsie Amy: Breads, White and Brown: Their Place in Thought and Social History, 20702

Widdowson, John: Wordmaps: A Dialect Atlas of England, 23793; Studies in Linguistic Geography: The Dialects of English in Britain and Ireland, 23794

Widem, P.: 'Social Casework in a British Day Hospital', 8684

Widgery, David: The Left in Britain, 1956–68, 1999

Widlake, Brian: In the City, 4288

Wiegand, W. A.: 'British Propaganda in American Public Libraries 1914–1917', 15216

Wieland, George Fred: *ed.* Changing Hospitals: A Report on the Hospital Internal Communications Project, 21355; *ed.* Standards for Morale: Cause and Effect in Hospitals, 21356

Wiender, R. S. P.: Drugs and Schoolchildren, 10579

Wiener, Joel H.: *ed.* Great Britain: Foreign Policy and the Span of Empire, 1689–1971: A Documentary History, 12485

Wiener, Martin J.: Between Two Worlds: The Political Thought of Graham Wallas, 2092; English Culture and the Decline of the Industrial Spirit, 1850–1980, 5416

Wiener, R. S. P.: 'The Administration and Evaluation of Research Units and Projects', 8789

Wigg, George [Baron]: George Wigg, 1332

Wigham, Eric Leonard: The Power to Manage: A History of the Engineering Employers Federation, 5494; Trade Unions, 6694; Strikes and the Government, 1893–1974, 6923; What's Wrong with the Unions?, 6924; Trade Unions, 6925

Wight, Martin: The Development of the Legislative Council, 1606–1945, 12472; 'Is the Commonwealth a Non-Hobbesian Institution?', 12524; The Gold Coast Legislative Council, 12744

Wightman, William Persehouse Delisle: 'Presidential Address: The Tyranny of Abstractions', 7119; The Emergence of Scientific Medicine, 21213; The Emergence of General Physiology, 22336

Wigley, Philip G.: 'Defining the First British Commonwealth: The Hankey Memorandum and the 1926 Imperial Conference', 12535; Canada and the Transition to Commonwealth: British-Canadian Relations, 1917–1926, 12648

Wilbraham, Anne: The Englishman's Food: A History of Five Centuries of English Diet, 20573

Wilcocks, Arthur John: Focus on Nurse Recruitment: A Snapshot from the Provinces, 21715

Wilcocks, Charles: Medical Advance, Public Health and Social Evolution, 22104

Wilcox, A. F.: 'Police 1964–1973', 10702

Wilcox, David: London: The Heartless City, 18333

Wilcox, Herbert: 'British Films, Past and Future', 24690

Wilcox, Michael: The Confederation of British Industry Predecessor Archive, 5491

Wild, Raymond: 'The Job Expectations of Immigrant Workers', 11419

Wildavsky, Aaron: The Private Government of Public Money, 808, 5528

Wilding, Norman William: An Encyclopedia of Parliament, 555

Wilding, Paul: 'Stereotypes of Male and Female Roles and their Influence on People's attitudes to One Parent Families', 7871; Ideology and Social Welfare, 8797; Motherless Families, 9942

Wildsmith, Osmond: A History of Wolverhampton Transport, 16353

Wiles, Paul: *ed.* Modern British Society: A Bibliography, 394; *ed.* Delinquency in Britain: Sociological Readings, 10266; The Sociology of Crime and Delinquency in Britain, 10267; Crime and Delinquency in Britain: Sociological Readings, 10622; Later edn: The Sociology of Crime and Delinquency in Britain, 10623; The Security Industry in the United Kingdom, 10883

Wilford, R.: The Welsh Veto: The Wales Act 1978 and the Referendum, 2577

Wiliam, Eurwyn: Home-made Homes: Dwellings of the Rural Poor in Wales, 19296; The Historical Farm Buildings of Wales, 19709

Wilkes, Peter: An Illustrated History of Traction Engines, 17089; An Illustrated History of Farming, 19413

Wilkie, Elaine: A History of the Council for the Education and Training of Health Visitors: An Account of its Establishment and Field of Activities, 1962–1975, 21735

Wilkie, Roy: 'The Ends of Industrial Sociology', 5652

Wilkins, A. F.: 'The Story of Radar', 7120

Wilkins, E. T.: 'Air Pollution Aspects of the London Fog of December 1952', 20038

Wilkins, Frances: Transport and Travel from 1930 to the 1980s, 16195

Wilkins, Harold Tom: Great English Schools, 23006

Wilkins, J.: 'The English Catholic Press', 11966

Wilkins, Leslie Thomas: The Adolescents in Britain, 8495; Consumerist Criminology, 10242; The Evaluation of Penal Measures, 10450; Probation and Parole: Selected Readings, 10494; Prediction Methods in Relation to Borstal Training, 10552; Delinquent Generations: Studies in the Causes of Delinquency and the Treatment of Offenders, 10567; Delinquent Generations, 10663; 'A Behavioural Theory of Drug Taking', 10838

Wilkins, Sir George Hubert: Flying the Arctic, 27182; Undiscovered Australia, 27183; Under the North Pole, 27184; Thoughts through Space, 27185

Wilkins, Warwick: Changes in Family Building Plans: A Follow up Study to 'How Many Children?', 9928

Wilkins-Jones, C.: *ed.* Centenary: A Hundred Years of County Government in Norfolk 1889–1989, 3364

Wilkinson, Alan G.: The Drawings of Henry Moore, 24042

Wilkinson, Alan: Dissent or Conform? War, Peace and the English Churches 1900–1945, 11851; The Church of England and the First World War, 11852

Wilkinson, Audine C.: 'The Road to Independence: Antigua and Barbuda: A Select Bibliography', 13058

Wilkinson, Ellen: The Town that Was Murdered: The Life-story of Jarrow, 18110

Wilkinson, Geoffrey: The IRC: An Experiment in Industrial Intervention, 4977

Wilkinson, George Stephen: Legal Aspects of Illegitimacy, 8399

Wilkinson, Henry Robert: Kingston-upon-Hull and Haltemprice: Social Area Analysis, 18024

Wilkinson, John Donald: ed. Catholic Anglicans Today, 11651

Wilkinson, John Thomas: 1662—and After: Three Centuries of English Nonconformity, 12002; Arthur Samuel Peake, 12093

Wilkinson, Lancelot Patrick: Bulmers of Hereford: A Century of Cider-Making, 6172, 20750; A Century of King's, 1873–1972, 23480; Kingsmen of a Century: 1873–1972, 23481

Wilkinson, Lise: An Introduction to the History of Virology, 22341; 'The Development of the Virus Concept as Reflected in Corpora of Studies on Individual Pathogens', 22342

Wilkinson, Mike: Regional Reports and Structure Plans in Scotland, 20289

Wilkinson, Paul: 'The Provisional I.R.A.: An Assessment in the Wake of the 1981 Hunger Strike', 2890; 'English Youth Movements, 1908–30', 8433

Wilkinson, Ronald K.: 'Differences in Earnings and the Distribution of Manpower in the U.K., 1948–1957', 3872; 'A Statistical Analysis of Attitudes to Moving: A Survey of Slum Clearances in Leeds', 9424, 18030, 18414; 'Rebuilding or Renovation?', 18527; 'The Finance of Improvements: A Study of Low Quality Housing in Three Yorkshire Towns', 18528; 'Determinants of Relative House Prices: A Case of Academic Astigmatism?', 18532; The Grand Theatre and Opera House Leeds, 1878–1978. First Hundred Years, 26167

Wilkinson, Rupert Hugh: Gentlemanly Power: British Leadership and the Public School Tradition: A Comparative Study in the Making of Rulers, 682; The Prefects: British Leadership and the Public School Tradition: A Comprehensive Study in the Making of Rulers, 9761; Governing Elites: Studies in Training and Selection, 9762; 'The Future of the Public Schools: A Reply', 23034; The Prefects: British Leadership and the Public School Tradition: A Comparative Study in the Making of Rulers, 23039; Winchester and the Public School Elite: A Statistical Analysis, 23086

Wilkinson-Latham, C.: The Royal Green Jackets, 15714; The South Wales Borderers, 15754

Wilkinson-Latham, John: British Cut and Thrust Weapons, 15497

Wilks, Stephen: Industrial Policy and the Motor Industry, 17403

Willats, E. C.: 'The Geographical Pattern of Population Changes in England and Wales, 1921–1951', 7299

Willatt, Sir Robert Hugh: The Arts Council of Great Britain: The First Twenty-five Years, 23758

Willcocks, Arthur John: 'A Survey of Social Research into the National Health Service', 21325; The Creation of the National Health Service: A Study of Pressure Groups and a Major Policy Decision, 21602

Willcocks, Diane M.: Private Lives in Public Places: A Research Based Critique of Residential Life in Local Authority Old People's Homes, 8639

Willcox, Philip H. A.: The Detective-Physician: The Life and Work of Sir William Willcox, 20908

Willcox, W. H. Temple: 'Projection or Publicity? Rival Concepts in the Pre-war Planning of the British Ministry of Information', 835

Willcox, Walter Temple: The 3rd (King's Own) Hussars in the Great War, 1914–1919, 15656

Willert, Sir Arthur: Aspects of British Foreign Policy, 13208; The Frontiers of England, 13209; Washington and other Memories, 13319

Willett, Shelagh M.: Lesotho, 12711

Willett, Terence Charles: Criminals on the Road: A Study of Serious Motoring Offences and those who commit them, 10234; Drivers after Sentence, 10235; The Motoring Offender: A Study of Serious Motoring Offenders and Offences in an English Police District, 17123

Willetts, Phoebe: Invisible Bars, 10219

Willey, Frederick Thomas [Baron]: An Enquiry into Teacher Training, 22732

William, Paul: Fairness, Collective Bargaining and Incomes Policy, 5822

Williams, Alan Lee: The Rise of the Social Democratic Party, 1853; Labour's Decline and the Social Democrats' Fall, 1854

Williams, Alan: Output Budgeting and the Contribution of Microeconomics to Efficiency in Government, 812; Current Issues in Cost-Benefit Analysis, 4767; Public Finance and Budget Policy, 4915; Efficiency in the Social Services, 8950

Williams, Allan: Rural Britain: A Social Geography, 19032

Williams, Alwyn Terrell Petre: The Anglican Tradition in the Life of England, 11574

Williams, Ann: Britain and France in the Middle East and North Africa, 1914–1967, 13833

Williams, Barrie: The Franciscan Revival in the Anglican Communion, 11668

Williams, Bruce E.: 'Government Scientific Policy and the Growth of the British Economy', 3640

Williams, C. Glyn: 'A Model of Collective Bargaining for U.K. and U.S. Manufacturing: A Comparative Study', 5804

Williams, Colin H.: 'Cultural Nationalism in Wales', 2604; National Separatism, 2605; 'Language Contact and Language Change

in Wales, 1901–1971: A Study in Historical Geolinguistics', 23828; 'Non-Violence and the Development of the Welsh Language Society, 1962–c.1974', 23829; 'Public Gain and Private Grief: The Rate of Language Loss among Welsh speakers between 1921 and 1981', 23830

Williams, D. Jeffrey: Capitalist Combination in the Coal Industry, 6256

Williams, D.: 'The Anatomy of a Crisis: Investment and Output in Britain 1958–1962', 4737

Williams, David Christopher: Locomotives of British Railways, 17063

Williams, David Glyndwr Tudor: 'Wales and Legislative Devolution', 2574; Keeping the Peace: The Police and Public Order, 10743; 'The Police and Law Enforcement', 10744

Williams, David Ivor: Experiments on Land Pollution, 20120

Williams, David Lloyd: Damned by Destiny: A Complete Account of all the World's Projects for Passenger Liners which never entered Service, 16585; Docks and Ports—I—Southampton, 16708

Williams, David: 'London and the 1931 Financial Crisis', 3570; 'Montagu Norman and Banking Policy in the 1920s', 4422

Williams, David: A History of Modern Wales, 1485–1939, 317, 2555

Williams, David: Not in the Public Interest, 763

Williams, David: Peter Brook: A Theatrical Casebook, 26122

Williams, David: Profit-sharing: Legal Aspects of Employee Share Schemes, 6035

Williams, Dorian: Horse of the Year: The Story of a Unique Horseshow, 27132

Williams, Dorothy Mary: Holyhead: The Story of a Port, 16690

Williams, E. G.: The Chester Society of Natural Science, 26530

Williams, E. T.: ed. The Dictionary of National Biography 6th Supplement [1941–1950], 17; ed. The Dictionary of National Biography 7th Supplement [1951–1960], 18; ed. The Dictionary of National Biography 8th Supplement [1961–1970], 19

Williams, Eddie: The Nutrition of Children, 20523; School Milk and Meals, 20524; School Dinners for all the World's Children, 20525

Williams, Emlyn: George: An Early Autobiography, 1905–1927, 25879, 26261; Emlyn: An Early Autobiography, 1927–1935, 26262

Williams, Eric: The Wooden Horse, 15047

Williams, Eric Eustace: Britain and the West Indies, 13015; History of the People of Trinidad and Tobago, 13066; Inward Hunger: The Education of a Prime Minister, 13072; ed. 'The Historical Background of the British West Indies Federation: Select Documents', 13092

Williams, Ernest Edwin: The New Public House, 20753

Williams, Francis, Baron Francis-Williams: A Pattern of Rulers, 960, 1568; A Prime Minister Remembers: The War and Post-war Memoirs of the Rt Hon Earl Attlee, Based on his Private Papers and on a Series of Recorded Conversations, 975; Fifty Years March: The Rise of the Labour Party, 1674; Magnificent Journey: The Rise of the Trade Unions, 6692; Dangerous Estate: The Anatomy of Newspapers, 25047; The Right to Know, 25060; Nothing so Strange, 25297; Journey into Adventure: The Story of the Workers Travel Association, 26990

Williams, Frank P.: Criminological Theory, 10147; No Fixed Address: Life on the Run for the Great Train Robbers, 10232

Williams, G. H.: Railways in Gwynedd, 16937

Williams, Gareth: George Ewart Evans, 26752; Fields of Praise: The Official History of the Welsh Rugby Union, 1881–1981, 27045

Williams, Gareth: The Academic Labour Market: Economic and Social Aspects of a Profession, 9837, 22545

Williams, Geoffrey Lee: Denis Healey and the Politics of Power, 1227; The Rise of the Social Democratic Party, 1853; Labour's Decline and the Social Democrats' Fall, 1854; Crisis in Procurement: A Case Study of the TSR-2, 15888

Williams, Lady Gertrude: Apprenticeship in Europe: The Lesson for Britain, 5956; The Changing Pattern of Women's Employment, 7695; The Marriage Rate and Women's Employment, 7696; ed. Caring for People: Staffing Residential Homes, 8853; The Price of Social Security, 8970; The Coming of the Welfare State, 8971

Williams, Gillian: ed. Controlling Women: The Normal and the Deviant, 7844

Williams, Glanmor: ed. Glamorgan County History 5: Industrial Glamorgan from 1700 to 1970, 3384

Williams, Glyn: Corporate Management and Financial Planning: The British Rail Experience, 16789

Williams, Glyn: ed. Social and Cultural Change in Contemporary Wales, 2589, 5328

Williams, Granville Llewellyn: Learning the Law, 22430

Williams, Sir Griffith: 'The First Ten Years of the Ministry of Education', 832

Williams, Guy Richard: London in the Country: The Growth of Suburbia, 18301; The Royal Parks of London, 19740

Williams, Gwylmor Prys: High Spirited Years: A Regional Analysis of Two Periods, 1954 to 1958 and 1961 to 1964, when Convictions for Drunkenness in England and Wales Rose and Fell to an Unusual Extent, 10879; Decade of Drunkenness: A Summary of Official Statistics of Pedestrian and Motorised Offences for the Ten Years before the Coming into Effect, from 1964 onwards, of Changes in the Licensing and Traffic Regulations, 10880; Drink in Great Britain, 1900 to 1979, 22140; Drink: Ups and Downs of Methodist Attitudes to Temperance, 22141; Chronic Alcoholics: A Report on the Incidence Apparent to Health Visitors and Probation Officers, 22144; Social Effects of Ending Resale Price Maintenance of Alcoholic Beverages, 1966

and 1967, England and Wales, 22145; Supermarket Off-Licences and the Growth of Drunkenness among Young Women and Young Persons since 1966, 22151

Williams, Gwyn Alfred: The Welsh in their History, 2552; 'Women Workers in Wales 1968–1982', 2553

Williams, Gwyndaf: Metropolitan Manchester: A Social Atlas, 18061

Williams, H. H.: ed. Liberal Points of View, 2167; ed. Liberalism and Some Problems of Today, 2168

Williams, Harcourt: ed. Vic-Wells: The Work of Lilian Baylis, 26113

Williams, Harley: 'The Morphology of State Medicine in Great Britain', 21025

Williams, Harry A.: Some Day I'll Find You: An Autobiography, 11822

Williams, Herbert: Railways in Wales, 16978

Williams, Howard: 'Three Types of Rural Welsh Community', 19295

Williams, Hubert Cecil Maurice: Public Health in a Seaport Town, 22105

Williams, Hugh Trevor: ed. Principles for British Agricultural Policy, 19503

Williams, Ioan: Emyr Humphreys, 25583

Williams, J. R.: 'The British General Election of 1951: Candidates and Parties', 2306

Williams, J. T.: ed. The Urban Road in Relation to the Conservation and Renewal of the Environment, 17129

Williams, Jac L.: 'Some Social Consequences of Grammar School Education in a Rural Area of Wales', 9470

Williams, James Eccles: The Derbyshire Miners: A Study in Industrial and Social History, 6902, 9649

Williams, James Geoffrey: Acquisitions and Mergers, 5544

Williams, Jennifer: Race, Community and Conflict: A Study of Sparkbrook, 11457

Williams, John: The Guns of Dakar: September 1940, 14821

Williams, John Hargreaves Harley: A Century of Public Health in Britain, 1832–1929, 22106

Williams, John Kyffin: Across the Straits: An Autobiography, 24084

Williams, John Lewis: Accidents and Ill-Health at Work, 4122

Williams, Karel: A Beveridge Reader, 9046; The Breakdown of Austin Rover: A Case-Study in the Failure of Business Strategies and Industrial Policy, 17427

Williams, Keith: Britons Awake! . . . Pt. 2. Straight Shooting, 11308

Williams, Lawrence John: Britain since 1945, 387; Britain and the World Economy, 1919–1970, 4802; 'Occupation in Wales, 1851–1971', 5344; ed. Modern South Wales: Essays in Economic History, 5380

Williams, Leonard Llewelyn Bulkeley: Middle Age and Old Age, 8556

Williams, Lincoln: Alcoholism Explained, 22147

Williams, M. E. W.: 'Choices in Oil Refining: The Case of BP, 1900–1960', 6522

Williams, M.: 'Britain and Rhodesia: The Economic Background to Sanctions', 12812

Williams, Marcia [Baroness Falkender]: Inside No. 10, 961

Williams, Maslyn: The Phosphaters: A History of the British Phosphate Commissioners and the Christmas Island Phosphate Commission, 12885

Williams, Michael: New Towns, 18995

Williams, Michael: The Venerable English College, Rome: A History 1539–1979, 11967

Williams, Morgan Watcyn: Creative Fellowship: An Outline of the History of Calvinistic Methodism in Wales, 12297

Williams, Neville: Royal Houses of Great Britain from Medieval to Modern Times, 455; The Royal Residences of Great Britain: A Social History, 456; A History of the Cayman Islands, 13047

Williams, P.: 'Building Societies and the Inner City', 4395

Williams, P.: 'Scarborough and Blackpool: An Analysis of some Votes at the Labour Party Conferences of 1960 and 1961', 1737

Williams, Penry Herbert: New College, Oxford, 1379–1979, 23569

Williams, Peter: 'The Government and Local Accountability since Layfield, 3265

Williams, Peter: A New History of the Organ from the Greeks to the Present Day, 24392

Williams, Peter: Not by Government Alone: The Role of British Non-Government Organisations in the Development Decade, 9180; Aid in the Commonwealth, 9181; ed. The Overseas Student Question: Studies for a Policy, 9882; 22573

Williams, Philip M.: Hugh Gaitskell, 1194; ed. Diary of Hugh Gaitskell, 1945–1956, 1195

Williams, Philip: The Practice of Educational Psychology, 22856

Williams, R. M.: 'Racial and Cultural Relations', 10905

Williams, R.: 'Administrative Modernisation in British Government', 866

Williams, R. R.: Defender of the Church of England: The Life of Bishop R. R. Williams, 11764

Williams, Raymond Henry: Culture and Society, 1780–1950, 323, 7590, 23724; 'Notes on Marxism in Britain since 1945', 2160; The Long Revolution, 9526, 23725; The Country and the City, 17852; Keywords: A Vocabulary of Culture and Society, 23723; 'The Press the People Want', 25048; Modern Tragedy, 26174; English Drama: Forms and Development: Essays in Honour of Muriel Clara Bradbrook, 26176; 'New English Drama', 26222

Williams, Robert: 'Unity of Command', 6808

Williams, Robert C.: Klaus Fuchs: Atom Spy, 16044

Williams, Robert Michael: British Population, 7393

Williams, Roger: The Nuclear Power Decisions: British Policies 1953–78, 6674

Williams, S.: 'Arts of a New Town', 20320

Williams, Sheila: 'The Growth of Trade Unionism in Banking, 1914–1927', 6890

Williams, Shirley: Politics is for People, 1334, 1837

Williams, Stephen: ed. 1939: The Communist Party of Great Britain and the War, 1931

Williams, Thomas Desmond: Ireland and the

War Years and After 1939–1951, 2705; *ed.* The Irish Struggle, 1916–1926, 2747; 'Negotiations Leading to the Anglo-Polish Agreement of 31 March 1939', 13898

Williams, Thomas Eifion Hopkins: Motorways in Urban Areas, 17112; *ed.* Urban Survival and Traffic: The Proceedings of a Symposium, 17124

Williams, Thomas George: The Main Currents of Social and Industrial Change 1870–1924, 3397

Williams, Thomas [Baron]: Digging for Britain, 1335

Williams, Trevor Illtyd: The Chemical Industry: Past and Present, 6209; A History of the British Gas Industry, 6400; A Biographical Dictionary of Scientists, 9810; Howard Florey: Penicillin and After, 22284

Williams, Val: Women Photographers: The Other Observers 1900 to the Present Day, 24713

Williams, W.: Population Problems of New Estates, with Special Reference to Norris Green, 9324

Williams, W. J.: The Smaller Firm and Technical Education, 23270; The Changing Pattern of Technical and Higher Education, 23271

Williams, W. M.: 'Mobility of General Practitioners during the First Few Years in General Practice', 9602

Williams, W. T.: *ed.* 'Science in Science Fiction', 7121

Williams, Sir William Emrys: Allen Lane: A Personal Portrait, 24987

Williams, William Morgan: *ed.* Occupational Choice: A Selection of Papers from the Sociological Review, 5902; Sociology, the Proper Study, 7977; The Country Craftsman: A Study of some Rural Crafts and the Rural Industries Organisation in England, 19094; A West Country Village, Ashworthy: Family, Kinship and Land, 19178; The Sociology of an English Village: Gosforth, 19189

Williams-Davies, John: Cider Making in Wales, 20749

Williams-Ellis, Sir Bertram Clough *and* Williams-Ellis, Mary Anabel Nassau: The Tank Corps, 15732; Architect Errant, 23875

Williamson, Arthur: *ed.* Violence and the Social Services in Northern Ireland, 2825, 8885

Williamson, Audrey May: Ballet of Three Decades, 24222; Old Vic Drama: A Twelve Years' Study of Plays and Players, 26144; Old Vic Drama 2, 1947–1957, 26145; Theatre of Two Decades, 26204; Contemporary Theatre, 1953–1956, 26205

Williamson, Bill: Class, Culture and Community: A Biographical Study of Social Change in Mining, 19216

Williamson, C.: 'Britain's New Colonial Policy, 1940–1951', 12560

Williamson, David G.: 'Cologne and the British', 13648; 'Great Britain and the Ruhr Crisis 1923–1924', 14245

Williamson, David: Lord Shaftesbury's Legacy: A Record of Eighty Years' Service by the Shaftesbury Society and Ragged School Union, 1824–1924, 8404; Ninety . . . not out: A Record of Ninety Years Child Welfare Work of the Shaftesbury Society and Ragged School Union, 8405

Williamson, Edward William: 'The Church in Wales', 12287

Williamson, Geoffrey: Inside Buchmanism: An Independent Inquiry into the Oxford Group Movement and Moral Rearmament, 12401

Williamson, George Scott: The Case for Action: A Survey of Everyday Life under Modern Industrial Conditions, with Special Reference to the Question of Health, 17713; Science, Synthesis and Sanity: An Inquiry into the Nature of Living, 17715

Williamson, Henry Raymond: British Baptists in China 1845–1952, 12368

Williamson, Hugh: Methods of Book Design: The Practice of an Industrial Craft, 25015

Williamson, Hugh: The Trade Unions, 6731

Williamson, J.: 'Threat of Racialism in Britain', 11163

Williamson, J. G.: 'British Mortality and the Value of Life 1781–1931', 7474

Williamson, John: A History of Morrison's Academy, Crieff, 23226

Williamson, John: The Financing Procedures of British Foreign Trade, 4808

Williamson, Joseph: Father Joe: The Autobiography of Joseph Williamson of Poplar and Stepney, 11823

Willings, David Richard: The Human Element in Management, 5482

Willink, Sir Henry: Report of the Committee to Consider the Future Numbers of Medical Practitioners and the Appropriate Intake of Medical Students, 20762

Willis, Carole: Race, Crime and Arrests, 10265

Willis, Eric: An Analysis of Industrial Change within the County Borough of Merthyr Tydfil, 1939–1969, 5354

Willis, F.: London General, 18347

Willis, J. R. M.: Tax Expenditures in the United Kingdom, 4858

Willis, John; The Parliamentary Powers of English Government Departments, 790

Willis, Kenneth George: Northern Region and Nation: A Short Migration Atlas 1960–1961. Papers on Migration and Mobility in Northern England, No. 4, 7270; The Economics of Town and Country Planning, 18802; Contemporary Issues in Town Planning, 18803

Willis, Paul E.: Learning to Labour: How Working Class Kids get Working Class Jobs, 9696

Willis, R. J. M.: An Accessions Tax, 4828

Willius, Frederick A.: A History of the Heart and the Circulation, 22337; Classics of Cardiology: A Collection of Classic Works on the Heart and Circulation, 22338

Willman, Paul: Innovation and Management Control: Labour Relations at British Leyland Cars, 17440

Willmot, G. F.: *ed.* York: A Survey, Prepared for the British Association, 18122

Willmott, Peter: Adolescent Boys of East London, 8429, 8496; *ed.* Sharing Inflation? Poverty Report, 9086; The Evolution of a Community: A Study of Dagenham after Forty Years, 9316, 18102; Whatever's Happening to London?: An Analysis of Changes in Population Structure and their Effects on Community Life, 9317, 18331; The Debate about Community: Papers from a Seminar on 'Community Social Policy', 9318; Friendship Networks and Social Support 1987, 9319; Local Government Decentralisation and Community, 9320; Planning and the Community, 9321; Community in Social Policy, 9322; 'Tendences de la société anglaise', 9498; Family and Kinship in East London, 10033; Family and Class in a London Suburb, 10034; The Symmetrical Family: A Study of Work and Leisure in a London Region, 10035; 'Kinship and Social Legislation', 10036; 'Some Social Characteristics of a Scottish and an English New Town', 18232; 'Some Social Trends', 18332; 'East Kilbride and Stevenage: Some Social Characteristics of a Scottish and an English New Town', 19015

Willmott, Phyllis: *ed.* The Social Workers, 8715; Consumer's Guide to the British Social Services, 8882; Lambeth, Inner Area Study, 9323; Growing up in a London Village [Lee, Kent]: Family Life between the Wars, 19194

Willoughby, G.: 'The Working Class Family in England', 10032

Wills, Alan: Great Western Steam through the Years, 16864

Wills, David: A Place Like Home: A Hostel for Disturbed Adolescents, 8497

Wills, Gordon: Sources of U.K. Marketing Information, 7256

Wills, John: Wilkinson and Riddell Limited, 1851–1951, 6237

Wills, William David: The Hawkspar Experiment: An Informal Account of the Training of Adolescents, 10501; Common Sense about Young Offenders, 10502; Throw away thy Rod, 10503; A Place Like Home: A Hostel for Disturbed Adolescents, 10504; Spare the Child: The Story of an Experimental Approved School, 10505

Willson, Francis Michael Glenn: *ed.* The Organisation of British Central Government, 1914–1956, 711; 'The Routes of Entry of New Members of the British Cabinet, 1868–1958', 740; 'Entry to the Cabinet, 1959–1968', 741; Administrators in Action: British Case Studies, 945; 'Some Career Patterns in British Politics: Whips in the House of Commons, 1906–1966', 1565; Governmental Services to the Sea-fish Industry of Great Britain, 19803

Willson, G. B.: Birth of a Spitfire: The Story of Beaverbrook's Ministry and its First 10,000,000, 15844

Willstatter, Richard: 'A Chemist's Retrospects and Perspectives', 7122

Wilmeth, Don B.: American and English Popular Entertainment. A Guide to Information Services, 26270

Wilmore, Albert: Industrial Britain, A Survey, 4954

Wilmot, Chester: The Struggle for Europe, 14975

Wilmot, Edward P.: The Labour Party: A Short History, 1679

Wilmot, John: Labour's Way to Control Banking and Finance, 4412

Wilmut, Roger: Kindly Leave the Stage! The Story of Variety, 1919–1960, 26268; From Fringe to Flying Circus: Celebrating a Unique Generation of Comedy 1960–1980, 26269; Tony Hancock: 'Artiste', 26316

Wilsher, M. J. D.: Glasgow Subway 1896–1977, 17022

Wilsher, Peter: The Pound in your Pocket, 1870–1970, 4717

Wilshere, John: Great Stretton: History, Parish Registers, Probate Inventories, 19334

Wilson, A. E.: Prime Minister of Mirth. The Biography of Sir George Robey, 26339

Wilson, A. T. M.: ed. Social Science Research and Industry, 5745

Wilson, A.: 'Recent Developments in Social Work', 8400

Wilson, A.: 'The District Audit Service', 3251

Wilson, Alan Geoffrey: 'Models in Urban Planning: A Synoptic Review of Recent Literature', 17767; Urban and Regional Models in Geography and Planning, 17848; Research for Regional Planning, 17851

Wilson, Alan Herries: Semiconductors and Metals: An Introduction to the Electron Theory of Metals, 7123

Wilson, Albert Edward: Christmas Pantomime: The Story of an English Institution, 26271

Wilson, Amrit: 'A Burning Fever: The Isolation of Asian Women in Britain', 11230

Wilson, Andrew N.: The Church in Crisis: A Critical Assessment of the Current State of the Church of England, 11601; Hilaire Belloc, 25378; C. S. Lewis: A Biography, 25668

Wilson, Andrew: The Concorde Fiasco, 17569

Wilson, Anne: Mixed Race Children: A Study of Identity, 8401

Wilson, Sir Arnold Talbot: Loyalties: Mesopotamia, 1914–1917: A Personal and Historical Record, 1544; Thoughts and Talks, 1935–1937, 1545; More Thoughts and Talks, 1546; Workmen's Compensation, 4028; Industrial Assurance: A Historical and Critical Study, 4029; Burial Reform and Funeral Costs, 4044; Old Age Pensions: An Historical and Critical Study, 4045; Gallantry: Its Public Recognition and Reward, in Peace and in War, at Home and Abroad, 9892

Wilson, Aubrey: The Marketing of Professional Services, 9777

Wilson, Brian Geoffrey: London United Tramways: A History, 1884–1933, 17231

Wilson, Brian: Bi-Confessionalism in a Confessional Party System: The Northern Ireland Alliance Party, 2817

Wilson, Bryan Ronald: The Social Context of the Youth Problem, 8535; The Youth Culture and the Universities, 9860, 22563; Sects and Society: A Sociological Study of Three Religious Groups in Britain, 12378; Patterns of Sectarianism: Organisation and Ideology in Social and Religious Movements, 12379; 'Becoming a Sectarian: Motivation and Commitment', 12380

Wilson, C. B.: ed. Environmental Quality, 19964

Wilson, C.: Economic Issues in Immigration: An Exploration of the Liberal Approach to Public Policy on Immigration, 11435

Wilson, Sir Charles Henry: ed. Economic History and the Historian: A Collection of Essays, 3544; Unilever 1945–1965: Challenge and Response in the Industrial Revolution, 6219; Men and Machines: A History of D. Napier & Son Engineers Ltd., 1808–1958, 6367; A Man and his Times: A Memoir of Sir Ellis Hunter, 6595; Australia 1788–1988: The Creation of a Nation, 12603; Conference on Industry and the Universities: Aspects of Interdependence, 23359; First with the News: The Story of W. H. Smith since 1972, 25008

Wilson, Charles McMoran [Baron Moran]: Churchill: The Struggle for Survival, 1940–1965, 988

Wilson, Conrad: Scottish Opera: The First Ten Years, 24567

Wilson, Constance Anne: Food and Drink in Britain from the Stone Age to Recent Times, 20570

Wilson, D. J.: 100 Years of the Association of Average Adjusters, 1869–1969, 4212

Wilson, David F.: Dockers: The Impact of Industrial Change, 16660

Wilson, David Jack: Power and Party Bureaucracy in Britain: Regional Organisation in the Conservative and Labour Parties, 1607

Wilson, David: ed. Sight and Sound: A Fiftieth Anniversary Collection, 24643

Wilson, Derek: Rothschild: A Story of Wealth and Power, 4472

Wilson, Des: Battle for Power, 1828; Pressure: The A to Z of Campaigning Britain, 2070; I Know it was the Place's Fault, 18698; Minority Report: A Diary of Protest 1970–73, 18699; The Lead Scandal: The Fight to Save Children from Damage by Lead in Petrol, 20169

Wilson, Desmond: 'The Churches and Violence in Ireland', 12166

Wilson, Dorothy J.: The Political Economy of the Welfare State, 9004

Wilson, Sir Duncan: Gilbert Murray OM 1855–1957, 26570

Wilson, Edward A.: The Ellesmere and Llangollen Canal: An Historical Background, 16416

Wilson, Elizabeth: Only Halfway to Paradise: Women in Post-war Britain, 1945–1968, 7649; 'The British Women's Movement', 7805; Women and the Welfare State, 9005

Wilson, Francesca M.: ed. Strange Island: Britain through Foreign Eyes, 1395–1940, 322; They Came as Strangers: The Story of Refugees to Great Britain, 11394

Wilson, Frank Richard: Journey to Work: Modal Split; A Study in Transportation, 16275; Railways in Guernsey, with Special Reference to the German Steam Railways, 16936; The British Tram, 17202

Wilson, G. K.: 'Planning: Lessons from the Ports', 16652

Wilson, Gail Graham: Social and Economic Statistics of North East England: Sub-regional and Local Authority Statistics of Population, Housing, Rateable Values and Employment, 5201; The Police: A Study in Manpower: The Evolution of the Service in England and Wales, 10699, 10748

Wilson, George B.: Alcohol and the Nation, 22142

Wilson, George Murray: ed. Fighting Tanks: An Account of the Royal Tank Corps in Action, 1916–1921, 15733

Wilson, Gladys: Quaker Worship: An Introductory Historical Study of the English Friends' Meeting, 12136

Wilson, Graham K.: Special Interests and Policy Making: Agricultural Policies and Politics in Britain and the United States of America, 1956–1970, 19573

Wilson, Harper Hubert: Pressure Group: The Campaign for Commercial Television, 2068, 24865; The Problem of Internal Security in Great Britain 1948–1953, 10884

Wilson, Harriet: Parents and Children in the Inner City, 8402; Poverty in Britain Today, 9056; Parents and Children in the Inner City, 10108; Delinquency and Child Neglect, 10596

Wilson, Henry Maitland, [Baron]: Eight Years Overseas, 1939–1947, 14789

Wilson, Hugh: Inner Area Study: Liverpool, 18032; Work Programme, 18033; Third Study Review, 18034; Vacant Land, 18035; Fourth Study Review, 18036; Social Area Analysis, 18037; Environmental Care Project, 18038; Change or Decay (final report), 18039; Getting a Job, 18040; Economic Development of the Inner Area, 18041; Inner Area Play (report of action projects on adventure playgrounds and play on wheels), 18042; Community Care of the Elderly, 18043; Single Parent Families, 18044; Exeter Town Centre Interim Report No. 1., 18869; Second Interim Report: Accommodation to be provided in the Guildhall Area, 18870

Wilson, Ian: Shipwrecks of the Ulster Coast, 16514

Wilson, J.: 'British Israelism', 12395

Wilson, [James] Harold [Baron]: Final Term: The Labour Government 1974–1976, 1061; Memoirs: The Making of a Prime Minister, 1916– 1994, 1061; Purpose in Politics: Selected Speeches, 1061; The Labour Government, 1964–1970: A Personal Record, 1061; The New Britain: Labour's Plans Outlined, Selected Speeches, 1061; New Deal for Coal, 1943; Post-War Economic Policies in Britain, 3618; United Kingdom Statistics, 6347; The Chariot of Israel: Britain, America and the State of Israel, 14359

Wilson, John Boyd: Equality, 9564; Philosophy and Practical Education, 22850

Wilson, John C.: 'Twenty Five Years' Change in Television', 7124

Wilson, John D.: Degrees of Excellence: The Academic Achievement Game, 22572

Wilson, John Stuart Gladstone: Monetary Policy and the Development of Money Markets, 4574

Wilson, John Veit: Parents and Children in the Inner City, 10108

Wilson, Keith M.: *ed.* Imperialism and Nationalism in the Middle East: The Anglo-Egyptian Experience, 1882–1982, 14399; A Study in the History and Politics of the 'Morning Post', 25146

Wilson, Kenneth: The Story of Dentistry, 9823

Wilson, L. M.: 'The Future of the Poor-Law Infirmary', 21484

Wilson, Leo: The Unequal Breadwinner: A New Perspective on Women and Social Security, 7792

Wilson, Leonard G.: 'The Clinical Definition of Scurvy and the Discovery of Vitamin C', 21026; Physiology of the Nervous System, 22316; 'Reflections on the History of Reflex Action', 22317; 'Somatic Functions of the Central Nervous System', 22318

Wilson, Mari: National Parties and Local Politics, 3144

Wilson, Mary C.: King Abdullah, Britain and the Making of Jordan, 14353

Wilson, Michael: Health is for People, 22107

Wilson, N.: 'The Local Government Service since the War', 3234

Wilson, Norman Scarlyn: Education in the Forces, 1939–1946: the Civilian Contribution, 23719

Wilson, Patrick: Murderess: A Study of the Women Executed in Britain since 1823, 7728

Wilson, Patrick: *ed.* Government and Politics of India and Pakistan 1885–1955: A Bibliography of Works in Western Languages, 13104

Wilson, Paul Alexander: The Professions, 9766; Britain and the United States: Problems in Co-operation, 14064

Wilson, Paul W.: 'The Gunpowder Mills of Westmorland and Furness', 7048

Wilson, Paul: A Britten Source Book, 24306

Wilson, R. H. L.: Pages in the History of Chest Surgery, 21141

Wilson, Richard George: *ed.* Entrepreneurship in Britain, 1750–1939, 5415; Greene King: A Business and Family History, 6158, 20745

Wilson, Robert Burdett: Sir Daniel Gooch: Memoirs and Diary, 17080

Wilson, Robert MacNair: The Beloved Physician, Sir James MacKenzie: A Biography, 20904

Wilson, Roger Burdett: Go Great Western: A History of Great Western Railway Publicity, 16869

Wilson, Roger Cowan: Difficult Housing Estates, 9347; Quaker Relief: An Account of the Relief Work of the Society of Friends, 1940–1948, 12150

Wilson, Ronald Eliot: Two Hundred Precious Metal Years: A History of the Sheffield Smelting Co. Ltd., 1760–1960, 6616

Wilson, Sandy: Ivor, 24483, 26078; I Could Be Happy: An Autobiography, 24489

Wilson, Sheila: The Theatre in the Fifties, 26199

Wilson, Stephen: *ed.* Alexander Cowan Wilson, 1866–1955: His Finances and His Causes, 4272

Wilson, Steve: British Motorcycles since 1950, 17182

Wilson, Theodore Allen: The First Summit: Roosevelt and Churchill at Placentia Bay 1941, 14047

Wilson, Thomas Bright: *ed.* Ulster under Home Rule: A Study of the Political and Economic Problems of Northern Ireland, 2929; *ed.* Ulster Divided, 2930; Planning and Growth, 3531; Inflation, 3996; Inflation, Unemployment and the Market, 4017; Policies for Regional Development, 5059; 'Scotland: A Financial and Industrial History', 5249; *ed.* Pensions, Inflation and Growth: A Comparative Study of the Elderly in the Welfare State, 8613; The Political Economy of the Welfare State, 9004

Wilson, Trevor Gordon: The Downfall of the Liberal Party, 1914–1935, 1810; 'Lord Bryce's Investigation into Alleged German Atrocities in Belgium, 1914–15', 13477; The Political Diaries of C. P. Scott, 25281

Wilson, William: Towards Industrial Democracy in Britain, 5460, 6030

Wilton, David: Falklands: The Air War, 16093

Wiltse, K. T.: 'Social Casework and Public Assistance', 8655

Wiltshire, H. C.: 'The Great Tradition in University Adult Education', 23650

Wimberley, H.: 'Conjugal Role Organisation and Social Networks in England and Japan', 10086

Wimperis, Virginia: The Unmarried Mother and Her Child, 7868

Winch, Donald Norman: Economics and Policy: A Historical Study, 3528, 6100; The Economic Advisory Council, 1930–1939, 6139

Winchester, David: 'Industrial Relations Research in Britain', 5832

Winchester, Simon: In Holy Terror: Reporting the Ulster Troubles, 2882

Winchester: Winchester College, 23085; Winchester and the Public School Elite: A Statistical Analysis, 23086; Sixth-centenary Essays, 23087

Wincott, Harold: The Business of Capitalism: A Selection of Unconventional Essays on Economic Problems of the 1960's, 3658

Wincott, Len: Invergordon Mutineer, 15298

Windeler, Robert: Julie Andrews: A Biography, 24473

Winder, George: Modern Rural Rides: An Account of a Ride through the Counties of Sussex, Hampshire and Wiltshire, with some Reference to the Agricultural Act of 1947 and to other Farming and Historical Matters, 19115

Winder, R.: 'Vacation Training of Undergraduate Engineers', 22511

Windle, Robert: British and American Economic History, 1850–1950, 3726

Windmuller, John P.: *ed.* Employers' Associations and Industrial Relations: A Comparative Study, 5837

Windrich, Elaine: The Rhodesia Problem: A Documentary Record 1923–1973, 12790; Britain and the Politics of Rhodesian Independence, 12804; British Labour's Foreign Policy, 13566

Windsor, Duchess of: The Heart Has its Reasons, 476

Windsor, John: 'Education and the Class Barrier', 22813

Winfield, Sir Percy Henry: *ed.* Penal Reform in England 1940, 10431

Wing, John Kenneth: 'Rehabilitation of Psychiatric Patients', 21847; Measurement and Classification of Psychiatric Symptoms, 21856; *ed.* Psychiatric Case Registers, 21857; Reasoning about Madness, 21873; *ed.* Evaluating a Community Psychiatric Service: The Camberwell Register, 1964–1971, 21874; *ed.* Early Childhood Autism: Clinical, Educational and Social Aspects, 21881

Wingate, Pauline: Newspaper History from the Seventeenth Century to the Present Day, 25072

Wingate, Sir Ronald: Lord Ismay: A Biography, 14765

Wingfield, A. J.: The Bolton Artillery: A History, 1860–1975, 15605

Wingfield-Stratford, Esmé Cecil: Beyond Empire, 377; The Squire and his Relations, 9741

Wingo, Lowdon: *ed.* Cities, Regions and Public Policy, 5063, 17835; *ed.* The Relevance to the U.S. of British and French Regional Population Strategies, 5064

Wingrove, Janet Madge: *ed.* The Handicapped Person in the Community, 21921

Winkel, H.: 'Boykott und Gegenboykott: zu den deutsch-englischen Handelsbeziehungen im Jahre 1933', 13689

Winkler, H. A.: Politische Weichenstellungen im Nachkriegsdeutschland 1945–1953, 14211

Winkler, Henry Ralph: 'Some Recent Writings on Twentieth Century Britain', 372; The League of Nations Movement in Great Britain, 13472; 'The Emergence of a Labour Foreign Policy in Great Britain, 1918–1929', 13548

Winks, Robin William: Malaysia: Selected Historical Readings, 12000

Winn, Godfrey Herbert: The Young Queen: The Life Story of Her Majesty Queen Elizabeth II, 509; The Younger Sister: an Intimate Portrait Study of H.R.H. Princess Margaret, 524

Winnett, Arthur Robert: Attempt Great Things: The Diocese of Guildford, 1927–1977, 11616

Winnicott, Clare: Child Care and Social Work: A Collection of Papers Written between 1954 and 1963, 8406

Winnicott, Donald Woods: The Child, the Family and the Outside World, 10080; The Family and Individual Development, 10081

Winnington-Ingram, Arthur Foley: Fifty Years Work in London, 1889–1939, 11767

Winsbury, R.: Thomson McLintock & Co.: The First Hundred Years 1877–1977, 4176

Winship, Janice: Advertising in Women's Magazines, 1956–1974, 4304; Femininity and Women's Magazines: A Case Study of Woman's Own: 'First in Britain for Women', 25194; Inside Women's Magazines, 25195

Winslow, C. E. A.: The Conquest of Epidemic Disease, 22357; Man and Epidemics, 22358

Winslow, T. E.: Forewarned is Forearmed: A History of the Royal Observer Corps, 15766

Winstedt, Sir Richard Olof: Britain and Malaya, 1786–1941, 12910

Winstone, H. E.: ed. English Catholic Worship: Liturgical Renewal in England since 1900, 11976

Winstone, H. V. F.: Gertrude Bell, 13814

Wint, Guy: The British in Asia, 13579; Middle East Crisis, 14368; Total War: Causes and Courses of the Second World War, 14703

Winter, Denis: Death's Men: Soldiers of the Great War, 14489

Winter, Jay Murray: Socialism and the Challenge of War: Ideas and Politics in Britain 1912–1918, 1694; 'Arthur Henderson, the Russian Revolution and the Reconstruction of the Labour Party', 1697, 13376; 'A Bibliography of the Published Writings of R.H. Tawney, 2145; ed. War and Economic Development: Essays in Memory of David Joslin, 3739, 26803; 'Some Aspects of the Demographic Consequences of the First World War in Britain', 7432; 'Britain's "Lost Generation" of the First World War', 7433; 'Unemployment, Nutrition and Infant Mortality in Britain', 7434; ed. The Working Class in Modern British History: Essays in Honour of Henry Pelling, 2548, 7434, 9630, 27120

Winter, Michael: 'Corporatism and Agriculture in the U.K.: The Case for the Milk Marketing Board', 20662

Winter, Paul D.: Atlas of Mortality from Selected Diseases in England and Wales, 22233

Winterton, Wilfred: Breath-Taking History, 22146

Wintle, F.: The Plymouth Blitz, 15145

Winton, J. R.: Lloyds Bank 1918–1969, 4499

Winton, John: Air Power at Sea, 1939–1945, 15013, 15422; The Forgotten Fleet, 15023; Find, Fix and Strike: The Fleet Air Arm at War, 1939–45, 15423

Wintour, Charles Vere: Pressures on the Press: An Editor Looks at Fleet Street, 25299; Celebration: Twenty Five Years of British Theatre, 26110

Wintour, Jim: The Housing Crisis Nationwide, 18754

Wintour, Patrick: Eddie Shah and the Newspaper Revolution, 25106

Winwood, Robert J.: A Guide to the British Food Manufacturing Industry, 20629

Winyard, Steve: The Case for a National Minimum Wage, 3953; Poor Farmworkers, Rich Farms, 9710; 'Cold Comfort Farm': A Study of Farm Workers and Low Pay, 19676

Wisden's Cricketers' Almanack: 1864+, 27095

Wisdom, Allen Sidney: Sewerage and Sewage Disposal, 20092

Wisdom, Thomas Henry: Triumph over Tunisia, Being the Story of the Part of the R.A.F. in the African Victory, 15942; Wings over Olympus: The Story of the R.A.F. in Libya and Greece, 15943

Wise, Ernie: There's No Answer to That: An Autobiography with Help from Michael Freedland, 26334

Wise, Mark: The Common Fisheries Policy of the European Community, 19833

Wise, Michael John: ed. R. O. Buchanan and Economic Geography, 26661

Wiseman, Anthony John Ley: Introduction to Crop Husbandry, 19698

Wiseman, Christopher: Beyond the Labyrinth: A Study of Edwin Muir's Poetry, 25725

Wiseman, Harry: From Rhodesia to Zimbabwe: The Politics of Transition, 12809

Wiseman, Herbert Victor: Parliament at Work: A Case-Book of Parliamentary Procedure, 647; 'Supply and Ways and Means: Procedural Changes in 1966', 659; Parliament and the Executive: an Analysis with Readings, 735; 'Regional Government in the United Kingdom', 2400; ed. Local Government in England 1958–69, 3165; Local Government at Work: A Case Study of a County Borough, 3329; Britain and the Commonwealth, 12580; 'Parliament and the University Grants Committee', 23329; 'University Extension Work since 1945', 23652

Wiseman, Jack: The Growth of Public Expenditure in the United Kingdom, 4757; 'Cost-benefit Analysis and Health Service Policy', 21598; An Annotated Bibliography of Health and Economics, 21634; Education for Democrats: A Study of the Financing of Education in a Free Society, 23201

Wiseman, Stephen: 'Higher Degrees in Education in British Universities', 22724; ed. Examinations and English Education, 22916

Wistow, Gerald: Whither State Welfare?: Policy Implementation in the Personal Social Services 1979–1980, 9007

Wistrich, Enid: Local Government Reorganisation: The First Years of Camden, 3310; The Politics of Transport, 16266

Witherick, M. E.: ed. Dimensions of Change in a Growth Area Southampton since 1960, 18083

Witherow, John: The Winter War: The Falklands, 16105

Withers, Charles W. J.: Gaelic in Scotland, 1698–1981: The Geographical History of a Language, 2462; Gaelic Scotland and the Transformation of a Culture Region, 2463

Withers, Hartley: Pioneers of British Life Assurance, 4222; The Quicksands of the City and a Way through for Investors, 4248; Stocks and Shares, 4249; Should the Banks be Nationalised?, 4419; The War and Lombard Street, 4420; National and Provincial Bank 1833–1933, 4502

Witkin, Robert W.: 'Social Class Influence on the Amount and Type of Positive Evaluation of School Lessons', 9507

Witt, F. H.: Pictorial History of Dentistry, 22405

Wittgenstein, Ludwig: Letters to C. K. Ogden, 26882

Witting, C.: ed. A History of Eltham College for the Sons of Missionaries, 23057

Wittke, Carl Frederick: The History of English Parliamentary Privilege, 646

Wittman, M.: 'Social Work Manpower for Mental Health Services in England', 8941

Witton, Alan M.: ed. Fleetbooks Series, 17281; ed. Buses of Greater Manchester, 17282; ed. Buses of South and East Yorkshire, 17283; ed. Buses of West Yorkshire, 17284; ed. Buses of Lancashire and Cumbria, 17285; ed. Buses of Mersey, North Wales and the Isle of Man, 17286; ed. Buses of the West Midlands, 17287; ed. Buses of the East Midlands, 17288; ed. Buses of North East England, 17289; ed. Buses of South Wales, 17290; ed. Buses of Eastern England, 17291; ed. Buses of South East England, 17292; ed. Buses of South West England and the Channel Islands, 17293; ed. Buses of Inner London, 17296; ed. Buses of Outer London, 17297; ed. Buses of South Central London, 17298

Wobbe, R. A.: Graham Greene: A Bibliography and Guide to Research, 25560

Wober, Mallory: Television Coverage of the 1983 General Election: Audiences, Appreciation and Public Opinion, 24901

Wodehouse, L.: ed. British Architects 1840–1975: A Guide to Information Sources, 23861

Wodehouse, P. G.: Wodehouse on Wodehouse, 25885

Wogan, Terry: Wogan on Wogan, 24917

Woglom, W. H.: Discoverers for Medicine, 21238

Wolf, David C.: 'To Secure a Convenience: Britain Recognises China 1950', 13634

Wolfe, Billy: Scotland Lives, 2506

Wolfe, James Nathaniel: ed. Government and Nationalism in Scotland: An Enquiry by Members of the University of Edinburgh, 2495; The Church of Scotland: An Economic Survey, 12240

Wolfe, Willard: 'A Century of Books on the History of Socialism in Britain, Part 1: Before 1950', 1663; 'Writings on the History of Socialism in Britain, Part 2: Since 1950', 1664

Wolfendale, Arnold Whittaker: The Search for the Neutrino, 7125

Wolfenden, J. H.: 'The Dawn of Hot Atom Chemistry', 7126

Wolfenden, Sir John Frederick: The Purpose and Influence of the British Building Society, 4361

Wolfers, Arnold: Britain and France between Two World Wars: Conflicting Strategies of Peace since Versailles, 14260

Wolff, L.: 'The Public Faces of Harold Nicolson: The Thirties', 1494

Wolff, Leon: In Flanders Fields: The 1917 Campaign, 14577

Wolff, Louis: Her Majesty Queen Mary: An Authoritative Portrait of a Great Lady in Her Years as Queen Mother, 475; Elizabeth and Philip, 509

Wolff, Michael: If Freedom Fail, 10347; Prison: The Penal Institutions of Britain: Prisons, Borstals, Detention Centres, Approved Schools and Remand Homes, 10430

Wolff, R. D.: The Economics of Colonialism: Britain and Kenya 1870–1930, 12838

Wolff, Sula: Children under Stress, 8397

Wolfram, Sybil: In-Laws and Out-Laws: Kinship and Marriage in England, 9972

Wolkowitz, Carol: Homeworking: Myths and Realities, 7644

Woll, B.: Perspectives on British Sign Language and Deafness, 21933

Wolman, Harold L.: Housing and Housing Policy in the U.S. and the U.K., 18765

Wolmar, Christian: Councils in Conflict: The Rise and Fall of the Municipal Left, 3230

Wolpert, S. A.: A New History of India, 13110

Wolpin, Kenneth I.: 'An Economic Analysis of Crime and Punishment in England and Wales, 1894–1967', 10228

Wolstenholme, Gordon Ethelbert Ward: ed. Immigration: Medical and Social Aspects, 11407

Wolters, Richard A.: The World of Silent Flight, 17543

Women's Voluntary Services: Report on 25 Years Work, WVS Civil Defence, 1938–1963, 9144

Womersley, Lewis: Inner Area Study: Liverpool, 18032; Work Programme, 18033; Third Study Review, 18034; Vacant Land, 18035; Fourth Study Review, 18036; Social Area Analysis, 18037; Environmental Care Project, 18038; Change or Decay (final report), 18039; Getting a Job, 18040; Economic Development of the Inner Area, 18041; Inner Area Play (report of action projects on adventure playgrounds and play on wheels), 18042; Community Care of the Elderly, 18043; Single Parent Families, 18044; Exeter Town Centre Interim Report No. 1., 18869; Second Interim Report: Accommodation to be Provided in the Guildhall Area, 18870

Wood, A.: 'History of the Cavendish Laboratory, Cambridge', 21028

Wood, Adrian: A Theory of Pay, 3944

Wood, Alan: The True History of Lord Beaverbrook, 1075; Mr Rank: A Study of J. Arthur Rank and British Films, 24659; Bertrand Russell: The Passionate Sceptic, 26868

Wood, Alfred Cecil: History of University College, Nottingham, 1881–1948, 23544

Wood, Bruce: The Process of Local Government Reform 1966–74, 3175; The Scope of Local Initiative: A Study of Cheshire County Council 1961–1974, 3350

Wood, C. L.: British Employment Statistics: A Guide to Sources and Methods, 5911

Wood, C. M.: The Geography of Pollution: A Study of Greater Manchester, 20059

Wood, Charles Lindley [Viscount Halifax]: ed. The Conversations at Malines, 1921–1925: Original Documents, 12312

Wood, Christopher Maxwell: Planning and Pollution: An Examination of the Role of Land Use Planning in the Protection of Environmental Quality, 20004; The Geography of Pollution: A Study of Greater Manchester, 20006

Wood, Clive: The Fight for Acceptance: A History of Contraception, 21065

Wood, David Neville: Decimal Currency for Britain, 4724

Wood, Derek: The Narrow Margin: The Battle of Britain and the Rise of Air Power, 1930–1940, 14816; Target England; an Illustrated History of the Battle of Britain, 14817; Attack Warning Red: The Royal Observer Corps and the Defence of Britain, 1925–1975, 15767

Wood, Diana: ed. The Church and Wealth, 12205, 12276

Wood, Douglas: Economic Aspects of Pigmeat Marketing, 20674

Wood, Edward Frederick Linley [Earl of Halifax]: Fullness of Days, 1217

Wood, Edward Geoffrey: Productivity for Profit, 5996

Wood, Ethel Mary: A History of the Polytechnic, 22526

Wood, Francis: 'The Fertility of the English Middle Classes: A Statistical Study', 7475

Wood, Geoffrey Bernard: Yorkshire Villages, 19149

Wood, Geoffrey E.: 'Money Substitutes and Monetary Policy in the United Kingdom, 1922–1974', 4632; Monetarism in the United Kingdom, 4636; The Financing Procedures of British Foreign Trade, 4808

Wood, H. C. S.: 'The Birth of a Vitamin', 21027

Wood, H. J.: Exploration and Discovery, 27179

Wood, Sir Henry: My Life of Music, 24441

Wood, Herbert Fairlie: Vimy!, 14578

Wood, Herbert George: Belief and Unbelief since 1850, 11880; Living Issues in Religious Thought from George Fox to Bertrand Russell, 11881; Henry T. Hodgkin: A Memoir, 12145; Terrot Reaveley Glover: A Biography, 26566

Wood, Ian: ed. Forward! Labour Politics in Scotland 1888–1988, 2513

Wood, J. R. T.: 'The Roles of Diefenbaker, Macmillan and Verwoerd in the Withdrawal of South Africa from the Commonwealth', 12721; The Welensky Papers: A History of the Federation of Rhodesia and Nyasaland, 12784

Wood, James L.: Aviation in Scotland, 17530

Wood, John: The Instrument of Advertising, 4329

Wood, John B.: ed. A Nation not Afraid: The Thinking of Enoch Powell, 1296; ed. Powell and the 1970 Election, 2236; How Much Inequality? An Inquiry into the 'Evidence', 9567

Wood, Sir John: 'Last Offer Arbitration', 5846

Wood, Jonathan: Classic Motor Cars, 17357; The Rolls-Royce, 17452

Wood, Leslie: The Miracle of the Movies, 24629

Wood, Michael: Ballet Rambert: 50 Years and On, 24242; The Sadler's Wells Ballet, 1931–1956: A Record of Twenty Five Years, 24243

Wood, Neal: Communism and British Intellectuals, 1928

Wood, Peter Anthony: Regional Problems, Problem Regions and Public Policy in the United Kingdom, 5127; The West Midlands, 5139; Employment Location in Regional Economic Planning: A Case Study of the West Midlands, 5223; Character of a Conurbation: A Computer Atlas of Birmingham and the Black Country, 17982; Housing and Migration of Labour in England and Wales, 18552

Wood, Peter Denis: ed. Essays in Geography for Austin Miller, 26664

Wood, Robert: A World in your Ear: The Broadcasting of an Era, 1923–64, 24721

Wood, Robert Francis: Fifty Years of Forestry Research: A Review of Work Conducted and Supported by the Forestry Commission 1920–1970, 19744; Forestry in the British Scene, 19745

Wood, Robert George Ernest: Railways in Essex [until 1923.], 16933

Wood, Stephen: Industrial Relations and Management Strategy, 5827; 'Redundancy and Female Employment', 5922

Wood, Susanne: 'The Coloured Population of Great Britain', 11047

Wood, Timothy: Computers in Britain: A Survey of the Use of Computing Equipment for Data Processing and Process Control in Great Britain, 7090

Wood, Victor: Pension Schemes, 3972; New Trends in Pensions, 3973; Pension Schemes Practice, 3974; Company Pension Schemes, 3975; Managing Pension Schemes: A Guide to Contemporary Pension Plans and the Social Security Act, 3976

Wood, William Wales: Banker and Customer, 4428

Woodall, Samuel James: The Manor House Hospital: A Personal Record, 21436

Woodbridge, Barry: Alfred North Whitehead: A Primary-secondary Bibliography, 26880

Woodburn, Stanley Woodburn: Singapore: The Chain of Disaster, 15078

Woodcock, George: Who Killed the British Empire?, 12587; The Crystal Spirit: A Critical Study of George Orwell, 25742

Woodford, F. Peter: The Ciba Foundation: An Analytic History, 1949–1974, 20765

Woodford, George P.: The Value of Standards for the External Residential Environment, 19958

Woodforde, John: The Story of the Bicycle, 17164

Woodhall, Maureen: Economic Aspects of Education: A Review of Research in Britain, 23205, 23315; Productivity Trends in British University Education, 1938–1962', 23312; 'Investment in Industrial Training: Effects of the Industrial Training Act on the Volume and Costs of Training', 23662

Woodhams, John: Funicular Railways, 16801; Old Lorries, 17468

Woodhead, Caroline: The U.K. Life Assurance Industry: A Study in Applied Economics, 4224

Woodhouse, Christopher Montague: Post-war Britain, 300; Something Ventured, 1551; British Foreign Policy since the Second World War, 13226; 'Great Britain's European Policy since the Second World War', 14148; The Struggle for Greece, 1941–1945, 14851

Woodhouse, Michael: Essays on the History of Communism in Britain, 1924

Woodhouse, Thomas: A Century's Progress in Jute Manufacture, 1833–1933, 6427

Wooding, Hugh: *ed.* Report of the Commission of Inquiry Appointed by the Governments of the United Kingdom and St. Christopher-Nevis-Anguilla to Examine the Anguilla Problem, 13059

Woodland, Christine: A Guide to the Papers of British Cabinet Ministers 1900–1951, 79, 963

Woodliffe, J. C.: 'State Participation in the Development of United Kingdom Offshore Petroleum Resources', 6503

Woodroofe, Kathleen: From Charity to Social Work in England and the United States, 8982

Woodruff, Sir Michael Francis Addison: The One and the Many: 'Patient Care in the World of Today' and 'The Cost of Progress', Two Lectures on Ethical Considerations Relating to the Practice of Medicine, 21258; And Ghosts Shall Drive You On, 21259; On Science and Surgery, 21260

Woodruffe, Brian J.: Rural Settlement Policies and Plans, 19062; Wiltshire Villages, 19148

Woods, Edward Sydney: Theodore, Bishop of Winchester, 11771

Woods, Frederick: A Bibliography of the Works of Sir Winston Churchill, 1001

Woods, Gerald: Art without Boundaries, 1950–1970, 23972

Woods, Grace E.: The Handicapped Child: Assessment and Management, 21899

Woods, Hilda M.: The Incidence of Industrial Accidents upon Individuals with Special Reference to Multiple Accidents, 4106

Woods, John A.: A Bibliography of Parliamentary Debates of Great Britain, 640

Woods, Katherine Seymour: Development of Country Towns in the South-West Midlands during the 1960s, 18893

Woods, Kevin J.: 'The National Health Service in London: A Review of the Impact of N.H.S. Policy since 1976', 21686

Woods, R. I.: 'The Causes of Rapid Mortality Decline in England and Wales 1861–1921', 7473

Woods, R.: 'Margaret Thatcher and Secondary Reorganisation', 22968

Woods, Robin: Robin Woods, an Autobiography, 11770

Woodside, Moxa: Patterns of Marriage: A Study of Marriage Relationships in the Urban Working Classes, 10027

Woodstock, Henry Iles: A History of Tobago, 13069

Woodward, David R.: 'David Lloyd George, a Negotiated Peace with Germany, and the Kühlmann Peace Kite of September 1917', 13380

Woodward, Sir Ernest Llewellyn: Great Britain and the War of 1914–1918, 14435; Short Journey, 26829

Woodward, Grace Steele *and* Woodward, Guy H.: The Secret of Sherwood Forest: Oil Production in England during World War II, 6513

Woodward, Ian: Glenda Jackson: A Study in Fire and Ice, 26057

Woodward, J.: 'The Falklands Experience', 16112

Woodward, J.: The Saleswoman, 4949

Woodward, J. H.: 'The Causes of Rapid Mortality Decline in England and Wales 1861–1921', 7473

Woodward, Judith: Regulating the Meat Product Industry, 20676

Woodward, Patricia J.: 'Homelessness Four Years On', 18514

Woodward, Peter: Condominium and Sudanese Nationalism, 14416

Woodward, Ralph Lee: Belize, 13021

Woodward, V. H.: 'Economic Policy and the Energy Supply Situation in Britain', 7207

Woodworth, David P.: Current British Periodicals: A Bibliographical Guide, 159

Woodworth, Robert Sessions: Contemporary Schools of Psychology, 22419

Wookey, Charles: Inflation, 4018

Wooldrige, Sidney William: *ed.* London essays in Geography, 26649

Woolf, Cecil: A Bibliography of Norman Douglas, 25478

Woolf, Leonard Sidney: Sowing: An Autobiography of the Years 1880–1904, 2126; Growing: An Autobiography of the Years 1904–1911, 2127; Beginning Again: An Autobiography of the Years 1911–1918, 2128; Downhill all the Way: An Autobiography of the Years 1919–1939, 2129

Woolf, Myra: Family Intentions, 7492; Families Five Years On, 7493; Government Social Survey. The Housing Survey in England and Wales, 1964, 18680

Woolford, A. J.: 'New Universities and Adult Education', 23697

Woollcombe, Kenneth J.: The Failure of the English Covenant, 12348

Woollcombe, Robert: The Campaigns of Wavell, 1939–1943, 14787

Woolley, Sir Richard: 'The Stars and the Structure of the Galaxy', 7127

Woolner, Alfred Herbert: Modern Industry in Britain, 4957

Woolnough, Brian: Black Magic: The Rise of the Black Footballer, 27073

Woolton, Frederick James [Earl]: The Memoirs of the Rt. Hon. the Earl of Woolton, 1336

Woolven, Gillian B.: The Warwick Guide to British Labour Periodicals 1790–1970: A Check-list, 1662; Publications of the Independent Labour Party, 1893–1932, 1875; A Bibliography of British Industrial Relations, 5568

Woolwich and District Invalid Children's Aid Association: Annual Report for Year Ending Dec. 31 1928, 8208; Annual Report 1936, 8209

Woosley, Janet: 'Stereotypical Reactions to Regional Accents', 9493

Wootton, Barbara Frances [Baroness]: In a World I Never Made: Autobiographical Reflections, 2131; Plan or No Plan?, 3533; Incomes Policy: An Inquest and a Proposal, 3819; The Social Foundations of Wage Policy: A Study of Contemporary British Wage and Salary Structure, 3894; Contemporary Britain: Three Lectures, 7599; Testament for Social Science: An Essay in the Application of Scientific Method to Human Problems, 7927; The Future of the Social Sciences: The Second Annual Lecture of the Research Students' Association, Delivered at Canberra on 18 October, 1961, 7928; Social Science and Social Pathology, 7929; 'The Image of the Social Worker', 8654; 'Is There a Welfare State? A Review of Recent Social Change in Britain', 9000; Crime and the Criminal Law: Reflections of a Magistrate and Social Scientist, 10171; Crime and Penal Policy: Reflections on Fifty Years' Experience, 10172; Social Science and Social Pathology, 10173

Wootton, J. Graham: Pressure Politics in Contemporary Britain, 2063; Workers, Unions and the State, 6876; The Politics of Influence: British Ex-servicemen, Cabinet Decisions and Cultural Change 1917–57, 15467; Official History of the British Legion, 15468

Woozley, A. D.: *ed.* History of the King's Dragoon Guards, 1938–1945, 15622

Worall, John: *ed.* Philosophical Papers of Imre Lakatos, 26852

Worcester, Richard: The Roots of Air Power, 15782; Roots of British Air Policy, 17653

Worcester: A History of the Worcester Royal Grammar School, 23001

Worcestershire County Council: Working Party on Gypsies: Report, 11351

Workers' Revolutionary Party, Pamphlet: Scargill, Solidarity and the Worker's Revolutionary Party, 1988; Studies in Dialectical Materialism, 1989

Worlock, David: Parliament and the People, 1780–1970, 554

Worlock, Derek: Better Together: Christian Partnership in a Hurt City, 11849

Wormald, E.: *ed.* Sex Differences in Britain, 7686

Worral, Geoff: Exeter Airport in Peace and War: A Pictorial History, 17675

Worrall, B. G.: The Making of the Modern Church: Christianity in England since 1800, 11558

Worrall, Stanley: Christians in Ulster 1968–1980, 12170

Worsdall, Frank: The Tenement: A Way of Life: A Social, Historical and Architectural Study of Housing in Glasgow, 18458

Worsfield, W. Basil: The War and Social Reform, 7550

Worskett, Roy: The Character of Towns: An Approach to Conservation, 18963

Worsley, Francis: 'ITMA' 1938–1948, 26320

Worsley, Peter: Problems of Modern Society: A Sociological Perspective, 8009; *ed.* Modern Sociology: Introductory Readings: Selected Readings, 8010

Worsley, Thomas Cuthbert: Television: The Ephemeral Art, 24857; The Fugitive Art: Dramatic Commentaries, 1947–1951, 25928

Worswick, George David Norman: 'Two Great Recessions: The 1980s and the 1930s in Britain', 3541; The British Economy 1945–1950, 3616; The British Economy in the 1950s, 3617; Profits in the British Economy, 1909–1938, 5982; *ed.* Keynes and the Modern World, 26605

Worth, Katharine Joyce: Revolutions in Modern English Drama, 26173

Worthington, Tom: New Agricultural Landscapes: Report of a Study Undertaken on Behalf of the Countryside Commission during 1972, 19560

Wortley, Ian: Industrial Relations, 5805

Worville, Roy: The Radio Universe: An Introduction to Radio Astronomy and Outer Space, 26431

Wouk, Jonathan: 'British Guiana: A Case Study in British Colonial and Foreign Policy', 13043

Wragg, David W.: Plane Talk: A Report on British Aviation Policy, 17654

Wragg, Edward Conrad: Teaching Teaching, 22740

Wragg, Richard: Post-war Trends in Employment, Productivity, Output, Labour Costs and Prices by Industry in the United Kingdom, 5915; A Study of the Passenger Transport Needs of Urban Wales, 16339

Wraith, Ronald Edward: The Consumer Cause: A Short Account of its Organisation, Power and Importance, 20465

Wray, Ian: Re-structuring the Regions: A Framework for Managing Regional Growth and Decline in the 1980's and 1990's, 5123

Wray, J. V. C.: 'Les syndicats et les jeunes travailleurs en Grande-Bretagne', 6754

Wray, Margaret: Location of Industry in Hertfordshire: Planning and Industry in the Post-war Period, 5159

Wren, Wilfrid John: Ports of the Eastern Counties, 16682

Wrench, Sir John Evelyn Leslie: Alfred, Lord Milner: The Man of No Illusions, 1854–1925, 1272; Geoffrey Dawson and our Times, 25228

Wright, A. D.: St Mary's Hospital and Paddington, 21437

Wright, Alan James: Airbus, 17612; British Airports, 17670

Wright, Andrew: Joyce Cary: A Preface to his Novels, 25442

Wright, Anthony Edgar Gartside: The Development of the Modern British Steel Industry, 6573

Wright, Anthony W.: 'Labour and the Lessons of 1931', 1713; *ed* Worlds of Labour: Essays in Birmingham Labour History, 1782, 2298; British Socialism: Socialist Thought from the 1880s to the 1960s, 2100; G. D. H. Cole and Socialist Democracy, 2125; R.H. Tawney, 2143

Wright, Bruce Stanley: The Frogmen of Burma: The Story of the Sea Reconnaissance Unit, 15404

Wright, Sir Denis: The English amongst the Persians during the Qajar Period, 1787–1921, 13851

Wright, E.: 'The British Referendum: The Constitutional Significance', 2394

Wright, Eric Olin: Class, Crisis and the State, 9562; Classes, 9563

Wright, Frank Joseph: The Evolution of Modern Industrial Organization, 4986,

5606; The Elements of Modern Industrial Organisation, 5607

Wright, Geoffrey Norman: Roads and Trackways of the Yorkshire Dales, 17160

Wright, Helena: Sex and Society, 9974

Wright, Henry Myles: 'The First Ten Years: Post War Planning and Development in England', 18797; Cambridge Planning Proposals, 18851

Wright, Hilton: Building for Daylight . . . With an Introductory Historical Note on English Window Design by John Gloag, 18628

Wright, Ian L.: Canals in Wales, 16395

Wright, J. E.: 'The Library of the Institution of Electrical Engineers in London', 7128

Wright, J. F. : Britain in the Age of Economic Management: An Economic History since 1939, 3454; 'British Economic Growth, 1688–1959', 3518

Wright, Jack: The Practice of Educational Psychology, 22856

Wright, K. G.: Economic Aspects of Health Services, 21632; Need and the N.H.S.: Economics and Social Choice, 21633

Wright, L. R.: *ed.* A Collection of Treaties and other Documents Affecting the States of Malaysia 1761–1963, 12899

Wright, Margaret Scott: Student Nurses in Scotland: Characteristics of Success and Failure, 23235

Wright, Martin: Making Good: Prisons, Punishment and Beyond, 10429; *comp.* Deprivation of Liberty for Young Offenders: A Select Bibliography on Approved Schools, Attendance Centres, Borstals, Detention Centres and Remand Homes, 1940–1965, 10499

Wright, Maurice: 'Ministers and Civil Servants: Relations and Responsibilities', 902

Wright, Michael: Management Buy-outs, 5548

Wright, Sir Michael: Disarm and Verify: An Explanation of the Central Difficulties and of National Policies, 13542

Wright, Monte D.: Most Probable Position: A History of Aerial Navigation to 1941, 27252

Wright, Myles: Lord Leverhulme's Unknown Venture: The Lever Chair and the Beginnings of Town and Regional Planning 1908–1940, 18789

Wright, Peter: The Language of British Industry, 23815; Cockney Dialect and Slang, 23816

Wright, Peter: Spycatcher: The Candid Autobiography of a Senior Intelligence Officer, 16058

Wright, Peter L.: The Coloured Worker in British Industry, with Special Reference to the Midlands and North of England, 11473

Wright, Reginald Charles: A Survey of Manpower Demand Forecasts for the Social Services, 8942

Wright, Robert: Dowding and the Battle of Britain, 14815, 15957

Wright, Ronald Selby: *ed.* Fathers of the Kirk: Some Leaders of the Church in Scotland from the Reformation to the Reunion, 12234; *ed.* Another Home, 12235

Wright, Tom: The Gardens of Britain 4: Kent, East and West Sussex and Surrey, 19885

Wright, V.: *ed.* The Politics of Steel: Western Europe and the Steel Industry in the Crisis Years, 1974–1984, 6581

Wright, Walter Dawson: Life and Commerce in Britain: An Approach to Social Geography, 5049

Wrigley, Chris J.: 'Symposium: Local Government', 3128; *ed.* A History of British Industrial Relations, 5576; *ed.* The Government and Industrial Relations in Britain 1910–1921, 5577; Warfare, Diplomacy and Politics: Essays in Honour of A. J. P. Taylor, 14129, 14346; A. J. P.Taylor; A Complete Annotated Bibliography and Guide to his Historical and other Writings, 26816

Wrigley, Edward Anthony: *ed.* An Introduction to Historical Demography, 7370; Population and History, 7402; Towns in Societies: Essays in Economic History and Historical Sociology, 17942

Wroe, Ashley: Social Work, Child Abuse and the Press, 8907

Wrong, Dennis Hume: 'Class Fertility Differences in England and Wales', 7486

Wrottesley, John: The Great Northern Railway vol. 3: The 20th Century to Grouping, 16848; The Midland and Great Northern Joint Railway, 16901

Wroughton History Group: Studies in the History of Wroughton Parish, 19363

Wroughton, John: Documents on British Political History, 284

Wyatt, H. V.: 'CATs and Robbins', 22496

Wyatt, Robert John: The Austin 1905–1952, 17423; The Austin Seven: The Motor for the Million 1922–1939, 17424

Wyatt, Stanley: A Study of Attitudes to Factory Work, 5635

Wyatt, Thomas William: Post-war Poverty and Unemployment Can Be Prevented, 9024

Wyatt, Woodrow: Confessions of an Optimist, 1552

Wycherley, Richard Newman: The Pageantry of Methodist Union: Being a Pictorial Record of Events Leading up to and Consummating in the Historic Uniting Conference of 1932, 12080

Wye College Department of Agricultural Economics: Researches in Farm Management 1923–1950, 19479

Wykeham, Sir Peter Guy: Fighter Command: A Study of Air Defence, 1914–1960, 14991, 15910

Wykes, Alan: Ale and Hearty: Gleanings from the History of Brews and Brewing, 20734

Wykes, George: A Short Economic and Social History of Twentieth Century Britain, 386

Wylie, D.: 'Confrontation over Kenya: The Colonial Office and its Critics, 1918–1940', 12826

Wylie, Gus: The Hebrides, 19261

Wylie, James H.: The Influence of British Arms, 15432

Wylly, Harold Carmichael: The Green Howards in the Great War, 1914–1918, 15639

Wymer, Norman: Harry Ferguson, 5499

Wyncoll, P.: The Nottingham Labour Movement, 1880–1939, 1779

Wyndham, Francis: Graham Greene, 25561

Wyndham, Humphrey: The Household Cavalry at War, 15652

Wynia, Gary W.: Argentina: Illusions and Realities, 16109

Wynn, Alfred Hearst Wynn Elias: Ambush, 14525

Wynn, Arthur and Wynn, Margaret: The Protection of Maternity and Infancy: A Study of the Services for Pregnant Women and Young Children in Finland with some Comparisons with Britain, 22108

Wynn, Margaret: Fatherless Families, 9946

Wynne, Greville: The Man from Moscow: The Story of Wynne and Penkovsky, 16060

Y.H.A. (England and Wales): Landscape and Forestry in Mid-Wales: A Land Use Survey, 19727, 20312

Yamaguchi, Mas: World Vegetables: Principles, Production and Nutritive Values, 20707

Yamey, Basil Selig: Resale Price Maintenance and Shoppers' Choice, 5033

Yardley, Alice: The Infant School, 23134

Yardley, D. C. M.: 'Local Ombudsmen in England: Recent Trends and Developments', 3254

Yass, Marion: Britain between the World Wars, 1918–1939, 299; The Great Depression, 3596

Yates, Alfred: Admission to Grammar Schools, 22980; The First Twenty Five Years: A Review of the N.F.E.R. 1946–1971, 23242

Year Book of Education, 22860

Yearbook of Education: 1959, 22492

Yearbook of the Churches of Christ in Great Britain and Ireland, 1846–1981, 12118

Yearbook of World Affairs: 1947+, 267

Year's Art 1880–1947: 1970+, 23935

Year's Work in Film: Annual 1949–, 24588

Yearwood, P. J.: '"Consistently with Honour": Great Britain, the League of Nations and the Corfu Crisis of 1923', 13483

Yelloly, Margaret A.: 'Factors Relating to an Adoption Decision by Mothers of Illegitimate Infants', 7870

Yeo, Stephen: ed. New Views of Co-operation, 2162

Yockney, John: ed. The Railways of South East Wales, 16974

Yoeli, M.: 'Sir Ronald Ross and the Evolution of Malarial Research', 20994

Yorke, Malcolm: Eric Gill: A Man of Flesh and Spirit, 24018

Young A.: 'Post-war Developments in the Coal Mining Industry, 6296

Young Fabian Group: Young Fabian Pamphlets, 21537

Young, A. D.: 'Dr. A. P. Thurston: A Review of his Contributions to Aeronautics, 7129

Young, A.: Recreation and Tourism in the Loch Lomond Area: A Report to the County Council of Dumbarton, 26946

Young, Agnes Freda: Social Services in British Industry, 5978, 8883

Young, Alison: The Reselection of MPs, 1787

Young, Allan: The Approach to Local Self-Government in British Guiana, 13038

Young, Andrew David: One Hundred Years of Leeds Tramways, 17229

Young, Arthur Primrose: The 'X' Documents: The Secret History of Foreign Office Contacts with German Resistance, 1937–1939, 13684

Young, [Charles] Kenneth: Stanley Baldwin, 977; Arthur James Balfour: The Happy Life of the Politician, Prime Minister, Statesman and Philosopher, 1848–1930, 980; Churchill and Beaverbrook: A Study in Friendship and Politics, 988, 1076; Sir Alec Douglas Home, 1004; Chapel: The Joyous Days and Prayerful Nights of the Non-conformists in their Hey-day, circa 1850–1950, 11998; Music's Great Days in the Spas and Watering Places, 24538; Arnold Bennett, 25390

Young, Donald: 'Brickmaking at Sandleheath, Hampshire', 7047

Young, Douglas: 'Social Class Differences in Conceptions of the Uses of Toys', 9484

Young, Sir Frank George: 'Biochemistry in Retrospect and Prospect', 26470

Young, Frederick Walter: The Story of the Staff College 1858–1958, 15775

Young, George Kennedy: Merchant Banking: Practice and Prospects, 4465

Young, George Malcolm: Stanley Baldwin, 977

Young, George Vaughan Chichester: Subject Guide and Chronological Table Relating to the Acts of the Tynwald, 1776–1975, 2614

Young, Howard Irving: 'British Studios in Wartime', 24647

Young, Hugo: The Crossman Affair, 761, 1168; The Thatcher Phenomenon, 1057; Thatcherism: Personality and Politics, 1058; One of Us: A Biography of Margaret Thatcher, 1059

Young, J. H.: Caesarian Section: The History and Development of the Operation from Earliest Times, 21089

Young, J.: A Dictionary of Ships of the Royal Navy of the Second World War, 15358

Young, James D.: 'Marxism and the Scottish National Question', 2501; The Rousing of the Scottish Working Class, 2515; Women and Popular Struggles: A History of British Working Class Women, 1560–1984, 7850

Young, James Harvey: Patent Medicines: An Early Example of Competitive Marketing, 7150

Young, Jimmy: A Short History of Ale, 20733

Young, Jock: Abortion on Demand, 7884; ed. Contemporary Social Problems in Britain, 8841; ed. Critical Criminology, 10145; The New Criminology: For a Social Theory of Deviance, 10146; Confronting Crime, 10279; The Manufacture of News: Social Problems, Deviance and the Mass Media, 10626, 25320; The Drugtakers: The Social Meaning of Drug Use, 10832, 22195

Young, John Harley: St Mary's Hospital, Manchester, 1790–1963, 21464

Young, John Wilson: 'Churchill, the Russians and the Western Alliance: The Three-Power Conference at Bermuda, December 1953', 14109; Britain, France and the Unity of Europe, 1945–1951, 14123, 14138; 'Churchill's "No" to Europe: The Rejection of European Union by Churchill's Post-war Government, 1951–1952', 14145; 'The Foreign Office, the French and the Post-War Division of Germany', 14194; 'The Foreign Office and the Departure of General de Gaulle, June 1945–January 1946', 14232

Young, Ken: ed. Half a Century of Municipal Decline 1935–1985, 3130; ed. New Directions for County Government, 3200; ed. National Interests and Local Government, 3219; 'The Changing Role and Responsibilities of Local Authority Chief Officers', 3247; Metropolitan London: Politics and Urban Change 1837–1981, 3280, 18924; Local Politics and the Rise of the Party: The London Municipal Society and the Conservative Intervention in Local Elections 1894–1963, 3301; 'The Conservative Strategy for London 1855–1975', 3302; ed. Ethnic Pluralism and Public Policy: Achieving Equality in the United States and Britain, 11082; Strategy and Conflict in Metropolitan Housing: Suburbia versus the Greater London Council 1965–1975, 18663

Young, Michael Dunlop: Labour's Plan for Plenty, 3621; 'The Distribution of Income within the Family', 3821; Lifeline Telephone Service for the Elderly: An Account of a Pilot Project in Hull, 8609; 'Old Age in London and San Francisco: Some Families Compared', 8630; ed. Poverty Report 1974: A Review of Policies and Problems in the Last Year, 9081; ed. Poverty Report 1975 etc, 9082; The Rise of the Meritocracy, 1870–2033 [sic]: An Essay on Education and Equality, 9523; 'In Search of an Explanation of Social Mobility', 9589; Family and Kinship in East London, 10033; Family and Class in a London Suburb, 10034; The Symmetrical Family: A Study of Work and Leisure in a London Region, 10035; Forecasting and the Social Sciences, 17798; The Elmhirsts of Dartington: The Creation of a Utopian Community, 23105

Young, Nigel: An Infantile Disorder? Crisis and Decline of the New Left, 2000, 2156; ed. Campaigning for Peace: British Peace Movements in the Twentieth Century, 13438

Young, Patricia: 'A Short History of the Chartered Society of Physiotherapy', 21732

Young, Percy Marshall: A History of British Music, 24282; Letters of Edward Elgar and Other Writings, 24335, 24339; Elgar OM: A Study of his Music, 24338; Future for English Music and Other Lectures, 24340; Alice Elgar: Enigma of a Victorian Lady, 24341; Vaughan Williams, 24374; The Choral Tradition: An Historical and Analytical Survey from the Sixteenth Century to the Present Day, 24397; A History of British Football, 27059; Bolton Wanderers, 27078; Football in Sheffield, 27079; Football on Merseyside, 27080; Manchester United, 27081

Young, Peter: The 1945 Revolution, 2295

Young, Peter: The British Army, 15441; The Machinery of War: An Illustrated History of Weapons, 15498

Young, Peter: The Power to Punish, 10396

Young, Richard A.: The Flying Bomb, 15205

Young, Ronald G.: The Search for Democracy: A Guide to and Polemic about Local Government in Scotland, 3179

Young, Stephen: ed. Industry, Policy and the Scottish Economy, 5277; Foreign Multinationals and the British Economy: Impact and Policy, 5565; Intervention in the Mixed Economy: The Evolution of British Industrial Policy, 1964–1972, 6111; 'The Implementation of Britain's National Steel Strategy at the Local Level', 6581

Young, Terence: Beacontree and Dagenham: The Story of the Growth of a Housing Estate, 9315

Young, Tim: Community Technical Aid: A Directory of Technical Aid Centres Serving Community Groups on London, 9426

Young, Warren: Community Service Orders, 10493

Younger, Calton: Ireland's Civil War, 2749: A State of Disunion, 2837; Arthur Griffith, 3055

Younger, Sir Kenneth Gilmour: The Changing Aims of British Foreign Policy, 13227; Changing Perspectives in British Foreign Policy, 13228; 'Britain and Europe, 1950: A Comment', 14142; 'Britain in Europe: The Impact on Foreign Policy', 14178

Younghusband, Dame Eileen Louise: Living with Handicap: The Report of a Working Party on Children with Special Needs. 1970, 8407, 21896; 'Trends in Social Work Education', 8663; 'Social Work Education in the World Today', 8664; 'Social Work in Public and Voluntary Agencies', 8665; New Developments in Casework, 8666; Readings in Social Work, 8668; Social Work and Social Values, 8669; Social Work in Britain, 1950–1975: A Follow-up Study, 8670; Study Group on Training for Community Work, 8671; Current Issues in Community Work: A Study by the Community Work Group, 8672; Working Party on Social Workers in the Local Authority Health and Welfare Services, 8673; Community Work and Social Change, 8674; The Newest Profession: A Short History of Social Work, 8675

Youngs, Frederick A.: Guide to the Local Administration Units of England, 3090

Youngson, Alexander John: The British Economy, 1920–1957, 3508

Youthaid: The Youth Opportunities Programme: Making It Work, 8545

Yudkin, John: This Nutrition Business, 20541; Nutrition, 20542; ed. The Diet of Man: Needs and Wants: International Symposium . . . , 20543; Pure, White and Deadly: The Problem of Sugar, 20544; Our Changing Fare, 20545; Changing Food Habits, 20546; ed. Sugar: Chemical, Biological and Nutritional Aspects of Sucrose, 20547

Yudkin, Solomon Simon: Working Mothers and their Children: A Study for the Council for Children's Welfare, 7688; The Health and Welfare of the Immigrant Child, 11050

Yuille, George: ed. History of the Baptists in Scotland from Pre-Reformation Times, 12256

Yule, William: ed. The Lead Debate: The Environment, Toxicology and Child Health, 20173

Yvard, P.: 'Literature and Society in the Fifties in Great Britain', 23783

Zabalza, A.: Women and Equal Pay: The Effects of Legislation on Female Employment and Wages in Britain, 7790

Zacune, J.: Drugs, Alcohol and Tobacco in Britain, 22189

Zametica, John: ed. British Officials and British Foreign Policy 1945–1950, 13249

Zander, Michael: Lawyers and the Public Interest, 9813

Zaretsky, Eli: Capitalism, the Family and Personal Life, 10105

Zebedee, Donald Henry John: Lincoln Diocesan Training College, 1862–1962, 22752

Zebel, Sydney Henry: Balfour: A Political Biography, 980

Zeeman, Bert: 'Britain and Western Europe 1945–1951: Opportunities Lost', 14139

Zellick, Graham: 'National Security, Official Information and the Law', 770

Zeman, Zbynek: Selling the War: Art and Propaganda in World War II, 15103

Zentner, Peter: Social Democracy in Britain: Must Labour Lose?, 1833

Zetland, George Dundas, Marquis: The Life of Lord Curzon, 1174

Zhigalov, I. I.: '[Neo-Fascism in Great Britain: Sources, Aims, Peculiarities]', 2048; 'The Problem of Great Britain's Participation in the 1956 Suez Crisis and its Reflection in Historical Literature', 14380

Zhivkova, Ludmila: Anglo-Turkish Relations, 1933–1939, 13842

Ziderman, Adrian: Manpower Training: Theory and Policy, 5948; 'Rates of Return on Investment in Education: Recent Results for Britain', 23209

Ziegler, Frank: The Story of 609 Squadron: Under the White Rose, 15931

Ziegler, Philip: Mountbatten: The Official Life, 15270; ed. Personal Diary of Admiral the Lord Louis Mountbatten, Supreme Allied Commander, South East Asia, 1943–1946, 15271; ed. From Shore to Shore: The Final Volume of Lord Mountbatten's Diaries, 15272; Diana Cooper, 26025

Zilliacus, Konni: The League of Nations Today: Its Growth, Record and Relation to British Foreign Policy, 13479; Inquest on Peace: An Analysis of the National Government's Foreign Policy, 13690; Why We Are Losing the Peace: The National Government's Foreign Policy, 13757

Ziman, John: 'The College System at Oxford and Cambridge', 23468

Zimmeck, M.: 'Strategies and Stratagems for the Employment of Women in the British Civil Service, 1919–1939', 948

Zimmerman, J. D.: 'A Chapter in English Church Reform: The Enabling Act of 1919', 11622

Zimmerman, Leo M.: Great Ideas in the History of Surgery, 21135

Zinberg, Dorothy: 'The Widening Gap: Attitudes of First Year Students and Staff towards Chemistry, Science, Careers and Commitment: An Informal Study of the Chemistry Department of an English University', 7130

Zinkin, Maurice and Zinkin, Taya: Britain and India: Requiem for Empire, 13108

Zinsser, Hans: Rats, Lice and History, 22376

Zionist Federation of Great Britain and Ireland: Aspects of Anglo-Jewish Life, 1856–1956: A Tercentenary Brochure, 12415

Zola, I. K.: 'Medicine as an Institution of Social Control', 21319

Zorzoli, G. B.: A Pictorial History of Inventions, 7141

Zubaida, Sami: ed. Race and Racialism, 11166

Zubatsky, David S.: Doctoral Dissertations in History and the Social Sciences in Latin America and the Caribbean Accepted by Universities in the United Kingdom 1920–1972, 12998

Zubrzycki, Jerzy: 'The Use of Inter-marriage Statistics as an Index of Assimilation', 10937; Polish Immigrants in Britain: A Study of Adjustment, 11371

Zuckerman, Harriet: 'Nobel Laureates in Science: Patterns of Productivity, Collaboration and Authorship', 7131

Zuckerman, Lady Joan: The Birmingham Heritage, 18014

Zuckerman, Solly [Baron]: Scientists and War, 15191; 'Growth of Higher Education', 23381; ed. Classics in Biology: A Course of Selected Readings by Authorities: With an Introductory Reading Guide, 26515

Zupnick, Elliott: 'Consumer Credit and Monetary Policy in the United States and the United Kingdom', 3720; Britain's Post-War Dollar Problem, 4621

Zurrer, Werner: Persien zwischen England und Russland 1918–1925: Grossmächteinflüsse und nationaler Wiederaufstieg am Beispiel des Iran, 13855

Zwehl, Konrad von: Die Deutschlandpolitik Englands von 1922–1924, 13647

Zweig, Ferdynand: Women's Life and Labour, 7674; The Planning of Free Societies, 8772; Labour, Life and Poverty, 9051; Men in the Pits, 9634; The British Worker, 9635; The Worker in an Affluent Society: Family Life and Industry, 9636; The Student in the Age of Anxiety: A Survey of Oxford and Manchester Students, 9857, 22556; The Cumbernauld Study, 18184

Zweig, Ronald W.: Britain and Palestine during the Second World War, 14320; 'The Political Uses of Military Intelligence: Evaluating the Threat of a Jewish Revolt against Britain during the Second World War', 14332

Zwerdling, Alex: Orwell and the Left, 25743

Zytaruk, George J.: ed. The Letters of D. H. Lawrence, 25630; The Quest for Rananim: D. H. Lawrence's Letters to S. S. Kotel, 1914–1930, 25648